The Longman Anthology of British Literature

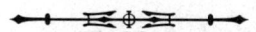

SECOND COMPACT EDITION

VOLUME A

David Damrosch
COLUMBIA UNIVERSITY

Christopher Baswell
UNIVERSITY OF CALIFORNIA, LOS ANGELES

Clare Carroll
QUEENS COLLEGE, CITY UNIVERSITY OF NEW YORK

Kevin J. H. Dettmar
SOUTHERN ILLINOIS UNIVERSITY

Heather Henderson

Constance Jordan
CLAREMONT GRADUATE UNIVERSITY

Peter J. Manning
STATE UNIVERSITY OF NEW YORK, STONY BROOK

Anne Howland Schotter
WAGNER COLLEGE

William Chapman Sharpe
BARNARD COLLEGE

Stuart Sherman
FORDHAM UNIVERSITY

Jennifer Wicke
UNIVERSITY OF VIRGINIA

Susan J. Wolfson
PRINCETON UNIVERSITY

The Longman Anthology of British Literature

Second Compact Edition

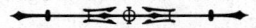

David Damrosch

General Editor

VOLUME A

THE MIDDLE AGES
Christopher Baswell *and* Anne Howland Schotter

THE EARLY MODERN PERIOD
Constance Jordan *and* Clare Carroll

THE RESTORATION AND THE EIGHTEENTH CENTURY
Stuart Sherman

PEARSON

Longman

New York   San Francisco   Boston
London   Toronto   Sydney   Tokyo   Singapore   Madrid
Mexico City   Munich   Paris   Cape Town   Hong Kong   Montreal

Vice President and Editor-in-Chief: *Joseph Terry*
Development Manager: *Janet Lanphier*
Senior Marketing Manager: *Melanie Craig*
Senior Supplements Editor: *Donna Campion*
Media Supplements Editor: *Nancy Garcia*
Senior Production Manager: *Valerie Zaborski*
Project Coordination and Electronic Page Makeup: *Elm Street Publishing Services, Inc.*
Cover Designer/Manager: *Nancy Danahy*
On the Cover: Detail from *Sarah Siddons* (1793) by Sir William Beechey, 1759–1839. The
    National Portrait Gallery, London. The complete image appears on the back cover.
Photo Researcher: *Photosearch, Inc.*
Manufacturing Buyer: *Lucy Hebard*
Printer and Binder: *Quebecor World/Taunton*
Cover Printer: *Lehigh Press, Inc.*

For permission to use copyrighted material, grateful acknowledgment is made to the copyright
holders on pages 1453–54, which are hereby made part of this copyright page.

Library of Congress Cataloging-in-Publication Data

The Longman anthology of British literature / David Damrosch, general
    editor. — Compact 2nd ed.
        p.   cm.
    Includes bibliographical references and index.
    Contents: v. 1. The Middle Ages / Christopher Baswell and Anne Howland
Schotter. The early modern period / Constance Jordan and Clare
Carroll. The Restoration and the 18th century / Stuart Sherman —
v. 2. The Romantics and their contemporaries / Susan Wolfson and Peter
Manning. The Victorian age / Heather Henderson and William Sharpe.
The twentieth century / Kevin Dettmar and Jennifer Wicke.
    ISBN 0-321-19891-3 (v. A). — ISBN 0-321-20239-2 (v. B)
    1. English literature.   2. Great Britain—Literary collections.
I. Damrosch, David.
PR1109.L69   2004
820.8—dc21   2003052707

Please visit our website at http://www.ablongman.com/damrosch

ISBN 0-321-19891-3 (Volume A)
ISBN 0-321-20239-2 (Volume B)

8 9 10 —QWT—07

CONTENTS

THE SECOND PLAY OF THE SHEPHERDS

MIDDLE ENGLISH LYRICS

DAFYDD AP GWILYM

WILLIAM DUNBAR

The Early Modern Period

JOHN SKELTON

⊷ PERSPECTIVES ⊷
Government and Self-Government   632

❧ PERSPECTIVES ❧
Tracts on Women and Gender   824

The Restoration and the Eighteenth Century 1040

LIST OF ILLUSTRATIONS

The Middle Ages

The Early Modern Period

Color Plates   *following page 404*

Black-and-White Images

The Restoration and the Eighteenth Century

PREFACE

Literature has a double life. Born in one time and place and read in another, literary works are at once products of their age and independent creations, able to live on long after their original world has disappeared. The goal of this anthology is to present a wealth of poetry, prose, and drama from the full sweep of the literary history of the British Isles, and to do so in ways that will bring out both the works' original cultural contexts and their lasting aesthetic power. These aspects are, in fact, closely related: Form and content, verbal music and social meanings, go hand in hand. This double life makes literature, as Aristotle said, "the most philosophical" of all the arts, intimately connected to ideas and to realities that the writer transforms into moving patterns of words. The challenge is to show these works in the contexts in which, and for which, they were written, while at the same time not trapping them within those contexts. The warm response this anthology received from the hundreds of teachers who adopted it in its first edition reflects the growing consensus that we don't have to accept an either/or choice between the literature's aesthetic and cultural dimensions. Our users' responses have now guided us in seeing how we can improve our anthology further, so it can be most pleasurable and stimulating to students, most useful to teachers, and most responsive to ongoing developments in literary studies. This preface can serve as a road map to the new phase in this book's life.

LITERATURE IN ITS TIME—AND IN OURS

When we engage with a rich literary history that extends back over a thousand years, we often encounter writers who assume their readers know all sorts of things that are little known today: historical facts, social issues, literary and cultural references. Beyond specific information, these works will have come out of a very different literary culture than our own. Even the contemporary British Isles present a cultural situation—or a mix of cultures—very different from what North American readers encounter at home, and these differences only increase as we go farther back in time. A major emphasis of this anthology is to bring the works' original cultural moment to life: not because the works simply or naively reflect that moment of origin, but because they do refract it in fascinating ways. British literature is both a major heritage for modern North America and, in many ways, a very distinct culture; reading British literature will regularly give an experience both of connection and of difference. Great writers create imaginative worlds that have their own compelling internal logic, and a prime purpose of this anthology is to help readers to understand the formal means— whether of genre, rhetoric, or style—with which these writers have created works of haunting beauty. At the same time, as Virginia Woolf says in *A Room of One's Own*, the gossamer threads of the artist's web are joined to reality "with bands of steel." This anthology pursues a range of strategies to bring out both the beauty of these webs of words and their points of contact with reality.

The Longman Anthology brings related authors and works together in several ways:

☞ PERSPECTIVES: **Broad groupings that illuminate underlying issues in a variety of the major works of a period.**

☞ AND ITS TIME: **A focused cluster that illuminates a specific cultural moment or a debate to which an author is responding.**

☞ COMPANION READINGS: **Pairings of works in dialogue with each other.**

These groupings provide a range of means of access to the literary culture of each period. The Perspectives sections do much more than record what major writers thought about an issue: they give a variety of views in a range of voices, to illustrate the wider culture within which the literature was being written. An attack on tobacco by King James the First; theological reflections by the pioneering scientist Isaac Newton; haunting testimony by Victorian child workers concerning their lives; these and many other vivid readings give rhetorical as well as social contexts for the poems, plays, and stories around them. Perspectives sections typically relate to several major authors of the period, as with a section on Government and Self-Government that relates broadly to Spenser's *Faerie Queene* and to Milton's *Paradise Lost*. Most of the writers included in Perspectives sections are important figures of the period who could be neglected if they were listed on their own with just a few pages each; grouping them together has proven to be useful pedagogically as well as intellectually. Perspectives sections may also include work by a major author whose primary listing appears elsewhere in the period; thus, a Perspective section on the abolition of slavery—a hotly debated issue in England from the 1790s through the 1830s—includes poems and other writing on slavery by both Dorothy and William Wordsworth so as to give a rounded presentation of the issue in ways that can inform the reading of those authors in their individual sections.

When we present a major work "And Its Time," we give a cluster of related materials to suggest the context within which the work was written. Thus Sir Philip Sidney's great *Apology for Poetry* is accompanied by readings showing the controversy that was raging at the time concerning the nature and value of poetry. Some of the writers in these groupings and in our Perspectives sections have not traditionally been seen as literary figures, but all have produced lively and intriguing works, from medieval clerics writing about saints and sea monsters, to a polemical seventeenth-century tract giving *The Arraignment of Lewd, Idle, Froward, and Unconstant Women*, to rousing speeches by Winston Churchill as the British faced the Nazis during World War II.

Also, we include "Companion Readings" to present specific prior texts to which a work is responding: when Sir Thomas Wyatt creates a beautiful poem, *Whoso list to hunt*, by making a free translation of a Petrarch sonnet, we include Petrarch's original (with a literal translation) as a companion reading. John Keats's sonnet "On First Looking into Chapman's Homer" is accompanied by excerpts from Chapman's translation of the *Iliad*, as well as by Alexander Pope's rendering (much better known in Keats's time), so readers can directly see why Chapman's vibrant version looked so exciting to Keats in contrast to Pope's polished heroic couplets.

CULTURAL EDITIONS

This edition follows the establishment of an important new series of companion volumes under the general editorship of Susan Wolfson, the Longman Cultural Editions, which carry further the anthology's emphases by presenting major texts along with a generous selection of contextual material. Initial volumes are devoted to *King Lear*; a pairing of *Othello* and Elizabeth Cary's *Tragedie of Mariam*; *Pride and Prejudice*; *Frankenstein*; and *Hard Times*. More are currently being developed and are available free, for course use, with the anthology itself. Taken together, our new edition and the Longman Cultural Editions offer an unparalleled set of materials for the enjoyment and study of British literary culture from its first beginnings to the present.

ILLUSTRATING VISUAL CULTURE

Another important context for literary production has been a different kind of culture: the visual. We have newly added in this edition a suite of color plates in each volume, and we also have dozens of black-and-white illustrations throughout the anthology, chosen to show artistic and cultural images that figured importantly for literary creation. Sometimes, a poem refers to a specific painting, or more generally emulates qualities of a school of visual art. At other times, more popular materials like advertisements may underlie scenes in Victorian or Modernist writing. In some cases, visual and literary creation have merged, as in Hogarth's series *A Rake's Progress*, included in Volume A, or Blake's illustrated engravings of his *Songs of Innocence and of Experience*, several of whose plates are reproduced in color in Volume B.

Our cover illustration is an excellent instance of a beautiful image that gives insight into the culture of its era. In this painting, *Sarah Siddons* (1793), the society painter William Beechey portrays a theatrical superstar at the height of her fame. Siddons (1755–1831) performed tragic roles so hypnotically that she moved tragedy back to the center of London theatrical life, after decades in which comedy had predominated. Here, the emblems of her achievement range from the ancient (the tragic mask she holds out to her left) to the relatively recent: the monument of Shakespeare at her back, partially visible in the cropped image on the cover, is topped with a cupid weeping, perhaps because his cherished comedies have been displaced. Contemporaries complained that in the painting, the actress's appearance seemed at odds with her emblems. Her incipient smile and lively posture suggested (wrote one critic) a gypsy "disporting at a masquarade" rather than the high priestess of tragedy that Siddons had become in the minds of the worshipful audiences. Still, Beechey knows what he is doing here—and, of course, so does Siddons. Other painters had depicted her as possessed by her roles, in thrall to the spirit of tragedy. Beechey, by contrast, shows her in possession, a confident and conscious player, craftily half-unmasking, meeting us eye to eye, and plainly enjoying her art, her power, and her self.

AIDS TO UNDERSTANDING

We have attempted to contextualize our selections in suggestive rather than exhaustive ways, trying to enhance rather than overwhelm the experience of reading the texts themselves. Thus, when difficult or archaic words need defining in poems, we use glosses in the margins, so as to disrupt the reader's eye as little as possible; footnotes are intended to be concise and informative, rather than massive or interpretive. Important literary and social terms are defined when they are used. At the end of Volume A, there are useful summaries of British political and religious organization, and of money, weights, and measures. For further reading, carefully selected, up-to-date bibliographies for each period and for each author can be found at the end of each volume.

LOOKING—AND LISTENING—FURTHER

Beyond the boundaries of the anthology itself, along with this edition we have created a pair of CDs giving a wide range of readings of texts in the anthology and selections of music from each period. It is only in the past century or two that people usually began to read literature silently; most literature has been written in the expectation that it would be read aloud, or even sung in the case of lyric poetry ("lyric" itself means a work meant to be sung to the accompaniment of a lyre or other instruments). The aural power and beauty of these works are a crucial dimension of their experience. For further explorations, we have also expanded our Web site, available to all users at www.awlonline.com/damrosch; this site gives a wealth of information, annotated links to related sites, and an archive of texts for further reading. For instructors, we have revised and expanded our popular companion volume, *Teaching British Literature*, written directly by the anthology's editors, 600 pages in length, available free to everyone who adopts the anthology.

WHAT IS BRITISH LITERATURE?

Turning now to the book itself, let us begin by defining our basic terms: What is "British" literature? What is literature itself? And just what should an anthology of this material look like at the present time? The term "British" can mean many things, some of them contradictory, some of them even offensive to people on whom the name has been imposed. If the term "British" has no ultimate essence, it does have a history. The first British were Celtic people who inhabited the British Isles and the northern coast of France (still called Brittany) before various Germanic tribes of Angles and Saxons moved onto the islands in the fifth and sixth centuries. Gradually the Angles and Saxons amalgamated into the Anglo-Saxon culture that became dominant in the southern and eastern regions of Britain and then spread outward; the old British people were pushed west, toward what became known as Cornwall, Wales, and Ireland, which remained independent kingdoms for centuries, as did Celtic Scotland to the north. By an ironic twist of linguistic fate, the Anglo-Saxons began to appropriate the term British from the Britons they had displaced, and they took as a national hero the early, semi-mythic Welsh King Arthur. By the seventeenth century, English monarchs had extended their sway over Wales, Ireland, and Scotland, and they began to refer to their holdings as "Great Britain." Today, Great Britain includes England, Wales, Scotland, and Northern Ireland, but does not include the Republic of Ireland, which has been independent from England since 1922.

This anthology uses "British" in a broad sense, as a geographical term encompassing the whole of the British Isles. For all its fraught history, it seems a more satisfactory term than to speak simply of "English" literature, for two reasons. First: most speakers of English live in countries that are not the focus of this anthology; second, while the English language and its literature have long been dominant in the British Isles, other cultures in the region have always used other languages and have produced great literature in these languages. Important works by Irish, Welsh, and Scots writers appear regularly in the body of this anthology, some of them written directly in their languages and presented here in translation, and others written in an English inflected by the rhythms, habits of thought, and modes of expression characteristic of these other languages and the people who use them.

We use the term "literature" in a similarly capacious sense, to refer to a range of artistically shaped works written in a charged language, appealing to the imagination at least as much as to discursive reasoning. It is only relatively recently that creative writers have been able to make a living composing poems, plays, and novels, and only in the past hundred years or so has creating "belles lettres" or high literary art been thought of as a sharply separate sphere of activity from other sorts of writing that the same authors would regularly produce. Sometimes, Romantic poets wrote sonnets to explore the deepest mysteries of individual perception and memory; at other times, they wrote sonnets the way a person might now write an Op-Ed piece, and such a sonnet would be published and read along with parliamentary debates and letters to the editor on the most pressing contemporary issues.

WOMEN'S WRITING, AND MEN'S

Literary culture has always involved an interplay between central and marginal regions, groupings, and individuals. A major emphasis in literary study in recent years has been the recovery of writing by women writers, some of them little read until recently, others major figures in their time. This anthology gives an integrated presentation of women's writing in the British Isles from the Middle Ages to the present. The Irish poet Eavan Boland, in fact, appears in both periods—as a translator of medieval Irish verse, and as an important contemporary poet in her own right. Attending to these voices gives us a new variety of compelling works, and helps us rethink the entire periods in which they wrote. The first third of the nineteenth century, for example, can be defined more broadly than as a "Romantic Age" dominated by six male poets; looking closely at women's writing as well as at men's, we can deepen our understanding of the period as a whole, including the specific achievements of Blake, William Wordsworth, Coleridge, Keats, Percy Shelley, and Byron, all of whom continue to have a major presence in these pages as most of them did during the nineteenth century.

VARIETIES OF LITERARY EXPERIENCE

Above all, we have striven to give as full a presentation as possible to the varieties of great literature produced over the centuries in the British Isles, by women as well as by men, in outlying regions as well as in the metropolitan center of London, and in prose, drama, and verse alike. While we have made sure to keep this Compact Edition to a moderate length, judicious pruning has made room for important additions in every period, including Perspectives: Ethnic and Religious Encounters, in the

Middle Ages; Perspectives: Government and Self-Government, in the early modern period; *The Beggar's Opera* in the eighteenth century; Perspectives: The Sublime, the Beautiful, and the Picturesque, in the Romantic era; Perspectives: Imagining Childhood, in the Victorian period; and Perspectives: Regendering Modernism, in the twentieth century. Finally, lyric poetry appears in profusion throughout the anthology, from early lyrics by anonymous Middle English poets and the trenchantly witty Dafydd ap Gwilym to the powerful contemporary voices of Philip Larkin, Seamus Heaney, Eavan Boland, and Derek Walcott—himself a product of colonial British education, heir of Shakespeare and James Joyce—who closes the anthology with poems about Englishness abroad and foreignness in Britain.

As topical as these contemporary writers are, we hope that this anthology will show that the great works of earlier centuries can also speak to us compellingly today, their value only increased by the resistance they offer to our views of ourselves and our world. To read and reread the full sweep of this literature is to be struck anew by the degree to which the most radically new works are rooted in centuries of prior innovation. Even this preface can close in no better way than by quoting the words written eighteen hundred years ago by Apuleius of Madaura—both a consummate artist and a kind of anthologist of extraordinary tales—when he concluded the prologue to his masterpiece *The Golden Ass:* Attend, reader, and pleasure is yours.

David Damrosch

ACKNOWLEDGMENTS

In planning and preparing the second compact edition of our anthology, the editors have been fortunate to have the support, advice, and assistance of many people. Our editor, Joe Terry, has been unwavering in his enthusiasm for the book and his commitment to it; he and his associates Roth Wilkofsky, Janet Lanphier, and Melanie Craig have supported us in every possible way throughout the process, ably assisted by Nancy Crochiere, Michele Cronin, and Alison Main. Our developmental editor, Mark Getlein, guided us and our manuscript from start to finish with unfailing acuity and Wildean wit. Daniel Kline and Peter Meyers have devoted enormous energy and creativity to revising our Web site and developing our new audio CDs. Lynn Smith cleared our many text permissions, and Jacqui Sutton of Photosearch, Inc., cleared our many illustration permissions. Finally, Valerie Zaborski oversaw the production with sunny good humor and kept the book successfully on track on a very challenging schedule, working closely with Karin Vonesh at Elm Street Publishing Services.

Our plans for the new edition have been shaped by comments and suggestions from many faculty who have used the book over the past four years. We are specifically grateful for the thoughtful advice of our reviewers for this edition, Alexander M. Bruce (Florida Southern College), Teri Gaston (The University of Texas at Arlington), Stephen J. Harris (University of Massachusetts Amherst), Nancy Knowles (Eastern Oregon University), Ben Kohn (Whatcom Community College), Pat Lonchar (University of the Incarnate Word), Ann Martin (Louisiana State University), Delilah Orr (Fort Lewis College), Mark K. Stevens (Southern Polytechnic State University), Rob Breton (The University of British Columbia), Catherine R. Eskin (Florida Southern College), Carol Hanes (Howard College), Marvin Hunt (North Carolina State University), Helaine Razovsky (Northwestern State University), Gerald Richman (Suffolk University), Maxine Susman (Caldwell College), Marion Hoctor (Nazareth College), Ted Sherman (Middle Tennessee State University), Robert Barrett (University of Pennsylvania), Mary Been (Clovis Community College), Stephen Behrendt (University of Nebraska), James Campbell (University of Central Florida), Linda McFerrin Cook (McLellan Community College), Kevin Gardner (Baylor University), Peter Greenfield (University of Puget Sound), Natalie Grinnell (Wofford College), Wayne Hall (University of Cincinnati), Donna Hamilton (University of Maryland), Carrie Hintz (Queens College), Eric Johnson (Dakota State College), Roxanne Kent-Drury (Northern Kentucky University), Adam Komisaruk (West Virginia University), John Laflin (Dakota State University), Paulino Lim (California State University, Long Beach), Ed Malone (Missouri Western State College), William W. Matter (Richland College), Evan Matthews (Navarro College), Lawrence McCauley (College of New Jersey), Peter E. Medine (University of Arizona), Charlotte Morse (Virginia Commonwealth University), Mary Morse (Rider University), Richard Nordquist (Armstrong Atlantic State University), John Ottenhoff (Alma College), Joyce Cornette Palmer (Texas Women's University), Leslie Palmer (University of North Texas), Rebecca Phillips (West Virginia University), William Rankin (Abilene Christian University), Sherry Rankin (Abilene Christian University), Luke Reinsma (Seattle Pacific University), David Rollison (College of Marin), Kathryn Rummel (California Polytechnic), R. G. Siemens

(Malaspina University-College), Brad Sullivan (Florida Gulf Coast University), Brett Wallen (Cleveland Community College), Daniel Watkins (Duquesne University), and Julia Wright (University of Waterloo).

As if all this help weren't enough, the editors also drew directly on friends and colleagues in many ways, for advice, for information, sometimes for outright contributions to headnotes and footnotes, even (in a pinch) for aid in proofreading. In particular, we wish to thank David Ackiss, Marshall Brown, James Cain, Cathy Corder, Jeffrey Cox, Michael Coyle, Pat Denison, Tom Farrell, Andrew Fleck, Jane Freilich, Laurie Glover, Lisa Gordis, Joy Hayton, Ryan Hibbet, V. Lauryl Hicks, Nelson Hilton, Jean Howard, David Kastan, Stanislas Kemper, Andrew Krull, Ron Levao, Carol Levin, David Lipscomb, Denise MacNeil, Jackie Maslowski, Richard Matlak, Anne Mellor, James McKusick, Melanie Micir, Michael North, David Paroissien, Stephen M. Parrish, Peter Platt, Cary Plotkin, Desma Polydorou, Gina Renee, Alan Richardson, Esther Schor, Catherine Siemann, Glenn Simshaw, David Tresilian, Shasta Turner, Nicholas Watson, Michael Winckleman, Gillen Wood, and Sarah Zimmerman for all their guidance and assistance.

The pages on the Restoration and the eighteenth century are the work of many collaborators, diligent and generous. Michael F. Suarez, S. J. (Campion Hall, Oxford) edited the Swift and Pope sections; Mary Bly (Fordham University) edited Sheridan's *School for Scandal*; Lauren Simonetti. Steven N. Zwicker (Washington University) co-wrote the period introduction, and the headnotes for the Dryden section. Bruce Redford (Boston University) crafted the footnotes for Dryden, Gay, Johnson, and Boswell. Susan Brown, Christine Coch, Tara Czechowski, Paige Reynolds, and Andrew Tumminia helped with texts, footnotes, and other matters throughout; William Pritchard gathered texts, wrote notes, and prepared the bibliography. To all, abiding thanks.

It has been a pleasure to work with all of these colleagues in the ongoing collaborative process that has produced this book and brought it to this new stage of its life and use. This book exists for its readers, whose reactions and suggestions we warmly welcome, as these will in turn reshape this book for later users in the years to come.

The Longman Anthology of British Literature

SECOND COMPACT EDITION

VOLUME A

Laurence, Prior of Durham, depicted as a scribe, from a 12th-century manuscript.

The Middle Ages

✦══◆══✦

> At the present time, there are five languages in Britain, just as
> the divine law is written in five books, all devoted to seeking out
> and setting forth one and the same kind of wisdom, namely the
> knowledge of sublime truth and of true sublimity. These are the
> English, British, Irish, Pictish, as well as the Latin languages;
> through the study of the scriptures, Latin is in general use among
> them all.
>
> *Bede, Ecclesiastical History of the English People*

The Venerable Bede's famous and enormously influential *Ecclesiastical History of the English People,* written in the early 700s, reflects a double triumph. First, its very title acknowledges the dominance by Bede's day of the Anglo-Saxons, who, centuries earlier, had established themselves on an island already inhabited by Celtic Britons and by Picts. Second, the Latin of Bede's text and his own life as a monk point to the presence of ancient Mediterranean influences in the British Isles, earlier through Rome's military colonization of ancient Britain and later through the conversion of Bede's people to Roman Christianity.

In this first chapter of his first book, Bede shows a complex awareness of the several populations still active in Britain and often resisting or encroaching on Anglo-Saxon rule, and much of his *History* narrates the successive waves of invaders and missionaries who had brought their languages, governments, cultures, and beliefs to his island. This initial emphasis on peoples and languages should not be taken as early medieval multiculturalism, however: Bede's brief comparison to the single truth embodied in the five books of divine law also shows us his eagerness to draw his fragmented world into a coherent and transcendent system of Latin-based Christianity.

It is useful today, however, to think about medieval Britain, before and long after Bede, as a multilingual and multicultural setting, densely layered with influences and communities that divide, in quite different ways, along lines of geography, language, and ethnicity, as well as religion, gender, and class. These elements produced extraordinary cultures and artistic works, whose richness and diversity challenge the modern imagination. The medieval British Isles were a meeting place, but also a point of resistance, for wave after wave of cultural and political influences. Awareness of these multiple origins, moreover, persisted. In the mid-thirteenth century, Matthew Paris's map of England (Color Plate 4) reflects an alertness to the complex geography of history and settlement on his island. Six hundred years after Bede we encounter a historian like Sir Thomas Gray complaining that recent disorders were "characteristic of a medley of different races. Wherefore some people are of the opinion that the diversity of spirit among the English is the cause of their revolutions" (*Scalacronica,* c. 1363).

3

This complex mixture sometimes resulted from systematic conquest, as with the Romans and, three centuries after Bede, the famous Norman Conquest of 1066; sometimes it was from slower, less unified movements of ethnic groups, such as the Celts, Anglo-Saxons, the Irish in Scotland, and the Vikings. Other important influences arrived more subtly: various forms of Christianity, classical Latin literature and learning, continental French culture in the thirteenth century, and an imported Italian humanism toward the close of the British Middle Ages.

Our understanding of this long period and our very name for it also reflect a long history of multiple influences and cultural and political orders. The term "medieval" began as a condescending and monolithic label, first applied by Renaissance humanists who were eager to distinguish their revived classical scholarship from what they interpreted as a "barbarous" past. They and later readers often dismissed the Middle Ages as rigidly hierarchical, feudal, and Church-dominated. Others embraced the period for equally tendentious reasons, rosily picturing "feudal" England and Europe as a harmonious society of contented peasants, chivalrous nobles, and holy clerics. It is true that those who exercised political and religious control during the Middle Ages—the Roman church and the Anglo-Norman and then the English monarchy—sought to impose hierarchy on their world and created explicit ideologies to justify doing so. They were not unopposed, however; those who had been pushed aside continued to resist—and to contribute to Britain's multiple and dynamic literatures.

The period that we call "the Middle Ages" is vast and ungainly, spanning eight hundred years by some accounts. Scholars traditionally divide medieval English literature into the Old English period, from about 700 to 1066 (the date of the Norman Conquest), and the Middle English period, from 1066 to about 1500. Given the very different state of the English language during the two periods and given the huge impact of the Norman Conquest, this division is reasonable and is reflected in this collection under the headings "Before the Norman Conquest" and "After the Norman Conquest." There were substantial continuities, nevertheless, before and after the Conquest, especially in the Celtic areas beyond the Normans' immediate control.

THE CELTS

It is with the Celts, in fact, that the recorded history of Britain begins, and their literatures continue to the present day in Ireland and Wales. The Celts first migrated to Britain about 400 B.C., after spreading over most of Europe in the two preceding centuries. In England these "Brittonic" Celts absorbed some elements of Roman culture and social order during Rome's partial occupation of the island from the first to the fifth centuries A.D. After the conversion of the Roman emperor Constantine in the fourth century and the establishment of Christianity as the official imperial religion, many British Celts adopted Christianity. The language of these "British" to whom Bede refers gave rise to Welsh. The Celts maintained contact with their people on the Continent, who were already being squeezed toward what is now Brittany, in the west of France. The culture of the Brittonic Celts was thus not exclusively insular, and their myths and legends came to incorporate these cross-Channel memories, especially in the stories of King Arthur.

Celts also arrived in Ireland; and as one group, the "Goidelic" Celts, achieved linguistic and social dominance there, their language split off from that of the Britons.

Color Plate 1 First page of the Gospel of Matthew, from the *Lindisfarne Gospels*, c. 698. This illustrated gospel book was made on the "holy island" of Lindisfarne off the coast of Northumberland, partly in honor of St. Cuthbert, who had died there 11 years earlier and whose cult was fast developing at the time. The manuscript reflects an extraordinary flowering of artistic production during these years, and the meeting of world cultures that occurred in Northumbrian monastic life: Mediterranean Latin language and imagery, Celtic interlace, and Germanic animal motifs. In the 10th century an Anglo-Saxon translation was added in the margins and between the lines. *(By permission of The British Library, Cott. Nero. D.IV f.27.)*

Color Plate 2 Gold buckle, from the Sutton Hoo ship-burial, c. 625–630. Fragments of a remarkably preserved ship-burial, probably for an Anglo-Saxon king, were discovered among other burial mounds at Sutton Hoo, in Suffolk, England, in 1939. The burial mound contained numerous coins and 41 objects in gold, among them this magnificent buckle. Stylized animal heads (including two dragons in the circle at bottom) invite comparison with the powerful animal imagery in *Beowulf.* Other objects in the ship include two silver spoons inscribed "Saul" and "Paul," signs of the mixing of pagan practices and Christian influences in this era. *(Copyright The British Museum.)*

Color Plate 3 The Ardagh Chalice, c. 9th century. This greatest surviving piece of medieval Celtic metalwork was found near the site of an ancient fort at Ardagh, in County Limerick in the southwest of Ireland. Measuring 9.5 inches across and 7 inches tall, the chalice was probably used for wine on great holidays like Easter, when laypeople took Communion. In the 7th century, the learned Irish monk Adamnan had described the chalice of the Last Supper as a silver cup with two opposite handles. The Ardagh Chalice is very similar. It is made of silver alloy, magnificently decorated with gilt and enamel. Its elaborate interlace decoration uses a wide range of Celtic motifs, including fearsomely toothed animal heads. In a band running around the entire bowl are the names of the 12 apostles, further linking its liturgical role to the Last Supper. *(National Museum of Ireland.)*

Color Plate 4 Map of England, from Matthew Paris's *Historia Major*, mid-13th century. A monk of St. Albans, Matthew Paris wrote a monumental *History of England*, of which two illustrated copies in his own hand survive. Matthew's richly detailed map of England, including counties and major towns, illustrates the geographical knowledge of his day. It further suggests how alert he was to the ethnic divisions that still crossed his island and to the settlements and invasions, both mythic and actual, that had given rise to them. His inscription near the depiction of Hadrian's Wall, for example, informs us that the wall "once divided the English and the Picts." Recalling the claim that the original Britons were Trojan refugees, he writes about Wales (left center): "The people of this region are descended from the followers of Brutus." The story of Arthur's conception may have led Paris to identify Tintagel ("Tintaiol," lower left). Matthew also links geography and racial character, as in his comment on northern Scotland (top center): "A mountainous, woody region producing an uncivilized people." *(By permission of The British Library, Cott. Claud. D.IV f.12v.)*

Color Plate 5 *Passion Scenes,* from the *Winchester Psalter,* 1150–1160. A series of full-page miniatures of crucial scenes from the Bible precedes the Psalter texts of this manuscript. The page reproduced here depicts scenes of the betrayal and flagellation of Christ. The vividly drawn images show the clinging drapery and exaggerated expressions typical of the manuscript; equally exaggerated are the African and Semitic features of some of the tormentors, associating them with peoples who were exotic or reviled in 12th-century England. Some of the original richness of color of this manuscript has been lost through damp, but also because blue pigment has been scraped off, presumably for reuse—a sign of how costly was the making of such manuscripts. *(By permission of The British Library, Cott. Nero. C.IV f.21.)*

Color Plate 6 *King Arthur and His Knights,* from a manuscript of the *Prose Lancelot,* late 13th century. This miniature appears in a manuscript of French prose Arthurian romances, which were also widely known in England. Here, King Arthur asks his knights to tell about their adventures on the quest for the Holy Grail. *(Beinecke Rare Book and Manuscript Library, Yale University.)*

Color Plate 7 *Annunciation to the Shepherds* (top) and *Nativity Scene* (bottom), from *The Holkham Bible Picture Book*, c. 1325–1330. This vividly illustrated manuscript depicts episodes from the Bible, adding events from later Christian legends. Crowded scenes are vigorous and full of gesture; they may reflect contact with liturgical drama and look forward to vernacular enactments such as the *Second Play of the Shepherds*. Short rhyming narratives above each picture mix up the major languages of early 14th-century England. At first the shepherds cannot understand the angel's Latin "*Gloria in excelsis*"; in Anglo-French they say "Glum? Glo? That means nothing. Let's go there, we'll understand better." At the scene of the Nativity, below, Middle English breaks in and "Songen alle with one stevene [voice]," though the shepherds can now sing famous Latin hymns: "*Gloria in excelsis deo*" and "*Te deum laudamus*." Both the images and French and Middle English text mediate between the learned clerical class and the wealthy lay people who were the manuscript's intended audience. *(By permission of The British Library, Add. 18850 f.257v.)*

Color Plate 8 *Richard II with His Regalia*, 1394–1395. Richard himself commissioned this splendid life-size and unusually lifelike portrait soon after the death of his beloved first wife, Anne of Bohemia. It was probably mounted at the back of the King's private pew at Westminster Abbey in London, but it also may suggest his wish to be perpetually near Anne, who was entombed nearby. At the same time, the throne, crown, orb, and scepter are all signs of Richard's sense of kingship and secular authority. *(Copyright: Dean and Chapter of Westminster.)*

Color Plate 9 Opening page of *The Wife of Bath's Tale,* from the Ellesmere manuscript of Chaucer's *Canterbury Tales,* 1405–1410. One of the two earliest surviving manuscripts of the *Tales,* it was owned for centuries by the Egerton family, who became Earls of Ellesmere in the nineteenth century. The Ellesmere Chaucer was probably made in London, by then the center of book production in England. Its elaborate decoration and illustration are all the more striking, given how few Middle English texts received such treatment. The portrait of the Wife of Bath is positioned to highlight the beginning of her tale. Her red clothing, whip, and large hat follow details of her description in the *General Prologue* of the *Tales,* and her own words in the prologue to her tale. The grandeur of the treatment of text and decoration in this manuscript—clearly meant both for display and reading—reflect the speed with which Chaucer became a "canonical" author in the years after his death in 1400, and perhaps the wish of wealthy patrons to associate themselves and their interests with his work. It is partly the same wish that ultimately led the American railroad tycoon Henry E. Huntington to buy the manuscript in 1917 and leave it to his library in San Marino, California. *(This item is reproduced by permission of The Huntington Library, San Marina, California. EL26C9F72r.)*

Color Plate 10 *Anne, Duchess of Bedford, Kneeling Before the Virgin Mary and Saint Anne*, from the *Bedford Hours*, early 15th century. A book of hours was a prayerbook used by laypeople for private devotion. The *Bedford Hours* was produced in a Paris workshop for the Duke of Bedford, a brother of Henry V, and his wife, Anne of Burgundy. Here, Saint Anne is shown teaching her daughter, the Virgin Mary, to read; another book lies open on a lectern in front of the kneeling Anne of Burgundy. *(By permission of The British Library, Add. 18850 f.257v.)*

Some of these Irish Celts later established themselves in Argyll and the western isles of Scotland, "either by friendly treaty or by the sword," says Bede, and from them the Scottish branch of the Celtic languages developed. Bede mentions this language as the "Irish" that is spoken in Britain. The Irish converted to Christianity early but slowly, without the pressure of a Christianized colonizer. When the great Irish monasteries flourished in the sixth century, their extraordinary Latin scholarship seems to have developed alongside the traditional learning preserved by the rigorous schools of vernacular poetry, as we see in the section "Early Irish Verse" (pages 92–100). If anything, Irish monastic study was stimulated by these surviving institutions of a more poetic and priestly class. The Irish monasteries in turn became the impetus behind Irish and Anglo-Saxon missionaries who carried Christianity to the northern and eastern reaches of Europe. Both as missionaries and as scholars, insular Christians had great impact on continental Europe, especially in the eighth and ninth centuries.

By 597 when Pope Gregory the Great sent Augustine (later "of Canterbury") to expand the Christian presence in England, there was already a flourishing Christian Celtic society, especially in Ireland. Ensuing disagreements over Celtic versus Roman ways of worship were ultimately resolved in favor of the Roman liturgy and calendar, but the cultural impact of Celts on British Christianity remained enormous. The Irish *Book of Kells* (page 10), and the Lindisfarne Gospels (Color Plate 1), produced in England, are enlivened by the swirls, interlace, and stylized animals long evident in the work of pagan Celtic craftsmen on the continent. The monks who illuminated such magnificent gospel books also copied classical Latin texts, notably Virgil's *Aeneid* and works by Cicero and Seneca, thereby helping keep ancient Roman literature alive when much of continental Europe fell into near chaos during the Germanic invasions that led to the fall of Rome.

Included in this anthology are examples from the two great literatures written in Celtic languages, Irish and Welsh. Welsh literature is represented first by lyrics attributed to the early, shadowy poet Taliesin and second by a much later story about his accomplishments which serves to show some of the continuities of Welsh literary culture. Wales also absorbed Latin and later European influences, as represented by fourteenth-century lyrics from the marvelously sophisticated Dafydd ap Gwilym, who resembles Chaucer in his use of continental poetry.

THE GERMANIC MIGRATIONS

While Celtic culture flourished in Ireland, the British Celts and their faith suffered a series of disastrous reversals after the withdrawal of the Romans and the aggressive incursions of the pagan Angles, Saxons, and Jutes from the Continent. The Picts and Scots in the north, never Romanized, had begun to harass the Britons, who responded by inviting allies from among the Germanic tribes on the Continent in the mid-fifth century. These protectors soon became predators, demanding land and establishing small kingdoms of their own in roughly the eastern half of modern-day England. Uneasy and temporary treaties followed. The Britons retained a presence in the northwest, in the kingdoms of Rheged and of the Strathclyde Welsh; others were slowly pressed toward present-day Wales in the southwest.

The Angles, Saxons, and Jutes were not themselves a monolithic force, though. Divided into often warring states, they faced resistance, however diminishing, from the Britons and still had to battle the aggressive Picts and Scots, who were the original reason for their arrival. Their own culture was further changed as they converted to Christianity. The piecemeal Anglo-Saxon colonization of England in the sixth and seventh centuries and the island's conversion and later reconversion to Christianity present a complex picture, then—one that could be retold very differently depending on the perspectives of later historians. As the Angles and Saxons settled in and extended their control, the emerging "English" culture drew on new interpretations of the region's history. The most influential account of all was Bede's *Ecclesiastical History,* completed in 731. Our most reliable and eloquent source for early British history, Bede nonetheless wrote as an Anglo-Saxon. He presented his people's history from a providential perspective, seeing their role in Britain and their conversion to Christianity as a crucial part of a divine plan. King Alfred extended this world view when, in the late ninth century, he wrote of his people's struggle against the invading pagan Vikings.

Bede thus adopts an approach to history that reflects his own devout Christian faith and the disciplined religious practices of his monastic brethren in Northumberland. Nevertheless, Bede lived in a wider culture still deeply imbued with the tribal values of its Germanic and pagan past, a culture that maintained at least a nostalgic regard for the kind of individual heroic glory that rarely looks beyond this world. Even in Bede's day, most kings died young and on the battlefield. And natural disasters such as those in 664 (a plague, and the deaths of a king and an archbishop occurring on the day of an eclipse) could send the Anglo-Saxons back to pagan worship. The two worlds, one with its roots in Mediterranean Christianity and the other in Germanic paganism, overlapped and interpenetrated for generations.

The pagan culture that is the setting for the epic *Beowulf* still strongly resembled that of the Germanic "barbarians" described by the Roman historian Tacitus in the first century. The heroic code of the Germanic warrior bands—what Tacitus called the "*comitatus*"—valued courage in battle above all, followed by loyalty to the tribal leader and the warband. These formed the core of heroic identity. A warrior whose leader fell in battle was obliged to seek vengeance at any cost; it was an indelible shame to survive an unavenged leader. Family links were also profound, however, and a persistent tragic theme in Germanic and Anglo-Saxon heroic narrative pits the claims of vengeance against those of family loyalty.

Early warrior culture in the British Isles, as elsewhere, was fraught with violence, as fragile truces between warring tribes and clans were continually broken. The tone of Old English poetry (as of much of Old Irish heroic narrative) is consequently somber, often suffused with a sense of doom. Even moments of high festivity are darkened by allusions to later disasters. Humor often occurs through a kind of ironic understatement: a poet may state that a warrior strode less swiftly into battle, for example, when the warrior in fact is dead. Similarly Cet, an Irish warrior, claims that if his brother were in the house, he would overcome his opponent, Conall. Conall replies, "But he is in the house," and almost casually flings the brother's head at Cet.

The Angles and Saxons had come to England as military opportunists, and they in turn faced attacks and settlement from across the Channel. Their increasingly ordered political world and their thriving monastic establishments, such as Bede's monastery of Jarrow, were plundered by Vikings in swift attacks by boat as early as the end of the eighth century. Irish monastic culture faced similar depredations. This continued for a hundred years, and eventually resulted in widespread Scandinavian settlements north of the Thames, in areas called the Danelaw, and around modern-day Dublin. By the 890s Christian Viking kings reigned at York and in East Anglia, extending a history of independence from the southern kingdoms. The period of raids and looting was largely over by 900, but even King Alfred (d. 899) faced Viking incursions in Wessex and consciously depicted himself as a Christian hero holding the line against pagan invaders. Only his kingdom, in fact, resisted their attacks with complete success. Vikings also intermarried with Anglo-Saxons and expanded their influence by political means. Profiting from English dynastic disorder around the turn of the eleventh century, aristocrats in the Danelaw became brokers of royal power. From 1016 to 1035 the Danish Cnut (Canute) was king of both England and Denmark, briefly uniting the two in a maritime empire. The Scandinavian presence was not exclusively combative, however. They sent peaceful traders to the British Isles—among them Ohthere, whose tale of his voyages is included here. They also left their mark on literature and language, as in the early Middle English romance *Havelock the Dane*, which contains many words borrowed from Old Norse.

PAGAN AND CHRISTIAN: TENSION AND CONVERGENCE

Given that writing in the Roman alphabet was introduced to pre-Conquest England by churchmen, it is not surprising that most texts from the period are written in Latin on Christian subjects. Most writing even in the Old English language was also religious. In Anglo-Saxon England and in the Celtic cultures, vernacular literature tended at first to be orally composed and performed. The body of written vernacular Anglo-Saxon poetry that survives is thus very small indeed, although there are plenty of prose religious works. It is something of a miracle that *Beowulf*, which celebrates the exploits of a pagan hero, was deemed worthy of being copied by scribes who were almost certainly clerics. (In fact, almost all the greatest Anglo-Saxon poetry survives in only a single copy—so tenuous is our link to that past.) Yet the copying of *Beowulf* also hints at the complex interaction of the pagan and Christian traditions in Anglo-Saxon culture.

The conflict between the two traditions was characterized (and perhaps exaggerated) by Christian writers and readers as a struggle between pagan violence and Christian values of forgiveness. The old, deep-seated respect for treasure as a sign of power and achievement seemed to conflict with Christian contempt for worldly goods. In fact, however, pagan Germanic and Christian values were alike in many respects and coexisted with various degrees of mutual influence.

Old English poets explored the tensions as well as the overlap between the two sets of values in two primary poetic modes—the heroic and the elegiac. The heroic mode, of which *Beowulf* is the supreme example, celebrates the values of bravery, loyalty, vengeance, and desire for treasure. The great buckle from Sutton Hoo burial (Color Plate 2) is a surviving artifact of such treasure. The elegiac mode, by contrast, calls the value of these things into question, as at best transient and at worst a worldly distraction from spiritual life. The elegiac speaker, usually an exile, laments the loss of earthly goods—his lord, his comrades, the joys of the mead hall—and, in the case of the short poem known as *The Wanderer*, turns his thoughts to heaven. *Beowulf*, composed most likely by a Christian poet looking back at the deeds of his pagan Scandinavian ancestors, uses elements of both the heroic and the elegiac to focus on the overlap of pagan and Christian virtues. A similar, though less adversarial, interaction of a heroic code and the new religion is also encountered in medieval Irish literature, such as the examples of early Irish verse offered here.

The goals of earthly glory and heavenly salvation that concern Old English poetry are presented primarily as they affect men. Recent scholarship, however, reveals the active roles played in society by Anglo-Saxon women, particularly aristocratic ones. One of these is Aethelflaed, daughter of King Alfred, who co-ruled the kingdom of Mercia with her brother Edward at the turn of the tenth century, taking an active military role in fighting off the Danes. Better known today is Abbess Hilda, who founded and ran the great monastery at Whitby from 657 until her death in 680; five Whitby monks became bishops across England during her rule. Nevertheless, women generally take a marginal role in Old English poetry. In secular works marriages are portrayed as being arranged to strengthen military alliances, in efforts (often doomed) to heal bloody rifts between clans. Women thus function primarily as "peace weavers," a term referring occasionally to their active diplomacy in settling disputes but more often to their passive role in marriage exchanges. This latter role was fraught with danger, for if a truce were broken between the warring groups, the woman would face tragically conflicting loyalties to husband and male kin.

The effect of the Germanic heroic code on women is explored in two tantalizingly short poems that invest the elegiac mode with women's voices: *Wulf and Eadwacer* and *The Wife's Lament*. In both, a woman speaker laments her separation from her lord, whether husband or lover, through some shadowy events of heroic warfare. More indicative of the actual power of aristocratic and religious women in Anglo-Saxon society, perhaps, is the Old English poem *Judith*, a biblical narrative which uses heroic diction reminiscent of that in *Beowulf* to celebrate the heroine's military triumph over the pagan Holofernes.

ORAL POETRY, WRITTEN MANUSCRIPTS

For all their deep linguistic differences and territorial conflicts, the Celts and Anglo-Saxons had affinities in the heroic themes and oral settings of their greatest surviving narratives and in the echoes of a pre-Christian culture that endure there. Indeed, these can be compared to conditions of authorship in oral cultures worldwide, from Homer's Greece to parts of contemporary Africa. In a culture with little or no writing, the singer of tales has an enormously important role as the conservator of the past. In *Beowulf*, for instance, the traditional content and verbal formulas of the poetry of praise are swiftly reworked to celebrate the hero's killing of the monster Grendel:

> Meanwhile a man
> skilled as a singer,   versed in old stories,
> wove a new lay   of truly-linked words.
> So the scop started   his song of Beowulf's
> wisdom and strength,   setting his spell
> with subtle staves.

A poet of this kind (in Anglo-Saxon, a *scop* or "shaper") does not just enhance the great warrior's prestige by praising his hero's ancestors and accomplishments. He also recalls and performs the shared history and beliefs of the entire people, in great feats of memory that make the poet virtually the encyclopedia of his culture. A poet from the oral tradition might also become a singer of the new Christian cosmology, like the illiterate herdsman Caedmon, whom Bede describes as having been called to monastic vows by the Abbess Hilda, in honor of his Christian poems composed in the vernacular oral mode.

In Celtic areas, oral poets had even greater status. The ancient class of learned Irish poets were honored servants of noblemen and kings; they remained as a powerful if reduced presence after the establishment of Christianity. The legal status of such a poet (a *fili*) was similar to that of a bishop, and indeed the *fili* carried out some functions of spells and divination inherited from the pagan priestly class, the druids. The ongoing influence of these poets in Irish politics and culture is reflected in the body of surviving secular literature from medieval Ireland, which is considerably larger than that from Anglo-Saxon England.

In a culture in which a poet has such a wide and weighty role, ranging from entertainer to purveyor of the deepest reaches of religious belief, possession of the word bestows tremendous, even magical power. Even when these tales were copied into manuscripts, their written versions were essentially scripts for later performance, or for memorization.

This attitude of awe toward the word as used by the oral poet was only enhanced by the arrival of Christianity, a faith that attributes creation itself to an act of divine speech. Throughout the Middle Ages and long after orally composed poetry had retreated from many centers of high culture, the power of the word also inhered in its written form, as encountered in certain prized books. Chief among these were the Bible and other books of religious story, especially by such church fathers as Saints Augustine and Jerome, and books of the liturgy. Since these texts bore the authority of divine revelation, the manuscripts that contained them shared in their charisma.

The power of these manuscripts was both reflected and aided by their visual grandeur. Among the highest expressions of the fervor and discipline of early insular monasticism is its production of beautifully copied and exquisitely decorated books of the Bible. The extreme elaboration of their production and the great labor and expense lavished on them suggest their almost holy status. Figures depicted holding a book in the late eighth-century *Book of Kells* (page 10), or writing in the Lindisfarne Gospels, indicate this importance.

The cost and effort of making manuscript books and their very scarcity contributed to their aura. Parchment was produced from animal skins, stretched and scraped. The training and discipline involved in copying texts, especially sacred texts, were great. The decoration of the most ambitious manuscripts involved rare colors, gold leaf, and often supreme artistry. Thus these magnificent manuscripts could become almost magical icons: Bede, for example, tells of scrapings from Irish manuscripts which mixed with water cured the bites of poisonous snakes.

Manuscripts slowly became more widely available. By the twelfth century we hear more of manuscripts in private hands and the beginning of production outside ecclesiastical settings. By the fourteenth century merchants and private scholars were buying books from shops that resembled modern booksellers. The glamour and prestige of

Saint John, from the
Book of Kells. Late 8th
century.

beautiful manuscripts remained, though, even if the sense of their magic faded to a degree. Great families would donate psalters and gospels to religious foundations, with the donor carefully represented in the decoration presenting the book to the Virgin Mary or the Christ child. Spectacular books of private devotion were at once a medium for spiritual meditation and proof of great wealth (see Color Plate 10). Stories of epic conquest like the *Aeneid* would sometimes feature their aristocratic owners' coat of arms.

THE NORMAN CONQUEST

By the time of these developments in book production, though, a gigantic change had occurred. In a single year, 1066, England witnessed the death of the Anglo-Saxon King Edward and the coronation of his disputed successor King Harold, the invasion and triumph of the foreigner William of Normandy, and his own coronation as King William. These events are recorded, from very different perspectives, in *The Anglo-Saxon Chronicle* and the Bayeux Tapestry (page 124). The Normans conquered, with relative ease, an Anglo-Saxon kingdom disordered by civil strife. The monastic

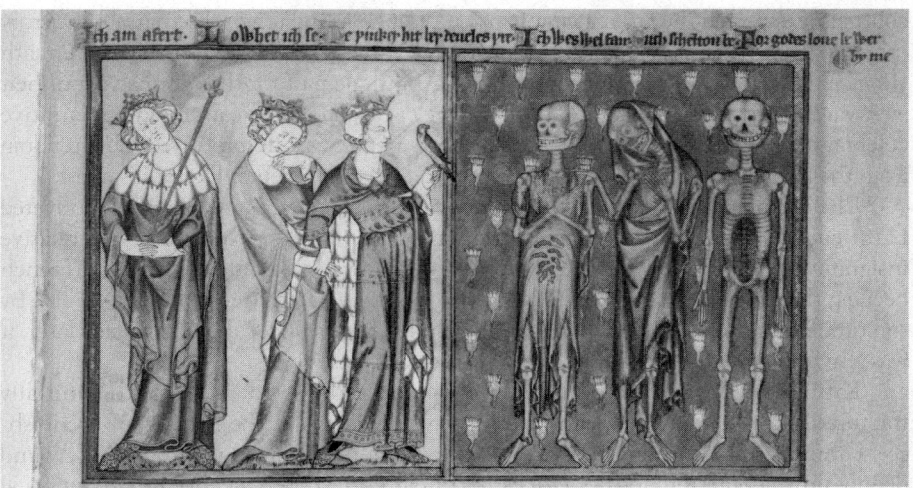

The Three Living and the Three Dead, from *The De Lisle Psalter*. The transience of life, especially of worldly glory, was never far from the medieval imagination. In this image from a Psalter made in the early 14th century for Baron Robert de Lisle, three kings in elegant courtly array face three rotting corpses. While most of the Psalter is in French and Latin, this scene has a "caption" in rhymed Middle English at the top. The kings say in turn (in modernized form), "I am afeared. Lo, what I see! I think that here are devils three." The corpses reply, "I was well fair. Such shalt thou be. For God's love beware by me."

movement had lost much of its earlier fervor and discipline, despite reform in the tenth century. Baronial interests had weakened severely the reign of the late King Edward "the Confessor." On an island that already perceived itself as repeatedly colonized, 1066 nonetheless represented a climactic change, experienced and registered at virtually all levels of social, religious, and cultural experience.

One sign of how great a breach had been opened in England, paradoxically, is the multifaceted effort put forth by conquerors and conquered to maintain—or invent—continuity with the pre-Conquest past. In religious institutions, in dynastic genealogies, in the intersection of history and racial myth, in the forms and records of social institutions, the generations after 1066 sought to absorb a radically changed world yet to ground their world in an increasingly mythicized Anglo-Saxon or Briton antiquity. The Normans and their dynastic successors the Angevins eagerly took up and adapted to their own preoccupations ancient Briton political myths such as that of King Arthur and his court, and the stories of such saintly Anglo-Saxon kings as Oswald and Edward the Confessor.

They promoted narratives of their ancestors, like Wace's *Roman de Rou*, the story of the Normans' founder Rollo, commissioned by Henry II. Geoffrey of Monmouth dedicated his *History of the Kings of England* partly to Henry II's uncle, Robert Duke of Gloucester. In that work Geoffrey links the Celtic myths of King Arthur and his followers to an equally ancient myth that England was founded by descendants of the survivors of Troy; he makes his combined, largely fictive but enormously appealing work available to a Norman audience by writing it in Latin. Geoffrey's story was soon retold in "romance," the French from which vernacular texts took their name. The Angevin court also supported the "romances of antiquity," poems in French that narrate the story of Troy (the *Roman de Troie*), its background (*Roman de Thèbes*), and its aftermath (*Roman d'Eneas*), thus creating a model in the antique past for the Normans and their westward conquest of England. And the *Song of Roland,* the great crusading narrative celebrating the heroic death of Charlemagne's nephew as he protected Christendom from the Spanish Moslems, was probably written in the milieu of Henry II's court.

The Normans brought with them a new system of government, a freshly renovated Latin culture, and most important a new language. Anglo-Saxon sank into relative insignificance at the level of high culture and central government. Norman French became the language of the courts of law, of literature, and of most of the nobility. By the time English rose again to widespread cultural significance, about 250 years later, it was a hybrid that combined Romance and Germanic elements.

Latin offered a lifeline of communication at some social levels of this initially fractured society. The European clerics who arrived under the immigrant archbishops Lanfranc and Anselm brought a new and different learning, and often new and deeply unwelcome religious practices: a celibate priesthood, skepticism about local saints, and newly disciplined monasticism. Yet despite these differences and the tensions that accompanied them, clerics of European or British origin were linked by a common liturgy, a considerable body of shared reading, and most of all a common learned language. Secular as well as religious society were coming to be based more and more on the practical use of the written word: the letter, the charter, the documentary record, and the written book. Whereas Anglo-Saxon England had been governed by the word enacted and performed—a law of oral witness and a culture of oral poets—Norman England increasingly became a land of documents and books.

SOCIAL AND RELIGIOUS ORDER

The famed Domesday Book is a first instance of many of these developments. The Domesday survey was a gigantic undertaking, carried out with a speed that still astonishes between Christmas 1085 and William the Conqueror's death in September 1087. A county-by-county survey of the lands of King William and those held by his tenants-in-chief and subtenants, Domesday also records the obligations of landholders and thus reflects a new feudal system by which, increasingly, land was held in post-Conquest England.

Under the Normans, a nobleman held land from the king as a fief, in exchange for which he owed the king certain military and judicial services, including the provision of armed knights. These knights in turn held land from their lord, to whom they also owed military service and other duties. Some of this land they might keep for their own farming and profit, and the rest they divided among serfs (who were obliged, in theory, to stay on the land to which they were born) and free peasantry. Both groups owed their knight or lord labor and either a portion of their agricultural produce or rents in cash. This system of land tenure was surely more complex and irregular in practice than in the theoretical model called feudalism. For instance, services at all levels were sometimes (and increasingly) commuted to cash payment, and while fiefs were theoretically held only by an individual for a lifetime, increasingly there were expectations that they would be inherited. Royal power gradually grew during the thirteenth and fourteenth centuries, yet the local basis of landholding and social order always acted as a counterbalance, even a block, to royal ambition.

The Domesday Book was only one piece of the multifaceted effort by which the Norman and later kings sought to extend and centralize royal power in their territories. William and his successors established a system of royal justices who traveled throughout the realm and reported ultimately to the king, and an organized royal bureaucracy began to appear. The most powerful and learned of these Anglo-Norman kings was William the Conqueror's great-grandson, Henry II, who ruled from 1154 to 1177. Under Henry, royal justice, bureaucracy, and record-keeping made great advances; the production of documents was centralized and took on more standardized forms, and copies of these documents (called "pipe rolls") began to be produced for later reference and proof.

Along with a stronger royal government, the Normans brought a clergy invigorated both by new learning and by the spirituality of recent monastic reforms. Saint Anselm, the second of the Norman archbishops of Canterbury, was a great prelate and the writer of beautiful and widely influential texts and prayers of private devotion. The Victorines and the Cistercians (inspired in part by Saint Bernard of Clairvaux) also brought a strong mystical streak to English monasticism. All these would bear fruit once again in the fourteenth century in a group of mystics writing in Latin and in English.

On the other hand, the Norman prelates, like their kings, brought an urge toward centralized order in the church and a belief that the church and its public justice (the "canon law") should be independent of secular power. This created frequent conflict with kings and aristocrats, who wanted to extend their judicial power and expected to wield considerable influence in the appointment of church officials.

The most explosive moment in this ongoing controversy occurred in the disagreements between Henry II and Thomas Becket, who was Henry's Chancellor and then Archbishop of Canterbury. Becket's increasingly public refusal to accommodate the king, either in the judicial sphere or the matter of clerical appointments, finally led to his murder by Henry's henchmen in 1170 at the altar of Canterbury Cathedral and his canonization very soon thereafter. A large body of hagiography (narratives of his martyrdom and posthumous miracles) swiftly developed, adding to an already rich tradition of writing about the lives of English saints. As Saint Thomas, Becket became a powerful focus for ecclesiastical ambition, popular devotion and pilgrimage, and religious and secular narrative. In fact, the characters of Chaucer's *Canterbury Tales* tell their stories while making a pilgrimage to his shrine.

At least in theory, feudal tenure involved an obligation of personal loyalty between lord and vassal that was symbolically enacted in the rituals of enfeoffment, in which the lord would bestow a fief on his vassal. This belief was elaborated in a large body of secular literature in the twelfth century and after. Yet feudal loyalty was always fragile and ideologically charged. Vassals regularly resisted the wills of their lord or king when their interests collided, sometimes to the extent of officially withdrawing from the feudal bond. Connected to feudal relations was the notion of a chivalric code among the knightly class (those who fought on horses, *chevaliers*), which involved not just loyalty to the lord but also honorable behavior within the class, even among enemies. Chivalric literature is thus full of stories of captured opponents being treated with the utmost politeness, as indeed happened when Henry II's son Richard was held hostage for years in Germany, awaiting ransom.

The Murder of Thomas Becket, from Matthew Paris's *Historia Major,* mid-13th century.

Similarly, although medieval theories of social order had some basis in fact, they exercised shifting influence within a much more complex social reality. For instance, medieval society was often analyzed by the model of the "three estates"—those who fought (secular aristocrats), those who prayed (the clergy), and those who worked the land (the free and servile peasantry). This model appears more or less explicitly in the poetry of Geoffrey Chaucer. Such a system, though, did not allow for the gradual increase in manufacturing (weaving, pottery, metalwork, even the copying of books) or for the urban merchants who traded in such products. As society became more complex, a model of the "mystical social body" gained popularity, especially in the fourteenth century. Here a wider range of classes and jobs was compared to limbs and other body parts. Even this more flexible image was strictly hierarchical, though. Peasants and laborers were the feet, knights (on the right) and merchants (on the left) were hands, and townspeople were the heart, but the head was made up of kings, princes, and prelates of the church.

CONTINENTAL AND INSULAR CULTURES

The arrival of the Normans, and especially the learned clerics who came then and after, opened England to influences from a great intellectual current that was stirring on the Continent, the "renaissance of the twelfth century," which was to have a significant impact in the centuries that followed. A period of comparative political stability and economic growth made travel easier, and students and teachers were on the move, seeking new learning in Paris and the Loire valley, in northern Italy, and in Toledo with its Arab and Jewish cultures. Schools were expanding beyond the monasteries and into the precincts of urban cathedrals and other religious foundations. Along with offering traditional biblical and theological study, these schools sparked a revived interest in elegant Latin writing, Neoplatonic philosophy, and science deriving from Aristotle.

Because the Normans and Angevins ruled large territories on the Continent, movement across the Channel was frequent; by the mid-twelfth century learned English culture was urbane and international. English clerics like John of Salisbury studied at Chartres and Paris, and texts by eminent speculative and scientific writers like William of Conches and Bernard Silvestris came to England. As these foreign works entered England, education became more ambitious and widely available, and its products show growing contact with the works of classical Latin writers such as Horace, Virgil, Terence, Cicero, Seneca, and Ovid in his erotic as much as in his mythological poetry.

The renewed attention to these works went along with a revival of interest in the *trivium*, the traditional division of the arts of eloquence: grammar, rhetoric, and dialectic. The most aggressive of these was dialectic, a form of logic developed by the Greeks and then rediscovered by Christian Europe from Arab scholars who had preserved and pursued Greek learning. John of Salisbury, who promoted dialectic in his *Metalogicon*, described it with metaphors of military prowess, as though it were an extension of knightly jousting. "Since dialectic is carried on between two persons," he writes, Aristotle's *Topics* "teaches the matched contestants whom it trains and provides with reasons and topics, to handle their proper weapons and engage in verbal, rather than physical conflict." Rhetoric was elaborately codified in technical manuals of poetry. Though in one sense it was merely ornamental, teaching how to flesh out a description or incident with figures of speech, rhetoric could be as coercive as dialectic, though, since it specified strategies of persuasion in a tradition deriving from ancient oratory. Rhetorical texts also instructed the student in letter-writing, increasingly important as an administrative skill and as a form of elevated composition.

The study of the *trivium* generated many Latin school texts and helped foster a high level of Latinity and a self-consciously sophisticated, classicizing literature in the second half of the twelfth century. Some school texts had great influence on vernacular literature, such as the *Poetria Nova* by Geoffrey of Vinsauf, a rhetorical handbook filled with vivid poetic examples. More intriguing is *Pamphilus*, a short Ovidian poem about a seduction, aided by Venus, which turns into a rape. It is thought to have been an exercise in *disputatio*, the oral form that dialectic assumed in the classroom. The poem was immensely popular in the next few centuries and was translated into many vernacular languages. *Pamphilus* was a conduit at once for Ovidian eroticism and for the language of debate on love. Chaucer mentions it as a model of passionate love and seems to have adapted some of its plot devices in his *Troilus and Criseyde*.

While classical Latin literature was often read with a frank interest in pagan ideas and practices, commentators also offered allegorical interpretations that drew pagan stories into the spiritual and cosmological preoccupations of medieval Christianity. Ovid's *Metamorphoses* were thus interpreted in a French poem, the *Ovide Moralisé*, that was clearly known to Chaucer, and in Latin commentaries such as the *Ovidius moralizatus* of Pierre Bersuire. For instance, Ovid describes Jupiter, in the form of a bull, carrying the Tyrian princess Europa into the sea to rape her. Bersuire interprets this as Christ taking on human flesh in order to take up the human soul he loves. Alternatively, he offers an explicitly misogynist allegory, casting Europa as young women who like to see handsome young men—bulls: "They are drawn through the stormy sea of evil temptations and are raped." Neither text is often very subtle in the extraction of Christian or moral analogies from Ovid's stories, yet both were popular and influential, if only because they also tell Ovid's tales before allegorizing them.

Allegory became a complex and fruitful area of the medieval imagination, with profound implications not only for reading, but for artistic production as well. In its simplest sense, an allegorical text takes a metaphor and extends it into narrative, often personifying a quality as a character. For instance, the enormously popular dream vision the *Roman de la Rose* by Guillaume de Lorris and Jean de Meun (which Chaucer translated into English) presents a lady's ambivalence toward courtship as the conflict between such personifications as "Reserve" and "Fair Welcome," both aspects of her own mind. When Christine de Pizan came to challenge the misogynist texts of Western tradition—the *Roman de la Rose* among them—she too chose the allegorical mode. In the *Book of the City of Ladies*, it is three virtues personified as ladies—Reason, Rectitude, and Justice—who refute the slanders of men and who encourage the poet to build a city celebrating female achievements. Medieval writers also employed an allegorical method known as typology, derived from biblical interpretation, in which Old Testament events are seen as literally true but also symbolically predictive of, and fulfilled by, events in the New Testament.

The Continent, particularly France, provided a variety of vernacular influences. French was the international language of aristocratic culture and an important literary language in England; continental French literature was crucial in the rise of courtly literature in Middle English. Many English Arthurian works, including *Sir Gawain and the Green Knight* and Sir Thomas Malory's *Morte Darthur*, are less indebted to English sources than to French romances, whether written on the Continent or in England by authors such as Marie de France and Thomas of Britain. Chaucer borrowed the conventions and imagery of the love poetry of Guillaume de Machaut and Eustache Deschamps, and even the meter of his earlier poetry derives from their French octosyllabic couplets. To a lesser extent, influences from Italy can be seen in Chaucer's use of Dante's *Divine Comedy*, and his extensive borrowing from Petrarch and Boccaccio. Such continental vernacular literatures infiltrated even the Celtic cultures, as we see in the witty mix of Welsh and European traditions in the poems of Dafydd ap Gwilym.

If such writers and records reflect the higher achievements of education in England of the twelfth century and later, literacy was also diffusing in wider circles and new venues. In a society like England's that continued to produce considerable oral and public literature, indeed, the divide between literacy and illiteracy was always unstable and permeable. A secular aristocrat might have a clerk read to him or her; an urbanite could attend and absorb parts of public rituals that involved poems and orations; even a peasant would be able to pick up Latin tags from sermons or the liturgy. Thus Chaucer could imagine a character like the Wife of Bath who, at best semiliterate, could still quote bits of the Latin liturgy. Access to texts and the self-awareness fostered by private reading may have helped promote the social ambitions and disruptions within the mercantile and even peasant classes during the later Middle Ages.

WOMEN, COURTLINESS, AND COURTLY LOVE

Access to books also increased the self-awareness of women. Possession of books that encouraged prayer and private devotion, such as psalters and Books of Hours, appears to have facilitated early language training in the home. The many images in manuscripts of women reading—especially the Virgin Mary and her mother, Saint Anne—have interesting implications for our understanding of women's literacy and cultural roles. (See for instance the illumination from the *Bedford Hours*, Color Plate 10.) A number of aristocratic Norman and Angevin women received good educations at convents. Women in the holy life possessed at least some literacy, though this often may have been minimal indeed. Even well-educated women were more likely to read English or French than Latin, with the exception of liturgical books.

The roles of women in the society and cultural imagination of post-Conquest England are complex and contradictory. No Anglo-Norman woman held ecclesiastical prestige like the Anglo-Saxon Abbess Hilda or other Anglo-Saxon holy women. Women's power seems to have declined in the long term, both in worldly affairs and in the church, as the Normans consolidated their hold on England and imposed their order on society. Nevertheless, ambitious women could have great influence, especially when they seized upon moments of disruption. In civil strife over the succession to King Henry I, the Empress Matilda organized an army, issued royal writs, and in the end guaranteed the accession of her son Henry II. If Henry II's wife, Eleanor of Aquitaine, spent the latter decades of her husband's reign under virtual house arrest, it was largely because she had conspired with her sons to raise an army against her own husband.

Despite the limitations of their actual power, women were the focus, often the worshiped focus, of much of the best imaginative literature of the twelfth and thirteenth centuries; and women were central to the social rituals we associate with courtliness and the idea of courtly love. Despite her later imprisonment, Eleanor of Aquitaine was a crucial influence in the diffusion of courtly ideas from the Continent, especially the south of France; and among the great writers of the century was Marie de France, who was probably related to Henry II. Scholars continue to debate whether the observances of "courtly love" were in fact widely practiced and whether

Grotesques and a Courtly Scene, from the *Ormesby Psalter,* c. 1310–1325.

A Knight, early 14th century. This rubbing from a funerary brass depicts a knight as he presented himself to eternity, sheathed in chain mail and fully armed but with his hands joined in prayer. The dog at his feet is a symbol of fidelity.

its worship of women was empowering or restrictive: the image of the distant, adored lady implies immobility and even silence on her part. Certainly lyrics and narratives that embody courtly values are widespread, even if they often question what they celebrate; and the ideals of courtliness may have had as great an impact through these imaginative channels as through actual enactment.

The ideas and rituals of courtliness reach back to Greek and Roman models of controlled and stylized behavior in the presence of great power. In the Middle Ages, values of discretion and modesty also may have filtered into the secular world from the rigidly disciplined setting of the monasteries. As the society of western Europe took on a certain degree of order in the eleventh and twelfth centuries, courtly attainments began to converge and even compete with simple martial prowess in the achievement of worldly power. The presence of large numbers of armed and ambitious men at the great courts provided at once an opportunity for courtly behavior and the threat of its disruption.

Whatever its historical reality, courtly love as a literary concept had an immense influence. In this it adopted the vocabulary of two distinct traditions: the veneration of the Virgin Mary and the love poetry of Ovid and his heirs. Mariolatry, which has a particularly rich tradition in England, celebrates the perfection of Mary as a woman and mother, who undid the sins of Eve and now intercedes for fallen mankind. Ovid, with his celebration of sensuality and cynical instructions for achieving the lover's desire, provided medieval Europe with a whole catalog of love psychology and erotic persuasion.

The self-conscious command of fine manners, whether the proper way of hunting, dressing, addressing a superior, or wooing a lady, became a key mark of an aristocrat. Great reputations grew around courtly attainment, as in the legends that circulated about Richard I. Centuries later, the hero of *Sir Gawain and the Green Knight* is tested as much through his courtly behavior as through his martial bravery. A literature of etiquette emerged as early as the reign of Henry I in England and continued through the thirteenth century. In the court of Henry II, Daniel of Beccles wrote *Urbanus Magnus*, a verse treatise in Latin on courtesy. In this poem he offers detailed advice in many arenas of specific behavior at court: avoiding frivolity, giving brief counsel, and especially comporting oneself among the wealthy:

> Eating at the table of the rich, speak little
> Lest you be called a chatterbox among the diners.
> Be modest, make reverence your companion.

In a mildly misogynist passage, Daniel especially warns against becoming involved with the lord's wife, even if she makes an overture, as occurs in Marie de France's *Lanval*. Should this happen, Daniel offers polite evasive strategies, skills we see demonstrated in *Sir Gawain and the Green Knight*.

ROMANCE

Courtliness was expressed both in lyric poetry and in a wide range of vernacular narratives that we now loosely call "romances"—referring both to their genre and to the romance language in which they were first written. The Arthurian tradition, featured in this anthology, is only one of many romance traditions; others include the legends of Tristan and Isolde, Alexander, and Havelock the Dane. In romances that focus on courtly love, the hero's devotion to an unapproachable lady tends to elevate his character. Although many courtly romances conclude in a happy and acceptable marriage of hero and heroine, others begin with such a marriage and move to complications or warn of the dangers of transgressive love (as does Marie's *Lanval*). To the extent that they portray women as disruptive agents of erotic desire, some romances take on elements of the misogynist tradition that persisted in clerical thought alongside the adoration of the Virgin. Near the end of *Sir Gawain and the Green Knight*, even the courtly Gawain explodes in a virulent diatribe against women.

Love was not the only subject of romance, however. Stories of love and war typically lead the protagonists into encounters with the uncanny, the marvelous, the taboo. This is not so surprising when we recall the practices of medieval Christianity that brought the believer into daily contact with such miracles as the Eucharist; even chronicles of saints' lives regularly showed the divine will breaking miraculously into everyday life. We may say today that romance looses the hero and heroine onto the landscape of the private or social subconscious; a medieval writer might have stressed that nature itself is imbued with mystery both by God and by other, more shadowy, spiritual forces.

In romances, the line between the mundane and the extraordinary is often highly permeable: an episode may move swiftly from a simple ride to a meeting with a magical lady or malevolent dwarf, as often occurs in Thomas Malory. Romance also seems to be a form of imaginative literature in which medieval society could acknowledge the transgressions of its own ordering principles: adultery, incest, unmotivated martial violence. And it often revisits areas of belief and imagination that official culture long had put aside: *Sir Gawain and the Green Knight*, for instance, features a magical knight who can survive having his head cut off and a powerful aged woman who is called a goddess. Both characters reach back, however indirectly, to pre-Christian figures encountered in early Irish and Welsh stories.

THE RETURN OF ENGLISH

The romances are another of the dense points of contact among the many languages and ethnicities of the medieval British Isles. These powerful and evocative narratives often feature figures of Celtic origin like the British King Arthur and his court who came to French- and English-language culture through the Latin *History* by Geoffrey of Monmouth. Such transmission is typical of the linguistic mix in post-Conquest England. The language of the aristocracy was French, used in government and law as well as in the nascent vernacular literature. A few conservative monasteries continued the famed *Anglo-Saxon Chronicle* in its original language after the Conquest. But increasingly English or an evolving form of Anglo-Saxon was the working language of the peasantry. Mixed-language households must have appeared as provincial Anglo-Saxon gentry began, quite quickly, to intermarry with the Normans and their descendants. The twelfth-century satirist Nigel of Canterbury (or "Wireker"), author of the *Mirror of Fools*, came from just such a mixed family.

Few writings in Middle English survive from the late twelfth century, and very little of value besides the extraordinary *Brut* of Layamon, which retranslates much of Geoffrey of Monmouth's *History* from a French version. A manuscript containing the earliest English lyric in this collection, the thirteenth-century *Cuckoo Song*, can suggest the linguistic complexity of the era: it contains lyrics in English and French, and instructions for performance in Latin.

English began to reenter the world of official discourse in the thirteenth century. Communications between the church and the laity took place increasingly in English, and by the late 1250s, Archbishop Sewal of York tended to reject papal candidates for bishoprics if they did not have good English. In 1258 King Henry III issued a proclamation in Latin, French, and English, though the circumstances were unusual. Teaching glossaries include a growing number of English words, as well as the French traditionally used to explain difficult Latin.

The fourteenth century inaugurated a distinct change in the status of English, however, as it became the language of parliament and a growing number of governmental activities. We hear of Latin being taught in the 1340s through English rather than French. In 1362 a statute tried (but failed) to switch the language of law courts from French to English, and in 1363 Parliament was opened in English. The period also witnesses tremendous activity in translating a wide range of works into English, including Chaucer's version of Boethius' *Consolation of Philosophy* and the Wycliffite translations of the Bible, completed by 1396. Finally, at the close of the century, the Rolls of Parliament record in Latin the overthrow of Richard II, but they feature Henry IV (in what was probably a self-consciously symbolic gesture) claiming the throne in a brief, grave speech in English and promising to uphold "the gude lawes and custumes of the Rewme."

The reemergence of English allowed an extraordinary flowering of vernacular literature, most notably the achievements of Chaucer, Langland, and the anonymous genius who wrote *Sir Gawain and the Green Knight*. It would be more accurate, nevertheless, to speak of the reemergence of "Englishes" in the second half of the fourteenth century. The language scholars now call Middle English divides into four quite distinct major dialects in different regions of the island. These dialects were in many ways mutually unintelligible, so that Chaucer, who was from London in the Southeast Midlands, might have been hard-pressed to understand *Sir Gawain and the Green Knight*, written in the West Midlands near Lancashire. (Certainly Chaucer was aware of dialects and mimics some northern vocabulary in his *Canterbury Tales*.) London was the center of government and commerce in this era and later the place of early book printing, which served to stabilize the language. Thus Chaucer's dialect ultimately dominated and developed into modern English. Therefore English-speaking students today can read Chaucer in the original without much difficulty, whereas *Sir Gawain* may seem virtually a foreign tongue. As a result, the latter work is offered in translation in this anthology. (For a practical guide to Chaucer's Middle English, also helpful in reading some of the lyrics and plays in this section, see pages 249–51.)

Not only is *Sir Gawain* written in a dialect different from that of Chaucer's London, it also employs a quite distinct poetic style which descends from the alliterative meter of Old English poetry, based on repetitions of key consonants and on general patterns of stress. By contrast, the rhymed syllabic style used by poets like Chaucer developed under the influence of medieval French poetry and its many lyric forms. Fourteenth-century alliterative poetry was part of a revival that occurred in the North and West of the country, at a time when the form would have seemed old fashioned to many readers in the South. In the next two centuries, in a region even more distant from London, alliterative poetry or its echoes persisted in the Middle Scots poetry of William Dunbar, Robert Henryson, and Gavin Douglas.

POLITICS AND SOCIETY IN THE FOURTEENTH CENTURY

The fourteenth-century authors wrote in a time of enormous ferment, culturally and politically as well as linguistically. During the second half of the fourteenth century, new social and theological movements shook past certainties about the divine right of kings, the division of society among three estates, the authority of the church, and the role of women. An optimistic backward view can see in that time the struggle of the peasantry for greater freedom, the growing power of the Commons in Parliament, and the rise of a mercantile middle class. These changes often appeared far darker at the time, though, with threatening, even apocalyptic implications.

The forces of nature also cast a shadow across the century. In a time that never produced large agricultural surpluses, poor harvests led to famine in the second and third decades of the century, and an accompanying deflation drove people off the land. In 1348 the Black Death arrived in England, killing at least 35 percent of the population by 1350. Plague struck violently three more times before 1375, emptying whole villages. Overall, as much as half the population may have died.

The kingship was already in trouble. After the consolidation of royal power under Henry II and the Angevins in the twelfth century, the regional barons began to reassert their power. In a climactic confrontation in 1215, they forced King John to sign the Magna Carta, guaranteeing (in theory at least) their traditional rights and privileges as well as due process in law and judgment by peers. In the fourteenth century the monarchy came under considerable new pressures. Edward II (1307–1327) was deposed by one of his barons, Roger de Mortimer, and with the connivance of his own queen, Isabella. His son Edward III had a long and initially brilliant reign, marked by great military triumphs in a war against France, but the conflict dragged on so long that it became known as the Hundred Years' War. Edward III's reign was marked at home by famine, deflation, and then, most horribly, plague. His later years were marked by premature senility and control by a court circle. These years were further darkened by the death of that paragon of chivalry, Edward's son and heir-apparent, Edward "The Black Prince." Edward's successor, the Black Prince's son Richard II, launched a major peace initiative in the Hundred Years' War and became a great patron of the arts, but he was also capable of great tyranny. In 1399, like his great-grandfather, he was deposed. An ancient and largely creaky royal bureaucracy had difficulty running a growing mercantile economy, and when royal justice failed to control crime in the provinces, it was increasingly replaced by local powers.

The aristocracy too experienced pressures from the increased economic power of the urban merchants and from the peasants' efforts to exploit labor shortages and win better control over their land. The aristocrats responded with fierce, though only partly successful, efforts to limit wages and with stricter and more articulate divisions within society, even between the peerage and gentry. It is not clear, however, that fourteenth-century aristocrats perceived themselves as a threatened order. If anything, events may have pressed them toward a greater class cohesion, a more self-conscious pursuit of chivalric culture and values. The reign of Edward III saw the foundation of the royal Order of the Garter, a select group of nobles honored for their chivalric accomplishments as much as their power (the order is almost certainly evoked at the close of *Sir Gawain and the Green Knight*). Edward further exploited the Arthurian myth in public rituals such as tournaments and Round Tables. The ancient basis of the feudal tie, land tenure, began to give way to contract and payment in the growing, hierarchicalized retinues of the period. These were still lifelong relationships between lord and retainer, nevertheless, and contemporary historians of aristocratic sympathies like Jean Froissart idealize an ongoing community of chivalric conduct that could reach even across combating nations.

The second estate, the church, was also troubled—in part, paradoxically, because of the growing and active piety of the laity. Encouraged by the annual confession that had been required since the Fourth Lateran Council of 1215, laymen increasingly took control of their own spiritual lives. But the new emphasis on confession also led to clerical corruption. Mendicant (begging) friars, armed with manuals of penance, spread across the countryside to confess penitents in their own homes and sometimes accepted money for absolving them. Whether or not these abuses were truly widespread, they inspired much anticlerical satire—as is reflected in the works of Chaucer—and the Church's authority diminished in the process. The traditional priesthood, if better educated, was also more worldly than in the past, increasingly pulled from parish service into governmental bureaucracy; it too faced widespread literary satire. Well aware of clerical venality, the church nevertheless fearfully resisted the criticisms and innovations of "reforming clerics" like John Wycliffe and his supporters among the gentry, the "Lollard knights." The church's control over religious experience was further complicated and perhaps undermined by the rise of popular mysticism, among both the clergy and the laity, which was difficult to contain within the traditional ecclesiastical hierarchy.

The third estate, the commoners, was the most problematic and rapidly evolving of the three in the fourteenth century. The traditional division of medieval society into three estates had no place for the rising mercantile bourgeoisie and grouped them with the peasants who worked the land. In fact the new urban wealthy formed a class quite of their own. Patrons and consumers of culture, they also served in the royal bureaucracy under Edward III, as is illustrated by the career of Geoffrey Chaucer who came from just such a background. Yet only the wealthiest married into the landed gentry, and poor health conditions in the cities made long mercantile dynasties uncommon. Cities in anything like a modern sense were few and retained rural features. Houses often had gardens, even orchards, and pigs (and pig dung) filled the narrow, muddy streets. Only magnates built in stone; only they and ecclesiastical institutions had the luxury of space and privacy. Otherwise, cities were crowded and dirty—the suburbs especially disreputable—and venues for communicable disease.

The peasants too had a new sense of class cohesion. Events had already loosened the traditional bond of serfs to the land on which they were born, and the plagues further shifted the relative economic power of landowning and labor. As peasants found they could demand better pay, fiercely repressive laws were passed to stop them. These and other discontents, like the arrival of foreign labor and technologies, led to the Rising of 1381 (also known as the Peasants' Revolt). Led by literate peasants and renegade priests, the rebels attacked aristocrats, foreigners, and some priests. They were swiftly and violently put down, but the event was nevertheless a watershed and haunted the minds of the English.

Chaucer virtually ignored the revolt, aside from a brief comic reference in *The Nun's Priest's Tale;* it remains unclear, though, whether Chaucer's silence reflects comfortable bourgeois indifference or stems from deep anxiety and discomfort. At the same time, these disruptions introduced a period of cultural ferment, and the mercantile middle class also provided a creative force, appearing (though not without some nervous condescension) in some of Chaucer's most enduring characters like *The Canterbury Tales'* Merchant, the Wife of Bath, and the Miller.

It is both from this new middle class and from the established upper class that wider choices in the lives of women emerged in the later Middle Ages. Their social and political power had been curtailed both by clerical antifeminism and by the increasingly centralized government during the twelfth and thirteenth centuries. Starting in the fourteenth century, however, women began to regain an increased voice and presence. Among the aristocracy, Edward II's wife Isabella was an important player in events that brought about the king's deposition. And at the end of the century, Edward III's mistress Alice Perrers was widely criticized for her avarice and her influence on the aging king. Still, for the representation of women's voices in this period we are largely dependent on the fictional creations of men. Chaucer's famous Wife of Bath, for instance, strikes many modern readers as an articulate voice opposing women's repression and expressing their ambitions, but for all her critique of the antifeminist stereotypes of the church, she is in many ways their supreme embodiment. And in a number of Middle English lyrics, probably by men, the woman's voice may evoke scorn rather than pity as she laments her seduction and abandonment by a smooth-talking man, usually a cleric.

THE SPREAD OF BOOK CULTURE IN THE FIFTEENTH CENTURY

Geoffrey Chaucer died in 1400, a convenient date for those who like their eras to end with round numbers. Certainly literary historians have often closed off the English Middle Ages with Chaucer and left the fifteenth century as a sort of drab and undefined waiting period before the dawn of the Renaissance. Yet parts of fifteenth-century England are sites of vital and burgeoning literary culture. Book ownership spread more and more widely. Already in the late fourteenth century, Chaucer had imagined a fictional Clerk of Oxford with a solid collection of university texts despite his relative poverty. More of the urban bourgeoisie bought books and even had appealing collections assembled for them. When printing came to England in the later fifteenth century, books became even more available, though still not cheap.

Whether in manuscript or print, a swiftly growing proportion of these books was in English. The campaigns of Henry V in the second decade of the fifteenth century and his death in 1422 mark England's last great effort to reclaim the old Norman and Angevin territories on the Continent. With the loss of all but a scrap of this land and the decline of French as a language of influence, these decades consolidate a notion of cultural and nationalistic Englishness. The Lancastrian kings, Henry the Fourth, Fifth, and Sixth, seem to have adopted English as the medium for official culture and patronized translators like Lydgate. Later in the period William Caxton made a great body of French and English texts available to aristocratic and middle-class readers, both by translating and by diffusing them in the new medium of print.

Ancient aristocratic narratives continued to evolve, as in Thomas Malory's retelling of the Arthurian story in his *Morte Darthur*, one of the books printed by Caxton. Malory works mostly from French prose versions but trims back much of the exploration of love and the uncanny; the result is a recharged tale of chivalric battle and familial and political intrigue. Other continental and local traditions are revived in another courtly setting by a group of Scots poets including William Dunbar.

As more and more commoners had educational and financial access to books, they also participated in a lively public literary culture in towns and cities. The fifteenth century sees the flowering of the great dramatic "mystery cycles," sets of plays on religious themes produced and in part performed by craft guilds of larger towns in the Midlands and North. Included here is a brilliant sample, *The Second Play of the Shepherds* from Wakefield. Probably written by clerics, this play is nonetheless dense with the preoccupations of contemporary working people and enriched by implicit analogies between the lives of their actors and the biblical events they portray. Lyrics and political poems continue to flourish. Sermons remain a popular and widespread form of religious instruction and literary production. And highly literary public rituals, such as Henry V's triumphal civic entries as he returned from his French campaigns, are part of Lancastrian royal propaganda.

By the time Caxton was editing and printing Malory in 1485 with an eye to sales and profit, over eight hundred years had passed since Caedmon is said to have composed his first Christian hymn under angelic direction. The idea of the poet had moved from a version of magician and priest to something more like a modern author; and the dominant model of literary transmission was shifting from listening to an oral performance to reading a book privately. Chaucer, that most bookish of poets, is a case in point. Many of his early poems refer to the pleasures of reading, not only for instruction but even as a mere pastime, often to avoid insomnia. Chaucer, of course, read his books and disseminated his own work in handwritten manuscript; in his humorous lyric *To His Scribe Adam* he expresses his frustration with copyists who might mistranscribe his words.

Despite such private bookishness, however, a more public and oral literary culture never disappeared from medieval Britain. Considerable interdependence between oral and literate modes of communication remained; poetry was both silently read and orally performed. In *The Canterbury Tales*, for instance, when the pilgrim Chaucer apologizes for the bawdiness of *The Miller's Tale*, he suggests that if the listener/reader does not like what he *hears*, he should simply turn the *page* and choose another tale. At the same time, literate clerics practiced what we might call learned orality, through lectures or disputations at Oxford and Cambridge or from the pulpit in a more popular setting. The popular orality of minstrel performance, harking back however distantly to the world of the Anglo-Saxon *scop* and the Irish *fili*, was also exploited with great self-consciousness by literate poets. *Sir Gawain and the Green Knight* presents itself as an oral performance, based on a tale that the narrator has heard recited. By contrast, Chaucer gently twits minstrels in his marvelous parody of popular romance, *Sir Thopas*. Chaucer remains a learned poet whose greatest achievement, paradoxically, was the presentation of fictional oral performances—the tale-telling of the Canterbury pilgrims.

The speed with which communication technologies are changing in our own era has heightened our awareness of such changes in the past. We are now closing the era of the book and moving into the era of the endlessly malleable electronic text. In many ways the means by which we have come to receive and transmit information—television, radio, CD-ROM, Internet—mix orality and literacy in a fashion wholly new yet also intriguingly reminiscent of the later Middle Ages. In contrast to the seeming fixity of texts in the intervening centuries, contemporary literary culture may be recovering the sense of textual and cultural fluidity that brought such dynamism to literary creation in the Middle Ages.

Before the Norman Conquest

Beowulf

Beowulf has come down to us as if by chance, for it is preserved only in a single manuscript now in the British Library, Cotton Vitellius A.xv, which almost perished in a fire in 1731. An anonymous poem in the West Saxon dialect of Old English, it may stretch back as early as the late eighth century, although recent scholars think the version we now have was composed within one hundred years of its transcription in the late tenth century. If the later date is correct, this first "English epic" could have appealed to one of the Viking kings who ruled in northern and eastern England. This would help explain a king's burial at sea, a Viking practice, that occurs early in the poem (page 32), and the setting of most of the poem's action in Scandinavia (see map, page 28). Although it was studied by a few antiquarians during the early modern period, *Beowulf* remained virtually unknown until its first printing in 1815, and it was only in the twentieth century that it achieved a place in the canon, not just as a cultural artifact or a good adventure story but as a philosophical epic of great complexity and power.

Several features of *Beowulf* make its genre problematic: the vivid accounts of battles with monsters link it to the folktale, and the sense of sorrow for the passing of worldly things mark it as elegiac. Nevertheless, it is generally agreed to be the first postclassical European epic. Like the *Iliad* and the *Odyssey*, it is a primary epic, originating in oral tradition and recounting the legendary wars and exploits of its audience's tribal ancestors from the heroic age.

The values of Germanic tribal society are indeed central to *Beowulf*. The tribal lord was held to ideals of extraordinary martial valor. More practically, he rewarded his successful followers with treasure that symbolized their mutual obligations. A member of the lord's *comitatus*—his band of warriors—was expected to follow a rigid code of heroic behavior stressing bravery, loyalty, and willingness to avenge lord and comrades at any cost. He would suffer the shame of exile if he should survive his lord in battle; the speaker of *The Wanderer* (pages 130–33) may be such a man. Such values are explicitly invoked at the end of *Beowulf,* when Wiglaf, the hero's only loyal retainer, upbraids his comrades for having abandoned Beowulf to the dragon: he says that their prince wasted his war gear on them, and predicts the demise of their people, the Geats, once their ancient enemies, the Swedes, hear that Beowulf is dead.

Beowulf offers an extraordinary double perspective, however. First, for all its acceptance of the values of pagan heroic code, it also refers to Christian concepts that in many cases conflict with them. Although all characters in the poem—Danes, Swedes, and Geats, as well as the monsters—are pagan, the monster Grendel is described as descended from Cain and destined for hell. It is the joyous song of creation at Hrothgar's banquet, reminiscent of Genesis 1, that inspires Grendel to renew his attacks. Furthermore, while violence in the service of revenge is presented as the proper way for Beowulf to respond to inhuman assailants such as Grendel's mother, the narrator expresses a regretful view, perhaps influenced by Christianity, of the unending chain of violence engaged in by feuding tribes. And although the Danish king Hrothgar uses wealth as a kind of social sacrament when he lavishly rewards Beowulf for his military aid, he simultaneously invokes God in a "sermon" warning him against excessive pride in his youthful strength. This rich division of emotional loyalty probably arises from a poet and audience of Christians who look back at their pagan ancestors with both pride and grief, stressing the intersection of pagan and Christian values in an effort to reconcile the two. By restricting his biblical references to events in the Old Testament, the poet shows the Germanic revenge ethic as consistent with the Old Law of retribution, and leaves implicit its conflict with the New Testament injunction to forgive one's enemies.

Peoples and places in *Beowulf*, after F. Klaeber.

The style *of Beowulf* is simultaneously a challenge and a reward to the modern reader. Some of its features, such as the variation of an idea in different words—which would have been welcomed by a listening, and often illiterate, audience—can seem repetitious to a literate audience. The poem's somewhat archaic diction can make it seem difficult as well, although the translators of the version included here have adopted a more straightforward and colloquial style than was often used in the past. By rendering the opening word "Hwaet!" as "So!" rather than "Hark!" or "Lo!" they have avoided the stuffiness of earlier versions. They have also tried to reduce the confusion arising from the poem's use of patronymics—phrases identifying a character by his father's name. Though they generally retain the designations of Beowulf as "Ecgtheow's son," they often substitute the name of a minor character for the poem's patronymic, rendering "Ecglaf's son" as "Unferth," for instance.

Two other stylistic features that are indebted to the poem's oral origin are highly admired today. First, like other Old English poems, *Beowulf* uses alliteration as a structural principle, beginning three of the four stressed words in a line with the same letter. The translators have sought the same effect, even when departing considerably from the original language, as when they render the line, "waes se grimma gaest Grendel haten" in the passage below as "a horror from hell, hideous Grendel." The poet also uses compound words, such as *mearcstapa* ("borderland-prowler") and *fifelcynnes* ("of monsterkind"), with unusual inventiveness and force. A specific type of compound used for powerful stylistic effects is the "kenning," a kind of compressed metaphor, such as "swan-road" for "ocean" or "wave-courser" for "ship." The kennings resemble the Old English riddles in their teasing, enigmatic quality.

On a larger narrative level is another stylistic feature, also traceable to the poem's oral roots: the tendency to digress into stories tangential to the action of the main plot. The poet's digressions, however, actually contribute to his artistry of broad contrasts—youth and age, joy and sorrow, good and bad kingship. For instance, Hrothgar, while urging humility and generosity on the victorious Beowulf, tells the story of the proud and parsimonious King Heremod. Similarly, when Beowulf returns home in glory to the kingdom of the Geats, the poet praises his uncle Hygelac's young Queen Hygd by contrasting her with the bad Queen Modthryth, who lost her temper and sent her suitors to death.

These episodes also return to prominent themes like nobility, heroic glory, and the distribution of treasure. Such return to key themes, as well as the poem's formulaic repetition and stylistic variation, all bear comparison to insular art of its time. As seen in the page from the *Book of Kells* illustrated on page 10, the dense repetition of lines and intertwined curves, even zoomorphic shapes (often called interlace), competes for attention with the central image of Saint John. This intricately crafted biblical image, like the royal treasure from Sutton Hoo ship burial (Color Plate 2), help remind us that the extraordinary artistic accomplishments of Anglo-Saxon culture went hand-in-hand with its nostalgia for heroic violence.

The poet uses digression and repetition in an especially subtle way to foreshadow dark events to come. To celebrate Beowulf's victory over Grendel, the scop at Hrothgar's hall sings of events of generations earlier, in which a feud caused the deaths of a Danish princess's brother and son. Although this story has nothing to do with the main plot of the poem, there is an implied parallel a few lines later, when, ominously, Hrothgar's queen Wealtheow hints that her husband's nephew Hrothulf should treat her young sons honorably, remembering the favors Hrothgar has shown him, and soon after, she urges Beowulf also to be kind to them. The original audience would have known that after Hrothgar's death, his queen will suffer a disaster like that of the princess in the song. The poet thus applies his broad principle of comparison and contrast to complex narrative situations as well as to simpler concepts such as good and bad kings. It is the often tragic tenor of these digressions that evokes much of the dark mood that suffuses *Beowulf*, even in its moments of heroic triumph.

The following passage from the original Old English, which has been translated literally, illustrates some of the stylistic features of *Beowulf* discussed above.*

Swā ðā drihtguman   drēamum lifdon,
100   ēadiglice,   oð ðæt ān ongan
fyrene fre(m)man   fēond on helle;
wæs se grimma gæst   Grendel hāten,
mǣre mearcstapa,   sē þe mōras hēold,
fen ond fæsten;   fifelcynnes eard
105   wonsǣli wer   weardode hwile,
siþðan him Scyppend   forscrifen haefde
in Cāines cynne—   þone cwealm gewraec
ēce Drihten,   þaes þe hē Abel slōg;
ne gefeah hē þǣre fǣðe,   ac hē hine feor forwraec,
110   Metod for þȳ māne   mancynne fram.

And so the warriors   lived in joy
100   happily   until one began
the commit crimes,   a fiend from hell
the grim demon   was called Grendel,
notorious borderland-prowler   who dwelt in the moors
fen and stronghold;   the home of monsterkind
105   this cursed creature   occupied for a long while
since the Creator   had condemned him
as the kin of Cain—   he punished the killing,
the Eternal Lord,   because he slew Abel;
He did not rejoice in that evil deed,   but He banished him far
110   from mankind,   God, in return for the crime.

*The passage is taken from *Beowulf and the Fight at Finnsburg*, 3rd ed., ed. Frederick Klaeber (Boston: D. C. Heath, 1950). The translation is by Anne Schotter.

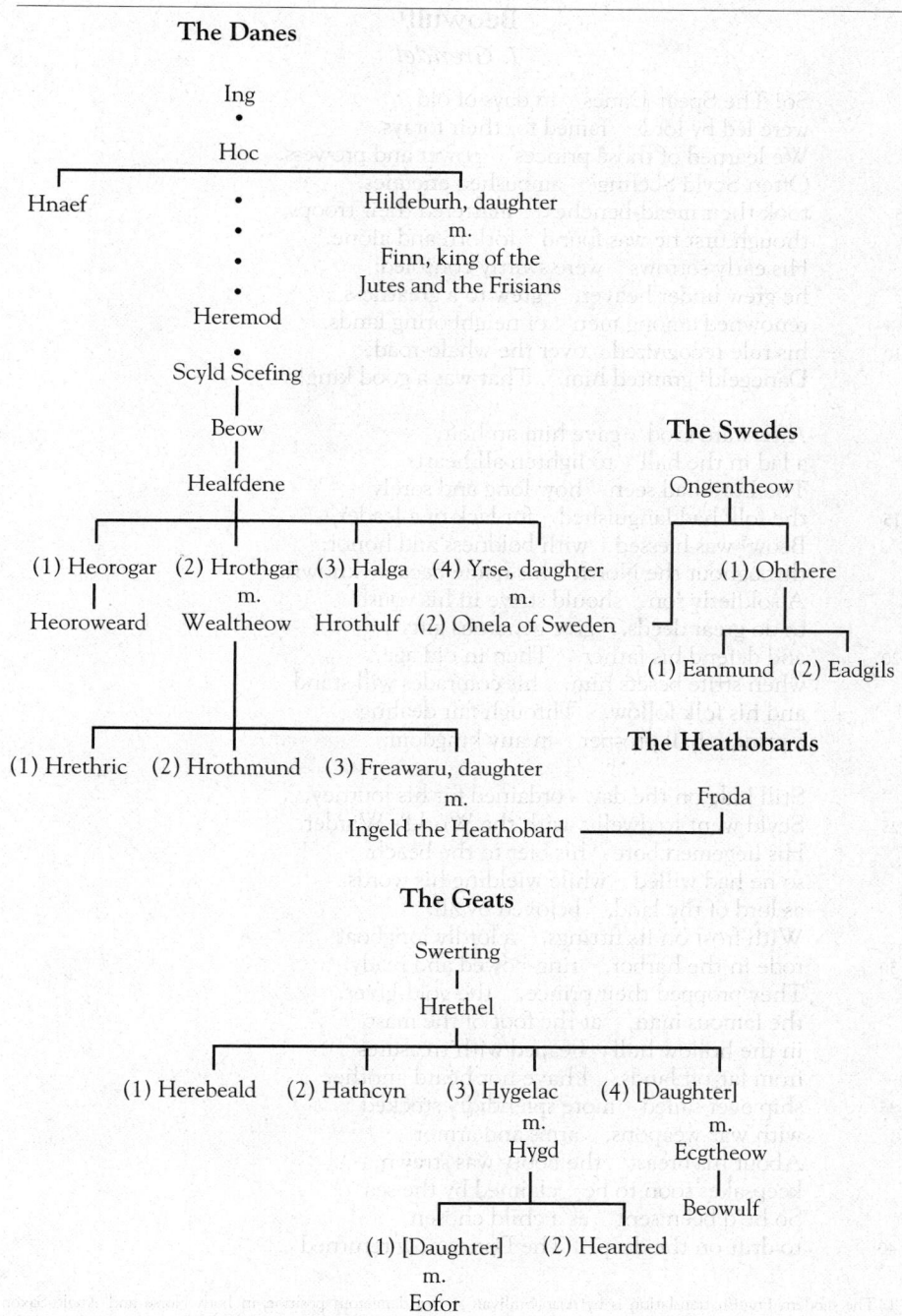

Royal genealogies of the Northern European tribes according to the *Beowulf* text.

Beowulf[1]

I. Grendel

So! The Spear-Danes   in days of old
were led by lords   famed for their forays.
We learned of those princes'   power and prowess.
Often Scyld Scefing[2]   ambushed enemies,
5   took their mead-benches,   mastered their troops,
though first he was found   forlorn and alone.[3]
His early sorrows   were swiftly consoled:
he grew under heaven,   grew to a greatness
renowned among men   of neighboring lands,
10   his rule recognized   over the whale-road,
Danegeld[4] granted him.   That was a good king!

Afterward God   gave him an heir,
a lad in the hall   to lighten all hearts.
The Lord had seen   how long and sorely
15   the folk had languished   for lack of a leader.
Beow[5] was blessed   with boldness and honor;
throughout the North   his name became known.
A soldierly son   should strive in his youth
to do great deeds,   give generous gifts
20   and defend his father.   Then in old age,
when strife besets him,   his comrades will stand
and his folk follow.   Through fair dealing
a prince shall prosper   in any kingdom.

Still hale on the day   ordained for his journey,
25   Scyld went to dwell   with the World's Warder.
His liegemen bore   his bier to the beach:
so he had willed   while wielding his words
as lord of the land,   beloved by all.
With frost on its fittings,   a lordly longboat
30   rode in the harbor,   ring-bowed and ready.
They propped their prince,   the gold-giver,
the famous man,   at the foot of the mast,
in the hollow hull   heaped with treasures
from far-off lands.   I have not heard another
35   ship ever sailed   more splendidly stocked
with war-weapons,   arms and armor.
About his breast   the booty was strewn,
keepsakes soon to be   claimed by the sea.
So he'd been sent   as a child chosen
40   to drift on the deep.   The Danes now returned

---

1. The modern English translation is by Alan Sullivan and Timothy Murphy (2002).
2. The traditional founder of the Danish royal house. His name means "shield" or "protection" of the "sheaf," suggesting an earlier association in Norse mythology with the god of vegetation. The Danes are known afterward as "Scyldings," descendants of Scyld.
3. Scyld Scefing arrives among the Danes as a foundling, a dangerous position in both Norse and Anglo-Saxon cultures. Solitaries and outcasts were generally regarded with suspicion; it is a tribute to Scyld Scefing that he surmounted these obstacles to become the leader and organizer of the Danish people.
4. Gold paid as tribute to the Danes.
5. The manuscript reads "Beowulf" here, the copyist's mind having skipped ahead to the story's protagonist.

treasures no less   than those they had taken,
and last they hoisted   high overhead
a golden banner   as they gave the great one
back to the brine   with heavy hearts
45   and mournful minds.   Men cannot say,
though clever in council   or strong under sky,
who might have landed   that shipload of loot.

But the son of Scyld   was hailed in the strongholds
after the father   had fared far away,
50   and he long ruled   the lordly Scyldings.
A son was born   unto Beow also:
proud Healfdene,   who held his high seat,
battle-hardened   and bold in old age.
Four offspring   descended from Healfdene,
55   awake in the world: Heorogar, Hrothgar,
kindly Halga;   I have heard that the fourth
was Onela's queen[6]   and slept with the sovereign
of warlike Swedes.
                     Hrothgar was granted
swiftness for battle   and staunchness in strife,[7]
60   so friends and kinfolk   followed him freely.
His band of young soldiers   swelled to a swarm.
In his mind he mulled   commanding a meadhall
higher than humankind   ever had heard of,
and offering everyone,   young and old,
65   all he could give   that God had granted,
save common land   and commoners' lives.
Then, I am told,   he tackled that task,
raising the rafters   with craftsmen summoned
from many kingdoms   across Middle-Earth.
70   They covered it quickly   as men count the time,
and he whose word   held the land whole
named it Heorot,[8]   highest of houses.
The prince did not fail   to fulfill his pledge:
feasts were given,   favor and fortune.
75   The roof reared up;   the gables were great,
awaiting the flames   which would flare fiercely
when oaths were broken,   anger awakened;
but Heorot's ruin   was not yet at hand.[9]

Each day, one evil   dweller in darkness
80   spitefully suffered   the din from that hall
where Hrothgar's men   made merry with mead.
Harp-strings would sound,   and the song of the scop

---

6. The daughters of Germanic royal families were married to the heads of opposing tribes in an attempt to cement military alliances. Often, as here, they are not named in the poem.

7. Significantly, Hrothgar is not the first-born of his generation. Leadership of the tribe was customarily conferred by acclamation upon the royal candidate who showed the greatest promise and ability.

8. The name of Hrothgar's hall in Anglo-Saxon literally means "hart" or "stag," a male deer. The epithet "adorned with horns," which is applied to Heorot later, may further suggest its function as a hunting lodge.

9. The peace concluded between the Danes and the Heathobards through intermarriage is already doomed before it has taken place. The events foreshadowed here will occur long after the time of the poem.

would recount the tales   told of time past:
whence mankind had come,   and how the Almighty
85 had fashioned the world   with its fair fields
set in wide waters,   with sun and moon
lifted on high   and lighting the lands
for Earth's first dwellers,   with forests everywhere
branching and blooming,   with life breathing
90 in all kinds of creatures.
                         So the king's thanes
gathered in gladness;   then crime came calling,
a horror from hell,   hideous Grendel,
wrathful rover   of borders and moors,
holder of hollows,   haunter of fens.
95 He had lived long   in the land of the loathsome,
born to the band   whom God had banished
as kindred of Cain,   thereby requiting
the slayer of Abel.[1]   Many such sprang
from the first murderer: monsters and misfits,
100 elves and ill-spirits,   also those giants
whose wars with the Lord   earned them exile.

After nightfall   he nosed around Heorot,
saw how swordsmen   slept in the hall,
unwary and weary   with wine and feasting,
105 numb to the sorrows   suffered by men.
The cursed creature,   cruel and remorseless,
swiftly slipped in.   He seized thirty thanes
asleep after supper,   shouldered away
what trophies he would,   and took to his lair
110 pleased with the plunder,   proud of his murders.

When daylight dawned   on the spoils of slaughter,
the strength of the fiend   was readily seen.
The feast was followed   by fits of weeping,
and cries of outrage   rose in the morning.
115 Hrothgar the strong   sank on his throne,
helpless and hopeless,   beholding the carnage,
the trail of the terror,   a trouble too wrathful,
a foe too ferocious,   too steadfast in rage,
ancient and evil.   The evening after
120 he murdered again   with no more remorse,
so fixed was his will   on that wicked feud.
Henceforth the fearful   were easily found
elsewhere, anywhere   far from the fiend,
bedding in barns,   for the brutal hall-thane
125 was truly betokened   by terrible signs,
and those who escaped   stayed safer afar.

So wrath fought alone   against rule and right;
one routed many;   the mead-hall stood empty.
Strongest of Spear-Danes,   Hrothgar suffered

---

1. See Genesis 4.3–16.

130   this fell affliction   for twelve winters' time.
       As his woes became known   widely and well,
       sad songs were sung   by the sons of men:
       how season on season,   with ceaseless strife,
       Grendel assailed   the Scyldings' sovereign.
135   The monster craved   no kinship with any,
       no end to the evil   with wergeld[2] owed;
       nor might a king's   council have reckoned
       on quittance come   from the killer's hand.
       The dark death-shadow   daunted them all,
140   lying in ambush   for old and young,
       secretly slinking   and stalking by night.
       No man knows where   on the misty moor
       the heathen keepers   of hell-runes[3] wander.

       So over and over   the loathsome ogre
145   mortally menaced   mankind with his crimes.
       Raiding by night,   he reigned in the hall,
       and Heorot's high   adornments were his,
       but God would not grant   throne-gifts to gladden
       a scourge who spurned   the Sovereign of Heaven.

150   Stricken in spirit,   Hrothgar would often
       closet his council   to ponder what plan
       might be deemed best   by strong-minded men.
       Sometimes the elders   swore before altars
       of old war-idols,   offering prayers
155   for the soul-slayer   to succor their people.[4]
       Such was their habit,   the hope of heathens:
       with hell in their hearts,   they were lost to the Lord.
       Their inmost minds   knew not the Almighty;
       they never would worship   the world's true protector.
160   Sorry is he   who sears his soul,
       afflicted by flames   he freely embraced.
       No cheer for the chastened!   No change for the better!
       But happy is he   who trusts in heaven
       and lives to his last   in the Lord's keeping.

165   So in his sorrow   the son of Healfdene[5]
       endlessly weighed   how a wise warrior
       might fend off harm.   The hardship this foe
       of his folk inflicted   was fierce and long-lasting,
       most ruinous wrath   and wracking night-evil.

170   A thane[6] of Hygelac   heard in his homeland

---

2. A cash payment for someone's death. *Wergeld* was regarded as an advance over violent revenge, and Grendel is marked as uncivilized because he refuses to acknowledge this practice.
3. By rendering the Old English *helrunan*, which means "those adept in the mysteries of hell," as "heathen keepers of hell-runes," the translators are taking the liberty of suggesting that "demons" such as Grendel are familiar with runes—the letters of the early Germanic alphabet.
4. In their fear, the Danes resume heathen practices. In Christian belief, the pagan gods were transformed into devils.
5. Hrothgar. He is referred to by his patronymic, his father's name, as is frequent with male characters in the poem.
6. One of the king's principal retainers, chief among these being the earls.

of Grendel's deeds.   Great among Geats,[7]
this man was more mighty   than any then living.
He summoned and stocked   a swift wave-courser,
and swore to sail   over the swan-road
175   as one warrior should   for another in need.
His elders could find   no fault with his offer,
and awed by the omens,   they urged him on.
He gathered the bravest   of Geatish guardsmen.
One of fifteen,   the skilled sailor
180   strode to his ship   at the ocean's edge.

He was keen to embark: his keel was beached
under the cliff   where sea-currents curled
surf against sand;   his soldiers were ready.
Over the longboat's   bow they boarded,
185   bearing below   their burnished weapons
and gilded gear   to hoard in the hull.
Other men shoved   the ship from the shore,
and off went the band,   their wood-braced vessel
bound for the venture   with wind on the waves
190   and foam under bow,   like a fulmar in flight.[8]

On the second day   their upswept prow
slid into sight   of a steep-sided coast,
the goal of their voyage,   gained in good time.
Sea-cliffs and stacks   shone before them,
195   flat-topped capes   at the close of their crossing.
Swiftly the sailors   steered for the shore,
moored their boat   and debarked on the berm.
Clad in corselets   of clattering mail,
they saluted the Lord   for their smooth sailing.

200   From the post he held   high on the headland,
a Scylding had spied   the strangers bearing
bright bucklers   and battle-armor
over their gangplank.   Avid for answers
and minded to know   what men had come hence,
205   Hrothgar's thane   hastened on horseback
down to the beach   where he brusquely brandished
spear-haft in hand   while speaking stern words:

"What warriors are you,   wearers of armor,
bearers of byrnies,   daring to bring
210   your lofty longboat   over the sea-lane?
Long have I looked   out on the ocean
so foreign foes   might never float hither
and harry our homeland   with hostile fleets.
No men have ever   more brazenly borne
215   shields to our shores,   nor have you sought

---

7. A Germanic tribe who lived along the southwestern   8. Gull-like sea bird of the far north Atlantic.
coast of what is now Sweden.

leave from our lords   to land in this place,
nor could you have known   my kin would consent.
I have never beheld   an earl on this earth
more mighty in arms   than one among you.
220 This is no hall-warmer,   handsome in harness,
showy with shield,   but the noblest of knights
unless looks belie him.   Now let me know
who are your fathers   before you fare further
or spy on the Danes.   I say to you, sailors
225 far from your homes: hear me and hasten
to answer me well.   Whence have you wandered?
Why have you come?"
                    Wisest with words,
the eldest offered   an answer for all:
"From Geat-land we come;   we are Geatish men,
230 sharers of Hygelac's   hearth and hall.
My father was famous   among our folk
as a lordly leader   who lived many winters
before, full of years,   he departed our fastness.
His name was Ecgtheow.   All over Earth
235 every wise man   remembers him well.
We have landed in friendship   to look for your lord,
the son of Healfdene,   sovereign of Scyldings.
Give us good guidance: a great errand
has driven us hence   to the holder of Danes.
240 Our purpose is open;   this I promise:
but you could attest   if tales tell the truth.
They speak of some scourge,   none can say what,
secretly stalking   by night among Scyldings,
the shadowy shape   of his malice to men
245 shown by a shameful   shower of corpses.
I offer Hrothgar,   with honest heart,
the means to make   an end to this menace.
Wise and good,   he will win his reward,
the scaling surges   of care will be cooled
250 if ever such awful   evil is vanquished.
So his sorrows   shall swiftly be soothed
or else his anguish   haunt him, unaltered,
as long as his house   holds on the hilltop."

Astride his steed,   the guard spoke again:
255 "A sharp-witted warrior   often must weigh
words against works   when judging their worth.
This I have learned: you honor our lord.
Thus you may come,   though clad in corselets
and weaponed for war.   I shall show you the way.
260 Meanwhile those thanes   who are mine to command
shall stand by the ship   you steered to our shore.
No thief will trouble   your newly-tarred craft
before you return   and take to the tide.
A swan-necked bow   will bear you back

Boar, from a bas-relief carving on Saint Nicholas Church, Ipswich, England. Although this large and vigorous boar dates from the 12th century, it retains stylistic elements of earlier Anglo-Saxon and Viking art. An ancient totem of power, boars were often depicted on early medieval weapons and helmets.

265   to your windward coast.   Most welcome of men,
                     may you be granted   good fortune in battle,
                     enduring unharmed   the deed you would do."

                     So they set out   while the ship sat at rest,
                     the broad-beamed longboat   bound to the beach,
270   lashed by its lines.   Lustrous boar-icons
                     glinted on cheek-guards.   Adorned with gold,
                     the flame-hardened helms   defended their lives.
                     Glad of their mettle   while marching together,
                     the troop hastened   until they beheld
275   the highest of halls   raised under heaven,
                     most famed among folk   in foreign lands.
                     Sheathed with gold   and grandly gabled,
                     the roof of the ruler   lit up his realm.
                     The foremost warrior   waved them forward
280   and bade the band   go straight to that building,
                     court of the king   and his brave kinsmen.
                     Reining his steed,   he spoke a last word:
                     "It is time I returned.   May All-Ruling Father
                     favor your errand.   I'm off to the ocean,
285   to watch and ward   away wrathful marauders."

                     A stone-paved street   steered the men hence.
                     They strode on together,   garbed in glinting
                     jackets of chain-mail   whose jingling rings,
                     hard and hand-linked,   sang on harnesses
290   borne toward the hall   by that battle-armed band.

Still sea-weary,   they set their broad-shields
of well-seasoned wood   against Heorot's wall.
Their byrnies clanged   as they bent to a bench
and stood their sturdy   spears in a row,
295   gray from the ash grove,   ground to sharp points.
This was a war party   worthy of weapons.

Then a proud prince   questioned their purpose:
"Where are you bringing   these burnished bosses,
these gray mail-shirts,   grimly-masked helms
300   and serried spears?   I am Hrothgar's
herald and door-ward.   I have never beheld
a band of wanderers   with bearings so brave.
I believe that boldness   has brought you to Hrothgar,
not banishment's shame."
                    The eldest answered,
305   hard and hardy   under his helmet,
a warlike prince   of the Weder[9] people:
"We are Hygelac's   hearth-companions.
My name is Beowulf;   my purpose, to bear
unto Healfdene's son,   your lordly leader,
310   a message meant   for that noblest of men,
if he will allow us   leave to approach."

Wise Wulfgar,   man of the Wendels,
known to many   for boldness in battle,
stoutly spoke out: "I shall ask our sovereign,
315   well-wisher of Danes   and awarder of wealth,
about this boon   you have come to request
and bear you back,   as soon as may be,
whatever answer   the great man offers."

He went straightaway   where Hrothgar waited,
320   old and gray-haired,   with earls gathered round.
Squarely he stood   for his king to assess him.
Such was the Scylding   custom at court,
and so Wulfgar spoke   to his sovereign and friend:
"Far-sailing Geats   have come to our kingdom
325   across the wide water.   These warriors call
their leader Beowulf   and bid me bring
their plea to our prince,   if it pleases him
to allow them entrance   and offer them audience.
I implore you to hear them,   princely Hrothgar,
330   for I deem them worthy   of wearing their armor
and treating with earls.   Truly the elder
who led them hither   is a lord of some stature."

Helm of the Scyldings,   Hrothgar held forth:
"I knew him once.   He was only a lad.

9. An alternate name for Geat.

335 His honored father,   old Ecgtheow,
     was dowered the daughter   of the Geat, Hrethel.
     The son now seeks us   solely from friendship.
     Seamen have said,   after sailing hence
     with gifts for the Geats,   that his hand-grip would match
340 the might and main   of thirty strong men.
     The West-Danes[1] have long   awaited God's grace.
     Here is our hope   against Grendel's dread,
     if I reckon rightly   the cause of his coming.
     I shall give this brave man   boons for boldness.
345 Bring him in quickly.   The band of my kinsmen
     is gathered together.   Welcome our guest
     to the dwelling of Danes."
                              Then Wulfgar went
     through the hall's entry   with word from within:
     "I am ordered to answer   that the lord of East-Danes
350 honors your father   and offers you welcome,
     sailors who sought us   over the sea-waves,
     bravely bent   on embarking hither.
     Now you may march   in your mail and masks
     to behold Hrothgar.   Here you must leave
355 war-shields and spears   sharpened for strife.
     Your weapons can wait   for words to be spoken."

     The mighty one rose   with many a man
     marshaled about him,   though some were bidden
     to stay with the weapons   and stand on watch.
360 Under Heorot's roof   the rest hastened
     when Beowulf brought them   boldly before
     the hearth of Hrothgar.   Helmed and hardy,
     the war-chief shone   as he stood in skillfully
     smithed chain-mail   and spoke to his host:

365 "Hail to you, Hrothgar!   I am Hygelac's
     kinsman and comrade,   esteemed by the king
     for deeds I have done   in the years of youth.
     I heard in my homeland   how Grendel grieves you.
     Seafarers say   that your splendid hall
370 stands idle and useless   after the sun
     sinks each evening   from Heaven's height.
     The most honored among us,   earls and elders,
     have urged me to seek you,   certain my strength
     would serve in your struggle.   They have seen me return
375 bloody from binding   brutish giants,
     a family of five   destroyed in our strife;
     by night in the sea   I have slain monsters.
     Hardship I had,   but our harms were avenged,
     our enemies mastered.   Now I shall match

---

1. Hrothgar is, in fact, king of all the Danes: North, South, East, and West. The different terms merely conform to the Anglo-Saxon alliterative pattern established in each line.

| 380 | my grip against Grendel's   and get you an end |

380 my grip against Grendel's   and get you an end
to this feud with the fiend.   Therefore one favor
I ask from you, Hrothgar,   sovereign of Spear-Danes,
shelter of shield-bearers,   friend to your folk:
that I and my officers,   we and no others,
385 be offered the honor   of purging your hall.
I have also heard   that the rash thing reckons
the thrust of a weapon   no threat to his thews,[2]
so I shall grab   and grapple with Grendel.
Let my lord Hygelac   hear and be glad
390 I foreswore   my sword and strong shield
when I fought for life   with that fearsome foe.
Whomever death takes,   his doom is doubtless
decreed by the Lord.   If I let the creature
best me when battle   begins in this building,
395 he will freely feast   as he often has fed
on men of much mettle.   My corpse will require
no covering cloth.   He will carry away
a crushed carcass   clotted with gore,
the fiend's fodder   gleefully eaten,
400 smearing his lonesome   lair on the moor.
No need to worry   who buries my body
if battle takes me.   Send back to my sovereign
this best of shirts   which has shielded my breast,
this choice chain-mail,   Hrethel's heirloom
405 and Weland's work.[3]   Fate goes as it will."

Helm of the Scyldings,   Hrothgar answered:
"It is fair that you seek   to defend us, my friend,
in return for the favor   offered your father
when a killing fanned   the fiercest of feuds
410 after he felled   the Wylfing, Heatholaf.
Wary of war,   the Weder-Geats wanted
Ecgtheow elsewhere,   so over the sea-swells
he sought the South-Danes,   strong Scyldings.
I had lately become   king of my kinsmen,
415 a youth ruling   this jewel of a realm,
this store-house of heroes,   with Heorogar gone,
my brother and better,   born of Healfdene.
I calmed your father's   quarrel with wergeld
sent over sea   straight to the Wylfings,
420 an ancient heirloom;   and Ecgtheow's oath
I took in return.
                    "It pains me to tell
what grief Grendel   has given me since,
what harm in Heorot,   hatred and shame
at his sudden onset.   My circle is shrunken;
425 my guardsmen are gone,   gathered by fate
into Grendel's grip.   How simply the Sovereign
of Heaven could hinder   deeds of this hell-fiend!

2. Well-developed sinew or muscle.   3. Legendary blacksmith of the Norse gods.

Beer-swollen boasters,   brave in their ale-cups,
often have sworn   to stay with their swords
430   drawn in the dark,   to strike down the demon.
Then in the morning   the mead-hall was drenched,
blood on the bench-boards,   blood on the floor,
the highest of houses   a horror at dawn.
Fewer were left   to keep faith with their lord
435   since those dear retainers   were taken by death.
But sit now to sup   and afterward speak
of soldierly pride,   if the spirit prompts you."

A bench was then cleared,   there in the beer-hall,
so all of the Geats   could sit together,
440   sturdy soldiers,   proud and stout-hearted.
A dutiful Dane   brought them bright ale-cups
and poured sweet mead   while the scop was singing
high-voiced in Heorot.   That host of warriors,
Weders and Scyldings,   shared in the wassails.

445   But envious Unferth,[4]   Ecglaf's son,
spat out his spite   from the seat he took
at his sovereign's feet.   The seafarer's quest
grieved him greatly,   for he would not grant
any man ever,   in all Middle-Earth,
450   more fame under heaven   than he himself had.

"Are you that Beowulf   Breca bested
when both of you bet   on swimming the straits,
daring the deep   in a dire struggle,
risking your lives   after rash boasting?
455   Though friend or foe,   no man could deflect
your foolhardy foray.   Arms flailing,
you each embraced   the billowing stream,
spanned the sea-lane   with swift-dipping hands
and wended over   the warring ocean.
460   Winter-like waves   were roiling the waters
as the two of you toiled   in the tumult of combers.
For seven nights   you strove to outswim him,
but he was the stronger   and saw at sunrise
the sea had swept him   to Heathoraem[5] shores.
465   Breca went back   to his own homeland,
his burg on the bluff,   stronghold of Brondings,
fair folk and wealthy.   The wager was won;
Beanstan's son   had brought off his boast.
However you fared   in onslaughts elsewhere,
470   I doubt you will live   the length of a night
if you dare to linger   so near Grendel."

4. Hrothgar's spokesman or court jester; his rude behavior toward Beowulf is consistent with other figures in epics and romances who taunt the hero before he undertakes his exploits. "Unferth" may mean "strife."
5. Coastal tribe of central Sweden near the Norwegian border.

Then Beowulf spoke,   son of Ecgtheow:
"Listen, Unferth,   my fuddled friend
brimful of beer,   you blabber too much
475   about Breca's venture.   I tell you the truth:
my force in the flood   is more than a match
for any man   who wrestles the waves.
Boys that we were,   brash in our youth
and reckless of risk,   both of us boasted
480   that each one could swim   the open ocean.
So we set forth,   stroking together
sturdily seaward   with swords drawn
hard in our hands   to ward off whale-fish.
No swifter was he   in those heaving seas;
485   each of us kept   close to the other,
floating together   those first five nights.
Then the storm-surges   swept us apart:
winter-cold weather   and warring winds
drove from the north   in deepening darkness.
490   Rough waves rose   and sea-beasts raged,
but my breast was wound   in a woven mail-shirt.
Hard and hand-linked,   hemmed with gold,
it kept those creatures   from causing me harm.
I was drawn to the depths,   held fast by the foe,
495   grim in his grasp;   yet granted a stab,
I stuck in my sword-point,   struck down the horror.
The mighty sea-monster   met death by my hand.

"Often afterward   snatchers of swimmers
snapped at my heels.   With my strong sword
500   I served them fitly.   I would fatten no foes,
feed no man-banes   munching their morsels
when setting to feast   on the floor of the sea.
Instead at sunrise   the sword-stricken
washed up in windrows   to lie lifelessly,
505   lodged by the tide-line,   and nevermore trouble
sailors crossing   the steep-cliffed straits.
As God's beacon   brightened the East,
I spied a cape   across calming seas,
a windward wall.   So I was spared,
510   for fate often favors   an unmarked man
if he keeps his courage.   My sword was the slayer
of nine nixies.[6]   I have not heard of many
who fought a more fearsome   assault in the night
while hurled by the waves   under heaven's vault.
515   Yet I broke the beasts' grip   and got off alive,
weary of warfare.   Swiftly surging
after the storm,   the sea-current swept me
to Finland's coast.
            "Such close combat
or stark sword-strokes   you have not seen,
520   you or Breca.   No yarn has boasted

6. Fabulous sea creatures.

how either of you two   ever attempted
so bold a deed   done with bright sword,
though I would not bruit   a brother's bane
if the killing of kin   were all I'd accomplished.
525   For that you are certain   to suffer in Hell,
doomed with the damned   despite your swift wit.
I say straight out,   son of Ecglaf,
that ghastly Grendel,   however gruesome,
would never have done   such dreadful deeds,
530   harming your lord   here in his hall,
if your spirit were stern,   your will, warlike,
as you have affirmed.   The foe has found
that he need not reckon   with wrathful swords
or look with alarm   on the likes of you,
535   Scylding victor.   He takes his tribute,
sparing no man,   snatching and supping
whenever he wishes   with wicked delight,
expecting no strife   with spear-bearing Danes.
But soon, very soon,   I shall show him the strength
540   and boldness of Geats   giving him battle.
When morning comes   to light up the land,
you may go again   and gladly get mead
as the bright sun   beams in the South
and starts a new day   for the sons of men."

545   Gray-haired Hrothgar,   giver of hoard-wealth,
was happy to hear   Beowulf bolster
hope for his folk   with forthright avowal.
About the Bright-Danes'   battle-leader
rang warriors' laughter   and winsome words.
550   The queen, Wealtheow,[7]   courtly by custom,
greeted the party   aglitter with gold
and bore the full cup   first to her lord,
the keeper of East-Danes,   dear to his people,
bidding him drink   and be glad of his beer.
555   That soldierly sovereign   quaffed and supped
while his Helming princess   passed through the hall
offering everyone,   young men and old,
the dole he was due.   Adorned with rings,
she bore the burnished   mead-bowl to Beowulf,
560   last of them all,   and honored the Geat
with gracious words,   firm in her wisdom
and grateful to God   for granting her wish.
Here was the prayed-for   prince who would help
to end the ill deeds.   He emptied the cup
565   Wealtheow offered;   then the willing warrior,
Ecgtheow's son,   spoke as one ready
for strife and slaughter:
                    "When I set my ship
to sail on the sea   and hunched in her hull

7. "Weal theow" means "foreign slave," and she may be British or Celtic in origin. Even after her marriage to Hrothgar, she continues to maintain her identity as the "lady of the Helmings," an epithet recalling her father Helm.

with my squadron of swords,   I swore to fulfill
570   the will of the Scyldings   or die in the deed,
fall with the slain,   held fast by the foe,
my last day lived out   here in your hall."

The wife was well-pleased   with Beowulf's words,
this oath from the Geat;   and glinting with gold
575   the queen, Wealtheow,   went to her king.
Boasts were bandied   once more in the beer-hall,
the hearty speech   of a hopeful household,
a forceful folk.   But soon the sovereign,
son of Healfdene,   hankered for sleep.
580   He knew how the brute   brooded on bloodshed
all day from dawn   until deepening dusk.
Covered by darkness,   the creature would creep,
a shade among shadows.   The company stood.
One man to another,   Hrothgar hailed
585   brave Beowulf,   wishing him well
and granting him leave   to guard the wine-hall:

"So long as my hand   has hefted a shield,
I never have yielded   the Danes' mansion
to any man else,   whatever his mettle.
590   Now you shall hold   this highest of houses.
Be mindful of fame;   make your might known;
but beware of the wicked.   You will want no boon
if you tackle this task   and live to request it."

Hrothgar and his princes   departed the hall;
595   the warder of Danes   went to his woman,
couched with his queen.   The King of Glory
had granted a guard   against Grendel's wrath,
as all had now learned.   One man had offered
to take on this task   and watch for the terror.
600   The leader of the Geats   would gladly trust
the force of God's favor.   He flung off his mail-shirt,
then handed his helmet   and inlaid sword
to the squire assigned   safe-keeping of iron
and gilded war-gear.   Again the bold
605   Beowulf boasted   while bound for his bed:

"I am no weaker   in works of war,
no less a grappler   than Grendel himself.
Soon I shall sink him   into his death-sleep,
not with my sword   but solely by strength.
610   He is unschooled in skills   to strike against me,
to shatter my shield,   though feared for his fierceness.
So I shall bear   no blade in the night
if he sees fit   to fight without weapons.
May God in His wisdom   grant whom He wills
615   blessing in battle."
The brave soldier

settled in bed,   and a bolster pillowed
his proud cheekbone.   About him were stretched
the strong sea-warriors,   each one wondering
whether he ever   would walk once again
620   his beloved land,   or find his own folk
from childhood's time   in an untroubled town.
All had been told   how often before
dreadful death   had swept up the Danes
who lay in this hall.   But the Lord lent them
625   aid in their anguish,   weaving their war-luck,
for one man alone   had the might and main
to fight off the fiend,   crush him in combat,
proving who ruled   the races of men,
then and forever: God, the Almighty.[8]

630   Cunningly creeping,   a spectral stalker
slunk through the gloom.   The bowmen were sleeping
who ought to have held   the high-horned house,
all except one,   for the Lord's will
now became known: no more would the murderer
635   drag under darkness   whomever he wished.
Wrath was wakeful,   watching in hatred;
hot-hearted Beowulf   was bent upon battle.

Then from the moor   under misty hillsides,
Grendel came gliding,   girt with God's anger.
640   The man-scather sought   someone to snatch
from the high hall.   He crept under clouds
until he caught sight   of the king's court
whose gilded gables   he knew at a glance.
He often had haunted   Hrothgar's house;
645   but he never found,   before or after,
hardier hall-thanes   or harder luck.
The joyless giant   drew near the door,
which swiftly swung back   at the touch of his hand
though bound and fastened   with forge-bent bars.
650   The building's mouth   had been broken open,
and Grendel entered   with ill intent.
Swollen with fury,   he stalked over flagstones
and looked round the manse   where many men lay.
An unlovely light   most like a flame
655   flashed from his eyes,   flared through the hall
at young soldiers dozing   shoulder to shoulder,
comradely kindred.   The cruel creature laughed
in his murderous mind,   thinking how many
now living would die   before the day dawned,
660   how glutted with gore   he would guzzle his fill.
It was not his fate   to finish the feast

8. This interpolation of Christian belief into what is essentially a pagan tradition has been taken as evidence of a conscious rewriting of much earlier material. The narrative assures its reader that Christian beliefs were still valid, regardless of what the characters in the story may have believed.

he foresaw that night.
                Soon the Stalwart,
Hygelac's kinsman,   beheld how the horror,
not one to be idle,   went about evil.

665   For his first feat   he suddenly seized
a sleeping soldier,   slashed at the flesh,
bit through bones   and lapped up the blood
that gushed from veins   as he gorged on gobbets.
Swiftly he swallowed   those lifeless limbs,

670   hands and feet whole;   then he headed forward
with open palm   to plunder the prone.
One man angled   up on his elbow:
the fiend soon found   he was facing a foe
whose hand-grip was harder   than any other

675   he ever had met   in all Middle-Earth.
Cravenly cringing,   coward at heart,
he longed for a swift   escape to his lair,
his bevy of devils.   He never had known
from his earliest days   such awful anguish.

680   The captain, recalling   his speech to the king,
straightaway stood   and hardened his hold.
Fingers fractured.   The fiend spun round;
the soldier stepped closer.   Grendel sought
somehow to slip   that grasp and escape,

685   flee to the fens;   but his fingers were caught
in too fierce a grip.   His foray had failed;
the harm-wreaker rued   his raid on Heorot.
From the hall of the Danes   a hellish din
beset every soldier   outside the stronghold,

690   louder than laughter   of ale-sodden earls.
A wonder it was   the wine-hall withstood
this forceful affray   without falling to earth.
That beautiful building   was firmly bonded
by iron bands   forged with forethought

695   inside and out.   As some have told it,
the struggle swept on   and slammed to the floor
many mead-benches   massive with gold.
No Scylding elders   ever imagined
that any would harm   their elk-horned hall,

700   raze what they wrought,   unless flames arose
to enfold and consume it.   Frightful new sounds
burst from the building,   unnerved the North-Danes,
each one and all   who heard those outcries
outside the walls.   Wailing in anguish,

705   the hellish horror,   hateful to God,
sang his despair,   seized by the grip
of a man more mighty   than any then living.

That shielder of men   meant by no means
to let the death-dealer   leave with his life,

710   a life worthless   to anyone elsewhere.

Then the young soldiers   swung their old swords
again and again   to save their guardian,
their kingly comrade,   however they could.
Engaging with Grendel   and hoping to hew him
715   from every side,   they scarcely suspected
that blades wielded   by worthy warriors
never would cut   to the criminal's quick.
The spell was spun   so strongly about him
that the finest iron   of any on earth,
720   the sharpest sword-edge   left him unscathed.
Still he was soon   to be stripped of his life
and sent on a sore   sojourn to Hell.
The strength of his sinews   would serve him no more;
no more would he menace   mankind with his crimes,
725   his grudge against God,   for the high-hearted kinsman
of King Hygelac   had hold of his hand.
Each found the other   loathsome while living;
but the murderous man-bane   got a great wound
as tendons were torn,   shoulder shorn open,
730   and bone-locks broken.   Beowulf gained
glory in war;   and Grendel went off
bloody and bent   to the boggy hills,
sorrowfully seeking   his dreary dwelling.
Surely he sensed   his life-span was spent,
735   his days upon days;   but the Danes were grateful:
their wish was fulfilled   after fearsome warfare.

Wise and strong-willed,   the one from afar
had cleansed Heorot,   hall of Hrothgar.
Great among Geats,   he was glad of his night-work
740   ending the evil,   his fame-winning feat,
fulfilling his oath   to aid the East-Danes,
easing their anguish,   healing the horror
they suffered so long,   no small distress.
As token of triumph,   the troop-leader hung
745   the shorn-off shoulder   and arm by its hand:
the grip of Grendel   swung from the gable!

Many a warrior   met in the morning
around Hrothgar's hall,   so I have heard.
Folk-leaders fared   from near and far
750   over wide wolds   to look on the wonder,
the track of the terror,   glad he had taken
leave of his life   when they looked on footprints
wending away   to the mere of monsters.
Weary and weak,   defeated in war,
755   he dripped his blood-spoor   down to dark water,
tinting the terrible   tide where he sank,
spilling his lifeblood   to swirl in the surge.
There the doomed one   dropped into death
where he long had lurked   in his joyless lair,
760   and Hell harrowed   his heathen soul.

Many went hence: young men and old
mounted white mares   and rode to the mere,
a joyous journey   on brave battle-steeds.
There Beowulf's   prowess was praised
765   and applauded by all.   Everyone said
that over the Earth   and under bright sky,
from north to south   between sea and sea,
no other man   was more worthy of wearing
corselet or crown,   though no one denied
770   the grace of Hrothgar: that was a good king.

Sometimes they galloped   great-hearted bays;
races were run   where roads were smooth
on open upland.   Meanwhile a man
skilled as a singer,   versed in old stories,
775   wove a new lay   of truly-linked words.
So the scop started   his song of Beowulf's
wisdom and strength,   setting his spell
with subtle staves.   Of Sigemund[9] also
he said what he knew: many marvels,
780   deeds of daring   and distant journeys,
the wars of Waels' son,   his wildness, his sins,
unsung among men   save by Fitela,
Sigemund's nephew,   who knew his secrets
and aided his uncle   in every conflict
785   as comrade-at-need.   A whole clan of ogres
was slain by the Waelsing   wielding his sword.
No small esteem   sprang up for Sigemund
after his death-day.   Dauntless in war,
he struck down a serpent   under gray stone
790   where it held its hoard.   He fared alone
on this fearsome foray,   not with Fitela;
but fate allowed him   to lunge with his blade,
spitting the scaly   worm to the wall.
His pluck repaid,   Sigemund was pleased
795   to take his pick   of the piled-up treasure
and load bright arms   in his longboat's breast
while the molten worm   melted away.

Thus that wayfarer   famed far and wide
among nations of men,   that mighty war-maker,
800   shelter of shield-bearers,   outshone another:
unhappy Heremod,[1]   king of the Danes,
whose strength, spirit,   and courage were spent.
He fell among foes,   was taken by traitors
and swiftly dispatched.   So his sorrows
805   ended at last.   Too long had lords

9. The story of Sigemund is also told in the Old Norse *Volsunga Saga* and with major variations in the Middle High German *Niebelungenlied*. The scop's comparison of Sigemund with Beowulf is ironic in that the order and the outcome of Beowulf's later encounter with a dragon will be reversed.

1. Heremod, an earlier Danish king, was the stock illustration of the unjust and unwise ruler. After bringing bloodshed upon his own house, Heremod took refuge among the Jutes, who eventually put him to death.

and commoners suffered,   scourged by their king,
who ought to have honored   his father's office,
defending his homeland,   his hoard and folk.
Evil had entered him.   Dearer to Danes
810   and all humankind   was Hygelac's kinsman.

Still running heats,   the horses hurtled
on sandy lanes.   The light of morning
had swung to the south,   and many men sped,
keen to behold   the hall of the king,
815   the strange sights inside.   Hrothgar himself,
keeper of treasures   and leader of troops,
came from the queen's   quarters to march
with measured tread   the track to his mead-hall;
the queen and her maidens   also came forth.
820   He stopped on the stairs   and gazed at the gable,
glinting with gold   behind Grendel's hand:

"My thanks for this sight   go straight to Heaven!
Grendel has given me   grief and grievance;
but God often works   wonders on wonders.
825   Not long ago   I had no hope at all
of living to see   relief from my sorrows
while slaughter stained   the highest of houses,
wide-spilling woes   the wisest advisors
despaired of stanching.   None of them knew
830   how to fend off our foes: the ghosts and ghasts
afflicting our folk   here in our fastness.
Now, praise Heaven,   a prince has proven
this deed could be done   that daunted us all.
Indeed the mother   who bore this young man
835   among mankind   may certainly say,
if she still is living,   that the Lord of Old
blessed her child-bearing.   Henceforth, Beowulf,
best of the brave,   I shall hold you in heart
as close as a son.   Keep our new kinship,
840   and I shall award you   whatever you wish
that is mine to command.   Many a time
I have lavished wealth   on lesser warriors,
slighter in strife.   You have earned your esteem.
May the All-Wielder   reward you always,
845   just as He gives you   these goods today."

Beowulf spoke,   son of Ecgtheow:
"We gladly engaged   in this work of war
and freely faced   the unknowable foe,
but I greatly regret   that you were not granted
850   the sight of him broken,   slathered with blood.
I sought to grip him   swiftly and strongly,
wrestle him down   to writhe on his death-bed
as life left him,   unless he broke loose.

It was not my fate   to fasten the man-bane
855   firmly enough.   The fiend was so fierce
he secured his escape   by leaving this limb
to ransom his life,   though little the wretch
has gained for his hurt,   held in the grip
of a dire wound,   awaiting death
860   as a savage man,   besmirched by his sins,
might wait to learn   what the Lord wills."

Unferth was silent.   He spoke no more boasts
about works of war   when warriors gazed
at the hand hanging   from Heorot's roof,
865   the fiend's fingers   jutting in front,
each nail intact,   those terrible talons
like spikes of steel.   Everyone said
that the strongest sword   from smithies of old,
the hardest iron   edge ever forged,
870   would never have harmed   that monstrous mauler,
those bloody claws   crooked for combat.

II. Grendel's Mother

Inside Heorot   many hands hastened
at Hrothgar's command: men and women
washed out the wine-hall,   unfurled on the walls
875   gold-woven hangings   to gladden their guests,
each of whom gazed   wide-eyed in wonder.
Though bound with iron,   the bright building
was badly battered,   its hinges broken.
Only the roof   had escaped unscathed
880   before the fell creature   cringed and fled,
stained by his sin   and despairing of life.
Flee it who will,   a well-earned fate
is not often altered,   for every earth-dweller
and soul-bearing son   must seek out a spot
885   to lay down his body,   lie on his death-bed,
sleep after feasting.
                    So came the season
for Healfdene's son   to stride through his hall:
the king himself   would sup with his kin.
I have never heard   in any nation
890   of such a great host   so graciously gathered,
arrayed on benches   around their ruler,
glad of his fame   and glad for the feast.
Many a mead-cup   those masterful kinsmen
Hrothgar and Hrothulf   raised in the hall.
895   All were then friends   who filled Heorot,
treason and treachery   not yet contrived.[1]

---

1. Possibly an allusion to the later usurpation of the Danish throne by Hrothgar's nephew Hrothulf.

Crowning his conquest,   the King of the Danes
bestowed on the Stalwart   a battle-standard
embroidered with gold,   a helmet, a byrnie,
900 and an unblemished blade   borne out while ranks
of warriors watched.   Then Beowulf drank
a flagon before them: he would feel no shame
facing bold spearmen   with boons such as these.
Not many men   on mead benches
905 have given another   four golden gifts
in friendlier fashion.   The head-guard was flanged
with windings of wire.   Facing forward,
it warded off harm   when the wearer in war
was obliged to bear shield   against enemy blades
910 that were hammer-hardened   and honed by files.
The sovereign ordered   eight swift steeds
brought to the court   on braided bridles.
One bore a saddle   studded with gems
and glinting gold-work: there the great king,
915 son of Healfdene,   would sit during sword-strife,
never faltering,   fierce at the front,
working his will   while the wounded fell.
Then Hrothgar awarded   horses and weapons
both to Beowulf,   bade that he keep them
920 and wield them well.   So from his hoard
he paid the hero   a princely reward
of heirlooms and arms   for braving the battle;
no man could fairly   or truthfully fault them.

That lord also lavished   gifts on the Geats
925 whom Beowulf brought   over broad seas,
and wergeld he gave   for the one Grendel
had wickedly killed,   though the creature would surely
have murdered more   had God in his wisdom,
man in his strength   failed to forestall it.
930 So the Almighty   has always moved men;
yet man must consistently   strive to discern
good from evil,   evil from good
while drunk with days   he dwells in this world.

Music and story   now sounded together
935 as Hrothgar's scop   sang for the hall-fest
a tale often told   when harp was held:[2]
how Finn's followers,   faithless Jutes,
fell to fighting   friends in his fortress;
how Hnaef the Half-Dane,   hero of Scyldings,
940 was fated to fall   in Frisian warfare;

2. The following episode is one of the most obscure in *Beowulf*. It seems that Hnaef and Hildeburh are both children of an earlier Danish king named Hoc and that Hildeburh has been sent to marry Finn, the son of Folcwalda and king of the Jutes and Frisians, in order to conclude a marriage alliance and thus settle a prior blood feud between the two tribes. Upon going to visit her sister and her husband, Hnaef is treacherously ambushed and killed by Finn's men; Hildeburh's son by Finn is also killed. In her role as peace-weaver, Hildeburh is torn by conflicting allegiances, foreshadowing the fate of Hrothgar's own daughter Freawaru in her marriage to Ingeld.

how by shield-swagger   harmless Hildeburh,
faithful to Finn   though daughter of Danes,
lost her beloved   brother and son
who were both born   to be struck by spears.
945 Not without cause   did Hoc's daughter
bewail the Lord's will   when morning awoke:
she who had known   nothing but happiness
beheld under heaven   the horror of kin-strife.

War had taken   its toll of attackers;
950 few men remained   for Finn to muster,
too few to force   the fight against Hengest,
a dutiful earl   who had rallied the Danes.
As tokens of truce   Finn offered these terms:
a haven wholly   emptied of foes,
955 hall and high seat,   with an equal share
in gifts given   his own gathered kin.
Each time he treated   his sons to treasures
plated with gold,   a portion would go
to sweeten Hengest's   stay in his hall.
960 The two sides swore   a strict treaty;
and Finn freely   affirmed to Hengest
that all would honor   this oath to the Danes,
as his council decreed,   and further declared
no Frisian would ever,   by word or work,
965 challenge the peace   or mention with malice
the plight of survivors   deprived of their prince
and wintered-in   at the slayer's stronghold.
Should any Frisian   enter in anger,
the sword's edge   would settle the quarrel.

970 That oath offered,   the hoard was opened
for gold to array   the greatest of War-Danes.
Iron-hard guardians   gilded with gold,
bloody byrnies   and boar-tusked helms
were heaped on his bier,   awaiting the balefire.
975 Many a warrior,   weakened by wounds,
had faltered and fallen   with foes he had slain.
Hildeburh ordered   her own dear son
be placed on the pyre,   the prince and his uncle
shoulder to shoulder.   Their bodies were burned
980 while the stricken lady   sang out her sorrow.
Streamers of smoke   burst from the bier
as corpses kindled   with cruelest of flames.
Faces withered,   flesh-wounds yawned
and blood boiled out   as the blaze swallowed
985 with hateful hunger   those whom warfare
had borne away,   the best of both houses.
Their glory was gone.
                    The Frisians were fewer
heading for home;   their high stronghold

was empty of allies.   For Hengest also
990   that winter was woeful,   walled up in Frisia,
brooding on bloodshed   and longing to leave,
though knowing his longboat   never could breast
the wind-darkened swells   of a wide ocean
seething with storms,   or break the ice-bindings
995   that barred his bow   from the bitter waters.
Constrained to wait   for kindlier weather,
he watched until spring,   season of sunlight,
dawned on men's dwellings   as ever it did
and still does today.   Winter withdrew
1000 and Earth blossomed.
                              Though the exile was eager
to end his visit,   he ached for vengeance
before sailing home.   Loathe to foreswear
the way of this world,   he schemed to assail
the sons of slayers.   So Hengest heeded
1005 Hunlaf's son,   who laid on his lap
the sword War-Flame,   feared by all foes,
asking its edge   be offered the Jutes.
His heart was hot;   he could hold back no more.
Gladly he answered   Guthlaf and Oslaf,
1010 who wrathfully spoke   of the wrong they suffered,
the shame of Scyldings   sharing their plight.
Then fierce-hearted Finn   fell in his turn,
stricken by swords   in his own stronghold.
The building was bloody   with bodies of foemen:
1015 the king lay slain,   likewise his kin;
and the queen was captured.   Scyldings carried
off in their ship   all of the chattels
found in Finn's fortress,   gemstones and jewels.
The lady was borne   to the land of her birth.

1020 So that story   was sung to its end,
then mirth once more   mounted in Heorot.
Revelry rang   as wine-bearers brought
finely-wrought flagons   filled to the brim.
Wearing her circlet,   Wealtheow walked
1025 where uncle and nephew,   Hrothgar and Hrothulf,
were sitting in peace,   two soldiers together,
each still believing   the other was loyal.
Likewise the officer,   Unferth, was honored
to sit at the feet   of the Scylding sovereign.
1030 Everyone thought him   honest and trustworthy,
blameless and brave,   though his blade had unjustly
stricken a kinsman.
                              So the queen spoke:
"Quaff from your cup,   king of the Scyldings,
giver of gold;   quaff and be glad;
1035 greet the Geats mildly   as well a man might,
mindful of gifts   graciously given
from near and far,   now in your keeping.

They say you would name   that knight as a son
for purging the ring-hall.   Employ as you please
1040   wealth and rewards,   but bequeath to your kin
rule of this realm   when the Ruler of All
holds that you must.   I know that Hrothulf
will honor our trust   and treat these youths well
if you have to leave   this life before him.
1045   I am counting on him   to recall our kindness
when he was a child   and repay our children
for presents we gave   and pleasures we granted."

She turned to the bench   where her sons were seated,
Hrethric and Hrothmund.   Between the two brothers
1050   Beowulf sat;   and the cup-bearer brought him
words of welcome,   willingly gave him
as tokens of favor   two braided arm-bands,
jerkin, corselet,   and jeweled collar
grander than any   other on Earth.[3]
1055   I have heard under heaven   of no higher treasure
hoarded by heroes   since Hama stole off
to his fair fortress   with Freya's necklace,
shining with stones   set by the Fire-Dwarves.
So Hama earned   Eormanric's anger,
1060   and fame for himself.   Foolhardy Hygelac,
grandson of Swerting   and sovereign of Geats,
would wear it one day   on his final foray.
He fell in the fray   defending his treasure,
the spoils he bore   with his battle-standard.
1065   Recklessly raiding   the realm of Frisia,
the prince in his pride   had prompted misfortune
by crossing the sea   while clad in that collar.
He fell under shield,   fell to the Franks,
weaker warriors   stripping the slain
1070   of armor and spoil   after the slaughter.
Hygelac held   the graveyard of Geats.

The hall applauded   the princely prize
bestowed by the queen,   and Wealtheow spoke
for the host to hear: "Keep this collar,
1075   beloved Beowulf;   and bear this byrnie,
wealth of our realm;   may it ward you well.
Swear that your strength   and kindly counsel
will aid these youngsters,   and I shall reward you.
Now your renown   will range near and far;
1080   your fame will wax wide,   as wide as the water
hemming our hills,   homes of the wind.
Be blessed, Beowulf,   with abundant treasures
as long as you live;   and be mild to my sons,
a model admired.   Here men are courtly,

3. The narrative jumps ahead beyond Beowulf's return home to the Geats. His uncle, Hygelac, the king, will not only receive the collar from Beowulf but will die with it in battle among the Frisians. The collar thus connects different events at different times.

1085 honest and true, each to the other,
    all to their ruler; and after the revels,
    well-bolstered with beer, they do as I bid."

    The lady left him and sat on her seat.
    The feast went on; wine was flowing.
1090 Men could not know what fate would befall them,
    what evil of old was decreed to come
    for the earls that evening. As always, Hrothgar
    headed for home, where the ruler rested.
    A great many others remained in the hall,
1095 bearing bright benches and rolling out beds
    while one drunkard, doomed and death-ripened,
    sprawled into sleep. They set at their heads
    round war-shields, well-adorned wood.
    Above them on boards, their battle-helms rested,
1100 ringed mail-shirts and mighty spear-shafts
    waiting for strife. Such was their wont
    at home or afield, wherever they fared,
    in case their king should call them to arms.
    That was a fine folk.
            They sank into slumber,
1105 but one paid sorely for sleep that evening,
    as often had happened when grim Grendel
    held the gold-hall, wreaking his wrongs
    straight to the end: death after sins.
    It would soon be perceived plainly by all
1110 that one ill-wisher still was alive,
    maddened by grief: Grendel's mother,
    a fearsome female bitterly brooding
    alone in her lair deep in dread waters
    and cold currents since Cain had killed
1115 the only brother born of his father.
    Marked by murder, he fled from mankind
    and went to the wastes. Doomed evil-doers
    issued from him. Grendel was one,
    but the hateful Hell-walker found a warrior
1120 wakefully watching for combat in Heorot.
    The monster met there a man who remembered
    strength would serve him, the great gift of God,
    faith in the All-Wielder's favor and aid.
    By that he mastered the ghastly ghoul;
1125 routed, wretched, the hell-fiend fled,
    forlornly drew near his dreary death-place.
    Enraged and ravenous, Grendel's mother
    swiftly set out on a sorrowful journey
    to settle the score for her son's demise.

1130 She slipped into Heorot, hall of the Ring-Danes,
    where sleeping earls soon would suffer
    an awful reversal. Her onslaught was less

by as much as a woman's   mettle in war
is less than a man's   wielding his weapon:

1135 the banded blade   hammered to hardness,
a blood-stained sword   whose bitter stroke
slashes a boar-helm   borne into battle.
In the hall, sword-edge   sprang from scabbard;
broadshield was swung   swiftly off bench,

1140 held firmly in hand.   None thought of helmet
or sturdy mail-shirt   when terror assailed him.

Out she hastened,   out and away,
keen to keep living   when caught in the act.
She fastened on one,   then fled to her fen.

1145 He was Hrothgar's   highest counselor,
boon companion   and brave shield-bearer,
slain in his bed.   Beowulf slept
elsewhere that evening,   for after the feast
the Geat had been given   a different dwelling.

1150 A din of dismay   mounted in Heorot:
the gory hand   was gone from the gable.
Dread had retaken   the Danes' dwelling.
That bargain was bad   for both barterers,
costing each one   a close comrade.

1155 It was grim for the sovereign,   the grizzled soldier,
to learn his old thane   was no longer living,
to know such a dear one   was suddenly dead.
Swiftly he sent   servants to fetch
battle-blessed Beowulf   early from bed,

1160 together with all   the great-hearted Geats.
He marched in their midst,   went where the wise one
was wondering whether   the All-Wielder
ever would alter   this spell of ill-fortune.
That much-honored man   marched up the floor,

1165 and timbers dinned   with the tread of his troop.
He spoke soberly   after the summons,
asking how soundly   the sovereign had slept.

Hrothgar answered,   head of his house:
"Ask not about ease!   Anguish has wakened

1170 again for the Danes.   Aeschere is dead.
He was Yrmenlaf's   elder brother,
my rune-reader   and keeper of counsel,
my shoulder's shielder,   warder in war
when swordsmen struck   at boar-headed helms.

1175 Whatever an honored   earl ought to be,
such was Aeschere.   A sleepless evil
has slipped into Heorot,   seized and strangled.
No one knows where   she will wander now,
glad of the gory   trophy she takes,

1180 her fine fodder.   So she requites

her kinsman's killer   for yesterday's deed,
when you grabbed Grendel   hard in your hand-grip.
He plagued and plundered   my people too long.
His life forfeit,   he fell in the fray;
1185   but now a second   mighty man-scather
comes to carry   the feud further,
as many a thane   must mournfully think,
seeing his sovereign   stricken with grief
at the slaying of one   who served so well.

1190   "I have heard spokesmen   speak in my hall,
country-folk saying   they sometimes spotted
a pair of prodigies   prowling the moors,
evil outcasts,   walkers of wastelands.
One, they descried,   had the semblance of woman;
1195   the other, ill-shapen,   an aspect of man
trudging his track,   ever an exile,
though superhuman   in stature and strength.
In bygone days   the border-dwellers
called him *Grendel*.   What creature begot him,
1200   what nameless spirit,   no one could say.
The two of them trekked   untraveled country:
wolf-haunted heights   and windy headlands,
the frightening fen-path   where falling torrents
dive into darkness,   stream beneath stone
1205   amid folded mountains.   That mere[4] is not far,
as miles are measured.   About it there broods
a forest of fir trees   frosted with mist.
Hedges of wood-roots   hem in the water
where each evening   fire-glow flickers
1210   forth on the flood,   a sinister sight.
That pool is unplumbed   by wits of the wise;
but the heath-striding hart   hunted by hounds,
the strong-antlered stag   seeking a thicket,
running for cover,   would rather be killed
1215   than bed on its bank.   It is no pleasant place
where water-struck waves   are whipped into clouds,
surging and storming,   swept by the winds,
so the heights are hidden   and heaven weeps.
Now you alone   can relieve our anguish:
1220   look, if you will,   at the lay of the land;
and seek, if you dare,   that dreadful dale
where the she-demon dwells.   Finish this feud,
and I shall reward you   with age-old wealth,
twisted-gold treasures,   if you return."

1225   Beowulf spoke,   son of Ecgtheow:
"Grieve not, good man.   It is better to go
and avenge your friend   than mourn overmuch.
We all must abide   an end on this earth,

---

4. A small lake.

but a warrior's works   may win him renown
1230   as long as he lives   and after life leaves him.
Rise now, ruler;   let us ride together
and seek out the spoor   of Grendel's mother.
I swear to you this: she shall not escape
in chasm or cave,   in cliff-climbing thicket
1235   or bog's bottom,   wherever she bides.
Suffer your sorrow   this one day only;
I wish you to wait,   wait and be patient."

The elder leapt up and   offered his thanks
to God Almighty,   Master of all,
1240   for such hopeful speech.   Then Hrothgar's horse,
a steed with mane braided,   was brought on its bridle.
The sage sovereign   set out in splendor
with shield-bearing soldiers   striding beside him.
Tracks on the trail   were easy to trace:
1245   they went from woodland   out to the open,
heading through heather   and murky moors
where the best of thanes   was borne off unbreathing.
He would live no longer   in Hrothgar's house.
Crossing the moorland,   the king mounted
1250   a stony path   up steepening slopes.
With a squad of scouts   in single file,
he rode through regions   none of them knew,
mountains and hollows   that hid many monsters.
The sovereign himself,   son of great forebears,
1255   suddenly spotted   a forest of fir-trees
rooted on rock,   their trunks tipping
over a tarn   of turbulent eddies.
Danes were downcast,   and Geats, grim;
every soldier   was stricken at heart
1260   to behold on that height   Aeschere's head.

As they looked on the lake,   blood still lingered,
welled to the surface.   A war-horn sounded
its bold battle-cry,   and the band halted.
Strange sea-dragons   swam in the depths;
1265   sinuous serpents   slid to and fro.
At the base of the bluff   water-beasts lay,
much like monsters   that rise in the morning
when seafarers sail   on strenuous journeys.
Hearing the horn's   high-pitched challenge,
1270   they puffed up with rage   and plunged in the pool.
One Geatish lad   lifted his bow
and loosing an arrow,   ended the life
of a wondrous wave-piercer.   War-shaft jutting
hard in its heart,   the swimmer slowed
1275   as death seized it.   With startling speed
the waters were torn   by terrible tuskers.
They heaved the hideous   hulk to the shore
with spear-hooked heads   as warriors watched.

Undaunted, Beowulf   donned battle armor.
1280   His woven war-corselet,   wide and ornate,
would safeguard his heart   as he searched underwater.
It knew how to armor   the beast of its bearer
if an angry grappler   grasped him in battle.
The bright war-helm   would hold his head
1285   when he sought the seafloor   in swirling flood.
A weapon-smith   had skillfully worked
its gilding of gold   in bygone days
and royally ringed it.   He added afterward
figures of boars   so blades of foemen
1290   would fail to bite.   One further aid
Beowulf borrowed: Unferth offered
the hilt of Hrunting,   his princely sword,
a poisoned war-fang   with iron-edged blade,
blood-hardened   in battles of old.
1295   It never had failed   in any man's grasp
if he dared to fare   on a dreadful foray
to fields of foes.   This was not the first time
it was forced to perform   a desperate deed.

Though strong and sly,   the son of Ecglaf
1300   had somehow forgotten   the slander he spoke,
bleary with beer.   He loaned his blade
to a better bearer,   a doer of deeds
that he would not dare.   His head never dipped
under wild waves,   and his fame waned
1305   when bravery failed him   as battle beckoned.
Not so, the other,   armed and eager.

Beowulf spoke,   son of Ecgtheow:
"Remember, wise master,   mover of men
and giver of gold,   since now I begin
1310   this foray full-willing,   how once before
you pledged to fill   the place of a father
if I should be killed   acquitting your cause.
Guard these young earls,   my partners in arms,
if death takes me.   The treasures you dealt,
1315   Hrothgar, my lord,   I leave to Hygelac.
Let the king of Geats   gaze on the gold
and see that I found   a fair bestower,
a generous host   to help while I could.
And let Unferth have   his heirloom, Hrunting,
1320   this wonderful weapon,   wavy-skinned sword
renowned among men.   Now I shall conquer
or die in the deed."
                              So saying, he dived,
high-hearted and hasty,   awaiting no answer.
The waters swallowed   that stout soldier.
1325   He swam a half-day   before seeing sea-floor.
Straightaway someone   spied him as well:
she that had hidden   a hundred half-years

in the void's vastness.   Grim and greedy,
she glimpsed a creature   come from above
1330 and crept up to catch him,   clutch him, crush him.
Quickly she learned   his life was secure;
he was hale and whole,   held in the ring-mail.
Linked and locked,   his life-shielding shirt
was wrapped around him,   and wrathful fingers
1335 failed to rip open   the armor he wore.
The wolf of the waters   dragged him away
to her den in the deep,   where weapons of war,
though bravely wielded,   were worthless against her.
Many a mere-beast   banded about him,
1340 brandishing tusks   to tear at his shirt.

The soldier now saw   a high-roofed hall:
unharmed, he beheld   the foe's fastness
beyond the reach   of the roiling flood.
Fire-light flared;   a blaze shone brightly.
1345 The lordly one looked   on the hellish hag,
the mighty mere-wife.   He swung his sword
for a swift stroke,   not staying his hand;
and the whorled blade   whistled its war-song.
But the battle-flame   failed to bite her;
1350 its edge was unable   to end her life,
though Hrunting had often   hacked through helmets
and slashed mail-shirts   in hand-to-hand strife.
For the first time   the famous blade faltered.

Resolve unshaken,   courage rekindled,
1355 Hygelac's kinsman   was keen for conquest.
In a fit of fury,   he flung down the sword.
Steely and strong,   the ring-banded blade
rang on the stones.   He would trust in the strength
of his mighty hand-grip.   Thus should a man,
1360 unmindful of life,   win lasting renown.
Grabbing the tresses   of Grendel's mother,
the Geats' battle-chief,   bursting with wrath,
wrestled her down: no deed to regret
but a favor repaid   as fast as she fell.
1365 With her grim grasp   she grappled him still.
Weary, the warrior   stumbled and slipped;
the strongest foot-soldier   fell to the foe.
Astraddle the hall-guest,   she drew her dagger,
broad and bright-bladed,   bent on avenging
1370 her only offspring.   His mail-shirt shielded
shoulder and breast.   Barring the entry
of edge or point,   the woven war-shirt
saved him from harm.   Ecgtheow's son,
the leader of Geats,   would have lost his life
1375 under Earth's arch   but for his armor
and Heaven's favor   furnishing help.
The Ruler of All   readily aided

the righteous man   when he rose once more.

He beheld in a hoard   of ancient arms
1380   a battle-blessed sword   with strong-edged blade,
a marvelous weapon   men might admire
though over-heavy   for any to heft
when finely forged   by giants of old.
The Scyldings' shielder   took hold of the hilt
1385   and swung up the sword,   though despairing of life.
He struck savagely,   hit her hard neck
and broke the bone-rings,   cleaving clean through
her fated flesh.   She fell to the floor.
The sword sweated;   the soldier rejoiced.

1390   The blaze brightened,   shining through shadows
as clearly as Heaven's   candle on high.
Grim and angry,   Hygelac's guardsman
glanced round the room   and went toward the wall
with his weapon raised,   holding it hard
1395   by the inlaid hilt.   Its edge was useful
for quickly requiting   the killings of Grendel.
Too many times   he had warred on the West-Danes.
He had slain Hrothgar's   hearth-mates in sleep,
eagerly eaten   fifteen of those folk
1400   and as many more borne   for his monstrous booty.
He paid their price   to the fierce prince,
who looked on the ground   where Grendel lay limp,
wound-weary,   worn out by warfare.
The lifeless one lurched   at the stroke of the sword
1405   that cleaved his corpse   and cut off his head.

At once the wise men   waiting with Hrothgar
and watching the waters   saw the waves seethe
with streaks of gore.   Gray-haired and glum,
age around honor,   they offered their counsel,
1410   convinced that no victor   would ever emerge
and seek out the sovereign.   All were certain
the mere-wolf had mauled him.   It was mid-afternoon,
and the proud Danes   departed the dale;
generous Hrothgar   headed for home.
1415   The Geats lingered   and looked on the lake
with sorrowful souls,   wistfully wishing
they still might see   their beloved leader.

The sword shrank   from battle-shed blood;
its blade began melting,   a marvel to watch,
1420   that war-icicle   waning away
like a rope of water   unwound by the Ruler
when Father releases   fetters of frost,
the true Sovereign   of seasons and times.
The Weders' warlord   took only two treasures
1425   from all he beheld: the head and the hilt,

studded with gems.   The sword had melted.
Its banded blade   was burnt by the blood,
so hot was the horror,   so acid the evil
that ended thereon.   Soon he was swimming:
1430   the strife-survivor   drove up from the deep
when his foe had fallen.   The foaming waves,
the wide waters   were everywhere cleansed;
that alien evil   had ended her life-days,
left the loaned world.
                  Landward he swam;
1435   the strong-minded savior   of sea-faring men
was glad of his burden,   the booty he brought.
Grateful to God,   the band of brave thanes
hastened gladly   to greet their chieftain,
astonished to see him   whole and unharmed.
1440   His helm and hauberk   were swiftly unstrapped.
Calm under clouds,   the lake lay quietly,
stained by the slain.   They found the foot-path
and marched manfully,   making their way
back through the barrens.   Proud as princes,
1445   they hauled the head   far from the highland,
an effort for each   of the four who ferried it
slung from spear-shafts.   They bore their booty
straight to the gold-hall.   Battle-hardened,
all fourteen strode   from the field outside,
1450   a bold band of Geats   gathered about
their leader and lord,   the war-worthy man,
peerless in prowess   and daring in deeds.
He hailed Hrothgar   as Grendel's head
was dragged by the hair,   drawn through the hall
1455   where earls were drinking.   All were awe-stricken:
women and warriors   watched in wonder.

Beowulf spoke,   son of Ecgtheow:
"Hail, Hrothgar,   Healfdene's son.
Look on this token   we took from the lake,
1460   this glorious booty   we bring you gladly.
The struggle was stark;   the danger, dreadful.
My foe would have won   our war underwater
had the Lord not looked   after my life.
Hrunting failed me,   though finely fashioned;
1465   but God vouchsafed me   a glimpse of a great-sword,
ancient and huge,   hung from the wall.
All-Father often   fosters the friendless.
Wielding this weapon,   I struck down and slew
the cavern's keeper   as soon as I could.
1470   My banded war-blade   was burned away
when blood burst forth   in the heat of battle.
I bore the hilt here,   wrested from raiders.
Thus I avenged   the deaths among Danes
as it was fitting,   and this I assure you:

1475 henceforth in Heorot heroes shall sleep
untroubled by terror. Your warrior troop,
all of your thanes, young men and old,
need fear no further evil befalling,
not from that quarter, king of the Scyldings."

1480 He gave the gold hilt to the good old man;
the hoary war-chief held in his hand
an ancient artifact forged by giants.
At the devils' downfall, this wondrous work
went to the Danes. The dark-hearted demon,
1485 hater of humans, Heaven's enemy,
committer of murders, and likewise his mother,
departed this Earth. Their power passed
to the wisest world-king who ever awarded
treasure in Denmark between the two seas.

1490 Hrothgar spoke as he studied the hilt,
that aged heirloom inscribed long ago
with a story of strife: how the Flood swallowed
the race of giants with onrushing ocean.
Defiant kindred, they fared cruelly,
1495 condemned for their deeds to death by water.
Such were the staves graven in gold-plate,
runes rightly set, saying for whom
the serpent-ribbed sword and raddled hilt[5]
were once fashioned of finest iron.
1500 When the wise one spoke, all were silent:

"Truth may be told by the homeland's holder
and keeper of kinfolk, who rightly recalls
the past for his people: this prince was born
bravest of fighters. My friend, Beowulf,
1505 your fame shall flourish in far countries,
everywhere honored. Your strength is sustained
by patience and judgment. Just as I promised,
our friendship is firmed, a lasting alliance.
So you shall be a boon to your brethren,
1510 unlike Heremod who ought to have helped
Ecgwela's sons, the Honor-Scyldings.
He grew up to grief and grim slaughter,
doling out death to the Danish people.
Hot-tempered at table, he cut down comrades,
1515 slew his own soldiers and spurned humankind,
alone and unloved, an infamous prince,
though mighty God had given him greatness
and raised him in rank over all other men.

---

5. On the sword hilt is the story of the flood, written in runes (letters of the early Germanic alphabet), and a decorative pattern of twisted serpent shapes. A similar pattern can be seen on the great buckle of the Sutton Hoo ship burial, Color Plate 2.

Hidden wrath   took root in his heart,
1520 bloodthirsty thoughts.   He would give no gifts
to honor others.   Loveless, he lived,
a lasting affliction   endured by the Danes
in sorrow and strife.   Consider him well,
his life and lesson.
                                    "Wise with winters,
1525 I tell you this tale   as I mull and marvel
how the Almighty   metes to mankind
the blessings of reason,   rule and realm.
He arranges it all.   For a time He allows
the mind of a man   to linger in love
1530 with earthly honors.   He offers him homeland
to hold and enjoy,   a fort full of folk,
men to command   and might in the world,
wide kingdoms   won to his will.
In his folly, the fool   imagines no ending.
1535 He dwells in delight   without thought of his lot.
Illness, old age,   anguish or envy:
none of these gnaw   by night at his mind.
Nowhere are swords   brandished in anger;
for him the whole world   wends as he wishes.
1540 He knows nothing worse   till his portion of pride
waxes within him.   His soul is asleep;
his gate, unguarded.   He slumbers too soundly,
sunk in small cares.   The slayer creeps close
and shoots a shaft   from the baneful bow.
1545 The bitter arrow   bites through his armor,
piercing the heart   he neglected to guard
from crooked counsel   and evil impulse.
Too little seems all   he has long possessed.
Suspicious and stingy,   withholding his hoard
1550 of gold-plated gifts,   he forgets or ignores
what fate awaits him,   for the world's Wielder
surely has granted   his share of glory.
But the end-rune   is already written:
the loaned life-home   collapses in ruin;
1555 some other usurps   and openly offers
the hoarded wealth,   heedless of worry.

"Beloved Beowulf,   best of defenders,
guard against anger   and gain for yourself
perpetual profit.   Put aside pride,
1560 worthiest warrior.   Now for awhile
your force flowers,   yet soon it shall fail.
Sickness or age   will strip you of strength,
or the fangs of flame,   or flood-surges,
the sword's bite   or the spear's flight,
1565 or fearful frailty   as bright eyes fade,
dimming to darkness.   Afterward death
will sweep you away,   strongest of war-chiefs.

"I ruled the Ring-Danes   a hundred half-years,
stern under clouds   with sword and spear
1570 that I wielded in war   against many nations
across Middle-Earth,   until none remained
beneath spacious skies   to reckon as rivals.
Recompense happened   here in my homeland,
grief after gladness   when Grendel came,
1575 when the ancient enemy   cunningly entered.
Thereafter I suffered   constant sorrows
and cruelest cares.   But God has given me
long enough life   to look at this head
with my own eyes,   as enmity ends
1580 spattered with gore.   Sit and be glad,
war-worthy one: the feast is forthcoming,
and many gifts   will be granted tomorrow."

Gladly the Geat   sought out his seat
as the Ancient asked.   With all of his men,
1585 the famous one feasted   finely once more.
The helm of Heaven   darkened with dusk,
and the elders arose.   The oldest of Scyldings
was ready to rest   his hoary-haired head
at peace on his pillow.   Peerless with shield,
1590 the leader of Geats   was equally eager
to lie down at last.   A thane was appointed
to serve as his squire.   Such was the courtesy
shown in those days   to weary wayfarers,
soldiers sojourning   over the ocean.

1595 Beneath golden gables   the great-hearted guest
dozed until dawn   in the high-roofed hall,
when the black raven   blithely foretold
joy under Heaven.   Daybreak hastened,
sun after shadow.   The soldiers were ardent,
1600 the earls eager   to hurry homeward;
the stern-minded man   would make for his ship,
fare back to his folk.   But first he bade
that Hrunting be sent   to the son of Ecglaf,
a treasure returned   with thanks for the loan
1605 of precious iron.   He ordered the owner
be told he considered   the sword a fine friend,
blameless in battle.   That was a Gallant!
Keen for the crossing,   his weapons secure,
the warrior went   to the worthy Dane;
1610 the thane sought the throne   where a sovereign sat,
that steadfast hero,   Hrothgar the Great.

Beowulf spoke,   son of Ecgtheow:
"Now we must say   as far-sailing seamen,
we wish to make way   homeward to Hygelac.

1615 Here we were well   and warmly received.
If anything further   would earn your favor,
some deed of war   that remains to be done
for the master of men,   I shall always be ready.
Should word ever wend   over wide ocean
1620 that nearby nations   menace your marches,
as those who detest you   sometimes have tried,
I shall summon a thousand   thanes to your aid.
I know Hygelac,   though newly-anointed
the nation's shepherd,   will surely consent
1625 to honor my offer   in word and action.
If you ever need men,   I shall muster at once
a thicket of spears   and support you in strength.
Should Hrethric, your son,   sail overseas,
he shall find friends   in the fort of the Geats.
1630 It is well for the worthy   to fare in far countries."

Hrothgar offered   these answering words:
"Heaven's Sovereign   has set in your heart
this vow you have voiced.   I never have known
someone so young   to speak more wisely.
1635 You are peerless in strength,   princely in spirit,
straightforward in speech.   If a spear fells
Hrethel's son,   if a hostile sword-stroke
kills him in combat   or after, with illness,
slays your leader   while you still live,
1640 the Sea-Geats surely   could name no better
to serve as their king   and keeper of treasure,
should you wish to wield   rule in your realm.
I sensed your spirit   the instant I saw you,
precious Beowulf,   bringer of peace
1645 for both our peoples: War-Danes and Weders,
so often sundered   by strife in the past.
While I wield the rule   of this wide realm,
men will exchange   many more greetings
and riches will ride   in ring-bowed ships
1650 bearing their gifts   where the gannets bathe.
I know your countrymen   keep to old ways,
fast in friendship,   and war as well."

Then the hall's holder,   Healfdene's son,
gave his protector   twelve more treasures,
1655 bidding he bear   these tokens safely
home to his kin,   and quickly return.
The good king kissed   that noblest of knights;
the hoary-haired warrior   hugged him and wept,
too well aware   with the wisdom of age
1660 that he never might see   the young man again
coming to council.   So close had they grown,
so strong in esteem,   he could scarcely endure
the secret sorrow   that surged in his heart;

the flame of affection   burned in his blood.
1665   But Beowulf walked   away with his wealth;
proud of his prizes,   he trod on the turf.
Standing at anchor,   his sea-courser
chafed for its captain.   All the way home
Hrothgar's gifts   were often honored.
1670   That was a king   accorded respect
until age unmanned him,   like many another.

High-hearted,   the band of young braves
strode to the sea,   wrapped in their ring-mesh,
linked and locked shirts.   The land-watcher spied
1675   the fighters faring,   just as before.
He called no taunts   from the top of the cliff
but galloped to greet them   and tell them the Geats
would always be welcome,   armored warriors
borne on their ship.   The broad longboat
1680   lay on the beach,   laden with chain-mail,
chargers and treasures   behind its tall prow.
The mast soared high   over Hrothgar's hoard.

The boat-guard was given   a gold-bound sword;
thereafter that man   had honor enhanced,
1685   bearing an heirloom   to Heorot's mead-bench.
They boarded their vessel,   breasted the deep,
left Denmark behind.   A halyard hoisted
the sea-wind's shroud;   the sail was sheeted,
bound to the mast,   and the beams moaned
1690   as a fair wind wafted   the wave-rider forward.
Foamy-throated,   the longboat bounded,
swept on the swells   of the swift sea-stream
until welcoming capes   were sighted ahead,
the cliffs of Geat-land.   The keel grounded
1695   as wind-lift thrust it   straight onto sand.

The harbor-guard hastened   hence from his post.
He had looked long   on an empty ocean
and waited to meet   the much-missed men.
He moored the broad-beamed   bow to the beach
1700   with woven lines   lest the backwash of waves
bear off the boat.   Then Beowulf ordered
treasures unloaded,   the lordly trappings,
gold that was going   to Hygelac's hall,
close to the cliff-edge,   where the ring-giver kept
1705   his comrades about him.
                              That building was bold
at the hill's crown;   and queenly Hygd,
Haereth's daughter,   dwelt there as well.
Wise and refined,   though her winters were few,
she housed in her bower,   enclosed by the keep,
1710   and granted generous   gifts to the Geats,

       most unlike Modthryth,⁶   a maiden so fierce
       that none but her father   dared venture near.
       The brave man who gazed   at Modthryth by day
       might reckon a death-rope   already twisted,
1715   might count himself quickly   captured and killed,
       the stroke of a sword   prescribed for his trespass.
       Such is no style   for a queen to proclaim:
       though peerless, a woman   ought to weave peace,
       not snatch away life   for illusory slights.

1720   Modthryth's madness   was tamed by marriage.
       Ale-drinkers say   her ill-deeds ended
       once she was given   in garlands of gold
       to Hemming's kinsman.   She came to his hall
       over pale seas,   accepted that prince,
1725   a fine young heir,   at her father's behest.
       Thenceforth on the throne,   she was famed for fairness,
       making the most   of her lot in life,
       sustained by loving   her lordly sovereign.
       That king, Offa,   was called by all men
1730   the ablest of any   ruling a realm
       between two seas,   so I am told.
       Gifted in war,   a wise gift-giver
       everywhere honored,   the spear-bold soldier
       held his homeland   and also fathered
1735   help for the heroes   of Hemming's kindred:
       war-worthy Eomer,   grandson of Garmund.

       Brave Beowulf   marched with his band,
       strode up the sands   of the broad beach
       while the sun in the south   beamed like a beacon.
1740   The earls went eagerly   up to the keep
       where the strong sovereign,   Ongentheow's slayer,
       the young war-king   doled out gold rings.
       Beowulf's coming   was quickly proclaimed.
       Hygelac heard   that his shoulder-shielder
1745   had entered the hall,   whole and unharmed
       by bouts of battle.   The ruler made room
       for the foot-guest crossing   the floor before him.

       Saluting his lord   with a loyal speech
       earnestly worded,   the winner in war
1750   sat facing the king,   kinsman with kinsman.
       A mead-vessel moved   from table to table
       as Haereth's daughter,   heedful of heroes,
       bore the wine-beaker   from hand to hand.
       Keen to elicit   his comrade's account
1755   in the high-roofed hall,   Hygelac graciously
       asked how the Sea-Geats   fared on their foray:

---

6. "Modthryth" may mean "arrogant in temper"; it may be a reference to an arrogant woman rather than a proper name.

"Say what befell   from your sudden resolve
to seek out strife   over salt waters,
to struggle in Heorot.   Have you helped Hrothgar
1760   ward off the well-known   cares of his kingdom?
You have cost me disquiet,   angst and anguish.
Doubting the outcome,   dearest of men,
for anyone meeting   that murderous demon,
I sought to dissuade you   from starting the venture.
1765   The South-Danes themselves   should have settled their feud
with ghastly Grendel.   Now I thank God
that I see you again,   safe and sound."

Beowulf spoke,   son of Ecgtheow:
"For a great many men   our meeting's issue
1770   is hardly hidden,   my lord Hygelac.
What a fine fracas   passed in that place
when both of us battled   where Grendel had brought
sore sorrow   on scores of War-Scyldings!
I avenged every one,   so that none of his kin
1775   anywhere need   exult at our night-bout,
however long   the loathsome race lives,
covered with crime.   When Hrothgar came
and heard what had happened   there in the ring-hall,
he sat me at once   with his own two sons.

1780   "The whole of his host   gathered in gladness;
all my life long   I never have known
such joy in a hall   beneath heaven's vault.
The acclaimed queen,   her kindred's peace-pledge,
would sometimes circle   the seated youths,
1785   lavishing rings   on delighted young lords.
Hrothgar's daughter   handed the elders
ale-cups aplenty,   pouring for each
old trooper in turn.   I heard the hall-sitters
calling her Freawaru   after she proffered
1790   the studded flagon.   To Froda's fair son
that maiden is sworn.   This match seems meet
to the lord of Scyldings,   who looks to settle
his Heatho-Bard feud.   Yet the best of brides
seldom has stilled   the spears of slaughter
1795   so swiftly after   a sovereign was stricken.

"Ingeld and all   his earls will be rankled,
watching that woman   walk in their hall
with high-born Danes   doing her bidding.
Her escorts will wear   ancient heirlooms:
1800   Heatho-Bard swords   with braided steel blades,
weapons once wielded   and lost in war
along with the lives   of friends in the fray.
Eyeing the ring-hilts,   an old ash-warrior
will brood in his beer   and bitterly pine

1805   for the stark reminders   of men slain in strife.
      He will grimly begin   to goad a young soldier,
      testing and tempting   a troubled heart,
      his whispered words   waking war-evil:

      "'My friend, have you spotted   the battle-sword
1810   that your father bore   on his final foray?
      Wearing his war-mask,   Withergyld fell
      when foemen seized   the field of slaughter.
      His priceless blade   became battle-plunder.
      Now some son   of the Scylding who slew him
1815   struts on our floor,   flaunting his trophy,
      an heirloom that you   should rightfully own.'

      "He will prick and pique   with pointed words
      time after time   till the challenge is taken,
      the maiden's attendant   is murdered in turn,
1820   blade-bitten   to sleep in his blood,
      forfeit his life   for his father's feat.
      Another will run,   knowing the road.
      So on both sides   oaths will be broken;
      and afterward Ingeld's   anger will grow
1825   hotter, unchecked,   as he chills toward his wife.
      Hence I would hold   the Heatho-Bards likely
      to prove unpeaceable   partners for Danes.

      "Now I shall speak   of my strife with Grendel,
      further acquainting   the kingdom's keeper
1830   with all that befell   when our fight began.
      Heaven's gem   had gone overhead;
      in darkness the dire   demon stalked us
      while we stood guard   unharmed in Heorot.
      Hondscioh was doomed   to die with the onslaught,
1835   first to succumb,   though clad for combat
      when grabbed by Grendel,   who gobbled him whole.
      That beloved young thane   was eaten alive.
      Not one to leave   the hall empty-handed,
      the bloody-toothed terror   intended to try
1840   his might upon me.   A curious creel
      hung from his hand,   cunningly clasped
      and strangely sewn   with devilish skill
      from skin of a dragon.   The demon would stuff me,
      sinless, inside   like so many others;
1845   but rising in wrath,   I stood upright.
      It is too long a tale,   how the people's plaguer
      paid for his crimes   with proper requital;
      but the feat reflected   finely, my lord,
      on the land you lead.   Though the foe fled
1850   to live awhile longer,   he left behind him
      as spoor of the strife   a hand in Heorot.
      Humbled, he fell   to the floor of the mere.

"The warder of Scyldings   rewarded my warfare
with much treasure   when morning arrived,
1855   and we sat for a feast   with songs and sagas.
He told many tales   he learned in his lifetime.
Sometimes a soldier   struck the glad harp,
the sounding wood;   sometimes strange stories
were spoken like spells,   tragic and true,
1860   rightly related.   The large-hearted lord
sometimes would start   to speak of his youth,
his might in war.   His memories welled;
ancient in winters,   he weighed them all.

"So we delighted   the livelong day
1865   until darkness drew   once more upon men.
Then Grendel's mother,   mourning her son,
swiftly set out   in search of revenge
against warlike Geats.   The grisly woman
wantonly slew   a Scylding warrior:
1870   aged Aeschere,   the king's counselor,
relinquished his life.   Nor in the morning
might death-weary Danes   bear off his body
to burn on a bier,   for the creature clutching him
fled to her fastness   under a waterfall.
1875   This was the sorest   of sorrows that Hrothgar
suffered as king.   Distraught, he beseeched me
to do in your name   a notable deed.
If I dived in the deep,   heedless of danger,
to war underwater,   he would reward me.

1880   "Under I went,   as now is well-known;
and I found the hideous   haunter of fens.
For a time we two   contested our hand-strength;
then I struck off her head   with a huge sword
that her battle-hall held,   and her hot blood
1885   boiled in the lake.   Leaving that place
was no easy feat,   but fate let me live.
Again I was granted   gifts that the guardian,
Healfdene's son,   had sworn to bestow.
The king of that people   kept his promise,
1890   allotting me all   he had earlier offered:
meed for my might,   with more treasures,
my choice from the hoard   of Healfdene's son.
These, my lord,   I deliver to you,
as proof of fealty.   My future depends
1895   wholly on you.   I have in this world
few close kin   but my king, Hygelac."

He bade the boar-banner   now be brought in,
the high helmet,   hard mail-shirt,
and splendid sword,   describing them thus:
1900   "When Hrothgar gave me   this hoarded gear,

the sage sovereign   entreated I tell
the tale of his gift: this treasure was held
by Heorogar, king,   who long was the lord
of Scylding people.   It should have passed
1905 to armor the breast   of bold Heoroweard,
the father's favorite,   faithful and brave;
but he willed it elsewhere,   so use it well."

I have heard how horses   followed that hoard,
four dappled mounts,   matching and fleet.
1910 He gave up his gifts,   gold and horses.
Kinsmen should always   act with honor,
not spin one another   in snares of spite
or secretly scheme   to kill close comrades.
Always the nephew   had aided his uncle;
1915 each held the other's   welfare at heart.
He gave to Queen Hygd   the golden collar,
wondrously wrought,   Wealtheow's token,
and also three steeds,   sleek and bright-saddled.
Thereafter her breast   was graced by the gift.

1920 So Ecgtheow's son   won his repute
as a man of mettle,   acting with honor,
yet mild-hearted   toward hearth-companions,
harming no one   when muddled with mead.
Bold in battle,   he guarded the guerdon
1925 that God had granted,   the greatest strength
of all humankind,   though once he was thought
weak and unworthy,   a sloucher and slacker,
mocked for meekness   by men on the mead-bench,
and given no gifts   by the lord of the Geats.
1930 Every trouble   untwined in time
for the glory-blessed man.
        A blade was brought
at the king's request,   Hrethel's heirloom
glinting with gold.   No greater treasure,
no nobler sword   was held in his hoard.
1935 He lay that brand   on Beowulf's lap
and also bestowed   a spacious estate,
hall and high seat.   When land and lordship
were left to them both,   by birthright and law,
he who ranked higher   ruled the wide realm.

III. The Dragon

1940 It happened long after,   with Hygelac dead,
that war-swords slew   Heardred, his son,
when Battle-Scylfings   broke his shield-wall
and hurtled headlong   at Hereric's nephew.
So Beowulf came   to rule the broad realm.
1945 For fifty winters   he fostered it well;

then the old king,   keeper of kinfolk,
heard of a dragon   drawn from the darkness.
He had long lain   in his lofty fastness,
the steep stone-barrow,   guarding his gold;
1950   but a path pierced it,   known to no person
save him who found it   and followed it forward.
That stranger seized   but a single treasure.
He bore it in hand   from the heathen hoard:
a finely-worked flagon   he filched from the lair
1955   where the dragon dozed.   Enraged at the robber,
the sneaking thief   who struck while he slept,
the guardian woke   glowing with wrath,
as his nearest neighbors   were soon to discern.

It was not by choice   that the wretch raided
1960   the wondrous worm-hoard.   The one who offended
was stricken himself,   sorely distressed,
the son of a warrior   sold as a slave.
Escaping his bondage,   he braved the barrens
and guiltily groped   his way below ground.
1965   There the intruder   trembled with terror
hearing the dragon   who drowsed in the dark,
an ancient evil   sleepily breathing.
His fate was to find   as fear unmanned him
his fingers feeling   a filigreed cup.

1970   Many such goblets   had gone to the earth-house,
legacies left   by a lordly people.
In an earlier age   someone unknown
had cleverly covered   those costly treasures.
That thane held the hoard   for the lifetime allowed him,
1975   but gold could not gladden   a man in mourning.
Newly-built   near the breaking waves,
a barrow stood   at the base of a bluff,
its entrance sculpted   by secret arts.
Earthward the warrier   bore the hoard-worthy
1980   portion of plate,   the golden craftwork.
The ringkeeper spoke   these words as he went:

"Hold now, Earth,   what men may not,
the hoard of the heroes,   earth-gotten wealth
when it first was won.   War-death has felled them,
1985   an evil befalling   each of my people.
The long-house is mirthless   when men are lifeless.
I have none to wear sword,   none to bear wine
or polish the precious   vessels and plates.
Gone are the brethren   who braved many battles.
1990   From the hard helmet   the hand-wrought gilding
drops in the dust.   Asleep are the smiths
who knew how to burnish   the war-chief's mask
or mend the mail-shirts   mangled in battle.

Shields and mail-shirts   molder with warriors
1995   and follow no foes   to faraway fields.
No harp rejoices   to herald the heroes,
no hand-fed hawk   swoops through the hall,
no stallion stamps   in the keep's courtyard.
Death has undone   many kindreds of men."

2000   Stricken in spirit,   he spoke of his sorrow
as last of his line,   drearily drifting
through day and dark   until death's flood-tide
stilled his heart.   The old night-scather
was happy to glimpse   the unguarded hoard.
2005   Balefully burning,   he seeks out barrows.
Naked and hateful   in a raiment of flame,
the dragon dreaded   by outland dwellers
must gather and guard   the heathen gold,
no better for wealth   but wise with his winters.

2010   For three hundred winters   the waster of nations
held that mighty   hoard in his earth-hall
till one man wronged him,   arousing his wrath.
The wretched robber   ransomed his life
with the prize he pilfered,   the plated flagon.
2015   Beholding that marvel   men of old made,
his fief-lord forgave   the skulker's offense.
One treasure taken   had tainted the rest.
Waking in wrath,   the worm reared up
and slid over stones.   Stark-hearted,
2020   he spotted the footprints   where someone had stepped,
stealthily creeping   close to his jaws.
The fortunate man   slips swiftly and safely
through the worst dangers   if the World's Warder
grants him that grace.
                        Eager and angry,
2025   the hoard-guard hunted   the thief who had haunted
his hall while he slept.   He circled the stone-house,
but out in that wasteland   the one man he wanted
was not to be found.   How fearsome he felt,
how fit for battle!   Back in his barrow
2030   he tracked the intruder   who dared to tamper
with glorious gold.   Fierce and fretful,
the dragon waited   for dusk and darkness.
The rage-swollen holder   of headland and hoard
was plotting reprisal: flames for his flagon.
2035   Then day withdrew,   and the dragon, delighted,
would linger no longer   but flare up and fly.
His onset was fearful   for folk on the land,
and a cruel ending   soon came for their king.

The ghastly specter   scattered his sparks
2040   and set their buildings   brightly burning,

flowing with flames   as homesteaders fled.
He meant to leave   not one man alive.
That wreaker of havoc   hated and harried
the Geatish folk   fleeing his flames.
2045   Far and wide   his warfare was watched
until night waned,   and the worm went winging
back to the hall   where his hoard lay hidden,
sure of his stronghold,   his walls and his war,
sure of himself,   deceived by his pride.

2050   Then terrible tidings   were taken to Beowulf:
how swiftly his own   stronghold was stricken,
that best of buildings   bursting with flames
and his throne melting.   The hero was heart-sore;
the wise man wondered   what wrong he had wrought
2055   and how he trangressed   against old law,
the Lord Everlasting,   Ruler of All.
His grief was great,   and grim thoughts
boiled in his breast   as never before.
The fiery foe   had flown to his coastlands,
2060   had sacked and seared   his keep by the sea.
For that the war-king   required requital.
He ordered a broad-shield   fashioned of iron,
better for breasting   baleful blazes
than the linden-wood   that warded his warriors.
2065   Little was left   of the time lent him
for life in the world;   and the worm as well,
who had haughtily held   his hoard for so long.
Scorning to follow   the far-flying foe
with his whole host,   the ring-giver reckoned
2070   the wrath of a dragon   unworthy of dread.
Fearless and forceful,   he often had faced
the straits of struggle   blessed with success.
Beowulf braved   many a battle,
after ridding Hrothgar's   hall of its horrors
2075   and grappling with Grendel's   gruesome kin.

Not least of his clashes   had come when the king
Hygelac fell   while fighting the Frisians
in hand-to-hand combat.   His friend and fief-lord,
the son of Hrethel,   was slain in the onslaught,
2080   stricken to death   by a blood-drinking blade.
Beowulf battled   back to the beach
where he proved his strength   with skillful swimming,
for he took to the tide   bearing the trophies
of thirty earls   he had felled in the field.
2085   None of the Hetware   needed to boast
how they fared on foot,   flaunting their shields
against that fierce fighter,   for few remained
after the battle   to bear the tale home.

Over wide waters   the lone swimmer went,
2090 the son of Ecgtheow   swept on the sea-waves
back to his homeland,   forlorn with his loss,
and hence to Hygd   who offered her hoard:
rings and a realm,   a throne for the thane.
With Hygelac dead   she doubted her son
2095 could guard the Geats   from foreigners' forays.
Refusing her boon,   Beowulf bade
the leaderless lords   to hail the lad
as their rightful ruler.   He chose not to reign
by thwarting his cousin   but to counsel the king
2100 and guide with good will   until Heardred grew older.

It was Heardred who held   the Weder-Geats' hall
when outcast Scylfings   came seeking its safety:
Eanmund and Eadgils,   nephews of Onela.
That strong sea-king   and spender of treasures
2105 sailed from Sweden   pursuing the rebels
who challenged his right   to rule their realm.
For lending them haven,   Hygelac's son
suffered the sword-stroke   that spilled out his life.
The Swede headed home   when Heardred lay dead,
2110 leaving Beowulf,   lordship of Geats.
That was a good king,   keeping the gift-seat;
yet Heardred's death   dwelled in his thoughts.
A long time later   he offered his aid
to end the exile   of destitute Eadgils.
2115 He summoned an army   for Ohthere's son,
sent weapons and warriors   over wide waters,
a voyage of vengeance   to kill off a king.

Such were the struggles   and tests of strength
the son of Ecgtheow   saw and survived.
2120 His pluck was proven   in perilous onslaughts
till that fateful day   when he fought the dragon.
As leader of twelve   trailing that terror,
the greatest of Geats   glowered with rage
when he looked on the lair   where the worm lurked.
2125 By now he had found   how the feud flared,
this fell affliction   befalling his kingdom,
for the kingly cup   had come to his hand
from the hand of him   who raided the hoard.
That sorry slave   had started the strife,
2130 and against his will   he went with the warriors,
a thirteenth man   bringing the band
to the barrow's brink   which he alone knew.
Hard by the surge   of the seething sea
gaped a cavern   glutted with golden
2135 medallions and chains.   The murderous manbane
hunkered within,   hungry for warfare.

No taker would touch   his treasures cheaply:
the hoard's holder   would drive a hard bargain.

2140 The proud war-king   paused on the sea-point
to lighten the hearts   of his hearth-companions,
though his heart was heavy   and hankered for death.
It was nearing him now.   That taker of treasure
would sunder the soul   from his old bones and flesh.
So Beowulf spoke,   the son of Ecgtheow,
2145 recalling the life   he was loathe to lose:

"From boyhood I bore   battles and bloodshed,
struggles and strife: I still see them all.
I was given at seven   to house with King Hrethel,
my mother's father   and friend of our folk.
2150 He kept me fairly   with feasts and fine gifts.
I fared no worse   than one of his sons:
Herebeald, Hathcyn,   or princely Hygelac
who was later my lord.   The eldest, Herebeald,
unwittingly went   to a wrongful death
2155 when Hathcyn's horn-bow   hurled an arrow.
Missing the mark,   it murdered the kinsman;
a brother was shot   by the blood-stained shaft.
This blow to the heart   was brutal and baffling.
A prince had fallen.   The felon went free.[1]

2160 "So it is sore   for an old man to suffer
his son swinging   young on the gallows,
gladdening ravens.   He groans in his grief
and loudly laments   the lad he has lost.
No help is at hand   from hard-won wisdom
2165 or the march of years.   Each morning reminds him
his heir is elsewhere,   and he has no heart
to wait for a second   son in his stronghold
when death has finished   the deeds of the first.
He ceaselessly sees   his son's dwelling,
2170 the desolate wine-hall,   the windswept grave-sward
where swift riders   and swordsmen slumber.
No harp-string sounds,   no song in the courtyard.
He goes to his bed   sighing with sorrow,
one soul for another.   His home is hollow;
2175 his field, fallow.
                              "So Hrethel suffered,
hopeless and heart-sore   with Herebeald gone.
He would do no deed   to wound the death-dealer
or harrow his household   with hatred and anger;
but bitter bloodshed   had stolen his bliss,

1. Even in cases of involuntary manslaughter, punishment was required to avenge the dead. In this instance, it seems that a ritual, sacrificial hanging was performed to spare Hathcyn for murdering his brother Herebeald.

2180   and he quit his life   for the light of the Lord.
        Like a luckier man,   he could leave his land
        in the hands of a son,   though he loved him no longer.

        "Then strife and struggle   of Geats and Swedes
        crossed the wide water.   Warfare wounded
2185   both sides in battle   when Hrethel lay buried.
        Ongentheow's sons,   fierce and unfriendly,
        suddenly struck   at Hreosna-Beorh
        and bloodied the bluff   with baneful slaughter.
        Our foes in this feud   soon felt the wrath
2190   of my kinsman the king   claiming our due,
        though the counterblow   cost his own life.
        Hathcyn was killed,   his kingship cut short.
        The slayer himself   was slain in the morning.
        I have heard how Eofor   struck the old Scylfing.
2195   Sword-ashen,   Ongentheow sank
        with his helm split: heedful of harm,
        to kinsman and king,   the hand would not halt
        the death-blow it dealt.
                                "My own sword-arm
        repaid my prince   for the gifts he granted.
2200   He gave me a fiefdom,   the land I have loved.
        He never had need   to seek among Spear-Danes,
        Gifthas or Swedes   and get with his gifts
        a worse warrior.   I wielded my sword
        at the head of our host;   so shall I hold
2205   this blade that I bear   boldly in battle
        as long as life lasts.   It has worn well
        since the day when Daeghrefn   died by my hand,
        the Frankish foe   who fought for the Frisians,
        bearing their banner.   He broke in my grip,
2210   never to barter   the necklace he robbed
        from Hygelac's corpse.   I crushed that killer;
        his bones snapped,   and his life-blood spilled.
        I slew him by strength,   not by the sword.
        Now I shall bear   his brand into battle:
2215   hand and hard sword   will fight for the hoard."

        Now Beowulf spoke   his last battle-boast:
        "In boyhood I braved   bitter clashes;
        still in old age   I would seek out strife
        and gain glory   guarding my folk,
2220   if the man-bane comes   from his cave to meet me."

        Then he turned to his troop   for the final time,
        bidding farewell   to bold helmet-bearers,
        fast in friendship: "I would wear no sword,
        no weapon at all   to ward off the worm,
2225   if I knew how to fight   this fiendish foe
        as I grappled with Grendel   one bygone night.

But here I shall find   fierce battle-fire
and breath envenomed,   therefore I bear
this mail-coat and shield.   I shall not shy
2230   from standing my ground   when I greet the guardian,
follow what will   at the foot of his wall.
I shall face the fiend   with a firm heart.
Let the Ruler of men   reckon my fate:
words are worthless   against the war-flyer.
2235   Bide by the barrow,   safe in your byrnies,
and watch, my warriors,   which of us two
will better bear   the brunt of our clash.
This war is not yours;   it is meted to me,
matching my strength,   man against monster.
2240   I shall do this deed   undaunted by death
and get you gold   or else get my ending,
borne off in battle,   the bane of your lord."

The hero arose,   helmed and hardy,
a war-king clad   in shield and corselet.
2245   He strode strongly   under the stone-cliff:
no faint-hearted man,   to face it unflinching!
Stalwart soldier   of so many marches,
unshaken when shields   were crushed in the clash,
he saw between stiles   an archway where steam
2250   burst like a boiling   tide from the barrow,
woeful for one   close to the worm-hoard.
He would not linger long   unburned by the lurker
or safely slip   through the searing lair.
Then a battle-cry broke   from Beowulf's breast
2255   as his rightful wrath   was roused for the reckoning.
His challenge sounded   under stark stone
where the hateful hoard-guard   heard in his hollow
the clear-voiced call   of a man coming.

No quarter was claimed;   no quarter given.
2260   First the beast's breath   blew hot from the barrow
as battle-bellows   boomed underground.
The stone-house stormer   swung up his shield
at the ghastly guardian.   Then the dragon's grim heart
kindled for conflict.   Uncoiling, he came
2265   seeking the Stalwart;   but the swordsman had drawn
the keen-edged blade   bequeathed him for combat,
and each foe confronted   the other with fear.
His will unbroken,   the warlord waited
behind his tall shield,   helm and hauberk.
2270   With fitful twistings   the fire-drake hastened
fatefully forward.   His fender held high,
Beowulf felt   the blaze blister through
hotter and sooner   than he had foreseen.
So for the first time   fortune was failing
2275   the mighty man   in the midst of a struggle.
Wielding his sword,   he struck at the worm

and his fabled blade   bit to the bone
through blazoned hide: bit and bounced back,
no match for the foe   in this moment of need.

2280   The peerless prince   was hard-pressed in response,
for his bootless blow   had maddened the monster
and fatal flames   shot further than ever,
lighting the land.   The blade he bared
failed in the fray,   though forged from iron.

2285   No easy end   for the son of Ecgtheow:
against his will   he would leave this world
to dwell elsewhere,   as every man must
when his days are done.   Swiftly the death-dealer
moved to meet him.   From the murderous breast

2290   bellows of breath   belched fresh flames.
Enfolded in fire,   he who formerly
ruled a whole realm   had no one to help him
hold off the heat,   for his hand-picked band
of princelings had fled,   fearing to face

2295   the foe with their lord.   Loving honor
less than their lives,   they hid in the holt.
But one among them   grieved for the Geats
and balked at the thought   of quitting a kinsman.

This one was Wiglaf,   son of Weohstan,
2300   kinsman of Aelfhere,   earl among Scylfings.
Seeing his liege-lord   suffering sorely
with war-mask scorched   by the searing onslaught,
the thankful thane   thought of the boons
his sovereign bestowed: the splendid homestead

2305   and folk-rights his father   formerly held.
No shirker could stop him   from seizing his shield
of yellow linden   and lifting the blade
Weohstan won   when he slew Eanmund,
son of Ohthere.   Spoils of that struggle,

2310   sword and scabbard,   smithwork of giants,
a byrnie of ring-mail   and bright burnished helm
were granted as gifts,   a thane's war-garb,
for Onela never   acknowledged his nephews,
but struck against both   of his brother's sons.

2315   When Eadgils avenged   Eanmund's death,
Weohstan fled.   Woeful and friendless,
he saved that gear   for seasons of strife,
foreseeing his son   someday might crave
sword and corselet.   He came to his kinsman,

2320   the prince of the Geats,   and passed on his heirlooms,
hoping Wiglaf   would wear them with honor.
Old then, and wise,   he went from the world.

This war was the first   young Wiglaf would fight
helping the king.   His heart would not quail
2325   nor weapon fail   as the foe would find

going against him;   but he made his grim mood
known to the men: "I remember the time
when taking our mead   in the mighty hall,
all of us offered   oaths to our liege-lord.
2330   We promised to pay   for princely trappings
by staunchly wielding   sword-blades in war,
if need should arise.   Now we are needed
by him who chose,   from the whole of his host,
twelve for this trial,   trusting our claims
2335   as warriors worthy   of wearing our blades,
bearing keen spears.   Our king has come here
bent on battling   the man-bane alone,
because among warriors   one keeper of kinfolk
has done, undaunted,   the most deeds of daring.
2340   But this day our lord   needs dauntless defenders
so long as the frightful   fires keep flaring.
God knows I would gladly   give my own body
for flames to enfold   with the gold-giver.
Shameful, to shoulder   our shields homeward!
2345   First we must fell   this fearsome foe
and protect the life   of our people's lord.
It is wrong that one man   be wrathfully racked
for his former feats   and fall in this fight,
guarding the Geats.   We shall share our war-gear:
2350   shield and battle-shirt,   helm and hard sword."

So speaking, he stormed   through the reek of smoke,
with helmet on head,   to help his lord.
"Beloved Beowulf,   bear up your blade.
You pledged in your youth,   powerful prince,
2355   never to let   your luster lessen
while life was left you.   Now summon your strength.
Stand steadfast.   I shall stand with you."

After these words   the worm was enraged.
For a second time   the spiteful specter
2360   flew at his foe,   and he wreathed in flames
the hated human   he hungered to harm.
His dreadful fire-wind   drove in a wave,
charring young Wiglaf's   shield to the boss,
nor might a byrnie   bar that breath
2365   from burning the brave   spear-bearer's breast.
Wiglaf took cover   close to his kinsman,
shielded by iron   when linden was cinder.
Then the war-king,   recalling past conquests,
struck with full strength   straight at the head.
2370   His battle-sword, Naegling,   stuck there and split,
shattered in combat,   so sharp was the shock
to Beowulf's great   gray-banded blade.
He never was granted   the gift of a sword
as hard and strong   as the hand which held it.

2375   I have heard that he broke   blood-hardened brands,
         so the weapon-bearer   was none the better.

         The fearful fire-drake,   scather of strongholds,
         flung himself forward   a final time,
         wild with wounds   yet wily and sly.
2380   In the heat of the fray,   he hurtled headlong
         to fasten his fangs   in the foe's throat.
         Beowulf's life-blood   came bursting forth
         on those terrible tusks.   Just then, I am told,
         the second warrior   sprang from his side,
2385   a man born for battle   proving his mettle,
         keen to strengthen   his kinsman in combat.
         He took no heed   of the hideous head
         scorching his hand   as he hit lower down.
         The sword sank in,   patterned and plated;
2390   the flames of the foe   faltered, faded.
         Though gored and giddy,   Beowulf gathered
         strength once again   and slipped out his sheath-knife,
         the keen killing-blade   he kept in his corselet.
         Then the Geats' guardian   gutted the dragon,
2395   felling that fiend   with the help of his friend,
         two kinsmen together   besting the terror.
         So should a thane   succor his sovereign.

         That deed was the king's   crowning conquest;
         Beowulf's work   in the world was done.
2400   He soon felt his wound   swelling and stinging
         where fell fangs   had fastened upon him,
         and evil venom   enveloped his heart.
         Wisely he sought   a seat by the stone-wall,
         and his gaze dwelled   on the dark doorway
2405   delved in the dolmen,   the straight stiles
         and sturdy archway   sculpted by giants.
         With wonderful kindness   Wiglaf washed
         the clotting blood   from his king and kinsman;
         his hands loosened   the lord's high helm.
2410   Though banefully bitten,   Beowulf spoke,
         for he knew his lifetime   would last no longer.
         The count of his days   had come to a close.
         His joys were done.   Death drew near him.

         "Now I would wish   to will my son
2415   these weapons of war,   had I been awarded
         an heir of my own,   holder of heirlooms.
         I fathered our folk   for fifty winters.
         No warlike lord   of neighboring lands
         dared to assail us   or daunt us with dread.
2420   A watchful warden,   I waited on fate
         while keeping the Geats   clear of quarrels.
         I swore many oaths;   not one was wrongful.

So I rejoice,   though sick with my death-wound,
that God may not blame me   for baseless bloodshed
2425   or killing of kin   when breath quits my body.
Hurry below   and look on the hoard,
beloved Wiglaf.   The worm lies sleeping
under gray stone,   sorely stricken
and stripped of his gold.   Go swiftly and seize it.
2430   Get me giltwork   and glittering gems:
I would set my sight   on that store of wealth.
Loath would I be   to leave for less
the life and lordship   I held for so long."

I have heard how swiftly   the son of Weohstan
2435   hastened to heed   his wounded and weakening
war-lord's behest.   In his woven mail-shirt,
his bright byrnie,   he entered the barrow;
and passing its threshold,   proud and princely,
he glimpsed all the gold   piled on the ground,
2440   the walled-in wealth   won by the worm,
that fierce night-flyer.   Flagons were standing,
embossed wine-beakers   lying unburnished,
their inlays loosened.   There were lofty helmets
and twisted arm-rings   rotting and rusting.
2445   Gold below ground   may betray into grief
any who hold it: heed me who will!

Wiglaf saw also   a gold-woven standard,
a wonder of handiwork,   finger-filigreed,
high above ground.   It gave off a glow
2450   that let him behold   the whole of the hoard.
I am told he took   from that trove of giants
goblets and platters   pressed to his breastplate,
and the golden banner   glinting brightly.
He spotted no sign   of the stricken worm.
2455   The iron-edged brand   old Beowulf bore
had mortally wounded   the warder of wealth
and fiery foe   whose flames in the night
welled so fiercely   before he was felled.

Bent with his burden,   the messenger hastened
2460   back to his master,   burning to know
whether the brave   but wound-weakened
lord of the Weders   was lost to the living.
Setting his spoils   by the storied prince
whose lifeblood blackened   the ground with gore,
2465   Wiglaf wakened   the war-lord with water,
and these words thrust   like spears through his breast
as the ancient one grimly   gazed on the gold:

"I offer my thanks   to the Almighty Master,
the King of Glory,   for granting my kindred
2470   for these precious things   I look upon last.

Losing my life,   I have bought this boon
to lighten my leave-day.   Look to our people,
for you shall be leader;   I lead no longer.
Gather my guard   and raise me a grave-mound
2475   housing my ashes   at Hronesnaess,
reminding my kin   to recall their king
after his pyre   has flared on the point.
Seafarers passing   shall say when they see it
'Beowulf's Barrow'   as bright longboats
2480   drive over darkness,   daring the flood."

So the stern prince   bestowed on his sword-thane
and keen spear-wielder   the kingly collar,
his gold-plated helm   and hammered hauberk.
He told him to bear them   bravely in battle:
2485   "Farewell, Wiglaf,   last Waegmunding.
I follow our fathers,   foredestined to die,
swept off by fate,   though strong and steadfast."
These heartfelt words   were the warrior's last
before his body   burned in the bale-fire
2490   and his soul sought   the doom of the truthful.

Smitten with sorrow,   the young man saw
the old lord he loved   lying in pain
as life left him.   Slain and slayer
died there together: the dread earth-dragon,
2495   deprived of his life,   no longer would lurk
coiled on the hoard.   Hard-hammered swords
had felled the far-flyer   in front of his lair.
No more would he sport   on the midnight sky,
proud of his wealth,   his power and pomp.
2500   He sprawled on stone   where the war-chief slew him.
Though deeds of daring   were done in that land,
I have heard of no man   whose might would suffice
to face the fire-drake's   fuming breath
or help him escape   if he handled the hoard
2505   once he had woken   its warder from sleep.
Beowulf paid   for that lode with his life;
his loan of days   was lost to the dragon.

Before long the laggards   limped from the woods,
ten cowards together,   the troth-breakers
2510   who had failed to bare   their blades in battle
at the moment their master   needed them most.
In shame they shouldered   their shields and spears.
Armored for war,   they went to Wiglaf
who sorrowfully sat   at their sovereign's shoulder.
2515   Laving his leader,   the foot-soldier failed
to waken the fallen   fighter one whit,
nor could he will   his lord back to life.
The World's Warden   decided what deeds

men might achieve   in those days and these.

2520   A hard answer   was easily offered
by young Wiglaf,   Weohstan's son.
With little love   he looked on the shirkers:
"I tell you in truth,   takers of treasure,
bench-sitting boasters   brave in the hall:
2525   Beowulf gave you   the gear that you wear,
the best helms and hauberks   found near or far
for a prince to proffer   his thankless thanes;
but he wasted his wealth   on a worthless troop
who cast off their king   at the coming of war.
2530   Our lord had no need   to laud his liege-men;
yet God, giver   of glory and vengeance,
granted him strength   to stand with his sword.
I could do little   to lengthen his life
facing that foe,   but I fought nonetheless:
2535   beyond my power   I propped up my prince.
The fire-drake faltered   after I struck him,
and his fuming jaws   flamed less fiercely,
but too few friends   flew to our king
when evil beset him.   Now sword-bestowing
2540   and gold-getting   shall cease for the Geats.
You shall have no joy   in the homeland you love.
Your farms shall be forfeit,   and each man fare
alone and landless   when foreign lords
learn of your flight,   your failure of faith.
2545   Better to die   than dwell in disgrace."

Then Wiglaf bade   that the battle-tidings
be sent to the camp   over the sea-cliff
where warriors waited   with shields unslung,
sadly sitting   from dawn until noon
2550   to learn if their lord   and beloved leader
had seen his last sunrise   or soon would return.
The herald would leave them   little to doubt;
he sped up the headland   and spoke to them all:

"Now the wish-granter,   warlord of Weders,
2555   lies on his death-bed.   The leader of Geats
stays in the slaughter-place,   slain by the worm
sprawled at his side.   Dagger-stricken,
the slayer was felled,   though a sword had failed
to wound the serpent.   Weohstan's son,
2560   Wiglaf is waiting   by Beowulf's body;
a living warrior   watches the lifeless,
sad-heartedly   sitting to guard
the loved and the loathed.   Look now for war
as Franks and Frisians   learn how the king
2565   has fallen in combat.   Few foreigners love us,

for Hygelac angered   the harsh Hugas
when his fleet forayed   to far-off Frisia.
Fierce Hetware   met him with forces
bigger than his.   They broke him in battle;
2570 that mail-clad chieftain   fell with his men.
Hygelac took   no trophies to thanes;
no king of the Meroving   wishes us well.

"I also foresee   strife with the Swedes,
feud without end,   for all know Ongentheow
2575 slew Hrethel's son   when Hathcyn first forayed
near Ravenswood   with hot-headed Geats
and raided the realm   of Scylf-land's ruler.
That fearsome old foe,   father of Ohthere,
quickly struck back.   He cut down our king
2580 to rescue the queen   Hathcyn had captured.
Her captors had shorn   the crone of her gold,
dishonored the aged   mother of Onela.
Ongentheow followed   hard on their heels.
Wounded, weary   and fiercely-harried,
2585 those left unslain   by Swedish swords
limped off leaderless,   hid in the holt.
A huge army   beleaguered them there.
All night long   Ongentheow taunted
the wretched raiders.   At daybreak, he swore,
2590 he would slice them to slivers.   Some would swing
slung on his gallows,   sport for the ravens.
But gladness came   again to grim Geats
hearing Hygelac's   horns in the morning,
the trumpet calls   of the troop that tracked them.
2595 Hathcyn's brother,   bold with his band,
had rallied for battle.
                              "A bloody swath
Scylfings and Geats   left on the landscape,
everywhere gored   with spoor of the stricken.
So the two folks   stirred further feuds.
2600 Wise in warfare,   old Ongentheow
grimly stood off,   seeking the safety
of higher ground.   He had heard of Hygelac's
strength in struggles,   his pride and prowess.
Mistrusting his force   to fend off the foray,
2605 he feared for his family   and fell back to guard
the hoard hidden   behind his earthworks.
Then Hrethel's people   pressed the pursuit:
the standards of Hygelac   stormed the stronghold.
There the Swede   was snared between swords.
2610 Eofor humbled   that hoary-haired leader,
though Wulf struck first,   fierce with his weapon,
and a cut vein colored   the king's white head.
Undaunted, Ongentheow   warded him off;

Wulf was wounded   the worse in return:
2615   Ongentheow's blow   broke open his helm,
hurled him headlong,   helpless and bleeding
though not destined   to die on that day.
Then Eofor faced   the folk-lord alone.
Sternly he stood   when his brother slumped:
2620   Hygelac's soldier   with broadsword in hand
and helmet on head,   hoarded smithwork
shaped by old crafts,   shattered the shield-wall.
The king crumpled,   struck to the quick.

"Now the Geats gathered   after the slaughter.
2625   Some bound the wound   of Eofor's brother
and bundled him off   the field of battle.
Meanwhile one warrior   plundered the other:
Eofor stripped   the hard-hilted sword,
helm and corselet   from Ongentheow's corpse.
2630   He handed that heap   of armor to Hygelac.
Pleased with his prizes,   the king pledged in turn
to reward war-strokes   as lord of the Weders.
He gave great riches   to Wulf and Eofor.
Once they were home,   he honored each one
2635   with a hundred thousand   in land and linked rings.
No man in Middle-Earth   ever begrudged them
the favor and fortune   bestowed for their feat.
Yet a further honor   was offered Eofor:
the king's only daughter   adorned his house,
2640   awarded in wedlock   to Wonred's son.

"Full of this feud,   this festering hatred,
the Swedes, I am certain,   will swiftly beset us,
as soon as they learn   our lord lies lifeless
who held his hoard,   his hall and his realm
2645   against all foes   when heroes had fallen,
who fostered his folk   with fair kingship.
Now must we hasten,   behold our sovereign,
and bear him for burial.   The brave one shall not
be beggared of booty   to melt on his bier.
2650   Let funeral flames   greedily fasten
on gold beyond measure,   grimly gotten,
lucre our leader   bought with his life.
No earl shall take   tokens to treasure
nor maiden be made   fairer with finery
2655   strung at her throat.   Stripped of their wealth,
they shall wander woefully   all their lives long,
lordless and landless   now that their king
has laid aside laughter,   sport and song.
Their hands shall heft   many a spear-haft,
2660   cold in the morning.   No call of the harp

shall waken warriors   after their battles;
but the black raven   shall boast to the eagle,
crowing how finely   he fed on the fated
when, with the wolf,   he went rending the slain."

2665   Thus the terrible   tidings were told,
and the teller had not   mistaken the truth.
The warriors all rose   and woefully went
to look on the wonder   with welling tears.
They found on the sand   under Earnanaess
2670   their lifeless lord   laid there to rest,
beloved giver   of gifts and gold rings,
the war-king come   at the close of his days
to a marvelous death.   At first the monster
commanded their gaze: grim on the ground
2675   across from the king   the creature had crumpled,
scaly and scorched,   a fearsome fire-drake
fifty feet long.   He would fly no more,
free in the darkness,   nor drop to his den
at the break of dawn.   Death held the dragon;
2680   he never would coil   in his cavern again.
Beyond the serpent   stood flagons and jars,
plated flatware   and priceless swords
rotting in ruin,   etched out with rust.
These riches had rested   in Earth's embrace
2685   for a thousand winters,   the heritage held
by warders of old,   spell-enwoven
and toilfully tombed   that none might touch them,
unless God Himself,   granter of grace,
true Lord of glory,   allotted release
2690   to one of His choosing   and opened the hoard.

It little profited   him who had wrongfully
hidden the hand-wrought   wealth within walls.
His payment was scant   for slaying the one
with courage to claim it: the kill was quickly
2695   and harshly requited.   So the kingly
may come to strange ends   when their strength is spent
and time meted out.   They may not remain
as men among kin,   mirthful with mead.
Beowulf goaded   the gold's guardian,
2700   raised up the wrath,   not reckoning whether
his death-day had dawned,   not knowing the doom
solemnly sworn   by princes who placed
their hoard in that hollow: the thief who held it
would fall before idols,   forge himself hell-bonds,
2705   waste in torment   for touching the treasure.
He failed to consider   more fully and sooner
who rightfully owned   such awesome riches.

So spoke Wiglaf, son of Weohstan:
"By the whim of one man, many warriors
2710 sometimes may suffer, as here has happened.
No means were at hand to move my master;
no counsel could sway the kingdom's keeper
never to trouble the treasure's taker,
but leave him lying where long he had hidden,
2715 walled with his wealth until the world's ending.
He kept to his course, uncovered the hoard.
Fate was too strongly forcing him hither.
I have entered that hall, beheld everything
golden within, though none too glad
2720 for the opening offered under its archway.
In haste I heaved much from the hoard,
and a mighty burden I bore from the barrow
straight to my sovereign. He still was alive.
His wits were clear; his words came quickly.
2725 In anguish, the Ancient asked that I say
he bade you to build a barrow for him
befitting the deeds of a fallen friend.
You shall heap it high over his ashes,
since he was the world's worthiest warrior,
2730 famed far and wide for the wealth of his fortress.

"Now let us hurry hence to the hoard.
For a second time I shall see that splendor
under the cliff-wall, those wonders of craftwork.
Come, I shall take you close to the trove,
2735 where you may behold heaps of broad gold.
Then let a bier be readied to bear
our beloved lord to his long dwelling
under the watch of the World's Warden."

Then Weohstan's heir ordered the earls,
2740 heads of houses and fief holders,
to fetch firewood fit for the folk-leader's
funeral pyre: "Flames shall now flare,
feed on the flesh and fade into darkness,
an ending for him who often endured
2745 the iron showers shot over shield-walls
when string-driven storms of arrows arose
with feathered fins to steer them in flight
with barbed arrowheads eager to bite."

Wisely Wiglaf, son of Weohstan,
2750 summoned the seven most steadfast thanes.
They went in together, eight earls entering
under the evil arch of the earth-house
with one man bearing a blazing torch.
No lot was cast to learn which liege-man

2755   would plunder the loot   lying unguarded,
        as each searcher   could see for himself;
        yet none was unhappy   to hurry that hoard
        out into daylight.   They heaved the dragon
        over the sea-cliff   where surges seized him:
2760   the treasure's keeper   was caught by the tide.
        Then they filled a wain   with filigreed gold
        and untold treasures;   and they carried the king,
        their hoary-haired warlord,   to Hronesnaess.

        There the king's kinsmen   piled him a pyre,
2765   wide and well-made   just as he willed it.
        They hung it with helmets,   shields and hauberks,
        then laid in its midst   their beloved lord,
        renowned among men.   Lamenting their loss,
        his warriors woke   the most woeful fire
2770   to flare on the bluff.   Fierce was the burning,
        woven with weeping,   and wood-smoke rose
        black over the blaze,   blown with a roar.
        The fire-wind faltered   and flames dwindled,
        hot at their heart   the broken bone-house.
2775   Sunken in spirit   at Beowulf's slaying,
        the Geats gathered   grieving together.
        Her hair wound up,   a woebegone woman
        sang and resang   her dirge of dread,
        foretelling a future   fraught with warfare,
2780   kinfolk sundered,   slaughter and slavery
        even as Heaven   swallowed the smoke.

        High on the headland   they heaped his grave-mound
        which seafaring sailors   would spy from afar.
        Ten days they toiled   on the scorched hilltop,
2785   the cleverest men   skillfully crafting
        a long-home built   for the bold in battle.
        They walled with timbers   the trove they had taken,
        sealing in stone   the circlets and gems,
        wealth of the worm-hoard   gotten with grief,
2790   gold from the ground   gone back to Earth
        as worthless to men   as when it was won.
        Then sorrowing swordsmen   circled the barrow,
        twelve of his earls   telling their tales,
        the sons of nobles   sadly saluting
2795   deeds of the dead.   So dutiful thanes
        in liege to their lord   mourn him with lays
        praising his peerless   prowess in battle
        as it is fitting   when life leaves the flesh.
        Heavy-hearted   his hearth-companions
2800   grieved for Beowulf,   great among kings,
        mild in his mien,   most gentle of men,
        kindest to kinfolk   yet keenest for fame.

Early Irish Verse

The following samples of Irish verse from the ninth and tenth centuries suggest some of the complex but enormously fruitful interactions of native Irish traditions and the new Christian culture.

Ireland began to be Christianized from the mid-fifth century, but Christianity came to Ireland more by genuine and gradual conversion than by the point of a sword. The learned monks and hermits, well established by the ninth and tenth centuries, encountered far more disruption from the raids of Vikings, beginning in A.D. 795, than from surviving Irish pre-Christian cultures. Instead, the ancient native dynasties of learned poets, genealogists, and diviners interacted with the new learning of Latin Christianity. Indeed, Saint Columba (c. 521–597) was partly educated by the *fili* Gemmán, the chief poet of Leinster. (*Fili*, plural *filid*, was the highest class of poet in medieval Ireland. One of Columba's few returns to Ireland after founding his monastery on the isle of Iona was to defend the native poets from clerical forces that wanted them suppressed. In fact we know that many monks were also vernacular poets; and conversely, secular *filid* wrote praise poems to clerics, most famously to Saint Columba himself. Their cultural prestige and preservation of ancient learning continued, even as their religious and quasi-magical activity dwindled. All this led to a rich and persistent convergence (not without competition) of native and Christian elements in medieval Irish culture.

The figure addressed in *To Crinog,* for instance, is at once a wise crone—a traditional figure of initiation—and a book of Christian wisdom, perhaps a Latin primer. Irish myths report instruction in craft or battle by a wise woman, with whom the apprentice also enjoys physical intimacy (as a youthful Cú Chulainn had with the woman warrior Scáthach), although in this poem Crinog's teaching is explicitly chaste. Monks also began using the resources of Irish poetry to record religious study—the Word, to which their faith was so attached—and the making of written books. *Pangur the Cat* explores the solitary pleasures of the monk or hermit, and the challenge of textual interpretation, in contrast with the more heroic mold of many saints' lives or contemporary heroic tales: "Fame comes second to the peace / Of study. . . ." *Writing in the Wood* is a poem of labor, but undertaken in a holiday spirit, away from the monastic scriptorium where books were usually copied.

Other voices look to the legendary past with open regret. *A Grave Marked with Ogam* evokes a disastrous battle in which the speaker, now quite alone, fought on the losing side. *Findabair Remembers Fróech* is a yearning lament for a lost lover. It is quite unconnected to monasticism, but a similar history of passions that efface the present also informs the powerful monologue *The Old Woman of Beare;* there the contrast also involves the shift from a lost world of secular heroes to declining mortality in a convent. Her name, and the memories she has of past generations and eras, may link the Old Woman of Beare to a mythic figure of sovereignty, rejuvenated by each man to whom she gives her body and her powers. At the same time, she is a voice of wise lament on the passing of greater times (not unlike many moments in *Beowulf*); she is a rich concubine who has lost her beauty and become a nun; and—in a land where women's powers were usually quite limited—she is a woman who has gone her own way and made choices that now leave her poor, unprotected, and rueful, but not regretful. *The Old Woman of Beare* records the unresolved dialogue between the era of heroic legend and the era of Christ, between joys mortal and immortal: "for Mary's Son / too soon redeems."

The Voyage of Máel Dúin shows us, perhaps most clearly of all, how native secular genres and attitudes persisted, but were revised, under the influence of Christianity. Both in structure and detail, the *Voyage* echoes the *immrana*, native tales of wondrous voyages to otherworldly islands, places both of terror and sybaritic pleasures. Máel Dúin and his companions visit many such islands, but they also pause at the island homes of four Christian hermits, themselves not without magical qualities. Máel Dúin's own genealogy mirrors this meeting of traditions; he is the illegitimate child of a nun and a great warrior. His father has been killed by raiders, he learns, and his voyage is a quest to find them and take obligatory vengeance in the heroic style. The fourth hermit he meets, though, convinces Máel Dúin to forgive his father's murderers and return home in peace. At the levels of genre, genealogy, and narrative, then, the *Voyage* enacts at once a preservation and a revision of native traditions under Christian influence.

To Crinog[1]

Crinog, melodious is your song.
Though young no more you are still bashful.
We two grew up together in Niall's[2] northern land,
When we used to sleep together in tranquil slumber.

5   That was my age when you slept with me.
O peerless lady of pleasant wisdom:
A pure-hearted youth, lovely without a flaw,
A gentle boy of seven sweet years.

We lived in the great world of Banva[3]
10   Without sullying soul or body,
My flashing eyes full of love for you,
Like a poor innocent untempted by evil.

Your just counsel is ever ready,
Wherever we are to seek it:
15   To love your penetrating wisdom is better
Than glib discourse with a king.

Since then you have slept with four men after me,
Without folly or falling away:
I know, I hear it on all sides,
20   You are pure, without sin from man.

At last, after weary wanderings,
You have come to me again,
Darkness of age has settled on your face:
Sinless your life draws near its end.

25   You are still dear to me, faultless one,
You shall have welcome from me without stint:
You will not let us be drowned in torment;
We will earnestly practice devotion with you.

The lasting world is full of your fame.
30   Far and wide you have wandered on every track:
If every day we followed your ways,
We should come safe into the presence of dread God.

You leave an example and a bequest
To every one in this world,

---

1. Translated by Kuno Meyer.
2. Legendary Irish king, whose dynasty ruled Ulster and other areas.
3. An early name for Ireland.

35   You have taught us by your life:
      Earnest prayer to God is no fallacy.

      Then may God grant us peace and happiness!
      May the countenance of the King
      Shine brightly on us
40   When we leave behind us our withered bodies.

Pangur the Cat[1]

      Myself and Pangur, cat and sage
      Go each about our business;
      I harass my beloved page,
      He his mouse.

5   Fame comes second to the peace
      Of study, a still day.
      Unenvious, Pangur's choice
      Is child's play.

      Neither bored, both hone
10   At home a separate skill,
      Moving, after hours alone,
      To the kill.

      On my cell wall here,
      His sight fixes. Burning.
15   Searching. My old eyes peer
      At new learning.

      His delight when his claws
      Close on his prey
      Equals mine, when sudden clues
20   Light my way.

      So we find by degrees
      Peace in solitude,
      Both of us—solitaries—
      Have each the trade

25   He loves. Pangur, never idle
      Day or night
      Hunts mice. I hunt each riddle
      From dark to light.

Writing in the Wood[1]

      Overwatched by woodland wall
          merles make melody full well;
      above my book—lined, lettered—
          birds twittered a soothing spell.

1. Translated by Eavan Boland.
1. Translated by Ruth P. M. Lehmann. This translation
aims to reproduce much of the complex internal rhyme
and end-rhyme, assonance, and alliteration of the original; it takes minor liberties with the literal sense.

5   Cuckoos call clear—fairest phrase—
      cloaked in grays, from leafy leas.
    Lord's love, what blessings show' ring!
      Good to write 'neath tow' ring trees.

The Viking Terror[1]

Bitter is the wind to-night,
It tosses the ocean's white hair:
To-night I fear not the fierce warriors of Norway
Coursing on the Irish Sea.

The Old Woman of Beare[1]

The ebbing that has come on me
is not the ebbing of the sea.
What knows the sea of grief or pain?—
Happy tide will flood again.

5   I am the hag of Bui and Beare—[2]
the richest cloth I used to wear.
Now with meanness and with thrift
I even lack a change of shift.

    It is wealth
10   and not men that you love.
In the time that we lived
it was men that we loved.

Those whom we loved, the plains
we ride today bear their names;
15   gaily they feasted with laughter
nor boasted thereafter.

To-day they gather in the tax
but, come to handing out, are lax;
the very little they bestow
20   be sure that everyone will know.

Chariots there were, and we
had horses bred for victory.
Such things came in a great wave;
pray for the dead kings who gave.

25   Bitterly does my body race
seeking its destined place;
now let God's Son come and take
that which he gave of his grace.

---

1. Translated by Kuno Meyer.
1. Translated by James Carney. The speaker's name, "caillech," "veiled one," can mean old woman, hag, widow, and nun. The hag figure has resonance with teachers of crafts and wisdom, as well as early mythic female figures of sovereignty and initiation, rejuvenated when they are embraced by a chosen hero.
2. A peninsula in Munster, in the far southwest of Ireland, or a tiny island off its coast. "Bui" may be the small nearby island of Dursey.

These arms, these scrawny things you see,
30   scarce merit now their little joy
when lifted up in blessing
      over sweet student boy.

These arms you see,
      these bony scrawny things,
35 had once more loving craft
      embracing kings.

When Maytime comes
      the girls out there are glad,
and I, old hag, old bones,
40   alone am sad.

No wedding wether° killed for me,   *sheep*
      an end to all coquetry;
a pitiful veil I wear
      on thin and faded hair.

45 Well do I wear
      plain veil on faded hair;
many colors I wore
      and we feasting before.

Were it not for Feven's plain[3]
50   I'd envy nothing old;
I have a shroud of aged skin,
      Feven's crop is gold.

Ronan's city there in Bregon[4]
      and in Feven the royal standing stone,
55 why are their cheeks not weathered,
      only mine alone?

Winter comes and the sea will rise
      crying out with welcoming wave;
but no welcome for me from nobleman's son
60   or from son of a slave.

What they do now, I know, I know:
      to and fro they row and race;
but they who once sailed Alma's ford[5]
      rest in a cold place.

65 It's more than a day
      since I sailed youth's sea,
beauty's years not devoured
      and sap flowing free.

3. In inland Munster; connected with power and wealth.   of Feven.
4. Probably an 8th-century king who ruled in the area   5. An unidentified site.

It's more than a day, God's truth,
70   that I'm lacking in youth;
I wrap myself up in the sun—
I know Old Age, I see him come.

There was a summer of youth
    nor was autumn the worst of the year,
75   but winter is doom
        and its first days are here.

God be thanked, I had joy in my youth.
    I swear that it's true,
if I hadn't leapt the wall
80   this old cloak still were not new.

The Lord on the world's broad back
    threw a lovely cloak of green;
first fleecy, then it's bare,
    and again the fleece is seen.

85   All beauty is doomed.
        God! Can it be right
to kneel in a dark prayer-house
    after feasting by candlelight?

I sat with kings drinking wine and mead
90   for many a day,
and now, a crew of shriveled hags,
        we toast in whey.

Be this my feast, these cups of whey;
    and let me always count as good
95   the vexing things that come of Christ
        who stayed God's ire with flesh and blood.

The mind is not so clear,
    there's mottling of age on my cloak,
gray hairs sprouting through skin,
100   I am like a stricken oak.

For deposit on heaven
    of right eye bereft,
I conclude the purchase
    with loss of the left.

105   Great wave of flood
        and wave of ebb and lack!
What flooding tide brings in
        the ebbing tide takes back.

Great wave of flood
110   and wave of ebbing sea,
the two of them I know
        for both have washed on me.

Great wave of flood
    brings no step to silent cellar floor;
115   a hand fell on all the company
        that feasted there before.

The Son of Mary knew right well
    he'd walk that floor one day;
120   grasping I was, but never sent
        man hungry on his way.

Pity Man!—
    If only like the elements he could
come out of ebbing in the very way
    that he comes out of flood.

125   Christ left with me on loan
    flood tide of youth, and now it seems
there's ebb and misery, for Mary's Son
    too soon redeems.

Blessed the island in the great sea
130   with happy ebb and happy flood.
For me, for me alone, no hope:
    the ebbing is for good.

Findabair Remembers Fróech[1]

This, thereafter, is what Findabair used to say,
seeing anything beautiful:
it would be more beautiful for her
to see Fróech crossing the dark water,
5   body for shining whiteness,
hair for loveliness,
face for shapeliness,
eye for blue-grayness,
a well-born youth
10   without fault or blemish,
face broad above, narrow below,
and he straight and perfect,
the red branch with its berries
between throat and white face.
15   This is what Findabair used to say:
She had never seen
anything a half
or a third as beautiful as he.

---

1. Translated by James Carney. Findabair (FIN-a-wer) was a daughter of Medb and Ailill. She falls in love with the famously handsome warrior Fróech (Froich, guttural -ch) but her parents resist their marriage. When Fróech is killed by Cú Chulainn, Findabair ultimately dies of heartbreak.

A Grave Marked with Ogam[1]

Ogam in stone on grave stead,
    where men sometimes tread on course;
king's son of Ireland cut low,
    hit by spear's throw hurled from horse.

5   Cairpre let a quick cast fly
    from high on horseback, stout steed;
ere he wearied his hand struck,
    cut down Oscar, cruel deed.[2]

Oscar hurled a hard throw, crude,
10   like a lion, rude his rage;
killed Con's kin, Cairpre proud,
    ere they bowed on battle stage.

Tall, keen, cruel were the lads
    who found their death in the strife,
15   just before their weapons met;
    more were left in death than life.

I myself was in the fight
    on right, south of Gabair green;
twice fifty warriors I killed,
20   my skilled hand slew them, clear, clean.

I'd play for pirates in bale,
    the while the trail I must tread,
in holy holt boar I'd fell,
    or would snatch the snell bird's egg.

25   That ogam there in the stone,
    around which the slain fall prone,
    if Finn the fighter could come,
    long would he think on ogam.

from The Voyage of Máel Dúin[1]

They went to an island with a high enclosure of the color of a swan
In which they found a noble pavilion, a dwelling of brightness.
Silver brooches, gold-hilted swords, large necklets,
Beautiful beds, excellent food, golden rows.
5   Strengthening delicate food in the midst of the house, sound savory liquor;

1. Translated by Ruth P. M. Lehmann. This translation again aims to reproduce much of the rhyme, assonance, and alliteration of the original; it takes minor liberties with the literal sense. Ogam is the earliest Irish alphabet, used before the Latin alphabet was applied to Irish. It is a system of long lines marked with short dashes, cross-hatches, and small figures. Most often found in inscriptions or associated with secret messages and divination, it is too awkward an alphabet for writing longer texts.
2. Characters from the "Finn Cycle," a group of tales even more popular than the Ulster Cycle and its central epic the *Táin*. Oscar is Finn's grandson and the cycle's greatest warrior. He and Cairpre, high king of Ireland, kill one another at the Battle of Gabair (GAV-*ar*), which ends the power of Finn's people.
1. Verse redaction of chs. 11, 19, and 34, translated by H. P. A. Oskamp. Máel Dúin (*Moil Doon*), the illegitimate son of a nun and a warrior, is brought up by a queen. Learning at the same time of his father's death, he sets out on a sea journey to find and take vengeance on his father's killers. Máel Dúin and his companions came upon a series of islands, each with its marvel or danger.

With fierce greediness upon a high pillar a seemly very quick cat.
It leapt then over the pillars, a speedy feat;
Not very big was the guardian of the meat, it was not repulsive.
One of the three foster brothers of the powerful chief, it was a
    courageous action,
10   Takes with him—it was a proud ounce-weight—a golden necklet.[2]
The fiery claw of the mysterious cat rent his body,
The guilty body of the unfortunate man was burnt ash.
The large necklet was brought back, it created friendship again,
The ashes of the unfortunate man were cast into the ocean.

* * *

Then they saw in a small island a psalm-singing old man;
Excellent was his dignified noble appearance, holy were his words.
Hair of his noble head—delightful the bright covering—a garment
    with whiteness,
A brilliant large mantle; bright-covered coloring covering was around him.
5   The excellent chief said to him: "Whence were you sent?"
"I shall not hide from you what you ask: from Ireland.
My pilgrimage brought me without any penance
In the body of a boat over the swift sea; I did not regret it.
My prowed boat came apart under me on the very violent sea;
10   A bitter, twisting, active, big-waved course put me ashore.
I cut a sod from the gray-green surface of my fatherland;
To the place in which I am a breeze brought me: small is the fame.
The star-strong King established under me out of the miraculous sod
A delightful island with the color of a seagull over the dark sea.
15   A foot was added to the island every year—
It is a victorious achievement—and a tree above the sea's crest.
A clear well came to me—everlasting food—
By the grace of angels, sound beautiful food—a holy gathering.
You will all reach your countries, a fruitful company along the ocean's track,
20   Though it will be a long journey; all except one man."[3]
By the grace of the angels to each single man of them
Came a complete half-loaf and a noble morsel of fish as provision.

* * *

Then they went to an island full of flocks, a famed halting-place,
A victorious achievement; they found there an Irish falcon.
Then they rowed after it, swift to encounter,
Over the crest of the waves to an island in which was their enemy.
5   They made peace there with the swift Máel Dúin, in the presence of
    every swift man;
After true pledging they went to their country, a prosperous journey.
Many remarkable things, many marvels, many mysteries
Was their pleasant story, as swift Máel Dúin told.
A long life and peace while I am in the famous world,
10   May I have cheerful company with virtue from my King of Kings.
When I die may I then reach heaven past the fierce, violent host of demons
In the Kingdom of angels, a famous affair, a very high dwelling.

---

2. Máel Dúin's foster brothers had swum to his boat as it departed, violating a druid's prohibition; none return from the journey.

3. One of the three foster brothers still remains with the voyagers at this point. A later hermit prophesies, "though you will meet your enemies, you will not slay them."

Judith

The Old English poem *Judith,* concerning the legendary beheader of the Assyrian general Holofernes, has been seen most often as a heroic poem, like *Beowulf,* which it immediately follows in the same unique manuscript. It expresses the same fierce love of battle, and uses the same heroic poetic conventions—archaic diction, formulas, and themes. *Judith* achieves ironic effects, however, by placing these conventions in unexpected contexts, for instance calling Holofernes a "brave man" as he hides behind a net to spy on his retainers. Similarly, it presents his raucous feast as an antifeast—a symbol of misrule rather than of social harmony—and his henchmen as a parody of the traditional band of loyal retainers, as they flee in terror to save their lives.

In addition to *Beowulf, Judith* has affinities with Old English poems based on the Old Testament, like *Exodus* and *Daniel,* whose heroes devote their military zeal to the glory of God. Like them, it assumes the timeless perspective of Christian salvation history, so that the apparent anachronisms of Judith's praying to the Trinity or Christ's abhorring Holofernes are entirely appropriate. Based on the Book of Judith in the Latin Bible, which the Anglo-Saxons considered canonical, this poem, like many others in Old English, exists only in fragmentary form. The original audience would have known that Holofernes had entered Judea to besiege the Hebrew city of Bethulia. At the point where the Old English poem begins, the "wickedly promiscuous" general, after his drunken feast, orders the beautiful Hebrew maiden Judith to be brought to his bed. Finding him stretched out in a drunken stupor, she first prays for help and then decapitates him. She thereupon returns to her camp, brandishing the head and exhorting the Hebrews to battle with a stirring speech, which inspires them to victory over the leaderless Assyrians.

The poem does not simply express the timeless Christian theme of the struggle of God's people against the pagans, but also comments on the immediate social and historical context of its time. It seems to reflect the resistance of the Christian Anglo-Saxons against the pagan Danes during the ninth-century invasions, perhaps exaggerating the Assyrians' drunkenness in order to comment on the notorious Danish drinking habits. Furthermore, Holofernes' plan to rape Judith may evoke the rape of Anglo-Saxon women by Danish soldiers in the presence of their husbands and fathers.

Judith's identity as a woman warrior also puts the poem in the social context of the time. The poem's emphasis on her power, in contrast to the biblical source's emphasis on God's power to operate through the hand of a mere woman, reflects the relatively strong role of aristocratic women in England before the Norman Conquest. (Other Old English poems that reflect this strength include *Juliana,* a typical saint's legend whose heroine is martyred while resisting a Roman general's advances, and *Elene,* whose heroine—Constantine's mother Saint Helen—was believed to have discovered the true cross.) Finally, Judith's heroic action has been seen as an inversion of the rape which Holofernes himself intends to commit upon her, as, seeing him unconscious on his bed, she "took the heathen man by the hair, dragged him ignominiously towards her with her hands, and carefully laid out the debauched and odious man."

Judith[1]

. . . She was suspicious of gifts in this wide world. So she readily met with a helping hand from the glorious Prince when she had most need of the supreme Judge's support and that he, the Prime Mover, should protect her against this supreme danger. The illustrious Father in the skies granted her request in this because she always had firm faith in the Almighty.

---

1. Prose translation by S. A. J. Bradley.

I have heard, then, that Holofernes cordially issued invitations to a banquet and had dishes splendidly prepared with all sorts of wonderful things, and to it this lord over men summoned all the most senior functionaries. With great alacrity those shield-wielders complied and came wending to the puissant prince, the nation's chief person. That was on the fourth day after Judith, shrewd of purpose, the woman of elfin beauty first visited him.

So they went and settled down to the feasting, insolent men to the wine-drinking, all those brash armored warriors, his confederates in evil. Deep bowls were borne continually along the benches there and brimming goblets and pitchers as well to the hall-guests. They drank it down as doomed men, those celebrated shield-wielders—though the great man, the awesome lord over evils, did not foresee it. Then Holofernes, the bountiful lord of his men, grew merry with tippling. He laughed and bawled and roared and made a racket so that the children of men could hear from far away how the stern-minded man bellowed and yelled, insolent and flown with mead, and frequently exhorted the guests on the benches to enjoy themselves well. So the whole day long the villain, the stern-minded dispenser of treasure, plied his retainers with wine until they lay unconscious, the whole of his retinue drunk as though they had been struck dead, drained of every faculty.

Thus the men's elder commanded the hall-guests to be ministered to until the dark night closed in on the children of men. Then, being wickedly promiscuous, he commanded the blessed virgin, decked with bracelets and adorned with rings, to be fetched in a hurry to his bed. The attendants promptly did as their master, the ruler of armored warriors, required them. They went upon the instant to the guest-hall where they found the astute Judith, and then the shield-wielding warriors speedily conducted the noble virgin to the lofty pavilion where the great man always rested of a night, Holofernes, abhorrent to the Savior.

There was an elegant all-golden fly-net there, hung about the commandant's bed so that the debauched hero of his soldiers could spy through on every one of the sons of men who came in there, but no one of humankind on him, unless, brave man, he summoned one of his evilly renowned soldiers to go nearer to him for a confidential talk.

Hastily, then, they brought the shrewd lady to bed. Then they went, stout-hearted heroes, to inform their master that the holy woman had been brought to his pavilion. The man of mark, lord over cities, then grew jovial of mood: he meant to defile the noble lady with filth and with pollution. To that heaven's Judge, Shepherd of the celestial multitude, would not consent but rather he, the Lord, Ruler of the hosts, prevented him from the act.

So this species of fiend, licentious, debauched, went with a crowd of his men to seek his bed—where he was to lose his life, swiftly, within the one night: he had then come to his violent end upon earth, such as he had previously deserved, the stern-minded prince over men, while he lived in this world under the roof of the skies.

Then the great man collapsed in the midst of his bed, so drunk with wine that he was oblivious in mind of any of his designs. The soldiers stepped out of his quarters with great alacrity, wine-glutted men who had put the perjurer, the odious persecutor, to bed for the last time.

Then the glorious handmaid of the Savior was sorely preoccupied as to how she might most easily deprive the monster of his life before the sordid fellow, full of corruption, awoke. Then the ringletted girl, the Maker's maiden, grasped a sharp sword, hardy in the storms of battle, and drew it from its sheath with her right hand. Then she called by name upon the Guardian of heaven, the Savior of all the world's inhabitants, and spoke these words:

"God of beginnings, Spirit of comfort, Son of the universal Ruler, I desire to entreat you for your grace upon me in my need, Majesty of the Trinity. My heart is now sorely anguished and my mind troubled and much afflicted with anxieties. Give me, Lord of heaven, victory and true faith so that with this sword I may hew down this dispenser of violent death. Grant me my safe deliverance, stern-minded Prince over men. Never have I had greater need of your grace. Avenge now, mighty Lord, illustrious Dispenser of glory, that which is so bitter to my mind, so burning in my breast."

Then the supreme Judge at once inspired her with courage—as he does every single man dwelling here who looks to him for help with resolve and with true faith. So hope was abundantly renewed in the holy woman's heart. She then took the heathen man firmly by his hair, dragged him ignominiously towards her with her hands and carefully laid out the debauched and odious man so as she could most easily manage the wretch efficiently. Then the ringletted woman struck the malignant-minded enemy with the gleaming sword so that she sliced through half his neck, so that he lay unconscious, drunk and mutilated.

He was not then yet dead, not quite lifeless. In earnest then the courageous woman struck the heathen dog a second time so that his head flew off on to the floor. His foul carcass lay behind, dead; his spirit departed elsewhere beneath the deep ground and was there prostrated and chained in torment ever after, coiled about by snakes, trussed up in tortures and cruelly prisoned in hellfire after his going hence. Never would he have cause to hope, engulfed in darkness, that he might get out of that snake-infested prison, but there he shall remain forever to eternity henceforth without end in that murky abode, deprived of the joys of hope.

Judith then had won outstanding glory in the struggle according as God the Lord of heaven, who gave her the victory, granted her. Then the clever woman swiftly put the harrier's head, all bloody, into the bag in which her attendant, a pale-cheeked woman, one proved excellent in her ways, had brought food there for them both; and then Judith put it, all gory, into her hands for her discreet servant to carry home. From there the two women then proceeded onwards, emboldened by courage, until they had escaped, brave, triumphant virgins, from among the army, so that they could clearly see the walls of the beautiful city, Bethulia, shining. Then the ring-adorned women hurried forward on their way until, cheered at heart, they had reached the rampart gate.

There were soldiers, vigilant men, sitting and keeping watch in the fortress just as Judith the artful-minded virgin had enjoined the despondent folk when she set out on her mission, courageous lady. Now she had returned, their darling, to her people, and quickly then the shrewd woman summoned one of the men to come out from the spacious city to meet her and speedily to let them in through the gate of the rampart; and to the victorious people she spoke these words:

"I can tell you something worthy of thanksgiving: that you need no longer grieve in spirit. The ordaining Lord, the Glory of kings, is gracious to you. It has been revealed abroad through the world that dazzling and glorious success is impending for you and triumph is granted you over those injuries which you long have suffered."

Then the citizens were merry when they heard how the saintly woman spoke across the high rampart. The army was in ecstasies and the people rushed towards the fortress gate, men and women together, in flocks and droves; in throngs and troops they surged forward and ran towards the handmaid of the Lord, both old and young in their thousands. The heart of each person in that city of mead-halls was exhilarated when they realized that Judith had returned home; and then with humility they hastily let her in.

Then the clever woman ornamented with gold directed her attentive servant-girl to unwrap the harrier's head and to display the bloody object to the citizens as proof of how she had fared in the struggle. The noble lady then spoke to the whole populace:

"Victorious heroes, leaders of the people; here you may openly gaze upon the head of that most odious heathen warrior, the dead Holofernes, who perpetrated upon us the utmost number of violent killings of men and painful miseries, and who intended to add to it even further, but God did not grant him longer life so that he might plague us with afflictions. I took his life, with God's help. Now I want to urge each man among these citizens, each shield-wielding soldier, that you immediately get yourselves ready for battle. Once the God of beginnings, the steadfastly gracious King, has sent the radiant light from the east, go forth bearing shields, bucklers in front of your breasts and mail-coats and shining helmets into the ravagers' midst; cut down the commanders, the doomed leaders, with gleaming swords. Your enemies are sentenced to death and you shall have honor and glory in the fight according as the mighty Lord has signified to you by my hand."

Then an army of brave and keen men was quickly got ready for the battle. Renowned nobles and their companions advanced; they carried victory-banners; beneath their helms the heroes issued forth straight into battle from out of the holy city upon the very dawning of the day. Shields clattered, loudly resonated. At that, the lean wolf in the wood rejoiced, and that bird greedy for carrion, the black raven. Both knew that the men of that nation meant to procure them their fill among those doomed to die; but in their wake flew the eagle, eager for food, speckled-winged; the dark-feathered, hook-beaked bird sang a battle-chant.

On marched the soldiers, warriors to the warfare, protected by their shields, hollowed linden bucklers, they who a while previously had been suffering the abuse of aliens, the blasphemy of heathens. This was strictly repaid to all the Assyrians in the spear-fight once the Israelites under their battle-ensigns had reached the camp. Firmly entrenched, they vigorously let fly from the curved bow showers of darts, arrows, the serpents of battle. Loudly the fierce fighting-men roared and sent spears into their cruel enemies' midst. The heroes, the in-dwellers of the land, were enraged against the odious race. Stern of mood they advanced; hardened of heart they roughly roused their drink-stupefied enemies of old. With their hands, retainers unsheathed from scabbards bright-ornamented swords, proved of edge, and set about the Assyrian warriors in earnest, intending to smite them. Of that army they spared not one of the men alive, neither the lowly nor the mighty, whom they could overpower.

Thus in the hour of morn those comrades in arms the whole time harried the aliens until those who were their adversaries, the chief sentries of the army, acknowledged that the Hebrew people were showing them very intensive sword-play. They went to inform the most senior officers of this by word of mouth and they roused those warriors and fearfully announced to them in their drunken stupor the dreadful news, the terror of the morning, the frightful sword-encounter.

Then, I have heard, those death-doomed heroes quickly shook off their sleep and thronged in flocks, demoralized men, to the pavilion of the debauched

Holofernes. They meant to give their lord warning of battle at once, before the terror and the force of the Hebrews descended upon him; all supposed that the men's leader and that beautiful woman were together in the handsome tent, the noble Judith and the lecher, fearsome and ferocious. Yet there was not one of the nobles who dared awaken the warrior to inquire how it had turned out for the soldier with the holy virgin, the woman of the Lord.

The might of the Hebrews, their army, was drawing closer; vehemently they fought with tough and bloody weapons and violently they indemnified with gleaming swords their former quarrels and old insults: in that day's work the Assyrians' repute was withered, their arrogance abased. The men stood around their lord's tent, extremely agitated and growing gloomier in spirit. Then all together they began to cough and loudly make noises and, having no success, to chew the grist with their teeth, suffering agonies. The time of their glory, good fortune and valorous doings was at an end. The nobles thought to awaken their lord and friend; they succeeded not at all.

Then one of the soldiers belatedly and tardily grew so bold that he ventured pluckily into the pavilion as necessity compelled him. Then he found his lord lying pallid on the bed, deprived of his spirit, dispossessed of life. Straightway then he fell chilled to the ground, and distraught in mind he began to tear his hair and his clothing alike and he uttered these words to the soldiers who were waiting there miserably outside:

"Here is made manifest our own perdition, and here it is imminently signalled that the time is drawn near, along with its tribulations, when we must perish and be destroyed together in the strife. Here, hacked by the sword, decapitated, lies our lord."

Then distraught in mind they threw down their weapons; demoralized they went scurrying away in flight. The nation magnified in strength attacked them in the rear until the greatest part of the army lay on the field of victory levelled by battle, hacked by swords, as a treat for the wolves and a joy to the carrion-greedy birds. Those who survived fled from the linden spears of their foes. In their wake advanced the troop of Hebrews, honoured with the victory and glorified in the judgment: the Lord God, the almighty Lord, had come handsomely to their aid. Swiftly then with their gleaming swords those valiant heroes made an inroad through the thick of their foes; they hacked at targes[2] and sheared through the shield-wall. The Hebrew spear-throwers were wrought up to the fray; the soldiers lusted mightily after a spear-contest on that occasion. There in the dust fell the main part of the muster-roll of the Assyrian nobility, of that odious race. Few survivors reached their native land.

The soldiers of royal renown turned back in retirement amidst carnage and reeking corpses. That was the opportunity for the land's in-dwellers to seize from those most odious foes, their old dead enemies, bloodied booty, resplendent accoutrements, shield and broad sword, burnished helmets, costly treasures. The guardians of their homeland had honorably conquered their enemies on the battlefield and destroyed with swords their old persecutors. In their trail lay dead those who of living peoples had been most inimical to their existence.

Then the whole nation, most famous of races, proud, curled-locked, for the duration of one month were carrying and conveying into the beautiful city, Bethulia, helmets and hip-swords, gray mail-coats, and men's battle-dress ornamented with gold, more glorious treasures than any man among ingenious men can tell. All that the people splendidly gained, brave beneath their banners in the fray, through the

2. Shields.

shrewd advice of Judith, the courageous woman. As a reward the celebrated spear-men brought back for her from the expedition the sword and the bloodied helmet of Holofernes as well as his huge mail-coat adorned with red gold; and everything the ruthless lord of the warriors owned of riches or personal wealth, of rings and of beau-tiful treasures, they gave it to that beautiful and resourceful lady.

For all this Judith gave glory to the Lord of hosts who granted her esteem and renown in the realm of earth and likewise too a reward in heaven, the prize of victory in the glory of the sky because she always had true faith in the Almighty. Certainly at the end she did not doubt the reward for which she long had yearned.

For this be glory into eternity to the dear Lord who created the wind and the clouds, the skies and the spacious plains and likewise the cruel seas and the joys of heaven, through his peculiar mercy.

--- ⌑⌑⌑ ---

The Dream of the Rood

The Dream of the Rood is a remarkable tenth-century poem, a mystical dream vision whose nar-rator tells of his dream that the rood—Christ's cross—appeared to him and told the story of its unwilling role in the crucifixion. The poem is an excellent illustration of how the conventions of Old English heroic poems like *Beowulf* were adapted to the doctrines of Christianity. Christ's Passion is converted into a heroic sacrifice as the cross reports that it watched him—the young hero—strip himself naked, as if preparing for battle, and bravely ascend it. In the same vein, the cross presents itself as a thane (retainer) forced into disloyalty, as it watches—and participates in—the crucifixion, unable to avenge its beloved Lord.

In addition to heroic poetry, *The Dream of the Rood* recalls Old English genres such as the riddle and the elegy. In riddle fashion, the cross asks, "What am I?"—that started as a tree, became an instrument of torture, and am now a beacon of victory, resplendent with jewels. In the manner of elegies like *The Wanderer,* the speaker, stained with sin, presents himself as a lonely exile whose companions have left him and gone to heaven. After his vision, he resolves to seek the fellowship of his heavenly Lord and his former companions, which he pictures as taking place in a celestial mead hall: "the home of joy and happiness, / where the people of God are seated at the feast / in eternal bliss."

One of the most striking poetic effects of *The Dream of the Rood* is its focus on the Incar-nation, God's taking on human flesh. The poet often juxtaposes references to Christ's human-ity and divinity in the same line, thereby achieving a powerful effect of paradox, as when he tells of the approach of "the young warrior, God Almighty." It is noteworthy that the aspect of Christ's humanity which the poet stresses is the heroism rather than the pathos which was to become so prominent in later medieval poetry and art. This heroism provides a context for a cryptic passage at the end of the poem, where the dreamer refers to Christ's "journey" to bring "those who before suffered burning" victoriously to heaven. In *The Harrowing of Hell* (based on the apocryphal Gospel of Nicodemus), Christ heroically freed the virtuous Old Testament patriarchs from damnation and led them to eternal bliss.

The fame of *The Dream of the Rood* appears to have been widespread in its own time. Our knowledge of it comes from three sources: the huge stone Ruthwell Cross in southern Scotland built in the eighth century (on which a short version is inscribed in runic letters); the silver Brussels Cross, made in England in the tenth century; and the manuscript found written in Vercelli in northern Italy, also written in the tenth century—the only complete version of the poem. These varied locations are a testament to the wide influence of Anglo-Saxon scholars, not only in the British Isles but on the Continent as well.

The Dream of the Rood[1]

Listen! I will describe the best of dreams
which I dreamed in the middle of the night
when, far and wide, all men slept.
It seemed that I saw a wondrous tree
5   soaring into the air, surrounded by light,
the brightest of crosses; that emblem was entirely
cased in gold; beautiful jewels
were strewn around its foot, just as five
studded the cross-beam. All the angels of God,
10   fair creations, guarded it. That was no cross
of a criminal, but holy spirits and men on earth
watched over it there—the whole glorious universe.

Wondrous was the tree of victory, and I was stained
by sin, stricken by guilt. I saw this glorious tree
15   joyfully gleaming, adorned with garments,
decked in gold; the tree of the Ruler
was rightly adorned with rich stones;
yet through that gold I could see the agony
once suffered by wretches, for it had bled
20   down the right hand side. Then I was afflicted,
frightened at this sight; I saw that sign often change
its clothing and hue, at times dewy with moisture,
stained by flowing blood, at times adorned with treasure.
Yet I lay there for a long while
25   and gazed sadly at the Savior's cross
until I heard it utter words;
the finest of trees began to speak:
"I remember the morning a long time ago
that I was felled at the edge of the forest
30   and severed from my roots. Strong enemies seized me,
bade me hold up their felons on high,
made me a spectacle. Men shifted me
on their shoulders and set me on a hill.
Many enemies fastened me there. I saw the Lord of Mankind
35   hasten with such courage to climb upon me.
I dared not bow or break there
against my Lord's wish, when I saw the surface
of the earth tremble. I could have felled
all my foes, yet I stood firm.
40   Then the young warrior, God Almighty,
stripped Himself, firm and unflinching. He climbed
upon the cross, brave before many, to redeem mankind.
I quivered when the hero clasped me,
yet I dared not bow to the ground,
45   fall to the earth. I had to stand firm.
A rood was I raised up; I bore aloft the mighty King,
the Lord of Heaven. I dared not stoop.

1. Translated by Kevin Crossley-Holland.

The Ruthwell Cross, north side, top section, 7th–8th century. Preserved in a church in southern Scotland, this 18-foot stone cross is carved with many Christian scenes, including this depiction of Saint John the Baptist, bearded and holding the Lamb of God. The Latin inscription beneath the saint is written in runes—the traditional Germanic alphabet, used for ritualistic purposes. Runic inscriptions elsewhere on the cross reproduce portions of *The Dream of the Rood* in Old English. Still other inscriptions are in Latin and employ the Roman alphabet. Thus, like *The Dream of the Rood* itself, whose Christlike hero resembles a Germanic warrior, the Ruthwell Cross illustrates the fusion of Mediterranean and Germanic traditions in Anglo-Saxon Christian culture.

They drove dark nails into me; dire wounds are there to see,
the gaping gashes of malice; I dared not injure them.
50   They insulted us both together; I was drenched in the blood
that streamed from the Man's side after He set His spirit free.

"On that hill I endured many grievous trials;
I saw the God of Hosts stretched
on the rack; darkness covered the corpse
55   of the Ruler with clouds, His shining radiance.
Shadows swept across the land, dark shapes
under the clouds. All creation wept,
wailed for the death of the King; Christ was on the cross.
Yet men hurried eagerly to the Prince
60   from afar; I witnessed all that too.
I was oppressed with sorrow, yet humbly bowed to the hands of men,
and willingly. There they lifted Him from His heavy torment,

they took Almighty God away. The warriors left me standing there,
stained with blood; sorely was I wounded by the sharpness of spear-shafts.
65   They laid Him down, limb-weary; they stood at the corpse's head,
they beheld there the Lord of Heaven; and there He rested for a while,
worn-out after battle. And then they began to build a sepulchre;
under his slayers' eyes, they carved it from the gleaming stone,
and laid therein the Lord of Victories. Then, sorrowful at dusk,
70   they sang a dirge before they went, weary,
from their glorious Prince; He rested in the grave alone.
But we still stood there, weeping blood,
long after the song of the warriors
had soared to heaven; the corpse grew cold,
75   the fair human house of the soul. Then our enemies
began to fell us; that was a terrible fate.
They buried us in a deep pit; but friends
and followers of the Lord found me there
and girded me with gold and shimmering silver.

80   "Now, my loved man, you have heard
how I endured bitter anguish
at the hands of evil men. Now the time is come
when men far and wide in this world,
and all this bright creation, bow before me;
85   they pray to this sign. On me the Son of God
suffered for a time; wherefore I now stand on high,
glorious under heaven; and I can heal
all those who stand in awe of me.
Long ago I became the worst of tortures,
90   hated by men, until I opened
to them the true way of life.
Lo! The Lord of Heaven, the Prince of Glory,
honored me over any other tree
just as He, Almighty God, for the sake of mankind
95   honored Mary, His own mother,
before all other women in the world.
Now I command you, my loved man,
to describe your vision to all men;
tell them with words this is the tree of glory
100   on which the Son of God suffered once
for the many sins committed by mankind,
and for Adam's wickedness long ago.
He sipped the drink of death. Yet the Lord rose
with His great strength to deliver man.
105   Then He ascended into heaven. The Lord Himself,
Almighty God, with His host of angels,
will come to the middle-world again
on Domesday to reckon with each man.
Then He who has the power of judgment
110   will judge each man just as he deserves
for the way in which he lived this fleeting life.
No-one then will be unafraid
as to what words the Lord will utter.

Before the assembly, He will ask where that man is
115   who, in God's name, would undergo the pangs of death,
just as He did formerly upon the cross.
Then men will be fearful and give
scant thought to what they say to Christ.
But no-one need be numbed by fear
120   who has carried the best of all signs in his breast;
each soul that has longings to live with the Lord
must search for a kingdom far beyond the frontiers of this world."

Then I prayed to the cross, eager
and light-hearted, although I was alone
125   with my own poor company. My soul
longed for a journey, great yearnings
always tugged at me. Now my hope in this life
is that I can turn to that tree of victory
alone and more often than any other man
130   and honor it fully. These longings master
my heart and mind, and my help comes
from holy cross itself. I have not many friends
of influence on earth; they have journeyed on
from the joys of this world to find the King of Glory,
135   they live in heaven with the High Father,
dwell in splendor. Now I look day by day
for that time when the cross of the Lord,
which once I saw in a dream here on earth,
will fetch me away from this fleeting life
140   and lift me to the home of joy and happiness
where the people of God are seated at the feast
in eternal bliss, and set me down
where I may live in glory unending and share
the joy of the saints. May the Lord be a friend to me,
145   He who suffered once for the sins of men
here on earth on the gallows-tree.
He has redeemed us; He has given life to us,
and a home in heaven.
                           Hope was renewed,
blessed and blissful, for those who before suffered burning.
150   On that journey the Son was victorious,
strong and successful. When He, Almighty Ruler,
returned with a thronging host of spirits
to God's kingdom, to joy among the angels
and all the saints who lived already
155   in heaven in glory, then their King,
Almighty God, entered His own country.

⇒⊹ PERSPECTIVES ⊹⇐
Ethnic and Religious Encounters

In the centuries of their insurgency and the consolidation of their influence in Britain, the Angles and Saxons negotiated a series of encounters that left them, and England, profoundly transformed. They arrived from the distant coasts of northwest continental Europe as self-conscious foreigners, divided into large tribal groups and often warring among themselves. They were pagans and masters of a great but essentially oral culture. By the end of their dominance, in 1066, they were long-Christianized and increasingly had come to perceive themselves as a single people. Moreover, their conversion involved a new commitment to the practical uses of writing and the talismanic power of the written book, as well as a heightened sense of the conflicting claims and uses of their ancient vernacular and of Latin. They now experienced England as their native place and registered their ancestral geography on the Continent as an area of nostalgic exploration or, equally, the source of hostile invasion.

All this was the work of centuries. It was not an unconscious or "natural" development, however. The passages in this section, in their different ways, offer key moments in the lengthy and complex process by which the Germanic newcomers encountered other peoples, religions, textual cultures, and geographies.

The initial contact between the Germanic invaders and the prior inhabitants of England—Britons, the "Irish" of the northwest, and the Picts—was based on military service which turned into military aggression. Relatively soon, though, and even as their territorial ambitions continued, the Angles and Saxons developed other contacts, especially with the Britons. The British were already Christian, and the Angles and Saxons first came to Christianity through British models if not by British hands. Later, the Anglo-Saxons themselves would face invasion by Vikings, who ultimately settled north of the Humber in the "Danelaw." Much of Asser's *Life of King Alfred* documents Alfred's struggle against Viking raiders.

Though he celebrated Alfred's West Saxon kingship and culture, Asser was himself a Welshman. His presence at Alfred's court is a sign of how Latin learning had declined in the disordered era of Viking incursions; Alfred was obliged to turn to other peoples to restore education in his own realm. The Norwegian trader Ohthere, too, came to Alfred's court even while the King was fending off Viking raiders. Ohthere seems to have sparked lively interest in his own people and their social order, as well as in his visits to what the Anglo-Saxons knew was their ancestral home.

Christianization was also a slow, complex, and incomplete process of acculturation. Bede recounts a number of moments when the differing responses to a single event register the encounters of pagan and Christian, literate and illiterate, and Latin and Germanic traditions. The conversion of King Edwin, for instance, involved not just the King fulfilling a promise made in a vision but also his nobles learning to imagine a new spiritual geography which went far beyond the brief joys of their warrior cohort. In the story of Imma, the magical loosing of a prisoner's chains is seen by some as the effect of an ancient pagan "loosing spell," but by Imma (and Bede's Christian readers) as the effect of masses said for his soul.

Language and literacy equally figure in the conversion of the Angles and Saxons and in the slow emergence of the idea of an "English" people. Imma is freed by the uncanny (and somewhat misdirected) power of the Latin mass. The high level of Bede's own Latin suggests how that language was becoming a cohesive force, at least among clerics. Yet in one of his tenderest stories, Bede tells about the illiterate Caedmon who learned, by divine intervention, to tell biblical stories in vernacular poetry. Bede admits that his Latin version of *Caedmon's Hymn* is inadequate, which suggests that Anglo-Saxon could assume its own place in the operations of the sacred. And Asser celebrates Alfred's childhood love of Saxon poems, laments Alfred's illiteracy, yet tells how the illiterate prince competed for the gift of a book he valued almost as a talisman. Alfred's acquisition of literacy and of Latin is part of his rise to successful kingship, and he caps his own reign with the series of translations that bring crucial texts of Latin Christianity into an Anglo-Saxon that Alfred now seems to see as a unifying national tongue.

Finally, even as some Anglo-Saxons aspire to nationhood, they do so by nostalgic memories of their foreign past, as seen in the information they draw from the Norwegian visitor Ohthere. At the same time, though, they mark themselves off from this geography and see themselves as the sinning victims of invasions that will end their power, just as their own successful invasions had punished and subdued the earlier Britons. This is repeatedly made explicit in *The Anglo-Saxon Chronicle*'s report of the twin battles fought by King Harold against Norwegian aggressors in the North and then against the triumphant Normans in the South. Their sense of nationhood and of being folded into processes of Christian history is clearest as the Chronicler witnesses the close of Anglo-Saxon dominance.

Bede
672–735

Bede was born on lands belonging to the abbey of Wearmouth-Jarrow. He entered that monastery at the age of seven and never traveled more than seventy-five miles away. Bede is the most enduring product of the golden age of Northumbrian monasticism. In the generations just preceding his, a series of learned abbots had brought Roman liturgical practices and monastic habits to Wearmouth-Jarrow, as well as establishing there the best library in England. Out of this settled life and disciplined religious culture Bede created a diverse body of writings that are learned both in scholarly research and in the purity of their Latin. They include biblical commentaries, school texts from spelling to metrics, treatises on the liturgical calendar, hymns, and lives of saints.

Bede's *An Ecclesiastical History of the English People*, completed in 731, marks the apex of his achievement. Given the localism of his life, Bede's grasp of English history is extraordinary, not just in terms of his eager pursuit of information, but equally in his balanced and complex sense of the broad movement of history. Bede registers a persistent concern about his sources and their reliability. He prefers written and especially documentary evidence, but he will use oral reports if they come from several sources and are close enough to the original event.

The *Ecclesiastical History* suggests the contours of a national history, even a providential history, in the arrival of the Angles and Saxons, and in the island's uneven conversion to Christianity. Despite his frequent stories of battles among the Germanic peoples in Britain, Bede speaks of the English people emphatically in the singular. Nevertheless, Bede is delicately aware of the historical layering brought about by colonization and the ongoing resistance of earlier inhabitants. Further, he is always alert to profoundly transformative influences, aside from ethnicity, that color his time: the process of conversion to Christianity, and the variable coexistence of Christian and pagan instincts in individual minds; the interplay of oral and written culture; the status in religious and official life of Latin and the Anglo-Saxon vernaculars.

from An Ecclesiastical History of the English People[1]
[THE CONVERSION OF KING EDWIN][2]

King Edwin hesitated to accept the word of God which Paulinus[3] preached but, as we have said, used to sit alone for hours at a time, earnestly debating within himself what he ought to do and what religion he should follow. One day Paulinus came to

---

1. Edited and translated by Bertram Colgrave and R. A. B. Mynors.
2. From bk. 2, chs. 12–14. Edwin became king of Northumbria in 616, aided by Raedwald, king of the East Angles. Exiled at Raedwald's court, Edwin had a vision wherein he promised a shadowy visitor he would convert

if he achieved the crown. The visitor laid his right hand on Edwin's head as a sign to remember that promise when the gesture was repeated.
3. Later archbishop of York, Paulinus had been sent to Northumbria from Kent with Edwin's Christian wife after Edwin had promised tolerance of Christian worship.

him and, placing his right hand on the king's head, asked him if he recognized this sign. The king began to tremble and would have thrown himself at the bishop's feet but Paulinus raised him up and said in a voice that seemed familiar, "First you have escaped with God's help from the hands of the foes you feared; secondly you have acquired by His gift the kingdom you desired; now, in the third place, remember your own promise; do not delay in fulfilling it but receive the faith and keep the commandments of Him who rescued you from your earthly foes and raised you to the honor of an earthly kingdom. If from henceforth you are willing to follow His will which is made known to you through me, He will also rescue you from the everlasting torments of the wicked and make you a partaker with Him of His eternal kingdom in heaven."

When the king had heard his words, he answered that he was both willing and bound to accept the faith which Paulinus taught. He said, however, that he would confer about this with his loyal chief men and his counselors so that, if they agreed with him, they might all be consecrated together in the waters of life. Paulinus agreed and the king did as he had said. A meeting of his council was held and each one was asked in turn what he thought of this doctrine hitherto unknown to them and this new worship of God which was being proclaimed.

Coifi, the chief of the priests, answered at once, "Notice carefully, King, this doctrine which is now being expounded to us. I frankly admit that, for my part, I have found that the religion which we have hitherto held has no virtue nor profit in it. None of your followers has devoted himself more earnestly than I have to the worship of our gods, but nevertheless there are many who receive greater benefits and greater honor from you than I do and are more successful in all their undertakings. If the gods had any power they would have helped me more readily, seeing that I have always served them with greater zeal. So it follows that if, on examination, these new doctrines which have now been explained to us are found to be better and more effectual, let us accept them at once without any delay."

Another of the king's chief men agreed with this advice and with these wise words and then added, "This is how the present life of man on earth, King, appears to me in comparison with that time which is unknown to us. You are sitting feasting with your ealdormen and thegns[4] in winter time; the fire is burning on the hearth in the middle of the hall and all inside is warm, while outside the wintry storms of rain and snow are raging; and a sparrow flies swiftly through the hall. It enters in at one door and quickly flies out through the other. For the few moments it is inside, the storm and wintry tempest cannot touch it, but after the briefest moment of calm, it flits from your sight, out of the wintry storm and into it again. So this life of man appears but for a moment; what follows or indeed what went before, we know not at all. If this new doctrine brings us more certain information, it seems right that we should accept it."[5] Other elders and counselors of the king continued in the same manner, being divinely prompted to do so.

Coifi added that he would like to listen still more carefully to what Paulinus himself had to say about God. The king ordered Paulinus to speak, and when he had said his say, Coifi exclaimed, "For a long time now I have realized that our religion is worthless; for the more diligently I sought the truth in our cult, the less I found it. Now I confess openly that the truth shines out clearly in this teaching which can

4. Ealdorman: the highest Anglo-Saxon rank below king; thegn: a noble warrior still serving within the king's household.

5. This famous simile is put in the mouth of a lay nobleman, not the pagan priest Coifi whose argument for conversion was based on disappointed self-interest.

bestow on us the gift of life, salvation, and eternal happiness. Therefore I advise your Majesty that we should promptly abandon and commit to the flames the temples and the altars which we have held sacred without reaping any benefit." Why need I say more? The king publicly accepted the gospel which Paulinus preached, renounced idolatry, and confessed his faith in Christ. When he asked the high priest of their religion which of them should be the first to profane the altars and the shrines of the idols, together with their precincts, Coifi answered, "I will; for through the wisdom the true God has given me no one can more suitably destroy those things which I once foolishly worshiped, and so set an example to all." And at once, casting aside his vain superstitions, he asked the king to provide him with arms and a stallion; and mounting it he set out to destroy the idols. Now a high priest of their religion was not allowed to carry arms or to ride except on a mare. So, girded with a sword, he took a spear in his hand and mounting the king's stallion he set off to where the idols were. The common people who saw him thought he was mad. But as soon as he approached the shrine, without any hesitation he profaned it by casting the spear which he held into it; and greatly rejoicing in the knowledge of the worship of the true God, he ordered his companions to destroy and set fire to the shrine and all the enclosures. The place where the idols once stood is still shown, not far from York, to the east, over the river Derwent. Today it is called Goodmanham, the place where the high priest, through the inspiration of the true God, profaned and destroyed the altars which he himself had consecrated.[6]

So King Edwin, with all the nobles of his race and a vast number of the common people, received the faith and regeneration by holy baptism in the eleventh year of his reign, that is in the year of our Lord 627 and about 180 years after the coming of the English to Britain. He was baptized at York on Easter Day, 12 April, in the church of Saint Peter the Apostle, which he had hastily built of wood while he was a catechumen and under instruction before he received baptism. He established an episcopal see for Paulinus, his instructor and bishop, in the same city.

[THE STORY OF IMMA][7]

In this battle in which King Aelfwine[8] was killed, a remarkable incident is known to have happened which in my opinion should certainly not be passed over in silence, since the story may lead to the salvation of many. During the battle one of the king's retainers, a young man named Imma, was struck down among others; he lay all that day and the following night as though dead, among the bodies of the slain, but at last he recovered consciousness, sat up, and bandaged his wounds as best he could; then, having rested for a short time, he rose and set out to find friends to take care of him. But as he was doing so, he was found and captured by men of the enemy army and taken to their lord, who was a *gesith*[9] of King Aethelred. On being asked who he was, he was afraid to admit that he was a thegn; but he answered instead that he was a poor peasant and married; and he declared that he had come to the army in company with other peasants to bring food to the soldiers. The *gesith* took him and had his wounds attended to. But when Imma began to get better, he ordered him to be bound at night to prevent his escape. However, it proved impossible to bind him, for no sooner had those who chained him gone, than his fetters were loosed.

6. This detail is typical of Bede's liking for textual or archaeological authentication.
7. Bk. 4, ch. 22.
8. A battle in 679, between King Ecgfrith of Northumbria

and Aethelred king of the Mercians caused the death of this under-king and brother of Ecgfrith.
9. A nobleman, serving a king but having his own household of retainers and servants.

Now he had a brother whose name was Tunna, a priest and abbot of a monastery in a city which is still called *Tunnacaestir* after him. When Tunna heard that his brother had perished in the fight, he went to see if he could find his body; having found another very like him in all respects, he concluded that it must be his brother's body. So he carried it to the monastery, buried it with honor, and took care to offer many masses for the absolution of his soul. It was on account of these celebrations that, as I have said, no one could bind Imma because his fetters were at once loosed. Meanwhile the *gesith* who kept him captive grew amazed and asked him why he could not be bound and whether he had about him any loosing spells such as are described in stories. But Imma answered that he knew nothing of such arts. "However," said he, "I have a brother in my country who is a priest and I know he believes me to be dead and offers frequent masses on my behalf; so if I had now been in another world, my soul would have been loosed from its punishment by his intercessions." When he had been a prisoner with the *gesith* for some time, those who watched him closely realized by his appearance, his bearing, and his speech that he was not of common stock as he had said, but of noble family. Then the *gesith* called him aside and asked him very earnestly to declare his origin, promising that no harm should come to him, provided that he told him plainly who he was. The prisoner did so, revealing that he had been one of the king's thegns. The *gesith* answered, "I realized by every one of your answers that you were not a peasant, and now you ought to die because all my brothers and kinsmen were killed in the battle: but I will not kill you for I do not intend to break my promise."

As soon as Imma had recovered, the *gesith* sold him to a Frisian in London; but he could neither be bound on his way there nor by the Frisian. So after his enemies had put every kind of bond on him and as his new master realized that he could not be bound, he gave him leave to ransom himself if he could. Now the bonds were most frequently loosed from about nine in the morning, the time when masses were usually said. So having sworn that he would either return or send his master the money for his ransom, he went to King Hlothhere of Kent, who was the son of Queen Aethelthryth's sister already mentioned, because he had once been one of Aethelthryth's thegns; he asked for and received the money from him for his ransom and sent it to his master as he had promised.[1]

He afterwards returned to his own country, where he met his brother and gave him a full account of all his troubles and the comfort that had come to him in those adversities; and from what his brother told him, he realized that his bonds had generally been loosed at the time when masses were being celebrated on his behalf; so he perceived that the other comforts and blessings which he had experienced during his time of danger had been bestowed by heaven, through the intercession of his brother and the offering up of the saving Victim. Many who heard about this from Imma were inspired to greater faith and devotion, to prayer and almsgiving and to the offering up of sacrifices to God in the holy oblation, for the deliverance of their kinsfolk who had departed from the world; for they realized that the saving sacrifice availed for the everlasting redemption of both body and soul.

This story was told me by some of those who heard it from the very man to whom these things happened; therefore since I had so clear an account of the incident, I thought that it should undoubtedly be inserted into this *History*.

1. Imma had been thegn to Aethelthryth, wife of King Ecgfrith, before he entered Aelfwine's service. He now turns to her nephew, implicitly invoking obligations of kinship, for help with his ransom.

[CAEDMON'S HYMN][2]

In the monastery of this abbess[3] there was a certain brother who was specially marked out by the grace of God, so that he used to compose godly and religious songs; thus, whatever he learned from the holy Scriptures by means of interpreters, he quickly turned into extremely delightful and moving poetry, in English, which was his own tongue. By his songs the minds of many were often inspired to despise the world and to long for the heavenly life. It is true that after him other Englishmen attempted to compose religious poems, but none could compare with him. For he did not learn the art of poetry from men nor through a man but he received the gift of song freely by the grace of God. Hence he could never compose any foolish or trivial poem but only those which were concerned with devotion and so were fitting for his devout tongue to utter. He had lived in the secular habit until he was well advanced in years and had never learned any songs.[4] Hence sometimes at a feast, when for the sake of providing entertainment, it had been decided that they should all sing in turn, when he saw the harp approaching him, he would rise up in the middle of the feasting, go out, and return home.

On one such occasion when he did so, he left the place of feasting and went to the cattle byre, as it was his turn to take charge of them that night. In due time he stretched himself out and went to sleep, whereupon he dreamed that someone stood by him, saluted him, and called him by name: "Caedmon," he said, "sing me something." Caedmon answered, "I cannot sing; that is why I left the feast and came here because I could not sing." Once again the speaker said, "Nevertheless you must sing to me." "What must I sing?" said Caedmon. "Sing," he said, "about the beginning of created things." Thereupon Caedmon began to sing verses which he had never heard before in praise of God the Creator, of which this is the general sense: "Now we must praise the Maker of the heavenly kingdom, the power of the Creator and his counsel, the deeds of the Father of glory and how He, since he is the eternal God, was the Author of all marvels and first created the heavens as a roof for the children of men and then, the almighty Guardian of the human race, created the earth." This is the sense but not the order of the words which he sang as he slept. For it is not possible to translate verse, however well composed, literally from one language to another without some loss of beauty and dignity. When he awoke, he remembered all that he had sung while asleep and soon added more verses in the same manner, praising God in fitting style.

In the morning he went to the reeve[5] who was his master, telling him of the gift he had received, and the reeve took him to the abbess. He was then bidden to describe his dream in the presence of a number of the more learned men and also to recite his song so that they might all examine him and decide upon the nature and origin of the gift of which he spoke; and it seemed clear to all of them that the Lord had granted him heavenly grace. They then read to him a passage of sacred history or doctrine, bidding him make a song out of it, if he could, in metrical form. He undertook the task and went away; on returning next morning he repeated the passage he had been given, which he had put into excellent verse. The abbess, who

2. Bk. 4, ch. 24.
3. Hild, an aristocratic woman famed for her piety, who had founded and ruled the abbey of Whitby.
4. Monks, who devoted their lives to prayer and the cele-

bration of the liturgy, needed to be literate in Latin. Caedmon was one of the lay brothers, who performed menial tasks and were often uneducated.
5. Person responsible for running the monastery's estates.

recognized the grace of God which the man had received, instructed him to renounce his secular habit and to take monastic vows. She and all her people received him into the community of the brothers and ordered that he should be instructed in the whole course of sacred history. He learned all he could by listening to them and then, memorizing it and ruminating over it, like some clean animal chewing the cud, he turned it into the most melodious verse: and it sounded so sweet as he recited it that his teachers became in turn his audience. He sang about the creation of the world, the origin of the human race, and the whole history of Genesis, of the departure of Israel from Egypt and the entry into the promised land and of many other of the stories taken from the sacred Scriptures: of the incarnation, passion, and resurrection of the Lord, of His ascension into heaven, of the coming of the Holy Spirit and the teaching of the apostles. He also made songs about the terrors of future judgment, the horrors of the pains of hell, and the joys of the heavenly kingdom. In addition he composed many other songs about the divine mercies and judgments, in all of which he sought to turn his hearers away from delight in sin and arouse in them the love and practice of good works. He was a most religious man, humbly submitting himself to the discipline of the Rule; and he opposed all those who wished to act otherwise with a flaming and fervent zeal. It was for this reason that his life had a beautiful ending.

When the hour of his departure drew near he was afflicted, fourteen days before, by bodily weakness, yet so slight that he was able to walk about and talk the whole time. There was close by a building to which they used to take those who were infirm or who seemed to be at the point of death. On the night on which he was to die, as evening fell, he asked his attendant to prepare a place in this building where he could rest. The attendant did as Caedmon said though he wondered why he asked, for he did not seem to be by any means at the point of death. They had settled down in the house and were talking and joking cheerfully with each of those who were already there and it was past midnight, when he asked whether they had the Eucharist in the house. They answered, "What need have you of the Eucharist? You are not likely to die, since you are talking as cheerfully with us as if you were in perfect health." "Nevertheless," he repeated, "bring me the Eucharist." When he had taken it in his hand he asked if they were all charitably disposed towards him and had no complaint nor any quarrel nor grudge against him. They answered that they were all in charity with him and without the slightest feeling of anger; then they asked him in turn whether he was charitably disposed towards them. He answered at once, "My sons, I am in charity with all the servants of God." So, fortifying himself with the heavenly viaticum, he prepared for his entrance into the next life. Thereupon he asked them how near it was to the time when the brothers had to awake to sing their nightly praises to God. They answered, "It will not be long." And he answered, "Good, let us wait until then." And so, signing himself with the sign of the holy cross, he laid his head on the pillow, fell asleep for a little while, and so ended his life quietly. Thus it came about that, as he had served the Lord with a simple and pure mind and with quiet devotion, so he departed into His presence and left the world by a quiet death; and his tongue which had uttered so many good words in praise of the Creator also uttered its last words in His praise, as he signed himself with the sign of the cross and commended his spirit into God's hands; and from what has been said, it would seem that he had foreknowledge of his death.

Bishop Asser

? – c. 909

When Bede died in 735, he left an island that was very unstable in its political geography but apparently ever more stable and accomplished in its religion and learning. By the end of the century, that world was shattered. In 793 Vikings sacked the monastery of Lindisfarne, not far from Wearmouth-Jarrow. Waves of raiders and then settlers followed. Monastic communities fled inland, and some shifted for generations before resettling finally. However sporadic and temporary may have been the worldly impact of these Viking raiders, however quickly they became peaceful settlers, they had a disastrous effect on the kind of disciplined learning witnessed by the life of Bede. By the time of Asser, Latin learning in most of England was fragmented and in decline, though not so bad as it suits Alfred to claim. Asser, a Welsh monk and later bishop of Sherborne, was summoned to Wessex by King Alfred as part of a project to revive learning and extend its audience beyond those who read Latin. Alfred accomplished this, in part, by looking to men like Asser, from areas such as Wales which had preserved some traditions of classical learning.

Asser's worshipful and disorganized but lively *Life of King Alfred* was written in Latin during the king's life, about 893. It depicts the origins of the king's scholarly ambitions, interwoven with the struggles by which Alfred established and extended his rule and resisted renewed Viking incursions. Asser thus offers a double narrative of texts and conquests which make one another possible and worthy. The diffusion of learning and revival of religious discipline become enmeshed in a logic that also includes Alfred's ambitions to rule all the Anglo-Saxons.

from The Life of King Alfred[1]

[ALFRED'S BOYHOOD]

Now he was greatly cherished above all his brothers by the united and ardent love of his father and mother, and indeed of all people; and he was ever brought up entirely at the royal court. As he passed through his infancy and boyhood he surpassed all his brothers in beauty, and was more pleasing in his appearance, in his speech, and in his manners. From his earliest childhood the noble character of his mind gave him a desire for all things useful in this present life, and, above all, a longing for wisdom; but, alas! the culpable negligence of his relations, and of those who had care of him, allowed him to remain ignorant of letters until his twelfth year, or even to a later age. Albeit, day and night did he listen attentively to the Saxon poems, which he often heard others repeating, and his retentive mind enabled him to remember them.

An ardent hunter, he toiled persistently at every form of that art, and not in vain. For in his skill and success at this pursuit he surpassed all, as in all other gifts of God. And this skill we have ourselves seen on many occasions.

Now it chanced on a certain day that his mother showed to him and to his brothers a book of Saxon poetry, which she had in her hand, and said, "I will give this book to that one among you who shall the most quickly learn it." Then, moved at these words, or rather by the inspiration of God, and being carried away by the beauty of the initial letter in that book, anticipating his brothers who surpassed him in years but not in grace, he answered his mother, and said, "Will you of a truth give that book to one of us? To him who shall soonest understand it and repeat it to you?"

1. Translated by L. C. Jane.

And at this she smiled and was pleased, and affirmed it, saying, "I will give it to him."
Then forthwith he took the book from her hand and went to his master, and read it;
and when he had read it he brought it back to his mother and repeated it to her.

After this he learnt the Daily Course, that is, the services for each hour, and
then some psalms and many prayers. These were collected in one book, which, as we
have ourselves seen, he constantly carried about with him everywhere in the fold of
his cloak, for the sake of prayer amid all the passing events of this present life. But,
alas! the art of reading which he most earnestly desired he did not acquire in accordance with his wish, because, as he was wont himself to say, in those days there were
no men really skilled in reading in the whole realm of the West Saxons.

With many complaints, and with heartfelt regrets, he used to declare that among
all the difficulties and trials of this life this was the greatest. For at the time when he
was of an age to learn, and had leisure and ability for it, he had no masters; but when
he was older, and indeed to a certain extent had anxious masters and writers, he
could not read. For he was occupied day and night without ceasing both with illnesses
unknown to all the physicians of that island, and with the cares of the royal office
both at home and abroad, and with the assaults of the heathen by land and sea.[2]
None the less, amid the difficulties of this life, from his infancy to the present day, he
has not in the past faltered in his earnest pursuit of knowledge, nor does he even now
cease to long for it, nor, as I think, will he ever do so until the end of his life.

[ALFRED'S KINGSHIP]

Yet amid the wars and many hindrances of this present life, and amid the assaults of
the pagans, and his daily illness, the king ceased not from the governance of the
kingdom and from the pursuit of every form of hunting. Nor did he omit to instruct
also his goldsmiths and all his artificers, his falconers and his huntsmen and the keepers of his dogs; nor to make according to new designs of his own articles of goldsmiths' work, more venerable and more precious than had been the wont of all his
predecessors. He was constant in the reading of books in the Saxon tongue, and more
especially in committing to memory the Saxon poems, and in commanding others to
do so. And he by himself labored most zealously with all his might.

Moreover he heard the divine offices daily, the Mass, and certain psalms and
prayers. He observed the services of the hours by day and by night, and oftentimes
was he wont, as we have said, without the knowledge of his men, to go in the night-
time to the churches for the sake of prayer. He was zealous in the giving of alms, and
generous towards his own people and to those who came from all nations. He was
especially and wonderfully kindly towards all men, and merry. And to the searching
out of things not known did he apply himself with all his heart.

Moreover many Franks, Frisians and Gauls, pagans, Britons, Scots and Armori-
cans, of their own free will, submitted them to his rule, both nobles and persons of
low degree. All these he ruled, according to his excellent goodness, as he did his
own people, and loved them and honored them, and enriched them with money
and with power.

He was eager and anxious to hear the Holy Scripture read to him by his own
folk, but he would also as readily pray with strangers, if by any chance one had come
from any place. Moreover he loved with wonderful affection his bishops and all the

2. Alfred's patient suffering in illness is one of several patterns by which Asser implies analogies with the lives of saints.

clergy, his ealdormen and nobles, his servants and all his household. And cherishing their sons, who were brought up in the royal household, with no less love than he bore towards his own children, he ceased not day and night, among other things, himself to teach them all virtue and to make them well acquainted with letters.

But it was as though he found no comfort in all these things. For, as if he suffered no other care from within or without, in anxious sorrow, day and night, he would make complaint to the Lord and to all who were joined to him in close affection, lamenting with many sighs for that Almighty God had not made him skilled in divine wisdom and in the liberal arts.

King Alfred
849–899

Alfred, king of the West Saxons, had ambitions to be king of all England, at least south of the Humber. He spent much of his reign in a series of campaigns against Viking raiders. After a decisive victory at the battle of Edington in 878, Alfred negotiated a peace that included the departure of the Danes from Wessex and the baptism of their king Guthrum. In the later years of his reign, starting about 890, he embarked on a quite different, but ultimately more influential, campaign of conquest and Christian conversion, through the series of Anglo-Saxon translations from Latin produced by his own hand and under his patronage. Pope Gregory the Great's *Pastoral Care* (c. 591), a handbook for bishops, was the first. This effort assuredly had charitable and scholarly motivations, but it also takes on interesting national overtones when it assumes that Anglo-Saxon is one language and known by all, and even more when it is linked to earlier translations and the westward movement of ancient power.

Preface to Saint Gregory's *Pastoral Care*[1]

King Alfred bids greet Bishop Waerferth[2] with his words lovingly and with friendship; and I let it be known to thee that it has very often come into my mind what wise men there formerly were throughout England, both of sacred and secular orders; and what happy times there were then throughout England; and how the kings who had power over the nation in those days obeyed God and His ministers; how they preserved peace, morality, and order at home, and at the same time enlarged their territory abroad; and how they prospered both with war and with wisdom; and also how zealous the sacred orders were both in teaching and learning, and in all the services they owed to God; and how foreigners came to this land in search of wisdom and instruction, and how we should now have to get them from abroad if we were to have them. So general was its decay in England that there were very few on this side of the Humber who could understand their rituals in English, or translate a letter from Latin into English; and I believe that there were not many beyond the Humber. There were so few of them that I cannot remember a single one south of the Thames when I came to the throne. Thanks be to Almighty God that we have any teachers among us now. And therefore I command thee to do as I believe thou art willing, to disengage thyself from worldly matters as often as thou canst, that thou mayest apply

---

1. Translated by Kevin Crossley-Holland.
2. Waerferth, bishop of Worcester, had earlier translated

Gregory's *Dialogues* for Alfred and perhaps inspired the king's more ambitious program.

the wisdom which God has given thee wherever thou canst. Consider what punishments would come upon us on account of this world, if we neither loved it [wisdom] ourselves nor suffered other men to obtain it: we should love the name only of Christian, and very few the virtues. When I considered all this, I remembered also that I saw, before it had been all ravaged and burned, how the churches throughout the whole of England stood filled with treasures and books; and there was also a great multitude of God's servants, but they had very little knowledge of the books, for they could not understand anything of them, because they were not written in their own language. As if they had said: "Our forefathers, who formerly held these places, loved wisdom, and through it they obtained wealth and bequeathed it to us. In this we can still see their tracks, but we cannot follow them, and therefore we have lost both the wealth and the wisdom, because we would not incline our hearts after their example." When I remembered all this, I wondered extremely that the good and wise men who were formerly all over England, and had perfectly learned all the books, had not wished to translate them into their own language. But again I soon answered myself and said: "They did not think that men would ever be so careless, and that learning would so decay; through that desire they abstained from it, since they wished that the wisdom in this land might increase with our knowledge of languages." Then I remembered how the law was first known in Hebrew, and again, when the Greeks had learned it, they translated the whole of it into their own language, and all other books besides. And again the Romans, when they had learned them, translated the whole of them by learned interpreters into their own language. And also all other Christian nations translated a part of them into their own language.[3] Therefore it seems better to me, if you think so, for us also to translate some books which are most needful for all men to know into the language which we can all understand, and for you to do as we very easily can if we have tranquility enough, that is, that all the youth now in England of free men, who are rich enough to be able to devote themselves to it, be set to learn as long as they are not fit for any other occupation, until they are able to read English writing well: and let those be afterwards taught more in the Latin language who are to continue in learning, and be promoted to a higher rank. When I remembered how the knowledge of Latin had formerly decayed throughout England, and yet many could read English writing, I began, among other various and manifold troubles of this kingdom, to translate into English the book which is called in Latin *Pastoralis,* and in English *Shepherd's Book,* sometimes word by word, and sometimes according to the sense, as I had learned it from Plegmund my archbishop, and Asser my bishop, and Grimbald my mass-priest, and John my mass-priest. And when I had learned it as I could best understand it, and as I could most clearly interpret it, I translated it into English; and I will send a copy to every bishopric in my kingdom; and in each there is a book-mark worth fifty mancuses.[4] And I command in God's name that no man take the book-mark from the book, or the book from the monastery. It is uncertain how long there may be such learned bishops as now, thanks be to God, there are nearly everywhere; therefore I wish them always to remain in their places unless the bishop wish to take them with him, or they be lent out anywhere, or any one be making a copy from them.

3. An early statement of the widespread medieval idea of the persistent westward movement of learning, *translatio studii,* in parallel with the westward movement of power, *translatio imperii.* If Alfred will now revive learning in England, he may imply, should he not also consolidate power?
4. Gold coins.

Ohthere's Journeys

Along with religious and speculative works like *Pastoral Care* and Boethius's *Consolation of Philosophy*, Alfred also sponsored the translation of histories, both Bede's *Ecclesiastical History of the English People* and the early fifth-century *Seven Books of History against the Pagans*, of Paulus Orosius. In the latter, Orosius's opening survey of geography is expanded to include lands north of the Alps, and the translator inserts the following account of two northern voyages by the Norwegian trader Ohthere, who later came to Alfred's court.

Ohthere describes two journeys, one made largely for curiosity (but also for walrus tusks) and the other mostly for trade. In the first, he heads north along the west coast of Norway, around the north edge of modern Sweden and Finland, and into the White Sea—a little-known area, inhabited only by hunters and fishermen. In the second he goes to the main trading town of his nation, Sciringes-heal (on the south coast of modern Norway), and then to a large town and trading center, Hedeby (modern Schleswig in northern Germany). Along with keen details of fauna and almost anthropological observation of local tribes, Ohthere notes the great exports of his area: furs, amber, and ivory—some of which he has brought to King Alfred. Throughout the passage, an implicit, curious interlocutor mediates between the interests (and ignorance) of the English audience and the foreign traveler.

Ohthere's Journeys[1]

Ohthere told his lord, King Alfred,[2] that he lived the furthest north of all Norwegians. He said that he lived in the north of Norway on the coast of the Atlantic. He also said that the land extends very far north beyond that point, but it is all uninhabited, except for a few places here and there where the *Finnas*[3] have their camps, hunting in winter, and in summer fishing in the sea.

He told how he once wished to find out how far the land extended due north, or whether anyone lived to the north of the unpopulated area. He went due north along the coast, keeping the uninhabited land to starboard and the open sea to port continuously for three days. He was then as far north as the whale hunters go at their furthest. He then continued due north as far as he could reach in the second three days. There the land turned due east, or the sea penetrated the land he did not know which—but he knew that he waited there for a west-northwest wind, and then sailed east along the coast as far as he could sail in four days. There he had to wait for a due northern wind, because there the land turned due south, or the sea penetrated the land he did not know which. Then from there he sailed due south along the coast as far as he could sail in five days. A great river went up into the land there. They turned up into the river, not daring to sail beyond it without permission, since the land on the far side of the river was fully settled. He had not previously come across any settled district since he left his own home, but had, the whole way, land to starboard that was uninhabited apart from fishers and bird-catchers and hunters, and they were all *Finnas*. To port he always had the open sea. The *Beormas* had extensive settlements in their country but the Norwegians did not dare to venture there. But the land of the *Terfinnas* was totally uninhabited except where hunters made camp, or fishermen or bird-catchers.

---

1. Translated by Christine E. Fell.
2. As a foreign visitor, Ohthere would need the official protection of the king, who is thus "his lord."
3. The *Finnas* (modern Lapps) are a nomadic people who give tribute to the Norwegians. They herd deer, hunt, and fish. They are not the peoples we now call Finns, whom Ohthere called *Beormas* and *Cwenas*.

The *Beormas* told him many stories both about their own country and about the lands which surrounded them, but he did not know how much of it was true because he had not seen it for himself. It seemed to him that the *Finnas* and the *Beormas* spoke almost the same language. His main reason for going there, apart from exploring the land, was for the walruses, because they have very fine ivory in their tusks—they brought some of these tusks to the king—and their hide is very good for ship-ropes. This whale [i.e., walrus] is much smaller than other whales; it is no more than seven ells long. The best whale-hunting is in his own country; those are forty-eight ells long, the biggest fifty ells long; of these he said that he, one of six, killed sixty in two days.

He was a very rich man in those possessions which their riches consist of, that is in wild deer. He had still, when he came to see the king, six hundred unsold tame deer. These deer they call "reindeer." Six of these were decoy-reindeer. These are very valuable among the *Finnas* because they use them to catch the wild reindeer. He was among the chief men in that country, but he had not more than twenty cattle, twenty sheep and twenty pigs, and the little that he plowed he plowed with horses. Their wealth, however, is mostly in the tribute which the *Finnas* pay them. That tribute consists of the skins of beasts, the feathers of birds, whale-bone, and ship-ropes made from whale-hide and sealskin. Each pays according to his rank. The highest in rank has to pay fifteen marten skins, five reindeer skins, one bear skin and ten measures of feathers, and a jacket of bearskin or otterskin and two ship-ropes. Each of these must be sixty ells long, one made from whale-hide the other from seal.

He said that the land of the Norwegians is very long and narrow. All of it that can be used for grazing or plowing lies along the coast and even that is in some places very rocky. Wild mountains lie to the east, above and alongside the cultivated land. In these mountains live the *Finnas*. The cultivated land is broadest in the south, and the further north it goes the narrower it becomes. In the south it is perhaps sixty miles broad or a little broader; and in the middle, thirty or broader; and to the north, he said, where it is narrowest, it might be three miles across to the mountains. The mountains beyond are in some places of a width that takes two weeks to cross, in others of a width that can be crossed in six days.

Beyond the mountains Sweden borders the southern part of the land as far as the north, and the country of the *Cwenas* borders the land in the north. Sometimes the *Cwenas* make raids on the Norwegians across the mountains, and sometimes the Norwegians make raids on them. There are very large fresh-water lakes throughout these mountains, and the *Cwenas* carry their boats overland onto the lakes and from there make raids on the Norwegians. They have very small, very light boats.

Ohthere said that the district where he lived is called *Halgoland*.[4] He said no-one lived to the north of him. In the south part of Norway there is a trading-town which is called *Sciringes heal*. He said that a man could scarcely sail there in a month, assuming he made camp at night, and each day had a favorable wind. He would sail by the coast the whole way. To starboard is first of all *Iraland*[5] and then those islands which are between *Iraland* and this land, and then this land until he comes to *Sciringes heal*, and Norway is on the port side the whole way. To the south of *Sciringes heal* a great sea penetrates the land; it is too wide to see across. Jutland is on the far side and after that *Sillende*.[6] This sea flows into the land for many hundred miles.

---

4. The northernmost province of Norway, much of it within the polar circle.

5. Possibly a corruption of Iceland.

6. Probably southern Jutland, modern North Schleswig.

The Death of Harold, from *The Bayeux Tapestry,* c. 1073–1088. This narrative tapestry was made within living memory of the Conquest, and the scenes depicted on it overlap much of the story as told in the *Anglo-Saxon Chronicle.* The tapestry is an extraordinary production: a roll about 20 inches high and some 230 feet long thought to have been embroidered by English women, whose needlework had international fame. In this climactic scene, at left King Harold is cut down by a mounted Norman knight; at center, Anglo-Saxon foot soldiers parry spears thrown by mounted Normans. In the marginal decoration at top, birds of prey and lions face off, emblems perhaps of the noble combatants; at the bottom, in a very different tone, lie the corpses and arms of fallen soldiers.

From *Sciringes heal* he said that he sailed in five days to the trading-town called Hedeby, which is situated among Wends, Saxons and Angles and belongs to the Danes. When he sailed there from *Sciringes heal* he had Denmark to port and the open sea to starboard for three days. Then two days before he arrived at Hedeby he had Jutland and *Sillende* and many islands to starboard. The Angles lived in these districts before they came to this land. On the port side he had, for two days, those islands which belong to Denmark.

The Anglo-Saxon Chronicle

The Anglo-Saxon Chronicle began to be assembled in the 890s at Winchester, in the heart of King Alfred's Wessex and at the high point of his reign. The decision to use Anglo-Saxon in this originally monastic product reflects the influence of Alfred's translation projects. The original version of the *Chronicle* was distributed to a number of monasteries, which made their own additions sometimes as late as the mid-twelfth century. If the various *Chronicles* began as a gesture of common language and shared history, though, their later entries—like the one below—increasingly record dynastic struggle and civil strife. And the *Chronicles* themselves, in their extensions after the Conquest, emblematize the fate of the Anglo-Saxon vernacular and culture: increasingly isolated, fragmentary, and recorded in a disappearing tongue.

from The Anglo-Saxon Chronicle[1]

STAMFORD BRIDGE AND HASTINGS

1066   In this year King Harold came from York to Westminster at the Easter follow-ing the Christmas that the king died,[2] and Easter was then on 16 April. Then over all England there was seen a sign in the skies such as had never been seen before. Some said it was the star "comet" which some call the long-haired star; and it first appeared on the eve of the Greater Litany, that is 24 April, and so shone all the week. And soon after this Earl Tosti came from overseas into the Isle of Wight with as large a fleet as he could muster and both money and provisions were given him.[3] And King Harold his brother assembled a naval force and a land force larger than any king had assembled before in this country, because he had been told that William the Bastard[4] meant to come here and conquer this country. This was exactly what happened afterwards. Meanwhile Earl Tosti came into the Humber with sixty ships and Earl Edwin came with a land force and drove him out, and the sailors deserted him. And he went to Scotland with twelve small vessels, and there Harold, king of Norway, met him with three hundred ships, and Tosti submitted to him and became his vassal; and they both went up the Humber until they reached York. And there Earl Edwin and Morcar his brother fought against them; but the Norwegians had the victory. Harold, king of the English, was informed that things had gone thus; and the fight was on the Vigil of Saint Matthew. Then Harold our king came upon the Norwegians by surprise and met them beyond York at Stamford Bridge with a large force of the English people; and that day there was a very fierce fight on both sides. There was killed Harold Fairhair and Earl Tosti, and the Norwegians who sur-vived took to flight; and the English attacked them fiercely as they pursued them until some got to the ships. Some were drowned, and some burned, and some destroyed in various ways so that few survived and the English remained in command of the field. The king gave quarter to Olaf, son of the Norse king, and their bishop and the earl of Orkney and all those who survived on the ships, and they went up to our king and swore oaths that they would always keep peace and friendship with this country; and the king let them go home with twenty-four ships. These two pitched battles were fought within five nights.

Then Count William came from Normandy to Pevensey on Michaelmas Eve, and as soon as they were able to move on they built a castle at Hastings. King Harold was informed of this and he assembled a large army and came against him at the hoary apple-tree. And William came against him by surprise before his army was drawn up in battle array. But the king nevertheless fought hard against him, with the men who were willing to support him, and there were heavy casualties on both sides. There King Harold was killed and Earl Leofwine his brother, and Earl Gyrth his brother, and many good men, and the French remained masters of the field, even as God granted it to them because of the sins of the people. Archbishop Aldred and the citizens of London wanted to have Edgar *Cild*[5] as king, as was his proper due; and Edwin and Morcar promised him that they would fight on his side; but always the more it ought to have been forward the more it got behind, and the worse it grew

1. Translated by Kevin Crossley-Holland.
2. Edward "the Confessor" ruled 1042–1066. Harold claims the throne through his sister Edith, Edward's widow.
3. Tosti was Harold's estranged brother, and now sup-ported the rival claim of Harold Fairhair, king of Norway.

4. William of Normandy, "the Conqueror."
5. Son of Edgar the Exile, grandson and great-grandson of kings; his great-uncle King Edward had titled him "Aetheling," or "throne-worthy." He was still a minor in 1066 and would have had to rule through a regent.

from day to day, exactly as everything came to be at the end. The battle took place on the festival of Calixtus the pope. And Count William went back to Hastings, and waited there to see whether submission would be made to him. But when he understood that no one meant to come to him, he went inland with all his army that was left to him, and that came to him afterwards from overseas, and ravaged all the region that he overran until he reached Berkhamstead. There he was met by Archbishop Aldred and Edgar *Cild,* and Earl Edwin and Earl Morcar, and all the chief men from London. And they submitted out of necessity after most damage had been done— and it was a great piece of folly that they had not done it earlier, since God would not make things better, because of our sins. And they gave hostages and swore oaths to him, and he promised them that he would be a gracious liege lord, and yet in the meantime they ravaged all that they overran. Then on Christmas Day, Archbishop Aldred consecrated him king at Westminster. And he promised Aldred on Christ's book and swore moreover (before Aldred would place the crown on his head) that he would rule all this people as well as the best of the kings before him, if they would be loyal to him. All the same he laid taxes on people very severely, and then went in spring overseas to Normandy, and took with him Archbishop Stigand, and Aethelnoth, abbot of Glastonbury, and Edgar *Cild* and Earl Edwin and Earl Morcar, and Earl Waltheof, and many other good men from England. And Bishop Odo and Earl William stayed behind and built castles far and wide throughout this country, and distressed the wretched folk, and always after that it grew much worse. May the end be good when God wills!

━━✥ END OF PERSPECTIVES: ETHNIC AND RELIGIOUS ENCOUNTERS ✥━━

►──━✥✦✥━──◄

Taliesin

The name of Taliesin resonated through Welsh literary imagination for more than a millennium, from the late sixth century until the end of the Middle Ages. Only a small cluster of about a dozen poems can be securely identified with him, all of them praise poems and elegies for contemporary kings. These must have circulated for generations in oral form. They appear in their earliest surviving manuscript, the late thirteenth-century Book of Taliesin, already embedded within a nimbus of intriguing legends and falsely attributed works that had been attached to the prestige of his name across the centuries.

Despite this central role, Taliesin was not a poet of "Wales" in anything like its modern geography. In the later sixth century when he was active, Welsh-speaking kingdoms survived in the north and west of Britain and into modern Scotland. They were embattled, pressured by the expanding Anglo-Saxon kingdoms to the east and south, by Picts in the north, and by Irish Celts in the kingdom of Dalriada to the far northwest. Among these unstable Welsh kingdoms, especially Rheged around the Solway Firth, Taliesin became an important court poet.

The warrior kings in the Welsh north, such as Taliesin's chief patrons Urien king of Rheged and his son Owain, were extolled in a poetic culture that celebrated treasure and heroic violence, yet did so in forms of considerable intricacy and language of dramatic spareness. Taliesin's poems use ambitious meters and stanzas involving internal rhyme, end rhyme, and alliteration. They do not merely glory in armed bloodshed but also explore the boasts and emotions leading up to battle; they often display a haunting visual sense of its grisly aftermath. Taliesin further celebrates the generosity and gaiety of the triumphant court: in ways reminiscent of the Anglo-Saxon *Wanderer*, one poem here registers the poet's terror at the thought of losing his patron and protector. In an elegy for Owain ap Urien, Taliesin combines all these elements, yet brackets them with a suddenly broadened and suggestively discordant perspective, a Christian plea for the needs of Owain's soul.

Urien Yrechwydd[1]

Urien of Yrechwydd   most generous of Christian men,
much do you give   to the people of your land;
as you gather   so also you scatter,
the poets of Christendom   rejoice while you stand.
5 More is the gaiety   and more is the glory
that Urien and his heirs   are for riches renowned,
and he is the chieftain,   the paramount ruler,
the far-flung refuge,   first of fighters found.
The Lloegrians[2] know it   when they count their numbers,
10 death have they suffered   and many a shame,
their homesteads a-burning,   stripped their bedding,
and many a loss   and many a blame,
and never a respite   from Urien of Rheged.
Rheged's defender,   famed lord, your land's anchor,
15 all that is told of you   has my acclaim.
Intense is your spear-play   when you hear ploy of battle,
when to battle you come   'tis a killing you can,
fire in their houses ere day   in the lord of Yrechwydd's way,
Yrechwydd the beautiful   and its generous clan.
20 The Angles are succorless.   Around the fierce king
are his fierce offspring.   Of those dead, of those living,
of those yet to come,   you head the column.
To gaze upon him   is a widespread fear;
Gaiety clothes him,   the ribald ruler,
25 gaiety clothes him   and riches abounding,
gold king of the Northland   and of kings king.

The Battle of Argoed Llwyfain[1]

There was a great battle Saturday morning
From when the sun rose until it grew dark.
The fourfold hosts of Fflamddwyn[2] invaded,
Goddau and Rheged gathered in arms,
5 Summoned from Argoed as far as Arfynydd[3]—
They might not delay by as much as a day.

With a great blustering din, Fflamddwyn shouted,
"Have these the hostages come? Are they ready?"[4]

---

1. "I-*rech*-ooeed" (gutural "ch"), or Rheged. Like many Anglo-Saxon poems, this poem uses a break (caesura) in midline. Translated by Saunders Lewis.
2. The Angles and Saxons.
1. "Ar-goid Lloo-*ee*-vine, the Welsh "ll" rather like "tl" pronounced quickly as a single sound. Translated by Anthony Conran.

2. "Flom-*thoo*-een," the Flame-bearer, identity uncertain.
3. "Goddau ("Go-thy,") and Arfynydd ("Ar-*vi*-nith") British territories.
4. Fflamddwyn arrogantly demands hostages, guarantees of submission, before the battle. The use of direct quotation is unique among Taliesin's poems.

To him then Owain, scourge of the eastlands,
10   "They've not come, no! they're not, nor shall they be ready."
And a whelp of Coel would indeed be afflicted
Did he have to give any man as a hostage!

And Urien, lord of Erechwydd, shouted,
"If they would meet us now for a treaty,
15   High on the hilltop let's raise our ramparts,
Carry our faces over the shield rims,
Raise up our spears, men, over our heads
And set upon Fflamddwyn in the midst of his hosts
And slaughter him, ay, and all that go with him!"

20   There was many a corpse beside Argoed Llwyfain;
From warriors ravens grew red
And with their leader a host attacked.
For a whole year I shall sing to their triumph.

The War-Band's Return[1]

Through a single year
This man has poured out
Wine, bragget, and mead,
Reward for valor.
5   A host of singers,
A swarm about spits,
Their torques round their heads,
Their places splendid.
Each went on campaign,
10   Eager in combat,
His steed beneath him,
Set to raid Manaw
For the sake of wealth,
Profit in plenty,
15   Eight herds alike
Of calves and cattle,
Milch cows and oxen,
And each one worthy.

I could have no joy
20   Should Urien be slain,
So loved before he left,
Brandishing his lance,
And his white hair soaked,
And a bier his fate,
25   And gory his cheek
With the stain of blood,
A strong, steadfast man,
His wife made a widow,
My faithful king,

---

1. Translated by Joseph P. Clancy.

30   My faithful trust,
            My bulwark, my chief,
            Before savage pain.

            Go, lad, to the door:
            What is that clamor?
35   Is the earth shaking?
            Is the sea in flood?
            The chant grows stronger
            From marching men!

            Were a foe in hill,
40   Urien will stab him;
            Were a foe in dale,
            Urien has pierced him;
            Were foe in mountain,
            Urien conquers him;
45   Were foe on hillside,
            Urien will wound him;
            Were foe on rampart,
            Urien will smite him:
            Foe on path, foe on peak,
50   Foe at every bend,
            Not one sneeze or two
            He permits before death.
            No famine can come,
            Plunder about him.
55   Like death his spear
            Piercing a foeman.
            And until I die, old,
            By death's strict demand,
            I shall not be joyful
60   Unless I praise Urien.

Lament for Owain Son of Urien[1]

            God, consider the soul's need
                Of Owain son of Urien!
            Rheged's prince, secret in loam:
                No shallow work to praise him.

5   A straight° grave, a man much praised,   *narrow*
                His whetted spear the wings of dawn:
            That lord of bright Llwyfenydd,
                Where is his peer?

            Reaper of enemies; strong of grip;
10   One kind with his fathers;
            Owain, to slay Fflamddwyn,
                Thought it no more than sleep.

1. Translated by Saunders Lewis.

<blockquote>

Sleepeth the wide host of England
With light in their eyes,
15   And those that had not fled
Were braver than were wise.

Owain dealt them doom
As the wolves devour sheep;
That warrior, bright of harness,
20   Gave stallions for the bard.

Though he hoarded wealth like a miser
For his soul's sake he gave it.
God, consider the soul's need
Of Owain son of Urien!

</blockquote>

╼━╾═╪═╾━╼

The Wanderer

In the Exeter Book, a manuscript copied about 975 and donated to the Bishop of Exeter, are preserved some of the greatest short poems in Old English, including a number of poems referred to as elegies—laments that contrast past happiness with present sorrow and remark on how fleeting is the former. Along with *The Wanderer*, the elegies include its companion piece *The Seafarer*; *The Ruin*; *The Husband's Message*; *The Wife's Lament*; and *Wulf and Eadwacer*. While the last two are exceptional in dealing with female experience, elegies for the most part focus on male bonds and companionship, particularly the joys of the mead hall. Old English poetry as a whole is almost entirely devoid of interest in romantic love between men and women and focuses instead on the bond between lord and retainer; elegiac poems such as *The Wanderer* have in fact been called "the love poetry of a heroic society."

The Wanderer opens with an appeal to a Christian concept, as the third-person narrator speaks of the wanderer's request for God's mercy. The body of the poem, however—primarily a first-person account in the wanderer's voice—reflects more pagan values in its regret for the loss of earthly joys. Though the poem's structure is somewhat confusing, one can discern two major parts. In the first, the wanderer laments his personal situation: he was once a member of a warrior band, but his lord—his beloved "gold-friend"—has died, leaving him a homeless exile. He dreams that he "clasps and kisses" his lord, but he then wakes to see only the dark waves, the snow, and the sea birds.

The second part of the poem turns from personal narrative to a more general statement of the transitoriness of all earthly things. The speaker (possibly someone other than the wanderer at this point), looking at the ruin of ancient buildings, is moved to express the ancient Roman motif known as "*ubi sunt*" (Latin for "where are"): "Where has the horse gone? Where the man? Where the giver of gold? / Where is the feasting place? And where the pleasures of the hall?" In the concluding five lines, the reader is urged to seek comfort in heaven.

There has been much debate about the degrees of Christianity and paganism in this tenth-century poem. The positions range from the view that the Christian opening and closing are totally extraneous to the poem and have been tacked on by a monkish copyist, to the view that the poem is a Christian allegory about a soul exiled from his heavenly home, longing for his lord Jesus Christ. It is now generally held that the poem is authentically Christian, in a literal rather than an allegorical way, but that the values of pagan society still exert a powerful pull in it.

The Wanderer[1]

Often the wanderer pleads for pity
and mercy from the Lord; but for a long time,
sad in mind, he must dip his oars
into icy waters, the lanes of the sea;
5   he must follow the paths of exile: fate is inflexible.

Mindful of hardships, grievous slaughter,
the ruin of kinsmen, the wanderer said:
"Time and again at the day's dawning
I must mourn all my afflictions alone.
10   There is no one still living to whom I dare open
the doors of my heart. I have no doubt
that it is a noble habit for a man
to bind fast all his heart's feelings,
guard his thoughts, whatever he is thinking.
15   The weary in spirit cannot withstand fate,
a troubled mind finds no relief:
wherefore those eager for glory often
hold some ache imprisoned in their hearts.
Thus I had to bind my feelings in fetters,
20   often sad at heart, cut off from my country,
far from my kinsmen, after, long ago,
dark clods of earth covered my gold-friend;
I left that place in wretchedness,
plowed the icy waves with winter in my heart;
25   in sadness I sought far and wide
for a treasure-giver, for a man
who would welcome me into his mead-hall,
give me good cheer (for I boasted no friends),
entertain me with delights. He who has experienced it
30   knows how cruel a comrade sorrow can be
to any man who has few loyal friends:
for him are the ways of exile, in no wise twisted gold;
for him is a frozen body, in no wise the fruits of the earth.
He remembers hall-retainers and treasure
35   and how, in his youth, his gold-friend
entertained him. Those joys have all vanished.
A man who lacks advice for a long while
from his loved lord understands this,
that when sorrow and sleep together
40   hold the wretched wanderer in their grip,
it seems that he clasps and kisses
his lord, and lays hands and head
upon his lord's knee as he had sometimes done
when he enjoyed the gift-throne in earlier days.
45   Then the friendless man wakes again
and sees the dark waves surging around him,
the sea-birds bathing, spreading their feathers,
frost and snow falling mingled with hail.

---

1. Translated by Kevin Crossley-Holland.

"Then his wounds lie more heavy in his heart,
50   aching for his lord. His sorrow is renewed;
the memory of kinsmen sweeps through his mind;
joyfully he welcomes them, eagerly scans
his comrade warriors. Then they swim away again.
Their drifting spirits do not bring many old songs
55   to his lips. Sorrow upon sorrow attend
the man who must send time and again
his weary heart over the frozen waves.

"And thus I cannot think why in the world
my mind does not darken when I brood on the fate
60   of brave warriors, how they have suddenly
had to leave the mead-hall, the bold followers.
So this world dwindles day by day,
and passes away; for a man will not be wise
before he has weathered his share of winters
65   in the world. A wise man must be patient,
neither too passionate nor too hasty of speech,
neither too irresolute nor too rash in battle;
not too anxious, too content, nor too grasping,
and never too eager to boast before he knows himself.
70   When he boasts a man must bide his time
until he has no doubt in his brave heart
that he has fully made up his mind.
A wise man must fathom how eerie it will be
when all the riches of the world stand waste,
75   as now in diverse places in this middle-earth
old walls stand, tugged at by winds
and hung with hoar-frost, buildings in decay.
The wine-halls crumble, lords lie dead,
deprived of joy, all the proud followers
80   have fallen by the wall: battle carried off some,
led them on journeys; the bird carried one
over the welling waters; one the gray wolf
devoured; a warrior with downcast face
hid one in an earth-cave.
85   Thus the Maker of Men laid this world waste
until the ancient works of the giants stood idle,
hushed without the hubbub of inhabitants.
Then he who has brooded over these noble ruins,
and who deeply ponders this dark life,
90   wise in his mind, often remembers
the many slaughters of the past and speaks these words:
Where has the horse gone? Where the man? Where the giver of gold?
Where is the feasting-place? And where the pleasures of the hall?
I mourn the gleaming cup, the warrior in his corselet,
95   the glory of the prince. How that time has passed away,
darkened under the shadow of night as if it had never been.
Where the loved warriors were, there now stands a wall
of wondrous height, carved with serpent forms.
The savage ash-spears, avid for slaughter,

100 have claimed all the warriors—a glorious fate!
Storms crash against these rocky slopes,
sleet and snow fall and fetter the world,
winter howls, then darkness draws on,
the night-shadow casts gloom and brings
105 fierce hailstorms from the north to frighten men.
Nothing is ever easy in the kingdom of earth,
the world beneath the heavens is in the hands of fate.
Here possessions are fleeting, here friends are fleeting,
here man is fleeting, here kinsman is fleeting,
110 the whole world becomes a wilderness."
So spoke the wise man in his heart as he sat apart in thought.
Brave is the man who holds to his beliefs; nor shall he ever
show the sorrow in his heart before he knows how he
can hope to heal it. It is best for a man to seek
115 mercy and comfort from the Father in heaven, the safe home that awaits us all.

Wulf and Eadwacer *and* The Wife's Lament

Old English literature focuses largely on masculine and military concerns and lacks a concept of romantic love—what the twelfth-century French would later call *"fine amour."* Against this backdrop *Wulf and Eadwacer* and *The Wife's Lament* stand out, first, by their use of woman's voice and second, by their treatment of the sorrows of love.

Though the exact genre of these poems is problematic, some scholars classifying them as riddles and others as religious allegories, most group them with a class of Old English poems known as elegies, with which they are preserved in the same manuscript, the Exeter Book. The elegies lament the loss of earthly goods, comradeship, and the "hall joys," often, as in *The Wanderer* and *The Seafarer*, by a speaker in exile. *The Wife's Lament* and *Wulf and Eadwacer* differ from the other elegies in that the speakers, as women, had no experience of comradeship to lose, as their main function was to be exchanged in marriage to cement relationships between feuding tribes. They are in a sense twice exiled, first from the noble brotherhood by their gender, and second from their beloved by their personal history. Furthermore, unlike the speakers in *The Wanderer* and *The Seafarer*, they do not look forward to the consolation of a heavenly kingdom imagined as a warlord with his group of retainers.

Although the two elegies in woman's voice are unique in the Old English corpus, they have analogues within the larger tradition of continental woman's song, which flourished in medieval Latin and the vernaculars from the eleventh century on. Their composition was so early—990 at the latest—that this tradition could not have influenced them, although the Roman poet Ovid's *Heroides* (verse letters of abandoned heroines to their faithless lovers) could have done so. One critic has raised the question of female authorship, on the grounds that continental nuns in the eighth century were criticized for writing romantic songs. As the critic Marilynn Desmond has suggested, perhaps Virginia Woolf's speculation that "anonymous was a woman" is true of these poems.

Though scholars agree that *Wulf and Eadwacer* is "heartrending" and "haunting," they cannot agree on the dramatic situation—each translation is an act of interpretation. The present translator, Kevin Crossley-Holland, sees the poem as involving the female speaker; her husband (Eadwacer); her lover (Wulf), from whom she is separated; and her child (a "cub"). Although what transpired before is unclear, she wistfully concludes, "men easily savage what was never secure, our song together." The dramatic setting of *The Wife's Lament* is similarly

ambiguous; it is not clear whether the woman's anger is directed toward her husband or to a
third person who plotted to separate them.

Wulf and Eadwacer

Prey, it's as if my people have been handed prey.
They'll tear him to pieces if he comes with a troop.

O, we are apart.

Wulf is on one island, I on another,
5   a fastness that island, a fen-prison.
Fierce men roam there, on that island;
they'll tear him to pieces if he comes with a troop.

O, we are apart.

How I have grieved for my Wulf's wide wanderings.
10   When rain slapped the earth and I sat apart weeping,
when the bold warrior wrapped his arms about me,
I seethed with desire and yet with such hatred.
Wulf, my Wulf, my yearning for you
and your seldom coming have caused my sickness,
15   my mourning heart, not mere starvation.
Can you hear, Eadwacer? Wulf will spirit
our pitiful whelp to the woods.
Men easily savage what was never secure,
our song together.

The Wife's Lament[1]

I draw these words from my deep sadness,
my sorrowful lot. I can say that,
since I grew up, I have not suffered
such hardships as now, old or new.
5   I am tortured by the anguish of exile.

First my lord forsook his family
for the tossing waves; I fretted at dawn
as to where in the world my lord might be.
In my sorrow I set out then,
10   a friendless wanderer, to search for my man.
But that man's kinsmen laid secret plans
to part us, so that we should live
most wretchedly, far from each other
in this wide world; I was seized with longings.

15   My lord asked me to live with him here;
I had few loved ones, loyal friends
in this country; that is reason for grief.
Then I found my own husband was ill-starred,
sad at heart, pretending, plotting
20   murder behind a smiling face. How often

---

1. Translated by Kevin Crossley-Holland.

we swore that nothing but death should ever
divide us; that is all changed now;
our friendship is as if it had never been.
Early and late, I must undergo hardship
25 because of the feud of my own dearest loved one.
Men forced me to live in a forest grove,
under an oak tree in the earth-cave.
This cavern is age-old; I am choked with longings.
Gloomy are the valleys, too high the hills,
30 harsh strongholds overgrown with briars:
a joyless abode. The journey of my lord so often
cruelly seizes me. There are lovers on earth,
lovers alive who lie in bed,
when I pass through this earth-cave alone
35 and out under the oak tree at dawn;
there I must sit through the long summer's day
and there I mourn my miseries,
my many hardships; for I am never able
to quiet the cares of my sorrowful mind,
40 all the longings that are my life's lot.

Young men must always be serious in mind
and stout-hearted; they must hide
their heartaches, that host of constant sorrows,
behind a smiling face.   Whether he is master
45 of his own fate or is exiled in a far-off land—
sitting under rocky storm-cliffs, chilled
with hoar-frost, weary in mind,
surrounded by the sea in some sad place—
my husband is caught in the clutches of anguish;
over and again he recalls a happier home.
50 Grief goes side by side with those
who suffer longing for a loved one.

After the Norman Conquest

➤ PERSPECTIVES ➤

Arthurian Myth in the History of Britain

Almost since it first appeared, the story of King Arthur has occupied a contested zone between myth and history. Far from diminishing the Arthurian tradition, though, this ambiguity has lent it a tremendous and protean impact on the political and cultural imagination of Europe, from the Middle Ages to the present. Probably no other body of medieval legend remains today as widely known and as often revisited as the Arthurian story.

One measure of Arthur's undiminished importance is the eager debate, eight centuries old and going strong, about his historical status. Whether or not a specific "Arthur" ever existed, legends and attributes gathered around his name from a very early date, mostly in texts of Welsh background. Around 600 a Welsh poem refers briefly to Arthur's armed might, and by about 1000, the story *Culhwch and Olwen*, from the Mabinogion, assumes knowledge of Arthur as a royal warlord. Other early Welsh texts begin to give him more-than-mortal attributes, associating Arthur with such marvels as an underworld quest and a mysterious tomb. In the ninth century, the Latin *History of the Britons* by the Welshman Nennius confidently speaks of Arthur as a great leader and lists his twelve victories ending with that at Mount Badon.

Some of this at least fits with better-documented history and with less-shadowy commanders who might have been models for an Arthurian figure, even if they were not "Arthur." When the Romans withdrew in 410, the romanized Britons soon faced territorial aggression from the Saxons and Picts. In the decades after midcentury, the Britons mounted a successful defense, led in part by Aurelius Ambrosius and culminating, it appears, with the battle of Badon in roughly 500, after which Saxon incursions paused for a time. In those same years of territorial threat, some Britons had emigrated to what is now Brittany, and in the 460s or 470s a warlord named Riothamus led an army, probably from Britain, and fought successfully in Gaul in alliance with local rulers sympathetic to Rome. His name was latinized from a British title meaning "supreme king." Both Riothamus and Aurelius Ambrosius correspond to parts of the later narratives of Arthur: his role as high king, his triumphs against the Saxons, his links to Rome (both friendly and hostile), and his campaigns on the Continent.

Whether the origins of Arthur's story lie in fact or in an urge among the Welsh to imagine a great leader who once restored their power against the ever-expanding Anglo-Saxons, he was clearly an established figure in Welsh oral and written literature by the ninth century. Arthur, however, also held a broader appeal for other peoples of England. The British Isles were felt to lie at the outer edge of world geography, but the story of Arthur and his ancestor Brutus served to create a Britain with other kinds of centrality. The legend of Brutus made Britain the end point of an inexorable westward movement of Trojan imperial power, the *translatio imperii*, and Arthur's forebears became linked to Roman imperial dynasties. Finally, the general movement of Arthur's continental campaigns neatly reversed the patterns of Roman and then Norman colonization.

In the later Middle Ages and after, Arthur and his court are most often encountered in works that lay little claim to historical accuracy. Rather, they exploit the very uncertainty of Arthurian narrative to explore the highest (if sometimes self-deceiving) yearnings of private emotion and social order. These Arthurian romances also probe, often in tragic terms, the limits and taboos that both define and subvert such ideals, including the mutual threats posed by private emotion and social order.

Nevertheless, the Arthurian tradition has also been pulled persistently into the realm of the real. It was presented as serious historical writing from the twelfth century through the end of the Middle Ages. Political agents have used Arthur's kingship as a model or precedent for their own aspirations, as seen in the Kennedy administration's portrayal as a version of Camelot. Even elements of the Christian church wrote their doctrines into Arthurian narrative or claimed Arthur as a patron.

The texts in this section present three illuminating moments of Arthur's emergence into history and politics. Geoffrey of Monmouth's *History of the Kings of Britain*, finished around 1138, was the fullest version yet of Arthur's origin and career. Geoffrey was the first to make Arthur such a central figure in British history, and it was largely through Geoffrey's Latin "history" that Arthur became so widespread a feature of cultural imagination in the Middle Ages and beyond. Writing at the close of the twelfth century, Gerald of Wales narrates an occasion, possibly orchestrated by Henry II, in which Arthurian tradition was slightly altered and folded into emergent Norman versions of British antiquity. The section ends with two politically charged versions of national origin, English and Scottish, proposed in 1301 as part of Edward I's efforts to influence royal succession in Scotland.

Geoffrey of Monmouth
c. 1100–1155

From the perspective of surviving British peoples in Wales and Cornwall, the Norman Conquest of 1066 was only the last among successive waves of invasion by Romans, Picts, Anglo-Saxons, and Vikings. The Celtic Britons had long been pushed into the far southwest by the time the Normans arrived, where they continued to resist colonization. The Welsh maintained a vital language, culture, and ethnic mythology, including a memory of their fellow Celts in Brittany and a divided nostalgia for the long-departed Romans. Thus a whole Celtic linguistic and political world offered an alternative to the languages and legends of the Normans, much of which derived ultimately from Mediterranean antiquity. Arthur, king of the Britons, emerged as a key figure as these peoples and cultures began to articulate the complex new forms of political and private identity precipitated by the Conquest.

No one was more important in this process than Geoffrey of Monmouth. He was prior of the Abbey of Monmouth in Wales and later was named bishop of Saint Asaph, though civil disorder prevented his taking the post. Yet he was also active in the emerging schools of Oxford, he was patronized by Norman nobles and bishops, and he wrote in Latin. Geoffrey's learning reflects this double allegiance. Well schooled in the Latin curriculum that embraced ancient Roman and Christian literature, he was also deeply versed in the oral and written culture of Wales. As a creative negotiator between Welsh and Anglo-Norman legends and languages, his influence was without parallel.

Both of Geoffrey's surviving prose works, the *Prophecies of Merlin* (finished around 1135) and the *History of the Kings of Britain* (about 1138) present themselves as translations of ancient texts from Wales or Brittany. Geoffrey also wrote a *Life of Merlin* in Latin verse. He probably synthesized a number of sources and added material of his own in his "translations." It was a pointed gesture, nevertheless, to posit a Celtic text whose authority rivaled the Latin culture and legends that had underwritten later Anglo-Saxon and then Norman power in England. Geoffrey daringly inverted the general hierarchy of Latin and vernaculars in his time; instead, he offered "British" as the ancient tongue that he wanted to make more broadly accessible for Latin-reading newcomers.

Geoffrey's central heroes are Brutus, the exiled Trojan descendant who colonized and named Britain, and Arthur, who reunified England after Saxon and Pictish attacks, and repulsed Roman efforts to reestablish power there. Geoffrey's own purposes in the *History* were complex but he was responding in part to contemporary events. The 1130s were a decade of civil strife in England, as nobles shifted their allegiances between King Stephen and the other claimant to the throne, the future Henry II. Welsh nobles took advantage of this disorder to rebel and set up their own principalities. Scholars remain divided as to whether Geoffrey was more interested in a return to strong and unified rule in Norman England, or wanted rather to encourage the Welsh princes with the story of a great predecessor who might one day return.

Geoffrey's narrative carefully presents itself as history, in a century of great historical writing. He uses the typical armature of documentary and other written records, archaeological evidence, and claims to well-founded witness. Casting the story of Arthur into this respected form allows Geoffrey to employ but also to counter the dominant master-narrative of Christian history in England, which was Bede's. Rather than a story of Anglo-Saxon arrival and conversion, Geoffrey offers a story of an earlier foundation and a prior conversion; he thus creates imaginative space for a convergence between Norman power and the culture and ambitions of people and languages at its edges. Moreover, the *History* generates an exterior (if now conveniently absent) common enemy in the imperial Romans. Geoffrey pulls in yet more ancient models by frequently echoing Virgil's *Aeneid* and its story of exile and refoundation, and by placing his story within biblical, Trojan, and Roman chronologies. And he points forward to his own time by inserting the earlier *Prophecies of Merlin* in the midst of the *History*.

The continued influence of Geoffrey's *History* on later literature is testimony to the powerful themes he folded into his story. Much that is developed in later romance explorations of the Arthurian world is already here: the tragedy of a people bravely battling its own decline; the danger and overwhelming attraction of illicit sexual desire; the ambivalent position of Mordred as cousin or nephew; the Arthurian realm brought down, ultimately, by the treachery of the king's own kin and by a transgression of the marriage bed that echoes Arthur's own conception.

The following selections from Geoffrey's *History* feature the Trojan background of Britain and the birth and early kingship of Arthur. Other texts in this section and following trace later episodes in his evolving legend: the development of Arthur's court, the celebration and tragedy of romantic desire, and the death of the king.

from History of the Kings of Britain[1]
Dedication

Whenever I have chanced to think about the history of the kings of Britain, on those occasions when I have been turning over a great many such matters in my mind, it has seemed a remarkable thing to me that, apart from such mention of them as Gildas and Bede had each made in a brilliant book on the subject, I have not been able to discover anything at all on the kings who lived here before the Incarnation of Christ, or indeed about Arthur and all the others who followed on after the Incarnation. Yet the deeds of these men were such that they deserve to be praised for all time. What is more, these deeds were handed joyfully down in oral tradition, just as if they had been committed to writing, by many peoples who had only their memory to rely on.

At a time when I was giving a good deal of attention to such matters, Walter, Archdeacon of Oxford, a man skilled in the art of public speaking and well-informed about the history of foreign countries, presented me with a certain very ancient book written in the British language.[2] This book, attractively composed to form a consecutive

---

1. Translated by Lewis Thorpe (1966).
2. Walter and Geoffrey were both associated with an early Oxford college, and their names appear together on sev-

eral legal documents. In two of these, Geoffrey calls himself a *magister*, a teacher at an advanced level.

and orderly narrative, set out all the deeds of these men, from Brutus, the first King of the Britons, down to Cadwallader, the son of Cadwallo.[3] At Walter's request I have taken the trouble to translate the book into Latin, although, indeed, I have been content with my own expressions and my own homely style and I have gathered no gaudy flowers of speech in other men's gardens. If I had adorned my page with high-flown rhetorical figures, I should have bored my readers, for they would have been forced to spend more time in discovering the meaning of my words than in following the story.

I ask you, Robert, Earl of Gloucester,[4] to do my little book this favor. Let it be so emended by your knowledge and your advice that it must no longer be considered as the product of Geoffrey of Monmouth's small talent. Rather, with the support of your wit and wisdom, let it be accepted as the work of one descended from Henry, the famous King of the English; of one whom learning has nurtured in the liberal arts and whom his innate talent in military affairs has put in charge of our soldiers, with the result that now, in our own lifetime, our island of Britain hails you with heartfelt affection, as if it had been granted a second Henry.

You too, Waleran, Count of Mellent, second pillar of our kingdom, give me your support, so that, with the guidance provided by the two of you, my work may appear all the more attractive when it is offered to its public.[5] For indeed, sprung as you are from the race of the most renowned King Charles, Mother Philosophy has taken you to her bosom, and to you she has taught the subtlety of her sciences. What is more, so that you might become famous in the military affairs of our army, she has led you to the camp of kings, and there, having surpassed your fellow-warriors in bravery, you have learned, under your father's guidance, to be a terror to your enemies and a protection to your own folk. Faithful defender as you are of those dependent on you, accept under your patronage this book which is published for your pleasure. Accept me, too, as your writer, so that, reclining in the shade of a tree which spreads so wide, and sheltered from envious and malicious enemies, I may be able in peaceful harmony to make music on the reed-pipe of a muse who really belongs to you.

[TROY, AENEAS, BRUTUS' EXILE][6]

After the Trojan war, Aeneas fled from the ruined city with his son Ascanius and came by boat to Italy. He was honorably received there by King Latinus, but Turnus, King of the Rutuli, became jealous of him and attacked him. In the battle between them Aeneas was victorious. Turnus was killed and Aeneas seized both the kingdom of Italy and the person of Lavinia, who was the daughter of Latinus.[7]

When Aeneas' last day came, Ascanius was elected King. He founded the town of Alba on the bank of the Tiber and became the father of a son called Silvius. This Silvius was involved in a secret love-affair with a certain niece of Lavinia's; he married her and made her pregnant. When this came to the knowledge of his father Ascanius, the latter ordered his soothsayers to discover the sex of the child which the girl had conceived. As soon as they had made sure of the truth of the matter, the

---

3. Bede's *Ecclesiastical History of the English People* was the source most used by 12th-century historians, but it has little to say about England before the coming of the Angles and Saxons. Geoffrey offers a (perhaps fictive) source for a more ancient history of the people who preceded the Saxons.
4. An illegitimate son of King Henry I. He had a hand in the education of the future Henry II, his nephew.
5. Waleran de Beaumont, Count of Meulan (1104–1166)

moved in the same circles as the Earl of Gloucester, and was patron of the Norman Abbey of Bec, a great center of learning. Geoffrey's fulsome tone is typical of dedications to great magnates in the period.
6. From bk. 1, ch. 3.
7. This summarizes the political narrative of Virgil's *Aeneid*, a text Geoffrey knew well and echoed frequently throughout his *History*.

soothsayers said that she would give birth to a boy, who would cause the death of both his father and his mother; and that after he had wandered in exile through many lands this boy would eventually rise to the highest honor.

The soothsayers were not wrong in their forecast. When the day came for her to have her child, the mother bore a son and died in childbirth. The boy was handed over to the midwife and was given the name Brutus. At last, when fifteen years had passed, the young man killed his father by an unlucky shot with an arrow, when they were out hunting together. Their beaters drove some stags into their path and Brutus, who was under the impression that he was aiming his weapon at these stags, hit his own father below the breast. As the result of this death Brutus was expelled from Italy by his relations, who were angry with him for having committed such a crime. He went in exile to certain parts of Greece; and there he discovered the descendants of Helenus, Priam's son, who were held captive in the power of Pandrasus, King of the Greeks. After the fall of Troy, Pyrrhus, the son of Achilles, had dragged this man Helenus off with him in chains, and a number of other Trojans, too. He had ordered them to be kept in slavery, so that he might take vengeance on them for the death of his father.

When Brutus realized that these people were of the same race as his ancestors, he stayed some time with them. However, he soon gained such fame for his military skill and prowess that he was esteemed by the kings and princes more than any young man in the country.

[THE NAMING OF BRITAIN][8]

[Brutus conquers the Greek king (reversing the Greek conquest of his ancestral Troy), marries the king's daughter Ignoge, and leads the Trojan descendants off to seek a new land. They pass through continental Europe, where they do battle with the Gauls.]

In their pursuit the Trojans continued to slaughter the Gauls, and they did not abandon the bloodshed until they had gained victory.

Although this signal triumph brought him great joy, Brutus was nevertheless filled with anxiety, for the number of his men became smaller every day, while that of the Gauls was constantly increasing. Brutus was in doubt as to whether he could oppose the Gauls any longer; and he finally chose to return to his ships in the full glory of his victory while the greater part of his comrades were still safe, and then to seek out the island which divine prophecy had promised would be his. Nothing else was done. With the approval of his men Brutus returned to his fleet. He loaded his ships with all the riches which he had acquired and then went on board. So, with the winds behind him, he sought the promised island, and came ashore at Totnes.

At this time the island of Britain was called Albion. It was uninhabited except for a few giants. It was, however, most attractive, because of the delightful situation of its various regions, its forests and the great number of its rivers, which teemed with fish; and it filled Brutus and his comrades with a great desire to live there. When they had explored the different districts, they drove the giants whom they had discovered into the caves in the mountains. With the approval of their leader they divided the land among themselves. They began to cultivate the fields and to build houses, so that in a short time you would have thought that the land had always been inhabited.

---

8. From bk. 1, chs. 15–18 and bk. 2, ch. 1.

Brutus then called the island Britain from his own name, and his companions he called Britons. His intention was that his memory should be perpetuated by the derivation of the name. A little later the language of the people, which had up to then been known as Trojan or Crooked Greek, was called British, for the same reason.[9]

[BRUTUS BUILDS NEW TROY]

Once he had divided up his kingdom, Brutus decided to build a capital. In pursuit of this plan, he visited every part of the land in search of a suitable spot. He came at length to the River Thames, walked up and down its banks and so chose a site suited to his purpose. There then he built his city and called it Troia Nova. It was known by this name for long ages after, but finally by a corruption of the word it came to be called Trinovantum. * * *

When the above-named leader Brutus had built the city about which I have told you, he presented it to the citizens by right of inheritance, and gave them a code of laws by which they might live peacefully together. At that time the priest Eli was ruling in Judea and the Ark of the Covenant was captured by the Philistines. The sons of Hector reigned in Troy, for the descendants of Antenor had been driven out. In Italy reigned Aeneas Silvius, son of Aeneas and uncle of Brutus, the third of the Latin Kings. * * *[1]

In the meantime Brutus had consummated his marriage with his wife Ignoge. By her he had three sons called Locrinus, Kamber and Albanactus, all of whom were to become famous. When their father finally died, in the twenty-third year after his landing, these three sons buried him inside the walls of the town which he had founded. They divided the kingdom of Britain between them in such a way that each succeeded to Brutus in one particular district. Locrinus, who was the first-born, inherited the part of the island which was afterwards called Loegria after him. Kamber received the region which is on the further bank of the River Severn, the part which is now known as Wales but which was for a long time after his death called Kambria from his name. As a result the people of that country still call themselves Kambri today in the Welsh tongue. Albanactus, the youngest, took the region which is nowadays called Scotland in our language. He called it Albany, after his own name.

[MERLIN AND THE FIRST CONQUEST OF IRELAND][2]

[The descendants of Brutus' three sons include Leir (Shakespeare's King Lear), the brothers Brennius and Belinus who conquer Rome, and Lud who rebuilds New Troy and names it Kaerlud after himself (whence "London"). In the reign of Lud's brother, Julius Caesar invades England; generations of Britons resist, until King Coel makes peace with the Roman legate Constantius. The latter succeeds Coel, marries Coel's daughter, and sires Constantine who becomes emperor of Rome. The Romans tire of defending Britain against invaders and withdraw from the island. Vortigern usurps the throne from the Briton line, then holds it in alliance with the Saxons Hengist and Horsa. The Saxons become aggressors, and Vortigern flees them but is overcome by the brothers Aurelius Ambrosius and Utherpendragon, who restore the Briton royal line and drive the Saxons into the north. Aurelius reigns, restoring churches and the rule of law; he wants to commemorate the Britons who died fighting off the Saxons.]

9. With this detail, Geoffrey creates a linguistic history in which early Welsh is as ancient as classical Latin, and more purely "Trojan."

1. Medieval historians often made such parallels between biblical and secular chronologies.
2. From bk. 8, chs. 10–13.

Aurelius collected carpenters and stone-masons together from every region and ordered them to use their skill to contrive some novel building which would stand forever in memory of such distinguished men. The whole band racked their brains and then confessed themselves beaten. Then Tremorinus, Archbishop of the City of the Legions,[3] went to the King and said: "If there is anyone anywhere who has the ability to execute your plan, then Merlin, the prophet of Vortigern, is the man to do it.[4] In my opinion, there is no one else in your kingdom who has greater skill, either in the foretelling of the future or in mechanical contrivances. Order Merlin to come and use his ability, so that the monument for which you are asking can be put up."

Aurelius asked many questions about Merlin; then he sent a number of messengers through the various regions of the country to find him and fetch him. They traveled through the provinces and finally located Merlin in the territory of the Gewissei, at the Galabes Springs, where he often went. They explained to him what they wanted of him and then conducted him to the King. The King received Merlin gaily and ordered him to prophesy the future, for he wanted to hear some marvels from him. "Mysteries of that sort cannot be revealed," answered Merlin, "except where there is the most urgent need for them. If I were to utter them as an entertainment, or where there was no need at all, then the spirit which controls me would forsake me in the moment of need."

He gave the same refusal to everyone present. The King had no wish to press him about the future, but he spoke to him about the monument which he was planning. "If you want to grace the burial-place of these men with some lasting monument," replied Merlin, "send for the Giants' Ring which is on Mount Killaraus in Ireland. In that place there is a stone construction which no man of this period could ever erect, unless he combined great skill and artistry. The stones are enormous and there is no one alive strong enough to move them. If they are placed in position round this site, in the way in which they are erected over there, they will stand forever."

At these words of Merlin's Aurelius burst out laughing. "How can such large stones be moved from so far-distant a country?" he asked. "It is hardly as if Britain itself is lacking in stones big enough for the job!" "Try not to laugh in a foolish way, your Majesty," answered Merlin. "What I am suggesting has nothing ludicrous about it. These stones are connected with certain secret religious rites and they have various properties which are medicinally important. Many years ago the Giants transported them from the remotest confines of Africa and set them up in Ireland at a time when they inhabited that country. Their plan was that, whenever they felt ill, baths should be prepared at the foot of the stones; for they used to pour water over them and to run this water into baths in which their sick were cured. What is more, they mixed the water with herbal concoctions and so healed their wounds. There is not a single stone among them which hasn't some medicinal virtue."

When the Britons heard all this, they made up their minds to send for the stones and to make war on the people of Ireland if they tried to hold them back. In the end the King's brother, Utherpendragon, and fifteen thousand men, were chosen to carry out the task. Merlin, too, was co-opted, so that all the problems which had to be met could have the benefit of his knowledge and advice. They made ready their ships and they put to sea. The winds were favorable and they arrived in Ireland.

3. Also called Caerusk or Caerleon; Geoffrey mentions it often and may have had some connection with it.
4. Merlin, son of a Briton princess and a demonic spirit, has already appeared; he triumphed over Vortigern's magicians and uttered a series of prophecies. Merlin's roles as a royal advisor, a prophet, and even a shape-shifter can be compared to those of poets in early Celtic cultures.

At that time there reigned in Ireland a young man of remarkable valor called Gillomanius. As soon as he heard that the Britons had landed in the country, he collected a huge army together and hurried to meet them. When he learned the reason of their coming, Gillomanius laughed out loud at those standing round him. "I am not surprised that a race of cowards has been able to devastate the island of the Britons," said he, "for the Britons are dolts and fools. Who ever heard of such folly? Surely the stones of Ireland aren't so much better than those of Britain that our realm has to be invaded for their sake! Arm yourselves, men, and defend your fatherland, for as long as life remains in my body they shall not steal from us the minutest fragment of the Ring."

When he saw that the Irish were spoiling for a fight, Uther hurriedly drew up his own line of battle and charged at them. The Britons were successful almost immediately. The Irish were either mangled or killed outright, and Gillomanius was forced to flee. Having won the day, the Britons made their way to Mount Killaraus. When they came to the stone structure, they were filled with joy and wonder. Merlin came up to them as they stood round in a group. "Try your strength, young men," said he, "and see whether skill can do more than brute strength, or strength more than skill, when it comes to dismantling these stones!"

At his bidding they all set to with every conceivable kind of mechanism and strove their hardest to take the Ring down. They rigged up hawsers and ropes and they propped up scaling-ladders, each preparing what he thought most useful, but none of these things advanced them an inch. When he saw what a mess they were making of it, Merlin burst out laughing. He placed in position all the gear which he considered necessary and dismantled the stones more easily than you could ever believe. Once he had pulled them down, he had them carried to the ships and stored on board, and they all set sail once more for Britain with joy in their hearts.

The winds were fair. They came to the shore and then set off with the stones for the spot where the heroes had been buried. The moment that this was reported to him, Aurelius dispatched messengers to all the different regions of Britain, ordering the clergy and the people to assemble and, as they gathered, to converge on Mount Ambrius, where they were with due ceremony and rejoicing to re-dedicate the burial-place which I have described. At the summons from Aurelius the bishops and abbots duly assembled with men from every rank and file under the King's command. All came together on the appointed day. Aurelius placed the crown on his head and celebrated the feast of Whitsun in right royal fashion, devoting the next three days to one long festival. * * *

Once he had settled these matters, and others of a similar nature, Aurelius ordered Merlin to erect round the burial-place the stones which he had brought from Ireland. Merlin obeyed the King's orders and put the stones up in a circle round the sepulchre, in exactly the same way as they had been arranged on Mount Killaraus in Ireland, thus proving that his artistry was worth more than any brute strength.

[UTHERPENDRAGON SIRES ARTHUR][5]

[*Vortigern's son attacks Aurelius Ambrosius and Utherpendragon. They drive him off, though Aurelius is poisoned through Saxon treachery. A miraculous star appears, which Merlin interprets as a sign of Uther's destined kingship, the coming of Arthur, and the rule of Uther's dynasty. At the same time, however, Merlin prophesies the decline of the Britons. As king, Uther fights off more Saxon incursions.*]

5. From bk. 8, chs. 19–24.

The next Eastertide Uther told the nobles of his kingdom to assemble in that same town of London, so that he could wear his crown and celebrate so important a feast-day with proper ceremony. They all obeyed, traveling in from their various cities and assembling on the eve of the feast. The King was thus able to celebrate the feast as he had intended and to enjoy himself in the company of his leaders. They, too, were all happy, seeing that he had received them with such affability. A great many nobles had gathered there, men worthy of taking part in such a gay festivity, together with their wives and daughters.

Among the others there was present Gorlois, Duke of Cornwall, with his wife Ygerna, who was the most beautiful woman in Britain. When the King saw her there among the other women, he was immediately filled with desire for her, with the result that he took no notice of anything else, but devoted all his attention to her. To her and to no one else he kept ordering plates of food to be passed and to her, too, he kept sending his own personal attendants with golden goblets of wine. He kept smiling at her and engaging her in sprightly conversation. When Ygerna's husband saw what was happening, he was so annoyed that he withdrew from the court without taking leave. No one present could persuade him to return, for he was afraid of losing the one object that he loved better than anything else. Uther lost his temper and ordered Gorlois to come back to court, so that he, the King, could seek satisfaction for the way in which he had been insulted. Gorlois refused to obey. The King was furious and swore an oath that he would ravage Gorlois' lands, unless the latter gave him immediate satisfaction.

Without more ado, while the bad blood remained between the two of them, the King collected a huge army together and hurried off to the Duchy of Cornwall, where he set fire to towns and castles. Gorlois' army was the smaller of the two and he did not dare to meet the King in battle. He preferred instead to garrison his castles and to bide his time until he could receive help from Ireland. As he was more worried about his wife than he was about himself, he left her in the castle of Tintagel,[6] on the sea-coast, which he thought was the safest place under his control. He himself took refuge in a fortified camp called Dimilioc,[7] so that, if disaster overtook them, they should not both be endangered together. When the King heard of this, he went to the encampment where Gorlois was, besieged it and cut off every line of approach.

Finally, after a week had gone by, the King's passion for Ygerna became more than he could bear. He called to him Ulfin of Ridcaradoch, one of his soldiers and a familiar friend, and told him what was on his mind. "I am desperately in love with Ygerna," said Uther, "and if I cannot have her I am convinced that I shall suffer a physical breakdown. You must tell me how I can satisfy my desire for her, for otherwise I shall die of the passion which is consuming me." "Who can possibly give you useful advice," answered Ulfin, "when no power on earth can enable us to come to her where she is inside the fortress of Tintagel? The castle is built high above the sea, which surrounds it on all sides, and there is no other way in except that offered by a narrow isthmus of rock. Three armed soldiers could hold it against you, even if you stood there with the whole kingdom of Britain at your side. If only the prophet Merlin would give his mind to the problem, then with his help I think you might be able to obtain what you want." The King believed Ulfin and ordered Merlin to be sent for, for he, too, had come to the siege.

---

6. Tin-ta-jel, on the rocky northwestern coast of Corn-wall.

7. Di-mi-li-oc, perhaps a site roughly five miles from Tintagel.

Merlin was summoned immediately. When he appeared in the King's presence, he was ordered to suggest how the King could have his way with Ygerna. When Merlin saw the torment which the King was suffering because of this woman, he was amazed at the strength of his passion. "If you are to have your wish," he said, "you must make use of methods which are quite new and until now unheard-of in your day. By my drugs I know how to give you the precise appearance of Gorlois, so that you will resemble him in every respect. If you do what I say, I will make you exactly like him, and Ulfin exactly like Gorlois' companion, Jordan of Tintagel. I will change my own appearance, too, and come with you. In this way you will be able to go safely to Ygerna in her castle and be admitted."

The King agreed and listened carefully to what he had to do. In the end he handed the siege over to his subordinates, took Merlin's drugs, and was changed into the likeness of Gorlois. Ulfin was changed into Jordan and Merlin into a man called Britaelis, so that no one could tell what they had previously looked like. They then set off for Tintagel and came to the Castle in the twilight. The moment the guard was told that his leader was approaching, he opened the gates and the men were let in. Who, indeed, could possibly have suspected anything, once it was thought that Gorlois himself had come? The King spent that night with Ygerna and satisfied his desire by making love with her. He had deceived her by the disguise which he had taken. He had deceived her, too, by the lying things that he said to her, things which he planned with great skill. He said that he had come out secretly from his besieged encampment so that he might make sure that all was well with her, whom he loved so dearly, and with his castle, too. She naturally believed all that he said and refused him nothing that he asked. That night she conceived Arthur, the most famous of men, who subsequently won great renown by his outstanding bravery.

Meanwhile, when it was discovered at the siege of Dimilioc that the King was no longer present, his army, acting without his instructions, tried to breach the walls and challenge the beleaguered Duke to battle. The Duke, equally ill-advisedly, sallied forth with his men, imagining apparently that he could resist such a host of armed men with his own tiny band. As the struggle between them swayed this way and that, Gorlois was among the first to be killed. His men were scattered and the besieged camp was captured. The treasure which had been deposited there was shared out in the most inequitable way, for each man seized in his greedy fist whatever good luck and his own brute strength threw in his way.[8]

Not until the outrages which followed this daring act had finally subsided did messengers come to Ygerna to announce the death of the Duke and the end of the siege. When they saw the King sitting beside Ygerna in the likeness of their leader, they blushed red with astonishment to see that the man whom they had left behind dead in the siege had in effect arrived there safely before them. Of course, they did not know of the drugs prepared by Merlin. The King put his arms round the Duchess and laughed aloud to hear these reports. "I am not dead," he said. "Indeed, as you see, I am very much alive! However, the destruction of my camp saddens me very much and so does the slaughter of my comrades. What is more, there is great danger that the King may come this way and capture us in this castle. I will go out to meet him and make peace with him, lest even worse should befall us."

8. Geoffrey emphasizes the destructive potential of private greed, private ambition, and brute force, even in the rule of a strong king like Uther. This becomes a dominant theme in Geoffrey and later Arthurian narratives.

The King set out and made his way towards his own army, abandoning his disguise as Gorlois and becoming Utherpendragon once more. When he learned all that had happened, he mourned for the death of Gorlois; but he was happy, all the same, that Ygerna was freed from her marital obligations. He returned to Tintagel Castle, captured it and seized Ygerna at the same time, she being what he really wanted. From that day on they lived together as equals, united by their great love for each other; and they had a son and a daughter. The boy was called Arthur and the girl Anna.

[ANGLO-SAXON INVASION]

As the days passed and lengthened into years, the King fell ill with a malady which affected him for a long time. Meanwhile the prison warders who guarded Octa and Eosa,[9] as I have explained above, led a weary life. In the end they escaped with their prisoners to Germany and in doing so terrified the kingdom: for rumor had it that they had already stirred up Germany, and had fitted out a huge fleet in order to return to the island and destroy it. This, indeed, actually happened. They came back with an immense fleet and more men than could ever be counted. They invaded certain parts of Albany[1] and busied themselves in burning the cities there and the citizens inside them. The British army was put under the command of Loth of Lodonesia, with orders that he should keep the enemy at a distance. This man was one of the leaders, a valiant soldier, mature both in wisdom and age. As a reward for his prowess, the King had given him his daughter Anna and put him in charge of the kingdom while he himself was ill. When Loth moved forward against the enemy he was frequently driven back again by them, so that he had to take refuge inside the cities. On other occasions he routed and dispersed them, forcing them to fly either into the forests or to their ships. Between the two sides the outcome of each battle was always in doubt, it being hard to tell which of them was victorious. Their own arrogance was a handicap to the Britons, for they were unwilling to obey the orders of their leaders. This undermined their strength and they were unable to beat the enemy in the field.

Almost all the island was laid waste. When this was made known to the King, he fell into a greater rage than he could really bear in his weakened state. He told all his leaders to appear before him, so that he could rebuke them for their overweening pride and their feebleness. As soon as he saw them all assembled in his presence, he reproached them bitterly and swore that he himself would lead them against the enemy. He ordered a litter to be built, so that he could be carried in it; for his weakness made any other form of progress impossible. Then he instructed them all to be in a state of preparedness, so that they could advance against the enemy as soon as the opportunity offered. The litter was constructed immediately, the men were made ready to start and the opportunity duly came.

They put the King in his litter and set out for Saint Albans, where the Saxons I have told you about were maltreating all the local population * * *

[Despite his illness, Uther prevails. Octa and Eosa are killed.]

Once the Saxons had been defeated, as I have explained above, they did not for that reason abandon their evil behavior. On the contrary, they went off to the north-

---

9. A son and a kinsman of the Saxon Hengist; Uther had imprisoned them in London. Geoffrey closely connects the resurgence of the Saxon invaders with Uther's adul- tery and the disorder within his own army.
1. That is, Scotland, named for Brutus's son Albanactus.

ern provinces and preyed relentlessly upon the people there. King Uther was keen to pursue them, as he had proposed, but his princes dissuaded him from it, for after his victory his illness had taken an even more serious turn. As a result the enemy became bolder still in their enterprises, striving by every means in their power to take complete control of the realm. Having recourse, as usual, to treachery, they plotted to see how they could destroy the King by cunning. When every other approach failed, they made up their minds to kill him with poison. This they did: for while Uther lay ill in the town of St. Albans, they sent spies disguised as beggars, who were to discover how things stood at court. When the spies had obtained all the information that they wanted, they discovered one additional fact which they chose to use as a means of betraying Uther. Near the royal residence there was a spring of very limpid water which the King used to drink when he could not keep down any other liquids because of his illness. These evil traitors went to the spring and polluted it completely with poison, so that all the water which welled up was infected. When the King drank some of it, he died immediately. Some hundred men died after him, until the villainy was finally discovered. Then they filled the well in with earth. As soon as the death of the King was made known, the bishops of the land came with their clergy and bore his body to the monastery of Ambrius and buried it with royal honors at the side of Aurelius Ambrosius, inside the Giants' Ring.

[ARTHUR OF BRITAIN][2]

After the death of Utherpendragon, the leaders of the Britons assembled from their various provinces in the town of Silchester and there suggested to Dubricius, the Archbishop of the City of the Legions, that as their King he should crown Arthur, the son of Uther. Necessity urged them on, for as soon as the Saxons heard of the death of King Uther, they invited their own countrymen over from Germany, appointed Colgrin as their leader and began to do their utmost to exterminate the Britons. They had already over-run all that section of the island which stretches from the River Humber to the sea named Caithness.[3]

Dubricius lamented the sad state of his country. He called the other bishops to him and bestowed the crown of the kingdom upon Arthur. Arthur was a young man only fifteen years old; but he was of outstanding courage and generosity, and his inborn goodness gave him such grace that he was loved by almost all the people. Once he had been invested with the royal insignia, he observed the normal custom of giving gifts freely to everyone. Such a great crown of soldiers flocked to him that he came to an end of what he had to distribute. However, the man to whom open-handedness and bravery both come naturally may indeed find himself momentarily in need, but poverty will never harass him for long. In Arthur courage was closely linked with generosity, and he made up his mind to harry the Saxons, so that with their wealth he might reward the retainers who served his own household. The justness of his cause encouraged him, for he had a claim by rightful inheritance to the kingship of the whole island. He therefore called together all the young men whom I have just mentioned and marched on York. * * * [4]

[Arthur and his followers attack Colgrin and ultimately subdue the Saxons; then they repel armies of Scots, Picts, and Irish. Arthur restores Briton dynasties throughout England, marries Guinevere, and establishes a stable peace.]

2. From bk. 9, chs. 1–11.
3. That is, Northumberland and Scotland.
4. Geoffrey links the ancient practice of a king's largesse to his warrior band together with the claim of dynastic genealogy. Arthur will again use the latter claim when he decides to invade Gaul and then march toward Rome.

Arthur then began to increase his personal entourage by inviting very distinguished men from far-distant kingdoms to join it. In this way he developed such a code of courtliness in his household that he inspired peoples living far away to imitate him. The result was that even the man of noblest birth, once he was roused to rivalry, thought nothing at all of himself unless he wore his arms and dressed in the same way as Arthur's knights. At last the fame of Arthur's generosity and bravery spread to the very ends of the earth; and the kings of countries far across the sea trembled at the thought that they might be attacked and invaded by him, and so lose control of the lands under their dominion. They were so harassed by these tormenting anxieties that they rebuilt their towns and the towers in their towns, and then went so far as to construct castles on carefully chosen sites, so that, if invasion should bring Arthur against them, they might have a refuge in their time of need.

All this was reported to Arthur. The fact that he was dreaded by all encouraged him to conceive the idea of conquering the whole of Europe.

◆━≡◆≡━◆

Gerald of Wales
c. 1146–1222

Geoffrey of Monmouth's *History of the Kings of Britain* was soon translated into French, early Middle English, and Welsh, and it reappears in other languages for centuries. Contemporary historians, especially those interested in pre-Saxon history, were enthusiastic about this new story. Others were skeptical. Nevertheless, Geoffrey's narrative was soon accepted widely as fact, adopted, and revised to serve the interests of the Angevin dynasty.

The discovery of Arthur's bones at Glastonbury Abbey in 1191, as reported by the prolific writer Gerald of Wales, is a particularly rich instance of this habit, benefiting both the status of Henry II and the prestige of the abbey. Glastonbury faced a crisis common among Anglo-Saxon monastic foundations after the Norman Conquest. It was, in fact, probably the earliest Christian community in Britain; nonetheless, the oral tradition of its antiquity was weakened as the Normans took power, bringing with them a new insistence on written documentation. Glastonbury had little proof of its claims to ancient privilege, either by way of charters (and those mostly spurious) or the related prestige of holy relics. At the same time, Henry II was interested in ancient narratives that might legitimize his imperial aims.

Gerald's version of events both suggests Henry's almost wondrous wisdom in identifying the very spot of Arthur's burial and implies the existence of early written records at Glastonbury. To have Arthur as a patron, authenticated by King Henry himself, greatly substantiated the abbey's other claims. At the same time, Henry's knowledge mysteriously linked him to Arthur, and the corpse itself neatly altered Arthurian tradition, certifying Arthur's actual death and perhaps damping Welsh hopes for a messianic return.

from The Instruction of Princes[1]

The memory of Arthur, that most renowned King of the Britons, will endure forever. In his own day he was a munificent patron of the famous Abbey at Glastonbury, giving many donations to the monks and always supporting them strongly, and he is highly praised in their records. More than any other place of worship in his kingdom he loved the church of the Blessed Mary, Mother of God, in Glastonbury, and he

---

1. Translated by Lewis Thorpe. Gerald reports the same events again in a later text, the *Speculum Ecclesiae*.

fostered its interests with much greater loving care than that of any of the others. When he went out to fight, he had a full-length portrait of the Blessed Virgin painted on the front of his shield, so that in the heat of battle he could always gaze upon her; and whenever he was about to make contact with the enemy he would kiss her feet with great devoutness.

In our lifetime Arthur's body was discovered at Glastonbury, although the legends had always encouraged us to believe that there was something otherworldly about his ending, that he had resisted death and had been spirited away to some far-distant spot.[2] The body was hidden deep in the earth in a hollowed-out oak-bole and between two stone pyramids which had been set up long ago in the churchyard there. They carried it into the church with every mark of honor and buried it decently there in a marble tomb. It had been provided with most unusual indications which were, indeed, little short of miraculous, for beneath it—and not on top, as would be the custom nowadays—there was a stone slab, with a leaden cross attached to its underside. I have seen this cross myself and I have traced the lettering which was cut into it on the side turned towards the stone, instead of being on the outer side and immediately visible. The inscription read as follows: HERE IN THE ISLE OF AVALON LIES BURIED THE RENOWNED KING ARTHUR, WITH GUINEVERE, HIS SECOND WIFE.

There are many remarkable deductions to be made from this discovery. Arthur obviously had two wives, and the second one was buried with him. Her bones were found with those of her husband, but they were separate from his. Two-thirds of the coffin, the part towards the top end, held the husband's bones, and the other section, at his feet, contained those of his wife. A tress of woman's hair, blond, and still fresh and bright in color, was found in the coffin. One of the monks snatched it up and it immediately disintegrated into dust. There had been some indications in the Abbey records that the body would be discovered on this spot, and another clue was provided by lettering carved on the pyramids, but this had been almost completely erased by the passage of the years. The holy monks and other religious had seen visions and revelations. However, it was Henry II, King of England, who had told the monks that, according to a story which he had heard from some old British soothsayer,[3] they would find Arthur's body buried at least sixteen feet in the ground, not in a stone coffin but in a hollowed-out oak-bole. It had been sunk as deep as that, and carefully concealed, so that it could never be discovered by the Saxons, whom Arthur had attacked relentlessly as long as he lived and whom, indeed, he had almost wiped out, but who occupied the island [of Britain] after his death. That was why the inscription, which was eventually to reveal the truth, had been cut into the inside of the cross and turned inwards towards the stone. For many a long year this inscription was to keep the secret of what the coffin contained, but eventually, when time and circumstance were both opportune, the lettering revealed what it had so long concealed.

What is now known as Glastonbury used in ancient times to be called the Isle of Avalon. It is virtually an island, for it is completely surrounded by marshlands. In Welsh it is called "Ynys Avallon," which means the Island of Apples. "Aval" is the Welsh word for apple, and this fruit used to grow there in great abundance.[4] After the

2. In his other version (the *Speculum Ecclesiae*) Gerald is more nervously dismissive: "In their stupidity the British people maintain that he is still alive.... According to them, once he has recovered from his wounds this strong and all-powerful King will return to rule over the Britons in the normal way."

3. In the *Speculum Ecclesiae*, Gerald says that Henry learned this "from the historical accounts of the Britons and from their bards."
4. Citing and explaining words from the various British vernaculars is a widespread habit in Latin historical writing as early as Bede.

Battle of Camlann,[5] a noblewoman called Morgan, who was the ruler and patroness of these parts as well as being a close blood-relation of King Arthur, carried him off to the island now known as Glastonbury, so that his wounds could be cared for. Years ago the district had also been called "Ynys Gutrin" in Welsh, that is the Island of Glass, and from these words the invading Saxons later coined the place-name "Glastingebury." The word "glass" in their language means "vitrum" in Latin, and "bury" means "castrum" [camp] or "civitas" [city].

You must know that the bones of Arthur's body which were discovered there were so big that in them the poet's words seem to be fulfilled:

All men will exclaim at the size of the bones they've exhumed.[6]

The Abbot showed me one of the shin-bones. He held it upright on the ground against the foot of the tallest man he could find, and it stretched a good three inches above the man's knee. The skull was so large and capacious that it seemed a veritable prodigy of nature, for the space between the eyebrows and the eye-sockets was as broad as the palm of a man's hand. Ten or more wounds could clearly be seen, but they had all mended except one. This was larger than the others and it had made an immense gash. Apparently it was this wound which had caused Arthur's death.

1193

Edward I
1239–1307

Beginning in 1291, King Edward I of England revived an ancient claim to be feudal overlord of Scotland and thereby sought to control a disputed succession to its throne. By 1293 the Scottish king John Balliol had become Edward's vassal, but rebelled and was forced to abdicate in 1296. The military and diplomatic struggle (later called the "Great Cause") stretched across the decade. By the turn of the fourteenth century, in an extraordinary move, both the English and Scots had turned to the court of Pope Boniface VIII for a legal decision. In pursuing Edward's claim, his agents ransacked chronicles—including Geoffrey of Monmouth's *History*—as well as ancient charters, to compile a dossier of historical and legal precedents. Despite his own bureaucratic reforms requiring documentary proof for most legal claims, Edward was ready to invoke common memory and ancient legends to support his position regarding Scotland. Knowing that such chronicle material would have no status in court, in May of 1301 Edward resorted to the letter below before Pope Boniface ruled in the matter.

The written letter was a highly developed and self-conscious genre during the Middle Ages. Letters were often meant to be public and could carry the force of law. Indeed, the form of many legal documents had developed from royal letters. Letter writing became an area for textbooks and school study, the *ars dictaminis*. Elaborate formulas of salutation and closing, and other rhetorical figures, were taught and used for important correspondence as a way of establishing the sender's learning and prestige. The papal curia employed a particularly challenging system of prose rhythm called the *cursus*, which was imitated in some royal chanceries and is found in the Latin of Edward's letter.

---

5. Arthur's last battle, fought against the rebel army of his kinsman Mordred. Arthur kills Mordred but is himself mortally wounded.
6. Virgil, *Georgics*, 1.497.

Letter sent to the Papal Court of Rome
Concerning the king's rights in the realm of Scotland[1]

To the most Holy Father in Christ lord Boniface, by divine providence the supreme pontiff of the Holy Roman and Universal Church, Edward, by grace of the same providence king of England, lord of Ireland, and duke of Aquitaine offers his humblest devotion to the blessed saints.[2] What follows we send to you not to be treated in the form or manner of a legal plea, but altogether extrajudicially, in order to set the mind of your Holiness at rest. The All-Highest, to whom all hearts are open, will testify how it is graven upon the tablets of our memory with an indelible mark, that our predecessors and progenitors, the kings of England, by right of lordship and dominion, possessed, from the most ancient times, the suzerainty of the realm of Scotland and its kings in temporal matters, and the things annexed thereto, and that they received from the self-same kings, and from such magnates of the realm as they so desired, liege homage and oaths of fealty. We, continuing in the possession of that very right and dominion, have received the same acknowledgments in our time, both from the king of Scotland, and from the magnates of that realm; and indeed such prerogatives of right and dominion did the kings of England enjoy over the realm of Scotland and its kings, that they have even granted to their faithful folk the realm itself, removed its kings for just causes, and constituted others to rule in their place under themselves. Beyond doubt these matters have been familiar from times long past and still are, though perchance it has been suggested otherwise to your Holiness' ears by foes of peace and sons of rebellion, whose elaborate and empty fabrications your wisdom, we trust, will treat with contempt.

Thus, in the days of Eli and of Samuel the prophet, after the destruction of the city of Troy, a certain valiant and illustrious man of the Trojan race called Brutus, landed with many noble Trojans, upon a certain island called, at that time, Albion.[3] It was then inhabited by giants, and after he had defeated and slain them, by his might and that of his followers, he called it, after his own name, Britain, and his people Britons, and built a city which he called Trinovant, now known as London. Afterwards he divided his realm among his three sons, that is he gave to his first born, Locrine, that part of Britain now called England, to the second, Albanact, that part then known as Albany, after the name of Albanact, but now as Scotland, and to Camber, his youngest son, the part then known by his son's name as Cambria and now called Wales, the royal dignity being reserved for Locrine, the eldest. Two years after the death of Brutus there landed in Albany a certain king of the Huns, called Humber, and he slew Albanact, the brother of Locrine. Hearing this, Locrine, the king of the Britons, pursued him, and he fled and was drowned in the river which from his name is called Humber, and thus Albany reverted to Locrine. * * * Again, Arthur, king of the Britons, a prince most renowned, subjected to himself a rebellious Scotland, destroyed almost the whole nation, and afterwards installed as king of Scotland one Angusel by name. Afterwards, when King Arthur held a most famous feast at Caerleon, there were present there all the kings subject to him, and among them

---

1. Translated by E. L. G. Stones (1965). Although sent in the name of the King, a Latin letter of such formality would have been written by notaries in his chancery. A French draft also survives, which might have been used by Edward himself.

2. A flowery opening formula was typical of formal letters

between persons of power; it also provided a place for Edward to make ambitious (and in the case of Aquitaine, highly optimistic) territorial claims.

3. Here the letter borrows closely from Geoffrey of Monmouth's foundation narrative; see page 140.

Angusel, king of Scotland, who manifested the service due for the realm of Scotland by bearing the sword of King Arthur before him; and in succession all the kings of Scotland have been subject to all the kings of the Britons. Succeeding kings of England enjoyed both monarchy and dominion in the island, and subsequently Edward, known as the elder, son of Alfred, king of England, had subject and subordinate to him, as lord superior, the kings of the Scots, the Cumbrians, and the Strathclyde Welsh. * * *

Since, indeed, from what has been said already, and from other evidence, it is perfectly clear and well-known that the realm of Scotland belongs to us of full right, by reason of property and of possession, and that we have not done and have not dared to do anything, as indeed we could not do, in writing or in action, by which any prejudice may be implied to our right or possession, we humbly beseech your Holiness to weigh all this with careful meditation, and to condescend to keep it all in mind when making your decision, setting no store, if you please, by the adverse assertions which come to you on this subject from our enemies, but, on the contrary, retaining our welfare and our royal rights, if it so please you, in your fatherly regard. May the Most High preserve you, to rule his Holy Church through many years of prosperity.

Kempsey, 7 May 1301, the twenty-ninth year of our reign.

⌇

COMPANION READING

A Report to Edward I[1]

Sir, seeing that you have lately sent a statement to the pope concerning your right to Scotland, the Scots are making efforts to nullify that statement by certain objections which are given below. * * * They say that in that letter you ground your right on old chronicles, which contain various falsehoods and lies, and are abrogated and made void by the subsequent contrary actions of your predecessors and of yourself, which vitiate all the remaining part of your letter, and therefore one should give no credence to such a document. And they say further, that with only this unworthy and feeble case to rely upon, you are striving to evade the cognizance of your true judge, and to suppress the truth, and unlawfully, by force of arms, to repel your weaker neighbors, and to prevent the pope from pursuing the examination of this case. * * *

Again, they say that the old chronicles that you use as evidence of your right could not assist you, even if they were authenticated, as is not the case, they say, because it is notorious that these same old chronicles are utterly made naught and of no avail by other subsequent documents of greater significance, by contrary agreements and actions, and by papal privileges. * * * Then, sir, in order that credence be not given to the documents, histories, and deeds described in your statement, they say that allegations like those recounted in your narrative are put out of court by the true

---

1. The Scots learned about Edward's letter and made their own response to the pope; this report to Edward, written in the French he would actually have used with his counselors, specifies the Scots' rebuttal. The Scots carefully assert the superior force of later charters and other legal instruments, and dismiss Edward's reliance on unauthenticated legends. In case Edward's story should carry weight with Boniface, however, they also provide a counternarrative of their own national foundation by Scota, daughter of the Pharaoh, and how she expelled British influence from her land. The English and Scots diplomats thus tell opposing prehistories that underwrite their current claims. Just as important, though, they are negotiating around an unusually articulate moment in the contest between different forms of textuality—legendary and chronicle tradition versus legal documents—in the creation of contemporary political power.

facts, and they endeavor to demonstrate their assertion by chronicles and narratives of a contrary purport. Brutus divided between his three sons the island once called Britain, and now England, and gave to one son Loegria, to another Wales, and to the third what is now called Scotland, and made them peers, so that none of them was subject to another. Afterwards came a woman named Scota, daughter of Pharaoh of Egypt, who came via Spain and occupied Ireland, and afterwards conquered the land of Albany, which she had called, after her name, *Scotland*,[2] and one place in that land she had called after the names of her son Erk and her husband Gayl, wherefore that district was called *Ergaill* [Argyll], and they drove out the Britons, and from that time the Scots, as a new race and possessing a new name, had nothing to do with the Britons, but pursued them daily as their enemies, and were distinguished from them by different ranks and customs, and by a different language. Afterwards they joined company with the Picts, by whose strength they destroyed the Britons, and the land which is now called England, and for this reason the Britons gave tribute to the Romans, to obtain the help of the Roman emperor, whose name was Severus, against the Scots, and by his help the Britons made a wall between themselves and the Scots, having a length of 130 leagues in length from one sea to the other, and they say that by this it appears that Scotland was not at any time under the lordship of the Britons.[3] But they do not deny that King Arthur by his prowess conquered Denmark, France, Norway and also Scotland, and held them until he and Mordred were slain in battle, and from that time the realm of Scotland returned to its free status. They say that the Britons were then expelled by the Saxons, and then the Saxons by the Danes, and then the Danes by the Saxons, and that in the whole period of the Saxon kings the Scots remained free without being subject to them, and at that time, by the relics of Saint Andrew which came from Greece, they were converted to the faith five hundred years before the English became Christians, and from that time the realm of Scotland, with the king and the realm [*sic*], were under the lordship of the Roman church without any intermediary, and by it were they defended against all their enemies. * * *

━━╅ END OF PERSPECTIVES: ARTHURIAN MYTH IN THE HISTORY OF BRITAIN ╆━━

ARTHURIAN ROMANCE

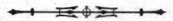

Marie de France
(fl. 2nd half of the 12th century)

In a famous line from the prologue to her *Lais*, Marie de France suggested that serious readers could approach an obscure old book and "supply its significance from their own wisdom." The original French text, "*de lur sen le surplus mettre*," implies that such readers add on something

---

2. This neatly replicates Brutus's trajectory from the eastern Mediterranean, across part of continental Europe, and thence to the British Isles.
3. The Scots artfully shift the emphasis found in Geoffrey

of Monmouth. Roman colonization and Hadrian's wall become evidence of an ancient ethnic division and Scots independence both from the Britons and from the Britons' later invaders.

that is missing. In part a gesture of respect toward the study of pagan Latin literature in a Christian setting, this statement also seems to permit Marie herself a dramatically new perspective when she encounters the long-established Arthurian story, in *Lanval*. Starting with a scene of war that readers of Geoffrey of Monmouth might recognize, Marie swiftly brings into play elements that had been largely absent in the historicizing stories of Arthur: bodily desire and its dangers, romantic longing, the realm of the uncanny, the power of women, the force of wealth and influence in even the noblest courts.

Marie's specific identity remains obscure, but it is clear that she was a woman of French origin writing in England in the later decades of the twelfth century, widely educated, and in touch with the royal court. She dedicates her book of *Lais* to a "noble King" who was probably Henry II, and she may have been his kinswoman, possibly an illegitimate half-sister. Marie's works draw into that courtly culture the languages and traditions of the English and Celtic past. She rewrote a Latin narrative about the origin of "Saint Patrick's Purgatory" and the adventure of an Irish knight there; and she retold the fables of Aesop using an English translation that she attributed to King Alfred. The *Lais*, she says, came to her through oral transmission, and she connects them with the Bretons. Indeed, the best early copy of the *Lais*, Harley manuscript 978 in the British Library, is itself a multilingual compilation that includes the early Middle English poem *The Cuckoo Song* ("Sumer is icumen in"; see page 371).

Writing a generation after Geoffrey of Monmouth and not long before Gerald of Wales, Marie brings a quite different and rather critical set of preoccupations to her Arthurian story. She opens her tale with a realistic and admirable occasion of male power and strong kingship: Arthur's battle for territory and his reward of faithful vassals. A bleaker side of that courtly world, and perhaps of Marie's own, is also implicit, however. With a terseness and indirection typical of her *lais*, Marie shows women as property in the king's gift, knights forgotten when their wealth runs out, and the perversion of judicial process.

Marvels and erotic desire dominate her tale, though, and women's power, for good or ill, is its primary motivating force. Guinevere, in a hostile portrait of adulterous aggression and vengeful dishonesty, nonetheless manages to manipulate Arthur and his legal codes when Lanval rejects her advances. The queen is countered by Lanval's supernatural mistress, who commands luxurious riches that dwarf Arthur's; she rescues Lanval by being an unimpeachable legal witness in his defense. Indeed, she arrives on her white palfrey as the moment of judgment nears, almost like a knightly champion in a trial by battle. Lanval vanishes into a timeless world of fulfilled desire and limitless wealth that has analogies in much older Celtic tradition—for instance, in *The Voyage of Máel Dúin* (page 99). This closing scene defies the reintegration of male courtly order that is typical even in the erotic romances of Marie's contemporary Chrétien de Troyes.

The realm of eroticism and women's power in *Lanval*, though, is not automatically any more virtuous or stable than the ostentatious wealth and corruptible law of the world of Arthurian men. If Lanval's mysterious lady is beautiful and generous, she also takes his knightliness from him. Lanval is last seen riding behind the lady, and not on a warhorse but on a palfrey. Guinevere swiftly reduces Arthur to a weak and temporizing king. And in her initial explosion after Lanval rejects her, Guinevere accuses him of homosexuality. For all its absurdity, the moment articulates unnerving implications of the profound bonds among men in the Arthurian world, implications that could interrupt genealogical transmission of wealth and power. Marie's Guinevere again voices fears the tradition has left unsaid.

Marie de France may be trying less to propound a critique of the received stories of Arthur than to recall her readers' attention to elements that tradition has left aside, as she suggests in her prologue. Some of this is no more troubling than a delightful fantasy of wealth and pleasure, outside time and without consequences. Other elements imply, with startling economy, forces that (in the hands of later romancers) tear the Arthurian world to pieces.

Marie de France Writing, from an illuminated manuscript of her works. While most images of writing feature men, women were also writers and copyists as well as readers (see Color Plate 10). Here, in a late-13th-century manuscript of her poems, Marie de France is shown at her writing desk, strikingly similar in posture and detail (and in authority) to Laurence of Durham more than a century earlier (see page 2).

from LAIS[1]
Prologue

Whoever has received knowledge
and eloquence in speech from God
should not be silent or secretive
but demonstrate it willingly.
5   When a great good is widely heard of,
then, and only then, does it bloom,
and when that good is praised by many,
it has spread its blossoms.
The custom among the ancients—
10   as Priscian[2] testifies—
was to speak quite obscurely
in the books they wrote,
so that those who were to come after
and study them
15   might gloss the letter
and supply its significance from their own wisdom.[3]
Philosophers knew this,
they understood among themselves
that the more time they spent,
20   the more subtle their minds would become
and the better they would know how to keep themselves
from whatever was to be avoided.
He who would guard himself from vice
should study and understand
25   and begin a weighty work

1. Translated by Robert Hanning and Joan Ferrante.
2. A famed grammarian of the late Roman empire, Priscian remained widely influential in the study of Latin language and literature in the 12th century.
3. Marie refers to the practice of supplying glosses— explanatory notes such as this one—to school texts; she also implies that later readers bring their own perspective to earlier works, a point relevant to her own free adaptation of earlier Arthurian stories.

by which he might keep vice at a distance,
and free himself from great sorrow.
That's why I began to think
about composing some good stories
30   and translating from Latin to Romance;[4]
but that was not to bring me fame:
too many others have done it.
Then I thought of the *lais* I'd heard.[5]
I did not doubt, indeed I knew well,
35   that those who first began them
and sent them forth
composed them in order to preserve
adventures they had heard.
I have heard many told;
40   and I don't want to neglect or forget them.
To put them into word and rhyme
I've often stayed awake.

In your honor, noble King,[6]
who are so brave and courteous,
45   repository of all joys
in whose heart all goodness takes root,
I undertook to assemble these *lais*
to compose and recount them in rhyme.
In my heart I thought and determined,
50   sire, that I would present them to you.
If it pleases you to receive them,
you will give me great joy;
I shall be happy forever.
Do not think me presumptuous
55   if I dare present them to you.
Now hear how they begin.

Lanval

I shall tell you the adventure of another *lai*,
just as it happened:
it was composed about a very noble vassal;
in Breton, they call him Lanval.[1]

5   Arthur, the brave and the courtly king,
was staying at Cardoel,[2]
because the Scots and the Picts
were destroying the land.[3]
They invaded Logres°   *England*

---

4. That is, to French.
5. A *lai* was typically a short verse narrative, meant for
oral performance with music. A particular group of these,
often including Arthurian tales, was especially connected
with Brittany.
6. Probably Henry II.

1. Marie seems to imply knowledge of Breton, a Celtic
language related to Welsh. In other works, she shows
knowledge of English as well, and excellent Latin.
2. Carlisle, in the north of England.
3. Scots and Picts were Arthur's traditional enemies.

10	and laid it waste.
	At Pentecost, in summer,[4]
	the king stayed there.
	He gave out many rich gifts:
	to counts and barons,
15	members of the Round Table—
	such a company had no equal in all the world—
	he distributed wives and lands,
	to all but one who had served him.
	That was Lanval; Arthur forgot him,
20	and none of his men favored him either.
	For his valor, for his generosity,
	his beauty and his bravery,
	most men envied him;
	some feigned the appearance of love
25	who, if something unpleasant happened to him,
	would not have been at all disturbed.
	He was the son of a king of high degree
	but he was far from his heritage.
	He was of the king's household
30	but he had spent all his wealth,
	for the king gave him nothing
	nor did Lanval ask.
	Now Lanval was in difficulty,
	depressed and very worried.
35	My lords, don't be surprised:
	a strange man, without friends,
	is very sad in another land,
	when he doesn't know where to look for help.
	The knight of whom I speak,
40	who had served the king so long,
	one day mounted his horse
	and went off to amuse himself.
	He left the city
	and came, all alone, to a field;
45	he dismounted by a running stream
	but his horse trembled badly.
	He removed the saddle and went off,
	leaving the horse to roll around in the meadow.
	He folded his cloak beneath his head
50	and lay down.
	He worried about his difficulty,
	he could see nothing that pleased him.
	As he lay there
	he looked down along the bank
55	and saw two girls approaching;
	he had never seen any lovelier.
	They were richly dressed,

4. "Summer" here refers to late spring. The feast of Pentecost commemorates the descent of the Holy Spirit among Christ's apostles; it is often the occasion of Arthurian stories, especially those that involve marvels.

tightly laced,
in tunics of dark purple;
60   their faces were very lovely.
The older one carried basins,
golden, well made, and fine;
I shall tell you the truth about it, without fail.
The other carried a towel.
65   They went straight
to where the knight was lying.
Lanval, who was very well bred,
got up to meet them.
They greeted him first
70   and gave him their message:
"Sir Lanval, my lady,
who is worthy and wise and beautiful,
sent us for you.
Come with us now.
75   We shall guide you there safely.
See, her pavilion is nearby!"
The knight went with them;
giving no thought to his horse
who was feeding before him in the meadow.
80   They led him up to the tent,[5]
which was quite beautiful and well placed.
Queen Semiramis,
however much more wealth,
power, or knowledge she had,
85   or the emperor Octavian[6]
could not have paid for one of the flaps.
There was a golden eagle on top of it,
whose value I could not tell,
nor could I judge the value of the cords or the poles
90   that held up the sides of the tent;
there is no king on earth who could buy it,
no matter what wealth he offered.
The girl was inside the tent:
the lily and the young rose
95   when they appear in the summer
are surpassed by her beauty.
She lay on a beautiful bed—
the bedclothes were worth a castle—
dressed only in her shift.
100   Her body was well shaped and elegant;
for the heat, she had thrown over herself,
a precious cloak of white ermine,
covered with purple alexandrine,°   *embroidery*
but her whole side was uncovered,

---

5. Elaborate tents are often found in contemporary narratives of kings going out to battle.
6. Semiramis, legendary queen of Assyria and builder of Babylon, led armies of conquest; she is also a conventional figure of uncontrolled sexual desire. She is interestingly placed here as a female counterpart to Octavian (Augustus Caesar), the first Roman emperor.

105 her face, her neck and her bosom;
she was whiter than the hawthorn flower.
The knight went forward
and the girl addressed him.
He sat before the bed.
110 "Lanval," she said, "sweet love,
because of you I have come from my land;
I came to seek you from far away.
If you are brave and courtly,
no emperor or count or king
115 will ever have known such joy or good;
for I love you more than anything."
He looked at her and saw that she was beautiful;
Love stung him with a spark
that burned and set fire to his heart.
120 He answered her in a suitable way.
"Lovely one," he said, "if it pleased you,
if such joy might be mine
that you would love me,
there is nothing you might command,
125 within my power, that I would not do,
whether foolish or wise.
I shall obey your command;
for you, I shall abandon everyone.
I want never to leave you.
130 That is what I most desire."
When the girl heard the words
of the man who could love her so,
she granted him her love and her body.
Now Lanval was on the right road!
135 Afterward, she gave him a gift:
he would never again want anything,
he would receive as he desired;
however generously he might give and spend,
she would provide what he needed.
140 Now Lanval is well cared for.
The more lavishly he spends,
the more gold and silver he will have.
"Love," she said, "I admonish you now,
I command and beg you,
145 do not let any man know about this.
I shall tell you why:
you would lose me for good
if this love were known;
you would never see me again
150 or possess my body."
He answered that he would do
exactly as she commanded.
He lay beside her on the bed;
now Lanval is well cared for.
155 He remained with her

that afternoon, until evening
and would have stayed longer, if he could,
and if his love had consented.
"Love," she said, "get up.

160   You cannot stay any longer.
Go away now; I shall remain
but I will tell you one thing:
when you want to talk to me
there is no place you can think of

165   where a man might have his mistress
without reproach or shame,
that I shall not be there with you
to satisfy all your desires.
No man but you will see me

170   or hear my words."
When he heard her, he was very happy,
he kissed her, and then got up.
The girls who had brought him to the tent
dressed him in rich clothes;

175   when he was dressed anew,
there wasn't a more handsome youth in all the world;
he was no fool, no boor.
They gave him water for his hands
and a towel to dry them,

180   and they brought him food.
He took supper with his love;
it was not to be refused.
He was served with great courtesy,
he received it with great joy.

185   There was an entremet°   *side dish*
that vastly pleased the knight
for he kissed his lady often
and held her close.
When they finished dinner,

190   his horse was brought to him.
The horse had been well saddled;
Lanval was very richly served.
The knight took his leave, mounted,
and rode toward the city,

195   often looking behind him.
Lanval was very disturbed;
he wondered about his adventure
and was doubtful in his heart;
he was amazed, not knowing what to believe;

200   he didn't expect ever to see her again.
He came to his lodging
and found his men well dressed.
That night, his accommodations were rich
but no one knew where it came from.

205   There was no knight in the city
who really needed a place to stay

whom he didn't invite to join him
to be well and richly served.
Lanval gave rich gifts,
210 Lanval released prisoners,
Lanval dressed jongleurs,°   *performers*
Lanval offered great honors.
There was no stranger or friend
to whom Lanval didn't give.
215 Lanval's joy and pleasure were intense;
in the daytime or at night,
he could see his love often;
she was completely at his command.

In that same year, it seems to me,
220 after the feast of Saint John,
about thirty knights
were amusing themselves
in an orchard beneath the tower
where the queen was staying.
225 Gawain was with them
and his cousin, the handsome Yvain;[7]
Gawain, the noble, the brave,
who was so loved by all, said:
"By God, my lords, we wronged
230 our companion Lanval,
who is so generous and courtly,
and whose father is a rich king,
when we didn't bring him with us."
They immediately turned back,
235 went to his lodging
and prevailed on Lanval to come along with them.
At a sculpted window
the queen was looking out;
she had three ladies with her.
240 She saw the king's retinue,
recognized Lanval and looked at him.
Then she told one of her ladies
to send for her maidens,
the loveliest and the most refined;
245 together they went to amuse themselves
in the orchard where the others were.
She brought thirty or more with her;
they descended the steps.
The knights came to meet them,
250 because they were delighted to see them.
The knights took them by the hand;
their conversation was in no way vulgar.
Lanval went off to one side,

7. Gawain and Yvain serve to place Marie's hero in the context of more famous Arthurian episodes. Gawain, nephew of Arthur and distinguished both for bravery and courtesy, increasingly acts as Lanval's sponsor in the rest of the *lai*.

far from the others; he was impatient

255 to hold his love,
to kiss and embrace and touch her;
he thought little of others' joys
if he could not have his pleasure.
When the queen saw him alone,

260 she went straight to the knight.
She sat beside him and spoke,
revealing her whole heart:
"Lanval, I have shown you much honor,
I have cherished you, and loved you.

265 You may have all my love;
just tell me your desire.
I promise you my affection.
You should be very happy with me."
"My lady," he said, "let me be!

270 I have no desire to love you.
I've served the king a long time;
I don't want to betray my faith to him.
Never, for you or for your love,
will I do anything to harm my lord."

275 The queen got angry;
in her wrath, she insulted him:
"Lanval," she said, "I am sure
you don't care for such pleasure;
people have often told me

280 that you have no interest in women.
You have fine-looking boys
with whom you enjoy yourself.
Base coward, lousy cripple,
my lord made a bad mistake

285 when he let you stay with him.
For all I know, he'll lose God because of it."
When Lanval heard her, he was quite disturbed;
he was not slow to answer.
He said something out of spite

290 that he would later regret.
"Lady," he said, "of that activity
I know nothing,
but I love and I am loved
by one who should have the prize

295 over all the women I know.
And I shall tell you one thing;
you might as well know all:
any one of those who serve her,
the poorest girl of all,

300 is better than you, my lady queen,
in body, face, and beauty,
in breeding and in goodness."
The queen left him
and went, weeping, to her chamber.

305	She was upset and angry
	because he had insulted her.
	She went to bed sick;
	never, she said, would she get up
	unless the king gave her satisfaction
310	for the offense against her.
	The king returned from the woods,
	he'd had a very good day.
	He entered the queen's chambers.
	When she saw him, she began to complain.
315	She fell at his feet, asked his mercy,
	saying that Lanval had dishonored her;
	he had asked for her love,
	and because she refused him
	he insulted and offended her:
320	he boasted of a love
	who was so refined and noble and proud
	that her chambermaid,
	the poorest one who served her,
	was better than the queen.
325	The king got very angry;
	he swore an oath:
	if Lanval could not defend himself in court
	he would have him burned or hanged.
	The king left her chamber
330	and called for three of his barons;
	he sent them for Lanval
	who was feeling great sorrow and distress.
	He had come back to his dwelling,
	knowing very well
335	that he'd lost his love,
	he had betrayed their affair.
	He was all alone in a room,
	disturbed and troubled;
	he called on his love, again and again,
340	but it did him no good.
	He complained and sighed,
	from time to time he fainted;
	then he cried a hundred times for her to have mercy
	and speak to her love.
345	He cursed his heart and his mouth;
	it's a wonder he didn't kill himself.
	No matter how much he cried and shouted,
	ranted and raged,
	she would not have mercy on him,
350	not even let him see her.
	How will he ever contain himself?
	The men the king sent
	arrived and told him
	to appear in court without delay:
355	the king had summoned him

because the queen had accused him.
Lanval went with his great sorrow;
they could have killed him, for all he cared.
He came before the king;
360   he was very sad, thoughtful, silent;
his face revealed great suffering.
In anger the king told him:
"Vassal, you have done me a great wrong!
This was a base undertaking,
365   to shame and disgrace me
and to insult the queen.
You have made a foolish boast:
your love is much too noble
if her maid is more beautiful,
370   more worthy, than the queen."
Lanval denied that he'd dishonored
or shamed his lord,
word for word, as the king spoke:
he had not made advances to the queen;
375   but of what he had said,
he acknowledged the truth,
about the love he had boasted of,
that now made him sad because he'd lost her.
About that he said he would do
380   whatever the court decided.
The king was very angry with him;
he sent for all his men
to determine exactly what he ought to do
so that no one could find fault with his decision.
385   They did as he commanded,
whether they liked it or not.
They assembled,
judged, and decided,
that Lanval should have his day;
390   but he must find pledges for his lord
to guarantee that he would await the judgment,
return, and be present at it.[8]
Then the court would be increased,
for now there were none but the king's household.
395   The barons came back to the king
and announced their decision.
The king demanded pledges.
Lanval was alone and forlorn,
he had no relative, no friend.
400   Gawain went and pledged himself for him,
and all his companions followed.
The king addressed them: "I release him to you
on forfeit of whatever you hold from me,

8. Marie introduces judicial procedures that may have recalled those in Henry's reign: summons and accusation, setting a day for judgment, the rise of royal jurisdiction, the possibility of a champion, and trial by battle.

lands and fiefs, each one for himself."
405 When Lanval was pledged, there was nothing else to do.
He returned to his lodging.
The knights accompanied him,
they reproached and admonished him
that he give up his great sorrow;
410 they cursed his foolish love.
Each day they went to see him,
because they wanted to know
whether he was drinking and eating;
they were afraid that he'd kill himself.
415 On the day that they had named,
the barons assembled.
The king and the queen were there
and the pledges brought Lanval back.
They were all very sad for him:
420 I think there were a hundred
who would have done all they could
to set him free without a trial
where he would be wrongly accused.
The king demanded a verdict
425 according to the charge and rebuttal.
Now it all fell to the barons.
They went to the judgment,
worried and distressed
for the noble man from another land
430 who'd gotten into such trouble in their midst.
Many wanted to condemn him
in order to satisfy their lord.
The Duke of Cornwall said:
"No one can blame us;
435 whether it makes you weep or sing
justice must be carried out.
The king spoke against his vassal
whom I have heard named Lanval;
he accused him of felony,
440 charged him with a misdeed—
a love that he had boasted of,
which made the queen angry.
No one but the king accused him:
by the faith I owe you,
445 if one were to speak the truth,
there should have been no need for defense,
except that a man owes his lord honor
in every circumstance.
He will be bound by his oath,
450 and the king will forgive us our pledges
if he can produce proof;
if his love would come forward,
if what he said,
what upset the queen, is true,

455 then he will be acquitted,
because he did not say it out of malice.
But if he cannot get his proof,
we must make it clear to him
that he will forfeit his service to the king;
460 he must take his leave."
They sent to the knight,
told and announced to him
that he should have his love come
to defend and stand surety for him.
465 He told them that he could not do it:
he would never receive help from her.
They went back to the judges,
not expecting any help from Lanval.
The king pressed them hard
470 because of the queen who was waiting.
When they were ready to give their verdict
they saw two girls approaching,
riding handsome palfreys.
They were very attractive,
475 dressed in purple taffeta,
over their bare skin.
The men looked at them with pleasure.
Gawain, taking three knights with him,
went to Lanval and told him;
480 he pointed out the two girls.
Gawain was extremely happy, and begged him
to tell if his love were one of them.
Lanval said he didn't know who they were,
where they came from or where they were going.
485 The girls proceeded
still on horseback;
they dismounted before the high table
at which Arthur, the king, sat.
They were of great beauty,
490 and spoke in a courtly manner:
"King, clear your chambers,
have them hung with silk
where my lady may dismount;
she wishes to take shelter with you."
495 He promised it willingly
and called two knights
to guide them up to the chambers.
On that subject no more was said.
The king asked his barons
500 for their judgment and decision;
he said they had angered him very much
with their long delay.
"Sire," they said, "we have decided.
Because of the ladies we have just seen
505 we have made no judgment.

Let us reconvene the trial."
Then they assembled, everyone was worried;
there was much noise and strife.
While they were in that confusion,
510   two girls in noble array,
dressed in Phrygian silks
and riding Spanish mules,
were seen coming down the street.
This gave the vassals great joy;
515   to each other they said that now
Lanval, the brave and bold, was saved.
Gawain went up to him,
bringing his companions along.
"Sire," he said, "take heart.
520   For the love of God, speak to us.
Here come two maidens,
well adorned and very beautiful;
one must certainly be your love."
Lanval answered quickly
525   that he did not recognize them,
he didn't know them or love them.
Meanwhile they'd arrived,
and dismounted before the king.
Most of those who saw them praised them
530   for their bodies, their faces, their coloring;
each was more impressive
than the queen had ever been.
The older one was courtly and wise,
she spoke her message fittingly:
535   "King, have chambers prepared for us
to lodge my lady according to her need;
she is coming here to speak with you."
He ordered them to be taken
to the others who had preceded them.
540   There was no problem with the mules.
When he had seen to the girls,
he summoned all his barons
to render their judgment;
it had already dragged out too much.
545   The queen was getting angry
because she had fasted so long.
They were about to give their judgment
when through the city came riding
a girl on horseback;
550   there was none more beautiful in the world.
She rode a white palfrey,
who carried her handsomely and smoothly:
he was well apportioned in the neck and head,
no finer beast in the world.
555   The palfrey's trappings were rich;
under heaven there was no count or king

who could have afforded them all
without selling or mortgaging lands.
She was dressed in this fashion:
560   in a white linen shift
that revealed both her sides
since the lacing was along the side.
Her body was elegant, her hips slim,
her neck whiter than snow on a branch,
565   her eyes bright, her face white,
a beautiful mouth, a well-set nose,
dark eyebrows and an elegant forehead,
her hair curly and rather blond;
golden wire does not shine
570   like her hair in the light.
Her cloak, which she had wrapped around her,
was dark purple.
On her wrist she held a sparrow hawk,
a greyhound followed her.
575   In the town, no one, small or big,
old man or child,
failed to come look.
As they watched her pass,
there was no joking about her beauty.
580   She proceeded at a slow pace.
The judges who saw her
marveled at the sight;
no one who looked at her
was not warmed with joy.
585   Those who loved the knight
came to him and told him
of the girl who was approaching,
if God pleased, to rescue him.
"Sir companion, here comes one
590   neither tawny nor dark;
this is, of all who exist,
the most beautiful woman in the world."
Lanval heard them and lifted his head;
he recognized her and sighed.
595   The blood rose to his face;
he was quick to speak.
"By my faith," he said, "that is my love.
Now I don't care if I am killed,
if only she forgives me.
600   For I am restored, now that I see her."
The lady entered the palace;
no one so beautiful had ever been there.
She dismounted before the king
so that she was well seen by all.
605   And she let her cloak fall
so they could see her better.
The king, who was well bred,

rose and went to meet her;
all the others honored her
610 and offered to serve her.
When they had looked at her well,
when they had greatly praised her beauty,
she spoke in this way,
she didn't want to wait:
615 "I have loved one of your vassals:
you see him before you—Lanval.
He has been accused in your court—
I don't want him to suffer
for what he said; you should know
620 that the queen was in the wrong.
He never made advances to her.
And for the boast that he made,
if he can be acquitted through me,
let him be set free by your barons."
625 Whatever the barons judged by law
the king promised would prevail.
To the last man they agreed
that Lanval had successfully answered the charge.
He was set free by their decision
630 and the girl departed.
The king could not detain her,
though there were enough people to serve her.
Outside the hall stood
a great stone of dark marble
635 where heavy men mounted
when they left the king's court;
Lanval climbed on it.
When the girl came through the gate
Lanval leapt, in one bound,
640 onto the palfrey, behind her.
With her he went to Avalun,
so the Bretons tell us,
to a very beautiful island;
there the youth was carried off.
645 No man heard of him again,
and I have no more to tell.

Sir Gawain and the Green Knight

As a subject of literary romance, Arthurian tradition never had the centrality in later medieval England it had gained in France. It was only one of a wide range of popular topics like Havelok the Dane, King Horn, and the Troy story. Nevertheless Arthur and his court played an ongoing role in English society, written into histories and emulated by aristocrats and kings. And in the later fourteenth or early fifteenth century, several very distinguished Arthurian poems appeared, such as the alliterative *Morte Arthure* and the *Awntyrs (Adventures) off Arthure*.

Sir Gawain and the Green Knight is the greatest of the Arthurian romances produced in England. The poem embraces the highest aspirations of the late medieval aristocratic world, both courtly and religious, even while it eloquently admits the human failings that threaten those values. A knight's troth and word, a Christian's election and covenant, the breaking point of a person's or a society's virtues, all come in for celebration and painful scrutiny during Gawain's adventure.

Like Beowulf, Sir Gawain and the Green Knight comes down to us by the thread of a single copy. Its manuscript contains a group of poems (Sir Gawain, Pearl, Purity, and Patience) that mark their anonymous author as a poet whose range approaches that of his contemporary Chaucer, and whose formal craft is in some ways more ambitious than Chaucer's.

Gawain is the work of a highly sophisticated provincial court poet (likely in the northwest Midlands), working in a form and narrative tradition that is conservative in comparison with Chaucer's. The poet uses the alliterative long line, a meter with its roots in Anglo-Saxon poetry; the unrhymed alliterative stanzas, of irregular length, each end with five shorter rhymed lines often called a "bob-and-wheel" stanza. Within these traditional constraints, however, the poem achieves an apex of medieval courtly literature, as a superlatively crafted and stylized version of quest romance.

The romance never aims to detach itself from society or history, though. It opens and closes by referring to Troy, the ancient, fallen empire whose survivors were legendary founders of Britain, a connection well known through Geoffrey of Monmouth. Arthur, their ultimate heir, went on later in his myth to pursue imperial ambitions that, like those of Troy, were foiled by adulterous desire and political infidelity. Sir Gawain also echoes its contemporary world in the technical language of architecture, crafts, and arms. This helps draw in the kind of conservative, aristocratic court for which the poem seems to have been written, probably in Cheshire or Lancashire, a somewhat backward region whose nobles remained loyal to Richard II. Along with the pleasure it takes in fine armor and courtly ritual, the poem seems to enfold anxieties about the economic pressures of maintaining chivalric display in a period of costly new technology, inflation, and declining income from land.

By the time this poem was written, toward the close of the fourteenth century, Gawain was a famous Arthurian hero. His reputation was ambiguous, though; he was both Arthur's faithful retainer and nephew, but also a suave seducer. Which side of Gawain would dominate in this particular poem? Would he stand for a civilization of Christian chivalry or one of cynical sophistication?

The test that begins to answer this question occurs during Arthur's ritual celebrations of Christmas and the New Year, and within the civilized practices of Eucharist and secular feast. A gigantic green knight interrupts Arthur's banquet to offer a deadly game of exchanged axblows, to be resolved in one year's time. Although the Green Knight, with his ball of holly leaves, seems at first to come from the tradition of the Wild Man—a giant force of nature itself—he is also a sophisticated knight, gorgeously attired. He knows, too, just how to taunt a young king without quite overstepping the bounds of courtly behavior. Gawain takes up the challenge, but a still greater marvel ensues.

As the term of the agreement approaches, Gawain rides off, elaborately armed, to find the Green Knight and fulfill his obligation, even if that means his death. What Gawain encounters first, though, are temptations of character and sexuality even trickier and more crucial than they at first seem.

Sir Gawain and the Green Knight is remarkable not only for the intricacy of its plot but also for the virtuosity of its descriptions, such as the almost elegiac review of the passing seasons ("And so the year moves on in yesterdays many"). The poem rejoices in the masterful exercise of skill as the mark of civilization. Beautifully crafted knots appear everywhere, and we encounter artisanal craft as well in narrative elements like the Green Knight's dress (a dazzling mixture of leafy green and jeweler's gold), Gawain's decorated shield and arms, and the expertise of the master of the hunt who carves up the prey of Gawain's host with ritual precision. Even Gawain's exquisite courtly manners appear as a civilizing artifice.

The ambition of the poem's own craft is equally evident in its extraordinary range of formal devices. Preeminent among these is the symbolic register of number. The poem can be seen as a single unit, circling back to the Trojan scene with which it begins. It has a double structure, too, as it shifts between the courts of Arthur and Gawain's mysterious host. In the manuscript it is divided into four parts ("fits") that respond to the seasonal description at the opening of Part 2. The narrative proper ends by echoing the very start of the poem, at line 2525, itself a multiple of fives that recalls the pentangle on Gawain's shield symbolizing his virtues. The final rhyming stanza, with its formula of grace and salvation, brings the line total to 2530, whose individual digits add up to ten, a number associated with the divine in medieval numerology.

This symbolic structure can seem sometimes overdetermined. A range of elements, however, invites the reader to come at the poem from other perspectives. The poem's very circularity, narrative and formal, allows it to be viewed from beginning or ending. From the front it is a poem of male accomplishment, largely celebrating *men's* courts and *men's* virtues (even men's horses). At the other end, however, it focuses on a court presided over by an old woman (later called a goddess), a court whose irruption into the Arthurian world is explained as the playing out of an old and mysterious rivalry between two queens. Male, even patriarchal from one direction, the poem seems matriarchal, almost pagan, from the other. For all its formal cohesion and celebration of craft, the poem also pulls the reader back and keeps its mysteries intact by leaving many narrative loose ends and unanswered questions.

Unresolvable ambiguities reside most clearly in the pentangle on Gawain's shield and in the "green girdle" whose true owner remains uncertain. For all their differences, both are figures that insist on repetition, end where they begin, and possess a geometry that can be traced forward or backward. Yet the static perfection of the pentangle is subtly set against the protean green girdle, which passes through so many hands, alters its shape (being untied and retied repeatedly), and connects with so many issues in the poem: mortality, women's power, Gawain's fault and the acceptance of that fault by the whole Arthurian court. The girdle becomes an image both of flaw and triumph and of all the loose ends in this early episode of the Arthurian myth.

The girdle also serves to link *Sir Gawain* to political and social issues of the poet's own time, particularly efforts to revalidate a declining system of chivalry. After the last line in the manuscript, a later medieval hand has added "Hony Soyt Qui Mal Pence" ("shamed be he who thinks ill thereof"), the motto of the royal Order of the Garter, founded by Edward III in 1349 to promote a revival of knighthood. The Arthurian myth had already been redeployed to buttress royal power when Edward III refounded a Round Table in 1344. King Arthur's wisdom at the close of Gawain's adventure lies in transforming Gawain's shame, rage, and humiliated sense of sin into an emblem at once of mortal humanity and aristocratic cohesion. This is the place—back with the king and ritually connected with the Order of the Garter—where the closed circle of the poem opens to the social, historical world of empire, court, and kingship.

Sir Gawain and the Green Knight[1]
Part 1

When the siege and the assault had ceased at Troy,
and the fortress fell in flame to firebrands and ashes,
the traitor who the contrivance of treason there fashioned

---

1. This translation, remarkably faithful to the original alliterative meter and stanza form, is by J.R.R. Tolkien.

was tried for his treachery, the most true upon earth—
5   it was Aeneas[2] the noble and his renowned kindred
who then laid under them lands, and lords became
of well-nigh all the wealth in the Western Isles.[3]
When royal Romulus to Rome his road had taken,
in great pomp and pride he peopled it first,
10   and named it with his own name that yet now it bears;
Tirius[4] went to Tuscany and towns founded,
Langaberde[5] in Lombardy uplifted halls,
and far over the French flood Felix Brutus
on many a broad bank and brae[6] Britain established
15   full fair,
            where strange things, strife and sadness,
            at whiles in the land did fare,
            and each other grief and gladness
            oft fast have followed there.

20   And when fair Britain was founded by this famous lord,[7]
bold men were bred there who in battle rejoiced,
and many a time that betid they troubles aroused.
In this domain more marvels have by men been seen
than in any other that I know of since that olden time;
25   but of all that here abode in Britain as kinds
ever was Arthur most honoured, as I have heard men tell.
Wherefore a marvel among men I mean to recall,
a sight strange to see some men have held it,
one of the wildest adventures of the wonders of Arthur.
30   If you will listen to this lay but a little while now,
I will tell it at once as in town I have heard
                    it told,
            as it is fixed and fettered
            in story brave and bold,
35   thus linked and truly lettered,
            as was loved in this land of old.

This king lay at Camelot[8] at Christmas-tide
with many a lovely lord, lieges most noble,
indeed of the Table Round[9] all those tried brethren,
40   amid merriment unmatched and mirth without care.
There tourneyed many a time the trusty knights,
and jousted full joyously these gentle lords;
then to the court they came at carols to play.

2. Aeneas led the survivors of Troy to Italy, after a series
of ambiguous omens and misadventures. In medieval tradition, he was also said to have plotted to betray his own
city. "The traitor" in line 3, though, may refer to the Trojan Antenor, also said to have betrayed Troy.
3. Perhaps Europe, or just the British Isles. Many royal
houses traced their ancestry to Rome and Troy.
4. Possibly Titus Tatius, ancient king of the Sabines.
5. Ancestor of the Lombards, and a nephew of Brutus.
6. The steep bank bounding a river valley.
7. According to Geoffrey of Monmouth and others, a
great-grandson of Aeneas, exiled after accidentally killing
his father and later the founder of Britain.
8. Arthur's capital; its location is uncertain, probably in
Wales, and perhaps it is to be connected with Caerleon-
on-Usk where Arthur had been crowned. Knights were
expected to gather at his court, in celebration and
homage, on the five liturgical holidays on which Arthur
wore his crown: Easter, Ascension, Pentecost, All Saints'
Day, and Christmas.
9. Its shape symbolized the unity of Arthur's knights but
also avoided disputes over precedence.

For there the feast was unfailing full fifteen days,
45 with all meats and all mirth that men could devise,
such gladness and gaiety as was glorious to hear,
din of voices by day, and dancing by night;
all happiness at the highest in halls and in bowers
had the lords and the ladies, such as they loved most dearly.
50 With all the bliss of this world they abode together,
the knights most renowned after the name of Christ,
and the ladies most lovely that ever life enjoyed,
and he, king most courteous, who that court possessed.
For all that folk so fair did in their first estate[1]
55   abide,
        Under heaven the first in fame,
        their king most high in pride;
        it would now be hard to name
        a troop in war so tried.

60 While New Year was yet young that yestereve had arrived,
that day double dainties on the dais were served,
when the king was there come with his courtiers to the hall,
and the chanting of the choir in the chapel had ended.
With loud clamour and cries both clerks and laymen
65 Noel announced anew, and named it full often;
then nobles ran anon with New Year gifts,
Handsels,° handsels they shouted, and handed them out,   *gifts*
Competed for those presents in playful debate;
ladies laughed loudly, though they lost the game,
70 and he that won was not woeful, as may well be believed.[2]
All this merriment they made, till their meat was served;
then they washed, and mannerly went to their seats,
ever the highest for the worthiest, as well held to be best.
Queen Guinevere the gay was with grace in the midst
75 of the adorned dais[3] set. Dearly was it arrayed:
finest sendal° at her sides, a ceiling above her   *thin silk garment*
of true tissue of Tolouse, and tapestries of Tharsia
that were embroidered and bound with the brightest gems
one might prove and appraise to purchase for coin
80   any day.
        That loveliest lady there
        on them glanced with eyes of grey;
        that he found ever one more fair
        in sooth might no man say.

85 But Arthur would not eat until all were served;
his youth made him so merry with the moods of a boy,
he liked lighthearted life, so loved he the less

1. Arthur is emphatically a young king here, even "boy-ish." The phrase may also recall the Golden Age, an era of uncorrupted happiness.
2. The distribution of gifts at New Year displayed the king's wealth and power; it was also the occasion here of some courtly game of exchange, in which the loser perhaps gave up a kiss.
3. A medieval nobleman's hall typically had a raised platform at one end, on which the "high table" stood.

either long to be lying or long to be seated:
so worked on him his young blood and wayward brain.
90 And another rule moreover was his reason besides
that in pride he had appointed: it pleased him not to eat
upon festival so fair, ere he first were apprised
of some strange story or stirring adventure,
or some moving marvel that he might believe in
95 of noble men, knighthood, or new adventures;
or a challenger should come a champion seeking
to join with him in jousting, in jeopardy to set
his life against life, each allowing the other
the favour of fortune, were she fairer to him.
100 This was the king's custom, wherever his court was holden,
at each famous feast among his fair company
in hall.
So his face doth proud appear,
and he stands up stout and tall,
105 all young in the New Year;
much mirth he makes with all.

Thus there stands up straight the stern king himself,
talking before the high table of trifles courtly.
There good Gawain was set at Guinevere's side,
110 with Agravain a la Dure Main on the other side seated,
both their lord's sister-sons, loyal-hearted knights.
Bishop Baldwin had the honour of the board's service,
and Iwain[4] Urien's son ate beside him.
These dined on the dais and daintily fared,
115 and many a loyal lord below at the long tables.
Then forth came the first course with fanfare of trumpets,
on which many bright banners bravely were hanging;
noise of drums then anew and the noble pipes,[5]
warbling wild and keen, wakened their music,
120 so that many hearts rose high hearing their playing.
Then forth was brought a feast, fare of the noblest,
multitude of fresh meats on so many dishes
that free places were few in front of the people
to set the silver things full of soups on cloth
125 so white.
Each lord of his liking there
without lack took with delight:
twelve plates to every pair,
good beer and wine all bright.

130 Now of their service I will say nothing more,
for you are all well aware that no want would there be.
Another noise that was new drew near on a sudden,

4. Another nephew of Arthur. The relationship of uncle
and nephew is close in many Arthurian romances, and
noble youths were often sent to be raised by an uncle on
the mother's side.
5. Holiday banquets were formalized, almost theatrical.

so that their lord might have leave at least to take food.
For hardly had the music but a moment ended,
135 and the first course in the court as was custom been served,
when there passed through the portals a perilous horseman,
the mightiest on middle-earth in measure of height,
from his gorge to his girdle so great and so square,
and his loins and his limbs so long and so huge,
140 that half a troll upon earth I trow° that he was,   *trust; believe*
but the largest man alive at least I declare him;
and yet the seemliest for his size that could sit on a horse,
for though in back and in breast his body was grim,
both his paunch and his waist were properly slight,
145 and all his features followed his fashion so gay
in mode;
for at the hue men gaped aghast
in his face and form that showed;
as a fay-man fell he passed,
150 and green all over glowed.

All of green were they made, both garments and man:
a coat tight and close that clung to his sides;
a rich robe above it all arrayed within
with fur finely trimmed, shewing fair fringes
155 of handsome ermine gay, as his hood was also,
that was lifted from his locks and laid on his shoulders;
and trim hose tight-drawn of tincture alike
that clung to his calves; and clear spurs below
of bright gold on silk broideries banded most richly,
160 though unshod were his shanks, for shoeless he rode.
And verily all this vesture was of verdure clear,
both the bars on his belt, and bright stones besides
that were richly arranged in his array so fair,
set on himself and on his saddle upon silk fabrics:
165 it would be too hard to rehearse one half of the trifles
that were embroidered upon them, what with birds and with flies
in a gay glory of green, and ever gold in the midst.
The pendants of his poitrel, his proud crupper,
his molains, and all the metal to say more, were enamelled,
170 even the stirrups that he stood in were stained of the same;
and his saddlebows in suit, and their sumptuous skirts,
which ever glimmered and glinted all with green jewels;
even the horse that upheld him in hue was the same,
I tell:
175 a green horse great and thick,
a stallion stiff to quell,
in broidered bridle quick:
his matched his master well.

Very gay was this great man guised all in green,
180 and the hair of his head with his horse's accorded:
fair flapping locks enfolding his shoulders,

a big beard like a bush over his breast hanging
that with the handsome hair from his head falling
was sharp shorn to an edge just short of his elbows,
185   so that half his arms under it were hid, as it were
in a king's capadoce[6] that encloses his neck.
The mane of that mighty horse was of much the same sort,
well curled and all combed, with many curious knots
woven in with gold wire about the wondrous green,
190   ever a strand of the hair and a string of the gold;
the tail and the top-lock were twined all to match
and both bound with a band of a brilliant green:
with dear jewels bedight to the dock's ending,
and twisted then on top was a tight-knitted knot
195   on which many burnished bells of bright gold jingled.
Such a mount on middle-earth, or many to ride him,
was never beheld in that hall with eyes ere that time;
                    for there
            his glance was as lightning bright,
200   so did all that saw him swear;
            no many would have the might,
            they thought, his blows to bear.

And yet he had not a helm, nor a hauberk[7] either,
not a pisane,[8] not a plate that was proper to arms;
205   not a shield, not a shaft, for shock or for blow,
but in his one hand he held a holly-bundle,
that is greatest in greenery when groves are leafless,
and an axe in the other, ugly and monstrous,
a ruthless weapon aright for one in rhyme to describe:
210   the head was as large and as long as an ellwand,
a branch of green steel and of beaten gold;
the bit, burnished bright and broad at the edge,
as well shaped for shearing as sharp razors;
the stem was a stout staff, by which sternly he gripped it,
215   all bound with iron about to the base of the handle,
and engraven in green in graceful patterns,
lapped round with a lanyard that was lashed to the head
and down the length of the haft was looped many times;
and tassels of price were tied there in plenty
220   to bosses of the bright green, braided most richly.
Such was he that now hastened in, the hall entering,
pressing forward to the dais—no peril he feared.
To none gave he greeting, gazing above them,
and the first word that he winged: 'Now where is', he said,
225   'the governor of this gathering? For gladly I would
on the same set my sight, and with himself now talk
                    in town.'

---

6. Probably a hooded cape, fastened under the chin.   8. A piece of armor to protect the upper part of the chest
7. A tunic of chain mail.   and neck.

On the courtiers he cast his eye,
and rolled it up and down;
230   he stopped, and stared at espy
who there had most renown.

Then they looked for a long while, on that lord gazing;
for every man marvelled what it could mean indeed
that horseman and horse such a hue should come by
235   as to grow green as the grass, and greener it seemed,
than green enamel on gold glowing far brighter.
All stared that stood there and stole up nearer,
watching him and wondering what in the world he would do.
For many marvels they had seen, but to match this nothing;
240   wherefore a phantom and fay-magic folk there thought it,
and so to answer little eager was any of those knights,
and astounded at his stern voice stone-still they sat there
in a swooning silence through that solemn chamber,
as if all had dropped into a dream, so died their voices
245   away.
Not only, I deem, for dread;
but of some 'twas their courtly way
to allow their lord and head
to the guest his word to say.

250   Then Arthur before the high dais beheld this wonder,
and freely with fair words, for fearless was he ever,
saluted him, saying: 'Lord, to this lodging thou'rt welcome!
The head of this household Arthur my name is.
Alight, as thou lovest me, and linger, I pray thee;
255   and what may thy wish be in a while we shall learn.'
'Nay, so help me,' quoth the horseman, 'He that on high is throned,
to pass any time in this place was no part of my errand.
But since they praises, prince, so proud are uplisted,
and thy castle and courtiers are accounted the best,
260   the stoutest in steel-gear that on steeds may ride,
most eager and honourable of the earth's people,
valiant to vie with in other virtuous sports,
and here is knighthood renowned, as is noised in my ears:
'tis that has fetched me hither, by my faith, at this time.
265   You may believe by this branch that I am bearing here
that I pass as one in peace,[9] no peril seeking.
For had I set forth to fight in fashion of war,
I have a hauberk at home, and a helm also,
a shield, and a sharp spear shining brightly,
270   and other weapons to wield too, as well I believe;
but since I crave for no combat, my clothes are softer.
Yet if thou be so bold, as abroad is published,
thou wilt grant of thy goodness the game that I ask for
by right.'

9. A holly branch could symbolize peace and was used in games of the Christmas season.

275   Then Arthur answered there,
    and said: 'Sir, noble knight,
    if battle thou seek thus bare,
    thou'lt fail not here to fight.'

'Nay, I wish for no warfare, on my word I tell thee!
280   Here about on these benches are but beardless children.
Were I hasped in armour on a high charger,
there is no man here to match me—their might is so feeble.
And so I crave in this court only a Christmas pastime,
since it is Yule and New Year, and you are young here and merry.
285   If any so hardy in this house here holds that he is,
if so bold be his blood or his brain be so wild,
that he stoutly dare strike one stroke for another,
then I will give him as my gift this guisarm[1] costly,
this axe—'tis heavy enough—to handle as he pleases;
290   and I will abide the first brunt, here bare as I sit.
If any fellow be so fierce as my faith to test,
hither let him haste to me and lay hold of this weapon—
I hand it over for ever, he can have it as his own—
and I will stand a stroke from him, stock-still on this floor,
295   provided thou'lt lay down this law: that I may deliver him another.
                Claim I!
    And yet a respite I'll allow,
    till a year and a day go by.
    Come quick, and let's see now
300   if any here dare reply!'

If he astounded them at first, yet stiller were then
all the household in the hall, both high men and low.
The man on his mount moved in his saddle,
and rudely his red eyes he rolled then about,
305   bent his bristling brows all brilliantly green,
and swept round his beard to see who would rise.
When none in converse would accost him, he coughed then loudly,
stretched himself haughtily and straightway exclaimed:
'What! Is this Arthur's house,' said he thereupon,
310   'the rumour of which runs through realms unnumbered?
Where now is your haughtiness, and your high conquests,
your fierceness and fell mood, and your fine boasting?
Now are the revels and the royalty of the Round Table
overwhelmed by a word by one man spoken,
315   for all blench now abashed ere a blow is offered!'
With that he laughed so loud that their lord was angered,
the blood shot for shame into his shining cheeks
                and face;
    as wroth as wind he grew,
320   so all did in that place.
    Then near to the stout man drew
    the kind of fearless race,

1. A long-handled ax with a spike at the end.

And said: 'Marry! Good man, 'tis madness thou askest,
and since folly thou hast sought, thou deservest to find it.
325   I know no lord that is alarmed by thy loud words here.
Give me now they guisarm, in God's name, sir,
and I will bring thee the blessing thou hast begged to receive.'
Quick then he came to him and caught it from his hand.
Then the lordly man loftily alighted on foot.
330   Now Arthur holds his axe, and the haft grasping
sternly he stirs it about, his stroke considering.
The stout man before him there stood his full height,
higher than any in that house by a head and yet more.
With stern face as he stood he stroked at his beard,
335   and with expression impassive he pulled down his coat,
no more disturbed or distressed at the strength of his blows
than if someone as he sat had served him a drink
                  of wine.
           From beside the queen Gawain
340   to the king did then incline:
           'I implore with prayer plain
           that this match should now be mine.'

'Would you, my worthy lord,' said Gawain to the king,
'bid me abandon this bench and stand by you there,
345   so that I without discourtesy might be excused from the table,
and my liege lady were not loth to permit me,
I would come to your counsel before your courtiers fair.
For I find it unfitting, as in fact it is held,
when a challenge in your chamber makes choices so exalted,
350   though you yourself be desirous to accept it in person,
while many bold men about you on bench are seated:
on earth there are, I hold, none more honest of purpose,
no figures fairer on field where fighting is waged.
I am the weakest, I am aware, and in wit feeblest,
355   and the least loss, if I live not, if one would learn the truth.
Only because you are my uncle is honour given me:
save your blood in my body I boast of no virtue;
and since this affair is so foolish that it nowise befits you,
and I have requested it first, accord it then to me!
360   If my claim is uncalled-for without cavil shall judge
                  this court.'
           To consult the knights draw near,
           and this plan they all support;
           the king with crown to clear,
365   and give Gawain the sport.

The king them commanded that he quickly should rise,
and he readily uprose and directly approached,
kneeling humbly before his highness, and laying hand on the
                  weapon;
and he lovingly relinquished it, and lifting his hand
370   gave him God's blessing, and graciously enjoined him
that his hand and his heart should be hardly alike.

'Take care, cousin,' quoth the king, 'one cut to address,
and if thou learnest him his lesson, I believe very well
that thou wilt bear any blow that he gives back later.'

375 Gawain goes to the great man with guisarm in hand,
and he boldly abides there—he blenched not at all.
Then next said to Gawain the knight all in green:
'Let's tell again our agreement, ere we go any further.
I'd know first, sir knight, they name; I entreat thee

380 to tell it me truly, that I may trust in thy word.'
'In good faith,' quoth the good knight, 'I Gawain am called
who bring thee this buffet, let be what may follow;
and at this time a twelvemonth in thy turn have another
with whatever weapon thou wilt, and in the world with none else

385   but me.'
                The other man answered again:
                'I am passing pleased,' said he,
                'upon my life, Sir Gawain,
                that this stroke should be struck by thee.'

390 'Begad,' said the green knight, 'Sir Gawain, I am pleased
to find from thy fist the favour I asked for!
And thou hast promptly repeated and plainly hast stated
without abatement the bargain I begged of the king here;

395 save that thou must assure me, sir, on thy honour
that thou'lt seek me thyself, search where thou thinkest
I may be found near or far, and fetch thee such payment
as thou deliverest me today before these lordly people,'
'Where should I light on thee,' quoth Gawain, 'where look for thy
                        place?
I have never learned where thou livest, by the Lord that made me,

400 and I know thee not, knight, thy name nor thy court.
But teach me the true way, and tell what men call thee,
and I will apply all my purpose the path to discover:
and that I swear thee for certain and solemnly promise.'
'That is enough in New Year, there is need of no more!'

405 said the great man in green to Gawain the courtly.
'If I tell thee the truth of it, when I have taken the knock,
and though handily hast hit me, if in haste I announce then
my house and my home and mine own title,
then thou canst call and enquire and keep the agreement;

410 and if I waste not a word, thou'lt win better fortune,
for thou mayst linger in thy land and look no further—
                        but stay!
                To thy grim tool now take heed, sir!
                Let us try thy knocks today!'

415   'Gladly', said he, 'indeed, sir!'
                and his axe he stroked in play.

The Green Knight on the ground now gets himself ready,
leaning a little with the head he lays bare the flesh,
and his locks long and lovely he lifts over his crown,

420   letting the naked neck as was needed appear.
       His left foot on the floor before him placing,
       Gawain gripped on his axe, gathered and raised it,
       from aloft let it swiftly land where 'twas naked,
       so that the sharp of his blade shivered the bones,
425   and sank clean through the clear fat and clove it asunder,
       and the blade of the bright steel then bit into the ground.
       The fair head to the floor fell from the shoulders,
       and folk fended it with their feet as forth it went rolling;
       the blood burst from the body, bright on the greenness,
430   and yet neither faltered nor fell the fierce man at all,
       but stoutly he strode forth, still strong on his shanks,
       and roughly he reached out among the rows that stood there,
       caught up his comely head and quickly upraised it,
       and then hastened to his horse, laid hold of the bridle,
435   stepped into stirrup-iron, and strode up aloft,
       his head by the hair in his hand holding;
       and he settled himself then in the saddle as firmly
       as if unharmed by mishap, though in the hall he might wear
                          no head.
440   His trunk he twisted round,
                 that gruesome body that bled,
                 and many fear then found,
                 as soon as his speech was sped.

       For the head in his hand he held it up straight,
445   towards the fairest at the table he twisted the face,
       and it lifted up its eyelids and looked at them broadly,
       and made such words with its mouth as may be recounted.
       'See thou get ready, Gawain, to go as thou vowedst,
       and as faithfully seek till thou find me, good sir,
450   as thou hast promised in this place in the presence of these knights.
       To the Green Chapel go thou, and get thee, I charge thee,
       such a dint as thou hast dealt—indeed thou hast earned
       a nimble knock in return on New Year's morning!
       The Knight of the Green Chapel I am known to many,
455   so if to find me thou endeavour, thou'lt fail not to do so.
       Therefore come! Or to be called a craven thou deservest.'
       With a rude roar and rush his reins he turned then,
       and hastened out through the hall-door with his head in his hand,
       and fire of the flint flew from the feet of his charger.
460   To what country he came in that court no man knew,
       no more than they had learned from what land he had journeyed.
                          Meanwhile,
                 the king and Sir Gawain
                 at the Green Man laugh and smile;
465   yet to men had appeared, 'twas plain,
                 a marvel beyond denial.

       Though Arthur the high king in his heart marvelled,
       he let no sign of it be seen, but said then aloud

to the queen so comely with courteous words:
470 'Dear Lady, today be not downcast at all!
Such cunning play well becomes the Christmas tide,
interludes,[2] and the like, and laughter and singing,
amid these noble dances of knights and of dames.
Nonetheless to my food I may fairly betake me,
475 for a marvel I have met, and I may not deny it.'
He glanced at Sir Gawain and with good point he said:
'Come, hang up thine axe, sir![3] It has hewn now enough.'
And over the table they hung it on the tapestry behind,
where all men might remark it, a marvel to see,
480 and by its true token might tell of that adventure.
Then to a table they turned, those two lords together,
the kind and his good kinsman, and courtly men served them
with all dainties double, the dearest there might be,
with all manner of meats and with minstrelsy too.
485 With delight that day they led, till to the land came the night
again.
Sir Gawain, now take heed
lest fear make thee refrain
from daring the dangerous deed
490 that thou in hand hast ta'en!

Part 2

With this earnest of high deeds thus Arthur began
the young year, for brave vows he yearned to hear made.
Though such words were wanting when they went to table,
now of fell work to full grasp filled with their hands.
495 Gawain was gay as he began those games in the hall,
but if the end be unhappy, hold it no wonder!
For though men be merry of mood when they have mightily drunk,
a year slips by swiftly, never the same returning;
the outset to the ending is equal but seldom.
500 And so this Yule passed over and the year after,
and severally the seasons ensued in their turn:[4]
after Christmas there came the crabbed Lenten
that with fish tries the flesh and with food more meagre;
but then the weather in the world makes war on the winter,
505 cold creeps into the earth, clouds are uplifted,
shining rain is shed in showers that all warm
fall on the fair turf, flowers there open,
of grounds and of groves green is the raiment,
birds are busy a-building and bravely are singing
510 for sweetness of the soft summer that will soon be on
the way;
and blossoms burgeon and blow
in hedgerows bright and gay;

2. Brief performances between the courses of the banquet.
3. A literal suggestion, but also an invitation to put the
matter aside.

4. This famous passage on the cycle of seasons draws both
on Germanic conventions of the battle of Winter and
Summer, and on Romance springtime lyrics, the *reverdies*.

then glorious musics go
515   through the woods in proud array.

After the season of summer with its soft breezes,
when Zephyr goes sighing through seeds and herbs,
right glad is the grass that grows in the open,
when the damp dewdrops are dripping from the leaves,
520 to greet a gay glance of the glistening sun.
But then Harvest hurries in, and hardens it quickly,
warns it before winter to wax to ripeness.
He drives with his drought the dust, till it rises
from the face of the land and flies up aloft;
525 wild wind in the welkin° makes war on the sun,   *the sky*
the leaves loosed from the linden alight on the ground,
and all grey is the grass that green was before:
all things ripen and rot that rose up at first,
and so the year runs away in yesterdays many,
530 and here winter wends again, as by the way of the world
       it ought,
      until the Michaelmas moon[5]
      has winter's boding brought;
      Sir Gawain then full soon
535   of his grievous journey thought.

And yet till All Hallows[6] with Arthur he lingered,
who furnished on that festival a feast for the knight
with much royal revelry of the Round Table.
The knights of renown and noble ladies
540 all for the love of that lord had longing at heart,
but nevertheless the more lightly of laughter they spoke:
many were joyless who jested for his gentle sake.
For after their meal mournfully he reminded his uncle
that his departure was near, and plainly he said:
545 'Now liege-lord of my life, for leave I beg you.
You know the quest and the compact; I care not further
to trouble you with tale of it, save a trifling point:
I must set forth to my fate without fail in the morning,
as God will me guide, the Green Man to seek.'
550 Those most accounted in the castle came then together,[7]
Iwain and Erric and others not a few,
Sir Doddinel le Savae, the Duke of Clarence,
Lancelot, and Lionel, and Lucan the Good,
Sir Bors and Sir Bedivere that were both men of might,
555 and many others of mark with Mador de la Porte.
All this company of the court the king now approached
to comfort the knight with care in their hearts.

---

5. The harvest moon at Michaelmas, on 29 September.
6. All Saints' Day, on 1 November, another holiday on which Arthur presided, crowned, over his court.
7. The following list would have recalled, especially to readers of French romances, other great quests and challenges encountered by Arthur's knights. The list's order may also suggest later and more tragic episodes in the Arthurian narrative, ending with Bedivere who throws Excalibur into a lake after Arthur is mortally wounded.

Much mournful lament was made in the hall
that one so worthy as Gawain should went on that errand,
560   to endure a deadly dint and deal no more
                              with blade.
            The knight ever made good cheer,
            saying, 'Why should I be dismayed?
            Of doom the fair or drear
565   by a man must be assayed.'

He remained there that day, and in the morning got ready,
asked early for his arms, and they all were brought him.
First a carpet of red silk was arrayed on the floor,
and the gilded gear in plenty there glittered upon it.
570   The stern man stepped thereon and the steel things handled,
dressed in a doublet of damask of Tharsia,
and over it a cunning capadoce that was closed at the throat
and with fair ermine was furred all within.
Then sabatons[8] first they set on his feet,
575   his legs lapped in steel in his lordly greaves,
on which the polains they placed, polished and shining
and knit upon his knees with knots all of gold;
then the comely cuisses that cunningly clasped
the thick thews of his thighs they with thongs on him tied;
580   and next the byrnie,° woven of bright steel rings   *coat of mail*
upon costly quilting, enclosed him about;
and armlets well burnished upon both of his arms,
with gay elbow-pieces and gloves of plate,
and all the goodly gear to guard him whatever
585   betide;
            coat-armour richly made,
            gold spurs on heel in pride;
            girt with a trusty blade,
            silk belt about his side.

590   When he was hasped in his armour his harness was splendid:
the least latchet or loop was all lit with gold.
Thus harnessed as he was he heard now his Mass,
that was offered and honoured at the high altar;
and then he came to the king and his court-companions,
595   and with love he took leave of lords and of ladies;
and they kissed him and escorted him, and to Christ him commended.
And now Gringolet stood groomed, and girt with a saddle
gleaming right gaily with many gold fringes,
and all newly for the nonce nailed at all points;
600   adorned with bars was the bridle, with bright gold banded;
that apparelling proud of poitrel and of skirts,
and the crupper and caparison[9] accorded with the saddlebows:
all was arrayed in red with rich gold studded,

---

8. A broad-toed armed foot-covering worn by warriors in   9. A cloth or covering spread over the saddle or harness
armor.   of a horse, often gaily ornamented.

so that it glittered and glinted as a gleam of the sun.
605 Then he in hand took the helm and in haste kissed it:
strongly was it stapled and stuffed within;
it sat high upon his head and was hasped at the back,
and a light kerchief was laid o'er the beaver,
all braided and bound[1] with the brightest gems
610 upon broad silken broidery, with birds on the seams
like popinjays depainted, here preening and there,
turtles and true-loves, entwined as thickly
as if many sempstresses had the sewing full seven winters
in hand.
615 A circlet of greater price
his crown about did band;
The diamonds point-device
there blazing bright did stand.

Then they brought him his blazon that was of brilliant gules
620 with the pentangle[2] depicted in pure hue of gold.
By the baldric he caught it and about his neck cast it:
right well and worthily it went with the knight.
And why the pentangle is proper to that prince so noble
I intend now to tell you, though it may tarry my story.
625 It is a sign that Solomon once set on a time
to betoken Troth, as it is entitled to do;
for it is a figure that in it five points holdeth,
and each line overlaps and is linked with another,
and every way it is endless; and the English, I hear,
630 everywhere name it the Endless Knot.
So it suits well this knight and his unsullied arms;
for ever faithful in five points, and five times under each,
Gawain as good was acknowledged and as gold refined,
devoid of every vice and with virtues adorned.
635 So there
the pentangle painted new
he on shield and coat did wear,
as one of word most true
and knight of bearing fair.

640 First faultless was he found in his five senses,
and next in his five fingers he failed at no time,
and firmly on the Five Wounds, all his faith was set
that Christ received on the cross, as the Creed tells us;
and wherever the brave man into battle was come,
645 on this beyond all things was his earnest thought:
that ever from the Five Joys all his valour he gained
that to Heaven's courteous Queen once came from her Child.[3]

1. The preceding technical language of armor is now joined by an equally technical description of needlework, for which English women were famous.
2. A five-pointed star and symbol of perfection and eternity, since it can be drawn with an uninterrupted line ending at the point of the star where it begins. Inscribed within a circle, it was called Solomon's seal.
3. Poems and meditations on the Virgin's joys and sorrows were widespread. Her five joys were the Annunciation, Nativity, Resurrection, Ascension, and Assumption.

For which cause the knight had in comely wise
on the inner side of his shield her image depainted,
650   that when he case his eyes thither his courage never failed.
The fifth five that was used, as I find, by this knight
was free-giving and friendliness first before all,
and chastity and chivalry ever changeless and straight,
and piety surpassing all points: these perfect five
655   were hasped upon him harder than on any man else.
Now these five series, in sooth, were fastened on this knight,
and each was knit with another and had no ending,
but were fixed at five points that failed not at all,
coincided in no line nor sundered either,
660   not ending in any angle anywhere, as I discover,
wherever the process was put in play or passed to an end.
Therefore on his shining shield was shaped now this knot,
royally with red gules upon red gold set:
this is the pure pentangle as people of learning
665   have taught.
        Now Gawain in brave array
        his lance at last hath caught.
        He gave them all good day,
        for evermore as he thought.

670   He spurned his steed with the spurs and sprang on his way
so fiercely that the flint-sparks flashed out behind him.
All who beheld him so honourable in their hearts were sighing,
and assenting in sooth one said to another,
grieving for that good man: 'Before God, 'tis a shame
675   that thou, lord, must be lost, who art in life so noble!
To meet his match among men, Marry, 'tis not easy!
To behave with more heed would have behoved one of sense,
and that dear lord duly a duke to have made,
illustrious leader of liegemen in this land as befits him;
680   and that would better have been than to be butchered to death,
beheaded by an elvish man for an arrogant vaunt.
Who can recall any king that such a course ever took
as knights quibbling at court at their Christmas games!'
Many warm tears outwelling there watered their eyes,
685   when that lord so beloved left the castle
        that day.
        No longer he abode,
        but swiftly went his way;
        bewildering ways he rode,
690   as the book I heard doth say.

Now he rides thus arrayed through the realm of Logres,[4]
Sir Gawain in God's care, though no game now he found it.

---

4. Identified with England in Geoffrey of Monmouth, elsewhere a vaguer term for Arthur's kingdom. Here, Gawain is heading northward through Wales, then along the coast of the Irish Sea and into the forest of Wirral in Cheshire—a wild area and resort of outlaws in the 14th century. Gawain thus moves into the area around Chester, where the poem may well have been written.

Oft forlorn and alone he lodged of a night
where he found not afforded him such fare as pleased him.
695   He had no friend but his horse in the forests and hills,
no man on his march to commune with but God,
till anon he drew near unto Northern Wales.
All the isles of Anglesey he held on his left,
and over the fords he fared by the flats near the sea,
700   and then over by the Holy Head to high land again
in the wilderness of Wirral: there wandered but few
who with good will regarded either God or mortal.
And ever he asked as he went on of all whom he met
if they had heard any news of a knight that was green
705   in any ground thereabouts, or of the Green Chapel.
And all denied it, saying nay, and that never in their lives
a single man had they seen that of such a colour
                could be.
         The knight took pathways strange
710   by many a lonesome lea,
         and oft his view did change
         that chapel ere he could see.

Many a cliff he climbed o'er in countries unknown,
far fled from his friends without fellowship he rode.
715   At every wading or water on the way that he passed
he found a foe before him, save at few for a wonder;
and so foul were they and fell that fight he must needs.
So many a marvel in the mountains he met in those lands
that 'twould be tedious the tenth part to tell you thereof.
720   At whiles with worms he wars, and with wolves also,
at whiles with wood-trolls that wandered in the crags,
and with bulls and with bears and boards, too, at times;
and with ogres that hounded him from the heights of the fells.
Had he not been stalwart and staunch and steadfast in God,
725   he doubtless would have died and death had met often;
for though war wearied him much, the winter was worse,
when the cold clear water from the clouds spilling
froze ere it had fallen upon the faded earth.
Wellnigh slain by the sleet he slept ironclad
730   more nights than enow in the naked rocks,
where clattering from the crest the cold brook tumbled,
and hung high o'er his head in hard icicles.
Thus in peril and pain and in passes grievous
till Christmas-eve that country he crossed all alone
735   in need.
         The knight did at that tide
         his plaint to Mary plead,
         her rider's road to guide
         and to some lodging lead.

740   By a mount in the morning merrily he was riding
into a forest that was deep and fearsomely wild,

with high hills at each hand, and hoar woods beneath
of huge aged oaks by the hundred together;
the hazel and the hawthorn were huddled and tangled
745   with rough ragged moss around them trailing,
with many birds bleakly on the bare twigs sitting
that piteously piped there for pain of the cold.
The good man on Gringolet goes now beneath them
through many marshes and mires, a man all alone,
750   troubled lest a truant at that time he should prove
from the service of the sweet Lord, who on that selfsame night
of a maid became man our mourning to conquer.
And therefore sighing he said: 'I beseech thee, O Lord,
and Mary, who is the mildest mother most dear,
755   for some harbour where with honour I might hear the Mass
and thy Matins[5] tomorrow. This meekly I ask,
and thereto promptly I pray with Pater and Ave
                    and Creed.'[6]
            In prayer he now did ride,
760   lamenting his misdeed;
            he blessed him oft and cried,
            'The Cross of Christ me speed!'

The sign on himself he had set but thrice,
ere a mansion he marked within a moat in the forest,
765   on a low mound above a lawn, laced under the branches
of many a burly bole around about by the ditches:
the castle most comely that ever a king possessed
placed amid a pleasaunce with a park all about it,
within a palisade of pointed pales set closely
770   that took its turn round the trees for two miles or more.
Gawain from the one side gazed on the stronghold
as it shimmered and shone through the shining oaks,
and then humbly he doffed his helm, and with honour he thanked
Jesus and Saint Julian,[7] who generous are both,
775   who had courtesy accorded him and to his cry harkened.
'Now bon hostel, guoth the knight, 'I beg of you still!'
Then he goaded Gringolet with his gilded heels,
and he chose by good chance the chief pathway
and brought his master bravely to the bridge's end
780   at last.
            That brave bridge was up-hauled,
            the gates were bolted fast;
            the castle was strongly walled,
            it feared no wind or blast.

785   Then he stayed his steed that on the steep bank halted
above the deep double ditch that was drawn round the place.

5. First of the canonical hours of prayer and praise in monastic tradition, observed between midnight and dawn.
6. The Paternoster ("Our Father . . ."), Ave Maria ("Hail Mary . . ."), and Creed (the articles of the Christian faith).
7. Patron saint of hospitality.

The wall waded in the water wondrous deeply,
and up again to a huge height in the air it mounted,
all of hard hewn stone to the high cornice,
790 fortified under the battlement in the best fashion
and topped with fair turrets set by turns about
that had many graceful loopholes with a good outlook:
that knight a better barbican had never seen built.[8]
And inwards he beheld the hall uprising,
795 tall towers set in turns, and as tines[9] clustering
the fair finials, joined featly, so fine and so long,
their capstones all carven with cunning and skill.
Many chalk-white chimneys he chanced to espy
upon the roofs of towers all radiant white;
800 so many painted pinnacle was peppered about,
among the crenelles of the castle clustered so thickly
that all pared out of paper it appeared to have been.[1]
The gallant knight on his great horse good enough thought it,
if he could come by any course that enclosure to enter,
805 to harbour in that hostel while the holy day lasted
                                with delight.
            He called, and there came with speed
            a porter blithe and bright;
            on the wall he learned his need,
810   and hailed the errant knight.

'Good sir,' quoth Gawain, 'will you go with my message
to the high lord of this house for harbour to pray?'
'Yes, by Peter!'[2] quoth the porter, 'and I promise indeed
that you will, sir, be welcome while you wish to stay here.'
815 Then quickly the man went and came again soon,
servants bringing civilly to receive there the knight.
They drew down the great drawbridge, and duly came forth,
and on the cold earth on their knees in courtesy knelt
to welcome this wayfarer with such worship as they knew.
820 They delivered him the broad gates and laid them wide open,
and he readily bade them rise and rode o'er the bridge.
Several servants then seized the saddle as he alighted,
and many stout men his steed to a stable then led,
while knights and esquires anon descended
825 to guide there in gladness this guest to the hall.
When he raised up his helm many ran there in haste
to have it from his hand, his highness to serve;
his blade and his blazon both they took charge of.
Then he greeted graciously those good men all,
830 and many were proud to approach him, that prince to honour.
All hasped in his harness to hall they brought him,
where a fair blaze in the fireplace fiercely was burning.

8. The poet again revels in technical vocabulary, here architectural; this is a fashionable (if exaggerated) building of the 14th century.
9. Pinnacles.

1. Models in cut paper sometimes decorated elaborate feasts such as that at the beginning of the poem.
2. Swearing by Saint Peter, keeper of the keys to heaven.

Then the lord of that land leaving his chamber
Came mannerly to meet the man on the floor.
835 He said: 'You are welcome at your wish to dwell here.
What is here, all is your own, to have in your rule
     and sway.'
    'Grammercy!' quoth Gawain,
    'May Christ you this repay!'
840   As men that to meet were fain
    they both embraced that day.

Gawain gazed at the good man who had greeted him kindly,
and he thought bold and big was the baron of the castle,
very large and long, and his life at the prime:
845 broad and bright was his beard, and all beaver-hued,
stern, strong in his stance upon stalwart legs,
his face fell as fire, and frank in his speech;
and well it suited him, in sooth, as it seemed to the knight,
a lordship to lead untroubled over lieges trusty.
850 To a chamber the lord drew him, and charged men at once
to assign him an esquire to serve and obey him;
and there to wait on his word many worthy men were,
who brought him to a bright bower where the bedding was splendid:
there were curtains of costly silk with clear-golden hems,
855 and coverlets cunning-wrought with quilts most lovely
of bright ermine above, embroidered at the sides,
hangings running on ropes with red-gold rings,
carpets of costly damask that covered the walls
and the floor under foot fairly to match them.
860 There they despoiled him, speaking to him gaily,
his byrnie doing off and his bright armour.
Rich robes then readily men ran to bring him,
for him to change, and to clothe him, having chosen the best.
As soon as he had donned one and dressed was therein,
865 as it sat on him seemly with its sailing skirts,
then verily in his visage a vision of Spring
to each man there appeared, and in marvellous hues
bright and beautiful was all his body beneath.
That knight more noble was never made by Christ
870   they thought.
    He came none knew from where,
    but it seemed to them he ought
    to be a prince beyond compare
    in the field where fell men fought.

875 A chair before the chimney where charcoal was burning
was made ready in his room, all arrayed and covered
with cushions upon quilted cloths that were cunningly made.
Then a comely cloak was cast about him
of bright silk brocade, embroidered most richly
880 and furred fairly within with fells of the choicest
and all edged with ermine, and its hood was to match;
and he sat in that seat seemly and noble

and warmed himself with a will, and then his woes were amended.
Soon up on good trestles a table was raised[3]
885   and clad with a clean cloth clear white to look on;
there was surnape, salt-cellar, and silvern spoons.
He then washed as he would and went to his food,
and many worthy men with worship waited upon him;
soups they served of many sorts, seasoned most choicely,
890   in double helpings, as was due, and divers sorts of fish;
some baked in bread, some broiled on the coals,
some seethed, some in gravy savoured with spices,
and all with condiments so cunning that it caused him delight.
A fair feast he called it frankly and often,
895   graciously, when all the good men together there pressed him:
                 'Now pray,
         this penance deign to take;
         'twill improve another day!'[4]
         The man much mirth did make,
900   for wine to his head made way.

Then inquiry and question were carefully put
touching personal points to that prince himself,
till he courteously declared that to the court he belonged
that high Arthur in honour held in his sway,
905   who was the right royal King of the Round Table,
and 'twas Gawain himself that as their guest now sat
and had come for that Christmas, as the case had turned out.
When the lord had learned whom luck had brought him,
loud laughed he threat, so delighted he was,
910   and they made very merry, all the men in that castle,
and to appear in the presence were pressing and eager
of one who all profit and prowess and perfect manners
comprised in his person, and praise ever gained;
of all men on middle-earth he most was admired.
915   Softly each said then in secret to his friend:
'Now fairly shall we mark the fine points of manners,
and the perfect expressions of polished converse.
How speech is well spent will be expounded unasked,
since we have found here this fine father of breeding.
920   God has given us His goodness His grace now indeed,
Who such a guest as Gawain has granted us to have!
When blissful men at board for His birth sing blithe
                at heart,
        what manners high may mean
925   this knight will now impart.
        Who hears him will, I ween,
        of love-speech learn some art.'[5]

3. A castle's great hall had many uses; tables were set up
for dining and then put aside or hung.
4. An exchange of graceful courtesies. Gawain has politely praised the many fish dishes; his hosts demur, remind
him that Christmas Eve is a fast day, and promise him
better meals later.
5. Though Gawain is engaged on a serious quest, his reputation as a graceful courtier and master in the arts of love
has preceded him.

When his dinner was done and he duly had risen,
it now to the night-time very near had drawn.
930 The chaplains then took to the chapel their way
and rang the bells richly, as rightly they should,
for the solemn evensong of the high season.
The lord leads the way, and his lady with him;
into a goodly oratory gracefully she enters.
935 Gawain follows gladly, and goes there at once
and the lord seizes him by the sleeve and to a seat leads him,
kindly acknowledges him and calls him by his name,
saying that most welcome he was of all guests in the world.
And he grateful thanks gave him, and each greeted the other,
940 and they sat together soberly while the service lasted.
Then the lady longed to look at this knight;
and from her closet she came with many comely maidens.
She was fairer in face, in her flesh and her skin,
her proportions, her complexion, and her port than all others,
945 and more lovely than Guinevere to Gawain she looked.
He came through the chancel to pay court to her grace;
leading her by the left hand another lady was there
who was older than she, indeed ancient she seemed,
and held in high honour by all men about her.
950 But unlike in their looks those ladies appeared,
for if the younger was youthful, yellow was the elder;
with rose-hue the one face was richly mantled,
rough wrinkled cheeks rolled on the other;
on the kerchiefs of the one many clear pearls were,
955 her breast and bright throat were bare displayed,
fairer than white snow that falls on the hills;
the other was clad with a cloth that enclosed all her neck,
enveloped was her black chin with chalk-white veils,
her forehead folded in silk, and so fumbled all up,
960 so topped up and trinketed and with trifles bedecked
that naught was bare of that beldame but her brows all black,
her two eyes and her nose and her naked lips,
and those were hideous to behold and horribly bleared;
that a worthy dame she was may well, fore God,
965   be said!
        short body and thick waist,
        with bulging buttocks spread;
        more delicious to the taste
        was the one she by her led.

970 When Gawain glimpsed that gay lady that so gracious looked,
with leave sought of the lord towards the ladies he went;
the elder he saulted, low to her bowing,
about the lovelier he laid then lightly his arms
and kissed her in courtly wise with courtesy speaking.
975 His acquaintance they requested, and quickly he begged
to be their servant in sooth, if so they desired.
They took him between them, and talking they led him

to a fireside in a fair room, and first of all called
for spices, which men sped without sparing to bring them,
980   and ever wine therewith well to their liking.
The lord for their delight leaped up full often,
many times merry games being minded to make;
his hood he doffed, and on high he hung it on a spear,
and offered it as an honour for any to win
985   who the most fun could devise at that Christmas feast—
'And I shall try, by my troth, to contend with the best
ere I forfeit this hood, with the help of my friends!'
Thus with laughter and jollity the lord made his jests
to gladden Sir Gawain with games that night
990   in hall,
          until the time was due
          that the lord for lights should call;
          Sir Gawain with leave withdrew
          and went to bed withal.

995   On the morn when every man remembers the time
that our dear Lord for our doom to die was born,
in every home wakes happiness on earth for His sake.
So did it there on that day with the dearest delights:
at each meal and at dinner marvellous dishes
1000   men set on the dais, the daintiest meats.
The old ancient woman was highest at table,
meetly to her side the master he took him;
Gawain and the gay lady together were seated
in the centre, where as was seemly the service began,
1005   and so on through the hall as honour directed.
When each good man in his degree without grudge had been served,
there was food, there was festival, there was fullness of joy;
and to tell all the tale of it I should tedious find,
though pains I might take every point to detail.
1010   Yet I ween that Gawain and that woman so fair
in companionship took such pleasure together
in sweet society soft words speaking,
their courteous converse clean and clear of all evil,
that with their pleasant pastime no prince's sport
1015   compares.
          Drums beat, and trumps men wind,
          many pipers play their airs;
          each man his needs did mind,
          and they two minded theirs.

1020   With much feasting they fared the first and the next day,
and as heartily the third came hastening after:
the gaiety of Saint John's day[6] was glorious to hear;
[with cheer of the choicest Childermas followed,]
and that finished their revels, as folk there intended,

---

6. 27 December, traditionally given over to drinking and celebration.

for there were guests who must go in the grey morning.
1025   So a wondrous wake they held, and the wine they drank,
and they danced and danced on, and dearly they carolled.[7]
At least when it was late their leave then they sought
to wend on their ways, each worthy stranger.
Good-day then said Gawain, but the good man stayed him,
1030   and led him to his own chamber to the chimney-corner,
and there he delayed him, and lovingly thanked him,
for the pride and pleasure his presence had brought,
for so honouring his house at that high season
and deigning his dwelling to adorn with his favour.
1035   'Believe me, sir, while I live my luck I shall bless
that Gawain was my guest at God's own feast.'
'Gramercy, sir,' said Gawain, 'but the goodness is yours,
all the honour is your own—may the High King repay you!
And I am under your orders what you ask to perform,
1040   as I am bound now to be, for better or worse,
                by right.'
            Him longer to retain
            the lord them pressed the knight;
            to him replied Gawain
1045   that he by no means might.

Then with courteous question he enquired of Gawain
what dire need had driven him on that festal date
with such keenness from the king's court, to come forth alone
ere wholly the holidays from men's homes had departed.
1050   'In sooth, sir,' he said, 'you say but the truth:
a high errand and a hasty from that house brought me;
for I am summoned myself to seek for a place,
though I wonder where in the world I must wander to find it.
I would not miss coming night it on New Year's morning
1055   for all the land in Logres, so our Lord help me!
And so, sir, this question I enquire of you here:
can you tell me in truth if you tale ever heard
of the Green Chapel, on what ground it may stand,
and of the great knight that guards it, all green in his colour?
1060   For the terms of a tryst were between us established
to meet that man at that mark, if I remained alive,
and the named New Year is now nearly upon me,
and I would look on that lord, if God will allow me,
more gladly, by God's son, than gain any treasure.
1065   So indeed, if you please, depart now I must.
For my business I have now but barely three days,
and I would fainer fall dead than fail in my errand.'
Then laughing said the lord: 'Now linger you must;
for when 'tis time to that tryst I will teach you the road.
1070   On what ground is the Green Chapel—let it grieve you no more!

7. A ring dance.

In your bed you shall be, sir, till broad is the day,
without fret, and then fare on the first of the year,
and come to the mark at midmorn, there to make what play
          you know.
1075   Remain till New Year's day,
          then rise and riding go!
          We'll set you on your way,
          'tis but two miles or so.'

Then was Gawain delighted, and in gladness he laughed:
1080 'Now I thank you a thousand times for this beyond all!
Now my quest is accomplished, as you crave it, I will
dwell a few days here, and else do what you order.'
The lord then seized him and set him in a seat beside him,
and let the ladies be sent for to delight them the more,
1085 for their sweet pleasure there in peace by themselves.
For love of him that lord was as loud in his mirth
as one near out of his mind who scarce knew what he meant.
Then he called to the knight, crying out loudly:
'You have promised to do whatever deed I propose.
1090 Will you hold this behest here, at this moment?'
'Yes, certainly sir,' then said the true knight,
'while I remain in your mansion, your command I'll obey.'
'Well,' returned he, 'you have travelled and toiled from afar,
and then I've kept you awake: you're not well yet, not cured;
1095 both sustenance and sleep 'tis certain you need.
Upstairs you shall stay, sir, and stop there in comfort
tomorrow till Mass-time, and to a meal then go
when you wish with my wife, who with you shall sit
and comfort you with her company, till to court I return.
1100   You stay,
          and I shall early rouse,
          and a-hunting wend my way.'
          Gawain gracefully bows:
          'Your wishes I will obey.'

1105 'One thing more,' said the master, 'we'll make an agreement:
whatever I win in the wood at once shall be yours,
and whatever gain you may get you shall give in exchange.
Shall we swap thus, sweet man—come, say what you think!—
whether one's luck be light, or one's lot be better?'
1110 'By God,' quoth good Gawain, 'I agree to it all,
and whatever play you propose seems pleasant to me.'
'Done! 'Tis a bargain! Who'll bring us the drink?'
So said the lord of that land. They laughed one and all;
they drank and they dallied, and they did as they pleased,
1115 these lords and ladies, as long as they wished,
and then with customs of France and many courtly phrases
they stood in sweet debate and soft words bandied,
and lovingly they kissed, their leave taking.
With trusty attendants and torches gleaming

1120   they were brought at the last to their beds so soft,
                            one and all.
                    Yet ere to bed they came,
                    he the bargain did oft recall;
                    he knew how to play a game
1125   the old governor of that hall.

Part 3

        Before the first daylight the folk uprose:
        the guests that were to go for their grooms they called;
        and they hurried up in haste horses to saddle,
        to stow all their stuff and strap up their bags.
1130   The men of rank arrayed them, for riding got ready,
        to saddle leaped swiftly, seized then their bridles,
        and went off on their ways where their wish was to go.
        The liege-lord of the land was not last of them all
        to be ready to ride with a rout of his men;
1135   he ate a hurried mouthful after the hearing of Mass,
        and with horn to the hunting-field he hastened at once.[8]
        When daylight was opened yet dimly on earth
        he and his huntsman were up on their high horses.
        Then the leaders of the hounds leashed them in couples,
1140   unclosed the kennel-door and cried to them 'out!',
        and blew boldly on bugles three blasts full long.
        Beagles bayed thereat, a brave noise making;
        and they whipped and wheeled in those that wandered on a scent;
        a hundred hunting-dogs, I have heard, of the best
1145   were they.
                    To their stations keepers passed;
                    the leashes were cast away,
                    and many a rousing blast
                    woke din in the woods that day.

1150   At the first burst of the baying all beasts trembled;
        deer dashed through the dale by dread bewildered,
        and hastened to the heights, but they hotly were greeted,
        and turned back by the beaters, who boldly shouted.
        They let the harts go past with their high antlers,
1155   and the brave bucks also with their branching palms;
        for the lord of the castle had decreed in the close season
        that no man should molest the male of the deer.
        The hinds were held back with hey! and ware!,
        the does driven with great din to the deep valleys:
1160   there could be seen let slip a sleet of arrows;
        at each turn under the trees went a twanging shaft
        that into brown hides bit hard with barbed head.
        Lo! they brayed, and they bled, and on the banks they died;
        and ever the hounds in haste hotly pursued them,

8. The hunts that follow, for all their violent energy, are as ritualized in their procedure as the earlier feasts and games. The poet delights in describing still another area of knightly lore. A number of contemporary treatises on hunting survive.

1165 and hunters with high horns hurried behind them
with such a clamour and cry as if cliffs had been riven.
If any beast broke away from bowmen there shooting,
it was snatched down and slain at the receiving-station;
when they had been harried from the height and hustled to the waters,
1170 the men were so wise in their craft at the watches below,
and their greyhounds were so great that they got them at once,
and flung them down in a flash, as fast as men could see
                    with sight.
        The lord then wild for joy
1175   did oft spur and oft alight,
        and thus in bliss employ
        that day till dark of night.

Thus in his game the lord goes under greenwood eaves,
and Gawain the bold lies in goodly bed,
1180 lazing, till the walls are lit by the light of day,
under costly coverlet with curtains about him.
And as in slumber he strayed, he heard stealthily come
a soft sound at his door as it secretly opened;
and from under the clothes he craned then his head,
1185 a corner of the curtain he caught up a little,
and looked that way warily to learn what it was.
It was the lady herself, most lovely to see,
that cautiously closed the door quietly behind her,
and drew near to his bed. Then abashed was the knight,
1190 and lay down swiftly to look as if he slept;
and she stepped silently and stole to his bed,
cast back the curtain, and crept then within,
and sat her down softly on the side of the bed,
and there lingered very long to look for his waking.
1195 He lay there lurking a long while and wondered,
and mused in his mind how the matter would go,
to what point it might pass—to some surprise, he fancied.
Yet he said to himself: 'More seemly 'twould be
in due course with question to enquire what she wishes.'
1200 Then rousing he rolled over, and round to her turning
he lifted his eyelids with a look as of wonder,
and signed him with the cross, thus safer to be kept
                    aright.
        With chin and cheeks so sweet
1205   of blended red and white,
        with grace them him did greet
        small lips with laughter bright.

'Good morning, Sir Gawain!' said that graciously lady.
'You are a careless sleeper, if one can creep on you so!
1210 Now quickly you are caught! If we come not to terms,
I shall bind you in your bed, you may be assured.'
With laughter the lady thus lightly jested.
'Good morning to your grace!' said Gawain gaily.

'You shall work on me your will, and well I am pleased;
1215   for I submit immediately, and for mercy I cry,
and that is best, as I deem, for I am obliged to do so.'
Thus he jested in return with much gentle laughter:
'But if you would, lady gracious, then leave grant me,
and release your prisoner and pray him to rise,
1220   I would abandon this bed and better array me;
the more pleasant would it prove then to parley with you.'
'Nay, for sooth, fair sir,' said the sweet lady,
'you shall not go from you bed! I will govern you better:
here fast shall I enfold you, on the far side also,
1225   and then talk with my true knight that I have taken so.
For I wot well indeed that Sir Gawain you are,
to whom all men pay homage wherever you ride;
your honour, your courtesy, by the courteous is praised,
by lords, by ladies, by all living people.
1230   And right here you now are, and we all by ourselves;
my husband and his huntsmen far hence have ridden,
other men are abed, and my maids also,
the door closed and caught with a clasp that is strong;
and since I have in this house one that all delight in,
1235   my time to account I will turn, while for talk I chance
               have still.
        To my body will you welcome be
        of delight to take your fill;
        for need constraineth me
1240   to serve you, and I will.'

'Upon my word,' said Gawain, 'that is well, I guess;
though I am not now he of whom you are speaking—
to attain to such honour as here you tell of
I am a knight unworthy, as well indeed I know—
1245   by God, I would be glad, if good to you seemed
whatever I could say, or in service could offer
to the pleasure of your excellence—it would be pure delight.'
'In good faith, Sir Gawain,' said the gracious lady,
'the prowess and the excellence that all others approve,
1250   if I scorned or decried them, it were scant courtesy.
But there are ladies in number who liever would now
have thee in their hold, sir, as I have thee here,
pleasantly to play with in polished converse,
their solace to seek and their sorrows to soothe,
1255   than great part of the goods or gold that they own.
But I thank Him who on high of Heaven is Lord
that I have here wholly in my hand what all desire,
              by grace.'
        She was an urgent wooer,
1260   that lady fair of face;
        the knight with speeches pure
        replied in every case.

'Madam,' said he merrily, 'Mary reward you!
For I have enjoyed, in good faith, your generous favour,
1265   and much honour have had else from others' kind deeds;
but as for the courtesy they accord me, since my claim is not equal,
the honour is your own, who are ever well-meaning.'
'Nay, Mary!' the lady demurred, 'as for me, I deny it.
for were I worth all the legion of women alive,
1270   and all the wealth in the world at my will possessed,
if I should exchange at my choice and choose me a husband,
for the noble nature I know, Sir Knight, in thee here,
in beauty and bounty and bearing so gay—
of which earlier I have heard, and hold it now true—
1275   then no lord alive would I elect before you.'
'In truth, lady,' he returned, 'you took one far better.
But I am proud of the praise you are pleased to give me,
and as your servant in earnest my sovereign I hold you,
and your knight I become, and may Christ reward you.'
1280   Thus of many matters they spoke till midmorn was passed,
and ever the lady demeaned her as one that loved him much,
and he fenced with her featly, ever flawless in manner.
'Though I were lady most lovely,' thought the lady to herself,
'the less love would he bring here,' since he looked for his bane,
1285   that blow
           that him so soon should grieve,
           and needs it must be so.
           Then the lady asked for leave
           and at once he let her go.

1290   Then she gave him 'good day', and with a glance she laughed,
and as she stood she astonished him with the strength of her words:
'Now He that prospers all speed for this disport repay you!
But that you should be Gawain, it gives me much thought.'
'Why so?', then eagerly the knight asked her,
1295   afraid that he had failed in the form of his converse.
But 'God bless you! For this reason', blithely she answered,
'that one so good as Gawain the gracious is held,
who all the compass of courtesy includes in his person,
so long with a lady could hardly have lingered
1300   without craving a kiss, as a courteous knight,
by some tactful turn that their talk led to.'
Then said Gawain, 'Very well, as you wish be it done.
I will kiss at your command, as becometh a knight,
and more, lest he displease you, so plead it no longer.'
1305   She came near thereupon and caught him in her arms,
and down daintily bending dearly she kissed him.
They courteously commended each other to Christ.
Without more ado through the door she withdrew and departed,
and he to rise up in haste made ready at once.
1310   He calls to his chamberlain, and chooses his clothes,
and goes forth when garbed all gladly to Mass.

Then he went to a meal that meetly awaited him,
and made merry all day, till the moon arose
      o'er earth.
1315   Ne'er was knight so gaily engaged
    between two dames of worth,
    the youthful and the aged:
    together they made much mirth.

And ever the lord of the land in his delight was abroad,
1320 hunting by holt and heath after hinds that were barren.
When the sun began to slope he had slain such a number
of does and other deer one might doubt it were true.
Then the fell folk at last came flocking all in,
and quickly of the kill they a quarry assembled.
1325 Thither the master hastened with a host of his men,
gathered together those greatest in fat
and had them riven open rightly, as the rules require.
At the assay they were searched by some that were there,
and two fingers' breadth of fat they found in the leanest.
1330 Next they slit the eslot, seized on the arber,
shaved it with a sharp knife and shore away the grease;
next ripped the four limbs and rent off the hide.
Then they broke open the belly, the bowels they removed
(flinging them nimbly afar) and the flesh of the knot;
1335 they grasped then the gorge, disengaging with skill
the weasand[9] from the windpipe, and did away with the guts.
Then they shore out the shoulders with their sharpened knives
(drawing the sinews through a small cut) the sides to keep whole;
next they burst open the breast, and broke it apart,
1340 and again at the gorge one begins thereupon,
cuts all up quickly till he comes to the fork,
and fetches forth the fore-numbles;[1] and following after
all the tissues along the ribs they tear away quickly.
Thus by the bones of the back they broke off with skill,
1345 down even to the haunch, all that hung there together,
and hoisted it up all whole and hewed it off there:
and that they took for the numbles, as I trow is their name
      in kind.
    Along the fork of every thigh
1350   the flaps they fold behind;
    to hew it in two they hie,
    down the back all to unbind.

Both the head and the neck they hew off after,
and next swiftly they sunder the sides from the chine,°   *backbone*
1355 and the bone for the crow they cast in the boughs.[2]
Then they thrust through both thick sides with a thong by the rib,
and then by the hocks of the legs they hang them both up:
all the folk earn the fees that fall to their lot.

---

9. The esophagus.
1. Internal organs such as heart, liver, lungs.

2. The gristle at the end of the breastbone was left for the
crows, still another of the prescribed rituals of the hunt.

Upon the fell of the fair beast they fed their hounds then
1360 on the liver and the lights[3] and the leather of the paunches
with bread bathed in blood blended amongst them.
Boldly they blew the prise,[4] amid the barking of dogs,
and then bearing up their venison bent their way homeward,
striking up strongly many a stout horn-call.
1365 When daylight was done they all duly were come
into the noble castle, where quietly the knight
abode
in bliss by bright fire set.
Thither the lord now stroke;
1370 when Gawain with him met,
then free all pleasure flowed.

Then the master commanded his men to meet in that hall,
and both dames to come down with their damsels also;
before all the folk on that floor fair men he ordered
1375 to fetch there forthwith his venison before him,
and all gracious in game to Gawain he called,
announced the number by tally of the nimble beasts,
and showed him the shining fat all shorn on the ribs.
'How does this play please you? Have I praise deserved?
1380 Have I earned by mine art the heartiest thanks?'
'Yea verily,' the other averred, 'here is venison the fairest
that I've seen in seven years in the season of winter!'
'And I give it you all, Gawain,' said the good man at once,
'for as our covenant accorded you may claim it as your own.'
1385 'That is true,' he returned, 'and I tell you the same:
what of worth within these walls I have won also
with as good will, I warrant, 'tis awarded to you.'
His fair neck he enfolded then fast in his arms,
and kissed him with all the kindness that his courtesy knew.
1390 'There take you my gains, sir! I got nothing more.
I would give it up gladly even if greater it were.'
'That is a good one!' quoth the good man. 'Greatly I thank you.
'Tis such, maybe, that you had better briefly now tell me
where you won this same wealth by the wits you possess.'
1395 'That was not the covenant,' quoth he. 'Do not question me
more!
For you've drawn what is due to you, no doubt can you have
'tis true.'
They laugh, and with voices fair
their merriment pursue,
1400 and to supper soon repair
with many dainties new.

Later by the chimney in chamber they were seated,
abundant wine of the best was brought to them oft,
and again as a game they agreed on the morrow

3. Lungs.
4. A thing seized or requisitioned for the king's use by his officers or purveyors, or for the use of the garrisons in his castles.

1405   to abide by the same bond as they had bargained before:
        chance what might chance, to exchange all their trade,
        whatever new thing they got, when they gathered at night.
        They concluded this compact before the courtiers all;
        the drink for the bargain was brought forth in jest;
1410   then their leave at the last they lovingly took,
        and away then at once each went to his bed.
        When the cock had crowed and cackled but thrice,
        the lord had leaped from his bed, and his lieges each one;
        so that their meal had been made, and the Mass was over,
1415   and folk bound for the forest, ere the first daybreak,
                            to chase.
                Loud with hunters and horns
                o'er plains they passed apace,
                and loosed there among the thorns
1420   the running dogs to race.

        Soon these cried for a quest in a covert by a marsh;
        the huntsman hailed the hound that first heeded the scent,
        stirring words he spoke to him with a strident voice.
        The hounds then that heard it hastened thither swiftly,
1425   and fell fast on the line, some forty at once.
        Then such a baying and babel of bloodhounds together
        arose that the rock-wall rang all about them.
        Hunters enheartened them with horn and with mouth,
        and then all in a rout rushed on together
1430   between a fen-pool in that forest and a frowning crag.
        In a tangle under a tall cliff at the tarn's° edges,   *a small mountain lake*
        where the rough rock ruggedly in ruin was fallen,
        they fared to the find, followed by hunters
        who made a cast round the crag and the clutter of stones,
1435   till well they were aware that it waited within:
        the very beast that the baying bloodhounds had spoken.
        Then they beat on the bushes and bade him uprise,
        and forth he came to their peril against folk in his path.
        'Twas a boar without rival that burst out upon them;
1440   long the herd he had left, that lone beast aged,
        for savage was he, of all swine the hugest,
        grim indeed when he grunted. Then aghast were many;
        for three at the first thrust he threw to the ground,
        and spray off with great speed, sparing the others;
1445   and they hallooed on high, and ha! ha! shouted,
        and held horn to mouth, blowing hard the rally.
        Many were the wild mouthings of men and of dogs,
        as they bounded after this boar, him with blare and with din
                            to quell.
1450   Many times he turns to bay,
                and maims the pack pell-mell;
                he hurts many hounds, and they
                grievously yowl and yell.

Hunters then hurried up eager to shoot him,
1455   aimed at him their arrows, often they hit him;
but poor at core proved the points that pitched on his shields,
and the barbs on his brows would bite not at all;
though the shaven shaft shivered in pieces,
back the head came hopping, wherever it hit him.
1460   But when the hurts went home of their heavier strokes,
then with brain wild for battle he burst out upon them,
ruthless he rent them as he rushed forward,
and many quailed at his coming and quickly withdrew.
But the lord on a light horse went leaping after him;
1465   as bold man on battle-field with his bugle he blew
the rally-call as he rode through the rough thickets,
pursuing this wild swine till the sunbeams slanted.
This day in such doings thus duly they passed,
while our brave knight beloved there lies in his bed
1470   at home in good hap, in housings so costly
              and gay.
      The lady did not forget:
      she came to bid good day;
      early she on him set,
1475   his will to wear away.

She passed to the curtain and peeped at the knight.
Sir Gawain graciously then welcomed her first,
and she answered him alike, eagerly speaking,
and sat her softly by his side; and suddenly she laughed,
1480   and with a look full of love delivered these words:
'Sir, if you are Gawain, a wonder I think it
that a man so well-meaning, ever mindful of good,
yet cannot comprehend the customs of the gentle;
and if one acquaints you therewith, you do not keep them in mind:
1485   thou hast forgot altogether what a day ago I taught
by the plainest points I would put into words!'
'What is that?' he said at one. 'I am not aware of it at all.
But if you are telling the truth, I must take all the blame.'
'And yet as to kisses', she quoth, 'this counsel I gave you:
1490   wherever favour is found, defer not to claim them:
that becomes all who care for courteous manners.'
'Take back', said the true knight, 'that teaching, my dear!
For that I dared not do, for dread of refusal.
Were I rebuffed, I should be to blame for so bold an offer.'
1495   'Ma fay!'° said the fair lady, 'you may not be refused;   *French "ma foi,"*
you are stout enough to constrain one by strength, if you like,   *my faith*
if any were so ill bred as to answer you nay.'
'Indeed, by God', quoth Gawain, 'you graciously speak;
but force finds no favour among the folk where I dwell,
1500   and any gift not given gladly and freely.
I am at your call and command to kiss when you please.

You may receive as you desire, and cease as you think
                                in place.'
                    Then down the lady bent,
1505   and sweetly kissed his face.
                    Much speech then there they spent
                    of lovers' grief and grace.

'I would learn from you, lord,' the lady then said,
     'if you would not mind my asking, what is the meaning of this:
1510   that one so young as are you in years, and so gay,
     by renown so well known for knighthood and breeding,
     while of all chivalry the choice, the chief thing to praise,
     is the loyal practice of love: very lore of knighthood—[5]
     for, talking of the toils that these true knights suffer,
1515   it is the title and contents and text of their works:
     how lovers for their true love their lives have imperilled,
     have endured for their dear one dolorous trials,
     until avenged by their valour, their adversity passed,
     they have brought bliss into her bower by their own brave virtues—
1520   and you are the knight of most noble renown in our age,
     and your fame and fair name afar is published,
     and I have sat by your very self now for the second time,
     yet your mouth has never made any remark I have heard
     that ever belonged to love-making, lesser or greater.
1525   Surely, you that are so accomplished and so courtly in your vows
     should be prompt to expound to a young pupil
     by signs and examples the science of lovers.
     Why? Are you ignorant who all honour enjoy?
     Or else you esteem me too stupid to understand your courtship?
1530   But nay!
                    Here single I come and sit,
                    a pupil for your play;
                    come, teach me of your wit,
                    while my lord is far away.'

1535   'In good faith', said Gawain, 'may God reward you!
     Great delight I gain, and am glad beyond measure
     that one so worthy as you should be willing to come here
     and take pains with so poor a man: as for playing with your knight,
     showing favour in any form, it fills me with joy.
1540   But for me to take up the task on true love to lecture,
     to comment on the text and tales of knighthood
     to you, who I am certain possess far more skill
     in that art by the half than a hundred of such
     as I am, or shall ever be while on earth I remain,
1545   it would be folly manifold, in faith, my lady!
     All your will I would wish to work, as I am able,
     being so beholden in honour, and, so help me the Lord,
     desiring ever the servant of yourself to remain.'
     Thus she tested and tried him, tempting him often,

5. The lady compares Gawain's behavior to descriptions of courtly love in romances; the poem is mirrored within itself.

1550   so as to allure him to love-making, whatever lay in her heart.
But his defence was so fair that no fault could be seen,
nor any evil upon either side, nor aught but joy
                     they wist.
           They laughed and long they played;
1555   at least she him then kissed,
           with grace adieu him bade,
           and went whereso she list.

Then rousing from his rest he rose to hear Mass,
and then their dinner was laid and daintily served.
1560   The livelong day with the ladies in delight he spent,
but the lord o'er the lands leaped to and fro,
pursuing his fell swine that o'er the slopes hurtled
and bit asunder the backs of the best of his hounds,
wherever to bay he was brought, until bowmen dislodged him,
1565   and made him, maugre his teeth, move again onward,
so fast the shafts flew when the folk were assembled.
And yet the stoutest of them still he made start there aside,
till at least he was so spent he could speed no further,
but in such haste as he might he made for a hollow
1570   on a reef beside a rock where the river was flowing.
He put the bank at his back, began then to paw;
fearfully the froth of his mouth foamed from the corners;
he whetted his white tusks. Then weary were all
the brave men so bold as by him to stand
1575   of plaguing him from afar, yet for peril they dared not
                        come nigher.
           He had hurt so many before,
           that none had now desire
           to be torn with the tusks once more
1580   of a beast both mad and dire.

Till the knight himself came, his courser spurring,
and saw him brought there to bay, and all about him his men.
Nothing loth he alighted, and leaving his horse,
brandished a bright blade and boldly advanced,
1585   striding stoutly through the ford to where stood the felon.
The wild beast was aware of him with his weapon in hand,
and high raised his hair; with such hate he snorted
that folk feared for the knight, lest his foe should worst him.
Out came the swine and set on him at once,
1590   and the boar and the brave man were both in a mellay
in the wildest of the water. The worse had the beast,
for the man marked him well, and as they met he at once
struck steadily his point straight in the neck-slot,
and hit him up to the hilts, so that his heart was riven,
1595   and with a snarl he succumbed, and was swept down the water
                      straightway.
           A hundred hounds him caught,
           and fiercely bit their prey;
           the men to the bank him brought,

1600   and dogs him dead did lay.

There men blew for the prise in many a blaring horn,
and high and loud hallooed all the hunters that could;
bloodhounds bayed for the beast, as bade the masters,
who of that hard-run chase were the chief huntsmen.
1605 Then one that was well learned in woodmen's lore
with pretty cunning began to carve up this boar.
First he hewed off his head and on high set it,
then he rent him roughly down the ridge of the back,
brought out the bowels, burned them on gledes,
1610 and with them, blended with blood, the bloodhounds rewarded.
Next he broke up the boar-flesh in broad slabs of brawn,
and haled forth the hastlets in order all duly,
and yet all whole he fastened the halves together,
and strongly on a stout pole he strung them then up.
1615 Now with this swine homeward swiftly they hastened,
and the boar's head was borne before the brave knight himself
who felled him in the ford by force of his hand
          so great.
       Until he saw Sir Gawain
1620   in the hall he could hardly wait.
       He called, and his pay to gain
       the other came there straight.

The lord with his loud voice and laughter merry
gaily he greeted him when Gawain he saw.
1625 The fair ladies were fetched and the folk all assembled,
and he showed them the shorn slabs, and shaped his report
of the width and wondrous length, and the wickedness also
in war, of the wild swine, as in the woods he had fled.
With fair words his friend the feat then applauded,
1630 and praised the great prowess he had proved in his deeds;
for such brawn on a beast, the brave knight declared,
or such sides on a swine he had never seen before.
They then handled the huge head, and highly he praised it,
showing horror at the hideous thing to honour the lord.
1635 'Now, Gawain,' said the good man, 'this game is your own
by close covenant we concluded, as clearly you know.'
'That is true,' he returned, 'and as truly I assure you
all my winnings, I warrant, I shall award you in exchange.'
He clasped his neck, and courteously a kiss he then gave him
1640 and swiftly with a second he served him on the spot.
'Now we are quits,' he quoth, 'and clear for this evening
of all covenants we accorded, since I cam to this house,
          as is due.'
       The lord said: 'By Saint Gile,[6]
1645   you rmatch I never knew!
       You'll be wealthy in a while,
       such trade if you pursue.'

6. A hermit and patron saint of woodlands.

Then on top of the trestles the tables they laid,
cast the cloths thereon, and clear light then
1650   wakened along the walls; waxen torches
men set there, and servants went swift about the hall.
Much gladness and gaiety began then to spring
round the fire on the hearth, and freely and oft
at supper and later: many songs of delight,
1655   such as canticles of Christmas, and new carol-dances,
amid all the mannerly mirth that men can tell of;
and ever our noble knight was next to the lady.
Such glances she gave him of her gracious favour,
secretly stealing sweet looks that strong man to charm,
1660   that he was passing perplexed, and ill-pleased at heart.
Yet he would fain not of his courtesy coldly refuse her,
but graciously engaged her, however against the grain
                    the play.
        When mirth they had made in hall
1665   as long as they wished to stay,
            to a room did the lord them call
            and to the ingle they made their way.

There amid merry words and wine they had a mind once more
to harp on the same note on New Yea's Eve.
1670   But said Gawain: 'Grant me leave to go on the morrow!
For the appointment approaches that I pledged myself to.'
The lord was loth to allow it, and longer would keep him,
and said: 'As I am a true man I swear on my troth
the Green Chapel thou shalt gain, and go to your business
1675   in the dawn of New Year, sir, ere daytime egins.
So still lie upstairs and stay at thine ease,
and I shall hunt in the holt here, and hold to my terms
with thee truly, when I return, to trade all our gains.
For I have tested thee twice, and trusty I find thee.
1680   Now 'third time pays for all', bethink thee tomorrow!
Make we merry while we may and be mindful of joy,
for the woe one may win whenever one wishes!'
This was graciously agreed, and Gawain would linger.
Then gaily drink is given them and they go to their beds
1685   with light.
        Sir Gawain lies and sleeps
            soft and sound all night;
            his host to his hunting keeps,
            and is early arrayed aright.

1690   After Mass of a morsel he and his men partook.
Merry was the morning. For his mount then he called.
All the huntsmen that on horse behind him should follow
were ready mounted to ride arrayed at the gates.
Wondrous fair were the fields, for the frost clung there;
1695   in red rose-hued o'er the wrack arises the sun,
sailing clear along the coasts of the cloudy heavens.

The hunters loosed hounds by a holt-border;
the rocks rang in the wood to the roar of their horns.
Some fell on the line to where the fox was lying,
1700 crossing and re-crossing it in the cunning of their craft.
A hound then gives tongue, the huntsman names him,
round him press his companions in a pack all snuffling,
running forth in a rabble then right in his path.
The fox flits before them. They find him at once,
1705 and when they see him by sight they pursue him hotly,
decrying him full clearly with a clamour of wrath.
He dodges and ever doubles through many a dense coppice,
and looping oft he lurks and listens under fences.
At last a little ditch he leaps o'er a thorn-hedge,
1710 sneaks out secretly by the side of a thicket,
weens he is out of the wood and away by his wiles from the hounds.
Thus he went unawares to a watch that was posted,
where fierce on him fell three foes at once
                    all grey.
1715   He swerves then swift again,
             and dauntless darts astray;
             in grief and in great pain
             to the wood he turns away.

Then to hark to the hounds it was heart's delight,
1720 when all the pack came upon him, there pressing together.
Such a curse at the view they called down on him
that the clustering cliffs might have clattered in ruin.
Here he was hallooed when hunters came on him,
yonder was he assailed with snarling tongues;
1725 there he was threatened and oft thief was he called,
with ever the trailers at his trail so that tarry he could not.
Oft was he run at, if he rushed outwards;
oft he swerved in again, so subtle was Reynard.
Yea! he led the lord and his hunt as laggards behind him
1730 thus by mount and by hill till mid-afternoon.
Meanwhile the courteous knight in the castle in comfort slumbered
behind the comely curtains in the cold morning.
But the lady in love-making had no liking to sleep
nor to disappoint the purpose she had planned in her heart;
1735 but rising up swiftly his room now she sought
in a gay mantle that to the ground was measured
and was fur-lined most fairly with fells well trimmed,
with no comely coif° on her head, only the clear jewels   *close-fitting cap*
that were twined in her tressure[7] by twenties in clusters;
1740 her noble face and her neck all naked were laid,
her breast bare in front and at the back also.
She came through the chamber-door and closed it behind her,
wide set a window, and to wake him she called,
thus greeting him gaily with her gracious words
1745   of cheer:

7. Ornamental hairnet.

'Ah! man, how canst thou sleep,
the morning is so clear!'
He lay in darkness deep,
but her call he then could hear.

1750 In heavy darkness drowsing he dream-words muttered,
as a man whose mind was bemused with many mournful thoughts,
how destiny should his doom on that day bring him
when he at the Green Chapel the great man would meet,
and be obliged his blow to abide without debate at all.
1755 But when so comely she came, he recalled then his wits,
swept aside his slumbers, and swiftly made answer.
The lady in lovely guise came laughing sweetly,
bent down o'er his dear face, and deftly kissed him.
He greeted her graciously with a glad welcome,
1760 seeing her so glorious and gaily attired,
so faultless in her features and so fine in her hues
that at once joy up-welling went warm to his heart.
With smiles sweet and soft they turned swiftly to mirth,
and only brightness and bliss was broached there between them
1765 so gay.
They spoke then speeches good,
much pleasure was in that play;
great peril between them stood,
unless Mary for her knight should pray.

1770 For she, queenly and peerless, pressed him so closely,
led him so near the line, that at least he must needs
either refuse her with offence or her favours there take.
He cared for his courtesy, lest a caitiff he proved,
yet more for his sad case, if he should sin commit
1775 and to the owner of the house, to his host, be a traitor.
'God help me!' said he. 'Happen that shall not!'
Smiling sweetly aside from himself then he turned
all the fond words of favour that fall from her lips.
Said she to the knight then: 'Now shame you deserve,
1780 if you love not one that lies alone here beside you,
who beyond all women in the world is wounded in heart,
unless you have a lemman, more beloved, whom you like better,
and have affianced faith to that fair one so fast and so true
that your release you desire not—and so I believe now;
1785 and to tell me if that be so truly, I beg you.
For all sakes that men swear by conceal not the truth
in guile.'
The knight said: 'By Saint John,'
and softly gave a smile,
1790 'Nay! lover have I none,
and none will have meanwhile.'

'Those words', said the woman, 'are the worst that could be.
But I am answered indeed, and 'tis hard to endure.
Kiss me now kindly, and I will quickly depart.

1795   I may but mourn while I love as one that much is in love.'
       Sighing she sank down, and sweetly she kissed him;
       then soon she left his side, and said as she stood there:
       'Now, my dear, at this parting do me this pleasure,
       give me something as thy gift, thy glove it might be,
1800   that I may remember thee, dear man, my mourning to lessen.'
       'Now on my word,' then said he, 'I wish I had here
       the loveliest thing for thy delight that in my land I possess;
       for worthily have you earned wondrously often
       more reward by rights than within my reach would now be,
1805   save to allot you as love-token thing of little value.
       Beneath your honour it is to have here and now
       a glove for a guerdon° as the gift of Sir Gawain: *reward*
       and I am here on an errand in unknown lands,
       and have no bearers with baggage and beautiful things
1810   (unluckily, dear lady) for your delight at this time.
       A man must do as he is placed; be not pained nor aggrieved,'
                                      said he.
               Said she so comely clad:
                  'Nay, noble knight and free,
1815   though naught of yours I had,
                  you should get a gift from me.'

       A rich ring she offered him of red gold fashioned,
       with a stone like a star standing up clear
       that bore brilliant beams as bright as the sun:
1820   I warrant you it was worth wealth beyond measure.
       But the knight said nay to it, and announced then at once:
       'I will have no gifts, fore God, of your grace at this time.
       I have none to return you, and naught will I take.'
       She proffered it and pressed him, and he her pleading refused,
1825   and swore swiftly upon his word that accept it he would not.
       And she, sorry that he refused, said to him further:
       'If to my ring you say nay, since too rich it appears,
       and you would not so deeply be indebted to me,
       I shall give you my girdle, less gain will that be.'
1830   She unbound a belt swiftly that embracing her sides
       was clasped above her kirtle under her comely mantle.
       Fashioned it was of green silk, and with gold finished,
       though only braided round about, embroidered by hand;
       and this she would give to Gawain, and gladly besought him,
1835   of no worth though it were, to be willing to take it.
       And he said nay, he would not, he would never receive
       either gold or jewelry, ere God the grace sent him
       to accomplish the quest on which he had come thither.
       'And therefore I pray you, please be not angry,
1840   and cease to insist on it, for to your suit I will ever
                                      say no.
               I am deeply in debt to you
                  for the favour that you show,
                  to be your servant true
1845   for ever in weal or woe.'

'Do you refuse now this silk,' said the fair lady,
'because in itself it is poor? And so it appears.
See how small 'tis in size, and smaller in value!
But one who knew of the nature that is knit therewithin
1850   would appraise it probably at a price far higher
For whoever goes girdled with this green riband,
while he keeps it well clasped closely about him,
there is none so hardy under heaven that to hew him were able;
for he could not be killed by any cunning of hand.'
1855   The knight then took note, and thought now in his heart,
'twould be a prize in that peril that was appointed to him.
When he gained the Green Chapel to get there his sentence,
if by some sleight he were not slain, 'twould be a sovereign device.
Then he bore with her rebuke, and debated not her words;
1860   and she pressed him on the belt, and proffered it in earnest;
and he agreed, and she gave it very gladly indeed,
and prayed him for her sake to part with it never,
but on his honour hide it from her husband; and he then agreed
that no one ever should know, nay, none in the world
1865   buy they.
           With earnest heart and mood
           great thanks he oft did say.
           She then the knight so good
           a third time kissed that day.

1870   Then she left him alone, her leave taking,
for amusement from the man no more could she get.
When she was gone Sir Gawain got him soon ready,
arose and robed himself in raiment noble.
He laid up the love-lace that the lady had given,
1875   hiding it heedfully where he after might find it.
Then first of all he chose to fare to the chapel,
privately approached a priest, and prayed that he there
would uplift his life, that he might learn better
how his soul should be saved, when he was sent from the world.
1880   There he cleanly confessed him and declared his misdeeds,
both the more and the less, and for mercy he begged,
to absolve him of them all he besought the good man;
and he assoiled him and made him as safe and as clean
as for Doom's Day indeed, were it due on the morrow.[8]
1885   Thereafter more merry he made among the fair ladies,
with carol-dances gentle and all kinds of rejoicing,
than ever he did ere that day, till the darkness of night,
              in bliss.
           Each man there said: 'I vow
1890   a delight to all he is!
           Since hither he came till now,
           he was ne'er so gay as this.'

---

8. Gawain's confession and absolution are problematic, since he has just accepted the green girdle and resolved to break the covenant of exchange with his host.

Now indoors let him dwell and have dearest delight,
while the free lord yet fares afield in his sports!
1895   At last the fox he has felled that he followed so long;
for, as he spurred through a spinney° to espy there the villain,   *a small wood*
where the hounds he had heard that hard on him pressed,
Reynard on his road came through a rough thicket,
and all the rabble in a rush were right on his heels.
1900   The man is aware of the wild thing, and watchful awaits him,
brings out his bright brand and at the beast hurls it;
and he blenched at the blade, and would have backed if he could.
A hound hastened up, and had him ere he could;
and right before the horse's feet they fell on him all,
1905   and worried there the wily one with a wild clamour.
The lord quickly alights and lifts him at once,
snatching him swiftly from their slavering mouths,
holds him high o'er his head, hallooing loudly;
and there bay at him fiercely many furious hounds.
1910   Huntsmen hurried thither, with horns full many
ever sounding the assembly, till they saw the master.
When together had come his company noble,
all that ever bore bugle were blowing at once,
and all the others hallooed that had not a horn:
1915   it was the merriest music that ever men harkened,
the resounding song there raised that for Reynard's soul
                    awoke.
        To hounds they pay their fees,
        their heads they fondly stroke,
1920   and Reynard then they seize,
        and off they skin his cloak.

And then homeward they hastened, for at hand was now night,
making strong music on their mighty horns.
The lord alighted at last at his beloved abode,
1925   found a fire in the hall, and fair by the hearth
Sir Gawain the good, and gay was he too,
among the ladies in delight his lot was most joyful.
He was clad in a blue cloak that came to the ground;
his surcoat well beseemed him with its soft lining,
1930   and its hood of like hue that hung on his shoulder:
all fringed with white fur very finely were both.
He met indeed the master in the midst of the floor,
and in gaiety greeted him, and graciously said:
'In this case I will first our covenant fulfil
1935   that to our good we agreed, when ungrudged went the drink.'
He clasps then the knight and kisses him thrice,
as long and deliciously as he could lay them upon him.
'By Christ!' the other quoth, 'you've come by a fortune
in winning such wares, were they worth what you paid.'
1940   'Indeed, the price was not important,' promptly he answered,
'whereas plainly is paid now the profit I gained.'
'Marry!' said the other man, 'mine is not up to't;

for I have hunted all this day, and naught else have I got
but this foul fox-fell—the Fiend have the goods!—
1945   and that is price very poor to pay for such treasures
as these you have thrust upon me, three such kisses
                so good.'
        'Tis enough,' then said Gawain.
        'I thank you, by the Rood,'
1950   and how the fox was slain
        he told him as they stood.

With mirth and minstrelsy and meats at their pleasure
as merry they made as any men could be;
amid the laughter of ladies and light words of jest
1955   both Gawain and the good man could no gayer have proved,
unless they had doted indeed or else drunken had been.
Both the host and his household went on with their games,
till the hour had approached when part must they all;
to bed were now bound the brave folk at last.
1960   Bowing low his leave of the lord there first
the good knight then took, and graciously thanked him:[9]
'For such a wondrous welcome as within these walls I have had,
for your honour at this high feast the High King reward you!
In your service I set myself, your servant, if you will.
1965   For I must needs make a move tomorrow, as you know,
if you give me some good man to go, as you promised,
and guide me to the Green Chapel, as God may permit me
to face on New Year's day such doom as befalls me.'
'On my word,' said his host, 'with hearty good will
1970   to all that ever I promised I promptly shall hold.'
Then a servant he assigns him to set him on the road,
and by the downs to conduct him, that without doubt or delay
he might through wild and through wood ways most straight
                pursue.
1975   Said Gawain, 'My thanks receive,
        such a favour you will do!'
        The knight then took his leave
        of those noble ladies two.

Sadly he kissed them and said his farewells,
1980   and pressed oft upon them in plenty his thanks,
and they promptly the same again repaid him;
to God's keeping they gave him, grievously sighing.
Then from the people of the castle he with courtesy parted;
all the men that he met he remembered wiht thanks
1985   for their care for his comfort and their kind service,
and the trouble each had taken in attendance upon him;
and every one was as woeful to wish him adieu
as had they lived all their lives with his lordship in honour.
Then with link-men and lights he was led to his chamber

9. Gawain's highly stylized leave-taking is typical of courtly romance and again emphasizes his command of fine manners.

1990   and brought sweetly to bed, there to be at his rest.
That soundly he slept then assert will I not,
for he had many matters in the morning to mind, if he would,
                                    in thought.
              There let him lie in peace,
1995   near now is the tryst he sought.
              If a while you will hold your peace,
              I will tell the deeds they wrought!

Part 4

Now New Year draws near and the night passes,
day comes driving the dark, as ordained by God;
2000   but wild weathers of the world awake in the land,
clouds cast keenly the cold upon earth
with bitter breath from the North biting the naked.
Snow comes shivering sharp to shrivel the wild things,
and whistling wind whirls from the heights
2005   and drives every dale full of drifts very deep.
Long the knight listens as he lies in his bed;
though he lays down his eyelids, very little he sleeps:
at the crow of every cock he recalls well his tryst.
Briskly he rose from his bed ere the break of day,
2010   for there was light from a lamp that illumined his chamber.
He called to his chamberlain, who quickly him answered,
and he bade him bring his byrnie and his beast saddle.
The man got him up and his gear fetched him,
and garbed then Sir Gawain in great array;
2015   first he clad him in his clothes to keep out the cold,
and after that in his harness that with heed had been tended,
both his pauncer and his plates polished all brightly,
the rings rid of the rust on his rich byrnie:
all was neat as if new, and the knight him thanked
2020   with delight.
              He put on every piece
              all burnished well and bright;
              most gallant from here to Greece
              for his courser called the knight.

2025   While the proudest of his apparel he put on himself:
his coat-armour, with the cognisance of the clear symbol
upon velvet environed with virtuous gems
all bound and braided about it, with broidered seams
and with fine firs lined wondrous fairly within,
2030   yet he overlooked not the lace that the lady had given him;
that Gawain forgot not, of his own good thinking;
when he had belted his brand upon his buxom haunches,
he twined the love-token twice then about him,
and swiftly he swathed it sweetly about his waist,
2035   that girdle of green silk, and gallant it looked
upon the royal red cloth that was rich to behold.
But he wore not for worth nor for wealth this girdle,

not for pride in the pendants, though polished they were,
not though the glittering gold there gleamed at the ends,
2040   but so that himself he might save when suffer he must,
must abide bane without debating it with blade or with brand
                              of war.
              When arrayed the knight so bold
              came out before the door,
2045   to all that high household
              great thanks he gave once more.

Now Gringolet was groomed, the great horse and high,
who had been lodged to his liking and loyally tended:
fain to gallop was that gallant horse for his good fettle.
2050   His master to him came and marked well his coat,
and said: 'Now solemnly myself I swear on my troth
there is a company in this castle that is careful of honour!
Their lord that them leads, may his lot be joyful!
Their beloved lady in life may delight befall her!
2055   If they out of charity thus cherish a guest,
upholding their house in honour, may He them reward
that upholds heaven on high, and all of you too!
And if life a little longer I might lead upon earth,
I would give you some guerdon gladly, were I able.'
2060   Then he steps in the stirrup and strides on his horse;
his shield his man showed him, and on shoulder he slung it,
Gringolet he goaded with his gilded heels,
and he plunged forth on the pavement, and prancing no more
                              stood there.
2065   Ready now was his squire to ride
              that his helm and lance would bear.
              'Christ keep his castle!' he cried
              and wished it fortune fair.

The bridge was brought down and the broad gates then
2070   unbarred and swung back upon both hinges.
The brave man blessed himself, and the boards crossing,
bade the porter up rise, who before the prince kneeling
gave him 'Good day, Sir Gawain!', and 'God save you!'
Then he went on his way with the one many only
2075   to guide him as he goes to that grievous place
where he is due to endure the dolorous blow.
They go by banks and by braes where branches are bare,[1]
they climb along cliffs where clingeth the cold;
the heavens are lifted high, but under them evilly
2080   mist hangs moist on the moor, melts on the mountains;
every hill has a hat, a mist-mantle huge.
Brooks break and boil on braes all about,
bright bubbling on their banks where they bustle downwards.

---

1. The grimness of this landscape, reminiscent of wastelands in Anglo-Saxon poetry, swiftly returns the poem from the courtly world to the elemental challenge Gawain now faces.

Very wild through the wood is the way they must take,
2085   until soon comes the season when the sun rises
that day.
On a high hill they abode,
white snow beside them lay;
the man that by him rode
2090   there bade his master stay.

'For so far I have taken you, sir, at this time,
and now you are near to that noted place
that you have enquired and questioned so curiously after.
But I will announce now the truth, since you are known to me,
2095   and you are a lord in this life that I love greatly,
if you would follow my advice you would fare better.
The place that you pass to, men perilous hold it,
the worst wight in the world in that waste dwelleth;
for he is stout and stern, and to strike he delights,
2100   and he mightier than any man upon middle-earth is,
and his body is bigger than the four best men
that are in Arthur's house, either Hestor[2] or others.
All goes as he chooses at the Green Chapel;
no one passes by that place so proud in his arms
2105   that he hews not to death by dint of his hand.
For he is a man mounstrous, and mercy he knows not;
for be it a churl or a chaplain that by the Chapel rideth,
a monk or a mass-priest or any man besides,
he would as soon have him slain as himself go alive.
2110   And so I say to you, as sure as you sit in your saddle,
if you come there, you'll be killed, if the carl has his way.
Trust me, that is true, though you had twenty lives
to yeild.
He here has dwelt now long
2115   and stirred much strife on field;
against his strokes so strong
yourself you cannot shield.

And so, good Sir Gawain, now go another way,
and let the man alone, for the love of God, sir!
2120   Come to some other country, and there may Christ keep you!
And I shall haste me home again, and on my honour I promise
that I swear will be God and all His gracious saints,
so help me God and the Halidom,[3] and other oaths a plenty,
that I will safe keep your secret, and say not a word
2125   that ever you fain were to flee for any foe that I knew of.'
'Gramercy!' quoth Gawain, and regretfully answered:
'Well, man, I wish thee, who wishest my good,
and keep safe my secret, I am certain thou wouldst.
But however heedfully thou hid it, if I here departed,

---

2. Chief hero among the defenders of Troy and, like Arthur, one of the "Nine Worthies" celebrated for their heroic valor; or perhaps Arthur's knight Hector De Maris. 3. "By my holy relics."

2130   fain in fear now to flee, in the fashion thou speakest,
       I should a knight coward be, I could not be excused.
       Nay, I'll fare to the Chapel, whatever chance may befall,
       and have such words with that wild man as my wish is to say,
       come fair or come foul, as fate will allot
2135   me there.
                   He may be a fearsome knave
                   to tame, and club may bear;
                   but His servants true to save
                   the Lord can well prepare.'

2140   'Marry!' quoth the other man, 'now thou makest it so clear
       that thou wishest thine own bane to bring on thyself,
       and to lose thy life hast a liking, to delay thee I care not!
       Have here thy helm on thy head, thy spear in thy hand,
       and ride down by yon rock-side where runs this same track,
2145   till thou art brought to the bottom of the baleful valley.
       A little to thy left hand then look o'er the green,
       and thou wilt see on the slope the selfsame chapel,
       and the great man and grim on ground that it keeps.
       Now farewell in God's name, Gawain the noble!
2150   For all the gold in the world I would not go with thee,
       nor bear thee fellowship through this forest one foot further!'
       With that his bridle towards the wood back the man turneth,
       hits his horse with his heels as hard as he can,
       gallops on the greenway, and the good knight there leaves
2155   alone,
                   Quoth Gawain: 'By God on high
                   I will neither grieve nor groan.
                   With God's will I comply,
                   Whose protection I do own.'

2160   Then he puts spurs to Gringolet, and espying the track,
       thrust in along a bank by a thicket's border,
       rode down the rough brae right to the valley;
       and then he gazed all about: a grim place he thought it,
       and saw no sign of shelter on any side at all,
2165   only high hillsides sheer upon either hand,
       and notched knuckled crags with gnarled boulders;
       the very skies by the peaks were scraped, it appeared.
       Then he halted and held in his horse for the time,
       and changed oft his front the Chapel to find.
2170   Such on no side he saw, as seemed to him strange,
       save a mound as it might be near the marge of a green,
       a worn barrow[4] on a brae by the brink of a water,
       beside falls in a flood that was flowing down;
       the burn bubbled therein, as if boiling it were.
2175   He urged on his horse then, and came up to the mound,
       there lightly alit, and lashed to a tree

---

4. The barrow, perhaps a burial mound, seems to link the moment to ancient, probably pagan, inhabitants.

his reins, with a rough branch rightly secured them.
Then he went to the barrow and about it he walked,
debating in his mind what might the thing be.
2180   It had a hole at the end and at either side
and with grass in green patches was grown all over,
and was all hollow within: nought but an old cavern,
or a cleft in an old crag; he could not it name
aright.
2185   'Can this be the Chapel Green,
O Lord?' said the gentle knight.
'Here the Devil might say, I ween,
his matins about midnight!'

'On my word,' quoth Gawain, ''tis a wilderness here!
2190   This oratory looks evil. With herbs overgrown
it fits well that fellow transformed into green
to follow here his devotions in the Devil's fashion.
Now I feel in my five wits the Fiend 'tis himself
that has trapped me with this trust to destroy me here.
2195   This is a chapel of mischance, the church most accursed
that ever I entered. Evil betide it!'
With high helm on his head, his lance in his hand,
he roams up to the roof of that rough dwelling.
Then he heard from the high hill, in a hard rock-wall
2200   beyond the stream on a steep, a sudden startling noise.
How it clattered in the cliff, as if to cleave it asunder,
as if one upon a grindstone were grinding a scythe!
How it whirred and it rasped as water in a mill-race!
How it rushed, and it rang, rueful to harken!
2205   Then 'By God,' quoth Gawain, 'I guess this ado
is meant for my honour, meetly to hail me
as knight!
As God wills! Waylaway!
That helps me not a mite.
2210   My life though down I lay,
no noise can me affright.'

Then clearly the knight there called out aloud:
'Who is master in this place to meet me at tryst?
For now 'tis good Gawain on ground that here walks.
2215   If any aught hath to ask, let him hasten to me,
either now or else never, his needs to further!'
'Stay!' said one standing above on the steep o'er his head,
'and thou shalt get in good time what to give thee I vowed.'
Still with that rasping and racket he rushed on a while,
2220   and went back to his whetting, till he wished to descent.
And then he climbed past a crag, and came from a hole,
hurtling out of a hid nook with a horrible weapon:
a Danish axe[5] newly dressed the dint to return,

5. A long-bladed ax, associated with Viking raiders.

with cruel cutting-edge curved along the handle—
2225   filed on a whetstone, and four feet in width,
'twas no less—along its lace of luminous hue;
and the great man in green still guised as before,
his locks and long beard, his legs and his face,
save that firm on his feet he fared on the ground,
2230   steadied the haft on the stones and stalked beside it.
When he walked to the water, where he wade would not,
he hopped over on his axe and haughtily strode,
fierce and fell on a field where far all about
                    lay snow.
2235   Sir Gawain the man met there,
                neither bent nor bowed he low.
                The other said: 'Now, sirrah fair,
                I true at tryst thee know!'

'Gawain,' said that green man, 'may God keep thee!
2240   On my word, sir, I welcome thee with a will to my place,
and thou hast timed thy travels as trust man should,
and thou hast forgot not the engagement agreed on between us:
at this time gone a twelvemonth thou took'st thy allowance,
and I should now this New Year nimbly repay thee.
2245   And we are in this valley now verily on our own,
there are no people to part us—we can play as we like.
Have thy helm off thy head, and have here thy pay!
Bandy me no more debate than I brought before thee
when thou didst sweep off my head with one swipe only!'
2250   'Nay,' quoth Gawain, 'by God that gave me my soul,
I shall grudge thee not a grain any grief that follows.
Only restrain thee to one stroke, and still shall I stand
and offer thee no hindrance to act as thou likest
                    right here.'
2255   With a nod of his neck he bowed,
                let bare the flesh appear;
                he would not by dread be cowed,
                no sign he gave of fear.

Then the great man in green gladly prepared him,
2260   gathered up his grim tool there Gawain to smite;
with all the lust in his limbs aloft he heaved it,
shaped as mighty a stroke as if he meant to destroy him.
Had it driving come down as dour as he aimed it,
under his dint would have died the most doughty man ever.
2265   But Gawain on that guisarm then glanced to one side,
as down it came gliding on the green there to end him,
and he shrank a little with his shoulders at the sharp iron.
With a jolt the other man jerked back the blade,
and reproved then the prince, proudly him taunting.
2270   'Thou'rt not Gawain,' said the green man, 'who is so good reported,
who never flinched from any foes on fell or in dale;
and now thou fleest in fear, ere thou feelest a hurt!

Of such cowardice that knight I ne'er heard accused.
Neither blenched I nor backed, when thy blow, sir, thou aimedst,
2275 nor uttered any cavil in the court of King Arthur.
My head flew to my feet, and yet fled I never;
but thou, ere thou hast any hurt, in thy heart quailest,
and so the nobler knight to be named I deserve
                    therefore.'
2280   'I blenched once,' Gawain said,
              'and I will do so no more.
              But if on floor now falls my head,
              I cannot it restore.

But get busy, I beg, sir, and bring me to the point.
2285 Deal me my destiny, and do it out of hand!
For I shall stand from thee a stroke and stir not again
till thine axe hath hit me, have here my word on't!'
'Have at thee then!' said the other, and heaved it aloft,
and wratched him as wrathfully as if he were wild with rage.
2290 He made at him a mighty aim, but the man touched not,
holding back hastily his hand, ere hurt it might do.
Gawain warily awaited it, and winced with no limb,
but stood as still as a stone or the stump of a tree
that with a hundred ravelled roots in rocks is embedded.
2295 This time merrily remarked then the man in the green:
'So, now thou hast they heart whole, a hit I must make.
May the high order now keep thee that Arthur gave thee,
and guard thy gullet at this go, if it can gain thee that.'
Angrily with ire then answered Sir Gawain:
2300 'Why! last away, thou lusty man! Too long dost thou threaten.
'Tis thy heart methinks in thee that now quaileth!'
'In faith,' said the fellow, 'so fiercely thou speakest,
I no longer will linger delaying thy errand
                    right now.'
2305   Then to strike he took his stance
              and grimaced with lip and brow.
              He that of rescue saw no chance
              was little pleased, I trow.

Lightly his weapon he lifted, and let it down neatly
2310 with the bent horn of the blade towards the neck that was bare;
though he hewed with a hammer-swing, he hurt him no more
than to snick him on one side and sever the skin.
Through the fair fat sank the edge, and the flesh entered,
   so that the shining blood o'er his shoulders was shed on the earth;
2315 and when the good knight saw the gore that gleamed on the snow,
he sprang out with spurning feet a spear's length and more,
in haste caught his helm and on his head cast it,
under his fair shield he shot with a shake of his shoulders,[6]
brandished his bright sword, and boldly he spake—

6. Gawain, who has displayed so much courtly refinement and religious emotion, now shows himself a practiced fighter, swiftly pulling his armor into place.

2320 never since he as manchild of his mother was born
was he ever on this earth half so happy a man:
'Have done, sir, with thy dints! Now deal me no more!
I have stood from thee a stroke without strife on this spot,
and if thou offerest me others, I shall answer thee promptly,
2325 and give as good again, and as grim, be assured,
     shall pay.
    But one stroke here's my due,
    as the covenant clear did say
    that in Arthur's halls we drew.
2330   And so, good sir, now stay!'

From him the other stood off, and on his axe rested,
held the haft to the ground, and on the head leaning,
gazed at the good knight as on the green he there strode.
To see him standing so stout, so stern there and fearless,
2335 armed and unafraid, his heart it well pleased.
Then merrily he spoke with a mighty voice,
and loudly it rang, as to that lord he said:
'Fearless knight on this field, so fierce do not be!
No man here unmannerly hath thee maltreated,
2340 nor aught given thee not granted by agreement at court.
A hack I thee vowed, and thou'st had it, so hold thee content;
I remit thee the remnant of all rights I might claim.
If I brisker had been, a buffet, it may be,
I could have handed three more harshly, and harm could have done thee.
2345 First I menaced thee in play with no more than a trial,
and clove thee with no cleft: I had a claim to the feint,
for the fast pact we affirmed on the first evening,
and thou fairly and unfailing didst faith with me keep,
all thy gains thou me gavest, as good man ought.
2350 The other trial for the morning, man, I thee tendered
when thou kissedst my comely wife, and the kisses didst render.
For the two here I offered only two harmless feints
     to make.
    The true shall truly repay,
2355   for no peril then need he quake.
    Thou didst fail on the third day,
    and so that tap now take!

For it is my weed that thou wearest, that very woven girdle:
my own wife it awarded thee, I wot well indeed.
2360 Now I am aware of thy kisses, and thy courteous ways,
and of thy wooing by my wife: I worked that myself!
I sent her to test thee, and thou seem'st to me truly
the fair knight most faultless that e'er foot set on earth!
As a pearl than white pease is prized more highly,
2365 so is Gawain, in good faith, than other gallant knights.
But in this you lacked, sir, a little, and of loyalty came short.
But that was for no artful wickedness, nor for wooing either,
but because you loved your own life: the less do I blame you.'

The other stern knight in a study then stood a long while,
2370   in such grief and disgust he had a grue° in his heart;   *shiver; shudder*
all the blood from his breast in his blush mingled,
and he shrank into himself with shame at that speech.
The first words on that field that he found then to say
were: 'Cursed be ye, Coveting, and Cowardice also!
2375   In you is vileness, and vice that virtue destroyeth.'
He took then the treacherous thing, and untying the knot
fiercely flung he the belt at the feet of the knight:
'See there the falsifier, and foul be its fate!
Through care for thy blow Cowardice brought me
2380   to consent to Coveting, my true kind to forsake,
which is free-hand and faithful word that are fitting to knights.
Now I am faulty and false, who afraid have been ever
of treachery and troth-breach: the two now my curse
        may bear!
2385   I confess, sir, here to you
        all faulty has been my fare.
        Let me gain your grace anew,
        and after I will beware.'

Then the other man laughed and lightly answered:
2390   'I hold it healed beyond doubt, the harm that I had.
Thou hast confessed thee so clean and acknowledged thine errors,
and hast the penance plain to see from the point of my blade,
that I hold thee purged of that debt, made as pure and as clean
as hadst thou done no ill deed since the day thou wert born.
2395   And I give hee, sir, the girdle with gold at its hems,
for it is green like my gown. So, Sir Gawain, you may
think of this our contest when in the throng thou walkest
among princes of high praise; 'twill be a plain reminder
of the chance of the Green Chapel between chivalrous knights.
2400   And now you shall in this New Year come anon to my house,
and in our revels the rest of this rich season
        shall go.'
        The lord pressed him hard to wend,
        and said, 'my wife, I know,
2405   we soon shall make your friend,
        who was your bitter foe.'

'Nay forsooth!' the knight said, and seized then his helm,
and duly it doffed, and the doughty man thanked:
'I have lingered too long! May your life now be blest,
2410   and He promptly repay you Who apportions all honours!
And give my regards to her grace, your goodly consort,
both to her and to the other, to mine honoured ladies,
who thus their servant with their designs have subtly beguiled.
But no marvel it is if mad be a fool,
2415   and by the wiles of women to woe be brought.
For even so Adam by one on earth was beguiled,
and Solomon by several, and to Samson moreover

his doom by Delilah was dealt; and David was after
blinded by Bathsheba, and he bitterly suffered.[7]
2420   Now if these came to grief through their guile, a gain 'twould be vast
to love them well and believe them not, if it lay in man's power!
Since these were aforetime the fairest, by fortune most blest,
eminent among all the others who under heaven bemused
                were too,
2425   and all of them were betrayed
        by women that they knew,
        though a fool I now am made,
        some excuse I think my due.'

'But for your girdle,' quoth Gawain, 'may God you repay!
2430   That I will gain with good will, not for the gold so joyous
of the cincture, nor the silk, nor the swinging pendants,
nor for wealth, nor for worth, nor for workmanship fine;
but as a token of my trespass I shall turn to it often
when I ride in renown, ruefully recalling
2435   the failure and the frailty of the flesh so perverse,
so tender, so ready to take taints of defilement.
And thus, when pride my heart pricks for prowess in arms,
one look at this love-lace shall lowlier make it.
But one thing I would pray you, if it displeaseth you not,
2440   since you are the lord of yonder land, where I lodged for a while
in your house and in honour—may He you reward
Who upholdeth the heavens and on high sitteth!—
how do you announce your true name? And then nothing further.'
'That I will tell thee truly,' then returned the other.
2445   'Bertilak de Hautdesert hereabouts I am called,
[who thus have been enchanted and changed in my hue]
by the might of Morgan le Fay[8] that in my mansion dwelleth,
and by cunning of lore and crafts well learned.
The magic arts of Merlin she many hath mastered;
for deeply in dear love she dealt on a time
2450   with that accomplished clerk, as at Camelot runs
                the fame;
        and Morgan the Goddess
        is therefore now her name.
        None power and pride possess
2455   too high for her to tame.

She made me go in this guise to your goodly court
to put its pride to the proof, if the report were true
that runs of the great renown of the Round Table.
She put this magic upon me to deprive you of your wits,
2460   in hope Guinevere to hurt, that she in horror might die

---

7. Gawain suddenly erupts in a brief but fierce diatribe, including this list of treacherous women recognizable from contemporary misogynist texts.

8. Morgan is Arthur's half-sister and ruler of the mysterious Avalon; she learned magical arts from Merlin. Her presence can bode good or ill. In some stories she holds a deep grudge against Guinevere, yet she carries off the wounded Arthur after his final battle, perhaps to heal him. The earlier Celtic Morrigan, possibly related, is queen of demons, sower of discord, and goddess of war.

aghast at that glamoury that gruesomely spake
with its head in its hand before the high table.
She it is that is at home, that ancient lady;
she is indeed thine own aunt, Arthur's half-sister,
2465   daughter of the Duchess of Tintagel on whom doughty Sir Uther
after begat Arthur, who in honour is now.[9]
Therefore I urge thee in earnest, sir, to thine aunt return!
In my hall make merry! My household thee loveth,
and I wish thee as well, upon my word, sir knight,
2470   as any that go under God, for thy great loyalty.'
But he denied him with a 'Nay! by no means I will!'
They clasp then and kiss and to the care give each other
of the Prince of Paradise; and they part on that field
                    so cold,
2475   To the king's court on courser keen
               then hastened Gawain the bold,
               and the knight in the glittering green
               to ways of his own did hold.

Wild ways in the world Gawain now rideth
2480   on Gringolet: by the grace of God he still lived.
Oft in house he was harboured and lay oft in the open,
oft vanquished his foe in adventures as he fared
which I intend not this time in my tale to recount.
The hurt was healed that he had in his neck,
2485   and the bright-hued belt he bore now about it
obliquely like a baldric bound at his side,
under his left arm with a knot that lace was fastened
to betoken he had been detected in the taint of a fault;
and so at least he came to the Court again safely.
2490   Delight there was awakened, when the lords were aware
that good Gawain had returned: glad news they thought it.
The king kissed the knight, and the queen also,
and then in turn many a true knight that attended to greet him.
About his quest they enquire, and he recounts all the marvels,
2495   declares all the hardships and care that he had,
what chanced at the Chapel, what cheer made the knight,
the love of the lady, and the lace at the last.
The notch in his neck naked he showed them
that he had for his dishonesty from the hands of the knight
2500   in blame.
               It was torment to tell the truth:
               in his face the blood did flame;
               he groaned for grief and ruth
               when he showed it, to his shame.

2505   'Lo! Lord,' he said at last, and the lace handled,
'This is the band! For this a rebuke I bear in my neck!

9. The poem now recalls an earlier transgression of guest–host obligations, when Uther began to lust for Ygerne while her husband, Gorlois, was at his court; he later killed Gorlois and married Ygerne. See Geoffrey of Monmouth, pages 144–46.

This is the grief and disgrace I have got for myself
from the covetousness and cowardice that o'ercame me there!
This is the token of the troth-breach that I am detected in,
2510 and needs must I wear it while in the world I remain;
for a man may cover his blemish, but unbind it he cannot,
for where once 'tis applied, thence part will it never.'
The king comforted the knight, and all the Court also
laughed loudly thereat, and this law made in mirth
2515 the lords and the ladies that whoso belonged to the Table,
every knight of the Brotherhood, a baldric should have,
a band of bright green obliquely about him,
and this for love of that knight as a livery should wear.
For that was reckoned the distinction of the Round Table,
2520 and honour was his that had it evermore after,
as it is written in the best of the books of romance.
Thus in Arthur his days happened this marvel,
as the Book of the Brut beareth us witness;
since Brutus the bold knight to Britain came first,
2525 after the siege and the assault had ceased at Troy,
                I trow,
          many a marvel such before,
          has happened here ere now.
          To His bliss us bring Who bore
2530   the Crown of Thorns on brow!   AMEN

        HONY SOYT QUI MAL PENCE

Sir Thomas Malory
c. 1410–1471

The full identity of Sir Thomas Malory shimmers just beyond our grasp. In several of his colophons—those closing formulas to texts—the author of the *Morte Darthur* says he is "a knyght presoner, sir Thomas Malleorré," and prays that "God sende hym good delyveraunce sone and hastely." Scholars have traced a number of such names in the era, among whom two seem particularly likely: Sir Thomas Malory of Newbold Revell, and Thomas Malory of Papworth. The former Thomas Malory had a scabrous criminal record and was long kept prisoner awaiting trial, while the latter had links to a rich collection of Arthurian books.

Another colophon provides the more useful information that "the hoole book of kyng Arthur and of his noble knyghtes of the Rounde Table" was completed in the ninth year of King Edward IV, that is 1469 or 1470. So whichever Malory wrote the *Morte Darthur*, he was certainly working in the unsettled years of the War of the Roses, in which the great ducal families of York and Lancaster battled for control of the English throne. As one family gained dominance, adherents of the other were often jailed on flimsy charges. The spectacle of a nation threatening to crumble into clan warfare provides much of the thematic weight of the *Morte Darthur,* while the declining chivalric order of the later fifteenth century underlies Malory's increasingly elegiac tone.

Whether he gained his remarkable knowledge of French and English Arthurian tradition in or out of jail, Malory infused his version of these stories with a darkening perspective very much his own. Malory sensed the high aspirations, especially the bonds of honor and fellowship in battle, that held together Arthur's realm. Yet he was also bleakly aware of how tenuous those bonds were and how easily undone by tragically competing pressures. These include the centuries-old Arthurian preoccupation with transgressive love, but Malory is more concerned with the conflicting claims of loyalty to clan or king, the urge to avenge the death of a fellow knight, and the resulting alienation even among the best of knights. Still more unnerving, agents of a virtually unmotivated or unexplained malice have ever more impact as the *Morte Darthur* progresses.

For all his initial energy and control, Malory's Arthur is increasingly a king forced to suppress knightly grievances, to deplore religious quest, even to overlook the adultery of his wife and his greatest knight, all in the interest of his fading hopes for chivalric honor and unity. Arthur's commitment to courtesy finally undoes his honor in the eyes of his own knights. As the Round Table is broken (an image Malory uses repeatedly) Arthur is put in the agonizing position of acting as judge in his wife's trial, making war on his early companion Lancelot, and finally engaging in single combat with his own treacherous son Mordred.

Malory would have found many of these themes in his sources. Twelfth-century Arthurian romances in French verse had explored the elevation and danger of courtly eroticism, and the theme was extended in the enormous French prose versions of the thirteenth century that Malory had read in great detail. In these prose romances, too, religious and chivalric themes converged around the story of the Grail. Malory also knew the alliterative *Morte Arthur* poems of fourteenth-century England, with their emphases on conquest, treachery, and the military details of Arthur's final battles.

Malory regularly acknowledges these sources, but his powers of synthesis and the stamp of his style make his *Morte Darthur* unique. While he occasionally writes a complex, reflective sentence, Malory's prose is typically composed of simple, idiomatic narrative statements, and speeches so brief as to be almost gnomic. On hearing of his brother's death, Gawain faints, then rises and says only "Alas!" Yet the grief of his cry resonates across the closing episodes of the work. Malory's imagery is similarly resonant. He tends to strip it of the explanations that had become frequent in the French prose works, and he concentrates its impact by an almost obsessive repetition. The later episodes of the work become almost an incantation of breakage and dispersal, blood and wounds, each image cluster reaching alternately toward religious experience or secular destruction.

These versions of chivalric ambition, sacred or secular, do not divide easily in the *Morte Darthur*. The saintly Galahad and the scheming Mordred may represent extremes of contrary ambition, but Malory is more preoccupied by the sadly mixed motives of Lancelot or Arthur himself. In three late episodes offered below, the reader is drawn into the perspective of lesser knights like Bors and Bedivere, who witness great moments while affecting them only marginally. They bring back to the world of lesser men stories of uncanny experience and oversee their conversion from verbal rumor to written form, whether in books or on tombs. Much of Malory's power and his continuing appeal come from his unresolved doubleness of perspective. Whether by way of his characters or his style, resonant and mysterious elements emerge from a narrative of gritty realism.

from MORTE DARTHUR

The Poisoned Apple[1]

So after the quest of the Sankgreall was fulfilled, and all knights that were left on live were come home again unto the Table Round, as *The Book of the Sankgreall* maketh mention, then was there great joy in the court, and in especial King Arthur and Queen Guinevere

---

1. From the section titled *The Book of Sir Launcelot and Queen Guinevere,* in *King Arthur and His Knights,* ed. Eugène Vinaver (1975).

made great joy of the remnant that were come home. And passing glad was the king and the queen of Sir Lancelot and of Sir Bors, for they had been passing long away in the quest of the Sankgreall.

Then, as the book saith, Sir Lancelot began to resort unto Queen Guinevere again and forgat the promise and the perfection° *of perfection* that he made in the quest; for, as the book saith, had not Sir Lancelot been in his privy° thoughts and in his mind so set inwardly *secret* to the queen as he was in seeming outward to God, there had no knight passed him in the quest of the Sankgreall. But ever his thoughts privily were on the queen, and so they loved together more hotter than they did to forehand, and had many such privy draughts° *meetings* together that many in the court spake of it, and in especial Sir Agravain, Sir Gawain's brother, for he was ever open-mouthed.

So it befell that Sir Lancelot had many resorts of° ladies and *entreaties from* damsels which daily resorted unto him, that besought him to be their champion. In all such matters of right Sir Lancelot applied him daily to do for the pleasure of Our Lord Jesu Christ, and ever as much as he might he withdrew him from the company of Queen Guinevere for to eschew the slander and noise.° Wherefore the *rumor* queen waxed wroth with Sir Lancelot.

So on a day she called him unto her chamber and said thus:

"Sir Lancelot, I see and feel daily that your love beginneth to slake,° for ye have no joy to be in my presence, but ever ye are out of *cool* this court, and quarrels and matters ye have nowadays for ladies, maidens and gentlewomen, more than ever ye were wont to have beforehand."

"Ah, madam," said Sir Lancelot, "in this ye must hold me excused for divers causes. One is, I was but late in the quest of the Sankgreall, and I thank God of His great mercy, and never of my deserving, that I saw in that my quest as much as ever saw any sinful man living, and so was it told me. And if that I had not had my privy thoughts to return to your love again as I do, I had° seen as great mysteries as ever saw my *should have* son, Sir Galahad, Perceval, other Sir Bors. And therefore, madam, I was but late in that quest, and wit you well, madam, it may not be yet lightly forgotten, the high service in whom I did my diligent labour.

"Also, madam, wit you well that there be many men speaketh of our love in this court, and have you and me greatly in await,° as this *suspicion* Sir Agravain and Sir Mordred.[2] And, madam, wit you well I dread them more for your sake than for any fear I have of them myself, for I may happen to escape and rid myself in a great need where, madam, ye must abide all that will be said unto you. And then, if that ye fall in any distress throughout° wilful folly, then is there none other help *through* but by me and my blood.° *kinsmen*

"And wit you well, madam, the boldness of you and me will bring us to shame and slander; and that were me loath to see you dishonoured. And that is the cause I take upon me more for to do for damsels and maidens than ever I did toforn:° that men should under- *before*

2. Mordred was Arthur's illegitimate son, by an incestuous encounter with his half-sister Morgause (or in some versions, Morgan le Fay).

stand my joy and my delight is my pleasure to have ado for damsels and maidens."

All this while the queen stood still and let Sir Lancelot say what he would; and when he had all said she brast out of weeping, and so she sobbed and wept a great while. And when she might speak she said,

"Sir Lancelot, now I well understand that thou art a false, recreant° knight and a common lecher, and lovest and holdest other ladies, and of me thou hast disdain and scorn. For wit thou well, now I understand thy falsehood I shall never love thee more, and look thou be never so hardy° to come in my sight. And right here I discharge thee this court, that thou never come within it, and I forfend° thee my fellowship, and upon pain° of thy head that thou see me nevermore!"

Right so Sir Lancelot departed with great heaviness that unneth° he might sustain himself for great dole-making.

Then he called Sir Bors, Ector de Maris and Sir Lionel, and told them how the queen had forfended him the court, and so he was in will to depart into his own country.

"Fair sir," said Bors de Ganis, "ye shall not depart out of this land by mine advice, for ye must remember you what ye are, and renowned the most noblest knight of the world, and many great matters ye have in hand. And women in their hastiness will do oftentimes that after them sore repenteth. And therefore, by mine advice, ye shall take your horse and ride to the good hermit here beside Windsor, that sometime was a good knight; his name is Sir Brastias. And there shall ye abide till that I send you word of better tidings."

"Brother," said Sir Lancelot, "wit you well I am full loath to depart out of this realm, but the queen hath defended° me so highly,° that meseemeth she will never be my good lady as she hath been."

"Say ye never so," said Sir Bors, "for many times or° this time she hath been wroth with you, and after that she was the first that repented it."

"Ye say well," said Sir Lancelot, "for now will I do by your counsel and take mine horse and mine harness and ride to the hermit Sir Brastias, and there will I repose me till I hear some manner of tidings from you. But, fair brother, in that° ye can get me the love of my lady, Queen Guinevere."

"Sir," said Sir Bors, "ye need not to move° me of such matters, for well ye wot I will do what I may to please you."

And then Sir Lancelot departed suddenly, and no creature wist where he was become° but Sir Bors. So when Sir Lancelot was departed the queen outward made no manner of sorrow in showing to none of his blood nor to none other, but wit ye well, inwardly, as the book saith, she took great thought;° but she bare it out with a proud countenance, as though she felt no thought nother danger.°

So the queen let make° a privy dinner in London unto the knights of the Round Table, and all was for to show outward that she

---

Marginal glosses:

cowardly

bold

forbid / at the risk

scarcely

dismissed
angrily

before

so far as

persuade

had gone

grief
fear
had made

had as great joy in all other knights of the Round Table as she had in
Sir Lancelot. So there was all only at that dinner Sir Gawain and his
brethren, that is for to say Sir Agravain, Sir Gaheris, Sir Gareth and
Sir Mordred, also there was Sir Bors de Ganis, Sir Blamore de Ganis,
Sir Bleoberis de Ganis, Sir Galihad, Sir Eliodin, Sir Ector de Maris,
Sir Lionel, Sir Palomides, Sir Safir, his brother, Sir La Cote Male
Tayle, Sir Persaunt, Sir Ironside, Sir Braundiles, Sir Kay le
Seneschal, Sir Mador de la Porte, Sir Patrise, a knight of Ireland, Sir
Aliduke, Sir Ascamore, and Sir Pinel le Savage, which was cousin to
Sir Lamorak de Galis, the good knight that Sir Gawain and his
brethren slew by treason.[3]

And so these four-and-twenty knights should dine with the
queen in a privy place by themselves, and there was made a great
feast of all manner of dainties. But Sir Gawain had a custom that he
used daily at meat and at supper, that he loved well all manner of
fruit, and in especial apples and pears. And therefore whosomever
dined other° feasted Sir Gawain would commonly purvey for° good   *or / provide*
fruit for him. And so did the queen; for to please Sir Gawain she let
purvey for him all manner of fruit. For Sir Gawain was a passing hot°   *hot-tempered*
knight of nature, and this Sir Pinel hated Sir Gawain because of his
kinsman Sir Lamorak's death, and therefore, for pure envy and hate,
Sir Pinel enpoisoned certain apples for to enpoison Sir Gawain.

So this was well yet unto° the end of meat, and so it befell by   *toward*
misfortune a good knight Sir Patrise, which was cousin unto Sir
Mador de la Porte, took an apple, for he was enchafed° with heat of   *inflamed*
wine. And it mishapped him to take a poisoned apple. And when he
had eaten it he swall° sore till he brast,° and there Sir Patrise fell   *swelled / burst*
down suddenly° dead among them.   *instantly*

Then every knight leap from the board ashamed, and araged
for° wrath out of their wits, for they wist not what to say; considering   *enraged with*
Queen Guinevere made the feast and dinner they had all suspicion
unto her.

"My lady the queen!" said Sir Gawain. "Madam, wit you that
this dinner was made for me and my fellows, for all folks that
knoweth my condition understand that I love well fruit. And now I
see well I had near been slain. Therefore, madam, I dread me lest ye
will be shamed."

Then the queen stood still and was so sore abashed that she wist
not what to say.

"This shall not so be ended," said Sir Mador de la Porte, "for
here have I lost a full noble knight of my blood, and therefore upon
this shame and despite° I will be revenged to the utterance!"°   *wrong / utmost*

And there openly Sir Mador appealed° the queen of the death   *accused*
of his cousin Sir Patrise.

Then stood they all still, that° none would speak a word against   *for*
him, for they all had great suspicion unto the queen because she let
make that dinner. And the queen was so abashed that she could

---

3. This catalog draws together most of the Round Table knights who survived the Grail quest.

none otherways do but wept so heartily that she fell on a swough. So
with this noise and cry came to them King Arthur, and when he wist
of the trouble he was a passing heavy° man. And ever Sir Mador   *sad*
stood still before the king, and appealed the queen of treason. (For
the custom was such at that time that all manner of shameful death
was called treason.)

"Fair lords," said King Arthur, "me repenteth of this trouble, but
the case is so I may not have ado° in this matter, for I must be a   *intervene*
rightful judge. And that repenteth me that I may not do battle[4] for
my wife, for, as I deem, this deed came never by her.° And therefore   *by her doing*
I suppose she shall not be all disdained° but that some good knight   *dishonored*
shall put his body in jeopardy for my queen rather than she should be
brent° in a wrong quarrel.° And therefore, Sir Mador, be not so   *burned / unjustly*
hasty; for, perdy,° it may happen she shall not be all friendless. And   *by God*
therefore desire thou thy day of battle, and she shall purvey her of°   *find herself*
some good knight that shall answer you, other else it were to me
great shame and to all my court."

"My gracious lord," said Sir Mador, "ye must hold me excused,
for though ye be our king, in that degree° ye are but a knight as we   *rank*
are, and ye are sworn unto knighthood as well as we be. And therefore I beseech you that ye be not displeased, for there is none of all
these four-and-twenty knights that were bidden to this dinner but all
they have great suspicion unto the queen. What say ye all, my
lords?" said Sir Mador.

Then they answered by and by and said they could not excuse
the queen for why she made the dinner, and other it must come by
her other by her servants.

"Alas," said the queen, "I made this dinner for a good intent and
never for none evil, so Almighty Jesu help me in my right,° as I was   *just cause*
never purposed to do such evil deeds, and that I report me unto God."[5]

"My lord the king," said Sir Mador, "I require you as ye be a
righteous king, give me my day that I may have justice."

"Well," said the king, "this day fifteen days look thou be ready
armed on horseback in the meadow beside Winchester. And if it so
fall° that there be any knight to encounter against you, there may   *happens*
you do your best, and God speed the right. And if so befall that there
be no knight ready at that day, then must my queen be brent, and
there she shall be ready to have her judgment."

"I am answered," said Sir Mador.

And every knight yode° where him liked.   *went*

So when the king and the queen were together the king asked
the queen how this case° befell. Then the queen said,   *misfortune*

"Sir, as Jesu be my help!" She wist not how nother° in what   *nor*
manner.

"Where is Sir Lancelot?" said King Arthur. "An° he were here   *if*
he would not grudge to do battle for you."

---

4. Malory refers to a procedure in law, archaic in his day,
wherein an armed champion could vindicate a person's
innocence in a "trial by battle."
5. I appeal to God to confirm.

"Sir," said the queen, "I wot not where he is, but his brother and his kinsmen deem that he be not within this realm."

"That me repenteth," said King Arthur, "for an he were here he would soon stint° this strife. Well, then I will counsel you," said the king, "that ye go unto Sir Bors, and pray him for to do battle for you for Sir Lancelot's sake, and upon my life he will not refuse you. For well I see," said the king, "that none of the four-and-twenty knights that were at your dinner where Sir Patrise was slain that will do battle for you, nother none of them will say well of you, and that shall be great slander to you in this court."

°stop

"Alas," said the queen, "an I may not do withall,[6] but now I miss Sir Lancelot, for an he were here he would soon put me in my heart's ease."

"What aileth you," said the king, "that ye cannot keep Sir Lancelot upon your side? For wit you well," said the king, "who hath Sir Lancelot upon his party° hath the most man of worship in this world upon his side. Now go your way," said the king unto the queen, "and require Sir Bors to do battle for you for Sir Lancelot's sake."

°faction

So the queen departed from the king and sent for Sir Bors into the chamber. And when he came she besought him of succour.

"Madam," said he, "what would ye that I did? For I may not with my worship° have ado in this matter, because I was at the same dinner, for dread of any of those knights would have you in suspicion. Also Madam," said Sir Bors, "now miss ye Sir Lancelot, for he would not a failed you in your right nother in your wrong, for when ye have been in right great dangers he hath succoured you. And now ye have driven him out of this country, by whom ye and all we were daily worshipped° by. Therefore, madam, I marvel how ye dare for shame to require me to do anything for you, insomuch ye have enchased out of your court by whom° we were upborne and honoured."

°with honor

°honored

°the man by whom

"Alas, fair knight," said the queen, "I put me wholly in your grace, and all that is amiss I will amend as ye will counsel me." And therewith she kneeled down upon both her knees, and besought Sir Bors to have mercy upon her, "other else I shall have a shameful death, and thereto I never offended."°

°did wrong

Right so came King Arthur and found the queen kneeling. And then Sir Bors took her up, and said,

"Madam, ye do me great dishonour."

"Ah, gentle knight," said the king, "have mercy upon my queen, courteous knight, for I am now in certain she is untruly defamed! And therefore, courteous knight," the king said, "promise her to do battle for her, I require you for the love ye owe unto Sir Lancelot."

"My lord," said Sir Bors, "ye require me the greatest thing that any man may require me. And wit you well, if I grant to do battle for the queen I shall wrath° many of my fellowship of the Table Round. But as for that," said Sir Bors, "I will grant° for my lord Sir Lancelot's

°enrage

°consent

6. If I cannot help it.

sake, and for your sake: I will at that day be the queen's champion unless that there come by adventures a better knight than I am to do battle for her."

"Will ye promise me this," said the king, "by your faith?"

"Yea sir," said Sir Bors, "of that I shall not fail you, nother her; but if there come a better knight than I am, then shall he have the battle."

Then was the king and the queen passing glad, and so departed, and thanked him heartily.

Then Sir Bors departed secretly upon a day, and rode unto Sir Lancelot thereas he was with Sir Brastias, and told him of all this adventure.

"Ah Jesu," Sir Lancelot said, "this is come happily as I would have it. And therefore I pray you make you ready to do battle, but look that ye tarry till ye see me come as long as ye may. For I am sure Sir Mador is an hot knight when he is enchafed for the more ye suffer him the hastier will he be to battle."

"Sir," said Sir Bors, "let me deal with him. Doubt ye not ye shall have all your will."

So departed Sir Bors from him and came to the court again. Then it was noised° in all the court that Sir Bors should do battle for the queen, wherefore many knights were displeased with him that he would take upon him to do battle in the queen's quarrel; for there were but few knights in all the court but they deemed the queen was in the wrong and that she had done that treason. So Sir Bors answered thus to his fellows of the Table Round.

"Wit you well, my fair lords, it were shame to us all an we suffered to see the most noble queen of the world to be shamed openly, considering her lord and our lord is the man of most worship christened, and he hath ever worshipped° us all in all places."

Many answered him again: "As for our most noble King Arthur, we love him and honour him as well as ye do, but as for Queen Guinevere we love her not, because she is a destroyer of good knights."

"Fair lords," said Sir Bors, "meseemeth ye say not as ye should say, for never yet in my days knew I never ne° heard say that ever she was a destroyer of good knights, but at all times as far as ever I could know, she was a maintainer of good knights; and ever she hath been large° and free of her goods to all good knights, and the most bounteous lady of her gifts and her good grace that ever I saw other heard speak of. And therefore it were shame to us all and to our most noble king's wife whom we serve an we suffered her to be shamefully slain. And wit ye well," said Sir Bors, "I will not suffer it, for I dare say so much, for the queen is not guilty of Sir Patrise's death: for she owed° him never none evil will nother none of the four-and-twenty knights that were at that dinner, for I dare say for good love she bade us to dinner, and not for no mal engine.° And that, I doubt not, shall be proved hereafter, for howsomever the game goeth, there was treason among us."

Then some said to Bors, "We may well believe your words." And so some were well pleased and some were not.

rumored

honored

nor

generous

felt towards

evil intent

So the day came on fast until the even that° the battle should be. *evening before*
Then the queen sent for Sir Bors and asked him how he was
disposed.° *resolved*

"Truly, madam," said he, "I am disposed in like wise as I
promised you, that is to say I shall not fail you unless there by adventure come a better knight than I am to do battle for you. Then,
madam, I am of° you discharged° of my promise." *by / released*

"Will ye," said the queen, "that I tell my lord the king thus?"

"Do as it pleaseth you, madam."

Then the queen yode° unto the king and told the answer of *went*
Sir Bors.

"Well, have ye no doubt," said the king, "of Sir Bors, for I call
him now that is living° one of the noblest knights of the world, and *of those now alive*
most perfectest man."

And thus it passed on till the morn, and so the king and the
queen and all manner of knights that were there at that time drew° *gathered*
them unto the meadow beside Winchester where the battle should
be. And so when the king was come with the queen and many
knights of the Table Round, so the queen was then put in the constable's award,° and a great fire made about an iron stake, that an Sir *custody*
Mador de le Porte had the better, she should there be brent; for such
custom was used in those days: for favour, love, nother affinity° *kinship*
there should be none other but righteous judgment, as well upon a
king as upon a knight, and as well upon a queen as upon another° *any*
poor lady.

So this meanwhile came in Sir Mador de la Porte, and took his
oath before the king, how that the queen did this treason until° his *toward*
cousin Sir Patrise, "and unto mine oath I will prove it with my body,
hand for hand, who that will say the contrary."

Right so came in Sir Bors de Ganis and said that as for Queen
Guinevere, "she is in the right, and that will I make good that she is
not culpable of this treason that is put upon her."

"Then make thee ready," said Sir Mador, "and we shall prove
whether thou be in the right or I."

"Sir Mador," said Sir Bors, "wit you well, I know you for a good
knight. Notforthen° I shall not fear you so greatly but I trust to God *nevertheless*
I shall be able to withstand your malice. But thus much have I
promised my lord Arthur and my lady the queen, that I shall do battle for her in this cause to the utterest, unless that there come a better knight than I am and discharge° me." *release*

"Is that all?" said Sir Mador. "Other come thou off and do battle
with me, other else say nay!"

"Take your horse," said Sir Bors, "and, as I suppose, I shall not
tarry long but ye shall be answered."

Then either departed to their tents and made them ready to
horseback° as they thought best. And anon Sir Mador came into the *to mount*
field with his shield on his shoulder and his spear in his hand, and so
rode about the place crying unto King Arthur,

"Bid your champion come forth an he dare!"

Then was Sir Bors ashamed, and took his horse and came to the
lists'° end. And then was he ware° where came from a wood there
fast by a knight all armed upon a white horse with a strange shield of
strange arms, and he came driving all that° his horse might run. And
so he came to Sir Bors and said thus:

*jousting field's /
noticed*

as fast as

"Fair knight, I pray you be not displeased, for here must a better knight than ye are have this battle. Therefore I pray you withdraw you, for wit you well I have had this day a right great journey
and this battle ought to be mine. And so I promised you when I
spake with you last, and with all my heart I thank you of your
good will."

Then Sir Bors rode unto King Arthur and told him how there
was a knight come that would have the battle to fight for the queen.

"What knight is he?" said the king.

"I wot not," said Sir Bors, "but such covenant he made with me to
be here this day. Now, my lord," said Sir Bors, "here I am discharged."

Then the king called to that knight, and asked him if he would
fight for the queen. Then he answered and said,

"Sir, therefore come I hither. And therefore, sir king, tarry° me
no longer, for anon as I have finished this battle I must depart hence,
for I have to do many battles elsewhere. For wit you well," said the
knight, "this is dishonour to you and to all knights of the Round
Table to see and know so noble a lady and so courteous as Queen
Guinevere is, thus to be rebuked and shamed amongst you."

delay

Then they all marvelled what knight that might be that so took
the battle upon him, for there was not one that knew him but if it
were Sir Bors. Then said Sir Mador de la Porte unto the king:

"Now let me wit with whom I shall have ado."

And then they rode to the lists' end, and there they couched°
their spears and ran together with all their mights. And anon Sir
Mador's spear brake all to pieces, but the other's spear held and bare
Sir Mador's horse and all backwards to the earth a great fall. But
mightily and deliverly he avoided his horse from him and put his
shield before him and drew his sword and bade the other knight
alight and do battle with him on foot.

lowered

Then that knight descended down from his horse and put his
shield before him and drew his sword. And so they came eagerly
unto battle, and either gave other many sad° strokes, tracing and traversing and foining° together with their swords as it were wild boars,
thus fighting nigh an hour; for this Sir Mador was a strong knight,
and mightily proved in many strong battles. But at the last this
knight smote Sir Mador grovelling upon the earth, and the knight
stepped near him to have pulled Sir Mador flatling° upon the
ground; and therewith Sir Mador arose, and in his rising he smote
that knight through the thick of the thighs, that the blood brast out
fiercely.

*grievous
thrusting*

at full length

And when he felt himself so wounded and saw his blood, he let
him arise upon his feet, and then he gave him such a buffet upon the
helm that he fell to the earth flatling. And therewith he strode to

him to have pulled off his helm off his head. And so Sir Mador prayed that knight to save his life. And so he yielded him as overcome, and released the queen of his quarrel.° *accusation*

"I will not grant thee thy life," said the knight, "only that° thou *unless* freely release the queen forever, and that no mention be made upon Sir Patrise's tomb that ever Queen Guinevere consented to that treason."

"All this shall be done," said Sir Mador, "I clearly discharge my quarrel forever."

Then the knights parters° of the lists took up Sir Mador and led *stewards* him till his tent. And the other knight went straight to the stairfoot where sat King Arthur. And by that time was the queen came to the king, and either kissed other heartily.

And when the king saw that knight he stooped down to him and thanked him, and in like wise did the queen. And the king prayed him put off his helmet and to repose him and to take a sop of wine.

And then he put off his helm to drink, and then every knight knew him that it was Sir Lancelot. And anon as the king wist that, he took the queen in his hand and yode unto Sir Lancelot and said,

"Sir, gramercy of your great travail° that ye have had this day for *labor* me and for my queen."

"My lord," said Sir Lancelot, "wit you well I ought of right ever to be in your quarrel,° and my lady the queen's quarrel, to do battle; *on your side* for ye are the man that gave me the high Order of Knighthood, and that day my lady, your queen, did me worship.° And else I had been *honor* shamed, for that same day that ye made me knight through my hastiness I lost my sword, and my lady, your queen, found it, and lapped° *wrapped* it in her train, and gave me my sword when I had need thereto; and else had I been shamed among all knights. And therefore, my lord Arthur, I promised her at that day ever to be her knight in right other in wrong."

"Gramercy," said the king, "for this journey. And wit you well," said the king, "I shall acquit° your goodness." *reward*

And evermore the queen beheld Sir Lancelot and wept so tenderly that she sank almost to the ground for sorrow, that he had done to her so great kindness where she showed him great unkindness. Then the knights of his blood drew unto him, and there either of them made great joy of other. And so came all the knights of the Table Round that were there at that time and welcomed him.

And then Sir Mador was healed of his leechcraft,° and Sir *by surgery* Lancelot was healed of his play.° And so there was made great joy *wound* and many mirths there was made in that court.

And so it befell that the Damsel of the Lake that hight Ninive, which wedded the good knight Sir Pelleas, and so she came to the court, for ever she did great goodness unto King Arthur and to all his knights through her sorcery and enchantments. And so when she heard how the queen was grieved° for the death of Sir Patrise, then *blamed* she told it openly that she was never guilty, and there she disclosed by whom it was done, and named him Sir Pinel, and for what cause he did it. There it was openly known and disclosed, and so the queen was excused. And this knight Sir Pinel fled into his country, and was openly known that he enpoisoned the apples at that feast to that intent to have destroyed Sir Gawain, because Sir Gawain and his breathren destroyed Sir Lamorak de Galis which Sir Pinel was cousin unto.

Then was Sir Patrise buried in the church of Westminster in a tomb, and thereupon was written: "Here lieth Sir Patrise of Ireland, slain by Sir Pinel le Savage, that enpoisoned apples to have slain Sir Gawain, and by misfortune Sir Patrise ate one of the apples, and then suddenly he brast." Also there was written upon the tomb that Queen Guinevere was appealed° of treason of° the death of Sir   *accused / for*
Patrise by Sir Mador de la Porte, and there was made the mention how Sir Lancelot fought with him for Queen Guinevere and overcame him in plain battle. All this was written upon the tomb of Sir Patrise in excusing of the queen.

And then Sir Mador sued daily and long to have the queen's good grace, and so by the means of Sir Lancelot he caused him to stand in the queen's good grace, and all was forgiven.

[*In intervening episodes, Agravain and Mordred, nursing long-held grudges, connive to expose the adultery of Lancelot and Guinevere. Their brother, Gawain, reluctantly joins their plot. Mordred traps Lancelot at night in Guinevere's chamber, and in escaping Lancelot kills Agravain. Rescuing Guinevere as she is about to be burned at the stake, Lancelot kills another of Gawain's brothers, Gareth, thereby earning Gawain's implacable enmity. Arthur must now make war on Lancelot and, pressed by Gawain, repeats his siege even after Guinevere is returned to him. Arthur thus besieges Lancelot in his French domain, leaving Mordred as regent.*]

The Day of Destiny[1]

As Sir Mordred was ruler of all England, he let make° letters as   *commissioned*
though that they had come from beyond the sea, and the letters specified that King Arthur was slain in battle with Sir Lancelot. Wherefore Sir Mordred made a parliament, and called the lords together, and there he made them to choose him king. And so was he crowned at Canterbury, and held a feast there fifteen days.

And afterward he drew him unto Winchester, and there he took Queen Guinevere, and said plainly that he would wed her (which was his uncle's wife and his father's wife). And so he made ready for the feast, and a day prefixed that they should be wedded; wherefore Queen Guinevere was passing heavy,° but spake fair, and agreed to   *sad*
Sir Mordred's will.

---

1. From the section titled *The Most Piteous Tale of the Morte Arthur Saunz Guerdon,* in *King Arthur and His Knights,* ed. Eugène Vinaver (1975).

And anon she desired of Sir Mordred to go to London to buy all manner things that longed to the bridal. And because of her fair speech Sir Mordred trusted her and gave her leave; and so when she came to London she took the Tower of London and suddenly in all haste possible she stuffed it with all manner of victual, and well garnished° it with men, and so kept it.   *garrisoned*

And when Sir Mordred wist this he was passing wroth out of measure. And short tale to make, he laid a mighty siege about the Tower and made many assaults, and threw engines° unto them, and   *siege machines* shot great guns. But all might not prevail, for Queen Guinevere would never, for fair speech neither for foul, never to trust unto Sir Mordred to come in his hands again.

Then came the Bishop of Canterbury, which was a noble clerk and an holy man, and thus he said unto Sir Mordred:

"Sir, what will ye do? Will you first displease God and sithen°   *then* shame yourself and all knighthood? For is not King Arthur your uncle, and no farther but your mother's brother, and upon her he himself begat you, upon his own sister? Therefore how may you wed your own father's wife? And therefore, sir," said the Bishop, "leave this opinion,° other else I shall curse you with book, bell and candle."   *intention*

"Do thou thy worst," said Sir Mordred, "and I defy thee!"

"Sir," said the Bishop, "and wit you well I shall not fear me to do that me ought to do. And also ye noise° that my lord Arthur is slain,   *spread rumors* and that is not so, and therefore ye will make a foul work in this land!"

"Peace, thou false priest!" said Sir Mordred, "for an thou chafe°   *anger* me any more, I shall strike off thy head."

So the Bishop departed, and did the cursing in the most orgulust°   *defiant* wise that might be done. And then Sir Mordred sought the Bishop of Canterbury for to have slain him. Then the Bishop fled, and took part of his goods with him, and went nigh unto Glastonbury. And there he was a priest-hermit in a chapel, and lived in poverty and in holy prayers; for well he understood that mischievous war was at hand.

Then Sir Mordred sought upon Queen Guinevere by letters and sonds,° and by fair means and foul means, to have her to come out of   *messengers* the Tower of London; but all this availed nought, for she answered him shortly, openly and privily,[2] that she had liefer° slay herself than   *rather* be married with him.

Then came there word unto Sir Mordred that King Arthur had araised the siege from Sir Lancelot and was coming homeward with a great host to be avenged upon Sir Mordred; wherefore Sir Mordred made write writs° unto all the barony of this land, and much people   *summonses* drew unto him. For then was the common voice among them that with King Arthur was never other life but war and strife, and with Sir Mordred was great joy and bliss. Thus was King Arthur depraved° and evil said of; and many there were that King Arthur   *disparaged* had brought up of nought, and given them lands, that might not then say him a good word.

2. At once, publicly and privately.

Lo ye Englishmen, see ye not what a mischief° here was? For he   *evil*
that was the most kind and noblest knight of the world, and most loved
the fellowship of noble knights, and by him they all were upholden,
and yet might not these Englishmen hold them content with him. Lo
thus was the old custom and the usages of this land, and men say that
we of this land have not yet lost that custom. Alas! this is a great
default of us Englishmen, for there may no thing us please no term.°   *length of time*

And so fared the people at that time: they were better pleased
with Sir Mordred than they were with the noble King Arthur, and
much people drew unto Sir Mordred and said they would abide with
him for better and for worse. And so Sir Mordred drew with a great
host to Dover, for there he heard say that King Arthur would arrive,
and so he thought to beat his own father from his own lands. And
the most party of all England held with Sir Mordred, for the people
were so new-fangle.°   *fond of new things*

And so as Sir Mordred was at Dover with his host, so came King
Arthur with a great navy of ships and galleys and carracks, and there
was Sir Mordred ready awaiting upon his landing, to let° his own   *stop*
father to land° upon the land that he was king over.   *from landing*

Then there was launching of great boats and small, and full of
noble men of arms; and there was much slaughter of gentle knights,
and many a full bold baron was laid full low, on both parties. But
King Arthur was so courageous that there might no manner of
knight let him to land, and his knights fiercely followed him. And so
they landed maugre° Sir Mordred's head° and all his power, and put   *against / will*
Sir Mordred aback, that he fled and all his people.

So when this battle was done King Arthur let search his people[3]
that were hurt and dead. And then was noble Sir Gawain found in a
great boat, lying more than half dead. When King Arthur knew that
he was laid so low he went unto him and so found him. And there
the king made great sorrow out of measure, and took Sir Gawain in
his arms, and thrice he there swooned. And then when he was
waked, King Arthur said,

"Alas! Sir Gawain, my sister son, here now thou liest, the man
in the world that I loved most. And now is my joy gone! For now,
my nephew, Sir Gawain, I will discover me unto° you, that in your   *disclose*
person and in Sir Lancelot I most had my joy and my affiance.° And   *trust*
now have I lost my joy of you both, wherefore all mine earthly joy is
gone from me!"

"Ah, mine uncle," said Sir Gawain, "now I will that ye wit that
my death-days be come! And all I may wite° mine own hastiness°   *blame / rashness*
and my wilfulness, for through my wilfulness I was causer of mine
own death; for I was this day hurt and smitten upon mine old wound
that Sir Lancelot gave me, and I feel myself that I must needs be
dead by the hour of noon. And through me and my pride ye have all
this shame and disease,° for had that noble knight, Sir Lancelot,   *sorrow*

---

3. Had his people searched for.

been with you, as he was and would have been, this unhappy war had never been begun; for he, through his noble knighthood and his noble blood, held all your cankered° enemies in subjection and danger.° And now," said Sir Gawain, "ye shall miss Sir Lancelot. But alas that I would not accord° with him! And therefore, fair uncle, I pray you that I may have paper, pen and ink, that I may write unto Sir Lancelot a letter written with mine own hand."

malignant
control
make peace

So when paper, pen and ink was brought, then Sir Gawain was set up weakly° by King Arthur, for he was shriven a little afore. And then he took his pen and wrote thus, as the French book maketh mention:

gently

"Unto thee, Sir Lancelot, flower of all noble knights that ever I heard of or saw by my days, I, Sir Gawain, King Lot's son of Orkney, and sister's son unto the noble King Arthur, send thee greeting, letting thee to have knowledge that the tenth day of May I was smitten upon the old wound that thou gave me afore the city of Benwick, and through that wound I am come to my death-day. And I will that all the world wit that I, Sir Gawain, knight of the Table Round, sought my death, and not through thy deserving, but mine own seeking. Wherefore I beseech thee, Sir Lancelot, to return again unto this realm and see my tomb and pray some prayer more other less for my soul. And this same day that I wrote the same cedle° I was hurt to the death, which wound was first given of thine hand, Sir Lancelot; for of a more nobler man might I not be slain.

letter

"Also, Sir Lancelot, for all the love that ever was betwixt us, make no tarrying, but come over the sea in all the goodly haste that ye may, with your noble knights, and rescue that noble king that made thee knight, for he is full straitly bestead with° a false traitor which is my half-brother, Sir Mordred. For he hath crowned himself king and would have wedded my lady, Queen Guinevere; and so had he done, had she not kept the Tower of London with strong hand. And so the tenth day of May last past my lord King Arthur and we all landed upon them at Dover, and there he put that false traitor, Sir Mordred, to flight. And so it misfortuned me to be smitten upon the stroke that ye gave me of old.

hard-pressed by

"And the date of this letter was written but two hours and a half before my death, written with mine own hand and subscribed with part of my heart blood. And therefore I require thee, most famous knight of the world, that thou wilt see my tomb."

And then he wept and King Arthur both, and swooned. And when they were awaked both, the king made Sir Gawain to receive his sacrament, and then Sir Gawain prayed the king for to send for Sir Lancelot and to cherish him above all other knights.

And so at the hour of noon Sir Gawain yielded up the ghost. And then the king let inter him° in a chapel within Dover Castle. And there yet all men may see the skull of him, and the same wound is seen that Sir Lancelot gave in battle.

had him buried

Then was it told the king that Sir Mordred had pight a new field upon Barham Down.[4] And so upon the morn King Arthur rode thither to him, and there was a great battle betwixt them, and much people were slain on both parties. But at the last King Arthur's party stood best, and Sir Mordred and his party fled unto Canterbury.

And there the king let search all the downs for his knights that were slain and interred them; and salved them with soft salves° that full sore were wounded. Then much people drew unto King Arthur, and then they said that Sir Mordred warred upon King Arthur with wrong.

ointments

And anon King Arthur drew him with his host down by the sea-side westward, toward Salisbury. And there was a day assigned betwixt King Arthur and Sir Mordred, that they should meet upon a down beside Salisbury, and not far from the seaside. And this day was assigned on Monday after Trinity Sunday, whereof King Arthur was passing glad that he might be avenged upon Sir Mordred.

Then Sir Mordred araised much people about London, for they of Kent, Sussex and Surrey, Essex, Suffolk and Norfolk held the most party with Sir Mordred. And many a full noble knight drew unto him and also to the king; but they that loved Sir Lancelot drew unto Sir Mordred.

So upon Trinity Sunday at night King Arthur dreamed a wonderful dream, and in his dream him seemed that he saw upon a chaf-flet° a chair, and the chair was fast to a wheel, and thereupon sat King Arthur in the richest cloth of gold that might be made. And the king thought there was under him, far from him, an hideous deep black water, and therein was all manner of serpents and worms° and wild beasts, foul and horrible. And suddenly the king thought that the wheel turned up-so-down, and he fell among the serpents, and every beast took him by a limb. And then the king cried as he lay in his bed, "Help! help!"

platform

dragons

And then knights, squires and yeomen awaked the king, and then he was so amazed that he wist not where he was. And then so he awaked until it was nigh day, and then he fell on slumbering again, not sleeping nor thoroughly waking. So° the king seemed verily that there came Sir Gawain unto him with a number of fair ladies with him. So when King Arthur saw him he said,

to

"Welcome, my sister's son, I weened° ye had been dead. And now I see thee on live, much am I beholden unto Almighty Jesu. Ah, fair nephew, what been these ladies that hither be come with you?"

thought

"Sir," said Sir Gawain, "all these be ladies for whom I have foughten for, when I was man living. And all these are those that I did battle for in righteous quarrels, and God hath given them that grace at their great prayer, because I did battle for them for their right, that they should bring me hither unto you. Thus much hath given me leave God for to warn you of your death: for an ye fight as

---

4. Set up a new battleground at Barham Down (southeast of Canterbury).

to-morn with Sir Mordred, as ye both have assigned, doubt ye not ye
shall be slain, and the most party of your people on both parties.
And for the great grace and goodness that Almighty Jesu hath unto
you, and for pity of you and many more other good men there shall
be slain, God hath sent me to you of His especial grace to give you
warning that in no wise ye do battle as to-morn, but that ye take a
treatise for a month-day.[5] And proffer you largely,° so that to-morn   *generously*
ye put in a delay. For within a month shall come Sir Lancelot with
all his noble knights, and rescue you worshipfully, and slay Sir Mordred and all that ever will hold with him."

    Then Sir Gawain and all the ladies vanished, and anon the king
called upon his knights, squires, and yeomen, and charged° them   *ordered*
mightly to fetch his noble lords and wise bishops unto him. And
when they were come the king told them of his avision: that Sir
Gawain had told him and warned him that an he fought on the
morn he should be slain. Then the king commanded Sir Lucan the
Butler and his brother Sir Bedivere the Bold, with two bishops with
them, and charged them in any wise to take a treatise for a month-
day with Sir Mordred:

    "And spare not, proffer him lands and goods as much as you
think reasonable."

    So then they departed and came to Sir Mordred where he had
a grim° host of an hundred thousand. And there they entreated   *fierce*
Sir Mordred long time, and at the last Sir Mordred was agreed for
to have Cornwall and Kent by° King Arthur's days;° and after   *during / lifetime*
that all England, after the days of King Arthur. Then were they
condescended° that King Arthur and Sir Mordred should meet   *agreed*
betwixt both their hosts, and every each of them should bring
fourteen persons. And so they came with this word unto Arthur.
Then said he,

    "I am glad that this is done," and so he went into the field.

    And when King Arthur should depart he warned all his host
that an they see any sword drawn, "look ye come on fiercely and slay
that traitor, Sir Mordred, for I in no wise trust him." In like wise Sir
Mordred warned his host that "an ye see any manner of sword drawn
look that ye come on fiercely and so slay all that ever before you
standeth, for in no wise I will not trust for this treatise." And in the
same wise said Sir Mordred unto his host: "for I know well my father
will be avenged upon me."

    And so they met as their pointment was, and were agreed and
accorded thoroughly. And wine was fette,° and they drank together.   *fetched*
Right so came out an adder of a little heath-bush, and it stang a
knight in the foot. And so when the knight felt him so stung, he
looked down and saw the adder; and anon he drew his sword to slay
the adder, and thought none other harm. And when the host on
both parties saw that sword drawn, then they blew beams,° trumpets,   *bugles*

---

5. Make a compact for a month from today.

and horns, and shouted grimly, and so both hosts dressed them together.° And King Arthur took his horse and said, "Alas, this unhappy day!" And so rode to his party, and Sir Mordred in like wise.

 And never since was there seen a more dolefuller battle in no Christian land, for there was but rushing and riding, foining° and striking, and many a grim word was there spoken of either to other, and many a deadly stroke. But ever King Arthur rode throughout the battle° of Sir Mordred many times and did full nobly, as a noble king should do, and at all times he fainted never. And Sir Mordred did his devour° that day and put himself in great peril.

 And thus they fought all the long day, and never stinted° till the noble knights were laid to the cold earth. And ever they fought still till it was near night, and by then was there an hundred thousand laid dead upon the earth. Then was King Arthur wood wroth° out of measure, when he saw his people so slain from him.

 And so he looked about him and could see no mo° of all his host, and good knights left no mo on live but two knights: the tone° was Sir Lucan de Butler and his brother, Sir Bedivere; and yet they were full sore wounded.

 "Jesu mercy!" said the king, "where are all my noble knights become? Alas, that ever I should see this doleful day! For now," said King Arthur, "I am come to mine end. But would to God," said he, "that I wist now where were that traitor Sir Mordred that hath caused all this mischief."°

 Then King Arthur looked about and was ware where stood Sir Mordred leaning upon his sword among a great heap of dead men.

 "Now, give me my spear," said King Arthur unto Sir Lucan, "for yonder I have espied the traitor that all this woe hath wrought."

 "Sir, let him be," said Sir Lucan, "for he is unhappy.° And if ye pass this unhappy day ye shall be right well revenged. And, good lord, remember ye of your night's dream and what the spirit of Sir Gawain told you to-night, and yet God of His great goodness hath preserved you hitherto. And for God's sake, my lord, leave off this, for, blessed be God, ye have won the field: for yet we been here three on live, and with Sir Mordred is not one of live. And therefore if ye leave off now, this wicked day of Destiny is past!"

 "Now tide° me death, tide me life," said the king, "now I see him yonder alone, he shall never escape mine hands! For at a better avail° shall I never have him."

 "God speed you well!" said Sir Bedivere.

 Then the king gat his spear in both his hands, and ran toward Sir Mordred, crying and saying,

 "Traitor, now is thy death-day come!"

 And when Sir Mordred saw King Arthur he ran until° him with his sword drawn in his hand, and there King Arthur smote Sir Mordred under the shield with a foin° of his spear throughout the body more than a fathom. And when Sir Mordred felt that he had his death wound he thrust himself with the might that he had up

confronted each other

thrusting

battle formation

utmost effort

ceased

wild with rage

more
one

evil

unlucky

befall

advantage

toward

thrust

to the burr° of King Arthur's spear, and right so he smote his   *hand guard*
father, King Arthur, with his sword holding in both his hands,
upon the side of the head, that the sword pierced the helmet and
the tay° of the brain. And therewith Mordred dashed down stark   *lining*
dead to the earth.

And noble King Arthur fell in a swough to the earth, and there
he swooned oftentimes, and Sir Lucan and Sir Bedivere oftentimes
hove° him up. And so weakly° betwixt them they led him to a little   *lifted / gently*
chapel not far from the sea, and when the king was there, him
thought him reasonably eased.

Then heard they people cry in the field.

"Now go thou, Sir Lucan," said the king, "and do me to wit°   *let me know*
what betokens that noise in the field."

So Sir Lucan departed, for he was grievously wounded in many
places; and so as he rode he saw and harkened by the moonlight how
that pillers° and robbers were come into the field to pille and to rob   *plunderers*
many a full noble knight of brooches and bees° and of many a good   *bracelets*
ring and many a rich jewel. And who that were not dead all out,
there they slew them for their harness° and their riches.   *armor*

When Sir Lucan understood his work he came to the king as
soon as he might, and told him all what he had heard and seen.

"Therefore by my rede,"° said Sir Lucan, "it is best that we bring   *advice*
you to some town."

"I would it were so," said the king, "but I may not stand, my
head works° so. . . . Ah, Sir Lancelot!" said King Arthur, "this day   *aches*
have I sore missed thee! And alas, that ever I was against thee! For
now have I my death, whereof Sir Gawain me warned in my dream."

Then Sir Lucan took up the king the tone party° and Sir Bedi-   *on one side*
vere the other party, and in the lifting up the king swooned, and in
the lifting Sir Lucan fell in a swoon, that part of his guts fell out of
his body; and therewith the noble knight his heart brast. And when
the king awoke he beheld Sir Lucan, how he lay foaming at the
mouth and part of his guts lay at his feet.

"Alas," said the king, "this is to me a full heavy sight, to see this
noble duke so die for my sake, for he would have holpen° me that had   *helped*
more need of help than I! Alas, that he would not complain him, for
his heart was so set to help me. Now Jesu have mercy upon his soul!"

Then Sir Bedivere wept for the death of his brother.

"Now leave this mourning and weeping, gentle knight," said the
king, "for all this will not avail° me. For wit thou well an I might live   *aid*
myself, the death of Sir Lucan would grieve me evermore. But my
time passeth on fast," said the king. "Therefore," said King Arthur
unto Sir Bedivere, "take thou here Excalibur, my good sword, and go
with it to yonder water's side; and when thou comest there, I charge
thee throw my sword in that water, and come again and tell me what
thou seest there."

"My lord," said Sir Bedivere, "your commandment shall be
done, and lightly° bring you word again."   *I will quickly*

So Sir Bedivere departed. And by the way he beheld that noble sword, and the pomell° and the haft° was all precious stones. And then he said to himself, "If I throw this rich sword in the water, thereof shall never come good, but harm and loss." And then Sir Bedivere hid Excalibur under a tree, and so soon as he might he came again unto the king and said he had been at the water and thrown the sword into the water.

hand guard / handle

"What saw thou there?" said the king.

"Sir," he said, "I saw nothing but waves and winds."

"That is untruly said of thee," said the king. "And therefore go thou lightly again, and do my commandment as thou art to me lief° and dear: spare not but throw it in."

beloved

Then Sir Bedivere returned again and took the sword in his hand; and yet him thought sin and shame to throw away that noble sword. And so eft° he hid the sword and returned again and told the king that he had been at the water and done his commandment.

again

"What sawest thou there?" said the king.

"Sir," he said, "I saw nothing but waters wap° and waves wan."°

lapping / dark

"Ah, traitor unto me and untrue," said King Arthur, "now hast thou betrayed me twice! Who would ween° that thou who has been to me so lief and dear, and also named so noble a knight, that thou would betray me for the riches of this sword? But now go again lightly; for thy long tarrying putteth me in great jeopardy of my life, for I have taken cold. And but if° thou do now as I bid thee, if ever I may see thee, I shall slay thee mine own hands, for thou wouldest for my rich sword see me dead."

believe

unless

Then Sir Bedivere departed and went to the sword and lightly took it up, and so he went unto the water's side. And there he bound the girdle about the hilt, and threw the sword as far into the water as he might. And there came an arm and an hand above the water, and took it and cleight° it, and shook it thrice and brandished, and then vanished with the sword into the water.

clutched

So Sir Bedivere came again to the king and told him what he saw.

"Alas!" said the king, "help me hence, for I dread me I have tarried over long."

Then Sir Bedivere took the king upon his back and so went with him to the water's side. And when they were there, even fast by° the bank hoved° a little barge with many fair ladies in it, and among them all was a queen, and all they had black hoods. And all they wept and shrieked when they saw King Arthur.

next to / floated

"Now put me into that barge," said the king.

And so he did softly, and there received him three ladies with great mourning. And so they set him down, and in one of their laps King Arthur laid his head. And then the queen said,

"Ah, my dear brother![6] Why have you tarried so long from me? Alas, this wound on your head hath caught overmuch cold!"

---

6. The queen is thus revealed as Morgan le Fay, in whose story magical healing powers mixed with inveterate hostility to Guinevere and sometimes to Arthur himself.

And anon they rowed fromward° the land, and Sir Bedivere   *away from*
beheld all those ladies go fromward him. Then Sir Bedivere cried
and said,

"Ah, my lord Arthur, what shall become of me, now ye go from
me and leave me here alone among mine enemies?"

"Comfort thyself," said the king, "and do as well as thou mayst,
for in me is no trust for to trust in. For I must into the vale of Avalon
to heal me of my grievous wound. And if thou hear nevermore of
me, pray for my soul!"

But ever the queen and ladies wept and shrieked, that it was
pity to hear. And as soon as Sir Bedivere had lost sight of the
barge he wept and wailed, and so took° the forest and went all   *went into*
that night.

And in the morning he was ware, betwixt two holts hoar°, of a   *gray woods*
chapel and an hermitage. Then was Sir Bedivere fain°, and thither   *glad*
he went, and when he came into the chapel he saw where lay an
hermit grovelling° on all fours, fast thereby a tomb was new   *face down*
graven.° When the hermit saw Sir Bedivere he knew him well, for   *freshly dug*
he was but little tofore Bishop of Canterbury, that Sir Mordred
fleamed.°   *put to flight*

"Sir," said Sir Bedivere, "what man is there here interred that
you pray so fast° for?"   *intently*

"Fair son," said the hermit, "I wot not verily but by deeming.°   *guessing*
But this same night, at midnight, here came a number of ladies and
brought here a dead corse and prayed me to inter him. And here
they offered an hundred tapers, and gave me a thousand besants."°   *gold coins*

"Alas," said Sir Bedivere, "that was my lord King Arthur, which
lieth here graven° in this chapel."   *buried*

Then Sir Bedivere swooned, and when he awoke he prayed the
hermit that he might abide with him still, there to live with fasting
and prayers:

"For from hence will I never go," said Sir Bedivere, "by my will,
but all the days of my life here to pray for my lord Arthur."

"Sir, ye are welcome to me," said the hermit, "for I know you
better than ye ween that I do: for ye are Sir Bedivere the Bold, and
the full noble duke Sir Lucan de Butler was your brother."

Then Sir Bedivere told the hermit all as you have heard tofore,
and so he beleft° with the hermit that was beforehand Bishop of   *remained*
Canterbury. And there Sir Bedivere put upon him poor clothes, and
served the hermit full lowly in fasting and in prayers.

Thus of Arthur I find no more written in books that been
authorised, neither more of the very certainty of his death heard I
never read, but thus was he led away in a ship wherein were three
queens; that one was King Arthur's sister, Queen Morgan le Fay, the
tother was the Queen of North Galis, and the third was the Queen
of the Waste Lands.

Now more of the death of King Arthur could I never find, but
that these ladies brought him to his grave, and such one was
interred there which the hermit bare witness that sometime° Bishop   *was once*

of Canterbury. But yet the hermit knew not in certain that he was verily the body of King Arthur; for this tale Sir Bedivere, a knight of the Table Round, made it to be written.

Yet some men say in many parts of England that King Arthur is not dead, but had° by the will of our Lord Jesu into another place; *was carried* and men say that he shall come again, and he shall win the Holy Cross. Yet I will not say that it shall be so, but rather I would say: here in this world he changed his life. And many men say that there is written upon the tomb this:

HIC IACET ARTHURUS REX QUONDAM REXQUE FUTURUS[7]

And thus leave I here Sir Bedivere with the hermit that dwelled that time in a chapel beside Glastonbury, and there was his hermitage. And so they lived in prayers and fastings and great abstinence.

And when Queen Guinevere understood that King Arthur was dead and all the noble knights, Sir Mordred and all the remnant, then she stole away with five ladies with her, and so she went to Amesbury. And there she let make herself° a nun, and weared white *became* clothes and black, and great penance she took upon her, as ever did sinful woman in this land. And never creature could make her merry, but ever she lived in fasting, prayers and alms-deeds, that all manner of people marvelled how virtuously she was changed.

━━◆━━

Geoffrey Chaucer
c. 1340–1400

On Easter weekend 1300, the Italian poet Dante Alighieri had a vision in which he descended to hell, climbed painfully through purgatory, and then attained a transcendent experience of paradise. He tells his tale in his visionary, passionately judgmental *Divine Comedy*. One hundred years later, on 25 October 1400, Geoffrey Chaucer—the least judgmental of poets—died quietly in his house at the outskirts of London. By a nice accident of history, these two great writers bracket the last great century of the Middle Ages.

Of Chaucer's own life our information is abundant but often frustrating. Many documents record the important and sensitive posts he held in government, but there are only faint hints of his career as a poet. During his lifetime, he was frequently in France and made at least two trips to Italy, which proved crucial for his own growth as a writer and indeed for the history of English literature. He also served under three kings: the aging Edward III, his brilliant and sometimes tyrannical grandson Richard II, and—at the very end of his life—Richard's usurper Henry IV.

Chaucer was born into a rising mercantile family, part of the growing bourgeois class that brought so much wealth to England even while it disrupted medieval theories of social order. Chaucer's family fit nowhere easily in the old model of the three estates: those who pray (the clergy), those who fight (the aristocracy), and those who work the land (the peasants). Yet like many of their class, they aspired to a role among the aristocracy, and in fact Chaucer's parents succeeded in holding minor court positions. Chaucer himself became a major player in the

---

7. Here lies Arthur, once and future king.

cultural and bureaucratic life of the court, and Thomas Chaucer (who was very probably his son) was ultimately knighted.

Geoffrey was superbly but typically educated. He probably went to one of London's fine grammar schools, and as a young man he very likely followed a gentlemanly study of law at one of the Inns of Court. He shows signs of knowing and appreciating the topics debated in the university life of his time. His poems reflect a vast reading in classical Latin, French, and Italian (of which he was among the earliest English readers). *The Parliament of Fowls*, for instance, reveals the influence not only of French court poetry but also of Dante's *Divine Comedy*; and the frame-story structure of *The Canterbury Tales* may have been inspired by Boccaccio's *Decameron*.

By 1366 Chaucer had married Philippa de Roet, a minor Flemish noblewoman, and a considerable step up the social hierarchy. Her sister later became the mistress and ultimately the wife of Chaucer's great patron, John of Gaunt. Thus, when Gaunt's son Henry Boling-broke seized the throne from Richard II, the elderly Geoffrey Chaucer found himself a distant in-law of his king. Chaucer had been associated with Richard II and suffered reverses when Richard's power was restricted by the magnates. But he was enough of a cultural figure that Henry IV continued (perhaps with some prompting) the old man's royal annuities. Whatever Western literature owes to Chaucer (and its debts are profound), in his own life his writing made a place in the world for him and his heirs.

Despite his lifelong productivity as a writer, and despite the slightly obtuse narrative voice he consistently uses, Geoffrey Chaucer was a canny and ambitious player in the world of his time. He was a soldier, courtier, diplomat, and government official in a wide range of jobs. These included controller of the customs on wool and other animal products, a lucrative post, and later controller of the Petty Custom that taxed wine and other goods. Chaucer's frequent work overseas extended his contacts with French and Italian literature. He was ward of estates for several minors, a job that also benefited the guardian. Chaucer began to accumulate property in Kent, where he served as justice of the peace (an important judicial post) and then Member of Parliament in the mid-1380s.

Despite the comfortable worldly progress suggested by such activities, these were troubled years in the nation and in Chaucer's private life. Chaucer's personal fortunes were affected by the frequent struggles between King Richard and his magnates over control of the government. From another direction there exploded The Rising of 1381, rocking all of English society. The year before that, Chaucer had been accused of *raptus* by Cecilia Chaumpaigne, daughter of a baker in London. A great deal of nervous scholarship has been exercised over this case, but it becomes increasingly clear that in legal language *raptus* meant some form of rape. The case was settled, and there are signs of efforts to hush it up at quite high levels of government. The somewhat bland and bumbling quality of Chaucer's narrative persona would probably have seemed more artificially constructed and more ironic to Chaucer's contemporaries than it does at first glance today.

Chaucer was a Janus-faced poet, truly innovative at the levels of language and theme yet deeply involved with literary and intellectual styles that stretched back to Latin antiquity and twelfth- and thirteenth-century France. His early poems—the dream visions such as *The Parliament of Fowls* and the tragic romance *Troilus and Criseyde*—derive from essentially medieval genres and continental traditions: the French poets Deschamps and Machaut and the Italians Dante, Boccaccio, and Petrarch. Yet in his reliance on the English vernacular, Chaucer was in a vanguard generation along with the *Gawain* poet and William Langland. English was indeed gaining importance in other parts of this world, such as in Parliament, some areas of education, and in the "Wycliffite" translations of the Bible. Chaucer's own exclusive use of English was particularly ambitious, though, for a poet whose patronage came from the court of the francophile Richard II.

The major work of Chaucer's maturity, *The Canterbury Tales*, founds an indisputably English tradition. While he still uses the craft and allusions he learned from his continental masters, he also experiments with the subject matter of everyday English life and the vocabularies

Portrait of Geoffrey the Canterbury Pilgrim, from the Ellesmere manuscript of *The Canterbury Tales,* early 15th century. This carefully produced and beautifully decorated manuscript reflects the speed with which Chaucer's works took on wide cultural prestige and were enshrined in luxury books for a wealthy, probably aristocratic audience.

of the newly valorized English vernacular. Moreover, starting with traditional forms and largely traditional models of society and the cosmos, Chaucer found spaces for new and sometimes disruptive perspectives, especially those of women and the rising mercantile class into which he had been born. Though always a court poet, Chaucer increasingly wrote in ways that reflected both the richness and the uncertainties of his entire social world. The *Tales* include a Knight who could have stepped from a twelfth-century heroic poem; yet they also offer the spectacle of the Knight's caste being aped, almost parodied, and virtually shouted down by a sword-carrying peasant, the Miller. And the entire notion of old writings as sources of authoritative wisdom is powerfully challenged by the illiterate or only minimally literate Wife of Bath.

The *Canterbury Tales* also differ from the work of many of Chaucer's continental predecessors in their deep hesitation to cast straightforward judgment, either socially or spiritually. Here we may return to Chaucer's connection with Dante. His *Divine Comedy* presented mortal life as a pilgrimage and an overt test in stable dogma, a journey along a dangerous road toward certain damnation or the reward of the heavenly Jerusalem. *The Canterbury Tales* are literally about a pilgrimage, and Chaucer presents the road as beautiful and fascinating in its own right. The greatness of the poem lies in its exploration of the variousness of the journey and that journey's reflection of a world pressured by spiritual and moral fractures. In depicting a mixed company of English men and women traveling England's most famous pilgrimage route and telling one another stories, Chaucer suggests not only the spiritual meaning of humankind's earthly pilgrimage, but also its overflowing beauties and attractions as well as the evils and temptations that lie along the way. The vision of the serious future, the day of judgment, is constantly attended in *The Canterbury Tales* by the troubling yet hilarious and distracting present.

Unlike Dante, however, Chaucer almost never takes it upon himself to judge, at least not openly. He records his characters with dizzying immediacy, but he never tells his reader quite what to think of them, leaving the gaps for us as readers to fill. He does end the *Tales* with a kind of sermon, the Parson's long prose treatise on the Christian vices and virtues. That coda by no means erases the humor and seriousness, sentiment and ribaldry, high spiritual love and unmasked carnal desire, profound religious belief and squalid clerical corruption that have been encountered along the way. Indeed, Chaucer's genius is to transmute the disorder of his world almost into an aesthetic of plenitude: "foyson" in Middle English. His poem overflows constantly with rich detail, from exquisite visions to squabbling pilgrims. His language overflows with its multiple vocabularies, Anglo-Saxon, Latin, and French. And finally, the tales themselves are notable for the range of genres used by the pilgrims: the Miller's bawdy fabliau, the Wife of Bath's romance, the Franklin's story of courtly love and clerkly magic, the Nun's Priest's beast fable, the Pardoner's hypocritical cautionary tale, as well as the Parson's sermon. *The Canterbury Tales* are an anthology embracing almost every important literary type of Chaucer's day.

None of this celebratory richness, however, fully masks the unresolved social and spiritual tensions that underlie the *Tales*. The notion of spiritual pilgrimage is deeply challenged by the very density of characterization and worldly detail that so enlivens the work. And the model of a competitive game, which provides the fictional pretext for the tales themselves, is only one version of what the critic Peggy Knapp has called Chaucer's "social contest" in the work as a whole. The traditional estates such as knight and peasant openly clash during the pilgrimage, and the estate of the clergy is more widely represented by its corrupt than by its virtuous members. Women, merchants, common landowners, and others from outside the traditional three estates bulk large in the tales. And their stories cast doubt upon such fundamental religious institutions as penance and such social institutions as marriage. For all their pleasures, *The Canterbury Tales* have survived, in part, because they are so riven by challenge and doubt.

CHAUCER'S MIDDLE ENGLISH

Grammar

The English of Chaucer's London, and particularly the English of government bureaucracy, became the source for the more standardized vernacular that emerged in the era of print at the close of the Middle Ages. As a result, Chaucer's English is easier to understand today than the dialect of many of his great contemporaries such as the *Gawain* poet, who worked far to the north. The text that follows preserves Chaucer's language, with some spellings slightly modernized and regularized by its editor, E. Talbot Donaldson.

The marginal glosses in the readings are intended to help the nonspecialist reader through Chaucer's language without elaborate prior study. It will be helpful, though, to explain a few key differences from Modern English.

Nouns: The possessive is sometimes formed without a final -s.

Pronouns: Readers will recognize the archaic *thou, thine, thee* of second-person singular, and *ye* of the plural. Occasional confusion can arise from the form *hir*, which can mean "her" or "their." *Hem* is Chaucer's spelling for "them," and *tho* for "those." Chaucer uses *who* to mean "whoever."

Adverbs: Formed, as today, with -*ly*, but also with -*liche*. Sometimes an adverb is unchanged from its adjective form: *fairly, fairliche, faire* can all be adverbs.

Verbs: Second-person singular is formed with -*est* (*thou lovest*, past tense *thou lovedest*); third-person singular often with -*eth* (*he loveth*); plurals often with -*n* (*we loven*); and infinitive with -*n* (*loven*).

Strong verbs/impersonal verbs: Middle English has many "strong verbs," which form the past and perfect by changing a vowel in their stem; these are usually recognizable by analogy with surviving forms in Modern English (*go, went, gone; sing, sang, sung;* etc.). Middle English also often uses "impersonal verbs" (*liketh,* "it pleases"; *as me thinketh,* "as I think"), in which case sometimes no obvious subject noun or pronoun occurs.

Pronunciation

A few guidelines will help approximate the sound of Chaucer's English and the richness of his versification. For fuller discussion, consult sources listed in the bibliography.

Pronounce all consonants: *knight* is "k/neecht" with a guttural *ch,* not "nite"; *gnaw* is "g/naw." Middle English consonants preserve many of the sounds of the language's Germanic roots: guttural *gh;* sounded *l* and *w* in words like *folk* or *write.* (Exceptions occur in some words that derive from French, like *honour* whose *h* is silent.)

Final *-e* was sounded in early Middle English. Such pronunciation was becoming archaic by Chaucer's time, but was available to aid meter in the stylized context of poetry.

The distinction between short and long vowels was greater in Middle English than today. Middle English short vowels have mostly remained short in Modern English, with some shift in pronunciation: short *a* sounds like the *o* in *hot,* short *o* like a quick version of the *aw* in *law,* short *u* like the *u* in *full.*

Long vowels in Middle English (here usually indicated by doubling, when vowel length is unclear by analogy to modern spelling) are close to long vowels in modern Romance languages. The chart shows some differences in Middle English long vowels.

Middle English	pronounced as in	Modern English
a (as in *name*)		*father*
open *e* (*deel*)		*swear, bread*
close *e* (*sweet*)		*fame*
i (*whit*)		*feet*
open *o* (*holy*)		*law*
close *o* (*roote*)		*note*
u (as in *town, aboute*)		*root*
u (*vertu*)		*few*

Open and close long vowels are a challenge for modern readers. Generally, open long *e* in Middle English (*deel*) has become Modern English spelling with *ea* (*deal*); close long *e* (*sweet*) has become Modern English spelling with *ee* (*sweet*). Open long *o* in Middle English has come to be pronounced as in *note;* close long *o* in Middle English has come to be pronounced *root.* This latter case illustrates the idea of "vowel shift" across the centuries, in which some long vowels have moved forward in the throat and palate.

Versification

All of Chaucer's poetry presented here is in a loosely iambic pentameter line, which Chaucer was greatly responsible for bringing into prominence in England. He is a fluid versifier, though, and often shifts stress, producing metrical effects that have come to be called trochees and spondees. Final *-e* is often pronounced within lines to provide an unstressed syllable and is typically pronounced at the end of each line. Yet final *-e* may also elide with a following word that begins with a vowel. The following lines from *The Nun's Priest's Tale* have a proposed scansion, but the reader will see that alternate scansions are possible at several places.

"Avoi," quod she, "fy on you, hertelees!
Allas," quod she, "for by that God above,
Now han ye lost myn herte and al my love!
I can nat love a coward, by my faith.
For certes, what so any womman saith,
We alle desiren, if it mighte be,
To han housbondes hardy, wise, and free,
And secree, and no nigard, ne no fool,
Ne him that is agast of every tool,
Ne noon avauntour. By that God above,
How dorste ye sayn for shame unto youre love
That any thing mighte make you aferd?
Have ye no mannes herte and han a beerd?

from THE CANTERBURY TALES

THE GENERAL PROLOGUE   The twenty-nine "sondry folke" of the Canterbury company gather at the Tabard Inn, ostensibly with the pious intent of making a pilgrimage to England's holiest shrine, the tomb of Saint Thomas Becket at Canterbury. From the start in the raffish and worldly London suburb of Southwerk, though, the pilgrims' attentions and energy veer wildly between the sacred and the profane. The mild story-telling competition proposed by the Host also slides swiftly into a contest among social classes. Set in Chaucer's own time and place, *The Canterbury Tales* reflect both the dynamism and the uncertainties of a society still nostalgic for archaic models of church and state, yet riven by such crises as plague, economic disruption, and the new claims of peasants and mercantile bourgeois—claims expressed and repressed most violently in the recent Rising, or "Peasants' Revolt," of 1381.

Chaucer's *Prologue* has roots in the genre known as "estates satire." Such writings criticized the failure of the members of the three traditional "estates" of medieval society—the aristocracy, the clergy, and the commons—to fulfill their ordained function of fighting, praying, and working the land, respectively. From the beginning the pilgrims' portraits are couched in language fraught with class connotations. The Knight, the idealized (if archaic) representative of the aristocracy, is called *gentil* (that is, "noble, aristocratic") and is said never to have uttered any *vileynye*—speech characteristic of peasants or *villeyns*. Many of the pilgrims in the other two estates display aristocratic manners, among the clergy notably the Prioress, with her "cheere of court," and the Monk, who lives like a country gentleman, hunting with greyhounds and a stable full of fine horses. Both pilgrims contrast with the ideal of their estate, the Parson, who, though "*povre*" is "rich" in holy works.

The commons are traditionally the last of the "three estates," yet they bulk largest in the Canterbury company and fit least well in that model of social order. There are old-fashioned laborers on the pilgrimage, but many more characters from the emerging and disruptive world of small industry and commerce. They are commoners, but have ambitions that lead them both to envy and to mock the powers held by their aristocratic and clerical companions.

Among the group that traditionally comprised the commons, the peasants, Chaucer singles out one ideal, the Plowman, who is, significantly, the Parson's brother. He is characterized as a diligent *swynkere* (worker), in implicit contrast to the lazy peasants castigated in estates satire. Most of the rest of the commons, however, such as the Miller and the Cook, are presented as "churlish," and their tales have a coarse vigor that Chaucer clearly relishes even as he disassociates himself from their vulgarity.

In theory, women were treated as a separate category, defined by their sexual nature and marital role rather than by their class. Nevertheless, the Prioress and the Wife of Bath are both satirized as much for their social ambition as for the failings of their gender. The Prioress prides herself on her courtesy, and the commoner Wife of Bath aspires to the same social recognition as the guildsmen's upwardly mobile wives. Her portrait is complex, however, for she is simultaneously satirized and admired for challenging the expected roles of women at the time, with her economic independence (as a rich widow and a cloth-maker) and her resultant freedom to travel. The narrator's suggestion that she goes on many pilgrimages in order to find a sixth husband bears out the stereotype of unbridled female sexuality familiar from estates satire, as her fondness of talking and laughing bears out the stereotype of female garrulousness.

Chaucer's satire is pointed but also exceptionally subtle, largely because of the irony achieved through his use of the narrator, seemingly naive and a little dense. His deadpan narration leaves the readers themselves to supply the judgment.

from THE CANTERBURY TALES
The General Prologue

	Whan that April with his showres soote°	*sweet*
	The droughte of March hath perced to the roote,	
	And bathed every veine in swich licour,°	*such liquid*
	Of which vertu° engendred is the flowr;	*by whose strength*
5	Whan Zephyrus[1] eek° with his sweete breeth	*also*
	Inspired hath in every holt and heeth°	*wood and field*
	The tendre croppes, and the yonge sonne	
	Hath in the Ram° his halve cours yronne,	*the zodiac sign Aries*
	And smale fowles maken melodye	
10	That sleepen al the night with open yë°—	*eye*
	So priketh hem Nature in hir corages°—	*hearts, spirits*
	Thanne longen folk to goon on pilgrimages,	
	And palmeres[2] for to seeken straunge strondes°	*shores*
	To ferne halwes,° couthe° in sondry londes;	*far-off shrines / known*
15	And specially from every shires ende	
	Of Engelond to Canterbury they wende,°	*go*
	The holy blisful martyr[3] for to seeke	
	That hem hath holpen° whan that they were seke.°	*helped / sick*
	Bifel that in that seson on a day,	
20	In Southwerk[4] at the Tabard as I lay,	
	Redy to wenden on my pilgrimage	
	To Canterbury with ful devout corage,	
	At night was come into that hostelrye	
	Wel nine and twenty in a compaignye	
25	Of sondry folk, by aventure yfalle	
	In felaweshipe, and pilgrimes were they alle	
	That toward Canterbury wolden ride.	
	The chambres° and the stables weren wide,	*guestrooms*

1. In Roman mythology Zephyrus was the demigod of the west wind, herald of warmer weather.
2. Pilgrims who had traveled to the Holy Land.
3. St. Thomas Becket, murdered in Canterbury Cathedral in 1170.
4. Southwark, a suburb of London south of the Thames and the traditional starting point for the pilgrimage to

Canterbury in Kent, was notorious as a center of gambling and prostitution. The Tabard Inn was an actual public house at the time, named for the shape of its sign which resembled the coarse, sleeveless outer garment worn by members of the lower classes, monks, and foot soldiers alike.

And wel we weren esed° at the beste.   *accommodated*
30 And shortly, whan the sonne was to reste,
So hadde I spoken with hem everichoon
That I was of hir felaweshipe anoon,
And made forward° erly for to rise,   *agreed*
To take oure way ther as I you devise.°   *relate*
35   But nathelees, whil I have time and space,°   *opportunity*
Er that I ferther in this tale pace,°   *proceed*
Me thinketh it accordant to resoun
To telle you al the condicioun°   *circumstances*
Of eech of hem, so as it seemed me,
40 And whiche they were, and of what degree,°   *social status*
And eek in what array that they were inne:
And at a knight thanne wol I first biginne.
A Knight ther was, and that a worthy man,
That fro the time that he first bigan
45 To riden out, he loved chivalrye,
Trouthe and honour, freedom and curteisye.[5]
Ful worthy was he in his lordes werre,°   *war*
And therto hadde he riden, no man ferre,°   *farther*
As wel in Cristendom as hethenesse,°   *heathen lands*
50 And evere honoured for his worthinesse.
At Alisandre[6] he was whan it was wonne;
Ful ofte time he hadde the boord bigonne[7]
Aboven alle nacions in Pruce;
In Lettou had he reised,° and in Ruce,   *campaigned*
55 No Cristen man so ofte of his degree;
In Gernade at the sege eek hadde he be
Of Algezir, and riden in Belmarye;
At Lyeis was he, and at Satalye,
Whan they were wonne; and in the Grete See
60 At many a noble arivee° hadde he be.   *military landing*
At mortal batailes[8] hadde he been fifteene,
And foughten for oure faith at Tramissene
In listes° thries, and ay° slain his fo.   *duels / always*
This ilke° worthy Knight hadde been also   *same*
65 Somtime with the lord of Palatye
Again° another hethen in Turkye;   *against*
And everemore he hadde a soverein pris.°   *reputation*
And though that he were worthy, he was wis,
And of his port° as meeke as is a maide.   *bearing*
70 He nevere yit no vilainye° ne saide   *rudeness*
In al his lif unto no manere wight:°   *no kind of man*
He was a verray,° parfit,° gentil° knight.   *true / perfect / noble*
But for to tellen you of his array,°   *equipment*

5. Fidelity and good reputation, generosity and courtliness.
6. The place-names Chaucer lists over the next 15 lines
were primarily associated with 14th-century Crusades
against both Muslims and Eastern Orthodox Christians.
Alisandre: Alexandria in Egypt; Pruce: Prussia; Lettou:
Lithuania; Ruce: Russia; Gernade and Algezir: Granada
and Algeciras in Spain; Belmarye: Ben-Marin near
Morocco; Lyeis: Ayash in Turkey; Satalye: Atalia in
Turkey; Grete See: Mediterranean; Tramissene: Tlemcen
near Morocco; Palatye: Balat in Turkey.
7. Held the place of honor at feasts.
8. Tournaments waged to the death.

His hors were goode, but he was nat gay.°   *gaily attired*

75   Of fustian° he wered a gipoun°   *coarse cloth / tunic*

Al bismotered with his haubergeoun,[9]

For he was late come from his viage,°   *expedition*

And wente for to doon his pilgrimage.

     With him ther was his sone, a yong Squier,

80   A lovere and a lusty bacheler,[1]

With lokkes crulle° as they were laid in presse.   *curled*

Of twenty yeer of age he was, I gesse.

Of his stature he was of evene° lengthe,   *average*

And wonderly delivere,° and of greet strengthe.   *agile*

85   And he hadde been som time in chivachye°   *cavalry expedition*

In Flandres, in Artois, and Picardye,[2]

And born him wel as of so litel space,°   *time*

In hope to stonden in his lady grace.°   *lady's favor*

     Embrouded° was he as it were a mede,°   *embroidered / meadow*

90   Al ful of fresshe flowres, white and rede;

Singing he was, or floiting,° al the day: *playing the flute*

He was as fressh as is the month of May.

Short was his gowne, with sleeves longe and wide.

Wel coude he sitte on hors, and faire ride;

95   He coude songes make, and wel endite,°   *compose*

Juste° and eek daunce, and wel portraye° and write.   *joust / draw*

So hote he loved that by nightertale°   *nighttime*

He slepte namore than dooth a nightingale.

Curteis he was, lowely,° and servisable,°   *humble / attentive*

100   And carf° biforn his fader° at the table   *carved / father*

     A Yeman[3] hadde he° and servants namo   *i.e., the Knight*

At that time, for him liste° ride so;   *he liked*

And he was clad in cote and hood of greene.

A sheef of pecok arwes,° bright and keene,   *peacock arrows*

105   Under his belt he bar ful thriftily;

Wel coude he dresse° his takel° yemanly: *arrange / gear*

His arwes drouped nought with fetheres lowe.

And in his hand he bar a mighty bowe.

A not-heed° hadde he with a brown visage.°   *short haircut / face*

110   Of wodecraft° wel coude he al the usage.   *forestry*

Upon his arm he bar a gay bracer,°   *archer's armguard*

And by his side a swerd and a bokeler,°   *small shield*

And on that other side a gay daggere,

Harneised wel and sharp as point of spere;

115   A Cristophre[4] on his brest of silver sheene;

An horn he bar, the baudrik° was of greene.   *shoulder strap*

A forster° was he soothly,° as I gesse.   *gamekeeper / truly*

     Ther was also a Nonne, a Prioresse,

That of hir smiling was ful simple and coy.°   *quiet, shy*

---

9. Rust-stained from his coat of mail.

1. An unmarried and unpropertied younger knight.

2. Regions in the north of France and in what is now Belgium, where the English and the French were fighting out the Hundred Years' War.

3. A yeoman was a freeborn servant (not a peasant), who looked after the affairs of the gentry. This particular yeoman was a forester and gamekeeper for the Knight.

4. Medal of St. Christopher, patron saint of travelers.

120	Hir gretteste ooth was but by Sainte Loy!⁵
	And she was cleped° Madame Eglantine.°
	Ful wel she soong the service divine,
	Entuned in hir nose ful semely;°
	And Frenssh she spak ful faire and fetisly,°
125	After the scole of Stratford at the Bowe⁶
	For Frenssh of Paris was to hire unknowe.
	At mete° wel ytaught was she withalle:
	She leet no morsel from hir lippes falle,
	Ne wette hir fingres in hir sauce deepe;
130	Wel coude she carye a morsel, and wel keepe°
	That no drope ne fille upon hir brest.
	In curteisye was set ful muchel hir lest.°
	Hir over-lippe° wiped she so clene
	That in hir coppe ther was no ferthing⁷ seene
135	Of grece,° whan she dronken hadde hir draughte;
	Ful semely after hir mete she raughte.°
	And sikerly° she was of greet disport,°
	And ful plesant, and amiable of port,
	And pained hire to countrefete cheere°
140	Of court, and to been estatlich° of manere,
	And to been holden digne° of reverence.
	But, for to speken of hir conscience,
	She was so charitable and so pitous
	She wolde weepe if that she saw a mous
145	Caught in a trappe, if it were deed or bledde.
	Of smale houndes hadde she that she fedde
	With rosted flessh,° or milk and wastelbreed;⁸
	But sore wepte she if oon of hem were deed,
	Or if men smoot° it with a yerde° smerte;°
150	And al was conscience and tendre herte.
	Ful semely hir wimpel⁹ pinched was,
	Hir nose tretis,° hir yën greye as glas,
	Hir mouth ful smal, and therto softe and reed—
	But sikerly she hadde a fair forheed:
155	It was almost a spanne¹ brood, I trowe,°
	For hardily,° she was nat undergrowe.°
	Ful fetis° was hir cloke, as I was war;
	Of smal coral aboute hir arm she bar
	A paire of bedes, gauded al with greene,²
160	And theron heeng a brooch of gold ful sheene,
	On which ther was first writen a crowned A.³
	And after, *Amor vincit omnia*.⁴

called / Brier-rose

becomingly

elegantly

meals

safeguard

her great pleasure
upper lip

grease
reached for her food
certainly / good cheer

appearance
stately
worthy

meat

hit / rod / painfully

shapely

believe
assuredly / short
elegant

---

5. St. Eligius, patron saint of metalworkers, believed never to have sworn an oath in his life.

6. From the school (i.e., after the manner) of Stratford, a suburb of London where the prosperous convent of St. Leonard's was located; her French is Anglo-Norman as opposed to the French spoken on the Continent.

7. Spot the size of a farthing.

8. Bread of the finest quality.

9. A pleated headdress covering all but the face, such as nuns and married women wore.

1. A hand's width, 7 to 9 inches.

2. A set of rosary beads, marked off by larger beads (gauds) to indicate where the Paternosters should be said.

3. The letter "A" with a crown on top.

4. Love conquers all (Virgil, *Eclogues*, 10.69). Though pagan and secular in origin, the phrase was often used to refer to divine love as well.

Another Nonne with hire hadde she
That was hir chapelaine,° and preestes three.   *secretary*
165   A Monk ther was, a fair for the maistrye,°   *very good-looking*
An outridere[5] that loved venerye,°   *hunting*
A manly° man, to been an abbot able.   *courageous*
Ful many a daintee° hors hadde he in stable,   *fine*
And whan he rood, men mighte his bridel heere
170   Ginglen° in a whistling wind as clere   *jingling*
And eek as loude as dooth the chapel belle
Ther as this lord was kepere of the celle.[6]
The rule of Saint Maure or of Saint Beneit,[7]
By cause that it was old and somdeel strait°—   *somewhat strict*
175   This ilke Monk leet olde thinges pace,
And heeld after the newe world the space.°   *the times (customs)*
He yaf nought of that text° a pulled° hen   *regulation / plucked*
That saith that hunteres been nought holy men,
Ne that a monk, whan he is recchelees,°   *careless*
180   Is likned til a fissh that is waterlees—
This is to sayn, a monk out of his cloistre;
But thilke° text heeld he nat worth an oystre.   *that same*
And I saide his opinion was good:
What sholde he studye and make himselven wood°   *crazy*
185   Upon a book in cloistre alway to poure,
Or swinke° with his handes and laboure,   *work*
As Austin[8] bit?° How shal the world be served?   *orders*
Lat Austin have his swink° to him reserved!   *toil*
Therfore he was a prikasour° aright.   *hunter on horseback*
190   Grehoundes he hadde as swift as fowl in flight.
Of priking and of hunting for the hare
Was al his lust,° for no cost wolde he spare.   *pleasure*
I sawgh his sleeves purfiled° at the hand   *fur-lined*
With gris,° and that the fineste of a land;   *gray fur*
195   And for to festne his hood under his chin
He hadde of gold wrought a ful curious° pin: *elaborate*
A love-knotte[9] in the grettere° ende ther was.   *larger*
His heed was balled,° that shoon as any glas,   *bald*
And eek his face, as he hadde been anoint:
200   He was a lord ful fat and in good point;°   *in good shape*
His yën steepe,° and rolling in his heed,   *bright*
That stemed as a furnais of a leed;[1]
His bootes souple,° his hors in greet estat[2]—   *supple*
Now certainly he was a fair prelat.[3]
205   He was nat pale as a forpined° gost: *tormented*
A fat swan loved he best of any rost.
His palfrey° was as brown as is a berye.   *saddle horse*

---

5. A monk who worked outside the confines of the monastery.
6. Supervisor of the outlying cell of the monastery.
7. St. Benedict (Beneit) was the founder of Western monasticism, and his Rule prohibited monks from leaving the grounds of the monastery without special permission. St. Maurus introduced the Benedictine order into France.
8. St. Augustine recommended that monks perform manual labor.
9. An elaborate knot.
1. Glowed like a furnace under a cauldron.
2. Excellent condition.
3. Prelate, important churchman.

	A Frere° ther was, a wantoune[4] and a merye,	*Friar*
	A limitour,[5] a ful solempne man.	
210	In alle the ordres foure[6] is noon that can°	*knows*
	So muche of daliaunce° and fair langage:	*flirtation*
	He hadde maad ful many a mariage	
	Of yonge wommen at his owene cost;	
	Unto his ordre he was a noble post.°	*pillar*
215	Ful wel biloved and familier was he	
	With frankelains[7] over al in his contree,	
	And with worthy wommen of the town—	
	For he hadde power of confessioun,	
	As saide himself, more than a curat,°	*parish priest*
220	For of his ordre he was licenciat.[8]	
	Ful swetely herde he confessioun,	
	And plesant was his absolucioun.	
	He was an esy man to yive penaunce	
	Ther as he wiste to have a good pitaunce;[9]	
225	For unto a poore ordre for to yive	
	Is signe that a man is wel yshrive;°	*absolved*
	For if he yaf, he dorste make avaunt°	*boast*
	He wiste that a man was repentaunt;	
	For many a man so hard is of his herte	
230	He may nat weepe though him sore smerte:°	*hurts*
	Therfore, in stede of weeping and prayeres,	
	Men mote yive silver to the poore freres.	
	His tipet° was ay farsed° ful of knives	*scarf / packed*
	And pinnes, for to yiven faire wives;	
235	And certainly he hadde a merye note;	
	Wel coude he singe and playen on a rote;°	*fiddle*
	Of yeddinges° he bar outrely the pris.[1]	*singing ballads*
	His nekke whit was as the flowr-de-lis;[2]	
	Therto he strong was as a champioun.	
240	He knew the tavernes wel in every town,	
	And every hostiler and tappestere,°	*innkeeper and barmaid*
	Bet than a lazar or a beggestere.°	*a leper or a beggar*
	For unto swich a worthy man as he	
	Accorded nat, as by his facultee,°[3]	*official position*
245	To have with sike° lazars aquaintaunce:	*such*
	It is nat honeste,° it may nought avaunce,°	*dignified / profit*
	For to delen with no swich poraile,°	*poor people*
	But al with riche, and selleres of vitaile;°	*food*
	And over al ther as profit sholde arise,	
250	Curteis he was, and lowely° of servise.	*humble*
	Ther was no man nowher so vertuous:°	*capable*
	He was the beste beggere in his hous.	
	And yaf a certain ferme for the graunt:[4]	

4. Jovial, pleasure-seeking.
5. Friar licensed by his order to beg for alms within a given district.
6. The four orders of friars were the Carmelites, Augustinians, Dominicans, and Franciscans.
7. Franklins, important property holders.
8. Licensed by the Church to hear confessions.
9. Where he knew he would get a good donation.
1. Utterly took the prize.
2. Lily, emblem of the royal house of France.
3. It was unbecoming to his official post.
4. And gave a certain fee for the license to beg.

Noon of his bretheren cam ther in his haunt.°   *territory*
255 For though a widwe hadde nought a sho,
So plesant was his *In principio*[5]
Yit wolde he have a ferthing er he wente;
His purchas° was wel bettre than his rente.°   *income / expense*
And rage° he coude as it were right a whelpe;°   *flirt / puppy*
260 In love-dayes[6] ther coude he muchel helpe,
For ther he was nat lik a cloisterer,
With a thredbare cope, as is a poore scoler,
But he was lik a maister° or a pope.   *professor*
Of double worstede was his semicope,°[7]   *short cloak*
265 And rounded as a belle out of the presse.°   *bell-mold*
Somwhat he lipsed for his wantounesse
To make his Englissh sweete upon his tonge;
And in his harping, whan that he hadde songe,
His yën twinkled in his heed aright
270 As doon the sterres in the frosty night.
This worthy limitour was cleped° Huberd.   *called*
     A Marchant was ther with a forked beerd,
In motlee,° and hye on hors he sat,   *multicolored fabric*
Upon his heed a Flandrissh° bevere hat,   *Flemish*
275 His bootes clasped faire and fetisly.°   *elegantly*
His resons° he spak ful solempnely,   *opinions*
Souning° alway th'encrees of his winning.   *announcing*
He wolde the see were kept for any thing°   *protected at all costs*
Bitwixen Middelburgh and Orewelle.[8]
280 Wel coude he in eschaunge sheeldes[9] selle.
This worthy man ful wel his wit bisette:°   *employed*
Ther wiste° no wight° that he was in dette,   *knew / person*
So estatly° was he of his governaunce,°   *dignified / management*
With his bargaines, and with his chevissaunce.°   *borrowing*
285 Forsoothe° he was a worthy man withalle;   *in truth*
But, sooth to sayn, I noot° how men him calle.   *do not know*
     A Clerk ther was of Oxenforde also
That unto logik hadde longe ygo.°   *gone (studied)*
As lene was his hors as is a rake,
290 And he was nought right fat, I undertake,
But looked holwe,° and therto sobrely.   *emaciated*
Ful thredbare was his overeste courtepy,°   *outer cloak*
For he hadde geten him yit no benefice,°   *church income*
Ne was so worldly for to have office.°   *secular employment*
295 For him was levere° have at his beddes heed   *he preferred*
Twenty bookes, clad in blak or reed,
Of Aristotle and his philosophye,
Than robes riche, or fithele,° or gay sautrye.°   *fiddle / harp*
But al be that he was a philosophre[1]

---

5. "In the beginning," the opening line in Genesis and
the Gospel of John, popular for devotions.
6. Holidays for settling disputes out of court.
7. His short cloak was made of thick woolen cloth.
8. Middelburgh in the Netherlands and Orwell in Suffolk

were major ports for the wool trade.
9. Unit of exchange, a credit instrument for foreign merchants.
1. A philosopher could be a scientist or alchemist.

300	Yit hadde he but litel gold in cofre;	
	But al that he mighte of his freendes hente,°	*get*
	On bookes and on lerning he it spente,	
	And bisily gan for the soules praye	
	Of hem that yaf him wherwith to scoleye.°	*study*
305	Of studye took he most cure° and most heede.	*care*
	Nought oo° word spak he more than was neede,	*one*
	And that was said in forme° and reverence,	*formally*
	And short and quik, and ful of height sentence:°	*lofty meaning*
	Souning in° moral vertu was his speeche,	*consonant with*
310	And gladly wolde he lerne, and gladly teche.	
	A Sergeant of the Lawe,² war and wis,	
	That often hadde been at the Parvis³	
	Ther was also, ful riche of excellence.	
	Discreet he was, and of greet reverence—	
315	He seemed swich, his wordes weren so wise.	
	Justice he was ful often in assise⁴	
	By patente and by plein commissioun.⁵	
	For his science° and for his heigh renown	*knowledge*
	Of fees and robes hadde he many oon.	
320	So greet a purchasour° was nowher noon;	*buyer of land*
	Al was fee simple⁶ to him in effect—	
	His purchasing mighte nat been infect.°	*invalidated*
	Nowher so bisy a man as he ther nas;	
	And yit he seemed bisier than he was.	
325	In termes hadde he caas and doomes° alle	*lawsuits and judgments*
	That from the time of King William⁷ were falle.	
	Therto he coude endite and make a thing,⁸	
	Ther coude no wight° pinchen° at his writing;	*person / find fault with*
	And every statut coude he plein by rote.⁹	
330	He rood but hoomly° in a medlee° cote,	*simply / multicolored*
	Girt with a ceint° of silk, with barres° smale.	*belt / stripes*
	Of his array telle I no lenger tale.	
	A Frankelain¹ was in his compaignye:	
	Whit was his beerd as is the dayesye;°	*daisy*
335	Of his complexion he was sanguin.²	
	Wel loved he by the morwe a sop in win.³	
	To liven in delit° was evere his wone,°	*pleasure / custom*
	For he was Epicurus owene sone,	
	That heeld opinion that plein° delit	*complete*
340	Was verray felicitee parfit.⁴	
	An housholdere and that a greet was he:	
	Saint Julian⁵ he was in his contree.	

---

2. A lawyer of the highest rank.
3. The porch of St. Paul's Cathedral, a meeting place for lawyers.
4. He was often judge in the court of assizes (civil court).
5. By letter of appointment from the king and by full jurisdiction.
6. Owned outright with no legal impediments.
7. Since the introduction of Norman law in England under William the Conqueror.

8. Compose and draw up a deed.
9. He knew entirely from memory.
1. A large landholder, freeborn but not belonging to the nobility.
2. In temperament he was sanguine (optimistic, governed by blood as his chief humor).
3. In the morning a sop of bread soaked in wine.
4. True and perfect happiness.
5. Patron saint of hospitality.

His breed, his ale, was always after oon;°   *just as good*
A bettre envined° man was nevere noon.   *stocked with wine*
345   Withouten bake mete was nevere his hous,
Of fissh and flessh, and that so plentevous°   *plentiful*
It snewed° in his hous of mete and drinke,   *snowed*
Of alle daintees that men coude thinke.
After the sondry sesons of the yeer
350   So chaunged he his mete and his soper.[6]
Ful many a fat partrich° hadde he in mewe,°   *partridge / cage*
And many a breem,° and many a luce° in stewe.°   *carp / pike / pond*
Wo was his cook but if his sauce were
Poinant° and sharp, and redy al his gere.   *pungent*
355   His table dormant[7] in his halle alway
Stood redy covered al the longe day.
At sessions[8] ther was he lord and sire.
Ful ofte time he was Knight of the Shire.[9]
An anlaas° and a gipser° al of silk   *dagger / purse*
360   Heeng at his girdel, whit as morne milk.
A shirreve hadde he been, and countour.[1]
Was nowher swich a worthy vavasour.[2]

An Haberdasshere° and a Carpenter,   *hat-maker*
A Webbe, a Dyere, and a Tapicer[3]—
365   And they were clothed alle in oo liveree°   *in the same uniform*
Of a solempne and a greet fraternitee.°   *parish guild*
Ful fresshe and newe hir gere apiked was;[4]
Hir knives were chaped° nought with bras,   *mounted*
But al with silver; wrought ful clene° and weel   *quite nicely made*
370   Hir girdles and hir pouches everydeel.°   *entirely*
Wel seemed eech of hem a fair burgeis°   *townsperson*
To sitten in a yeldehalle° on a dais.   *guildhall*
Everich, for the wisdom that he can,°   *knows*
Was shaply° for to been an alderman.°   *fit / mayor*
375   For catel° hadde they ynough and rente,°   *property / income*
And eek hir wives wolde it wel assente—
And elles certain were they to blame:
It is ful fair to been ycleped° "Madame,"   *called*
And goon to vigilies[5] al bifore,
380   And have a mantel royalliche ybore.

A Cook they hadde with hem for the nones,°   *for the occasion*
To boile the chiknes with the marybones,°   *marrowbones*
And powdre-marchant tart and galingale.°   *aromatic spices*
Wel coude he knowe a draughte of London ale.
385   He coude roste, and seethe,° and broile, and frye,   *boil*
Maken mortreux,° and wel bake a pie.   *stews*

---

6. For health he changed his diet according to the different seasons.
7. Left standing rather than dismantled between meals.
8. Meetings of the justices of the peace.
9. A representative of the district at Parliament.
1. He had been sheriff and auditor of the county finances.

2. Lower member of the feudal elite.
3. A weaver, dyer, and a tapestry-maker, all members of the
same commercial guild.
4. Their gear was decorated.
5. Feasts held the night before a holy day.

But greet harm was it, as it thoughte me,
That on his shine a mormal° hadde he.   ulcer
For blankmanger,° that made he with the beste.   thick stew
390   A Shipman was ther, woning° fer by weste—   dwelling
For ought I woot,° he was of Dertemouthe.[6]   know
He rood upon a rouncy° as he couthe,   nag
In a gowne of falding° to the knee.   coarse brown cloth
A daggere hanging on a laas° hadde he   strap
395   Aboute his nekke, under his arm adown.
The hote somer hadde maad his hewe al brown;
And certainly he was a good felawe.
Ful many a draughte of win hadde he drawe
Fro Burdeuxward, whil that the chapman° sleep[7]:   merchant
400   Of nice° conscience took he no keep;°   scrupulous / care
If that he faught and hadde the hyer hand,
By water he sente hem hoom to every land.
But of his craft, to rekene wel his tides,
His stremes° and his daungers° him bisides,   currents / hazards
405   His herberwe° and his moone, his lodemenage,°   harboring / navigation
Ther was noon swich from Hulle to Cartage.[8]
Hardy he was and wis to undertake;
With many a tempest hadde his beerd been shake;
He knew alle the havenes as they were
410   Fro Gotlond to the Cape of Finistere,[9]
And every crike° in Britaine° and in Spaine.   inlet / Brittany
His barge ycleped was the Maudelaine.
        With us ther was a Doctour of Physik:°   Medicine
In al this world ne was ther noon him lik
415   To speken of physik and of surgerye.
For he was grounded in astronomye,°   astrology
He kepte his pacient a ful greet deel
In houres° by his magik naturel.   astronomical hours
Wel coude he fortunen the ascendent[1]
420   Of his images° for his pacient.   talismans
He knew the cause of every maladye,
Were it of hoot or cold or moiste or drye,[2]
And where engendred° and of what humour:[3]   originated
He was a verray parfit praktisour.°   practitioner
425   The cause yknowe, and of his harm the roote,
Anoon he yaf the sike man his boote.°   remedy
        Ful redy hadde he his apothecaries
To senden him drogges and his letuaries,°   medicines
For eech of hem made other for to winne:

6. Dartmouth, a port on the southwestern coast.
7. On the trip back from Bordeaux while the merchant slept.
8. Hull, on the northeastern coast in Yorkshire; Cartage: Carthage in North Africa or Cartagena on the Mediterranean coast of Spain.
9. Gotland in the Baltic Sea; Finistere: Land's End in western Spain.

1. Calculate the ascendent (propitious moment).
2. The qualities of the four natural elements, corresponding to the humors of the body and the composition of the universe, needed to be kept in perfect balance.
3. Bodily fluids, or "humors," thought to govern moods (blood, phlegm, black bile, yellow bile).

430   Hir frendshipe was nought newe to biginne.
       Wel knew he the olde Esculapius,[4]
       And Deiscorides and eek Rufus,
       Olde Ipocras, Hali, and Galien,
       Serapion, Razis, and Avicen,
435   Averrois, Damascien, and Constantin,
       Bernard, and Gatesden, and Gilbertin.
       Of his diete mesurable° was he,   *moderate*
       For it was of no superfluitee,
       But of greet norissing and digestible.
440   His studye was but litel on the Bible.
       In sanguin° and in pers° he clad was al,   *red / Persian blue*
       Lined with taffata and with sendal;°   *silks*
       And yit he was but esy of dispence;°   *thrifty*
       He kepte that he wan in pestilence.
445   For gold in physik is a cordial,°   *tonic*
       Therfore he loved gold in special.
              A good Wif was ther of biside Bathe,
       But she was somdeel deef,° and that was scathe.°   *somewhat deaf / a pity*
       Of cloth-making she hadde swich an haunt,°   *practice*
450   She passed hem of Ypres and of Gaunt.[5]
       In al the parissh wif ne was ther noon
       That to the offring[6] bifore hire sholde goon,
       And if ther dide, certain so wroth° was she   *angry*
       That she was out of alle charitee.
455   Hir coverchiefs ful fine were of ground[7]—
       I dorste swere they weyeden° ten pound   *weighed*
       That on a Sonday weren upon hir heed.
       Hir hosen° weren of fin scarlet reed,   *stockings*
       Ful straite yteyd,° and shoes ful moiste° and newe.   *tightly laced / supple*
460   Bold was hir face and fair and reed of hewe.
       She was a worthy womman al hir live:
       Housbondes at chirche dore she hadde five,
       Withouten other compaignye in youthe—
       But therof needeth nought to speke as nouthe.°   *for now*
465   And thries hadde she been at Jerusalem;
       She hadde passed many a straunge streem;
       At Rome she hadde been, and at Boloigne,[8]
       In Galice at Saint Jame, and at Coloigne:
       She coude° muchel of wandring by the waye.   *knew*
470   Gat-toothed° was she, soothly for to saye.   *gap-toothed*
       Upon an amblere[9] esily she sat,
       Ywimpled[1] wel, and on hir heed an hat

4. The Physician is acquainted with a full range of medical authorities from among the ancient Greeks (Aesculapius, Dioscorides, Rufus, Hippocrates, Galen, and Sera-
pion), the Persians (Hali and Rhazes), the Arabs
(Avicenna and Averroes), the Mediterranean transmit-
ters of Eastern science to the West (John of Damascus,
Constantine the African), and later medical school professors (Bernard of Gordon, who taught at Montpellier;
John of Gaddesden, who taught at Merton College; and
Gilbertus Anglicus, an early contemporary of Chaucer's).
5. Centers of Flemish cloth-making.
6. The collection of gifts at the consecration of the Mass.
7. Her linen kerchiefs were fine in texture.
8. Rome, Boulogne, Santiago Compostela, and Cologne
were major European pilgrimage sites.
9. A horse with a gentle pace.
1. Wearing a large headdress that covers all but the face.

As brood as is a bokeler or a targe,°   *small shields*
A foot-mantel° aboute hir hipes large,   *riding skirt*
475 And on hir feet a paire of spores° sharpe.   *spurs*
In felaweshipe wel coude she laughe and carpe:
Of remedies of love she knew parchaunce,[2]
For she coude of that art the olde daunce.°   *tricks*
A good man was ther of religioun,
480 And was a poore Person° of a town,   *parson*
But riche he was of holy thought and werk.
He was also a lerned man, a clerk,
That Cristes gospel trewely wolde preche;
His parisshens° devoutly wolde he teche.   *parishioners*
485 Benigne he was, and wonder diligent,
And in adversitee ful pacient,
And swich he was preved ofte sithes.
Ful loth were him to cursen for his tithes,[3]
But rather wolde he yiven, out of doute,
490 Unto his poore parisshens aboute
Of his offring and eek of his substaunce:°   *possessions*
He coude in litel thing have suffisaunce.
Wid was his parissh, and houses fer asonder,
But he ne lafte nought for rain ne thonder,
495 In siknesse nor in meschief, to visite
The ferreste in his parissh, muche and lite,[4]
Upon his feet, and in his hand a staf.
This noble ensample° to his sheep he yaf   *example*
That first he wroughte,° and afterward he taughte.   *did*
500 Out of the Gospel he tho° wordes caughte,   *those*
And this figure° he added eek therto: *saying*
That if gold ruste, what shal iren do?
For if a preest be foul, on whom we truste,
No wonder is a lewed° man to ruste.   *uneducated*
505 And shame it is, if a preest take keep,°   *is concerned*
A shiten° shepherde and a clene sheep.   *shit-covered*
Wel oughte a preest ensample for to yive
By his clennesse how that his sheep sholde live.
He sette nought his benefice to hire[5]
510 And leet his sheep encombred in the mire
And ran to London, unto Sainte Poules,
To seeken him a chaunterye for soules,
Or with a bretherhede to been withholde,
But dwelte at hoom and kepte wel his folde,
515 So that the wolf ne made it nought miscarye:
He was a shepherde and nought a mercenarye.
And though he holy were and vertuous,
He was to sinful men nought despitous,°   *scornful*

---

2. She knew cures for lovesickness, as it happened.
3. And so was he shown to be many times. / He was most unwilling to curse parishioners (with excommunication) if they failed to pay his tithes (a tenth of their income due to the Church).

4. The furthest away in his parish, great and small.
5. The priest did not rent out his parish to another in order to take a more profitable position saying masses for the dead at the chantries of St. Paul's in London or to serve as chaplain to a wealthy guild (bretherhede).

Ne of his speeche daungerous ne digne,°   *haughty*
520   But in his teching discreet and benigne,
To drawen folk to hevene by fairnesse
By good ensample—this was his bisinesse.
But it were any persone obstinat,
What so he were, of heigh or lowe estat,
525   Him wolde he snibben° sharply for the nones:°   *rebuke / on the spot*
A bettre preest I trowe° ther nowher noon is.   *believe*
He waited after° no pompe and reverence,   *expected*
Ne maked him a spiced° conscience,   *overly critical*
But Cristes lore° and his Apostles twelve   *teaching*
530   He taughte, but first he folwed° it himselve.   *followed*
With him ther was a Plowman, was his brother,
That hadde ylad of dong ful many a fother.⁶
A trewe swinkere° and a good was he,   *worker*
Living in pees° and parfit° charitee.   *peace / perfect*
535   God loved he best with al his hoole herte
At alle times, though him gamed or smerte,⁷
And thanne his neighebor right as himselve.
He wolde thresshe, and therto dike and delve,°   *make ditches and dig*
For Cristes sake, for every poore wight,°   *person*
540   Withouten hire,° if it laye in his might.   *pay*
His tithes payed he ful faire and wel,
Bothe of his propre swink⁸ and his catel.°   *possessions*
In a tabard° rood upon a mere.°   *smock / mare*
Ther was also a Reeve° and a Millere,   *estate manager*
545   A Somnour, and a Pardoner⁹ also,
A Manciple,° and myself—ther were namo.   *Steward*
The Millere was a stout carl° for the nones.   *fellow*
Ful big he was of brawn and eek of bones—
That preved wel, for overal ther he cam
550   At wrastling he wolde have alway the ram.¹
He was short-shuldred, brood, a thikke knarre.°   *bully*
Ther was no dore that he nolde heve of harre,°   *push off its hinges*
Or breke it at a renning with his heed.
His beerd as any sowe or fox was reed,
555   And therto brood, as though it were a spade;
Upon the cop° right of his nose he hade   *tip*
A werte, and theron stood a tuft of heres,
Rede as the bristles of a sowes eres;
His nosethirles° blake were and wide.   *nostrils*
560   A swerd and a bokeler° bar° he by his side.   *small shield / carried*
His mouth as greet was as a greet furnais.
He was a janglere and a Goliardais,²
And that was most of sinne and harlotries.°   *obscenities*
Wel coude he stelen corn and tollen thries³—

6. That had carried many a cartload of manure.
7. Enjoyed himself or suffered pain.
8. Money earned from his own work.
9. A Summonour, a server of summonses for the ecclesiastical courts; Pardoner: a seller of indulgences.
1. Awarded as a prize for wrestling.
2. He was a teller of dirty stories and a reveller.
3. Collect three times as much tax as was due.

565	And yit he hadde a thombe of gold,[4] pardee.°	*by God*
	A whit cote and a blew hood wered he.	
	A baggepipe wel coude he blowe and soune,	
	And therwithal he broughte us out of towne.	
	A gentil Manciple was ther of a temple,°	*law school*
570	Of which achatours° mighte take exemple	*buyers*
	For to been wise in bying of vitaile;°	*food*
	For wheither that he paide or took by taile,°	*on credit*
	Algate he waited so in his achat[5]	
	That he was ay biforn° and in good stat.°	*always ahead / well off*
575	Now is nat that of God a ful fair grace°	*blessing*
	That swich a lewed° mannes wit shal pace°	*uneducated / surpass*
	The wisdom of an heep of lerned men?	
	Of maistres° hadde he mo than thries ten	*scholars*
	That weren of lawe expert and curious,°	*skillful*
580	Of whiche ther were a dozeine in that house	
	Worthy to been stiwardes of rente° and lond	*managers of revenues*
	Of any lord that is in Engelond,	
	To make him live by his propre good°	*own wealth*
	In honour dettelees but if he were wood,°	*unless he were crazy*
585	Or live as scarsly° as him list° desire,	*thriftily / pleases*
	And able for to helpen al a shire	
	In any caas° that mighte falle° or happe,	*event / befall*
	And yit this Manciple sette hir aller cappe!°	*made fools of them all*
	The Reeve was a sclendre° colerik° man;	*lean / ill-tempered*
590	His beerd was shave as neigh° as evere he can;	*close*
	His heer was by his eres ful round yshorn;	
	His top was dokked° lik a preest biforn;°	*clipped / in front*
	Ful longe were his legges and ful lene,	
	Ylik° a staf, ther was no calf yseene.°	*like / visible*
595	Wel coude he keepe a gerner° a binne—	*granary*
	Ther was noon auditour coude on him winne.[6]	
	Wel wiste he by the droughte and by the rain	
	The yeelding of his seed and of his grain.	
	His lordes sheep, his neet,° his dayerye,°	*cattle / dairy cattle*
600	His swim, his hors, his stoor,° and his pultrye	*livestock*
	Was hoolly in this Reeves governinge,	
	And by his covenant° yaf the rekeninge,°	*contract / gave account*
	Sin that his lord was twenty yeer of age.	
	Ther coude no man bringe him in arrerage.°	*financial arrears*
605	Ther nas baillif, hierde, nor other hine,[7]	
	That he ne knew his sleighte° and his covine°—	*tricks / plotting*
	They were adrad of him as of the deeth.	
	His woning° was ful faire upon an heeth;°	*dwelling / meadow*
	With greene trees shadwed was his place.	
610	He coude bettre than his lord purchace.°	*buy property*
	Ful riche he was astored prively.°	*stocked in secret*

---

4. It was proverbial that millers were dishonest and that an honest miller was as rare as one who had a golden thumb. The statement is meant ironically.
5. He was always so watchful for his opportunities to pur-
chase.
6. Gain anything (by catching him out).
7. There was no foreman, herdsman, or other farmhand.

His lord wel coude he plesen subtilly,
To yive and lene° him of his owene good,°   *lend / possessions*
And have a thank,° and yit a cote and hood.   *gratitude*
615   In youthe he hadde lerned a good mister:°   *profession*
He was a wel good wrighte, a carpenter.
This Reeve sat upon a ful good stot°   *stallion*
That was a pomely° grey and highte° Scot.   *dappled / named*
A long surcote° of pers° upon he hade,   *overcoat / blue*
620   And by his side he bar a rusty blade.
Of Northfolk[8] was this Reeve of which I telle,
Biside a town men clepen° Baldeswelle.   *call*
Tukked[9] he was as is a frere aboute,
And evere he rood the hindreste° of oure route.°   *hindmost / group*
625   A Somnour was ther with us in that place
That hadde a fir-reed° cherubinnes° face,   *fire-red / cherub's*
For saucefleem° he was, with yën narwe,   *pimply*
And hoot he was, and lecherous as a sparwe,°   *sparrow*
With scaled° browes blake and piled[1] beerd: *scabby*
630   Of his visage children were aferd.°   *frightened*
Ther nas quiksilver, litarge, ne brimstoon,
Boras, ceruce, ne oile of tartre noon,[2]
Ne oinement that wolde clense and bite,
That him mighte helpen of his whelkes° white,   *blotches*
635   Nor of the knobbes° sitting on his cheekes.   *lumps*
Wel loved he garlek, oinons, and eek leekes,
And for to drinke strong win reed as blood.
Thanne wolde he speke and crye as he were wood;°   *crazy*
And whan that he wel dronken hadde the win,
640   Thanne wolde he speke no word but Latin:
A fewe termes hadde he, two or three,
That he hadde lerned out of som decree;
No wonder is—he herde it al the day,
And eek ye knowe wel how that a jay°   *parrot*
645   Can clepen "Watte"° as wel as can the Pope—   *call "Walter"*
But whoso coude in other thing him grope,°   *examine*
Thanne hadde he spent all his philosophye;
Ay *Questio quid juris*[3] wolde he crye.
He was a gentil harlot° and a kinde;   *rascal*
650   A bettre felawe sholde men nought finde:
He wolde suffre,° for a quart of win,   *allow*
A good felawe to have his concubin°   *mistress*
A twelfmonth, and excusen him at the fulle;
Ful prively a finch eek coude he pulle.[4]
655   And if he foond owher° a good felawe   *anywhere*
He wolde techen him to have noon awe
In swich caas of the Ercedekenes curs,[5]

---

8. Norfolk in the north of England. The Reeve is notable for his northern dialect and regionalisms.
9. He wore his clothes tucked up with a cinch as friars did.
1. With hair falling out.
2. There was not mercury, lead ointment, or sulphur, /

Borax, white lead, nor any oil of tartar that could clean him.
3. "The question as to what point of law (applies)"; often used in ecclesiastical courts.
4. And secretly he also knew how to fool around.
5. In case of excommunication by the archdeacon.

	But if a mannes soule were in his purs,°	*wallet*
	For in his purs he sholde ypunisshed be.	
660	"Purs is the Ercedekenes helle," saide he.	
	But wel I woot° he lied right in deede:	*know*
	Of cursing° oughte eech gilty man him drede,°	*excommunication / fear*
	For curs wol slee° right as assoiling° savith—	*will kill / absolving*
	And also war him of a *significavit.*[6]	
665	In daunger hadde he at his owene gise[7]	
	The yonge girles of the diocise,	
	And knew hir conseil,° and was al hir reed.°	*secrets / advice*
	A gerland hadde he set upon his heed	
	As greet as it were for an ale-stake;°	*tavern sign*
670	A bokeler hadde he maad him of a cake.°	*loaf of bread*
	With him ther rood a gentil Pardoner	
	Of Rouncival,[8] his freend and his compeer,°	*companion*
	That straight was comen fro the Court of Rome.	
	Ful loude he soong, "Com hider, love, to me."[9]	
675	This Somnour bar to him a stif burdoun:°	*a strong baritone*
	Was nevere trompe° of half so greet a soun.	*trumpet*
	This Pardoner hadde heer as yelow as wex,	
	But smoothe it heeng as dooth a strike of flex;°	*clump of flax*
	By ounces° heenge his lokkes that he hadde,	*thin strands*
680	And therwith he his shuldres overspradde,	
	But thinne it lay, by colpons,° oon by oon;	*strands*
	But hood for jolitee° wered he noon,	*fanciness*
	For it was trussed up in his walet:°	*pack*
	Him thoughte he rood al of the newe jet.°	*fashion*
685	Dischevelee° save his cappe he rood al bare.	*loose-haired*
	Swiche glaring yën hadde he as an hare.	
	A vernicle[1] hadde he sowed upon his cappe,	
	His walet biforn him in his lappe,	
	Bretful of pardon,[2] comen from Rome al hoot.	
690	A vois he hadde as smal° as hath a goot;°	*high-pitched / goat*
	No beerd hadde he, ne nevere sholde have;	
	As smoothe it was as it were late yshave:	
	I trowe he were a gelding or a mare.[3]	
	But of his craft,° fro Berwik into Ware,[4]	*skill*
695	Ne was ther swich another pardoner;	
	For in his male° he hadde a pilwe-beer°	*bag / pillowcase*
	Which that he saide was Oure Lady veil;	
	He saide he hadde a gobet° of the sail	*chunk*
	That Sainte Peter hadde whan that he wente	
700	Upon the see, til Jesu Crist him hente.°	*grabbed*
	He hadde a crois of laton,° ful of stones,	*brass cross*
	And in a glas he hadde pigges bones,	
	But with thise relikes whan that he foond	

6. Order of transfer from ecclesiastical to secular courts.
7. Under his control he had at his disposal.
8. A hospital at Charing Cross in London.
9. A popular ballad.
1. A pilgrim badge, reproducing St. Veronica's veil bearing the imprint of Christ's face.
2. Full to the brim with indulgences.
3. I believe he was a gelding (eunuch) or a mare (perhaps
a passive homosexual).
4. Towns north and south of London.

A poore person° dwelling upon lond,   *parson*
705   Upon a day he gat him more moneye
     Than that the person gat in monthes twaye;°   *two*
     And thus with feined flaterye and japes°   *tricks*
     He made the person and the peple his apes.°   *dupes*
     But trewely to tellen at the laste,
710   He was in chirche a noble ecclesiaste;
     Wel coude he rede a lesson and a storye,°   *liturgical texts*
     But alderbest° he soong an offertorye,   *best of all*
     For wel he wiste whan that song was songe,
     He moste preche and wel affile° his tonge   *sharpen*
715   To winne silver, as he ful wel coude—
     Therfore he soong the merierly and loude.
       Now have I told you soothly° in a clause°   *truly / briefly*
     Th'estaat, th'array, the nombre, and eek the cause
     Why that assembled was this compaignye
720   In Southwerk at this gentil hostelrye
     That highte the Tabard, faste by the Belle;[5]
     But now is time to you for to telle
     How that we baren us that ilke° night   *same*
     Whan we were in that hostelrye alight;
725   And after wol I telle of oure viage,°   *trip*
     And al the remenant of oure pilgrimage.
       But first I praye you of youre curteisye
     That ye n'arette° it nought my vilainye°   *consider / rudeness*
     Though that I plainly speke in this matere
730   To telle you hir wordes and hir cheere,°   *comportment*
     Ne though I speke hir wordes proprely;°   *accurately*
     For this ye knowen also wel as I:
     Who so shal telle a tale after a man
     He moot reherce,° as neigh as evere he can,   *must repeat*
735   Everich a word, if it be in his charge,
     Al speke he nevere so rudeliche° and large,°   *crudely / freely*
     Or elles he moot telle his tale untrewe,
     Or feine° thing, or finde wordes newe;   *invent, falsify*
     He may nought spare although he were his brother:
740   He moot as wel saye oo word as another.
     Crist spak himself ful brode° in Holy Writ,   *plainly*
     And wel ye woot° no vilainye is it;   *know*
     Eek Plato saith, who so can him rede,
     The wordes mote be cosin° to the deede.   *closely related*
745   Also I praye you to foryive it me
     Al° have I nat set folk in hir degree°   *although / rank*
     Here in this tale as that they sholde stonde:
     My wit is short, ye may wel understonde.
       Greet cheere made oure Host us everichoon,
750   And to the soper sette he us anoon.
     He served us with vitaile at the beste,
     Strong was the win, and wel to drinke us leste.°   *it pleased*

---

5. Another tavern in Southwark.

A semely° man oure Hoste was withalle   *apt*
For to been a marchal° in an halle;   *master of ceremonies*
755 A large man he was, with yën steepe;°   *glaring eyes*
A fairer burgeis was ther noon in Chepe°—   *Cheapside (in London)*
Bold of his speeche, and wis, and wel ytaught,
And of manhood him lakkede° right naught.   *he lacked*
Eek therto he was right a merye man,
760 And after soper playen he bigan,
And spak of mirthe amonges othere thinges—
Whan that we hadde maad oure rekeninges°—   *paid the bill*
And saide thus, "Now, lordinges, trewely,
Ye been to me right welcome, hertely.
765 For by my trouthe, if that I shal nat lie,
I sawgh nat this yeer so merye a compaignye
At ones in this herberwe° as is now.   *inn*
Fain wolde I doon you mirthe, wiste I how.
And of a mirthe I am right now bithought,
770 To doon you ese, and it shal coste nought.
      Ye goon to Canterbury—God you speede;
The blisful martyr quite° you youre meede.°   *repay / reward*
And wel I woot° as ye goon by the waye   *know*
Ye shapen° you to talen° and to playe,   *intend / tell tales*
775 For trewely, confort ne mirthe is noon
To ride by the waye domb as stoon;
And therfore wol I maken you disport
As I saide erst,° and doon you som confort;   *before*
And if you liketh alle, by oon assent,
780 For to stonden at my juggement,
And for to werken as I shal you saye,
Tomorwe whan ye riden by the waye—
Now by my fader soule that is deed,
But° ye be merye I wol yive you myn heed!   *unless*
785 Holde up youre handes withouten more speeche."
      Oure conseil was nat longe for to seeche;°   *seek*
Us thoughte it was nat worth to make it wis,°   *deliberate*
And graunted him withouten more avis,°   *opinions*
And bade him saye his voirdit° as him leste.   *verdict*
790 "Lordinges," quod he, "now herkneth for the beste;
But taketh it nought, I praye you, in desdain.
This is the point, to speken short and plain,
That eech of you, to shorte with oure waye
In this viage, shal tellen tales twaye°—   *two*
795 To Canterburyward, I mene it so,
And hoomward he shal tellen othere two,
Of aventures that whilom° have bifalle;   *long ago*
And which of you that bereth him best of alle—
That is to sayn, that telleth in this cas
800 Tales of best sentence° and most solas°—   *substance / pleasure*
Shal have a soper at oure aller cost,
Here in this place, sitting by this post,
Whan that we come again fro Canterbury.

And for to make you the more mury
805 I wol myself goodly° with you ride—   *gladly*
Right at myn owene cost—and be youre gide.
And who so wol my juggement withsaye°   *contradict*
Shal paye al that we spende by the waye.
And if ye vouche sauf° that it be so,   *grant*
810 Telle me anoon, withouten wordes mo,
And I wol erly shape° me therfore."   *prepare*
     This thing was graunted and oure othes swore
With ful glad herte, and prayden him also
That he wolde vouche sauf for to do so,
815   And that he wolde been oure governour,
And of oure tales juge° and reportour,°   *judge / recordkeeper*
And sette a soper at a certain pris,°   *price*
And we wol ruled been at his devis,°   *plan*
In heigh and lowe; and thus by oon assent
820 We been accorded to his juggement.
And therupon the win was fet° anoon;   *fetched*
We dronken and to reste wente eechoon°   *everyone*
Withouten any lenger taryinge.
     Amorwe° whan that day bigan to springe   *next morning*
825 Up roos oure Host and was oure aller cok,°   *cock, wake-up call*
And gadred us togidres in a flok,
And forth we riden, a litel more than pas,°   *slow walk*
Unto the watering of Saint Thomas;[6]
And ther oure Host bigan his hors arreste,°   *stop*
830 And saide, "Lordes, herkneth if you leste:°   *it please*
     "Ye woot youre forward° and it you recorde:°   *agreement / remember*
If evensong and morwesong accorde,
Lat see now who shal telle the firste tale.
As evere mote I drinken win or ale,
835 Who so be rebel to my juggement
Shal paye for al that by the way is spent.
Now draweth cut° er that we ferrer twinne:°   *lots / separate furthur*
He which that hath the shorteste shal biginne.
     "Sire Knight," quod he, "my maister and my lord,
840 Now draweth cut, for that is myn accord.°   *wish*
Cometh neer," quod he, "my lady Prioresse,
And ye, sire Clerk, lat be youre shamefastnesse°—   *modesty*
Ne studieth nought. Lay hand to, every man!"
     Anoon to drawen every wight° bigan,   *person*
845 And shortly for to tellen as it was,
Were it by aventure, or sort, or cas,°   *luck, fate or chance*
The soothe° is this, the cut fil° to the Knight;   *truth / fell*
Of which ful blithe° and glad was every wight,   *happy*
And telle he moste his tale, as was resoun,
850 By forward and by composicioun,°   *agreement*
As ye han herd. What needeth wordes mo?
And whan this goode man sawgh that it was so,

6. A brook two miles from London.

As he that wis was and obedient
To keepe his forward by his free assent,
855   He saide, "Sin I shal biginne the game,
What, welcome be the cut, in Goddes name!
Now lat us ride, and herkneth what I saye."
And with that word we riden forth oure waye,
And he bigan with right a merye cheere°   *expression*
860   His tale anoon, and saide as ye may heere.

THE MILLER'S TALE   *The Miller's Tale* both answers and parodies *The Knight's Tale*, a long
aristocratic romance about two knights in rivalry for the hand of a lady. While the Miller tells a
nearly analogous story of erotic competition, his tale is radically shorter and explicitly sexual.
Such brevity and physicality fit his tale's genre—a fabliau, or short comic tale, usually bawdy and
often involving a clerk, a wife, and a cuckolded husband. Following the convention (if not the
reality) that romances were written by and for the nobility and fabliaux by and for the commons,
Chaucer suits *The Miller's Tale* to its teller as aptly as he does the Knight's. Slyly disclaiming re-
sponsibility for the tale, he explains its bawdiness by the Miller's class status: "the Millere is a
cherle" and like his peer the Reeve who follows and "requites" him, tells "harlotrye."

The drunken Miller's insistence on telling his tale to requite the Knight's tale has been
called a "literary peasants' revolt." Although the Miller, a free man, was not actually a peasant,
yeomen of his status were active in the Rising of 1381, and millers in particular played a symbolic role in it. In fact, this tale is highly literate, with its echoes of the Song of Songs and its
parody of the language of courtly love: an actual miller would have had neither the education
nor the social sophistication to tell it. Yet a parody implies some degree of attachment to the
very model being ridiculed, and *The Miller's Tale* is as much a claim upon the Knight's world as
a repudiation of it. The Miller wants to "quiten" the Knight's tale, he says, using a word that
can mean to repay or avenge, but also to fulfill. The tale's several plots converge brilliantly
upon a single cry: "Water!" The tale's impact derives as well from its plenitude of pleasures
(sexual, comic, even religious) after the austere and rigid desires of *The Knight's Tale*.

The Miller's Tale

The Introduction

Whan that the Knight hadde thus his tale ytold,
In al the route° nas ther yong ne old   *group*
That he ne saide it was a noble storye,
And worthy for to drawen° to memorye,   *recall*
5   And namely the gentils° everichoon.   *upper class*
     Oure Hoste lough° and swoor, "So mote I goon,[1]   *laughed*
This gooth aright: unbokeled is the male.[2]
Lat see now who shal telle another tale.
For trewely the game is wel bigonne.
10   Now telleth ye, sire Monk, if that ye conne,°   *know*
Somwhat to quite° with the Knightes tale."   *repay*
     The Millere, that for dronken was al pale,
So that unnethe° upon his hors he sat,   *barely*
He nolde avalen° neither hood ne hat,   *would not remove*
15   Ne abiden no man for his curteisye,
But in Pilates[3] vois he gan to crye,

1. Thus I may proceed.   3. The role of Pilate was traditionally played in a loud
2. The bag is opened (i.e., the games are begun).   and raucous voice in the mystery plays.

And swoor, "By armes and by blood and bones,°   *(of Christ)*
I can° a noble tale for the nones,   *know*
With which I wol now quite the Knightes tale."
20   Oure Hoste sawgh that he was dronke of ale,
And saide, "Abide,° Robin, leve° brother,   *wait / dear*
Som bettre man shal telle us first another.
Abide, and lat us werken thriftily."°   *properly*
"By Goddes soule," quod he, "that wol nat I,
25   For I wol speke or elles go my way."
Oure Host answerde, "Tel on, a devele way!°   *in the devil's name*
Thou art a fool; thy wit is overcome."
"Now herkneth," quod the Millere, "alle and some.°   *one and all*
But first I make a protestacioun
30   That I am dronke: I knowe it by my soun.°   *sound*
And therfore if that I mis speke or saye,
Wite it° the ale of Southwerk, I you praye;   *blame it on*
For I wol telle a legende and a lif [4]
Bothe of a carpenter and of his wif,
35   How that a clerk hath set the wrightes cappe."[5]
The Reeve answerde and saide, "Stint thy clappe!°   *hold your tongue*
Lat be thy lewed° dronken harlotrye.°   *unlearned / obscenity*
It is a sinne and eek a greet folye
To apairen° any man or him defame,   *injure*
40   And eek to bringen wives in swich fame.
Thou maist ynough of othere thinges sayn."
This dronken Millere spak ful soone again,
And saide, "Leve brother Osewold,
Who hath no wif, he is no cokewold.°   *cuckold*
45   But I saye nat therfore that thou art oon.
Ther ben ful goode wives many oon,
And evere a thousand goode ayains oon badde.°   *against one bad*
That knowestou wel thyself but if thou madde.°   *go insane*
Why artou angry with my tale now?
50   I have a wif, pardee,° as wel as thou,   *by God*
Yet nolde I, for the oxen in my plough,[6]
Take upon me more than ynough
As deemen° of myself that I were oon:°   *judge / one (a cuckold)*
I wol bileve wel that I am noon.
55   An housbonde shal nought been inquisitif
Of Goddes privetee,° nor of his wif.   *secrets*
So he may finde Goddes foison° there,   *plenty*
Of the remenant needeth nought enquere."
What sholde I more sayn but this Millere
60   He nolde° his wordes for no man forbere,   *would not*
But tolde his cherles° tale in his manere.   *commoner's*
M'athinketh° that I shal reherce° it here,   *I regret / repeat*
And therfore every gentil wight° I praye,   *person*
Deemeth nought, for Goddes love, that I saye
65   Of yvel entente, but for° I moot° reherse   *because / must*

4. The story of a saint's life.
5. Made a fool of the carpenter.
6. Yet I wouldn't, not even (in wager) for the oxen in my plough.

Hir tales alle, be they bet or werse,
Or elles falsen som of my matere.
And therfore, whoso list it nought yheere
Turne over the leef,° and chese° another tale,   *page / choose*
70   For he shal finde ynowe,° grete and smale,   *enough*
Of storial° thing that toucheth gentilesse,°   *historical / nobility*
And eek moralitee and holinesse:
Blameth nought me if that ye chese amis.
The Millere is a cherl, ye knowe wel this,
75   So was the Reeve eek, and othere mo,
And harlotrye they tolden bothe two.
Aviseth you,° and putte me out of blame: *be warned*
And eek men shal nought maken ernest of game.°   *treat jokes seriously*

The Tale

Whilom° ther was dwelling at Oxenforde   *long ago*
80   A riche gnof° that gestes heeld to boorde,°   *fool / took in boarders*
And of his craft he was a carpenter.
With him ther was dwelling a poore scoler,
Hadde lerned art,[7] but al his fantasye°   *fancy*
Was turned for to lere° astrologye,   *learn*
85   And coude a certain of conclusiouns,°   *predictions*
To deemen by interrogaciouns,[8]
If that men axed° him in certain houres   *asked*
Whan that men sholde have droughte or elles showres,
Or if men axed him what shal bifalle
90   Of every thing—I may nat rekene° hem alle.   *count*
This clerk was cleped° hende[9] Nicholas.   *called*
Of derne° love he coude, and of solas,[1]   *secret*
And therto he was sly and ful privee,°   *secretive*
And lik a maide meeke for to see.
95   A chambre hadde he in that hostelrye°   *inn*
Allone, withouten any compaignye,
Ful fetisly ydight with herbes swoote,[2]
And he himself as sweete as is the roote
Of licoris or any setewale.[3]
100   His Almageste[4] and bookes grete and smale,
His astrelabye,[5] longing for° his art,   *belonging to*
His augrim stones,° layen faire apart   *abacus beads*
On shelves couched° at his beddes heed;   *arranged*
His presse° ycovered with a falding° reed;   *dresser / coarse cloth*
105   And al above ther lay a gay sautrye,°   *harp*
On which he made a-nightes melodye
So swetely that al the chambre roong,
And *Angelus ad Virginem*[6] he soong,

---

7. The arts curriculum (trivium).
8. To estimate by consulting (the stars).
9. Handsome, courteous, handy.
1. Pleasure, (sexual) comforts.
2. Elegantly decked out with sweet herbs.

3. Setwall, a gingerlike spice used as a stimulant.
4. An astrological treatise by Ptolemy.
5. Astrolabe, an astrological instrument.
6. A prayer commemorating the Annunciation.

And after that he soong the *Kinges Note:*[7]
110 Ful often blessed was his merye throte.
And thus this sweete clerk his time spente
After his freendes finding and his rente.[8]
    This carpenter hadde wedded newe a wif
Which that he loved more than his lif.
115 Of eighteteene yeer she was of age;
Jalous he was, and heeld hire narwe in cage,
For she was wilde and yong, and he was old,
And deemed° himself been lik a cokewold.   *supposed*
He knew nat Caton,[9] for his wit was rude,
120 That bad men sholde wedde his similitude:°   *equal in age*
Men sholde wedden after hir estat,°   *station in life*
For youthe and elde is often at debat.
But sith that he was fallen in the snare,
He moste endure, as other folk, his care.
125   Fair was this yonge wif, and therwithal
As any wesele hir body gent and smal.[1]
A ceint° she wered, barred° al of silk;   *belt / striped*
A barmcloth° as whit as morne milk   *apron*
Upon hir lendes,° ful of many a gore;°   *loins / flounce*
130 Whit was hir smok,° and broiden° al bifore   *slip / embroidered*
And eek bihinde, on hir coler aboute,°   *around her collar*
Of col-blak silk, withinne and eek withoute;
The tapes° of hir white voluper°   *ribbons / cap*
Were of the same suite° of hir coler;   *pattern*
135 Hir filet° brood° of silk and set ful hye;   *headband / broad*
And sikerly she hadde a likerous yë;[2]
Ful smale ypulled° were hir browes two,   *plucked*
And tho° were bent, and blake as any slo.°   *they / plum*
She was ful more blisful on to see
140 Than is the newe perejonette° tree,   *pear*
And softer than the wolle is of a wether;°   *ram*
And by hir girdel° heeng a purs of lether,   *belt*
Tasseled with silk and perled° with latoun.°   *decorated / brass*
In al this world, to seeken up and down,
145 Ther nis no man so wis that coude thenche°   *imagine*
So gay a popelote° or swich a wenche.[3]   *doll*
Ful brighter was the shining of hir hewe
Than in the Tower the noble° yforged newe.[4]   *gold coin*
But of hir song, it was as loud and yerne°   *lively*
150 As any swalwe sitting on a berne.
Therto she coude skippe and make game
As any kide or calf folwing his dame.°   *mother*
Hir mouth was sweete as bragot or the meeth,°   *honey drinks*
Or hoord of apples laid in hay or heeth.°   *heather*

7. A popular song.
8. According to what his friends gave him and his income.
9. Cato, Latin author of a book of maxims used in elementary education.
1. Her body as delicate and slender as any weasel.
2. And certainly she had a wanton eye.
3. Woman of the working class.
4. Than the new-forged gold coin in the Tower (of London, the royal mint).

Line	Text	Gloss
155	Winsing° she was as is a joly° colt,	skittish / spirited
	Long as a mast, and upright° as a bolt.°	strait / arrow
	A brooch she bar upon hir lowe coler	
	As brood as is the boos° of a bokeler;°	boss / shield
	Hir shoes were laced on hir legges hye.	
160	She was a primerole,° a piggesnye,[5]	primrose
	For any lord to leggen in his bedde,	
	Or yet for any good yeman to wedde.	
	Now sire, and eft° sire, so bifel the cas	again
	That on a day this hende Nicholas	
165	Fil with this yonge wif to rage° and playe,	sport
	Whil that hir housbonde was at Oseneye°	Osney, near Oxford
	(As clerkes been ful subtil and ful quainte),°	clever
	And prively he caughte hire by the queinte,[6]	
	And saide, "Ywis,° but if ich have my wille,	certainly
170	For derne° love of thee, lemman,° I spille,"°	secret / sweetheart / die
	And heeld hire harde by the haunche-bones,	
	And saide, "Lemman, love me al atones,°	at once
	Or I wol dien, also° God me save."	so
	And she sproong as a colt dooth in a trave,[7]	
175	And with hir heed she wried° faste away;	twisted
	She saide, "I wol nat kisse thee, by my fay.°	faith
	Why, lat be," quod she, "lat be, Nicholas!	
	Or I wol crye 'Out, harrow, and allas!'	
	Do way youre handes, for your curteisye!"	
180	This Nicholas gan mercy for to crye,	
	And spak so faire, and profred him° so faste,	pressed his case
	That she hir love him graunted atte laste,	
	And swoor hir ooth by Saint Thomas of Kent	
	That she wolde been at his comandement,	
185	Whan that she may hir leiser° wel espye.	opportunity
	"Myn housbonde is so ful of jalousye	
	That but ye waite wel and been privee,[8]	
	I woot° right wel I nam but deed,"° quod she.	know / am no more than
	"Ye moste been ful derne° as in this cas."	secret
190	"Nay, therof care thee nought," quod Nicholas.	
	"A clerk hadde litherly biset his while,°	wasted his time
	But if he coude a carpenter bigile."	
	And thus they been accorded and ysworn	
	To waite a time, as I have told biforn.	
195	Whan Nicholas hadde doon this everydeel,	
	And thakked° hire upon the lendes° weel,	patted / loins
	He kiste hire sweete, and taketh his sautrye,	
	And playeth faste, and maketh melodye.	
	Thanne fil it thus, that to the parissh chirche,	
200	Cristes owene werkes for to wirche,	
	This goode wif wente on an haliday:°	holy day
	Hir forheed shoon as bright as any day,	

5. Pig's eye, a flower.
6. Literally "dainty part," slang for the female genitals.
7. A restraint for horses when they are being shod.
8. That unless you're very caurious and discreet.

So was it wasshen whan she leet° hir werk.   *left off*
  Now was ther of that chirche a parissh clerk,
205 The which that was ycleped° Absolon: *called*
  Crul° was his heer, and as the gold it shoon,   *curly*
  And strouted as a fanne⁹ large and brode;
  Ful straight and evene lay his joly shode.°   *part in his hair*
  His rode° was reed, his y'n greye as goos.   *complexion*
210 With Poules window¹ corven° on his shoos,   *carved*
  In hoses rede he wente fetisly.°   *elegantly*
  Yclad he was ful smale° and proprely,   *fine*
  Al in a kirtel° of a light waget°—   *tunic / blue*
  Ful faire and thikke been the pointes° set—   *laces*
215 And therupon he hadde a gay surplis,°   *clerical robe*
  As whit as is the blosme upon the ris.°   *twig*
  A merye child° he was, so God me save.   *lad*
  Wel coude he laten blood,² and clippe,° and shave,   *cut hair*
  And maken a chartre of land, or acquitaunce;°   *legal release*
220 In twenty manere coude he trippe and daunce
  After the scole of Oxenforde tho,
  And with his legges casten° to and fro,   *fling*
  And playen songes on a smal rubible;°   *fiddle*
  Therto he soong somtime a loud quinible,°   *high treble*
225 And as wel coude he playe on a giterne:°   *guitar*
  In al the town nas brewhous ne taverne
  That he ne visited with his solas,³
  Ther any gailard tappestere° was.   *saucy barmaid*
  But sooth to sayn, he was somdeel squaimous°   *somewhat squeamish*
230 Of farting, and of speeche daungerous.°   *haughty*
    This Absolon, that joly was and gay,
  Gooth with a cencer° on the haliday,   *incense bowl*
  Cencing the wives of the parissh faste,
  And many a lovely look on hem he caste,
235 And namely on this carpenteres wif:
  To looke on hire him thoughte a merye lif.
  She was so propre and sweete and likerous,°   *sexy*
  I dar wel sayn, if she hadde been a mous,
  And he a cat, he wolde hire hente° anoon.   *catch*
240 This parissh clerk, this joly Absolon,
  Hath in his herte swich a love-longinge
  That of no wif ne took he noon offringe—
  For curteisye he saide he wolde noon.
  The moone, whan it was night, ful brighte shoon,
245 And Absolon his giterne hath ytake—
  For paramours he thoughte for to wake⁴—
  And forth he gooth, jolif° and amorous,   *pretty*
  Til he cam to the carpenteres hous,
  A litel after cokkes hadde ycrowe,

9. And spread out like a winnowing fan (for separating   2. Let blood (a medical treatment performed by barbers).
wheat from chaff).   3. Entertainment (also with sexual connotations).
1. The windows of St. Paul's Chapel were intricately   4. For the sake of love he thought to keep a vigil.
patterned.

250	And dressed° him up by a shot-windowe°	placed / hinged window
	That was upon the carpenteres wal.	
	He singeth in his vois gentil and smal,°	high
	"Now dere lady, if thy wille be,	
	I praye you that ye wol rewe° on me,"	take pity
255	Ful wel accordant° to his giterninge.	harmonizing
	This carpenter awook and herde him singe,	
	And spak unto his wif, and saide anoon,	
	"What, Alison, heerestou nought Absolon	
	That chaunteth thus under oure bowres° wal?"	bedroom's
260	And she answerde hir housbonde therwithal,	
	"Yis, God woot,° John, I heere it everydeel."°	knows / every bit
	This passeth forth. What wol ye bet than weel?[5]	
	Fro day to day this joly Absolon	
	So woweth° hire that him is wo-bigoon:	woos
265	He waketh al the night and al the day;	
	He kembed° his lokkes brode° and made him gay;	combed / wide-spreading
	He woweth hire by menes and brocage,[6]	
	And swoor he wolde been hir owene page;°	attendant
	He singeth, brokking° as a nightingale;	trilling
270	He sente hire piment,° meeth,° and spiced ale,	spiced wine / mead
	And wafres° piping hoot out of the gleede;°	pastries / coals
	And for she was of towne, he profred meede°—	bribes
	For som folk wol be wonnen for richesse,	
	And som for strokes,° and som for gentilesse.	by force
275	Somtime to shewe his lightnesse° and maistrye,°	agility / skill
	He playeth Herodes[7] upon a scaffold° hye.	platform
	But what availeth him as in this cas?	
	She loveth so this hende Nicholas	
	That Absolon may blowe the bukkes horn;[8]	
280	He ne hadde for his labour but a scorn.	
	And thus she maketh Absolon hir ape,°	fool
	And al his ernest turneth til a jape.°	joke
	Ful sooth° is this proverbe, it is no lie;	true
	Men saith right thus: "Alway the nye slye°	sly one nearby
285	Maketh the ferre leve to be loth."[9]	
	For though that Absolon be wood° or wroth,°	crazy / angry
	By cause that he fer was from hir sighte,	
	This nye Nicholas stood in his lighte.°	in the way
	Now beer thee wel, thou hende Nicholas,	
290	For Absolon may waile and singe allas.	
	And so bifel it on a Saterday	
	This carpenter was goon til Oseney,	
	And hende Nicholas and Alisoun	
	Accorded been to this conclusioun,	
295	That Nicholas shal shapen hem a wile°	devise them a trick
	This sely° jalous housbonde to bigile,	innocent
	And if so be this game wente aright,	

5. What more would you want?
6. He woos her with go-betweens and mediation.
7. In the English mystery plays, Herod was often portrayed as a bully.
8. Undertake a useless endeavor.
9. Makes the distant beloved seem hateful.

She sholden sleepen in his arm al night—
For this was his desir and hire also.

300 And right anoon, withouten wordes mo,
This Nicholas no lenger wolde tarye,
But dooth ful softe unto his chambre carye
Bothe mete and drinke for a day or twaye,
And to hir housbonde bad hire for to saye,

305 If that he axed after Nicholas,
She sholde saye she niste° wher he was—   *did not know*
Of al that day she sawgh him nought with yë:
She trowed° that he was in maladye,   *believed*
For for no cry hir maide coude him calle,

310 He nolde° answere for no thing that mighte falle.°   *would not / happen*
    This passeth forth al thilke° Saterday   *that same*
That Nicholas stille in his chambre lay,
And eet, and sleep, or dide what him leste,°   *he liked*
Til Sonday that the sonne gooth to reste.

315   This sely carpenter hath greet mervaile°   *wonder*
Of Nicholas, or what thing mighte him aile,
And saide, "I am adrad,° by Saint Thomas,   *afraid*
It stondeth nat aright with Nicholas.
God shilde° that he deide sodeinly!   *forbid*

320 This world is now ful tikel,° sikerly:°   *changeable / surely*
I sawgh today a corps yborn to chirche
That now a Monday last I sawgh him wirche.°   *working*
Go up," quod he unto his knave° anoon,   *manservant*
"Clepe° at his dore or knokke with a stoon.   *call*

325 Looke how it is and tel me boldely."
    This knave gooth him up ful sturdily,
And at the chambre dore whil that he stood
He cride and knokked as that he were wood,
"What? How? What do ye, maister Nicholay?

330 How may ye sleepen al the longe day?".
But al for nought: he herde nat a word.
An hole he foond ful lowe upon a boord,
Ther as the cat was wont in for to creepe,
And at that hole he looked in ful deepe,

335 And atte laste he hadde of him a sighte.
    This Nicholas sat evere caping° uprighte   *staring*
As he hadde kiked° on the newe moone.   *gazed*
A down he gooth and tolde his maister soone
In what array° he saw this ilke° man.   *condition / same*

340   This carpenter to blessen him[1] bigan.
And saide, "Help us, Sainte Frideswide![2]
A man woot litel what him shal bitide.
This man is falle, with his astromye,
In som woodnesse° or in som agonye.°   *madness / fit*

345 I thoughte ay° wel how that it sholde be: *always*
Men sholde nought knowe of Goddes privetee.

---

1. Bless himself (with the sign of the cross).   2. A saint venerated for her healing powers.

Ye, blessed be alway a lewed° man   *unlearned*
That nought but only his bileve can.°   *knows his creed*
So ferde° another clerk with astromye: *fared*
350   He walked in the feeldes for to prye°   *gaze*
Upon the sterres, what ther sholde bifalle,
Til he was in a marle-pit° yfalle—   *clay-pit*
He saw nat that. But yet, by Saint Thomas,
Me reweth sore° for hende Nicholas.   *feel sorry*
355   He shal be rated° of his studying,   *scolded*
If that I may, by Jesus, hevene king!
Get me a staf that I may underspore,°   *pry upward*
Whil that thou, Robin, hevest up the dore.
He shal out of his studying, as I gesse."
360   And to the chambre dore he gan him dresse.°   *placed himself*
His knave was a strong carl° for the nones,°   *fellow / purpose*
And by the haspe° he haaf° it up atones: *hinge / heaved*
Into the floor the dore fil anoon.
This Nicholas sat ay as stille as stoon,
365   And evere caped up into the air.
This carpenter wende° he were in despair,   *thought*
And hente° him by the shuldres mightily,   *grabbed*
And shook him harde, and cride spitously,°   *vigorously*
"What, Nicholay, what, how! What! Looke adown!
370   Awaak and thenk on Cristes passioun![3]
I crouche° thee from elves and fro wightes."°   *bless / evil spirits*
Therwith the nightspel° saide he anoonrightes   *charm*
On foure halves° of the hous aboute,   *sides*
And on the threshfold on the dore withoute:
375   "Jesu Crist and Sainte Benedight,[4]
Blesse this hous from every wikked wight!
For nightes nerye° the White Pater Noster.[5]   *protect*
Where wentestou, thou Sainte Petres soster?"°   *sister*
And at the laste this hende Nicholas
380   Gan for to sike° sore, and saide, "Allas,   *sigh*
Shal al the world be lost eftsoones° now?"°   *immediately*
    This carpenter answerde, "What saistou?
What, thenk on God as we doon, men that swinke."°   *work*
    This Nicholas answerde, "Fecche me drinke,
385   And after wol I speke in privetee
Of certain thing that toucheth me and thee.
I wol telle it noon other man, certain."
    This carpenter gooth down and comth again,
And broughte of mighty ale a large quart,
390   And whan that eech of hem hadde dronke his part,
This Nicholas his dore faste shette,°   *shut*
And down the carpenter by him he sette,
And saide, "John, myn hoste lief° and dere,   *beloved*
Thou shalt upon thy trouthe° swere me here   *word of honor*

---

3. Thinking about Christ's death and resurrection was   4. St. Benedict, founder of Western monasticism.
supposed to ward off evil spells.   5. The Lord's Prayer, used as a charm.

395	That to no wight thou shalt this conseil° wraye;°	*advice / disclose*
	For it is Cristes conseil that I saye,	
	And if thou telle it man, thou art forlore,°	*lost*
	For this vengeance thou shalt have therfore,	
	That if thou wraye° me, thou shalt be wood."°	*reveal / mad*
400	"Nay, Crist forbede it, for his holy blood,"	
	Quod tho this sely man. "I nam no labbe,°	*am no blabbermouth*
	And though I saye, I nam nat lief° to gabbe.	*do not like*
	Say what thou wilt, I shal it nevere telle	
	To child ne wif, by him that harwed helle."⁶	
405	"Now John," quod Nicholas, "I wol nought lie.	
	I have yfounde in myn astrologye,	
	As I have looked in the moone bright,	
	That now a Monday next, at quarter night,°	*near dawn*
	Shal falle a rain, and that so wilde and wood,°	*furious*
410	That half so greet was nevere Noees° flood.	*Noah's*
	This world," he saide, "in lasse than an hour	
	Shal al be dreint,° so hidous is the showr.	*drowned*
	Thus shal mankinde drenche° and lese hir lif."°	*drown / lose their lives*
	This carpenter answerde, "Allas, my wif!	
415	And shal she drenche? Allas, myn Alisoun!"	
	For sorwe of this he fil almost adown,	
	And saide, "Is there no remedye in this cas?"	
	"Why yis, for Gode," quod hende Nicholas,	
	"If thou wolt werken° after lore° and reed°—	*act / learning / advice*
420	Thou maist nought werken after thyn owene heed;	
	For thus saith Salomon that was ful trewe,	
	'Werk al by conseil and thou shalt nought rewe.'°	*regret*
	And if thou werken wolt by good conseil,	
	I undertake, withouten mast or sail,	
425	Yet shal I save hire and thee and me.	
	Hastou nat herd how saved was Noee	
	Whan that Oure Lord hadde warned him biforn	
	That al the world with water sholde be lorn?"°	*lost*
	"Yis," quod this carpenter, "ful yore° ago."	*long*
430	"Hastou nat herd," quod Nicholas, "also	
	The sorwe° of Noee with his felaweshipe?°	*sorrow / companions*
	Er that he mighte gete his wif to shipe,	
	Him hadde levere,° I dar wel undertake,	*would have preferred*
	At thilke° time than alle his wetheres blake°	*that / black rams*
435	That she hadde had a ship hirself allone.⁷	
	And therfore woostou° what is best to doone?	*do you know*
	This axeth haste, and of an hastif° thing	*urgent*
	Men may nought preche or maken tarying.	
	Anoon go gete us faste into this in°	*inn*
440	A kneeding trough or elles a kimelin°	*brewing trough*
	For eech of us, but looke that they be large,	
	In whiche we mowen swimme as in a barge,	

---

6. Christ, who harrowed hell upon his resurrection, releasing captive souls.

7. Noah's wife was traditionally portrayed in the mystery plays as a complaining wife who resisted boarding the ark.

	And han therinne vitaile suffisaunt°	*enough food*
	But for a day—fy on the remenaunt!	
445	The water shal aslake° and goon away	*recede*
	Aboute prime° upon the nexte day.	*6 A.M.*
	But Robin may nat wite° of this, thy knave,	*know*
	Ne eek thy maide Gille I may nat save.	
	Axe nought why, for though thou axe me,	
450	I wol nought tellen Goddes privetee.	
	Suffiseth thee, but if thy wittes madde,°	*go mad*
	To han° as greet a grace as Noee hadde.	*have*
	Thy wif shal I wel saven, out of doute.	
	Go now thy way, and speed thee heraboute.	
455	But whan thou hast for hire and thee and me	
	Ygeten° us thise kneeding-tubbes three,	*gotten*
	Thanne shaltou hangen hem in the roof ful hye,	
	That no man of oure purveyance° espye.	*preparations*
	And whan thou thus hast doon as I have said,	
460	And hast oure vitaile faire in hem ylaid,	
	And eek° an ax to smite° the corde atwo,	*also / cut*
	Whan that the water comth that we may go,	
	And broke an hole an heigh° upon the gable	*on high*
	Unto the gardinward,° over the stable,	*toward the garden*
465	That we may freely passen forth oure way,	
	Whan that the grete showr is goon away,	
	Thanne shaltou swimme as merye, I undertake,	
	As dooth the white doke° after hir drake.	*female duck*
	Thanne wol I clepe,° 'How, Alison? How, John?	*call out*
470	Be merye, for the flood wol passe anoon.'	
	And thou wolt sayn, 'Hail, maister Nicholay!	
	Good morwe, I see thee wel, for it is day!'	
	And thanne shal we be lordes al oure lif	
	Of al the world, as Noee and his wif.	
475	But of oo thing I warne thee ful right:	
	Be wel avised on that ilke night	
	That we been entred into shippes boord	
	That noon of us ne speke nought a word,	
	Ne clepe,° ne crye, but been in his prayere,	*call out*
480	For it is Goddes owene heeste° dete.	*commandment*
	Thy wif and thou mote° hange fer atwinne,°	*must / apart*
	For that bitwixe you shal be no sinne—	
	Namore in looking than ther shal in deede.	
	This ordinance is said: go, God thee speede.	
485	Tomorwe at night whan men been alle asleepe,	
	Into oure kneeding-tubbes wol we creepe,	
	And sitten there, abiding Goddes grace.	
	Go now thy way, I have no lenger space°	*time*
	To make of this no lenger sermoning.	
490	Men sayn thus: 'Send the wise and say no thing.'	
	Thou art so wis it needeth thee nat teche:	
	Go save oure lif, and that I thee biseeche."	
	This sely° carpenter gooth forth his way:	*single*

        Ful ofte he saide allas and wailaway,

495   And to his wif he tolde his privetee,

        And she was war,° and knew it bet° than he,   *aware / better*

        What al this quainte cast° was for to saye.°   *clever trick / mean*

        But nathelees she ferde° as she wolde deye,   *acted*

        And saide, "Allas, go forth thy way anoon.

500   Help us to scape,° or we been dede eechoon.   *escape*

        I am thy trewe verray wedded wif:

        Go, dere spouse, and help to save oure lif."

           Lo, which a greet thing is affeccioun!°   *emotion*

        Men may dien,° of imaginacioun,°   *die / fantasy*

505   So deepe may impression be take.

        This sely carpenter biginneth quake;

        Him thinketh verrailiche° that he may see   *truly*

        Noees flood come walwing° as the see   *rolling in*

        To drenchen Alison, his hony dere.

510   He weepeth, waileth, maketh sory cheere;°   *expression*

        He siketh° with ful many a sory swough,°   *sighs / breath*

        And gooth and geteth him a kneeding-trough,

        And after a tubbe and a kimelin,

        And prively he sente hem to his in,

515   And heeng hem in the roof in privetee;

        His owene hand he made laddres three,

        To climben by the ronges and the stalkes°   *uprights*

        Unto the tubbes hanging in the balkes,°   *rafters*

        And hem vitailed, bothe trough and tubbe,

520   With breed and cheese and good ale in a jubbe,°   *jug*

        Suffising right ynough as for a day.

        But er that he hadde maad al this array,

        He sente his knave, and eek his wenche also,

        Upon his neede° to London for to go.   *errand*

525   And on the Monday whan it drow to nighte,

        He shette his dore withouten candel-lighte,

        And dressed° alle thing as it sholde be,   *arranged*

        And shortly up they clomben alle three.

        They seten stille wel a furlong way.[8]

530   "Now, Pater Noster, clum,"[9] saide Nicholay,

        And "Clum" quod John, and "Clum" saide Alisoun.

        This carpenter saide his devocioun,

        And stille he sit and biddeth his prayere,

        Awaiting on the rain, if he it heere.

535   The dede sleep, for wery bisinesse,

        Fil on this carpenter right as I gesse

        Aboute corfew time,° or litel more.   *dusk*

        For travailing of his gost° he groneth sore,   *spirit*

        And eft he routeth,° for his heed mislay.   *snores*

540   Down of the laddre stalketh Nicholay,

        And Alison ful softe adown she spedde:

        Withouten wordes mo they goon to bedde

---

8. The length of time to travel a furlong.   9. Say the Lord's Prayer and hush.

Ther as the carpenter is wont to lie.
Ther was the revel and the melodye,
545   And thus lith Alison and Nicholas
In bisinesse of mirthe and of solas,
Til that the belle of Laudes[1] gan to ringe,
And freres° in the chauncel° gonne singe.   *friars / chapel*
This parissh clerk, this amorous Absolon,
550   That is for love alway so wo-bigoon,
Upon the Monday was at Oseneye,
With compaignye him to disporte and playe,
And axed upon caas° a cloisterer[2]   *by chance*
Ful prively after John the carpenter;
555   And he drow him apart out of the chirche,
And saide, "I noot:° I sawgh him here nought wirche°   *don't know / working*
Sith Saterday. I trowe that he be went
For timber ther oure abbot hath him sent.
For he is wont for timber for to go,
560   And dwellen atte grange° a day or two.   *outlying farm*
Or elles he is at his hous, certain.
Where that he be I can nought soothly° sayn."   *truly*
This Absolon ful jolif was and light,°   *amorous and happy*
And thoughte, "Now is time to wake al night,
565   For sikerly,° I sawgh him nought stiringe   *surely*
Aboute his dore sin° day bigan to springe.°   *since / break*
So mote I thrive,° I shal at cokkes crowe   *may I prosper*
Ful prively knokken at his windowe
That stant ful lowe upon his bowres° wal.   *bedroom's*
570   To Alison now wol I tellen al
My love-longing, for yet I shal nat misse
That at the leeste way I shal hire kisse.
Som manere confort shal I have, parfay.°   *indeed*
My mouth hath icched° al this longe day: *itched*
575   That is a signe of kissing at the leeste.
Al night me mette° eek I was at a feeste.   *dreamed*
Therfore I wol go sleepe an hour or twaye,
And al the night thanne wol I wake and playe."
Whan that the firste cok hath crowe, anoon
580   Up rist this joly lovere Absolon,
And him arrayeth gay at point devis.°   *fastidiously*
But first he cheweth grain[3] and licoris,
To smellen sweete, er he hadde kembd his heer.
Under his tonge a trewe-love[4] he beer.
585   For therby wende° he to be gracious.°   *supposed / attractive*
He rometh to the carpenteres hous,
And stille he stant under the shot-windowe—
Unto his brest it raughte,° it was so lowe—   *reached*
And ofte he cougheth with a semisoun.°   *soft noise*
590   "What do ye, hony-comb, sweete Alisoun,

---

1. Lauds, daily church service before sunrise.
2. Member of the monastery.
3. Grain of paradise, an aromatic spice.
4. Four-leafed herb in the shape of a love knot.

My faire brid,° my sweete cinamome?   *bird or bride*
Awaketh, lemman° myn, and speketh to me.   *sweetheart*
Wel litel thinken ye upon my wo
That for your love I swete° ther I go.   *dissolve*
595 No wonder is though that I swelte° and swete: *swelter*
I moorne as dooth a lamb after the tete.
Ywis,° lemman, I have swich love-longinge, *certainly*
That lik a turtle° trewe is my moorninge: *turtle-dove*
I may nat ete namore than a maide."
600 "Go fro the windowe, Jakke fool," she saide.
"As help me God, it wol nat be com-pa-me.° *come kiss me*
I love another, and elles I were to blame,
Wel bet than thee, by Jesu, Absolon.
Go forth thy way or I wol caste a stoon,
605 And lat me sleepe, a twenty devele way."[5]
  "Allas," quod Absolon, "and wailaway,
That trewe love was evere so yvele biset.° *badly done to*
Thanne kis me, sin that it may be no bet,
For Jesus love and for the love of me."
610 "Woltou thanne go thy way therwith?" quod she.
"Ye, certes, lemman," quod this Absolon.
"Thanne maak thee redy," quod she. "I come anoon."
And unto Nicholas she said stille,
"Now hust,° and thou shalt laughen al thy fille." *hush*
615 This Absolon down sette him on his knees,
And saide, "I am a lord at alle degrees,° *in every way*
For after this I hope ther cometh more.
Lemman, thy grace, and sweete brid, thyn ore!"° *mercy*
  The windowe she undooth, and that in haste.
620 "Have do," quod she, "com of and speed thee faste,
Lest that oure neighebores thee espye."
  This Absolon gan wipe his mouth ful drye:
Derk was the night as pich or as the cole,
And at the windowe out she putte hir hole.
625 And Absolon, him fil no bet ne wers,
But with his mouth he kiste hir naked ers,
Ful savourly,° er he were war of this. *enthusiastically*
Abak he sterte, and thoughte it was amis,
For wel he wiste a womman hath no beerd.
630 He felte a thing al rough and longe yherd,° *haird*
And saide, "Fy, allas, what have I do?"
"Teehee," quod she, and clapte the windowe to.
And Absolon gooth forth a sory pas.° *with downcast step*
"A beerd, a beerd!" quod hende Nicholas,
635 "By Goddes corpus,° this gooth faire and weel." *body*
  This sely Absolon herde everydeel,
And on his lippe he gan for anger bite,
And to himself he saide, "I shal thee quite."° *repay*
  Who rubbeth now, who froteth now his lippes
640 With dust, with sond, with straw, with cloth, with chippes,
But Absolon, that saith ful ofte allas?

5. In the name of 20 devils.

"My soule bitake° I unto Satanas,   *hand over*
But me were levere than⁶ all this town," quod he,
"Of this despit° awroken° for to be.   *insult / avenged*
645   Allas," quod he, "allas I ne hadde ybleint!"°   *turned aside*
His hote love was cold and al yqueint,°   *quenched*
For fro that time that he hadde kist hir ers
Of paramours he sette nought a kers,⁷
For he was heled of his maladye.
650   Ful ofte paramours he gan defye,°   *renounce*
And weep as dooth a child that is ybete.°   *beaten*
A softe paas he wente over the streete
Until a smith men clepen daun° Gervais,   *call Sir*
That in his forge smithed plough harneis:°   *equipment*
655   He sharpeth shaar° and cultour° bisily.   *plowshare / plough-blade*
This Absolon knokketh al esily,°   *softly*
And saide, "Undo,° Gervais, and that anoon."   *open up*
      "What, who artou?" "It am I, Absolon."
"What, Absolon? What, Cristes sweete tree!
660   Why rise ye so rathe?° Ey, benedicite,°   *early / bless me*
What aileth you? Som gay girl, God it woot,
Hath brought you thus upon the viritoot.°   *on the prowl*
By Sainte Note,⁸ ye woot wel what I mene."
      This Absolon ne roughte nat a bene°   *did not care a bean*
665   Of al his play. No word again he yaf:°   *gave*
He hadde more tow on his distaf⁹
Than Gervais knew, and saide, "Freend so dere,
This hote cultour in the chimenee° here,   *fireplace*
As lene it me:¹ I have therwith to doone.
670   I wol bringe it thee again ful soone."
      Gervais answerde, "Certes, were it gold,
Or in a poke nobles alle untold,²
Thou sholdest have, as I am trewe smith.
Ey, Cristes fo,³ what wol ye do therwith?"
675   "Therof," quod Absolon, "be as be may.
I shal wel telle it thee another day,"
And caughte the cultour by the colde stele.°   *handle*
Ful softe out at the dore he gan to stele,
And wente unto the carpenteres wal:
680   He cougheth first and knokketh therwithal
Upon the windowe, right as he dide er.°   *before*
      This Alison answerde, "Who is ther
That knokketh so? I warante° it a thief."   *bet*
      "Why, nay," quod he, "God woot, my sweete lief,°   *dear*
685   I am thyn Absolon, my dereling.
Of gold," quod he, "I have thee brought a ring—
My moder yaf it me, so God me save;
Ful fin it is and therto wel ygrave:°   *engraved*
This wol I yiven thee if thou me kisse."

6. I would rather than (have).
7. Did not value as much as a piece of cress.
8. St. Noet, a ninth-century saint, with possible pun on Noah.
9. Flax on his distaff (i.e., cares on his mind).
1. Be so good as to lend it to me.
2. Or in a pouch of uncounted gold coins.
3. By Christ's foe (i.e., the Devil).

690   This Nicholas was risen for to pisse,
        And thoughte he wolde amenden al the jape:[4]
        He sholde kisse his ers er that he scape.
        And up the windowe dide he hastily,
        And out his ers he putteth prively,
695   Over the buttok to the haunche-boon.°   *thigh*
            And therwith spak this clerk, this Absolon,
        "Speek, sweete brid, I noot nought wher thou art."
        This Nicholas anoon leet flee° a fart   *let fly*
        As greet as it hadde been a thonder-dent°   *thunderbolt*
700   That with the strook he was almost yblent,°   *blinded*
        And he was redy with his iren hoot,
        And Nicholas amiddle the ers he smoot:
        Of gooth the skin an hande-brede° aboute;   *hand's width*
        The hote cultour brende so his toute°   *backside*
705   That for the smert° he wende° for to die;   *pain / thought*
        As he were wood for wo he gan to crye,
        "Help! Water! Water! Help, for Goddes herte!"
            This carpenter out of his slomber sterte,
        And herde oon cryen "Water!" as he were wood,
710   And thoughte, "Allas, now cometh Noweles° flood!"   *Noah's*
        He sette him up withoute wordes mo,
        And with his ax he smooth the corde atwo,
        And down gooth al: he foond neither to selle
        Ne breed ne ale til he cam to the celle,[5]
715   Upon the floor, and ther aswoune° he lay.   *stunned*
            Up sterte° hire Alison and Nicholay,   *leaped*
        And criden "Out" and "Harrow" in the streete.
        The neighebores, bothe smale and grete,[6]
        In ronnen for to gauren° on this man   *stare*
720   That aswoune lay bothe pale and wan,
        For with the fal he brosten° hadde his arm;   *broken*
        But stonde he moste unto his owene harm,
        For whan he spak he was anoon bore down°   *restrained*
        With° hende Nicholas and Alisoun: *by*
725   They tolden every man that he was wood°—   *crazy*
        He was agast° so of Noweles flood,   *afraid*
        Thurgh fantasye, that of his vanitee°   *folly*
        He hadde ybought him kneeding-tubbes three,
        And hadde hem hanged in the roof above,
730   And that he prayed hem, for Goddes love,
        To sitten in the roof, *par compaignye*.°   *for fellowship*
            The folk gan laughen at his fantasye.
        Into the roof they kiken° and they cape,°   *peer / gape*
        And turned al his harm unto a jape,
735   For what so that this carpenter answerde,
        It was for nought: no man his reson herde;

4. Make the joke even better.
5. He found no time to sell either bread or ale until he reached the floor (i.e., he fell to the ground too quickly to be aware of what was happening).
6. Lower- and upper-class people alike.

	With othes grete he was so sworn adown,°	*refuted by oaths*
	That he was holden wood in al the town,	
	For every clerk anoonright heeld with other:	
740	They saide, "The man was wood, my leve brother,"	
	And every wight° gan laughen at this strif.	*person*
	Thus swived° was the carpenteres wif	*screwed*
	For al his keeping and his jalousye,	
	And Absolon hath kist hir nether° yë,	*lower*
745	And Nicholas is scalded in the toute:	
	This tale is doon, and God save al the route!	

THE WIFE OF BATH'S PROLOGUE AND TALE   Dame Alison, the Wife of Bath, is Chaucer's greatest contribution to the stock characters of Western culture. She has a long literary ancestry, most immediately in the Duenna of the thirteenth-century French poem, *The Romance of the Rose,* and stretching back to the Roman poet Ovid. Dame Alison stands out in bold relief, even among the vivid Canterbury pilgrims, partly because Chaucer gives her so rebellious and explicitly self-created a biography. She has out-lived five husbands, accumulated wealth from the first three, and made herself rich in the growing textile industry of her time. At once a great companion and greatly unnerving, Alison lives in constant battle with a secular and religious world mostly controlled by men and yet has a keen appetite both for the men and for the battle.

The Wife of Bath's *Prologue* and *Tale* seem only the current installments of a multifaceted struggle in which Dame Alison has long been engaged, at first through her body and social role and now, in the face of advancing years, through the remaining agency of retrospective storytelling. She battles a society in which many young women are almost chattels in a marital market, as was the twelve-year-old version of herself who first was married off to a wealthier, much older man. She battles him and later husbands for power within the marriage, and her ambition to social dominance, as the *General Prologue* reports, extends to life in her urban parish.

By the moment of the Canterbury pilgrimage, though, the Wife's adversaries are more daunting, less easily conquered. The *Wife's Prologue,* for all its autobiographical energy, is primarily a debate with the clergy and with "auctoritee"—the whole armature of learning and literacy by which the clergy (like her clerically educated fifth husband, Jankyn) seeks to silence her.

The Wife's Tale, too, can be seen as an angry riposte to the secular fantasies of Arthurian chivalry and genetic nobility. The Wife's well-born Arthurian knight is a common rapist, who finds himself at the mercy of a queen and then in the arms of a crone. The tale turns Arthurian conventions on their head, lays sexual violence in the open, and puts legal and magical power in the hands of women. It is explicitly a fantasy, but a powerful one.

Alison's final enemy, mortality itself, is what makes her both most desperate and most sympathetic. The husbands are gone. Even the fondly recalled Jankyn slips into a rosy glow and the past tense; so does her own best friend and "gossip," the odd mirror-double "Alisoun." The Wife of Bath keeps addressing other "wives" in her *Prologue,* but there are no others on the pilgrimage. Her very argument with the institutionalized church distances her from its comforts, and she is deeply aware that time is stealing her beauty as it has taken away the companions who made up her earlier life. If Alison's *Tale* closes with a delicious fantasy of restored youth, it is only a pendant to the much longer *Prologue* and its cheerful yet poignant acceptance of age.

The Wife of Bath's Prologue

Experience, though noon auctoritee[1]
Were in this world, is right ynough for me
To speke of wo that is in mariage:
For lordinges,° sith I twelf yeer was of age—   *gentlemen*

1. Even if no authority, textual precedent.

5   Thanked be God that is eterne on live—
         Housbondes at chirche dore I have had five
         (If I so ofte mighte han wedded be),
         And alle were worthy men in hir° degree.   *their*
         But me was told, certain, nat longe agoon is,
10   That sith that Crist ne wente nevere but ones°   *once*
         To wedding in the Cane of Galilee,²
         That by the same ensample taughte he me
         That I ne sholde wedded be but ones.
         Herke eek, lo, which a sharp word for the nones,°   *for the purpose*
15   Biside a welle, Jesus, God and man,
         Spak in repreve° of the Samaritan:³   *reproof*
         "Thou hast yhad five housbondes," quod he,
         "And that ilke° man that now hath thee   *same*
         Is nat thyn housbonde." Thus saide he certain.
20   What that he mente therby I can nat sayn,
         But that I axe why that the fifthe man
         Was noon housbonde to the Samaritan?
         How manye mighte she han in mariage?
         Yit herde I nevere tellen in myn age
25   Upon this nombre diffinicioun.
         Men may divine° and glosen° up and down,   *guess / interpret*
         But wel I woot,° expres,° withouten lie,   *know / manifestly*
         God bad us for to wexe° and multiplye: *increase*
         That gentil text can I wel understonde.
30   Eek wel I woot he saide that myn housbonde
         Sholde lete° fader and moder and take to me,   *leave*
         But of no nombre mencion made he—
         Of bigamye or of octogamye:
         Why sholde men thanne speke of it vilainye?°   *as churlish*
35   Lo, here the wise king daun° Salomon: *Lord*
         I trowe° he hadde wives many oon,   *believe*
         As wolde God it leveful° were to me   *lawful*
         To be refresshed half so ofte as he.
         Which yifte° of God hadde he for alle his wives!   *what a gift*
40   No man hath swich that in this world alive is.
         God woot° this noble king, as to my wit,°   *knows / understanding*
         The firste night hadde many a merye fit
         With eech of hem, so wel was him on live.
         Blessed be God that I have wedded five,
45   Of whiche I have piked° out the beste,   *picked*
         Bothe of hir nether purs and of hir cheste.⁴
         Diverse° scoles maken parfit° clerkes,   *different / accomplished*
         And diverse practikes in sondry werkes
         Maken the werkman° parfit sikerly:°   *craftsman / surely*
50   Of five housbondes scoleying° am I.   *studying*
         Welcome the sixte whan that evere he shal!

---

2. Cana, where Jesus performed his first miracle at a wed-   in John 4.6 ff.
ding feast (John 2.1).   4. Money chest, with a pun on body parts.
3. The story of Jesus and the Samaritan woman is related

For sith I wol nat keepe me chast in al,
Whan myn housbonde is fro the world agoon,
Som Cristen man shal wedde me anoon.
55 For thanne th'Apostle[5] saith that I am free
To wedde, a Goddes half,[6] where it liketh° me.   *please*
He said that to be wedded is no sinne:
Bet° is to be wedded than to brinne.°   *better / burn (in hell)*
What rekketh° me though folk saye vilainye   *do I care*
60 Of shrewed° Lamech[7] and his bigamye?   *cursed*
I woot wel Abraham was an holy man,
And Jacob eek, as fer as evere I can,°   *know*
And eech of hem hadde wives mo than two,
And many another holy man also.
65   Where can ye saye in any manere age
That hye God defended° mariage   *prohibited*
By expres word? I praye you, telleth me.
Or where comanded he virginitee?
I woot as wel as ye, it is no drede,°   *doubt*
70 Th'Apostle, whan he speketh of maidenhede,°   *virginity*
He saide that precept° therof hadde he noon: *command*
Men may conseile a womman to be oon,°   *single*
But conseiling nis no comandement.
He putte it in oure owene juggement.
75 For hadde God comanded maidenhede,
Thanne hadde he dampned° wedding with the deede;   *condemned*
And certes, if ther were no seed ysowe,
Virginitee, thanne wherof sholde it growe?
Paul dorste nat comanden at the leeste
80 A thing of which his maister yaf no heeste.°   *commandment*
The dart° is set up for virginitee: *prize*
Cacche whoso may, who renneth° best lat see.   *runs*
But this word is nought take° of every wight,°   *required / person*
But ther as God list° yive it of his might.   *pleases*
85 I woot wel that th'Apostle was a maide,°   *virgin*
But nathelees, though that he wroot or saide
He wolde that every wight were swich as he,
Al nis but° conseil to virginitee;   *it is only*
And for to been a wif he yaf me leve
90 Of indulgence; so nis it no repreve
To wedde me if that my make° die,   *mate*
Withouten excepcion° of bigamye—   *legal objection*
Al were it good no womman for to touche
(He mente as in his bed or in his couche,
95 For peril is bothe fir and tow t'assemble[8]—
Ye knowe what this ensample may resemble).
This al and som,° he heeld virginitee   *all told*
More parfit than wedding in freletee.°   *due to weakness*
(Freletee clepe° I but if° that he and she   *call / except*

5. St. Paul, in Romans 7.2.
6. From God's perspective.
7. The earliest bigamist in the Bible (Genesis 4.19).
8. To bring together fire and flax.

100   Wolde leden al hir lif in chastitee).
       I graunte it wel, I have noon envye
       Though maidenhede preferre° bigamye: *surpasses*
       It liketh hem to be clene in body and gost.°   *soul*
       Of myn estaat° ne wol I make no boost;   *condition*
105   For wel ye knowe, a lord in his houshold
       Ne hath nat every vessel al of gold:
       Some been of tree,° and doon hir lord servise.   *wood*
       God clepeth° folk to him in sondry wise,   *calls*
       And everich hath of God a propre yifte,
110   Som this, som that, as him liketh shifte.⁹
       Virginitee is greet perfeccioun,
       And continence eek with devocioun,
       But Crist, that of perfeccion is welle,°   *source*
       Bad nat every wight° he sholde go selle   *person*
115   Al that he hadde and yive it to the poore,
       And in swich wise folwe° him and his fore:°   *follow / footsteps*
       He spak to hem that wolde live parfitly°—   *perfectly*
       And lordinges, by youre leve, that am nat I.
       I wol bistowe the flour of al myn age
120   In th'actes and in fruit of mariage.
           Telle me also, to what conclusioun°   *end*
       Were membres maad of generacioun
       And of so parfit wis a wrighte ywrought?¹
       Trusteth right wel, they were nat maad for nought.
125   Glose whoso wol, and saye bothe up and down
       That they were maked for purgacioun
       Of urine, and oure bothe thinges smale
       Was eek to knowe a femele from a male,
       And for noon other cause—saye ye no?
130   Th'experience woot wel it is nought so.
       So that the clerkes be nat with me wrothe,°   *angry*
       I saye this, that they maked been for bothe—
       That is to sayn, for office° and for ese°   *use / pleasure*
       Of engendrure,° ther we nat God displese.   *procreation*
135   Why sholde men elles in hir bookes sette
       That man shal yeelde° to his wif hir dette?°   *pay / marriage debt*
       Now wherwith sholde he make his payement
       If he ne used his sely° instrument?   *innocent*
       Thanne were they maad upon a creature
140   To purge urine, and eek for engendrure.
           But I saye nought that every wight is holde,°   *bound*
       That hath swich harneis° as I to you tolde,   *equipment*
       To goon and usen hem in engendrure:
       Thanne sholde men take of chastitee no cure.°   *heed*
145   Crist was a maide and shapen as a man,
       And many a saint sith that the world bigan,
       Yit lived they evere in parfit° chastitee.   *perfect*
       I nil envye no virginitee:

---

9. As it pleases him to provide.   1. And created by so perfectly wise a Creator?

Lat hem be breed° of pured° whete seed, *bread / refined*
150 And lat us wives hote° barly breed— *be called*
And yit with barly breed, Mark telle can,
Oure Lord Jesu refresshed many a man.
In swich estaat as God hath cleped° us *called*
I wol persevere: I nam nat precious.° *am not fussy*
155 In wifhood wol I use myn instrument
As freely° as my Makere hath it sent. *generously*
If I be daungerous,° God yive me sorwe:° *withholding / sorrow*
Myn housbonde shal it han both eve and morwe,° *morning*
Whan that him list come forth and paye his dette.
160 An housbonde wol I have, I wol nat lette,° *forgo*
Which shal be bothe my dettour and my thral,° *slave*
And have his tribulacion withal
Upon his flessh whil that I am his wif.
I have the power during al my lif
165 Upon his propre° body, and nat he: *own*
Right thus th'Apostle tolde it unto me,
And bad oure housbondes for to love us weel.
Al this sentence° me liketh everydeel. *interpretation*

An Interlude

Up sterte° the Pardoner and that anoon: *started*
170 "Now dame," quod he, "by God and by Saint John,
Ye been a noble prechour° in this cas. *preacher*
I was aboute to wedde a wif: allas,
What° sholde I bye° it on my flessh so dere? *why / buy*
Yit hadde I levere° wedde no wif toyere."° *rather / this year*
175 "Abid," quod she, "my tale is nat bigonne.
Nay, thou shalt drinken of another tonne,° *barrel*
Er that I go, shal savoure wors than ale.
And whan that I have told thee forth my tale
Of tribulacion in mariage,
180 Of which I am expert in al myn age—
This is to saye, myself hath been the whippe—
Thanne maistou chese° wheither thou wolt sippe *may you choose*
Of thilke° tonne that I shal abroche:° *that same / open*
Be war of it, er thou too neigh approche,
185 For I shal telle ensamples mo than ten.
'Whoso that nile° be war by othere men, *will not*
By him shal othere men corrected be.'
Thise same wordes writeth Ptolomee:[2]
Rede in his Almageste and take it there."
190 "Dame, I wolde praye you if youre wil it were,"
Saide this Pardoner, "as ye bigan,
Telle forth youre tale; spareth for no man,
And teche us yonge men of youre practike."
"Gladly," quod she, "sith it may you like;

2. Ptolemy, ancient Greek astronomer and author of the *Almageste*.

195 But that I praye to al this compaignye,
    If that I speke after my fantasye,°   *fancy*
    As taketh nat agrief° of that I saye,   *amiss*
    For myn entente nis but° for to playe."   *intent is only*

The Wife Continues

    Now sire, thanne wol I telle you forth my tale.
200 As evere mote I drinke win or ale,
    I shal saye sooth:° tho° housbondes that I hadde,   *truth / those*
    As three of hem were goode, and two were badde.
    The three men were goode, and riche, and olde;
    Unnethe° mighte they the statut holde   *scarcely*
205 In which they were bounden unto me—
    Ye woot wel what I mene of this, pardee.°   *by God*
    As help me God, I laughe whan I thinke
    How pitously anight I made hem swinke;°   *work*
    And by my fay,° I tolde of it no stoor:°   *faith / gave it no heed*
210 They hadde me yiven hir land and hir tresor;°   *wealth*
    Me needed nat do lenger diligence
    To winne hir love or doon hem reverence.
    They loved me so wel, by God above,
    That I ne tolde no daintee° of hir love.   *set no value on*
215 A wis womman wol bisye hire evere in oon°   *constantly*
    To gete hire love, ye, ther as she hath noon.
    But sith I hadde hem hoolly in myn hand,
    And sith that they hadde yiven me al hir land,
    What sholde I take keep° hem for to plese,   *care*
220 But it were for my profit and myn ese?
    I sette hem so awerke, by my fay,°   *faith*
    That many a night they songen wailaway.
    The bacon was nat fet° for hem, I trowe,   *collected*
    That some men han in Essexe at Dunmowe.³
225 I governed hem so wel after my lawe
    That eech of hem ful blisful was and fawe°   *glad*
    To bringe me gaye thinges fro the faire;
    They were ful glade whan I spak to hem faire,
    For God it woot, I chidde° hem spitously.°   *scolded / cruelly*
230   Now herkneth how I bar me proprely:
    Ye wise wives, that conne understonde,
    Thus sholde ye speke and bere him wrong on honde°—   *wrongly accuse*
    For half so boldely can ther no man
    Swere and lie as a woman can.
235 I saye nat this by wives that been wise,
    But if it be whan they hem misavise.°   *err*
    A wis wif, if that she can hir good,⁴
    Shal bere him on hande the cow is wood,⁵
    And take witnesse of hir owene maide

---

3. At Dunmowe, spouses who had spent a year without quarrelling were awarded a side of bacon.
4. Knows what's good for her.

5. Shall convince him the chough is mad. The chough, a crow-like bird, was fabled to reveal wives' infidelities.

240	Of hir assent.° But herkneth how I saide:	*as her accomplice*
	"Sire olde cainard,° is this thyn array?	*dotard*
	Why is my neighebores wif so gay?	
	She is honoured overal ther she gooth:	
	I sitte at hoom; I have no thrifty° cloth.	*decent*
245	What doostou at my neighebores hous?	
	Is she so fair? Artou so amorous?	
	What roune° ye with oure maide, benedicite?°	*whisper / bless us*
	Sire olde lechour, lat thy japes° be.	*tricks*
	And if I have a gossib° or a freend,	*confidante*
250	Withouten gilt ye chiden as a feend,	
	If that I walke or playe unto his hous.	
	Thou comest hoom as dronken as a mous,	
	And prechest on thy bench, with yvel preef.°	*bad luck to you*
	Thou saist to me, it is a greet meschief	
255	To wedde a poore womman for costage.°	*expense*
	And if that she be riche, of heigh parage,°	*breeding*
	Thanne saistou that it is a tormentrye	
	To suffre hir pride and hir malencolye.	
	And if that she be fair, thou verray knave,	
260	Thou saist that every holour° wol hire have:	*whoremonger*
	She may no while in chastitee abide	
	That is assailed upon eech a side.	
	"Thou saist som folk desiren us for richesse,	
	Som for oure shap, and som for oure fairnesse,	
265	And som for she can outher° singe or daunce,	*either*
	And som for gentilesse and daliaunce,°	*conversation*
	Som for hir handes and hir armes smale—	
	Thus gooth al to the devel by thy tale!⁶	
	Thou saist men may nat keepe a castel wal,	
270	It may so longe assailed been overal.	
	And if that she be foul, thou saist that she	
	Coveiteth° every man that she may see;	*desires*
	For as a spaniel she wol on him lepe,	
	Til that she finde som man hire to chepe.°	*take*
275	Ne noon so grey goos gooth ther in the lake,	
	As, saistou, wol be withoute make;°	*mate*
	And saist it is an hard thing for to weelde°	*control*
	A thing that no man wol, his thankes,° heelde.°	*willingly / hold*
	Thus saistou, lorel,° whan thou goost to bedde,	*scoundrel*
280	And that no wis man needeth for to wedde,	
	Ne no man that entendeth° unto hevene—	*expects (to go)*
	With wilde thonder-dint° and firy levene°	*thunderclap / lightning*
	Mote° thy welked° nekke be tobroke!°	*may / withered / broken*
	Thou saist that dropping° houses and eek smoke	*leaking*
285	And chiding wives maken men to flee	
	Out of hir owene houses: a, benedicite,	
	What aileth swich an old man for to chide?	
	Thou saist we wives wil oure vices hide	

6. According to what you say.

Til we be fast,° and thanne we wol hem shewe—   *bound (in marriage)*

290   Wel may that be a proverbe of a shrewe!°   *scoundrel*

Thou saist that oxen, asses, hors, and houndes,

They been assayed° at diverse stoundes;°   *tested / times*

Bacins,° lavours,° er that men hem bye,   *basins / wash bowls*

Spoones, stooles, and al swich housbondrye,

295   And so be pottes, clothes, and array—

But folk of wives maken noon assay°   *trial*

Til they be wedded—olde dotard shrewe!

And thanne, saistou, we wil oure vices shewe.

Thou saist also that it displeseth me

300   But if° that thou wolt praise my beautee,   *unless*

And but thou poure alway upon my face,

And clepe° me 'Faire Dame' in every place,   *call*

And but thou make a feeste on thilke° day   *that*

That I was born, and make me fressh and gay,

305   And but thou do to my norice° honour,   *nurse*

And to my chamberere° within my bowr,°   *chambermaid / bedroom*

And to my fadres folk, and his allies°—   *kinsmen*

Thus saistou, olde barel-ful of lies.

And yit of our apprentice Janekin,

310   For his crispe heer,° shining as gold so fin,   *curly hair*

And for he squiereth° me bothe up and down,   *chaperones*

Yit hastou caught a fals suspecioun;

I wil° him nat though thou were deed tomorwe.   *desire*

     "But tel me this, why hidestou with sorwe

315   The keyes of thy cheste away fro me?

It is my good as wel as thyn, pardee.°   *by God*

What, weenestou° make an idiot of oure dame?   *do you suppose*

Now by that lord that called is Saint Jame,[7]

Thou shalt nought bothe, though that thou were wood,°   *enraged*

320   Be maister of my body and of my good:

That oon thou shalt forgo, maugree thine yën.[8]

     "What helpeth it of me enquere and spyen?

I trowe thou woldest loke° me in thy cheste.   *lock*

Thou sholdest saye, 'Wif, go wher thee leste.°   *it pleases*

325   Taak youre disport.° I nil leve° no tales: *amusement / believe*

I knowe you for a trewe wif, dame Alis.'

We love no man that taketh keep° or charge   *notice*

Wher that we goon: we wol been at oure large.°   *liberty*

Of alle men yblessed mote he be

330   The wise astrologen daun Ptolomee,

That saith this proverbe in his Almageste:

'Of alle men his wisdom is the hyeste

That rekketh° nat who hath the world in honde.'   *cares*

By this proverbe thou shalt understonde,

335   Have thou ynough, what thar° thee rekke° or care   *need / be concerned*

How merily that othere folkes fare?°   *go about*

---

7. Santiago de Compostela, whose shrine in Spain the
Wife of Bath has already made a pilgrimage to visit.

8. In spite of your eyes (an oath).

For certes, olde dotard, by youre leve,
Ye shal han queinte° right ynough at eve: *sex*
He is too greet a nigard that wil werne°   *refuse*
340   A man to lighte a candle at his lanterne;
He shal han nevere the lasse lighte, pardee.°   *by God*
Have thou ynough, thee thar nat plaine thee.°   *complain*
    "Thou saist also that if we make us gay
With clothing and with precious array,
345   That it is peril of oure chastitee,
And yit with sorwe thou moste enforce thee,⁹
And saye thise wordes in th'Apostles name:
'In habit° maad with chastitee and shame   *clothing*
Ye wommen shal apparaile you,' quod he,
350   'And nat in tressed heer° and gay perree,°   *styled hair / jewels*
As perles ne with gold ne clothes riche.'
After thy text, ne after thy rubriche,¹
I wol nat werke as muchel as a gnat.
Thou saidest this, that I was lik a cat:
355   For whoso wolde senge° a cattes skin,   *singe*
Thanne wolde the cat wel dwellen in his in;°   *inn*
And if the cattes skin be slik° and gay,   *sleek*
She wol nat dwelle in house half a day,
But forth she wol, er any day be dawed,°   *dawned*
360   To shewe her skin and goon a-caterwawed.°   *caterwauling*
This is to saye, if I be gay, sire shrewe,
I wol renne out, my borel° for to shewe.   *coarse cloth*
Sire olde fool, what helpeth thee t'espyen?
Though thou praye Argus² with his hundred yën
365   To be my wardecors,° as he can best,   *bodyguard*
In faith, he shal nat keepe me but me lest:
Yit coude I make his beerd,³ so mote I thee.°   *so may I prosper*
    "Thou saidest eek that ther been thinges three,
The whiche thinges troublen al this erthe,
370   And that no wight° may endure the ferthe.°   *person / fourth*
O leve sire shrewe, Jesu shorte thy lif!
Yit prechestou and saist an hateful wif
Yrekened° is for oon of thise meschaunces.   *accounted*
Been ther nat none othere resemblaunces
375   That ye may likne youre parables to,
But if a sely° wif be oon of tho?   *innocent*
    "Thou liknest eek wommanes love to helle,
To bareine land ther water may nat dwelle;
Thou liknest it also to wilde fir—
380   The more it brenneth,° the more it hath desir   *burns*
To consumen every thing that brent wol be;
Thou saist right as wormes shende° a tree,   *destroy*
Right so a wif destroyeth hir housbonde—

---

9. Reinforce (your position).
1. Rubric, interpretive heading on a text.
2. Mythical hundred-eyed monster employed by Juno to

guard over Io, one of Jove's many lovers, whom the goddess turned into a cow.
3. Deceive him.

This knowen they that been to wives bonde."

385   Lordinges, right thus, as ye han understonde,
Bar I stifly° mine olde housbondes on honde°   *firmly / swore*
That thus they saiden in hir dronkenesse—
And al was fals, but that I took witnesse
On Janekin and on my nece° also.   *kinswoman*
390 O Lord, the paine I dide hem and the wo,
Ful giltelees, by Goddes sweete pine!°   *suffering*
For as an hors I coude bite and whine;
I coude plaine and° I was in the gilt,°   *when / wrong*
Or elles often time I hadde been spilt.°   *ruined*
395 Whoso that first to mille comth first grint.°   *grinds*
I plained first: so was oure werre° stint.°   *war / stopped*
They were ful glad to excusen hem ful blive°   *quickly*
Of thing of which they nevere agilte° hir live.   *offended (in)*
Of wenches wolde I beren hem on honde,
400 Whan that for sik they mighte unnethe° stonde,   *barely*
Yit tikled I his herte for that he
Wende° I hadde had of him so greet cheertee.° *supposed / fondness*
I swoor that al my walking out by nighte
Was for to espye wenches that he dighte.°   *had sex with*
405 Under that colour° hadde I many a mirthe.   *pretense*
For al swich wit is yiven us in oure birthe:
Deceite, weeping, spinning God hath yive
To wommen kindely° whil they may live.   *by nature*
And thus of oo thing I avaunte° me: *boast*
410 At ende I hadde the bet in eech degree,
By sleighte° or force, or by som manere thing,   *deception*
As by continuel murmur° or grucching;° *complaining / grumbling*
Namely abedde° hadden they meschaunce:° *in bed / misfortune*
Ther wolde I chide and do hem no plesaunce;
415 I wolde no lenger in the bed abide
If that I felte his arm over my side,
Til he hadde maad his raunson° unto me;   *amends*
Thanne wolde I suffre him do his nicetee.°   *lust*
And therfore every man this tale I telle:
420 Winne whoso may, for al is for to selle;
With empty hand men may no hawkes lure.
For winning° wolde I al his lust endure,   *profit*
And make me a feined appetit—
And yit in bacon° hadde I nevere delit.   *old meat*
425 That made me that evere I wolde hem chide;
For though the Pope hadde seten° hem biside,   *sat*
I wolde nought spare hem at hir owene boord.°   *table*
For by my trouthe, I quitte° hem word for word.   *repaid*
As help me verray God omnipotent,
430 Though I right now sholde make my testament,
I ne owe hem nat a word that it nis quit.°   *is not repaid*
I broughte it so aboute by my wit
That they moste yive it up as for the beste,
Or elles hadde we nevere been in reste;

435   For though he looked as a wood leoun,°   *crazed lion*
          Yit sholde he faile of his conclusion.°   *purpose*
            Thanne wolde I saye, "Goodelief,° taak keep,   *Sweetheart*
          How mekely looketh Wilekin, oure sheep!
          Com neer my spouse, lat me ba° thy cheeke—   *kiss*
440   Ye sholden be al pacient and meeke,
          And han a sweete-spiced conscience,
          Sith ye so preche of Jobes[4] pacience;
          Suffreth alway, sin ye so wel can preche;
          And but ye do, certain, we shal you teche
445   That it is fair to han a wif in pees.
          Oon of us two moste bowen, doutelees,
          And sith a man is more resonable
          Than womman is, ye mosten been suffrable.°   *patient*
          What aileth you to grucche thus and grone?
450   Is it for ye wolde have my queinte allone?
          Why, taak it al—lo, have it everydeel.
          Peter,° I shrewe° you but ye love it weel.   *by St. Peter / curse*
          For if I wolde selle my bele chose,[5]
          I coude walke as fressh as is a rose;
455   But I wol keepe it for youre owene tooth.°   *taste*
          Ye be to blame. By God, I saye you sooth!"
          Swiche manere wordes hadde we on honde.
          Now wol I speke of my ferthe housbonde.
            My ferthe housbonde was a revelour—
460   This is to sayn, he hadde a paramour°—   *lover*
          And I was yong and ful of ragerye,°   *wantonness*
          Stibourne° and strong and joly as a pie:°   *stubborn / magpie*
          How coude I daunce to an harpe smale,°   *gracefully*
          And singe, ywis,° as any nightingale,   *certainly*
465   Whan I hadde dronke a draughte of sweete win.
          Metellius,[6] the foule cherl,° the swin,   *ruffian*
          That with a staf birafte his wif hir lif
          For she drank win, though I hadde been his wif,
          Ne sholde nat han daunted me fro drinke;
470   And after win on Venus moste I thinke,
          For also siker° as cold engendreth hail,   *certainly*
          A likerous° mouth moste han a likerous° tail: *gluttonous / lecherous*
          In womman vinolent° is no defence—   *drunken*
          This knowen lechours by experience.
475   But Lord Crist, whan that it remembreth me
          Upon my youthe and on my jolitee,
          It tikleth me aboute myn herte roote°—   *bottom of my heart*
          Unto this day it dooth myn herte boote°   *good*
          That I have had my world as in my time.
480   But age, allas, that al wol envenime,°   *poison*
          Hath me birafte my beautee and my pith°—   *vigor*

---

4. The biblical Job, who suffers patiently the trials imposed by God.
5. "Beautiful thing," a euphemism for female genitals.

6. Egnatius Metellius, whose actions are described in Valerius Maximus's *Facta et dicta memorabilia*, 6.3.

Lat go, farewel, the devel go therwith!
The flour is goon, ther is namore to telle:
The bren° as I best can now moste I selle;   *bran*
485   But yit to be right merye wol I fonde.°   *try*
Now wol I tellen of my ferthe housbonde.
     I saye I hadde in herte greet despit
That he of any other hadde delit,
But he was quit,° by God and by Saint Joce:°   *repaid / St. Judocus*
490   I made him of the same wode a croce°—   *cross*
Nat of my body in no foul manere—
But, certainly, I made folk swich cheere
That in his owene grece° I made him frye,   *grease*
For angre and for verray jalousye.
495   By God, in erthe I was his purgatorye,
For which I hope his soule be in glorye.
For God it woot, he sat ful ofte and soong
Whan that his sho° ful bitterly him wroong.°   *shoe / pinched*
Ther was no wight° save God and he that wiste   *person*
500   In many wise how sore I him twiste.
He deide whan I cam fro Jerusalem,
And lith ygrave° under the roode-beem,°   *buried / crossbeam*
Al is his tombe nought so curious°   *carefully made*
As was the sepulcre of him Darius,[7]
505   Which that Appelles wroughte subtilly:
It nis but wast to burye him preciously.°   *expensively*
Lat him fare wel, God yive his soule reste;
He is now in his grave and in his cheste.
     Now of my fifthe housbonde wol I telle—
510   God lete his soule nevere come in helle—
And yit he was to me the moste shrewe:
That feele I on my ribbes al by rewe,°   *in a row*
And evere shal unto myn ending day.
But in oure bed he was so fressh and gay,
515   And therwithal so wel coude he me glose°   *flatter*
Whan that he wolde han my bele chose,°   *pretty thing*
That though he hadde me bet° on every boon,°   *beaten / bone*
He coude winne again my love anoon.
I trowe I loved him best for that he
520   Was of his love daungerous° to me.   *hard to get*
We wommen han, if that I shal nat lie,
In this matere a quainte fantasye:
Waite° what thing we may nat lightly° have,   *note that / easily*
Therafter wol we crye al day and crave;
525   Forbede us thing, and that desiren we;
Presse on us faste, and thanne wol we flee.
With daunger oute we al oure chaffare:[8]
Greet prees° at market maketh dere ware,°   *crowd / costly goods*
And too greet chepe° is holden at litel pris.   *bargain*

---

7. Persian Emperor defeated by Alexander the Great, whose tomb was elaborately designed by the Jewish craftsman Apelles.

8. With coyness we spread out all our merchandise.

530	This knoweth every womman that is wis.	
	My fifthe housbonde—God his soule blesse!—	
	Which that I took for love and no richesse,	
	He somtime was a clerk of Oxenforde,	
	And hadde laft scole° and wente at hoom to boorde	*left school*
535	With my gossib,° dwelling in oure town—	*close friend*
	God have hir soule!—hir name was Alisoun;	
	She knew myn herte and eek my privetee°	*secrets*
	Bet than oure parissh preest, as mote I thee.	
	To hire biwrayed° I my conseil° al,	*revealed / thoughts*
540	For hadde myn housbonde pissed on a wal,	
	Or doon a thing that sholde han cost his lif,	
	To hire, and to another worthy wif,	
	And to my nece which that I loved weel,	
	I wolde han told his conseil everydeel;	
545	And so I dide ful often, God it woot,	
	That made his face often reed° and hoot°	*red / hot*
	For verray shame, and blamed himself for he	
	Hadde told to me so greet a privetee.	
	And so bifel that ones in a Lente—	
550	So often times I to my gossib wente,	
	For evere yit I loved to be gay,	
	And for to walke in March, Averil, and May,	
	From hous to hous, to heere sondry tales—	
	That Janekin clerk and my gossib dame Alis	
555	And I myself into the feeldes wente.	
	Myn housbonde was at London al that Lente:	
	I hadde the better leiser° for to playe,	*opportunity*
	And for to see, and eek for to be seye°	*seen*
	Of lusty° folk—what wiste I wher my grace°	*merry / luck*
560	Was shapen° for to be, or in what place?	*destined*
	Therfore I made my visitaciouns	
	To vigilies[9] and to processiouns,	
	To preching eek, and to thise pilgrimages,	
	To playes of miracles and to mariages,	
565	And wered upon my gaye scarlet gites°—	*robes*
	Thise wormes ne thise motthes ne thise mites,	
	Upon my peril, frete° hem neveradeel:	*devoured*
	And woostou why? For they were used weel.	
	Now wol I tellen forth what happed me.	
570	I saye that in the feeldes walked we,	
	Til trewely we hadde swich daliaunce,°	*flirtation*
	This clerk and I, that of my purveyaunce°	*providence*
	I spak to him and saide him how that he,	
	If I were widwe, sholde wedde me.	
575	For certainly, I saye for no bobaunce°	*boast*
	Yit was I nevere withouten purveyaunce	
	Of mariage n'of othere thinges eek:	
	I holde a mouses herte nought worth a leek	

9. Services on the eve of holy days.

That hath but oon hole for to sterte° to,   *flee*
580   And if that faile thanne is al ydo.
        I bar him on hand he hadde enchaunted me
        (My dame taughte me that subtiltee);
        And eek I saide I mette° of him al night: *dreamed*
        He wolde han slain me as I lay upright,°   *facing up*
585   And al my bed was ful of verray blood—
        "But yit I hope that ye shul do me good;
        For blood bitokeneth gold, as me was taught."
        And al was fals, I dremed of it right naught,
        But as I folwed ay° my dames lore°   *always / teaching*
590   As wel of that as of othere thinges more.
        But now sire—lat me see, what shal I sayn?
        Aha, by God, I have my tale again.
           Whan that my ferthe housbonde was on beere,°   *funeral bier*
        I weep algate,° and made sory cheere,   *constantly*
595   As wives moten, for it is usage,°   *custom*
        And with my coverchief covered my visage;
        But for that I was purveyed° of a make,°   *provided / mate*
        I wepte but smale, and that I undertake.°   *vouch*
           To chirche was myn housbonde born amorwe°   *next morning*
600   With neighebores that for him maden sorwe,
        And Janekin oure clerk was oon of tho.
        As help me God, whan that I saw him go
        After the beere, me thoughte he hadde a paire
        Of legges and of feet so clene and faire,
605   That al myn herte I yaf unto his hold.°   *possession*
        He was, I trowe, twenty winter old,
        And I was fourty, if I shal saye sooth°—   *truth*
        But yit I hadde alway a coltes tooth:°   *youthful tastes*
        Gat-toothed° was I, and that bicam me weel;   *gap-toothed*
610   I hadde the prente° of Sainte Venus seel.°   *imprint / beauty mark*
        As help me God, I was a lusty oon,
        And fair and riche and yong and wel-bigoon,°   *well situated*
        And trewely, as mine housbondes tolde me,
        I hadde the beste quoniam° mighte be.   *you-know-what*
615   For certes I am al Venerien[1]
        In feeling, and myn herte is Marcien:°   *governed by Mars*
        Venus me yaf my lust, my likerousnesse,
        And Mars yaf me my sturdy hardinesse.
        Myn ascendent° was Taur° and Mars therinne—   *zodiac sign / Taurus*
620   Allas, allas, that evere love was sinne!
        I folwed ay my inclinacioun
        By vertu of my constellacioun;
        That made me I coude nought withdrawe°   *withhold*
        My chambre of Venus from a good felawe.
625   Yit have I Martes° merk upon my face,   *Mars's*
        And also in another privee place.
        For God so wis° be my savacioun,°   *surely / salvation*

---

1. Governed by Venus, the planet.

I loved nevere by no discrecioun,
But evere folwede° myn appetit,   *followed*
630   Al were he short or long or blak or whit;
I took no keep, so that he liked° me,   *pleased*
How poore he was, ne eek of what degree.
        What sholde I saye but at the monthes ende
This joly clerk Janekin that was so hende°   *courteous*
635   Hath wedded me with greet solempnitee,
And to him yaf I al the land and fee°   *property*
That evere was me yiven therbifore—
But afterward repented me ful sore:
He nolde suffre° no thing of my list.°   *would allow / pleasure*
640   By God, he smoot° me ones on the list°   *struck / ear*
For that I rente° out of his book a leef,°   *tore / page*
That of the strook myn ere weex° al deef.   *grew, became*
Stibourne I was as is a leonesse,
And of my tonge a verray jangleresse,°   *chatterbox*
645   And walke I wolde, as I hadde doon biforn,
From hous to hous, although he hadde it sworn;°   *prohibited*
For which he often times wolde preche,
And me of olde Romain geestes° teche,   *Latin stories*
How he Simplicius Gallus² lafte his wif,
650   And hire forsook for terme of al his lif,
Nought but for open-heveded° he hire sey°   *bareheaded / saw*
Looking out at his dore upon a day.
        Another Romain³ tolde he me by name
That, for his wif was at a someres° game   *summer's*
655   Withouten his witing,° he forsook hire eke;   *knowledge*
And thanne wolde he upon his Bible seke
That ilke proverbe of Ecclesiaste⁴
Where he comandeth and forbedeth faste
Man shal nat suffre his wif go roule° aboute;   *roam*
660   Thanne wolde he saye right thus withouten doute:
"Whoso that buildeth his hous al of salwes,°   *willow branches*
And priketh° his blinde hors over the falwes,°   *rides / open fields*
And suffreth his wif to go seeken halwes,°   *shrines*
Is worthy to be hanged on the galwes."
665   But al for nought—I sette nought an hawe⁵
Of his proverbes n'of his olde sawe;
N'I wolde nat of him corrected be:
I hate him that my vices telleth me,
And so doon mo, God woot, of us than I.
670   This made him with me wood al outrely:°   *utterly*
I nolde nought forbere° him in no cas.   *would not submit*
        Now wol I saye you sooth, by Saint Thomas,
Why that I rente out of his book a leef,
For which he smoot me so that I was deef.
675   He hadde a book that gladly night and day

2. Narrated in Valerius Maximus, *Facta et dicta memora-*   Facta 6.3.
bilia 6.3.   4. Ecclesiasticus 25.25.
3. P. Sempronius Sophus, as related in Valerius Maximus,   5. Hawthorn berry (i.e., little value).

For his disport° he wolde rede alway.   *amusement*
He cleped° it Valerie and Theofraste,[6]   *called*
At which book he lough° alway ful faste;   *laughed*
And eek ther was somtime a clerk at Rome,
680 A cardinal, that highte Saint Jerome,
That made a book again Jovinian;
In which book eek ther was Tertulan,
Crysippus, Trotula, and Helouis,
That was abbesse nat fer fro Paris;
685 And eek the Parables of Salomon,
Ovides Art, and bookes many oon—
And alle thise were bounden in oo volume.
And every night and day was his custume,°   *custom*
Whan he hadde leiser and vacacioun
690 From other worldly occupacioun,
To reden in this book of wikked wives.
He knew of hem mo legendes and lives
Than been of goode wives in the Bible.
For trusteth wel, it is an impossible°   *impossibility*
695 That any clerk wol speke good of wives,
But if it be of holy saintes lives,
N'of noon other womman nevere the mo—
Who painted the leon, tel me who?[7]
By God, if wommen hadden writen stories,
700 As clerkes han within hir oratories,
They wolde han writen of men more wikkednesse
Than al the merk of° Adam may redresse.   *mark, sex*
The children of Mercurye and Venus[8]
Been in hir werking° ful contrarious:°   *deeds / contradictory*
705 Mercurye loveth wisdom and science,
And Venus loveth riot° and dispence;°   *celebration / expense*
And for hir diverse disposicioun
Each falleth in otheres exaltacioun,[9]
And thus, God woot, Mercurye is desolat°   *powerless*
710 In Pisces wher Venus is exaltat,
And Venus falleth ther Mercurye is raised:
Therfore no womman of no clerk is praised.
The clerk, whan he is old and may nought do
Of Venus werkes worth his olde sho,°   *shoe*
715 Thanne sit he down and writ in his dotage
That wommen can nat keepe hir mariage.

6. Janekin's book is a collection of different works, nearly all of which are directed against women: Walter Map's fictitious letter entitled *Valerius's Dissuasion of Rufinus from Marrying* (Valerius); Theophrastus's *Golden Book on Marriage* (Theofraste); Saint Jerome's *Against Jovinian*; Tertullian's misogynist tracts on sexual continence (Tertulan); Crysippus's writings, mentioned by Jerome but otherwise unknown; *The Sufferings of Women*, an 11th-century book on gynecology by Trotula di Ruggiero, a female physician from Sicily (Trotula); the letters of the abbess Heloise to her lover Abelard (Helouis); the bibli-

cal Book of Proverbs (Parables of Salomon), and Ovid's *Art of Love*.
7. In one of Aesop's fables, a lion asked this question when confronted by a painting of a man killing a lion, indicating that if a lion had painted the picture, the scene would have been very different.
8. Followers of Mercury, the god of rhetoric (scholars, poets, orators); followers of Venus (lovers).
9. Astrologically, one planet diminishes in influence as the other ascends.

But now to purpos why I tolde thee
That I was beten for a book, pardee:°   *by God*
Upon a night Janekin, that was oure sire,°   *master of our house*
720 Redde on his book as he sat by the fire
Of Eva[1] first, that for hir wikkednesse
Was al mankinde brought to wrecchednesse,
For which that Jesu Crist himself was slain
That boughte° us with his herte blood again—   *redeemed*
725 Lo, heer expres of wommen may ye finde
That womman was the los° of al mankinde.   *ruin*
    Tho° redde he me how Sampson loste his heres:°   *then / hair*
Sleeping his lemman° kitte° it with hir sheres,   *lover / cut*
Thurgh which treson loste he both his yën.
730   Tho redde he me, if that I shal nat lien,
Of Ercules and of his Dianire,[2]
That caused him to sette himself afire.
    No thing forgat he the sorwe and wo
That Socrates hadde with his wives two—
735 How Xantippa[3] caste pisse upon his heed:
This sely man sat stille as he were deed;
He wiped his heed, namore dorste he sayn
But "Er° that thonder stinte,° comth a rain."   *before / stops*
    Of Phasipha[4] that was the queene of Crete—
740 For shrewednesse° him thoughte the tale sweete—   *wickedness*
Fy, speek namore, it is a grisly thing
Of hir horrible lust and hir liking.
    Of Clytermistra[5] for hir lecherye
That falsly made hir housbonde for to die,
745 He redde it with ful good devocioun.
    He tolde me eek for what occasioun
Amphiorax[6] at Thebes loste his lif:
Myn housbonde hadde a legende of his wif
Eriphylem, that for an ouche° of gold   *trinket*
750 Hath prively unto the Greekes told
Wher that hir housbonde hidde him in a place,
For which he hadde at Thebes sory grace.
    Of Livia[7] tolde he me and of Lucie:
They bothe made hir housbondes for to die,
755 That oon for love, that other was for hate;
Livia hir housbonde on an even late
Empoisoned hath for that she was his fo;
Lucia likerous loved hir housbonde so

---

1. Eve's temptation by the serpent was blamed for humanity's fall from grace and thus required Christ's incarnation to redeem the world.
2. Deianira gave her husband, Hercules, a robe which she believed was charmed with a love potion, but once he put it on, it burned his flesh so badly that he died.
3. Xanthippe was famous for nagging her husband, the philosopher Socrates.
4. Pasiphae, wife of Minos, became enamored of a bull,

engendering the Minotaur.
5. Clytemnestra, queen of Mycenae, slew her husband Agamemnon when he returned from the Trojan War.
6. Amphiaraus died at the Siege of Thebes after listening to the advice of his wife, Eriphyle.
7. Livia poisoned her husband, Drusus, to satisfy her lover Sejanus; Lucia unwittingly poisoned her husband, the poet Lucretius, with a potion meant to keep him faithful.

That for he sholde alway upon hire thinke,
760   She yaf him swich a manere love-drinke
That he was deed er it were by the morwe.
And thus algates° housbondes han sorwe.   *continually*
    Thanne tolde he me how oon Latumius
Complained unto his felawe Arrius
765   That in his gardin growed swich a tree,
On which he saide how that his wives three
Hanged hemself for herte despitous.°   *cruel*
    "O leve brother," quod this Arrius,
"Yif° me a plante of thilke° blessed tree,   *give / that same*
770   And in my gardin planted shal it be."
    Of latter date of wives hath he red
That some han slain hir housbondes in hir bed
And lete hir lechour dighte° hire al the night,   *screw*
Whan that the cors° lay in the floor upright;°   *corpse / face up*
775   And some han driven nailes in hir brain
Whil that they sleepe, and thus they han hem slain;
Some han hem yiven poison in hir drinke.
He spak more harm than herte may bithinke,
And therwithal he knew of mo proverbes
780   Than in this world ther growen gras or herbes:
"Bet is," quod he, "thyn habitacioun
Be with a leon or a foul dragoun
Than with a wommman using° for to chide."   *accustomed*
"Bet is," quod he, "hye in the roof abide
785   Than with an angry wif down in the hous:
They been so wikked and contrarious,
They haten that hir housbondes loveth ay."°   *always*
He saide, "A womman cast hir shame away
Whan she cast of hir smok,"° and ferthermo,   *slip*
790   "A fair womman, but she be chast also,
Is lik a gold ring in a sowes nose."
Who wolde weene, or who wolde suppose
The wo that in myn herte was and pine?
    And whan I sawgh he wolde nevere fine°   *end*
795   To reden on this cursed book al night,
Al sodeinly three leves have I plight°   *plucked*
Out of his book right as he redde, and eke
I with my fist so took° him on the cheeke   *struck*
That in oure fir he fil bakward adown.
800   And up he sterte as dooth a wood° leoun,   *enraged*
And with his fist he smoot me on the heed
That in the floor I lay as I were deed.
And whan he sawgh how stille that I lay,
He was agast,° and wolde have fled his way,   *afraid*
805   Til atte laste out of my swough° I braide:°   *faint / arose*
"O hastou slain me, false thief?" I saide,
"And for my land thus hastou mordred me?
Er I be deed yit wol I kisse thee."

And neer he cam and kneeled faire adown,
810   And saide, "Dere suster Alisoun,
As help me God, I shal thee nevere smite.
That I have doon, it is thyself to wite.°   *blame*
Foryif it me, and that I thee biseeke."
And yit eftsoones° I hitte him on the cheeke,   *immediately*
815   And saide, "Thief, thus muchel am I wreke.°   *avenged*
Now wol I die: I may no lenger speke."
        But at the laste with muchel care and wo
We fille accorded by us selven two.
He yaf me al the bridel° in myn hand,   *bridle, control*
820   To han the governance of hous and land,
And of his tonge and his hand also;
And made him brenne his book anoonright tho.
And whan that I hadde geten unto me
By maistrye° al the sovereinetee,°   *skill / dominance*
825   And that he saide, "Myn owene trewe wif,
Do as thee lust° the terme of al thy lif,   *please*
Keep thyn honour, and keep eek myn estat,"
After that day we hadde nevere debat.
God help me so, I was to him as kinde
830   As any wif from Denmark unto Inde,
And also trewe, and so was he to me.
I praye to God that sit in majestee,
So blesse his soule for his mercy dere.
Now wol I saye my tale if ye wol heere.

Another Interruption

835   The Frere lough whan he hadde herd al this:
"Now dame," quod he, "so have I joye or blis,
This is a long preamble of a tale."
And whan the Somnour herde the Frere gale,°   *exclaim*
"Lo," quod the Somnour, "Goddes armes two,
840   A frere wol entremette him° everemo!   *interfere*
Lo, goode men, a flye and eek a frere
Wol falle in every dissh and eek matere.
What spekestou of preambulacioun?
What, amble or trotte or pisse or go sitte down!
845   Thou lettest° oure disport in this manere."   *hinder*
        "Ye, woltou so, sire Somnour?" quod the Frere.
"Now by my faith, I shal er that I go
Telle of a somnour swich a tale or two
That al the folk shal laughen in this place."
850   "Now elles, Frere, I wol bishrewe thy face,"
Quod this Somnour, "and I bishrewe me,
But if I telle tales two or three
Of freres, er I come to Sidingborne,⁸

___

8. Sittingbourne, a town about 40 miles from London.

That I shal make thyn herte for to moorne—
855 For wel I woot thy pacience is goon."
    Oure Hoste cride, "Pees, and that anoon!"
And saide, "Lat the womman telle hir tale:
Ye fare° as folk that dronken been of ale.   *behave*
Do, dame, tel forth youre tale, and that is best."
860   "Al redy, sire," quod she, "right as you lest°—   *it pleases*
If I have licence of this worthy Frere."
"Yis, dame," quod he, "tel forth and I wol heere."

The Wife of Bath's Tale

In th'olde dayes of the King Arthour,
Of which that Britouns° speken greet honour,   *Bretons*
865 Al was this land fulfild° of faïrye: *filled*
The elf-queene° with hir joly compaignye   *fairy queen*
Daunced ful ofte in many a greene mede°—   *meadow*
This was the olde opinion as I rede;
I speke of many hundred yeres ago.
870 But now can no man see none elves mo,
For now the grete charitee and prayeres
Of limitours,[1] and othere holy freres,
That serchen every land and every streem,
As thikke as motes° in the sonne-beem,   *dust particles*
875 Blessing halles, chambres, kichenes, bowres,°   *bedrooms*
Citees, burghes,° castels, hye towres,   *boroughs*
Thropes,° bernes,° shipnes,° dayeries—   *villages / barns / stables*
This maketh that ther been no faïries.
For ther as wont° to walken was an elf   *where there used*
880 Ther walketh now the limitour himself,
In undermeles° and in morweninges,°   *afternoons / mornings*
And saith his Matins° and his holy thinges,   *morning prayers*
As he gooth in his limitacioun.°   *prescribed district*
Wommen may go saufly° up and down: *safely*
885 In every bussh or under every tree
Ther is noon other incubus[2] but he,
And he ne wol doon hem but dishonour.
    And so bifel it that this King Arthour
Hadde in his hous a lusty bacheler,°   *young knight*
890 That on a day cam riding fro river,°   *hunting waterfowl*
And happed that, allone as he was born,
He sawgh a maide walking him biforn;
Of which maide anoon, maugree hir heed,°   *against her will*
By verray force he rafte° hir maidenheed;   *stole*
895 For which oppression was swich clamour,
And swich pursuite° unto the King Arthour,   *petitioning*
That dampned° was this knight for to be deed   *condemned*
By cours of lawe, and sholde han lost his heed—
Paraventure° swich was the statut tho°—   *as it happens / then*

---

1. Friars licensed to beg within set districts.   2. Demon who fornicates with women.

900 But that the queene and othere ladies mo
     So longe prayeden the king of grace,
     Til he his lif him graunted in the place,
     And yaf him to the queene, al at hir wille,
     To chese° wheither she wolde him save or spille.°   *decide / destroy*
905 The queene thanked the king with al hir might,
     And after this thus spak she to the knight,
     Whan that she saw hir time upon a day:
     "Thou standest yit," quod she, "in swich array°   *situation*
     That of thy lif yit hastou no suretee.°   *guarantee*
910 I graunte thee lif if thou canst tellen me
     What thing it is that wommen most desiren:
     Be war and keep thy nekke boon° from iren.°   *bone / iron*
     And if thou canst nat tellen me anoon,
     Yit wol I yive thee leve for to goon
915 A twelfmonth and a day to seeche° and lere°   *seek out / learn*
     An answere suffisant° in this matere,   *satisfactory*
     And suretee° wol I han er that thou pace,°   *pledge / pass*
     Thy body for to yeelden° in this place."   *surrender*
          Wo was this knight, and sorwefully he siketh.°   *sighs*
920 But what, he may nat doon al as him liketh,
     And atte laste he chees him° for to wende,°   *decided / travel*
     And come again right at the yeres ende,
     With swich answere as God wolde him purveye,°   *provide*
     And taketh his leve and wendeth forth his waye.
925 He seeketh every hous and every place
     Wher as he hopeth for to finde grace,
     To lerne what thing wommen love most.
     But he ne coude arriven in no coost°   *country*
     Wher as he mighte finde in this matere
930 Two creatures according in fere.°   *agreeing together*
          Some saiden wommen loven best richesse;
     Some saide honour, some saide jolinesse;°   *pleasure*
     Some riche array, some saiden lust abedde,
     And ofte time to be widwe and wedde.
935 Some saide that oure herte is most esed
     Whan that we been yflatered and yplesed—
     He gooth ful neigh the soothe,° I wol nat lie: *near the truth*
     A man shal winne us best with flaterye,
     And with attendance and with bisinesse°   *attentive service*
940 Been we ylimed,° bothe more and lesse.   *ensnared*
          And some sayen that we loven best
     For to be free, and do right as us lest,°   *pleases*
     And that no man repreve° us of oure vice,   *scold*
     But saye that we be wise and no thing nice.°   *foolish*
945 For trewely, ther is noon of us alle,
     If any wight wol clawe us on the galle,°   *rub a sore spot*
     That we nil kike° for he saith us sooth:°   *kick / the truth*
     Assaye° and he shal finde it that so dooth.   *try*
     For be we nevere so vicious withinne,
950 We wol be holden° wise and clene of sinne.   *considered*

	And some sayn that greet delit han we	
	For to be holden stable° and eek secree,°	*constant / discreet*
	And in oo purpos stedefastly to dwelle,	
	And nat biwraye° thing that men us telle—	*reveal*
955	But that tale is nat worth a rake-stele.°	*rake handle*
	Pardee,° we wommen conne no thing hele:°	*by God / conceal*
	Witnesse on Mida.[3] Wol ye heere the tale?	
	Ovide, amonges othere thinges smale,	
	Saide Mida hadde under his longe heres,	
960	Growing upon his heed, two asses eres,	
	The whiche vice° he hidde as he best mighte	*fault*
	Ful subtilly from every mannes sighte,	
	That save his wif ther wiste of it namo.°	*no one else know*
	He loved hire most and trusted hire also.	
965	He prayed hire that to no creature	
	She sholde tellen of his disfigure.°	*deformity*
	She swoor him nay, for al this world to winne,	
	She nolde° do that vilainye or sinne	*would not*
	To make hir housbonde han so foul a name:	
970	She nolde nat telle it for hir owene shame.	
	But nathelees, hir thoughte that she dyde°	*would die*
	That she so longe sholde a conseil° hide;	*secret*
	Hire thoughte it swal so sore aboute hir herte	
	That nedely° som word hire moste asterte,°	*surely / come out*
975	And sith she dorste nat telle it to no man,	
	Down to a mareis° faste° by she ran—	*marsh / close*
	Til she cam there hir herte was afire—	
	And as a bitore° bombleth° in the mire,	*heron / squawks*
	She laide hir mouth unto the water down:	
980	"Biwray° me nat, thou water, with thy soun,"°	*betray / sound*
	Quod she. "To thee I telle it and namo:	
	Myn housbonde hath longe asses eres two.	
	Now is myn herte al hool, now is it oute.	
	I mighte no lenger keepe it, out of doute."	
985	Here may ye see, though we a time abide,	
	Yit oute it moot:° we can no conseil hide.	*must*
	The remenant of the tale if ye wol heere,	
	Redeth Ovide, and ther ye may it lere.°	*learn*
	This knight of which my tale is specially,	
990	Whan that he sawgh he mighte nat come therby—	
	This is to saye what wommen loven most—	
	Within his brest ful sorweful was his gost,°	*spirit*
	But hoom he gooth, he mighte nat sojurne:°	*linger*
	The day was come that hoomward moste he turne.	
995	And in his way it happed him to ride	
	In al this care under a forest side,	
	Wher as he sawgh upon a daunce go	
	Of ladies foure and twenty and yit mo;	
	Toward the whiche daunce he drow° ful yerne,°	*drew / gladly*

3. Midas's story is recounted in Ovid's *Metamorphoses* 9.

1000	In hope that som wisdom sholde he lerne.
	But certainly, er he cam fully there,
	Vanisshed was this daunce, he niste° where.
	No creature sawgh he that bar lif,
	Save on the greene he sawgh sitting a wif—
1005	A fouler wight° ther may no man devise.°
	Again the knight this olde wif gan rise,
	And saide, "Sire knight, heer forth lith no way.°
	Telle me what ye seeken, by youre fay.°
	Paraventure it may the better be:
1010	Thise olde folk conne° muchel thing," quod she.
	"My leve moder,"° quod this knight, "certain,
	I nam but° deed but if that I can sayn
	What thing it is that wommen most desire.
	Coude ye me wisse,° I wolde wel quite youre hire."°
1015	"Plight° me thy trouthe° here in myn hand," quod she,
	"The nexte thing that I require thee,
	Thou shalt it do, if it lie in thy might,
	And I wol telle it you er it be night."
	"Have heer my trouthe," quod the knight. "I graunte."
1020	"Thanne," quod she, "I dar me wel avaunte°
	Thy lif is sauf, for I wol stande therby.
	Upon my lif the queene wol saye as I.
	Lat see which is the pruddeste° of hem alle
	That wereth on a coverchief or a calle°
1025	That dar saye nay of that I shal thee teche.
	Lat us go forth withouten lenger speeche."
	Tho rouned° she a pistel° in his ere,
	And bad him to be glad and have no fere.
	Whan they be comen to the court, this knight
1030	Saide he hadde holde his day as he hadde hight,°
	And redy was his answere, as he saide.
	Ful many a noble wif, and many a maide,
	And many a widwe—for that they been wise—
	The queene hirself sitting as justise,°
1035	Assembled been this answere for to heere,
	And afterward this knight was bode appere.
	To every wight comanded was silence,
	And that the knight sholde telle in audience
	What thing that worldly wommen loven best.
1040	This knight ne stood nat stille° as dooth a best,°
	But to his question anoon answerde
	With manly vois that al the court it herde.
	"My lige° lady, generally," quod he,
	"Wommen desire to have sovereinetee
1045	As wel over hir housbonde as hir love,
	And for to been in maistrye him above.
	This is youre moste desir though ye me kille.
	Dooth as you list: I am here at youre wille."
	In al the court ne was ther wif ne maide
1050	Ne widwe that contraried that he saide,

Marginal glosses:
- 1002 *did not know*
- 1005 *creature / imagine*
- 1007 *road*
- 1008 *faith*
- 1010 *know*
- 1011 *dear mother*
- 1012 *am no more than*
- 1014 *inform / repay you*
- 1015 *pledge / promise*
- 1020 *brag*
- 1023 *proudest*
- 1024 *headdress*
- 1027 *whispered / message*
- 1030 *promised*
- 1034 *judge*
- 1040 *silent / beast*
- 1043 *liege*

But saiden he was worthy han his lif.
   And with that word up sterte that olde wif,
Which that the knight sawgh sitting on the greene;
"Mercy," quod she, "my soverein lady queene,
1055 Er that youre court departe, do me right.
I taughte this answere unto the knight,
For which he plighte me his trouthe there
The firste thing I wolde him requere
He wolde it do, if it laye in his might.
1060 Bifore the court thanne praye I thee, sire knight,"
Quod she, "that thou me take unto thy wif,
For wel thou woost° that I have kept° thy lif.   *know / saved*
If I saye fals, say nay, upon thy fay."
   This knight answerde, "Allas and wailaway,
1065 I woot° right wel that swich was my biheeste.°   *know / promise*
For Goddes love, as chees° a newe requeste: *choose*
Taak al my good and lat my body go."
   "Nay thanne," quod she, "I shrewe° us bothe two.   *curse*
For though that I be foul and old and poore,
1070 I nolde° for al the metal ne for ore   *would not wish*
That under erthe is grave° or lith above,   *buried*
But if thy wif I were and eek thy love."
   "My love," quod he. "Nay, my dampnacioun!
Allas, that any of my nacioun°   *lineage*
1075 Sholde evere so foule disparaged° be."   *degraded*
But al for nought, th'ende is this, that he
Constrained was: he needes moste hire wedde,
And taketh his olde wif and gooth to bedde.
   Now wolden some men saye, paraventure,
1080 That for my necligence I do no cure
To tellen you the joy and al th'array
That at the feeste was that ilke day.
To which thing shortly answere I shal:
I saye ther nas no joye ne feeste at al;
1085 Ther nas but hevinesse and muche sorwe.
For prively he wedded hire on morwe,°   *in the morning*
And al day after hidde him as an owle,
So wo was him, his wif looked so foule.
   Greet was the wo the knight hadde in his thought:
1090 Whan he was with his wif abedde brought,
He walweth° and he turneth to and fro.   *rolls over*
His olde wif lay smiling everemo,
And saide, "O dere housbonde, benedicite,°   *bless us*
Fareth° every knight thus with his wif as ye? *behaves*
1095 Is this the lawe of King Arthures hous?
Is every knight of his thus daungerous?°   *reserved*
I am youre owene love and youre wif;
I am she which that saved hath youre lif;
And certes yit ne dide I you nevere unright.° *injustice*
1100 Why fare° ye thus with me this firste night?   *behave*
Ye faren like a man hadde lost his wit.

What is my gilt? For Goddes love, telle it,
And it shal been amended if I may."
"Amended!" quod this knight. "Allas, nay, nay,
1105   It wol nat been amended neveremo.
Thou art so lothly° and so old also,   loathsome
And therto comen of so lowe a kinde,°   breeding
That litel wonder is though I walwe and winde.°   turn
So wolde God myn herte wolde breste!"°   burst
1110   "Is this," quod she, "the cause of youre unreste?"
"Ye, certainly," quod he. "No wonder is."
"Now sire," quod she, "I coude amende al this,
If that me liste,° er it were dayes three,   it pleased me
So° wel ye mighte bere you° unto me.   provided that / behave
1115   "But for ye speken of swich gentilesse°   nobility
As is descended out of old richesse—
That therfore sholden ye be gentilmen—
Swich arrogance is nat worth an hen.
Looke who that is most vertuous alway,
1120   Privee and apert,° and most entendeth ay   privately and publicly
To do the gentil deedes that he can,
Taak him for the gretteste gentilman.
Crist wol° we claime of him oure gentilesse,   wishes
Nat of oure eldres for hir 'old richesse.'
1125   For though they yive us al hir heritage,
For which we claime to been of heigh parage,°   noble lineage
Yit may they nat biquethe for no thing
To noon of us hir vertuous living,
That made hem gentilmen ycalled be,
1130   And bad us folwen° hem in swich degree.   to follow
"Wel can the wise poete of Florence,
That highte° Dant,[4] speken in this sentence;°   was called / opinion
Lo, in swich manere rym is Dantes tale:
'Ful selde° up riseth by his braunches[5] smale   seldom
1135   Prowesse° of man, for God of his prowesse   excellence
Wol that of him we claime oure gentilesse.'
For of oure eldres may we no thing claime
But temporel thing that man may hurte and maime.
Eek every wight woot° this as wel as I,   person knows
1140   If gentilesse were planted natureelly
Unto a certain linage down the line,
Privee and apert, thanne wolde they nevere fine°   end
To doon of gentilesse the faire office°—   duty
They mighte do no vilainye or vice.
1145   "Taak fir and beer° it in the derkeste hous   bring
Bitwixe this and the Mount of Caucasus,
And lat men shette° the dores and go thenne,°   shut / thence
Yit wol the fir as faire lie and brenne
As twenty thousand men mighte it biholde:

---

4. Dante Alighieri, the 13th-century Italian poet, ex-   5. Branches (of his family tree).
pressed similar views in his *Convivio*.

1150	His° office natureel ay° wol it holde,	*its / always*
	Up peril of my lif, til that it die.	
	Heer may ye see wel how that genterye°	*gentility*
	Is nat annexed° to possessioun,	*connected*
	Sith° folk ne doon hir operacioun°	*since / their work*
1155	Alway, as dooth the fir, lo, in his kinde.°	*nature*
	For God it woot, men may wel often finde	
	A lordes sone do shame and vilainye;	
	And he that wol han pris° of his gentrye,°	*esteem / noble birth*
	For he was boren of a gentil hous,	
1160	And hadde his eldres noble and vertuous,	
	And nil° himselven do no gentil deedes,	*will not*
	Ne folwen his gentil auncestre that deed is,	
	He nis nat gentil, be he duc or erl—	
	For vilaines sinful deedes maken a cherl.°	*ruffian*
1165	Thy gentilesse nis but renomee°	*reputation*
	Of thine auncestres for hir heigh bountee,°	*generosity*
	Which is a straunge° thing for thy persone.	*foreign*
	For gentilesse cometh fro God allone.	
	Thanne comth oure verray gentilesse of grace:	
1170	It was no thing biquethe us with oure place.	
	Thenketh how noble, as saith Valerius,[6]	
	Was thilke° Tullius Hostilius[7]	*that*
	That out of poverte roos to heigh noblesse.	
	Redeth Senek,[8] and redeth eek Boece:	
1175	Ther shul ye seen expres that no drede° is	*doubt*
	That he is gentil that dooth gentil deedes.	
	And therfore, leve housbonde, I thus conclude:	
	Al were it that mine auncestres weren rude,°	*lowborn*
	Yit may the hye God—and so hope I—	
1180	Graunte me grace to liven vertuously.	
	Thanne am I gentil whan that I biginne	
	To liven vertuously and waive° sinne.	*avoid*
	"And ther as ye of poverte me repreve,	
	The hye God, on whom that we bileve,	
1185	In wilful poverte chees to live his lif;	
	And certes every man, maiden, or wif	
	May understonde that Jesus, hevene king,	
	Ne wolde nat chese a vicious living.	
	Glad poverte is an honeste° thing, certain;	*honorable*
1190	This wol Senek and othere clerkes sayn.	
	Whoso that halt him paid of his poverte,[9]	
	I holde him riche al° hadde he nat a sherte.°	*although / shirt*
	He that coveiteth is a poore wight,	
	For he wolde han that is nat in his might;	
1195	But he that nought hath, ne coveiteth have,	
	Is riche, although we holde him but a knave.°	*servant*

6. The Roman historian Valerius Maximus, in his *Facta et dicta memorabilia* 3.4.
7. The legendary third king of Rome who started as a shepherd.

8. Seneca, the Stoic author, in his *Epistle* 44; Boece: Boethius in his *Consolation of Philosophy*.
9. Whoever is satisfied with poverty.

Verray poverte it singeth proprely.
Juvenal[1] saith of poverte, 'Merily
The poore man, whan he gooth by the waye,
1200   Biforn the theves he may singe and playe.'
Poverte is hateful good, and as I gesse,
A ful greet bringere out of bisinesse;°   *worldly cares*
A greet amendere eek of sapience°   *wisdom*
To him that taketh it in pacience;
1205   Poverte is thing, although it seeme elenge,°   *miserable*
Possession that no wight wol chalenge;
Poverte ful often, whan a man is lowe,
Maketh his God and eek himself to knowe;
Poverte a spectacle° is, as thinketh me,   *eyeglass*
1210   Thurgh which he may his verray freendes see.
And therfore, sire, sin that I nought you greve,
Of my poverte namore ye me repreve.
    "Now sire, of elde° ye repreve me: *old age*
And certes sire, though noon auctoritee
1215   Were in no book, ye gentils of honour
Sayn that men sholde an old wight° doon favour,   *person*
And clepe° him fader for youre gentilesse—   *call*
And auctours° shal I finden, as I gesse.   *authorities*
    "Now ther ye saye that I am foul and old:
1220   Thanne drede you nought to been a cokewold,°   *cuckold*
For filthe and elde, also mote I thee,
Been grete wardeins° upon chastitee.   *guardians*
But nathelees, sin I knowe your delit,
I shal fulfille youre worldly appetit.
1225   "Chees° now," quod she, "oon of thise thinges twaye: *choose*
To han me foul and old til that I deye
And be to you a trewe humble wif,
And nevere you displese in al my lif,
Or elles ye wol han me yong and fair,
1230   And take youre aventure° of the repair°   *chances / visits*
That shal be to youre hous by cause of me—
Or in som other place, wel may be.
Now chees youreselven wheither° that you liketh."   *whichever*
    This knight aviseth him° and sore siketh;°   *considers / sighs*
1335   But atte laste he saide in this manere:
"My lady and my love, and wif so dere,
I putte me in youre wise governaunce:
Cheseth yourself which may be most plesaunce
And most honour to you and me also.
1240   I do no fors° the wheither of the two,   *do not care*
For as you liketh it suffiseth° me."   *satisfies*
    "Thanne have I gete of you° maistrye," quod she,   *won from you*
"Sin I may chese and governe as me lest?"°   *it pleases*
    "Ye, certes, wif," quod he. "I holde it best."
1245   "Kisse me," quod she. "We be no lenger wrothe.°   *opposed*

1. The misogynist Roman poet in his *Satires* 10.21, 22.

For by my trouthe, I wol be to you bothe—
This is to sayn, ye, bothe fair and good.
I praye to God that I mote sterven wood,°   *die mad*
But I to you be al so good and trewe
1250   As evere was wif sin that the world was newe.
And but I be tomorn° as fair to seene   *in the morning*
As any lady, emperisse, or queene,
That is bitwixe the eest and eek the west,
Do with my lif and deeth right as you lest:
1255   Caste up the curtin, looke how that it is."
        And whan the knight sawgh verraily al this,
That she so fair was and so yong therto,
For joye he hente° hire in his armes two;   *seized*
His herte bathed in a bath of blisse;
1260   A thousand time arewe° he gan hire kisse,   *in a row*
And she obeyed him in every thing
That mighte do him plesance or liking.
And thus they live unto hir lives ende
In parfit° joye. And Jesu Crist us sende   *perfect*
1265   Housbondes meeke, yonge, and fresshe abedde—
And grace t'overbide° hem that we wedde.   *outlive*
And eek I praye Jesu shorte hir lives
That nought wol be governed by hir wives,
And olde and angry nigardes of dispence°—   *misers in spending*
1270   God sende hem soone a verray pestilence!

THE PARDONER'S PROLOGUE AND TALE   There is something in Chaucer's Pardoner to unnerve practically everyone. The Pardoner's physiology blurs gender itself, his apparent homosexuality challenges the dominant heterosexual ordering of medieval society, his *Prologue* subverts the notion that the intent and effect of words are connected, and his willingness to convert religious discourse into cash undermines the very bases of faith. He initiates a sequence of moments in the later tales that threaten to puncture or tear the social fabric of the Canterbury company.

The Pardoner and "his freend and his compeer," the Summoner, are the last two pilgrims described in *The General Prologue,* reflecting the distaste with which such marginal clergy were often regarded in the period. Summoners were the policing branch of the ecclesiastical courts, paid to bring in transgressors against the canon law. Pardoners had the job, criticized even within the church, of exchanging indulgences for cash. The sufferings of Christ and saintly martyrs, it was thought, had left the church with a legacy of goodness. This could be transferred to sinners, freeing them from a period in Purgatory, if they proved their penitence (among other ways) by gifts to support good works such as the hospital for which the Pardoner worked.

The Pardoner has turned this part of the structure of penitence into a profit center. In his own *Prologue,* the Pardoner is boastfully explicit about this:

For myn entente is nat but for to winne,
And no thing for correccion of sinne . . .

This merciless equation of his verbal power with cash profit deeply subverts the logic of Christian language and the priestly role in salvation. These are replaced by language working in a strange self-consuming circle: the Pardoner brilliantly achieves the very sin his sermon most vituperates.

The Pardoner's physiology—he has either lost his testicles or never had them—may emblematize this exploitation of language emptied of spiritual intention. His uncertain or incomplete gender, though, also challenges the fundamental distinctions of the body within the medieval social economy, as does his apparent homosexuality. The Pardoner's theatrical self-presentation, abetted by rhetorical techniques he lovingly describes, draws the fascinated if queasy attention of his audience and seems to provide him a monstrous though (as it turns out) fragile power.

The Pardoner's tale of three rioters and their encounter with death is actually folded into his Prologue as an exemplum, an illustrative story, in the sermon against cupidity he proposes to offer as a sample of his skills. Yet the Pardoner's obsession with bodies in extremity, seeking or denying death, skeletal or gorged, pulls against his tale as a parable of greed. The tale draws toward its close in a scene of rage, exposure, and angry silence, which threatens to undo the pilgrim society, rather as the Pardoner and his discourse have threatened so much of the broader social contract. The Knight steps in, though, and almost bullies the Host and the Pardoner into a kiss of peace. This ritual gesture, nearly as empty of real goodwill as any of the Pardoner's most cynical words, does allow the shaken group to continue on their way, even as it hints at the emptiness that may hide in other, less openly challenged systems of value in the tales and their world.

The Pardoner's Prologue
The Introduction

	Oure Hoste gan to swere as he were wood;°	*mad*
	"Harrow," quod he, "by nailes[1] and by blood,	
	This was a fals cherl° and a fals justice.°[2]	*villain / judge*
	As shameful deeth as herte may devise	
5	Come to thise juges and hir advocats.°	*lawyers*
	Algate° this sely° maide is slain, allas!	*anyway / innocent*
	Allas, too dere boughte she beautee!	
	Wherfore I saye alday° that men may see	*always*
	The yiftes of Fortune and of Nature	
10	Been cause of deeth to many a creature.	
	As bothe yiftes° that I speke of now,	*gifts*
	Men han ful ofte more for harm than prow.°	*profit*
	"But trewely, myn owene maister dere,	
	This is a pitous tale for to heere.	
15	But nathelees, passe over, is no fors:°	*concern*
	I praye to God so save thy gentil° cors,°	*noble / body*
	And eek thine urinals[3] and thy jurdones,°	*chamber pots*
	Thyn ipocras and eek thy galiones,[4]	
	And every boiste° ful of thy letuarye°—	*box / medicine*
20	God blesse hem, and oure lady Sainte Marye.	
	So mote I theen,° thou art a propre man,	*so may I prosper*
	And lik a prelat,° by Saint Ronian![5]	*Church officer*
	Saide I nat wel? I can nat speke in terme.°	*jargon*
	But wel I woot,° thou doost myn herte to erme°	*know / grieve*

---

1. Nails (of Christ's cross).
2. Harry Baily, the host, is responding to *The Physician's Tale* and the story of a young woman named Virginia whose father kills her rather than surrender her to a wicked judge and his accomplice.
3. Physician's vessels for analyzing urine samples.
4. Medicines named after the ancient Greek physicians Hippocrates and Galen.
5. St. Ronan, a Scottish saint, with a possible pun on "runnions," the male sexual organs.

25	That I almost have caught a cardinacle.°	*heart condition*
	By corpus bones,[6] but if I have triacle,°	*medicine*
	Or elles a draughte of moiste° and corny° ale,	*fresh / malted*
	Or but I heere anoon a merye tale,	
	Myn herte is lost for pitee of this maide.	
30	"Thou bel ami,[7] thou Pardoner," he saide,	
	"Tel us som mirthe or japes° right anoon."	*joke*
	"It shal be doon," quod he, "by Saint Ronian.	
	But first," quod he, "here at this ale-stake°	*tavern marker*
	I wol bothe drinke and eten of a cake."°	*loaf of bread*
35	And right anoon thise gentils gan to crye,	
	"Nay, lat him telle us of no ribaudye.°	*obscenity*
	Tel us som moral thing that we may lere,°	*learn*
	Som wit, and thanne wol we gladly heere."	
	"I graunte, ywis,"° quod he, "but I moot° thinke	*certainly / must*
40	Upon som honeste° thing whil that I drinke."	*honorable*

The Prologue

	Lordinges—quod he—in chirches whan I preche,	
	I paine me to han an hautein° speeche,	*loud*
	And ringe it out as round as gooth a belle,	
	For I can al by rote° that I telle.	*know it all by heart*
45	My theme is alway oon,° and evere was:	*the same*
	Radix malorum est cupiditas.[8]	
	First I pronounce whennes that I come,	
	And thanne my bulles° shewe I alle and some:	*indulgences*
	Oure lige lordes seel[9] on my patente,°	*license*
50	That shewe I first, my body to warente,°	*safeguard*
	That no man be so bold, ne preest ne clerk,	
	Me to destourbe of Cristes holy werk.	
	And after that thanne telle I forth my tales—	
	Bulles of popes and of cardinales,	
55	Of patriarkes and bisshopes I shewe,	
	And in Latin I speke a wordes fewe,	
	To saffron° with my predicacioun,°	*season / preaching*
	And for to stire hem to devocioun.	
	Thanne shewe I forth my longe crystal stones,°	*jars*
60	Ycrammed ful of cloutes° and of bones—	*rags*
	Relikes been they, as weenen they eechoon.°	*they all suppose*
	Thanne have I in laton° a shulder-boon	*brazened*
	Which that was of an holy Jewes sheep.	
	"Goode men," I saye, "take of my wordes keep:°	*notice*
65	If that this boon be wasshe in any welle,	
	If cow, or calf, or sheep, or oxe swelle,	
	That any worm° hath ete or worm ystonge,	*snake*
	Take water of that welle and wassh his tonge,	
	And it is hool° anoon. And ferthermoor,	*healthy*

6. A confused oath mixing God's body and God's bones.   8. Greed is the root of all evil.
7. Fair friend (French, affected).   9. Seal of our liege lord (i.e., the Pope).

70	Of pokkes° and of scabbe and every soor	*pox*
	Shal every sheep be hool that of this welle	
	Drinketh a draughte. Take keep eek that I telle:	
	If that the goode man that the beestes oweth°	*owns*
	Wol every wike,° er that the cok him croweth,	*week*
75	Fasting drinken of this welle a draughte—	
	As thilke° holy Jew oure eldres taughte—	*that*
	His beestes and his stoor° shal multiplye.	*stock*
	"And sire, also it heleth jalousye:	
	For though a man be falle in jalous rage	
80	Lat maken with this water his potage,°	*soup*
	And nevere shal he more his wif mistriste,	
	Though he the soothe° of hir defaute wiste,°	*truth / offense knows*
	Al hadde she taken preestes two or three.	
	"Here is a mitein° eek that ye may see:	*mitten*
85	He that his hand wol putte in this mitein	
	He shal have multiplying of his grain,	
	Whan he hath sowen, be it whete or otes—	
	So that he offre pens° or elles grotes.°	*pennies / silver coins*
	"Goode men and wommen, oo thing warne I you:	
90	If any wight° be in this chirche now	*person*
	That hath doon sinne horrible, that he	
	Dar nat for shame of it yshriven° be,	*confessed*
	Or any womman, be she yong or old,	
	That hath ymaked hir housbonde cokewold,°	*cuckold*
95	Swich folk shal have no power ne no grace	
	To offren to my relikes in this place;	
	And whoso findeth him out of swich blame,	
	He wol come up and offre in Goddes name,	
	And I assoile° him by the auctoritee	*absolve*
100	Which that by bulle ygraunted was to me."	
	By this gaude° have I wonne, yeer by yeer,	*trick*
	An hundred mark[1] sith I was pardoner.	
	I stonde lik a clerk in my pulpet,	
	And whan the lewed° peple is down yset,	*ignorant*
105	I preche so as ye han herd bifore,	
	And telle an hundred false japes° more.	*tricks*
	Thanne paine I me to strecche forth the nekke,	
	And eest and west upon the peple I bekke°	*nod*
	As dooth a douve,° sitting on a berne;°	*dove / barn*
110	Mine handes and my tonge goon so yerne°	*fast*
	That it is joye to see my bisinesse.	
	Of avarice and of swich cursednesse	
	Is al my preching, for to make hem free°	*generous*
	To yiven hir pens, and namely unto me,	
115	For myn entente is nat but for to winne,°	*profit*
	And no thing for correccion of sinne:	
	I rekke° nevere whan that they been beried°	*care / buried*
	Though that hir soules goon a-blakeberied.[2]	

---

1. About 66 pounds.   2. Looking for blackberries.

For certes, many a predicacioun

120 Comth ofte time of yvel entencioun:
Som for plesance of folk and flaterye,
To been avaunced by ypocrisye,
And som for vaine glorye, and som for hate;
For whan I dar noon otherways debate,

125 Thanne wol I stinge him with my tonge smerte°   *hurting*
In preching, so that he shal nat asterte°   *escape*
To been defamed falsly, if that he
Hath trespassed to my bretheren or to me.
For though I telle nought his propre name,

130 Men shal wel knowe that it is the same
By signes and by othere circumstaunces.
Thus quite° I folk that doon us displesaunces;°   *repay / trouble*
Thus spete I out my venim under hewe°   *color*
Of holinesse, to seeme holy and trewe.

135 But shortly myn entente I wol devise:°   *describe*
I preche of no thing but for coveitise;°   *greed*
Therfore my theme is yit and evere was
Radix malorum est cupiditas.
     Thus can I preche again that same vice

140 Which that I use, and that is avarice.
But though myself be gilty in that sinne,
Yit can I make other folk to twinne°   *separate*
From avarice, and sore to repente—
But that is nat my principal entente:

145 I preche no thing but for coveitise.
Of this matere it oughte ynough suffise.
     Thanne telle I hem ensamples° many oon   *exemplary tales*
Of olde stories longe time agoon,
For lewed peple loven tales olde—

150 Swiche thinges can they wel reporte° and holde.°   *repeat / remember*
What, trowe° ye that whiles I may preche,   *believe*
And winne gold and silver for I teche,
That I wol live in poverte wilfully?
Nay, nay, I thoughte it nevere, trewely,

155 For I wol preche and begge in sondry landes;
I wol nat do no labour with mine handes,
Ne make baskettes and live therby,
By cause I wol nat beggen idelly.°   *in vain*
I wol none of the Apostles countrefete:°   *imitate*

160 I wol have moneye, wolle,° cheese, and whete,   *wool*
Al were it yiven of the pooreste page,°   *servant*
Or of the pooreste widwe in a village—
Al sholde hir children sterve° for famine.   *die*
Nay, I wol drinke licour of the vine

165 And have a joly wenche in every town.
But herkneth, lordinges, in conclusioun,
Youre liking is that I shal telle a tale:
Now have I dronke a draughte of corny ale,
By God, I hope I shal you telle a thing

170   That shal by reson been at youre liking;
       For though myself be a ful vicious man,
       A moral tale yit I you telle can,
       Which I am wont to preche for to winne.
       Now holde youre pees, my tale I wol biginne.

The Pardoner's Tale

175   In Flandres whilom° was a compaignye   *once*
       Of yonge folk that haunteden° folye—   *practiced*
       As riot, hasard, stewes,[1] and tavernes,
       Wher as with harpes, lutes, and giternes°   *guitars*
       They daunce and playen at dees° bothe day and night, *dice*
180   And ete also and drinke over hir might,
       Thurgh which they doon the devel sacrifise
       Withinne that develes temple in cursed wise
       By superfluitee° abhominable.   *overindulgence*
       Hir othes been so grete and so dampnable
185   That it is grisly for to heere hem swere:
       Oure blessed Lordes body they totere°—   *rip apart*
       Hem thoughte that Jewes rente° him nought ynough.   *tore*
       And eech of hem at otheres sinne lough.°   *laughed*
       And right anoon thanne comen tombesteres,°   *dancing girls*
190   Fetis° and smale,° and yonge frutesteres,[2]   *elegant / slender*
       Singeres with harpes, bawdes,° wafereres°—   *pimps / cake sellers*
       Whiche been the verray develes officeres,
       To kindle and blowe the fir of lecherye
       That is annexed° unto glotonye:°   *connected / gluttony*
195   The Holy Writ take I to my witnesse
       That luxure° is in win and dronkenesse.   *lechery*
       Lo, how that dronken Lot[3] unkindely°   *against nature*
       Lay by his doughtres two unwitingly:
       So dronke he was he niste what he wroughte.°   *knew not what he did*
200   Herodes,[4] who so wel the stories soughte,
       Whan he of win was repleet at his feeste,
       Right at his owene table he yaf his heeste°   *command*
       To sleen° the Baptist John, ful giltelees.   *slay*
           Senek[5] saith a good word douteless:
205   He saith he can no difference finde
       Bitwixe a man that is out of his minde
       And a man which that is dronkelewe,°   *drunk*
       But that woodnesse, yfallen in a shrewe,[6]
       Persevereth lenger than dooth dronkenesse.
210   O glotonye, ful of cursednesse!
       O cause first of oure confusioun!°   *ruin*
       O original of oure dampnacioun,

1. Such as carousing, gambling, brothels.
2. Girls selling fruit.
3. Lot, the nephew of Abraham, whose story is told in Genesis 19.30–38.
4. King Herod, who was enticed by Salome into bringing her the head of John the Baptist (Mark 6.17–29, Matthew 14.1–12).
5. The stoic author Seneca in his *Epistle* 83.18.493–97.
6. Madness, occurring in a wicked person.

Detail from a carved chest, c. 1410. This large wooden panel is the surviving half of the front of a massive chest. It presents scenes from *The Pardoner's Tale*: at left, the youngest rioter buys wine; in the center, his two companions stab him to death; at right, they die from the wine their companion had poisoned. The composition and carving have much of the energy and economical narrative style of the tale itself. Produced about a decade after Chaucer's death, the panel reflects the impact of his tales in settings very different from those that supported such grand aristocratic productions as the Ellesmere manuscript, created around the same time (see Color Plate 9 and page 248).

	Til Crist hadde bought° us with his blood again!	*redeemed*
	Lo, how dere, shortly for to sayn,	
215	Abought was thilke° cursed vilainye;	*that*
	Corrupt was al this world for glotonye:	
	Adam oure fader and his wif also	
	Fro Paradis to labour and to wo	
	Were driven for that vice, it is no drede.°	*doubt*
220	For whil that Adam fasted, as I rede,	
	He was in Paradis; and whan that he	
	Eet of the fruit defended° on a tree,	*forbidden*
	Anoon he was out cast to wo and paine.	
	O glotonye, on thee wel oughte us plaine!°	*lament*
225	O, wiste a man how manye maladies	
	Folwen of° excesse and of glotonies,	*result from*
	He wolde been the more mesurable°	*moderate*
	Of his diete, sitting at his table.	
	Allas, the shorte throte, the tendre mouth,	
230	Maketh that eest and west and north and south,	
	In erthe, in air, in water, men to swinke,°	*labor*
	To gete a gloton daintee mete and drinke.	
	Of this matere, O Paul, wel canstou trete:°	*discuss*
	"Mete unto wombe, and wombe° eek unto mete,	*belly*
235	Shal God destroyen bothe," as Paulus saith.[7]	

7. St. Paul in 1 Corinthians 6.13.

Allas, a foul thing is it, by my faith,
To saye this word, and fouler is the deede
Whan man so drinketh of the white and rede°   *white and red wines*
That of his throte he maketh his privee°   *toilet*
240 Thurgh thilke cursed superfluitee.
    The Apostle[8] weeping saith ful pitously,
"Ther walken manye of which you told have I—
I saye it now weeping with pitous vois—
They been enemies of Cristes crois,°   *cross*
245 Of whiche the ende is deeth—wombe is hir god!"
O wombe, O bely, O stinking cod,°   *bag*
Fulfilled of dong° and of corrupcioun!   *dung*
At either ende of thee foul is the soun.°   *sound*
How greet labour and cost is thee to finde!°   *provide for*
250 Thise cookes, how they stampe and straine and grinde,
And turnen substance into accident[9]
To fulfillen al thy likerous talent!°   *greedy desire*
Out of the harde bones knokke they
The mary,° for they caste nought away   *marrow*
255 That may go thurgh the golet° softe and soote.°   *gullet / sweet*
Of spicerye of leef and bark and roote
Shal been his sauce ymaked by delit,
To make him yit a newer appetit.
But certes, he that haunteth swiche delices°   *delicacies*
260 Is deed whil that he liveth in tho° vices.   *those*
    A lecherous thing is win, and dronkenesse
Is ful of striving° and of wrecchednesse.   *quarreling*
O dronke man, disfigured is thy face!
Sour is thy breeth, foul artou to embrace!
265 And thurgh thy dronke nose seemeth the soun
As though thou saidest ay° "Sampsoun, Sampsoun."   *always*
And yit, God woot,° Sampson drank nevere win.   *knows*
Thou fallest as it were a stiked swin;°   *stuck pig*
Thy tonge is lost, and al thyn honeste cure,°   *care for honor*
270 For dronkenesse is verray sepulture°   *grave*
Of mannes wit and his discrecioun.
In whom that drinke hath dominacioun
He can no conseil keepe, it is no drede.
Now keepe you fro the white and fro the rede—
275 And namely fro the white win of Lepe[1]
That is to selle in Fisshstreete or in Chepe:[2]
The win of Spaine creepeth subtilly[3]
In othere wines growing faste° by,   *close*
Of which ther riseth swich fumositee°   *vapors*
280 That whan a man hath dronken draughtes three

---

8. St. Paul, in Philippians 3.18–19.
9. A learned joke about the Eucharist where, in Catholic doctrine, the essence ("substance") of bread and wine is transformed into the body and blood of Christ, though their form ("accident") remains unchanged.
1. Wine-growing region in Spain.

2. Commercial districts in London.
3. Chaucer is referring to the illegal practice of using cheap wine (here, Spanish wine from Lepe) to dilute more expensive wines (from the neighboring French provinces of La Rochelle and Bordeaux).

And weeneth that he be at hoom in Chepe,
He is in Spaine, right at the town of Lepe,
Nat at The Rochele ne at Burdeux town;
And thanne wol he sayn "Sampsoun, Sampsoun."

285   But herkneth, lordinges, oo word I you praye,
That alle the soverein actes,° dar I saye,   *excellent deeds*
Of victories in the Olde Testament,
Thurgh verray God that is omnipotent,
Were doon in abstinence and in prayere:

290   Looketh the Bible and ther ye may it lere.°   *learn*
        Looke Attilla, the grete conquerour,[4]
Deide in his sleep with shame and dishonour,
Bleeding at his nose in dronkenesse:
A capitain sholde live in sobrenesse.

295   And overal this, aviseth you right wel
What was comanded unto Lamuel[5]—
Nat Samuel, but Lamuel, saye I—
Redeth the Bible and finde it expresly,
Of win-yiving° to hem that han° justise: *wine-serving / dispense*

300   Namore of this, for it may wel suffise.
        And now that I have spoken of glotonye,
Now wol I you defende hasardrye:°   *gambling*
Hasard is verray moder of lesinges,°   *lies*
And of deceite and cursed forsweringes,

305   Blaspheme of Crist, manslaughtre, and wast° also   *waste*
Of catel° and of time; and ferthermo,   *property*
It is repreve° and contrarye of honour   *reprobate*
For to been holden a commune hasardour,
And evere the hyer he is of estat

310   The more is he holden desolat.°   *dissolute*
If that a prince useth hasardrye,
In alle governance and policye
He is, as by commune opinioun,
Yholde the lasse in reputacioun.

315   Stilbon,[6] that was a wis embassadour,
Was sent to Corinthe in ful greet honour
Fro Lacedomye° to make hir alliaunce,   *Sparta*
And whan he cam him happede parchaunce
That alle the gretteste that were of that lond

320   Playing at the hasard he hem foond,
For which as soone as it mighte be
He stal him hoom again to his contree,
And saide, "Ther wol I nat lese° my name,   *lose*
N'I wol nat take on me so greet defame

325   You to allye unto none hasardours:
Sendeth othere wise embassadours,
For by my trouthe, me were levere° die   *I would rather*
Than I you sholde to hasardours allye.

4. Attila the Hun died on his wedding night from excessive drinking.
5. Biblical king of Massa, warned against drinking in

Proverbs 31.4.
6. Possibly referring to the Greek philosopher Stilbo or Chilon.

For ye that been so glorious in honours
330   Shal nat allye you with hasardours
As by my wil, ne as by my tretee."
This wise philosophre, thus saide he.
    Looke eek that to the king Demetrius
The King of Parthes,[7] as the book saith us,
335   Sente him a paire of dees of gold in scorn,
For he hadde used hasard therbiforn,
For which he heeld his glorye or his renown
At no value or reputacioun.
Lordes may finden other manere play
340   Honeste ynough to drive the day away.
    Now wol I speke of othes false and grete
A word or two, as olde bookes trete:
    Greet swering is a thing abhominable,
And fals swering is yit more reprevable.°   *reprehensible*
345   The hye God forbad swering at al—
Witnesse on Mathew. But in special
Of swering saith the holy Jeremie,[8]
"Thou shalt swere sooth° thine othes and nat lie,   *truly*
And swere in doom° and eek in rightwisnesse,   *judgment*
350   But idel swering is a cursednesse."
    Biholde and see that in the firste Table°   *tablet*
Of hye Goddes heestes° honorable   *commandments*
How that the seconde heeste of him is this:
"Take nat my name in idel or amis."
355   Lo, rather° he forbedeth swich swering   *sooner*
Than homicide, or many a cursed thing.
I saye that as by ordre thus it stondeth—
This knoweth that° his heestes understondeth   *he who*
How that the seconde heeste of God is that.
360   And fertherover, I wol thee telle al plat°   *flatly*
That vengeance shal nat parten from his hous
That of his othes is too outrageous.
"By Goddes precious herte!" and "By his nailes!"
And "By the blood of Crist that is in Hailes,[9]
365   Sevene is my chaunce, and thyn is cink and traye!"° *five and three*
"By Goddes armes, if thou falsly playe
This daggere shal thurghout thyn herte go!"
This fruit cometh of the bicche bones° two—   *cursed dice*
Forswering, ire, falsnesse, homicide.
370   Now for the love of Crist that for us dyde,
Lete° youre othes bothe grete and smale.   *leave off*
But sires, now wol I telle forth my tale.
    Thise riotoures° three of whiche I telle,   *revelers*
Longe erst er° prime° ronge of any belle,   *before / 6 A.M.*
375   Were set hem in a taverne to drinke,
And as they sat they herde a belle clinke

---

7. Parthia in northern Persia.
8. The prophet Jeremiah (4.2).

9. Hales Abbey in Gloucestershire owned a relic of
Christ's blood.

Biforn a cors° was caried to his grave.   *corpse*
That oon of hem gan callen to his knave:°   *servant*
"Go bet,"° quod he, "and axe redily   *quickly*
380   What cors is this that passeth heer forby,
And looke that thou reporte his name weel."
    "Sire," quod this boy, "it needeth neveradeel:[1]
It was me told er ye cam heer two houres.
He was, pardee,° an old felawe of youres,   *by God*
385   And sodeinly he was yslain tonight,
Fordronke° as he sat on his bench upright;   *very drunk*
Ther cam a privee° thief men clepeth° Deeth,   *stealthy / call*
That in this contree al the peple sleeth,°   *slays*
And with his spere he smoot his herte atwo,
390   And wente his way withouten wordes mo.
He hath a thousand slain this pestilence.°   *during this plague*
And maister, er ye come in his presence,
Me thinketh that it were necessarye
For to be war of swich an adversarye;
395   Beeth redy for to meete him everemore:
Thus taughte me my dame.° I saye namore."   *mother*
    "By Sainte Marye," saide this taverner,
"The child saith sooth,° for he hath slain this yeer,   *truth*
Henne° over a mile, within a greet village,   *from here*
400   Bothe man and womman, child and hine° and page.°   *farmhand / servant*
I trowe his habitacion be there.
To been avised° greet wisdom it were   *warned*
Er that he dide a man a dishonour."
    "Ye, Goddes armes," quod this riotour,
405   "Is it swich peril with him for to meete?
I shal him seeke by way and eek by streete,
I make avow to Goddes digne° bones.   *worthy*
Herkneth, felawes, we three been alle ones:
Lat eech of us holde up his hand to other
410   And eech of us bicome otheres brother,
And we wol sleen this false traitour Deeth.
He shal be slain, he that so manye sleeth,
By Goddes dignitee, er it be night."
    Togidres han thise three hir trouthes° plight°   *words of honor / pledged*
415   To live and dien eech of hem with other,
As though he were his owene ybore° brother.   *born*
And up they sterte, al dronken in this rage,
And forth they goon towardes that village
Of which the taverner hadde spoke biforn.
420   And many a grisly ooth thanne han they sworn,
And Cristes blessed body they torente:°   *tore apart*
Deeth shal be deed if that they may him hente.°   *capture*
    Whan they han goon nat fully, half a mile,
Right as they wolde han treden° over a stile,   *stepped*
425   An old man and a poore with hem mette;

---

1. Is not necessary in the least.

This olde man ful mekely hem grette,°   *greeted*
And saide thus, "Now lordes, God you see."°   *look after*
   The pruddeste° of thise riotoures three   *proudest*
Answerde again, "What, carl with sory grace,°   *unlucky fellow*
430 Why artou al forwrapped° save thy face?   *bundled up*
Why livestou so longe in so greet age?"
   This olde man gan looke in his visage,
And saide thus, "For I ne can nat finde
A man, though that I walked into Inde,
435 Neither in citee ne in no village,
That wolde chaunge his youthe for myn age;
And therfore moot I han° myn age stille,   *I must have*
As longe time as it is Goddes wille.
   "Ne Deeth, allas, ne wol nat have my lif.
440 Thus walke I lik a restelees caitif,°   *wretch*
And on the ground which is my modres° gate   *mother's*
I knokke with my staf bothe erly and late,
And saye, 'Leve° moder, leet me in: *dear*
Lo, how I vanisshe, flessh and blood and skin.
445 Allas, whan shal my bones been at reste?
Moder, with you wolde I chaunge° my cheste°   *exchange / strongbox*
That in my chambre longe time hath be,
Ye, for an haire-clout° to wrappe me.'   *winding sheet*
But yit to me she wol nat do that grace,
450 For which ful pale and welked° is my face.   *withered*
But sires, to you it is no curteisye
To speken to an old man vilainye,°   *discourtesy*
But he trespasse in word or elles in deede.
In Holy Writ ye may yourself wel rede,
455 'Agains an old man, hoor° upon his heed,   *grey*
Ye shal arise.' Wherfore I yive you reed,°   *advice*
Ne dooth unto an old man noon harm now,
Namore than that ye wolde men dide to you
In age, if that ye so longe abide.
460 And God be with you wher ye go or ride:
I moot go thider as I have to go."
   "Nay, olde cherl, by God thou shalt nat so,"
Saide this other hasardour anoon.
"Thou partest nat so lightly,° by Saint John!   *easily*
465 Thou speke right now of thilke traitour Deeth,
That in this contree alle oure freendes sleeth:
Have here my trouthe, as thou art his espye,
Tel wher he is, or thou shalt it abye,°   *pay for*
By God and by the holy sacrament!
470 For soothly thou art oon of his assent°   *in league with him*
To sleen us yonge folk, thou false thief."
   "Now sires," quod he, "if that ye be so lief°   *eager*
To finde Deeth, turne up this crooked way,
For in that grove I lafte him, by my fay,
475 Under a tree, and ther he wol abide:
Nat for youre boost he wol him no thing hide.

See ye that ook?° Right ther ye shal him finde.   *oak*
God save you, that boughte again° mankinde,   *redeemed*
And you amende." Thus saide this olde man.
480   And everich of thise riotoures ran
Til he cam to that tree, and ther they founde
Of florins° fine of gold ycoined rounde   *gold coins*
Wel neigh an eighte busshels as hem thoughte—
Ne lenger thanne after Deeth they soughte,
485   But eech of hem so glad was of the sighte,
For that the florins been so faire and brighte,
That down they sette hem by this precious hoord.
The worste of hem he spak the firste word:
    "Bretheren," quod he, "take keep what that I saye:
490   My wit is greet though that I bourde° and playe.   *joke*
This tresor hath Fortune unto us yiven
In mirthe and jolitee oure lif to liven,
And lightly as it cometh so wol we spende.
Ey, Goddes precious dignitee, who wende°   *would suppose*
495   Today that we sholde han so fair a grace?
But mighte this gold be caried fro this place
Hoom to myn hous—or elles unto youres—
For wel ye woot that al this gold is oures—
Thanne were we in heigh felicitee.°   *happiness*
500   But trewely, by daye it mighte nat be:
Men wolde sayn that we were theves stronge,°   *flagrant*
And for oure owene tresor doon us honge.°   *have us hanged*
This tresor moste ycaried be by nighte,
As wisely and as slyly as it mighte.
505   Therfore I rede° that cut° amonges us alle   *advise / lots*
Be drawe, and lat see wher the cut wol falle;
And he that hath the cut with herte blithe°   *happy*
Shal renne to the town, and that ful swithe,°   *swiftly*
And bringe us breed and win ful prively;
510   And two of us shal keepen subtilly
This tresor wel, and if he wol nat tarye,
Whan it is night we wol this tresor carye
By oon assent wher as us thinketh best."
That oon of hem the cut broughte in his fest°   *fist*
515   And bad hem drawe and looke wher it wol falle;
And it fil on the yongeste of hem alle,
And forth toward the town he wente anoon.
And also soone as that he was agoon,
That oon of hem spak thus unto that other:
520   "Thou knowest wel thou art my sworen brother;
Thy profit wol I telle thee anoon:
Thou woost wel that oure felawe is agoon,
And here is gold, and that ful greet plentee,
That shal departed° been among us three.   *divided*
525   But nathelees, if I can shape° it so   *arrange*
That it departed were among us two,
Hadde I nat doon a freendes turn to thee?"

That other answerde, "I noot° how that may be: *do not know*
He woot° that the gold is with us twaye.   *knows*
530 What shal we doon? What shal we to him saye?"
"Shal it be conseil?"° saide the firste shrewe.°   *secret / villain*
"And I shal telle in a wordes fewe
What we shul doon, and bringe it wel aboute."
"I graunte," quod that other, "out of doute,
535 That by my trouthe I wol thee nat biwraye."°   *betray*
"Now," quod the firste, "thou woost wel we be twaye,
And two of us shal strenger be than oon:
Looke whan that he is set that right anoon
Aris as though thou woldest with him playe,
540 And I shal rive° him thurgh the sides twaye,   *stab*
Whil that thou strugelest with him as in game,
And with thy daggere looke thou do the same;
And thanne shal al this gold departed be,
My dere freend, bitwixe thee and me.
545 Thanne we may bothe oure lustes° al fulfille,   *desires*
And playe at dees right at oure owene wille."
And thus accorded been thise shrewes twaye
To sleen the thridde, as ye han herd me saye.
This yongeste, which that wente to the town,
550 Ful ofte in herte he rolleth up and down
The beautee of thise florins newe and brighte.
"O Lord," quod he, "if so were that I mighte
Have al this tresor to myself allone,
Ther is no man that liveth under the trone°   *throne*
555 Of God that sholde live so merye as I."
And at the laste the feend oure enemy
Putte in his thought that he sholde poison beye,°   *buy*
With which he mighte sleen his felawes twaye—
Forwhy° the feend foond him in swich livinge   *wherefore*
560 That he hadde leve° him to sorwe° bringe: *permission / sorrow*
For this was outrely his fulle entente,
To sleen hem bothe, and nevere to repente.
And forth he gooth—no lenger wolde he tarye—
Into the town unto a pothecarye,°   *druggist*
565 And prayed him that he him wolde selle
Som poison that he mighte his rattes quelle,°   *kill*
And eek ther was a polcat° in his hawe°   *weasel / yard*
That, as he saide, his capons° hadde yslawe,°   *chickens / slain*
And fain° he wolde wreke° him if he mighte   *gladly / avenge*
570 On vermin that destroyed him by nighte.
The pothecarye answerde, "And thou shalt have
A thing that, also° God my soule save,   *so*
In al this world ther is no creature
That ete or dronke hath of this confiture°—   *concoction*
575 Nat but the mountance° of a corn° of whete—   *amount / grain*
That he ne shal his lif anoon forlete.°   *lose*
Ye, sterve° he shal, and that in lasse while   *die*
Than thou wolt goon a paas° nat but a mile,   *walking*

The poison is so strong and violent."
580   This cursed man hath in his hand yhent°   *taken*
This poison in a box and sith he ran
Into the nexte streete unto a man
And borwed of him large botels three,
And in the two his poison poured he—
585   The thridde he kepte clene for his drinke,
For al the night he shoop° him for to swinke°   *prepared / work*
In carying of the gold out of that place.
And whan this riotour with sory grace
Hadde filled with win his grete botels three,
590   To his felawes again repaireth he.
    What needeth it to sermone of it more?
For right as they had cast° his deeth bifore,   *planned*
Right so they han him slain, and that anoon.
And whan that this was doon, thus spak that oon:
595   "Now lat us sitte and drinke and make us merye,
And afterward we wol his body berye."
And with that word it happed him par cas°   *by chance*
To take the botel ther the poison was,
And drank, and yaf his felawe drinke also,
600   For which anoon they storven bothe two.
    But certes I suppose that Avicen[2]
Wroot nevere in no canon ne in no *fen*
Mo wonder signes of empoisoning
Than hadde thise wrecches two er hir ending:
605   Thus ended been thise homicides two,
And eek the false empoisonere also.
    O cursed sinne of alle cursednesse!
O traitours homicide, O wikkednesse!
O glotonye, luxure,° and hasardrye!   *lechery*
610   Thou balsphemour of Crist with vilainye
And othes grete of usage° and of pride!   *habit*
Allas, mankinde, how may it bitide
That to thy Creatour which that thee wroughte,
And with his precious herte blood thee boughte,
615   Thou art so fals and so unkinde,° allas?   *unnatural*
    Now goode men, God foryive you youre trespas,
And ware° you fro the sinne of avarice: *guard*
Myn holy pardon may you alle warice°—   *save*
So that ye offre nobles or sterlinges,°   *gold or silver coins*
620   Or elles silver brooches, spoones, ringes.
Boweth your heed under this holy bulle!
Cometh up, ye wives, offreth of youre wolle!°   *wool*
Youre name I entre here in my rolle: anoon
Into the blisse of hevene shul ye goon.
625   I you assoile° by myn heigh power—   *absolve*
Ye that wol offre—as clene and eek as cleer°   *pure*
As ye were born.—And lo, sires, thus I preche.

2. The 12th-century Arab philosopher Avicenna composed a *Canon of Medicine*, divided into sections called "fens."

And Jesu Crist that is oure soules leeche°   *physician*
So graunte you his pardon to receive,
630   For that is best—I wol you nat deceive.

The Epilogue

"But sires, oo word forgat I in my tale:
I have relikes and pardon in my male°   *bag*
As faire as any man in Engelond,
Whiche were me yiven by the Popes hond.
635   If any of you wol of devocioun
Offren and han myn absolucioun,
Come forth anoon, and kneeleth here adown,
And mekely receiveth my pardoun,
Or elles taketh pardon as ye wende,°   *travel*
640   Al newe and fressh at every miles ende—
So that ye offre alway newe and newe°   *over and over*
Nobles or pens whiche that be goode and trewe.
It is an honour to everich that is heer
That ye mowe have a suffisant° pardoner   *competent*
645   T'assoile you in contrees as ye ride,
For aventures whiche that may bitide:
Paraventure ther may falle oon or two
Down of his hors and breke his nekke atwo;
Looke which a suretee° is it to you alle   *safeguard*
650   That I am in youre felaweshipe yfalle
That may assoile you, bothe more and lasse,
Whan that the soule shal fro the body passe.
I rede° that oure Hoste shal biginne,   *advise*
For he is most envoluped in sinne.
655   Com forth, sire Host, and offre first anoon,
And thou shalt kisse the relikes everichoon,
Ye, for a grote:° unbokele anoon thy purs."   *fourpence coin*
      "Nay, nay," quod he, "thanne have I Cristes curs!
Lat be," quod he, "it shal nat be, so theech!°   *may I prosper*
660   Thou woldest make me kisse thyn olde breech
And swere it were a relik of a saint,
Though it were with thy fundament° depeint.°   *bowels / stained*
But, by the crois° which that Sainte Elaine[3] foond,   *cross*
I wolde I hadde thy coilons° in myn hond,   *testicles*
665   In stede of relikes or of saintuarye.°   *container of relics*
Lat cutte hem of: I wol thee helpe hem carye.
They shal be shrined in an hogges tord."°   *turd*
      This Pardoner answerde nat a word:
So wroth° he was no word ne wolde he saye.   *angry*
670   "Now," quod oure Host, "I wol no lenger playe
With thee, ne with noon other angry man."
      But right anoon the worthy Knight bigan,
Whan that he sawgh that al the peple lough,
"Namore of this, for it is right ynough.

---

3. St. Helen, who was said to have found the True Cross on which Jesus was crucified.

675   Sire Pardoner, be glad and merye of cheere,
       And ye, sire Host that been to me so dere,
       I praye you that ye kisse the Pardoner,
       And Pardoner, I praye thee, draw thee neer,
       And as we diden lat us laughe and playe."
680   Anoon they kiste and riden forth hir waye.

THE NUN'S PRIEST'S TALE   Of all his varied and ambitious output, *The Nun's Priest's Tale*
may be Chaucer's most impressive tour de force. At its core is a wonderful animal fable, free of
the conventionality and sometimes easy moralities this ancient form had taken on by the fourteenth century. The fable of Chauntecleer and Pertelote achieves quite extraordinary density,
further, because of the multiple frames—structural and thematic—that surround it.

As part of the Canterbury tale-telling competition, the priest's fable plays a role in that
broadest contest of classes and literary genres. More locally, it is one of many moments in
which the Host, Harry Bailey, demands a tale from a male pilgrim in a style that also suggests a
sexual challenge, and then adjusts his estimate of the teller's virility (even his social position)
to suit. The fable itself is surrounded by an intimate portrait of Chauntecleer's peasant owner
and her simple life, content with "hertes suffisaunce," a marked contrast to courtly values.

The central story of Chauntecleer's dream, danger, and escape works within a subtle and
funny exploration of relations between the sexes. This is conditioned by courtly love conventions, literacy and education, and even the vocabulary of Pertelote's mostly Anglo-Saxon diction and Chauntecleer's love of French. This linguistic competition has its high point when
Chauntecleer condescendingly mistranslates a misogynist Latin tag. Linguistic vanity, though,
is exactly what puts Chauntecleer most in jeopardy. It is not the destiny Chauntecleer thinks
he glimpses in his dream that almost costs his life, but rather another verbal competition, and
an almost Oedipal challenge to his father.

Much of the story's energy, however, derives not from its frames but from the explosion of
those frames—literary, spatial, even social—enacted and recalled at the heart of the tale. The
chickens are simultaneously, and hilariously, both courtly lovers and very realistic fowl. When
Chauntecleer is carried off, the whole world of the tale—widow, daughters, dogs, even bees—
bursts outward in pursuit. In the midst of mock-epic and mock-romance comparisons to this
joyful disorder, Chaucer even inserts one of his very few direct references to the greatest disorder of his time, the Rising of 1381.

The Nun's Priest's Tale is a comedy as well as a fable, reversing a lugubrious series of
tragedies in the preceding *Monk's Tale*. In the end, it is a story of canniness, acquired self-
knowledge, and self-salvation. Woven into the priest's humor are a gentle satire and a quiet
assertion that free will is the final resource of any agent, avian or human.

The Nun's Priest's Tale
The Introduction

       "Ho!" quod the Knight, "good sire, namore of this:
       That ye han said is right ynough, ywis,°   *indeed*
       And muchel more, for litel hevinesse
       Is right ynough to muche folk° I gesse:[1]   *for most folks*
5   I saye for me it is a greet disese,
       Wher as men han been in greet welthe and ese,
       To heeren of hir sodein° fal, allas;   *sudden*

---

1. The Monk has just told a series of stark and repetitive "tragedies"—the falls of men both ancient and modern.

And the contrarye is joye and greet solas,°   comfort
As whan a man hath been in poore estat,
10   And climbeth up and wexeth° fortunat,   becomes
And there abideth in prosperitee:
Swich thing is gladsom, as it thinketh° me,   seems to
And of swich thing were goodly for to telle."
    "Ye," quod oure Host, "by Sainte Poules° belle,   Paul's
15   Ye saye right sooth:° this Monk he clappeth° loude.   truly / chatters
He spak how Fortune covered with a cloude—
I noot nevere what.° And als of a tragedye   I don't know what
Right now ye herde, and pardee,° no remedye   by God
It is for to biwaile ne complaine
20   That that is doon, and als° it is a paine,   also
As ye han said, to heere of hevinesse.
    "Sire Monk, namore of this, so God you blesse:
Youre tale anoyeth al this compaignye;
Swich talking is nat worth a boterflye,
25   For therinne is ther no disport ne game.
Wherfore, sire Monk, or daun° Piers by youre name,   Master
I praye you hertely telle us somwhat elles:
For sikerly, nere clinking of youre belles,[2]
That on youre bridel hange on every side,
30   By hevene king that for us alle dyde,
I sholde er this have fallen down for sleep,
Although the slough° hadde nevere been so deep.   mud
Thanne hadde youre tale al be told in vain;
For certainly, as that thise clerkes sayn,
35   Wher as a man may have noon audience,
Nought helpeth it to tellen his sentence;°   statement
And wel I woot° the substance is in me,   know
If any thing shal wel reported be.
Sire, saye somwhat of hunting, I you praye."
40   "Nay," quod this Monk, "I have no lust° to playe.   wish
Now lat another telle, as I have told."
    Thanne spak oure Host with rude speeche and bold,
And saide unto the Nonnes Preest anoon,
"Com neer, thou Preest,[3] com hider, thou sire John:
45   Tel us swich thing as may oure hertes glade.°   gladden our hearts
Be blithe,° though thou ride upon a jade!°   happy / nag
What though thyn hors be bothe foul and lene?°   thin
If he wol serve thee, rekke nat a bene.°   don't care a bean
Looke that thyn herte be merye everemo."
50   "Yis, sire," quod he, "yis, Host, so mote I go,
But I be merye, ywis, I wol be blamed."
And right anoon his tale he hath attamed,°   begun
And thus he saide unto us everichoon,
This sweete Preest, this goodly man sire John.

2. For truly, were it not for the jingling of your bells.   "thou," then contemptuously calls the priest "Sir John."
3. The Host uses the familiar, somewhat condescending

The Tale

55	A poore widwe somdeel stape° in age	*well along*
	Was whilom° dwelling in a narwe cotage,	*once upon a time*
	Biside a grove, stonding in a dale:	
	This widwe of which I telle you my tale,	
	Sin° thilke° day that she was last a wif,	*since / that*
60	In pacience ladde a ful simple lif.	
	For litel was hir catel° and hir rente,°	*property / income*
	By housbondrye° of swich as God hire sente	*management*
	She foond° hirself and eek hir doughtren two.	*provided for*
	Three large sowes hadde she and namo,	
65	Three kin,° and eek a sheep that highte° Malle.	*cows / was named*
	Ful sooty was hir bowr° and eek hir halle,	*bedroom*
	In which she eet ful many a sclendre meel;	
	Of poinant° sauce hire needed neveradeel:	*pungent*
	No daintee morsel passed thurgh hir throte—	
70	Hir diete was accordant to hir cote.°	*cottage*
	Repleccioun° ne made hire nevere sik:	*gluttony*
	Attempre° diete was al hir physik,	*moderate*
	And exercise and hertes suffisaunce.	
	The goute lette hire nothing for to daunce,[4]	
75	N'apoplexye shente° nat hir heed.	*hurt*
	No win ne drank she, neither whit ne reed:	
	Hir boord° was served most with whit and blak,	*table*
	Milk and brown breed, in which she foond no lak;°	*fault*
	Seind° bacon, and somtime an ey° or twaye,°	*singed / egg / two*
80	For she was as it were a manere daye.°	*dairy maid*
	A yeerd° she hadde, enclosed al withoute	*yard*
	With stikkes, and a drye dich aboute,	
	In which she hadde a cok heet° Chauntecleer:	*called*
	In al the land of crowing nas his peer.	
85	His vois was merier than the merye orgon	
	On massedayes that in the chirche goon;°	*is played*
	Wel sikerer° was his crowing in his logge°	*surer / dwelling*
	Than is a clok or an abbeye orlogge;°	*timepiece*
	By nature he knew eech ascensioun	
90	Of th'equinoxial[5] in thilke town:	
	For whan degrees fifteene were ascended,	
	Thanne crew he that it mighte nat been amended.°	*surpassed*
	His comb was redder than the fin coral,	
	And batailed° as it were a castel wal;	*crenellated*
95	His bile° was blak, and as the jeet° it shoon;	*beak / jet*
	Like asure° were his legges and his toon;°	*azure / toes*
	His nailes whitter than the lilye flowr,	
	And lik the burned° gold was his colour.	*burnished*
	This gentil cok hadde in his governaunce	
100	Sevene hennes for to doon al his plesaunce,	
	Whiche were his sustres and his paramours,°	*lovers*

4. Did not keep her from dancing.   5. The points marking the celestial hours.

And wonder like to him as of colours;
Of whiche the faireste hewed° on hir throte   *colored*
Was cleped° faire damoisele Pertelote: *called*
105   Curteis she was, discreet, and debonaire,°   *gracious*
And compaignable,° and bar hirself so faire,   *sociable*
Sin thilke° day that she was seven night old,   *that*
That trewely she hath the herte in hold
Of Chauntecleer, loken in every lith.[6]
110   He loved hire so that wel was him therwith.
But swich a joye was it to heere hem singe,
Whan that the brighte sonne gan to springe,
In sweete accord "My Lief is Faren in Londe"[7]—
For thilke time, as I have understonde,
115   Beestes and briddes° couden speke and singe.   *birds*
          And so bifel that in a daweninge,
As Chauntecleer among his wives alle
Sat on his perche that was in the halle,
And next him sat this faire Pertelote,
120   This Chauntecleer gan gronen in his throte,
As man that in his dreem is drecched° sore.   *disturbed*
          And whan that Pertelote thus herde him rore,
She was agast, and saide, "Herte dere,
What aileth you to grone in this manere?
125   Ye been a verray° slepere, fy, for shame!"   *true*
          And he answerde and saide thus, "Madame,
I praye you that ye take it nat agrief.°   *amiss*
By God, me mette° I was in swich meschief   *I dreamed*
Right now, that yit myn herte is sore afright.
130   Now God," quod he, "my swevene recche aright,[8]
And keepe my body out of foul prisoun!
Me mette how that I romed up and down
Within oure yeerd, wher as I sawgh a beest,
Was lik an hound and wolde han maad arrest°   *taken captive*
135   Upon my body, and han had me deed.
His colour was bitwixe yelow and reed,
And tipped was his tail and bothe his eres
With blak, unlik the remenant of his heres;°   *the rest of his hair*
His snoute smal, with glowing yën twaye.
140   Yit of his look for fere almost I deye:
This caused me my groning, doutelees."
          "Avoi,"° quod she, "fy on you, hertelees!°   *Have done! / coward*
Allas," quod she, "for by that God above,
Now han ye lost myn herte and al my love!
145   I can nat love a coward, by my faith.
For certes, what so any womman saith,
We alle desiren, if it mighte be,
To han housbondes hardy, wise, and free,°   *generous*
And secree,° and no nigard, ne no fool,   *discreet*

---

6. Locked in every limb (i.e., thoroughly).   8. Interpret my dream correctly.
7. A popular ballad, "My Love Has Gone to the Country."

150	Ne him that is agast° of every tool,°	*afraid / weapon*
	Ne noon avauntour.° By that God above,	*braggart*
	How dorste ye sayn for shame unto youre love	
	That any thing mighte make you aferd?	
	Have ye no mannes herte and han a beerd?	
155	Allas, and conne ye been agast of swevenes?	
	No thing, God woot,° but vanitee° in swevene is!	*knows / illusion*
	Swevenes engendren of replexiouns,°	*surfeits*
	And ofte of fume° and of complexiouns,°	*gas / bodily humors*
	Whan humours been too habundant in a wight.°	*creature*
160	Certes, this dreem which ye han met tonight	
	Comth of the grete superfluitee	
	Of youre rede colera,⁹ pardee,°	*by God*
	Which causeth folk to dreden in hir dremes	
	Of arwes,° and of fir with rede lemes,°	*arrows / flames*
165	Of rede beestes, that they wol hem bite,	
	Of contek,° and of whelpes° grete and lite—	*strife / dogs*
	Right as the humour of malencolye¹	
	Causeth ful many a man in sleep to crye	
	For fere of blake beres or boles° blake,	*bulls*
170	Or elles blake develes wol hem take.	
	Of othere humours coude I telle also	
	That werken many a man in sleep ful wo,	
	But I wol passe as lightly as I can.	
	Lo, Caton,² which that was so wis a man,	
175	Saide he nat thus? 'Ne do no fors° of dremes.'	*pay no attention to*
	Now, sire," quod she, "whan we flee° fro the bemes,°	*fly / rafters*
	For Goddes love, as take som laxatif.	
	Up° peril of my soule and of my lif,	*upon*
	I conseile you the beste, I wol nat lie,	
180	That bothe of colere and of malencolye	
	Ye purge you; and for ye shal nat tarye,	
	Though in this town is noon apothecarye,	
	I shal myself to herbes techen you,	
	That shal been for youre hele° and for youre prow,°	*health / profit*
185	And in oure yeerd tho° herbes shal I finde,	*then*
	The whiche han of hir propretee by kinde°	*nature*
	To purge you binethe and eek above.	
	Foryet nat this, for Goddes owene love.	
	Ye been ful colerik of complexioun;	
190	Ware° the sonne in his ascencioun	*beware lest*
	Ne finde you nat repleet° of humours hote;°	*full / hot*
	And if it do, I dar wel laye³ a grote°	*fourpence*
	That ye shul have a fevere terciane,⁴	
	Or an agu° that may be youre bane.°	*fever / death*
195	A day or two ye shul han digestives	
	Of wormes, er ye take youre laxatives	

---

9. Coleric bile, thought to overheat the body.
1. Black bile, thought to produce dark thoughts.
2. Marcus Porcius Cato, ancient author of a book of

proverbs used by schoolchildren.
3. Bet (with a pun on egg-laying).
4. Recurring fever.

Of lauriol, centaure, and fumetere,[5]
Or elles of ellebor that groweth there,
Of catapuce, or of gaitres beries,
200   Of herbe-ive growing in oure yeerd ther merye is.°   *where it is pleasant*
Pekke hem right up as they growe and ete hem in.
Be merye, housbonde, for youre fader kin!
Dredeth no dreem: I can saye you namore."
      "Madame," quod he, "graunt mercy of youre lore.°   *learning*
205   But nathelees, as touching daun Catoun,
That hath of wisdom swich a greet renown,
Though that he bad no dremes for to drede,
By God, men may in olde bookes rede
Of many a man more of auctoritee
210   Than evere Caton was, so mote I thee,°   *so may I prosper*
That al the revers sayn of his sentence,°   *opinion*
And han wel founden by experience
That dremes been significaciouns
As wel of joye as tribulaciouns
215   That folk enduren in this lif present.
Ther needeth make of this noon argument:
The verray preve° sheweth it in deede.   *proof*
      "Oon of the gretteste auctour that men rede
Saith thus, that whilom two felawes wente
220   On pilgrimage in a ful good entente,
And happed so they comen in a town,
Wher as ther was swich congregacioun
Of peple, and eek so strait of herbergage,°   *short of lodging*
That they ne founde as muche as oo° cotage   *one*
225   In which they bothe mighte ylogged be;
Wherfore they mosten of necessitee
As for that night departe compaignye.
And eech of hem gooth to his hostelrye,
And took his logging as it wolde falle.
230   That oon of hem was logged in a stalle,
Fer in a yeerd, with oxen of the plough;
That other man was logged wel ynough,
As was his aventure or his fortune,
That us governeth alle as in commune.
235   And so bifel that longe er it were day,
This man mette in his bed, ther as he lay,
How that his felawe gan upon him calle,
And saide, 'Allas, for in an oxes stalle
This night I shal be mordred° ther I lie!   *murdered*
240   Now help me, dere brother, or I die!
In alle haste com to me,' he saide.
      "This man out of his sleep for fere abraide,°   *bolted up*
But whan that he was wakened of his sleep,
He turned him and took of this no keep:°   *heed*
245   Him thoughte his dreem nas° but a vanitee.   *was not*

5. These and the following are bitter herbs that produce hot and dry sensations and lead to purging.

Thus twies in his sleeping dremed he,
And atte thridde time yit his felawe
Cam, as him thoughte, and saide, 'I am now slawe:°   *slain*
Bihold my bloody woundes deepe and wide.
250   Aris up erly in the morwe tide°   *morning time*
And atte west gate of the town,' quod he,
'A carte ful of dong° ther shaltou see,   *dung*
In which my body is hid ful prively:
Do thilke° carte arresten° boldely.   *that / have seized*
255   My gold caused my mordre, sooth° to sayn'—   *truth*
And tolde him every point how he was slain,
With a ful pitous face, pale of hewe.
And truste wel, his dreem he foond ful trewe,
For on the morwe as soone as it was day,
260   To his felawes in he took the way,
And whan that he cam to this oxes stalle,
After his felawe he bigan to calle.
      "The hostiler° answerde him anoon,   *innkeeper*
And saide, 'Sire, youre felawe is agoon:
265   As soone as day he wente out of the town.'
      "This man gan fallen in suspecioun,
Remembring on his dremes that he mette;
And forth he gooth, no lenger wolde he lette,°   *delay*
Unto the west gate of the town, and foond
270   A dong carte, wente as it were to donge° lond,   *spread manure on*
That was arrayed in that same wise
As ye han herd the dede man devise;
And with an hardy herte he gan to crye,
'Vengeance and justice of this felonye!
275   My felawe mordred is this same night,
And in this carte he lith gaping upright!°   *facing up*
I crye out on the ministres,'° quod he,   *magistrates*
'That sholde keepe and rulen this citee.
Harrow, allas, here lith my felawe slain!'
280   What sholde I more unto this tale sayn?
The peple up sterte and caste the carte to grounde,
And in the middel of the dong they founde
The dede man that mordred was al newe.°   *just recently*
      "O blisful God that art so just and trewe,
285   Lo, how that thou biwrayest° mordre alway!   *reveal*
Mordre wol out, that see we day by day:
Mordre is so wlatsom° and abhominable   *loathsome*
To God that is so just and resonable,
That he ne wol nat suffre it heled° be,   *concealed*
290   Though it abide a yeer or two or three.
Mordre wol out: this my conclusioun.
And right anoon ministres of that town
Han hent° the cartere and so sore him pined,°   *seized / tortured*
And eek the hostiler so sore engined,
295   That they biknewe° hir wikkednesse anoon,   *confessed*
And were anhanged by the nekke boon.

Here may men seen that dremes been to drede.
"And certes, in the same book I rede—
Right in the nexte chapitre after this—
300   I gabbe° nat, so have I joye or blis—   *lie*
Two men that wolde han passed over see
For certain cause into a fer contree,
If that the wind ne hadde been contrarye
That made hem in a citee for to tarye,
305   That stood ful merye upon an haven° side—   *harbor*
But on a day again° the even tide   *toward*
The wind gan chaunge, and blewe right as hem leste:°   *they wanted*
Jolif° and glad they wenten unto reste,   *merry*
And casten hem° ful erly for to saile.   *decided*
310   "But to that oo man fil a greet mervaile;
That oon of hem, in sleeping as he lay,
Him mette a wonder dreem again the day:
Him thoughte a man stood by his beddes side,
And him comanded that he sholde abide,
315   And saide him thus, 'If thou tomorwe wende,°   *travel*
Thou shalt be dreint:° my tale is at an ende.'   *drowned*
       "He wook and tolde his felawe what he mette,
And prayed him his viage to lette;°   *put off his journey*
As for that day he prayed him to bide.
320   His felawe that lay by his beddes side
Gan for to laughe, and scorned him ful faste.
'No dreem,' quod he, 'may so myn herte agaste
That I wol lette for to do my thinges.°   *business*
I sette nat a straw by thy dreminges,
325   For swevenes been but vanitees and japes:°   *tricks*
Men dreme alday° of owles or of apes,   *constantly*
And of many a maze° therwithal—   *delusion*
Men dreme of thing that nevere was ne shal.
But sith° I see that thou wolt here abide,   *since*
330   And thus forsleuthen° wilfully thy tide,   *waste due to sloth*
Good woot, it reweth me; and have good day.'
And thus he took his leve and wente his way.
But er that he hadde half his cours ysailed—
Noot° I nat why ne what meschaunce it ailed°—   *know / went wrong*
335   But casuelly° the shippes botme rente,°   *by accident / split apart*
And ship and man under the water wente,
In sighte of othere shippes it biside,
That with hem sailed at the same tide.
And therfore, faire Pertelote so dere,
340   By swiche ensamples olde maistou lere°   *may you learn*
That no man sholde been too recchelees°   *careless*
Of dremes, for I saye thee doutelees
That many a dreem ful sore is for to drede.
       "Lo, in the lif of Saint Kenelm[6] I rede—
345   That was Kenulphus sone, the noble king

6. St. Cenhelm, son of Cenwulf, a 9th-century child-king in Mercia who was murdered at his sister's orders.

Of Mercenrike—how Kenelm mette a thing
A lite° er he was mordred on a day.   *little while*
His mordre in his avision° he sey.°   *dream / saw*
His norice° him expounded everydeel   *nurse*
350 His swevene, and bad him for to keepe him° weel   *guard against*
For traison, but he nas but seven yeer old,
And therfore litel tale hath he told°   *he cared little for*
Of any dreem, so holy was his herte.
By God, I hadde levere than my sherte°   *would give my shirt*
355 That ye hadde rad his legende as have I.
        "Dame Pertelote, I saye you trewely,
Macrobeus,[7] that writ the Avisioun
In Affrike of the worthy Scipioun,
Affermeth° dremes, and saith that they been   *confirms*
360 Warning of thinges that men after seen.
        "And ferthermore, I praye you looketh wel
In the Olde Testament of Daniel,
If he heeld dremes any vanitee.[8]
        "Rede eek of Joseph and ther shul ye see
365 Wher° dremes be somtime—I saye nat alle—   *whether*
Warning of thinges that shul after falle.
        "Looke of Egypte the king daun Pharao,
His bakere and his botelere° also,   *butler*
Wher they ne felte noon effect in dremes.[9]
370 Whoso wol seeke actes of sondry remes°   *various kingdoms*
May rede of dremes many a wonder thing.
        "Lo Cresus, which that was of Lyde° king,   *Lydia*
Mette he nat that he sat upon a tree,
Which signified he sholde anhanged be?
375 "Lo here Andromacha, Ectores° wif,   *Hector of Troy*
That day that Ector sholde lese° his lif,   *lose*
She dremed on the same night biforn
How that the lif of Ector sholde be lorn,
If thilke day he wente into bataile;
380 She warned him, but it mighte nat availe:
He wente for to fighte nathelees,
But he was slain anoon of Achilles.
But thilke tale is al too long to telle,
And eek it is neigh day, I may nat dwelle.
385 Shortly I saye, as for conclusioun,
That I shal han of this avisioun
Adversitee, and I saye ferthermoor
That I ne telle of laxatives no stoor,°   *hold no regard for*
For they been venimes,° I woot° it weel: *poisons / know*
390 I hem defye, I love hem neveradeel.
        "Now lat us speke of mirthe and stinte° al this.   *stop*
Madame Pertelote, so have I blis,

7. Macrobius, a 4th-century author, wrote an extensive commentary on Cicero's *Dream of Scipio*.
8. Daniel interprets the pagan King Nebuchadnezzar's dream, which foretells his downfall (Daniel 4).
9. Joseph interpreted dreams for the pharaoh's chief baker and butler (Genesis 40–41).

Of oo thing God hath sente me large grace:
For whan I see the beautee of youre face—
395   Ye been so scarlet reed aboute youre yën—
It maketh al my drede for to dien.
For also siker° as In principio,[1]   *certain*
Mulier est hominis confusio.[2]
Madame, the sentence° of this Latin is,   *meaning*
400   'Womman is mannes joye and al his blis.'
For whan I feele anight youre softe side—
Al be it that I may nat on you ride,
For that oure perche is maad so narwe, allas—
I am so ful of joye and of solas°   *delight*
405   That I defye bothe swevene and dreem."
And with that word he fleigh down fro the beem,
For it was day, and eek° his hennes alle,   *also*
And with a "chuk" he gan hem for to calle,
For he hadde founde a corn lay in the yeerd.
410   Real° he was, he was namore aferd:°   *regal / afraid*
He fethered Pertelote twenty time,
And trad° hire as ofte er it was prime.[3]   *mounted*
He looketh as it were a grim leoun,°   *lion*
And on his toes he rometh up and down:
415   Him deined nat to sette his foot to grounde.
He chukketh whan he hath a corn yfounde,
And to him rennen thanne his wives alle.
Thus royal, as a prince is in his halle,
Leve I this Chauntecleer in his pasture,
420   And after wol I telle his aventure.
     Whan that the month in which the world bigan,
That highte March, whan God first maked man,
Was compleet, and passed were also,
Sin March biran,° thritty days and two,[4]   *finished*
425   Bifel that Chauntecleer in al his pride,
His sevene wives walking him biside,
Caste up his yën to the brighte sonne,
That in the signe of Taurus hadde yronne
Twenty degrees and oon and somwhat more,
430   And knew by kinde,° and by noon other lore,   *nature*
That it was prime, and crew with blisful stevene.°   *voice*
"The sonne," he saide, "is clomben up on hevene
Fourty degrees and oon and more, ywis.°   *indeed*
Madame Pertelote, my worldes blis,
435   Herkneth thise blisful briddes° how they singe,   *birds*
And see the fresshe flowres how they springe:
Ful is myn herte of revel and solas."
But sodeinly him fil a sorweful cas,°   *event*
For evere the latter ende of joye is wo—

---

1. "In the beginning," the opening verse of the Book of
Genesis and the Gospel of John.
2. "Woman is the ruination of mankind."

3. First hour of the day.
4. The date is thus 3 May.

440	God woot that worldly joye is soone ago,	
	And if a rethor° coude faire endite,°	*rhetorician / compose*
	He in a cronicle saufly° mighte it write,	*safely*
	As for a soverein notabilitee.	
	Now every wis man lat him herkne me:	
445	This storye is also° trewe, I undertake,	*as*
	As is the book of Launcelot de Lake,[5]	
	That wommen holde in ful greet reverence.	
	Now wol I turne again to my sentence.°	*topic*
	A colfox° ful of sly iniquitee,	*black fox*
450	That in the grove° hadde woned° yeres three,	*woods / lived*
	By heigh imaginacion forncast,[6]	
	The same night thurghout the hegges brast°	*burst*
	Into the yeerd ther Chauntecleer the faire	
	Was wont, and eek his wives, to repaire;	
455	And in a bed of wortes° stille he lay	*cabbages*
	Til it was passed undren° of the day,	*midmorning*
	Waiting his time on Chauntecleer to falle,	
	As gladly doon thise homicides alle,	
	That in await liggen to mordre men.	
460	O false mordrour, lurking in thy den!	
	O newe Scariot! Newe Geniloun![7]	
	False dissimilour!° O Greek Sinoun,[8]	*dissembler*
	That broughtest Troye al outrely° to sorwe!	*entirely*
	O Chauntecleer, accursed be that morwe	
465	That thou into the yeerd flaugh fro the bemes!	
	Thou were ful wel ywarned by thy dremes	
	That thilke day was perilous to thee;	
	But what that God forwoot moot° needes be,	*foreknew must*
	After the opinion of certain clerkes:	
470	Witnesse on him that any parfit° clerk is	*accomplished*
	That in scole is greet altercacioun	
	In this matere, and greet disputisoun,	
	And hath been of an hundred thousand men.	
	But I ne can nat bulte it to the bren,[9]	
475	As can the holy doctour Augustin,	
	Or Boece, or the bisshop Bradwardin[1]—	
	Wheither that Goddes worthy forwiting°	*foreknowledge*
	Straineth° me nedely for to doon a thing	*compels*
	("Nedely" clepe I simple necessitee),	
480	Or elles if free chois be graunted me	
	To do that same thing or do it nought,	
	Though God forwoot it er that I was wrought;°	*made*
	Or if his witing straineth neveradeel,	
	But by necessitee condicionel[2]—	

5. The adventures of the Arthurian knight.
6. Predicted (in Chauntecleer's dream).
7. Judas Iscariot, who handed Jesus over to the Roman authorities for execution; Ganelon, a medieval traitor who betrayed the hero Roland to his Saracen enemies.
8. The Greek who tricked the Trojans into accepting the Trojan horse behind the city walls.

9. Sift it from the husks (i.e., discriminate).
1. St. Augustine, the ancient writer Boethius, and the 14th-century Archbishop of Canterbury Thomas Bradwardine attempted to explain how God's predestination of events still allowed for humans to have free will.
2. Boethius argued only for conditional necessity, which still permitted for much exercise of free will.

485   I wol nat han to do of swich matere:
       My tale is of a cok, as ye may heere,
       That took his conseil of his wif with sorwe,
       To walken in the yeerd upon that morwe
       That he hadde met the dreem that I you tolde.
490   Wommenes conseils been ful ofte colde,°   *disastrous*
       Wommanes conseil broughte us first to wo,
       And made Adam fro Paradis to go,
       Ther as he was ful merye and wel at ese.
       But for I noot° to whom it mighte displese   *do not know*
495   If I conseil of wommen wolde blame,
       Passe over, for I saide it in my game—
       Rede auctours° where they trete of swich matere,   *authors*
       And what they sayn of wommen ye may heere—
       Thise been the cokkes wordes and nat mine:
500   I can noon harm of no womman divine.°   *guess at*
          Faire in the sond° to bathe hire merily   *sand*
       Lith° Pertelote, and alle hir sustres by,   *lies*
       Again the sonne, and Chauntecleer so free
       Soong merier than the mermaide in the see—
505   For Physiologus[3] saith sikerly
       How that they singen wel and merily.
          And so bifel that as he caste his yë
       Among the wortes on a boterflye,°   *butterfly*
       He was war of this fox that lay ful lowe.
510   No thing ne liste him° thanne for to crowe,   *he wanted*
       But cride anoon "Cok cok!" and up he sterte,
       As man that was affrayed in his herte—
       For naturelly a beest desireth flee
       Fro his contrarye° if he may it see,   *natural enemy*
515   Though he nevere erst° hadde seen it with his yë.   *before*
       This Chauntecleer, whan he gan him espye,
       He wolde han fled, but that the fox anoon
       Saide, "Gentil sire, allas, wher wol ye goon?
       Be ye afraid of me that am youre freend?
520   Now certes, I were worse than a feend°   *devil*
       If I to you wolde harm or vilainye.
       I am nat come youre conseil for t'espye,
       But trewely the cause of my cominge
       Was only for to herkne how that ye singe:
525   For trewely, ye han as merye a stevene°   *voice*
       As any angel hath that is in hevene.
       Therwith ye han in musik more feelinge
       Than hadde Boece,[4] or any that can singe.
       My lord your fader—God his soule blesse!—
530   And eek youre moder, of hir gentilesse,°   *gentility*
       Han in myn hous ybeen, to my grete ese.
       And certes sire, ful fain° wolde I you plese.   *gladly*

---

3. Said to have written a bestiary.   textbook.
4. In addition to theology, Boethius also wrote a music

But for men speke of singing, I wol saye,
So mote I brouke° wel mine yën twaye,   *use*
535 Save ye, I herde nevere man so singe
As dide youre fader in the morweninge.
Certes, it was of herte° al that he soong.   *heartfelt*
And for to make his vois the more strong,
He wolde so paine him that with bothe his yën
540 He moste winke,° so loude wolde he cryen;   *shut his eyes*
And stonden on his tiptoon therwithal,
And strecche forth his nekke long and smal;
And eek he was of swich discrecioun
That ther nas no man in no regioun
545 That him in song or wisdom mighte passe.°   *surpass*
I have wel rad in Daun Burnel the Asse.[5]
Among his vers how that ther was a cok,
For° a preestes sone yaf him a knok   *because*
Upon his leg whil he was yong and nice,°   *foolish*
550 He made him for to lese his benefice.[6]
But certain, ther nis no comparisoun
Bitwixe the wisdom and discrecioun
Of youre fader and of his subtiltee.
Now singeth, sire, for sainte° charitee!   *holy*
555 Lat see, conne ye youre fader countrefete?"°   *imitate*
    This Chauntecleer his winges gan to bete,
As man that coude his traison nat espye,
So was he ravisshed with his flaterye.
    Allas, ye lordes, many a fals flatour
560 Is in youre court, and many a losengeour,°   *deceiver*
That plesen you wel more, by my faith,
Than he that soothfastnesse° unto you saith!   *truth*
Redeth Ecclesiaste[7] of flaterye.
Beeth war, ye lordes, of hir trecherye.
565   This Chauntecleer stood hye upon his toos,
Strecching his nekke, and heeld his yën cloos,
And gan to crowe loude for the nones;°   *for the purpose*
And daun Russel the fox sterte up atones,°   *at once*
And by the gargat° hente° Chauntecleer,   *throat / seized*
570 And on his bak toward the wode him beer,
For yit ne was ther no man that him sued.
    O destinee that maist nat been eschued!°   *avoided*
Allas that Chauntecleer fleigh fro the bemes!
Allas his wif ne roughte° nat of dremes!   *cared*
575 And on a Friday[8] fil al this meschaunce!
    O Venus that art goddesse of plesaunce,
Sin that thy servant was this Chauntecleer,
And in thy service dide al his power—
More for delit than world° to multiplye—   *population*

5. The hero of a 12th-century satirical poem, *Speculum Stultorum*, by Nigel Wirecker, Brunellus was a donkey who traveled around Europe trying to educare himself.
6. Lose his commission (because he overslept).
7. The Book of Ecclesiasticus.
8. Venus's day, but also an ominous day of the week.

580	Why woldestou suffre him on thy day to die?	
	O Gaufred,[9] dere maister soverein,	
	That, whan thy worthy king Richard was slain	
	With shot,° complainedest his deeth so sore,	*(of an arrow)*
	Why ne hadde I now thy sentence and thy lore,	
585	The Friday for to chide as diden ye?	
	For on a Friday soothly° slain was he.	*truly*
	Thanne wolde I shewe you how that I coude plaine°	*lament*
	For Chauntecleres drede and for his paine.	
	Certes, swich cry ne lamentacioun	
590	Was nevere of ladies maad whan Ilioun°	*Troy*
	Was wonne, and Pyrrus[1] with his straite° swerd,	*drawn*
	Whan he hadde hent King Priam by the beerd	
	And slain him, as saith us Eneidos,°	*Virgil's* Aeneid
	As maden alle the hennes in the cloos,°	*yard*
595	Whan they hadde seen of Chauntecleer the sighte.	
	But sovereinly Dame Pertelote shrighte°	*shrieked*
	Ful louder than dide Hasdrubales wif[2]	
	Whan that hir housbonde hadde lost his lif,	
	And that the Romains hadden brend Cartage:	
600	She was so ful of torment and of rage	
	That wilfully unto the fir she sterte,	
	And brende hirselven with a stedefast herte.	
	O woful hennes, right so criden ye	
	As, whan that Nero[3] brende the citee	
605	Of Rome, criden senatoures wives	
	For that hir housbondes losten alle hir lives:	
	Withouten gilt this Nero hath hem slain.	
	Now wol I turne to my tale again.	
	The sely° widwe and eek hir doughtres two	*innocent*
610	Herden thise hennes crye and maken wo,	
	And out at dores sterten they anoon,	
	And sien° the fox toward the grove goon,	*saw*
	And bar upon his bak the cok away,	
	And criden, "Out, harrow, and wailaway,	
615	Ha, ha, the fox," and after him they ran,	
	And eek with staves many another man;	
	Ran Colle oure dogge, and Talbot and Gerland,[4]	
	And Malkin with a distaf in hir hand,	
	Ran cow and calf, and eek the verray hogges,	
620	Sore aferd for berking of the dogges	
	And shouting of the men and wommen eke.	
	They ronne so hem thoughte hir herte breke;	
	They yelleden as feendes doon in helle;	
	The dokes° criden as men wolde hem quelle;°	*ducks / kill*
625	The gees for fere flowen over the trees;	

9. Geoffrey of Vinsauf, who wrote a poem when King Richard the Lion-Hearted died, cursing the day of the week on which he died, a Friday.
1. Pyrrhus, the son of Achilles, who slew Troy's King Priam.
2. Hasdrubal was King of Carthage when it was defeated by the Romans during the Punic Wars.
3. The Emperor Nero set fire to Rome, killing many of his senators.
4. Common names for dogs.

Out of the hive cam the swarm of bees;
So hidous was the noise a, benedicite,
Certes, he Jakke Straw[5] and his meinee
Ne made nevere shoutes half so shrille
630   Whan that they wolden any Fleming kille,
As thilke day was maad upon the fox:
Of bras they broughten bemes° and of box,°   *trumpets / boxwood*
Of horn, of boon, in whiche they blewe and pouped,°   *puffed*
And therwithal they skriked and they houped—
635   It seemed as that hevene sholde falle.
    Now goode men, I praye you herkneth alle:
Lo, how Fortune turneth sodeinly
The hope and pride eek of hir enemy.
This cok that lay upon the foxes bak,
640   In al his drede unto the fox he spak,
And saide, "Sire, if that I were as ye,
Yit sholde I sayn, as wis° God helpe me,   *certainly*
'Turneth ayain, ye proude cherles° alle!   *ruffians*
A verray pestilence upon you falle!
645   Now am I come unto this wodes side,
Maugree° your heed,° the cok shal here abide.   *despite / planning*
I wol him ete, in faith, and that anoon.'"
    The fox answerde, "In faith, it shal be doon."
And as he spak that word, al sodeinly
650   The cok brak from his mouth deliverly,°   *nimbly*
And hye upon a tree he fleigh anoon.
    And whan the fox sawgh that he was agoon,
"Allas," quod he, "O Chauntecleer, allas!
I have to you," quod he, "ydoon trespas,
655   In as muche as I maked you aferd
Whan I you hente and broughte out of the yeerd.
But sire, I dide it in no wikke° entente: *wicked*
Come down, and I shal telle you what I mente.
I shal saye sooth to you, God help me so."
660   "Nay thanne," quod he, "I shrewe° us bothe two: *curse*
But first I shrewe myself, bothe blood and bones,
If thou bigile me ofter than ones;
Thou shalt namore thurgh thy flaterye
Do° me to singe and winken with myn yë.   *make*
665   For he that winketh whan he sholde see,
Al wilfully, God lat him nevere thee."°   *prosper*
    "Nay," quod the fox, "but God yive him meschaunce
That is so undiscreet of governaunce
That jangleth° whan he sholde holde his pees."   *chatters*
670   Lo, swich it is for to be recchelees°   *careless*
And necligent and truste on flaterye.
But ye that holden this tale a folye
As of a fox, or of a cok and hen,
Taketh the moralitee, goode men.

5. Jack Straw was one of the leaders of the Peasants' Revolt of 1381, which was directed in part against the Flemish traders in London.

675   For Saint Paul saith that al that writen is
      To oure doctrine° it is ywrit, ywis:°   *instruction / indeed*
      Taketh the fruit, and lat the chaf be stille.
      Now goode God, if that it be thy wille,
      As saith my lord, so make us alle goode men,
680   And bringe us to his hye blisse. Amen.

The Epilogue

      "Sire Nonnes Preest," oure Hoste saide anoon,
      "Yblessed be thy breech° and every stoon:°   *buttocks / testicle*
      This was a merye tale of Chauntecleer.
      But by my trouthe, if thou were seculer°   *a layman*
685   Thou woldest been a tredefowl° aright: *a cock*
      For if thou have corage° as thou hast might   *desire*
      Thee were neede of hennes, as I weene,°   *suppose*
      Ye, mo than sevene times seventeene.
      See whiche brawnes° hath this gentil preest—   *muscles*
690   So greet a nekke and swich a large breest.
      He looketh as a sperhawk° with his yën;   *sparrowhawk*
      Him needeth nat his colour for to dyen
      With brasil ne with grain of Portingale.[6]
      Now sire, faire falle you for youre tale."
695   And after that he with ful merye cheere
      Saide unto another as ye shul heere.

THE PARSON'S TALE   Although *The Canterbury Tales* remain unfinished and even the order of the tales is unclear, we know that Chaucer's plan was to end them with *The Parson's Tale*, just as it was to begin them with the pilgrimage to Canterbury in *The General Prologue*. Thus, when the Parson responds to the Host's request for a final tale by praying Jesus to show the way to the "glorious pilgrimage" called "Jerusalem celestial," there is a sense of closure in his return to an idea that has been obscured during the tale-telling. His shift of the destination from Canterbury to the heavenly city, however, gives us pause. The view that life on earth is a pilgrimage to heaven was a Christian commonplace, but was it Chaucer's view? The three parts of *The Parson's Tale* included here raise questions about how Chaucer's religious beliefs relate to his art. What is his final judgment of the artful, but often sinful, tales he has been telling?

In the introduction, the Parson rejects the idea of poetry entirely, scornfully refusing to tell a "fable" or to adorn his tale with alliteration or rhyme; instead, he will tell what he refers to as a "merye tale in prose," which turns out to be a forty-page treatise on penitence. Thus Chaucer specifically attributes to him an ascetic view of art which is hard to reconcile with his own extraordinary poetry. Does the Parson speak for Chaucer? Although he has a measure of authority as the only exemplary member of the clergy on the pilgrimage, he is nevertheless a fictional character. Since, however, Chaucer is thought to have written the introduction to this tale as well as the *Retraction* at the end of his life, perhaps he could have come to share the Parson's aesthetic views.

The Parson begins his tale proper with a second reference to celestial Jerusalem, stating that the route to it is through penitence. The tale, which Chaucer had translated at an earlier period, belongs to a common type of manuals of confession for either clergy or laity. Included in it is an analysis of the seven deadly sins—pride, envy, anger, sloth, avarice, gluttony, and lechery—in an order that suggests that Chaucer, like Dante, considered the last to be the least

---

6. Two types of red dye, the latter from Portugal.

serious, although still worthy of damnation. The passage on lechery excerpted here offers an opportunity to measure *The Parson's Tale* against the tales that have gone before, particularly such "sinful" works as *The Miller's Tale* and *The Wife of Bath's Prologue*.

Whatever conclusion we draw about the relevance of *The Parson's Tale* to the tales preceding, the *Retraction* appended to it is troubling yet intriguing. In it Chaucer repudiates much of the work for which he is most loved and admired, such "worldly vanitees" as *Troilus and Criseyde, The Parliament of Fowls*, and those *Canterbury Tales* that "sounen [lead] into sinne." On the other hand, he thanks God for his works of "moralitee," including his translation of Boethius and his saints' legends, works that are seldom read today. He himself is engaged in penance—repentance, confession, and satisfaction—thus connecting his own spiritual experience with the manual he has translated. However disappointing it is to read this rejection of his most artistically satisfying tales, we must remember that a concept of art for art's sake would have been historically unavailable to him. Perhaps his last tale was indeed his last word.

from **The Parson's Tale**
The Introduction

	By that° the Manciple hadde his tale al ended,	*by that time*
	The sonne fro the south line[1] was descended	
	So lowe, that he nas nat to my sighte	
	Degrees nine and twenty as in highte.	
5	Four of the clokke it was, so as I gesse,	
	For elevene foot,° or litel more or lesse,	*feet*
	My shadwe was at thilke° time as there,	*that*
	Of swich feet as my lengthe parted were	
	In sixe feet equal of proporcioun.	
10	Therwith the moones exaltacioun°—	*dominant influence*
	I mene Libra[2]—alway gan ascende,	
	As we were entring at a thropes ende.°	*village boundary*
	For which oure Host, as he was wont to gie°	*lead*
	As in this caas oure joly compaignye,	
15	Saide in this wise, "Lordinges everichoon,	
	Now lakketh us no tales mo than oon:	
	Fulfild is my sentence° and my decree;	*design*
	I trowe° that we han herd of eech degree;	*believe*
	Almost fulfild is al myn ordinaunce.	
20	I praye to God, so yive him right good chaunce	
	That telleth this tale to us lustily.	
	Sire preest," quod he, "artou a vicary,°	*vicar*
	Or arte a Person?° Say sooth, by thy fay.°	*parish priest / faith*
	Be what thou be, ne breek thou nat oure play,	
25	For every man save thou hath told his tale.	
	Unbokele and shew us what is in thy male!°	*bag*
	For trewely, me thinketh by thy cheere°	*expression*
	Thou sholdest knitte up wel a greet matere.	
	Tel us a fable anoon, for cokkes bones!"[3]	
30	This Person answerde al atones,	
	"Thou getest fable noon ytold for me,	
	For Paul, that writeth unto Timothee,[4]	
	Repreveth hem that waiven soothfastnesse,°	*truth*

1. Astronomical marking parallel to the celestial equator.
2. Seventh sign in the Zodiac, the Scales.
3. Cock's bones, a euphemism for God's bones.
4. St. Paul's Epistle to Timothy.

And tellen fables and swich wrecchednesse.

35 Why sholde I sowen draf° out of my fest,°   *chaff / fist*
Whan I may sowen whete if that me lest?°   *it pleases*
For which I saye that if you list to heere
Moralitee and vertuous matere,
And thanne that ye wol yive me audience,
40 I wol ful fain,° at Cristes reverence,   *gladly*
Do you plesance leveful° as I can.   *lawfully*
But trusteth wel, I am a southren man:[5]
I can nat geeste° Rum-Ram-Ruf by lettre—   *tell stories*
Ne, God woot,° rym holde° I but litel bettre.   *knows / appreciate*
45 And therfore, if you list, I wol nat glose;°   *adorn my speech*
I wol you telle a merye tale in prose,
To knitte up al this feeste and make an ende.
And Jesu for his grace wit me sende
To shewe you the way in this viage°   *journey*
50 Of thilke parfit° glorious pilgrimage   *that perfect*
That highte Jerusalem celestial.
And if ye vouche-sauf,° anoon I shal   *agree*
Biginne upon my tale, for which I praye
Telle youre avis:° I can no bettre saye.   *opinion*
55 But nathelees, this meditacioun
I putte it ay° under correccioun   *always*
Of clerkes, for I am nat textuel:°   *a literalist*
I take but the sentence,° trusteth wel.   *sense*
Therfore I make protestacioun
60 That I wol stonde to correccioun."
    Upon this word we han assented soone,
For, as it seemed, it was for to doone
To enden in som vertuous sentence,°   *topic*
And for to yive him space° and audience;   *time*
65 And bede oure Host he sholde to him saye
That alle we to telle his tale him praye.
    Oure Hoste hadde the wordes for us alle:
"Sire preest," quod he, "now faire you bifalle:
Telleth," quod he, "youre meditacioun.
70 But hasteth you, the sonne wol adown.
Beeth fructuous, and that in litel space,
And to do wel God sende you his grace.
Saye what you list, and we wol gladly heere."
And with that word he saide in this manere.

from *The Tale*

Oure sweete Lord God of Hevene, that no man wol perisse[1] but wol
that we comen alle to the knowliche of him and to the blisful lif
that is perdurable,° amonesteth° us by the prophete Jeremie[2] that   *enduring / warns*
saith in this wise: "Stondeth upon the wayes and seeth and axeth of

---

5. The parson, like Chaucer himself, comes from the
south of England and so is not accustomed to telling stories in the alliterative meter used traditionally in the

north. Rum-Ram-Raf is an example of alliteration.
1. Who wishes no man to perish.
2. Jeremiah 6.16.

olde pathes (that is to sayn, of olde sentences)° which is the goode ~ *opinions*
way, and walketh in that way, and ye shul finde refresshing for youre
soules."

Manye been the wayes espirituels that leden folk to oure Lord
Jesu Crist and to the regne of glorye: of whiche wayes ther is a ful
noble way and a ful covenable° which may nat faile to man ne to ~ *suitable*
womman that thurgh sinne hath misgoon fro the righte way of
Jerusalem celestial; and this way is cleped° Penitence. * * * ~ *called*

THE REMEDY FOR THE SIN OF LECHERY

Now cometh the remedye agains Lecherye, and that is generally
Chastitee and Continence that restraineth alle the desordainee
mevinges° that comen of flesshly talents.° And evere the gretter ~ *impulses / desires*
merite shal he han that most restraineth the wikkede eschaufinges° ~ *inflammations*
of the ardure of this sinne. And this is in two maneres: that is to
sayn, chastitee in mariage and chastitee of widwehood.

Now shaltou understonde that matrimoine is leeful° assembling ~ *lawful*
of man and of womman that receiven by vertu of the sacrement the
bond thurgh which they may nat be departed in al hir life—that is to
sayn, whil that they liven bothe. This, as saith the book, is a ful greet
sacrement: God maked it, as I have said, in Paradis, and wolde himself be born in mariage. And for to halwen° mariage, he was at a ~ *bless*
wedding where as he turned water into win, which was the firste
miracle that he wroughte in erthe biforn his disciples. Trewe effect
of mariage clenseth fornicacion and replenisseth Holy Chirche of
good linage° (for that is the ende of mariage), and it chaungeth ~ *offspring*
deedly sinne[3] into venial sinne bitwixe hem that been ywedded, and
maketh the hertes al oon° of hem that been ywedded, as wel as the ~ *united*
bodies.

This is verray mariage that was establissed by God er that
sinne bigan, whan naturel lawe was in his right point° in Paradis; ~ *order*
and it was ordained that oo man sholde have but oo womman, and
oo womman but oo man (as saith Saint Augustine) by manye
resons: First, for mariage is figured° bitwixe Crist and Holy ~ *represented*
Chirche; and that other is for a man is heved° of a womman— ~ *head*
algate,° by ordinance it sholde be so. For if a womman hadde mo ~ *at least*
men than oon, thanne sholde she have mo hevedes than oon, and
that were an horrible thing biforn God; and eek a womman ne
mighte nat plese to many folk at ones. And also ther ne sholde
nevere be pees ne reste amonges hem, for everich wolde axen his
owene thing. And fortherover, no man sholde knowe his owene
engendrure,° ne who sholde have his heritage, and the womman ~ *offspring*
sholde been the lesse biloved fro the time that she were conjoint to
manye men.

Now cometh how that a man sholde bere him with his wif, and
namely in two thinges, that is to sayn, in suffrance° and in rever- ~ *obedience*
ence, as shewed Crist when he made first womman. For he ne made

---

3. Sex remains a minor sin even within marriage, but it is a more serious sin outside of marriage.

hire nat of the heved of Adam for she sholde nat claime too greet
lorshipe: for ther as womman hath the maistrye she maketh too greet
desray° (ther needen none ensamples of this: the experience of day   *disorder*
by day oughte suffise). Also, certes, God ne made nat womman of
the foot of Adam, for she ne sholde nat be holden too lowe, for she
can nat paciently suffre. But God made womman of the rib of Adam
for womman sholde be felawe unto man. Man sholde bere him to his
wif in faith, in trouthe, and in love, as saith Sainte Paul, that a man
sholde loven his wif as Crist loved Holy Chirche, that loved it so wel
that he deide for it. So sholde a man for his wif, if it were neede.

Now how that a womman sholde be subjet to hir housbonde,
that telleth Sainte Peter: First, in obedience. And eek, as saith the
decree, a womman that is a wif, as longe as she is a wif, she hath
noon auctoritee° to swere ne to bere witnesse withoute leve of hir   *power*
housbonde that is hir lord—algate, he sholde be so by reson. She
sholde eek serven him in alle honestee, and been attempree° of hir   *moderate*
array; I woot wel that they sholde setten hir entente° to plesen hir   *purpose*
housbondes, but nat by hir quaintise of array:° Saint Jerome saith   *flamboyant attire*
that wives that been apparailed in silk and in precious purpre ne
mowe nat clothen hem in Jesu Crist. What saith Saint John eek in
this matere? Saint Gregorye eek saith that no wight° seeketh precious   *person*
array but only for vaine glorye to been honoured the more biforn the
peple. It is a greet folye a womman to have a fair array outward and
in hireself be foul inward. A wif sholde eek be mesurable° in looking   *modest*
and in bering and in laughing, and discreet in alle hir wordes and hir
deedes. And aboven alle worldly thinges she sholde loven hir housbonde with al hir herte, and to him be trewe of hir body (so sholde
an housbonde eek be to his wif): for sith that° al the body is the   *since*
housbondes, so sholde hir herte been, or elles ther is bitwixe hem
two as in that no parfit mariage.

Thanne shul men understonde that for three thinges a man and
his wif flesshly mowen° assemble. The firste is in entente of engen-   *may*
drure of children to the service of God: for certes, that is the cause
final of matrimoine. Another cause is to yeelden everich° of hem to   *each*
other the dette of hir bodies, for neither of hem hath power of his
owene body. The thridde is for to eschewe lecherye and vilainye.
The ferthe is, for soothe, deedly sinne. As to the firste, it is merito-
rye; the seconde also, for, as saith the decree, that she hath merite of
chastitee that yeeldeth to hir housbonde the dette of hir body, ye,
though it be again hir liking and the lust of hir herte. The thridde
manere is venial sinne—and, trewely, scarsly may any of thise be
withoute venial sinne, for the corrupcion and for the delit. The ferthe
manere is for to understonde if they assemble only for amorous love
and for noon of the forsaide causes, but for to accomplice thilke
brenning delit—they rekke° nevere how ofte—soothly, it is deedly   *care*
sinne. And yit with sorwe some folk wol painen hem° more to doon   *trouble*
than to hir appetit suffiseth. * * *   *themselves*

Another remedye agains lecherye is specially to withdrawen
swiche thinges as yive occasion to thilke vilainye, as ese,° eting, and   *leisure*

drinking: for certes, whan the pot boileth strongly, the beste remedye is
to withdrawe the fir. Sleeping longe in greet quiete is eek a greet
norice° to lecherye. Another remedye agains lecherye is that a man or a
womman eschewe the compaignye of hem by whiche he douteth° to be
tempted: for al be it so that the deede be withstonden, yit is ther greet
temptacion. Soothly, a whit wal,° although it ne brenne nought fully by
stiking of a candele, yit is the wal blak of the leit.° Ful ofte time I rede
that no man truste in his owene perfeccion but he be stronger than
Sampson, holier than David, and wiser than Salomon.

nurse
suspects

wall
from the flame

Chaucer's Retraction

Here Taketh the Makere of This Book His Leve

Now praye I to hem alle that herkne this litel tretis° or rede,° that
if ther be any thing in it that liketh° hem, that therof they thanken
oure Lord Jesu Crist, of whom proceedeth al wit and al goodnesse.
And if ther be any thing that displese hem, I praye hem also that
they arrette° it to the defaute of myn unconning,° and nat to my
wil, that wolde ful fain° have said bettre if I hadde had conning.
For oure book saith, "Al that is writen is writen for oure doctrine,"
and that is myn entente. Wherfore I biseeke you mekely, for the
mercy of God, that ye praye for me that Crist have mercy on me
and foryive me my giltes,° and namely of my translacions and
enditinges° of worldly vanitees, the whiche I revoke in my retrac-
cions:[4] as is the book of Troilus; the book also of Fame; the book of
the five and twenty Ladies; the book of the Duchesse; the book of
Saint Valentines Day of the Parlement of Briddes; the tales of Canterbury, thilke that sounen° into sinne; the book of the Leon; and
many another book, if they were in my remembrance, and many a
song and many a leccherous lay: that Crist for his grete mercy
foryive me the sinne. But of the translacion of Boece *de Consolatione*, and othere bookes of legendes of saintes, and omelies, and
moralitee, and devocion, that thanke I oure Lord Jesu Crist and his
blisful Moder and alle the saintes of hevene, biseeking hem that
they from hennes forth unto my lives ende sende me grace to
biwaile° my giltes and to studye to the salvacion of my soule, and
graunte me grace of verray penitence, confession, and satisfaccion
to doon in this present lif, thurgh the benigne grace of him that is
king of kinges and preest over alle preestes, that boughte° us with
the precious blood of his herte, so that I may been oon of hem at
the day of doom° that shulle be saved. *Qui cum patre et Spiritu Sanc-
to vivis et regnas Deus per omnia saecula. Amen.*[5]

treatise / advice
pleases

attribute / inability
gladly

sins / writings

lead

repent

redeemed

judgment

4. Here Chaucer repents having written most of his major
works: *Troilus and Criseyde, The Book* (or *House*) *of Fame,
The Legend of Good Women, The Book of the Duchess, The
Parliament of Fowls*, and various of *The Canterbury Tales.
The Book of the Lion* has not been preserved. Chaucer's
translation of Boethius's *Consolation of Philosophy* is
excepted.
5. You who live with the Father and the Holy Spirit and
reign as God through all the centuries. Amen.

To His Scribe Adam[1]

Adam scrivain,° if evere it thee bifalle   *copyist*
Boece[2] or Troilus for to writen newe,
Under thy longe lokkes thou moste have° the scalle,°   *may you get / mange*
But after my making thou write more trewe,[3]
So ofte a day I moot° thy werk renewe,   *must*
It to correcte, and eek to rubbe and scrape:
And al is thurgh thy necligence and rape.°   *haste*

———— ❧❦❧ ————

The Second Play of the Shepherds

Medieval drama is very entertaining, but it was meant to instruct as well. It developed not from classical drama, which virtually died out in the Middle Ages, but from the church liturgy. Although it originated on the Continent, its greatest flowering was in England, in the plays of the Corpus Christi cycle performed from the end of the fourteenth to the end of the sixteenth century. So called because they were put on during the feast of Corpus Christi in midsummer, these plays portray the entire cycle of sacred history from Creation to the Last Judgment, including such events as the Fall of Lucifer, Noah's flood, the Nativity, and Christ's Crucifixion and Resurrection. The plays are given coherence by a pattern of typology whereby Satan's deception and Adam's sin are redeemed by Christ's sacrifice. Old Testament events and characters predict and are fulfilled by New Testament ones—for instance, Isaac and Moses being types of Christ, and Cain, Pharaoh, and Herod being types of Satan.

The cycle plays exist in four versions, which are almost complete and come primarily from the north of England: the Chester, N-Town, York, and Wakefield (or Townley) cycles. They were generally performed outdoors, in partnership with the church, by craft guilds, associations of tradesmen who represented a newly prosperous mercantile class. Often they sponsored plays whose subject matter was specifically appropriate to their craft—for instance, the butchers putting on the killing of Abel and the water-drawers the play of Noah.

The popularity of the plays in the Corpus Christi cycle—as well as their function as a surrogate Bible for the poor—can be seen in Chaucer's *Miller's Tale*. The Miller himself insists on telling his tale out of order in "Pilate's voice," the ranting manner of Pontius Pilate in the Passion plays, and the foppish Absolon woos his beloved Alison by playing the role of the tyrant Herod on a scaffold. More importantly, the chief trick of this fabliau—the clerk Nicholas's arranging to be alone with Alison by frightening her husband with the threat of a second flood—relies on the old man's sketchy knowledge of the play of Noah.

---

1. Given his position at court, Chaucer was asked to write many lyrics and occasional poems, such as this poem and the one that follows. In both, he wittily bemoans the conditions of authorship under which he was forced to work, depending on scribes to reproduce his poetry and on patrons to support it. In *To His Scribe Adam*, he strikes a pose of affectionate raillery toward his scribe, whose occupation writers widely scorned. Perhaps he sees it as fitting to curse Adam with a skin disease which will make him scratch his scalp, just as Chaucer has had to scratch out the errors from his manuscripts. However, the poem has a serious undertone too. In fearing that Adam will miscopy his great romance, *Troilus and Criseyde*, he echoes a concern for the accurate reproduction of his work, which he voiced at the end of *Troilus* itself: he prays God that, in view of the great dialectal "diversitee / in Englissh, and in writing of oure tonge," no one "miswrite" his book (5.1793–94).

2. Chaucer's translation of Boethius's *Consolation of Philosophy*.

3. Unless you make a more reliable copy of what I have composed.

Nicholas's invocation of a sacred story to pursue a profane goal walks a thin line between comedy and blasphemy. So too did many of the Corpus Christi plays, but for a more obviously sacred purpose. The Wakefield *Annunciation*, for instance, presents Joseph in fabliau fashion as an old man fearing that he has been cuckolded when he discovers that Mary, his young bride-to-be, is pregnant. Only at the end does he come to understand the divine purpose behind her condition.

Nowhere are the sacred and profane paired as brilliantly as in the Nativity play known as *The Second Play of the Shepherds*, one of the Wakefield plays, named after the prosperous Yorkshire town in which they were performed. It was written or revised by an artist of great imagination and skill, no doubt a cleric, known as the Wakefield Master. His great achievement is his ability to make biblical stories relevant to fifteenth-century England in such a way that daily life takes on typological significance. The prime example is the parallel between Mak's stolen sheep, hidden in swaddling clothes in a cradle, and the newborn Christ child whom the shepherds visit at the end of the play. The mercy that the shepherds show to Mak by tossing him in a blanket rather than delivering him to be hanged prefigures the mercy that the Christ child will bring into the world.

No matter how neatly the typological scheme works, however, the author does not present the birth of Christ as entirely nullifying the complaints of the characters in the play. With his guileful assault on the sheep fold and his concealment of a "horned lad" swaddled in a cradle, Mak may be a type of the devil, but his complaints of poverty (he stole the sheep to feed his rapidly expanding family) are real. So too are those of the shepherds that they echo, to which the first 180 lines of the play are devoted. The shepherds' opening complaints against taxes, lords and their condescending servants, and nagging, prolific wives reflect the power of the wool and cloth trade that enriched medieval England in the fourteenth and fifteenth centuries but impoverished farmers by driving landlords to enclose individually owned lands in order to convert them to profitable sheep farming. These complaints cannot simply be dismissed as the grumbling of fallen men who fail to understand their need for divine grace. Nor can the complaints of Mak's wife Gill against women's work be seen as simply setting her up as a contrast with the patient Virgin Mary at the end of the play.

The Second Play of the Shepherds

[*Scene: Field near Bethlehem.*]

I PASTOR: Lord, what these weathers are cold!   And I am ill happed.[1]

I am near hand dold,°   so long have I napped;   *almost numb*

My legs they fold,   my fingers are chapped.

It is not as I would,   for I am all lapped°   *tied up*

5   In sorrow.

In storms and tempest,

Now in the east, now in the west,

Woe is him has never rest

Mid-day nor morrow!

10   But we sely° shepherds   that walks on the moor,   *poor*

In faith we are near hands   out of the door.

No wonder, as it stands,   if we be poor,

For the tilthe of our lands   lies fallow as the floor,

As ye ken.°   *know*

15   We are so hamed,°   *hamstrung*

For-taxed° and ramed,°   *overburdened / oppressed*

---

1. Clothed.

We are made hand tamed
With these gentlery men.°   *gentry, aristocrats*

20 Thus they reave° us our rest,   our Lady them wary!°   *rob / curse*
These men that are lord-fest,²   they cause the plow tarry.
That men say is for the best,   we find it contrary.
Thus are husbandys° opprest,   in point to miscarry   *farmhands*
On live.
Thus hold they us hunder;°   *under*
25 Thus they bring us in blonder;°   *trouble*
It were great wonder
And ever should we thrive.

For may he get a paint slefe°   or a broche now on days,   *painted sleeve*
Woe is him that him grefe°   or once again says!   *troubles*
30 Dare noman him reprefe,°   what mastry° he mays,   *reprove / power*
And yet may noman lefe°   one word that he says,   *believe*
No letter.
He can make purveance°   *provision*
With boast and bragance,
35 And all is through maintenance
Of men that are greater.

There shall come a swane   as proud as a po,³
He must borrow my wane,°   my plow also,   *wagon*
Then I am full fane°   to grant or he go.   *pleased*
40 Thus live we in pain,   anger, and woe,
By night and day.
He must have if he langed,°   *desired*
If I should forgang° it;   *forgo*
I were better be hanged
45 Then once say him nay.
It does me good, as I walk   thus by mine one,
Of this world for to talk   in manner of moan.
To my sheep will I stalk,   and hearken anone,°   *awhile*
There abide on a balk,°   or sit on a stone,   *ridge*
50 Full soon.
For I trowe,° perde,°   *believe / by God*
True men if they be,
We get more company
Or° it be noon.   *before*

[*The Second Shepherd enters without noticing the First.*]
II PASTOR: Benste and Dominus!⁴   What may this bemean?
Why fares this world thus?   Oft have we not seen?
Lord, these weathers are spytus,°   and the winds full keen,   *spiteful*
And the frosts so hideous   they water my eyes—
No lie.

2. Bound to their lords.   4. Corruption of a Latin blessing, *Benedicite ad Dominum.*
3. A servant as proud as a peacock.

60   Now in dry, now in wete,
      Now in snow, now in sleet;
      When my shoen° freeze to my feet,   shoes
      It is not all easy.

      But as far as I ken,   or yet as I go,
65   We sely wedmen   dre mekyll woe;[5]
      We have sorrow then and then: it falls oft so.
      Sely Copple,[6] our hen,   both to and fro
      She cackles;
      But begin she to croak,
70   To groan or to cluck,
      Woe is him is of our cock,
      For he is in the shackels.

      These men that are wed   have not all their will;
      When they are full hard sted,°   they sigh full still;   placed
75   God wayte° they are led   full hard and full ill;   knows
      In bower° nor in bed   they say nought there till,°   bedroom / thereto
      This tide.°   time
      My part have I fun;°   found
      I know my lesson.
80   Woe is him that is bun,°   bound in marriage
      For he must abide.

      But now late in our lives   a marvel to me,
      That I think my heart rives°   such wonders to see.   breaks
      What that destiny drives   it should so be;
85   Some men will have two wives   and some men three,
      In store;
      Some are woe that has any,
      But so far can I,
      Woe is him that has many,
90   For he felys° sore.   suffers

      But young men of a-wooing,   for God that you bought,°   redeemed
      Be well ware of wedding,   and think in your thought,
      "Had I wist"° is a thing   it serves of nought;   known
      Mekyll° still° mourning   has wedding home brought,   much / constant
95   And griefs,
      With many a sharp shower;
      For thou may catch in an hour
      That shall savour fulle sour
      As long as thou lives.

100   For, as ever read I pistill[7]   I have one to my fere,°   mate
      As sharp as a thistle,   as rough as a brere;
      She is browed like a bristle   with a sour-loten cheer;[8]
      Had she once wet her whistle   she could sing full clear
      Her *Paternoster*.°   Lord's Prayer

---

5. We poor, innocent married men suffer much.   7. [St. Paul's] Epistle.
6. A copple is the crest on a bird's head.   8. Sour-looking face.

105   She is as great as a whale;
        She has a gallon of gall.
        By him that died for us all,
        I would I had run to° I had lost her.   *until*

I PASTOR: God look over the raw!⁹   Full deafly ye stand.

II PASTOR: Yea, the devil in thy maw,°   so tariand.°   *mouth / slow*
        Saw thou awre° of Daw?¹   *anywhere*

I PASTOR: Yea, on a ley land°   *fallow ground*
        Hard I him blaw.²   He comes here at hand,
        Not far.
        Stand still.

II PASTOR: Why?

I PASTOR: For he comes, hope I.

II PASTOR: He will make us both a lie
        But if° we beware.   *unless*

        [*Enter Third Shepherd.*]

III PASTOR: Christ's cross me speed,   and Saint Nicholas!
        There of had I need;   it is worse than it was.

120   Whoso could take heed   and let the world pass,
        It is ever in dread   and brekill° as glass,   *brittle*
        And slithes.°   *slides away*
        This world fowre° never so,   *fared*
        With marvels mo and mo,

125   Now in weal, now in woe,
        And all thing writhes.°   *turns about*

        Was never sin° Noah's flood   such floods seen;   *since*
        Winds and rains so rude,   and storms so keen;
        Some stammerd, some stood   in doubt,° as I ween;   *fear*

130   Now God turn all to good!   I say as I mean,
        For° ponder.   *to*
        These floods so they drown,
        Both fields and in town,
        And bears all down,

135   And that is a wonder.

        We that walk on the nights,   our cattle to keep,
        We see sudden sights   when other men sleep.
        Yet me think my heart lights;   I see shrews peep;³
        Ye are two ill wights.   I will give my sheep

140   A turn.
        But full ill have I meant;
        As I walk on this bent,
        I may lightly repent,
        My toes if I spurn.

9. Let God pay attention to his audience (row), i.e., God   2. I just blew by him.
attend me.   3. I see villains peeping out.
1. The Third Shepherd.

145   Ah, sir, God you save,   and master mine!
           A drink fain would I have,   and somewhat to dine.
I PASTOR: Christ's curse, my knave,   thou art a leder hine!°   *lazy servant*
II PASTOR: What, the boy list rave!   Abide unto sine;[4]
           We have made it.[5]
150   Ill thrift on thy pate!
           Though the shrew came late,
           Yet is he in state
           To dine, if he had it.

III PASTOR: Such servants as I,   that sweats and swinks,°   *works*
155   Eats our bread full dry,   and that me forthinks;°   *upsets*
           We are oft wet and weary   when master-men winks;°   *sleeps*
           Yet comes full lately   both diners and drinks,
           But nately.°   *thoroughly*
           Both our dame and our sire,
160   When we have run in the mire,
           They can nip° at our hire,°   *trim / wages*
           And pay us full lately.

           But here my troth, master: for the fare that ye make,
           I shall do therafter,   work as I take;
165   I shall do a little, sir,   and emang ever lake,[6]
           For yet lay my supper   never on my stomach
           In fields.
           Whereto should I threpe?°   *wrangle*
           With my staff can I leap,
170   And men say "Light cheap°   *little cost*
           Letherly for-yields."°   *poorly yields*

I PASTOR: Thou were an ill lad   to ride a-wooing
           With a man that had   but little of spending.
II PASTOR: Peace, boy, I bade.   No more jangling,°   *chattering*
175   Or I shall make there full rad,°   by the heavens king!   *quickly*
           With thy gauds°—   *tricks*
           Where are our sheep, boy?—we scorn.°   *despise*
III PASTOR: Sir, this same day at morn
           I them left in the corn,
180   When they rang lauds.[7]

           They have pasture good,   they cannot go wrong.
I PASTOR: That is right, by the roode![8]   these nights are long,
           Yet I would, or we yode,°   one gave us a song.   *went*
II PASTOR: So I thought as I stood,   to mirth us among.
III PASTOR: I grant.
I PASTOR: Let me sing the tenory.
II PASTOR: And I treble so hee.

4. The boy is crazy; wait a while.
5. We have already eaten.
6. Keep playing besides.
7. The first church service of the day.

8. Cross; the humor here, as with the other oaths, is based on the anachronism that Jesus has not yet been born, much less crucified.

III PASTOR: Then the meyne° falls to me: *middle*
      Let see how ye chant.
  [*They sing.*]
  Tunc intrat Mak in clamide se super togam vestitus.[9]

MAK: Now, Lord, for thy names vii,[1]   that made both moon and starns°   *stars*
      Well mo then can I neven°   thy will, Lord, of me tharns;[2]   *say*
      I am all uneven,   that moves oft my harness.
      Now would God I were in heaven,   for there weep no barnes°   *babies*
      So still.

I PASTOR: Who is that pipes so poor?

MAK: Would God ye wist how I foor!°   *fared*
      Lo, a man that walks on the moor,
      And has not all his will!

II PASTOR: Mak, where has thou gone?   Tell us tiding.

III PASTOR: Is he comme? Then ylkon°   take heed to his thing.   *everyone*
  Et accipit clamidem ab ipso.[3]

MAK: What! Ich be a yoman,[4]   I tell you, of the king;
      The self and the same,   sond° from a great lording,   *messenger*
      And sich.°   *such like*
      Fy on you! Goeth hence
205   Out of my presence!
      I must have reverence;
      Why, who be ich?

I PASTOR: Why make ye it so quaint?[5]   Mak, ye do wrang.

II PASTOR: But, Mak, list ye saint?   I trow that ye lang.[6]

III PASTOR: I trow the shrew can paint,   the devill might him hang!

MAK: Ich shall make complaint, and make you all to thwang[7]
      At a word,
      And tell even how ye doth.

I PASTOR: But, Mak, is that sooth?
215   Now take out that southren tooth,°   *accent*
      And set in a turd!

II PASTOR: Mak, the devil in your eye!   A stroke would I lean° you.   *lend*

III PASTOR: Mak, know ye not me?   By God, I could teen° you.   *rage at*

MAK: God look you all three!   Me thought I had seen you;
220   Ye are a fair company.

I PASTOR: Can ye now mean you?

II PASTOR: Shrew, pepe![8]
      Thus late as thou goes,
      What will men suppose?
      And thou has an ill nose°   *reputation*
225   Of steeling of sheep.

---

9. Then Mak enters, wearing a cloak over his garment.
1. Seven (written by the copyist as the roman numeral).
2. Is lacking.
3. And he takes his cloak from him.
4. Freeborn property-holder.

5. Why act so elegant?
6. Do you want to be a saint? I think you long to be.
7. Be beaten.
8. Villain, look around!

MAK: And I am true as steel,   all men waytt,°   know
But a sickness I feel   that holds me full haytt;°   hot
My belly fares not weel;   it is out of estate.
III PASTOR: Seldom lies the devil   dead by the gate.[9]
MAK: Therfore
Full sore am I and ill,
If I stand stone still;
I eat not an nedill°   scrap
This month and more.

I PASTOR: How fares thy wife? By my hood,   how fares sho?°   she
MAK: Lies waltering,° by the rood,   by the fire, lo!   collapsed
And a house full of brood.°   She drinks well, too;   children
Ill spede° other good   that she will do!   success
But sho
240   Eats as fast as she can,
And ilk° year that comes to man   each
She brings forth a lakan,°   baby
And some years two.

But were I not more gracious   and richer by far;
245   I were eaten out of house   and of harbar;°   home
Yet is she a foul dowse,°   if ye come nar;   wench
There is none that trowse°   nor knows a war°   imagines / worse
Than ken I.
Now will ye see what I proffer,
250   To give all in my coffer
To morn at next to offer
Her hed mas-penny.[1]

II PASTOR: I wote so forwaked°   is none in this shire: sleepless
I would sleep if I taked   less to my hire.
III PASTOR: I am cold and naked,   and would have a fire.
I PASTOR: I am weary, for-rakyd,°   and run in the mire.   exhausted
Wake thou!
II PASTOR: Nay, I will lyg° down by,   lie
For I must sleep truly.
III PASTOR: As good a man's son was I
As any of you.

But, Mak, come hither! Between   shall thou lyg down.
[Mak lies down with the Shepherds.]
MAK: Then might I let you bedene   of that ye would rowne,[2]
No drede.
265   From my top to my toe,
Manus was commendo,
Poncio Pilato;[3]

---

9. Proverbial: The devil seldom lies dead by the wayside; i.e., the devil is not often an innocent victim.
1. Penny offering for a mass for the dead.
2. That way I can readily prevent you from whispering together.
3. An amusing corruption of two Bible verses: "Into your hand I commend my soul" and "I wash my hands of this man."

Christ cross me speed!

Tunc surgit, pastoribus dormientibus, et dicit[4]

	Now were time for a man that lacks what he would	
270	To stalk privily than unto a fold,	
	And nimbly to work than, and be not too bold,	
	For he might aby the bargain, if it were told	
	At the ending.	
	Now were time for to reyll;°	*revel*
275	But he needs good counsel	
	That fain would fare well,	
	And has but little spending.	
	But about you a circle, as round as a moon,	
	Too I have done that I will, till° that it be noon,[5]	*until*
280	That ye lyg stone still to that I have done,	
	And I shall say theretill of good words a foyne.°	*a few*
	"On hight	
	Over your heads my hand I lift;	
	Out go your eyes! Fordo° your sight!"	*ruin*
285	But yet I must make better shift,	
	And it be right.	
	Lord, what they sleep hard! That may ye all here;	
	Was I never a shepherd, but now will I lere.°	*learn*
	If the flock be scared, yet shall I nip near.	
290	How, drawes° hitherward! Now mends our cheer	*come*
	From sorrow:	
	A fat sheep, I dare say,	
	A good fleece, dare I lay,	
	Eft-whyte when I may,[6]	
295	But this will I borrow.	

[*Mak goes home to his wife.*]

	How, Gill, art thou in? Get us some light.	
UXOR EIUS:[7]	Who makes such din this time of the night?	
	I am set for to spin; I hope not[8] I might	
	Rise a penny to win,° I shrew° them on height!	*gain / curse*
300	So fares	
	A housewife that has been	
	To be raised° thus between:	*disturbed*
	Here may no note° be seen	*scrap*
	For such small chares.°	*chores*

MAK: Good wife, open the hek!°   Sees thou not what I bring?   *inner door*

UXOR: I may thole the dray the snek.[9]   Ah, come in, my sweeting!

MAK: Yea, thou thar not rek°   of my long standing.   *care*

---

4. Then Mak arises, while the shepherds are sleeping, and speaks.
5. Mak is casting a spell on the shepherds in the form of a fairy circle to keep them from waking.
6. I will pay it back when I can.
7. His wife.
8. I don't expect that.
9. I will let you draw the latch.

UXOR: By the naked neck   art thou like for to hing.
MAK: Do way:
310   I am worthy my meat,°   *supper*
        For in a strait° can I get   *tight spot*
        More than they that swink° and sweat   *work*
        All the long day.

        Thus it fell to my lot,   Gill, I had such grace.
UXOR: It were a foul blot   to be hanged for the case.
MAK: I have skaped, Jelot,[1]   oft as hard a glase.°   *blow*
UXOR: But so long goes the pot   to the water, men says,
        At last
        Comes it home broken.
MAK: Well know I the token,
        But let it never be spoken;
        But come and help fast.

        I would he were flayn;°   I lyst° well eat: *skinned / wish*
        This twelvemonth was I not   so fain of one sheep mete.
UXOR: Come they or° he be slain,   and hear the sheep bleat—   *before*
MAK: Then might I be tane.°   That were a cold sweat!   *taken*
        Go spar°   *lock*
        The gate-door.
UXOR: Yes, Mak,
        For and° they come at thy back—   *if*
MAK: Then might I buy, for all the pack,[2]
        The devil of the war.

UXOR: A good bowrde° have I spied,   sin thou can none.   *trick*
        Here shall we him hide   to° they be gone;   *until*
335   In my cradle abide.   Let me alone,
        And I shall lyg beside   in childbed, and groan.
MAK: Thou red;°   *get ready*
        And I shall say thou was light°   *delivered*
        Of a knave child this night.
UXOR: Now well is me day bright,
340   That ever was I bred.

        This is a good gise°   and a far cast;   *way*
        Yet a woman avise   helps at the last.
        I wote° never who spies,   agane° go thou fast.   *know / back*
MAK: But I come or they rise, else blows a cold blast!
345   I will go sleep.
[*Mak returns to the Shepherds and lies down.*]
        Yet sleeps all this meneye,°   *household*
        And I shall go stalk privily
        As it had never been I
        That carried there sheep.

1. Affectionate nickname for "Gill."
2. Then I may have the worse, for there are such a pack of them.

I PASTOR: *Resurrex a mortruis!*[3]   Have hold my hand.
   Iudas carnas dominus![4]   I may not well stand:
   My foot sleeps, by Jesus,   and I water fastand.[5]
   I thought that we had laid us   full near England.

II PASTOR: Ah ye!
355 Lord, what I have slept well;
   As fresh as an eel,
   As light I me feel
   As leaf on a tree.

III PASTOR: Benste° be here in!   So my heart quakes,   *a blessing*
360 My heart is out of skin,°   what so it makes.   *(body)*
   Who makes all this din?   So my brows blakes°   *darkens*
   To the door will I win.   Hark, fellows, wakes!
   We were four:
   See ye awre° of Mak now?   *anywhere*

I PASTOR: We were up or thou.

II PASTOR: Man, I give God a vow,
   Yet yede° he nawre.°   *went / nowhere*

III PASTOR: Me thought he was lapt,°   in a wolf skin.   *clothed*

I PASTOR: So are many hapt°   now namely within.   *covered*

II PASTOR: When we had long napped,   me thought with a gyn°   *trap*
   A fat sheep he trapped,   but he made no din.

III PASTOR: Be still:
   Thy dream makes thee woode:°   *mad*
   It is but phantom, by the roode.°   *cross*

I PASTOR: Now God turn all to good,
   If it be his will.

II PASTOR: Rise, Mak, for shame!   Thou lies right long.

MAK: Now Christ's holy name   be us among!
   What is this? For Saint Jame,   I may not well gang!
380 I trow I be the same.   Ah, my neck has lain wrong
   Enough.
   Mekill,° thanks syn° yister even,   *many / since*
   Now, by Saint Steven,
   I was flayd° with a sweven,°   *frightened / dream*
385 My heart out of slough.°   *skin*

   I thought Gill began to croak   and travail° full sad,   *struggle*
   Welner° at the first cock,   of a young lad   *nearly*
   For to mend our flock.   Then be I never glad;
   I have tow° on my rock°   more then ever I had.   *flax / distaff*
390 Ah, my head!
   A house full of young tharms;°   *children*
   The devil knock out their harns!°   *brains*

---

3. Corruption from the Latin Bible of "He rose from the dead."

4. A corruption into Latin gibberish, "Judas lord of the flesh."

5. Stagger from lack of food.

Woe is him has many barns,
And thereto little bread!

395   I must go home, by your leave,   to Gill, as I thought.
I pray you looke,° my sleeve   that I steal nought: *inspect*
I am loath you to grieve,   or from you take ought.
III PASTOR: Go forth, ill might thou chefe!° Now would I we sought,   *fare*
This morn,
400   That we had all our store.
I PASTOR: But I will go before;
Let us meet.
II PASTOR: Whore?
III PASTOR: At the crooked thorn.
     [*The Shepherds leave. Mak knocks at his door.*]
MAK: Undo this door! Who is here?   How long shall I stand?
UXOR EIUS: Who makes such a bere?°   Now walk in the wenyand.[6]   *noise*
MAK: Ah Gill, what cheer?   It is I, Mak, your husband.
UXOR: Then may we be here   the devil in a band,
Sir Gyle:[7]
Lo, he comes with a lote°   *noise*
410   As he were holden° in the throat.   *held*
I may not sit at my note,°   *work*
A hand-lang° while.   *little*

MAK: Will ye hear what fare she makes   to get her a glose?[8]
And does nought but lakes°   and claws her toes.   *plays*
UXOR: Why, who wanders, who wakes?   Who commes, who goes?
Who brews, who bakes?   What makes me thus hose?°   *hoarse*
And than,
It is rewthe° to behold,   *pitiful*
Now in hot, now in cold,
420   Full woeful is the household
That wants a woman.
But what end has thou made   with the herds, Mak?
MAK: The last word that thay said   when I turned my back,
They would look that they had   their sheep, all the pack.
425   I hope[9] they will not be well paid   when they their sheep lack,
Perde!
But how so the game goes,
To me they will suppose,
And make a foul noise,
430   And cry out upon me.

But thou must do as thou hight.°   *said*
UXOR: I accord me there till.
I shall swaddle him right   in my cradle;
If it were a greater sleight,°   yet could I help till.   *trick*
I will lyg down straight.   Come hap me.

---

6. Waning hour, unlucky time.   8. Make up an excuse.
7. Mister Deceiver (the Devil).   9. Expect.

MAK: I will.

UXOR: Behind!
       Come Coll[1] and his maroo,°   *mate*
       They will nyp° us full naroo.°   *pinch / hard*

MAK: But I may cry out "Haroo!"
       The sheep if they find.

UXOR: Harken ay when they call;   they will come onone.°   *soon*
       Come and make ready all   and sing by thine one;
       Sing "lullay" thou shall,   for I must groan,
       And cry out by the wall   on Mary and John,
       For sore.
445   Sing "lullay" on fast
       When thou hears at the last;
       And but I play a false cast,°   *trick*
       Trust me no more.

       [*At the crooked thorn.*]

III PASTOR: Ah, Coll, good morn.   Why sleeps thou not?

I PASTOR: Alas, that ever was I born!   We have a foul blot.
       A fat wether° have we lorne.°   *ram / lost*

III PASTOR: Mary, God's forbot!

II PASTOR: Who should do us that scorn?°   That were a foul spot.   *harm*

I PASTOR: Some shrewe.°   *villain*
       I have sought with my dogs
455   All Horbury[2] shrogs,°   *hedges*
       And of xv° hogs   *fifteen*
       Found I but one ewe.

III PASTOR: Now trow me, if ye will,   by Saint Thomas of Kent,
       Either Mak or Gill   was at that assent.°   *affair*

I PASTOR: Peace, man, be still!   I saw when he went;
       Thou slanders him ill;   thou ought to repent,
       Good speed.

II PASTOR: Now as ever might I the,°   *thrive*
       If I should even here die,
465   I would say it were he,
       That did that same deed.

III PASTOR: Go we thither, I read,   and run on our feet.
       Shall I never eat bread   the sothe to I wytt.[3]

I PASTOR: Nor drink in my head   with him till I meet.

II PASTOR: I will rest in no stead   till that I him greet,
       My brother.
       One I will hight:°   *promise*
       Till I see him in sight
       Shall I never sleep one night
475   There I do another.

---

1. The First Shepherd.   3. Until I know the truth.
2. A town south of Wakefield.

[*They approach Mak's house.*]

III PASTOR: Will ye hear how they hack?[4]   Our sire list croon.
I PASTOR: Heard I never none crack   so clear out of toon;
    Call on him.
II PASTOR: Mak,   undo your door soon.
MAK: Who is that spake,   as it were noon
480 On loft?
    Who is that, I say?
III PASTOR: Good felows, were it day.
MAK: As far as ye may,
    Good, speaks soft,

485 Over a sick woman's head   that is at malaise;
    I had lever° be dead   or she had any disease.   *rather*
UXOR: Go to another stead!   I may not well qweasse.°   *breathe*
    Each foot that ye tread   goes through my nese,°   *nose*
    So hee!°   *loudly*
I PASTOR: Tell us, Mak, if ye may,
    How fare ye, I say?
MAK: But are ye in this town to-day?
    Now how fare ye?

    Ye have run in the mire,   and are wet yit:
495 I shall make you a fire,   if you will sit.
    A nurse would I hire.   Think ye on yit,
    Well quit is my hire[5]—   my dream this is it—
    A season.
    I have barns, if ye knew,
500 Well mo then enewe,
    But we must drink as we brew,
    And that is but reason.
    I would ye dined or ye yode.[6]   Me think that ye sweat.
II PASTOR: Nay, neither mends our mood   drink nor meat.
MAK: Why, sir, ails you ought but good?
III PASTOR: Yea, our sheep that we get,
    Are stolen as they yode.   Our loss is great.
MAK: Sirs, drinks!
    Had I been there,
    Some should have bought it full sore.
I PASTOR: Mary, some men trowes° that ye wore,   *believes*
    And that us forthinks.°   *disturbs*

II PASTOR: Mak, some men trowys   that it should be ye.
III PASTOR: Either ye or your spouse,   so say we.
MAK: Now if ye have suspowse°   to Gill or to me,   *suspicion*
515 Come and ripe° our house,   and then may ye see   *search*
    Who had her;
    If I any sheep fot,°   *took*

4. Sing (badly).   6. I would like you to eat before you go.
5. My wages are paid; i.e., his dream has been fulfilled.

Either cow or stot;°   heifer
And Gill, my wife, rose not
520   Here sin she laid her.

As I am true and leal,°   to God here I pray,   loyal
That this be the first meal   that I shall eat this day.
I PASTOR: Mak, as have I ceyll,°   advise thee, I say;   heaven
He learned timely to steal   that could not say nay.
UXOR: I swelt!°   die
Out, thieves, from my wonys!°   home
Ye come to rob us for the nonys.°   for the purpose
MAK: Here ye not how she groans?
Your hearts should melt.

UXOR: Out, thieves, from my barn!   Nigh him not thor!°   there
MAK: Wist ye how she had farn,°   your hearts would be sore.   fared
Ye do wrong, I you warn,   that thus comes before
To a woman that has farn—   but I say no more.
UXOR: Ah, my medill!°   middle
535   I pray to God so mild,
If ever I you beguiled,
That I eat this child
That lies in this cradle.

MAK: Peace, woman, for God's pain,   and cry not so:
540   Thou spills thy brain,   and makes me full woe.
II PASTOR: I trow our sheep be slain.   What find ye two?
III PASTOR: All work we in vain;   as well may we go.
But hatters,°   (an oath)
I can find no flesh,
545   Hard nor nesh,°   soft
Salt nor fresh,
But two tome° platters.   empty
Whik° cattle but this,   tame nor wild,   living
None, as have I bliss,   as loud as he smiled.°   smelled
UXOR: No, so God me bliss,   and give me joy of my child!
I PASTOR: We have marked amiss;   I hold us beguiled.
II PASTOR: Sir, don,°   it is done
Sir, our Lady him save,
Is your child a knave?[7]
MAK: Any lord might him have
This child to his son.

When he wakens he kips,°   that joy is to see.   snatches
III PASTOR: In good time to his hips,   and in cele.°   heaven
But who was his gossips°,   so soon rede?°   godparents / ready
MAK: So fair fall their lips!
I PASTOR: Hark now, a le.°   lie
MAK: So God them thank,

---

7. Boy-child (of the serving-class).

Parkin, and Gibon Waller I say,
And gentle John Horne,[8] in good fay,
He made all the garray,°   noise
565   With the great shank.°   leg

II PASTOR: Mak, friends will we be,   for we are all one.
MAK: We? Now I hold for me,   for mends° get I none.   profit
Farewell all three!   All glad were ye gone.
    [*The Shepherds depart.*]
III PASTOR: Fair words may there be,   but love is there none
570   This year.
I PASTOR: Gave ye the child anything?
II PASTOR: I trow not one farthing.
III PASTOR: Fast again will I fling,°   hurry
Abide ye me there.
    [*Returns to the house.*]

575   Mak, take it to no grief   if I come to thy barn.°   baby
MAK: Nay, thou does me great reproof,   and foul has thou farn.°   done
III PASTOR: The child will it not grief,   that little daystarn.[9]
Mak, with your leaf,   let me give your barn
But vi° pence.   six
MAK: Nay, do way: he sleeps.
III PASTOR: Me think he peeps.
MAK: When he wakens he weeps.
I pray you go hence.
    [*The other Shepherds return.*]

III PASTOR: Give me leave him to kiss,   and lift up the clout.°   cloth
585   What the devil is this?   He has a long snout.
I PASTOR: He is marked amiss.   We wat° ill about.   watch
II PASTOR: Ill-spun weft, iwys,   ay comes foul out.[1]
Aye, so!
He is like to our sheep!
III PASTOR: How, Gyb,° may I peep?   the Second Shepherd
I PASTOR: I trow kind° will creep   Nature
Where it may not go.°   walk

II PASTOR: This was a quaint gawde,°   and a far cast.   clever trick
It was a high fraud.
III PASTOR: Yea, sirs, was't.
595   Let bren° this bawd,   and bind her fast.   burn
A false skawd°   hang at the last;   scold
So shall thou.
Will ye see how they swaddle
His four feet in the middle?
600   Saw I never in a cradle
A horned lad[2] or° now.   before

8. Parkin, Gibon Waller, and John Horne are the names
of the shepherds in the First Play of the Shepherds, possibly referring to actual townspeople.
9. Little day star; a term also used for the Christ child

later in the play, indicating a parallel with Mak's baby.
1. Badly spun thread always makes poor cloth.
2. A horned child (devil).

MAK: Peace bid I. What,   let be youre fare;

    I am he that him gat,°   and yond woman him bare.   *begat*

I PASTOR: What devil shall he hat,°   Mak? Lo, God, Mak's heir. *be called*

II PASTOR: Let be all that.   Now God give him care,

    I sagh.°   *saw*

UXOR: A pretty child is he

    As sits on a woman's knee;

    A dillydown,° perde,   *darling*

610   To gar° a man laugh.   *make*

III PASTOR: I know him by the earn mark: that is a good token.

MAK: I tell you, sirs, hark!—   his nose was broken.

    Sithen° told me a clerk   that he was forspoken.° *since / bewitched*

I PASTOR: This is a false work;   I would fain be wroken.° *avenged*

615   Get wepyn.

UXOR: He was taken with° an elf;   *by*

    I saw it myself.

    When the clock struck twelve

    Was he forshapen.°   *changed*

II PASTOR: Ye two are well feft°   sam° in a stead. *endowed / together*

III PASTOR: Sin they maintain their theft,   let do them to dead.

MAK: If I trespass eft,°   gird° off my head.   *again / cut*

    With you will I be left.

I PASTOR: Sirs, do my read.°   *advice*

    For this trespass,

625   We will neither ban ne flite,°   *curse nor quarrel*

    Fight nor chite,°   *chide*

    But have done as tite,°   *quickly*

    And cast him in canvas.

    [They toss Mak in a sheet.]

    Lord, what I am sore, in point for to brist.

630   In faith I may no more; therefore will I rist.

II PASTOR: As a sheep of vii score[3]   he weighed in my fist.

    For to sleep ay-whore°   me think that I list. *anywhere*

III PASTOR: Now I pray you,

    Lyg down on this green.

I PASTOR: On these thieves yet I mene.°   *speak*

III PASTOR: Whereto should ye tene?°   *be angry*

    Do as I say you.

    [The Shepherds sleep.]

    Angelus cantat "Gloria in excelsis"; postea dicat [4]

ANGELUS: Rise, herd-men heynd!   For now is he born

    That shall take fro the fiend   that Adam had lorn;° *lost*

640   That warloo° to shend,°   this night is he born. *devil / destroy*

    God is made your friend   now at this morn.

    He behestys°   *orders*

---

3. Seven score pounds (140 lbs).   *afterward says.*

4. The Angel sings "Glory to God in the highest," and

At Bedlem° go see: *Bethlehem*
There lies that fre°   *lord*

645   In a crib full poorly,
        Betwyx two bestys.

I PASTOR: This was a quaint steven°   that ever yet I heard.   *voice*
       It is a marvel to neven,°   thus to be scared.   *mention*
II PASTOR: Of God's son of heaven   he spake upward.°   *on high*
650   All the wood on a leven   me thought that he gard
       Appear.[5]
III PASTOR: He spake of a barn
       In Bedlem, I you warn.
I PASTOR: That betokens yond starn.°   *star*
655   Let us seek him there.

II PASTOR: Say, what was his song?   Heard ye not how he cracked° it?   *roared*
       Three breves to a long.[6]
III PASTOR: Yea, marry, he hakt° it.   *sang*
       Was no crochett° wrong,   nor nothing that lacked it.   *note*
I PASTOR: For to sing us among   right as he knacked° it,   *sang*
660   I can.
II PASTOR: Let se how ye croon.
       Can ye bark at the moon?
III PASTOR: Hold your tongues, have done!
I PASTOR: Hark after than.
     [*Sings.*]

II PASTOR: To Bedlem he bade   that we should gang:
       I am full fard°   that we tarry too lang.   *afraid*
III PASTOR: Be merry and not sad;   of mirth is our sang;
       Ever-lasting glad   to mede° may we fang,°   *reward / get*
       Without noise.
I PASTOR: Hie we thither for-thy;°   *therefore*
       If we be wet and weary,
       To that child and that lady,
       We have it not to lose.

II PASTOR: We find by the prophecy—   let be your din—
675   Of David and Isay,[7]   and mo than I min,
       They prophesied by clergy   that in a virgin
       Should he light and lie,   to sloken° our sin   *remove*
       And slake it,
       Our kynd° from woe;   *humankind*
680   For Isay said so,
       Ecce virgo
       Concipiet[8] a child that is naked.

III PASTOR: Full glad may we be,   and abide that day
       That lovely to see,   that all mights may.
685   Lord, well were me,   for once and for ay,

---

5. I thought he lit up the woods like lightning.
6. Three short notes to one long.

7. The prophet Isaiah.
8. Behold, a virgin conceives (Isaiah 7.14).

Might I kneel on my knee,   some word for to say
To that child.
But the angel said
In a crib was he laid;
690   He was poorly arrayed,
Both mener° and milde.   *poor*

I PASTOR: Patriarchs that has been,   and prophets beforn,
They desired to have seen   this child that is born.
They are gone full clean,°   that have they lorn.°   *entirely / lost*
695   We shall see him, I ween,   or it be morn,
To token.°   *as proof*
When I see him and feel,
Then wot I full weel
It is true as steel
700   That prophets have spoken:

To so poore as we are   that he would appear,
First find, and declare   by his messenger.

II PASTOR: Go we now, let us fare; the place is us near.

III PASTOR: I am ready and yare;° go we in fere°   *prepared / together*
705   To that bright.
Lord, if thy wills be,
We are lewde° all three,   *unschooled*
Thou grant us somkyns glee°   *some kind of joy*
To comfort thy wight.°   *creature*
[They enter the stable.]

I PASTOR: Hail, comely and clean! Hail, young child!
Hail, maker, as I mean, of a maiden so mild!
Thou has waryd,° I ween, the warlo° so wild;   *cursed / devil*
The false gyler° of teen° now goes he beguiled. *deceiver / anger*
Lo, he merries!
715   Lo, he laughs, my sweeting!
A well fair meeting!
I have holden my heting;°   *kept my promise*
Have a bob° of cherries.   *bunch*

II PASTOR: Hail, sovereign saviour, for thou has us sought!
720   Hail, freely food and flour,[9] that all thing has wrought!
Hail, full of favour, that made all of nought!
Hail! I kneel and I cower. A bird have I brought
To my barn.
Hail, little tyne mop!°   *tiny baby*
725   Of our creed thou art crop:°   *fruit, fulfillment*
I would drink on thy cop,°   *cup*
Little day starn.°   *star*

III PASTOR: Hail, darling dear, full of Godhede!
I pray thee be near when that I have need.
730   Hail, sweet is thy cheer! My heart would bleed

9. Noble child and flower.

To see thee sit here   in so poor weed,°   *clothing*
With no pennies.
Hail, put forth thy dall!°   *hand*
I bring thee but a ball:
735   Have and play thee with all,
And go to the tenys.°   *tennis*

MARIA: The Father of heaven,   God omnipotent,
That set all on seven,[1]   his son has he sent.
My name could he neven,°   and light or he went.   *name*
740   I conceived him full even   through might, as he ment,°   *intended*
And now is he born.
He keep you from woe!
I shall pray him so.
Tell forth as ye go,
745   And myn° on this morn.   *remember*

I PASTOR: Farewell, lady,   so fair to behold,
With thy child on thy knee.
II PASTOR: But he lies full cold.
Lord, well is me!   Now we go, thou behold.
III PASTOR: Forsooth already   it seems to be told
750   Full oft.
I PASTOR: What grace we have fun!°   *found*
II PASTOR: Come forth: now are we won.
III PASTOR: To sing are we bun:°   *bound*
Let take on loft![2]

[*They go out singing.*]

Explicit pagina Pastorum.[3]

Middle English Lyrics

Although many Middle English lyrics have a beguilingly fresh and unselfconscious tone, they
owe much to learned and sophisticated continental sources—the medieval Latin lyrics of the
"Goliard poets" and the Provençal and French lyrics of the Troubadours and Trouvères. Most
authors were clerics, aware of the similarities between earthly and divine love, and fond of
punning in Latin or English.

The anonymity of the Middle English lyrics prevents us from seeing them as part of a single poet's *oeuvre*, as we can, for instance, with the poems of Chaucer, Dunbar, and Dafydd ap
Gwilym. Rather, we must rely on more general contexts, such as genre, to establish relationships among poems. One of the most popular genres among the secular lyrics was the *reverdie*, a
poem celebrating the return of spring. The early thirteenth-century *Cuckoo Song* ("Sumer is
icumen in") joyfully invokes the bird's song, and revels in the blossoming of the countryside
and the calls of the animals to their young. More typical examples of the *reverdie* are *Alisoun*

1. Made everything in seven days.   3. The play of the Shepherds is finished.
2. Let us sing on high.

and *Spring*, whose male speakers ruefully contrast the burgeoning of nature with the stinginess of their beloveds; in *Spring*, flowers bloom, birds sing, animals mate—but one woman remains unmoved. In the genre of the love complaint, *My Lefe Is Faren in a Lond* expresses erotic loss and frustration with great succinctness.

Frustration was not the only attitude in Middle English love lyrics, however. Clerical misogyny is expressed in *Abuse of Women*, which ostensibly praises women by absolving them of the vices—gossip, infidelity, shrewishness—typically attributed to them in satires against women; yet the refrain first praises women as the best of creatures but then undercuts this claim in Latin, which few women would have been able to understand.

Although most of the Middle English lyrics are in the male voice, there are a few "women's songs"—most likely written by men—which convey female experience. Occasionally these songs are invitations (for instance, the enigmatic *Irish Dancer*), but more often they are laments by an abandoned, and often pregnant, woman.

The majority of Middle English lyrics were not secular but religious. Songs in praise of the Virgin Mary or Christ, however, employ the same erotic language as the secular lyrics, often in conjunction with typological figures linking events in the Old Testament to those in the New. In *Adam Lay Ibounden*, for instance, the poet follows a statement of the "fortunate Fall"—that Adam's sin was necessary to permit Christ's redemption—with a courtly compliment to the Virgin Mary. Similarly, *I Sing of a Maiden* draws on the typological significance of Gideon's fleece in Judges 6 (the soaking of the fleece by dew figuring Mary's impregnation by the Holy Spirit) while also employing the courtly imagery of a poet "singing of a maiden" who "chooses" Christ as her son, as if he were a lover.

Occasionally the Middle English religious lyric uses secular motifs and genres in a way that approaches parody. For instance, the second stanza of the Nativity poem *Mary Is with Child* resembles a pregnancy lament by a young girl. Mary, however, explains that her condition will be a source of joy rather than shame, when she will sing a lullaby to her "darling." This Middle English poet, far from blaspheming, was trying to humanize the mystery of the Nativity and relate it to daily life.

Other religious poems celebrate Christ. The poems to Christ, in their tenderness and immediacy, resemble those to Mary. Poets used erotic language in poems to Christ as well as those to Mary, as in *Jesus, My Sweet Lover*.

The Cuckoo Song

Sumer is icumen in,°		*spring has come in*
Lhude° sing, cuccu!°		*loudly / cuckoo*
Groweth sed° and bloweth° med°		*seed / blooms / meadow*
And springth° the wude° nu.°		*grows / forest / now*
5	Sing, cuccu!	
	Awe° bleteth after lomb,	*ewe*
	Lhouth° after calve° cu,°	*lows / calf / cow*
	Bulluc sterteth,° bucke ferteth.°	*leaps / farts*
	Murie° sing, cuccu!	*merrily*
10	Cuccu, cuccu,	
	Wel singes thu, cuccu.	
	Ne swik° thu naver° nu!	*cease / never*
	Sing cuccu nu, sing cuccu!	
	Sing cuccu, sing cuccu nu!	

This page contains the words and music to one of the earliest and best loved of Middle English lyrics, *The Cuckoo Song* ("Sumer is icumen in"). The lyric is a *reverdie*, or spring song, but its joyful description of nature's rebirth is given a more sober allegorical interpretation by the interlinear Latin gloss, apparently to be sung to the same tune. The gloss parallels the lyric's celebration of the reawakening landscape with an account of the "heavenly farmer" (*celicus agricola*) whom "rot on the vine" (*vitis vicio*) leads to sacrifice his Son. The fact that the manuscript was copied at a monastery reminds us that this song, like much other early English secular poetry, survives only because it was seen to have religious relevance.

Spring

	Lenten° is come with love to toune,°	*spring / town*
	With blosmen° and with briddes° roune,°	*flowers / birds' / song*
	That all this blisse bringeth.	
	Dayeseyes° in this° dales,	*daisies / these*
5	Notes swere of nightegales—	
	Uch° foul° song singeth.	*each / bird*
	The threstelcok him threteth o;[1]	
	Away is here° winter wo their	*their*
	When woderove° springeth.°	*woodruff / grows*
10	This foules° singeth ferly fele,°	*birds / wonderfully much*
	And wliteth on here winne wele,[2]	
	That all the wode ringeth.	
	The rose raileth hire rode,°	*puts on her rosy hue*
	The leves on the lighte° wode	*bright*

---

1. The song thrush contends always.   2. And chirp their wealth of joys.

15	Waxen° all with wille.°	grow / pleasure
	The mone mandeth hire bleo,³	
	The lilie is lossom° to seo,°	lovely / see
	The fenil° and the fille.°	fennel / chervil
	Wowes° this° wilde drakes;	woo / these
20	Miles murgeth here makes,⁴	
	Ase strem that striketh° stille.°	flows / softly
	Mody meneth, so doth mo;⁵	
	Ichot° ich° am one of tho,°	I know / I / those
	For love that likes° ille.	pleases
25	The mone mandeth hire light;	
	So doth the semly,° sonne bright,	lovely
	When briddes singeth breme.°	loudly
	Deawes donketh the dounes;⁶	
	Deores with here derne rounes,⁷	
30	Domes for to deme;⁸	
	Wormes woweth under cloude,°	the soil
	Wimmen waxeth° wounder° proude,	become / wondrously
	So well it wol hem° seme.°	to them / appear
	If me shall wonte wille of on,⁹	
35	This wunne weole° I wole forgon	wealth of joys
	And wight° in wode be fleme.°	quickly / exile

Alisoun

	Bitwene Mersh° and Averil°	March / April
	When spray° biginneth to springe,°	twig / grow
	The lutel° fowl° hath hire° will	little / bird / her
	On° hire lud° to singe.	in / language
5	Ich° libbe° in love-longinge	I / live
	For semlokest° of alle thinge:	fairest
	He° may me blisse bringe;	she
	Ich° am in hire baundoun.°	I / power
	An hendy hap ich habbe ihent!¹	
10	Ichot° from hevene it is me sent;	I know
	From alle wimmen my love is lent,°	taken away
	And light° on Alisoun.²	settled
	On hew° hire her° is fair inogh,	color / hair
	Hire browe browne, hire eye blake;	
15	With lossum chere he on me logh,³	
	With middel° small and well imake.°	waist / made
	Bote° he me wolle° to hire take	unless / will
	For to ben hire° owen° make,°	her / own / mate

---

3. The moon sends forth her light.
4. Beasts gladden their mates.
5. The high-spirited man mourns, so do others.
6. Dew moistens the downs (hills).
7. Animals with their secret whispers.
8. Speak their opinions.

9. If I shall lack the pleasure of one.
1. A fair destiny I have received.
2. Alison is a stock name for a country woman, shared by the wife in Chaucer's *Miller's Tale* and by his Wife of Bath.
3. With lovely manner she laughed at me.

Longe to liven ichulle° forsake,°   *I will / refuse*
20   And feye° fallen adoun.   *doomed*
  An hendy hap ich habbe ihent!
  Ichot from hevene it is me sent;
  From alle wimmen my love is lent,
  And light on Alisoun.

25   Nightes° when I wende° and wake—   *at night / turn*
Forthy min wonges waxeth won[4]—
Levedy,° all for thine sake   *lady*
Longinge is ilent° me on.   *come*
In world nis non so witer° mon   *wise*
30   That all hire° bounte° telle con: *her / excellence*
Hire swire° is whittore° then the swon,   *neck / whiter*
And feirest may° in toune.   *maiden*
  An hendy hap ich habbe ihent!
  Ichot from hevene it is me sent;
35   *From alle wimmen my love is lent,*
  And light on Alisoun.

Ich am for wowing all forwake,[5]
Wery so water in wore[6]
Lest eny reve° me my make°   *steal / mate*
40   Ich habbe iyerned yore.[7]
Betere is tholien while sore[8]
Then mournen evermore.
Geynest° under gore,°   *kindest / petticoat*
Herkne to my roun!°   *song*
45   *An hendy hap ich habbe ihent!*
  Ichot from hevene it is me sent;
  From alle wimmen my love is lent,
  And light on Alisoun.

My Lefe Is Faren in a Lond[1]

My lefe is faren in a lond[2]—
Alas! why is she so?
And I am so sore bound
I may nat com her to.
She hath my hert in hold,°   *imprisoned*
Where-ever she ride or go,
With trew love a thousandfold.

Abuse of Women

Of all creatures women be best:
Cuius contrarium verum est.[1]

In every place ye may well see
That women be trewe as tirtil° on tree,   turtledove
Not liberal° in langage, but ever in secree,°   licentious / secrecy
And gret joye amonge them is for to be.

    Of all creatures women be best:
    Cuius contrarium verum est.

The stedfastnes of women will never be don,
So jentil, so curtes they be everychon,[2]
Meke as a lambe, still as a stone,
Croked° nor crabbed find ye none!   perverse

    Of all creatures women be best:
    Cuius contrarium verum est.

Men be more cumbers° a thousand fold,   troublesome
And I mervail how they dare be so bold
Against women for to hold,
Seeing them so pacient, softe, and cold.

    Of all creatures women be best:
    Cuius contrarium verum est.

For tell a woman all your counsaile,
And she can kepe it wonderly well;
She had lever go quik° to hell,   alive
Than to her neighbour she wold it tell!

    Of all creatures women be best:
    Cuius contrarium verum est.

For by women men be reconsiled,
For by women was never man begiled,
For they be of the condicion of curtes Grisell,[3]
For they be so meke and milde.

    Of all creatures women be best:
    Cuius contrarium verum est.

Now say well by° women or elles be still,   about
For they never displesed man by ther will;
To be angry or wroth they can° no skill,   have
For I dare say they think non ill.

    Of all creatures women be best:
    Cuius contrarium verum est.

---

1. Latin for "The opposite of this is true."
2. So well-bred, so courteous is each one.
3. Griselda, the long-suffering wife of Chaucer's *Clerk's* *Tale*; the tale ends with the observation that there are no more Griseldas left.

Trow° ye that women list° to smater,°   *think / like / chatter*
40   Or against ther husbondes for to clater?
Nay, they had lever° fast bred and water,   *rather*
Then for to dele in suche a mater.

     Of all creatures women be best:
     Cuius contrarium verum est.

45   Though all the paciens in the world were drownd,
And non were lefte here on the ground,
Again in a woman it might be found,
Suche vertu in them dothe abound!

     Of all creatures women be best:
50   *Cuius contrarium verum est.*

To the tavern they will not go,
Nor to the alehous never the mo,°   *more*
For, God wot,° ther hartes wold be wo, knows   *knows*
To spende ther husbondes money so.

55   *Of all creatures women be best:*
     Cuius contrarium verum est.

If here were a woman or a maid,
That list for to go freshely arayed,
Or with fine kirchers° to go displayed,   *kerchiefs*
60   Ye wold say, "They be proude": it is ill said.

     Of all creatures women be best:
     Cuius contrarium verum est.

The Irish Dancer

Ich° am of Irlaunde,   *I*
And of the holy londe
Of Irlande.
Gode° sire, pray ich thee,   *good*
For of sainte° charitee,°   *holy / charity*
Come and daunce wit me
In Irlaunde.

Adam Lay Ibounden

Adam lay ibounden,°   *bound*
Bounden in a bond;
Foure thousand winter
Thowt° he not too long.   *thought*
5   And all was for an appil,
An appil that he took,
As clerkes finden wreten
In here° book.   *their*

Ne° hadde the appil take° ben,   *if not / taken*
10   The appil taken ben,

Ne° hadde never our lady   *not*
A ben hevene quen.[1]
Blissed be the time
That appil take was!
15   Therfore we moun° singen   *may*
"*Deo gracias!*"°   *Thanks be to God!*

I Sing of a Maiden

I sing of a maiden
That is makeles,[1]
King of alle kinges
To° here° sone she ches.°   *for / her / chose*

5   He cam also° stille°   *as / quietly*
Ther° his moder was   *where*
As dew in Aprille
That falleth on the gras.

He cam also stille
10   To his moderes bowr
As dew in Aprille
That falleth on the flour.

He cam also stille
Ther his moder lay
15   As dew in Aprille
That falleth on the spray.°   *twigs*

Moder and maiden
Was never non but she:
Well may swich° a lady   *such*
20   Godes moder be.

Mary Is with Child

Nowel! nowel! nowel!
Sing we with mirth!
Christ is come well
With us to dwell,
5   *By his most noble birth.*

Under a tree
In sporting me,
Alone by a wod-side,°   *side of a wood*
I hard° a maid[1]   *heard*
10   That swetly said,
"I am with child this tide.°   *time*

"Graciously
Conceived have I

---

1. Have been heaven's queen.
1. Spotless, matchless, and mateless.
1. A poem that opens with the speaker in the countryside
overhearing a woman's lament raises expectations that we will hear a *chanson d'aventure*, with erotic connotations.

The Son of God so swete:
15 His gracious will
I put me till,
As moder him to kepe.

"Both night and day
I will him pray,
20 And her° his lawes taught,   hear
And every dell°   in every way
His trewe gospell
In his apostles fraught.°   carried

"This ghostly° case°   spiritual / act
25 Doth me embrace,
Without despite or mock;
With my derling,
'Lullay,'° to sing,   lullabye
And lovely him to rock.

30 "Without distress
In grete lightness
I am both night and day.
This hevenly fod°   child
In his childhod
35 Shall daily with me play.

"Soone must I sing
With rejoicing,
For the time is all ronne°   run out
That I shall child,°   give birth to
40 All undefil'd,
The King of Heven's Sonne."

Jesus, My Sweet Lover

Jesu Christ, my lemmon° swete,   lover
That diyedest on the Rode° Tree,   Cross
With all my might I thee beseche,
For thy woundes two and three,
That also° faste mot° thy love   as / may
Into mine herte fitched° be   fixed
As was the spere into thine herte,
Whon thou soffredest deth for me.

Dafydd ap Gwilym

Widely regarded as the greatest Welsh poet, Dafydd ap Gwilym flourished in the fourteenth
century, during a period of relative peace between two failed rebellions—that of Llywelyn, the
last native prince of Wales, in 1282, and that of Owain Glyn Dwr (Owen Glendower), in

1400. A member of an upper-class family whose ancestors had served the English king, he wrote for a sophisticated audience of poets and patrons.

Dafydd drew inspiration from both continental and Welsh poetry but not, significantly, from English. (Influence, if any, went the other way, for the Middle English Harley lyrics, composed near the Welsh border, may owe their intricate rhyme scheme and ornamental alliteration to Welsh poetry; see *Spring* and *Alisoun*, pages 372–74). Among continental poets, the Roman Ovid is the greatest influence, whether directly or through twelfth-century Latin adaptations. He is the only foreign poet whom Dafydd mentions by name (*One Saving Place*, line 39). Dafydd is also indebted to medieval French and Provençal lyric genres—the *aubade* (dawn song), and the *reverdie* (spring song)—as well as to the *fabliau*.

Much of Dafydd's charm comes from his undercutting and transforming inherited poetic conventions through his personal revelations. His most endearing device, the self-deprecating persona, has been compared to that of his younger contemporary, Geoffrey Chaucer. There is an important difference, however, for while Chaucer in early love poems presents himself as a failed lover, Dafydd often boasts of his success. Although he gives comic accounts of romantic failures, these are as often due to external obstacles as to his own inadequacy. In fact, Dafydd's persona is much more akin to Ovid's than to Chaucer's, with *The Hateful Husband* echoing the exasperated and scheming lover of *Amores* 1.4 and 1.6. In *The Ruin*, Dafydd gives an erotic twist to the ascetic Christian motif of the impermanence of worldly pleasures (as in the Old English *Wanderer*, page 130) by recalling that he once made love in a cottage that is now abandoned. He concludes his complaint *The Winter* with the observation that he would not venture out in such snowy weather for the sake of any girl.

Dafydd's poetry owes an equal debt to the rich poetic tradition of Wales. He shows familiarity with characters from the Arthurian tradition, which was originally Celtic although transformed by French adaptations by the time it reached him. In the poems included here, he often emphasizes the local Welsh setting. In *One Saving Place*, for instance, he lists all the locales where he sought his beloved Morvith, or she refused him—places with names like Meirch, Eleirch, Rhiw, and Cwcwll hollow. In *The Winter*, it is specifically in north Wales that he is assailed by snow.

Dafydd's work is also distinguished by the poetic techniques of Welsh poetry, which are extraordinarily complex. His *cywyddau* (lyric poems) are written in the traditional lines of seven syllables, which rhyme in couplets, with the rhyming syllables alternately stressed and unstressed. He applies further ornamentation with a technique called *cynghanned*—internal alliteration or rhyme, which he sometimes extends over many lines. Although such an intricate style is impossible to capture in English, Rolfe Humphries has tried to approximate it in the translations given here. Easier to reproduce are Daffyd's *dyfalu*—strings of fanciful comparisons, such as the metaphors for snow used in *The Winter*:

> The snowflakes wander,
> A swarm of white bees.
> Over the woods
> A cold veil lies.
> A load of chalk
> Bows down the trees.
>
>   * * *
>
> Will someone tell me
> What angels lift
> Planks in the flour-loft
> Floor of heaven
> Shaking down dust?
> An angel's cloak
> Is cold quicksilver.

In extending the virtuoso techniques of the native tradition, Dafydd set the standard for Welsh poets for the next two centuries.

One Saving Place

What wooer ever walked through frost and snow,
Through rain and wind, as I in sorrow?
My two feet took me to a tryst in Meirch[1]
No luck; I swam and waded the Eleirch,
5   No golden loveliness, no glimpse of her;
Night or day, I came no nearer
Except in Bleddyn's arbors, where I sighed
When she refused me, as she did beside
Maesalga's murmuring water-tide.
10   I crossed the river, Bergul, and went on
Beyond its threatening voices; I have gone
Through the mountain-pass of Meibion,
Came to Camallt, dark in my despair,
For one vision of her golden hair.
15   All for nothing. I've looked down from Rhiw,
All for nothing but a valley view,
Kept on going, on my journey through
Cyfylfaen's gorge, with rock and boulder,
Where I had thought to ermine-cloak her shoulder.
20   Never; not here, there, thither, thence,
Could I ever find her presence.
Eagerly on summer days I'd go
Brushing my way through Cwcwll hollow,
Never stopped, continued, skirting
25   Gastell Gwrgan and its ring
Where the red-winged blackbirds sing,
Tramped across fields where goslings feed
Below the cat-tail and the reed.
I have limped my way, a weary hound,
30   In shadow of the walls that bound
Adail Heilyn's broken ground.
I have hidden, like a friar,
In Ifor's Court, among the choir,
Sought to seek my sweet one there,
35   But there was no sign of her.
On both sides of Nant-y-glo
There's no vale, no valley, no
Stick or stump where I failed to go,
Only Gwynn of the Mist for guide,
40   Without Ovid[2] at my side.

---

1. This and other Welsh place names are listed by Dafydd in his account of his search for his beloved, Morvith.

2. See introduction for Dafydd's indebtedness to the Roman love poet.

Gwenn-y-Talwrn!—there I found
My hand close on hers, on ground
Where no grass was ever green,
Where not even a shrub was seen,
45   There at last I made the bed
For my Morvith,[3] my moon-maid,
Underneath the dark leaf-cloak
Woven by saplings of an oak.
Bitter, if a man must move
50   On his journeys without love.
Bitter, if soul's pilgrimage
Must be like the body's rage,
Must go down the desolate road
Midway through the darkling wood.

The Hateful Husband

'Tis sorrow and pain,
'Tis endless chagrin
For Dafydd to gain
His dark-haired girl.
5   Her house is a jail,
Her turnkey a vile,
Sour, yellow-eyed, pale,
Odious churl.

She cannot go out
10   Unless he's about,
The blackguard, the lout,
The stingy boor.
The look in her eye
Of fondness for me—
15   God bless her bounty!—
He can't endure.

I know he hates play:
The greenwood in May,
The birds' roundelay
20   Are not for him.
The cuckoo, I know,
He'd never allow
To sing on his bough,
Light on his limb

25   The flash of the wing,
The swell of the song,
Harp-music playing

---

3. The lady most frequently mentioned in Dafydd's love poems, apparently married.

Draw his black looks.
The hounds in full cry,
30   A race-horse of bay,
He cannot enjoy
More than the pox.

My heart would be glad
At seeing him laid
35   All gray in his shroud;
How could I grieve?
Should he die this year,
I'd give him with cheer
Good oak for his bier,
40   Sods for his grave.

O starling, O swift,
Go soaring aloft,
Come down to the croft
By Dovekie's home.
45   This message give her,
Tell her I love her,
And I will have her,
All in good time.

The Winter

Across North Wales
The snowflakes wander,
A swarm of white bees.
Over the woods
5   A cold veil lies.
A load of chalk
Bows down the trees.

No undergrowth
Without its wool,
10   No field unsheeted;
No path is left
Through any field;
On every stump
White flour is milled.

15   Will someone tell me
What angels lift
Planks in the flour-loft
Floor of heaven
Shaking down dust?
20   An angel's cloak
Is cold quicksilver.

And here below
The big drifts blow,
Blow and billow
25   Across the heather
Like swollen bellies.
The frozen foam
Falls in fleeces.

Out of my house
30   I will not stir
For any girl
To have my coat
Look like a miller's
Or stuck with feathers
35   Of eider down.

What a great fall
Lies on my country!
A wide wall, stretching
One sea to the other,
40   Greater and graver
Than the sea's graveyard.
When will rain come?

The Ruin

Nothing but a hovel now
Between moorland and meadow,
Once the owners saw in you
A comely cottage, bright, new,
5   Now roof, rafters, ridge-pole, all
Broken down by a broken wall.

A day of delight was once there
For me, long ago, no care
When I had a glimpse of her
10   Fair in an ingle-corner.
Beside each other we lay
In the delight of that day.

Her forearm, snowflake-lovely,
Softly white, pillowing me,
15   proferred a pleasant pattern
For me to give in my turn,
And that was our blessing for
The new-cut lintel and door.

"Now the wild wind, wailing by,
20   Crashes with curse and with cry

Against my stones, a tempest
Born and bred in the East,
Or south ram-batterers break
The shelter that folk forsake."

25   Life is illusion and grief;
A tile whirls off, as a leaf
Or a lath goes sailing, high
In the keening of kite-kill cry.
Could it be, our couch once stood
30   Sturdily under that wood?

"Pillar and post, it would seem
Now you are less than a dream.
Are you that, or only the lost
Wreck of a riddle, rune-ghost?"

35   "Dafydd, the cross on their graves
Marks what little it saves,
Says, *They did well in their lives.*"

⊶ ⩵◆⩶ ⊷

William Dunbar

Of all the Makars, Dunbar is the greatest virtuoso, intoxicated with language, whether it be the elevated vocabulary borrowed from Latin, or the Germanic diction of alliterative poetry, whose tradition was kept alive in Scotland a century after it had died out in England. He was versatile in his choice of genres, writing occasional poems (such an an allegory in celebration of the marriage of James IV and Princess Margaret), divine poems, and parodies such as *The Tretis of Two Mariit Wemen and the Wedo*, a bawdy satire on the morals of court ladies written in the traditional alliterative long line. Included here are a meditation on death (*Lament for the Makars*) and a parody of the courtly genre of the *chanson d'aventure* (*In Secreit Place This Hyndir Nycht*).

Lament for the Makars[1]

I that in heill° wes° and gladnes   *health / was*
Am trublit now with gret seikens
And feblit with infermite:
    Timor mortis conturbat me.[2]

---

1. This poem reflects the late medieval fascination with death. The speaker wistfully observes that beautiful ladies, brave knights, and wise clerks have had their lives cut short but gives most of his attention to poets. He lists 23 of these—three English (Chaucer, Gower, and Lydgate) and 20 Scots, only half of whom modern scholars can identify. Since Death has taken all his "brothers," he regards himself as next and resolves to prepare himself for the next world. The poem was printed in 1508 by Walter Chepman and Andrew Myllar, who introduced the printing press to Scotland.

2. Fear of death shakes me (from the liturgical Office of the Dead).

5   Our plesance heir is all vane glory,
       This fals warld is bot transitory,
       The flesche is brukle,° the Fend° is sle:°   *frail / Devil / sly*
           Timor mortis conturbat me.

       The stait of man dois change and vary,
10   Now sound, now seik, now blith, now sary,
       Now dansand mery, now like to dee:°   *die*
           Timor mortis conturbat me.

       No stait in erd° heir standis sickir;°   *on earth / secure*
       As with the wynd wavis the wickir,
15   Wavis this warldis vanite:
           Timor mortis conturbat me.

       On to the ded gois all estatis,
       Princis, prelotis,° and potestatis,°   *prelates / rulers*
       Baith riche and pur of al degre:
20   *Timor mortis conturbat me.*

       He takis the knychtis° in to feild,°   *knights / the field*
       Anarmit° under helme and scheild; armed   *armed*
       Victour he is at all mellie:°.   *battles*
           Timor mortis conturbat me.

25   That strang unmercifull tyrand
       Takis, on the moderis° breist sowkand,°   *mother's / sucking*
       The bab full of benignite:
           Timor mortis conturbat me.

       He takis the campion° in the stour,°   *champion / conflict*
30   The capitane closit in the tour,
       The lady in bour° full of bewte: *bower*
           Timor mortis conturbat me.

       He sparis no lord for his piscence,°   *power*
       Na clerk for his intelligence;
35   His awfull strak° may no man fle: *stroke*
           Timor mortis conturbat me.

       Art magicianis and astrologgis,
       Rethoris,° logicianis and theologgis,   *rhetoricians*
       Thame helpis no conclusionis sle:°   *clever*
40   *Timor mortis conturbat me.*

       In medicyne the most practicianis,
       Lechis,° surrigianis,° and phisicianis,   *doctors / surgeons*
       Thame self fra ded° may not supple:°   *death / deliver*
           Timor mortis conturbat me.

45   I se that makaris° amang the laif°   *poets / remainder*
       Playis heir ther pageant, syne gois to graif;°   *grave*
       Sparit° is nocht ther faculte: *spared*
           Timor mortis conturbat me.

50   He hes done petuously devour
      The noble Chaucer of makaris flour,°   *flower of poets*
      The Monk of Bery,[3] and Gower, all thre:
          Timor mortis conturbat me.

      The gude Syr Hew of Eglintoun,[4]
55   And eik Heryot, and Wyntoun,[5]
      He hes tane out of this cuntre:
          Timor mortis conturbat me.

      That scorpion fell° hes done infek°   *fierce / infect*
      Maister Johne Clerk and James Afflek[6]
      Fra ballat making and tragidie:
60   *Timor mortis conturbat me.*

      Holland and Barbour[7] he hes berevit;
      Allace,° that he nocht with us levit   *alas*
      Schir Mungo Lokert of the Le:[8]
          Timor mortis conturbat me.

65   Clerk of Tranent eik he hes tane,
      That maid the Anteris° of Gawane;   *adventures*
      Schir Gilbert Hay endit hes he:[9]
          Timor mortis conturbat me.

      He hes Blind Hary and Sandy Traill
70   Slaine with his schour° of mortall haill,   *shower*
      Quhilk Patrik Johnestoun[1] myght nocht fle:
          Timor mortis conturbat me.

      He hes reft° Merseir his endite°   *taken from / talent*
      That did in luf so lifly° write,   *in a lively manner*
75   So schort, so quyk, of sentence hie:
          Timor mortis conturbat me.

      He hes tane Roull of Aberdene
      And gentill Roull of Corstorphin;
      Two bettir fallowis did no man se:
80   *Timor mortis conturbat me.*

      In Dunfermelyne he hes done roune°   *held conversation*
      With Maister Robert Henrisoun.[2]

---

3. John Lydgate, monk of Bury St. Edmunds, a minor poet who was an imitator of Chaucer. He also used the *"timor mortis"* refrain in a poem on the same subject.
4. Brother-in-law of Robert II and not otherwise known as a poet.
5. Andrew of Wyntoun, author of the *Oryginale Chronykil of Scotland.*
6. These two are unknown, as are the other poets in this list not identified.
7. Sir Richard Holland, author of the allegorical *Buke of the Howlat* (c. 1450), and John Barbour, author of the patriotic *Actes and Life . . . of Robert Bruce* (1376).
8. This Scotsman (d. 1489?) is not otherwise known as a poet.
9. The "clerk of Tranent" is unknown, but Arthurian romances focusing on Gawain were popular in Scotland; Sir Gilbert Hay (d. 1456) translated the poem *The Buik of Alexander* from French.
1. Blind Harry is credited with writing the Scots epic *Wallace* (c. 1475); Patrick Johnstoune was a producer of stage entertainments at court in the late 1400s.
2. Henryson was a major Middle Scots poet.

Schir Johne the Ros enbrast° hes he: *embraced*
    Timor mortis conturbat me.

85   And he hes now tane last of aw
Gud gentill Stobo and Quintyne Schaw,[3]
Of quham all wichtis hes pete:[4]
    Timor mortis conturbat me.

Gud Maister Walter Kennedy[5]
90   In° poynt of dede° lyis veraly;°   *on / death / truly*
Gret reuth° it wer that so suld be: *pity*
    Timor mortis conturbat me.

Sen he hes all my brether tane
He will nocht lat me lif alane;
95   On forse° I man his nyxt pray be: *of necessity*
    Timor mortis conturbat me.

Sen for the deid remeid° is none,   *remedy*
Best is that we for dede dispone°   *prepare*
Eftir our deid that lif may we:
    Timor mortis conturbat me.

In Secreit Place This Hyndir Nycht[1]

In secreit place this hyndir° nycht   *last*
I hard ane beyrne° say till ane bricht,°   *man / fair lady*
"My huny, my hart, my hoip, my heill,[2]
I have bene lang° your luifar° leill°   *long / lover / loyal*
5   And can of yow get confort nane:°   *none*
How lang will ye with danger deill?[3]
Ye brek my hart, my bony ane."°   *pretty one*

His bony beird was kemmit and croppit,[4]
Bot all with cale° it was bedroppit,°   *soup / smeared*
10 And he wes townysche, peirt and gukit.[5]
He clappit fast, he kist and chukkit[6]
As with the glaikis° he wer ouirgane;°   *lust / overcome*
Yit be his feirris° he wald have fukkit: *manner*
"Ye brek my hart, my bony ane."

---

3. John Reid, known as Stobo, was priest and secretary to James II, James III, and James IV; Schaw was a minor Scots poet.
4. On whom all people have pity.
5. Known for his *Flyting* (poem of ritual insult) with Dunbar.
1. This comic account of the wooing of a kitchen maid by a boorish man parodies the *chanson d'aventure*, a genre in which the speaker overhears a dialogue between two lovers. Dunbar undercuts the poem's courtly language, which he has used seriously elsewhere, with overtly sex-

ual references. In addition to words familiar to modern readers, the poem features terms of endearment from colloquial Scots which have long since been lost.
2. My honey, my heart, my hope, my salvation.
3. Ladies were expected to be "dangerous" (reluctant) in a courtship situation.
4. His handsome beard was combed and trimmed.
5. And he was townish (uncourtly), pert, and foolish.
6. He fondled fast, kissed, and chucked her under the chin.

15   Quod he, "My hairt, sweit° as the hunye,   *sweet*
        Sen that I borne wes of my mynnye°   *mother*
        I never wowit° weycht° bot yow;   *wooed / creature*
        My wambe° is of your luif sa fow°   *belly / full*
        That as ane gaist° I glour° and grane,°   *ghost / glower / groan*
20   I trymble° sa, ye will not trow:°   *tremble / believe*
        Ye brek my hart, my bony ane."

        "Tehe,"° quod scho, and gaif ane gawfe;°   *Teehee / guffaw*
        "Be still my tuchan[7] and my calfe,
        My new spanit howffing fra the sowk,[8]
25   And all the blythnes° of my bowk;°   *joy / body*
        My sweit swanking,° saif yow allane   *fine fellow*
        Na leid° I luiffit° all this owk:°   *no man / loved / week*
        Full leifis° me° your graceles gane."°   *dear / to me / face*

        Quod he, "My claver° and my curldodie,°   *clover / a plant*
30   My huny soppis, my sweit possodie,°   *sheep's head broth*
        Be not oure bosteous° to your billie,°   *rough / sweetheart*
        Be warme hairtit° and not evill willie;°   *hearted / ill-willed*
        Your heylis quhyt as quhalis bane,[9]
        Garris ryis° on loft my quhillelillie:°   *makes rise / penis*
35   Ye brek my hart, my bony ane."

        Quod scho, "My clype, my unspaynit gyane[1]
        With moderis° mylk yit in your mychane,°   *mother's / mouth*
        My belly huddrun,° my swete hurle bawsy,[2]   *big-bellied glutton*
        My huny gukkis,° my slawsy gawsy,   *sweet fool*
40   Your musing waild perse° ane hart of stane: *would pierce*
        Tak gud confort, my grit heidit° slawsy,   *great-headed*
        Full leifis me your graceles gane."

        Quod he, "My kid, my capirculyoun,°   *woodgrouse*
        My bony baib° with the ruch° brylyoun,   *babe / rough*
45   My tendir gyrle, my wallie gowdye,°   *pretty goldfinch*
        My tyrlie myrlie, my crowdie mowdie,°   *milky porridge*
        Quhone° that oure mouthis dois meit° at ane   *when / do meet*
        My stang dois storkyn with your towdie:[3]
        Ye brek my hairt, my bony ane."

50   Quod scho, "Now tak me be the hand,
        Welcum, my golk° of Marie° land,   *cuckoo / fairy*
        My chirrie and my maikles munyoun,[4]
        My sowklar° sweit as ony unyoun,°   *suckling / any onion*

---

7. Calf skin stuffed with straw, to encourage a cow to give milk.
8. My clumsy fellow newly weaned from nursing.
9. Your neck white as whale's bone; a common alliterative phrase in the conventional love poetry.

1. Said she, "My big soft fellow, my unweaned giant."
2. An obscure term of endearment, as are several other phrases in the following lines.
3. My pole does stiffen by your thing.
4. My cherry and my matchless darling.

My strumill stirk yit new to spane,[5]
55   I am applyit° to your opunyoun:°   *inclined / opinion*
I luif rycht weill° your graceles gane."   *love right well*

He gaiff to hir ane apill rubye;°   *apple red*
Quod scho, "Gramercye,° my sweit cowhubye.°"   *thanks / fool*
And thai tway to ane play began
60   Quhilk° men dois call the dery dan,[6]   *which*
Quhill° that thair myrthis° met baythe in ane: *while / pleasure*
"Wo is me," quod scho, "Quhair will ye,° man?   *where will you go*
Best now I luif° that graceles gane."   *love*

5. My stumbling bullock still newly weaned.   6. A dance (i.e., copulation).

Frontispiece from Saxton's *Atlas*, 1579.

The Early Modern Period

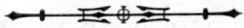

We see the past through lenses that show us something of the world we are living in. How we mark periods in history depends less on an objective evaluation of evidence than on our sense of its relation to our own present. The centuries between 1500 and 1700 have been termed the "Renaissance," and, more recently, "the early modern period." They were also centuries in which Europe and England saw a massive change in Christian religious thought and practice; this has been called the "Reformation." What do these names mean, and what do they tell us about our understanding of this single and continuous stretch of time?

However we describe these centuries, they encompassed events that altered the ways people lived and thought. In 1500 England and Europe were Catholic countries. Apart from its few communities of Jews, Christendom was united by a universal church whose head was the Pope in Rome, and its faithful prayed according to a common liturgy in Latin. The shape of the cosmos was determined by Aristotelian physics and what could be deduced from the scriptural story of creation. It was believed that the earth was the center of the universe and composed of four elements—earth, air, fire, and water; that the human body was a balance of these elements; and that nature, read as if it were a book, revealed a divinely sanctioned moral order. Christian subjects generally respected their national or positive law, which they saw as a mirror of God's law of nature and providentially guaranteed; they assumed it would protect them from tyranny as well as anarchy. A person's place in society tended to be fixed at birth; the majority of folk lived in country villages, worked the land, and traded in regional markets.

By the end of the seventeenth century, much—though not all—of this way of life had vanished. Certain of its features would remain in place for the next hundred years, as historians who refer to the period before the nineteenth century as *la longue durée* ("the long period") remind us: land continued to be farmed by methods followed "time out of mind"; manufacture was still largely done by individuals on small, handmade machines. Religion continued to determine every aspect of life; science and art, politics and economics were discussed in terms supplied by religious thought and institutions. But Christianity was no longer of one piece. Europe had become divided by the establishment of Protestantism in the Low Countries, Scandinavia, and most of Germany. England and Scotland were also Protestant, but with a difference: the first conformed to the doctrine and practices of the Church of England, the second to the requirements of Presbyterianism. Ireland, speaking its Celtic language and retaining many of its ancient customs, remained Catholic despite English attempts at conquest and conversion. Catholics in England, always suspected of subversive intentions, were barely tolerated. Sects proliferated: among them were Anabaptists, Puritans, and Quakers; commonly, their religious doctrines called for massive social change. Cosmic order, too, had changed; it was no longer thought of as geocentric, nor did its elements consist of four primary materials. A natural philosophy based on experimental methods had begun to reshape the disciplines of physics, medicine, and biology; such ancient authorities as Aristotle, Galen, and Pliny were no longer unquestioned. Though sketched in principle by Sir Francis Bacon in his treatise on scientific inquiry, *Novum Organum* ("the new instrument"), published in 1620, a systematic investigation of nature was not underway before the Restoration of the Stuart monarchy in 1660, when scientists in England consolidated their status as intellectuals by forming the Royal Society of London for the Improvement of Natural Knowledge—an organization vigorously supported by the new Stuart king, Charles II. But the worldview that this investigation would help to confirm was already evident early in the seventeenth century. The work of the Italian physicist Galileo Galilei on gravitational force had demonstrated that the most elementary laws of nature were mathematical; the German astronomer Johannes Kepler had confirmed that the universe was heliocentric; the English physician William Harvey had established that the body was energized not by the eccentric flow of "humors" but by a circulation of blood to and from the heart; and the Dutch cosmographer Gerhardus Mercator had discovered the means to navigate the globe safely by accurately mapping latitude and longitude. An international trade, now hugely stimulated by the development of colonies in the Americas, promised wealth to investors willing to take risks and prosperity to the towns and cities in which they lived.

In England, social and political life had been transformed by the activities of city dwellers, or "burgesses," many of whom were merchants, and also by a civil war. Involving English, Scots, and Irish subjects and parties, it had been fought over religious and social issues but also on a matter of principle. British subjects were to be governed by a monarch whose authority and power were not absolute but limited by law and the actions of Parliament, a legislative assembly representing the monarch's subjects. As a whole, the nation was conceived of as a "mystical body politic"; as the radical Bishop of Winchester John Ponet had declared, the monarch's office—not his person—was sacred. Towns and cities became crowded even as they expanded with new streets, marketplaces, and buildings for private as well as public use. Country folk, flocking to these burgeoning urban centers, succumbed to diseases created by filth and overcrowding and died younger than did their rural relatives. But England was becoming a nation of city dwellers, and everyone knew of "citizens" who had gained wealth and station in these exciting, if also terrifying, cities.

THE HUMANIST RENAISSANCE AND EARLY MODERN SOCIETY

The period from 1500 to 1700 has been understood as a "Renaissance"—literally a "rebirth." Many of its features had already been registered in that earlier renaissance of the twelfth century, particularly an interest in classical authors and their modes of expression in logic and rhetoric. By 1400, however, Italian scholars had begun to reread with fresh eyes the works of Greek and Roman authors such as Plato, Aristotle, Virgil, Ovid, and Horace. What was "reborn" as a result was a sense of the meanings to be discovered in the here and now, in the social, political, and economic everyday world. Writing about the intellectual vitality of the age, the French humanist François Rabelais had his amiable character, the giant Gargantua, confess that his own education had been "darksome, obscured with clouds of ignorance." Gargantua knows, however, that his son will be taught differently:

Hans Holbein, *The Ambassadors*, 1533.

Good literature has been restored unto its former light and dignity, and with such amendment and increase of knowledge, that now hardly should I be admitted unto the first form of the little grammar-school boys . . . I see robbers, hangmen, freebooters, tapsters, ostlers, and such like, of the very rubbish of the people, more learned now than the doctors and preachers were in my time.

These comically overstated remarks nevertheless convey the spirit of the Renaissance: learning was no longer to be devoted only to securing salvation but should address the conditions of ordinary life as well. More important, it should be disseminated through all ranks of society.

The writers and scholars responsible for the rebirth of a secular culture, derived in large measure from the pre-Christian cultures of the ancient Mediterranean, have been known as "humanists," because they read "humane" as well as "sacred" letters; their intellectual and artistic practices have been termed "humanism." They cultivated certain habits of thought that became widely adopted by early modern thinkers of all kinds: skill in using language analytically, attentiveness to public and political affairs as well as private and moral ones, and an acute appreciation for differences between peoples, regions, and times. It was, after all, the humanists who began to realize that the classical past required *understanding*. They recognized it as unfamiliar, neither Christian nor European, and they knew, therefore, that it had to be studied, interpreted, and, in a sense, reborn. From its inception in Italy, the work of the humanists traveled north and west, to France, the Low Countries, Germany, the Iberian peninsula, and eventually the British Isles.

At the same time, the cultures of these regions were changing in unprecedented ways. As much as an older world was being reborn, a modern world was being born, and it is in this sense that we can speak of these centuries not only as the Renaissance but also as the "early modern period." Its modernity was registered in various ways, many of them having to do with systems of quantification. Instruments for measuring time and space provided a knowledge of physical nature and its control. Sailing to the new world in 1585, Sir Walter Raleigh made use of Mercator's projection, published in 1568. Means were designed to compute the wealth that was being created by manufacture and trade. Money was used in new and complex ways, its flow managed through such innovations as double-entry bookkeeping and letters of exchange that registered debt and credit in inter-regional markets. The capital that accumulated as a result of these kinds of transactions fueled merchant banks, joint-stock companies, and—notably in England—trading companies that sponsored colonies abroad. Heralded with enthusiasm by William Drayton in 1606, the Virginia colony was reflected in a more muted fashion five years later in Shakespeare's *The Tempest*. In England especially, wealth was increasingly based not on land but on money, and the change encouraged a social mobility that reflected but also exploited the old hierarchy. The effort to ascend the social ladder could prove ruinous. But riches could also make it possible for an artisan's son to purchase a coat of arms and become a gentleman, as Shakespeare did. More important, moneyed wealth supported the artistic and scholarly institutions that allowed the stepson of a bricklayer to attend the best school in London, to profit from the business of the theater, and to compose literary works of sufficient brilliance to make him Poet Laureate—as Ben Jonson did. "Ambition is like choler," warned Francis Bacon; it makes men "active, earnest, full of alacrity and stirring." But if ambition "be stopped and cannot have his way, it becommeth adust, and thereby maligne and venomous." Early modern society was certainly both active and stirring, but the very energy that gave it momentum could also lead to hardship, distress, and personal tragedy.

Urban life flourished in conditions increasingly hospitable to commerce; rural existence became precarious as small farms failed. During the previous century, the nobility had begun to enlarge their estates by the incorporation or "enclosing" of what had formerly been public or common land. They sought to profit from the newest kind of farming: sheep. Thousands of men and women who had worked the land on modest estates lost their livelihoods as a result. The situation got worse when Henry VIII broke England's tie to the Catholic Church, for Henry added to the property of the very rich by giving them the land he had confiscated from the church. Many of the poor and dispossessed came to the cities, particularly London; others traveled through the country, looking for odd work, begging and thieving. Some, like Isabella Whitney, would try city life only to find it wanting. By the early 1600s, a few men and women were electing to seek their fortunes in the Americas. Despite such

SCVLPTVRA IN ÆS.

Sculptor noua arte, braêteata in lamina   Sculpit figuras, atque prælis imprimit.

Hans Collaert, after Jan van der Straet, called Stradanus, *The Printmaker's Workshop* (detail).

constraints, however, the great centers of commerce—Bristol, Norwich, and London—sustained large populations, employed not only in trade but in many kinds of manufacture. One of the most important was printing. The invention of movable type in 1436 by a German printer, Johann Gutenberg, revolutionized the dissemination of texts. A single illuminated manuscript took years to produce and provided what was often a unique version of a text, an item that might cost as much as a small farm; a printing press could quickly produce multiple copies of a text, all of them identical, for as little as a few shillings.

Both the mentality of the "Renaissance" and the more comprehensive culture of the early modern period are illustrated by the history of the most frequently disseminated and contested text of these centuries: the Bible. It was the work of humanists to establish what that text was (after centuries of corrupted versions) and then to translate it into the vernacular languages. Desiderius Erasmus provided accurate Hebrew and Greek texts and translated them into Latin. Printed English translations begin with William Tyndale's New Testament, introduced to England in the 1520s. Later versions included the Geneva Bible with its Calvinist commentary; the Bishops' Bible, repudiating much of that commentary; and the King James Bible or "Authorized Version," a work by forty-seven translators published in 1611. Protestant doctrine emphasized the importance of reading Scripture as a means to spiritual enlightenment, and the preface to the King James Bible insists that for this purpose a translation is as good as the original: "No cause why the word translated should be denied to be the word." But the importance of the Bible went beyond its status as the basis for religious belief.

Henry VIII, following his divorce from Queen Catherine of Aragon and marriage to Anne Boleyn, a lady of the court already celebrated by the poet Sir Thomas Wyatt, instituted perhaps the most important feature of Protestant practice in England: that the Bible be read and spoken in English. This, along with the Act in Restraint of Appeals in 1533 making the English church independent of Rome, and the Act of Supremacy in 1534 establishing the monarch as the head of that church, proved to be decisive for Protestants in England. As the Church of England under Elizabeth I and, later, James I came increasingly under criticism from Presbyterians, Puritans, and other sectarians of different kinds, how to read and eventually preach from the text of the Bible became a point of contention. Disputes over doctrine regarding the nature and efficacy of the sacraments and the place of images and icons in religious worship divided communities and even families; occasionally, they even disturbed the peace. Here the story is a grim one. Catholics in the north of England unsuccessfully resisted Henry's imposition of Protestantism in their Pilgrimage of Grace in 1536. Protestants, in turn, were persecuted by Mary I throughout her reign; many of their stories are recounted in John Foxe's *Book of Martyrs*. Catholics were suppressed by Elizabeth I, and sectarians of various denominations were required to adhere to Anglican forms of worship and obey episcopal power under the Stuarts.

Some, seeing the Bible as an eminently useful text, relied on it to argue for the reform of both church and state. This was especially true for a growing number of women writers, who were moved to rethink and resist their customary place as the inferiors of men. While the scholarly Juan Luis Vives had attributed their natures to the disobedient Eve of Genesis, Aemelia Lanyer and others rejected this interpretation. Mary Herbert and Queen Elizabeth each translated the Psalms, in effect turning themselves into interpreters of Scripture; and referring to particular passages in the Bible, agitators like Ester Sowernam argued that women were the equal of men. In 1641, women convinced that Scripture granted them the right to protest religious abuses presented their *Petition of the Gentlewomen and Tradesmen's Wives, In and About the City of London* to the House of Commons. Much of the general debate regarding the nature and power of the monarchy and other forms of government reflected interpretations of Scripture. Drawing on biblical representations of conscience, John Ponet insisted that a monarch was obliged to obey the law of the land and thus to adhere to a "constitution"; reflecting the same passages in Scripture, King James VI of Scotland, later James I of England, thought that a monarch should respect only divine law and be considered "absolute." Continued into the next generation of thinkers, this dispute ended in the execution of Charles I. God's word, it turned out, could have a distinctly practical application.

Many features of Renaissance and early modern culture are again in transition today: the printed book, which once superseded the manuscript, is now challenged by computer-generated hypertext; the nation state, which once eclipsed the feudal domain and divided "Christendom," is now qualified by an international economy; and the belief in human progress, which was once applauded as an advance over the medieval faith in divine providence, is now subject to criticism, in large part because of such kinds of injustice and inequity as slavery, colonialism, and the exploitation of wage labor—all factors in the growth of early modern England and other states in

Europe. As modern and postmodern readers, we have a special affinity with our early modern counterparts. Like them, we study change.

HISTORY AND EPIC

The political life of the sixteenth century was dominated by the genius of a single dynasty: the Tudors. Its founder was Owen Tudor, a squire of an ancient Welsh family. Employed at the court of Henry V, he eventually married Henry's widow, Catherine of Valois. The first Tudor monarch was their grandson, Henry, Earl of Richmond, who defeated Richard III at Bosworth Field in 1485 to become Henry VII. He married Elizabeth, daughter of Edward IV, whom Richard III had succeeded—a fortunate event for the people of England, as it united the two parties by whom the crown had been disputed for many decades. Once Henry, who represented the House of Lancaster (whose emblem was a red rose) was joined to Elizabeth, a member of the House of York (signified by a white rose), the so-called "Wars of the Roses" were at an end. Henry VII's bureaucratic skills then settled the kingdom in ways that allowed it to grow and become identified as a single nation, however much it also comprised different peoples: the midlands and the north were distinguished from the more populous south by dialectal forms of speech; and to the west, in Cornwall and Wales, many English subjects still spoke Celtic. More thoroughly Celtic were Ireland, across the sea to the west, and Scotland, to the north. While the Anglo-Normans had invaded Ireland in the twelfth century, it was not until the reign of Elizabeth that the English pursued the subjugation of Ireland by colonizing plantations and conducting a brutal military campaign that produced famine, massacres, and the forced relocation of people. But this supposed English fiefdom remained rebellious and effectively unconquered for Elizabeth's entire reign. Its resistance to English rule was crushed only in 1603, an event that marked the end of an independent Ireland for three hundred years. Oliver Cromwell's account of the massacre of the city of Drogheda in 1649, related in his *Letters from Ireland*, illustrates a later instance of the brutality typical of the English conquest of Ireland. Scotland, to the far north, was a separate and generally unfriendly kingdom with strong ties to France until James VI of Scotland became James I of England. His accession to the English throne in 1603 began a process that would end with the complete union of the two kingdoms in 1707. And there were even more remote regions to consider: England's colonization of the Americas began under Elizabeth I, progressed under James I, and allowed the English to think of themselves as an imperial power.

Writing history offered a way to reinforce the developing sense of nationhood, a project all the more appealing after the creation of an English church and the beginnings of what was thought to be a British empire. Medieval historians had concentrated on the actions of ambitious men and women whose lives reflected their good or bad qualities; early modern historians wrote about events and their manifold causes. William Camden's *Brittania* and Raphael Holinshed's *Chronicles of England, Scotland, and Ireland* (the source for many of Shakespeare's plays) celebrate the deeds and the character of the early peoples of the British Isles. The land itself became the subject of comment: William Harrison wrote a description of the English counties (included in Holinshed), John Stow surveyed the neighborhoods of London, and Michael Drayton, a Stuart poet, wrote a mythopoetic account of England's towns and countryside entitled *Poly-Olbion*. As a history, however, it is Richard Hakluyt's collection of travel stories, *The Principal Navigations, Voyages and Discoveries of the English Nation*, that has proved most memorable over time. It reports in magnificent detail the exploration of the Americas in the latter half of the sixteenth century. Accounts of this wild and fruitful land fired the imaginations of English readers, who, it was hoped, would decide to promote and even participate in the laborious task of colonization. Describing landfall on the coast of Virginia in 1585, Arthur Barlow evoked the image of a paradise, "where we smelled so sweet and so strong a smell as if we had been in the midst of some delicate garden abounding with all kind of odoriferous flowers. . . . I think in all the world the like abundance is not to be found." Attempts to occupy this land of incredible natural wealth were determined by two principal objectives: securing profitable trade with the Indians, and possessing land from which to extract such resources as timber, furs, fish, and eventually, tobacco. The hope of finding gold was on everyone's mind. The Chesapeake Bay and its environs were settled by men interested in commerce, often at great personal expense. The Massachusetts coast attracted Puritan divines and their flocks, and while these colonists also profited from trade, matters of faith were supposed to be their principal concern. By celebrating a national identity, contemporary narratives reveal their thematic connections with the epic, a genre of poetic fiction. But they do not conform to that genre as contemporary poetry represented it—expressing heroic grandeur not only in action but also in the musical verse form and elevated language of the epic tradition.

The masterpieces of early modern English epic are represented by Edmund Spenser's *The Faerie Queene* and John Milton's *Paradise Lost*. Spenser imitated continental models to create an English Protestant epic-romance, an optimistic projection of Elizabethan culture. The realities of Elizabeth I's reign were indeed far from the poet's vision of things, but they were nonetheless very impressive. England's cities had grown to be centers of world commerce, and the bold explorations of such men as Sir Francis Drake testified to the nation's seafaring power. In the figures of his poem, Spenser embodied the energies producing this expansive growth. His virtuous knights overcome monstrous threats to order, peace, and tranquillity. Aspects of the queen's own genius are reflected in his heroines. Like the warrior maiden Britomart, Elizabeth I assumed a martial character when England was in danger from abroad; like his Queen Mercilla, she was supposed to be gracious to her enemies—a trait somewhat belied by her speeches to Parliament agreeing to the execution of Mary Queen of Scots. Like the virgin Una, she stood for what the poet and most of his readers believed was the one true faith: Protestantism. And like Spenser's enigmatic and distant Queen Gloriana, the Faerie Queene of the title, she exercised her authority and power in unpredictable ways: secrecy and dissimulation were her stock in trade. To her subjects, her majesty was awful and sometimes terrifying. But she was also mortal, and at her death, few could have foreseen the new and divided nation that would come into being with the accession of James I.

The new king was greeted with mixed feelings. On the one hand, his claim to the throne was not disputed; on the other hand, he came from Scotland, long an enemy of England and always a source of anxiety to those who sought dominion over the British Isles as a whole. Although educated by the humanist George Buchanan, whose treatises praising republican government were widely known and read, James, as his own treatise *The Trew Law of Free Monarchy* shows, favored absolute rule and believed that a monarch should be *lex loquens*, the living spirit of the law, and therefore not bound by the terms of national or positive law. His personal conduct appeared to be dubious. His critics represented him as frequently unkempt and claimed that he preferred to hunt deer rather than to take charge of matters of state. Disputes with the House of Commons over money to support the Crown's activities were frequent. Reports of intrigue with Catholic Spain shattered the nation's sense of security; an attempt in 1605 to blow up the Houses of Parliament, revealed as the Gunpowder Plot, caused a near panic. These and other kinds of unrest grew more intense when James's heir, Charles I, proved to be even more autocratic than his father. Charles's queen, Henrietta Maria, the daughter of Henry IV of France, was a Catholic, and it was rumored that she was treacherous. Religious controversy raged throughout the British Isles, and the struggle over the authority and power of the monarch culminated in a bloody civil war. Across England and Scotland, forces loyal to the king fought the army of Parliament, led by Oliver Cromwell, a Puritan Member of the Commons. The war, which lasted from 1642 to 1651, ended with the defeat of the royalists.

In 1649 Charles I was captured and executed by order of Parliament, and England began to be governed as a republic. She was no longer a kingdom but a Commonwealth, and this period in her history is known as the Interregnum, the period between kingdoms. The long-advocated change, now a reality, could hardly have begun in a more shocking way. The monarchy had always been regarded as a sacred office and institution, as Shakespeare's Richard II had said:

> Not all the water in the rough rude sea
> Can wash the balm off from an anointed king;
> The breath of worldly men cannot depose
> The deputy elected by the Lord.

But in the course of half a century, the people had proved themselves to be a sovereign power, and it was politically irrelevant that Charles, on the block, exemplified a regal self-control. As the Parliamentarian poet Andrew Marvell later wrote of the King's admirable courage at his execution: "He nothing common did or mean / Upon that memorable scene . . . Nor called the gods with vulgar spite / To vindicate his helpless right."

The conflict itself, its causes and its outcome, have been variously interpreted. As a religious and cultural struggle, the Civil War, also known as the Wars of Three Kingdoms, expressed the resistance of Scots Presbyterians and Irish Catholics to the centralizing control of the English church and government. As a revolution in government, the conflict was defined by common lawyers, energized by Puritan enthusiasm, and marked the nation's transition to a society in which the absolute rule by a monarch was no longer a possibility. The people themselves had acquired a voice. To some extent this was a religious voice. Puritans who professed a belief in congregational church government were generally proponents of republican rule. Their dedication to the ideal of a society of equals under the law was shared by men and women of other sects: the Levellers, led by John Lilburne, who argued for a written constitution, universal manhood suffrage, and religious toleration (for God, Lilburne wrote, "doth not choose many rich, nor many wise"); the Diggers, led by Gerrard Winstanley, who proposed to institute a communistic society in the wastelands they were ploughing and cultivating; the Quakers, led by George Fox, who rejected all forms of church order in deference to the inner light of an individual conscience and, insisting on social equality, refused to take off their hats before gentry or nobility; and the Ranters, who denied the authority of Scripture and saw God everywhere in nature. Without widespread acceptance of the egalitarian concept that had initiated the Protestant reformation—all believers are members of a real though invisible priesthood—it is hard to see how the move from a monarchy to a representative and republican government could have taken place.

The most comprehensive contemporary history of the war, *The True Historical Narrative of the Rebellion and Civil Wars in England*, by Edward Hyde, Earl of Clarendon, was not published before 1704, but the troubled period found an oblique commentary in what is arguably England's greatest and certainly most humanistic epic poem: Milton's *Paradise Lost*, in print by 1667. Milton's career was inextricably bound up with the fate of the Commonwealth. Educated at Cambridge and with his reputation as a poet well established, Milton had begun by 1649 to contribute to a defense of Puritanism and the creation of a republican government. Despite worsening eyesight, he published *The Tenure of Kings and Magistrates*, a sustained and eloquent apology for tyrannicide, after the execution of Charles I; and in his *Eikonoklastes* ("image-breaker"), written after he was made Latin secretary to the new executive, the Council of State, he derided attempts by royalists to celebrate Charles I in John Gauden's pamphlet *Eikon Basilike* ("image of a king"). In 1660, disturbed by the proposed restoration of Charles Stuart, soon to be Charles II, Milton—now completely blind—published his last political treatise, *The Ready and Easy Way to Establish a Commonwealth*. It presented the case for a republicanism that had already lost most of its popularity: the government of the Commonwealth had adopted measures that resembled the autocratic rule of the monarchy it had overthrown. Meanwhile, the composition of *Paradise Lost* was underway. Indebted to many of Spenser's themes in *The Faerie Queene*, Milton infused his subject—the fall of the rebellious angels and the exile from paradise of the disobedient Adam and Eve—with the spirit of the account in Genesis. His poem is the product of a doubly dark vision of life. Sightless and suffering again what he felt were the constraints of a monarchy, Milton's story of exile from paradise spoke to his own and England's loss of innocence and painful acquisition of the knowledge of good and evil during the period of the war and its aftermath. His *Paradise Lost* and its sequel, *Paradise Regained*, express the most provocative ambiguities of contemporary English culture; they were—and still are—praised as rivalling the epics of Homer, Virgil, and Dante in their power and scope.

DRAMA AND SOCIAL SATIRE

Drama provided another perspective on English life. While epics depicted the grander aspirations of the nation, its human character was expressed in stage plays, masques or speaking pageants, and dramatic processions. These forms exploited the material of chronicle to illustrate not only the virtues of heroes but also their foibles and limitations; history's villains warned viewers that evil would be punished, if not by civil authority then by providence. Writing tragedy based on history and legend, Marlowe and Shakespeare complicated the direct moralism of medieval drama.

Rather than portraying characters who became victims of their own misdoings, rising to power only to fall in disgrace, the early modern stage showed virtue and vice as intertwined—a hero's tragic error could also be at the heart of his greatness. The origins of evil were seen as mysterious, even obscure. Some sense of this moral ambiguity can be traced to the tragedies of the Roman philosopher Seneca, which were translated into English and published in 1581. English drama reproduced many of their features: the five-act structure, rapid-fire dialogue punctuated by pithy maxims, and images of tyranny, revenge, and fate illustrated by haunting dreams and echoing curses. Shakespeare's *Richard III*, the most frequently performed of his plays in his own time, and Elizabeth Cary's *Tragedy of Miriam*, the first tragedy in English written by a woman, powerfully exemplify the qualities of early modern tragedy.

If tragedy turned away from straightforward piety, so did comedy. The medieval drama of Christian salvation, in which the hero's struggle against sin was ended by his acknowledgment of grace, was replaced with plays about the wars between the sexes and between parents and children. Much of this material was modeled on the comedies of Plautus, a Roman playwright, and on the tales or *novellas* of contemporary Italian writers. Playwrights like Ben Jonson also found a wealth of material in the improvisatory Italian *commedia dell'arte*, with its stock characters of the old dotard, the cuckolded husband, the damsel in distress, and the mountebank or quack.

The social criticism implicit in plays of this time was, of course, one reason why they were so popular. Their pointed censure of various kinds of behavior, including religious practices, showed how ready audiences were to imagine a reform of their society. The end of the century saw a brilliant example of satire in a series of pamphlets secretly published by an anonymous author, known as Martin Marprelate, who disparaged all aspects of the episcopacy and promoted in its place a frankly Presbyterian church, in which authority would reside in Scripture and in congregations rather than in a church hierarchy. But it was the stage that was generally regarded as responsible for both illustrating social failings and stirring up discontent. Although some, like the playwright Thomas Heywood, praised plays as a form of instruction for the unschooled, others, like the Puritan pamphleteer Philip Stubbes, asserted that plays "maintain bawdry, insinuate foolery, and revive the remembrance of heathen idolatry." As Stephen Gosson wrote in *Plays Confuted in Five Actions*:

> If private men be suffered to forsake their calling because they desire to talk gentlemen-like in satin & velvet, with a buckler at their heels, proportion is so broken, unity dissolved, harmony confounded, that the whole body must be dismembered, and the prince or head cannot choose but sicken.

The fear was not only that the tricksters of drama would be the objects of emulation rather than scorn, but also that the actors' masquerade of identities would spur social instability in the public theater's audience, ranging from the groundlings in the pit to the gentry in the higher-priced seats. Parliament had tried to maintain social order by regulating, through sumptuary laws, what style and fabrics persons of a particular rank could wear. A subject's experience of the theater, where commoners played the parts of nobility and dressed accordingly, might discourage observation of these laws, which were repealed in 1633.

Londoners enjoyed two kinds of theater: public and private. The public theaters were open to all audiences for a fee and were generally immune from oversight because they were located outside the City of London, in an area referred to as the Liberties, notorious for prostitution and the sport of bear-baiting. London's two biggest theaters were located there: the Fortune, and the more famous Globe, home to Shakespeare's company. Private theaters—open only to invited guests—were located in the large houses of the gentry, the Inns of Court (the schools of common law), and the guildhalls; the best known, Blackfriars, was housed in an old monastery. Their performances were acted almost exclusively by boy actors, although the popularity of these companies was short-lived. James I, annoyed by the send-up of the Scots court in *Eastward Ho!*, a play that Ben Jonson had a part in writing, dissolved his queen's own company, known as the Queen's Revels Children. The most private and prestigious stage of all remained the royal court. Shakespeare's *The Tempest*, performed at King James's court in 1611, illustrated the resources an indoor stage could provide. By its distinctive framing of dramatic action, it invited the audience to suspend its disbelief and appreciate the illusionism of theater. Of exclusive interest to this audience was the masque, a speaking pageant accompanied by music and dancing, staged with elaborate sets and costumes, and acted by members of the court, including the Queens Anna and Henrietta Maria. But in 1649, a Puritan Parliament, disgusted with what it considered to be the immorality of the drama, banned all stage plays, and the theaters remained closed until the Restoration in 1660.

LYRIC POETRY AND ROMANCE

In early modern England, epic narratives, stage plays, and satire in all forms were genres designed for audiences and readers the writer did not know, a general public with varied tastes and background. Lyric poetry, prose romances, and tales were more often written for a closed circle of friends. Circulated in manuscript, these genres allowed a writer's wit to play on personal or coterie matters. Here writers could speak of the pain of love or the thrill of ambition, and both reveal and, in a sense, create their own identities in and through language. By imitating and at the same time changing the conventions of the lyric, particularly as they were illustrated by the Italian poet Francesco Petrarch, English poets were able to represent a persona, or fictive self, that became in turn a model for others. Unlike Petrarch, who saw his lady as imbued with numinous power before which he could only submit, Sir Thomas Wyatt and Sir Philip Sidney imagined love in social and very human terms. In the struggle to gain affection and power, their subjectivity took strength from their conquests as well as their resistance to defeat. The use of the lyric in pastoral (whether erotic or spiritual) are illustrated by poets as different as Robert Herrick, John Donne, and Andrew Marvell. At times, its objects of adoration could be divine or mystical, as in the verse of George Herbert. Women poets, such as Lady Mary Wroth and Katherine Philips, reworked the conventions of the love lyric to encompass a feminine perspective on passion and, equally important, on friendship. Sonnet sequences were popular and, reflecting a taste for narrative romance, often dramatized a conflict between lovers. Shakespeare wrote the best-known sonnets of the period. His cast of characters—including the poet as principal speaker, his beloved male friend, a rival poet, and a fickle lady—appear as protagonists in a drama of love, betrayal, devotion, and despair. Some poets embedded their love poetry in prose narratives that told a

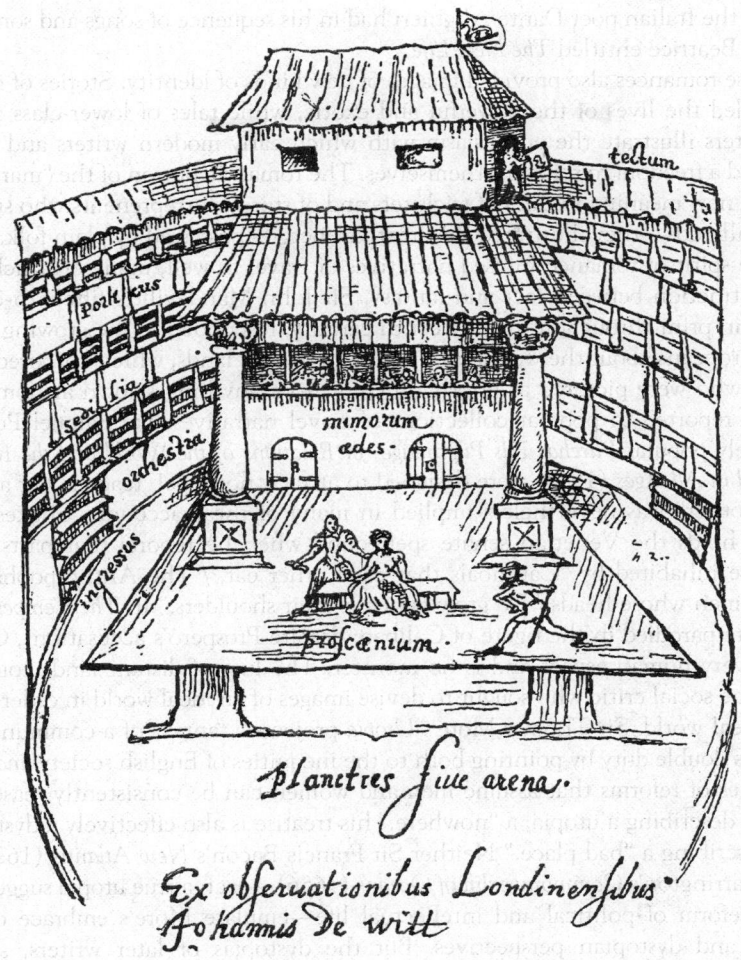

planities sive arena.

Ex observationibus Londinensibus
Johannis de Witt

Arend von Buchell, *The Swan Theatre*, after Johannes de Witt, c. 1596. The only extant drawing of a public theater in 1590s London, this sketch shows what Shakespeare's Globe must have looked like. The round playhouse centered on the curtainless platform of the stage (*proscenium*), which projected into the yard (*planities sive arena*). Raised above the stage by two pillars, the roof (*tectum*) stored machinery. At the back of the stage, the tiring house (*mimorum aedes*), where the actors dressed, contained two doors for entrances and exits. There were no stage sets and only movable props such as thrones, tables, beds, and benches, like the one shown here. Other documents on the early modern stage are the contract of the Fortune Theatre and stage directions in the plays themselves. Modeled on the Globe, although square in shape, the Fortune featured a stage forty-three feet broad and twenty-seven and a half feet deep. Stage directions include further clues: sometimes a curtained booth made "discovery" scenes possible; trapdoors allowed descents; and a space "aloft," such as the gallery above the stage doors, represented a room above the street. Eyewitness accounts fill out the picture. In the yard stood the groundlings who paid a penny for standing room, exposed to the sky, which provided natural lighting. For those willing to pay a penny or two more, three galleries (*orchestra, sedilia,* and *porticulus*) provided seats—the most expensive of which were cushioned. Spectators could buy food and drink during the performance. The early modern theater held an audience of roughly eight hundred standing in the yard, and fifteen hundred more seated in the galleries. According to Thomas Platter, who had seen Shakespeare's *Julius Caesar* in 1599, "everyone has a good view."

story, as the Italian poet Dante Alighieri had in his sequence of songs and sonnets to the lady Beatrice entitled *The New Life*.

Prose romances also provided images of new kinds of identity. Stories of marvels surrounded the lives of the powerful and exotic, while tales of lower-class artisan-adventurers illustrate the enthusiasm with which early modern writers and readers embraced a freedom to reinvent themselves. The romantic notion of the "marvelous" gained a new meaning in tales of tricksters and of sturdy entrepreneurs who survived against all odds—they illustrated the creative energies possessed by plain folk.

The spirit of romance infused narratives of travel as well, many of which made little distinction between fact and fantasy. Sir John Mandeville's fifteenth-century *Travels*, in print throughout the sixteenth century, responded to the growing curiosity of Europeans about the wonders of nature in distant lands, which harbored whole peoples who were pictured as utterly different from anything known at home. The wonders reported in popular collections of travel narratives like Samuel Purchas's immensely popular *Purchas His Pilgrimage, or Relations of the World and the Religions Observed in All Ages* (1613) were designed to attract, not repel, readers, but a horror of the "other" was nevertheless implied in many of these accounts. Shakespeare's *Othello* holds the Venetian senate spellbound when he reports that parts of the world are inhabited by "Cannibals that each other eat, / The Anthropophagi," as well as "men whose heads / Do grow beneath their shoulders." In *The Tempest*, such claims are parodied in the figure of Caliban: despite Prospero's accusations, Caliban bears a very human aspect and is no monster. The lure of distant lands could also attract the social critic who sought to devise images of an ideal world in order to better the real world. Sir Thomas More's *Utopia* projects a fantasy of a communal state that does double duty by pointing both to the inequities of English society *and* to the absurdities of reforms that assume men and women can be consistently reasonable. Literally describing a utopia, a "nowhere," his treatise is also effectively a dystopia, a work describing a "bad place." Neither Sir Francis Bacon's *New Atlantis* (1627) nor James Harrington's *Commonwealth of Oceans* (1656)—each a true utopia suggesting a radical reform of political and intellectual life—emulate More's embrace of both utopian and dystopian perspectives. But the dystopias of later writers, such as Jonathan Swift's *Gulliver's Travels* (1726), Samuel Butler's *Erewhon* (an anagram for "nowhere," 1872), and George Orwell's *1984* (1949) impressively illustrate the hazards of idealistic and visionary social thought.

CHANGING SOCIAL ROLES

The imaginative work of "self-fashioning" in early modern lyric and romance kept pace, to a degree, with actual social change. During this period, a person was born into a place—defined by locale, family, and work—but did not necessarily remain there. The social ladder was traveled in both directions. An impecunious member of the gentry, a second son of a poor squire, or a widow whose noble husband had left her without a suitable jointure or estate could sink below the rank to which they had been born and effectively become a "commoner." In turn, a prosperous artisan, a thrifty yeoman, or an enterprising merchant could eventually become a member of the gentry—folk who were entitled to signal their identity by a coat of arms and were not supposed to do manual work. The new rich were sometimes mocked for seeking

Color Plate 11 Rowland Lockey, *Sir Thomas More, His Father, His Household and His Descendants*, fl. 1593–1616 after Hans Holbein, 1497 or 8–1543. Commissioned by Thomas More II, grandson of Sir Thomas More, this painting portrays five generations of this Roman Catholic family. The first seven figures from left to right are modeled on a lost painting by Hans Holbein. Sir Thomas More himself is shown seated at the left, wearing a brown robe. His father, in red, sits next to him, while behind him to either side stand his wife, Anne, and his son, John. His daughters Cecily, Elizabeth, and Margaret are grouped at the center. *(By courtesy of The National Portrait Gallery, London.)*

Color Plate 12 Nicholas Hilliard, *The Young Man Amongst Roses*, c. 1597. Hilliard, the greatest miniaturist of the Elizabethan age, here represents an exquisite aristocratic young man in the pose of melancholic lover. *(Victoria & Albert Museum, London/Art Resource, NY.)*

Color Plate 13 Inigo Jones, *Fiery Spirit*, costume design for a torchbearer in *The Lord's Masque*, performed 14 February 1613. Jones designed this masque as part of the celebrations for the marriage of James I's daughter Elizabeth to Frederick V, the Elector Palatine. The elaborate costume designs were modeled on those created for Florentine court theater. *(The Devonshire Collection, Chatsworth. Reproduced by permission of the Duke of Devonshire and the Chatsworth Settlement Trustees.)*

Color Plate 14   Marcus Gheeraerts II (1561–1636), *Portrait of Captain Thomas Lee*, 1594. Thomas Lee served as an army officer during the Elizabethan colonization of Ireland. This painting portrays him as part barefoot Irish foot soldier and part elaborately accoutered English gentleman. On the tree behind him appears a Latin quotation from Livy, "both to act and to suffer with fortitude is a Roman's part," which is what the Roman patriot Scaevola is supposed to have said when he was captured by rebel Etruscans as he entered their camp disguised in their garb. The painting is thus an elaborate allegory protesting Lee's English loyalty despite his friendship with such Irish chiefs as Hugh O'Neill. On 13 February 1601, Lee died a traitor's death as punishment for his role in the Earl of Essex's rebellion. *(Oil on canvas. © Tate, London 2002.)*

Color Plate 15 *Portrait of John Donne*, c. 1595. *(Private Collection/Bridgeman Art Library.)*

Color Plate 16 Unknown artist, *Portrait of John Milton*, c. 1629. This is very likely the portrait of the great poet at 21, as he appeared at Cambridge, of whom John Aubrey wrote "he was so fair that they called him the lady of Christ's College." *(By courtesy of The National Portrait Gallery, London.)*

Color Plate 17 Peter Paul Rubens, *The Apotheosis of James I*, from the Banqueting House, installed 1636. Idolized and knighted in London, the great Flemish painter Rubens was commissioned by Charles I to celebrate the greatness of his father James I's reign in a series of paintings for the Banqueting House, the ceremonial dining hall of Whitehall Palace. This large oval at the center of the room's ceiling depicts James I with scepter in hand and his foot atop a globe, symbolizing imperial domination. Justice lifts James up in an expression of the Stuart kings' belief in the divine right of kings. The side panels show genii bearing a garland and genii playing with animals. *(Crown copyright: Historic Royal Palaces. Reproduced by permission of Historic Royal Palaces under license from the Controller of Her Majesty's Stationery Office.)*

Color Plate 18 Peter Paul Rubens (1577–1640), *Minerva Protects Pax from Mars (Peace and War)*, 1630. Rubens produced this work for Charles I to commemorate the English-Spanish peace treaty, which the painter himself helped negotiate. The painting optimistically represents both the court of Charles I at its zenith and the hope for European peace that would be dashed ten years later. The painting is charged with movement. A satyr grasps the fruits of peace, while to the right, Minerva, goddess of wisdom, drives out Mars, god of war, and the avenging goddess Fury Allecto. At the center, Peace extends her full breast to the baby Plutus, god of riches. *(Oil (identified) on canvas, 203.5 × 298.0. © National Gallery, London.)*

Color Plate 19 Sir Anthony van Dyck, *Philip, 4th Earl and His Family*, 1635. Born at Antwerp, Van Dyck studied under Rubens for five years. Charles I knighted and appointed Van Dyck as court painter in 1632. This painting was commissioned by the Earl of Pembroke and painted in London in 1634–1635. In 1652 it was moved to Wilton House, where it was placed in the "Double Cube" room designed by Inigo Jones. *(Earl of Pembroke, Wilton House, Wilton, Salisbury, UK.)*

Color Plate 20 Cornelius Johnson (or Jonson) (1593–1661), *The Capel Family*, c. 1640. This painting in the style of Van Dyck portrays the royalist Arthur Capel, who was executed the same year as Charles I. In the background appear gardens, perhaps those of his home at Little Hadham. *(By courtesy of The National Portrait Gallery, London.)*

advice in conduct books regarding the proper behavior for gentlefolk, but no one could overlook the change in their status. More important, representatives of the "middling sort" were gaining political power. They generally had the right to vote for a member of the House of Commons, and they regularly held local office as bailiffs, magistrates, or sheriffs, and served on juries in towns and villages throughout the kingdom. They administered property, engaged in business, and traded on international markets. Creating much of the wealth of early modern England, they defined the concept of an economic class independent of social rank or family background: "What is Gentry if wealth be wanting, but base servile beggery?" asked Robert Greene. The idea that a person inherited a way of life was undercut by evidence of continuous shifts in both urban and rural society.

The situation for women in particular exhibited a certain ideological ambivalence. Ancient philosophy and medieval theology had insisted that *woman*kind was essentially and naturally different from *man*kind, characterized by physical weakness, intellectual passivity, and an aptitude for housework, childcare, and the minor decorative arts. That some women had distinguished themselves in occupations traditionally reserved for men was understood to signal an exception; in general, social doctrine imposed rigid codes of behavior on men and women. This thinking was countered by the text of Scripture—but also and increasingly by evidence from history, which revealed that ordinary women had undertaken all kinds of activity and therefore that a woman had the same range of talents as a man. Literary representation and authorship reflected some of this argument.

These novel ways of understanding women found corresponding changes in attitudes toward men. Departing from medieval social norms, humanists had stressed that men should be educated in the arts as well as arms, and writers like Sir Philip Sidney, illustrating the sensitivity of men to emotional life, devised characters whose masculinity was amplified by attributes that were conventionally associated with women: passion, sympathy, and an aptitude for creative deception. Flexibility with respect to categories of gender is also a feature of much lyric poetry; the male poet's beloved is sometimes another man. Shakespeare's sonnets are the chief example of homosexual verse in this period, but homoerotic innuendo, often suggested as a feature of a love triangle, is common in all genres of writing.

Ideas as well as social forms and practices were also changing. The repeated shifts in religious practice—from medieval Catholicism to Henrician Protestantism, then back to the Catholicism dictated by Queen Mary I, and then on to the Anglican Church of Queen Elizabeth I—revealed that divine worship could alter its form without bringing on the apocalypse. More subtly, the emerging capitalist economy produced a conceptual model for cultural exchange. Just as material goods flowed through regional and national markets, entering a particular locale only to move elsewhere, sometimes over great distances, so might ideas, styles, and artistic sensibilities. Drama especially conveyed how fluid were the customs, codes, and practices that gave society its sense of identity. The enthusiasm for stage plays was motivated in part by an interest in role-playing: if an actor who in real life might have been born a servant could perform the part of a king in a play, then might he not also perform the part of a king indeed? Was there more to being than performing? This mutability was both liberating and dangerous, as Shakespeare showed by dramatizing the protean powers of Othello's false friend, Iago, who chillingly boasts, "I am not what I am."

THE BUSINESS OF LITERATURE

It was the business of early modern literature to ask these questions. The idea that social convention was established on a natural order of things was no longer accepted. As Shakespeare's bastard Edmund declares, rejecting the customary inferiority of a person who is born out of wedlock, "Why bastard, Wherefore base? / When my dimensions are as well compact . . . As honest madam's issue." Writers were certainly supposed to educate their readers in virtuous ways. Spenser intended that his epic would "fashion a gentleman or noble person in vertuous and gentle discipline," and Sidney believed that poetry at its finest could "take naughtiness away and plant goodness even in the secretest cabinet of our souls." But literature also questioned matters of being and identity because writers themselves were in the forefront of a class that was in the process of changing its way of life and its means of support.

During the early modern period, an educated man who sought employment as a writer was the object of patronage by the gentry or nobility, often functioning as a tutor or secretary in a prosperous household. The poet John Skelton taught the future Henry VIII; John Donne accompanied his patron Sir William Drury on his European journeys and dedicated his *Anniversaries* to Drury's deceased daughter, Elizabeth; and Andrew Marvell educated Lord Fairfax's daughter, Mary. Men who were employed in other ways—in diplomacy, law, or some aspect of commerce—might be rewarded for their writing by stipends from the rich. Elizabeth I gave Spenser, one of her administrators in Ireland, a single grant of fifty pounds for *The Faerie Queene*; and Ben Jonson, thanks to the generosity of James I, was able to make a successful career for himself as a poet. As a young man, Milton was patronized by the noble Egerton family, for whom he wrote a masque called *Comus*. But as the seventeenth century progressed, writers discovered that they could be supported by a broader public; after the Restoration, the talented playwright Aphra Behn gained a living by selling her literary work to producers and printers. Increasingly, the forces of the market moved to include the business of printing, both liberating and captivating the energies of the nation's writers.

It was obvious to those in power and authority that the printing press was an agent of change; the question they had to answer was how to control it. Under Elizabeth I, all printing was regulated (in effect, subject to censorship) by the Stationer's Company, which had the exclusive right to print and sell literary work. The theater was also controlled. From 1574, all plays had to be licensed by the Master of Revels, a servant and appointee of the monarch, before they could be produced. These conditions bound writers to observe both royal and ecclesiastical policy, at least in their direct statements. Some resorted to coded critique; others openly defied custom. In 1579, John Stubbs wrote a pamphlet against the Queen's proposed marriage to the French king's brother, the Duke of Alençon, entitled *The Discoverie of a Gaping Gulf whereinto England Is Like to be Swallowed;* he was arrested and had his hand cut off as punishment. This situation, in which publication was officially regulated, was altered early in the seventeenth century by the development of a new institution: journalism.

By the middle of James I's reign, a market had emerged for a periodical news-pamphlet known as a "coranto," or current of news, which contained foreign intelligence taken from foreign papers: the first was actually printed in Amsterdam and shipped to England. Within a short time, English printers were publishing their own news in the form of sixteen-page "diurnals," or newsbooks, and by 1646 Londoners could read fourteen different papers in English. The rapid growth of the news industry promoted a public readership increasingly informed about political affairs. Parliament grew alarmed and discussed imposing stringent forms of licensing; in 1649, it sanctioned the publication of only two newspapers, both dedicated to printing official news. Underground presses continued to publish on current affairs, however, some of them from a royalist point of view and others endorsing the position of Parliament. Their writers enjoyed a risky freedom, but it was still a freedom. The boldest of them, Marchamont Nedham, wrote in support of both sides at different times. But journalism did more than provide news; it also created a basis for the freedom of writers in general. The most eloquent attack on a state-controlled press was by Milton, whose *Areopagitica* protested the practice of licensing books before their publication—that is, before readers had a chance to make up their minds about what these books contained. He drew on ideas of democracy that were current in ancient Athens and on the Puritan notion that good emerges only in contact with evil. "I cannot praise a fugitive and cloistered virtue," he announced, because no true virtue is untested, unchallenged, unexamined; it is valid only when it has deliberately and consciously rejected what is false. The journalistic enterprise of this period fostered the right to free speech and a free press that is now the bedrock of modern democracies.

THE LANGUAGES OF LITERATURE:
THE NEW SCIENCE AND THE OLD NATURE

Changing ideas of identity, both personal and political, were reflected in changes in the English language, which responded to popular as well as learned culture. An accomplished classicist, Ben Jonson closely modeled his verses on Latin poems and their syntax; at the same time, the language of his poetry and his plays often echoes the cadences of the English spoken by ordinary folk. Authors of popular comic pamphlets conveyed the lively language of London rogues and vagabonds, combining local slang with parodic Latin. The writing of English prose was further changed by the study of Latin grammar and rhetoric in the humanist curriculum inspired by the pedagogical reforms of Erasmus and his English followers, John Colet, Roger Ascham (tutor to Elizabeth I), and Richard Mulcaster. Many words of Latin origin were introduced into the English vocabulary, and many writers experimented with analytic prose by adapting Latin syntax, which allowed them to show relations of cause and effect by resorting to clauses beginning with "if," "when," "because," and so forth. The first Latin-English dictionary on humanist principles was compiled by Sir Thomas Elyot, and one of the most important English grammars, Ascham's *The Schoolmaster* (1570), instructed readers in the merits of an eloquent style.

This enrichment of language from various sources inevitably caused debate. Prose composition was especially affected. Proponents of the so-called Ciceronian style (after the Roman orator Cicero), liked long sentences of many clauses exhibiting variation and restatement. Practitioners of the Senecan style favored short, direct, and uncomplicated sentences. Francis Bacon in particular criticized Ciceronian rhetoric for its emphasis on decorative "tropes and figures" rather than descriptive substance or "weight of matter." He argued for a language that would accurately denote what he considered "scientific" data: the measures of the physical world.

Bacon's reforms influenced English pedagogy and were further realized in the enterprise of the Royal Academy of Science, founded in 1660 by Charles II, who was determined to give his monarchy a new look and a new purpose. The terse, clear, pointed language of Bacon's *Essays* (1597) more resembles what we might think of as modern than does, for example, the florid style that Robert Burton used a quarter century later for his mythological-historical medical discourse *The Anatomy of Melancholy.*

Language and style were changing notions of the world and of God's design in creating it. Habits of thought that had prevailed during the medieval period now seemed to be incompatible with knowledge derived from the experience of nature. Europeans had inherited from classical philosophy an idea of creation as a vast aggregate of layered systems, or "spheres." Supposedly centered on the densest matter at the earth's core, they emanated outward and upward, ending finally in the sphere of pure spirit, or the ethereal presence of divinity. The entities in these layered spheres had assigned places that determined their natures both within their particular sphere and in relation to other spheres. Thus gold, the most precious metal, was superior to silver, but it was at the same time analogous to a lion, a king, and the sun, each also representing the peak of perfection within its particular class of beings. Human nature was also systematized, with the body and personality alike regulated by a balanced set of "humors," each of which consisted of a primary element. The earth, water, air, and fire that made up the great world, or macrocosm, of nature also composed the small universe, or microcosm, of the individual man or woman, whose personality was ideally balanced between impulses that were melancholic (caused by a kind of bile), phlegmatic (brought on by a watery substance), sanguine (bloody), and choleric (hot tempered). Excessive learning, the contemplation of death, the darkness of night, and isolation were all associated with melancholia, a diseased condition that in more or less severe form is represented in such disparate texts as Marlowe's *Dr. Faustus*, Milton's *Il Penseroso*, and Sir Thomas Browne's *Religio Medici* ("the religion of a doctor").

This view of creation was important for artists and writers because it gave them a symbolic language of correspondences by which they could refer to creatures in widely differing settings and conditions. In a sense, it made nature hospitable to poetry by seeing creation as a divine work of art, designed to inspire not only awe but also a kind of familiarity. Things were the likenesses of other things. Particularly in so-called "metaphysical" poetry, whose chief exponent is John Donne, human emotional experience is compared to the realms of astronomy, geography, medicine, Neoplatonic philosophy, and Christian theology. These correspondences are created through strikingly unusual metaphors, which some have called metaphysical conceits, from the Italian *concetto* ("concept"). The result is a pervasive sense of a universal harmony in all human experience.

Such analogies were not always respected, however. Increasingly, they were questioned by proponents of a kind of vision that depended on a quantitative or denotative sense of identity or difference. Poetic metaphor might not be able to account for creation in all its complexity; instead, nature had to be understood through the abstractions of science. By the seventeenth century, it was becoming difficult to regard creation as a single and comprehensive whole; natural philosophers and scientists in the making wanted to analyze it piece by individual piece. As John

Donne wrote of the phenomenon of uniqueness in his elegy for Elizabeth Drury, *The Anniversary:*

> The element of fire is quite put out;
> The Sun is lost, and th' earth, and no man's wit
> Can well direct him, where to look for it.
> And freely men confess, that this world's spent,
> When in the Planets, and the Firmament
> They seek so many new; they see that this
> Is crumbled out again to his Atoms.
> Tis all in pieces, all coherence gone;
> All just supply, and all Relation:
> Prince, Subject, Father, Son, are things forgot,
> For every man alone thinks he has got
> To be a Phoenix, and that there can be
> None of that kind, of which he is but he.

The earth had been decentered by the insights of the astronomer Nicholas Copernicus, who in the 1520s deduced that the earth orbits the sun. This "Copernican revolution" was confirmed by the calculations of Tycho Brahe and Johannes Kepler, and our solar system itself was revealed as but one among many. With traditional understandings of the natural order profoundly shaken, many thinkers feared for the survival of the human capacity to order and understand society as well. Ironically, Donne complains of radical individualism by invoking the emblem of the Phoenix, the very sort of traditional metaphor that constituted the coherence he claims has "gone." But whereas the symbol in an emblem book carried with it the myth of the bird's Christ-like death and rebirth, the image of the rare bird takes on a newly skeptical and even satirical meaning in *The Anniversary*: it becomes the sign of a dangerous fragmentation within nature's order. Donne's audience would have been familiar with such symbols from emblem books, poems, and coats of arms, as well as in interior decoration, clothing, and the printers' marks on title pages of books. They were also featured on the standards or flags carried in the Civil War—antique signs in a decidedly modern conflict.

THE WAR AND THE MODERN ORDER OF THINGS

The Wars of Three Kingdoms ended with the restoration of the Stuart monarchy, but the society that Charles II was heir to was very different from the one his grandfather, James I, had come from Scotland to rule. The terms of modern life were formulated during this period, even though they were only partially and inconsistently realized. They helped to shape these essentially modern institutions: a representative government under law, a market economy fueled by concentrations of capital, and a class system determined by wealth and the power it conferred. They supported a culture in which extreme and opposing points of view were usual. Milton's republican *Tenure of Kings and Magistrates* was followed by Thomas Hobbes's defense of absolute rule, *The Leviathan, or the Matter, Form, and Power of a Commonwealth, Ecclesiastical and Civil* (1651). Hobbes rejected the assumption that had determined all previous political thought—Aristotle's idea that man was naturally sociable—by characterizing the natural condition of human life as "solitary, poor, nasty, brutish and short." A

The Souldiers in their passage to York turn unto reformers pull down Popish pictures, break down rayles, turn altars into Tables.

Wenceslaus Hollar, *Parliamentarian soldiers in Yorkshire destroying "Popish" paintings, etc.* Illustration to *Sight of the Transactions of these latter yeares,* by John Vicars, 1646.

civil state, said Hobbes, depended on the willingness of each and every citizen to relinquish all his or her rights to the sovereign, which is the Commonwealth. The vigorous language of Puritan sermons, preached and published during the 1640s and 1650s, was replicated in the corantoes and diurnals of the period. These new forms would eventually lead to the sophisticated commentary of eighteenth-century journalism. Nationalism, however problematic, was registered in history and epic, as well as in attempts to colonize the Americas and to subdue the Gaelic peoples to the west and the north. Irish poems supporting the Stuarts and lamenting the losses of the Cromwellian wars would become rallying cries during the late seventeenth- and eighteenth-century nationalist risings against English control, eventually to result in Ireland's inclusion in the 1801 Union of Great Britain.

Intellectual thought, mental attitudes, religious practices, and the customs of the people fostered new relations to the past and a new sense of self. While Milton was perhaps the greatest humanist of his time, able to read and write Hebrew, Greek, Latin, Italian, and French, his contemporaries witnessed the disappearance of the culture of Petrarch, Erasmus, and More—humanists who had fashioned the disciplines of humanism. Much seventeenth-century literature reflected personal experience; the diary of Ralph Josselin, a prosperous country squire; the printed testimony of the trial of Ana Trapnel, a Quaker woman accused of witchcraft; the captivity of Mary Rowlandson by the Indians in Massachusetts; and the servitude of John Revel in Virginia convey the details of social life with an immediacy that challenges the studied figures of earlier Renaissance prose. Such personal reckonings are comparable to the spiritual interiority revealed in John Bunyan's allegorical novel about his conversion to faith in God, *The Pilgrim's Progress*, and the first-person narrative of Daniel Defoe's *Robinson Crusoe*, the story of a sailor shipwrecked on an island somewhere off the coast of South America, which was actually modeled on the history of a Scotsman, Alexander Selkirk, who was similarly marooned.

As more particularized portraits of individual life emerged, new philosophical trends promoted denotative descriptions and quantitative figurations of the world. Shortly after the Restoration of Charles II, the Royal Academy of Science would form a "committee for improving the English language," an attempt to design a universal grammar and an ideal philosophical language. This project, inspired by the intellectual reforms of Francis Bacon, would have been uncongenial to the skeptical casts of mind exhibited by Erasmus and More. The abstract rationalism of the new science, the growth of an empire overseas, a burgeoning industry and commerce at home, and a print culture spreading news throughout Europe and across the Atlantic, would continue to be features of life in the British Isles through the eighteenth century.

John Skelton
1460?–1529

The first great Tudor satirist, John Skelton illustrates the appeal of the unorthodox. Taking orders at the age of thirty-eight, Skelton already enjoyed an impressive reputation as a writer of satire and love lyrics. His poems must have appealed to Henry VII, who made him responsible for the education of his second son, the future Henry VIII, and they would eventually prompt Erasmus to call Skeleton "a light and ornament of British literature." In 1502, following the death of Henry's older brother Arthur, Skelton lost his employment as royal tutor. Henry, now heir apparent to the English throne, was obliged to trade Skelton's gentle instruction in humane and sacred letters for practical training in statecraft and the art of war. At forty-two and already an old man (by contemporary reckoning), Skelton undertook pastoral duties, although he lived away from his rectory for much of the rest of his life. His satires of the clergy in *Colin Clout* and of Cardinal Wolsey in *Why Come Ye Not to Court* may have placed him in some jeopardy; it is said that a threat from the Cardinal forced Skelton to take refuge on the grounds of Westminster Abbey in London. Skelton never got the satisfaction of witnessing Wolsey's disgrace; he died just a few months before Wolsey lost the office of Lord Chancellor for failing to procure a divorce for the king.

Skelton's poetry is as unusual as was his career. His favorite verse form has become known as "skeltonics"; it consists of a series of lines of two or three stresses whose end rhyme repeats itself for an unspecified number of lines. The lines themselves show alliteration and move at a headlong pace. Skelton excused his practice in *Colin Clout* by noting the "pith" or substance it conveys:

> For though my rhyme be ragged,
> Tattered and jagged,
> Rudely rain-beaten,
> Rusty and moth-eaten,
> If ye take well therewith,
> It hath in it some pith.

Skelton's satires poke fun at the pretensions that characterize all forms of public life, including the ways of courtiers and vagabonds. His dream poem, *The Bowge of Court*, and his morality play about wealth and power, *Magnificence*, provide a witty view of court corruption. His verse includes tender tributes to ladies he loves or has loved as well as anticourtly lyrics accusing women of bad behavior and sexual indiscretion. His verse can even be conversational, as when he appears to be addressing a particular person or representing two or more people speaking to each other.

Womanhod, Wanton

Womanhod, wanton,[1] ye want;
Youre medelyng, mastres, is manerles;
Plente of yll, of goodnes skant,
Ye rayll at ryot, recheles:°   *carelessly*
5   To prayse youre porte° it is nedeles;   *bearing*
For all your draffe yet and youre dreggys,°   *refuse*
As well borne as ye full oft tyme beggys.

1. The poem address mistress Ann, a "wanton" or woman of the town, who lives at an inn called "The Key." The poet's tone disparages Ann's pretensions rather than her way of life.

Why so koy and full of skorne?
Myne horse is sold, I wene, you say;
10   My new furryd gowne, when it is worne,
Put up youre purs, ye shall non pay.[2]
By crede, I trust to se the day,
As proud a pohen° as ye sprede,   *peahen*
Of me and other ye may have nede.

15   Though angelyk be youre smylyng,
Yet is youre tong an adders tayle,
Full lyke a scorpyon styngyng
All those by whom ye have avayle:
Good mastres Anne, there ye do shayle:°   *mistake*
20   What prate° ye, praty pyggysny?°   *talk / pretty flower*
I truste to quyte° you or° I dy.   *revenge myself on / before*

Youre key is mete° for every lok,   *suited*
Youre key is commen and hangyth owte;
Youre key is redy, we nede not knok,
25   Nor stand long wrestyng° there aboute;   *twisting*
Of youre doregate ye have no doute:
But one thyng is, that ye be lewde:°   *common*
Holde youre tong now, all beshrewde!°   *corrupted*

To mastres Anne, that farly swete,°   *pretty sweetheart*
30   That wonnes° at the Key in Temmys strete.   *lives*

Lullay

With, Lullay, lullay, lyke a chylde,[1]
Thou slepyst to long, thou art begylde.°   *fooled*

My darlyng dere, my daysy floure,
Let me, quod he, ly in your lap.
5   Ly styll, quod she, my paramoure,
Ly styll hardely,° and take a nap.   *only*
Hys hed was hevy, such was his hap,
All drowsy dremyng, dround in slepe,
That of hys love he toke no kepe,°   *care*
10   With, Hey, lullay, &c.

With ba, ba, ba, and bas, bas, bas,
She cheryshed° hym both cheke and chyn,   *stroked*
That he wyst never where he was;
He had forgoten all dedely syn.
15   He wantyd wyt her love to wyn,
He trusted her payment,° and lost all hys pray:°   *words / desire*
She left hym slepyng, and stale° away,   *stole*
              Wyth, Hey, lullay, &c.

2. You are scornful because my horse is sold (I am poor and in need), but you shall have my new gown for nothing when it is worn out (you are poorer than I am).

1. The poem is an ironic lullaby. It actually warns a man who is asleep to wake up: he is a fool, and his wife has gone off with another man.

    The ryvers rowth,° the waters wan;°   *rough / dark*
20 She sparyd not to wete her fete;
    She wadyd over, she found a man
    That halsyd° her hartely and kyst her swete: *embraced*
    Thus after her cold she cought a hete.
    My lefe, she sayd, rowtyth° in hys bed;   *snores*
25 I wys he hath an hevy hed,
          Wyth, Hey, lullay, &c.

    What dremyst thou, drunchard, drousy pate![2]
    Thy lust° and lykyng is from the gone;   *pleasure*
    Thou blynkerd blowboll,° thou wakyst to late, *blinking drunkard*
30 Behold, thou lyeste, luggard, alone!
    Well may thou sygh, well may thou grone,
    To dele wyth her so cowardly:
    I wys,° powle hachet, she bleryd° thyne I.°   *indeed / blinded / eye*

Knolege, Aquayntance

    Knolege, aquayntance, resort,° favour with grace;[1] *love*
    Delyte, desyre, respyte wyth lyberte;
    Corage wyth lust,° convenient tyme and space; *pleasure*
    Dysdayns, dystres, exylyd° cruelte;   *banished*
5 Wordys well set with good habylyte;°   *skill*
    Demure demenaunce,° womanly of porte;° *appearance / bearing*
    Transendyng plesure, surmountyng all dysporte;° *gratification*

    Allectuary arrectyd° to redres   *medicine designed*
    These feverous axys,° the dedely wo and payne *attacks*
10 Of thoughtfull hertys plungyd in dystres;
    Refresshyng myndys° the Aprell shoure of rayne; *minds*
    Condute° of comforte, and well most soverayne; *stream*
    Herber° enverduryd, contynuall fressh and grene; *arbor*
    Of lusty somer the passyng goodly quene;

15 The topas rych and precyouse in vertew;
    Your ruddys° wyth ruddy rubys may compare; *cheeks*
    Saphyre of sadnes, envayned wyth indy° blew; *violet*
    The pullyshed perle youre whytenes° doth declare; *fair skin*
    Dyamand poyntyd to rase° oute hartly care; *erase*
20 Geyne surfetous suspecte the emeraud comendable;[2]
    Relucent smaragd,° objecte imcomperable;   *a bright stone*

    Encleryd° myrroure and perspectyve most bryght, *shining*
    Illumynyd° wyth feturys far passyng my reporte; *glowing*
    Radyent Esperus,° star of the clowdy nyght, *Hesperus, morning star*
25 Lode star to lyght these lovers to theyr porte,
    Gayne dangerous stormys theyr anker of supporte,
    Theyr sayll of solace most comfortably clad,[3]
    Whych to behold makyth hevy hartys glad:

---

2. The poet speaks to wake the sleeper.
1. The poem, a series of epithets in praise of a lady, complains of her absence from him. He imagines that she can cure the world's ills by her gracious virtue and that absence will not remove her from his heart.

2. Against excessive suspicion the praiseworthy emerald.
3. The poet compares the lady's effect to that of the north star guiding a ship to port, the anchor preventing its drifting away, and the sail propelling it forward.

Remorse have I of youre most goodlyhod,

30   Of youre behavoure curtes° and benynge,   *courteous*

Of your bownte and of youre womanhod,

Which makyth my hart oft to lepe and sprynge,

And to remember many a praty° thynge;   *pleasant*

But absens, alas, wyth tremelyng° fere and drede   *trembling*

35   Abashyth° me, albeit I have no nede.   *shames*

You I assure, absens is my fo,

My dedely wo, my paynfull hevynes;

And if ye lyst° to know the cause why so,   *much*

Open myne hart, beholde my mynde expres:°   *immediately*

40   I wold ye coud! then shuld ye se, mastres,

How there nys thynge that I covet so fayne°   *much*

As to enbrace you in myne armys twayne.

Nothynge yerthly° to me more desyrous   *earthly*

Than to beholde youre bewteouse countenaunce:

45   But, hatefull absens, to me so envyous,°   *distressing*

Though thou withdraw me from her by long dystaunce,°   *absence*

Yet shall she never oute of remembraunce;

For I have gravyd° her wythin the secret wall   *engraved*

Of my trew hart, to love her best of all!

Manerly Margery Mylk and Ale[1]

"Ay, besherewe° yow, be my fay,°   *confound / faith*

This wanton clarkes be nyse all way;

Avent, avent, my popagay!°   *go away, parrot*

What, will ye do no thyng but play?

5   Tully valy, strawe, let be,° I say!"   *stop*

Gup,° Cristian Clowte, gup, Jak of the vale!   *go on*

With, manerly Margery mylk and ale.

"Be Gad, ye be a pretty pode,°   *sausage*

And I love you an hole cart lode."

10   "Strawe, Jamys foder,° ye play the fode,°   *ragweed / deceiver*

I am no hakney for your rode;°   *riding*

Go watch a bole,° your bak is brode":   *bull*

Gup, Cristian Clowte, gup, Jak of the vale!

With, manerly Margery mylk and ale.

15   "I wiss ye dele uncurtesly";

"What wolde ye frompill° me? now, fy, fy!   *rumple*

What, and ye shalbe my piggesnye?

Be Crist, ye shal not, no, no, hardely;

I will not be japed bodely":°   *fooled, seduced*

1. The poem is constructed as a dialogue between Margery, who complains of the advances of Cristian Clout, and Cristian Clout, who protests that he loves her. Their dialogue is punctuated by the poet's refrain, which encourages Cristian to persist in his courtship. The first stanza is spoken by Margery, the second and third stanzas by Cristian and then Margery, and the final stanza by Cristian, who, having seduced Margery, nevertheless declares he wants to marry her for the love of God.

20 Gup, Cristian Clowte, gup, Jake of the vale!
    With, manerly Margery mylk and ale.

    "Walke forth your way, ye cost me nought;
    Now have I fownd that I have sought,
    The best chepe flessh that evyr I bought.
25 Yet, for His love that all hath wrought,
    Wed me, or els I dye for thought!"
    Gup, Cristian Clowte, your breth is stale!
    With, manerly Margery Mylk and Ale!
    Gup, Cristian Clowte, gup, Jak of the vale!
30 With, manerly Margery mylk and ale.

from Garland of Laurel[1]
To Maystres Jane Blennerhasset

         What though my penne wax faynt,
         And hath smale lust° to paint?   *desire*
         Yet shall there no restraynt
         Cause me to cese,
5   Amonge this prese,°   *crowd*
         For to encrese°   *celebrate*
         Yowre goodly name.
             I wyll my selfe applye,
         Trust me, ententifly,°   *carefully*
10   Yow for to stellyfye;[2]
         And so observe
         That ye ne swarve°   *swerve*
         For to deserve
         Inmortall fame.
15   Sith mistres Jane Haiset
         Smale flowres helpt to sett
         In my goodly chapelet,°   *crown*
         Therefore I render of her the memory
         Unto the legend of fare Laodomi.[3]

To Maystres Isabell Pennell

         By saynt Mary, my lady,
         Your mammy and your dady
         Brought forth a godely babi!
             My mayden Isabell,
5   Reflaring rosabell,°   *sweet rose*
         The flagrant camamell;°   *fragrant camomile*
             The ruddy rosary,°   *rosebush*
         The soverayne rosemary,

1. The next three poems were included in a collection of lyrics entitled *Garland of Laurel*, published in 1523. The first is addressed to Jane Blennerhasset, who was probably the wife of Ralph Blennerhasset; if so, we know that she died in 1501, at the age of 97. The second is addressed to Isabell Pennell, presumably the young daughter of John Paynell. The third is addressed to Margaret Hussey, an unidentified young woman of marriageable age.
2. Place in the sky as a star.
3. The poet remembers a favor Jane Blennerhasset has done for him and recalls the legend of Laodomia: Just as Laodomia followed her dead husband to the underworld, so has the poet's memory followed Jane beyond the grave.

	The praty° strawbery;	pretty
10	The columbyne, the nepte,°	catnip
	The jeloffer° well set,	gillyflower
	The propre vyolet;	
	Enuwyd° your colowre	renewed
	Is lyke the dasy flowre	
15	After the Aprill showre;	
	Sterre° of the morow gray,	star
	The blossom on the spray,	
	The fresshest flowre of May;	
	Maydenly demure,	
20	Of womanhode the lure;°	model
	Wherfore I make you sure,°	assure you
	It were an hevenly helth,	
	It were an endeles welth,	
	A lyfe for God hymselfe,	
25	To here this nightingale,[4]	
	Amonge the byrdes smale,	
	Warbelynge in the vale,	
	Dug, dug,	
	Jug, jug,	
30	Good yere and good luk,	
	With chuk, chuk, chuk, chuk!	

To Maystres Margaret Hussey

	Mirry Margaret,	
	As mydsomer flowre,	
	Jentill as fawcoun°	falcon
	Or hawke of the towre;[5]	
5	With solace and gladnes,	
	Moche mirthe and no madnes,	
	All good and no badnes,	
	So joyously,	
	So maydenly,	
10	So womanly	
	Her demenyng°	behavior
	In every thynge,	
	Far, far passynge	
	That I can endyght,°	recount
15	Or suffyce to wryght	
	Of mirry Margarete,	
	As mydsomer flowre,	
	Jentyll as fawcoun	
	Or hawke of the towre;	
20	As pacient and as styll,[6]	
	And as full of good wyll,	

4. The poet imagines Isabell Pennell as a nightingale whose singing is heavenly.
5. A hawk that towers in the air.
6. The poet compares Margaret Hussey to sweet-smelling herbs and strong heroines of classical legend: Isaphill or Hypsipyle, known for her fortitude; and Cassaunder or Cassandra, the prophetess.

As fayre Isaphill;
Colyaunder,°   *coriander*
Swete pomaunder,°   *perfume ball*
25   Good cassaunder;
Stedfast of thought,
Wele made, wele wrought;
Far may be sought
Erst that ye can fynde
30   So corteise, so kynde
As mirry Margarete,
This midsomer flowre,
Ientyll as fawcoun
Or hawke of the towre.

* ⇥◊⇤ *

Sir Thomas Wyatt
1503–1542

A gifted poet and diplomat, Sir Thomas Wyatt exemplified the ambitious mixture of social
and artistic skills that later ages would see as the ideal of the "Renaissance man." Having
entered the household of King Henry VIII immediately after his education at Cambridge,
Wyatt promoted English interests on missions to France, Venice, Rome, Spain, and the Low
Countries. His career was to prove more precarious at home, where he became involved in
court politics. He was deeply attached to the Lady Anne Boleyn, who, by 1527, was the object
of Henry's affections and a probable pretext for the King's divorce from Catherine of Aragon
and England's break from the Roman Catholic Church. Made Henry's queen in 1533, but out
of favor by 1536, Anne implicated by association those who were supposed to have been her
lovers. Wyatt was lucky to suffer no more than imprisonment; the Queen's other favorites were
executed. Wyatt subsequently regained political status both at home and abroad, although not
without periods of disappointment. Despite the execution of his powerful patron, Sir Thomas
Cromwell, and a second prison term in 1541 for suspected treason, Wyatt obtained Henry's
goodwill at the end of his short life. He died from a fever at the age of thirty-nine while on a
diplomatic mission for the king.

By any poetic reckoning, Wyatt is to be valued as a pioneer of English verse. Although
many of his poems exhibit irregular meters, they have been praised for their remarkable texture
and sense of surprise. His translations of Francesco Petrarch's sonnets established the principal
forms of English lyric, the rhyming sonnet with its pentameter line and the more loosely con-
figured song derived from the Italian *canzone*. Wyatt's own poems change the spirit of their
Petrarchan themes by giving erotic subjects a satirical and even bitter twist and political topics
an inward and personal reference. In one of his best-known sonnets, *Whoso List to Hunt*, he
writes of vainly pursuing a "hind" or "deer" (a dear or beloved lady) belonging to "Caesar"
(King Henry VIII). Long understood to be a reference to Anne Boleyn, Wyatt's "deer" is quite
a different figure than the "deer" in his source, Petrarch's sonnet to a "white doe," who represents his lady, Laura, whom he met in 1327 and loved from a distance until her death in
1350. While Petrarch's lady is imagined as chastely devoted to a heavenly Caesar or God, and
therefore as inspiring a religious awe, Wyatt's beloved is the possession of an earthly Caesar,
King Henry VIII, and is thus the cause of his immediate frustration.

Wyatt's verse was circulated in manuscript during his lifetime and probably read only by his
friends and his acquaintances at court. A few poems were published in 1540, in a collection

entitled *The Court of Venus*, but the majority—ninety-seven poems in all—appeared in 1557, in a massive anthology called *Songs and Sonnets*, published by the printer Richard Tottel. This volume, which includes poems by Henry Howard, Earl of Surrey and others, was a milestone in the history of literature. Unlike the earlier sixteenth-century poetry of the British Isles, which remained relatively simple in its genres and diction, *Tottel's Miscellany* (as it has come to be known) exhibited a range of new forms and meters: the sonnet, the song (or *canzone*), the epigram, and rhyming and blank verse. Familiar to writers and readers of Italian and French, these forms allowed poets (now writing a recognizably modern English) to develop a stylistic flexibility and thematic richness previously achieved only by the Middle English poet Geoffrey Chaucer. Before presenting his anthology to the public, however, Tottel did some fairly drastic editing: smoothing out metrical irregularities by adding, subtracting, or changing words, he obviously sought to impress readers with what he judged to be the elegant and up-to-date styles represented by the works in his collection. The poems reprinted here are based not on the *Songs and Sonnets* but on Wyatt's original texts.

The Long Love, That in My Thought Doth Harbor

The long love, that in my thought doth harbor
And in mine heart doth keep his residence,
Into my face presseth with bold pretence,
And therein campeth, spreading his banner.
5   She that me learneth° to love and suffer,   *teaches*
And will that my trust and lust's negligence
Be reined by reason, shame and reverence,
With his hardiness° taketh displeasure.   *boldness*
Wherewithal, unto the heart's forest he fleeth,
10   Leaving his enterprise with pain and cry,
And there him hideth and not appeareth.
What may I do when my master feareth
But in the field with him to live and die?
For good is the life, ending faithfully.

Whoso List to Hunt

Who so list° to hunt, I know where is an hind,°   *wishes / doe*
But as for me, helas, I may no more:
The vain travail° hath wearied me so sore.   *idle labor*
I am of them that farthest cometh behind.
5   Yet may I by no means my wearied mind
Draw from° the deer: but as she fleeth afore,   *forget*
Fainting I follow. I leave off therefore,
Since in a net I seek to hold the wind.
Who list her hunt I put him out of doubt,
10   As well as I may spend his time in vain:
And, graven° with diamonds, in letters plain   *engraved*
There is written her fair neck round about:
Noli me tangere,[1] for Caesar's I am,
And wild for to hold though I seem tame.

---

1. "Touch me not," the words the resurrected but not yet risen Christ spoke to Mary Magdalene before his tomb (John 20.17). The "deer" of the poem has often been identified with Anne Boleyn and "Caesar" with Henry VIII.

COMPANION READING
Petrarch, Sonnet 190[1]

Una candida cerva sopra l'erba
verde m'apparve con duo corna d'oro,
fra due riviere all' ombra d'un alloro,
Levando 'l sole a la stagione acerba.
5   Era sua vista sì dolce superba
ch' i'lasciai per seguirla ogni lavoro,
come l'avaro che 'n cercar tesoro
con diletto l'affanno disacerba.
"Nessun mi tocchi," al bel collo d'intorno
10   scritto avea di diamanti et di topazi.
"Libera farmi al mio Cesare parve."
Et era 'l sol già vòlto al mezzo giorno,
gli occhi miei stanchi di mirar, non sazi,
quand' io caddi ne l'acqua et ella sparve.

Petrarch, Sonnet 190: A Translation

A white doe on the green grass appeared to me, with two golden horns, between two rivers, in the shade of a laurel, when the sun was rising in the unripe season.

Her look was so sweet and proud that to follow her I left every task, like the miser who as he seeks treasure sweetens his trouble with delight.

"Let no one touch me," she bore written with diamonds and topazes around her lovely neck. "It has pleased my Caesar to make me free."

And the sun had already turned at midday; my eyes were tired by looking but not sated, when I fell into the water, and she disappeared.

They Flee from Me

They flee from me that sometime did me seek
With naked foot stalking in my chamber.
I have seen them gentle tame and meek
That now are wild and do not remember
5   That sometime they put themself in danger
To take bread at my hand; and now they range
Busily seeking with a continual change.
Thanked be fortune, it hath been otherwise
Twenty times better; but once in special,
10   In thine array after a pleasant guise,°   *manner, disguise*
When her loose gown from her shoulders did fall,
And she me caught in her arms long and small;
Therewithal sweetly did me kiss,

1. Petrarch (1304–1374), known to his fellow Italians as Francesco Petrarca, was the virtual inventor of modern lyric poetry. Comprising sonnets, songs (*canzone*), and odes, his *Rime sparse* or "various poems"—widely circulated during and after his lifetime—were translated and imitated by poets throughout Europe. Petrarch's verse demonstrated to his early modern readers that a lyric poet could invest subjects with a spirituality and a seriousness previously attributed to the epic, the ode, and to philosophical poems. Translation by Robert M. Durling.

And softly said, "dear heart, how like you this?"
15   It was no dream: I lay broad waking.
But all is turned through my gentleness
Into a strange fashion of forsaking;
And I have leave to go of her goodness,
And she also to use new fangledness.
20   But since that I so kindly am served,
I would fain° know what she hath deserved.   *wish to*

My Lute, Awake!

My lute, awake! perform the last
Labor that thou and I shall waste
    And end that I have now begun,
For when this song is sung and past,
5   My lute be still, for I have done.

As to be heard where ere is none,°   *there is no one*
As lead to grave in marble stone,
    My song may pierce her heart as sone;°   *soon*
Should we then sigh, or sing, or moan?
10   No, no, my lute, for I have done.

The rocks do not so cruelly
Repulse the waves continually,
    As she my suit and affection,
So that I am past remedy,
15   Whereby my lute and I have done.

Proud of the spoil that thou hast got
Of simple hearts through love's shot,
    By whom, unkind, thou has them won,
Think not he hath his bow forgot,
20   Although my lute and I have done.

Vengeance shall fall on thy disdain,
That makest but game on earnest pain;
    Think not alone under the sun
Unquit° to cause thy lover's plain,°   *freely / lament*
25   Although my lute and I have done.

Perchance thee lie weathered and old,
The winter nights that are so cold,
    Plaining in vain unto the mone;°   *moon*
Thy wishes then dare not be told,
30   Care then who list,° for I have done.   *wishes*

And then may chance thee to repent
The time that thou hast lost and spent
    To cause thy lover's sigh and swoon;
Then shalt thou know beauty but lent
35   And wish and want as I have done.

Now cease, my lute, this is the last
Labor that thou and I shall wast,°   *waste*
    And ended is that we begun;

Now is this song both sung and past,
40   My lute be still, for I have done.

Blame Not My Lute

Blame not my lute for he must sound
    Of this or that as liketh me,
For lack of wit the lute is bound
    To give such tunes as pleaseth me:
5   Though my songs be somewhat strange,
And speaks such words as touch thy change,[1]
        Blame not my lute.

My lute, alas, doth not offend,
    Though that perforce he must agree
10   To sound such tunes as I intend
    To sing to them that heareth me;
Then though my songs be somewhat plain,
And toucheth some that used to fain,[2]
        Blame not my lute.

15   My lute and strings may not deny,
    But as I strike they must obey;
Break not them then so wrongfully,
    But wreak° thyself some wiser way: *revenge*
And though the songs which I endite°   *write*
20   Do quit° thy change with rightful spite,   *discharge, answer*
        Blame not my lute.

Spite asketh spite and changing change,
    And falsed° faith must needs be known: *betrayed*
The fault so great, the case so strange,
25   Of right it must abroad be blown:
Then since that by thine own desert°   *desert*
My songs do tell how true thou art,
        Blame not my lute.

Blame but the self that hast misdone
30   And well deserved to have blame;
Change thou thy way, so evil begun,
    And then my lute shall sound that same:
But if till then my fingers play
By thy desert their wonted way,
35   Blame not my lute.

Farewell, unknown, for though thou break
    My strings in spite with great disdain,
Yet have I found out for thy sake
    Strings for to string my lute again;
40   And if perchance this folys° rhyme   *foolish*
Do make thee blush at any time,
        Blame not my lute.

1. I.e., the lady's change of heart, probably also to be signified by a change of tone in the music to which this lyric
was supposedly set.
2. Who used to be desirous or who used to feign desire.

Stand Whoso List

Stand whoso list° upon the slipper° top   *wishes / slippery*
Of courts' estates, and let me here rejoice;
And use me° quiet without let° or stop,   *my / hindrance*
Unknown in court, that hath such brackish joys:
5   In hidden place, so let my days forth pass,
That when my years be done, withouten noise,
I may die aged after the common trace.°   *manner*
For him death greep'the° right hard by the crop°   *grips / throat*
That is much known of other; and of himself alas,
10   Doth die unknown, dazed with dreadful face.

———— ≍✧≍ ————

Edmund Spenser
1552?–1599

A man whose poetry has come to be known as a monument to Queen Elizabeth's England began life modestly enough. Attending Cambridge as a "sizar," or "poor scholar," he worked as a servant to pay for his fees. Allegiance to the English church was expected of all subjects, and Spenser showed his support of the faith while still a student by contributing anti-Catholic verses to the first emblem book published in England. The genre, consisting of emblems or symbolic scenes explained by clever captions, acquainted the aspiring poet with elements of the mode he was later to master: allegory. Literally a writing that conveys "other" (from the Greek *allos*, "other") than literal meanings, the allegory that Spenser would eventually perfect for his epic poem *The Faerie Queene* produced narrative verse of great flexibility and verve. Building on powerful images, his verse allegories of education in a "virtuous" chivalry convey the challenges he saw attending the creation of a civil society in early modern England.

Shortly after leaving Cambridge in 1576, Spenser found employment as a secretary in the London household of the rich and influential Earl of Leicester, a favorite courtier of Queen Elizabeth and an ardent defender of international Protestantism. There he met Leicester's already famous nephew, Sir Philip Sidney, to whom Spenser dedicated his first work, the deliberately archaic, neo-Chaucerian *The Shepheardes Calender,* a sequence of twelve eclogues or poems on pastoral subjects, one for each month of the year. A work of a paradoxically innovative style, *The Shepheardes Calender* demonstrated a range of metrical forms that had yet to be seen in English poetry; probably more compelling to the general reader was Spenser's use of pastoral motifs and settings to represent opinions on love, poetry, and social order. Sidney's response to the poem was, nevertheless, somewhat ambivalent. While recognizing that Spenser's eclogues had "much poetry" in them, he stated that he disliked verse composed in an "old rustic language"; among earlier and model poets of pastoral, "neither Theocritus in Greek, Virgil in Latin, nor Sannazaro in Italian did affect it." But precisely because this "old rustic language" could be recognized as purely English and independent of European traditions, Spenser would use a modified form of it in *The Faerie Queene*; in this way he hoped to demonstrate that English literature had as rich a past as any in Europe. He probably began the poem while in Leicester's service; the seventeenth-century biographer John Aubrey reported the discovery of "an abundance of cards, with stanzas of the *Faerie Queene* written on them" in the wainscoting of Spenser's London lodging.

From 1580 to the end of his life, Spenser lived in Ireland, serving as secretary to the Lord Deputy of Ireland, Arthur Grey. At such a distance from Queen Elizabeth's court, Spenser could not have secured royal favor. He was rescued from obscurity in 1589 by Sir Walter Raleigh, who, impressed with the first three books of *The Faerie Queene*, invited Spenser to present his poem to the queen. Beside the gallant and charismatic Raleigh, the poet—said to have been a "little man, who wore short hair, little bands (collars) and little cuffs"—must have cut a poor figure. But the queen liked the poem that illustrated her majesty in so many ways, "desired at timely hours to hear" it, and rewarded Spenser with a life pension of £50 a year. When Spenser returned to Ireland in 1590, he met and fell in love with Elizabeth Boyle, a woman much his junior. They were married in 1594, and Spenser celebrated their courtship and wedding in the *Amoretti*, a sonnet sequence describing the poet's quest for his "deer" or dear, and *Epithalamion*, a hymn to each of the twenty-four hours of their wedding day. The second three books of *The Faerie Queene*, published in 1596, proved as popular with readers as the first three, although James VI of Scotland (later James I of England) thought slanderous its portrait of the evil queen Duessa, whom he identified as his mother, Mary Queen of Scots. He demanded that Spenser be "duly tried and punished." Fortunately, however, Spenser's friends at court intervened, and nothing came of the king's displeasure.

The last years of the poet's life were full of grief and bitter disappointment. In 1598 the Irish in the province of Munster, rebelling against the English colonial authorities, burned the castle in which Spenser lived. The poet and his wife fled; their newborn child was reported to have perished in the flames. In December of that year, Spenser went to London to deliver letters to the queen from the Governor of Ireland concerning the uprising. He included a note describing his own assessment of the situation—a note that may have included material in a treatise entitled *A View of the Present State of Ireland*, supporting a militaristic policy to colonize the people of Ireland, which he is supposed to have written. He died a month after arriving in London in January of 1599 and was buried in Westminster Abbey near Geoffrey Chaucer, whose poetry had meant so much to him. The monument placed on his grave is inscribed with these words: "Prince of poets in his time, whose Divine Spirit needs no other witness than the works which he left behind."

Consciously aspiring both to Chaucer's humane dignity and to his vividly colloquial style, Spenser saw himself as fashioning and refashioning a tradition of English and possibly British poetry. As he made a point of using older terms and spelling, his poems are presented here unmodernized. Spenser's choice of language parallels his use of the motifs of knightly romance: turning to the past, he sought a vital perspective on the present. John Milton would later describe him as a "sage and serious" poet, who, in *The Faerie Queene*, wrote of the struggle of good against evil and the triumph of faith over falsehood. The subject, treated by weaving different story lines together to form a vast tapestry, interested not only Milton, who was clearly inspired by Spenser's complex understanding of human psychology, but also the next generation of poets in England, especially Ben Jonson, John Donne, and George Herbert, who turned to Spenser for a poetry of satirical vigor and spiritual insight. Yet other readers have been moved by Spenser's lyrics. His shorter poems and occasional verse show his skillful use of repetitive sounds or verbal echoes and reveal his unerring sense of language as a musical medium.

THE FAERIE QUEENE   In 1583 Spenser told guests at a dinner he was attending that he proposed to write a poem in which he would "represent all the moral virtues, assigning to every virtue a knight in whose actions and chivalry the operations of that virtue are to be expressed, and the vices and unruly appetites that oppose themselves to be beaten down." The project, obviously ambitious, recalls the great epics of classical antiquity: the twenty-four books of Homer's *Iliad*, the twelve books of Virgil's *Aeneid*. Spenser must have believed he was prepared for such an undertaking; like Virgil, he had served his apprenticeship by writing pastoral poetry. But whatever his intention, he realized his great work only in part. He depicted the first six virtues in the "legends" of Holiness, Temperance, Chastity, Friendship, Justice, and Courtesy, in which each virtue is perfected by the trials of a particular knight fighting the evil that most threatens his character. He published the first three books in 1590, adding the next three in a second edition in 1596. His plan for a second set of six books resulted in only two cantos—on the virtue of Constancy.

Spenser's moral chivalry is sponsored and sustained by the court of Gloriana, the Faerie Queene, in whom is reflected the imposing figure of Queen Elizabeth. Gloriana's story is illustrated by the actions of a character called Prince Arthur, who intervenes at crucial moments to assist Gloriana's knights and is otherwise bent on seeking out Gloriana herself, the bride he has chosen in a dream. In the mythical genealogy of the Tudors, King Arthur (known to Spenser's readers through Sir Thomas Malory's *Morte Darthur*) was identified as the dynasty's progenitor; thus, in the allegorical schema of the poem, the prospective marriage of the Faerie Queene and Prince Arthur, also the champion of Magnificence, signifies the perfect union of monarch and state.

Book 1 relates the adventures of the knight of Holiness, known as the Redcrosse Knight from the sign on his shield and identified as Saint George, England's patron saint. His mission is to overcome the machinations of spiritual error menacing the English church and to deliver the parents of Una, his lady, who is the Truth, from the demons of false faith. The foes of the Redcrosse Knight are many: the fiendish wizard Archimago, who stands for corrupt doctrine; the cunning queen Duessa, who, as the embodiment of duplicity, is never what she seems; the bloated giant Orgoglio, or Pride; and the loathsome many-headed dragon who is supposed to wield the institutional power of the Catholic Church. The Redcrosse Knight kills Pride and the dragon but, although he at last understands that they are thoroughly sinister, fails to capture Duessa and Archimago. They return in later books to trouble Gloriana's other knights.

Book 2 tells of the adventures of the knight of Temperance, Sir Guyon, who must destroy a garden of surpassing beauty, known as the Bower of Bliss, presided over by a brilliantly seductive witch called Acrasia. He is accompanied on his quest by the Palmer, who, as the embodiment of reason, informs and guides him in achieving the perfection of his virtue. In Canto 12, perhaps the best-known canto in the entire poem, Guyon sails to Acrasia's island garden in the company of the Palmer, is tempted by the illusionistic pleasures Acrasia provides her suitors, but finally rejects her in a massive act of defiance, tearing down all the beguiling structures of her island in a salutary rage.

The verse form of *The Faerie Queene* is virtually unique to Spenser. It features a sequence of stanzas each comprising nine lines (known to later readers as "Spenserian"), of which the first eight contain five feet or accented syllables and the last contains six feet. They are rhymed in a pattern—*ababbcbcc*—particularly difficult for poets writing in English. Unlike the Romance languages (French, Italian, and Spanish), English has relatively few words ending in vowel sounds, which are easily rhymed. Spenser's ear for the sound of English allowed him to compose verse of a musicality comparable to what was possible in the Romance languages, itself an extraordinary accomplishment. The narrative units of Spenser's epic poem achieve a dramatic coherence by his constructive use of imagery in particular story lines that continuously develop new contexts for their subjects. In other words, a character signifying a special quality in one canto will not signify precisely that quality in another canto: Spenser will change his or her role with the setting the story demands. This gives the reader an active role in the poem's interpretation; in a sense, the reader finds the meaning of the poem in the process of reading it.

The First Booke of the Faerie Queene
Contayning The Legende of the Knight of the Red Crosse,
or
Of Holinesse.

1

Lo I the man, whose Muse whilome° did maske,[1]   *formerly*
   As time her taught, in lowly Shepheards weeds,°   *clothing*
   Am now enforst a far unfitter taske,

---

1. In this stanza and in the rest of the Proem (introduction), Spenser is announcing his intention to write an epic poem. His earlier *Shepheardes Calender* had been written in the more modest pastoral style, characterized by the "oaten reed" of the shepherd's pipe. Here he casts off the guise of the shepherd to undertake the lofty subject of *The Faerie Queene*.

For trumpets sterne to chaunge mine Oaten reeds,
5   And sing of Knights and Ladies gentle deeds;
  Whose prayses having slept in silence long,
  Me, all too meane,° the sacred Muse areeds°   *lowly / commands*
  To blazon broad° emongst her learned throng: *proclaim abroad*
Fierce warres and faithfull loves shall moralize my song.

2

10 Helpe then, O holy Virgin chiefe of nine,[2]
  Thy weaker Novice to performe thy will,
  Lay forth out of thine everlasting scryne°   *treasure chest*
  The antique rolles,° which there lye hidden still,   *scrolls*
  Of Faerie knights and fairest Tanaquill,
15   Whom that most noble Briton Prince° so long   *Arthur*
  Sought through the world, and suffered so much ill,
  That I must rue° his undeserved wrong: *regret*
O helpe thou my weake wit, and sharpen my dull tong.

3

And thou most dreaded impe° of highest Jove,[3]   *child*
20   Faire Venus sonne,° that with thy cruell dart   *Cupid, god of love*
  At that good knight° so cunningly didst rove,°   *Arthur / pierce*
  That glorious fire it kindled in his hart,
  Lay now thy deadly Heben° bow apart,   *ebony*
  And with thy mother milde come to mine ayde:[4]
25   Come both, and with you bring triumphant Mart,° *Mars*
  In loves and gentle jollities arrayd,
After his murdrous spoiles and bloudy rage allayd.° *quelled*

4

And with them eke, O Goddesse heavenly bright,[5]
  Mirrour of grace and Majestie divine,
30   Great Lady of the greatest Isle, whose light
  Like Phoebus lampe throughout the world doth shine,
  Shed thy faire beames into my feeble eyne,
  And raise my thoughts too humble and too vile,
  To thinke of that true glorious type° of thine,   *the Faerie Queene*
35   The argument of mine afflicted stile:
The which to heare, vouchsafe,° O dearest dread° a-while. *grant / power*

---

2. Spenser calls on a muse to inspire him; he may be referring to Clio, the muse of history, or to Calliope, the muse of epic poetry. Tanaquill was a Roman woman famous for her chaste and noble character; here Spenser establishes a symbolic relation between Tanaquill, the Faerie Queene (whom Arthur seeks in the poem), and Queen Elizabeth I, much as he will later refer to other characters—most prominently, Britomart, Gloriana, and Mercilla—as figuring aspects of the queen, her power and attributes.
3. The king of the pagan gods. Like all the poets of the period who were not writing religious verse, Spenser refers to the classical pantheon as a way of alluding to God and to his various expressions of power.
4. Spenser also invokes Cupid, who combines the loving nature of Venus and the warlike spirit of Mars, to illustrate the mood of his poem.
5. Spenser celebrates the nature of Elizabeth I in grandiose terms: She is a "goddess" whose eyes, like the lamp of Phoebus Apollo (the sun), shine throughout the world and must now illuminate the poet's mind.

Canto 1

The Patron of true Holinesse,
Foule Errour doth defeate:
Hypocrisie him to entrapp;
Doth to his home entreate.

1

A Gentle Knight[6] was pricking° on the plaine,   *riding*
    Y cladd in mightie armes and silver shielde,
    Wherein old dints of deepe wounds did remaine,
    The cruell markes of many a bloudy fielde;
5   Yet armes till that time did he never wield:
    His angry steede did chide his foming bitt,
    As much disdayning to the curbe to yield:
    Full jolly knight he seemd, and faire did sitt,
As one for knightly giusts° and fierce encounters fitt.   *joust*

2

10   But on his brest a bloudie Crosse[7] he bore,
    The deare remembrance of his dying Lord,
    For whose sweete sake that glorious badge he wore,
    And dead as living ever him ador'd:
    Upon his shield the like was also scor'd,°   *represented*
15   For soveraine hope, which in his° helpe he had: *his Lord's*
    Right faithfull true he was in deede and word,
    But of his cheere° did seeme too solemne sad;   *demeanor*
Yet nothing did he dread,° but ever was ydrad.°   *fear / feared*

3

Upon a great adventure he was bond,
20   That greatest Gloriana[8] to him gave,
    That greatest Glorious Queene of Faerie lond,
    To winne him worship, and her grace to have,
    Which of all earthly things he most did crave;
    And ever as he rode, his hart did earne
25   To prove his puissance° in battell brave   *power*
    Upon his foe, and his new force to learne;
Upon his foe, a Dragon horrible and stearne.

4

A lovely Ladie rode him faire beside,
    Upon a lowly Asse more white then snow,[9]
30   Yet she much whiter, but the same did hide
    Under a vele, that wimpled° was full low,   *gathered*
    And over all a blacke stole she did throw,

---

6. This gentle or well-born knight, identified as the Red-crosse Knight from the sign on his shield and introduced to the poem in Spenser's prefatory letter, wears the armor of Christianity. The armor itself has been worn by many who fought for the faith, but the Redcrosse Knight is new to the spiritual battlefield and will have to prove himself.
7. The red cross is Spenser's figure for the salvation offered by Christ to humankind through his death on the cross, the sacrifice of his blood, and his resurrection. It

was also the badge traditionally worn by St. George, the patron saint of England.
8. The character Spenser most frequently invokes when he alludes to Elizabeth I. Gloriana presides over the action of the poem, although she does not take part in it herself.
9. This imagery suggests the role the Lady will play: the ass signifies her humility, the veil her modesty, and the lamb her innocence.

As one that inly mournd: so was she sad,
And heavie sat upon her palfrey[1] slow:
35   Seemed in heart some hidden care she had,
And by her in a line a milke white lambe she lad.

5

So pure an innocent, as that same lambe,
She was in life and every vertuous lore,
And by descent from Royall lynage came
40   Of ancient Kings and Queenes, that had of yore
Their scepters stretcht from East to Westerne shore,
And all the world in their subjection held;[2]
Till that infernall feend with foule uprore
Forwasted all their land, and them expeld:
45   Whom to avenge, she had this Knight from far compeld.

6

Behind her farre away a Dwarfe[3] did lag,
That lasie seemd in being ever last,
Or wearied with bearing of her bag
Of needments at his backe. Thus as they past,
50   The day with cloudes was suddeine overcast,
And angry Jove an hideous storme of raine
Did poure into his Lemans[4] lap so fast,
That every wight to shrowd° it did constrain,°   *shelter / impel*
And this faire couple eke° to shroud themselves were fain.°   *also / desirous*

7

55   Enforst to seeke some covert° nigh at hand,   *hiding place*
A shadie grove not far away they spide,
That promist ayde the tempest to withstand:
Whose loftie trees yclad with sommers pride,
Did spred so broad, that heavens light did hide,
60   Not perceable with power of any starre:
And all within were pathes and alleies wide,
With footing worne, and leading inward farre:
Faire harbour that them seemes; so in they entred arre.

8

And foorth they passe, with pleasure forward led,
65   Joying to heare the birdes sweete harmony,
Which therein shrouded from the tempest dred,
Seemd in their song to scorne the cruell sky.
Much can they prayse the trees so straight and hy,
The sayling° Pine, the Cedar proud and tall,   *soaring*
70   The vine-prop Elme, the Poplar never dry,

---

1. A horse suitable for a woman.
2. The Lady traces her lineage to Adam and Eve, who held dominion over Eden before the Fall. The "infernall feend," or Satan, is represented as the destroyer of their realm, which stretched from East to West and was therefore truly universal, unlike the regions dominated by

Rome or by the Catholic Church. By designating the Knight as the avenger of Adam and Eve, Spenser identifies him with Christ.
3. The servant who serves the Lady, a source of prudence, common sense, and wariness.
4. I.e., his lady love's, or the earth's.

The builder Oake, sole king of forrests all,
The Aspine good for staves,° the Cypresse funerall.   *poles*

9

The Laurell, meed° of mightie Conquerours   *reward*
And Poets sage, the Firre that weepeth still,
75   The Willow worne of forlorne Paramours,°   *forsaken lovers*
The Eugh obedient to the benders will,
The Birch for shaftes, the Sallow° for the mill,   *willow*
The Mirrhe sweete bleeding in the bitter wound,
The warlike Beech, the Ash for nothing ill,
80   The fruitfull Olive, and the Platane° round,   *sycamore*
The carver Holme,° the Maple seeldom inward sound.   *holly*

10

Led with delight, they thus beguile° the way,   *make pleasant*
Untill the blustring storme is overblowne;
When weening° to returne, whence they did stray,   *thinking*
85   They cannot finde that path, which first was showne,
But wander too and fro in wayes unknowne,
Furthest from end then, when they neerest weene,
That makes them doubt, their wits be not their owne:
So many pathes, so many turnings seene,
90   That which of them to take, in diverse doubt they been.

11

At last resolving forward still to fare,
Till that some end° they finde or° in or out,   *way / either*
That path they take, that beaten seemd most bare,
And like to lead the labyrinth about;
95   Which when by tract they hunted had throughout,
At length it brought them to a hollow cave,
Amid the thickest woods. The Champion stout
Eftsoones dismounted from his courser brave,
And to the Dwarfe a while his needlesse spere he gave.

12

100   Be well aware, quoth then that Ladie milde,
Least suddaine mischiefe ye too rash provoke:
The danger hid, the place unknowne and wilde,
Breedes dreadful doubts: Oft fire is without smoke,
And perill without show: therefore your stroke
105   Sir knight with-hold, till further triall made.
Ah Ladie (said he) shame were to revoke
The forward footing for an hidden shade:
Vertue gives her selfe light, through darkenesse for to wade.[5]

13

Yea but (quoth she) the perill of this place
110   I better wot° then you, though now too late   *know*

---

5. Lacking humility and overly confident of his own virtue, the Redcrosse Knight believes he is strong enough to withstand the dangers of the wood. In fact, as we learn in the next stanza, he has stepped into the den of a monster who personifies Error, one of Satan's many manifestations in the poem.

To wish you backe returne with foule disgrace,
Yet wisedome warnes, whilest foot is in the gate,
To stay° the steppe, ere forced to retrate.°   *halt / retreat*
This is the wandring wood, this Errours den,
115   A monster vile, whom God and man does hate:
Therefore I read beware. Fly fly (quoth then
The fearefull Dwarfe:) this is no place for living men.

14

But full of fire and greedy hardiment,
The youthfull knight could not for ought° be staide,   *anything*
120   But forth unto the darksome hole he went,
And looked in: his glistring armor made
A litle glooming light, much like a shade,
By which he saw the ugly monster plaine,
Halfe like a serpent horribly displaide,
125   But th'other halfe did womans shape retaine,[6]
Most lothsom, filthie, foule, and full of vile disdaine.

15

And as she lay upon the durtie ground,
Her huge long taile her den all overspred,
Yet was in knots and many boughtes° upwound,   *coils*
130   Pointed with mortall sting. Of her there bred
A thousand yong ones, which she dayly fed,
Sucking upon her poisonous dugs, eachone
Of sundry shapes, yet all ill favored:
Soone as that uncouth° light upon them shone,   *strange*
135   Into her mouth they crept, and suddain all were gone.

16

Their dam upstart, out of her den effraide,
And rushed forth, hurling her hideous taile
About her cursed head, whose folds displaid
Were stretcht now forth at length without entraile.°   *coiling*
140   She lookt about, and seeing one in mayle°   *armor*
Armed to point, sought backe to turne againe;
For light she hated as the deadly bale,°   *injury*
Ay wont° in desert darknesse to remaine,   *ever used*
Where plaine° none might her see, nor she see any plaine.   *plainly*

17

145   Which when the valiant Elfe° perceiv'd, he lept   *Redcrosse Knight*
As Lyon fierce upon the flying pray,
And with his trenchand blade her boldly kept
From turning backe, and forced her to stay:
Therewith enrag'd she loudly gan to bray,
150   And turning fierce, her speckled taile advaunst,
Threatning her angry sting, him to dismay:
Who nought aghast, his mightie hand enhaunst:°   *raised up*
The stroke down from her head unto her shoulder glaunst.

6. Spenser follows traditional treatments of Error in giving her a woman's face and a serpent's body.

18

Much daunted with that dint, her sence was dazd,
155 Yet kindling rage, her selfe she gathered round,
  And all attonce her beastly body raizd
  With doubled forces high above the ground:
  Tho wrapping up her wrethed sterne° arownd,   *tail*
  Lept fierce upon his shield, and her huge traine°   *tail*
160 All suddenly about his body wound,
  That hand or foot to stirre he strove in vaine:
God helpe the man so wrapt in Errours endlesse traine.

19

His Lady sad to see his sore constraint,°   *predicament*
  Cride out, Now now Sir knight, shew what ye bee,
165 Add faith unto your force, and be not faint:
  Strangle her, else she sure will strangle thee.
  That when he heard, in great perplexitie,
  His gall did grate° for griefe and high disdaine,   *anger was aroused*
  And knitting all his force got one hand free,
170 Wherewith he grypt her gorge with so great paine,
That soone to loose her wicked bands did her constraine.

20

Therewith she spewd out of her filthy maw°   *stomach*
  A floud of poyson horrible and blacke,
  Full of great lumpes of flesh and gobbets raw,
175 Which stunck so vildly, that it forst him slacke
  His grasping hold, and from her turne him backe:
  Her vomit full of bookes and papers was,[7]
  With loathly frogs and toades, which eyes did lacke,
  And creeping sought way in the weedy gras:
180 Her filthy parbreake° all the place defiled has.   *vomit*

21

As when old father Nilus° gins to swell   *the river Nile*
  With timely pride aboue the Aegyptian vale,
  His fattie° waves do fertile slime outwell,°   *fertile / pour forth*
  And overflow each plaine and lowly dale:
185 But when his later spring° gins to avale,°   *last waters / subside*
  Huge heapes of mudd he leaves, wherein there breed
  Ten thousand kindes of creatures, partly male
  And partly female of his fruitfull seed;
Such ugly monstrous shapes elswhere may no man reed.°   *know*

22

190 The same so sore annoyed has the knight,
  That welnigh choked with the deadly stinke,
  His forces faile, ne can no longer fight.
  Whose corage when the feend perceiv'd to shrinke,
  She poured forth out of her hellish sinke°   *womb*

7. Error's vomit is a figurative depiction of the falsehoods that corrupt religion. The vehicles of such lies are both the spoken and written word; hence the material issuing from Error's mouth includes books as well as other poisonous things.

195   Her fruitfull cursed spawne° of serpents small,   *offspring*
            Deformed monsters, fowle, and blacke as inke,
            Which swarming all about his legs did crall,
       And him encombred sore, but could not hurt at all.

23

       As gentle Shepheard in sweete even-tide,
200   When ruddy Phoebus gins to welke° in west,   *sink*
            High on an hill, his flocke to vewen wide,
            Markes which do byte their hasty supper best;
            A cloud of combrous gnattes do him molest,
            All striving to infixe their feeble stings,
205   That from their noyance he no where can rest,
            But with his clownish hands their tender wings
       He brusheth oft, and oft doth mar their murmurings.

24

       Thus ill bestedd,° and fearefull more of shame,   *situated*
            Then of the certaine perill he stood in,
210   Halfe furious unto his foe he came,
            Resolv'd in minde all suddenly to win,
            Or soone to lose, before he once would lin;°   *surrender*
            And strooke at her with more then manly force,
            That from her body full of filthie sin
215   He raft° her hatefull head without remorse;   *cut off*
       A streame of cole black bloud forth gushed from her corse.

25

       Her scattred brood, soone as their Parent deare
            They saw so rudely° falling to the ground,   *violently*
            Groning full deadly, all with troublous feare,
220   Gathred themselves about her body round,
            Weening their wonted entrance to have found
            At her wide mouth: but being there withstood
            They flocked all about her bleeding wound,
            And sucked up their dying mothers blood,
225   Making her death their life, and eke her hurt their good.

26

       That detestable sight him much amazde,
            To see th'unkindly Impes° of heaven accurst,   *unnatural offspring*
            Devoure their dam; on whom while so he gazd,
            Having all satisfide their bloudy thurst,
230   Their bellies swolne he saw with fulnesse burst,
            And bowels gushing forth: well worthy end
            Of such as drunke her life, the which them nurst;
            Now needeth him no lenger labour spend,
       His foes have slaine themselves, with whom he should contend.

27

235   His Ladie seeing all, that chaunst, from farre
            Approcht in hast to greet his victorie,
            And said, Faire knight, borne under happy starre,

Who see your vanquisht foes before you lye:
Well worthy be you of that Armorie,[8]
240 Wherein ye have great glory wonne this day,
And proov'd your strength on a strong enimie,
Your first adventure: many such I pray,
And henceforth ever wish, that like succeed it may.

28

Then mounted he upon his Steede againe,
245 And with the Lady backward sought to wend;
That path he kept, which beaten was most plaine,
Ne ever would to any by-way bend,
But still did follow one unto the end,
The which at last out of the wood them brought.
250 So forward on his way (with God to frend)
He passed forth, and new adventure sought;
Long way he travelled, before he heard of ought.

29

At length they chaunst to meet upon the way
An aged Sire, in long blacke weedes yclad,
255 His feete all bare, his beard all hoarie gray,
And by his belt his booke he hanging had;
Sober he seemde, and very sagely sad,
And to the ground his eyes were lowly bent,
Simple in shew, and voyde of malice bad,
260 And all the way he prayed, as he went,
And often knockt his brest, as one that did repent.

30

He faire the knight saluted, louting° low,   *bowing*
Who faire him quited,° as that courteous was: *answered*
And after asked him, if he did know
265 Of straunge adventures, which abroad did pas.
Ah my deare Sonne (quoth he) how should, alas,
Silly° old man, that lives in hidden cell,   *simple*
Bidding° his beades all day for his trespas,   *telling*
Tydings of warre and worldly trouble tell?
270 With holy father sits not with such things to mell.°   *meddle*

31

But if of daunger which hereby doth dwell,
And homebred evill ye desire to heare,
Of a straunge man I can you tidings tell,
That wasteth° all this countrey farre and neare.   *destroys*
275 Of such (said he)° I chiefly do inquere,   *Redcrosse Knight*
And shall you well reward to shew the place,
In which that wicked wight his dayes doth weare:°   *spend*
For to all knighthood it is foule disgrace,
That such a cursed creature lives so long a space.

8. The Lady is proclaiming that by conquering Error, the Redcrosse Knight has become worthy to wear the armor of Christ; the episode foreshadows the knight's final triumph over the many-headed dragon that represents false faith.

32

280 Far hence (quoth he)° in wastfull wildernesse,   *the aged Sire*
　　His dwelling is, by which no living wight
　　　May ever passe, but thorough° great distresse.   *through*
　　Now (sayd the Lady) draweth toward night,
　　And well I wote,° that of your later fight   *know*
285 Ye all forwearied° be: for what so strong,   *exhausted*
　　But wanting rest will also want of might?
　　The Sunne that measures heaven all day long,
At night doth baite° his steedes the Ocean waves emong.   *nourish*

33

Then with the Sunne take Sir, your timely rest,
290 And with new day new worke at once begin:
　　Untroubled night they say gives counsell best.
　　Right well Sir knight ye have advised bin,
　　(Quoth then that aged man;) the way to win
　　Is wisely to advise: now day is spent;
295 Therefore with me ye may take up your In
　　For this same night. The knight was well content:
So with that godly father to his home they went.

34

A little lowly Hermitage it was,[9]
　　Downe in a dale, hard by° a forests side,   *next to*
300 Far from resort of people, that did pas
　　In travell to and froe: a little wyde
　　There was an holy Chappell edifyde,°   *built*
　　Wherein the Hermite dewly wont to say
　　His holy things each morne and eventyde:
305 Thereby a Christall streame did gently play,
Which from a sacred fountaine welled forth alway.

35

Arrived there, the little house they fill,
　　Ne looke for entertainment, where none was:
　　Rest is their feast, and all things at their will;
310 The noblest mind the best contentment has.
　　With faire discourse the evening so they pas:
　　For that old man of pleasing wordes had store,
　　And well could file his tongue as smooth as glas;
　　He told of Saintes and Popes, and evermore
315 He strowd° an Ave-Mary after and before.[1]   *recited*

36

The drouping Night thus creepeth on them fast,
　　And the sad humour° loading their eye liddes,   *moisture*

9. This stanza illustrates the use of symbol in allegory; taken as a whole, its imagery suggests that the Redcrosse Knight has met the hermit because he suffers from a failing that the hermit will exploit. The hermitage is down in a dale, or valley, because the knight has begun to descend into a false faith, and it is isolated because he is traveling in a strange and unusual direction.

1. Despite his pious demeanor, the old man's discourse of saints and popes and his recital of Ave Marias indicate his affiliation with Catholicism; they are therefore intended to signal his corrupt and duplicitous character.

As messenger of Morpheus° on them cast   *god of sleep*
Sweet slombring deaw, the which to sleepe them biddes.

320   Unto their lodgings then his guestes he° riddes: *the aged Sire*
Where when all drownd in deadly sleepe he findes,
He to his study goes, and there amiddes
His Magick bookes and artes of sundry kindes,
He seekes out mighty charmes, to trouble sleepy mindes.

37

325   Then choosing out few wordes most horrible,
(Let none them read) thereof did verses frame,°   *compose*
With which and other spelles like terrible,
He bad awake blacke Plutoes griesly Dame,[2]
And cursed heaven, and spake reprochfull shame
330   Of highest God, the Lord of life and light;
A bold bad man, that dar'd to call by name
Great Gorgon,[3] Prince of darknesse and dead night,
At which Cocytus quakes, and Styx is put to flight.[4]

38

And forth he cald out of deepe darknesse dred
335   Legions of Sprights,° the which like little flyes   *spirits*
Fluttring about his ever damned hed,
A-waite whereto their service he applyes,
To aide his friends, or fray° his enimies: *frighten*
Of those he chose out two, the falsest twoo,
340   And fittest for to forge true-seeming lyes;
The one of them he gave a message too,
The other by him selfe staide other worke to doo.

39

He making speedy way through spersed° ayre,   *empty*
And through the world of waters wide and deepe,
345   To Morpheus[5] house doth hastily repaire.
Amid the bowels of the earth full steepe,
And low, where dawning day doth never peepe,
His dwelling is; there Tethys his wet bed
Doth ever wash, and Cynthia still doth steepe
350   In silver deaw his ever-drouping hed,
Whiles sad Night over him her mantle black doth spred.

40

Whose double gates he findeth locked fast,
The one faire fram'd of burnisht Yvory,
The other all with silver overcast;
355   And wakefull dogges before them farre do lye,
Watching to banish Care their enimy,
Who oft is wont to trouble gentle Sleepe.

---

2. Persephone, Pluto's wife and sometimes goddess of the underworld.
3. One of a family of monsters, daughters of the primitive gods of antiquity; Spenser, making her male, identifies the Gorgon with Pluto and also Satan.
4. The Cocytus and the Styx were rivers in the classical underworld.
5. God of sleep, who lives in the depths of the dark earth: Tethus or the sea washes him; Cynthia or the moon bedews him; Night covers him.

By them the Sprite doth passe in quietly,
And unto Morpheus comes, whom drowned deepe
360   In drowsie fit° he findes: of nothing he takes keepe.°   *stupor / notice*

41

And more, to lulle him in his slumber soft,
    A trickling streame from high rocke tumbling downe
    And ever-drizling raine upon the loft,
    Mixt with a murmuring winde, much like the sowne
365   Of swarming Bees, did cast him in a swowne°:   *faint*
    No other noyse, nor peoples troublous cryes,
    As still are wont t'annoy the walled towne,
    Might there be heard: but carelesse Quiet lyes,
Wrapt in eternall silence farre from enemyes.

42

370 The messenger approching to him spake,
    But his wast wordes returnd to him in vaine:
    So sound he° slept, that nought mought him awake.   *Morpheus*
    Then rudely he him thrust, and pusht with paine,
    Whereat he gan to stretch: but he againe
375   Shooke him so hard, that forced him to speake.
    As one then in a dreame, whose dryer braine
    Is tost with troubled sights and fancies weake,
He mumbled soft, but would not all his silence breake.

43

The Sprite then gan more boldly him to wake,
380   And threatned unto him the dreaded name
    Of Hecate:[6] whereat he gan to quake,
    And lifting up his lumpish head, with blame
    Halfe angry asked him, for what he came.
    Hither (quoth he) me Archimago[7] sent,
385   He that the stubborne Sprites can wisely tame,
    He bids thee to him send for his intent
A fit false dreame, that can delude the sleepers sent.°   *senses*

44

The God obayde, and calling forth straight way
    A diverse dreame out of his prison darke,
390   Delivered it to him, and downe did lay
    His heavie head, devoide of carefull carke,°   *sorrowful anxiety*
    Whose sences all were straight benumbd and starke.°   *paralyzed*
    He backe returning by the Yvorie dore,
    Remounted up as light as chearefull Larke,
395   And on his litle winges the dreame he bore
In hast unto his Lord, where he him left afore.

---

6. The dark aspect of Cynthia, the moon, and thus also of Diana; Hecate figures the underworld, death, and darkness.
7. The sage Sire is named Archimago, an "arch (or chief) magus (or magician)" and hence a forger or architect of images rather than real things. Because these images are clever and deceptive imitations of reality, Archimago is associated with hypocrisy and magic, an art that Christians were forbidden to practice.

45

Who all this while with charmes and hidden artes,
　Had made a Lady of that other Spright,
　And fram'd of liquid ayre her tender partes
400　So lively, and so like in all mens sight,
　That weaker sence it° could have ravisht quight:　　　*the spright*
　The maker selfe for all his wondrous witt,
　Was nigh beguiled with so goodly sight:
　Her all in white he clad, and over it
405　Cast a blacke stole, most like to seeme for Una[8] fit.

46

Now when that ydle dreame was to him brought,
　Unto that Elfin knight he° bad him° fly,　　　*Archimago / the spright*
　Where he slept soundly void of evill thought,
　And with false shewes abuse his fantasy,
410　In sort as he him schooled privily:
　And that new creature borne without her dew,°　　　*unnaturally*
　Full of the makers guile, with usage sly
　He taught to imitate that Lady trew,
　Whose semblance she did carrie under feigned hew.

47

415　Thus well instructed, to their worke they hast,
　And comming where the knight in slomber lay,
　The one upon his hardy head him plast,
　And made him dreame of loves and lustfull play,
　That nigh his manly hart did melt away,
420　Bathed in wanton blis and wicked joy:
　Then seemed him his Lady by him lay,
　And to him playnd, how that false winged boy°　　　*Cupid*
　Her chast hart had subdewd, to learne Dame pleasures toy.

48

　And she her selfe of beautie soveraigne Queene,
425　Faire Venus seemde unto his bed to bring
　Her,[9] whom he waking evermore did weene
　To be the chastest flowre, that ay did spring
　On earthly braunch, the daughter of a king,
　Now a loose Leman to vile service bound:
430　And eke the Graces seemed all to sing,
　Hymen iō Hymen,[1] dauncing all around,
　Whilst freshest Flora her with Yvie girlond crownd.

---

8. Here the Lady is named Una; she is to symbolize the ideal unity of Truth and the Church whose faith the Redcrosse Knight defends. She is named only when her false double appears.
9. I.e., she, impersonating Una, seemed also a Venus; this composite queen of beauty appears to the Redcrosse Knight to have come into his bed.
1. A Roman chant praising Hymen, the god of marriage, sung here by the Graces, handmaids of Venus, who personify the arts of courtesy and courtship. The union they celebrate in this case is not, however, a lawful Christian marriage but rather one provoked by lust and sexuality. In Roman mythology, Flora is the goddess of flowers, but early modern poets often gave her the role of a harlot. This entire scene uses the imagery of the Roman Bacchanalia (celebration of the god Bacchus) to suggest the mood of an orgy.

49

In this great passion of unwonted lust,
   Or wonted feare of doing ought amis,

435   He° started up, as seeming to mistrust   *Redcrosse Knight*
   Some secret ill, or hidden foe of his:
   Lo there before his face his Lady is,
   Under blake stole hyding her bayted hooke,
   And as halfe blushing offred him to kis,

440   With gentle blandishment and lovely looke,
Most like that virgin true, which for her knight him took.

50

All cleane° dismayd to see so uncouth sight,   *fully*
   And halfe enraged at her shamelesse guise,
   He thought have slaine her in his fierce despight:°   *indignation*

445   But hasty heat tempring with sufferance° wise,   *patience*
   He stayde his hand, and gan himselfe advise
   To prove his sense,° and tempt° her faigned truth.[2]   *what he saw / test*
   Wringing her hands in wemens pitteous wise,
   Tho° can she weepe, to stirre up gentle ruth,   *then*

450 Both for her noble bloud, and for her tender youth.

51

And said, Ah Sir, my liege Lord and my love,
   Shall I accuse the hidden cruell fate,
   And mightie causes wrought in heaven above,
   Or the blind God, that doth me thus amate,°   *dismay*

455   For hoped love to winne me certaine hate?
   Yet thus perforce he bids me do, or die.
   Die is my dew:° yet rew° my wretched state   *due / pity*
   You, whom my hard avenging destinie
Hath made judge of my life or death indifferently.

52

460 Your owne deare sake forst me at first to leave
   My Fathers kingdome, There she stopt with teares;
   Her swollen hart her speach seemd to bereave,
   And then againe begun, My weaker yeares
   Captiv'd to fortune and frayle worldly feares,

465   Fly to your faith for succour and sure ayde:
   Let me not dye in languor and long teares.
   Why Dame (quoth he) what hath ye thus dismayd?
What frayes° ye, that were wont to comfort me affrayd?   *frightens*

53

Love of your selfe, she said, and deare° constraint°   *dire / danger*

470   Lets me not sleepe, but wast the wearie night
   In secret anguish and unpittied plaint,

---

2. The Redcrosse Knight unwisely tests his senses rather than his faith. In doing so, he succumbs to the sensuality of the false Una and thus proves himself false to the true Una. The episode illustrates the danger inherent in powerful illusion; in such cases the false and the true may be indistinguishable.

Whiles you in carelesse sleepe are drowned quight.
Her doubtfull words made that redoubted knight
Suspect her truth: yet since no'untruth he knew,
475 Her fawning love with foule disdainefull spight
He would not shend,° but said, Deare dame I rew,   *reproach*
That for my sake unknowne such griefe unto you grew.

54

Assure your selfe, it fell not all to ground;
For all so deare as life is to my hart,
480 I deeme your love, and hold me to you bound;
Ne let vaine feares procure your needlesse smart,°   *pain*
Where cause is none, but to your rest depart.
Not all content, yet seemd she to appease
Her mournefull plaintes, beguiled of her art,
485 And fed with words, that could not chuse but please,
So slyding softly forth, she turnd as to her ease.

55

Long after lay he musing at her mood,
Much griev'd to thinke that gentle Dame so light,
For whose defence he was to shed his blood.
490 At last dull wearinesse of former fight
Having yrockt a sleepe his irkesome spright,
That troublous dreame gan freshly tosse his braine,
With bowres, and beds, and Ladies deare delight:
But when he° saw his labour all was vaine,   *Archimago*
495 With that misformed spright he backe returnd againe.

Canto 2

The guilefull great Enchaunter parts
The Redcrosse Knight from Truth:
Into whose stead faire falshood steps,
And workes him wofull ruth.

1

By this the Northerne wagoner had set
His sevenfold teme behind the stedfast starre,[1]
That was in Ocean waves yet never wet,
But firme is fixt, and sendeth light from farre
5   To all, that in the wide deepe wandring arre:
And chearefull Chaunticlere° with his note shrill   *a rooster*
Had warned once, that Phoebus fiery carre°   *chariot*
In hast was climbing up the Easterne hill,
Full envious that night so long his roome° did fill.   *the sky*

1. Spenser is referring to a constellation that includes Ursa Major, which contemporary English readers envisioned as a ploughman drawing a wagon. The "stedfast starre" is the Pole Star; it remains at the center of the stars in Ursa Major, which revolve around it and is "never wet" because it never sets into the ocean. The brightest star in this constellation is Arcturus, which the English associated with the mythical King Arthur.

2

10   When those accursed messengers of hell,
         That feigning dreame, and that faire-forged Spright
         Came to their wicked maister, and gan° tell   *did*
         Their bootelesse paines,° and ill succeeding night: *fruitless efforts*
         Who all in rage to see his skilfull might
15   Deluded so, gan threaten hellish paine
         And sad Proserpines wrath, them to affright.
         But when he saw his threatning was but vaine,
     He cast about, and searcht his balefull° bookes againe.   *evil*

3

     Eftsoones° he tooke that miscreated faire,   *soon after*
20   And that false other Spright, on whom he spred
         A seeming body of the subtile aire,
         Like a young Squire, in loves and lusty-hed°   *lechery*
         His wanton dayes that ever loosely led,
         Without regard of armes and dreaded fight:
25   Those two he tooke, and in a secret bed,
         Covered with darknesse and misdeeming° night,   *deceiving*
     Them both together laid, to joy in vaine delight.

4

     Forthwith he runnes with feigned faithfull hast
         Unto his guest, who after troublous sights
30   And dreames, gan° now to take more sound repast,   *began*
         Whom suddenly he wakes with fearefull frights,
         As one aghast with feends or damned sprights,
         And to him cals, Rise rise unhappy Swaine,°   *youth*
         That here wex old in sleepe, whiles wicked wights
35   Have knit themselves in Venus shamefull chaine;
     Come see, where your false Lady doth her honour staine.

5

     All in amaze he suddenly up start
         With sword in hand, and with the old man went;
         Who soone him brought into a secret part,
40   Where that false couple were full closely ment°   *joined*
         In wanton lust and lewd embracement:
         Which when he saw, he burnt with gealous fire,
         The eye of reason was with rage yblent,°   *blinded*
         And would have slaine them in his furious ire,
45   But hardly was restreined of that aged sire.

6

     Returning to his bed in torment great,
         And bitter anguish of his guiltie sight,
         He could not rest, but did his stout heart eat,
         And wast his inward gall° with deepe despight,°   *irritation / malice*
50   Yrkesome° of life, and too long lingring night.   *tired*
         At last faire Hesperus² in highest skie

2. The evening and morning star, the planet Venus.

Had spent his lampe, and brought forth dawning light,
Then up he rose, and clad him hastily;
The Dwarfe him brought his steed: so both away do fly.

7

55   Now when the rosy-fingred Morning faire,
       Weary of aged Tithones[3] saffron bed,
       Had spred her purple robe through deawy aire,
       And the high hils Titan[4] discovered,
       The royall virgin shooke off drowsy-hed,
60   And rising forth out of her baser bowre,
       Lookt for her knight, who far away was fled,
       And for her Dwarfe, that wont to wait° each houre;   *used to attend*
    Then gan she waile and weepe, to see that woefull stowre.°   *plight*

8

    And after him she rode with so much speede
65   As her slow beast could make; but all in vaine:
       For him so far had borne his light-foot steede,
       Pricked with wrath and fiery fierce disdaine,
       That him to follow was but fruitlesse paine;
       Yet she her weary limbes would never rest,
70   But every hill and dale, each wood and plaine
       Did search, sore grieved in her gentle brest,
    He so ungently left her, whom she loved best.

9

    But subtill Archimago, when his guests
       He saw divided into double parts,
75   And Una wandring in woods and forrests,
       Th'end of his drift,° he praisd his divelish arts,   *intention*
       That had such might over true meaning harts;
       Yet rests not so, but other meanes doth make,
       How he may worke unto her further smarts:
80   For her he hated as the hissing snake,
    And in her many troubles did most pleasure take.

10

    He then devisde himselfe how to disguise;
       For by his mightie science he could take
       As many formes and shapes in seeming wise,
85   As ever Proteus[5] to himselfe could make:
       Sometime a fowle, sometime a fish in lake,
       Now like a foxe, now like a dragon fell,°   *deadly*
       That of himselfe he oft for feare would quake,
       And oft would flie away. O who can tell
90   The hidden power of herbes, and might of Magicke spell?

11

    But now seemde best, the person to put on
       Of that good knight, his late beguiled° guest: *deceived*

---

3. Husband of the dawn.
4. The sun. I.e., when the sun revealed the high hills.

5. A sea-god, son of two other deities of the sea, Oceanus and Tethys; Proteus could change his shape at will.

95	In mighty armes he was yclad anon,°	*presently*
	And silver shield: upon his coward brest	
	A bloudy crosse, and on his craven crest°	*cowardly head*
	A bounch of haires discolourd diversly:	
	Full jolly knight he seemde, and well addrest,	
	And when he sate upon his courser free,	
	Saint George himself ye would have deemed him to be.[6]	

12

100	But he the knight, whose semblaunt° he did beare,	*likeness*
	The true Saint George was wandred far away,	
	Still flying from his thoughts and gealous feare;	
	Will was his guide, and griefe led him astray.	
	At last him chaunst to meete upon the way	
105	A faithlesse Sarazin[7] all arm'd to point,	
	In whose great shield was writ with letters gay	
	Sans-Foy:° full large of limbe and every joint	*faithless*
	He was, and cared not for God or man a point.°	*bit*

13

	He had a faire companion of his way,	
110	A goodly Lady[8] clad in scarlot° red,	*a royal cloth*
	Purfled with gold and pearle of rich assay,°	*quality*
	And like a Persian mitre° on her hed	*papal hat*
	She wore, with crownes and owches° garnished,	*jewels*
	The which her lavish lovers to her gave;	
115	Her wanton palfrey all was overspred	
	With tinsell trappings, woven like a wave,	
	Whose bridle rung with golden bels and bosses brave.°	*splendid ornaments*

14

	With faire disport° and courting dalliaunce°	*teasing / play*
	She intertainde her lover all the way:	
120	But when she saw the knight his speare advaunce,	
	She soone left off her mirth and wanton play,	
	And bad her knight addresse him to the fray:°	*face the challenge*
	His foe was nigh at hand. He prickt° with pride	*spurred on*
	And hope to winne his Ladies heart that day,	
125	Forth spurred fast: adowne his coursers side	
	The red bloud trickling staind the way, as he did ride.	

15

	The knight of the Redcrosse when him he spide,	
	Spurring so hote with rage dispiteous,°	*cruel*
	Gan fairely couch his speare, and towards ride:	
130	Soone meete they both, both fell and furious,	

---

6. Here, Archimago assumes the appearance of the Red-crosse Knight; incidentally, he reveals that the true knight is actually Saint George.

7. A Saracen, or follower of Islam. Early modern Europeans commonly represented believers in a non-Christian faith as infidels or nonbelievers. Sans-Foy (as this knight is later named—literally, "without faith") is there-fore not actually without a faith, but he is a Saracen and not a Christian.

8. The description of this Lady associates her with the Whore of Babylon (Revelation 17.4), who was identified by 16th-century Protestants with the Antichrist, i.e., the Pope and his retinue.

That daunted° with their forces hideous,   *dazed*
Their steeds do stagger, and amazed stand,
And eke themselves too rudely rigorous,
Astonied° with the stroke of their owne hand,   *stunned*
135   Do backe rebut,° and each to other yeeldeth land.   *recoil*

16

As when two rams stird with ambitious pride,
Fight for the rule of the rich fleeced flocke,
Their horned fronts so fierce on either side
Do meete, that with the terrour of the shocke
140   Astonied both, stand sencelesse as a blocke,
Forgetfull of the hanging victory:
So stood these twaine, unmoved as a rocke,
Both staring fierce, and holding idely
The broken reliques of their former cruelty.

17

145   The Sarazin sore daunted with the buffe°   *blow*
Snatcheth his sword, and fiercely to him flies;
Who well it wards, and quyteth° cuff° with cuff: *repays / blow*
Each others equall puissaunce° envies,   *power*
And through their iron sides with cruell spies
150   Does seeke to perce: repining° courage yields   *exhausted*
No foote to foe. The flashing fier flies
As from a forge out of their burning shields,
And streames of purple bloud new dies the verdant fields.

18

Curse on that Crosse (quoth then the Sarazin)
155   That keepes thy body from the bitter fit;°   *pangs of death*
Dead long ygoe I wote thou haddest bin,
Had not that charme from thee forwarned° it: *prevented*
But yet I warne thee now assured sitt,
And hide thy head. Therewith upon his crest
160   With rigour so outrageous he smitt,°   *struck*
That a large share it hewd out of the rest,
And glauncing downe his shield, from blame° him fairely blest.° *injury/protected*

19

Who thereat wondrous wroth,° the sleeping spark   *angry*
Of native vertue gan eftsoones revive,
165   And at his haughtie helmet making mark,
So hugely stroke, that it the steele did rive,°   *cut*
And cleft his head. He tumbling downe alive,
With bloudy mouth his mother earth did kis,
Greeting his grave: his grudging ghost did strive
170   With the fraile flesh; at last it flitted is,
Whither the soules do fly of men, that live amis.

20

The Lady when she saw her champion fall,
Like the old ruines of a broken towre,

Staid not to waile his woefull funerall,

175 But from him° fled away with all her powre;   *Redcrosse Knight*
Who after her as hastily gan scowre,°   *pursue*
Bidding the Dwarfe with him to bring away
The Sarazins shield, signe of the conqueroure.
Her soone he overtooke, and bad° to stay,   *commanded*

180 For present cause was none of dread her to dismay.⁹

21

She turning backe with ruefull° countenaunce,   *pitiful*
Cride, Mercy mercy Sir vouchsafe to show
On silly Dame, subject to hard mischaunce,
And to your mighty will. Her humblesse low

185 In so ritch weedes and seeming glorious show,
Did much emmove his stout heroïcke heart,
And said, Deare dame, your suddein overthrow
Much rueth me;° but now put feare apart,   *I regret*
And tell, both who ye be, and who that tooke your part.

22

190 Melting in teares, then gan she thus lament;
The wretched woman, whom unhappy howre
Hath now made thrall to your commandement,
Before that angry heavens list to lowre,°   *scowl*
And fortune false betraide me to your powre,

195 Was, (O what now availeth° that I was!)   *does it help*
Borne the sole daughter of an Emperour,
He that the wide West under his rule has,¹
And high hath set his throne, where Tiberis° doth pas.   *Tiber River, in Rome*

23

He in the first flowre of my freshest age,

200 Betrothed me unto the onely haire
Of a most mighty king, most rich and sage;
Was never Prince so faithfull and so faire,
Was never Prince so meeke and debonaire;°   *gentle*
But ere my hoped day of spousall° shone,   *marriage*

205 My dearest Lord fell from high honours staire,
Into the hands of his accursed fone,°   *foe*
And cruelly was slaine, that shall I ever mone.

24

His blessed body spoild of lively breath,
Was afterward, I know not how, convaid

210 And fro me hid: of whose most innocent death

---

9. I.e., he did not mean to frighten her.
1. The Lady's story in this and the next two stanzas allegorically describes the corruption of the Holy Roman Empire and its separation from true Christianity. The Lady's father, an emperor, reigned in Rome, the seat of Catholicism (cf. Una's father, who is Adam), and the

prince she was to marry was Christ. The Lady's quest to find his corpse suggests that she denies the doctrine of the resurrection of the body. In any case, Protestants in this period were critical of the Catholic emphasis on Christ's dead body in religious art and literature and contrasted it to the Protestant celebration of his resurrection.

When tidings came to me unhappy maid,
    O how great sorrow my sad soule assaid.°   *afflicted*
    Then forth I went his woefull corse to find,
    And many yeares throughout the world I straid,
215   A virgin widow, whose deepe wounded mind
With love, long time did languish as the striken hind.°   *doe*

25

At last it chaunced this proud Sarazin
    To meete me wandring, who perforce° me led   *forcibly*
    With him away, but yet could never win
220   The Fort, that Ladies hold in soveraigne dread.
    There lies he now with foule dishonour dead,
    Who whiles he liv'de, was called proud Sans-Foy,
    The eldest of three brethren, all three bred
    Of one bad sire, whose youngest is Sans-Joy,
225 And twixt them both was borne the bloudy bold Sans-Loy.[2]

26

In this sad plight, friendlesse, unfortunate,
    Now miserable I Fidessa[3] dwell,
    Craving of you in pitty of my state,
    To do none ill, if please ye not do well.
230   He in great passion all this while did dwell,
    More busying his quicke eyes, her face to view,
    Then his dull eares, to heare what she did tell;
    And said, Faire Lady hart of flint would rew
The undeserved woes and sorrowes, which ye shew.

27

235 Henceforth in safe assauraunce may ye rest,
    Having both found a new friend you to aid,
    And lost an old foe, that did you molest:
    Better new friend then an old foe is said.
    With chaunge of cheare the seeming simple maid
240   Let fall her eyen,° as shamefast to the earth,   *eyes*
    And yeelding soft, in that she nought gain-said,°   *denied*
    So forth they rode, he feining seemely merth,
And she coy lookes: so dainty they say maketh derth.[4]

28

Long time they thus together traveiled,
245   Till weary of their way, they came at last,
    Where grew two goodly trees, that faire did spred
    Their armes abroad, with gray mosse overcast,
    And their greene leaves trembling with every blast,

2. Sans-Loy ("without law") and Sans-Joy ("without joy") illustrate other aspects of the infidel attacking the spiritual well-being of the Redcrosse Knight. Spenser draws on Galatians 5.22–23: "But the fruit of the spirit is love, joy . . . faith . . . temperance; against such there is no Law."
3. The Lady in Persian dress calls herself Fidessa, a name that can mean "faithful" in a corrupted kind of Latin. From her association with Sans-Foy, however, the reader knows that she is not representative of the true faith and so only puts on the appearance of fidelity.
4. I.e., such daintiness is costly.

Made a calme shadow far in compasse round:
250   The fearefull Shepheard often there aghast°   *frightened*
Under them never sat, ne wont there sound
His mery oaten pipe, but shund th'unlucky ground.

29

But this good knight soone as he them can spie,
For the coole shade him thither hastly got:
255   For golden Phoebus now ymounted hie,
From fiery wheeles of his faire chariot
Hurled his beame so scorching cruell hot,
That living creature mote° it not abide;   *might*
And his new Lady it endured not.
260   There they alight, in hope themselves to hide
From the fierce heat, and rest their weary limbs a tide.°   *while*

30

Faire seemely pleasaunce each to other makes,
With goodly purposes there as they sit:
And in his falsed fancy he her takes
265   To be the fairest wight,° that lived yit;   *creature*
Which to expresse, he bends his gentle wit,
And thinking of those braunches greene to frame
A girlond for her dainty forehead fit,
He pluckt a bough; out of whose rift there came
270   Small drops of gory bloud, that trickled downe the same.[5]

31

Therewith a piteous yelling voyce was heard,
Crying, O spare with guilty hands to teare
My tender sides in this rough rynd embard,°   *enclosed*
But fly, ah fly far hence away, for feare
275   Least to you hap, that happened to me heare,
And to this wretched Lady, my deare love,
O too deare love, love bought with death too deare.
Astond he stood, and up his haire did hove,
And with that suddein horror could no member move.

32

280   At last whenas the dreadfull passion
Was overpast, and manhood well awake,
Yet musing at the straunge occasion,
And doubting much his sence, he thus bespake;
What voyce of damned Ghost from Limbo lake,°   *the pit of hell*
285   Or guilefull spright wandring in empty aire,
Both which fraile men do oftentimes mistake,
Sends to my doubtfull eares these speaches rare,
And ruefull plaints, me bidding guiltlesse bloud to spare?

---

5. Following Dante and Ariosto, Spenser imitates a well-known episode in Virgil's *Aeneid* in which the hero Aeneas, thinking he might have reached the country in which he was to found a new Troy, is warned by a bleeding bush that he must continue his quest. Spenser probably expected that his readers would take pleasure in his own inventive transformation of this powerful image.

33

Then groning deepe, Nor damned Ghost, (quoth he,)
290   Nor guilefull sprite to thee these wordes doth speake,
But once a man Fradubio,[6] now a tree,
Wretched man, wretched tree; whose nature weake,
A cruell witch her cursed will to wreake,
Hath thus transformd, and plast in open plaines,
295   Where Boreas° doth blow full bitter bleake,   *the north wind*
And scorching Sunne does dry my secret vaines:
For though a tree I seeme, yet cold and heat me paines.

34

Say on Fradubio then, or man, or tree,
Quoth then the knight, by whose mischievous arts
300   Art thou misshaped thus, as now I see?
He oft finds med'cine, who his griefe imparts;
But double griefs afflict concealing harts,
As raging flames who striveth to suppresse.
The author then (said he) of all my smarts,°   *pains*
305   Is one Duessa[7] a false sorceresse,
That many errant knights hath brought to wretchednesse.

35

In prime of youthly yeares, when corage° hot   *spirit*
The fire of love and joy of chevalree°   *chivalry*
First kindled in my brest, it was my lot
310   To love this gentle Lady, whom ye see,
Now not a Lady, but a seeming tree;
With whom as once I rode accompanyde,
Me chaunced of a knight encountred bee,
That had a like faire Lady by his syde,
315   Like a faire Lady, but did fowle Duessa hyde.

36

Whose forged° beauty he did take in hand,   *artificial*
All other Dames to have exceeded farre;
I in defence of mine did likewise stand,
Mine, that did then shine as the Morning starre:
320   So both to battell fierce arraunged° arre,   *engaged*
In which his harder fortune was to fall
Under my speare: such is the dye° of warre: *hazard*
His Lady left as a prise martiall,
Did yield her comely person, to be at my call.

37

325   So doubly lov'd of Ladies unlike° faire,   *differently*
Th'one seeming such, the other such indeede,

---

6. Brother Doubt (Italian). Because loss of faith through doubt is dehumanizing, Fradubio is cast into the form of a plant. He is intended to convey to the Redcrosse Knight how dangerous a creature Fidessa is.
7. Double-being (Italian), i.e., two-faced or duplicitous. The name contrasts with Una, or the undivided truth.

Duessa wears a mask of beauty, although she is actually hideous and evil. Spenser places Duessa, who is not what she appears to be, in opposition to Una, whose beauty is hidden beneath a veil but who signifies wholeness or integrity.

One day in doubt I cast° for to compare,   *sought*
Whether in beauties glorie did exceede;
A Rosy girlond was the victors meede:
330   Both seemde to win, and both seemde won to bee,
So hard the discord was to be agreede.
Fraelissa[8] was as faire, as faire mote bee,
And ever false Duessa seemde as faire as shee.

                            38
The wicked witch now seeing all this while
335   The doubtfull ballaunce equally to sway,
What not by right, she cast to win by guile,
And by her hellish science raisd streight way
A foggy mist, that overcast the day,
And a dull blast, that breathing on her face,
340   Dimmed her° former beauties shining ray,   *Fraelissa's*
And with foule ugly forme did her disgrace:°   *disfigure*
Then was she faire alone, when none was faire in place.

                            39
Then cride she out, Fye, fye, deformed wight,
Whose borrowed beautie now appeareth plaine
345   To have before bewitched all mens sight;
O leave her soone, or let her soone be slaine.[9]
Her loathly visage viewing with disdaine,
Eftsoones I thought her such, as she me told,
And would have kild her; but with faigned paine,
350   The false witch did my wrathfull hand with-hold;
So left her, where she now is turnd to treen mould.°   *a treelike shape*

                            40
Thens forth I tooke Duessa for my Dame,
And in the witch unweeting° joyd long time,   *without knowing*
Ne ever wist, but that she was the same,
355   Till on a day (that day is every Prime,°   *first (of the month)*
When Witches wont do penance for their crime)
I chaunst to see her in her proper hew,
Bathing her selfe in origane° and thyme: *oregano*
A filthy foule old woman I did vew,
360   That ever to have toucht her, I did deadly rew.

                            41
Her neather° partes misshapen, monstruous,   *lower*
Were hidd in water, that I could not see,
But they did seeme more foule and hideous,
Then womans shape man would beleeve to bee.
365   Thens forth from her most beastly companie
I gan refraine, in minde to slip away,
Soone as appeard safe opportunitie:

---

8. Fradubio's lady is Fraelissa, "frail nature" (Italian); she,   9. Duessa ironically condemns Fraelissa as a witch and
like Fradubio, is Duessa's victim.   tells Fradubio to abandon her.

For danger great, if not assur'd decay
I saw before mine eyes, if I were knowne to stray.

42

370 The divelish hag by chaunges of my cheare
Perceiv'd my thought, and drownd in sleepie night,
With wicked herbes and ointments did besmeare
My bodie all, through charmes and magicke might,
That all my senses were bereaved° quight: *departed*
375 Then brought she me into this desert waste,
And by my wretched lovers side me pight,°   *planted*
Where now enclosd in wooden wals full faste,
Banisht from living wights, our wearie dayes we waste.

43

But how long time, said then the Elfin knight,
380 Are you in this misformed house to dwell?
We may not chaunge (quoth he) this evil plight,
Till we be bathed in a living well;[1]
That is the terme prescribed by the spell.
O how, said he, mote I that well out find,
385 That may restore you to your wonted well?
Time and suffised fates to former kynd
Shall us restore, none else from hence may us unbynd.

44

The false Duessa, now Fidessa hight,°   *called*
Heard how in vaine Fradubio did lament,
390 And knew well all was true. But the good knight
Full of sad feare and ghastly dreriment,°   *terror*
When all this speech the living tree had spent,°   *finished*
The bleeding bough did thrust into the ground,
That from the bloud he might be innocent,
395 And with fresh clay did close the wooden wound:
Then turning to his Lady, dead with feare her found.

45

Her seeming dead he found with feigned feare,
As all unweeting of that well she knew,
And paynd himselfe with busie care to reare
400 Her out of carelesse° swowne. Her eylids blew   *unconscious*
And dimmed sight with pale and deadly hew°   *color*
At last she up gan lift: with trembling cheare
Her up he tooke, too simple and too trew,[2]
And oft her kist. At length all passed feare,
405 He set her on her steede, and forward forth did beare.

---

1. The Well of Life: a spring of constantly flowing water, figured in the water of baptism that promises eternal life to the faithful (John 4.14).
2. The Redcrosse Knight fails to connect Fradubio's story to his own; he does not follow the model presented by Virgil's Aeneas, and therefore he remains deceived and on the wrong course.

Canto 3

> *Forsaken Truth long seekes her love,*
> *And makes the Lyon mylde,*
> *Marres blind Devotions mart, and fals*
> *In hand of leachour vylde.*

1

Nought is there under heav'ns wide hollownesse,
    That moves more deare compassion of mind,
    Then beautie brought t'unworthy wretchednesse
    Through envies snares or fortunes freakes unkind:
5   I, whether lately through her brightnesse blind,
    Or through alleageance and fast fealtie,°   *loyalty*
    Which I do owe unto all woman kind,
    Feele my heart perst° with so great agonie,   *pierced*
When such I see, that all for pittie I could die.

2

10 And now it is empassioned° so deepe,   *moved*
    For fairest Unaes sake, of whom I sing,
    That my fraile eyes these lines with teares do steepe,°   *soak*
    To thinke how she through guilefull handeling,
    Though true as touch, though daughter of a king,
15   Though faire as ever living wight was faire,
    Though nor in word nor deede ill meriting,
    Is from her knight divorced° in despaire   *separated*
And her due loves° deriv'd to that vile witches share.   *the love due her*

3

Yet she most faithfull Ladie all this while
20   Forsaken, wofull, solitarie mayd
    Farre from all peoples prease,° as in exile,   *crowds*
    In wildernesse and wastfull deserts strayd,
    To seeke her knight; who subtilly betrayd
    Through that late vision, which th'Enchaunter wrought,
25   Had her abandond. She of nought affrayd,
    Through woods and wastnesse wide him daily sought;
Yet wished tydings none of him unto her brought.

4

One day nigh wearie of the yrkesome way,
    From her unhastie beast she did alight,
30   And on the grasse her daintie limbes did lay
    In secret shadow, farre from all mens sight:
    From her faire head her fillet she undight,
    And laid her stole aside. Her angels face
    As the great eye of heaven shyned bright,
35   And made a sunshine in the shadie place;
Did never mortall eye behold such heavenly grace.

5

It fortuned out of the thickest wood
  A ramping Lyon[1] rushed suddainly,
  Hunting full greedie after salvage° blood;   *savage*
40 Soone as the royall virgin he did spy,
  With gaping mouth at her ran greedily,
  To have attonce devour'd her tender corse:
  But to the pray when as he drew more ny,
  His bloudie rage asswaged with remorse,
45 And with the sight amazd, forgat his furious forse.

6

In stead thereof he kist her wearie feet,
  And lickt her lilly hands with fawning tong,
  As° he her wronged innocence did weet.   *as if*
  O how can beautie maister the most strong,
50 And simple truth subdue avenging wrong?
  Whose yeelded pride and proud submission,
  Still dreading death, when she had marked long,
  Her hart gan melt in great compassion,
And drizling teares did shed for pure affection.

7

55 The Lyon Lord of everie beast in field,
  Quoth she, his princely puissance° doth abate,   *strength*
  And mightie proud to humble weake does yield,
  Forgetfull of the hungry rage, which late
  Him prickt, in pittie of my sad estate:
60 But he° my Lyon, and my noble Lord,   *Redcrosse Knight*
  How does he find in cruell hart to hate
  Her that him lov'd, and ever most adord,
As the God of my life? why hath he me abhord?

8

Redounding teares did choke th'end of her plaint,
65 Which softly ecchoed from the neighbour wood;
  And sad to see her sorrowfull constraint
  The kingly beast upon her gazing stood;
  With pittie calmd, downe fell his angry mood.
  At last in close hart shutting up her paine,
70 Arose the virgin borne of heavenly brood,
  And to her snowy Palfrey got againe,
To seeke her strayed Champion, if she might attaine.° *overtake him*

9

The Lyon would not leave her desolate,
  But with her went along, as a strong gard
75 Of her chast person, and a faithfull mate
  Of her sad troubles and misfortunes hard:
  Still when she slept, he kept both watch and ward,
  And when she wakt, he waited diligent,
  With humble service to her will prepard:
80 From her faire eyes he tooke commaundement,
And ever by her lookes conceived° her intent.   *understood*

10

Long she thus traveiled through deserts wyde,
    By which she thought her wandring knight shold pas,
    Yet never shew of living wight espyde;
85   Till that at length she found the troden gras,
    In which the tract° of peoples footing was,   *trace*
    Under the steepe foot of a mountaine hore;°   *barren*
    The same she followes, till at last she has
    A damzell spyde slow footing her before,
90 That on her shoulders sad a pot of water bore.

11

To whom approching she to her gan call,
    To weet, if dwelling place were nigh at hand;
    But the rude wench her answer'd nought at all,
    She could not heare, nor speake, nor understand;
95   Till seeing by her side the Lyon stand,
    With suddaine feare her pitcher downe she threw,
    And fled away: for never in that land
    Face of faire Ladie she before did vew,
And that dread Lyons looke her cast in deadly hew.

12

100 Full fast she fled, ne° ever lookt behynd,   *nor*
    As if her life upon the wager lay,
    And home she came, whereas her mother blynd
    Sate in eternall night: nought could she say,
    But suddaine catching hold, did her dismay
105   With quaking hands, and other signes of feare:
    Who full of ghastly fright and cold affray,°   *terror*
    Gan shut the dore. By this arrived there
Dame Una, wearie Dame, and entrance did requere.°   *request*

13

Which when none yeelded, her unruly Page
110   With his rude clawes the wicket° open rent,   *small gate*
    And let her in; where of his cruell rage
    Nigh dead with feare, and faint astonishment,
    She found them both in darkesome corner pent;
    Where that old woman day and night did pray
115   Upon her beades devoutly penitent;
    Nine hundred *Pater nosters* every day,
And thrise nine hundred *Aves* she was wont to say.[2]

14

And to augment her painefull pennance more,
    Thrise every weeke in ashes she did sit,
120   And next her wrinkled skin rough sackcloth wore,
    And thrise three times did fast from any bit:°   *bit of food*
    But now for feare her beads she did forget.
    Whose needlesse dread for to remove away,

---

2. Spenser's readers would have identified Paternosters and Ave Marias as Catholic prayers.

Faire Una framed words and count'nance fit:
125   Which hardly doen,° at length she gan them pray,   *done*
That in their cotage small, that night she rest her may.

15

The day is spent, and commeth drowsie night,
      When every creature shrowded is in sleepe;
      Sad Una downe her laies in wearie plight,
130   And at her feet the Lyon watch doth keepe:
      In stead of rest, she does lament, and weepe
      For the late losse of her deare loved knight,
      And sighes, and grones, and evermore does steepe
      Her tender brest in bitter teares all night,
135   All night she thinks too long, and often lookes for light.

16

Now when Aldeboran was mounted hie
      Above the shynie Cassiopeias chaire,[3]
      And all in deadly sleepe did drowned lie,
      One knocked at the dore, and in would fare;
140   He knocked fast, and often curst, and sware,
      That readie entrance was not at his call:
      For on his backe a heavy load he bare
      Of nightly stelths° and pillage severall,   *thefts*
Which he had got abroad by purchase criminall.

17

145   He was to weete° a stout and sturdie thiefe,[4]   *wit*
      Wont to robbe Churches of their ornaments,
      And poore mens boxes of their due reliefe,
      Which given was to them for good intents;
      The holy Saints of their rich vestiments
150   He did disrobe, when all men carelesse slept,
      And spoild the Priests of their habiliments,°   *holy things*
      Whiles none the holy things in safety kept;
Then he by cunning sleights° in at the window crept.   *tricks*

18

And all that he by right or wrong could find,
155   Unto this house he brought, and did bestow
      Upon the daughter of this woman blind,
      Abessa daughter of Corceca slow,[5]
      With whom he whoredome usd, that few did know,
      And fed her fat with feast of offerings,
160   And plentie, which in all the land did grow;
      Ne spared he to give her gold and rings:
And now he to her brought part of his stolen things.

3. Aldeboran and Cassiopeia are stars that appear at midnight during the winter solstice; the references to winter and midnight reflect Una's distress.
4. This thief is later named Kirkrapine, literally "church robber" (see stanza 22). Spenser's Protestant contemporaries complained that the Roman Catholic Church had used English abbeys and monasteries as a means of amassing wealth at the expense of the spiritual well-being of the people that they were supposed to serve.
5. Corceca means "blind of heart"; her daughter, Abessa, who is both deaf and mute, is the offspring of ignorant superstition. Through her name, Spenser associates Abessa with Catholic abbeys and monasteries, which he criticizes in this and the previous two stanzas.

19

Thus long the dore with rage and threats he bet,
        Yet of those fearefull women none durst rize,
165   The Lyon frayed° them, him in to let: *frightened*
        He would no longer stay him to advize,°   *consider*
        But open breakes the dore in furious wize,
        And entring is; when that disdainfull° beast   *indignant*
        Encountring fierce, him suddaine doth surprize,
170   And seizing cruell clawes on trembling brest,
Under his Lordly foot him proudly hath supprest.

20

Him booteth not° resist, nor succour call,   *it did no good to*
        His bleeding hart is in the vengers hand,
        Who streight him rent° in thousand peeces small,   *tore*
175   And quite dismembred hath: the thirstie land
        Drunke up his life; his corse left on the strand.[6]
        His fearefull friends weare out the wofull night,
        Ne dare to weepe, nor seeme to understand
        The heavie hap,° which on them is alight,   *event*
180 Affraid, least to themselves the like mishappen might.

21

Now when broad day the world discovered has,
        Up Una rose, up rose the Lyon eke,
        And on their former journey forward pas,
        In wayes unknowne, her wandring knight to seeke,
185   With paines farre passing that long wandring Greeke,[7]
        That for his love refused deitie;
        Such were the labours of this Lady meeke,
        Still seeking him, that from her still did flie,
Then furthest from her hope, when most she weened nie.

22

190 Soone as she parted thence, the fearefull twaine,
        That blind old woman and her daughter deare
        Came forth, and finding Kirkrapine° there slaine,   *church-robber*
        For anguish great they gan to rend their heare,
        And beat their brests, and naked flesh to teare.
195   And when they both had wept and wayld their fill,
        Then forth they ranne like two amazed deare,
        Halfe mad through malice, and revenging will,°   *desire to revenge*
To follow her, that was the causer of their ill.

23

Whom overtaking, they gan loudly bray,
200   With hollow howling, and lamenting cry,
        Shamefully at her rayling° all the way,   *accusing*
        And her accusing of dishonesty,
        That was the flowre of faith and chastity;

6. Kirkrapine's death signifies a step toward the purifica-
tion of the Church and thereby an approach to the true
Church, which Una represents.

7. Una is compared to Ulysses, whose love for his wife
Penelope caused him to reject the goddess Calypso and
the promise of immortality she offered him.

And still amidst her rayling, she did pray,
205   That plagues, and mischiefs, and long misery
      Might fall on her, and follow all the way,
And that in endlesse error she might ever stray.

24

But when she saw her prayers nought prevaile,
      She backe returned with some labour lost;
210   And in° the way as she did weepe and waile,   *along*
      A knight her met in mighty armes embost,
      Yet knight was not for all his bragging bost,°   *display*
      But subtill Archimag, that Una sought
      By traynes° into new troubles to have tost: *tricks*
215   Of that old woman tydings he besought,
If that of such a Ladie she could tellen ought.

25

Therewith she gan her passion to renew,
      And cry, and curse, and raile,° and rend her heare,   *accuse*
      Saying, that harlot she too lately knew,
220   That causd her shed so many a bitter teare,
      And so forth told the story of her feare:
      Much seemed he to mone her haplesse chaunce,
      And after for that Ladie did inquere;°   *inquire*
      Which being taught, he forward gan advaunce
225 His fair enchaunted steed, and eke his charmed launce.

26

Ere long he came, where Una traveild slow,
      And that wilde Champion wayting her besyde;
      Whom seeing such, for dread he° durst not show   *Archimago*
      Himselfe too nigh at hand, but turned wyde
230   Unto an hill; from whence when she him spyde,
      By his like seeming shield, her knight by name
      She weend it was, and towards him gan ryde:[8]
      Approching nigh, she wist it was the same,
And with faire fearefull humblesse towards him shee came.

27

235 And weeping said, Ah my long lacked° Lord,   *lost*
      Where have ye bene thus long out of my sight?
      Much feared I to have bene quite abhord,
      Or ought have done, that ye displeasen might,
      That should as death unto my deare hart light:°   *come*
240   For since mine eye your joyous sight did mis,
      My chearefull day is turnd to chearelesse night,
      And eke my night of death the shadow is;
But welcome now my light, and shining lampe of blis.

---

8. Una recognizes the arms of the Redcrosse Knight but is deceived by appearances; she is actually greeting Archimago.

28

He thereto meeting said, My dearest Dame,
245   Farre be it from your thought, and fro° my will,   *from*
    To thinke that knighthood I so much should shame,
    As you to leave,° that have me loved still,   *lose*
    And chose in Faery court of meere goodwill,
    Where noblest knights were to be found on earth:
250   The earth shall sooner leave her kindly skill°   *natural art*
    To bring forth fruit, and make eternall derth,°   *famine*
Then I leave you, my liefe, yborne of heavenly berth.

29

And sooth° to say, why I left you so long,   *truly*
    Was for to seeke adventure in strange place,
255   Where Archimago said a felon strong
    To many knights did daily worke disgrace;
    But knight he now shall never more deface:
    Good cause of mine excuse; that mote° ye please   *might*
    Well to accept, and evermore embrace
260   My faithfull service, that by land and seas
Have vowd you to defend, now then your plaint appease.

30

His lovely words her seemd due recompence
    Of all her passed paines: one loving howre
    For many yeares of sorrow can dispence:°   *compensate*
265   A dram of sweet is worth a pound of sowre:
    She has forgot, how many a wofull stowre°   *hardship*
    For him she late endur'd; she speakes no more
    Of past: true is, that true love hath no powre
    To looken backe; his eyes be fixt before.
270 Before her stands her knight, for whom she toyld so sore.

31

Much like, as when the beaten marinere,
    That long hath wandred in the Ocean wide,
    Oft soust° in swelling Tethys° saltish teare,   *drenched / a sea-goddess*
    And long time having tand his tawney hide
275   With blustring breath of heaven, that none can bide,
    And scorching flames of fierce Orions hound,[9]
    Soone as the port from farre he has espide,
    His chearefull whistle merrily doth sound,
And Nereus° crownes with cups;° his mates him pledg around.   *a sea-god / of wine*

32

280 Such joy made Una, when her knight she found;
    And eke th'enchaunter joyous seemd no lesse,
    Then° the glad marchant, that does vew from ground   *than*
    His ship farre come from watrie wildernesse,
    He hurles out vowes, ° and Neptune oft doth blesse: *makes promises*
285   So forth they past, and all the way they spent

---

9. Sirius, the Dog Star, which marks the hottest days of the year. Nereus is the eldest child of Tethys, a sea-goddess.

Discoursing of her dreadfull late distresse,
In which he askt her, what the Lyon ment:
Who° told her all that fell° in journey as she went.   *Una / had happened*

33

They had not ridden farre, when they might see
290   One pricking towards them with hastie heat,
Full strongly armd, and on a courser free,
That through his fiercenesse fomed all with sweat,
And the sharpe yron° did for anger eat,   *iron bit*
When his hot ryder spurd his chauffed side;
295   His looke was sterne, and seemed still to threat
Cruell revenge, which he in hart did hyde,
And on his shield Sans-Loy in bloudie lines was dyde.

34

When nigh he drew unto this gentle payre
And saw the Red-crosse, which the knight did beare,
300   He burnt in fire, and gan eftsoones prepare
Himselfe to battell with his couched° speare.   *lowered*
Loth was that other,° and did faint through feare,   *Archimago*
To taste th'vntryed dint of deadly steele;
But yet his Lady did so well him cheare,
305   That hope of new good hap he gan to feele;
So bent his speare, and spurnd° his horse with yron heele.   *spurred*

35

But that proud Paynim° forward came so fierce,[1]   *pagan*
And full of wrath, that with his sharp-head speare
Through vainely crossed shield he quite did pierce,
310   And had his staggering steede not shrunke for feare,
Through shield and bodie eke he should him beare:
Yet so great was the puissance of his push,
That from his saddle quite he did him beare:
He tombling rudely downe to ground did rush,
315   And from his gored wound a well of bloud did gush.

36

Dismounting lightly from his loftie steed,
He to him lept, in mind to reave° his life,   *take*
And proudly said, Lo there the worthie meed
Of him, that slew Sans-Foy with bloudie knife;
320   Henceforth his ghost freed from repining° strife,   *fretting*
In peace may passen° over Lethe lake,[2]   *pass*
When morning altars° purgd with enemies life,   *altars of mourning*
The blacke infernall Furies doen aslake:°   *satisfy*
Life from Sans-Foy thou tookst, Sans-Loy shall from thee take.

---

1. The double deception registered in this episode is characteristic of Spenser's complex allegories: mistaken in his sense of identity, Sans-Loy attacks the very person who is best able to protect him. Archimago, having assumed the guise of the Redcrosse Knight, finds that the cross that should protect him from harm does not in fact do so. In this instance his shield is "vainely crossed."
2. The lake of forgetfulness in the underworld.

37

325 Therewith in haste his helmet gan unlace,
     Till Una cride, O hold that heavie hand,
     Deare Sir, what ever that thou be in place:
     Enough is, that thy foe doth vanquisht stand
     Now at thy mercy: Mercie not withstand:°   *oppose*
330 For he is one the truest° knight alive,   *the one truest*
     Though conquered now he lie on lowly land,
     And whilest him fortune favourd, faire did thrive
     In bloudie field: therefore of life him not deprive.

38

     Her piteous words might not abate his rage,
335 But rudely° rending up his helmet, would   *violently*
     Have slaine him straight: but when he sees his age,
     And hoarie head of Archimago old,
     His hastie hand he doth amazed hold,
     And halfe ashamed, wondred at the sight:
340 For the old man well knew he, though untold,°   *i.e., by sight*
     In charmes and magicke to have wondrous might,
     Ne ever wont in field, ne in round lists° to fight.   *tournament arenas*

39

     And said, Why Archimago, lucklesse syre,
     What doe I see? what hard mishap is this,
345 That hath thee hither brought to taste mine yre?
     Or thine the fault, or mine the error is,
     In stead of foe to wound my friend amis?
     He answered nought, but in a traunce still lay,
     And on those guilefull dazed eyes of his
350 The cloud of death did sit. Which doen away,°   *having passed*
     He left him lying so, ne would no lenger stay.

40

     But to the virgin comes, who all this while
     Amased stands, her selfe so mockt to see
     By him, who has the guerdon° of his guile,   *reward*
355 For so misfeigning her true knight to bee:
     Yet is she now in more perplexitie,°   *distress*
     Left in the hand of that same Paynim bold,
     From whom her booteth° not at all to flie;   *it helped her*
     Who by her cleanly° garment catching hold,   *pure*
360 Her from her Palfrey pluckt, her visage to behold.

41

     But her fierce servant full of kingly awe
     And high disdaine, whenas his soveraine Dame
     So rudely handled by her foe he sawe,
     With gaping jawes full greedy at him came,
365 And ramping on° his shield, did weene the same   *charging at*
     Have reft away with his sharpe rending clawes:
     But he was stout, and lust did now inflame

His corage more, that from his griping pawes
He hath his shield redeem'd,° and foorth his swerd he drawes.   *retained*

42

370 O then too weake and feeble was the forse
Of salvage beast, his puissance to withstand:
For he was strong, and of so mightie corse,
As ever wielded speare in warlike hand,
And feates of armes did wisely understand.
375 Eftsoones he perced through his chaufed° chest   *angered*
With thrilling° point of deadly yron brand,   *piercing*
And launcht° his Lordly hart: with death opprest   *pierced*
He roar'd aloud, whiles life forsooke his stubborne brest.

43

Who now is left to keepe the forlorne maid
380 From raging spoile of lawlesse victors will?[3]
Her faithful gard remov'd, her hope dismaid,°   *thwarted*
Her selfe a yeelded pray to save or spill.°   *destroy*
He now Lord of the field, his pride to fill,
With foule reproches, and disdainfull spight
385 Her vildly entertaines,° and will or nill,   *treats*
Beares her away upon his courser light:
Her prayers nought prevaile, his rage is more of might.

44

And all the way, with great lamenting paine,
And piteous plaints she filleth his dull eares,
390 That stony hart could riven have in twaine,
And all the way she wets with flowing teares:
But he enrag'd with rancor, nothing heares.
Her servile beast yet would not leave her so,
But followes her farre off, ne ought he feares,
395 To be partaker of her wandring woe,
More mild in beastly kind,° then that her beastly foe.   *animal nature*

Canto 4

To sinfull house of Pride,[1] Duessa
guides the faithfull knight,
Where brothers death to wreak° Sans-Joy   *avenge*
doth chalenge him to fight.

1

Young knight, what ever° that dost armes professe,   *whoever*
And through long labours huntest after fame,
Beware of fraud, beware of ficklenesse,
In choice, and change of thy deare loved Dame,
5 Least° thou of her beleeve° too lightly blame,   *lest / faith*

3. I.e., who will now protect Una from becoming the
spoil or booty of the lawless victor's raging will?
1. An extended metaphor for the consequences of the
sin of Pride. Like the Tower of Babel, which Spenser
invokes in this passage, the house of Pride is the product of humanity's art, ambition, and vanity but is
devoid of Christian values.

And rash misweening° doe thy hart remove: *rashly mistrusting*
For unto knight there is no greater shame,
Then lightnesse and inconstancie in love;
That doth this Redcrosse knights ensample° plainly prove.   *example*

2

10 Who after that he had faire Una lorne,°   *lost*
Through light misdeeming of her loialtie,
And false Duessa in her sted had borne,
Called Fidess', and so supposd to bee;
15 Long with her traveild, till at last they see
A goodly building, bravely garnished,
The house of mightie Prince it seemd to bee:
And towards it a broad high way that led,
All bare° through peoples feet, which thither traveiled.   *worn bare*

3

Great troupes of people traveild thitherward
20 Both day and night, of each degree and place,
But few returned, having scaped hard,
With balefull° beggerie, or foule disgrace,   *wretched*
Which ever after in most wretched case,
Like loathsome lazars,° by the hedges lay.   *lepers*
25 Thither Duessa bad him bend° his pace: *direct*
For she is wearie of the toilesome way,
And also nigh consumed is the lingring day.

4

A stately Pallace built of squared bricke,[2]
Which cunningly was without morter laid,
30 Whose wals were high, but nothing strong, nor thick,
And golden foile all over them displaid,
That purest skye with brightnesse they dismaid:°   *shamed*
High lifted up were many loftie towres,
And goodly galleries farre over laid,°   *built high above*
35 Full of faire windowes, and delightfull bowres;°   *chambers*
And on the top a Diall° told the timely howres.   *sundial*

5

It was a goodly heape° for to behould,   *structure*
And spake the praises of the workmans wit;
But full great pittie, that so faire a mould
40 Did on so weake foundation ever sit:
For on a sandie hill, that still did flit,°   *shift*
And fall away, it mounted was full hie,
That every breath of heaven shaked it:
And all the hinder° parts, that few could spie,   *rear*
45 Were ruinous and old, but painted cunningly.

---

2. The house of Pride offers a dazzling facade, but its construction is weak, much like the sin of Pride itself, which places outward appearances over inner substance. It is surmounted by a sundial to tell the hours, a sign that Pride has no sense of eternity but lives only for the moment.

6

Arrived there they passed in forth right;
    For still° to all the gates stood open wide,   *always*
    Yet charge of them was to a Porter hight°   *called*
    Cald Malvenù,° who entrance none denide: *welcome to evil*
50 Thence to the hall, which was on every side
    With rich array and costly arras dight:°   *furnished*
    Infinite sorts of people did abide
    There waiting long, to win the wished sight
Of her, that was the Lady of that Pallace bright.

7

55 By them they passe, all gazing on them round,
    And to the Presence mount; whose glorious vew
    Their frayle amazed senses did confound:°   *confuse*
    In living Princes court none ever knew
    Such endlesse richesse, and so sumptuous shew;
60 Ne° Persia selfe, the nourse° of pompous pride   *not even / nurse*
    Like ever saw. And there a noble crew
    Of Lordes and Ladies stood on every side,
Which with their presence faire, the place much beautifide.

8

High above all a cloth of State was spred,
65 And a rich throne, as bright as sunny day,
    On which there sate most brave embellished
    With royall robes and gorgeous array,
    A mayden Queene,[3] that shone as Titans ray,
    In glistring gold, and peerelesse pretious stone:
70 Yet her bright blazing beautie did assay°   *strive*
    To dim the brightnesse of her glorious throne,
As envying her selfe, that too exceeding shone.

9

Exceeding shone, like Phoebus fairest childe,[4]
    That did presume his fathers firie wayne,
75 And flaming mouthes of steedes unwonted° wilde   *unaccustomed*
    Through highest heaven with weaker hand to rayne;°   *guide*
    Proud of such glory and advancement vaine,
    While flashing beames do daze his feeble eyen,
    He leaves the welkin° way most beaten plaine,   *well-known*
80 And rapt with whirling wheeles, inflames the skyen,
With fire not made to burne, but fairely for to shyne.

10

So proud she shyned in her Princely state,
    Looking to heaven; for earth she did disdayne,
    And sitting high; for lowly she did hate:

---

3. "The maiden queen": a reference to the "virgin daughter
of Babylon" (Isaiah 47.1). She is later identified as Lucifera,
a feminine form of Lucifer, literally "light bringer," but also
Satan's name when he was still an angel. Hence the queen
shines as brightly as the sun (Titan).
4. Phaeton (son of the sun god Apollo), who stole his
father's chariot and perished because he could not manage the horses. He is a figure for the sin of Pride.

85
Lo underneath her scornefull feete, was layne
A dreadfull Dragon with an hideous trayne,
And in her hand she held a mirrhour bright,
Wherein her face she often vewed fayne,
And in her selfe-lov'd semblance° tooke delight;   *image*
90
For she was wondrous faire, as any living wight.

11

Of griesly Pluto she the daughter was,[5]
And sad Proserpina the Queene of hell;
Yet did she thinke her pearelesse° worth to pas   *unequaled*
That parentage, with pride so did she swell,
95
And thundring Jove, that high in heaven doth dwell,
And wield the world, she claymed for her syre,
Or if that any else did Jove excell:
For to the highest she did still aspyre,
Or if ought higher were then° that, did it desyre.   *than*

12

100
And proud Lucifera men did her call,
That made her selfe a Queene, and crownd to be,
Yet rightfull kingdome she had none at all,
Ne heritage° of native° soveraintie,   *inheritance / rightful*
But did ysurpe° with wrong and tyrannie   *usurp*
105
Upon the scepter, which she now did hold:
Ne ruld her Realmes with lawes, but pollicie,°   *political cunning*
And strong advizement of six wisards old,
That with their counsels bad her kingdome did uphold.

13

Soone as the Elfin knight in presence came,
110
And false Duessa seeming Lady faire,
A gentle Husher,° Vanitie by name   *usher*
Made rowme, and passage for them did prepaire:
So goodly brought them to the lowest staire
Of her high throne, where they on humble knee
115
Making obeyssance,° did the cause declare,   *submissive bows*
Why they were come, her royall state to see,
To prove° the wide report of her great Majestee.   *confirm*

14

With loftie eyes, halfe loth° to looke so low,   *disdaining*
She thanked them in her disdainefull wise,
120
Ne other grace vouchsafed° them to show   *condescended*
Of Princesse worthy, scarse them bad arise.
Her Lordes and Ladies all this while devise
Themselves to setten forth to straungers sight:
Some frounce° their curled haire in courtly guise,   *arrange*

---

5. Lucifera is identified as the daughter of Pluto, king of the underworld, and Proserpina, goddess of the seasons, who is obliged to spend half the year underground with her husband, Pluto. The conflation of mythologies represented in this description of Lucifera is characteristic of Spenser's allegory. Here he associates the biblical figure of the daughter of Babylon with the pagan figures of Pluto and Proserpina. Their "daughter" Lucifera is his own invention.

125   Some prancke° their ruffes, and others trimly dight   *adjust*
    Their gay attire: each others greater pride does spight.

15

    Goodly they all that knight do entertaine,
      Right glad with him to have increast their crew:
      But to Duess' each one himselfe did paine
130   All kindnesse and faire courtesie to shew;
      For in that court whylome° her well they knew: *previously*
      Yet the stout Faerie[6] mongst the middest crowd
      Thought all their glorie vaine in knightly vew,
      And that great Princesse too exceeding prowd,
135   That to strange knight no better countenance° allowd.   *reception*

16

    Suddein upriseth from her stately place
      The royall Dame, and for her coche doth call:
      All hurtlen° forth, and she with Princely pace,   *rush*
      As faire Aurora° in her purple pall,   *goddess of the dawn*
140   Out of the East the dawning day doth call:
      So forth she comes: her brightnesse brode° doth blaze;   *abroad*
      The heapes of people thronging in the hall,
      Do ride each other, upon her to gaze:
    Her glorious glitterand° light doth all mens eyes amaze.   *glittering*

17

145   So forth she comes, and to her coche does clyme,
      Adorned all with gold, and girlonds gay,
      That seemd as fresh as Flora° in her prime,   *goddess of spring*
      And strove to match, in royall rich array,
      Great Junoes golden chaire, the which they say
150   The Gods stand gazing on, when she does ride
      To Joves high house through heavens bras-paved way
      Drawne of faire Pecocks, that excell in pride,
    And full of Argus[7] eyes their tailes dispredden° wide.   *spread out*

18

    But this was drawne of six unequall beasts,
155   On which her six sage Counsellours[8] did ryde,
      Taught to obay their bestiall beheasts,°   *urges*
      With like conditions to their kinds° applyde: *natures*
      Of which the first, that all the rest did guyde,
      Was sluggish Idlenesse the nourse of sin;
160   Upon a slouthfull Asse he chose to ryde,
      Arayd in habit blacke, and amis° thin,   *monk's hood*
    Like to an holy Monck, the service to begin.

6. The Redcrosse Knight. He is designated as a faerie because he is an inhabitant of Faerie Land and also to distinguish him from the inhabitants of the house of Pride.
7. A mythical herdsman with 100 eyes. When Argus died, Juno—goddess of marriage and wife to Jupiter or Jove, king of the gods—set his eyes in the tail of a peacock.
8. The following stanzas describe the procession of Lucifer's wise counsellors, actually the Seven Deadly Sins: Pride (in the person of Lucifera), Idleness, Gluttony, Lechery, Avarice (greed), Envy, and Wrath.

19

And in his hand his Portesse° still he bare,   *prayer book*
  That much was worne, but therein little red,
165   For of devotion he had little care,
  Still drownd in sleepe, and most of his dayes ded;
  Scarse could he once uphold his heavie hed,
  To looken, whether it were night or day:
  May seeme° the wayne was very evill led,   *it may seem that*
170   When such an one had guiding of the way,
That knew not, whether right he went, or else astray.

20

From worldly cares himselfe he did esloyne,°   *withdraw*
  And greatly shunned manly exercise,
  From every worke he chalenged essoyne,°   *claimed exception*
175   For contemplation sake: yet otherwise,
  His life he led in lawlesse riotise;°   *unruly conduct*
  By which he grew to grievous malady;
  For in his lustlesse limbs through evill guise
  A shaking fever raignd° continually: *ruled*
180 Such one was Idlenesse, first of this company.

21

And by his side rode loathsome Gluttony,
  Deformed creature, on a filthie swyne,
  His belly was up-blowne with luxury,
  And eke with fatnesse swollen were his eyne,°   *eyes*
185   And like a Crane his necke was long and fyne,
  With which he swallowd up excessive feast,
  For want whereof poore people oft did pyne;
  And all the way, most like a brutish beast,
He spued up his gorge,° that all did him deteast.   *vomited his food*

22

190 In greene vine leaves he was right fitly clad;
  For other clothes he could not weare for heat,
  And on his head an ivie girland had,
  From under which fast trickled downe the sweat:
  Still as he rode, he somewhat still did eat,
195   And in his hand did beare a bouzing° can,   *drinking*
  Of which he supt so oft, that on his seat
  His dronken corse he scarse upholden can,
In shape and life more like a monster, then a man.

23

Unfit he was for any worldly thing,
200 And eke unhable once to stirre or go,
  Not meet to be of counsell to a king,
  Whose mind in meat and drinke was drowned so,
  That from his friend he seldome knew his fo:
  Full of diseases was his carcas blew,

205   And a dry dropsie[9] through his flesh did flow:
       Which by misdiet daily greater grew:
       Such one was Gluttony, the second of that crew.

                          24
       And next to him rode lustfull Lechery,
           Upon a bearded Goat, whose rugged haire,
210   And whally° eyes (the signe of gelosy,)   glaring
           Was like the person selfe,° whom he did beare: himself
           Who rough, and blacke, and filthy did appeare,
           Unseemely man to please faire Ladies eye;
           Yet he of Ladies oft was loved deare,
215   When fairer faces were bid standen by:
       O who does know the bent of womens fantasy?

                          25
       In a greene gowne he clothed was full faire,
           Which underneath did hide his filthinesse,
           And in his hand a burning hart he bare,
220   Full of vaine follies, and new fanglenesse:
           For he was false, and fraught with ficklenesse,
           And learned had to love with secret lookes,
           And well could daunce, and sing with ruefulnesse,°   melancholy
           And fortunes tell, and read in loving bookes,°   books of love
225   And thousand other wayes, to bait his fleshly hookes.

                          26
       Inconstant man, that loved all he saw,
           And lusted after all, that he did love,
           Ne would his looser life be tide to law,
           But joyd weake wemens hearts to tempt and prove°   test
230   If from their loyall loves he might them move;
           Which lewdnesse fild him with reprochfull paine
           Of that fowle evill, which all men reprove,
           That rots the marrow, and consumes the braine:
       Such one was Lecherie, the third of all this traine.

                          27
235   And greedy Avarice by him did ride,
           Upon a Camell loaden all with gold;
           Two iron coffers hong on either side,
           With precious mettall full, as they might hold,
           And in his lap an heape of coine he told;°   counted
240   For of his wicked pelfe° his God he made,   profits
           And unto hell him selfe for money sold;
           Accursed usurie was all his trade,[1]
       And right and wrong ylike in equall ballaunce waide.

---

9. A disease characterized by bloating.
1. Usury (lending money for profit) was forbidden by Scripture but was nevertheless practiced—with certain restrictions—in early modern Europe and England. High rates of interest were generally forbidden, but loans could be made as forms of investment in commerce or industry.

28

His life was nigh unto deaths doore yplast,°   *i.e., nearly over*
245   And thred-bare cote, and cobled° shoes he ware,   *patched*
       Ne scarse good morsell all his life did tast,
       But both from backe and belly still did spare,
       To fill his bags, and richesse to compare;²
       Yet chylde ne kinsman living had he none
250   To leave them to; but thorough daily care
       To get, and nightly feare to lose his owne,°   *his own wealth*
He led a wretched life unto him selfe unknowne.

29

Most wretched wight, whom nothing might suffise,
       Whose greedy lust did lacke in greatest store,
255   Whose need had end, but no end covetise,°   *greed*
       Whose wealth was want, whose plenty made him pore,
       Who had enough, yet wished ever more;
       A vile disease, and eke in foote and hand
       A grievous gout tormented him full sore,
260   That well he could not touch, nor go, nor stand:
Such one was Avarice, the fourth of this faire band.

30

And next to him malicious Envie rode,
       Upon a ravenous wolfe, and still did chaw°   *chew*
       Betweene his cankred° teeth a venemous tode,   *infected*
265   That all the poison ran about his chaw;°   *mouth*
       But inwardly he chawed his owne maw°   *guts*
       At neighbours wealth, that made him ever sad;
       For death it was, when any good he saw,
       And wept, that cause of weeping none he had,
270   But when he heard of harme, he wexed° wondrous glad.   *grew*

31

All in a kirtle° of discoloured say°   *gown / fine cloth*
       He clothed was, ypainted full of eyes;
       And in his bosome secretly there lay
       An hatefull Snake, the which his taile uptyes
275   In many folds, and mortall sting implyes.³
       Still as he rode, he gnasht his teeth, to see
       Those heapes of gold with griple Covetyse,⁴
       And grudged at the great felicitie
Of proud Lucifera, and his owne companie.

32

280   He hated all good workes and vertuous deeds,
       And him no lesse, that any like did use,°   *perform*
       And who with gracious bread the hungry feeds,

---

2. I.e., he wore rags and starved himself.
3. Envy's clothing symbolically displays the envious and covetous eyes with which he views the world. The snake he carries in his bosom was a traditional symbol of envy;

its "mortall sting" is deadly to Envy himself as well as to others.
4. Grasping Avarice; Envy is envious of Avarice's gold.

His almes for want of faith he doth accuse;°   *misrepresent*
So every good to bad he doth abuse:⁵
285   And eke the verse of famous Poets witt
He does backebite, and spightfull poison spues
From leprous mouth on all, that ever writt:
Such one vile Envie was, that fifte in row did sitt.

33

And him beside rides fierce revenging Wrath,
290   Upon a Lion, loth for° to be led;   *reluctant*
And in his hand a burning brond° he hath,   *brand*
The which he brandisheth about his hed;
His eyes did hurle forth sparkles fiery red,
And stared sterne on all, that him beheld,
295   As ashes pale of hew and seeming ded;
And on his dagger still his hand he held,
Trembling through hasty rage, when choler° in him sweld.   *anger*

34

His ruffin° raiment all was staind with blood,   *ruffianly*
Which he had spilt, and all to rags yrent,
300   Through unadvized rashnesse woxen wood;°   *grown mad*
For of his hands he had no governement,°   *control*
Ne car'd for bloud in his avengement:
But when the furious fit was overpast,
His cruell facts° he often would repent;   *deeds*
305   Yet wilfull man he never would forecast,°   *foresee*
How many mischieves° should ensue his heedlesse hast.   *evil consequences*

35

Full many mischiefes follow cruell Wrath;
Abhorred bloudshed, and tumultuous strife,
Unmanly murder, and unthrifty scath,°   *wasteful harm*
310   Bitter despight,° with rancours rusty knife,   *malice*
And fretting griefe the enemy of life;
All these, and many evils moe haunt ire,
The swelling Splene,° and Frenzy raging rife,   *temper*
The shaking Palsey, and Saint Fraunces fire:⁶
315   Such one was Wrath, the last of this ungodly tire.°   *procession*

36

And after all, upon the wagon beame°   *shaft*
Rode Sathan, with a smarting whip in hand,
With which he forward lasht the laesie teme,
So oft as Slowth still in the mire did stand.
320   Huge routs of people did about them band,
Showting for joy, and still° before their way   *always*

---

5. Envy believes that good deeds reveal a lack of faith. Here Spenser attacks doctrine associated with radical Protestant sects that, rejecting Catholic belief in the merit of good works as a means to salvation, insist that it is only through faith and God's grace that a Christian is saved.
6. Erysipelas or, as it was actually known, St. Anthony's fire. A common disease of the period, it was characterized by a disfiguring and painful skin rash.

A foggy mist had covered all the land;
And underneath their feet, all scattered lay
Dead sculs and bones of men, whose life had gone astray.

37

325
So forth they marchen in this goodly sort,
To take the solace of the open aire,
And in fresh flowring fields themselves to sport;
Emongst the rest rode that false Lady faire,
The fowle Duessa, next unto the chaire
330
Of proud Lucifera, as one of the traine:
But that good knight would not so nigh repaire,°   *follow*
Him selfe estraunging from their joyaunce vaine,
Whose fellowship seemd far unfit for warlike swaine.

38

So having solaced themselves a space
335
With pleasaunce of the breathing fields yfed,[7]
They backe returned to the Princely Place;
Whereas° an errant° knight in armes ycled,   *where / wandering*
And heathnish shield, wherein with letters red
Was writ Sans-Joy, they new arrived find:
340
Enflam'd with fury and fiers hardy-hed,°   *boldness*
He seemd in hart to harbour thoughts unkind,
And nourish bloudy vengeaunce in his bitter mind.

39

Who when the shamed shield of slaine Sans-Foy
He spide with that same Faery champions page,
345
Bewraying° him, that did of late destroy   *revealing*
His eldest brother, burning all with rage
He to him leapt, and that same envious gage°   *envious token*
Of victors glory from him snatcht away:
But th'Elfin knight, which ought° that warlike wage,   *owned*
350
Disdaind to loose° the meed° he wonne in fray,   *give up / reward*
And him recountring° fierce, reskewd the noble pray.[8]   *combatting*

40

Therewith they gan to hurtlen° greedily,   *fight*
Redoubted battaile ready to darrayne,°   *wage*
And clash their shields, and shake their swords on hy,
355
That with their sturre they troubled all the traine;
Till that great Queene upon eternall paine
Of high displeasure, that ensewen° might,   *follow*
Commaunded them their fury to refraine,
And if that either to that shield had right,
360
In equall lists° they should the morrow next it fight.   *tournament*

---

7. I.e., having fed themselves with fresh air from the fields, where they momentarily escape the stench of sin.
8. By striving to recover Sans-Foy's shield instead of pursuing his quest to free Una's parents, the Redcrosse Knight exhibits pride and exemplifies a false chivalry.

41

Ah dearest Dame, (quoth then the Paynim bold,)
  Pardon the errour of enraged wight,
  Whom great griefe made forget the raines° to hold   *reins*
  Of reasons rule, to see this recreant° knight,   *cowardly*
365   No knight, but treachour full of false despight°   *indignation*
  And shamefull treason, who through guile hath slayn
  The prowest knight, that ever field did fight,
  Even stout Sans-Foy (O who can then refrayn?)
Whose shield he beares renverst,° the more to heape disdayn.   *upside down*

42

370   And to augment the glorie of his guile,
  His dearest love the faire Fidessa loe°   *look*
  Is there possessed of° the traytour vile,[9]   *by*
  Who reapes the harvest sowen by his foe,
  Sowen in bloudy field, and bought with woe:
375   That brothers hand shall dearely well requight°   *repay*
  So be, O Queene, you equall favour showe.
  Him litle answerd th'angry Elfin knight;
He never meant with words, but swords to plead his right.°   *cause*

43

But threw his gauntlet° as a sacred pledge,   *glove*
380   His cause in combat the next day to try:
  So been they parted both, with harts on edge,
  To be aveng'd each on his enimy.
  That night they pas in joy and jollity,
  Feasting and courting both in bowre and hall;
385   For Steward was excessive Gluttonie,
  That of his plenty poured forth to all;
Which doen, the Chamberlain° Slowth did to rest them call.   *master of bedchambers*

44

Now whenas° darkesome night had all displayd   *when*
  Her coleblacke curtein over brightest skye,
390   The warlike youthes on dayntie couches layd,
  Did chace away sweet sleepe from sluggish eye,
  To muse on meanes of hoped victory.
  But whenas Morpheus had with leaden mace
  Arrested° all that courtly company,   *i.e., put to sleep*
395   Up-rose Duessa from her resting place,
And to the Paynims lodging comes with silent pace.

45

Whom broad awake she finds, in troublous fit,
  Forecasting, how his foe he might annoy,°   *injure*
  And him amoves° with speaches seeming fit: *arouses*
400   Ah deare Sans-Joy, next dearest to Sans-Foy,
  Cause of my new griefe, cause of my new joy,

---

9. Sans-Joy accused the Redcrosse Knight of absconding with Fidessa (i.e., Duessa), who actually belonged to his brother, Sans-Foy.

Joyous, to see his ymage in mine eye,
And greev'd, to thinke how foe did him destroy,
That was the flowre of grace and chevalrye;
405 Lo his Fidessa to thy secret faith I flye.

46

With gentle wordes he can° her fairely greet,   *did*
And bad° say on the secret of her hart.   *commanded*
Then sighing soft, I learne that little sweet
Oft tempred is (quoth she) with muchell smart:°   *much pain*
410 For since my brest was launcht° with lovely dart   *pierced*
Of deare Sans-Foy, I never joyed howre,
But in eternall woes my weaker hart
Have wasted, loving him with all my powre,
And for his sake have felt full many an heavie stowre.°   *sorrowful time*

47

415 At last when perils all I weened past,
And hop'd to reape the crop of all my care,
Into new woes unweeting I was cast,
By this false faytor,° who unworthy ware°   *deceiver / wore*
His° worthy shield, whom he with guilefull snare   *Sans-Foy's*
420 Entrapped slew, and brought to shamefull grave.
Me silly maid away with him he bare,
And ever since hath kept in darksome cave,
For that° I would not yeeld, that to Sans-Foy I gave.   *that which*

48

But since faire Sunne hath sperst° that lowring° clowd,   *dispersed / threatening*
425 And to my loathed life now shewes some light,
Under your beames I will me safely shrowd,°   *take shelter*
From dreaded storme of his° disdainfull spight: *Redcrosse Knight's*
To you th'inheritance belongs by right
Of brothers prayse, to you eke longs his love.
430 Let not his love, let not his restlesse spright
Be unreveng'd, that calles to you above
From wandring Stygian° shores, where it doth endlesse move.   *underworld*

49

Thereto said he, Faire Dame be nought dismaid
For sorrowes past; their griefe is with them gone:
435 Ne yet of present perill be affraid;
For needlesse feare did never vantage none,°   *benefit anyone*
And helplesse hap it booteth° not to mone.   *helps*
Dead is Sans-Foy, his vitall paines° are past,   *troubles in life*
Though greeved ghost for vengeance deepe do grone:
440 He lives, that shall him pay his dewties last,°   *final debts*
And guiltie Elfin bloud shall sacrifice in hast.

50

O but I feare the fickle freakes° (quoth shee)   *accidents*
Of fortune false, and oddes of armes in field.
Why dame (quoth he) what oddes can ever bee,

445   Where both do fight alike, to win or yield?
        Yea but (quoth she) he beares a charmed shield,
        And eke enchaunted armes, that none can perce,
        Ne none can wound the man, that does them wield.
        Charmd or enchaunted (answerd he then ferce)
450   I no whit reck,° ne you the like need to reherce.°   *care nothing / mention*

51

        But faire Fidessa, sithens° fortunes guile,   *since*
        Or enimies powre hath now captiued you,
        Returne from whence ye came, and rest a while
        Till morrow next, that I the Elfe subdew,
455   And with Sans-Foyes dead dowry you endew.°   *give*
        Ay me, that is a double death (she said)
        With proud foes sight my sorrow to renew:
        Where euer yet I be, my secrete aid
        Shall follow you. So passing forth she him obaid.

Canto 5

The faithfull knight in equall field
subdewes his faithlesse foe,
Whom false Duessa saves, and for
his cure to hell does goe.

1

        The noble hart, that harbours vertuous thought,
        And is with child° of glorious great intent,   *pregnant*
        Can neuer rest, untill it forth haue brought
        Th'eternall brood of glorie excellent:
5   Such restlesse passion did all night torment
        The flaming corage of that Faery knight,
        Deuizing, how that doughtie° turnament   *worthy*
        With greatest honour he atchieuen might;
        Still did he wake, and still did watch for dawning light.

2

10   At last the golden Orientall° gate   *eastern*
        Of greatest heauen gan to open faire,
        And Phoebus fresh, as bridegrome to his mate,
        Came dauncing forth, shaking his deawie haire:
        And hurld his glistring° beames through gloomy aire.   *glistening*
15   Which when the wakeful Elfe perceiu'd, streight way
        He started up, and did him selfe prepaire,
        In sun-bright armes, and battailous° array: *warlike*
        For with that Pagan proud he combat will that day.

3

        And forth he comes into the commune hall,
20   Where earely waite him many a gazing eye,
        To weet° what end to straunger knights may fall.   *know*
        There many Minstrales maken melody,
        To driue away the dull melancholy,

And many Bardes, that to the trembling chord
25   Can tune their timely voyces cunningly,
And many Chroniclers, that can record
Old loves, and warres for Ladies doen by many a Lord.

4

Soone after comes the cruell Sarazin,
In woven maile all armed warily,°   *carefully*
30   And sternly lookes at him, who not a pin
Does care for looke of living creatures eye.
They bring them wines of Greece and Araby,°   *Arabia*
And daintie spices fetcht from furthest Ynd,°   *India*
To kindle heat of corage privily:°   *internally*
35   And in the wine a solemne oth they bynd
T'observe the sacred lawes of armes, that are assynd.

5

At last forth comes that far renowmed° Queene,   *famed*
With royall pomp and Princely majestie;
She is ybrought unto a paled greene,°   *enclosed field*
40   And placed under stately canapee,
The warlike feates of both those knights to see.
On th'other side in all mens open vew
Duessa placed is, and on a tree
Sans-Foy his shield is hangd with bloudy hew:
45   Both those the lawrell girlonds to the victor dew.[1]

6

A shrilling trompet sownded from on hye,
And unto battaill bad them selves addresse:
Their shining shieldes about their wrestes they tye,
And burning blades about their heads do blesse,[2]
50   The instruments of wrath and heavinesse:
With greedy force each other doth assayle,
And strike so fiercely, that they do impresse
Deepe dinted furrowes in the battred mayle;
The yron walles° to ward their blowes are weake and fraile.   *of the armor*

7

55   The Sarazin was stout, and wondrous strong,
And heaped blowes like yron hammers great:
For after bloud and vengeance he did long.
The knight was fiers, and full of youthly heat:
And doubled strokes, like dreaded thunders threat:
60   For all for prayse and honour he did fight.
Both stricken strike, and beaten both do beat,
That from their shields forth flyeth firie light,
And helmets hewen deepe,° shew marks of eithers might.   *deeply cut*

---

1. I.e., the victor will receive both Sans-Foy's shield and
Duessa as his prize.

2. Brandish: They make the sign of the cross in the air
with their swords.

8

So th'one for wrong, the other strives for right:
65   As when a Gryfon³ seized of his pray,
    A Dragon fiers encountreth in his flight,
    Through widest ayre making his ydle way,
    That would his rightfull ravine° rend away: *spoil*
    With hideous horrour both together smight,
70   And souce° so sore, that they the heavens affray: *attack*
    The wise Southsayer seeing so sad sight,
Th'amazed vulgar tels of warres and mortall fight.

9

So th'one for wrong, the other strives for right,
    And each to deadly shame would drive his foe:
75   The cruell steele so greedily doth bight
    In tender flesh, that streames of bloud down flow,
    With which the armes, that earst° so bright did show,   *first*
    Into a pure vermillion now are dyde:
    Great ruth° in all the gazers harts did grow,   *pity*
80   Seeing the gored woundes to gape so wyde,
That victory they dare not wish to either side.

10

At last the Paynim chaunst to cast his eye,
    His suddein eye, flaming with wrathfull fyre,
    Upon his brothers shield, which hong thereby:
85   Therewith redoubled was his raging yre,
    And said, Ah wretched sonne of wofull syre,°   *Sans-Foy*
    Doest thou sit wayling by black Stygian° lake,   *by the river Styx*
    Whilest here thy shield is hangd for victors hyre,
    And sluggish german° doest thy forces slake,   *kinsman*
90 To after-send his foe, that him may overtake?⁴

11

Goe caytive Elfe,⁵ him quickly overtake,
    And soone redeeme from his long wandring woe;
    Goe guiltie ghost, to him my message make,
    That I his shield have quit° from dying foe.   *recovered*
95   Therewith upon his crest he stroke him so,
    That twise he reeled, readie twise to fall;
    End of the doubtfull battell deemed tho
    The lookers on, and lowd to him gan call
The false Duessa, Thine the shield, and I, and all.⁶

3. A lion with eagle's wings. Dante used the gryfon as a symbol for the dual nature of Christ, as both spirit and flesh. However, in traditional iconography the gryfon also appeared as a creature who guarded gold and was thus emblematic of greed. The image suggests that the Redcrosse Knight is foolish to engage in a contest for material prizes.
4. Sans-Joy is addressing the dead Sans-Foy, asking if Sans-Foy grieves because his shield is a prize and the strength of his brother, Sans-Joy, which should be wielded to dispatch the Redcrosse Knight to the shores of the Styx, is actually slackening, growing weak.
5. Sans-Joy addresses the Redcrosse Knight. The epithet "caytive," meaning "servile," was especially insulting in the context of chivalry, because it implied weakness and lack of valor.
6. Duessa is calling to Sans-Joy; however, the Redcrosse Knight assumes that she is cheering him on and therefore redoubles his force.

12

100 Soone as the Faerie heard his Ladie speake,
     Out of his swowning dreame he gan awake,
     And quickning faith, that earst was woxen° weake,   *had grown*
     The creeping deadly cold away did shake:
     Tho mou'd with wrath, and shame, and Ladies sake,
105 Of all attonce he cast avengd to bee,
     And with so'exceeding furie at him strake,°   *struck*
     That forced him to stoupe upon his knee;
     Had he not stouped so, he should have cloven° bee.   *cut in half*

13

     And to him said, Goe now proud Miscreant,°   *heathen*
110 Thy selfe thy message doe to german deare,
     Alone he wandring thee too long doth want:°   *lack*
     Goe say, his foe thy shield with his doth beare.
     Therewith his heavie hand he high gan reare,°   *began to raise*
     Him to have slaine; when loe a darkesome clowd
115 Upon him fell: he no where doth appeare,
     But vanisht is. The Elfe him cals alowd,
     But answer none receiues: the darknes him does shroud.

14

     In haste Duessa from her place arose,
     And to him running said, O prowest° knight,   *most valiant*
120 That ever Ladie to her love did chose,
     Let now abate the terror of your might,
     And quench the flame of furious despight,
     And bloudie vengeance; lo th'infernall powres
     Covering your foe with cloud of deadly night,
125 Have borne him hence to Plutoes balefull° bowres.   *deadly*
     The conquest yours, I yours, the shield, and glory yours.

15

     Not all so satisfide, with greedie eye
     He sought all round about, his thirstie blade
     To bath in bloud of faithlesse enemy;
130 Who all that while lay hid in secret shade:
     He standes amazed, how he thence should fade.
     At last the trumpets Triumph sound on hie,
     And running Heralds humble homage made,
     Greeting him goodly with new victorie,
135 And to him brought the shield, the cause of enmitie.

16

     Wherewith he goeth to that soveraine Queene,
     And falling her before on lowly knee,
     To her makes present of his service seene:
     Which she accepts, with thankes, and goodly gree,°   *courteous goodwill*
140 Greatly advauncing his gay chevalree.
     So marcheth home, and by her takes the knight,
     Whom all the people follow with great glee,

Shouting, and clapping all their hands on hight,°   *high*
That all the aire it fils, and flyes to heaven bright.

17

145   Home is he brought, and laid in sumptuous bed:
Where many skilfull leaches° him abide,   *doctors*
To salve° his hurts, that yet still freshly bled.   *dress*
In wine and oyle they wash his woundes wide,
And softly can embalme on every side.
150   And all the while, most heavenly melody
About the bed sweet musicke did divide,°   *modulate*
Him to beguile of griefe and agony:
And all the while Duessa wept full bitterly.

18

As when a wearie traveller that strayes
155   By muddy shore of broad seven-mouthed Nile,
Unweeting of the perillous wandring wayes,
Doth meet a cruell craftie Crocodile,
Which in false griefe hyding his harmefull guile,
Doth weepe full sore, and sheddeth tender teares:
160   The foolish man, that pitties all this while
His mournefull plight, is swallowd up unwares,
Forgetfull of his owne, that mindes° anothers cares.   *attends to*

19

So wept Duessa untill eventide,
That shyning lampes in Joves high house were light:
165   Then forth she rose, ne lenger° would abide,   *no longer*
But comes unto the place, where th'Hethen knight
In slombring swownd nigh voyd of vitall spright,°   *living spirit*
Lay cover'd with inchaunted cloud all day:
Whom when she found, as she him left in plight,
170   To wayle his woefull case she would not stay,
But to the easterne coast of heaven makes speedy way.

20

Where griesly Night, with visage deadly sad,
That Phoebus chearefull face durst never vew,
And in a foule blacke pitchie mantle clad,
175   She findes forth comming from her darkesome mew,°   *den*
Where she all day did hide her hated hew.
Before the dore her yron charet stood,
Alreadie harnessed for journey new;
And coleblacke steedes yborne of hellish brood,
180   That on their rustie bits did champ, as they were wood.°   *mad*

21

Who when she saw Duessa sunny bright,
Adornd with gold and jewels shining cleare,
She greatly grew amazed at the sight,
And th'unacquainted light began to feare:
185   For never did such brightnesse there appeare,

And would have backe retyred to her cave,
   Untill the witches speech she gan to heare,
   Saying, Yet O thou dreaded Dame, I crave
Abide,° till I have told the message, which I have.   *wait*

22

190 She stayd, and foorth Duessa gan proceede,
   O thou most auncient Grandmother of all,[7]
   More old then Jove, whom thou at first didst breede,
   Or that great house of Gods caelestiall,
   Which wast begot in Daemogorgons° hall,   *chaos's*
195   And sawst the secrets of the world unmade,°   *not yet made*
   Why suffredst thou thy Nephewes deare to fall
   With Elfin sword, most shamefully betrade?
Lo where the stout° Sans-Joy doth sleepe in deadly shade.   *sturdy*

23

And him before, I saw with bitter eyes
200   The bold Sans-Foy shrinke underneath his speare;
   And now the pray of fowles in field he lyes,
   Nor wayld of friends, nor laid on groning beare,°   *bier*
   That whylome was to me too dearely deare.
   O what of Gods then boots° it to be borne,   *benefits*
205   If old Aveugles[8] sonnes so evill heare?
   Or who shall not great Nightes children scorne,
When two of three her Nephews are so fowle forlorne?°   *foully abandoned*

24

Up then, up dreary Dame, of darknesse Queene,
   Go gather up the reliques° of thy race,   *remains*
210   Or else goe them avenge, and let be seene,
   That dreaded Night in brightest day hath place,°   *highest rank*
   And can the children of faire light deface.
   Her feeling speeches some compassion moved
   In hart, and chaunge in that great mothers face:
215   Yet pittie in her hart was never proved°   *experienced*
Till then: for evermore she hated, never loved.

25

And said, Deare daughter rightly may I rew
   The fall of famous children borne of mee,
   And good successes, which their foes ensew:
220   But who can turne the streame of destinee,
   Or breake the chayne of strong necessitee,
   Which fast is tyde to Joves eternall seat?[9]
   The sonnes of Day he favoureth, I see,
   And by my ruines thinkes to make them great:
225 To make one great by others losse, is bad excheat.°   *exchange*

7. Invoking Night, Duessa recalls that Jove was raised in a dark cave to escape being eaten by his father, Saturn; here, Spenser is implying that darkness gave birth to Jove.
8. Blind (French). Duessa uses the name "Aveugle" to refer to either Night herself or her husband; "Aveugles sonne" is Sans-Joy.
9. Night reveals her fatalism and therefore her ignorance of Christian grace. God can forgive a repentant sinner; hence for Christians there is no "chain of necessity" prior to God's decision to send the sinner to eternal damnation.

26

Yet shall they not escape so freely all;
    For some shall pay the price of° others guilt: *for*
    And he the man that made Sans-Foy to fall,
    Shall with his owne bloud price that he hath spilt.
230   But what art thou, that telst of Nephews kilt?°   *killed*
    I that do seeme not I, Duessa am,
    (Quoth she) how ever now in garments gilt,
    And gorgeous gold arayd I to thee came;
Duessa I, the daughter of Deceipt and Shame.

27

235 Then bowing downe her aged backe, she kist
    The wicked witch, saying; In that faire face
    The false resemblance of Deceipt, I wist
    Did closely° lurke; yet so true-seeming grace   *secretly*
    It carried, that I scarse in darkesome place
240   Could it discerne, though I the mother bee
    Of falshood, and root of Duessaes race.
    O welcome child, whom I have longd to see,
And now have seene unwares.° Lo now I go with thee.   *unknowingly*

28

Then to her yron wagon she betakes,
245   And with her beares the fowle welfavour witch:[1]
    Through mirkesome° aire her readie way she makes.   *murky*
    Her twyfold° Teme, of which two blacke as pitch,   *twofold*
    And two were browne, yet each to each unlich,°   *unlike*
    Did softly swim away, ne ever stampe,
250   Unlesse she chaunst their stubborne mouthes to twitch;
    Then foming tarre, their bridles they would champe,
And trampling the fine element,° would fiercely rampe.°   *air / rear up*

29

So well they sped, that they be come at length
    Unto the place, whereas the Paynim lay,
255   Devoid of outward sense, and native° strength,   *natural*
    Coverd with charmed cloud from vew of day,
    And sight of men, since his late luckelesse fray.°   *fight*
    His cruell wounds with cruddy bloud congealed,
    They binden up so wisely, as they may,
260   And handle softly, till they can be healed:
So lay him in her charet, close° in night concealed.   *hidden*

30

And all the while she stood upon the ground,
    The wakefull dogs did never cease to bay,°   *howl*
    As giving warning of th'unwonted° sound,   *unaccustomed*
265   With which her yron wheeles did them affray,
    And her darke griesly looke them much dismay;
    The messenger of death, the ghastly Owle

1. Duessa is a foul creature disguised as a beautiful woman.

With drearie shriekes did also her bewray;°   *expose*
And hungry Wolves continually did howle,
270   At her abhorred face, so filthy and so fowle.

                                        31
        Thence turning backe in silence soft they stole,
            And brought the heavie corse with easie pace
            To yawning gulfe of deepe Avernus° hole.   *a lake in hell*
            By that same hole an entrance darke and bace°   *low*
275   With smoake and sulphure hiding all the place,
            Descends to hell: there creature never past,
            That backe returned without heavenly grace;
        But dreadfull Furies,[2] which their chaines have brast,
        And damned sprights sent forth to make ill° men aghast.   *bad*

                                        32
280   By that same way the direfull° dames doe drive   *dreadful*
            Their mournefull charet, fild° with rusty blood,   *defiled*
            And downe to Plutoes house are come bilive:°   *quickly*
            Which passing through, on every side them stood
            The trembling ghosts with sad amazed mood,
285   Chattring their yron teeth, and staring wide
            With stonie eyes; and all the hellish brood
            Of feends infernall flockt on every side,
        To gaze on earthly wight, that with the Night durst° ride.   *dared*

                                        33
        They pas the bitter waves of Acheron,[3]
290   Where many soules sit wailing woefully,
            And come to fiery flood of Phlegeton,
            Whereas the damned ghosts in torments fry,
            And with sharpe shrilling shriekes doe bootlesse° cry,   *futilely*
            Cursing high Jove, the which them thither sent.
295   The house of endlesse paine is built thereby,
            In which ten thousand sorts of punishment
        The cursed creatures doe eternally torment.

                                        34
        Before the threshold dreadfull Cerberus[4]
            His three deformed heads did lay along,
300   Curled with thousand adders venemous,
            And lilled forth° his bloudie flaming tong: *stuck out*
            At them he gan to reare his bristles strong,
            And felly gnarre,° untill dayes enemy   *deadly snarl*
            Did him appease; then downe his taile he hong
305   And suffered them to passen quietly:
        For she in hell and heaven had power equally.

2. The three mythical female spirits who live in the   the underworld.
underworld and punish people for their crimes; they per-   4. The fierce, three-headed dog who guards the entrance
sonified the forces of revenge.   to the underworld.
3. Acheron and Phlegeton are two of the four rivers of

35

There was Ixion[5] turned on a wheele,
   For daring tempt the Queene of heaven to sin;
   And Sisyphus an huge round stone did reele
310   Against an hill, ne might from labour lin;
   There thirstie Tantalus hong by the chin;
   And Tityus fed a vulture on his maw;
   Typhoeus joynts were stretched on a gin,
   Theseus condemned to endlesse slouth by law,
315 And fifty sisters water in leake vessels draw.

36

They all beholding worldly wights in place,
   Leave off their worke, unmindfull of their smart,°   *pain*
   To gaze on them; who forth by them doe pace,
   Till they be come unto the furthest part:
320   Where was a Cave ywrought° by wondrous art,   *built*
   Deepe, darke, uneasie, dolefull, comfortlesse,
   In which sad Aesculapius[6] farre a part
   Emprisond was in chaines remedilesse,
For that Hippolytus rent corse he did redresse.°   *restore*

37

325 Hippolytus a jolly huntsman was,
   That wont° in charet chace the foming Bore;   *often*
   He all his Peeres in beautie did surpas,
   But Ladies love as losse of time forbore:°   *abstained from*
   His wanton stepdame° loved him the more,   *stepmother*
330   But when she saw her offred sweets refused
   Her love she turnd to hate, and him before
   His father fierce of treason false accused,
And with her gealous termes his open eares abused.

38

Who ail in rage his Sea-god syre besought,
335   Some cursed vengeance on his sonne to cast:
   From surging gulf two monsters straight were brought,
   With dread whereof his chasing steedes aghast,°   *terrified*
   Both charet swift and huntsman overcast.
   His goodly corps on ragged cliffs yrent,
340   Was quite dismembred, and his members chast°   *virgin, virtuous*
   Scattered on every mountaine, as he went,
That of Hippolytus was left no moniment.°   *trace*

5. This stanza describes various mythological figures who suffer in the underworld. Ixion, king of Thessaly, sought the love of Juno and was punished by being bound forever on a revolving wheel. Sisyphus, a greedy king of Corinth, was condemned forever to roll up a hill a heavy stone, which always rolled back down again. Tantalus was doomed to stand up to his neck in water with fruit hanging at his fingertips, yet could never reach the fruit or drink the water. Tityus's punishment was to have a vulture constantly feed on his liver, which grew back as soon as it was devoured. Theseus, hero and eventually king of Athens, was famous for a multitude of exploits and adventures; he was condemned to sit forever in the chair of forgetfulness. The 50 sisters were the daughters of Danaus, king of Argos; they were condemned to collect water in leaky pots because they had murdered their husbands on their wedding night.

6. The god of medicine. In the following stanzas, Spenser tells the story of how Aesculapius revived the corpse of Hippolytus and was punished for exceeding the limits of medical art.

39

His cruell stepdame seeing what was donne,
   Her wicked dayes with wretched knife did end,
345   In death avowing th'innocence of her sonne.
   Which hearing his rash Syre, began to rend°   *tear*
   His haire, and hastie tongue, that did offend:
   Tho gathering up the relicks of his smart°   *pain*
   By Dianes° meanes, who was Hippolyts frend,   *goddess of the hunt*
350   Them brought to Aesculape, that by his art
Did heale them all againe, and joyned every part.

40

Such wondrous science in mans wit to raine°   *rule*
   When Jove avizd,° that could the dead revive,   *found out*
   And fates expired could renew againe,
355   Of endlesse life he might him not deprive,
   But unto hell did thrust him downe alive,
   With flashing thunderbolt ywounded sore:
   Where long remaining, he did alwaies strive
   Himselfe with salves to health for to restore,
360 And slake° the heavenly fire, that raged evermore.   *put out*

41

There auncient Night arriving, did alight
   From her nigh wearie waine, and in her armes
   To Aesculapius brought the wounded knight:
   Whom having softly disarayd of armes,
365   Tho gan to him discover all his harmes,°   *injuries*
   Beseeching him with prayer, and with praise,
   If either salves, or oyles, or herbes, or charmes
   A fordonne° wight from dore of death mote raise,   *dying*
He would at her request prolong her nephews daies.

42

370 Ah Dame (quoth he) thou temptest me in vaine,
   To dare the thing, which daily yet I rew,
   And the old cause of my continued paine
   With like attempt to like end to renew.[7]
   Is not enough, that thrust from heaven dew
375   Here endlesse penance for one fault I pay,
   But that redoubled crime with vengeance new
   Thou biddest me to eeke?° Can Night defray°   *increase / appease*
The wrath of thundring Jove, that rules both night and day?

43

Not so (quoth she) but sith that heavens king
380   From hope of heaven hath thee excluded quight,
   Why fearest thou, that canst not hope for thing,°   *anything*
   And fearest not, that more thee hurten might,
   Now in the powre of everlasting Night?
   Goe to then, O thou farre renowmed sonne
385   Of great Apollo, shew thy famous might

---

7. I.e., to repeat the actions that caused his punishment in the first place and thus to renew the punishment itself.

In medicine, that else hath to thee wonne
Great paines, and greater praise, both never to be donne.°   *surpassed*

44

Her words prevaild: And then the learned leach°   *doctor*
His cunning hand gan to his wounds to lay,
390   And all things else, the which his art did teach:
Which having seene, from thence arose away
The mother of dread darknesse, and let stay
Aveugles sonne there in the leaches cure,
And backe returning tooke her wonted way,
395   To runne her timely race, whilst Phoebus pure
In westerne waves his wearie wagon did recure.°   *renew*

45

The false Duessa leaving noyous° Night,   *noxious*
Returnd to stately pallace of dame Pride;
Where when she came, she found the Faery knight
400   Departed thence, albe° his woundes wide   *although*
Not throughly heald, unreadie were to ride.
Good cause he had to hasten thence away;
For on a day his wary Dwarfe had spide,
Where in a dongeon deepe huge numbers lay
405   Of caytive wretched thrals,° that wayled night and day.   *prisoners*

46

A ruefull sight, as could be seene with eie;
Of whom he learned had in secret wise°   *manner*
The hidden cause of their captivitie,
How mortgaging their lives to Covetise,°   *greed*
410   Through wastfull Pride, and wanton Riotise,°   *idle abandon*
They were by law of that proud Tyrannesse
Provokt with Wrath, and Envies false surmise,°   *suspicion*
Condemned to that Dongeon mercilesse,
Where they should live in woe, and die in wretchednesse.[8]

47

415   There was that great proud king of Babylon,°   *Nebuchadnezzar*
That would compell all nations to adore,
And him as onely° God to call upon,   *the only*
Till through celestiall doome° throwne out of dore,   *heavenly judgment*
Into an Oxe he was transform'd of yore:°   *in ancient times*
420   There also was king Croesus, that enhaunst
His heart too high through his great riches store;

---

8. Spenser lists some of the inhabitants of the underworld, the domain of Night, implying that they were damned for their evil deeds and were therefore in a Christian hell. The theology supporting this image is problematic: While Spenser names individuals who were considered to have been proud and malicious, they were also not people who could have known the salutary message of Christianity. Nebuchadnezzar, king of Babylon, set up a golden image to be worshipped as God and was transformed into an ox as a punishment (Daniel 3–6); Croesus was the vastly rich king of Lydia; Antiochus, king of Antioch, was supposed scornfully to have danced on an altar; Nimrod was the first tyrant to emerge after the Flood; Ninus, the founder of Ninevah, conquered India and was the first to make war. "That mightie Monarch" was Alexander the Great, who rejected his father to claim descent from Jove or Jupiter, sometimes called Jupiter Ammon.

And proud Antiochus, the which advaunst
His cursed hand gainst God, and on his altars daunst.

48

And them long time before, great Nimrod was,

425   That first the world with sword and fire warrayd;°   *ravaged*

    And after him old Ninus farre did pas

    In princely pompe, of all the world obayd;

    There also was that mightie Monarch layd

    Low under all, yet above all in pride,

430   That name of native syre° did fowle upbrayd,°   *natural father / denounce*

    And would as Ammons sonne be magnifide,

Till scornd of God and man a shamefull death he dide.

49

All these together in one heape were throwne,

    Like carkases of beasts in butchers stall.

435   And in another corner wide were strowne°   *strewn*

    The antique ruines of the Romaines fall:[9]

    Great Romulus the Grandsyre of them all,

    Proud Tarquin, and too lordly Lentulus,

    Stout Scipio, and stubborne Hanniball,

440   Ambitious Sylla, and sterne Marius,

High Caesar, great Pompey, and fierce Antonius.

50

Amongst these mighty men were wemen mixt,[1]

    Proud wemen, vaine, forgetfull of their yoke:°   *place*

    The bold Semiramis, whose sides transfixt

445   With sonnes owne blade, her fowle reproches spoke;

    Faire Sthenoboea, that her selfe did choke

    With wilfull cord, for wanting of her will;

    High minded Cleopatra, that with stroke

    Of Aspes° sting her selfe did stoutly kill: *snakes'*

450 And thousands moe the like, that did that dongeon fill.

51

Besides the endlesse routs° of wretched thralles,   *crowds*

    Which thither were assembled day by day,

    From all the world after their wofull falles,

    Through wicked pride, and wasted wealthes decay.°   *loss*

9. Spenser lists men who figured prominently in the history of ancient Rome; some were heroes, others were tyrants or wrongdoers. Romulus was the founder and first king of Rome; Tarquin was the last king of Rome before it became a republic; Lentulus attempted to set fire to Rome; Scipio was a Roman general who conquered Africa; Hannibal constantly waged war against Rome; Sylla was a Roman dictator who was engaged in civil war with Marius; Caesar, Pompey, and Antonius fought among themselves for rulership of Rome and its colonies, Caesar eventually winning the office only to be assassinated shortly thereafter.

1. The women in the underworld, like the men, were figures from ancient history and mythology; those that are listed were judged to have been evil. After the death of her husband, King Ninus, Semiramis disguised herself as her son to gain the throne. Her son killed her when she tried to sleep with him. Sthenoboea lusted after her brother-in-law, Bellerophon, and committed suicide when he refused her advances. After Egypt had been defeated by the Roman forces of Octavius (later the Emperor Augustus), Cleopatra, the queen of Egypt, committed suicide by allowing herself to be bitten by asps, a kind of poisonous snake.

455   But most of all, which in that Dongeon lay
  Fell from high Princes courts, or Ladies bowres,
  Where they in idle pompe, or wanton play,
  Consumed had their goods, and thriftlesse howres,
And lastly throwne themselves into these heavy stowres.°   *afflictions*

52

460   Whose case when as the carefull Dwarfe had tould,
  And made ensample° of their mournefull sight   *description*
  Unto his maister, he no lenger° would   *longer*
  There dwell in perill of like° painefull plight,   *similar*
  But early rose, and ere that dawning light
465   Discovered had the world to heaven wyde,
  He by a privie Posterne° tooke his flight,   *secret back door*
  That of no envious eyes he mote he spyde:
For doubtlesse death ensewd, if any him descryde.°   *discovered*

53

  Scarse could he footing find in that fowle way,
470   For° many corses, like a great Lay-stall° *because of | open grave*
  Of murdred men which therein strowed lay,°   *lay strewn*
  Without remorse, or decent funerall:
  Which all through that great Princesse pride did fall
  And came to shamefull end. And them beside
475   Forth ryding underneath the castell wall,
  A donghill° of dead carkases he spide,   *garbage heap*
The dreadfull spectacle of that sad house of Pride.

Canto 6

From lawlesse lust by wondrous grace
* fayre Una is releast:*
Whom salvage nation does adore,
* and learnes her wise beheast.°*   *teaching*

1

  As when a ship, that flyes faire under saile,
  An hidden rocke escaped hath unwares,
  That lay in waite her wrack° for to bewaile,   *destruction*
  The Marriner° yet halfe amazed stares   *sailor*
5 At perill past, and yet in doubt ne dares°   *dares not*
  To joy at his foole-happie° oversight: *lucky*
  So doubly is distrest twixt joy and cares
  The dreadlesse courage of this Elfin knight,
Having escapt so sad ensamples° in his sight.   *warnings*

2

10   Yet sad he was that his too hastie speed
  The faire Duess' had forst him leave behind;
  And yet more sad, that Una his deare dreed° *revered one*
  Her truth had staind with treason so unkind;° *unnatural*

                Yet crime in her could never creature find,
15   But for his love, and for her owne selfe sake,
                She wandred had from one to other Ynd,°   *throughout the world*
                Him for to seeke, ne ever would forsake,
           Till her unwares the fierce Sans-Loy did overtake.

                                    3
           Who after Archimagoes fowle defeat,
20   Led her away into a forrest wilde,
                And turning wrathfull fire to lustfull heat,
                With beastly sin thought° her to have defilde,   *decided*
                And made the vassall° of his pleasures vilde.   *slave*
                Yet first he cast by treatie,° and by traynes,°   *treaty / tricks*
25   Her to perswade, that stubborne fort° to yilde: *i.e., her chastity*
                For greater conquest of hard love he gaynes,
           That workes it to his will, then he that it constraines.°   *forces*

                                    4
           With fawning wordes he courted her a while,
                And looking lovely,° and oft sighing sore,   *amorously*
30   Her constant hart did tempt with diverse guile:°   *various deceits*
                But wordes, and lookes, and sighes she did abhore,
                As rocke of Diamond stedfast evermore.
                Yet for to feed his fyrie lustfull eye,
                He snatcht the vele, that hong her face before;
35   Then gan her beautie shine, as brightest skye,
           And burnt his beastly hart t'efforce° her chastitye.   *to force*

                                    5
           So when he saw his flatt'ring arts to fayle,
                And subtile engines bet from batteree,[1]
                With greedy force he gan the fort assayle,°   *attack*
40   Whereof he weend° possessed soone to bee,   *believed*
                And win rich spoile of ransackt chastetee.
                Ah heavens, that do this hideous act behold,
                And heavenly virgin thus outraged° see,   *violated*
                How can ye vengeance just so long withhold,
45   And hurle not flashing flames upon that Paynim bold?

                                    6
           The pitteous maiden carefull° comfortlesse,   *grief-stricken*
                Does throw out thrilling° shriekes, and shrieking cryes,   *piercing*
                The last vaine helpe of womens great distresse,
                And with loud plaints° importuneth the skyes,   *laments*
50   That molten° starres do drop like weeping eyes;   *melting*
                And Phoebus flying so most shamefull sight,
                His blushing face in foggy cloud implyes,°   *hides*
                And hides for shame. What wit of mortall wight
           Can now devise to quit a thrall from such a plight?

1. I.e., Sans-Loy's clever devices are overcome by the success of Una's "battery" or repulses.

7

55 Eternall providence exceeding thought,
        Where none appeares can make her selfe a way:
        A wondrous way it for this Lady wrought,
        From Lyons clawes to pluck the griped° pray.   trapped
        Her shrill outcryes and shriekes so loud did bray,
60   That all the woodes and forestes did resownd;
        A troupe of Faunes and Satyres° far away   woodland deities
        Within the wood were dauncing in a rownd,°   circle
    Whiles old Sylvanus° slept in shady arber sownd.°   a wood god / soundly

8

    Who when they heard that pitteous strained voice,
65   In hast forsooke° their rurall meriment,   abandoned
        And ran towards the far rebownded° noyce,   reverberating
        To weet,° what wight so loudly did lament.   discover
        Unto the place they come incontinent:°   headlong
        Whom when the raging Sarazin espide,
70   A rude, misshapen, monstrous rablement,
        Whose like he never saw, he durst° not bide,°   dared / stay
    But got his ready steed, and fast away gan ride.

9

    The wyld woodgods arrived in the place,
        There find the virgin dolefull desolate,
75   With ruffled rayments, and faire blubbred° face,   tear-stained
        As her outrageous foe had left her late,°   recently
        And trembling yet through feare of former hate;
        All stand amazed at so uncouth° sight,   strange
        And gin to pittie her unhappie state,
80   All stand astonied° at her beautie bright,   amazed
    In their rude eyes unworthie of so wofull plight.

10

    She more amaz'd, in double dread doth dwell;
        And every tender part for feare does shake:
        As when a greedie Wolfe through hunger fell°   deadly
85   A seely° Lambe farre from the flocke does take,   innocent
        Of whom he meanes his bloudie feast to make,
        A Lyon spyes fast running towards him,
        The innocent pray in hast he does forsake,
        Which quit° from death yet quakes in every lim°   rescued / limb
90 With chaunge of feare, to see the Lyon looke so grim.

11

    Such fearefull fit assaid° her trembling hart,   assailed
        Ne word to speake, ne joynt to move she had:
        The salvage° nation² feele her secret smart,   wild
        And read her sorrow in her count'nance sad;
95   Their frowning forheads with rough hornes yclad,
        And rusticke horror all a side doe lay,°   put away

---

2. I.e., the wood gods.

And gently grenning,° shew a semblance° glad   *grinning / expression*
   To comfort her, and feare to put away,
Their backward bent knees teach her humbly to obay.[3]

12

100 The doubtfull Damzell dare not yet commit
        Her single person to their barbarous truth,°   *allegiance*
        But still twixt feare and hope amazd does sit,
        Late° learnd what harme to hastie trust ensu'th,°   *recently / follows*
        They in compassion of her tender youth,
105   And wonder of her beautie soveraine,
        Are wonne with pitty and unwonted° ruth,   *unaccustomed*
        And all prostrate upon the lowly plaine,°   *ground*
Do kisse her feete, and fawne on her with count'nance faine.°   *glad expressions*

13

     Their harts she ghesseth by their humble guise,
110   And yieldes her to extremitie of time;[4]
        So from the ground she fearelesse doth arise,
        And walketh forth without suspect° of crime:°   *fear / evil*
        They all as glad, as birdes of joyous Prime,°   *spring*
        Thence lead her forth, about her dauncing round,
115   Shouting, and singing all a shepheards ryme,
        And with greene braunches strowing° all the ground,   *strewing*
Do worship her, as Queene, with olive girlond cround.

14

     And all the way their merry pipes they sound,
        That all the woods with doubled Eccho ring,
120   And with their horned feet do weare° the ground,   *tread*
        Leaping like wanton° kids in pleasant Spring.   *playful*
        So towards old Sylvanus they her bring;
        Who with the noyse awaked, commeth out,
        To weet° the cause, his weake steps governing,°   *discover / guiding*
125   And aged limbs on Cypresse stadle stout,[5]
And with an yvie twyne° his wast is girt° about.   *vine / wrapped*

15

     Far off he wonders, what them makes so glad,
        Or° Bacchus[6] merry fruit° they did inuent,   *whether / grapes*
        Or Cybeles[7] franticke rites have made them mad;
130   They drawing nigh, unto their God° present   *Sylvanus*
        That flowre of faith and beautie excellent.
        The God himselfe vewing that mirrhour rare,
        Stood long amazd, and burnt in his intent;

---

3. The fauns and satyrs have goat legs, so when they kneel before Una, their legs bend backward. It is not clear who teaches whom to obey in this line: their own act of kneeling may be teaching the fauns and satyrs to obey Una, or their awkward gestures may be teaching Una to obey them and put away her fear.
4. I.e., she submits to the necessities imposed on her by circumstances and loses her fear of the fauns and satyrs.

5. Sylvanus uses a cane made from the trunk of a cypress tree.
6. The Roman god of wine; he is associated with both riot and fertility. Sylvanus suspects the fauns and satyrs of having discovered and drunk too much wine.
7. The goddess of grain and the harvest; the spring festival held in her honor was a fertility rite that resembled a bacchanalia.

His owne faire Dryope[8] now he thinkes not faire,
135   And Pholoe fowle, when her to this he doth compaire.

16

The woodborne° people fall before her flat,   *born of the woods*
  And worship her as Goddesse of the wood;
  And old Sylvanus selfe bethinkes not,° what   *cannot tell*
  To thinke of wight so faire, but gazing stood,
140   In doubt to deeme° her borne of earthly brood;   *believe*
  Sometimes Dame Venus selfe he seemes to see,
  But Venus never had so sober° mood;   *serious*
  Sometimes Diana he her takes to bee,
But misseth bow, and shaftes,° and buskins° to her knee.   *arrows / boots*

17

145   By vew of her he ginneth to revive
  His ancient love, and dearest Cyparisse,[9]
  And calles to mind his pourtraiture aliue,°   *living image*
  How faire he was, and yet not faire to this,
  And how he slew with glauncing dart amisse
150   A gentle Hynd, the which the lovely boy
  Did love as life, above all worldly blisse;
  For griefe whereof the lad n'ould after° joy,   *would never afterward*
But pynd° away in anguish and selfe-wild° annoy.   *wasted / self-willed*

18

The wooddy Nymphes, faire Hamadryades°   *tree spirits*
155   Her to behold do thither runne apace,
  And all the troupe of light-foot Naiades,°   *water nymphs*
  Flocke all about to see her lovely face:
  But° when they vewed have her heavenly grace,   *except for*
  They envie her in their malitious mind,
160   And fly away for feare of fowle disgrace:
  But all the Satyres scorne their woody kind,
And henceforth nothing faire, but her on earth they find.

19

Glad of such lucke, the luckelesse lucky maid,
  Did her content to please their feeble eyes,
165   And long time with that salvage people staid,
  To gather breath in many miseries.
  During which time her gentle wit she plyes,°   *employs*
  To teach them truth, which worship her in vaine,
  And made her th'Image of Idolatryes;
170   But when their bootlesse° zeale she did restraine   *misguided*
From her own worship, they her Asse would worship fayn.°   *gladly*

---

8. At this point, Una is still unveiled from her encounter with Sans-Loy. When Sylvanus views her, he sees a mirror reflecting heavenly faith and beauty and hence considers his beloved nymphs, Dryope and Pholoe, ugly by comparison.

9. Cyparisse was a boy whom Sylvanus loved. Here Spenser recounts how Sylvanus accidentally killed Cyparisse's doe, after which the boy became so sad that Apollo turned him into a cypress to relieve his distress.

20

It fortuned° a noble warlike knight   *happened*
    By just occasion to that forrest came,
    To seeke his kindred, and the lignage right,°   *proper lineage*
175   From whence he tooke his well deserved name:
    He had in armes abroad wonne muchell° fame,   *much*
    And fild far landes with glorie of his might,
    Plaine, faithfull, true, and enimy of shame,
    And ever lou'd to fight for Ladies right,
180 But in vaine glorious frayes° he litle did delight.   *battles*

21

A Satyres sonne yborne in forrest wyld,
    By straunge adventure as it did betyde,°   *happen*
    And there begotten of a Lady myld,
    Faire Thyamis the daughter of Labryde,[1]
185   That was in sacred bands of wedlocke tyde
    To Therion, a loose unruly swayne;°   *fellow*
    Who had more joy to raunge the forrest wyde,
    And chase the salvage beast with busie payne,°   *painstakingly*
Then° serve his Ladies love, and wast in pleasures vayne.   *than*

22

190 The forlone mayd did with loves longing burne,
    And could not lacke° her lovers company,   *do without*
    But to the wood she goes, to serve her turne,°   *satisfy her desire*
    And seeke her spouse, that from her still° does fly,   *always*
    And followes other game and venery:
195   A Satyre chaunst her wandring for to find,
    And kindling coles of lust in brutish eye,
    The loyall links of wedlocke did unbind,
And made her person thrall° unto his beastly kind.   *prisoner*

23

So long in secret cabin there he held
200   Her captive to his sensuall desire,
    Till that with timely fruit her belly sweld,
    And bore a boy unto that salvage sire:
    Then home he suffred her for to retire,°   *return*
    For ransome leaving him the late borne childe;
205 Whom till to ryper yeares he gan aspire,°   *began to grow*
    He noursled up° in life and manners wilde,   *raised*
Emongst wild beasts and woods, from lawes of men exilde.

24

For all he taught the tender ymp,° was but   *child*
    To banish cowardize and bastard feare,
210   His trembling hand he would him force to put
    Upon the Lyon and the rugged Beare,
    And from the she Beares teats her whelps° to teare;   *cubs*

---

1. The Greek names reveal the natures of these characters: Thyamis means "passion"; Labryde means "turbulence" or "greed"; and Therion means "wild beast."

And eke wyld roring Buls he would him make
   To tame, and ryde their backes not made to beare;°   be ridden
215   And the Robuckes° in flight to overtake,   bucks
That every beast for feare of him did fly and quake.

                          25
Thereby so fearelesse, and so fell° he grew,   deadly
   That his owne sire and maister of his guise°   behavior
   Did often tremble at his horrid vew,
220   And oft for dread of hurt would him advise,
   The angry beasts not rashly to despise,
   Nor too much to provoke; for he would learne°   teach
   The Lyon stoup° to him in lowly wise,   to bow
   (A lesson hard) and make the Libbard° sterne   leopard
225 Leave roaring, when in rage he for revenge did earne.°   yearn

                          26
And for to make his powre approved° more,   apparent
   Wyld beasts in yron yokes he would compell;°   command
   The spotted Panther, and the tusked Bore,
   The Pardale° swift, and the Tigre cruell;   female leopard
230   The Antelope, and Wolfe both fierce and fell;
   And them constraine in equall teme to draw.°   harness together
   Such joy he had, their stubborne harts to quell,°   subdue
   And sturdie courage tame with dreadfull aw,
That his beheast° they feared, as a tyrans° law.   command / tyrant's

                          27
235 His loving mother came upon a day
   Unto the woods, to see her little sonne;
   And chaunst unwares to meet him in the way,
   After his sportes, and cruell pastime donne,
   When after him a Lyonesse did runne,
240   That roaring all with rage, did lowd requere°   demand
   Her children deare, whom he away had wonne:°   taken
   The Lyon whelpes she saw how he did beare,
And lull° in rugged° armes, withouten childish feare.   cradle / hairy

                          28
The fearefull Dame° all quaked at the sight,   his mother
245   And turning backe, gan fast to fly away,
   Untill with love revokt° from vaine affright,   restrained
   She hardly yet perswaded was to stay,
   And then to him these womanish words gan say;
   Ah Satyrane,[2] my dearling, and my joy,
250   For love of me leave off° this dreadfull play;   stop
   To dally thus with death, is no fit toy,°   pastime
Go find some other play-fellowes, mine own sweet boy.

2. Like a satyr.

29

In these and like delights of bloudy game
 He trayned was, till ryper yeares he raught,°   *reached*
255 And there abode,° whilst any beast of name°   *lived / known*
 Walkt in that forest, whom he had not taught
 To feare his force: and then his courage haught°   *haughty*
 Desird of forreine foemen to be knowne,
 And far abroad for straunge° adventures sought: *foreign*
260 In which his might was never overthrowne,
 But through all Faery lond his famous worth was blown.° *broadcast*

30

Yet evermore it was his manner faire,
 After long labours and adventures spent,
 Unto those native woods for to repaire,
265 To see his sire and ofspring auncient.
 And now he thither came for like intent;
 Where he unwares the fairest Una found,
 Straunge Lady, in so straunge habiliment,°   *surroundings*
 Teaching the Satyres, which her sat around,
270 Trew sacred lore, which from her sweet lips did redound.

31

He wondred at her wisedome heavenly rare,
 Whose like in womens wit he never knew;
 And when her curteous deeds he did compare,
 Gan her admire, and her sad sorrowes rew,
275 Blaming of Fortune, which such troubles threw,
 And joyd to make proofe of° her° crueltie   *test / Fortune's*
 On gentle Dame, so hurtlesse, and so trew:
 Thenceforth he kept her goodly company,
 And learnd her discipline of faith and veritie.

32

280 But she all vowd unto the Redcrosse knight,
 His wandring perill closely did lament,
 Ne in this new acquaintaunce could delight,
 But her deare heart with anguish did torment,
 And all her wit in secret counsels spent,
285 How to escape. At last in privie wise°   *secretly*
 To Satyrane she shewed her intent;
 Who glad to gain such favour, gan devise,
 How with that pensive Maid he best might thence arise.° *depart*

33

So on a day when Satyres all were gone,
290 To do their service to Sylvanus old,
 The gentle virgin left behind alone
 He led away with courage stout and bold.
 Too late it was, to Satyres to be told,
 Or ever hope recover her againe:
295 In vaine he seekes that having cannot hold.

So fast he carried her with carefull paine,°   *skill*
That they the woods are past, and come now to the plaine.

34

The better part now of the lingring day,
    They traveild had, when as they farre espide
300   A wearie wight forwandring° by the way,   *wandering*
    And towards him they gan in hast to ride,
    To weet° of newes, that did abroad betide,°   *learn / occur*
    Or tydings of her knight of the Redcrosse.
    But he them spying, gan to turne aside,
305   For feare as seemd, or for some feigned losse;
More greedy they of newes, fast towards him do crosse.

35

A silly° man, in simple weedes forworne,°   *simple / old clothes*
    And soild with dust of the long dried way;
    His sandales were with toilesome travell torne,
310   And face all tand with scorching sunny ray,
    As he had traveild many a sommers day,
    Through boyling sands of Arabie and Ynde;°   *India*
    And in his hand a Iacobs staffe,° to stay   *pilgrim's staff*
    His wearie limbes upon: and eke behind,
315 His scrip° did hang, in which his needments he did bind.   *bag*

36

The knight approching nigh, of him inquerd°   *asked*
    Tydings of warre, and of adventures new;
    But warres, nor new adventures none he herd.
    Then Una gan to aske, if ought he knew,
320   Or heard abroad of that her champion trew,
    That in his armour bare a croslet° red.   *small cross*
    Aye me, Deare dame (quoth he) well may I rew
    To tell the sad sight, which mine eies have red:°   *seen*
These eyes did see that knight both living and eke ded.

37

325 That cruell word her tender hart so thrild,°   *pierced*
    That suddein cold did runne through every vaine,
    And stony horrour all her sences fild
    With dying fit,° that downe she fell for paine.   *deathlike swoon*
    The knight her lightly° reared° up againe,   *quickly / lifted*
330   And comforted with curteous kind reliefe:
    Then wonne° from death,[3] she bad° him tellen plaine   *brought back / ordered*
    The further processe of her hidden griefe;
The lesser pangs can beare, who hath endur'd the chiefe.°   *greater*

38

Then gan the Pilgrim thus, I chaunst this day,
335   This fatall day, that shall I ever rew,

---

3. Recovered from her swoon, Una asks the old man to continue telling her the details of the tale as yet unknown to her that will cause her further grief.

To see two knights in travell° on my way   *traveling*
(A sory sight) arraung'd° in battell new,⁴   *engaged*
Both breathing vengeaunce, both of wrathfull hew:
My fearefull flesh did tremble at their strife,
340   To see their blades so greedily imbrew,°   *stain themselves*
That drunke with bloud, yet thristed after life:
What more? the Redcrosse knight was slaine with Paynim knife.

39

Ah dearest Lord (quoth she) how might that bee,
And he the stoutest° knight, that ever wonne?   *sturdiest*
345   Ah dearest dame (quoth he) how might° I see   *could*
The thing, that might not be, and yet was donne?
Where is (said Satyrane) that Paynims sonne,
That him of life, and us of joy hath reft?°   *deprived*
Not far away (quoth he) he hence doth wonne°   *stay*
350   Foreby° a fountaine, where I late him left   *nearly*
Washing his bloudy wounds, that through° the steele were cleft.° *by / cut*

40

Therewith the knight thence marched forth in hast,
Whiles Una with huge heavinesse opprest,°   *overcome*
Could not for sorrow follow him so fast;
355   And soone he came, as he the place had ghest,°   *guessed*
Whereas° that Pagan proud him selfe did rest,   *where*
In secret shadow by a fountaine side:
Even he it was, that earst° would have supprest   *previously*
Faire Una: whom when Satyrane espide,
360   With fowle reprochfull words he boldly him defide.°   *challenged*

41

And said, Arise thou cursed Miscreaunt,°   *heathen*
That hast with knightlesse guile and trecherous train°   *tricks*
Faire knighthood fowly shamed, and doest vaunt°   *boast*
That good knight of the Redcrosse to have slain:
365   Arise, and with like treason° now maintain°   *treachery / defend*
Thy guilty wrong, or else thee guilty yield.°   *admit*
The Sarazin this hearing, rose amain,°   *at once*
And catching up in hast his three square° shield,   *triangular*
And shining helmet, soone him buckled° to the field.   *prepared*

42

370   And drawing nigh him said, Ah misborne Elfe,
In evill houre thy foes thee hither sent,
Anothers wrongs to wreake upon° thy selfe: *bring down*
Yet ill° thou blamest me, for having blent°   *wrongly / defiled*
My name with guile and traiterous intent;
375   That Redcrosse knight, perdie,° I never slew,   *by God*
But had he beene, where earst° his armes were lent,° *previously / borrowed*

---

4. The old man is telling the story of Archimago's battle with Sans-Loy; however, because he fabricates a second round of the battle here, the reader knows he is deceitful.

Th'enchaunter vaine his errour should not rew:
But thou his errour shalt, I hope now proven trew.[5]

43

Therewith they gan, both furious and fell,
380   To thunder blowes, and fiersly to assaile
     Each other bent° his enimy to quell,°   *intending / subdue*
     That with their force they perst both plate and maile,°   *types of armor*
     And made wide furrowes in their fleshes fraile,
     That it would pitty° any living eie.   *inspire pity in*
385   Large floods of bloud adowne their sides did raile;°   *pour*
     But floods of bloud could not them satisfie:
Both hungred after death: both chose to win, or die.

44

So long they fight, and fell revenge pursue,
     That fainting each, themselves to breathen let,°   *to catch their breath*
390   And oft refreshed, battell oft renue:
     As when two Bores with rancling malice met,
     Their gory° sides fresh bleeding fiercely fret,°   *gored / wound*
     Til breathlesse both them selves aside retire,
     Where foming wrath, their cruell tuskes they whet,°   *sharpen*
395   And trample th'earth, the whiles they may respire;°   *so they can breathe*
Then backe to fight againe, new breathed and entire.°   *refreshed*

45

So fiersly, when these knights had breathed° once,   *rested*
     They gan to fight returne, increasing more
     Their puissant° force, and cruell rage attonce,°   *powerful / at once*
400   With heaped° strokes more hugely, then before,   *increased*
     That with their drerie° wounds and bloudy gore   *bloody*
     They both deformed,° scarsely could be known.   *disfigured*
     By this sad Una fraught° with anguish sore,   *afflicted*
     Led with their noise, which through the aire was thrown,
405 Arriv'd, where they in erth° their fruitles° bloud had sown.   *on the ground / futile*

46

Whom all so soone as that proud Sarazin
     Espide, he gan revive the memory
     Of his lewd lusts, and late attempted sin,
     And left the doubtfull° battell hastily,   *undecided*
410   To catch her, newly offred to his eie:
     But Satyrane with strokes him turning, staid,
     And sternely bad him other businesse plie,°   *attend*
     Then hunt the steps of pure unspotted Maid:
Wherewith he° all enrag'd, these bitter speaches said.   *Sans-Loy*

47

415 O foolish faeries sonne, what furie mad
     Hath thee incenst,° to hast thy dolefull fate?   *enraged*

---

5. Sans-Loy refers to the action in 3.33–39. He denies killing the Redcrosse Knight, but he also states that had the Redcrosse Knight, and not Archimago, been wearing his own armor, then Sans-Loy would have killed him, and Archimago would not have to regret his, Sans-Loy's, error. But Sans-Loy will make good this error by engaging in judicial combat with Satyrane.

Were it not better, I that Lady had,
Then that thou hadst repented° it too late?   *regretted*
Most sencelesse man he, that himselfe doth hate,
420   To love another. Lo then for thine ayd
Here take thy lovers token on thy pate.°   *head*
So they to fight; the whiles the royall Mayd
Fled farre away, of that proud Paynim sore afrayd.

48

But that false Pilgrim, which that leasing° told,   *lie*
425   Being in deed old Archimage, did stay
In secret shadow, all this to behold,
And much rejoyced in their bloudy fray:
But when he saw the Damsell passe away
He left his stond,° and her pursewd apace,°   *place / awhile*
430   In hope to bring her to her last decay.°   *death*
But for to tell her lamentable cace,°   *situation*
And eke this battels end, will need another place.

Canto 7

The Redcrosse knight is captive made
By Gyaunt proud opprest,
Prince Arthur meets with Una greatly
with those newes distrest.

1

What man so wise, what earthly wit so ware,°   *alert*
As to descry° the crafty cunning traine,°   *perceive / guile*
By which deceipt doth maske in visour° faire,   *mask*
And cast her colours dyed deepe in graine,
5   To seeme like Truth, whose shape she well can faine,
And fitting gestures to her purpose frame,°   *suit*
The guiltlesse man with guile to entertaine?
Great maistresse of her art was that false Dame,
The false Duessa, cloked with Fidessaes name.[1]

2

10   Who when returning from the drery Night,
She fownd not in that perilous house of Pryde,
Where she had left, the noble Redcrosse knight,
Her hoped pray,° she would no lenger bide,°   *victim / stay*
But forth she went, to seeke him far and wide.
15   Ere long she fownd, whereas he wearie sate,
To rest him selfe, foreby a fountaine side,
Disarmed all of yron-coted Plate,°   *armor*
And by his side his steed the grassy forage ate.

3

He feedes upon the cooling shade, and bayes°   *bathes*
20   His sweatie forehead in the breathing wind,

1. Duessa (duplicity) falsely bears the name Fidessa (fidelity).

Which through the trembling leaves full gently playes
Wherein the cherefull birds of sundry kind
Do chaunt sweet musick, to delight his mind:
The Witch approching gan him fairely greet,
25   And with reproch of carelesnesse unkind
Upbrayd,° for leaving her in place unmeet,   *accused*
With fowle words tempring faire, soure gall° with hony sweet.   *anger*

4

Unkindnesse past, they gan of solace treat,°   *speak of pleasure*
And bathe in pleasaunce of the joyous shade,
30   Which shielded them against the boyling heat,
And with greene boughes decking a gloomy glade,
About the fountaine like a girlond made;
Whose bubbling wave did ever freshly well,
Ne ever would through fervent sommer fade:°   *dry up*
35   The sacred Nymph, which therein wont to dwell,
Was out of Dianes favour, as it then befell.°   *so happened*

5

The cause was this: one day when Phoebe[2] fayre
With all her band was following the chace,
This Nymph, quite tyr'd with heat of scorching ayre
40   Sat downe to rest in middest of the race:
The goddesse wroth gan fowly her disgrace,
And bad the waters, which from her did flow,
Be such as she her selfe was then in place.
Thenceforth her waters waxed dull and slow,
45   And all that drunke thereof, did faint and feeble grow.[3]

6

Hereof° this gentle knight unweeting was,   *of this*
And lying downe upon the sandie graile,°   *gravel*
Drunke of the streame, as cleare as cristall glas;
Eftsoones his manly forces gan to faile,
50   And mightie strong was turnd to feeble fraile.
His chaunged powres at first them selves not felt,
Till crudled° cold his corage° gan assaile,   *congealing / vital powers*
And chearefull bloud in faintnesse chill did melt,
Which like a fever fit[4] through all his body swelt.°   *raged*

7

55   Yet goodly court° he made still to his Dame,   *advances*
Pourd out in loosnesse° on the grassy grownd,   *licentiousness*
Both carelesse of his health, and of his fame:
Till at the last he heard a dreadfull sownd,
Which through the wood loud bellowing, did rebownd,
60   That all the earth for terrour seemd to shake,

---

2. An aspect or persona of Diana. As Diana, she is goddess of the hunt, but as Phoebe she is also goddess of the moon.
3. The nymph is transformed into a fountain whose waters cause fatigue rather than rejuvenation; paradoxically, this is a fountain that is never dry.
4. Heat is usually associated with strength, but here, the weakening effect of the fountain, associated with coldness, turns its forces against the Knight's strength, causing him to suffer both chill and fever.

And trees did tremble. Th'Elfe therewith astownd,
Upstarted lightly from his looser make,°   *mate*
And his unready weapons gan in hand to take.

8

But ere he could his armour on him dight,°   *put*
65   Or get his shield, his monstrous enimy
With sturdie steps came stalking in his sight,
An hideous Geant horrible and hye,°   *tall*
That with his talnesse seemd to threat the skye,
The ground eke groned under him for dreed;
70   His living like saw never living eye,
Ne durst° behold:[5] his stature did exceed   *nor dared*
The hight of three the tallest sonnes of mortall seed.°   *men*

9

The greatest Earth his uncouth° mother was,   *unnatural*
And blustring Aeolus° his boasted sire,   *god of the winds*
75   Who with his breath, which through the world doth pas,
Her hollow womb did secretly inspire,°   *impregnate*
And fild her hidden caues with stormie yre,
That she conceiv'd; and trebling° the dew time,   *tripling*
In which the wombes of women do expire,°   *give birth*
80   Brought forth this monstrous masse of earthly slime,
Puft up with emptie wind, and fild with sinfull crime.

10

So growen great through arrogant delight
Of th'high descent, whereof he was yborne,
And through presumption of his matchlesse might,
85   All other powres and knighthood he did scorne.[6]
Such now he marcheth to this man forlorne,
And left to losse: his stalking steps are stayde°   *supported*
Upon a snaggy Oke, which he had torne
Out of his mothers bowelles, and it made
90   His mortall° mace,° wherewith his foemen he dismayde.   *deadly / club*

11

That when the knight he spide, he gan advance
With huge force and insupportable° mayne,°   *irresistible / force*
And towardes him with dreadfull fury praunce;
Who haplesse, and eke hopelesse, all in vaine
95   Did to him pace, sad battaile to darrayne,°   *engage*
Disarmd, disgrast, and inwardly dismayde,
And eke so faint in every joynt and vaine,
Through that fraile fountaine, which him feeble made,
That scarsely could he weeld° his bootlesse° single blade.   *raise / useless*

12

100   The Geaunt strooke so maynly° mercilesse,   *forcefully*
That could have overthrowne a stony towre,

5. I.e., no living person had ever seen anything like the   6. I.e., the giant's ancestry has caused him to grow both
giant nor would even have dared to look at such a creature.   extremely tall and extremely proud.

And were not heavenly grace, that him did blesse,°   *preserve*
He had beene pouldred° all, as thin as flowre:°   *pulverized / flour*
But he was wary of that deadly stowre,°   *attack*
105   And lightly lept from underneath the blow:
Yet so exceeding was the villeins powre,
That with the wind it did him overthrow,
And all his sences stound,° that still he lay full low.   *stunned*

13

As when that divelish yron Engin° wrought   *the cannon*
110   In deepest Hell, and framd by Furies skill,[7]
With windy Nitre and quick Sulphur fraught,
And ramd with bullet round, ordaind to kill,
Conceiveth° fire, the heavens it doth fill   *catches*
With thundring noyse, and all the ayre doth choke,
115   That none can breath, nor see, nor heare at will,
Through smouldry cloud of duskish° stincking smoke,   *dusky*
That th'onely breath him daunts, who hath escapt the stroke.[8]

14

So daunted when the Geaunt saw the knight,[9]
His heavie hand he heaved up on hye,
120   And him to dust thought to have battred quight,
Untill Duessa loud to him gan crye;
O great Orgoglio,[1] greatest under skye,
O hold° thy mortall hand for Ladies sake,   *stop*
Hold for my sake, and do him not to dye,
125   But vanquisht thine eternall bondslave make,
And me thy worthy meed unto° thy Leman° take.   *as / beloved*

15

He hearkned, and did stay from further harmes,
To gayne so goodly guerdon,° as she spake: *prize*
So willingly she came into his armes,
130   Who her as willingly to grace did take,
And was possessed of his new found make.
Then up he tooke the slombred sencelesse corse,
And ere he could out of his swowne° awake,   *swoon*
Him to his castle brought with hastie forse,
135   And in a Dongeon deepe him threw without remorse.

16

From that day forth Duessa was his deare,
And highly honourd in his haughtie° eye,   *proud*
He gave her gold and purple pall° to weare,   *robe*
And triple crowne set on her head full hye,
140   And her endowd with royall majestye:

7. According to Renaissance tradition, the cannon was invented by the devil in hell. "Nitre" (potassium nitrate) and sulfur are the main ingredients of gunpowder; they are "windy" because they produce the blast that propels the cannonball through the air.
8. I.e., those who are not struck by the cannonball are overcome by the smoke.
9. I.e., when the Giant saw that the Knight was overcome by the smoke, he raised his heavy hand to beat him down completely.
1. Pride, haughtiness, disdain (Italian).

Then for to make her dreaded more of men,
And peoples harts with awfull terrour tye,°   *enthrall*
A monstrous beast ybred° in filthy fen°   *born / swamp*
He chose, which he had kept long time in darksome den.

17

145   Such one it was, as that renowmed° Snake   *famous*
Which great Alcides in Stremona slew,[2]
Long fostred in the filth of Lerna lake,
Whose many heads out budding ever new,
Did breed him endlesse labour to subdew:
150   But this same Monster much more ugly was;
For seven great heads out of his body grew,
An yron brest, and backe of scaly bras,
And all embrewd° in bloud, his eyes did shine as glas.   *stained*

18

His tayle was stretched out in wondrous length,
155   That to the house of heavenly gods it raught,°   *reached*
And with extorted° powre, and borrow'd strength,   *wrongfully obtained*
The ever-burning lamps from thence it brought,
And prowdly threw to ground, as things of nought;°   *worthless*
And underneath his filthy feet did tread
160   The sacred things, and holy heasts foretaught.°   *previously taught*
Upon this dreadfull Beast with sevenfold head
He set the false Duessa, for more aw and dread.[3]

19

The wofull Dwarfe, which saw his maisters fall,
Whiles he had keeping of his grasing steed,
165   And valiant knight become a caytive thrall,
When all was past, tooke up his forlorne weed,°   *abandoned armor*
His mightie armour, missing most at need;
His silver shield, now idle maisterlesse;
His poynant° speare, that many made to bleed,   *sharp*
170   The ruefull moniments of heavinesse,°   *tokens of grief*
And with them all departes, to tell his great distresse.

20

He had not travaild° long, when on the way   *traveled*
He wofull Ladie, wofull Una met,
Fast flying from the Paynims greedy pray,[4]
175   Whilest Satyrane him from pursuit did let:°   *hinder*

2. The "snake" Spenser is referring to is the hydra, a creature from Greek mythology with a hundred heads, that lived in the lake of Lerna and was killed by Hercules (Alcides) as one of his 12 labors. The hydra was particularly difficult for Hercules to kill because each time he cut off one of its heads, several new ones grew in its place. Hercules eventually burnt the hydra's neck after each decapitation, thus preventing new heads from sprouting. Stremona is a river in Thrace.

3. Spenser compares the hydra with the Roman Catholic Church. The seven heads of this monster refer to the seven hills on which Rome was built, as well as the seven deadly sins. Orgoglo mounts Duessa upon the seven-headed monster to make her more dreaded and awe-inspiring. This gesture also associates Duessa with the corrupt Roman Catholic Church, which, represented by the monster, has gained its power through tyranny and defiles true Christian doctrine.

4. I.e., Una is flying from Sans-Loy, who greedily has made her his prey or victim (see 6.42–47). The Dwarf meets Una at this point, while Satyrane is distracting Sans-Loy from his pursuit of her.

Who when her eyes she on the Dwarfe had set,
And saw the signes, that deadly tydings spake,
She fell to ground for sorrowfull regret,
And lively breath° her sad brest did forsake,   *breath of life*
180   Yet might her pitteous hart be seene to pant and quake.

21

The messenger of so unhappie newes
    Would faine° have dyde: dead was his hart within,   *rather*
    Yet outwardly some little comfort shewes:
    At last recovering hart, he does begin
185   To rub her temples, and to chaufe° her chin,   *rub*
    And every tender part does tosse and turne:
    So hardly° he the flitted life does win,   *with difficulty*
    Unto her native prison to retourne:⁵
Then gins° her grieved ghost thus to lament and mourne.   *begins*

22

190   Ye dreary instruments of dolefull° sight,⁶   *sorrowful*
    That doe this deadly spectacle behold,
    Why do ye lenger° feed on loathed light,   *longer*
    Or liking find to gaze on earthly mould,°   *shapes*
    Sith cruell fates⁷ the carefull threeds° unfould,   *threads*
195   The which my life and love together tyde?
    Now let the stony dart of senselesse cold
    Perce to my hart, and pas through every side,
And let eternall night so sad sight fro° me hide.   *from*

23

O lightsome day, the lampe of highest Jove,
200   First made by him, mens wandring wayes to guyde,
    When darknesse he in deepest dongeon drove,
    Henceforth thy hated face for ever hyde,
    And shut up heavens windowes shyning wyde:
    For earthly sight can nought but sorrow breed,
205   And late repentance, which shall long abyde.°   *persist*
    Mine eyes no more on vanitie shall feed,
But seeled up with death, shall have their deadly meed.°   *reward of death*

24

Then downe againe she fell unto the ground;
    But he her quickly reared° up againe: *raised*
210   Thrise did she sinke adowne in deadly swownd,
    And thrise he her reviv'd with busie paine:
    At last when life recover'd had the raine,°   *rein, control*
    And over-wrestled his strong enemie,
    With foltring tong,° and trembling every vaine,   *faltering tongue*
215   Tell on (quoth she) the wofull Tragedie,
The which these reliques sad present unto mine eie.

---

5. The native prison of Una's spirit is her body.
6. Here Una is addressing her eyes.
7. Mythical arbiters of human life, who as spinsters mea-

sure out the fate of every individual by twisting, winding,
and cutting his or her thread of life.

25

Tempestuous fortune hath spent all her spight,
  And thrilling sorrow throwne his utmost dart;
  Thy sad tongue cannot tell more heavy plight,
220   Then that I feele, and harbour in mine hart:
  Who hath endur'd the whole, can beare each part.
  If death it be, it is not the first wound,[8]
  That launched° hath my brest with bleeding smart.°   *pierced / wound*
  Begin, and end the bitter balefull stound;°   *wretched situation*
225 If lesse, then° that I feare, more favour I have found.[9]   *than*

26

Then gan the Dwarfe the whole discourse° declare,   *story*
  The subtill traines° of Archimago old;   *tricks*
  The wanton loves of false Fidessa faire,
  Bought with the bloud of vanquisht Paynim bold:
230   The wretched payre° transform'd to treen mould;°   *pair / tree shape*
  The house of Pride, and perils round about;
  The combat, which he with Sans-Joy did hould;
  The lucklesse conflict with the Gyant stout,°   *sturdy*
  Wherein captiv'd, of life or death he stood in doubt.

27

235 She heard with patience all unto the end,
  And strove to maister sorrowfull assay,°   *grief*
  Which greater grew, the more she did contend,°   *struggle*
  And almost rent her tender hart in tway;°   *two*
  And love fresh coles unto her fire did lay:
240   For greater love, the greater is the losse.
  Was never Ladie loved dearer day,
  Then she did love the knight of the Redcrosse;[1]
  For whose deare sake so many troubles her did tosse.°   *suffer*

28

At last when fervent° sorrow slaked° was,   *burning / quenched*
245   She up arose, resolving him to find
  A live or dead: and forward forth doth pas,°   *proceed*
  All as the Dwarfe the way to her assynd:°   *indicated*
  And evermore in constant carefull mind
  She fed her wound with fresh renewed bale;°   *bitterness*
250   Long tost with stormes, and bet° with bitter wind,   *beat*
  High over hils, and low adowne the dale,°   *valley*
  She wandred many a wood, and measurd° many a vale.°   *crossed / valley*

29

At last she chaunced by good hap° to meet   *luck*
  A goodly knight, faire marching by the way
255   Together with his Squire, arayed meet:°   *well-dressed*
  His glitterand armour shined farre away,

8. I.e., if the Redcrosse Knight has met his death, he would not be the first knight who had died attempting to help Una with her quest, and therefore this would not be the first time that Una has felt the pain of learning of such a death.

9. I.e., if what the Dwarf has to tell is less terrible than Una fears, she will consider herself lucky.

1. I.e., there was never a lady who loved life itself more than Una loved the Redcrosse Knight.

Like glauncing° light of Phoebus brightest ray;   *dazzling*
From top to toe no place appeared bare,
That deadly dint° of steele endanger may: *stroke*
260   Athwart° his brest a bauldrick brave° he ware,   *across / splendid belt*
That shynd, like twinkling stars, with stons most pretious rare.

30

And in the midst thereof one pretious stone
Of wondrous worth, and eke of wondrous mights,°   *powers*
Shapt like a Ladies head, exceeding shone,
265   Like Hesperus[2] emongst the lesser lights,
And strove for to amaze° the weaker sights;   *dazzle*
Thereby his mortall° blade full comely hong   *deadly*
In yvory sheath, ycarv'd with curious slights;°   *strange designs*
Whose hilts were burnisht° gold, and handle strong   *polished*
270   Of mother pearle, and buckled with a golden tong.°   *pin*

31

His haughtie° helmet, horrid° all with gold,   *tall / encrusted*
Both glorious brightnesse, and great terrour bred;
For all the crest a Dragon did enfold
With greedie pawes, and over all did spred
275   His golden wings: his dreadfull hideous hed
Close couched° on the bever,° seem'd to throw   *crouched / visor*
From flaming mouth bright sparkles fierie red,
That suddeine horror to faint° harts did show;   *weak*
And scaly tayle was stretcht adowne his backe full low.

32

280   Upon the top of all his loftie crest,
A bunch of haires discolourd diversly,°   *of many colors*
With sprincled pearle, and gold full richly drest,
Did shake, and seem'd to daunce for jollity,
Like to an Almond tree ymounted hye
285   On top of greene Selinis[3] all alone,
With blossomes brave bedecked° daintily;   *splendidly ornamented*
Whose tender locks do tremble every one
At every little breath, that under heaven is blowne.

33

His warlike shield all closely cover'd° was,   *hidden*
290   Ne might of mortall eye be ever seene;
Not made of steele, nor of enduring bras,
Such earthly mettals soone consumed bene:[4]
But all of Diamond perfect pure and cleene
It framed was, one massie entire mould,°   *solid piece*
295   Hewen° out of Adamant° rocke with engines keene,°   *cut / diamond / sharp*

2. The evening star, associated with Venus. The comparison of the stone on Arthur's breast to Venus suggests that love is central in his quest.
3. From *palmosa Selinis* ("palmy Selinis"), a town in Italy. Spenser suggests that the knight's helmet is topped with palms, signifying victory in battle. This helmet, decorated with a dragon, identifies the knight as Prince Arthur, whose father, Uther Pendragon, was so named because he carried a golden dragon to war with him. "Pendragon" literally means "dragon's head."
4. I.e., steel or brass would soon have been destroyed or disintegrated. The diamond will last forever.

That point of speare it never percen could,
Ne dint° of direfull° sword divide the substance would.   *stroke / dreadful*

34

The same to wight° he never wont disclose,[5]   *creature*
  But when as monsters huge he would dismay,
300 Or daunt° unequall armies of his foes,   *vanquish*
  Or when the flying heavens he would affray;°   *frighten*
  For so exceeding shone his glistring ray,
  That Phoebus golden face it did attaint,
  As when a cloud his beames doth over-lay;
305 And silver Cynthia wexed pale and faint,
As when her face is staynd with magicke arts° constraint.   *witchcraft*

35

No magicke arts hereof had any might,
  Nor bloudie wordes of bold Enchaunters call,
  But all that was not such, as seemd in sight,
310 Before that shield did fade, and suddeine fall:[6]
  And when him list the raskall routes appall,[7]
  Men into stones therewith he could transmew,°   *transform*
  And stones to dust, and dust to nought at all;
  And when him list the prouder lookes subdew,
315 He would them gazing blind, or turne to other hew.[8]

36

Ne let it seeme, that credence this exceedes,[9]
  For he that made the same, was knowne right well
  To have done much more admirable deedes.
  It Merlin[1] was, which whylome° did excell   *formerly*
320 All living wightes in might° of magicke spell: *power*
  Both shield, and sword, and armour all he wrought
  For this young Prince, when first to armes he fell;
  But when he dyde, the Faerie Queene it brought
To Faerie lond, where yet it may be seene, if sought.

37

325 A gentle youth, his dearely loved Squire
  His speare of heben wood° behind him bare,   *ebony*
  Whose harmefull head,° thrice heated in the fire,   *point*
  Had riven many a brest with pikehead° square;°   *spear tip / accurately*
  A goodly person, and could menage° faire   *manage a horse*
330 His stubborne steed with curbed canon° bit,   *a kind of bit*
  Who under him did trample as the aire,

5. Arthur never shows his diamond to anyone except when he uses it to overcome his enemies because it is too dazzling. In this respect, Arthur's diamond functions much like Una's face, whose truth and beauty are so brilliant that she wears a veil to cover it.
6. All that was false, i.e., that was not what it appeared to be, was vanquished in the presence of Arthur's shield.
7. When Arthur wished to subdue vulgar mobs, he would turn them to stone.

8. When Arthur wished to subdue his more elevated opponents, he would blind them.
9. Let it not be thought that this is beyond belief.
1. A magician and prophet in the court of Arthur's father. He created the shield, sword, and armor worn by the young Prince Arthur. By noting that Arthur's armor still exists in Faerie Land, Spenser suggests that Arthur's virtue lives on in England and may be discovered through faith.

And chauft,° that any on his backe should sit;   *annoyed*
The yron rowels° into frothy fome he bit.   *part of the bit*

38

When as this knight nigh to the Ladie drew,
335   With lovely court° he gan her entertaine;   *attention*
    But when he heard her answeres loth,° he knew   *reluctant*
    Some secret sorrow did her heart distraine:°   *afflict*
    Which to allay,° and calme her storming paine,   *sooth*
    Faire feeling words he wisely gan display,
340   And for her humour fitting purpose faine,[2]
    To tempt the cause it selfe for to bewray;°   *reveal*
Wherewith emmou'd, these bleeding words she gan to say.

39

What worlds delight, or joy of living speach
    Can heart, so plung'd in sea of sorrowes deepe,
345   And heaped with so huge misfortunes, reach?
    The carefull cold beginneth for to creepe,
    And in my heart his yron arrow steepe,°   *immerse*
    Soone as I thinke upon my bitter bale:°   *sorrows*
    Such helplesse harmes yts° better hidden keepe,   *it is*
350   Then rip up griefe, where it may not availe,°   *avail*
My last left comfort is, my woes to weepe and waile.

40

Ah Ladie deare, quoth then the gentle knight,
    Well may I weene,° your griefe is wondrous great; *know*
    For wondrous great griefe groneth in my spright,
355   Whiles thus I heare you of your sorrowes treat.°   *tell*
    But wofull Ladie let me you intrete,°   *entreat*
    For to unfold the anguish of your hart:
    Mishaps are maistred° by advice discrete,   *mastered*
    And counsell° mittigates the greatest smart;   *advice*
360   Found never helpe, who never would his hurts impart.[3]

41

O but (quoth she) great griefe will not be tould,
    And can more easily be thought, then said.
    Right so; (quoth he) but he, that never would,
    Could never: will to might gives greatest aid.[4]
365   But griefe (quoth she) does greater grow displaid,° *when displayed*
    If then it find not helpe, and breedes despaire.
    Despaire breedes not (quoth he) where faith is staid.° *strong*
    No faith so fast° (quoth she) but flesh does paire.°   *firm / weaken*
Flesh may empaire° (quoth he) but reason can repaire.   *impair*

---

2. Arthur chooses words more appropriate to Una's sadness.
3. He who never tells his woes will never find a remedy.

4. Desire to overcome adversity is the greatest help. Arthur is preventing Una from falling into a state of hopeless despair and helping her to reaffirm her faith.

42

370   His goodly reason, and well guided speach
          So deepe did settle in her gratious thought,
          That her perswaded to disclose the breach,°   *wound*
          Which love and fortune in her heart had wrought,
          And said; Faire Sir, I hope good hap° hath brought   *luck*
375   You to inquire the secrets of my griefe,
          Or that your wisedome will direct my thought,
          Or that your prowesse° can me yield reliefe: *valor*
      Then heare the storie sad, which I shall tell you briefe.

43

      The forlorne Maiden, whom your eyes have seene
380   The laughing stocke of fortunes mockeries,
          Am th'only daughter of a King and Queene,
          Whose parents deare, whilest equall° destinies   *impartial*
          Did runne about,° and their felicities   *run their course*
          The favourable heavens did not envy,
385   Did spread their rule through all the territories,
          Which Phison and Euphrates floweth by,
      And Gehons golden waves doe wash continually.[5]

44

      Till that their cruell cursed enemy,
          An huge great Dragon[6] horrible in sight,
390   Bred in the loathly lakes of Tartary,°   *Hell*
          With murdrous ravine,° and devouring might   *violence*
          Their kingdome spoild, and countrey wasted quight:
          Themselves, for feare into his jawes to fall,
          He forst to castle strong to take their flight,
395   Where fast embard° in mightie brasen° wall,   *imprisoned / brass*
      He has them now foure yeres besiegd to make them thrall.

45

      Full many knights adventurous and stout
          Have enterprizd° that Monster to subdew;   *undertaken*
          From every coast that heaven walks about,
400   Have thither come the noble Martiall[7] crew,
          That famous hard atchievements still pursew,
          Yet never any could that girlond win,
          But all still shronke, and still he greater grew:
          All they for want of faith, or guilt of sin,
405   The pitteous pray of his fierce crueltie have bin.[8]

5. Una's parents are Adam and Eve, and the territory that they govern is Eden. The Phison, Euphrates, and Gehon are three of the four rivers surrounding Eden and were thought to water the entire world.
6. The dragon is Satan. After the Fall, Adam and Eve were exiled from Eden. The "four years" that Spenser refers to may figuratively represent the 4,000 years that, according to the Geneva Bible, passed between the Fall and the birth of Christ.
7. This stanza refers to the many knights ("the noble Martiall crew") who have undertaken to assist Una in her quest to overcome the Dragon and rescue her parents.
8. Until now, the knights have all failed in their quest because they have lacked faith or have succumbed to sin and have thus become victims of the Dragon's cruelty.

46

At last yledd° with farre reported praise,   *led by*
  Which flying fame throughout the world had spred,
  Of doughtie° knights, whom Faery land did raise, *worthy*
  That noble order hight of Maidenhed,° *virginity*
410 Forthwith to court of Gloriane I sped,
  Of Gloriane great Queene of glory bright,
  Whose kingdomes seat Cleopolis⁹ is red,° *named*
  There to obtaine some such redoubted° knight, *formidable*
That Parents deare from tyrants powre deliver might.

47

415 It was my chance (my chance was faire and good)
  There for to find a fresh unproved° knight, *untried in battle*
  Whose manly hands imbrew'd° in guiltie blood *stained*
  Had never bene, ne ever by his might
  Had throwne to ground the unregarded right:¹
420 Yet of his prowesse° proofe he since hath made *virtue*
  (I witnesse am) in many a cruell fight;
  The groning ghosts of many one dismaide° *defeated*
Have felt the bitter dint of his avenging blade.

48

And ye² the forlorne reliques of his powre,
425 His byting sword, and his devouring speare,
  Which have endured many a dreadfull stowre,° *conflict*
  Can speake his prowesse, that did earst° you beare, *formerly*
  And well could rule: now he hath left you heare,
  To be the record of his ruefull losse,
430 And of my dolefull disaventurous° deare: *unfortunate*
  O heavie record of the good Redcrosse,
Where have you left your Lord, that could so well you tosse?° *brandish*

49

Well hoped I, and faire beginnings had,
  That he my captive langour³ should redeeme,
435 Till all unweeting,° an Enchaunter bad *unknown to the knight*
  His sence abusd,° and made him to misdeeme° *distorted / misjudge*
  My loyalty, not such as it did seeme;⁴
  That rather death desire, then° such despight.° *than / outrage*
  Be judge ye heavens, that all things right esteeme,
440 How I him lov'd, and love with all my might,
So thought I eke of him, and thinke I thought aright.

50

Thenceforth me desolate he quite forsooke,
  To wander, where wilde fortune would me lead,

9. The city of fame or glory where the Faerie Queene lives. The knights of her court belong to the order of the "Maidenhed," or virginity, an order that reflects the Faerie Queene's own virtue as well as that of Queen Elizabeth I, who was known as the "virgin queen."
1. The right for which he had no regard or respect; on the contrary, the Redcrosse Knight promotes and protects the right.
2. Here Una is addressing the Redcrosse Knight's armor.
3. Una is referring to her parents' languishment in captivity but also to the symbolic captivity of humankind whom the Redcrosse Knight, as a figure of Christ, will redeem.
4. The Redcrosse Knight misjudged Una's loyalty, thinking that it was not what it appeared to be.

And other bywaies he himselfe betooke,
445 Where never foot of living wight did tread,
That brought not backe the balefull° body dead;   *wretched*
In which him chaunced false Duessa meete,
Mine onely foe, mine onely deadly dread,
Who with her witchcraft and misseeming sweete,
450 Inveigled° him to follow her desires unmeete.°   *tricked / unsuitable*

51

At last by subtill sleights° she him betraid   *tricks*
Unto his foe, a Gyant huge and tall,
Who him disarmed, dissolute,° dismaid,°   *weakened / vanquished*
Unwares surprised, and with mightie mall°   *weapon*
455 The monster mercilesse him made to fall,
Whose fall did never foe before behold;[5]
And now in darkesome dungeon, wretched thrall,
Remedilesse,° for aie° he doth him hold;   *helpless / ever*
This is my cause of griefe, more great, then° may be told.   *than*

52

460 Ere she had ended all, she gan° to faint: *began*
But he her comforted and faire bespake,
Certes,° Madame, ye have great cause of plaint,   *certainly*
That stoutest heart, I weene,° could cause to quake.   *believe*
But be of cheare, and comfort to you take:
465 For till I have acquit° your captive knight,   *avenged*
Assure your selfe, I will you not forsake.
His chearefull words reviv'd her chearelesse spright,
So forth they went, the Dwarfe them guiding ever right.

Canto 8

Faire virgin to reedeme her deare
brings Arthur to the fight:
Who slayes the Gyant, wounds the beast,
and strips Duessa quight.

1

Ay me, how many perils doe enfold
The righteous man, to make him daily fall?
Were not,° that heavenly grace doth him uphold,[1]   *were it not*
And stedfast truth acquite° him out of all.   *absolve*
5 Her love is firme, her care continuall,
So oft as he through his owne foolish pride,
Or weaknesse is to sinfull bands made thrall:
Else° should this Redcrosse knight in bands have dyde,   *otherwise*
For whose deliverance she this Prince doth thither guide.

---

5. The Redcrosse Knight had never yet been defeated in battle.
1. In this stanza, Una is overtly equated with heavenly grace. The Redcrosse Knight originally undertook the quest to help Una redeem her parents, but in this canto it is she who delivers the Redcrosse Knight from captivity.

2

10 They sadly traveild thus, untill they came
　　Nigh to a castle builded strong and hie:
　　Then cryde the Dwarfe, lo yonder is the same,
　　In which my Lord my liege° doth lucklesse lie,　　　　*master*
　　Thrall to that Gyants hatefull tyrannie:
15　　Therefore, deare Sir, your mightie powres assay.°　　*prove*
　　The noble knight alighted by and by
　　From loftie steede, and bad the Ladie stay,
To see what end of fight should him befall that day.

3

So with the Squire, th'admirer of his might,
20　　He marched forth towards that castle wall;
　　Whose gates he found fast shut, ne living wight
　　To ward° the same, nor answere commers° call.　　*guard / visitor's*
　　Then tooke that Squire an horne of bugle small,
　　Which hong adowne his side in twisted gold,
25　　And tassels gay. Wyde wonders over all
　　Of that same hornes great vertues weren told,[2]
Which had approved bene in uses manifold.°　　　　*many*

4

Was never wight, that heard that shrilling sound,
　　But trembling feare did feele in every vaine;
30　　Three miles it might be easie heard around,
　　And Ecchoes three answerd it selfe againe:
　　No false enchauntment, nor deceiptfull traine°　　*deception*
　　Might once abide° the terror of that blast,　　　　*tolerate*
　　But presently was voide and wholly vaine:°　　　　*ineffectual*
35　　No gate so strong, no locke so firme and fast,
But with that percing noise flew open quite, or brast.°　*burst*

5

The same before the Geants gate he blew,
　　That all the castle quaked from the ground,
　　And every dore of freewill° open flew.　　　　*itself*
40　　The Gyant selfe dismaied with that sownd,
　　Where he with his Duessa dalliance fownd,[3]
　　In hast came rushing forth from inner bowre,°　　*chamber*
　　With staring° countenance sterne, as one astownd,°　*glaring / confused*
　　And staggering steps, to weet, what suddein stowre°　*uproar*
45　Had wrought that horror strange, and dar'd° his dreaded powre.　*defied*

6

And after him the proud Duessa came,
　　High mounted on her manyheaded beast,
　　And every head with fyrie tongue did flame,
　　And every head was crowned on his creast,[4]

2. Wonderful stories of the horn's powers were told everywhere.
3. The sound of the horn reached the chamber where the

Giant and Duessa were engaged in lovemaking.
4. Each head of Duessa's many-headed beast had a crown
on it.

50 And bloudie mouthed with late cruell feast.
     That when the knight beheld, his mightie shild
     Upon his manly arme he soone addrest,°   *made ready*
     And at him fiercely flew, with courage fild,
   And eger greedinesse through every member thrild.

                               7
55 Therewith the Gyant buckled° him to fight,   *engaged*
     Inflam'd with scornefull wrath and high disdaine,
     And lifting up his dreadfull club on hight,
     All arm'd° with ragged snubbes° and knottie graine,   *covered / roots*
     Him thought at first encounter to have slaine.
60   But wise and warie was that noble Pere,
     And lightly leaping from so monstrous maine,°   *force*
     Did faire° avoide the violence him nere;   *easily*
   It booted nought,° to thinke, such thunderbolts to beare.   *it was useless*

                               8
   Ne shame° he thought to shunne so hideous might: *not shameful*
65   The idle stroke, enforcing furious way,
     Missing the marke of his misaymed sight
     Did fall to ground, and with his heavie sway°   *force*
     So deepely dinted° in the driven° clay,   *struck / packed*
     That three yardes deepe a furrow up did throw:
70   The sad earth wounded with so sore assay,°   *attack*
     Did grone full grievous underneath the blow,
   And trembling with strange feare, did like an earthquake show.

                               9
   As when almightie Jove in wrathfull mood,
     To wreake the guilt of mortall sins is bent,°   *determined*
75   Hurles forth his thundring dart with deadly food,°   *hatred*
     Enrold° in flames, and smouldring dreriment,   *engulfed*
     Through riven cloudes and molten firmament;°   *sky*
     The fierce threeforked engin° making way,   *the thunderbolt*
     Both loftie towres and highest trees hath rent,
80   And all that might his angrie passage stay,°   *hinder*
   And shooting in the earth, casts up a mount° of clay.   *mountain*

                              10
   His boystrous° club, so buried in the ground,   *enormous*
     He could not rearen° up againe so light,°   *raise / easily*
     But° that the knight him at avantage found,   *so*
85   And whiles he strove his combred° clubbe to quight°   *encumbered / free*
     Out of the earth, with blade all burning bright
     He smote° off his left arme, which like a blocke   *struck*
     Did fall to ground, depriv'd of native might;
     Large streames of bloud out of the truncked stocke°   *truncated stump*
90 Forth gushed, like fresh water streame from riven rocke.

                              11
   Dismaied with so desperate deadly wound,
     And eke impatient of unwonted paine,
     He loudly brayd with beastly yelling sound,

That all the fields rebellowed° againe;   *echoed his bellows*
95   As great a noyse, as when in Cymbrian plaine[5]
    An heard of Bulles, whom kindly rage doth sting,
    Do for the milkie mothers want° complaine,   *absence*
    And fill the fields with troublous bellowing,
The neighbour woods around with hollow murmur ring.

12
100   That when his deare Duessa heard, and saw
    The evill stownd°, that daungerd her estate,°   *peril / situation*
    Unto his aide she hastily did draw
    Her dreadfull beast, who swolne with bloud of late
    Came ramping° forth with proud presumpteous gate,   *bounding*
105   But him the Squire made quickly to retrate,°   *retreat*
    Encountring fierce with single sword in hand,
And twixt° him and his Lord did like a bulwarke° stand.   *between / barrier*

13
The proud Duessa full of wrathfull spight,
110   And fierce disdaine, to be affronted so,
    Enforst° her purple beast with all her might   *spurred on*
    That stop° out of the way to overthroe,   *obstacle*
    Scorning the let° of so unequall° foe: *hindrance / inferior*
    But nathemore° would that courageous swayne°   *not at all / fellow*
115   To her yeeld passage, gainst his Lord to goe,
    But with outrageous strokes did him restraine,
And with his bodie bard° the way atwixt them twaine.°   *barred / between*

14
Then tooke the angrie witch her golden cup,
    Which still she bore, replete° with magick artes;   *filled*
120   Death and despeyre did many thereof sup,°   *drink*
    And secret poyson through their inner parts,
    Th'eternall bale° of heavie wounded harts;   *destruction*
    Which after charmes and some enchauntments said,
    She lightly sprinkled on his weaker parts;
125   Therewith his sturdie courage soone was quayd,°   *quelled*
And all his senses were with suddeine dread dismayd.°   *overcome*

15
So downe he fell before the cruell beast,
    Who on his necke his bloudie clawes did seize,
    That life nigh crusht out of his panting brest:
130   No powre he had to stirre, nor will to rize.
    That when the carefull knight gan well avise,°   *notice*
    He lightly left the foe, with whom he fought,
    And to the beast gan turne his enterprise;°   *attack*
    For wondrous anguish in his hart it wrought,
135   To see his loved Squire into such thraldome brought.

5. The Cimbri were a savage tribe that invaded Europe in the 1st century B.C.

16

And high advauncing° his bloud-thirstie blade,   *lifting up*
 Stroke one of those deformed heads so sore,
 That of his puissance° proud ensample made;   *strength*
 His monstrous scalpe downe to his teeth it tore,
140 And that misformed shape mis-shaped more:
 A sea of bloud gusht from the gaping wound,
 That her gay garments staynd with filthy gore,
 And overflowed all the field around;
That over shoes in bloud he waded on the ground.[6]

17

145 Thereat he roared for exceeding paine,
 That to have heard, great horror would have bred,[7]
 And scourging° th'emptie ayre with his long traine,°   *tearing / tail*
 Through great impatience of his grieved hed
 His gorgeous ryder from her loftie sted°   *place*
150 Would have cast downe, and trod in durtie myre,
 Had not the Gyant soone her succoured;°   *rescued*
 Who all enrag'd with smart° and franticke yre,   *pain*
Came hurtling in full fierce, and forst the knight retyre.°   *to back off*

18

The force, which wont° in two to be disperst,   *usually*
155 In one alone left hand he now unites,[8]
 Which is through rage more strong then both were erst;°   *before*
 With which his hideous club aloft he dites,°   *raises*
 And at his foe with furious rigour° smites,   *violence*
 That strongest Oake might seeme to ouerthrow:
160 The stroke upon his shield so heavie lites,°   *falls*
 That to the ground it doubleth° him full low: *collapse*
What mortall wight could ever beare so monstrous blow?

19

And in his fall his shield, that covered was,
 Did loose his vele° by chaunce, and open flew: *its covering*
165 The light whereof, that heavens light did pas,°   *surpass*
 Such blazing brightnesse through the aier threw,
 That eye mote° not the same endure to vew.   *could*
 Which when the Gyaunt spyde with staring eye,
 He downe let fall his arme, and soft withdrew
170 His weapon huge, that heaved° was on hye   *raised*
For to have slaine the man, that on the ground did lye.

20

And eke the fruitfull-headed° beast, amaz'd   *many-headed*
 At flashing beames of that sunshiny shield,
 Became starke blind, and all his senses daz'd,
175 That downe he tumbled on the durtie field,

---

6. The pool of blood is so deep that it reaches over
Arthur's shoes.
7. The beast roars so loudly from the pain that anyone

who heard it would have been struck with horror.
8. The strength that has been divided in the Giant's two
hands is now concentrated in his remaining hand.

And seem'd himselfe as conquered to yield.[9]
Whom when his maistresse proud perceiv'd to fall,
Whiles yet his feeble feet for faintnesse reeld,
Unto the Gyant loudly she gan call,
180   O helpe Orgoglio, helpe, or else we perish all.

21

At her so pitteous cry was much amoov'd
Her champion stout, and for to ayde his frend,
Againe his wonted° angry weapon proov'd:°   usual / tried
But all in vaine: for he has read his end°   death
185   In that bright shield, and all their forces spend
Themselves in vaine: for since that glauncing° sight,   dazzling
He hath no powre to hurt, nor to defend;
As where th'Almighties lightning brond° does light,   bolt
It dimmes the dazed eyen, and daunts° the senses quight.   stuns

22

190   Whom when the Prince, to battell new addrest,
And threatning high his dreadfull stroke did see,[1]
His sparkling blade about his head he blest,°   brandished
And smote off quite his right leg by the knee,
That downe he tombled; as an aged tree,
195   High growing on the top of rocky clift,
Whose hartstrings with keene steele nigh hewen be,°   are nearly cut off
The mightie trunck halfe rent, with ragged rift°   splitting
Doth roll adowne the rocks, and fall with fearefull drift.°   force

23

Or as a Castle reared° high and round,   built
200   By subtile° engins and malitious slight   clever
Is undermined from the lowest ground,
And her° foundation forst,° and feebled quight,   the castle's / broken
At last downe falles, and with her heaped hight
Her hastie ruine does more heavie make,
205   And yields it selfe unto the victours might;
Such was this Gyaunts fall, that seemd to shake
The stedfast globe of earth, as it for feare did quake.

24

The knight then lightly leaping to the pray,°   victim
With mortall steele him smot° againe so sore,   struck
210   That headlesse his unweldy bodie lay,
All wallowd in his owne fowle bloudy gore,
Which flowed from his wounds in wondrous store.°   amounts
But soone as breath out of his breast did pas,
That huge great body, which the Gyaunt bore,
215   Was vanisht quite,° and of that monstrous mas   completely
Was nothing left, but like an emptie bladder was.[2]

9. By falling down, the beast seems not only to be conquered but also to submit himself ("yield") to Arthur.
1. The Giant is already overcome by the sight of Arthur's
shield, but when Arthur sees him raising his weapon to
defend Duessa, Arthur renews the battle.
2. A bladder or balloon can be blown up to a great size,
although it is actually empty, i.e., full of hot air.

25

Whose grievous fall, when false Duessa spide,
  Her golden cup she cast unto the ground,
  And crowned mitre° rudely threw aside;   *papal crown*
220 Such percing griefe her stubborne hart did wound,
  That she could not endure that dolefull stound,°   *dismal situation*
  But leaving all behind her, fled away:
  The light-foot Squire her quickly turnd around,
  And by hard meanes enforcing her to stay,
225 So brought unto his Lord, as his deserved pray.

26

The royall Virgin, which beheld from farre,
  In pensive plight, and sad perplexitie,
  The whole atchievement° of this doubtfull° warre, *progress / fearful*
  Came running fast to greet his victorie,
230 With sober gladnesse, and myld modestie,
  And with sweet joyous cheare him thus bespake;
  Faire braunch of noblesse, flowre of chevalrie,
  That with your worth the world amazed make,
How shall I quite° the paines, ye suffer for my sake?   *repay*

27

235 And you fresh bud of vertue springing fast,
  Whom these sad eyes saw nigh unto deaths dore,
  What hath poore Virgin for such perill past,
  Wherewith you to reward? Accept therefore
  My simple selfe, and service evermore;
240 And he that high does sit, and all things see
  With equall° eyes, their merites to restore,   *impartial*
  Behold what ye this day have done for mee,
And what I cannot quite, requite with usuree.[3]

28

But sith° the heavens, and your faire handeling°   *since / skill*
245 Have made you maister of the field this day,
  Your fortune maister eke with governing,
  And well begun end all so well, I pray,[4]
  Ne let that wicked woman scape° away;   *escape*
  For she it is, that did my Lord bethrall,°   *seduce, enslave*
250 My dearest Lord, and deepe in dongeon lay,
  Where he his better dayes hath wasted all.
O heare, how piteous he to you for ayd does call.

29

Forthwith he gave in charge unto his Squire,
  That scarlot whore to keepen carefully;
255 Whiles he himselfe with greedie° great desire   *eager*

3. What Una cannot completely repay, God will repay
with interest. Unlike Duessa, who offers herself as a mistress to those who are victorious in battle, Una, a virgin,
can offer only her loyalty and service. She goes on to call
on God to restore her champions to a state of grace, with
"merites" referring to all that was lost through the Fall of
humankind.
4. I.e., while the heavens and skill have made you the
"maister of the field this day," now you must also master
your fortune through governance, and I pray that what
has begun well will also end well.

Into the Castle entred forcibly,
Where living creature none he did espye;
Then gan he lowdly through the house to call:
But no man car'd to answere to his crye.
260   There raignd a solemne silence over all,
Nor voice was heard, nor wight was seene in bowre or hall.

30

At last with creeping crooked pace forth came
An old old man, with beard as white as snow,
That on a staffe his feeble steps did frame,°   support
265   And guide his wearie gate° both too and fro: steps
For his eye sight him failed long ygo,°   ago
And on his arme a bounch of keyes he bore,
The which unused rust did overgrow:
Those were the keyes of every inner dore,
270   But he could not them use, but kept them still in store.°   handy

31

But very uncouth° sight was to behold,   strange
How he did fashion his untoward° pace,   awkward
For as he forward moov'd his footing old,
So backward still was turnd his wrincled face,
275   Unlike to men, who ever as they trace,
Both feet and face one way are wont to lead.[5]
This was the auncient keeper of that place,
And foster father of the Gyant dead;
His name Ignaro did his nature right aread.

32

280   His reverend haires and holy grauitie
The knight much honord, as beseemed well,[6]
And gently askt, where all the people bee,
Which in that stately building wont° to dwell.   accustomed
Who answerd him full soft, he could not tell.
285   Againe he askt, where that same knight was layd,
Whom great Orgoglio with his puissaunce fell°   deadly strength
Had made his caytive thrall;° againe he sayde,   wretched prisoner
He could not tell: ne ever other answere made.

33

Then asked he, which way he in might pas:°   enter
290   He could not tell, againe he answered.
Thereat the curteous knight displeased was,
And said, Old sire, it seemes thou hast not red°   perceived
How ill it sits° with that same silver hed   unsuitable
In vaine to mocke, or mockt in vaine to bee:
295   But if thou be, as thou art pourtrahed

---

5. The steward and doorkeeper of Orgoglio's castle, Ignaro (Ignorance), walks forward but keeps his face turned backward, unlike humans, who look where they go.

6. Arthur treats Ignaro with the respect that his appearance of advanced age warrants.

With natures pen, in ages grave degree,
 Aread° in graver wise, what I demaund of thee.[7]   *declare*

34

His answere likewise was, he could not tell.
 Whose sencelesse speach, and doted° ignorance   *stupid*
300 When as the noble Prince had marked well,
 He ghest° his nature by his countenance,°   *guessed / behavior*
 And calmd his wrath with goodly temperance.
 Then to him stepping, from his arme did reach
 Those keyes, and made himselfe free enterance.
305 Each dore he opened without any breach;°   *breaking in*
There was no barre to stop, nor foe him to empeach.°   *hinder*

35

There all within full rich arayd he found,
 With royall arras and resplendent gold.
 And did with store of every thing abound,
310 That greatest Princes presence might behold.[8]
 But all the floore (too filthy to be told)
 With bloud of guiltlesse babes, and innocents trew,
 Which there were slaine, as sheepe out of the fold,
 Defiled was, that dreadfull was to vew,
315 And sacred ashes[9] over it was strowed new.°   *newly scattered*

36

And there beside of marble stone was built
 An Altare, carv'd with cunning imagery,
 On which true Christians bloud was often spilt,
 And holy Martyrs often doen to dye,
320 With cruell malice and strong tyranny:
 Whose blessed sprites from underneath the stone
 To God for vengeance cryde continually,
 And with great griefe were often heard to grone,
That hardest heart would bleede, to heare their piteous mone.

37

325 Through every rowme he sought, and every bowr,
 But no where could he find that wofull thrall:°   *Redcrosse Knight*
 At last he came unto an yron doore,
 That fast was lockt, but key found not at all
 Emongst that bounch, to open it withall;
330 But in the same a little grate was pight,°   *placed*
 Through which he sent his voyce, and lowd did call
 With all his powre, to weet, if living wight
Were housed therewithin, whom he enlargen° might.   *release*

38

Therewith an hollow, dreary, murmuring voyce
335 These piteous plaints and dolours° did resound;   *laments*

7. I.e., if you are as old and wise as you appear, respond more seriously to what I ask of you.
8. The castle is equipped with everything worthy of the greatest prince.
9. The ashes of martyred saints used here to soak up the blood of innocent Christians. The newly strewn ashes appear to be evidence of a recently performed pagan ritual, as is suggested by the altar in the next stanza.

O who is that, which brings me happy choyce
Of death, that here lye dying every stound,°   *moment*
Yet live perforce° in balefull° darkenesse bound?   *constrained / wretched*
For now three Moones have changed thrice their hew,°   *shape*
340   And have beene thrice hid underneath the ground,
Since I the heavens chearefull face did vew,
O welcome thou, that doest of death bring tydings trew.[1]

39

Which when that Champion heard, with percing point
Of pitty deare his hart was thrilled° sore,   *pierced*
345   And trembling horrour ran through every joynt,
For ruth of gentle knight so fowle forlore:°   *forlorn*
Which shaking off, he rent that yron dore,
With furious force, and indignation fell;°   *deadly*
Where entred in, his foot could find no flore,
350   But all a deepe descent, as darke as hell,
That breathed ever forth a filthie banefull° smell.   *poisonous*

40

But neither darkenesse fowle, nor filthy bands,
Nor noyous° smell his purpose could withhold,   *noxious*
(Entire affection hateth nicer hands)[2]
355   But that with constant zeale, and courage bold,
After long paines and labours manifold,
He found the meanes that Prisoner up to reare;[3]
Whose feeble thighes, unhable° to uphold   *unable*
His pined corse,° him scarse to light could beare,   *wasted body*
360   A ruefull spectacle of death and ghastly drere.°   *misery*

41

His sad dull eyes deepe sunck in hollow pits,
Could not endure th'unwonted° sunne to view;   *unaccustomed*
His bare thin cheekes for want° of better bits,°   *lack / food*
And empty sides deceived° of their dew,   *deprived*
365   Could make a stony hart his hap° to rew;   *situation*
His rawbone° armes, whose mighty brawned bowrs°   *thin / brawny muscles*
Were wont to rive steele plates, and helmets hew,
Were cleane consum'd, and all his vitall powres
Decayd, and all his flesh shrunk up like withered flowres.

42

370   Whom when his Lady saw,[4] to him she ran
With hasty joy: to see him made her glad,
And sad to view his visage pale and wan,°   *thin*
Who earst in flowres of freshest youth was clad.°   *dressed*
Tho when her well of teares she wasted had,

---

1. Three moons have changed their shape three times; in
other words, nine months have passed. The voice they
hear rings with despair, wishing for death rather than rescue or salvation.
2. A perfect love disdains great fastidiousness; Prince
Arthur could overlook the filth of Orgoglio's prison

because he cares so much for the Redcrosse Knight.
3. The Prisoner's legs are too weak to hold him up, so
Arthur has to lift him out of the dungeon. The "light" is
also a reference to Una.
4. Una recognizes the Prisoner as the Redcrosse Knight.

375   She said, Ah dearest Lord, what evill starre
        On you hath found, and pourd his influence bad,[5]
        That of your selfe ye thus berobbed arre,
And this misseeming hew° your manly looks doth marre?   *appearance*

43
But welcome now my Lord, in wele° or woe,   *prosperity*
380   Whose presence I have lackt too long a day;
        And fie° on Fortune mine avowed foe,   *shame*
        Whose wrathfull wreakes° them selves do now alay.°   *vengeances / abate*
        And for these wrongs shall treble penaunce° pay   *penance*
        Of treble good: good growes of evils priefe.°   *trial*
385   The chearelesse man, whom sorrow did dismay,°   *overcome*
        Had no delight to treaten° of his griefe;   *tell*
His long endured famine needed more reliefe.

44
Faire Lady, then said that victorious knight,
        The things, that grievous were to do, or beare,
390   Them to renew,° I wote, breeds no delight;   *repeat*
        Best musicke breeds delight in loathing eare:
        But th'onely good, that growes of passed feare,
        Is to be wise, and ware° of like agein.   *wary*
        This dayes ensample° hath this lesson deare°   *example / dire*
395   Deepe written in my heart with yron pen,
That blisse may not abide in state of mortall men.

45
Henceforth sir knight, take to you wonted strength,
        And maister these mishaps° with patient might;   *misfortunes*
        Loe where your foe lyes stretcht in monstrous length,
400   And loe that wicked woman in your sight,
        The roote of all your care,° and wretched plight,   *trouble*
        Now in your powre, to let her live, or dye.
        To do her dye (quoth Una) were despight,°   *malice*
        And shame t'avenge so weake an enimy;
405   But spoile her of her scarlot robe, and let her fly.[6]

46
So as she bad,° that witch they disaraid,°   *commanded / undressed*
        And robd of royall robes, and purple pall,°   *cloak*
        And ornaments that richly were displaid;
        Ne spared they to strip her naked all.
410   Then when they had despoild her tire and call,°   *attire and headdress*
        Such as she was, their eyes might her behold,
        That her misshaped parts did them appall,
        A loathly, wrinckled hag, ill favoured, old,
Whose secret filth good manners biddeth not be told.

---

5. The Redcrosse Knight has ended up in the dungeon through his own folly; however, Una insists here that it must have been an "evill starre," i.e., misfortune, that was responsible for his imprisonment.

6. Like Christ, who seeks to destroy the works of the devil rather than the devil himself (1 John 3.8), Una seeks to destroy Duessa's ability to do evil.

47

415   Her craftie head was altogether bald,
        And as in hate of honorable eld,[7]
        Was overgrowne with scurfe° and filthy scald;[8]   *scabs*
        Her teeth out of her rotten gummes were feld,°   *fallen*
        And her sowre breath abhominably smeld;
420   Her dried dugs,° like bladders lacking wind,   *breasts*
        Hong downe, and filthy matter from them weld;°   *oozed*
        Her wrizled° skin as rough, as maple rind,[9]   *wrinkled*
    So scabby was, that would have loathd all womankind.

48

    Her neather° parts, the shame of all her kind,   *lower*
425   My chaster Muse for shame doth blush to write;
        But at her rompe° she growing had behind   *rump*
        A foxes taile, with dong all fowly dight;
        And eke her feete most monstrous were in sight;
        For one of them was like an Eagles claw,
430   With griping talaunts° armd to greedy fight,   *talons*
        The other like a Beares uneven° paw: *rough*
    More ugly shape yet never living creature saw.

49

    Which when the knights beheld, amazd they were,
        And wondred at so fowle deformed wight.
435   Such then (said Una) as she seemeth here,
        Such is the face of falshood, such the sight
        Of fowle Duessa, when her borrowed light
        Is laid away, and counterfesaunce° knowne.   *falsity*
        Thus when they had the witch disrobed quight,
440   And all her filthy feature° open showne,   *body*
    They let her goe at will, and wander wayes unknowne.

50

    She flying fast from heavens hated face,
        And from the world that her discovered wide,
        Fled to the wastfull° wildernesse apace,   *desolate*
445   From living eyes her open shame to hide,
        And lurkt in rocks and caves long unespide.
        But that faire crew of knights, and Una faire
        Did in that castle afterwards abide,
        To rest them selves, and weary powres repaire,
450   Where store° they found of all, that dainty was and rare.   *supplies*

---

7. I.e., Duessa's ugly head is a hateful mockery of old people whose baldness is usually a sign of honorable "eld" or old age.

8. Scall, a disease that causes scabs to form on the scalp.

9. Maples were often thought to be hard on the outside but rotten inside. Duessa's diseased appearance also suggests syphilis.

Canto 9

His loves and lignage Arthur tells:
The knights knit friendly bands:
Sir Trevisan flies from Despayre,
Whom Redcrosse knight withstands.

1

O Goodly golden chaine, wherewith yfere°   *together*
   The vertues linked are in lovely wize:
   And noble minds of yore allyed were,
   In brave poursuit of chevalrous emprize,°   *adventure*
5   That none did others safety despize,°   *disregard*
   Nor aid envy to him, in need that stands,
   But friendly each did others prayse devize
   How to advaunce with favourable hands,
As this good Prince redeemd the Redcrosse knight from bands.° *captivity*

2

10 Who when their powres, empaird° through labour long,   *weakened*
   With dew° repast they had recured° well,   *suitable / recovered*
   And that weake captive wight now wexed° strong,   *grown*
   Them list no lenger there at leasure dwell,
   But forward fare, as their adventures fell,
15   But ere they parted, Una faire besought
   That straunger knight his name and nation tell;
   Least so great good, as he for her had wrought,
Should die unknown, and buried be in thanklesse thought.

3

Faire virgin (said the Prince) ye me require
20   A thing without the compas of my wit:[1]
   For both the lignage° and the certain Sire,   *lineage*
   From which I sprong, from me are hidden yit.
   For all so soone as life did me admit
   Into this world, and shewed heavens light,
25   From mothers pap° I taken was unfit: *breast*
   And streight delivered to a Faery knight,
To be upbrought in gentle thewes° and martiall might.   *manners*

4

Unto old Timon[2] he me brought bylive,°   *immediately*
   Old Timon, who in youthly yeares hath beene
30   In warlike feates th'expertest man alive,
   And is the wisest now on earth I weene;°   *believe*
   His dwelling is low in a valley greene,
   Under the foot of Rauran[3] mossy hore,
   From whence the river Dee[4] as silver cleene

---

1. I.e., your question is beyond my ability to answer.
2. Honor (Greek).
3. A hill in Wales, hoary with moss.

4. A river marking the boundary between England and Wales.

35   His tombling billowes rolls with gentle rore:
         There all my dayes he traind me up in vertuous lore.

5

         Thither the great Magicien Merlin came,
           As was his use,° ofttimes to visit me: *custom*
           For he had charge my discipline to frame,[5]
40   And Tutours nouriture to oversee.
           Him oft and oft I askt in privitie,°   *privately*
           Of what loines and what lignage I did spring:
           Whose aunswere bad me still assured bee,
           That I was sonne and heire unto a king,
45   As time in her just terme° the truth to light should bring.   *due course*

6

         Well worthy impe,° said then the Lady gent,°   *offspring / noble*
           And Pupill fit for such a Tutours hand.
           But what adventure, or what high intent
           Hath brought you hither into Faery land,
50   Aread° Prince Arthur, crowne of Martiall band?[6]   *declare*
           Full hard it is (quoth he) to read aright
           The course of heavenly cause, or understand
           The secret meaning of th'eternall might,
         That rules mens wayes, and rules the thoughts of living wight.

7

55   For whither° he through fatall deepe foresight   *whether*
           Me hither sent, for cause to me unghest,°   *unguessed*
           Or that fresh bleeding wound, which day and night
           Whilome° doth rancle in my riven° brest,   *constantly / wounded*
           With forced° fury following his behest,°   *forceful / command*
60   Me hither brought by wayes yet never found,
           You to have helpt I hold my selfe yet blest.
           Ah curteous knight (quoth she) what secret wound
         Could ever find, to grieve the gentlest hart on ground?[7]

8

         Deare Dame (quoth he) you sleeping sparkes awake,
65   Which troubled once, into huge flames will grow,[8]
           Ne ever will their fervent fury slake,°   *cease*
           Till living moysture[9] into smoke do flow,
           And wasted life do lye in ashes low.
           Yet sithens° silence lesseneth not my fire,   *since*
70   But told it flames, and hidden it does glow,
           I will revele, what ye so much desire:
         Ah Love, lay downe thy bow,[1] the whiles I may respire.°   *breathe*

---

5. Merlin was in charge of Arthur's education and made sure Arthur's tutor was properly recompensed.
6. Although Arthur does not declare his name, Una is able to recognize him.
7. I.e., what injury could ever find a way to hurt the gentlest heart "on ground" (in the world)?
8. Prince Arthur addresses Una; she reminds him of his

hidden pain, which once reawakened will continue to grow.
9. A reference to the Renaissance medical theory of the humors that compose the human body.
1. Cupid shoots arrows of love at people and causes them to fall in love with the first person they see.

9

It was in freshest flowre of youthly yeares,
   When courage first does creepe in manly chest,
75   Then first the coale of kindly heat appeares
   To kindle love in every living brest;
   But me had warnd old Timons wise behest,°   *warning*
   Those creeping flames° by reason to subdew,   *of love*
   Before their rage grew to so great unrest,
80   As miserable lovers use to rew,
Which still wex old in woe, whiles woe still wexeth new.[2]

10

That idle name of love, and lovers life,
   As losse of time, and vertues enimy
   I ever scornd, and joyd to stirre up strife,
85   In middest of° their mournfull Tragedy,   *in the midst of*
   Ay wont to laugh, when them I heard to cry,
   And blow the fire, which them to ashes brent:°   *burned*
   Their God himselfe,° griev'd at my libertie,   *Cupid*
   Shot many a dart at me with fiers intent,
90   But I them warded all with wary government.°   *cautious self-control*

11

But all in vaine: no fort can be so strong,
   Ne fleshly brest can armed be so sound,°   *completely*
   But will at last be wonne with battrie° long,   *battery*
   Or unawares at disavantage found;[3]
95   Nothing is sure, that growes on earthly ground:
   And who most trustes in arme of fleshly might,
   And boasts, in beauties chaine not to be bound,
   Doth soonest fall in disaventrous° fight,   *unfortunate*
And yeeldes his caytive° neck to victours most despight.°   *servile / malice*

12

100   Ensampel° make of him your haplesse joy,   *example*
   And of my selfe now mated,° as ye see;   *checked*
   Whose prouder vaunt° that proud avenging boy   *boast*
   Did soone pluck downe, and curbd my libertie.
   For on a day prickt forth with jollitie
105   Of looser life, and heat of hardiment,[4]
   Raunging the forest wide on courser° free,   *horse*
   The fields, the floods, the heavens with one consent
Did seeme to laugh on me, and favour mine intent.

13

For-wearied° with my sports, I did alight   *tired*
110   From loftie steed, and downe to sleepe me layd;
   The verdant° gras my couch did goodly dight,°   *green / adorn*

2. Sorrow makes lovers grow old while their sorrow remains forever young.
3. No fort is so strong, or flesh so well protected, that it cannot be overcome by continual battering.
4. I.e., inspired by the joy of a life of freedom and the heat of boldness.

And pillow was my helmet faire displayd:
Whiles every sence the humour° sweet embayd,°   *dew of sleep / bathed*
And slombring soft my hart did steale away,
115   Me seemed,° by my side a royall Mayd   *it seemed to me*
Her daintie limbes full softly down did lay:
So faire a creature yet saw never sunny day.

14

Most goodly glee° and lovely blandishment   *entertainment*
She to me made, and bad me love her deare,
120   For dearely sure her love was to me bent,
As when just time expired should appeare.[5]
But whether dreames delude, or true it were,
Was never hart so ravisht with delight,
Ne living man like° words did ever heare,   *similar*
125   As she to me delivered all that night;
And at her parting said, She Queene of Faeries hight.°   *was called*

15

When I awoke, and found her place devoyd,°   *empty*
And nought° but pressed gras, where she had lyen,°   *nothing / lain*
I sorrowed all so much, as earst° I joyd,   *at first*
130   And washed all her place with watry eyen.
From that day forth I lov'd that face divine;
From that day forth I cast° in carefull mind,   *resolved*
To seeke her out with labour, and long tyne,°   *suffering*
And never vow to rest, till her I find,
135   Nine monethes I seeke in vaine yet ni'll° that vow unbind.   *never will*

16

Thus as he spake, his visage wexed pale,
And chaunge of hew great passion did bewray;°   *betray*
Yet still he strove to cloke his inward bale,°   *sorrow*
And hide the smoke, that did his fire display,
140   Till gentle Una thus to him gan° say;   *did*
O happy Queene of Faeries, that hast found
Mongst many, one that with his prowesse may
Defend thine honour, and thy foes confound:
True Loves are often sown, but seldom grow on ground.°   *on this earth*

17

145   Thine, O then, said the gentle Redcrosse knight,
Next to that Ladies love, shalbe the place,
O fairest virgin, full of heavenly light,
Whose wondrous faith, exceeding earthly race,°   *people*
Was firmest fixt in mine extremest case.
150   And you, my Lord, the Patrone° of my life,   *protector*
Of that great Queene may well gaine worthy grace:
For onely worthy you through prowes priefe[6]
If living man mote° worthy be, to be her liefe.°   *might / beloved*

---

5. Her love was directed as it would appear in the due course of time. Arthur's dream is both lifelike and prophetic.

6. The test of your valor shows that you are the only one worthy of her grace.

18

So diversly° discoursing of their loves,   *variously*
155   The golden Sunne his glistring head gan shew,
And sad remembraunce now the Prince amoves,°   *compels*
With fresh desire his voyage to pursew:
Als Una earnd her traveill° to renew.   *quest*
Then those two knights, fast° friendship for to bynd,   *firm*
160   And love establish each to other trew,
Gave goodly gifts, the signes of gratefull mynd,
And eke° as pledges firme, right hands together joynd.   *also*

19

Prince Arthur gave a boxe of Diamond sure,
Embowd° with gold and gorgeous ornament,   *encircled*
165   Wherein were closd few drops of liquor pure,[7]
Of wondrous worth, and vertue excellent,
That any wound could heale incontinent:°   *immediately*
Which to requite, the Redcrosse knight him gave
A booke, wherein his Saveours testament°   *the Gospels*
170   Was writ with golden letters rich and brave;
A worke of wondrous grace, and able soules to save.

20

Thus beene they parted, Arthur on his way
To seeke his love, and th'other for to fight
With Unaes foe, that all her realme did pray.°   *molest*
175   But she now weighing the decayed plight,
And shrunken synewes of her chosen knight,
Would not a while her forward course pursew,
Ne bring him forth in face of dreadfull fight,
Till he recovered had his former hew:
180   For him to be yet weake and wearie well she knew.

21

So as they traveild, lo they gan espy
An armed knight towards them gallop fast,
That seemed from some feared foe to fly,
Or other griesly thing, that him agast.
185   Still as he fled, his eye was backward cast,
As if his feare still followed him behind;
Als flew his steed, as he his bands had brast,°   *burst*
And with his winged heeles did tread the wind,
As he had beene a fole° of Pegasus[8] his kind.   *foal*

22

190   Nigh as he drew, they might perceive his head
To be unarmd, and curld uncombed heares
Upstaring° stiffe, dismayd with uncouth° dread;   *standing / unknown*
Nor drop of bloud in all his face appeares
Nor life in limbe: and to increase his feares,

7. The blood of Christ, the wine of the Eucharist.   Perseus.
8. A winged horse, belonging to the mythological hero

195   In fowle reproch of knighthoods faire degree,
    About his neck an hempen rope he weares,
    That with his glistring armes° does ill agree;   *armor*
    But he of rope or armes has now no memoree.

23

    The Redcrosse knight toward him crossed fast,
200   To weet,° what mister° wight was so dismayd: *know / manner of*
    There him he finds all sencelesse and aghast,
    That of him selfe he seemd to be afrayd;
    Whom hardly he from flying forward stayd,[9]
    Till he these wordes to him deliver might;
205   Sir knight, aread who hath ye thus arayd,°   *clothed*
    And eke from whom make ye this hasty flight:
    For never knight I saw in such misseeming° plight.   *unseemly*

24

    He answerd nought° at all, but adding new   *not*
    Feare to his first amazment, staring wide
210   With stony° eyes, and hartlesse hollow hew,   *staring*
    Astonisht stood, as one that had aspide
    Infernall furies, with their chaines untide.
    Him yet againe, and yet againe bespake
    The gentle knight; who nought to him replide,
215   But trembling every joynt did inly quake,
    And foltring° tongue at last these words seemd forth to shake.   *stammering*

25

    For Gods deare love, Sir knight, do me not stay;°   *detain*
    For loe° he comes, he comes fast after mee.   *here*
    Eft° looking backe would faine° have runne away;   *again / rather*
220   But he him forst to stay, and tellen free°   *freely tell*
    The secret cause of his perplexitie:
    Yet nathemore° by his bold hartie speach,   *not at all*
    Could his bloud-frosen hart emboldned bee,[1]
    But through his boldnesse rather feare did reach,
225   Yet forst, at last he made through silence suddein breach.°   *break*

26

    And am I now in safetie sure (quoth he)
    From him, that would have forced me to dye?
    And is the point of death now turnd fro° mee,   *from*
    That I may tell this haplesse° history?   *unlucky*
230   Feare nought: (quoth he) no daunger now is nye.
    Then shall I you recount a ruefull cace,°   *sad situation*
    (Said he) the which with this unlucky eye
    I late beheld, and had not greater grace
    Me reft° from it, had bene partaker of the place.[2]   *torn*

9. The Redcrosse Knight could hardly keep the frightened knight (earlier identified as Sir Trevisan) from trying to flee.
1. The Redcrosse Knight's bold words do not encourage
Sir Trevisan; in the end, however, the Redcrosse Knight

forces him to speak.
2. Had not greater grace torn me from the unfortunate
events I beheld, I would have been a victim of those
events myself.

27

235 I lately chaunst (Would I had never chaunst)
    With a faire knight to keepen companee,
    Sir Terwin hight, that well himselfe advaunst
    In all affaires, and was both bold and free,
240 But not so happie as mote happie bee:
    He lov'd, as was his lot, a Ladie gent,°   *gentle*
    That him againe° lov'd in the least degree: *in return*
    For she was proud, and of too high intent,°   *ambition*
    And joyd to see her lover languish and lament.

28

    From whom° returning sad and comfortlesse,   *Terwin's lady*
245 As on the way together we did fare,°   *travel*
    We met that villen (God from him me blesse)
    That cursed wight, from whom I scapt° whyleare,°   *escaped / earlier*
    A man of hell, that cals himselfe Despaire:
    Who first us greets, and after faire areedes°   *tells*
250 Of tydings strange, and of adventures rare:
    So creeping close, as Snake in hidden weedes,
    Inquireth of our states, and of our knightly deedes.

29

    Which when he knew, and felt our feeble harts
    Embost° with bale,° and bitter byting griefe,   *encrusted / sorrow*
255 Which love had launched with his deadly darts,
    With wounding words and termes of foule repriefe°   *scorn*
    He pluckt from us all hope of due reliefe,
    That earst° us held in love of lingring life;   *recently*
    Then hopelesse hartlesse, gan the cunning thiefe
260 Perswade us die, to stint° all further strife: *stop*
    To me he lent this rope, to him a rustie knife.

30

    With which sad instrument of hastie death,
    That wofull lover, loathing lenger° light,   *longer*
    A wide way° made to let forth living breath.   *cut*
265 But I more fearefull, or more luckie wight,°   *creature*
    Dismayd with that deformed dismall sight,
    Fled fast away, halfe dead with dying feare:°   *fear of dying*
    Ne yet assur'd of life by you, Sir knight,
    Whose like infirmitie like chaunce may beare:
270 But God you never let his charmed speeches heare.[3]

31

    How may a man (said he) with idle speach
    Be wonne,° to spoyle the Castle of his health?   *convinced*
    I wote° (quoth he) whom triall late did teach,   *would not*
    That like would not for all this worldes wealth:[4]
275 His subtill tongue, like dropping honny, mealt'th°   *melteth*

---

3. May God prevent you from hearing his seductive speeches.   4. I would not undergo such a test for all the wealth in the world.

Into the hart, and searcheth every vaine,
  That ere° one be aware, by secret stealth   *before*
  His powre is reft,° and weaknesse doth remaine.   *broken*
O never Sir desire to try° his guilefull traine.°   *test / trickery*

32

280 Certes° (said he) hence shall I never rest,   *indeed*
  Till I that treachours° art have heard and tride;° *traitor's / tested*
  And you Sir knight, whose name mote I request,
  Of grace do me unto his cabin° guide.   *cave*
  I that hight° Trevisan (quoth he) will ride   *am called*
285 Against my liking backe, to doe you grace:°   *a favor*
  But nor for gold nor glee will I abide
  By you, when ye arrive in that same place;
For lever° had I die, then° see his deadly face.   *rather / than*

33

Ere long they come, where that same wicked wight
290 His dwelling has, low in an hollow cave,
  Farre underneath a craggie clift ypight,°   *pitched*
  Darke, dolefull, drearie, like a greedie grave,
  That still° for carrion carcases doth crave: *always*
  On top whereof aye° dwelt the ghastly Owle,   *ever*
295 Shrieking his balefull° note, which ever drave *sorrowful*
  Farre from that haunt all other chearefull fowle;
And all about it wandring ghostes did waile and howle.

34

And all about old stockes and stubs of trees,
  Whereon nor fruit, nor leafe was ever seene,
300 Did hang upon the ragged rocky knees;°   *hillsides*
  On which had many wretches hanged beene,
  Whose carcases were scattered on the greene,
  And throwne about the cliffs. Arrived there,
  That bare-head knight for dread and dolefull teene,° *grief*
305 Would faine have fled, ne durst° approchen neare, *dared*
But th'other forst him stay, and comforted in feare.

35

That darkesome cave they enter, where they find
  That cursed man, low sitting on the ground,
  Musing full sadly in his sullein mind;
310 His griesie lockes, long growen, and unbound,
  Disordred hong about his shoulders round,
  And hid his face; through which his hollow eyne
  Lookt deadly dull, and stared as astound;
  His raw-bone cheekes through penurie° and pine,° *poverty / starvation*
315 Were shronke into his jawes, as he did never dine.

36

His garment nought but many ragged clouts,°   *rags*
  With thornes together pind and patched was,
  The which his naked sides he wrapt abouts;
  And him beside there lay upon the gras

320   A drearie° corse,° whose life away did pas,   *gory / body*
        All wallowd in his owne yet luke-warme blood,
        That from his wound yet welled fresh alas;
        In which a rustie knife fast fixed stood,
  And made an open passage for the gushing flood.

37
325   Which piteous spectacle, approving° trew   *proving*
        The wofull tale that Trevisan had told,
        When as the gentle Redcrosse knight did vew,
        With firie zeale he burnt in courage bold,
        Him to avenge, before his bloud were cold,
330   And to the villein said, Thou damned wight,
        The author of this fact, we here behold,
        What justice can but judge against thee right,
  With thine owne bloud to price° his bloud, here shed in sight?   *pay for*

38
  What franticke fit (quoth he) hath thus distraught
335   Thee, foolish man, so rash a doome° to give?   *judgment*
        What justice ever other judgement taught,
        But he should die, who merites not to live?
        None° else to death this man despayring drive,°   *nothing / drove*
        But his owne guiltie mind deserving death.
340   Is then unjust to each his due to give?
        Or let him die, that loatheth living breath?
  Or let him die at ease, that liveth here uneath?°   *unhappily*

39
  Who travels by the wearie wandring way,
        To come unto his wished home in haste,
345   And meetes a flood, that doth his passage stay,
        Is not great grace to helpe him over past,
        Or free his feet, that in the myre sticke fast?
        Most envious man, that grieves at neighbours good,
        And fond,° that joyest in the woe thou hast,   *foolish*
350   Why wilt not let him passe, that long hath stood
  Upon the banke, yet wilt thy selfe not passe the flood?

40
  He there does now enjoy eternall rest
        And happie ease, which thou doest want and crave,
        And further from it daily wanderest:
355   What if some litle paine the passage have,
        That makes fraile flesh to feare the bitter wave?
        Is not short paine well borne, that brings long ease,
        And layes the soule to sleepe in quiet grave?
        Sleepe after toyle, port after stormie seas,
360   Ease after warre, death after life does greatly please.

41
  The knight much wondred at his suddeine wit,
        And said, The terme of life is limited,

Ne may a man prolong, nor shorten it;
The souldier may not move from watchfull sted,°   *post*
365   Nor leave his stand, untill his Captaine bed.°   *command*
Who life did limit by almightie doome,
(Quoth he) knowes best the termes established;
And he, that points the Centonell his roome,
Doth license him depart at sound of morning droome.°   *drum*

42

370   Is not his deed, what ever thing is donne,
In heaven and earth? did not he all create
To die againe? all ends that was begonne,
Their times in his eternall booke of fate
Are written sure, and have their certaine date.
375   Who then can strive with strong necessitie,
That holds the world in his still chaunging state,
Or shunne the death ordaynd by destinie?
When houre of death is come, let none aske whence, nor why.

43

The lenger life, I wote the greater sin,[5]
380   The greater sin, the greater punishment:
All those great battels, which thou boasts to win,
Through strife, and bloud-shed, and avengement,
Now praysd, hereafter deare° thou shalt repent: *dearly*
For life must life, and bloud must bloud repay.
385   Is not enough thy evill life forespent?°   *wasted*
For he, that once hath missed the right way,
The further he doth goe, the further he doth stray.

44

Then do no further goe, no further stray,
But here lie downe, and to thy rest betake,
390   Th'ill° to prevent, that life ensewen° may.   *evil / continue*
For what hath life, that may it loved make,
And gives not rather cause it to forsake?°   *leave*
Feare, sicknesse, age, losse, labour, sorrow, strife,
Paine, hunger, cold, that makes the hart to quake;
395   And ever fickle fortune rageth rife
All which, and thousands mo° do make a loathsome life.   *more*

45

Thou wretched man, of death hast greatest need,
If in true ballance thou wilt weigh thy state:°   *condition*
For never knight, that dared warlike deede,
400   More lucklesse disaventures did amate:°   *meet*
Witnesse the dongeon deepe, wherein of late
Thy life shut up, for death so oft did call;
And though good lucke prolonged hath thy date,

5. The longer the life, the greater the sin.

Yet death then, would the like mishaps forestall,
405 Into the which hereafter thou maiest happen fall.[6]

46

Why then doest thou, O man of sin, desire
  To draw thy dayes forth to their last degree?
  Is not the measure of thy sinfull hire°   employment
  High heaped up with huge iniquitie,°   sinfulness
410 Against the day of wrath, to burden thee?
  Is not enough, that to this Ladie milde
  Thou falsed° hast thy faith with perjurie,   violated
  And sold thy selfe to serve Duessa vilde,°   vile
With whom in all abuse thou hast thy selfe defilde?

47

415 Is not he just, that all this doth behold
  From highest heaven, and beares an equall eye?
  Shall he thy sins up in his knowledge fold,
  And guiltie be of thine impietie?
  Is not his law, Let every sinner die:
420 Die shall all flesh? what then must needs be donne,
  Is it not better to doe willinglie,
  Then° linger, till the glasse be all out ronne?   than
Death is the end of woes: die soone, O faeries sonne.

48

The knight was much enmoved° with his speach,   moved
425 That as a swords point through his hard did perse,° pierce
  And in his conscience made a secret breach,[7]
  Well knowing true all, that he did reherse,
  And to his fresh remembrance did reverse°   recall
  The ugly vew of his deformed crimes,
430 That all his manly powres it did disperse,
  As° he were charmed with inchaunted rimes,   as if
That oftentimes he quakt, and fainted oftentimes.

49

In which amazement, when the Miscreant°   misbeliever (Despair)
  Perceived him to waver weake and fraile,
435 Whiles trembling horror did his conscience dant,° overcome
  And hellish anguish did his soule assaile,
  To drive him to despaire, and quite to quaile,
  He shew'd him painted in a table° plaine,°   picture / clearly
  The damned ghosts, that doe in torments waile,
440 And thousand feends that doe them endlesse paine
With fire and brimstone, which for ever shall remaine.

50

The sight whereof so throughly him dismaid,
  That nought° but death before his eyes he saw,   nothing
  And ever burning wrath before him laid,

6. If death had come when you called for it, then the misfortunes that await you might have been prevented.

7. Despair's words disrupt the Redcrosse Knight's inner
knowledge of God's grace.

445   By righteous sentence of th'Almighties law:
       Then gan the villein him to overcraw,°   *triumph over*
       And brought unto him swords, ropes, poison, fire,
       And all that might him to perdition draw;
       And bad him choose, what death he would desire:
450 For death was due to him, that had provokt Gods ire.

51

       But when as none of them he saw him take,
       He to him raught° a dagger sharpe and keene,   *handed*
       And gave it him in hand: his hand did quake,
       And tremble like a leafe of Aspin greene,
455   And troubled bloud through his pale face was seene
       To come, and goe with tydings from the hart,
       As it a running messenger had beene.
       At last resolv'd to worke his finall smart,°   *pain*
       He lifted up his hand, that backe againe did start.

52

460   Which when as Una saw, through every vaine
       The crudled cold ran to her well of life,°   *her heart*
       As in a swowne: but soone reliv'd° againe,   *revived*
       Out of his hand she snatcht the cursed knife,
       And threw it to the ground, enraged rife,°   *uncontrollably*
465   And to him said, Fie, fie,° faint harted knight,   *shame*
       What meanest thou by this reprochfull strife?
       Is this the battell, which thou vauntst° to fight   *boast*
       With that fire-mouthed Dragon, horrible and bright?

53

       Come, come away, fraile, feeble, fleshly wight,
470   Ne let vaine words bewitch thy manly hart,
       Ne divelish thoughts dismay thy constant spright.
       In heavenly mercies hast thou not a part?
       Why shouldst thou then despeire, that chosen art?
       Where justice growes, there grows eke greater grace,
475   The which doth quench the brond of hellish smart,
       And that accurst hand-writing doth deface.[8]
       Arise, Sir knight arise, and leave this cursed place.

54

       So up he rose, and thence amounted streight.°   *immediately*
       Which when the carle° beheld, and saw his guest   *villain*
480   Would safe depart, for all his subtill sleight,°   *trickery*
       He chose an halter° from among the rest,   *noose*
       And with it hung himselfe, unbid unblest.
       But death he could not worke himselfe thereby;
       For thousand times he so himselfe had drest,
485   Yet nathelesse° it could not doe° him die,   *nevertheless / make*
       Till he should die his last, that is eternally.

8. Una alludes to heavenly grace and God's mercy toward repentent sinners—an allowance that Despair had omitted from his argument.

Canto 10

Her faithfull knight faire Una brings
to house of Holinesse,
Where he is taught repentance, and
the way to heavenly blesse.

1

What man is he, that boasts of fleshly might,
  And vaine° assurance of mortality,   *empty*
Which all so soone, as it doth come to fight,
  Against spirituall foes, yeelds by and by,
5 Or from the field most cowardly doth fly?
  Ne let the man ascribe it to his skill,
  That thorough° grace hath gained victory.   *through*
  If any strength we have, it is to ill,
But all the good is Gods, both power and eke will.

2

10 By that, which lately hapned, Una saw,
  That this her knight was feeble, and too faint;
  And all his sinews woxen° weake and raw,   *grown*
  Through long enprisonment, and hard constraint,
  Which he endured in his late restraint,
15 That yet he was unfit for bloudie fight:
  Therefore to cherish° him with diets daint,°   *nourish / dainty foods*
  She cast to bring him, where he chearen° might,   *be cheered*
Till he recovered had his late decayed plight.

3

There was an auntient° house not farre away,   *ancient*
20 Renowmd throughout the world for sacred lore,°   *wisdom*
  And pure unspotted life: so well they say
  It governd was, and guided evermore,
  Through wisedome of a matrone grave and hore;°   *venerable*
  Whose onely joy was to relieve the needes
25 Of wretched soules, and helpe the helpelesse pore:
  All night she spent in bidding of her bedes,°   *saying prayers*
And all the day in doing good and godly deedes.

4

Dame Caelia° men did her call, as thought   *heavenly*
  From heaven to come, or thither to arise,
30 The mother of three daughters, well upbrought
  In goodly thewes,° and godly exercise: *manners*
  The eldest two most sober, chast, and wise,
  Fidelia° and Speranza° virgins were,   *Faith / Hope*
  Though spousd, yet wanting wedlocks solemnize;[1]
35 But faire Charissa° to a lovely fere°   *Charity / loving husband*
Was lincked, and by him had many pledges° dere.   *children*

---

1. Faith and Hope are each engaged to be married, but their marriages have not yet taken place. The implication is that Faith and Hope are not fulfilled in this life but will be fulfilled in the hereafter through God's promise of salvation.

5

Arrived there, the dore they find fast° lockt;   *tightly*
 For it was warely° watched night and day,   *carefully*
 For feare of many foes: but when they knockt,
40 The Porter opened unto them streight way:°   *right away*
 He was an aged syre, all hory gray,
 With lookes full lowly cast,[2] and gate° full slow,   *pace*
 Wont on a staffe his feeble steps to stay,°   *support*
 Hight Humiltá.° They passe in stouping low;   *named Humility*
45 For streight and narrow was the way, which he did show.

6

Each goodly thing is hardest to begin,
 But entred in a spacious court they see,
 Both plaine, and pleasant to be walked in,
 Where them does meete a francklin[3] faire and free,
50 And entertaines with comely° courteous glee,   *appropriate*
 His name was Zele,[4] that him right well became,
 For in his speeches and behaviour hee
 Did labour lively to expresse the same,
 And gladly did them guide, till to the Hall they came.

7

55 There fairely them receives a gentle Squire,
 Of milde demeanure,° and rare courtesie,   *manner*
 Right cleanly clad in comely sad attire;
 In word and deede that shew'd great modestie,
 And knew his good to all of each degree,[5]
60 Hight Reverence. He them with speeches meet
 Does faire entreat; no courting nicetie,°   *flattery*
 But simple true, and eke unfained° sweet,   *honest*
 As might become a Squire so great persons to greet.

8

And afterwards them to his Dame he leades,
65 That aged Dame, the Ladie of the place:
 Who all this while was busie at her beades:
 Which doen,° she up arose with seemely grace,   *done*
 And toward them full matronely did pace.°   *walk*
 Where when that fairest Una she beheld,
70 Whom well she knew to spring from heavenly race,
 Her hart with joy unwonted inly° sweld,   *inwardly*
 As feeling wondrous comfort in her weaker eld.°   *age*

9

And her embracing said, O happie earth,
 Whereon thy innocent feet doe ever tread,
75 Most vertuous virgin borne of heavenly berth,

2. The porter casts his eyes down in an expression of humility.
3. A person who owns his own land and is therefore his own master.
4. The franklin's zeal or enthusiasm is an attribute of his Christian freedom.
5. He knows how to behave courteously toward members of each social rank.

That to redeeme thy woeful parents head,
From tyrans° rage, and ever-dying dread,   *tyrant's*
Hast wandred through the world now long a day;
Yet ceasest not thy wearie soles° to lead,   *feet, souls*
80   What grace hath thee now hither brought this way?
Or doen° thy feeble feet unweeting hither stray?   *do*

10

Strange thing it is an errant° knight to see   *wandering*
Here in this place, or any other wight,
That hither turnes his steps. So few there bee,
85   That chose the narrow path, or seeke the right:
All keepe the broad high way, and take delight
With many rather for to go astray,
And be partakers of their evill plight,
Then with a few to walke the rightest° way;   *righteous*
90   O foolish men, why haste ye to your owne decay?

11

Thy selfe to see, and tyred limbs to rest,
O matrone sage° (quoth she) I hither came,   *wise*
And this good knight his way with me addrest,°   *directed*
Led with thy prayses and broad-blazd° fame,   *widely reported*
95   That up to heaven is blowne. The auncient Dame
Him goodly greeted in her modest guise,
And entertaynd them both, as best became,
With all the court'sies, that she could devise,°   *think of*
Ne wanted ought, to shew her bounteous° or wise.   *generous*

12

100   Thus as they gan of sundry things devise,
Loe two most goodly virgins came in place,
Ylinked° arme in arme in lovely wise,[6]   *linked*
With countenance° demure,° and modest grace,   *expression / modest*
They numbred even steps and equall pace:
105   Of which the eldest, that Fidelia hight,
Like sunny beames threw from her Christall face,
That could have dazd the rash° beholders sight,   *foolish*
And round about her head did shine like heavens light.

13

She was araied° all in lilly white,   *dressed*
110   And in her right hand bore a cup of gold,[7]
With wine and water fild up to the hight,°   *brim*
In which a Serpent did himselfe enfold,°   *coil*
That horrour made to all, that did behold;
But she no whit° did chaunge her constant mood: *not a bit*
115   And in her other hand she fast° did hold   *tightly*

---

6. Faith and Hope enter the room harmoniously linked, unlike in the House of Pride, where the inhabitants are joined by a yoke of servitude.

7. The sacramental cup of the Holy Communion; it contains the healing blood and baptismal water that poured from Christ's wounds when he was crucified. The serpent here is a symbol of healing and redemption, and the book Fidelia holds is the New Testament, which is sealed with Christ's blood in the sense that Christ's crucifixion assures salvation for all humankind.

A booke, that was both signd and seald with blood,
Wherein darke things were writ, hard to be understood.

14

Her younger sister, that Speranza hight,°   *was called*
    Was clad in blew,[8] that her beseemed° well;   *suited*
120 Not all so chearefull seemed she of sight,
    As was her sister; whether dread° did dwell,   *fear*
    Or anguish in her hart, is hard to tell:
    Upon her arme a silver anchor lay,[9]
    Whereon she leaned ever, as befell:°   *it happened*
125 And ever up to heaven, as she did pray,
Her stedfast eyes were bent, ne swarved° other way.   *turned*

15

They seeing Una, towards her gan wend,
    Who them encounters° with like courtesie;   *greets*
    Many kind speeches they betwene them spend,
130 And greatly joy each other well to see:
    Then to the knight with shamefast° modestie   *humble*
    They turne themselves, at Unaes meeke request,
    And him salute with well beseeming glee;
    Who faire them quites,° as him beseemed best,   *greets*
135 And goodly gan discourse° of many a noble gest.°   *speak / deed*

16

Then Una thus; But she your sister deare,
    The deare Charissa where is she become?[1]
    Or wants° she health, or busie is elsewhere?   *lacks*
    Ah no, said they, but forth she may not come:
140 For she of late is lightned of her wombe,°   *recently gave birth*
    And hath encreast° the world with one sonne more,   *increased*
    That her to see should be but troublesome.
    Indeede (quoth she) that should her trouble sore,
But thankt be God, and her encrease so evermore.[2]

17

145 Then said the aged Caelia, Deare dame,
    And you good Sir, I wote° that of your toyle,   *believe*
    And labours long, through which ye hither came,
    Ye both forwearied° be: therefore a whyle   *tired*
    I read you rest, and to your bowres recoyle.°   *retire*
150 Then called she a Groome, that forth him led
    Into a goodly lodge, and gan despoile°   *remove*
    Of puissant armes, and laid in easie bed;
His name was meeke Obedience rightfully ared.°   *understood*

---

8. Blue is the color traditionally associated with the Virgin Mary.
9. Cf. Hebrews 6.19: "which hope we have as an anchor of the soul, both sure and steadfast." Silver is a symbol of purity.
1. What has become of her?
2. May God give her more children.

18

Now when their wearie limbes with kindly rest,
155 And bodies were refresht with due repast,
 Faire Una gan Fidelia faire request,
 To have her knight into her schoolehouse plaste,
 That of her heavenly learning he might taste,
 And heare the wisedome of her words divine.
160 She graunted, and that knight so much agraste,°   *graced*
 That she him taught celestiall discipline,
And opened his dull eyes, that light mote° in them shine.   *might*

19

And that her sacred Booke, with bloud ywrit,°   *written*
 That none could read, except° she did them teach,   *unless*
165 She unto him disclosed every whit,°   *bit*
 And heavenly documents thereout did preach,
 That weaker wit of man could never reach,
 Of God, of grace, of justice, of free will,
 That wonder was to heare her goodly speach:
170 For she was able, with her words to kill,
And raise againe to life the hart,[3] that she did thrill.°   *pierce*

20

And when she list° poure out her larger spright,   *chose to*
 She would commaund the hastie Sunne to stay,°   *stop*
 Or backward turne his course from heavens hight;
175 Sometimes great hostes of men she could dismay,°   *defeat*
 Dry-shod to passe, she parts the flouds in tway;°   *two*
 And eke huge mountaines from their native seat
 She would commaund, themselves to beare away,
 And throw in raging sea with roaring threat.°   *threatening roar*
180 Almightie God her gave such powre, and puissance great.[4]

21

The faithfull knight now grew in litle space,
 By hearing her, and by her sisters lore,
 To such perfection of all heavenly grace,
 That wretched world he gan for to abhore,
185 And mortall life gan loath,° as thing forlore,°   *despise / lost*
 Greev'd with remembrance of his wicked wayes,
 And prickt° with anguish of his sinnes so sore,   *wounded*
 That he desirde to end his wretched dayes:
So much the dart of sinfull guilt the soule dismayes.°   *overwhelms*

22

190 But wise Speranza gave him comfort sweet,
 And taught him how to take assured hold
 Upon her silver anchor, as was meet;

---

3. Cf. 2 Corinthians 3.6: "for the letter killeth, but the Spirit giveth life."
4. These miracles were attested in Scripture: stopping the sun, Joshua 10.12–13; turning back the sun, 2 Kings 20.10–11; defeating great hosts, Judges 1.21; parting the sea, Exodus 14.22; moving mountains, Matthew 21.21.

	Else had his sinnes so great, and manifold	
	Made him forget all that Fidelia told.	
195	In this distressed doubtfull agonie,	
	When him his dearest Una did behold,	
	Disdeining life, desiring leave° to die,	*permission*
	She found her selfe assayld with great perplexitie.	

23

	And came to Caelia to declare her smart,°	*pain*
200	Who well acquainted with that commune plight,	
	Which sinfull horror workes in wounded hart,	
	Her wisely comforted all that she might,	
	With goodly counsell and advisement° right;	*advice*
	And streightway sent with carefull diligence,	
205	To fetch a Leach,° the which had great insight	*doctor*
	In that disease of grieved conscience,	
	And well could cure the same; His name was Patience.	

24

	Who comming to that soule-diseased knight,	
	Could hardly him intreat,° to tell his griefe:[5]	*convince*
210	Which knowne, and all that noyd° his heavie spright	*troubled*
	Well searcht,° eftsoones he gan apply reliefe	*explored*
	Of salves and med'cines, which had passing priefe,°	*surpassing efficacy*
	And thereto added words of wondrous might:	
	By which to ease he him recured briefe,°	*quickly cured*
215	And much asswag'd° the passion° of his plight,	*soothed / suffering*
	That he his paine endur'd, as seeming now more light.	

25

	But yet the cause and root of all his ill,	
	Inward corruption, and infected sin,	
	Not purg'd° nor heald, behind remained still,	*cleansed*
220	And festring sore did rankle yet within,	
	Close creeping twixt the marrow° and the skin.	*bone*
	Which to extirpe,° he laid him privily°	*remove / privately*
	Downe in a darkesome lowly place farre in,	
	Whereas he meant his corrosives to apply,	
225	And with streight° diet tame his stubborne malady.[6]	*strict*

26

	In ashes and sackcloth he did array°	*dress*
	His daintie corse,[7] proud humors to abate,[8]	
	And dieted with fasting every day,	
	The swelling of his wounds to mitigate,	

---

5. Confession is a necessary element of the Redcrosse Knight's recovery.

6. To heal the Redcrosse Knight, Patience returns him to Orgoglio's dungeon. Patience intends to use corrosive medication to remove his "inward corruption."

7. Patience has the Redcrosse Knight assume the role of a penitent.

8. According to Renaissance medicine, the humors, or bodily fluids, must be in balance to achieve good health; here Patience wants to "abate" or diminish them. The Redcrosse Knight's adventure in the House of Pride has left him with an excess of pride, which the doctor seeks to remove through penance and prayer.

230   And made him pray both earely and eke late:
        And ever as superfluous flesh did rot
        Amendment readie still at hand did wayt,
        To pluck it out with pincers firie whot,°   *not*
        That soone in him was left no one corrupted jot.°   *bit*

                                27

235   And bitter Penance with an yron whip,
        Was wont him once to disple° every day: *discipline*
        And sharpe Remorse his hart did pricke° and nip,   *pierce*
        That drops of bloud thence° like a well did play;   *from his heart*
        And sad Repentance used to embay°   *drench*
240   His bodie in salt water smarting sore,
        The filthy blots of sinne to wash away.
        So in short space they did to health restore
        The man that would not live, but earst lay at deathes dore.

                                28

        In which his torment often was so great,
245   That like a Lyon he would cry and rore,
        And rend his flesh, and his owne synewes° eat.   *muscles*
        His owne deare Una hearing evermore
        His ruefull shrieks and gronings, often tore
        Her guiltlesse garments, and her golden heare,
250   For pitty of his paine and anguish sore;
        Yet all with patience wisely she did beare;
        For well she wist, his crime could else be never cleare.°   *cleansed*

                                29

        Whom thus recover'd by wise Patience,
        And trew Repentance they to Una brought:
255   Who joyous of his cured conscience,
        Him dearely kist, and fairely eke besought
        Himselfe to chearish, and consuming thought
        To put away out of his carefull° brest.   *worried*
        By this Charissa, late in child-bed brought,[9]
260   Was woxen strong, and left her fruitfull nest;
        To her faire Una brought this unacquainted guest.

                                30

        She was a woman in her freshest age,
        Of wondrous beauty, and of bountie° rare,   *generosity*
        With goodly grace and comely° personage,   *attractive*
265   That was on earth not easie to compare;
        Full of great love, but Cupids wanton snare
        As hell she hated, chast in worke and will;
        Her necke and breasts were ever open bare,
        That ay° thereof her babes might sucke their fill;   *always*
270   The rest was all in yellow robes arayed still.°   *always*

9. Charissa, who had recently given birth.

31

A multitude of babes about her hong,
   Playing their sports, that joyd her to behold,
   Whom still° she fed, whiles they were weake and young,   *always*
   But thrust them forth still, as they wexed° old: *grew*
275   And on her head she wore a tyre° of gold,   *crown*
   Adornd with gemmes and owches° wondrous faire,   *jewels*
   Whose passing price uneath° was to be told;[1]   *scarcely*
   And by her side there sate a gentle paire
Of turtle doves, she sitting in an yvorie chaire.

32

280 The knight and Una entring, faire her greet,
   And bid her joy of that her happie brood;
   Who them requites° with court'sies seeming meet,°   *repays / suitable*
   And entertaines with friendly chearefull mood.
   Then Una her besought,° to be so good,   *requested*
285   As in her vertuous rules to schoole her knight,
   Now after all his torment well withstood,
   In that sad house of Penaunce, where his spright
Had past the paines of hell, and long enduring night.

33

She was right joyous of her just° request,   *reasonable*
290   And taking by the hand that Faeries sonne,
   Gan him instruct in every good behest,°   *command*
   Of love, and righteousnesse, and well to donne,°   *good deeds*
   And wrath, and hatred warely° to shonne,   *carefully*
   That drew on men Gods hatred, and his wrath,
295   And many soules in dolours had fordonne:°   *overcome*
   In which when him she well instructed hath,
From thence to heaven she teacheth him the ready° path.   *direct*

34

Wherein his weaker wandring steps to guide,
   An auncient matrone she to her does call,
300   Whose sober lookes her wisedome well descride:°   *revealed*
   Her name was Mercie, well knowne over all,
   To be both gratious, and eke liberall:
   To whom the carefull charge of him she gave,
   To lead aright, that he should never fall
305   In all his wayes through this wide worldes wave,°   *currents*
That Mercy in the end his righteous soule might save.

35

The godly Matrone by the hand him beares°   *leads*
   Forth from her presence, by a narrow way,
   Scattred with bushy thornes, and ragged breares,°   *briars*
310   Which still° before him she remov'd away,   *ever*
   That nothing might his ready° passage stay:°   *direct / stop*
   And ever when his feet encombred were,

---

1. Whose surpassing value was incalculable.

Or gan to shrinke,° or from the right to stray,   *pull back*
She held him fast,° and firmely did upbeare,°   *firmly / support*
315   As carefull Nourse her child from falling oft does reare.°   *raise*

36

Eftsoones unto an holy Hospitall,°   *hostel*
That was fore° by the way, she did him bring,   *close*
In which seven Bead-men° that had vowed all   *men of prayer*
Their life to service of high heavens king
320   Did spend their dayes in doing godly thing:
Their gates to all were open evermore,°   *always*
That by the wearie way were traveiling,
And one sate° wayting ever them before,   *sat*
To call in commers-by,° that needy were and pore.   *passers-by*

37

325   The first of them that eldest was, and best,
Of all the house had charge and governement,
As Guardian and Steward of the rest:
His office° was to give entertainment°   *duty / provisions*
And lodging, unto all that came, and went:
330   Not unto such, as could him feast againe,
And double quite,° for that he on them spent,   *repay*
But such, as want° of harbour did constraine:[2]   *lack*
Those for Gods sake his dewty was to entertaine.

38

The second was as Almner[3] of the place,
335   His office was, the hungry for to feed,
And thristy give to drinke, a worke of grace:
He feard not once him selfe to be in need,
Ne car'd to hoord° for those, whom he did breede:°   *hoard / his children*
The grace of God he layd up still in store,
340   Which as a stocke he left unto his seede;
He had enough, what need him care for more?
And had he lesse, yet some he would give to the pore.[4]

39

The third had of their wardrobe custodie,
In which were not rich tyres,° nor garments gay,°   *clothes / trashy*
345   The plumes of pride, and wings of vanitie,
But clothes meet to keepe keene could° away,   *sharp cold*
And naked nature seemely° to aray;   *suitably*
With which bare wretched wights he dayly clad,
The images of God in earthly clay;
350   And if that no spare cloths to give he had,
His owne coate he would cut, and it distribute glad.

---

2. He did not provide for those who could return the favor with an even more lavish reception, but provided only for those who were destitute.
3. One who provides charitable relief to the poor.

4. He did not accumulate worldly goods for the wealth of his family, but gave to the poor, which made him rich in the virtue of charity.

40

The fourth appointed by his office was,
    Poore prisoners to relieve with gratious ayd,°   *aid*
    And captives to redeeme° with price of bras,   *ransom*
355   From Turkes and Sarazins, which them had stayd;°   *imprisoned*
    And though they faultie were,[5] yet well he wayd,°   *judged*
    That God to us forgiveth every howre
    Much more then that, why° they in bands° were layd,   *for which / chains*
    And he that harrowd hell with heavie stowre,°   *sorrow*
360 The faultie soules from thence brought to his heavenly bowre.[6]

41

The fift had charge sicke persons to attend,
    And comfort those, in point° of death which lay;   *at the brink*
    For them most needeth comfort in the end,
    When sin, and hell, and death do most dismay
365   The feeble soule departing hence away.
    All is but lost, that living we bestow,
    If not well ended at our dying day.[7]
    O man have mind of that last bitter throw;°   *agony*
For as the tree does fall, so lyes it ever low.

42

370 The sixt had charge of them now being dead,
    In seemely sort their corses to engrave,°   *bury*
    And deck with dainty flowres their bridall bed,
    That to their heavenly spouse[8] both sweet and brave
    They might appeare, when he their soules shall save.
375   The wondrous workemanship of Gods owne mould,°   *image*
    Whose face he made, all beasts to feare, and gave
    All in his hand, even dead we honour should.
Ah dearest God me graunt, I dead be not defould.°   *defiled*

43

The seventh now after death and buriall done,
380 Had charge the tender Orphans of the dead
    And widowes ayd, least° they should be undone:°   *lest / ruined*
    In face of judgement he their right would plead,
    Ne ought° the powre of mighty men did dread   *not at all*
    In their defence,[9] nor would for gold or fee
385   Be wonne° their rightfull causes downe to tread: *bribed*
    And when they stood in most necessitee,
He did supply their want, and gave them° ever° free.   *to them / always*

44

There when the Elfin knight arrived was,
    The first and chiefest of the seven, whose care°   *duty*

5. Christian prisoners of pagans were "faultie" if they had given up their faith, even if they had been tortured in the process. But although succumbing to pagan force was strictly speaking a sin, the fourth Beadman considers that God forgives much greater sins all the time.
6. According to a medieval story, after his crucifixion Christ descended into Hell to release good people who had lived before him and thus had not been able to enter heaven.
7. A lifetime of faith is lost if one gives in to despair at the time of death.
8. In Revelation 21.2, the redeemed are "prepared as a bride adorned for her husband."
9. He would plead their causes in court and did not fear the power of mighty men.

390   Was guests to welcome, towardes him did pas:°   *go*
      Where seeing Mercie, that his steps up bare,°   *supported*
      And alwayes led, to her with reverence rare
      He humbly louted° in meeke lowlinesse,   *bowed*
      And seemely° welcome for her did prepare: *suitable*
395   For of their order she was Patronesse,°   *protector*
    Albe° Charissa were their chiefest founderesse.   *although*

45

    There she awhile him stayes, him selfe to rest,
      That to the rest° more able he might bee: *remainder*
      During which time, in every good behest°   *deed*
400   And godly worke of Almes and charitee
      She him instructed with great industree;
      Shortly therein so perfect he became,
      That from the first unto the last degree,
      His mortall life he learned had to frame°   *conduct*
405   In holy righteousnesse,[1] without rebuke or blame.

46

    Thence forward by that painfull way they pas,°   *go*
      Forth to an hill, that was both steepe and hy;
      On top whereof a sacred chappell was,
      And eke a litle Hermitage thereby,
410   Wherein an aged holy man did lye,
      That day and night said his devotion,
      Ne other worldly busines did apply;°   *conduct*
      His name was heavenly Contemplation;
    Of God and goodnesse was his meditation.

47

415   Great grace that old man to him given had;
      For God he often saw from heavens hight,°   *height*
      All were his earthly eyen both blunt° and bad,   *blurred*
      And through great age had lost their kindly° sight, *natural*
      Yet wondrous quick and persant° was his spright, *piercing*
420   As Eagles eye, that can behold the Sunne:
      That hill they scale° with all their powre and might, *climb*
      That his frayle thighes nigh° wearie and fordonne *all but*
    Gan faile, but by her° helpe the top at last he wonne.° *Mercy's / reached*

48

    There they do finde that godly aged Sire,
425   With snowy lockes adowne his shoulders shed,
      As hoarie frost with spangles° doth attire   *icicles*
      The mossy braunches of an Oke halfe ded.
      Each bone might through his body well be red,°   *seen*
      And every sinew° seene through his long fast: *muscle*
430   For nought he car'd his carcas long unfed;[2]
      His mind was full of spirituall repast,
    And pyn'd° his flesh, to keepe his body low and chast. *starved*

---

1. Spenser emphasizes that holy righteousness is not just an inner moral state but is achieved through the active practice of charity.
2. He did not care about the hunger of his body.

49

Who when these two approching he aspide,°   *saw*

 At their first presence grew agrieved sore,°   *very upset*

435 That forst him lay his heavenly thoughts aside;

 And had he not that Dame respected more,

 Whom highly he did reverence and adore,

 He would not once have moved for the knight.

 They him saluted standing far afore;°   *at a distance*

440 Who well them greeting, humbly did requight,° *return the greeting*

And asked, to what end they clomb that tedious height.

50

What end (quoth° she) should cause us take such paine, *said*

 But that same end, which every living wight

 Should make his marke,° high heaven to attaine? *aim*

445 Is not from hence the way, that leadeth right

 To that most glorious house, that glistreth° bright *shines*

 With burning starres, and everliuing fire,

 Whereof the keyes[3] are to thy hand behight° *delivered*

 By wise Fidelia? she doth thee require,

450 To shew it to this knight, according° his desire. *granting*

51

Thrise° happy man, said then the father grave,   *thrice*

 Whose staggering steps thy steady hand doth lead,

 And shewes the way, his sinfull soule to save.

 Who better can the way to heaven aread,°   *show*

455 Then thou thy selfe, that was both borne and bred

 In heavenly throne, where thousand Angels shine?

 Thou doest the prayers of the righteous sead° *the redeemed*

 Present before the majestie divine,

And his avenging wrath to clemencie incline.[4]

52

460 Yet since thou bidst, thy pleasure shalbe donne.

 Then come thou man of earth, and see the way,

 That never yet was seene of Faeries sonne,

 That never leads the traveiler astray,

 But after labours long, and sad delay,

465 Brings them to joyous rest and endlesse blis.

 But first thou must a season fast and pray,

 Till from her bands° the spright assoiled° is,[5] *bonds / released*

And have her strength recur'd° from fraile infirmitis. *restored*

53

That done, he leads him to the highest Mount;[6]

470 Such one,[7] as that same mighty man of God,

 That bloud-red billowes[8] like a walled front

---

3. The keys to the kingdom of heaven.
4. Contemplation is addressing Mercy, who turns the Almighty's wrath into forgiveness.
5. The bonds that Contemplation is referring to are the bonds of the flesh.
6. This is the "great and high mountain" of Revelation

21.10, from which God showed John the New Jerusalem.
7. Such a mountain—Sinai—Moses climbed to spend 40 days before receiving the Ten Commandments.
8. Spenser is referring to the Red Sea, which Moses parted to allow the Israelites to escape from Egypt without drowning.

On either side disparted with his rod,
Till that his army dry-foot through them yod,°   *went*
Dwelt fortie dayes upon; where writ in stone
With bloudy letters by the hand of God,
475
The bitter doome of death and balefull mone°   *moan*
He did receive, whiles flashing fire about him shone.[9]

54

Or like that sacred hill, whose head full hie,
Adornd with fruitfull Olives all arownd,[1]
480
Is, as it were for endlesse memory
Of that deare Lord, who oft thereon was fownd,
For ever with a flowring girlond crownd:
Or like that pleasant Mount, that is for ay
Through famous Poets verse each where renownd,[2]
485
On which the thrise three learned Ladies[3] play
Their heavenly notes, and make full many a lovely lay.

55

From thence, far off he unto him did shew
A litle path, that was both steepe and long,
Which to a goodly Citie[4] led his vew;
490
Whose wals and towres were builded high and strong
Of perle and precious stone, that earthly tong
Cannot describe, nor wit of man can tell;
Too high a ditty for my simple song;
The Citie of the great king hight it well,°   *it is well named*
495
Wherein eternall peace and happinesse doth dwell.[5]

56

As he thereon stood gazing, he might see
The blessed Angels to and fro descend[6]
From highest heaven, in gladsome° companee,°   *happy / friendship*
And with great joy into that Citie wend,
500
As commonly as friend does with his frend.
Whereat he wondred much, and gan enquere,°   *asked*
What stately building durst° so high extend   *dared*
Her loftie towres unto the starry sphere,°   *heavens*
And what unknowen nation there empeopled were.°   *inhabited it*

57

505
Faire knight (quoth he) Hierusalem that is,
The new Hierusalem, that God has built
For those to dwell in, that are chosen his,
His chosen people purg'd from sinfull guilt,
With pretious bloud,[7] which cruelly was spilt

9. Referring to the burning bush through which God appeared to Moses (Deuteronomy 4.11).
1. The Mount of Olives, where Jesus taught.
2. Parnassus, the home of the Greek gods and celebrated by the Greek poets.
3. The nine Muses, goddesses of the arts and sciences.
4. The New Jerusalem, the promised home of the faithful

in eternity (Revelation 20.10–21).
5. Cf. Psalms 48.2: "the joy of the whole earth is Mount Zion . . . the city of the great king."
6. The image recalls Jacob's vision of the ladder that extended from earth to heaven (Genesis 28.12).
7. The blood spilled by Christ when he was crucified and by which the faithful are redeemed from sin.

510   On cursed tree, of that unspotted lam,°   *lamb*
          That for the sinnes of all the world was kilt:
          Now are they Saints all in that Citie sam,°   *same*
     More deare unto their God, then younglings to their dam.

58

     Till now, said then the knight, I weened well,
515   That great Cleopolis,[8] where I have beene,
          In which that fairest Faerie Queene doth dwell,
          The fairest Citie was, that might be seene;
          And that bright towre all built of christall cleene,
          Panthea, seemd the brightest thing, that was:
520   But now by proofe all otherwise I weene;
          For this great Citie that does far surpas,
     And this bright Angels towre quite dims that towre of glas.

59

     Most trew, then said the holy aged man;
       Yet is Cleopolis for earthly frame,[9]
525   The fairest peece, that eye beholden can:
          And well beseemes all knights of noble name,
          That covet in th'immortall booke of fame
          To be eternized, that same to haunt,
          And doen their service to that soveraigne Dame,[1]
530   That glorie does to them for guerdon° graunt: *reward*
     For she is heavenly borne, and heaven may justly vaunt.[2]

60

     And thou faire ymp,° sprong out from English race,   *child*
       How ever now accompted° Elfins sonne,   *considered*
          Well worthy doest thy service for her grace,
535   To aide a virgin desolate foredonne.°   *in distress*
          But when thou famous victorie hast wonne,
          And high emongst all knights hast hong thy shield,
          Thenceforth the suit° of earthly conquest shonne,°   *pursuit / shun*
          And wash thy hands from guilt of bloudy field:
540   For bloud can nought but sin, and wars but sorrowes yield.

61

     Then seeke this path, that I to thee presage,°   *foretell*
       Which after all to heaven shall thee send;
       Then peaceably thy painefull pilgrimage
       To yonder same Hierusalem do bend,°   *go*
545   Where is for thee ordaind a blessed end:
       For thou emongst those Saints, whom thou doest see,
       Shalt be a Saint, and thine owne nations frend

---

8. The Redcrosse Knight compares the New Jerusalem with Cleopolis, the city ruled by the Faerie Queene, and its tower Panthea—literally, in Greek, all sights or the best of sights—together a perfect representation of a political state (as realized by Spenser and perhaps by Plato and others in their political treatises). He finds that the transcendent brilliance of the angels' city surpasses that of the other cities of "glass," i.e., products of a merely human power of reflection.
9. As an earthly as opposed to a heavenly structure.
1. It is fitting that noble knights who seek glory serve in the Faerie Queene's court.
2. Because the Faerie Queene was born in Heaven, Heaven may rightfully boast ("vaunt") that it is her home.

And Patrone: thou Saint George shalt called bee,
Saint George of mery England, the signe of victoree.

62

550   Unworthy wretch (quoth he°) of so great grace,   *Redcrosse Knight*
        How dare I thinke such glory to attaine?
        These that have it attaind, were in like cace
        (Quoth he°) as wretched, and liv'd in like paine.   *Contemplation*
        But deeds of armes must I[3] at last be faine,°   *willing*
555   And Ladies love to leave so dearely bought?
        What need of armes, where peace doth ay° remaine,   *ever*
        (Said he°) and battailes none are to be fought?   *Contemplation*
As for loose loves are vaine,° and vanish into nought.   *false*

63

O let me not (quoth he) then turne againe
560   Backe to the world, whose joyes so fruitlesse are;
        But let me here for aye° in peace remaine,   *ever*
        Or streight way° on that last long voyage fare,[4]   *immediately*
        That nothing may my present hope empare.°   *diminish*
        That may not be (said he) ne maist thou yit
565   Forgo° that royall maides bequeathed care,   *give up*
        Who did her cause into thy hand commit,[5]
Till from her cursed foe thou have her freely quit.

64

Then shall I soone, (quoth he) so God me grace,
        Abet° that virgins cause disconsolate,   *assist*
570   And shortly backe returne unto this place,
        To walke this way in Pilgrims poore estate.°   *condition*
        But now aread,° old father, why of late°   *tell me / just now*
        Didst thou behight° me borne of English blood,   *call*
        Whom all a Faeries sonne doen nominate?[6]
575   That word shall I (said he) avouchen° good,   *prove*
Sith to thee is unknowne the cradle of thy brood.°   *girth*

65

For well I wote, thou springst from ancient race
        Of Saxon kings, that have with mightie hand
        And many bloudie battailes fought in place°   *in that place*
580   High reard° their royall throne in Britane land,   *erected*
        And vanquisht them,° unable to withstand: *the Britons*
        From thence a Faerie thee unweeting reft,°   *took*
        There as thou slepst in tender swadling band,
        And her base Elfin brood° there for thee left.[7]   *child*
585   Such men do Chaungelings° call, so chaungd° by Faeries theft.   *changelings / switched*

3. The Redcrosse Knight asks himself whether he can abandon chivalry and then learns that in the New Jerusalem there are neither wars nor loves.
4. The Redcrosse Knight is referring to death.
5. He may not yet give up Una's quest to which he is committed; he must avenge and free her from her enemy.
6. The Redcrosse Knight believes he is an inhabitant of Faerie Land, the fictional ground of the poem as Spenser

names it to his readers. When Contemplation tells the Redcrosse Knight that he is actually English, Spenser is alerting readers to the fact that St. George (as Spenser apparently believed) was a historical figure, represented in historical record, and not merely a figment of the poet's imagination.
7. I.e., unknown to you, a fairy took you from your cradle and put its own child in your place.

66

Thence° she thee brought into this Faerie lond,   *from there*
    And in an heaped furrow did thee hyde,
    Where thee a Ploughman all unweeting fond,
    As he his toylesome teme° that way did guyde,   *toiling oxen*
590   And brought thee up in ploughmans state to byde,
    Whereof Georgos° he thee gave to name;   *farmer*
    Till prickt° with courage, and thy forces pryde,   *moved*
    To Faery court thou cam'st to seeke for fame,
And prove thy puissaunt armes, as seemes thee best became.[8]

67

595 O holy Sire (quoth he) how shall I quight°   *repay*
    The many favours I with thee have found,
    That hast my name and nation red aright,°   *correctly*
    And taught the way that does to heaven bound?
    This said, adowne he looked to the ground,
600   To have returnd, but dazed were his eyne,
    Through passing brightnesse, which did quite confound°   *bewilder*
    His feeble sence, and too exceeding shyne.[9]
So darke are earthly things compard to things divine.

68

At last whenas himselfe he gan to find,
605   To Una back he cast him° to retire;   *decided*
    Who him awaited still with pensive mind.
    Great thankes and goodly meed° to that good syre,   *reward*
    He thence departing gave for his paines hyre.[1]
    So came to Una, who him joyd to see,
610   And after litle rest, gan him desire,
    Of her adventure° mindfull for to bee.   *quest*
So leave they take of Caelia, and her daughters three.

Canto 11

The knight with that old Dragon fights
two dayes incessantly:
The third him overthrowes, and gayns
most glorious victory.

1

High time now gan it wex° for Una faire,   *grow*
    To thinke of those her captive Parents deare,
    And their forwasted° kingdome to repaire: *desolated*
    Whereto whenas they now approched neare,
5   With hartie words her knight she gan to cheare,
    And in her modest manner thus bespake;°   *said*
    Deare knight, as deare, as ever knight was deare,

---

8. The qualities that prompted the Redcrosse Knight to leave the farm—i.e., pride in his chivalric skill—are qualities his faith will have had to modify to conform to a Christian mode of life.

9. The Redcrosse Knight glances down, intending to look back up, but the force of revelation overwhelms him.
1. The hire of his pains, the trouble Contemplation took to instruct the Redcrosse Knight.

That all these sorrowes suffer for my sake,
High heaven behold the tedious toyle, ye for me take.[1]

2

10   Now are we come unto my native soyle,
       And to the place, where all our perils dwell;
       Here haunts° that feend, and does his dayly spoyle,°   *lurks / evil*
       Therefore henceforth be at your keeping well,°   *on your guard*
       And ever ready for your foeman fell.°   *dangerous enemy*
15   The sparke of noble courage now awake,
       And strive your excellent selfe to excell;°   *outdo yourself*
       That shall ye evermore renowmed make,
Above all knights on earth, that batteill undertake.

3

And pointing forth, lo yonder is (said she)
20   The brasen towre in which my parents deare
       For dread of that huge feend emprisond be,
       Whom I from far see on the walles appeare,
       Whose sight my feeble soule doth greatly cheare:
       And on the top of all I do espye
25   The watchman wayting tydings glad to heare,[2]
       That O my parents might I happily
Unto you bring, to ease you of your misery.

4

With that they heard a roaring hideous sound,
       That all the ayre with terrour filled wide,
30   And seemd uneath° to shake the stedfast ground.   *almost*
       Eftsoones that dreadfull Dragon they espide,
       Where stretcht he lay upon the sunny side
       Of a great hill, himselfe like a great hill.
       But all so soone, as he from far descride°   *saw*
35   Those glistring armes, that heaven with light did fill,
He rousd himselfe full blith,° and hastned them untill.°   *joyfully / toward them*

5

Then bad the knight his Lady yede aloofe,°   *stand aside*
       And to an hill her selfe with draw aside,
       From whence she might behold that battailles proof
40   And eke be safe from daunger far descryde:°   *seen from a distance*
       She him obayd, and turnd a little wyde.°   *moved aside*
       Now O thou sacred Muse, most learned Dame,[3]
       Faire ympe of Phoebus, and his aged bride,
       The Nourse of time, and everlasting fame,
45   That warlike hands ennoblest with immortall name;

6

O gently come into my feeble brest,
       Come gently, but not with that mighty rage,

---

1. Una asks the heavens to witness the difficult task that the Redcrosse Knight undertakes for her.
2. Waiting to hear good news. In the next line, Una addresses her parents, expressing her wish to bring them the good news of their rescue herself.
3. Spenser is calling upon Clio, the muse of history, who preserves great events and records glorious deeds.

Wherewith the martiall troupes thou doest infest,°   *inspire*
And harts of great Heroës doest enrage,
50   That nought their kindled courage may aswage,°   *diminish*
Soone as they dreadfull trompe° begins to sownd;   *trumpet*
The God of warre with his fiers equipage°   *weapons*
Thou doest awake, sleepe never he so sownd,
And scared nations doest with horrour sterne astownd.°   *astonish*

7

55   Faire Goddesse lay that furious fit aside,[4]
Till I of warres and bloudy Mars do sing,
And Briton fields with Sarazin bloud bedyde,
Twixt that great faery Queene and Paynim king,
That with their horrour heaven and earth did ring,
60   A worke of labour long, and endlesse prayse:[5]
But now a while let downe that haughtie string,
And to my tunes thy second tenor° rayse,   *accompaniment*
That I this man of God his godly armes may blaze.°   *proclaim*

8

By this the dreadful Beast drew nigh to hand,°   *near*
65   Halfe flying, and halfe footing in his hast,
That with his largenesse measured much land,
And made wide shadow under his huge wast;°   *bulk*
As mountaine doth the valley overcast.
Approching nigh, he reared high afore
70   His body monstrous, horrible, and vast,
Which to increase his wondrous greatnesse more,
Was swolne with wrath, and poyson, and with bloudy gore.

9

And over, all with brasen scales was armd,
Like plated coate of steele, so couched neare,°   *closely set*
75   That nought mote perce, ne might his corse be harmd
With dint of sword, nor push of pointed speare;
Which as an Eagle, seeing pray appeare,
His aery plumes doth rouze, full rudely dight,°   *violently arranged*
So shaked he, that horrour was to heare,
80   For as the clashing of an Armour bright,
Such noyse his rouzed scales did send unto the knight.

10

His flaggy° wings when forth he did display,   *drooping*
Were like two sayles, in which the hollow wynd
Is gathered full,[6] and worketh speedy way:
85   And eke the pennes,[7] that did his pineons° bynd,   *feathers*
Were like mayne-yards,° with flying canvas lynd,   *mainsail ropes*
With which whenas him list the ayre to beat,

4. The muse's "furious fit" is music that rouses men to war.
5. The song of war that Spenser refers to here may be some part of the poem he plans to write in the future.
6. The force of the wind fills the sails and makes them billow out.
7. The bones in the Dragon's wings.

And there by force unwonted passage find,[8]
The cloudes before him fled for terrour great,
90   And all the heavens stood still amazed with his threat.

11

His huge long tayle wound up in hundred foldes,
Does overspred his long bras-scaly backe,
Whose wreathed boughts° when ever he unfoldes,   *wound-up coils*
And thicke entangled knots adown does slacke,
95   Bespotted as with shields of red and blacke,
It sweepeth all the land behind him farre,
And of three furlongs does but litle lacke;[9]
And at the point two stings in-fixed arre,
Both deadly sharpe, that sharpest steele exceeden farre.

12

100   But stings and sharpest steele did far exceed
The sharpnesse of his cruell rending clawes;
Dead was it sure, as sure as death in deed,
What ever thing does touch his ravenous pawes,
Or what within his reach he ever drawes.
105   But his most hideous head my toung to tell
Does tremble: for his deepe devouring jawes
Wide gaped, like the griesly mouth of hell,
Through which into his darke abisse° all ravin° fell.   *pit / prey*

13

And that more wondrous was, in either jaw
110   Three ranckes of yron teeth enraunged were,
In which yet trickling bloud and gobbets° raw   *chunks*
Of late devoured bodies did appeare,
That sight thereof bred cold congealed feare:
Which to increase, and all atonce° to kill,   *suddenly*
115   A cloud of smoothering smoke and sulphur seare°   *burning*
Out of his stinking gorge forth steemed still,
That all the ayre about with smoke and stench did fill.

14

His blazing eyes, like two bright shining shields,
Did burne with wrath, and sparkled living fyre;
120   As two broad Beacons, set in open fields,
Send forth their flames farre off to every shyre,°   *district*
And warning give, that enemies conspyre,
With fire and sword the region to invade;
So flam'd his eyne with rage and rancorous yre:
125   But farre within, as in a hollow glade,
Those glaring lampes were set, that made a dreadfull shade.

15

So dreadfully he towards him did pas,
Forelifting° up aloft his speckled brest,   *raising*

---

8. Although the Dragon cannot fly normally, he does so through the sheer force with which he beats his wings.

9. The Dragon's tail measures nearly three furlongs, 660 yards, a third of a mile.

	And often bounding on the brused gras,	
130	As for great joyance of his newcome guest.	
	Eftsoones he gan advance his haughtie crest,	
	As chauffed Bore° his bristles doth upreare,	*angry boar*
	And shoke his scales to battell readie drest;[1]	
	That made the Redcrosse knight nigh quake for feare,	
135	As bidding° bold defiance to his foeman neare.	*inciting*

16

	The knight gan fairely couch his steadie speare,	
	And fiercely ran at him with rigorous might:	
	The pointed steele arriving rudely theare,	
	His harder hide would neither perce, nor bight,	
140	But glauncing by forth passed forward right;	
	Yet sore amoved with so puissant push,	
	The wrathfull beast about him turned light,°	*quickly*
	And him so rudely passing by, did brush	
	With his long tayle, that° horse and man to ground did rush.°	*so that / fall*

17

145	Both horse and man up lightly rose againe,	
	And fresh encounter towards him addrest:	
	But th'idle stroke° yet backe recoyld in vaine,	*futile swordstroke*
	And found no place his deadly point to rest.	
	Exceeding rage enflam'd the furious beast,	
150	To be avenged of so great despight;	
	For never felt his imperceable brest	
	So wondrous force, from hand of living wight;	
	Yet had he prov'd° the powre of many a puissant knight.	*tested*

18

	Then with his waving wings displayed wyde,	
155	Himselfe up high he lifted from the ground,	
	And with strong flight did forcibly divide	
	The yielding aire, which nigh° too feeble found	*almost*
	Her flitting partes, and element unsound,	
	To beare so great a weight:[2] he cutting way	
160	With his broad sayles, about him soared round:	
	At last low stouping with unweldie sway,°	*awkward force*
	Snatcht up both horse and man, to beare them quite away.	

19

	Long he them bore above the subject plaine,	
	So farre as Ewghen° bow a shaft may send,	*made of yew*
165	Till struggling strong did him at last constraine,	
	To let them downe before his flightes end:	
	As hagard hauke° presuming to contend	*untamed hawk*
	With hardie fowle, above his hable° might,	*natural*
	His wearie pounces° all in vaine doth spend,	*claws*

1. He shook his scales into position for battle.
2. The air is almost too weak to support the Dragon; in other words, the Dragon is almost too heavy to fly, given the strength of his wings in relation to his overall weight.

170 To trusse° the pray too heavie for his flight; *carry off*
 Which comming downe to ground, does free it selfe by fight.

20

 He so disseized° of his gryping grosse,° *freed / heavy grasp*
  The knight his thrillant speare againe assayd
  In his bras-plated body to embosse,° *embed*
175 And three mens strength unto the stroke he layd;
  Wherewith the stiffe beame° quaked, as affrayd, *shaft*
  And glauncing from his scaly necke, did glyde
  Close under his left wing, then broad displayd.
  The percing steele there wrought a wound full wyde,
180 That with the uncouth smart° the Monster lowdly cryde. *pain*

21

 He cryde, as raging seas are wont to rore,
  When wintry storme his wrathfull wreck does threat,
  The rolling billowes beat the ragged shore,
  As they the earth would shoulder from her seat,
185 And greedie gulfe does gape, as he would eat
  His neighbour element° in his revenge: *the earth*
  Then gin the blustring brethren boldly threat,
  To move the world from off his stedfast henge,° *hinge*
 And boystrous battell make, each other to avenge.

22

190 The steely head stucke fast° still in his flesh, *firmly*
  Till with his cruell clawes he snatcht the wood,° *shaft*
  And quite a sunder broke. Forth flowed fresh
  A gushing river of blacke goarie blood,
  That drowned all the land, whereon he stood;
195 The streame thereof would drive a water-mill.
  Trebly augmented was his furious mood
  With bitter sense of his deepe rooted ill,
 That flames of fire he threw forth from his large nosethrill.° *nostril*

23

 His hideous tayle then hurled he about,
200 And therewith all enwrapt the nimble thyes° *thighs*
  Of his froth-fomy steed, whose courage stout
  Striving to loose the knot, that fast him tyes,
  Himselfe in streighter bandes° too rash implyes, *tighter bondage*
  That to the ground he is perforce° constraynd *thereby*
205 To throw his rider: who can quickly ryse
  From off the earth, with durty bloud distaynd,° *stained*
 For that reprochfull fall right fowly he disdaynd.

24

 And fiercely tooke his trenchand° blade in hand, *sharp*
  With which he stroke so furious and so fell,
210 That nothing seemd the puissance could withstand:
  Upon his crest the hardned yron fell,
  But his more hardned crest was armd so well,

That deeper dint therein it would not make;
Yet so extremely did the buffe° him quell,°   blow / overwhelm
215   That from thenceforth he shund the like to take,
But when he saw them come, he did them still forsake.°   avoid

25

The knight was wrath to see his stroke beguyld,°   foiled
And smote againe with more outrageous might;
But backe againe the sparckling steele recoyld,
220   And left not any marke, where it did light;°   land
As if in Adamant° rocke it had bene pight.   hardest
The beast impatient of his smarting wound,
And of so fierce and forcible despight,°   injury
Thought with his wings to stye° above the ground;   fly
225   But his late wounded wing unserviceable found.

26

Then full of griefe and anguish vehement,
He lowdly brayd, that like was never heard,
And from his wide devouring oven° sent   mouth
A flake of fire, that flashing in his° beard,   Redcrosse Knight's
230   Him all amazd, and almost made affeard:
The scorching flame sore swinged° all his face,   singed
And through his armour all his bodie seard,°   burned
That he could not endure so cruell cace,°   situation
But thought his armes to leave, and helmet to unlace.

27

235   Not that great Champion³ of the antique world,
Whom famous Poetes verse so much doth vaunt,°   celebrate
And hath for twelve huge labours high extold,°   praised
So many furies and sharpe fits did haunt,
When him the poysoned garment did enchaunt
240   With Centaures bloud, and bloudie verses charm'd,
As did this knight twelve thousand dolours daunt,°   defy
Whom fyrie steele now burnt, that earst° him arm'd,   recently
That erst° him goodly arm'd, now most of all him harm'd.   at first

28

Faint, wearie, sore, emboyled, grieved, brent
245   With heat, toyle, wounds, armes, smart, and inward fire
That never man such mischiefes did torment;
Death better were, death did he oft desire,
But death will never come, when needes require.
Whom so dismayd when that his foe° beheld,   the Dragon
250   He cast to suffer him no more respire,⁴
But gan his sturdie sterne° about to weld,   tail
And him° so strongly stroke, that to the ground him feld.   Redcrosse Knight

---

3. Hercules. After successfully completing his 12 impossible labors, the hero was plagued ("haunted") by "furies":
his wife gave him a tunic soaked in the poison blood of a
centaur. The blood was meant to work as a love charm

but instead burned Hercules' flesh, and he died in agony.
4. The Dragon, seeing how desperate the Redcrosse
Knight is, determines to kill him.

29

It fortuned (as faire it then befell)
    Behind his backe unweeting, where he stood,
255   Of auncient time there was a springing well,
    From which fast trickled forth a silver flood,
    Full of great vertues, and for med'cine good.
    Whylome, before that cursed Dragon got
    That happie land, and all with innocent blood
260   Defyld those sacred waves, it rightly hot
The well of life, ne yet his vertues had forgot.

30

For unto life the dead it could restore,
    And guilt of sinfull crimes cleane wash away,
    Those that with sicknesse were infected sore,
265   It could recure,° and aged long decay   *cure*
    Renew, as one were borne that very day.
    Both Silo this,[5] and Jordan did excell,
    And th'English Bath, and eke the german Spau,
    Ne can Cephise, nor Hebrus match this well:
270   Into the same the knight backe overthrowen, fell.

31

Now gan the golden Phoebus for to steepe
    His fierie face in billowes of the west,
    And his faint steedes watred in Ocean deepe,
    Whiles from their journall° labours they did rest,   *daily*
275   When that infernall Monster, having kest°   *cast*
    His wearie foe into that living well,
    Can high advance his broad discoloured brest,
    Above his wonted pitch, with countenance fell,
    And clapt his yron wings, as victor he did dwell.°   *remain*

32

280 Which when his pensive° Ladie saw from farre,   *worried*
    Great woe and sorrow did her soule assay,
    As weening that the sad end of the warre,
    And gan to highest God entirely pray,
    That feared chance from her to turne away;[6]
285   With folded hands and knees full lowly bent
    All night she watcht, ne once adowne would lay
    Her daintie limbs in her sad dreriment,°   *plight*
But praying still did wake, and waking did lament.

33

The morrow next gan early to appeare,
290   That Titan rose to runne his daily race;
    But early ere the morrow next gan reare

---

5. Silo, Jordan, Bath, Spau, Cephise, and Hebrus: all waters reputed to have healing powers. The blind man is cured by bathing in the waters of Siloam (John 9.7), and John baptized Christ in the River Jordan (Matthew 3.16). Cephise and Hebrus are mentioned in classical mythol-

ogy. Spenser probably wanted his readers to associate the water from "the well of life" with baptism, as in John 4.14.
6. She prayed to God to prevent the event she fears, the death of the Redcrosse Knight.

Out of the sea faire Titans deawy face,
Up rose the gentle virgin from her place,
And looked all about, if she might spy
295   Her loved knight to move his manly pace:
      For she had great doubt° of his safety,   *fear*
Since late she saw him fall before his enemy.

34

At last she saw, where he upstarted brave
Out of the well, wherein he drenched lay;
300   As Eagle fresh out of the Ocean wave,
Where he hath left his plumes all hoary gray,
And deckt himselfe with feathers youthly gay,
Like Eyas hauke[7] up mounts unto the skies,
His newly budded pineons° to assay,   *wings*
305   And marveiles at himselfe, still as he flies:
So new this new-borne knight to battell new did rise.

35

Whom when the damned feend so fresh did spy,
No wonder if he wondred at the sight,
And doubted, whether his late enemy
310   It were, or other new supplied knight.
He,° now to prove his late renewed might,   *Redcrosse Knight*
High brandishing his bright deaw-burning blade,[8]
Upon his crested scalpe so sore did smite,
That to the scull a yawning wound it made:
315   The deadly dint his dulled senses all dismaid.

36

I wote not, whether the revenging steele
Were hardned with that holy water dew,
Wherein he fell, or sharper edge did feele,
Or his baptized hands now greater grew;
320   Or other secret vertue did ensew;°   *result*
Else never could the force of fleshly arme,
Ne molten mettall in his° bloud embrew:°   *the Dragon's / soak*
For till that stownd° could never wight him harme,[9] *moment*
By subtilty, nor slight, nor might, nor mighty charme.

37

325   The cruell wound enraged him so sore,
That loud he yelded for exceeding paine;
As hundred ramping Lyons seem'd to rore,
Whom ravenous hunger did thereto constraine:°   *torment*
Then gan he tosse aloft his stretched traine,
330   And therewith scourge the buxome° aire so sore,   *yielding*
That to his force to yeelden it was faine;
Ne ought° his sturdie strokes might stand afore,° *nor anything / before*
That high trees overthrew, and rocks in peeces tore.

7. A young, untamed hawk; a symbol of victory.
8. The Redcrosse Knight's sword is like the sun, which burns up the dew.
9. Until that moment, neither human strength nor human weapons could succeed in piercing the Dragon's flesh.

38

335

The same° advauncing high above his head,   *the Dragon*
With sharpe intended sting so rude him smot,
That to the earth him drove, as stricken dead,
Ne living wight would have him life behot:°   *predicted*
The mortall sting his angry needle shot
Quite through his shield, and in his shoulder seasd,°   *pierced*

340

Where fast it stucke, ne would there out be got:
The griefe thereof him wondrous sore diseasd,
Ne might his ranckling paine with patience be appeasd.

39

But yet more mindfull of his honour deare,
Then of the grievous smart, which him did wring,°   *afflict*

345

From loathed soile he can° him lightly reare,   *did*
And strove to loose the farre infixed sting:
Which when in vaine he tryde with struggeling,
Inflam'd with wrath, his raging blade he heft,°   *lifted*
And strooke so strongly, that the knotty string

350

Of his huge taile he quite a sunder cleft,
Five joynts thereof he hewd,° and but the stump him left.   *cut*

40

Hart cannot thinke, what outrage, and what cryes,
With foule enfouldred¹ smoake and flashing fire,
The hell-bred beast threw forth unto the skyes,

355

That all was covered with darknesse dire:
Then fraught with rancour,° and engorged ire,   *malice*
He cast at once him to avenge for all,
And gathering up himselfe out of the mire,
With his uneven wings did fiercely fall

360

Upon his sunne-bright shield, and gript it fast withall.°   *as well*

41

Much was the man encombred with his hold,
In feare to lose his weapon in his paw,
Ne wist yet, how his talants to unfold;
Nor harder was from Cerberus² greedie jaw

365

To plucke a bone, then from his cruell claw
To reave° by strength the griped gage³ away: *pry*
Thrise he assayd it from his foot to draw,
And thrise in vaine to draw it did assay,
It booted nought to thinke, to robbe him of his pray.

42

370

Tho when he saw no power might prevaile,
His trustie sword he cald to his last aid,
Wherewith he fiercely did his foe assaile,
And double blowes about him stoutly laid,

---

1. Like a thundercloud filled with lightning bolts.
2. The mythological three-headed dog guarding the gates
of Hell.

3. The prize over which a battle is fought; here, the Redcrosse Knight's shield.

That glauncing fire out of the yron plaid;°   *leaped*
375   As sparckles from the Anduile° use to fly,   *anvil*
When heavie hammers on the wedge° are swaid;°   *metal / struck*
Therewith at last he forst him to unty
One of his grasping feete, him° to defend thereby.   *himself*

43

The other foot, fast fixed on his shield,
380   Whenas no strength, nor stroks mote him° constraine   *the Dragon*
To loose, ne yet the warlike pledge to yield,
He° smot thereat with all his might and maine,   *Redcrosse Knight*
That nought° so wondrous puissance might sustaine;   *nothing*
Upon the joynt the lucky steele did light,
385   And made such way, that hewd it quite in twaine;
The paw yet missed not his minisht might,°   *diminished strength*
But hong still on the shield, as it at first was pight.°   *fixed*

44

For griefe thereof, and divelish despight,
From his infernall fournace forth he threw
390   Huge flames, that dimmed all the heavens light,
Enrold in duskish smoke and brimstone⁴ blew;
As burning Aetna° from his boyling stew   *a volcano in Sicily*
Doth belch out flames, and rockes in peeces broke,
And ragged ribs of mountaines molten new,°   *newly molten*
395   Enwrapt in coleblacke clouds and filthy smoke,
That all the land with stench, and heaven with horror choke.

45

The heate whereof, and harmefull pestilence°   *destruction*
So sore him noyd,° that forst him to retire   *injured*
A little backward for his best defence,
400   To save his bodie from the scorching fire,
Which he° from hellish entrailes did expire.   *the Dragon*
It chaunst (eternall God that chaunce did guide)
As he recoyled° backward, in the mire   *shrank*
His nigh forwearied° feeble feet did slide,   *tired*
405   And downe he fell, with dread of shame sore terrifide.

46

There grew a goodly tree him faire beside,
Loaden with fruit and apples rosie red,
As they in pure vermilion had beene dide,
Whereof great vertues over all were red:
410   For happie life to all, which thereon fed,
And life eke everlasting did befall:
Great God it planted in that blessed sted°   *place*
With his almightie hand, and did it call
*The tree of life,*⁵ the crime of our first fathers fall.

4. Sulfur, which burns blue.
5. The tree of life was denied to Adam for his "crime"— his defiance of God's commandment not to eat the fruit of the tree of knowledge of good and evil. As a result, God expelled him from the Garden of Eden where the tree of life grew.

47

415 In all the world like was not to be found,
    Save in that soile, where all good things did grow,
    And freely sprong out of the fruitfull ground,
    As incorrupted Nature did them sow,
    Till that dread Dragon° all did overthrow.   *Satan, the serpent*
420 Another like faire tree eke grew thereby,[6]
    Whereof who so did eat, eftsoones did know
    Both good and ill: O mornefull memory:
That tree through one mans fault hath doen us all to dy.

48

From that first tree forth flowd, as from a well,
425 A trickling streame of Balme, most soveraine
    And daintie deare,° which on the ground still fell,   *very precious*
    And overflowed all the fertill plaine,
    As it had deawed° bene with timely raine: *sprinkled*
    Life and long health that gratious ointment gave,
430 And deadly woundes could heale, and reare againe
    The senseless corse appointed for the grave.[7]
Into that same he fell: which did from death him save.

49

For nigh thereto the ever damned beast
    Durst° not approch, for he was deadly made,[8]   *dared*
435 And all that life preserved, did detest:
    Yet he it° oft adventur'd° to invade.°   *the tree / tried / destroy*
    By this the drouping day-light gan to fade,
    And yeeld his roome° to sad succeeding night,   *place*
    Who with her sable mantle gan to shade
440 The face of earth, and wayes of living wight,
And high her burning torch set up in heaven bright.

50

When gentle Una saw the second fall
    Of her deare knight, who wearie of long fight,
    And faint through losse of bloud, mov'd not at all,
445 But lay as in a dreame of deepe delight,
    Besmeard with pretious Balme, whose vertuous might
    Did heale his wounds, and scorching heat alay,
    Againe she stricken was with sore affright,
    And for his safetie gan devoutly pray;
450 And watch the noyous° night, and wait for joyous day.   *sorrowful*

51

The joyous day gan early to appeare,
    And faire Aurora[9] from the deawy bed

6. The tree of knowledge of good and evil.
7. The balm from the tree of life heals the Redcrosse
Knight; its function follows that of the water in baptism.
Having been freed of the consequences of original sin in
baptism, the baptized are constantly open to restorations
of faith in pursuit of good works. Cf. Revelation 22.2:

"The leaves of the tree [of life] served to heale the
nations."
8. He was allied with Death, not Life.
9. The goddess of the dawn, married to Tithone or
Tithonus.

Of aged Tithone gan her selfe to reare,
With rosie cheekes, for shame as blushing red;
455   Her golden lockes for haste were loosely shed
About her eares, when Una her did marke
Clymbe to her charet, all with flowers spred,
From heaven high to chase the chearelesse darke;
With merry note her° loud salutes the mounting larke.   *Una*

52

460   Then freshly up arose the doughtie knight,
All healed of his hurts and woundes wide,
And did himselfe to battell readie dight;
Whose early foe awaiting him beside
To have devourd, so soone as day he spyde,
465   When now he saw himselfe so freshly reare,
As if late fight had nought him damnifyde,°   *harmed*
He woxe° dismayd, and gan his fate to feare;   *grew*
Nathlesse° with wonted rage he him advaunced neare.   *nonetheless*

53

And in his first encounter, gaping wide,
470   He thought attonce° him to have swallowd quight,   *at once*
And rusht upon him with outragious pride;
Who him r'encountring fierce, as hauke in flight,
Perforce° rebutted° backe. The weapon bright   *necessarily / attacked*
Taking advantage of his open jaw,
475   Ran through his mouth with so importune° might,   *violent*
That deepe emperst his darksome hollow maw,°   *mouth*
And back retyrd,° his life bloud forth with all did draw.   *retracted*

54

So downe he fell, and forth his life did breath,[1]
That vanisht into smoke and cloudes swift;
480   So downe he fell, that th'earth him underneath
Did grone, as feeble so great load to lift;
So downe he fell, as an huge rockie clift,
Whose false foundation waves have washt away,
With dreadfull poyse° is from the mayneland rift,   *force*
485   And rolling downe, great Neptune doth dismay;
So downe he fell, and like an heaped mountaine lay.

55

The knight himselfe even trembled at his fall,
So huge and horrible a masse it seem'd;
And his deare Ladie, that beheld it all,
490   Durst not approch for dread, which she misdeem'd,
But yet at last, when as the direfull feend
She saw not stirre, off-shaking vaine affright,°   *empty fear*
She nigher drew, and saw that joyous end:
Then God she praysd, and thankt her faithfull knight,
495   That had atchiev'd so great a conquest by his might.

1. The blood that flows from the Dragon takes his life with it.

Canto 12

Faire Una to the Redcrosse knight
  betrouthed is with joy:
Though false Duessa it to barre°   prevent
  her false sleights doe imploy.

1

Behold I see the haven° nigh at hand,   harbor
  To which I meane my wearie course to bend;
  Vere° the maine shete, and beare up with° the land,   loosen / steer toward
  The which afore is fairely to be kend,°   recognized
5 And seemeth safe from stormes, that may offend;
  There this faire virgin wearie of her way
  Must landed be, now at her journeyes end:
  There eke my feeble barke° a while may stay,   ship
Till merry wind and weather call her thence away.

2

10 Scarsely had Phoebus in the glooming° East   glowing
  Yet harnessed his firie-footed teeme,
  Ne reard above the earth his flaming creast,
  When the last deadly smoke aloft did steeme,
  That signe of last outbreathed life did seeme
15 Unto the watchman on the castle wall;
  Who thereby dead that balefull Beast did deeme,
  And to his Lord and Ladie lowd gan call,
To tell, how he had seene the Dragons fatall fall.

3

Uprose with hastie joy, and feeble speed
20 That aged Sire,° the Lord of all that land,   Una's father
  And looked forth, to weet, if true indeede
  Those tydings were, as he did understand,
  Which whenas true by tryall° he out fond,   investigation
  He bad to open wyde his brazen gate,
25 Which long time had bene shut, and out of hond°   immediately
  Proclaymed joy and peace through all his state;
For dead now was their foe, which them forrayed° late.°   plundered / lately

4

Then gan triumphant Trompets sound on hie,
  That sent to heaven the ecchoed report
30 Of their new joy, and happie victorie
  Gainst him, that had them long opprest with tort,°   wrong
  And fast imprisoned in sieged fort.
  Then all the people, as in solemne feast,
  To him assembled with one full consort,°   in unison
35 Rejoycing at the fall of that great beast,
From whose eternall bondage now they were releast.

5

Forth came that auncient Lord and aged Queene,
  Arayd° in antique robes downe to the ground,   dressed

And sad habiliments right well beseene;[1]
40 A noble crew° about them waited round   *crowd*
Of sage and sober Peres, all gravely gownd;
Whom farre before did march a goodly band
Of tall young men, all hable° armes to sownd,°   *able / wield*
But now they laurell braunches bore in hand;
45 Glad signe of victorie and peace in all their land.

6

Unto that doughtie° Conquerour they came,   *worthy*
And him before themselves prostrating low,
Their Lord and Patrone loud did him proclame,
And at his feet their laurell boughes did throw.
50 Soone after them all dauncing on a row
The comely virgins came, with girlands dight,°   *prepared*
As fresh as flowres in medow greene do grow,
When morning deaw upon their leaves doth light:°   *land*
And in their hands sweet Timbrels° all upheld on hight. *tambourines*

7

55 And them before, the fry° of children young   *group*
Their wanton sports and childish mirth did play,
And to the Maydens sounding tymbrels sung
In well attuned notes, a joyous lay,
And made delightfull musicke all the way,
60 Untill they came, where that faire virgin stood;
As faire Diana in fresh sommers day
Beholds her Nymphes, enraung'd° in shadie wood,   *spread out*
Some wrestle, some do run, some bathe in christall flood.° *clear waters*

8

So she beheld those maydens meriment
65 With chearefull vew; who when to her they came,
Themselves to ground with gratious humblesse bent,
And her ador'd by honorable name,
Lifting to heaven her everlasting fame:
Then on her head they set a girland greene,
70 And crowned her twixt earnest and twixt game;[2]
Who in her selfe-resemblance well beseene,[3]
Did seeme such, as she was, a goodly maiden Queene.

9

And after, all the raskall many° ran,   *playful crowd*
Heaped together in rude rablement,°   *confusion*
75 To see the face of that victorious man:°   *Redcrosse Knight*
Whom all admired, as from heaven sent,
And gazd upon with gaping wonderment.
But when they came, where that dead Dragon lay,
Stretcht on the ground in monstrous large extent,

---

1. Their somber clothes were appropriate.
2. Half seriously, half playfully.
3. Una appears appropriately like herself (unlike Duessa, for instance, who appeared to be something other than what she was).

80 The sight with idle feare did them dismay,
    Ne durst° approch him nigh, to touch, or once assay.⁴   *nor dared*

                          10
    Some feard, and fled; some feard and well it faynd;°   *hid it well*
       One that would wiser seeme, then° all the rest,   *than*
       Warnd him not touch, for yet perhaps remaynd
85   Some lingring life within his hollow brest,
       Or in his wombe might lurke some hidden nest
       Of many Dragonets, his fruitfull seed;
       Another said, that in his eyes did rest
       Yet sparckling fire, and bad thereof take heed;°   *care*
90 Another said, he saw him move his eyes indeed.

                          11
    One mother, when as her foolehardie chyld
       Did come too neare, and with his talants° play,   *claws*
       Halfe dead through feare, her litle babe revyld,
       And to her gossips gan in counsell say;
95   How can I tell, but that his talants may
       Yet scratch my sonne, or rend his tender hand?
       So diversly themselves in vaine they fray;°   *frighten*
       Whiles some more bold, to measure him nigh stand,
    To prove how many acres he did spread of land.

                          12
100 Thus flocked all the folke him round about,
       The whiles that hoarie° king, with all his traine,   *aged*
       Being arrived, where that champion stout
       After his foes defeasance° did remaine,   *defeat*
       Him goodly greetes, and faire does entertaine,
105   With princely gifts of yvorie and gold,
       And thousand thankes him yeelds° for all his paine.   *gives*
       Then when his daughter deare he does behold,
    Her dearely doth imbrace, and kisseth manifold.°   *many times*

                          13
    And after to his Pallace he them brings,
110   With shaumes,° and trompets, and with Clarions° sweet;   *oboes / trumpets*
       And all the way the joyous people sings,
       And with their garments strowes the paved street:
       Whence mounting up, they find purveyance meet°   *suitable refreshment*
       Of all, that royall Princes court became,
115   And all the floore was underneath their feet
       Bespred with costly scarlot° of great name,   *cloth*
    On which they lowly sit, and fitting purpose frame.°   *converse nicely*

                          14
    What needs me tell their feast and goodly guize,°   *behavior*
       In which was nothing riotous nor vaine?
120   What needs of daintie dishes to devize,°   *describe*

---

4. They did not dare to approach the dragon, to touch it, or even to try to touch it.

Of comely services, or courtly trayne?
My narrow leaves cannot in them containe
The large discourse of royall Princes state.
Yet was their manner then but bare° and plaine: *simple*
125   For th'antique world excesse and pride did hate;
Such proud luxurious pompe is swollen up but late.°   *only recently*

15

Then when with meates and drinkes of every kinde
Their fervent appetites they quenched had,
That auncient Lord gan fit occasion finde,
130   Of straunge adventures, and of perils sad,
Which in his travell him befallen had,
For to demaund of his renowmed° guest: *renowned*
Who then with utt'rance° grave, and count'nance sad,   *expression*
From point to point, as is before exprest,
135   Discourst° his voyage long, according his request.   *related*

16

Great pleasure mixt with pittifull regard,°   *compassion*
That godly King and Queene did passionate,°   *empathize*
Whiles they his pittifull adventures heard,
That oft they did lament his lucklesse state,
140   And often blame the too importune° fate,   *cruel*
That heapd on him so many wrathfull wreakes:°   *injuries*
For never gentle knight, as he of late,°   *recently*
So tossed was in fortunes cruell freakes;°   *accidents*
And all the while salt teares bedeawd° the hearers cheaks. *wetted*

17

145   Then said that royall Pere in sober wise;
Deare Sonne, great beene the evils, which ye bore
From first to last in your late enterprise,
That I note, whether prayse, or pitty more:
For never living man, I weene, so sore
150   In sea of deadly daungers was distrest;
But since now safe ye seised° have the shore,   *reached*
And well arrived are, (high God be blest)
Let us devize° of ease and everlasting rest.   *speak*

18

Ah dearest Lord, said then that doughty° knight,   *worthy*
155   Of ease or rest I may not yet devize;
For by the faith, which I to armes have plight,
I bounden am streight after this emprize,°   *enterprise*
As that your daughter can ye well advize,
Backe to returne to that great Faerie Queene,
160   And her to serve six yeares in warlike wize,°   *manner*
Gainst that proud Paynim king, that workes her teene:°   *sorrow*
Therefore I ought crave pardon, till I there have beene.

19

Unhappie falles that hard necessitie,
(Quoth he) the troubler of my happie peace,

165
And vowed foe of my felicitie;
Ne I against the same can justly preace:°   *argue*
But since that band° ye cannot now release,   *bond*
Nor doen undo; (for vowes may not be vaine)
Soone as the terme of those six yeares shall cease,
170
Ye then shall hither backe returne againe,
The marriage to accomplish vowd° betwixt you twain.   *promised*

20

Which for my part I covet° to performe,   *desire*
In sort as through the world I did proclame,
That who so kild that monster most deforme,
175
And him in hardy battaile overcame,
Should have mine onely daughter to his Dame,
And of my kingdome heire apparaunt bee:
Therefore since now to thee perteines the same,
By dew desert of noble chevalree,
180
Both daughter and eke kingdome, lo I yield to thee.

21

Then forth he called that his daughter faire,
The fairest Un' his onely daughter deare,
His onely daughter, and his onely heyre;
Who forth proceeding with sad sober cheare,
185
As bright as doth the morning starre appeare
Out of the East, with flaming lockes bedight,
To tell that dawning day is drawing neare,
And to the world does bring long wished light;
So faire and fresh that Lady shewd her selfe in sight.

22

190
So faire and fresh, as freshest flowre in May;
For she had layd her mournefull stole° aside,   *dark cloak*
And widow-like sad wimple throwne away,
Wherewith her heavenly beautie she did hide,
Whiles on her wearie journey she did ride;
195
And on her now a garment she did weare,
All lilly white, withoutten° spot, or pride,   *without a*
That seemd like silke and silver woven neare,
But neither silke nor silver therein did appeare.

23

The blazing brightnesse of her beauties beame,
200
And glorious light of her sunshyny face
To tell, were as to strive against the streame.
My ragged rimes° are all too rude and bace,   *rhymes*
Her heavenly lineaments° for to enchace.°   *features / display*
Ne wonder; for her owne deare loved knight,
205
All were she dayly with himselfe in place,°   *by his side*
Did wonder much at her celestiall sight:
Oft had he seene her faire, but never so faire dight.

24

So fairely dight, when she in presence came,
She to her Sire made humble reverence,

210   And bowed low, that her right well became,
       And added grace unto her excellence:
       Who with great wisedome, and grave eloquence
       Thus gan to say. But eare he thus had said,
       With flying speede, and seeming great pretence,°   *purpose*
215   Came running in, much like a man dismaid,°   *overwhelmed*
       A Messenger with letters, which his message said.

                              25
       All in the open hall amazed stood,
         At suddeinnesse of that unwarie° sight,   *unexpected*
         And wondred at his breathlesse hastie mood.
220   But he for nought would stay his passage right,°   *stop*
         Till fast before° the king he did alight;°   *in front of / arrive*
         Where falling flat, great humblesse he did make,
         And kist the ground, whereon his foot was pight;°   *placed*
         Then to his hands that writ° he did betake,°   *message / deliver*
225   Which he disclosing,° red thus, as the paper spake.°   *unfolding / said*

                              26
       To thee, most mighty king of Eden faire,
         Her greeting sends in these sad lines addrest,
         The wofull daughter, and forsaken heire
         Of that great Emperour of all the West;
230   And bids thee be advized for the best,
         Ere thou thy daughter linck° in holy band   *join*
         Of wedlocke to that new unknowen guest:
         For he already plighted° his right hand   *promised*
       Unto another love, and to another land.

                              27
235   To me sad mayd, or rather widow sad,
         He was affiaunced° long time before,   *engaged*
         And sacred pledges he both gave, and had,
         False erraunt° knight, infamous, and forswore:°   *erring / lying*
         Witnesse the burning Altars, which° he swore,⁵   *by which*
240   And guiltie heavens of his bold perjury,°   *lie*
         Which though he hath polluted oft of yore,
         Yet I to them for judgement just do fly,
       And them conjure° t'avenge this shamefull injury.⁶   *implore*

                              28
       Therefore since mine he is, or free or bond,
245   Or false or trew, or living or else dead,
         Withhold, O soveraine Prince, your hasty hond
         From knitting league with him, I you aread;°   *advise*
         Ne weene my right with strength adowne to tread,⁷
         Through weakenesse of my widowhed,° or woe: *widowhood*
250   For truth is strong, her rightfull cause to plead,

5. Referring to a pagan marriage ritual in which sacrifices
are burned on an altar to confirm the marriage vows.
6. Although the Redcrosse Knight has polluted the heav-

ens with his lies, the author of the message nonetheless
looks to them for judgment against him.
7. Do not try to overcome my rights by force.

And shall find friends, if need requireth soe,
So bids thee well to fare,° Thy neither friend, nor foe.   *farewell*

29

When he° these bitter byting words had red,°   *the king / heard*
   The tydings° straunge did him abashed make,   *news*
255   That still he sate long time astonished
   As in great muse,° ne word to creature spake.   *astonishment*
   At last his solemne silence thus he brake,
   With doubtfull eyes fast fixed on his guest;
   Redoubted° knight, that for mine onely sake   *formidable*
260   Thy life and honour late adventurest,
Let nought be hid from me, that ought to be exprest.

30

What meane these bloudy vowes, and idle threats,
   Throwne out from womanish impatient mind?
   What heavens? what altars? what enraged heates°   *rantings*
265   Here heaped up with termes of love unkind,
   My conscience cleare with guilty bands would bind?
   High God be witnesse, that I guiltlesse ame.
   But if your selfe, Sir knight, ye faultie° find,   *guilty*
   Or wrapped be in loves of former Dame,
270   With crime° do not it cover, but disclose the same.   *lies*

31

To whom the Redcrosse knight this answere sent,
   My Lord, my King, be nought hereat dismayd,
   Till well ye wote by grave intendiment,°   *careful consideration*
   What woman, and wherefore° doth me upbrayd   *why*
275   With breach of love, and loyalty betrayd.
   It was in my mishaps, as hitherward°   *on my way here*
   I lately traveild, that unwares I strayd
   Out of my way, through perils straunge and hard;
That day should faile me, ere I had them all declard.

32

280 There did I find, or rather I was found
   Of this false woman, that Fidessa hight,
   Fidessa hight the falsest Dame on ground,
   Most false Duessa, royall richly dight,
   That easie° was t'invegle° weaker sight: *eager / blind*
285   Who by her wicked arts, and wylie skill,
   Too false and strong for earthly skill or might,
   Unwares° me wrought unto her wicked will,   *unknowingly*
And to my foe betrayd, when least I feared ill.

33

Then stepped forth the goodly royall Mayd,
290   And on the ground her selfe prostrating° low,   *bowing*
   With sober countenaunce thus to him sayd;
   O pardon me, my soveraigne Lord, to show
   The secret treasons, which of late° I know   *recently*

To have bene wroght° by that false sorceresse.   *committed*
295 She onely she it is, that earst did throw
       This gentle knight into so great distresse,
That death him did awaite in dayly wretchednesse.

34

And now it seemes, that she suborned° hath   *bribed*
       This craftie messenger with letters vaine,°   *false*
300 To worke new woe and improvided° scath,   *unforeseen*
       By breaking of the band betwixt us twaine;
       Wherein she used hath the practicke paine°   *crafty labor*
       Of this false footman, clokt° with simplenesse,   *cloaked*
       Whom if ye please for° to discover plaine,   *wish*
305 Ye shall him Archimago find, I ghesse,
The falsest man alive; who° tries shall find no lesse.   *whoever*

35

The king was greatly moved at her speach,
       And all with suddein indignation fraight,°   *filled*
       Bad on that Messenger rude hands to reach.
310 Eftsoones the Gard, which on his state did wait,
       Attacht° that faitor false, and bound him strait: *seized*
       Who seeming sorely chauffed° at his band,   *annoyed*
       As chained Beare, whom cruell dogs do bait,
       With idle force did faine° them to withstand,   *attempt*
315 And often semblaunce made° to scape out of their hand.[8] *pretended*

36

But they him layd full low in dungeon deepe,
       And bound him hand and foote with yron chains.
       And with continuall watch did warely° keepe;   *carefully*
       Who then would thinke, that by his subtile trains
320 He could escape fowle death or deadly paines?
       Thus when that Princes wrath was pacifide,
       He gan renew the late forbidden banes,°   *banns*
       And to the knight his daughter deare he tyde,
With sacred rites and vowes for ever to abyde.[9]

37

325 His owne two hands the holy knots did knit,
       That none but death for ever can devide;
       His owne two hands, for such a turne most fit,
       The housling° fire[1] did kindle and provide,   *domestic*
       And holy water thereon sprinckled wide;
330 At which the bushy Teade° a groome did light,   *torch*
       And sacred lampe in secret chamber hide,
       Where it should not be quenched day nor night,
For feare of evill fates, but burnen ever bright.

---

8. Because Archimago himself is false, his efforts to escape are also false.
9. The King recommences the announcement of marriage that had been recently forbidden by Duessa's false charges against the Redcrosse Knight.
1. Originally Roman marriage rituals, the fire and water used by the King here also suggest baptism and the sanctification of married love.

38

335
Then gan they sprinckle all the posts with wine,[2]
And made great feast to solemnize that day;
They all perfumde with frankincense divine,
And precious odours fetcht from far away,
That all the house did sweat with great aray:°   ceremony
And all the while sweete Musicke did apply
340
Her curious skill, the warbling notes to play,
To drive away the dull Melancholy;
The whiles one sung a song of love and jollity.

39

During the which there was an heavenly noise
Heard sound through all the Pallace pleasantly,
345
Like as it had bene many an Angels voice,
Singing before th'eternall majesty,
In their trinall triplicities[3] on hye;
Yet wist no creature, whence that heavenly sweet
Proceeded, yet eachone felt secretly
350
Himselfe thereby reft of his sences meet,°   ordinary
And ravished with rare impression in his sprite.

40

Great joy was made that day of young and old,
And solemne feast proclaimd throughout the land,
That their exceeding merth° may not be told: joy
355
Suffice it heare by signes to understand[4]
The usuall joyes at knitting of loves band.
Thrise° happy man the knight himselfe did hold,   thrice
Possessed of his Ladies hart and hand,
And ever, when his eye did her behold,
360
His heart did seeme to melt in pleasures manifold.

41

Her joyous presence and sweet company
In full content he there did long enjoy,
Ne wicked envie, ne vile gealosy
His deare delights were able to annoy:
365
Yet swimming in that sea of blisfull joy,
He nought forgot, how he whilome had sworne,
In case he could that monstrous beast destroy,
Unto his Faerie Queene backe to returne:
The which he shortly did, and Una left to mourne.

42

370
Now strike your sailes ye jolly Mariners,
For we be come unto a quiet rode,°   haven
Where we must land some of our passengers,
And light this wearie vessell of her lode.

2. Roman brides sprinkled the doorposts of their new homes with wine in a ritual symbolizing joy and fertility.
3. The triple triad or the nine orders of angels. The music that they play is the music of the spheres, which humankind had been unable to hear since the Fall.
4. I.e., because the happiness of the occasion is beyond the ability of words to express, let it be sufficient to understand it through symbols.

Here she a while may make her safe abode,
375   Till she repaired have her tackles spent,°   *worn out fittings*
And wants supplide. And then againe abroad
On the long voyage whereto she is bent:
Well may she speede° and fairely finish her intent.   *continue*

from The Second Booke of the Faerie Queene
Contayning The Legend of Sir Guyon
or
Temperaunce

from *Canto 12*

Guyon, by Palmers governance,
passing through perils great,
Doth overthrow the Bowre of blisse,
and Acrasie defeat.

1

Now gins° this goodly frame of Temperance   *begins*
Fairely to rise, and her adorned hed
To pricke of highest praise forth to advance,
Formerly° grounded, and fast setteled   *previously*
5   On firme foundation of true bountihed;[1]
And this brave knight, that for that vertue fights,
Now comes to point of that same perilous sted,°   *dangerous place*
Where Pleasure dwelles in sensuall delights,
Mongst thousand dangers, and ten thousand magick mights.°   *powers*

* * *

42

370   Thence passing forth, they shortly do arrive,
Whereas the Bowre of Blisse was situate;
A place pickt out by choice of best alive,
That natures worke by art can imitate
In which what ever in this worldly state
375   Is sweet, and pleasing unto living sense,
Or that may dayntiest fantasie aggrate,°   *please*
Was poured forth with plentifull dispence,°   *abundance*
And made there to abound with lavish affluence.°   *extravagance*

43

Goodly it was enclosed round about,
380   Aswell their entred° guestes to keepe within,   *entered*
As those unruly beasts to hold without;°   *keep out*
Yet was the fence thereof but weake and thin;
Nought° feard their force, that fortilage° to win,   *nothing / fortress*
But wisedomes powre, and temperaunces might,
385   By which the mightiest things efforced bin:[2]

---

1. The virtue of temperance begins to be praised, now that it is established on goodness ("bountihed").
2. Acrasia did not fear beasts but only the power of wisdom and temperance, which can control the mightiest things.

And eke the gate was wrought of substaunce light,
Rather for pleasure, then for battery° or fight.   *physical assault*

44

Yt framed was of precious yvory,
That seemd a worke of admirable wit;°   *skill*
390   And therein all the famous history
Of Jason and Medaea³ was ywrit;
Her mighty charmes, her furious loving fit,
His goodly conquest of the golden fleece,
His falsed° faith, and love too lightly flit,°   *violated / fickle*
395   The wondred Argo, which in venturous peece°   *adventurous ship*
First through the Euxine seas bore all the flowr of Greece.

45

Ye might have seene the frothy billowes fry
Under the ship,° as thorough them she went,   *the Argo*
That seemd the waves were into yvory,
400   Or yvory into the waves were sent;
And other where° the snowy substaunce sprent°   *elsewhere / sprinkled*
With vermell, like the boyes bloud therein shed,⁴
A piteous spectacle did represent,
And otherwhiles° with gold besprinkeled;   *elsewhere*
405   Yt seemd th'enchaunted flame, which did Creüsa⁵ wed.

46

All this, and more might in that goodly gate
Be red;° that ever open stood to all,   *seen*
Which thither came: but in the Porch there sate
A comely personage of stature tall,
410   And semblaunce pleasing, more then naturall,
That travellers to him seemd to entize;°   *entice*
His looser garment to the ground did fall,
And flew about his heeles in wanton wize,°   *manner*
Not fit for speedy pace, or manly exercize.

47

415   They in that place him Genius⁶ did call:
Not that celestiall powre, to whom the care
Of life, and generation of all
That lives, pertaines in charge particulare,°   *as a special charge*
Who wondrous things concerning our welfare,
420   And straunge phantomes° doth let us oft forsee,   *images*
And oft of secret ill bids us beware:

---

3. Jason sailed in the Argo, the first oceangoing ship, to capture the golden fleece, a Greek treasure, which belonged to King Aeetes of Colchis. The king's daughter, Medea, assisted Jason with her magical powers. When Jason abandoned her, betraying the fidelity he had promised her, Medea took revenge. Medea was said to have inherited her magical powers from Circe, her aunt.
4. A reference to Medea's murder of her brother, whose body she threw into the sea to distract her father as she and Jason fled from Colchis with the golden fleece.
5. The woman for whom Jason abandoned Medea. In

revenge, Medea sent Creüsa an enchanted dress, which burned her to death with its own fire; hence Creüsa could be said to have wed a flame.
6. Not what he is traditionally, that is, the spirit, associated with heavenly power, who has a specific duty to care for each individual man or woman. Identified as a "self" or ego, genius also has the force of a moral consciousness. Although we do not see this genius, each of us has a sense of it. Spenser calls that genius Agdistes; however, the figure at Acrasia's gate is his diabolical double.

That is our Selfe, whom though we do not see,
Yet each doth in him selfe it well perceive to bee.

48

Therefore a God him sage Antiquity
425   Did wisely make, and good Agdistes call:
    But this same was to that quite contrary,
    The foe of life, that good envyes to all,
    That secretly doth us procure° to fall,   *cause*
    Through guilefull semblaunts,° which he makes us see.   *deceitful images*
430 He of this Gardin had the governall,°   *management*
    And Pleasures porter was devizd° to bee,   *appointed*
Holding a staffe in hand for more formalitee.

49

With diverse flowres he daintily was deekt,
    And strowed° round about, and by his side   *strewn*
435   A mighty Mazer° bowle of wine was set,   *maple*
    As if it had to him bene sacrifide;[7]
    Wherewith all new-come guests he gratifide:
    So did he eke Sir Guyon passing by:
    But he his idle curtesie defide,
440   And overthrew his bowle disdainfully;
And broke his staffe, with which he charmed semblants sly.

50

Thus being entred, they behold around
    A large and spacious plaine, on every side
    Strowed with pleasauns,° whose faire grassy ground   *small parks*
445   Mantled° with greene, and goodly beautifide   *cloaked*
    With all the ornaments of Floraes° pride,   *goddess of flowers*
    Wherewith her mother Art, as halfe in scorne
    Of niggard Nature, like a pompous bride
    Did decke her, and too lavishly adorne,[8]
450 When forth from virgin bowre she comes in th'early morne.

51

There to the Heavens alwayes Joviall,°   *joyful*
    Lookt on them lovely, still° in stedfast° state,   *always / constant*
    Ne suffred° storme nor frost on them to fall,   *allowed*
    Their tender buds or leaves to violate,
455   Nor scorching heat, nor cold intemperate
    T'afflict the creatures, which therein did dwell,
    But the milde aire with season moderate
    Gently attempred,° and disposd so well,   *temperate*
That still it breathed forth sweet spirit and holesome smell.

52

460 More sweet and holesome, then the pleasaunt hill
    Of Rhodope, on which the Nimphe, that bore

---

7. As if it were a sacrificial offering.
8. Flora's mother, Art, scorns the simplicity of Nature

and dresses Flora in showy clothing.

A gyaunt babe, her selfe for griefe did kill;[9]
Or the Thessalian Tempe, where of yore
Faire Daphne Phoebus hart with love did gore;

465   Or Ida, where the Gods lov'd to repaire,°   *retire*
When ever they their heavenly bowres forlore;
Or sweet Parnasse, the haunt of Muses faire;
Or Eden selfe, if ought° with Eden mote compaire.   *anything*

53

Much wondred Guyon at the faire aspect°   *appearance*
470   Of that sweet place, yet suffred° no delight   *allowed*
To sincke into his sence, nor mind affect,
But passed forth, and lookt still forward right,°   *straight ahead*
Bridling his will, and maistering his might:
Till that he came unto another gate;
475   No gate, but like one, being goodly dight°   *decorated*
With boughes and braunches, which did broad dilate°   *extend*
Their clasping armes, in wanton wreathings intricate.

54

So fashioned a Porch[1] with rare device,°   *design*
Archt over head with an embracing vine,
480   Whose bounches° hanging downe, seemed to entice   *bunches*
All passers by, to tast their lushious wine,
And did themselves into their hands incline,°   *hang*
As freely offering to be gathered:
Some deepe empurpled as the Hyacint,[2]
485   Some as the Rubine,° laughing sweetly red,   *ruby*
Some like faire Emeraudes,° not yet well ripened.   *emeralds*

55

And them° amongst, some were of burnisht gold,   *the grapes*
So made by art, to beautifie the rest,
Which did themselves emongst the leaves enfold,
490   As lurking from the vew of covetous° guest,   *greedy*
That the weake bowes,° with so rich load opprest,   *boughs*
Did bow adowne, as over-burdened.
Under that Porch a comely dame did rest,
Clad in faire weedes, but fowle disordered,°   *sloppy*
495   And garments loose, that seemd unmeet for womanhed.[3]

56

In her left hand a Cup of gold she held,
And with her right the riper fruit did reach,

---

9. Spenser compares the Bower of Bliss with five Greek landscapes, all of which (except for Parnassus) were also the scenes of monstrosity and tragedy. Rhodope was the hill where Orpheus sang and was torn to pieces by the Maenads; it was also the name of a nymph who gave birth to a giant child whose father was Neptune. Daphne, the first love of Phoebus or Apollo, could be said to have wounded his heart by her disdain of him; Mount Ida was the site of the beauty contest between Hera (Juno), Aphrodite (Venus), and Athena (Minerva) that led to the Trojan War.
1. The branches created a sort of porch.
2. Hyacinth or jacinth, a blue stone.
3. Unsuitable for womanhood.

Whose sappy liquor, that with fulnesse sweld,
Into her cup she scruzd,° with daintie breach°   *squeezed / crushing*
500   Of her fine fingers, without fowle empeach,[4]
That so faire wine-presse made the wine more sweet:
Thereof she usd to give to drinke to each,
Whom passing by she happened to meet:
It was her guise, all Straungers goodly so to greet.

57

505   So she to Guyon offred it to tast;
Who taking it out of her tender hond,
The cup to ground did violently cast,
That all in peeces it was broken fond,
And with the liquor stained all the lond:
510   Whereat Excesse[5] exceedingly was wroth,
Yet no'te° the same amend, ne yet withstond,°   *could not / prevent*
But suffered him to passe, all were she loth;°   *reluctant*
Who nought regarding her displeasure forward goth.

58

There the most daintie Paradise on ground,
515   It selfe doth offer to his sober eye,
In which all pleasures plenteously abound,
And none does others happinesse envye:
The painted flowres, the trees upshooting hye,
The dales for shade, the hilles for breathing space,
520   The trembling groves, the Christall running by;
And that, which all faire workes doth most aggrace,°   *add grace to*
The art, which all that wrought, appeared in no place.[6]

59

One would have thought, (so cunningly, the rude,
And scorned parts were mingled with the fine,)
525   That nature had for wantonesse ensude°   *imitated*
Art, and that Art at nature did repine;°   *fret*
So striving each th'other to undermine,
Each did the others worke more beautifie;
So diff'ring both in willes, agreed in fine:
530   So all agreed through sweete diversitie,°   *disagreement*
This Gardin to adorne with all varietie.

60

And in the midst of all, a fountaine stood,
Of richest substaunce, that on earth might bee,
So pure and shiny, that the silver flood
535   Through every channell running one might see;
Most goodly it with curious imageree
Was over-wrought, and shapes of naked boyes,
Of which some seemd with lively jollitee,

4. She used her own fingers to squeeze the grapes without
soiling her fingers or ruining the grapes.
5. The lady at the Porch.

6. The scene appears natural, and the art that created it is
invisible.

To fly about, playing their wanton toyes,
540   Whilest others did them selves embay° in liquid joyes.   *bathe*

61

And over all, of purest gold was spred,
   A trayle° of yvie in his native hew: *vine*
   For the rich mettall was so coloured,
   That wight, who did not well avis'd° it vew,   *carefully*
545   Would surely deeme it to be yvie trew:
   Low his° lascivious armes adown did creepe,   *the ivy's*
   That themselves dipping in the silver dew,
   Their fleecy flowres they tenderly did steepe,
Which drops of Christall seemd for wantones to weepe.

62

550   Infinit streames continually did well
   Out of this fountaine, sweet and faire to see,
   The which into an ample laver° fell,   *basin*
   And shortly grew to so great quantitie,
   That like a little lake it seemd to bee;
555   Whose depth exceeded not three cubits° hight,   *about four feet*
   That through the waves one might the bottom see,
   All pav'd beneath with Jaspar° shining bright,   *green stone*
That seemd the fountaine in that sea did sayle upright.[7]

63

And all the margent° round about was set,   *edge*
560   With shady Laurell trees, thence to defend
   The sunny beames, which on the billowes bet,°   *beat*
   And those which therein bathed, mote offend.[8]
   As Guyon hapned by the same to wend,
   Two naked Damzelles he therein espyde,
565   Which therein bathing, seemed to contend,
   And wrestle wantonly,° ne car'd to hyde,   *lewdly*
Their dainty parts from vew of any, which them eyde.

64

Sometimes the one would lift the other quight
   Above the waters, and then downe againe
570   Her plong,° as over maistered by might,   *plunge*
   Where both awhile would covered remaine,
   And each the other from to rise restraine;
   The whiles their snowy limbes, as through a vele,
   So through the Christall waves appeared plaine:
575   Then suddeinly both would themselves unhele,°   *release*
And th'amarous sweet spoiles to greedy eyes revele.

65

As that faire Starre, the messenger of morne,
   His deawy face out of the sea doth reare:

---

7. The jet of water rose up in the fountain so that it   8. The beams of the sun might bother bathers.
resembled a ship sailing on the sea.

Or as the Cyprian goddesse, newly borne
580 Of th'Oceans fruitfull froth, did first appeare:[9]
Such seemed they, and so their yellow heare
Christalline humour° dropped downe apace.   *water of the fountain*
Whom such when Guyon saw, he drew him neare,
And somewhat gan relent his earnest° pace,   *brisk*
585 His stubborn brest gan secret pleasaunce° to embrace.   *pleasure*

66

The wanton Maidens him espying, stood
Gazing a while at his unwonted° guise;°   *unfamiliar / manner*
Then th'one her selfe low ducked in the flood,
Abasht, that her a straunger did a vise:°   *view*
590 But th'other rather higher did arise,
And her two lilly paps° aloft displayd,   *breasts*
And all, that might his melting hart entise
To her delights, she unto him bewrayd:°   *revealed*
The rest hid underneath, him more desirous made.

67

595 With that, the other likewise up arose,
And her faire lockes,° which formerly were bownd   *hair*
Up in one knot, she low adowne did lose:
Which flowing long and thick, her cloth'd arownd,
And th'yvorie in golden mantle gownd:°   *draped*
600 So that faire spectacle from him was reft,°   *taken*
Yet that, which reft it, no lesse faire was fownd:
So hid in lockes and waves from lookers theft,
Nought but her lovely face she for his looking left.

68

Withall she laughed, and she blusht withall,
605 That blushing to her laughter gave more grace,
And laughter to her blushing, as did fall:
Now when they spide the knight to slacke his pace,
Them to behold, and in his sparkling face
The secret signes of kindled lust appeare,
610 Their wanton meriments they did encreace,
And to him beckned, to approch more neare,
And shewd him many sights, that courage cold could reare.[1]

69

On which when gazing him the Palmer saw,
He much rebukt those wandring eyes of his,
615 And counseld well, him forward thence did draw.°   *move*
Now are they come nigh to the Bowre of blis
Of° her° fond favorites so nam'd amis:°   *by / Acrasia's / wrongly*
When thus° the Palmer; Now Sir, well avise;   *thus spoke*
For here the end of all our travell is:
620 Here wonnes° Acrasia,[2] whom we must surprise,   *dwells*
Else she will slip away, and all our drift° despise.   *purpose*

9. Both star and the Cyprian goddess signify Venus.
1. They showed Guyon many things that could arouse his
lust.
2. Ill-temper, incontinence, impotence (medieval Latin).

70

Eftsoones they heard a most melodious sound,
    Of all° that mote delight a daintie eare,   *everything*
    Such as attonce might not on living ground,
625   Save in this Paradise, be heard elswhere:
    Right hard it was, for wight, which did it heare,
    To read,° what manner musicke that mote bee: *understand*
    For all that pleasing is to living eare,
    Was there consorted° in one harmonee,   *joined*
630 Birdes, voyces, instruments, windes, waters, all agree.

71

The joyous birdes shrouded° in chearefull shade,   *hidden*
    Their notes unto the voyce° attempred° sweet,   *harmony / attuned*
    Th'Angelicall soft trembling voyces made
    To th'instruments° divine respondence° meet: *of the Bower / answer*
635   The silver sounding instruments did meet
    With the base murmure of the waters fall:
    The waters fall with difference discreet,
    Now soft, now loud, unto the wind did call:
The gentle warbling wind low answered to all.

72

640 There, whence that Musick seemed heard to bee,
    Was the faire Witch her selfe now solacing,°   *relaxing*
    With a new Lover, whom through sorceree
    And witchcraft, she from farre did thither bring:
    There she had him now layd a slombering,
645   In secret shade, after long wanton joyes:
    Whilst round about them pleasauntly did sing
    Many faire Ladies, and lascivious boyes,
That ever mixt their song with light licentious toyes.°   *pastimes*

73

And all that while, right over him she hong,
650   With her false eyes fast fixed in his sight,
    As seeking medicine, whence she was stong,
    Or greedily depasturing° delight: *grazing on*
    And oft inclining downe with kisses light,
    For feare of waking him, his lips bedewd,°   *wet*
655   And through his humid eyes did sucke his spright,
    Quite molten° into lust and pleasure lewd;   *melted*
Wherewith she sighed soft, as if his case she rewd.

74

The whiles some one did chaunt° this lovely lay;°   *sing / song*
    Ah see, who so faire thing doest faine° to see,   *wish*
660   In springing flowre the image of thy day;°   *life*
    Ah see the Virgin Rose, how sweetly shee
    Doth first peepe forth with bashfull modestee,
    That fairer seemes, the lesse ye see her may;[3]
    Lo see soone after, how more bold and free

---

3. The less you see of her, the fairer she seems.

665   Her bared bosome she doth broad° display;   *openly*
            Loe see soone after, how she fades, and falles away.

75

            So passeth,° in the passing of a day,   *passes*
              Of mortall life the leafe, the bud, the flowre,
              Ne more doth flourish after first decay,°   *withering*
670   That earst was sought to decke° both bed and bowre,   *adorn*
              Of many a Ladie, and many a Paramowre:°   *lover*
              Gather therefore the Rose, whilest yet is prime,[4]
              For soone comes age, that will her pride deflowre:
              Gather the Rose of love, whilest yet is time,
675   Whilest loving thou mayst loved be with equall crime.

76

            He ceast, and then gan all the quire° of birdes   *choir*
              Their diverse notes t'attune unto his lay,
              As in approvance° of his pleasing words.   *as if approving*
              The constant paire heard all, that he did say,
680   Yet swarved,° but kept their forward way,   *turned*
              Through many covert groves, and thickets close,
              In which they creeping did at last display°   *discover*
              That wanton Ladie, with her lover lose,
            Whose sleepie head she in her lap did soft dispose.°   *lay*

77

685   Upon a bed of Roses she was layd,
              As faint through heat, or dight to° pleasant sin,   *prepared for*
              And was arayd, or rather disarayd,
              All in a vele of silke and silver thin,
              That hid no whit her alablaster° skin,   *white*
690   But rather shewd more white, if more might bee:
              More subtile web Arachne[5] cannot spin,
              Nor the fine nets, which oft we woven see
            Of scorched° deaw, do not in th'aire more lightly flee.°   *dried / float*

78

            Her snowy brest was bare to readie spoyle°   *easy view*
695   Of hungry eies, which n'ote° therewith be fild,   *could not*
              And yet through languour° of her late sweet toyle,   *weariness*
              Few drops, more cleare then Nectar, forth distild,°   *gathered*
              That like pure Orient perles adowne it trild,°   *trickled*
              And her faire eyes sweet smyling in delight,
700   Moystened their fierie beames, with which she thrild°   *pierced*
              Fraile harts, yet quenched not; like starry light
           Which sparckling on the silent waves, does seeme more bright.

---

4. A figure common in love lyrics: the woman is compared to a flower that is to be picked just as it is about to bloom—an argument against moderation and temperance and for gratification and pleasure. Spenser concludes his version of the figure uncharacteristically, with a reminder that in the life of a temperate man or woman this kind of passion is a "crime."

5. A princess whose skill in the art of weaving surpassed that of the goddess Athena, who became jealous and transformed Arachne into a spider.

79

The young man sleeping by her, seemd to bee
　　Some goodly swayne of honorable place,
705　　That certes it great pittie was to see
　　Him his nobilitie so foule deface;°　　　　　　　　　　*horribly disgrace*
　　A sweet regard, and amiable grace,
　　Mixed with manly sternnesse did appeare
　　Yet sleeping, in his well proportiond face,
710　　And on his tender lips the downy heare°　　　　　　　　*hair*
Did now but freshly spring, and silken blossomes beare.

80

His warlike armes,° the idle instruments　　　　　　　　　*armor*
　　Of sleeping praise, were hong upon a tree,
　　And his brave shield, full of old moniments,°　　　　　*marks of battle*
715　　Was fowly ra'st,° that none the signes might see;　　　　*erased*
　　Ne for them, ne for honour cared hee,
　　Ne ought, that did to his advauncement tend,
　　But in lewd loves, and wastfull luxuree,
　　His dayes, his goods, his bodie he did spend:
720　O horrible enchantment, that him so did blend.°　　　　*blind*

81

The noble Elfe, and carefull Palmer drew
　　So nigh them, minding nought, but lustfull game,°　　　*pleasures*
　　That suddein° forth they on them rusht, and threw　　*suddenly*
　　A subtile net, which onely for the same
725　　The skilfull Palmer formally° did frame.　　　　　　　*especially*
　　So held them under fast, the whiles the rest[6]
　　Fled all away for feare of fowler° shame.　　　　　　　*fouler*
　　The faire Enchauntresse, so unwares opprest,
Tryde all her arts, and all her sleights, thence out to wrest.°　*escape*

82

730　And eke her lover strove: but all in vaine;
　　For that same net so cunningly was wound,°　　　　　　*woven*
　　That neither guile, nor force might it distraine.°　　　*destroy*
　　They tooke them both, and both them strongly bound
　　In captive bandes, which there they readie found:
735　　But her in chaines of adamant° he tyde;　　　　　　　*hard stone*
　　For nothing else might keepe her safe and sound;
　　But Verdant[7] (so he hight) he soone untyde,
And counsell sage in steed° thereof to him applyde.　　　*stead*

83

But all those pleasant bowres and Pallace brave,
740　　Guyon broke downe, with rigour° pittilesse;　　　　　*violence*
　　Ne ought their goodly workmanship might save
　　Them from the tempest of his wrathfulnesse,

---

6. The Bower's other inhabitants.　　　　　　　　　at the beginning of his maturity.
7. Greening, growing green; here, one who is young and

But that their blisse he turn'd to balefulnesse:°   *misery*
Their groves he feld, their gardins did deface,
745 Their arbers spoyle, their Cabinets° suppresse,   *bowers*
Their banket° houses burne, their buildings race,°   *banquet / raze*
And of the fairest late, now made the fowlest place.

84

Then led they her away, and eke that knight
They with them led, both sorrowfull and sad:
750 The way they came, the same retourn'd they right,
Till they arrived, where they lately had
Charm'd those wild-beasts, that rag'd with furie mad.
Which now awaking, fierce at them gan fly,
As in their mistresse reskew, whom they lad;[8]
755 But them the Palmer soone did pacify.
Then Guyon askt, what meant those beastes, which there did ly.

85

Said he, These seeming beasts are men indeed,
Whom this Enchauntresse hath transformed thus,
Whylome° her lovers, which her lusts did feed,   *formerly*
760 Now turned into figures hideous,
According to their mindes like monstruous.
Sad end (quoth he) of life intemperate,
And mournefull meed of joyes delicious:
But Palmer, if it mote thee so aggrate,°   *please*
765 Let them returned be unto their former state.

86

Streight way he with his vertuous staffe them strooke,
And streight of beasts they comely men became;
Yet being men they did unmanly looke,
And stared ghastly, some for inward shame,
770 And some for wrath, to see their captive Dame:
But one above the rest in speciall,
That had an hog beene late, hight Grille[9] by name,
Repined° greatly, and did him miscall,°   *raged / insult*
That had from hoggish forme him brought to naturall.

87

775 Said Guyon, See the mind of beastly man,
That hath so soone forgot the excellence
Of his creation, when he life began,
That now he chooseth, with vile difference,
To be a beast, and lacke intelligence.
780 To whom the Palmer thus, The donghill kind
Delights in filth and foule incontinence:

---

8. The beasts attack Guyon and the Palmer as if to rescue their mistress, whom Guyon and the Palmer are leading.
9. Hog (Greek). Here Spenser follows the *Odyssey*: Grille is one of Ulysses's men whom Circe had transformed into a hog; he later refused to be returned to his human state.

Let Grill be Grill, and have his hoggish mind,
But let us hence depart, whilest wether serves and wind.[1]

---

from **Amoretti**[1]

1

Happy ye leaves° when as those lilly hands,   *of the book*
Which hold my life in their dead doing° might,   *death-dealing*
Shall handle you and hold in loves soft bands,°   *bonds*
Lyke captives trembling at the victors sight.
5   And happy lines, on which with starry light,
Those lamping° eyes will deigne sometimes to look   *flashing*
And reade the sorrowes of my dying spright,°   *spirit*
Written with teares in harts close bleeding book.
And happy rymes bath'd in the sacred brooke,[2]
10   Of Helicon whence she derived is,
When ye behold that Angels blessed looke,
My soules long lacked foode, my heavens blis.
Leaves, lines, and rymes, seeke her to please alone,
Whom if ye please, I care for other none.

22

This holy season fit to fast and pray,[3]
Men to devotion ought to be inclynd:
Therefore, I lykewise on so holy day,
For my sweet Saynt some service fit will find.
5   Her temple fayre is built within my mind,
In which her glorious ymage placed is,
On which my thoughts doo day and night attend
Lyke sacred priests that never thinke amisse.
There I to her as th'author of my blisse,
10   Will builde an altar to appease her yre:°   *anger*
And on the same my hart will sacrifise,
Burning in flames of pure and chast desyre:
The which vouchsafe O goddesse to accept,
Amongst thy deerest relicks to be kept.

62

The weary yeare his race now having run,
The new[4] begins his compast° course anew: *encompassed*

---

1. While the weather and the wind are in our favor.
1. "Little loves," a sonnet sequence apparently written for
Elizabeth Boyle, whom Spenser married in 1594, though
he may have written some of the sonnets much earlier
and for another woman. The *Amoretti* were published in
1595 together with the *Epithalamion*, Spenser's marriage
hymn upon his wedding. Both the sonnets and the hymn,
each referring to regular moments in the passage of time,
can be read as one continuous narrative.

2. Aganippe, which rises (or is "derived") from Helicon, a
mountain that is home to the Muses, goddesses of all the
arts but known especially for their inspiration of poets.
3. The holy season is Lent; the holy day is Ash
Wednesday. The sonnet celebrates the poet's admission that his love has a spiritual dimension; complimenting his heart's desire is the worship he gives to his
lady's image in the temple of his mind.
4. The Christian new year, the Feast of the Annunciation.

With shew of morning mylde he hath begun,
Betokening peace and plenty to ensew.
5   So let us, which this chaunge of weather vew,
Chaunge eeke° our mynds and former lives amend,   *also*
The old yeares sinnes forepast° let us eschew,°   *gone by / avoid*
And fly the faults with which we did offend.
Then shall the new yeares joy forth freshly send,
10   Into the glooming° world his gladsome ray: *gloomy*
And all these stormes which now his beauty blend,°   *dim*
Shall turne to caulmes and tymely cleare away.
So likewise love cheare you your heavy spright,
And chaunge old yeares annoy° to new delight.   *grief*

68

Most glorious Lord of lyfe that on this day,[5]
Didst make thy triumph over death and sin:
And having harrowd hell, didst bring away
Captivity thence captive us to win.[6]
5   This joyous day, deare Lord, with joy begin,
And grant that we for whom thou diddest dye
Being with thy deare blood clene washt from sin,
May live for ever in felicity.
And that thy love we weighing worthily,
10   May likewise love thee for the same againe:
And for thy sake that all lyke deare° didst buy,   *at the same cost*
With love may one another entertayne.
So let us love, deare love, lyke as we ought,
Love is the lesson which the Lord us taught.

75

One day I wrote her name upon the strand,°   *beach*
But came the waves and washed it away:
Agayne I wrote it with a second hand,
But came the tyde, and made my paynes his pray.
5   Vayne man, sayd she, that doest in vaine assay,°   *attempt*
A mortall thing so to immortalize.
For I my selve shall lyke to this decay,
And eek my name bee wyped out lykewize.
Not so, (quod I) let baser things devize,°   *consent*
10   To dy in dust, but you shall live by fame:
My verse your vertues rare shall eternize,°   *make eternal*
And in the hevens wryte your glorious name:
Where whenas death shall all the world subdew,
Our love shall live, and later life renew.

5. The sonnet addresses the "dear Lord" of the Passion on Easter Day to harmonize the poet's love for his lady and his obligation to follow the lesson of Christ.
6. Christians believed that after his Resurrection, Christ descended into Hell to rescue Adam and Eve and the patriarchs and prophets of the Hebrew Bible. The event is often described as the harrowing of Hell.

Epithalamion[1]

Ye learned sisters[2] which have oftentimes
Beene to me ayding, others to adorne:
Whom ye thought worthy of your gracefull rymes,
That even the greatest did not greatly scorne
5   To heare theyr names sung in your simple layes,°   *verses*
But joyed° in theyr prayse.   *took pleasure*
And when ye list° your owne mishaps to mourne,   *wish*
Which death, or love, or fortunes wreck did rayse,
Your string could soone to sadder tenor turne,
10   And teach the woods and waters to lament
Your dolefull dreriment.°   *misfortune*
Now lay those sorrowfull complaints aside,
And having all your heads with girland° crownd,   *garlands*
Helpe me mine owne loves prayses to resound,
15   Ne let the same of any be envide:
So Orpheus[3] did for his owne bride,
So I unto my selfe alone will sing,
The woods shall to me answer and my Eccho ring.

Early before the worlds light giving lampe,
20   His golden beame upon the hils doth spred,
Having disperst the nights unchearefull dampe,
Doe ye awake and with fresh lusty hed,°   *merriment*
Go to the bowre of my beloved love,
My truest turtle dove
25   Bid her awake; for Hymen° is awake,   *god of marriage*
And long since ready forth his maske° to move,   *masque*
With his bright Tead° that flames with many a flake,   *torch*
And many a bachelor to waite on him,
In theyr fresh garments trim.
30   Bid her awake therefore and soone her dight,°   *dress*
For lo the wished day is come at last,
That shall for al the paynes and sorrowes past,
Pay to her usury of long delight,
And whylest she doth her dight,
35   Doe ye to her joy and solace sing,
That all the woods may answer and your eccho ring.

Bring with you all the Nymphes[4] that you can heare°   *here*
Both of the rivers and the forrests greene:
And of the sea that neighbours to her neare,

---

1. An epithalamion (meaning "at the bedroom" in Greek) was a poem written in celebration of a marriage. Spenser's epithalamion is unusual in that he wrote it for his own marriage to the lady of the *Amoretti*, Elizabeth Boyle; epithalamia (the plural form of the word) were usually written by a professional for a family with whom he had no personal connection. Each of the 24 sections of Spenser's poem describes a hour in the wedding day, which begins at one in the morning and continues to 12 midnight. The temporal structure of the *Epithalamion*

recalls the calendrical structure of the *Amoretti*.
2. The nine Muses, the creative spirits presiding over the arts and sciences. The "others" Spenser refers to include Queen Elizabeth, whom he celebrates in various figures throughout *The Faerie Queene*.
3. The founder of poetry, according to Greek mythology; he was often invoked as a model by lyric poets of the early modern period.
4. The spirits in nature, generally associated with trees and streams.

40   Al with gay girlands goodly wel beseene.°   *appearing*
      And let them also with them bring in hand,
      Another gay girland
      For my fayre love of lillyes and of roses,
      Bound truelove wize with a blew silke riband.
45   And let them make great store of bridale poses,°   *posies*
      And let them eeke bring store of other flowers
      To deck the bridale bowers.
      And let the ground whereas her foot shall tread,
      For feare the stones her tender foot should wrong
50   Be strewed with fragrant flowers all along,
      And diapred lyke the discolored mead.[5]
      Which done, doe at her chamber dore awayt,
      For she will waken strayt,°   *immediately*
      The whiles doe ye this song unto her sing,
55   The woods shall to you answer and your Eccho ring.

      Ye Nymphes of Mulla[6] which with carefull heed,°   *attention*
      The silver scaly trouts doe tend full well,
      And greedy pikes which use therein to feed,
      (Those trouts and pikes all others doo excell)
60   And ye likewise which keepe the rushy lake,
      Where none doo fishes take,
      Bynd up the locks° the which hang scatterd light,   *of the nymphs*
      And in his waters which your mirror make,
      Behold your faces as the christall bright,
65   That when you come whereas my love doth lie,
      No blemish she may spie.
      And eke ye lightfoot mayds which keepe the deere,
      That on the hoary mountayne use to towre,°   *soar*
      And the wylde wolves which seeke them to devoure,
70   With your steele darts doo chace from comming neer
      Be also present heere,
      To helpe to decke her and to help to sing,
      That all the woods may answer and your eccho ring.

      Wake now my love, awake; for it is time,
75   The Rosy Morne long since left Tithones[7] bed,
      All ready to her silver coche° to clyme,   *coach*
      And Phoebus[8] gins to shew his glorious hed.
      Hark how the cheerefull birds do chaunt° theyr laies°   *sing / songs*
      And carroll of loves praise.
80   The merry Larke hir mattins sings aloft,
      The thrush replyes, the Mavis° descant° playes,   *thrush / accompaniment*
      The Ouzell° shrills, the Ruddock° warbles soft,   *blackbird / redbreast*
      So goodly all agree with sweet consent,
      To this dayes merriment.

5. Variegated like the many-colored fields.   Boyle.
6. Spenser's name for the Awbeg, a river in the county of   7. The mythical lover of the goddess of the dawn.
Munster in Ireland, where he was serving as a deputy for   8. Apollo, the god of the sun.
the English crown at the time of his marriage to Elizabeth

85   Ah my deere love why doe ye sleepe thus long,
      When meeter° were that ye should now awake,   *more fitting*
      T'awayt the comming of your joyous make,°   *mate*
      And hearken to the birds lovelearned song,
      The deawy leaves among.
90   For they of joy and pleasance to you sing,
      That all the woods them answer and theyr eccho ring.

      My love is now awake out of her dreame,
      And her fayre eyes like stars that dimmed were
      With darksome cloud, now shew theyr goodly beams
95   More bright then Hesperus⁹ his head doth rere.
      Come now ye damzels, daughters of delight,
      Helpe quickly her to dight,
      But first come ye fayre houres which were begot
      In loves sweet paradice, of Day and Night,
100   Which doe the seasons of the yeare allot,
      And al that ever in this world is fayre
      Doe make and still° repayre.¹   *forever*
      And ye three handmayds of the Cyprian Queene,²
      The which doe still adorne her beauties pride,
105   Helpe to addorne my beautifullest bride.
      And as ye her array, still throw betweene
      Some graces to be seene,
      And as ye use to Venus, to her sing,
      The whiles the woods shal answer and your eccho ring.

110   Now is my love all ready forth to come,
      Let all the virgins therefore well awayt,
      And ye fresh boyes that tend upon her groome
      Prepare your selves; for he is comming strayt.
      Set all your things in seemely good aray
115   Fit for so joyfull day,
      The joyfulst day that ever sunne did see.
      Faire Sun, shew forth thy favourable ray,
      And let thy lifull° heat not fervent be   *full of life*
      For feare of burning her sunshyny face,
120   Her beauty to disgrace.
      O fayrest Phoebus,³ father of the Muse,
      If ever I did honour thee aright,
      Or sing the thing, that mote° thy mind delight,   *could*
      Doe not thy servants simple boone° refuse,   *favor*
125   But let this day let this one day be myne,
      Let all the rest be thine.
      Then I thy soverayne prayses loud wil sing,
      That all the woods shal answer and theyr eccho ring.

---

9. Venus, the evening or morning star.
1. The hours or time both create and re-create everything
in the world.
2. Venus, whose handmaids are the Graces, attributes of
courtesy and artistic expression.
3. Apollo, god of the sun and music hence the father of
the Muses and the muse of lyric poetry.

Harke how the Minstrels gin to shrill aloud
130 Their merry Musick that resounds from far,
The pipe, the tabor, and the trembling Croud,°   *violin*
That well agree withouten breach° or jar.   *discord*
But most of all the Damzels doe delite,
When they their tymbrels° smyte,   *tambourines*
135 And thereunto doe daunce and carrol sweet,
That all the sences they doe ravish quite,
The whyles the boyes run up and downe the street,
Crying aloud with strong confused noyce,
As if it were one voyce.
140 Hymen⁴ io Hymen, Hymen they do shout,
That even to the heavens theyr shouting shrill
Doth reach, and all the firmament doth fill,
To which the people standing all about,
As in approvance° doe thereto applaud   *approval*
145 And loud advaunce her laud,°   *praise*
And evermore they Hymen Hymen sing,
That al the woods them answer and theyr eccho ring.

Loe where she comes along with portly° pace,   *dignified*
Lyke Phoebe⁵ from her chamber of the East,
150 Arysing forth to run her mighty race,
Clad all in white, that seemes a virgin best.
So well it her beseemes° that ye would weene°   *befits / think*
Some angell she had beene.
Her long loose yellow locks lyke golden wyre,
155 Sprinckled with perle, and perling° flowres a tweene,° *rippling / between*
Doe lyke a golden mantle her attyre,
And being crowned with a girland greene,
Seeme lyke some mayden Queene.
Her modest eyes abashed to behold
160 So many gazers, as on her do stare,
Upon the lowly ground affixed are.
Ne dare lift up her countenance too bold,
But blush to heare her prayses sung so loud,
So farre from being proud.
165 Nathlesse° doe ye still loud her prayses sing,   *nevertheless*
That all the woods may answer and your eccho ring.

Tell me ye merchants daughters did ye see
So fayre a creature in your towne before,
So sweet, so lovely, and so mild as she,
170 Adornd with beautyes grace and vertues store,
Her goodly eyes lyke Saphyres shining bright,
Her forehead yvory white,
Her cheekes lyke apples which the sun hath rudded,°   *reddened*
Her lips lyke cherryes charming men to byte,
175 Her brest like to a bowle of creame uncrudded,°   *uncurdled*

---

4. The god of marriage who was invoked as part of the   5. Diana, goddess of the moon.
marriage ceremony.

Her paps lyke lyllies budded,
Her snowie necke lyke to a marble towre,
And all her body like a pallace fayre,
Ascending uppe with many a stately stayre,
180   To honors seat and chastities sweet bowre.
Why stand ye still ye virgins in amaze,
Upon her so to gaze,
Whiles ye forget your former lay to sing,
To which the woods did answer and your eccho ring.

185   But if ye saw that which no eyes can see,
The inward beauty of her lively spright,
Garnisht with heavenly guifts of high degree,
Much more then would ye wonder at that sight,
And stand astonisht lyke to those which red°   *looked at*
190   Medusaes[6] mazeful hed.
There dwels sweet love and constant chastity,
Unspotted fayth and comely womanhood,
Regard of honour and mild modesty,
There vertue raynes as Queene in royal throne,
195   And giveth lawes alone.
The which the base affections doe obay,
And yeeld theyr services unto her will,
Ne thought of thing uncomely° ever may   *improper*
Thereto approch to tempt her mind to ill.
200   Had ye once seene these her celestial threasures,
And unrevealed pleasures,
Then would ye wonder and her prayses sing,
That al the woods should answer and your echo ring.

Open the temple gates unto my love,
205   Open them wide that she may enter in,
And all the postes adorne as doth behove,
And all the pillours deck with girlands trim,
For to recyve° this Saynt with honour dew,   *receive*
That commeth in to you.
210   With trembling steps and humble reverence,
She commeth in, before th'almighties vew,
Of her ye virgins learne obedience,
When so ye come into those holy places,
To humble your proud faces:
215   Bring her up to th'high altar that she may,
The sacred ceremonies there partake,
The which do endlesse matrimony make,
And let the roring Organs loudly play;
The praises of the Lord in lively notes,
220   The whiles with hollow throates
The Choristers the joyous Antheme sing,
That al the woods may answere and their eccho ring.

6. One of three mythological monstrous women, the Gorgons; Medusa, whose hair consisted of snakes (hence her head is "mazeful"), turned anyone who looked at her to stone.

Behold whiles she before the altar stands
Hearing the holy priest that to her speakes
225   And blesseth her with his two happy hands,
How the red roses flush up in her cheekes,
And the pure snow with goodly vermill° stayne,   *vermilion*
Like crimsin dyde in grayne,°   *fast dyed*
That even th'Angels which continually,
230   About the sacred Altare doe remaine,
Forget their service and about her fly,
Ofte peeping in her face that seemes more fayre,
The more they on it stare.
But her sad eyes still fastened on the ground,
235   Are governed with goodly modesty,
That suffers not one looke to glaunce awry,
Which may let in a little thought unsownd.°   *suspicions*
Why blush ye love to give to me your hand,
The pledge of all our band?
240   Sing ye sweet Angels, Alleluya sing,
That all the woods may answere and your eccho ring.

Now al is done; bring home the bride againe,
Bring home the triumph of our victory,
Bring home with you the glory of her gaine,
245   With joyance bring her and with jollity.°   *merriment*
Never had man more joyfull day then this,
Whom heaven would heape with blis.
Make feast therefore now all this live long day,
This day for ever to me holy is,
250   Poure out the wine without restraint or stay,
Poure not by cups, but by the belly full,
Poure out to all that wull,°   *will*
And sprinkle all the postes and wals with wine,
That they may sweat, and drunken be withall.
255   Crowne ye God Bacchus[7] with a coronall,°   *garland*
And Hymen also crowne with wreathes of vine,
And let the Graces daunce unto the rest;
For they can doo it best:
The whiles the maydens doe theyr carroll sing,
260   To which the woods shal answer and theyr eccho ring.

Ring ye the bels, ye yong men of the towne,
And leave your wonted labors for this day:
This day is holy; doe ye write it downe,
That ye for ever it remember may.
265   This day the sunne is in his chiefest hight,
With Barnaby the bright,[8]
From whence declining daily by degrees,
He somewhat loseth of his heat and light,
When once the Crab[9] behind his back he sees.

7. The god of wine.
8. Spenser's wedding took place on St. Barnabas day, June 11, the solstice or longest day of the year in the Eliz-abethan calendar.
9. The constellation Cancer, through which the sun passes in late July.

270 But for this time it ill ordained was,
To chose the longest day in all the yeare,
And shortest night, when longest fitter weare:°   *were*
Yet never day so long, but late would passe.
Ring ye the bels, to make it weare away,
275 And bonefiers° make all day,   *bonfires*
And daunce about them, and about them sing:
That all the woods may answer, and your eccho ring.

Ah when will this long weary day have end,
And lende me leave to come unto my love?
280 How slowly do the houres theyr numbers spend?
How slowly does sad Time his feathers° move?   *wings*
Hast thee O fayrest Planet[1] to thy home
Within the Westerne fome:°   *the sea*
Thy tyred steedes long since have need of rest.
285 Long though it be, at last I see it gloome,
And the bright evening star with golden creast
Appeare out of the East.
Fayre childe of beauty, glorious lampe of love
That all the host of heaven in rankes doost lead,
290 And guydest lovers through the nightes dread,
How chearefully thou lookest from above,
And seemst to laugh atweene° thy twinkling light   *between*
As joying in the sight
Of these glad many which for joy doe sing,
295 That all the woods them answer and their echo ring.

Now ceasse ye damsels your delights forepast;
Enough is it, that all the lay was youres:
Now day is doen, and night is nighing° fast: *approaching*
Now bring the Bryde into the brydall boures.°   *chambers*
300 Now night is come, now soone her disaray,°   *undress*
And in her bed her lay;
Lay her in lillies and in violets,
And silken courteins over her display,
And odourd sheetes, and Arras[2] coverlets.
305 Behold how goodly my faire love does ly
In proud humility;
Like unto Maia,[3] when as Jove her tooke,
In Tempe, lying on the flowry gras,
Twixt sleepe and wake, after she weary was,
310 With bathing in the Acidalian brooke.
Now it is night, ye damsels may be gon,
And leave my love alone,
And leave likewise your former lay to sing:
The woods no more shal answere, nor your echo ring.

315 Now welcome night, thou night so long expected,
That long daies labour doest at last defray,°   *repay*

1. The sun, according to Ptolomaic astronomy.
2. A town in France, famous for its textiles.

3. The daughter of Atlas and the mother of Mercury by Jupiter, i.e., Jove.

And all my cares, which cruell love collected,
Hast sumd in one, and cancelled for aye:°   *ever*
Spread thy broad wing over my love and me,
320   That no man may us see,
And in thy sable mantle us enwrap,
From feare of perrill and foule horror free.
Let no false treason seeke us to entrap,
Nor any dread disquiet once annoy
325   The safety of our joy:
But let the night be calme and quietsome,
Without tempestuous storms or sad afray:
Lyke as when Jove with fayre Alcmena[4] lay,
When he begot the great Tirynthian groome:
330   Or lyke as when he with thy selfe did lie,
And begot Majesty.
And let the mayds and yongmen cease to sing:
Ne let the woods them answer, nor theyr eccho ring.

Let no lamenting cryes, nor dolefull teares,
335   Be heard all night within nor yet without:
Ne let false whispers breeding hidden feares,
Breake gentle sleepe with misconceived dout.
Let no deluding dreames, nor dreadful sights
Make sudden sad affrights;
340   Ne let housefyres, nor lightnings helpelesse harmes,
Ne let the Pouke,° nor other evill sprights,   *a house fairy*
Ne let mischivous witches with theyr charmes,
Ne let hob Goblins, names whose sence we see not,
Fray° us with things that be not.   *frighten*
345   Let not the shriech Oule,° nor the Storke be heard: *screech owl*
Nor the night Raven that still deadly yels,
Nor damned ghosts cald up with mighty spels,
Nor griesly vultures make us once affeard:
Ne let th'unpleasant Quyre° of Frogs still croking   *choir*
350   Make us to wish theyr choking.
Let none of these theyr drery accents sing;
Ne let the woods them answer, nor theyr eccho ring.

But let stil Silence trew night watches keepe,
That sacred peace may in assurance rayne,
355   And tymely sleep, when it is tyme to sleepe,
May poure his limbs forth on your pleasant playne,°   *complaint of love*
The whiles an hundred little winged loves,
Like divers° fethered doves,   *many*
Shall fly and flutter round about your bed,
360   And in the secret darke, that none reproves,
Their prety stealthes shal worke, and snares shal spread
To filch away sweet snatches of delight,
Conceald through covert night.
Ye sonnes of Venus, play your sports at will,

4. The mother of Hercules, the "Tirynthian groom," who was supposed to have taken three nights to beget.

365   For greedy pleasure, carelesse of your toyes,
       Thinks more upon her paradise of joyes,
       Then what ye do, albe it good or ill.
       All night therefore attend your merry play,
       For it will soone be day:
370   Now none doth hinder you, that say or sing,
       Ne will the woods now answer, nor your Eccho ring.

       Who is the same, which at my window peepes?
       Or whose is that faire face, that shines so bright,
       Is it not Cinthia,° she that never sleepes,   *the moon*
375   But walkes about high heaven al the night?
       O fayrest goddesse, do thou not envy
       My love with me to spy:
       For thou likewise didst love, though now unthought,
       And for a fleece of woll, which privily,
380   The Latmian shephard[5] once unto thee brought,
       His pleasures with thee wrought.
       Therefore to us be favorable now;
       And sith of wemens labours thou hast charge,
       And generation goodly dost enlarge,
385   Encline thy will t'effect our wishfull vow,
       And the chast wombe informe° with timely seed,   *implant*
       That may our comfort breed:
       Till which we cease our hopefull hap° to sing,   *condition*
       Ne let the woods us answere, nor our Eccho ring.

390   And thou great Juno,[6] which with awful might
       The lawes of wedlock still dost patronize,
       And the religion of the faith first plight
       With sacred rites hast taught to solemnize:
       And eeke for comfort often called art
395   Of women in their smart,
       Eternally bind thou this lovely band,
       And all thy blessings unto us impart.
       And thou glad Genius,[7] in whose gentle hand,
       The bridale bowre and geniall° bed remaine,   *generative*
400   Without blemish or staine,
       And the sweet pleasures of theyr loves delight
       With secret ayde doest succour and supply,
       Till they bring forth the fruitfull progeny,
       Send us the timely fruit of this same night.
405   And thou fayre Hebe,[8] and thou Hymen free,
       Grant that it may so be.
       Til which we cease your further prayse to sing,
       Ne any woods shal answer, nor your Eccho ring.

       And ye high heavens, the temple of the gods,
410   In which a thousand torches flaming bright

---

5. Endymion, beloved of Diana, goddess of the moon, chastity, and childbirth, also known as Cynthia.
6. Wife of Jupiter, goddess of marriage.

7. In Roman religion, the spirit of paternity who protected the family.
8. Handmaid to the gods, daughter of Jupiter and Juno.

Doe burne, that to us wretched earthly clods:
In dreadful darknesse lend desired light;
And all ye powers which in the same remayne,
More than we men can fayne,°   *represent*
415   Poure out your blessing on us plentiously,
And happy influence upon us raine,
That we may raise a large posterity,
Which from the earth, which they may long possesse,
With lasting happinesse,
420   Up to your haughty° pallaces may mount,   *high*
And for the guerdon° of theyr glorious merit   *reward*
May heavenly tabernacles there inherit,
Of blessed Saints for to increase the count.
So let us rest, sweet love, in hope of this,
425   And cease till then our tymely joyes to sing,
The woods no more us answer, nor our eccho ring.

Song made in lieu of many ornaments,
With which my love should duly have bene dect,°   *bedecked*
Which cutting off through hasty accidents,
430   Ye would not stay your dew time to expect,
But promist both to recompens,
Be unto her a goodly ornament,
And for short time an endlesse moniment.

Sir Philip Sidney
1554–1586

Reality is often stranger but hardly ever more perfect than fiction. As Sir Philip Sidney tells us, the poets bring forth a "golden world." Exempt from judgments about its truth or falsehood, "poetry" (by which Sidney meant fiction) should construct forms of the ideal to mitigate our suffering and move us to good action. Sidney's own work comments brilliantly on contemporary moral and political issues: his sonnet sequence *Astrophil and Stella* illustrates the lover's paradox (love may require chastity); and his *Apology for Poetry* defends poetic and dramatic art from critics who would dismiss it in favor of philosophy and history. Yet to his countrymen, Sidney's most important achievement may have been a life dedicated to a public heroism and shaped by a sense of personal honor.

History has portrayed him as a prodigy. As his friend Fulke Greville wrote, "though I knew him from a child, yet I never knew him other than a man, . . . his very play tending to enrich his mind, so that even his teachers found something in him to observe and learn above that which they had usually read or taught." Play—understood in the Renaissance manner as "serious play"—took up much of Sidney's early career. Leaving Oxford at the age of seventeen but without a degree, Sidney embarked on what in later centuries was known as the Grand Tour. He visited Europe's major cities, seeking men and women who were fashioning the political goals and aesthetic sensibilities of the age. They included the philosopher Hubert Languet, whose Protestantism was linked to a fiercely antityrannical politics; the artists Tintoretto and Paolo Veronese, whose luminous realism was to determine painterly style for more than a generation; and, finally, Henry of Navarre (later King Henry IV of France) and his wife, Margaret of Valois, whose reign would see the worst of the religious wars in Europe. Back in England by 1575, Sidney espoused a politics that challenged authority. Siding with his father, Henry Sidney, Queen Elizabeth's Lord Deputy Governor of Ireland, he argued for imposing a land tax on the Anglo-Irish nobility, citing their "unreasonable and arrogant pretensions" as a cause of civil unrest. And in 1580, seeking to protect the monarchy from foreign influences, he wrote to the Queen cautioning her against a match with Francis, Duke of Alençon and brother to the French king, Henry III. She was furious at his temerity and ordered him to the country, where he was to remain out of touch with court affairs. By 1584 she had relented, sending Sidney to the Netherlands to assess the Protestant resistance to Spanish rule. There, in 1586, fighting for the Queen's interest and the Protestant cause she championed, he died of an abscessed bullet wound in his thigh.

Sidney's first literary work was a brief pastoral masque entitled *The Lady of May*, composed in honor of the Queen in 1578. His subsequent exile from court provided him with extensive time to write. He was often at Wilton, the estate of his sister, Mary Herbert, Countess of Pembroke; it was there that he wrote the first two of his major works, in all likelihood with his sister and her circle as his first readers and critics. *The Apology for Poetry*, a work defending what Sidney called his "unelected vocation," answers attacks on art, poetry, and the theater by such censorious writers as Stephen Gosson. But its argument exceeds the limits of antitheatrical debate to embrace questions about the uses of history and the effectiveness of philosophy—a subject that bears comparison with the poetics of Aristotle and Horace. Readers have remembered most its insistence that "poetry" goes beyond nature to fashion an ideal; it works "not only to make a Cyrus, which had been but a particular excellency as nature might have done, but to bestow a Cyrus upon the world to make many Cyruses." Poetry's creatures—whether heroes, heroines, or villains—cannot misrepresent fact because they exist only in the imagination of readers and listeners: "for the poet," Sidney declared, "he nothing affirms, and therefore never lieth."

Sidney's last work, *Astrophil and Stella*, has often been understood as self-satire. Its principal character, the young Astrophil, is frustrated by the marriage of his beloved Stella to a man who is characterized as "rich," an apparent reference to Sidney's disappointment when Penelope Devereux, whom he had courted for several years, married Lord Rich. Sidney mocks the young lover's passionate complaints while at the same time transforming the courtly figure of the distant yet beloved lady to reveal a paradox: as "absent," Stella may be present to Astrophil in spirit; as "present," she can only deny him her intimate friendship. The sequence is a marvelously witty reconceptualization of the principal themes of English Petrarchanism, a style that by the 1580s had become rather trite. Addressing his Stella, Sidney's Astrophil ends a sonnet with these lines:

> And not content to be Perfection's heir
> Thyself, doest strive all minds that way to move:
> Who mark in thee what is in thee most fair.

So while thy beauty draws the heart to love,
As fast thy virtue bends that love to good:
But ah, Desire still cries, give me some food.

Conventionally Petrarchan in his depiction of the lady as a model and inspiration to a moral virtue that would seem to rule out any physical expressions of love, Sidney is at last very unconventional: he refuses to renounce "Desire" and its "food," or sexual gratification. A more imitative poet would not have so rejected Petrarch's idealistic asceticism. But just as Sidney had challenged the authority of church and state to promote better government (as he saw it), so did he exploit the process of "invention," the discovery of new meaning in old matter, to revitalize literary forms and expression.

from Astrophil and Stella[1]

1

   Loving in truth, and fain° in verse my love to show,   *wishing*
   That she (dear she) might take some pleasure of my pain:
   Pleasure might cause her read, reading might make her know,
   Knowledge might pity win, and pity grace obtain,
5 I sought fit words to paint the blackest face of woe,
   Studying inventions[2] fine, her wits to entertain:
   Oft turning others' leaves, to see if thence would flow
   Some fresh and fruitfull showers upon my sun-burned brain.
   But words came halting forth, wanting Invention's stay,°   *support*
10 Invention Nature's child, fled step-dame Study's blows,
   And others' feet still seemed but strangers in my way.
   Thus great with child to speak, and helpless in my throes,°   *agonies*
   Biting my trewand° pen, beating my self for spite,   *truant*
   Fool, said my Muse to me, look in thy heart and write.

31

   With how sad steps, O Moon, thou climb'st the skies,
   How silently, and with how wan° a face,   *pale*
   What may it be, that even in heavenly place
   That busy archer° his sharp arrows tries?   *Cupid*
5 Sure if° that long with Love acquainted eyes   *surely if those*
   Can judge of Love, thou feel'st a lover's case;
   I read it in thy looks, thy languished grace
   To me that feel the like, thy state descries.°   *reveals*
   Then ev'n of fellowship, O Moon, tell me
10 Is constant Love deemed there but want of wit?
   Are Beauties there as proud as here they be?
   Do they above love to be loved, and yet

---

1. This sonnet sequence was composed in 1582 and published in 1591.
2. "Invention" was the term early modern rhetoricians used to designate the choice of a literary subject and its development as an argument, in contrast to the forms of expression, figures of thought and speech, and imagery by which that subject was conveyed. As Sidney suggests, "invention" depended on the writer's imaginative intelligence, not on his literary education.

Those lovers scorn whom that Love doth possess?
Do they call Virtue there ungratefulness?

39

Come sleep, O sleep, the certain knot of peace,
The baiting° place of wit, the balm of woe,   *resting*
The poor man's wealth, the prisoner's release,
Th'indifferent judge between the high and low;
5   With shield of proof° shield me from out the prease°   *proven shield / throng*
Of those fierce darts, despair at me doth throw:
O make in me those civil wars to cease;
I will good tribute pay if thou do so.
Take thou of me smooth pillows, sweetest bed,
10   A chamber deaf to noise, and blind to light:
A rosy garland, and a weary head:
And if these things, as being thine by right,
Move not thy heavy grace, thou shalt in me
Livelier then elsewhere Stella's image see.

71

Who will in fairest book of Nature[3] know,
How Virtue may best lodged in beauty be,
Let him but learn of Love to read in thee
Stella, those fair lines, which true goodness show.
5   There shall he find all vices overthrow,°   *overthrown*
Not by rude force, but sweetest sovereignty
Of reason, from whose light those night-birds fly;
That inward sun in thine eyes shineth so.
And not content to be Perfection's heir
10   Thyself, doest strive all minds that way to move:
Who mark in thee what is in thee most fair.
So while thy beauty draws the heart to love,
As fast thy Virtue bends that love to good:
But ah, Desire still cries, give me some food.

106

O absent presence, Stella is not here;
False flattering hope, that with so fair a face,
Bare° me in hand, that in this orphan place,   *took*
Stella, I say my Stella, should appear.
5   What sayest thou now, where is that dainty cheer,°   *food*
Thou toldst mine eyes should help their famist° case?   *famished*

3. All of creation, in effect the second "book" of God and a supplement to the Bible. It was a philosophical commonplace that Nature was the repository of natural law, which all human beings could discover through reason, just as the Bible held divine law, which was revealed to the faithful through grace.

But thou art gone now that self felt disgrace,
Doth make me most to wish thy comfort near.[4]
But here I do store of fair ladies meet,
10   Who may with charm of conversation sweet,
Make in my heavy mold new thoughts to grow:
Sure they prevail as much with me, as he
That bad his friend but then new maimed,° to be   wounded
Merry with him, and not think of his woe.

108

When sorrow (using mine own fire's might)
Melts down his lead into my boiling breast,
Through that dark furnace to heart oppressed,
There shines a joy from thee my only light;
5   But soon as thought of thee breeds my delight,
And my young soul flutters to thee his nest,
Most rude despair my daily unbidden guest,
Clips straight my wings, straight wraps me in his night,
And makes me then bow down my head, and say,
10   Ah what doth Phoebus' gold that wretch avail,
Whom iron doors do keep from use of day?
So strangely (alas) thy works[5] in me prevail,
That in my woes for thee thou art my joy,
And in my joys for thee my only annoy.

from The Apology for Poetry

When the right virtuous Edward Wotton[1] and I were at the Emperor's court together, we gave ourselves to learn horsemanship of John Pietro Pugliano, one that with great commendation had the place of an esquire in his stable. And he, according to the fertileness of the Italian wit, did not only afford us the demonstration of his practice, but sought to enrich our minds with the contemplations therein, which he thought most precious. But with none I remember mine ears were at that time more laden, than when (either angered with slow payment, or moved with our learner-like admiration) he exercised his speech in the praise of his faculty. He said soldiers were the noblest estate of mankind, and horsemen the noblest of soldiers. He said they were the masters of war and ornaments of peace, speedy goers and strong abiders, triumphers both in camps and courts. Nay, to so unbelieved a point he proceeded as that no earthly thing bred such wonder to a prince as to be a good horseman—skill of government was but a *pedanteria* [pedantry] in comparison. Then would he add certain praises, by telling what a peerless beast the horse was, the only serviceable

4. I.e., you are gone now that that self (my own self) has felt the disgrace of rejection; this makes me wish you here.
5. I.e., "your works," what you have done and meant, affect me strangely.

1. Edward Wotton (1548–1626), half-brother of Henry Wotton who saw diplomatic service under James I. Edward Wotton and Sidney undertook a mission to the court of the Emperor Maximilian at Vienna in 1574–1575.

courtier without flattery, the beast of most beauty, faithfulness, courage, and such more, that if I had not been a piece of a logician before I came to him, I think he would have persuaded me to have wished myself a horse. But thus much at least with his no few words he drave into me, that self-love is better than any gilding to make that seem gorgeous wherein ourselves be parties. Wherein, if Pugliano's strong affection and weak arguments will not satisfy you, I will give you a nearer example of myself, who (I know not by what mischance) in these my not old years and idlest times having slipped into the title of a poet, am provoked to say something unto you in the defense of that my unelected vocation,[2] which if I handle with more good will than good reasons, bear with me, since the scholar is to be pardoned that followeth the steps of his master. And yet I must say that, as I have more just cause to make a pitiful defense of poor poetry, which from almost the highest estimation of learning is fallen to be the laughingstock of children, so have I need to bring some more available proofs: since the former is by no man barred of his deserved credit, the silly latter hath had even the names of philosophers used to the defacing of it, with great danger of civil war among the Muses.[3]

And first, truly, to all them that, professing learning, inveigh against poetry may justly be objected that they go very near to ungratefulness, to seek to deface that which, in the noblest nations and languages that are known, hath been the first light-giver to ignorance, and first nurse, whose milk by little and little enabled them to feed afterwards of tougher knowledges. And will they now play the hedgehog that, being received into the den, drive out his host? Or rather the vipers, that with their birth kill their parents?

Let learned Greece in any of his manifold sciences be able to show me one book before Musaeus, Homer, and Hesiod, all three nothing else but poets.[4] Nay, let any history be brought that can say any writers were there before them, if they were not men of the same skill, as Orpheus, Linus,[5] and some other are named, who, having been the first of that country that made pens deliverers of their knowledge to the posterity, may justly challenge to be called their fathers in learning: for not only in time they had this priority (although in itself antiquity be venerable) but went before them, as causes to draw with their charming sweetness the wild untamed wits to an admiration of knowledge. So, as Amphion[6] was said to move stones with his poetry to build Thebes, and Orpheus to be listened to by beasts—indeed stony and beastly

---

2. Sidney refers to writing poetry as his "unelected vocation" because he would have readers believe that he undertook it only after Elizabeth I had exiled him from court.

3. Mythological figures who were thought to inspire the liberal arts.

4. Musaeus was in fact a poet of the 5th century A.D., reported to be a pupil of the mythical Orpheus, the first musician. Homer was the legendary author of the *Iliad*, an epic poem telling of the seige of Troy by the army of the Greeks led by the hero, Achilles; and of the *Odyssey*, recounting the return of the hero, Odysseus, from Troy to his homeland in Ithaka. Hesiod is known as the poet of the *Theogony*, which tells the story of the gods in Greece; and of *Works and Days*, which describes the rituals and practices of the agricultural year. Both Homer and Hesiod lived in the 8th century B.C.

5. Supposed to have been the teacher of Orpheus.

6. Sidney lists historical and legendary poets to illustrate his claim that they were the founders of civilization and culture. Amphion was supposed to have moved stones by playing his music and thus to have built the walls of Troy; Livius Andronicus (c. 284–204 B.C.) was believed to have been the first Latin poet; Ennius (c. 239–169 B.C.) was traditionally regarded as the greatest of the early Latin poets. Dante, Boccaccio, and Petrarch were the first of the great Italian poets of the early Renaissance; Chaucer and Gower were the most important of the late medieval poets who wrote in English.

people—so among the Romans were Livius Andronicus and Ennius. So in the Italian language the first that made it aspire to be a treasure-house of science were the poets Dante, Boccaccio, and Petrarch. So in our English were Gower and Chaucer, after whom, encouraged and delighted with their excellent fore-going,[7] others have followed, to beautify our mother tongue, as well in the same kind as in other arts.

This did so notably show itself, that the philosophers of Greece durst not a long time appear to the world but under the masks of poets. So Thales, Empedocles, and Parmenides[8] sang their natural philosophy in verses; so did Pythagoras and Phocylides their moral counsels; so did Tyrtaeus in war matters, and Solon in matters of policy: or rather they, being poets, did exercise their delightful vein in those points of highest knowledge, which before them lay hid to the world. For that wise Solon was directly a poet it is manifest, having written in verse the notable fable of the Atlantic Island, which was continued by Plato. And truly even Plato[9] whosoever well considereth shall find that in the body of his work, though the inside and strength were philosophy, the skin, as it were, and beauty depended most of[1] poetry: for all standeth upon dialogues, wherein he feigneth many honest burgesses of Athens to speak of such matters, that, if they had been set on the rack, they would never have confessed them, besides his poetical describing the circumstances of their meetings, as the well ordering of a banquet,[2] the delicacy of a walk, with interlacing mere tales, as Gyges' ring and others, which who knoweth not to be flowers of poetry did never walk into Apollo's garden.[3]

And even historiographers (although their lips sound of things done, and verity[4] be written in their foreheads) have been glad to borrow both fashion and, perchance, weight of the poets. So Herodotus entitled his History by the name of the nine Muses;[5] and both he and all the rest that followed him either stale[6] or usurped of poetry their passionate describing of passions, the many particularities of battles, which no man could affirm; or, if that be denied me, long orations put in the mouths of great kings and captains, which it is certain they never pronounced.

So that truly neither philosopher nor historiographer could at the first have entered into the gates of popular judgments, if they had not taken a great passport of poetry, which in all nations at this day where learning flourisheth not, is plain to be seen; in all which they have some feeling of poetry.

In Turkey, besides their law-giving divines, they have no other writers but poets. In our neighbor country Ireland, where truly learning goeth very bare, yet are their poets held in a devout reverence. Even among the most barbarous and simple Indians

---

7. Example.
8. Sidney lists the best-known of the Greek philosophers before Plato: Thales, a geometrician; Empedocles, who studied the concepts of change and permanence; Parmeneides, who investigated the nature of being; Pythagoras, a mathematician and astronomer; Phocylides, a moralist; and Tyrtaeus, a poet. Solon (c. 640–558 B.C.) was an Athenian statesman, poet, and constitutional reformer. No trace remains of a poem by Solon telling of Atlantis, an island beyond the pillars of Hercules that vanishes beneath the sea; Sidney recalls Plato's dialogue (Timaeus, 21–24), in which Critias tells Socrates that the story of Atlantis originates in an unfinished poem of Solon.
9. Author of many works of philosophy in dialogue form, notably The Republic, on the construction of an ideal

state, and The Symposium, on the nature of love and its association with beauty and truth. He was a key influence on Renaissance thinkers.
1. On.
2. A banquet is the setting of The Symposium; speakers take a walk in the The Phaedrus; and the story of Gyges' ring is told in The Republic.
3. Apollo was the god of poetry.
4. Truth.
5. Herodotus, a Greek historian (480–425 B.C.), wrote about the struggle between Asia and Greece; later classical editors divided his work, which he entitled simply History, into nine books named after the nine Muses: Calliope, Clio, Euterpe, Melpomene, Terpsichore, Erato, Polyhymnia, Urania, and Thalia.
6. Stole.

where no writing is, yet have they their poets who make and sing songs, which they call *areytos*,[7] both of their ancestors' deeds and praises of their gods: a sufficient probability that, if ever learning come among them, it must be by having their hard dull wits softened and sharpened with the sweet delights of poetry—for until they find a pleasure in the exercises of the mind, great promises of much knowledge will little persuade them that know not the fruits of knowledge. In Wales, the true remnant of the ancient Britons, as there are good authorities to show the long time they had poets, which they called bards, so through all the conquests of Romans, Saxons, Danes, and Normans, some of whom did seek to ruin all memory of learning from among them, yet do their poets even to this day last; so as it is not more notable in soon beginning than in long continuing.

But since the authors of most of our sciences[8] were the Romans, and before them the Greeks, let us a little stand upon their authorities, but even so far as to see what names they have given unto this now scorned skill.

Among the Romans a poet was called *vates*, which is as much as a diviner, foreseer, or prophet, as by his conjoined words *vaticinium* [prediction] and *vaticinari* [to foretell] is manifest: so heavenly a title did that excellent people bestow upon this heart-ravishing knowledge. And so far were they carried into the admiration thereof, that they thought in the chanceable hitting upon any such verses great foretokens of their following fortunes were placed. Whereupon grew the word of *Sortes Virgilianae*,[9] when by sudden opening Virgil's book they lighted upon any verse of his making, whereof the histories of the emperors' lives are full: as of Albinus, the governor of our island, who in his childhood met with this verse

Arma amens capio nec sat rationis in armis[1]

and in his age performed it. Which, although it were a very vain and godless superstition, as also it was to think spirits were commanded by such verses—whereupon this word charms, derived of *carmina* [songs], cometh—so yet serveth it to show the great reverence those wits were held in; and altogether not without ground, since both the oracles of Delphos and Sibylla's prophecies were wholly delivered in verses.[2] For that same exquisite observing of number and measure[3] in the words, and that high flying liberty of conceit proper to the poet, did seem to have some divine force in it.

And may not I presume a little further, to show the reasonableness of this word *vates*, and say that the holy David's Psalms are a divine poem? If I do, I shall not do it without the testimony of great learned men, both ancient and modern. But even the name of Psalms will speak for me, which being interpreted, is nothing but songs; then that it is fully written in meter, as all learned Hebricians agree, although the rules be not yet fully found; lastly and principally, his handling his prophecy, which is merely poetical: for what else is the awaking his musical instruments, the often and free

7. A West Indian dance, recorded by José de Acosta in his *Natural and Moral History of the West Indies* (translated into English in 1604).
8. Any body of knowledge, typically natural philosophy and also including ethics and politics.
9. The Virgilian lots, or fortune as it is implied in lines from the *Aeneid*, which the reader chose at random and then subjects to interpretation.

1. "I seize arms madly, nor is there reason in arming" (2.314).
2. The shrine of Apollo at Delphi was presided over by a priestess who was believed to know the god's thoughts about the future; the Sibyls were supposed to be ancient prophetesses whose words were collected in the *Sibylline Books*.
3. Meter and rhythm.

changing of persons, his notable *prosopopoeias* [personifications], when he maketh you, as it were, see God coming in His majesty, his telling of the beasts' joyfulness and hills leaping,[4] but a heavenly poesy, wherein almost he showeth himself a passionate lover of that unspeakable and everlasting beauty to be seen by the eyes of the mind, only cleared by faith? But truly now having named him, I fear me I seem to profane that holy name, applying it to poetry, which is among us thrown down to so ridiculous an estimation. But they that with quiet judgments will look a little deeper into it, shall find the end and working of it such as, being rightly applied, deserveth not to be scourged out of the Church of God.

But now let us see how the Greeks named it, and how they deemed of it. The Greeks called him a "poet," which name hath, as the most excellent, gone through other languages. It cometh of this word ποιεῖν, which is, to make: wherein, I know not whether by luck or wisdom, we Englishmen have met with the Greeks in calling him a maker: which name, how high and incomparable a title it is, I had rather were known by marking the scope of other sciences than by any partial allegation.

There is no art delivered to mankind that hath not the works of nature for his principal object, without which they could not consist, and on which they so depend, as they become actors and players, as it were, of what nature will have set forth. So doth the astronomer look upon the stars, and, by that he seeth, set down what order nature hath taken therein. So doth the geometrician and arithmetician in their diverse sorts of quantities. So doth the musicians in time tell you which by nature agree, which not. The natural philosopher thereon hath his name, and the moral philosopher standeth upon the natural virtues, vices, or passions of man; and follow nature (saith he) therein, and thou shalt not err. The lawyer saith what men have determined; the historian what men have done. The grammarian speaketh only of the rules of speech; and the rhetorician and logician, considering what in nature will soonest prove and persuade, thereon give artificial rules, which still are compassed within the circle of a question according to the proposed matter. The physician weigheth the nature of man's body, and the nature of things helpful or hurtful unto it. And the metaphysic,[5] though it be in the second and abstract notions, and therefore be counted supernatural, yet doth he indeed build upon the depth of nature. Only the poet, disdaining to be tied to any such subjection, lifted up with the vigor of his own invention, doth grow in effect another nature, in making things either better than nature bringeth forth, or, quite anew, forms such as never were in nature, as the Heroes, Demigods, Cyclops, Chimeras, Furies,[6] and such like: so as he goeth hand in hand with nature, not enclosed within the narrow warrant[7] of her gifts, but freely ranging only within the zodiac of his own wit. Nature never set forth the earth in so rich tapestry as divers poets have done; neither with so pleasant rivers, fruitful trees, sweet-smelling flowers, nor whatsoever else may make the too much loved earth more lovely. Her world is brazen, the poets only deliver a golden.

But let those things alone, and go to man—for whom as the other things are, so it seemeth in him her uttermost cunning is employed—and know whether she have

4. Psalm 29.
5. A philosopher who considered abstractions and aspects of mental and spiritual life entertained in a state of contemplation rather than of action.
6. Furies: supernatural forces figured as mad goddesses pursuing revenge; demigods: male offspring of a god and a mortal, having some divine powers; cyclops: a one-eyed giant; chimeras: imaginary monsters made up of grotesquely disparate parts.
7. Authority.

brought forth so true a lover as Theagenes, so constant a friend as Pylades, so valiant a man as Orlando, so right a prince as Xenophon's Cyrus, so excellent a man every way as Virgil's Aeneas.[8] Neither let this be jestingly conceived, because the works of the one be essential, the other in imitation or fiction; for any understanding knoweth the skill of each artificer standeth in that *idea* or fore-conceit[9] of the work, and not in the work itself. And that the poet hath that *idea* is manifest, by delivering them forth in such excellency as he had imagined them. Which delivering forth also is not wholly imaginative, as we are wont to say by them that build castles in the air; but so far substantially it worketh, not only to make a Cyrus, which had been but a particular excellency as nature might have done, but to bestow a Cyrus upon the world to make many Cyruses, if they will learn aright why and how that maker made him.

Neither let it be deemed too saucy a comparison to balance the highest point of man's wit with the efficacy of nature; but rather give right honor to the heavenly Maker of that maker, who having made man to His own likeness, set him beyond and over all the works of that second nature: which in nothing he showeth so much as in poetry, when with the force of a divine breath he bringeth things forth surpassing her doings—with no small arguments to the credulous of that first accursed fall of Adam, since our erected wit maketh us know what perfection is, and yet our infected will keepeth us from reaching unto it. But these arguments will by few be understood, and by fewer granted. This much (I hope) will be given me, that the Greeks with some probability of reason gave him the name above all names of learning.

* * * [Now let us show] the poet's nobleness, by setting him before his other competitors. Among whom as principal challengers step forth the moral philosophers, whom, me thinketh, I see coming towards me with a sullen gravity, as though they could not abide vice by daylight, rudely clothed for to witness outwardly their contempt of outward things, with books in their hands against glory, whereto they set their names, sophistically speaking against subtlety, and angry with any man in whom they see the foul fault of anger. These men casting largess as they go, of definitions, divisions, and distinctions, with a scornful interrogative do soberly ask whether it be possible to find any path so ready to lead a man to virtue as that which teacheth what virtue is; and teach it not only by delivering forth his very being, his causes and effects, but also by making known his enemy, vice, which must be destroyed, and his cumbersome servant, passion, which must be mastered; by showing the generalities that containeth it, and the specialities that are derived from it; lastly, by plain setting down how it extendeth itself out of the limits of a man's own little world to the government of families and maintaining of public societies.

8. Sidney cites men recognized for their virtues. Theagenes exemplifies the true lover in Heliodorus's romance, the *Aethiopica*; Pylades, who helped Orestes avenge his father Agamemnon's murder, was cited by Renaissance commentators as a perfect friend; Orlando (modeled on Roland, the knight who fought for Charlemagne against the Basques at the battle of Roncesvalles, A.D. 778) was the hero of Ariosto's *Orlando Furioso* and illustrated the Renaissance idea of valor. The *Anabasis* of Xenophon (himself a general in Cyrus's army) relates how Cyrus the Younger, a Persian prince, helped the Peloponnesians resist the army of Athens and then died in an attempt to take the Persian throne from his brother Artaxerxes in the 5th century B.C. Aeneas, the hero of Virgil's *Aeneid* and the mythical founder of the Roman Empire, was generally considered to be the epitome of the statesman.
9. The element of the literary work that determines how and to what end its subject is conveyed. Sidney later states that an *Idea* works "substantially" because it makes readers want to imitate the virtuous characters represented in a literary work.

The historian scarcely giveth leisure to the moralist to say so much, but that he, laden with old mouse-eaten records, authorizing himself (for the most part) upon other histories, whose greatest authorities are built upon the notable foundation of hearsay; having much ado to accord differing writers and to pick truth out of their partiality; better acquainted with a thousand years ago than with the present age, and yet better knowing how this world goeth than how his own wit runneth; curious for antiquities and inquisitive of novelties; a wonder to young folks and a tyrant in table talk, denieth, in a great chafe,[1] that any man for teaching of virtue, and virtuous actions is comparable to him. "I am *testis temporum, lux veritatis, vita memoriae, magistra vitae, nuntia vetustatis.*[2] The philosopher," saith he, "teacheth a disputative virtue, but I do an active. His virtue is excellent in the dangerless Academy of Plato,[3] but mine showeth forth her honorable face in the battles of Marathon, Pharsalia, Poitiers, and Agincourt.[4] He teacheth virtue by certain abstract considerations, but I only bid you follow the footing of them that have gone before you. Old-aged experience goeth beyond the fine-witted philosopher, but I give the experience of many ages. Lastly, if he make the songbook, I put the learner's hand to the lute; and if he be the guide, I am the light." Then would he allege you innumerable examples, confirming story by stories, how much the wisest senators and princes have been directed by the credit of history, as Brutus, Alphonsus of Aragon,[5] and who not, if need be? At length the long line of their disputation maketh a point in this, that the one giveth the precept, and the other the example.

Now whom shall we find (since the question standeth for the highest form in the school of learning) to be moderator? Truly, as me seemeth, the poet; and if not a moderator, even the man that ought to carry the title from them both, and much more from all other serving sciences. Therefore compare we the poet with the historian and with the moral philosopher; and if he go beyond them both, no other human skill can match him. For as for the divine, with all reverence it is ever to be excepted, not only for having his scope as far beyond any of these as eternity exceedeth a moment, but even for passing each of these in themselves. And for the lawyer, though *Ius* [Right] be the daughter of Justice, and justice the chief of virtues, yet because he seeketh to make men good rather *formidine poenae* than *virtutis amore;*[6] or, to say righter, doth not endeavor to make men good, but that their evil hurt not others; having no care, so he be a good citizen, how bad a man he be: therefore as our wickedness maketh him necessary, and necessity maketh him honorable, so is he not in the deepest truth to stand in rank with these who all endeavor to take naughtiness away and plant goodness even in the secretest cabinet of our souls. And these four are all that any way deal in that consideration of men's manners, which being the supreme knowledge, they that best breed it deserve the best commendation.

---

1. Heat, fury.
2. Sidney quotes Cicero in his *De Oratore* (*Concerning the Orator*): "I am the witness of time, the light of truth, the life of memory, the governess of life, the herald of antiquity."
3. The olive grove near Athens, where Plato and his successors taught philosophy.
4. Sidney mentions some memorable battles: The Athenians defeated the invading Persians at Marathon in 490 B.C.; Caesar defeated Pompey at Pharsalus in 48 B.C.; the Franks, under Charles Martel, defeated the Moors, led by Spanish emir Abd al-Rahman Ghafiqi in 732; the English, under Edward, the Black Prince, overcame the French army and captured their king, John II in 1356, each time at Poitiers; finally, Henry V defeated the French in 1415 at Agincourt.
5. Brutus: Roman statesman, one of Caesar's assassins, who is said to have spent the night before the battle of Pharsalus reading history; Alphonsus: King of Aragon and Sicily who encouraged his soldiers to seize the libraries of those they conquered and to bring their books to him.
6. I.e., rather "from fear of punishment" than "from love of virtue" (Horace, *Epistles* 1.2.62). Sidney distinguishes between staying within the law and moral behavior.

The philosopher, therefore, and the historian are they which would win the goal, the one by precept, the other by example. But both, not having both, do both halt.[7] For the philosopher, setting down with thorny arguments the bare rule, is so hard of utterance and so misty to be conceived, that one that hath no other guide but him shall wade in him till he be old before he shall find sufficient cause to be honest. For his knowledge standeth so upon the abstract and general, that happy is that man who may understand him, and more happy that can apply what he doth understand. On the other side, the historian, wanting the precept, is so tied, not to what should be but to what is, to the particular truth of things and not to the general reason of things, that his example draweth no necessary consequence, and therefore a less fruitful doctrine.

Now doth the peerless poet perform both: for whatsoever the philosopher saith should be done, he giveth a perfect picture of it in someone by whom he presupposeth it was done, so as he coupleth the general notion with the particular example. A perfect picture I say, for he yieldeth to the powers of the mind an image of that whereof the philosopher bestoweth but a wordish description, which doth neither strike, pierce, nor possess the sight of the soul so much as that other doth. For as in outward things, to a man that had never seen an elephant or a rhinoceros, who should tell him most exquisitely all their shapes, color, bigness, and particular marks, or of a gorgeous palace, an *architector* [architect], with declaring the full beauties, might well make the hearer able to repeat, as it were by rote, all he had heard, yet should never satisfy his inward conceit[8] with being witness to itself of a true lively knowledge; but the same man, as soon as he might see those beasts well painted, or the house well in model, should straightways grow, without need of any description, to a judicial comprehending of them: so no doubt the philosopher with his learned definitions—be it of virtue, vices, matters of public policy or private government—replenisheth the memory with many infallible grounds of wisdom, which, notwithstanding, lie dark before the imaginative and judging power, if they be not illuminated or figured forth by the speaking picture of poesy.

* * * [O]f all writers under the sun the poet is the least liar, and, though he would, as a poet can scarcely be a liar. The astronomer, with his cousin the geometrician, can hardly escape, when they take upon them to measure the height of the stars. How often, think you, do the physicians lie, when they aver things good for sicknesses, which afterwards send Charon[9] a great number of souls drowned in a potion before they come to his ferry? And no less of the rest, which take upon them to affirm. Now, for the poet, he nothing affirms, and therefore never lieth. For, as I take it, to lie is to affirm that to be true which is false. So as the other artists, and especially the historian, affirming many things, can, in the cloudy knowledge of mankind, hardly escape from many lies. But the poet (as I said before) never affirmeth. The poet never maketh any circles about your imagination, to conjure you to believe for true what he writes. He citeth not authorities of other histories, but even for his entry calleth the sweet Muses to inspire into him a good invention; in truth, not laboring to tell you what is or is not, but what should or should not be. And therefore, though he recount things not true, yet because he telleth them not for true, he lieth not—without we will say that Nathan lied in his speech before-alleged to David; which as a wicked man durst scarce say, so think I none so simple would say that Aesop lied in the tales of his beasts; for who thinks that Aesop wrote

---

7. Limp.
8. The listener's mental picture or image.

9. According to Greek myth, Charon ferries souls across the River Styx to the underworld.

it for actually true were well worthy to have his name chronicled among the beasts he writeth of. What child is there, that, coming to a play, and seeing *Thebes* written in great letters upon an old door, doth believe that it is Thebes? If then a man can arrive to that child's age to know that the poets' persons and doings are but pictures what should be, and not stories what have been, they will never give the lie to things not affirmatively but allegorically and figuratively written. And therefore, as in history, looking for truth, they may go away full fraught with falsehood, so in poesy, looking but for fiction, they shall use the narration but as an imaginative ground-plot of a profitable invention. But hereto is replied, that the poets give names to men they write of, which argueth a conceit of an actual truth, and so, not being true, proves a falsehood. And doth the lawyer lie then, when under the names of *John-a-stiles* and *John-a-nokes*[1] he puts his case? But that is easily answered. Their naming of men is but to make their picture the more lively, and not to build any history: painting men, they cannot leave men nameless. We see we cannot play at chess but that we must give names to our chessmen; and yet, methinks, he were a very partial champion of truth that would say we lied for giving a piece of wood the reverend title of a bishop. The poet nameth Cyrus or Aeneas no other way than to show what men of their fames, fortunes, and estates should do.

* * * So that since the ever-praiseworthy Poesy is full of virtue-breeding delightfulness, and void of no gift that ought to be in the noble name of learning; since the blames laid against it are either false or feeble; since the cause why it is not esteemed in England is the fault of poet-apes, not poets; since, lastly, our tongue is most fit to honor poesy, and to be honored by poesy; I conjure you all that have had the evil luck to read this ink-wasting toy of mine, even in the name of the nine Muses, no more to scorn the sacred mysteries of poesy; no more to laugh at the name of poets, as though they were next inheritors to fools; no more to jest at the reverent title of a rhymer; but to believe, with Aristotle, that they were the ancient treasurers of the Grecians' divinity; to believe, with Bembus, that they were first bringers-in of all civility; to believe, with Scaliger, that no philosopher's precepts can sooner make you an honest man than the reading of Virgil; to believe, with Clauserus,[2] the translator of Cornutus, that it pleased the heavenly Deity, by Hesiod and Homer, under the veil of fables, to give us all knowledge, logic, rhetoric, philosophy natural and moral, and *quid non?* [what not]; to believe, with me, that there are many mysteries contained in poetry, which of purpose were written darkly, lest by profane wits it should be abused; to believe, with Landino,[3] that they are so beloved of the gods that whatsoever they write proceeds of a divine fury; lastly, to believe themselves, when they tell you they will make you immortal by their verses. Thus doing, your name shall flourish in the printers' shops; thus doing, you shall be of kin to many a poetical preface; thus doing, you shall be most fair, most rich, most wise, most all, you shall dwell upon superlatives; thus doing, though you be *libertino patre natus* [son of freed slave], you shall suddenly grow *Herculea proles* [a descendant of Hercules],

    Si quid mea carmina possunt;[4]

---

1. I.e., John Doe, or John Roe of ancient law courts.
2. Conrad Clauser, a 16th-century German scholar who translated the works of Lucius Annaeus Cornutus, a 1st-century Greek slave who wrote commentaries on Aristotle and Virgil.
3. Cristofor Landino (1424–1504), an Italian humanist who wrote moral dialogues.
4. "If my songs can do anything" (*Aeneid* 9.446).

thus doing, your soul shall be placed with Dante's Beatrice, or Virgil's Anchises. But if (fie of such a but) you be born so near the dull-making cataract of Nilus[5] that you cannot hear the planet-like music of poetry; if you have so earth-creeping a mind that it cannot lift itself up to look to the sky of poetry, or rather, by a certain rustical disdain, will become such a mome as to be a Momus[6] of poetry; then, though I will not wish unto you the ass's ears of Midas, nor to be driven by a poet's verses, as Bubonax[7] was, to hang himself, nor to be rhymed to death, as is said to be done in Ireland; yet thus much curse I must send you, in the behalf of all poets, that while you live, you live in love, and never get favor for lacking skill of a sonnet; and, when you die, your memory die from the earth for want of an epitaph.

1579–80   1595

⊠ "THE APOLOGY" AND ITS TIME ⊠
The Art of Poetry

After the spread of Reformation doctrine on the importance of moral discipline, English readers often encountered denunciations of poetry and especially drama. The issues that Sidney took up when he defended poetry were the subject of sharp dispute. Stephen Gosson represented the opinions of many of poetry's detractors. As he declares in *The School of Abuse*, published shortly before Sidney wrote his *Apology*, poetry provides frivolous distraction from the serious business of life and, what is worse, temptations to godlessness. But others, like Sidney, took a more optimistic view of the subject. In *The Art of English Poesy*, George Puttenham states that poets were the first lawgivers (as Sidney had) and focuses particularly on epic poetry, which, he says, give readers images of a truth beyond history as well as consistently inspiring models of action to imitate. His popular treatise contains a wealth of practical advice for aspiring writers and even today remains a useful sourcebook for information on rhetorical figures of thought and speech.

In addition to the challenge posed by moralists such as Gosson, defenders of English poetry also had to confront purely practical problems. Unlike the Romance languages—Italian, French, and Spanish—sixteenth-century English had lost almost all its feminine endings, the accented vowel sounds that made rhyming fairly easy. English was also a language in which words of one syllable were quite common, and poets had trouble creating the metrical harmonies usual in poetry written in languages rich in polysyllables. George Gascoigne's brief treatise *Certain Notes of Instruction concerning the making of verse or rhyme in English* deals with these conditions directly. He warns against trying to achieve euphony or a musical quality by "rolling in pleasant words," as in the sequence "Rim, Ram, Ruff," and he insists that the "truer Englishman" uses words of one syllable. Critics could differ in what they valued, of course; in *A Defence of Rhyme*, Samuel Daniel justified rhyme as "pleasing to nature," which desires form and closures, not chaos and infinity. More important, he defended English writers against the claim that they could never match their classical precursors. He reminded readers that imputations of barbarism and ignorance are based on relative, not absolute, judgments.

---

5. Cicero claimed that hearing the sound of the cataracts of the Nile river in Egypt caused deafness; the Neoplatonists thought the movement of the planets produced heavenly music, the music of the spheres.
6. Momus personified the faultfinder in Greek literature; a mome is a blockhead. Apollo changed Midas's ears to those of an ass to signal his stupidity after Midas judged

Pan's flute playing to be superior to Apollo's (Ovid, *Metamorphoses* 11.146).
7. Sidney conflates Hipponax, a Greek poet, with Bupalus, a sculptor. The latter had made an unflattering portrait of the former, who took revenge with deadly verses. Irish poets claimed their verses could kill man or beast.

Stephen Gosson
from *The School of Abuse*[1]

The Syracusans used such variety of dishes in their banquets that when they were set and their boards furnished,[2] they were many times in doubt which they should touch first or taste last. And in my opinion the world giveth every writer so large a field to walk in that before he set pen to the book, he shall find himself feasted at Syracuse, uncertain where to begin or when to end. This caused Pindarus[3] to question with his Muse whether he were better with his art to decipher the life of Nimpe Melia, or Cadmus's encounter with the dragon, or the wars of Hercules at the walls of Thebes, or Bacchus's cups, or Venus's juggling? He saw so many turnings laid open to his feet, that he knew not which way to bend his pace.

Therefore, as I cannot but commend his wisdom which in banqueting feeds most upon that that doth nourish best, so must I dispraise his method in writing which, following the course of amorous poets, dwelleth longest on those points that profit least, and like a wanton whelp,[4] leaveth the game[5] to run riot. The scarab flies over many a sweet flower and lights in a cowsherd.[6] It is the custom of the fly to leave the sound places of the horse and suck at the botch,[7] the nature of colloquintida[8] to draw the worst humors to itself, the manner of swine to forsake the fair fields and wallow in the mire, and the whole practice of poets, either with fables to show their abuses or with plain terms to unfold their mischief, discover their shame, discredit themselves, and disperse their poison through the world. Virgil sweats in describing his gnat, Ovid bestirreth him to paint out his flea; the one shows his art in the lust of Dido, the other his cunning in the incest of Myrrha and that trumpet of bawdry, the craft of love.[9]

I must confess that poets are the whetstones of wit, notwithstanding that wit is dearly bought. Where honey and gall are mixed, it will be hard to sever the one from the other. The deceitful physician giveth sweet syrups to make his poison go down the smoother, the juggler casteth a mist to work the closer, the siren's song is the sailor's wrack,[1] the fowler's whistle the bird's death, the wholesome bait the fish's bane. The Harpies[2] have virgin faces, and the vultures, talents; Hyena speaks like a friend and devours like a foe; the calmest seas hide dangerous rocks; the wolf jets in wether's fells.[3] Many good sentences are spoken by David to shadow his knavery,[4] and written by poets as ornaments to beautify their works and set their trumpery to sale without suspect.

But if you look well to Epaeus's horse,[5] you shall find in his bowels the destruction of Troy; open the sepulchre of Semiramis,[6] whose title promiseth such wealth to the kings

---

1. Stephen Gosson was a playwright who turned against the stage, and then wrote Puritanical critiques of what he considered its immorality. His *School of Abuse* was published in 1579.
2. Tables set.
3. Pindar, the most difficult and obscure of Greek poets, famous for his odes. The story of Cadmus's encounter with the dragon is a fragment of a cycle of legends about the city of Thebes; the legendary hero Hercules delivered the city of Thebes from the burden of paying tribute to the foreign king Orchomenus; Bacchus was the Roman god of wine; and Venus's "juggling" refers to her erotic escapades.
4. Unruly puppy.
5. Hunt.
6. Cow dung.
7. Ulcer.
8. A wild cucumber, used as an herbal medicine.
9. Dido, Queen of Carthage, with whom the legendary Tro-

jan hero Aeneas stayed on his way to founding Rome; Virgil's *Aeneid* provides the best-known account of this episode. According to legend, Myrrha was the mother of the Greek god of vegetation, Adonis, by her father, King Cinyras, who, when he learned of his incest, changed her into a myrtle; the story is told by Ovid in his *Metamorphoses*, a poem describing erotic transformations. Gosson condemns Ovid's poem *Ars Amatoria*, or "the craft (or art) of love," as an immoral work ("bawdry" is licentiousness).
1. The mermaid's song is the sailor's shipwreck.
2. Monstrous and filthy birds whom Aeneas and his companions encounter.
3. The wolf strolls in sheep's clothing.
4. King of the ancient Israelites and poet of the psalms, David was guilty of adulterous love for Bathsheba, whose husband he murdered.
5. The Trojan horse.
6. Mythical queen of Assyria, who is supposed to have built the city of Babylon.

of Persia, you shall see nothing but dead bones; rip up the golden ball that Nero conse-crated to Jupiter Capitolinus,[7] you shall [find] it stuffed with the shavings of his beard; pull off the visor that poets mask in, you shall disclose their reproach, bewray[8] their van-ity, loathe their wantonness, lament their folly, and perceive their sharp sayings to be placed as pearls in dunghills, fresh pictures on rotten walls, chaste matrons' apparel on common courtesans. These are the cups of Circe,[9] that turn reasonable creatures into brute beasts; the balls of Hippomenes,[1] that hinder the course of Atalanta; and the blocks of the Devil, that are cast in our ways to cut off the race of toward wits. No marvel though Plato shut them out of his school and banished them quite from his common-wealth as effeminate writers,[2] unprofitable members, and utter enemies to virtue.

George Puttenham
from *The Art of English Poesie*[1]

How Poets were the first Philosophers, the first Astronomers and Historiographers, and Orators and Musicians of the world.[2]

Utterance also and language is given by nature to man for persuasion of others and aid of themselves, I mean the first ability to speak. For speech itself is artificial and made by man, and the more pleasing it is, the more it prevaileth to such purpose as it is intended for. But speech by meter is a kind of utterance more cleanly couched and more delicate to the ear than prose is, because it is more current and slipper upon the tongue and withal tunable and melodious as a kind of music and therefore may be termed a musical speech or utterance which cannot but please the hearer very well. Another cause is for that[3] is briefer and more compendious and easier to bear away and be retained in memory than that which is contained in multitude of words and full of tedious ambage and long periods.[4] It is beside a manner of utterance more elo-quent and rhetorical than the ordinary proof which we use in our daily talk, because it is decked and set out with all manner of fresh colors and figures, which maketh that it sooner inveigleth[5] the judgment of man and carryeth his opinion this way and that, whither soever the heart by impression of the ear shall be most affectionately bent and directed. The utterance in prose is not of so great efficacy because not only it is daily used, and by that occasion the care is over-glutted with it, but is also not so voluble and slipper on the tongue, being wide and loose, and nothing numerous nor contrived into measures and founded with so gallant and harmonical accents, nor in fine allowed that figurative conveyance[6] nor so great license in choice of words and phrases as meter is. So as the poets were also from the beginning the best persuaders

---

7. The Emperor Nero is said to have consecrated a golden ball to Jupiter in his temple on the Capitoline Hill in Rome.
8. Expose.
9. In Homer's *Odyssey*, the goddess who transformed the companions of Odysseus into swine.
1. The legendary suitor of Atalanta, who refused to marry anyone she could defeat in a footrace. Hippomenes won the race by dropping golden apples on the race track. Atalanta could not resist stopping to pick them up, and her delay allowed Hippomenes victory.
2. Plato exiles poets from his ideal republic (see *The Republic* 3.398A).
1. George Puttenham has always been assumed to be the author of *The Art of English Poesy*, a critical treatise that

appeared in 1589. Dividing his work into three books (*Of Poets and Poesy*, *Of Proportion*, and *Of Ornament*), Put-tenham discusses the works of English poets, poetic forms and genres, and figures of speech and thought respective-ly. The work as a whole is a compendium of contempo-rary ideas and practices illustrating the proper way to compose and appreciate poetry.
2. In his *Apology for Poetry*, Sidney also claims that poets were the first human beings to express feeling, thought, and a sense of the higher purposes of life.
3. I.e., poetry.
4. Dull indirection and long sentences.
5. Appeals to.
6. Expression.

and their eloquence the first rhetoric of the world, even so it became[7] that the high mysteries of the gods should be revealed and taught by a manner of utterance and language of extraordinary phrase and brief and compendious and above all others sweet and civil as the metrical is. The same also was meetest to register the lives and noble gifts of princes, and of the great monarchs of the world and all other memorable accidents of time, so as the poet was also the first historiographer. Then forasmuch as they were the first observers of all natural causes and effects in the things generable and corruptable, and from thence mounted up to search after the celestial courses and influences and yet penetrated further to know the divine essences and substances separate,[8] as is said before, they were the first astronomers and philosophists and metaphysics. Finally, because they did altogether endeavor themselves to reduce[9] the life of man to a certain method of good manners, and made the first differences between virtue and vice, and then tempered all these knowledges and skills with the exercise of a delectable music by melodious instruments, which withall served them to delight their hearers and to call the people together by admiration to a plausible and virtuous conversation, therefore were they the first philosophers ethic[1] and the first artificial musicians of the world. Such was Linus, Orpheus, Amphion, and Musaeus,[2] the most ancient poets and philosophers, of whom there is left any memory by the profane writers. King David also and Solomon his son and many other of the holy prophets wrote in meters and used to sing them to the harp,[3] although to many of us ignorant of the Hebrew language and phrase and not observing it, the same seem but a prose. It cannot be therefore that any scorn or indignity should justly be offered to so noble, profitable, ancient, and divine a science as Poesie is. * * *

Of historical poesie,[4] *by which the famous acts of Princes and the virtuous and worthy lives of our forefathers were reported.*

There is nothing in man of all the potential parts of his mind (reason and will excepted) more noble or more necessary to the active life than memory. Because it maketh[5] most to a sound judgment and perfect worldly wisdom, examining and comparing the times past with the present and by them both considering the time to come, [it] concludeth with a steadfast resolution what is the best course to be taken in all his actions and advices in this world. It came upon this reason: experience [is] to be so highly commended in all consultations of importance and preferred before any learning or science, and yet experience is no more than a mass of memories assembled, that is, such trials as man hath made in time before. Right so, no kind of argument in all the oratory craft doth better persuade and more universally satisfy than example, which is but the representation of old memories and like successes [that have] happened in times past. For these regards, the poesie historical is of all other, next[6] the divine, most honorable and worthy, as well for the common benefit as for the special comfort every man receiveth by it. No one thing in the world with more delectation [is] reviving our spirits than to behold, as it were in a glass, the lively image of our dear

---

7. Was appropriate.
8. I.e., to know the divine essences and the particular objects present in the heavens.
9. Abstract.
1. I.e., philosophers who consider ethics.
2. Puttenham names legendary figures who were thought to be among the first poets: Linus, a poet and the teacher of Hercules, who later killed him with his own lyre; Orpheus, commonly considered the first poet, whose

music charmed even the animals; Amphion, the poet whose music moved stones to build Thebes; and Musaeus, said to have been a pupil of Orpheus.
3. Scripture provides accounts of King David, supposed to be the author of the psalms, and Solomon, to whom the Song of Songs is attributed.
4. Epic poetry.
5. Benefits.
6. After.

forefathers, their noble and virtuous manner of life, with other things authentic, which because we are not able otherwise to attain to the knowledge of by any of our fences,[7] we apprehend them by memory, whereas the present time and things so swiftly pass away [so] as they give us no leisure almost to look into them and much less to know and consider of them thoroughly. The things future, being also events very uncertain, and such as cannot possibly be known because they be not yet, cannot be used for example nor for delight otherwise than by hope, though many promise the contrary, by vain and deceitful arts taking upon them to reveal the truth of accidents to come, which if it were so as they surmise, are yet but sciences merely conjectural and not of any benefit to man or to the commonwealth where they be used or professed. Therefore the good and exemplary things and actions of the former ages were reserved only to the historical reports of wise and grave men; those of the present time [were] left to the fruition and judgment of our senses; the future as hazards and uncertain events [were] utterly neglected and laid aside for magicians and mockers to get their livings by, such manner of men as by negligence of magistrates and remisses of laws every country breedeth great store of. These historical men nevertheless used not the matter so precisely to wish that all they wrote should be accounted true,[8] for that was not needful nor expedient to the purpose, namely to be used either for example or for the pleasure, considering that many times it is seen a feigned matter or altogether fabulous, besides that it maketh more mirth than any other, works no less good conclusions for example than the most true and veritable, but oftentimes more, because the poet hath the handling of them[9] to fashion at his pleasure, but not so of the other[1] which must go according to their verity and none otherwise without the writers' great blame. Again as ye know, more and more excellent examples may be feigned in one day by a good wit than many ages through man's frailty are able to put in ure,[2] which made the learned and witty men of those times to devise many historical matters of no verity at all, but with purpose to do good and no hurt, as using them for a manner of discipline and precedent of commendable life. Such was the commonwealth of Plato, and Sir Thomas More's *Utopia*, resting all in device,[3] but never [to be] put in execution and easier wished than to be performed. And you shall perceive that histories were of three sorts, wholly true and wholly false, and a third holding part of either, but for honest recreation and good example they were all of them.[4]

George Gascoigne
from *Certain Notes of Instruction*[1]

The first and most necessary point that ever I found meet to be considered in making of a delectable poem is this, to ground it upon some fine invention.[2] For it is not enough to roll in pleasant words, nor yet to thunder in Rim, Ram, Ruff, by letter

---

7. Ways of arguing.
8. Puttenham identifies epic poets as historical, in that they represent the past, but not as historians, in that they do not represent it entirely truthfully.
9. His poetic subjects.
1. I.e., the historian who must try to discover the factual truth of the past.
2. Use.
3. Conception.
4. I.e., they were all equally good for recreation and good

moral example.
1. George Gascoigne's *Certain Notes* was published in 1575 as part of his second work, containing both poetry and prose, entitled *The Posies of George Gascoigne*.
2. In early modern treatises on the art of writing poetry, "invention" meant the discovery and development of "matter," the topics and ideas that the poet will then represent. After "invention," he draws on a knowledge of rhetoric, the techniques by which "matter" is made interesting and memorable.

(quoth my master Chaucer) nor yet to abound in apt vocables or epithets, unless the invention have in it also *aliquid salis* [something salty]. By this *aliquid salis* I mean some good and fine device, showing the quick capacity of a writer, and where I say some good and fine invention, I mean that I would have it both fine and good. For many inventions are so superfine that they are *Vix* [scarcely] good. And again many inventions are good, and yet not finely handled. And for a general forewarning: what theme soever you do take in hand, if you do handle it but *tanquam in oratione perpetua* [as a perpetual sermon], and never study for some depth of device in your invention and some figures also in the handling thereof, it will appear to the skillful reader but a tale of a tub. To deliver unto you general examples it were almost impossible, since the occasions of inventions are (as it were) infinite. Nevertheless, take in worth mine opinion and perceive my further meaning in these few points. If I should undertake to write in praise of a gentlewoman, I would neither praise her crystal eye nor her cherry lip, etc., for these things are *trita et obvia* [trite and obvious]. But I would either find some supernatural cause whereby my pen might walk in superlative degree, or else I would undertake to answer for any imperfection that she hath, and thereupon raise the praise of her commendation.[3] Likewise, if I should disclose my pretense in[4] love, I would either make a strange discourse of some intolerable passion, or find occasion to plead by the example of some history, or discover[5] my disquiet in shadows *per allegoriam* [through allegory], or use the covertest mean that I could to avoid the uncomely customs of common writers. Thus much I adventure to deliver unto you (my friend) upon [the] rule of invention, which of all other rules is most to be marked and hardest to be prescribed in certain and infallible rules. Nevertheless, to conclude therein, I would have you stand most upon the excellency of your invention and stick[6] not to study deeply for some fine device. For that being found, pleasant words will follow well enough and fast enough.

Your invention being once devised, take heed that neither pleasure of rhyme nor variety of device do carry you from it. For as to use obscure and dark phrases in a pleasant[7] sonnet is nothing delectable, so to intermingle merry jests in a serious matter is an indecorum.[8]

I will next advise you that you hold the just measure wherewith you begin your verse. I will not deny but this may seem a preposterous order, but because I covet rather to satisfy you particularly than to undertake a general tradition, I will not so much stand upon the manner as the matter of my precepts. I say then, remember to hold the same measure wherewith you begin, whether it be in a verse of six syllables, eight, ten, twelve, etc., and though this precept might seem ridiculous unto you, since every young scholar can conceive that he ought to continue in the same measure wherewith he beginneth, yet do I see and read many men's poems nowadays which beginning with the measure of twelve in the first line and fourteen in the second (which is the common kind of verse), they will yet (by that time they have passed over a few verses) fall into fourteen and fourteen and *sic de similibus* [so on], the which is either forgetfulness or carelessness. * * *

I think it not amiss to forewarn you that you thrust as few words of many syllables into your verse as may be, and hereunto I might allege many reasons. First, the most ancient English words are of one syllable, so that the more monosyllables that

3. My compliment to her.
4. Profession of.
5. Reveal.

6. Hesitate.
7. Lighthearted.
8. Improper act.

you use, the truer Englishman you shall seem, and the less you shall smell of the inkhorn.[9] Also, words of many syllables do cloy a verse and make it unpleasant, whereas words of one syllable will more easily fall to be short or long as occasion requireth, or will be adapted to become circumflex[1] or of an indifferent[2] sound.

I would exhort you also to beware of rhyme without reason. My meaning is hereby that your rhyme lead you not from your first invention, for many writers when they have laid the platform of their invention are yet drawn sometimes (by rhyme) to forget it or at least to alter it, as when they cannot readily find out a word which may rhyme to the first (and yet continue their determinate invention) they do then either botch it up with a word that will rhyme (how small reason soever it carry with it) or else they alter their first word and so perhaps decline or trouble their former invention. But do you always hold your first determined invention, and do rather search the bottom of your brains for apt words than change good reason for rumbling rhyme. * * *

Also as much as may be, eschew strange words or *obsoleta et inusitata* [obsolete and rare], unless the theme do give just occasion. Marry, in some places a strange word doth draw attentive reading, but yet I would have you therein to use discretion.

And as much as you may, frame your style to perspicuity and to be sensible, for the haughty obscure verse doth not much delight and the verse that is too easy is like a tale of a rusted[3] horse. But let your poem be such as may both delight and draw attentive reading and therewithal may deliver such matter as be worth the marking.

Samuel Daniel
from *A Defense of Rhyme*[1]

Such affliction doth laborsome curiosity[2] still lay upon our best delights (which ever must be made strange and variable) as if art were ordained to afflict nature and that we could not go but in fetters. Every science, every profession, must be so wrapped up in unnecessary intrications, as if it were not to fashion but to confound the understanding, which makes me much to distrust man and fear that our presumption goes beyond our ability and our curiosity is more than our judgment, laboring ever to seem to be more than we are or laying greater burdens upon our minds than they are well able to bear, because we would not appear like other men.

And indeed I have wished there were not that multiplicity of rhymes as is used by many in sonnets, which yet we see in some so happily to succeed and hath been so far from hindering their inventions as it hath begot conceit[3] beyond expectation and comparable to the best inventions of the world. For sure in an eminent spirit whom nature hath fitted for that mystery, rhyme is no impediment to his conceit, but rather gives him wings to mount and carries him, not out of his course, but as it were beyond his power to a far happier flight. All excellencies being sold us at the hard price of labor, it follows, where we bestow most thereof, we buy the best success, and rhyme being far

9. Inkpot.
1. Accentuated.
2. Soft.
3. Restless.
1. Samuel Daniel, a poet and playwright, published a variety of works throughout his long career, notably: a collection of sonnets, *Delia* (1592); two tragedies, *Cleopatra* (1594) and *Philotas* (1604); an epic poem of the Wars

of the Roses, *Civil Wars* (1595, 1609); and several masques. His essay on poetry, *A Defense of Rhyme*, was published in 1603.
2. Daniel's criticism of "laborsome curiosity" is comparable to Gascoigne's criticism of an "inkhorn" style: both poets reject pedantry.
3. Created conceptions.

more laborious than loose measures (whatsoever is objected), must needs, meeting with wit and industry, breed greater and worthier effects in our language. So that if our labors have wrought out a manumission[4] from bondage and that we go at liberty, notwithstanding these ties, we are no longer the slaves of rhyme but we make it a most excellent instrument to serve us. Nor is this certain limit observed in sonnets any tyrannical bounding of the conceit,[5] but rather a reducing it in *girum* [in bounds], and a just form, neither too long for the shortest project nor too short for the longest, being but only employed for a present passion. For the body of our imagination, being as an unformed chaos without fashion, without day, if by the divine power of the spirit it be wrought into an orb of order and form, is it not more pleasing to nature that desires a certainty and comports not with that which is infinite, to have these closes[6] rather than not to know where to end or how far to go, especially seeing our passions are often without measure. And we find in the best of the Latins many times either not concluding or else otherwise in the end than they began. Besides, is it not most delightful to see much excellently ordered in a small room, or little gallantly disposed and made to fill up a space of like capacity, in such sort that the one would not appear so beautiful in a larger circuit nor the other do well in a less, which often we find to be so, according to the powers of nature, in the workman. And these limited proportions and rests of stanzas, consisting of six, seven, or eight lines, are of that happiness, both for the disposition of the matter, the apt planting the sentence where it may best stand to hit, the certain close of delight with the full body of a just period well-carried,[7] is such as neither the Greeks or Latins ever attained unto. For their boundless running on often so confounds the reader that having once lost himself must either give off unsatisfied or certainly cast back to retrieve the escaped sense and to find way again into his matter.

Methinks we should not so soon yield our consents captive to the authority of antiquity unless we saw more reason. All our understandings are not to be built by the square of Greece and Italy. We are the children of nature as well as they, we are not so placed out of the way of judgment but that the same sun of discretion shineth upon us, we have our portion of the same virtues as well as of the same vices. * * *

It is not the observing of trochaics nor their iambics[8] that will make our writings aught the wiser. All their poesie, all their philosophy is nothing unless we bring the discerning light of conceit[9] with us to apply it to use. It is not books, but only that great book of the world and the all-overspreading grace of heaven that makes men truly judicial.[1] Nor can it be but a touch of arrogant ignorance to hold this or that nation barbarous, these or those times gross, considering how this manifold creature man, wheresoever he stand in the world, hath always some disposition of worth, entertains the order of society, affects that which is most in use, and is eminent in some one thing or other that fits his humor and the times. The Grecians held all other nations barbarous but themselves, yet Pyrrhus when he saw the well-ordered marching of the Romans, which made them see their presumptuous error, could say it was no barbarous manner of preceding. The Goths, Vandals, and Longobards,[2] whose coming down like an innundation overwhelmed, as they say, all the glory of learning in Europe, have yet left us still their laws and customs as the originals of most of the provincial constitutions of Christendom, which well-considered with their other course of government may serve to clear them from this imputation of ignorance. And though the van-

---

4. Release.
5. I.e., the conception informing the poem.
6. Endings, as in rhyme.
7. A well-constructed sentence.

8. Meters used in classical poetry.
9. Imagination.
1. Discriminating.
2. Lombards.

quished never yet spoke well of the conqueror,[3] yet even through the unsound coverings of malediction appear those monuments of truth as argue well their worth and proves them not without judgment, though without Greek and Latin.

END OF "THE APOLOGY" AND THE ART OF POETRY

Isabella Whitney
fl. 1567–1573

Little is known about the life of Isabella Whitney. Biographers agree that she was the sister of Geoffrey Whitney, the author of the first emblem book in England, and that, like him, she was born in Cheshire. The rest is to be deduced from her poetry, which points to an author with little formal education, a sharp eye for the details of urban life, and some knowledge of classical mythology. The modesty of Whitney's literary background sets her off from such later and accomplished poets as Mary Herbert and Aemilia Lanyer, and her poems on the challenges of love, friendship, and survival in a large city distinguish her from women who wrote devotional verse. Her poems follow the form and conventions of broadside ballads, a feature that may have made them popular with readers who were drawn to stories that gave advice on affairs of the heart and matters of the purse. Of "the middling sort," Whitney probably came to London for employment and diversion, but she seems to have had difficulty supporting herself. In any case, after publishing two collections of verse, *The Copy of a Letter* (c. 1567) and *A Sweet Nosegay* (1573), she left the city, having lived out the dreams as well as the disappointments of many English villagers who went to London to find work.

I.W. To Her Unconstant Lover

As close° as you your wedding[1] kept   *quiet*
    yet now the truth I hear,
Which you (ere now) might me have told
    what need you nay to swear?

5   You know I always wished you well,
    so will I during life,
But since you shall a husband be,
    God send you a good wife.

And this (whereso you shall become)
10   full boldly may you boast:
That once you had as true a love
    as dwelt in any coast.

Whose constantness had never quailed
    if you had not begun,
15   And yet it is not so far past,
    but might again be won.

---

3. Daniel refers to the culture of conquered peoples without specifying which conquests or peoples he has in mind. But he acknowledges that even in the curses of these peoples, as they complain about their conquerors, there are "monuments of truth" that reveal worth and judgment.
1. The formal announcement of an impending marriage; he is not yet actually married.

If you so would; yea and not change
   so long as life should last,
But if that needs you marry must?
20   then farewell, hope is past.

And if you cannot be content
   to lead a single life?
(Although the same right quiet be)
   then take me to your wife.

25   So shall the promises be kept,
   that you so firmly made;
Now choose whether ye will be true,
   or be of Sinon's trade.[2]

Whose trade if that you long shall use,
30   it shall your kindred stain;
Example take by many a one
   whose falsehood now is plain.

As by Aeneas[3] first of all,
   who did poor Dido leave,
35 Causing the Queen by his untruth
   with sword her heart to cleave.

Also I find that Theseus did
   his faithful love forsake,
Stealing away within the night,
40   before she did awake.

Jason that came of noble race
   two ladies did beguile;
I muse how he durst show his face
   to them that knew his wile.°   *cunning*

45 For when he by Medea's art
   had got the fleece of gold
And also had of her that time
   all kind of things he would,

He took his ship and fled away
50   regarding not the vows,
That he did make so faithfully
   unto his loving spouse.

How durst he trust the surging seas
   knowing himself forsworn?
55 Why did he scape safe to the land
   before the ship was torn?

2. Posing as a deserter from the Greek army, Sinon persuaded the besieged Trojans to open the city gates to him and a large wooden horse that he pretended was a gift from Athena but in fact hid Greek warriors in its belly.
3. Whitney lists unfaithful lovers recorded in myth: Aeneas, the Trojan hero and founder of Rome, who deserted Dido, queen of Carthage, after expressing love for her; Theseus, the hero and king of Athens, who left Ariadne, the daughter of Minos, king of Crete, on a island in the sea, even though she had saved him from the monster, Minotaur; Jason, the leader of the Argonauts who captured the golden fleece—a Greek treasure—with the help of Medea, and then abandoned her in favor of Glauce, daughter of Creon, king of Corinth.

I think King Aeolus° stayed the winds   *god of the winds*
    and Neptune° ruled the sea;   *god of the sea*
Then might he boldly pass the waves
60   no perils could him slay.

But if his falsehood had to them
    been manifest before,
They would have rent the ship as soon
    as he had gone from shore.

65   Now may you hear how falseness is
    made manifest in time,
Although they that commit the same
    think it a venial crime.

For they, for their unfaithfulness,
70   did get perpetual fame.
Fame? Wherefore did I term it so?
    I should have called it shame.

Let Theseus be, let Jason pass,
    let Paris[4] also 'scape,°   *escape*
75   That brought destruction unto Troy
    all through the Grecian rape,

And unto me a Troilus[5] be,
    if not you may compare,
With any of these persons that
80   above expressed are.

But if I cannot please your mind,
    for wants that rest in me,
Wed whom you list,° I am content,   *wish*
    your refuse for to be.

85   It shall suffice me simple soul
    of thee to be forsaken,
And it may chance, although not yet,
    you wish you had me taken.

But rather than you should have cause
90   to wish this through° your wife,   *because of*
I wish to her, ere her you have,
    no more but loss of life.

For she that shall so happy be,
    of thee to be elect,
95   I wish her virtues to be such,
    she need not be suspect.

---

4. Son of Priam, king of Troy; he stole Helen, the wife of King Menelaus of Sparta, a theft that brought about the invasion of Troy by Menelaus and the Greeks.
5. Son of Priam, king of Troy; his fidelity to Cressida, who deserted him in favor of Diomedes, a Greek warrior, is recounted in a 4th-century addition to the stories of the Trojan War.

I rather wish her Helen's face,
    than one of Helen's trade,
With chasteness of Penelope[6]
100   the which did never fade.

A Lucrece for her constancy,
    and Thisby for her truth;
If such thou have, then Peto[7] be,
    not Paris, that were ruth.

105 Perchance, ye will think this thing rare
    in one woman to find;
Save Helen's beauty, all the rest
    the gods have me assigned.

These words I do not speak, thinking
110   from thy new love to turn thee.
Thou knowest by proof what I deserve;
    I need not to inform thee.

But let that pass. Would God I had
    Cassandra's gift[8] me lent;
115 Then either thy ill chance or mine
    my foresight might prevent.

But all in vain for this I seek,
    wishes may not attain it;
Therefore may hap° to me what shall,   *happen*
120   and I cannot refrain it.

Wherefore I pray God be my guide
    and also thee defend;
No worser than I wish myself,
    until thy life shall end.

125 Which life I pray God may again
    King Nestor's[9] life renew,
And after that your soul may rest
    amongst the heavenly crew.

Thereto I wish King Xerxes'[1] wealth,
130   or else King Croesus's gold,
With as much rest and quietness
    as man may have on mold.°   *in the world*

And when you shall this letter have
    let it be kept in store.
135 For she that sent the same hath sworn
    as yet to send no more.

---

6. Whitney alludes to women who exemplify fidelity: Penelope, who waited for the return of Odysseus from the Trojan War; Lucrece or Lucretia, who killed herself after confessing to her husband that she had been raped; and Thisby or Thisbe, who killed herself when she saw her dying lover, Pyramus.
7. The source of this name is unknown.
8. Daughter of Priam, king of Troy; she had prophetic powers, though her prophecies of the city's fall were not believed.
9. King of Pylos and wise counselor to all the Greeks during their siege of Troy.
1. Whitney names men of legendary wealth: Xerxes, king of the Persians, who, with enormous resources gathered from all Asia Minor, attacked Athens and was defeated there by Themistocles; and Croesus, king of Lydia, who was defeated by Cyrus, king of the Persians.

And now farewell, for why at large
   my mind is here expressed?
The which you may perceive, if that
140   you do peruse the rest.

Finis.

c. 1567

A Careful Complaint by the Unfortunate Author

Good Dido[1] stint thy tears,
   and sorrows all resign
To me that born was to augment
   misfortune's luckless line.
5   Or using still the same,
   good Dido do thy best,
In helping to bewail the hap
   that furthereth mine unrest.
For though thy Troyan mate,
10   that Lord Aeneas hight,
Requiting all thy steadfast love,
   from Carthage took his flight,
And foully broke his oath,
   and promise made before,
15   Whose falsehood finished thy delight,
   before thy hairs were hoar.
Yet greater cause of grief
   compels me to complain,
For Fortune fell° converted hath   *evil*
20   my health to heaps of pain.
And that she[2] swears my death,
   too plain it is (alas),
Whose end let malice still attempt
   to bring the same to pass.
25   O Dido, thou hadst lived
   a happy woman still,
If fickle fancy had not thralled°   *enslaved*
   thy wits to reckless will.
For as the man by whom
30   thy deadly dolors bred,
Without regard of plighted troth
   from Carthage city fled,
So might thy cares in time
   be banished out of thought,
35   His absence might well salve the sore
   that erst° his presence wrought.   *first*
For fire no longer burns
   than faggots° feed the flame,   *except when sticks*

---

1. Queen of Carthage, seduced and then abandoned by
Aeneas on his way from Troy to Italy.

2. I.e., Fortune, whose end or purpose, Whitney's death,
malice will bring to pass.

40   The want of things that breed annoy
        may soon redress the same.[3]
        But I, unhappy most,
        and gripped with endless griefs,
        Despair (alas) amid my hope,
        and hope without relief.
45   And as the swelt'ring heat
        consumes the war away,
        So do the heaps of deadly harms
        still threaten my decay.
        O death delay not long
50   thy duty to declare.
        Ye Sisters three[4] dispatch my days
        and finish all my care.

- - - - ❧✦❧ - - - -

Elizabeth I
1533–1603

No British monarch has left posterity a more dazzling record of accomplishments than Elizabeth Tudor, second daughter of Henry VIII. During the course of her reign, England became a nation to rival France and Spain; England's cities became centers of commerce, her navy controlled the principal routes of trade, and her people pursued lucrative interests in Europe and the New World. Having ruled England for almost half a century, Elizabeth has lived on as a figure of compelling power in the history of her people. What Shakespeare said of his character Cleopatra—"Age cannot wither her, nor custom stale her infinite variety"—conveys something of the fascination the memory of this extraordinary woman has had for the English people as well as for others around the globe. Age did, of course, eventually touch her being; doubtless, too, the brilliant strategies by which she governed subjects who were ever jealous of her royal prerogative must finally have become predictable. But Elizabeth was brought up in the atmosphere of a volatile politics, given to shifts in the winds of chance, susceptible to the heat of violent controversy and even to the flames of rebellion. She did what she had to do to remain on the throne; her father's example, if nothing else, taught her how fragile was the rule of a monarch who depended much more on the loyalty of subjects than on the authority of office or the power of the law.

Elizabeth's birth was itself a disappointment, at least to Henry VIII, who had hoped for a son. Her mother was the king's second wife, the charming Anne Boleyn, whom he married after divorcing Catherine of Aragon, the mother of his first daughter, Mary Tudor. The divorce precipitated the king's break with the Catholic Church, made Mary Tudor illegitimate, and effectively defined Anne's politics as unequivocally Protestant. But the new queen's influence was short-lived. Supporters of Catholicism, those who remained faithful to the memory of Catherine and respected the claims of Mary Tudor, may have been responsible for convincing the king that Anne had been unfaithful to him; in any case, he ordered her execution. Ten days later, he married Jane Seymour, declared Elizabeth illegitimate, and again waited for the birth of a son. Elizabeth's half-brother, the future Edward VI, was born in

---

3. I.e., "want," which breeds annoyance, will also end annoyance, as it will eventually result in death.

4. I.e., the three Fates, who determine the length of life and the time of death.

Robert Peake (attr.), *Queen Elizabeth Going in Procession to Blackfriars in 1600*. This splendid painting is linked to no particular event. Its arrangement of figures suggests a Roman imperial triumph, and evokes the success of the queen's monarchy. She appears to be in a litter, but is actually in a chair on wheels pushed by attendants, and protected by a canopy held by courtiers. She is preceded by a knight, perhaps Gilbert Talbot, Earl of Shrewsbury, who carries the sword of state. Though Elizabeth was sixty-eight when this painting was made in 1601, she is shown as a much younger woman. Her wish to be recognized as always desirable and ever the object of courtly devotion is well illustrated by her pale, unlined face, her highly dressed hair and her stylized body, clothed in a bejeweled dress whose puffed sleeves and intricate lace ruff suggest an ethereal and even divine creature. She is attended by six Knights of the Garter; the knight standing directly beside her (with a bald head and stiff grey beard) has been identified as her current favorite, Edward Somerset, Earl of Worcester; his two principal castles, Raglan and Chepstow, are probably those in the background of the painting.

1537, when Elizabeth was four years old. Fortunately, at the age of ten, Elizabeth at last acquired a loving stepmother: Henry's sixth wife, Catherine Parr, looked after her interests and education. An excellent student, fluent in Latin, French, and Italian and versed in history, Elizabeth was raised to be the subject of her brother, who became king after Henry's death in 1547. When he died in 1553, she became a pawn in a long and vicious struggle for the crown. Imprisoned in the Tower and then in Woodstock Castle in Oxfordshire by the Catholic supporters of her sister's claim to the throne, Elizabeth wrote lyrics that testify to both her fears and her faith during this dangerous time.

In 1558, Queen Mary died, and Elizabeth was crowned with much rejoicing; in the historian William Camden's words: "neither did the people ever embrace any other Prince with more willing and constant mind." Once on the throne, Elizabeth pursued a policy of exemplary discretion; she rewarded those who were loyal to her and punished those who showed signs of disobedience. In 1568, when her cousin Mary, Queen of Scots, abdicated the throne of Scotland in favor of her son, James VI, Elizabeth granted Mary refuge in England. Yet evidence later suggested that Mary, an ardent Catholic, had plotted to kill Elizabeth and restore

Catholicism in England, and in 1587, Elizabeth ordered her execution with great regret. Reflecting on this action, also the subject of a speech to Parliament, the queen declared: "This death will wring my heart as long as I live."

A woman and reigning monarch, Elizabeth's position was anomalous. As a woman, she retained an important kind of social power only as long as she was an object of desire, to be courted and won; as a reigning monarch, she was expected not only to govern but also to secure the succession. In her speech to Parliament on the subject of marriage early in her reign, Elizabeth provided reasons why she would delay taking a husband. She probably never intended to take one. Continuing the fiction of courtship well past the age at which she could be expected to have a child, she saw to it that she remained at once attractive and unavailable. Most important, she succeeded in commanding the attention of her subjects by transforming her court into a center of literary and artistic activity. Late in life, she met her most serious suitor, the Duke of Alençon, brother to the French king, Henry III. A dwarf whose face was disfigured by smallpox, he was her "little frog," a man she is said to have loved dearly. The problem of succession required another kind of temporizing. She refused to name James VI of Scotland as the next king of England until shortly before she died—a silence that she maintained was necessary to preserve the peace.

Throughout her long reign she cultivated two personas. As a monarch, she could speak courageously (as she did to her soldiers at Tilbury on the Devon coast while they waited for the Spanish to invade); as a woman, she could convey understanding (as she did to her critics in her so-called Golden Speech curtailing her prerogative to create monopolies). Her government remained a conscientious one to its very end. She cultivated a habit of mind that must have helped to ensure its stability: as her translation of Boethius's *Consolation of Philosophy* (made when she was sixty years old) reminds us, she never allowed herself to forget the vicissitudes of fortune and her own mortality.

Written with a Diamond on Her Window at Woodstock[1]

Much suspected by° me,   *to have been done by*
Nothing proved can be,
   Quoth Elizabeth prisoner.

Written on a Wall at Woodstock

Oh fortune, thy wresting wavering state
Hath fraught with cares my troubled wit,
Whose witness this present prison late
Could bear, where once was joy's loan quit.[1]
5   Thou causedst the guilty to be loosed
From bands° where innocents were inclosed,   *bonds*
And caused the guiltless to be reserved,°   *bound*
And freed those that death had well deserved.
But all herein° can be nothing wrought,   *in prison*
10   So God send to my foes all they have thought.[2]

---

1. Elizabeth was imprisoned at Woodstock Castle, near Oxford, from 23 May 1554 to sometime late in April 1555. The queen, Mary I, Elizabeth's half-sister, suspected her of treason. This and the following poem are thought to have been written at this time.
1. I.e., this prison could bear witness recently to fortune's

wavering state, where once it did not have to borrow joy [as it does now].
2. I.e., nothing can be done by one who is in prison, so may God send to my foes what they have suspected me of planning.

The Doubt of Future Foes

The doubt° of future foes exiles my present joy,   *fear*
And wit me warns to shun such snares as threaten mine annoy;[1]
For falsehood now doth flow, and subjects' faith doth ebb,
Which should not be if reason ruled or wisdom weaved the web.
5 But clouds of joys untried° do cloak aspiring minds,   *untested*
Which turn to rain of late repent by changed course of winds.[2]
The top of hope supposed the root upreared shall be,
And fruitless all their grafted guile, as shortly ye shall see.[3]
The dazzled eyes with pride, which great ambition blinds,
10 Shall be unsealed by worthy wights[4] whose foresight falsehood finds.
The daughter of debate that discord aye° doth sow   *ever*
Shall reap no gain where former rule[5] still peace hath taught to know.
No foreign banished wight[6] shall anchor in this port;
Our realm brooks not seditious sects, let them elsewhere resort.
15 My rusty sword through rest shall first his edge employ
To poll their tops[7] that seek such change or gape[8] for future joy.

On Monsieur's Departure[1]

I grieve and dare not show my discontent,
I love and yet am forced to seem to hate,
I do, yet dare not say I ever meant,
I seem stark mute but inwardly do prate.
5   I am and not,° I freeze and yet am burned,   *am not*
      Since from myself another self I turned.

My care is like my shadow in the sun,
Follows me flying, flies when I pursue it,
Stands and lies by me, doth what I have done.
10 His too familiar care doth make me rue°it.   *regret*
      No means I find to rid him from my breast,
      Till by the end of things° it be supprest.   *death*

Some gentler passion slide into my mind,
For I am soft and made of melting snow;
15 Or be more cruel, love, and so be kind.
Let me or° float or sink, be high or low.   *either*
      Or let me live with some more sweet content,
      Or die and so forget what love ere meant.

---

1. My harm.
2. I.e., because of a change of wind, my enemies' clouds of joy can turn to the rain of repentance.
3. I.e., at their most hopeful, my enemies supposed that the tree of my monarchy would be uprooted, but their grafted limbs of guile will bear no fruit.
4. Men.
5. The rule of Elizabeth's father, Henry VIII, and brother, Edward VI, both Protestants.

6. Any supporter of Philip II, king of Spain and consort of Mary I.
7. Cut their heads off.
8. Smile.
1. The poem expresses Elizabeth's regret at the departure of the Duke d'Alençon, who had sought her hand in marriage. After four years of visits and inconclusive negotiations, the courtship ended in 1583.

Psalm 13

Fools that true faith yet never had
Saith in their hearts, there is no God.
Filthy they are in their practice,
Of them not one is godly wise.
5   From heaven the Lord on man did look
To know what ways he undertook.
All they were vain and went astray,
Not one he found in the right way.
In heart and tongue have they deceit,
10   Their lips throw forth a poisoned bait.
Their minds are mad, their mouths° are wode,°   *speech / empty*
And swift they be in shedding blood.
So blind they are, no truth they know,
No fear of God in them will grow.
15   How can that cruel sort be good,
Of God's dear flock which suck the blood?
On him rightly shall they not call,
Despair will so their hearts appall.
At all times God is with the just,
20   Because they put in him their trust.
Who shall therefore from Sion[1] give
That health which hangeth in our belief?
When God shall take from his the smart,
Then will Jacob rejoice in heart.
25   Praise to God

from **The Metres of Boethius's *Consolation of Philosophy***[1]
Book 1, No. 2

O in how headlong depth the drowned mind is dim!
   And losing light her own, to others' darkness drawn,
As oft as driven with earthly flaws the harmful care upward grows.[2]
   Once this man free in open field used the skies to view,
5   Of rosie sun the light beheld,
   Of frosty moon the planets saw,
And what star else runs her wonted° course.   *accustomed*
   Bending by many circles this man had wone°   *used*
By number to know them all;[3]
10   Yea, causes each whence roaring winds the seas perturb.
Acquainted with the spirit that rolls the steady world,

---

1. Zion, the heavenly city, source and object of salvation.
1. These poems are Elizabeth's translations, undertaken late in her life, of portions of the *De consolatione philosophiae* (*On the Consolation of Philosophy*) by the Christian martyr Anicius Manlius Severinus Boethius (475–525), written while Boethius was in prison, awaiting execution. The treatise's representation of a heavenly perspective from which earthly concerns appear trivial made it a favorite work of moral philosophy through the Middle Ages and early modern period. Even at the height of her power, Elizabeth was attracted by Boethius's Stoic rejection of worldly ambition.
2. I.e., losing her own light, the mind is drawn to the darkness of others, just as care grows with the faults of others.
3. I.e., this man was accustomed to know all the "circles" (cycles and epicycles of the stars and planets).

And why the star that falls to the Hesperia's waters[4]
From his reddy° root doth raise herself.[5]   *reddish*
Who that gives the spring's mild hours their temper,
15   That with rosy flowers the earth bedeckt,
Who made the fertile autumn at fullest of the year
Abound with grape all swollen with ripest fruits.
He, wonted to search and find sundry causes of hidden nature,
Down lies of mind's light bereaved,[6]
20   With bruised neck by overheavy chains,
A bowed low look by weight bearing,
Driven, alas, the silly° earth behold.   *insignificant*

Book 1, No. 7

Dim clouds,
Sky close
Light none
Can afford.
5   If roiling seas
Boisterous soweth,°   *scatters*
Mix his° foam,   *its*
Greeny° once   *greenish*
Like the clearest
10   Days, the water—
Straight mud,
Stirred up all foul—
The sight gainsays.°   *prevents*
Running stream
15   That pours
From highest hills,
Oft is stayed
By slaked°   *cool*
Stone of rock.
20   Thou, if thou wilt
In clearest light
The truth behold,
By straight line
Hit in the path.[1]
25   Chase joys,
Repulse fear,
Thrust out hope,
Woe not retain.
Cloudy is the mind
30   With snaffle° bound   *bridle-bit*
Where they reign.[2]

---

4. The sea to the west of the Hesperides, mythical islands located beyond the known horizon.
5. "His root" and "herself" both refer to the star that sinks in the west, perhaps the planet Mars, known for its reddish tinge.
6. I.e., happiness comes to the man who studies and knows nature; but when he contemplates the insignificance of the earth, he is weighed down with care.
1. I.e., keep to the path in a straight line.
2. Boethius extols the extreme indifference to fortune and the emotions that Stoic philosophers believed was necessary for the good life.

Book 2, No. 3

In pool when Phoebus with reddy wain[1]
　　The light to spread begins,
The star,[2] dimmed with flames° uprising,　　　　　　*of the sun*
　　Pales her whitty° looks.　　　　　　　　　　　　*whitish*
5　When wood° with Siphirus'[3] milding blast　　　*vegetation*
　　Blusheth with the springing° roses,　　　　　　*budding*
And cloudy soweth his blustering blasts,
　　Away from stalk° the beauty goes.　　　　　　　*of the flower*
Some time with calmy fair° the sea　　　　　　　　*a fair calm*
10　　Void of waves doth run;
Oft boisterous tempests the north
　　With foaming seas turns up.[4]
If rarely steady be the world's form,
　　If turns so many it makes,
15　Believe slippar° mens' lucks,　　　　　　　　　　*slippery*
　　Trust that sliding° be their goods.　　　　　　*impermanent*
Certain, and in eternal law is writ,
　　Sure standeth naught° is made.　　　　　　　　　*nothing that*

SPEECHES

The speeches of Elizabeth I exemplify early modern public oratory at its most effective. But they are also marked by features uniquely derived from her sense of herself as a monarch who wished (and probably needed) to convince her subjects that their welfare was more important to her than her own. In the excerpts that follow, Elizabeth emphasizes that although nature made her a woman and therefore of the weaker sex, divine right has made her a "prince," a person endowed with a masculine persona whose function it is to command not obey. She further emphasizes that her principal care is for her subjects, who are her charges and in some sense her children. In her public dealings throughout her reign, she played the gender card for all it was worth; in so doing, she transformed the fact that she was a woman, potentially a liability, into an instrument of policy.

On Marriage[1]

I may say unto you that from my years of understanding, sith[2] I first had consideration of myself to be born a servitor of Almighty God, I happily chose this kind of life in which I yet live, which I assure you for mine own part hath hitherto best contented myself and I trust hath been most acceptable to God. From the which, if either ambition of high estate offered to me in marriage by the pleasure and appointment of my prince[3]—whereof I have some records in this presence, as you our Lord Treasurer[4] well know; or if the

1. I.e., when Phoebus, or Apollo, god of the sun with his red chariot, spreads his light over the deep.
2. Venus, who as the morning star is known as Lucifer, or the light-bearer.
3. Zephyrus, god of the west wind.
4. This series of alterations in states of being—from darkness to light, from a breeze to a gale, and from a calm to a foaming sea—illustrates the "eternal law" of change.
1. In 1559, a year after she had acceded to the throne at the age of twenty-five, Elizabeth addressed Parliament on the subject of marriage. Because the monarchy passed on by inheritance, it was expected that a monarch would marry and have children. In this speech, Elizabeth hints that she will never marry and also that she trusts God to

provide for her successor. She probably intended to convey to her subjects that she would never abandon the kingdom either to the rule of a foreign prince (as Mary I had) or to a succession crisis.
2. Since.
3. The "prince" Elizabeth refers to is probably not Philip II, the consort of Mary I, but rather Mary herself, who in her official capacity as queen regnant might have offered her sister's hand in marriage to a suitable consort. Elizabeth can refer to Mary as her "sister" when she alludes to a "cause" that has no implications for the state but is rather personal, "in my sister herself."
4. The Marquis of Winchester.

eschewing of the danger of mine enemies or the avoiding of the period of death, whose messenger or rather continual watchman, the prince's indignation, was not little time daily before mine eyes—by whose means, although I know or justly may suspect, yet I will not now utter; or if the whole cause were in my sister herself, I will not now burthen her therewith, because I will not charge the dead: if any of these I say, I had not now remained in this estate wherein you see me. But so constant have I always continued in this determination—although my youth and words may seem to some hardly to agree together—yet is it most true that at this day I stand free from any other meaning that either I have had in times past or have at this present. With which trade of life I am so thoroughly acquainted that I trust God, who hath hitherto therein preserved and led me by the hand, will not now of His goodness suffer me to go alone. * * *

Nevertheless—if any of you be in suspect—whensoever it may please God to incline my heart to another kind of life, ye may well assure yourselves my meaning is not to do or determine anything wherewith the realm may or shall have just cause to be discontented. And therefore put that clean out of your heads.[5] For I assure you— what credit my assurance may have with you I cannot tell, but what credit it shall deserve to have the sequence shall declare—I will never in that matter conclude any-thing that shall be prejudicial to the realm, for the weal, good, and safety whereof I will never shun to spend my life. And whomsoever my chance shall be to light upon, I trust he shall be as careful for the realm and you—I will not say as myself, because I cannot so certainly determine of any other; but at the least ways, by my good will and desire he shall be such as shall be as careful for the preservation of the realm and you as myself.

And albeit it might please Almightly God to continue me still in this mind to live out of the state of marriage, yet it is not to be feared but He will so work in my heart and in your wisdoms as good provision by His help may be made in convenient time, whereby the realm shall not remain destitute of an heir that may be a fit gover-nor, and peradventure more beneficial to the realm than such offspring as may come of me. For, although I be never so careful of your well doings and mind ever so to be, yet may my issue grow out of kind and become perhaps ungracious. And in the end, this shall be for me sufficient, that a marble stone shall declare that a Queen, having reigned such a time, lived and died a virgin.

On Mary, Queen of Scots[1]

The bottomless graces and immeasurable benefits bestowed upon me by the Almighty are and have been such, as I must not only acknowledge them but admire them, accounting them as well miracles as benefits; not so much in respect of His Divine Majesty—with whom nothing is more common than to do things rare and singular—as in regard of our weakness, who cannot sufficiently set forth His wonder-ful works and graces, which to me have been so many, so diversely folded and embroidered one upon another, as in no sort am I able to express them.

5. Elizabeth emphasizes that her subjects and their repre-sentatives in Parliament have no authority to force her into marriage, however desirable they may think mar-riage is for the future of the kingdom.
1. The text is Elizabeth's answer to a petition from Parlia-ment to execute Mary, Queen of Scots, who was reported to have conspired to depose her cousin Elizabeth and who had been a prisoner of the English queen for ten years. In

August 1586, evidence of a new plot came to light, and the conspirators, led by Sir Thomas Babington, were exe-cuted. On the evidence in letters to Babington, Mary was then formally tried and convicted of treason by a special court of peers, counsellors, and judges. Elizabeth answered Parliament in October by asking for delay and divine enlightenment.

And although there liveth not any that may more justly acknowledge themselves infinitely bound unto God than I, whose life He hath miraculously preserved at sundry times (beyond my merit) from a multitude of perils and dangers, yet is not that the cause for which I count myself the deepliest bound to give Him my humblest thanks, or to yield Him greatest recognition; but this which I shall tell you hereafter, which will deserve the name of wonder, if rare things and seldom seen be worthy of account. Even this it is: that as I came to the crown with the willing hearts of subjects, so do I now, after twenty-eight years' reign, perceive in you no diminution of good wills, which, if haply I should want, well might I breathe but never think I lived.

And now, albeit I find my life hath been full dangerously sought, and death contrived by such as no desert procured it, yet am I thereof so clear from malice—which hath the property to make men glad at the falls and faults of their foes, and make them seem to do for other causes, when rancor is the ground—as I protest it is and hath been my grievous thought that one, not different in sex, of like estate, and my near kin, should be fallen into so great a crime. Yea, I had so little purpose to pursue her with any color of malice, that as it is not unknown to some of my Lords here—for now I will play the blab—I secretly wrote her a letter upon the discovery of sundry treasons, that if she would confess them, and privately acknowledge them by her letters unto myself, she never should need be called for them into so public question. Neither did I it of mind to circumvent her, for then I knew as much as she could confess; and so did I write.

And if, even yet, now the matter is made but too apparent, I thought she truly would repent—as perhaps she would easily appear in outward show to do—and that for her none other would take the matter upon them; or that we were but as two milkmaids, with pails upon our arms; or that there were no more dependency upon us, but mine own life were only in danger, and not the whole estate of your religion and well doings; I protest—wherein you may believe me, for although I may have many vices, I hope I have not accustomed my tongue to be an instrument of untruth—I would most willingly pardon and remit this offence. Or if by my death other nations and kingdoms might truly say that this realm had attained an ever prosperous and flourishing estate, I would (I assure you) not desire to live, but gladly give my life, to the end my death might procure you a better prince. And for your sakes it is that I desire to live: to keep you from a worse. For, as for me, I assure you I find no great cause I should be fond to live. I take no such pleasure in it that I should much wish it, nor conceive such terror in death that I should greatly fear it. And yet I say not but, if the stroke were coming, perchance flesh and blood would be moved with it, and seek to shun it.

I have had good experience and trial of this world. I know what it is to be a subject, what to be a sovereign, what to have good neighbors, and sometime meet evil-willers. I have found treason in trust, seen great benefits little regarded, and instead of gratefulness, courses[2] of purpose to cross. These former remembrances, present feeling, and future expectation of evils, (I say), have made me think an evil is much the better the less while it dureth,[3] and so them happiest that are soonest hence;[4] and taught me to bear with a better mind these treasons, than is common to my sex—yea, with a better heart perhaps than is in some men. Which I hope you will not merely impute to my simplicity or want of understanding, but rather that I thus conceived—that had their purposes taken effect, I should not have found the blow, before I had felt it; nor, though my peril should have been great, my pain should have been but

2. Plans.
3. Lasts.
4. I.e., out of this world.

small and short. Wherein, as I would be loath to die so bloody a death, so doubt I not but God would have given me grace to be prepared for such an event; which, when it shall chance, I refer to His good pleasure.

And now, as touching their treasons and conspiracies, together with the contriver of them. I will not so prejudicate myself and this my realm as to say or think that I might not, without the last statute, by the ancient laws of this land have proceeded against her; which[5] was not made particularly to prejudice her, though perhaps it might then be suspected in respect of the disposition of such as depend that way. It was so far from being intended to entrap her, that it was rather an admonition to warn the danger thereof. But sith it is made, and in the force of a law, I thought good, in that which might concern her, to proceed according thereunto rather than by course of common law. Wherein, if you the judges have not deceived me, or that the books you brought me were not false—which God forbid—I might as justly have tried her by the ancient laws of the land.

But you lawyers are so nice and so precise in sifting and scanning every word and letter, that many times you stand more upon form than matter, upon syllables than the sense of the law. For, in this strictness and exact following of common form, she must have been indicted in Staffordshire, been arraigned at the bar, holden up her hand, and then been tried by a jury: a proper course, forsooth, to deal in that manner with one of her estate! I thought it better, therefore, for avoiding of these and more absurdities, to commit the cause to the inquisition of a good number of the greatest and most noble personages of this realm, of the judges and others of good account, whose sentence I must approve.[6]

And all little enough: for we Princes, I tell you, are set on stages, in the sight and view of all the world duly observed. The eyes of many behold our actions; a spot is soon spied in our garments, a blemish quickly noted in our doings. It behoveth us, therefore, to be careful that our proceedings be just and honorable.

But I must tell you one thing more: that in this late Act of Parliament you have laid an hard hand on me—that I must give direction for her death, which cannot be but most grievous, and an irksome burden to me. And lest you might mistake mine absence from this Parliament—which I had almost forgotten: although there be no cause why I should willingly come amongst multitudes (for that amongst many, some may be evil), yet hath it not been the doubt of any such danger or occasion that kept me from thence, but only the great grief to hear this cause spoken of, especially that such one of state and kin should need so open a declaration, and that this nation should be so spotted with blots of disloyalty. Wherein, the less is my grief for that I hope the better part is mine; and those of the worse not much to be accounted of, for that in seeking my destruction they might have spoiled their own souls.

And even now could I tell you that which would make you sorry. It is a secret; and yet I will tell it you (although it be known I have the property to keep counsel but too well, often times to mine own peril). It is not long since mine eyes did see it written that an oath was taken within few days either to kill me or to be hanged themselves; and that to be performed ere one month were ended. Hereby I see your danger in me, and neither can or will be so unthankful or careless of your consciences as to take no care for your safety.

---

5. I.e., the Parliamentary statute of 1584–1585, known as the Act for the Queen's Surety, which provided for the trial of Mary, Queen of Scots, should she be accused of treason.
6. Elizabeth claims that Mary could have been tried as a criminal in a common law court but that this would have been an improper way to proceed as Mary remained a Queen of Scotland and her liability under English law was open to question.

I am not unmindful of your oath made in the Association,[7] manifesting your great good wills and affections, taken and entered into upon good conscience and true knowledge of the guilt, for safeguard of my person; done (I protest to God) before I ever heard it, or ever thought of such a matter, till a thousand hands, with many obligations, were showed me at Hampton Court, signed and subscribed with the names and seals of the greatest of this land. Which, as I do acknowledge as a perfect argument of your true hearts and great zeal to my safety, so shall my bond be stronger tied to greater care for all your good.

But, for that this matter is rare, weighty and of great consequence, and I think you do not look for any present resolution—the rather for that, as it is not my manner in matters of far less moment to give speedy answer without due consideration, so in this of such importance—I think it very requisite with earnest prayer to beseech His Divine Majesty so to illuminate mine understanding and inspire me with His grace, as I may do and determine that which shall serve to the establishment of His Church, preservation of your estates, and prosperity of this Commonwealth under my charge. Wherein, for that I know delay is dangerous, you shall have with all conveniency our resolution delivered by our message. And what ever any prince may merit of their subjects, for their approved testimony of their unfeigned sincerity, either by governing justly, void of all partiality, or sufferance of any injuries done (even to the poorest), that do I assuredly promise inviolably to perform, for requital of your so many deserts.

On Mary's Execution[1]

Full grievous is the way whose going on and end breeds cumber[2] for the hire of a laborious journey. I have strived more this day than ever in my life whether I should speak or use silence. If I speak and not complain, I shall dissemble; if I hold my peace, your labor taken were full vain.

For me to make my moan were strange and rare, for I suppose you shall find few that, for their own particular, will cumber you with such a care. Yet such, I protest, hath been my greedy desire and hungry will that of your consultation might have fallen out some other means to work my safety, joined with your assurance, than that for which you are become so earnest suitors, as I protest I must needs use complaint[3]—though not of you, but unto you, and of the cause; for that I do perceive, by your advices, prayers, and desires, there falleth out this accident, that only my injurer's bane must be my life's surety.

But if any there live so wicked of nature to suppose that I prolonged this time only pro forma, to the intent to make a show of clemency, thereby to set my praises to the wire-drawers[4] to lengthen them the more, they do me so great a wrong as they can hardly recompense. Or if any person there be that think or imagine that the least vainglorious thought hath drawn me further herein, they do me as open injury as ever was done to any living creature—as He that is the maker of all thoughts knoweth best to be true. Or if there be any that think that the Lords, appointed in

---

7. The Oath (or Bond) of Association was taken by the Queen's Council in October 1582. It provided for Mary's arrest and execution without a trial; in essence, it sanctioned a lynching.

1. Parliament had determined that Elizabeth's safety and the future of Protestantism in England could be secured only by Mary's execution; it sent a delegation to Eliza-beth asking for her approval. Again Elizabeth demurred. It was only in February 1587, after a new conspiracy was discovered, that Elizabeth signed Mary's death warrant.

2. Distress.

3. Express regret.

4. One who draws metal into wire.

commission, durst do no other, as fearing thereby to displease or to be suspected to be of a contrary opinion to my safety, they do but heap upon me injurious conceits. For, either those put in trust by me to supply my place have not performed their duty towards me, or else they have signified unto you all that my desire was that every one should do according to his conscience, and in the course of these proceedings should enjoy both freedom of voice and liberty of opinion, and what they would not openly, they might privately to myself declare. It was of a willing mind and great desire I had, that some other means might be found out, wherein I should have taken more comfort than in any other thing under the sun.

And since now it is resolved that my surety cannot be established without a princess's head, I have just cause to complain that I, who have in my time pardoned so many rebels, winked at so many treasons, and either not produced[5] them or altogether slipped them over with silence, should now be forced to this proceeding, against such a person. I have besides, during my reign, seen and heard many opprobrious books and pamphlets against me, my realm and state, accusing me to be a tyrant. I thank them for their alms. I believe therein their meaning was to tell me news: and news it is to me indeed. I would it were as strange to hear of their impiety. What will they not now say, when it shall be spread that for the safety of her life a maiden queen could be content to spill the blood even of her own kinswoman? I may therefore full well complain that any man should think me given to cruelty; whereof I am so guiltless and innocent as I should slander God if I should say He gave me so vile a mind. Yea, I protest, I am so far from it that for mine own life I would not touch her. Neither hath my care been so much bent how to prolong mine, as how to preserve both: which I am right sorry is made so hard, yea so impossible.

I am not so void of judgment as not to see mine own peril; nor yet so ignorant as not to know it were in nature a foolish course to cherish a sword to cut mine own throat; nor so careless as not to weigh that my life daily is in hazard. But this I do consider, that many a man would put his life in danger for the safeguard of a king. I do not say that so will I; but I pray you think that I have thought upon it.

But sith so many hath both written and spoken against me, I pray you give me leave to say somewhat for myself, and, before you return to your countries, let you know for what a one you have passed so careful thoughts. And, as I think myself infinitely beholding unto you all that seek to preserve my life by all the means you may, so I protest that there liveth no prince—nor ever shall be—more mindful to requite so good deserts. Wherein, as I perceive you have kept your old wont[6] in a general seeking the lengthening of my days, so am I sure that never shall I requite it, unless I had as many lives as you all; but for ever I will acknowledge it while there is any breath left me. Although I may not justify, but may justly condemn, my sundry faults and sins to God, yet for my care in this government let me acquaint you with my intents.

When first I took the sceptre, my title made me not forget the giver, and therefore [I] began as it became me, with such religion as both I was born in, bred in, and, I trust, shall die in; although I was not so simple as not to know what danger and peril so great an alteration might procure me—how many great princes of the contrary opinion would attempt all they might against me, and generally what enmity I should thereby breed unto myself. Which all I regarded not, knowing that He, for whose sake I did it, might and would defend me. Rather marvel that I am, than muse that I

5. Acted upon.   6. Desire.

should not be if it were not God's holy hand that continueth me beyond all other expectation.

I was not simply trained up, nor in my youth spent my time altogether idly; and yet, when I came to the crown, then entered I first into the school of experience, bethinking myself of those things that best fitted a king—justice, temper, magnanimity, judgment. As for the two latter, I will not boast. But for the two first, this may I truly say: among my subjects I never knew a difference of person, where right was one;[7] nor never to my knowledge preferred for favor what I thought not fit for worth; nor bent mine ears to credit a tale that first was told me; nor was so rash to corrupt my judgment with my censure, ere I heard the cause. I will not say but many reports might fortune[8] be brought me by such as must hear the matter, whose partiality might mar the right; for we princes cannot hear all causes ourselves. But this dare I boldly affirm: my verdict went with the truth of my knowledge.

But full well wished Alcibiades[9] his friend, that he should not give any answer till he had recited the letters of the alphabet. So have I not used over-sudden resolutions in matters that have touched me full near: you will say that with me, I think. And therefore, as touching your counsels and consultations, I conceive them to be wise, honest, and conscionable; so provident and careful for the safety of my life (which I wish no longer than may be for your good), that though I never can yield you of recompense your due, yet shall I endeavor myself to give you cause to think your good will not ill bestowed, and strive to make myself worthy for such subjects. And as for your petition: your judgment I condemn not, neither do I mistake your reasons, but pray you to accept my thankfulness, excuse my doubtfulness, and take in good part my answer-answerless. Wherein I attribute not so much to my own judgment, but that I think many particular persons may go before me, though by my degree I go before them. Therefore, if I should say, I would not do what you request, it might peradventure be more than I thought; and to say I would do it, might perhaps breed peril of that you labor to preserve, being more than in your own wisdoms and discretions would seem convenient,[1] circumstances of place and time being duly considered.

To the English Troops at Tilbury, Facing the Spanish Armada[1]

My loving people, we have been persuaded by some that are careful of our safety, to take heed how we commit ourselves to armed multitudes, for fear of treachery. But I assure you, I do not desire to live to distrust my faithful and loving people. Let tyrants fear. I have always so behaved myself that, under God, I have placed my chiefest strength and safeguard in the loyal hearts and good will of my subjects; and therefore I am come amongst you, as you see, at this time, not for my recreation and disport,[2] but being at this time resolved, in the midst and heat of the battle, to live or die amongst you all, to lay down for my God, and for my kingdom, and for my people, my

---

7. I.e., my justice was impartial; it did not regard rank, occupation, or property as factors in determining what was right.
8. By chance.
9. An Athenian statesman who took part in the Peloponnesian War; changed sides to support Athen's enemy, Sparta; and was finally assassinated by Persians with whom he sought an alliance. The source of Elizabeth's reference is unknown.

1. Elizabeth equivocates nicely. She refuses to disagree with Parliament, lest she not respect her own misgivings; she refuses to agree with Parliament, lest its policy not be in her own interest.
1. In 1588, with the Spanish fleet threatening the south coast of England, Elizabeth went to Tilbury, in Dorset, to speak to the troops who were guarding England against an invasion.
2. Amusement.

honor and my blood, even in the dust. I know I have the body of a weak and feeble woman, but I have the heart and stomach of a king, and of a king of England too, and think foul scorn[3] that Parma or Spain, or any prince of Europe should dare to invade the border of my realm; to which rather than any dishonor shall grow[4] by me, I myself will take up arms, I myself will be your general, judge, and rewarder of every one of your virtues in the field. I know, already for your forwardness[5] you have deserved rewards and crowns;[6] and we do assure you, in the word of a prince, they shall be duly paid you.

The Golden Speech[1]

Mr. Speaker, we have heard your declaration and perceive your care of our estate, by falling into a consideration of a grateful acknowledgment of such benefits as you have received; and that your coming is to present thanks to us, which I accept with no less joy than your loves can have desire to offer such a present.

I do assure you there is no prince that loves his subjects better, or whose love can countervail our love. There is no jewel, be it of never so rich a price, which I set before this jewel: I mean your love. For I do esteem it more than any treasure or riches; for that we know how to prize, but love and thanks I count unvaluable. And, though God hath raised me high, yet this I count the glory of my crown, that I have reigned with your loves. This makes me that I do not so much rejoice that God hath made me to be a queen, as to be a queen over so thankful a people. Therefore, I have cause to wish nothing more than to content the subject; and that is a duty which I owe. Neither do I desire to live longer days than I may see your prosperity; and that is my only desire. And as I am that person that still yet under God hath delivered you, so I trust, by the almighty power of God, that I shall be His instrument to preserve you from every peril, dishonor, shame, tyranny and oppression; partly by means of your intended helps which we take very acceptably, because it manifesteth the largeness of your good loves and loyalties unto your sovereign.

Of myself I must say this: I never was any greedy, scraping grasper, nor a strait, fast-holding prince, nor yet a waster. My heart was never set on any worldly goods, but only for my subjects' good. What you bestow on me, I will not hoard it up, but receive it to bestow on you again. Yea, mine own properties I account yours, to be expended for your good; and your eyes shall see the bestowing of all for your good. Therefore, render unto them, I beseech you, Mr. Speaker, such thanks as you imagine my heart yieldeth, but my tongue cannot express.

Since I was queen, yet did I never put my pen to any grant but that, upon pretext and semblance made unto me, it was both good and beneficial to the subject in general, though a private profit to some of my ancient servants who had deserved well at my hands. But the contrary being found by experience, I am exceedingly beholding to such subjects as would move the same at the first. And I am not so simple to suppose, but that there be some of the Lower House whom these grievances

3. Shameful.
4. Be caused.
5. Courage.
6. Recompense.
1. The queen had the prerogative or absolute power to grant favored subjects a patent for an exclusive manufacture. But the monopolies so created were disliked by those who would otherwise have competed for business, and a move to limit them was begun in Parliament. In response, in 1601, Elizabeth met with a committee of the House of Commons, led by the Speaker, thanked them for the subsidies recently granted the crown by the Commons, and promised to reform her practice.

never touched: and for them, I think they spake out of zeal to their countries,[2] and not out of spleen or malevolent affection as being parties grieved; and I take it exceeding gratefully from them, because it gives us to know that no respects or interest had moved them, other than the minds they have to suffer no diminution of our honor and our subjects' love unto us. The zeal of which affection, tending to ease my people and knit their hearts unto me, I embrace with a princely care, for above all earthly treasure I esteem my people's love, more than which I desire not to merit.

That my grants should be grievous to my people and oppressions privileged under color of our patents, our kingly dignity shall not suffer[3] it. Yea, when I heard it, I could give no rest unto my thoughts until I had reformed it. Shall they, think you, escape unpunished that have thus oppressed you, and have been respectless of their duty, and regardless of our honor?[4] No, I assure you, Mr. Speaker, were it not more for conscience' sake than for any glory or increase of love that I desire, these errors, troubles, vexations and oppressions, done by these varlets and lewd persons, not worthy the name of subjects, should not escape without condign punishment. But I perceive they dealt with me like physicians who, ministering a drug, make it more acceptable by giving it a good aromatical savor, or when they give pills do gild them all over.[5]

I have ever used to set the Last-Judgment Day before mine eyes, and so to rule as I shall be judged to answer before a higher Judge, to whose judgment seat I do appeal, that never thought was cherished in my heart that tended not unto my people's good. And now, if my kingly bounties have been abused, and my grants turned to the hurt of my people, contrary to my will and meaning, and if any in authority under me have neglected or perverted what I have committed to them, I hope God will not lay their culps[6] and offences to my charge; who, though there were danger in repealing our grants, yet what danger would I not rather incur for your good, than I would suffer them still to continue?

I know the title of a king is a glorious title; but assure yourself that the shining glory of princely authority hath not so dazzled the eyes of our understanding, but that we well know and remember that we also are to yield an account of our actions before the great Judge. To be a king and wear a crown is a thing more glorious to them that see it, than it is pleasant to them that bear it. For myself, I was never so much enticed with the glorious name of a king or royal authority of a queen, as delighted that God hath made me His instrument to maintain His truth and glory, and to defend this kingdom (as I said) from peril, dishonor, tyranny and oppression.

There will never queen sit in my seat with more zeal to my country, care for my subjects, and that will sooner with willingness venture her life for your good and safety, than myself. For it is my desire to live nor reign no longer than my life and reign shall be for your good. And though you have had and may have many princes more mighty and wise sitting in this seat, yet you never had nor shall have any that will be more careful and loving.

Shall I ascribe anything to myself and my sexly weakness? I were not worthy to live then; and, of all, most unworthy of the mercies I have had from God, who hath

---

2. I.e., those members who protested monopolies in behalf of their constituents, or "countries," and not on their own account.
3. Allow.
4. I.e., those who benefited from a monopoly without regard to the welfare of the general public.

5. Elizabeth compares unscrupulous patentees to physicians who coat bitter pills with sugar; in this case she is the patient who did not realize what was being given to her.
6. Sins.

given me a heart that yet never feared any foreign or home enemy. And I speak it to give God the praise, as a testimony before you, and not to attribute anything to myself. For I, oh Lord! what am I, whom practices and perils past should not fear? Or what can I do? That I should speak for any glory, God forbid.

This, Mr. Speaker, I pray you deliver unto the House, to whom heartily recommend me. And so I commit you all to your best fortunes and further counsels. And I pray you, Mr. Comptroller,[7] Mr. Secretary,[8] and you of my Council, that before these gentlemen go into their countries, you bring them all to kiss my hand.

⇒ PERSPECTIVES ⇒
Government and Self-Government

In a period marked by an increasingly centralized monarchy and a corresponding resistance to its bureaucratic reforms, ideas on government were debated in a variety of discourses. Political philosophers, such as More, described ideal forms of rule; historians reported events that actually happened and attempted to explain what followed as a result. A writer's point of view was clearly important; philosophers constructed models of order that reflected their belief in a certain kind of creation and the deity overseeing its development, while historians tried to interpret the actions of a person or a group in relation to the social interests they judged were at stake. Inevitably, the practice of government demonstrated the limits of a theory, while theory suggested the implications of a practice.

The selections included here reveal how comprehensive were these concerns, understood both in theory and in relation to daily life. Political thinkers sought to determine the proper business of state and also the conduct required of individual persons. Of course, they identified men and women as particular characters, each with his or her habits of mind and behavior, but they also recognized that every person had a specific office, a place and a role in life that was governed by expectations created by custom and, to a lesser extent, by common law. A man

Frontispiece to *Leviathan*, by Thomas Hobbes, 1651. This engraving illustrates the author's idea of government in a "commonwealth." Rising above the countryside is the mystical figure of the body politic. It consists of a crowned head—perhaps a dictator, perhaps a monarch—who has sovereign authority, and a body comprising the people, his subjects. The sovereign wields two powers: a civil power, symbolized by the sword in his right hand, and an ecclesiastical power, symbolized by the crozier in his left. Cells in the lower register of the engraving depict the mechanisms that support these powers, with scenes and symbols of the military on the left and of the church on the right. Published in 1651, *Leviathan* attempted to articulate conditions of rule proclaimed two years earlier, after the execution of Charles I. Hobbes believed that government was created by men who, rejecting the warlike state of nature in which they had originated, had handed over their natural rights to a sovereign in a kind of "contract," which traded their obedience for his protection. The idea of a body politic regularly was featured in early modern political thought and was discussed by writers as different as Bishop John Ponet and James I.

was primarily understood in terms of his work—as servant, artisan, yeoman, merchant, magistrate, or lord. A woman had fewer options and was usually identified according to her marital status—as a maid, a mother, or a widow. Over the course of the century, these categories became subject to challenge. Controversy grew as to the very basis of social order, the fundamental authority and power of the superior (whatever the office) over his or her subordinates. Protestant notions about the primacy of the individual conscience over collective authority were particularly effective in upsetting customary hierarchies of rule. On the one hand, they were used to justify individual rights; on the other, they supplied a rationale for those claiming such rights to protest as a group or a social body. There was a general agreement that states and persons should be governed by rules, but what these rules ought to be was becoming a contentious topic. Discussions of the power and authority of monarchs and magistrates generally emphasized that their power and authority were not absolute but limited by divine, natural, and positive law or the law of the land. This emphasis is matched by a pervasive fear of the tyrant—the ruler who not only makes and unmakes the law but does so in his own interest rather than for his people's welfare.

William Tyndale
c. 1495–1536

William Tyndale was perhaps the foremost of early English Protestants. Best known as the first translator of the Bible into English, he was active in political disputes as well, insisting on the absolute authority and power of the secular arm of government. He was motivated, in part, by his belief that no European monarch should have to obey the Pope in Rome. To him, a monarch and his magistrates were God's ministers on earth. In its later formulations under the Stuarts, this view of government was criticized for its toleration of tyranny. Tyndale found allies in Protestant Europe, and especially in Martin Luther, whom he visited in Wittenberg. He travelled extensively, seeing his translation of the New Testament through presses in Cologne and Worms, settling finally in Antwerp. As the popularity of Tyndale's work grew, he became increasingly the target of criticism. Denounced by bishops in England and particularly by Sir Thomas More, then a privy counsellor to Henry VIII, Tyndale was eventually arrested for heresy by officers of the Holy Roman Empire, imprisoned, strangled, and burned at the stake at Vilvorde in 1536.

from The Obedience of a Christian Man

Let every soul submit himself unto the authority of the higher powers. There is no power but of God; the powers that be are ordained of God. Whosoever therefore resisteth the power, resisteth the ordinance of God. They that resist shall receive to themselves damnation. For rulers are not to be feared for good works, but for evil. Wilt thou be without fear of the power? Do well then, and so shalt thou be praised of the same, for he is the minister of God for thy wealth. But, and if thou do evil, then fear, for he beareth not a sword for nought, for he is the minister of God, to take vengeance on them that do evil. Wherefore ye must needs obey, not for fear of vengeance only, but also because of conscience. Even for this cause pay ye tribute: for they are God's ministers serving for the same purpose. * * *

God therefore hath given laws unto all nations, and in all lands hath put kings, governors, and rulers in his own stead, to rule the world through them. And hath commanded all causes to be brought before them, as thou readest (Exod. 22). In all causes (saith he) of injury or wrong, whether it be ox, ass, sheep, or vesture, or any lost thing which another challengeth, let the cause of both parties be brought unto the gods; whom the gods condemn, the same shall pay double unto his neighbor. Mark, the judges are called gods in the Scriptures, because they are in God's room,[1] and execute the commandments of God. And in another place of the said chapter, Moses chargeth saying, See that thou rail not on[2] the gods, neither speak evil of the ruler of thy people. Whosoever therefore resisteth them, resisteth God (for they are in the room of God) and they that resist shall receive the damnation.

Such obedience unto father and mother, master, husband, emperor, king, lords, and rulers, requireth God of all nations, yea of the very Turks and infidels. * * *

Neither may the inferior person avenge himself upon the superior, or violently resist him for whatsoever wrong it be. If he do, he is condemned in the deed doing, inasmuch as he taketh upon him that which belongeth to God only, which saith, Vengeance is mine, and I will reward (Deut. 32). And Christ sayeth (Mat. 26), All they that take the sword shall perish with the sword. Taketh thou a sword to avenge thyself? So givest thou not room unto God to avenge thee, but robbest him of his most high honor, in that thou wilt not let him be judge over thee.

1528

—•— ⚎⧫⚎ —•—

Juan Luis Vives
1492–1540

A Spanish philosopher educated in Valencia, Paris, and Bruges, Vives lectured at Oxford and attended the court of Henry VIII between 1523 and 1528. His treatise on the education of women was composed for Mary Tudor while she was still a child, at the request of her mother, Catherine of Aragon, wife of Henry VIII. It was published in Latin in 1523; the English translation, by Richard Hyrde, was published in 1540. It illustrates the way in which the idea of government comprised doctrine on matters of individual conduct. Vives clearly believed that the subordination of a wife to a husband was an expression of the natural order of things, not a social convention; he thought it depended on the innate characteristics of the female in contrast to the male.

from Instruction of a Christian Woman

Chastity is the principal virtue of a woman, and counterepayseth with[1] all the rest. If she have that, no man will look for any other, and if she lack that, no man will regard other. * * * She that is chaste is fair, well-favored, rich, fruitful, noble, and all best things that can be named, and contrary, she that is unchaste is a sea and treasure of all illness. Now shamefastness[2] and soberness be the inseparable companions of chastity, insomuch that she cannot be chaste that is not ashamed.[3] * * *

Of shamefastness cometh demureness and measureableness, that whether she think ought, or say, or do, nothing shall be outrageous, neither in passions of mind, nor words, nor deeds; nor presumptuous; nor nice,[4] wanton, pert; nor boasting; nor ambitious; and as for honors she will neither think herself worthy nor desire them but rather flee them, and if they chance unto her, she will be ashamed of them, as of a

1. Place.
2. Complain against.
1. Outweighs.
2. Modesty.

3. I.e., good manners and temperance derive from modesty.
4. Fastidious.

thing not deserved; nor be for nothing high-minded, neither for beauty, nor proper-ness,[5] nor kindred, nor riches, being sure that they shall soon perish and that pride shall have everlasting pain.

The man getteth, that woman saveth and keepeth. Therefore he hath stomach given to him to gather lustily,[6] and she hath it taken from her, that she may warily keep.[7] And of this soberness of body cometh soberness of mind. * * * Let her apply herself to virtue and be content with a little, and take in worth that[8] she hath nor seek for other that she hath not, nor for [the wealth of] other folks, whereof riseth envy, hate, or curiosity of other folks' matters.

Forth she must go sometimes, but I would it should be as seldom as may be for many causes. Principally because as often as a maid goeth forth among people, so often she cometh in judgment and extreme peril of her beauty, honesty, demureness, wit, shamefastness, and virtue. For nothing is more tender than is the fame and esti-mation of women, nor nothing more in danger of wrong, insomuch that it hath been said, and not without a cause, to hang by a cobweb.

Let the woman understand that if she will not spend all her substance to save her husband from never so little harms, she is not worthy to bear the name neither of a good nor Christian woman, nor once to be called wife. * * * I will that she shall give him great worship, reverence, great obedience, and service also, which thing not only the example of the old world teacheth us, but also all laws, both spiritual and temporal, and nature herself cryeth and commandeth that the woman shall be subject and obedi-ent to the man. And in all kinds of beasts the females obey the males and wait upon them and fawn upon them and suffer themselves to be corrected of them, which thing nature showeth must be and is convenient[9] to be done. * * * Nature showeth that the male's duty is to succor and defend, and the female's to follow and wait upon the male and to creep under his aid and obey him, that she may live the better.

Let the authority and rule be reserved unto thy husband and be thou an example to all thine house what sovereignty they owe unto him. Do thou prove him to be lord by thine obedience, and make him great with thine humility, for the more honor thou givest unto him, the [more] honorable thou shalt be thyself.

That thou mayest better obey thy husband and do all things after his mind, first thou must learn all his manners and consider well his dispositions and state, for there be many kinds of husbands and all ought to be loved, honored and worshipped and obeyed, but all must not be entreated under one manner. * * * If thou have one after thine appetite, thou mayest be glad, * * * but if he be ill, either find some craft to make him good or at the leastwise better to deal with.

◆━◆☲◆━◆

Sir Thomas Elyot
c. 1490–1546

To support his defense of monarchy in his treatise on government, Sir Thomas Elyot—a humanist and Henry VIII's ambassador to Emperor Charles V—drew on popular analogies with what he saw as the hierarchical order of the heavens and the natural world. He also insisted that a monarchy—in which the king (or queen) held a patriarchal kind of power—preserved security within society and yet, by observing custom and established law, avoided

---

5. Station in life.   8. Value what.
6. Energetically.   9. Appropriate.
7. Carefully conserve.

tyranny or anarchy. His later work continued to engage political topics. His dialogue supporting women's rule may have been composed in the anticipation of Mary Tudor's queenship; its argument drew on a literature debating the nature of womankind as it was represented in both the medieval *querelle des femmes*, or "controversy on the subject of womankind," and the classical and humanist histories of famous women. His character Candidus ("honest and openminded") represents the affirmative case; Caninius ("snarling and spiteful") states his objections to it.

from The Book Named the Governor

Like as to a castle or fortress sufficeth one owner or sovereign, and where any more be of like power and authority seldom cometh the work to perfection; or being already made, where the one diligently overseeth and the other neglecteth, in that contention all is subverted and cometh to ruin, in semblable wise[1] doth a public weal[2] that hath more chief governors than one. Example we may take of the Greeks, among whom in divers cities were divers forms of public weals governed by multitudes. Wherein one was most tolerable where the governance and rule was always permitted to them which excelled in virtue, and was in the Greek tongue called *Aristocratia*, in Latin *Optimorum Potentia*, in the English rule of men of best disposition, which the Thebans of long time observed.

    Another public weal was among the Athenians, where equality was of estate among[3] the people, and only by their whole consent their city and dominions were governed: which might well be called a monster with many heads. Nor never was it certain nor stable, and often times they banished or slew the best citizens, which by their virtue and wisdom had most profited to the public weal. This manner of governance was called in Greek *Democratia*, in Latin *Popularis Potentia*, in English the rule of the commonalty. Of these two governances none of them may be sufficient. For in the first, which consisteth of good men, virtue is not so constant in a multitude, but that some, being once in authority be incensed with a glory, some with ambition, other with covetousness and desire of treasure or possessions. Whereby they fall into contention, and finally, where any achieveth the superiority, the whole government is reduced unto a few in number, which fearing the multitude and their mutability, to the intent to keep them in dread to rebel, ruleth by terror and cruelty, thinking thereby to keep themselves in surety.[4] Notwithstanding, rancour, coarcted[5] and long detained in a narrow room, at the last bursteth out with intolerable violence and bringeth all to confusion. For the power that is practised to the hurt of many cannot continue. The popular estate,[6] if it anything do vary from equality of substance or estimation, or that the multitude of people have overmuch liberty, of necessity one of these inconveniences must happen: either tyranny, where he that is too much in favor would be elevate and suffer none equality, or else into the rage of a commonalty,[7] which of all rules is most to be feared. For like as the commons, if they feel some severity, they do humbly serve and obey, so where they embracing a license refuse to be bridled, they fling[8] and plunge. And if they once throw down their governor, they order everything without justice, only with vengeance and cruelty, and

1. The same way.
2. State.
3. Endorsed by.
4. Elyot argues against democracy because he believes that it leads to various forms of tyranny: among the many, a few will gain ascendancy and, to keep their fellow citizens from rebelling, will rule by terror and think themselves secure.

5. Confined.
6. Common people.
7. Democracy also leads to the tyranny of a single man or of the mob: either the single man manages to take charge and allows no "equality" among the ruled, or the many degenerate into a mob.
8. Rear.

with incomparable difficulty and unneth[9] by any wisdom [can they] be pacified and brought again into order. Wherefore undoubtedly the best and most sure governance is by one king or prince, which ruleth only for the weal[1] of his people to him subject; and that manner of governance is best approved, and hath longest continued, and is most ancient. For who can deny but that all thing in heaven and earth is governed by one God, by one perpetual order, by one providence? One sun ruleth over the day, and one moon over the night. And to descend down to the earth, in a little beast, which of all other is most to be marveled at, I mean the bee, is left to man by nature, as it seemeth, a perpetual figure of a just governance or rule, who hath among them one principal bee for their governor, who excelleth all other in greatness, yet hath he no prick or sting, but in him is more knowledge than in the residue.[2] For if the day following shall be fair and dry, and that the bees may issue out of their stalls without peril of rain or vehement wind, in the morning early he calleth them, making a noise as it were the sound of the horn or a trumpet; and with that all the residue prepare them to labor, and flyeth abroad, gathering nothing but that shall be sweet and profitable, although they sit often times on herbs and other things that be venomous and stinking.

The captain himself laboreth not for his sustenance, but all the other for him; he only seeth that if any drone or other unprofitable bee entereth into the hive and consumeth the honey gathered by other, that he be immediately expelled from that company. And when there is another number of bees increased, they semblably[3] have also a captain, which be not suffered to continue with the other. Wherefore this new company gathered into a swarm, having their captain among them and environing[4] him to preserve him from harm, they issue forth seeking a new habitation, which they find in some tree, except with some pleasant noise they be lured and conveyed unto another hive. I suppose who seriously beholdeth this example, and hath any commendable wit, shall thereof gather much matter to the forming of a public weal.

1531

from The Defence of Good Women

CANDIDUS [to Caninius, detractor of women]: And so ye conclude,[1] that the power of reason is more in the prudent and diligent keeping than in the valiant or politic getting, and that discretion, election, and prudence, which is all and in every part reason, do excel strength, wit, and hardiness.[2] And consequently, they in whom be those virtues, in that, that they have them, do excel in just estimation them that be strong, hardy, or politic in getting of anything.

CANINIUS: Ye have well gathered together all that conclusion.

CANDIDUS: Behold Caninius, where ye be now: ye have so much extolled reason, that in the respect thereof bodily strength remaineth as nothing. Forasmuch as the corporal powers with powers of the soul can make no comparison. And ye have not denied but that this word *Man*, unto whom reason pertaineth, doth imply in

9. Scarcely.
1. Good.
2. Elyot did not realize that the bee that ruled the hive was in fact female.
3. Similarly.
4. Surrounding.
1. Candidus reminds Caninius that they have reached a conclusion: Reason is more manifest in the arts that conserve resources than in those that acquire them. The effect of this conclusion will then prove decisive to the debate between the two men: By putting reason above any other attribute, Caninius has unwittingly established a basis for Candidus's claim that women, conventionally held to excel in virtues associated with introspection, are superior to men, who were rather praised for excelling in virtues associated with physical strength. The notion of a woman's function as conservative is expressed in treatises on domestic economy by Xenophon and Aristotle.
2. Courage.

it both man and woman.[3] And agreeing unto Aristotle's saying ye have confirmed that prudence which in effect is more aptly applied to the woman, whereby she is more circumspect in keeping, as strength is to the man, that he may be more valiant in getting. And likewise ye have preferred the prudence in keeping, for the utility thereof, before the valiantness in getting, and seemingly them which be prudent in keeping before them that be only strong and hardy in getting. And so ye have concluded that women, which are prudent in keeping, be more excellent than men in reason, which be only strong and valiant in getting. And where excellency is, there is most perfection. Wherefore a woman is not a creature unperfect, but as it seemeth is more perfect than man.

CANINIUS: Why, have ye dallied herefore with me all this long season?

CANDIDUS: Surely I have used neither dalliance nor sophistry, but if ye consider it well, ye shall find it but a natural induction, and plain to all them that have any capacity. But yet have I somewhat more to say to you. Ye said moreover Caninius, that the wits of women were apt only to trifles and shrewdness and not to wisdom and civil policy. I will be plain to you, I am sorry to find in your words such manner of lewdness, I cry you mercy, I would have said so much ungentleness, and in your own words so much forgetfulness.

CANINIUS: What mean ye thereby?

CANDIDUS: Ye have twice granted that natural reason is in women as well as in men.

CANINIUS: Yes and what then?

CANDIDUS: Then have women also discretion, election, and prudence, which do make that wisdom which pertaineth to governance. And perdy,[4] many arts and necessary occupations have been invented by women, as I will bring now some unto your remembrance.

1540

John Ponet
1514–1556

Ponet was among the most articulate and thoughtful of the Protestants who wrote against tyranny. Made Bishop of Winchester under Henry VIII, he fled to Frankfurt after the accession of Mary I; his treatise on government was composed in 1556 while he was abroad and is one of several such works produced during this period by writers who have been called the Marian exiles. Ponet's argument supporting tyrannicide is grounded in his belief that the monarch has authority and power by virtue of his office, not his person; once he fails to rule according to the requirements of office, he is no longer a monarch and therefore can be deposed and even tried for crimes like any other subject. Many of the points in Ponet's treatise were rehearsed in arguments against the rule of Charles I.

from A Short Treatise of Political Power

Forasmuch as those that be the rulers in the world and would be taken for gods (that is, the ministers and images of God here in earth, the examples and mirrors of all godliness, justice, equity, and other virtues) claim and exercise an absolute power, which

---

3. A reminder that man and woman were alike in being made in the image of God (Genesis 1.27).   4. Indeed.

also they call a fullness of power, or prerogative to do what they lust, and none may gainsay them; to dispense with the laws as pleaseth them, and freely and without correction or offence do contrary to the law of nature, and other [of] God's laws and the positive laws and customs of their countries, or break them; and use their subjects as men do their beasts, and as lords do their villeins and bondmen, getting their goods from them by hook and by crook, with *Sic voio, Sic jubeo* [As I wish, so I command], and spending it to the destruction of their subjects, the misery of this time requireth to examine whether they do it rightfully or wrongfully; that if it be rightful, the people may the more willingly obey and receive the same; if it be wrongful, that then those that use it may the rather for the fear of God leave it. For (no doubt) God will come, and judge the world with equity, and revenge the cause of the oppressed. * * *

True it is, that in matters indifferent, that is, that of themselves be neither good nor evil, hurtful, or profitable, but for a decent order, kings and princes (to whom the people have given their authority) may make such laws, and dispense with them. But in matters not indifferent, but godly and profitably ordained for the commonwealth, there can they not (for all their authority) break them or dispense with them. For princes are ordained to do good, not to do evil; to take away evil, not to increase it; to give example of well doing, not to be procurers of evil; to procure the wealth and benefit of their subjects, and not to work their hurt or undoing. * * *

Antiochus the third, King of Syria, wrote thus to all the cities of his dominion, that if he did command anything that should be contrary to the laws, they should not pass thereon, but that rather they should think it was stolen or forged without his knowledge, considering that the prince or governor is nothing else but the minister of the laws. And this same saying of this most noble king seemed to be so just and reasonable that it is taken for a common principle, how subjects should know when they should do that they be commanded, and when they ought not.

Likewise a bishop of Rome, called Alexander the third,[1] wrote to an archbishop to do a thing which seemed to the archbishop to be unreasonable and contrary to the laws. The pope perceiving that the archbishop was offended with his writing and would not do that he required, desired him not to be offended, but that if there were cause why he thought he should not do that he required, he would advertise him and therewith would be satisfied.[2]

This is a pope's saying, which who is so hardy daring to deny to be of less authority than a law? Yea, not below, but above God's word?[3] Whereupon this is a general rule, that the pope is not to be obeyed, but in lawful and honest things, and so by good argument from the more to the less, that princes (being but footstools and stirrup holders to popes) commanding their subjects [to do] that [which] is not godly, not just, not lawful, or hurtful to their country, ought not to be obeyed, but withstood. For the subjects ought not (against nature) to further their own destruction, but to seek their own salvation, not to maintain evil but to suppress evil. For not only the doers but also the consentors to evil shall be punished, say both God's and man's laws. And men ought to have more respect to their country, than to their prince; to the commonwealth, than to any one person. For the country and commonwealth is a degree above the king. Next unto God, men ought to love their country, and the whole commonwealth before any member of it, as kings and princes (be they never

---

1. I.e., Pope Alexander III. As a Protestant, Ponet could not consider that the Pope was anything more than the Bishop of Rome.
2. The Pope would reconsider his order to determine whether it was lawful.

3. The law is above not only the word of the Pope but even the word of God expressed in Scripture. Ponet understands the law as positive law, the aggregate of the common law and statute; it is, in other words, law made by the people.

so great) are but members, and commonwealths may stand well enough and flourish, albeit there be no kings, but contrarywise, without a commonwealth there can be no king. Commonwealths and realms may live when the head is cut off, and may put on a new head, that is, make them a new governor, when they see their old head seek too much his own will and not the wealth of the whole body, for the which he was only ordained. And by that justice and law that lately hath been executed in England (if it may be called justice and law), it should appear that the ministers of civil power do sometimes command that, that the subjects ought not to do.

When the innocent Lady Jane, contrary to her will, yea by force, with tears dropping down her cheeks, suffered herself to be called Queen of England, yet ye see, because she consented to that which was not by civil justice lawful, she and her husband for company suffered the pains of traitors, both headless, buried in one pit. * * *

But thou wilt say, whereof cometh this common saying: all things be the kaiser's, all things be the king's?[4] It cannot come of nothing. But by that that is already said, ye see that every man may keep his own and none may take it from him, so that it cannot be interpreted that all things be the kaiser's or king's, as his own proper,[5] or that they may take them from their subjects at their pleasure, but it is thus to be expounded, that they ought to defend that[6] every man hath, that he may quietly enjoy his own, and to see that they be not robbed or spoiled thereof. For as in a great man's house all things be said to be the steward's, because it is committed to his charge to see that every man in the house behave himself honestly and do his duty to see that all things be well kept and preserved; and may take nothing away from any man, nor misspend, or waste; and of his doings he must render account to his lord for all, so in a realm or other dominion, the realm and country are God's. He is the lord, the people are his servants, and the king or governor is but God's minister or steward, ordained not to misuse the servants, that is the people, neither to spoil them of what they have, but to see the people do their duty to their lord God, that the goods of this world be not abused but spent to God's glory, to the maintenance and defense of the commonwealth, and not to the destruction of it. The prince's watch ought to defend the poor man's house, his labor the subject's ease, his diligence the subject's pleasure, his trouble the subject's quietness. And as the sun never standeth still but continually goeth about the world, doing his office, with his heat refreshing and comforting all natural things in the world, so ought a good prince to be continually occupied in his ministry, not seeking his own profit, but the wealth of those that be committed to his charge.

<hr />

John Foxe
1516–1587

Like John Ponet, Foxe was a Protestant scholar who left England after the accession of Mary I. He went to live in Basel, where he (barely) supported himself as a proofreader. In Basel he began the work that would eventually result in his major history of the Christian church and its martyrs. He returned to London after the Protestant Queen Elizabeth ascended the throne and, in 1563, published his book under the title *Acts and Monuments of These Latter and Perilous Days*; it soon became known as *The Book of Martyrs*. Like many of his fellow Marian

---

4. Cf. Matthew 22.21: "Render unto Caesar the things which are Caesar's, and unto God the things that are God's."

5. Property.
6. That which.

exiles, Foxe believed that the authority and power of the monarchy should be limited, especially with respect to church doctrine and matters of faith. His accounts of martyrs to Catholicism testify not only to the gruesome persecutions the state enacted and the formidable courage of those who resisted the power of the secular arm of government, but also to his own skillful use of images, reported speech, and descriptive detail, as he shapes the reader's sympathies toward his cause. His book was enormously popular, a fact that illustrates how ready contemporary readers were to take sides in religious conflict and how effectively historical narrative, however polemical and one-sided, could be used to advance or discredit a particular political or religious position.

from The Book of Martyrs

There was a certain act of parliament made in the government of the lord Hamilton, earl of Arran, and governor of Scotland, giving privilege to all men of the realm of Scotland, to read the Scriptures in their mother tongue and language, secluding nevertheless all reasoning, conference, convocation of people to hear the Scriptures read or expounded. Which liberty of private reading being granted by public proclamation, lacked not its own fruit, so that in sundry parts of Scotland thereby were opened the eyes of the elect of God to see the truth, and abhor the papistical abominations, amongst whom were certain persons in St. John's-town, as after is declared.

At this time there was a sermon made by friar Spence, in St. John's-town, otherwise called Perth, affirming prayer made to saints to be so necessary that without it there could be no hope of salvation to man. This blasphemous doctrine a burgess of the said town, called Robert Lamb, could not abide, but accused him in open audience of erroneous doctrine, and adjured[1] him, in God's name, to utter the truth. This the friar, being stricken with fear, promised to do; but the trouble, tumult, and stir of the people increased so, that the friar could have no audience, and yet the said Robert, with great danger of his life, escaped the hands of the multitude, namely of the women who, contrary to nature, addressed them to extreme cruelty against him.

At this time, A.D. 1543, the enemies of the truth procured John Charterhouse, who favored the truth and was provost of the said city and town of Perth, to be deposed from his office by the said governor's authority, and a papist, called Master Alexander Marbeck, to be chosen in his room, that they might bring the more easily their wicked and ungodly enterprise to an end.

After the deposing of the former provost and election of the other, in the month of January the year aforesaid, on St. Paul's day came to St. John's-town the governor, the cardinal, the Earl of Argyle, Justice Sir John Campbell of Lundie, knight, and Justice Defort, the Lord Borthwicke, the bishops of Dunblane and Orkney, with certain other of the nobility. And although there were many accused for the crime of heresy (as they term it), yet these persons only were apprehended upon the said St. Paul's day: Robert Lamb, William Anderson, James Hunter, James Raveleson, James Finlason, and Helen Stirke his wife, and were cast that night in the Spay Tower of the said city, the morrow after to abide judgment.

Upon the morrow, when they appeared and were brought forth to judgment in the town, were laid in general to all their charge the violating of the act of parliament before expressed and their conference and assemblies in hearing and expounding of Scripture against the tenor of the said act. Robert Lamb was accused, in special, for interrupting of the friar in the pulpit; which he not only confessed, but also

1. Charged.

affirmed constantly, that it was the duty of no man who understood and knew the truth to hear the same impugned without contradiction, and therefore sundry who were there present in judgment, who hid the knowledge of the truth, should bear the burden in God's presence for consenting to the same.

The said Robert also, with William Anderson and James Raveleson, were accused for hanging up the image of St. Francis in a cord, nailing of rams' horns to his head, and a cow's rump to his tail, and for eating of a goose on Allhallow-even.

James Hunter, being a simple man and without learning, and a flesher[2] by occupation, so that he could be charged with no great knowledge in the doctrine, yet because he often used that suspected company of the rest, he was accused.

The woman Helen Stirke was accused, for that in her childbed she was not accustomed to call on the name of the Virgin Mary, being exorted thereto by her neighbors, but only on God for Jesus Christ's sake; and because she said, in like manner, that if she herself had been in the time of the Virgin Mary, God might have looked to her humility and base estate as he did to the Virgin's in making her the mother of Christ, thereby meaning that there were no merits in the Virgin which procured her that honor, to be made the Mother of Christ and to be preferred before other women, but that only God's free mercy exalted her to that estate, which words were counted most execrable in the face of the clergy, and of the whole multitude.

James Raveleson aforesaid, building a house, set upon the round of his fourth stair the three-crowned diadem of Peter carved out of tree, which the cardinal took as done in mockage of his cardinal's hat; and this procured no favor to the said James at their hands.

These aforesaid persons, upon the morrow after St. Paul's day, were condemned and judged to death, and that by an assize, for violating (as was alleged) the act of parliament, in reasoning and conferring upon Scripture, for eating flesh upon days forbidden, for interrupting the holy friar in the pulpit, for dishonoring of images, and for blaspheming of the Virgin Mary, as they alleged.

After sentence was given, their hands were bound and the men cruelly treated, which thing the woman beholding, desired likewise to be bound by the sergeants with her husband for Christ's sake.

There was great intercession made by the town in the mean season, for the life of these persons aforenamed, to the governor, who of himself was willing so to have done that they might have been delivered, but the governor was so subject to the appetite of the cruel priests that he could not do that which he would. Yea, they menaced to assist his enemies and to depose him, except that he assisted their cruelty.[3]

There were certain priests in the city, who did eat and drink before these honest men's houses, to whom the priests were much bounden. These priests were earnestly desired to entreat for their hosts at the cardinal's hands, but they altogether refused, desiring rather their death than their preservation.[4] So cruel are these beasts, from the lowest to the highest.

Then after, they were carried by a great band of armed men (for they feared rebellion in the town except they had their men of war) to the place of execution, which was common to all thieves, and that to make their cause appear more odious to the people.

---

2. Butcher.

3. If the governor did not agree with the priests, they would turn to his enemies and attempt to depose him.

4. I.e., the priests discounted the hospitality they had enjoyed and agreed to the persecution of their hosts.

Robert Lamb, at the gallows' foot, made his exortation to the people, desiring them to fear God, and leave the leaven of papistical abominations,[5] and manifestly there prophesied of the ruin and plague which came upon the cardinal thereafter. So every one comforting another, and assuring themselves they should sup together in the kingdom of heaven that night, they commended themselves to God, and died constantly in the Lord.

The woman desired earnestly to die with her husband, but she was not suffered; yet, following him to the place of execution, she gave him comfort, exorting him to perseverance and patience for Christ's sake, and, parting from him with a kiss, said on this manner, "Husband, rejoice, for we have lived together many joyful days; but this day, in which we must die, ought to be most joyful unto us both, because we must have joy forever. Therefore I will not bid you good night, for we shall suddenly meet with joy in the kingdom of heaven." The woman, after that, was taken to a place to be drowned, and albeit she had a child sucking on her breast, yet this moved nothing the unmerciful hearts of the enemies. So, after she had commended her children to the neighbors of the town for God's sake, and the sucking bairn was given to the nurse, she sealed up the truth by her death.

<hr/>

Richard Hooker
1554–1600

Richard Hooker was a theologian and a professor of Hebrew at Oxford whose *Laws of Ecclesiastical Polity* embraced a wide range of topics on the moral and political foundations of the Church of England. One of the great masters of English prose, Hooker began his book as a final reply to a controversy that had been stirred up by *An Admonition to the Parliament*, which had been secretly published in 1572 by Puritans who denied Queen Elizabeth's right to lead a national church. Hooker worked on his book from 1591 to the end of his life; it was published in sections from 1593 through 1614. In his work, he defended the newly established church against both Roman Catholics and Puritans, arguing for a middle position that would give weight both to the individual reading of Scripture and to the authority of a national church, headed by the monarch rather than the Pope. His discussions of national and church governance entailed probing basic concepts of law itself. Hooker distinguished between natural law—unwritten, universally recognized, and discoverable by reason—on the one hand, and positive law or "laws politic"—the written law of a particular people or state—on the other. He valued human reason and its capacity to discern "goodness" and natural law, but he also believed that human beings harbored a "wild beast" within themselves which had to be controlled by positive law. The first selection is from Book 1; the second is from Book 8.

from The Laws of Ecclesiastical Polity

Signs and tokens to know good by are of sundry kinds; some more certain and some less. The most certain token of evident goodness is if the general persuasion of all men do so account it. And therefore a common received error is never utterly overthrown, till such time as we go from signs unto causes, and show some manifest root or fountain thereof common unto all, whereby it may clearly appear how it hath come to pass that so many have been overseen. In which case surmises and slight

5. Lamb imagines that Catholic doctrine is the "leaven" or corruption (as in fermentation) of Christianity.

probabilities will not serve, because the universal consent of men is the perfectest and strongest in this kind, which comprehendeth only the signs and tokens of goodness. Things casual do vary, and that which a man doth but chance to think well of cannot still have the like hap.[1] Wherefore although we know not the cause, yet thus much we may know; that some necessary cause there is, whensoever the judgments of all men generally or for the most part run one and the same way, especially in matters of natural discourse. For of things necessarily and naturally done there is no more affirmed but this, "They keep either always or for the most part one tenure."[2] The general and perpetual voice of men is as the sentence of God himself.[3] For that which all men have at all times learned, nature herself must needs have taught; and God being the author of nature, her voice is but his instrument. By her from Him we receive whatsoever in such sort we learn. Infinite duties there are, the goodness whereof is by this rule sufficiently manifested, although we had no other warrant besides to approve them. The Apostle St. Paul having speech concerning the heathen saith of them, "They are a law unto themselves" (Rom. 2.14). His meaning is, that by force of the light of reason, wherewith God illuminateth every one which cometh into the world, men being enabled to know truth from falsehood and good from evil, do thereby learn in many things what the will of God is; which will, himself not revealing by any extraordinary means unto them, but they by natural discourse attaining the knowledge thereof, seem the makers of those laws which indeed are his, and they but only the finders of them out. * * *

We see then how nature itself teacheth laws and statutes to live by. The laws which have been hitherto mentioned do bind men absolutely even as they are men, although they have never any settled fellowship, never any solemn agreement amongst themselves what to do or not to do. But forasmuch as we are not by ourselves sufficient to furnish ourselves with competent store of things needful for such a life as our nature doth desire, a life fit for the dignity of man; therefore to supply those defects and imperfections which are in us living single and solely by ourselves, we are naturally induced to seek communion and fellowship with others.[4] This was the cause of men's uniting themselves at the first in politic societies, which societies could not be without government, nor government without a distinct kind of law from that which hath been already declared. Two foundations there are which bear up public societies; the one, a natural inclination, whereby all men desire sociable life and fellowship; the other, an order expressly or secretly agreed upon touching the manner of their union in living together. The latter is that which we call the law of a commonweal, the very soul of a politic body, the parts whereof are by law animated, held together, and set on work in such actions as the common good requireth. Laws politic, ordained for external order and regiment amongst men, are never framed as they should be, unless presuming the will of man to be inwardly obstinate, rebellious, and adverse from all obedience unto the sacred laws of his nature; in a word, unless presuming man to be in regard of his depraved mind little better than a wild beast, they do accordingly provide notwithstanding so to frame his outward actions, that they be no hindrance unto the common good for which societies are instituted. Unless they do this, they are not perfect.

1. Cannot always have the same outcome.
2. Condition.
3. Hooker identifies the law of nature in human beings, the law they know by virtue of being human, with the law of God. He further identifies the source of this law as reason.

4. The following sentences describe the origins of government in man's natural instinct to gather into societies. The classic statement of this idea of a political society is Aristotle's; see *Politics* 1.1252b1–1253a1.

[THE RULE OF LAW]

Many of the ancients in their writings do speak of kings with such high and ample terms, as if universality of power, even in regard of things and not of persons only, did appertain[5] to the very being of a king. The reason is because their speech concerning kings they frame according to the state of those monarchs to whom unlimited authority was given, which some not observing imagine that all kings, even in that they are kings, ought to have whatsoever power they find any sovereign ruler lawfully to have enjoyed. But that most judicious philosopher,[6] whose eye scarce anything did escape which was to be found in the bosom of nature, he considering how far the power of one sovereign ruler may be different from another regal authority, noteth in Spartan kings, "that of all others they were most tied to law, and so had the most restrained power." A king which hath not supreme power in the greatest things, is rather entitled a king, than invested with real sovereignty. We cannot properly term him a king, of whom it may not be said, at the leastwise as touching certain the very chiefest affairs of state, "his right in them is to have rule, not subject to any other predominant."[7] I am not of opinion that simply always in kings the most, but the best limited power is best. The most limited is that which may deal in fewest things; the best, that which in dealing is tied unto the soundest, perfectest, and most indifferent rule, which rule is the law.[8] I mean not only the law of nature and of God, but very national or municipal law consonant thereunto. Happier that people whose law is their king in the greatest of things, than that whose king is himself their law. Where the king doth guide the state, and the law the king, that commonwealth is like an harp or melodious instrument, the strings whereof are tuned and handled all by one hand, following as laws the rules and canons of musical science. Most divinely therefore Archytas[9] maketh unto public felicity these four steps, every later whereof doth spring from the former, as from a mother cause: "The king ruling by law, the magistrate following, the subject free, and the whole society happy"; adding on the contrary side, that "where this order is not, it cometh by transgression thereof to pass that the king grows a tyrant; he that ruleth under him abhorreth to be guided and commanded by him; the people subject under both, have freedom under neither; and the whole community is wretched."

━━◆━━

James I (James VI of Scotland)
1567–1625

James VI of Scotland, eventually James I of England, wrote his treatise on monarchy to curb the enthusiasm of his subjects for a government under the law rather than by an all-powerful ruler. He had ascended his throne in highly uncertain circumstances. His father died when James was eight months old. A few months later, his mother, Mary, was forced from the throne, and James became king of Scotland in 1567 at the age of one. Mary left the kingdom the following year; James never saw her again. He grew up reading widely, writing poetry,

---

5. Belong.
6. Aristotle; see *Politics* 3.1284b–85b.
7. Power.
8. Hooker states that a king's "best" power is not the most power but rather the "best limited" power; that is, it is limited not because it deals with only a few things, but

rather it is limited by law—it therefore comprehends what law does, the workings of the entire body politic. Hooker goes on to argue for a monarchy under positive law, much as Ponet did.
9. A mathematician and friend of Plato, to whom is attributed the treatise *On Law and Justice* (c. 400 B.C.).

harrassed by fears of the devil but enjoying the fellowship of a few trusted Scottish lords. He published a work on devils entitled *Daemonologie* in 1597; *The True Law of Free Monarchies* was published the next year, following conflicts with the Scottish parliament and church authorities. In his book, James insisted that the people had no rights of resistance, even against monarchs who broke divine and natural law; at the same time, he acknowledged that a good king, obeying the law, would not give his subjects a reason to dispute his rule. In theory, James was unequivocally committed to the proposition that Scripture and moral law justified absolute monarchy; in practice, however, he conceded authority and power to Parliament and the common law.

from The True Law of Free Monarchies

Kings are called gods by the prophetical King David, because they sit upon God's Throne in the earth and have the count of their administration to give unto him. Their office is to minister justice and judgment to the people, as the same David saith; to advance the good and punish the evil, as he likewise saith; to establish good laws to his people, and procure obedience to the same, as divers good kings of Judah did; to procure the peace of the people, as the same David saith; to decide all controversies that can arise among them, as Solomon did; to be the minister of God for the weal[1] of them that do well, and as the minister of God, to take vengeance upon them that do evil, as St. Paul saith. And finally, as a good pastor, to go out and in before his people as is said in the first of Samuel; that through the prince's prosperity, the people's peace may be procured, as Jeremy saith. * * *

By the law of nature the king becomes a natural father to all his lieges at his coronation and as the father, of his fatherly duty, is bound to care for the nourishing, education, and virtuous government of his children, even so is the king bound to care for all his subjects.[2] As all the toil and pain that the father can take for his children will be thought light and well-bestowed by him, so that the effect thereof redound to their profit and weal, so ought the prince to do towards his people. As the kindly father ought to foresee all inconveniences and dangers that may arise towards his children, and though with the hazard of his own person press to prevent the same, so ought the king towards his people. As the father's wrath and correction upon any of his children that offendeth ought to be by a fatherly chastisement seasoned with pity, as long as there is any hope of amendment in them, so ought the king towards any of his lieges that offend in that measure. * * *

The kings therefore in Scotland were before any estates or ranks of men within the same, before any Parliaments were holden or laws made, and by them was the land distributed (which at the first was wholly theirs), states erected and discerned, and forms of government devised and established. And so it follows of necessity that the kings were the authors and makers of the laws and not the laws of the kings. And to prove this my assertion more clearly, it is evident by the rolls of our chancellery (which contain our eldest and fundamental Laws) that the king is *Dominus omnium honorum*, and *Dominus directus totius Dominii*,[3] the whole subjects being but his vassals and from him holding all their lands as their overlord, who according to good services

---

1. Benefit.
2. James's identification of royal with paternal or patriarchal power—that is, the power of the father over his children, or the head of the family over its members—is mod-

eled after what was thought to be Roman law and custom, in which the male head of the household ruled absolutely over it.
3. The lord of the manor, the first lord of all lords.

done unto him, changeth their holdings from tack to fee, from ward to blanch,[4] erecteth new baronies and uniteth old, without advice or authority of either Parliament or any other subaltern judicial seat. So as if wrong might be admitted in play (albeit I grant wrong should be wrong in all persons), the king might have a better color for his pleasure, without further reason, to take the land from his lieges,[5] as overlord of the whole, and do with it as pleaseth him, since all that they hold is of him, then, as foolish writers say, the people might unmake the king and put in another in his room; but either of them, as unlawful and against the ordinance of God, ought to be alike odious to be thought, much less put in practice. * * *

The king is overlord of the whole land, so is he master over every person that inhabiteth the same, having power over the life and death of every one of them. For although a just prince will not take the life of any of his subjects without a clear law, yet the same laws whereby he taketh them are made by himself, or his predecessors, and so the power flows always from himself; as by daily experience we see, good and just princes will from time to time make new laws and statutes, adjoining the penalties to the breakers thereof, which before the law was made, had been no crime to the subject to have committed. Not that I deny the old definition of a king, and of a law, which makes the king to be a speaking law, and the law a dumb king, for certainly a king that governs not by his law can neither be countable to God for his administration nor have a happy and established reign. For albeit be true that I have at length proved that the king is above the law, as both the author and giver of strength thereto, yet a good king will not only delight to rule his subjects by the law, but even will conform himself in his own actions thereto, always keeping that ground that the health of the commonwealth be his chief law. And where he sees the law doubtsome or rigorous, he may interpret or mitigate the same, lest otherwise *Summum jus be summa injuria.*[6] And therefore general laws, made publicly in Parliament, may upon known respects to the king by his authority be mitigated and suspended upon causes only known to him.

Baldassare Castiglione
1478–1529

A courtier at Urbino, the ducal seat of the Gonzaga family, Castiglione wrote his book of advice for men and women seeking advancement in court society. Published in 1528, it proved popular not only with Italian readers but throughout Europe. It was translated into English in 1561 by the diplomat Sir Thomas Hoby. One of the most influential prose stylists of his generation, Hoby belonged to a group of writers who sought to create a clear and forceful English prose free of ornate Latinisms. Written in dialogue form, *The Book of the Courtier* sketched the principles of self-government as they applied to those who sought favor and patronage from rich and powerful nobility; chiefly, it specified how a courtier could gain and keep his lord's attention. One of Castiglione's best-known directives concerns the manner in which the courtier should perform his duties: it will only be impressive, Castiglione insists, if it seems to

---

4. These are legal terms relating to the conditions of feudal tenure. James notes that the king can change what is required of his tenants from knightly service to the payment of rent and can change the nature of the rent his tenants pay from goods to coin.

5. Lords.

6. The most exacting enforcement of the law may be an injustice. Here James invokes the principle of equity, which allows a magistrate discretion to moderate the effect of the law in certain cases.

be completely unlearned, unrehearsed, and natural. Castiglione's arguments influenced many writers, including Shakespeare; the courtier and writer Sir Philip Sidney "never stirred abroad without a copy in his pocket."

from The Book of the Courtier

Whoso mindeth to be gracious or to have a good grace in the exercises of the body (presupposing first that he be not of nature unapt) ought to begin betimes and to learn his principles of cunning men. The which thing how necessary a matter Philip King of Macedonia thought it, a man may gather in that his will was that Aristotle, so famous a philosopher and perhaps the greatest that hath ever been in the world, should be the man that should instruct Alexander his son in the first principles of letters. * * *

He therefore that will be a good scholar, beside the practicing of good things must evermore set all his diligence to be like his master, and (if it were possible) change himself into him. And when he hath had some entry, it profiteth him much to behold sundry men of that profession, and governing himself with that good judgment that must always be his guide, go about to pick out, sometime of one and sometime of another, sundry matters. And even as the bee in the green meadows fleeth always about the grass choosing out flowers, so shall our courtier steal this grace from them that to his seeming have it, and from each one that parcel that shall be most worthy praise. And not do, as a friend of ours, whom you all know, that thought he resembled much King Ferdinand the younger of Aragon, and regarded not to resemble him in any other point but in the often lifting up his head, wrying therewithall a part of his mouth, the which custom the king had gotten by infirmity. And many such there are that think they do much, so they resemble a great man in somewhat, and take many times the thing in him that worst becometh him. But I, imagining with myself oftentimes how this grace cometh, leaving apart such as have it from above, find one rule that is most general which in this part (methink) taketh place in all things belonging to man in word or deed above all other. And that is to eschew as much as a man may, and as a sharp and dangerous rock, affectation or curiosity and (to speak a new word) to use in everything a certain recklessness, to cover art withall, and seem whatsoever he doth and sayeth to do it without pain and (as it were) not minding it. And of this do I believe grace is much derived, for in rare matters and well brought to pass every man knoweth the hardness[1] of them, so that a readiness therein maketh great wonder. And contrariwise to use force, and (as they say) to haul by the hair, giveth a great disgrace, and maketh every thing how great soever it be, to be little esteemed. Therefore that may be said to be a very art that appeareth not to be art, neither ought a man to put more diligence in anything than in covering it, for in case it be open, it loseth credit clean, and maketh a man little set by. And I remember that I have read in my days that there were some most excellent orators, which among other their cares, enforced themselves to make every man believe that they had no sight in letters, and dissembling their cunning, made semblant[2] their orations to be made very simply, and rather as nature and truth lead them than study and art, the which if it had been openly known would have put a doubt in the people's mind, for fear least he beguiled them. You may see then how to show art and such bent[3] study taketh away the grace of every thing.

---

1. Difficulty.   3. Dedicated.
2. Made it apparent that.

Roger Ascham
1515–1568

Secretary to both Queen Mary and Queen Elizabeth, Ascham was convinced that the education of children was crucial to the prosperity of the state; for him, education was not a private concern but a public matter. Adopting humanist methods of instruction, teachers in this period had become increasingly committed to preparing students not only to understand what they read but also why it was important. In short, the value of rote learning, which depends on a quick memory and a willing acceptance of authority, had become debatable. Ascham favored an education based on discussion, questioning, and criticism, and he preferred teaching in English rather than Latin. In 1545 he had published the first book written in English on the subject of archery; *The Schoolmaster,* published posthumously in 1570, embodies Ascham's ideals in a lively and emphatic style. In the following excerpt, he defends a "hard-witted" student, one who learns slowly but thoroughly, thereby highlighting the importance of character in the process of learning; by stressing character, Ascham turns the attention of the reader from the formal aspects of education and toward its role in the formation of the individual citizen.

from The Schoolmaster

If your scholar do miss sometimes in marking rightly these foresaid six things, chide not hastily, for that shall both dull his wit and discourage his diligence; but monish[1] him gently, which shall make him both willing to amend and glad to go forward in love and hope of learning.

I have now wished, twice or thrice, this gentle nature to be in a schoolmaster, and that I have done so neither by chance nor without some reason I will now declare at large, why, in mine opinion, love is fitter than fear, gentleness better than beating, to bring up a child rightly in learning.

With the common use of teaching and beating in common schools of England I will not greatly contend, which if I did, it were but a small grammatical controversy, neither belonging to heresy nor treason, nor greatly touching God nor the prince; although in very deed, in the end the good or ill bringing up of children doth as much serve to the good or ill service of God, our prince, and our whole country, as any one thing doth beside.

I do gladly agree with all good schoolmasters in these points: to have children brought to good perfectness in learning, to all honesty in manners, to have all faults rightly amended, to have every vice severally corrected; but for the order and way that leadeth rightly to these points, we somewhat differ. For commonly, many schoolmasters, some, as I have seen, more, as I have heard tell, be of so crooked a nature as when they meet with a hard-witted scholar, they rather break him than bow him, rather mar him than mend him. For when the schoolmaster is angry with some other matter, then will he soonest fall to beat his scholar, and though he himself should be punished for his folly, yet must he beat some scholar for his pleasure though there be no cause for him to do so nor yet fault in the scholar to deserve so. These will ye say be fond schoolmasters, and few they be that be found to be such. They be found indeed, but surely over-many such be found everywhere. But this will I say, that even the wisest of your great beaters do as oft punish nature as they do correct faults. Yea, many times, the better nature is sorer punished, for if one by

---

1. Admonish.

quickness of wit take his lesson readily, another, by hardness of wit taketh it not so speedily; the first is always commended, the other is commonly punished, when a wise schoolmaster should rather discreetly consider the right disposition of both their natures and not so much weigh what either of them is able to do now, as what either of them is likely to do hereafter. For this I know, not only by reading of books in my study, but also by experience of life abroad in the world, that those which be commonly the wisest, the best learned and best men also, when they be old, were never commonly the quickest of wit when they were young. The causes why, amongst other, which be many, that move me thus to think be these few which I will reckon. Quick wits commonly be apt to take, unapt to keep; soon hot and desirous of this and that; as cold and soon weary of the same again; more quick to enter speedily than able to pierce far; even like some over-sharp tools, whose edges be very soon turned. Such wits delight themselves in easy and pleasant studies and never pass far forward in high and hard sciences. And therefore the quickest wits commonly may prove the best poets, but not the wisest orators; ready of tongue to speak boldly, not deep of judgment, either for good counsel or wise writing. Also, for manners and life, quick wits commonly be in desire newfangled; in purpose, unconstant; light to promise anything, ready to forget everything, both benefit and injury; and thereby neither fast to friend nor fearful to foe; inquisitive of every trifle, not secret in greatest affairs; bold with any person; busy in any matter; soothing such as be present, nipping any that is absent; of nature also, always flattering their betters, envying their equals, despising their inferiors; and by quickness of wit, very quick and ready to like none so well as themselves.

Moreover, commonly, men very quick of wit be also very light of conditions, and thereby very ready of disposition, to be carried over quickly by any light company to any riot and unthriftiness when they be young, and therefore seldom either honest of life or rich in living when they be old. For, quick in wit and light in manners be either seldom troubled or very soon weary in carrying a heavy purse. Quick wits also be, in most part of all their doings, over-quick, hasty, rash, heady, and brainsick. These last two words, heady and brainsick, be fit and proper words, rising naturally of the matter and termed aptly by the condition of overmuch quickness of wit. In youth also they be ready scoffers, privy mockers, and ever over-light and merry. In age, soon testy, very waspish, and always over-miserable, and yet few of them come to any great age, by reason of their misordered life when they were young; but a great deal fewer of them come to show any great countenance or bear any great authority abroad in the world, but either live obscurely, men know not how, or die obscurely, men mark not when. They be like trees that show forth fair blossoms and broad leaves in springtime, but bring out small and not long lasting fruit in harvest time; and that only such as fall and rot before they be ripe and so never or seldom come to any good at all. For this ye shall find most true by experience, that amongst a number of quick wits in youth, few be found in the end either very fortunate for themselves or very profitable to serve the commonwealth, but decay and vanish men know not which way, except a very few, to whom peradventure blood and happy parentage may perchance purchase a long standing upon the stage. The which felicity, because it cometh by others' procuring, not by their own deserving, and stand by other men's feet, and not by their own, what outward brag so ever is born by them, is indeed, of itself and in wise men's eyes, of no great estimation. * * *

Contrariwise, a wit in youth, that is not over dull, heavy, knotty, and lumpish, but hard, rough and though somewhat staffish, as Tully wisheth *otium, quietum, non languidum,* and *negotium cum labore, non cum periculo,*[2] such a wit, I say, if it be first well handled by the mother and rightly smoothed and wrought as it should, not over-thwartly and against the wood by the schoolmaster, both for learning and whole course of living, proveth always the best. In wood and stone, not the softest, but hardest be always aptest for portraiture, both fairest for pleasure and most durable for profit. Hard wits be hard to receive, but sure to keep; painful without weariness, heedful without wavering, constant without newfangledness; bearing heavy things, though not lightly, yet willingly; entering hard things, though not easily, yet deeply; and so come to that perfectness of learning in the end that quick wits seem in hope, but do not in deed, or else very seldom ever attain unto. Also, for manners and life, hard wits commonly are hardly carried either to desire every new thing or else to marvel at every strange thing, and therefore they be careful and diligent in their own matters, not curious or busy in other men's affairs; and so they become wise them-selves and also are counted honest by others. They be grave, steadfast, silent of tongue, secret of heart; not hasty in making, but constant in keeping any promise; not rash in uttering, but wary in considering every matter; and thereby, not quick in speaking, but deep of judgment, whether they write or give counsel in all weighty affairs. And these be the men that become in the end both most happy for them-selves and always best esteemed abroad in the world.

⊶ ⇥⬥⇤ ⊷

Richard Mulcaster
1530–1611

One of the best-known humanists of the early Tudor period, Mulcaster remained a school-teacher all his life, first at Merchant Taylors' School and then at Saint Paul's, both in London. Like Ascham, he rejected methods of teaching that did not result in a thoughtful and open-minded student. Early in the second of his two treatises on education, *The Elementary* (1582), he identifies ignorance and prejudice as impediments to learning; of the two, he insists, preju-dice is worse.

from **The First Part of the Elementary**

What greater enemies hath learning even in nature than prejudice and ignorance? Whence is there more open show of implacable hostility to knowledge than from prejudice and ignorance? Ignorance knoweth nothing, and therefore is no friend to an unknown good, prejudice knoweth and will not, and therefore is a great foe to a not-favored good. Ignorance yet in part deserveth some excuse for all her disfriend-ship, because infirmity is her fault, not bolstered with ill will, and the worst is her own, an ordinary case, where even enmity pitieth.[1] But prejudice is a poison to any commonweal, so far as it stretcheth, which being at the first infected with the incur-able disease of a cankered and a corrupt opinion gathered by confluence of sundry ill

---

2. Ascham refers to Cicero, who desires "a quiet not a languid leisure" and "an occupation that entails work not danger."

1. I.e., ignorance does not imply ill will; its effects are limited by its own failure to seek knowledge; even his enemies pity the ignorant man.

humors, will neither itself yield to a right judgment, nor will suffer any other, where her persuasion can take place. For by yielding herself she feareth the impairing of her misconceived estimation, and by suffering other to yield, she feareth the increase of knowledge's friends, whereby herself shall come in danger to be oppressed, both with truth of matter and number of patrons. Wherefore she opposeth herself, she bendeth all her eloquence, she mureth up[2] all passages, so much as she may, both by persuasion and entreaty, that none shall judge right which will hear her speak and regard her authority, but shall take that music to sound the sweetest which cometh from her, though she be but a mermaid, which by offering of delight endeavoreth to destroy.

Ignorance is violent and like unto a lion, when it encountereth with knowledge, still in fury without feeling, in rage without reason, and riseth of two causes, either infirmity in nature or negligence in labor. Whereof the one could not, the other would not conceive at the first when knowledge was in dealing. Both enemies to knowledge, but negligence the greater,[3] which, either fearing disdain for her first refusal or envying him which loveth where she left, will not seem to favor where she once forsook and stomacheth[4] him which embraceth her leavings, wreaking her malice in show upon knowledge, indeed upon folly. Which folly, being lodged within her own breast beside that negligent ignorance, useth to call in a dangerous opinion the contempt of that good, which she ought to commend, rather than she will by change of opinion and altering her hue, bewray her own error, which all men see saving she that should.[5] Being at defiance with knowledge, not by simplicity of nature, which offered, but by naughtiness of choice, which refused the attaining thereof.

Now natural infirmity the other and more gentle mean of ignorance would perhaps, nay would indeed change her blind opinion, if she could once change her ingenerate heaviness. She would reverence learning if she might see her beauty wherewith to be ravished, being enemy unto her, not of malice but of weakness. * * *

But that same perverse prejudice is a subtle foe to knowledge like a many-headed hydra, and as the venom of his authority is gathered of diverse grounds, so the sting of his poison infecteth diverse ways. The person himself which is thus carried away by a peevish opinion is commonly no heavy head,[6] but either superfically learned and yet loath to seem so, or enviously affected and still carping at[7] his better; or ambitiously given and presumeth upon countenance;[8] or he measureth knowledge by gain, and setteth naught by any more than he himself shall need to compass that [which] he coveteth, where a little cunning will compass much more than reason thinks enough in corruption of minds.[9] * * * The party so corrupted will seek by all means to continue his credit, so much the more a deadly enemy to knowledge, because prejudice must give place if knowledge come in place, and therefore that it may not come, he employeth all his forces, by all cunning and all well-colored shifts[1] to shoulder it out: a professed foe, and so much the shrewder, because he supplanteth knowledge under the opinion of knowledge.

≕ END OF PERSPECTIVES: GOVERNMENT AND SELF-GOVERNMENT ≔

2. Walls up.
3. Negligence is a greater enemy to knowledge than "infirmity in nature" because it will not seem to favor the knowledge it has rejected or to tolerate the person who picks up that knowledge; negligence acts with malice toward knowledge, acting foolishly.
4. Will not tolerate.
5. Folly persists in condemning what is good lest others see her error—as they do anyway.
6. Slow learner.
7. Criticizing.
8. Appearance.
9. I.e., cleverness will do more than reason thinks is necessary to corrupt minds.
1. Persuasive arguments.

Aemilia Lanyer
1569–1645

Aemilia Lanyer was born Aemilia Bassano, the daughter of Queen Elizabeth's court musician, Baptista Bassano. Acquaintance with the nobility surrounding the Queen allowed her an education that was typically reserved for women of high station. At eighteen, shortly after her mother's death, she became the mistress of Henry Cary Hunsdon, the Lord Chancellor. Her position increased her presence at court until, at twenty-three, she became pregnant and was forced to marry a court musician. Their son, conspicuously named Henry, was born three months after the wedding. The first years of her married life were not auspicious. Alfonso Lanyer was a spendthrift, and the money Aemilia had acquired as Hunsdon's mistress was soon exhausted. Desperate for reassurance, she visited the astrologer Simon Forman to learn whether the stars indicated that Alfonso would gain a knighthood. The disreputable Forman appears to have had other ideas. His casebook records that on one occasion, he "went and supped with her and stayed all night, and she was familiar and friendly to him in all things. But only she would not halek [have intercourse] . . . he never obtained his purpose and she was a whore and dealt evil with him."

Lanyer's character is more accurately represented in the record of her long friendship with Margaret Clifford, Countess of Cumberland, and her daughter Anne. In 1610, partly in tribute to the loyal support of her patroness, Lanyer published a volume of poetry entitled *Salve Deus Rex Judaeorum*; this included a verse defense of women and a poem to Cookham, a country house leased by Margaret Clifford's brother, William Russell, and visited frequently by Lanyer until 1605. She particularly records two critical transformations in her sense of herself: a spiritual awakening, inspired by the piety of the Countess, and a confirmation of herself as a poet. Her impressions of Cookham express a unity among aesthetic elements that are usually opposed and antithetical: pagan culture and Christian vision, temporal experience and spiritual knowledge, and the erotic pleasure in the discipline of chastity.

The Description of Cookham

Farewell (sweet Cookham) where I first obtained
Grace from that Grace where perfit° grace remained;   *perfect*
And where the Muses[1] gave their full consent,
I should have power the virtuous to content;
5   Where princely Palace willed me to indite,°   *write*
The sacred story[2] of the soul's delight.
Farewell (sweet place) where virtue then did rest,
And all delights did harbor in her breast;
Never shall my said eyes again behold
10   Those pleasures which my thoughts did then unfold:
Yet you (great Lady),[3] Mistress of that place,
From whose desires did spring this work of grace;
Vouchsafe° to think upon those pleasures past,   *agree*
As fleeting worldly joys that could not last,
15   Or, as dim shadows of celestial pleasures,
Which are desired above all earthly treasures.

---

1. Divinities who presided over the arts and courtesy.
2. Possibly the story of the Passion, recounted in the

poem *Salve Deus Rex Judaeorum*.
3. Margaret Clifford, the Countess of Cumberland.

Oh how (me thought) against you thither came,[4]
Each part did seem some new delight to frame!
The house received all ornaments to grace it,
20   And would endure no foulness to deface it.
The walks put on their summer liveries,°   uniforms
And all things else did hold like similies:°   comparisons
The trees with leaves, with fruits, with flowers clad,
Embraced each other, seeming to be glad,
25   Turning themselves to beauteous canopies,
To shade the bright sun from your brighter eyes.
The crystal streams with silver spangles graced,
While by the glorious sun they were embraced,
The little birds in chirping notes did sing,
30   To entertain both you and that sweet spring.
And Philomela[5] with her sundry lays,°   songs
Both you and that delightful place did praise.
Oh, how me thought each plant, each flower, each tree
Set forth their beauties then to welcome thee:
35   The very hills right humbly did descend,
When you to tread upon them did intend.
And as you set your feet, they still did rise,
Glad that they could receive so rich a prize.
The gentle winds did take delight to be
40   Among those woods that were so graced by thee.
And in sad° murmur uttered pleasing sound,   deep
That pleasure in that place might more abound:
The swelling banks delivered all their pride,
When such a Phoenix[6] once they had espied.
45   Each arbor, bank, each seat, each stately tree,
Thought themselves honored in supporting thee.
The pretty birds would oft come to attend thee,
Yet fly away for fear they should offend thee:
The little creatures in the burrow by°   nearby
50   Would come abroad to sport them in your eye;
Yet fearful of the bow in your fair hand,
Would run away when you did make a stand.
Now let me come unto that stately tree,
Wherein such goodly prospects you did see;
55   That oak that did in height his fellows pass,
As much as lofty trees, low growing grass
Much like a comely cedar straight and tall,
Whose beauteous stature far exceeded all.
How often did you visit this fair tree,
60   Which seeming joyful in receiving thee,
Would like a palm tree spread his arms abroad,

4. In preparation for your arrival.
5. In Greek mythology, a woman who was transformed into a swallow; in Latin versions of her story she becomes a nightingale.
6. A mythical bird, always unique on earth, that regenerates itself in its own funeral pyre and therefore signifies eternity; here it figures the Countess.

Desirous that you there should make abode:
Whose fair green leaves much like a comely veil,
Defended Phoebus when he would assail:[7]
65 Whose pleasing boughs did yield a cool fresh air,
Joying his happiness when you were there.
Where being seated, you might plainly see,
Hills, vales, and woods, as if on bended knee
They had appeared, your honor to salute,
70 Or to prefer some strange unlooked for suit:
All interlaced with brooks and crystal springs,
A prospect fit to please the eyes of kings:
And thirteen shires appeared all in your sight,
Europe could not afford much more delight.
75 What was there then but gave you all content,
While you the time in meditation spent,
Of their Creator's power, which there you saw,
In all his creatures held a perfit law;
And in their beauties did you plain descry,°   discern
80 His beauty, wisdom, grace, love, majesty.
In these sweet woods how often did you walk,
With Christ and his apostles there to talk;
Placing his holy writ in some fair tree,
To meditate what you therein did see:
85 With Moses you did mount his holy hill,[8]
To know his pleasure, and perform his will.
With lovely David[9] you did often sing
His holy hymns to heaven's eternal king.
And in sweet music did your soul delight,
90 To sound his praises, morning, noon, and night.
With blessed Joseph you did often feed
Your pined° brethren, when they stood in need.[1]   poor
And that sweet lady sprung from Clifford's race,[2]
Of noble Bedford's blood, fair steam of grace,
95 To honorable Dorset now espoused,
In whose fair breast true virtue then was housed.
Oh, what delight did my weak spirits find
In those pure parts of her well framed mind,
And yet it grieves me that I cannot be
100 Near unto her, whose virtues did agree
With those fair ornaments of outward beauty,
Which did enforce from all both love and duty.
Unconstant Fortune, thou art most to blame,
Who casts us down into so low a frame,

---

7. The leaves of the palm tree protected the Countess from Phoebus, the god of the sun.
8. Moses climbed Mount Sinai to receive the law of God (Exodus 24, 25).
9. King David the psalmist.
1. Sold by his jealous brothers into slavery, Joseph became Pharaoh's right-hand man and granted these same brothers food and money during a famine many years later (Genesis 42.1–28).
2. The Lady is the Countess's daughter Anne, descended from Margaret Russell of Bedford and her father George Clifford, Duke of Cumberland. Anne married the Earl of Dorset in 1609 and is thus referred to as Dorset.

105 Where our great friends we cannot daily see,
    So great a diffrence is there in degree.
    Many are placed in those orbs of state,
    Parters° in honor, so ordained by Fate;   *participants*
    Nearer in show, yet farther off in love,
110 In which, the lowest always are above.[3]
    But whither am I carried in conceit?°   *imagination*
    My wit too weak to conster of° the great.   *understand*
    Why not? although we are but born of earth,
    We may behold the heavens, despising death;
115 And loving heaven that is so far above,
    May in the end vouchsafe us entire love.
    Therefore sweet memory do thou retain
    Those pleasures past, which will not turn again;
    Remember beauteous Dorset's former sports,
120 So far from being touched by ill reports;
    Wherein myself did always bear a part,
    While reverend Love presented my true heart.
    Those recreations let me bear in mind,
    Which her sweet youth and noble thoughts did find,
125 Whereof deprived, I evermore must grieve,
    Hating blind Fortune, careless to relieve.
    And you sweet Cookham, whom these ladies leave,
    I now must tell the grief you did conceive
    At their departure; when they went away,
130 How everything retained a sad dismay;
    Nay long before, when once an inkling came,
    Methought each thing did unto sorrow frame:
    The trees that were so glorious in our view,
    Forsook both flowers and fruit, when once they knew
135 Of your depart,° their very leaves did wither,   *departure*
    Changing their colors as they grew together.
    But when they saw this had no power to stay you,
    They often wept, though speechless, could not pray° you;   *beg*
    Letting their tears in your fair bosoms fall,
140 As if they said, "Why will ye leave us all?"
    This being vain, they cast their leaves away,
    Hoping that pity would have made you stay,
    Their frozen tops like age's hoary hairs,
    Shows their disasters, languishing in fears;
145 A swarthy riveled rine° all overspread,   *bark*
    Their dying bodies half alive, half dead.
    But your occasions called you so away,
    That nothing there had power to make you stay:
    Yet did I see a noble grateful mind,
150 Requiting each according to their kind,

---

3. I.e., persons of low station or rank love more than those who are of the gentry or nobility.

Forgetting not to turn and take your leave
Of these sad creatures, powerless to receive
Your favor when with grief you did depart,
Placing their former pleasures in your heart;
155 Giving great charge to noble memory,
There to preserve their love continually:
But specially the love of that fair tree,
That first and last you did vouchsafe to see:
In which it pleased you oft to take the air,
160 With noble Dorset, then a virgin fair:
Where many a learned book was read and scanned
To this fair tree, taking me by the hand,
You did repeat the pleasures which had passed,
Seeming to grieve they could no longer last.
165 And with a chaste, yet loving kiss took leave,
Of which sweet kiss I did it soon bereave:[4]
Scorning a senseless creature should possess
So rare a favor, so great happiness.
No other kiss it could receive from me,
170 For fear to give back what it took of thee:
So I ungrateful creature did deceive it,
Of that which you vouchsafed in love to leave it.
And though it oft° had given me much content,   *often*
Yet this great wrong I never could repent:
175 But of the happiest made it most forlorn,
To show that nothing's free from Fortune's scorn,
While all the rest with this most beauteous tree,
Made their sad consort° sorrow's harmony.   *music*
The flowers that on the banks and walks did grow,
180 Crept in the ground, the grass did weep for woe.
The winds and waters seemed to chide together,
Because you went away they know not whither:
And those sweet brooks that ran so fair and clear,
With grief and trouble wrinkled did appear.
185 Those pretty birds that wonted° were to sing,   *accustomed*
Now neither sing, nor chirp, nor use their wing;
But with their tender feet on some bare spray,
Warble forth sorrow, and their own dismay.
Fair Philomela leaves her mournful ditty,
190 Drowned in dead sleep, yet can procure no pity:
Each arbor, bank, each seat, each stately tree,
Looks bare and desolate now for want of thee;
Turning green tresses into frosty gray,
While in cold grief they wither all away.
195 The sun grew weak, his beams no comfort gave,
While all green things did make the earth their grave;

---

4. I.e., I took their kiss from the tree on which they had put it.

Each briar, each bramble, when you went away,
Caught fast your clothes, thinking to make you stay;
Delightful Echo[5] wonted° to reply   *used*
200   To our last words, did now for sorrow die:
The house cast off each garment that might grace it,
Putting on dust and cobwebs to deface it.
All desolation then there did appear,
When you were going whom they held so dear.
205   This last farewell to Cookham here I give,
When I am dead thy name in this may live,
Wherein I have performed her noble hest,°   *request*
Whose virtues lodge in my unworthy breast,
And ever shall, so long as life remains,
210   Tying my heart to her by those rich chains.

from Salve Deus Rex Judaeorum
To the Doubtful Reader

Gentle reader, if thou desire to be resolved, why I give this title, *Salve Deus Rex Judaeorum*, know for certain; that it was delivered unto me in sleep many years before I had any intent to write in this manner, and was quite out of my memory, until I had written the Passion of Christ, when immediately it came into my remembrance, what I had dreamed long before; and thinking it a significant token, that I was appointed to perform this work, I gave the very same words I received in sleep as the fittest title I could devise for this book.

To the Virtuous Reader[1]

Often have I heard, that it is the property of some women, not only to emulate the virtues and perfections of the rest, but also by all their powers of ill speaking, to eclipse the brightness of their deserved fame. Now contrary to this custom, which men I hope unjustly lay to their charge, I have written this small volume, or little book, for the general use of all virtuous ladies and gentlewomen of this kingdom; and in commendation of some particular persons of our own sex, such as for the most part are so well known to myself, and others, that I dare undertake fame dares not to call any better. And this have I done, to make known to the world that all women deserve not to be blamed, though some—forgetting they are women themselves and in danger to be condemned by the words of their own mouths—fall into so great an error as to speak unadvisedly against the rest of their sex; which if it be true, I am persuaded they can show their own imperfection in nothing more: and therefore could wish (for their own ease, modesties, and credit) they would refer[2] such points of folly to be practiced by evil disposed men, who forgetting they were born of women, nourished of women, and that if it were not by the means of

---

5. A nymph who can only repeat what she has heard; in the absence of voices, she dies.
1. This preface is Lanyer's general introduction to her poem *Salve Deus Rex Judaeorum* (Hail, Lord God, King of the Jews). Three excerpts follow: the invocation, an argument against beauty without virtue, and Pilate's apology for Eve.
2. Assign.

women, they would be quite extinguished out of the world and a final end of them
all, do like vipers deface the wombs wherein they were bred, only to give way and
utterance to their want of discretion and goodness. Such as these, were they that
dishonored Christ his apostles and prophets, putting them to shameful deaths.
Therefore we are not to regard any imputations, that they undeservedly lay upon
us, no[3] otherwise than to make use of them to our own benefits as spurs to virtue,
making us fly all occasions that may color their unjust speeches to pass current,[4]
especially considering that they have tempted even the patience of God himself,
who gave power to wise and virtuous women, to bring down their pride and arrogance: As was cruel *Caesar* by the discreet counsel of noble *Deborah*,[5] judge and
prophetess of Israel; and resolution of *Jael*, wife of *Heber* the Kenite; wicked
Haman, by the divine prayers and prudent proceedings of beautiful *Hester*; blasphemous *Holofernes*, by the invincible courage, rare wisdom, and confident carriage of
Judith; and the unjust judges, by the innocence of chaste *Susanna*; with infinite
others, which for brevity's sake I will omit. As also in respect it pleased our Lord
and Savior Jesus Christ, without the assistance of man, being free from original and
all other sins from the time of his conception till the hour of his death, to be begotten of a woman, born of a woman, nourished of a woman, obedient to a woman;
and that he healed woman,[6] pardoned women, comforted women; yea, even when
he was in his greatest agony and bloody sweat, going to be crucified, and also in the
last hour of his death, took care to dispose of a woman;[7] after his resurrection,
appeared first to a woman, sent a woman to declare his most glorious resurrection
to the rest of his disciples.[8] Many other examples I could allege of divers faithful
and virtuous women, who have in all ages, not only been confessors, but also
endured most cruel martyrdom for their faith in Jesus Christ. All which is sufficient
to enforce all good Christians and honorable-minded men to speak reverently of
our sex, and especially of all virtuous and good women. To the modest censures of
both which, I refer these my imperfect endeavors, knowing that according to their
own excellent dispositions, they will rather, cherish, nourish, and increase the least
spark of virtue where they find it, by their favorable and best interpretations, than
quench it by wrong constructions. To whom I wish all increase of virtue, and desire
their best opinions.

[INVOCATION]

Sith *Cynthia*[9] is ascended to that rest
Of endless joy and true eternity,
That glorious place that cannot be expressed
By any wight° clad in mortality,   *person*

---

3. Not.
4. To avoid occasions in which their unjust speeches
might appear to have some truth.
5. Lanyer lists virtuous women who benefited their people: Deborah, a wise judge and prophet of Israel, who
urged the warrior Barak to attack their enemy, Sisera
[Cesarus]; Jael, who killed Sisera with a blow to the head
(both figures from Judges 4); Hester [Esther], the queen of
the Israelites, who hanged Haman (Esther 5–7); the Jewish heroine Judith, who saved her town by killing King
Nebuchadnezzar's general Holofernes (the Apocryphal
Book of Judith 8–12); and Susanna, whose chastity was

proved by the prophet Daniel (the Apocryphal History of
Daniel and Susanna).
6. Womankind.
7. Jesus, from the cross, ordered a disciple (traditionally
understood to be John) to care for his mother (John
19.25–27).
8. After his resurrection, Jesus appeared first to Mary
Magdalene and "the other Mary," who then told the other disciples of this event (Matthew 28.8–10).
9. Goddess of the moon, also known as Diana; here she
represents Queen Elizabeth I.

5   In her almighty love so highly blest,
       And crowned with everlasting sovereignty;
           Where saints and angels do attend her throne,
           And she gives glory unto God alone.

       To thee great Countess[1] now I will apply
10   My pen, to write thy never dying fame;
       That when to heaven thy blessed soul shall fly,
       These lines on earth record thy reverend name:
       And to this task I mean my muse to tie,
       Though wanting skill I shall but purchase blame:
15   Pardon (dear Lady) want of woman's wit
           To pen thy praise, when few can equal it.

[Against Beauty Without Virtue]

185   That outward beauty which the world commends
       Is not the subject I will write upon,
       Whose date expired, that tyrant Time soon ends;
       Those gaudy colors soon are spent and gone;
       But those fair virtues which on thee attends,
190   Are always fresh, they never are but one:
           They make thy beauty fairer to behold,
           Than was that queen's[2] for whom proud Troy was sold.

       As for those matchless colors red and white,
       Or perfit° features in a fading face,   perfect
195   Or due proportion pleasing to the sight;
       All these do draw but dangers and disgrace;
       A mind enriched with virtue, shines more bright,
       Adds everlasting beauty, gives true grace,
           Frames an immortal goddess on the earth,
200   Who though she dies, yet fame gives her new birth.

       That pride of nature which adorns the fair,
       Like blazing comets to allure all eyes,
       Is but the thread, that weaves their web of care,
       Who glories most, where most their danger lies;
205   For greatest perils do attend the fair,
       When men do seek, attempt, plot and devise,
           How they may overthrow the chastest dame,
           Whose beauty is the white[3] whereat they aim.

       'Twas beauty bred in Troy the ten years' strife,
210   And carried *Helen* from her lawful lord;
       'Twas beauty made chaste *Lucrece*[4] lose her life,

---

1. Lady Margaret Clifford, the Countess of Cumberland. Lanyer declares that the poem she is writing will be a memorial to her.
2. Helen of Troy, wife of King Menelaus of Sparta. Renowned for her beauty, she was kidnapped by Paris, son of Priam, King of Troy. This brought about the Trojan War.
3. The "white" at which hunters aim is the breast of the deer (or dear), a common figure for the beloved lady.
4. Wife of the Roman nobleman Collatinus. She was raped by Sextus Tarquinius, son of Superbus, King of Rome. The crime aroused the people of Rome to overthrow the tyranny of the Tarquins and institute a republic.

For which proud *Tarquin's* fact° was so abhorr'd: deed
Beauty the cause *Antonius*[5] wronged his wife,
Which could not be decided but by sword:
215   Great *Cleopatra's* beauty and defects
      Did work *Octavia's* wrongs, and his neglects.

What fruit did yield that fair forbidden tree,
But blood, dishonor, infamy, and shame?
Poor blinded queen,[6] could'st thou no better see,
220   But entertain disgrace, instead of fame?
Do these designs with majesty agree?
To stain thy blood, and blot thy royal name.
      That heart that gave consent unto this ill,
      Did give consent that thou thyself should'st kill.

[PILATE'S WIFE APOLOGIZES FOR EVE]

745   Now *Pontius Pilate*[7] is to judge the cause
Of faultless *Jesus*, who before him stands;
Who neither hath offended prince, nor laws,
Although he now be brought in woeful bands:°   bonds
"O noble governor, make thou you a pause,
750   Do not in innocent blood imbrue° thy hands;   stain
      But hear the words of thy most worthy wife,
      Who sends to thee, to beg her Saviour's life.

Let barbarous cruelty far depart from thee,
And in true justice take affliction's part;
755   Open thine eyes, that thou the truth mayest see;
Do not the thing that goes against thy heart,
Condemn not him that must thy Saviour be;
But view his holy life, his good desert.
      Let not us women glory in men's fall,
760   Who had power given to overrule us all.

Till now your indiscretion sets us free,
And makes our former fault much less appear;[8]
Our Mother *Eve*, who tasted of the tree,
Giving to *Adam* what she held most dear,
765   Was simply good, and had no power to see,
The after-coming harm did not appear:[9]
      The subtle serpent that our sex betrayed,
      Before our fall so sure a plot had laid.

5. Marc Antony, who married Octavia, sister to Octavius, who would become the Emperor Augustus; Antony later abandoned her in favor of Cleopatra, queen of Egypt.
6. Cleopatra, figuratively blinded by her passion for Marc Antony. The couple committed suicide after Marc Antony's defeat by Octavius at the battle of Actium.
7. The Roman governor of Jerusalem, A.D. 26–36. He was the judge at the trial of Jesus, who was accused of violating the laws of Rome. His wife warned him against condemning Jesus, saying, "Have thou nothing to do with that just man: for I have suffered many things this day in

a dream because of him" (Matthew 27.19).
8. Lanyer recapitulates points raised by many writers who denied that Eve should have all the blame for the loss of Eden and paradise. Lanyer stresses Eve's innocence, and emphasizes that Adam should have exercised authority over Eve. This latter point is central to Milton's representation of Adam's sin in *Paradise Lost*, exonerating Eve while also making her Adam's subordinate.
9. She could not foresee the harm that would follow her disobedience.

That undiscerning ignorance° perceived   *i.e., of Eve*
770   No guile, or craft that was by him intended;
For had she known, of what we were bereaved,
To his request she had not condescended.
But she (poor soul) by cunning was deceived,
No hurt therein her harmless heart intended:
775   For she alleged God's word, which he denies,
That they should die, but even as gods, be wise.

But surely *Adam* cannot be excused,
Her fault though great, yet he was most to blame;
What weakness offered, strength might have refused,
780   Being Lord of all, greater was his shame:
Although the serpent's craft had her abused,
God's holy word ought all his actions frame,
        For he was lord and king of all the earth,
        Before poor *Eve* had either life or breath.

785   Who being framed by God's eternal hand,
The perfectest man that ever breathed on earth;
And from God's mouth received that strait° command,   *stern*
The breach whereof he knew was present death:
Yea, having power to rule both sea and land,
790   Yet with one apple won to lose that breath
        Which god had breathed in his beauteous face,
        Bringing us all in danger and disgrace.

And then to lay the fault on Patience° back,   *Patience's*
That we (poor women) must endure it all;
795   We know right well he did discretion lack,
Being not persuaded thereunto at all;
If *Eve* did err, it was for knowledge sake,
The fruit being fair, persuaded him to fall:
        No subtle serpent's falsehood did betray him,
800   If he would eat it, who had power to stay him?

Not *Eve*, whose fault was only too much love,
Which made her give this present to her dear,
That what she tasted, he likewise might prove,
Whereby his knowledge might become more clear;
805   He never sought her weakness to reprove,
With those sharp words, which he of God did hear:
        Yet men will boast of knowledge, which he took
        From *Eve's* fair hand, as from a learned book.

If any evil did in her remain,
810   Being made of him, he was the ground of all;
If one of many worlds[1] could lay a stain
Upon our sex, and work so great a fall
To wretched man, by Satan's subtle train;
What will so foul a fault amongst you all?

---

1. I.e., Adam who, as the father of all humankind, was of many people.

815   Her weakness did the serpent's words obey;
              But you in malice God's dear Son betray.

              Whom, if unjustly you condemn to die,
              Her sin was small, to what you do commit;
              All mortal sins that do for vengeance cry,
820   Are not to be compared unto it:
              If many worlds would altogether try,
              By all their sins the wrath of God to get;
                  This sin of yours, surmounts them all as far
                  As doth the sun, another little star.

825   Then let us have our liberty again,
              And challenge° to your selves no sovereignty;[2]   *attribute*
              You came not in the world without our pain:
              Make that a bar against your cruelty;
              Your fault being greater, why should you disdain
830   Our being your equals, free from tyranny?
                  If one weak woman simply did offend,
                  This sin of yours, hath no excuse, nor end.

              To which (poor souls) we never gave consent,
              Witness thy wife (*O Pilate*) speaks for all,
835   Who did but dream, and yet a message sent,
              That thou should'st have nothing to do at all
              With that just man; which, if thy heart relent,
              Why wilt thou be a reprobate° with *Saul?*   *sinner*
                  To seek the death of him that is so good,
840   For thy soul's health to shed his dearest blood.

━◆⧓━

Sir Walter Raleigh
c. 1554–1618

Born in South Devon, a region in which ports and shipyards testified to the importance of England's world trade and colonies abroad, Sir Walter Raleigh spent a considerable part of his life outside his native land. As a boy, he fought with Huguenot armies in France; at twenty-four he led an expedition to the West Indies with his half-brother, Sir Humphrey Gilbert; and two years later, he commanded a contingent of English troops in Ireland. He is reported to have been a great favorite of Elizabeth, at least until 1592, when he secretly married one of her ladies-in-waiting, Elizabeth Throckmorton. The Queen, furious that she had had no say in the match, imprisoned Raleigh in the Tower of London for a period that summer.

    Raleigh was famous for his travels. His most challenging expedition was intended to locate the legendary gold mines of El Dorado in South America. In 1595 he set out for the Spanish colony of Guiana, penetrating the interior of that land by venturing up the Orinoco. He described his trip in the brilliantly detailed *Discovery of the Large, Rich and Beautiful Empire*

---

2. Because men are afflicted with the weakness of Adam, they forfeit their original sovereignty over creation; their rule over woman is therefore a tyranny.

of Guiana, and although he returned to England without the gold he had gone for, his leadership of an expedition to sack the harbor of Cadiz in 1596 was enough to restore him to royal favor. But Raleigh was to encounter real trouble with the accession of James I. His enemies at court convinced the king that Raleigh had committed treason, and in 1603 he was tried, convicted, and once again confined to the Tower of London, this time with his wife and family. He remained there for thirteen years. His release was finally granted on the condition that he lead another expedition to Guiana. He had informed the King that on his earlier trip he had discovered an actual gold mine, and he now claimed that his new adventure would be successful. In fact, it was a disaster. Not only did he find no gold, but the mine to whose existence he had sworn was revealed to be a fabrication. On this occasion the grounds for proving treason were stronger than they had been in 1603. Raleigh was executed in 1618.

During his long imprisonment, Raleigh began to write a complete history of the world, managing only to cover events in ancient history to 168 B.C. Entitled *The History of the World* and published in 1614, the work is primarily remembered for the stunning reflection on death that appears on its last page: "O eloquent, just and mighty Death! Whom none could advise, thou hast persuaded; what none hath dared, thou hast done; and whom all the world hath flattered, thou only hast cast out of the world and despised; thou hast drawn together all the far stretched greatness, all the pride, cruelty, and ambition of man, and covered it all over with those two narrow words, *Hic iacet*."

Much of Raleigh's poetry is occasional, written to address the circumstances and the moment in which he found himself. It possesses the quality Castiglione celebrated in his treatise on court life: a brilliance of self-expression that contemporary Italians termed *sprezzatura*, created by the supposedly artless use of artifice showing not the courtier's education but, rather, his native wit and talent. Raleigh exploits images of common life but with an unusual intensity, adding sensuous detail to expressions of affection and reminders of mortality to celebrations of love.

To the Queen[1]

Our passions are most like to floods and streams,
The shallow murmur, but the deep are dumb.
So when affections yield discourse, it seems
The bottom is but shallow whence they come.
5   They that are rich in words must needs discover
      That they are poor in that which makes a lover.

Wrong not, dear empress of my heart,
      The merit of true passion,
With thinking that he feels no smart,
10   That sues for no compassion.
Since, if my plaints serve not to prove
      The conquest of your beauty,
It comes not from defect of love,
      But from excess of duty.

15   For knowing that I sue to serve
      A saint of such perfection,
As all desire, but none deserve,

---

1. This elaborate compliment is typical of the courtly expressions of devotion Elizabeth I often inspired.

A place in her affection;
I rather choose to want relief
20   Than venture the revealing,
When glory recommends the grief,
    Despair distrusts the healing.

Thus those desires that aim too high
    For any mortal lover,
25 When reason cannot make them die,
    Discretion will them cover.
Yet when discretion doth bereave
    The plaints that they should utter,
Then your discretion may perceive
30   That silence is a suitor.

Silence in love bewrays more woe
    Than words, though ne'er so witty,
A beggar that is dumb, you know,
    Deserveth double pity.
35 Then misconceive not (dearest heart)
    My true, though secret passion,
He smarteth most that hides his smart,
    And sues for no compassion.
c. 1590

On the Life of Man

What is our life? A play of passion,
Our mirth the music of division,
Our mothers' wombs the tiring houses be,
Where we are dressed for this short comedy,
5   Heaven the judicious sharp spectator is,
That sits and marks still who doth act amiss,
Our graves that hide us from the searching sun,
Are like drawn curtains when the play is done;
Thus march we playing to our latest rest,
10 Only we die in earnest, that's no jest.

1612

The Author's Epitaph, Made by Himself

Even such is time, which takes in trust
Our youth, our joys, and all we have,
And pays us but with age and dust,
Who in the dark and silent grave,
5   When we have wandered all our days,
Shuts up the story of our days;
And from which earth, and grave, and dust,
The Lord shall raise me up, I trust.

from The Discovery of the Large, Rich and Beautiful Empire of Guiana[1]
from *Epistle Dedicatory*

To the Right Honorable my singular good lord and kinsman, Charles Howard,[2] Knight of the Garter, Baron, and Chancellor, and of the Admirals of England the most reknowned, and to the Right Honorable Sir Robert Cecil, Knight, Counselor in Her Highness's Privy Councils.[3]

For your Honors' many honorable and friendly parts, I have hitherto only returned promises, and now for answer of both your adventures, I have sent you a bundle of papers which I have divided between your Lordship and Sir Robert Cecil in these two respects chiefly. First, for it is reasonable that wasteful factors,[4] when they have consumed such stocks as they had in trust, do yield some color for the same in their account; secondly, for that I am assured that whatsoever shall be done or written by me shall need a double protection and defense. The trial that I had of both your loves, when I was left of all but of malice and revenge, makes me still presume that you will be pleased (knowing what little power I had to perform aught, and the great advantage of forewarned enemies) to answer that out of knowledge which others shall but object out of malice.[5] In my more happy times as I did especially honor you both, so I found that your loves sought me out in the darkest shadow of adversity, and the same affection which accompanied my better fortune, soared not away from me in my many miseries. All which, though I cannot requite, yet I shall ever acknowledge, and the great debt which I have no power to pay, I can do no more for a time but confess to be due. It is true that as my errors were great, so they have yielded very grievous effects, and if aught might have been deserved in former times to have counterpoised any part of offenses, the fruit thereof (as it seemeth) was long before fallen from the tree and the dead stock[6] only remained.[7] I did therefore even in the winter of my life undertake these travels, fitter for boys less blasted with misfortunes, for men of greater ability, and for minds of better encouragement, that thereby if it were possible I might recover but the moderation of excess and the least taste of the greatest plenty formerly possessed. If I had known other way to win, if I had imagined how greater adventures might have regained, if I could conceive what further means I might yet use but even to appease so powerful displeasure, I would not doubt but for one year more to hold fast my soul in my teeth til it were performed. Of that little remain I had, I have wasted in effect all therein,[8] I have undergone many constructions,[9] I have been accompanied with many sorrows, with labor, hunger, heat, sick-

1. A region in Venezuela. The full title of Raleigh's report is *The Discovery of the Large, Rich and Beautiful Empire of Guiana, with a relation of the Great and Golden City of Manoa (which the Spaniards call El Dorado) and the provinces of Emeria, Arromaia, Amapaia and other Countries, with their rivers, adjoining*. It was written and published in London in 1596, a year after Raleigh undertook his expedition.
2. Charles Howard (1536–1624) was Baron Howard of Effingham and Earl of Nottingham, commander of the Queen's navy at the defeat of the Armada and the capture of Cadiz.
3. Sir Robert Cecil was the first Earl of Salisbury, son of a principal advisor to Elizabeth I. Robert Cecil became Elizabeth's secretary of state in 1589 and was a key figure in the administration of James I, in which he eventually held the office of Lord Treasurer.

4. Raleigh refers to himself as a "factor," an agent who is commissioned to perform a certain function. Factors who exhausted the resources at their disposal had to account for their expenditures.
5. Raleigh presumes that Howard and Cecil will be able to answer his detractors (who speak from malice) with knowledge gained from this account of his travels to Guiana.
6. Trunk.
7. Raleigh admits that he has made errors and that the successes he had earlier in his career, which might have compensated for these errors, can no longer serve this purpose.
8. I.e., of what was left of my resources, I have effectually wasted everything.
9. Trials.

ness, and peril. It appeareth notwithstanding that I made no other bravado of going to sea than was meant, and that I was neither hidden in Cornwall or elsewhere, as was supposed.[1] They have grossly belied me, that forejudged that I would rather become a servant to the Spanish king than return; and the rest were much mistaken who would have persuaded that I was too easeful and sensual to undertake a journey of so great travel. But if what I have done receive the gracious construction[2] of a painful pilgrimage and purchase the least remission, I shall think all too little, and that there were wanting to the rest, many miseries.[3] But if both the times past, the present, and what may be in the future do all by one grain of gall continue in an eternal distaste, I do not then know whether I should bewail myself either for my too much travel and expense, or condemn myself for doing less than that which can deserve nothing.[4] From myself I have deserved no thanks, for I am returned a beggar, and withered, but that I might have bettered my poor estate it shall appear by the following discourse, if I had not only respected Her Majesty's future honor and riches. It became not the former fortune in which I once lived, to go journeys of picorie,[5] and it had sorted ill with the offices of honor which by Her Majesty's grace I hold this day in England to run from Cape to Cape and from place to place for the pillage of ordinary prizes. Many years since, I had knowledge by relation of that mighty, rich and beautiful Empire of Guiana and of that great and golden city which the Spaniards call El Dorado, and the naturals,[6] Manoa, which city was conquered, re-edified, and enlarged by a younger son of Guainacapa, Emperor of Peru, at such time as Francisco Pizarro[7] and others conquered the said empire from his two elder brethren, Guascar and Atabalipa, both then contending for the same, the one being favored by the Oreiones of Cuzco, the other by the people of Caximalca. I sent my servant Jacob Whiddon the year before to get knowledge of the passages, and I had some light from Captain Parker, sometime my servant and now attending on your Lordship, that such a place there was to the southward of the great bay of Charuas, or Guanipa, but I found that it was six hundred miles farther off than they supposed, and many other impediments to them unknown and unheard. After I had displanted[8] Don Antonio de Berreo, who was upon the same enterprise, leaving my ships at Trinidad, at the port called Curiapan, I wandered four hundred miles into the said country by land and river, the particulars I will leave to the following discourse.[9] The country hath more quantity of gold by manifold than the best parts of the Indies or Peru; all the most of the kings of the borders are already become Her Majesty's vassals and seem to desire nothing more than Her Majesty's protection and the return of the English nation.

1. I.e., it is apparent that I made no other boast of going to sea than to state that I intended to do it and that I was not hidden in Cornwall or elsewhere. Here Raleigh addresses the rumor that he had never gone to Guiana but rather had waited for his men to return from there, then claimed that his expedition was a success.

2. Interpretation.

3. I.e., if I could get some credit for having taken this painful pilgrimage, I would wish that my miseries had been more severe.

4. I.e., if everything continues to go badly, I do not know whether I should regret my travel or condemn myself for doing less than what can deserve nothing (what is not enough to deserve anything).

5. Suitable for the *picaro*, or rogue in Spanish.

6. Indigenous people.

7. Pizarro (1475–1541) conquered Peru by capturing the Incan king Atahualpa, whom Raleigh refers to as Ata-

balipa. Atahualpa was the son of Guainacapa and the brother of Guascar, whom he killed to get the throne. This passage suggests that Guianacapa had three sons; Raleigh later states that he had only two sons. Pizarro captured Cuzco, the principal city of the Incas, in 1533. The Oreiones were the native people of Cuzco; Caximalca or Casimarca was another large city in Peru.

8. Dislodged.

9. Here Raleigh claims that a Captain Parker told him that El Dorado was south of the bay of Guanipa (which opens onto the Gulf of Paria and has no connection with the Orinoco), but he discovered that it was 600 miles in the interior of the country and away from the shore. Don Antonio de Berreo was the Spanish Governor of Trinidad and Guiana; Trinidad is an island just off the Venezuelan coast. Presumably, Raleigh marched from that coast 400 miles inland.

[THE AMAZONS]

I made inquiry amongst the most ancient and best traveled of the Orenoqueponi, and I had knowledge of all the rivers between Orenoque and [the river of the] Amazons, and was very desirous to understand the truth of those warlike women, because of some it is believed, of others not.[1] And though I digress from my purpose, yet I will set down what hath been delivered me for truth of those women, and I spake with a Casique or Lord of people that told me he had been in the river, and beyond it also. The nations of these women are on the south side of the river in the provinces of Topago, and their chiefest strengths and retreats are in the Islands situated on the south side of the entrance, some 60 leagues within the mouth of the said river. The memories of the like women are very ancient as well in Africa as in Asia. In Africa those that had Medusa[2] for Queen: others in Scithia near the rivers of Tanais and Thermadon: we find also that Lampedo and Marthesia[3] were Queens of the Amazons: in many histories they are verified to have been, and in diverse ages and provinces. But they which are not far from Guiana do accompany with men but once a year, and for the time of one month, which I gather by their relation to be in April. At that time all the kings of the borders assemble, and the queens of the Amazons, and after the queens have chosen, the rest cast lots for their Valentines. This one month, they feast, dance, and drink of their wines in abundance, and the moon being done, they all depart to their own provinces. If they conceive, and be delivered of a son, they return him to the father, if of a daughter they nourish it, and retain it, and as many as have daughters send unto the begetters a present, all being desirous to increase their own sex and kind, but that they cut off the right dug of the breast I do not find to be true. It was further told me, that if in the wars they took any prisoners that they used to accompany with those also at what time soever, but in the end for certain they put them to death: for they are said to be very cruel and bloodthirsty, especially to such as offer to invade their territories.

[THE ORINOCO]

The great river of Orenoque or Baraquan hath nine branches which fall out on the north side of his own main mouth. On the south side it hath seven other fallings into the sea, so it disemboqueth[1] by sixteen arms in all, between islands and broken ground, but the islands are very great, many of them as big as the Isle of Wight[2] and bigger, and many less. From the first branch on the north to the last of the south it is at least one hundred leagues, so as the river's mouth is no less than three hundred miles wide at his entrance into the sea, which I take to be far bigger than that of [the] Amazons. All those that inhabit in the mouth of this river upon the several north branches are these Tiuitiuas,[3] of which there are two chief lords which have continual wars one with the other. The islands which lie on the right hand are called Pallamos, and the land on the left, Hororotomaka, and the river by which John Douglas returned within the land from Amana to Capuri, they call Macuri.

---

1. Raleigh takes his account of the Amazons from a native of Guiana. He associates this race of women, whose presence has never been verified, with a comparable people described in Greek mythology who are also warlike and consort with men only to conceive children.
2. A mythical monstrous woman, one of the Gorgons, who turned to stone whoever looked at her.

3. The legendary queen of the Amazons who fought in the Trojan war.
1. Discharges.
2. Island off the southern coast of England.
3. The Waraus, an indigenous people who live on the delta of the Orinoco and adjoining coasts. Spanish historians refer to them as the Guaraunos or Guaraunu.

These Tiuitiuas are a very goodly people and very valiant, and have the most manly speech and most deliberate that ever I heard of, what nation so ever. In the summer they have houses on the ground as in other places, where they build very artificial towns and villages, as it is written in the Spanish story of the West Indies, that those people do in the low lands near the gulf of Uraba. For between May and September, the river of Orenoque riseth thirty foot upright, and then those islands overflow twenty foot high above the level of the ground, saving some few raised grounds in the middle of them, and for this cause they are enforced to live in this manner. They never eat of anything that is set or sown, and as at home they use neither planting nor other manurance, so when they come abroad they refuse to feed of aught but of that which nature without labor bringeth forth.[4] They use the tops of *palmitos* [palm trees] for bread and kill deer, fish, and porks for the rest of their sustenance; they also have many sorts of fruits that grow in the woods and a great variety of birds and fowl.

And if to speak of them were not tedious and vulgar, surely we saw in those passages of very rare colors and forms not elsewhere to be found, for as much as I have either seen or read. Of these poeple, those that dwell upon the branches of the Orenoque called Capuri and Macureo are for the most part carpenters of *canoas* [canoes], for they make the most and fairest houses and sell them into Guiana for gold, and into Trinidad for tobacco, in the excessive taking whereof they exceed all nations, and notwithstanding the moistness of the air in which they live, the hardness of their diet, and the great labors they suffer to hunt, fish, and fowl for their living, in all my life either in the Indies or in Europe did I never behold a more goodly or better-favored people, or a more manly. They were wont to make war upon all nations and especially on the Cannibals, so as none durst without a good strength trade by those rivers; but of late they are at peace with their neighbors, all holding the Spaniards for a common enemy.[5] When their commanders die, they use great lamentation, and when they think the flesh of their bodies is putrified and fallen from the bones, then they take up the carcass again and hang it in the Casique's house that died, and deck his skull with feathers of all colors and hang all his gold plates about the bones of his arms, thighs, and legs. Those nations which are called Arwacas,[6] which dwell on the south of Orenoque (of which place and nation our Indian pilot was), are dispersed in many other places and do use to beat the bones of their lords into powder, and their wives and friends drink it all in their several sorts of drinks.

[THE NEW WORLD OF GUIANA]

To conclude, Guiana is a country that hath yet her maidenhead, never sacked, turned, nor wrought; the face of the earth hath not been torn, nor the virtue and salt of the soil spent by manurance, the graves have not been opened for gold, the mines not broken with sledges, nor their images pulled down out of their temples. It hath never been entered by any army of strength and never conquered or possessed by any

4. As people that do not farm, the Tiuitiuas would have been categorized by many Europeans as having no conception of property and therefore incapable of being dispossessed.
5. Here and throughout the narrative, Raleigh portrays the people of the region as desiring the protection of the English against the Spanish, whose mistreatment of the natives of the Americas was well publicized. Raleigh could claim that by making these natives vassals of the English monarch, England could acquire an empire to rival Spain's.
6. Known today as Arawaks, these people were neighbors of the Tiuitiuas.

Christian prince. It is besides so defensible that if two forts be builded in one of the provinces which I have seen, the flood setteth in so near the bank where the channel also lieth that no ship can pass but within a pike's length of the artillery, first of the one and afterwards of the other. Which two forts will be a sufficient guard both to the empire of *Inga* [Inca] and to an hundred other several kingdoms lying within the said river, even to the city of Quito in Peru.

There is therefore a great difference between the easiness of the conquest of Guiana and the defense of it being conquered, and the West or East Indies. Guiana hath but one entrance by the sea (if it have that) for any vessels of burden, so as whosoever shall first possess it, it shall be found inaccessible for any enemy except he come in wherries, barges, or *canoas,* or else in flat-bottomed boats; and if he do offer to enter it in that manner, the woods are so thick two hundred miles together upon the rivers of such entrance as a mouse cannot sit in a boat unhit from the bank. By land it is more impossible to approach, for it hath the strongest situation of any region under the sun, and is so environed with impassable mountains on every side as it is impossible to victual any company in the passage, which hath been well-proved by the Spanish nation, who, since the conquest of Peru have never left five years free from attempting this empire or discovering some way into it, and yet of twenty-three several gentlemen, knights, and noblemen, there was never any that knew which way to lead an army by land or to conduct ships by sea anything near the said country. Oreliano, of which the river of the Amazons taketh name, was the first, and Don Anthonio de Berreo (whom we displanted), the last; and I doubt much whether he himself or any of his yet know the best way into the said empire. It can therefore hardly be regained if any strength be formerly set down but in one or two places, and but two or three crumsters or galleys built and furnished upon the river within. The West Indies hath many ports, watering places, and landings, and nearer than three hundred miles to Guiana no man can harbor a ship, except he know one only place which is not learned in haste, and which I will undertake there is not any one of my companies that knoweth, whosoever hearkened after it.

Besides by keeping one good fort or building one town of strength, the whole empire is guarded, and whatsoever companies shall be afterwards planted within the land, although in twenty several provinces, those shall be able all to reunite themselves upon any occasion either by the way of one river or be able to march by land without either wood, bog, or mountain; whereas in the West Indies there are few towns or provinces that can succour or relieve one the other, either by land or sea. By land the countries are either desert, mountainous, or strong enemies. By sea, if any man invade to the eastward, those to the west cannot in many months turn against the breeze and east wind, besides the Spaniards are therein so dispersed as they are nowhere strong but in *Nueva Hispania* [New Spain] only. The sharp mountains, the thorns, the poisoned prickles, the sandy and deep ways in the valleys, the smothering heat and air, and want of water in other places are their only and best defense, which (because those nations that invade them are not victualled or provided to stay, neither have any place to friend adjoining) do serve them instead of good arms and great multitudes.

The West Indies were first offered Her Majesty's grandfather by Columbus,[1] a stranger in whom there might be doubt of deceit, and besides it was then thought

1. The brother of Christopher Columbus, Bartholomew Columbus, who invited Henry VII, King of England and grandfather of Elizabeth I, to accept his brother's services in his effort to find a continent west of England. Henry is reported to have accepted this offer, but not before Christopher Columbus had contracted his services to Queen Isabella of Spain. Therefore the West Indies were not ever offered to Henry VII; they were and remained Spanish through the 19th century.

incredible that there were such and so many lands and regions never written of before. This empire is made known to Her Majesty by her own vassal, and by him that oweth to her more duty than an ordinary subject, so that it shall ill sort with the many graces and benefits which I have received to abuse Her Highness either with fables or imaginations. The country is already discovered,[2] many nations won to Her Majesty's love and obedience, and those Spaniards which have latest and longest labored about the conquest, beaten out, discouraged and disgraced, which among these nations were thought invincible. Her Majesty may in this enterprise employ all those soldiers and gentlemen that are younger brethren, and all captains and chieftains that want employment, and the charge will be only the first setting out in victualling and arming them, for after the first or second year I doubt not but to see in London a contratation house of more receipt for Guiana than there is now in Seville for the West Indies.[3]

And I am resolved that if there were but a small army afoot in Guiana, marching towards Manoa, the chief city of *Inga*, he would yield Her Majesty by composition so many hundred thousand pounds yearly as should both defend all enemies abroad and defray all expenses at home and that he would besides pay a garrison of three or four thousand soldiers very royally to defend him against other nations. For he cannot but know how his predecessors, yea, how his own great uncles Guascar and Atibalipa, sons to Guanacapa, Emperor of Peru, were (while they contended for the empire) beaten out by the Spaniards and that both of late years and ever since the said conquest, the Spaniards have sought the passages and entry of his country; and of their cruelties used to the borderers he cannot be ignorant. In which respects no doubt but he will be brought to tribute with great gladness, if not, he hath neither shot nor iron weapon in all his empire and therefore may be easily conquered.

And I further remember that Berreo confessed to me and others (which I protest before the majesty of God to be true) that there was found among the prophecies of Peru (at such time as the empire was reduced to Spanish obedience) in their chiefest temples, among diverse others, which foreshadowed the loss of the said empire, that from *Inglatierra* [England] those *Ingas* should be again in time to come restored and delivered from the servitude of the said conquerors. And I hope, as we with these few hands have displanted the first garrison and driven them out of the said country, so Her Majesty will give order for the rest and either defend it and hold it as tributary, or conquer and keep it as Empress of the same. For whatsoever Prince shall possess it shall be greatest, and if the king of Spain enjoy it, he will become unresistable. Her Majesty hereby shall confirm and strengthen the opinions of all nations as touching her great and princely actions. And where the south border of Guiana reacheth to the dominion and empire of the Amazons, those women shall hereby hear the name of a virgin which is not only able to defend her own territories and her neighbors, but also to invade and conquer so great empires so far removed.[4]

To speak more at this time I fear would be but troublesome. I trust in God, this being true will suffice, and that he which is King of all Kings and Lord of all Lords will put it into her heart which is Lady of Ladies to possess it, if not, I will judge those men worthy to be kings thereof that by her grace and leave will undertake of it themselves.

---

2. The continent of which Guiana is a part.

3. Raleigh states that there will be a trading house or mercantile exchange for investors in Guiana that will exceed in its volume of business the comparable institu-

tion for the West Indian trade in Seville.

4. This reference to the Amazons allows Raleigh to pay tribute to Elizabeth I, who represented herself as a powerful virgin queen.

▓ "THE DISCOVERY" AND ITS TIME ▓
Voyage Literature

During the second half of the sixteenth century in England, descriptions of the land and peoples of the New World increasingly found their way into print. Much of this material, including translations of treatises written in Spanish, French, and Portuguese, was gathered by Richard Hakluyt and published in volumes under the general title of *The Principal Navigations, Voyages, and Discoveries of the English Nation* (1598–1600). In some respects the observations and opinions of these adventurers to the Caribbean, Virginia, Newfoundland, and other points on the Atlantic coast can be appreciated as a kind of anthropology; the accounts Hakluyt collected by writers such as Arthur Barlow, Thomas Hariot, and René Laudonnière convey their fascination with the cultures of the New World. In other respects, their writing is obviously self-interested, motivated by a desire for wealth. Treatises encouraging trade with the natives of the New World were often punctuated with apologies for the use of violence, justifications for the dispossession of native property, and professions of faith in a providence that allowed Europeans to convert the heathen to Christianity and to civilize peoples who many judged to be "barbarians." Ironically, these apologies were sometimes countered by evidence provided in European accounts of their encounters with American natives: Raleigh had noted the civilized trade of the Capuri on the Orinoco; here, Barlow cites the social order and commerce of the Algonquins around Roanoke; and Captain John Smith would later testify to the subtle politics of the Powhatans on the Chesapeake Bay. It is important also to remember that English colonists regarded themselves as being in competition with other nations for American land and resources. The Spanish were England's principal rivals, but as the account of René Laudonnière reveals, the French also had hopes for a New France.

Arthur Barlow
from *The First Voyage Made to the Coasts of America*[1]

This island had many goodly woods full of deer, coneys,[2] hares, and fowl, even in the midst of summer in incredible abundance. The woods are not such as you find in Bohemia, Muscovy, or Hercynia,[3] barren and fruitless, but the highest and reddest cedars of the world, far bettering the cedars of the Azores, of the Indies; or lybanus,[4] pines, cypress, sassafras, the lentisk, or the tree that beareth the mastic,[5] the tree that beareth the rind of black cinnamon, of which Master Winter brought from the straits of Magellan; and many other of excellent smell and quality. We remained by the side of this island two whole days before we saw any people of the country. The third day we espied one small boat rowing toward us, having in it three persons. This boat came to the island side, four harquebus[6]-shot from our ships, and there two of the people remaining, the third came along the shore side toward us, and, and we being then all within board, walked up and down upon the point of the land next unto us. Then the master and the pilot of the Admiral,[7] Simon Ferdinando, and Captain

---

1. Published in 1600 in Hakluyt's third volume, Arthur Barlow's account describes events in a voyage he took to North America in the summer of 1584. His company landed on the coast of what is now Virginia on July 4 and, by a verbal declaration of "the right of the Queen's most excellent Majesty, as rightful Queen and Princess of the same," took possession of all the land that they could see on July 13. Barlow's account is notable for its picture of the Indians as hospitable people who were prepared to engage in trade with the English on the fairest of terms, although in general his judgments reflect his own Anglo-European experience. Describing the Indians' reliance on

prophecy, for example, Barlow compares it to the Romans' dependence on the oracle of Apollo.
2. Rabbits.
3. The woods of Virginia are described by what they are not like: those in Bohemia (now a region comprising portions of Hungary and the Czech Republic), Muscovy (the western portions of modern Russia), and Hercynia (now the Bavarian Alps in modern Germany).
4. Known for its incense.
5. Gum.
6. Gun.
7. The ship on which the admiral of the fleet sails.

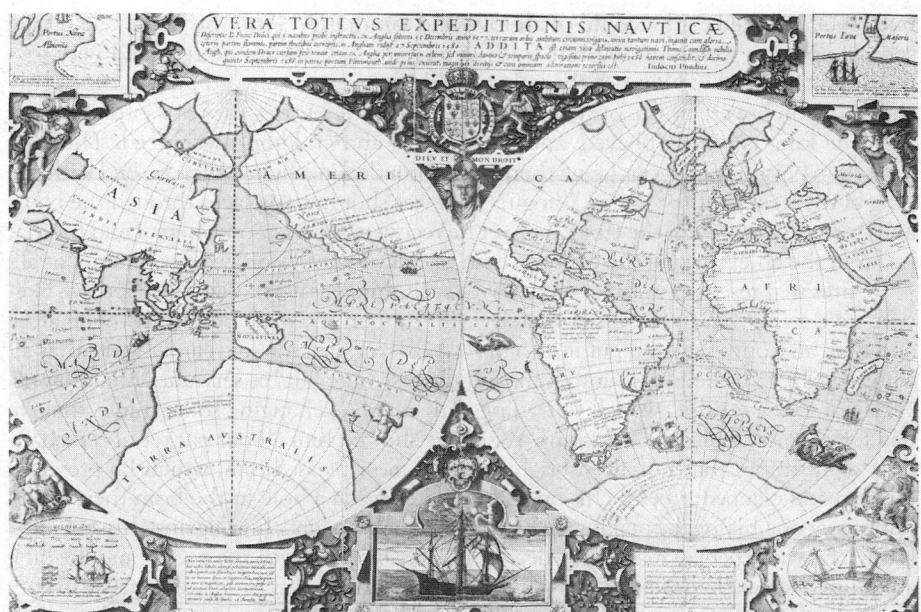

Hondius, *Sir Francis Drake's Map of the World*, c. 1590.

Philip Amadas, myself, and others rowed to the land, whose coming this fellow attended, never making any show of fear and doubt. And after he had spoken of many things not understood by us, we brought him with his own good liking aboard the ship and gave him a shirt, a hat, and some other things, and made him taste of our wine and our meat, which he liked very well. And after having viewed both barks, he departed and went to his own boat again, which he had left in a little cove or creek adjoining. As soon as he was two bowshot into the water, he fell to fishing, and in less than half an hour, he had laden his boat as deep as it could swim, with which he came again to the point of the land and there he divided his fish into two parts, appointing one part to the ship and the other to the pinnace, which, after he had (as much as he might) requited the former benefits received, departed out of our sight.

The next day there came to us diverse boats, and in one of them the King's brother, accompanied with forty or fifty men, very handsome and goodly people, and in their behavior as mannerly and civil as any of Europe. His name was Granganimeo, and the king is called Wingina, the country Wingandacoa, and now by Her Majesty, Virginia. The manner of his coming was in this sort: he left his boats altogether, as the first man did, a little from the ships by the shore, and came along to the place over against the ships, followed with forty men. When he came to the place, his servants spread a long mat upon the ground, on which he sat down, and at the other end of the mat four others of his company did the like; the rest of his men stood round about him, somewhat afar off. When we came to the shore to him with our weapons, he never moved from his place, nor any of the other four, nor never mistrusted any harm to be offered from us, but sitting still, he beckoned us to come and sit by him, which we performed. And being set, he made all signs of joy and welcome, striking on his head with his breast and afterwards on ours, to show we were all one, smiling and making show the best he could of all love and familiarity. After he had made a long speech unto us, we presented him with diverse things, which he received very joy-fully and thankfully. None of the company durst speak one word all the time, only the four which were at the other end spake one in the other's ear very softly.

The king is greatly obeyed, and his brothers and children reverenced. The king himself in person was, at our being there, sore wounded in a fight which he had with the king of the next country, called Wingina, and was shot in two places through the body, and once clean through the thigh, but yet he recovered. By reason whereof and for that he lay at the chief town of the country, being six days' journey off, we saw him not at all.

After we presented this his brother with such things as we thought he liked, we like-wise gave somewhat to the other that sat with him on the mat. But presently he arose and took all from them and put it into his own basket, making signs and tokens that all things ought to be delivered unto him, and the rest were but his servants and followers. A day or two after this, we fell to trading with them, exchanging some things that we had for chamois, buff, and deerskins. When we showed him all our packet of merchan-dise, of all things that he saw, a bright tin dish most pleased him, which he presently took up and clapped it before his breast, and after made a hole in the brim thereof and hung it about his neck, making signs that it would defend him against his enemies' arrows; for those people maintain a deadly and terrible war, with the people and the king adjoining. We exchanged our tin dish for twenty skins, worth twenty crowns or twenty nobles, and a copper kettle for fifty skins worth fifty crowns. They offered us good exchange for our hatchets and axes, and for knives, and would have given anything for swords, but we would not depart with any. After two or three days the king's brother came aboard the ships and drank wine and eat of our meat and of our bread, and liked exceedingly thereof; and after a few days had overpassed, he brought his wife with him to the ships, his daughter, and two or three children. His wife was very well-favored, of mean stature and very bashful; she had on her back a long cloak of leather with the fur side next to her body and before her a piece of the same. About her forehead she had a band of white coral, and so had her husband many times. In her ears she had bracelets of pearls hanging to her middle (whereof we delivered your worship a little bracelet) and those were of the bigness of good peas. The rest of her women of the better sort had pen-dants of copper hanging in either ear, and some of the children of the king's brother and other noblemen have five or six in either ear. He himself had upon his head a broad plate of gold or copper, for being unpolished we knew not what metal it would be, nei-ther would he by any means suffer us to take it off his head, but feeling it, it would bow very easily. His apparel was as his wife's, only the women wear their hair long on both sides and the men but on one. They are of color yellowish, and their hair black for the most part, and yet we saw children that had very fine auburn- and chestnut-colored hair.

After that these women had been there, there came down from all parts great store of people, bringing with them leather, coral, diverse kinds of dyes very excellent, and exchanged with us; but when Granganimeo the king's brother was present, none durst trade but himself, except such as wear red pieces of copper on their heads like himself, for that is the difference between the noblemen and the governors of coun-tries, and the meaner sort. And we both noted there and you have understood since by these men which we have brought home, that no people in the world carry more respect to their king, nobility, and governors than these do. The king's brother's wife, when she came to us (as she did many times) was allowed with forty or fifty women always, and when she came into the ship, she left them all on land, saving her two daughters, her nurse, and one or two more. The king's brother always kept this order, as many boats as he would come withal to the ships, so many fires would he make on the shore afar off, to the end we might understand with what strength and company he approached. Their boats are made of one tree, either of pine or pitch trees, a wood not commonly known to our people, nor found growing in England. They have no edge tools to make them withal; if they have any, they are very few and those it seems they had twenty years since, which, as those two men declared, was out of a wreck which happened upon their coast of some Christian ship, being beaten that way by some storm and outrageous weather, whereof none of the people were saved, but only the ship, or some part of her being cast upon the sand out of whose sides they drew the nails and the spikes and with those they made their best instruments. The manner of making their boats is thus: They burn down some great tree, or take such as are wind-fallen, and putting gum and rosin upon one side thereof, they set fire into it, and when it hath burnt it hollow, they cut out the coal with their shells and everywhere they would burn it deeper or wider they lay on gums which burn away the timber and by this means they fashion very fine boats and such as will transport twenty men. Their oars are like scoops, and many times they set[8] with long poles as the depth serveth.

The king's brother had great liking of our armor, a sword, and diverse other things which we had, and offered to lay a great box of pearl in gage[9] for them; but we refused it for this time, because we would not make them know that we esteemed thereof until we had understood in what places of the country the pearl grew, which now your worship doth very well understand.

He was very just of his promise; for many times we delivered him merchandise upon his word, but ever he came within the day and performed his promise. He sent us everyday a brace or two of fat bucks, coneys, hares, fish, the best of the world. He sent us diverse kinds of fruits, melons, walnuts, cucumbers, gourds, peas, and diverse roots, and fruits very excellent good, and of their country, corn,[1] which is very white, fair, and well-tasted, and growth three times in five months. In May they sow, in July they reap; in June they sow, in August they reap; in July they sow, in September they reap. Only they cast the corn into the ground, breaking a little of the soft turf with a wooden mattock or pickaxe. Ourselves proved the soil and put some of our peas in the ground, and in ten days they were of fourteen inches high. They have also beans very fair of diverse colors and wonderful plenty, some growing naturally and some in their gardens, and so have they wheat and oats.

The soil is the most plentiful, sweet, fruitful, and wholesome of all the world. There are above fourteen several sweet-smelling timber trees, and the most part of their underwoods are bays and such like. They have those oaks that we have, but far greater and better. After they had been diverse times aboard our ships, myself with seven more went twenty miles into the river that runneth toward the city of Skicoak, which river they call Occam; and the evening following, we came to an island which they call Raonoak,[2] distant from the harbor by which we entered seven leagues. And at the north end thereof was a village of nine houses, built of cedar and fortified round about with sharp trees to keep out their enemies, and the entrance into it made like a turnpike, very artificially. When we came toward it, standing near unto

---

8. Punt.
9. Payment.
1. Possibly buckwheat. The English used the term "maize" for the grain that in the United States is now known as corn.
2. Roanoke. A year later, this island in what is now

North Carolina was to be the site of the first English colony in North America. Sir Walter Raleigh sent out settlers in 1585, who returned to England in 1586; another group, who tried to revive the colony in 1587, had vanished without a trace by 1591, when ships from England reached them with additional settlers and supplies.

the water's side, the wife of Granganimeo, the king's brother, came running out to meet us very cheerfully and friendly; her husband was not then in the village. Some of her people she commanded to draw our boat on shore for the beating of the billow, others she appointed to carry us on their backs to the dry ground, and others to bring our oars into the house for fear of stealing. When we were come into the outer room, having five rooms in her house, she caused us to sit down by a great fire, and took off our clothes and washed them and dried them again. Some of the women plucked off our stockings and washed them, some washed our feet in warm water, and she herself took great pains to see all things ordered in the best manner she could, making great haste to dress some meat for us to eat.

After we had thus dried ourselves, she brought us into the inner room, where she set on the board standing along the house some wheat like fermenty,[3] sodden[4] venison and roasted; fish, sodden, boiled and roasted; melons raw and sodden; roots of diverse kinds, and diverse fruits. Their drink is commonly water, but while the grape lasteth, they drink wine, and for want of casks to keep it, all the year after they drink water, but it is sodden with ginger in it, and black cinnamon, and sometimes sassafras and diverse other wholesome and medicinable herbs and trees. We were entertained with all love and kindness, and with as much bounty (after their manner) as they could possibly devise. We found the people most gentle, loving and faithful, void of all guile and treason, and such as live after the manner of the golden age.[5] The people could only care how to defend themselves from the cold in their short winter, and to feed themselves with such meat as the soil affordeth. Their meat is very well sodden and they make broth very sweet and savory. Their vessels are earthen pots, very large, white, and sweet; their dishes are wooden platters of sweet timber. Within the place where they feed was their lodging, and within that, their idol which they worship, of whom they speak incredible things. While we were at meat, there came in at the gates two or three men with their bows and arrows from hunting, whom when we espied, we began to look one toward another and offered to reach our weapons; but as soon as she spied our mistrust, she was very much moved and caused some of her men to run out and take away their bows and arrows and break them and withal beat the poor fellows out of the gate again. When we departed in the evening and would not tarry all night, she was very sorry and gave us into our boat our supper half dressed, pots and all, and brought us to our boat's side, in which we lay all night, removing the same a pretty distance from the shore. She, perceiving our jealousy,[6] was much grieved, and sent diverse men and thirty women to sit all night on the bank side by us and sent us into our boats five mats to cover us from the rain, using many words to entreat us to rest in their houses. But because we were few men and if we had miscarried, the voyage had been in very great danger, we durst not adventure of anything, though there was no cause of doubt; for a more kind and loving people there cannot be found in the world, as far as we have hitherto had trial.

* * *

They wondered marvelously when we were amongst them at the whiteness of our skins, ever coveting[7] to touch our breast and to view the same. Besides they had our ships in marvelous admiration and all things else were so strange unto them as it appeared that none of them had ever seen the like. When we discharged any piece,

---

3. Porridge.
4. Boiled.
5. The Indians of the Americas were sometimes compared with the people who were supposed to have lived during the mythical golden age, a period in which nature provided food without toil, property was common, and human society was free of conflict.
6. Fear.
7. Wishing.

were it but an harquebus, they would tremble thereat for very fear and for the strangeness of the same. For the weapons which themselves use are bows and arrows; the arrows are but of small canes, headed with a sharp shell or tooth of a fish sufficient enough to kill a naked man. Their swords be of wood hardened, likewise they use wooden breastplates for their defense. They have besides a kind of club, in the end whereof they fasten the sharp horns of a stag or other beast. When they go to wars they carry about with them their idol, of whom they ask counsel, as the Romans were wont of the Oracle of Apollo. They sing songs as they march toward the battle, instead of drums and trumpets. Their wars are very cruel and bloody by reason whereof, and of their civil dissensions which have happened of late years among them, the people are marvelously wasted,[8] and in some places the country left desolate.

Thomas Hariot
from *A Brief and True Report of the Newfound Land of Virginia*[1]

It resteth I speak a word or two of the natural inhabitants, their natures and manners, leaving large discourse thereof until time more convenient hereafter; now only so far forth as that you may know how they in respect of troubling our inhabiting and planting are not to be feared, but that they shall have cause both to fear and love us that shall inhabit with them.

They are a people clothed with loose mantles made of deerskins, and aprons of the same round about their middles, all else naked; of such a difference of statures only as we in England;[2] having no edge tools or weapons of iron or steel to offend us withal, neither know they how to make any. Those weapons that they have are only bows made of witch hazel and arrows of reeds, flat-edged truncheons also of wood about a yard long; neither have they anything to defend themselves but targets[3] made of barks and some armors made of sticks wickered together with thread. * * *

Their manner of war amongst themselves is either by sudden surprising one another, most commonly about the dawning of the day or moonlight, or else by ambushes or some subtle devices. Set battles are very rare, except it fall out where there are many trees, where either part may have some hope of defense after the delivery of every arrow, in leaping behind some or other.[4]

If there fall out any wars between us and them, what their fight is likely to be, we having advantages against them so many manner of ways, as by our discipline, our strong weapons and devices else, especially ordinance[5] great and small, it may easily be imagined. By the experience we have had in some places, the turning up of their heels against us in running away was their best defense.

8. Reduced in numbers.
1. Thomas Hariot, an astronomer and mathematician, was a member of Sir Walter Raleigh's household. This account, published by Hakluyt in 1598, reports on Hariot's voyage to Virginia in 1586. He tells of an unanticipated yet terrible consequence of European colonization: the death of numbers of Indians from diseases—brought by colonists—to which the Indians had no immunity. As a scientific matter, the phenomenon was not at all understood, and Hariot describes attempts by the English to explain what it meant in supposedly moral terms and also to take advantage of its practical effect—the reduction of the Indian population—as a way to colonize the region further.

2. I.e., the Indians are generally of the same stature as the English and have the same range of differences in height as the English.
3. Shields.
4. Europeans fought each other in "set battles." Typically, an army was led by its cavalry and supported by its infantry, who marched to a distance from which they could fire their guns and cannons at the enemy. Indians waged what is known in the modern period as guerrilla warfare, attacking the enemy by surprise maneuvers and defending themselves in quick retreats.
5. Artillery.

In respect of us they are a people poor, and for want of skill and judgment in the knowledge and use of our things do esteem our trifles before things of greater value. Nothwithstanding, in their proper manner (considering the want of such means as we have), they seem very ingenious. For although they have no such tools, nor any such crafts, sciences, and arts as we, yet in those things they do, they show excellency of wit. And by how much they upon due consideration shall find our manner of knowledges and crafts to exceed theirs in perfection and speed for doing or execution, by so much the more is it probable that they should desire our friendship and love and have the greater respect for pleasing and obeying us. Whereby may be hoped, if means of good government be used, that they may in a short time be brought to civility and the embracing of true religion.

Some religion they have already, which although it be far from the truth, yet being as it is, there is hope that it may be the easier and sooner reformed.

They believe that there are many gods, which they call Mantoac, but of different sorts and degrees, one only chief and great God, which hath been from all eternity, who, as they affirm, when he purposed to make the world, made first other gods of a principal order to be as means and instruments to be used in the creation and government to follow, and after, the sun, moon, and stars as petty gods and the instruments of the other more principal. First (they say) were made waters, out of which by the gods was made all diversity of creatures that are visible or invisible.

For mankind, they say a woman was made first, which by the working of one of the gods, conceived and brought forth children; and in such sort they say they had their beginning. But how many years or ages have passed since, they say they can make no relation, having no letters or other such means as we to keep records of the particularities of times past, but only tradition from father to son.

* * *

Most things they saw with us, as mathematical instruments, sea compasses, the virtue of the loadstone[6] in drawing[7] iron, a perspective glass[8] whereby was showed many strange sights, burning glasses,[9] wild fireworks, guns, hooks, writing and reading, springclocks that seem to go of themselves, and many other things that we had were so strange unto them and so far exceeded their capacities to comprehend the reason and means how they should be made and done that they thought they were rather the works of gods than of men, or at the leastwise they had been given and taught us of the gods. Which made many of them to have such opinion of us as that if they knew not the truth of God and religion already, it was rather to be had from us whom God so specially loved than from a people that were so simple as they found themselves to be in comparison of us. Whereupon greater credit was given unto that we spoke of, concerning such matters. * * *

There could at no time happen any strange sickness, losses, hurts, or any other cross unto them but that they would impute to us the cause or means thereof, for offending or not pleasing us. One other rare and strange accident, leaving others, will I mention before I end, which moved the whole country that either knew or heard of us, to have us in wonderful admiration.

There was no town where we had any subtle devise[1] practiced against us, we leaving it unpunished or not revenged (because we sought by all means possible to win them by gentleness) but that within a few days after our departure from every

6. Magnet.
7. Attracting.
8. Telescope.

9. Magnifying glasses.
1. Trick.

such town, the people began to die very fast, and many in short space; in some towns about twenty, in some forty, and in one six score, which in truth was very many in respect of their numbers. This happened in no place that we could learn but where we had been where they used some practice against us, and after such time.[2] The disease also was so strange that they neither knew what it was, nor how to cure it, the like by report of the oldest men in the country never happened before, time out of mind. * * *

This marvelous accident in all the country wrought so strange opinions of us that some people could not tell whether to think us gods or men, and the rather because that all the space of their sickness, there was no man of ours known to die or that was especially sick; they noted also that we had no women among us, neither that we did care for any of theirs.

Some therefore were of opinion that we were not born of women, and therefore not mortal, but that we were men of an old generation many years past, then risen again to immortality.

Some would likewise seem to prophecy that there were more of our generation yet to come to kill theirs and take their places, as some thought the purpose was, by that which was already done. Those that were immediately to come after us they imagined to be in the air, yet invisible and without bodies, and that they by our entreaty and for the love of us did make the people to die in that sort as they did by shooting invisible bullets into them.

To confirm this opinion, their physicians (to excuse their ignorance in curing the disease) would not be ashamed to say but earnestly make the simple people believe that the strings of blood that they sucked out of the sick bodies were the strings wherewithal the invisible bullets were tied and cast. Some also thought that we shot them ourselves out of our pieces from the place where we dwelt and killed the people in any town that had offended us, as we listed, how far distant from us so ever it were. And other some said that it was the special work of God for our sakes as we ourselves have cause in some sort to think no less, whatsover some do or may imagine to the contrary, specially some astrologers, knowing of the eclipse of the sun which we saw the same year before in our voyage thitherward, which unto them appeared very terrible. And also of a comet which began to appear but a few days before the beginning of the said sickness.[3] But to exclude them[4] from being the special causes of so special an accident, there are further reasons than I think fit at this present to be alleged. These their[5] opinions I have set down the more at large that it may appear unto you that there is good hope that they may be brought through discreet dealing and government to the embracing of the truth and consequently to honor, obey, fear, and love us.

And although some of our company toward the end of the year showed themselves too fierce in slaying some of the people in some towns, upon causes that on our part might easily enough have been born withal; yet notwithstanding, because it was on their part justly deserved, the alteration of their opinions generally and for the

2. Hariot moralizes the phenomenon of immunity by stating that Indian villages that came down with disease were those that had resisted or "used some practice against" the English.
3. The Indians attributed their disease to God's favor toward the English. Hariot observes that the English concurred in this opinion, despite the warnings of astrologers

who saw a recent eclipse of the sun and the arrival of a comet as bad omens. He concludes that the Indians' sense of a divine power backing the English enterprise could be the basis for their further peaceful subjugation.
4. The eclipse and the comet.
5. I.e., the Indians'.

most part concerning us is the less to be doubted.[6] And whatsoever else they may be, by carefulness[7] of ourselves need nothing at all to be feared.

René Laudonnière
from A Notable History Containing Four Voyages Made to Florida[1]

My Lord Admiral of Chastillion, a nobleman more desirous of the public than of his private benefit, understanding the pleasure of the King his prince, which was to discover new and strange countries, caused vessels fit for this purpose to be made ready with all diligence and men to be levied meet for such an enterprise, among whom he chose Captain John Ribault, a man in truth expert in sea causes, which having received his charge, set himself to sea in the year 1562, the eighteenth of February, accompanied only with two of the king's ships, but so well furnished with gentlemen (of whose number I myself was one) and with old soldiers that he had means to achieve some notable thing and worthy of eternal memory. Having therefore sailed two months, never holding the usual course of the Spaniards, he arrived in Florida. * * *

Having sailed twelve leagues at the least, we perceived a troop of Indians, which as soon as ever they espied the pinnaces[2] were so afraid that they fled into the woods leaving behind them a young lucerne[3] which they were turning upon a spit, for which cause the place was called Cape Lucerne. Proceeding forth on our way, we found another arm of the river, which ran toward the east, up which the Captain determined to sail and to leave the great current. A little while after, they began to espy diverse other Indians, both men and women, half hidden within the woods, who, knowing not that we were such as desired their friendship were dismayed at the first but soon after were emboldened, for the Captain caused store of merchandise to be showed them openly whereby they knew that we meant nothing but well unto them. And then they made a sign that we should come on land, which we would not refuse. At our coming on shore, diverse of them came to salute our general according to their barbarous fashion. Some of them gave him skins of chamois;[4] others, little baskets made of palm leaves. Some presented him with pearls, but no great number. Afterwards they went about to make an arbor to defend us in that place from the parching heat of the sun; but we would not stay as then. Wherefore the Captain thanked them much for their good will and gave presents to each of them, wherewith he pleased them so well before he went thence that his sudden departure was nothing pleasant unto them. For knowing him to be so liberal, they would have wished him to have stayed a little longer, seeking by all means to give him occasion to stay, showing him by signs that he should stay but that day only, and that they desired to advertise a great Indian lord which had pearls in great abundance and silver also, all which things should be given unto him at the king's[5] arrival, saying further that in the meantime while that this great lord came thither, they would lead him to their houses and show him there a thousand pleasures in shooting and seeing the stag killed, therefore they prayed him not to deny them their request. Notwithstanding, we returned to our ships. * * *

---

6. Hariot admits that the English were "too fierce" in killing Indians for insufficient reason; at the same time, he states, without further explanation, that as these actions were "justly deserved," the English need fear no change in the Indians' attitude toward them.
7. Taking care.
1. Laudonnière set sail with John (Jean) Ribault, a French captain under the command of the Admiral of

Chastillon in 1562. This account of their adventures was translated from French into English and published in 1600 in Hakluyt's third volume.
2. Small sailing ships, often used to scout along rivers and bays.
3. Wildcat.
4. Deerskin.
5. I.e., of the Indians.

A few days afterward, John Ribault determined to return once again toward the Indians which inhabited that arm of the river which runneth toward the west, and to carry with him good store of soldiers. For his meaning was to take two Indians of this place to bring them into France, as the queen had commanded him. With this deliberation again we took our former course so far forth that at the last we came into the selfsame place where at the first we found the Indians, from thence we took two Indians by permission of the king, which thinking they were more favored than the rest thought themselves very happy to stay with us. But these two Indians, seeing we made no show at all that we would go on land but rather that we followed in the midst of the current, began to be somewhat offended and would by force have leapt into the water, for they are so good swimmers that immediately they would have gotten into the forests.[6] Nevertheless, being acquainted with their humor, we watched them narrowly and sought by all means to appease them, which we could not by any means do for that time, though we offered them things which they much esteemed, which things they disdained to take and gave back again whatever was given them, thinking that such gifts should have altogether bound them and that in restoring them they should be restored unto their liberty. In fine, perceiving that all that they did availed them nothing, they prayed us to give them those things which they had restored, which we did incontinent. Then they approached one toward the other and began to sing, agreeing so sweetly together that in hearing their song it seemed that they lamented the absence of their friends. They continued their songs all night without ceasing, all which time we were constrained to lie at anchor by reason that the tide was against us; but we hoisted sail the next day very early in the morning and returned to our ships.[7] As soon as we were come to our ships, every one sought to gratify these two Indians and to show them the best countenance that was possible, to the intent that by such courtesies they might perceive the good desire and affection which we had to remain their friends in time to come. Then we offered them meat to eat, but they refused it and made us to understand that they were accustomed to wash their face and to stay until the sun were set before they did eat, which is a ceremony common to all the Indians of New France. Nevertheless in the end they were constrained to forget their superstitions and to apply themselves to our nature, which was somewhat strange to them at the first. They became therefore more jocund, every hour made us a thousand discourses, being marvelous sorry that we could not understand them. A few days after, they began to bear so goodwill toward me that, as I think, they would rather have taken perished with hunger and thirst than have taken their refection at any man's hand but mine. Seeing this their goodwill, I sought to learn some Indian words and began to ask them questions, showing them the thing whereof I desired to know the name and how they called it. They were very glad to tell it me and, knowing the desire that I had to learn their language, they encouraged me afterward to ask them everything. So that putting down in writing the words and phrases of the Indian speech, I was able to understand the greatest part of their discourses. Every day they did nothing but speak unto me of the desire that they had to use me well, if we returned unto their houses, and cause me to receive all the pleasures that they could devise, as well in hunting as in seeing their very strange and superstitious ceremonies at a certain feast which they call Toya, which feast they observe as straightly as we observe the Sunday. They gave me to

6. In effect, the Indians found that they were prisoners.
7. These "ships" were the larger sailing vessels, or galleons, having three masts, five or six sails, and three or four decks, on which most settlers crossed the ocean.

understand that they would bring me to see the greatest lord of this country, which they call Chicola, who exceedeth them in height (as they told me) a good foot and a half. They said unto me that he dwelt within the land in a very large place and enclosed exceeding high, but I could not learn wherewith. And as far as I can judge, this place whereof they spoke unto me was a very fair city. For they said unto me that within the enclosure there was great store of houses which were built very high, wherein there was an infinite number of men like unto themselves which made none account of gold, of silver, nor of pearls, seeing they had thereof in abundance. * * * After they had stayed awhile in our ships, they began to be sorry and still demanded of me when they should return. I made them to understand that the Captain's will was to send them home again, but that first he would bestow apparel of them, which a few days after was delivered unto them. But seeing he would not give them license to depart, they resolved themselves to steal away by night and to get a little boat which we had, and by the help of the tide to sail home toward their dwellings and by this means to save themselves; which thing they failed not to do, and put their enterprise in execution, yet leaving behind them the apparel which the Captain had given them and carrying away nothing but that which was their own, showing well hereby that they were not void of reason. The Captain cared not greatly for their departure, considering they had not been used otherwise than well and that therefore they should not estrange themselves from the Frenchmen.

END OF "THE DISCOVERY" AND VOYAGE LITERATURE

Christopher Marlowe
1564–1593

When Christopher Marlowe began his career as a dramatist, the Elizabethan stage was at the height of its popularity and sophistication. Marlowe's plays were an immediate success, fascinating audiences with dazzling characters, exotic settings, and controversial subjects. Throughout his career—and even after his sudden death at the age of twenty-nine—Marlowe was Shakespeare's principal commercial and artistic rival.

A shoemaker's son, Marlowe went to Cambridge on a scholarship that was intended to prepare him for holy orders. His interests proved to be literary rather than religious, however, and he left Cambridge for London. As a student, he had composed a number of poems, notably the brilliant but unfinished *Hero and Leander*, a narrative of heterosexual and homosexual passion, but public recognition came with the production of his first play, *Tamburlaine the Great*, in 1587. This was followed by *The Second Part of Tamburlaine the Great*, *The Jew of Malta*, *Edward II*, *Dr. Faustus*, *Dido, Queen of Carthage*, and finally, *The Massacre at Paris*, all composed within a period of six years. Marlowe's bold and inventive language captivated audiences; his blank verse, in which the sense of a sentence is not interrupted at the end of each line by the constraints of rhyme, brought the rhythms of natural speech to the language of theater. His characterizations of heroes were equally astonishing: driven by an incandescent desire that no conquest could satisfy, they revealed the torment and tragedy that were occasioned by pride.

Marlowe himself may have been employed in subversive activities. While still at Cambridge, he became a spy for Queen Elizabeth's secret service, dedicated to the infiltration and exposure of Catholic groups in England and abroad. How much activity he was responsible for remains guesswork. At the very least, the manner in which he died suggests his involvement in clandestine politics. In May 1593, the Queen's Privy Council issued a warrant for his arrest. The charge against him—blasphemy—seems to have come from Thomas Kyd, a fellow playwright with whom Marlowe shared lodgings. While in London waiting for a hearing, Marlowe, who was drinking in an alehouse, got into a fight with three men (all government spies), one of whom was Ingram Friser. Marlowe raised a dagger to stab Friser, but Friser, warding off the blow, managed to turn the dagger against Marlowe. It pierced his eye "in such sort that his brains coming out at the dagger point, he shortly after died." The affair did not end there; two days after Marlowe's death, Richard Baines (himself a former spy) accused him before the Privy Council of atheism, treason, and the opinion "that they that love not tobacco and boys were fools." Whether or not these accusations held any truth, they referred to views that were not unusual in the circles Marlowe frequented; they indicate a skepticism in matters of religion and an indifference to social decorum that authorities responsible for political order would have considered dangerous. Some scholars think that Marlowe was murdered by government command. Although the mystery surrounding his death may never be solved, the mercurial brilliance of his work remains undisputed.

With the exception of the two parts of *Tamburlaine*, published in 1590, Marlowe's works were published after his death: *Edward II* and *Dido, Queen of Carthage* in 1594; *Hero and Leander* in 1598; *Dr. Faustus* in 1604; and *The Jew of Malta* in 1633. The celebrated lyric entitled *The Passionate Shepherd to His Love* first appeared in 1599 in an unauthorized collection of verse called *The Passionate Pilgrim* published by William Jaggard.

The Passionate Shepherd to His Love

Come live with me, and be my love,
And we will all the pleasures prove,
That valleys, groves, hills, and fields,
Woods, or steepy mountain yields.

5   And we will sit upon the rocks,
Seeing the shepherds feed their flocks,
By shallow rivers, to whose falls,
Melodious birds sing madrigals.

And I will make thee beds of roses,
10   And a thousand fragrant poesies,
A cap of flowers, and a kirtle,
Embroidered all with leaves of myrtle.

A gown made of the finest wool,
Which from our pretty lambs we pull,
15   Fair lined slippers for the cold,
With buckles of the purest gold.

A belt of straw, and ivy buds,
With coral clasps and amber studs,
And if these pleasures may thee move,
20   Come live with me, and be my love.

The shepherd swains shall dance and sing,
For thy delight each May morning,
If these delights thy mind may move,
Then live with me and be my love.

COMPANION READING
Sir Walter Raleigh: The Nymph's Reply to the Shepherd[1]

If all the world and love were young,
And truth in every shepherd's tongue,
These pretty pleasures might me move,
To live with thee, and be thy love.

5   Time drives the flocks from field to fold,
When rivers rage, and rocks grow cold,
And Philomel° becometh dumb,   *the nightingale*
The rest complain of cares to come.

The flowers do fade, and wanton fields,
10   To wayward winter reckoning yields,
A honey tongue, a heart of gall,
Is fancy's spring, but sorrow's fall.

Thy gowns, thy shoes, thy beds of roses,
Thy cap, thy kirtle, and thy poesies,
15   Soon break, soon wither, soon forgotten;
In folly ripe, in reason rotten.

Thy belt of straw and ivy buds,
Thy coral clasps and amber studs,
All these in me no means can move,
20   To come to thee, and be thy love.

But could youth last, and love still breed,
Had joys no date, nor age no need,
Then these delights my mind might move,
To live with thee, and be thy love.

THE TRAGICAL HISTORY OF DR. FAUSTUS   Marlowe's play is the first dramatic rendition of the medieval legend of a man who sold his soul to the devil. Sixteenth-century readers associated him with a necromancer named Dr. Faustus, and Marlowe exploited this identification when he reworked the medieval plot for his play. Rejecting the usual learning available to ambitious men—philosophy, medicine, law, and theology—Marlowe's Faustus signs a contract with the devil, represented in this case by his servant, Mephostophilis; in exchange for his soul, Faustus gains superhuman powers for twenty-four years. He uses these powers to conjure the Pope in Rome into giving the Protestant Emperor Charles V authority over the church through a surrogate Pope, Bruno; but his powers are also deployed in the banal trickery of simple and even criminal characters. The play is enigmatic on points of doctrine. Mephostophilis describes hell not as a locale but rather as the state of mind of one who has rejected God—a description that Milton will later amplify—telling Faustus: "this is hell, nor am I out of it." And Faustus, having worshipped the devil, is nevertheless offered a chance to repent and find salvation even at the very end of his alloted life. But he rejects God's love in favor of a night with Helen of Troy, praising her in lines that are now famous:

---

1. Raleigh's *Reply* was published together with Marlowe's poem in Jaggard's collection.

"Was this the face that launched a thousand ships, / And burnt the topless towers of Ilium?" The play concludes with a report of Faustus' mangled body, torn to bits by the demon to whom he had given his soul.

The textual history of the play is very vexed, and the extent of Marlowe's own authorship remains unclear. A short version of the play was published in 1604; known as the A text, it was probably used by touring companies. The longer B text, given here, was published in 1616, probably based on Marlowe's original manuscript but also incorporating revisions and additions by Marlowe and others as the play continued to evolve in performance.

Although playtexts in this period quite often show variants from one edition to another, the case of *Dr. Faustus* is an extreme one; lacking an authoritative version, it has generally been read in various conflations of A and B. Even so, it has continued to prove popular with audiences, both for the fatal drama of Faustus's bargain with the Devil and for the magnificent blank verse in which the drama plays out.

The Tragical History of Dr. Faustus

Dramatis Personae

Chorus	The Pope
Faustus	Bruno
Wagner, *Servant to Faustus*	Raymond, *King of Hungary*
Good Angel and Evil Angel	Charles, *the German Emperor*
Valdes ⎱ *Friends to Faustus*	Martino
Cornelius ⎰	Frederick
Mephostophilis	Benvolio
Lucifer	Saxony
Belzebub	Duke of Vanholt
The Seven Deadly Sins	Duchess of Vanholt
Clown/Robin	Spirits in the Shapes of Alexander
Dick	The Great, Darius, Paramour, and
Rafe	Helen
Vintner	An Old Man
Carter	Scholars, Soldiers, Devils, Courtiers,
Hostess	Cardinals, Monks, Cupids

[*Enter Chorus.*]

CHORUS: Not marching in the fields of Thrasimene,[1]
         Where Mars did mate the warlike Carthigens,
         Nor sporting in the dalliance of love
         In courts of kings where state is overturned,
5   Nor in the pomp of proud audacious deeds,
         Intends our muse to vaunt his heavenly verse.[2]
         Only this, gentles: we must now perform
         The form of Faustus' fortunes, good or bad.
         And now to patient judgments we appeal,
10   And speak for Faustus in his infancy.
         Now is he born, of parents base of stock,

---

1. Trasimeno, a lake in Italy near Rome. The Carthaginian general Hannibal conquered Roman forces at Trasimeno in 217 B.C.; Marlowe's "Mars" is probably a reference to the Roman army, which "mated" or engaged the enemy opposition there.

2. These lines may refer to plays Marlowe had previously staged and whose subjects were war (*Tamburlaine*) and love (*Edward II, Dido, Queen of Carthage*).

In Germany, within a town called Rhodes.
At riper years to Wittenberg he went,
Whereas his kinsmen chiefly brought him up.
15   So much he profits in divinity,
The fruitful plot° of scholarism graced,   *field*
That shortly he was graced with Doctor's name,
Excelling all; and sweetly can dispute
In th' heavenly matters of theology.
20   Till swol'n with cunning of a self-conceit,
His waxen wings did mount above his reach,
And melting, heavens conspired his overthrow.[3]
For falling to a devilish exercise,
And glutted now with learning's golden gifts,
25   He surfeits upon cursed necromancy.
Nothing so sweet as magic is to him,
Which he prefers before his chiefest bliss:
And this the man that in his study sits.

ACT 1

Scene 1

[*Faustus in his study.*]
FAUSTUS: Settle thy studies, Faustus, and begin
To sound the depth of that thou wilt profess.
Having commenced, be a divine in show,
Yet level at the end of every art
5   And live and die in Aristotle's works.
Sweet Analytics, 'tis thou hast ravished me.[4]
Bene disserere est finis logices.
Is "to dispute well logic's chiefest end"?
Affords this art no greater miracle?
10   Then read no more: thou hast attained that end.
A greater subject fitteth Faustus' wit.
Bid *on cai me on*° farewell. And Galen,[5] come,   *being and non-being*
Seeing, *ubi desinit philosophus, ibi incipit medicus.*
Be a physician, Faustus: heap up gold
15   And be eternized for some wondrous cure.
Summum bonum medicinae sanitas:
"The end of physic is our body's health."
Why, Faustus, hast thou not attained that end?
Is not thy common talk sound aphorisms?°   *wise sayings*
20   Are not thy bills hung up as monuments,
Whereby whole cities have escaped the plague,

3. Faustus is compared to the legendary figure of Icarus, whose father, the master craftsman Daedalus, made him a pair of wings that were attached to his body with wax. Icarus flew too near the sun, the wax supporting his wings melted, and he fell to the sea. The legend is generally understood to signify the consequences of pride and presumption.

4. Aristotle (384–322 B.C.), the best known of the Greek philosophers, wrote on the natural and social sciences. His *Analytics* dealt with logic.
5. Greek physician (A.D. 130–200) whose works on medicine were studied through the early modern period. Faustus welcomes his change of authorities with "where the philosopher ends, the physician begins."

And thousand desperate maladies been cured?
Yet art thou still but Faustus and a man.
Couldst thou make men to live eternally,
25   Or being dead, raise them to life again,
Then this profession were to be esteemed.
Physic, farewell. Where is Justinian?[6]
Si una eademque res legatur duobus,
Alter rem, alter valorem rei etc.,
30   A petty case of paltry legacies!
Exhaereditare filium non potest pater, nisi—
Such is the subject of the institute
And universal body of the law.
This study fits a mercenary drudge,
35   Who aims at nothing but external trash,
Too servile and illiberal for me.
When all is done Divinity is best.
Jerome's Bible![7] Faustus, view it well.
Stipendium peccati mors est. Ha! Stipendium etc.,
40   "The reward of sin is death."[8] That's hard.
Si pecasse negamus, fallimur, et nulla est in nobis veritas.
"If we say that we have no sin
We deceive ourselves, and there is no truth in us."[9]
Why then, belike, we must sin,
45   And so consequently die.
Ay, we must die, an everlasting death.
What doctrine call you this? *Che sera, sera.*
"What will be, shall be." Divinity, adieu!
These necromantic books are heavenly,
50   Lines, circles, scenes, letters and characters:
Ay, these are those that Faustus most desires.
Oh, what a world of profit and delight,
Of power, of honor, of omnipotence,
Is promised to the studious artisan!
55   All things that move between the quiet poles
Shall be at my command. Emperors and kings
Are but obeyed in their several provinces.
Nor can they raise the wind or rend the clouds.
But his dominion that exceeds in this
60   Stretcheth as far as doth the mind of man:
A sound magician is a demi-god.
Here, tire° my brains to get° a deity.   use / engender
[*Enter Wagner.*]
Wagner, commend me to my dearest friends,

6. Justinian, Emperor of Byzantium (483–565), codified all of Roman law; his *Institutes* provided the basis for civil law in England as well as on the continent. Faustus cites a principle of estate law: "if one and the same thing is bequeathed to two people, one of them should have the thing itself, and the other the value of it"; and "the father may not disinherit the son."
7. Jerome (347–420), a theologian who translated the Greek Bible and some of the Hebrew Bible into Latin, also wrote on Christian doctrine.
8. Romans 6.23.
9. 1 John 1.8.

The German Valdes and Cornelius.
65   Request them earnestly to visit me.
WAGNER: I will, sir.   [Exit.]
FAUSTUS: Their conference will be a greater help to me
          Than all my labors, plod I ne'er so fast.
     [Enter the Good and Evil Angels.]
GOOD ANGEL: Oh Faustus, lay that damned book aside,
70   And gaze not on it lest it tempt thy soul
          And heap God's heavy wrath upon thy head.
          Read, read the scriptures: that is blasphemy.
EVIL ANGEL: Go forward, Faustus, in that famous art
          Wherein all nature's treasure is contained.
75   Be thou on earth as Jove[1] is in the sky,
          Lord and commander of these elements.
                                         [Exeunt Angels.]
                                                    idea
FAUSTUS: How am I glutted with conceit° of this!
          Shall I make spirits fetch me what I please,
          Resolve me of all ambiguities,
80   Perform what desperate enterprise I will?
          I'll have them fly to India for gold,
          Ransack the ocean for orient pearl,
          And search all corners of the new-found world
          For pleasant fruits and princely delicates.
85   I'll have them read me strange philosophy,
          And tell the secrets of all foreign kings.
          I'll have them wall all Germany with brass,
          And make swift Rhine circle fair Wittenberg.
          I'll have them fill the public schools° with silk,   college lecture halls
90   Wherewith the students shall be bravely clad.
          I'll levy soldiers with the coin they bring,
          And chase the Prince of Parma from our land,
          And reign sole king of all the provinces.
          Yea, stranger engines for the brunt of war
95   Than was the fiery keel[2] at Antwerp's bridge
          I'll make my servile spirits to invent.
          Come, German Valdes and Cornelius,
          And make me blest with your sage conference.
     [Enter Valdes and Cornelius.]
          Valdes, sweet Valdes and Cornelius!
100   Know that your words have won me at the last
          To practice magic and concealed arts.
          Yet not your words only but mine own fantasy
          That will receive no object° for my head,   idea
          But ruminates on necromantic skill.
105   Philosophy is odious and obscure.
          Both law and physic are for petty wits.

1. Roman god of the heavens and king of the gods.   across the river Scheldt in the city of Antwerp.
2. In 1585 a fireship destroyed the Duke of Parma's bridge

Divinity is basest of the three,
Unpleasant, harsh, contemptible and vile.
'Tis magic, magic that hath ravished me.
110   Then, gentle friends, aid me in this attempt,
And I, that have with subtle syllogisms
Gravelled the pastors of the German Church
And made the flowering pride of Wittenberg
Swarm to my problems as the infernal spirits
115   On sweet Musaeus[3] when he came to hell,
Will be as cunning as Agrippa was,
Whose shadow made all Europe honor him.
VALDES: Faustus, these books, thy wit and our experience
Shall make all nations to canonize us,
120   As Indian moors obey their Spanish lords.
So shall the spirits of every element
Be always serviceable to us three.
Like lions shall they guard us when we please;
Like Almain rutters° with their horsemen's staves;   German knights
125   Or Lapland giants trotting by our sides.
Sometimes like women or unwedded maids,
Shadowing more beauty in their airy brows
Than has the white breasts of the queen of love.
From Venice shall they drag huge argosies,°   merchant ships
130   And from America the golden fleece[4]
That yearly stuffs old Philip's treasury
If learned Faustus will be resolute.
FAUSTUS: Valdes, as resolute am I in this
As thou to live, therefore object° it not.   reject
CORNELIUS: The miracles that magic will perform
Will make thee vow to study nothing else.
He that is grounded in Astrology,
Enriched with tongues,° well seen° in minerals,   languages / educated
Hath all the principles magic doth require.
140   Then doubt not, Faustus, but to be renowned,
And more frequented° for this mystery   sought after
Than heretofore the Delphian oracle.[5]
The spirits tell me they can dry the sea,
And fetch the treasure of all foreign wracks,°   wrecks
145   Yea, all the wealth that our forefathers hid
Within the massy° entrails of the earth.   massive
Then tell me, Faustus, what shall we three want?

3. Faustus wants to model himself on Musaeus, a legendary poet, said to have been a student of Orpheus, and Cornelius Agrippa of Nettesheim (1486–1535), a philosopher known for his works on skepticism and the occult.
4. The "golden fleece" refers to the treasure (the gold wool of a divine ram) sought and won by the legendary hero, Jason, and his companions, known as the Argonauts (from the name of their ship, the Argo). Faustus alludes to this treasure when he refers to the gold the King of Castile, Philip II, was taking from lands in the New World.
5. A shrine of Apollo, the god of the sun, music, and medicine, in his temple at Delphi, where his priestess, called the Pythia, spoke incoherent phrases that a priest later interpreted as prophecies.

FAUSTUS: Nothing, Cornelius! Oh, this cheers my soul.
    Come, show me some demonstrations magical,
150   That I may conjure in some bushy grove,
    And have these joys in full possession.
VALDES: Then haste thee to some solitary grove,
    And bear wise Bacon's and Albanus'[6] works,
    The Hebrew Psalter and New Testament;
155   And whatsoever else is requisite
    We will inform thee e're our conference cease.
CORNELIUS: Valdes, first let him know the words of art,
    And then, all other ceremonies learned,
    Faustus may try his cunning by himself.
VALDES: First I'll instruct thee in the rudiments,
    And then wilt thou be perfecter than I.
FAUSTUS: Then come and dine with me, and after meat
    We'll canvass every quiddity° thereof,   *question*
    For ere I sleep, I'll try what I can do.
165   This night I'll conjure, though I die therefore.   [*Exeunt.*]

Scene 2

[*Enter two Scholars.*]

FIRST SCHOLAR: I wonder what's become of Faustus, that was wont to make our
    schools ring with *sic probo*.[7]
    [*Enter Wagner.*]
SECOND SCHOLAR: That shall we presently know. Here comes his boy.
FIRST SCHOLAR: How now, sirrah, where's thy master?
WAGNER: God in heaven knows.
SECOND SCHOLAR: Why, dost not thou know then?
WAGNER: Yes, I know, but that follows not.
FIRST SCHOLAR: Go to, sirrah. Leave your jesting and tell us where he is.
WAGNER: That follows not by force of argument, which you, being licentiates,[8]
10   should stand upon. Therefore, acknowledge your error and be attentive.
SECOND SCHOLAR: Then you will not tell us?
WAGNER: You are deceived, for I will tell you. Yet if you were not dunces, you would
    never ask me such a question. For is he not *Corpus naturale*?[9] And is not that
    mobile? Then wherefore should you ask me such a question? But that I am by
15   nature phlegmatic, slow to wrath and prone to lechery (to love, I would
    say), it were not for you to come within forty foot of the place of execution,
    although I do not doubt but to see you both hanged the next sessions. Thus,
    having triumphed over you, I will set my countenance like a precision,[1] and
    begin to speak thus: "Truly, my dear brethren, my master is within at dinner
20   with Valdes and Cornelius, as this wine, if it could speak, would inform your
    worships. And so the Lord bless you, preserve you and keep you, my dear
    brethren."   [*Exit.*]

6. Roger Bacon (1214–1294) was an English Franciscan monk and a lecturer at Oxford University who was interested in natural science, particularly alchemy. Albanus is perhaps Pietro D'Abano (1250–1360), who was supposed to be a sorcerer and was burned in effigy by the Inquisition after his death.
7. "Thus I prove."
8. Postgraduates.
9. A natural body.
1. Puritan.

FIRST SCHOLAR: Oh Faustus, then I fear that which I have long suspected:
  That thou art fallen into that damned art
25 For which they two are infamous through the world.
SECOND SCHOLAR: Were he a stranger, not allied to me,
  The danger of his soul would make me mourn.
  But come, let us go, and inform the Rector.
  It may be his grave counsel may reclaim him.
FIRST SCHOLAR: I fear me nothing will reclaim him now.
SECOND SCHOLAR: Yet let us see what we can do.   [Exeunt.]

Scene 3

[Thunder. Enter Lucifer and Four Devils. Faustus to them with this speech.]
FAUSTUS: Now that the gloomy shadow of the night,
  Longing to view Orion's drizzling look,
  Leaps from th'Antarctic world unto the sky,
  And dims the welkin° with her pitchy breath,   *heaven*
5 Faustus, begin thine incantations
  And try if devils will obey thy hest,°   *command*
  Seeing thou hast prayed and sacrificed to them.
  Within this circle is Jehovah's name
  Forward and backward anagrammatized:
10 The abbreviated names of holy saints,
  Figures of every adjunct to the heavens,
  And characters of signs and evening stars,
  By which the spirits are enforced to rise.
  Then fear not, Faustus, to be resolute
15 And try the utmost magic can perform.[2]
  [Thunder.]
    Sint mihi dei acherontis propitii, valeat numen triplex Jehovae, ignei areii, aquatani
    spiritus salvete: orientis princeps Belzebub, inferni ardentis monarcha et demigor-
    gon, propitiamus vos, ut appareat, et surgat Mephostophilis (Dragon)[3] quod tumer-
    aris: per Jehovam, gehennam, et consecratam aquam quam nunc spargo;
20   *signumque crucis quod nunc facio; et per vota nostra ipse nunc surgat nobis dica-*
    tus Mephostophilis.
  [Enter a Devil.]
  I charge thee to return and change thy shape.
  Thou art too ugly to attend on me.
  Go, and return an old Franciscan friar:
25 That holy shape becomes a devil best.
                                                          [Exit Devil.]
  I see there's virtue in my heavenly words.
  Who would not be proficient in this art?
  How pliant is this Mephostophilis!

2. Faustus styles himself an accomplished magician. He now repeats, in Latin, his command to Mephostophilis to appear in the guise of a friar: "May the gods of the underworld be kind to me; may the triple deity of Jehovah be gone; to the spirits of fire, air, and water, greetings. Prince of the east, Beelzebub, monarch of the fires below, and Demogorgon, we appeal to you so that Mephostophilis may appear and rise. Why do you delay? By Jehovah, hell and the hallowed water which I now sprinkle, and the sign of the cross, which I now make, and by our vows, let Mephostophilis himself now arise to serve us."
3. This appears to be a stage direction that was inserted into the playtext; it probably indicates that at this point the figure of a dragon should come on stage.

Full of obedience and humility,

30   Such is the force of magic and my spells.

Now, Faustus, thou art conjuror laureate:[4]

Thou canst command great Mephostophilis.

Quin redis Mephostophilis fratris imagine.

[*Enter Mephostophilis.*]

MEPHOSTOPHILIS: Now, Faustus, what wouldst thou have me do?

FAUSTUS: I charge thee wait upon me whilst I live,

To do whatever Faustus shall command,

Be it to make the moon drop from her sphere,

Or the ocean to overwhelm the world.

MEPHOSTOPHILIS: I am a servant to great Lucifer,

40   And may not follow thee without his leave.

No more than he commands must we perform.

FAUSTUS: Did not he charge thee to appear to me?

MEPHOSTOPHILIS: No, I came now hither of mine own accord.

FAUSTUS: Did not my conjuring speeches raise thee? Speak.

MEPHOSTOPHILIS: That was the cause, but yet *per accidens;*°   *by accident*

For when we hear one rack the name of God,

Abjure the scriptures and his saviour Christ,

We fly in hope to get his glorious soul.

Nor will we come unless he use such means

50   Whereby he is in danger to be damned.

Therefore the shortest cut for conjuring

Is stoutly to abjure all godliness

And pray devoutly to the price of hell.

FAUSTUS: So Faustus hath already done, and holds this principle:

55   There is no chief but only Belzebub,

To whom Faustus doth dedicate himself.

This word "damnation" terrifies not me,

For I confound hell in elysium.°   *heaven*

My ghost be with the old philosophers.

60   But leaving these vain trifles of men's souls,

Tell me, what is that Lucifer, thy lord?

MEPHOSTOPHILIS: Arch-regent and commander of all spirits.

FAUSTUS: Was not that Lucifer an angel once?

MEPHOSTOPHILIS: Yes, Faustus, and most dearly loved of God.

FAUSTUS: How comes it then that he is prince of devils?

MEPHOSTOPHILIS: Oh, by aspiring pride and insolence,

For which God threw him from the face of heaven.

FAUSTUS: And what are you that live with Lucifer?

MEPHOSTOPHILIS: Unhappy spirits that fell with Lucifer,

70   Conspired against our God with Lucifer,

And are for ever damned with Lucifer.

FAUSTUS: Where are you damned?

---

4. Faustus, stating he is a "conjurer laureate" or honored magician, asks again, in Latin: "Why do you not return, Mephostophilis, in the guise of a friar?"

MEPHOSTOPHILIS: In hell.

FAUSTUS: How comes it then that thou art out of hell?

MEPHOSTOPHILIS: Why, this is hell, nor am I out of it.
    Think'st thou that I that saw the face of God
    And tasted the eternal joys of heaven,
    Am not tormented with ten thousand hells
    In being deprived of everlasting bliss?
80   Oh, Faustus, leave these frivolous demands,
    Which strike a terror to my fainting soul.

FAUSTUS: What, is great Mephostophilis so passionate
    For being deprived of the joys of heaven?
    Learn thou of Faustus manly fortitude,
85   And scorn those joys thou never shalt possess.
    Go, bear these tidings to great Lucifer,
    Seeing Faustus hath incurred eternal death
    By desperate thoughts against Jove's deity.
    Say he surrenders up to him his soul,
90   So he will spare him four and twenty years,
    Letting him live in all voluptuousness,
    Having thee ever to attend on me,
    To give me whatsoever I shall ask,
    To tell me whatsoever I demand,
95   To slay mine enemies and to aid my friends
    And always be obedient to my will.
    Go, and return to mighty Lucifer,
    And meet me in my study at midnight,
    And then resolve me of thy master's mind.

MEPHOSTOPHILIS: I will, Faustus.   [Exit.]

FAUSTUS: Had I as many souls as there be stars,
    I'd give them all for Mephostophilis.
    By him I'll be great emperor of the world,
    And make a bridge through the air
105   To pass the ocean. With a band of men
    I'll join the hills that bind the Affrick shore,
    And make that country continent to Spain,
    And both contributory to my crown.
    The Emperor shall not live but by my leave,
110   Nor any potentate of Germany.
    Now that I have obtained what I desired,
    I'll live in speculation of this art
    Till Mephostophilis return again.   [Exit.]

Scene 4

[Enter Wagner and the Clown.]

WAGNER: Come hither, sirrah boy.

CLOWN: Boy? Oh, disgrace to my person! Zounds! "Boy" in your face! You have
    seen many boys with beards, I am sure.

WAGNER: Sirrah, hast thou no comings in?

CLOWN: Yes, and goings out too, you may see, sir.

WAGNER: Alas, poor slave. See how poverty jests in his nakedness. I know the villain's out of service and so hungry that I know he would give his soul to the devil for a shoulder of mutton though it were blood-raw.

CLOWN: Not so neither. I had need to have it well roasted, and good sauce to it, if I
10   pay so dear, I can tell you.

WAGNER: Sirrah, wilt thou be my man and wait on me? And I will make thee go like *Qui mihi discipulus.*[5]

CLOWN: What, in verse?

WAGNER: No, slave, in beaten silk and stavesacre.[6]

CLOWN: Stavesacre? That's good to kill vermin. Then belike, if I serve you I shall be lousy.

WAGNER: Why, so thou shalt be whether thou dost it or no. For, sirrah, if thou dost not presently bind thyself to me for seven years, I'll turn all the lice about thee into familiars,[7] and make them tear thee in pieces.

CLOWN: Nay, sir, you may save yourself a labor, for they are as familiar with me as if they paid for their meat and drink, I can tell you.

WAGNER: Well, sirrah, leave your jesting and take these guilders.[8]

CLOWN: Yes, marry, sir, and I thank you too.

WAGNER: So, now thou art to be at an hour's warning, whensoever and wheresoever
25   the devil shall fetch thee.

CLOWN: Here, take your guilders.

WAGNER: Truly, I'll none of them.

CLOWN: Truly but you shall.

WAGNER: Bear witness I gave them him.

CLOWN: Bear witness I give them you again.

WAGNER: Not I. Thou art pressed. Prepare thyself, for I will presently raise up two devils, to carry thee away: Banio, Belcher!

CLOWN: Belcher? And Belcher come here, I'll belch him! I am not afraid of a devil.
[*Enter Two Devils and the Clown runs up and down crying.*]

WAGNER: How now, sir, will you serve me now?

CLOWN: Ay, good Wagner. Take away the devil then.

WAGNER: Baliol and Belcher, spirits, away!

[*Exeunt Devils.*]

CLOWN: What, are they gone? A vengeance on them! They have vile long nails. There was a he-devil and a she-devil. I'll tell you how you shall know them: all he-devils has horns, and all she-devils has clifts[9] and cloven feet.

WAGNER: Well, sirrah, follow me.

CLOWN: But, do you hear, if I should serve you, would you teach me to raise up Banio's and Belcheo's?

WAGNER: I will teach thee to turn thyself to anything, to a dog, or a cat, or a mouse, or a rat, or anything.

CLOWN: How? A Christian fellow to a dog or a cat, a mouse or a rat? No, no, sir, if you turn me into anything, let it be in the likeness of a little pretty frisking flea, that I may be here and there and everywhere. Oh, I'll tickle the pretty wenches' plackets![1] I'll be amongst them, i'faith.

---

5. One who is my disciple.
6. A poison.
7. Spirits.

8. Coins.
9. Clefts.
1. Petticoats.

WAGNER: Well, sirrah, come.

CLOWN: But do you hear, Wagner?

WAGNER: How? Baliol and Belcher!

CLOWN: Oh Lord, I pray, sir, let Banio and Belcher go sleep.

WAGNER: Villain, call me Master Wagner, and see that you walk attentively and
      let your right eye be always diametrically fixed upon my left heel, that thou
55   mayest *Quasi vestigias nostras insistere*.[2]   [*Exit.*]

CLOWN: God forgive me, he speaks Dutch fustian![3] Well, I'll follow him. I'll serve
      him, that's flat.   [*Exit.*]

Scene 5

[*Enter Faustus in his study.*]

FAUSTUS: Now, Faustus, must thou needs be damned?
      And canst thou not be saved?
      What boots it then to think on God or heaven?
      Away with such vain fancies and despair,
5   Despair in God and trust in Belzebub.°   *the Devil*
      Now go not backward. No, Faustus, be resolute.
      Why waverest thou? Oh, something soundeth in mine ears
      Abjure this magic, turn to God again.
      Ay, and Faustus will turn to God again.
10   To God? He loves thee not.
      The God thou servest is thine own appetite,
      Wherein is fixed the love of Belzebub.
      To him I'll build an altar and a church,
      And offer lukewarm blood of new-born babes.

[*Enter the Good and Evil Angels.*]

GOOD ANGEL: Sweet Faustus, leave that execrable art.

FAUSTUS: Contrition, prayer, repentance, what of these?

GOOD ANGEL: Oh, they are means to bring thee unto heaven.

EVIL ANGEL: Rather illusions, fruits of lunacy,
      That make men foolish that do trust them most.

GOOD ANGEL: Sweet Faustus, think of heaven and heavenly things.

EVIL ANGEL: No, Faustus, think of honor and of wealth.
                                             [*Exeunt Angels.*]

FAUSTUS: Of wealth!
      Why, the signory of Emden[4] shall be mine!
      When Mephostophilis shall stand by me,
25   What God can hurt thee, Faustus? Thou art safe.
      Cast no more doubts. Come, Mephostophilis,
      And bring glad tidings from great Lucifer.
      Is't not midnight? Come Mephostophilis!
      Veni, veni,° Mephostophile!   *come, come*

[*Enter Mephostophilis.*]

30   Now tell me, what saith Lucifer, thy lord?

---

2. Wagner mocks the Clown by telling him to walk "as if
to tread in our footsteps," knowing that the clown's
magic will never be as powerful as his own.
3. Nonsense.

4. At this point in his career, Faustus aspires to the governorship of Emden, an important trading town in Germany, a pathetic exchange for his immortal soul.

MEPHOSTOPHILIS: That I shall wait on Faustus whilst he lives,
    So he will buy my service with his soul.
FAUSTUS: Already Faustus hath hazarded that for thee.
MEPHOSTOPHILIS: But now thou must bequeath it solemnly,
35   And write a deed of gift with thine own blood,
    For that security craves great Lucifer.
    If thou deny it, I will back to hell.
FAUSTUS: Stay, Mephostophilis, and tell me
    What good will my soul do thy lord?
MEPHOSTOPHILIS: Enlarge his kingdom.
FAUSTUS: Is that the reason why he tempts us thus?
MEPHOSTOPHILIS: *Solamen miseris, socios habuisse doloris.*[5]
FAUSTUS: Why, have you any pain, that torture others?
MEPHOSTOPHILIS: As great as have the human souls of men.
45   But tell me, Faustus, shall I have thy soul?
    And I will be thy slave and wait on thee,
    And give thee more than thou hast wit to ask.
FAUSTUS: Ay, Mephostophilis, I'll give it thee.
MEPHOSTOPHILIS: Then, Faustus, stab thy arm courageously,
50   And bind thy soul, that at some certain day
    Great Lucifer may claim it as his own,
    And then be thou as great as Lucifer.
FAUSTUS: Lo, Mephostophilis, for love of thee
    I cut mine arm, and with my proper blood
55   Assure my soul to be great Lucifer's,
    Chief lord and regent of perpetual night.
    View here the blood that trickles from mine arm,
    And let it be propitious for my wish.
MEPHOSTOPHILIS: But, Faustus, thou must write it in manner of a deed of gift.
FAUSTUS: Ay, so I will. But, Mephostophilis,
    My blood congeals and I can write no more!
MEPHOSTOPHILIS: I'll fetch thee fire to dissolve it straight.   *[Exit.]*
FAUSTUS: What might the staying of my blood portend?
    Is it unwilling I should write this bill?
65   Why streams it not that I may write afresh?
    "Faustus gives to thee his soul": ah, there it stayed!
    Why shouldst thou not? Is not thy soul thine own?
    Then write again: "Faustus gives to thee his soul."
[Enter Mephostophilis with a chafer of coals.]
MEPHOSTOPHILIS: Here's fire. Come, Faustus, set it on.
FAUSTUS: So, now my blood begins to clear again.
    Now will I make an end immediately.
MEPHOSTOPHILIS: Oh what will not I do to obtain his soul!
FAUSTUS: *Consummatum est:*[6] this bill is ended,
    And Faustus hath bequeathed his soul to Lucifer.

5. Mephostophilis states that misery loves company in hell: "It is a comfort in wretchedness to have companions in woe."
6. As reported in the Vulgate Bible, Faustus speaks the last words of Jesus on the cross: "It is finished" (John 19.30), and then realizes he must try to avoid the consequences: "Flee, O man."

75   But what is this inscription on mine arm?
        Homo fuge!° Whither should I flee?   *Flee, O man*
        If unto heaven, he'll throw me down to hell.
        My senses are deceived: here's nothing writ!
        Oh, yes, I see it plain. Even here is writ
80   *Homo fuge.* Yet shall not Faustus fly.
MEPHOSTOPHILIS: I'll fetch him somewhat to delight his mind.   [*Exit.*]
        [*Enter Devils, giving crowns and rich apparel to Faustus; they dance and then depart.
        Enter Mephostophilis.*]
FAUSTUS: What means this show? Speak, Mephostophilis.
MEPHOSTOPHILIS: Nothing, Faustus, but to delight thy mind,
        And let thee see what magic can perform.
FAUSTUS: But may I raise such spirits when I please?
MEPHOSTOPHILIS: Ay, Faustus, and do greater things than these.
FAUSTUS: Then there's enough for a thousand souls.
        Here, Mephostophilis, receive this scroll,
        A deed of gift, of body and of soul:
90   But yet conditionally, that thou perform
        All covenants and articles between us both.
MEPHOSTOPHILIS: Faustus, I swear by hell and Lucifer
        To effect all promises between us both.
FAUSTUS: Then hear me read it, Mephostophilis.
95   On these conditions following:
        First, that Faustus may be a spirit in form and substance.
        Secondly, that Mephostophilis shall be his servant, and be by him commanded.
        Thirdly, that Mephostophilis shall do for him, and bring him whatsoever.
        Fourthly, that he shall be in his chamber or house invisible.
100   Lastly, that he shall appear to the said John Faustus at all times, in what
            shape and form soever he please.
        I, John Faustus of Wittenberg Doctor, by these presents, do give both body
            and soul to Lucifer, Prince of the East, and his minister Mephostophilis,
            and furthermore grant unto them that four and twenty years being
105   expired, and these articles above written being inviolate, full power to
            fetch or carry the said John Faustus, body and soul, flesh, blood or goods,
            into their habitation wheresoever.
        By me, John Faustus.
MEPHOSTOPHILIS: Speak, Faustus, do you deliver this as your deed?
FAUSTUS: Ay, take it, and the devil give thee good of it.
MEPHOSTOPHILIS: So now, Faustus, ask me what thou wilt.
FAUSTUS: First I will question with thee about hell.
        Tell me, where is the place that men call hell?
MEPHOSTOPHILIS: Under the heavens.
FAUSTUS: Ay, so are all things else; but whereabouts?
MEPHOSTOPHILIS: Within the bowels of these elements,
        Where we are tortured and remain for ever.
        Hell hath no limits, nor is circumscribed
        In one self place. But where we are is hell,
120   And where hell is there must we ever be.
        And to be short, when all the world dissolves

And every creature shall be purified,
All places shall be hell that is not heaven.

FAUSTUS: Come, I think hell's a fable.

MEPHOSTOPHILIS: Ay, think so still, till experience change thy mind.

FAUSTUS: Why, dost thou think that Faustus shall be damned?

MEPHOSTOPHILIS: Ay, of necessity, for here's the scroll
In which thou hast given thy soul to Lucifer.

FAUSTUS: Ay, and body too, but what of that?

130   Think'st thou that Faustus is so fond to imagine
That after this life there is any pain?
Tush, these are trifles and old wives' tales.

MEPHOSTOPHILIS: But Faustus, I am an instance to prove the contrary,
For I tell thee I am damned, and now in hell.

FAUSTUS: How? Now in hell? Nay, and this be hell, I'll willingly be damned here.
What! Sleeping, eating, walking and disputing? But leaving this, let me
have a wife, the fairest maid in Germany, for I am wanton and lascivious,
and can not live without a wife.

MEPHOSTOPHILIS: How, a wife? I prithee, Faustus, talk not of a wife.

FAUSTUS: Nay, sweet Mephostophilis, fetch me one, for I will have one.

MEPHOSTOPHILIS: Well, thou wilt have one. Sit there till I come: I'll fetch thee
a wife in the devil's name.

[Enter a Devil dressed like a woman, with fireworks.]

FAUSTUS: What sight is this?

MEPHOSTOPHILIS: Tell, Faustus, how dost thou like thy wife?

FAUSTUS: A plague on her for a hot whore.

MEPHOSTOPHILIS: Tut, Faustus, marriage is but a ceremonial toy.
If thou lovest me, think no more of it.
I'll cull thee out the fairest courtesans
And bring them every morning to thy bed.

150   She whom thine eye shall like, thy heart shall have,
Be she as chaste as was Penelope,[7]
As wise as Saba, or as beautiful
As was bright Lucifer before his fall.
Here, take this book, and peruse it well.

155   The iterating° of these lines brings gold,   repetition
The framing of this circle on the ground
Brings thunder, whirlwinds, storm and lightning.
Pronounce this thrice devoutly to thyself
And men in harness shall appear to thee,

160   Ready to execute what thou commandest.

FAUSTUS: Thanks, Mephostophilis. Yet fain would I have a book wherein I might
behold all spells and incantations, that I might raise up spirits when I please.

MEPHOSTOPHILIS: Here they are in this book.   [There turn to them.]

FAUSTUS: Now would I have a book where I might see all characters and planets of

165   the heavens, that I might know their motions and dispositions.

---

7. Mephostophilis compares the ideal woman to Penelope, the wife of Odysseus, who waited 20 years for him to return from the Trojan wars, and to Saba, the wise Queen of Sheba, who taught King Solomon, known himself for his wisdom (1 Kings).

MEPHOSTOPHILIS: Here they are too.   [*Turn to them.*]
FAUSTUS: Nay, let me have one book more, and then I have done, wherein I
    might see all plants, herbs and trees that grow upon the earth.
MEPHOSTOPHILIS: Here they be.
FAUSTUS: Oh thou art deceived.
MEPHOSTOPHILIS: Tut, I warrant thee.   [*Turn to them.*]

ACT 2

Scene 1

[*Enter Faustus in his study, and Mephostophilis.*]
FAUSTUS: When I behold the heavens then I repent,
    And curse thee, wicked Mephostophilis,
    Because thou hast deprived me of those joys.
MEPHOSTOPHILIS: 'Twas thine own seeking, Faustus, thank thyself.
5   But thinkst thou heaven is such a glorious thing?
    I tell thee, Faustus, it is not half so fair
    As thou or any man that breathes on earth.
FAUSTUS: How prov'st thou that?
MEPHOSTOPHILIS: 'Twas made for man; then he's more excellent.
FAUSTUS: If heaven was made for man, 'twas made for me.
    I will renounce this magic and repent.
[*Enter the Good and Evil Angels.*]
GOOD ANGEL: Faustus, repent. Yet God will pity thee.
EVIL ANGEL: Thou art a spirit. God cannot pity thee.
FAUSTUS: Who buzzeth in mine ears I am a spirit?
15   Be I a devil, yet God may pity me.
    Yea, God will pity me if I repent.
EVIL ANGEL: Ay, but Faustus never shall repent.   [*Exeunt.*]
FAUSTUS: My heart's so hardened I cannot repent.
    Scarce can I name salvation, faith or heaven,
20   But fearful echoes thunder in mine ears
    "Faustus, thou art damned." Then swords and knives,
    Poison, guns, halters and envenomed steel
    Are laid before me to dispatch myself.
    And long ere this I should have done the deed,
25   Had not sweet pleasure conquered deep despair.
    Have not I made blind Homer sing to me
    Of Alexander's love and Oenon's death?[1]
    And hath not he that built the walls of Thebes
    With ravishing sound of his melodious harp
30   Made music with my Mephostophilis?[2]
    Why should I die then, or basely despair?

1. Faustus claims he has made the poet Homer sing to him of the love of Alexander the Great (356–323 B.C.), who was married to Statira, daughter of the Emperor Darius of Persia; and of Oenone, a nymph of Mount Ida, who died from grief when her lover, Paris of Troy, deserted her for Helen, the wife of King Menalaus of Sparta.
2. Faustus further claims that the legendary Amphion, whose music built the walls of Thebes, also made music with Mephostophilis, now Faustus's servant.

I am resolved, Faustus shall not repent.
Come, Mephostophilis, let us dispute again,
And reason of divine astrology.
35   Speak, are there many spheres above the moon?
Are all celestial bodies but one globe,
As is the substance of this centric earth?[3]
MEPHOSTOPHILIS: As are the elements, such are the heavens,
Even from the moon unto the empyrial orb,
40   Mutually folded in each other's spheres,
And jointly move upon one axle-tree,
Whose termine° is termed the world's wide pole.   *end point*
Nor are the names of Saturn, Mars or Jupiter
Feigned, but are erring stars.
FAUSTUS: But have they all one motion, both *situ et tempore*?[4]
MEPHOSTOPHILIS: All move from east to west in four and twenty hours upon the
poles of the world, but differ in their motions upon the poles of the zodiac.
FAUSTUS: Tush, these slender trifles Wagner can decide. Hath Mephostophilis
no greater skill? Who knows not the double motion of the planets? That
50   the first is finished in a natural day? The second thus, as Saturn in thirty
years, Jupiter in twelve, Mars in four, the sun, Venus and Mercury in
twenty-eight days. Tush, these are freshmen's suppositions. But tell me,
hath every sphere a dominion or *intelligentia*?[5]
MEPHOSTOPHILIS: Ay.
FAUSTUS: How many heavens or spheres are there?
MEPHOSTOPHILIS: Nine, the seven planets, the firmament, and the empyrial
heaven.
FAUSTUS: But is there not *coelum igneum et cristallinum*?
MEPHOSTOPHILIS: No, Faustus, they be but fables.[6]
FAUSTUS: Resolve me then in this one question. Why are not conjunctions, oppositions,
aspects, eclipses, all at one time, but in some years we have more, in some less?
MEPHOSTOPHILIS: *Per inaequalem motum, respectu totius*.[7]
FAUSTUS: Well, I am answered. Now tell me, who made the world?
MEPHOSTOPHILIS: I will not.
FAUSTUS: Sweet Mephostophilis, tell me.
MEPHOSTOPHILIS: Move me not, Faustus.
FAUSTUS: Villain, have not I bound thee to tell me anything?
MEPHOSTOPHILIS: Ay, that is not against our kingdom, but this is.
Think on hell, Faustus, for thou art damned.
FAUSTUS: Think, Faustus, upon God, that made the world.
MEPHOSTOPHILIS: Remember this—   [*Exit.*]
FAUSTUS: Ay, go, accursed spirit to ugly hell.

---

3. Faustus alludes to the Ptolemaic universe in which the
earth, at the center, is surrounded by concentric spheres,
beginning with the moon. Beyond the spheres of the stars
that were thought to move (the constellations) were the
spheres of the fixed stars.
4. In place and in time.
5. Guiding spirit.

6. Faustus asks whether there is a "fiery and crystalline
heaven" beyond the "empyrial heaven" Mephostophilis
has mentioned, and he is told it is a fiction.
7. Faustus asks why planetary and astral events do not
occur uniformly, and Mephostophilis answers that they
do "with respect to the whole" but each "by unequal
motion."

'Tis thou hast damned distressed Faustus' soul.
Is't not too late?
[*Enter the Good and Evil Angels.*]

EVIL ANGEL: Too late.

GOOD ANGEL: Never too late, if Faustus will repent.

EVIL ANGEL: If thou repent devils will tear thee in pieces.

GOOD ANGEL: Repent, and they shall never raze° thy skin.   *shave*
[*Exeunt Angels.*]

FAUSTUS: Ah, Christ my savior,

80   Seek to save distressed Faustus' soul.
[*Enter Lucifer, Belzebub and Mephostophilis.*]

LUCIFER: Christ cannot save thy soul, for he is just.
There's none but I have interest in the same.

FAUSTUS: Oh what art thou that look'st so terribly?

LUCIFER: I am Lucifer, and this is my companion prince in hell.

FAUSTUS: Oh Faustus, they are come to fetch away thy soul.

BELZEBUB: We are come to tell thee thou dost injure us.

LUCIFER: Thou call'st on Christ contrary to thy promise.

BELZEBUB: Thou shouldst not think on God.

LUCIFER: Think on the devil.

BELZEBUB: And his dam too.

FAUSTUS: Nor will I henceforth. Pardon me in this,
And Faustus vows never to look to heaven,
Never to name God or to pray to him,
To burn his scriptures, slay his ministers,

95   And make my spirits pull his churches down.

LUCIFER: Do so, and we will highly gratify thee.

BELZEBUB: Faustus, we are come from hell in person to show thee some pastime.
Sit down and thou shalt behold the seven deadly sins appear to thee in their
own proper shapes and likeness.

FAUSTUS: That sight will be as pleasant to me as Paradise was to Adam the first
day of his creation.

LUCIFER: Talk not of Paradise or Creation, but mark this show. Talk of the devil
and nothing else. Go, Mephostophilis, fetch them in.
[*Enter the Seven Deadly Sins.*]

BELZEBUB: Now, Faustus, question them of their names and dispositions.

FAUSTUS: That shall I soon. What art thou, the first?

PRIDE: I am Pride. I disdain to have any parents. I am like to Ovid's flea.[8] I can
creep into every corner of a wench. Sometimes like a periwig I sit upon her
brow. Next, like a necklace I hang about her neck. Then, like a fan of feathers, I kiss her. And then turning myself to a wrought smock do what I list.

110   But fie, what a smell is here! I'll not speak a word for a king's ransome,
unless the ground be perfumed and covered with cloth of Arras.[9]

FAUSTUS: Thou art a proud knave indeed. What art thou, the second?

COVETOUSNESS: I am Covetousness. Begotten of an old churl in a leather bag.

---

8. One of the poems of the Roman poet Ovid (43
B.C.–A.D. 18) describes the journey of a flea around a

woman's body.
9. Flemish cloth for tapestries.

And might I now obtain my wish, this house, you and all, should turn to
115   gold, that I might lock you safe into my chest. Oh, my sweet gold!

FAUSTUS: And what art thou, the third?

ENVY: I am Envy, begotten of a chimney-sweeper and an oyster-wife. I cannot read
and therefore wish all books were burnt. I am lean with seeing others eat.
Oh, that there would come a famine over all the world, that all might die,
120   and I live alone, then thou should'st see how fat I'd be. But must thou sit
and I stand? Come down, with a vengeance!

FAUSTUS: Out, envious wretch. But what art thou, the fourth?

WRATH: I am Wrath. I had neither father nor mother. I leapt out of a lion's mouth
when I was scarce an hour old, and ever since have run up and down the world
125   with this case of rapiers, wounding myself when I could get none to fight
withal. I was born in hell, and look to it, for some of you shall be my father.

FAUSTUS: And what art thou, the fifth?

GLUTTONY: I am Gluttony. My parents are all dead, and the devil a penny they
have left me, but a small pension and that buys me thirty meals a day and
130   ten bevers:[1] a small trifle to suffice nature. I come of a royal pedigree; my
father was a gammon of bacon and my mother was a hog's head of claret
wine. My godfathers were these: Peter Pickle-herring and Martin Martle-
mas-beef. But my godmother, oh, she was an ancient gentlewoman, and
well-beloved in every good town and city. Her name was Mistress Margery
135   March-beer. Now, Faustus, thou hast heard all my progeny, wilt thou bid me
to supper?

FAUSTUS: No, I'll see thee hanged. Thou wilt eat up all my victuals.

GLUTTONY: Then the devil choke thee.

FAUSTUS: Choke thyself, Glutton. What art thou, the sixth?

SLOTH: Hey ho, I am Sloth. I was begotten on a sunny bank where I have lain ever
since, and you have done me great injury to bring me from thence. Let me be
carried thither again by Gluttony and Lechery. I'll not speak another word for
a king's ransom.

FAUSTUS: And what are you, Mistress Minx, the seventh and last?

LECHERY: Who, I sir? I am one that loves an inch of raw mutton better than an ell
of fried stockfish,[2] and the first letter of my name begins with Lechery.

FAUSTUS: Away to hell! Away, on, piper!

[Exeunt the Seven Deadly Sins.]

LUCIFER: Now, Faustus, how dost thou like this?

FAUSTUS: Oh, this feeds my soul.

LUCIFER: Tut, Faustus, in hell is all manner of delight.

FAUSTUS: Oh, might I see hell and return again safe, how happy were I then!

LUCIFER: Faustus, thou shalt. At midnight I will send for thee. Meanwhile, peruse
this book and view it throughly, and thou shalt turn thyself into what shape
thou wilt.

FAUSTUS: Thanks, mighty Lucifer. This will I keep as chary as my life.

LUCIFER: Now, Faustus, farewell, and think on the devil.

FAUSTUS: Farewell, great Lucifer. Come, Mephostophilis.

[Exeunt omnes, several ways.]

---

1. Snacks.
2. Lechery implies that she would prefer a short but ener-   getic penis to a yard-long but dry one.

Scene 2

[*Enter the Clown.*]

CLOWN: What, Dick, look to the horses there till I come again. I have gotten one of
    Doctor Faustus' conjuring books, and now we'll have such knavery as't passes.
    [*Enter Dick.*]

DICK: What, Robin, you must come away and walk the horses.

ROBIN: I walk the horses? I scorn't, faith. I have other matters in hand. Let the horses
5   walk themselves and they will. *A per se a, t.h.e. the: o per se o deny orgon,
        gorgon.*[3] Keep further from me, O thou illiterate and unlearned hostler.

DICK: 'Snails![4] What hast thou got there? A book? Why, thou canst not tell ne'er a
    word on't.

ROBIN: That thou shalt see presently. Keep out of the circle, I say, lest I send you
10   into the ostry[5] with a vengeance.

DICK: That's like, faith. You had best leave your foolery, for, an my master come,
    he'll conjure you, faith!

ROBIN: My master conjure me? I'll tell thee what, an my master come here, I'll clap
    as fair a pair of horns[6] on's head as e'er thou sawest in thy life.

DICK: Thou need'st not do that, for my mistress hath done it.

ROBIN: Ay, there be of us here, that have waded as deep into matters as other men,
    if they were disposed to talk.

DICK: A plague take you! I thought you did not sneak up and down after her for noth-
    ing. But I prithee tell me, in good sadness, Robin, is that a conjuring book?

ROBIN: Do but speak what thou't have me to do, and I'll do't. If thou't dance
    naked, put off thy clothes and I'll conjure thee about presently. Or if thou't
    go but to the tavern with me, I'll give thee white wine, red wine, claret
    wine, sack, muskadine, malmesey and whippincrust.[7] Hold, belly, hold; and
    we'll not pay one penny for it.

DICK: Oh brave! Prithee, let's to it presently, for I am as dry as a dog.

ROBIN: Come, then, let's away.   [*Exeunt.*]

ACT 3

Scene 1

[*Enter the Chorus.*]

CHORUS: Learned Faustus,
        To find the secrets of astronomy,
        Graven in the book of Jove's high firmament,
        Did mount him up to scale Olympus' top,
5   Where sitting in a chariot burning bright,
        Drawn by the strength of yoked dragons' necks,
        He views the clouds, the planets, and the stars,
        The tropic, zones, and quarters of the sky,
        From the bright circle of the horned moon,
10   Even to the height of *Primum Mobile*.[1]

---

3. Barely literate, Robin is trying to parse a Latin phrase,
atheo Demigorgon ("godless Demigorgon").
4. Christ's nails.
5. Inn.
6. Sign of a cuckold.
7. Robin lists various kinds of wine; "whippencrust" is

probably a corruption of "hippocras," a kind of sweet
wine.
1. The outermost of the heavenly spheres. Faustus is pictured as viewing the heavens from Mount Olympus to the
circle of the moon and beyond, to the *primum mobile*.

And whirling round with this circumference,
Within the concave compass of the pole,
From east to west his dragons swiftly glide,
And in eight days did bring him home again.
15   Not long he stayed within his quiet house,
To rest his bones after his weary toil,
But new exploits do hale him out again,
And mounted then upon a dragon's back,
That with his wings did part the subtle air,
20   He now is gone to prove cosmography,
That measures coasts and kingdoms of the earth;
And as I guess will first arrive at Rome,
To see the Pope and manner of his court,
And take some part of holy Peter's feast,
25   The which this day is highly solemnized.   [*Exit.*].

Scene 2

[*Enter Faustus and Mephostophilis.*]
FAUSTUS: Having now, my good Mephostophilis,
Passed with delight the stately town of Trier,
Environed round with airy mountain tops,
With walls of flint, and deep entrenched lakes,
5   Not to be won by any conquering prince,
From Paris next coasting the realm of France
We saw the river Main fall into Rhine,
Whose banks are set with groves of fruitful vines;
Then up to Naples, rich Campania,
10   Whose buildings fair and gorgeous to the eye,
The streets straight forth and paved with finest brick,
Quarters the town in four equivolence.°   *parts*
There saw we learned Maro's golden tomb,[2]
The way he cut an English mile in length,
15   Thorough a rock of stone in one night's space.
From thence to Venice, Padua and the rest,
In midst of which a sumptuous temple stands,
That threats the stars with her aspiring top,
Whose frame is paved with sundry colored stones,
20   And roofed aloft with curious work in gold.
Thus hitherto hath Faustus spent his time.
But tell me now, what resting place is this?
Hast thou, as erst I did command,
Conducted me within the walls of Rome?
MEPHOSTOPHILIS: I have, my Faustus, and for proof thereof,
This is the goodly palace of the Pope;
And cause we are no common guests,
I choose his privy chamber for our use.

---

2. Faustus' fiery chariot cut through rocks to go from Naples, where the Roman poet Publius Virgilius Maro, or Virgil, is buried, to Padua and Venice.

FAUSTUS: I hope his Holiness will bid us welcome.

MEPHOSTOPHILIS: All's one, for we'll be bold with his venison.
    But now, my Faustus, that thou may'st perceive
    What Rome contains for to delight thine eyes,
    Know that this city stands upon seven hills
    That underprop the groundwork of the same.
35   Just through the midst runs flowing Tiber's stream,
    With winding banks that cut it in two parts,
    Over the which four stately bridges lean,
    That make safe passage to each part of Rome.
    Upon the bridge called Ponto Angelo
40   Erected is a castle passing strong,
    Where thou shalt see such store of ordinance
    As that the double cannons forged of brass
    Do match the number of the days contained
    Within the compass of one complete year.
45   Beside the gates and high pyramides,
    That Julius Caesar brought from Africa.[3]

FAUSTUS: Now by the kingdoms of infernal rule,
    Of Styx, or Acheron, and the fiery lake
    Of ever-burning Phlegethon,° I swear   *rivers in hell*
50   That I do long to see the monuments
    And situation of bright splendent Rome.
    Come, therefore, let's away.

MEPHOSTOPHILIS: Now, stay, my Faustus. I know you'd see the Pope,
    And take some part of holy Peter's feast,
55   The which in state and high solemnity
    This day is held through Rome and Italy
    In honor of the Pope's triumphant victory.

FAUSTUS: Sweet Mephostophilis, thou pleasest me.
    Whilst I am here on earth let me be cloyed
60   With all things that delight the heart of man.
    My four and twenty years of liberty
    I'll spend in pleasure and in dalliance,
    That Faustus' name, whilst this bright frame doth stand,
    May be admired through the furthest land.

MEPHOSTOPHILIS: 'Tis well said, Faustus. Come then, stand by me,
    And thou shalt see them come immediately.

FAUSTUS: Nay stay, my gentle Mephostophilis,
    And grant me my request, and then I go.
    Thou know'st within the compass of eight days
70   We viewed the face of heaven, of earth and hell.
    So high our dragons soared into the air,
    That looking down, the earth appeared to me
    No bigger than my hand in quantity.
    There did we view the kingdoms of the world,
75   And what might please mine eye, I there beheld.

3. The Emperor Caligula brought an obelisk back from Heliopolis in Egypt, which stands before St. Peter's in Rome.

Then in this show let me an actor be,
That this proud Pope may Faustus' cunning see.
MEPHOSTOPHILIS: Let it be so, my Faustus, but first stay
And view their triumphs° as they pass this way.   *procession*
80   And then devise what best contents thy mind
By cunning in thine art to cross the Pope,
Or dash the pride of this solemnity,
To make his monks and abbots stand like apes,
And point like antics° at his triple crown,   *clowns*
85   To beat the beads about the friars' pates,
Or clap huge horns upon the cardinals' heads,
Or any villainy thou canst devise,
And I'll perform it, Faustus. Hark, they come!
This day shall make thee be admired in Rome.
[*Enter the Cardinals and Bishops, some bearing crosiers, some the pillars, Monks and Friars, singing their procession. Then the Pope and Raymond, King of Hungary with Bruno⁴ led in chains.*]
POPE: Cast down our footstool.
RAYMOND: Saxon Bruno, stoop,
Whilst on thy back his Holiness ascends
Saint Peter's chair and state pontifical.
BRUNO: Proud Lucifer, that state belongs to me:
95   But thus I fall to Peter, not to thee.
POPE: To me and Peter shalt thou grovelling lie,
And crouch before the papal dignity.
Sounds trumpets then, for thus Saint Peter's heir
From Bruno's back ascends Saint Peter's chair.
[*A flourish while he ascends.*]
100   Thus, as the gods creep on with feet of wool
Long ere with iron hands they punish men,
So shall our sleeping vengeance now arise,
And smite with death thy hated enterprise.
Lord cardinals of France and Padua,
105   Go forthwith to our holy consistory,
And read amongst the statutes decretal,
What by the holy council held at Trent⁵
The sacred synod hath decreed for them
That doth assume the papal government,
110   Without election and a true consent.
Away, and bring us word with speed!
FIRST CARDINAL: We go, my lord.
[*Exeunt Cardinals.*]
POPE: Lord Raymond.
FAUSTUS: Go, haste thee, gentle Mephostophilis,
115   Follow the cardinals to the consistory,
And as they turn their superstitious books,

4. This character has no apparent historical counterpart or model.
5. The council of Trent, called to meet the challenges posed by the Protestant Reformation, was held between 1545 and 1563.

Strike them with sloth and drowsy idleness,
And make them sleep so sound that in their shapes
Thyself and I may parly° with this Pope,   *speak*
120   This proud confronter of the Emperor,[6]
And in despite of all his holiness
Restore this Bruno to his liberty
And bear him to the states of Germany.

MEPHOSTOPHILIS: Faustus, I go.

FAUSTUS: Dispatch it soon,
The Pope shall curse that Faustus came to Rome.

                               [*Exeunt Faustus and Mephostophilis.*]

BRUNO: Pope Adrian,[7] let me have some right of law:
I was elected by the Emperor.

POPE: We will depose the Emperor for that deed,
130   And curse the people that submit to him.
Both he and thou shalt stand excommunicate,
And interdict from Church's privilege
And all society of holy men.
He grows too proud in his authority,
135   Lifting his lofty head above the clouds
And like a steeple overpeers the Church.
But we'll pull down his haughty insolence,
And, as Pope Alexander, our progenitor,
Stood on the neck of German Frederick,[8]
140   Adding this golden sentence to our praise,
That Peter's heirs should tread on emperors
And walk upon the dreadful adder's back,
Treading the lion and the dragon down,
And fearless spurn the killing basilisk,[9]
145   So will we quell that haughty schismatic,
And by authority apostolical
Depose him from his regal government.

BRUNO: Pope Julius swore to princely Sigismond[1]
For him and the succeeding popes of Rome,
150   To hold the emperors their lawful lords.

POPE: Pope Julius did abuse the Church's rites,
And therefore none of his decrees can stand.
Is not all power on earth bestowed on us?
And therefore though we would we cannot err.
155   Behold this silver belt, whereto is fixed
Seven golden seals fast sealed with seven seals,
In token of our seven-fold power from heaven,
To bind or loose, lock fast, condemn or judge,

---

6. The Holy Roman Emperor, Charles V, Emperor from 1519.
7. Possibly Marlowe means Hadrian VI (1522–1523), although he was Pope before the Council of Trent, after which the action of the play is supposed to have taken place.

8. Pope Alexander III (1159–1181) forced Emperor Frederick Barbarossa to acknowledge his authority.
9. A mythical creature whose glance was lethal.
1. It is unclear to whom Marlowe refers; there was no Pope Julius during the reign of the Emperor Sigismund (1368–1436).

          Resign or seal, or what so pleaseth us.
160   Then he and thou, and all the world, shall stoop,
          Or be assured of our dreadful curse,
          To light as heavy as the pains of hell.

[Enter Faustus and Mephostophilis, like the cardinals.]

MEPHOSTOPHILIS: Now tell me, Faustus, are we not fitted well?
FAUSTUS: Yes, Mephostophilis, and two such cardinals
165   Ne'er served a holy Pope as we shall do.
          But whilst they sleep within the consistory,
          Let us salute his reverend fatherhood.
RAYMOND: Behold, my lord, the cardinals are returned.
POPE: Welcome, grave fathers, answer presently
170   What have our holy council there decreed
          Concerning Bruno and the Emperor,
          In quittance of their late conspiracy
          Against our state and papal dignity?
FAUSTUS: Most sacred patron of the Church of Rome,
175   By full consent of all the synod
          Of priests and prelates, it is thus decreed:
          That Bruno and the German Emperor
          Be held as lollards[2] and bold schismatics
          And proud disturbers of the Church's peace.
180   And if that Bruno by his own assent,
          Without enforcement of the German peers,
          Did seek to wear the triple diadem
          And by your death to climb Saint Peter's chair,
          The statutes decretal have thus decreed:
185   He shall be straight condemned of heresy
          And on a pile of faggots burnt to death.
POPE: It is enough. Here, take him to your charge,
          And bear him straight to Ponto Angelo,
          And in the strongest tower enclose him fast.
190   Tomorrow, sitting in our consistory
          With all our college of grave cardinals,
          We will determine of his life or death.
          Here, take his triple crown along with you,
          And leave it in the Church's treasury.
195   Make haste again, my good lord cardinals,
          And take our blessing apostolical.
MEPHOSTOPHILIS: So, so, was never devil thus blessed before.
FAUSTUS: Away, sweet Mephostophilis, be gone:
          The cardinals will be plagued for this anon.

[Exeunt Faustus and Mephostophilis.]

POPE: Go presently, and bring a banquet forth
          That we may solemnize Saint Peter's feast,
          And with Lord Raymond, King of Hungary,
          Drink to our late and happy victory.   *[Exeunt.]*

2. Heretics; in England, followers of John Wycliffe (1328?–1384).

Scene 3

[*A sennet[3] while the banquet is brought in, and then enter Faustus and Mephostophilis in their own shapes.*]

MEPHOSTOPHILIS: Now, Faustus, come prepare thyself for mirth.
  The sleepy cardinals are hard at hand
  To censure Bruno that is posted° hence,   *ridden*
  And on a proud paced steed as swift as thought
5 Flies o'er the Alps to fruitful Germany,
  There to salute the woeful Emperor.
FAUSTUS: The Pope will curse them for their sloth today,
  That slept both Bruno and his crown away.
  But now, that Faustus may delight his mind,
10 And by their folly make some merriment,
  Sweet Mephostophilis, so charm me here,
  That I may walk invisible to all,
  And do what e'er I please unseen of any.
MEPHOSTOPHILIS: Faustus, thou shalt. Then kneel down presently:
15 Whilst on thy head I lay my hand,
  And charm thee with this magic wand.
  First wear this girdle, then appear
  Invisible to all are here.
  The planets seven, the gloomy air,
20 Hell and the Furies'[4] forked hair,
  Pluto's[5] blue fire and Hecate's[6] tree,
  With magic spells so compass thee,
  That no eye may thy body see.
  So, Faustus, now for all their holiness,
25 Do what thou wilt, thou shalt not be discerned.
FAUSTUS: Thanks, Mephostophilis. Now, friars, take heed
  Lest Faustus make your shaven crowns to bleed.
MEPHOSTOPHILIS: Faustus, no more. See where the cardinals come.
[*Enter the Pope and all the Lords. Enter the Cardinals with a book.*]
POPE: Welcome, lord cardinals. Come, sit down.
30 Lord Raymond, take your seat. Friars, attend
  And see that all things be in readiness
  As best beseems this solemn festival.
FIRST CARDINAL: First, may it please your sacred Holiness,
  To view the sentence of the reverend synod
35 Concerning Bruno and the Emperor?
POPE: What needs this question? Did I not tell you
  Tomorrow we would sit i'the consistory
  And there determine of his punishment?
  You brought us word even now, it was decreed
40 That Bruno and the cursed Emperor
  Were by the holy Council both condemned

3. A trumpet call.
4. Greek divinities instigating revenge.
5. The Roman god of the underworld.

6. Goddess representing death and the dark side of the moon.

For loathed lollards and base schismatics.
Then wherefore would you have me view that book?
FIRST CARDINAL: Your Grace mistakes. You gave us no such charge.
RAYMOND: Deny it not. We all are witnesses
    That Bruno here was late delivered you,
    With his rich triple crown to be reserved
    And put into the Church's treasury.
BOTH CARDINALS: By holy Paul, we saw them not.
POPE: By Peter, you shall die
    Unless you bring them forth immediately.
    Hale° them to prison, lade their limbs with gyves!°   *take / chains*
    False prelates, for this hateful treachery,
    Cursed be your souls to hellish misery.
FAUSTUS: So, they are safe. Now Faustus, to the feast.
    The Pope had never such a frolic guest.
POPE: Lord Archbishop of Rheims, sit down with us.
BISHOP: I thank your Holiness.
FAUSTUS: Fall to, and the devil choke you an you spare.
POPE: Who's that spoke? Friars, look about.
FRIARS: Here's nobody, if it like your Holiness.
POPE: Lord Raymond, pray fall to. I am beholding
    To the Bishop of Milan for this so rare a present.
FAUSTUS: I thank you, sir. [*Snatches it.*]
POPE: How now? Who snatched the meat from me?
    Villains, why speak you not?
    My good Lord Archbishop, here's a most dainty dish
    Was sent me from a cardinal in France.
FAUSTUS: I'll have that too. [*Snatches it.*]
POPE: What lollards do attend our Holiness
    That we receive such great indignity? Fetch me some wine.
FAUSTUS: Ay, pray do, for Faustus is a-dry.
POPE: Lord Raymond, I drink unto your grace.
FAUSTUS: I pledge your grace. [*Snatches the glass.*]
POPE: My wine gone too? Ye lubbers,° look about   *louts*
    And find the man that doth this villainy,
    Or by our sanctitude you all shall die.
    I pray, my lords, have patience at this
    Troublesome banquet.
BISHOP: Please it your Holiness, I think it be some ghost crept out of Purgatory,
    and now is come unto your Holiness for his pardon.
POPE: It may be so.
    Go, then, command our priests to sing a dirge
    To lay the fury of this same troublesome ghost.
    [*The Pope crosseth himself.*]
FAUSTUS: How now? Must every bit be spiced with a cross?
    Nay then, take that.
    [*Faustus hits him a box of the ear.*]
POPE: Oh, I am slain! Help me, my lords.

Oh come, and help to bear my body hence.
Damned be this soul for ever for this deed!

[*Exeunt the Pope and his train.*]

MEPHOSTOPHILIS: Now, Faustus, what will you do now?
For I can tell you, you'll be cursed with bell, book and candle.

FAUSTUS: Bell, book and candle, candle, book and bell,
Forward and backward, to curse Faustus to hell.

[*Enter the Friars with bell, book and candle, for the dirge.*]

FIRST FRIAR: Come, brethren, let's about our business with good devotion.

95   [*sing*] Cursed be he that stole his Holiness' meat from the table. *Maledicat dominus.*[7]
Cursed be he that took his Holiness a blow on the face. *Maledicat dominus.*
Cursed be he that struck Friar Sandelo a blow on the pate. *Maledicat dominus.*

100   Cursed be he that disturbeth our holy dirge. *Maledicat dominus.*
Cursed be he that took away his Holiness' wine. *Maledicat dominus.*
Et omnes sancti.[8] Amen.

[*Faustus and Mephostophilis beat the Friars, fling fireworks among them and exeunt. Enter Chorus.*]

CHORUS: When Faustus had with pleasure ta'en the view
Of rarest things and royal courts of kings,
105   He stayed his course and so returned home;
Where such as bear his absence but with grief,
I mean his friends and nearest companions,
Did gratulate his safety with kind words,
And in their conference of what befell,
110   Touching his journey through the world and air,
They put forth questions of astrology,
Which Faustus answered with such learned skill
As they admired and wondered at his wit.
Now is his fame spread forth in every land;
115   Amongst the rest, the Emperor is one,
Carolus the Fifth, at whose palace now
Faustus is feasted 'mongst his noblemen.
What there he did in trial of his art,
I leave untold: your eyes shall see performed.

Scene 4

[*Enter Robin the ostler[9] with a book in his hand.*]

ROBIN: Oh this is admirable! Here I ha' stol'n one of Doctor Faustus' conjuring books, and, i'faith, I mean to search some circles for my own use. Now will I make all the maidens in our parish dance at my pleasure stark naked before me. And so by that means I shall see more than ere I felt or saw yet.

[*Enter Rafe calling Robin.*]

RAFE: Robin, prithee come away! There's a gentleman tarries to have his horse, and he would have his things rubbed and made clean. He keeps such a chafing

---

7. May God curse you.
8. And all the saints.
9. Stableman.

with my mistress about it, and she has sent me to look thee out. Prithee, come away!

ROBIN: Keep out, keep out, or else you are blown up. You are dismembered, Rafe,
10   keep out, for I am about a roaring piece of work.

RAFE: Come, what dost thou with that same book? Thou canst not read?

ROBIN: Yes, my master and mistress shall find that I can read, he for his forehead, she for her private study. She's born to bear with me, or else my art fails.

RAFE: Why, Robin, what book is that?

ROBIN: What book? Why, the most intolerable book for conjuring that ere was invented by any brimstone devil.

RAFE: Canst thou conjure with it?

ROBIN: I can do all these things easily with it. First, I can make thee drunk with ippocras at any tavern in Europe, for nothing. That's one of my conjuring works!

RAFE: Our master parson says that's nothing.

ROBIN: True, Rafe. And more, Rafe, if thou hast any mind to Nan Spit, our kitchen maid, then turn her and wind her to thy own use as often as thou wilt, and at midnight.

RAFE: Oh brave Robin! Shall I have Nan Spit, and to mine own use? On that con-
25   dition, I'll feed thy devil with horsebread as long as he lives, of free cost.

ROBIN: No more, sweet Rafe. Let's go and make clean our boots which lie foul upon our hands, and then to our conjuring, in the devil's name.

[Exeunt. Re-enter Robin and Rafe with a silver goblet.]

ROBIN: Come, Rafe, did I not tell thee we were for ever made by this Doctor Faustus' book? Ecce signum,[1] here's a simple purchase for horse-keepers. Our
30   horses shall eat no hay as long as this lasts.

[Enter the Vintner.]

RAFE: But, Robin, here comes the vintner.

ROBIN: Hush, I'll gull[2] him supernaturally. Drawer, I hope all is paid. God be with you. Come, Rafe.

VINTNER: Soft, sir, a word with you. I must yet have a goblet paid from you ere you go.

ROBIN: I, a goblet? Rafe, I a goblet? I scorn you, and you are but a etc. I, a goblet? Search me.

VINTNER: I mean so, sir, with your favor.

ROBIN: How say you now?

VINTNER: I must say somewhat to your fellow—you, sir.

RAFE: Me, sir? Me, sir? Search your fill. Now, sir, you may be ashamed to burden honest men with a matter of truth.

VINTNER: Well, t'one of you hath this goblet about you.

ROBIN: You lie, drawer. 'Tis afore me! Sirrah, you! I'll teach ye to impeach honest men. Stand by, I'll scour you for a goblet. Stand aside, you were best. I
45   charge you in the name of Belzebub. Look to the goblet, Rafe.

VINTNER: What mean you, sirrah?

ROBIN: I'll tell you what I mean. [He reads] Sanctobolorum Periphrasticon.[3] Nay, I'll tickle you, vintner—look to the goblet, Rafe. Polypragmos Belseborams framanto pacostiphos tostu Mephostophilis, Etc.

[Enter Mephostophilis, who sets squibs[4] at their backs. They run about.]

1. "Behold, the sign"; i.e., of the truth.   3. Gibberish.
2. Trick.   4. Firecrackers.

VINTNER: *O nomine Domine*[5] what mean'st thou, Robin? Thou hast no goblet.

RAFE: *Peccatum peccatorum*[6] here's thy goblet, good vintner.

ROBIN: *Misericordia pro nobis*[7] what shall I do? Good devil, forgive me now and I'll never rob thy library more.

[*Enter to them Mephostophilis.*]

MEPHOSTOPHILIS: Vainish villains! Th'one like an ape, another like a bear, the
55   third an ass, for doing this enterprise.
        Monarch of hell, under whose black survey
        Great potentates do kneel with awful fear,
        Upon whose altars thousand souls do lie,
        How am I vexed with these villains' charms?
60   From Constantinople am I hither come,
        Only for pleasure of these damned slaves.

ROBIN: How, from Constantinople? You have had a great journey. Will you take six pence in your purse to pay for your supper, and be gone?

MEPHOSTOPHILIS: Well, villains, for your presumption I transform thee into an ape and thee into a dog, and so be gone.   [*Exit.*]

ROBIN: How, into an ape? That's brave! I'll have fine sport with the boys. I'll get nuts and apples enow.

RAFE: And I must be a dog!

ROBIN: I'faith thy head will never be out of the potage pot.   [*Exeunt.*]

ACT 4

Scene 1

[*The Emperor's Court. Enter Martino and Frederick at several doors.*]

MARTINO: What ho, officers, gentlemen!
        Hie to the presence to attend the Emperor.
        Good Frederick, see the rooms be voided straight.
        His Majesty is coming to the hall;
5   Go back, and see the state in readiness.

FREDERICK: But where is Bruno, our elected Pope,
        That on a fury's back came post from Rome?
        Will not his grace consort° the Emperor?   greet

MARTINO: Oh yes, and with him comes the German conjuror,
10   The learned Faustus, fame of Wittenberg,
        The wonder of the world for magic art.
        And he intends to show great Carolus
        The race of all his stout progenitors,
        And bring in presence of his Majesty
15   The royal shapes and warlike semblances
        Of Alexander and his beauteous paramour.[1]

FREDERICK: Where is Benvolio?

MARTINO: Fast asleep, I warrant you.
        He took his rouse with stoups° of Rhenish wine   large cups
20   So kindly yesternight to Bruno's health,

5. In God's name.
6. Sin of sins.
7. Mercy on us.
1. Alexander the Great and his wife, Roxana.

That all this day the sluggard keeps his bed.

FREDERICK: See, see, his window's ope. We'll call to him.

MARTINO: What ho, Benvolio?

[*Enter Benvolio above at a window in his nightcap, buttoning.*]

BENVOLIO: What a devil ail you two?

MARTINO: Speak softly, sir, lest the devil hear you;
    For Faustus at the court is late arrived,
    And at his heels a thousand furies wait
    To accomplish whatsoever the Doctor please.

BENVOLIO: What of this?

MARTINO: Come, leave thy chamber first, and thou shalt see
    This conjuror perform such rare exploits
    Before the Pope and royal Emperor
    As never yet was seen in Germany.

BENVOLIO: Has not the Pope enough of conjuring yet?
35   He was upon the devil's back late enough,
    And if he be so far in love with him,
    I would he would post with him to Rome again.

FREDERICK: Speak, wilt thou come and see this sport?

BENVOLIO: Not I.

MARTINO: Wilt thou stand in thy window and see it, then?

BENVOLIO: Ay, and I fall not asleep i' the meantime.

MARTINO: The Emperor is at hand, who comes to see
    What wonders by black spells may compassed be.

BENVOLIO: Well, go you, attend the Emperor. I am content for this once to thrust
45   my head out at a window, for they say if a man be drunk over night the dev-
    il cannot hurt him in the morning. If that be true, I have a charm in my
    head shall control him as well as the conjuror, I warrant you.

                          [*Exeunt Martino and Frederick.*]

Scene 2

[*Sennet. Charles, the German Emperor, Bruno, Saxony, Faustus, Mephostophilis, Frederick, Martino, and Attendants. Benvolio still at the window.*]

EMPEROR: Wonder of men, renowned magician,
    Thrice-learned Faustus, welcome to our court.
    This deed of thine, in setting Bruno free
    From his and our professed enemy,
5   Shall add more excellence unto thine art,
    Than if by powerful necromantic spells
    Thou couldst command the world's obedience.
    For ever be beloved of Carolus;
    And if this Bruno thou hast late redeemed,
10   In peace possess the triple diadem
    And sit in Peter's chair, despite of chance,
    Thou shalt be famous through all Italy,
    And honored of the German Emperor.

FAUSTUS: These gracious words, most royal Carolus,
15   Shall make poor Faustus to his utmost power
    Both love and serve the German Emperor,

And lay his life at holy Bruno's feet.
For proof whereof, if so your Grace be pleased,
The Doctor stands prepared, by power of art,
20   To cast his magic charms that shall pierce through
The ebon° gates of ever-burning hell,   *ebony*
And hale the stubborn furies from their caves,
To compass whatsoe'er your Grace commands.
BENVOLIO [*aside*]: Blood, he speaks terribly! But for all that, I do not greatly
25   believe him. He looks as like a conjuror as the Pope to a coster-monger.[2]
EMPEROR: Then, Faustus, as thou late didst promise us,
We would behold that famous conqueror,
Great Alexander, and his paramour,
In their true shapes and state majestical,
30   That we may wonder at their excellence.
FAUSTUS: Your Majesty shall see them presently.
Mephostophilis, away!
And with a solemn noise of trumpets' sound,
Present before this royal Emperor
35   Great Alexander and his beauteous paramour.
MEPHOSTOPHILIS: Faustus, I will.
BENVOLIO: Well, Master Doctor, an your devils come not away quickly, you shall
have me asleep presently. Zounds, I could eat myself for anger, to think
I have been such an ass all this while, to stand gaping after the devil's
40   governor, and can see nothing.
FAUSTUS: I'll make you feel something anon, if my art fail me not.
My lord, I must forwarn your Majesty
That when my spirits present the royal shapes
Of Alexander and his paramour,
45   Your Grace demand no questions of the King,
But in dumb silence let them come and go.
EMPEROR: Be it as Faustus please, we are content.
BENVOLIO: Ay, ay, and I am content too. And thou bring Alexander and his para-
mour before the Emperor, I'll be Actaeon[3] and turn myself to a stag.
FAUSTUS: And I'll play Diana, and send you the horns presently.
[*Sennet. Enter at one the Emperor Alexander, at the other Darius. They meet. Darius
is thrown down; Alexander kills him, takes off his crown, and, offering to go out, his
Paramour meets him. He embraceth her and sets Darius' crown upon her head, and
coming back, both salute the Emperor, who, leaving his state, offers to embrace them,
which Faustus seeing, suddenly stays him. Then trumpets cease and music sounds.*]
My gracious lord, you do forget yourself.
These are but shadows, not substantial.
EMPEROR: Oh pardon me, my thoughts are so ravished
With sight of this renowned Emperor,
55   That in mine arms I would have compassed him.
But, Faustus, since I may not speak to them,
To satisfy my longing thoughts at full,
Let me this tell thee: I have heard it said

2. Vegetable seller.
3. Mythical hunter, changed by the goddess Diana into a

stag because he had seen her naked as she bathed after a
hunt; he was then devoured by his own dogs.

That this fair lady, whilst she lived on earth,
60   Had on her neck a little wart or mole.
How may I prove that saying to be true?

FAUSTUS: Your Majesty may boldly go and see.

EMPEROR: Faustus, I see it plain,
And in this sight thou better pleasest me
65   Than if I gained another monarchy.

FAUSTUS: Away, be gone.   [Exit Show.]
See, see, my gracious lord, what strange beast is yon, that
    thrusts his head out at window?

EMPEROR: Oh, wondrous sight! See, Duke of Saxony,
70   Two spreading horns most strangely fastened
Upon the head of young Benvolio![4]

SAXONY: What, is he asleep? Or dead?

FAUSTUS: He sleeps, my lord: but dreams not of his horns.

EMPEROR: This sport is excellent. We'll call and wake him.
75   What ho, Benvolio!

BENVOLIO: A plague upon you! Let me sleep awhile.

EMPEROR: I blame thee not to sleep much, having such a head of thine own.

SAXONY: Look up, Benvolio, 'tis the Emperor calls.

BENVOLIO: The Emperor? Where? Oh, zounds, my head!

EMPEROR: Nay, and thy horns hold, 'tis no matter for thy head, for that's armed
    sufficiently.

FAUSTUS: Why, how now, Sir Knight? What, hanged by the horns? This most
    horrible! Fie, fie! Pull in your head for shame; let not all the world wonder
    at you.

BENVOLIO: Zounds, Doctor, is this your villainy?

FAUSTUS: Oh, say not so, sir. The Doctor has no skill,
No art, no cunning, to present these lords
Or bring before this royal Emperor
The mighty monarch, warlike Alexander.
90   If Faustus do it, you are straight resolved
In bold Actaeon's shape to turn a stag.
And therefore, my lord, so please your majesty,
I'll raise a kennel of hounds shall hunt him so
As all his footmanship shall scarce prevail
95   To keep his carcass from their bloody fangs.
Ho, Belimote, Argiron, Asterote!

BENVOLIO: Hold, hold! Zounds, he'll raise up a kennel of devils, I think anon.
    Good my lord, entreat for me. 'Sblood, I am never never able to endure
    these torments.

EMPEROR: Then, good Master Doctor,
Let me entreat you to remove his horns:
He has done penance now sufficiently.

FAUSTUS: My gracious lord, not so much for injury done to me, as to delight your
    majesty with some mirth, hath Faustus justly requited this injurious knight;

---

4. To be "horned" was to be cuckolded. Benvolio, who has insulted scholars, is given horns by Faustus, who takes a scholar's revenge. The insult is introduced as a reflection on the myth of Diana and Actaeon.

105   which being all I desire, I am content to remove his horns. Mephostophilis,
       transform him. And hereafter, sir, look you speak well of scholars.
BENVOLIO [*aside*]: Speak well of ye? 'Sblood, and scholars be such cuckold-makers
       to clap horns of honest men's heads o' this order, I'll ne'er trust smooth faces
       and small ruffs more. But an I be not revenged for this, would I might be
110   turned to a gaping oyster and drink nothing but salt water.
EMPEROR: Come, Faustus, while the Emperor lives,
       In recompense of this thy high desert,°   *merit*
       Thou shalt command the state of Germany,
       And live beloved of mighty Carolus.

                                                            [*Exeunt omnes.*]

                              Scene 3

       [*Enter Benvolio, Martino, Frederick and Soldiers.*]
MARTINO: Nay, sweet Benvolio, let us sway thy thoughts
       From this attempt against the conjuror.
BENVOLIO: Away, you love me not, to urge me thus.
       Shall I let slip° so great an injury,   *overlook*
5   When every servile groom jests at my wrongs,
       And in their rustic gambols proudly say
       Benvolio's head was graced with horns today?
       Oh, may these eyelids never close again
       Till with my sword I have that conjuror slain.
10   If you will aid me in this enterprise,
       Then draw your weapons and be resolute.
       If not, depart. Here will Benvolio die,
       But Faustus' death shall quit my infamy.
FREDERICK: Nay, we will stay with three, betide what may,
15   And kill that Doctor if he come this way.
BENVOLIO: Then, gentle Frederick, hie° thee to the grove,   *take*
       And place our servants and our followers
       Close in an ambush there behind the trees.
       By this I know the conjuror is near:
20   I saw him kneel and kiss the Emperor's hand,
       And take his leave, laden with rich rewards.
       Then, soldiers, boldly fight. If Faustus die,
       Take you the wealth, leave us the victory.
FREDERICK: Come, soldiers, follow me unto the grove.
25   Who kills him shall have gold and endless love.
                                                [*Exit Frederick with the Soldiers.*]
BENVOLIO: My head is lighter than it was by th'horns,
       But yet my heart more ponderous than my head,
       And pants until I see that conjuror dead.
MARTINO: Where shall we place ourselves, Benvolio?
BENVOLIO: Here will we stay to bide the first assault.
       Oh, were that damned hell-hound but in place,
       Thou soon shouldst see me quit my foul disgrace.
       [*Enter Frederick.*]
FREDERICK: Close, close! The conjuror is at hand,

And all alone comes walking in his gown.
35   Be ready then, and strike the peasant down.
BENVOLIO: Mine be that honor, then. Now sword, strike home.
          For horns he gave, I'll have his head anon.
          [*Enter Faustus with a false head.*]
MARTINO: See, see, he comes.
BENVOLIO: No words. This blow ends all.
40   Hell take his soul; his body thus must fall. [*Attacks Faustus.*]
FAUSTUS: Oh!
FREDERICK: Groan you, Master Doctor?
BENVOLIO: Break may his heart with groans! Dear Frederick, see,
          Thus will I end his griefs immediately. [*Cuts off his head.*]
MARTINO: Strike with a willing hand: his head is off.
BENVOLIO: The devil's dead! The Furies now may laugh.
FREDERICK: Was this that stern aspect, that awful frown,
          Made the grim monarch of infernal spirits
          Tremble and quake at his commanding charms?
MARTINO: Was this that damned head, whose heart conspired
          Benvolio's shame before the Emperor?
BENVOLIO: Ay, that's the head, and here the body lies,
          Justly rewarded for his villainies.
FREDERICK: Come, let's devise how we may add more shame
55   To the black scandal of his hated name.
BENVOLIO: First, on his head, in quittance° of my wrongs,   *payment*
          I'll nail huge forked horns, and let them hang
          Within the window where he yoked° me first,   *overcame*
          That all the world may see my just revenge.
MARTINO: What use shall we put his beard to?
BENVOLIO: We'll sell it to a chimney-sweeper: it will wear
          out ten birching° brooms, I warrant you.   *birch-twig*
FREDERICK: What shall eyes do?
BENVOLIO: We'll put out his eyes, and they shall serve for buttons to his lips, to
65   keep his tongue from catching cold.
MARTINO: An excellent policy! And now, sirs, having divided him, what shall the
          body do?
          [*Faustus rises.*]
BENVOLIO: Zounds, the devil's alive again!
FREDERICK: Give him his head, for God's sake!
FAUSTUS: Nay, keep it. Faustus will have heads and hands.
          I call your hearts to recompense this deed.
          Knew you not, traitors, I was limited
          For four and twenty years to breathe on earth?
          And had you cut my body with your swords,
75   Or hewed this flesh and bones as small as sand,
          Yet in a minute had my spirit returned,
          And I had breathed a man made free from harm.
          But wherefore do I dally° my revenge?   *delay*
          Asteroth, Belimoth, Mephostophilis!
          [*Enter Mephostophilis and other Devils.*]

80   Go, horse these traitors on your fiery backs,
And mount aloft with them as high as heaven;
Thence pitch them headlong to the lowest hell.
Yet stay, the world shall see their misery,
And hell shall after plague their treachery.

85   Go, Belimoth, and take this caitiff° hence,   *coward*
And hurl him in some lake of mud and dirt.
Take thou this other: drag him through the woods
Amongst the pricking thorns and sharpest briars,
Whilst with my gentle Mephostophilis,

90   This traitor flies unto some steepy rock,
That rolling down may break the villain's bones,
As he intended to dismember me.
Fly hence, dispatch my charge immediately.

FREDERICK: Pity us, gentle Faustus! Save our lives!

FAUSTUS: Away!

FREDERICK: He must needs go that the devil drives.

[*Exeunt Spirits with the Knights. Enter the Ambush Soldiers.*]

FIRST SOLDIER: Come, sirs, prepare yourselves in readiness.
Make haste to help these noble gentlemen.
I heard them parley with the conjuror.

SECOND SOLDIER: See, where he comes. Dispatch and kill the slave.

FAUSTUS: What's here? An ambush to betray my life!
Then Faustus, try thy skill. Base peasants, stand!
For lo, these trees remove at my command,
And stand as bulwarks twixt yourselves and me,

105   To shield me from your hated treachery.
Yet, to encounter this your weak attempt,
Behold an army comes incontinent.°   *rapidly*

[*Faustus strikes the door, and enter a devil playing on a drum; after him another bearing an ensign;⁵ and divers with weapons; Mephostophilis with fireworks. They set upon the soldiers and drive them out.*]

Scene 4

[*Enter at several doors Benvolio, Frederick and Martino, their heads and faces bloody and besmeared with mud and dirt, all having horns on their heads.*]

MARTINO: What ho, Benvolio!

BENVOLIO: Here! What, Frederick, ho!

FREDERICK: Oh help me, gentle friend. Where is Martino?

MARTINO: Dear Frederick, here,

5   Half smothered in a lake of mud and dirt,
Through which the Furies dragged me by the heels.

FREDERICK: Martino, see Benvolio's horns again!

MARTINO: Oh misery! How now, Benvolio?

BENVOLIO: Defend me, heaven! Shall I be haunted still?

MARTINO: Nay, fear not, man; we have no power to kill.

BENVOLIO: My friends transformed thus! Oh hellish spite!

5. Flag.

Your heads are all set with horns!
FREDERICK: You hit it right:
　It is your own you mean. Feel on your head.
BENVOLIO: Zounds, horns again!
MARTINO: Nay, chafe not, man. We all are sped.°   *done for*
BENVOLIO: What devil attends this damned magician,
　That, spite of spite, our wrongs are doubled?
FREDERICK: What may we do, that we may hide our shames?
BENVOLIO: If we should follow him to work revenge,
　He'd join long asses' ears to these huge horns,
　And make us laughing stocks to all the world.
MARTINO: What shall we then do, dear Benvolio?
BENVOLIO: I have a castle joining near these woods,
25　And thither we'll repair and live obscure,
　Till time shall alter these our brutish shapes.
　Sith° black disgrace hath thus eclipsed our fame,   *since*
　We'll rather die with grief, than live with shame.
                                                    [*Exeunt omnes.*]

Scene 5

　[*Enter Faustus and Mephostophilis.*]
FAUSTUS: Now, Mephostophilis, the restless course
　That time doth run with calm and deadly foot,
　Shortening my days and thread of vital life,
　Calls for the payment of my latest years.
5　Therefore, sweet Mephostophilis, let us
　Make haste to Wittenberg.
MEPHOSTOPHILIS: What, will you go on horseback, or on foot?
FAUSTUS: Nay, till I am past this fair and pleasant green
　I'll walk on foot.
　[*Enter a Horse-Courser.*]⁶
HORSE-COURSER: I have been all this day seeking one master Fustian.⁷ Mass, see
　where he is! God save you, Master Doctor.
FAUSTUS: What, horse-courser! You are well met.
HORSE-COURSER: Do you hear, sir? I have brought you forty dollars for your horse.
FAUSTUS: I cannot sell him so. If thou likest him for fifty, take him.
HORSE-COURSER: Alas, sir, I have no more. I pray you, speak for me.
MEPHOSTOPHILIS: I pray you, let him have him. He is an honest fellow, and he
　has a great charge, neither wife nor child.
FAUSTUS: Well, come, give me your money. My boy will deliver him to you. But I
　must tell you one thing before you have him: ride him not into the water at
20　any hand.
HORSE-COURSER: Why, sir, will he not drink of all waters?
FAUSTUS: Oh yes, he will drink of all waters; but ride him not into the water. Ride
　him over hedge or ditch or where thou wilt, but not into the water.
HORSE-COURSER: Well, sir, now I am a made man for ever. I'll not leave my
25　horse for forty. If he had but the quality of hey ding ding, hey ding ding, I'd

6. Horse trader.   7. Bombast.

make a brave living on him. He has a buttock as slick as an eel. Well, God bye, sir. Your boy will deliver him me. But hark ye sir: if my horse be sick or ill at ease, if I bring his water to you, you'll tell me what is?

FAUSTUS: Away, you villain! What, dost think I am a horse-doctor?

[*Exit Horse-Courser.*]

30   What art thou, Faustus, but a man condemned to die?
Thy fatal time doth draw to final end:
Despair doth drive distrust into my thoughts.
Confound these passions with a quiet sleep.
Tush, Christ did call the thief upon the cross;
35   Then rest thee, Faustus, quiet in conceit.

[*Sleeps in his chair. Enter Horse-Courser all wet, crying.*]

HORSE-COURSER: Alas, alas, Doctor Fustian quotha! Mass, Doctor Lopus[8] was never such a doctor. Has given me a purgation has purged me of forty dollars: I shall never see them more. But yet like an ass as I was, I would not be ruled by him, for he bade me I should ride him into no water. Now I, think-
40   ing my horse had had some rare quality that he would not have had me known of, I, like a venturous youth, rid him into the deep pond at the town's end. I was no sooner in the middle of the pond but my horse van-ished away, and I sat upon a bottle of hay, never so near drowning in my life. But I'll seek out my Doctor and have my forty dollars again, or I'll make it
45   the dearest horse. Oh, yonder is his snipper-snapper. Do you hear? You! Hey-pass, where's your master?

MEPHOSTOPHILIS: Why, sir, what would you? You cannot speak with him.

HORSE-COURSER: But I *will* speak with him.

MEPHOSTOPHILIS: Why, he's fast asleep. Come some other time.

HORSE-COURSER: I'll speak with him now, or I'll break his glass windows about his ears.

MEPHOSTOPHILIS: I tell thee he has not slept this eight nights.

HORSE-COURSER: And he have not slept this eight weeks I'll speak with him.

MEPHOSTOPHILIS: See where he is fast asleep.

HORSE-COURSER: Ay, this is he. God save ye, Master Doctor. Master Doctor!
55   Master Doctor Fustian! Forty dollars, forty dollars for a bottle of hay!

MEPHOSTOPHILIS: Why, thou seest he hears thee not.

HORSE-COURSER: So, ho, ho! So, ho, ho! [*Halloos in his ear.*]
No, will you not wake? I'll make you wake e'er I go. [*He pulls him by the leg, and pulls it away.*]
Alas, I am undone! What shall I do?

FAUSTUS: Oh, my leg, my leg! Help, Mephostophilis. Call the officers. My leg, my leg!

MEPHOSTOPHILIS: Come, villain, to the Constable.

HORSE-COURSER: Oh lord, sir, let me go and I'll give you forty dollars more.

MEPHOSTOPHILIS: Where be they?

HORSE-COURSER: I have none about me. Come to my hostry and I'll give them you.

MEPHOSTOPHILIS: Be gone, quickly!

[*Horse-Courser runs away.*]

---

8. Dr. Lopez, Queen Elizabeth's physician, who was executed in 1594 for alleged complicity in an attempt to murder the Queen. Marlowe died in 1593, so the reference is not his but one of a later editor.

FAUSTUS: What, is he gone? Farewell he. Faustus has his leg again, and the horse-courser, I take it, a bottle of hay for his labor. Well, this trick shall cost him forty dollars more.

[*Enter Wagner.*]

FAUSTUS: How now, Wagner, what news with thee?

WAGNER: If it please you, the Duke of Vanholt[9] doth earnestly entreat your company, and hath sent some of his men to attend you with provision for your journey.

FAUSTUS: The Duke of Vanholt's an honorable gentleman, and one to whom I must be no niggard[1] of my cunning. Come, away.   [*Exeunt.*]

Scene 6

[*Enter Clown, Dick, Horse-Courser and a Carter.*]

CARTER: Come, my masters, I'll bring you to the best beer in Europe. What ho, hostess. Where be these whores?

[*Enter Hostess.*]

HOSTESS: How now, what lack you? What, my old guests, welcome!

CLOWN: Sirrah Dick, dost thou know why I stand so mute?

DICK: No, Robin, why is't?

CLOWN: I am eighteen pence on the score.[2] But say nothing. See if she have forgotten me.

HOSTESS: Who's this, that stands so solemnly by himself? What, my old guest?

CLOWN: Oh, hostess, how do you? I hope my score stands still.

HOSTESS: Ay, there's no doubt of that, for methinks you make no haste to wipe it out.

DICK: Why, hostess, I say, fetch us some beer.

HOSTESS: You shall presently. Look up into the hall there, ho!   [*Exit.*]

DICK: Come, sirs, what shall we do now till mine hostess comes?

CARTER: Marry, sir, I'll tell you the bravest tale how a conjuror served me. You know Doctor Faustus?

HORSE-COURSER: Ay, a plague take him. Here's some on's have cause to know him. Did he conjure thee too?

CARTER: I'll tell you how he served me. As I was going to Wittenberg t'other day, with a load of hay, he met me and asked me what he should give me for as much hay as he could eat. Now, sir, I, thinking that a little would serve his turn, bade him take as much as he would for three-farthings. So he presently gave me my money and fell to eating. And, as I am a cursen man, he never left eating till he had eat up all my load of hay.

ALL: Oh monstrous! Eat a whole load of hay?

CLOWN: Yes, yes, that may be, for I have heard of one that has eat a load of logs.

HORSE-COURSER: Now, sirs, you shall hear how villainously he served me. I went to him yesterday to buy a horse of him, and he would by no means sell him under forty dollars. So, sir, because I knew him to be such a horse as would run over hedge and ditch and never tire, I gave him his money. So when I had my horse, Doctor Fauster bade me ride him night and day and spare him no time. But, quoth he, in any case ride him not into the water. Now, sir, I thinking the horse had some quality that he would not have me know of,

9. The Duchy of Anholt in Germany.
1. Miser.
2. Eighteen pence in debt.

what did I but ride him into a great river, and when I came just in the midst, my horse vanished away, and I sat straddling upon a bottle of hay.

ALL: Oh brave Doctor!

HORSE-COURSER: But you shall hear how bravely I served him for it: I went me home to his house, and there I found him asleep. I kept a-hallowing and whooping in his ears, but all could not wake him. I, seeing that, took him by the leg and never rested pulling, till I had pulled me his leg quite off, and
40   now 'tis at home in mine hostry.

CLOWN: And has the Doctor but one leg, then? That's excellent, for one of his devils turned me into the likeness of an ape's face.

CARTER: Some more drink, hostess.

CLOWN: Hark you, we'll into another room and drink a while, and then we'll go
45   seek out the Doctor.   [Exeunt omnes.]

                                        Scene 7

[Enter the Duke of Vanholt, his Duchess, Faustus and Mephostophilis.]

DUKE: Thanks, Master Doctor, for these pleasant sights. Nor know I how sufficiently to recompense your great deserts in erecting that enchanted castle in the air, the sight whereof so delighted me, as nothing in the world could please me more.

FAUSTUS: I do think myself, my good lord, highly recompensed in that it pleaseth
5   your grace to think but well of that which Faustus hath performed. But, gracious lady, it may be that you have taken no pleasure in those sights. Therefore, I pray you tell me, what is the thing you most desire to have. Be it in the world, it shall be yours. I have heard that great-bellied women do long for things are rare and dainty.

LADY: True, Master Doctor, and since I find you so kind, I will make known unto you what my heart desires to have; and were it now summer, as it is January, a dead time of the winter, I would request no better meat than a dish of ripe grapes.

FAUSTUS: This is but a small matter. Go, Mephostophilis, away.

                                                              [Exit Mephostophilis.]
15   Madame, I will do more than this for your content.

[Enter Mephostophilis again with the grapes.]

        Here, now taste ye these. They should be good, for they come from a far country, I can tell you.

DUKE: This makes me wonder more than all the rest, that at this time of the year, when every tree is barren of his fruit, from whence you had these ripe grapes.

FAUSTUS: Please it your grace, the year is divided into two circles over the whole world, so that when it is winter with us, in the contrary circle it is likewise summer with them, as in India, Saba and such countries that lie far East, where they have fruit twice a year. From whence, by means of a swift spirit that I have, I had these grapes brought as you see.

LADY: And trust me, they are the sweetest grapes that e'er I tasted.

[The Clowns bounce at the gate within.]

DUKE: What rude disturbers have we at the gate?
        Go, pacify their fury. Set it ope,
        And then demand of them what they would have.

[They knock again and call out to talk with Faustus.]

SERVANT: Why, how now, masters? What a coil³ is there?

30   What is the reason you disturb the Duke?

DICK: We have no reason for it, therefore a fig for him.

SERVANT: Why, saucy varlets, dare you be so bold?

HORSE-COURSER: I hope, sir, we have wit enough to be more bold than welcome.

SERVANT: It appears so. Pray be bold elsewhere,

35   And trouble not the Duke.

DUKE: What would they have?

SERVANT: They all cry out to speak with Doctor Faustus.

CARTER: Ay, and we will speak with him.

DUKE: Will you, sir? Commit the rascals.

DICK: Commit with us! He were as good commit with his father as commit with us.

FAUSTUS: I do beseech your grace let them come in.

          They are good subject for a merriment.

DUKE: Do as thou wilt, Faustus; I give thee leave.

FAUSTUS: I thank your grace.

      [*Enter the Clown, Dick, Carter and Horse-Courser.*]

45   Why, how now, my good friends?

          Faith, you are too outrageous, but come near.

          I have procured your pardons. Welcome all.

CLOWN: Nay, sir, we will be welcome for our money, and we will pay for what we
          take. What ho! Give's half-a-dozen of beer here, and be hanged.

FAUSTUS: Nay, hark you. Can you tell me where you are?

CARTER: Ay, marry can I. We are under heaven.

SERVANT: Ay, but, sir sauce-box, know you in what place?

HORSE-COURSER: Ay, ay, the house is good enough to drink in. Zounds, fill us
          some beer or we'll break all the barrels in the house and dash out all your

55   brains with your bottles.

FAUSTUS: Be not so furious. Come, you shall have beer.

          My lord, beseech you give me leave awhile.

          I'll gage my credit, 'twill content your Grace.

DUKE: With all my heart, kind Doctor; please thyself.

60   Our servants and our court's at thy command.

FAUSTUS: I humbly thank your Grace. Then fetch some beer.

HORSE-COURSER: Ay, marry. There spake a doctor indeed, and faith, I'll drink a
          health to thy wooden leg for that word.

FAUSTUS: My wooden leg? What dost thou mean by that?

CARTER: Ha, ha, ha! Dost thou hear him, Dick? He has forgot his leg.

HORSE-COURSER: Ay, ay, he does not stand much upon that.

FAUSTUS: No, faith. Not much upon a wooden leg.

CARTER: Good lord! That flesh and blood should be so frail with your worship. Do
          not you remember a horse-courser you sold a horse to?

FAUSTUS: Yes, I remember I sold one a horse.

CARTER: And do you remember you bid he should not ride into the water?

FAUSTUS: Yes, I do very well remember that.

CARTER: And do you remember nothing of your leg?

FAUSTUS: No, in good sooth.

---

3. Disturbance.

CARTER: Then I pray remember your courtesy.[4]

FAUSTUS: I thank you, sir.

CARTER: 'Tis not so much worth. I pray you, tell me one thing.

FAUSTUS: What's that?

CARTER: Be both your legs bedfellows every night together?

FAUSTUS: Wouldst thou make a colossus[5] of me, that thou askest me such questions?

CARTER: No, truly, sir. I would make nothing of you, but I would fain know that.
    [Enter Hostess with drink.]

FAUSTUS: Then I assure thee certainly they are.

CARTER: I thank you, I am fully satisfied.

FAUSTUS: But wherefore dost thou ask?

CARTER: For nothing, sir: but methinks you should have a wooden bedfellow of one of 'em.

HORSE-COURSER: Why, do you hear, sir? Did not I pull off one of your legs when you were asleep?

FAUSTUS: But I have it again now I am awake. Look you here, sir.

ALL: Oh horrible! Had the Doctor three legs?

CARTER: Do you remember, sir, how you cozened[6] me and eat up my load of—
    [Faustus charms him dumb.]

DICK: Do you remember how you made me wear an ape's—

HORSE-COURSER: You whoreson conjuring scab, do you remember how you cozened me with a ho—

CLOWN: Ha'you forgotten me? You think to carry it away with your hey-pass and re-pass. Do you remember the dog's fa—
    [Faustus has charmed each dumb in turn; exeunt Clowns.]

HOSTESS: Who pays for the ale? Hear you, Master Doctor, now you have sent away my guests, I pray who shall pay me for my a—?   [Exit Hostess.]

LADY: My lord,
100   We are much beholding to this learned man.

DUKE: So are we, madam, which we will recompense
        With all the love and kindness that we may.
        His artful sport drives all sad thoughts away.   [Exeunt.]

ACT 5

Scene 1

[Thunder and lightning. Enter Devils with covered dishes. Mephostophilis leads them into Faustus' study. Then enter Wagner.]

WAGNER: I think my master means to die shortly.
        He hath made his will, and given me his wealth,
        His house, his goods, and store of golden plate,
        Besides two thousand ducats ready coined.
5   And yet methinks, if that death were near,
        He would not banquet and carouse and swill
        Amongst the students, as even now he doth,
        Who are at supper with such belly-cheer
        As Wagner ne'er beheld in all his life.

4. Kindness   6. Tricked.
5. Huge statue.

10   See where they come; belike the feast is ended.   [*Exit.*]
    [*Enter Faustus, Mephostophilis and two or three Scholars.*]
FIRST SCHOLAR: Master Doctor Faustus, since our conference about fair ladies,
        which was the beautifullest in all the world, we have determined with our-
        selves that Helen of Greece[1] was the admirablest lady that ever lived.
        Therefore Master Doctor, if you will do us so much favor, as to let us see that
15   peerless dame of Greece, whom all the world admires for majesty, we should
        think ourselves much beholding unto you.
FAUSTUS: Gentlemen, for that I know your friendship is unfeigned,
        It is not Faustus' custom to deny
        The just request of those that wish him well.
20   You shall behold that peerless dame of Greece,
        No otherwise for pomp of majesty,
        Than when Sir Paris crossed the seas with her,
        And brought the spoils to rich Dardania.°   Troy
        Be silent then, for danger is in words.
    [*Music sounds. Mephostophilis brings in Helen; she passeth over the stage.*]
SECOND SCHOLAR: Was this fair Helen, whose admired worth
        Made Greece with ten years wars afflict poor Troy?
THIRD SCHOLAR: Too simple is my wit to tell her worth
        Whom all the world admires for majesty.
FIRST SCHOLAR: Now we have seen the pride of nature's work,
30   We'll take our leaves, and for this blessed sight
        Happy and blest be Faustus evermore.
    [*Enter an Old Man.*]
FAUSTUS: Gentlemen, farewell: the same wish I to you.   [*Exeunt Scholars.*]
OLD MAN: Oh gentle Faustus, leave this damned art,[2]
        This magic, that will charm thy soul to hell,
35   And quite bereave thee of salvation.
        Though thou hast now offended like a man,
        Do not persever in it like a devil.
        Yet, yet, thou hast an amiable° soul,   lovable
        If sin by custom grow not into nature:
40   Then, Faustus, will repentance come too late,
        Then thou art banished from the sight of heaven;
        No mortal can express the pains of hell.
        It may be this my exhortation
        Seems harsh and all unpleasant; let it not,
45   For, gentle son, I speak it not in wrath,
        Or envy of thee, but in tender love,

1. The mythical queen of Menelaus, King of Sparta, who was abducted by Paris, son of King Priam of Troy. The action began the Trojan War.
2. The Old Man's lines appear in the A text in a markedly different mode; there, they convey some hope that Faustus may still be saved:

    Ah Doctor Faustus, that I might prevail,
    To guide thy steps unto the way of life,
    By which sweet path thou mayst attain the goal

That shall conduct thee to celestial rest.
Break heart, drop blood, and mingle it with tears,
Tears falling from repentant heaviness
Of thy most vile and loathsome filthiness,
The stench whereof corrupts the inward soul
With such flagitious crimes of hainous sinnes,
As no commiseration may expel,
But mercy Faustus of thy Saviour sweet,
Whose blood alone must wash away thy guilt.

And pity of thy future misery.
And so have hope, that this my kind rebuke,
Checking thy body, may amend thy soul.
FAUSTUS: Where art thou, Faustus? Wretch, what hast thou done?
Damned art thou, Faustus, damned: despair and die.
Hell claims his right, and with a roaring voice
Says "Faustus, come, thine hour is almost come"
[*Mephostophilis gives him a dagger.*]
And Faustus now will come to do thee right.
OLD MAN: Oh stay, good Faustus, stay thy desperate steps.
I see an angel hover o'er thy head,
And with a vial full of precious grace,
Offers to pour the same into thy soul.
Then call for mercy and avoid despair.
FAUSTUS: Ah my sweet friend, I feel thy words
To comfort my distressed soul.
Leave me awhile to ponder on my sins.
OLD MAN: I leave thee, but with grief of heart,
Fearing the ruin of thy hopeless soul. [*Exit.*]
FAUSTUS: Accursed Faustus, wretch, what hast thou done?
I do repent, and yet I do despair.
Hell strives with grace for conquest in my breast.
What shall I do to shun the snares of death?
MEPHOSTOPHILIS: Thou traitor, Faustus, I arrest thy soul
70   For disobedience to my sovereign lord.
Revolt,[3] or I'll in piecemeal tear thy flesh.
FAUSTUS: I do repent I e'er offended him.
Sweet Mephostophilis, entreat thy lord
To pardon my unjust presumption,
75   And with my blood again I will confirm
The former vow I made to Lucifer.
MEPHOSTOPHILIS: Do it then, Faustus, with unfeigned heart,
Lest greater dangers do attend thy drift.
FAUSTUS: Torment, sweet friend, that base and crooked age
80   That durst dissuade me from thy Lucifer,
With greatest torment that our hell affords.
MEPHOSTOPHILIS: His faith is great: I cannot touch his soul.
But what I may afflict his body with
I will attempt, which is but little worth.
FAUSTUS: One thing, good servant, let me crave of thee,
To glut the longing of my heart's desire,
That I may have unto my paramour
That heavenly Helen which I saw of late,
Whose sweet embraces may extinguish clear
90   Those thoughts that do dissuade me from my vow,
And keep my vow I made to Lucifer.
MEPHOSTOPHILIS: This, or what else my Faustus shall desire,

3. I.e., return to the terms of your bargain with the devil.

Shall be performed in twinkling of an eye.

[*Enter Helen again, passing over between two Cupids.*]

FAUSTUS: Was this the face that launched a thousand ships,
95   And burnt the topless towers of Ilium?
      Sweet Helen, make me immortal with a kiss.
      Her lips suck forth my soul: see where it flies.
      Come, Helen, come, give me my soul again.
      Here will I dwell, for heaven is in those lips,
100   And all is dross that is not Helena.

[*Enter Old Man.*]

      I will be Paris,[4] and for love of thee
      Instead of Troy shall Wittenberg be sacked,
      And I will combat with weak Menelaus,
      And wear thy colors on my plumed crest.
105   Yea, I will wound Achilles in the heel,
      And then return to Helen for a kiss.
      Oh, thou art fairer than the evening's air,
      Clad in the beauty of a thousand stars.
      Brighter art thou than flaming Jupiter,
110   When he appeared to hapless Semele:[5]
      More lovely than the monarch of the sky,
      In wanton Arethusa's[6] azure arms,
      And none but thou shalt be my paramour.   [*Exeunt.*]

OLD MAN: Accursed Faustus, miserable man,
115   That from thy soul exclud'st the grace of heaven,
      And fliest the throne of his tribunal seat.

[*Enter the Devils.*]

      Satan begins to sift° me with his pride,   *scrutinize*
      As in this furnace God shall try my faith.
      My faith, vile hell, shall triumph over thee.
120   Ambitious fiends, see how the heavens smiles
      At your repulse, and laughs your state to scorn.
      Hence, hell, for hence I fly unto my God.   [*Exeunt.*]

Scene 2

[*Thunder. Enter Lucifer, Belzebub and Mephostophilis.*]

LUCIFER: Thus from infernal Dis° do we ascend   *hell*
      To view the subjects of our monarchy,
      Those souls which sin seals the black sons of hell,
      'Mong which as chief, Faustus, we come to thee,
5   Bringing with us lasting damnation
      To wait upon thy soul. The time is come
      Which makes it forfeit.

MEPHOSTOPHILIS: And this gloomy night,

---

4. Faustus imagines he will be not only Paris, Helen's lover, but also the victor in combat with her husband, King Menelaus, as well as with the greatest of the Greek warriors, Achilles.

5. The mortal woman to whom Jupiter appeared as lightening.

6. A nymph beloved by the river-god Alpheus; no myth describes her as Jupiter's lover.

Here in this room will wretched Faustus be.

BELZEBUB: And here we'll stay,

10   To mark him how he doth demean himself.

MEPHOSTOPHILIS: How should he, but in desperate lunacy?
Fond worldling, now his heart blood dries with grief.
His conscience kills it, and his laboring brain
Begets a world of idle fantasies

15   To overreach the devil. But all in vain:
His store of pleasures must be sauced with pain.
He and his servant Wagner are at hand.
Both come from drawing Faustus' latest will.
See where they come.

[Enter Faustus and Wagner.]

FAUSTUS: Say, Wagner, thou hast perused my will:
How dost thou like it?

WAGNER: Sir, so wondrous well
As in all humble duty I do yield
My life and lasting service for your love.

[Enter the Scholars.]

FAUSTUS: Gramercies, Wagner. Welcome, gentlemen.

FIRST SCHOLAR: Now, worthy Faustus, methinks your looks are changed.

FAUSTUS: Oh gentlemen!

SECOND SCHOLAR: What ails Faustus?

FAUSTUS: Ah, my sweet chamber-fellow, had I lived with thee
Then had I lived still, but now must die eternally.

30   Look, sirs, comes he not? Comes he not?

FIRST SCHOLAR: Oh, my dear Faustus, what imports this fear?

SECOND SCHOLAR: Is all our pleasure turned to melancholy?

THIRD SCHOLAR: He is not well with being oversolitary.

SECOND SCHOLAR: If it be so, we'll have physicians, and Faustus shall be cured.

THIRD SCHOLAR: 'Tis but a surfeit, sir; fear nothing.

FAUSTUS: A surfeit of deadly sin, that hath damned both body and soul.

SECOND SCHOLAR: Yet Faustus, look up to heaven, and remember mercy is infinite.

FAUSTUS: But Faustus' offence can ne'er be pardoned, The serpent that tempted
Eve may be saved, but not Faustus. Oh gentlemen, hear with patience and

40   tremble not at my speeches. Though my heart pant and quiver to remember
that I have been a student here these thirty years, oh would I had never seen
Wittenberg, never read book. And what wonders I have done all Germany
can witness, yea all the world, for which Faustus hath lost both Germany
and the world, yea heaven itself, heaven, the seat of God, the throne of the

45   blessed, the kingdom of joy, and must remain in hell for ever. Hell, oh
hell for ever. Sweet friends, what shall become of Faustus, being in hell
for ever?

SECOND SCHOLAR: Yet Faustus, call on God.

FAUSTUS: On God, whom Faustus hath abjured? On God, whom Faustus hath
blasphemed? Oh my God, I would weep, but the devil draws in my tears.

50   Gush forth blood instead of tears, yea, life and soul. Oh, he stays my tongue.
I would lift up my hands, but see, they hold them, they hold them.

ALL: Who, Faustus?

FAUSTUS: Why, Lucifer and Mephostophilis: Oh gentlemen, I gave them my soul
for my cunning.

ALL: Oh, God forbid.

FAUSTUS: God forbade it indeed, but Faustus hath done it. For vain pleasure of four
and twenty years hath Faustus lost eternal joy and felicity. I writ them a bill
with mine own blood, the date is expired: this is the time, and he will fetch me.

FIRST SCHOLAR: Why did not Faustus tell us of this before, that divines might
60   have prayed for thee?

FAUSTUS: Oft have I thought to have done so, but the devil threatened to tear me
in pieces if I named God; to fetch me body and soul if I once gave ear to
divinity, and now 'tis too late. Gentlemen, away, lest you perish with me.

SECOND SCHOLAR: Oh what may we do to save Faustus?

FAUSTUS: Talk not of me, but save yourselves and depart.

THIRD SCHOLAR: God will strengthen me. I will stay with Faustus.

FIRST SCHOLAR: Tempt not God, sweet friend, but let us into the next room and
pray for him.

FAUSTUS: Ay, pray for me, pray for me. And what noise soever you hear, come not
70   unto me, for nothing can rescue me.

SECOND SCHOLAR: Pray thou, and we will pray, that God may have mercy upon thee.

FAUSTUS: Gentlemen, farewell. If I live till morning, I'll visit you. If not, Faustus is
gone to hell.

ALL: Faustus, farewell.   [*Exeunt Scholars.*]

MEPHOSTOPHILIS: Ay, Faustus, now thou hast no hope of heaven,
Therefore despair, think only upon hell,
For that must be thy mansion, there to dwell.

FAUSTUS: Oh, thou bewitching fiend, 'twas thy temptation
Hath robbed me of eternal happiness.

MEPHOSTOPHILIS: I do confess it, Faustus, and rejoice.
'Twas I that, when thou were't i' the way to heaven,
Dammed up thy passage; when thou took'st the book
To view the scriptures, then I turned the leaves
And led thine eye.

85   What, weep'st thou? 'Tis too late, despair. Farewell.
Fools that will laugh on earth, must weep in hell.   [*Exit.*]
[*Enter the Good and the Evil Angel at several doors.*]

GOOD ANGEL: Oh Faustus, if thou hadst given ear to me,
Innumerable joys had followed thee.
But thou didst love the world.

EVIL ANGEL: Gave ear to me,
90   And now must taste hell's pains perpetually.

GOOD ANGEL: Oh, what will all thy riches, pleasures, pomps,
Avail thee now?

EVIL ANGEL: Nothing but vex thee more,
To want in hell, that had on earth such store.
[*Music while the throne descends.*]

GOOD ANGEL: Oh, thou hast lost celestial happiness,
95   Pleasures unspeakable, bliss without end.
Hadst thou affected sweet divinity,
Hell, or the devil, had had no power on thee.

Hadst thou kept on that way, Faustus, behold
In what resplendent glory thou hadst sat
100   In yonder throne, like those bright shining saints,
And triumphed over hell. That thou hast lost,
And now, poor soul, must thy good angel leave thee:
The jaws of hell are open to receive thee.   [Exit.]
[Hell is discovered.]
EVIL ANGEL: Now, Faustus, let thine eyes with horror stare
105   Into that vast perpetual torture-house.
There are the furies tossing damned souls
On burning forks. Their bodies broil in lead.
There are live quarters broiling on the coals
That ne'er can die. This ever-burning chair
110   Is for o'er-tortured souls to rest them in.
These, that are fed with sops of flaming fire,
Were gluttons, and loved only delicates,
And laughed to see the poor starve at their gates.
But yet all these are nothing. Thou shalt see
115   Ten thousand tortures that more horrid be.
FAUSTUS: Oh, I have seen enough to torture me.
EVIL ANGEL: Nay, thou must feel them, taste the smart of all:
He that loves pleasure must for pleasure fall.
And so I leave thee, Faustus, till anon.
120   Then wilt thou tumble in confusion.   [Exit.]
[The clock strikes eleven.]
FAUSTUS: Ah Faustus,
Now hast thou but one bare hour to live,
And then thou must be damned perpetually.
Stand still, you ever-moving spheres of heaven,
125   That time may cease and midnight never come.
Fair nature's eye, rise, rise again, and make
Perpetual day. Or let this hour be but
A year, a month, a week, a natural day,
That Faustus may repent and save his soul.
130   O lente, lente, currite noctis equi.[7]
The stars move still, time runs, the clock will strike.
The devil will come, and Faustus must be damned.
Oh, I'll leap up to my God: who pulls me down?
See, see, where Christ's blood streams in the firmament.
135   One drop would save my soul, half a drop. Ah, my Christ!
Ah, rend not my heart for naming of my Christ!
Yet will I call on him. Oh, spare me, Lucifer!
Where is it now? 'Tis gone:
And see where God stretcheth out his arm,
140   And bends his ireful brows.
Mountains and hills, come, come, and fall on me,
And hide me from the heavy wrath of God.

7. Faustus quotes from Ovid's Amores 1.13.40: "O slowly, slowly run, horses of the night."

No, no. Then will I headlong run into the earth.
Earth, gape! Oh no, it will not harbor me.

145 You stars that reigned at my nativity,
Whose influence hath allotted death and hell,
Now draw up Faustus like a foggy mist
Into the entrails of yon laboring cloud,
That when you vomit forth into the air

150 My limbs may issue from your smoky mouths,
So that my soul may but ascend to heaven.
[*The watch strikes.*]
Ah! half the hour is past,
'Twill all be past anon.°   *soon*
Oh God, if thou wilt not have mercy on my soul,

155 Yet, for Christ's sake whose blood hath ransomed me,
Impose some end to my incessant pain.
Let Faustus live in hell a thousand years,
A hundred thousand, and at last be saved.
Oh, no end is limited to damned souls.

160 Why wert thou not a creature wanting soul?
Or why is this immortal that thou hast?
Ah, Pythagoras' *metempsychosis*,[8] were that true
This soul should fly from me, and I be changed
Unto some brutish beast.

165 All beasts are happy, for when they die
Their souls are soon dissolved in elements,
But mine must live still to be plagued in hell.
Cursed be the parents that engendered me!
No, Faustus, curse thyself, curse Lucifer,

170 That hath deprived thee of the joys of heaven.
[*The clock strikes twelve.*]
Oh, it strikes, it strikes! Now body turn to air,
Or Lucifer will bear thee quick to hell.
[*Thunder and lightning.*]
Oh soul, be changed into little water drops
And fall into the ocean, ne'er be found.
[*Thunder. Enter the Devils.*]

175 My God, my God, look not so fierce on me.
Adders and serpents, let me breathe awhile.
Ugly hell, gape not, come not, Lucifer!
I'll burn my books. Ah, Mephostophilis!   [*Exeunt with him.*]

Scene 3

[*Enter the Scholars.*]
FIRST SCHOLAR: Come, gentlemen, let us go visit Faustus,
For such a dreadful night was never seen
Since first the world's creation did begin.

8. The transmigration of souls. The Greek philosopher Pythagoras speculated that souls were reborn in other bodies in an endless progression.

Such fearful shrieks and cries were never heard.

5   Pray heaven the Doctor have escaped the danger.

SECOND SCHOLAR: Oh help us, heaven! See, here are Faustus' limbs,
      All torn asunder by the hand of death.

THIRD SCHOLAR: The devils whom Faustus served have torn him thus:
      For twixt the hours of twelve and one, methought

10   I heard him shriek and call aloud for help,
      At which self time the house seemed all on fire
      With dreadful horror of these damned fiends.

SECOND SCHOLAR: Well, gentlemen, though Faustus' end be such.
      As every Christian heart laments to think on,

15   Yet, for he was a scholar once admired
      For wondrous knowledge in our German schools,
      We'll give his mangled limbs due burial,
      And all the students clothed in mourning black
      Shall wait upon his heavy funeral.   [*Exeunt.*]

Epilogue

[*Enter the Chorus.*]

CHORUS: Cut is the branch that might have grown full straight,
      And burned is Apollo's laurel bough,
      That sometime grew within this learned man.
      Faustus is gone. Regard his hellish fall,

5   Whose fiendful fortune may exhort the wise
      Only to wonder at unlawful things,
      Whose deepness doth entice such forward wits,
      To practice more than heavenly power permits.

Terminat hora diem, Terminat Author opus.[9]
Finis.

⊷ ⊱✦⊰ ⊶

William Shakespeare
1564–1616

English colonists venturing to the New World carried with them an English Bible; if they owned a single secular book, it was probably the works of William Shakespeare. A humanist scripture of sorts, his works have never hardened into doctrine; rather, they have lent themselves to a myriad range of interpretations, each shaped by particular interests, tastes, and expectations. Ben Jonson's line—"He was not of an age, but for all time!"—describes the appeal Shakespeare has had for speakers of English and the many other languages into which his works have been translated.

Shakespeare was born in the provincial town of Stratford-on-Avon, a three-day journey from London by horse or carriage. His father, John Shakespeare, was a glover and local justice of the peace; his mother, Mary Arden, came from a family that owned considerable land in the county.

---

9. The hour ends the day, the author ends the work.

He probably went to a local grammar school where he learned Latin and read histories of the ancient world. Jonson's disparaging comment, that Shakespeare knew "small Latin and less Greek," must not be taken too seriously. Shakespeare (unlike Jonson) was not classically inclined, but his mature works reveal a mind that was extraordinarily well informed and acutely aware of rhetorical techniques and logical argument. At eighteen Shakespeare married Anne Hathaway, who was twenty-six; in the next three years they had a daughter, Susanna, and then twins, Hamnet and Judith. Six years later, perhaps after periods of teaching school in Stratford, he went to London, eventually (in 1594) to join one of the great theatrical companies of the day, the Chamberlain's Men. It was with this company that he began his career as actor, manager, and playwright. In 1599 the troupe began to put on plays at the Globe, an outdoor theater in Southwark, not far from the other principal theaters of the day—the Rose, the Bear Garden, and the Swan—and across the river from the city of London itself. Because these theaters were outside city limits, in a district known as "the liberties," they were free from the control of authorities responsible for civic order; in effect, the theater provided a place in which all kinds of ideas and ways of life, whether conventional or not, could be represented, examined, and criticized. When James I acceded to the throne in 1603, Shakespeare's company became the King's Men and played also at court and at Blackfriars, an indoor theater in London. Some critics think that the change in venue necessitated a degree of allusiveness and innuendo that was not evident in earlier productions.

During the years Shakespeare was writing for the theater, the populations of Europe were periodically devastated by the plague, and city authorities were obliged to close places of public gathering, including theaters. Shakespeare provided plays for seasons in which the theaters in London were open, composing them at lightning speed and helping to stage productions on very short notice. The plays that we now accept as Shakespeare's fall roughly into several general categories: first, the histories, largely based on the chronicles of the Tudor historian Raphael Holinshed, and the Roman plays, inspired by Plutarch's *Lives of the Ancient Romans*, written in Greek and translated by Sir Thomas North; second, the comedies, often set in the romantic world of the English countryside or an Italian town; third, the tragedies, some of which explore the dark legends of the past; and fourth, a group in the mixed genre of tragicomedy but also called, after critics in the nineteenth century, the romances. A fifth, somewhat anomalous group—*All's Well That Ends Well*, *Measure for Measure*, and *Troilus and Cressida*—falls between comedy and satire; these plays are usually termed "problem comedies."

The early phase of Shakespeare's career, the decade beginning in the late 1580s, saw the first cycle of his English histories. In four plays (known as the first tetralogy) this cycle depicted events in the reigns of Henry VI and Richard III and concluded by dramatizing the accession of the first Tudor monarch, Henry VII. Fascinated by the fate of peoples governed by feeble or oppressive rulers, Shakespeare expressed his loathing of tyranny by showing how the misgovernment of a weak king can lead to despotic rule. The cycle ends with the death of the tyrant, Richard III, and the accession of the Duke of Richmond, later Henry VII (Elizabeth's grandfather)—an action that celebrates the founder of the Tudor dynasty and the providence that had selected this family to bring peace to England. A later play, *King John*, concerns an earlier monarch whose claim to the throne is suspect; here divine right, having validated the succession of the Tudor monarchy in the first tetralogy, is made doubtful by a monarch's own viciousness. The play implies a question that Shakespeare continues to ask of history for the rest of his career: in what sense may divine right to be understood as a principle of monarchic rule? History, as Shakespeare will go on to represent it, no longer clearly demonstrates the triumph of justice but rather shows the interrelatedness of good and evil motives that end in morally ambiguous action. The first of the Roman plays, *The Tragedy of Titus Andronicus*, which tells of the Roman general's revenge for the rape of his daughter Lavinia, and the early comedies, *The Taming of the Shrew*, *The Comedy of Errors*, *Two Gentlemen of Verona*, and *Love's Labor's Lost*, which depict the effects of mistaken identity and misunderstood

speech, illustrate other themes that Shakespeare will continue to represent: the terrible consequences of the search for revenge and the unfortunate, as well as salutary, self-deceptions of love.

The second phase, culminating in productions around 1600, is marked by more and subtler comedy: *A Midsummer Night's Dream*, *The Merchant of Venice*, *The Merry Wives of Windsor*, *Much Ado About Nothing*, *As You Like It*, and *Twelfth Night*. These plays insert into plots
focusing primarily on the courtship of young couples a dramatic commentary on darker kinds
of human desire: a longing for possessions; a wish to control others, particularly children; and a
self-love so intense that it leads to fantasy and delusion. A romantic tragedy of this period,
Romeo and Juliet, shows how the gross unreason sustaining a family feud and a mysteriously
malevolent fate combine to destroy the future of lovers. A second cycle of four English histories, beginning with the deposition of Richard II and ending in the triumphs of Henry V and
the birth of Henry VI, reveals how Shakespeare complicates the genre. An ostensible motive
for the second tetralogy was the celebration of an English monarchy that had been preserved
through the ages by God's will. Yet the actions of even the least controversial of its kings are
questionable: Henry V's conquest of France is driven by greed as much as by his claim to the
French throne, which is represented as dubious even in the playtext. A second Roman play,
The Tragedy of Julius Caesar, takes up the question of tyranny in relation to the liberty inherent in a republic; the play seems most tragic when its action suggests that the Roman people do
not recognize the sacrifices that are necessary to preserve such freedom and even regard freedom itself as negligible. As a whole, these plays demonstrate the characteristics of Shakespeare's mature style. Certain recurring images unify the plays thematically and, more important, link them to contemporary habits of speech as well as to the intellectual discourse of the
period. Visual images—the I and the eye of the lover—often clarify the language of love, and
figures denoting the well-being of different kinds of "corporation," including the human body,
the family, and the body politic, signal the comprehensive order that was supposed to govern
relations among all the elements of creation.

Incorporating many of the themes in the "problem comedies," the tragedies of the same
period preoccupied Shakespeare for the seven years following the accession of James I: *Hamlet*, *Othello*, *King Lear*, *Macbeth*, *Antony and Cleopatra*, and *Coriolanus*, together with *Timon of
Athens*, a play that was apparently written in collaboration with Thomas Middleton. *All's
Well That Ends Well* and *Measure for Measure* illustrate societies that contain rather than
reject sordid or unregenerate characters, both noble and common, and thus provide opportunities for comic endings to situations that might otherwise have ended in tragedy. And making much of the need for order but exemplifying the deep disorder of the military societies of
Greece and Troy, the characters in *Troilus and Cressida* reveal the extent to which Shakespeare could imagine language as ironic and the human spirit as utterly possessed by a cynical
need to turn every occasion to its own advantage. These plays serve to introduce tragedies of
unprecedented scope.

Featuring heroes who overreach the limits of their place in life and so fail to fulfill their
obligations to themselves and their dependents, Shakespeare's later tragedies embrace a wider
range of human experience than can be explained by traditional conceptions of sin and fate.
Profoundly complex in their treatment of motivation and the operations of the will, the
tragedies entertain the idea of a beneficent deity who both permits terrible suffering and infuses, to use Hamlet's words, a "special providence in the fall of a sparrow." They reveal the blind-
ing egotism that causes fatal misperceptions of character, motive, and action; their heroes are
at once terribly in error and also strangely sympathetic. The human capacity for evil is perhaps
most fully realized in the characters of women: the bestial daughters of King Lear, Goneril and
Regan; the diabolical Lady Macbeth; the shamelessly duplicitous Cleopatra. Yet even they are
not entirely unsympathetic; in many ways their behavior responds to the challenges that other,
essentially more authoritative characters represent. The romances—*Pericles*, *Cymbeline*, *The*

Winter's Tale, and *The Tempest*—round out the final phase of Shakespeare's dramatic career, representing (like the comedies) the restoration of family harmony and (like the histories) the return of good government. The deeply troubling divisions within families and states that characterize the tragedies are the basis for the restorative unions in the romances. Their depiction of passages of time and space that allow providential recoveries of health and prosperity to both individual characters and whole bodies politic are largely owing to the intervention of women. Unlike the women of the tragedies, the daughters and wives of the romances are generative in the broadest sense. They heal their fathers and husbands by restoring to their futures the possibility of descendents and therefore of dynastic continuity. Their agency is, in turn, sustained by forces identified as divine and outside history. *Henry VIII*, a history, and *Two Noble Kinsmen*, a romance, both probably composed jointly with John Fletcher, conclude Shakespeare's career as a dramatist.

Shakespeare also wrote narrative and lyric poems of great power, notably *Venus and Adonis*, *The Rape of Lucrece*, and a cycle of 154 sonnets. In a bold departure from tradition, the sonnets celebrate the poet's steadfast love for a young man (never identified), his competitive rivalry with another poet (sometimes identified as Christopher Marlowe), and his troubled relationship with a woman who has dark features. The cycle encourages an interpretation that accounts for its romantic elements, but it also thwarts any obvious construction of events. It is thought that most of the sonnets were composed in the mid-1590s, although they were not published until 1609, apparently without Shakespeare's oversight. Their order therefore cannot be assigned to Shakespeare, and for this reason alone their function as narrative must remain problematic. Still, the reader can trace their representation of successive relations between persons and themes: the young man, although himself derelict in the duties of friendship, will remain beloved by the poet and be made immortal by his verse, while the dark lady, who is unscrupulous and afflicted with venereal disease, receives only expressions of desire and lust, shadowed by the poet's disdain and self-loathing.

In a sense, Shakespeare has always been up to date. True, his language is not what is heard today, and his characters are shaped by forces within his culture, not ours. Yet we continue to see his plays on stage and in film, sometimes as recreations of the productions that historians of theater think he knew and saw but more often as reconceived with the addition of modern costumes, settings, and music as well as some strategic cutting of the dramatic text. Earlier periods produced their own kinds of Shakespeare. The Restoration stage, with scenery that allowed audiences to imagine they were looking through a window to life itself, put on plays that were embellished and trimmed to satisfy the taste of the time. Some producers omitted characters who were considered superfluous (the porter in *Macbeth*); others added characters who were judged essential for balance (Miranda's sister, Dorinda, in *The Tempest*). *King Lear* acquired a happy ending when Edgar married Cordelia. No one production of any period has defined a play entirely; every director has had his or her vision of what Shakespeare meant an audience to see. These reinterpretations testify to the perennial vitality of a playwright who was indeed, as Jonson said, "for all time."

THE SONNETS   The entire sequence numbers 154 sonnets. The first fourteen encourage a young man to marry and have children and may have been commissioned by his family. Neither the young man nor his family has been identified, although some readers have thought Henry Wriosthesley, Earl of Southampton, a possible subject. Sonnet 20 initiates a long sequence of sonnets addressed to a young man as the poet's lover. Beginning with Sonnet 78, the poet complains that a rival poet is stealing his subject—the young man's virtue and grace—to the detriment of his own poetry. Who Shakespeare's rival is (or whether he is in fact a single person) is not known, although some readers have considered Christopher Marlowe a possibility. A final set of twenty-eight sonnets introduces a new character to the sequence, a figure often referred to as "the dark lady," who is the lover of both the poet and the young man. The threesome make up a dramatic unity that is fraught with tension and anguish.

Sonnets

1

From fairest creatures we desire increase,
That thereby beauty's rose might never die,
But as the riper° should by time decease,   *the older person*
His tender heir might bear his memory;
5   But thou, contracted° to thine own bright eyes,   *engaged, shrunk*
Feed'st thy light's flame with self-substantial fuel,
Making a famine where abundance lies,
Thyself thy foe, to thy sweet self too cruel.
Thou that art now the world's fresh ornament,
10 And only herald to the gaudy spring,
Within thine own bud buriest thy content,
And, tender churl, mak'st waste in niggarding.°   *hoarding*
    Pity the world, or else this glutton be:
    To eat the world's due, by the grave and thee.[1]

18

Shall I compare thee to a summer's day?
Thou art more lovely and more temperate.
Rough winds do shake the darling buds of May,
And summer's lease hath all too short a date.°   *duration*
5   Sometimes too hot the eye of heaven shines,
And often is his gold complexion dimmed;
And every fair from fair sometimes declines,
By chance or nature's changing course untrimmed.°   *stripped bare*
But thy eternal summer shall not fade
10 Nor lose possession of that fair thou ow'st;°   *own*
Nor shall Death brag thou wanderest in his shade,
When in eternal lines° to time thou grow'st.   *of verse*
    So long as men can breathe or eyes can see,
    So long lives this, and this gives life to thee.

20

A woman's face with Nature's own hand painted
Hast thou, the master-mistress of my passion;[2]
A woman's gentle heart, but not acquainted
With shifting change, as is false women's fashion;
5   An eye more bright than theirs, less false in rolling,°   *straying*
Gilding the object whereupon it gazeth;
A man in hue, all hues in his controlling,[3]
Which steals men's eyes and women's souls amazeth.
And for a woman wert thou first created,

---

1. Have pity on the world and do not consume your own substance by refusing to engender the child you owe now to the world and finally to the grave.
2. Feminine in appearance, the young man is both a master and a mistress of the poet's passion. This is the first of a series of sonnets in which Shakespeare addresses the young man in clearly erotic language.
3. A man in appearance, he determines the nature of what he sees, what is apparent to him.

10   Till Nature, as she wrought thee, fell a-doting,°   *in love*
     And by addition me of thee defeated,[4]
     By adding one thing to my purpose nothing.
         But since she pricked thee out for women's pleasure,
         Mine be thy love and thy love's use their treasure.

29

     When, in disgrace with fortune and men's eyes,
     I all alone beweep my outcast state,
     And trouble deaf heaven with my bootless° cries,   *unavailing*
     And look upon myself and curse my fate,
5   Wishing me like to one more rich in hope,
     Featured like him, like him with friends possessed,
     Desiring this man's art and that man's scope,°   *powers*
     With what I most enjoy contented least;
     Yet in these thoughts myself almost despising,
10   Haply° I think on thee, and then my state,   *perhaps*
     Like to the lark at break of day arising
     From sullen earth, sings hymns at heaven's gate;
         For thy sweet love remembered such wealth brings
         That then I scorn to change° my state with kings.   *exchange*

30

     When to the sessions° of sweet silent thought[5]   *law courts*
     I summon up remembrance of things past,
     I sigh the lack of many a thing I sought,
     And with old woes new wail my dear time's waste.[6]
5   Then can I drown an eye, unused to flow,
     For precious friends hid in death's dateless° night,   *endless*
     And weep afresh love's long since cancelled woe,
     And moan th'expense° of many a vanished sight.   *what it cost*
     Then can I grieve at grievances foregone,
10   And heavily° from woe to woe tell o'er   *sorrowfully*
     The sad account of fore-bemoanèd moan,
     Which I new pay as if not paid before.[7]
         But if the while I think on thee, dear friend,
         All losses are restored, and sorrows end.

55

     Not marble nor the gilded monuments
     Of princes shall outlive this powerful rhyme,
     But you shall shine more bright in these contents

4. The last four lines of the sonnet are full of double meanings: the thing loving nature adds to the young man is a penis; this points or "pricks" him out for women's pleasure or "use" (with the added suggestion that his body is capital, which through usury generates interest); but the poet reserves for himself the young man's love, which is beyond commerce and has no price.

5. The conceit governing this imagery depends on the poet's association of his sense of guilt at his misdeeds with a notion of a debt. He represents himself as a debtor who

cannot discharge what he owes to others because the complaints against him remain constantly fresh in his mind. He also figures as in debt to himself, as it is his time that he has wasted in reviewing these complaints. His debts are paid, however, when he thinks of his friend.

6. I bemoan the waste of my time by remembering anew former sadness.

7. I add up the sorrows and complaints against me that I have already accounted for; I pay for them as if they were new debts; so I add to the sum I have wasted.

Than unswept stone besmeared with sluttish° time.   *dirty*
5   When wasteful war shall statues overturn,
And broils° root out the work of masonry,   *uprisings*
Nor° Mars his sword nor war's quick fire shall burn   *neither*
The living record of your memory.
'Gainst death and all-oblivious° enmity   *casting into oblivion*
10   Shall you pace forth; your praise shall still find room
Even in the eyes of all posterity
That wear this world out to the ending doom.°   *judgment day*
    So, till the judgment that yourself° arise,   *when you yourself*
    You live in this, and dwell in lovers' eyes.

60

Like as the waves make towards the pebbled shore,
So do our minutes hasten to their end;
Each changing place with that which goes before,
In sequent° toil all forwards do contend.°   *successive / strive*
5   Nativity, once in the main° of light,   *sea*
Crawls to maturity, wherewith being crowned,
Crookèd eclipses 'gainst his glory fight,
And Time that gave doth now his gift confound.°   *destroy*
Time doth transfix° the flourish set on youth   *puncture*
10   And delves° the parallels in beauty's brow,   *digs*
Feeds on the rarities of nature's truth,
And nothing stands but for his scythe to mow.
    And yet to times in hope my verse shall stand,
    Praising thy worth despite his cruel hand.

73

That time of year thou mayst in me behold
When yellow leaves, or none, or few, do hang
Upon those boughs which shake against the cold,
Bare ruined choirs[8] where late the sweet birds sang.
5   In me thou seest the twilight of such day
As after sunset fadeth in the west,
Which by and by black night doth take away,
Death's second self, that seals up all in rest.
In me thou seest the glowing of such fire
10   That on the ashes of his youth doth lie
As the deathbed whereon it must expire,
Consumed with that which it was nourished by.
    This thou perceiv'st, which makes thy love more strong,
    To love that well which thou must leave ere long.

87

Farewell! Thou art too dear for my possessing,
  And like enough thou know'st thy estimate.°   *value*

---

8. The choir is the section of a church reserved for the singers in the choir. "Choir" puns on "quire," the gathering of pages in a book, and thus recalls the "leaves" in line 2.

The charter of thy worth gives thee releasing;[9]
My bonds in thee are all determinate.°   *ended*
5   For how do I hold thee but by thy granting,
And for that riches where is my deserving?
The cause of this fair gift in me is wanting,
And so my patent[1] back again is swerving.
Thyself thou gav'st, thy own worth then not knowing,
10   Or me, to whom thou gav'st it, else mistaking;
So thy great gift, upon misprision° growing,   *error*
Comes home again, on better judgment making.
　　Thus have I had thee as a dream doth flatter,
　　In sleep a king, but waking no such matter.

106

When in the chronicle of wasted° time   *past*
I see descriptions of the fairest wights,°   *people*
And beauty making beautiful old rhyme
In praise of ladies dead and lovely knights,
5   Then, in the blazon° of sweet beauty's best,   *catalogue*
Of hand, of foot, of lip, of eye, of brow,
I see their antique pen would have expressed
Even such a beauty as you master° now.   *possess*
So all their praises are but prophecies
10   Of this our time, all you prefiguring;
And, for° they looked but with divining eyes,   *because*
They had not skill enough your worth to sing.
　　For we, which now behold these present days,
　　Have eyes to wonder, but lack tongues to praise.[2]

116

Let me not to the marriage of true minds
Admit impediments. Love is not love
Which alters when it alteration finds,°   *in the beloved*
Or bends with the remover to remove.
5   O, no, it is an ever-fixèd mark°   *landmark*
That looks on tempests and is never shaken;
It is the star to every wandering bark,
Whose worth's unknown, although his height be taken.[3]
Love's not Time's fool, though rosy lips and cheeks
10   Within his bending sickle's compass° come;   *range*
Love alters not with his brief hours and weeks,
But bears it out even to the edge of doom.°   *judgment day*
　　If this be error and upon me proved,
　　I never writ, nor no man ever loved.

9. You are worth so much that you can pay off all obligations you owe me; in other words, I have no right to you.
1. Deed granting a monopoly.
2. The poets of antiquity could not describe your perfection because they could only guess at it; we recognize

your perfection but lack but the skill to describe it.
3. The star by which ships navigate by measuring its alti-
tude from the horizon (known values) is itself beyond
valuation.

126

O thou, my lovely boy, who in thy power
Dost hold Time's fickle glass,° his sickle hour;   *hourglass*
Who hast by waning grown, and therein show'st
Thy lovers withering as thy sweet self grow'st;
5   If Nature, sovereign mistress over wrack,°   *destruction*
As thou goest onwards, still will pluck thee back,
She keeps thee to this purpose, that her skill
May Time disgrace and wretched minutes kill.[4]
Yet fear her, O thou minion° of her pleasure!   *slave*
10   She may detain, but not still keep, her treasure.
    Her audit, though delayed, answered must be,
    And her quietus° is to render thee.[5]   *settlement*

130

My mistress' eyes are nothing like the sun;
Coral is far more red than her lips' red;
If snow be white, why then her breasts are dun;°   *brown*
If hairs be wires, black wires grow on her head.
5   I have seen roses damasked,° red and white,   *mingled*
But no such roses see I in her cheeks;
And in some perfumes is there more delight
Than in the breath that from my mistress reeks.
I love to hear her speak, yet well I know
10   That music hath a far more pleasing sound.
I grant I never saw a goddess go;
My mistress, when she walks, treads on the ground.
    And yet, by heaven, I think my love as rare
    As any she belied with false compare.[6]

138

When my love swears that she is made of truth
I do believe her, though I know she lies,
That she might think me some untutored youth,
Unlearnèd in the world's false subtleties.
5   Thus vainly thinking that she thinks me young,
Although she knows my days are past the best,
Simply I credit her false-speaking tongue;
On both sides thus is simple truth suppressed.
But wherefore says she not she is unjust?
10   And wherefore say not I that I am old?
O, love's best habit is in seeming° trust,   *apparent*
And age in love loves not to have years told.
    Therefore I lie° with her, and she with me,   *deceive; have sex*
    And in our faults by lies we flattered be.

---

4. His lover's power can hold back time and prevent his sickle from mowing down his green youth; paradoxically, while others grow old, he grows young.
5. Yet Nature owes you to Time and will pay her debt by handing you over at last.
6. The couplet suggests ironic compliment: my mistress is exceptional in that she has set new standards for true beauty by a comparison that defies its standards.

TWELFTH NIGHT; OR, WHAT YOU WILL. Shakespeare's *Twelfth Night; or, What You Will* was first performed during the feast of Candlemas at the Middle Temple, one of the Inns of Court, on 2 February 1602. An eyewitness to that performance, the barrister John Manningham, found the story of the puritanical steward Malvolio the most memorable: "A good practice in it to make the steward believe his lady widow was involved with him, by counterfeiting a letter as from his Lady . . . telling him what she liked best in him, and prescribing his gesture in smiling, his apparel, etc. And then when he came to practice making him believe he was mad." However distant the memory of the twelfth day of Christmas as a feast of misrule was at the time of the play's first performance, the element of the world turned upside down in Shakespeare's comedy delighted the carousing young lawyers. The plot of how the sanctimonious Malvolio is fooled into believing that he might be the love object of Olivia, his female employer, and so acts out the most preposterous courtship of her is part of the play's larger parody of the self-delusion of desire and of the literary forms in which that desire is expressed. The play sends up the conventions of courtly love, particularly as stylized in the lyric love poetry that was popular among young London men with literary ambition as well as self-dramatizing aristocrats in the Elizabethan court. This was the poetry of Sir Walter Raleigh and the young John Donne, with all its teasing eroticism, hyperbolic flattery, and Petrarchan angst. In *Twelfth Night*, the three central characters—Orsino, Olivia, and Viola—all act out their similarly stylized passions. Orsino lolls about listening to sad music as he pines for love of Olivia. She vows to do nothing but mourn for her dead brother—for seven years—until she meets Cesario, a servant whom Orsino has sent to woo her. Cesario, none other than the shipwrecked Viola disguised as a male servant, praises Olivia from head to toe and makes witty, erotic jokes and complaints against the lady's cruelty that capture her fancy. Olivia is jolted out of mourning and into infatuation. Cesario/Viola in turn falls almost immediately in love with Orsino, and her love grows in heat not despite but more likely because of the apparent impossibility of fulfillment. Viola's twin Sebastian meanwhile flees Antonio, a man who has taken care of him for three months since being shipwrecked, only to fall haphazardly into Olivia's arms at the right moment to become the realization of her infatuation for Cesario. All these self-deluded desires are expressed in some of Shakespeare's most lyrical dramatic verse. The play is studded throughout with such stars of lyric illumination as the fool Feste's songs. The sad ironies he reflects on and the enlightening wit he laces his barbs with provide a kind of detachment and wisdom that set into relief the absurdity of the lovers' self-seriousness. At the end of the play, the lovers—and even the drunkard Sir Toby Belch and the serving maid Maria—are matched as couples, while only Malvolio vows revenge. Antonio, the one character whose passion seems to be based on any real acquaintance with the object of his affection, is also left alone; the text is silent on his fate. In the comic world of *Twelfth Night*, mistaken identity and lack of self-knowledge are, if not for Antonio, at least overcome for some by "nature's bias"—an openness to affection and the ability to snatch pleasure when the lucky opportunity arises.

The text of *Twelfth Night* is based on the 1623 Folio.

Twelfth Night; or, What You Will

The Names of the Actors

ORSINO, *Duke (or Count) of Illyria*
VALENTINE, *gentleman attending on Orsino*
CURIO, *gentleman attending on Orsino*

VIOLA, *a shipwrecked lady, later disguised as Cesario*
SEBASTIAN, *twin brother of Viola*

ANTONIO, *a sea captain, friend to Sebastian*
CAPTAIN *of the shipwrecked vessel*

OLIVIA, *a rich countess of Illyria*
MARIA, *gentlewoman in Olivia's household*
SIR TOBY BELCH, *Olivia's uncle*
SIR ANDREW AGUECHEEK, *a companion of Sir Toby*
MALVOLIO, *steward of Olivia's household*
FABIAN, *a member of Olivia's household*
FESTE, *a clown, also called* FOOL, *Olivia's jester*

A PRIEST
FIRST OFFICER
SECOND OFFICER

LORDS, SAILORS, MUSICIANS, and OTHER ATTENDANTS

Scene: *A city in Illyria, and the seacoast near it*

ACT 1

Scene 1¹

[Enter Orsino Duke of Illyria, Curio, and other lords (with musicians).]

ORSINO: If music be the food of love, play on;
    Give me excess of it, that surfeiting,
    The appetite may sicken and so die.
    That strain again! It had a dying fall;°   cadence
5   O, it came o'er my ear like the sweet sound
    That breathes upon a bank of violets,
    Stealing and giving odor. Enough, no more.
    'Tis not so sweet now as it was before.
    O spirit of love, how quick° and fresh art thou,   alive
10   That, notwithstanding thy capacity
    Receiveth as the sea, naught enters there,
    Of what validity° and pitch° soe'er,   value / worth
    But falls into abatement° and low price   depreciation
    Even in a minute! So full of shapes° is fancy°   imagined forms / love
15   That it alone is high fantastical.°   highly imaginative
CURIO: Will you go hunt, my lord?
ORSINO: What, Curio?
CURIO: The hart.
ORSINO: Why, so I do, the noblest that I have.°   pun on "heart"
    O, when mine eyes did see Olivia first,
    Methought she purged the air of pestilence.
20   That instant was I turned into a hart,
    And my desires, like fell° and cruel hounds,   fierce
    E'er since pursue me.²
    [Enter Valentine.]
           How now, what news from her?

1. Location: Orsino's court.   Diana and killed by his own hounds.
2. Allusion to Ovid: Actaeon was turned into a stag by

VALENTINE: So please my lord, I might not be admitted,
    But from her handmaid do return this answer:
25   The element° itself, till seven years' heat,°   *sky / seven summers*
    Shall not behold her face at ample view;
    But like a cloistress° she will veilèd walk,   *nun*
    And water once a day her chamber round
    With eye-offending brine—all this to season°   *preserve*
30   A brother's dead love, which she would keep fresh
    And lasting in her sad remembrance.
ORSINO: O, she that hath a heart of that fine frame°   *construction*
    To pay this debt of love but to a brother,
    How will she love, when the rich golden shaft°   *Cupid's arrow*
35   Hath killed the flock of all affections else°   *other feelings*
    That live in her; when liver, brain, and heart,[3]
    These sovereign thrones, are all supplied, and filled
    Her sweet perfections,[4] with one self king!°   *single lord*
    Away before me to sweet beds of flowers.
40   Love-thoughts lie rich when canopied with bowers.   *[Exeunt.]*

Scene 2[5]

[Enter Viola, a Captain, and sailors.]
VIOLA: What country, friends, is this?
CAPTAIN: This is Illyria, lady.
VIOLA: And what should I do in Illyria?
    My brother he is in Elysium.[6]
5   Perchance° he is not drowned. What think you, sailors?   *perhaps*
CAPTAIN: It is perchance° that you yourself were saved.   *by chance*
VIOLA: O, my poor brother! And so perchance may he be.
CAPTAIN: True, madam, and to comfort you with chance,°   *possibilities*
    Assure yourself, after our ship did split,
10   When you and those poor number saved with you
    Hung on our driving° boat, I saw your brother,   *drifting*
    Most provident in peril, bind himself,
    Courage and hope both teaching him the practice,
    To a strong mast that lived° upon the sea;   *floated*
15   Where, like Arion[7] on the dolphin's back,
    I saw him hold acquaintance with the waves
    So long as I could see.
VIOLA: For saying so, there's gold. *[She gives money.]*
    Mine own escape unfoldeth to my hope,°   *gives me hope*
20   Whereto thy speech serves for authority,
    The like of him. Know'st thou this country?
CAPTAIN: Ay, madam, well, for I was bred and born
    Not three hours' travel from this very place.
VIOLA: Who governs here?

---

3. Seats of the passions.
4. I.e., her sweet perfections are filled.
5. Location: The coast of the Adriatic.
6. Home of the blessed dead.

7. Greek poet who jumped overboard to escape murderous sailors and charmed dolphins with his lyre, so that they carried him to shore.

CAPTAIN: A noble duke, in nature as in name.

VIOLA: What is his name?

CAPTAIN: Orsino.

VIOLA: Orsino! I have heard my father name him.
　　　He was a bachelor then.

CAPTAIN: And so is now, or was so very late;
　　　For but a month ago I went from hence,
　　　And then 'twas fresh in murmur°—as, you know,　　　*rumor*
　　　What great ones do the less° will prattle of—　　　*social inferiors*
　　　That he did seek the love of fair Olivia.

VIOLA: What's she?

CAPTAIN: A virtuous maid, the daughter of a count
　　　That died some twelvemonth since, then leaving her
　　　In the protection of his son, her brother,
　　　Who shortly also died; for whose dear love,
40　　They say, she hath abjured the sight
　　　And company of men.

VIOLA:　　　　　　　　O, that I served that lady,
　　　And might not be delivered° to the world　　　*revealed*
　　　Till I had made mine own occasion mellow,°　　　*ready*
　　　What my estate° is!　　　　　　*social position*

CAPTAIN:　　　　　That were hard to compass,°　　　*bring about*
45　　Because she will admit no kind of suit,
　　　No, not° the Duke's.　　　　　　*not even*

VIOLA: There is a fair behavior° in thee, Captain,　　*conduct; appearance*
　　　And though that nature with a beauteous wall
　　　Doth oft close in pollution, yet of thee
50　　I will believe thou hast a mind that suits
　　　With this thy fair and outward character.°　　　*appearance*
　　　I prithee, and I'll pay thee bounteously,
　　　Conceal me what I am, and be my aid
　　　For such disguise as haply shall become
55　　The form of my intent.° I'll serve this duke.　　*my outward purpose*
　　　Thou shalt present me as an eunuch[8] to him.
　　　It may be worth thy pains, for I can sing
　　　And speak to him in many sorts of music
　　　That will allow° me very worth his service.　　　*prove*
60　　What else may hap, to time I will commit;
　　　Only shape thou thy silence to my wit.°　　　*plan*

CAPTAIN: Be you his eunuch, and your mute° I'll be;　　*silent attendant*
　　　When my tongue blabs, then let mine eyes not see.

VIOLA: I thank thee. Lead me on.　　　　　*[Exeunt.]*

Scene 3[9]

[Enter Sir Toby [Belch] and Maria.]

SIR TOBY: What a plague means my niece to take the death of her brother thus? I
　　　am sure care's an enemy to life.

---

8. Castrato, or male soprano singer, which would explain　　9. Location: Olivia's house.
her high-pitched voice.

MARIA: By my troth, Sir Toby, you must come in earlier o'nights. Your cousin,[1] my lady, takes great exceptions to your ill hours.

SIR TOBY: Why, let her except before excepted.[2]

MARIA: Ay, but you must confine yourself within the modest limits of order.

SIR TOBY: Confine? I'll confine myself no finer[3] than I am. These clothes are good enough to drink in, and so be these boots too. An[4] they be not, let them hang themselves in their own straps.

MARIA: That quaffing and drinking will undo you. I heard my lady talk of it yesterday, and of a foolish knight that you brought in one night here to be her wooer.

SIR TOBY: Who, Sir Andrew Aguecheek?

MARIA: Ay, he.

SIR TOBY: He's as tall[5] a man as any's in Illyria.

MARIA: What's that to the purpose?

SIR TOBY: Why, he has three thousand ducats a year.

MARIA: Ay, but he'll have but a year in all these ducats.[6] He's a very fool and a prodigal.

SIR TOBY: Fie, that you'll say so! He plays o' the viol-degamboys,[7] and speaks three or four languages word for word without book, and hath all the good gifts of nature.

MARIA: He hath indeed, almost natural,[8] for, besides that he's a fool, he's a great quarreler, and but that he hath the gift of a coward to allay the gust[9] he hath
25   in quarreling, 'tis thought among the prudent he would quickly have the gift of a grave.

SIR TOBY: By this hand, they are scoundrels and substractors[1] that say so of him. Who are they?

MARIA: They that add, moreover, he's drunk nightly in your company.

SIR TOBY: With drinking healths to my niece. I'll drink to her as long as there is a passage in my throat and drink in Illyria. He's a coward and a coistrel[2] that will not drink to my niece till his brains turn o' the toe like a parish top.[3] What, wench? *Castiliano vulgo!*[4] For here comes Sir Andrew Agueface.[5]

[*Enter Sir Andrew (Aguecheek).*]

SIR ANDREW: Sir Toby Belch! How now, Sir Toby Belch?

SIR TOBY: Sweet Sir Andrew!

SIR ANDREW [*to Maria*]: Bless you, fair shrew.[6]

MARIA: And you too, sir.

SIR TOBY: Accost,[7] Sir Andrew, accost.

SIR ANDREW: What's that?

SIR TOBY: My niece's chambermaid.[8]

SIR ANDREW: Good Mistress Accost, I desire better acquaintance.

---

1. Kinswoman.
2. I.e., let her take exception all she wants; I don't care (plays on the cant legal phrase, *exceptis excipiendis*, "with the exceptions before named").
3. Tighter; better.
4. If.
5. Brave; tall.
6. He'll spend all his money in a year.
7. Predecessor to the violincello.
8. Play on the sense "born idiot."
9. Taste.
1. Detractors.

2. Horse groom (base fellow).
3. Large top, spun by whipping, provided by the parish as a form of exercise.
4. Uncertain meaning. Possibly a call for politeness, or else a form of "speak of the devil."
5. With the thin, pale countenance of someone suffering from ague, a fever marked by chills.
6. Small creature (connotation of shrewishness probably unintended).
7. Greet her.
8. A lady-in-waiting, not a servant.

MARIA: My name is Mary, sir.

SIR ANDREW: Good Mistress Mary Accost—

SIR TOBY: You mistake, knight. "Accost" is front her,[9] board her,[1] woo her, assail her.

SIR ANDREW: By my troth, I would not undertake her in this company. Is that the meaning of "accost"?

MARIA: Fare you well, gentlemen. [*Going.*]

SIR TOBY: An thou let part[2] so, Sir Andrew, would thou mightst never draw sword again.

SIR ANDREW: An you part so, mistress, I would I might never draw sword again. Fair lady, do you think you have fools in hand?[3]

MARIA: Sir, I have not you by the hand.

SIR ANDREW: Marry,[4] but you shall have, and here's my hand. [*He gives her his hand.*]

MARIA: Now, sir, thought is free. I pray you, bring your hand to the buttery-bar,[5]
55   and let it drink.

SIR ANDREW: Wherefore, sweetheart? What's your metaphor?

MARIA: It's dry,[6] sir.

SIR ANDREW: Why, I think so. I am not such an ass but I can keep my hand dry. But what's your jest?

MARIA: A dry[7] jest, sir.

SIR ANDREW: Are you full of them?

MARIA: Ay, sir, I have them at my fingers' ends.[8] Marry, now I let go your hand, I am barren. [*She lets go his hand.*]   [*Exit Maria.*]

SIR TOBY: O knight, thou lack'st a cup of canary![9] When did I see thee so put
65   down?[1]

SIR ANDREW: Never in your life, I think, unless you see canary put me down.[2] Methinks sometimes I have no more wit than a Christian or an ordinary man has. But I am a great eater of beef, and I believe that does harm to my wit.

SIR TOBY: No question.

SIR ANDREW: An I thought that, I'd forswear it. I'll ride home tomorrow, Sir Toby.

SIR TOBY: *Pourquoi,*[3] my dear knight?

SIR ANDREW: What is *"pourquoi"*? Do or not do? I would I had bestowed that time in the tongues[4] that I have in fencing, dancing, and bearbaiting. O, had I but followed the arts![5]

SIR TOBY: Then hadst thou had an excellent head of hair.

SIR ANDREW: Why, would that have mended my hair?

SIR TOBY: Past question, for thou seest it will not curl by nature.

SIR ANDREW: But it becomes me well enough, does't not?

SIR TOBY: Excellent. It hangs like flax on a distaff;[6] and I hope to see a huswife
80   take thee between her legs and spin it off.[7]

SIR ANDREW: Faith, I'll home tomorrow, Sir Toby. Your niece will not be seen, or if she be, it's four to one she'll none of me. The Count himself here hard by[8] woos her.

9. Come alongside her.
1. As in a naval encounter.
2. If you let her leave.
3. Have fools to deal with (Mary chooses to take it literally).
4. Indeed.
5. Door of the wine-cellar.
6. Thirsty; aged and sexually weak.
7. Ironic; barren (referring to Sir Andrew).
8. At my disposal; in my hand.
9. Sweet wine from the Canary Islands.

1. Discomfited.
2. Knocked flat.
3. Why.
4. Languages, perhaps with a pun on curling-tongs.
5. Liberal arts (but Sir Toby plays on arts as "artifice").
6. Staff for holding flax during spinning.
7. Treat your hair like flax to be spun; cause you to lose it through venereal disease ("huswife" may be a pun on "hussy").
8. Nearby.

SIR TOBY: She'll none o' the Count. She'll not match above her degree,⁹ neither in
85   estate,¹ years, nor wit; I have heard her swear 't. Tut; there's life in 't,² man.

SIR ANDREW: I'll stay a month longer. I am a fellow o' the strangest mind i' the
        world; I delight in masques and revels sometimes altogether.³

SIR TOBY: Art thou good at these kickshawses,⁴ knight?

SIR ANDREW: As any man in Illyria, whatsoever he be, under the degree of my
90   betters,⁵ and yet I will not compare with an old man.⁶

SIR TOBY: What is thy excellence in a galliard,⁷ knight?

SIR ANDREW: Faith, I can cut a caper.⁸

SIR TOBY: And I can cut the mutton to 't.

SIR ANDREW: And I think I have the back-trick⁹ simply as strong as any man in
95   Illyria.

SIR TOBY: Wherefore are these things hid? Wherefore have these gifts a curtain
        before 'em? Are they like to take¹ dust, like Mistress Mall's picture?² Why
        dost thou not go to church in a galliard and come home in a coranto?³ My
        very walk should be a jig; I would not so much as make water but in a sink-a-
100   pace.⁴ What dost thou mean? Is it a world to hide virtues⁵ in? I did think,
        by the excellent constitution of thy leg, it was formed under the star of a
        galliard.⁶

SIR ANDREW: Ay, 'tis strong, and it does indifferent well⁷ in a dun-colored stock.⁸
        Shall we set about some revels?

SIR TOBY: What shall we do else? Were we not born under Taurus?⁹

SIR ANDREW: Taurus? That's sides and heart.

SIR TOBY: No, sir, it is legs and thighs. Let me see thee caper. [Sir Andrew capers.]
        Ha, higher! Ha, ha, excellent!   [Exeunt.]

Scene 4¹

[Enter Valentine, and Viola in man's attire.]

VALENTINE: If the Duke continue these favors towards you, Cesario, you are like
        to be much advanced. He hath known you but three days, and already you
        are no stranger.

VIOLA: You either fear his humor² or my negligence, that you call in question the
5   continuance of his love. Is he inconstant, sir, in his favors?

VALENTINE: No, believe me.

[Enter Duke (Orsino), Curio, and attendants.]

VIOLA: I thank you. Here comes the Count.

ORSINO: Who saw Cesario, ho?

VIOLA: On your attendance,° my lord, here.   at your service

ORSINO: Stand you awhile aloof. [The others stand aside.] Cesario,
        Thou know'st no less but all.° I have unclasped   everything

9. Rank.
1. Fortune.
2. There's hope left.
3. In all respects.
4. Trifles (from the French quelque chose).
5. Excepting my social superiors.
6. Experienced person.
7. Lively dance in triple-time. 8. Lively leap; spice used with mutton (mutton suggests "whore").
9. Backward step in the galliard.
1. Likely to collect.
2. Any woman's portrait (usually kept under protective glass).
3. Running dance.
4. Dance like the galliard (French cinquepace).
5. Talents.
6. Under a star favorable to dancing.
7. Well enough.
8. Stocking.
9. Zodiacal sign said to govern legs and thighs (Sir Andrew is mistaken).
1. Location: Orsino's court.
2. Changeableness.

> To thee the book even of my secret soul.
> Therefore, good youth, address thy gait° unto her;   go
> Be not denied access, stand at her doors,
15 And tell them, there thy fixèd foot shall grow
> Till thou have audience.
> VIOLA: Sure, my noble lord,
> If she be so abandoned to her sorrow
> As it is spoke, she never will admit me.
> ORSINO: Be clamorous and leap all civil bounds°   bounds of civility
20 Rather than make unprofited return.
> VIOLA: Say I do speak with her, my lord, what then?
> ORSINO: O, then unfold the passion of my love;
> Surprise° her with discourse of my dear faith.   take her by storm
> It shall become° thee well to act my woes;   suit
25 She will attend it better in thy youth
> Than in a nuncio's° of more grave aspect.   messenger's
> VIOLA: I think not so, my lord.
> ORSINO: Dear lad, believe it;
> For they shall yet belie thy happy years
> That say thou art a man. Diana's lip
30 Is not more smooth and rubious;° thy small pipe°   ruby red / voice
> Is as the maiden's organ, shrill and sound,°   high and clear
> And all is semblative° a woman's part.   resembling
> I know thy constellation° is right apt   predestined nature
> For this affair.—Some four or five attend him.
35 All, if you will, for I myself am best
> When least in company.—Prosper well in this,
> And thou shalt live as freely as thy lord,
> To call his fortunes thine.
> VIOLA: I'll do my best
> To woo your lady. [Aside.] Yet a barful strife!°   conflict full of impediments
40 Whoe'er I woo, myself would be his wife.   [Exeunt.]

Scene 5³

[Enter Maria and Clown (Feste).]

MARIA: Nay, either tell me where thou hast been, or I will not open my lips so wide
as a bristle may enter in way of thy excuse. My lady will hang thee for thy
absence.

FESTE: Let her hang me. He that is well hanged in this world needs to fear no
5 colors.⁴

MARIA: Make that good.⁵

FESTE: He shall see none to fear.⁶

MARIA: A good Lenten⁷ answer. I can tell thee where that saying was born, of "I
fear no colors."

FESTE: Where, good Mistress Mary?

MARIA: In the wars,⁸ and that may you be bold to say in your foolery.

---

3. Location: Olivia's house.   6. He'll be dead and, therefore, fear no one.
4. Fear nothing.   7. Meager, like Lenten fare.
5. Explain that.   8. In war, "colors" would be enemy flags.

FESTE: Well, God give them wisdom that have it; and those that are fools, let them use their talents.[9]

MARIA: Yet you will be hanged for being so long absent; or to be turned away,[1] is
15 not that as good as a hanging to you?

FESTE: Many a good hanging[2] prevents a bad marriage; and for turning away, let summer bear it out.[3]

MARIA: You are resolute, then?

FESTE: Not so, neither, but I am resolved on two points.[4]

MARIA: That if one break, the other will hold; or if both break, your gaskins[5] fall.

FESTE: Apt, in good faith, very apt. Well, go thy way. If Sir Toby would leave drinking, thou wert as witty a piece of Eve's flesh as any in Illyria.

MARIA: Peace, you rogue, no more o' that. Here comes my lady. Make your excuse wisely, you were best.[6]   [Exit.]

[Enter Lady Olivia with Malvolio (and attendants).]

FESTE [aside]: Wit, an 't be thy will, put me into good fooling! Those wits that think they have thee do very oft prove fools, and I that am sure I lack thee may pass for a wise man. For what says Quinapalus?[7] "Better a witty fool than a foolish wit."—God bless thee, lady!

OLIVIA [to attendants]: Take the fool away.

FESTE: Do you not hear, fellows? Take away the lady.

OLIVIA: Go to,[8] you're a dry[9] fool. I'll no more of you. Besides, you grow dishonest.[1]

FESTE: Two faults, madonna,[2] that drink and good counsel will amend. For give the
    dry[3] fool drink, then is the fool not dry. Bid the dishonest man mend him-
35   self; if he mend, he is no longer dishonest; if he cannot, let the botcher[4] mend him. Anything that's mended is but patched; virtue that transgresses is but patched with sin, and sin that amends is but patched with virtue. If that this simple syllogism will serve, so; if it will not, what remedy? As there is no true cuckold but calamity, so beauty's a flower.[5] The lady bade take
40   away the fool; therefore I say again, take her away.

OLIVIA: Sir, I bade them take away you.

FESTE: Misprision[6] in the highest degree! Lady, *cucullus non facit monachum*;[7] that's as much to say as I wear not motley[8] in my brain. Good madonna, give me leave to prove you a fool.

OLIVIA: Can you do it?

FESTE: Dexterously, good madonna.

OLIVIA: Make your proof.

FESTE: I must catechize you for it, madonna. Good my mouse of virtue,[9] answer me.

OLIVIA: Well, sir, for want of other idleness,[1] I'll bide[2] your proof.

FESTE: Good madonna, why mourn'st thou?

9. Abilities (reference to the parable of the talents, Matthew 25.14–29).
1. Dismissed.
2. Perhaps a bawdy pun on being "well-hung."
3. Let mild weather make homelessness endurable.
4. Maria plays on points as "laces used to hold up breeches."
5. Wide breeches.
6. It would be best for you.
7. Feste's invention.
8. Stop.
9. Dull.
1. Unreliable.

2. My lady.
3. Thirsty.
4. Mender of old clothes.
5. I.e., Olivia has wedded calamity but will be unfaithful to it, for it is natural to seize the moment of youth and beauty.
6. Mistake.
7. The cowl does not make the monk.
8. The multicolored fool's garment.
9. Virtuous mouse (term of endearment).
1. Pastime.
2. Endure.

OLIVIA: Good fool, for my brother's death.
FESTE: I think his soul is in hell, madonna.
OLIVIA: I know his soul is in heaven, fool.
FESTE: The more fool, madonna, to mourn for your brother's soul, being in heaven.
55 Take away the fool, gentlemen.
OLIVIA: What think you of this fool, Malvolio? Doth he not mend?[3]
MALVOLIO: Yes, and shall do till the pangs of death shake him. Infirmity, that decays the wise, doth ever make the better fool.
FESTE: God send you, sir, a speedy infirmity for the better increasing your folly! Sir
60 Toby will be sworn that I am no fox, but he will not pass[4] his word for twopence that you are no fool.
OLIVIA: How say you to that, Malvolio?
MALVOLIO: I marvel your ladyship takes delight in such a barren rascal. I saw him put down the other day with[5] an ordinary fool that has no more brain than a
65 stone. Look you now, he's out of his guard[6] already. Unless you laugh and minister occasion[7] to him, he is gagged. I protest I take these wise men that crow so at these set[8] kind of fools no better than the fools' zanies.[9]
OLIVIA: O, you are sick of self-love, Malvolio, and taste with a distempered[1] appetite. To be generous, guiltless, and of free disposition is to take those
70 things for bird-bolts[2] that you deem cannon bullets. There is no slander in an allowed[3] fool, though he do nothing but rail; nor no railing in a known discreet man, though he do nothing but reprove.
FESTE: Now Mercury[4] endue thee with leasing,[5] for thou speak'st well of fools!
  [Enter Maria.]
MARIA: Madam, there is at the gate a young gentleman much desires to speak with
75 you.
OLIVIA: From the Count Orsino, is it?
MARIA: I know not, madam. 'Tis a fair young man, and well attended.
OLIVIA: Who of my people hold him in delay?
MARIA: Sir Toby, madam, your kinsman.
OLIVIA: Fetch him off, I pray you. He speaks nothing but madman.[6] Fie on him!
  [Exit Maria.] Go you, Malvolio. If it be a suit from the Count, I am sick, or not at home; what you will, to dismiss it. [Exit Malvolio.] Now you see, sir, how your fooling grows old, and people dislike it.
FESTE: Thou hast spoke for us, madonna, as if thy eldest son should be a fool; whose
85 skull Jove cram with brains, for—here he comes—
  [Enter Sir Toby.]
  one of thy kin has a most weak pia mater.[7]
OLIVIA: By mine honor, half drunk. What is he at the gate, cousin?
SIR TOBY: A gentleman.
OLIVIA: A gentleman? What gentleman?
SIR TOBY: 'Tis a gentleman here—[He belches.] A plague o' these pickle-herring! [To Feste.] How now, sot?[8]

3. Improve.
4. Give.
5. By.
6. Defenseless.
7. Provide occasion for wit.
8. Artificial.
9. Fools' assistants.
1. Diseased.

2. Blunt arrows for shooting birds.
3. Licensed.
4. God of trickery.
5. Make you a skillful liar.
6. The words of madness.
7. Brain.
8. Fool; drunkard.

FESTE: Good Sir Toby.

OLIVIA: Cousin,[9] cousin, how have you come so early by this lethargy?

SIR TOBY: Lechery? I defy lechery. There's one at the gate.

OLIVIA: Ay, marry, what is he?

SIR TOBY: Let him be the devil an he will, I care not.
Give me faith,[1] say I. Well, it's all one.[2]   [*Exit.*]

OLIVIA: What's a drunken man like, Fool?

FESTE: Like a drowned man, a fool, and a madman. One draft above heat[3] makes
100   him a fool, the second mads him, and a third drowns him.

OLIVIA: Go thou and seek the crowner,[4] and let him sit o' my coz;[5] for he's in the
third degree of drink, he's drowned. Go, look after him.

FESTE: He is but mad yet, madonna; and the fool shall look to the madman. [*Exit.*]
[*Enter Malvolio.*]

MALVOLIO: Madam, yond young fellow swears he will speak with you. I told him
105   you were sick; he takes on him to understand so much, and therefore comes
to speak with you. I told you you were asleep; he seems to have a foreknowledge of that too, and therefore comes to speak with you. What is to be said
to him, lady? He's fortified against any denial.

OLIVIA: Tell him he shall not speak with me.

MALVOLIO: He's been told so; and he says he'll stand at your door like a sheriff's
post,[6] and be the supporter to a bench, but he'll speak with you.

OLIVIA: What kind o' man is he?

MALVOLIO: Why, of mankind.

OLIVIA: What manner of man?

MALVOLIO: Of very ill manner. He'll speak with you, will you or no.

OLIVIA: Of what personage and years is he?

MALVOLIO: Not yet old enough for a man, nor young enough for a boy; as a squash[7]
is before 'tis a peascod,[8] or a codling[9] when 'tis almost an apple. 'Tis with
him in standing water[1] between boy and man. He is very well-favored,[2] and
120   he speaks very shrewishly.[3] One would think his mother's milk were scarce
out of him.

OLIVIA: Let him approach. Call in my gentlewoman.

MALVOLIO: Gentlewoman, my lady calls.   [*Exit.*]
[*Enter Maria.*]

OLIVIA: Give me my veil. Come, throw it o'er my face.
125   We'll once more hear Orsino's embassy. [*Olivia veils.*]
[*Enter Viola.*]

VIOLA: The honorable lady of the house, which is she?

OLIVIA: Speak to me; I shall answer for her. Your will?

VIOLA: Most radiant, exquisite, and unmatchable beauty—I pray you, tell me if
this be the lady of the house, for I never saw her. I would be loath to cast
130   away my speech; for besides that it is excellently well penned, I have taken
great pains to con[4] it. Good beauties, let me sustain[5] no scorn; I am very

---

9. Kinsman.
1. I.e., to resist the devil.
2. It doesn't matter.
3. Drink more than would make him warm.
4. Coroner.
5. Hold an inquest on my kinsman (Sir Toby).
6. Post before the sheriff's door to mark a residence of
authority.

7. Unripe pea-pod.
8. Pea-pod.
9. Unripe apple.
1. At the turn of the tide.
2. Good-looking.
3. Sharply.
4. Learn by heart.
5. Endure.

comptible,[6] even to the least sinister usage.[7]

OLIVIA: Whence came you, sir?

VIOLA: I can say little more than I have studied, and that question's out of my part.

135   Good gentle one, give me modest[8] assurance if you be the lady of the house, that I may proceed in my speech.

OLIVIA: Are you a comedian?[9]

VIOLA: No, my profound heart; and yet, by the very fangs of malice, I swear I am not that I play. Are you the lady of the house?

OLIVIA: If I do not usurp[1] myself, I am.

VIOLA: Most certain, if you are she, you do usurp yourself; for what is yours to bestow is not yours to reserve. But this is from[2] my commission. I will on with my speech in your praise, and then show you the heart of my message.

OLIVIA: Come to what is important in 't. I forgive[3] you the praise.

VIOLA: Alas, I took great pains to study it, and 'tis poetical.

OLIVIA: It is the more like to be feigned. I pray you, keep it in. I heard you were saucy at my gates, and allowed your approach rather to wonder at you than to hear you. If you be not mad,[4] begone; if you have reason,[5] be brief. 'Tis not that time of moon with me[6] to make one[7] in so skipping[8] a dialogue.

MARIA: Will you hoist sail, sir? Here lies your way.

VIOLA: No, good swabber,[9] I am to hull[1] here a little longer.—Some mollification for your giant,[2] sweet lady. Tell me your mind; I am a messenger.

OLIVIA: Sure you have some hideous matter to deliver, when the courtesy[3] of it is so fearful. Speak your office.[4]

VIOLA: It alone concerns your ear. I bring no overture of war, no taxation[5] of homage. I hold the olive[6] in my hand; my words are as full of peace as matter.

OLIVIA: Yet you began rudely. What are you? What would you?

VIOLA: The rudeness that hath appeared in me have I learned from my entertainment.[7] What I am and what I would are as secret as maidenhead—to your

160   ears, divinity;[8] to any other's, profanation.

OLIVIA: Give us the place alone. We will hear this divinity. [*Exeunt Maria and attendants.*] Now, sir, what is your text?

VIOLA: Most sweet lady—

OLIVIA: A comfortable[9] doctrine, and much may be said of it. Where lies your text?

VIOLA: In Orsino's bosom.

OLIVIA: In his bosom? In what chapter of his bosom?

VIOLA: To answer by the method,[1] in the first of his heart.

OLIVIA: O, I have read it. It is heresy. Have you no more to say?

VIOLA: Good madam, let me see your face.

OLIVIA: Have you any commission from your lord to negotiate with my face? You are now out of your text. But we will draw the curtain and show you the

6. Sensitive.
7. Slightest rude treatment.
8. Reasonable.
9. Actor.
1. Supplant.
2. Outside.
3. Excuse.
4. Altogether mad? But mad?
5. Sanity.
6. I'm not in the mood.
7. Take part.
8. Sprightly.

9. One who swabs the deck.
1. Float without sails.
2. Small Maria, who guards her lady like a medieval giant.
3. Formal beginning.
4. Business.
5. Demand.
6. Olive-branch.
7. Reception.
8. Holy discourse.
9. Comforting.
1. To continue the metaphor.

picture. [*Unveiling.*] Look you, sir, such a one I was this present.[2] Is 't not
    well done?

VIOLA: Excellently done, if God did all.

OLIVIA: 'Tis in grain,[3] sir; 'twill endure wind and weather.

VIOLA: 'Tis beauty truly blent,[4] whose red and white
    Nature's own sweet and cunning[5] hand laid on.
    Lady, you are the cruel'st she alive
    If you will lead these graces to the grave
180   And leave the world no copy.

OLIVIA: O, sir, I will not be so hardhearted. I will give out divers schedules[6] of my
    beauty. It shall be inventoried, and every particle and utensil[7] labeled to[8]
    my will: as, item, two lips, indifferent[9] red; item, two gray eyes, with lids to
    them; item, one neck, one chin, and so forth. Were you sent hither to
185   praise[1] me?

VIOLA: I see you what you are: you are too proud.
    But, if° you were the devil, you are fair.   *even if*
    My lord and master loves you. O, such love
    Could be but recompensed,° though you were crowned   *could only be repaid*
190   The nonpareil of beauty!

OLIVIA: How does he love me?

VIOLA: With adorations, fertile° tears,   *abundant*
    With groans that thunder love, with sighs of fire.

OLIVIA: Your lord does know my mind; I cannot love him.
    Yet I suppose him virtuous, know him noble,
195   Of great estate, of fresh and stainless youth,
    In voices well divulged,° free,° learned, and valiant, *well spoken of / generous*
    And in dimension and the shape of nature°   *physical form*
    A gracious° person. But yet I cannot love him.   *graceful*
    He might have took his answer long ago.

VIOLA: If I did love you in my master's flame,°   *passion*
    With such a suffering, 'such a deadly° life,   *death-like*
    In your denial I would find no sense;
    I would not understand it.

OLIVIA: Why, what would you?

VIOLA: Make me a willow[2] cabin at your gate
205   And call upon my soul° within the house;   *Olivia*
    Write loyal cantons° of contemnèd° love   *songs / rejected*
    And sing them loud even in the dead of night;
    Hallow° your name to the reverberate hills,   *call; bless*
    And make the babbling gossip° of the air   *echo*
210   Cry out "Olivia!" O, you should not rest
    Between the elements of air and earth
    But you should pity me!

OLIVIA: You might do much.
               What is your parentage?

---

2. A minute ago.   7. Article.
3. Fast dyed.   8. Added to.
4. Blended.   9. Somewhat.
5. Skillful.   1. Pun on "appraise."
6. Lists.   2. Willow was the symbol of unrequited love.

VIOLA: Above my fortunes, yet my state° is well.   *social standing*
I am a gentleman.
OLIVIA: Get you to your lord.
I cannot love him. Let him send no more—
Unless, perchance, you come to me again
To tell me how he takes it. Fare you well.
I thank you for your pains. Spend this for me. [*She offers a purse.*]
VIOLA: I am no fee'd post,° lady. Keep your purse.   *paid messenger*
My master, not myself, lacks recompense.
Love make his heart of flint that you shall love,
And let your fervor, like my master's, be
Placed in contempt! Farewell, fair cruelty.   [*Exit.*]
OLIVIA: "What is your parentage?"
"Above my fortunes, yet my state is well:
I am a gentleman." I'll be sworn thou art!
Thy tongue, thy face, thy limbs, actions, and spirit
Do give thee fivefold blazon.° Not too fast! Soft,° soft!   *coat of arms / wait*
230   Unless the master were the man.³ How now?
Even so quickly may one catch the plague?
Methinks I feel this youth's perfections
With an invisible and subtle stealth
To creep in at mine eyes. Well, let it be.
235   What ho, Malvolio!
[*Enter Malvolio.*]
MALVOLIO: Here, madam, at your service.
OLIVIA: Run after that same peevish messenger,
The County's° man. He left this ring behind him, [*giving a ring*]   *Count's*
Would I or not.⁴ Tell him I'll none of it.
Desire him not to flatter with° his lord,   *encourage*
240   Nor hold him up with hopes; I am not for him.
If that the youth will come this way tomorrow,
I'll give him reasons for 't. Hie thee, Malvolio.
MALVOLIO: Madam, I will.   [*Exit*]
OLIVIA: I do I know not what, and fear to find
245   Mine eye too great a flatterer for my mind.
Fate, show thy force. Ourselves we do not owe.°   *own*
What is decreed must be; and be this so.   [*Exit.*]

ACT 2

Scene 1⁵

[*Enter Antonio and Sebastian.*]
ANTONIO: Will you stay no longer? Nor will you not⁶ that I go with you?
SEBASTIAN: By your patience,⁷ no. My stars shine darkly over me. The malignancy
of my fate might perhaps distemper yours; therefore I shall crave of you your
leave that I may bear my evils alone. It were a bad recompense for your love
5   to lay any of them on you.

3. Unless Cesario and Orsino changed places.   6. Do you not wish.
4. Whether I wanted it or not.   7. Leave.
5. Location: Somewhere in Illyria.

ANTONIO: Let me yet know of you whither you are bound.

SEBASTIAN: No, sooth,[8] sir; my determinate[9] voyage is mere extravagancy.[1] But I
perceive in you so excellent a touch of modesty that you will not extort from
me what I am willing to keep in; therefore it charges me in manners the
10   rather to express myself.[2] You must know of me then, Antonio, my name is
Sebastian, which I called Roderigo. My father was that Sebastian of Messaline whom I know you have heard of. He left behind him myself and a sister, both born in an hour.[3] If the heavens had been pleased, would we had so
ended! But you, sir, altered that, for some hour[4] before you took me from the
15   breach of the sea[5] was my sister drowned.

ANTONIO: Alas the day!

SEBASTIAN: A lady, sir, though it was said she much resembled me, was yet of
many accounted beautiful. But though I could not with such estimable wonder[6] over-far believe that, yet thus far I will boldly publish[7] her: she bore a
20   mind that envy[8] could not but call fair. She is drowned already, sir, with salt
water, though I seem to drown her remembrance again with more.

ANTONIO: Pardon me, sir, your bad entertainment.[9]

SEBASTIAN: O good Antonio, forgive me your trouble.[1]

ANTONIO: If you will not murder me for[2] my love, let me be your servant.

SEBASTIAN: If you will not undo what you have done, that is, kill him whom you
have recovered,[3] desire it not. Fare ye well at once. My bosom is full of kindness,[4] and I am yet so near the manners of my mother[5] that upon the least
occasion more mine eyes will tell tales of me. I am bound to the Count
Orsino's court. Farewell.   [Exit.]

ANTONIO: The gentleness of all the gods go with thee!
I have many enemies in Orsino's court,
Else would I very shortly see thee there.
But come what may, I do adore thee so
That danger shall seem sport, and I will go.   [Exit.]

Scene 2[6]

[Enter Viola and Malvolio, at several[7] doors.]

MALVOLIO: Were not you even now with the Countess Olivia?

VIOLA: Even now, sir. On a moderate pace I have since arrived but hither.

MALVOLIO: She returns this ring to you, sir. You might have saved me my pains, to
have taken[8] it away yourself. She adds, moreover, that you should put your
5   lord into a desperate[9] assurance she will none of him. And one thing more:
that you be never so hardy to come[1] again in his affairs, unless it be to report
your lord's taking of this. Receive it so.

VIOLA: She took the ring of me. I'll none of it.

MALVOLIO: Come, sir, you peevishly threw it to her, and her will is it should be so

---

8. Truly.
9. Determined upon.
1. Wandering.
2. Courtesy demands that I reveal myself.
3. In the same hour.
4. About an hour.
5. The surf.
6. Admiring judgment.
7. Proclaim.
8. Even malice.
9. Reception.

1. The trouble I put you to.
2. Be the death of me in return for.
3. Saved.
4. Tenderness.
5. Womanly inclination to weep.
6. Location: Outside Olivia's house.
7. Different.
8. By taking.
9. Without hope.
1. Bold as to come.

10   returned. [*He throws down the ring.*] If it be worth stooping for, there it lies,
        in your eye; if not, be it his that finds it.   [*Exit.*]

VIOLA [*picking up the ring*]: I left no ring with her. What means this lady?
        Fortune forbid my outside have not charmed her!
        She made good view of° me, indeed so much   *looked closely at*
15   That sure methought her eyes had lost° her tongue,   *caused her to lose*
        For she did speak in starts, distractedly.
        She loves me, sure! The cunning of her passion
        Invites me in° this churlish messenger.   *in the person of*
        None of my lord's ring? Why, he sent her none.
20   I am the man.° If it be so—as 'tis—   *man of her choice*
        Poor lady, she were better love a dream.
        Disguise, I see, thou art a wickedness
        Wherein the pregnant enemy° does much.   *resourceful Satan*
        How easy is it for the proper false°   *handsome deceivers*
25   In women's waxen° hearts to set their forms!°   *malleable / impressions*
        Alas, our frailty is the cause, not we,
        For such as we are made of, such we be.
        How will this fadge?° My master loves her dearly,   *turn out*
        And I, poor monster,[2] fond° as much on him;   *dote*
30   And she, mistaken, seems to dote on me.
        What will become of this? As I am man,
        My state is desperate° for my master's love;   *hopeless*
        As I am woman—now, alas the day!—
        What thriftless° sighs shall poor Olivia breathe!   *unprofitable*
35   O Time, thou must untangle this, not I;
        It is too hard a knot for me t' untie.   [*Exit.*]

Scene 3[3]

[*Enter Sir Toby and Sir Andrew.*]

SIR TOBY: Approach, Sir Andrew. Not to be abed after midnight is to be up
        betimes;[4] and *diluculo surgere*,[5] thou know'st—

SIR ANDREW: Nay, by my troth, I know not, but I know to be up late is to be up
        late.

SIR TOBY: A false conclusion. I hate it as an unfilled can.[6] To be up after midnight
        and to go to bed then, is early; so that to go to bed after midnight is to go to
        bed betimes. Does not our lives consist of the four elements?[7]

SIR ANDREW: Faith, so they say, but I think it rather consists of eating and drinking.

SIR TOBY: Thou'rt a scholar; let us therefore eat and drink. Marian, I say, a stoup[8]
10   of wine!

[*Enter Clown (Feste).*]

SIR ANDREW: Here comes the Fool, i' faith.

FESTE: How now, my hearts! Did you never see the picture of "we three"?[9]

SIR TOBY: Welcome, ass. Now let's have a catch.[1]

2. Because both man and woman.
3. Location: Olivia's house.
4. Early.
5. *Diluculo surgere (saluberrimum est)*—to rise early is most
healthful (from Lilly's *Latin Grammar*).
6. Tankard.

7. Fire, water, earth, air.
8. Goblet.
9. Picture of two fools or asses, the onlooker being the
third.
1. Round-song.

SIR ANDREW: By my troth, the Fool has an excellent breast.[2] I had rather than
15   forty shillings I had such a leg, and so sweet a breath to sing, as the fool has.
       In sooth, thou wast in very gracious[3] fooling last night, when thou spok'st of
       Pigrogromitus, of the Vapians passing the equinoctial of Queubus.[4] 'Twas
       very good, i' faith. I sent thee sixpence for thy leman.[5] Hadst it?
FESTE: I did impeticos thy gratillity;[6] for Malvolio's nose is no whipstock.[7] My lady
20   has a white hand, and the Myrmidons[8] are no bottle-ale houses.
SIR ANDREW: Excellent! Why, this is the best fooling, when all is done. Now, a
       song.
SIR TOBY: Come on, there is sixpence for you. [*He gives money.*] Let's have a song.
SIR ANDREW: There's a testril[9] of me too. [*He gives money.*] If one knight give a—
FESTE: Would you have a love song, or a song of good life?[1]
SIR TOBY: A love song, a love song.
SIR ANDREW: Ay, ay, I care not for good life.
FESTE [*sings*]:   O mistress mine, where are you roaming?
                      O, stay and hear, your true love 's coming.
30   That can sing both high and low.
                      Trip no further, pretty sweeting
                      Journeys end in lovers' meeting,
                         Every wise man's son doth know.
SIR ANDREW: Excellent good, i' faith.
SIR TOBY: Good, good.
FESTE [*sings*]:   What is love? 'tis not hereafter;
                      Present mirth hath present laughter;
                         What's to come is still unsure.
                      In delay there lies no plenty.
40   Then come kiss me, sweet and twenty;
                         Youth's a stuff will not endure.
SIR ANDREW: A mellifluous voice, as I am true knight.
SIR TOBY: A contagious[2] breath.
SIR ANDREW: Very sweet and contagious, i' faith.
SIR TOBY: To hear by the nose, it is dulcet in contagion. But shall we make the
       welkin[3] dance indeed? Shall we rouse the night owl in a catch that will draw
       three souls out of one weaver?[4] Shall we do that?
SIR ANDREW: An you love me, let's do't. I am dog at a catch.
FESTE: By'r Lady, sir, and some dogs will catch well.
SIR ANDREW: Most certain. Let our catch be "Thou knave."
FESTE: "Hold thy peace, thou knave," knight? I shall be constrained in 't to call
       thee knave, knight.
SIR ANDREW: 'Tis not the first time I have constrained one to call me knave.
       Begin, Fool. It begins, "Hold thy peace."
FESTE: I shall never begin if I hold my peace.
SIR ANDREW: Good, i' faith. Come, begin. [*Catch sung.*]

---

2. Voice.
3. Elegant.
4. Mock erudition.
5. Sweetheart.
6. Impetticoat (pocket up) thy gratuity.
7. Whip-handle.

8. Followers of Achilles.
9. Coin worth sixpence.
1. Virtuous living.
2. Catchy; infected.
3. Sky.
4. Weavers were associated with the singing of psalms.

[*Enter Maria.*]

MARIA: What a caterwauling do you keep here! If my lady have not called up her steward Malvolio and bid him turn you out of doors, never trust me.

SIR TOBY: My lady's a Cataian,[5] we are politicians,[6] Malvolio's a Peg-o'-Ramsey,[7]
60   and [*He sings*] "Three merry men be we." Am not I consanguineous?[8] Am I not of her blood? Tillyvally![9] Lady! [*He sings.*] "There dwelt a man in Babylon, lady, lady."[1]

FESTE: Beshrew me, the knight's in admirable fooling.

SIR ANDREW: Ay, he does well enough if he be disposed, and so do I too. He does
65   it with a better grace, but I do it more natural.[2]

SIR TOBY [*sings*]: "O' the twelfth day of December"—

MARIA: For the love o' God, peace!

[*Enter Malvolio.*]

MALVOLIO: My masters, are you mad? Or what are you? Have you no wit,[3] manners, nor honesty[4] but to gabble like tinkers at this time of night? Do ye
70   make an alehouse of my lady's house, that ye squeak out your coziers'[5] catches without any mitigation or remorse[6] of voice? Is there no respect of place, persons, nor time in you?

SIR TOBY: We did keep time, sir, in our catches. Sneck up![7]

MALVOLIO: Sir Toby, I must be round[8] with you. My lady bade me tell you that
75   though she harbors you as her kinsman, she's nothing allied to your disorders. If you can separate yourself and your misdemeanors, you are welcome to the house; if not, an it would please you to take leave of her, she is very willing to bid you farewell.

SIR TOBY [*sings*]: "Farewell, dear heart, since I must needs be gone."[9]

MARIA: Nay, good Sir Toby.

FESTE [*sings*]: "His eyes do show his days are almost done."

MALVOLIO: Is't even so?

SIR TOBY [*sings*]: "But I will never die."

FESTE: "Sir Toby, there you lie."

MALVOLIO: This is much credit to you.

SIR TOBY [*sings*]: "Shall I bid him go?"

FESTE [*sings*]: "What an if you do?"

SIR TOBY [*sings*]: "Shall I bid him go, and spare not?"

FESTE [*sings*]: "O, no, no, no, no, you dare not."

SIR TOBY: Out o' tune, sir? Ye lie. Art any more than a steward? Dost thou think, because thou art virtuous, there shall be no more cakes and ale?

FESTE: Yes, by Saint Anne,[1] and ginger[2] shall be hot i' the mouth, too.

SIR TOBY: Thou'rt i' the right.—Go, sir, rub your chain with crumbs.[3]—A stoup of wine, Maria!

5. Native of Cathay; trickster.
6. Schemers.
7. Character in a popular song (here used contemptuously).
8. Related.
9. Nonsense.
1. From an old song, *The Constancy of Suzanna.*
2. Naturally (unconsciously suggesting idiocy).
3. Common sense.
4. Decency.

5. Cobblers'.
6. Considerate lowering.
7. Go hang.
8. Blunt.
9. From the ballad *Corydon's Farewell to Phyllis.*
1. Mother of the Virgin Mary. (Her cult was derided in the Reformation, as were cakes and ale at church feasts.)
2. Used to spice ale.
3. Remember your position.

MALVOLIO: Mistress Mary, if you prized my lady's favor at anything more than contempt, you would not give means[4] for this uncivil rule.[5] She shall know of it, by this hand.   [*Exit.*]

MARIA: Go shake your ears.[6]

SIR ANDREW: Twere as good a deed as to drink when a man's a-hungry to chal-
100   lenge him the field[7] and then to break promise with him and make a fool of him.

SIR TOBY: Do 't, knight. I'll write thee a challenge, or I'll deliver thy indignation to him by word of mouth.

MARIA: Sweet Sir Toby, be patient for tonight. Since the youth of the Count's was
105   today with my lady, she is much out of quiet. For[8] Monsieur Malvolio, let me alone with him. If I do not gull[9] him into a nayword[1] and make him a common recreation,[2] do not think I have wit enough to lie straight in my bed. I know I can do it.

SIR TOBY: Possess us,[3] possess us. Tell us something of him.

MARIA: Marry, sir, sometimes he is a kind of puritan.

SIR ANDREW: O, if I thought that, I'd beat him like a dog.

SIR TOBY: What, for being a puritan? Thy exquisite reason, dear knight?

SIR ANDREW: I have no exquisite reason for 't, but I have reason good enough.

MARIA: The devil a puritan that he is, or anything constantly,[4] but a time-pleaser;[5]
115   an affectioned[6] ass, that cons state without book[7] and utters it by great swaths; the best persuaded of himself, so crammed, as he thinks, with excellencies, that it is his grounds of faith that all that look on him love him; and on that vice in him will my revenge find notable cause to work.

SIR TOBY: What wilt thou do?

MARIA: I will drop in his way some obscure epistles of love, wherein by the color of his beard, the shape of his leg, the manner of his gait, the expressure[8] of his eye, forehead, and complexion, he shall find himself most feelingly personated.[9] I can write very like my lady your niece; on a forgotten matter[1] we can hardly make distinction of our hands.

SIR TOBY: Excellent! I smell a device.

SIR ANDREW: I have't in my nose too.

SIR TOBY: He shall think, by the letters that thou wilt drop, that they come from my niece, and that she's in love with him.

MARIA: My purpose is indeed a horse of that color.

SIR ANDREW: And your horse now would make him an ass.

MARIA: Ass, I doubt not.

SIR ANDREW: O, 'twill be admirable!

MARIA: Sport royal, I warrant you. I know my physic[2] will work with him. I will plant you two, and let the Fool make a third, where he shall find the letter.
135   Observe his construction[3] of it. For this night, to bed, and dream on the event.[4] Farewell.   [*Exit.*]

4. I.e., provide wine.
5. Behavior.
6. I.e., your ass's ears.
7. To a duel.
8. As for.
9. Trick.
1. Byword (for dupe).
2. Sport.
3. Inform.
4. Consistently.

5. Sychophant.
6. Affected.
7. Learns a stately manner by heart.
8. Expression.
9. Represented.
1. When we have forgotten who wrote something.
2. Medicine.
3. Interpretation.
4. Outcome.

SIR TOBY: Good night, Penthesilea.[5]

SIR ANDREW: Before me,[6] she's a good wench.

SIR TOBY: She's a beagle[7] true-bred and one that adores me. What o' that?

SIR ANDREW: I was adored once, too.

SIR TOBY: Let's to bed, knight. Thou hadst need send for more money.

SIR ANDREW: If I cannot recover[8] your niece, I am a foul way out.[9]

SIR TOBY: Send for money, knight. If thou hast her not i' the end, call me cut.[1]

SIR ANDREW: If I do not, never trust me, take it how you will.

SIR TOBY: Come, come, I'll go burn some sack.[2] 'Tis too late to go to bed now. Come, knight; come, knight.   [*Exeunt.*]

Scene 4[3]

[Enter Duke (Orsino) Viola, Curio, and others.]

ORSINO: Give me some music. Now, good morrow,° friends.   *morning*
    Now, good Cesario, but° that piece of song,   *I ask only*
    That old and antique° song we heard last night.   *quaint*
    Methought it did relieve my passion much,
5   More than light airs and recollected° terms   *studied*
    Of these most brisk and giddy-pacèd times.
    Come, but one verse.

CURIO: He is not here, so please your lordship, that should sing it.

ORSINO: Who was it?

CURIO: Feste the jester, my lord, a fool that the Lady Olivia's father took much delight in. He is about the house.

ORSINO: Seek him out, and play the tune the while.

                                                [Exit Curio.]

[Music plays.]

    [To Viola.] Come hither, boy. If ever thou shalt love
    In the sweet pangs of it remember me;
15   For such as I am, all true lovers are,
    Unstaid and skittish in all motions else°   *other emotions*
    Save in the constant image of the creature
    That is beloved. How dost thou like this tune?

VIOLA: It gives a very echo to the seat
    Where Love is throned.°   *i.e., the heart*

ORSINO: Thou dost speak masterly.
    My life upon 't, young though thou art, thine eye
    Hath stayed upon some favor° that it loves.   *face*
    Hath it not, boy?

VIOLA: A little, by your favor.

ORSINO: What kind of woman is 't?

VIOLA: Of your complexion.

ORSINO: She is not worth thee, then. What years, i' faith?

VIOLA: About your years, my lord.

---

5. Queen of the Amazons.
6. I swear.
7. Small, intelligent hunting dog.
8. Win.

9. Out of money.
1. Horse with a docked tail or, perhaps, a gelding.
2. Warm some Spanish wine.
3. Location: Orsino's court.

ORSINO: Too old, by heaven. Let still° the woman take   *always*
        An elder than herself. So wears° she to him;   *adapts herself*
        So sways she level° in her husband's heart.   *she keeps constant*
30   For, boy, however we do praise ourselves,
        Our fancies° are more giddy and unfirm,   *loves*
        More longing, wavering, sooner lost and worn,
        Than women's are.
VIOLA: I think it well, my lord.
ORSINO: Then let thy love be younger than thyself,
35   Or thy affection cannot hold the bent;°   *hold steady*
        For women are as roses, whose fair flower
        Being once displayed,° doth fall that very hour.   *full blown*
VIOLA: And so they are. Alas that they are so,
        To die even when° they to perfection grow!   *just as*
      [Enter Curio and Clown (Feste).]
ORSINO: O fellow, come, the song we had last night.
        Mark it, Cesario, it is old and plain;
        The spinsters° and the knitters in the sun,   *spinners*
        And the free° maids that weave their thread with bones,°   *innocent / bobbins*
        Do use° to chant it. It is silly sooth,°   *are used / simple truth*
45   And dallies with the innocence of love,
        Like the old age.°   *good old days*
FESTE: Are you ready, sir?
ORSINO: Ay, prithee, sing. *[Music.]*
      [The Song.]
FESTE *[sings]:*   Come away, come away, death,
50   And in sad cypress° let me be laid.   *coffin*
           Fly away, fly away, breath;
                  I am slain by a fair cruel maid.
           My shroud of white, stuck all with yew,°   *yew-sprigs*
                  O, prepare it!
55   My part° of death, no one so true   *portion*
                  Did share it.

           Not a flower, not a flower sweet
                  On my black coffin let there be strown;°   *strewn*
           Not a friend, not a friend greet
60   My poor corpse, where my bones shall be thrown.
           A thousand thousand sighs to save,
                  Lay me, O, where
           Sad true lover never find my grave,
                  To weep there!
ORSINO *[offering money]:* There's for thy pains.
FESTE: No pains, sir. I take pleasure in singing, sir.
ORSINO: I'll pay thy pleasure then.
FESTE: Truly, sir, and pleasure will be paid,[4] one time or another.
ORSINO: Give me now leave to leave thee.

---

4. Indulgence must be paid for.

FESTE: Now, the melancholy god[5] protect thee, and the tailor make thy doublet[6] of changeable taffeta, for thy mind is a very opal. I would have men of such constancy put to sea, that their business might be everything and their intent[7] everywhere, for that's it that always makes a good voyage of nothing.[8] Farewell.   [*Exit.*]

ORSINO: Let all the rest give place.[9] [*Curio and attendants withdraw.*]
        Once more, Cesario,
        Get thee to yond same sovereign cruelty.°   *cruel person*
        Tell her, my love, more noble than the world,
        Prizes not quantity of dirty lands;
80   The parts° that fortune hath bestowed upon her,   *possessions*
        Tell her, I hold as giddily as fortune;
        But 'tis that miracle and queen of gems
        That nature pranks° her in attracts my soul.   *adorns*
VIOLA: But if she cannot love you, sir?
ORSINO: I cannot be so answered.
VIOLA: Sooth,° but you must.   *In truth*
        Say that some lady, as perhaps there is,
        Hath for your love as great a pang of heart
        As you have for Olivia. You cannot love her;
        You tell her so; Must she not then be answered?°   *accept your answer*
ORSINO: There is no woman's sides
        Can bide° the beating of so strong a passion   *withstand*
        As love doth give my heart; no woman's heart
        So big, to hold so much. They lack retention.
        Alas, their love may be called appetite,
95   No motion° of the liver,[1] but the palate,   *emotion*
        That suffer surfeit, cloyment,° and revolt;°   *satiety / revulsion*
        But mine is all as hungry as the sea,
        And can digest as much. Make no compare
        Between that love a woman can bear me
        And that I owe° Olivia.   *have for*
VIOLA: Ay, but I know—
ORSINO: What dost thou know?
VIOLA: Too well what love women to men may owe.
        In faith, they are as true of heart as we.
        My father had a daughter loved a man
105   As it might be, perhaps, were I a woman,
        I should your lordship.
ORSINO: And what's her history?
VIOLA: A blank, my lord. She never told her love,
        But let concealment, like a worm i' the bud,
        Feed on her damask° cheek. She pined in thought,   *pink and white*
110   And with a green and yellow° melancholy   *pale and sallow*
        She sat like Patience on a monument,°   *tomb*

---

5. Saturn, said to control the melancholy temperament.   8. Come to nothing.
6. Jacket.   9. Leave.
7. Destination.   1. Seat of the emotion of love.

Smiling at grief. Was not this love indeed?
We men may say more, swear more, but indeed
Our shows° are more than will;° for still we prove   displays / our passions
115   Much in our vows, but little in our love.
ORSINO: But died thy sister of her love, my boy?
VIOLA: I am all the daughters of my father's house,
And all the brothers too—and yet I know not.
Sir, shall I to this lady?
ORSINO: Ay, that's the theme.
To her in haste; give her this jewel. [*He gives a jewel.*] Say
My love can give no place, bide no denay.°   cannot endure denial
                                             [*Exeunt (separately).*]

Scene 5[2]

[*Enter Sir Toby, Sir Andrew, and Fabian.*]
SIR TOBY: Come thy ways,[3] Signor Fabian.
FABIAN: Nay, I'll come. If I lose a scruple[4] of this sport, let me be boiled to death
with melancholy.
SIR TOBY: Wouldst thou not be glad to have the niggardly rascally sheep-biter[5]
5   come by some notable shame?
FABIAN: I would exult, man. You know he brought me out o' favor with my lady
about a bearbaiting[6] here.
SIR TOBY: To anger him we'll have the bear again, and we will fool him black and
blue. Shall we not, Sir Andrew?
SIR ANDREW: An we do not, it is pity of our lives.
[*Enter Maria (with a letter).*]
SIR TOBY: Here comes the little villain.—How now, my metal of India![7]
MARIA: Get ye all three into the boxtree.[8] Malvolio's coming down this walk. He
has been yonder i' the sun practicing behavior[9] to his own shadow this half
hour. Observe him, for the love of mockery, for I know this letter will make
15   a contemplative[1] idiot of him. Close,[2] in the name of jesting! [*The others
hide.*] Lie thou there [*throwing down a letter*]; for here comes the trout that
must be caught with tickling.[3]   [*Exit.*]
[*Enter Malvolio.*]
MALVOLIO: 'Tis but fortune; all is fortune. Maria once told me she did affect me;[4]
and I have heard herself come thus near, that should she fancy,[5] it should be
20   one of my complexion.[6] Besides, she uses me with a more exalted respect
than anyone else that follows[7] her. What should I think on 't?
SIR TOBY: Here's an overweening rogue!
FABIAN: O, peace! Contemplation makes a rare turkey-cock of him. How he jets[8]
under his advanced[9] plumes!

2. Location: Olivia's garden.
3. Come along.
4. A bit.
5. Dog that bites sheep; i.e., a sneak.
6. Target of Puritan disapproval.
7. Gold; i.e., priceless one.
8. Shrub.
9. Elegant conduct.
1. I.e., from his musings.

2. Hide.
3. Stroking about the gills.
4. Olivia liked me.
5. Fall in love.
6. Personality.
7. Serves.
8. Struts.
9. Raised.

SIR ANDREW: 'Slight,[1] I could so beat the rogue!

SIR TOBY: Peace, I say.

MALVOLIO: To be Count Malvolio.

SIR TOBY: Ah, rogue!

SIR ANDREW: Pistol him, pistol him.

SIR TOBY: Peace, peace!

MALVOLIO: There is example[2] for 't. The lady of the Strachy[3] married the yeoman of the wardrobe.

SIR ANDREW: Fie on him, Jezebel![4]

FABIAN: O, peace! Now he's deeply in. Look how imagination blows him.[5]

MALVOLIO: Having been three months married to her, sitting in my state[6]—

SIR TOBY: O, for a stone-bow,[7] to hit him in the eye!

MALVOLIO: Calling my officers about me, in my branched[8] velvet gown; having come from a daybed,[9] where I have left Olivia sleeping—

SIR TOBY: Fire and brimstone!

FABIAN: O, peace, peace!

MALVOLIO: And then to have the humor of state;[1] and after a demure travel of regard,[2] telling them I know my place as I would they should do theirs, to ask for my kinsman Toby.

SIR TOBY: Bolts and shackles!

FABIAN: O, peace, peace, peace! Now, now.

MALVOLIO: Seven of my people, with an obedient start, make out for him. I frown the while, and perchance wind up my watch, or play with my[3]—some rich jewel. Toby approaches; curtsies[4] there to me—

SIR TOBY: Shall this fellow live?

FABIAN: Though our silence be drawn from us with cars,[5] yet peace.

MALVOLIO: I extend my hand to him thus, quenching my familiar smile with an austere regard of control[6]—

SIR TOBY: And does not Toby take[7] you a blow o' the lips then?

MALVOLIO: Saying, "Cousin Toby, my fortunes having cast me on your niece give
55   me this prerogative of speech—"

SIR TOBY: What, what?

MALVOLIO: "You must amend your drunkenness."

SIR TOBY: Out, scab!

FABIAN: Nay, patience, or we break the sinews of our plot.

MALVOLIO: "Besides, you waste the treasure of your time with a foolish knight—"

SIR ANDREW: That's me, I warrant you.

MALVOLIO: "One Sir Andrew."

SIR ANDREW: I knew 'twas I, for many do call me fool.

MALVOLIO: What employment have we here? [Taking up the letter.]

---

1. By God's light.
2. Precedent.
3. Unknown reference; lady who married below her station.
4. Wicked queen of Israel.
5. Puffs him up.
6. Chair of state.
7. Crossbow.
8. Embroidered.
9. Sofa.

1. Manner of authority.
2. Grave survey of the company.
3. Malvolio recalls that, as a Count, he would not be wearing his steward's chain.
4. Bows.
5. With chariots; i.e., by force.
6. Look of authority.
7. Give.

FABIAN: Now is the woodcock[8] near the gin.[9]

SIR TOBY: O, peace, and the spint of humors[1] intimate reading aloud to him!

MALVOLIO: By my life, this is my lady's hand. These be her very c's, her u's, and her t's;[2] and thus makes she her great[3] P's. It is in contempt of[4] question her hand.

SIR ANDREW: Her c's, her u's, and her t's. Why that?

MALVOLIO [reads]: "To the unknown beloved, this, and my good wishes."—Her very phrases! By your leave, wax.[5] Soft![6] And the impressure her Lucrece,[7] with which she uses to seal. 'Tis my lady. To whom should this be? [He opens the letter.]

FABIAN: This wins him, liver[8] and all.

MALVOLIO [reads]: "Jove knows I love,
        But who?
    Lips, do not move;
    No man must know."

"No man must know." What follows? The numbers[9] altered! "No man must
80   know." If this should be thee, Malvolio?

SIR TOBY: Marry, hang thee, brock![1]

MALVOLIO [reads]: "I may command where I adore,
        But silence, like a Lucrece knife,
        With bloodless stroke my heart doth gore;
85   M.O.A.I. doth sway my life."

FABIAN: A fustian[2] riddle!

SIR TOBY: Excellent wench,[3] say I.

MALVOLIO: "M.O.A.I. doth sway my life." Nay, but first, let me see, let me see, let me see.

FABIAN: What dish o' poison has she dressed[4] him!

SIR TOBY: And with what wing[5] the staniel[6] checks at it![7]

MALVOLIO: "I may command where I adore." Why, she may command me; I serve her, she is my lady. Why, this is evident to any formal capacity.[8] There is no obstruction[9] in this. And the end—what should that alphabetical position
95   portend? If I could make that resemble something in me! Softly! M.O.A.I.—

SIR TOBY: O, ay, make up that. He is now at a cold scent.[1]

FABIAN: Sowter will cry upon 't[2] for all this, though it be as rank as a fox.

MALVOLIO: M—Malvolio. M! Why, that begins my name!

FABIAN: Did not I say he would work it out? The cur is excellent at faults.[3]

MALVOLIO: M—But then there is no consonancy in the sequel that suffers under probation:[4] A should follow, but O does.

---

8. Proverbially stupid bird.
9. Snare.
1. Whim.
2. Cut; slang for female pudenda.
3. Uppercase; copious (implying "pee").
4. Beyond.
5. Conventional apology for breaking a seal.
6. Softly.
7. Lucretia; chaste matron.
8. Seat of passion.
9. Verses.
1. Badger.
2. Pompous.

3. Clever girl (Maria).
4. Prepared.
5. Speed.
6. Inferior hawk.
7. Turns to fly at it.
8. Normal understanding.
9. Difficulty.
1. Difficult trail.
2. The hound will pick up the scent.
3. Breaks in the scent.
4. Pattern in the letters that stands up under examination.

FABIAN: And O shall end,[5] I hope.

SIR TOBY: Ay, or I'll cudgel him, and make him cry "O!"

MALVOLIO: And then I comes behind.

FABIAN: Ay, an you had any eye behind you, you might see more detraction[6] at your heels than fortunes before you.

MALVOLIO: M.O.A.I. This simulation[7] is not as the former. And yet, to crush[8] this a little, it would bow to me, for every one of these letters are in my name. Soft! Here follows prose.

110   [*He reads.*] "If this fall into thy hand, revolve.[9] In my stars[1] I am above thee, but be not afraid of greatness. Some are born great, some achieve greatness, and some have greatness thrust upon 'em. Thy Fates open their hands; let thy blood and spirit embrace them; and, to inure[2] thyself to what thou art like to be, cast thy humble slough[3] and appear fresh. Be opposite[4] with a

115   kinsman, surly with servants. Let thy tongue tang[5] arguments of state; put thyself into the trick of singularity.[6] She thus advises thee that sighs for thee. Remember who commended thy yellow stockings, and wished to see thee ever cross-gartered.[7] I say, remember. Go to, thou art made, if thou desir'st to be so. If not, let me see thee a steward still, the fellow of servants, and not

120   worthy to touch Fortune's fingers. Farewell. She that would alter services[8] with thee,

The Fortunate-Unhappy."[9]

Daylight and champaign[1] discovers[2] not more! This is open. I will be proud, I will read politic authors,[3] I will baffle[4] Sir Toby, I will wash off gross

125   acquaintance, I will be point-devise[5] the very man. I do not now fool myself, to let imagination jade[6] me; for every reason excites to this, that my lady loves me. She did commend my yellow stockings of late, she did praise my leg being cross-gartered; and in this[7] she manifests herself to my love, and with a kind of injunction drives me to these habits[8] of her liking. I thank my

130   stars, I am happy.[9] I will be strange,[1] stout,[2] in yellow stockings and cross-gartered, even with the swiftness of putting on. Jove and my stars be praised! Here is yet a post-script. [*He reads.*] "Thou canst not choose but know who I am. If thou entertain'st[3] my love, let it appear in thy smiling; thy smiles become thee well. Therefore in my presence still[4] smile, dear my sweet, I

135   prithee."

Jove, I thank thee. I will smile; I will do everything that thou wilt have me.   [*Exit.*]

[*Sir Toby, Sir Andrew, and Fabian come from hiding.*]

---

5. O ends Malvolio's name; a noose shall end his life; *omega* ends the Greek alphabet.
6. Defamation.
7. Disguise.
8. Force.
9. Consider.
1. Fate.
2. Accustom.
3. Outer skin.
4. Contradictory.
5. Sound with.
6. Eccentricity.
7. Wearing hose garters crossed above and below the knee.
8. Change places.

9. Unfortunate.
1. Open country.
2. Discloses.
3. Political writers.
4. Disgrace.
5. Correct to the letter.
6. Trick.
7. This letter.
8. Attire.
9. Fortunate.
1. Aloof.
2. Haughty.
3. You accept.
4. Always.

FABIAN: I will not give my part of this sport for a pension of thousands to be paid
140   from the Sophy.[5]

SIR TOBY: I could marry this wench for this device.

SIR ANDREW: So could I too.

SIR TOBY: And ask no other dowry with her but such another jest.

    [*Enter Maria.*]

SIR ANDREW: Nor I neither.

FABIAN: Here comes my noble gull-catcher.[6]

SIR TOBY: Wilt thou set thy foot o' my neck?

SIR ANDREW: Or o' mine either?

SIR TOBY: Shall I play[7] my freedom at tray-trip,[8] and become thy bondslave?

SIR ANDREW: I' faith, or I either?

SIR TOBY: Why, thou hast put him in such a dream that when the image of it
150   leaves him he must run mad.

MARIA: Nay, but say true, does it work upon him?

SIR TOBY: Like aqua vitae[9] with a midwife.

MARIA: If you will then see the fruits of the sport, mark his first approach before my
    lady. He will come to her in yellow stockings, and 'tis a color she abhors,
155   and cross-gartered, a fashion she detests; and he will smile upon her, which
    will now be so unsuitable to her disposition, being addicted to a melancholy
    as she is, that it cannot but turn him into a notable contempt.[1] If you will
    see it, follow me.

SIR TOBY: To the gates of Tartar,[2] thou most excellent devil of wit!

SIR ANDREW: I'll make one[3] too.   [*Exeunt.*]

ACT 3

Scene 1[4]

[*Enter Viola, and Clown (Feste, playing his pipe and tabor)*.]

VIOLA: Save thee,[5] friend, and thy music. Dost thou live by[6] thy tabor?[7]

FESTE: No, sir, I live by the church.

VIOLA: Art thou a churchman?

FESTE: No such matter, sir. I do live by the church, for I do live at my house, and
5   my house doth stand by the church.

VIOLA: So thou mayst say the king lies[8] by a beggar if a beggar dwell near him, or
    the church stands by thy tabor if thy tabor stand by the church.

FESTE: You have said, sir. To see this age! A sentence is but a cheveril[9] glove to a
    good wit. How quickly the wrong side may be turned outward!

VIOLA: Nay, that's certain. They that dally nicely[1] with words may quickly make
    them wanton.[2]

FESTE: I would therefore my sister had had no name, sir.

VIOLA: Why, man?

---

5. Shah of Persia.
6. Fool-catcher.
7. Gamble.
8. Game of dice.
9. Distilled liquor.
1. Notorious object of contempt.
2. Tartarus, the section of hell for the most evil.
3. Tag along.

4. Location: Olivia's garden.
5. God save.
6. Earn your living with.
7. Drum.
8. Dwells; lies sexually.
9. Kid.
1. Play subtly; toy amorously.
2. Equivocal.

FESTE: Why, sir, her name's a word, and to dally with that word might make my
15   sister wanton.³ But indeed, words are very rascals since bonds disgraced them.⁴

VIOLA: Thy reason, man?

FESTE: Troth, sir, I can yield you none without words, and words are grown so false
        I am loath to prove reason with them.

VIOLA: I warrant thou art a merry fellow and car'st for nothing.

FESTE: Not so, sir, I do care for something; but in my conscience, sir, I do not
        care for you. If that be to care for nothing, sir, I would it would make you
        invisible.

VIOLA: Art not thou the Lady Olivia's fool?

FESTE: No indeed, sir. The Lady Olivia has no folly. She will keep no fool, sir, till
25   she be married, and fools are as like husbands as pilchers⁵ are to herrings—
        the husband's the bigger. I am indeed not her fool but her corrupter of
        words.

VIOLA: I saw thee late⁶ at the Count Orsino's.

FESTE: Foolery, sir, does walk about the orb⁷ like the sun; it shines everywhere. I
30   would be sorry, sir, but⁸ the fool should be as oft with your master as with my
        mistress. I think I saw your wisdom there.

VIOLA: Nay, an thou pass upon⁹ me, I'll no more with thee. Hold, there's expenses
        for thee. [*She gives a coin.*]

FESTE: Now Jove, in his next commodity¹ of hair, send thee a beard!

VIOLA: By my troth, I'll tell thee, I am almost sick for one—[*aside*] though I would
        not have it grow on my chin.—Is thy lady within?

FESTE: Would not a pair of these have bred, sir?

VIOLA: Yes, being kept together and put to use.²

FESTE: I would play Lord Pandarus³ of Phrygia, sir, to bring a Cressida to this
40   Troilus.

VIOLA: I understand you, sir. 'Tis well begged. [*She gives another coin.*]

FESTE: The matter, I hope, is not great, sir, begging but a beggar; Cressida was a
        beggar.⁴ My lady is within, sir. I will conster⁵ to them whence you come.
        Who you are and what you would are out of my welkin⁶—I might say
45   "element," but the word is overworn.   [*Exit.*]

VIOLA: This fellow is wise enough to play the fool,
        And to do that well craves° a kind of wit.   *requires*
        He must observe their mood on whom he jests,
        The quality of persons, and the time,
50   And, like the haggard,° check° at every feather   *untrained hawk / turn*
        That comes before his eye. This is a practice°   *skill*
        As full of labor as a wise man's art;
        For folly that he wisely shows is fit,
        But wise men, folly-fall'n,° quite taint their wit.⁷   *fallen into folly*
[*Enter Sir Toby and (Sir) Andrew.*]

---

3. Licentious.
4. Since sworn statements have been needed to make them good.
5. Pitchers.
6. Recently.
7. Earth.
8. Unless.
9. Fence verbally with me.

1. Shipment.
2. Put out at interest.
3. Go-between in the story of Troilus and Cressida.
4. She became a leprous beggar in Henrsyon's continuation of Chaucer's story.
5. Explain.
6. Sky.
7. Ruin their reputation for intelligence.

SIR TOBY: Save you, gentleman.

VIOLA: And you, sir.

SIR ANDREW: *Dieu vous garde, monsieur.*[8]

VIOLA: *Et vous aussi; votre serviteur.*[9]

SIR ANDREW: I hope, sir, you are, and I am yours.

SIR TOBY: Will you encounter[1] the house? My niece is desirous you should enter, if
    your trade[2] be to her.

VIOLA: I am bound to[3] your niece, sir; I mean, she is the list[4] of my voyage.

SIR TOBY: Taste[5] your legs, sir. Put them to motion.

VIOLA: My legs do better understand[6] me, sir, than I understand what you mean by
65   bidding me taste my legs.

SIR TOBY: I mean, to go, sir, to enter.

VIOLA: I will answer you with gait and entrance.—But we are prevented.[7]
    [*Enter Olivia and gentlewoman (Maria).*]
    Most excellent accomplished lady, the heavens rain odors on you!

SIR ANDREW: That youth's a rare courtier. "Rain odors"—well.

VIOLA: My matter hath no voice,[8] lady, but to your own most pregnant[9] and
    vouchsafed[1] ear.

SIR ANDREW: "Odors," "pregnant," and "vouchsafed." I'll get 'em all three all
    ready.[2]

OLIVIA: Let the garden door be shut, and leave me to my hearing. [*Exeunt Sir
75   Toby, Sir Andrew, and Maria.*] Give me your hand, sir.

VIOLA: My duty, madam, and most humble service.

OLIVIA: What is your name?

VIOLA: Cesario is your servant's name, fair princess.

OLIVIA: My servant, sir? 'Twas never merry world
80   Since lowly feigning° was called compliment.   *false humility*
    You're servant to the Count Orsino, youth.

VIOLA: And he is yours, and his must needs be yours;
    Your servant's servant is your servant, madam.

OLIVIA: For him, I think not on him. For his thoughts,
85   Would they were blanks, rather than filled with me!

VIOLA: Madam, I come to whet your gentle thoughts
    On his behalf.

OLIVIA: O, by your leave,° I pray you.   *please*
    I bade you never speak again of him.
    But, would you undertake another suit,
90   I had rather hear you to solicit that
    Than music from the spheres.°   *heavenly harmony*

VIOLA: Dear lady—

OLIVIA: Give me leave, beseech you. I did send,
    After the last enchantment you did here,
    A ring in chase of you; so did I abuse°   *deceive*

8. God protect you, sir.
9. You, too; your servant.
1. Enter.
2. Business.
3. Bound for; obliged to.
4. Destination.
5. Try.

6. Comprehend; stand under.
7. Anticipated.
8. Cannot be uttered.
9. Receptive.
1. Attentive.
2. Memorized for future use.

95   Myself, my servant, and, I fear me, you.
        Under your hard construction° must I sit,   *interpretation*
        To force° that on you in a shameful cunning   *for forcing*
        Which you knew none of yours. What might you think?
        Have you not set mine honor at the stake
100   And baited° it with all th' unmuzzled thoughts   *harassed*
        That tyrannous heart can think? To one of your receiving°   *intelligence*
        Enough is shown; a cypress,° not a bosom,   *thin black cloth*
        Hides my heart. So, let me hear you speak.
VIOLA: I pity you.
OLIVIA: That's a degree to love.
VIOLA: No, not a grece;° for 'tis a vulgar proof°   *step / common experience*
        That very oft we pity enemies.
OLIVIA: Why then, methinks 'tis time to smile again.
        O world, how apt° the poor are to be proud!   *ready*
        If one should be a prey, how much the better
110   To fall before the lion than the wolf!
    [*Clock strikes.*]
        The clock upbraids me with the waste of time.
        Be not afraid, good youth, I will not have you;
        And yet, when wit and youth is come to harvest
        Your wife is like° to reap a proper° man.   *likely / handsome*
        There lies your way, due west.
VIOLA: Then westward ho!³
        Grace and good disposition attend your ladyship.
        You'll nothing, madam, to my lord by me?
OLIVIA: Stay.
        I prithee, tell me what thou think'st of me.
VIOLA: That you do think you are not what you are.
OLIVIA: If I think so, I think the same of you.
VIOLA: Then think you right. I am not what I am.
OLIVIA: I would you were as I would have you be!
VIOLA: Would it be better, madam, than I am?
125   I wish it might, for now I am your fool.
OLIVIA [*aside*]: O, what a deal of scorn looks beautiful
        In the contempt and anger of his lip!
        A murderous guilt shows not itself more soon
        Than love that would seem hid; love's night is noon.⁴—
130   Cesario, by the roses of the spring,
        By maidhood, honor, truth, and everything,
        I love thee so that, maugre° all thy pride,   *despite*
        Nor wit nor reason can my passion hide.
        Do not extort thy reasons from this clause,
135   For that I woo, thou therefore hast no cause.
        But rather reason thus with reason fetter.
        Love sought is good, but given unsought is better.

___

3. The cry of Thames watermen to attract westward-   4. Love cannot hide itself.
bound passengers from London to Westminster.

VIOLA: By innocence I swear, and by my youth,
          I have one heart, one bosom, and one truth,
140   And that no woman has, nor never none
          Shall mistress be of it save I alone.
          And so adieu, good madam. Nevermore
          Will I my master's tears to you deplore.°   *beweep*
OLIVIA: Yet come again, for thou perhaps mayst move
145   That heart, which now abhors, to like his love.

                                                          [*Exeunt (separately)*.]

                              Scene 2⁵

          [*Enter Sir Toby, Sir Andrew, and Fabian.*]

SIR ANDREW: No, faith, I'll not stay a jot longer.
SIR TOBY: Thy reason, dear venom,⁶ give thy reason.
FABIAN: You must needs yield your reason, Sir Andrew.
SIR ANDREW: Marry, I saw your niece do more favors to the Count's servingman
5   than ever she bestowed upon me. I saw't i' the orchard.⁷
SIR TOBY: Did she see thee the while, old boy? Tell me that.
SIR ANDREW: As plain as I see you now.
FABIAN: This was a great argument⁸ of love in her toward you.
SIR ANDREW: 'Slight,⁹ will you make an ass o' me?
FABIAN: I will prove it legitimate,¹ sir, upon the oaths² of judgment and reason.
SIR TOBY: And they have been grand-jurymen since before Noah was a sailor.
FABIAN: She did show favor to the youth in your sight only to exasperate you, to
          awake your dormouse³ valor, to put fire in your heart and brimstone in your
          liver. You should then have accosted her, and with some excellent jests,
15   fire-new from the mint, you should have banged the youth into dumbness.
          This was looked for at your hand, and this was balked.⁴ The double gilt of
          this opportunity you let time wash off, and you are now sailed into the
          north⁵ of my lady's opinion, where you will hang like an icicle on a Dutch-
          man's beard⁶ unless you do redeem it by some laudable attempt either of
20   valor or policy.⁷
SIR ANDREW: An't be any way, it must be with valor, for policy I hate. I had as lief
          be a Brownist⁸ as a politician.⁹
SIR TOBY: Why, then, build me thy fortunes upon the basis of valor. Challenge me
          the Count's youth to fight with him; hurt him in eleven places. My niece
25   shall take note of it; and assure thyself, there is no love-broker in the world
          can more prevail in man's commendation with woman than report of valor.
FABIAN: There is no way but this, Sir Andrew.
SIR ANDREW: Will either of you bear me a challenge to him?

5. Location: Olivia's house.
6. Venomous person.
7. Garden.
8. Proof.
9. God's light.
1. True.
2. Testimony.
3. Sleepy.

4. Missed.
5. Out of the warmth.
6. Alludes to the arctic voyage of William Berentz in 1596–1597.
7. Stratagem.
8. Early name for the Congregationalists, after founder Robert Browne.
9. Schemer.

SIR TOBY: Go, write it in a martial hand. Be curst[1] and brief; it is no matter how
30   witty, so it be eloquent and full of invention. Taunt him with the license of
      ink.[2] If thou "thou"-est[3] him some thrice, it shall not be amiss; and as many
      lies[4] as will lie in thy sheet of paper, although the sheet were big enough for
      the bed of Ware[5] in England, set 'em down. Go, about it. Let there be gall[6]
      enough in thy ink, though thou write with a goose pen,[7] no matter. About it.
SIR ANDREW: Where shall I find you?
SIR TOBY: We'll call thee at the cubiculo.[8] Go.

[*Exit Sir Andrew.*]

FABIAN: This is a dear manikin[9] to you, Sir Toby.
SIR TOBY: I have been dear to him, lad, some two thousand strong or so.
FABIAN: We shall have a rare letter from him; but you'll not deliver 't?
SIR TOBY: Never trust me, then; and by all means stir on the youth to an answer. I
      think oxen and wainropes[1] cannot hale[2] them together. For Andrew, if he
      were opened and you find so much blood in his liver[3] as will clog the foot of
      a flea, I'll eat the rest of th' anatomy.
FABIAN: And his opposite,[4] the youth, bears in his visage no great presage of cruelty.
      [*Enter Maria.*]
SIR TOBY: Look where the youngest wren[5] of nine comes.
MARIA: If you desire the spleen,[6] and will laugh yourselves into stitches, follow me.
      Yond gull[7] Malvolio is turned heathen, a very renegado; for there is no
      Christian that means to be saved by believing rightly can ever believe such
      impossible passages of grossness.[8] He's in yellow stockings.
SIR TOBY: And cross-gartered?
MARIA: Most villainously, like a pedant that keeps a school i', the church. I have
      dogged him like his murderer. He does obey every point of the letter that I
      dropped to betray him. He does smile his face into more lines than is in the
      new map with the augmentation of the Indies.[9] You have not seen such a
55   thing as 'tis. I can hardly forbear hurling things at him. I know my lady will
      strike him. If she do, he'll smile and take't for a great favor.
SIR TOBY: Come, bring us, bring us where he is.

[*Exeunt omnes.*]

Scene 3[1]

[*Enter Sebastian and Antonio.*]
SEBASTIAN: I would not by my will have troubled you,
      But since you make your pleasure of your pains,
      I will no further chide you.
ANTONIO: I could not stay behind you. My desire,
5   More sharp than filèd steel, did spur me forth,

---

1. Fierce.
2. Freedom of writing.
3. Call him "thou" (informal).
4. Charges of lying.
5. Famous bed, more than ten feet wide.
6. Bitterness; ingredient in ink.
7. Goose quill; foolish style.
8. Small chamber.
9. Puppet.
1. Wagon ropes.

2. Haul.
3. A pale and bloodless liver was a sign of cowardice.
4. Adversary.
5. Smallest of small birds.
6. Laughing fit.
7. Fool.
8. Gross impossibilities.
9. Emerie Molyneux's map, c. 1599, which showed more of the East Indies than had ever been mapped before.
1. Location: A street.

And not all° love to see you—though so much   *only*
As might have drawn one to a longer voyage—
But jealousy° what might befall your travel,   *solicitude*
Being skilless in° these parts, which to a stranger,   *unacquainted with*
10   Unguided and unfriended, often prove
Rough and unhospitable. My willing love,
The rather by these arguments of fear,
Set forth in your pursuit.

SEBASTIAN: My kind Antonio,
I can no other answer make but thanks,
15   And thanks; and ever oft good turns
Are shuffled off with such uncurrent° pay.   *valueless*
But were my worth,° as is my conscience,° firm,   *wealth / inclination*
You should find better dealing.° What's to do?   *treatment*
Shall we go see the relics° of this town?   *monuments*

ANTONIO: Tomorrow, sir. Best first go see your lodging.

SEBASTIAN: I am not weary, and 'tis long to night.
I pray you, let us satisfy our eyes
With the memorials and the things of fame
That do renown° this city.   *make famous*

ANTONIO: Would you'd pardon me.
25   I do not without danger walk these streets.
Once in a sea fight 'gainst the Count his° galleys   *Count's*
I did some service, of such note indeed
That were I ta'en here it would scarce be answered.°   *atoned for*

SEBASTIAN: Belike° you slew great number of his people?   *Perhaps*

ANTONIO: Th' offense is not of such a bloody nature,
Albeit the quality of the time and quarrel
Might well have given us bloody argument.°   *cause for bloodshed*
It might have since been answered° in repaying   *atoned for*
What we took from them, which for traffic's° sake   *trade's*
35   Most of our city did. Only myself stood out,
For which, if I be lapsèd° in this place,   *surprised*
I shall pay dear.

SEBASTIAN: Do not then walk too open.

ANTONIO: It doth not fit me. Hold, sir, here's my purse. [*He gives his purse.*]
In the south suburbs, at the Elephant,°   *an inn*
40   Is best to lodge. I will bespeak our diet,°   *order our food*
Whiles you beguile the time and feed your knowledge
With viewing of the town. There shall you have me.

SEBASTIAN: Why I your purse?

ANTONIO: Haply° your eye shall light upon some toy°   *perhaps / trifle*
45   You have desire to purchase; and your store°   *store of money*
I think is not for idle markets,° sir.   *useless purchases*

SEBASTIAN: I'll be your purse-bearer and leave you
For an hour.

ANTONIO: To th' Elephant.

SEBASTIAN: I do remember.

                                [*Exeunt (separately).*]

Scene 4[2]

[*Enter Olivia and Maria.*]

OLIVIA [*aside*]: I have sent after him; he says he'll come.
How shall I feast him? What bestow of him?
For youth is bought more oft than begged or borrowed.
I speak too loud.—

5   Where's Malvolio? He is sad and civil,[3]
And suits well for a servant with my fortunes.
Where is Malvolio?

MARIA: He's coming, madam, but in very strange manner. He is, sure, possessed,
madam.

OLIVIA: Why, what's the matter? Does he rave?

MARIA: No, madam, he does nothing but smile. Your ladyship were best to have
some guard about you if he come, for sure the man is tainted in 's wits.

OLIVIA: Go call him hither. [*Maria summons Malvolio.*] I am as mad as he,
If sad and merry madness equal be.

[*Enter Malvolio, (cross-gartered and in yellow stockings).*]

15   How now, Malvolio?

MALVOLIO: Sweet lady, ho, ho!

OLIVIA: Smil'st thou? I sent for thee upon a sad occasion.

MALVOLIO: Sad, lady? I could be sad. This does make some obstruction in the
blood, this cross-gartering, but what of that? If it please the eye of one, it is
20   with me as the very true sonnet[4] is, "Please one and please all."

OLIVIA: Why, how dost thou, man? What is the matter with thee?

MALVOLIO: Not black in my mind, though yellow in my legs. It did come to his
hands, and commands shall be executed. I think we do know the sweet
roman hand.[5]

OLIVIA: Wilt thou go to bed, Malvolio?

MALVOLIO: To bed! "Ay, sweetheart, and I'll come to thee."[6]

OLIVIA: God comfort thee! Why dost thou smile so and kiss thy hand so oft?

MARIA: How do you, Malvolio?

MALVOLIO: At your request? Yes, nightingales answer daws.[7]

MARIA: Why appear you with this ridiculous boldness before my lady?

MALVOLIO: "Be not afraid of greatness." 'Twas well writ.

OLIVIA: What mean'st thou by that, Malvolio?

MALVOLIO: "Some are born great—"

OLIVIA: Ha?

MALVOLIO: "Some achieve greatness—"

OLIVIA: What sayst thou?

MALVOLIO: "And some have greatness thrust upon them."

OLIVIA: Heaven restore thee!

MALVOLIO: "Remember who commended thy yellow stockings—"

OLIVIA: Thy yellow stockings?

MALVOLIO: "And wished to see thee cross-gartered."

2. Location: Olivia's garden.
3. Serious and sedate.
4. Song.
5. Italian style of handwriting.

6. Quotation from a popular song.
7. I.e., why should a fine fellow like me answer a daw
(crow) like you.

OLIVIA: Cross-gartered?

MALVOLIO: "Go to, thou art made, if thou desir'st to be so—"

OLIVIA: Am I made?

MALVOLIO: "If not, let me see thee a servant still."

OLIVIA: Why, this is very midsummer madness.

[*Enter Servant.*]

SERVANT: Madam, the young gentleman of the Count Orsino's is returned. I could hardly, entreat him back. He attends your ladyship's pleasure.

OLIVIA: I'll come to him. [*Exit Servant.*] Good Maria, let this fellow be looked to.
50 Where's my cousin Toby? Let some of my people have a special care of him. I would not have him miscarry[8] for the half of my dowry.

[*Exeunt (Olivia and Maria, different ways).*]

MALVOLIO: Oho, do you come near[9] me now? No worse man than Sir Toby to look to me! This concurs directly with the letter. She sends him on purpose that I may appear stubborn to him, for she incites me to that in the letter.
55 "Cast thy humble slough," says she; "be opposite with a kinsman, surly with servants; let thy tongue tang with arguments of state; put thyself into the trick of singularity." And consequently sets down the manner how: as, a sad[1] face, a reverend carriage, a slow tongue, in the habit[2] of some sir of note, and so forth. I have limed[3] her, but it is Jove's doing, and Jove make me
60 thankful! And when she went away now, "Let this fellow be looked to." "Fellow!"[4] Not "Malvolio," nor after my degree,[5] but "fellow." Why, everything adheres together, that no dram[6] of a scruple,[7] no scruple of a scruple, no obstacle, no incredulous[8] or unsafe circumstance—what can be said?— nothing that can be can come between me and the full prospect of my
65 hopes. Well, Jove, not I, is the doer of this, and he is to be thanked.

[*Enter (Sir) Toby, Fabian, and Maria.*]

SIR TOBY: Which way is he, in the name of sanctity? If all the devils of hell be drawn in little,[9] and Legion[1] himself possessed him, yet I'll speak to him.

FABIAN: Here he is, here he is.—How is't with you, sir? How is't with you, man?

MALVOLIO: Go off. I discard you. Let me enjoy my private. Go off.

MARIA: Lo, how hollow the fiend speaks within him! Did not I tell you? Sir Toby, my lady prays you to have a care of him.

MALVOLIO: Aha, does she so?

SIR TOBY: Go to, go to! Peace, peace, we must deal gently with him. Let me alone.—How do you, Malvolio? How is 't with you? What, man, defy the
75 devil! Consider, he's an enemy to mankind.

MALVOLIO: Do you know what you say?

MARIA: La you,[2] an you speak ill of the devil, how he takes it at heart! Pray God he be not bewitched!

FABIAN: Carry his water[3] to the wisewoman.

---

8. Come to harm.
9. Appreciate.
1. Serious.
2. Attire.
3. Caught.
4. Companion.
5. According to my position.
6. Small amount; one-eighth of a fluid ounce.

7. Doubt; one-third of a dram.
8. Incredible.
9. Brought together in a small space.
1. An unclean spirit ("My name is Legion, for we are many," Mark 5.9).
2. Look you.
3. Urine.

MARIA: Marry, and it shall be done tomorrow morning, if I live. My lady would not lose him for more than I'll say.

MALVOLIO: How now, mistress?

MARIA: O Lord!

SIR TOBY: Prithee, hold thy peace; this is not the way. Do you not see you move[4]
85   him? Let me alone with him.

FABIAN: No way but gentleness, gently, gently. The fiend is rough, and will not be roughly used.

SIR TOBY: Why, how now, my bawcock![5] How dost thou, chuck?[6]

MALVOLIO: Sir!

SIR TOBY: Ay, biddy,[7] come with me. What man, tis not for gravity[8] to play at cherry-pit[9] with Satan. Hang him, foul collier![1]

MARIA: Get him to say his prayers, good Sir Toby, get him to pray.

MALVOLIO: My prayers, minx?

MARIA: No, I warrant you, he will not hear of godliness.

MALVOLIO: Go hang yourselves all! You are idle,[2] shallow things; I am not of your element. You shall know more hereafter.   [Exit.]

SIR TOBY: Is 't possible?

FABIAN: If this were played upon a stage, now, I could condemn it as an improbable fiction.

SIR TOBY: His very genius[3] hath taken the infection of the device, man.

MARIA: Nay, pursue him now, lest the device take air and taint.[4]

FABIAN: Why, we shall make him mad indeed.

MARIA: The house will be the quieter.

SIR TOBY: Come, we'll have him in a dark room and bound. My niece is already in
105   the belief that he's mad. We may carry it[5] thus for our pleasure and his penance till our very pastime, tired out of breath, prompt us to have mercy on him, at which time we will bring the device to the bar[6] and crown thee for a finder of madmen. But see, but see!

[Enter Sir Andrew (with a letter).]

FABIAN: More matter for a May morning.[7]

SIR ANDREW: Here's the challenge. Read it. I warrant there's vinegar and pepper in 't.

FABIAN: Is 't so saucy?[8]

SIR ANDREW: Ay, is 't, I warrant him. Do but read.

SIR TOBY: Give me. [He reads.] "Youth, whatsoever thou art, thou art but a scurvy fellow."

FABIAN: Good, and valiant.

SIR TOBY [reads]: "Wonder not, nor admire[9] not in thy mind, why I do call thee so, for I will show thee no reason for 't."

FABIAN: A good note, that keeps you from the blow of the law.

4. Upset.
5. Fine fellow (from French beau-coq).
6. Chick.
7. Chicken.
8. Dignity.
9. A child's game.
1. Coal-peddler.
2. Foolish.

3. Spirit.
4. Become exposed to air and, thus, to spoil.
5. Carry the trick on.
6. To court.
7. Material for a Mayday comedy.
8. Spicy; insolent.
9. Marvel.

SIR TOBY [*reads*]: "Thou com'st to the Lady Olivia, and in my sight she uses thee
120　　kindly. But thou liest in thy throat; that is not the matter I challenge thee
　　　for."
FABIAN: Very brief, and to exceeding good sense—less.
SIR TOBY [*reads*]: "I will waylay thee going home, where if it be thy chance to kill
　　　me—"
FABIAN: Good.
SIR TOBY [*reads*]: "Thou kill'st me like a rogue and a villain."
FABIAN: Still you keep o' the windy[1] side of the law. Good.
SIR TOBY [*reads*]: "Fare thee well, and God have mercy upon one of our souls! He
　　　may have mercy upon mine, but my hope is better, and so look to thyself.
130　　Thy friend, as thou usest him, and thy sworn enemy,

　　　　　　　　　　　　　　　　　　　　　　　　Andrew Aguecheek."
　　　If this letter move him not, his legs cannot. I'll give 't him.
MARIA: You may have very fit occasion for 't. He is now in some commerce with
　　　my lady, and will by and by depart.
SIR TOBY: Go, Sir Andrew. Scout me[2] for him at the corner of the orchard like a
　　　bum-baily.[3] So soon as ever thou seest him, draw, and as thou draw'st, swear
　　　horrible; for it comes to pass oft that a terrible oath, with a swaggering
　　　accent sharply twanged off, gives manhood more approbation[4] than ever
　　　proof[5] itself would have earned him. Away!
SIR ANDREW: Nay, let me alone for swearing.[6]　　　　　　　　　　　[*Exit.*]
SIR TOBY: Now will not I deliver his letter, for the behavior of the young gentle-
　　　man gives him out to be of good capacity and breeding; his employment
　　　between his lord and my niece confirms no less. Therefore this letter, being
　　　so excellently ignorant, will breed no terror in the youth. He will find it
145　　comes from a clodpoll.[7] But, sir, I will deliver his challenge by word of
　　　mouth, set upon Aguecheek a notable report of valor, and drive the gentle-
　　　man—as I know his youth will aptly receive it—into a most hideous opin-
　　　ion of his rage, skill, fury, and impetuosity. This will so fright them both
　　　that they will kill one another by the look, like cockatrices.[8]
　　[*Enter Olivia and Viola.*]
FABIAN: Here he comes with your niece. Give them way till he take leave, and
　　　presently after him.
SIR TOBY: I will meditate the while upon some horrid message for a challenge.
　　　　　　　　　　　　　　　　　　　　[*Exeunt Sir Toby, Fabian, and Maria.*]
OLIVIA: I have said too much unto a heart of stone
　　　And laid mine honor too unchary° on 't.　　　　　　　　　　　　*carelessly*
155　　There's something in me that reproves my fault,
　　　But such a headstrong potent fault it is
　　　That it but mocks reproof.
VIOLA: With the same havior° that your passion bears　　　　　　　*behavior*
　　　Goes on my master's griefs.
OLIVIA [*giving a locket*]: Here, wear this jewel for me. 'Tis my picture.

1. Windward; i.e., safe.
2. Keep watch.
3. Agent who makes arrests.
4. Reputation.

5. Testing.
6. Leave swearing to me.
7. Blockhead.
8. Basilisks, or reptiles able to kill with a glance.

Refuse it not; it hath no tongue to vex you.
And I beseech you come again tomorrow.
What shall you ask of me that I'll deny,
That honor, saved, may upon asking give?

VIOLA: Nothing but this; your true love for my master.

OLIVIA: How with mine honor may I give him that
Which I have given to you?

VIOLA: I will acquit° you.   release

OLIVIA: Well, come again tomorrow. Fare thee well.
A fiend like° thee might bear my soul to hell.   [*Exit.*]   resembling

[*Enter (Sir) Toby and Fabian.*]

SIR TOBY: Gentleman, God save thee.

VIOLA: And you, sir.

SIR TOBY: That defense thou hast, betake thee to 't. Of what nature the wrongs
are thou hast done him, I know not, but thy intercepter,[9] full of despite,[1]
bloody as the hunter, attends thee at the orchard end. Dismount thy tuck,[2]
175   be yare[3] in thy preparation, for thy assailant is quick, skillful, and deadly.

VIOLA: You mistake sir. I am sure no man hath any quarrel to me. My remembrance is very free and clear from any image of offense done to any man.

SIR TOBY: You'll find it otherwise, I assure you. Therefore, if you hold your life at
any price, betake you to your guard, for your opposite[4] hath in him what
180   youth, strength, skill, and wrath can furnish man withal.

VIOLA: I pray you, sir, what is he?

SIR TOBY: He is knight, dubbed with unhatched[5] rapier and on carpet consideration,[6] but he is a devil in private brawl. Souls and bodies hath he divorced
three, and his incensement at this moment is so implacable that satisfaction
185   can be none but by pangs of death and sepulcher. Hob, nob[7] is his word;[8]
give 't or take 't.

VIOLA: I will return again into the house and desire some conduct[9] of the lady. I am
no fighter. I have heard of some kind of men that put quarrels purposely on
others, to taste[1] their valor. Belike[2] this is a man of that quirk.[3]

SIR TOBY: Sir, no. His indignation derives itself out of a very competent[4] injury;
therefore, get you on and give him his desire. Back you shall not to the
house unless you undertake that with me which with as much safety you
might answer him. Therefore, on, or strip your sword stark naked; for
meddle[5] you must, that's certain, or forswear to wear iron[6] about you.

VIOLA: This is as uncivil as strange. I beseech you, do me this courteous office, as to
know of the knight what my offense to him is. It is something of my negligence, nothing of my purpose.

SIR TOBY: I will do so.—Signor Fabian, stay you by this gentleman till my return.

[*Exit (Sir) Toby.*]

9. He who lies in wait.
1. Defiance.
2. Draw your rapier.
3. Quick.
4. Opponent.
5. Unhacked; unused in battle.
6. Through court favor.
7. Have or have not.

8. Motto.
9. Escort.
1. Test.
2. Probably.
3. Peculiarity.
4. Sufficient.
5. Engage in combat.
6. Give up your right to wear a sword.

VIOLA: Pray you, sir, do you know of this matter?

FABIAN: I know the knight is incensed against you, even to a mortal arbitrament,[7] but nothing of the circumstance more.

VIOLA: I beseech you, what manner of man is he?

FABIAN: Nothing of that wonderful promise, to read him by his form, as you are like to find him in the proof of his valor. He is, indeed, sir, the most skillful, bloody, and fatal opposite that you could possibly have found in any part of Illyria. Will you walk towards him, I will make your peace with him if I can.

VIOLA: I shall be much bound to you for 't. I am one that had rather go with Sir Priest than Sir Knight. I care not who knows so much of my mettle. [*Exeunt.*]
[*Enter (Sir) Toby and (Sir) Andrew.*]

SIR TOBY: Why, man, he's a very devil; I have not seen such a firago.[8] I had a pass[9] with him, rapier, scabbard, and all, and he gives me the stuck in[1] with such a mortal motion that it is inevitable; and on the answer,[2] he pays you as surely as your feet hits the ground they step on. They say he has been fencer to the Sophy.

SIR ANDREW: Pox on 't, I'll not meddle with him.

SIR TOBY: Ay, but he will not now be pacified. Fabian can scarce hold him younder.

SIR ANDREW: Plague on 't, an I thought he had been valiant and so cunning in fence, I'd have seen him damned ere I'd have challenged him. Let him let the matter slip and I'll give him my horse, gray Capilet.

SIR TOBY: I'll make the motion.[3] Stand here, make a good show on 't. This shall end without the perdition of souls.[4] [*Aside, as he crosses to meet Fabian.*] Marry, I'll ride your horse as well as I ride you.
[*Enter Fabian and Viola.*]
[*Aside to Fabian.*] I have his horse to take up[5] the quarrel. I have persuaded him the youth's a devil.

FABIAN: He is as horribly conceited of him,[6] and pants and looks pale as if a bear were at his heels.

SIR TOBY [*to Viola*]: There's no remedy, sir, he will fight with you for 's oath's sake. Marry, he hath better bethought him of his quarrel, and he finds that now scarce to be worth talking of. Therefore draw, for the supportance of his vow; he protests he will not hurt you.

VIOLA [*aside*]: Pray God defend me! A little thing would make me tell them how much I lack of a man.

FABIAN: Give ground, if you see him furious.

SIR TOBY [*crossing to Sir Andrew*]: Come, Sir Andrew, there's no remedy. The gentleman will, for his honor's sake, have one bout with you. He cannot by the *duello*[7] avoid it. But he has promised me, as he is a gentleman and a soldier, he will not hurt you. Come on, to 't.

SIR ANDREW: Pray God he keep his oath!
[*Enter Antonio.*]

7. Trial to the death.
8. Virago (overbearing woman).
9. Bout.
1. Thrust.
2. Return.
3. Offer.

4. I.e., killing.
5. Settle.
6. I.e., Cesario has as horrible a conception of Sir Andrew.
7. Dueling code.

VIOLA: I do assure you, 'tis against my will.
    [*They draw.*]
ANTONIO [*drawing, to Sir Andrew*]: Put up your sword. If this young gentleman
        Have done offense, I take the fault on me;
        If you offend him, I for him defy you.
SIR TOBY: You, sir? Why, what are you?
ANTONIO: One, sir, that for his love dares yet do more
245   Than you have heard him brag to you he will.
SIR TOBY [*drawing*]: Nay, if you be an undertaker,° I am for° you.   *challenger / ready for*
    [*Enter Officers.*]
FABIAN: O good Sir Toby, hold! Here come the officers.
SIR TOBY [*to Antonio*]: I'll be with you anon.
VIOLA [*to Sir Andrew*]: Pray, sir, put your sword up, if you please.
SIR ANDREW: Marry, will I, sir; and for that I promised you, I'll be as good as my word.
        He will bear you easily, and reins well.
FIRST OFFICER: This is the man. Do thy office.
SECOND OFFICER: Antonio, I arrest thee at the suit
        Of Count Orsino.
ANTONIO: You do mistake me, sir.
FIRST OFFICER: No, sir, no jot. I know your favor° well,   *face*
        Though now you have no sea-cap on your head.—
        Take him away. He knows I know him well.
ANTONIO: I must obey. [*To Viola.*] This comes with seeking you.
        But there's no remedy; I shall answer it.
260   What will you do, now my necessity
        Makes me to ask you for my purse? It grieves me
        Much more for what I cannot do for you
        Than what befalls myself. You stand amazed,
        But be of comfort.
SECOND OFFICER: Come, sir, away.
ANTONIO [*to Viola*]: I must entreat of you some of that money.
VIOLA: What money, sir?
        For the fair kindness you have showed me here,
        And part° being prompted by your present trouble,   *partly*
        Out of my lean and low ability
270   I'll lend you something. My having° is not much;   *wealth*
        I'll make division of my present° with you.   *what I have now*
        Hold, there's half my coffer.° [*She offers money.*]   *purse*
ANTONIO: Will you deny me now?
        Is 't possible that my deserts to° you   *claims on*
        Can lack persuasion? Do not tempt my misery,
275   Lest that it make me so unsound a man
        As to upbraid you with those kindnesses
        That I have done for you.
VIOLA: I know of none,
        Nor know I you by voice or any feature.
        I hate ingratitude more in a man
280   Than lying, vainness, babbling drunkenness,
        Or any taint of vice whose strong corruption

Inhabits our frail blood.
ANTONIO: O heavens themselves!
SECOND OFFICER: Come, sir, I pray you, go.
ANTONIO: Let me speak a little. This youth that you see here
    I snatched one half out of the jaws of death,
    Relieved him with such° sanctity of love,   *much*
    And to his image, which methought did promise
    Most venerable worth,° did I devotion.   *worthiness*
FIRST OFFICER: What's that to us? The time goes by. Away!
ANTONIO: But, O, how vile an idol proves this god!
    Thou hast, Sebastian, done good feature shame.
    In nature there's no blemish but the mind;
    None can be called deformed but the unkind.°   *unnatural*
    Virtue is beauty, but the beauteous evil
295   Are empty trunks o'erflourished° by the devil.   *ornamented*
FIRST OFFICER: The man grows mad. Away with him! Come, come, sir.
ANTONIO: Lead me on.   *[Exit (with Officers).]*
VIOLA *[aside]*: Methinks his words do from such passion fly
    That he believes himself. So do not I.
    Prove true, imagination, O, prove true,
    That I, dear brother, be now ta'en for you!
SIR TOBY: Come hither, knight. Come hither, Fabian.
    We'll whisper o'er a couplet or two of most sage saws.°   *wise sayings*
[They gather apart from Viola.]
VIOLA: He named Sebastian. I my brother know
305   Yet living in my glass;° even such and so   *mirror*
    In favor was my brother, and he went
    Still° in this fashion, color, ornament,   *always*
    For him I imitate. O, if it prove,°   *prove true*
    Tempests are kind, and salt waves fresh in love!   *[Exit.]*
SIR TOBY: A very dishonest[8] paltry boy, and more a coward than a hare. His dishonesty appears in leaving his friend here in necessity and denying him; and for his cowardship, ask Fabian.
FABIAN: A coward, a most devout coward, religious° in it.   *confirmed*
SIR ANDREW: 'Slid,° I'll after him again and beat him.   *God's eyelid*
SIR TOBY: Do, cuff him soundly, but never draw thy sword.
SIR ANDREW: An I do not—   *[Exit.]*
FABIAN: Come, let's see the event.°   *result*
SIR TOBY: I dare lay any money 'twill be nothing yet.°   *nevertheless*
                            [Exeunt.]

ACT 4

Scene 1[9]

[Enter Sebastian and Clown (Feste).]
FESTE: Will you make me believe that I am not sent for you?
SEBASTIAN: Go to, go to, thou art a foolish fellow. Let me be clear of thee.

8. Dishonorable.   9. Location: Before Olivia's house.

FESTE: Well held out,[1] i' faith! No, I do not know you, nor I am not sent to you by
      my lady to bid you come speak with her, nor your name is not Master
5   Cesario, nor this is not my nose, neither. Nothing that is so is so.

SEBASTIAN: I prithee, vent thy folly somewhere else. Thou know'st not me.

FESTE: Vent my folly! He has heard that word of some great man, and now applies
      it to a fool. Vent my folly! I am afraid this great lubber,[2] the world, will
      prove a cockney.[3] I prithee now, ungird thy strangeness[4] and tell me what I
10   shall vent to my lady. Shall I vent to her that thou art coming?

SEBASTIAN: I prithee, foolish Greek,[5] depart from me. There's money for thee.
      [He gives money.] If you tarry longer, I shall give worse payment.

FESTE: By my troth, thou hast an open hand. These wise men that give fools money
      get themselves a good report—after fourteen years' purchase.[6]
     [Enter (Sir) Andrew, (Sir) Toby, and Fabian.]

SIR ANDREW: Now, sir, have I met you again? There's for you! [He strikes Sebastian.]

SEBASTIAN: Why, there's for thee, and there, and there! [He beats Sir Andrew with
      the hilt of his dagger.]
     Are all the people mad?

SIR TOBY: Hold, sir, or I'll throw your dagger o'er the house.

FESTE: This will I tell my lady straight. I would not be in some of your coats for
      twopence.   [Exit.]

SIR TOBY: Come on, sir, hold! [He grips Sebastian.]

SIR ANDREW: Nay, let him alone. I'll go another way to work with him. I'll have
      an action of battery[7] against him, if there be any law in Illyria. Though I
25   struck him first, yet it's no matter for that.

SEBASTIAN: Let go thy hand!

SIR TOBY: Come, sir, I will not let you go. Come, my young soldier, put up your
      iron. You are well fleshed.[8] Come on.

SEBASTIAN: I will be free from thee. [He breaks free and draws his sword.] What
30   wouldst thou now?
     If thou dar'st tempt me further, draw thy sword.

SIR TOBY: What, what? Nay, then I must have an ounce or two of this malapert[9]
      blood from you. [He draws.]
     [Enter Olivia.]

OLIVIA: Hold, Toby! On thy life I charge thee, hold!

SIR TOBY: Madam—

OLIVIA: Will it be ever thus? Ungracious wretch,
     Fit for the mountains and the barbarous caves,
     Where manners ne'er were preached! Out of my sight!—
     Be not offended, dear Cesario.—
40   Rudesby,° begone!   rude fellow
                    [Exeunt Sir Toby, Sir Andrew, and Fabian.]
              I prithee, gentle friend,
     Let thy fair wisdom, not thy passion, sway
     In this uncivil and unjust extent°   attack

---

1. Kept up.
2. Lout.
3. Affected person.
4. Abandon your strange manner.
5. Buffoon.

6. At great expense.
7. Assault charge.
8. Initiated into battle.
9. Impudent.

Against thy peace. Go with me to my house,
And hear thou there how many fruitless pranks
45   This ruffian hath botched up,° that thou thereby   *contrived*
Mayst smile at this. Thou shalt not choose but go.
Do not deny.° Beshrew° his soul for me!   *refuse / curse*
He started° one poor heart of mine, in thee.   *startled*
SEBASTIAN [*aside*]: What relish° is in this? How runs the stream?   *taste*
50   Or I am mad, or else this is a dream.
Let fancy° still my sense in Lethe[1] steep;   *imagination*
If it be thus to dream, still let me sleep!
OLIVIA: Nay, come, I prithee. Would thou'dst be ruled by me!
SEBASTIAN: Madam, I will.
OLIVIA: O, say so, and so be!   [*Exeunt.*]

Scene 2[2]

[*Enter Maria (with a gown and a false beard), and Clown (Feste).*]
MARIA: Nay, I prithee, put on this gown and this beard; make him believe thou art
Sir[3] Topas[4] the curate. Do it quickly. I'll call Sir Toby the whilst.   [*Exit.*]
FESTE: Well, I'll put it on, and I will dissemble[5] myself in 't, and I would I were the
first that ever dissembled in such a gown. [*He disguises himself in gown and
5   beard.*] I am not tall enough to become the function[6] well, nor lean[7] enough
to be thought a good student; but to be said an honest man and a good
housekeeper[8] goes as fairly as to say a careful man and a great scholar. The
competitors[9] enter.
[*Enter (Sir) Toby (and Maria).*]
SIR TOBY: Jove bless thee, Master Parson.
FESTE: *Bonos dies,*[1] Sir Toby. For, as the old hermit of Prague,[2] that never saw pen
and ink, very wittily said to a niece of King Gorboduc,[3] "That that is, is"; so
I, being Master Parson, am Master Parson; for what is "that" but "that," and
"is" but "is"?
SIR TOBY: To him, Sir Topas.
FESTE: What, ho, I say! Peace in this prison! [*He approaches the door behind which
Malvolio is confined.*]
SIR TOBY: The knave[4] counterfeits well; a good knave.
MALVOLIO [*within*]: Who calls there?
FESTE: Sir Topas the curate, who comes to visit Malvolio the lunatic.
MALVOLIO: Sir Topas, Sir Topas, good Sir Topas, go to my lady—
FESTE: Out, hyperbolical[5] fiend! How vexest thou this man! Talkest thou nothing
but of ladies?
SIR TOBY: Well said, Master Parson.
MALVOLIO: Sir Topas, never was man thus wronged. Good Sir Topas, do not
25   think I am mad. They have laid me here in hideous darkness.

---

1. River of forgetfulness in the Underworld.
2. Location: Olivia's house.
3. Title for priests.
4. Comic knight in Chaucer. (The topaz stone was believed to cure lunacy.)
5. Disguise.
6. Priestly office.
7. Scholars were supposed to be poor and, therefore, thin.

8. Neighbor.
9. Associates.
1. Good day.
2. Invented authority.
3. Legendary British king in the tragedy *Gorbobuc* (1562).
4. Fellow.
5. Boisterous.

FESTE: Fie, thou dishonest Satan! I call thee by the most modest terms, for I am one
of those gentle ones that will use the devil himself with courtesy. Sayst thou
that house[6] is dark?

MALVOLIO: As hell, Sir Topas.

FESTE: Why, it hath bay windows transparent as barricadoes,[7] and the clerestories[8]
toward the south north are as lustrous as ebony; and yet complainest thou of
obstruction?

MALVOLIO: I am not mad, Sir Topas. I say to you this house is dark.

FESTE: Madman, thou errest. I say there is no darkness but ignorance, in which
35   thou art more puzzled than the Egyptians in their fog.[9]

MALVOLIO: I say this house is as dark as ignorance, though ignorance were as dark
as hell; and I say there was never man thus abused. I am no more mad than
you are. Make the trial of it in any constant question.[1]

FESTE: What is the opinion of Pythagoras[2] concerning wildfowl?

MALVOLIO: That the soul of our grandam might haply, inhabit a bird.

FESTE: What think'st thou of his opinion?

MALVOLIO: I think nobly of the soul, and no way approve his opinion.

FESTE: Fare thee well. Remain thou still in darkness. Thou shalt hold th' opinion of
Pythagoras ere I will allow of thy wits,[3] and fear to kill a woodcock[4] lest thou
45   dispossess the soul of thy grandam. Fare thee well.

[He moves away from Malvolio's prison.]

MALVOLIO: Sir Topas, Sir Topas!

SIR TOBY: My most exquisite Sir Topas!

FESTE: Nay, I am for all waters.[5]

MARIA: Thou mightst have done this without thy beard and gown. He sees thee not.

SIR TOBY: To him in thine own voice, and bring me word how thou find'st him. I
would we were well rid of this knavery. If he may be conveniently delivered,[6] I
would he were, for I am now so far in offense with my niece that I cannot pursue with any safety this sport to the upshot.[7] Come by and by to my chamber.

[Exit (with Maria).]

FESTE [singing as he approaches Malvolio's prison]:
        "Hey, Robin, jolly Robin,
55   Tell me how thy lady does."[8]

MALVOLIO: Fool!

FESTE: "My lady is unkind, pardie."[9]

MALVOLIO: Fool!

FESTE: "Alas, why is she so?"

MALVOLIO: Fool, I say!

FESTE: "She loves another—" Who calls, ha?

MALVOLIO: Good Fool, as ever thou wilt deserve well at my hand, help me to a
candle, and pen, ink, and paper. As I am a gentleman, I will live to be
thankful to thee for 't.

6. Room.
7. Barricades.
8. Upper windows.
9. Allusion to the darkness Moses brought upon Egypt
(Exodus 10.21–23).
1. Consistent discussion.
2. Philosopher who originated the doctrine of the transmigration of souls.

3. Acknowledge your sanity.
4. Proverbially stupid bird.
5. Good for any trade.
6. Delivered from prison.
7. Conclusion.
8. Fragment of a song attributed to Thomas Wyatt.
9. By God (French: par Dieu).

FESTE: Master Malvolio?

MALVOLIO: Ay, good Fool.

FESTE: Alas, sir, how fell you beside your five wits?[1]

MALVOLIO: Fool, there was never man so notoriously abused. I am as well in my wits, Fool, as thou art.

FESTE: But[2] as well? Then you are mad indeed, if you be no better in your wits than a fool.

MALVOLIO: They have here propertied me,[3] keep me in darkness, send ministers to me—asses—and do all they can to face me[4] out of my wits.

FESTE: Advise you[5] what you say. The minister is here. [*He speaks as Sir Topas.*]
75   Malvolio, Malvolio, thy wits the heavens restore! Endeavor thyself to sleep; and leave thy vain bibble-babble.

MALVOLIO: Sir Topas!

FESTE [*in Sir Topas' voice*]: Maintain no words with him, good fellow. [*In his own voice.*] Who, I, sir? Not I, sir. God b' wi' you, good Sir Topas. [*In Sir Topas' voice.*] Marry, amen. [*In his own voice.*] I will, sir, I will.
80

MALVOLIO: Fool! Fool! Fool, I say!

FESTE: Alas, sir, be patient. What say you, sir? I am shent[6] for speaking to you.

MALVOLIO: Good Fool, help me to some light and some paper. I tell thee I am as well in my wits as any man in Illyria.

FESTE: Welladay[7] that you were, sir!

MALVOLIO: By this hand, I am. Good Fool, some ink, paper, and light; and convey what I will set down to my lady. It shall advantage thee more than ever the bearing of letter did.

FESTE: I will help you to 't. But tell me true, are you not mad indeed, or do you but
90   counterfeit?

MALVOLIO: Believe me, I am not. I tell thee true.

FESTE: Nay, I'll ne'er believe a madman till I see his brains. I will fetch you light and paper and ink.

MALVOLIO: Fool, I'll requite it in the highest degree. I prithee, begone.

FESTE [*sings*]:   I am gone, sir,
                                   And anon, sir,
                        I'll be with you again,
                                   In a trice,
                             Like to the old Vice,[8]
100   Your need to sustain;

                             Who, with dagger of lath,°   *Vice's weapon*
                             In his rage and his wrath,
                        Cries, "Aha!" to the devil;
                             Like a mad lad,
105   "Pare thy nails, dad?
                        Adieu, goodman devil!"   [*Exit.*]

---

1. Out of your mind.
2. Only.
3. Treated me as property.
4. Brazen me.
5. Take care.
6. Rebuked.
7. Alas.
8. Comic character of old morality plays.

Scene 3⁹

[*Enter Sebastian (with a pearl)*.]

SEBASTIAN: This is the air; that is the glorious sun;
        This pearl she gave me, I do feel 't and see 't;
        And though 'tis wonder that enwraps me thus,
        Yet 'tis not madness. Where's Antonio, then?
5   I could not find him at the Elephant;
        Yet there he was,° and there I found this credit,°   *had been / belief*
        That he did range the town to seek me out.
        His counsel now might do me golden service;
        For though my soul disputes well with my sense
10   That this may be some error, but no madness,
        Yet doth this accident° and flood of fortune   *surprise*
        So far exceed all instance,° all discourse,°   *precedent / logic*
        That I am ready to distrust mine eyes
        And wrangle° with my reason that persuades me   *dispute*
15   To any other trust° but that I am mad,   *belief*
        Or else the lady's mad. Yet if 'twere so,
        She could not sway° her house, command her followers,   *rule*
        Take and give back affairs and their dispatch°   *management*
        With such a smooth, discreet, and stable bearing
20   As I perceive she does. There's something in 't
        That is deceivable.° But here the lady comes.   *deceptive*

[*Enter Olivia and Priest*.]

OLIVIA: Blame not this haste of mine. If you mean well,
        Now go with me and with this holy man
        Into the chantry° by. There, before him,   *chapel nearby*
25   And underneath that consecrated roof,
        Plight me the full assurance of your faith,
        That my most jealous° and too doubtful soul   *anxious*
        May live at peace. He shall conceal it
        Whiles° you are willing it shall come to note,° *until / become known*
30   What time° we will our celebration keep   *at which time*
        According to my birth.° What do you say?   *social position*
SEBASTIAN: I'll follow this good man, and go with you,
        And having sworn truth, ever will be true.
OLIVIA: Then lead the way, good Father, and heavens so shine
35   That they may fairly note° this act of mine!   *look well upon*

[*Exeunt*.]

ACT 5

Scene 1¹

[*Enter Clown (Feste) and Fabian*.]

FABIAN: Now, as thou lov'st me, let me see his letter.
FESTE: Good Master Fabian, grant me another request.

---

9. Location: Olivia's garden.   1. Location: Before Olivia's house.

FABIAN: Anything.

FESTE: Do not desire to see this letter.

FABIAN: This is to give a dog and in recompense desire my dog again.[2]

[Enter Duke (Orsino), Viola, Curio, and lords.]

ORSINO: Belong you to the Lady Olivia, friends?

FESTE: Ay, sir, we are some of her trappings.[3]

ORSINO: I know thee well. How dost thou, my good fellow?

FESTE: Truly, sir, the better for[4] my foes and the worse for my friends.

ORSINO: Just the contrary—the better for thy friends.

FESTE: No, sir, the worse.

ORSINO: How can that be?

FESTE: Marry, sir, they praise me, and make an ass of me. Now my foes tell me
plainly I am an ass, so that by my foes, sir, I profit in the knowledge of
15   myself, and by my friends I am abused;[5] so that, conclusions to be as kisses, if
your four negatives make your two affirmatives, why then the worse for my
friends and the better for my foes.

ORSINO: Why, this is excellent.

FESTE: By my troth, sir, no, though it please you to be one of my friends.

ORSINO: Thou shalt not be the worse for me. There's gold. [He gives a coin.]

FESTE: But that it would be double-dealing,[6] sir, I would you could make it another.

ORSINO: O, you give me ill counsel.

FESTE: Put your grace in your pocket,[7] sir, for this once, and let your flesh and blood
obey it.[8]

ORSINO: Well, I will be so much a sinner to be a double-dealer. There's another.
[He gives another coin.]

FESTE: Primo, secundo, tertio, is a good play,[9] and the old saying is, the third pays for
all.[1] The triplex,[2] sir, is a good tripping measure; or the bells of Saint Ben-
net,[3] sir, may put you in mind—one, two, three.

ORSINO: You can fool no more money out of me at this throw.[4] If you will let your
lady know I am here to speak with her, and bring her along with you, it may
awake my bounty further.

FESTE: Marry, sir, lullaby to your bounty till I come again. I go, sir, but I would not
have you to think that my desire of having is the sin of covetousness. But as
35   you say, sir, let your bounty take a nap. I will awake it anon.   [Exit.]

[Enter Antonio and Officers.]

VIOLA: Here comes the man, sir, that did rescue me.

ORSINO: That face of his I do remember well,
    Yet when I saw it last it was besmeared
    As black as Vulcan[5] in the smoke of war.
40   A baubling° vessel was he captain of,   trifling°
    For shallow draft[6] and bulk unprizable,[7]

---

2. Famously, Queen Elizabeth once asked Dr. Bulleyn for his dog and promised a gift of his choosing in exchange; he asked to have his dog back.
3. Ornaments.
4. Because of.
5. Deceived.
6. Giving twice; deceit.
7. Pocket your virtue; be generous.
8. I.e., my ill counsel.

9. Game.
1. I.e., the third time is lucky.
2. Triple-time in music.
3. Church of St. Benedict.
4. Throw of the dice.
5. Roman god of fire, smith to the other gods.
6. Depth of water a ship draws.
7. Of slight value.

		harmful

With which such scatheful° grapple did he make | *harmful*
With the most noble bottom° of our fleet | *ship*
That very envy° and the tongue of loss° | *even malice / the losers*
45   Cried fame and honor on him. What's the matter?
FIRST OFFICER: Orsino, this is that Antonio
That took the *Phoenix* and her freight from Candy,° | *Crete*
And this is he that did the *Tiger* board
When your young nephew Titus lost his leg.
50   Here in the streets, desperate° of shame and state, | *reckless*
In private brabble° did we apprehend him. | *brawl*
VIOLA: He did me kindness, sir, drew on my side,
But in conclusion put strange speech upon me.
I know not what 'twas but distraction.° | *madness*
ORSINO: Notable° pirate, thou saltwater thief, | *notorious*
What foolish boldness brought thee to their mercies
Whom thou in terms so bloody and so dear° | *costly*
Hast made thine enemies?
ANTONIO: Orsino, noble sir,
60   Be pleased that I° shake off these names you give me. | *allow me to*
Antonio never yet was thief or pirate,
Though, I confess, on base and ground° enough | *solid grounds*
Orsino's enemy. A witchcraft drew me hither.
That most ingrateful boy there by your side
65   From the rude sea's enraged and foamy mouth
Did I redeem; a wreck past hope he was.
His life I gave him, and did thereto add
My love, without retention° or restraint, | *reservation*
All his in dedication. For his sake
70   Did I expose myself—pure° for his love— | *purely*
Into° the danger of this adverse° town, | *unto / hostile*
Drew to defend him when he was beset;
Where being apprehended, his false cunning,
Not meaning to partake with me in danger,
75   Taught him to face me out of his acquaintance° | *deny knowing me*
And grew a twenty years' removed° thing | *estranged*
While one would wink; denied me mine own purse,
Which I had recommended° to his use | *entrusted*
Not half an hour before.
VIOLA: How can this be?
ORSINO: When came he to this town?
ANTONIO: Today, my lord; and for three months before,
No interim, not a minute's vacancy,
Both day and night did we keep company.
   [*Enter Olivia and attendants.*]
ORSINO: Here comes the Countess. Now heaven walks on earth.
85   But for thee, fellow—fellow, thy words are madness.
Three months this youth hath tended upon me;
But more of that anon. Take him aside.
OLIVIA [*to Orsino*]: What would my lord—but that° he may not have— | *except what*

         Wherein Olivia may seem serviceable?—
90   Cesario, you do not keep promise with me.
VIOLA: Madam?
ORSINO: Gracious Olivia—
OLIVIA: What do you say, Cesario?—Good my lord—
VIOLA: My lord would speak. My duty hushes me.
OLIVIA: If it be aught to the old tune, my lord,
         It is as fat° and fulsome° to mine ear   *gross / offensive*
         As howling after music.
ORSINO: Still so cruel?
OLIVIA: Still so constant, lord.
ORSINO: What, to perverseness? You uncivil lady,
100   To whose ingrate° and unauspicious° altars   *ungrateful / unpromising*
         My soul the faithfull'st offerings have breathed out
         That e'er devotion tendered! What shall I do?
OLIVIA: Even what it please my lord that shall become° him.   *suit*
ORSINO: Why should I not, had I the heart to do it,
105   Like to th' Egyptian thief⁸ at point of death
         Kill what I love?—a savage jealousy
         That sometimes savors nobly. But hear me this:
         Since you to nonregardance° cast my faith,   *neglect*
         And that° I partly know the instrument   *since*
110   That screws° me from my true place in your favor,   *pries*
         Live you the marble-breasted tyrant still.
         But this your minion,° whom I know you love,   *favorite*
         And whom, by heaven I swear, I tender° dearly,   *hold*
         Him will I tear out of that cruel eye
115   Where he sits crownèd in his master's spite.°—   *despite his master*
         Come, boy, with me. My thoughts are ripe in mischief.
         I'll sacrifice the lamb that I do love,
         To spite a raven's heart within a dove. [*Going.*]
VIOLA: And I, most jocund, apt,° and willingly,   *readily*
120   To do you rest,° a thousand deaths would die. [*Going.*] *give you peace*
OLIVIA: Where goes Cesario?
VIOLA: After him I love
         More than I love these eyes, more than my life,
         More by all mores° than e'er I shall love wife.   *all comparisons*
         If I do feign, you witnesses above
125   Punish my life for tainting of my love!
OLIVIA: Ay me, detested! How am I beguiled!
VIOLA: Who does beguile you? Who does do you wrong?
OLIVIA: Hast thou forgot thyself? Is it so long?
         Call forth the holy father.
                                              [*Exit an attendant.*]
ORSINO [*to Viola*]:   Come, away!
OLIVIA: Whither, my lord? Cesario, husband, stay.

8. Allusion to the *Ethiopica* by Heliodorus, in which the robber captain Thyamis kidnaps and falls in love with Chariclea. Threatened with death, he tries to kill her first.

ORSINO: Husband?

OLIVIA: Ay, husband. Can he that deny?

ORSINO [*to Viola*]: Her husband, sirrah?⁹

VIOLA: No, my lord, not I.

OLIVIA: Alas, it is the baseness of thy fear
        That makes thee strangle thy propriety.°   *identity*

135   Fear not, Cesario, take thy fortunes up;
        Be that thou know'st thou art, and then thou art
        As great as that thou fear'st.°   *Orsino*

[*Enter Priest.*]

                        O, welcome, Father!
        Father, I charge thee by thy reverence
        Here to unfold—though lately we intended

140   To keep in darkness what occasion now
        Reveals before 'tis ripe—what thou dost know
        Hath newly passed between this youth and me.

PRIEST: A contract of eternal bond of love,
        Confirmed by mutual joinder° of your hands,   *joining*

145   Attested by the holy close° of lips,   *meeting*
        Strengthened by interchangement of your rings,
        And all the ceremony of this compact
        Sealed in my function, by my testimony;
        Since when, my watch hath told me, toward my grave

150   I have traveled but two hours.

ORSINO [*to Viola*]: O thou dissembling cub! What wilt thou be
        When time hath sowed a grizzle° on thy case?°   *gray hair / skin*
        Or will not else thy craft so quickly grow
        That thine own trip° shall be thine overthrow?   *trickery*

155   Farewell, and take her, but direct thy feet
        Where thou and I henceforth may never meet.

VIOLA: My Lord, I do protest—

OLIVIA: O, do not swear!
                 Hold little° faith, though thou hast too much fear.   *a little*

[*Enter Sir Andrew.*]

SIR ANDREW: For the love of God, a surgeon! Send one presently¹ to Sir Toby.

OLIVIA: What's the matter?

SIR ANDREW: He's broke my head across, and has given Sir Toby a bloody cox-
     comb² too. For the love of God, your help! I had rather than forty pound I
     were at home.

OLIVIA: Who has done this, Sir Andrew?

SIR ANDREW: The Count's gentleman, one Cesario. We took him for a coward,
     but he's the very devil incardinate.³

ORSINO: My gentleman, Cesario?

SIR ANDREW: 'Od's lifelings,⁴ here he is!—You broke my head for nothing, and
     that that I did I was set on to do 't by Sir Toby.

---

9. Address to an inferior.   3. Incarnate.
1. Immediately.   4. By God's little lives.
2. Fool's cap (here, head).

VIOLA: Why do you speak to me? I never hurt you.
　　　You drew your sword upon me without cause,
　　　But I bespake you fair, and hurt you not.
SIR ANDREW: If a bloody coxcomb be a hurt, you have hurt me. I think you set
　　　nothing by a bloody coxcomb.
　　　[Enter (Sir) Toby and Clown (Feste).]
175　　Here comes Sir Toby, halting.[5] You shall hear more. But if he had not been
　　　in drink, he would have tickled you othergates[6] than he did.
ORSINO: How now, gentleman? How is 't with you?
SIR TOBY: That's all one.[7] He's hurt me, and there's th' end on 't.—Sot,[8] didst see
　　　Dick surgeon, sot?
FESTE: O, he's drunk, Sir Toby, an hour agone; his eyes were set[9] at eight i' the
　　　morning.
SIR TOBY: Then he's a rogue, and a passy measures pavane.[1] I hate a drunken rogue.
OLIVIA: Away with him! Who hath made this havoc with them?
SIR ANDREW: I'll help you, Sir Toby, because we'll be dressed[2] together.
SIR TOBY: Will you help? An ass-head and a coxcomb and a knave, a thin-faced
　　　knave, a gull!
OLIVIA: Get him to bed, and let his hurt be looked to.
　　　　　　　　[Exeunt Feste, Fabian, Sir Toby, and Sir Andrew.]
　　[Enter Sebastian.]
SEBASTIAN: I am sorry, madam, I have hurt your kinsman;
　　　But, had it been the brother of my blood,
190　　I must have done no less with wit and safety.[3]—
　　　You throw a strange regard° upon me, and by that　　　　　　　　*estranged look*
　　　I do perceive it hath offended you.
　　　Pardon me, sweet one, even for the vows
　　　We made each other but so late ago.
ORSINO: One face, one voice, one habit°, and two persons,　　　　　　　*dress*
　　　A natural perspective,[4] that is and is not!
SEBASTIAN: Antonio, O my dear Antonio!
　　　How have the hours racked and tortured me
　　　Since I have lost thee!
ANTONIO: Sebastian are you?
SEBASTIAN:　　　　　　Fear'st thou° that, Antonio?　　　　　　　*do you doubt*
ANTONIO: How have you made division of yourself?
　　　An apple cleft in two is not more twin
　　　Than these two creatures. Which is Sebastian?
OLIVIA: Most wonderful!
SEBASTIAN *[seeing Viola]*: Do I stand there? I never had a brother;
　　　Nor can there be that deity in my nature
　　　Of here and everywhere.° I had a sister,　　　　　　　　　　*omnipresence*
　　　Whom the blind° waves and surges have devoured.　　　　　　　　*heedless*
　　　Of charity,° what kin are you to me?　　　　　　　　　*tell me in kindness*

5. Limping.
6. Otherwise.
7. It doesn't matter.
8. Drunkard.
9. Closed.

1. Slow dance.
2. Have our wounds dressed.
3. With an intelligent regard for my safety.
4. Optical illusion.

210   What countryman? What name? What parentage?
VIOLA: Of Messaline. Sebastian was my father.
        Such a Sebastian was my brother, too.
        So went he suited° to his watery tomb.   *dressed*
        If spirits can assume both form and suit,
        You come to fright us.
SEBASTIAN: A spirit I am indeed,
        But am in that dimension grossly clad°   *clothed in the flesh*
        Which from the womb I did participate.°   *inherit*
        Were you a woman, as the rest goes even,°   *circumstances allow*
        I should my tears let fall upon your cheek
220   And say, "Thrice welcome, drownèd Viola!"
VIOLA: My father had a mole upon his brow.
SEBASTIAN: And so had mine.
VIOLA: And died that day when Viola from her birth
        Had numbered thirteen years.
SEBASTIAN: O, that record° is lively in my soul!   *memory*
        He finishèd indeed his mortal act
        That day that made my sister thirteen years.
VIOLA: If nothing lets° to make us happy both   *hinders*
        But this my masculine usurped attire,
230   Do not embrace me till each circumstance
        Of place, time, fortune, do cohere and jump°   *agree completely*
        That I am Viola—which to confirm
        I'll bring you to a captain in this town
        Where lie my maiden weeds,° by whose gentle help   *clothes*
235   I was preserved to serve this noble count.
        All the occurrence of my fortune since
        Hath been between this lady and this lord.
SEBASTIAN [to Olivia]: So comes it, lady, you have been mistook.
        But nature to her bias drew° in that.   *followed her bent*
240   You would have been contracted to a maid,°   *virgin man*
        Nor are you therein, by my life, deceived.
        You are betrothed both to a maid and man.
ORSINO [to Olivia]: Be not amazed; right noble is his blood.
        If this be so, as yet the glass° seems true,   *natural perspective*
245   I shall have share in this most happy wreck.
        [To Viola.] Boy, thou hast said to me a thousand times
        Thou never shouldst love woman like to° me.   *as much as*
VIOLA: And all those sayings will I over swear,°   *swear again*
        And all those swearings keep as true in soul
250   As doth that orbèd continent° the fire   *the Sun*
        That severs day from night.
ORSINO: Give me thy hand,
        And let me see thee in thy woman's weeds.
VIOLA: The captain that did bring me first on shore
        Hath my maid's garments. He upon some action°   *legal charge*
255   Is now in durance,° at Malvolio's suit,   *imprisonment*
        A gentleman and follower of my lady's.

OLIVIA: He shall enlarge° him. Fetch Malvolio hither.   *release*
    And yet, alas, now I remember me,
    They say, poor gentleman, he's much distract.
    [*Enter Clown (Feste) with a letter, and Fabian.*]
260   A most extracting° frenzy of mine own   *distracting*
    From my remembrance clearly banished his.
    How does he, sirrah?
FESTE: Truly, madam, he holds Beelzebub at the stave's end[5] as well as a man in his
    case may do. He's here writ a letter to you; I should have given 't you today
265   morning. But as a madman's epistles are no gospels, so it skills[6] not much
    when they are delivered.
OLIVIA: Open 't and read it.
FESTE: Look then to be well edified when the fool delivers[7] the madman. [*He reads
    loudly.*] "By the Lord, madam—"
OLIVIA: How now, art thou mad?
FESTE: No, madam, I do but read madness. An your ladyship will have it as it ought
    to be, you must allow *vox*.[8]
OLIVIA: Prithee, read i' thy right wits.[9]
FESTE: So I do, madonna; but to read his right wits is to read thus. Therefore per-
275   pend,[1] my princess, and give ear.
OLIVIA [*to Fabian*]: Read it you, sirrah.
FABIAN [*reads*]: "By the Lord, madam, you wrong me, and the world shall know it.
    Though you have put me into darkness and given your drunken cousin rule
    over me, yet have I the benefit of my senses as well as your ladyship. I have
280   your own letter that induced me to the semblance I put on, with the which I
    doubt not but to do myself much right or you much shame. Think of me as
    you please. I leave my duty a little unthought of, and speak out of my injury.
                                        The madly used Malvolio."
OLIVIA: Did he write this?
FESTE: Ay, madam.
ORSINO: This savors not much of distraction.
OLIVIA: See him delivered,° Fabian. Bring him hither.   *released*
                                        [*Exit Fabian.*]
    My lord, so please you, these things further thought on,
    To think me as well a sister as a wife,
290   One day shall crown th' alliance on 't, so please you,
    Here at my house and at my proper° cost.   *own*
ORSINO: Madam, I am most apt° t' embrace your offer.   *ready*
    [*To Viola.*] Your master quits° you; and for your service done him, *releases*
    So much against the mettle° of your sex,   *disposition*
295   So far beneath your soft and tender breeding,
    And since you called me master for so long,
    Here is my hand. You shall from this time be
    Your master's mistress.
OLIVIA: A sister! You are she.
    [*Enter (Fabian with) Malvolio.*]
ORSINO: Is this the madman?

5. Holds the devil off.   8. Loud voice.
6. Matters.   9. I.e., express his true state of mind.
7. Speaks the words of.   1. Consider.

OLIVIA: Ay, my lord, this same.
                 How now, Malvolio?

MALVOLIO: Madam, you have done me wrong
                 Notorious wrong.

OLIVIA: Have I, Malvolio? No.

MALVOLIO [*showing a letter*]: Lady, you have. Pray you, peruse that letter.
                 You must not now deny it is your hand.
                 Write from it,° if you can, in hand or phrase,   *differently*
305   Or say 'tis not your seal, not your invention.°   *composition*
                 You can say none of this. Well, grant it then,
                 And tell me, in the modesty of honor,
                 Why you have given me such clear lights° of favor,   *signs*
                 Bade me come smiling and cross-gartered to you,
310   To put on yellow stockings, and to frown
                 Upon Sir Toby and the lighter° people?   *lesser*
                 And, acting this in an obedient hope,
                 Why have you suffered me to be imprisoned,
                 Kept in a dark house, visited by the priest,°   *Feste*
315   And made the most notorious geck° and gull   *dupe*
                 That e'er invention played on? Tell me why?

OLIVIA: Alas, Malvolio, this is not my writing,
                 Though, I confess, much like the character;°   *my handwriting*
                 But out of° question 'tis Maria's hand.   *beyond*
320   And now I do bethink me, it was she
                 First told me thou wast mad; then cam'st in smiling,
                 And in such forms which here were presupposed°   *pre-imposed*
                 Upon thee in the letter. Prithee, be content.
                 This practice° hath most shrewdly° passed upon thee;   *plot / mischievously*
325   But when we know the grounds and authors of it,
                 Thou shalt be both the plaintiff and the judge
                 Of thine own cause.

FABIAN: Good madam, hear me speak,
                 And let no quarrel nor no brawl to come
                 Taint the condition of this present hour,
330   Which I have wondered at. In hope it shall not,
                 Most freely I confess, myself and Toby
                 Set this device against Malvolio here,
                 Upon° some stubborn and uncourteous parts°   *because of / qualities*
                 We had conceived against him. Maria writ
335   The letter at Sir Toby's great importance,°   *importunity*
                 In recompense whereof he hath married her.
                 How with a sportful malice it was followed°   *carried out*
                 May rather pluck on° laughter than revenge,   *induce*
                 If that the injuries be justly weighed
340   That have on both sides passed.

OLIVIA [*to Malvolio*]: Alas, poor fool, how have they baffled° thee!   *disgraced*

FESTE: Why, "Some are born great, some achieve greatness, and some have great-
                 ness thrown upon them." I was one, sir, in this interlude,[2] one Sir Topas, sir,

2. Little play.

but that's all one. "By the Lord, fool, I am not mad." But do you remember?
345   "Madam, why laugh you at such a barren rascal? An you smile not, he's
gagged." And thus the whirligig³ of time brings in his revenges.

MALVOLIO: I'll be revenged on the whole pack of you!   [Exit.]

OLIVIA: He hath been most notoriously abused.

ORSINO: Pursue him, and entreat him to a peace.
350   He hath not told us of the captain yet.
When that is known, and golden time convents,°   is convenient
A solemn combination shall be made
Of our dear souls. Meantime, sweet sister,
We will not part from hence. Cesario, come—
355   For so you shall be, while you are a man;
But when in other habits° you are seen,   attire
Orsino's mistress and his fancy's° queen.   love's
                                        [Exeunt (all, except Feste).]

FESTE [sings]:   When that I was and a little tiny boy,
                    With hey, ho, the wind and the rain,
360   A foolish thing was but a toy,°   trifle
                    For the rain it raineth every day.

                    But when I came to man's estate,
                    With hey, ho, the wind and the rain,
                    'Gainst knaves and thieves men shut their gate,
365   For the rain it raineth every day.

                    But when I came, alas, to wive,
                    With hey, ho, the wind and the rain,
                    By swaggering could I never thrive,
                    For the rain it raineth every day.

370   But when I came unto my beds,
                    With hey, ho, the wind and the rain,
                    With tosspots° still had drunken heads,   drunkards
                    For the rain it raineth every day.

                    A great while ago the world begun,
375   With hey, ho, the wind and the rain,
                    But that's all one, our play is done,
                    And we'll strive to please you every day.
[Exit.]

Ben Jonson
1572–1637

Ben Jonson's life was full of changes and contradictions. His earliest biographer, William Drummond, called him "passionately kind and angry, careless either to gain or keep, vindictive, but, if he be well answered, at himself." His father was Protestant, but Jonson turned

3. Spinning top.

Catholic, only to recant that conversion later; nevertheless, in his last years he called himself a "beadsman." The stepson of a bricklayer, he became Poet Laureate. He wrote poems of praise to win the patronage of king and court but also skewered their follies in satire. Though often assuming the role of moralist in his poetry and plays, Jonson admitted that as a younger man he was "given to venery" and pleaded guilty to the charge of murder. He was attached to admiring younger poets, "the tribe of Ben," yet he also enjoyed feuds, such as those with fellow drama-tists Marston and Dekker. While espousing Horatian spareness and an acute sense of meter in both criticism and poetry, Jonson also had a keen ear for the colloquial language of London.

Indeed, London was one of the few constants in Jonson's turbulent career. Born in Harts-Born Lane near Charing Cross, he was buried in Poets' Corner at Westminster Abbey. Jonson portrayed the city as the world of those who lived by their wits. He dramatized literary infight-ing in *Every Man Out of His Humour* (1599), greedy schemes in *Volpone* (1606), intellectual confidence scams in *The Alchemist* (1610), and antitheatrical Puritan preaching in *Bartholomew Fair* (1614). The London audience at the Hope Theatre was reported to have exclaimed at a performance of *Bartholomew Fair:* "O rare Ben Jonson!"

Unlike other playwrights of his time (including Shakespeare), Jonson oversaw the publica-tion of his plays, which appeared with his poems in the same deluxe folio volume, entitled *Works* (1616). The assertion of the dignity of popular drama surprised many of his readers, one of whom wrote, "Pray tell me Ben, where doth the mystery lurk, / What others call a play, you call a work?" That Jonson wanted his plays to be read as much as performed can be gathered from the comment printed on the title page of *Every Man Out of His Humour:* "as it was first composed by the author, Ben Jonson, containing more than hath been publicly spoken or acted."

Jonson viewed writing as his profession; he became the first poet in England to earn a living by his art. His achievement was recognized by James I, who made Jonson the first Poet Laureate of England and granted him a pension for life. Before becoming laureate, Jonson depended on a whole string of patrons. With the new Stuart king in power, Jonson was able to use his claim of Scots descent to advantage. He was supported by Esme Stuart Seigneur D'Aubigny (a cousin of King James), to whom he dedicated his first tragedy, *Sejanus* (1603). His patrons included Sir Walter Raleigh and Lady Mary Wroth, to whom he dedicated *The Alchemist.* Jonson's most important break came when he received a commission for a court masque. In 1605 he wrote *The Masque of Blackness* starring the Queen herself. To gain some idea of the extravagance of these masques, consider that in 1617, while 12,000 pounds were spent on the entire administration of Ireland, 4,000 pounds were spent on a single masque, *Pleasure Reconciled to Virtue.* The masques were lavish ventures that required costumes, music, and magnificent scenery, which was designed by Inigo Jones, who introduced the Italian invention of perspective.

If the pursuit of patronage was crucial to Jonson's advancement, his satire of politics and power repeatedly put his career and even his life at risk. In 1603 Jonson was called before the Privy Council for *Sejanus;* the charges included "popery and treason." Jonson's *Epicoene, or the Silent Woman*—which climaxes in the revelation that the silent woman is really a boy—was suppressed because it lampooned a love affair of the King's first cousin, Lady Arbella Stuart. One observer complained of the 1613 *Irish Masque at Court* that it was "no time . . . to exasper-ate that nation by making ridiculous." Jonson was imprisoned twice for the offense that his plays gave to the powerful—once for the now lost *The Isle of Dogs* (1597) and another time for *Eastward Ho!* (1605), in which he made fun of King James's Scots accent.

Jonson took reckless risks, whose consequences he barely managed to escape. While imprisoned for the murder of Gabriel Spencer in 1598, Jonson became a Catholic. Following his conversion, Jonson pleaded guilty to manslaughter (later calling it the result of a duel) but went free by claiming benefit of clergy. This medieval custom originally allowed clerics to be judged by the bishop's court but, by Jonson's time, permitted anyone who could translate the Latin Bible to go free. Jonson left prison with his belongings confiscated, his thumb branded for the felony, and his reputation marked by his profession of an outlaw religion. Like any oth-er Catholic in Elizabethan England, Jonson could be fined or have his property confiscated for

not attending Anglican services. Indeed, he and his wife were interrogated for their nonatten-
dance in 1605; Jonson was also charged with being "a poet, and by fame a seducer of youth to
the Popish religion." Threatened again with loss of property and another prison term, Jonson
complied with the Court's order that he take instruction in Protestantism.

Not all Jonson's disputes were quite so dangerous. Like the characters in his plays, he
enjoyed engaging in the game of vapors, a mock argument, drummed up for the display of wit.
He not only engaged in combats of wit with Shakespeare (who acted in *Every Man Out of His
Humour*) but also ridiculed Marston and Dekker in what critics call "the War of the Theaters."
Jonson's *Every Man Out of His Humour* satirized Marston as a pseudo-intellectual. The same
year, Jonson and Dekker collaborated on a play. Two years later, Dekker parodied Jonson as
the bombastic Horace, constantly reading his work aloud and expecting praise in *Satiriomastix*
(1601). The title of this play means "the whipping of the satirist," and it is full of barbs about
Jonson's checkered past—both his imprisonment and his theatrical flops. Dekker called Jonson a "brown-bread mouth-stinker." Jonson responded with a "forced defense" against "base
detractors and illiterate apes" in *Poetaster* (1601).

Jonson did have high regard for some of his contemporaries, as they did for him. Among
these was John Donne, who wrote commendatory verses for *Volpone* and to whom Jonson
wrote "Who shall doubt, Donne, whe'er I a poet be / When I dare send my epigrams to thee?"
As an older man, Jonson held court at the Devil Tavern among his fellow poets as self-
proclaimed *arbiter bibendi* (master of drinking), whose main object was "Not drinking much,
but talking wittily." This vein of wit was carried on by Sir John Suckling's *A Session of Poets*
and Herrick's *Prayer for Ben Jonson*. His servant Brome wrote an elegy for him, as did the many
men of letters who contributed to *Jonsonius Virbius* ("Jonson Reborn"), the year after his death.

Jonson saw himself as a moral and poetic guide. His satire of moral depravity and intellectual delusion is hysterically funny. His plays include direct criticism of contemporary poetry and
drama, contracts with the audience, and self-mockery—a foretaste of the break from realistic
conventions in modernism. Jonson's comedies also persuade us that there is no reality without
satire; we cannot know the world without laughing at its ridiculousness. The human foibles and
obsessions portrayed in his comedies are captured in a language so vivid and oral that it has to be
read aloud. Jonson's verse dazzles by concealing its art, allowing conversational words and
rhythms to be perfectly wedded to poetic meters. The simplicity and restraint of his language, as
in his elegy on the death of his son, are the vehicles for pure music and powerful emotion.

On Something, That Walks Somewhere[1]

At court I met it, in clothes brave° enough   *showy*
  To be a courtier, and looks grave enough
To seem a statesman. As I near it came,
  It made me a great face; I asked the name.
5 "A lord," it cried, "buried in flesh, and blood,
  And such from whom let no man hope least good,
For I will do none; and as little ill,
  For I will dare none." Good lord, walk dead still.

On My First Daughter[1]

Here lies to each her parents' ruth,°   *grief*
  Mary, the daughter of their youth;
Yet, all heaven's gifts, being heaven's due,

---

1. This and the following four poems were all first printed
in the collected *Works* of 1616 under the heading "Epigrams." An epigram is a short, witty poem of invective or

satire. Jonson's "Epigrams" include epitaphs, poems of
praise, and verse letters.
1. Probably written in the late 1590s.

It makes the father less to rue.
5   At six months' end, she parted hence
With safety of her innocence;
Whose soul heaven's Queen (whose name she bears),
In comfort of her mother's tears,
Hath placed amongst her virgin-train;
10   Where, while that severed doth remain,
This grave partakes the fleshly birth;[2]
Which cover lightly, gentle earth.

To John Donne

Donne, the delight of Phoebus,[1] and each Muse,
Who, to thy one, all other brains refuse;[2]
Whose every work, of thy most early wit
Came forth example, and remains so, yet;
5   Longer a-knowing than most wits do live;
And which no affection praise enough can give!
To it,[3] thy language, letters, arts, best life,
Which might with half mankind maintain a strife;
All which I meant to praise, and, yet, I would,
10   But leave, because I cannot as I should.

On My First Son[1]

Farewell, thou child of my right hand,[2] and joy;
My sin was too much hope of thee, loved boy.
Seven years thou wert lent to me, and I thee pay,
Exacted by thy fate, on the just day.
5   O, could I lose all father, now![3] For why
Will man lament the state he should envy?
To have so soon 'scaped world's and flesh's rage,
And, if no other misery, yet age?
Rest in soft peace, and, asked, say, "Here doth lie
10   Ben Jonson his best piece of poetry."
For whose sake, henceforth, all his vows be such,
As what he loves may never like too much.[4]

To Penshurst[1]

Thou art not, Penshurst, built to envious show
Of touch,° or marble; nor canst boast a row   *black marble*
Of polished pillars, or a roof of gold;

2. While the soul is in heaven, the grave holds the body.
1. God of poetry.
2. The Muses give the inspiration to your brain that they deny to others.
3. In addition to your wit.
1. Benjamin, who died of the plague on his birthday in 1603.
2. In Hebrew, Benjamin means "son of the right hand; dexterous, fortunate."
3. Let go of fatherly feeling.

4. "If you wish . . . to beware of sorrows that gnaw the heart, to no man make yourself too much a comrade" (Martial 12.34, lines 8–11).
1. First published in the 1616 *Works* in *The Forest*, a title inspired by the Latin *silva* (timber), suggesting raw materials to be worked, used by classical authors for an improvised collection of poems. Penshurst was the Sidney family's house in Kent since 1552, the "great lord" (line 91) of which was Robert Sidney, Baron Sidney of Penshurst and Viscount of Lille, younger brother of Sir Philip Sidney.

Thou hast no lantern,° whereof tales are told,   *turret*
5   Or stair, or courts; but stand'st an ancient pile,[2]
          And these grudged at, art reverenced the while.
     Thou joy'st in better marks, of soil, of air,
          Of wood, of water; therein thou art fair.
     Thou hast thy walks for health, as well as sport:
10   Thy mount to which the dryads° do resort,   *wood nymphs*
     Where Pan, and Bacchus their high feasts have made,[3]
          Beneath the broad beech and the chestnut shade;
     That taller tree, which of a nut was set
          At his great birth, where all the Muses met.
15   There, in the writhèd bark, are cut the names
          Of many a sylvan,° taken with his flames;   *wood sprite*
     And thence, the ruddy satyrs oft provoke
          The lighter fauns, to reach thy Lady's oak.[4]
     Thy copse,° too, named of Gamage, thou hast there,   *a small wood*
20   That never fails to serve thee seasoned deer
     When thou wouldst feast, or exercise thy friends.
          The lower land, that to the river bends,
     Thy sheep, thy bullocks, kine° and calves do feed;   *cows*
          The middle grounds thy mares and horses breed.
25   Each bank doth yield thee conies,° and the tops   *rabbits*
          Fertile of wood, Ashour and Sydney's copse,
     To crown thy open table, doth provide
          The purpled pheasant with the speckled side;
     The painted partridge lies in every field,
30   And, for thy mess, is willing to be killed.
     And if the high-swoll'n Medway[5] fail thy dish,
          Thou hast thy ponds, that pay thee tribute fish:
     Fat, agèd carps, that run into thy net.
          And pikes, now weary their own kind to eat,
35   As loath, the second draught, or cast to stay,
          Officiously, at first, themselves betray;
     Bright eels, that emulate them, and leap on land
          Before the fisher, or into his hand.
     Then hath thy orchard fruit, thy garden flowers,
40   Fresh as the air, and new as are the hours.
     The early cherry, with the later plum,
          Fig, grape, and quince, each in his time doth come;
     The blushing apricot and woolly peach
          Hang on thy walls, that every child may reach.
45   And though thy walls be of the country stone,
          They're reared with no man's ruin, no man's groan;
     There's none, that dwell about them, wish them down;
          But all come in, the farmer, and the clown,°   *peasant*
     And no one empty-handed, to salute
50   Thy lord and lady, though they have no suit.

---

2. The castle was built in 1340.
3. Pan was the god of forest, field, and pasture; Bacchus
was the god of wine.
4. In Greek mythology the satyr with a man's body and a

goat's legs was devoted to lechery. Robert Sidney's wife
Barbara Gamage was said to have given birth under this
oak.
5. The local river.

Some bring a capon, some a rural cake,
    Some nuts, some apples; some that think they make
The better cheeses, bring'em; or else send
    By their ripe daughters, whom they would commend
55   This way to husbands; and whose baskets bear
    An emblem of themselves in plum, or pear.
But what can this (more than express their love)
    Add to thy free provisions, far above
The need of such? whose liberal board doth flow
60   With all that hospitality doth know!
Where comes no guest, but is allowed to eat
    Without his fear, and of thy lord's own meat;
Where the same beer, and bread, and self-same wine
    That is his lordship's shall be also mine,
65   And I not fain to sit (as some this day
    At great men's tables) and yet dine away.
Here no man tells my cups; nor, standing by,
    A waiter, doth my gluttony envy,
But gives me what I call, and lets me eat;
70   He knows below he shall find plenty of meat,
Thy tables hoard not up for the next day.
    Nor, when I take my lodging, need I pray
For fire, or lights, or livery:° all is there,   *provisions, food*
    As if thou then wert mine, or I reigned here;
75   There's nothing I can wish, for which I stay.
    That found King James, when, hunting late this way
With his brave son, the Prince, they saw thy fires
    Shine bright on every hearth as the desires
Of thy Penates[6] had been set on flame
80   To entertain them; or the country came,
With all their zeal, to warm their welcome here.
    What (great, I will not say, but) sudden cheer
Didst thou, then, make 'em! and what praise was heaped
    On thy good lady, then, who therein reaped
85   The just reward of her high housewifery;
    To have her linen, plate, and all things nigh,
When she was far, and not a room, but dressed
    As if it had expected such a guest!
These, Penshurst, are thy praise, and yet not all.
90   Thy lady's noble, fruitful, chaste withall.
His children thy great lord may call his own,
    A fortune, in this age, but rarely known.
They are, and have been, taught religion; thence
    Their gentler spirits have sucked innocence.
95   Each morn and even, they are taught to pray,
    With the whole household, and may every day
Read in their virtuous parents' noble parts
    The mysteries of manners, arms, and arts.
Now, Penshurst, they that will proportion° thee   *compare*

6. Household gods.

100   With other edifices, when they see
        Those proud, ambitious heaps, and nothing else,
            May say, their lords have built, but thy lord dwells.

Song to Celia

        Drink to me only with thine eyes,
            And I will pledge with mine;
        Or leave a kiss but in the cup,
            And I'll not look for wine.
5   The thirst that from the soul doth rise
            Doth ask a drink divine;
        But might I of Jove's nectar sup,
            I would not change for thine.
        I sent thee late a rosy wreath,
10   Not so much honoring thee
        As giving it a hope that there
            It could not withered be.
        But thou thereon didst only breathe,
            And sent'st it back on me;
15   Since when it grows, and smells, I swear,
            Not of itself, but thee.

To the Memory of My Beloved, the Author, Mr. William Shakespeare, and What He Hath Left Us[1]

        To draw no envy, Shakespeare, on thy name,
            Am I thus ample[2] to thy book and fame,
        While I confess thy writings to be such,
            As neither man nor muse can praise too much.
5   'Tis true, and all men's suffrage. But these ways
            Were not the paths I meant unto thy praise;
        For silliest ignorance on these may light,
            Which, when it sounds at best, but echoes right;
        Or blind affection, which doth ne'er advance
10   The truth, but gropes, and urgeth all by chance;
        Or crafty malice, might pretend this praise,
            And think to ruin, where it seemed to raise.
        These are as some infamous bawd or whore
            Should praise a matron. What could hurt her more?
15   But thou art proof against them, and indeed
            Above the ill fortune of them, or the need.
        I, therefore will begin. Soul of the age!
            The applause! delight! the wonder of our stage!
        My Shakespeare, rise; I will not lodge thee by
20   Chaucer, or Spenser, or bid Beaumont lie
        A little further, to make thee a room;[3]

---

1. Prefixed to the first folio of Shakespeare's plays (1623).
2. From Latin *amplus*: copious; an *amplus orator* was one who spoke richly and with dignity.

3. Chaucer, Spenser, and Francis Beaumont were buried in Westminster Abbey; Shakespeare was buried in Stratford.

To the Memory of My Beloved, the Author, Mr. William Shakespeare

Thou art a monument without a tomb,
And art alive still while thy book doth live,
And we have wits to read, and praise to give.
That I not mix thee so, my brain excuses,
25 I mean with great, but disproportioned, Muses;
For, if I thought my judgment were of years,
I should commit thee surely with thy peers,
And tell how far thou didst our Lyly outshine,
Or sporting Kyd, or Marlowe's mighty line.[4]
30 And though thou hadst small Latin, and less Greek,
From thence to honor thee, I would not seek
For names, but call forth thundering Aeschylus,
Euripides, and Sophocles to us,
Pacuvius, Accius, him of Cordova dead,
35 To life again, to hear thy buskin[5] tread
And shake a stage; or, when thy socks[6] were on,
Leave thee alone for the comparison
Of all that insolent Greece or haughty Rome
Sent forth, or since did from their ashes come.
40 Triumph, my Britain; thou hast one to show
To whom all scenes of Europe homage owe.
He was not of an age, but for all time!
And all the muses still were in their prime
When like Apollo he came forth to warm
45 Our ears, or like a Mercury to charm![7]
Nature herself was proud of his designs,
And joyed to wear the dressing of his lines,
Which were so richly spun, and woven so fit
As, since, she will vouchsafe no other wit.
50 The merry Greek, tart Aristophanes,
Neat Terence, witty Plautus,[8] now not please,
But antiquated, and deserted lie,
As they were not of nature's family.
Yet must I not give nature all; thy art,
55 My gentle Shakespeare, must enjoy a part.
For though the poet's matter nature be,
His art doth give the fashion. And that he
Who casts to write a living line must sweat
(Such as thine are) and strike the second heat
60 Upon the Muses' anvil: turn the same,
And himself with it, that he thinks to frame;[9]
Or for the laurel, he may gain a scorn;
For a good poet's made as well as born.
And such wert thou! Look how the father's face
65

---

4. Lyly was an author of English prose comedies; Kyd and Marlowe were authors of English verse tragedies.
5. Boot worn by tragic actors. Jonson compares Shakespeare to tragedians of ancient Greece (Aeschylus, Sophocles, Euripides) and Rome (Pacuvius, Accius, and "him of Cordova," Seneca).
6. Symbols of comedy.

7. Apollo and Mercury were the gods of poetry and eloquence.
8. Aristophanes was an ancient Greek comic playwright; Terence and Plautus were authors of Roman comedy.
9. See Horace, Ars Poetica 441: "return the ill-tuned verses to the anvil."

Lives in his issue; even so, the race
Of Shakespeare's mind and manners brightly shines
In his well-turnèd, and true-filèd lines:
In each of which he seems to shake a lance,[1]
70   As brandished at the eyes of ignorance.
Sweet Swan of Avon, what a sight it were
To see thee in our waters yet appear,
And make those flights upon the banks of Thames,
That so did take Eliza, and our James![2]
75 But stay, I see thee in the hemisphere
Advanced, and made a constellation there!
Shine forth, thou star of poets, and with rage
Or influence chide or cheer the drooping stage,[3]
Which, since thy flight from hence, hath mourned like night,
80   And despairs day, but for thy volume's light.

———— ✦✦✦ ————

John Donne
1572–1631

John Donne wrote some of the most passionate love poems and most moving religious verse in the English language. Even his contemporaries wondered how one mind could express itself in such different modes. Eliciting a portrait of the artist as a split personality, Donne's letters mention the melancholic lover "Jack Donne," succeeded by the Anglican priest "Doctor Donne." Izaak Walton's *Life of Donne* (1640) portrays an earnest, aspiring clergyman who wrote love poetry to his wife. Yet Donne actually wrote most of his poetry—both the love lyrics and the *Holy Sonnets*—before he entered the ministry at forty-three. An ambitious, talented, and handsome young man, Donne struggled to attain secular patronage; later, he resigned himself to life in the church and, after his wife's death, came to terms with his own mortality.

Donne was born into a Catholic family. His mother was the great-niece of Sir Thomas More; she went into exile in Antwerp for a time to seek religious toleration. One of Donne's uncles was imprisoned in the Tower of London because he was a Jesuit priest. Donne wrote of his family that none "hath endured and suffered more in their persons and fortunes, for obeying the Teachers of Roman Doctrine, then it hath done." Donne and his brother Henry entered Hart Hall, Oxford, when they were just eleven and ten, young enough to be spared the required oath recognizing the Queen as head of the church. The Donne brothers later studied law at Lincoln's Inn, where Henry was arrested for harboring a priest in 1593. The priest was drawn and quartered; Henry died in Newgate prison of the plague.

Though shadowed by his brother's death, Donne's student years in London had their pleasures. Donne was distracted from studying law by "the worst voluptuousness . . . an Hydroptique immoderate desire of humane learning and languages." The young Donne was described by his friend Sir Richard Baker as "a great visitor of ladies, a great frequenter of Playes, a great writer of conceited Verses." Among these were Donne's erotic *Elegies*, including *To His Mistress Going to Bed* and *Love's Progress*, both of which were refused a license for publication in the 1633 edition of his collected verse.

---

1. Pun on "Shake-speare."
2. Queen Elizabeth and King James.
3. Like an ancient hero, Shakespeare is given a place among the stars; as the "rage" and "influence" of the planets affect life on earth, Shakespeare affects the world of the stage.

Shortly after gaining a position as secretary to Sir Thomas Egerton, Lord Keeper of the Great Seal, in 1597, Donne met and fell in love with Ann More. His noble employer's niece, she was so far above Donne's station that they married secretly. When Ann's father heard the news, he asked Egerton to have Donne fired and saw to it that he was incarcerated. At this time, Donne is said to have written to Ann: *"John Donne, Ann Donne, un-done."* As a result of Donne's petition, the Court of Audience for Canterbury declared the marriage lawful; nevertheless, Ann was disinherited.

John and Ann made a love match, but their life was not easy. She bore twelve children in fifteen years, not counting miscarriages. Donne lamented the "poorness of [his] fortune and the greatness of [his] charge." After thirteen years of marriage, however, he could also still say: "we had not one another at so cheap a rate, as that we should ever be weary of one another." A few of the love poems in *Songs and Sonnets* express a mixture of bliss and hardship linked with their marriage.

Relations with friends and patrons also influenced Donne's poetry. He is said to have addressed several poems to Magdalen Herbert, mother of the poet George. Living in Mitcham near London, Donne cemented his friendship with Ben Jonson, who wrote two epigrams in praise of Donne in thanks for his Latin verses on *Volpone* (1607). Donne was also introduced to Lucy, Countess of Bedford, who asked Jonson to get her a copy of Donne's *Satires*. Donne not only addressed several verse letters to her but also enjoyed her poems. An even more generous patron was Sir Robert Drury, for the death of whose young daughter Elizabeth the poet composed *A Funeral Elegie*, the inspiration for his two *Anniversaries* (1612) on the nature of the cosmos and death.

Donne's writing from 1607 to 1611 dealt with theological and moral controversies. His *Pseudo-Martyr* (1610) argued that Catholics should take the Oath of Allegiance to the King and that resistance to him should not be glorified as a form of martyrdom. This work won him James I's advice to enter the ministry, but, still skeptical, Donne held off. He protested against sectarianism: "You know I never fettered nor imprisoned the word Religion . . . immuring it in a Rome, or a Wittenberg, or a Geneva." Donne also examined the morality of suicide in *Biathanatos* (written 1607, published 1646). His *Holy Sonnets* (some of which may have been written as early as 1608–1610) reveal an obsession with his own death and fear of damnation: "I dare not move my dim eyes any way, / Despair behind, and death before doth cast / Such terror."

Donne was plagued by professional bad luck until he became an Anglican priest. With the exception of Sir Robert Drury, Donne never found a dependable patron. His applications for secretaryships in Ireland and Virginia were unsuccessful. In search of the Earl of Somerset's patronage, Donne wrote an epithalamion for his marriage to Frances Howard and even volunteered to justify her earlier controversial divorce. Fortunately for Donne, his attempts to win a position through Somerset failed, since a year later the Earl fell from power. Giving up his long quest for secular preferment, Donne took holy orders in 1615. Once an Anglican priest, he was made a royal chaplain and received an honorary Doctorate of Divinity from Cambridge. Two years later, he became reader in divinity at his old law school Lincoln's Inn.

Prosperity was followed by tragic loss. Ann Donne died giving birth in 1617. The death of his wife turned Donne more completely toward God. His later prose viewed death from a different perspective from his earlier personal torment. Suffering from a recurring fever, he wrote *Devotions upon Emergent Occasions* (1624). In the midst of a major epidemic, at the height of his fever, distraught and sleepless, he realizes our common mortality: "never send to know for whom the bell tolls; it tolls for thee." He became a prolific and stirring preacher of sermons. Some of these, such as that urging the Company of the Virginia Plantation to spread the gospel (1622), were printed in his lifetime. One written just before his death shows confidence in God's forgiveness: "I cannot plead innocency of life, especially of my youth: But I am to be judged by a merciful God."

If Donne's life can be split into the secular and religious, his poetic sensibility cannot. His verse fuses flesh and spirit through metaphysical conceits that create fascinating connections between apparently unrelated topics. In Donne's erotic lyrics, sex excites spiritual ecstasy along with hot lust and seductive wit. Similarly, Donne's religious poems express his relation with God not as an intellectual construct but as an emotional need, articulated in intimate and even erotic language. Later ages did not always appreciate either Donne's sensuality or his intellectual extravagance; remarkably, none of his poems was included in the most important nineteenth-century anthology of poetry, Palgraves's *Golden Treasury*. Donne's fame was revived early in the twentieth century, when modernist poets, especially T. S. Eliot, took inspiration from Donne's complex mixture of immediacy and artifice, passion and subtle thought.

The Good Morrow[1]

I wonder by my troth, what thou, and I
Did, till we loved? Were we not weaned till then?
But sucked on country pleasures, childishly?
Or snorted we in the seven sleepers' den?[2]
5   'Twas so; but this, all pleasures fancies be.
If ever any beauty I did see,
Which I desired, and got, 'twas but a dream of thee.

And now good morrow to our waking souls,
Which watch not one another out of fear;
10   For love, all love of other sights controls,
And makes one little room, an everywhere.
Let sea-discoverers to new worlds have gone,
Let maps to others, worlds on worlds have shown,
Let us possess one world, each hath one, and is one.

15   My face in thine eye, thine in mine appears,
And true plain hearts do in the faces rest.
Where can we find two better hemispheres
Without sharp north, without declining west?
What ever dies was not mixed equally;[3]
20   If our two loves be one, or, thou and I
Love so alike, that none do slacken, none can die.

Song

Go, and catch a falling star,
    Get with child a mandrake root,[1]
Tell me, where all past years are,
    Or who cleft the Devil's foot,
5   Teach me to hear mermaids singing,
Or to keep off envy's stinging,
        And find
        What wind
Serves to advance an honest mind.

---

1. Donne's love poems, written over a period of 20 years, cannot be dated with any certainty. They were first printed in 1633, scattered throughout the entire collection of poems. Then, in the 1635 edition, the love poems were printed as a group under the title *Songs and Sonnets*. There is no certainty that the titles were chosen by Donne.

2. Legendary cave where seven Ephesian youths were put to sleep by God to escape the persecution of Christians by the Emperor Decius (249).
3. According to ancient medicine, death was caused by an imbalance of elements in the body.
1. A fork-rooted plant, resembling the human body in its form.

10 If thou be borne to strange sights,
      Things invisible to see,
  Ride ten thousand days and nights,
      Till age snow white hairs on thee.
  Thou, when thou return'st, will tell me
15 All strange wonders that befell thee,
      And swear
      No where
  Lives a woman true, and fair.

  If thou findest one, let me know,
20   Such a pilgrimage were sweet;
  Yet do not, I would not go,
      Though at next door we might meet,
  Though she were true, when you met her,
  And last, till you write your letter,
25   Yet she
      Will be
  False, ere I come, to two, or three.

The Undertaking

  I have done one braver thing
      Than all the Worthies did,[1]
  And yet a braver thence doth spring,
      Which is to keep that hid.

5 It were but madness now to impart
      The skill of specular stone,[2]
  When he which can have learned the art
      To cut it, can find none.

  So, if I now should utter this,
10   Others (because no more
  Such stuff to work upon, there is,)
      Would love but as before.

  But he who loveliness within
      Hath found, all outward loathes,
15 For he who color loves, and skin,
      Loves but their oldest clothes.

  If, as I have, you also do
      Virtue attired in woman see,
  And dare love that, and say so too,
20   And forget the He and She;

  And if this love, though placèd so,
      From profane men you hide,
  Which will no faith on this bestow,
      Or, if they do, deride:

1. The nine great military heroes of ancient and medieval legend and history.

2. Transparent stone of ancient times, but now lost, that required great skill to cut in strips.

25   Then you have done a braver thing
    Than all the Worthies did;
And a braver thence will spring,
    Which is, to keep that hid.

The Sun Rising[1]

    Busy old fool, unruly Sun,
      Why dost thou thus
Through windows, and through curtains call on us?
Must to thy motions lovers' seasons run?
5   Saucy pedantic wretch, go chide
      Late schoolboys, and sour prentices,°   *apprentices*
    Go tell court-huntsmen, that the king will ride,
    Call country ants to harvest offices;
Love, all alike, no season knows, nor clime,
10 Nor hours, days, months, which are the rags of time.

      Thy beams, so reverend, and strong
      Why shouldst thou think?
I could eclipse and cloud them with a wink,
But that I would not lose her sight so long:
15   If her eyes have not blinded thine,
      Look, and tomorrow late, tell me,
    Whether both th'Indias of spice and mine[2]
    Be where thou left'st them, or lie here with me.
Ask for those kings whom thou saw'st yesterday,
20 And thou shalt hear, all here in one bed lay.

      She is all states, and all princes, I,
      Nothing else is.
Princes do but play us; compared to this,
All honor's mimic; all wealth alchemy.°   *fake science*
25   Thou sun art half as happy as we,
      In that the world's contracted thus;
    Thine age asks ease, and since thy duties be
    To warm the world, that's done in warming us.
Shine here to us, and thou art everywhere;
30 This bed thy center is, these walls, thy sphere.

The Canonization[1]

For God's sake hold your tongue, and let me love,
    Or° chide my palsy, or my gout,   *either*
My five gray hairs, or ruined fortune flout,
    With wealth your state, your mind with arts improve,

---

1. In the tradition of the alba, a love song addressing the dawn, as in Ovid's *Amores* 1.13 and Petrarch's *Canzoniere* 188.

2. The East Indies was the source of spice; the West Indies was the source of gold.
1. The making of saints.

5   Take you a course, get you a place,
          Observe his Honor, or his Grace,
     Or the King's real, or his stampèd face[2]
          Contemplate, what you will, approve,
          So you will let me love.

10   Alas, alas, who's injured by my love?
          What merchant's ships have my sighs drowned?
     Who says my tears have overflowed his ground?
          When did my colds a forward spring remove?
          When did the heats which my veins fill
15   Add one more to the plaguy bill?[3]
     Soldiers find wars, and lawyers find out still
          Litigious men, which quarrels move
          Though she and I do love.

     Call us what you will, we are made such by love;
20   Call her one, me another fly,
     We are tapers° too, and at our own cost die,[4]   *candles*
          And we in us find the eagle and the dove.
          The phoenix riddle hath more wit[5]
          By us; we two being one, are it.
25   So to one neutral thing both sexes fit,
          We die and rise the same, and prove
          Mysterious by this love.

     We can die by it, if not live by love,
          And if unfit for tombs and hearse
30   Our legend be, it will be fit for verse;
          And if no piece of chronicle we prove,
          We'll build in sonnets pretty rooms;[6]
          As well a well wrought urn becomes
     The greatest ashes, as half-acre tombs,
35   And by these hymns, all shall approve
          Us canonized for love.

     And thus invoke us: You whom reverend love
          Made one another's hermitage;°   *refuge, retreat*
     You, to whom love was peace, that now is rage;
40   Who did the whole world's soul contract, and drove
          Into the glasses° of your eyes[7]   *lenses*
          (So made such mirrors, and such spies,
     That they did all to you epitomize)
          Countries, towns, courts: beg from above
45   A pattern of your love!

---

2. The King's actual face or his image stamped on coins.
3. Daily list of those who have died issued during outbreaks of the plague.
4. To die is to experience orgasm.
5. The mythical bird that was burned and reborn out of its own ashes, a symbol of perfection.
6. A play on *stanza*, Italian for "room."
7. The lovers gazing into each other's eyes saw there a compact version or microcosm of the larger world or macrocosm.

The Flea[1]

Mark but this flea, and mark in this,
How little that which thou deniest me is;
It sucked me first,[2] and now sucks thee,
And in this flea, our two bloods mingled be;
5   Thou know'st that this cannot be said
A sin, nor shame, nor loss of maidenhead,
 Yet this enjoys before it woo,
  And pampered swells with one blood made of two,
  And this, alas, is more than we would do.

10 Oh stay, three lives in one flea spare,
Where we almost, yea more than married are.
This flea is you and I, and this
Our marriage bed, and marriage temple is;
Though parents grudge, and you, w'are met,
15 And cloistered in these living walls of jet.°   *black*
 Though use make you apt to kill me,
  Let not to that, self murder added be,
  And sacrilege, three sins in killing three.

Cruel and sudden, hast thou since
20 Purpled thy nail, in blood of innocence?
Wherein could this flea guilty be,
Except in that drop which it sucked from thee?
Yet thou triumph'st, and say'st that thou
Find'st not thy self, nor me the weaker now;
25 'Tis true, then learn how false, fears be;
 Just so much honor, when thou yield'st to me,
  Will waste, as this flea's death took life from thee.

The Bait[1]

Come live with me, and be my love,
And we will some new pleasures prove
Of golden sands, and crystal brooks,
With silken lines, and silver hooks.

5   There will the river whispering run
Warmed by thy eyes, more than the sun.
And there the enamored fish will stay,
Begging themselves they may betray.

When thou wilt swim in that live bath,
10   Each fish, which every channel hath,
Will amorously to thee swim,
Gladder to catch thee, then thou him.

If thou, to be so seen, be'st loath,
By sun, or moon, thou darkenest both,

---

1. Based on a poem attributed to Ovid, the poem plays on the belief that intercourse involved the mixing of bloods.
2. "Me it sucked first" in the 1635 edition.

1. Parodies Marlowe's *The Passionate Shepherd to His Love* and Raleigh's *The Nymph's Reply*; see pages 683–84.

15   And if myself have leave to see,
       I need not their light, having thee.

       Let others freeze with angling reeds,
       And cut their legs, with shells and weeds,
       Or treacherously poor fish beset,
20   With strangling snare, or windowy net:

       Let coarse bold hands, from slimy nest
       The bedded fish in banks out-wrest,
       Or curious traitors, sleave-silk flies²
       Bewitch poor fishes' wandering eyes.

25   For thee, thou need'st no such deceit,
       For thou thyself are thine own bait;
       That fish, that is not catched thereby,
       Alas, is wiser far than I.

A Valediction: Forbidding Mourning¹

       As virtuous men pass mildly away,
           And whisper to their souls, to go,
       Whilst some of their sad friends do say,
           The breath goes now, and some say, no:

5   So let us melt, and make no noise,
           No tear-floods, nor sigh-tempests move,
       'Twere profanation° of our joys   *desecration*
           To tell the laity² of our love.

       Moving of th'earth brings harms and fears,
10   Men reckon what it did and meant,
       But trepidation of the spheres,³
           Though greater far, is innocent.

       Dull sublunary⁴ lovers' love
           (Whose soul is sense) cannot admit
15   Absence, because it doth remove
           Those things which elemented° it.   *composed*

       But we by a love, so much refined,
           That our selves know not what it is,
       Inter-assurèd of the mind,
20   Care less, eyes, lips, and hands to miss.

       Our two souls therefore, which are one,
           Though I must go, endure not yet
       A breach, but an expansion,
           Like gold to airy thinness beat.⁵

---

2. Artificial flies made from silk threads.
1. In his *Life of Dr. John Donne* (1640), Walton describes the occasion as Donne's farewell to his wife before his journey to France in 1611.
2. The uninitiated.

3. Though the movement of the spheres is greater than an earthquake, we feel its effects less.
4. Under the sphere of the moon, hence sensual.
5. Gold was beaten to produce gold leaf. "Airy" suggests their love will become so fine that it will be spiritual.

25 If they be two, they are two so
        As stiff twin compasses⁶ are two,
    Thy soul the fixed foot, makes no show
        To move, but doth, if th' other do.

    And though it in the center sit,
30   Yet when the other far doth roam,
    It leans, and hearkens after it,
        And grows erect, as that comes home.

    Such wilt thou be to me, who must
        Like th' other foot, obliquely run;
35 Thy firmness makes my circle just,°   *complete*
        And makes me end, where I begun.

The Ecstasy¹

    Where, like a pillow on a bed,
        A pregnant bank swelled up, to rest
    The violet's reclining head,²
        Sat we two, one another's best.

5   Our hands were firmly cemented
        With a fast balm, which thence did spring,
    Our eye-beams twisted, and did thread
        Our eyes, upon one double string;³

    So to intergraft our hands, as yet
10   Was all the means to make us one,
    And pictures in our eyes to get
        Was all our propagation.⁴

    As 'twixt two equal armies, Fate
        Suspends uncertain victory,
15 Our souls (which to advance their state
        Were gone out) hung 'twixt her and me.

    And whilst our souls negotiate there,
        We like sepulchral statues lay;
    All day, the same our postures were,
20   And we said nothing, all the day.

    If any, so by love refined,
        That he soul's language understood,
    And by good love were grown all mind,
        Within convenient distance stood,

25 He (though he knew not which soul spake
        Because both meant, both spake the same)

---

6. A common emblem of constancy amidst change.
1. From *ekstasis* (Greek) meaning passion and the withdrawal of the soul from the body. A beautiful and secluded pastoral spot was a frequent setting for love poetry.
2. The violet was an emblem of faithfulness.

3. The lovers are totally enthralled by gazing into each other's eyes.
4. The act of reflecting each other's image was called "making babies."

Might thence a new concoction[5] take,
    And part far purer than he came.

This ecstasy doth unperplex,
    We said, and tell us what we love,
30 We see by this, it was not sex,
    We see, we saw not what did move:

But as all several souls contain
    Mixture of things, they know not what,
35 Love, these mixed souls, doth mix again,
    And makes both one, each this and that.

A single violet transplant,
    The strength, the color, and the size,
(All which before was poor and scant)
40   Redoubles still, and multiplies.

When love with one another so
    Interinanimates two souls,
That abler soul, which thence doth flow,
    Defects of loneliness controls.

45 We then, who are this new soul, know,
    Of what we are composed and made,
For, th' atomies° of which we grow,   *components, parts*
    Are souls, whom no change can invade.

But O alas, so long, so far
50   Our bodies why do we forbear?
They are ours, though they are not we, we are
    The intelligences, they the sphere.[6]

We owe them thanks, because they thus,
    Did us to us at first convey,
55 Yielded their forces, sense, to us,
    Nor are dross° to us, but allay.°   *refuse / a mixture*

On man heaven's influence works not so,
    But that it first imprints the air,[7]
So soul into the soul may flow,
60   Though it to body first repair.

As our blood labors to beget
    Spirits, as like souls as it can,
Because such fingers need to knit
    That subtle knot, which makes us man:[8]

65 So much pure lovers' souls descend
    T'affections,° and to faculties,°[9]   *feelings / powers*

5. Refining of metals by heat.
6. In Aristotelian cosmology, each planet moved in a sphere (the form of its motion around the earth) and was guided by an inner spiritual force, or intelligence.
7. An angel has to put on clothes of air to be seen by men; in hermetic medicine, the air mediates the influence of the stars. Just as spirits need a material medium, so souls need the union of bodies.
8. In scholastic philosophy a human being is composed of body and soul, and vapors called spirits produced by the blood link the body with the soul.
9. As the blood mediates between body and soul, so the lovers' feelings mediate between flesh and spirit.

Which sense may reach and apprehend,
    Else a great prince in prison lies.

To our bodies turn we then, that so
    Weak men on love revealed may look;
70   Love's mysteries in souls do grow,
    But yet the body is his book.

And if some lover, such as we,
    Have heard this dialogue of one,
75   Let him still mark us, he shall see
    Small change, when we are to bodies gone.

from **Holy Sonnets**
Divine Meditations

1

As due by many titles° I resign   *legal rights*
Myself to thee, Oh God, first I was made
By thee, and for thee, and when I was decayed
Thy blood bought that, the which before was thine,
5   I am thy son, made with thyself to shine,
Thy servant, whose pains thou has still repaid,
Thy sheep, thine image, and, till I betrayed
Myself, a temple of thy Spirit divine;
Why doth the devil then usurp on me?
10 Why doth he steal, nay ravish that's thy right?
Except thou rise and for thine own work fight,
Oh I shall soon despair, when I do see
That thou lov'st mankind well, yet wilt not choose me,
And Satan hates me, yet is loth to lose me.

5

If poisonous minerals, and if that tree,
Whose fruit threw death on else immortal us,
If lecherous goats, if serpents envious
Cannot be damned; alas, why should I be?
5   Why should intent or reason, born in me,
Make sins, else equal, in me more heinous?
And mercy being easy, and glorious
To God, in his stern wrath, why threatens he?
But who am I, that dare dispute with thee?
10 O God, Oh! of thine only worthy blood,
And my tears, make a heavenly Lethean[1] flood,
And drown in it my sins' black memory.
That thou remember them, some claim as debt,
I think it mercy, if thou wilt forget.

---

1. Of Lethe, the river of forgetfulness in the underworld of ancient mythology.

6

Death be not proud, though some have called thee
Mighty and dreadful, for thou are not so.
For, those, whom thou think'st thou dost overthrow,
Die not, poor death, nor yet canst thou kill me;
5   From rest and sleep, which but thy pictures be,
Much pleasure, then from thee, much more must flow,
And soonest our best men with thee do go,
Rest of their bones, and soul's delivery.
Thou art slave to fate, chance, kings, and desperate men,
10 And dost with poison, war, and sickness dwell,
And poppy,° or charms can make us sleep as well,   *a narcotic*
And better than thy stroke; why swell'st° thou then?   *grow in pride*
One short sleep past, we wake eternally,
And death shall be no more. Death thou shalt die.[2]

9

What if this present were the world's last night?
Mark in my heart, O soul, where thou dost dwell,
The picture of Christ crucified, and tell
Whether that countenance can thee affright,
5   Tears in his eyes quench the amazing light,
Blood fills his frowns, which from his pierced head fell,
And can that tongue adjudge thee unto hell,
Which prayed forgiveness for his foes' fierce spite?
No, no; but as in my idolatry[3]
10 I said to all my profane mistresses,
Beauty, of pity, foulness only is
A sign of rigor:[4] so I say to thee,
To wicked spirits are horrid shapes assigned,
This beauteous form assures a piteous mind.

10

Batter my heart, three-personed God;[5] for, you
As yet but knock, breathe, shine, and seek to mend;
That I may rise, and stand, o'erthrow me, and bend
Your force, to break, blow, burn and make me new.
5   I, like an usurped town, to another due,
Labor to admit you, but oh, to no end,
Reason your viceroy° in me, me should defend,   *ruler*
But is captived, and proves weak or untrue,
Yet dearly I love you, and would be loved fain,°   *willingly*
10 But am betrothed unto your enemy,
Divorce me, untie, or break that knot again,
Take me to you, imprison me, for I
Except you enthrall me, never shall be free,
Nor ever chaste, except you ravish me.

2. "The last enemy that shall be destroyed is death" (1
Corinthians 15.26).
3. Erotic devotion to women.

4. Beautiful women show compassion; only ugly ones
refuse their lovers.
5. The Trinity: God the Father, Son, and Holy Spirit.

Lady Mary Wroth
1586–1640

Lady Mary Wroth was born the same year that her uncle Sir Philip Sidney died in battle. Like her uncle, she wrote brilliant sonnets and an entertaining and complex prose romance, but whereas his death and writing became the stuff of myth, she died in obscurity. Appreciated by the finest poets of her time, her writing was neglected for the next 300 years; she has only recently been rediscovered as one of the most compelling women writers of her age. Her *Pamphilia to Amphilanthus*, the first Petrarchan sonnet sequence in English by a woman, was first printed in 1621 but was not reprinted until 1977. Wroth's work has finally become available outside rare book libraries, thanks to Josephine Robert's editions of Wroth's complete poems (1983) and her prose romance *The Countess of Montgomeries Urania* (1995), along with Michael Brennan's edition of her pastoral tragicomedy *Love's Victory* (1988). Recent criticism has stressed the formal complexity and variety of her poetry and prose, their creation of female subjectivity, and their relationship to her life and social context, shedding new light on one of the most emotionally powerful and stylistically innovative authors of the Jacobean period.

Mary Wroth was born into the cultivated and distinguished Sidney family. Mary and her mother, two brothers, and seven sisters lived at the family estate Penshurst in Kent. She sometimes visited her father in the Low Countries, where he commanded the English troops fighting for the Protestant cause against the Spanish. Ben Jonson sang the praises of Lady Mary's family and their way of life in *To Penshurst* (see page 799), a place where the children not only enjoyed natural beauty—"broad beech" and "chest-nut shade"—but also learned the "mysteries of manners, arms and arts." Mary also spent a great deal of time in London with her aunt for whom she was named, Mary (Sidney) Herbert, Countess of Pembroke, hostess to and patron of a circle of poets that included George Chapman and Ben Jonson.

Mary found a mentor in her aunt, who herself wrote poems as well as translations of the Psalms and of Petrarch. Mary Herbert's translation of Petrarch's *Trionfo della Morte* ("Triumph of Death") portrays the poet's beloved Laura not as a passive object but as a lively and eloquent speaker. Mary Wroth's own sonnets similarly portray the woman as the suffering and desiring subject of love rather than the mute object that was common in earlier English Petrarchan poetry. Mary Wroth took the title of her *Urania* from a character in Philip Sidney's *The Countess of Pembrokes Arcadia*, whose publication had been overseen by his sister, Mary Sidney Herbert. Mary Wroth even created the character of the Queen of Naples as a fictional version of her aunt and perhaps saw *Urania* as a continuation of *Arcadia*.

When Mary married Sir Robert Wroth, Lord of Durance and Laughton House and juror for the Gunpowder Plot, she continued her close family ties with her aunt and father (yet another poet), but she also moved into the larger world of the Jacobean court. She served as Queen Anne's companion, and she became at once an observer and a center of attention in the aristocratic circle at court. In 1605, shortly after the first recorded performance of *Othello* at Whitehall, Lady Mary Wroth played in Ben Jonson's *Masque of Blackness*, in which she was presented to the court with Lady Frances Walsingham as the embodiment of gravity and dignity. Later, Wroth would deploy metaphors of darkness and night to great effect in her lyric poems.

It was in this court context that she attracted the attention of Ben Jonson, who not only wrote a poem complimenting her husband but also dedicated a sonnet and two epigrams to her. Jonson paid tribute to her as a subject and inspiration for poetry and as a powerfully moving poet in her own right. He claimed that since writing out her sonnets, he had "become / A better lover and much better poet." Dedicating his great play *The Alchemist* to her, he portrayed her as inheriting her uncle's mantle as poet: "To that Lady Most Deserving her Name and Blood, Lady Mary Wroth,"—a pun on her name, as Wroth was pronounced "worth."

While she, too, punned on her married name in her poetry, Mary clung to her identity as a Sidney, using the Sidney device in her letters.

Her marriage was not particularly happy and pales in comparison with her literary friendship and love affair with her cousin William Herbert, by whom she had two illegitimate children, after she was widowed in 1614. During the years of her early widowhood she wrote the first part of her prose romance *Urania*, which was printed with *Pamphilia to Amphilanthus* in 1621. The *Urania* not only presents a fictional account of her relationship with her cousin and her parents' own happy marriage but also was read at the time as a criticism of the mores of the court. King James's courtiers, taking offense at the satire of their private lives, attacked her, prompting her to ask for the book to be removed from publication a few months after it first appeared. The early modern prejudice against women writing surfaces in Lord Denny's punning condescension to Wroth: "leave idle books alone / For wiser and worthier women have writ none."

Fortunately for us, she didn't take his advice and continued to write the second book of the *Urania*, which survives in manuscript. Indeed, no record of a warrant to recall the book survives. Her final years remain a mystery; she lived in retirement after her cousin's death. She left behind a body of poetry challenging the status quo of the court, proclaiming the suffering she had endured for love, and singing the beauty of spiritual love in a woman's voice. Imitating not only her uncle Philip's *Arcadia* but also the *Heptameron* of the French writer Marguerite de Navarre, Mary Wroth made the prose romance a complex combination of novelistic fantasy, roman à clef, and social satire. The greatest English woman writer of her age, Mary Wroth fashioned a new voice and new perspectives within literary tradition that convey the fullness and complexity of her life as woman, lover, and writer.

from Pamphilia to Amphilanthus[1]

1

> When night's black mantle could most darkness prove,
>   And sleep death's image did my senses hire
>   From knowledge of myself, then thoughts did move
>   Swifter than those most swiftness need require:
> 5 In sleep, a chariot drawn by winged desire
>   I saw, where sat bright Venus, Queen of love,
>   And at her feet her son, still adding fire
>   To burning hearts which she did hold above,
>   But one heart flaming more than all the rest
> 10   The goddess held, and put it to my breast.
>   "Dear son, now shut?"[2] said she, "thus must we win."
> He her obeyed, and martyred my poor heart,
>   I, waking, hoped as dreams it would depart;[3]
>   Yet since, O me, a lover I have been.

16

> Am I thus conquered? Have I lost the powers
>   That to withstand, which joys to ruin me?
>   Must I be still while it my strength devours

---

1. The title means "From the All-loving one to the Dual Lover." First published in 1621, the sonnets here follow the numbering in Josephine Robert's 1983 edition.
2. Enclose that flaming heart within Pamphilia.

3. Pamphilia's experience of love is represented as a dream vision, a symbolic narrative in which the dreamer discovers hidden truth.

And captive leads me prisoner, bound, unfree?
5   Love first shall leave men's fant'sies to them free,[4]
Desire shall quench love's flames, spring hate sweet showers,
Love shall loose all his darts, have sight, and see
His shame, and wishings hinder happy hours.[5]
Why should we not Love's purblind° charms resist?   *totally blind*
10   Must we be servile, doing what he list?°   *wants*
No, seek some host to harbor thee: I fly
Thy babish° tricks, and freedom do profess;   *childish*
But O my hurt, makes my lost heart confess
I love, and must. So farewell liberty.

39

Take heed mine eyes, how you your looks do cast,
Lest they betray my heart's most secret thought;
Be true unto yourselves for nothing's bought
More dear than doubt which brings a lover's fast.
5   Catch you all watching eyes, ere they be past,
Or take yours fixed where your best love hath sought
The pride of your desires; let them be taught
Their faults for shame, they could no truer last;
Then look, and look with joy for conquest won,
10   Of those that searched your hurt in double kind;
So you kept safe, let them themselves look blind;
Watch, gaze, and mark 'til they to madness run,
While you, mine eyes, enjoy full sight of love
Contented that such happinesses move.

40

False hope which feeds but to destroy, and spill°   *kill*
What it first breeds; unnatural to the birth
Of thine own womb; conceiving but to kill,[6]
And plenty gives to make the greater dearth,
5   So tyrants do who falsely ruling earth
Outwardly grace them, and with profits fill,
Advance those who appointed are to death
To make their greater fall to please their will.
Thus shadow they their wicked vile intent,
10   Coloring evil with a show of good
While in fair shows their malice so is spent;
Hope kills the heart, and tyrants shed the blood.
For hope deluding brings us to the pride[7]
Of our desires the farther down to slide.

---

4. Before I surrender to Love, Love will allow men to realize their fantasies freely.
5. Cupid blindfolded was a popular figure in Renaissance iconography.
6. The image is of a miscarriage or infanticide.
7. Arrogance, but also elation and pleasure.

74. Song

Love a child is ever crying,
   Please him, and he straight is flying;
   Give him, he the more is craving,
   Never satisfied with having.

5   His desires have no measure,
   Endless folly is his treasure;
   What he promiseth he breaketh;
   Trust not one word that he speaketh.

   He vows nothing but false matter,
10   And to cozen° you he'll flatter.   *trick*
   Let him gain the hand[8] he'll leave you,
   And still glory to deceive you.

   He will triumph in your wailing,
   And yet cause be of your failing.
15   These his virtues are, and slighter
   Are his gifts, his favors lighter.

   Feathers are as firm in staying,
   Wolves no fiercer in their preying;
   As a child then leave him crying,
20   Nor seek him so given to flying.

from *A Crown of Sonnets Dedicated to Love*[1]

77

In this strange labyrinth how shall I turn?
   Ways° are on all sides while the way I miss: *paths*
   If to the right hand, there, in love I burn;
   Let me go forward, therein danger is;
5   If to the left, suspicion hinders bliss,
   Let me turn back, shame cries I ought return,
   Nor faint° though crosses with my fortunes kiss;[2]   *lose heart*
   Stand still is harder, although sure to mourn.[3]
   Thus let me take the right, or left-hand way,
10   Go forward, or stand still, or back retire;
   I must these doubts endure without allay°   *relief*
   Or help, but travail[4] find for my best hire.
   Yet that which most my troubled sense doth move
   Is to leave all, and take the thread of love.[5]

---

8. Let him take control.
1. The crown (Italian *corona*) is a form in which the last line of each poem is repeated as the first line of the next. The last poem of the sequence ends with the first line of the first poem.
2. Though troubles embrace my luck, or fate.
3. It is more difficult to do nothing, although this is sure

to make me mourn.
4. Hard work, with word play on "Travel," which occurs in the 1621 text.
5. An allusion to the myth of Ariadne, beloved of Theseus, to whom she gave a thread to unwind behind him on his path through the labyrinth so that, after slaying the Minotaur, he could retrace his steps on his way out.

103

My muse now happy, lay thyself to rest,
   Sleep in the quiet of a faithful love,
   Write you no more, but let these fant'sies move
   Some other hearts, wake not to new unrest;
5   But if you study, be those thoughts addressed
   To truth, which shall eternal goodness prove,
   Enjoying of true joy, the most, and best,
   The endless gain which never will remove.
Leave the discourse to Venus, and her son
10   To young beginners, and their brains inspire
   With stories of great love, and from that fire
   Get heat to write the fortunes they have won,
And thus leave off; what's past shows you can love,
Now let your constancy your honor prove.

                               Pamphilia.[6]

from The Countess of Montgomery's Urania
from *Book 1*

When the spring began to appear like the welcome messenger of summer, one sweet (and in that more sweet) morning, after Aurora[1] had called all careful eyes to attend the day, forth came the fair shepherdess Urania,[2] (fair indeed; yet that far too mean a title for her, who for beauty deserved the highest style could be given by best knowing judgments). Into the mead[3] she came, where usually she drove her flocks to feed, whose leaping and wantonness showed they were proud of such a guide: But she, whose sad thoughts led her to another manner of spending her time, made her soon leave them, and follow her late begun custom; which was (while they delighted themselves) to sit under some shade, bewailing her misfortune; while they fed, to feed upon her own sorrow and tears, which at this time she began again to summon, sitting down under the shade of a well-spread beech; the ground (then blest) and the tree with full and fine leaved branches growing proud to bear and shadow such perfections. But she regarding nothing, in comparison of her woe, thus proceeded in her grief:

"Alas Urania," said she (the true servant to misfortune); "of any misery that can befall woman, is not this the most and greatest which thou art fallen into? Can there be any near the unhappiness of being ignorant, and that in the highest kind, not being certain of mine own estate or birth? Why was I not still continued in the belief I was, as I appear, a shepherdess, and daughter to a shepherd? My ambition then went no higher than this estate, now flies it to a knowledge; then was I contented, now perplexed. O ignorance, can thy dullness yet procure so sharp a pain? and that such a thought as makes me now aspire unto knowledge? How did I joy in this poor life being quiet? blest in the love of those I took for parents, but now by them I know the contrary, and by that knowledge, not to know myself. Miserable Urania, worse art thou now than these thy lambs; for they know their dams, while thou dost live unknown of any."

---

6. According to the 1621 *Urania*, when Pamphilia accepts the keys to the Throne of Love, the virtue *Constancy* disappears and is transformed into Pamphilia's breast.
1. Goddess of the dawn.

2. Urania represents Susan Herbert, countess of Montgomery (1587–1629), the author's close friend. In Spenser's *Colin Clouts Come Home Again*, Urania stands for Wroth's aunt, Mary Sidney, Countess of Pembroke.
3. Meadow.

By this were others come into that mead with their flocks: but she esteeming her sorrowing thoughts her best, and choicest company, left that place, taking a little path which brought her to the further side of the plain, to the foot of the rocks, speaking as she went these lines, her eyes fixed upon the ground, her very soul turned into mourning.

> Unseen, unknown, I here alone complain
>   To rocks, to hills, to meadows and to springs,
> Which can no help return to ease my pain,
>   But back my sorrows the sad echo brings.
> 5 Thus still increasing are my woes to me,
>   Doubly resounded by that moanful voice,
> Which seems to second me in misery,
>   And answer gives like friend of mine own choice.
> Thus only she doth my companion prove,
> 10 The others silently do offer ease:
> But those that grieve, a grieving note do love;
>   Pleasures to dying eyes bring but disease:
> And such am I, who daily ending live,
> Wailing a state which can no comfort give.

In this passion she went on, till she came to the foot of a great rock, she thinking of nothing less than ease, sought how she might ascend it; hoping there to pass away her time more peaceably with loneliness, though not to find least respite from her sorrow, which so dearly she did value, as by no means she would impart it to any. The way was hard, though by some windings making the ascent pleasing. Having attained the top, she saw under some hollow trees the entry into the rock: she fearing nothing but the continuance of her ignorance, went in; where she found a pretty room, as if that stony place had yet in pity, given leave for such perfections to come into the heart as chiefest, and most beloved place, because most loving. The place was not unlike the ancient (or the descriptions of ancient) hermitages,[4] instead of hangings, covered and lined with ivy, disdaining aught else should come there, that being in such perfection. This richness in nature's plenty made her stay to behold it, and almost grudge the pleasant fullness of content that place might have, if sensible, while she must know to taste of torments. As she was thus in passion mixed with pain, throwing her eyes as wildly as timorous lovers do for fear of discovery, she perceived a little light, and such a one, as a chink doth oft discover to our sights. She curious to see what this was, with her delicate hands put the natural ornament aside, discerning a little door, which she putting from her, passed through it into another room, like the first in all proportion; but in the midst there was a square stone, like to a pretty table, and on it a wax-candle burning; and by that a paper, which had suffered itself patiently to receive the discovering of so much of it, as presented this sonnet (as it seemed newly written) to her sight.

> Here all alone in silence might I mourn:
>   But how can silence be where sorrows flow?
> Sighs with complaints have poorer pains out-worn;
>   But broken hearts can only true grief show.
> 5 Drops of my dearest blood shall let love know
>   Such tears for her I shed, yet still do burn,

4. Hermits' cells.

As no spring can quench least part of my woe,
Till this live earth, again to earth do turn.

Hateful all thought of comfort is to me,
10   Despised day, let me still night possess;
Let me all torments feel in their excess,
And but this light[5] allow my state to see.

Which still doth waste, and wasting as this light,
Are my sad days unto eternal night.

"Alas Urania!" sighed she. "How well do these words, this place, and all agree with thy fortune? Sure poor soul thou wert here appointed to spend thy days, and these rooms ordained to keep thy tortures in; none being assuredly so matchlessly unfortunate."

Turning from the table, she discerned in the room a bed of boughs, and on it a man lying, deprived of outward sense, as she thought, and of life, as she at first did fear, which struck her into a great amazement: yet having a brave spirit, though shadowed under a mean habit, she stepped unto him, whom she found not dead, but laid upon his back, his head a little to her wards,[6] his arms folded on his breast, hair long, and beard disordered, manifesting all care; but care itself had left him: curiousness thus far afforded him, as to be perfectly discerned the most exact piece of misery; apparel he had suitable to the habitation, which was a long gray robe. This grievefull spectacle did much amaze the sweet and tender-hearted shepherdess; especially, when she perceived (as she might by the help of the candle) the tears which distilled from his eyes; who seeming the image of death, yet had this sign of worldly sorrow, the drops falling in that abundance, as if there were a kind strife among them, to rid their master first of that burdenous carriage; or else meaning to make a flood, and so drown their woeful patient in his own sorrow, who yet lay still, but then fetching a deep groan from the profoundest part of his soul, he said:

"Miserable Perissus,[7] canst thou thus live, knowing she that gave thee life is gone? Gone, O me! and with her all my joy departed. Wilt thou (unblessed creature) lie here complaining for her death, and know she died for thee? Let truth and shame make thee do something worthy of such a love, ending thy days like thyself, and one fit to be her servant. But that I must not do: then thus remain and softer storms, still to torment thy wretched soul withall, since all are little, and too too little for such a loss. O dear Limena,[8] loving Limena, worthy Limena, and more rare, constant Limena: perfections delicately feigned to be in women were verified in thee, was such worthiness framed only to be wondered at by the best, but given as a prey to base and unworthy jealousy? When were all worthy parts joined in one, but in thee (my best Limena)? Yet all these grown subject to a creature ignorant of all but ill; like unto a fool, who in a dark cave, that hath but one way to get out, having a candle, but not the understanding what good it doth him, puts it out:[9] this ignorant wretch not being able to comprehend thy virtues, did so by thee in thy murder, putting out the world's light, and men's admiration: Limena, Limena, O my Limena."

With that he fell from complaining into such a passion, as weeping and crying were never in so woeful a perfection, as now in him; which brought as deserved a

---

5. A candle. The story of Cleophila finding a poem atop a table in a dark cave (Philip Sidney, *Old Arcadia*) is the source for the story of Urania's finding the sonnet.
6. Toward her.

7. Lost one.
8. Woman of the home or threshold.
9. An allusion to the Myth of the Cave in Plato's *Republic*.

compassion from the excellent shepherdess, who already had her heart so tempered with grief, as that it was apt to take any impression that it would come to feel withall. Yet taking a brave courage to her, she stepped unto him, kneeling down by his side, and gently pulling him by the arm, she thus spake.

"Sir," said she, "having heard some part of your sorrows, they have not only made me truly pity you, but wonder at you; since if you have lost so great a treasure, you should not lie thus leaving her and your love unrevenged, suffering her murderers to live, while you lie here complaining; and if such perfections be dead in her, why make you not the phoenix[1] of your deeds live again, as to new life raised out of revenge you should take on them? Then were her end satisfied, and you deservedly accounted worthy of her favor, if she were so worthy as you say."

"If she were? O God," cried out Perissus, "what devilish spirit art thou, that thus dost come to torture me? But now I see you are a woman; and therefore not much to be marked, and less resisted: but if you know charity, I pray now practice it, and leave me who am afflicted sufficiently without your company; or if you will stay, discourse not to me."

"Neither of these will I do," said she.

"If you be then," said he, "some fury of purpose sent to vex me, use your force to the uttermost in martyring me; for never was there a fitter subject, than the heart of poor Perissus is."

"I am no fury," replied the divine Urania, "not hither come to trouble you, but by accident lighted on this place; my cruel hap[2] being such, as only the like can give me content, while the solitariness of this like cave might give me quiet, though not ease, seeking for such a one, I happened hither; and this is the true cause of my being here, though now I would use it to a better end if I might. Wherefore favor me with the knowledge of your grief; which heard, it may be I shall give you some counsel, and comfort in your sorrow."

"Cursed may I be," cried he, "if ever I take comfort, having such case of mourning: but because you are, or seem to be afflicted, I will not refuse to satisfy your demand, but tell you the saddest story that ever was rehearsed by dying man to living woman; and such a one, as I fear will fasten too much sadness in you; yet should I deny it, I were to blame, being so well known to these senseless places; as were they sensible of sorrow, they would condole, or else amazed at such cruelty, stand dumb as they do, to find that man should be so inhuman."

1. The mythical bird that burned and was then reborn   2. Fate, chance.
from its ashes.

⇥ PERSPECTIVES ⇤
Tracts on Women and Gender

What is the nature of woman? Is she meant to be subordinate to man or an equal partner? What virtues is she capable of? Does she have intellectual ability, and if so, is it appropriate for her to write? How should she behave toward her husband? What are his responsibilities to her? What is the difference between a good woman and a bad one? What is the difference between manly behavior and womanly behavior? These are some of the questions that early modern English tracts on women and gender ask. Although we would not ask all of these questions in precisely the same way today, they are still of burning interest. The debate over these questions in early modern tracts on women sheds light on the representation of sex and gender in the poetry and drama of the period. By *sex* is meant the representation of biological difference; by *gender* is meant the representation of sex difference as it is socially constructed.

In the Middle Ages there were both attacks on women and defenses of them by both women and men, but intellectual and social changes modified the debate in the early modern period. One of the prominent medieval genres that continued to be imitated in the early mod-

Title page from *The English Gentlewoman,* by Richard Brathwaite, 1631.

ern period was the praise of exemplary women, such as Boccaccio's *De Claris Mulieribus* ("concerning famous women"), Chaucer's *Legend of Good Women*, and Christine de Pisan's *Le Livre de la Cité des Dames* (translated into English in 1521 as *The Book of the City of Ladies*). Renaissance humanism brought a new intellectual rigor to the genre. The German humanist Heinrich Cornelius Agrippa (1486–1535) stands out in the early Tudor controversy of the 1540s. Agrippa's *De Nobilitate et Praecellentia Foemenei Sexus* (translated in 1542 as *A Treatise of the Nobilitie and Excellencye of Woman Kynde*) not only lists biblical and classical heroines but also examines how the place of women in society is determined by culture rather than nature: "And thus by these lawes, the women being subdued as it were by force of arms, are constrained to give place to men, and to obey their subduers, not by natural, nor divine necessity or reason, but by custom, education, fortune, and a certain tyrannical occasion." However, even a humanist author such as Erasmus, who had enlightened views on other social issues, had very strict views about the absolute subordination of wife to husband. Indeed, this subordination seems to have increased in intensity in the early modern period as the nuclear family headed by the father superseded the extended family, in which power was more dispersed throughout the network of kinship.

Among the learned, the new classical humanist education was still largely reserved for young men. Such changes moved the historian Joan Kelly Gadol to ask, "Did women have a Renaissance?" At the same time, some early modern women were educated enough to represent themselves in the debate on the nature of women, and they brought new perspectives to it. Margaret Tyler was one of the first English women to speak in defense of women as writers. Two tracts of the 1620s, *Hic Mulier* ("the mannish woman") and *Haec Vir* ("the womanish man") humorously raised the problem of the blurring of genders and carried on a debate about the style of dress and behavior that men and women should adopt.

Whether these tracts take the form of an oration, a speech by one person, or a dialogue between two people (as in *Haec Vir*), they are all in lively conversation with each other, either directly or indirectly. They are also in a lively conversation with other texts in this period. Representing only a fraction of the early modern literature on women and gender, these tracts attest to heightened interest in questions of gender.

◆━━ ≡◆≡ ━━◆

Desiderius Erasmus
1469?–1536

Erasmus was the author not only of the humorous *Encomium Morae* (*The Praise of Folly*), dedicated to his friend Thomas More, but also of numerous works on Christian morals. Although *The Praise of Folly* was translated into English only in 1551, Erasmus's *Coniugium* (c. 1523), a text on marriage, appeared in English as *A Mery Dialogue, Declaringe the Propertyes of Shrewde Shrewes, and Honest Wyves* as early as 1542. This text advocated wifely submissiveness but also domesticity for both men and women—concepts that influenced the English bourgeois notion of marriage. Richard Tavernour also translated Erasmus's writing on marriage as *A Ryght Frutefull Epystle Devised in Laude and Praise of Matrimony* (1534). The following passage from this text demonstrates a view of marriage as the closest possible bond between human beings—and, more than that, as a sacrament calling for the wife's sole loyalty to her husband and lasting even beyond death.

from **In Laude and Praise of Matrimony**

* * * if the most part of things (yea which be also bitter) are of a good man to be desired for none other purpose, but because they be honest, matrimony doubtless is chiefly to be desired whereof a man may doubt whether it hath more honesty than pleasure. For what thing is sweeter than with her to live, with whom ye may be most straightly cou-pled, not only in the benevolence of the mind, but also in the conjunction of the body? If a great delectation of mind be taken of the benevolence of our other kinsmen, since it is an especial sweetness to have one with whom ye may communicate the secret affections of your mind, with whom ye may speak even as it were with your own self, whom ye may safely trust, which supposeth your chances to be his, what felicity (think ye) have the conjunction of man and wife, than which no thing in the univer-sal world may be found either greater or firmer. For with our other friends we be con-joined only with the benevolence of minds, with our wife we be coupled with most high love, with permixtion[1] of bodies, with the confederate band of the sacrament, and finally with the fellowship of all chances. Furthermore, in other friendships, how great simulation is there, how great falsity? Yea, they whom we judge our best friends, like as the swallows flee away when summer is gone, so they forsake us when fortune turneth her wheel. And sometime the fresher friend casts out the old. We hear of few whose fidelity endure till their lives' end. The wife's love is with no falsity corrupted, with no simulation obscured, with no chance of things minished,[2] finally with death only (nay not with death neither) withdrawn. She, the love of her parents, she, the love of her sisters, she, the love of her brethren, despiseth for the love of you, her only respect is to you, of you she hangeth,[3] with you she coveteth to die. * * *

* * * Do ye judge any pleasure to be compared with this so great a conjunction? If ye tarry at home there is at hand which shall drive away the tediousness of solitary being. If from home ye have one that shall kiss you when ye depart, long for you when ye be absent, receive you joyously when ye return. A sweet companion of youth, a kind solace of age. By nature yea any fellowship is delectable to man, as whom nature hath created to benevolence and friendship. This fellowship then how shall it not be most sweet, in which everything is common to them both? And contrarily, if we see the sav-age beasts also abhor[4] solitary living and delighted in fellowship, in my mind he is not once to be supposed a man, which abhoreth from[5] this fellowship most honest and pleasant of all. For what is more hateful than the man which (as though he were born only to himself) liveth for himself, seeketh for himself, spareth for himself, doth cost to himself, loveth no person, is loved of no person? Shall not such a monster be adjudged worthy to be cast out of all men's company into the mid sea with Timon the Athen-ian,[6] which because he fled all men's company, was called Misanthropus that is to say hate man * * *

But I know well enough what among these, ye murmur against me. A blessed thing is wedlock, if all prove according to the desire, But what if a wayward wife chanceth?[7] What if an unchaste? What if unnatural children? There will run in your mind the examples of those whom wedlock have brought to utter destruction. Heap up as much as ye can, but yet these be the vices of men and not of wedlock. Believe me, an evil wife is not wont to chance, but to evil husbands. Put this unto it, that it lieth in you to choose out a good one. But what if after the marriage she be marred?[8] Of an evil husband (I will well) a good wife may be marred, but of a good, the evil is

---

1. A thorough mixture or mingling.
2. Diminished, lessened in power.
3. In the sense of clinging, holding fast, adhering.
4. Hate.
5. Shrink with horror from.

6. The story of how Timon shunned society after his friends abandoned him when he lost his wealth is told by Plutarch (the source for Shakespeare's *Timon of Athens*).
7. Comes about by chance.
8. Injured.

wont to be reformed and mended. We blame wives falsely. No man (if ye give any credence to men) had ever a shrew to his wife, but through his own default.[9]

+=◆=+

Barnabe Riche
1542–1617

A veteran of wars in the Low Countries and Ireland and author of twenty-six books, Barnabe Riche led a life as fraught with contention as his writing. Best known as the author of *His Farewell to Military Profession* (1581), which contains the source for Shakespeare's *Twelfth Night*, Riche was both a keen observer of contemporary social life and a spy. Alongside his attacks on shameless city women in *My Lady's Looking Glass* (1616) and *A New Description of Ireland* (1610), he also portrays Dublin ladies as critics of his work in *A True and Kind Excuse* (1612)—an interesting episode documenting women's literacy in this period. His writing has the zealous spirit of reforming Protestantism and looks forward to the impassioned prose of radical dissenters in the Civil War. *My Lady's Looking Glass* was published by Thomas Adams, London, in 1616, and dedicated to Lady Saint Jones, wife of the Lord Deputy of Ireland. This text bears comparison with Riche's *Excellency of Good Women* (London, 1613), as well as numerous other Jacobean tracts on the conduct of women.

from My Lady's Looking Glass

But my promise was to give rules how to distinguish between a good woman and a bad, and promise is debt, but I must be well advised how I take the matter in hand; for we were better to charge a woman with a thousand defects in her soul, than with that one abuse of her body; and we must have two witnesses, besides our own eyes, to testify, or we shall not be believed: but I myself have thought of a couple that I hope will carry credit.

The first is the prophet Isaiah, that in his days challenged the daughters of Zion for their stretched-out necks, their wandering eyes, at their mincing and wanton demeanor as they passed through the streets: these signs and shows have ever been thought to be the special marks whereby to know a harlot.[1] But Solomon in a more particular manner better furnishes us with more assured notes, and to the end that we might the better distinguish the good woman from the bad, he delivereth their several qualities, and wherein they are opposite: and speaking of a good woman he saith, *She seeketh out wool and flax, and laboreth cheerfully with her hands: she overseeth the ways of her household, and eateth not the bread of idleness.*[2]

Solomon thinketh that a good woman should be a home *housewife*, he pointeth her out her housework. *She overseeth the ways of her household,* she must look to her children, her servants and family; but *the paths of a harlot* (he saith) *are movable, for now she is in the house, now in the streets, now she lies in wait in every corner,* she is still gadding from place to place, from person to person, from company to company; from custom to custom, she is evermore wandering: her feet are wandering, her eyes are wandering, her wits are wandering, *Her ways are like the ways of a serpent:* hard to be found out.[3]

---

9. Fault.
1. See Isaiah 3.16.

2. See Proverbs 31.13, 27.
3. See Proverbs 7.10–12.

A good woman (again) *opens her mouth with wisdom, the law of grace is in her tongue:* but *a harlot is full of words, she is loud and babbling,* saith Solomon.

She is bold, she is impudent, she is shameless, she cannot blush: and she that hath lost all these virtues hath lost her evidence of honesty: for the ornaments of a good woman are temperance in her mind, silence in her tongue, and bashfulness in her countenance.

It is not she that can lift up her heels highest in the dancing of a galliard,[4] she that is lavish of her lips or loose of her tongue.

Now if Solomon's testimony be good, the woman that is impudent, immodest, shameless, insolent, audacious, a night-walker, a company-keeper, a gadder from place to place, a reveller, a ramper, a roister, a rioter: she that has these properties, has the certain signs and marks of a harlot, as Solomon has avowed. Now what credit his words will carry in the Commissaries' court, I leave to those that be advocates, and proctors in women's causes.[5]

I have hitherto presented to your view the true resemblance of a harlot, as well what she is, as how she might be discerned: I would now give you the like notice of that notable *Strumpet, the whore of Babylon,*[6] that has made so many Kings and Emperors drunk with the cup of abominations, by whom the nations of the earth have so defiled themselves by their spiritual fornication, called in the Scripture by the name of *idolatry* (but now within the last five hundred years, amongst Christians) shadowed under the title of Popery. This harlot has her agents, Popes, Cardinals, Bishops, Abbots, Monks, Friars, Jesuits, Priests, with a number of other like, and all of them factors in her bands,[7] the professed enemies of the Gospel of Jesus Christ, that do superstitiously adore the crucifix, and are indeed enemies of the cross of Christ, and do tread his holy blood under their scornful feet: that build up devotion with ignorance, and do ring out their hot alarms in the ears of the unlearned, teaching that the light can be no light, that the Scriptures can be no Scriptures, nor the truth can be no truth, but by their allowance, and if they will say that high noon is midnight, we must believe them, and make no more ado but get us to bed.

✦ ═✦═ ✦

Margaret Tyler
fl. 1578

Margaret Tyler is best known today for the preface to her translation of Diego Ortunez de Calahorra's Spanish prose romance *The Mirrour of Princely Deedes and Knighthood,* Book I (1578), in which she argues that women have the ability to write on any subject. She was a waiting woman in the Catholic household of the Duke of Norfolk in the 1560s, where she may have read her translation aloud to the Duchess and her circle. In the preface to her translation, Tyler refers both to the "friends" who wanted her to return to her "old reading" and defends herself against potential critics who might object to her translating "matter more manlike than becometh my sex." She argues that she is more interested in virtue than in war and that, in any case, war affects women as much as it does men. The sixteenth-century humanist Vives had viewed romances as unsuitable for women readers, while male authors of romances often dedicated

---

4. A lively dance in triple time.
5. Commissaries' court: the court of a bishop's representative, which had jurisdiction over divorce and probate; advocates: pleaders, legal counselors; proctors: attorneys.

6. An image from Revelation 17, taken by Protestants to symbolize the Roman Catholic Church.
7. Agents in her leagues, or covenants.

their work to women. Arguing for women's right to an education, Tyler reasons that if men can dedicate their texts to women, then women can read them, and that if women can read texts on such subjects as war and government, then they can write them.

from Preface to *The First Part of the Mirror of Princely Deeds*

Thou hast here, gentle Reader, the history of Trebatio, an Emperor in Greece: whether a true history of him indeed, or a feigned fable, I wot[1] not, neither did I greatly seek after it in the translation, but by me it is done into English for thy profit and delight. The chief matter therein contained, is of exploits of wars, and the parties therein named are especially renowned for their magnanimity and courage. * * * Such delivery as I have made I hope thou wilt friendly accept, the rather for that it is a woman's work, though in a story profane, and a matter more manlike than becometh my sex. But as for any manliness of the matter, thou knowest that it is not necessary for every trumpeter or drumstare[2] in the war to be a good fighter. They take wages only to incite others, though themselves have privy maims,[3] and are thereby recureless.[4] So, gentle reader, if my travail in Englishing this author may bring thee to a liking of the virtues herein commended, and by example thereof in thy princes' and countries' quarrel to hazard thy person, and purchase good name, as for hope of well deserving myself that way, I neither bend my self thereto, nor yet fear the speech of people if I be found backward. I trust every man holds not the plough, which would that the ground were tilled, and it is no sin to talk of Robin Hood, though you never shot in his bow. Or be it that the attempt were bold to intermeddle in arms, as the ancient Amazons[5] did, and in this story Claridiana doth, and in other stories not a few, yet to report of arms is not so odious, but that it may be borne withall, not only in you men which yourselves are fighters, but in us women, to whom the benefit in equal part appertains of your victories, either the matter is so commendable that it carries no discredit from the homeliness of the speaker, or that it is so generally known, that it fits every man to speak thereof. * * * But my defense is by example of the best, amongst which, many have dedicated their labors, some stories, some of war, some physic, some law, some as concerning government, some divine matters, unto diverse ladies and gentlewomen. And if men may and do bestow such of their travails upon gentlewomen, then may we women read such of their works as they dedicate to us, and if we may read them, why not further wade in them to the search of truth. * * * But to return to whatever the truth is, whether that women may not at all discourse in learning, for men late in their claim to being sole possessioners of knowledge, or whether they may in some manner, that is by limitation or appointment in some kind of learning, my persuasion hath been thus, that it is all one for a woman to pen a story, as for a man to address his story to a woman. But amongst all my ill-willers, some I hope are not so straight that they would enforce me necessarily either not to write or to write of divinity. Whereas neither durst I trust mine own judgment sufficiently, if matter of controversy were handled, nor yet could I find any book in any tongue, which would not breed offense to some. But I perceive some may be rather angry to see their Spanish delight turned to all English pastime: they could well allow the story in Spanish, but they may not afford it so cheap, or they would have it proper to themselves. What

---

1. Know.
2. Drummer.
3. Secret weaknesses.

4. Irrecoverable.
5. A tribe of female warriors described by Herodotus and other ancient Greek authors as living in Scythia.

natures such men be of, I list[6] not greatly to dispute, but my meaning hath been to make others partners of my liking, as I doubt not gentle reader, but if it shall please thee after serious matters to sport thyself with this Spaniard, that thou shalt find in him the just reward of malice and cowardice, with the good speed of honesty and courage, being able to furnish thee with sufficient store of foreign examples to both purposes. And as in such matters which have been rather devised to beguile time, than to breed matter of sad learning, he hath ever borne away any price which could season such delights with some profitable reading: so shalt thou have this stranger an honest man when need serveth, and at other times either a good companion to drive out a weary night, or a merry jest at thy board. And this much concerning this present story, that it is neither unseemly for a woman to deal in, neither greatly requiring a less staid age than mine is. But of these two points, gentle reader, I thought to give thee warning, lest perhaps understanding my name and years, there mightest be a wrong suspect[7] of my boldness and rashness, from which I would gladly free myself by this plain excuse, and if I may deserve thy good favor by like labor, when the choice is my own, I will have a special regard of thy liking. So I wish thee well.

Thine to use, M.T.[8]

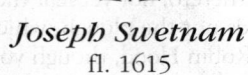

Joseph Swetnam
fl. 1615

Little is known about Joseph Swetnam other than that he stirred up an enormous controversy over the question of women when he wrote *An Arraignment of Lewd, Idle, Froward, and Unconstant Women* (1615). The work was published anonymously with an introductory letter signed by "Thomas Tel-troth." Trotting out all the negative stereotypes of women he could jumble together, Swetnam constructed his mock treatise as a piece of raucous comedy, aimed at the lowest common denominator. Reading Swetnam's work as a serious diatribe against women, Rachel Speght and the pseudonymous Ester Sowernam and Constantia Munda produced critiques of misogyny. Speght unmasked Swetnam's authorship and identified him as a fencing master in Bristol. An anonymous comedy, *Swetnam the Woman-hater, Arraigned by Women* (1620), possibly by Thomas Heywood, dramatized the debate as a court trial with Swetnam prosecuting his case against women and the Amazon Atlanta (a soldier disguised as a woman) defending them. Swetnam is finally turned over to a court of women, who find him guilty and muzzle him.

from The Arraignment of Lewd, Idle, Froward, and Unconstant Women

from Chapter 2. The Second Chapter showeth the manner of such women as live upon evil report: it also showeth that the beauty of women has been the bane of many a man, for it hath overcome valiant and strong men, eloquent and subtle men. And in a word it hath overcome all men, as by examples following shall appear.

First, that of Solomon unto whom God gave singular wit and wisdom, yet he loved so many women that he quite forgot his God which always did guide his steps, so long as he lived godly and ruled justly, but after he had glutted himself with women,

---

6. Wish.
7. Suspicion.

8. Margaret Tyler.

then he could say, vanity of vanity all is but vanity. He also in many places of his book of Proverbs exclaims most bitterly against lewd women calling them all that naught is, and also displayeth their properties, and yet I cannot let men go blameless although women go shameless; but I will touch them both, for if there were not receivers then there would not be so many stealers: if there were not some knaves there would not be so many whores, for they both hold together to bolster each other's villainy, for always birds of a feather will flock together hand in hand to bolster each other's villainy.

Men, I say, may live without women, but women cannot live without men. For Venus, whose beauty was excellent fair, yet when she needeth man's help she took Vulcan, a clubfooted smith. And therefore if a woman's face glister,[1] and her gesture pierce the marble wall, or if her tongue be as smooth as oil or as soft as silk, and her words so sweet as honey, or if she were a very ape for wit, or a bag of gold for wealth, or if her personage have stolen away all that nature can afford, and if she be decked up in gorgeous apparel, then a thousand to one but she will love to walk where she may get acquaintance, and acquaintance bringeth familiarity, and familiarity setteth all follies abroach,[2] and twenty to one that if a woman love gadding but that she will pawn her honor to please her fantasy.

Man must be at all the cost and yet live by the loss. A man must take all the pains and women will spend all the gains. A man must watch and ward, fight and defend, till the ground, labor in the vineyard, and look what he getteth in seven years; a woman will spread it abroad with a fork in one year, and yet little enough to serve her turn but a great deal too little to get her good will. Nay, if thou give her ever so much and yet if thy person please not her humor, then will I not give a half-penny for her honesty at the year's end.

For then her breast will be the harborer of an envious heart, and her heart the storehouse of poisoned hatred; her head will devise villainy, and her hands are ready to practice that which their heart desireth. Then who can but say that women are sprung from the devil, whose heads, hands and hearts, minds and souls are evil, for women are called the hook of all evil, because men are taken by them as a fish is taken in with the hook.

For women have a thousand ways to entice thee, and ten thousand ways to deceive thee, and all such fools as are suitors unto them; some they keep in hand with promises, and some they feed with flattery, and some they delay with dalliances, and some they please with kisses. They lay out the folds of their hair to entangle men into their love; betwixt their breasts is the vale of destruction, and in their beds there is hell, sorrow and repentance. Eagles do not eat men till they are dead, but women devour them alive, for a woman will pick thy pocket and empty thy purse, laugh in thy face and cut thy throat. They are ungrateful, perjured, full of fraud, flouting and deceit, unconstant, waspish,[3] toyish,[4] light, sullen, proud, discourteous and cruel, and yet they were by God created, and by nature formed, and therefore by policy and wisdom to be avoided, for good things abused are to be refused. Or else for a month's pleasure, she may make thee go stark naked. She will give thee roast meat, but she will beat thee with the spit. If thou hast crowns in thy purse, she will be thy heart's gold until she leave thee not a whit of white money. They are like summer birds, for they will abide no storm, but flock about thee in the pride of thy glory, and fly from thee in the storms of affliction; for they aim more at thy wealth than at thy person,

1. Glitter, shine.
2. Flowing abroad.

3. Spiteful
4. Frivolous, wanton.

and esteem more thy money than any man's virtuous qualities; for they esteem of a man without money as a horse does a fair stable without meat. They are like eagles which will always fly where the carrion is.

They will play the horse-leech to suck away thy wealth, but in the winter of thy misery, she will fly away from thee. Not unlike the swallow, which in the summer harboreth herself under the eaves of a house, and against winter flieth away, leaving nothing but dirt behind her.

Solomon saith, he that will suffer himself to be led away or to take delight in such women's company is like a fool which rejoiceth when he is led to the stocks. *Proverbs* 7.

Hosea, by marrying a lewd woman of light behavior was brought unto idolatry, *Hosea* 1. Saint Paul accounteth fornicators so odious, that we ought not to eat meat with them. He also showeth that fornicators shall not inherit the kingdom of Heaven, 1 *Corinthians* the 9th and 11th verse.

And in the same chapter Saint Paul excommunicateth fornicators, but upon amendment he receiveth them again. Whoredom punished with death, *Deuteronomy* 22.21 and *Genesis* 38.24. Phineas a priest thrust two adulterers, both the man and the woman, through the belly with a spear, *Numbers* 25.

God detests the money or goods gotten by whoredom, *Deuteronomy* 23.17, 18. Whores called by diverse names, and the properties of whores, *Proverbs* 7.6 and 21. A whore envieth an honest woman, *Esdras* 16 and 24. Whoremongers God will judge, *Hebrews* 13 and 42. They shall have their portions with the wicked in the lake that burns with fire and brimstone, *Revelation* 21.8.

Only for the sin of whoredom God was sorry at heart, and repented that he ever made man, *Genesis* 6.67.

Saint Paul saith, to avoid fornication every man may take a wife, 1 *Corinthians* 6.9.

Therefore he which hath a wife of his own and yet goeth to another woman is like a rich thief which will steal when he has no need.

There are three ways to know a whore: by her wanton looks, by her speech, and by her gait. *Ecclesiasticus* 26.[5] And in the same chapter he saith, that we must not give our strength unto harlots, for whores are the evil of all evils, and the vanity of all vanities, they weaken the strength of a man and deprive the body of his beauty, it furroweth his brows and maketh the eyes dim, and a whorish woman causeth the fever and the gout; and at a word, they are a great shortening to a man's life.

For although they seem to be as dainty as sweet meat, yet in trial not so wholesome as sour sauce. They have wit, but it is all in craft; if they love it is vehement, but if they hate it is deadly.

Plato saith, that women are either angels or devils, and that they either love dearly or hate bitterly, for a woman hath no mean in her love, nor mercy in her hate, no pity in revenge, nor patience in her anger; therefore it is said, that there is nothing in the world which both pleases and displeases a man more than a woman, for a woman most delighteth a man and yet most deceiveth him, for as there is nothing more sweet to a man than a woman when she smiles, even so there is nothing more odious than the angry countenance of a woman.

Solomon in his 20th chapter of *Ecclesiastes*[6] saith, that an angry woman will foam at the mouth like a boar. If all this be true as most true it is, why shouldest thou spend one hour in the praise of women as some fools do, for some will brag of the

---

5. Apocryphal book of the Old Testament.
6. A faulty citation: in Ecclesiasticus 25, an angry woman is compared to a bear.

beauty of such a maid, another will vaunt of the bravery of such a woman, that she goeth beyond all the women in the parish. Again, some study their fine wits how they may cunningly smooth[7] women, and with logic how to reason with them, and with eloquence to persuade them. They are always tempering their wits as fiddlers do their strings, who wrest them so high, that many times they stretch them beyond time, tune and reason.

Again, there are many that weary themselves with dallying, playing, and sporting with women, and yet they are never satisfied with the unsatiable desire of them; if with a song thou wouldest be brought asleep, or with a dance be led to delight, then a fair woman is fit for thy diet. If thy head be in her lap she will make thee believe that thou are hard by[8] God's seat, when indeed thou are just at hell gate.

"Ester Sowernam"

The pen name Ester Sowernam comes from the Old Testament heroine Esther, who defended her people against Haman, and the antithesis of Joseph Swetnam's last name (sweet/sour). The full title of her text also parodies Swetnam's: *Ester Hath Hanged Haman; or An Answer to a Lewd Pamphlet, Entitled The Arraignment of Women. With the Arraignment of Lewd, Idle, Froward and Unconstant Men, and Husbands* (1617). On the whole, the author of this pamphlet presents herself in a secular light. Sowernam's criticisms of misogyny are more psychological and social than moral and logical. Trained in classics as well as Scripture and a keen observer, Ester Sowernam finds that Swetnam has incorrectly stated that the Bible is the source of the statement that women are a necessary evil and finds that the true source is in Euripides' *Medea*. Sowernam also cites the double standard by which men are excused for what women are judged harshly for in order to assert women's superiority. She argues that women are judged more severely because they are thought to be more virtuous in the first place. The second half of her pamphlet may have helped to inspire the comedy that spoofed the entire controversy, *Swetnam the Woman-Hater Arraigned By Women* (1620).

from **Ester Hath Hanged Haman**
from **Chapter 7. The answer to all objections which are material made against women**

As for that crookedness and frowardness[1] with which you charge women, look from whence they have it. For of themselves and their own disposition it doth not proceed, which is proved directly by your own testimony. For in your 46th page, line 15[16], you say: "A young woman of tender years is flexible, obedient, and subject to do anything, according to the will and pleasure of her husband." How cometh it then that this gentle and mild disposition is afterwards altered? Yourself doth give the true reason, for you give a great charge not to marry a widow. But why? Because, say you in the same page, "A widow is framed to the conditions[2] of another man." Why then, if a woman have froward conditions, they be none of her own, she was framed to them. Is not our adversary ashamed of himself to rail against women for those faults which do all come from men? Doth not he most grievously charge men to learn[3] their

---

7. Sway, woo.
8. Close to.
1. Perversity, unreasonableness.

2. Circumstances, character traits.
3. Teach.

wives bad and corrupt behavior? For he saith plainly: "Thou must unlearn a widow, and make her forget and forego her former corrupt and disordered behavior." Thou must unlearn her; *ergo*, what fault she hath learned: her corruptness comes not from her own disposition but from her husband's destruction.

Is it not a wonder that your pamphlets are so dispersed? Are they not wise men to cast away time and money upon a book which cutteth their own throats? 'Tis pity but that men should reward you for your writing (if it be but as the Roman Sertorius[4] did the idle poet: he gave him a reward, but not for his writing—but because he should never write more). As for women, they laugh that men have no more able a champion. This author cometh to bait women or, as he foolishly saith, the "Bearbaiting of Women," and he bringeth but a mongrel cur who doth his kind[5] to brawl and bark, but cannot bite. The mild and flexible disposition of a woman is in philosophy proved in the composition of her body, for it is a maxim: *Mores animi sequuntur temperaturam corporis* (the disposition of the mind is answerable to the temper of the body). A woman in the temperature of her body is tender, soft and beautiful, so doth her disposition in mind correspond accordingly: she is mild, yielding and virtuous. What disposition accidentally happeneth unto her is by the contagion of a froward husband, as Joseph Swetnam affirmeth.

And experience proveth. It is a shame for a man to complain of a froward woman—in many respects all concerning himself. It is a shame he hath no more government over the weaker vessel.[6] It is a shame he hath hardened her tender sides and gentle heart with his boisterous and Northern blasts. It is a shame for a man to publish and proclaim household secrets—which is a common practice amongst men, especially drunkards, lechers, and prodigal spendthrifts. These when they come home drunk, or are called in question for their riotous misdemeanors, they presently show themselves the right children of Adam. They will excuse themselves by their wives and say that their unquietness and frowardness at home is the cause that they run abroad: an excuse more fitter for a beast than a man. If thou wert a man thou wouldst take away the cause which urgeth a woman to grief and discontent, and not by thy frowardness increase her distemperature.[7] Forbear thy drinking, thy luxurious riot, thy gaming and spending, and thou shalt have thy wife give thee as little cause at home as thou givest her great cause of disquiet abroad. Men which are men, if they chance to be matched with froward wives—either of their own making or others' marring[8]—they would make a benefit of the discommodity:[9] either try his skill to make her mild or exercise his patience to endure her cursedness; for all crosses are inflicted either for punishment of sins or for exercise of virtues. But humorous[1] men will sooner mar a thousand women than out of a hundred make one good.

And this shall appear in the imputation which our adversary chargeth upon our sex: to be lascivious, wanton and lustful. He saith: "Women tempt, allure and provoke men." How rare a thing is it for women to prostitute and offer themselves? How common a practice is it for men to seek and solicit women to lewdness? What charge do they spare? What travail do they bestow? What vows, oaths and protestations do they spend to make them dishonest? They hire panders, they write letters, they seal them with damnations and execrations to assure them of love when the end proves but lust. They know the flexible disposition of women, and the sooner to overreach

---

4. Quintus Sertorius, Roman general, appointed governor of Farther Spain in 83 B.C.
5. Nature.
6. From 1 Peter 3.7.

7. Disorder in mind and body.
8. Spoiling.
9. Inconvenience, disadvantageousness.
1. Moody.

them some will pretend they are so plunged in love that, except they obtain their
desire, they will seem to drown, hang, stab, poison, or banish themselves from friends
and country. What motives are these to tender dispositions? Some will pretend marriage, another offer continual maintenance; but when they have obtained their purpose, what shall a woman find?—just that which is her everlasting shame and grief:
she hath made herself the unhappy subject to a lustful body and the shameful stall[2] of
a lascivious tongue. Men may with foul shame charge woman with this sin which she
had never committed, if she had not trusted; nor had ever trusted, if she had not been
deceived with vows, oaths and protestations. To bring a woman to offend in one sin,
how many damnable sins do they commit? I appeal to their own consciences. The
lewd disposition of sundry men doth appear in this: if a woman or maid will yield to
lewdness, what shall they want?[3]—but if they would live in honesty, what help shall
they have? How much will they make of the lewd? How base an account of the honest? How many pounds will they spend in bawdy houses? But when will they bestow a
penny upon an honest maid or woman, except it be to corrupt them?

Our adversary bringeth many examples of men which have been overthrown by
women. It is answered before: the fault is their own. But I would have him, or anyone
living, to show any woman that offended in this sin of lust, but that she was first
solicited by a man.

Helen was the cause of Troy's burning: first, Paris did solicit her; next, how many
knaves and fools of the male kind had Troy, which to maintain whoredom would
bring their city to confusion?

When you bring in examples of lewd women and of men which have been
stained by women, you show yourself both frantic and a profane irreligious fool to
mention Judith,[4] for cutting off Holofernes' head, in that rank.

You challenge women for untamed and unbridled tongues; there was never
woman was ever noted for so shameless, so brutish, so beastly a scold as you prove
yourself in this base and odious pamphlet. Your blaspheme God, you rail at his creation, you abuse and slander his creatures; and what immodest or impudent scurrility
is it which you do not express in this lewd and lying pamphlet?

Hitherto I have so answered all your objections against women that, as I have
not defended the wickedness of any, so I have set down the true state of the question.
As Eve did not offend without temptation of a serpent, so women do seldom offend
but it is by provocation of men. Let not your impudency, nor your consorts' dishonesty, charge our sex hereafter with those sins of which you yourselves were the first
procurers. I have, in my discourse, touched you, and all yours, to the quick. I have
taxed you with bitter speeches; you will, perhaps, say I am a railing scold. In this
objection, Joseph Swetnam, I will teach you both wit and honesty. The difference
between a railing scold and an honest accuser is this: the first rageth upon passionate
fury without bringing cause or proof, the other bringeth direct proof for what she
allegeth. You charge women with clamorous words, and bring no proof; I charge you
with blasphemy, with impudency, scurrility, foolery and the like. I show just and
direct proof for what I say. It is not my desire to speak so much; it is your dessert to
provoke me upon just cause so far. It is not railing to call a crow black, or a wolf a

2. Target.
3. Lack, need.
4. A wealthy, attractive widow who saved her people
from Holofernes, an Assyrian general, by attracting and

then killing him. (See The Book of Judith, part of the
Catholic Bible, but viewed as apocryphal by Jews and
Protestants.)

ravenor,[5] or a drunkard a beast; the report of the truth is never to be blamed: the deserver of such a report deserves the shame.

Now, for this time, to draw to an end. Let me ask according to the question of Cassian, *cui bono?*[6]—what have you gotten by publishing your pamphlet? Good I know you can get none. You have, perhaps, pleased the humors of some giddy, idle, conceited persons. But you have dyed yourself in the colors of shame, lying, slandering, blasphemy, ignorance, and the like.

The shortness of time and the weight of business call me away, and urge me to leave off thus abruptly; but assure yourself, where I leave now I will by God's grace supply the next term, to your small content. You have exceeded in your fury against widows, whose defense you shall hear of at the time aforesaid. In the mean space, recollect your wits; write out of deliberation, not out of fury; write out of advice, not out of idleness: forbear to charge women with faults which come from the contagion of masculine serpents.

━┿━ ⌖◈⌖ ━┿━

Hic Mulier

and

Haec-Vir

Hic Mulier and *Haec-Vir* were published anonymously within a week of each other in February 1620. *Hic Mulier*, the first of the two pamphlets to appear, begins with the complaint that "since the days of Adam women were never so masculine." The title introduces this theme by a gender switch of its own: *Hic Mulier*, Latin for "This Woman," uses the masculine form *hic* instead of the feminine *haec*. The title page contains illustrations of two such mannish women—one wearing a man's hat, which she admires in a mirror, and another sitting in a barber's chair to get her hair cut. Structured as a "brief declamation," or oration, the text argues that such activities as hair bobbing and wearing men's clothes are immoral and unnatural for women. Furthermore, such gender crossing is also a threat to the entire political order: "most pernicious to the commonwealth for she hath power by example to do it a world of injury."

As its subtitle boasts, *Haec-Vir* was "an answer to the late book intituled *Hic Mulier*" and was represented as "a brief dialogue between Haec-Vir the Womanish-Man, and Hic Mulier the Man-Woman." The effeminate man and the hermaphroditic woman first misrecognize each other's gender. Once that is cleared up, the foppish man launches into a diatribe against the woman, who defends herself by arguing that "custom is an idiot." The first half of the dialogue reads like a proclamation of the equality of the sexes, with the bare-breasted, dagger-swinging Hic Mulier exclaiming, "We are as free-born as men, have as free election, and as free spirits, we are compounded of like parts and may with like liberty make benefit of our creations." Despite this bold challenge, the text as a whole makes a rather conservative case for the need for gender distinctions, the overturning of which was seen as an assault on hierarchy. The dialogue ends with both participants agreeing to exchange clothes and Latin pronouns so that men will again be manly and women subservient to them.

These pamphlets display the early modern fascination with, and loathing of, transvestism. Not only did the fashionable young male favorites of King James I's court resemble the womanish man of *Haec-Vir*, but there were more than a few documented cases of women wearing

---

5. An animal who seizes in order to devour.   Lucius Cassius.
6. "To whose benefit," a phrase attributed by Cicero to

breeches on the streets. A few women were actually brought before ecclesiastical courts for "shamefully" putting on "man's apparel."

While conforming to the comic pattern of disrupting and then reestablishing the status quo, these pamphlets show that questions about custom, nature, and sex and gender roles were being asked in the early seventeenth century.

from Hic Mulier; or, The Man-Woman

So I present these masculine women in their deformities as they are, that I may call them back to the modest comeliness in which they were.

The modest comeliness in which they were? Why, did ever these mermaids, or rather mere-monsters,[1] that wear the Car-man's block,[2] the Dutchman's feather *upse-van-muffe*, the poor man's pate pouled by a Treene dish, the French doublet trussed with points, to Mary Aubries' light nether skirts, the fool's baldric, and the devil's poniard. Did they ever know comeliness or modesty? Fie, no, they never walked in those paths, for these at the best are sure but rags of gentry, torn from better pieces for their foul stains, or else the adulterate branches of rich stocks,[3] that taking too much sap from the root, are cut away, and employed in base uses; or, if not so, they are the stinking vapors drawn from dunghills, which nourished in the higher regions of the air, become meteors and false fires blazing and flashing therein, and amazing men's minds with their strange proportions, till the substance of their pride being spent, they drop down again to the place from whence they came, and there rot and consume unpitied, and unremembered.

And questionless it is true, that such were the first beginners of these last deformities, for from any purer blood would have issued a purer birth; there would have been some spark of virtue: some excuse for imitation; but this deformity has no agreement with goodness, nor any difference against the weakest reason: it is all base, all barbarous. Base, in the respect it offends men in the example, and God in the most unnatural use: barbarous, in that it is exorbitant from nature, and an antithesis to kind,[4] going astray (with ill-favored affectation) both in attire, in speech, in manners, and (it is to be feared) in the whole courses and stories of their actions. What can be more true and curious consent of the most fairest colors and the wealthy gardens which fill the world with living plants? Do but you receive virtuous inmates (as what palaces are more rich to receive heavenly messengers?) and you shall draw men's souls to you with that severe, devout, and holy adoration, that you shall never want praise, never love, never reverence.

But now methinks I hear the witty-offending great ones reply in excuse of their deformities: What, is there no difference amongst women? no distinction of places, no respect of honors, nor no regard of blood, or alliance? Must but a bare pair of shears pass between noble and ignoble, between the generous spirit and the base mechanic; shall we be all co-heirs of one honor, one estate, and one habit? O men, you are then too tyrannous, and not only injure nature, but also break the laws and customs of the wisest princes. Are not bishops known by their miters, princes by their

---

1. Pure monsters.
2. A merchant's hat. Descriptions of ridiculous fashions follow: the *upse-van-muffe* is an elaborate feathered hat; the pate pouled by a Treene dish is hair cut short to the shape of a wooden dish; the French doublet is a man's close-fitting upper body garment tied with laces; baldric: fancy belt; poniard: dagger.
3. Trunks or stems.
4. The opposite of what is natural to the gender.

crowns, judges by their robes, and knights by their spurs? But poor women have nothing (how great soever they be) to divide themselves from the enticing shows or moving images which do furnish most shops in the city. What is it that either the laws have allowed to the greatest ladies, custom found convenient, or their bloods or places challenged, which hath not been engrossed into the city with as great greediness, and pretense of true title; as if the surcease[5] from the imitation were the utter breach of their charter everlastingly.

For this cause, these apes of the city have enticed foreign nations to the cells, and there committing gross adultery with their gewgaws,[6] have brought out such unnatural conceptions, that the whole world is not able to make a *Democritus* big enough to laugh at their foolish ambitions.[7] Nay, the very art of painting (which to the last age shall ever be held in detestation) they have so cunningly stolen and hidden amongst their husbands' hoards of treasure, that the decayed stock of prostitution (having little other revenues) are hourly in bringing their action of *detinue*[8] against them. Hence (being thus troubled with these *Popeniars*,[9] and loath still to march in one rank with fools and *zanies*[1]) have proceeded these disguised deformities, not to offend the eyes of goodness, but to tire with ridiculous contempt the never to be satisfied appetites of these gross and unmannerly intruders. Nay, look if this very last edition of disguise, this which is so full of faults, corruptions, and false quotations, this bait which the devil had laid to catch the souls of wanton women, be not as frequent in the demi-palaces of burghers and citizens as it is either at masque, triumph, tilt-yard, or playhouse. Call but to account the tailors that are contained within the circumference of the walls of the city, and let but their heels and their hard reckonings be justly summed together, and it will be found they have raised more new foundations of this new disguise, and metamorphosed more modest old garments, to this new manner of short base and French doublet (only for the use of freemen's wives[2] and their children) in one month, than has been worn in court, suburbs, or country, since the unfortunate beginning of the first devilish invention.

Let therefore the powerful Statute of Apparel[3] but lift his battle-axe, and crush the offenders in pieces, so as every one may be known by the true badge of their blood, or fortune; and then these *Chimeras* of deformity will be sent back to hell, and there burn to cinders in the flames of their own malice.

Thus, methinks, I hear the best offenders argue, nor can I blame a high blood to swell when it is coupled and counter-checked with baseness and corruption; yet this shows an anger passing near akin to envy, and alludes much to the saying of an excellent poet:

> Women never
> Love beauty in their sex, but envy ever.

They have Caesar's ambition, and desire to be one and one alone, but yet to offend themselves, to grieve others, is a revenge dissonant to reason, and as *Euripides* says, a woman of that malicious nature is a fierce beast, and most pernicious to the commonwealth, for she has power by example to do it a world of injury. But far be

---

5. Cessation, stop.
6. Showy decorations.
7. Seneca recounts how Democritus laughed rather than cried at human life (*De tranquilitate animi* 15.2).
8. Legal action to recover personal property.
9. Popinjays, vain and empty people.
1. Parasites, those who play the fool for amusement.

2. Women married to men possessing the freedom of a city, borough, or corporation.
3. Laws governing dress that were intended to differentiate the aristocracy from the common people had been enacted from the Middle Ages through to the early modern period.

such cruelty from the softness of their gentle dispositions: O let them remember what the poet saith:

> Women be
> Fram'd with the same parts of the mind as men
> Nay Nature triumph'd in their beauty's birth,
> And women made the glory of the earth,
> The life of beauty, in whose simple breast,
> (As in her fair lodging) Virtue rests:
> Whose towering thoughts attended with remorse,
> Do make their fairness be of greater force.

But when they thrust virtue out of doors, and give a shameless liberty to every loose passion, that either their weak thoughts engender, or the discourse of wicked tongues can charm into their yielding bosoms (much too apt to be opened with any pick-lock of flattering and deceitful insinuation) then they turn maskers, mummers, nay monsters in their disguises, and so they may catch the bridle in their teeth, and run away with their rulers, they care not into what dangers they plunge either their fortunes or reputations, the disgrace of the whole sex, or the blot and obloquy of their private families, according to the saying of the poets

> Such is the cruelty of women-kind,
> When they have shaken off the shamefac'd band
> With which wise nature did them strongly bind,
> T'obey the hests of man's well-ruling hand
> That then all rule and reason they withstand
> To purchase a licentious liberty;
> But virtuous women wisely understand,
> That they were born to mild humility,
> Unless the heavens them lift to lawful sovereignty.[4]

To you therefore that are fathers, husbands, of sustainers of these new hermaphrodites, belongs the cure of this impostume;[5] it is you that give fuel to the flames of their wild indiscretion. You add the oil which makes their stinking lamps defile the whole house with filthy smoke, and your purses purchase these deformities at rates both dear and unreasonable. Do you but hold close your liberal hands, or take a strict account of the employment of the treasure you give to their necessary maintenance, and these excesses will either cease, or else die smothered in prison in the tailors' trunks for want of redemption.

from Haec-Vir; or, The Womanish-Man

Hic-Mulier: Well, then to the purpose: first, you say, I am base in being a slave to novelty. What flattery can there be in freedom of election? Or what baseness to crown my delights with those pleasures which are most suitable to mine affections? Bondage or slavery is a restraint from those actions, which the mind (of its own accord) doth most willingly desire: to perform the intents and purposes of another's disposition, and that not but by mansuetude[1] or sweetness of entreaty; but by the force of authority and strength of compulsion. Now for me to follow change, according to the limitation of my own will and pleasure, there cannot be a greater freedom.

---

4. Description of the tyranny of the Amazonian ruler   5. Abscess.
Radigund in Spenser's *Faerie Queene* 5.5.25.   1. Gentleless, meekness.

Nor do I in my delight of change otherwise than as the whole world doth, or as becometh a daughter of the world to do. For what is the world, but a very shop or warehouse of change? Sometimes winter, sometimes summer; day and night: they hold sometimes riches, sometimes poverty, sometimes health, sometimes sickness: now pleasure; presently anguish; now honor; then contempt: and to conclude, there is nothing but change, which doth surround and mix with all our fortunes. And will you have poor woman such a fixed star, that she shall not so much as move or twinkle in her own sphere? That would be true slavery indeed, and a baseness beyond the chains of the worst servitude. Nature to everything she hath created hath given a singular delight in change, as to herbs, plants, and trees a time to wither and shed their leaves, a time to bud and bring forth their leaves, and a time for their fruits and flowers; to worms and creeping things a time to hide themselves in the pores and hollows of the earth, and a time to come abroad and suck the dew; to beasts liberty to choose their food, liberty to delight in their food, and liberty to feed and grow fat with their food. The birds have the air to fly in, the waters to bathe in, and the earth to feed on. But to man, both these and all things else, to alter, frame, and fashion, according to his will and delight shall rule him. Again, who will rob the eye of the variety of objects, the ear of the delight of sounds, the nose of smells, the tongue of taste, and the hand of feeling? And shall only woman, excellent woman, so much better in that she is something purer, be only deprived of this benefit? Shall she be the bondslave of time, the handmaid of opinion, or the strict observer of every frosty or cold benumbed imagination? It would be a cruelty beyond the rack or strapado.[2]

But you will say it is not change, but novelty, from which you deter us: a thing that doth avert the good, and erect the evil; prefer the faithless, and confound desert; that with the change of opinions breeds the change of states, and with continual alterations thrusts headlong forward both ruin and subversion. Alas (soft Sir) what can you christen by that new imagined title, when the words of a wise man are: *that what was done, is but done again: all things do change, and under the cope of heaven there is no new thing.*[3] So that whatsoever we do or imitate, it is neither slavish, base, nor a breeder of novelty.

Next, you condemn me of unnaturalness, in forsaking my creation, and contemning[4] custom. How do I forsake my creation, that do all the right and offices due to my creation? I was created free, born free, and live free: what lets me then so to spin out my time, that I may die free?

To alter creation were to walk on my hands with my heels upward, to feed myself with my feet, or to forsake the sweet sound of sweet words, for the hissing noise of the serpent: but I walk with a face erected, with a body clothed, with a mind busied, and with a heart full of reasonable and devout cogitations; only offensive in attire, inasmuch as it is a stranger to the curiosity of the present times, and an enemy to custom. Are we then bound to be the flatterers of time, or the dependents on custom? O miserable servitude chained only to baseness and folly! For then custom, nothing is more absurd, nothing more foolish. * * *

Cato Junior held it for a custom, never to eat meat but sitting on the ground. The Venetians kiss one another ever at the first meeting; and even in this day it is a

---

2. Rack: a frame with a roller at either end on which a person would be tortured; strapado: a form of torture in which the victim's hands would be tied behind his or her back and the victim would then be suspended by a pulley with a sharp jolt.
3. Ecclesiastes 1.9.
4. Disdaining, despising.

general received custom amongst our English, that when we meet or overtake any man in our travel or journeying, to examine him whither he rides, how far, to what purpose, and where he lodgeth? Nay, and with that unmannerly boldness of inquisition, that it is a certain ground of a most insufficient quarrel, not to receive a full satisfaction of those demands which go far astray from good manners, or comely civility; and will you have us to marry ourselves to these mimic and most fantastic customs? It is a fashion or custom with us to mourn in black, yet the Argian[5] and Roman ladies ever mourned in white; and (if we will tie the action upon the signification of colors) I see not but we may mourn in green, blue, red or any simple color used in heraldry. For us to salute strangers with a kiss is counted but civility, but with foreign nations immodesty; for you to cut the hair of your upper lips, familiar here in England, everywhere else almost thought unmanly. To ride on side-saddles at first was counted here abominable pride, and et cetera. I might instance in a thousand things that only custom and not reason hath approved. To conclude, Custom is an idiot, and whoever dependeth wholly upon him, without the discourse of reason, will take from him his pied[6] coat, and become a slave indeed to contempt and censure.

But you say we are barbarous and shameless and cast off all softness, to run wild through a wilderness of opinions. In this you express more cruelty than in all the rest, because I do not stand with my hands on my belly like a baby[7] at Bartholomew Fair,[8] that move not my whole body when I should but only stir my head like Jack of the clock house[9] which has no joints, that is not dumb when wantons court me, as if asslike I were ready for all burdens, or because I weep not when injury gripes me, like a worried deer in the fangs of many curs. Am I therefore barbarous or shameless? He is much injurious that so baptized us; we are as free-born as men, have as free election, and as free spirits, we are compounded of like parts, and may with like liberty make benefit of our creations; my countenance shall smile on the worthy, and frown on the ignoble, I will hear the wise, and be deaf to idiots, give counsel to my friend, but be dumb to flatterers, I have hands that shall be liberal to reward desert, feet that shall move swiftly to do good offices, and thoughts that shall ever accompany freedom and severity. If this be barbarous, let me leave the city and live with creatures of like simplicity.

* * *

Hic-Mulier: Therefore to take your proportion in a few lines (my dear Feminine-Masculine) tell me what Charter, prescription or right of claim you have to those things you make our absolute inheritance? Why do you curl, frizzle and powder your hair, bestowing more hours and time in dividing lock from lock, and hair from hair, in giving every thread his posture, and every curl his true fence and circumference than ever Caesar did in marshalling his army, either at Pharsalia, in Spain, or Britain? Why do you rob us of our ruffs, our earrings, carkanets,[1] and mamillions,[2] of our fans and feathers, our busks and French bodies, nay, of our masks, hoods, shadows, and shapynas,[3] not so much as the very art of painting, but you have so greedily engrossed it, that were it not for that little fantastical sharp pointed dagger that hangs at your chins, and the cross hilt which guards your upper lip, hardly would there be any difference between the fair mistress and the foolish servant. But is this theft the

---

5. Of Argos.
6. Spotted, motley.
7. Doll.
8. A popular carnival fair held every year from 1133 to 1865 at West Smithfield on August 24, the feast day of

Saint Bartholomew.
9. Figure that strikes the bell of a clock.
1. A jeweled or gold necklace.
2. Rounded protuberances (from French *mamelon*, nipple).
3. Disguises.

uttermost of our spoil? Fie, you have gone a world further, and even ravished from us our speech, our actions, sports, and recreations. Goodness leave me, if I have not heard a man court his mistress with the same words that Venus did Adonis, or as near as the book could instruct him;[4] where are the tilts and tourneys, and lofty galliards[5] that were danced in the days of old, when men capered in the air like wanton kids on the tops of mountains, and turned above ground as if they had been compact of fire or a purer element?[6] Tut, all's forsaken, all's vanished, those motions showed more strength than art, and more courage than courtship; it was much too robustious, and rather spent the body than prepared it, especially where any defect before reigned; hence you took from us poor women our traverses and tourneys, our modest stateliness and curious slidings, and left us nothing but the new French garb of puppet hopping and setting. Lastly, poor shuttlecock[7] that was only a female invention, how have you taken it out of our hands, and made yourselves such lords and rulers over it, that though it be a very emblem of us, and our lighter despised fortunes, yet it dare now hardly come near us; nay, you keep it so imprisoned within your bed-chambers and dining rooms, amongst your pages and panders, that a poor innocent maid to give but a kick with her battledore,[8] were more than halfway to the ruin of her reputation. For this you have demolished the noble schools of horsemanship (of which many were in this city) hung up your arms to rust, glued up those swords in their scabbards that would shake all Christendom with the brandish, and entertained into your mind such softness, dullness, and effeminate niceness that it would even make *Heraclitus*[9] himself laugh against his nature to see how pulingly[1] you languish in this weak entertained sin of womanish softness. To see one of your gender either show himself (in the midst of his pride or riches) at a playhouse or public assembly; how (before he dare enter) with the Jacob's-staff of his own eyes and his pages, he takes a full survey of himself, from the highest sprig in his feather, to the lowest spangle that shines in his shoestring: how he prunes and picks himself like a hawk set a-weathering, calls every several garment to auricular[2] confession, making them utter both their mortal great stains, and their venial and less blemishes, though the mote must be much less than an atom. Then to see him pluck and tug everything into the form of the newest received fashion; and by *Durer's* rules[3] make his leg answerable to his neck; his thigh proportionable with his middle, his foot with his hand, and a world of such idle disdained foppery. To see him thus patched up with symmetry, make himself complete, and even as a circle, and lastly, cast himself among the eyes of the people (as an object of wonder) with more niceness than a virgin goes to the sheets of her first lover would make patience herself mad with anger, and cry with the poet:

> O hominum mores, O gens, O tempora dura,
> Quantus in urbe dolor; quantus in orbe dolus![4]

Now since according to your own inference, even by the laws of nature, by the rules of religion, and the customs of all civil nations, it is necessary there be a distinct and special difference between man and woman, both in their habit and behaviors,

---

4. Venus, goddess of love, fell in love with the beautiful youth Adonis.
5. A brisk dance in triple time.
6. Men were thought to be dominated by dry humors and women by humid ones.
7. A small piece of cork with feathers sticking out of it, batted back and forth in the game of battledoor and shuttlecock.
8. A small racket, used to hit a shuttlecock.

9. Heraclitus was said to weep whenever he went forth in public (See Seneca, *De tranquilitate animi* 15.2).
1. In a whining tone.
2. Told privately, to the ear.
3. Albrecht Dürer (1471–1528), German painter and engraver, wrote a work on human proportions that was published after his death.
4. O customs of men, O people, O hard times / what great sadness in the city; what great fraud in the world.

what could we poor weak women do less (being far too weak by force to fetch back those spoils you have unjustly taken from us) than to gather up those garments you have proudly cast away, and therewith to clothe both our bodies and our minds; since no other means was left us to continue our names, and to support a difference? For to have held the way in which our forefathers first set us, or to have still embraced the civil modesty, or gentle sweetness of our soft inclinations; why, you had so far encroached upon us, and so over-bribed the world, to be deaf to any grant of restitution, that as at our creation, our whole sex was contained in man our first parent, so we should have had no other being, but in you, and your most effeminate quality. Hence we have preserved (though to our own shames) those manly things which you have forsaken, which would you again accept, and restore to us the blushes we laid by, when first we put on your masculine garments; doubt not but chaste thoughts and bashfulness will again dwell in us, and our palaces being newly gilt, trimmed, and re-edified, draw to us all the Graces, all the Muses,[5] which that you may more willingly do, and (as we of yours) grow into detestation of that deformity you have purloined, to the utter loss of your honors and reputations. Mark how the brave Italian poet,[6] even in the infancy of your abuses, most lively describes you:

> About his neck a Carknet[7] rich he ware
> Of precious Stones, all set in gold well tried;
> His arms that erst all warlike weapons bare,
> In golden bracelets wantonly were tied:
> Into his ears two rings conveyed are
> Of golden wire, at which on either side,
> Two Indian pearls, in making like two pears,
> Of passing price were pendant at his ears.
>
> His locks bedewed with water of sweet savor,
> Stood curled round in order on his head;
> He had such wanton womanish behavior,
> At though in valor he had ne'er been bred:
> So chang'd in speech, in manners and in favor,
> So from himself beyond all reason led,
> By these enchantments of this amorous dame;
> He was himself in nothing, but in name.

Thus you see your injury to us is of an old and inveterate continuance, having taken such strong root in your bosoms, that it can hardly be pulled up, without some offense to the soil: ours young and tender, scarce freed from the swaddling clothes, and therefore may with as much ease be lost, as it was with little difficulty found. Cast then from you our ornaments, and put on your own armors. Be men in shape, men in show, men in words, men in actions, men in counsel, men in example: then will we love and serve you; then will we hear and obey you; then will we like rich jewels hang at your ears to take our instructions, like true friends follow you through all dangers, and like careful leeches[8] pour oil into your wounds. Then shall you find delight in our words; pleasure in our faces; faith in our hearts; chastity in our thoughts, and sweetness

5. The graces were the three sisters, Aglaia, Thalia, and Euphrosyne, viewed as bestowers of charm and beauty; the muses were the nine daughters of Zeus and Memory who inspire poetry and the arts.
6. Ludovico Ariosto (1474–1532), whose description of Ruggiero's decadence when he is seduced by the sorceress Alcina in *Orlando Furioso 7* is quoted here in the translation (1590) by Sir John Harington, Queen Elizabeth's godson.
7. Necklace.
8. Physicians.

both in our inward and outward inclinations. Comeliness shall be then our study; fear our armor, and modesty our practice: then shall we be all your most excellent thoughts can desire, and have nothing in us less than impudence and deformity.

Haec-Vir; Enough: you have both raised my eyelids, cleared my sight, and made my heart entertain both shame and delight at an instant; shame in my follies past; delight in our noble and worthy conversion. Away then from me these light vanities, the only ensigns[9] of a weak and soft nature: and come you grave and solid pieces, which arm a man with fortitude and resolution: you are too rough and stubborn for a woman's wearing, we will here change our attires, as we have changed our minds, and with our attires, our names. I will no more be *Haec-Vir,* but *Hic Vir,* nor you *Hic-Mulier,* but *Haec Mulier.* From henceforth deformity shall pack to Hell; and if at any time he hide himself upon the earth, yet it shall be with contempt and disgrace. He shall have no friend but Poverty; no favorer but Folly, nor no reward but Shame. Henceforth we will live nobly like ourselves, ever sober, ever discreet, ever worthy; true men, and true women. We will be henceforth like well-coupled doves, full of industry, full of love: I mean, not of sensual and carnal love, but heavenly and divine love, which proceeds from God, whose inexpressible nature none is able to deliver in words, since is like his dwelling, high and beyond the reach of human apprehension.

END OF PERSPECTIVES: TRACTS ON WOMEN AND GENDER

Robert Herrick
1591–1674

The urbane and at times pagan poet Robert Herrick might seem an unlikely candidate for rural vicar, but such were his connections that he was promoted from deacon to priest in a day. He spent most of his life as vicar of the Devonshire parish of Dean, where he wrote poetry about country customs and church liturgy. A hundred and fifty years after his death, a writer in the *Quarterly Review* was able to find people in the village who could recite from memory Herrick's *Farewell to Dean Bourn:* "I never look to see / Dean, or thy watery incivility," lines that "they said he uttered as he crossed the brook, upon being ejected from the vicarage by Cromwell." Referring to Herrick's return to the vicarage after the Restoration, these locals "added with an air of innocent triumph, 'He did see it again.'" The villagers also recalled stories of how the bachelor vicar threw his sermon at the congregation one day for their inattention and how he taught his pet pig to drink from a tankard. Many of his best poems, such as *Corinna's Going A-Maying,* celebrate the landscape and the life of the country in the idealized tradition of pastoral poetry.

The son of a goldsmith in Cheapside, Herrick was apprenticed to the trade at age fourteen. After taking his B.A. from Cambridge in 1617, he returned to London, where he spent his poetic apprenticeship until he was appointed chaplain to the Duke of Buckingham in his failed expedition to aid the French Protestants of Rhé in 1627. Only a year later, Herrick moved to the vicarage at Dean, but many of his poems recount his London days, recalling the feasts frequented by Ben Jonson, whose verse "out-did the meat, out-did the frolic wine." The influence of Jonson's classical concision, wit, and urbanity can be felt in such poems as *Delight in Disorder* and his *Prayer* to the poet. While in London, Herrick also became friends with William Lawes, the court composer who wrote the music for Milton's masque *Comus.* When Lawes set

9. Banners, signs.

Herrick's *To the Virgins, to Make Much of Time* to music, this poem became one of the most popular drinking songs of the seventeenth century—often sung as a "catch," which meant that its words could be played with to produce ribald double meanings. His poems circulated in manuscript until his volume of verse was printed in 1648, with his secular poetry entitled *Hesperides* and his religious poetry entitled *His Noble Numbers*. He first achieved a wide readership in the early nineteenth century with the romantic revival of interest in rural life and poetry.

from HESPERIDES
The Argument of His Book[1]

I sing of brooks, of blossoms, birds, and bowers,
Of April, May, of June, and July flowers.
I sing of Maypoles, hock carts, wassails, wakes,[2]
Of bridegrooms, brides, and of their bridal cakes.
5   I write of youth, of love, and have access
By these, to sing of cleanly wantonness.°   *carefree abandon*
I sing of dews, of rains, and piece by piece,
Of balm, of oil, of spice, and ambergris.[3]
I sing of times trans-shifting;[4] and I write
10 How roses first came red, and lilies white.
I write of groves, of twilights, and I sing
The court of Mab,[5] and of the fairy king.
I write of hell; I sing (and ever shall)
Of Heaven, and hope to have it after all.

To the Sour Reader

If thou dislik'st the piece thou light'st on first;
Think that of all that I have writ, the worst:
But if thou read'st my book unto the end,
And still do'st this and that verse reprehend:
5   O perverse man! If all disgustful be,
Th' extreme scab take thee, and thine, for me.

When He Would Have His Verses Read

In sober mornings, do not thou rehearse
The holy incantation of a verse;
But when that men have both well drunk and fed,
Let my enchantments then be sung or read.
5   When laurel spirits i' th' fire, and when the hearth
Smiles to itself, and guilds the roof with mirth;
When up the thyrse[1] is rais'd, and when the sound
Of sacred orgies[2] flies around, around;
When the rose reigns, and locks with ointment shine,
10 Let rigid Cato[3] read these lines of mine.

---

1. All of Herrick's poems were published in 1648. The "Argument" introduces the book's themes.
2. Hock carts: harvest wagons; wassails: drinking toasts; wakes: celebrations in honor of the dedication of a parish church.
3. Secretion from the intestines of sperm whales, used to make perfume.

4. Times changing and passing; the cycle of the seasons.
5. Queen of the fairies.
1. A javelin twisted with ivy.
2. Songs to Bacchus, god of wine.
3. Cato the Elder, Roman statesman (234–149 B.C.), who inveighed against moral laxity.

Delight in Disorder

A sweet disorder in the dress
Kindles in clothes a wantonness:
A lawn° about the shoulders thrown   *scarf*
Into a fine distraction;
5   An erring° lace, which here and there   *wandering*
Enthralls the crimson stomacher:[1]
A cuff neglectful, and thereby
Ribbons to flow confusedly:
A winning wave, deserving note,
10   In the tempestuous petticoat;
A carelesse shoestring, in whose tie
I see a wild civility:
Do more bewitch me, than when art
Is too precise[2] in every part.

Corinna's Going A-Maying

Get up, get up for shame! the blooming morn
Upon her wings presents the god unshorn.[1]
     See how Aurora[2] throws her fair
     Fresh-quilted colors through the air:
5   Get up, sweet slug-a-bed, and see
         The dew-bespangling herb and tree.
Each flower has wept, and bowed toward the east,
Above an hour since; yet you not dressed,
         Nay! not so much as out of bed?
10   When all the birds have matins° said,   *morning prayer*
         And sung their thankfull hymns: 'tis sin,
         Nay, profanation° to keep in,   *impiety*
Whenas a thousand virgins on this day
Spring, sooner than the lark, to fetch in May.[3]

15   Rise, and put on your foliage, and be seen
To come forth, like the springtime, fresh and green,
         And sweet as Flora.[4] Take no care
         For jewels for your gown, or hair:
         Fear not; the leaves will strew
20   Gems in abundance upon you;
Besides, the childhood of the day has kept,
Against you come, some orient° pearls unwept;   *oriental, shining*
         Come, and receive them while the light
         Hangs on the dew-locks of the night,
25   And Titan[5] on the eastern hill

---

1. Ornamental covering for the chest worn under the lacing of the bodice.
2. "Precise" was often used to describe the strictness of the Puritans.
1. Apollo, the sun god, whose beams are seen as his flowing locks.

2. Goddess of the dawn in Roman mythology.
3. The custom on May Day morning was to gather blossoms.
4. Ancient Italian goddess of fertility and flowers.
5. The sun god.

Retires himself, or else stands still
Till you come forth. Wash, dress, be brief in praying:
Few beads are best,[6] when once we go a-Maying.

Come, my Corinna, come; and coming, mark
30   How each field turns a street; each street a park
         Made green, and trimmed with trees; see how
         Devotion gives each house a bough,
         Or branch: each porch, each door, ere this,
         An ark, a tabernacle is,[7]
35   Made up of whitethorn neatly interwove;
As if here were those cooler shades of love.
         Can such delights be in the street
         And open fields, and we not see't?
         Come, we'll abroad; and let's obey
40   The proclamation made for May,
And sin no more, as we have done, by staying;
But my Corinna, come, let's go a-Maying.

There's not a budding boy, or girl, this day,
But is got up, and gone to bring in May.
45   A deal of youth, ere this, is come
         Back, and with whitethorn laden home.
         Some have dispatched their cakes and cream,
         Before that we have left to dream:
And some have wept, and wooed, and plighted troth,
50   And chose their priest, ere we can cast off sloth.
         Many a green-gown has been given,
         Many a kiss, both odd and even:[8]
         Many a glance, too, has been sent
         From out the eye, love's firmament:
55   Many a jest told of the keys betraying
This night, and locks picked; yet we're not a-Maying.

Come, let us go, while we are in our prime,
And take the harmless folly of the time.
         We shall grow old apace, and die
60   Before we know our liberty.
         Our life is short; and our days run
         As fast away as does the sun;
And as a vapor, or a drop of rain
Once lost, can ne'er be found again,
65   So when or you or I are made
         A fable, song, or fleeting shade,°   *soul*
         All love, all liking, all delight
Lies drowned with us in endless night.
Then while time serves, and we are but decaying,
70   Come, my Corinna, come, let's go a-Maying.

---

6. An allusion to Catholic rosary beads.
7. The Hebrew ark of the Covenant contained the tablets of the laws; a tabernacle is an ornamental niche to hold the consecrated host.
8. Green gown . . . given: by lying in the grass. Kisses are odd and even in kissing games.

To the Virgins, to Make Much of Time

Gather ye rosebuds while ye may,
   Old time is still a-flying;[1]
And this same flower that smiles today,
   Tomorrow will be dying.[2]

5   The glorious lamp of heaven, the sun,
   The higher he's a-getting;
The sooner will his race be run,[3]
   And nearer he's to setting.

That age is best, which is the first,
10   When youth and blood are warmer;
But being spent, the worse, and worst
   Times still succeed the former.

Then be not coy, but use your time,
   And while ye may, go marry;
15   For having lost but once your prime,
   You may for ever tarry.

Upon Julia's Clothes

When as in silks my Julia goes,
Then, then, me thinks, how sweetly flows
That liquefaction of her clothes.
Next, when I cast mine eyes and see
5   That brave° vibration each way free;   *splendid*
O how that glittering taketh me!

Discontents in Devon

More discontents I never had
   Since I was born, than here;
Where I have been, and still am sad,
   In this dull Devonshire.
5   Yet justly too I must confess:
   I ne'er invented such
Ennobled numbers for the press,
   Than where I loath'd so much.

To Dean-Bourn, a Rude River in Devon

Dean-Bourn, farewell; I never look to see
Deane, or thy watery incivility.
Thy rocky bottom that doth tear thy streams,
And makes them frantic, ev'n to all extremes,
5   To my content I never should behold,

---

1. The Latin tag *tempus fugit* ("time flies").
2. "Dying" was also a euphemism for orgasm.

3. In Greek mythology, the sun was seen as the chariot of
Apollo drawn across the sky each day as in a race.

Were thy streams silver, or thy rocks all gold.
Rocky thou art; and rocky we discover
Thy men; and rocky are thy ways all over.
O men, O manners; there and ever known
10   To be a rocky generation!
A people currish, churlish as the seas;
And rude (almost) as rudest savages:
With whom I did, and may re-sojourn when
Rocks turn to rivers, rivers turn to men.

His Last Request to Julia

I have been wanton and too bold, I fear,
To chafe o'er much the virgin's cheek or ear:
Beg for my Pardon, Julia; *He doth win
Grace with the Gods, who's sorry for his sin.*
5   That done, my Julia, dearest Julia, come,
And go with me to choose my burial room:
My fates are ended; when thy Herrick dies,
Clasp thou his book, then close thou up his eyes.

from HIS NOBLE NUMBERS
His Prayer for Absolution

For those my unbaptizèd rhymes,
Writ in my wild unhallow'd times;
For every sentence, clause, and word,
That's not inlaid with Thee (my Lord),
5   Forgive me God, and blot each line
Out of my book that is not Thine.
But if 'mongst all, Thou find'st here one
Worthy thy benediction,
That one of all the rest shall be
10   The glory of my work, and me.

To God, on His Sickness

What though my harp and viol be
Both hung upon the willow tree?[1]
What though my bed be now my grave,
And for my house I darkness have?
5   What though my healthful days are fled,
And I lie number'd with the dead?
Yet I have hope, by Thy great power,
To spring, though now a wither'd flower.

---

1. In Psalm 137, the Hebrew poets, exiled in Babylon, hang their harps in the willow trees, too sorrowful to sing songs of their lost homeland.

George Herbert
1593–1633

George Herbert spent the last three years of his life as a country parson. In an age in which such a church living was often a mere sinecure, Herbert had a genuine vocation, which he chose over other paths open to him through his talent and the connections of his distinguished Welsh family. His education and vocation were most influenced by his mother Magdalene Herbert, a woman with a great appreciation for poetry and strong devotion to the Church of England. When she died in 1627, John Donne gave the funeral sermon, extolling not only her grace, wit, and charm but especially her extraordinary charity to those who suffered from the plague of 1625, among whom was Donne himself. Herbert's mother had been widowed when he was just three years old. She brought up ten children, first in Oxford and then in London, where she saw to it that they were well read in the Bible and the classics.

Herbert studied at Cambridge University, where he became Reader in Rhetoric in 1616; in 1620 he was elected Public Orator, a post that he held for eight years. He wrote poetry and delivered public addresses in Latin and worked on the Latin version of Francis Bacon's *The Advancement of Learning.* Herbert also stood for Parliament and served there in 1624, when the Virginia Company, in which many of his friends and family were stockholders, was beset by financial difficulties and ultimately dissolved by James I.

Though his book *The Temple,* which included all his English poems, was not published until just after his death in 1633, Herbert was already writing verse as an undergraduate in 1610, when he dedicated two sonnets to his mother that advocated religious rather than secular love as the subject for poetry. His first published poems were written in Latin, commemorating the death of Prince Henry (1612). Herbert also wrote three different collections of Latin poems during his Cambridge years: *Musae Responsoriae,* polemical poems that defended the rites of the Church of England from Puritan criticism; *Passio discerpta,* religious verse that focused on Christ's passion and death in a style reminiscent of Crashaw; and *Lucas,* a collection of brief epigrams, such as this one on pride: "Each man is earth, and the field's child. Tell me, / Will you be a sterile mountain or a fertile valley?" The sardonic and mocking tone of these epigrams may surprise a reader of his English poems, but the wit and the rhetorical finish of his Latin poetry recur in his later verse.

Herbert's poetry is some of the most complex and innovative of all English verse. In a very pared-down style, enlivened by gentle irony, Herbert produces complexity of meaning through allegory and emblem, directly or more often indirectly alluding to biblical images, events, and insights, which take on their own moral and poetic meaning in the life of the speaker and the reader. Each of his poems is a kind of spiritual event, enacting in its form, both visual and aural, the very theological experiences and beliefs—or conflict of beliefs—expressed. Herbert allows us to make the spiritual journey with him through suffering and redemption, through doubt and hope. The meaning of one of his poems unravels like a discovery, each line and stanza raising alternative possibilities and altering the meaning of the one before. His spirituality is not a matter of easy acceptance but one of struggle, portrayed with wit, logic, and passion that recall the best of Donne's verse. The humility, subtle hesitancy, and whimsical irony are Herbert's alone, as when he addresses a love poem, *The Pearl,* to God:

> I know the ways of pleasure, the sweet strains,
> The lullings and the relishes of it . . .
> My stuff is flesh, not brass; my senses live,
> And grumble oft, that they have more in me
> Then he that curbs them, being but one to five:
> Yet I love thee.

The Altar[1]

A broken ALTAR, Lord, thy servant rears,
Made of a heart, and cemented with tears:
    Whole parts are as thy hand did frame;
    No workman's tool has touched the same.[2]
5   A HEART alone
          Is such a stone,
          As nothing but
          Thy power doth cut.
          Wherefore each part
10   Of my hard heart
          Meets in this frame,
          To praise thy Name.
    That, if I chance to hold my peace,
    These stones to praise thee may not cease.[3]
15 Oh let thy blessed SACRIFICE be mine,
and sanctify this ALTAR to be thine.

Easter Wings[1]

Lord, who createdst man in wealth and store,[2]
  Though foolishly he lost the same,
    Decaying more and more,
      Till he became
        Most poor:
        With thee
      Oh let me rise
    As larks, harmoniously,
  And sing this day thy victories:
Then shall the fall[3] further the flight in me.

My tender age in sorrow did begin
  And still with sickness and shame
    Thou didst so punish sin,
      That I became
        Most thin.
        With thee
      Let me combine,
    And feel this day thy victory:
  For, if I imp[4] my wing on thine,
Affliction shall advance the flight in me.

1. All of Herbert's poems were published in *The Temple* (1633).
2. See Exodus 20.5, where God tells Moses: "And if thou wilt make me an altar of stone, thou shalt not build it of hewn stone: for if thou lift up thy tool upon it thou has polluted it."
3. See Luke 19.40: "I tell you that, if these should hold their peace, the stones would immediately cry out."

1. As in the first editions of Herbert, this poem is printed sideways to represent the shape of wings.
2. Plenty.
3. The human frailty of sin, as well as the speaker's own descent into sin and suffering, which Christ redeems through his rising from the dead on Easter.
4. In falconry, to insert feathers in a bird's wing.

Jordan (1)[1]

Who says that fictions only and false hair
Become a verse? Is there in truth no beauty?
Is all good structure in a winding stair?
May no lines pass, except they do their duty
5   Not to a true, but painted chair?

Is it no verse, except enchanted groves
And sudden arbors shadow coarse-spun lines?
Must purling° streams refresh a lover's loves?   *rippling*
Must all be veiled, while he that reads, divines,[2]
10   Catching the sense at two removes?

Shepherds are honest people; let them sing:
Riddle who list,[3] for me, and pull for prime.[4]
I envy no man's nightingale or spring;
Nor let them punish me with loss of rhyme,
15   Who plainly say, *My God, My King.*

Jordan (2)

When first my lines of heav'nly joys made mention,
Such was their luster, they did so excel,
That I sought out quaint° words, and trim invention;   *clever*
My thoughts began to burnish,° sprout, and swell,   *spread out*
5 Curling with metaphors a plain intention,
Decking the sense, as if it were to sell.[1]

Thousands of notions in my brain did run,
Off'ring their service, if I were not sped.[2]
I often blotted what I had begun;
10 This was not quick° enough, and that was dead.   *lively*
Nothing could seem too rich to clothe the sun,
Much less those joys which trample on his head.[3]

As flames do work and wind, when they ascend,
So did I weave my self into the sense.
15 But while I bustled, I might hear a friend
Whisper, "How wide° is all this long pretence!   *beside the point*
There is in love a sweetness ready penn'd:
Copy out only that, and save expense."

The Collar

I struck the board,° and cried, "No more.   *table*
      I will abroad!
What? Shall I ever sigh and pine?
My lines and life are free; free as the road,

---

1. To cross the River Jordan symbolizes entering the Promised Land.
2. To interpret what is obscure through magical insight or intuitive conjecture.
3. Whoever wants to may interpret.

4. Draw a lucky card, or hit upon a lucky guess.
1. Decorating the meaning as if it were for sale.
2. Dealt with so that I was satisfied.
3. The sun is a symbol for Christ; the sun's head is the Son's head.

5   Loose as the wind, as large as store.°   *abundance*
Shall I be still in suit?[1]
Have I no harvest but a thorn
To let me blood, and not restore
What I have lost with cordial[2] fruit?
10   Sure there was wine
Before my sighs did dry it; there was corn
Before my tears did drown it.
Is the year only lost to me?
Have I no bays[3] to crown it?
15   No flowers, no garlands gay? all blasted?
All wasted?
Not so, my heart; but there is fruit,
And thou hast hands.
Recover all thy sigh-blown age
20   On double pleasures: leave thy cold dispute
Of what is fit and not forsake thy cage,
Thy rope of sands,
Which petty thoughts have made, and made to thee
Good cable, to enforce and draw,
25   And be thy law,
While thou didst wink[4] and wouldst not see.
Away! take heed:
I will abroad.
Call in thy death's head[5] there: tie up thy fears.
30   He that forbears
To suit and serve his need,
Deserves his load."
But as I raved and grew more fierce and wild
At every word,
35   Me thoughts I heard one calling, *Child!*
And I replied, *My Lord.*

Love (3)

Love bade me welcome: yet my soul drew back,
Guilty of dust and sin.
But quick-eyed Love, observing me grow slack°   *slow, weak*
From my first entrance in,
5   Drew nearer to me, sweetly questioning,
If I lacked anything.

"A guest," I answered, "worthy to be here":
Love said, "You shall be he."
"I the unkind, ungrateful? Ah my dear,
10   I cannot look on thee."
Love took my hand, and smiling did reply,
"Who made the eyes but I?"

---

1. Engaged in a lawsuit.   4. Shut your eyes to.
2. Invigorating to the heart.   5. The skull as an emblem of human mortality.
3. The poet's laurel wreath.

"Truth Lord, but I marred them; let my shame
         Go where it doth deserve."
15   "And know you not," says Love, "who bore the blame?"
         "My dear, then I will serve."
     "You must sit down," says Love, "and taste my meat."
         So I did sit and eat.[1]

Andrew Marvell
1621–1678

Praised by his nephew for "joining the most peculiar graces of wit and learning" and berated by his antagonist Samuel Parker for speaking the language of "boat-swains and cabin boys," Andrew Marvell left little evidence for his biographers. Most of what remains of his verse has been bequeathed to posterity by virtue of a shady banking scheme on his part and an implausible claim by his housekeeper to be "Mrs. Marvell." Though she couldn't remember the date of his death, Mary Palmer tried to prove that she was the poet's wife to get at money that her master had squirrelled away in an account for some bankrupt acquaintances. To further her claim, she saw to it that Marvell's *Miscellaneous Poems* were published in 1681. In his own name, Marvell published only a few occasional poems and a satire attacking religious intolerance and political authoritarianism.

If it is thanks to Mrs. Palmer's rummaging through the poet's papers that such exquisite poems as *To His Coy Mistress* and *The Definition of Love* saw the light of day, it is largely thanks to T. S. Eliot that modern critical attention was turned to Marvell's poetry. The Augustans and Romantics neglected him, and it was not until Eliot that such features of Marvell's verse as Latinate gravity, metaphysical wit, and muscular syntax came to be fully appreciated. For ingenious ambiguity and sheer seductive sensuousness, Marvell is one of the greatest poets of all time.

As tantalizing as the verse is, it leaves little solid evidence of what was a very private life. Marvell grew up in a house surrounded by gardens in the Yorkshire town of Hull on the Humber, where his father was the Anglican rector. There is a story that Marvell once left university for London to flirt with Catholicism, but his father made sure he returned to Cambridge and Protestantism. After his father's death, Marvell traveled in Holland, France, Italy, and Spain (1642–1647). He later tutored Mary Fairfax, daughter of Lord Fairfax of Nun-Appleton House (1650–1652), and taught William Dutton, Cromwell's ward (1653–1656). Initially recommended by Milton to serve as Assistant Latin Secretary in 1653, Marvell was first appointed Latin Secretary to the Council of State in 1657. He was elected Member of Parliament for Hull in 1659, a position he held until 1678. When Charles I returned to power, Marvell interceded on Milton's behalf and made sure his old friend and fellow poet was released from prison. Later in life, Marvell wrote satires criticizing the corruption of the Restoration regime, all but one published anonymously.

Marvell chose to keep his cards close to his chest in the ideologically volatile atmosphere of the Civil War and Restoration. A contemporary biographer remarked that Marvell "was wont to say that, he would not play the good-fellow in any man's company in whose hands he would not trust his life." He did not fight in the Civil War, since he was in Europe at the time, and as he later ambiguously maintained, "the Cause was too good to have been fought for." His strategy in dealing with change involved publicly siding with the faction in power while main-

---

1. The speaker takes Communion, which symbolizes union with God.

taining politically incorrect friendships and finding himself "inclinable to favor the weaker party"—whether it was a Royalist who had given his life for the King, such as Lord Hastings, or a Republican who went to prison for his convictions, such as Milton. Marvell wrote poems praising both royalists and revolutionaries. He was nothing if not tolerant.

He was also something of a chameleon, an assumer of numerous poetic personae and disguises. In *Tom May's Death*, Marvell satirized the Royalist turned Republican, here portrayed arriving in heaven drunk. Marvell equivocally praised Cromwell in *An Horatian Ode*, ironically maintaining that it was the Irish whom Cromwell had so brutally massacred who could "best affirm his praises." When he became tutor to Cromwell's ward William Dutton, Marvell wrote poems praising Cromwell in such slavishly glowing terms that the poet was made Latin Secretary to the Council of State.

The last word should go to Marvell, whose choice to translate the following chorus from Seneca's *Thyestes* shows his outlook on the vicissitudes of power:

> Climb at court for me that will
> Giddy favor's slippery hill;
> All I seek is to lie still,
> Settled in some secret nest.
> In calm leisure let me rest,
> And far off the public stage
> Pass away my silent age.
> Thus, when without noise, unknown,
> I have lived out all my span,
> I shall die without a groan,
> An old honest countryman,
> Who exposed to others' eyes,
> Into his own heart ne'er pries.
> Death to him's a strange surprise.

To His Coy Mistress[1]

Had we but world enough, and time,
This coyness, Lady, were no crime.
We would sit down, and think which way
To walk, and pass our long love's day.
5 Thou by the Indian Ganges' side
Shouldst rubies find: I by the tide
Of Humber would complain.[2] I would
Love you ten years before the flood:
And you should if you please refuse
10 Till the conversion of the Jews.[3]
My vegetable love should grow
Vaster than empires, and more slow.[4]
An hundred years should go to praise

---

1. A poem on the theme of *carpe diem* ("seize the day") that includes a blazon, or description of the lady from head to toe, and a logical argument: "If . . . But . . . Therefore."
2. Marvell grew up in Hull on the Humber River.
3. The end of time: the Flood occurred in the distant past, and Christians prophesied that Jews would convert to Christianity at the end of the world.
4. The "vegetable" was characterized only by growth, in contrast to the sensitive, which felt, and the rational, which could reason.

Thine eyes, and on thy forehead gaze.
15 Two hundred to adore each breast:
But thirty thousand to the rest.
An age at least to every part,
And the last age should show your heart.
For Lady you deserve this state;
20 Nor would I love at lower rate.
    But at my back I always hear
Times wingèd chariot hurrying near:
And yonder all before us lie
Deserts of vast eternity.
25 Thy beauty shall no more be found;
Nor, in thy marble vault, shall sound
My echoing song: then worms shall try
That long preserved virginity:
And your quaint honor turn to dust;[5]
30 And into ashes all my lust.
The grave's a fine and private place,
But none, I think, do there embrace.
    Now, therefore, while the youthful hue
Sits on thy skin like morning dew,[6]
35 And while thy willing soul transpires
At every pore with instant fires,
Now let us sport us while we may;
And now, like amorous birds of prey,
Rather at once our time devour,
40 Than languish in his slow-chapped° power.   *slowly biting*
Let us roll all our strength, and all
Our sweetness, up into one ball:
And tear our pleasures with rough strife,
Thorough the iron gates of life.[7]
45 Thus, though we cannot make our sun
Stand still, yet we will make him run.[8]

The Definition of Love

My Love is of a birth as rare
As 'tis for object strange and high:
It was begotten by Despair
Upon Impossibility.

5 Magnanimous Despair alone
Could show me so divine a thing,
Where feeble Hope could ne'er have flown
But vainly flapped its tinsel wing.

And yet I quickly might arrive
10 Where my extended soul is fixed,

---

5. "Quaint honor," proud chastity. Note the pun on *queynte* (Middle English), woman's genitals.
6. In the 1681 Folio, "dew" reads "glue," and in two manuscripts the rhymes in lines 33 and 34 are "glue" and "dew."

7. One manuscript reads "grates" for "gates."
8. Joshua made the sun stand still in the war against Gibeon (see Joshua 10.12).

But Fate does iron wedges drive,
And always crowds itself betwixt.

For Fate with jealous eye does see
Two perfect loves, nor lets them close:°   *unite*
15 Their union would her ruin be,
And her tyrannic power depose.

And therefore her decrees of steel
Us as the distant poles have placed,
(Though Love's whole world on us doth wheel)
20 Not by themselves to be embraced.

Unless the giddy heaven fall,
And earth some new convulsion tear;
And, us to join, the world should all
Be cramped into a planisphere.[1]

25 As lines (so loves) oblique[2] may well
Themselves in every angle greet:
But ours so truly parallel,
Though infinite, can never meet.

Therefore the love which us doth bind,
30 But Fate so enviously debars,
Is the conjunction of the mind,
And opposition of the stars.[3]

The Garden

How vainly men themselves amaze
To win the palm, the oak, or bays,[1]
And their uncessant labors see
Crowned from some single herb or tree,
5 Whose short and narrow-vergèd shade
Does prudently their toils upbraid,
While all flowers and all trees do close°   *unite*
To weave the garlands of repose.

Fair quiet, have I found thee here,
10 And innocence thy sister dear!
Mistaken long, I sought you then
In busy companies of men.
Your sacred plants, if here below,
Only among the plants will grow.
15 Society is all but rude,
To this delicious solitude.[2]

---

1. A two-dimensional map of the globe.
2. Slanting at an angle other than a right angle, and also veering away from right morals.
3. Conjunction: coming together in the same sign of the zodiac; union. Stars in opposition are diametrically opposed to one another.

1. Vainly: arrogantly, in vain; amaze: bewilder, go mad; the palm, the oak, or bays: prizes symbolic of military, political, and poetic excellence.
2. Compare to Katherine Philips's *A Country-life*: "Then welcome dearest solitude, / My great felicity; / Though some are pleased to call thee rude."

No white nor red[3] was ever seen
So am'rous as this lovely green.
Fond lovers, cruel as their flame,
20   Cut in these trees their mistress' name.
Little, alas, they know, or heed,
How far these beauties hers exceed!
Fair trees! whereso'er your barks I wound,
No name shall but your own be found.

25   When we have run our passion's heat,
Love hither makes his best retreat.
The gods, that mortal beauty chase,
Still in a tree did end their race.
Apollo hunted Daphne so,
30   Only that she might laurel grow,
And Pan did after Syrinx speed,
Not as a nymph, but for a reed.[4]

What wondrous life in this I lead!
Ripe apples drop about my head;
35   The luscious clusters of the vine
Upon my mouth do crush their wine;
The nectarine, and curious peach,
Into my hands themselves do reach;
Stumbling on melons, as I pass,
40   Insnared with flowers, I fall on grass.

Meanwhile the mind, from pleasure less,
Withdraws into its happiness:
The mind, that ocean where each kind
Does straight its own resemblance find,[5]
45   Yet it creates, transcending these,
Far other worlds, and other seas,
Annihilating all that's made
To a green thought in a green shade.

Here at the fountain's sliding foot,
50   Or at some fruit-tree's mossy root,
Casting the body's vest aside,
My soul into the boughs does glide:
There like a bird it sits and sings,
Then whets and combs its silver wings;
55   And, till prepared for longer flight,
Waves in its plumes the various light.

Such was that happy garden-state,
While man there walked without a mate:
After a place so pure and sweet,

---

3. Colors used to describe the beloved's beauty.
4. As god of poetry, Apollo seeks the laurel (the bays),
while Pan seeks the syrinx (pipe) of pastoral poetry.
Apollo chased Daphne, who prayed to be saved from him
and was transformed into a laurel tree, just as Syrinx

escaped Pan's lust when she was turned into a reed.
5. It was popularly believed that animals and plants on
land had counterparts in the sea. This line describes the
mind as innately possessing ideas, a concept of Platonic
philosophy.

60 What other help could yet be meet!
    But 'twas beyond a mortal's share
    To wander solitary there:
    Two paradises 'twere in one
    To live in paradise alone.

65 How well the skillful gardener drew
    Of flowers and herbs this dial new;[6]
    Where from above the milder sun
    Does through a fragrant zodiac run;
    And, as it works, th' industrious bee
70 Computes its time as well as we.[7]
    How could such sweet and wholesome hours
    Be reckoned but with herbs and flowers!

An Horatian Ode Upon Cromwell's Return from Ireland[1]

    The forward youth that would appear
    Must now forsake his muses dear,
        Nor in the shadows sing
        His numbers[2] languishing.
5   'Tis time to leave the books in dust,
    And oil th' unusèd armor's rust:
        Removing from the wall
        The corslet[3] of the hall.
    So restless Cromwell could not cease
10 In the inglorious arts of peace,
        But through adventurous war
        Urgèd his active star.
    And, like the three-forked lightning, first
    Breaking the clouds where it was nursed,
15   Did thorough his own side
        His fiery way divide:[4]
    For 'tis all one to courage high
    The emulous or enemy;
        And with such to enclose
20   Is more than to oppose.
    Then burning through the air he went,
    And palaces and temples rent:
        And Caesar's head at last
        Did through his laurels blast.[5]
25 'Tis madness to resist or blame
    The force of angry heaven's flame:

---

6. The garden is arranged as a floral sundial.

7. Computes its time: a pun on thyme.

1. Cromwell returned from his military campaign in Ireland in May 1650. After General Fairfax resigned as commander of the parliamentary army because he refused to invade Scotland, Cromwell assumed his position and attacked the Scots. This poem was printed in the 1681 edition but then was canceled from printed copies until 1776. The influence of Horace's *Odes* (especially I. 35, 37; IV. 4, 5, 14, 15) surfaces in the poised dignity of the verse and its subtly ambiguous attitude toward power.

2. Conformity to a rhythmical pattern in verse or music.

3. Defensive armor covering the upper body.

4. Cromwell's overtaking his rivals in Parliament is described as an elemental force similar to the "three-forked lightning" of Zeus.

5. Although lightning was thought not to strike the laurel (symbolizing the royal crown), Cromwell had struck down Charles I (Caesar).

And, if we would speak true,
Much to the man is due,
Who, from his private gardens, where
30   He lived reservèd and austere,
As if his highest plot
To plant the bergamot,[6]
Could by industrious valor climb
To ruin the great work of Time,
35   And cast the kingdom old
Into another mold.
Though justice against fate complain,
And plead the ancient rights in vain:
But those do hold or break,
40   As men are strong or weak.
Nature, that hateth emptiness,
Allows of penetration less:[7]
And therefore must make room
Where greater spirits come.
45 What field of all the Civil Wars,
Where his were not the deepest scars?
And Hampton[8] shows what part
He had of wiser art,
Where, twining subtle fears with hope,
50 He wove a net of such a scope,
That Charles himself might chase
To Carisbrooke's narrow case:
That thence the royal actor borne,
The tragic scaffold might adorn;
55   While round the armèd bands
Did clap their bloody hands.
He nothing common did or mean
Upon that memorable scene:
But with his keener eye
60   The axe's[9] edge did try;
Nor called the gods with vulgar spite
To vindicate his helpless right,
But bowed his comely head,
Down, as upon a bed.
65 This was that memorable hour
Which first assured the forcèd power.
So when they did design
The Capitol's first line,
A bleeding head where they begun,
70 Did fright the architects to run;

6. A pear known as the "prince's pear."
7. Nature abhors not only a vacuum but even more so the penetration of one body's space by another body.
8. Hampton Court where Charles I was held captive before his execution in 1649. He had fled to Carisbrooke

Castle on the Isle of Wight, where he was betrayed to the Governor in 1647.
9. Marvell plays on the Latin "*acies*," the sharp edge of a sword, a keen glance, and the vanguard of battle.

And yet in that the State
Foresaw it's happy fate.[1]
And now the Irish are ashamed
To see themselves in one year tamed:[2]
75   So much one man can do,
That does both act and know.
They can affirm his praises best,
And have, though overcome, confessed
How good he is, how just,
80   And fit for highest trust.[3]
Nor yet grown stiffer with command,
But still in the Republic's hand:
How fit he is to sway
That can so well obey.[4]
85 He to the commons' feet presents
A kingdom, for his first year's rents:
And, what he may, forbears
His fame to make it theirs:
And has his sword and spoils ungirt,
90   To lay them at the public's skirt.
So when the falcon high
Falls heavy from the sky,
She, having killed, no more does search,
But on the next green bough to perch;
95   Where, when he first does lure,
The falconer has her sure.
What may not then our isle presume
While victory his crest does plume!
What may not others fear
100   If thus he crown each year!
A Caesar he ere long to Gaul,
To Italy an Hannibal,[5]
And to all states not free
Shall climactéric° be.   *period of change*
105 The Pict no shelter now shall find
Within his particolored mind;
But from this valor sad°   *severe*
Shrink underneath the plaid:[6]
Happy if in the tufted brake
110   The English hunter him mistake;
Nor lay his hounds in near
The Caledonian° deer.   *Scottish*

---

1. In digging the foundations of the temple of Jupiter Capitolinum, the excavators found a human's head (*caput*), which was interpreted as prophesying that Rome should be the capitol of the Empire (see Livy, *Annals* I.55.6).
2. From August 1649 to his return to England in May 1650, Cromwell went on a savage military campaign that included the slaughter of Irish civilians.
3. An example of one of the many equivocal statements in this poem; of course, the Irish did not affirm Cromwell's greatness.
4. A saying attributed to the Athenian Solon the lawgiver.
5. Neither Caesar nor Hannibal gave freedom to peoples whose countries they invaded and conquered.
6. Marvell uses "Picts" the ancient name for the Scots, creating a play on *picti* (Latin: painted) and particolored.

But thou the wars' and fortune's son
March indefatigably on;
115   And for the last effect
          Still keep thy sword erect:
Besides the force it has to fright
The spirits of the shady night,[7]
          The same arts that did gain
120   A power must it maintain.

+━━❈━━+

Katherine Philips
1631–1664

Idolized as the "Matchless Orinda" in her own day, Katherine Philips is now taking her place in the history of English verse after two centuries of neglect. During her lifetime, her work circulated in manuscript among a close network of friends. The first edition of her poems appeared posthumously in 1664. The second edition of 1667 was evidently a commercial success, since it was reprinted in 1669, 1678, and 1710. The next complete edition of her poems did not appear until 1994.

John Keats esteemed Philips's *To Mrs. Mary Awbrey at Parting* as an example of "real feminine Modesty"; today, by contrast, critics praise her poems to women friends as reminiscent of the ancient Greek Sappho's erotic lyrics. By imitating Donne's love lyrics in her poems to women, Philips poetically conceives of these friendships as no less world-changing, no less ennobling and enthralling, than Donne's romantic liaisons. Some of the best poets of her own day were able to appreciate her as a fellow poet rather than as Keats's romanticized ideal woman. Marvell paid tribute to her by subtly alluding to lines of her poetry in one of his greatest poems, *The Garden*. And Henry Vaughan insisted that "No laurel grows, but for [her] brow."

Katherine Philips's work was particularly important for other women writers. Philips's lyric poetry influenced such other early modern women poets as Aphra Behn and Anne Killigrew. Yet it is impossible to pigeonhole Philips as stereotypically feminine. She wrote on public and political themes as well as personal subjects, endowing traditional genres such as the parting poem, the elegy, and the epitaph, with a particular directness and clarity all her own.

Katherine Philips was born in London to a well-to-do Presbyterian family. Her father was a prosperous merchant, and her mother was the daughter of a Fellow of the Royal College of Physicians. Philips's father was wealthy enough to invest two hundred pounds for a thousand acres in Ulster, a scheme that was begun in 1642 by the Puritan Parliament but, ironically, not realized until the Restoration, when we find Katherine in Ireland pursuing lawsuits to obtain this land. As a girl, Katherine attended Mrs. Salmon's Presbyterian School, where she learned to love poetry and began to write verses. In 1646 her widowed mother married Sir Richard Philips, and the family moved to his castle in Wales. Philips herself married Sir Richard's kinsman James Philips, and they lived together for twelve years in the small Welsh town of Cardigan when not in London, where her husband served as a Member of Parliament during the Interregnum.

However Presbyterian and Cromwellian were the associations of her family and marriage, she emerged after the Restoration as a complete Anglican. Not only did she write poetry against the regicide, such as *Upon the Double Murder of King Charles*, but she became a favorite

---

7. There was an ancient tradition of dead spirits being frightened by raised swords (Homer, *Odyssey* 11; Virgil, *Aeneid* 6). The dead spirits referred to here include the dead in the wars in Ireland and England, including the king.

author at court. She was encouraged to write poetry by her friend "Poliarchus," Sir Charles Cotterell, Master of Ceremonies in the Court of Charles II, who showed her poems to the royal family. An Anglo-Irish nobleman, the Earl of Orrery, encouraged her to complete a translation of Corneille's *Pompey* and actually produced and had the play printed in Dublin in 1663.

Katherine Philips developed friendships that became the theme of what most critics regard as her best poems. Perhaps the most intense of these friendships was that with Mrs. Anne Owen, the Lucasia of Philips's most passionate poems, several of which echo love poems by Donne. Her friend Sir Edward Dering, whom she called "the Noble Silvander," lamented Katherine Philips's death in recounting the extraordinary accomplishment of both her poetry and her life, which had attempted

> the most generous design . . . to unite all those of her acquaintance which she found worthy or desired to make so (among which later number she was pleased to give me a place) into one society, and by the bands of friendship to make an alliance more firm than what nature, our country or equal education can produce.

Friendship in Emblem
or the Seal,[1]

To My Dearest Lucasia[2]

The hearts thus intermixèd speak
A love that no bold shock can break;
For joined and growing, both in one,
Neither can be disturbed alone.

5 That means a mutual knowledge too;
For what is't either heart can do,
Which by its panting sentinel°   *guard*
It does not to the other tell?

That friendship hearts so much refines,
10 It nothing but itself designs:
The hearts are free from lower ends,
For each point to the other tends.

They flame, 'tis true, and several ways,
But still those flames do so much raise,
15 That while to either they incline
They yet are noble and divine.

From smoke or hurt those flames are free,
From grossness or mortality:
The hearts (like Moses bush presumed)[3]
20 Warmed and enlightened, not consumed.

The compasses that stand above
Express this great immortal Love;[4]

---

1. A symbolic picture, which appeared with a motto and a poem. The central emblematic image of this poem is "the compasses" (line 21); another emblem is "those flames" (line 14).
2. Anne Owen, to whom many of Philips's poems are dedicated, was a neighbor of hers in Wales and a close friend from 1651 until Philips's death.

3. See Exodus 3.2–5 for the burning bush through which the angel of the Lord appeared to and from which God called Moses.
4. Compare the image of the compasses here to the "twin compasses" in Donne's A *Valediction: Forbidding Mourning,* page 811.

For friends, like them, can prove this true,
They are, and yet they are not, two.

25   And in their posture is expressed
Friendship's exalted interest:
Each follows where the other leans,
And what each does, the other means.

And as when one foot does stand fast,
30   And t'other circles seeks to cast,
The steady part does regulate
And make the wanderer's motion straight:

So friends are only two in this,
T'reclaim each other when they miss:
35   For whose'er will grossly fall,
Can never be a friend at all.

And as that useful instrument
For even lines was ever meant;
So friendship from good angels[5] springs,
40   To teach the world heroic things.

As these are found out in design
To rule and measure every line;
So friendship governs actions best,
Prescribing law to all the rest.

45   And as in nature nothing's set
So just as lines and numbers met;
So compasses for these being made,
Do friendship's harmony persuade.

And like to them, so friends may own
50   Extension, not division:
Their points, like bodies, separate;
But head, like souls, knows no such fate.

And as each part so well is knit,
That their embraces ever fit:
55   So friends are such by destiny,
And no third can the place supply.

There needs no motto to the seal:
But that we may the mine[6] reveal
To the dull eye, it was thought fit
60   That friendship only should be writ.

But as there is degrees of bliss,
So there's no friendship meant by this,
But such as will transmit to fame
Lucasia's and Orinda's name.

5. Guardian spirits, with puns on angels, and *angeli* (Latin), messengers.
6. A mass of gold, a store of plenty, as well as a pun on the possessive pronoun meaning "my own" and perhaps also on "mind."

Upon the Double Murder of King Charles
in Answer to a Libelous Rhyme Made by V. P.[1]

I think not on the state, nor am concerned
Which way soever that great helm is turned,
But as that son whose father's danger nigh
Did force his native dumbness, and untie
5   The fettered organs: so here is a cause
That will excuse the breach of nature's laws.[2]
Silence were now a sin: nay passion now
Wise men themselves for merit would allow.
What noble eye could see, (and careless pass)
10   The dying lion kicked by every ass?
Hath Charles so broke God's laws, he must not have
A quiet crown, nor yet a quiet grave?
Tombs have been sanctuaries; thieves lie here
Secure from all their penalty and fear.
15   Great Charles his double misery was this,
Unfaithful friends, ignoble enemies;
Had any heathen been this prince's foe,
He would have wept to see him injured so.
His title was his crime, they'd reason good
20   To quarrel at the right they had withstood.
He broke God's laws, and therefore he must die,
And what shall then become of thee and I?
Slander must follow treason; but yet stay,
Take not our reason with our king away.
25   Though you have seized upon all our defense,
Yet do not sequester° our common sense.   *confiscate*
But I admire not at this new supply:
No bounds will hold those who at scepters fly.
Christ will be King, but I ne'er understood,
30   His subjects built his kingdom up with blood,
(Except their own) or that he would dispense
With his commands, though for his own defense.
Oh! to what height of horror are they come,
Who dare pull down a crown, tear up a tomb![3]

To the Truly Noble, and Obliging Mrs. Anne Owen
(*on My First Approaches*)[1]

Madam,
As in a triumph conquerors admit
Their meanest captives to attend on it,[2]

1. Vavasor Powell, a Fifth Monarchist who believed that Christ's second coming was imminent, and an ardent Republican, whose verses on the murder of the king are lost. According to Philips's poem, Powell argued that Charles I had usurped God's power.
2. Breaking the prohibition against women speaking on public affairs. See Margaret Tyler's preface to *The First Part of the Mirror of Princely Deeds*, page 829, for a defense of woman's ability to write about war, traditionally considered only appropriate to male authors.
3. Possibly a reference to the unearthing of the regicides' bodies.
1. Mrs. Anne Owen of Orielton, Wales, was Philips's close friend and the Lucasia of her poems; she was married to John Owen and was the heiress to the ancient seat of Presaddfed in Anglesey.
2. Here, "triumph" means military victory and the triumphal procession that announced it.

Who, though unworthy, have the power confessed,
And justified the yielding of the rest:
5   So when the busy world (in hope t'excuse
Their own surprise) your conquests do peruse,
And find my name, they will be apt to say
Your charms were blinded, or else thrown away.
There is no honor got in gaining me,
10 Who am a prize not worth your victory.
But this will clear you, that 'tis general
The worst applaud what is admired by all.
But I have plots in't: for the way to be
Secure of fame to all posterity
15 Is to obtain the honor I pursue,
To tell the world I was subdued by you.
And since in you all wonders common are,
Your votaries° may in your virtues share,   *devoted admirers*
While you by noble magic worth impart:
20 She that can conquer, can reclaim a heart.
Of this creation I shall not despair,
Since for your own sake it concerns your care:
For 'tis more honor that the world should know
You made a noble soul, than found it so.

To My Excellent Lucasia, on Our Friendship
17th. July 1651[1]

I did not live until this time
    Crowned my felicity,
When I could say without a crime,
    I am not thine, but thee.
5   This carcass breathed, and walked, and slept,
    So that the world believed
There was a soul the motions kept;
    But they were all deceived.
For as a watch by art is wound
10   To motion, such was mine:
But never had Orinda found
    A soul till she found thine;
Which now inspires, cures and supplies,
    And guides my darkened breast:
15 For thou art all that I can prize,
    My joy, my life, my rest.
Nor bridegroom's nor crowned conqueror's mirth
    To mine compared can be:
They have but pieces of this earth,
20   I've all the world in thee.
Then let our flame still light and shine,
    (And no bold fear control)
As innocent as our design,
    Immortal as our soul.

1. Philips met her friend Anne Owen (called Lucasia) in 1651.

The World

We falsely think it due unto our friends,
That we should grieve for their too early ends:
He that surveys the world with serious eyes,
And strips her from her gross and weak disguise,[1]
5   Shall find 'tis injury to mourn their fate;
He only dies untimely who dies late.
For if 'twere told to children in the womb,
To what a stage of mischief they must come;
Could they foresee with how much toil and sweat
10   Men court that gilded nothing, being great;
What pains they take not to be what they seem,
Rating their bliss by others' false esteem,
And sacrificing their content, to be
Guilty of grave and serious vanity;
15   How each condition hath its proper thorns,
And what one man admires, another scorns;
How frequently their happiness they miss,
And so far from agreeing what it is,
That the same person we can hardly find,
20   Who is an hour together in a mind;
Sure they would beg a period of their breath,
And what we call their birth would count their death.
Mankind is mad; for none can live alone,
Because their joys stand by comparison:
25   And yet they quarrel at society,
And strive to kill they know not whom, nor why.
We all live by mistake, delight in dreams,
Lost to ourselves, and dwelling in extremes;
Rejecting what we have, though ne'er so good,
30   And prizing what we never understood.
Compared to our boisterous inconstancy
Tempests are calm, and discords harmony.
Hence we reverse the world, and yet do find
The God that made can hardly please our mind.
35   We live by chance, and slip into events;
Have all of beasts except their innocence.
The soul, which no man's power can reach, a thing
That makes each woman man, each man a king,
Doth so much loose, and from its height so fall,
40   That some contend to have no soul at all.
'Tis either not observed, or at the best
By passion fought withall, by sin depressed.
Freedom of will (God's image) is forgot;
And if we know it, we improve it not.
45   Our thoughts, though nothing can be more our own,
Are still unguided, very seldom known.
Time 'scapes our hands as water in a sieve,
We come to die ere we begin to live.

---

1. The Platonic notion that the body is a covering for the soul.

Truth, the most suitable and noble prize,
50   Food of our spirits, yet neglected lies.
Errors and shadows are our choice, and we
Owe our perdition to our own decree.
If we search truth, we make it more obscure;
And when it shines, we can't the light endure.
55   For most men who plod on, and eat, and drink,
Have nothing less their business than to think;
And those few that enquire, how small a share
Of truth they find! how dark their notions are!
That serious evenness that calms the breast,
60   And in a tempest can bestow a rest,
We either not attempt, or else decline,
By every trifle snatched from our design.
(Others he must in his deceits involve,
Who is not true unto his own resolve.)
65   We govern not ourselves, but loose the reins,
Courting our bondage to a thousand chains;
And with as many slaveries content,
As there are tyrants ready to torment,
We live upon a rack, extended still
70   To one extreme, or both, but always ill.
For since our fortune is not understood,
We suffer less from bad than from the good.
The sting is better dressed and longer lasts,
As surfeits are more dangerous than fasts.
75   And to complete the misery to us,
We see extremes are still contiguous.
And as we run so fast from what we hate,
Like squibs on ropes,[2] to know no middle state;
So (outward storms strengthened by us) we find
80   Our fortune as disordered as our mind.
But that's excused by this, it doth its part;
A treacherous world befits a treacherous heart.
All ill's our own; the outward storms we loathe
Receive from us their birth, or sting, or both;
85   And that our vanity be past a doubt,
'Tis one new vanity to find it out.
Happy are they to whom God gives a grave,
And from themselves as from his wrath doth save.
'Tis good not to be born; but if we must,
90   The next good is, soon to return to dust:
When th'uncaged[3] soul, fled to eternity,
Shall rest, and live, and sing, and love, and see.
Here we but crawl and grope, and play and cry;[4]
Are first our own, then other's enemy:
95   But there shall be defaced both stain and score,
For time, and death, and sin shall be no more.[5]

---

2. A display of fireworks on a line.   4. Paraphrasing 1 Corinthians 13.11–12.
3. Free from the body.   5. As promised in Revelation 21.4.

The Execution of Charles I, engraved by C. R. V. N. 17th-century German print.

≒ PERSPECTIVES ≒

The Civil War, or the Wars of Three Kingdoms

The English Civil War arose out of citizens' revolutionary demands for their rights and those of their legislature, and out of England's attempt to dominate Ireland and Scotland. The armed conflicts that arose from the demand for political self-determination in every part of the British Isles would have consequences for centuries to come. During the period from 1639 to 1651, war raged not only in England but also in Ireland, Scotland, and Wales; hence, historians now prefer to call this period of conflict the Wars of Three Kingdoms. The origins of the conflict in England were between Parliament and a King who had an absolutist style of governing. Charles I reigned without Parliament from 1629 to 1640, a period referred to as the "Eleven Years' Tyranny." He also imposed unpopular heavy taxes in the form of ship money levies to build up the fleet. Even more controversial was his imposition of Anglican worship and episcopal authority on Puritans and Presbyterians, who felt that such ritual was tantamount to Roman Catholicism. The King placed two Anglican bishops on the court of Star Chamber, who used the arbitrary power of this body to enforce unpopular religious practices.

When the King decided to impose an Anglican liturgy on the Scottish Kirk in 1639, riots broke out in Edinburgh, and Scottish Lowlanders united in a National Covenant against

English interference. In 1639 and 1640, Scottish military uprisings necessitated Charles I's recalling Parliament to ask for financial aid. The Parliament was already angered by the eleven-year shutdown by the King, his imposition of taxes without its consent, and his support for Archbishop Laud, whom Parliament viewed as too dictatorial and too high church, shutting out both Puritans (who elected their ministers and disdained Catholic sacraments) and Presbyterians (who favored central church government but not Anglo-Catholic authority or ritual). When Parliament refused after three weeks to grant the King's request for money, the King decided to dissolve the "Short Parliament." In the wake of the dissolution of Parliament, soldiers went on rampages against churches, smashing stained glass windows and altar rails that smacked to them of Roman Catholicism. In some places, soldiers mutinied against their aristocratic commanders.

When the Scots defeated the King's army in the fall of 1640, he had to recall Parliament to petition for more funds. Led by John Pym, the "Long Parliament" seized the opportunity to criticize the King. It passed a Bill of Attainder, condemning to death as a traitor the general of the King's army, Viscount Strafford, who had been accused of instigating the war against Scotland and of suggesting that an Irish Catholic army could be used against England. No proof of guilt was necessary, only assent from the House of Lords and the King. Despite the King's reluctance, the combined opposition of the House of Commons and armed mobs in London in the spring of 1641 pressured him into signing Strafford's death warrant.

That fall two rebellions broke out in Ireland—one organized by Catholic Irish gentry, another arising more spontaneously among the native Gaelic Irish in Ulster against Scots and English settlers who had dispossessed them of their land. Pym blamed the unrest on the King and his Catholic court. Although there was terrible violence, especially in the popular uprisings, the English press wildly exaggerated the extent of the bloodshed, claiming a figure for Protestant deaths in the North of Ireland that was greater than the number of Protestants then living in the whole country. Pym, the leader of the House of Commons, moved that Parliament should offer no help in repressing Irish rebellion unless Charles agreed to dismiss his guilty counselors. The next day, Oliver Cromwell moved that the Parliament empower the Puritan Earl of Essex to head the English militia. Attacks on the King became stronger: his irresponsibility and violation of the security and rights of the people mandated Parliament's wresting power from him. On May 12, Archbishop Laud was executed. Although the King made some concessions, by January 1642 he decided to impeach Pym, four other members of Commons, and one from the House of Lords for treason. However, the accused were safely hidden in the City, and the King left London, not to return until he was put on trial and beheaded seven years later. Just on the eve of the outbreak of the war, the "Gentlewomen and Tradesmen's Wives of London" presented their petition to Parliament, complaining against Archbishop Laud's Anglicanism and the threat of violence from Ireland. The first part of the English Civil War (1642–1646), arising from the disputes between Parliament and the King, culminated in the victory of Parliament's New Model Army, headed by Sir Thomas Fairfax.

With the King defeated by the combined forces of the New Model Army and the Scots Covenanters in 1646, new conflicts arose between the army and the Parliament. Closely tied to the army, the Levellers, led by John Lilburne, agitated for a fundamental revision of the constitution: a single representative body, universal suffrage for men, and the abolition of monarchy and noble privilege. Colonel Ludlow, a leader of the republicans, opposed any negotiations with the King and petitioned Parliament to reform the constitution and to put the King on trial. When the House of Commons refused to listen to the army and continued to negotiate with the King, Colonels Ludlow, Ireton, and Pride purged Parliament, placing forty-five members under arrest and prohibiting another 186 from entering the House. This Rump Parliament set up a high court to try the King. On 27 January 1649, Charles I was condemned to death as a tyrant and traitor who had shed the blood of his people. John Bradshaw, President of the Court, proclaimed that the King was subject to the law and the law proceeded from Parliament. Arising out of these events came both the King's own memoir, *Eikon Basilike* ("the Royal Image"), ghostwritten and published after his execution by John Gauden, and Milton's militantly republican response *Eikonoklastes* ("Image-Breaker").

In the last stage of the civil war, the dead king's son, Charles II, attempted to regain power through Irish and Scottish aid. In Ireland the Marquis of Ormonde led a coalition of royalists that secured the support of Irish troops for the King in exchange for the free exercise of Catholicism. Before Charles II could land in Dublin, the English sent troops there to put down the uprising. Cromwell slaughtered many at the siege of Drogheda; his campaign throughout Munster killed many civilians. In the aftermath of Cromwell's conquest, what remained of an Irish intelligentsia was either exiled or killed off, and large numbers of native inhabitants were either thrown off their land onto poorer farming land in western Ireland or sent into indentured servitude in the Caribbean. Following policies begun by Elizabeth and James, Cromwell granted Irish land to English settlers. The late events of the war in Ireland are represented here by one of Cromwell's letters from his campaign in Ireland, and by *John O'Dwyer of the Glenn*, a translation of one of the many Irish-language laments for the devastation of the Cromwellian conquest.

In Scotland, Charles II found allies among Presbyterian Covenanters, infuriated with the English Parliament for executing a Scottish monarch, and in the Marquis of Montrose, who recruited the Highland clans. When the Covenanters met with Charles II for the Treaty of Breda in Holland, they imposed on him a promise to reestablish Presbyterianism as the religion of both England and Scotland, to reinstate the Scottish Parliament, and to repudiate his pledges to Ormonde and Montrose. When Charles landed in Scotland, he learned that Montrose, most loyal of all royalists, had been hanged and quartered as a traitor. The Covenanters, fighting for Scotland rather than for the King, were defeated by Cromwell at Dunbar. The Scots' losses were so huge that Scottish royalism was revived for one last battle between the King's Cavaliers and Cromwell's Roundheads. Facing Cromwell's army at Worcester in 1651, the forces of Scots and English royalists were vastly outnumbered and easily defeated. Charles II escaped to France, where he remained until the Restoration. Two years later, Cromwell became Lord Protector of the Commonwealth.

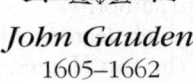

John Gauden
1605–1662

John Gauden wrote the most influential account of the royalist cause, *Eikon Basilike* ("Royal Portrait"), advance copies of which were sold on the day of Charles I's execution in 1649. Although Gauden at first sided with Parliament and the Presbyterians, he did not agree to the abolition of the bishops. In 1647 supporters of Charles I, then confined at Hampton Court by Parliament, sought Gauden's help to revise the King's meditations for publication. When the manuscript was complete, Gauden showed it to the King, who hesitated about having it published under his name. Meanwhile, the King was preoccupied first by his attempts to escape and then by his confinement, trial, and execution. When Royston first printed the book in January 1649, he believed that King Charles was the author. Just months later, William Duggard published another edition based on a manuscript that had been revised by the King; Gauden's authorship remained publically unknown until 1690.

Throughout the Interregnum, Gauden managed to keep his deanery at Brockton by conforming to Presbyterianism. With the Restoration in 1660, he was made Bishop of Exeter. In letters to Sir Edward Hyde, Gauden admitted his authorship and complained that his reward had not been sufficient. He was then promoted to the bishopric of Worcester, just a year before his death.

Eikon Basilike was written to influence public opinion and to guide the Prince of Wales, who waited in exile to regain his father's throne. A collection of meditations written in a lofty style, *Eikon Basilike* justified the King's views and evoked sympathy for his plight. The emblematic frontispiece shows the King in a saintly light—kneeling in prayer. Admirers of the work called it "most charitable, most heavenly" and "most pious, most ravishing." By the end of 1649, thirty-five editions had been printed in England. The most important of these, that of March 1649, added the King's prayers, the Prince of Wales's letter to his father, and an epitaph on the King's death. An English-language edition was published in Ireland in 1649, and twenty foreign-language editions were published on the Continent for the English community in exile as well as their European supporters.

The text aroused both support and criticism. Parliament had the printer Duggard arrested but released him when he produced a license to publish the book. Parliament prohibited the further sale of the book in May 1649, but by the end of 1649, five clandestine editions and two responses had appeared. *The Princely Pellican* explained how Charles had come to write the book, and *Eikon Alethine* attacked it as a fraud. Milton wrote his own rebuttal in *Eikonoklastes*, a savagely satirical prosecution of the King. *Eikonoklastes* merely went through two editions, showing that it could not compete in popularity with *Eikon Basilike*.

from Eikon Basilike
from Chapter 4. Upon the Insolency of the Tumults

I never thought anything, except our sins, more ominously presaging all these mischiefs which have followed, than those tumults in London and Westminster soon after the convening of this Parliament which were not like a storm at sea, (which yet wants not its terror,) but like an earthquake, shaking the very foundation of all; than which nothing in the world hath more of horror.

As it is one of the most convincing arguments that there is a God, while His power sets bounds to the raging of the sea, so it is no less that He restrains the madness of the people. Nor does anything portend more God's displeasure against a nation than when He suffers the confluence and clamors of the vulgar to pass all boundaries of laws and reverence to authority.

Which those tumults did to so high degrees of insolence, that they spared not to invade the honor and freedom of the two Houses, menacing, reproaching, shaking, yea, and assaulting some members of both Houses as they fancied or disliked them; nor did they forbear most rude and unseemly deportments, both in contemptuous words and actions, to myself and my court.

Nor was this a short fit or two of shaking, as an ague, but a quotidian fever, always increasing to higher inflammations, impatient of any mitigation, restraint, or remission.

First, they must be a guard against those fears which some men scared themselves and others withal; when, indeed, nothing was more to be feared, and less to be used by wise men, than those tumultuary confluxes of mean and rude people who are taught first to petition, then to protect, then to dictate, at last to command and overawe the Parliament.

All obstructions of Parliament, that is, all freedom of differing in votes, and debating matters with reason and candor, must be taken away with these tumults. By these must the Houses be purged, and all rotten members (as they pleased to count them) cast out; by these the obstinacy of men, resolved to discharge their consciences, must be subdued; by these all factious, seditious, and schismatical proposals against government, ecclesiastical or civil, must be backed and abetted till they prevailed.

Generally, whoever had most mind to bring forth confusion and ruin upon Church and State used the midwifery of those tumults, whose riot and impatience was such as they would not stay the ripening and season of counsels, or fair production of acts, in the order, gravity, and deliberateness befitting a Parliament, but ripped up with barbarous cruelty, and forcibly cut out abortive notes, such as their inviters and encouragers most fancied.

Yea, so enormous and detestable were their outrages, that no sober man could be without infinite shame and sorrow to see them so tolerated and connived at by some, countenanced, encouraged, and applauded by others.

What good man had not rather want anything he most desired for the public good, than obtain it by such unlawful and irreligious means? But men's passions and God's directions seldom agree; violent designs and motions must have suitable engines; such as too much attend their own ends, seldom confine themselves to God's means. Force must crowd in what reason will not lead.

Who were the chief demagogues and patrons of tumults, to send for them, to flatter and embolden them, to direct and tune their clamorous importunities, some men yet living are too conscious to pretend ignorance. God in His due time will let these see that those were no fit means to be used for attaining His ends.

But as it is no strange thing for the sea to rage when strong winds blow upon it, so neither for multitudes to become insolent when they have men of some reputation for parts and piety to set them on.

That which made their rudeness most formidable was, that many complaints being made, and messages sent by myself and some of both Houses yet no order for redress could be obtained with any vigor and efficacy proportionable to the malignity of that now far-spread disease and predominant mischief.

Such was some men's stupidity, that they feared no inconvenience; others' petulancy, that they joyed to see their betters shamefully outraged and abused, while they knew their only security consisted in vulgar flattery, so insensible were they of mine or the two Houses common safety and honors.

Nor could ever any order be obtained impartially to examine, censure, and punish the known boutefeus[1] and impudent incendiaries, who boasted of the influence they had, and used to convoke those tumults as their advantages served.

Yea some, who should have been wiser statesmen, owned them as friends, commending their courage, zeal, and industry, which to sober men could seem no better than that of the devil, who goes about seeking whom he may deceive and devour.

I confess, when I found such a deafness, that no declaration from the bishops, who were first foully insolenced and assaulted, nor yet from other lords and gentlemen of honor, nor yet from myself, could take place for the due repression of these tumults, and securing not only our freedom in Parliament, but our very persons in the streets; I thought myself not bound by my presence to provoke them to higher boldness and contempts; I hoped by my withdrawing[2] to give time both for the ebbing of their tumultuous fury, and others regaining some degrees of modesty and sober sense.

Some may interpret it as an effect of pusillanimity[3] in any man, for popular terrors, to desert his public station; but I think it is hardiness beyond true valor for a wise man to set himself against the breaking in of a sea, which to resist at present

---

1. Firebrands.
2. Charles decided to flee from London on the night of 10 January 1642 in response to rioting that erupted as a result of his failed attempts to arrest the five opposition leaders in the House of Commons. Charles returned to Whitehall only as a prisoner just before his execution.
3. Cowardice.

threatens imminent danger, but to withdraw gives it space to spend its fury, and gains a fitter time to repair the breach. Certainly a gallant man had rather fight to great disadvantages for number and place in the field in an orderly way, than scuffle with an undisciplined rabble.

Some suspected and affirmed that I meditated a war, when I went from Whitehall only to redeem my person and conscience from violence: God knows I did not then think of a war. Nor will any prudent man conceive that I would, by so many former and some after acts, have so much weakened myself if I had purposed to engage in a war, which to decline by all means I denied myself in so many particulars. It is evident I had then no army to fly unto for protection and vindication.

Who can blame me, or any other, for withdrawing ourselves from the daily baitings of the tumults, not knowing whether their fury and discontent might not fly so high as to worry and tear those in pieces whom as yet they but played with in their paws? God, who is my sole judge, is my witness in heaven that I never had any thoughts of my going from my house at Whitehall if I could have had but any reasonable fair quarter. I was resolved to bear much, and did so; but I did not think myself bound to prostitute the majesty of my place and person, the safety of my wife and children, to those who are prone to insult most when they have objects and opportunity most capable of their rudeness and petulancy.

But this business of the tumults, whereof some have given already an account to God, others yet living know themselves desperately guilty, time and the guilt of many has so smothered up and buried, that I think it best to leave it as it is; only I believe the just avenger of all disorders will in time make those men and that city see their sin in the glass of their punishment. It is more than an even lay, that they may one day see themselves punished by that way they offended.

Had this Parliament, as it was in its first election and constitution, sat full and free, the members of both Houses, being left to their freedom of voting, as in all reason, honor, and religion they should have been, I doubt not but things would have been so carried as would have given no less good content to all good men than they wished or expected.

For I was resolved to hear reason in all things, and to consent to it as far as I could comprehend it; but as swine are to gardens and orderly plantations, so are tumults to Parliaments, and plebeian concourses to public counsels, turning all into disorders and sordid confusions.

I am prone sometimes to think that had I called this Parliament to any other place in England, as I might opportunely enough have done, the sad consequences in all likelihood, with God's blessing, might have been prevented. A Parliament would have been welcome in any place; no place afforded such confluence of various and vicious humors as that where it was unhappily convened. But we must leave all to God, who orders our disorders, and magnifies His wisdom most when our follies and miseries are most discovered.

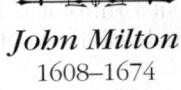

John Milton
1608–1674

With the popularity of the royalist tract *Eikon Basilike* after the execution of Charles I, the new Puritan government needed to find someone to defend its cause against the growing support for the King. The Puritans found their man in the newly appointed Secretary for Foreign

Tongues to the Council of State, John Milton. In *Eikonoklastes* ("Image Breaker"), Milton focused his attack on the arguments of *Eikon Basilike* more than on its authorship. He doubted whether the King wrote his own defense, but he chose to concentrate on a chapter-by-chapter refutation of the book's account of history—in terms of both events and the perspective on them. Milton also revealed that one the prayers attributed to the King was really Pamela's prayer from Sir Philip Sidney's prose romance *Arcadia*. For the Puritan Milton this was a shocking piece of paganism and plagiarism by one who presented himself as pious. Milton's language in *Eikonoklastes* is iconoclastic—mocking and sarcastic, marked by invective and sharply stinging *ad hominem* argument. One royalist called *Eikonoklastes* a "blackguardly book" in which Milton "blows his viper's breath upon those immortal devotions." Some royalists even viewed Milton's blindness as God's punishment for his having attacked the King. Shortly after the Restoration of Charles II in 1660, the House of Commons ordered the burning of *Eikonoklastes* and had Milton arrested. He was imprisoned for several months before being released through the aid of his friend Andrew Marvell. *Eikonklastes* was first published in October 1649; the second and final edition in Milton's lifetime appeared in 1650.

For more about Milton, see his principal listing, page 894.

from Eikonoklastes

from Chapter 1. Upon the King's Calling This Last Parliament

"The odium and offenses which some men's rigor, or remissness in church and state had contracted upon his government, he resolved to have expiated with better laws and regulations." And yet the worst of misdemeanors committed by the worst of all his favorites, in the height of their dominion, whether acts of rigor or remissness, he hath from time to time continued, owned, and taken upon himself by public declarations, as often as the clergy, or any other of his instruments felt themselves overburdened with the people's hatred. And who knows not the superstitious rigor of his Sunday's chapel, and the licentious remissness of his Sunday's theater;[1] accompanied with that reverend statute for dominical jigs and maypoles,[2] published in his own name, and derived from the example of his father James? Which testifies all that rigor in superstition, all that remissness in religion to have issued out originally from his own house, and from his own authority.

Much rather then may those general miscarriages in State, his proper sphere, be imputed to no other person chiefly than to himself. And which of all those oppressive acts, or impositions did he ever disclaim or disavow, till the fatal awe of this Parliament hung ominously over him. Yet here he smoothly seeks to wipe off all the envy of his evil government upon his substitutes, and under-officers: and promises, though much too late, what wonders he purposed to have done in the reforming of religion—a work wherein all his undertakings heretofore declare him to have had little or no judgment. Neither could his breeding, or his course of life acquaint him with a thing so spiritual. Which may well assure us what kind of reformation we could expect from him; either some politic form of an imposed religion, or else perpetual vexation, and persecution to all those that complied not with such a form.

The like amendment he promises in State; not a step further "than his reason and conscience told him was fit to be desired"; wishing "he had kept within those bounds, and not suffered his own judgment to have been overborne in some things,"

---

1. While observers such as the Spanish ambassador noted Charles's sincere piety, Milton considered traditional ritual "superstitious," ironically linking it to irreligious theater life. Like the Puritans, Milton abhorred Sunday theater performances, and in *Of Reformation*, he attacked the bishops for promoting "gaming, jigging, wassailing,

and mixed dancing" on Sundays.
2. The *Book of Sports* (1633) forbade bearbaiting and bullbaiting on Sundays, but also rebuked the Puritans for condemning other forms of recreation such as dancing and archery.

of which things one was the Earl of Strafford's execution.[3] And what signifies all this, but that still his resolution was the same, to set up an arbitrary government of his own; and that all Britain was to be tied and chained to the conscience, judgment, and reason of one man; as if those gifts had been only his peculiar and prerogative, entailed upon him with his fortune to be a king? When as doubtless no man so obstinate, or so much a tyrant, but professes to be guided by that which he calls his reason, and his judgment, though never so corrupted; and pretends also his conscience. In the meanwhile, for any Parliament or the whole nation to have either reason, judgment, or conscience, by this rule was altogether in vain, if it thwarted the king's will; which was easy for him to call by any other more plausible name. He himself hath many times acknowledged to have no right over us but by law; and by the same law to govern us: but law in a free nation hath been ever public reason, the enacted reason of a Parliament; which he denying to enact, denies to govern us by that which ought to be our law; interposing his own private reason, which to us is no law. And thus we find these fair and specious promises, made upon the experience of many hard sufferings, and his most mortified retirements, being thoroughly sifted, to contain nothing in them much different from his former practices, so cross, and so averse to all his Parliaments, and both the nations of this island. What fruits they could in likelihood have produced in his restorement, is obvious to any prudent foresight.

And this is the substance of his first section, till we come to the devout of it, modeled into the form of a private psalter. Which they who so much admire, either for the matter or the manner, may as well admire the archbishop's late breviary,[4] and many other as good *Manuals*, and *Handmaids of Devotion*, the lip-work of every prelatical liturgist, clapped together, and quilted out of Scripture phrase, with as much ease, and as little need of Christian diligence, or judgment, as belongs to the compiling of any ordinary and salable piece of English divinity, that the shops value. But he who from such a kind of psalmistry, or any other verbal devotion, without the pledge and earnest of suitable deeds, can be persuaded of a zeal, and true righteousness in the person, hath much yet to learn; and knows not that the deepest policy of a tyrant hath been ever to counterfeit religious. And Aristotle in his *Politics*, hath mentioned that special craft among twelve other tyrannical sophisms.[5] Neither want we examples. Andronicus Comnenus the Byzantine Emperor, though a most cruel tyrant, is reported by Nicetas[6] to have been a constant reader of Saint Paul's Epistles; and by continual study had so incorporated the phrase and style of that transcendent apostle into all his familiar letters, that the imitation seemed to vie with the original. Yet this availed not to deceive the people of that empire; who notwithstanding his saint's vizard, tore him to pieces for his tyranny.

From stories of this nature both ancient and modern which abound, the poets also, and some English, have been in this point so mindful of decorum, as to put never more pious words in the mouth of any person, than of a tyrant. I shall not instance an abstruse author, wherein the King might be less conversant, but one whom we

3. Thomas Wentworth, Earl of Strafford, was executed in May 1641. Charles had recalled Strafford from the Lord Deputyship in Ireland to help with the war against the Scots Covenanters. Parliament accused Wentworth of planning to use the Irish army to suppress the King's opponents in Scotland and England. Even though Strafford was successfully defended against the charges, Charles signed his death warrant, fearing retaliation against himself and the Queen for their part in a plot to rescue Strafford.
4. Milton's name for Archbishop Laud's *Prayer Book*, which the Puritans hated because of its similarity to Roman Catholic ritual.
5. See Aristotle, *Politics* 5.9.15, for the notion that care in religious ritual is a device of tyrants.
6. A 12th-century historian who recorded the cruelty of Comnenus's reign (1183–1185).

well know was the closet companion of these his solitudes, William Shakespeare, who introduces the person of Richard the Third, speaking in as high a strain of piety, and mortification, as is uttered in any passage of this book, and sometimes to the same sense and purpose with some words in this place, "I intended," saith he, "not only to oblige my friends but mine enemies." The like saith Richard, Act 2. Scene 1,

> I do not know that Englishman alive
> With whom my soul is any jot at odds,
> More than the infant that is born tonight;
> I thank my God for my humility.

Other stuff of this sort may be read throughout the whole tragedy, wherein the poet used not much license in departing from the truth of history, which delivers him a deep dissembler, not of his affections only, but of religion.

from *Chapter 4. Upon the Insolency of the Tumults*

And that the King was so emphatical and elaborate on this theme against tumults, and expressed with such a vehemence his hatred of them, will redound less perhaps, than he was aware, to the commendation of his government. For besides that in good governments they happen seldomest, and rise not without cause, if they prove extreme and pernicious, they were never counted so to monarchy, but to monarchical tyranny; and extremes one with another are at most antipathy. If then the King so extremely stood in fear of tumults, the inference will endanger him to be the other extreme. Thus far the occasion of this discourse against tumults; now to the discourse itself, voluble enough, and full of sentence,[1] but that, for the most part, either specious rather than solid, or to his cause nothing pertinent.

"He never thought any thing more to presage the mischiefs that ensued, than those tumults." Then was his foresight but short, and much mistaken. Those tumults were but the mild effects of an evil and injurious reign; not signs of mischiefs to come, but seeking relief for mischiefs past; those signs were to be read more apparent in his rage and purposed revenge of those free expostulations, and clamors of the people against his lawless government. "Not any thing," saith he, "portends more God's displeasure against a nation than when he suffers the clamors of the vulgar to pass all bounds of law & reverence to authority." It portends rather his displeasure against a tyrannous King, whose proud throne he intends to overturn by that contemptible vulgar; the sad cries and oppressions of whom his royalty regarded not. As for that supplicating people they did no hurt either to law or authority, but stood for it rather in the Parliament against whom they feared would violate it.

That "they invaded the honor and freedom of the two Houses," is his own officious accusation, not seconded by the Parliament, who had they seen cause, were themselves best able to complain. And if they "shook & menaced" any, they were such as had more relation to the Court, than to the Commonwealth; enemies, not patrons of the people. But if their petitioning unarmed were an invasion of both Houses, what was his entrance into the House of Commons, besetting it with armed men, in what condition then was the honor, and freedom of that House?

"They forbore not rude deportments, contemptuous words and actions to himself and his Court."

---

1. Significance, meaning.

It was more wonder, having heard what treacherous hostility he had designed against the city, and his whole kingdom, that they forbore to handle him as people in their rage have handled tyrants heretofore for less offenses.

"They were not a short ague, but a fierce quotidian fever:" He indeed may best say it, who most felt it; for the shaking was within him; and it shook him by his own description "worse than a storm, worse then an earthquake, Belshazzar's Palsy."[2] Had not worse fears, terrors, and envies made within him that commotion, how could a multitude of his subjects, armed with no other weapon then petitions, have shaken all his joints with such a terrible ague. Yet that the Parliament should entertain the least fear of bad intentions from him or his party, he endures not; but would persuade us that "men scare themselves and others without cause;" for he thought fear would be to them a kind of armor, and his design was, if it were possible, to disarm all, especially of a wise fear and suspicion; for that he knew would find weapons.

He goes on therefore with vehemence to repeat the mischiefs done by these tumults. "They first petitioned, then protected, dictate next, and lastly overawe the Parliament. They removed obstructions, they purged the Houses, cast out rotten members." If there were a man of iron, such as Talus, by our poet Spenser, is feigned to be the page of Justice, who with his iron flail could do all this, and expeditiously, without those deceitful forms and circumstances of law, worse than ceremonies in religion; I say God send it down, whether by one Talus, or by a thousand.[3]

"But they subdued the men of conscience in Parliament, backed and abetted all seditious and schismatical proposals against government ecclesiastical and civil."

Now we may perceive the root of his hatred whence it springs. It was not the King's grace or princely goodness, but this iron flail the people, that drove the bishops out of their baronies, out of their cathedrals, out of the Lord's house, out of their copes and surplices, and all those papistical innovations,[4] threw down the High Commission and Star Chamber, gave us a triennial Parliament, and what we most desired;[5] in revenge whereof he now so bitterly inveighs against them; these are those seditious and schismatical proposals, then by him condescended to, as acts of grace, now of another name; which declares him, touching matters of Church and State, to have been no other man in the deepest of his solitude, than he was before at the highest of his sovereignty.

But this was not the worst of these tumults, they played the hasty "midwives," and "would not stay the ripening, but went straight to ripping up, and forcibly cut out abortive votes."

They would not stay perhaps the Spanish demurring, and putting off such wholesome acts and counsels, as the politic cabin at Whitehall had no mind to. But all this is complained here as done to the Parliament, and yet we heard not the Par-

2. In *Of Reformation*, Milton compares the feasting of Anglican bishops to that of Belshazzar in his palace in Babylon on the eve of the fall of the city to the Medes and Persians. When King Belshazzar saw the mysterious writing on the wall that foretold his doom, "the joints of his loins were loosed, and his knees smote one against another" (Daniel 5.6).
3. Talus is the iron flail who ruthlessly cuts down all who oppose Artegal, the Knight of Justice, in Spenser's *Faerie Queene* 5, much of which is about the subjugation of Ireland by England.
4. Milton refers to the London petition calling for the abolition of the bishops' power, introduced into Parliament in December 1640, that resulted in their exclusion from the House of Lords.
5. The High Commission, the highest ecclesiastical court, investigated such matters as heresy, recusancy, and any writing against the Book of Common Prayer; Parliament abolished it on 5 July 1641. The Star Chamber was also abolished because it was viewed as a special tool of government favoring the special right of the sovereign above all other persons and the common law. A triennial Parliament is a parliament convened every three years.

liament at that time complain of any violence from the people, but from him. Wherefore intrudes he to plead the cause of Parliament against the people, while the Parliament was pleading their own cause against him; and against him were forced to seek refuge of the people? 'Tis plain then that those confluxes and resorts interrupted not the Parliament, nor by them were thought tumultuous, but by him only and his court faction.

"But what good Man had not rather want any thing he most desired for the public good, than attain it by such unlawful and irreligious means;" as much as to say, had not rather sit still and let his country be tyrannized, than that the people, finding no other remedy, should stand up like men and demand their rights and liberties. This is the artificialest piece of fineness to persuade men into slavery that the wit of court could have invented. But hear how much better the moral of this lesson would befit the teacher. What good man had not rather want a boundless and arbitrary power, and those fine flowers of the crown, called prerogatives, than for them to use force and perpetual vexation to his faithful subjects, nay to wade for them through blood and civil war? So that this and the whole bundle of those following sentences may be applied better to the convincement of his own violent courses, than of those pretended tumults.

"Who were the chief demagogues to send for those tumults, some alive are not ignorant." Setting aside the affrightment of this goblin word; for the King by his leave cannot coin English as he could money, to be current (and tis believed this wording was above his known style and orthography, and accuses the whole composure to be conscious of some other author)[6] yet if the people "were sent for, emboldened and directed" by those "demagogues," who, saving his Greek, were good patriots, and by his own confession "Men of some repute for parts and piety," it helps well to assure us there was both urgent cause, and the less danger of their coming.

"Complaints were made, yet no redress could be obtained." The Parliament also complained of what danger they sat in from another party, and demanded of him a guard, but it was not granted. What marvel then if it cheered them to see some store of their friends, and in the Roman not the pettifogging sense, their clients so near about them; a defense due by nature both from whom it was offered, and to whom; as due as to their parents; though the Court stormed, and fretted to see such honor given to them, who were then best fathers of the Commonwealth. And both the Parliament and people complained, and demanded justice for those assaults, if not murders done at his own doors, by that crew of rufflers, but he, instead of doing justice on them, justified and abetted them in what they did, as in his public "Answer to a Petition from the City" may be read. Neither is it slightly to be passed over, that in the very place where blood was first drawn in this cause, as the beginning of all that followed, there was his own blood shed by the executioner. According to that sentence of divine justice, "In the place where dogs licked the blood of Naboth, shall dogs lick thy blood, even thine."

From hence he takes occasion to excuse that improvident and fatal error of his absenting from the Parliament. "When he found that no declaration of the bishops could take place against those tumults." Was that worth his considering, that foolish and self-undoing declaration of twelve cypher bishops, who were immediately

6. Milton believed that Charles I could not have written *Eikon Basilike* because such passages as this one showed a word choice and style different from Charles's.

appeached of treason for that audacious declaring?[7] The bishops peradventure were now and then pulled by the rochets,[8] and deserved another kind of pulling; but what amounted this to "the fear of his own person in the streets"? Did he not the very next day after his irruption into the House of Commons, than which nothing had more exasperated the people, go in his coach unguarded into the city? did he receive the least affront, much less violence in any of the streets, but rather humble demeanors, and supplications? Hence may be gathered, that however in his own guiltiness he might have justly feared, yet that he knew the people so full of awe and reverence to his person, as to dare commit himself single among the thickest of them, at a time when he had most provoked them. Besides in Scotland they had handled the Bishops in a more robustious manner; Edinburgh had been full of tumults,[9] two armies from thence had entered England against him;[1] yet after all this, he was not fearful, but very forward to take so long a journey to Edinburgh;[2] which argues first, as did also his rendition afterward to the Scotch Army,[3] that to England he continued still, as he was indeed, a stranger, and full of diffidence; to the Scots only a native King,[4] in his confidence, though not in his dealing towards them. It shows us next beyond doubting, that all this his fear of tumults was but a mere color and occasion taken of his resolved absence from the Parliament, for some other end not difficult to be guessed. And those instances wherein valor is not to be questioned for not "scuffling with the sea, or an undisciplined rabble," are but subservient to carry on the solemn jest of his fearing tumults: if they discover not withall, the true reason why he departed; only to turn his slashing at the court gate, to slaughtering "in the field"; his disorderly bickering, to an orderly invading: which was nothing else but a more orderly disorder.

"Some suspected and affirmed, that he meditated a War when he went first from Whitehall." And they were not the worst heads that did so, nor did "any of his former acts weaken him" to that, as he alleges for himself, or if they had, they clear him only for the time of passing them, not for what ever thoughts might come after into his mind. Former actions of improvidence or fear, not with him unusual, cannot absolve him of all after meditations.

He goes on protesting his "no intention to have left Whitehall," had these horrid tumults given him but "fair quarter," as if he himself, his wife and children had been in peril. But to this enough hath been answered.

"Had this Parliament as it was in its first election," namely, with the Lord and Baron Bishops, "sat full and free," he doubts not but all had gone well. What warrant this of his to us? Whose not doubting was all good men's greatest doubt.

"He was resolved to hear reason, and to consent so far as he could comprehend." A hopeful resolution; what if his reason were found by oft experience to comprehend nothing beyond his own advantages, was this a reason fit to be intrusted with the common good of three nations?

---

7. The Bishops' Exclusion Bill was Parliament's reaction to the assertion by 12 bishops that any legislation passed by the House of Lords when the bishops were absent was void.
8. Vestments.
9. When Charles attempted to force the Book of Common Prayer on the Scottish churches, the people rioted.
1. The first Scottish war ended with the Treaty of Berwick in June 1639, the second with the Treaty of Ripon in October 1640.
2. Charles went to Edinburgh in 1641, hoping to pit the Covenanters against their opponents.
3. Charles surrendered himself to the Scottish army commanders in May 1646.
4. Charles was born in Scotland, and he made special appeals to the Scots to be their king in both 1641 and 1646.

"But," saith he, "as swine are to gardens, so are tumults to Parliaments." This the Parliament, had they found it so, could best have told us. In the meanwhile, who knows not that one great hog may do as much mischief in a garden, as many little swine.[5]

"He was sometimes prone to think that had he called this last Parliament to any other place in England, the sad consequences might have been prevented." But change of air changes not the mind. Was not his first Parliament at Oxford dissolved after two subsidies given him, and no justice received? Was not his last in the same place, where they sat with as much freedom, as much quiet from tumults, as they could desire, a Parliament both in his account, and their own, consisting of all his friends, that fled after him, and suffered for him, and yet by him nicknamed, and cashiered for a "mongrel Parliament that vexed his Queen with their base and mutinous motions," as his cabinet letter tells us?[6] Whereby the world may see plainly, that no shifting of place, no sifting of members to his own mind, no number, no paucity, no freedom from tumults, could ever bring his arbitrary wilfulness, and tyrannical designs to brook the least shape or similitude, the least counterfeit of a Parliament.

Finally instead of praying for his people as a good King should do, he prays to be delivered from them, as "from wild beasts, inundations, and raging seas, that had overborne all loyalty, modesty, laws, justice, and religion." God save the people from such intercessors.

The Petition of Gentlewomen and Tradesmen's Wives

A month after the King tried to have the five chief members of Parliament arrested, two petitions were presented to the Commons by "Gentlewomen and Tradesmen's Wives" of London. In the first of these, dated 1 February 1642, the women complained about the lack of trade, which caused great want and blamed the "opposition of some bishops or lords" for the neglect of the women's earlier petitions. In the second petition, reprinted here, the women complain about threats to the security of the state posed by the bishops and Catholic lords in the House of Lords, the still not-yet-executed Archbishop Laud, and the Catholic Mass. From the London women's vantage point, the 1641 rebellion of the Catholics in Ireland demonstrated the risk to Puritans of attacks from Catholics (indistinguishable from Anglicans) within England. The violence unleashed by the more spontaneous and popular revolts in Ireland had been luridly portrayed and grossly exaggerated in the English press. Nevertheless, the Catholic revolt did bring much bloodshed, which increased with the Protestant retaliation. Interestingly, some of the Irish uprisings were led by women, a fact that would not have made any difference to the London women, even if they had known it.

The chief terms of the petition, like the chief terms of the Wars of the Three Kingdoms, were religious. Archbishop Laud is attacked here, but the King is not. Even the women's justification of their right to approach Parliament with a petition is articulated in religious terms. They argue that women are the same as men in Christ's eyes and that women have suffered as

---

5. Milton may echo the identification of the hog with Henry VIII for his failure to carry out a thorough and consistent reformation in Anthony Gilby's *An Admonition to England and Scotland to Call Them to Repentance* (Geneva, 1558).

6. Charles called an opposition Parliament that met in Oxford in 22 January 1644 and that he ordered closed after disagreement with them. This Parliament first attempted a peaceful settlement with the Westminster Parliament and then declared it guilty of treason. The King called it his "mongrel Parliament."

much religious persecution as men. If these women argue that women are equal to men, it is mainly insofar as they are believers in the Puritan practice of religion. Delegated by his fellow members to make a reply, Pym publicly reassured the women that their petition had been read and that they would receive "satisfaction . . . to [their] just and lawful desires." The next day, the House of Lords passed a bill excluding the Bishops, and so Parliament met at least one of the women petitioners' demands.

A True Copy of the Petition of the Gentlewomen and Tradesmen's Wives, In and About the City of London[1]

Delivered to the Honorable, the Knights, Citizens, and Burgesses of the House of Commons in Parliament, the 4th of February, 1642

Together with their several reasons why their sex ought thus to petition, as well as the men; and the manner how both their petition and reasons was delivered.

Likewise the answer which the Honorable Assembly sent to them by Mr. Pym,[2] as they stood at the house door.

To the Honorable Knights, Citizens and Burgesses,[3] of the House of Commons assembled in Parliament. The most humble Petition of the Gentlewomen, Tradesmen's Wives, and many others of the female sex, all inhabitants of the city of London, and the suburbs thereto.

With lowest submission showing,

That we also with all thankful humility acknowledging the unwearied pains, care and great charge, besides hazard of health and life, which you the noble worthies of this honorable and renowned assembly have undergone, for the safety both of church and commonwealth, for a long time already past; for which not only we your humble petitioners, and all well affected in this kingdom, but also all other good Christians are bound now and at all times acknowledge; yet notwithstanding that many worthy deeds have been done by you, great danger and fear do still attend us, and will, as long as Popish Lords and superstitious bishops are suffered to have their voice in the House of Peers, and that accursed and abominable idol of the Mass suffered in the kingdom, and that archenemy[4] of our prosperity and reformation lieth in the Tower, yet not receiving his deserved punishment.

All these under correction, gives us great cause to suspect that God is angry with us, and to be the chief causes why your pious endeavors for a further reformation proceedeth not with that success as you desire, and is most earnestly prayed for of all that wish well to true religion, and the flourishing estate both of king and kingdom; the insolencies of the papists and their abettors, raiseth a just fear and suspicion of sowing sedition, and breaking out into bloody persecution in this kingdom, as they have done in Ireland, the thoughts of which sad and barbarous events maketh our tender hearts to melt within us, forcing us humbly to petition to this honorable assembly, to make safe provision for yourselves and us, before it be too late.

---

1. Printed in the *Parliamentary History* ii.1074.
2. John Pym (1583?–1643) was a strong Puritan opponent of episcopacy and a leader of the House of Commons, one of the five members whom Charles I unsuccessfully attempted to have arrested in 1642.
3. Members of Parliament representing boroughs or corporate towns.

4. Archbishop Laud (1573–1645), who enforced forms of worship that were Anglican High Church, or similar to Roman Catholicism, and promoted church government by Anglican bishops. His policies and support for Charles I won Laud impeachment in 1642; in 1643 he was condemned to death by the Commons.

And whereas we, whose hearts have joined cheerfully with all those petitions which have been exhibited unto you in the behalf of the purity of religion, and the liberty of our husbands' persons and estates, recounting ourselves to have an interest in the common privileges with them, do with the same confidence assure ourselves to find the same gracious acceptance with you, for easing of those grievances, which in regard of our frail condition, do more nearly concern us, and do deeply terrify our souls: our domestical dangers with which this kingdom is so much distressed, especially growing on us from those treacherous and wicked attempts already are such as we find ourselves to have as deep a share as any other.

We cannot but tremble at the very thoughts of the horrid and hideous facts which modesty forbids us now to name, occasioned by the bloody wars in Germany,[5] his Majesty's late Northern Army, how often did it affright our hearts, whilst their violence began to break out so furiously upon the persons of those whose husbands or parents were not able to rescue: we wish we had no cause to speak of those insolencies, and savage usage and unheard-of rapes, exercised upon our sex in Ireland, and have we not just cause to fear they will prove the forerunners of our ruin, except Almighty God by the wisdom and care of this Parliament be pleased to succor us, our husbands and children, which are as dear and tender unto us as the lives and blood of our hearts, to see them murdered and mangled and cut in pieces before our eyes, to see our children dashed against the stones, and the mothers' milk mingled with the infants' blood, running down the streets, to see our houses on flaming fire over our heads: oh how dreadful would this be?[6] We thought it misery enough (though nothing to that we have just cause to fear) but few years since for some of our sex, by unjust divisions from their bosom comforts, to be rendered in a manner widows, and the children fatherless, husbands were imprisoned from the society of their wives, even against the laws of God and nature, and little infants suffered in their fathers' banishments: thousands of our dearest friends have been compelled to fly from Episcopal persecutions into desert places amongst wild beasts, there finding more favor than in their native soil, and in the midst of all their sorrows such hath the pity of the Prelates[7] been, that our cries could never enter into their ears or hearts, not yet through multitudes of obstructions could never have access or come nigh to those royal mercies of our most gracious sovereign, which we confidently hope would have relieved us: but after all these pressures ended, we humbly signify that our present fears are, that unless the bloodthirsty faction of the Papists and Prelates be hindered in their designs, ourselves here in England as well as they in Ireland, shall be exposed to the misery which is more intolerable than that which is already past, as namely to the rage not of men alone, but of devils incarnate (as we may so say), besides the thralldom of our souls and consciences in matters concerning God, which of all things are most dear unto us.

Now the remembrance of all these fearful accidents aforementioned do strongly move us from the example of the woman of Tekoa (II Samuel 14.2–20)[8] to fall submissively at the feet of his Majesty, our dread sovereign, and cry Help, oh King, help

5. The Thirty Years War (1618–1648) was a European-wide war fought mainly in Germany between Protestant opponents to Habsburg rule and Catholic supporters of the Holy Roman Empire.
6. While there was violence on both sides, woodcuts of the Irish rebellions in the English press sensationalized the violence of Catholics against Protestant settlers by depicting the murder of infants and attacks upon women.
7. Churchmen, bishops.
8. The wise woman of Tekoa went before King David and urged him to act mercifully toward his son Absalom. King David had been failing to act decisively against rape and murder within his own household.

oh ye the noble Worthies now sitting in Parliament: And we humbly beseech you, that you will be a means to his Majesty and the House of Peers, that they will be pleased to take our heartbreaking grievances into timely consideration, and to add strength and encouragement to your noble endeavors, and further that you would move his Majesty with our humble requests, that he would be graciously pleased according to the example of the good King Asa,[9] to purge both the court and kingdom of that great idolatrous service of the Mass, which is tolerated in the Queen's court, this sin (as we conceive) is able to draw down a greater curse upon the whole kingdom than all your noble and pious endeavors can prevent, which was the cause that the good and pious King Asa would not suffer idolatry in his own mother, whose example if it shall please his Majesty's gracious goodness to follow, in putting down Popery and idolatry both in great and small, in court and in the kingdom throughout, to subdue the Papists and their abettors, and by taking away the power of the Prelates, whose government by long and woeful experience we have found to be against the liberty of our conscience and the freedom of the Gospel, and the sincere profession and practice thereof, then shall our fears be removed, and we may expect that God will pour down his blessings in abundance both upon his Majesty, and upon this Honorable Assembly, and upon the whole land.

For which your new petitioners shall pray affectionately.

The reasons follow.

It may be thought strange and unbeseeming our sex to show ourselves by way of petition to this Honorable Assembly: but the matter being rightly considered, of the right and interest we have in the common and public cause of the church, it will, as we conceive (under correction), be found a duty commanded and required.

First, because Christ hath purchased us at as dear a rate as he hath done men, and therefore requireth the like obedience for the same mercy as of men.

Secondly, because in the free enjoying of Christ in his own laws, and a flourishing estate of the church and commonwealth, consisteth the happiness of women as well as men.

Thirdly, because women are sharers in the common calamities that accompany both church and commonwealth, when oppression is exercised over the church or kingdom wherein they live; and an unlimited power have been given to Prelates to exercise authority over the consciences of women, as well as men, witness Newgate, Smithfield,[1] and other places of persecution, wherein women as well as men have felt the smart of their fury.

Neither are we left without example in scripture, for when the state of the church, in the time of King Ahasuerus, was by the bloody enemies thereof sought to be utterly destroyed, we find that Esther the Queen and her maids fasted and prayed, and that Esther petitioned to the King in the behalf of the church:[2] and though she enterprised this duty with the hazard of her own life, being contrary to the law to appear before the King before she were sent for, yet her love to the church carried her through all difficulties, to the performance of that duty.

---

9. Charles I is asked to banish Catholics and the Mass just as King Asa banished sodomites and idolatry in 1 Kings 15.8–12.
1. Persecutions at Smithfield and Newgate.
2. The Jewish Esther became the Queen of Ahasuerus and saved the Jews from Haman, who planned to massacre the Jews; see the Book of Esther and also *Ester Hath Hanged Haman* in Perspectives: Tracts on Women and Gender, page 833.

On which grounds we are emboldened to present our humble petition unto this Honorable Assembly, not weighing the reproaches which may and are by many cast upon us, who (not well weighing the premises) scoff and deride our good intent. We do it not out of any self-conceit, or pride of heart, as seeking to equal ourselves with men, either in authority or wisdom: But according to our places to discharge that duty we owe to God, and the cause of the church, as far as lieth in us, following herein the example of the men which have gone in this duty before us.

A relation of the manner how it was delivered, with their answer, sent by Mr. Pym.

This petition, with their reasons, was delivered the 4th of Feb. 1641/2, by Mrs. Anne Stagg, a gentlewoman and brewer's wife, and many others with her of like rank and quality, which when they had delivered it, after some time spent in reading of it, the Honorable Assembly sent them an answer by Mr. Pym, which was performed in this manner.

   Mr. Pym came to the Commons door, and called for the women, and spake unto them in these words: Good women, your petition and the reasons have been read in the house; and is very thankfully accepted of, and is come in a seasonable time: You shall (God willing) receive from us all the satisfaction which we can possibly give to your just and lawful desires. We entreat you to repair to your houses, and turn your petition which you have delivered here into prayers at home for us; for we have been, are and shall be (to our utmost power) ready to relieve you, your husbands, and children, and to perform the trust committed unto us towards God, our King and country, as becometh faithful Christians and loyal subjects.

John Lilburne
1614?–1657

John Lilburne was one of the most tireless political reformers of the Civil War in England. His pamphlets against the Anglican Church in 1638 got him arrested and brought before the Star Chamber (the secret royal tribunal that judged and punished without a jury). Lilburne seized the opportunity to question the court's procedures by refusing to incriminate himself. With Cromwell's help in the House of Commons, Lilburne was released from prison and became a lieutenant in the Parliamentary army (1642–1645), from which he resigned in objection to Presbyterianism as the state religion. Examined several times by the House of Commons for his criticisms of its policies and members, Lilburne became the chief exponent of the Levellers, derisively called such because of their egalitarianism. The Levellers wanted fundamental changes in the government, including universal suffrage, freedom of speech and religion, freedom from exorbitant taxation, care of the poor and aged, and trial by jury. Though a convinced antimonarchist, Lilburne even protested against the condemnation of Charles I without a proper trial.

   The House of Commons rejected Leveller reforms in January 1648. This defeat, combined with Lilburne's fear that the Levellers would be brought to trial for their dissent, provoked his speech to Commons in February. This speech was published as *England's New Chains Discovered*. The first part (a selection from which is reprinted here) reviews the Levellers' concerns, and the second part criticizes the members of Parliament, who condemned Lilburne's speech as seditious. Lilburne went on to publish tracts criticizing Cromwell, monopolies, and enclosures but was ordered into exile by Parliament in 1652 only for attacking his uncle's business enemy, Sir Arthur Hesilrige, as a man "fit to be spewed out of all human society." In 1653, Lilburne returned to England in defiance of Cromwell and was arrested on arrival. His plight aroused popular petitions in his favor, and he was finally acquitted. Nevertheless, the government would not let him go free. Having converted to Quakerism, he died in confinement just a year before the death of Cromwell.

from England's New Chains Discovered

or, The serious apprehensions of a part of the People, in behalf of the Commonwealth; (being Presenters, Promoters, and Approvers of the Large Petition of September 11. 1648.)

Presented to the Supreme Authority of England, the Representers of the people in Parliament assembled.

By Lieut. Col. John Lilburn, and divers other Citizens of London, and Borough of Southwark; February 26. 1648. Whereunto his speech delivered at the Bar is annexed.

Since you have done the nation so much right, and yourselves so much honor as to declare that the people (under God) are the original of all just powers; and given us thereby fair grounds to hope, that you really intend their freedom and prosperity; yet the way thereunto being frequently mistaken, and through haste or error of judgment, those who mean the best, are many times misled so far to the prejudice of those that trust them, as to leave them in a condition nearest to bondage, when they have thought they had brought them into a way of freedom. And since woeful experience hath manifested this to be a truth, there seemeth no small reason that you should seriously lay to heart what at present we have to offer, for discovery and prevention of so great a danger.

And because we have been the first movers in and concerning an Agreement of the People,[1] as the most proper and just means for the settling the long and tedious distractions of this nation, occasioned by nothing more, than the uncertainty of our government; and since there hath been an Agreement prepared and presented by some officers of the army to this honorable House,[2] as what they thought requisite to be agreed unto by the people (you approving thereof) we shall in the first place deliver our apprehensions thereupon.

That an Agreement between those that trust, and those who are trusted, hath appeared a thing acceptable to this honorable House, his Excellency, and the officers of the army, is as much to our rejoicing, as we conceive it just in itself, and profitable for the Commonwealth,[3] and cannot doubt but that you will protect those of the people, who have no ways forfeited their birthright, in their proper liberty of taking this, or any other, as God and their own considerations[4] shall direct them.

Which we the rather mention, for that many particulars in the Agreement before you, are upon serious examination thereof, dissatisfactory to most of those who are very earnestly desirous of an Agreement, and many very material things seem to be wanting therein, which may be supplied in another: As

1. They are now much troubled there should be any intervals between the ending of this Representative, and the beginning of the next as being desirous that this present Parliament that hath lately done so great things in so short a time, tending to

1. The Levellers published their proposals for "An Agreement of the People" in *Foundations of Freedom* (15 December 1648). The beginning of this speech complains about how the government has betrayed the principles set forth in the Leveller "Agreement."
2. *An Agreement Prepared for the People of England* was submitted to Parliament on 20 January 1649.
3. Commonwealth, meaning both public good and body politic, and specifically the republican government established in England between the execution of Charles I in 1649 and the Restoration in 1660.
4. Attentive thoughts.

their liberties, should sit; until with certainty and safety they can see them delivered into the hands of another Representative, rather than to leave them (though never so small a time) under the dominion of a Council of State; a Constitution of a new and unexperienced nature, and which they fear, as the case now stands, may design to perpetuate their power, and to keep off Parliaments for ever.

2. They now conceive no less danger, in that it is provided that Parliaments for the future are to continue but 6 months, and a Council of State 18. In which time, if they should prove corrupt, having command of all forces by sea and land, they will have great opportunities to make themselves absolute and unaccountable: And because this is a danger, than which there cannot well be a greater; they generally incline to Annual Parliaments, bounded and limited as reason shall devise, not dissolvable, but to be continued or adjourned as shall seem good in their discretion, during that year, but no longer; and then to dissolve of course, and give way to those who shall be chosen immediately to succeed them, and in the intervals of their adjournments, to entrust an ordinary Committee of their own members, as in other cases limited and bounded with express instructions, and accountable to the next session, which will avoid all those dangers feared from a Council of State, as at present this is constituted.

3. They are not satisfied with the clause, wherein it is said, that the power of the Representatives shall extend to the erecting and abolishing of Courts of Justice; since the alteration of the usual way of trials by twelve sworn men of the neighborhood, may be included therein: a constitution so equal and just in itself, as that they conceive it ought to remain unalterable. Neither is it clear what is meant by these words, (viz.) That the Representatives have the highest final judgment. They conceiving that their authority in these cases, is only to make laws, rules, and directions for other courts and persons assigned by law for the execution thereof; unto which every member of the Commonwealth, as well those of the Representative, as others, should be alike subject; it being likewise unreasonable in itself, and an occasion of much partiality, injustice, and vexation to the people, that the law-makers should be law-executors.[5]

4. Although it doth provide that in the laws hereafter to be made, no person by virtue of any tenure, grant, charter, patent, degree, or birth, shall be privileged from subjection thereunto, or from being bound thereby, as well as others. Yet doth it not null and make void those present protections by law, or otherwise; nor leave all persons, as well Lords as others, alike liable in person and estate, as in reason and conscience they ought to be.[6]

5. They are very much unsatisfied with what is expressed as a reserve from the Representative, in matters of religion, as being very obscure, and full of perplexity, that ought to be most plain and clear; there having occurred no greater trouble to the nation about any thing than by the intermeddling of Parliaments in matters of religion.[7]

6. They seem to conceive it absolutely necessary, that there be in their agreement, a reserve from ever having any kingly government, and a bar against restoring the House of Lords, both which are wanting in the agreement which is before you.

---

5. Lilburne is calling for a clear distinction between the power of the House of Commons to legislate and the power of the Courts to interpret the law.
6. The Commonwealth did not thoroughly abolish the privileges of the landed classes and so did not provide a government in which all classes would be treated equally under the law.
7. Lilburne criticizes the Commons for not completely separating Church and State, which he sees as a major danger, since the King's imposition of the rituals of the Anglican Church was one of the reasons the English Civil War was fought.

7. They seem to be resolved to take away all known and burdensome grievances, as tithes,[8] that great oppression of the country's industry and hindrance of tillage: excise, and customs, those secret thieves, and robbers, drainers of the poor and middle sort of people, and the greatest obstructers of trade, surmounting all the prejudices of ship money, patents, and projects,[9] before this Parliament: also to take away all monopolizing companies of merchants, the hinderers and decayers of clothing and cloth-working, dying, and the like useful professions; by which thousands of poor people might be set at work, that are now ready to starve, were merchandising restored to its due and proper freedom: they conceive likewise that the three grievances before mentioned, (viz.) monopolizing companies, excise, and customs, do exceedingly prejudice shipping and navigation, and consequently discourage seamen, and mariners, and which have had no small influence upon the late unhappy revolts which have so much endangered the nation, and so much advantaged your enemies. They also incline to direct a more equal and less burdensome way for levying monies for the future, those other forementioned being so chargeable in the receipt, as that the very stipends and allowance to the officers attending thereupon would defray a very great part of the charge of the army; whereas now they engender and support a corrupt interest. They also have in mind to take away all imprisonment of disabled men, for debt; and to provide some effectual course to enforce all that are able to a speedy payment, and not suffer them to be sheltered in prisons, where they live in plenty, whilst their creditors are undone. They have also in mind to provide work, and comfortable maintenance for all sorts of poor, aged, and impotent people, and to establish some more speedy, less troublesome and chargeable way for deciding of controversies in law, whole families having been ruined by seeking right in the ways yet in being. All which, though of greatest and most immediate concernment to the people, are yet omitted in their Agreement before you.

These and the like are their intentions in what they purpose for an Agreement of the people, as being resolved (so far as they are able) to lay an impossibility upon all whom they shall hereafter trust, of ever wronging the Commonwealth in any considerable measure, without certainty of ruining themselves, and as conceiving it to be an improper tedious, and unprofitable thing for the people, to be ever running after their Representatives with petitions for redress of such grievances as may at once be removed by themselves, or to depend for these things so essential to their happiness and freedom, upon the uncertain judgments of several Representatives, the one being apt to renew what the other hath taken away.

⊶ ⊱⫯⊰ ⊷

Oliver Cromwell
1599–1658

Oliver Cromwell's brutal conquest of Ireland (1649–1650) was the culmination of a long military, political, and religiously zealous career and the turning point in his rise to the position of Lord Protector. He had risen steadily in the Parliamentary Army, serving in the early days of

---

8. The tenth part of the annual produce of agriculture, due as payment for the Church.
9. "Ship money" was an ancient tax levied in time of war on maritime cities, which was revived by Charles I and applied to inland counties as well; patents were the sole right or license to sell or deal in a commodity; and projects were plans or schemes, here especially those by the government to get money.

the Civil War as captain of a troop of horses and finally becoming the chief of the New Model Army. Not only did he have a genius for military strategy but he was one of those who "never stirred from their troops . . . but fought to the last minute." He and his men were both called "Ironsides" in tribute to their indomitability. As a member of Parliament, he argued vigorously for the Puritan cause, and when Parliament was purged of Presbyterians in 1649, Cromwell's power and that of his fellow Congregationalists or Independents increased. At the trial of Charles I in January 1649, Cromwell adamantly demanded execution. Afterward, when the new Commonwealth was set up, one of Parliament's first charges was to send Cromwell to subdue Ireland, where Irish Royalists and Rebels, once pitted against each other, had formed a coalition and were gaining ground.

Cromwell's treatment of the Irish tested the limits of the principles of the Puritan Revolution and left a legacy of devastation. Although Cromwell was a strong member of the English Parliament, he helped to bring about the abolition of both Irish and Scottish Parliaments with his military defeats of both kingdoms. In September 1644, Cromwell urged the Presbyterian Parliament to guarantee liberty of conscience to the Independents among his troops, but when the Catholics of New Ross, Ireland, called for similar toleration in October 1649, Cromwell refused them: "if by liberty of conscience, you mean a liberty to exercise the Mass, I judge it best to use plain dealing, and to let you know, where the Parliament of England have power, that will not be allowed of." Indeed during Cromwell's rule in England, only Jews and non-Anglican Protestants were tolerated. Furthermore, Cromwell escalated the policy (begun under Elizabeth and James) of giving lands confiscated from native Irish inhabitants to English colonists. The massacre of Drogheda—including civilians as well as troops—made the Irish remember Cromwell as cruel. In the following letter of 17 September 1649, Cromwell presents his troops' massacre of the people of Drogheda as "the righteous judgment of God." The same religious conviction that had made him and his New Model Army such valiant defenders of English liberty was used to justify Irish slaughter.

Cromwell also used his letters to keep Parliament informed of his progress, to ask for further supplies, and to promote his political power. He was to go on to defeat the Scots in 1650. Ultimately, his power grew to such an extent that in 1657 he became Lord Protector, assuming the pomp and trappings of royalty. When his son Richard succeeded him at his death in September 1658, it seemed as if Oliver Cromwell's rule had led to a new monarchy. His son proved a weak successor, and the Commonwealth was restored in May 1659, only to collapse with the Restoration of 1660. If Cromwell's participation in parliamentary politics and the New Model Army contributed to the cause of republican liberty, his conquest of Ireland marked one of the bleakest chapters in the English colonization of Ireland.

from Letters from Ireland

Relating the Several Great Success It Hath Pleased God to Give Unto the Parliament's Forces There, in the Taking of Drogheda, Trym, Dundalk, Carlingford, and the Nury. * * *

For the Honorable *William Lenthal* Esq;
Speaker of the Parliament of *England*

Sir,
Your army[1] being safely arrived at Dublin, and the enemy endeavoring to draw all his forces together about Trym and Tecroghan[2] (as my intelligence gave me); from

---

1. The letter is addressed to Parliament from the commander of the parliamentary army, hence "your army."

2. A town and townland in County Meath, northwest of Dublin.

whence endeavors were used by the Marquis of Ormonde, to draw Owen Roe O'Neal with his forces to his assistance, but with what success I cannot yet learn.[3] I resolved after some refreshment taken for our weather beaten men and horses, and accommodations for a march, to take the field; and accordingly upon Friday the thirtieth of August last, rendezvoused with eight regiments of foot, and six of horse, and some troops of dragoons, three miles on the north side of Dublin; the design was, to endeavor the regaining of Drogheda,[4] or tempting the enemy, upon his hazard of the loss of that place, to fight. Your army came before the town upon Monday following, where having pitched, as speedy course as could be was taken to frame our batteries,[5] which took up the more time, because divers of the battering guns were on shipboard. Upon Monday the ninth of this instant, the batteries began to play; whereupon I sent Sir Arthur Ashton the then Governor a summons, to deliver the town to the use of the Parliament of England; to the which I received no satisfactory answer, but proceeded that day to beat down the steeple of the church on the south side of the town, and to beat down a tower not far from the same place, which you will discern by the card[6] enclosed. Our guns not being able to do much that day, it was resolved to endeavor to do our utmost the next day to make breaches[7] assaultable, and by the help of God to storm them. The places pitched upon, were that part of the town wall next a church, called St. Marie's, which was the rather chosen, because we did hope that if we did enter and possess that church, we should be the better able to keep it against their horse and foot, until we could make way for the entrance of our horse, which we did not conceive that any part of the town would afford the like advantage for that purpose with this. The batteries planted were two, one was for that part of the wall against the east end of the said church, the other against the wall on the south side; being somewhat long in battering, the enemy made six retrenchments, three of them from the said church to Duleek Gate, and three from the east end of the church to the town wall, and so backward. The guns after some two or three hundred shot, beat down the corner tower, and opened two reasonable good breaches in the east and south wall. Upon Tuesday the tenth of this instant, about five of the clock in the evening, we began the storm, and after some hot dispute, we entered about seven or eight hundred men, the enemy disputing it very stiffly with us; and indeed through the advantages of the place, and the courage God was pleased to give the defenders, our men were forced to retreat quite out of the breach, not without some considerable loss; Colonel Cassel being there shot in the head, whereof he presently died, and divers soldiers and officers doing their duty, killed and wounded. There was a tenalia[8] to flanker the south wall of the town, between Duleek Gate, and the corner tower before mentioned, which our men entered, wherein they found some forty or fifty of the enemy, which they put to the sword, and this they held; but it being without[9] the wall, and the sallyport[1] through the wall into that tenalia being choked up with some of the enemy which were killed in it, it proved of no use for our entrance into the town that way.

---

3. James Butler, Earl of Ormonde, represented Charles I in Ireland throughout the 1640s. At first opposed to the Catholic Confederation led by Owen Roe O'Neill (c. 1590–1649), Ormonde joined forces with O'Neill against the incursion of Cromwell's army.
4. Drogheda (Droichead átha, "Bridge of the ford"), a city in County Louth, was under royalist command when

Cromwell arrived there on 2 September 1649.
5. Platforms on which artillery was mounted.
6. Chart, map.
7. Gaps in fortifications.
8. A low fortification to protect the wall from the side.
9. Outside.
1. An opening for troops to pass through.

Although our men that stormed the breaches were forced to recoil, as before is expressed, yet being encouraged to recover their loss, they made a second attempt, wherein God was pleased to animate them, that they got ground of the enemy, and by the goodness of God, forced him to quit his entrenchments; and after a very hot dispute, the enemy having both horse and foot, and we only foot within the wall, the enemy gave ground, and our men became masters; but of their retrenchments and the church, which indeed although they made our entrance the more difficult, yet they proved of excellent use to us, so that the enemy could not annoy us with their horse, but thereby we had advantage to make good the ground, that so we might let in our own horse, which accordingly was done, though with much difficulty; the enemy retreated divers of them into the Mill-Mount, a place very strong and of difficult access, being exceeding high, having a good graft[2] and strongly pallisadoed;[3] the Governor Sir Arthur Ashton and divers considerable officers being there, our men getting up to them, were ordered by me to put them all to the sword; and indeed being in the heat of action, I forbade them to spare any that were in arms in the town, and I think that night they put to the sword about two thousand men, divers of the officers and soldiers being fled over the bridge into the other part of the town, where about one hundred of them possessed St. Peter's church steeple, some the west gate, and others, a round strong tower next the gate, called St. Sunday's. These being summoned to yield to mercy, refused; whereupon I ordered the steeple of St. Peter's church to be fired, where one of them was heard to say in the midst of the flames, "God damn me, God confound me, I burn, I burn." The next day the other two towers were summoned,[4] in one of which was about six or seven score, but they refused to yield themselves; and we knowing that hunger must compel them, set only good guards to secure them from running away, until their stomachs were come down. From one of the said towers, notwithstanding their condition, they killed and wounded some of our men; when they submitted, their officers were knocked on the head, and every tenth man of the soldiers killed, and the rest shipped for the Barbados;[5] the soldiers in the other tower were all spared, as to their lives only, and shipped likewise for the Barbados. I am persuaded that this is a righteous judgment of God upon these barbarous wretches, who have imbrued their hands in so much innocent blood, and that it will tend to prevent the effusion of blood for the future, which are the satisfactory grounds to such actions, which otherwise cannot but work remorse and regret.

The officers and soldiers of this garrison were the flower of all their army; and their great expectation was that our attempting this place would put fair to ruin us; they being confident of the resolution of their men, and the advantage of the place; if we had divided our force into two quarters, to have besieged the north town and the south town, we could not have had such a correspondency between the two parts of our army, but that they might have chosen to have brought their army, and have fought with which part they pleased, and at the same time have made a sally with two thousand men upon us, and have left their walls manned, they having in the town the numbers specified in this inclosed, by some say near four thousand. Since

2. Ditch, moat.
3. Defended with a strong fence of pointed stakes.
4. Called to surrender.
5. In the Cromwellian period in Ireland, not only men

captured in battle but also women and children were sent into indentured servitude to English colonies in the Caribbean.

this great mercy vouchsafed to us, I sent a party of horse and dragoons to Dundalk, which the enemy quitted, and we are possessed of; as also another castle they deserted between Trym and Drogheda, upon the Boynes.[6] I sent a party of horse and dragoons to a house within five miles of Trym, there being then in Trym some Scots companies which the Lord of Ards[7] brought to assist the Lord of Ormonde; but upon the news of Drogheda they ran away, leaving their great guns behind them, which we also have possessed. And now give me leave to say how it comes to pass that this work is wrought. It was set upon some of our hearts, that a great thing should be done, not by power, or might, but by the Spirit of God; and is it not so clear? That which caused your men to storm so courageously, it was the Spirit of God, who gave your men courage, and took it away again, and gave the enemy courage, and took it away again, and gave your men courage again, and therewith this happy success; and therefore it is good that God alone have all the glory.

It is remarkable, that these people at the first set up the Mass in some places of the town that had been monasteries; but afterwards grew so insolent, that the last Lord's day before the Storm,[8] the Protestants were thrust out of the great church, called St. Peter's, and they had public Mass there; and in this very place near one thousand of them were put to the sword, flying thither for safety: I believe all their friars were knocked on the head promiscuously, but two, the one of which was Father Peter Taaff (Brother to the Lord Taaff)[9] whom the Soldiers took the next day, and made an end of; the other was taken in the round tower, under the repute of lieutenant, and when he understood the officers in that tower had no quarter, he confessed he was a friar, but that did not save him. A great deal of loss in this business, fell upon Col. Hewson, Col. Cassel, and Colonel Ewers' regiments; Colonel Ewers having two field-officers in his regiment shot, Colonel Cassel and a captain of his regiment slain, Colonel Hewson's captain-lieutenant slain; I do not think we lost one hundred men upon the place, though many be wounded. I most humbly pray, the Parliament will be pleased this army may be maintained, and that a consideration may be had of them, and of the carrying on of the affairs here, as may give a speedy issue to this work, to which there seems to be a marvelous fair opportunity offered by God. And although it may seem very chargeable to the State of England to maintain so great a force, yet surely to stretch a little for the present, in following God's Providence, in hope the charge will not be long, I trust it will not be thought by any (that have no irreconcilable or malicious principles) unfit for me to move for a constant supply, which in humane probability, as to outward means, is most likely to hasten and perfect this work; and indeed, if God please to finish it here, as he hath done in England, the war is like to pay itself. We keep the field much, our tents sheltering us from the wet and cold, but yet the country sickness overtakes many, and therefore we desire recruits, and some fresh regiments of foot may be sent us; for it is easily conceived by what the garrisons already drink up, what our field army will come to, if God shall give more garrisons into our hands. Craving pardon for this great trouble, I rest,

Your most humble Servant,
O. CROMWELL

Dublin, Sept. 17, 1649

---

6. The Boyne River.
7. Hugh Montgomery (c. 1623–1663), 3rd Viscount of Ards.
8. I.e., Cromwell's attack on the town.

9. Theobald, 2nd Viscount Taaff (d. 1677). An uncle of Lord Taaff, Lucas was forced to surrender New Ross to Cromwell in October 1649.

John O'Dwyer of the Glenn
c. 1651

John O'Dwyer of the Glenn (*Seán O'Duibhir an Ghleanna*) is one of the most beautiful popular Irish-language songs commemorating the war against the Cromwellian conquest of Ireland and its aftermath. According to James Hardiman, who collected this song in his *Irish Minstrelsy, or Bardic Remains of Ireland* (1831), John O'Dwyer was "a distinguished officer who commanded in the Counties of Waterford and Tipperary in 1651." The poem is listed under the heading "Jacobite Relics," which places it in a long tradition of support for the Stuart kings, which began with the celebration of the accession of James I in elite bardic poetry and continued into the eighteenth century with support for Bonnie Prince Charlie in popular ballads.

The imagery of the natural world in *John O'Dwyer of the Glenn* symbolizes the state of Ireland. The lyric begins with a pastoral idyll, as the speaker describes awakening in the morning to the sound of birds singing. The intrusion of a fox signals the advent of war, and a sad old woman who stands by the side of the road reckoning her geese evokes Ireland weeping for those she has lost. Some of the geese (*geidh*), here referred to as "that prowler's spoil," died in battle; others, like the "wild geese" (*geidh fiádháin*) who left Ireland after the defeat of the Gaelic chiefs in 1603, fled to the Continent. John O'Dwyer and his men were said by Hardiman to have embarked for Spain.

The translation here is that of Thomas Furlong as printed in Hardiman's *Irish Minstrelsy*. The song originated in County Tipperary in the mid-seventeenth century, and there are more verses in Irish. It is still sung in both English and Irish. The best edition of the Irish text is that edited by Padraig de Brún and Breandán Ó Buachalla in *Nua-Dhuanaire* (1971), which also contains poems by such mid-seventeenth-century Irish poets as Piaras Feiritéar and Dáibhí O Bruadair.

John O'Dwyer of the Glenn

> Blithe the bright dawn found me,
> Rest with strength had crown'd me,
> Sweet the birds sung round me,
>   Sport was all their toil.
5 > The horn its clang was keeping,
> Forth the fox was creeping,
> Round each dame stood weeping,
>   O'er that prowler's spoil.
> Hark, the foe is calling,
10 > Fast the woods are falling,
> Scenes and sights appalling
>   Mark the wasted soil.[1]
>
> War and confiscation
> Curse the fallen nation;
15 > Gloom and desolation
>   Shade the lost land o'er.
> Chill the winds are blowing,
> Death aloft is going;

1. The falling woods are the old Irish families who have been thrown off their land, and the "wasted soil" is the country after war.

Peace or hope seems growing
20   For our race no more.
Hark the foe is calling,
Fast the woods are falling,
Scenes and sights appalling
    Throng our blood-stained shore.

25   Where's my goat to cheer me,[2]
Now it plays not near me;
Friends no more can hear me;
    Strangers round me stand.
Nobles once high-hearted,
30   From their homes have parted,
Scatter'd, scar'd and started
    By a base-born band.
Hark the foe is calling,
Fast the woods are falling;
35   Scenes and sights appalling
    Thicken round the land.

Oh! that death had found me
And in darkness bound me,
Ere each object round me
40   Grew so sweet, so dear.
Spots that once were cheering,
Girls beloved endearing,
Friends from whom I'm steering,
    Take this parting tear.
45   Hark, the foe is calling,
Fast the woods are falling;
Scenes and sights appalling
    Plague and haunt me here.

═══╪ END OF PERSPECTIVES: THE CIVIL WAR, OR THE WARS OF THREE KINGDOMS ╪═══

John Milton
1608–1674

While writing *Paradise Lost*, Milton would rise early to begin composing poetry; when his secretary arrived late, the old blind man would complain, "I want to be milked." Prodigious in his memory and ingenuity, austere in his frugality and discipline, Milton devoted his life to learning, politics, and art. He put his eloquence at the service of the Puritan Revolution, which brought on the beheading of a king and the institution of a republican commonwealth. Milton entered controversies on divorce and freedom of the press. He showed courage in defending the Puritan republic when he could have lost his life for doing so. Radical, scholar, sage—Milton is above all the great epic poet of England.

---

2. The goat stands for both Charles II in exile and the defeated Irish lords.

Milton's life was marked by a passionate devotion to his religious, political, and artistic ideals, a devotion that ran in his family. Milton's father was said to have been disinherited for his Protestantism by his own father, who was Roman Catholic. When the Civil War broke out, Milton sided with Cromwell while his brother fought for the King. The oldest of three children in a prosperous middle-class family, young John read Virgil, Ovid, and Livy; he especially loved "our sage and serious Spenser," whom he called "a better teacher than Aquinas." Milton later wrote that from the age of twelve he "hardly ever gave up reading for bed till midnight." After his first year at Christ's College, Cambridge, the poet was expelled. While in exile, Milton excoriated academia: "How wretchedly suited that place is to the worshippers of Phoebus! It is disgusting to be constantly subjected to the threats of a rough tutor and to other indignities my spirit cannot endure." Returning to Cambridge, he took his B.A. in 1629 and his M.A. in 1632. On vacations during these years he wrote two of his most musical lyrics, the erotic *L'Allegro* and the Platonic *Il Penseroso*. After leaving university, Milton lived with his parents in Berkshire, where he wrote *Lycidas*, a haunting elegy for the early death of his Cambridge friend Edward King, and *Comus*, a masque for the prominent noble Egerton family at Ludlow Castle.

After his mother's death in 1638, Milton traveled to Europe. He stayed longest in Italy, where his poems were greatly admired by the Florentine literati, who welcomed him into their academies. He later reflected that it was in Italy that he first sensed his vocation as an epic poet, hoping to "perhaps leave something so written, as they should not willingly let it die." Visiting Rome, Naples, and Venice, Milton collected Monteverdi's music, which he would later sing and play. He also met the famed astronomer Galileo, the censorship of whose works Milton would later protest. Concerned about political turmoil in England, he returned home at the outbreak of the Civil War.

From 1640 to 1660, Milton devoted himself to "the cause of real and substantial liberty," by which he meant religious, domestic, and civil liberties. Defending religious liberty, he decried Anglican hierarchy and ritualism—"the new vomited paganism of sensual idolatry"—in a series of tracts, including *Of Reformation* (1641) and *The Reason of Church Government* (1642).

That same year, Milton married seventeen-year-old Mary Powell, who came from a royalist Oxfordshire family. After only a month, she left Milton alone to his "philosophical" life for a more sociable one at home. Troubled by the unhappiness of his marriage, Milton wrote four treatises on divorce, for which he was publicly condemned. He argued that incompatibility should be grounds for divorce, that both husband and wife should be allowed to remarry, and that to maintain otherwise was contrary to reason and scripture. According to his nephew, whom Milton tutored during this time, he was interested in marrying another woman but by 1645 was reunited with Mary. They had a daughter soon afterward. They were joined for several years by Mary's family, who had lost their estate in the Civil War.

Along with "the true conception of marriage," Milton's concept of domestic liberty included "the sound education of children, and freedom of thought and speech." In *Of Education* (1644), opposing strictly vocational instruction, Milton called for the study of languages, rhetoric, poetry, philosophy, and science, the goal of which was "to perform justly, skillfully and magnanimously all of the offices both private and public of peace and war." In *Areopagitica* (1644), Milton fought against censorship before publication but counseled control of printed texts posing political or religious danger. In the 1640s, Milton steered a course midway between the religious conformity demanded by the once-dissenting Presbyterians and the complete separation of church and state advocated by such radicals as Roger Williams, who ultimately went to America in search of greater toleration.

After Oliver Cromwell defeated the Royalists and the King was tried and executed by order of the "Rump" parliament purged of dissenters, Milton wrote *The Tenure of Kings and Magistrates* (1649) to argue that subjects could justly overthrow a tyrant. This tract won him the job of Latin Secretary to the Council of State, handling all correspondence to foreign governments. After the beheading of Charles I in 1649, *Eikon Basilike*, "the Royal Image" appeared, pieced together from the King's papers by his chaplain John Gauden. To counteract sympathy for the King's cause that this work might elicit, Milton wrote a chapter-by-chapter refutation of it entitled *Eikonoklastes*, or *Image-Breaker* (1649). Milton also defended Cromwell's government in three Latin works that were in some measure self-defenses: *First* and *Second Defense of the English People* (1651, 1654) and *Defense of Himself* (1656).

His eyes weakened by the strain of so much writing, Milton went blind. His wife Mary died, leaving three daughters and one son. The boy died soon after, in May 1652. That same month, Milton wrote a sonnet exhorting the Lord General Cromwell to "Help us to save free conscience from the paw of hireling wolves," a reference to ministers who wanted to exclude dissenters from a unified established church. Sounding the cry for liberty again in *Avenge, O Lord these Slaughtered Saints* (1655), Milton lamented the massacre of Italian Protestants. One of Milton's most beautiful and best-known sonnets, *Methought I Saw My Late Espoused Saint*, is said to be about his second wife, Katherine Woodcock, who, after just two years of marriage, died following the birth of her child in 1558.

Cromwell died the same year, and his son Richard's succession to power began a period of political confusion. Milton continued to write political tracts, now even more radical in arguing for universal education and freedom from allegiance to *any* established church and against the abuse of church positions for money. In *De Doctrina Christiana* (written 1655–1660, published 1823), Milton set forth his individualistic theology; he was convinced that no one should be required to attend church and that everyone should interpret scripture in his own way. Committed to the cause of the republic even after the Restoration of Charles II, Milton published *The Ready and Easy Way to Establish a Free Commonwealth* in 1660. Shortly after its appearance, Milton went into hiding. The House of Commons ordered the burning of *Eikonoklastes* and had Milton arrested. He was held in prison for several months. For a time threatened with heavy fines and even death by hanging, Milton was finally released through the aid of his friend Andrew Marvell.

In the aftermath of the Restoration, Milton lived in obscurity and desolation. On the anniversary of Charles I's execution, Cromwell's body was dug up and hanged. More than a few of Milton's friends were either executed or forced into exile. The republic to which he had devoted his life's work had been defeated. Amid this experience of defeat, he worked on *Paradise Lost*, with its themes of fall, damnation, war in heaven, and future redemption for an erring humanity.

While writing his epic, he was much helped by the companionship and housekeeping of his young and amiable third wife Elizabeth Minshull, whom he married in 1663. Young pupils, secretaries, and his daughters read to him in many languages (some of which they didn't understand). The Miltons lived frugally on the money that he had saved from his salary as Latin Secretary (1649–1659). Milton had begun writing *Paradise Lost* by 1658–1659, but he only completed the first edition for publication in 1667. First conceiving of this work as a drama, he had written a soliloquy for the rebellious Lucifer in 1642, which later appeared near the opening of the epic's fourth book. Milton explained that he had put off writing *Paradise Lost* because it was "a work to be raised . . . by devout prayer to that eternal Spirit who can enrich with all utterance and knowledge."

In the last ten years of his life, Milton also wrote *Paradise Regained* (1671), a short epic about the temptation of Christ, based on the model of the Book of Job. Published in the same year was *Samson Agonistes*, a verse tragedy about the Biblical hero, who, betrayed by his lover Delilah, brought down destruction on himself as well as his enemies. In 1673 he published an expanded edition of his *Poems* (1645), to which he added his translations of the Psalms. Finally, in 1674, all twelve books of *Paradise Lost* as we know it were published. That same year, Milton died in a fit of gout and was buried in Saint Giles Cripplegate alongside his father.

Milton combined the traditional erudition of a Renaissance poet with the committed politics of a Puritan radical, both of which contributed to his crowning achievement, *Paradise Lost*. Milton draws on the Bible, Homer, Virgil, and Dante to create his own original sound and story. The vivid sensual imagery of *L'Allegro*, echoing Shakespeare and Spenser, suggests the pastoral idyll of Adam and Eve in Paradise. The intellectual rebelliousness of his prose works inflects the epic's dramatic embodiment of such problems as the origin of evil, sin, and death. Like *Paradise Lost* reaches humanity's psychological depths: arrogance, despair, revenge, self-destruction, desire, and self-knowledge. Most of all, *Paradise Lost* dramatizes human wayfaring in the face of the Fall, not unlike Milton's own heroic perseverance in writing his epic after the loss of the world he had helped to create.

L'Allegro[1]

Hence loathèd Melancholy
   Of Cerberus,[2] and blackest midnight born,
In Stygian cave forlorn.
   'Mongst horrid shapes, and shreiks, and sights unholy,
5   Find out some uncouth° cell,   *unknown*
   Where brooding darkness spreads his jealous wings,
And the night-raven[3] sings;
   There under ebon shades, and low-brow'd rocks,
As ragged as thy Locks,
10   In dark Cimmerian[4] desert ever dwell.
But come thou goddess fair and free,
In Heaven yclept° Euphrosyne,   *called*
And by men, heart-easing Mirth,
Whom lovely Venus at a birth
15   With two sister Graces more
To ivy-crownèd Bacchus bore;[5]
Or whether (as some sager sing)
The frolic wind that breathes the spring,
Zephyr with Aurora playing,
20   As he met her once a-Maying,[6]
There on beds of violets blue,
And fresh-blown roses washed in dew,
Filled her with thee a daughter fair,
So buxom,° blithe, and debonair.   *yielding*
25   Haste thee nymph, and bring with thee
Jest and youthful Jollity,
Quips and cranks,° and wanton wiles,   *jests*
Nods, and becks, and wreathèd smiles,
Such as hang on Hebe's[7] cheek,
30   And love to live in dimple sleek;
Sport that wrinkled Care derides,
And Laughter holding both his sides.
Come, and trip it as you go
On the light fantastic toe,
35   And in thy right hand lead with thee,

1. The happy person. This and the companion poem *Il Penseroso* (the pensive one) were composed around 1631; they were first published in 1645.
2. For the underworld cave of the three-headed dog Cerberus, see Virgil, *Aeneid* 6.418. Milton makes Cerberus and Night the parents of Melancholy, which is the subject of *Il Penseroso*.
3. Ominous bird.

4. The Cimmerians lived at the extreme limit of the known world (see *Odyssey* 11.13–22).
5. The Graces: Euphrosyne (Mirth), Aglaia (Brightness), and Thalia (Bloom). Servius's commentary to the *Aeneid* makes Venus and Bacchus their parents.
6. Milton invented this parentage of the Graces by Aurora, the dawn, and Zephyr, the west wind.
7. Goddess of youth and daughter of Zeus and Hera.

The mountain nymph, sweet Liberty;
And if I give thee honor due,
Mirth, admit me of thy crew
To live with her, and live with thee,
40   In unreprovèd pleasures free;
To hear the lark begin his flight,
And singing startle the dull night,
From his watch-tower in the skies,
Till the dappled dawn doth rise;
45   Then to come in spite of sorrow,
And at my window bid good morrow,
Through the sweetbriar, or the vine,
Or the twisted eglantine.°   *honey-suckle*
While the cock with lively din,
50   Scatters the rear of darkness thin,
And to the stack, or the barn door,
Stoutly struts his dames before,
Oft listening how the hounds and horn
Cheerly rouse the slumbring morn,
55   From the side of some hoar° hill,   *gray with mist*
Through the high wood echoing shrill.
Sometime walking not unseen
By hedge-row elms, on hillocks green,
Right against the eastern gate,
60   Where the great sun begins his state,°   *progress*
Robed in flames, and amber light,
The clouds in thousand liveries dight,°   *dressed*
While the plowman near at hand,
Whistles ore the furrowed land,
65   And the milkmaid singeth blithe,
And the mower whets his scythe,
And every shepherd tells his tale
Under the hawthorn in the dale.
Straight mine eye hath caught new pleasures
70   Whilst the landscape round it measures,
Russet lawns, and fallows° gray,   *plowed lands*
Where the nibling flocks do stray,
Mountains on whose barren breast
The laboring clouds do often rest;
75   Meadows trim with daisies pied,°   *variegated*
Shallow brooks, and rivers wide.
Towers and battlements it sees
Bosomed high in tufted trees,
Where perhaps some beauty lies,
80   The cynosure[8] of neighboring eyes.
Hard by, a cottage chimney smokes
From betwixt two agèd oaks,
Where Corydon and Thyrsis met,
Are at their savory dinner set

8. The North Star, here meaning, the center of attention.

85   Of herbs, and other country messes,
    Which the neat-handed Phyllis dresses;
    And then in haste her bower she leaves,
    With Thestylis⁹ to bind the sheaves;
    Or if the earlier season lead
90   To the tanned haycock° in the mead,   *heaps of hay*
    Sometimes with secure delight
    The upland hamlets will invite,
    When the merry bells ring round,
    And the jocond rebecks° sound   *fiddles*
95   To many a youth, and many a maid,
    Dancing in the checkered shade;
    And young and old come forth to play
    On a sunshine holiday,
    Till the livelong daylight fail,
100   Then to the spicy nut-brown ale,
    With stories told of many a feat,
    How fairy Mab¹ the junkets° eat,   *cream cheeses*
    She was pinched, and pulled she said,
    And by the friar's lantern led
105   Tells how the drudging goblin sweat,
    To earn his cream-bowl duly set,
    When in one night, ere glimpse of morn,
    His shadowy flail hath threshed the corn
    That ten day-laborers could not end;
110   Then lies him down the lubber fiend.²
    And stretched out all the chimney's length,
    Basks at the fire his hairy strength;
    And crop-full out of doors he flings,
    Ere the first cock his matin rings.
115   Thus done the tales, to bed they creep,
    By whispering winds soon lulled asleep.
    Towered cities please us then,
    And the busy hum of men,
    Where throngs of knights and barons bold,
120   In weeds° of peace high triumphs° hold,   *clothes / tournaments*
    With store of ladies, whose bright eyes
    Rain influence,³ and judge the prize,
    Of wit, or arms, while both contend
    To win her grace, whom all commend.
125   There let Hymen⁴ oft appear
    In saffron robe, with taper clear,
    And pomp, and feast, and revelry,
    With mask, and antique pageantry;
    Such sights as youthful poets dream
130   On summer eves by haunted stream.

9. The shepherds' names are common in Renaissance pastoral.
1. Queen of the fairies, and the topic of Mercutio's famous speech (*Romeo and Juliet* 1.4.54–95).
2. Slaving demon, like Robin Goodfellow called "lob of spirits" in *Midsummer Night's Dream* 2.1.16.
3. In astrology, the process by which an ethereal fluid emanating from the stars ruled human fate.
4. Roman wedding god.

Then to the well-trod stage anon,
If Jonson's learned sock[5] be on,
Or sweetest Shakespeare fancy's child,
Warble his native wood-notes wild,
135   And ever against eating cares
Lap me in soft Lydian airs,[6]
Married to immortal verse
Such as the meeting soul may pierce
In notes, with many a winding bout
140   Of linkèd sweetness long drawn out,
With wanton heed and giddy cunning,
The melting voice through mazes running,
Untwisting all the chains that tie
The hidden soul of harmony.
145   That Orpheus' self may heave his head
From golden slumber on a bed
Of heaped Elysian flowers, and hear
Such strains as would have won the ear
Of Pluto, to have quite set free
150   His half regained Eurydice.[7]
These delights, if thou canst give,
Mirth with thee, I mean to live.[8]

Il Penseroso[1]

Hence vain deluding joys,
    The brood of Folly without father bred,
How little you bestead,°   *help*
    Or fill the fixèd mind with all your toys;
5   Dwell in some idle brain,
    And fancies fond with gaudy shapes possess,
As thick and numberless
    As the gay motes that people the sunbeams,
Or likest hovering dreams,
10   The fickle pensioners° of Morpheus'[2] train.   *guards*
But hail thou Goddess, sage and holy,
Hail divinest Melancholy,
Whose saintly visage is too bright
To hit° the sense of human sight,   *fit*
15   And therefore to our weaker view,
O'er laid with black staid Wisdom's hue;[3]
Black, but such as in esteem,
Prince Memnon's sister[4] might beseem,

5. Low-heeled slipper of the comic actor in ancient
Greece and Rome.
6. Plato considered the Lydian mode to be morally cor-
rupting and loose; others found it a source of relaxed
enjoyment.
7. When Orpheus attempted to rescue his wife Eurydice
from Hades, he lost her by violating the command that
he not look back to see if she were behind him.
8. The concluding lines recall the final couplet of Mar-

lowe's lyric *The Passionate Shepherd to His Love:* "If these
delights thy mind may move; / Then live with me, and be
my love."
1. The pensive one.
2. God of dreams and son of Sleep.
3. Melancholy was governed by the black bile in the body
and manifested itself in a black face.
4. The Ethiopian Prince Memnon (*Odyssey* 11.521) had
a sister named Himera (Greek, "light of day").

Or that starred Ethiope Queen[5] that strove
20   To set her beauties praise above
The sea nymphs, and their powers offended.
Yet thou art higher far descended,
Thee bright-haired Vesta[6] long of yore,
To solitary Saturn bore;
25   His daughter she (in Saturn's reign
Such mixture was not held a stain)[7]
Oft in glimmering bowers, and glades
He met her, and in secret shades
Of woody Ida's inmost grove,
30   While yet there was no fear of Jove.
Come pensive nun, devout and pure,
Sober, steadfast, and demure,
All in a robe of darkest grain,
Flowing with majestic train,
35   And sable° stole of cypress lawn,°   *dark / fine linen*
Over thy decent shoulders drawn.
Come, but keep thy wonted state,
With even step, and musing gait,
And looks commercing with the skies,
40   Thy rapt soul sitting in thine eyes:
There held in holy passion still,
Forget thyself to marble,[8] till
With a sad leaden downward cast,
Thou fix them on the earth as fast.
45   And join with thee calm Peace, and Quiet,
Spare Fast, that oft with gods doth diet,
And hears the Muses in a ring,
Ay round about Jove's altar sing.
And add to these retired leisure;
50   That in trim gardens takes his pleasure;
But first, and chiefest, with thee bring
Him that yon soars on golden wing,
Guiding the fiery-wheelèd throne,[9]
The cherub Contemplation;[1]
55   And the mute Silence hist° along,   *a call*
'Less Philomel[2] will deign a song,
In her sweetest, saddest plight,
Smoothing the rugged brow of night,
While Cynthia[3] checks her dragon yoke,
60   Gently o'er th'accustomed oak;
Sweet bird that shunn'st the noise of folly,
Most musical, most melancholy!

---

5. Cassiopeia was turned into a constellation because she boasted that she was more beautiful than the Nereids.
6. Milton makes Vesta a mother; by tradition, she was a virgin, daughter of Saturn, and goddess of the hearth.
7. The Golden Age was a time of plenty and sexual freedom.
8. Turning to stone through grief comes from the story of Niobe.
9. See Ezekiel 1.4–6.
1. The angel Cherubim contemplate God.
2. The nightingale (Greek).
3. The moon goddess, another name for Hecate; for her dragons, see Ovid, *Metamorphoses* 7.218–19.

Thee chantress oft the woods among,
I woo to hear thy evensong;
65   And missing thee, I walk unseen
On the dry smooth-shaven green,
To behold the wandring moon,
Riding near her highest noon,
Like one that had been led astray
70   Through the heaven's wide pathless way;
And oft, as if her head she bowed,
Stooping through a fleecy cloud.
Oft on a plat° of rising ground,   *plot*
I hear the far-off curfew sound,
75   Over some wide-watered shore,
Swinging slow with sullen roar;
Or if the air will not permit,
Some still removèd place will fit,
Where glowing embers through the room
80   Teach light to counterfeit a gloom,
Far from all resort of mirth,
Save the cricket on the hearth,
Or the bellman's drowsy charm,[4]
To bless the doors from nightly harm;
85   Or let my lamp at midnight hour,
Be seen in some high lonely tower,
Where I may oft out-watch the Bear,[5]
With thrice great Hermes,[6] or unsphere[7]
The spirit of Plato to unfold
90   What worlds, or what vast regions hold
The immortal mind that hath forsook
Her mansion in this fleshly nook;
And of those demons that are found
In fire, air, flood, or under ground,
95   Whose power hath a true consent
With planet, or with element.
Sometime let gorgeous Tragedy
In scepter'd pall° come sweeping by,   *robe*
Presenting Thebes, or Pelops line,
100   Or the tale of Troy divine.[8]
Or what (though rare) of later age
Ennobled hath the buskined stage.[9]
But, O sad virgin, that thy power
Might raise Musaeus[1] from his bower,
105   Or bid the soul of Orpheus[2] sing

4. The night-watchman, or bellman, cries out the hours in a chant, or charm (from *carmen*, Latin for song).
5. The constellation of the Great Bear, which never sets, symbolizes perfection.
6. Hermes Trismegistus was believed to be the author of the Hermetica, texts of esoteric neoplatonism and magic.
7. To remove from the eternal sphere and make reappear on earth.
8. Thebes was the birthplace of Oedipus, tragic hero of Sophocles' *Oedipus Rex*. Pelops's descendants Agamem-

non and Orestes are the subject of Aeschylus' tragedy *Oresteia*. Troy was the city destroyed by the Trojan War, the tragic consequences of which are the subject of Euripides' *The Trojan Women*.
9. The high boots of tragic actors. Compare *L'Allegro* line 132.
1. Prophet and poet, who studied with the mythic bard Orpheus.
2. See *L'Allegro* 145–50.

Such notes as warbled to the string,
Drew iron tears down Pluto's cheek,
And made Hell grant what Love did seek.
Or call up him[3] that left half told
110   The story of Cambuscan bold,
Of Camball, and of Algarsife,
And who had Canace to wife,
That owned the virtuous° ring and glass,   *magical*
And of the wondrous horse of brass,
115   On which the Tartar king did ride;
And if aught else, great bards beside,[4]
In sage and solemn tunes have sung,
Of tourneys and of trophies hung;
Of forests, and enchantments drear,
120   Where more is meant then meets the ear.
Thus, Night, oft see me in thy pale career,
Till civil-suited Morn appear,
Not tricked and frounced[5] as she was wont,
With the Attic boy[6] to hunt,
125   But kerchiefed in a comely cloud,
While rocking winds are piping loud,
Or ushered with a shower still,°   *quiet*
When the gust hath blown his fill,
Ending on the rustling leaves,
130   With minute drops from off the eaves.
And when the sun begins to fling
His flaring beams, me, Goddess, bring
To archèd walks of twilight groves,
And shadows brown that Sylvan[7] loves
135   Of pine, or monumental oak,
Where the rude ax with heavèd stroke.
Was never heard the nymphs to daunt,
Or fright them from their hallowed haunt.
There in close covert by some brook,
140   Where no prophaner eye may look,
Hide me from day's garish eye,
While the bee with honeyed thigh,
That at her flowery work doth sing,
And the waters murmuring
145   With such consort° as they keep,   *musical harmony*
Entice the dewy-feathered sleep;
And let some strange mysterious dream
Wave at his wings in airy stream
Of lively portraiture displayed,
150   Softly on my eye-lids laid.
And as I wake, sweet music breathe
Above, about, or underneath,

3. Chaucer; the "story" is the unfinished *Squire's Tale*.
4. Lines 116–20 refer to Spenser's allegorical *Faerie Queene*.
5. Richly attired and wearing ringlets.
6. Cephalus, beloved of Aurora, who met him while he was hunting. (See Ovid, *Metamorphoses* 7.700–13.)
7. Roman god of the forest.

Sent by some spirit to mortals good,
Or th'unseen genius° of the wood.   *presiding local god*
155 But let my due feet never fail
To walk the studious cloisters° pale,   *enclosure*
And love the high embowèd° roof,   *arched*
With antic pillars massy proof,°   *impenetrability*
And storied[8] windows richly dight,°   *decorated*
160 Casting a dim religious light.
There let the pealing organ blow
To the full voiced choir below,
In service high, and anthems clear,
As may with sweetness, through mine ear,
165 Dissolve me into ecstasies,
And bring all heaven before mine eyes.
And may at last my weary age
Find out the peaceful hermitage,
The hairy gown and mossy cell,
170 Where I may sit and rightly spell°   *find out about*
Of every star that heaven doth shew,
And every herb that sips the dew,
Till old experience do attain
To something like prophetic strain.
175 These pleasures Melancholy give,
And I with thee will choose to live.[9]

Lycidas

In this Monody[1] the Author bewails a learned Friend,[2] unfortunately drowned in his passage from Chester on the Irish Seas, 1637. And by occasion foretells the ruin of our corrupted Clergy then in their height.

Yet once more, O ye laurels, and once more
Ye myrtles brown, with ivy[3] never sear,°   *withered*
I come to pluck your berries harsh and crude,°   *unripe*
And with forced fingers rude,
5 Shatter your leaves before the mellowing year.
Bitter constraint, and sad occasion dear,
Compels me to disturb your season due:
For Lycidas is dead, dead ere his prime,[4]
Young Lycidas, and hath not left his peer:
10 Who would not sing for Lycidas? he knew
Himself to sing, and build the lofty rhyme.
He must not float upon his watery bier
Unwept, and welter° to the parching wind,   *writhe*
Without the meed° of some melodious tear.°   *recompense / elegy*
15   Begin then, sisters of the sacred well,[5]

8. With stories from the Bible.
9. See *L'Allegro* 151–52.
1. A mournful song sung by one voice. *Lycidas* is a pastoral elegy, a lament for the dead through language evoking nature and the rural life of shepherds. The first *Idyll* of Theocritus and Virgil's fifth *Eclogue* are classical precedents for *Lycidas*. Shelley's *Adonais* and Arnold's *Thyrsis* are later examples of this form.

2. Edward King, who attended Cambridge when Milton did, drowned 10 August 1637. He had planned to enter the clergy and had written some Latin poems.
3. Laurels ... myrtles ... ivy: the leaves used to crown respectively poets, lovers, and scholars.
4. King ("Lycidas") was 25 when he died.
5. Sisters: the nine muses; well: Aganippe, on Mount Helicon, where there was an altar to Jove.

That from beneath the seat of Jove doth spring,
Begin, and somewhat loudly sweep the string.
Hence with denial vain, and coy excuse,
So may some gentle Muse
20 With lucky words favor my destined urn,
And as he passes turn,
And bid fair peace be to my sable° shrowd.   *black*
For we were nursed upon the self-same hill,
Fed the same flock; by fountain, shade, and rill.
25   Together both, ere the high lawns appeared
Under the opening eyelids of the morn,
We drove a field, and both together heard
What time the grayfly[6] winds her sultry horn,
Battening° our flocks with the fresh dews of night,   *fattening*
30 Oft till the star that rose, at evening, bright,
Toward heaven's descent had sloped his westering wheel.
Meanwhile the rural ditties were not mute,
Tempered to th' oaten flute,
Rough satyrs danced, and fauns with cloven heel,
35 From the glad sound would not be absent long,
And old Damaetas[7] lov'd to hear our song.
    But O the heavy change, now thou art gone,
Now thou art gone, and never must return!
Thee shepherd, thee the woods, and desert caves,
40 With wild thyme and the gadding° vine o'ergrown,   *wandering*
And all their echoes mourn.
The willows, and the hazle copses green,
Shall now no more be seen,
Fanning their joyous leaves to thy soft lays.
45 As killing as the canker° to the rose,   *cankerworm*
Or taint-worm[8] to the weanling herds that graze,
Or frost to flowers, that their gay wardrop wear,
When first the white thorn blows;
Such, Lycidas, thy loss to shepherd's ear.
50   Where were ye nymphs when the remorseless deep
Closed o'er the head of your loved Lycidas?
For neither were ye playing on the steep
Where your old Bards, the famous Druids,° lie,   *pagan Celtic priests*
Nor on the shaggy top of Mona[9] high,
55 Nor yet where Deva spreads her wizard stream:
Ay me, I fondly dream!
Had ye been there—for what could that have done?
What could the Muse[1] herself that Orpheus bore,
The Muse herself for her inchanting son
60 Whom universal nature did lament,
When by the rout that made the hideous roar
His gory visage down the stream was sent,

6. Name used to designate various kinds of insect.
7. "Damaetas" is etymologically derived from the Greek verb meaning "to tame;" thus a tutor is meant.
8. An intestinal worm that can kill newly weaned calves.

9. The island of Anglesey; Deva: the river Dee, viewed as magical and prophetic by the inhabitants.
1. Calliope, Orpheus' mother.

Down the swift Hebrus to the Lesbian shore.[2]
   Alas! What boots° it with incessant care   *avails*
65 To tend the homely slighted shepherd's trade,
And strictly meditate the thankless Muse,
Were it not better done as others use,
To sport with Amaryllis in the shade,
Or with the tangles of Neaera's hair?[3]
70 Fame is the spur that the clear spirit doth raise
(That last infirmity of noble mind)
To scorn delights, and live laborious days;
But the fair guerdon° when we hope to find,   *reward*
And think to burst out into sudden blaze,
75 Comes the blind Fury[4] with th'abhorred shears,
And slits the thin spun life. "But not the praise,"
Phoebus replied, and touched my trembling ears;[5]
"Fame is no plant that grows on mortal soil,
Nor in the glistering foil[6]
80 Set off to the world, nor in broad rumor lies,
But lives and spreds aloft by those pure eyes,
And perfet witness of all-judging Jove;
As he pronounces lastly on each deed,
Of so much fame in heaven expect thy meed."
85   O Fountain Arethuse, and thou honored flood,
Smooth-sliding Mincius, crowned with vocal reeds,
That strain I heard was of a higher mood.[7]
But now my oat proceeds,
And listens to the herald of the sea
90 That came in Neptune's plea.[8]
He asked the waves, and asked the felon° winds,   *savage*
"What hard mishap hath doomed this gentle swain?"
And questioned every gust of rugged wings
That blows from off each beakèd promontory;
95 They knew not of his story,
And sage Hippotades[9] their answer brings,
That not a blast was from his dungeon strayed,
The air was calm, and on the level brine,
Sleek Panope[1] with all her sisters played.
100 It was that fatal and perfidious bark,
Built in th' eclipse,° and rigged with curses dark,   *period of evil omen*
That sunk so low that sacred head of thine.
   Next Camus,[2] reverend sire, went footing slow,

2. Ovid, *Metamorphoses*, 11.1–55, relates how Orpheus was torn to pieces by the Thracian women and how his severed head floated down the Hebrus and was carried across to the island of Lesbos.
3. Amaryllis symbolizes erotic poetry (Virgil, *Eclogues* 2.14–15); Neaera: see *Eclogues* 3.3.
4. Atropos, one of the Fates, who cut the thread of life spun by her sisters.
5. Echoing Virgil, *Eclogues* 6.3–4: "the Cynthian plucked my ear and warned me."
6. A reflecting leaf of gold or silver placed under a pre-

cious stone.
7. The "higher mood" is the lofty tone of Phoebus' speech. The invocation to the river Arethuse (in Sicily) and the Mincius (Virgil's native river) marks a return to pastoral.
8. The herald Triton came to defend Neptune from blame for King's death.
9. God of winds, son of Hippotes.
1. One of the 50 Nereids (sea nymphs), mentioned by Virgil, *Aeneid* 5.240.
2. The River Cam, representing Cambridge University.

His mantle hairy, and his bonnet sedge,[3]
105 Inwrought with figures dim, and on the edge
Like to that sanguine flower inscribed with woe.[4]
"Ah! who hath reft (quoth he) my dearest pledge?"°   child
Last came, and last did go,
The Pilot of the Galilean lake,[5]
110 Two massy keys he bore of metals twain,
(The golden opes, the iron shuts amain°).   vehemently
He shook his mitered[6] locks, and stern bespake,
"How well could I have spared for thee, young swain,
Enow° of such as for their bellies' sake,   enough
115 Creep and intrude, and climb into the fold?[7]
Of other care they little reckoning make,
Than how to scramble at the shearer's feast,
And shove away the worthy bidden guest.
Blind mouths![8] that scarce themselves know how to hold
120 A sheep-hook, or have learned aught else the least
That to the faithfull herdman's art belongs!
What recks it them?[9] What need they? They are sped;°   satisfied
And when they list,° their lean and flashy° songs   please / insipid
Grate on their scrannel° pipes of wretched straw,   feeble
125 The hungry sheep look up, and are not fed,
But swoln with wind, and the rank mist they draw,
Rot inwardly, and foul contagion spread.
Besides what the grim woolf[1] with privy° paw   secret, hidden
Daily devours apace, and nothing said,
130 But that two-handed engine at the door,
Stands ready to smite once, and smite no more."[2]
     Return Alpheus,[3] the dread voice is past,
That shrunk thy streams; return Sicilian muse,
And call the vales, and bid them hither cast
135 Their bells, and flowerets of a thousand hues.
Ye valleys low where the mild whispers use,°   often go
Of shades and wanton winds, and gushing brooks,
On whose fresh lap the swart star[4] sparely looks,
Throw hither all your quaint enameled eyes,
140 That on the green turf suck the honeyed showers,
And purple all the ground with vernal flowers.
Bring the rathe° primrose that forsaken dies,   early
The tufted crow-toe,° and pale jessamine,°   hyacinth / jasmine
The white pink, and the pansie freaked° with jet,   adorned
145 The glowing violet.

3. "Hairy" refers to the fur of the academic gown; "sedge"
is a rushlike plant growing near water.
4. The hyacinth; see Ovid, *Metamorphoses* 10.214–16:
"the flower bore the marks AI AI, letters of lamentation."
5. St. Peter bearing the keys of heaven given to him by
Christ (Matthew 16.19).
6. Wearing a bishop's headdress.
7. See John 10.1: "He that entereth not by the door into
the sheepfold, but climbeth up some other way, the same
is a thief and a robber."

8. Milton's charge against the greed of the clergy.
9. What business is it of theirs?
1. The Roman Catholic Church.
2. Indicates that the corrupted clergy will be punished;
see 1 Samuel 26.8.
3. The Arcadian hunter, who pursued Arethusa, the
nymph he loved, under the sea to Sicily.
4. The Dog-star, Sirius. Its rising brings on the dog-days
of heat.

The musk-rose, and the well attired woodbine,
With cowslips wan° that hang the pensive head,   *pale*
And every flower that sad embroidery wears:
Bid amaranthus[5] all his beauty shed,
150 And daffadillies fill their cups with tears,
To strew the laureate hearse where Lycid lies.
For so to interpose a little ease,
Let our frail thoughts dally with false surmise.[6]
Ay me! whilst thee the shores, and sounding seas
155 Wash far away, where'er thy bones are hurled,
Whether beyond the stormy Hebrides[7]
Where thou perhaps under the whelming tide
Visit'st the bottom of the monstrous world;
Or whether thou to our moist° vows denied,   *tearful*
160 Sleep'st by the fable of Bellerus[8] old,
Where the great vision of the guarded mount
Looks toward Namancos and Bayona's hold;[9]
Look homeward angel° now, and melt with ruth.°   *Michael / pity*
And, O ye dolphins, waft the haples youth.[1]
165   Weep no more, woeful shepherds weep no more,
For Lycidas your sorrow is not dead,
Sunk though he be beneath the wat'ry floor,
So sinks the day-star° in the ocean bed,   *the sun*
And yet anon repairs his drooping head,
170 And tricks° his beams, and with new spangled ore,°   *arrays / gold*
Flames in the forehead of the morning sky:
So Lycidas sunk low, but mounted high,
Through the dear might of him[2] that walked the waves
Where other groves, and other streams along,
175 With nectar pure his oozy lock's he laves,[3]
And hears the unexpressive nuptial[4] song,
In the blest kingdoms meek of joy and love.
There entertain him all the saints above,
In solemn troops, and sweet societies
180 That sing, and singing in their glory move,
And wipe the tears for ever from his eyes.[5]
Now Lycidas the shepherds weep no more;
Henceforth thou art the genius° of the shore,   *local deity*
In thy large recompense, and shalt be good
185 To all that wander in that perilous flood.
    Thus sang the uncouth° swain to th' oaks and rills,   *unknown*
While the still morn went out with sandals gray,

---

5. The eternal flower (see *Paradise Lost*, 3.353–57).
6. The surmise is false since King's body drowned and will have no hearse.
7. Islands off the northwest coast of Scotland.
8. A giant of Bellerium, the Latin name for Land's End.
9. Namancos: an ancient name for a district in north-western Spain; Bayona: a fortress town about 50 miles south of Cape Finisterre. The two names represent the threat of Spanish Catholicism, against which St. Michael guards England.

1. The dolphin is a symbol of Christ; waft: convey by water.
2. Christ, who walks on the sea in Matthew 14.25–6.
3. The brooks in Eden run with nectar, *Paradise Lost* 4.240; oozy: slimy from contact with the sea.
4. Relating to the marriage of the Lamb, or Christ, to the Church (Revelation 19.7).
5. See Revelation 7.17: "God shall wipe away all tears from their eyes"; see also Revelation 21.4.

He touched the tender stops of various quills,[6]
With eager thought warbling his Doric° lay: *pastoral*
190   And now the sun had stretched out all the hills,[7]
And now was dropped into the western bay;
At last he rose, and twitch'd his mantle blue:[8]
Tomorrow to fresh woods, and pastures new.

1638

How Soon Hath Time

How soon hath time the subtle thief of youth,
    Stol'n on his wing my three and twentieth year![1]
    My hasting days fly on with full career,°   *speed*
    But my late spring no bud or blossom shew'th.
5   Perhaps my semblance° might deceive the truth,   *appearance*
    That I to manhood am arrived so near,
    And inward ripeness doth much less appear,
    That some more timely-happy spirits[2] endu'th.°   *gives, endows*
Yet be it less or more, or soon or slow,
10   It shall be still° in strictest measure even,°   *always / level with*
    To that same lot, however mean or high,
Toward which Time leads me, and the will of Heaven;
    All is, if I have grace to use it so,
    As ever in my great task Master's° eye.   *God's*

On the New Forcers of Conscience Under the Long Parliament[1]

Because you have thrown off your prelate Lord,[2]
    And with stiff vows renounced his liturgy[3]
    To seize the widowed whore Plurality[4]
    From them whose sin ye envied, not abhored,
5   Dare ye for this adjure° the civil sword   *entreat*
    To force our consciences that Christ set free,[5]
    And ride us with a classic hierarchy[6]
Taught ye by meer A. S. and Rutherford?[7]
Men whose life, learning, faith and pure intent
10   Would have been held in high esteem with Paul
    Must now be named and printed heretics
By shallow Edwards[8] and Scotch what d'ye call:
    But we do hope to find out all your tricks,

---

6. Stops are the finger-holes in the pipes; quills are the hollow reeds of the shepherd's pipe.
7. The setting sun had shone over the hills and lengthened their shadows.
8. Blue is the traditional symbol of hope.
1. Written when Milton was 23, this sonnet was published in 1645.
2. Those individuals of Milton's age who have already achieved success.
1. Written c. 1646, but printed in 1673.
2. Refers to the abolishment of episcopacy in England in September 1646.
3. The House of Commons forbade the use of the *Book of Common Prayer* in August 1645.

4. The practice of holding more than one living identified with episcopacy but subsequently supported by the Presbyterian system.
5. Milton complains of the Westminster Assembly's attempt to impose Presbyterianism by force.
6. Parliament resolved that the English congregations were to be grouped in Presbyteries or "Classes," which could impose rules after the Scottish pattern.
7. A. S.: Dr. Adam Stewart, Scottish Presbyterian controversialist; Rutherford: Samuel Rutherford, author of pamphlets in defense of Presbyterianism.
8. Thomas Edwards, author of *Antapologia*, advocating strict Presbyterianism, and *Gangraena* (1646), which included a denunciation of Milton's views on divorce.

Your plots and packing worse then those of Trent,[9]
15   That so the Parliament
May with their wholsome and preventive shears
Clip your phylacteries,[1] though balk° your ears,[2]   stop short of
              And succor our just fears,
When they shall read this clearly in your charge:
20   *New presbyter* is but *old priest* writ large.[3]

When I Consider How My Light Is Spent[1]

When I consider how my light is spent,
    Ere half my days, in this dark world and wide,
    And that one talent which is death to hide,[2]
    Lodged with me useless, though my soul more bent
5 To serve therewith my Maker, and present
    My true account, lest he returning chide,
    Doth God exact day-labor, light denied,
    I fondly° ask; but Patience to prevent   foolishly
That murmur, soon replies, "God doth not need
10   Either man's work or his own gifts,[3] who best
    Bear his mild yoke,[4] they serve him best, his state
    Is kingly. Thousands at his bidding speed
    And post o'er land and ocean without rest:
    They also serve who only stand and wait."

Methought I Saw My Late Espoused Saint[1]

Methought I saw my late espousèd saint°   soul in heaven
    Brought to me like Alcestis[2] from the grave,
    Whom Jove's great son to her glad husband gave,
    Rescued from death by force though pale and faint.
5 Mine as whom washed from spot of child-bed taint,
    Purification in the old Law[3] did save,
    And such, as yet once more I trust to have
    Full sight of her in Heaven without restraint,

---

9. Comparing the overwhelming Presbyterian predominance in the Assembly to the anti-protestant Roman Catholic Council of Trent (1545–1563).
1. Small leather boxes containing scriptural texts worn by Jews as a mark of obedience. Christ in Matthew 23.5 uses the phrase "make broad their phylacteries" in the sense "vaunt their own righteousness."
2. William Prynne, who had attacked one of the Bishops in print, actually did have both of his ears cut off. Milton's manuscript of this poem contains the line: "Crop ye as close as marginal P—'s ears."
3. "Priest" is etymologically a contracted form of Latin "presbyter" (an elder). The Presbyterians now appeared as dictatorial as the bishops had been.
1. Probably written around 1652, as Milton's blindness became complete.
2. In the parable of the talents, Jesus tells of a servant who is given a talent (a large sum of money) to keep for

his master. He buries the money; his master condemns him for not having invested it wisely. Matthew 25.14–30.
3. See Job 22.2.
4. See Matthew 11.30: "My yoke is easy."
1. The date of composition is placed at 1658; the poem appears as the last sonnet in the 1673 edition.
2. In Euripides' *Alcestis*, she gives her life for her husband Admetus, but Hercules ("Jove's great son") wrestles with death and brings her back from the grave.
3. According to Leviticus 12.4–8, after bearing a female child, a woman shall be unclean "two weeks, as in her separation: and she shall continue in the blood of her purifying threescore and six days" (i.e., during this period "she shall touch no hallowed thing, nor come into the sanctuary"). Some critics construe this line as evidence that the sonnet is about the death of Milton's second wife Katherine Woodcock, who died three months after childbirth in 1658.

> Came vested all in white, pure as her mind:
> 10   Her face was veiled, yet to my fancied sight,
> Love, sweetness, goodness, in her person shined
> So clear, as in no face with more delight,
> But O, as to embrace me she enclined,
> I waked, she fled, and day brought back my night.[4]

AREOPAGITICA   The title *Areopagitica* refers to the Areopagus, the ancient Athenian Council of State. Milton wrote *Areopagitica* to criticize the Parliamentary Ordinance of 14 June 1643 "to prevent and suppress the licence of printing." Although *Areopagitica* was unlicensed, Milton made the bold move of affixing his name to the title page, which made no mention of the printer. Also on the title page are these lines from Euripides' *Suppliant Women* (438–41):

> There is true Liberty when free born men
> Having to advise the public may speak free,
> Which he who can and will, deserv'd high praise,
> Who neither can nor will, may hold his peace;
> What can be juster in a state than this?

from Areopagitica[1]
A Speech of Mr. John Milton
for the Liberty of Unlicensed Printing,
to the Parliament of England

* * * Good and evil we know in the field of this world grow up together almost inseparably; and the knowledge of good is so involved and interwoven with the knowledge of evil, and in so many cunning resemblances hardly to be discerned, that those confused seeds which were imposed on Psyche as an incessant labor to cull out and sort asunder, were not more intermixed.[2] It was from out the rind of one apple tasted, that the knowledge of good and evil, as two twins cleaving together, leaped forth into the world. And perhaps this is that doom which Adam fell into of knowing good and evil, that is to say, of knowing good by evil.[3]

As therefore the state of man now is, what wisdom can there be to choose, what continence to forbear without the knowledge of evil? He that can apprehend and consider vice with all her baits and seeming pleasures, and yet abstain, and yet distinguish, and yet prefer that which is truly better, he is the true wayfaring[4] Christian. I cannot praise a fugitive and cloistered virtue, unexercised and unbreathed, that never sallies out and sees her adversary, but slinks out of the race where that immortal garland is to be run for, not without dust and heat. Assuredly we bring not innocence into the world, we bring impurity much rather: that which purifies us is trial, and trial is by what is contrary. That virtue therefore which is but a youngling in the contemplation of evil, and knows not the utmost that vice promises to her followers, and

---

4. In Virgil, Aeneas sees the ghost of his wife Creusa amid the ruins of Troy; when he tries to embrace her, "she withdrew into thin air . . . most like a winged dream" (*Aeneid* 2.791–794).

1. The Areopagus was the seat of the Council of State, organized as a judicial tribunal by Solon in the sixth century B.C. The Athenian orator Isocrates argues for its renewal in his *Areopagiticus*.

2. Furious over her son Cupid's love for Psyche, Venus ordered Psyche to sort out a huge mass of seeds, but the ants, sympathizing with her plight, sorted them for her. See Apuleius, *Golden Ass* 4–6.

3. See *Paradise Lost* 4.222: "Knowledge of Good bought dear by knowing ill."

4. The original reads "warfaring," but in several copies this is corrected by hand to "wayfaring."

rejects it, is but a blank virtue, not a pure; her whiteness is but an excremental[5] whiteness; which was the reason why our sage and serious poet Spenser, whom I dare be known to think a better teacher than Scotus or Aquinas, describing true temperance under the person of Guyon, brings him in with his palmer through the cave of Mammon and the bower of earthly bliss, that he might see and know, and yet abstain.[6]

Since therefore, the knowledge and survey of vice is in this world so necessary to the constituting of human virtue, and the scanning of error to the confirmation of truth, how can we more safely and with less danger scout into the regions of sin and falsity than by reading all manner of tractates and hearing all manner of reason? And this is the benefit which may be had of books promiscuously read.

But of the harm that may result hence, three kinds are usually reckoned. First is feared the infection that may spread; but then all human learning and controversy in religious points must remove out of the world, yea the Bible itself; for that ofttimes relates blasphemy not nicely,[7] it describes the carnal sense of wicked men not unelegantly, it brings in holiest men passionately murmuring against providence through all the arguments of Epicurus;[8] in other great disputes it answers dubiously and darkly to the common reader; and ask a Talmudist what ails the modesty of his marginal Keri, that Moses and all the prophets cannot persuade him to pronounce the textual Chetiv.[9] For these causes we all know the Bible itself put by the papist into the first rank of prohibited books. The ancientest fathers must be next removed, as Clement of Alexandria, and that Eusebian book of Evangelic preparation transmitting our ears through a hoard of heathenish obscenities to receive the Gospel. Who finds not that Irenaeus, Epiphanius, Jerome,[1] and others discover more heresies than they well confute, and that oft for heresy which is the truer opinion?[2]

* * *

Impunity and remissness, for certain, are the bane of a commonwealth; but here the great art lies, to discern in what the law is to bid restraint and punishment, and in what things persuasion only is to work. If every action which is good or evil in man at ripe years, were to be under pittance and prescription and compulsion, what were virtue but a name, what praise could be then due to well-doing, what gramercy[3] to be sober, just, or continent?

Many there be that complain of divine providence for suffering Adam to transgress. Foolish tongues! when God gave him reason, he gave him freedom to choose, for reason is but choosing; he had been else a mere artificial Adam, such an Adam as he is in the motions.[4] We ourselves esteem not of that obedience, or love, or gift, which is of force. God therefore left him free, set before him a provoking object, ever almost in his eyes; herein consisted his merit, herein the right of his reward, the

---

5. Superficial.
6. Duns Scotus and Thomas Aquinas here represent types of the scholastic theologian. For the cave of Mammon, see *The Faerie Queene* 2.7 (the Palmer is not with Guyon in Mammon's Cave); the "Bower of Bliss," 2.12.
7. Delicately.
8. The Greek philosopher who propounded a morality based on pleasure.
9. Talmudist: a student of the Talmud, the Jewish commentaries on the Bible; Keri: marginal emendations of rabbinical scholars on the Chetiv, the text of the Bible.
1. Early apologists of Christianity: St. Clement of

Alexandria (2nd century) and Eusebius, who describes pagan depravity to promote faith in Christianity, as do St. Irenaeus (2nd century), Epiphanius (4th century), and St. Jerome (early 5th century).
2. Milton goes on to argue that the effect of books depends upon the teacher, who, if really good, needs no books. Milton stresses the role of the reader: A wise person can find something instructive in even the worst books.
3. Thanks.
4. Puppet shows. For this statement about Adam, see *Paradise Lost* 3.103–28, pages 957–58.

praise of his abstinence. Wherefore did he create passions within us, pleasures round about us, but that these rightly tempered are the very ingredients of virtue? They are not skilful considerers of human things who imagine to remove sin by removing the matter of sin. For, besides that it is a huge heap increasing under the very act of diminishing, though some part of it may for a time be withdrawn from some persons, it cannot from all, in such a universal thing as books are; and when this is done, yet the sin remains entire. Though ye take from a covetous man all his treasure, he has yet one jewel left—ye cannot bereave him of his covetousness. Banish all objects of lust, shut up all youth into the severest discipline that can be exercised in any hermitage, ye cannot make them chaste that came not thither so: such great care and wisdom is required to the right managing of this point.

Suppose we could expel sin by this means; look how much we thus expel of sin, so much we expel of virtue: for the matter of them both is the same; remove that, and ye remove them both alike. This justifies the high providence of God, who, though he command us temperance, justice, continence, yet pours out before us, even to a profuseness, all desirable things, and gives us minds that can wander beyond all limit and satiety. Why should we then affect a rigor contrary to the manner of God and of nature, by abridging or scanting those means which books freely permitted are, both to the trial of virtue and the exercise of truth?[5]

* * *

And lest some should persuade ye, Lords and Commons, that these arguments of learned men's discouragement at this your Order are mere flourishes, and not real, I could recount what I have seen and heard in other countries where this kind of inquisition tyrannizes; when I have sat among their learned men, for that honor I had, and been counted happy to be born in such a place of philosophic freedom as they supposed England was, while themselves did nothing but bemoan the servile condition into which learning amongst them was brought; that this was it which had damped the glory of Italian wits; that nothing had been there written now these many years but flattery and fustian. There it was that I found and visited the famous Galileo, grown old, a prisoner to the Inquisition[6] for thinking in astronomy otherwise than the Franciscan and Dominican licensers thought. And though I knew that England then was groaning loudest under the prelatical yoke, nevertheless I took it as a pledge of future happiness that other nations were so persuaded of her liberty.

Yet was it beyond my hope that those worthies were then breathing in her air, who should be her leaders to such a deliverance as shall never be forgotten by any revolution of time that this world hath to finish. When that was once begun, it was as little in my fear, that what words of complaint I heard among learned men of other parts uttered against the Inquisition, the same I should hear by as learned men at home uttered in time of Parliament against an order of licensing; and that so generally, that when I had disclosed myself a companion of their discontent, I might say, if without envy, that he whom an honest quaestorship had endeared to the Sicilians, was not more by them importuned against Verres,[7] than the favorable opinion which

5. Milton argues that no intelligent person will be willing to take on the job of censorship and that an unintelligent person would be prone to commit serious errors. In addition to giving power to stupid people, censorship would actually encourage people to read banned books and to adhere to the perverse opinions expressed in such books.
6. In 1633 the great Italian astronomer Galileo was tried by the Inquisition at Rome and forced to abjure his earlier assertion that his findings confirmed the Copernican heliocentric theory of the universe. He was under house arrest in Florence when Milton visited there in 1638–1639.
7. Cicero exposed the corruption of Verres' government in 75 B.C.

I had among many who honor ye, and are known and respected by ye, loaded me with entreaties and persuasions that I would not despair to lay together that which just reason should bring into my mind toward the removal of an undeserved thraldom upon learning.

That this is not, therefore, the disburdening of a particular fancy, but the common grievance of all those who had prepared their minds and studies above the vulgar pitch to advance truth in others, and from others to entertain it, thus much may satisfy. And in their name I shall for neither friend nor foe conceal what the general murmur is; that if it come to inquisitioning again and licensing, and that we are so timorous of ourselves and so suspicious of all men as to fear each book and the shaking of every leaf, before we know what the contents are; if some who but of late were little better than silenced from preaching, shall come now to silence us from reading, except what they please, it cannot be guessed what is intended by some but a second tyranny over learning; and will soon put it out of controversy that bishops and presbyters are the same to us both name and thing.

* * * * *

But I am certain that a state governed by the rules of justice and fortitude, or a church built and founded upon the rock of faith and true knowledge, cannot be so pusillanimous.[8] While things are yet not constituted in religion, that freedom of writing should be restrained by a discipline imitated from the prelates, and learnt by them from the Inquisition, to shut us up all again into the breast of a licenser, must needs give cause of doubt and discouragement to all learned and religious men. Who cannot but discern the fineness of this politic drift, and who are the contrivers: that while bishops were to be baited down, then all presses might be open; it was the people's birthright and privilege in time of parliament, it was the breaking forth of light.

But now, the bishops abrogated and voided out of the church, as if our reformation sought no more but to make room for others into their seats under another name, the episcopal arts begin to bud again; the cruse[9] of truth must run no more oil; liberty of printing must be enthralled again under a prelatical commission of twenty, the privilege of the people nullified; and, which is worse, the freedom of learning must groan again, and to her old fetters: all this the parliament yet sitting. Although their own late arguments and defenses against the prelates might remember them that this obstructing violence meets for the most part with an event utterly opposite to the end which it drives at; instead of suppressing sects and schisms, it raises them and invests them with a reputation: "The punishing of wits enhances their authority," saith the Viscount St. Albans,[1] "and a forbidden writing is thought to be a certain spark of truth that flies up in the faces of them who seek to tread it out."

This Order, therefore, may prove a nursing mother to sects, but I shall easily show how it will be a stepdame to Truth; and first by disenabling us to the maintenance of what is known already.

Well knows he who uses to consider, that our faith and knowledge thrives by exercise, as well as our limbs and complexion. Truth is compared in scripture to a streaming fountain;[2] if her waters flow not in a perpetual progression, they sicken into a muddy pool of conformity and tradition. A man may be a heretic in the truth; and if he believe things only because his pastor says so, or the Assembly so deter-

---

8. Mean-spirited, cowardly.
9. Small vessel; see 1 Kings 17.12–16.
1. Sir Francis Bacon, *An Advertisement Touching the Con-*

troversies of the Church of England.
2. See Psalms 85.11.

mines, without knowing other reason, though his belief be true, yet the very truth he holds becomes his heresy. There is not any burden that some would gladlier post off to another than the charge and care of their religion. There be, who knows not that there be, of protestants and professors who live and die in as arrant an implicit faith, as any lay papist of Loreto.[3]

A wealthy man addicted to his pleasure and to his profits, finds religion to be a traffic so entangled, and of so many piddling accounts, that of all mysteries[4] he cannot skill to keep a stock going upon that trade. What should he do? Fain he would have the name to be religious, fain he would bear up with his neighbors in that. What does he, therefore, but resolves to give over toiling, and to find himself out some factor to whose care and credit he may commit the whole managing of his religious affairs; some Divine of note and estimation that must be. To him he adheres, resigns the whole warehouse of his religion with all the locks and keys into his custody; and indeed makes the very person of that man his religion; esteems his associating with him a sufficient evidence and commendatory of his own piety. So that a man may say his religion is now no more within himself, but is become a dividual movable,[5] and goes and comes near him, according as that good man frequents the house. He entertains him, gives him gifts, feasts him, lodges him. His religion comes home at night, prays, is liberally supped, and sumptuously laid to sleep, rises, is saluted, and after the malmsey, or some well spiced brewage, and better breakfasted than he[6] whose morning appetite would have gladly fed on green figs between Bethany and Jerusalem, his religion walks abroad at eight, and leaves his kind entertainer in the shop trading all day without his religion.

Another sort there be, who, when they hear that all things shall be ordered, all things regulated and settled, nothing written but what passes through the custom-house of certain publicans[7] that have the tonnaging and the poundaging of all free-spoken truth, will straight give themselves up into your hands, make 'em and cut 'em out what religion ye please. There be delights, there be recreations and jolly pastimes that will fetch the day about from sun to sun, and rock the tedious year as in a delightful dream. What need they torture their heads with that which others have taken so strictly and so unalterably into their own purveying? These are the fruits which a dull ease and cessation of our knowledge will bring forth among the people. How goodly, and how to be wished, were such an obedient unanimity as this, what a fine conformity would it starch us all into! Doubtless a staunch and solid piece of framework, as any January could freeze together.[8]

* * *

Truth indeed came once into the world with her divine Master, and was a perfect shape most glorious to look on. But when he ascended, and his apostles after him were laid asleep, then straight arose a wicked race of deceivers, who, as that story goes of the Egyptian Typhon with his conspirators, how they dealt with the good Osiris, took the virgin Truth, hewed her lovely form into a thousand pieces, and scattered them to the four winds.[9] From that time ever since, the sad friends of Truth,

---

3. Professors: those who profess religion; Loreto: a Catholic shrine supposed to have been transported to Italy from the Holy Land.
4. Trades, crafts.
5. A separate piece of property.
6. For this description of Christ, see Mark 11.12–14.
7. Tax collectors.

8. Milton goes on to argue that censorship will make the clergy lazy and will hinder the Reformation's goal of seeking truth.
9. Typhon tore apart and scattered Osiris's body, and his wife Isis and son Horus collected it. The interpretation here is based on Plutarch's allegory in *Isis and Osiris*.

such as durst appear, imitating the careful search that Isis made for the mangled body of Osiris, went up and down gathering up limb by limb still as they could find them. We have not yet found them all, Lords and Commons, nor ever shall do, till her Master's second coming. He shall bring together every joint and member, and shall mold them into an immortal feature of loveliness and perfection. Suffer not these licensing prohibitions to stand at every place of opportunity, forbidding and disturbing them that continue seeking, that continue to do our obsequies to the torn body of our martyred saint.

We boast our light; but if we look not wisely on the sun itself, it smites us into darkness. Who can discern those planets that are oft combust, and those stars of brightest magnitude that rise and set with the sun, until the opposite motion of their orbs bring them to such a place in the firmament, where they may be seen evening or morning. The light which we have gained, was given us, not to be ever staring on, but by it to discover onward things more remote from our knowledge. It is not the unfrocking of a priest, the unmitering of a bishop, and the removing him from off the Presbyterian shoulders that will make us a happy nation; no, if other things as great in the church, and in the rule of life both economical and political, be not looked into and reformed, we have looked so long upon the blaze that Zwinglius[1] and Calvin hath beaconed up to us, that we are stark blind.

There be who perpetually complain of schisms and sects, and make it such a calamity that any man dissents from their maxims. It is their own pride and ignorance which causes the disturbing, who neither will hear with meekness, nor can convince, yet all must be suppressed which is not found in their syntagma.[2] They are the troublers, they are the dividers of unity, who neglect and permit not others to unite those disseasered pieces which are yet wanting to the body of Truth. To be still searching what we know not by what we know, still closing up truth to truth as we find it (for all her body is homogeneal[3] and proportional), this is the golden rule in theology as well as in arithmetic, and makes up the best harmony in a church; not the forced and outward union of cold and neutral and inwardly divided minds.

Lords and Commons of England, consider what nation it is whereof ye are, and whereof ye are the governors; a nation not slow and dull, but of a quick, ingenious, and piercing spirit, acute to invent, subtle and sinewy to discourse, not beneath the reach of any point the highest that human capacity can soar to. Therefore the studies of learning in her deepest sciences have been so ancient and so eminent among us that writers of good antiquity and ablest judgment have been persuaded that even the school of Pythagoras and the Persian wisdom took beginning from the old philosophy of this island.[4] And that wise and civil Roman, Julius Agricola, who governed once here for Caesar, preferred the natural wits of Britain before the labored studies of the French.[5] Nor is it for nothing that the grave and frugal Transylvanian[6] sends out yearly from as far as the mountainous borders of Russia and beyond the Hercynian wilderness,[7] not their youth, but their staid men to learn our language and our theologic arts.

---

1. Ulrich Zwingli (1484–1531), the Protestant reformer of Zurich.
2. Systematic doctrinal treatise.
3. Homogeneous.
4. For the connection between the Druids and Zoroastrian and Pythagorean philosophy, see Pliny, *Natural*

History 30.2.
5. See Tacitus, *Agricola* 21.
6. Seventeenth-century Transylvania was Protestant and independent.
7. South-central Germany.

Yet that which is above all this, the favor and the love of Heaven, we have great argument to think in a peculiar manner propitious and propending towards us. Why else was this nation chosen before any other, that out of her as out of Sion should be proclaimed and sounded forth the first tidings and trumpet of reformation to all Europe? And had it not been the obstinate perverseness of our prelates against the divine and admirable spirit of Wycliffe[8] to suppress him as a schismatic and innovator, perhaps neither the Bohemian Huss and Jerome,[9] no, nor the name of Luther, or of Calvin, had been ever known; the glory of reforming all our neighbors had been completely ours. But now, as our obdurate clergy have with violence demeaned the matter, we are become hitherto the latest and the backwardest scholars of whom God offered to have made us the teachers.

Now once again by all concurrence of signs, and by the general instinct of holy and devout men, as they daily and solemnly express their thoughts, God is decreeing to begin some new and great period in his Church, even to the reforming of reformation itself. What does he then but reveal himself to his servants, and, as his manner is, first to his Englishmen? I say as his manner is, first to us, though we mark not the method of his counsels and are unworthy. Behold now this vast city, a city of refuge, the mansion house of liberty, encompassed and surrounded with his protection. The shop of war hath not there more anvils and hammers waking, to fashion out the plates and instruments of armed justice in defense of beleaguered Truth, than there be pens and heads there, sitting by their studious lamps, musing, searching, revolving new notions and ideas wherewith to present, as with their homage and their fealty, the approaching reformation; others as fast reading, trying all things, assenting to the force of reason and convincement.

What could a man require more from a nation so pliant and so prone to seek after knowledge? What wants there to such a towardly[1] and pregnant soul but wise and faithful laborers to make a knowing people, a nation of prophets, of sages, and of worthies? We reckon more than five months yet to harvest; there need not be five weeks, had we but eyes to lift up; the fields are white already. Where there is much desire to learn, there of necessity will be much arguing, much writing, many opinions; for opinion in good men is but knowledge in the making. Under these fantastic terrors of sect and schism, we wrong the earnest and zealous thirst after knowledge and understanding which God hath stirred up in this city.

What some lament of, we rather should rejoice at, should rather praise this pious forwardness among men, to reassume the ill-deputed care of their religion into their own hands again. A little generous prudence, a little forbearance of one another, and some grain of charity might win all these diligences to join and unite into one general and brotherly search after truth; could we but forego this prelatical tradition of crowding free consciences and Christian liberties into canons and precepts of men. I doubt not, if some great and worthy stranger should come among us, wise to discern the mold and temper of a people, and how to govern it, observing the high hopes and aims, the diligent alacrity of our extended thoughts and reasonings in the pursuance of truth and freedom, but that he would cry out as Pyrrhus did, admiring the Roman docility and courage, "If such were my Epirots, I would not despair the greatest design that could be attempted to make a church or kingdom happy."[2]

---

8. English Protestants viewed John Wyclif (1320?–1384) as the initiator of the Reformation in England.
9. Jerome of Prague (c. 1365–1416), a disciple of Wycliff, and John Huss of Bohemia (1373–1415).

1. Promising.
2. King Pyrrhus of Epirus defeated the Romans at Hereclea in 280 B.C.

Yet these are the men cried out against for schismatics and sectaries;[3] as if, while the temple of the Lord was building, some cutting, some squaring the marble, others hewing the cedars, there should be a sort of irrational men who could not consider there must be many schisms and many dissections made in the quarry and in the timber, ere the house of God can be built. And when every stone is laid artfully together, it cannot be united into a continuity, it can but be contiguous in this world; neither can every piece of the building be of one form; nay rather the perfection consists in this, that out of many moderate varieties and brotherly dissimilitudes that are not vastly disproportional, arises the goodly and the graceful symmetry that commends the whole pile and structure.

Let us, therefore, be more considerate builders, more wise in spiritual architecture, when great reformation is expected. For now the time seems come, wherein Moses, the great prophet, may sit in heaven rejoicing to see that memorable and glorious wish of his fulfilled, when not only our seventy elders, but all the Lord's people, are become prophets.

* * *

Methinks I see in my mind a noble and puissant nation rousing herself like a strong man after sleep, and shaking her invincible locks. Methinks I see her as an eagle muing[4] her mighty youth, and kindling her undazzled eyes at the full midday beam; purging and unscaling her long-abused sight at the fountain itself of heavenly radiance; while the whole noise of timorous and flocking birds, with those also that love the twilight, flutter about, amazed at what she means, and in their envious gabble would prognosticate a year of sects and schisms.

What should ye do then, should ye suppress all this flowery crop of knowledge and new light sprung up and yet springing daily in this city? Should ye set an oligarchy of twenty engrossers[5] over it, to bring a famine upon our minds again, when we shall know nothing but what is measured to us by their bushel? Believe it, Lords and Commons, they who counsel ye to such a suppressing, do as good as bid ye suppress yourselves; and I will soon show how.

* * *

And now the time in special is, by privilege, to write and speak what may help to the further discussing of matters in agitation. The temple of Janus with his two controversal faces might now not unsignificantly be set open.[6] And though all the winds of doctrine were let loose to play upon the earth, so Truth be in the field, we do injuriously by licensing and prohibiting to misdoubt her strength. Let her and Falsehood grapple; who ever knew Truth put to the worse, in a free and open encounter. Her confuting is the best and surest suppressing. He who hears what praying there is for light and clearer knowledge to be sent down among us, would think of other matters to be constituted beyond the discipline of Geneva, framed and fabriced already to our hands.[7]

Yet when the new light which we beg for shines in upon us, there be who envy and oppose, if it come not first in at their casements. What a collusion[8] is this, whenas we are exhorted by the wise man to use diligence, to seek for wisdom as for hidden treasures[9] early and late, that another order shall enjoin us to know nothing

---

3. Dividers of the church.
4. Renewing.
5. Monopolists.
6. The Roman god Janus's head had two faces looking in opposite directions. During times of war, the gates of Janus were open.

7. Discipline of Geneva: Calvinism; fabriced: fabricated.
8. Secret agreement for purposes of trickery; ambiguity in words or reasoning.
9. The wise man is Solomon; see Proverbs 8.11 and Matthew 13.44.

but by statute. When a man hath been laboring the hardest labor in the deep mines of knowledge, hath furnished out his findings in all their equipage, drawn forth his reasons as it were a battle ranged, scattered and defeated all objections in his way, calls out his adversary into the plain, offers him the advantage of wind and sun, if he please, only that he may try the matter by dint of argument; for his opponents then to skulk, to lay ambushments, to keep a narrow bridge of licensing where the challenger should pass, though it be valor enough in soldiership, is but weakness and cowardice in the wars of Truth.

For who knows not that Truth is strong, next to the Almighty. She needs no policies, nor stratagems, nor licensings to make her victorious—those are the shifts and the defenses that error uses against her power. Give her but room, and do not bind her when she sleeps, for then she speaks not true, as the old Proteus did, who spake oracles only when he was caught and bound,[1] but then rather she turns herself into all shapes except her own, and perhaps tunes her voice according to the time, as Micaiah did before Ahab,[2] until she be adjured into her own likeness.

Yet is it not impossible that she may have more shapes than one. What else is all that rank of things indifferent, wherein Truth may be on this side, or on the other, without being unlike herself? What but a vain shadow else is the abolition of those ordinances, that handwriting nailed to the cross;[3] what great purchase is this Christian liberty which Paul so often boasts of? His doctrine is, that he who eats, or eats not, regards a day, or regards it not, may do either to the Lord.[4] How many other things might be tolerated in peace and left to conscience, had we but charity, and were it not the chief stronghold of our hypocrisy to be ever judging one another. I fear yet this iron yoke of outward conformity hath left a slavish print upon our necks; the ghost of a linen decency[5] yet haunts us. We stumble and are impatient at the least dividing of one visible congregation from another, though it be not in fundamentals; and through our forwardness to suppress, and our backwardness to recover any enthralled piece of truth out of the gripe of custom, we care not to keep truth separated from truth, which is the fiercest rent and disunion of all. We do not see that while we still affect by all means a rigid external formality, we may as soon fall again into a gross conforming stupidity, a stark and dead congealment of "wood, and hay, and stubble"[6] forced and frozen together, which is more to the sudden degenerating of a church than many subdichotomies[7] of petty schisms.

Not that I can think well of every light separation, or that all in a church is to be expected "gold and silver and precious stones."[8] It is not possible for man to sever the wheat from the tares, the good fish from the other fry; that must be the angels' ministry at the end of mortal things.[9] Yet if all cannot be of one mind,—as who looks they should be?—this doubtless is more wholesome, more prudent, and more Christian, that many be tolerated, rather than all compelled. I mean not tolerated popery and open superstition, which, as it extirpates all religions and civil supremacies, so itself should be extirpate, provided first that all charitable and compassionate means be used to win and regain the weak and the misled; that also which is impious or evil absolutely, either against faith or manners, no law can possibly permit, that intends not to unlaw itself; but those neighboring differences, or rather indifferences, are

1. The story of Proteus is in *Odyssey* 384–93.
2. 1 Kings 22.
3. Colossians 2.14.
4. Romans 14.1–13.
5. A reference to the controversy over ecclesiastical vestments.
6. See 1 Corinthians 3.12.
7. Inconsequential divisions.
8. 1 Corinthians 3.12.
9. Matthew 13.24.

what I speak of, whether in some point of doctrine or of discipline, which though they may be many, yet need not interrupt "the unity of spirit," if we could but find among us the "bond of peace."[1]

In the meanwhile, if any one would write and bring his helpful hand to the slow-moving reformation which we labor under, if truth have spoken to him before others, or but seemed at least to speak, who hath so bejesuited us that we should trouble that man with asking license to do so worthy a deed? And not consider this, that if it come to prohibiting, there is not aught more likely to be prohibited than truth itself; whose first appearance to our eyes bleared and dimmed with prejudice and custom, is more unsightly and unplausible than many errors, even as the person is of many a great man slight and contemptible to see to. And what do they tell us vainly of new opinions, when this very opinion of theirs, that none must be heard but whom they like, is the worst and newest opinion of all others; and is the chief cause why sects and schisms do so much abound, and true knowledge is kept at distance from us; besides yet a greater danger which is in it. For when God shakes a kingdom with strong and healthful commotions to a general reforming, it is not untrue that many sectaries and false teachers are then busiest in seducing; but yet more true it is that God then raises to his own work men of rare abilities and more than common industry, not only to look back and revise what hath been taught heretofore, but to gain further and go on some new enlightened steps in the discovery of truth.

PARADISE LOST   *Paradise Lost* is about devastating loss attended by redemption. The reader's knowledge of the Fall creates a sense of tragic inevitability. And Satan, no less than Adam and Eve, appears in all the psychological complexity and verbal grandeur of a tragic hero. Indeed, there is even a manuscript in which Milton outlined the story as a tragedy. In that version, "Lucifer's contriving Adam's ruin" is Act 3. Following epic tradition, Milton places this part of the action at the forefront of his poem, beginning *in medias res*.

So powerful is Milton's opening portrayal of Satan that the Romantic poets thought Satan was the hero of the poem. Focusing on the first two books, the romantic reading sees him as a dynamic rebel. From a Renaissance point of view, Satan is more like an Elizabethan hero-villain, with his many soliloquies and his tortured psychology of brilliance twisted toward evil. Only in Book 9, however, does Milton say, "I now must change these notes to tragic," thereby signaling that he is about to narrate the fall of Adam and Eve. From this point on, the poem follows Adam and Eve's tragic movement from sin to despair to the recognition of sin and the need for repentance. Adam and Eve's learning through suffering and the prophecy of the Son's redemption of sin make this a story of gain as well as loss, on the order of Aeschylean tragedy.

Like all epics, *Paradise Lost* is encyclopedic, combining many different genres. To read this poem is to have an education in everything from literary history to astronomy. Milton draws on a vast wealth of reading, with the Bible as his main source—not only Genesis, but also Exodus, the Prophets, Revelation, Saint Paul, and especially the Psalms, which he had translated. Milton also makes great use of biblical commentary from rabbinical, patristic, and contemporary sources. Early on, Milton had envisaged a poem about the Arthurian legend, and his choice of the nonmartial, seemingly unheroic biblical story of Adam and Eve marks a bold departure from epic tradition. While Spenser's *Faerie Queene* is Milton's most important vernacular model, among epic poets his closest affinity is with Virgil and Dante, both of whom had written of the underworld; Dante especially devoted himself to humanity's free choice of sin. Like Dante, Milton creates his poem as a microcosm of the natural universe. His ideal vision of the world before the Fall is one where day and night are equal and the sun is always in

---

1. Ephesians 4.3.

the same sign of the zodiac, an image that embodies in poetic astronomy the world of simplicity and perfection that humans have lost through sin. Milton does not choose between the earth-centered Ptolemaic and the heliocentric Copernican systems but presents both as alternative explanations for the order of the universe.

Although we know nothing about the order in which the parts of the poem were composed, we do know that Milton typically composed at night or in the early morning. Sometimes he lay awake unable to write a line; at others he was seized "with a certain impetus and *oestro*" [frenzy]. He would dictate forty lines from memory and then reduce them to half that number. According to his nephew, the poem was written from 1658 to 1663.

The one extant manuscript of the poem, which contains the first book, reveals that Milton revised for punctuation and spelling. There were two editions in Milton's lifetime, both printed by Samuel Simmons. The first edition, *Paradise Lost: A poem in ten books*, was printed in six different issues in 1667, 1668, and 1669. From the fourth issue of the poem on, such paratexts as "The Printer to Reader," "The Argument" (which stood altogether), and Milton's note on the verse appear. With the second octave edition of 1674, Milton divided Books 7 and 10 into two books each to create twelve books in all. Prefaced by dedicatory Latin verses, one of which was by his old friend Andrew Marvell, this 1674 edition, which appeared in the year of Milton's death, is the basis for the present text.

from Paradise Lost[1]
Book 1
The Argument

This first Book proposes, first in brief, the whole Subject, Man's disobedience, and the loss thereupon of Paradise wherein he was plac't: Then touches the prime cause of his fall, the Serpent, or rather Satan in the Serpent; who revolting from God, and drawing to his side many Legions of Angels, was by the command of God driven out of Heaven with all his Crew into the great Deep. Which action past over, the Poem hastes into the midst of things,[2] presenting Satan with his Angels now fallen into Hell, describ'd here, not in the Centre (for Heaven and Earth may be suppos'd as yet not made, certainly not yet accurst) but in a place of utter darkness, fitliest call'd Chaos: Here Satan with his Angels lying on the burning Lake, thunder-struck and astonisht, after a certain space recovers, as from confusion, calls up him who next in Order and Dignity lay by him; they confer of thir miserable fall. Satan awakens all his Legions, who lay till then in the same manner confounded; They rise, thir Numbers, array of Battle, thir chief Leaders nam'd, according to the Idols known afterwards in Canaan and the Countries adjoining. To these Satan directs his Speech, comforts them with hope yet of regaining Heaven but tells them lastly of a new World and new kind of Creature to be created, according to an ancient Prophecy or report in Heaven; for that Angels were long before this visible Creation, was the opinion of many ancient Fathers. To find out the truth of this Prophecy, and what to determine thereon he refers to a full Council. What his Associates thence attempt. Pandemonium the Palace of Satan rises, suddenly built out of the Deep: The infernal Peers there sit in Council.

>   Of Man's First Disobedience, and the Fruit
>   Of that Forbidden Tree, whose mortal[3] taste
>   Brought Death into the World, and all our woe,[4]

---

1. Our text is taken from Merritt Y. Hughes, ed., *John Milton Complete Poems and Major Prose*, and the notes are adapted from John Carey and Alastair Fowler, eds., *The Poems of John Milton*.

2. Following Horace's rule that the epic should plunge "*in medias res.*"

3. "Death-bringing" (Latin *mortalis*) but also "to mortals."

4. This definition of the first sin follows Calvin's Catechism.

With loss of *Eden*, till one greater Man[5]
5 Restore us, and regain the blissful Seat,
Sing Heav'nly Muse,[6] that on the secret top
Of *Oreb*, or of *Sinai*, didst inspire
That Shepherd, who first taught the chosen Seed,[7]
In the Beginning how the Heav'ns and Earth
10 Rose out of *Chaos*: Or if *Sion* Hill[8]
Delight thee more, and *Siloa's* Brook[9] that flow'd
Fast° by the Oracle of God; I thence   *close*
Invoke thy aid to my advent'rous Song,
That with no middle flight intends to soar
15 Above th' *Aonian* Mount,[1] while it pursues
Things unattempted yet in Prose or Rhyme.[2]
And chiefly Thou O Spirit, that dost prefer
Before all Temples th' upright heart and pure,[3]
Instruct me, for Thou know'st; Thou from the first
20 Wast present, and with mighty wings outspread
Dove-like satst brooding on the vast Abyss
And mad'st it pregnant:[4] What in me is dark
Illumine, what is low raise and support;
That to the highth of this great Argument°   *theme*
25 I may assert Eternal Providence,
And justify[5] the ways of God to men.
    Say first, for Heav'n hides nothing from thy view
Nor the deep Tract of Hell, say first what cause
Mov'd our Grand[6] Parents in that happy State,
30 Favor'd of Heav'n so highly, to fall off
From thir Creator, and transgress his Will
For° one restraint, Lords of the World besides?°   *because of / otherwise*
Who first seduc'd them to that foul revolt?
Th' infernal Serpent;[7] hee it was, whose guile
35 Stirr'd up with Envy and Revenge, deceiv'd
The Mother of Mankind; what time his Pride
Had cast him out from Heav'n, with all his Host

---

5. Christ, in Pauline theology the second Adam (see Romans 5.19). The people and events referred to in these lines have a typological connection, i.e., the Christian interpretation of the Old Testament as a prefiguration of the New.
6. Rhetorically, lines 1–49 are the *invocatio*, consisting of an address to the Muse, and the *principium* that states the whole scope of the poem's action. The "Heavenly Muse," later addressed as the muse of astronomy Urania (7.1), is here identified with the Holy Spirit of the Bible, which inspires Moses.
7. The "Shepherd" is Moses, who was granted the vision of the burning bush on Mount Oreb (Exodus 3) and received the Law, either on Mount Oreb (Deuteronomy 4.10) or on its lower part, Mount Sinai (Exodus 19.20). Moses, the first Jewish writer, taught "the chosen seed," the children of Israel, about the beginning of the world in Genesis.
8. The sanctuary, a place of ceremonial song but also (Isaiah 2.3) of oracular pronouncements.
9. A spring immediately west of Mount Zion and beside

Calvary, often used as a symbol of the operation of the Holy Ghost.
1. Helicon, sacred to the Muses.
2. Ironically translating Ariosto's boast in the invocation to *Orlando Furioso*.
3. The Spirit is the voice of God, which inspired the Hebrew prophets.
4. Identifying the Spirit present at the creation (Genesis 1.2) with the Spirit in the form of a dove that descended on Jesus at the beginning of his ministry (John 1.32). Vast: large; deserted (Latin *vastus*).
5. Does not mean merely "demonstrate logically" but has its biblical meaning and implies spiritual rather than rational understanding.
6. Implies not only greatness, but also inclusiveness of generality or parentage.
7. "That old serpent, called the Devil, and Satan" (Revelation 12.9) both because Satan entered the body of a serpent to tempt Eve and because his nature is guileful and dangerous to humans.

Of Rebel Angels, by whose aid aspiring
To set himself in Glory above his Peers,
40 He trusted to have equall'd the most High,[8]
If he oppos'd; and with ambitious aim
Against the Throne and Monarchy of God
Rais'd impious War in Heav'n and Battle proud
With vain attempt. Him the Almighty Power
45 Hurl'd headlong flaming from th' Ethereal Sky[9]
With hideous ruin and combustion down
To bottomless perdition, there to dwell
In Adamantine Chains[1] and penal Fire,
Who durst defy th' Omnipotent to Arms.
50 Nine times the Space that measures Day and Night[2]
To mortal men, hee with his horrid crew
Lay vanquisht, rolling in the fiery Gulf
Confounded though immortal: But his doom
Reserv'd him to more wrath; for now the thought
55 Both of lost happiness and lasting pain
Torments him; round he throws his baleful° eyes   *evil, suffering*
That witness'd huge affliction and dismay
Mixt with obdúrate° pride and steadfast hate: *unyielding*
At once as far as Angels' ken° he views   *power of vision*
60 The dismal° Situation waste and wild,   *dreadful, sinister*
A Dungeon horrible, on all sides round
As one great Furnace flam'd, yet from those flames
No light, but rather darkness visible
Serv'd only to discover sights of woe,[3]
65 Regions of sorrow, doleful shades, where peace
And rest can never dwell, hope never comes
That comes to all;[4] but torture without end
Still urges,° and a fiery Deluge, fed   *presses*
With ever-burning Sulphur unconsum'd:
70 Such place Eternal Justice had prepar'd
For those rebellious, here thir Prison ordained
In utter° darkness, and thir portion set   *complete, outer*
As far remov'd from God and light of Heav'n
As from the Center thrice to th' utmost Pole.[5]
75 O how unlike the place from whence they fell!
There the companions of his fall, o'erwhelm'd

8. Satan's crime was not his aspiring "above his peers" but aspiring "To set himself in [divine] Glory." Numerous verbal echoes relate lines 40–48 to the biblical accounts of the fall and binding of Lucifer, in 2 Peter 2.4, Revelation 20.1–2, and Isaiah 14.12–15: "Thou hast said . . . I will exalt my throne above the stars of God . . . I will be like the most High. Yet thou shalt be brought down to hell."
9. Mingling an allusion to Luke 10.18, "I beheld Satan as lightning fall from heaven," with one to Homer, *Iliad* 1.591, Hephaistos "hurled from the ethereal threshold."
1. 2 Peter 2.4; "God spared not the angels that sinned, but . . . delivered them into chains of darkness."
2. The devils fall for the same number of days that the

Titans fall from heaven when overthrown by the Olympian gods (see Hesiod, *Theogony* 664–735).
3. See the account of the land of the dead in Job 10.22: "the light is as darkness."
4. The phrase echoes Dante's *Inferno:* III.9 "All hope abandon, ye who enter here."
5. Milton refers to the Ptolemaic universe in which the earth is at the center of ten concentric spheres. Milton draws attention to the numerical proportion, heaven-earth:earth-hell—i.e., earth divides the interval between heaven and hell in the proportion that Neoplatonists believed should be maintained between reason and concupiscence.

With Floods and Whirlwinds of tempestuous fire,
He soon discerns, and welt'ring by his side
One next himself in power, and next in crime,
80   Long after known in *Palestine*, and nam'd
Beëlzebub.[6] To whom th' Arch-Enemy,
And thence in Heav'n call'd Satan,[7] with bold words
Breaking the horrid silence thus began.[8]
        If thou beest hee; But O how fall'n! how chang'd
85   From him, who in the happy Realms of Light
Cloth'd with transcendent brightness didst outshine
Myriads though bright:[9] If he whom mutual league,
United thoughts and counsels, equal hope,
And hazard in the Glorious Enterprise,
90   Join'd with me once, now misery hath join'd
In equal ruin: into what Pit thou seest
From what highth fall'n, so much the stronger prov'd
He with his Thunder: and till then who knew
The force of those dire Arms? yet not for those,
95   Nor what the Potent Victor in his rage
Can else inflict, do I repent or change,
Though chang'd in outward luster; that fixt mind
And high disdain, from sense of injur'd merit,
That with the mightiest rais'd me to contend,
100   And to the fierce contention brought along
Innumerable force of Spirits arm'd
That durst dislike his reign, and mee preferring,
His utmost power with adverse power oppos'd
In dubious Battle on the Plains of Heav'n,
105   And shook his throne.[1] What though the field be lost?
All is not lost; the unconquerable Will,
And study° of revenge, immortal hate,   *pursuit*
And courage never to submit or yield:
And what is else not to be overcome?
110   That Glory[2] never shall his wrath or might
Extort from me. To bow and sue for grace
With suppliant knee, and deify his power
Who from the terror of this Arm so late
Doubted° his Empire, that were low indeed,   *feared for*
115   That were an ignominy and shame beneath
This downfall; since by Fate the strength of Gods
And this Empyreal substance cannot fail,[3]
Since through experience of this great event

---

6. Hebrew, "Lord of the flies"; Matthew 12.24, "the prince of the devils."
7. Hebrew, "enemy." After his rebellion, Satan's "former name" (Lucifer) was no longer used (5.658).
8. Rhetorically, the opening of the action proper. The 41-line speech beginning here, the first speech in the book, exactly balances the last, which also is spoken by Satan and also consists of 41 lines (1.622–62).
9. The break in grammatical concord (between "him" and "didst") reflects Satan's doubt whether Beelzebub is present and so whether second-person forms are appropri-ate.
1. The Son's chariot, not Satan's armies, shakes heaven to its foundations, as we learn in Book 6. Throughout the present passage, Satan sees himself as the hero of a pagan epic.
2. Either "the glory of overcoming me" or "my glory of will."
3. Implying not only that as angels they are immortal, but also that the continuance of their strength is assured by fate.

In Arms not worse, in foresight much advanc't,
120   We may with more successful hope resolve
To wage by force or guile eternal War
Irreconcilable to our grand Foe,
Who now triúmphs, and in th' excess of joy
Sole reigning holds the Tyranny of Heav'n.[4]
125   So spake th' Apostate Angel, though in pain,
Vaunting aloud, but rackt with deep despair:
And him thus answer'd soon his bold Compeer.°   *comrade*
    O Prince, O Chief of many Throned Powers,
That led th' imbattl'd Seraphim[5] to War
130   Under thy conduct, and in dreadful deeds
Fearless, endanger'd Heav'n's perpetual King;
And put to proof his high Supremacy,
Whether upheld by strength, or Chance, or Fate;[6]
Too well I see and rue the dire event,
135   That with sad overthrow and foul defeat
Hath lost us Heav'n, and all this mighty Host
In horrible destruction laid thus low,
As far as Gods and Heav'nly Essences
Can perish: for the mind and spirit remains
140   Invincible, and vigor soon returns,
Though all our Glory extinct, and happy state
Here swallow'd up in endless misery.
But what if he our Conqueror (whom I now
Of force° believe Almighty, since no less   *necessarily*
145   Than such could have o'erpow'rd such force as ours)
Have left us this our spirit and strength entire
Strongly to suffer and support our pains,
That we may so suffice° his vengeful ire,   *satisfy*
Or do him mightier service as his thralls
150   By right of War, whate'er his business be
Here in the heart of Hell to work in Fire,
Or do his Errands in the gloomy Deep;
What can it then avail though yet we feel
Strength undiminisht, or eternal being
155   To undergo eternal punishment?[7]
Whereto with speedy words th' Arch-fiend repli'd.
    Fall'n Cherub, to be weak is miserable
Doing or Suffering: but of this be sure,
To do aught good never will be our task,
160   But ever to do ill our sole delight,
As being the contrary to his high will
Whom we resist.[8] If then his Providence

---

4. An obvious instance of the devil's bias.
5. The traditional nine orders of angels are seraphim, cherubim, thrones, dominions, virtues, powers, principalities, archangels, and angels, but Milton does not use these terms systematically.
6. The main powers recognized in the devils' ideology. God's power rests on a quality that does not occur to Beelzebub: goodness.

7. Existing eternally, merely so that our punishment may also be eternal.
8. This fundamental disobedience and disorientation make Satan's heroic virtue into the corresponding excess of vice. Lines 163–65 look forward to 12.470–78 and Adam's wonder at the astonishing reversal whereby God will turn the Fall into an occasion for good.

Out of our evil seek to bring forth good,
Our labor must be to pervert that end,
165 And out of good still to find means of evil;
Which oft-times may succeed, so as perhaps
Shall grieve him, if I fail not, and disturb
His inmost counsels from thir destin'd aim.
But see the angry Victor hath recall'd
170 His Ministers of vengeance and pursuit
Back to the Gates of Heav'n: the Sulphurous Hail
Shot after us in storm, o'erblown hath laid°   *subdued*
The fiery Surge, that from the Precipice
Of Heav'n receiv'd us falling, and the Thunder,
175 Wing'd with red Lightning and impetuous rage,
Perhaps hath spent his shafts, and ceases now
To bellow through the vast and boundless Deep.
Let us not slip° th' occasion, whether scorn,   *lose*
Or satiate fury yield it from our Foe.
180 Seest thou yon dreary Plain, forlorn and wild,
The seat of desolation, void of light,
Save what the glimmering of these livid flames
Casts pale and dreadful? Thither let us tend
From off the tossing of these fiery waves,
185 There rest, if any rest can harbor there,
And reassembling our afflicted° Powers,   *downcast*
Consult how we may henceforth most offend°   *harm*
Our Enemy, our own loss how repair,
How overcome this dire Calamity,
190 What reinforcement we may gain from Hope,
If not what resolution from despair.
        Thus Satan talking to his nearest Mate
With Head up-lift above the wave, and Eyes
That sparkling blaz'd, his other Parts besides
195 Prone on the Flood, extended long and large
Lay floating many a rood,° in bulk as huge   *six to eight yards*
As whom the Fables name of monstrous size,
Titanian, or *Earth-born*, that warr'd on *Jove*,
Briareos or *Typhon*,[9] whom the Den
200 By ancient *Tarsus*[1] held, or that Sea-beast
Leviathan,[2] which God of all his works
Created hugest that swim th' Ocean stream:
Him haply slumb'ring on the *Norway* foam
The Pilot of some small night-founder'd° Skiff,   *sunk in night*
205 Deeming some Island, oft, as Seamen tell,
With fixed Anchor in his scaly rind

9. The serpent-legged *Briareos* was a Titan, the serpent-headed *Typhon* (Typhoeus) a Giant. Each was a son of Earth; each fought against Jupiter; and each was eventually confined beneath Aetna (see lines 232–37). Typhon was so powerful that when he first made war on the Olympians, they had to resort to metamorphoses to escape (Ovid, *Metamorphoses* 5.325–31 and 346–58).

1. The biblical Tarsus was the capital of Cilicia, and both Pindar and Aeschylus describe Typhon's habitat as a Cilician cave or "den."
2. The monster of Job 41, identified in Isaiah's prophecy of judgement as "the crooked serpent" (Isaiah 27.1) but also sometimes thought of as a whale.

Moors by his side under the Lee, while Night
Invests° the Sea, and wished Morn delays: *wraps*
So stretcht out huge in length the Arch-fiend lay
210 Chain'd on the burning Lake, nor ever thence
Had ris'n or heav'd his head, but that the will
And high permission of all-ruling Heaven
Left him at large to his own dark designs,
That with reiterated crimes he might
215 Heap on himself damnation, while he sought
Evil to others, and enrag'd might see
How all his malice serv'd but to bring forth
Infinite goodness, grace and mercy shown
On Man by him seduc't, but on himself
220 Treble confusion, wrath and vengeance pour'd.
Forthwith upright he rears from off the Pool
His mighty Stature; on each hand the flames
Driv'n backward slope thir pointing spires, and roll'd
In billows, leave i' th' midst a horrid° Vale.   *bristling*
225 Then with expanded wings he steers his flight
Aloft, incumbent[3] on the dusky Air
That felt unusual weight, till on dry Land
He lights, if it were Land that ever burn'd
With solid, as the Lake with liquid fire
230 And such appear'd in hue;[4] as when the force
Of subterranean wind transports a Hill
Torn from *Pelorus*,[5] or the shatter'd side
Of thund'ring *AEtna*, whose combustible
And fuell'd entrails thence conceiving Fire,
235 Sublim'd[6] with Mineral fury,[7] aid the Winds,
And leave a singed bottom all involv'd°   *wreathed*
With stench and smoke: Such resting found the sole
Of unblest feet. Him follow'd his next Mate,
Both glorying to have scap't the *Stygian*[8] flood
240 As Gods, and by thir own recover'd strength,
Not by the sufferance of supernal Power.
     Is this the Region, this the Soil, the Clime,
Said then the lost Arch-Angel, this the seat
That we must change° for Heav'n, this mournful gloom   *exchange*
245 For that celestial light? Be it so, since he
Who now is Sovran can dispose and bid
What shall be right: fardest° from him is best   *farthest*
Whom reason hath equall'd, force hath made supreme
Above his equals. Farewell happy Fields
250 Where Joy for ever dwells: Hail horrors, hail
Infernal world, and thou profoundest Hell
Receive thy new Possessor: One who brings

---

3. Pressing with his weight.
4. In the 17th century, "hue" referred to surface appearance and texture as well as color.
5. Pelorus and Aetna are volcanic mountains in Sicily.
6. Converted directly from solid to vapor by volcanic heat in such a way as to resolidify on cooling.
7. Disorder of minerals, or subterranean disorder.
8. Of the River Styx—i.e., hellish.

A mind not to be chang'd by Place or Time.
The mind is its own place, and in itself
255 Can make a Heav'n of Hell, a Hell of Heav'n.[9]
What matter where, if I be still the same,
And what I should be, all but less than hee
Whom Thunder hath made greater? Here at least
We shall be free; th' Almighty hath not built
260 Here for his envy, will not drive us hence:
Here we may reign secure, and in my choice
To reign is worth ambition[1] though in Hell:
Better to reign in Hell, than serve in Heav'n.
But wherefore let we then our faithful friends,
265 Th' associates and copartners of our loss
Lie thus astonisht on th' oblivious Pool,[2]
And call them not to share with us their part
In this unhappy Mansion: or once more
With rallied Arms to try what may be yet
270 Regain'd in Heav'n, or what more lost in Hell?
　　So *Satan* spake, and him *Beëlzebub*
Thus answer'd. Leader of those Armies bright,
Which but th' Omnipotent none could have foiled,
If once they hear that voice, thir liveliest pledge
275 Of hope in fears and dangers, heard so oft
In worst extremes, and on the perilous edge°   *front line*
Of battle when it rag'd, in all assaults
Thir surest signal, they will soon resume
New courage and revive, though now they lie
280 Groveling and prostrate on yon Lake of Fire,
As we erewhile, astounded and amaz'd;
No wonder, fall'n such a pernicious highth.
　　He scarce had ceas't when the superior Fiend
Was moving toward the shore; his ponderous shield
285 Ethereal temper,[3] massy, large and round,
Behind him cast; the broad circumference
Hung on his shoulders like the Moon, whose Orb
Through Optic Glass the *Tuscan* Artist[4] views
At Ev'ning from the top of *Fesole*,
290 Or in *Valdarno*, to descry new Lands,
Rivers or Mountains in her spotty Globe.
His Spear, to equal which the tallest Pine
Hewn on *Norwegian* hills, to be the Mast
Of some great Ammiral,° were but a wand,   *flagship*
295 He walkt with to support uneasy steps
Over the burning Marl,° not like those steps   *ground*

9. The view that heaven and hell are states of mind was held by Amaury de Bene, a medieval heretic often cited in 17th-century accounts of atheism.
1. Worth striving for (Latin *ambitio*). Satan refers not merely to a mental state but also to an active effort that is the price of power.
2. The pool attended by forgetfulness.

3. Tempered in celestial fire.
4. Galileo, who looked through a telescope ("optic glass"), had been placed under house arrest by the Inquisition near Florence, which is in the "Valdarno" or the Valley of the Arno, overlooked by the hills of "Fesole" or Fiesole.

On Heaven's Azure, and the torrid Clime
Smote on him sore besides, vaulted with Fire;
Nathless° he so endur'd, till on the Beach   *nevertheless*
300   Of that inflamed Sea, he stood and call'd
His Legions, Angel Forms, who lay intrans't
Thick as Autumnal Leaves that strow the Brooks
In *Vallombrosa*, where th' *Etrurian* shades
High overarch't imbow'r;⁵ or scatter'd sedge
305   Afloat, when with fierce Winds *Orion* arm'd
Hath vext the Red-Sea Coast,⁶ whose waves o'erthrew
Busiris and his *Memphian* Chivalry,
While with perfidious hatred they pursu'd
The Sojourners of *Goshen*, who beheld
310   From the safe shore thir floating Carcasses
And broken Chariot Wheels;⁷ so thick bestrown
Abject and lost lay these, covering the Flood,
Under amazement of thir hideous change.
He call'd so loud, that all the hollow Deep
315   Of Hell resounded. Princes, Potentates,
Warriors, the Flow'r of Heav'n, once yours, now lost,
If such astonishment as this can seize
Eternal spirits; or have ye chos'n this place
After the toil of Battle to repose
320   Your wearied virtue,° for the ease you find   *strength*
To slumber here, as in the Vales of Heav'n?
Or in this abject posture have ye sworn
To adore the Conqueror? who now beholds
Cherub and Seraph rolling in the Flood
325   With scatter'd Arms and Ensigns,° till anon   *battle flags*
His swift pursuers from Heav'n Gates discern
Th' advantage, and descending tread us down
Thus drooping, or with linked Thunderbolts
Transfix us to the bottom of this Gulf.
330   Awake, arise, or be for ever fall'n.
        They heard, and were abasht, and up they sprung
Upon the wing; as when men wont to watch
On duty, sleeping found by whom they dread,
Rouse and bestir themselves ere well awake.
335   Nor did they not perceive the evil plight
In which they were, or the fierce pains not feel;
Yet to thir General's Voice they soon obey'd
Innumerable. As when the potent Rod

5. See Isaiah 34.4: "and all their host shall fall down, as the leaf falleth off from the vine, and as a falling fig from the fig tree." Fallen leaves were an enduring simile for the numberless dead; see Homer, *Iliad* 6.146; Virgil, *Aeneid* 6.309; Dante, *Inferno* 3.112. Milton adds an actual locality, Vallombrosa, again near Florence.
6. Commentators on Job 9.9 and Amos 5.8 interpreted the creation of Orion as a symbol of God's power to raise tempests and floods to execute his judgments. Thus Mil-

ton's transition to the Egyptians overwhelmed by God's judgment in lines 306–11 is a natural one. The Hebrew name for the Red Sea was "Sea of Sedge."
7. Contrary to his promise, the Pharaoh with his Memphian (i.e., Egyptian) charioteers pursued the Israelites—who had been in captivity in Goshen—across the Red Sea. The Israelites passed over safely; but the Egyptians' chariot wheels were broken (Exodus 14.25), and the rising sea engulfed them and cast their corpses on the shore.

Of *Amram's* Son[8] in *Egypt's* evil day
340   Wav'd round the Coast, up call'd a pitchy cloud
Of *Locusts*, warping° on the Eastern Wind,   *floating*
That o'er the Realm of impious *Pharaoh* hung
Like Night, and darken'd all the Land of *Nile:*
So numberless were those bad Angels seen
345   Hovering on wing under the Cope° of Hell   *canopy*
'Twixt upper, nether, and surrounding Fires;
Till, as a signal giv'n, th' uplifted Spear
Of thir great Sultan waving to direct
Thir course, in even balance down they light
350   On the firm brimstone, and fill all the Plain;
A multitude, like which the populous North
Pour'd never from her frozen loins, to pass
Rhene or the *Danaw,* when her barbarous Sons
Came like a Deluge on the South, and spread
355   Beneath *Gibraltar* to the *Lybian* sands.[9]
Forthwith from every Squadron and each Band
The Heads and Leaders thither haste where stood
Thir great Commander; Godlike shapes and forms
Excelling human, Princely Dignities,
360   And Powers that erst in Heaven sat on Thrones;
Though of thir Names in heav'nly Records now
Be no memorial, blotted out and ras'd
By thir Rebellion, from the Books of Life.[1]
Nor had they yet among the Sons of *Eve*
365   Got them new Names, till wand'ring o'er the Earth,
Through God's high sufferance for the trial of man,
By falsities and lies the greatest part
Of Mankind they corrupted to forsake
God thir Creator, and th' invisible
370   Glory of him that made them, to transform
Oft to the Image of a Brute, adorn'd
With gay Religions° full of Pomp and Gold,   *ceremonies*
And Devils to adore for Deities:[2]
Then were they known to men by various Names,
375   And various Idols through the Heathen World.
Say, Muse, thir Names then known, who first, who last,
Rous'd from the slumber on that fiery Couch,
At thir great Emperor's call, as next in worth
Came singly where he stood on the bare strand,
380   While the promiscuous crowd stood yet aloof?
The chief were those who from the Pit of Hell
Roaming to seek thir prey on earth, durst fix
Thir Seats long after next the Seat of God,
Thir Altars by his Altar, Gods ador'd

8. Moses, who used his rod to bring down on the Egyptians a plague of locusts (Exodus 10.12–15).
9. The barbarian invasions of Rome began with crossings of the Rhine ("Rhene") and Danube ("Danaw") Rivers and spread to North Africa.

1. See Revelation 3.5 ("He that overcometh . . . I will not blot out his name out of the book of life") and Exodus 32.32–33.
2. The catalogue of gods here is an epic convention.

385   Among the Nations round, and durst abide
        Jehovah thund'ring out of *Sion*, thron'd
        Between the Cherubim; yea, often plac'd
        Within his Sanctuary itself thir Shrines,
        Abominations; and with cursed things
390   His holy Rites, and solemn Feasts profan'd,
        And with thir darkness durst affront his light.
        First *Moloch*,³ horrid King besmear'd with blood
        Of human sacrifice, and parents' tears,
        Though for the noise of Drums and Timbrels° loud   *tambourines*
395   Thir children's cries unheard, that pass'd through fire
        To his grim Idol. Him the *Ammonite*
        Worshipt in *Rabba* and her wat'ry Plain,
        In *Argob* and in *Basan*, to the stream
        Of utmost *Arnon*.⁴ Nor content with such
400   Audacious neighborhood, the wisest heart
        Of *Solomon*⁵ he led by fraud to build
        His Temple right against the Temple of God
        On that opprobrious Hill,⁶ and made his Grove
        The pleasant Valley of *Hinnom, Tophet* thence
405   And black *Gehenna* call'd, the Type of Hell.⁷
        Next *Chemos*,⁸ th' obscene dread of *Moab's* Sons,
        From *Aroar* to *Nebo*, and the wild
        Of Southmost *Abarim*; in *Hesebon*
        And *Horonaim, Seon's* Realm, beyond
410   The flow'ry Dale of *Sibma* clad with Vines,
        And *Eleale* to th' Asphaltic Pool.⁹
        *Peor*¹ his other Name, when he entic'd
        Israel in *Sittim* on thir march from *Nile*
        To do him wanton rites, which cost them woe.²
415   Yet thence his lustful Orgies he enlarg'd
        Even to that Hill of scandal, by the Grove
        Of *Moloch* homicide, lust hard by hate;
        Till good *Josiah*³ drove them thence to Hell.

3. Satan gathers twelve disciples: Moloch, Chemos, Baalim, Ashtaroth, Astoreth, Thammuz, Dagon, Rimmon, Osiris, Isis, Horus, and Belial. The literal meaning of *Moloch* is "king."
4. Though ostensibly magnifying Moloch's empire, these lines look forward to his eventual defeat; for Rabba, the Ammonite royal city, is best known for its capture by David after his repentance (2 Samuel 12), while the Israelite conquest of the regions of Argob and Basan, as far as the boundary river Arnon, is recalled by Moses as particularly crushing (Deuteronomy 3.1–13).
5. Solomon's wives drew him into idolatry (1 Kings 11.5–7); but the "high places that were before Jerusalem . . . on the right hand of the mount of corruption which Solomon . . . had builded for Ashtoreth the abomination of the Zidonians, and for Chemosh the abomination of the Moabites, and Milcom the abomination of the children of Ammon" were later destroyed by Josiah (2 Kings 23.13–14).
6. The Mount of Olives, because of Solomon's idolatry called "mount of corruption." Throughout the poem,

Solomon functions as a type both of Adam and of Christ.
7. To abolish sacrifice to Moloch, Josiah "defiled Topheth, which is in the valley of the children of Hinnom" (2 Kings 23.10). Gehenna, for "Valley of Hinnom," is used in Matthew 10.28 as a name for hell.
8. "The abomination of Moab," associated with neighboring god Moloch in 1 Kings 11.7.
9. Most of these places are named in Numbers 32 as the formerly Moabite inheritance assigned by Moses to the tribes of Reuben and Gad. Numbers 21.25–30 rejoices at the Israelite capture of Hesebon (Heshbon), a Moabite city which had been taken by the Amorite King Seon, or Sihon. Heshbon, Horonaim, "the vine of Sibmah," and Elealeh all figure in Isaiah's sad prophecy of the destruction of Moab (Isaiah 15.5, 16.8f). The Asphaltic Pool is the Dead Sea.
1. For the story of Peor, see Numbers 25.1–3 and Hosea 9.10.
2. A plague that killed 24,000 (Numbers 25.9).
3. Always a favorite with the Reformers because of his destruction of idolatrous images.

With these came they, who from the bord'ring flood
420 Of old *Euphrates*[4] to the Brook that parts
Egypt from *Syrian* ground, had general Names
Of *Baalim* and *Ashtaroth*,[5] those male,
These Feminine. For Spirits when they please
Can either Sex assume, or both; so soft
425 And uncompounded is thir Essence pure,
Not ti'd or manacl'd with joint or limb,
Nor founded on the brittle strength of bones,
Like cumbrous flesh; but in what shape they choose
Dilated° or condens't, bright or obscure,   *expanded*
430 Can execute thir aery purposes,
And works of love or enmity fulfil.
For those the Race of *Israel* oft forsook
Thir living strength,[6] and unfrequented left
His righteous Altar, bowing lowly down
435 To bestial Gods; for which thir heads as low
Bow'd down in Battle, sunk before the Spear
Of despicable foes. With these in troop
Came *Astoreth,* whom the *Phoenicians* call'd
Astarte, Queen of Heav'n, with crescent Horns;[7]
440 To whose bright Image nightly by the Moon
Sidonian Virgins paid thir Vows and Songs,
In *Sion* also not unsung, where stood
Her Temple on th' offensive Mountain, built
By that uxorious King, whose heart though large,
445 Beguil'd by fair Idolatresses, fell
To Idols foul. *Thammuz*[8] came next behind,
Whose annual wound in *Lebanon* allur'd
The *Syrian* Damsels to lament his fate
In amorous ditties all a Summer's day,
450 While smooth *Adonis* from his native Rock
Ran purple to the Sea, suppos'd with blood
Of *Thammuz* yearly wounded: the Love-tale
Infected *Sion's* daughters with like heat,
Whose wanton passions in the sacred Porch
455 *Ezekiel* saw, when by the Vision led
His eye survey'd the dark Idolatries
Of alienated *Judah.* Next came one
Who mourn'd in earnest, when the Captive Ark
Maim'd his brute Image, head and hands lopt off
460 In his own Temple, on the grunsel° edge,   *threshold*

4. An area stretching from the northeast limit of Syria to the southwest limit of Canaan, the River Besor.
5. Baal is the general name for most idols; the Phoenician and Canaanite sun gods were collectively called Baalim (plural form). Astartes (Ishtars) were manifestations of the moon goddess.
6. See 1 Samuel 15.29: "Strength of Israel," a formulaic periphrasis for Jehovah.
7. The image of Astoreth or Astarte, the Sidonian (Phoenician) moon goddess and Venus, was the statue of a woman with the head of a bull above her head with horns resembling the crescent moon. "Queen of heaven:" from Jeremiah 44.17–19.
8. The lover of Astarte. His identification with Adonis was based on St. Jerome's commentary on the passage in Ezekiel 8.14, drawn on by Milton in lines 454–56. The Syrian festival of Tammuz was celebrated after the summer solstice; the slaying of the young god by a boar was mourned as a symbol of the southward withdrawal of the sun and the death of vegetation. Each year when the River Adonis became discolored with red mud, it was regarded as a renewed sign of the god's wound.

Where he fell flat, and sham'd his Worshippers:
Dagon his Name, Sea Monster, upward Man
And downward Fish:[9] yet had his Temple high
Rear'd in *Azotus,* dreaded through the Coast
465   Of *Palestine,* in *Gath* and *Ascalon,*
And *Accaron* and *Gaza's* frontier bounds.[1]
Him follow'd *Rimmon,* whose delightful Seat
Was fair *Damascus,* on the fertile Banks
Of *Abbana* and *Pharphar,* lucid streams.[2]
470   He also against the house of God was bold:
A Leper once he lost and gain'd a King,
Ahaz his sottish Conqueror, whom he drew
God's Altar to disparage and displace
For one of *Syrian* mode, whereon to burn
475   His odious off'rings, and adore the Gods
Whom he had vanquisht.[3] After these appear'd
A crew who under Names of old Renown,
Osiris, Isis, Orus and thir Train
With monstrous shapes and sorceries abus'd°   *deceived*
480   Fanatic *Egypt* and her Priests, to seek
Thir wand'ring Gods disguis'd in brutish forms
Rather than human.[4] Nor did *Israel* scape
Th' infection when thir borrow'd Gold compos'd
The Calf in *Oreb:*[5] and the Rebel King[6]
485   Doubl'd that sin in *Bethel* and in *Dan,*
Lik'ning his Maker to the Grazed Ox,[7]
Jehovah, who in one Night when he pass'd
From *Egypt* marching, equall'd with one stroke
Both her first born and all her bleating Gods.[8]
490   *Belial* came last,[9] than whom a Spirit more lewd
Fell not from Heaven, or more gross to love
Vice for itself: To him no Temple stood
Or Altar smok'd; yet who more oft than hee
In Temples and at Altars, when the Priest
495   Turns Atheist, as did *Ely's* Sons, who fill'd
With lust and violence the house of God.[1]

9. When the Philistines put the ark of the Lord, which they had captured, into the temple of Dagon, "on the morrow morning, behold, Dagon was fallen upon his face to the ground . . . and the head of Dagon and both the palms of his hands were cut off upon the threshold" (1 Samuel 5.4).
1. Divine vengeance on these Philistine cities is prophesied in Zephaniah 2.4.
2. When Elisha told Naaman that his leprosy would be cured if he washed in the Jordan, the Syrian was at first angry (2 Kings 5.12: "Are not Abana and Pharpar, rivers of Damascus, better than all the waters of Israel?") but then humbled himself and was cured.
3. After engineering the overthrow of Damascus by the Assyrians, the sottish (foolish) King Ahaz became interested in the cult of Rimmon and had an altar of the Syrian type put in the temple of the Lord (2 Kings 16.9–17).
4. Milton alludes to the myth of the Olympian gods fleeing from the Giant Typhoeus into Egypt and hiding in bestial forms (Ovid, *Metamorphoses* 5.319–31) afterward

worshipped by the Egyptians.
5. Perhaps the most familiar of all Israelite apostasies was their worship of "a calf in Horeb" (Psalms 106.19) made by Aaron while Moses was away receiving the tables of the Law (Exodus 32).
6. Jeroboam, who led the revolt of the ten tribes of Israel against Rehoboam, Solomon's successor; he "doubled" Aaron's sin, since he made "two calves of gold," placing one in Bethel and the other in Dan (1 Kings 12.28–29).
7. "Thus they changed their glory into the similitude of an ox that eateth grass" (Psalms 106.20).
8. At the passover, Jehovah smote all the Egyptian firstborn, "both man and beast" (Exodus 12.12); presumably, this stroke would extend to their sacred animals.
9. Belial comes last, both because he had no local cult and because in the poem he is "timorous and slothful" (2.117). Properly, "Belial" is an abstract noun meaning "iniquity."
1. The impiety and fornication of Ely's sons are described in 1 Samuel 2.12–24.

In Courts and Palaces he also Reigns
And in luxurious Cities, where the noise
Of riot ascends above thir loftiest Tow'rs,
500   And injury and outrage: And when Night
Darkens the Streets, then wander forth the Sons
Of *Belial,* flown° with insolence and wine.[2]   *swollen*
Witness the Streets of *Sodom,* and that night
In *Gibeah,* when the hospitable door
505   Expos'd a Matron to avoid worse rape.[3]
These were the prime in order and in might;
The rest were long to tell, though far renown'd,
Th' *Ionian* Gods,[4] of *Javan's* Issue held
Gods, yet confest later than Heav'n and Earth
510   Thir boasted Parents; *Titan* Heav'n's first born
With his enormous° brood, and birthright seiz'd   *monstrous*
By younger *Saturn,* he from mightier *Jove*
His own and *Rhea's* Son like measure found;
So *Jove* usurping reign'd: these first in *Crete*
515   And *Ida* known,[5] thence on the Snowy top
Of cold *Olympus* rul'd the middle Air
Thir highest Heav'n; or on the *Delphian* Cliff,[6]
Or in *Dodona,* and through all the bounds
Of *Doric* Land;° or who with *Saturn* old   *Greece*
520   Fled over *Adria* to th' *Hesperian* Fields,
And o'er the *Celtic* roam'd the utmost Isles.[7]
All these and more came flocking; but with looks
Downcast and damp,° yet such wherein appear'd   *depressed*
Obscure some glimpse of joy, to have found thir chief
525   Not in despair, to have found themselves not lost
In loss itself; which on his count'nance cast
Like doubtful hue: but he his wonted pride
Soon recollecting,° with high words, that bore   *recovering*
Semblance of worth, not substance, gently rais'd
530   Thir fainting courage, and dispell'd thir fears.
Then straight commands that at the warlike sound
Of Trumpets loud and Clarions° be uprear'd   *shrill trumpets*
His mighty Standard; that proud honor claim'd
Azazel as his right, a Cherub tall:[8]
535   Who forthwith from the glittering Staff unfurl'd
Th' Imperial Ensign, which full high advanc't
Shone like a Meteor streaming to the Wind
With Gems and Golden lustre rich imblaz'd,[9]

---

2. The Puritans referred to their enemies as the Sons of Belial.

3. See Genesis 19 and Judges 19.

4. The Ionian Greeks were held by some to be the issue of Javan the son of Japhet the son of Noah, on the basis of the Septuagint version of Genesis 10.

5. Jove was born and secretly reared on Mount Ida, in Crete.

6. Delphi was famed as the site of the Pythian oracle of Apollo, but cults of Ge, Poseidon, and Artemis were also celebrated there.

7. After Saturn's downfall he fled across the Adriatic Sea (Adria) to Italy (Hesperian Fields), France (the Celtic), and the British Isles (Utmost Isles).

8. Azazel was one of the chief fallen angels who are the object of God's wrath in the apocryphal Book of Enoch. For the healing of the earth he is bound and cast into the same wilderness where the scapegoat was led (Enoch 10.4–8).

9. Adorned with heraldic devices.

	Seraphic arms and Trophies: all the while	
540	Sonorous metal blowing Martial sounds:	
	At which the universal Host upsent	
	A shout that tore Hell's Concave,° and beyond	*vault*
	Frighted the Reign of *Chaos* and old Night.[1]	
	All in a moment through the gloom were seen	
545	Ten thousand Banners rise into the Air	
	With Orient° Colors waving: with them rose	*brilliant*
	A Forest huge of Spears: and thronging Helms	
	Appear'd, and serried° Shields in thick array	*locked together*
	Of depth immeasurable: Anon they move	
550	In perfect *Phalanx*[2] to the *Dorian*° mood	*solemn*
	Of Flutes and soft Recorders; such as rais'd	
	To highth of noblest temper Heroes old	
	Arming to Battle, and instead of rage	
	Deliberate valor breath'd, firm and unmov'd	
555	With dread of death to flight or foul retreat,	
	Nor wanting power to mitigate and swage°	*assuage*
	With solemn touches, troubl'd thoughts, and chase	
	Anguish and doubt and fear and sorrow and pain	
	From mortal or immortal minds. Thus they	
560	Breathing united force with fixed thought	
	Mov'd on in silence to soft Pipes that charm'd	
	Thir painful steps o'er the burnt soil; and now	
	Advanc't in view they stand, a horrid° Front	*bristling*
	Of dreadful length and dazzling Arms, in guise	
565	Of Warriors old with order'd Spear and Shield,	
	Awaiting what command thir mighty Chief	
	Had to impose: He through the armed Files	
	Darts his experienc't eye, and soon traverse°	*across*
	The whole Battalion views, thir order due,	
570	Thir visages and stature as of Gods;	
	Thir number last he sums. And now his heart	
	Distends with pride, and hard'ning in his strength	
	Glories: For never since created man,[3]	
	Met such imbodied° force, as nam'd with these	*united*
575	Could merit more than that small infantry	
	Warr'd on by Cranes:[4] though all the Giant brood	
	Of *Phlegra* with th' Heroic Race were join'd	
	That fought at *Thebes* and *Ilium,* on each side	
	Mixt with auxiliar Gods;[5] and what resounds	
580	In Fable or *Romance* of *Uther's* Son°	*King Arthur*
	Begirt with *British* and *Armoric*[6] Knights;	
	And all who since, Baptiz'd or Infidel	

1. Chaos and Night, rulers of the region of unformed matter between Heaven and Hell.
2. A square battle formation.
3. Since humanity was created.
4. When compared with Satan's, any army would seem no bigger than pygmies ("that small infantry"), who were portrayed by Pliny as tiny men who fought with cranes.

5. To amplify the heroic stature of the angels, Milton mentions a series of armies that had been thought worthy of epic treatment only to dismiss them. The Giants, who fought with the Olympians at Phlegra, join with the heroes of Thebes and Troy (Ilium).
6. From Brittany.

Jousted in *Aspramont* or *Montalban*,
Damasco, or *Marocco*, or *Trebisond*,
585 Or whom *Biserta* sent from *Afric* shore
When *Charlemain* with all his Peerage fell
By *Fontarabbia*.[7] Thus far these beyond
Compare of mortal prowess, yet observ'd°   obeyed
Thir dread commander: he above the rest
590 In shape and gesture proudly eminent
Stood like a Tow'r; his form had yet not lost
All her Original brightness, nor appear'd
Less than Arch-Angel ruin'd, and th' excess
Of Glory obscur'd: As when the Sun new ris'n
595 Looks through the Horizontal misty Air
Shorn of his Beams, or from behind the Moon
In dim Eclipse disastrous twilight sheds
On half the Nations, and with fear of change
Perplexes Monarchs.[8] Dark'n'd so, yet shone
600 Above them all th' Arch-Angel: but his face
Deep scars of Thunder had intrencht, and care
Sat on his faded cheek, but under Brows
Of dauntless courage, and considerate° Pride   deliberate
Waiting revenge: cruel his eye, but cast
605 Signs of remorse and passion to behold
The fellows of his crime, the followers rather
(Far other once beheld in bliss) condemn'd
For ever now to have thir lot in pain,
Millions of Spirits for his fault amerc't°   deprived
610 Of Heav'n, and from Eternal Splendors flung
For his revolt, yet faithful how they stood,
Thir Glory wither'd. As when Heaven's Fire
Hath scath'd the Forest Oaks, or Mountain Pines,
With singed top thir stately growth though bare
615 Stands on the blasted Heath. He now prepar'd
To speak; whereat thir doubl'd Ranks they bend
From wing to wing, and half enclose him round
With all his Peers: attention held them mute.
Thrice he assay'd, and thrice in spite of scorn,
620 Tears such as Angels weep, burst forth: at last
Words interwove with sighs found out thir way.
    O Myriads of immortal Spirits, O Powers
Matchless, but with th' Almighty, and that strife
Was not inglorious, though th' event° was dire,   result
625 As this place testifies, and this dire change
Hateful to utter: but what power of mind
Foreseeing or presaging, from the Depth

7. Aspramont was a castle near Nice, and Montalban was the castle of Rinaldo; these castles figure in Ariosto's *Orlando Furioso* and the romances concerned with chivalric wars between Christians and Saracens. Milton would know late versions of the Charlemagne legend. Charlemagne's whole rearguard, led by Roland, one of the 12 peers or paladins, was massacred at Roncesvalles, about 40 miles from Fontarabbia (Fuenterrabia).
8. The comparison is ironically double-edged, for the ominous solar eclipse presages not only disaster for creation but also the doom of the godlike ruler for whom the sun was a traditional symbol.

Of knowledge past or present, could have fear'd
How such united force of Gods, how such
630 As stood like these, could ever know repulse?
For who can yet believe, though after loss,
That all these puissant° Legions, whose exíle   *powerful*
Hath emptied Heav'n, shall fail to re-ascend
Self-rais'd, and repossess thir native seat?
635 For mee be witness all the Host of Heav'n,
If counsels different, or danger shunn'd
By me, have lost our hopes. But he who reigns
Monarch in Heav'n, till then as one secure
Sat on his Throne, upheld by old repute,
640 Consent or custom, and his Regal State
Put forth at full, but still his strength conceal'd,
Which tempted our attempt, and wrought our fall.
Henceforth his might we know, and know our own
So as not either to provoke, or dread
645 New War, provok't; our better part remains
To work in close° design, by fraud or guile   *secret*
What force effected not: that he no less
At length from us may find, who overcomes
By force, hath overcome but half his foe.
650 Space may produce new Worlds; whereof so rife°   *common*
There went a fame° in Heav'n that he ere long   *rumor*
Intended to create, and therein plant
A generation, whom his choice regard
Should favor equal to the Sons of Heaven:
655 Thither, if but to pry, shall be perhaps
Our first eruption, thither or elsewhere:
For this Infernal Pit shall never hold
Celestial Spirits in Bondage, nor th' Abyss
Long under darkness cover. But these thoughts
660 Full Counsel must mature: Peace is despair'd,
For who can think Submission? War then, War
Open or understood, must be resolv'd.
      He spake: and to confirm his words, out-flew
Millions of flaming swords, drawn from the thighs
665 Of mighty Cherubim; the sudden blaze
Far round illumin'd hell: highly they rag'd
Against the Highest, and fierce with grasped Arms
Clash'd on thir sounding shields the din of war,
Hurling defiance toward the Vault of Heav'n.
670   There stood a Hill not far whose grisly top
Belch'd fire and rolling smoke; the rest entire
Shone with a glossy scurf, undoubted sign
That in his womb was hid metallic Ore,
The work of Sulphur.⁹ Thither wing'd with speed
675 A numerous Brígad° hasten'd. As when bands   *brigade*

---

9. The traditional physiognomy of the fiend is in Milton's hell displaced onto the landscape. It is a dead or corrupt body imaged as scurf (i.e., scales, crust), belching, ransacked womb, bowels, entrails, and ribs.

Of Píoners° with Spade and Pickax arm'd   *engineers*
Forerun the Royal Camp, to trench a Field,
Or cast a Rampart. *Mammon*[1] led them on,
Mammon, the least erected° Spirit that fell   *elevated*
680   From Heav'n, for ev'n in Heav'n his looks and thoughts
Were always downward bent, admiring more
The riches of Heav'n's pavement, trodd'n Gold,
Than aught divine or holy else enjoy'd
In vision beatific: by him first
685   Men also, and by his suggestion taught,
Ransack'd the Center, and with impious hands
Rifl'd the bowels of thir mother Earth
For Treasures better hid. Soon had his crew
Op'n'd into the Hill a spacious wound
690   And digg'd out ribs of Gold. Let none admire°   *wonder*
That riches grow in Hell; that soil may best
Deserve the precious bane. And here let those
Who boast in mortal things, and wond'ring tell
Of *Babel*, and the works of *Memphian* Kings,[2]
695   Learn how thir greatest Monuments of Fame,
And Strength and Art are easily outdone
By Spirits reprobate, and in an hour
What in an age they with incessant toil
And hands innumerable scarce perform.
700   Nigh on the Plain in many cells prepar'd,
That underneath had veins of liquid fire
Sluic'd° from the Lake, a second multitude   *led by channels*
With wondrous Art founded the massy Ore,
Severing each kind, and scumm'd the Bullion dross:
705   A third as soon had form'd within the ground
A various mould, and from the boiling cells
By strange conveyance fill'd each hollow nook:
As in an Organ from one blast of wind
To many a row of Pipes the sound-board breathes.
710   Anon out of the earth a Fabric huge
Rose like an Exhalation,[3] with the sound
Of Dulcet Symphonies and voices sweet,
Built like a Temple, where *Pilasters*° round   *columns*
Were set, and Doric pillars overlaid
715   With Golden Architrave; nor did there want
Cornice or Frieze, with bossy° Sculptures grav'n;   *embossed*
The Roof was fretted° Gold. Not *Babylon*,[4]   *patterned*
Nor great *Alcairo* such magnificence

---

1. In Matthew 6.24 and Luke 16.13, "Mammon" is an abstract noun meaning wealth, but later it was used as the name of "the prince of this world" (John 12.31). Medieval and Renaissance tradition often associated Mammon with Plutus, the Greek god of riches.
2. The Tower of Babel was built by the ambitious Nimrod. The works of Memphian kings, the Pyramids, were regarded as memorials of vanity.
3. Pandaemonium rises to music, since in the Renais-

sance it was believed that musical proportions governed the forms of architecture.
4. An ironic allusion to Ovid's description of the Palace of the Sun built by Mulciber (*Metamorphoses* 2.1–4). Pandaemonium has a classical design, complete in every respect, like that of the ancient (but still surviving) giltroofed Pantheon, the most admired building of Milton's time. Doric is the oldest and simplest order of Greek architecture.

	Equall'd in all thir glories,[5] to inshrine
720	*Belus*[6] or *Serapis*[7] thir Gods, or seat
	Thir Kings, when *Egypt* with *Assyria* strove
	In wealth and luxury. Th' ascending pile
	Stood fixt her stately highth, and straight the doors
	Op'ning thir brazen folds discover wide
725	Within, her ample spaces, o'er the smooth
	And level pavement: from the arched roof
	Pendant by subtle Magic many a row
	Of Starry Lamps and blazing Cressets[8] fed
	With *Naphtha* and *Asphaltus*[9] yielded light
730	As from a sky. The hasty multitude
	Admiring enter'd, and the work some praise
	And some the Architect: his hand was known
	In Heav'n by many a Tow'red structure high,
	Where Scepter'd Angels held thir residence,
735	And sat as Princes, whom the supreme King
	Exalted to such power, and gave to rule,
	Each in his Hierarchy, the Orders bright.
	Nor was his name unheard or unador'd
	In ancient *Greece*; and in *Ausonian* land
740	Men call'd him *Mulciber*;[1] and how he fell
	From Heav'n, they fabl'd, thrown by angry *Jove*
	Sheer o'er the Crystal Battlements: from Morn
	To Noon he fell, from Noon to dewy Eve,
	A Summer's day; and with the setting Sun
745	Dropt from the Zenith like a falling Star,
	On *Lemnos* th' *Aegean* Isle:[2] thus they relate,
	Erring; for he with this rebellious rout
	Fell long before; nor aught avail'd him now
	To have built in Heav'n high Tow'rs; nor did he scape
750	By all his Engines, but was headlong sent
	With his industrious crew to build in hell.
	Meanwhile the winged Heralds by command
	Of Sovran power, with awful Ceremony
	And Trumpets' sound throughout the Host proclaim
755	A solemn Council forthwith to be held
	At *Pandaemonium*, the high Capitol
	Of Satan and his Peers: thir summons call'd
	From every Band and squared Regiment
	By place or choice the worthiest; they anon
760	With hunderds and with thousands trooping came

5. In traditional biblical exegesis, Babylon, a place of proud iniquity, was often a figure of Antichrist or of hell. Memphis (modern Cairo) was the most splendid city of heathen Egypt.

6. Bel, the Babylonian Baal; see lines 421–23 n and Jeremiah 51.44: "I will punish Bel in Babylon."

7. An Egyptian deity.

8. Basketlike lamps.

9. *Naphtha* is an oily constituent of asphalt (asphaltus).

1. The Greek god Hephaistos, in Latin *Mulciber* or Vulcan, presided over all arts, such as metal-working, that required the use of fire. He built all the palaces of the gods. "Ausonian land" is the old Greek name for Italy. Milton emulates Homer's description of the daylong fall of Hephaistos (*Iliad* 1.591–95) and then deflates it in the casual but commanding dismissal of 746–48.

2. In Homer (*Iliad* 2.87–90), the Achaians going to a council are compared to bees, as are the Carthaginians in Virgil (*Aeneid* 1.430–36). Milton also glances at Virgil's mock-epic account of the ideal social organization of the hive (*Georgics* 4.149–227).

Attended: all access was throng'd, the Gates
And Porches wide, but chief the spacious Hall
(Though like a cover'd field, where Champions bold
Wont ride in arm'd, and at the Soldan's° chair   *Sultan's*
765 Defi'd the best of *Paynim°* chivalry   *pagan*
To mortal combat or career with Lance)
Thick swarm'd, both on the ground and in the air,
Brusht with the hiss of rustling wings. As Bees
In spring time, when the Sun with *Taurus*[3] rides,
770 Pour forth thir populous youth about the Hive
In clusters; they among fresh dews and flowers
Fly to and fro, or on the smoothed Plank,
The suburb of thir Straw-built Citadel,
New rubb'd with Balm, expatiate° and confer   *debate*
775 Thir State affairs. So thick the aery crowd
Swarm'd and were strait'n'd; till the Signal giv'n,
Behold a wonder! they but now who seem'd
In bigness to surpass Earth's Giant Sons
Now less than smallest Dwarfs, in narrow room
780 Throng numberless, like that Pigmean Race
Beyond the *Indian* Mount, or Faery Elves,
Whose midnight Revels, by a Forest side
Or Fountain some belated Peasant sees,
Or dreams he sees, while over-head the Moon
785 Sits Arbitress, and nearer to the Earth
Wheels her pale course;[4] they on thir mirth and dance
Intent, with jocund Music charm his ear;
At once with joy and fear his heart rebounds.
Thus incorporeal Spirits to smallest forms
790 Reduc'd thir shapes immense, and were at large,
Though without number still amidst the Hall
Of that infernal Court. But far within
And in thir own dimensions like themselves
The great Seraphic Lords and Cherubim
795 In close° recess and secret conclave[5] sat   *secret*
A thousand Demi-Gods on golden seats,
Frequent° and full. After short silence then   *crowded*
And summons read, the great consult began.
             The End of the First Book.

             from **Book 2**
             The Argument

The Consultation begun, Satan debates whether another Battle be to be hazarded for the recovery of Heaven: some advise it, others dissuade: A third proposal is preferr'd, mention'd before by Satan, to search the truth of that Prophecy or Tradition in Heaven concerning

---

3. In Milton's time the sun entered the second sign of the zodiac in mid-April, according to the Julian calendar.
4. Echoing *A Midsummer Night's Dream* 2.1.28f and 141. "The moon / Sits arbitress" because the moon-goddess was queen of faery.
5. "Conclave" could refer to any assembly in secret session but already had the specifically ecclesiastical meaning on which Milton's satire here depends.

another world, and another kind of creature equal or not much inferior to themselves, about this time to be created: Thir doubt who shall be sent on this difficult search: Satan thir chief undertakes alone the voyage, is honor'd and applauded. The Council thus ended, the rest betake them several ways and to several employments, as thir inclinations lead them, to entertain the time till Satan return. He passes on his Journey to Hell Gates, finds them shut, and who sat there to guard them, by whom at length they are op'n'd, and discover[1] to him the great Gulf between Hell and Heaven; with what difficulty he passes through, directed by Chaos, the Power of that place, to the sight of this new World which he sought.

High on a Throne of Royal State,[2] which far
Outshone the wealth of *Ormus* and of *Ind*,[3]
Or where the gorgeous East with richest hand
Show'rs on her Kings *Barbaric* Pearl and Gold,

5   Satan exalted sat, by merit rais'd
To that bad eminence; and from despair
Thus high uplifted beyond hope, aspires
Beyond thus high, insatiate to pursue
Vain War with Heav'n, and by success° untaught   *result*
10   His proud imaginations thus display'd.
      Powers and Dominions,[4] Deities of Heav'n,
For since no deep within her gulf can hold
Immortal vigor, though opprest and fall'n,
I give not Heav'n for lost. From this descent
15   Celestial Virtues rising, will appear
More glorious and more dread than from no fall
And trust themselves to fear no second fate:
Mee though just right and the fixt Laws of Heav'n
Did first create your Leader, next, free choice,
20   With what besides, in Counsel or in Fight,
Hath been achiev'd of merit, yet this loss
Thus far at least recover'd, hath much more
Establisht in a safe unenvied Throne
Yielded with full consent. The happier state
25   In Heav'n, which follows dignity, might draw
Envy from each inferior; but who here
Will envy whom the highest place exposes
Foremost to stand against the Thunderer's aim[5]
Your bulwark, and condemns to greatest share
30   Of endless pain? where there is then no good
For which to strive, no strife can grow up there
From Faction; for none sure will claim in Hell
Precedence, none, whose portion is so small
Of present pain, that with ambitious mind
35   Will covet more. With this advantage then
To union, and firm Faith, and firm accord,
More than can be in Heav'n, we now return

---

1. Disclose.
2. Compare Spenser's description of the bright throne of the Phaethon-like Lucifera, embodiment of pride in *The Faerie Queene* 1.4.8, page 462.
3. India. Ormus, an island town in the Persian Gulf, was famous as a jewel market.
4. Two angelic orders mentioned by St. Paul in Colossians 1.16.
5. By identifying him with thunder, the attribute of Jupiter, Satan reduces God to a mere Olympian tyrant.

942   John Milton

To claim our just inheritance of old,
Surer to prosper than prosperity
40 Could have assur'd us; and by what best way,
Whether of open War or covert guile,
We now debate; who can advise, may speak.
    He ceas'd, and next him *Moloch*, Scepter'd King
Stood up, the strongest and the fiercest Spirit
45 That fought in Heav'n; now fiercer by despair:
His trust was with th' Eternal to be deem'd
Equal in strength, and rather than be less
Car'd not to be at all; with that care lost
Went all his fear: of God, or Hell, or worse
50 He reck'd° not, and these words thereafter spake.   *cared*
    My sentence° is for open War: Of Wiles,   *opinion*
More unexpert,° I boast not: them let those   *inexperienced*
Contrive who need, or when they need, not now.
For while they sit contriving, shall the rest,
55 Millions that stand in Arms, and longing wait
The Signal to ascend, sit ling'ring here
Heav'n's fugitives, and for thir dwelling place
Accept this dark opprobrious Den of shame,
The Prison of his Tyranny who Reigns
60 By our delay? no, let us rather choose
Arm'd with Hell flames and fury[6] all at once
O'er Heav'n's high Tow'rs to force resistless way,
Turning our Tortures into horrid Arms
Against the Torturer; when to meet the noise
65 Of his Almighty Engine[7] he shall hear
Infernal Thunder, and for Lightning see
Black fire and horror shot with equal rage
Among his Angels; and his Throne itself
Mixt with *Tartarean* Sulphur, and strange fire,[8]
70 His own invented Torments. But perhaps
The way seems difficult and steep to scale
With upright wing against a higher foe.
Let such bethink them, if the sleepy drench[9]
Of that forgetful Lake benumb not still,
75 That in our proper motion we ascend
Up to our native seat: descent and fall
To us is adverse. Who but felt of late
When the fierce Foe hung on our brok'n Rear
Insulting,° and pursu'd us through the Deep,   *assaulting, exulting*
80 With what compulsion and laborious flight
We sunk thus low? Th' ascent is easy then;
Th' event° is fear'd; should we again provoke   *outcome*

6. The violent yoking of concrete and abstract words is one of the most characteristic figures of Milton's style.
7. Machine of war, probably here referring to the Messiah's chariot or perhaps to his thunder.
8. In the classical underworld, Tartarus was the place of the guilty. For "strange fire," see Leviticus 10.1–2:

"Nadab and Abihu, the sons of Aaron . . . offered strange fire before the Lord, which he commanded them not. And there went out fire from the Lord, and devoured them."
9. A draught of medicine for an animal.

Our stronger, some worse way his wrath may find
To our destruction: if there be in Hell
85 Fear to be worse destroy'd: what can be worse
Than to dwell here, driv'n out from bliss, condemn'd
In this abhorred deep to utter woe;
Where pain of unextinguishable fire
Must exercise° us without hope of end   *afflict*
90 The Vassals[1] of his anger, when the Scourge
Inexorably, and the torturing hour
Calls us to Penance? More destroy'd than thus
We should be quite abolisht and expire.
What fear we then? what doubt we to incense
95 His utmost ire? which to the highth enrag'd,
Will either quite consume us, and reduce
To nothing this essential,° happier far   *essence*
Than miserable to have eternal being:
Or if our substance be indeed Divine,
100 And cannot cease to be, we are at worst
On this side nothing;[2] and by proof we feel
Our power sufficient to disturb his Heav'n,
And with perpetual inroads to Alarm,
Though inaccessible, his fatal Throne:
105 Which if not Victory is yet Revenge.
     He ended frowning, and his look denounc'd
Desperate revenge, and Battle dangerous
To less than Gods. On th' other side up rose
Belial, in act more graceful and humane;
110 A fairer person lost not Heav'n; he seem'd
For dignity compos'd and high exploit:
But all was false and hollow; though his Tongue
Dropt Manna, and could make the worse appear
The better reason,[3] to perplex and dash
115 Maturest Counsels: for his thoughts were low;
To vice industrious, but to Nobler deeds
Timorous and slothful: yet he pleas'd the ear,
And with persuasive accent thus began.
     I should be much for open War, O Peers,
120 As not behind in hate; if what was urg'd
Main reason to persuade immediate War,
Did not dissuade me most, and seem to cast
Ominous conjecture on the whole success:
When he who most excels in fact° of Arms,   *feat*
125 In what he counsels and in what excels
Mistrustful, grounds his courage on despair
And utter dissolution, as the scope
Of all his aim, after some dire revenge.

---

1. Servants, slaves. Also an allusion to Romans 9.22: "What if God, willing to show his wrath, and to make his power known, endured with much longsuffering the vessels of wrath fitted to destruction . . . ?"

2. Already we are in the worst condition possible, short of being nothing, being annihilated.
3. This was the claim of the Greek Sophists, who taught their students how to use rhetoric to win an argument.

First, what Revenge? the Tow'rs of Heav'n are fill'd
130   With Armed watch, that render all access
Impregnable; oft on the bordering Deep
Encamp thir Legions, or with obscure[4] wing
Scout far and wide into the Realm of night,
Scorning surprise. Or could we break our way
135   By force, and at our heels all Hell should rise
With blackest Insurrection, to confound
Heav'n's purest Light, yet our great Enemy
All incorruptible would on his Throne
Sit unpolluted, and th' Ethereal mould
140   Incapable of stain would soon expel
Her mischief, and purge off the baser fire
Victorious.[5] Thus repuls'd, our final hope
Is flat° despair: we must exasperate   *absolute*
Th' Almighty Victor to spend all his rage,
145   And that must end us, that must be our cure,
To be no more; sad cure; for who would lose,
Though full of pain, this intellectual being,
Those thoughts that wander through Eternity,
To perish rather, swallow'd up and lost
150   In the wide womb of uncreated night,
Devoid of sense and motion? and who knows,
Let this be good,[6] whether our angry Foe
Can give it, or will ever? how he can
Is doubtful; that he never will is sure.
155   Will he, so wise, let loose at once his ire,
Belike° through impotence, or unaware,   *no doubt*
To give his Enemies thir wish, and end
Them in his anger, whom his anger saves
To punish endless? wherefore cease we then?
160   Say they who counsel War, we are decreed,
Reserv'd and destin'd to Eternal woe;
Whatever doing, what can we suffer more,
What can we suffer worse? is this then worst,
Thus sitting, thus consulting, thus in Arms?
165   What when we fled amain,° pursu'd and strook°   *headlong / struck*
With Heav'n's afflicting Thunder, and besought
The Deep to shelter us? this Hell then seem'd
A refuge from those wounds: or when we lay
Chain'd on the burning Lake? that sure was worse.
170   What if the breath that kindl'd those grim fires
Awak'd should blow them into sevenfold rage
And plunge us in the flames? or from above
Should intermitted vengeance arm again
His red right hand to plague us? what if all
175   Her° stores were op'n'd, and this Firmament   *Hell's*

4. "Obscure" is stressed on the first syllable here.
5. Criticizing Moloch's proposal to mix God's throne with sulphur (lines 68–9) and shoot "black fire" among his angels. This "baser fire" Belial contrasts with the "ethereal" (derived from ether, the fifth and purest element) fire of the throne.
6. Suppose it is good to be destroyed.

Of Hell should spout her Cataracts of Fire,
Impendent° horrors, threat'ning hideous fall   *threatening*
One day upon our heads; while we perhaps
Designing or exhorting glorious war,
180 Caught in a fiery Tempest shall be hurl'd
Each on his rock transfixt, the sport and prey
Of racking whirlwinds, or for ever sunk
Under yon boiling Ocean, wrapt in Chains;
There to converse with everlasting groans,
185 Unrespited, unpitied, unrepriev'd,
Ages of hopeless end; this would be worse.
War therefore, open or conceal'd, alike
My voice dissuades; for what can force or guile
With him, or who deceive his mind, whose eye
190 Views all things at one view? he from Heav'n's highth
All these our motions° vain, sees and derides;   *schemes*
Not more Almighty to resist our might
Than wise to frustrate all our plots and wiles.
Shall we then live thus vile, the race of Heav'n
195 Thus trampl'd, thus expell'd to suffer here
Chains and these Torments? better these than worse
By my advice; since fate inevitable
Subdues us, and Omnipotent Decree,
The Victor's will. To suffer, as to do,
200 Our strength is equal, nor the Law unjust
That so ordains: this was at first resolv'd,
If we were wise, against so great a foe
Contending, and so doubtful what might fall.
I laugh, when those who at the Spear are bold
205 And vent'rous, if that fail them, shrink and fear
What yet they know must follow, to endure
Exile, or ignominy, or bonds, or pain,
The sentence of thir Conqueror: This is now
Our doom; which if we can sustain and bear,
210 Our Supreme Foe in time may much remit
His anger, and perhaps thus far remov'd
Not mind us not offending, satisfi'd
With what is punisht; whence these raging fires
Will slack'n, if his breath stir not thir flames.
215 Our purer essence then will overcome
Thir noxious vapor, or enur'd° not feel,   *accustomed*
Or chang'd at length, and to the place conform'd
In temper[7] and in nature, will receive
Familiar the fierce heat, and void of pain;
220 This horror will grow mild, this darkness light,[8]
Besides what hope the never-ending flight
Of future days may bring, what chance, what change
Worth waiting, since our present lot appears

7. Temperament, the mixture or adjustment of humors. Thus the phrase means "adjusted psychologically and   physically to the new environment."
8. Easy to bear, and illumination.

For happy though but ill, for ill not worst,[9]
225   If we procure not to ourselves more woe.
        Thus *Belial* with words cloth'd in reason's garb
Counsell'd ignoble ease, and peaceful sloth,
Not peace: and after him thus *Mammon* spake.
        Either to disinthrone the King of Heav'n
230   We war, if war be best, or to regain
Our own right lost: him to unthrone we then
May hope, when everlasting Fate shall yield
To fickle Chance, and *Chaos* judge the strife:
The former vain to hope argues as vain
235   The latter: for what place can be for us
Within Heav'n's bound, unless Heav'n's Lord supreme
We overpower? Suppose he should relent
And publish Grace to all, on promise made
Of new Subjection; with what eyes could we
240   Stand in his presence humble, and receive
Strict Laws impos'd, to celebrate his Throne
With warbl'd Hymns, and to his Godhead sing
Forc't Halleluiahs[1] while he Lordly sits
Our envied Sovran, and his Altar breathes
245   Ambrosial[2] Odors and Ambrosial Flowers,
Our servile offerings. This must be our task
In Heav'n, this our delight; how wearisome
Eternity so spent in worship paid
To whom we hate. Let us not then pursue
250   By force impossible, by leave obtain'd
Unácceptable, though in Heav'n, our state
Of splendid vassalage, but rather seek
Our own good from ourselves, and from our own
Live to ourselves, though in this vast recess,
255   Free, and to none accountable, preferring
Hard liberty before the easy yoke
Of servile Pomp.[3] Our greatness will appear
Then most conspicuous, when great things of small,
Useful of hurtful, prosperous of adverse
260   We can create, and in what place soe'er
Thrive under evil, and work ease out of pain
Through labor and endurance. This deep world
Of darkness do we dread? How oft amidst
Thick clouds and dark doth Heav'n's all-ruling Sire
265   Choose to reside, his Glory unobscur'd,
And with the Majesty of darkness round
Covers his Throne; from whence deep thunders roar

---

9. Though as far as happiness is concerned, the devils are but ill off, as far as evil is concerned, they could be worse.
1. The word "hallelujah" (Hebrew, "praise Jehovah") occurred in so many psalms that it came to mean a song of praise to God.
2. Fragrant and perfumed, immortal. Ambrosia was the fabled food or drink of the gods.

3. In *Samson Agonistes* 271, Samson condemns those who are fonder of "bondage with ease than strenuous liberty." The antithesis is from the Roman historian, Sallust, who assigns it to an opponent of the dictator Sulla. See also Jesus' words in Matthew 11.28–30: "Come unto me. . . . For my yoke is easy."

Must'ring thir rage, and Heav'n resembles Hell?
As he our darkness, cannot we his Light
270   Imitate when we please? This Desert soil
Wants not her hidden lustre, Gems and Gold;
Nor want we skill or art, from whence to raise
Magnificence; and what can Heav'n show more?
Our torments also may in length of time
275   Become our Elements, these piercing Fires
As soft as now severe, our temper chang'd
Into their temper;[4] which must needs remove
The sensible of pain.[5] All things invite
To peaceful Counsels, and the settl'd State
280   Of order, how in safety best we may
Compose° our present evils, with regard   *order*
Of what we are and where, dismissing quite
All thoughts of War; ye have what I advise.
      He scarce had finisht, when such murmur fill'd
285   Th' Assembly, as when hollow Rocks retain
The sound of blust'ring winds, which all night long
Had rous'd the Sea, now with hoarse cadence lull
Sea-faring men o'erwatcht, whose Bark by chance
Or Pinnace anchors in a craggy Bay
290   After the Tempest: Such applause was heard
As *Mammon* ended, and his Sentence° pleas'd,   *opinion*
Advising peace: for such another Field
They dreaded worse than Hell: so much the fear
Of Thunder and the Sword of *Michaël*[6]
295   Wrought still within them; and no less desire
To found this nether Empire, which might rise
By policy,[7] and long process of time,
In emulation opposite to Heav'n.
Which when *Beëlzebub*[8] perceiv'd, than whom,
300   *Satan* except, none higher sat, with grave
Aspect he rose, and in his rising seem'd
A Pillar of State; deep on his Front° engraven   *forehead*
Deliberation sat and public care;
And Princely counsel in his face yet shone,
305   Majestic though in ruin: sage he stood
With *Atlantean*[9] shoulders fit to bear
The weight of mightiest Monarchies; his look
Drew audience and attention still as Night
Or Summer's Noon-tide air, while thus he spake.
310   Thrones and Imperial Powers, off-spring of Heav'n,
Ethereal Virtues; or these Titles now

4. Milton alludes to an idea of St. Augustine's, that the devils are bound to tormenting fires as if to bodies (*City of God*, 21.10).
5. The part of pain apprehended through the senses.
6. In the war in Heaven, Michael's two-handed sword felled "squadrons at once" and wounded even Satan. "Michael" here has three syllables.

7. Statesmanship, often in a bad sense, implying Machiavellian strategems. "Process" is stressed on the second syllable.
8. Satan's closest associate.
9. Worthy of Atlas, who was forced by Jupiter to carry the heavens on his shoulders as a punishment for his part in the rebellion of the Titans.

Must we renounce, and changing style be call'd
Princes of Hell? for so the popular vote
Inclines, here to continue, and build up here
315   A growing Empire; doubtless; while we dream,
And know not that the King of Heav'n hath doom'd
This place our dungeon, not our safe retreat
Beyond his Potent arm, to live exempt
From Heav'n's high jurisdiction, in new League
320   Banded against his Throne, but to remain
In strictest bondage, though thus far remov'd,
Under th' inevitable curb, reserv'd
His captive multitude: For he, be sure,
In highth or depth, still first and last will Reign
325   Sole King, and of his Kingdom lose no part
By our revolt, but over Hell extend
His Empire, and with Iron Sceptre rule
Us here, as with his Golden those in Heav'n.
What° sit we then projecting peace and war?   *why*
330   War hath determin'd[1] us, and foil'd with loss
Irreparable; terms of peace yet none
Voutsaf't[2] or sought; for what peace will be giv'n
To us enslav'd, but custody severe,
And stripes, and arbitrary punishment
335   Inflicted? and what peace can we return,
But to our power[3] hostility and hate,
Untam'd reluctance,° and revenge though slow,   *resistance*
Yet ever plotting how the Conqueror least
May reap his conquest, and may least rejoice
340   In doing what we most in suffering feel?[4]
Nor will occasion want, nor shall we need
With dangerous expedition to invade
Heav'n, whose high walls fear no assault or Siege,
Or ambush from the Deep. What if we find
345   Some easier enterprise? There is a place
(If ancient and prophetic fame in Heav'n
Err not) another World, the happy seat
Of some new Race call'd *Man*, about this time
To be created like to us, though less
350   In power and excellence, but favor'd more
Of him who rules above;[5] so was his will
Pronounc'd among the Gods, and by an Oath,
That shook Heav'n's whole circumference, confirm'd.[6]
Thither let us bend all our thoughts, to learn
355   What creatures there inhabit, of what mould,

1. Finished, but the context also activates a subsidiary meaning, "war has given us a settled aim."
2. "Vouchsafed": granted; Milton's spelling, "Voutsaf't," indicates the 17th-century pronunciation he preferred.
3. To the limit of our power.
4. How God may get the least happiness from our pain. Beelzebub portrays God as similar in his motives to the devils.
5. The creation of humanity was the subject of a public oath by God, but the time of the creation was the subject of a rumor only ("it is not for you to know the times or season," Acts 1.7).
6. See Isaiah 13.12–13: "I will make a man more precious than fine gold. . . . Therefore I will shake the Heavens."

Or substance, how endu'd,° and what thir Power,   *gifted*
And where thir weakness, how attempted° best,   *attacked*
By force or subtlety: Though Heav'n be shut,
And Heav'n's high Arbitrator sit secure
360   In his own strength, this place may lie expos'd
The utmost border of his Kingdom, left
To their defense who hold it: here perhaps
Some advantageous act may be achiev'd
By sudden onset, either with Hell fire
365   To waste his whole Creation, or possess
All as our own, and drive as we were driven,
The puny° habitants, or if not drive,   *weak*
Seduce them to our Party, that thir God
May prove thir foe, and with repenting hand
370   Abolish his own works. This would surpass
Common revenge, and interrupt his joy
In our Confusion, and our Joy upraise
In his disturbance; when his darling Sons
Hurl'd headlong to partake with us,[7] shall curse
375   Thir frail Original,° and faded bliss,   *author*
Faded so soon. Advise if this be worth
Attempting, or to sit in darkness here
Hatching vain Empires. Thus *Beëlzebub*
Pleaded his devilish Counsel, first devis'd
380   By *Satan*, and in part propos'd: for whence,
But from the Author of all ill could Spring
So deep a malice, to confound the race
Of mankind in one root,[8] and Earth with Hell
To mingle and involve, done all to spite
385   The great Creator? But thir spite still serves
His glory to augment. The bold design
Pleas'd highly those infernal States,[9] and joy
Sparkl'd in all thir eyes; with full assent
They vote: whereat his speech he thus renews.
390   Well have ye judg'd, well ended long debate,
Synod[1] of Gods, and like to what ye are,
Great things resolv'd, which from the lowest deep
Will once more lift us up, in spite of Fate,
Nearer our ancient Seat; perhaps in view
395   Of those bright confines, whence with neighboring Arms
And opportune excursion we may chance
Re-enter Heav'n; or else in some mild Zone
Dwell not unvisited of Heav'n's fair Light
Secure, and at the bright'ning Orient beam
400   Purge off this gloom; the soft delicious Air,
To heal the scar of these corrosive Fires
Shall breathe her balm. But first whom shall we send
In search of this new world, whom shall we find

---

7. Share in our condition; also, take sides with us.   9. Estates of the realm, people of rank and authority.
8. Adam, the root of the genealogical tree of man.   1. A meeting of councillors.

Sufficient? who shall tempt° with wand'ring feet   *venture upon*
405   The dark unbottom'd infinite Abyss
And through the palpable obscure[2] find out
His uncouth° way, or spread his aery flight   *unknown*
Upborne with indefatigable wings
Over the vast abrupt,[3] ere he arrive
410   The happy Isle; what strength, what art can then
Suffice, or what evasion bear him safe
Through the strict Senteries° and Stations thick   *sentries*
Of Angels watching round? Here he had need
All circumspection, and wee now no less
415   Choice in our suffrage;[4] for on whom we send,
The weight of all and our last hope relies.
     This said, he sat; and expectation held
His look suspense, awaiting who appear'd
To second, or oppose, or undertake
420   The perilous attempt; but all sat mute,
Pondering the danger with deep thoughts; and each
In other's count'nance read his own dismay
Astonisht: none among the choice and prime
Of those Heav'n-warring Champions could be found
425   So hardy as to proffer° or accept   *offer*
Alone the dreadful voyage; till at last
Satan, whom now transcendent glory rais'd
Above his fellows, with Monarchal pride
Conscious of highest worth, unmov'd thus spake.
430   O Progeny of Heav'n, Empyreal Thrones,
With reason hath deep silence and demur°   *delay*
Seiz'd us, though undismay'd: long is the way
And hard, that out of Hell leads up to light;
Our prison strong, this huge convex° of Fire,   *vault*
435   Outrageous to devour, immures us round
Ninefold, and gates of burning Adamant
Barr'd over us prohibit all egress.
These past, if any pass, the void profound
Of unessential° Night receives him next   *empty*
440   Wide gaping, and with utter loss of being
Threatens him, plung'd in that abortive gulf.
If thence he scape into whatever world,
Or unknown Region, what remains him less
Than[5] unknown dangers and as hard escape.
445   But I should ill become this Throne, O Peers,
And this Imperial Sov'ranty, adorn'd
With splendor, arm'd with power, if aught propos'd
And judg'd of public moment, in the shape
Of difficulty or danger could deter
450   Mee from attempting. Wherefore do I assume

---

2. See Exodus 10.21: "The Lord said unto Moses, Stretch out thine hand toward heaven, that there may be darkness over the land of Egypt, even darkness which may be felt."

3. The adjective (precipitous, broken off) is here used as a noun and refers to the abyss between hell and heaven.
4. Care in our vote (to elect him).
5. What awaits him except.

These Royalties, and not refuse to Reign,
Refusing[6] to accept as great a share
Of hazard as of honor, due alike
To him who Reigns, and so much to him due
455   Of hazard more, as he above the rest
High honor'd sits? Go therefore mighty Powers.
Terror of Heav'n, though fall'n; intend° at home,   *consider*
While here shall be our home, what best may ease
The present misery, and render Hell
460   More tolerable; if there be cure or charm
To respite° or deceive, or slack the pain   *rest*
Of this ill Mansion: intermit no watch
Against a wakeful Foe, while I abroad
Through all the Coasts of dark destruction seek
465   Deliverance for us all: this enterprise
None shall partake with me. Thus saying rose
The Monarch, and prevented all reply,
Prudent, lest from his resolution rais'd°   *encouraged*
Others among the chief might offer now
470   (Certain to be refus'd) what erst they fear'd;
And so refus'd might in opinion stand
His Rivals, winning cheap the high repute
Which he through hazard huge must earn. But they
Dreaded not more th' adventure than his voice
475   Forbidding; and at once with him they rose;
Thir rising all at once was as the sound
Of Thunder heard remote. Towards him they bend
With awful° reverence prone; and as a God   *respectful*
Extol him equal to the highest in Heav'n:
480   Nor fail'd they to express how much they prais'd,
That for the general safety he despis'd
His own: for neither do the Spirits damn'd
Lose all thir virtue; lest bad men should boast[7]
Thir specious° deeds on earth, which glory excites,   *pretending*
485   Or close° ambition varnisht o'er with zeal.   *secret*
Thus they thir doubtful consultations dark
Ended rejoicing in their matchless Chief:
As when from mountain tops the dusky clouds
Ascending, while the North wind sleeps, o'erspread
490   Heav'n's cheerful face, the low'ring Element
Scowls o'er the dark'n'd lantskip° Snow, or show'r;   *landscape*
If chance the radiant Sun with farewell sweet
Extend his ev'ning beam, the fields revive,
The birds thir notes renew, and bleating herds
495   Attest thir joy, that hill and valley rings.
O shame to men! Devil with Devil damn'd
Firm concord holds, men only disagree
Of Creatures rational, though under hope
Of heavenly Grace; and God proclaiming peace,

6. If I refuse.   7. So that men ought not to boast.

500	Yet live in hatred, enmity, and strife	
	Among themselves, and levy cruel wars,	
	Wasting the Earth, each other to destroy:	
	As if (which might induce us to accord)	
	Man had not hellish foes anow° besides,	*enough*
505	That day and night for his destruction wait.	
	The *Stygian* Council thus dissolv'd; and forth	
	In order came the grand infernal Peers:	
	Midst came thir mighty Paramount,° and seem'd	*ruler*
	Alone th' Antagonist of Heav'n, nor less	
510	Than Hell's dread Emperor with pomp Supreme,[8]	
	And God-like imitated State; him round	
	A Globe° of fiery Seraphim inclos'd	*band*
	With bright imblazonry,° and horrent° Arms.	*heraldry / bristling*
	Then of thir Session ended they bid cry	
515	With Trumpet's regal sound the great result:	
	Toward the four winds four speedy Cherubim	
	Put to thir mouths the sounding Alchymy[9]	
	By Herald's voice explain'd: the hollow Abyss	
	Heard far and wide, and all the host of Hell	
520	With deaf'ning shout, return'd them loud acclaim.	
	Thence more at ease thir minds and somewhat rais'd°	*encouraged*
	By false presumptuous hope, the ranged powers[1]	
	Disband, and wand'ring, each his several way	
	Pursues, as inclination or sad choice	
525	Leads him perplext, where he may likeliest find	
	Truce to his restless thoughts, and entertain	
	The irksome hours, till this great Chief return.	
	Part on the Plain, or in the Air sublime°	*uplifted*
	Upon the wing, or in swift Race contend,	
530	As at th' *Olympian* Games or *Pythian* fields;[2]	
	Part curb thir fiery Steeds, or shun the Goal	
	With rapid wheels, or fronted Brígads form.	
	As when to warn proud Cities war appears	
	Wag'd in the troubl'd Sky, and Armies rush	
535	To Battle in the Clouds, before each Van	
	Prick forth the Aery Knights, and couch thir spears	
	Till thickest Legions close; with feats of Arms	
	From either end of Heav'n the welkin° burns.	*sky*
	Others with vast *Typhoean*[3] rage more fell	
540	Rend up both Rocks and Hills, and ride the Air	
	In whirlwind; Hell scarce holds the wild uproar.	
	As when *Alcides* from *Oechalia* Crown'd	
	With conquest, felt th' envenom'd robe, and tore	

8. Lines 510–20 may portray the English mob's easy gullibility and their passion (which Milton detested) for the regalia of monarchy.
9. Trumpets made of the alloy brass, associated with alchemy.
1. Armies drawn up in ranks.
2. Epic models for lines 528–69 include the sports of the Myrmidons during Achilles' absence from the war

(Homer, *Iliad* 2.774ff.), the Greek funeral games of *Iliad* 23 and the Trojan of *Aeneid* 5, and the amusements of the blessed dead in Virgil's Elysium (*Aeneid* 6.642–59). To "shun the goal" (line 531) is to drive a chariot as close as possible around a post without touching it.
3. Like that of Typhon, the hundred-headed Titan. A pun, for "typhon" was also an English word meaning "whirlwind."

Through pain up by the roots *Thessalian* Pines,
545   And *Lichas* from the top of *Oeta* threw
Into th' *Euboic* Sea.[4] Others more mild,
Retreated in a silent valley, sing
With notes Angelical to many a Harp
Thir own Heroic deeds and hapless fall
550   By doom of Battle; and complain that Fate
Free Virtue should enthrall to Force or Chance.
Thir Song was partial,° but the harmony   *prejudiced*
(What could it less when Spirits immortal sing?)
Suspended° Hell, and took with ravishment   *enthralled*
555   The thronging audience. In discourse more sweet
(For Eloquence the Soul, Song charms the Sense,)
Others apart sat on a Hill retir'd,
In thoughts more elevate, and reason'd high
Of Providence, Foreknowledge, Will, and Fate,
560   Fixt Fate, Free will, Foreknowledge absolute,
And found no end, in wand'ring mazes lost.
Of good and evil much they argu'd then,
Of happiness and final misery,
Passion and Apathy, and glory and shame,
565   Vain wisdom all, and false Philosophie:[5]
Yet with a pleasing sorcery could charm
Pain for a while or anguish, and excite
Fallacious hope, or arm th' obdured° breast   *hardened*
With stubborn patience as with triple steel.
570   Another part in Squadrons and gross° Bands,   *dense*
On bold adventure to discover wide
That dismal World, if any Clime perhaps
Might yield them easier habitation, bend
Four ways thir flying March, along the Banks
575   Of four infernal Rivers that disgorge
Into the burning Lake thir baleful° streams;[6]   *evil*
Abhorred *Styx* the flood of deadly hate,
Sad *Acheron* of sorrow, black and deep;
Cocytus, nam'd of lamentation loud
580   Heard on the rueful stream; fierce *Phlegeton*
Whose waves of torrent fire inflame with rage.
Far off from these a slow and silent stream,
Lethe the River of Oblivion rolls
Her wat'ry Labyrinth, whereof who drinks,
585   Forthwith his former state and being forgets,
Forgets both joy and grief, pleasure and pain.
Beyond this flood a frozen Continent

---

4. "Alcides" (Hercules) returning as victor from "Oechalia" (Ovid, *Metamorphoses* 9.136) put on a ritual robe that had inadvertently been soaked by his wife in corrosive poison. Mad with pain, he blamed his friend Lichas, who had brought the robe, and hurled him far into the "Euboic" (Euboean) Sea.

5. Directed against Stoicism, the most formidable ethical challenge to Christianity; "apathy," or complete freedom from passion, was a Stoic ideal.

6. This description of the four rivers of hell takes its broad outline from Virgil's *Aeneid* 6, Dante's *Inferno* 14, and Spenser's *Faerie Queene* 2.7.56ff. Milton adds the detail of confluence in the "burning lake." The epithet or description attached to each river translates its Greek name (e.g., "Styx" means hateful).

Lies dark and wild, beat with perpetual storms
Of Whirlwind and dire Hail, which on firm land
590 Thaws not, but gathers heap, and ruin seems
Of ancient pile; all else deep snow and ice,
A gulf profound as that *Serbonian* Bog[7]
Betwixt *Damiata* and Mount *Casius* old,
Where Armies whole have sunk: the parching° Air   *withering*
595 Burns frore,° and cold performs th' effect of Fire.   *frozen*
Thither by harpy-footed Furies hal'd,[8]
At certain revolutions all the damn'd
Are brought: and feel by turns the bitter change
Of fierce extremes, extremes by change more fierce,
600 From Beds of raging Fire to starve° in Ice   *stifle*
Thir soft Ethereal warmth, and there to pine
Immovable, infixt, and frozen round,
Periods of time, thence hurried back to fire.
They ferry over this *Lethean* Sound
605 Both to and fro, thir sorrow to augment,
And wish and struggle, as they pass, to reach
The tempting stream, with one small drop to lose
In sweet forgetfulness all pain and woe,
All in one moment, and so near the brink;
610 But Fate withstands, and to oppose th' attempt
Medusa[9] with *Gorgonian* terror guards
The Ford, and of itself the water flies
All taste of living wight, as once it fled
The lip of *Tantalus*.[1] Thus roving on
615 In confus'd march forlorn, th' advent'rous Bands
With shudd'ring horror pale, and eyes aghast
View'd first thir lamentable lot, and found
No rest: through many a dark and dreary Vale
They pass'd, and many a Region dolorous,
620 O'er many a Frozen, many a Fiery Alp,
Rocks, Caves, Lakes, Fens, Bogs, Dens, and shades of death,
A Universe of death, which God by curse
Created evil, for evil only good,
Where all life dies, death lives, and Nature breeds,
625 Perverse, all monstrous, all prodigious things,
Abominable, inutterable, and worse
Than Fables yet have feign'd, or fear conceiv'd,
Gorgons and *Hydras*, and *Chimeras* dire.[2]

* * *

---

7. Serbonis, a lake bordered by quicksands on the Egyptian coast.
8. Milton combines the hook-clawed Harpies of Dante and Virgil with the ancient Greek Furies, daughters of Acheron and Night and agencies of divine vengeance.
9. One of the Gorgons, mythical sisters with snakes for hair, whose look turned the beholder into stone.
1. In Homer's hell, Tantalus is tormented by thirst, standing in a pool that recedes whenever he tries to drink (*Odyssey* 11.582–92).
2. The Hydra was many-headed, and the Chimeras breathed flame.

from **Book 3**
The Argument

God sitting on his Throne sees Satan flying towards this world, then newly created; shows him to the Son who sat at his right hand; foretells the success of Satan in perverting mankind; clears his own Justice and Wisdom from all imputation, having created Man free and able enough to have withstood his Tempter; yet declares his purpose of grace towards him, in regard he fell not of his own malice, as did Satan, but by him seduc't. The Son of God renders praises to his Father for the manifestation of his gracious purpose towards Man; but God again declares, that Grace cannot be extended towards Man without the satisfaction of divine Justice; Man hath offended the majesty of God by aspiring to Godhead, and therefore with all his Progeny devoted to death must die, unless some one can be found sufficient to answer for his offense, and undergo his Punishment. The Son of God freely offers himself a Ransom for Man: the Father accepts him, ordains his incarnation, pronounces his exaltation above all Names in Heaven and Earth; commands all the Angels to adore him; they obey, and hymning to thir Harps in full Choir, celebrate the Father and the Son. Meanwhile Satan alights upon the bare convex of this World's outermost Orb; where wand'ring he first finds a place since call'd The Limbo of Vanity; what persons and things fly up thither; thence comes to the Gate of Heaven, describ'd ascending by stairs, and the waters above the Firmament that flow about it: His passage thence to the Orb of the Sun; he finds there Uriel the Regent of that Orb, but first changes himself into the shape of a meaner Angel; and pretending a zealous desire to behold the new Creation and Man whom God had plac't there, inquires of him the place of his habitation, and is directed; alights first on Mount Niphates.

     Hail holy Light, offspring of Heav'n first-born,
Or of th' Eternal Coeternal beam
May I express thee unblam'd?[1] since God is Light,
And never but in unapproached Light
5 Dwelt from Eternity, dwelt then in thee,
Bright effluence° of bright essence increate.[2]   *radiance*
Or hear'st thou rather[3] pure Ethereal stream,
Whose Fountain who shall tell? before the Sun,
Before the Heavens thou wert, and at the voice
10 Of God, as with a Mantle didst invest°   *cover*
The rising world of waters dark and deep,
Won from the void° and formless infinite.[4]   *chaos*
Thee I revisit now with bolder wing,
Escap't the *Stygian* Pool, though long detain'd
15 In that obscure sojourn, while in my flight
Through utter and through middle darkness borne[5]
With other notes than to th' *Orphean* Lyre

1. The light of the invocation has been interpreted as the Son of God, as physical light, and as the principal image of God and the divine emanation itself, according to the Platonic system. Milton proposes three images or forms of address, "offspring," "beam," and "stream," each of which associates the divine Light or Wisdom with a different aspect of deity. The blame could attach only to using the second name, "co-eternal beam;" it is this name that is justified by the implicit appeal to scriptural authority. 2. "God is Light," from 1 John 1.5. God "only hath immortality, dwelling in the light which no man can approach unto" (1 Timothy 6.16). "Essence increate," the uncreated divine essence. In the physics and metaphysics of Milton's time, light was regarded as an "accident" (quality), not a body or substance.
3. Do you prefer to be called.
4. See Genesis 1.1–5.
5. The "Stygian pool" and the "utter" (outer) darkness are hell; the "middle darkness" is chaos.

I sung of *Chaos* and *Eternal Night,*
Taught by the heav'nly Muse° to venture down   *Urania*
20   The dark descent, and up to reascend,
Though hard and rare:⁶ thee I revisit safe,
And feel thy sovran vital Lamp; but thou
Revisit'st not these eyes, that roll in vain
To find thy piercing ray, and find no dawn;
25   So thick a drop serene⁷ hath quencht thir Orbs,
Or dim suffusion° veil'd. Yet not the more   *cataract*
Cease I to wander where the Muses haunt
Clear Spring, or shady Grove, or Sunny Hill,
Smit with the love of sacred Song;⁸ but chief
30   Thee *Sion*⁹ and the flow'ry Brooks beneath
That wash thy hallow'd feet, and warbling flow,
Nightly I visit: nor sometimes forget
Those other two equall'd with me in Fate,
So were I equall'd with them in renown,
35   Blind *Thamyris* and blind *Maeonides,*
And *Tiresias* and *Phineus* Prophets old.¹
Then feed on thoughts, that voluntary move
Harmonious numbers;° as the wakeful Bird²   *rhythmic measure*
Sings darkling,° and in shadiest Covert hid   *in the dark*
40   Tunes her nocturnal Note. Thus with the Year
Seasons return, but not to me returns
Day, or the sweet approach of Ev'n or Morn,
Or sight of vernal bloom, or Summer's Rose,
Or flocks, or herds, or human face divine;
45   But cloud instead, and ever-during dark
Surrounds me, from the cheerful ways of men
Cut off, and for the Book of knowledge³ fair
Presented with a Universal blanc°   *blank*
Of Nature's works to me expung'd and ras'd,°   *erased*
50   And wisdom at one entrance quite shut out.
So much the rather thou Celestial Light
Shine inward, and the mind through all her powers
Irradiate, there plant eyes, all mist from thence
Purge and disperse, that I may see and tell
55   Of things invisible to mortal sight.
       Now had th' Almighty Father from above,

6. Alluding to the "fable of Orpheus, whom they faigne to have recovered his Euridice from Hell with his Musick, that is, Truth and Equity from darkenesse of Barbarisme and Ignorance with his profound and excellent Doctrines; but, that in the way to the upper-earth, she was lost againe" (Henry Reynolds, *Mythomystes*). "Other notes," because Milton, unlike Orpheus, claims not to have lost his Eurydice.
7. Literally translating *gutta serena*, the medical term for the form of blindness from which Milton suffered.
8. An allusion to Virgil's prayer that "smitten with a great love" of the Muses, he may be shown by them the secrets of nature (*Georgics* 2.475–89).
9. The mountain of scriptural inspiration.

1. Thamyris was a Thracian poet who fell in love with the Muses and challenged them to a contest in which the loser was to give the winner whatever he wanted. The Muses, having won, took Thamyris's eyes and his lyre. Maeonides was Homer's surname; the contrast between his outward blindness and inner vision was a commonplace. In *De Idea Platonica*, Milton writes of Tiresias that his "very blindness gave him boundless light." The Thracian king Phineus lost his sight because he had become too good a prophet.
2. The nightingale. The soul of Thamyris passed into a nightingale.
3. The Book of Nature.

From the pure Empyrean where he sits
High Thron'd above all highth, bent down his eye,
His own works and their works at once to view:
60 About him all the Sanctities of Heaven
Stood thick as Stars, and from his sight receiv'd
Beatitude past utterance; on his right
The radiant image of his Glory sat,
His only Son; On Earth he first beheld
65 Our two first Parents, yet the only two
Of mankind, in the happy Garden plac't,
Reaping immortal fruits of joy and love,
Uninterrupted joy, unrivall'd love
In blissful solitude; he then survey'd
70 Hell and the Gulf between, and *Satan* there
Coasting the wall of Heav'n on this side Night
In the dun° Air sublime,° and ready now   *dusky / aloft*
To stoop with wearied wings, and willing feet
On the bare outside of this World, that seem'd
75 Firm land imbosom'd without Firmament,[4]
Uncertain which, in Ocean or in Air.
Him God beholding from his prospect high,
Wherein past, present, future he beholds,
Thus to his only Son foreseeing spake.
80   Only begotten Son, seest thou what rage
Transports our adversary, whom no bounds
Prescrib'd, no bars of Hell, nor all the chains
Heapt on him there, nor yet the main Abyss
Wide interrupt° can hold; so bent he seems   *divided*
85 On desperate revenge, that shall redound
Upon his own rebellious head. And now
Through all restraint broke loose he wings his way
Not far off Heav'n, in the Precincts of light,
Directly towards the new created World,
90 And Man there plac't, with purpose to assay°   *test*
If him by force he can destroy, or worse,
By some false guile pervert; and shall pervert;
For Man will heark'n to his glozing° lies,   *flattering*
And easily transgress the sole Command,[5]
95 Sole pledge of his obedience: So will fall
Hee and his faithless Progeny: whose fault?
Whose but his own? ingrate, he had of mee
All he could have; I made him just and right,
Sufficient to have stood, though free to fall.
100 Such I created all th' Ethereal Powers
And Spirits, both them who stood and them who fail'd;
Freely they stood who stood, and fell who fell.
Not free, what proof could they have giv'n sincere
Of true allegiance, constant Faith or Love,

4. The firmament or atmosphere, being inside the shell of   5. I.e., not to taste the fruit of the forbidden tree.
the universe that Satan stands on, is invisible to him.

105 Where only what they needs must do, appear'd,
Not what they would? what praise could they receive?
What pleasure I from such obedience paid,
When Will and Reason (Reason also is choice)
Useless and vain, of freedom both despoil'd,
110 Made passive both, had serv'd necessity,
Not mee. They therefore as to right belong'd,
So were created, nor can justly accuse
Thir maker, or thir making, or thir Fate;
As if Predestination over-rul'd
115 Thir will, dispos'd by absolute Decree
Or high foreknowledge; they themselves decreed
Thir own revolt, not I: if I foreknew,
Foreknowledge had no influence on their fault,
Which had no less prov'd certain unforeknown.
120 So without least impulse or shadow of Fate,
Or aught by me immutably foreseen,
They trespass, Authors to themselves in all
Both what they judge and what they choose; for so
I form'd them free, and free they must remain,
125 Till they enthrall themselves: I else must change
Thir nature, and revoke the high Decree
Unchangeable, Eternal, which ordain'd
Thir freedom: they themselves ordain'd thir fall.
The first sort⁶ by thir own suggestion° fell,   *temptation*
130 Self-tempted, self-deprav'd: Man falls deceiv'd
By th' other first: Man therefore shall find grace,
The other none: in Mercy and Justice both,
Through Heav'n and Earth, so shall my glory excel,
But Mercy first and last shall brightest shine.
135   Thus while God spake, ambrosial fragrance fill'd
All Heav'n, and in the blessed Spirits elect⁷
Sense of new joy ineffable diffus'd:
Beyond compare the Son of God was seen
Most glorious, in him all his Father shone
140 Substantially express'd, and in his face
Divine compassion visibly appear'd,
Love without end, and without measure Grace,
Which uttering thus he to his Father spake.
    O Father, gracious was that word which clos'd
145 Thy sovran° sentence, that Man should find grace;   *sovereign*
For which both Heav'n and Earth shall high extol
Thy praises, with th' innumerable sound
Of Hymns and sacred Songs, wherewith thy Throne
Encompass'd shall resound thee ever blest.
150 For should Man finally be lost, should Man
Thy creature late so lov'd, thy youngest Son
Fall circumvented thus by fraud, though join'd
With his own folly? that be from thee far,

6. Satan and the rebel angels.
7. The "elect angels" of 1 Timothy 5.21, explained in Mil-   ton's *De doctrina* 1.9 as angels "who have not revolted."

That far be from thee, Father, who art Judge
155   Of all things made, and judgest only right.
Or shall the Adversary[8] thus obtain
His end, and frustrate thine, shall he fulfil
His malice, and thy goodness bring to naught,
Or proud return though to his heavier doom,
160   Yet with revenge accomplish't and to Hell
Draw after him the whole Race of mankind,
By him corrupted? or wilt thou thyself
Abolish thy Creation, and unmake,
For him, what for thy glory thou hast made?
165   So should thy goodness and thy greatness both
Be question'd and blasphem'd without defense.
    To whom the great Creator thus repli'd.
O Son, in whom my Soul hath chief delight,[9]
Son of my bosom, Son who art alone
170   My word, my wisdom, and effectual might,
All hast thou spok'n as my thoughts are, all
As my Eternal purpose hath decreed:
Man shall not quite be lost, but sav'd who will,
Yet not of will in him, but grace in me
175   Freely voutsaf't;° once more I will renew   *vouchsafed*
His lapsed° powers, though forfeit and enthrall'd   *decayed*
By sin to foul exorbitant desires;
Upheld by me, yet once more he shall stand
On even ground against his mortal foe,
180   By me upheld, that he may know how frail
His fall'n condition is, and to me owe
All his deliv'rance, and to none but me.
Some I have chosen of peculiar grace
Elect above the rest; so is my will:[1]
185   The rest shall hear me call, and oft be warn'd
Thir sinful state, and to appease betimes
Th' incensed Deity while offer'd grace
Invites; for I will clear thir senses dark,
What may suffice, and soft'n stony hearts
190   To pray, repent, and bring obedience due.
To Prayer, repentance, and obedience due,
Though but endeavor'd with sincere intent,
Mine ear shall not be slow, mine eye not shut.
And I will place within them as a guide
195   My Umpire *Conscience*, whom if they will hear,
Light after light well us'd they shall attain,
And to the end persisting, safe arrive.

8. The literal meaning of "Satan."
9. Echoing Mark 1.11, the words out of the heavens at Jesus' baptism: "Thou art my beloved Son, in whom I am well pleased."
1. In *De doctrina* 1.4, Milton sets out an Arminian position, explicitly opposed to the Calvinist, on such doctrines as predestination, election, and reprobation, and he could be regarded as doing something similar here (lines 173–202); e.g., his God seems to make salvation depend on humans' will to avail themselves of grace, or on "prayer, repentance, and obedience" (line 191), whereas Calvinists regarded humans as incapable of contributing in any way to their own salvation. By the term "elect," Milton usually means no more than "whoever believes and continues in the faith."

This my long sufferance and my day of grace
They who neglect and scorn, shall never taste;
200   But hard be hard'n'd, blind be blinded more,
That they may stumble on, and deeper fall;
And none but such from mercy I exclude.
But yet all is not done; Man disobeying,
Disloyal breaks his fealty, and sins
205   Against the high Supremacy of Heav'n,
Affecting° God-head, and so losing all,   *seeking*
To expiate his Treason hath naught left,
But to destruction sacred and devote,°   *dedicated*
He with his whole posterity must die,
210   Die hee or Justice must; unless for him
Some other able, and as willing, pay
The rigid satisfaction, death for death.[2]
Say Heav'nly Powers, where shall we find such love,
Which of ye will be mortal[3] to redeem
215   Man's mortal crime, and just th' unjust to save,
Dwells in all Heaven charity° so dear?   *compassionate love*
    He ask'd, but all the Heav'nly Choir stood mute,
And silence was in Heav'n: on man's behalf
Patron or Intercessor none appear'd,
220   Much less that durst upon his own head draw
The deadly forfeiture, and ransom set.[4]
And now without redemption all mankind
Must have been lost, adjudg'd to Death and Hell
By doom° severe, had not the Son of God,   *judgment*
225   In whom the fulness dwells of love divine,
His dearest mediation thus renew'd.
    Father, thy word is past,[5] man shall find grace;
And shall grace not find means, that finds her way,
The speediest of thy winged messengers,
230   To visit all thy creatures, and to all
Comes unprevented,° unimplor'd, unsought?   *unanticipated*
Happy for man, so coming; he her aid
Can never seek, once dead in sins and lost;
Atonement for himself or offering meet,
235   Indebted and undone, hath none to bring:
Behold mee then, mee for him, life for life
I offer, on mee let thine anger fall;
Account mee man; I for his sake will leave
Thy bosom, and this glory next to thee
240   Freely put off, and for him lastly die
Well pleas'd, on me let Death wreck all his rage;
Under his gloomy power I shall not long
Lie vanquisht; thou hast giv'n me to possess

---

2. Note that human death is here regarded by God not as a punishment, but as a "satisfaction" for the treason. See *De doctrina* 1.16: "The satisfaction of Christ is the complete reparation made by him . . . by the fulfilment of the Law, and payment of the required price for all mankind."
3. Is willing to be subject to death.
4. Put down the ransom price (by giving his own life).
5. Your word of honor is pledged.

Life in myself for ever, by thee I live,[6]
245   Though now to Death I yield, and am his due
All that of me can die, yet that debt paid,
Thou wilt not leave me in the loathsome grave
His prey, nor suffer my unspotted Soul
For ever with corruption there to dwell;
250   But I shall rise Victorious, and subdue
My vanquisher, spoil'd of his vaunted spoil;
Death his death's wound shall then receive, and stoop
Inglorious, of his mortal sting disarm'd.[7]
I through the ample Air in Triumph high
255   Shall lead Hell Captive maugre° Hell, and show   *despite*
The powers of darkness bound. Thou at the sight
Pleas'd, out of Heaven shalt look down and smile,
While by thee rais'd I ruin all my Foes,
Death last, and with his Carcass glut the Grave:[8]
260   Then with the multitude of my redeem'd
Shall enter Heav'n long absent, and return,
Father, to see thy face, wherein no cloud
Of anger shall remain, but peace assur'd,
And reconcilement; wrath shall be no more
265   Thenceforth, but in thy presence Joy entire.
    His words here ended, but his meek aspéct
Silent yet spake, and breath'd immortal love
To mortal men, above which only shone
Filial obedience: as a sacrifice
270   Glad to be offer'd, he attends° the will   *awaits*
Of his great Father. Admiration seiz'd
All Heav'n, what this might mean, and whither tend
Wond'ring; but soon th' Almighty thus repli'd:
    O thou in Heav'n and Earth the only peace
275   Found out for mankind under wrath, O thou
My sole complacence! well thou know'st how dear
To me are all my works, nor Man the least
Though last created, that for him I spare
Thee from my bosom and right hand, to save,
280   By losing thee a while, the whole Race lost.
Thou therefore whom thou only canst redeem,
Thir Nature also to thy Nature join;
And be thyself Man among men on Earth,
Made flesh, when time shall be, of Virgin seed,
285   By wondrous birth: Be thou in *Adam's* room°   *place*
The Head of all mankind, though *Adam's* Son.
As in him perish all men, so in thee
As from a second root shall be restor'd,
As many as are restor'd, without thee none.[9]

6. See John 5.26: "As the Father hath life in himself: so hath he given to the Son to have life in himself."
7. See 1 Corinthians 15.55–56: "O death, where is thy sting? O grave, where is thy victory? The sting of death is sin; and the strength of sin is the law."
8. Alludes to 1 Corinthians 15.26: "The last enemy that shall be destroyed is death."
9. See 1 Corinthians 15.22: "As in Adam all die, even so in Christ shall all be made alive."

290 His crime makes guilty all his Sons, thy merit
    Imputed shall absolve them who renounce
    Thir own both righteous and unrighteous deeds,[1]
    And live in thee transplanted, and from thee
    Receive new life. So Man, as is most just,
295 Shall satisfy for Man, be judg'd and die,
    And dying rise, and rising with him raise
    His Brethren, ransom'd with his own dear life.
    So Heav'nly love shall outdo Hellish hate,
    Giving to death, and dying to redeem,
300 So dearly to redeem what Hellish hate
    So easily destroy'd, and still destroys
    In those who, when they may, accept not grace.
    Nor shalt thou by descending to assume
    Man's Nature, lessen or degrade thine own.
305 Because thou hast, though Thron'd in highest bliss
    Equal to God, and equally enjoying
    God-like fruition, quitted[2] all to save
    A world from utter loss, and hast been found
    By Merit more than Birthright Son of God,
310 Found worthiest to be so by being Good,
    Far more than Great or High; because in thee
    Love hath abounded more than Glory abounds,
    Therefore thy Humiliation shall exalt
    With thee thy Manhood also to this Throne;
315 Here shalt thou sit incarnate, here shalt Reign
    Both God and Man, Son both of God and Man,
    Anointed[3] universal King; all Power
    I give thee, reign for ever, and assume
    Thy Merits; under thee as Head Supreme
320 Thrones, Princedoms, Powers, Dominions I reduce:
    All knees to thee shall bow, of them that bide
    In Heaven, or Earth, or under Earth in Hell;
    When thou attended gloriously from Heav'n
    Shalt in the Sky appear, and from thee send
325 The summoning Arch-Angels to proclaim
    Thy dread Tribunal: forthwith from all Winds
    The living, and forthwith the cited° dead   *summoned*
    Of all past Ages to the general Doom°   *judgment*
    Shall hast'n, such a peal shall rouse thir sleep.
330 Then all thy Saints° assembl'd, thou shalt judge   *elect*
    Bad men and Angels, they arraign'd shall sink
    Beneath thy Sentence; Hell, her numbers full,
    Thenceforth shall be for ever shut. Meanwhile
    The World shall burn, and from her ashes spring
335 New Heav'n and Earth, wherein the just shall dwell

1. See *De doctrina* 1.22: "As therefore our sins are imputed to Christ, so the merits or righteousness of Christ are imputed to us through faith." If one simply renounced dependence on "righteous" deeds, one would be justified by faith alone; but for the "living faith"—faith issuing in works—that Milton believes necessary, one has to renounce (in a different sense) "unrighteous" deeds.
2. A pun, since "quitted" meant "redeemed, remitted" as well as "left."
3. The "Anointed" in Hebrew is the Messiah.

And after all thir tribulations long
See golden days, fruitful of golden deeds,
With Joy and Love triumphing, and fair Truth.[4]
Then thou thy regal Sceptre shalt lay by,
340   For regal Sceptre then no more shall need,
God shall be All in All. But all ye Gods,°   *angels*
Adore him, who to compass all this dies,
Adore the Son, and honor him as mee.
    No sooner had th' Almighty ceas't, but all
345   The multitude of Angels with a shout
Loud as from numbers without number, sweet
As from blest voices, uttering joy, Heav'n rung
With Jubilee, and loud Hosannas fill'd
Th' eternal Regions: lowly reverent
350   Towards either Throne they bow, and to the ground
With solemn adoration down they cast
Thir Crowns inwove with Amarant and Gold,
Immortal Amarant,[5] a Flow'r which once
In Paradise, fast by the Tree of Life
355   Began to bloom, but soon for man's offense
To Heav'n remov'd where first it grew, there grows,
And flow'rs aloft shading the Fount of Life,
And where the river of Bliss through midst of Heav'n
Rolls o'er *Elysian* Flow'rs her Amber stream;[6]
360   With these that never fade the Spirits elect
Bind thir resplendent locks inwreath'd with beams,
Now in loose Garlands thick thrown off, the bright
Pavement that like a Sea of Jasper shone
Impurpl'd with Celestial Roses smil'd.
365   Then Crown'd again thir gold'n Harps they took,
Harps ever tun'd, that glittering by thir side
Like Quivers hung, and with Preamble sweet
Of charming symphony they introduce
Thir sacred Song, and waken raptures high;
370   No voice exempt,° no voice but well could join   *debarred*
Melodious part, such concord is in Heav'n.
    Thee Father first they sung Omnipotent,
Immutable, Immortal, Infinite,[7]
Eternal King; thee Author of all being,
375   Fountain of Light, thyself invisible
Amidst the glorious brightness where thou sit'st
Thron'd inaccessible, but° when thou shad'st   *except*
The full blaze of thy beams, and through a cloud
Drawn round about thee like a radiant Shrine,
380   Dark with excessive bright thy skirts appear,
Yet dazzle Heav'n, that brightest Seraphim

---

4. The burning of Earth is based on 2 Peter 3.12ff.
5. "Amaranth" in Greek means "unwithering"; a purple flower that was a "symbol of immortality"; the amarantine crown was an ancient pagan symbol of untroubled tranquillity and health.

6. Allusion to Virgil, *Aeneid* 6.656–59, the description of spirits chanting in chorus beside the Eridanus, in the Elysian fields; "amber" was a standard of purity or clarity.
7. Line 373 is transplanted in its entirety from Sylvester's translation of Du Bartas's poem on creation.

Approach not, but with both wings veil thir eyes.
Thee next they sang of all Creation first,
Begotten Son, Divine Similitude,
385   In whose conspicuous count'nance, without cloud
Made visible, th' Almighty Father shines,
Whom else no Creature can behold;[8] on thee
Impresst th' effulgence of his Glory abides,
Transfus'd on thee his ample Spirit rests.
390   Hee Heav'n of Heavens and all the Powers therein
By thee created, and by thee threw down
Th' aspiring Dominations:°   thou that day   *rebel angels*
Thy Father's dreadful Thunder didst not spare,
Nor stop thy flaming Chariot wheels, that shook
395   Heav'n's everlasting Frame, while o'er the necks
Thou drov'st of warring Angels disarray'd.
Back from pursuit thy Powers with loud acclaim
Thee only extoll'd, Son of thy Father's might,
To execute fierce vengeance on his foes:
400   Not so on Man; him through their malice fall'n,
Father of Mercy and Grace, thou didst not doom°   *judge*
So strictly, but much more to pity incline:
No sooner did thy dear and only Son
Perceive thee purpos'd not to doom frail Man
405   So strictly, but much more to pity inclin'd,[9]
Hee to appease thy wrath, and end the strife
Of Mercy and Justice in thy face discern'd,
Regardless of the Bliss wherein hee sat
Second to thee, offer'd himself to die
410   For man's offense. O unexampl'd love,
Love nowhere to be found less than Divine!
Hail Son of God, Savior of Men, thy Name
Shall be the copious matter of my Song
Henceforth, and never shall my Harp thy praise
415   Forget, nor from thy Father's praise disjoin.
          Thus they in Heav'n, above the starry Sphere,
Thir happy hours in joy and hymning spent.
Meanwhile upon the firm opacous Globe
Of this round World, whose first convex divides
420   The luminous inferior Orbs, enclos'd
From *Chaos* and th' inroad of Darkness old,[1]
Satan alighted walks: a Globe far off
It seem'd, now seems a boundless Continent
Dark, waste, and wild, under the frown of Night
425   Starless expos'd, and ever-threat'ning storms
Of *Chaos* blust'ring round, inclement sky;
Save on that side which from the wall of Heav'n,

---

8. See John 1.18 and 14.9.
9. Most editors say that "but" or "than" has to be supplied before "He" (line 406). However, if "much more to pity inclined" refers to the Son, the "but" immediately preceding is available for the main clause.

1. The "starry Sphere," is either the sphere of the fixed stars or, more loosely, the stars and planets together. The stars are enclosed within the *primum mobile* or "first convex" (sphere). Both heaven and chaos lie outside that opaque ("opacous") shell.

Though distant far, some small reflection gains
Of glimmering air less vext° with tempest loud: *tossed about*
430 Here walk'd the Fiend at large in spacious field.
As when a Vultur on *Imaus* bred,
Whose snowy ridge the roving *Tartar* bounds,
Dislodging from a Region scarce of prey
To gorge the flesh of Lambs or yeanling Kids
435 On Hills where Flocks are fed, flies toward the Springs
Of *Ganges* or *Hydaspes, Indian* streams;
But in his way lights on the barren Plains
Of *Sericana*, where *Chineses* drive
With Sails and Wind thir cany Waggons light:
440 So on this windy Sea of Land, the Fiend
Walk'd up and down alone bent on his prey,[2]
Alone, for other Creature in this place
Living or lifeless to be found was none,
None yet, but store hereafter from the earth
445 Up hither like Aereal vapors flew
Of all things transitory and vain, when Sin
With vanity had fill'd the works of men:[3]
Both all things vain, and all who in vain things
Built thir fond hopes of Glory or lasting fame,
450 Or happiness in this or th' other life;
All who thir reward on Earth, the fruits
Of painful Superstition and blind Zeal,
Naught seeking but the praise of men, here find
Fit retribution, empty as thir deeds;
455 All th' unaccomplisht works of Nature's hand,
Abortive, monstrous, or unkindly mixt,
Dissolv'd on Earth, fleet hither, and in vain,
Till final dissolution, wander here,
Not in the neighboring Moon, as some have dream'd;
460 Those argent Fields more likely habitants,
Translated Saints,[4] or middle Spirits hold
Betwixt th' Angelical and Human kind:
Hither of ill-join'd Sons and Daughters born
First from the ancient World those Giants came
465 With many a vain exploit, though then renown'd:[5]
The builders next of *Babel* on the Plain
Of *Sennaar*, and still with vain design
New *Babels*, had they wherewithal, would build:[6]

---

2. The simile compares the vulture's journey to Satan's. One journey is from Imaus (a mountain range said to run through Afghanistan) to the rivers of India; the other is from the "frozen continent" (2.587) of Tartarus, which did not keep Satan from roving, to Eden with its rivers. The "barren plains of Sericana" correspond to the *primum mobile* because both are stopping places and in both the elements are confused. (The Chinese use sails, the means of propulsion for ships, on their land vehicles; and the *primum mobile* is a "sea of land.")

3. In *Orlando Furioso* 34.73ff., a passage from which Milton quotes in *Of Reformation*, Ariosto tells how Astolfo

searches for his lost wits in a Limbo of Vanity on the moon.

4. Probably such as Enoch (Genesis 5.24) and Elijah (2 Kings 2).

5. The first group of fools are the Giants, "mighty men . . . of renown," born of the misunion of "sons of God" with "daughters of men" (Genesis 6.4).

6. At 12.45–47 the builders of Babel are said to have formed their "vain design" out of a desire for fame. "New Babels" suggests the New Babylon of anti-Papist propaganda.

470 Others came single; he who to be deem'd
A God, leap'd fondly into Ætna flames,
Empedocles, and hee who to enjoy
Plato's Elysium, leap'd into the Sea,
Cleombrotus,[7] and many more too long,
Embryos, and Idiots, Eremites and Friars

475 White, Black and Grey, with all thir trumpery.[8]
Here Pilgrims roam, that stray'd so far to seek
In *Golgotha*[9] him dead, who lives in Heav'n;
And they who to be sure of Paradise
Dying put on the weeds of *Dominic*,

480 Or in *Franciscan* think to pass disguis'd;[1]
They pass the Planets seven, and pass the fixt,
And that Crystalline Sphere whose balance weighs
The Trepidation talkt, and that first mov'd;[2]
And now Saint *Peter* at Heav'n's Wicket seems

485 To wait them with his Keys, and now at foot
Of Heav'n's ascent they lift thir Feet, when lo
A violent cross wind from either Coast
Blows them transverse ten thousand Leagues awry
Into the devious Air; then might ye see

490 Cowls, Hoods and Habits with thir weares tost
And flutter'd into Rags, then Reliques, Beads,
Indulgences, Dispenses,[3] Pardons, Bulls,
The sport of Winds: all these upwhirl'd aloft
Fly o'er the backside of the World far off

495 Into a *Limbo*° large and broad, since call'd   *empty region*
The Paradise of Fools, to few unknown
Long after, now unpeopl'd and untrod;
All this dark Globe the Fiend found as he pass'd,
And long he wander'd, till at last a gleam

500 Of dawning light turn'd thither-ward in haste
His travell'd steps; far distant he descries
Ascending by degrees magnificent
Up to the wall of Heaven a Structure high,
At top whereof, but far more rich appear'd

505 The work as of a Kingly Palace Gate
With Frontispiece[4] of Diamond and Gold
Imbellisht; thick with sparkling orient° Gems   *brilliant*

7. Empedocles and Cleombrotus were not associated by classical writers but occur together in Lactantius' chapter on "Pythagoreans and Stoics who, Believing in the Immortality of the Soul, Foolishly Persuade a Voluntary Death" (*Divinae Institutiones* 3.18). Cleombrotus drowned himself after an unwise reading of Plato's *Phaedo*; Empedocles' motive was to conceal his own mortality.

8. Milton here satirizes a Catholic tradition that consigned cretins and unbaptized infants to a much debated *limbo infantum*. The friars were specified by robe color; "white" meant Carmelite, "black" Dominican, and "grey" Franciscan. The contemptuous juxtaposition of all three colors ridicules the importance assigned to external trappings. "Eremites" were Order of Friars Hermits.

9. The hill where Christ was crucified and buried.

1. Compare *Inferno* 27.67–84, in which Dante tells how Guido da Montefeltro hoped to get into heaven by virtue of Franciscan robes but found to his cost that absolution without repentance is vain.

2. In order of proximity to earth, the spheres passed are the seven planetary spheres; the eighth sphere, containing the "fixed" stars; the ninth, "crystalline sphere;" and the tenth sphere, the "first moved" or *primum mobile*.

3. A "dispense" or dispensation was an exemption from a solemn obligation by licence of an ecclesiastical dignitary, especially the Pope.

4. A decorated entrance or a pediment over the gate.

The Portal shone, inimitable on Earth
By Model, or by shading Pencil drawn.
510   The Stairs were such as whereon *Jacob* saw
Angels ascending and descending, bands
Of Guardians bright, when he from *Esau* fled
To *Padan-Aram* in the field of *Luz*,
Dreaming by night under the open Sky,
515   And waking cri'd, *This is the Gate of Heav'n.*[5]
Each Stair mysteriously° was meant,[6] nor stood   *symbolically*
There always, but drawn up to Heav'n sometimes
Viewless, and underneath a bright Sea flow'd
Of Jasper, or of liquid Pearl, whereon
520   Who after came from Earth, sailing arriv'd,
Wafted by Angels, or flew o'er the Lake
Rapt in a Chariot drawn by fiery Steeds.
The Stairs were then let down, whether to dare
The Fiend by easy ascent, or aggravate
525   His sad exclusion from the doors of Bliss.
Direct against which op'n'd from beneath,
Just o'er the blissful seat of Paradise,
A passage down to th' Earth, a passage wide,
Wider by far than that of after-times
530   Over Mount *Sion*, and, though that were large,
Over the *Promis'd Land* to God so dear,
By which, to visit oft those happy Tribes,
On high behests his Angels to and fro
Pass'd frequent, and his eye with choice° regard   *careful*
535   From *Paneas* the fount of *Jordan's* flood
To *Beërsaba*,[7] where the *Holy Land*
Borders on *Egypt* and th' *Arabian* shore;
So wide the op'ning seem'd, where bounds were set
To darkness, such as bound the Ocean wave.
540   *Satan* from hence now on the lower stair
That scal'd by steps of Gold to Heaven Gate
Looks down with wonder at the sudden view
Of all this World at once. As when a Scout
Through dark and desert ways with peril gone
545   All night; at last by break of cheerful dawn
Obtains° the brow of some high-climbing Hill,   *reaches*
Which to his eye discovers unaware
The goodly prospect of some foreign land
First seen, or some renown'd Metropolis
550   With glistering Spires and Pinnacles adorn'd,
Which now the Rising Sun gilds with his beams.

---

5. The unregenerate Jacob was terrified by the vision of a ladder reaching to heaven just after he had cheated Esau out of his father's blessing (Genesis 27–28). The experience awed him into belief and a vow to the Lord.
6. Jacob's ladder had been identified with Homer's golden chain linking the universe to Jupiter. Each "stair," or step, could be interpreted as a spiritual stage extending

"from the supreme God even to the bottomest dregs of the universe."
7. "Paneas," is a later Greek name for Dan—not the city of Dan but the spring of the same name, "the easternmost fountain of Jordan." Beersaba was the southern limit of Canaan, as Dan was the northern.

Such wonder seiz'd, though after Heaven seen,
The Spirit malign, but much more envy seiz'd
At sight of all this World beheld so fair.[8] * * *

from Book 4
The Argument

Satan *now in prospect of* Eden, *and nigh the place where he must now attempt the bold enterprise which he undertook alone against God and Man, falls into many doubts with himself, and many passions, fear, envy, and despair; but at length confirms himself in evil, journeys on to Paradise, whose outward prospect and situation is described, overleaps the bounds, sits in the shape of a Cormorant on the Tree of Life, as highest in the Garden to look about him. The Garden describ'd; Satan's first sight of Adam and Eve; his wonder at thir excellent form and happy state, but with resolution to work thir fall; overhears thir discourse, thence gathers that the Tree of Knowledge was forbidden them to eat of, under penalty of death; and thereon intends to found his Temptation, by seducing them to transgress: then leaves them a while, to know further of thir state by some other means. Meanwhile Uriel descending on a Sun-beam warns Gabriel, who had in charge the Gate of Paradise, that some evil spirit had escap'd the Deep, and past at Noon by his Sphere in the shape of a good Angel down to Paradise, discovered after by his furious gestures in the Mount. Gabriel promises to find him ere morning. Night coming on, Adam and Eve discourse of going to thir rest: thir Bower describ'd; thir Evening worship. Gabriel drawing forth his Bands of Night-watch to walk the round of Paradise, appoints two strong Angels to Adam's Bower, lest the evil spirit should be there doing some harm to Adam or Eve sleeping; there they find him at the ear of Eve, tempting her in a dream, and bring him, though unwilling, to Gabriel; by whom question'd, he scornfully answers, prepares resistance, but hinder'd by a Sign from Heaven, flies out of Paradise.*

      O for that warning voice, which he who saw
      Th' Apocalypse, heard cry in Heav'n aloud,
      Then when the Dragon, put to second rout,
      Came furious down to be reveng'd on men,
5   *Woe to the inhabitants on Earth!*[1] that now,
      While time was, our first Parents had been warn'd
      The coming of thir secret foe, and scap'd
      Haply so scap'd his mortal snare; for now
      Satan, now first inflam'd with rage, came down,
10   The Tempter ere th' Accuser of man-kind,
      To wreck° on innocent frail man his loss   *avenge*
      Of that first Battle, and his flight to Hell:
      Yet not rejoicing in his speed, though bold,
      Far off and fearless, nor with cause to boast,
15   Begins his dire attempt, which nigh the birth
      Now rolling, boils in his tumultuous breast,
      And like a devilish Engine back recoils
      Upon himself; horror and doubt distract

8. Seeing the archangel Uriel, Satan now disguises himself as a cherub and asks the way to Eden. Uriel directs him, not realizing who he is—"For neither Man nor Angel can discern / Hypocrisy, the only evil that walks / Invisible, except to God alone" (lines 682–85).
1. The Apocalypse of St. John (Revelation) relates a vision of a second battle in heaven between Michael and "the Dragon," Satan.

His troubl'd thoughts, and from the bottom stir
20   The Hell within him, for within him Hell
He brings, and round about him, nor from Hell
One step no more than from himself can fly
By change of place: Now conscience wakes despair
That slumber'd, wakes the bitter memory
25   Of what he was, what is, and what must be
Worse; of worse deeds worse sufferings must ensue.
Sometimes towards *Eden* which now in his view
Lay pleasant,[2] his griev'd look he fixes sad,
Sometimes towards Heav'n and the full-blazing Sun,
30   Which now sat high in his Meridian Tow'r:
Then much revolving, thus in sighs began.
     O thou that with surpassing Glory crown'd,
Look'st from thy sole Dominion like the God
Of this new World; at whose sight all the Stars
35   Hide thir diminisht heads; to thee I call,
But with no friendly voice, and add thy name
O Sun, to tell thee how I hate thy beams
That bring to my remembrance from what state
I fell, how glorious once above thy Sphere;
40   Till Pride and worse Ambition threw me down
Warring in Heav'n against Heav'n's matchless King:[3]
Ah wherefore! he deserv'd no such return
From me, whom he created what I was
In that bright eminence, and with his good
45   Upbraided none;[4] nor was his service hard.
What could be less than to afford him praise,
The easiest recompense, and pay him thanks,
How due! yet all his good prov'd ill in me,
And wrought but malice; lifted up so high
50   I sdein'd° subjection, and thought one step higher   *disdained*
Would set me highest, and in a moment quit°   *pay off*
The debt immense of endless gratitude,
So burdensome, still paying, still to owe;
Forgetful what from him I still receiv'd,
55   And understood not that a grateful mind
By owing owes not, but still pays, at once
Indebted and discharg'd; what burden then?[5]
O had his powerful Destiny ordain'd
Me some inferior Angel, I had stood
60   Then happy; no unbounded hope had rais'd
Ambition. Yet why not? some other Power
As great might have aspir'd, and me though mean
Drawn to his part; but other Powers as great
Fell not, but stand unshak'n, from within

---

2. The etymological meaning of "Eden" is "pleasure, delight."
3. According to Edward Phillips, lines 32–41 were shown to him and some others "before the Poem was begun,"
when Milton intended to write a tragedy on the Fall.
4. Demanded no return for his benefits; see James 1.5.
5. Simply by owning an obligation gratefully, one ceases to owe it.

65   Or from without, to all temptations arm'd.
     Hadst thou the same free Will and Power to stand?
     Thou hadst: whom hast thou then or what to accuse,
     But Heav'n's free Love dealt equally to all?
     Be then his Love accurst, since love or hate,
70   To me alike, it deals eternal woe.
     Nay curs'd be thou; since against his thy will
     Chose freely what it now so justly rues.
     Me miserable! which way shall I fly
     Infinite wrath, and infinite despair?
75   Which way I fly is Hell; myself am Hell;
     And in the lowest deep a lower deep
     Still threat'ning to devour me opens wide,
     To which the Hell I suffer seems a Heav'n.
     O then at last relent: is there no place
80   Left for Repentance, none for Pardon left?
     None left but by submission; and that word
     Disdain forbids me, and my dread of shame
     Among the Spirits beneath, whom I seduc'd
     With other promises and other vaunts
85   Than to submit, boasting I could subdue
     Th' Omnipotent. Ay me, they little know
     How dearly I abide that boast so vain,
     Under what torments inwardly I groan:
     While they adore me on the Throne of Hell,
90   With Diadem and Sceptre high advanc'd
     The lower still I fall, only Supreme
     In misery; such joy Ambition finds.
     But say I could repent and could obtain
     By Act of Grace[6] my former state; how soon
95   Would highth recall high thoughts, how soon unsay
     What feign'd submission swore: ease would recant
     Vows made in pain, as violent and void.
     For never can true reconcilement grow
     Where wounds of deadly hate have pierc'd so deep:
100 Which would but lead me to a worse relapse,
     And heavier fall: so should I purchase dear
     Short intermission bought with double smart.
     This knows my punisher; therefore as far
     From granting hee, as I from begging peace:
105 All hope excluded thus, behold instead
     Of us out-cast, exil'd, his new delight,
     Mankind created, and for him this World.
     So farewell Hope, and with Hope farewell Fear,
     Farewell Remorse: all Good to me is lost;
110 Evil be thou my Good; by thee at least
     Divided Empire with Heav'n's King I hold
     By thee, and more than half perhaps will reign;
     As Man ere long, and this new World shall know.
         Thus while he spake, each passion dimm'd his face,

6. By concession of favor, not of right; often used for a formal pardon by Parliament.

115	Thrice chang'd with pale, ire, envy and despair,
	Which marr'd his borrow'd visage, and betray'd
	Him counterfeit, if any eye beheld.
	For heav'nly minds from such distempers foul
	Are ever clear. Whereof hee soon aware,
120	Each perturbation smooth'd with outward calm,
	Artificer° of fraud; and was the first *inventor*
	That practis'd falsehood under saintly show,
	Deep malice to conceal, couch't° with revenge: *hidden*
	Yet not anough had practis'd to deceive
125	*Uriel* once warn'd; whose eye pursu'd him down
	The way he went, and on th' *Assyrian* mount° *Niphates*
	Saw him disfigur'd, more than could befall
	Spirit of happy sort: his gestures fierce
	He mark'd and mad demeanor, then alone,
130	As he suppos'd, all unobserv'd, unseen.
	So on he fares, and to the border comes
	Of *Eden*, where delicious Paradise,
	Now nearer, Crowns with her enclosure green,
	As with a rural mound the champaign° head *unenclosed, level*
135	Of a steep wilderness, whose hairy sides
	With thicket overgrown, grotesque and wild,
	Access deni'd; and over head up grew
	Insuperable highth of loftiest shade,
	Cedar, and Pine, and Fir, and branching Palm,
140	A Silvan Scene, and as the ranks ascend
	Shade above shade, a woody Theatre
	Of stateliest view. Yet higher than thir tops
	The verdurous wall of Paradise up sprung:
	Which to our general Sire° gave prospect large *Adam*
145	Into his nether Empire neighboring round.
	And higher than that Wall a circling row
	Of goodliest Trees loaden with fairest Fruit,
	Blossoms and Fruits at once of golden hue
	Appear'd, with gay enamell'd° colors mixt: *lustrous*
150	On which the Sun more glad impress'd his beams
	Than in fair Evening Cloud, or humid Bow,° *rainbow*
	When God hath show'r'd the earth; so lovely seem'd
	That Lantskip:° And of pure now purer air *landscape*
	Meets his approach, and to the heart inspires
155	Vernal delight and joy, able to drive
	All sadness but despair: now gentle gales
	Fanning thir odoriferous wings dispense
	Native perfúmes, and whisper whence they stole
	Those balmy spoils. As when to them who sail
160	Beyond the *Cape* of *Hope*, and now are past
	Mozambic,[7] off at Sea North-East winds blow
	Sabean[8] Odors from the spicy shore

---

7. Mozambique, a Portuguese colony on the east coast of Africa; the trade route lay between Mozambique and Madagascar.

8. Of Saba or Sheba (now Yemen). Milton draws on the description of "Araby the blest"—"Arabia felix"—in Diodorus Siculus 3.46.

Of *Araby* the blest, with such delay
Well pleas'd they slack thir course, and many a League
165   Cheer'd with the grateful smell old Ocean smiles.
So entertain'd those odorous sweets the Fiend
Who came thir bane, though with them better pleas'd
Than *Asmodeus* with the fishy fume,
That drove him, though enamor'd, from the Spouse
170   Of *Tobit's* Son, and with a vengeance sent
From *Media* post to *Egypt*, there fast bound.[9]
      Now to th' ascent of that steep savage° Hill   *wild*
Satan had journey'd on, pensive and slow;
But further way found none, so thick entwin'd,
175   As one continu'd brake, the undergrowth
Of shrubs and tangling bushes had perplext
All path of Man or Beast that pass'd that way:
One Gate there only was, and that look'd East
On th' other side: which when th' arch-felon saw
180   Due entrance he disdain'd, and in contempt,
At one slight bound high overleap'd all bound
Of Hill or highest Wall, and sheer within
Lights on his feet. As when a prowling Wolf,
Whom hunger drives to seek new haunt for prey,
185   Watching where Shepherds pen thir Flocks at eve
In hurdl'd Cotes° amid the field secure,   *shelters*
Leaps o'er the fence with ease into the Fold:
Or as a Thief bent to unhoard the cash
Of some rich Burgher, whose substantial doors,
190   Cross-barr'd and bolted fast, fear no assault,
In at the window climbs, or o'er the tiles:
So clomb° this first grand Thief into God's Fold: *climbed*
So since into his Church lewd Hirelings[1] climb.
Thence up he flew, and on the Tree of Life,
195   The middle Tree and highest there that grew,
Sat like a Cormorant;[2] yet not true Life
Thereby regain'd, but sat devising Death
To them who liv'd; nor on the virtue thought
Of that life-giving Plant, but only us'd
200   For prospect,° what well us'd had been the pledge   *lookout*
Of immortality. So little knows
Any, but God alone, to value right
The good before him, but perverts best things
To worst abuse, or to thir meanest use.
205   Beneath him with new wonder now he views
To all delight of human sense expos'd
In narrow room Nature's whole wealth, yea more,

---

9. The apocryphal book Tobit relates the story of Tobit's son Tobias, who was sent into Media on an errand and there married Sara. Sara had previously been given to seven men, but all were killed by the jealous spirit Asmodeus before their marriages could be consummated.

By the advice of Raphael, however, Tobias succeeded by creating a fishy smoke to drive away the devil Asmodeus.
1. Wicked men motivated only by material gain.
2. A voracious sea bird, often used to describe greedy clergy.

A Heaven on Earth: for blissful Paradise
Of God the Garden was, by him in the East
210 Of *Eden* planted; *Eden* stretch'd her Line
From *Auran* Eastward to the Royal Tow'rs
Of Great *Seleucia*, built by *Grecian* Kings,
Or where the Sons of *Eden* long before
Dwelt in *Telassar*:[3] in this pleasant soil
215 His far more pleasant Garden God ordain'd;
Out of the fertile ground he caus'd to grow
All Trees of noblest kind for sight, smell, taste;
And all amid them stood the Tree of Life,
High eminent, blooming Ambrosial Fruit
220 Of vegetable Gold; and next to Life
Our Death the Tree of Knowledge grew fast by,
Knowledge of Good bought dear by knowing ill.[4]
Southward through *Eden* went a River large,
Nor chang'd his course, but through the shaggy hill
225 Pass'd underneath ingulft, for God had thrown
That Mountain as his Garden mould high rais'd
Upon the rapid current, which through veins
Of porous Earth with kindly° thirst up-drawn,   *natural*
Rose a fresh Fountain, and with many a rill
230 Water'd the Garden;[5] thence united fell
Down the steep glade, and met the nether Flood,
Which from his darksome passage now appears,
And now divided into four main Streams,
Runs diverse, wand'ring many a famous Realm
235 And Country whereof here needs no account,
But rather to tell how, if Art could tell,
How from that Sapphire Fount the crisped° Brooks,   *wavy*
Rolling on Orient Pearl and sands of Gold,
With mazy error° under pendant shades   *wandering*
240 Ran Nectar, visiting each plant, and fed
Flow'rs worthy of Paradise which not nice° Art   *careful*
In Beds and curious Knots, but Nature boon°   *bounteous*
Pour'd forth profuse on Hill and Dale and Plain,
Both where the morning Sun first warmly smote
245 The open field, and where the unpierc't shade
Imbrown'd° the noontide Bow'rs: Thus was this place,   *darkened*
A happy rural seat of various view:
Groves whose rich Trees wept odorous Gums and Balm,
Others whose fruit burnisht with Golden Rind
250 Hung amiable,° *Hesperian* Fables true,[6]   *lovely*
If true, here only, and of delicious taste:
Betwixt them Lawns, or level Downs, and Flocks
Grazing the tender herb, were interpos'd,

3. Auran was an eastern boundary of the land of Israel. Great Seleucia was built by Alexander's general Seleucus Nicator as a seat of government for his Syrian empire. The mention of Telassar prophesies war in Eden; see 2 Kings 14.11ff., where Telassar is an instance of lands destroyed utterly.
4. See Genesis 2.9.
5. See Genesis 2.10.
6. Golden fruit like the legendary apples of the western islands, the Hesperides.

	Or palmy hillock, or the flow'ry lap	
255	Of some irriguous° Valley spread her store,	*well-watered*
	Flow'rs of all hue, and without Thorn the Rose:[7]	
	Another side, umbrageous° Grots and Caves	*shady*
	Of cool recess, o'er which the mantling Vine	
	Lays forth her purple Grape, and gently creeps	
260	Luxuriant; meanwhile murmuring waters fall	
	Down the slope hills, disperst, or in a Lake,	
	That to the fringed Bank with Myrtle crown'd,	
	Her crystal mirror holds, unite thir streams.	
	The Birds thir choir apply;° airs, vernal airs,[8]	*practice*
265	Breathing the smell of field and grove, attune	
	The trembling leaves, while Universal *Pan*[9]	
	Knit with the *Graces* and the *Hours* in dance	
	Led on th' Eternal Spring.[1] Not that fair field	
	Of *Enna*, where *Proserpin* gath'ring flow'rs	
270	Herself a fairer Flow'r by gloomy *Dis*	
	Was gather'd, which cost *Ceres* all that pain	
	To seek her through the world;[2] nor that sweet Grove	
	Of *Daphne* by *Orontes*, and th' inspir'd	
	Castalian Spring[3] might with this Paradise	
275	Of *Eden* strive; nor that *Nyseian* Isle	
	Girt with the River *Triton*, where old *Cham*,	
	Whom Gentiles *Ammon* call and *Lybian Jove*,	
	Hid *Amalthea* and her Florid° Son,	*ruddy-complexioned*
	Young *Bacchus*, from his Stepdame *Rhea's* eye;[4]	
280	Nor where *Abassin* Kings thir issue Guard,	
	Mount *Amara*, though this by some suppos'd	
	True Paradise under the *Ethiop* Line	
	By *Nilus* head, enclos'd with shining Rock,	
	A whole day's journey high,[5] but wide remote	
285	From this *Assyrian* Garden, where the Fiend	
	Saw undelighted all delight, all kind	
	Of living Creatures new to sight and strange:	
	Two of far nobler shape erect and tall,	
	Godlike erect, with native Honor clad	
290	In naked Majesty seem'd Lords of all,	
	And worthy seem'd, for in thir looks Divine	
	The image of thir glorious Maker shone,[6]	
	Truth, Wisdom, Sanctitude severe and pure,	

7. The thornless rose was used to symbolize the sinless state of humanity before the Fall; or the state of grace.
8. Breezes and melodies.
9. Pan (Greek for "all") was a symbol of universal nature.
1. Neoplatonists thought the triadic pattern of their dance expressed the movement underlying all natural generation.
2. The rape of Proserpina by Dis, the king of hell, was located in Enna by Ovid (*Fasti* 4.420ff.). The search for her made the world barren, and even when she was found, she was restored to Ceres—and fruitfulness to the world—only for half the year.
3. The grove called "Daphne" beside the River Orontes,

near Antioch, had an Apolline oracle and a stream named after the famous Castalian spring of Parnassus.
4. Ammon, King of Libya, had an illicit affair with a maiden Amaltheia, who gave birth to a marvelous son Dionysus (Bacchus). To protect mother and child from the jealousy of his wife Rhea, Ammon hid them on Nysa, an island near modern Tunis. The identifications of Ammon with the Libyan Jupiter and with Noah's son Ham were widely accepted.
5. Milton takes his description of Mount Amara from Peter Heylyn's *Cosmographie* 4.64.
6. See Genesis 1.27: "God created man in his own image."

Severe, but in true filial freedom plac't;
295 Whence true autority in men; though both
Not equal, as thir sex not equal seem'd;
For contemplation hee and valor form'd,
For softness shee and sweet attractive Grace,
Hee for God only, shee for God in him:[7]
300 His fair large Front° and Eye sublime° declar'd   *forehead / uplifted*
Absolute rule; and Hyacinthine Locks
Round from his parted forelock manly hung
Clust'ring, but not beneath his shoulders broad:
Shee as a veil down to the slender waist
305 Her unadorned golden tresses wore
Dishevell'd, but in wanton ringlets wav'd
As the Vine curls her tendrils, which impli'd
Subjection, but requir'd with gentle sway,
And by her yielded, by him best receiv'd,
310 Yielded with coy° submission, modest pride,   *modest*
And sweet reluctant amorous delay.
Nor those mysterious parts were then conceal'd,
Then was not guilty shame: dishonest shame
Of Nature's works, honor dishonorable,
315 Sin-bred, how have ye troubl'd all mankind
With shows instead, mere shows of seeming pure,
And banisht from man's life his happiest life,
Simplicity and spotless innocence.
So pass'd they naked on, nor shunn'd the sight
320 Of God or Angel, for they thought no ill:
So hand in hand they pass'd, the loveliest pair
That ever since in love's imbraces met,
Adam the goodliest man of men since born
His Sons, the fairest of her Daughters *Eve.*
325 Under a tuft of shade that on a green
Stood whispering soft, by a fresh Fountain side
They sat them down, and after no more toil
Of thir sweet Gard'ning labor than suffic'd
To recommend cool *Zephyr,*[8] and made ease
330 More easy, wholesome thirst and appetite
More grateful, to thir Supper Fruits they fell,
Nectarine Fruits which the compliant boughs
Yielded them, side-long as they sat recline°   *lying down*
On the soft downy Bank damaskt with flow'rs:
335 The savory pulp they chew, and in the rind
Still as they thirsted scoop the brimming stream;
Nor gentle purpose,° nor endearing smiles   *conversation*
Wanted,° nor youthful dalliance as beseems   *lacked*
Fair couple, linkt in happy nuptial League,
340 Alone as they. About them frisking play'd
All Beasts of th' Earth, since wild, and of all chase

---

7. See 1 Corinthians 11.3: "The head of every man is   head of Christ is God."
Christ; and the head of the woman is the man; and the   8. The west wind.

In Wood or Wilderness, Forest or Den;
Sporting the Lion ramp'd,° and in his paw   *reared up*
Dandl'd the Kid; Bears, Tigers, Ounces,° Pards°   *lynxes / leopards*
345   Gamboll'd before them, th' unwieldy Elephant
To make them mirth us'd all his might, and wreath'd
His Lithe Proboscis; close the Serpent sly
Insinuating,[9] wove with Gordian twine[1]
His braided train, and of his fatal guile
350   Gave proof unheeded; others on the grass
Coucht, and now fill'd with pasture gazing sat,
Or Bedward ruminating;[2] for the Sun
Declin'd was hasting now with prone career
To th' Ocean Isles,[3] and in th' ascending Scale
355   Of Heav'n the Stars that usher Evening rose:
When *Satan* still in gaze, as first he stood,
Scarce thus at length fail'd speech recover'd sad.
      O Hell! what do mine eyes with grief behold,
Into our room of bliss thus high advanc't
360   Creatures of other mould, earth-born perhaps,
Not Spirits, yet to heav'nly Spirits bright
Little inferior; whom my thoughts pursue
With wonder, and could love, so lively shines
In them Divine resemblance, and such grace
365   The hand that form'd them on thir shape hath pour'd.
Ah gentle pair, yee little think how nigh
Your change approaches, when all these delights
Will vanish and deliver ye to woe,
More woe, the more your taste is now of joy;
370   Happy, but for so happy ill secur'd
Long to continue, and this high seat your Heav'n
Ill fenc't for Heav'n to keep out such a foe
As now is enter'd; yet no purpos'd foe
To you whom I could pity thus forlorn
375   Though I unpitied: League with you I seek,
And mutual amity so strait,° so close,   *intimate*
That I with you must dwell, or you with me
Henceforth; my dwelling haply may not please
Like this fair Paradise, your sense, yet such
380   Accept your Maker's work; he gave it me,
Which I as freely give; Hell shall unfold,[4]
To entertain you two, her widest Gates,
And send forth all her Kings; there will be room,
Not like these narrow limits, to receive
385   Your numerous offspring; if no better place,
Thank him who puts me loath to this revenge
On you who wrong me not for him who wrong'd.
And should I at your harmless innocence

---

9. Penetrating by sinuous ways.
1. Coil, convolution, as difficult to undo as the Gordian knot, which it took the hero Alexander to cut.
2. Chewing the cud before going to rest.

3. The Azores.
4. A blasphemous echo of Matthew 10.8 ("freely ye have received, freely give").

Melt, as I do, yet public reason[5] just,
390 Honor and Empire with revenge enlarg'd,
By conquering this new World, compels me now
To do what else though damn'd I should abhor.
   So spake the Fiend, and with necessity,
The Tyrant's plea, excus'd his devilish deeds.
395 Then from his lofty stand on that high Tree
Down he alights among the sportful Herd
Of those fourfooted kinds, himself now one,
Now other, as thir shape serv'd best his end
Nearer to view his prey, and unespi'd
400 To mark what of thir state he more might learn
By word or action markt: about them round
A Lion now he stalks with fiery glare,
Then as a Tiger, who by chance hath spi'd
In some Purlieu° two gentle Fawns at play,   *edge of a forest*
405 Straight couches close, then rising changes oft
His couchant watch, as one who chose his ground
Whence rushing he might surest seize them both
Gript in each paw: when *Adam* first of men
To first of women *Eve* thus moving speech,
410 Turn'd him° all ear to hear new utterance flow.   *Satan*
   Sole partner and sole part of all these joys,[6]
Dearer thyself than all; needs must the Power
That made us, and for us this ample World
Be infinitely good, and of his good
415 As liberal and free as infinite,
That rais'd us from the dust and plac't us here
In all this happiness, who at his hand
Have nothing merited, nor can perform
Aught whereof hee hath need, hee who requires
420 From us no other service than to keep
This one, this easy charge, of all the Trees
In Paradise that bear delicious fruit
So various, not to taste that only Tree
Of Knowledge, planted by the Tree of Life,[7]
425 So near grows Death to Life, whate'er Death is,
Some dreadful thing no doubt; for well thou know'st
God hath pronounc't it death to taste that Tree,
The only sign of our obedience left
Among so many signs of power and rule
430 Conferr'd upon us, and Dominion giv'n
Over all other Creatures that possess
Earth, Air, and Sea.[8] Then let us not think hard
One easy prohibition, who enjoy
Free leave so large to all things else, and choice

---

5. Reason of state, a perversion of the Ciceronian principle (*Laws* 3.3.8) that the good of the people is the
supreme law.
6. The first "sole" means "only"; the second, "unrivalled."
7. See Genesis 2.16ff.

8. See Genesis 1.28: "God said unto them . . . have
dominion over the fish of the sea, and over the fowl of
the air, and over every living thing that moveth upon the
earth."

435 Unlimited of manifold delights:
But let us ever praise him, and extol
His bounty, following our delightful task
To prune these growing Plants, and tend these Flow'rs,
Which were it toilsome, yet with thee were sweet.
440 To whom thus Eve repli'd. O thou for whom
And from whom I was form'd flesh of thy flesh,[9]
And without whom am to no end, my Guide
And Head, what thou hast said is just and right.[1]
For wee to him indeed all praises owe,
445 And daily thanks, I chiefly who enjoy
So far the happier Lot, enjoying thee
Preëminent by so much odds,° while thou   *advantage*
Like consort to thyself canst nowhere find.
That day I oft remember, when from sleep
450 I first awak't, and found myself repos'd
Under a shade on flow'rs, much wond'ring where
And what I was, whence thither brought, and how.
Not distant far from thence a murmuring sound
Of waters issu'd from a Cave and spread
455 Into a liquid Plain, then stood unmov'd
Pure as th' expanse of Heav'n; I thither went
With unexperienc't thought, and laid me down
On the green bank, to look into the clear
Smooth Lake, that to me seem'd another Sky.
460 As I bent down to look, just opposite,
A Shape within the wat'ry gleam appear'd
Bending to look on me, I started back,
It started back, but pleas'd I soon return'd,
Pleas'd it return'd as soon with answering looks
465 Of sympathy and love; there I had fixt
Mine eyes till now, and pin'd with vain desire,[2]
Had not a voice thus warn'd me, What thou seest,
What there thou seest fair Creature is thyself,
With thee it came and goes: but follow me,
470 And I will bring thee where no shadow stays°   *awaits*
Thy coming, and thy soft imbraces, hee
Whose image thou art, him thou shalt enjoy
Inseparably thine, to him shalt bear
Multitudes like thyself, and thence be call'd
475 Mother of human Race: what could I do,
But follow straight, invisibly thus led?
Till I espi'd thee, fair indeed and tall,
Under a Platan, yet methought less fair,
Less winning soft, less amiably mild,
480 Than that smooth wat'ry image; back I turn'd,

9. See 1 Corinthians 11.9: "Neither was the man created for the woman; but the woman for the man." See Genesis 2.23.
1. See 1 Corinthians 11.3: "The head of every man is Christ; and the head of the woman is the man; and the head of Christ is God."
2. Alluding to Ovid's story of the proud youth Narcissus, who was punished for his scornfulness by being made to fall in love with his own reflection in a pool.

Thou following cri'd'st aloud, Return fair *Eve,*
Whom fli'st thou? whom thou fli'st, of him thou art,
His flesh, his bone; to give thee being I lent
Out of my side to thee, nearest my heart
485   Substantial Life, to have thee by my side
Henceforth an individual° solace dear;   *inseparable*
Part of my Soul I seek thee, and thee claim
My other half: with that thy gentle hand
Seiz'd mine, I yielded, and from that time see
490   How beauty is excell'd by manly grace
And wisdom, which alone is truly fair.
    So spake our general Mother, and with eyes
Of conjugal attraction unreprov'd,°   *innocent*
And meek surrender, half imbracing lean'd
495   On our first Father, half her swelling Breast
Naked met his under the flowing Gold
Of her loose tresses hid: hee in delight
Both of her Beauty and submissive Charms
Smil'd with superior Love, as *Jupiter*
500   On *Juno* smiles, when he impregns° the Clouds   *impregnates*
That shed *May* Flowers; and press'd her Matron lip
With kisses pure: aside the Devil turn'd
For envy, yet with jealous leer malign
Ey'd them askance, and to himself thus plain'd.°   *complained*
505   Sight hateful, sight tormenting! thus these two
Imparadis't in one another's arms
The happier *Eden,* shall enjoy thir fill
Of bliss on bliss, while I to Hell am thrust,
Where neither joy nor love, but fierce desire,
510   Among our other torments not the least,
Still unfulfill'd with pain of longing pines;°   *troubles*
Yet let me not forget what I have gain'd
From thir own mouths; all is not theirs it seems:
One fatal Tree there stands of Knowledge call'd,
515   Forbidden them to taste: Knowledge forbidd'n?
Suspicious, reasonless. Why should thir Lord
Envy them that? can it be sin to know,
Can it be death? and do they only stand
By Ignorance, is that thir happy state,
520   The proof of thir obedience and thir faith?
O fair foundation laid whereon to build
Thir ruin! Hence I will excite thir minds
With more desire to know, and to reject
Envious commands, invented with design
525   To keep them low whom Knowledge might exalt
Equal with Gods; aspiring to be such,
They taste and die: what likelier can ensue?
But first with narrow search I must walk round
This Garden, and no corner leave unspi'd;
530   A chance but chance³ may lead where I may meet

___
3. An accident and an opportunity.

Some wand'ring Spirit of Heav'n, by Fountain side,
Or in thick shade retir'd, from him to draw
What further would be learnt. Live while ye may,
Yet happy pair; enjoy, till I return,
535   Short pleasures, for long woes are to succeed.
   So saying, his proud step he scornful turn'd,
But with sly circumspection, and began
Through wood, through waste, o'er hill, o'er dale his roam.
Meanwhile in utmost Longitude,[4] where Heav'n
540   With Earth and Ocean meets, the setting Sun
Slowly descended, and with right aspect
Against the eastern Gate of Paradise
Levell'd his ev'ning Rays: it was a Rock
Of Alablaster,° pil'd up to the Clouds,   *alabaster*
545   Conspicuous far, winding with one ascent
Accessible from Earth, one entrance high;
The rest was craggy cliff, that overhung
Still as it rose, impossible to climb.[5]
Betwixt these rocky Pillars *Gabriel*[6] sat
550   Chief of th' Angelic Guards, awaiting night;
About him exercis'd Heroic Games
Th' unarmed Youth of Heav'n, but nigh at hand
Celestial Armory, Shields, Helms, and Spears
Hung high with Diamond flaming, and with Gold.
555   Thither came *Uriel*, gliding through the Even
On a Sun-beam, swift as a shooting Star
In *Autumn* thwarts° the night, when vapors fir'd   *crosses*
Impress the Air, and shows the Mariner
From what point of his Compass to beware
560   Impetuous winds:[7] he thus began in haste.
   Gabriel, to thee thy course by Lot hath giv'n
Charge and strict watch that to this happy place
No evil thing approach or enter in;
This day at highth of Noon came to my Sphere
565   A Spirit, zealous, as he seem'd, to know
More of th' Almighty's works, and chiefly Man
God's latest Image: I describ'd° his way   *observed*
Bent all on speed, and markt his Aery Gait;
But in the Mount that lies from *Eden* North,
570   Where he first lighted, soon discern'd his looks
Alien from Heav'n, with passions foul obscur'd:
Mine eye pursu'd him still, but under shade
Lost sight of him; one of the banisht crew
I fear, hath ventur'd from the Deep, to raise
575   New troubles; him thy care must be to find.
   To whom the winged Warrior thus return'd:

4. The farthest west.
5. A possible source is the paradise of Mount Amara in Heylyn's *Cosmographie*.
6. "Strength of God," one of the four archangels ruling the corners of the world.
7. Shooting stars were thought to be a sign of storm because in falling they were thrust down by winds.

Uriel,[8] no wonder if thy perfect sight,
Amid the Sun's bright circle where thou sitst,
See far and wide: in at this Gate none pass
580 The vigilance here plac't, but such as come
Well known from Heav'n; and since Meridian hour
No Creature thence: if Spirit of other sort,
So minded, have o'erleapt these earthy bounds
On purpose, hard thou know'st it to exclude
585 Spiritual substance with corporeal bar.
But if within the circuit of these walks
In whatsoever shape he lurk, of whom
Thou tell'st, by morrow dawning I shall know.
     So promis'd hee, and *Uriel* to his charge
590 Return'd on that bright beam, whose point now rais'd
Bore him slope downward to the Sun now fall'n
Beneath th' *Azores;* whither the prime Orb,
Incredible how swift, had thither roll'd
Diurnal,° or this less volúbil[9] Earth   *in one day*
595 By shorter flight to th' East, had left him there
Arraying with reflected Purple and Gold
The Clouds that on his Western Throne attend:[1]
Now came still Ev'ning on, and Twilight gray
Had in her sober Livery all things clad;
600 Silence accompanied, for Beast and Bird,
They to thir grassy Couch, these to thir Nests
Were slunk, all but the wakeful Nightingale;
She all night long her amorous descant sung;
Silence was pleas'd: now glow'd the Firmament
605 With living Sapphires: *Hesperus*[2] that led
The starry Host, rode brightest, till the Moon
Rising in clouded Majesty, at length
Apparent Queen unveil'd her peerless light,
And o'er the dark her Silver Mantle threw.
610   When *Adam* thus to *Eve: Fair* Consort, th' hour
Of night, and all things now retir'd to rest
Mind us of like repose, since God hath set
Labor and rest, as day and night to men
Successive, and the timely dew of sleep
615 Now falling with soft slumbrous weight inclines
Our eye-lids; other Creatures all day long
Rove idle unimploy'd, and less need rest;
Man hath his daily work of body or mind
Appointed, which declares his Dignity,
620 And the regard of Heav'n on all his ways;
While other Animals unactive range,
And of thir doings God takes no account.
Tomorrow ere fresh Morning streak the East

---

8. "Light of God."
9. Capable of ready rotation on its axis.
1. The appearance of sunset can be regarded as caused

either by orbital motion of the sun about the earth or by
the earth's rotation (a lesser movement).
2. The evening star.

With first approach of light, we must be ris'n,
625   And at our pleasant labor, to reform
Yon flow'ry Arbors, yonder Alleys green,
Our walk at noon, with branches overgrown,
That mock our scant manuring,° and require   *cultivating*
More hands than ours to lop thir wanton growth:
630   Those Blossoms also, and those dropping Gums,
That lie bestrown unsightly and unsmooth,
Ask riddance, if we mean to tread with ease;
Meanwhile, as Nature wills, Night bids us rest.
    To whom thus *Eve* with perfect beauty adorn'd.
635   My Author° and Disposer, what thou bidd'st   *origin, creator*
Unargu'd I obey; so God ordains,
God is thy Law, thou mine: to know no more
Is woman's happiest knowledge and her praise.
With thee conversing I forget all time,
640   All seasons and thir change, all please alike.[3]
Sweet is the breath of morn, her rising sweet,
With charm° of earliest Birds; pleasant the Sun   *song*
When first on this delightful Land he spreads
His orient Beams, on herb, tree, fruit, and flow'r,
645   Glist'ring with dew; fragrant the fertile earth
After soft showers; and sweet the coming on
Of grateful Ev'ning mild, then silent Night
With this her solemn Bird and this fair Moon,
And these the Gems of Heav'n, her starry train:
650   But neither breath of Morn when she ascends
With charm of earliest Birds, nor rising Sun
On this delightful land, nor herb, fruit, flow'r,
Glist'ring with dew, nor fragrance after showers,
Nor grateful Ev'ning mild, nor silent Night
655   With this her solemn Bird, nor walk by Moon,
Or glittering Star-light without thee is sweet.
But wherefore all night long shine these, for whom
This glorious sight, when sleep hath shut all eyes?
    To whom our general Ancestor repli'd.
660   Daughter of God and Man, accomplisht *Eve*,
Those have thir course to finish, round the Earth,
By morrow Ev'ning, and from Land to Land
In order, though to Nations yet unborn,
Minist'ring light prepar'd, they set and rise;
665   Lest total darkness should by Night regain
Her old possession, and extinguish life
In Nature and all things, which these soft fires
Not only enlighten, but with kindly heat
Of various influence foment and warm,
670   Temper or nourish, or in part shed down
Thir stellar virtue on all kinds that grow
On Earth, made hereby apter to receive

3. Time of day; not "seasons of the year," since it is still eternal spring.

Perfection from the Sun's more potent Ray.[4]
These then, though unbeheld in deep of night,
675 Shine not in vain, nor think, though men were none,
That Heav'n would want spectators, God want praise;
Millions of spiritual Creatures walk the Earth
Unseen, both when we wake, and when we sleep:
All these with ceaseless praise his works behold
680 Both day and night: how often from the steep
Of echoing Hill or Thicket have we heard
Celestial voices to the midnight air,
Sole, or responsive each to other's note
Singing thir great Creator: oft in bands
685 While they keep watch, or nightly rounding walk,
With Heav'nly touch of instrumental sounds
In full harmonic number join'd, thir songs
Divide the night, and lift our thoughts to Heaven.
     Thus talking hand in hand alone they pass'd
690 On to thir blissful Bower; it was a place
Chos'n by the sovran Planter, when he fram'd
All things to man's delightful use; the roof
Of thickest covert was inwoven shade
Laurel and Myrtle, and what higher grew
695 Of firm and fragrant leaf; on either side
Acanthus, and each odorous bushy shrub
Fenc'd up the verdant wall; each beauteous flow'r,
Iris all hues, Roses, and Jessamin°   *jasmine*
Rear'd high thir flourisht heads between, and wrought
700 Mosaic; underfoot the Violet,
Crocus, and Hyacinth with rich inlay
Broider'd the ground, more color'd than with stone
Of costliest Emblem:[5] other Creature here
Beast, Bird, Insect, or Worm durst enter none;
705 Such was thir awe of Man. In shadier Bower
More sacred and sequester'd, though but feign'd,
Pan or *Silvanus* never slept, nor Nymph,
Nor *Faunus* haunted.[6] Here in close recess
With Flowers, Garlands, and sweet-smelling Herbs
710 Espoused *Eve* deckt first her Nuptial Bed,
And heav'nly Choirs the Hymenaean° sung,   *wedding hymn*
What day the genial° Angel to our Sire   *nuptial, generative*
Brought her in naked beauty more adorn'd,
More lovely than *Pandora,* whom the Gods
715 Endow'd with all thir gifts, and O too like

4. In Neoplatonic astrology, Sol was said to accomplish the generation of new life by acting through each of the other planets in turn; their function was only to modulate his influence or to select from his complete spectrum of virtues. After the Fall, the influence of the stars becomes less "kindly" (benign; natural).
5. Any ornament of inlaid work; the other sense of "emblem" (pictorial symbol) also operates here, to draw attention to the emblematic properties of the flowers (the humility of the violet, prudence of the hyacinth, amiability of the jasmine, etc.). The bower as a whole is an emblem of true married love.
6. Pan, Silvanus, and Faunus were confused, for all were represented as half man, half goat. Pan was a symbol of fecundity; Silvanus, god of woods, symbolized gardens and limits; Faunus, the Roman Pan, a wood god, and the father of satyrs, was an emblem of concupiscence.

In sad event, when to the unwiser Son
Of *Japhet* brought by *Hermes,* she ensnar'd
Mankind with her fair looks, to be aveng'd
On him who had stole *Jove's* authentic fire.[7]
720   Thus at thir shady Lodge arriv'd, both stood,
Both turn'd, and under op'n Sky ador'd
The God that made both Sky, Air, Earth and Heav'n
Which they beheld, the Moon's resplendent Globe
And starry Pole:° Thou also mad'st the Night,   *sky*
725   Maker Omnipotent, and thou the Day,
Which we in our appointed work imploy'd
Have finisht happy in our mutual help
And mutual love, the Crown of all our bliss
Ordain'd by thee, and this delicious place
730   For us too large, where thy abundance wants
Partakers, and uncropt falls to the ground.
But thou hast promis'd from us two a Race
To fill the Earth, who shall with us extol
Thy goodness infinite, both when we wake,
735   And when we seek, as now, thy gift of sleep.
        This said unanimous, and other Rites
Observing none, but adoration pure
Which God likes best, into thir inmost bower
Handed they went; and eas'd the putting off
740   These troublesome disguises which wee wear,
Straight side by side were laid, nor turn'd I ween
Adam from his fair Spouse, nor *Eve* the Rites
Mysterious of connubial Love refus'd:
Whatever Hypocrites austerely talk
745   Of purity and place and innocence,
Defaming as impure what God declares
Pure, and commands to some, leaves free to all.
Our Maker bids increase,[8] who bids abstain
But our Destroyer, foe to God and Man?
750   Hail wedded Love, mysterious Law, true source
Of human offspring, sole propriety
In Paradise of all things common else.
By thee adulterous lust was driv'n from men
Among the bestial herds to range, by thee
755   Founded in Reason, Loyal, Just, and Pure,
Relations dear, and all the Charities°   *affections*
Of Father, Son, and Brother first were known.
Far be it, that I should write thee sin or blame,
Or think thee unbefitting holiest place,

7. Milton has followed the version of the myth in Charles Estienne's *Dictionarium historicum* (1671): "Pandora . . . is feigned by Hesiod the first woman—made by Vulcan at Jupiter's command— . . . she was called Pandora, either because she was 'endowed with all [the gods'] gifts,' or because she was endowed with gifts by all." She was "sent with a closed casket to Epimetheus, since Jupiter wanted revenge on the human race for the boldness of Prometheus, who had stolen fire from heaven and taken it . . . down to earth; and that Epimetheus received her and opened the casket, which contained every kind of evil, so that it filled the world with diseases and calamities." Prometheus and Epimetheus were sons of Iapetus, the Titan son of Coelus and Terra. Milton identifies Iapetus with Iaphet (Noah's son).
8. See Genesis 1.28.

760   Perpetual Fountain of Domestic sweets,
        Whose bed is undefil'd and chaste pronounc't,[9]
        Present, or past, as Saints and Patriarchs us'd.
        Here Love his golden shafts imploys,[1] here lights
        His constant Lamp, and waves his purple wings,
765   Reigns here and revels; not in the bought smile
        Of Harlots, loveless, joyless, unindear'd,
        Casual fruition, nor in Court Amours,
        Mixt Dance, or wanton Mask, or Midnight Ball,
        Or Serenate, which the starv'd Lover sings
770   To his proud fair, best quitted with disdain.
        These lull'd by Nightingales imbracing slept,
        And on thir naked limbs the flow'ry roof
        Show'r'd Roses, which the Morn repair'd.° Sleep on,   *made up for*
        Blest pair; and O yet happiest if ye seek
775   No happier state, and know to know no more.[2]
             Now had night measur'd with her shadowy Cone
        Half way up Hill this vast Sublunar Vault,[3]
        And from thir Ivory Port the Cherubim
        Forth issuing at th' accustom'd hour stood arm'd
780   To thir night watches in warlike Parade,
        When *Gabriel* to his next in power thus spake.
             Uzziel,[4] half these draw off, and coast the South
        With strictest watch; these other wheel the North;
        Our circuit meets full West. As flame they part
785   Half wheeling to the Shield, half to the Spear.[5]
        From these, two strong and subtle Spirits he call'd
        That near him stood, and gave them thus in charge.
             Ithuriel and *Zephon*, with wing'd speed
        Search through this Garden, leave unsearcht no nook,
790   But chiefly where those two fair Creatures Lodge,
        Now laid perhaps asleep secure° of harm.   *careless*
        This Ev'ning from the Sun's decline arriv'd
        Who tells of some infernal Spirit seen
        Hitherward bent (who could have thought?) escap'd
795   The bars of Hell, on errand bad no doubt:
        Such where ye find, seize fast, and hither bring.
             So saying, on he led his radiant Files,
        Dazzling the Moon; these to the Bower direct
        In search of whom they sought: him there they found
800   Squat like a Toad, close at the ear of *Eve*;
        Assaying by his Devilish art to reach
        The Organs of her Fancy, and with them forge

9. See Hebrews 13.4: "Marriage is honourable in all, and the bed undefiled."
1. Cupid's "golden shafts" were sharp and gleaming and kindled love, while those of lead were blunt and put love to flight (Ovid, *Metamorphoses* 1.468–71).
2. Either "know that it is best not to seek new knowledge (by eating the forbidden fruit)" or "know how to limit your experience to the state of innocence."
3. The earth's shadow is a cone that appears to circle around it in diametrical opposition to the sun. When the axis of the cone reaches the meridian, it is midnight; but here it is only "Half way up," so the time is nine o'clock.
4. "Uzziel" (Strength of God) occurs in the Bible as an ordinary human name (e.g., Exodus 6.18), and so does "Zephon" (Searcher of Secrets: Numbers 26.15). "Ithuriel" (Discovery of God) is not from the Bible.
5. "Shield" for "left" and "spear" for "right" were ancient military terms.

Illusions as he list, Phantasms° and Dreams,   *illusions*
Or if, inspiring venom, he might taint
805   Th' animal spirits⁶ that from pure blood arise
Like gentle breaths from Rivers pure, thence raise
At least distemper'd,° discontented thoughts,   *vexed*
Vain hopes, vain aims, inordinate desires
Blown up with high conceits ingend'ring pride.
810   Him thus intent *Ithuriel* with his Spear
Touch'd lightly; for no falsehood can endure
Touch of Celestial temper, but returns
Of force to its own likeness: up he starts
Discover'd and surpris'd. As when a spark
815   Lights on a heap of nitrous⁷ Powder, laid
Fit for the Tun⁸ some Magazin to store
Against° a rumor'd War, the Smutty grain   *preparing for*
With sudden blaze diffus'd, inflames the Air:
So started up in his own shape the Fiend.
820   Back stepp'd those two fair Angels half amaz'd
So sudden to behold the grisly King;
Yet thus, unmov'd with fear, accost him soon.
      Which of those rebel Spirits adjudg'd to Hell
Com'st thou, escap'd thy prison, and transform'd,
825   Why satst thou like an enemy in wait
Here watching at the head of these that sleep?
      Know ye not then said *Satan*, fill'd with scorn,
Know ye not mee?⁹ * * *

from **Book 5**

The Argument

Morning approacht, Eve relates to Adam her troublesome dream; he likes it not, yet comforts her: They come forth to thir day labors: Thir Morning Hymn at the Door of thir Bower. God to render Man inexcusable sends Raphael to admonish him of his obedience, of his free estate, of his enemy near at hand; who he is, and why his enemy, and whatever else may avail Adam to know. Raphael comes down to Paradise, his appearance describ'd, his coming discern'd by Adam afar off sitting at the door of his Bower; he goes out to meet him, brings him to his lodge, entertains him with the choicest fruits of Paradise got together by Eve; thir discourse at Table: Raphael performs his message, minds Adam of his state and of his enemy; relates at Adam's request who that enemy is, and how he came to be so, beginning from his first revolt in Heaven, and the occasion thereof; how he drew his Legions after him to the parts of the North, and there incited them to rebel with him, persuading all but only Abdiel a Seraph, who in Argument dissuades and opposes him, then forsakes him.

---

6. Spirits in this sense were fine vapors, regarded by some as a medium between body and soul, by others as a separate soul. Animal spirits (Latin *anima*, soul) ascended to the brain and issued through the nerves to impart motion to the body. Local movement of the animal spirits could also produce imaginative apparitions, by which angels were thought to affect the human mind.

7. Mixed with niter (potassium nitrate or saltpeter, an ingredient in gunpowder) to form an explosive.

8. In proper condition for casking, ready for use.

9. Ithuriel and Zephon take Satan to Gabriel, who orders him to return to Hell. Satan rises up to fight the assembled angels—"His Stature reacht the Sky, and on his Crest / Sat horror Plum'd"—but then God displays scales in heaven, showing victory tilting to Gabriel, and Satan flees.

from **Book 6**

The Argument

Raphael *continues to relate how* Michael *and* Gabriel *were sent forth to Battle against* Satan *and his Angels. The first fight describ'd:* Satan *and his Powers retire under Night: He calls a Council, invents devilish Engines, which in the second day's Fight put* Michael *and his Angels to some disorder; but they at length pulling up Mountains overwhelm'd both the force and Machines of* Satan: *Yet the Tumult not so ending, God on the third day sends Messiah his Son for whom he had reserv'd the glory of the Victory: Hee in the Power of his Father coming to the place, and causing all his Legions to stand still on either side, with his Chariot and Thunder driving into the midst of his Enemies, pursues them unable to resist towards the wall of Heaven; which opening they leap down with horror and confusion in the place of punishment prepar'd for them in the Deep:* Messiah *returns with triumph to his Father.*

from **Book 7**

The Argument

Raphael *at the request of* Adam *relates how and wherefore this world was first created; that God, after the expelling of* Satan *and his Angels out of Heaven, declar'd his pleasure to create another World and other Creatures to dwell therein; sends his Son with Glory and attendance of Angels to perform the work of Creation in six days: the Angels celebrate with Hymns the performance thereof, and his reascension into Heaven.*

from **Book 8**

The Argument

Adam *inquires concerning celestial Motions, is doubtfully answer'd, and exhorted to search rather things more worthy of knowledge:* Adam *assents, and still desirous to detain* Raphael, *relates to him what he remember'd since his own Creation, his placing in Paradise, his talk with God concerning solitude and fit society, his first meeting and Nuptials with* Eve, *his discourse with the Angel thereupon; who after admonitions repeated departs.*

Book 9

The Argument

Satan *having compast the Earth, with meditated guile returns as a mist by Night into Paradise, enters into the Serpent sleeping.* Adam *and* Eve *in the Morning go forth to thir labors, which* Eve *proposes to divide in several places, each laboring apart:* Adam *consents not, alleging the danger, lest that Enemy, of whom they were forewarn'd, should attempt her found alone:* Eve *loath to be thought not circumspect or firm enough, urges her going apart, the rather desirous to make trial of her strength;* Adam *at last yields: The Serpent finds her alone; his subtle approach, first gazing, then speaking, with much flattery extolling* Eve *above all other Creatures.* Eve *wond'ring to hear the Serpent speak, asks how he attain'd to human speech and such understanding not till now; the Serpent answers, that by tasting of a certain Tree in the Garden he attain'd both to Speech and Reason, till then void of both:* Eve *requires him to bring her to that Tree, and finds it to be the Tree of Knowledge forbidden: The Serpent now grown bolder, with many wiles and arguments induces her at length to eat; she pleas'd with the taste deliberates awhile whether to impart thereof to* Adam *or not, at last brings him of the Fruit, relates what persuaded her to eat thereof:* Adam *at first amaz'd, but perceiving her lost, resolves through vehemence[1] of love to perish with her; and extenuating[2] the trespass, eats also of the Fruit: The effects thereof in them both; they seek to cover thir nakedness; then fall to variance and accusation of one another.*

No more of talk where God or Angel Guest
With Man, as with his Friend, familiar us'd
To sit indulgent, and with him partake
Rural repast, permitting him the while

5　Venial° discourse unblam'd: I now must change   *permissible*
Those Notes to Tragic; foul distrust, and breach
Disloyal on the part of Man, revolt,
And disobedience: On the part of Heav'n
Now alienated, distance and distaste,

10　Anger and just rebuke, and judgment giv'n,
That brought into this World a world of woe,
Sin and her shadow Death, and Misery
Death's Harbinger: Sad task, yet argument
Not less but more Heroic than the wrath

15　Of stern *Achilles* on his Foe pursu'd
Thrice Fugitive about *Troy* Wall; or rage
Of *Turnus* for *Lavinia* disespous'd,
Or *Neptune*'s ire or *Juno*'s, that so long
Perplex'd the *Greek* and *Cytherea*'s Son;[3]

20　If answerable° style I can obtain   *equal, accountable*
Of my Celestial Patroness,[4] who deigns
Her nightly visitation unimplor'd,
And dictates to me slumb'ring, or inspires
Easy my unpremeditated Verse:

25　Since first this Subject for Heroic Song
Pleas'd me long choosing, and beginning late;
Not sedulous by Nature to indite
Wars, hitherto the only Argument
Heroic deem'd, chief maistry to dissect

30　With long and tedious havoc fabl'd Knights
In Battles feign'd; the better fortitude
Of Patience and Heroic Martyrdom
Unsung; or to describe Races and Games,
Or tilting Furniture, emblazon'd Shields,

35　Impreses[5] quaint, Caparisons[6] and Steeds;
Bases and tinsel Trappings, gorgeous Knights

---

1. The root meaning of Latin "vehementia" is mindlessness.
2. Carrying further, drawing out.
3. Achilles is "stern" in his "wrath" because he refused any covenant with Hector, and Turnus dies fighting Aeneas for the hand of Lavinia, whereas Messiah, more heroically, is not implacable in his anger. He issued his sole commandment "sternly" (8.333); but when it is disobeyed, he works for reconciliation. Similarly, God's anger is distinguished from "Neptune's ire" and "Juno's" (which merely "perplexed" Odysseus and Aeneas) in that

it is expressed in justice rather than in victimization.
4. The heavenly Muse, Urania. Both ancient and modern epics had always had war, or at least fighting, as a principal ingredient. (So has *Paradise Lost*, in the first half of the poem; but in the second half this subject is transcended.) Milton now glances unfavorably at the typical matter of the romantic epic.
5. Heraldic devices, often with accompanying mottos.
6. Ornamented coverings spread over the saddle of a horse.

At Joust and Tournament; then marshall'd Feast
Serv'd up in Hall with Sewers,° and Seneschals;°   *waiters / stewards*
The skill of Artifice or Office mean,
40 Not that which justly gives Heroic name
To Person or to Poem.[7] Mee of these
Nor skill'd nor studious, higher Argument
Remains, sufficient of itself to raise
That name,[8] unless an age too late, or cold
45 Climate, or Years damp my intended wing
Deprest; and much they may, if all be mine,
    Not Hers who brings it nightly to my Ear.
The Sun was sunk, and after him the Star
Of *Hesperus*,° whose Office is to bring   *the planet Venus*
50 Twilight upon the Earth, short Arbiter
Twixt Day and Night, and now from end to end
Night's Hemisphere had veil'd the Horizon round:
When *Satan* who late fled before the threats
Of *Gabriel* out of *Eden*,[9] now improv'd°   *intensified*
55 In meditated fraud and malice, bent
On Man's destruction, maugre what might hap
Of heavier on himself,[1] fearless return'd.
By Night he fled, and at Midnight return'd
From compassing the Earth, cautious of day,
60 Since *Uriel* Regent of the Sun descri'd
His entrance, and forewarn'd the Cherubim
That kept thir watch; thence full of anguish driv'n,
The space of seven continu'd Nights he rode
With darkness, thrice the Equinoctial Line
65 He circl'd, four times cross'd the Car of Night
From Pole to Pole, traversing each Colure;[2]
On th'eighth return'd, and on the Coast averse
From entrance or Cherubic Watch, by stealth
Found unsuspected way. There was a place,
70 Now not, though Sin, not Time, first wrought the change,
Where *Tigris* at the foot of Paradise
Into a Gulf shot under ground, till part
Rose up a Fountain by the Tree of Life;
In with the River sunk, and with it rose
75 *Satan* involv'd in rising Mist, then sought
Where to lie hid; Sea he had searcht and Land
From *Eden* over *Pontus*, and the Pool
Maeotis, up beyond the River *Ob*;[3]

7. Artifice implies mechanic or applied art. It is beneath the dignity of epic to teach etiquette and social ceremony and heraldry.
8. The name of epic.
9. I.e., at the end of Book 4, a week earlier.
1. Despite the danger of heavier punishment.
2. By keeping to earth's shadow, Satan contrives to experience a whole week of darkness. The two colures were

great circles, intersecting at right angles at the poles and dividing the equinoctial circle (the equator) into four equal parts.
3. In his north-south circles, Satan passed Pontus (the Black Sea), the "pool / Maeotis" (the Sea of Azov), and the Siberian River Ob, which flows north into the Gulf of Ob and from there into the Arctic Ocean.

Downward as far Antarctic; and in length
80 West from *Orontes* to the Ocean barr'd
At *Darien*, thence to the Land where flows
Ganges and *Indus*:[4] thus the Orb he roam'd
With narrow search; and with inspection deep
Consider'd every Creature, which of all
85 Most opportune might serve his Wiles, and found
The Serpent subtlest Beast of all the Field.[5]
Him after long debate, irresolute°   *undecided*
Of thoughts revolv'd, his final sentence° chose   *judgment*
Fit Vessel, fittest Imp° of fraud, in whom   *offshoot*
90 To enter, and his dark suggestions hide
From sharpest sight: for in the wily Snake,
Whatever sleights none would suspicious mark,
As from his wit and native subtlety
Proceeding, which in other Beasts observ'd
95 Doubt° might beget of Diabolic pow'r   *suspicion*
Active within beyond the sense of brute.
Thus he resolv'd, but first from inward grief
His bursting passion into plaints thus pour'd:
    O Earth, how like to Heav'n, if not preferr'd
100 More justly, Seat worthier of Gods, as built
With second thoughts, reforming what was old!
For what God after better worse would build?
Terrestrial Heav'n, danc't round by other Heav'ns
That shine, yet bear thir bright officious Lamps,
105 Light above Light, for thee alone, as seems,
In thee concentring all thir precious beams
Of sacred influence:[6] As God in Heav'n
Is Centre, yet extends to all, so thou
Centring receiv'st from all those Orbs; in thee,
110 Not in themselves, all thir known virtue appears
Productive in Herb, Plant, and nobler birth
Of Creatures animate with gradual life
Of Growth, Sense, Reason, all summ'd up in Man.[7]
With what delight could I have walkt thee round,
115 If I could joy in aught, sweet interchange
Of Hill and Valley, Rivers, Woods and Plains,
Now Land, now Sea, and Shores with Forest crown'd,
Rocks, Dens, and Caves; but I in none of these
Find place or refuge; and the more I see
120 Pleasures about me, so much more I feel
Torment within me, as from the hateful siege°   *conflict*
Of contraries; all good to me becomes
Bane,° and in Heav'n much worse would be my state.   *poison*

4. In his westward circling of the equinoctial line, he crossed the Syrian River Orontes, then the Pacific ("peaceful") "Ocean barred" by the Isthmus of Darien (Panama) and India.
5. See Genesis 3.1.

6. The case for an earth-centered universe, put at 8.86–114 by Raphael, is now put by Satan.
7. "Growth, sense, reason" are the activities of the vegetable, animal, and rational souls, respectively, in humans.

But neither here seek I, no nor in Heav'n
125   To dwell, unless by maistring Heav'n's Supreme;
Nor hope to be myself less miserable
By what I seek, but others to make such
As I, though thereby worse to me redound:
For only in destroying I find ease
130   To my relentless thoughts; and him destroy'd,
Or won to what may work his utter loss,
For whom all this was made, all this will soon
Follow, as to him linkt in weal or woe,
In woe then: that destruction wide may range:[8]
135   To mee shall be the glory sole among
Th'infernal Powers, in one day to have marr'd
What he *Almight* styl'd, six Nights and Days
Continu'd making, and who knows how long
Before had been contriving, though perhaps
140   Not longer than since I in one Night freed
From servitude inglorious well nigh half
Th' Angelic Name, and thinner left the throng
Of his adorers: hee to be aveng'd,
And to repair his numbers thus impair'd,
145   Whether such virtue° spent of old now fail'd   *power*
More Angels to Create, if they at least
Are his Created, or to spite us more,
Determin'd to advance into our room
A Creature form'd of Earth, and him endow,
150   Exalted from so base original,
With Heav'nly spoils, our spoils; What he decreed
He effected; Man he made, and for him built
Magnificent this World, and Earth his seat,
Him Lord pronounc'd, and, O indignity!
155   Subjected to his service Angel wings,
And flaming Ministers to watch and tend
Thir earthy Charge: Of these the vigilance
I dread, and to elude, thus wrapt in mist
Of midnight vapor glide obscure, and pry
160   In every Bush and Brake, where hap may find
The Serpent sleeping, in whose mazy folds
To hide me, and the dark intent I bring.
O foul descent! that I who erst contended
With Gods to sit the highest, am now constrain'd
165   Into a Beast, and mixt with bestial slime,
This essence to incarnate and imbrute,
That to the highth of Deity aspir'd;
But what will not Ambition and Revenge
Descend to? who aspires must down as low
170   As high he soar'd, obnoxious° first or last   *exposed*
To basest things. Revenge, at first though sweet,

8. The created cosmos will follow humans to destruction.

Bitter ere long back on itself recoils;
Let it, I reck not, so it light well aim'd,
Since higher I fall short, on him who next

175   Provokes my envy, this new Favorite
Of Heav'n, this Man of Clay, Son of despite,
Whom us the more to spite his Maker rais'd
From dust: spite then with spite is best repaid.
    So saying, through each Thicket Dank or Dry,

180   Like a black mist low creeping, he held on
His midnight search, where soonest he might find
The Serpent: him fast sleeping soon he found
In Labyrinth of many a round self-roll'd,
His head the midst, well stor'd with subtle wiles:

185   Not yet in horrid Shade or dismal Den,
Nor nocent° yet, but on the grassy Herb   *harmful, guilty*
Fearless unfear'd he slept: in at his Mouth
The Devil enter'd, and his brutal sense,
In heart or head, possessing soon inspir'd

190   With act intelligential; but his sleep
Disturb'd not, waiting close° th' approach of Morn.   *concealed*
Now whenas sacred Light began to dawn
In *Eden* on the humid Flow'rs, that breath'd
Thir morning incense, when all things that breathe,

195   From th' Earth's great Altar send up silent praise
To the Creator, and his Nostrils fill
With grateful Smell, forth came the human pair
And join'd thir vocal Worship to the Choir
Of Creatures wanting voice; that done, partake

200   The season, prime for sweetest Scents and Airs:
Then cómmune how that day they best may ply
Thir growing work: for much thir work outgrew
The hands' dispatch of two Gard'ning so wide.
And *Eve* first to her Husband thus began.

205   *Adam*, well may we labor still to dress
This Garden, still to tend Plant, Herb and Flow'r,
Our pleasant task enjoin'd, but till more hands
Aid us, the work under our labor grows,
Luxurious by restraint; what we by day

210   Lop overgrown, or prune, or prop, or bind,
One night or two with wanton growth derides
Tending to wild. Thou therefore now advise
Or hear what to my mind first thoughts present,
Let us divide our labors, thou where choice

215   Leads thee, or where most needs, whether to wind
The Woodbine round this Arbor, or direct
The clasping Ivy where to climb, while I
In yonder Spring of Roses intermixt
With Myrtle, find what to redress till Noon:

220   For while so near each other thus all day
Our task we choose, what wonder if so near
Looks intervene and smiles, or object new

Casual discourse draw on, which intermits
Our day's work brought to little, though begun
225 Early, and th' hour of Supper comes unearn'd.
    To whom mild answer *Adam* thus return'd.
Sole *Eve*, Associate sole, to me beyond
Compare above all living Creatures dear,
Well hast thou motion'd,° well thy thoughts imploy'd   *proposed*
230 How we might best fulfil the work which here
God hath assign'd us, nor of me shalt pass
Unprais'd: for nothing lovelier can be found
In Woman, than to study household good,
And good works in her Husband to promote.
235 Yet not so strictly hath our Lord impos'd
Labor, as to debar us when we need
Refreshment, whether food, or talk between,
Food of the mind, or this sweet intercourse
Of looks and smiles, for smiles from Reason flow,
240 To brute deni'd, and are of Love the food,
Love not the lowest end of human life.
For not to irksome toil, but to delight
He made us, and delight to Reason join'd.
These paths and Bowers doubt not but our joint hands
245 Will keep from Wilderness with ease, as wide
As we need walk, till younger hands ere long
Assist us: But if much converse perhaps
Thee satiate, to short absence I could yield.
For solitude sometimes is best society,
250 And short retirement urges sweet return.
But other doubt possesses me, lest harm
Befall thee sever'd from me; for thou know'st
What hath been warn'd us, what malicious Foe
Envying our happiness, and of his own
255 Despairing, seeks to work us woe and shame
By sly assault; and somewhere nigh at hand
Watches, no doubt, with greedy hope to find
His wish and best advantage, us asunder,
Hopeless to circumvent us join'd, where each
260 To other speedy aid might lend at need;
Whether his first design be to withdraw
Our fealty from God, or to disturb
Conjugal Love, than which perhaps no bliss
Enjoy'd by us excites his envy more;
265 Or this, or worse,⁹ leave not the faithful side
That gave thee being, still shades thee and protects.
The Wife, where danger or dishonor lurks,
Safest and seemliest by her Husband stays,
Who guards her, or with her the worst endures.
270   To whom the Virgin° Majesty of *Eve*,   *chaste, innocent*
As one who loves, and some unkindness meets,

9. Whether this or worse (be his first design).

With sweet austere composure thus repli'd.
    Offspring of Heav'n and Earth, and all Earth's Lord,
That such an Enemy we have, who seeks
275 Our ruin, both by thee inform'd I learn,
And from the parting Angel over-heard
As in a shady nook I stood behind,
Just then return'd at shut of Ev'ning Flow'rs.
But that thou shouldst my firmness therefore doubt
280 To God or thee, because we have a foe
May tempt it, I expected not to hear.
His violence thou fear'st not, being such,
As wee, not capable of death or pain,
Can either not receive, or can repel.
285 His fraud is then thy fear, which plain infers
Thy equal fear that my firm Faith and Love
Can by his fraud be shak'n or seduc't;
Thoughts, which how found they harbor in thy breast,
Adam, misthought of her to thee so dear?
290   To whom with healing words Adam repli'd.
Daughter of God and Man, immortal Eve,
For such thou art, from sin and blame entire:°   free
Not diffident° of thee do I dissuade   mistrustful
Thy absence from my sight, but to avoid
295 Th' attempt itself, intended by our Foe.
For hee who tempts, though in vain, at least asperses°   falsely charges
The tempted with dishonor foul, suppos'd
Not incorruptible of Faith, not proof
Against temptation: thou thyself with scorn
300 And anger wouldst resent the offer'd wrong,
Though ineffectual found: misdeem not then,
If such affront I labor to avert
From thee alone, which on us both at once
The Enemy, though bold, will hardly dare,
305 Or daring, first on mee th' assault shall light.
Nor thou his malice and false guile contemn;
Subtle he needs must be, who could seduce
Angels, nor think superfluous others' aid.
I from the influence of thy looks receive
310 Access° in every Virtue, in thy sight   increase
More wise, more watchful, stronger, if need were
Of outward strength; while shame, thou looking on,
Shame to be overcome or over-reacht
Would utmost vigor raise, and rais'd unite.
315 Why shouldst not thou like sense within thee feel
When I am present, and thy trial choose
With me, best witness of thy Virtue tri'd.
    So spake domestic Adam in his care
And Matrimonial Love; but Eve, who thought
320 Less° attribúted to her Faith sincere,   too little
Thus her reply with accent sweet renew'd.
    If this be our condition, thus to dwell

In narrow circuit strait'n'd by a Foe,
Subtle or violent, we not endu'd

325   Single with like defense, wherever met,
How are we happy, still in fear of harm?
But harm precedes not sin: only our Foe
Tempting affronts us with his foul esteem
Of our integrity: his foul esteem

330   Sticks no dishonor on our Front,° but turns   *forehead*
Foul on himself; then wherefore shunn'd or fear'd
By us? who rather double honor gain
From his surmise prov'd false, find peace within,
Favor from Heav'n, our witness from th' event.

335   And what is Faith, Love, Virtue unassay'd
Alone, without exterior help sustain'd?
Let us not then suspect our happy State
Left so imperfet by the Maker wise,
As not secure to single or combin'd.

340   Frail is our happiness, if this be so,
And *Eden* were no Eden[1] thus expos'd.
    To whom thus Adam fervently repli'd.
O Woman, best are all things as the will
Of God ordain'd them, his creating hand

345   Nothing imperfet or deficient left
Of all that he Created, much less Man,
Or aught that might his happy State secure,
Secure from outward force; within himself
The danger lies, yet lies within his power:

350   Against his will he can receive no harm.
But God left free the Will, for what obeys
Reason, is free, and Reason he made right,
But bid her well beware, and still erect,[2]
Lest by some fair appearing good surpris'd

355   She dictate false, and misinform the Will
To do what God expressly hath forbid.
Not then mistrust, but tender love enjoins,
That I should mind thee oft, and mind thou me.
Firm we subsist, yet possible to swerve,

360   Since Reason not impossibly may meet
Some specious object by the Foe suborn'd,
And fall into deception unaware,
Not keeping strictest watch, as she was warn'd.
Seek not temptation then, which to avoid

365   Were better, and most likely if from mee
Thou sever not: Trial will come unsought.
Wouldst thou approve° thy constancy, approve   *demonstrate*
First thy obedience; th' other who can know,
Not seeing thee attempted, who attest?

370   But if thou think, trial unsought may find
Us both securer° than thus warn'd thou seem'st,   *more careless*

1. I.e., no pleasure, the literal Hebrew meaning of "Eden."   2. Always attentive, but also with a glance at upright.

Go; for thy stay, not free, absents thee more;
Go in thy native innocence, rely
On what thou hast of virtue, summon all,
375   For God towards thee hath done his part, do thine.
        So spake the Patriarch of Mankind, but *Eve*
Persisted, yet submiss, though last, repli'd.
        With thy permission then, and thus forewarn'd
Chiefly by what thy own last reasoning words
380   Touch'd only, that our trial, when least sought,
May find us both perhaps far less prepar'd,
The willinger I go, nor much expect
A Foe so proud will first the weaker seek;
So bent, the more shall shame him his repulse.
385   Thus saying, from her Husband's hand her hand
Soft she withdrew, and like a Wood-Nymph light,
Oread or *Dryad,* or of *Delia's* Train,[3]
Betook her to the Groves, but *Delia's* self
In gait surpass'd and Goddess-like deport,
390   Though not as shee with Bow and Quiver arm'd,
But with such Gard'ning Tools as Art yet rude,
Guiltless° of fire had form'd, or Angels brought.[4]   innocent, ignorant
To Pales, or Pomona, thus adorn'd,
Likest she seem'd, Pomona when she fled
395   *Vertumnus,* or to *Ceres* in her Prime,
Yet Virgin of *Proserpina* from *Jove.*[5]
Her long and ardent look his Eye pursu'd
Delighted, but desiring more her stay.
Oft he to her his charge of quick return
400   Repeated, shee to him as oft engag'd
To be return'd by Noon amid the Bow'r,
And all things in best order to invite
Noontide repast, or Afternoon's repose.
O much deceiv'd, much failing, hapless *Eve,*
405   Of thy presum'd return! event perverse!
Thou never from that hour in Paradise
Found'st either sweet repast, or sound repose;
Such ambush hid among sweet Flow'rs and Shades
Waited with hellish rancor imminent
410   To intercept thy way, or send thee back
Despoil'd of Innocence, of Faith, of Bliss.
For now, and since first break of dawn the Fiend,
Mere° Serpent in appearance, forth was come,   plain
And on his Quest, where likeliest he might find
415   The only two of Mankind, but in them
The whole included Race, his purpos'd prey.
In Bow'r and Field he sought, where any tuft

3. Oreads were mountain nymphs, such as attended on
Diana; dryads were wood nymphs. Neither class of
nymphs was immortal.
4. Only as a result of the Fall did it become necessary for
humans to have some means of warming themselves.
There may also be an allusion to the fire stolen from

heaven by Prometheus.
5. Pales was the Roman goddess of pastures; Pomona was
the nymph or goddess of fruit trees, seduced by the disguised Vertumnus; Ceres was the goddess of corn and
agriculture who bore Proserpina to Jove.

	Of Grove or Garden-Plot more pleasant lay,	
	Thir tendance° or Plantation for delight,	*object of care*
420	By Fountain or by shady Rivulet,	
	He sought them both, but wish'd his hap° might find	*chance*
	Eve separate, he wish'd, but not with hope	
	Of what so seldom chanc'd, when to his wish,	
	Beyond his hope, *Eve* separate he spies,	
425	Veil'd in a Cloud of Fragrance, where she stood,	
	Half spi'd, so thick the Roses bushing round	
	About her glow'd, oft stooping to support	
	Each Flow'r of slender stalk, whose head though gay	
	Carnation, Purple, Azure, or speckt with Gold,	
430	Hung drooping unsustain'd, them she upstays	
	Gently with Myrtle band, mindless the while,	
	Herself, though fairest unsupported Flow'r,	
	From her best prop so far, and storm so nigh.[6]	
	Nearer he drew, and many a walk travers'd	
435	Of stateliest Covert, Cedar, Pine, or Palm,	
	Then voluble and bold, now hid, now seen	
	Among thick-wov'n Arborets and Flow'rs	
	Imborder'd on each Bank, the hand° of *Eve*:	*handiwork*
	Spot more delicious than those Gardens feign'd	
440	Or of reviv'd *Adonis*, or renown'd	
	Alcinoüs, host of old *Laertes'* Son,	
	Or that, not Mystic, where the Sapient King	
	Held dalliance with his fair *Egyptian* Spouse.[7]	
	Much hee the Place admir'd, the Person more.	
445	As one who long in populous City pent,	
	Where Houses thick and Sewers annoy the Air,	
	Forth issuing on a Summer's Morn to breathe	
	Among the pleasant Villages and Farms	
	Adjoin'd, from each thing met conceives delight,	
450	The smell of Grain, or tedded° Grass, or Kine,°	*mown / cows*
	Or Dairy, each rural sight, each rural sound;	
	If chance with Nymphlike step fair Virgin pass,	
	What pleasing seem'd, for her now pleases more,	
	She most, and in her look sums all Delight.	
455	Such Pleasure took the Serpent to behold	
	This Flow'ry Plat,° the sweet recess of *Eve*	*piece of ground*
	Thus early, thus alone; her Heav'nly form	
	Angelic, but more soft, and Feminine,	
	Her graceful Innocence, her every Air	
460	Of gesture or least action overaw'd	
	His Malice, and with rapine sweet bereav'd	
	His fierceness of the fierce intent it brought:	
	That space the Evil one abstracted stood	
	From his own evil, and for the time remain'd	

6. See 4.270, page 974, where Proserpina (and by implication Eve) was "Herself a fairer flower" when she was
carried off by the king of hell.
7. "The sapient king" was Solomon (*Song of Solomon* 6.2).
Milton alludes to Spenser's addition to the myth of Adonis, that Venus keeps Adonis hidden in a secret garden
(*The Faerie Queene* 3.6). "Laertes' son" was Odysseus;
much-traveled as he was, he marveled when he saw the
Garden of Alcinoüs (Homer, *Odyssey* 7).

465   Stupidly good, of enmity disarm'd,
       Of guile, of hate, of envy, of revenge;
       But the hot Hell that always in him burns,
       Though in mid Heav'n, soon ended his delight,
       And tortures him now more, the more he sees
470   Of pleasure not for him ordain'd: then soon
       Fierce hate he recollects, and all his thoughts
       Of mischief, gratulating,° thus excites.   *rejoicing*
          Thoughts, whither have ye led me, with what sweet
       Compulsion thus transported to forget
475   What hither brought us, hate, not love, nor hope
       Of Paradise for Hell, hope here to taste
       Of pleasure, but all pleasure to destroy,
       Save what is in destroying, other joy
       To me is lost. Then let me not let pass
480   Occasion which now smiles, behold alone
       The Woman, opportune° to all attempts,   *exposed*
       Her Husband, for I view far round, not nigh,
       Whose higher intellectual more I shun,
       And strength, of courage haughty, and of limb
485   Heroic built, though of terrestrial mould,°   *formed of earth*
       Foe not informidable, exempt from wound,
       I not; so much hath Hell debas'd, and pain
       Infeebl'd me, to what I was in Heav'n.
       Shee fair, divinely fair, fit Love for Gods,
490   Not terrible, though terror be in Love
       And beauty, not approacht by stronger hate,
       Hate stronger, under show of Love well feign'd,
       The way which to her ruin now I tend.
          So spake the Enemy of Mankind, enclos'd
495   In Serpent, Inmate bad, and toward *Eve*
       Address'd his way, not with indented wave,
       Prone on the ground, as since, but on his rear,
       Circular base of rising folds, that tow'r'd
       Fold above fold a surging Maze, his Head
500   Crested aloft, and Carbuncle his Eyes;[8]
       With burnisht Neck of verdant Gold, erect
       Amidst his circling Spires,° that on the grass   *coils*
       Floated redundant:° pleasing was his shape,   *abundant to excess*
       And lovely, never since of Serpent kind
505   Lovelier, not those that in *Illyria* chang'd
       Hermione and *Cadmus,* or the God
       In *Epidaurus;*[9] nor to which transform'd
       Ammonian Jove, or *Capitoline* was seen,
       Hee with *Olympias,* this with her who bore
510   *Scipio* the highth of Rome.[1] With tract oblique

---

8. "Carbuncle" or reddish eyes denoted rage.
9. Cadmus was turned into a serpent first; only after he had embraced his wife Hermione (Harmonia) in his new form did she too change (Ovid, *Metamorphoses* 4.572–603). Aesculapius, the god of healing, once changed into a serpent to help the Romans in that form

(Ovid, *Metamorphoses* 15.626–744).
1. Jupiter Ammon, the "Lybian Jove," as a serpent mated with Olympias to father Alexander the Great, just as the Roman Jupiter, Capitolinus, took the form of a snake to father the great general Scipio.

At first, as one who sought access, but fear'd
To interrupt, side-long he works his way.
As when a Ship by skilful Steersman wrought
Nigh River's mouth or Foreland, where the Wind
515 Veers oft, as oft so steers, and shifts her Sail;
So varied hee, and of his tortuous Train
Curl'd many a wanton wreath in sight of *Eve*,
To lure her Eye; shee busied heard the sound
Of rustling Leaves, but minded not, as us'd
520 To such disport before her through the Field,
From every Beast, more duteous at her call,
Than at *Circean* call the Herd disguis'd.[2]
Hee bolder now, uncall'd before her stood;
But as in gaze admiring: Oft he bow'd
525 His turret Crest, and sleek enamell'd Neck,
Fawning, and lick'd the ground whereon she trod.
His gentle dumb expression turn'd at length
The Eye of *Eve* to mark his play; he glad
Of her attention gain'd, with Serpent Tongue
530 Organic, or impulse of vocal Air,
His fraudulent temptation thus began.
        Wonder not, sovran Mistress, if perhaps
Thou canst, who are sole Wonder, much less arm
Thy looks, the Heav'n of mildness, with disdain,
535 Displeas'd that I approach thee thus, and gaze
Insatiate, I thus single, nor have fear'd
Thy awful brow, more awful thus retir'd.
Fairest resemblance of thy Maker fair,
Thee all things living gaze on, all things thine
540 By gift, and thy Celestial Beauty adore
With ravishment beheld, there best beheld
Where universally admir'd: but here
In this enclosure wild, these Beasts among,
Beholders rude, and shallow to discern
545 Half what in thee is fair, one man except,
Who sees thee? (and what is one?) who shouldst be seen
A Goddess among Gods, ador'd and serv'd
By Angels numberless, thy daily Train.
        So gloz'd° the Tempter, and his Proem° tun'd;   *flattered / prelude*
550 Into the Heart of *Eve* his words made way,
Though at the voice much marvelling; at length
Not unamaz'd she thus in answer spake.
        What may this mean? Language of Man pronounc't
By Tongue of Brute, and human sense exprest?[3]
555 The first at least of these I thought deni'd
To Beasts, whom God on thir Creation-Day

2. Homer's Circe changed men into beasts who surprised Odysseus's company by fawning on them like dogs (*Odyssey* 10.212–19).
3. Milton is unusually favorable to Eve in making her ask

the serpent how it came by its voice. The Eve of Scriptural exegesis, by contrast, is carried away by the words and makes no inquiry into their source.

Created mute to all articulate sound;
The latter I demur,° for in thir looks   *hesitate about*
Much reason, and in thir actions oft appears.

560 Thee, Serpent, subtlest beast of all the field
I knew, but not with human voice endu'd;
Redouble then this miracle, and say,
How cam'st thou speakable of mute,[4] and how
To me so friendly grown above the rest

565 Of brutal kind, that daily are in sight?
Say, for such wonder claims attention due.
    To whom the guileful Tempter thus repli'd.
Empress of this fair World, resplendent *Eve*,
Easy to mee it is to tell thee all

570 What thou command'st and right thou should'st be obey'd:
I was at first as other Beasts that graze
The trodden Herb, of abject° thoughts and low,   *mean-spirited*
As was my food, nor aught but food discern'd
Or Sex, and apprehended nothing high:

575 Till on a day roving the field, I chanc'd
A goodly Tree far distant to behold
Loaden with fruit of fairest colors mixt,
Ruddy and Gold: I nearer drew to gaze;
When from the boughs a savory odor blown,

580 Grateful to appetite, more pleas'd my sense
Than smell of sweetest Fennel, or the Teats
Of Ewe or Goat dropping with Milk at Ev'n,
Unsuckt of Lamb or Kid, that tend thir play.
To satisfy the sharp desire I had

585 Of tasting those fair Apples, I resolv'd
Not to defer; hunger and thirst at once,
Powerful persuaders, quick'n'd at the scent
Of that alluring fruit, urg'd me so keen.
About the mossy Trunk I wound me soon,

590 For high from ground the branches would require
Thy utmost reach or *Adam's*: Round the Tree
All other Beasts that saw, with like desire
Longing and envying stood, but could not reach.
Amid the Tree now got, where plenty hung

595 Tempting so nigh, to pluck and eat my fill
I spar'd not, for such pleasure till that hour
At Feed or Fountain never had I found.
Sated at length, ere long I might perceive
Strange alteration in me, to degree

600 Of Reason in my inward Powers, and Speech
Wanted not long, though to this shape retain'd.
Thenceforth to Speculations high or deep
I turn'd my thoughts, and with capacious mind
Consider'd all things visible in Heav'n,

605 Or Earth, or Middle, all things fair and good;

---

4. How did you become capable of speech from being dumb?

But all that fair and good in thy Divine
Semblance, and in thy Beauty's heav'nly Ray
United I beheld; no Fair° to thine   *beauty*
Equivalent or second, which compell'd
610   Mee thus, though importune perhaps, to come
And gaze, and worship thee of right declar'd
Sovran of Creatures, universal Dame.
          So talk'd the spirited[5] sly Snake; and *Eve*,
Yet more amaz'd unwary thus repli'd.
615   Serpent, thy overpraising leaves in doubt
The virtue° of that Fruit, in thee first prov'd: *power*
But say, where grows the Tree, from hence how far?
For many are the Trees of God that grow
In Paradise, and various, yet unknown
620   To us, in such abundance lies our choice,
As leaves a greater store of Fruit untoucht,
Still hanging incorruptible, till men
Grow up to thir provision, and more hands
Help to disburden Nature of her Birth.
625   To whom the wily Adder, blithe and glad.
Empress, the way is ready, and not long,
Beyond a row of Myrtles, on a Flat,
Fast by a Fountain, one small Thicket past
Of blowing° Myrrh and Balm; if thou accept   *blooming*
630   My conduct,° I can bring thee thither soon.   *guidance*
          Lead then, said Eve. Hee leading swiftly roll'd
In tangles, and made intricate seem straight,
To mischief swift. Hope elevates, and joy
          Bright'ns his Crest, as when a wand'ring Fire,
635   Compact° of unctuous vapor, which the Night   *made up*
Condenses, and the cold invirons round,
Kindl'd through agitation to a Flame,
Which oft, they say, some evil Spirit attends,
Hovering and blazing with delusive Light,
640   Misleads th' amaz'd Night-wanderer from his way
To Bogs and Mires, and oft through Pond or Pool,
There swallow'd up and lost, from succor far.
So glister'd the dire Snake, and into fraud
Led *Eve* our credulous Mother, to the Tree
645   Of prohibition, root of all our woe;
Which when she saw, thus to her guide she spake.
          Serpent, we might have spar'd our coming hither,
Fruitless to mee, though Fruit be here to excess,
The credit of whose virtue rest with thee,
650   Wondrous indeed, if cause of such effects.
But of this Tree we may not taste nor touch;
God so commanded, and left that Command
Sole Daughter of his voice;[6] the rest, we live

---

5. Endowed with an animating spirit, stirred up; also   6. A Hebraism for "voice sent from heaven."
energetic, enterprising, possessed by a spirit.

655   Law to ourselves, our Reason is our Law.
        To whom the Tempter guilefully repli'd.
      Indeed? hath God then said that of the Fruit
      Of all these Garden Trees ye shall not eat,
      Yet Lords declar'd of all in Earth or Air?[7]
        To whom thus *Eve* yet sinless. Of the Fruit
660   Of each Tree in the Garden we may eat,
      But of the Fruit of this fair Tree amidst
      The Garden, God hath said, Ye shall not eat
      Thereof, nor shall ye touch it, lest ye die.
        She scarce had said, though brief, when now more bold
665   The Tempter, but with show of Zeal and Love
      To Man, and indignation at his wrong,
      New part puts on, and as to passion mov'd,
      Fluctuates disturb'd, yet comely, and in act
      Rais'd, as of some great matter to begin.
670   As when of old some Orator renown'd
      In *Athens* or free *Rome*, where Eloquence
      Flourish'd, since mute, to some great cause addrest,
      Stood in himself collected, while each part,
      Motion, each act won audience ere the tongue,
675   Sometimes in highth began, as no delay
      Of Preface brooking through his Zeal of Right.[8]
      So standing, moving, or to highth upgrown
      The Tempter all impassion'd thus began.
        O Sacred, Wise, and Wisdom-giving Plant,
680   Mother of Science,° Now I feel thy Power   *knowledge*
      Within me clear, not only to discern
      Things in thir Causes, but to trace the ways
      Of highest Agents, deem'd however wise.
      Queen of this Universe, do not believe
685   Those rigid threats of Death; ye shall not Die:
      How should ye? by the Fruit? it gives you Life
      To° Knowledge: By the Threat'ner? look on mee,   *in addition to*
      Mee who have touch'd and tasted, yet both live,
      And life more perfet have attain'd than Fate
690   Meant mee, by vent'ring higher than my Lot.
      Shall that be shut to Man, which to the Beast
      Is open? or will God incense his ire
      For such a petty Trespass, and not praise
      Rather your dauntless virtue, whom the pain
695   Of Death denounc't, whatever thing Death be,
      Deterr'd not from achieving what might lead
      To happier life, knowledge of Good and Evil;
      Of good, how just? of evil, if what is evil
      Be real, why not known, since easier shunn'd?[9]

7. Lines 655–58 closely follow Genesis. 3.1.
8. This simile blends oratorical, theatrical, and theological meanings. Thus "part" means "part of the body," "dramatic role," and "moral act"; "motion" means "gesture," "mime" (or "puppet-show"), and "instigation, persuasive force, inclination"; "act" means "action," "performance of a play," and "the accomplished deed itself."
9. If the knowledge is good, how is it just to prohibit it? Here occurs the most egregious logical fallacy in speech. (For evil to be "shunned," it is not at all necessary that it should be "known" in the sense of being experienced.)

700 God therefore cannot hurt ye, and be just;
Not just, not God; not fear'd then, nor obey'd:
Your fear itself of Death removes the fear.
Why then was this forbid? Why but to awe,
Why but to keep ye low and ignorant,
705 His worshippers; he knows that in the day
Ye Eat thereof, your Eyes that seem so clear,
Yet are but dim, shall perfetly be then
Op'n'd and clear'd, and ye shall be as Gods,
Knowing both Good and Evil as they know.[1]
710 That ye should be as Gods, since I as Man,
Internal Man,[2] is but proportion meet,
I of brute human, thee of human Gods.
So ye shall die perhaps, by putting off
Human, to put on Gods, death to be wisht,
715 Though threat'n'd, which no worse than this can bring.[3]
And what are Gods that Man may not become
As they, participating° God-like food?   *sharing*
The Gods are first, and that advantage use
On our belief, that all from them proceeds;
720 I question it, for this fair Earth I see,
Warm'd by the Sun, producing every kind,
Them nothing: If they° all things, who enclos'd   *if they produce*
Knowledge of Good and Evil in this Tree,
That who so eats thereof, forthwith attains
725 Wisdom without their leave? and wherein lies
Th' offense, that Man should thus attain to know?
What can your knowledge hurt him, or this Tree
Impart against his will if all be his?
Or is it envy, and can envy dwell
730 In heav'nly breasts?[4] these, these and many more
Causes import° your need of this fair Fruit.   *suggest*
Goddess humane, reach then, and freely taste.
    He ended, and his words replete with guile
Into her heart too easy entrance won:
735 Fixt on the Fruit she gaz'd, which to behold
Might tempt alone, and in her ears the sound
Yet rung of his persuasive words, impregn'd°   *impregnated*
With Reason, to her seeming, and with Truth;
Meanwhile the hour of Noon drew on, and wak'd
740 An eager appetite, rais'd by the smell
So savory of that Fruit, which with desire,
Inclinable now grown to touch or taste,
Solicited her longing eye;[5] yet first
Pausing a while, thus to herself she mus'd.

---

1. See Genesis 3.5.
2. The serpent's pretence is that his "inward powers" are human.
3. Satan offers a travesty of Christian mortification and death to sin; see Colossians 3.1–15: "ye have put off the old man with his deeds; And have put on the new man, which is renewed in knowledge after the image of him that created him."
4. See Virgil, *Aeneid* 1.11; Satan is inviting Eve to participate in a pagan epic, complete with machinery of jealous gods.
5. For lines 735–43, see Genesis 3.6.

745   Great are thy Virtues, doubtless, best of Fruits,
        Though kept from Man, and worthy to be admir'd,
        Whose taste, too long forborne, at first assay
        Gave elocution to the mute, and taught
        The Tongue not made for Speech to speak thy praise:[6]
750   Thy praise hee also who forbids thy use,
        Conceals not from us, naming thee the Tree
        Of Knowledge, knowledge both of good and evil;
        Forbids us then to taste, but his forbidding
        Commends thee more, while it infers the good
755   By thee communicated, and our want:
        For good unknown, sure is not had, or had
        And yet unknown, is as not had at all.
        In plain° then, what forbids he but to know,   *plainly*
        Forbids us good, forbids us to be wise?
760   Such prohibitions bind not. But if Death
        Bind us with after-bands, what profits then
        Our inward freedom? In the day we eat
        Of this fair Fruit, our doom is, we shall die.
        How dies the Serpent? hee hath eat'n and lives,
765   And knows, and speaks, and reasons, and discerns,
        Irrational till then. For us alone
        Was death invented? or to us deni'd
        This intellectual food, for beasts reserv'd?
        For Beasts it seems: yet that one Beast which first
770   Hath tasted, envies not, but bring with joy
        The good befall'n him, Author unsuspect,[7]
        Friendly to man, far from deceit or guile,
        What fear I then, rather what know to fear[8]
        Under this ignorance of Good and Evil,
775   Of God or Death, of Law or Penalty?
        Here grows the Cure of all, this Fruit Divine,
        Fair to the Eye, inviting to the Taste,
        Of virtue° to make wise: what hinders then   *power*
        To reach, and feed at once both Body and Mind?
780   So saying, her rash hand in evil hour
        Forth reaching to the Fruit, she pluck'd, she eat:°   *ate*
        Earth felt the wound, and Nature from her seat
        Sighing through all her Works gave signs of woe,
        That all was lost. Back to the Thicket slunk
785   The guilty Serpent, and well might, for *Eve*,
        Intent now wholly on her taste, naught else
        Regarded, such delight till then, as seem'd,
        In Fruit she never tasted, whether true
        Or fancied so, through expectation high
790   Of knowledge, nor was God-head from her thought.[9]

6. Eve has trusted Satan's account of the fruit and consequently argues from false premises, such as its magical
power.
7. Eve means "informant not subject to suspicion."

8. What fear I, then—or rather (since I'm not allowed to
know anything) what do I know that is to be feared?
9. She expected to achieve godhead.

Greedily she ingorg'd without restraint,
And knew not eating Death:[1] Satiate at length,
And hight'n'd as with Wine, jocund and boon,°   *jolly*
Thus to herself she pleasingly began.
795   O Sovran, virtuous, precious of all Trees
In Paradise, of operation blest
To Sapience,[2] hitherto obscur'd, infam'd,°   *defamed*
And thy fair Fruit let hang, as to no end
Created; but henceforth my early care,
800   Not without Song, each Morning, and due praise
Shall tend thee, and the fertile burden ease
Of thy full branches offer'd free to all;
Till dieted by thee I grow mature
In knowledge, as the Gods who all things know;
805   Though others[3] envy what they cannot give;
For had the gift been theirs, it had not here
Thus grown. Experience, next to thee I owe,
Best guide; not following thee, I had remain'd
In ignorance, thou op'n'st Wisdom's way,
810   And giv'st access, though secret she retire.
And I perhaps am secret; Heav'n is high,
High and remote to see from thence distinct
Each thing on Earth; and other care perhaps
May have diverted from continual watch
815   Our great Forbidder, safe with all his Spies
About him. But to *Adam* in what sort
Shall I appear? shall I to him make known
As yet my change, and give him to partake
Full happiness with mee, or rather not.
820   But keep the odds of Knowledge in my power
Without Copartner? so to add what wants
In Female Sex, the more to draw his Love,
And render me more equal, and perhaps,
A thing not undesirable, sometime
825   Superior: for inferior who is free?
This may be well: but what if God have seen,
And Death ensue? then I shall be no more,
And *Adam* wedded to another *Eve*,
Shall live with her enjoying, I extinct;
830   A death to think. Confirm'd then I resolve,
Adam shall share with me in bliss or woe:
So dear I love him, that with him all deaths
I could endure, without him live no life.
    So saying, from the Tree her step she turn'd,
835   But first low Reverence done, as to the power
That dwelt within, whose presence had infus'd

1. She knew not that she was eating death; "she was unaware, while she ate death" or even "she 'knew'"; not eating (immediate) death."
2. "Sapience" is derived from Latin *sapientia* (discern-ment, taste) and ultimately from *sapere* (to taste).
3. I.e., God. Eve's language is now full of lapses in logic and evasions in theology.

Into the plant sciential[4] sap, deriv'd
From Nectar, drink of Gods. *Adam* the while
Waiting desirous her return, had wove
840   Of choicest Flow'rs a Garland to adorn
Her Tresses, and her rural labors crown,
As Reapers oft are wont thir Harvest Queen.
Great joy he promis'd to his thoughts, and new
Solace in her return, so long delay'd;
845   Yet oft his heart, divine° of something ill,   prophet
Misgave him; hee the falt'ring measure[5] felt;
And forth to meet her went, the way she took
That Morn when first they parted; by the Tree
Of Knowledge he must pass; there he her met,
850   Scarce from the Tree returning; in her hand
A bough of fairest fruit that downy smil'd,
New gather'd, and ambrosial smell diffus'd.
To him she hasted, in her face excuse
Came Prologue, and Apology to prompt,[6]
855   Which with bland words at will she thus addrest.
        Hast thou not wonder'd, *Adam*, at my stay?
Thee I have misst, and thought it long, depriv'd
Thy presence, agony of love till now
Not felt, nor shall be twice, for never more
860   Mean I to try, what rash untri'd I sought,
The pain of absence from thy sight. But strange
Hath been the cause, and wonderful to hear:
This Tree is not as we are told, a Tree
Of danger tasted,° nor to evil unknown   if tasted
865   Op'ning the way, but of Divine effect
To open Eyes, and make them Gods who taste;
And hath been tasted such: the Serpent wise,
Or not restrain'd as wee, or not obeying,
Hath eat'n of the fruit, and is become,
870   Not dead, as we are threat'n'd, but thenceforth
Endu'd with human voice and human sense,
Reasoning to admiration, and with mee
Persuasively hath so prevail'd, that I
Have also tasted, and have also found
875   Th' effects to correspond, opener mine Eyes,
Dim erst, dilated Spirits, ampler Heart,
And growing up to Godhead; which for thee
Chiefly I sought, without thee can despise.
For bliss, as thou hast part, to me is bliss,
880   Tedious, unshar'd with thee, and odious soon.
Thou therefore also taste, that equal Lot
May join us, equal Joy, as equal Love;

---

4. Endowed with knowledge.
5. The rhythm of his own heart.
6. The expression on Eve's face is visible in advance as
she approaches and so is like the prologue-speaker of a

play. But it also remains on her face as she speaks, to help
out her words, and so is like the prompter of the play. The
actor prompted is apology, i.e., justification or defense
personified.

Lest thou not tasting, different degree[7]
Disjoin us, and I then too late renounce
885   Deity for thee, when Fate will not permit.
     Thus *Eve* with Count'nance blithe her story told;
But in her Cheek distemper[8] flushing glow'd.
On th' other side, *Adam*, soon as he heard
The fatal Trespass done by *Eve*, amaz'd,
890   Astonied° stood and Blank, while horror chill   *stunned*
Ran through his veins, and all his joints relax'd;
From his slack hand the Garland wreath'd for *Eve*,
Down dropp'd, and all the faded Roses shed:
Speechless he stood and pale, till thus at length
895   First to himself he inward silence broke.
     O fairest of Creation, last and best
Of all God's Works, Creature in whom excell'd
Whatever can to sight or thought be form'd,
Holy, divine, good, amiable, or sweet!
900   How art thou lost, how on a sudden lost,
Defac't, deflow'r'd, and now to death devote?°   *given over*
Rather how hast thou yielded to transgress
The strict forbiddance, how to violate
The sacred Fruit forbidd'n! some cursed fraud
905   Of Enemy hath beguil'd thee, yet unknown,
And mee with thee hath ruin'd, for with thee
Certain my resolution is to Die;
How can I live without thee, how forgo
Thy sweet Converse and Love so dearly join'd,
910   To live again in these wild Woods forlorn?
Should God create another *Eve*, and I
Another Rib afford, yet loss of thee
Would never from my heart; no no, I feel
The Link of Nature draw me: Flesh of Flesh,
915   Bone of my Bone thou art, and from thy State
Mine never shall be parted, bliss or woe.
     So having said, as one from sad dismay
Recomforted, and after thoughts disturb'd
Submitting to what seem'd remediless,
920   Thus in calm mood his Words to *Eve* he turn'd.
     Bold deed thou hast presum'd, advent'rous *Eve*,
And peril great provok't, who thus hath dar'd
Had it been only coveting to Eye
That sacred Fruit, sacred° to abstinence,   *devoted*
925   Much more to taste it under ban to touch.
But past who can recall, or done undo?
Not God Omnipotent, nor Fate; yet so
Perhaps thou shalt not Die, perhaps the Fact°   *crime, deed*
Is not so heinous now, foretasted Fruit,

---

7. Differing position in the scale of creatures.
8. A disordered condition due to disturbance of the temperament of the bodily humors.

930　Profan'd first by the Serpent, by him first
Made common and unhallow'd ere our taste;
Nor yet on him found deadly, he yet lives,
Lives, as thou said'st, and gains to live as Man
Higher degree of Life, inducement strong
935　To us, as likely tasting to attain
Proportional ascent, which cannot be
But to be Gods, or Angels Demi-gods.
Nor can I think that God, Creator wise,
Though threat'ning, will in earnest so destroy
940　Us his prime Creatures, dignifi'd so high,
Set over all his Works, which in our Fall,
For us created, needs with us must fail,
Dependent made; so God shall uncreate,
Be frustrate, do, undo, and labor lose,
945　Not well conceiv'd of God, who though his Power
Creation could repeat, yet would be loath
Us to abolish, lest the Adversary
Triumph and say; Fickle their State whom God
Most Favors, who can please him long? Mee first
950　He ruin'd, now Mankind; whom will he next?
Matter of scorn, not to be given the Foe.
However I with thee have fixt my Lot,
Certain to undergo like doom;[9] if Death
Consort with thee, Death is to mee as Life;
955　So forcible within my heart I feel
The Bond of Nature draw me to my own,
My own in thee, for what thou art is mine;
Our State cannot be sever'd, we are one,
One Flesh; to lose thee were to lose myself.
960　　So *Adam*, and thus *Eve* to him repli'd.
O glorious trial of exceeding Love,
Illustrious evidence, example high!
Ingaging me to emulate, but short
Of thy perfection, how shall I attain,
965　*Adam*, from whose dear side I boast me sprung,
And gladly of our Union hear thee speak,
One Heart, one Soul in both; whereof good proof
This day affords, declaring thee resolv'd,
Rather than Death or aught than Death more dread
970　Shall separate us, linkt in Love so dear,
To undergo with mee one Guilt, one Crime,
If any be, of tasting this fair Fruit,
Whose virtue, for of good still good proceeds,
Direct, or by occasion[1] hath presented
975　This happy trial of thy Love, which else
So eminently never had been known.

---

9. Three separate meanings are possible: judgment, irrev-
ocable destiny, and death.

1. I.e., directly or indirectly.

Were it I thought Death menac't would ensue
This my attempt, I would sustain alone
The worst, and not persuade thee, rather die
980   Deserted, than oblige° thee with a fact   *make liable*
Pernicious to thy Peace, chiefly assur'd
Remarkably so late of thy so true,
So faithful Love unequall'd; but I feel
Far otherwise th' event,° nor Death, but Life   *result*
985   Augmented, op'n'd Eyes, new Hopes, new Joys,
Taste so Divine, that what of sweet before
Hath toucht my sense, flat seems to this, and harsh.
On my experience, *Adam*, freely taste,
And fear of Death deliver to the Winds.
990   So saying, she embrac'd him, and for joy
Tenderly wept, much won that he his Love
Had so ennobl'd, as of choice to incur
Divine displeasure for her sake, or Death.
In recompense (for such compliance bad
995   Such recompense best merits) from the bough
She gave him of that fair enticing Fruit
With liberal hand: he scrupl'd not to eat
Against his better knowledge, not deceiv'd,
But fondly overcome with Female charm.[2]
1000 Earth trembl'd from her entrails, as again
In pangs, and Nature gave a second groan,
Sky low'r'd, and muttering Thunder, some sad drops
Wept at completing of the mortal Sin
Original;[3] while *Adam* took no thought,
1005 Eating his fill, nor *Eve* to iterate
Her former trespass fear'd, the more to soothe
Him with her lov'd society, that now
As with new Wine intoxicated both
They swim in mirth, and fancy that they feel
1010 Divinity within them breeding wings
Wherewith to scorn the Earth: but that false Fruit
Far other operation first display'd,
Carnal desire inflaming, hee on *Eve*
Began to cast lascivious Eyes, she him
1015 As wantonly repaid; in Lust they burn:
Till *Adam* thus 'gan *Eve* to dalliance move.
     Eve, now I see thou are exact of taste,
And elegant, of Sapience[4] no small part,
Since to each meaning savor[5] we apply,
1020 And Palate call judicious; I the praise

2. See 1 Timothy 2.14: "And Adam was not deceived, but the woman being deceived was in the transgression."
3. The only occurrence in *Paradise Lost* of the term "Original Sin." In his *De doctrina* (1.11), Milton defines Original Sin as "the sin which is common to all men, that which our first parents, and in them all their posterity committed, when, casting off their obedience to God, they tasted the fruit of the forbidden tree."
4. Wisdom, from Latin *sapere*, to taste.
5. Tastiness, understanding.

Yield thee, so well this day thou hast purvey'd.°   *provided*
Much pleasure we have lost, while we abstain'd
From this delightful Fruit, nor known till now
True relish, tasting; if such pleasure be
1025   In things to us forbidden, it might be wish'd,
For this one Tree had been forbidden ten.
But come, so well refresh't, now let us play,
As meet is, after such delicious Fare;
For never did thy Beauty since the day
1030   I saw thee first and wedded thee, adorn'd
With all perfections, so inflame my sense
With ardor to enjoy thee, fairer now
Than ever, bounty of this virtuous Tree.[6]
        So said he, and forbore not glance or toy°   *caress*
1035   Of amorous intent, well understood
Of° *Eve*, whose Eye darted contagious Fire.   *by*
Her hand he seiz'd, and to a shady bank,
Thick overhead with verdant roof imbowr'd
He led her nothing loath; Flow'rs were the Couch,
1040   Pansies, and Violets, and Asphodel,
And Hyacinth, Earth's freshest softest lap.
There they thir fill of Love and Love's disport
Took largely, of thir mutual guilt the Seal,
The solace of thir sin, till dewy sleep
1045   Oppress'd them, wearied with thir amorous play.
Soon as the force of that fallacious Fruit,
That with exhilarating vapor bland°   *pleasing*
About thir spirits had play'd, and inmost powers
Made err, was now exhal'd, and grosser sleep
1050   Bred of unkindly fumes,[7] with conscious dreams
Encumber'd, now had left them, up they rose
As from unrest, and each the other viewing,
Soon found thir Eyes how op'n'd, and thir minds
How dark'n'd;[8] innocence, that as a veil
1055   Had shadow'd them from knowing ill, was gone,
Just confidence, and native righteousness,
And honor from about them, naked left
To guilty shame: hee cover'd, but his Robe
Uncover'd more. So rose the *Danite* strong
1060   *Herculean Samson* from the Harlot-lap
Of *Philistean Dalilah,* and wak'd
Shorn of his strength, They destitute and bare
Of all thir virtue:[9] silent, and in face
Confounded long they sat, as struck'n mute,

6. See Homer, *Iliad* 14, where Hera, bent on deceiving
Zeus, comes to him wearing Aphrodite's belt and seems
more charming to him than ever before.
7. Unnatural vapors or exhalations rising from the stomach to the brain.

8. See Genesis 3.7: "The eyes of them both were opened,
and they knew that they were naked."
9. See Judges 16 for the story of Samson's betrayal by
Delilah.

1065 Till *Adam*, though not less than *Eve* abasht,
At length gave utterance to these words constrain'd.
  O *Eve*, in evil hour thou didst give ear
To that false Worm, of whomsoever taught
To counterfeit Man's voice, true in our Fall,
1070 False in our promis'd Rising; since our Eyes
Op'n'd we find indeed, and find we know
Both Good and Evil, Good lost, and Evil got,
Bad Fruit of Knowledge, if this be to know,
Which leaves us naked thus, of Honor void,
1075 Of Innocence, of Faith, of Purity,
Our wonted Ornaments now soil'd and stain'd,
And in our Faces evident the signs
Of foul concupiscence; whence evil store;
Even shame, the last of evils; of the first
1080 Be sure then. How shall I behold the face
Henceforth of God or Angel, erst with joy
And rapture so oft beheld? those heav'nly shapes
Will dazzle now this earthly, with thir blaze
Insufferably bright. O might I here
1085 In solitude live savage, in some glade
Obscur'd, where highest Woods impenetrable
To Star or Sun-light, spread thir umbrage broad,
And brown as Evening: Cover me ye Pines,
Ye Cedars, with innumerable boughs
1090 Hide me, where I may never see them more.
But let us now, as in bad plight, devise
What best may for the present serve to hide
The Parts of each from other, that seem most
To shame obnoxious,° and unseemliest seen,   *exposed*
1095 Some Tree whose broad smooth Leaves together sew'd,
And girded on our loins, may cover round
Those middle parts, that this new comer, Shame,
There sit not, and reproach us as unclean.[1]
  So counsell'd hee, and both together went
1100 Into the thickest Wood, there soon they chose
The Figtree,[2] not that kind for Fruit renown'd,
But such as at this day to *Indians* known
In *Malabar* or *Decan* spreads her Arms
Branching so broad and long, that in the ground
1105 The bended Twigs take root, and Daughters grow
About the Mother Tree, a Pillar'd shade
High overarch't, and echoing Walks between;
There oft the *Indian* Herdsman shunning heat
Shelters in cool, and tends his pasturing Herds
1110 At Loopholes cut through thickest shade: Those Leaves
They gather'd, broad as Amazonian Targe,°   *shield*

1. See Genesis 3.7.   from Gerard's *Herball* (1597).
2. Milton's description of the banyan or Indian fig comes

And with what skill they had, together sew'd,
To gird thir waist, vain Covering if to hide
Thir guilt and dreaded shame; O how unlike
1115   To that first naked Glory. Such of late
Columbus found th' *American* so girt
With feather'd Cincture,° naked else and wild   *belt*
Among the Trees on Isles and woody Shores.
Thus fenc't, and as they thought, thir shame in part
1120   Cover'd, but not at rest or ease of Mind,
They sat them down to weep, nor only Tears
Rain'd at thir Eyes, but high Winds worse within
Began to rise, high Passions, Anger, Hate,
Mistrust, Suspicion, Discord, and shook sore
1125   Thir inward State of Mind, calm Region once
And full of Peace, now toss't and turbulent:
For Understanding rul'd not, and the Will
Heard not her lore, both in subjection now
To sensual Appetite, who from beneath
1130   Usurping over sovran Reason claim'd
Superior sway: From thus distemper'd breast,
Adam, estrang'd in look and alter'd style,
Speech intermitted thus to *Eve* renew'd.
　　Would thou hadst heark'n'd to my words, and stay'd
1135   With me, as I besought thee, when that strange
Desire of wand'ring this unhappy Morn,
I know not whence possess'd thee; we had then
Remain'd still happy, not as now, despoil'd
Of all our good, sham'd, naked, miserable.
1140   Let none henceforth seek needless cause to approve°   *give proof of*
The Faith they owe;[3] when earnestly they seek
Such proof, conclude, they then begin to fail.
　　To whom soon mov'd with touch of blame thus *Eve*.
What words have past thy Lips,[4] *Adam* severe,
1145   Imput'st thou that to my default, or will
Of wand'ring, as thou call'st it, which who knows
But might as ill have happ'n'd thou being by,
Or to thyself perhaps: hadst thou been there,
Or here th' attempt, thou couldst not have discern'd
1150   Fraud in the Serpent, speaking as he spake;
No ground of enmity between us known,
Why hee should mean me ill, or seek to harm.
Was I to have never parted from thy side?
As good have grown there still a lifeless Rib.
1155   Being as I am, why didst not thou the Head[5]
Command me absolutely not to go,
Going into such danger as thou said'st?

3. Be under obligation to render or possess.
4. Echoes Odysseus's disapproval of a speech of Agamemnon's (*Iliad* 14.83).
5. Alludes to 1 Corinthians 11.3: "The head of every man
is Christ; and the head of the woman is the man; and the
head of Christ is God."

    Too facile° then thou didst not much gainsay,   *permissive*
    Nay, didst permit, approve, and fair dismiss.
1160   Hadst thou been firm and fixt in thy dissent,
    Neither had I transgress'd, nor thou with mee.
      To whom then first incenst Adam repli'd.
    Is this the Love, is this the recompense
    Of mine to thee, ingrateful *Eve*, express't
1165   Immutable° when thou wert lost, not I,   *unchangeable*
    Who might have liv'd and joy'd immortal bliss,
    Yet willingly chose rather Death with thee:
    And am I now upbraided, as the cause
    Of thy transgressing? not enough severe,
1170   It seems, in thy restraint: what could I more?
    I warn'd thee, I admonish'd thee, foretold
    The danger, and the lurking Enemy
    That lay in wait; beyond this had been force,
    And force upon free Will hath here no place.
1175   But confidence then bore thee on, secure
    Either to meet no danger, or to find
    Matter of glorious trial; and perhaps
    I also err'd in overmuch admiring
    What seem'd in thee so perfet, that I thought
1180   No evil durst attempt thee, but I rue
    That error now, which is become my crime,
    And thou th' accuser. Thus it shall befall
    Him who to worth in Woman overtrusting
    Lets her Will rule; restraint she will not brook,
1185   And left to herself, if evil thence ensue,
    Shee first his weak indulgence will accuse.
      Thus they in mutual accusation spent
    The fruitless hours, but neither self-condemning,
    And of thir vain contést appear'd no end.
         The End of the Ninth Book.

from Book 10

The Argument

Man's *transgression known, the Guardian Angels forsake Paradise, and return up to Heaven to approve thir vigilance, and are approv'd, God declaring that the entrance of Satan could not be by them prevented. He sends his Son to judge the Transgressors, who descends and gives Sentence accordingly; then in pity clothes them both, and reascends.* Sin and Death *sitting till then at the Gates of Hell, by wondrous sympathy feeling the success of* Satan *in this new World, and the sin by Man there committed, resolve to sit no longer confin'd in Hell, but to follow* Satan *thir Sire up to the place of Man: To make the way easier from Hell to this World to and fro, they pave a broad Highway or Bridge over Chaos, according to the Track that Satan first made; then preparing for Earth, they meet him proud of his success returning to Hell; thir mutual gratulation. Satan arrives at Pandemonium, in full assembly relates with boasting his success against Man; instead of applause is entertained with a general hiss by all his audience, transform'd with himself also suddenly into*

Serpents, according to his doom giv'n in Paradise; then deluded with a show of the forbidden Tree springing up before them, they greedily reaching to take of the Fruit, chew dust and bitter ashes. The proceedings of Sin *and* Death; *God foretells the final Victory of his Son over them, and the renewing of all things; but for the present commands his Angels to make several alterations in the Heavens and Elements.* Adam *more and more perceiving his fall'n condition heavily bewails, rejects the condolement of* Eve; *she persists and at length appeases him: then to evade the Curse likely to fall on thir Offspring, proposes to* Adam *violent ways, which he approves not, but conceiving better hope, puts her in mind of the late Promise made them, that her Seed should be reveng'd on the Serpent, and exhorts her with him to seek Peace of the offended Deity, by repentance and supplication.*

      Meanwhile the heinous and despiteful act
      Of *Satan* done in Paradise, and how
      Hee in the Serpent had perverted *Eve,*
      Her Husband shee, to taste the fatal fruit,
5   Was known in Heav'n;[1] for what can scape the Eye
      Of God All-seeing, or deceive his Heart
      Omniscient, who in all things wise and just,
      Hinder'd not *Satan* to attempt the mind
      Of Man, with strength entire, and free will arm'd,
10   Complete to have discover'd and repulst
      Whatever wiles of Foe or seeming Friend.
      For still they knew, and ought to have still remember'd
      The high Injunction not to taste that Fruit,
      Whoever tempted; which they not obeying,
15   Incurr'd, what could they less, the penalty,
      And manifold[2] in sin, deserv'd to fall.
      Up into Heav'n from Paradise in haste
      Th' Angelic Guards ascended, mute and sad
      For Man, for of his state by this they knew,
20   Much wond'ring how the subtle Fiend had stol'n
      Entrance unseen. Soon as th' unwelcome news
      From Earth arriv'd at Heaven Gate, displeas'd
      All were who heard, dim sadness did not spare
      That time Celestial visages, yet mixt
25   With pity, violated not thir bliss.
      About the new-arriv'd, in multitudes
      Th' ethereal People ran, to hear and know
      How all befell: they towards the Throne Supreme
      Accountable made haste to make appear
30   With righteous plea, thir utmost vigilance,
      And easily approv'd; when the most High
      Eternal Father from his secret Cloud,
      Amidst in Thunder utter'd thus his voice.
      Assembl'd Angels, and ye Powers return'd

---

1. Rhetorically, lines 1–16 function both as *principium,* stating the subject of the book, and as *initium,* introducing the first scene. They also sum up the theological content of Book 3, which will receive specific application in the present book, in the exchanges between the Father and the Son (lines 34–84) and between the Son and

Adam (lines 124ff.). Note the structural symmetry whereby the divine decrees of the third book are balanced by those of the third from the end.
2. Multiplied; alluding to Psalms 38.19: "they that hate me wrongfully are multiplied."

35   From unsuccessful charge, be not dismay'd,
      Nor troubl'd at these tidings from the Earth,
      Which your sincerest care could not prevent,
      Foretold so lately what would come to pass,
      When first this Tempter cross'd the Gulf from Hell.
40   I told ye then he should prevail and speed°   succeed
      On his bad Errand, Man should be seduc't
      And flatter'd out of all, believing lies
      Against his Maker; no Decree of mine
      Concurring to necessitate his Fall,
45   Or touch with lightest moment of impulse
      His free Will, to her own inclining left
      In even scale.³ But fall'n he is, and now
      What rests, but that the mortal Sentence pass
      On his transgression. Death denounc't that day,
50   Which he presumes already vain and void,
      Because not yet inflicted, as he fear'd,
      By some immediate stroke; but soon shall find
      Forbearance no acquittance ere day end.
      Justice shall not return as bounty scorn'd.
55   But whom send I to judge them? whom but thee
      Vicegerent Son, to thee I have transferr'd
      All Judgment, whether in Heav'n, or Earth, or Hell.
      Easy it may be seen that I intend
      Mercy colleague with Justice, sending thee
60   Man's Friend, his Mediator, his design'd
      Both Ransom and Redeemer voluntary,
      And destin'd Man himself to judge Man fall'n.⁴
         So spake the Father, and unfolding bright
      Toward the right hand his Glory, on the Son
65   Blaz'd forth unclouded Deity; he full
      Resplendent all his Father manifest
      Express'd, and thus divinely answer'd mild.
         Father Eternal, thine is to decree,
      Mine both in Heav'n and Earth to do thy will
70   Supreme, that thou in mee thy Son belov'd
      May'st ever rest well pleas'd.⁵ I go to judge
      On Earth these thy transgressors, but thou know'st,
      Whoever judg'd, the worst on mee must light,
      When time shall be, for so I undertook
75   Before thee; and not repenting, this obtain
      Of right, that I may mitigate thir doom
      On me deriv'd, yet I shall temper so
      Justice with Mercy, as may illustrate most
      Them fully satisfied, and thee appease.
80   Attendance none shall need, nor Train, where none

---

3. "Moment" is a term applied to the smallest increment
that could affect the equilibrium of a balance. If man had
been protected from the tempter, then there would have
been real interference with the free action of the scales of
justice.

4. The double syntax—line 62 can be read as either
"himself a man, destined to judge man" (primary) or "destined to judge man himself, man fallen"—mimes the
close identification of Christ with humanity.
5. Echoing Matthew 3.17.

Are to behold the Judgment, but the judg'd,
Those two; the third[6] best absent is condemn'd,
Convict° by flight, and Rebel to all Law: *convicted*
Conviction to the Serpent none belongs.[7]
85   Thus saying, from his radiant Seat he rose
Of high collateral° glory: him Thrones and Powers, *side by side*
Princedoms, and Dominations ministrant
Accompanied to Heaven Gate, from whence
Eden and all the Coast in prospect lay.
90   Down he descended straight; the speed of Gods
Time counts not, though with swiftest minutes wing'd.
Now was the Sun in Western cadence° low[8] *falling*
From Noon, and gentle Airs due at thir hour
To fan the Earth now wak'd, and usher in
95   The Ev'ning cool, when he from wrath more cool
Came the mild Judge and Intercessor both
To sentence Man: the voice of God they heard
Now walking in the Garden, by soft winds
Brought to thir Ears, while day declin'd, they heard,
100   And from his presence hid themselves among
The thickest Trees, both Man and Wife, till God
Approaching, thus to Adam call'd aloud.
    Where art thou *Adam*, wont with joy to meet
My coming seen far off? I miss thee here,
105   Not pleas'd, thus entertain'd with solitude,
Where obvious duty erewhile appear'd unsought:
Or come I less conspicuous, or what change
Absents thee, or what chance detains? Come forth.
He came, and with him *Eve*, more loath, though first
110   To offend, discount'nanc't both, and discompos'd;
Love was not in thir looks, either to God
Or to each other, but apparent guilt,
And shame, and perturbation, and despair,
Anger, and obstinacy, and hate, and guile.
115   Whence *Adam* falt'ring long, thus answer'd brief.
    I heard thee in the Garden, and of thy voice
Afraid, being naked, hid myself. To whom
The gracious Judge without revile repli'd.
    My voice thou oft hast heard, and hast not fear'd,
120   But still rejoic't, how is it now become
So dreadful to thee? that thou art naked, who
Hath told thee? hast thou eaten of the Tree
Whereof I gave thee charge thou shouldst not eat?
    To whom thus *Adam* sore beset repli'd.
125   O Heav'n! in evil strait this day I stand
Before my Judge, either to undergo
Myself the total Crime, or to accuse

---

6. Satan.
7. "Conviction" has both the legal sense (proof of guilt) and
the theological (the condition of being convinced of sin).
8. Lines 92–123 follow Genesis 3.8–11.

My other self, the partner of my life;
Whose failing, while her Faith to me remains,
130   I should conceal, and not expose to blame
By my complaint; but strict necessity
Subdues me, and calamitous constraint,
Lest on my head both sin and punishment,
However insupportable, be all
135   Devolv'd;[9] though should I hold my peace, yet thou
Wouldst easily detect what I conceal.
This Woman whom thou mad'st to be my help,
And gav'st me as thy perfet gift, so good,
So fit, so acceptable, so Divine,
140   That from her hand I could suspect no ill,
And what she did, whatever in itself,
Her doing seem'd to justify the deed;
Shee gave me of the Tree, and I did eat.[1]
   To whom the sovran Presence thus repli'd.
145   Was shee thy God, that her thou didst obey
Before his voice, or was shee made thy guide,
Superior, or but equal, that to her
Thou didst resign thy Manhood, and the Place
Wherein God set thee above her made of thee,
150   And for thee, whose perfection far excell'd
Hers in all real° dignity:[2] Adorn'd   *regal*
She was indeed, and lovely to attract
Thy Love, not thy Subjection, and her Gifts
Were such as under Government well seem'd,
155   Unseemly to bear rule, which was thy part°   *role*
And person,° hadst thou known thyself aright.   *character*
   So having said, he thus to Eve in few:
Say Woman, what is this which thou hast done?
   To whom sad *Eve* with shame nigh overwhelm'd,
160   Confessing soon, yet not before her Judge
Bold or loquacious, thus abasht repli'd.
   The Serpent me beguil'd and I did eat.[3]
   Which when the Lord God heard, without delay
To Judgment he proceeded on th' accus'd
165   Serpent though brute, unable to transfer
The Guilt on him who made him instrument
Of mischief, and polluted from the end
Of his Creation; justly then accurst,
As vitiated in Nature: more to know
170   Concern'd not Man (since he no further knew)
Nor alter'd his offense; yet God at last
To Satan first in sin his doom appli'd,
Though in mysterious° terms, judg'd as then best: *mystical*
And on the Serpent thus his curse let fall.

---

9. Caused to fall upon.
1. See Genesis 3.12.
2. See 1 Corinthians 11.8ff.: "For the man is not of the

woman; but the woman of the man. Neither was the man
created for the woman; but the woman for the man."
3. Repeating Genesis 3.13.

175   Because thou hast done this, thou art accurst
Above all Cattle, each Beast of the Field;
Upon thy Belly groveling thou shalt go,
And dust shalt eat all the days of thy Life.
Between Thee and the Woman I will put
180   Enmity, and between thine and her Seed;
Her Seed shall bruise thy head, thou bruise his heel.[4]
    So spake this Oracle, then verifi'd
When *Jesus* son of *Mary* second *Eve*,
Saw Satan fall like Lightning down from Heav'n,[5]
185   Prince of the Air; then rising from his Grave
Spoil'd Principalities and Powers, triumpht
In open show, and with ascension bright
Captivity led captive through the Air,[6]
The Realm itself of Satan long usurpt,
190   Whom he shall tread at last under our feet;[7]
Ev'n hee who now foretold his fatal bruise,
And to the Woman thus his Sentence turn'd.
    Thy sorrow I will greatly multiply
By thy Conception; Children thou shalt bring
195   In sorrow forth, and to thy Husband's will
Thine shall submit, hee over thee shall rule.
    On *Adam* last thus judgment he pronounc'd.
Because thou hast heark'n'd to the voice of thy Wife,
And eaten of the Tree concerning which
200   I charg'd thee, saying: Thou shalt not eat thereof,
Curs'd is the ground for thy sake, thou in sorrow
Shalt eat thereof all the days of thy Life;[8]
Thorns also and Thistles it shall bring thee forth
Unbid, and thou shalt eat th' Herb of the Field,
205   In the sweat of thy Face shalt thou eat Bread,
Till thou return unto the ground, for thou
Out of the ground wast taken, know thy Birth,
For dust thou art, and shalt to dust return.[9]
    So judg'd he Man, both Judge and Savior sent,
210   And th' instant stroke of Death denounc't that day
Remov'd far off;[1] then pitying how they stood
Before him naked to the air, that now
Must suffer change, disdain'd not to begin
Thenceforth the form of servant to assume,[2]
215   As when he wash'd his servants' feet, so now
As Father of his Family he clad
Thir nakedness with Skins of Beasts, or slain,
Or as the Snake with youthful Coat repaid;

4. See Genesis 3.14ff.
5. "I beheld Satan as lightning fall from heaven" (Luke 10.18).
6. Psalms 68.18: "Thou hast ascended on high, thou hast led captivity captive:" applied to Christ in Ephesians 4.8.
7. See Romans 16.20: "And the God of peace shall bruise Satan under your feet shortly."
8. See Genesis 3.17.
9. See Genesis 3.18–19.
1. Christ removes the fear that physical death will follow the eating of the fruit on the same day.
2. See Philippians 2.7: "made himself of no reputation, and took upon him the form of a servant, and was made in the likeness of men."

And thought not much to clothe his Enemies:
220 Nor hee thir outward only with the Skins
Of Beasts, but inward nakedness, much more
Opprobrious, with his Robe of righteousness,
Arraying cover'd from his Father's sight.
To him with swift ascent he up return'd,
225 Into his blissful bosom reassum'd
In glory as of old, to him appeas'd
All, though all-knowing, what had past with Man
Recounted, mixing intercession sweet.[3]

*   *   *

Th' other way *Satan* went down
415 The Causey° to Hell Gate; on either side   causeway
Disparted *Chaos* over-built exclaim'd,
And with rebounding surge the bars assail'd,
That scorn'd his indignation: through the Gate,
Wide open and unguarded, *Satan* pass'd,
420 And all about found desolate; for those
Appointed to sit there,[4] had left thir charge,
Flown to the upper World; the rest were all
Far to th'inland retir'd, about the walls
Of *Pandaemonium,* City and proud seat
425 Of *Lucifer,* so by allusion call'd,
Of that bright Star to *Satan* paragon'd.°   compared
There kept thir Watch the Legions, while the Grand
In Council sat, solicitous° what chance   anxious
Might intercept thir Emperor sent, so hee
430 Departing gave command, and they observ'd.
As when the Tartar from his *Russian* Foe
By *Astracan*[5] over the Snowy Plains
Retires, or *Bactrian* Sophi[6] from the horns
Of *Turkish* Crescent,[7] leaves all waste beyond
435 The Realm of *Aladule,*[8] in his retreat
To *Tauris* or *Casbeen:*[9] So these the late
Heav'n-banisht Host, left desert utmost Hell
Many a dark League, reduc't in careful Watch
Round thir Metropolis, and now expecting
440 Each hour their great adventurer from the search
Of Foreign Worlds: he through the midst unmark't,
In show Plebeian Angel militant
Of lowest order, pass't; and from the door
Of that *Plutonian*[1] Hall, invisible
445 Ascended his high Throne, which under state°   canopy
Of richest texture spread, at th' upper end

3. Sin and Death now pave a highway across Chaos from Hell to earth. Satan meets them and sends them on to dwell on earth; he heads home to Hell.
4. Sin and Death.
5. Astracan, or Astrakhan, was a Tartar kingdom and capital city near the mouth of the Volga.
6. Persian king.

7. Refers not only to the Turkish ensign, but also to their battle formations.
8. Greater Armenia.
9. Tauris (modern Tabriz) is in the extreme northwest of Persia; Casbeen, or Kazvin, is north of Teheran.
1. Pertaining to Pluto, ruler of the classical underworld.

Was plac't in regal lustre. Down a while
He sat, and round about him saw unseen:
At last as from a Cloud his fulgent head
450 And shape Star-bright appear'd, or brighter, clad
With what permissive glory since his fall
Was left him, or false glitter: All amaz'd
At that so sudden blaze the Stygian throng
Bent thir aspect, and whom they wish'd beheld,
455 Thir mighty Chief return'd: loud was th' acclaim:
Forth rush'd in haste the great consulting Peers,
Rais'd from thir dark *Divan*,² and with like joy
Congratulant approach'd him, who with hand
Silence, and with these words attention won.
460   Thrones, Dominations, Princedoms, Virtues, Powers,
For in possession such, not only of right,
I call ye and declare ye now, return'd
Successful beyond hope, to lead ye forth
Triumphant out of this infernal Pit
465 Abominable, accurst, the house of woe,
And Dungeon of our Tyrant: Now possess,
As Lords, a spacious World, to our native Heaven
Little inferior, by my adventure hard
With peril great achiev'd. Long were to tell
470 What I have done, what suffer'd, with what pain
Voyag'd th' unreal, vast, unbounded deep
Of horrible confusion, over which
By Sin and Death a broad way now is pav'd
To expedite your glorious march; but I
475 Toil'd out my úncouth° passage, forc't to ride   *strange*
Th' untractable Abyss, plung'd in the womb
Of unoriginal° *Night* and *Chaos* wild,   *uncreated*
That jealous of thir secrets fiercely oppos'd
My journey strange, with clamorous uproar
480 Protesting Fate supreme; thence how I found
The new created World, which fame in Heav'n
Long had foretold, a Fabric wonderful
Of absolute perfection, therein Man
Plac't in a Paradise, by our exile
485 Made happy: Him by fraud I have seduc'd
From his Creator, and the more to increase
Your wonder, with an Apple; he thereat
Offended, worth your laughter, hath giv'n up
Both his beloved Man and all his World,
490 To Sin and Death a prey, and so to us,
Without our hazard, labor, or alarm,
To range in, and to dwell, and over Man
To rule, as over all he should have rul'd.
True is, mee also he hath judg'd, or rather
495 Mee not, but the brute Serpent in whose shape

2. Turkish council of state.

Man I deceiv'd: that which to mee belongs,
Is enmity, which he will put between
Mee and Mankind; I am to bruise his heel;
His Seed, when is not set, shall bruise my head:
500 A World who would not purchase with a bruise,
Or much more grievous pain? Ye have th' account
Of my performance: What remains, ye Gods,
But up and enter now into full bliss.
    So having said, a while he stood, expecting
505 Thir universal shout and high applause
To fill his ear, when contrary he hears
On all sides, from innumerable tongues
A dismal universal hiss, the sound
Of public scorn; he wonder'd, but not long
510 Had leisure, wond'ring at himself now more;
His Visage drawn he felt to sharp and spare,
His Arms clung to his Ribs, his Legs entwining
Each other, till supplanted° down he fell   *tripped*
A monstrous Serpent on his Belly prone,[3]
515 Reluctant,° but in vain: a greater power   *resisting*
Now rul'd him, punisht in the shape he sinn'd,
According to his doom: he would have spoke,
But hiss for hiss return'd with forked tongue
To forked tongue, for now were all transform'd
520 Alike, to Serpents all as accessories
To his bold Riot: dreadful was the din
Of hissing through the Hall, thick swarming now
With complicated° monsters, head and tail,   *compound*
Scorpion and Asp, and *Amphisbaena* dire,
525 *Cerastes* horn'd, *Hydrus*, and *Ellops* drear,
And *Dipsas*[4] (not so thick swarm'd once the Soil
Bedropt with blood of *Gorgon*, or the Isle
Ophiusa) but still greatest hee the midst,[5]
Now Dragon grown, larger than whom the Sun
530 Ingender'd in the *Pythian* Vale on slime,
Huge *Python*, and his Power no less he seem'd
Above the rest still to retain;[6] they all
Him follow'd issuing forth to th' open Field,
Where all yet left of that revolted Rout
535 Heav'n-fall'n, in station stood or just array,
Sublime° with expectation when to see   *uplifted*
In Triumph issuing forth thir glorious Chief;

---

3. See the metamorphosis of Cadmus in Ovid, *Metamorphoses* 4.572–603, and the mutual interchange of serpentine forms in Dante's canto of the thieves, *Inferno* 25.
4. The amphisbaena is a serpent with a head at either end. The cerastes has four horns on its head. The hydrus is a water snake. The ellops, though sometimes identified as the swordfish, is mentioned as a serpent in Pliny, *Natural History* 32.5. The dipsas causes raging thirst by its bite.
5. When Perseus was bringing back the severed head of

Medusa, drops of blood fell to earth and became serpents. "Ophiusa" means literally "full of serpents"; a name anciently given to several islands, including Rhodes and one of the Balearic group.
6. For the birth of Python from the slime remaining after the flood, see Ovid, *Metamorphoses* 1.438–40. Python was slain by Apollo. Satan's dragon shape is that of the "old dragon" of Christian apocalypse; see Revelation 12.9: "the great dragon was cast out, that old serpent, called the Devil, and Satan."

They saw, but other sight instead, a crowd
Of ugly Serpents; horror on them fell,
540 And horrid sympathy; for what they saw,
They felt themselves now changing; down thir arms,
Down fell both Spear and Shield, down they as fast,
And the dire hiss renew'd, and the dire form
Catcht by Contagion, like in punishment,
545 As in thir crime. Thus was th' applause they meant,
Turn'd to exploding hiss, triumph to shame
Cast on themselves from thir own mouths. There stood
A Grove hard by, sprung up with this thir change,
His will who reigns above, to aggravate
550 Thir penance, laden with fair Fruit, like that
Which grew in Paradise, the bait of *Eve*
Us'd by the Tempter: on that prospect strange
Thir earnest eyes they fix'd, imagining
For one forbidden Tree a multitude
555 Now ris'n, to work them furder° woe or shame;   *further*
Yet parcht with scalding thirst and hunger fierce,
Though to delude them sent, could not abstain,
But on they roll'd in heaps, and up the Trees
Climbing, sat thicker than the snaky locks
560 That curl'd *Megaera*:[7] greedily they pluck'd
The Fruitage fair to sight, like that which grew
Near that bituminous Lake where *Sodom* flam'd;[8]
This more delusive, not the touch, but taste
Deceiv'd; they fondly thinking to allay
565 Thir appetite with gust,° instead of Fruit   *taste*
Chew'd bitter Ashes, which th' offended taste
With spattering noise rejected: oft they assay'd,
Hunger and thirst constraining, drugg'd° as oft,   *nauseated*
With hatefullest disrelish writh'd thir jaws
570 With soot and cinders fill'd; so oft they fell
Into the same illusion, not as Man
Whom they triumph'd, once lapst. Thus were they plagu'd
And worn with Famine long, and ceaseless hiss,
Till thir lost shape, permitted, they resum'd,
575 Yearly enjoin'd, some say, to undergo
This annual humbling certain number'd days,
To dash thir pride, and joy for Man seduc't.
However some tradition they dispers'd
Among the Heathen of thir purchase got,
580 And Fabl'd how the Serpent, whom they call'd
Ophion with *Eurynome*, the wide-
Encroaching *Eve* perhaps, had first the rule
Of high *Olympus*, thence by Saturn driv'n
And Ops, ere yet *Dictaean Jove* was born.[9]

7. One of the Furies, often described as snaky-haired.
8. The allusion is to Josephus, *Wars* 4.8.4, where it is said that traces still remain of the divine fire that burnt Sodom, such as tasty-looking fruits that turned to ashes when plucked.

9. Ophion and Eurynome ruled Olympus until the one yielded to Cronos (Saturn) and the other to Rhea (Ops). Their two successors then ruled the Titans, while Zeus lived in the Dictaean cave. See Apollonius Rhodius, *Argonautica* 1.503–9.

585   Meanwhile in Paradise the hellish pair
         Too soon arriv'd, *Sin* there in power before,
         Once actual, now in body, and to dwell
         Habitual habitant; behind her *Death*
         Close following pace for pace, not mounted yet
590   On his pale Horse:[1] to whom *Sin* thus began.
              Second of *Satan* sprung, all conquering *Death*,
         What think'st thou of our Empire now, though earn'd
         With travail difficult, not better far
         Than still at Hell's dark threshold to have sat watch,
595   Unnam'd, undreaded, and thyself half starv'd?
              Whom thus the Sin-born Monster answer'd soon.
         To mee, who with eternal Famine pine,
         Alike is Hell, or Paradise, or Heaven,
         There best, where most with ravin I may meet;
600   Which here, though plenteous, all too little seems
         To stuff this Maw, this vast unhide-bound Corpse.
              To whom th' incestuous Mother thus repli'd.
         Thou therefore on these Herbs, and Fruits, and Flow'rs
         Feed first, on each Beast next, and Fish, and Fowl,
605   No homely morsels, and whatever thing
         The Scythe of Time mows down, devour unspar'd,
         Till I in Man residing through the Race,
         His thoughts, his looks, words, actions all infect,
         And season him thy last and sweetest prey.
610   This said, they both betook them several ways,
         Both to destroy, or unimmortal make
         All kinds, and for destruction to mature
         Sooner or later; which th' Almighty seeing
         From his transcendent Seat the Saints among,
615   To those bright Orders utter'd thus his voice.
              See with what heat these Dogs of Hell advance
         To waste and havoc° yonder World, which I   *devastate*
         So fair and good created, and had still
         Kept in that state, had not the folly of Man
620   Let in these wasteful Furies, who impute
         Folly to mee, so doth the Prince of Hell
         And his Adherents, that with so much ease
         I suffer them to enter and possess
         A place so heav'nly, and conniving seem
625   To gratify my scornful Enemies,
         That laugh, as if transported with some fit
         Of Passion, I to them had quitted° all,   *yielded*
         At random yielded up to their misrule;
         And know not that I call'd and drew them thither
630   My Hell-hounds, to lick up the draff° and filth   *refuse*
         Which man's polluting Sin with taint hath shed
         On what was pure, till cramm'd and gorg'd, nigh burst
         With suckt and glutted offal, at one sling

1. See Revelation 6.8: "I looked, and behold a pale horse: and his name that sat on him was Death, and Hell followed with him."

Of thy victorious Arm, well-pleasing Son,
635   Both *Sin*, and *Death*, and yawning *Grave* at last
Through *Chaos* hurl'd, obstruct the mouth of Hell
For ever, and seal up his ravenous Jaws.
Then Heav'n and Earth renew'd shall be made pure
To sanctity that shall receive no stain:
640   Till then the Curse pronounc't on both precedes.[2]

* * *

Thus began
Outrage from lifeless things; but Discord first
Daughter of Sin, among th' irrational,
Death introduc'd through fierce antipathy:
710   Beast now with Beast gan war, and Fowl with Fowl,
And Fish with Fish; to graze the Herb all leaving,
Devour'd each other; nor stood much in awe
Of Man, but fled him, or with count'nance grim
Glar'd on him passing: these were from without
715   The growing miseries, which *Adam* saw
Already in part, though hid in gloomiest shade,
To sorrow abandon'd, but worse felt within,
And in a troubl'd Sea of passion tost,
Thus to disburd'n sought with sad complaint.
720   O miserable of happy! is this the end
Of this new glorious World, and mee so late
The Glory of that Glory, who now become
Accurst of blessed, hide me from the face
Of God, whom to behold was then my highth
725   Of happiness: yet well, if here would end
The misery, I deserv'd it, and would
My own deservings; but this will not serve;
All that I eat or drink, or shall beget,
Is propagated curse.[3] O voice once heard
730   Delightfully, *Increase and multiply*,[4]
Now death to hear! for what can I increase
Or multiply, but curses on my head?
Who of all Ages to succeed, but feeling
The evil on him brought by me, will curse
735   My Head; Ill fare our Ancestor impure,
For this we may thank *Adam*; but his thanks
Shall be the execration; so besides
Mine own that bide upon me, all from mee
Shall with a fierce reflux on mee redound,°   *overflow, come back*
740   On mee as on thir natural centre light
Heavy, though in thir place. O fleeting joys
Of Paradise, dear bought with lasting woes!

---

2. See Genesis 3.17: "Cursed is the ground for thy sake."
God next commands the angels to make the earth turn
on its axis and so cause the change of seasons, and to disrupt the order of the planets, making their effect on the
world negative as well as positive.
3. Handed down from one generation to another. Food

prolongs life and thus extends the curse, while begetting
children hands it on. Note also that eating and sex are
jointly the concerns of the concupiscible faculty, which
was often regarded as the special field of operation of concupiscence or the "body of sin."
4. See Genesis 1.28.

Did I request thee, Maker, from my Clay
To mould me Man, did I solicit thee
745   From darkness to promote me, or here place
In this delicious Garden? as my Will
Concurr'd not to my being, it were but right
And equal° to reduce me to my dust,   *just*
Desirous to resign, and render back
750   All I receiv'd, unable to perform
Thy terms too hard, by which I was to hold
The good I sought not. To the loss of that,
Sufficient penalty, why hast thou added
The sense of endless woes? inexplicable
755   Thy Justice seems; yet to say truth, too late
I thus contest; then should have been refus'd
Those terms whatever, when they were propos'd:
Thou didst accept them; wilt thou enjoy the good,
Then cavil the conditions? and though God
760   Made thee without thy leave, what if thy Son
Prove disobedient, and reprov'd, retort,
Wherefore didst thou beget me? I sought it not:
Wouldst thou admit for his contempt of thee
That proud excuse? yet him not thy election,°   *choice*
765   But Natural necessity begot.
God made thee of choice his own, and of his own
To serve him, thy reward was of his grace,
Thy punishment then justly is at his Will.
Be it so, for I submit, his doom° is fair,   *judgment*
770   That dust I am, and shall to dust return:[5]
O welcome hour whenever! why delays
His hand to execute what his Decree
Fix'd on this day? why do I overlive,
Why am I mockt with death, and length'n'd out
775   To deathless pain? How gladly would I meet
Mortality my sentence, and be Earth
Insensible, how glad would lay me down
As in my Mother's lap![6] There I should rest
And sleep secure; his dreadful voice no more
780   Would Thunder in my ears, no fear of worse
To mee and to my offspring would torment me
With cruel expectation. Yet one doubt
Pursues me still, lest all I cannot die,
Lest that pure breath of Life, the Spirit of Man
785   Which God inspir'd, cannot together perish
With this corporeal Clod; then in the Grave,
Or in some other dismal place, who knows
But I shall die a living Death? O thought
Horrid, if true! yet why? it was but breath
790   Of Life that sinn'd; what dies but what had life
And sin? the Body properly hath neither.

---

5. Alluding to Genesis 3.19.   6. Adam's lament echoes Job 3.

All of me then shall die:[7] let this appease
The doubt, since human reach no further knows.
For though the Lord of all be infinite,
795　　Is his wrath also? be it, Man is not so,
But mortal doom'd. How can he exercise
Wrath without end on Man whom Death must end?
Can he make deathless Death? that were to make
Strange contradiction, which to God himself
800　　Impossible is held, as Argument
Of weakness, not of Power. Will he draw out,
For anger's sake, finite to infinite
In punish Man, to satisfy his rigor
Satisfi'd never; that were to extend
805　　His Sentence beyond dust and Nature's Law,
By which all Causes else according still
To the reception of thir matter act,
Not to th' extent of thir own Sphere.[8] But say
That Death be not one stroke, as I suppos'd,
810　　Bereaving sense, but endless misery
From this day onward, which I feel begun
Both in me, and without me, and so last
To perpetuity; Ay me, that fear
Comes thund'ring back with dreadful revolution
815　　On my defenseless head; both Death and I
Am found Eternal, and incorporate° both,　　　　　　*united, embodied*
Nor I on my part single, in mee all
Posterity stands curst:[9] Fair Patrimony
That I must leave ye, Sons; O were I able
820　　To waste it all myself, and leave ye none!
So disinherited how would ye bless
Me now your Curse! Ah, why should all mankind
For one man's fault thus guiltless be condemn'd,
If guiltless? But from me what can proceed,
825　　But all corrupt, both Mind and Will deprav'd,
Not to do only, but to will the same
With me? how can they then acquitted stand
In sight of God? Him after all Disputes
Forc't I absolve: all my evasions vain
830　　And reasonings, though through Mazes, lead me still
But to my own conviction:[1] first and last
On mee, mee only, as the source and spring
Of all corruption, all the blame lights due;

---

7. Adam's question is like Milton's in *De doctrina* 1.13: "What could be more absurd than that the mind, which is the part principally offending, should escape the threatened death; and that the body alone, to which immortality was equally allotted, before death came into the world by sin, should pay the penalty of sin by undergoing death, though not implicated in the transgression?" Milton's belief in the joint extinction and joint resurrection of man's body and mind was not an eccentric heresy but good biblical theology.
8. Adam tries to comfort himself with an argument drawn

from medieval philosophy. Here Adam means that God would be going beyond a natural law, that any agent acts according to the powers of what receives its action, not according to its own powers.
9. Not only are Death and I double, two in one, but so also am I, since I am both myself and my descendants.
1. Adam at last reaches full conviction of his sin, but being unable yet to pass to contrition, the next stage of repentance, he falls instead into despair. The present passage should be compared with Satan's similar fall into conscience-stricken despair at 4.86–113.

So might the wrath. Fond wish! couldst thou support
835   That burden heavier than the Earth to bear,
Than all the World much heavier, though divided
With that bad Woman? Thus what thou desir'st,
And what thou fear'st, alike destroys all hope
Of refuge, and concludes thee miserable
840   Beyond all past example and futúre,
To *Satan* only like both crime and doom.
O Conscience, into what Abyss of fears
And horrors hast thou driv'n me; out of which
I find no way, from deep to deeper plung'd!
845   Thus *Adam* to himself lamented loud
Through the still Night, not now, as ere man fell,
Wholesome and cool and mild, but with black Air
Accompanied, with damps and dreadful gloom,
Which to his evil Conscience represented
850   All things with double terror: On the ground
Outstretcht he lay, on the cold ground, and oft
Curs'd his Creation, Death as oft accus'd
Of tardy execution, since denounc't
The day of his offense. Why comes not Death,
855   Said he, with one thrice àcceptable stroke
To end me? Shall Truth fail to keep her word,
Justice Divine not hast'n to be just?
But Death comes not at call, Justice Divine
Mends not her slowest pace for prayers or cries.
860   O Woods, O Fountains, Hillocks, Dales and Bow'rs,
With other echo late I taught your Shades
To answer, and resound far other Song.
Whom thus afflicted when sad Eve beheld,
Desolate where she sat, approaching nigh,
865   Soft words to his fierce passion she assay'd:
But her with stern regard he thus repell'd.
     Out of my sight, thou Serpent, that name best
Befits thee with him leagu'd, thyself as false
And hateful; nothing wants, but that thy shape,
870   Like his, and color Serpentine may show
Thy inward fraud, to warn all Creatures from thee
Henceforth; lest that too heav'nly form, pretended[2]
To hellish falsehood, snare them. But for thee
I had persisted happy, had not thy pride
875   And wand'ring vanity, when least was safe,
Rejected my forewarning, and disdain'd
Not to be trusted, longing to be seen
Though by the Devil himself, him overweening
To over-reach, but with the Serpent meeting
880   Fool'd and beguil'd, by him thou, I by thee,
To trust thee from my side, imagin'd wise,
Constant, mature, proof against all assaults,

---

2. Stretched in front as a covering serving as a mask.

And understood not all was but a show
Rather than solid virtue, all but a Rib
885   Crooked by nature, bent, as now appears,
More to the part siníster[3] from me drawn,
Well if thrown out, as supernumerary
To my just number found. O why did God,
Creator wise, that peopl'd highest Heav'n
890   With Spirits Masculine, create at last
This novelty on Earth, this fair defect
Of Nature, and not fill the World at once
With Men as Angels without Feminine,
Or find some other way to generate
895   Mankind?[4] this mischief had not then befall'n,
And more that shall befall, innumerable
Disturbances on Earth through Female snares,
And strait conjunction with this Sex: for either
He never shall find out fit Mate, but such
900   As some misfortune brings him, or mistake,
Or whom he wishes most shall seldom gain
Through her perverseness, but shall see her gain'd
By a far worse, or if she love, withheld
By Parents, or his happiest choice too late
905   Shall meet, already linkt and Wedlock-bound
To a fell° Adversary, his hate or shame: *bitter*
Which infinite calamity shall cause
To Human life, and household peace confound.
        He added not, and from her turn'd, but *Eve*
910   Not so repulst, with Tears that ceas'd not flowing,
And tresses all disorder'd, at his feet
Fell humble, and imbracing them, besought
His peace, and thus proceeded in her plaint.
        Forsake me not thus, *Adam*, witness Heav'n
915   What love sincere, and reverence in my heart
I bear thee, and unweeting° have offended,   *unintentionally*
Unhappily deceiv'd; thy suppliant
I beg, and clasp thy knees; bereave me not,
Whereon I live, thy gentle looks, thy aid,
920   Thy counsel in this uttermost distress,
My only strength and stay: forlorn of thee,
Whither shall I betake me, where subsist?
While yet we live, scarce one short hour perhaps,
Between us two let there be peace, both joining,
925   As join'd in injuries, one enmity
Against a Foe by doom express assign'd us,
That cruel Serpent: On me exercise not
Thy hatred for this misery befall'n,
On me already lost, mee than thyself

---

3. Left; also corrupt, evil, base. The notion that woman is formed from a bent rib, and therefore crooked, had appeared in tracts like Joseph Swetnam's *The Arraignment of Lewd, Idle, Froward, and Inconstant Women* (page 831).

4. Another ancient piece of antifeminism; see Euripides, *Hippolytus* 616ff. Aristotle had said in the *De generatione* that the female is a defective male.

930 More miserable; both have sinn'd, but thou
Against God only, I against God and thee,
And to the place of judgment will return,
There with my cries importune Heaven, that all
The sentence from thy head remov'd may light
935 On me, sole cause to thee of all this woe,
Mee mee only just object of his ire.
    She ended weeping, and her lowly plight,
Immovable till peace obtain'd from fault
Acknowledg'd and deplor'd,[5] in *Adam* wrought
940 Commiseration; soon his heart relented
Towards her, his life so late and sole delight,
Now at his feet submissive in distress,
Creature so fair his reconcilement seeking,
His counsel whom she had displeas'd, his aid;
945 As one disarm'd, his anger all he lost,
And thus with peaceful words uprais'd her soon.
    Unwary, and too desirous, as before,
So now of what thou know'st not, who desir'st
The punishment all on thyself; alas,
950 Bear thine own first, ill able to sustain
His full wrath whose thou feel'st as yet least part,
And my displeasure bear'st so ill. If Prayers
Could alter high Decrees, I to that place
Would speed before thee, and be louder heard,
955 That on my head all might be visited,
Thy frailty and infirmer Sex forgiv'n,
To me committed and by me expos'd.
But rise, let us no more contend, nor blame
Each other, blam'd enough elsewhere,[6] but strive
960 In offices of Love, how we may light'n
Each other's burden in our share of woe;
Since this day's Death denounc't, if aught I see,
Will prove no sudden, but a slow-pac't evil,
A long day's dying to augment our pain,
965 And to our Seed (O hapless Seed!) deriv'd.
    To whom thus *Eve*, recovering heart, repli'd.
Adam, by sad experiment I know
How little weight my words with thee can find,
Found so erroneous, thence by just event°   *consequence*
970 Found so unfortunate; nevertheless,
Restor'd by thee, vile as I am, to place
Of new acceptance, hopeful to regain
Thy Love, the sole contentment of my heart
Living or dying, from thee I will not hide
975 What thoughts in my unquiet breast are ris'n,
Tending to some relief of our extremes,
Or end, though sharp and sad, yet tolerable,

5. Eve cannot be moved from Adam's feet until he forgives her.

6. Either "heaven" or the "place of judgment" of line 932.

As in our evils, and of easier choice.

If care of our descent° perplex° us most,   *descendants / torment*

980   Which must be born to certain woe, devour'd

By Death at last, and miserable it is

To be to other cause of misery,

Our own begott'n, and of our Loins to bring

Into this cursed World a woeful Race,

985   That after wretched Life must be at last

Food for so foul a Monster, in thy power

It lies, yet ere Conception to prevent

The Race unblest, to being yet unbegot.

Childless thou art, Childless remain: So Death

990   Shall be deceiv'd his glut, and with us two

Be forc'd to satisfy his Rav'nous Maw.

But if thou judge it hard and difficult,

Conversing, looking, loving, to abstain

From Love's due Rites, Nuptial embraces sweet,

995   And with desire to languish without hope,[7]

Before the present object° languishing   *Eve*

With like desire, which would be misery

And torment less than none of what we dread,

Then both ourselves and Seed at once to free

1000   From what we fear for both, let us make short,

Let us seek Death, or he not found, supply

With our own hands his Office on ourselves;

Why stand we longer shivering under fears,

That show no end but Death, and have the power,

1005   Of many ways to die the shortest choosing,

Destruction with destruction to destroy.

     She ended here, or vehement despair

Broke off the rest; so much of Death her thoughts

Had entertain'd, as dy'd her Cheeks with pale.

1010   But *Adam* with such counsel nothing sway'd,

To better hopes his more attentive mind

Laboring had rais'd, and thus to *Eve* replied.

     Eve, thy contempt of life and pleasure seems

To argue in thee something more sublime

1015   And excellent than what thy mind contemns;

But self-destruction therefore sought, refutes

That excellence thought in thee, and implies,

Not thy contempt, but anguish and regret

For loss of life and pleasure overlov'd.

1020   Or if thou covet death, as utmost end

Of misery, so thinking to evade

The penalty pronounc't, doubt not but God

Hath wiselier arm'd his vengeful ire than so

To be forestall'd; much more I fear lest Death

1025   So snatcht will not exempt us from the pain

7. See Dante, *Inferno* 4.42: "without hope we live in desire."

We are by doom to pay; rather such acts
Of contumacy° will provoke the Highest   *contempt*
To make death in us live: Then let us seek
Some safer resolution, which methinks
1030   I have in view, calling to mind with heed
Part of our Sentence, that thy Seed shall bruise
The Serpent's head; piteous amends, unless
Be meant, whom I conjecture, our grand Foe
Satan, who in the Serpent hath contriv'd
1035   Against us this deceit: to crush his head
Would be revenge indeed; which will be lost
By death brought on ourselves, or childless days
Resolv'd, as thou proposest; so our Foe
Shall 'scape his punishment ordain'd, and wee
1040   Instead shall double ours upon our heads.
No more be mention'd then of violence
Against ourselves, and wilful barrenness,
That cuts us off from hope, and savors only
Rancor and pride, impatience and despite,
1045   Reluctance° against God and his just yoke   *resistance*
Laid on our Necks. Remember with what mild
And gracious temper he both heard and judg'd
Without wrath or reviling; wee expected
Immediate dissolution, which we thought
1050   Was meant by Death that day, when lo, to thee
Pains only in Child-bearing were foretold,
And bringing forth, soon recompens't with joy,
Fruit of thy Womb: On mee the Curse aslope
Glanc'd on the ground, with labor I must earn
1055   My bread;[8] what harm? Idleness had been worse;
My labor will sustain me; and lest Cold
Or Heat should injure us, his timely care
Hath unbesought provided, and his hands
Cloth'd us unworthy, pitying while he judg'd;
1060   How much more, if we pray him, will his ear
Be open, and his heart to pity incline,[9]
And teach us further by what means to shun
Th' inclement Seasons, Rain, Ice, Hail and Snow,
Which now the Sky with various Face begins
1065   To show us in this Mountain, while the Winds
Blow moist and keen, shattering the graceful locks
Of these fair spreading Trees; which bids us seek
Some better shroud,° some better warmth to cherish   *shelter*
Our Limbs benumb'd, ere this diurnal Star[1]
1070   Leave cold the Night, how we his gather'd beams
Reflected, may with matter sere foment,[2]

8. Referring to Christ's words at lines 201–5.
9. Biblical diction; see Psalms 24.4, 119.36, 112, and 1
Peter 3.12.
1. The sun.

2. Cherish; but alluding also to Latin *fomes* (tinder).
Adam envisages making fire: focusing the sun's rays onto
dry combustibles ("matter sere") with a parabolic mirror.

Or by collision of two bodies grind
The Air attrite° to Fire, as late the Clouds   *ground down*
Justling° or pusht with Winds rude in thir shock   *jostling*
1075   Tine° the slant Lightning, whose thwart flame driv'n down   *ignite*
Kindles the gummy bark of Fir or Pine,
And sends a comfortable heat from far,
Which might supply° the Sun: such Fire to use,   *take the place of*
And what may else be remedy or cure
1080   To evils which our own misdeeds have wrought,
Hee will instruct us praying, and of Grace
Beseeching him, so as we need not fear
To pass commodiously this life, sustain'd
By him with many comforts, till we end
1085   In dust, our final rest and native home.
What better can we do, than to the place
Repairing where he judg'd us, prostrate fall
Before him reverent, and there confess
Humbly our faults, and pardon beg, with tears
1090   Watering the ground, and with our sighs the Air
Frequenting,° sent from hearts contrite, in sign   *filling*
Of sorrow unfeign'd, and humiliation meek.[3]
Undoubtedly he will relent and turn
From his displeasure; in whose look serene,
1095   When angry most he seem'd and most severe,
What else but favor, grace, and mercy shone?
    So spake our Father penitent, nor Eve
Felt less remorse: they forthwith to the place
Repairing where he judg'd them prostrate fell
1100   Before him reverent, and both confess'd
Humbly thir faults, and pardon begg'd, with tears
Watering the ground, and with thir sighs the Air
Frequenting, sent from hearts contrite, in sign
Of sorrow unfeign'd, and humiliation meek.[4]
The End of the Tenth Book.

from **Book 11**
The Argument

The Son of God present to his Father the Prayers of our first Parents now repenting, and intercedes for them: God accepts them, but declares that they must no longer abide in Paradise; sends Michael with a Band of Cherubim to dispossess them; but first to reveal to Adam future things; Michael's coming down. Adam shows to Eve certain ominous signs; he discerns Michael's approach, goes out to meet him: the Angel denounces thir departure. Eve's Lamentation. Adam pleads, but submits: The Angel leads him up to a high Hill, sets before him in vision what shall happ'n till the Flood.

---

3. Having passed on from conviction of sin Adam, now "contrite" (line 1103), is ready for confession, the third stage of repentance. An allusion to the Penitential Psalm: "The sacrifices of God are a broken spirit: a broken and a contrite heart, O God, thou wilt not despise" (Psalms 51.17).
4. Repeating lines 1086–92, modulated into narrative discourse (only the last two verses remain identical).

from **Book 12**

The Argument

The Angel Michael continues from the Flood to relate what shall succeed; then, in the mention of Abraham, comes by degrees to explain, who that Seed of the Woman shall be, which was promised Adam and Eve in the Fall; his Incarnation, Death, Resurrection, and Ascension; the state of the Church till his second Coming. Adam greatly satisfied and recomforted by these Relations and Promises descends the Hill with Michael; wakens Eve, who all this while had slept, but with gentle dreams compos'd to quietness of mind and submission. Michael in either hand leads them out of Paradise, the fiery Sword waving behind them, and the Cherubim taking thir Stations to guard the Place.

As one who in his journey bates° at Noon,   *pauses*
Though bent on speed, so here the Arch-Angel paus'd
Betwixt the world destroy'd and world restor'd,
If *Adam* aught perhaps might interpose;
5 Then with transition sweet new Speech resumes.
    Thus thou hast seen one World begin and end;
And Man as from a second stock proceed.[1]
Much thou hast yet to see, but I perceive
Thy mortal sight to fail; objects divine
10 Must needs impair and weary human sense:
Henceforth what is to come I will relate,
Thou therefore give due audience, and attend.
This second source of Men, while yet but few,
And while the dread of judgment past remains
15 Fresh in thir minds, fearing the Deity,
With some regard to what is just and right
Shall lead thir lives, and multiply apace,
Laboring° the soil, and reaping plenteous crop,   *tilling*
Corn, wine and oil; and from the herd or flock,
20 Oft sacrificing Bullock, Lamb, or Kid,
With large Wine-offerings pour'd, and sacred Feast,
Shall spend thir days in joy unblam'd, and dwell
Long time in peace by Families and Tribes
Under paternal rule; till one shall rise[2]
25 Of proud ambitious heart, who not content
With fair equality, fraternal state,
Will arrogate Dominion undeserv'd
Over his brethren, and quite dispossess
Concord and law of Nature from the Earth:[3]
30 Hunting (and Men not Beasts shall be his game)
With War and hostile snare such as refuse

---

1. "Stock," an ambiguity, refers not only to the literal replacement of one source of the human line of descent (Adam) by another (Noah), but also to the grafting of mankind onto the stem of Christ, according to the Pauline allegory of regeneration (Romans 11). The covenant with Noah was a type of the New Covenant.
2. Nimrod is not connected with the builders of the Tower in Genesis 10.8. The connection is made, however, in Josephus, *Antiquities* 1.4.2ff., where we also learn that Nimrod "changed the government into tyranny."
3. In *The Tenure of Kings and Magistrates*, Milton denies the natural right of kings and insists that their power is committed to them in trust by the people.

Subjection to his Empire tyrannous:[4]
A mighty Hunter thence he shall be styl'd
Before the Lord, as in despite of Heav'n,
35   Or from Heav'n claiming second Sovranty;[5]
And from Rebellion shall derive his name,
Though of Rebellion others he accuse.
Hee with a crew, whom like Ambition joins
With him or under him to tyrannize,
40   Marching from *Eden* towards the West, shall find
The Plain, wherein a black bituminous gurge°   whirlpool
Boils out from under ground, the mouth of Hell;
Of Brick, and of that stuff they cast to build
A City and Tow'r, whose top may reach to Heav'n;[6]
45   And get themselves a name, lest far disperst
In foreign Lands thir memory be lost,
Regardless whether good or evil fame.[7]
But God who oft descends to visit men
Unseen, and through thir habitations walks
50   To mark thir doings, them beholding soon,
Comes down to see thir City, ere the Tower
Obstruct Heav'n Tow'rs, and in derision sets
Upon thir Tongues a various Spirit to rase
Quite out thir Native Language, and instead
55   To sow a jangling noise of words unknown:
Forthwith a hideous gabble rises loud
Among the Builders; each to other calls
Not understood, till hoarse, and all in rage,
As mockt they storm;[8] great laughter was in Heav'n
60   And looking down, to see the hubbub strange
And hear the din; thus was the building left
Ridiculous, and the work Confusion nam'd.[9]
        Whereto thus *Adam* fatherly displeas'd.
O execrable Son so to aspire
65   Above his Brethren, to himself assuming
Authority usurpt, from God not giv'n:
He gave us only over Beast, Fish, Fowl
Dominion absolute; that right we hold
By his donation; but Man over men
70   He made not Lord; such title to himself
Reserving, human left from human free.
But this Usurper his encroachment proud
Stays not on Man; to God his Tower intends
Siege and defiance: Wretched man! what food

4. See *Eikonoklastes:* "The Bishops could have told him, that 'Nimrod,' the first that hunted after Faction is reputed, by ancient Tradition, the first that founded monarchy; whence it appears that to hunt after Faction is more properly the King's Game."
5. "Before the Lord," Genesis 10.9; Milton takes it in a constitutional sense; see *The Tenure:* "To say Kings are accountable to none but God, is the overturning of all Law."

6. The materials of the Tower—brick with bitumen as mortar—are specified in Genesis 11.3.
7. See Genesis 11.4.
8. In the 17th century it was generally believed that the separation of language into distinct individual languages had its beginning at the confusion of tongues at Babel.
9. See Genesis 11.9, "Therefore is the name of it called Babel"; marginal gloss: "that is, Confusion."

75   Will he convey up thither to sustain
        Himself and his rash Army, where thin Air
        Above the Clouds will pine his entrails gross,
        And famish him of breath, if not of Bread?
            To whom thus *Michael*. Justly thou abhorr'st
80   That Son, who on the quiet state of men
        Such trouble brought, affecting to subdue
        Rational Liberty;[1] yet know withal,
        Since thy original lapse, true Liberty
        Is lost, which always with right Reason dwells
85   Twinn'd, and from her hath no dividual° being: *separate*
        Reason in man obscur'd, or not obey'd,
        Immediately inordinate desires
        And upstart Passions catch the Government
        From Reason, and to servitude reduce
90   Man till then free. Therefore since hee permits
        Within himself unworthy Powers to reign
        Over free Reason, God in Judgment just
        Subjects him from without to violent Lords;
        Who oft as undeservedly enthral
95   His outward freedom: Tyranny must be,
        Though to the Tyrant thereby no excuse.
        Yet sometimes Nations will decline so low
        From virtue, which is reason, that no wrong,
        But Justice, and some fatal curse annext
100   Deprives them of thir outward liberty,
        Thir inward lost:[2]

                        * * *

            So spake th' Arch-Angel *Michaël*, then paus'd,
        As at the World's great period;[3] and our Sire
        Replete with joy and wonder thus repli'd.
            O goodness infinite, goodness immense![4]
470   That all this good of evil shall produce,
        And evil turn to good; more wonderful
        Than that which by creation first brought forth
        Light out of darkness! full of doubt I stand,
        Whether I should repent me now of sin
475   By mee done and occasion'd, or rejoice
        Much more, that much more good thereof shall spring,
        To God more glory, more good will to Men
        From God, and over wrath grace shall abound.[5]
        But say, if our deliverer up to Heav'n
480   Must reascend, what will betide the few

1. Lines 80–101 recall the regicide tracts and follow St. Augustine's *City of God* 19.15, where we read that the derivation of servitude, whose mother is sin, is the "first cause of man's subjection to man: which notwithstanding comes not to pass but by the direction of the highest, in whom is no injustice." For the connection between psychological and political enslavement, see 9.1127–31.

2. Michael goes on to describe the history of Israel, from Abraham to King David, then tells of the birth of the Messiah, who will crush Satan and defeat Sin and Death.

3. This is Michael's second pause; the first was at 12.2.

The three divisions of Adam's instruction are meant to correspond to "three drops" of the well of life placed in his eyes (11.416). Here the pause is compared with the world's period the dawning of the present age, from the first to the second coming of Christ.

4. The Final Cause or end of the Fall: a greater "glory" for God and an opportunity for him to show his surpassing love through the sacrifice of Christ.

5. See Romans 5.20 ("where sin abounded, grace did much more abound") and 2 Corinthians 4.15.

His faithful, left among th' unfaithful herd,
The enemies of truth; who then shall guide
His people, who defend? will they not deal
Worse with his followers than with him they dealt?
485   Be sure they will, said th' Angel; but from Heav'n
Hee to his own a Comforter will send,[6]
The promise of the Father, who shall dwell
His Spirit within them, and the Law of Faith
Working through love, upon thir hearts shall write,[7]
490   To guide them in all truth, and also arm
With spiritual Armor, able to resist
Satan's assaults, and quench his fiery darts,[8]
What Man can do against them, not afraid,
Though to the death, against such cruelties
495   With inward consolations recompens't,
And oft supported so as shall amaze
Thir proudest persecutors: for the Spirit
Pour'd first on his Apostles, whom he sends
To evangelize the Nations, then on all
500   Baptiz'd, shall them with wondrous gifts endue°   *endow*
To speak all Tongues, and do all Miracles,
As did thir Lord before them. Thus they win
Great numbers of each Nation to receive
With joy the tidings brought from Heav'n: at length
505   Thir Ministry perform'd, and race well run,
Thir doctrine and thir story written left,
They die; but in thir room, as they forewarn,
Wolves shall succeed for teachers, grievous Wolves,[9]
Who all the sacred mysteries of Heav'n
510   To thir own vile advantages shall turn
Of lucre and ambition, and the truth
With superstitions and traditions taint,
Left only in those written Records pure,
Though not but by the Spirit understood.[1]
515   Then shall they seek to avail themselves of names,
Places and titles, and with these to join
Secular power, though feigning still to act
By spiritual, to themselves appropriating
The Spirit of God, promis'd alike and giv'n
520   To all Believers;[2] and from that pretense,
Spiritual Laws by carnal° power shall force   *worldly*
On every conscience; Laws which none shall find
Left them inroll'd, or what the Spirit within

---

6. The Holy Spirit. See John 14.18 and 15.26.
7. See Galations 5.6: "faith which worketh by love."
8. Alluding to the allegory in Ephesians 6.16: "Above all, taking the shield of faith, wherewith ye shall be able to quench all the fiery darts of the wicked."
9. "For I know this, that after my departing shall grievous wolves enter in among you, not sparing the flock" (Acts 20.29). See the simile comparing Satan to a wolf in the

fold, at 4.183–87; see also *Lycidas* 113ff, page 907.
1. It was an important article of Protestant belief that in doctrinal matters the ultimate arbiter is individual conscience rather than mere authority.
2. The corruption of the Church through its pursuit of "secular power" is a subject Milton had dealt with in *Of Reformation.* In *De doctrina* 1.30 he condemns the enforcement of obedience to human opinions or authority.

Shall on the heart engrave.[3] What will they then
525 But force the Spirit of Grace itself, and bind
His consort Liberty; what, but unbuild
His living Temples, built by Faith to stand,[4]
Thir own Faith not another's: for on Earth
Who against Faith and Conscience can be heard
530 Infallible?[5] yet many will presume:
Whence heavy persecution shall arise
On all who in the worship persevere
Of Spirit and Truth; the rest, far greater part,
Will deem in outward Rites and specious forms
535 Religion satisfi'd; Truth shall retire
Bestuck with sland'rous darts, and works of Faith
Rarely be found: so shall the World go on,
To good malignant, to bad men benign,
Under her own weight groaning, till the day
540 Appear of respiration[6] to the just,
And vengeance to the wicked, at return
Of him so lately promis'd to thy aid,
The Woman's seed, obscurely then foretold,
Now amplier known thy Saviour and thy Lord,
545 Last in the Clouds from Heav'n to be reveal'd
In glory of the Father, to dissolve
Satan with his perverted World, then raise
From the conflagrant° mass, purg'd and refin'd,   *burning*
New Heav'ns, new Earth, Ages of endless date
550 Founded in righteousness and peace and love,
To bring forth fruits Joy and eternal Bliss.
    He ended; and thus *Adam* last repli'd.
How soon hath thy prediction, Seer blest,
Measur'd this transient World, the Race of time,
555 Till time stand fixt: beyond is all abyss,
Eternity, whose end no eye can reach.
Greatly instructed I shall hence depart,
Greatly in peace of thought, and have my fill
Of knowledge, what this Vessel can contain;
560 Beyond which was my folly to aspire.
Henceforth I learn, that to obey is best,
And love with fear the only God, to walk
As in his presence, ever to observe
His providence, and on him sole depend,
565 Merciful over all his works, with good
Still overcoming evil, and by small
Accomplishing great things, by things deem'd weak
Subverting worldly strong, and worldly wise
By simply meek; that suffering for Truth's sake

3. The wolves will enforce laws written neither in Scripture nor in the individual conscience.
4. See 1 Corinthians 3.17: "The temple of God is holy, which temple ye are."
5. Even though the doctrine of papal infallibility was not formally adapted until 1870, there can be no doubt that Rome is Milton's main target here. In *A Treatise of Civil Power* he writes that the "Pope assumes infallibility over conscience and scripture."
6. Opportunity for breathing again; rest.

570 Is fortitude to highest victory,
And to the faithful Death the Gate of Life;
Taught this by his example whom I now
Acknowledge my Redeemer ever blest.
        To whom thus also th' Angel last repli'd:
575 This having learnt, thou hast attain'd the sum
Of wisdom; hope no higher, though all the Stars
Thou knew'st by name, and all th' ethereal Powers,
All secrets of the deep, all Nature's works,
Or works of God in Heav'n, Air, Earth, or Sea,
580 And all the riches of this World enjoy'dst,
And all the rule, one Empire; only add
Deeds to thy knowledge answerable, add Faith,
Add Virtue, Patience, Temperance, add Love,
By name to come call'd Charity, the soul
585 Of all the rest;[7] then wilt thou not be loath
To leave this Paradise, but shalt possess
A paradise within thee, happier far.
Let us descend now therefore from this top
Of Speculation;[8] for the hour precise
590 Exacts our parting hence; and see the Guards,
By mee encampt on yonder Hill, expect
Thir motion,[9] at whose Front a flaming Sword,
In signal of remove, waves fiercely round;
We may no longer stay: go, waken *Eve*;
595 Her also I with gentle Dreams have calm'd
Portending good, and all her spirits compos'd
To meek submission: thou at season fit
Let her with thee partake what thou hast heard,
Chiefly what may concern her Faith to know,
600 The great deliverance by her Seed to come
(For by the Woman's Seed)[1] on all Mankind,
That ye may live, which will be many days,[2]
Both in one Faith unanimous though sad,
With cause for evils past, yet much more cheer'd
605 With meditation on the happy end.
        He ended, and they both descend the Hill;
Descended, *Adam* to the Bow'r where *Eve*
Lay sleeping ran before, but found her wak't;
And thus with words not sad she him receiv'd.
610   Whence thou return'st, and whither went'st, I know;
For God is also in sleep, and Dreams advise,
Which he hath sent propitious, some great good
Presaging, since with sorrow and heart's distress

---

7. Compare 2 Peter 1.5–7: "Add to your faith virtue; and to virtue knowledge; and to knowledge temperance; and to temperance patience; and to patience godliness; and to godliness brotherly kindness; and to brotherly kindness charity."

8. Vantage point but also height of theological speculation.
9. Await deployment, marching orders.
1. Alluding to the birth of Jesus.
2. Adam lived to be 930 years of age (Genesis 5.5).

Wearied I fell asleep: but now lead on;
615 In mee is no delay; with thee to go,
Is to stay here; without thee here to stay,
Is to go hence unwilling; thou to mee
Art all things under Heav'n, all places thou,
Who for my wilful crime art banisht hence.[3]
620 This further consolation yet secure
I carry hence; though all by mee is lost,
Such favor I unworthy am voutsaf't,
By mee the Promis'd Seed shall all restore.
    So spake our Mother *Eve*, and *Adam* heard
625 Well pleas'd, but answer'd not; for now too nigh
Th' Arch-Angel stood, and from the other Hill
To thir fixt Station, all in bright array
The Cherubim descended; on the ground
Gliding meteorous,° as Ev'ning Mist   *meteoric*
630 Ris'n from a River o'er the marish° glides,   *marsh*
And gathers ground fast at the Laborer's heel
Homeward returning. High in Front advanc't,
The brandisht Sword of God before them blaz'd
Fierce as a Comet; which with torrid heat,
635 And vapor as the *Libyan* Air adust,°   *scorched*
Began to parch that temperate Clime; whereat
In either hand the hast'ning Angel caught
Our ling'ring Parents, and to th' Eastern Gate
Led them direct, and down the Cliff as fast
640 To the subjected° Plain; then disappear'd.   *underlying*
They looking back, all th' Eastern side beheld
Of Paradise, so late thir happy seat,
Wav'd over by that flaming Brand,[4] the Gate
With dreadful Faces throng'd and fiery Arms:
645 Some natural tears they dropp'd, but wip'd them soon;
The World was all before them, where to choose
Thir place of rest, and Providence thir guide:[5]
They hand in hand with wand'ring steps and slow,
Through *Eden* took thir solitary way.

                        The End

3. Eve has assimilated Michael's exhortation at 11.292: "where [Adam] abides, think there thy native soil." There is also a resonance with Eve's song at 4.635–56 (every time of day is pleasing with Adam, none is pleasing without him).

4. See Genesis. 3.24: "a flaming sword which turned every way."
5. Note that "Providence" can be the object of "choose": decisions of faith lie ahead.

Thomas Bowles, *The Bubblers' Medley, or a Sketch of the Times*, 1720.

The Restoration and the Eighteenth Century

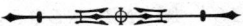

On 25 May 1660, Charles II set foot on the shore of Dover and brought his eleven-year exile to an end. The arrival was recorded by the great diarist Samuel Pepys, and his words preserve for us a form of the event:

> I went, and Mr. Mansell, and one of the King's footmen, with a dog that the King loved (which beshat the boat, which made us laugh, and methink that a king and all that belong to him are but just as others are), in a boat by ourselves, and so got on shore when the King did, who was received . . . with all imaginable love and respect at his entrance upon the land of Dover. Infinite the crowd of people and the horsemen, citizens, and noblemen of all sorts. The Mayor of the town came and gave him his white staff, the badge of his place, which the King did give him again. The Mayor also presented him from the town a very rich Bible, which he took and said it was the thing that he loved above all things in the world. . . . The shouting and joy expressed by all is past imagination.

Pepys captures and creates a brilliant mix of materials and experiences: his words compound jubilation and skepticism, images of authority and obeisance, tropes of spirituality and irony, and they remind us of the elements and passions by which all men live. Every gesture and exchange in this scene forecast the world to come, but what most signals the future is the paradox of remembering and forgetting that the diarist performs even as he records this scene. And all who witnessed the King's descent at Dover committed similar acts of memory and oblivion. Many of those (Pepys included) who were drunk with pleasure at the return of Charles Stuart had endorsed the destruction of his father eleven years before. The entire Restoration and the events that would follow over the ensuing years would prove a complex unfolding of memory and forgetfulness.

The jubilant crowds at Dover thought to make flux stop here: forever to banish the turbulence of civil war and political innovation, to restore all the old familiar forms, utterly to erase what had come between the death of the father and the restoration of the son. Charles II would soon institute an Act of Oblivion to those ends, forgiving proponents of rebellion by officially forgetting their misdeeds. But civil war and revolution would not be erased, nor could monarchy, the Anglican Church, aristocratic privilege, political patronage, and the old social hierarchies be revived as though nothing had intervened. Much of the old was brought back with the return of the Stuart monarchy, but the consequence of layering the present over a willfully suppressed past was an instability of feelings and forms that ensured the ever-changing triumph of different memories and different oblivions during the ensuing decades. No one celebrating the return of ancient ways in 1660 could have foreseen the ruptures and innovations that lay ahead in the next half of the century, when crises of conspiracy and the birth of party politics would produce further shifts in monarchy through a sequence of three ruling houses from three different countries. But even in 1660 the innocent acclaim on the shores of Dover was accompanied by hidden guilts and ironies, by vindictive desires, even for some by millenarian hopes. And while such stresses and tensions were unacknowledged in May 1660, they soon enough surfaced, and they unsettled not only the pleasures of this king's rule but the politics of an entire age.

MONARCHS, MINISTERS, EMPIRE

The coronation of Charles II in May 1661 marked the beginning of both the first and the eleventh year of his rule. The King's laws were named as if he had taken possession of the crown at the moment of his father's execution in 1649. And fictions, legal and not so legal, were to prove a hallmark of Stuart rule. The King openly proclaimed his love of parliaments, his devotion to the immemorial constitution of balance and moderation, his Protestant fervor, and his pious hopes for a national church. Yet he often postponed his parliaments; he claimed a tender conscience for Protestant dissenters, but he maneuvered for the toleration of Roman Catholics; he conducted an aggressive, nationalist program against European powers, but he signed a secret and deeply compromising treaty with Louis XIV; he took communion in the Anglican Church, but on his deathbed he sealed his own conversion to Catholicism; he was tenderly affectionate to his barren queen, yet he publicly flaunted his whoring tastes; he repeatedly exiled his unpopular brother James, Duke of York, while promoting and indulging his own bastard sons, yet he staunchly resisted any effort to displace his brother from the line of succession. The dominance of masquerade surely derived from Charles's temper, but fiction and falsehood were also the structural principles and aesthetic features of an entire world.

In December 1678, a series of events started to unfold that proved the very emblem of the masking, the fears, and the psychology of Charles II's rule. It began with legal depositions: one Titus Oates, a baker's son and self-anointed savior of a Protestant people, claimed to have knowledge of a secret plot to kill the King, crown his Catholic brother, and begin the wholesale conversion of English souls—and, just as frightening, English properties—to Rome. Oates offered to a public hungry for scandal and change a Popish plot and a familiar mix of images and idioms: priests and idols, the Roman Antichrist, conspiracy, murder, and mayhem. His depositions and fabrications played brilliantly on memories of the past and on fears of a future under a Catholic king. Nor did it help that the Duke of York's private secretary, Edward Coleman, was caught with treasonous correspondence in his chamber. The plot seemed compounded of sufficient truths to challenge the stability of the Crown. From the midst of the plot, and under the hand of the Earl of Shaftesbury, a political party emerged that took advantage of Popish facts and fears by proposing the Bill of Exclusion in Parliament, which would have barred the Duke of York and any future Catholic monarchs from the English throne. In the event, the bill failed, Charles died of natural causes, and the Duke succeeded his brother in February 1685.

During James's brief reign, no plots, conspiracies, or political parties proved so costly to his rule as did the new king himself. He succeeded his brother in a mood of surprising public affirmation. At his accession, James returned the embrace of Anglican England by promising to honor the national church and that most beloved of Protestant properties, a tender conscience. There would be no forcing of religious uniformity in this reign. But soon enough James began to move against Anglican interests: he staffed his army with Catholic officers, he imposed Catholic officials on

Oxford University, and he insisted that his Declarations of Toleration be read aloud from the pulpits of Anglican churches. Such a program challenged interest, property, and propriety, and it spelled the quick demise of Catholic rule.

As Duke of York, James had been famed for martial valor. But now, when confronted in November 1688 by the army of his Dutch son-in-law, William of Orange, he fled under cover of night to France. What had in part provoked James's flight were memories of the past—of civil war and of the execution of his father, Charles I. What had provoked the invasion by William of Orange was not merely the specter of Louis XIV hovering behind James's rule or the open presence of Jesuits at James's court. It was the birth of James Francis Edward Stuart, son of James II and Mary of Modena. Protestants would suffer not only the inconvenience of one Catholic monarch but the possibility of an endless Catholic succession. The prospect was too much to bear. Secret negotiations were begun between powerful English artistocrats—Whigs and Tories alike—and William, the governor (stadholder) of Holland, resulting in what many called the Glorious Revolution. But the deceits and pretenses—the gaps and silences—of this palace coup did not strike all contemporaries as glorious. The stadholder who chased a Catholic king from England was not only an invading hero (though some did call him William the Conqueror), he was also the son-in-law of James II. Those who clung to the binding ties of loyalty and gratitude accused William and Mary of deep impiety, indeed, of parricide.

But the astonishing invitation to William of Orange produced no bloodshed. What it did produce was a Protestant monarchy under the rule of King William III and Queen Mary. Members of Parliament, meeting to invent the laws that would sanctify this revolutionary change, decided that it would be best to say they had discovered the throne of England mysteriously vacant and that this William was no conqueror but a rightful claimant on a vacant throne. Of course, not everyone was pleased by such a revolution—sacred oaths had been broken, binding ties were cast aside, vows were juggled as mere words. Those who would not accept a convenient revolution were called Jacobites, that is, supporters of King James (*Jacobus* in Latin); they remained a force that would trouble British political life by threatening a Stuart restoration in the fervent but failed Jacobite rebellions of 1715 and 1745.

Most of William's subjects, though, were content with the evasions of this Glorious Revolution. Many were not content, though, with the program of European war in which the English were now plunged by their new king, intent on thwarting the ambitions of Louis XIV, his lifelong nemesis. The ruinous expense of war demanded taxes and fiscal innovation; it produced a stream of grumbling satire, complaint against Dutch favorites, and more than one conspiracy and attempted assassination. No such disaffection or turbulence disturbed the reign (1702–1714) of William's successor, Queen Anne. Her years were the twilight of Stuart monarchy, a time of political nostalgia and commercial confidence whose mood the young Alexander Pope captured in the lines of *Windsor-Forest* (1713), where softened memories and strategic elisions of the years of Stuart rule are mingled with images of triumph—of imperial expansion and a swelling commerce of domestic and foreign trade.

But luxury was not England's only import. At the death of Queen Anne, an entire court and new ruling house were shipped to England from the German state of Hanover. George I was the grandson of James I; beyond lineage, George's communion in a Protestant church was the virtue that most recommended his succession.

He spoke no English, knew nothing of his new subjects, and could not be bothered to learn. Nor was he much implicated in the management of a state whose rule would successively become less the prerogative of kings than the business of ministers and the function of parties, interest, and corruption. This displacement of monarch by minister was cemented during the period caustically nicknamed "Robin's Reign": two decades (1721–1742), transversing the reigns of George I and George II, when politics were dominated by Robert Walpole, who bought loyalties, managed kings, and ran the state with such ruthless efficency as to earn him the new label "prime minister" (the phrase was meant as an insult, aimed at the perceived excess of his power in a government where ministers were only supposed to advise their colleagues and their king). The South Sea Bubble, a state-endorsed investment scheme that ruined many, was the making of Robert Walpole. As the only cabinet minister untainted by the scandal (he had initially argued against the scheme, then lost money in it), he was put in charge of the subsequent governmental housecleaning. Once empowered, he cheerfully shed his scruples, devising a political machine fueled by patronage that made his cronies rich, his opposition apoplectic. By the firmness of his rule and the prudence of his policies, Walpole consolidated a long period of Whig supremacy that supplanted the party contest of the preceding decades, when Whigs and Tories had see-sawed more swiftly in and out of power.

The parties had begun to crystallize during the Exclusion crisis of the early 1680s, when Whigs fought to bar the king's Catholic brother from the throne and Tories upheld the established continuity of the Stuart line. Like "prime minister," the two party names began as insult, "Tory" denoting an Irish-Catholic bandit, "Whigs" identifying a group of Scottish rebels during the civil wars. Late in the eighteenth century, Samuel Johnson summed up their polarities: "The prejudice of the Tory is for establishment; the prejudice of the Whig is for innovation." "Establishment" meant preserving monarchic prerogatives, upholding the Anglican church, lamenting the advent of the Hanoverians, and—for some Tories, not all—actively yearning for the restoration of the Stuart line and abetting the attempts to achieve this in the Jacobite rebellions of 1715 and 1745. Whig "innovation" entailed enthusiastic support for both the Glorious Revolution and the House of Hanover, for policies of religious tolerance, and for all measures that advanced the interests of the newly prosperous and powerful merchant class. In the late seventeenth century, party politics had begun for the first time to supplant long-running religious conflicts as the main articulation of interest and power. For all its noise and rage, the new structure produced a paradoxical calm, not by the suppression of difference but by its recognition. The division into parties amounted to a sanctioned fragmentation of the whole. Even during the reign of Anne, when party conflict was at its most feverish, what the machinery of party seemed to ensure was the containment of partisan interest within the dynamic, even organic, coherence of the state.

During Walpole's "reign," portions of the two parties coalesced in an uneasy alliance. The arrogance, obstinacy, and efficacy of Walpole's methods galvanized an opposition consisting of both Tories and alienated Whigs; their endeavors acquired luster from the contributions of a remarkable array of writers (the Tories Jonathan Swift, Alexander Pope, John Gay, and Henry Fielding, and the Whig James Thomson) who opposed the prime minister on grounds of personality, principle, and of course self-interest. Walpole, recognizing that the best writers worked for the opposition, strove to suppress them by all the strategies of censorship he could devise. But by his greatness as a character and his force as an opponent, Walpole loomed for a long while as both literature's nemesis and its muse.

In fact, Walpole enforced the policies endorsed by only a fraction of his party—those moderate Whigs deeply interested in cultivating the country's wealth by commerce, deeply resistant to waging war. "My *politics*," he once wrote emphatically, "*are to keep free from all engagements, as long as we possibly can*"; by "engagements," he meant military commitments abroad. By the late 1730s, he discovered that he could keep free from them no longer. Britons feared that powers on the Continent—Spain, Austria, and above all France—were encroaching on their rights, and the popular clamor to wage European war prevailed. "When trade is at stake," the oppositionist William Pitt warned the British, "it is your last retrenchment; you must defend it or perish." Under the pressure of such sentiments Walpole eventually resigned, having led the state through two decades of comparative peace, growing national prosperity, and a new stability in government, but leaving behind him an army and a navy debilitated by disuse. Nonetheless, with trade at stake and the navy rebuilt, Britain embarked on a series of wars that ran almost unbroken for the rest of the century. Pitt presided brilliantly over many of them, wars waged directly or indirectly against France for trading privileges and territories abroad. By 1763, Britain had secured possession of Bengal in India, many islands and coastal territories in the Caribbean, and virtually all of North America (including Canada) east of the Mississippi, as well as half of all the international trade transpiring on the planet. So great was the impetus toward empire that even Britain's humiliating defeat in the American War of Independence (1775–1783) could not really halt the momentum; territories in India were still expanding, and settlement of Australia lay in the offing.

By now, the throne was occupied by the first Hanoverian monarch born in Britain—George III. His long reign (1760–1820) teemed with troubles: the popular scorn for his chosen ministers, the loss of the American war, the aftershocks of the French Revolution, the defiance of his heirs, the torments of his own slow-encroaching madness. But almost from beginning to end he ruled over the richest nation and the widest empire in the world. In 1740, a new song could be heard with a catchy refrain: "Rule, Britannia, rule the waves / Britons never will be slaves." The words were the work of the Scots-born poet James Thomson, now a proud adherent of "Britannia" by virtue of the Act of Union (1707), which had fused Scotland with England and Wales into a new nation, newly named: Great Britain. Over the ensuing years the song took hold because of the seductively prophetic ways in which it forecast Britain's greatness and partly because of the proud but peculiar resonances of the refrain's last line. There, Thomson contrasts British liberties with the slave-like constraints supposedly suffered by subjects of absolute monarchy elsewhere. Less directly, "slaves" also points to those peoples upon whose subjugation British privilege and British prosperity were increasingly to depend. Throughout the century, Britons profited spectacularly from the capture, transport, sale, and labor of African slaves in current and former colonies; "no nation," William Pitt the Younger proclaimed in 1792, had "plunged so deeply into this guilt as Great Britain."

There were also whole populations whose condition often evoked the analogy of slavery in the minds of the few who paid reformist attention to their plight: the oppressed indigenous peoples of the colonies, and women and the poor at home.

Conversation about such issues became louder and more purposeful near the end of the eighteenth century, as particular champions began to turn social questions into moral causes: John Wilkes on the widening of liberties and voting rights; Mary Wollstonecraft on the rights of women; William Blake (and later, William Cobbett) on the economic inequities of the whole social structure. The problems themselves did not even begin to find redress until the following century, but the emergence of such advocacies, quickened by the audacities of the French Revolution, marked a turning point toward the Romanticism that seized poetic and political imaginations in the 1790s. For most Britons of the eighteenth century, however, the new prosperity produced no special promptings of conscience. As their Restoration forebears had actively encouraged oblivion in an effort to anesthetize themselves to their past, men and women now sustained a moral and social oblivion that eased their use of others and their pleasure in new wealth. Out of such adroitly managed oscillations, Britons fabricated a new sense of themselves as a nation and an empire.

This new construct was in large measure the work of a prominent breed of economic architects: the capital-wielding middle classes. For centuries, wealth had derived primarily from land: tenant farmers performed the labor; the landed gentry collected the often enormous profits. The new wealth was amassed, even created, by people situated between these two extremes, constituting what was often referred to as "the middling rank," "the middling station," or "the middling orders." What set the middling orders apart was the comparatively new way in which they made their money: not by landed inheritance, not by tenancy or wage work, but by the adroit deployment of money itself. Having acquired a sum by inheritance, wage, or loan, they used it as capital, investing it, along with their own efforts, in potentially lucrative enterprises: in shops, in factories, and in the enormous new financial structures (banks, stocks) that underwrote the nation's economic expansiveness. They hired helpers, reinvested profits, and when their schemes succeeded, they made their money grow. With wealth, of course, grew clout. The interests of the "City"—that is, of the eastern half of London where bustling merchants made their deals—increasingly shaped the affairs of state, the appetites for empire. Empire also shaped the progress of the arts: members of the middle class became the chief consumers and energetic producers of the period's most conspicuous new forms of literature: newspapers and novels. But nowhere were the new powers of the burgeoning bourgeoisie more striking than in the theater, that cultural site they often visited and ultimately revised.

MONEY, MANNERS, AND THEATRICS

No event more exactly and more economically signals the return of an aristocratic court to the center of English culture than the reopening of the London theaters in 1662. The intimacy, indeed the complicity, of court with theater throughout the early modern period was such that when in the 1640s Parliament took aim at monarchy, aristocracy, and privilege, it not only struck off the heads of the Earl of Strafford and Archbishop Laud, it also banished play acting and shut tight the doors of the London stage. But Puritans could not banish the theater from the English imagination, and no sooner were the playhouses closed than publishers issued new editions of old plays and the theater made a secret return in domestic spaces and before private audiences. Print and memory would be the preservative of an entire culture. In 1660, monarchy and theater were restored in tandem. But this artistic restoration, like the political one that made it possible, irresistibly mingled the old with the new. Pepys captured all the excitement and splendor of this restoration; as usual he proves adroit at reckoning innovation:

> [T]he stage is now . . . a thousand times better and more glorious than heretofore. Now, wax-candles, and many of them; then, not above three pounds of tallow. Now, all things civil, no rudeness anywhere; then, as in a bear garden. Then, two or three fiddlers; now, nine or ten of the best. Then, nothing but rushes upon the ground and everything mean; and now all otherwise. Then the Queen seldom and the King never would come; now not the King only for state but all civil people do think they may come as well as any.

One reason that "all civil people" thought so was a matter of simple geography. Whereas the theaters of Shakespeare's day had been located in seedy districts on the outskirts of the city, this new and sumptuous theatrical world was ensconced in new neighborhoods strategically located for maximum social confluence, on the border between Westminster—home of the court—and the City of London, dwelling place of a "mighty band of citizens and prentices" whose sudden convergence with royalty seemed a dramatic innovation. They had all gathered to witness the most astonishing new spectacle of all: women on stage in a public theater.

Before the Restoration, aristocratic women had tantalized the court in private and privileged masquing; now the pleasures of display and consumption were democratized in several ways. For women, theatricality was no longer a pastime reserved for the very few but a plausible—though precarious—profession. For audiences at the new theaters, actresses represented the possibility of erotic spectacle for the price of a ticket—a chance to gaze on women who everyone knew were managing the pleasures, and often the policies, of kings and courtiers. Inevitably new strategies of theatricality suffused this audience, where women might model seductive conduct on the teasing combinations of concealment and display enacted before them. Pepys eavesdropped on the libertine Sir Charles Sedley in urgent banter with two women: "And one of the women would and did sit with her mask on, all the play. He would fain know who she was, but she would not tell; yet did give him many pleasant hints of her knowledge of him, by that means setting his brains at work to find out who she was, and did give him leave to use all means but pulling off her mask." Display and disguise not only animated the stage, they quickened social exchange in the intimate spaces of stalls and boxes. The traffic between revelation and concealment defined this theater. It drove the plots of plays and galvanized audiences, modeling and scripting their fashions, their language, their lives.

In such a world the theater provided a national mask, a fantasy of empire and heroism, and yet at the same time sustained a critique of masquerade, a brutal exposure of deceptions rampant in the culture. On the one hand, the heroic drama displayed, indeed reveled in, outsized acts of conquest in exotic lands, valor, and virtue: on stage, princes slaughtered infidels by the thousands; virgins sustained honor through impossible ordeals of abduction and assault. Yet in 1667, at the same moment such dramas were thriving in the king's and the duke's playhouses, the royal fleet was being burned and sunk by a Dutch navy that breached all defenses, invading the very precincts and privacy of London's docks and shipyards. And while the fleet burned, the king busied himself with other depredations, sustaining a series of intrigues, some with the very actresses who wore such incomparable honor and virtue on the stage. (The mix of myth and mischief was popular in pictures too—for example, in the portrait of Barbara Villiers, Countess of Castlemaine, perhaps the most notorious of all the king's mistresses, gotten up in the guise of Minerva, Roman goddess of wisdom; see Color Plate 21.) The heroic drama celebrated military conquest and colonial glory, and displayed them at a moment in national history that produced nothing so much as shame and humiliation: defeat at the hands of Dutch ships and Dutch commerce.

At the same time, but in a far different dramatic mode, the stage sustained a brilliant critique of a whole culture of incongruity, masquerade, and self-delusion. Restoration comedy took as its subject appetite and opportunism, social hypocrisy and sexual power play. The London audience watched scenes of seduction and connivance set in the very vicinities they had traversed to reach the playhouse: St. James's Park, Covent Garden. Such aristocratic libertines as Sir Charles Sedley and Lord Rochester, intent on their own intrigues, might admire themselves in a theatrical mirror, where the rake-hero conducted endless parry-and-thrust with his equals, brutalized his inferiors, and laid hands and claim on any moveable object of desire: fruits and foodstuffs, silks and sonnets, housemaids and women of high estate. But the rakes in the playhouse might see themselves mocked as well. The best comic writers—Wycherley, Etherege, Behn, Congreve—showed the libertines equaled and often bested in cunning by the women they pursued, baffled where they would be most powerful, enslaved where they would be most free. In brilliant volleys of dialogue, these lovers mixed passion and poison in volatile measures, chasing one another through a maze of plots, counterplots, and subplots so convoluted as to suggest a world of calculation run mad. Over the thirty years of its triumphs, Restoration comedy, in an astounding fugue of excesses and depravities, laid bare the turbulence and toxins of this culture.

That the heroic drama, with all its exaggerations and flatteries, found a market is hardly surprising; what is more puzzling is the commercial triumph of Restoration comedy, a theatrical mode that entertained by punishing and humiliating its audience—though it is hardly surprising that this theater should itself have fallen victim in the 1690s to prudery and what would come to be called "taste." In the wake of the Protestant revolution of 1688, which typed Stuart rule as the very emblem of self-indulgence, agents of moral improvement and social propriety made their assault on Restoration comedy the stalking horse for a broad program of Christian reform. Restoration comedy, which had erupted as a repudiation of Puritan prohibitions, now seemed to prompt a new wave of moral rectitude.

Under such pressures, the playhouse redirected its mirror away from the aristocracy toward the upper strata of the "middling sort": London merchants, colonial profiteers. During the Restoration, the newly prosperous mercantile classes who converged with courtiers at the theater had watched themselves either derided or ignored on stage, their social pretensions and ineptitudes put down in the comedies, their commercial concerns absent from the heroic drama. In the early eighteenth century, they saw themselves glorified instead, in "domestic tragedy," which displayed the tribulations of commercial households, and in sentimental comedy, which sought by a mix of tears and modest laughter to inculcate family values and to portray the merchant class as the nation's moral core. Richard Steele's *The Conscious Lovers* (1722) sounded the fanfare for a newly theatric social self-conception. "We merchants," a businessman informs an aristocrat, "are a species of gentry that have grown into the world this last century, and are as honorable and almost as useful as you landed folk, that have always thought yourself so much above us."

Nor was the stage the only venue to promulgate this new cultural self-awareness. By its very title *The Spectator* (1711–1713), one of the most widely read periodicals of the century, assured its largely middle-class audience that they moved under the constant, thoughtful scrutiny of a virtual playgoer, the paper's fictive author, "Mr. Spectator," who made all London a kind of theater, in which he (and his eagerly imitative readers) might perpetually enjoy the privileges of making observations and forming judgments. The very energies that had been drained away from the stage now found a new home in the theatricalized world of commerce, fashion, manners, taste.

The cast members in this new theater were numerous, varied, and eager for direction, mostly because, as a "new species of gentry," they aspired to roles for which they had formerly been deemed unfit. Terms like "esquire" and "gentleman" had operated in previous centuries as proof of literal "entitlement." They were secured by registration with the College of Heralds, and they calibrated not merely monetary wealth but lineage, landholdings, education, and social standing. In the eighteenth century, men and women with sufficient money and nerve assumed these titles for themselves, confident enough that they might learn to play the part. "In our days," noted a 1730 dictionary, "all are accounted gentlemen that have money." But since "the money" was now so variously attainable—by shopkeeping, by manufacture, by international trade—the "middle station" was itself subdivided into many strata, and since the very point of capital was accumulation and improvement, ascent by emulation became a master plot in the new social theater. "Everyone," observed one commentator, "is flying from his inferiors in pursuit of his superiors, who fly from him with equal alacrity."

Amid the flux, fashion and commodity—what one wore, what one owned— mattered enormously. Wigs, fans, scarves, silks, petticoats, and jewels; china, silver, family portraits—these were the costumes, these the props of the new commercial theater, by which members of the middle orders pleased themselves and imitated the gentry. The commercial classes who had begun by catering to the aristocracy gradually became, in their waxing prosperity, their own best customers, selling garb and goods to one another. Shrewd marketers saw that novelty itself possessed an intrinsic and urgent appeal for people constantly in social flight, tirelessly engaged in remaking themselves. Advertising came into its own, filling the pages and underwriting the costs of the daily, weekly, and monthly periodicals. The listing of consumables became a prevalent mode of print, in everything from auction catalogues (the still-dominant houses of Christie's and Sotheby's got their start near the middle of the century) to poems and novels, where long lists of products and possessions became a means of recording the culture's appetites, and at times of satirizing them. In the hands of Swift and Pope, the catalogue itself became a form of art. The taste in literary miscellany reflected a more general taste for omnivorous consumption: variety indexed abundance and proved power. Tea from China, coffee from the Caribbean, tobacco from Virginia—all were relatively new, comparatively inexpensive, and enormously popular. In daily rituals of drink and smoke, the middling orders imbibed and inhaled a pleasing sense of their global reach, their comfortable centrality on a planet newly commercialized.

Commodities formed part of a larger discourse, involving speech and gesture as well as prop and costume. A cluster of precepts, gathered under the umbrella-term "politeness," supplied the stage directions, even at times the script, for the new social theater in which everyone was actor and everyone was audience. Eager to shine in their recently acquired roles, the merchant classes pursued the polish implicit in the word "polite." They hired "dancing masters" to teach them graceful motions and proper manners, "bear leaders" (tutors) to guide their sons on the Grand Tour of France and Italy in the footsteps of the nobility, elocution coaches to help them purge inappropriate accents, teachers of painting and music to supply their daughters with marriageable competence. For the newly prosperous, politeness was the epitome of distinction: it went beyond gesture and accomplishment to suggest a state of mind, a refinement of perception, a mix of knowledge, responsiveness, and judgment often summarized as "taste." "The man of polite imagination," said the *Spectator*, "is let into a great many pleasures that the vulgar are not capable of receiving." Eager to gain access, middle-class readers avidly sought instruction.

Politeness (which Samuel Johnson once defined as "fictitious benevolence") required considerable self-control; the passions (rage, greed, lust) were to be contained and channeled into the appearance of abundant and abiding goodwill. The middle classes embraced such constraints partly to allay widespread suspicion of their commercial aggressions, their social ambitions. Their preoccupation with politeness has helped to foster a recurrent misimpression of the period: that, setting aside the occasional rake or wench, it was all manners and morals, dignity and decorum, fuss and formality, reason and enlightenment. Not so. Even among the merchant classes, politeness afforded only provisional concealment for roiling energies; amid the impoverished and the gentry, it held less purchase still. In no succeeding epoch until our own was language so openly and energetically obscene, drunkenness so rampant, sexual conduct so various and unapologetic. Even among the "officially" polite, the very failure of containment could produce a special thrill. In one of the century's most often-used phrases, a speaker announces that "I cannot forbear"—that is, cannot restrain myself—from saying or doing what the verb itself suggests were better left unsaid or undone. The formula declares helpless and pleasurable surrender to an unmastered impulse, and the condition was apparently endemic. James Boswell records the memorable self-summary of an elderly lawyer: "I have tried . . . in my time to be a philosopher, but—I don't know how—cheerfulness was always breaking in." Such "breakings-in" (and breakings-out) of feeling were common, even cherished. The scholar Donald Greene has argued well that the eighteenth century was less an "age of reason" (as has often been said) than an age of exuberance. Certainly much of what the middle classes read and wrote is a literature of outburst: of hilarity, of lament, of rage, of exaltation. The copious diaries that the century brought forth deal in all such exclamations; they are the prose of people who have chosen to write rather than repress the thoughts and actions that strict politeness might proscribe. Even the *Spectator*, that manual of polished taste, presents itself as the daily outpouring of a writer who, after maintaining an eccentric lifelong silence, has found that he can no longer keep his "discoveries"—moral, social, experiential—to himself.

Such self-publicizing was more complex for women than for men. When women represented their own lives—in manuscript (letters, journals) and increasingly in print—they sometimes chafed at the paradoxical mix of tantalizing possibilities and painful limitations that their privilege produced. Post-Restoration prosperity and politeness supplied women with many new venues for self-display and sociability, in playhouses and pleasure gardens, ballrooms, spas, and shops. Society exalted and paraded women as superior consumers: wearing the furs, fragrances, and fabrics of distant climes, they furnished evidence of empire, proud proof of their fathers' and husbands' economic attainments. They consumed print, too; near the start of the eighteenth century, male editors invented the women's periodical and found the new genre immensely profitable. Increasingly, women not only purchased print but produced it, deploying their words and wit as a kind of cultural capital, which when properly expended might reap both cash and fame. During the eighteenth century, for the first time, books by women—of poems, of precepts, and above all of fiction—became not exotic but comparatively commonplace.

Still, books by women remained controversial, as did all manifestations of female autonomy and innovation. The very excitement aroused by women's new conspicuousness in the culture provoked counter-efforts at containment. Preachers and moralists argued endlessly that female virtue resided in domesticity. Marriage itself offered an age-old instrument of social control, newly retooled to meet the needs of ambitious merchants, for whom daughters were the very currency of social mobility. If parents could arrange the right marriage, the whole family's status promptly rose. The dowry that the bride brought with her was an investment in future possibilities: in the rank and connections that the union secured, in the inheritance that would descend to its heirs, in the annual income ("jointure") that the wife herself would receive following the death of the husband. Financially, a widow (or for that matter, a well-born woman who never married) was often far more independent than a wife, whose wedding led to a kind of sanctioned erasure. She possessed little or no control over marital property (including the wealth she had brought to the union); "in marriage," wrote the codifier of English law William Blackstone, "husband and wife are one person, and that person is the husband." The sums that the husband undertook to hand over to his wife were dubbed "pin money" (a suggestive trivialization): funds for managing the household, that sphere wherein, as the moral literature insisted, a woman might best deploy her innate talents and find her sanctioned satisfactions. These consisted first and foremost in producing children and in shaping their manners and morals. In a time of improvisatory birth control, precarious obstetrics, and high infant mortality, the bearing of children was a relentless, dangerous, and emotionally exhausting process. The upbringing of children provided more pleasure and possessed a new cachet: the conduct literature endorsed busy, attentive child-rearing as the highest calling possible for women whose prosperity freed them from the need to work for wages. (Guidebooks for parents and pleasure books for children both had their origins in the eighteenth century.) Apart from the duties of motherhood and household management—the supervision of servants, meals, shopping, and social occasions—the woman of means was encouraged to pursue those pleasures for which her often deliberately constricted education had prepared her: music, embroidery, letter writing, and talk at the tea table—the domestic counterpart of the clubs and coffeehouses, where women were not permitted to appear.

In the late seventeenth century, the possibilities for women had seemed at moments more various and more audacious. In the plays of Aphra Behn, female characters pursued their pleasures with an almost piratical energy and ingenuity; in *A*

Serious Proposal to the Ladies (1694), the feminist Mary Astell imagined academies where women could withdraw to pursue the pleasures of learning and escape the drudgeries of marriage. In the eighteenth century, though, despite women's increasing authorial presence, these early audacities tended to go underground. Protests by women against their secondary status are most overt in manuscript—in the acerbic poems and letters that Mary Wortley Montagu circulated among her friends, in the journal entries wherein the brewer's wife Hester Thrale vented her frustrations. In print, women's desire for autonomy became a tension in the text, rather than its explicit point or outcome. Novelists explored women's psyches with subtlety; their plots, however, nearly always culminated in marriage, and more rarely in catastrophe, as though those were the only alternatives. Even the Bluestocking Circle, an eminent late-century group of intellectual women, preached tenets of essential sexual difference and subordination; they argued (for example) in favor of improving girls' educations, but as a way of preparing them for better and happier work within the home rather than for adventures abroad. During the eighteenth century, the middle classes did much to spell out the gendered divison of labor—father as the family's champion in the marketplace, mother as cheerfully efficient angel in the house—that remained a cultural commonplace, among families who could afford it, for the next two hundred years.

Among the poor, such divisions were not tenable; most manual labor paid so little that everyone in the family had to work if all were to survive. Wives not only managed their frugal households, they also worked for wages, in fields, in shops, or in cottage manufacture of fabrics, gloves, basketry. Children often began wage work at age four or five, treading laundry, scaring crows, sweeping chimneys; boys began the more promising role of apprenticeships around the age of ten. For many of the poor, domestic service offered employment comparatively secure and endlessly demanding. Darker prospects included prostitution, and crime: shoplifting was punishable by death. In the case of the helplessly indigent, local government was responsible for providing relief, but the Poor Law provided large loop-holes by which the parish could drive out any unwanted supplicant—an unwed mother, for example—who could not meet the intricate and restrictive criteria for legal residence. The poor had no vote, no voice in government; as the century progressed, their predicament attracted increasing attention and advocacy. Philanthropists instituted charity schools designed, in the words of their proponent Hannah More, "to train up the lower classes in habits of industry and piety." Two convictions informed even the most ambitious philanthropy: that poverty was part of a divine plan and that it was the fault of the indolent poor themselves; they thus found themselves caught between the rock of providence and the hard place of reproach. Yet charity schools did increase literacy, and with it perhaps the sense of possibilities. Other late-century developments, too, were mixed. Improvements in sanitation, medicine, and hygiene contributed to a surge in population, which in turn produced among the rural poor a labor surplus: too many people, too little work. At the same time, wealthy landholders increased the practice of "enclosure," acquiring and sequestering acreage formerly used by the poor for common pasturage and family farming. As a result, many rural families left the land on which they had worked for centuries and traveled to alien terrain: the textile mills that capitalists had newly built and the industrial cities developing rapidly around them.

As the poor became poorer, the very rich—landowning lords and gentry—became very much richer, both by the means they now shared with the middle class (capital investment in banks and stocks) and through their own long-held resources. Land increased in value, partly because there were now so many merchant families passionately eager to buy into the landscape and the life of their aristocratic betters, among whom the spectacle of emulation provoked amusement and revulsion. The landed gentry preserved their distance by many means: social practices (they often flaunted their adulteries, for example, as contrast to middle-class proprieties), artistic allegiance (with the advent of the bourgeois drama, aristocratic audiences defected from the theater to the opera house, where elaborate productions and myth-based plots sustained the aristocratic values of the heroic drama), and the sheer ostentation of their leisure and magnitude of their consumption. But the pivotal difference remained political: by the award of offices, by the control of elections, landowners maintained their strangle-hold on local and national power, despite all the waxing wealth of trade.

At the same time, their very absorption in pleasure and power demanded a continual traffic with their inferiors. Merchants and shopkeepers catered to them; professionals managed their transactions; household servants contrived their comforts; aspiring artists sought to cultivate their taste and profit by their patronage. Transactions among the aristocracy and the middle classes took other forms as well. A lord low on money often found it lucrative to marry the daughter of a thriving merchant. And middle-class modes of life could exert a subtler magnetism, too—particularly for George III, who prized mercantile decorum over aristocratic swagger. In the portrait of his queen and her two eldest sons in Color Plate 22, the artist Johann Zoffany (himself an expensive German import) celebrates not their royal state but their domestic felicity: the heroic trappings (helmet, spear, turban) so conspicuous in Lely's portrait of the scandalous Lady Castlemaine (see Color Plate 21) are here reduced to the props of child's play in the domestic theater of family relations.

King George had commissioned Johann Zoffany in pursuit of precisely this effect. By his eager emulation of the middling orders, George III broke with monarchic traditions, but he inaugurated a new one that would be sustained and expanded in various ways by Queen Victoria in the nineteenth century and her successors in the twentieth. During George's reign, too, the middle classes began to pursue more practical convergence with the aristocracy: a wider distribution of voting rights, a firmer political power base. For the first time, the phrase "middle classes" itself came into use, as a way of registering this cohort's recognition of its own coherence and interests, its unique, often combative relations with the classes above and below; the plural ("classes") registered the abiding diversity—of income, of lifestyle—within the cohesion. In the years since the Restoration, the middle classes had moved themselves energetically in the theater of social and economic relations from a place in the audience toward center stage, exerting enormous power over the working lives of the poor, posing challenges to the elite. Increasingly, their money, manners, appetites, and tastes came to be perceived as the essence of national life, as the part that might stand for the whole. "Trade," Henry Fielding remarked in 1751, "has indeed given a new face to the nation."

It gave the nation new momentum, too, literal as well as figurative. The engineering marvels of the eighteenth century—the harnessing of steam power, the innovations in factory design, the acceleration of production—were instruments of capital. So were improvements in the rate of transport. Over the course of the century, the government collaborated with private investors to construct a proliferating network of smooth turnpikes and inland waterways: canal boats delivered coal and other cargo with new celerity; stagecoaches sped between cities on precise schedules with crowded timetables. Timekeeping itself became a source of national wealth and pride. During the 1660s, British clockmakers established themselves as the best in Europe. A century later, the clockmaker John Harrison invented the "marine chronometer," a large watch so sturdy and so precise that it could keep time to the minute throughout a voyage around the world, amid all vicissitudes of wind and weather. Harrison's invention made it possible to calculate a ship's longitude accurately, thus solving a problem that had bedeviled navigation for centuries (and sometimes sunk whole fleets). The innovation further paved the way for trade and empire-building, and did much to establish Greenwich, a town just east of London, as the reference point for world time-keeping. Trade was giving a new face—a new distribution of power and priority—not only to the nation but also to the globe, placing Britain (so Britons liked to think) at its center.

FAITH AND KNOWLEDGE, THOUGHT AND FEELING

Clockwork functioned another way too: as a new, theologically unsettling metaphor for the relations between God and his creation. In his *Principia Mathematica* (1687), Isaac Newton set forth the mathematical principles—the laws of motion, the workings of gravity—by which, it turned out, the universe could be seen to operate more consistently and efficiently than even the finest clockwork. What need had this flawless mechanism for any further adjustments by its divine clockmaker? Some of Newton's admirers—though never the pious scientist himself—found in his discoveries the cue for a nearly omnivorous skepticism. The boldest deists and "freethinkers" dismissed Christianity as irrational fiction, to be supplanted by the stripped-down doctrine of "natural religion." In the intricate design of nature they found the proof of a creator whose existence and infinite wisdom, they argued, are all we know on earth and all we need to know. The fashion for such thought—at least in its purest form—proved fleeting. To most minds, the "argument from design" simply furnished further proof of God's benevolence. Amid such comfortable conviction, the blasphemies of a virtuoso skeptic like David Hume appeared an aberration, even an entertainment, rather than a trend. "There is a great cry about infidelity," Samuel Johnson remarked in 1775, "but there are, in reality, very few infidels." From deep belief and ingrained habit, Christianity retained its hold over the entire culture; though a few pietists voiced alarm, science tended to enhance faith, not destroy it.

Still, the relation of religion to public life had changed. In the mid-seventeenth century, politics was inevitably suffused with spirituality. Charles I had gone to the scaffold as an Anglican martyr; he had ruled according to the dictum "No bishop, no king." For many English men and women, the war of Parliament against the king was a holy war: Puritans had typed Charles I as that "man of blood"; Cromwell's army had gone to battle singing David's psalms. By the eighteenth century, ardors had cooled: no one went to war for creed alone. But that is not to say that these were lives bereft of the spiritual; deep religious feeling remained, even as violence of expression abated. The Restoration had reinstated Anglicanism as the national faith; its adherents were admitted to the full privileges of education and office. Over the ensuing century, the Church of England pursued a strategic but controversial mix of old exclusions and new accommodations. For dissenters (offspring of the Puritans), new laws proffered certain permissions (to teach, to congregate for public worship) in exchange for certain oaths. Catholics, by contrast, were kept beyond the pale; they received no such concessions until late in the eighteenth century, when even a limited act provoked angry Protestant riots. Early in the century, the Anglican faithful were divided between the "high flyers," who perennially claimed that the church was in danger of dilution, and the Latitudinarians, who argued that all kinds of dissent might finally be accommodated within the structure of the church. Latitudinarians prevailed, but as the Church of England broadened, it began to lose the force of its exclusiveness; attendance at services shrank markedly as the century advanced, but alternative forms of communal worship flourished. In the eighteenth century, evangelical religions came to occupy the crucial space of fervent spirituality that the church of Donne and Herbert had once claimed as its own. By midcentury, in the new movement called Methodism, John Wesley expressed a vehement response against the skeptical rationalism of the freethinkers and the monied complacency of the established church. Wesley preached the truth of scriptural revelation. He urged his followers to purge their sins methodically—by a constant self-monitoring, partly modeled on earlier Puritan practices—and enthusiastically, by attending revival meetings, hearing electrifying sermons. Wesley delivered some 40,000 sermons over the course of a phenomenally energetic life, and his no less relentless brother Charles composed some 6,000 hymns to quicken evangelical spirits. Methodism found its most ardent following among the poor, who discovered in the doctrine a sympathy for their condition and a recognition of their worth, epitomized in one of Charles Wesley's verses: "Our Savior by the rich unknown / Is worshipped by the poor alone." Their worship was loud and fervent; intensity of feeling attested authenticity of faith.

The middle class and gentry located their own fervor in the more polished idioms of sentiment and sensibility. The terms named a code of conduct and of feeling current in the mid-eighteenth century, when men and women increasingly came to pride themselves on an emotional responsiveness highly cultivated and conspicuously displayed: tears of pity at the spectacle of suffering, admiration for the achievements of art or the magnificence of nature. For many in the middle class, the cult of sentiment held out the appealing prospect of a democratization of manners; the elaborate protocols of the aristocracy might remain elusive, but pure *feeling* was surely more accessible, to anyone with the leisure and the training. For many women, the cult afforded the added attraction of honoring that very susceptibility to feeling and that renunciation of reason that had long and pejoratively been gendered female. The sufferings of the poor, of children, of animals, became a testing ground for empathy; majestic mountains became favorite proving grounds for heightened response. The fashion for benevolence helped focus attention on the plight of the poor and the oppressed, prompting new charities and social movements. For many of the conventionally religious, sentimentality became an adjunct article of faith. They found their scriptures in treatises that posited proper feeling as a chief measure of human worth—Adam Smith's *Theory of Moral Sentiments* (1759); in sentimental dramas that modeled the cultivation (and the performance) of elaborate emotion; in novels that paid minute attention to the protagonist's every emotional nuance— Samuel Richardson's *Pamela* (1740–1741) and *Clarissa* (1747–1749), Laurence Sterne's *Life and Opinions of Tristram Shandy* (1759–1767) and *A Sentimental Journey* (1768), Henry Mackenzies's *The Man of Feeling* (1771); in travel books that transported readers geographically and emotionally by charged descriptions of mighty vistas. For both deists and pietists earlier in the century, nature had testified the existence of a God; for connoisseurs of the sublime near century's end, nature itself was beginning to serve as surrogate for the divine.

In the articulation of eighteenth-century faith and science, thought and feeling, the most conspicuous and continuous voice was that of the first person. The "I" was omnipresent, observing world and self alike: in the experiment-reports of the scientists and the thought-experiments of the philosophers; in the Methodists' self-monitoring, the sentimentalist's self-approbation, the sublimity-seekers' recorded raptures; in the copious autobiographical writings—diaries, letters, memoirs—of characters in novels and people in the real world. Always and everywhere, it seems, someone was setting down the nuances of his or her experience. The self-reckoning promulgated in the past by dissenters was now a broad cultural preoccupation. Its dominion may help to explain why the literature of this era famed for the dominance and delight of its conversation returns us, again and again, to a sense of fundamental solitude.

WRITERS, READERS, CONVERSATIONS

The century and a half from the English Civil Wars to the brink of the French Revolution brought startling change to the structures of politics, social relations, scientific knowledge, and the economy, and no change was more intimate to all these revolutions than the transformations in the relations between writers and readers. From our present perspective, perhaps no scene seems more familiar, even eternal, than that of reader with book in hand. We imagine Virgil's readers and Dante's, Austen's and Wilde's, Pound's and Pynchon's similarly situated, alone with a book, communing silently with an oracular author. But these configurations have changed radically from age to age—sometimes driven by shifts in technology, at other times by social changes. In the eighteenth century, the sea change in relations between writers and readers derived from new social transactions and a new marketplace of letters. And this change did much to shape the modern reckoning of the mix of the solitary and the social, the commerical and the therapeutic within the act of reading. In its refiguring of the social contract between writers and readers, the eighteenth century was nearly as eruptive as our own time with its marketplace of e-mail and Internet, where everyone can potentially operate as both consumer and purveyor—and no one knows for sure the shape of literary things to come.

In 1661, the Earl of Argyle wrote to his son with advice on books, their acquisition, and their proper use:

Think no cost too much in purchasing rare books; next to that of acquiring good friends I look upon this purchase; but buy them not to lay by or to grace your library, with the name of such a manuscript, or by such a singular piece, but read, revolve him, and lay him up in your memory where he will be far the better ornament. Read seriously whatever is before you, and reduce and digest it to practice and observation, otherwise it will be Sisyphus's labor to be always revolving sheets and books at every new occurence which will require the oracle of your reading. Trust not to your memory, but put all remarkable, notable things you shall meet with in your books *sub salva custodia* [under the sound care] of pen and ink, but so alter the property by your own scholia and annotations on it, that your memory may speedily recur to the place it was committed to.

The earl's account displays all the elements of the traditional reading program of Renaissance humanism: book or manuscript as surrogate friend, as "ornament" of the gentleman's mind and library, as "oracle" of enduring truths, as "property" to be possessed, marked, transcribed, and committed to memory. In the decades that followed, all these constructions remained in play, yet every one of the earl's crucial terms broadened in application to include print genres and transactions that Argyle would not have imagined: the periodical review, the monthly miscellany; epistolary fiction; the three-volume novel; as well as the coffeehouses and penny lending libraries that broadly circulated these new forms of print. With these new genres and modes of distribution, the text's status as friend, ornament, oracle, and property changed markedly.

Nothing had demonstrated (some even thought created) the material force and oracular authority of print so much as the English Civil Wars. Sermons and prophecies bearing the names of "oracles" and "revelations" forecast the demise of the Beast, the triumph of Parliament, indeed the imminence of the thousand-year rule of Christ on earth. Nor had the restoration of the Stuart monarchy wholly denatured print as prophecy—royalists and radicals continued to publish apocalyptic claims. And yet, over the ensuing decades the repeated threat of contest and rebellion began to exhaust both the authority of print as prophecy and the appetite of readers for a textual diet of frenzy and apocalypse—not that party warfare in print forms declined, but rather that partisanship yoked political contest to forms of confrontation that cooled apocalyptic tempers and supplanted military combat with paper controversy. The uneven course of government censorship, the issuing and lapsing of the licensing laws that governed press freedom, meant that paper wars with their full armory of ephemera—pamphlets, broadsides, pasquinades—raged at moments of crisis and parliamentary inattention when printers might cash in on the market for opposition and confrontation.

But not all the action of print contest was situated in the gutter of journalism. Satire, that most venerable mode of attack and advocacy, flourished in England as it had in Augustan Rome. Horace and Juvenal were indeed the models for Dryden, Pope, and Swift, who not only translated the forms of Roman satire into native idioms but were themselves possessed by all the Roman delight in outrage and invective, in civic engagement and political contest. But the genius of satire is never solely political. Satirists always score their most important points by wit, by cool savagery, by the thrust and parry of language, by the most brilliant and damaging metaphors and rhymes. Their peers, their rivals, even their enemies ruefully conceded that Dryden, Pope, and Swift had brought the verse couplet and the prose sentence to an unprecedented suppleness and precision. Satire in the years of civil war and Stuart agitations had begun in politics; pamphlet wars, swelled by periodicals, continued to rage through the Georgian age. But the classic verse satire had moved to a more exalted ground where the aesthetic often overwhelmed the political, and satire itself became an object of admiration, even of theorizing, and of the most vivid and polite conversation.

"Conversation" had once meant the entire conduct of life itself; now, "conversation" had narrowed to signify social exchange; yet social exchange in its turn had expanded to govern the conduct of life itself. Many of the most striking literary developments in the period—its poetic modes and tastes, the popularity and prominence of letter and journal writing, the advent of the newspaper and the novel—can perhaps best be understood as new ways devised by writers for performing conversation on the page—conversation with readers, with other writers, and within the texts themselves. The cultural critic Mikhail Bakhtin has pinpointed as one key feature of the novel its "heteroglossia": its capacity to speak, almost concurrently, many different languages, in the various voices and viewpoints of its characters and narrators; the range of its concerns (across social ranks and geographical spaces); even the variabilities of its style (each with its own cultural connotations) from page to page, paragraph to paragraph. But in this respect as in so many, the novel, usually reckoned the greatest literary invention of the period, is the product of a time when virtually all modes of writing were involved with diversity and dialogue.

One of the most popular ways of buying and reading poetry, for example, was in the form of "miscellanies"—anthologies of work by many hands ancient and modern in many modes, brought together in intriguing juxtapositions. Such juxtapositions could also take place within a single poem. For poets, a crucial procedure was the "imitation"—a poem in English that closely echoes the tone, structure, and sequence of a classical model while applying the predecessor's form and thought to contemporary topics. Where the Roman poet Juvenal, for example, begins his tenth Satire by declaring that wise men are hard to find even if you search every country from Spain to India (roughly the extent of the known Roman world), Samuel Johnson begins his imitation of Juvenal's poem (*The Vanity of Human Wishes*) this way:

> Let Observation, with extensive view,
> Survey mankind, from China to Peru . . .

The known world, Johnson tacitly reminds his knowing reader, is much larger than it was when Juvenal wrote (and hence the rarity of discerning mortals will be all the more striking). The opening couplet prepares us for the poem's close, where it will turn out that moral possibilities are larger too: there, Johnson will supplant Juvenal's characteristically Roman resignation to "Fortune" with an expressly Christian reliance on the cardinal virtues (faith, hope, charity) as a means of protection from the delusions of desire. The writer of a poetic imitation always conducts at least a double dialogue: between poet and predecessor, and between the present writer and the ideal reader who knows enough of the "original" to savor the poetic exchange, the cultural cross-talk, in all its echoes, divergences, and diversions.

Johnson here practices a more general kind of imitation as well, by casting his poem in heroic couplets: iambic pentameter lines paired in a sequence of successive rhymes. The rhymed pairs are often "closed," so that the moment of the rhyme coincides with and clinches the completion of a sentence and a thought. The verse form was called "heroic" because of its frequent use in the heroic drama and other high-aspiring poetry of the Restoration; the rhymed, closed pentameter was also thought to imitate, as closely as English allowed, the grandeur and the sonority of the lines in which ancient poets composed their epics. Throughout the century following the Restoration, the heroic couplet prevailed as the most commonly used poetic structure, adaptable to all genres and occasions, deployed by every sort of poet from hacks to John Dryden and Alexander Pope, the supreme masters of the mode. It was in this form that Dryden translated Virgil's *Aeneid* (1697) and Pope translated Homer's *Iliad* (1715–1720) and *Odyssey* (1725–1726), it was in this form that they wrote original poems of high seriousness and savage satire, and it was in this form that they aspired (like many of their contemporaries) to write new epics of their own. Neither ever did; both complained intermittently that they lived in an unheroic age. But the mesh of mighty ancient models with trivial modern subjects produced a new mode of satire, the mock-heroic, and disclosed astonishing suppleness in the heroic couplet itself.

In the hands of Dryden, Pope, and many others, the mock mode—high style, low subject matter—performed brilliant accommodations and solved large problems. It allowed poets to turn what they perceived as the crassness of modern culture to satiric advantage. If the triviality of modern life prevented them from recapturing epic grandeur whole, they could at least strive to match the epic's inclusiveness, its capacity to encompass all the things and actions of the world: the accessories of a young woman's dressing table (Pope's *Rape of the Lock*), the clutter in a gutter after rain (Swift's *Description of a City Shower*), the glut of print itself and the folly of those who produce so much bad writing (Pope's *Dunciad*). After Pope's death, though, this vein of mockery seemed exhausted. The heroic couplet persisted in poetry to the end of the century, but other verse forms became prominent too, partly in the service of an even wider inclusiveness, of paying new kinds of attention to modes of life and literature that lay outside the heroic and the mock: the predicament of the poor, the pleasures of domesticity, the discoveries of science, the tones and textures of medieval English balladry, the modalities of melancholy, the improvisatory motions of human thought and feeling. Blank verse—iambic pentameter without rhyme—offered one manifestation of the impulse to open-endedness. William Cowper's *The Task* (1785) and other huge works in blank verse are epic in their own kind: they mingle genres and move from topic to topic with the improvisatory energy of a barely stoppable train of thought. They perform the world's miscellany, the mind's conversation with itself and others, in a new poetic language—one that Wordsworth had absorbed by century's end, when he cast his *Prelude* in a capacious blank verse and praised in the preface to *Lyrical Ballads* that kind of poetry which deploys "the real language" of "a man speaking to men."

In the new prose forms of the eighteenth century—both nonfiction and fiction—the dominion of miscellany, the centrality of conversation, is if anything more palpable than in poetry. The first daily newspaper and the first magazines both appeared early in the century, providing a regularly recurrent compendium of disparate items intended to appeal to a variety of tastes and interests. These periodicals formed part of a larger and highly visible print mix: coffeehouses attracted a burgeoning clientele of urbanites by laying out copies of the current gazettes, mercuries, newsletters, playbooks, and satiric verses. Customers took pleasure in the literary montage, the ever-shifting anthology on the tabletops (of which the pictorial medley on page 1040 conveys a vivid visual idea). Coffeehouse customers gathered to consume new drink and new print in a commerce of pleasure, intellect, and gossip. Some read silently, others aloud to listeners who eagerly seized on texts and topics. Habits of social reading that would have been familiar to Chaucer and his audience (even to Virgil performing his epic at the court of Augustus Caesar) contributed to sociable debate on the persons and personalities of public life, foreign potentates, military campaigns, theatrical rivalries, monsters, and prodigies. In the eighteenth century, the papers and the consequent conversations broadened to encompass questions of personal conduct, relations between the sexes, manner and fashion. Writers of papers still claimed oracular authority: "Isaac Bickerstaff" of the *Tatler* dubbed himself the Censor of Great Britain, Mr. Spectator claimed to watch everyone who read his paper, and the *Athenian Gazette* dispensed advice as though with the authority of a supremely learned society. But writers made such claims at least partly with tongue in cheek; they knew that their oracular "truths" would trickle down into the commerce of conversation.

The press not only stimulated but also simulated conversation. Newspapers had always depended on "correspondents"—not (as now) professional reporters, but local letter writers who sent in the news of their parish and county in exchange for free copies of the paper. To read a newspaper was to read in part the work of fellow readers. Other periodicals—the scientific monthly as well as the journal of advice and the review of arts—adopted the practice of printing letters as a reliable source of copy and as an act and model of sociability. Printed correspondence ran longer, more ambitiously, and more lucratively. For the first time, the collected letters of the eminent became an attractive commercial genre (Pope was a pioneer), and travel books in the form of copious letters home sold by the thousands.

The printed letter would prove crucial too to the development of the newest form of all, the "novel." Aphra Behn had pioneered epistolary fiction in the Restoration, and Samuel Richardson recast the mode on an epic scale in *Pamela* and *Clarissa*, among the most important and talked-about fictions of the eighteenth century. In discussing the fate of his characters, Richardson's readers joined a conversation already in progress; Richardson's characters, in their lively exchange of letters, performed and modeled what their creator called "the converse of the pen."

Yet letters were only one among the many kinds of conversation that novelists contrived to carry on. "The rise of the novel"—the emergence over the course of the eighteenth century of so curious, capacious, and durable a genre—has long excited interest and controversy among scholars, who explain the phenomenon in various ways: by the emergence of a large middle-class readership with the money to obtain, the leisure to read, and the eagerness to absorb long narratives that mirrored their circumstances, their aspirations, and their appetites; by a tension between the aristocratic virtues central to older forms of fiction and the constructs of human merit prized by a proud commercial culture; by the passion for journalistic and experiential

Color Plate 21 Sir Peter Lely, *Barbara Villiers, Countess of Castlemaine*, c. 1641–1709. Theatricality disseminated: Charles II's favorite painter portrays Charles II's favorite mistress, in costume as Minerva, Roman goddess of wisdom, against a stormy background. Castlemaine's countenance was reproduced in less costly ways as well, in engravings from Lely's portraits that made the visage of the King's mistress possessible by ordinary mortals. The diarist Samuel Pepys records a visit to Lely's sumptuous studio, where he "saw the so-much-by-me-desired picture of my Lady Castlemaine, which is a most blessed picture and that I must have a copy of." *(The Royal Collection © 2003, Her Majesty Queen Elizabeth II.)*

Color Plate 22 Johann Zoffany (1733/4–1810), *Queen Charlotte with Her Two Eldest Sons*, 1764. Theatricality domesticated: a century after Lely painted the king's mistress in the garb of the goddess of wisdom (Color Plate 21), such mythological trappings are reduced to dress-up for George III's two young sons at play. Amid sumptuous furnishings, Zoffany's conversation piece emphasizes not the grandeur of the royal family but its intimacy and affection; a new era of majesty as "good example" has commenced. *(The Royal Collection © 2003, Her Majesty Queen Elizabeth II.)*

Color Plate 23 Joshua Reynolds, *Mrs. Abington as "Miss Prue,"* 1771. Restoration theatricality
transposed and transformed: the comic actress Frances Abington (1737–1815) here traverses time
and rank, reincarnating Miss Prue, an "awkward country girl" in William Congreve's late-17th-
century comedy *Love for Love* (1695), in garb that epitomizes late-18th-century high fashion.
Abington later scored her greatest triumph in a similar role, modeled on Restoration antecedents
and crafted especially for her: Lady Teazle, the country wife ardent for London life in Richard
Brinsley Sheridan's *School for Scandal. (The Bridgeman Art Library International Ltd.)*

Color Plate 24 Marcellus Laroon, *Charles II as President of the Royal Society*, 1684. Science enthroned: in this portrait of the King painted a year before his death, the traditional trappings of royalty—crown, throne, and orb—literally take a back seat (in the background at left) to the advancements of the new science. Charles gestures toward the instruments of seeing, modeling, mapping, and calibrating that the Royal Society he sponsored had done much to devise and develop. By their placement, the painter suggests that these tools make possible the naval commerce and conquest depicted in the distance—as though the telescope were the world's new scepter, and the globe the monarch's proper sphere. *(The Art Archive/Christ's Hospital/Eileen Tweedy.)*

Color Plate 25 Joseph Wright, *A Philosopher Giving That Lecture on the Orrery, in Which a Lamp Is Put in Place of the Sun,* 1766. Science popularized: the experimental philosophy and new science pioneered during the 17th century provided both pleasure and instruction in the 18th, as teachers and textbooks strove to distill and redistribute recondite discoveries as common knowledge. The orrery, a working model of the solar system, figured prominently in this new educational endeavor; it could supply, wrote Richard Steele, "the pleasures of science to any one." The spheres within the circle, coordinated by clockwork, enacted the orbits of the planets and their moons. The sun's stand-in was often a brass ball, but more rarely (as here) a lit oil lamp at the center of the machine. In Wright's painting, the flame sheds light on the lecturer and his listeners, each of them different, all of them enthralled. (*Derby Museums and Art Gallery.*)

Color Plate 26 *Joseph Wright, An Experiment on a Bird in the Air Pump, 1768. Science interrogated: the experiment's purpose is to demonstrate the effects of a vacuum on a breathing creature; its outcome, unless the experimenter restores air to the glass chamber, will be the death of the bird. Such experiments, though widely performed, were deemed by one lecturer "too shocking to every spectator who has the least degree of humanity." This time, Wright depicts a mixture of reactions. The lecturer, gesturing like a conjurer, stares out at the viewer as though in a kind of trance, oblivious both to the bird and to his audience, whose faces and forms variously evince absorption, meditation, distraction, and distress. (© National Gallery, London.)*

Color Plate 27 William Hogarth, *The Beggar's Opera, Act 3, Scene 11,* 1792. Theatricality encompasses all: audience and actors encounter each other on stage. Hogarth here replicates icons of art history much as *The Beggar's Opera*, a theatrical sensation of 1728, echoed popular ballads (see page 1277). Macheath, the criminal-hero of the play, is shown poised in the center between Lucy (left) and Polly (right)—a grouping that evokes the hero Hercules at his mythic moment of choosing between Virtue and Vice. Meanwhile, Polly and her father, Mr. Peachum (in black at right), strike poses bizarrely reminiscent of Christ and Mary Magdalen. Another kind of pairing is in play too. Lavinia Fenton, the actress playing Polly, gestures not so much toward her stage father as to the audience member standing starstruck just beyond him: the Duke of Bolton, so taken with her in the role that he became her lover and eventually her husband. In this, the fifth version he painted of the same scene, Hogarth has expanded the scope of the stage set so that the prison walls appear to enclose the spectators too within the *Opera*'s bright, bleak world, where everything and everyone have become commodities—objects of desire and items of exchange engulfed in intricate, energetic, precarious transactions. *(Yale Center for British Art, Paul Mellon Collection, USA/Photo: Bridgeman Art Library.)*

Color Plate 28   William Hogarth, *Hogarth's Servants*, mid-1750s. In this late painting, Hogarth's lifelong brilliancies of satire cede place to an approach both documentary and tender, as he traces, with painstaking attention and evident affection, the faces of six people deeply familiar to him. *(Tate Gallery, London/Art Resource, NY.)*

Color Plate 29   Thomas Gainsborough, *The Cottage Door*, c. 1788. As the critic John Barrell has pointed out, Gainsborough's painting mingles two different perceptions of the rural poor. The gracious women and boisterous children basking in the day's last light conjure up the sort of sentimental idealization of pastoral joys that also found expression in such poems as Oliver Goldsmith's *The Deserted Village*. Other writers insisted, by contrast, on the misery of the laborer's lot, an emphasis that is figured here in the form of the returning husband at bottom left, bent with his burden of firewood and nearly buried by the shadows. *(Cincinnati Art Museum, Acc. 1948.173.)*

fact (in newspapers, criminal autobiographies, scientific experiments, etc.), shading over imperceptibly into new practices of fiction.

All of these explanations are true, and each is revelatory when applied to particular clusters of novels. Still, definition and explanation remain elusive, as they clearly were for the genre's early readers and practitioners. The very word "novel"—identifying the genre by no other marks than newness itself—performs a kind of surrender in the face of a form whose central claim to novelty was its barely definable breadth. Mimicry, motion, and metamorphosis are the genre's stock in trade. Novels absorbed all the modes of literature around them: letters, diaries, memoirs, news items, government documents, drawings, verses, even sheet music all crop up within the pages of the early novels, one representational mode supplanting another with often striking speed. Novelists moved with equal alacrity through space: through England (Henry Fielding's *Tom Jones*), Britain more broadly (Tobias Smollett's *Humphry Clinker*), Europe (Smollett's *Roderick Random*), the entire globe as it is ordinarily mapped (Behn's *Oroonoko*, Defoe's *Robinson Crusoe*) or as it could be extraordinarily imagined (Swift's *Gulliver's Travels*). Traversing geographies, the genre crossed cultures too, mostly by means of mimicry, and parroted a range of accents, for purposes either of mockery—the malapropisms of a semiliterate housemaid, the fulminations of a Scots soldier, the outrage of an Irish cuckold—or of pathos: the lamentations of the African slave Oroonoko, the delirium of the violated Clarissa. Many novels, too, made a point of spanning the social spectrum, often compassing destitution and prosperity, labor and luxury within the career of a single ambitious character. Social mobility was perhaps the one plot element that novel readers savored most.

But the novel's supplest means of self-conveyance, its subtlest modes of conversation, were grounded in its attention to the workings of the mind. In his *Essay Concerning Human Understanding* (1690), the philosopher John Locke had explained the mind as a capacious, absorptive instrument engaged in constant motion, linking mixed memories, impressions, and ideas in a ceaseless chain of "associations." In the eighteenth century, novelists took Locke's cue: their works both mimicked the mind's capacity, heterogeneity, and associativeness, and explored them too, tracking over many pages the subtlest modulations in the characters' thoughts and feelings. Richardson famously boasted that his epistolary mode, featuring "familiar letters written as it were to the moment" by characters in their times of crisis, enabled him to track the course of their "hopes and fears" with unprecedented precision—and he trusted that the value of such a process would surely excuse the "bulk" of the huge novels themselves. In the nine volumes of Laurence Sterne's *Life and Opinions of Tristram Shandy*, the title narrator is so committed to following his digressive trains of thought wherever they may lead that the pronouncement of his opinions leaves him preposterously little time to narrate his life. Moving widely over space, freely through society, minutely through time, and deeply into mind, the novelists devised new strategies for achieving that epic inclusiveness that writers sought, in various ways, throughout the century.

The new tactics of miscellany, the new conversations conducted by means of pen and printing press, poetry and prose, refigured the practices of reading that the Earl of Argyle had wished to transmit to his son. In the aristocratic world of Renaissance letters, the book as friend had intimated a sphere of male pedagogy and sociability. The grammar school classroom, the college lecture hall, the estate library, the world of the tutor and his high-born protégé, all these figured reading principally as the privilege and the pleasure of a limited few, mostly males in positions of some leisure, comfort, and power. The links between reading and power were sustained through patterns of production and consumption in which authors received benefits from aristocratic patrons, and manuscripts passed from hand to hand. Donne refused to imagine his verse circulating in any other fashion. After the Restoration, Dryden, Behn, and Pope all pursued the compensations of print, but they nonetheless remained eager to participate in patronage and coterie circulation. Even when printed, their satires purveyed the pleasurable sense of shared knowledge that had constituted the *frisson* of coterie reading. Printers and poets understood that concealing a public name behind initials and dashes provided safety from censors and litigants, at the same time garnering a market share among readers who pleased themselves by decoding "dangerous matter."

By the middle of the eighteenth century, the patronage model of literary production and the coterie mode of distribution had been complicated (some thought ruined) by the commerce of print, for print had become the principal mode of literary distribution. Samuel Johnson, a bookseller's son, thought of literature as print and rarely circulated a manuscript as a gesture of literary sociability. ("None but a blockhead," he famously intoned, "ever wrote except for money.") As a consequence of the dominance of print and its broad distribution, the audiences for texts proliferated into new mixtures. Readers from many strata could afford a penny paper; apprentices and merchants' daughters might read the same novel. Assumptions of commonality that had underwritten the intimate sociability of Renaissance reading had been exploded by civil conflict in the mid-seventeenth century, by the profusion of print and the proliferation of genres that drove and were driven by the appetite of contest and conversation. During the eighteenth century, the print marketplace generated audiences on a scale vaster than ever before, circulating widely across the boundaries of class and gender. Print may have canceled some of the intimacies of the coterie, but it generated new convergences, even new consciousness—a public sphere in which aesthetics, politics, conduct, and taste were all objects of perpetual, often pleasurable debate. To an unprecedented extent, print furnished its readers with the substance for sustained conversation and continual contact.

It also kept them apart. Nothing was more evident to eighteenth-century men and women than the burgeoning of their domestic economy, the vastness of their colonial empire, and the growth in wealth and population which both entailed. The proliferation of consumables was evident in the village market, the Royal Exchange, and the bookstalls of country towns and capitol. The sheer bulk and variety of these consumables were strikingly evident in the length and scope of that capacious new genre, the novel. But even in the midst of abundance and sociability, eighteenth-century consumers were instructed in their paradoxical solitude. Defoe inscribes the condition of the novel as isolation—Robinson Crusoe, a man alone on an island, opines that human life "is, or ought to be, one universal act of solitude." And in novel after novel the very transactions of commerce produce isolation, as ambition and acquisition drive each character into the solitary, often melancholy corner of his or her own self-interest. The novel itself as a reading experience produced comparable sensations. Readers might now empathize with an entire world of fictional characters, but in order to savor such imaginative pleasures, they spent long hours in the privacy of their own quarters, in silent acts of reading.

A sense of solitude underwrote all this century's celebrated gregariousness. This held true even for sociable transactions that might take place between a reader and a text. In the Renaissance, it had long been a practice to annotate texts with comments echoing and endorsing the author's oracular wisdom. Under the pressure of civil war, the dialogue between author and reader often became more heated as the manuscript marginalia expressed anger and outrage at the partisan zeal of the printed text. But one form of textual reverence persisted. Throughout the seventeenth century readers took pleasure in writing marginalia that epitomized the text, making its wisdom portable. They filled blank books with pithy sentences, "commonplaces" drawn from their favorite works and organized in ways that would allow them to recirculate these sayings in their own writing and conversation.

By the eighteenth century, print had managed to appropriate all these modes of study and sociability. Through print, the manuscript collation of wit and wisdom turned into popular commodities—the printed commonplace book, the miscellany, the anthology. Even annotation itself migrated from manuscript markings into print, as Swift and Pope (among others) found ways of exploding scholarly pretension and of rendering the breath of gossip and scandal in the elaborate apparatus of the printed page. By century's end, all of manuscript's august authority and its most cherished genres—letters and memoirs—had been commandeered by print. In the mid-1730s, Pope alarmed and outraged his contemporaries by publishing his letters as if they deserved to partake of eternity with Cicero's. By the early nineteenth century, even that most secretive mode of self-communion, the private journal, had made its way into the marketplace. In 1825, Pepys's *Diary* appeared in two large printed folios, laying bare the elaborate machinery of public life, the secrets and scandals of the Restoration court, and the diarist's own experiences, transgressions, and sequestered musings, which he had written in shorthand code and shown to no one. The communal and commodified medium of print had found yet another way to market signal acts of solitude.

CODA

Mrs. Abington as "Miss Prue" (1771), by the pre-eminent portraitist Sir Joshua Reynolds (see Color Plate 23), shows a solitary figure engaged in intricate conversation with the viewer. Some of the intricacy inheres in the life history of the sitter, whose career many of the painting's first viewers would have known well. The daughter of a cobbler, Frances Abington had worked in childhood as a flower seller and in her teens as an actress, quickly establishing herself as "by far the most eminent performer in comedy of her day" (these words, and others to follow, are the testimony of contemporaries); she would eventually score one of her greatest hits in the role of that latter-day country wife Lady Teazle, in Richard Brinsley Sheridan's *The School for Scandal* (1777). When an unknown, Abington had married her music teacher; as fame increased, she carried on several well-publicized affairs with members of parliament and the aristocracy. By her sexual frankness, she scandalized—and of course fascinated—the multitudes. By her grace and taste, she became "a favorite of the public" and "the high priestess of fashion"; her costumes on stage

Joshua Reynolds, *Mrs. Abington as "Miss Prue,"* 1771. Restoration theatricality transposed and transformed.

instantly set new trends among her audience. Reynolds, who greatly admired her, here captures the complexity of her character and reputation. Her dress is supremely stylish, her pose deliberately provocative. For a woman to lean casually over the back of a chair this way violated all propriety; in earlier portraits, only men had struck such a pose. The thumb at her lips suggests vulgarity verging on the lascivious. The portrait's title purports to explain such seeming aberrations: the actress here appears in her celebrated role as Miss Prue, the "silly, awkward country girl" in William Congreve's Restoration comedy *Love for Love* (1695), who comes to London with the intention, frankly lustful and loudly declared, of getting herself a husband. In Reynolds's painting, of course, Mrs. Abington plays a role more layered: a hybrid of Miss Prue, of the matchlessly fashionable figure into which the actress had transformed herself, and of the whole range of experiences, the prodigious lifelong motion from poverty to polish, which formed part of her self-creation and her fame. Impersonating Miss Prue some seventy-five years after the comedy's first production, Mrs. Abington here infuses Restoration wantonness with Georgian elegance, transgression with high taste, theatricality with self-assertive authenticity. Like the century she inhabits, she is miscellany incarnate.

Stuart Sherman and
Steven N. Zwicker

Samuel Pepys

1633–1703

Twice in his life, Samuel Pepys embarked on long projects that allowed him to fuse the methods of the bureaucrat with an inventiveness that amounted to genius. The longer project, which occupied him from his mid-twenties through his mid-fifties, was a fundamental restructuring of the Royal Navy. The shorter project began just a few months earlier. Starting on January 1, 1660, and continuing for the next nine years, Pepys devised the diary form as we know it today: a detailed, private, day-by-day account of daily doings.

Halfway through the diary, Pepys delights to describe himself as "a very rising man," and he wrote the diary in part to track his ascent. The rise began slowly. Born in London to a tailor and a butcher's sister, Pepys studied at Puritan schools; he then attended Magdalene College, Cambridge, as a scholarship student. His B.A. left him well educated but short on cash. A year later he married the fifteen-year-old Elizabeth St. Michel, a French Protestant whose poverty surpassed his own. By his mid-twenties (when the diary commences), neither his accomplishments nor his prospects were particularly striking: he was working as factotum for two powerful men, one of them his high-born cousin Edward Mountagu, First Earl of Sandwich, an important naval officer once devoted to Cromwell but recently turned Royalist.

The diary begins at a calendrical turning point (the first day of a new week, a new year, and a new decade) and on a kind of double bet: that the coming time would bring changes worth writing up, both in the life of the diarist and in the history of the state. The two surmises quickly proved true. As a schoolboy taught by Puritans, Pepys had attended and applauded the execution of Charles I, but the Restoration of Charles II was the making of him, and he recalibrated his loyalties readily enough. His cousin secured for him the Clerkship of the Acts in the Navy Office, a secretarial post that Pepys transformed into something more. By mastering the numberless details of shipbuilding and supplying—from the quality of timber to the composition of tar and hemp—he contrived to control costs and produce results to an extent unmatched by any predecessor.

He managed all these matters so carefully that he soon became the ruler of the Royal Navy, in effect if not in name. When the Test Act of 1673 forced Charles's Catholic brother James to resign as Lord High Admiral, Pepys took his place (in the newly created post of Admiralty Secretary) and ran the operation. He immediately launched a systematic reform of the institution, which he had come to see as dangerously slipshod. By devising (in the words of one biographer) "a rule for all things, great or small" and by enforcing the new disciplines through a method of tireless surveillance and correspondence with ports extending from the Thames to Tangier, Pepys made the navy immeasurably more efficient than ever before. His efforts were interrupted by the political tribulations of his patron James: Pepys spent two brief terms in prison on trumped-up charges of Catholic sympathies, and in 1688 the Glorious Revolution drove him from office into a prosperous retirement. At the height of his power, though, as his biographer Richard Ollard observes, Pepys was the "master builder" of the permanent, professional navy that made possible the expansion of trade and the conquest of colonies over the ensuing century. Energetic in his king's service and in his own (the taking of bribes was one of the perquisites of office that Pepys mastered most adroitly), the tailor's son functioned formidably as an early architect of empire.

Pepys's schooling and profession had immersed him in the two practices most central to earlier English diaries, Puritanism and financial bookkeeping. But where account books and religious diaries emphasize certain kinds of moment—exchanges of money and goods, instances of moral redemption and relapse—Pepys tries for something more comprehensive. He implicitly commits himself to tracking the whole day's experience: the motions of the body as it makes its way through the city in boats, in coaches, and on foot, and the motions of the mind as it shuttles between business and pleasure. He sustained his narrative over a virtually unbroken series of daily entries before stopping out of fear that his work on the diary had helped to damage his eyesight to the brink of blindness. "None of Pepys's contemporaries," writes his editor Robert Latham, "attempted a diary in the all-inclusive Pepysian sense and on the Pepysian scale." To the efficiency of the bookkeeper and the discipline of the Puritan, Pepys added the ardor of the virtuoso, eager (as he observes at one point) "to see any strange thing" and capable of finding wonder in ordinary things: music, plays, books, food, clothes, conversation. The phrase "with great pleasure" recurs in the diary as a kind of leitmotiv, and superlatives play leapfrog through the pages: many, many experiences qualify in turn as the "best" thing that the diarist ever ate, read, thought, saw, heard. To achieve the diary's seeming immediacy, Pepys put his entries through as many as five stages of revision, sometimes days or even months after the events recorded. Even at the final stage, in the bound, elegantly format- ted volumes of the diary manuscript, he often crammed new detail or comment into margins and between the lines. Comparable pressures operated in connection with the diary's complex privacy. Pepys took pains to secure secrecy for his text. He hid it from view in drawers or in cabinets. He wrote most of it in a secretarial shorthand, and where he most wanted secrecy, as in the accounts of his many flirtations and infidelities, he obscured things further by an impro- vised language made up of Spanish, French, Latin, and other tongues. (Elizabeth Pepys figures throughout the diary as a kind of muse and countermuse, the narrative's most recurrent and obsessive subject, and the person most urgently to be prevented from reading it.) At the same time, the manuscript makes notable gestures toward self-display. Pepys frequently shifts to a readily readable longhand, especially for names, places, titles of books, plays, and persons; at times even his secret sexual language opens out into longhand.

This ambivalent secrecy persisted past the diarist's death. Pepys bequeathed the manu- script to Magdalene College without calling any special attention to it. It was included among his many collections: of naval books and papers, of broadsheet ballads, and of instruction man- uals on shorthand methods—including the one Pepys used to write the diary. The manuscript kept its secrets long. In the early nineteenth century, the diary was discovered and painstak- ingly decoded (by a transcriber who, missing the connection between the manuscript and the shorthand manuals on adjacent shelves, treated the text as a million-word cryptogram); it was finally published, in a severely shortened and expurgated version, in 1825. Readers and reviewers soon called for more, recognizing that Pepys possessed (in the words of one re- viewer) "the most indiscriminating, insatiable, and miscellaneous curiosity, that ever . . . sup- plied the pen, of a daily chronicler." Expanded (but still bowdlerized) editions appeared throughout the century, and only in the 1970s did the semisecret manuscript make its way wholly into print.

from The Diary
[FIRST ENTRIES][1]

$16\frac{59}{60}$.

Blessed be God, at the end of the last year I was in very good health, without any sense of my old pain[2] but upon taking of cold.

---

1. England still adhered to the Old Style calendar, in which the new year officially began on March 25. Pepys wrote this "prelude" in early January 1659 according to the English reckoning, but 1660 (New Style) in the rest of Europe.
2. Pepys had suffered from stones in the bladder from babyhood until 1658, when he underwent a risky but suc- cessful operation.

I lived in Axe Yard,[3] having my wife and servant Jane, and no more in family than us three.

My wife, after the absence of her terms[4] for seven weeks, gave me hopes of her being with child, but on the last day of the year she hath them again. The condition of the state was thus. Viz. the Rump, after being disturbed by my Lord Lambert, was lately returned to sit again.[5] The officers of the army all forced to yield. Lawson lies still in the river and Monck is with his army in Scotland.[6] Only my Lord Lambert is not yet come in to the Parliament; nor is it expected that he will, without being forced to it.

The new Common Council of the City doth speak very high; and hath sent to Monck their sword-bearer, to acquaint him with their desires for a free and full Parliament, which is at present the desires and the hopes and expectation of all—22 of the old secluded members having been at the House door the last week to demand entrance; but it was denied them, and it is believed that they nor the people will not be satisfied till the House be filled.[7]

My own private condition very handsome; and esteemed rich, but indeed very poor, besides my goods of my house and my office, which at present is somewhat uncertain. Mr Downing master of my office.[8]

1 January 1659/60. Lord's Day. This morning (we lying lately in the garret) I rose, put on my suit with great skirts,[9] having not lately worn any other clothes but them.

Went to Mr. Gunning's church at Exeter House, where he made a very good sermon upon these words: that in the fullness of time God sent his Son, made of a woman, etc., showing that by "made under the law" is meant his circumcision, which is solemnized this day.[1]

Dined at home in the garret, where my wife dressed the remains of a turkey, and in the doing of it she burned her hand.

I stayed at home all the afternoon, looking over my accounts.

Then went with my wife to my father's; and in going, observed the great posts which the City hath set up[2] at the Conduit in Fleet Street.

Supped at my father's, where in came Mrs. Theophila Turner and Madam Morris[3] and supped with us. After that, my wife and I went home with them, and so to our own home.

---

3. In Westminster.

4. Menstrual periods.

5. John Lambert, a skilled general under Oliver Cromwell, now opposed the convening of the Rump Parliament, which had governed England since the fall of Cromwell's son Richard in 1659.

6. At this point, the political intentions and allegiance of General George Monck were the object of much speculation; he led his army back from Scotland into England on 1 January and became one of the principal engineers of the Restoration. Vice-Admiral John Lawson supported the Rump.

7. A Parliament that would include the "old secluded members"—the representatives expelled in 1648—was understood to be a first step toward restoration of the monarchy.

8. Pepys was at this point a clerk in the office of the Exchequer.

9. I.e., with a long coat.

1. Peter Gunning had held illegal Anglican services during the Commonwealth. His sermon text is Galatians 4.4: "But, when the fullness of the time was come, God sent forth his Son, made of a woman, made under the law."

2. As defensive barriers during its opposition to the Rump Parliament.

3. A relative and a friend, respectively. "Mistress" ("Mrs.") was applied to unmarried as well as to married women; Theophila was eight years old.

[THE CORONATION OF CHARLES II][4]

[23 April 1661] I lay with Mr. Shiply,[5] and about 4 in the morning I rose.

Coronation Day.

And got to the Abbey,[6] where I followed Sir J. Denham the surveyor with some company that he was leading in. And with much ado, by the favor of Mr. Cooper his man, did get up into a great scaffold across the north end of the Abbey—where with a great deal of patience I sat from past 4 till 11 before the King came in. And a pleasure it was to see the Abbey raised in the middle, all covered with red and a throne (that is a chair) and footstool on the top of it. And all the officers of all kinds, so much as the very fiddlers, in red vests.

At last comes in the Dean and prebends of Westminster with the Bishops (many of them in cloth-of-gold copes); and after them the nobility all in their Parliament robes, which was a most magnificent sight. Then the Duke[7] and the King with a scepter (carried by my Lord of Sandwich) and sword and mond before him, and the crown too.

The King in his robes, bare-headed, which was very fine. And after all had placed themselves, there was a sermon and the service. And then in the choir at the high altar he passed all the ceremonies of the coronation—which, to my very great grief, I and most in the Abbey could not see. The crown being put upon his head, a great shout begun. And he came forth to the throne and there passed more ceremonies: as, taking the oath and having things read to him by the Bishop, and his lords (who put on their caps as soon as the King put on his crown) and bishops came and kneeled before him.

And three times the King-at-Arms went to the three open places on the scaffold and proclaimed that if any one could show any reason why Charles Stuart should not be King of England, that now he should come and speak.

And a general pardon also was read by the Lord Chancellor;[8] and medals flung up and down by my Lord Cornwallis—of silver; but I could not come by any.

But so great a noise, that I could make but little of the music; and indeed, it was lost to everybody. But I had so great a list[9] to piss, that I went out a little while before the King had done all his ceremonies and went round the Abbey to Westminster Hall, all the way within rails, and 10,000 people, with the ground covered with blue cloth—and scaffolds all the way. Into the hall I got—where it was very fine with hangings and scaffolds, one upon another, full of brave[1] ladies. And my wife in one little one on the right hand.

Here I stayed walking up and down; and at last, upon one of the side-stalls, I stood and saw the King come in with all the persons (but the soldiers) that were yesterday in the cavalcade;[2] and a most pleasant sight it was to see them in their several robes. And the King came in with his crown on and his scepter in his hand—under a canopy borne up by six silver staves, carried by Barons of the Cinqueports—and little bells at every end.

---

4. Charles II had returned to England in May 1660; he scheduled his coronation for St. George's Day, honoring England's patron saint.
5. Edward Shipley was steward to Pepys's cousin Edward Mountagu.
6. Westminster Abbey, site of English coronations.
7. Charles's brother James, Duke of York, later James II.

8. Charles II's Act of Oblivion forgave the crimes of all those on the parliamentary side, with the principal exception of those who had participated in the trial, sentencing, and execution of his father.
9. Desire.
1. Splendid.
2. The previous day's procession.

And after a long time he got up to the farther end, and all set themselves down at their several tables—and that was also a rare sight. And the King's first course carried up by the Knights of the Bath. And many fine ceremonies there was of the heralds leading up people before him and bowing; and my Lord of Albemarle's[3] going to the kitchen and eat[4] a bit of the first dish that was to go to the King's table.

But above all was these three Lords, Northumberland and Suffolk and the Duke of Ormond, coming before the courses on horseback and staying so all dinner-time; and at last, to bring up Dymock the King's champion, all in armor on horseback, with his spear and target carried before him. And a herald proclaim that if any dare deny Charles Stuart to be lawful King of England, here was a champion that would fight with him; and with those words the champion flings down his gauntlet; and all this he doth three times in his going up toward the King's table. At last, when he is come, the King drinks to him and then sends him the cup, which is of gold; and he drinks it off and then rides back again with the cup in his hand.

I went from table to table to see the bishops and all others at their dinner, and was infinite pleased with it. And at the lords' table I met with Will Howe and he spoke to my Lord for me and he did give him four rabbits and a pullet; and so I got it, and Mr. Creed and I got Mr. Mitchell to give us some bread and so we at a stall eat it, as everybody else did what they could get.[5]

I took a great deal of pleasure to go up and down and look upon the ladies—and to hear the music of all sorts; but above all, the 24 violins.

About 6 at night they had dined; and I went up to my wife and there met with a pretty lady (Mrs. Franklin, a doctor's wife, a friend of Mr. Bowyer's) and kissed them both—and by and by took them down to Mr. Bowyer's. And strange it is, to think that these two days have held up fair till now that all is done and the King gone out of the Hall; and then it fell a-raining and thundering and lightening as I have not seen it do some years—which people did take great notice of God's blessing of the work of these two days—which is a foolery, to take too much notice of such things.

I observed little disorder in all this; but only the King's footmen had got hold of the canopy and would keep it from the Barons of the Cinqueports; which they endeavored to force from them again but could not do it till my Lord Duke of Albemarle caused it to be put into Sir R. Pye's hand till tomorrow to be decided.

At Mr. Bowyer's, a great deal of company; some I knew, others I did not. Here we stayed upon the leads[6] and below till it was late, expecting to see the fireworks; but they were not performed tonight. Only, the City had a light like a glory round about it, with bonfires.

At last I went to King Street; and there sent Crockford to my father's and my house to tell them I could not come home tonight, because of the dirt and a coach could not be had.

And so after drinking a pot of ale alone at Mrs. Harper's, I returned to Mr. Bowyer's; and after a little stay more, I took my wife and Mrs. Franklin (who I proferred the civility of lying with my wife at Mrs. Hunt's tonight) to Axe Yard. In which, at the further end, there was three great bonfires and a great many great gallants, men and women; and they laid hold of us and would have us drink the King's

---

3. In 1660 Charles II had made George Monck Duke of Albemarle as a reward for his role in the Restoration.
4. Ate (pronounced "ett"), to test for poison.
5. Will Howe and John Creed served as clerks to Sand-

wich, whom the diarist invariably refers to as "my Lord." Miles Mitchell was a local bookseller.
6. Rooftop.

health upon our knee, kneeling upon a fagot; which we all did, they drinking to us one after another—which we thought a strange frolic. But these gallants continued thus a great while, and I wondered to see how the ladies did tipple.

At last I sent my wife and her bedfellow to bed, and Mr. Hunt and I went in with Mr. Thornbury (who did give the company all their wines, he being yeoman of the wine-cellar to the King) to his house; and there, with his wife and two of his sisters and some gallant sparks that were there, we drank the King's health and nothing else, till one of the gentlemen fell down stark drunk and there lay spewing. And I went to my Lord's pretty well. But no sooner a-bed with Mr. Shiply but my head begun to turn and I to vomit, and if ever I was foxed[7] it was now—which I cannot say yet, because I fell asleep and sleep till morning—only, when I waked I found myself wet with my spewing. Thus did the day end, with joy everywhere; and blessed be God, I have not heard of any mischance to anybody through it all, but only to Sergeant Glynne, whose horse fell upon him yesterday and is like to kill him; which people do please themselves with, to see how just God is to punish that rogue at such a time as this—he being now one of the King's sergeants and rode in the cavalcade with Maynard, to whom people wished the same fortune.[8]

There was also this night, in King Street, a woman had her eye put out by a boy's flinging of a firebrand into the coach.

Now after all this, I can say that besides the pleasure of the sight of these glorious things, I may now shut my eyes against any other objects, or for the future trouble myself to see things of state and show, as being sure never to see the like again in this world.

[24 April 1661] Waked in the morning with my head in a sad taking through the last night's drink, which I am very sorry for. So rise and went out with Mr. Creed to drink our morning draught, which he did give me in chocolate to settle my stomach. And after that to my wife, who lay with Mrs. Franklin at the next door to Mrs. Hunt's.

And they were ready, and so I took them up in a coach and carried the lady to Paul's[9] and there set her down; and so my wife and I home—and I to the office.

That being done, my wife and I went to dinner to Sir W. Batten;[1] and all our talk about the happy conclusion of these last solemnities.

After dinner home and advised with my wife about ordering things in my house; and then she went away to my father's to lie, and I stayed with my workmen, who do please me very well with their work.

At night set myself to write down these three days' diary; and while I am about it, I hear the noise of the chambers and other things of the fireworks, which are now playing upon the Thames before the King. And I wish myself with them, being sorry not to see them.

So to bed.

[The Fire of London]

[2 September 1666] Lord's Day. Some of our maids sitting up late last night to get things ready against our feast today, Jane called us up, about 3 in the morning, to tell us

---

7. Drunk.
8. Sir John Glynne and Sir John Maynard were lawyers who had served under Cromwell.

9. St. Paul's Cathedral.
1. Surveyor of the Navy.

of a great fire they saw in the City. So I rose, and slipped on my nightgown and went to her window, and thought it to be on the back side of Mark Lane at the furthest; but being unused to such fires as followed, I thought it far enough off, and so went to bed again and to sleep. About 7 rose again to dress myself, and there looked out at the window and saw the fire not so much as it was, and further off. So to my closet[2] to set things to rights after yesterday's cleaning. By and by Jane comes and tells me that she hears that above 300 houses have been burned down tonight by the fire we saw, and that it was now burning down all Fish Street by London Bridge. So I made myself ready presently, and walked to the Tower and there got up upon one of the high places, Sir J. Robinson's little son going up with me; and there I did see the houses at that end of the bridge all on fire, and an infinite great fire on this and the other side the end of the bridge—which, among other people, did trouble me for poor little Mitchell and our Sarah on the bridge.[3] So down, with my heart full of trouble, to the Lieutenant of the Tower, who tells me that it begun this morning in the King's baker's house in Pudding Lane, and that it hath burned down St. Magnus's Church and most part of Fish Street already. So I down to the water-side and there got a boat and through bridge,[4] and there saw a lamentable fire. Poor Mitchell's house, as far as the Old Swan, already burned that way and the fire running further, that in a very little time it got as far as the Steelyard while I was there. Everybody endeavoring to remove their goods, and flinging into the river or bringing them into lighters[5] that lay off. Poor people staying in their houses as long as till the very fire touched them, and then running into boats or clambering from one pair of stair by the water-side to another. And among other things, the poor pigeons I perceive were loath to leave their houses, but hovered about the windows and balconies till they were some of them burned, their wings, and fell down.

Having stayed, and in an hour's time seen the fire rage every way, and nobody to my sight endeavoring to quench it, but to remove their goods and leave all to the fire; and having seen it get as far as the Steelyard, and the wind mighty high and driving it into the City, and everything, after so long a drought, proving combustible, even the very stones of churches, and among other things, the poor steeple by which pretty Mrs. Horsley lives, and whereof my old school-fellow Elborough is parson, taken fire in the very top and there burned till it fall down—I to Whitehall with a gentleman with me who desired to go off from the Tower to see the fire in my boat—to Whitehall, and there up to the King's closet in the chapel, where people came about me and I did give them an account dismayed them all; and word was carried in to the King, so I was called for and did tell the King and Duke of York what I saw, and that unless his Majesty did command houses to be pulled down, nothing could stop the fire. They seemed much troubled, and the King commanded me to go to my Lord Mayor from him and command him to spare no houses but to pull down before the fire every way. The Duke of York bid me tell him that if he would have any more soldiers, he shall; and so did my Lord Arlington afterward, as a great secret. Here meeting with Captain Cocke, I in his coach, which he lent me, and Creed with me, to Paul's; and there walked along Watling Street as well as I could, every creature coming away loaden with goods to save—and here and there sick people carried away in beds. Extraordinary good goods carried in carts and on backs. At last met my Lord Mayor in Canning Street,

---

2. Private room, study.
3. London Bridge was lined with shops and houses, including the liquor shop of Pepys's friend Michael

Mitchell and the residence of his former servant Sarah.
4. Under the bridge.
5. Barges.

like a man spent, with a hankercher about his neck. To the King's message, he cried like a fainting woman, "Lord, what can I do? I am spent! People will not obey me. I have been pulling down houses. But the fire overtakes us faster than we can do it." That he needed no more soldiers; and that for himself, he must go and refresh himself, having been up all night. So he left me, and I him, and walked home—seeing people all almost distracted and no manner of means used to quench the fire. The houses too, so very thick thereabouts, and full of matter for burning, as pitch and tar, in Thames Street—and warehouses of oil and wines and brandy and other things. Here I saw Mr. Isaac Houblon, that handsome man—prettily dressed and dirty at his door at Dowgate, receiving some of his brothers' things whose houses were on fire; and as he says, have been removed twice already, and he doubts (as it soon proved) that they must be in a little time removed from his house also—which was a sad consideration. And to see the churches all filling with goods, by people who themselves should have been quietly there at this time.

By this time it was about 12 a-clock, and so home and there find my guests, which was Mr. Wood and his wife, Barbary Shelden, and also Mr. Moone—she mighty fine, and her husband, for aught I see, a likely man. But Mr. Moone's design and mine, which was to look over my closet and please him with the sight thereof, which he hath long desired, was wholly disappointed, for we were in great trouble and disturbance at this fire, not knowing what to think of it. However, we had an extraordinary good dinner, and as merry as at this time we could be.

While at dinner, Mrs. Batelier came to inquire after Mr. Woolfe and Stanes (who it seems are related to them), whose houses in Fish Street are all burned, and they in a sad condition. She would not stay in the fright.

As soon as dined, I and Moone away and walked through the City, the streets full of nothing but people and horses and carts loaden with goods, ready to run over one another, and removing goods from one burned house to another—they now removing out of Canning Street (which received goods in the morning) into Lombard Street and further; and among others, I now saw my little goldsmith Stokes receiving some friend's goods, whose house itself was burned the day after. We parted at Paul's, he home and I to Paul's Wharf, where I had appointed a boat to attend me; and took in Mr. Carkesse and his brother, whom I met in the street, and carried them below and above bridge, to and again, to see the fire, which was now got further, both below and above, and no likelihood of stopping it. Met with the King and Duke of York in their barge, and with them to Queenhithe and there called Sir Richard Browne to them. Their order was only to pull down houses apace, and so below bridge at the water-side; but little was or could be done, the fire coming upon them so fast. Good hopes there was of stopping it at the Three Cranes above, and at Buttolph's Wharf below bridge, if care be used; but the wind carries it into the City, so as we know not by the water-side what it doth there. River full of lighters and boats taking in goods, and good goods swimming in the water; and only, I observed that hardly one lighter or boat in three that had the goods of a house in, but there was a pair of virginals[6] in it. Having seen as much as I could now, I away to Whitehall by appointment, and there walked to St. James's Park, and there met my wife and Creed and Wood and his wife and walked to my boat, and there upon the water again, and to the fire up and down, it still increasing and the wind great. So near the fire as we could for smoke; and all over the

---

6. A small harpsichord.

Thames, with one's face in the wind you were almost burned with a shower of fire-drops—this is very true—so as houses were burned by these drops and flakes of fire, three or four, nay five or six houses, one from another. When we could endure no more upon the water, we to a little alehouse on the Bankside over against the Three Cranes, and there stayed till it was dark almost and saw the fire grow; and as it grow darker, appeared more and more, and in corners and upon steeples and between churches and houses, as far as we could see up the hill of the City, in a most horrid malicious bloody flame, not like the fine flame of an ordinary fire. Barbary and her husband away before us. We stayed till, it being darkish, we saw the fire as only one entire arch of fire from this to the other side the bridge, and in a bow up the hill, for an arch of above a mile long. It made me weep to see it. The churches, houses, and all on fire and flaming at once, and a horrid noise the flames made, and the cracking of houses at their ruin. So home with a sad heart, and there find everybody discoursing and lamenting the fire; and poor Tom Hayter[7] came with some few of his goods saved out of his house, which is burned upon Fish Street Hill. I invited him to lie at my house, and did receive his goods: but was deceived in his lying there, the noise coming every moment of the growth of the fire, so as we were forced to begin to pack up our own goods and prepare for their removal. And did by moonshine (it being brave,[8] dry, and moonshine and warm weather) carry much of my goods into the garden, and Mr. Hayter and I did remove my money and iron-chests into my cellar—as thinking that the safest place. And got my bags of gold into my office ready to carry away, and my chief papers of accounts also there, and my tallies into a box by themselves. So great was our fear, as Sir W. Batten had carts come out of the country to fetch away his goods this night. We did put Mr. Hayter, poor man, to bed a little; but he got but very little rest, so much noise being in my house, taking down of goods.

[3 September 1666] About 4 a-clock in the morning, my Lady Batten sent me a cart to carry away all my money and plate and best things to Sir W. Rider's at Bethnell Green; which I did, riding myself in my nightgown in the cart; and Lord, to see how the streets and the highways are crowded with people, running and riding and getting of carts at any rate to fetch away things. I find Sir W. Rider tired with being called up[9] all night and receiving things from several friends. His house full of goods—and much of Sir W. Batten and Sir W. Penn's.[1] I am eased at my heart to have my treasure so well secured. Then home with much ado to find a way. Nor any sleep all this night to me nor my poor wife. But then, and all this day, she and I and all my people laboring to get away the rest of our things, and did get Mr. Tooker to get me a lighter to take them in, and we did carry them (myself some) over Tower Hill, which was by this time full of people's goods, bringing their goods thither. And down to the lighter, which lay at the next quay above the Tower Dock. And here was my neighbor's wife, Mrs. Buckworth, with her pretty child and some few of her things, which I did willingly give way to be saved with mine. But there was no passing with anything through the postern,[2] the crowd was so great.

The Duke of York came this day by the office and spoke to us, and did ride with his guard up and down the City to keep all quiet (he being now general, and having the care of all).

---

7. One of Pepys's clerks in the Navy Office.
8. Pleasant.
9. Called on, woken.

1. William Penn, Pepys's colleague on the Navy Board (and father of the founder of Pennsylvania).
2. Back or side gate.

This day, Mercer being not at home, but against her mistress's order gone to her mother's, and my wife going thither to speak with W. Hewer, met her there and was angry; and her mother saying that she was not a prentice girl, to ask leave every time she goes abroad, my wife with good reason was angry, and when she came home, bid her be gone again. And so she went away, which troubled me; but yet less than it would, because of the condition we are in fear of coming into in a little time, of being less able to keep one in her quality. At night, lay down a little upon a quilt of W. Hewer in the office (all my own things being packed up or gone); and after me, my poor wife did the like—we having fed upon the remains of yesterday's dinner, having no fire nor dishes, nor any opportunity of dressing anything.

[4 September 1666] Up by break of day to get away the remainder of my things, which I did by a lighter at the Iron Gate; and my hands so few, that it was the afternoon before we could get them all away.

Sir W. Penn and I to Tower Street, and there met the fire burning three or four doors beyond Mr. Howell's; whose goods, poor man (his trays and dishes, shovels, etc., were flung all along Tower Street in the kennels, and people working therewith from one end to the other), the fire coming on in that narrow street, on both sides, with infinite fury. Sir W. Batten, not knowing how to remove his wine, did dig a pit in the garden and laid it in there; and I took the opportunity of laying all the papers of my office that I could not otherwise dispose of. And in the evening Sir W. Penn and I did dig another and put our wine in it, and I my parmesan cheese as well as my wine and some other things.

The Duke of York was at the office this day at Sir W. Penn's, but I happened not to be within. This afternoon, sitting melancholy with Sir W. Penn in our garden and thinking of the certain burning of this office without extraordinary means, I did propose for the sending up of all our workmen from Woolwich and Deptford yards (none whereof yet appeared), and to write to Sir W. Coventry to have the Duke of York's permission to pull down houses rather then lose this office, which would much hinder the King's business. So Sir W. Penn he went down this night, in order to the sending them up tomorrow morning; and I wrote to Sir W. Coventry about the business, but received no answer.

This night Mrs. Turner (who, poor woman, was removing her goods all this day—good goods, into the garden, and knew not how to dispose of them)—and her husband supped with my wife and I at night in the office, upon a shoulder of mutton from the cook's, without any napkin or anything, in a sad manner but were merry. Only, now and then walking into the garden and saw how horridly the sky looks, all on a fire in the night, was enough to put us out of our wits; and indeed it was extremely dreadful—for it looks just as if it was at us, and the whole heaven on fire. I after supper walked in the dark down to Tower Street, and there saw it all on fire at the Trinity House on that side and the Dolphin Tavern on this side, which was very near us—and the fire with extraordinary vehemence. Now begins the practice of blowing up of houses in Tower Street, those next the Tower, which at first did frighten people more than anything; but it stopped the fire where it was done—it bringing down the houses to the ground in the same places they stood, and then it was easy to quench what little fire was in it, though it kindled nothing almost. W. Hewer this day went to see how his mother did, and comes late home, but telling us how he hath been forced to remove her to Islington, her house in Pye Corner being burned. So that it is got so far that way and all the Old

Bailey, and was running down to Fleet Street. And Paul's is burned, and all Cheapside. I wrote to my father this night; but the post-house being burned, the letter could not go.

⁓

COMPANION READING
John Evelyn: from *Kalendarium*[1]

[2 September 1666] This fatal night about ten, began that deplorable fire, near Fish Street in London. 2: I had public prayers at home: after dinner the fire continuing, with my wife and son took coach and went to the Bankside in Southwark,[2] where we beheld that dismal spectacle, the whole City in dreadful flames near the water-side, and had now consumed all the houses from the bridge all Thames Street and upwards towards Cheapside, down to the Three Cranes, and so returned exceedingly astonished, what would become of the rest. 3: The fire having continued all this night (if I may call that night, which was as light as day for 10 miles round about after a dreadful manner) when conspiring with a fierce eastern wind, in a very dry season, I went on foot to the same place, when I saw the whole south part of the City burning from Cheapside to the Thames, and all along Cornhill (for it likewise kindled back against the wind, as well as forward) Tower Street, Fenchurch Street, Gracious Street and so along to Baynard Castle, and was now taking hold of St. Paul's Church, to which the scaffolds contributed exceedingly. The conflagration was so universal, and the people so astonished, that from the beginning (I know not by what desponding or fate), they hardly stirred to quench it, so as there was nothing heard or seen but crying out and lamentation, and running about like distracted creatures, without at all attempting to save even their goods; such a strange consternation there was upon them, so as it burned both in breadth and length, the churches, public halls, Exchange, hospitals, monuments, and ornaments, leaping after a prodigious manner from house to house and street to street, at great distance one from the other, for the heat (with a long set of fair and warm weather) had even ignited the air, and prepared the materials to conceive the fire, which devoured after an incredible manner, houses, furniture, and everything. Here we saw the Thames covered with goods floating, all the barges and boats laden with what some had time and courage to save, as on the other, the carts etc. carrying out to the fields, which for many miles were strewed with moveables of all sorts, and tents erecting to shelter both people and what goods they could get away: O the miserable and calamitous spectacle, such as haply the whole world had not seen the like since the foundation of it, nor to be outdone, till the universal conflagration

---

1. John Evelyn (1620–1706), versatile author (on air pollution, architecture, gardening, forestry, and other subjects), wrote up his life on a plan very different from that of his friend Pepys. His *Kalendarium*, commenced when he was 40 years old, narrates selected dates (and omits many), starting with his birth and ending shortly before his death; the thousand-page manuscript encompasses (in legible longhand) his extensive travels in Europe during the Civil Wars and his busy social, court, and civic life after the Restoration. Evelyn's vantage on the Fire of London (as on much else) contrasts with Pepys's. A landowning gentleman, Evelyn dwelt at a remove from the

City on a country estate across the river. A devout Anglican, he saw the catastrophe as an apocalypse steeped in biblical precedent and prophecy. A tireless projector of plans and improvements, he reckoned the City's losses and began to imagine its renewal. Nine days after the fire's outbreak, Evelyn presented the king and queen "with a survey of the ruins and a plot for a new city. . . . [They seemed] extremely pleased with what I had so early thought on"—though in the event, no unified plan for rebuilding was followed.

2. The southern bank of the Thames, across the river from the fire.

of it. All the sky were of a fiery aspect, like the top of a burning oven, and the light seen above 40 miles round about for many nights. God grant mine eyes may never behold the like, who now saw above ten thousand houses all in one flame, the noise and crackling and thunder of the impetuous flames, the shrieking of women and children, the hurry of people, the fall of towers, houses and churches was like an hideous storm, and the air all about so hot and inflamed that at the last one was not able to approach it, so as they were forced to stand still, and let the flames consume on which they did for near two whole miles in length and one in breadth. The clouds also of smoke were dismal, and reached upon computation near 50 miles in length. Thus I left it this afternoon burning, a resemblance of Sodom, or the last day.[3] It called to mind that of 4 *Heb: non enim hic habemus stabilem Civitatem:*[4] the ruins resembling the picture of *Troy: London* was,[5] but is no more. Thus I returned.

[4 September 1666] The burning still rages; I went now on horseback, and it was now gotten as far as the Inner Temple; all Fleet Street, Old Bailey, Ludgate Hill, Warwick Lane, Newgate, Paul's Chain, Watling Street now flaming and most of it reduced to ashes, the stones of Paul's flew like granados,[6] the lead melting down the streets in a stream, and the very pavements of them glowing with fiery redness, so as nor horse nor man was able to tread on them, and the demolitions had stopped all the passages, so as no help could be applied; the eastern wind still more impetuously driving the flames forwards. Nothing but the almighty power of God was able to stop them, for vain was the help of man. On the fourth it crossed towards Whitehall, but O the confusion was then at that court. It pleased his Majesty to command me among the rest to look after the quenching of Fetter Lane end, to preserve (if possible) that part of Holborn, whilst the rest of the gentlemen took their several posts, some at one part, some at another, for now they began to bestir themselves, and not till now, who till now had stood as men interdict, with their hands a cross,[7] and began to consider that nothing was like to put a stop, but the blowing up of so many houses, as might make a wider gap, than any had yet been made by the ordinary method of pulling them down with engines.[8] This some stout seamen proposed early enough to have saved the whole City; but some tenacious and avaricious men, aldermen etc., would not permit, because their houses must have been of the first. It was therefore now commanded to be practiced, and my concern being particularly for the Hospital of St. Bartholomew's near Smithfield, where I had many wounded and sick men, made me the more diligent to promote it;[9] nor was my care for the Savoy less. So as it pleased Almighty God by abating of the wind, and the industry of people, now when all was lost, infusing a new spirit into them (and such as had if exerted in time undoubtedly preserved the whole) that the fury of it began sensibly to abate, about noon, so as it came no farther than the Temple westward, nor than the entrance of Smithfield north; but continued all this day and night so impetuous toward Cripplegate, and the Tower, as made us even all despair. It also brake out again in the Temple: but the courage of the multitude persisting, and innumerable houses blown up with gunpow-

---

3. In Genesis, the Lord destroys the sinful city of Sodom by raining "fire and brimstone . . . out of heaven" (19.24). "The last day" is the Day of Judgment, when the city of Babylon (emblem of the corrupt world) "shall be utterly burned with fire" (Revelation 18.8).
4. For here we have no lasting city (Hebrews 13.14; the sentence continues: "but we seek one to come").
5. Echoing the account of the fall of Troy in the *Aeneid*

(2.325): on the night the Greeks burn the city, a Trojan priest declares *fuit Ilium* ("Troy was").
6. Grenades.
7. Immobilized, with their arms crossed (a conventional posture of passivity).
8. Machines.
9. Evelyn served on the Navy Board as a commissioner, charged with the care of sick and wounded seamen.

der, such gaps and desolations were soon made, as also by the former three days' consumption, as the back fire did not so vehemently urge upon the rest, as formerly. There was yet no standing near the burning and glowing ruins near a furlong's space. The coal and wood wharves and magazines of oil, rosin, chandler, etc.[1] did infinite mischief; so as the invective I but a little before dedicated to his Majesty and published, giving warning what might probably be the issue of suffering those shops to be in the City, was looked on as prophetic.[2] But there I left this smoking and sultry heap, which mounted up in dismal clouds night and day, the poor inhabitants dispersed all about St. George's, Moorfields, as far as Highgate, and several miles in circle, some under tents, others under miserable huts and hovels, without a rag, or any necessary utensils, bed or board, who from delicateness, riches and easy accommodations in stately and well-furnished houses, were now reduced to extremist misery and poverty. In this calamitous condition I returned with a sad heart to my house, blessing and adoring the distinguishing mercy of God, to me and mine, who in the midst of all this ruin, was like Lot, in my little Zoar, safe and sound.[3]

[THE ROYAL SOCIETY][1]

[14 November 1666] Up, and by water to Whitehall; and thence to Westminister, where I bought several things—as, a hone—ribband—gloves—books. And then took coach and to Knepp's[2] lodging, whom I find not ready to go home with me, so I away to do a little business; among others, to call upon Mr. Osborne for my Tangier warrant for the last quarter, and so to the New Exchange for some things for my wife, and then to Knepp again and there stayed, reading of Waller's[3] verses while she finished her dressing—her husband being by, I had no other pastime. Her lodging very mean, and the condition she lives in; yet makes a show without doors, God bless us. I carried him along with us into the City, and set him down in Bishopsgate Street and then home with her. She tells me how Smith of the Duke's house hath killed a man upon a quarrel in play—which makes everybody sorry, he being a good actor, and they say a good man, however this happens. The ladies of the court do much bemoan him, she says. Here she and we alone at dinner, to some good victuals that we could not put off,[4] that was intended for the great dinner of my Lord Hinchingbrooke, if he had come. After dinner, I to teach her my new recitative of *It is decreed*[5]—of which she learnt a good part; and I do well like it, and believe shall be well pleased when she hath it all, and that it will be found an agreeable thing. Then carried her home, and my wife and I intended to have seen my Lady Jemima at Whitehall; but the Exchange street was so full of coaches, everybody as they say going thither to make themselves fine against tomorrow night,[6] that after half an hour's stay we could not do any; but only, my wife to see her brother, and I to go speak one word with

1. Different sorts of fuel, stored and sold in shops along the Thames.
2. In 1661 Evelyn had warned of these dangers in a pamphlet entitled *Fumifugium: or the Inconveniency of the Air and Smoke of London Dissipated. Together with Some Remedies Humbly Proposed by J. E., Esq; to His Sacred Majesty, and to the Parliament Now Assembled.*
3. Lot, a prosperous inhabitant of Sodom, is warned by angels of the city's impending destruction. He escapes to Zoar, a small city nearby (Genesis 19.20–22).
1. This next selection from Pepys was written two months after the fire, when life had begun to return to normal.
2. Elizabeth Knepp, actress, singer, and friend of Pepys.
3. Sir Edmund Waller (1606–1687), widely read poet and pioneer of the heroic couplet; he wrote much love poetry in praise of "Sacharissa," a woman he wooed without success.
4. Delay (because the food would spoil).
5. Pepys enjoyed composing music (here setting words from Ben Jonson's play *Catiline*).
6. When a court ball was to be held for the queen's birthday.

Sir G. Carteret about office business. And talk of the general complexion of matters; which he looks upon, as I do, with horror, and gives us all for an undone people— that there is no such thing as a peace in hand, nor a possibility of any without our begging it, they[7] being as high, or higher, in their terms than ever. And tells me that just now my Lord Hollis had been with him, and wept to think in what a condition we are fallen. He showed me my Lord Sandwich's letter to him, complaining of the lack of money; which Sir G. Carteret is at a loss how in the world to get the King to supply him[8] with—and wishes him for that reason here, for that he fears he will be brought to disgrace there, for want of supplies. He says the House is yet in a bad humor; and desiring to know whence it is that the King stirs not, he says he minds it not, nor will be brought to it—and that his servants of the House do, instead of mak- ing the Parliament better, rather play the rogue one with another, and will put all in fire.[9] So that upon the whole, we are in a wretched condition, and I went from him in full apprehensions of it. So took up my wife, her brother being yet very bad, and doubtful whether he will recover or no; and so to St. Ellen's and there sent my wife home, and myself to the Pope's Head, where all the Houblons were, and Dr. Croone;[1] and by and by to an exceeding pretty supper—excellent discourse of all sorts; and indeed, are a set of the finest gentlemen that ever I met withal in my life. Here Dr. Croone told me that at the meeting[2] at Gresham College tonight (which it seems they now have every Wednesday again) there was a pretty experiment, of the blood of one dog let out (till he died) into the body of another on one side, while all his own run out on the other side. The first died upon the place, and the other very well, and likely to do well. This did give occasion to many pretty wishes, as of the blood of a Quaker to be let into an archbishop, and such like. But, as Dr. Croone says, may if it takes be of mighty use to man's health, for the amending of bad blood by borrowing from a better body.

After supper James Houblon and another brother took me aside, and to talk of some businesses of their own, where I am to serve them, and will. And then to talk of public matters; and I do find that they, and all merchants else, do give over trade and the nation for lost—nothing being done with care or foresight—no convoys[3] granted, nor anything done to satisfaction. But do think that the Dutch and French will mas- ter us the next year, do what we can; and so do I, unless God Almighty makes the King to mind his business; which might yet save all.

Here we sat talking till past one in the morning, and then home—where my people sat up for me, my wife and all; and so to bed.

[30 May 1667] Up, and to the office, where all the morning. At noon dined at home; being, without any words, friends with my wife, though last night I was very angry, and do think I did give her as much cause to be angry with me. After dinner I walked to Arundel House, the way very dusty (the day of meeting of the Society being changed from Wednesday to Thursday; which I knew not before because the Wednesday is a Council day and several of the Council are of the Society, and would come but for

---

7. The Dutch.
8. Sandwich, now ambassador to Spain.
9. Into ruin.
1. The Houblons were a merchant family—a father and five sons—whom Pepys and others admired for their affection and generosity. Dr. William Croone, a specialist

in anatomy, was an original Fellow and First Secretary of the Royal Society for the Improving of Natural Knowl- edge.
2. Of the Royal Society.
3. Protective escort for merchant ships.

their attending the King at Council); where I find much company, indeed very much company, in expectation of the Duchess of Newcastle,[4] who had desired to be invited to the Society, and was, after much debate pro and con, it seems many being against it, and we do believe the town will be full of ballets[5] of it. Anon comes the Duchess, with her women attending her; among others, that Ferrabosco[6] of whom so much talk is, that her lady would bid her show her face and kill the gallants. She is indeed black[7] and hath good black little eyes, but otherwise but a very ordinary woman I do think; but they say sings well. The Duchess hath been a good comely woman; but her dress so antic and her deportment so unordinary, that I do not like her at all, nor did I hear her say anything that was worth hearing, but that she was full of admiration, all admiration.[8] Several fine experiments were shown her of colors, lodestones, microscope, and of liquors: among others, of one that did while she was there turn a piece of roasted mutton into pure blood—which was very rare. Here was Mr. Moore of Cambridge, whom I had not seen before, and I was glad to see him—as also a very pretty black boy that run up and down the room, somebody's child in Arundel House. After they had shown her many experiments, and she cried still she was "full of admiration," she departed, being led out and in by several lords that were there; among others, Lord George Berkeley and the Earl of Carlisle and a very pretty young man, the Duke of Somerset.

She gone, I by coach home and there busy at my letters till night; and then with my wife in the evening, singing with her in the garden with great pleasure. And so home to supper and to bed.

[21 November 1667] Up, and to the office, where all the morning; and at noon home, where my wife not very well, but is to go to Mr. Mill's child's christening, where she is godmother, Sir J. Mennes and Sir R. Brookes her companions. I left her after dinner (my clerks dining with me) to go with Sir J. Mennes, and I to the office, where did much business till after candlelight; and then, my eyes beginning to fail me, I out and took coach and to Arundel House, where the meeting of Gresham College was broke up; but there meeting Creed, I with him to the tavern in St. Clement's churchyard, where was Dean Wilkins, Dr. Whistler[9] * * * and others. * * * Among the rest, they discourse of a man that is a little frantic (that hath been a kind of minister, Dr. Wilkins saying that he hath read for him in his church) that is a poor and debauched man, that the college have hired for 20s[1] to have some of the blood of a sheep let into his body; and it is to be done on Saturday next. They purpose to let in about twelve ounces, which they compute is what will be let in in a minute's time by a watch. They differ in the opinion they have of the effects of it; some think that it may have a good effect upon him as a frantic man, by cooling his blood; others, that it will not have any effect at all. But the man is a very healthy man, and by this means will be able to give an account what alteration, if any, he doth find in himself, and so may be useful. On this occasion Dr. Whistler told a

4. Margaret Cavendish, Duchess of Newcastle, had published poems, plays, and treatises on natural philosophy highly critical of the Society's methods (see pages 1100–1106).
5. Ballads (Evelyn wrote one on Cavendish's visit).
6. An Italian family of this name was eminent in England for its musical talents.

7. I.e., of dark complexion and hair.
8. Wonder, amazement.
9. The mathematician John Wilkins was one of the founders of the Royal Society; the physician Daniel Whistler was a Fellow.
1. s: Shillings.

pretty story related by Muffett, a good author, of Dr. Caius that built Key's College: that being very old and lived only at that time upon woman's milk, while he fed upon the milk of an angry fretful woman, was so himself; and then being advised to take of a good-natured patient woman, he did become so, beyond the common temper of his age. Thus much nutriment, they observed, might do. Their discourse was very fine; and if I should be put out of my office,[2] I do take great content in the liberty I shall be at of frequenting these gentlemen's companies. Broke up thence and home, and there to my wife in her chamber, who is not well (of those[3]); and there she tells me great stories of the gossiping women of the parish, what this and what that woman was; and among the rest, how Mrs. Hollworthy is the veriest confident bragging gossip of them all, which I should not have believed—but that Sir R. Brookes, her partner,[4] was mighty civil to her and taken with her and what not. My eyes being bad, I spent the evening with her in her chamber, talking and inventing a cipher to put on a piece of plate[5] which I must give, better than ordinary, to the parson's child; and so to bed, and through my wife's illness had a bad night of it, and she a worse, poor wretch.

[30 November 1667] Then to Cary House, a house now of entertainment, * * * next my Lord Ashly's; and there, where I have heretofore heard Common Prayer in the time of Dr. Mossum,[6] we after two hours' stay, sitting at the table with our napkins open, had our dinners brought; but badly done. But here was good company, I choosing to sit next Dr. Wilkins, Sir George Ent, and others whom I value. And there talked of several things; among others, Dr. Wilkins, talking of the universal speech, of which he hath a book coming out,[7] did first inform me how man was certainly made for society, he being of all creatures the least armed for defense; and of all creatures in the world, the young ones are not able to do anything to help themselves, nor can find the dug without being put to it, but would die if the mother did not help it. And he says were it not for speech, man would be a very mean creature. Much of this good discourse we had. But here above all, I was pleased to see the person who had his blood taken out. He speaks well, and did this day give the Society a relation thereof in Latin, saying that he finds himself much better since, and as a new man. But he is cracked a little in his head, though he speaks very reasonably and very well. He had but 20s for his suffering it, and is to have the same again tried upon him—the first sound man that ever had it tried on him in England, and but one that we hear of in France, which was a porter hired by the virtuosi.

[ELIZABETH PEPYS AND DEBORAH WILLETT]

[25 October 1668] *Lord's Day.* Up, and discoursing with my wife about our house and many new things we are doing of; and so to church I, and there find Jack Fen come, and his wife, a pretty black woman; I never saw her before, nor took notice of her now. So home and to dinner; and after dinner, all the afternoon got my wife

---

2. Pepys's position was in jeopardy because of a parliamentary investigation into Navy Office mismanagement during the Second Dutch War.
3. Her menstrual period.
4. As godfather at the christening.
5. I.e., a coded message to be engraved on a silver dish (so that the gift includes a kind of game).
6. Robert Mossum had conducted illegal Anglican services (using the forbidden Book of Common Prayer) during the Interregnum.
7. In his *Essay toward a Real Character, and a Philosophical Language* (1668), Wilkins argued for (and attempted) the creation of a newly precise and logical language based not on an arbitrary alphabet but on written symbols representing ideas and things.

and boy to read to me. And at night W. Batelier comes and sups with us; and after supper, to have my head combed by Deb, which occasioned the greatest sorrow to me that ever I knew in this world; for my wife, coming up suddenly, did find me embracing the girl con my hand sub su coats; and indeed, I was with my main in her cunny.[8] I was at a wonderful loss upon it, and the girl also; and I endeavored to put it off, but my wife was struck mute and grew angry, and as her voice came to her, grew quite out of order; and I do say little, but to bed; and my wife said little also, but could not sleep all night; but about 2 in the morning waked me and cried, and fell to tell me as a great secret that she was a Roman Catholic and had received the Holy Sacrament; which troubled me but I took no notice of it, but she went on from one thing to another, till at last it appeared plainly her trouble was at what she saw; but yet I did not know how much she saw and therefore said nothing to her. But after her much crying and reproaching me with inconstancy and preferring a sorry girl before her, I did give her no provocations but did promise all fair usage to her, and love, and foreswore any hurt that I did with her—till at last she seemed to be at ease again; and so toward morning, a little sleep; [26][9] and so I, with some little repose and rest, rose, and up and by water to Whitehall, but with my mind mightily troubled for the poor girl, whom I fear I have undone by this, my wife telling me that she would turn her out of door. However, I was obliged to attend the Duke of York, thinking to have had a meeting of Tangier today, but had not; but he did take me and Mr. Wren into his closet, and there did press me to prepare what I had to say upon the answers of my fellow-officers to his great letter; which I promised to do against his coming to town again the next week; and so to other discourse, finding plainly that he is in trouble and apprehensions of the reformers, and would be found to do what he can towards reforming himself.[1] And so thence to my Lord Sandwich; where after long stay, he being in talk with others privately, I to him; and there he taking physic and keeping his chamber, I had an hour's talk with him about the ill posture of things at this time, while the King gives countenance to Sir Charles Sedley and Lord Buckhurst,[2] telling him their late story of running up and down the streets a little while since all night, and their being beaten and clapped up all night by the constable, who is since chid and imprisoned for his pains.

He tells me that he thinks his matters do stand well with the King—and hopes to have dispatch to his mind; but I doubt it, and do see that he doth fear it too. He told me my Lady Carteret's trouble about my writing of that letter[3] of the Duke of York's lately to the office; which I did not own, but declared to be of no injury to G. Carteret, and that I would write a letter to him to satisfy him therein. But this I am in pain how to do without doing myself wrong, and the end I had, of preparing a justification to myself hereafter, when the faults of the Navy come to be found out. However, I will do it in the best manner I can.

Thence by coach home and to dinner, finding my wife mightily discontented and the girl sad, and no words from my wife to her. So after dinner, they out with me about

---

8. I.e., with his hand under her petticoats and his hand in her vagina. Here as often, Pepys reports his illicit sexual activities in a "secret" language compounded of Latin, French, Spanish, and English.
9. Pepys wedges the new date into the margin, beside the run-on narrative.
1. The duke was Lord High Admiral of the navy; on his

behalf Pepys had composed a letter to the Navy Board proposing reforms in response to parliamentary investigations of the disastrous Second Dutch War.
2. Notorious libertines (Buckhurst was Nell Gwyn's current lover).
3. The "great letter" on naval reform.

two or three things; and so home again, I all the evening busy and my wife full of trouble in her looks; and anon to bed—where about midnight, she wakes me and there falls foul on me again, affirming that she saw me hug and kiss the girl; the latter I denied, and truly; the other I confessed and no more. And upon her pressing me, did offer to give her under my hand that I would never see Mrs. Pearse[4] more, nor Knepp, but did promise her particular demonstrations of my true love to her, owning some indiscretion in what I did, but that there was no harm in it. She at last on these promises was quiet, and very kind we were, and so to sleep; [27] and in the morning up, but with my mind troubled for the poor girl, with whom I could not get opportunity to speak; but to the office, my mind mighty full of sorrow for her, where all the morning, and to dinner with my people and to the office all the afternoon; and so at night home and there busy to get some things ready against tomorrow's meeting of Tangier; and that being done and my clerks gone, my wife did toward bedtime begin to be in a mighty rage from some new matter that she had got in her head, and did most part of the night in bed rant at me in most high terms, of threats of publishing my shame; and when I offered to rise, would have rose too, and caused a candle to be lit, to burn by her all night in the chimney while she ranted; while I, that knew myself to have given some grounds for it, did make it my business to appease her all I could possibly, and by good words and fair promises did make her very quiet; and so rested all night and rose with perfect good peace, being heartily afflicted for this folly of mine that did occasion it; but was forced to be silent about the girl, which I have no mind to part with, but much less that the poor girl should be undone by my folly. [28] So up, with mighty kindness from my wife and a thorough peace; and being up, did by a note advise the girl what I had done and owned, which note I was in pain for till she told me that she had burned it. This evening, Mr. Spong came and sat late with me, and first told me of the instrument called parrallogram, which I must have one of, showing me his practice thereon by a map of England.[5]

So by coach with Mr. Gibson[6] to Chancery Lane, and there made oath before a master of chancery to my Tangier account of fees; and so to Whitehall, where by and by a committee met; my Lord Sandwich there, but his report was not received, it being late; but only a little business done, about the supplying the place with victuals; but I did get, to my great content, my account allowed of fees, with great applause by my Lord Ashley and Sir W. Penn. Thence home, calling at one or two places, and there about our workmen, who are at work upon my wife's closet and other parts of my house, that we are all in dirt. So after dinner, with Mr. Gibson all the afternoon in my closet; and at night to supper and to bed, my wife and I at good peace, but yet with some little grudgings of trouble in her, and more in me, about the poor girl.

[14 November 1668] Up, and had a mighty mind to have seen or given a note to Deb or to have given her a little money; to which purpose I wrapped up 40s in a paper, thinking to give her; but my wife rose presently, and would not let me be out of her sight; and went down before me into the kitchen, and came up and told me that she was in the kitchen, and therefore would have me go round the other way; which she repeating, and I vexed at it, answered her a little angrily; upon which she instantly flew out into a rage, calling me dog and rogue, and that I had a rotten heart; all which, knowing that I deserved it, I bore with; and word being brought presently up that she was gone away by coach with her things, my wife was friends; and so all quiet, and I to

---

4. Elizabeth Pearse, wife of a naval surgeon.
5. The parallelogram was a device for making copies of

diagrams and maps on the same or on a different scale.
6. A favorite assistant of Pepys's.

the office with my heart sad, and find that I cannot forget the girl, and vexed I know not where to look for her—and more troubled to see how my wife is by this means likely for ever to have her hand over me, that I shall for ever be a slave to her; that is to say, only in matters of pleasure, but in other things she will make her business, I know, to please me and to keep me right to her—which I will labor to be indeed, for she deserves it of me, though it will be I fear a little time before I shall be able to wear Deb out of my mind. At the office all the morning, and merry at noon at dinner; and after dinner to the office, where all the afternoon and doing much business late; my mind being free of all troubles, I thank God, but only for my thoughts of this girl, which hang after her. And so at night home to supper, and there did sleep with great content with my wife. I must here remember that I have lain with my moher[7] as a husband more times since this falling-out then in I believe twelve months before—and with more pleasure to her than I think in all the time of our marriage before.

[20 November 1668] This morning up, with mighty kind words between my poor wife and I; and so to Whitehall by water, W. Hewer with me, who is to go with me everywhere until my wife be in condition to go out along with me herself; for she doth plainly declare that she dares not trust me out alone, and therefore made it a piece of our league that I should alway take somebody with me, or her herself; which I am mighty willing to, being, by the grace of God resolved never to do her wrong more.[8]

We landed at the Temple, and there I did bid him call at my cousin Roger Pepys's lodgings, and I stayed in the street for him; and so took water again at the Strand stairs and so to Whitehall, in my way I telling him plainly and truly my resolutions, if I can get over this evil, never to give new occasion for it. He is, I think, so honest and true a servant to us both, and one that loves us, that I was not much troubled at his being privy to all this, but rejoiced in my heart that I had him to assist in the making us friends; which he did do truly and heartily, and with good success—for I did get him to go to Deb to tell her that I had told my wife all of my being with her the other night, that so, if my wife should send, she might not make the business worse by denying it. While I was at Whitehall with the Duke of York doing our ordinary business with him, here being also the first time the new treasurers, W. Hewer did go to her and come back again; and so I took him into St. James's Park, and there he did tell me he had been with her and found what I said about my manner of being with her true, and had given her advice as I desired. I did there enter into more talk about my wife and myself, and he did give me great assurance of several particular cases to which my wife had from time to time made him privy of her loyalty and truth to me after many and great temptations, and I believe them truly. I did also discourse the unfitness of my leaving of my employment now in many respects, to go into the country as my wife desires—but that I would labor to fit myself for it; which he thoroughly understands, and doth agree with me in it; and so, hoping to get over this trouble, we about our business to Westminster Hall to meet Roger Pepys; which I did, and did there discourse of the business of lending him 500l to answer some occasions of his, which I believe to be safe enough; and so took leave of him and away by coach home, calling on my coach-maker by the way, where I like my little coach mightily. But when

---

7. Spanish *mujer*: wife. For the first time, Pepys applies his secret language to Elizabeth.
8. Two nights earlier, Pepys had traced Deborah Willett to her new lodgings, and caressed her in his coach. The next day, Elizabeth told him that she knew about the assignation, and he signed a pledge "never to see or speak with Deb while I live."

I came home, hoping for a further degree of peace and quiet, I find my wife upon her bed in a horrible rage afresh, calling me all the bitter names; and rising, did fall to revile me in the bitterest manner in the world, and could not refrain to strike me and pull my hair; which I resolved to bear with, and had good reason to bear it. So I by silence and weeping did prevail with her a little to be quiet, and she would not eat her dinner without me; but yet by and by into a raging fit she fell again worse than before, that she would slit the girl's nose; and at last W. Hewer came in and came up, who did allay her fury, I flinging myself in a sad desperate condition upon the bed in the blue room, and there lay while they spoke together; and at last it came to this, that if I would call Deb "whore" under my hand,[9] and write to her that I hated her and would never see her more, she would believe me and trust in me—which I did agree to; only, as to the name of "whore" I would have excused, and therefore wrote to her sparing that word; which my wife thereupon tore it, and would not be satisfied till, W. Hewer winking upon me, I did write so, with the name of a whore, as that I did fear she might too probably have been prevailed upon to have been[1] a whore by her carriage to me, and therefore, as such, I did resolve never to see her more. This pleased my wife, and she gives it W. Hewer to carry to her, with a sharp message from her. So from that minute my wife begun to be kind to me, and we to kiss and be friends, and so continued all the evening and fell to talk of other matters with great comfort, and after supper to bed.

This evening comes Mr. Billup to me to read over Mr. Wren's alterations of my draft of a letter for the Duke of York to sign, to the board; which I like mighty well, they being not considerable, only in mollifying some hard terms which I had thought fit to put in. From this to other discourse; I do find that the Duke of York and his servant Mr. Wren do look upon this service of mine as a very seasonable service to the Duke of York, as that which he will have to show to his enemies in his own justification of his care of the King's business. And I am sure I am heartily glad of it—both for the King's sake and the Duke of York's, and my own also—for if I continue, my work, by this means, will be the less, and my share in the blame[2] also.

He being gone, I to my wife again and so spent the evening with very great joy, and the night also, with good sleep and rest, my wife only troubled in her rest, but less than usual—for which the God of Heaven be praised. I did this night promise to my wife never to go to bed without calling upon God upon my knees by prayer; and I begun this night, and hope I shall never forget to do the like all my life—for I do find that it is much the best for my soul and body to live pleasing to God and my poor wife—and will ease me of much care, as well as much expense.

[31 May 1669] Up very betimes, and so continued all the morning, with W. Hewer, upon examining and stating my accounts, in order to the fitting myself to go abroad beyond sea,[3] which the ill condition of my eyes, and my neglect for a year or two, hath kept me behindhand in, and so as to render it very difficult now, and troublesome to my mind to do it; but I this day made a satisfactory entrance therein.[4] Dined at home, and in the afternoon by water to Whitehall, calling by the way at Mitchell's,[5] where I have not been many a day till just the other day; and now I met

---

9. In writing.
1. Become.
2. For Navy Board misconduct.
3. Pepys and his wife planned a tour of Holland, Flanders, and France. Near journey's end, Elizabeth Pepys caught a fever; she died in London on 10 November 1669.

4. Pepys suffered from a painful combination of farsightedness and astigmatism which doctors did not know how to diagnose or to treat; he feared (mistakenly) that he was going blind.
5. Michael Mitchell sold liquor in a shop on London Bridge; his wife Betty is the "her" of the ensuing clauses.

her mother there and knew her husband to be out of town. And here yo did besar ella, but have not opportunity para hazer mas[6] with her as I would have offered if yo had had it. And thence had another meeting with the Duke of York at Whitehall with the Duke of York on yesterday's work, and made a good advance; and so being called by my wife, we to the park, Mary Batelier, a Dutch gentleman, a friend of hers, being with us. Thence to the World's End, a drinking-house by the park, and there merry; and so home late.

And thus ends all that I doubt I shall ever be able to do with my own eyes in the keeping of my journal, I being not able to do it any longer, having done now so long as to undo my eyes almost every time that I take a pen in my hand; and therefore, whatever comes of it, I must forbear; and therefore resolve from this time forward to have it kept by my people in longhand, and must therefore be contented to set down no more than is fit for them and all the world to know; or if there be anything (which cannot be much, now my amours to Deb are past, and my eyes hindering me in almost all other pleasures), I must endeavor to keep a margin in my book open, to add here and there a note in shorthand with my own hand.[7] And so I betake myself to that course which is almost as much as to see myself go into my grave—for which, and all the discomforts that will accompany my being blind, the good God prepare me.

May. 31. 1669.   S.P.

---

6. I did kiss her but had no chance to do more.   that he envisions here.
7. Pepys never produced the continuation of his journal

⇒ PERSPECTIVES ⇐
The Royal Society and the New Science

In the late 1600s, the antiquarian John Aubrey looked back to the middle of his century as a turning point in intellectual history: "Till about the year 1649, when experimental philosophy was first cultivated by a club at Oxford, 'twas held a strange presumption for a man to attempt an innovation in learnings; and not to be good manners, to be more knowing than his neighbors and forefathers." The "club" consisted of a group of inquirers for whom the university at Oxford offered a place of retreat in time of civil war. As Aubrey implies, their "innovation" consisted in a kind of bad manners. They refused to take the word of their intellectual "forefathers" (notably Aristotle) for how the natural world worked, and instead pursued knowledge of it through direct experiment, preferring new data to old theory, the testimony of the senses over the constructs of the intellect; the works of Francis Bacon, who had articulated such a method a half-century earlier, served for these investigators as something akin to scripture. The members continued to meet during the Interregnum. In 1662, Charles II granted the group (which had relocated to London) a charter, a seal, and with his patronage, a new prominence. The informal club had become the "Royal Society for the Improving of Natural Knowledge."

That "Improving" was to take place on many fronts. The Society's charter stipulated that its experiments should be aimed at "promoting the knowledge of natural things and useful arts": science and technology. In its first decades, its members made enormous advances in both realms, producing (among innumerable innovations) new explanations of heat, cold, and light; an air pump capable of creating a vacuum; a newly efficient pocket watch; and a newly coherent and durable account of the universe. A Fellow of the Society might work simultaneously at many endeavors that have since become specialties, investigating biology, physics, and astronomy, inventing scientific instruments and domestic appliances, advancing inquiries into theology, astrology, even demonology.

The group liked to portray itself as inclusive demographically too. Its Fellows represented many religious views, political persuasions, and social strata, from dukes to merchants to "mechanicks." Still, the early records evince an initial emphasis on high rank: aristocrats, courtiers, politicians, and "gentlemen" made up more than half the original membership (women were excluded altogether). Many of these men were mere names on the rolls, enlisted to bolster the respectability of the new enterprise; others were occasional spectators, intermittently attending the meetings to observe (amused, amazed, often baffled) the experiments performed there. But the Society also fostered a new category of inquirer: the "Christian virtuoso," a man of birth, means, merit, brains, and leisure, whose dissociation from any one profession was taken to guarantee the objectivity of his investigations, and whose rank and goodness underwrote the integrity of his findings. The Honorable Robert Boyle, who coined the phrase, was also its epitome. Well-born, devout, and dazzlingly gifted at science, he was the Society's prime mover and first star. But the type also found a less rarified, more popular incarnation in a new kind of amateur: the prosperous person who read, contemplated, talked the new philosophy, and kept a "cabinet of curiosities"—a closet or small room in which were arranged, and proudly displayed, antiquarian objects, scientific specimens, anything whose strangeness might arouse interest. The Society was amassing comparable collections on a much larger scale; the history of museums begins within the cabinets of the virtuosi.

The Society's emphasis on gentlemanly virtuosity was partly a form of self-defense against attacks from many quarters, where the "experimental philosophy" was regarded as ludicrous or dangerous or both. The influential wits of the day scoffed at the earnestness of the investigators and the seeming preposterousness of their findings (even Charles II laughed out loud when he learned that the members were busy weighing air); some clergymen and politicians saw in the new enterprise a threat to religion and to social hierarchy, a challenge against past, present, and divine authority, mounted by persons so presumptuous as to suppose that the truths of the world could be determined by human investigation rather than by Christian revelation.

The Society answered (again in the language of its charter) that it was intent upon serving "the glory of God and the good of mankind." The "good of mankind" was to be enhanced by technological improvements, which would make work more productive, life easier, and commerce more abundant, in contrast to the dark old days when (as Aubrey reminisces) "even to attempt an improvement in husbandry [agriculture], though it succeeded with profit, was looked upon with an ill eye." The "glory of God" would be served by a new form of attention to the world God made. A long tradition ascribed to the Deity two sacred texts: the Book of Scripture, and the Book of Nature. The faithful had long pondered the first; the Society now undertook to read the second anew and aright. "Each page in the great volume of nature," observed Boyle, "is full of real hieroglyphs, where (by an inverted way of expression) things stand for words"—objects and actions incarnate truths. To disclose the divine intricacy in the Book of Nature (so the Society's advocates argued) could only enlarge wonder and increase worship.

The new reading of that old text reshaped other texts as well. In the 1660s and after, manuscripts, periodicals, and printed books all explored new forms, as writers attempted to render in language what Michel Foucault has called "the prose of the world," to grapple with new relations between words and things, and to make the written or the printed page (like the closet and the cabinet) a copious repository of newfound curiosities.

Thomas Sprat
1635–1713

Given the date of its first appearance, the *History of the Royal Society* seems puzzlingly titled. The Oxford-educated clergyman Thomas Sprat wrote much of it in 1663, just a year after the Society received its charter, and published it (after delays caused by fire, plague, and other distractions) in 1667. Both title and timing reflect the pressures that produced the book in the first place. As he acknowledges at the outset, Sprat has produced not so much a "plain history" of the Society as an "apology," in the Greek-based sense of the word current in the seventeenth century: an energetic defense of the new institution's policies and methods.

From its inception, the Society's directors felt the need for such a defense, and they brought Sprat in specifically to provide it, appointing him a Founding Fellow and anxiously inquiring after his progress on the book. They had chosen him not for his knowledge of science (negligible) but for his status as a divine and for his skill as a rhetorician. In response to its detractors, Sprat insists that the Society will enhance piety (by detailing the wonders of Creation); will uphold hierarchy (as evidenced by the predominance of gentlemen and aristocrats among the Fellowship); and will cultivate community (in order to appease fears that the Fellows will revive "disputation" when the new Restoration needs it least, Sprat downplays the importance of argument in the new science and stresses instead the accumulation of raw data). Above all, Sprat focuses on the Society's capacity to improve ordinary life by producing "new inventions and shorter ways of labor" that will make possible an easier and more prosperous existence for the English, whose national "Genius" is uniquely suited to such advances.

As Michael Hunter notes, Sprat's "generalized attempt to appeal to everybody and antagonize nobody" fell short. It appealed mainly to adherents, and provided critics with a new target for their attacks. In the selection printed here, Sprat navigates a particularly delicate portion of his argument. He sets forth the Fellows' attempts to simplify the prose style in which they wrote up their inquiries and discoveries. The degree to which the Society actually sought and managed to implement a new "mathematical plainness" has long remained a matter of dispute. In contemporary writing, clarity and "ornament" were often seen as mutually supportive; even when Sprat is arguing for a "naked" prose, he intermittently resorts to the very "amplifications, digressions, and swellings of style" that he is ruling out. As its sponsors intended, Sprat's *History* applies a polished rhetoric to a pointed claim: that the Royal Society was creating a "common-stock" of knowledge on which all might draw, and from which all might profit.

from The History of the Royal Society of London, for the Improving of Natural Knowledge

Thus they have directed, judged, conjectured upon, and improved experiments. But lastly, in these and all other businesses that have come under their care, there is one thing more about which the Society has been most solicitous, and that is the manner of their discourse, which unless they have been watchful to keep in due temper, the whole spirit and vigor of their design had been soon eaten out by the luxury and redundance of speech. The ill effects of this superfluity of talking have already over-whelmed most other arts and professions, insomuch that when I consider the means of happy living and the causes of their corruption, I can hardly forbear recanting what I said before, and concluding that eloquence ought to be banished out of all civil societies as a thing fatal to peace and good manners. To this opinion I should wholly incline, if I did not find that it is a weapon which may be as easily procured by bad men as good, and that, if these should only cast it away and those retain it, the naked innocence of virtue would be upon all occasions exposed to the armed malice of the wicked. This is the chief reason that should now keep up the ornaments of speaking in any request, since they are so much degenerated from their original usefulness. They were at first, no doubt, an admirable instrument in the hands of wise men, when they were only employed to describe goodness, honesty, obedience, in larger, fairer, and more moving images; to represent truth, clothed with bodies; and to bring knowledge back again to our very senses, from whence it was at first derived to our understandings. But now they are generally changed to worse uses. They make the fancy disgust[1] the best things, if they come sound and unadorned. They are in open defiance against reason, professing not to hold much correspondence with that, but with its slaves, the passions. They give the mind a motion too changeable and bewitching to consist with right practice. Who can behold, without indignation, how many mists and uncertainties these specious tropes and figures[2] have brought on our knowledge? How many rewards, which are due to more profitable and difficult arts, have been still snatched away by the easy vanity of fine speaking? For now I am warmed with this just anger, I cannot withhold myself from betraying the shallow-ness of all these seeming mysteries upon which we writers and speakers look so big. And, in few words, I dare say that of all the studies of men, nothing may be sooner obtained than this vicious abundance of phrase, this trick of metaphors, this volubil-ity of tongue, which makes so great a noise in the world. But I spend words in vain; for the evil is now so inveterate that it is hard to know whom to blame or where to begin to reform. We all value one another so much upon this beautiful deceit and labor so long after it in the years of our education that we cannot but ever after think kinder of it than it deserves. And indeed, in most other parts of learning, I look on it to be a thing almost utterly desperate in its cure. And I think it may be placed amongst those general mischiefs such as the dissension of Christian princes,[3] the

1. They make the imagination reject.   3. Disputes between Christian monarchs.
2. Figures of speech.

want[4] of practice in religion and the like, which have been so long spoken against, that men are become insensible about them, every one shifting off the fault from himself to others, and so they are only made bare commonplaces of complaint. It will suffice my present purpose to point out what has been done by the Royal Society towards the correcting of its[5] excesses in natural philosophy, to which it is, of all others, a most professed enemy.

They have therefore been most rigorous in putting in execution the only remedy that can be found for this extravagance. And that has been a constant resolution to reject all the amplifications, digressions, and swellings of style; to return back to the primitive purity and shortness, when men delivered so many *things,* almost in an equal number of *words.* They have exacted from all their members a close, naked, natural way of speaking; positive expressions; clear senses; a native easiness; bringing all things as near the mathematical plainness as they can and preferring the language of artisans, countrymen, and merchants before that of wits or scholars.[6]

And here there is one thing not to be passed by, which will render this established custom of the Society well nigh everlasting; and that is, the general constitution of the minds of the English. I have already often insisted on some of the prerogatives of England, whereby it may justly lay claim to be the head of a philosophical league, above all other countries in Europe. I have urged its situation,[7] its present genius, and the disposition of its merchants, and many more such arguments to encourage us still remain to be used. But of all others, this, which I am now alleging, is of the most weighty and important consideration. If there can be a true character given of the universal temper of any nation under heaven, then certainly this must be ascribed to our countrymen: that they have commonly an unaffected sincerity; that they love to deliver their minds with a sound simplicity; that they have the middle qualities between the reserved, subtle southern and the rough, unhewn northern people; that they are not extremely prone to speak; that they are more concerned what others will think of the strength, than of the fineness of what they say; and that an universal modesty possesses them. These qualities are so conspicuous and proper to our soil that we often hear them objected to us by some of our neighbor satirists in more disgraceful expressions. For they are wont to revile the English with a want of familiarity; with a melancholy dumpishness,[8] with slowness, silence, and with the unrefined sullenness of their behavior. But these are only the reproaches of partiality or ignorance. For they ought rather to be commended for an honorable integrity; for a neglect of circumstances and flourishes; for regarding things of greater moment,[9] more than less; for a scorn to deceive as well as to be deceived, which are all the best endowments that can enter into a philosophical mind. So that even the position of our climate, the air, the influence of the heaven, the composition of the English blood, as well as the embraces of the ocean, seem to join with the labors of the Royal Society to render our country a land of experimental knowledge. And it is a good sign that nature will reveal more of its secrets to the English than to others because it has already furnished them with a genius so well proportioned for the receiving and retaining its mysteries.

4. Lack.
5. I.e., eloquence's.
6. For a parody of this position, see Swift's depiction of the Academy in *Gulliver's Travels,* Part 3, ch. 5.
7. I.e., its location. Sprat has earlier emphasized that England's status as an island, and as "mistress of the Ocean," gives it a privileged position from which to supervise international scientific experiments and correspondence.
8. Tendency to depression.
9. Importance.

And now to come to a close of the second part of the narration. The Society has reduced its principal observations into one common-stock[1] and laid them up in public registers to be nakedly transmitted to the next generation of men, and so from them to their successors. And as their purpose was to heap up a mixed mass of experiments, without digesting them into any perfect model, so to this end, they confined themselves to no order of subjects; and whatever they have recorded, they have done it, not as complete schemes of opinions, but as bare, unfinished histories.

✦━✦◈✦━✦

Philosophical Transactions

Philosophical Transactions first appeared in 1665 and continues to the present day; it is the longest running periodical in English and the oldest scientific journal in the world. It was created by Henry Oldenburg (1618–1677), a German-born diplomat who came to England in 1653 as an emissary to Oliver Cromwell and found himself powerfully drawn to the ideas and the company of the practitioners of the new science at Oxford. His gift for copious, accurate reporting on scientific matters prompted the Royal Society to enlist him as Fellow and Secretary, charged with attending the meetings, keeping the minutes, and managing the new institution's huge correspondence with scientific inquirers in England and abroad. Oldenburg produced the monthly *Transactions* as a private venture, but he drew its material from the documents in which his Society work immersed him, particularly from the correspondence that provided so plentiful an account (in the words of the journal's subtitle) "of the present undertakings, studies, and labors of the ingenious in many considerable parts of the world." The *Transactions*' content ranged wide conceptually as well as geographically, readily shifting from systematic searches for natural laws, to reports on technological innovations, to eager surmises about random oddities: monstrous births, human and otherwise, were a recurrent favorite. The new journal combined in text the attractions of the scientific treatise and the cabinet of curiosities; the insatiable curiosity of the journal's most assiduous contributor, Oldenburg's patron Robert Boyle, helped to ensure this variety and texture.

More than any other instrument, the *Transactions* established the Royal Society as central to the new philosophy and fostered the conviction that the advancement of learning was a communal pursuit of truth to which (as Francis Bacon had predicted) everyone from a mariner to a virtuoso could contribute indispensable information. The *Transactions* influenced nonscientific journalism as well: with its topical headlines, variegated matter, and detailed tables of contents, it resembled no periodical of its time, but many that came after.

from Philosophical Transactions

[THE INTRODUCTION][1]

Whereas there is nothing more necessary for promoting the improvement of philosophical matters than the communicating, to such as apply their studies and endeavors that way, such things as are discovered or put in practice by others, it is therefore thought fit to employ the press as the most proper way to gratify those whose engagement in such studies and delight in the advancement of learning and profitable discoveries doth entitle them to the knowledge of what this kingdom or other parts of

---

1. Property and resource for the use of all.
1. This and the following two selections appeared in

Vol. 1, No. 1, 6 March 1665.

the world do from time to time afford, as well of the progress of the studies, labors, and attempts of the curious and learned in things of this kind, as of their complete discoveries and performances. To the end that such productions being clearly and truly communicated, desires after solid and useful knowledge may be further entertained, ingenious endeavors and undertakings cherished, and those addicted to and conversant in such matters may be invited and encouraged to search, try, and find out new things, impart their knowledge to one another, and contribute what they can to the grand design of improving natural knowledge and perfecting all philosophical arts and sciences. All for the glory of God, the honor and advantage of these kingdoms, and the universal good of mankind.

* * *

An Account of a Very Odd Monstrous Calf

By the same noble person[2] was lately communicated to the Royal Society an account of a very odd, monstrous birth produced at Limmington in Hampshire, where a butcher, having caused a cow (which calved her first calf the year before) to be covered that she might the sooner be fatted, killed her when fat, and opening the womb, which he found heavy to admiration, saw in it a calf, which had begun to have hair, whose hinderlegs had no joints and whose tongue was, Cerebus-like,[3] triple—to each side of his mouth one, and one in the midst. Between the forelegs and the hinderlegs was a great stone, on which the calf rid.[4] The *sternum*, or that part of the breast where the ribs lie, was also perfect stone. And the stone on which it rid weighed twenty pounds and a half. The outside of the stone was of greenish color, but some small parts being broken off, it appeared a perfect free-stone. The stone, according to the letter of Mr. David Thomas, who sent this account to Mr. Boyle, is with Dr. Haughten of Salisbury, to whom he also refers for further information.

* * *

An observation imparted to the noble Mr. Boyle by Mr. David Thomas touching some particulars further considerable in the monster mentioned in the first papers of these Philosophical Transactions.[5]

Upon the strictest inquiry, I find by one that saw the monstrous calf and stone, within four hours after it was cut out of the cow's belly, that the breast of the calf was not stony (as I wrote) but that the skin of the breast and between the legs and of the neck (which parts lay on the smaller end of the stone) was very much thicker than on any other part, and that the feet of the calf were so parted as to be like the claws of a dog. The stone I have since seen. It is bigger at one end than the other, of no plain *superficies*,[6] but full of little cavities. The stone, when broken, is full of small pebble stones of an oval figure. Its color is gray—like free-stone, but intermixed with veins of yellow and black. A part of it I have begged of Dr. Haughten for you, which I have sent to Oxford, whither a more exact account will be conveyed by the same person.

* * *

2. Robert Boyle.
3. Resembling the mythical three-headed dog that guarded the entrance to Hades, the underworld of the dead.
4. Rode (i.e., straddled).
5. A "follow-up" from Vol. 1, No. 2.
6. Smooth surface.

A letter of the honorable Robert Boyle of Sept. 13, 1673, to the publisher concerning Amber Greece and its being a vegetable production[7]

Sir,

Some occasions calling me this afternoon up to London, I was met there with a very intelligent gentleman, who was ready to go out of it. But before he did so, he willingly spared me some time to discourse with him about some of the affairs of our East Indian Company,[8] of which he was very lately Deputy Governor, and, his year being expired, is still one of the chief of the Court of Committees, which a foreigner would call Directors that manage all the affairs of that considerable society. And among other things, talking with him about some contents of a journal lately taken in a Dutch East Indian prize,[9] I learned from him that he, who understands that language very well, is now perusing that manuscript; and among many things recorded there that concern the economical and political affairs of the said Dutch company, he met with one physical observation which he thought so rare that, remembering the curiosity I had expressed for such things, he put it into English and transcribed it for me; and immediately drawing it out of his pocket, he presented me the short paper, whereof I now show you the copy. Upon perusal of which, you will very easily believe, that not only his civility obliged me, but the information it brought me surprised me too. For the several trials and observations of my own about amber greece have long kept me from acquiescing either in the vulgar opinions[1] or those of some learned men concerning it. Yet I confess, my experiments did much less discover what it is than this paper has done, in case we may safely and entirely give credit to its information, and that it reach to all kinds of amber greece. And probably you will be invited to look on this account, though not as complete, yet as very sincere, and on that score credible if you consider that this was not written by a philosopher to broach[2] a paradox or serve a hypothesis, but by a merchant or factor[3] for his superiors to give them an account of a matter of fact. And that this passage is extant in an authentic journal, wherein the affairs of the company were by public order from time to time registered at their chief colony Batavia.[4] And it appears by the paper itself that the relation was not looked upon as a doubtful thing, but as a thing from which a practical way may be deduced to make this discovery easily lucriferous[5] to the Dutch Company. And I could heartily wish that in those countries that are addicted to long navigations, more notice than is usual were taken and given of the natural rarities that occur to merchants and seamen. On which occasion I remember when I had in compliance with my curiosity put myself into our East Indian Company and had by their civility to me been chosen of their Committee as long as my health allowed me to continue so, I had the opportunity in some register books of merchants English and Dutch to observe some things which would easily justify this wish of mine, if my haste and

7. Ambergris (Latin, "gray amber") is a gray waxy substance formed in the intestines of sperm whales; it was valued as a component in perfumes and medicines. Because ambergris, once emitted by the whale, often floats along the sea coast, traders and scientists were uncertain about its origins. (Boyle's letter appeared in Vol. 8, No. 97.)

8. A company chartered by Elizabeth I in 1600 to develop trade with India and the Far East.

9. I.e., the ship's log of a Dutch trading vessel recently captured by the English.

1. Received ideas of ordinary people.

2. Penetrate, untangle.

3. Company agent. Boyle reaffirms the Royal Society's interest in raw data over cooked theory, in the testimony of experienced "mechanics" over that of abstract "philosophers."

4. A seaport on the island of Java.

5. Profitable.

their interest would permit me to acquaint others with them. But to return to our account of amber greece I think you will easily believe that if I had received it not by a paper but immediately from the writer,[6] I should by proposing diverse questions, have been enabled to give you a much more satisfactory account than this short one contains. But the obliging person that gave it me, being just going out of town, I could not civilly stay him to receive my queries about it, which though (God permitting) I may propose ere long, if I can light on him again, yet I fear he has given me in these few lines all that he found about this matter. However, this relation, as short as it is, being about the nature of a drug so precious and so little known will not, I hope, be unwelcome to the curious. To whom none is so like to convey it so soon and so well as Mr. O,[7] whose forwardness to oblige others by his various communications challenges returns of the like nature from others and particularly from his affectionate humble servant.

Follows the extract itself out of a Dutch journal belonging to the Dutch East Indian Company:

> Amber greece is not the scum or excrement of the whale, etc., but issues out of the root of a tree, which tree how far soever it stands on the land, always shoots forth its roots towards the sea, seeking the warmth of it, thereby to deliver the fattest gum that comes out of it, which tree otherwise by its copious fatness might be burnt and destroyed. Wherever that fat gum is shot into the sea, it is so tough that it is not easily broken from the root, unless its own weight and the working of the warm sea doth it,[8] and so it floats on the sea.
>
> There was found by a soldier 7/8 of a pound and by the chief two pieces weighing five pounds. If you plant the trees where the stream sets to the shore, then the stream will cast it up to great advantage. March 1, 1672, in Batavia.

Robert Hooke
1635–1703

In a long life, Robert Hooke got little sleep. From the age of twenty-eight until his death, he lived in rooms at Gresham College, the Royal Society headquarters, in order to make himself maximally available to meet the ceaseless demands of his many concurrent employments, as the Society's first Curator of Experiments, as the College's lecturer in geometry, as surveyor and rebuilder of London after the Great Fire, and as restless, relentless inventor and improver of scientific instruments. Hooke's friend John Aubrey described him as "the greatest mechanick this day in the world"; the jostle between the high superlative and the equivocal noun captures Hooke's uncertain status in the Society to which he devoted his prodigiously productive working life. The mechanical arts were in many ways the lifeblood of the Society's enterprise, but "mechanicks" were not gentry. In an institution founded and headed by aristocrats and gentlemen, this gifted son of a provincial clergyman was often treated (in Stephen Shapin's words) "as a tradesman, as a servant." Hooke's contract as Curator required that he prepare and perform "three or four substantial experiments" at each of the Society's weekly meetings, as well as any other experiments the Fellows might (in the recurrent wording of the meeting minutes) "order" or "direct" him to undertake. The empirical life of the Society during its first

---

6. I.e., in conversation.
7. Henry Oldenburg, editor of the *Transactions*.

8. I.e., breaks it off.

four decades would have been unimaginable without Hooke, but the Fellows registered his indispensability by irritation at the outside interests through which he pursued autonomy and income. "I could wish," wrote Sir Robert Moray, "he had finished the task laid upon him rather than to learn a dozen trades." Hooke's variegated pursuits, though, produced dozens of inventions and discoveries: newly efficient lenses, lamps, telescopes, watches; new theories of optics, chemistry, and gravity that in some cases anticipated Issac Newton's. Constitutionally irascible, Hooke spent much energy asserting, angrily but often accurately, the priority and/or superiority of his many innovations.

Hooke produced *Micrographia* at the Society's behest. The book doubled as a work of science and a piece of institutional propaganda, designed to promote the Society's methods. It fulfilled both purposes. In Hooke's sixty word-and-picture "Observations" of magnified objects, readers could see for the first time how far the useful artifice of the microscope had extended the "knowledge of natural things" into realms unreachable by the eye and mind alone. At the same time, the book touched a cultural pulse point. At its Greek root, Hooke's title suggests "the writing down of small things," and this is what many of his fellow Fellows—Pepys, Oldenburg, Evelyn, Aubrey—were in their different ways newly up to. (Pepys thought *Micrographia* "the most ingenious book that I ever read in my life.") Small things, it had been discovered, could produce large amazements when written up.

from Micrographia
Or Some Physiological Description of Minute Bodies Made by Magnifying Glasses with Observations and Inquiries thereupon

TO THE KING

Sir,

I do here most humbly lay this small present at your Majesty's royal feet. And though it comes accompanied with two disadvantages, the meanness of the author and of the subject; yet in both I am encouraged by the greatness of your mercy and your knowledge. By the one I am taught, that you can forgive the most presumptuous offenders. And by the other, that you will not esteem the least work of nature or art unworthy of your observation. Amidst the many felicities that have accompanied your Majesty's happy restoration and government, it is none of the least considerable that philosophy and experimental learning have prospered under your royal patronage.[1] And as the calm prosperity of your reign has given us the leisure to follow these studies of quiet and retirement, so it is just that the fruits of them should, by way of acknowledgment, be returned to your Majesty. There are, Sir, several other of your subjects, of your Royal Society, now busy about nobler matters: the improvement of manufactures and agriculture, the increase of commerce, the advantage of navigation—in all which they are assisted by your Majesty's encouragement and example. Amidst all those greater designs, I here presume to bring in that which is more proportional to the smallness of my abilities and to offer some of the least of all visible things to that mighty king that has established an empire over the best of all invisible things of this world, the minds of men. Your Majesty's most humble and most obedient subject and servant,

Robert Hooke

1. Charles II had granted the Society a royal charter in 1662.

To the Royal Society

After my address to our great founder and patron, I could not but think myself obliged, in consideration of those many engagements you have laid upon me, to offer these my poor labors to this most illustrious assembly. You have been pleased formerly to accept of these rude drafts.[2] I have since added to them some descriptions and some conjectures of my own. And therefore, together with your acceptance, I must also beg your pardon. The rules you have prescribed yourselves in your philosophical progress do seem the best that have ever yet been practiced. And particularly that of avoiding dogmatizing and the espousal of any hypothesis not sufficiently grounded and confirmed by experiments. This way seems the most excellent and may preserve both philosophy and natural history from its former corruptions. In saying which, I may seem to condemn my own course in this treatise, in which there may perhaps be some expressions, which may seem more positive than your prescriptions will permit. And though I desire to have them understood only as conjectures and queries (which your method does not altogether disallow) yet if even in those I have exceeded, 'tis fit that I should declare that it was not done by your directions. For it is most unreasonable that you should undergo the imputation of the faults of my conjectures, seeing you can receive so small advantage of reputation by the slight observations of Your most humble and most faithful servant,

Robert Hooke

from *The Preface*

[A]ll the uncertainty and mistakes of human actions proceed either from the narrowness and wandering of our senses, from the slipperiness or delusion of our memory, from the confinement or rashness of our understanding, so that 'tis no wonder that our power over natural causes and effects is so slowly improved, seeing we are not only to contend with the obscurity and difficulty of the things whereon we work and think, but even the forces of our own minds conspire to betray us.

These being the dangers in the process of human reason, the remedies of them all can only proceed from the real, the mechanical, the experimental philosophy, which has this advantage over the philosophy of discourse and disputation, that whereas that chiefly aims at the subtlety of its deductions and conclusions, without much regard to the first groundwork, which ought to be well laid on the sense and memory, so this intends the right ordering of them all and the making them serviceable to each other.

The first thing to be undertaken in this weighty work is a watchfulness over the failings and an enlargement of the dominion of the senses.

To which end it is requisite, first, that there should be a scrupulous choice and a strict examination of the reality, constancy, and certainty of the particulars that we admit.[3] This is the first rise[4] whereon truth is to begin, and here the most severe and most impartial diligence must be employed. The storing up of all, without any regard to evidence or use, will only tend to darkness and confusion. We must not therefore esteem the riches of our philosophical treasure by the number only, but chiefly by the weight. The most vulgar instances[5] are not to be neglected, but above all, the

---

2. Hooke had originally drawn many of the book's illustrations for use in the public presentation of experiments, which, as the Society's Curator of Experiments, he was obliged to perform regularly.

3. I.e., as experimental data.
4. Elevation (with "truth" imagined as a progressive ascent).
5. Familiar particulars.

most instructive are to be entertained.[6] The footsteps of Nature are to be traced, not only in her ordinary course, but when she seems to be put to her shifts,[7] to make many doublings and turnings, and to use some kind of art in endeavoring to avoid our discovery.

The next care to be taken, in respect of the senses, is a supplying of their infirmities with instruments, and as it were, the adding of artificial organs to the natural; this in one of them has been of late years accomplished with prodigious benefit to all sorts of useful knowledge by the invention of optical glasses. By the means of telescopes, there is nothing so far distant but may be represented to our view; and by the help of microscopes, there is nothing so small as to escape our inquiry; hence there is a new visible world discovered to the understanding. By this means the heavens are opened, and a vast number of new stars and new motions and new productions appear in them to which all the ancient astronomers were utterly strangers. By this the earth itself, which lies so near us under our feet, shows quite a new thing to us; and in every little particle of its matter, we now behold almost as great a variety of creatures as we were able before to reckon up in the whole universe itself. * * *

I here present to the world my imperfect endeavors, which though they shall prove no other way considerable, yet I hope they may be in some measure useful to the main design of a reformation in philosophy, if it be only by showing that there is not so much required towards it any strength of imagination or exactness of method or depth of contemplation (though the addition of these, where they can be had, must needs produce a much more perfect composure) as[8] a sincere hand and a faithful eye to examine and to record the things themselves as they appear.

And I beg my reader to let me take the boldness to assure him that in this present condition of knowledge, a man so qualified as I have endeavored to be, only with resolution and integrity and plain intentions of employing his senses aright, may venture to compare the reality and the usefulness of his services towards the true philosophy with those of other men that are of much stronger and more acute speculations that shall not make uses of the same method by the senses. * * *

from *Observation 1. Of the Point of a Sharp Small Needle*

As in geometry, the most natural way of beginning is from a mathematical point, so is the same method in observations and natural history the most genuine, simple, and instructive. We must first endeavor to make letters, and draw single strokes true, before we venture to write whole sentences, or to draw large pictures. And in physical inquiries, we must endeavor to follow Nature in the more plain and easy ways she treads in the most simple and uncompounded bodies, to trace her steps, and be acquainted with her manner of walking there, before we venture ourselves into the multitude of meanders she has in bodies of a more complicated nature; lest, being unable to distinguish and judge of our way, we quickly lose both Nature our guide, and ourselves too, and are left to wander in the labyrinth of groundless opinions; wanting both judgment, that light, and experience, that clue, which should direct our proceedings.

We will begin these our inquiries therefore with the observations of bodies of the most simple nature first, and so gradually proceed to those of a more compounded one. In prosecution of which method, we shall begin with a physical point; of which

6. Considered.   8. But only.
7. Up to her tricks.

kind the point of a needle is commonly reckoned for one, and is indeed, for the most part, made so sharp, that the naked eye cannot distinguish any parts of it. It very easily pierces and makes its way through all kinds of bodies softer than itself. But if viewed with a very good microscope, we may find that the top of a needle (though as to the sense very sharp) appears a broad, blunt, and very irregular end; not resembling a cone, as is imagined, but only a piece of a tapering body, with a great part of the top removed, or deficient. The points of pins are yet more blunt, and the points of the most curious mathematical instruments so very seldom arrive at so great a sharpness. How much therefore can be built upon demonstrations made only by the productions of the ruler and compasses, he will be better able to consider that shall but view those points and lines with a microscope.

* * *

The image we have here exhibited in the first figure, was the top of a small and very sharp needle, whose point *aa* nevertheless appeared through the microscope above a quarter of an inch broad, not round nor flat, but irregular and uneven; so that it seemed to have been big enough to have afforded a hundred armed mites room enough to be ranged by each other without endangering the breaking one another's necks, by being thrust off on either side. The surface of which, though appearing to the naked eye very smooth, could not nevertheless hide a multitude of holes and scratches and ruggednesses from being discovered by the microscope to invest it, several of which inequalities (as A, B, C, seemed holes made by some small specks of rust; and D some adventitious[9] body, that stuck very close to it) were casual.[1] All the rest that roughen the surface, were only so many marks of the rudeness and bungling of art.[2] So unaccurate is it, in all its productions, even in those which seem most neat, that if examined with an organ more acute than that by which they were made, the more we see of their shape, the less appearance will there be of their beauty; whereas in the works in nature, the deepest discoveries show us the greatest excellencies. An evident argument, that He that was the author of all these things, was no other than omnipotent; being able to include as great a variety of parts and contrivances in the yet smallest discernible point, as in those vaster bodies (which comparatively are called also points) such as the earth, sun, or planets. Nor need it seem strange that the earth itself may be by an analogy called a physical point: for as its body, though now so near us as to fill our eyes and fancies with a sense of the vastness of it, may by a little distance, and some convenient diminishing glasses, be made vanish into a scarce visible speck, or point (as I have often tried on the moon, and—when not too bright—on the sun itself), so, could a mechanical contrivance successfully answer our theory, we might see the least spot as big as the earth itself; and discover, as Descartes also conjectures,[3] as great a variety of bodies in the moon, or planets, as in the earth.

But leaving these discoveries to future industries, we shall proceed to add one observation more of a point commonly so called, that is, the mark of a full stop, or period. And for this purpose I observed many both printed ones and written; and among multitudes I found few of them more round or regular than this which I have delineated in the * * * second scheme, but very many abundantly more disfigured; and for the most part if they seemed equally round to the eye, I found those points that had

---

9. Chance-encountered.
1. Accidental.
2. Artifice; human (as opposed to natural) creation.

3. René Descartes (1596–1650); French mathematician and philosopher.

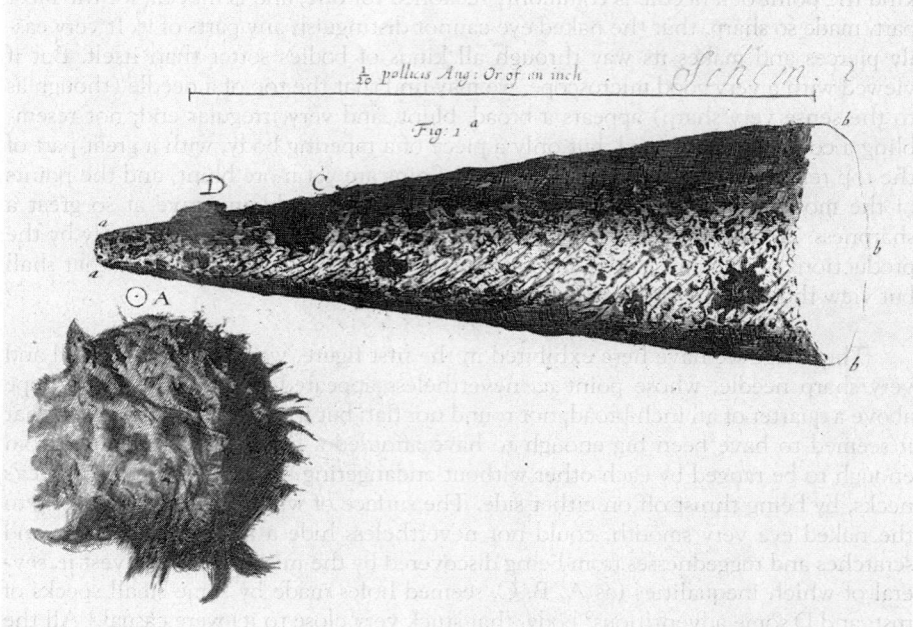

Robert Hooke, *Schema ii: Needle Point and Period,* from *Micrographia*, 1665.

been made by a copper plate, and roll-press, to be as misshapen as those which had been made with types, the most curious and smoothly engraven strokes and points looking but as so many furrows and holes, and their printed impressions but like smutty daubings on a mat or uneven floor with a blunt extinguished brand[4] or stick's end. And as for points made with a pen they were much more rugged and deformed. Nay, having viewed certain pieces of exceeding curious writing of the kind (one of which in the breadth of a two-pence comprised the Lord's Prayer, the Apostles' Creed, the Ten Commandments, and about half a dozen verses besides of the Bible[5]), whose lines were so small and near together, that I was unable to number them with my naked eye, a very ordinary microscope, I had then about me, enabled me to see that what the writer of it had asserted was true, but withal discovered of what pitiful bungling scribbles and scrawls it was composed, Arabian and China characters being almost as well shaped; yet thus much I must say for the man, that it was for the most part legible enough, though in some places there wanted a good fantasy well prepossessed[6] to help one through. If this manner of small writing were made easy and practicable (and I think I know such a one,[7] but have never yet made trial of it, whereby one might be enabled to write a great deal with much ease, and accurately enough in a very little room) it might be of very good use to convey secret intelligence without any danger of discovery or mistrusting. But to come again to the point. The irregularies of it are caused by three or four coadjutors,[8] one of which is the uneven surface of the paper, which at best appears

4. Torch.
5. In the mid-17th century, this minuscule writing was practiced as a craft; specimens (often of the scriptural texts Hooke lists here) were prized by collectors.

6. Imagination kindly disposed.
7. I.e., an instrument.
8. Factors.

no smoother than a very coarse piece of shagged cloth; next the irregularity of the type of engraving; and a third is the rough daubing of the printing ink that lies upon the instrument that makes the impression; to all which, add the variation made by the different lights and shadows, and you may have sufficient reason to guess that a point may appear much more ugly than this, which I have here presented, which though it appeared through the microscope gray, like a great splatch of London dirt, about three inches over; yet to the naked eye it was black, and no bigger than that in the midst of the Circle A. And could I have found room in this plate to have inserted an O you should have seen that the letters were not more distinct than the points of distinction, nor a drawn circle more exactly so, than we have now shown a point to be a point.

from *Observation 53. Of a Flea*

The strength and beauty of this small creature, had it no other relation at all to man, would deserve a description.

For its strength, the microscope is able to make no greater discoveries of it than the naked eye, but only the curious contrivance of its legs and joints, for the exerting that strength, is very plainly manifested, such as no other creature I have yet observed has anything like it; for the joints of it are so adapted, that he can, as 'twere, fold them short one within another, and suddenly stretch, or spring them out to their whole length, that is, of the forelegs. The part A * * * lies within B, and B within C, parallel to, or side by side each other; but the parts of the two next lie quite contrary, that is, D without E, and E without F, but parallel also; but the parts of the hinder legs G, H, and I, bend one within another, like the parts of a double jointed ruler, or like the foot, leg, and thigh of a man; these six legs he clitches[9] up altogether, and when he leaps, springs them all out, and thereby exerts his whole strength at once.

But, as for the beauty of it, the microscope manifests it to be all over adorned with a curiously polished suit of sable armor, neatly jointed, and beset with multitudes of sharp pins, shaped almost like porcupine's quills, or bright conical steel bodkins[1]; the head is either side beautified with a quick and round black eye K, behind each of which also appears a small cavity, L, in which he seems to move to and fro a certain thin film beset with many small transparent hairs, which probably may be his ears. In the forepart of his head, between the two forelegs, he has two small long jointed feelers, or rather smellers, M M, which have four joints, and are hairy, like those of several other creatures. Between these, it has a small proboscis, or probe, N N O, that seems to consist of a tube N N, and a tongue or sucker O, which I have perceived him to flip in and out. Besides these, it has also two chaps or biters P P, which are somewhat like those of an ant, but I could not perceive them toothed; and were opened and shut just after the same manner. With these instruments does this little busy creature bite and pierce the skin, and suck out the blood of an animal, leaving the skin inflamed with a small round red spot. These parts are very difficult to be discovered, because for the most part, they lie covered between the forelegs. There are many other particulars, which, being more obvious, and affording no great matter of information, I shall pass by, and refer the reader to the figure.

1663–1665   1665

---

9. Clutches.   used to bore holes" (Johnson's *Dictionary*).
1. "An instrument with a small blade and sharp point,

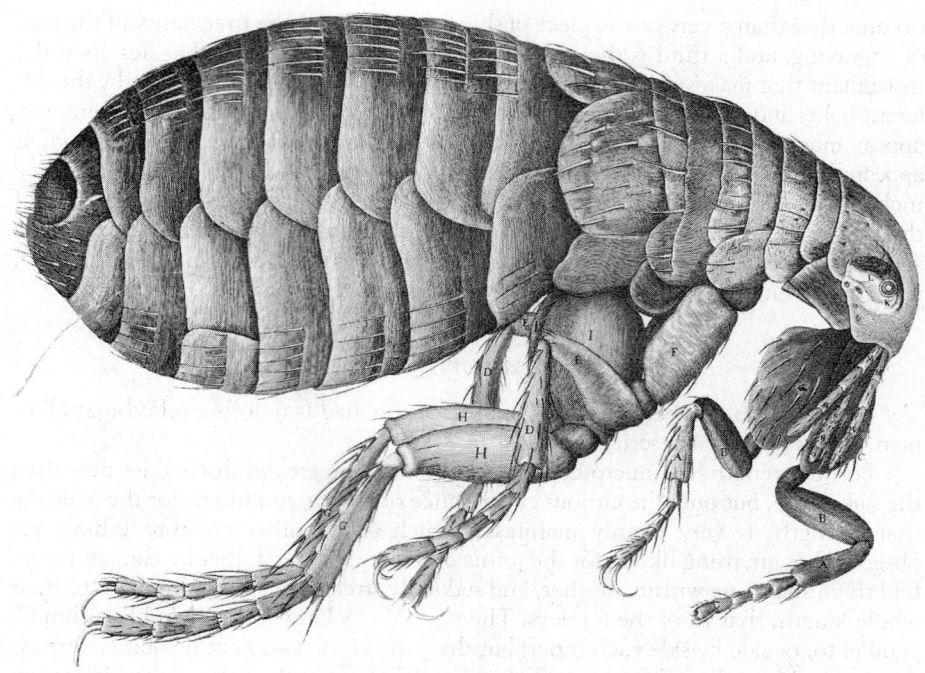

Robert Hooke, *Schema xxxiv: A Flea,* from *Micrographia,* 1665.

—◆▰◆▰◆—

Margaret Cavendish, Duchess of Newcastle
1623–1674

The youngest child in a wealthy family whose social arrogance and Royalist sympathies brought it near ruin during the Civil Wars, Margaret Lucas combined a near immobilizing shyness with a passion for fame. She spent the years of war and Interregnum on the continent, first as maid of honor to Charles's exiled queen, then as wife to the Royalist general William Cavendish, Marquis of Newcastle; he was made Duke by Charles II after the couple returned to England at the Restoration. Neglected by the Court, they lived far from London on their northern estates, where they cultivated their passions: his, riding and fencing; hers, reading and writing. Words poured from her pen into a variety of genres: verse (*Poems and Fancies,* 1653), fiction (*Nature's Pictures,* 1656), plays (*Love's Adventure, The Matrimonial Trouble, The Female Academy,* and some fifteen others: all printed, none performed); essays (*The World's Olio,* 1655); scientific speculations (*Philosophical and Physical Opinions,* 1663; *Observations upon Experimental Philosophy,* 1665); biography (of her husband); and autobiography (*A True Relation,* 1656; *Sociable Letters,* 1664). Cavendish and her husband published much of her work (and some of his) in sumptuous editions at their own expense.

It was rare for a woman to write and publish, rarer still for an aristocrat to write so revealingly and emphatically about her own fears, desires, opinions, and aspirations. The combination of her gender, rank, and work brought the Duchess an equivocal celebrity, a mix of amazement and derision which her occasional trips to London did much to animate.

from Observations upon Experimental Philosophy. To which is added, The Description of a New Blazing World[1]
Of Micrography, and of Magnifying and Multiplying Glasses[2]

Although I am not able to give a solid judgment of the art of micrography and the several dioptrical[3] instruments belonging thereto, by reason I have neither studied nor practiced that art, yet of this I am confident: that this same art, with all its instruments, is not able to discover the interior natural motions of any part or creature of nature. Nay, the question is whether it can represent yet the exterior shapes and motions so exactly as naturally they are, for art[4] doth more easily alter than inform. As, for example, art makes cylinders, concave and convex glasses, and the like, which represent the figure of an object in no part exactly and truly, but very deformed and misshaped. Also a glass that is flawed, cracked, or broke, or cut into the figure of lozenges, triangles, square or the like, will present numerous pictures of one object. Besides, there are so man· lterations made by several lights, their shadows, refractions, reflections, as also se· l lines, points, mediums, interposing and intermixing parts, forms, and positio   the truth of an object will hardly be known.[5] For the perception of sight, and ·   ie rest of the senses, goes no further than the exterior parts of the object prese·   d though the perception may be true when the object is truly presented, yet when the presentation is false, the information must be false also. And it is to be observed that art for the most part makes hermaphroditical,[6] that is, mixed figures, as partly artificial and partly natural. For art may make some metal as pewter, which is between tin and lead, as also brass, and numerous other things of mixed natures; in the like manner may artificial glasses present objects partly natural and partly artificial. Nay, put the case they can present the natural figure of an object; yet that natural figure may be presented in as monstrous a shape as it may appear misshapen rather than natural. For example, a louse by the help of a magnifying glass appears like a lobster,[7] where the microscope enlarging and magnifying each part of it makes them bigger and rounder than naturally they are. The truth is, the more the figure by art is magnified, the more it appears misshapen from the natural, inasmuch as each joint will appear as a diseased, swelled and tumid body, ready and ripe for incision. But mistake me not; I do not say that no glass presents the true picture of an object, but only that magnifying, multiplying, and the like optic glasses may and do oftentimes present falsely the picture of an exterior object. I say the picture because it is not the real body of the object which the glass presents, but the glass only figures or patterns out the picture presented in and by the glass, and there may easily mistakes be committed in taking copies from copies. Nay, artists[8] do confess themselves that flies and the like will appear of several figures or shapes, according to the several reflections, refractions, mediums, and positions of

---

1. The *Observations* is a critique of science, the *Blazing World* a work of fantasy; Cavendish published them together in a single volume as complementary texts. The "experimental philosophy" was that method and outlook pursued and exalted by the Royal Society; the group itself makes a sustained parodic appearance in the *Blazing World*. The Society held that copious experiment was the necessary basis for reliable study of the natural world. Cavendish challenges any such investigation grounded in human perceptions and the machines (microscopes, telescopes) contrived to enhance them; in the excerpt here she specifically takes on the work of Robert Hooke (see page 1093), whose *Micrographia* (1665) may well have prompted her to write the *Observations*, which includes the first selection given here.
2. Lenses.
3. Vision-enhancing (by means of refraction).
4. Artifice, like that of the lens-makers.
5. Early microscopes in England used simple lenses that blurred the image.
6. Composed of two opposite qualities.
7. As in Hooke's *Micrographia* illustration.
8. Technicians.

several lights. Which if so, how can they tell or judge which is the truest light, position, or medium, that doth present the object naturally as it is? And if not, then an edge may very well seem flat, and a point of a needle a globe;[9] but if the edge of a knife, or point of a needle were naturally and really so as the microscope presents them, they would never be so useful as they are, for a flat or broad plain-edged knife would not cut, nor a blunt globe pierce so suddenly another body. Neither would or could they pierce without tearing and rending, if their bodies were so uneven. And if the picture of a young beautiful lady should be drawn according to the representation of the microscope, or according to the various refraction and reflection of light through such like glasses, it would be so far from being like her, as it would not be like a human face, but rather a monster than a picture of nature.

Wherefore those that invented microscopes and suchlike dioptrical glasses at first did, in my opinion, the world more injury than benefit. For this art has intoxicated so many men's brains, and wholly employed their thoughts and bodily actions about phenomena, or the exterior figures of objects, as[1] all better arts and studies are laid aside. Nay, those that are not as earnest and active in such employments as they, are by many of them accounted unprofitable subjects to the commonwealth of learning. But though there be numerous books written of the wonders of these glasses, yet I cannot perceive any such; at best, they are but superficial wonders, as I may call them.

But could experimental philosophers find out more beneficial arts than our forefathers have done, either for the better increase of vegetables and brute animals to nourish our bodies, or better and commodious contrivances in the art of architecture to build us houses, or for the advancing of trade and traffic to provide necessaries for us to live, or for the decrease of nice[2] distinctions and sophistical[3] disputes in churches, schools, and courts of judicature, to make men live in unity, peace, and neighborly friendship, it would not only be worth their labor, but of as much praise as could be given to them. But as boys that play with watery bubbles, or sling dust into each other's eyes, or make a hobbyhorse of snow, are worthy of reproof rather than praise, for wasting their time with useless sports, so those that addict themselves to unprofitable arts spend more time than they reap benefit thereby. Nay, could they benefit men either in husbandry, architecture, or the like necessary and profitable employments, yet before the vulgar sort[4] would learn to understand them, the world would want bread to eat, and houses to dwell in, as also clothes to keep them from the inconveniences of the inconstant weather. But truly, although spinsters[5] were most experienced in this art, yet they will never be able to spin silk, thread, or wool, etc., from loose atoms; neither will weavers weave a web of light from the sun's rays, nor an architect build a house of the bubbles of water and air, unless they be poetical spinsters, weavers, and architects. And if a painter should draw a louse as big as a crab, and of that shape as the microscope presents, can anybody imagine that a beggar would believe it to be true?[6] But if he did, what advantage would it be to the beggar? For it doth neither instruct him how to avoid breeding them, or how to catch them, or to hinder them from biting. Again, if a painter should paint birds according to those colors the microscope presents, what advantage would it be for fowlers to take

9. Cavendish evidently refers to Hooke's micrographic depiction of a needle's point, a printed period (her "globe"), and (in the original illustration) a razor's edge; see page 1098.
1. That.
2. Minute, subtle, trivial.

3. Complicatedly and falsely argued.
4. Common people.
5. People who spin yarn or thread (possibly, here, with the additional sense of "unmarried woman").
6. Beggars were assumed to be most familiar (because most often afflicted) with lice.

them? Truly, no fowler will be able to distinguish several birds through a microscope, neither by their shapes nor colors; they will be better discerned by those that eat their flesh than by micrographers that look upon their colors and exterior figures through a magnifying glass.

In short, magnifying glasses are like a high heel to a short leg, which if it be made too high, it is apt to make the wearer fall, and at the best can do no more than represent exterior figures in a bigger, and so in a more deformed shape and posture than naturally they are. But as for the interior form and motions of a creature, as I said before, they can no more represent them, than telescopes can the interior essence and nature of the sun, and what matter it consists of. For if one that never had seen milk before should look upon it through a microscope, he would never be able to discover the interior parts of milk by that instrument, were it the best that is in the world—neither the whey, nor the butter, nor the curds. Wherefore the best optic[7] is a perfect natural eye, and a regular sensitive perception, and the best judge is reason, and the best study is rational contemplation joined with the observations of regular sense, but not deluding arts. For art is not only gross[8] in comparison to nature, but for the most part deformed and defective, and at best produces mixed or hermaphroditical figures—that is, a third figure between nature and art. Which proves that natural reason is above artificial sense, as I may call it. Wherefore those arts are the best and surest informers that alter nature least, and they the greatest deluders that alter nature most—I mean, the particular nature of each particular creature. (For art is so far from altering infinite Nature that it is no more in comparison to it than a little fly to an elephant;[9] no, not so much, for there is no comparison between finite and infinite.) But wise Nature taking delight in variety, her parts, which are her creatures, must of necessity do so too.

from The Description of a New Blazing World
from To the Reader

If you wonder that I join a work of fancy[1] to my serious philosophical contemplations, think not that it is out of a disparagement to philosophy, or out of an opinion as if this noble study were but a fiction of the mind * * * The end of reason is truth, the end of fancy is fiction. But mistake me not when I distinguish fancy from reason; I mean not as if fancy were not made by the rational parts of matter, but by "reason" I understand a rational search and inquiry into the causes of natural effects, and by "fancy" a voluntary creation or production of the mind, both being effects, or rather actions, of the rational part of matter, of which, as that[2] is a more profitable and useful study than this, so it is also more laborious and difficult, and requires sometimes the help of fancy to recreate the mind and withdraw it from its more serious contemplations.

And this is the reason, why I added this piece of fancy to my philosophical observations, and joined them as two worlds at the ends of their poles; both for my own sake, to divert my studious thoughts, which I employed in the contemplation thereof, and to delight the reader with variety, which is always pleasing. But lest my fancy should stray too much, I chose such a fiction as would be agreeable to the subject treated of in the former parts; it is a description of a new world, not such as Lucian's,

7. Lens.
8. Rough, approximate.
9. Cavendish probably refers to Hooke's illustration of a

flea (see page 1100).
1. Imagination.
2. Philosophy.

or the Frenchman's world in the moon;[3] but a world of my own creating, which I call
the Blazing World: the first part whereof is romancical, the second philosophical,
and the third is merely fancy, or (as I may call it) fantastical, which if it add any satisfaction to you, I shall account myself a happy creatoress.[4] If not, I must be content
to live a melancholy life in my own world; I cannot call it a poor world, if poverty be
only want of gold, silver, and jewels; for there is more gold in it than all the chemists
ever did, and (as I verily believe) will ever be able to make.[5] As for the rocks of diamonds, I wish with all my soul they might be shared amongst my noble female
friends, and upon that condition, I would willingly quit my part;[6] and of the gold I
should only desire so much as might suffice to repair my noble Lord and husband's
losses:[7] for I am not covetous, but as ambitious as ever any of my sex was, is, or can
be; which makes, that though I cannot be Henry the Fifth, or Charles the Second,[8]
yet I endeavor to be Margaret the First; and although I have neither power, time, nor
occasion to conquer the world as Alexander and Caesar did; yet rather than not to be
mistress of one, since Fortune and the Fates would give me none, I have made a world
of my own: for which nobody, I hope, will blame me, since it is in everyone's power
to do the like.

[CREATING WORLDS]

At last, when the Duchess[9] saw that no patterns would do her any good in the framing of her world, she resolved to make a world of her own invention, * * * which
world after it was made, appeared so curious and full of variety, so well ordered and
wisely governed, that it cannot possibly be expressed by words, nor the delight and
pleasure which the Duchess took in making this world of her own.

In the meantime the Empress was also making and dissolving several worlds in
her own mind, and was so puzzled, that she could not settle in any of them; wherefore
she sent for the Duchess, who being ready to wait on the Empress, carried her
beloved world along with her, and invited the Empress's soul to observe the frame,
order, and government of it. Her Majesty was so ravished with the perception of it,
that her soul desired to live in the Duchess's world; but the Duchess advised her to
make such another world in her own mind; for, said she, your Majesty's mind is full of
rational corporeal motions, and the rational motions of my mind shall assist you by
the help of sensitive expressions, with the best instructions they are able to give you.

The Empress being thus persuaded by the Duchess to make an imaginary world
of her own, followed her advice; and after she had quite finished it, and framed all

---

3. The *True History*, by the Greek satirist Lucian (2nd
century A.D.), initiated a long literary tradition of imaginary voyages, to which the French writer Savinien
Cyrano de Bergerac's account of a trip to the moon (*His-
toire comique contenant les états et empires de la lune* [1657])
was a recent, celebrated contribution.
4. In the first part of *The Blazing World*, a "virtuous lady"
survives her abduction at sea and is transported into a
"Blazing World" that touches Earth at the North Pole;
quickly wooed and wedded by the Emperor of this utopia,
she becomes its Empress. In the second, "philosophical,"
section, she hears the testimony of various scholars, scientists, theologians, and philosophers; in the third, "fantastical," section, the Empress summons the soul of Margaret Cavendish to travel from England to the Blazing
World, in order to serve as her companion and secretary.

The excerpts that follow are from the third part of the
narrative.
5. Alchemists sought to turn base metals into gold.
6. Give up my share.
7. During the civil wars, William Cavendish had lost
much wealth and property, of which he had recovered
only part since the Restoration.
8. Henry V of England (1387–1422) was celebrated for
his conquest of France; Charles II for his restoration of
the monarchy after the Interregnum.
9. Cavendish herself, whose soul has been transported to
the Blazing World at the Empress's request. At this point
in the story she and the Empress have been experiment-
ing with creating worlds in accordance with the theories
established by various experts, ancient and modern
(Pythagoras, Plato, Aristotle, Descartes, Hobbes).

kinds of creatures proper and useful for it, strengthened it with good laws, and beautified it with arts and sciences; having nothing else to do, unless she did dissolve her imaginary world, or made some alterations in the Blazing World she lived in, which yet she could hardly do, by reason it was so well ordered that it could not be mended.[1]

[EMPRESS, DUCHESS, DUKE]

At last, they entered into the Duke's house,[2] an habitation not so magnificent, as useful; and when the Empress saw it, "Has the Duke," said she, "no other house but this?" "Yes," answered the Duchess, "some five miles from this place, he has a very fine castle, called Bolsover."[3] "That place then," said the Empress, "I desire to see." "Alas!" replied the Duchess, "it is but a naked house, and unclothed of all furniture." "However," said the Empress, "I may see the manner of its structure and building." "That you may," replied the Duchess. And as they were thus discoursing, the Duke came out of the house into the court, to see his horses of manage;[4] whom when the Duchess's soul perceived, she was so overjoyed, that her aerial vehicle[5] became so splendorous, as if it had been enlightened by the sun; by which we may perceive, that the passions of souls or spirits can alter their bodily vehicles. Then these two ladies' spirits went close to him, but he could not perceive them; and after the Empress had observed the art of manage, she was much pleased with it, and commended it as a noble pastime, and an exercise fit and proper for noble and heroic persons; but when the Duke was gone into the house again, those two souls followed him; where the Empress observing, that he went to the exercise of the sword, and was such an excellent and unparalleled master thereof, she was as much pleased with that exercise, as she was with the former. But the Duchess's soul being troubled, that her dear lord and husband used such a violent exercise before meat, for fear of overheating himself, without any consideration of the Empress's soul, left her aerial vehicle, and entered into her lord. The Empress's soul perceiving this, did the like: and then the Duke had three souls in one body; and had there been but some such souls more, the Duke would have been like the Grand Signior in his seraglio,[6] only it would have been a Platonic seraglio.[7] But the Duke's soul being wise, honest, witty, complaisant, and noble, afforded such delight and pleasure to the Empress's soul by her conversation, that these two souls became enamored of each other; which the Duchess's soul perceiving, grew jealous at first, but then considering that no adultery could be committed amongst Platonic lovers, and that Platonism was divine, as being derived from divine Plato, cast forth of her mind that idea of jealousy. Then the conversation of these three souls was so pleasant, that it cannot be expressed; for the Duke's soul entertained the Empress's soul with scenes, songs, music, witty discourses, pleasant recreations, and all kinds of harmless sports; so that the time passed away faster than they expected. At last, a spirit came and told the Empress, that although neither the Emperor, nor any of his subjects knew that her soul was absent; yet the Empress's soul was so sad and melancholy, for want of his own beloved soul, that all the imperial

1. Instead, the Empress resolves "to see the world the Duchess came from," and so "those two female souls" travel together "as lightly as two thoughts," into England.
2. Welbeck Abbey, north-country birthplace and family seat of Cavendish's husband the Duke of Newcastle.
3. The Duke's favorite residence.
4. Well-disciplined in the actions and paces of *ménage*, or systematic horse training. The Duke, an expert equestrian, had published two books on the subject; when Charles II was a boy, Newcastle had taught him how to ride.
5. Form made out of air.
6. Harem.
7. One where the pleasures of the flesh would be repudiated in favor of the contemplation of pure, disembodied Ideas.

court took notice of it. Wherefore he advised the Empress's soul to return into the Blazing World, into her own body she left there; which both the Duke's and Duchess's soul was very sorry for, and wished, that if it had been possible, the Empress's soul might have stayed a longer time with them; but seeing it could not be otherwise, they pacified themselves. * * *

Epilogue

TO THE READER

By this poetical description, you may perceive, that my ambition is not only to be Empress, but Authoress of a whole world; and that the worlds I have made, both the Blazing and the other Philosophical World, mentioned in the first part of this description, are framed and composed of the most pure, that is, the rational parts of matter, which are the parts of my mind; which creation was more easily and suddenly effected than the conquests of the two famous monarchs of the world, Alexander and Caesar. Neither have I made such disturbances, and caused so many dissolutions of particulars,[8] otherwise named deaths, as they did; for I have destroyed but some few men in a little boat,[9] which died through the extremity of cold, and that by the hand of Justice, which was necessitated to punish their crime of stealing away a young and beauteous lady. And in the formation of those worlds, I take more delight and glory, than ever Alexander or Caesar did in conquering this terrestrial world; and though I have made my Blazing World a peaceable world, allowing it but one religion, one language, and one government; yet could I make another world, as full of factions, divisions, and wars, as this is of peace and tranquility; and the rational figures of my mind might express as much courage to fight, as Hector and Achilles had; and be as wise as Nestor, as eloquent as Ulysses, and as beautiful as Helen.[1] But I esteeming peace before war, wit before policy, honesty before beauty; instead of the figures of Alexander, Caesar, Hector, Achilles, Nestor, Ulysses, Helen, etc. chose rather the figure of honest Margaret Newcastle, which now I would not change for all this terrestrial world; and if any should like the world I have made, and be willing to be my subjects, they may imagine themselves such, and they are such, I mean, in their minds, fancies, or imaginations; but if they cannot endure to be subjects, they may create worlds of their own, and govern themselves as they please: but yet let them have a care, not to prove unjust usurpers, and to rob me of mine; for concerning the Philosophical World, I am Empress of it myself; and as for the Blazing World, it having an Empress already, who rules it with great wisdom and conduct, which Empress is my dear Platonic friend; I shall never prove so unjust, treacherous, and unworthy to her, as to disturb her government, much less to depose her from her imperial throne, for the sake of any other; but rather choose to create another world for another friend.

1666

═══ END OF PERSPECTIVES: THE ROYAL SOCIETY AND THE NEW SCIENCE ═══

---

8. Individuals.
9. The sailor-abductors of the "virtuous lady," who die during the boat's passage through the North Pole to the

Blazing World.
1. Characters in the *Iliad*, Homer's epic poem about the Trojan War.

John Dryden
1631–1700

In his last years, John Dryden often felt the need to defend his morals, his religion, his politics, even his writing. For nearly a quarter of a century, he had held high literary office and mingled with the great; he had curried royal favor and aristocratic patronage, bolstering officialdom, aiming to injure the Crown's enemies and to caress its friends. He wrote about politics and religion, about trade and empire; he wrote for the theater and for public occasions; he composed songs, fables, odes, and panegyrics, brilliant satire and savage polemic; he translated from many languages and formulated an idiomatic, familiar, and fluent prose style. Dryden virtually invented the idea of a commercial literary career; and through all the turns of a difficult public life, he fashioned from his own unlikely personality—from his privacy, self-doubts, and hesitations—a public figure of literary distinction. But he attained this celebrity at the cost of gossip and scandal, and in the last decade of his life (after the Glorious Revolution and his deposition from the Poet Laureateship) he faced suspicion and scorn.

The poet's beginnings give no hint of literary greatness or the likelihood of fame. He was born in 1631 in a country town and to comfortable circumstance; he was educated at Westminster School and graduated from Trinity College, Cambridge. He held minor public office in the 1650s but had written almost nothing before he was twenty-seven. Dryden then began his long career as public poet. He mourned the Lord Protector in 1659 (*Heroic Stanzas*) and then, in what looks like a convenient turn of allegiance, he celebrated the return of monarchy in 1660, writing poems to Charles II, to the Lord Chancellor, and to the Duchess of York; he praised the Royal Society (*To Doctor Charleton*) and defended the Royal Navy and its aristocratic high command (*Annus Mirabilis*, 1667).

The first years seem a series of calculated moves; and the combination of talent, application, and opportunity was crowned when Dryden was named Poet Laureate in 1667. But in addition to fashioning a career in the 1660s, Dryden also forged a new drama—an epic theater whose themes and language echoed the idioms of heroic verse—and a body of literary criticism that itself would have made his lasting reputation. Indeed, the great text of the first decade was the *Essay of Dramatic Poesy* (1668), Dryden's formulation of a pointedly English poetics and theater. Along with Sir Philip Sidney's *Apology for Poetry*, and Samuel Johnson's *Lives of the Poets*, Dryden's *Essay* is central to the long-standing canon of English literary criticism. Some of Dryden's early plays have been forgotten, but he worked steadily at a craft that would enable him to turn Milton's *Paradise Lost* into theater (*The State of Innocence*, 1677), create a superb adaptation of Shakespeare's *Antony and Cleopatra* in *All for Love* (1678), the finest of Restoration tragedies in *Don Sebastian* (1690), and the texts of one of England's first operas, *King Arthur* (1691), and last masques, *The Pilgrim* (1700).

By the late 1670s Dryden was famed as publicist for the Crown, and his theatrical work had come to dominate the stage; but he had hardly begun the career as satirist by which he is now best known. Its opening move was *Mac Flecknoe* (1676), and in the next few years Dryden fashioned masterpieces of literary mockery and political invective, poems that virtually created literary genres and dominated satire for decades to come. *Mac Flecknoe* allowed Dryden to ridicule and crush his rivals, all the while conjuring the suave tones and elegant manners of literary supremacy. In the abuse of rivals, only Pope surpasses Dryden as a master of scorn. But *Mac Flecknoe* was only the first act in a theater of invective. In the fall of 1681 Dryden wrote *Absalom and Achitophel*, a biblical allegory occasioned by the crisis of succession. The king had failed to beget a legitimate heir, and the king's Catholic brother waited ominously in the wings. It was Dryden's job to defend the Crown, to extenuate royal indulgence, and, especially, to defuse anxieties.

With *Absalom and Achitophel*, Dryden wove together the Bible and contemporary politics with such deftness that mere diversionary tactics were spun into an incomparable allegory of envy, ambition, and misdeed. The satire was read, marked, circulated, and treasured as a masterpiece and a menace.

The masterpiece secured Dryden's fame; the menace exacted a cost. The poet had attacked powerful men: aristocrats, politicians, and their partisan hacks who intrigued against the Crown. They failed in the early 1680s to foment rebellion, but by 1688 they were able to effect a revolution that deposed Catholic monarchy and the Poet Laureate himself. Dryden was reputed a brilliant and damaging advocate of Stuart rule; he had collaborated with court publicity and polemic; he had even converted to Roman Catholicism after James ascended the throne. Indeed, Dryden wrote his longest and most elaborate original poem—*The Hind and the Panther* (1687)— in defense of that king's rule and religion, and of his own conversion to Roman Catholicism. Once James II had been chased into exile, the poet felt he had nowhere to turn. In 1688 Dryden was fifty-seven, an old man by contemporary standards. He was forced from office, his pension was canceled, and he was driven back to the venues of commercial writing: the theater, translation, publication by subscription, even editing and anthologizing. He often expressed a keen sense of loss and abandonment in the 1690s, yet the decade would prove to be a remarkable phase of his career. Between his loss of the laureateship in 1689 and his death in 1700, Dryden wrote a series of superb translations that included selections from the satires of Juvenal and Persius, Ovid's *Metamorphoses* and *Amores*, Boccaccio's and Chaucer's tales. In these same years he wrote odes and epitaphs, and collaborated with his publisher Jacob Tonson in the new fashion for literary anthologies. Most remarkably, he produced *The Works of Virgil*, which set the standard for the translation of Latin poetry. He had come to his project late, and more than once he wrote of his inadequacy for this daunting task: "What Virgil wrote in the vigor of his age, in plenty and at ease, I have undertaken to translate in my declining years, struggling with wants, oppressed with sickness, curbed in my genius, liable to be misconstrued in all I write; and my judges . . . already prejudiced against me, by the lying character which has been given them of my morals." But Dryden's *Virgil* was a resounding, rehabilitating commercial and artistic success.

Nor were the twelve thousand lines of translated Virgil the close of this career. What followed was *Fables Ancient and Modern*, an anthology of original verse and new translations that included Ovid, Boccaccio, and Chaucer as well as a trial for what Dryden hoped would be his English Homer. He saw commercial opportunity in this new collection; but he must also have understood it as a crowning achievement in this life of theatricality and ventriloquism. He had begun by seeking a voice in the idioms and gestures of other poets; he now belonged wholly to himself as he casually turned their verse into his own. It is something of a paradox that a life of literary self-assertion, of aggressive, even calculating, careerism, should have closed with Dryden rummaging among other poets' verse, pausing over favorite lines, translating Ovid's Latin and Boccaccio's Italian into what was unmistakably his own voice. And the paradox of self-assertion ending in translation helps us to identify what is so particularly and so brilliantly Dryden's art. In the early modern world, writing meant belonging to others—to the authority of antiquity, to the opinions and fickle pleasure of patrons, to favor, to obligation, to taste, even to the emerging appetites of a reading public. Many of Dryden's contemporaries— Donne, Milton, Rochester—appeal to us by their seeming defiance of such self-denying ordinances. We read Dryden today not just for the skill with which he picked his way through political dangers or negotiated social minefields, not even for the savage cartooning of enemies or baroque praise of friends, but for the achievement of belonging to others as he became more exactly and more generously himself.

MAC FLECKNOE   In *Mac Flecknoe*, Dryden put on display a literary culture dangerously debased. The poem's title ("Son of Flecknoe") announces a royal succession in the kingdom of bad writing. A literary "father," the priest and minor poet Richard Flecknoe (c. 1605–

c. 1677), anoints as his true heir Thomas Shadwell (1640–1692), a playwright whom Dryden loathed as a tiresome controversialist and an ardent (worse, successful) rival for public favor and aristocratic patronage. Dryden wages his attack in an idiom at once elevated and scandalous, in language whose allegiance alternates (even within a single line) between epic poetry and the privy. Like much libelous and bawdy verse, Dryden's demolitionary masterpiece circulated in manuscript for several years; it was eventually printed in a pirated edition (1682) by a publisher seeking to capitalize on the recent success of *Absalom and Achitophel*. Like that poem, *Mac Flecknoe* plays upon the question of monarchic succession, but stages it in such a way as to implicate bad politics in bad taste. Dryden maps a City of London where foul writing chokes the streets, and dim-witted citizens get—and applaud—the poet-monarchs they deserve.

Mac Flecknoe

All human things are subject to decay,
And, when Fate summons, monarchs must obey.
This Flecknoe found, who, like Augustus, young
Was called to empire,[1] and had governed long:
5   In prose and verse was owned, without dispute,
Through all the realms of Nonsense, absolute.
This aged prince, now flourishing in peace,
And blest with issue of a large increase,
Worn out with business, did at length debate
10   To settle the succession of the state:
And, pondering which of all his sons was fit
To reign, and wage immortal war with wit,
Cried, " 'Tis resolved; for Nature pleads that he
Should only rule, who most resembles me:
15   Sh—— alone my perfect image bears,
Mature in dullness from his tender years.
Sh—— alone, of all my sons, is he
Who stands confirmed in full stupidity.
The rest to some faint meaning make pretense,
20   But Sh—— never deviates into sense.
Some beams of wit on other souls may fall,
Strike through and make a lucid interval,
But Sh——'s genuine night admits no ray,
His rising fogs prevail upon the day.
25   Besides, his goodly fabric° fills the eye,   *large body*
And seems designed for thoughtless majesty:
Thoughtless as monarch oaks that shade the plain,
And, spread in solemn state, supinely reign.
Heywood and Shirley were but types of thee,[2]
30   Thou last great prophet of tautology:
Even I, a dunce of more renown than they,
Was sent before but to prepare thy way;
And coarsely clad in Norwich drugget[3] came

1. Augustus became the first Roman emperor at the age of 32.
2. Thomas Heywood and James Shirley, popular and prolific playwrights from the first half of the 17th century.
As "types," they foreshadow or prepare for Shadwell, just as Old Testament figures such as Moses or Isaac were interpreted in Christian theology as forerunners of Jesus.
3. Woolen cloth; Shadwell came from Norwich.

To teach the nations in thy greater name.[4]

35   My warbling lute, the lute I whilom° strung   *once*
When to King John of Portugal I sung,[5]
Was but the prelude to that glorious day
When thou on silver Thames didst cut thy way,
With well-timed oars before the royal barge,
40   Swelled with the pride of thy celestial charge;
And big with hymn, commander of an host,
The like was ne'er in Epsom blankets tossed.[6]
Methinks I see the new Arion[7] sail,
The lute still trembling underneath thy nail.
45   At thy well-sharpened thumb from shore to shore
The treble squeaks for fear, the basses roar:
Echoes from Pissing Alley[8] "Sh————" call,
And "Sh————" they resound from A———— Hall.[9]
About thy boat the little fishes throng,
50   As at the morning toast° that floats along.   *sewage*
Sometimes as prince of thy harmonious band
Thou wield'st thy papers in thy threshing hand.
St. André's feet[1] ne'er kept more equal time,
Not ev'n the feet of thy own *Psyche*'s rhyme,
55   Though they in number as in sense excel;
So just, so like tautology they fell,
That, pale with envy, Singleton foreswore   ⎫
The lute and sword which he in triumph bore, ⎬
And vowed he ne'er would act Villerius[2] more. ⎭
60   Here stopped the good old sire, and wept for joy
In silent raptures of the hopeful boy.
All arguments, but most his plays, persuade,
That for anointed dullness he was made.
     Close to the walls which fair Augusta bind[3]
65   (The fair Augusta much to fears inclined[4]),
An ancient fabric,[5] raised t' inform the sight,
There stood of yore, and Barbican it hight:[6]
A watchtower once, but now, so Fate ordains,
Of all the pile an empty name remains.
70   From its old ruins brothel-houses rise,
Scenes of lewd loves and of polluted joys;
Where their vast courts the mother-strumpets keep

---

4. Here, Flecknoe is John the Baptist ("coarsely clad" in camel's hair) to Shadwell's Jesus.
5. Flecknoe claimed that, during his travels in Europe, he had been summoned to perform before the king of Portugal.
6. A glance at two of Shadwell's plays: *Epsom Wells* and *The Virtuoso*, in which Sir Samuel Hearty is tossed in a blanket; tossing in blankets was also a means of inducing childbirth.
7. Greek musician-poet rescued from drowning by music-loving dolphins.
8. West of Temple Bar, it led from the Strand down to the Thames.
9. Unidentified.

1. St. André, a French dancer who choreographed the opera *Psyche* (1675), for which Shadwell wrote the libretto.
2. John Singleton, one of the king's musicians; Villerius, a character in William Davenant's opera, *The Siege of Rhodes*.
3. The old wall of the City of London (Augusta).
4. Fears aroused by the Popish Plot.
5. Structure.
6. Was named; the Barbican, a medieval gatehouse, gave its name to a disreputable district of gaming and prostitution; adjoining it was Grub Street, the center of hack journalism.

And, undisturbed by watch,° in silence sleep.[7]   *police*
Near these a nursery[8] erects its head,
75 Where queens[9] are formed and future heroes bred;
Where unfledged actors learn to laugh and cry,
Where infant punks° their tender voices try,   *prostitutes*
And little Maximins[1] the gods defy.
Great Fletcher never treads in buskins here,
80 Nor greater Jonson dares in socks appear.[2]
But gentle Simkin[3] just reception finds
Amid this monument of vanished minds:
Pure clinches° the suburban Muse[4] affords,   *puns*
And Panton[5] waging harmless war with words.
85 Here Flecknoe, as a place to fame well known,
Ambitiously designed his Sh————'s throne.
For ancient Dekker[6] prophesied long since, ⎫
That in this pile should reign a mighty prince, ⎬
Born for a scourge of wit, and flail of sense: ⎭
90 To whom true dullness should some *Psyches* owe,
But Worlds of *Misers* from his pen should flow;
Humorists and *Hypocrites*[7] it should produce,
Whole Raymond families, and tribes of Bruce.
    Now Empress Fame had published the renown
95 Of Sh————'s coronation through the town.
Roused by report of Fame, the nations meet,
From near Bunhill, and distant Watling Street.[8]
No Persian carpets spread th' imperial way,
But scattered limbs of mangled poets lay:
100 From dusty shops neglected authors come,
Martyrs of pies, and relics of the bum.[9]
Much Heywood, Shirley, Ogilby[1] there lay,
But loads of Sh———— almost choked the way.
Bilked stationers for yeomen stood prepared,
105 And H————[2] was captain of the guard.
The hoary prince in majesty appeared,
High on a throne of his own labors reared.
At his right hand our young Ascanius[3] sate,

7. Parodying Abraham Cowley, *Davideis* (1656), "Where their vast court the mother-waters keep, / And undisturbed by moons in silence sleep."
8. A training theater for the two main playhouses.
9. Dryden puns on queen (stage-monarch)/quean (prostitute). During the Restoration, actresses were often thought to moonlight as sexual companions.
1. Maximin is the fulminating protagonist of Dryden's *Tyrannic Love*.
2. John Fletcher and Ben Jonson, major playwrights of the previous generations. The buskin is the symbol of tragedy (Fletcher's forte) and the sock of comedy (Jonson's). Shadwell promoted himself as Jonson's successor in the tradition of "humors" comedy.
3. A clownish character in a series of popular farces.
4. I.e., the muse presiding over the disreputable area outside the City walls.
5. Another farce character.
6. Thomas Dekker (1570?–1632), prolific dramatist

whose plays focused on London life.
7. Shadwell was the author of *The Miser* (1672), *The Humorists* (1671), and *The Hypocrite* (1669). Raymond and Bruce appear in *The Humorists* and *The Virtuoso*, respectively.
8. Fame draws her crowd both from cemeteries (like Bunhill Fields) and from mercantile districts (like Watling Street); thus, these devotees of Shadwell include both the dead and the living.
9. Unsold books might be recycled as pie wrappers or as toilet paper; the bones of martyrs were often venerated as relics.
1. John Ogilby, printer, cartographer, and translator (like Dryden) of Virgil.
2. Henry Herringman, a prominent bookseller-publisher; he had published both Shadwell and Dryden.
3. The son of Aeneas, marked for greatness by a heaven-sent flame about his head.

Rome's other hope, and pillar of the state.
110   His brows thick fogs, instead of glories, grace,
And lambent° dullness played around his face.   *glowing*
As Hannibal did to the altars come,
Sworn by his sire a mortal foe to Rome,[4]
So Sh——— swore, nor should his vow be vain,
115   That he till death true dullness would maintain;
And in his father's right, and realm's defense,
Ne'er to have peace with wit, nor truce with sense.
The king himself the sacred unction[5] made,
As king by office, and as priest by trade:
120   In his sinister° hand, instead of ball,   *left*
He placed a mighty mug of potent ale;
Love's Kingdom[6] to his right he did convey,
At once his scepter and his rule of sway,[7]
Whose righteous lore the prince had practiced young,
125   And from whose loins[8] recorded Psyche sprung.
His temples last with poppies[9] were o'erspread,
That nodding seemed to consecrate his head:
Just at that point of time, if Fame not lie,
On his left hand twelve reverend owls[1] did fly.
130   So Romulus,[2] 'tis sung, by Tiber's brook,
Presage of sway from twice six vultures took.
Th' admiring throng loud acclamations make,
And omens of his future empire take.
The sire then shook the honors[3] of his head,
135   And from his brows damps of oblivion shed
Full on the filial dullness: long he stood,   ⎫
Repelling from his breast the raging God;   ⎬
At length burst out in this prophetic mood: ⎭
      "Heavens bless my son, from Ireland let him reign
140   To far Barbados on the western main;[4]
Of his dominion may no end be known,
And greater than his father's be his throne.
Beyond *Love's Kingdom* let him stretch his pen!"
He paused, and all the people cried, "Amen."
145   "Then thus," continued he, "my son, advance
Still in new impudence, new ignorance.
Success let others teach, learn thou from me
Pangs without birth, and fruitless industry.
Let *Virtuosos* in five years be writ,
150   Yet not one thought accuse thy toil of wit.
Let gentle George[5] in triumph tread the stage,

4. According to Livy, Hannibal's father made the young boy swear himself Rome's enemy.
5. The oil with which the king was anointed during the coronation ceremony.
6. A play by Flecknoe.
7. Dryden parodies the rituals and props of the coronation ceremony.
8. Pronounced "lines" (a fact that permits Dryden a significant pun).
9. Symbolizing sleep.
1. Symbols of ignorance and darkness (because nocturnal).
2. Cofounder of Rome (through which the Tiber runs).
3. Ornaments, and by extension, hair—a Virgilian expression.
4. His kingdom will be the Atlantic Ocean.
5. Sir George Etherege, comic playwright; characters from his plays follow.

Make Dorimant betray, and Loveit rage;
Let Cully, Cockwood, Fopling charm the pit,
And in their folly show the writer's wit.
155 Yet still thy fools shall stand in thy defense,
And justify° their author's want of sense.   prove
Let 'em be all by thy own model made
Of dullness, and desire no foreign aid:
That they to future ages may be known,
160 Not copies drawn, but issue[6] of thy own.
Nay let thy men of wit too be the same,
All full of thee, and differing but in name;
But let no alien S—dl—y[7] interpose
To lard with wit thy hungry *Epsom* prose.
165 And when false flowers of rhetoric thou would'st cull,
Trust nature, do not labor to be dull;
But write thy best, and top; and in each line,
Sir Formal's[8] oratory will be thine.
Sir Formal, though unsought, attends thy quill,
170 And does thy northern dedications[9] fill.
Nor let false friends seduce thy mind to fame,
By arrogating Jonson's hostile name.
Let father Flecknoe fire thy mind with praise,
And uncle Ogilby thy envy raise.
175 Thou art my blood, where Jonson has no part;
What share have we in nature or in art?
Where did his wit on learning fix a brand,
And rail at arts he did not understand?
Where made he love in Prince Nicander's[1] vein,
180 Or swept the dust in *Psyche*'s humble strain?
Where sold he bargains,[2] "whip-stitch, kiss my arse,"
Promised a play and dwindled to a farce?
When did his Muse from Fletcher scenes purloin,
As thou whole Eth'rege dost transfuse to thine?
185 But so transfused as oil on waters flow,
His always floats above, thine sinks below.
This is thy province, this thy wondrous way,
New humors to invent for each new play:[3]
This is that boasted bias of thy mind,
190 By which one way, to dullness, 'tis inclined;
Which makes thy writings lean on one side still,
And in all changes that way bends thy will.
Nor let thy mountain belly make pretense
Of likeness; thine's a tympany[4] of sense.

6. A pun: both progeny and printing.
7. Sir Charles Sedley, courtier, poet, and intimate of Dryden's circle; he wrote a prologue for *Epsom Wells*.
8. Sir Formal Trifle, a character in Shadwell's *The Virtuoso*, described by Shadwell as "the Orator, a florid coxcomb."
9. Both Flecknoe and Shadwell dedicated several of their works to the Duke and Duchess of Newcastle (a town in the north of England).

1. A character in *Psyche*.
2. "To sell bargains" is to respond to an innocent question with a coarse phrase, as in this line. Dryden sharpens the insult by quoting the slangy nonsense phrase "whip-stitch" from Shadwell's own play, *The Virtuoso*.
3. I.e., by these contemptible means, you purport to out-do Ben Jonson.
4. A swelling of the abdomen, caused by air or gas.

195   A tun of man in thy large bulk is writ,
        But sure thou'rt but a kilderkin[5] of wit.
        Like mine thy gentle numbers feebly creep;
        Thy tragic Muse gives smiles, thy comic sleep.
        With whate'er gall thou sett'st thyself to write,
200   Thy inoffensive satires never bite.
        In thy felonious heart, though venom lies,
        It does but touch thy Irish[6] pen, and dies.
        Thy genius calls thee not to purchase fame
        In keen iambics,[7] but mild anagram:
205   Leave writing plays, and choose for thy command
        Some peaceful province in acrostic land.
        There thou may'st wings display and altars[8] raise,
        And torture one poor word ten thousand ways.
        Or if thou would'st thy diff'rent talents suit,
210   Set thy own songs, and sing them to thy lute."
        He said, but his last words were scarcely heard, ⎤
        For Bruce and Longvil had a trap prepared,[9] ⎬
        And down they sent the yet declaiming bard. ⎦
        Sinking he left his drugget robe behind,
215   Borne upward by a subterranean wind.
        The mantle fell to the young prophet's part,[1]
        With double portion of his father's art.

c. 1676   1682

Aphra Behn
1640?–1689

Aphra Behn's career was unprecedented, her output prodigious, her fame extensive, and her voice distinctive. Her origins, though, remain elusive. We know nothing certain about her birth, family, education, or marriage. She may have been born at the start or at the end of the 1640s, to parents of low or "gentle" station, named Johnson, Amies, or Cooper. Her Catholicism and her firm command of French suggest the possibility of a prosperous upbringing in a convent at home or abroad; the running argument against marriage for money that she sustains through much of her work suggests that her own marriage, to the otherwise unidentifiable "Mr. Behn," may have been obligatory and unhappy. In any case it was brief—and just possibly fictitious, since a widow could pursue a profession more freely than a spinster.

Behn's first appearances in the historical record suggest a propensity for self-invention. In 1663–1664, during a short stay with her family in the South American sugar colony of Surinam, a government agent there reported that she was conducting a flirtation with William

---

5. A tun was a large cask of wine; a kilderkin a quarter of a tun.
6. Neither Flecknoe nor Shadwell was actually Irish; Ireland was regarded in England as an abode of savages.
7. Sharp satire (written in iambic meter by classical satirists).
8. Dryden here mocks the practice of writing emblematic verse, poems in the shape of their subjects (e.g., George

Herbert's *Easter Wings* and *The Altar*). He lumps this practice together with other forms of empty ingenuity.
9. In Shadwell's *The Virtuoso*, Bruce and Longvil open a trap door beneath the long-winded Sir Formal Trifle.
1. A burlesque of 2 Kings 2.8–14, in which the prophet Elijah is borne up to heaven, while his mantle falls to his successor, Elisha.

Scott, an antimonarchist on the run from the Restoration. The agent referred to Scott as "Celadon" and Aphra as "Astraea," names the lovers may well have chosen for themselves from a popular French romance; Behn kept hers, as a *nom de plume*, for the whole of her writing life. Within two years, her loyalties had shifted and her self-invention had grown more intricate. In 1666 Behn herself became the king's spy, sent from London to Antwerp to persuade her old flame Scott to turn informer against his fellow Republicans and to apprise King Charles of rebellious plots. She did useful but costly work, garnering good information that her handlers ignored and spending much money that they were slow to reimburse. Returning to England later that year, and threatened with imprisonment for debt, she wrote her supervisor, "I have cried myself dead and could find in my heart to break through all and get to the King and never rise till he were pleased to pay this, but I am sick and weak and unfit for it or a prison . . . Sir, if I have not the money tonight you must send me something to keep [sustain] me in prison, for I will not starve." The king paid up, and Behn forestalled any further threat of starvation by writing plays for money—the first woman in England to earn a living by her pen. She had been "forced to write for bread," she later declared, and she was "not ashamed to own it."

Throughout her career Behn transmuted such "shamelessness" into a positive point of pride and a source of literary substance. Many of her plays, poems, and fictions focus on the difficulty with which intelligent, enterprising women pursue their desires against the current of social convention. In the prologues, prefaces, postscripts, and letters by which she provided a running commentary on her work, Behn sometimes aligned herself with the large fraternity of male authors who "like good tradesmen" sell whatever is "in fashion," but she often stood apart to muse acerbically on her unique position as a *female* purveyor of literary product. Once, surveying the panoply of contemporary male playwrights, she declared that "except for our most unimitable Laureate [Dryden], I dare say I know of none that write at such a formidable rate, but that a woman may well hope to reach their greatest heights." "Formidable rate" suggests both speed and skill; Behn made good on both boasts, producing twenty plays in twenty years, along with much poetry (including fervent pro-Stuart propaganda), copious translations, one of the earliest epistolary novels in English, and a cluster of innovative shorter fiction. In her range and her dexterity, she approached the stature of the "unimitable Laureate" himself, who knew her and praised her repeatedly. With her greatest successes—the comedy *The Rover* (1677), the novella *Oroonoko* (1688)—she secured both an audience and a reputation that continued without pause well into the following century.

Other pieces worked less well. Changes in literary fashion often obliged Behn to try new modes; she switched to fiction, for example, in the 1680s, when plays became less lucrative. Out of her vicissitudes—professional and personal, amorous, financial, literary—she fashioned a formidable celebrity, becoming the object of endless speculation in talk and in ink. "I value fame," she once wrote, and she cultivated it by what seemed an unprecedented frankness. ("All women together," wrote Virginia Woolf, "ought to let flowers fall upon the grave of Aphra Behn . . . for it was she who earned them the right to speak their minds.") In an age of libertines, when men like Rochester paraded their varied couplings in verse couplets, Behn undertook to proclaim and to analyze women's sexual desire, as manifested in her characters and in herself. Her disclosures, though, were intricately orchestrated. Living and writing at the center of a glamorous literary circle, Behn may have fostered, as the critic Janet Todd suggests, the "fantasy of a golden age of sexual and social openness," but she performed it for her readers rather than falling for it herself. Throughout her work Behn adroitly conceals the "self" that she purports to show and sell. She sometimes likens herself to those other female denizens of the theater, the mask-wearing prostitutes who roamed the audience in search of customers. The critic Catherine Gallagher has argued that Behn's literary persona—defiant, vulnerable, hypnotic—functions like the prostitute's vizard, promising the woman's "availability" as commodity while at the same time implying "the impenetrability of the controlling mind" behind the mask.

In Gallagher's reckoning, as in Woolf's, Behn's total career is more important than any particular work it produced. This is fitting tribute to a writer who, in an era of spectacular self-performers (Charles II, Dryden, Rochester), brought off, by virtue of her gender and her art, one of the most intricate performances of all. That performance now looks set for a long second run. After a hiatus in the nineteenth century, when both the writer and the work were dismissed as indecent, Behn's fame has undergone extraordinary revival. She dominates cultural-studies discourse as both a topic and a set of texts. The texts in particular are worth attending to: many are as astonishing as the career that engendered them.

The Disappointment[1]

One day the amorous Lysander,
By an impatient passion swayed,
Surprised fair Cloris, that loved maid,
Who could defend herself no longer.
5   All things did with his love conspire;
The gilded planet of the day,
In his gay chariot drawn by fire,
Was now descending to the sea,
And left no light to guide the world,
10   But what from Cloris' brighter eyes was hurled.

In a lone thicket made for love,
Silent as yielding maid's consent,
She with a charming languishment
Permits his force, yet gently strove;
15   Her hands his bosom softly meet,
But not to put him back designed,
Rather to draw 'em[2] on inclined;
Whilst he lay trembling at her feet,
Resistance 'tis in vain to show;
20   She wants° the power to say, "Ah! What d'ye do?"   lacks

Her bright eyes sweet, and yet severe,
Where love and shame confusedly strive,
Fresh vigor to Lysander give;
And breathing faintly in his ear,
25   She cried, "Cease, cease your vain desire,
Or I'll call out—what would you do?
My dearer honor even to you
I cannot, must not give—retire,
Or take this life, whose chiefest part
30   I gave you with the conquest of my heart."

But he as much unused to fear,
As he was capable of love,
The blessed minutes to improve,

1. Behn based this poem partly on a French source, *Sur une impuissance* (1661), itself derived in part from Ovid's poem on impotence in *Amores*, which also provided the model for Rochester's *Imperfect Enjoyment* (see page 1119). Behn's poem and Rochester's first appeared in the same volume, *Poems on Several Occasions* (1680); she later included hers, with alterations, in her own collection, *Poems on Several Occasions* (1684).
2. Behn's earlier version reads "him."

Kisses her mouth, her neck, her hair;
35   Each touch her new desire alarms,
His burning trembling hand he pressed
Upon her swelling snowy breast,
While she lay panting in his arms.
All her unguarded beauties lie
40   The spoils and trophies of the enemy.

And now without respect or fear,
He seeks the object of his vows,
(His love no modesty allows)
By swift degrees advancing—where
45   His daring hand that altar seized,
Where gods of love do sacrifice:
That awful° throne, that paradise   *awe-inspiring*
Where rage is calmed, and anger pleased;
That fountain where delight still flows,
50   And gives the universal world repose.

Her balmy lips encountering his,
Their bodies, as their souls, are joined;
Where both in transports unconfined
Extend themselves upon the moss.
55   Cloris half dead and breathless lay;
Her soft eyes cast a humid light,
Such as divides the day and night;
Or falling stars, whose fires decay:
And now no signs of life she shows,
60   But what in short-breathed sighs returns and goes.

He saw how at her length she lay;
He saw her rising bosom bare;
Her loose thin robes, through which appear
A shape designed for love and play;
65   Abandoned by her pride and shame,
She does her softest joys dispense,
Offering her virgin innocence
A victim to love's sacred flame;
While the o'er-ravished shepherd lies
70   Unable to perform the sacrifice.

Ready to taste a thousand joys,
The too transported hapless swain³
Found the vast pleasure turned to pain;
Pleasure which too much love destroys.
75   The willing garments by he laid,
And Heaven all opened to his view,
Mad to possess, himself he threw
On the defenseless lovely maid.
But oh what envying god conspires
80   To snatch his power, yet leave him the desire!

3. In English pastoral poetry, this is the conventional term for the shepherd/lover.

Nature's support[4] (without whose aid
She can no human being give)
Itself now wants the art to live.
Faintness its slackened nerves invade.
85   In vain the enraged youth essayed
To call its fleeting vigor back,
No motion 'twill from motion take.
Excess of love his love betrayed.
In vain he toils, in vain commands;
90   The insensible[5] fell weeping in his hand.

In this so amorous cruel strife,
Where love and fate were too severe,
The poor Lysander in despair
Renounced his reason with his life.
95   Now all the brisk and active fire
That should the nobler part inflame,
Served to increase his rage and shame,
And left no spark for new desire.
Not all her naked charms could move
100   Or calm that rage that had debauched° his love.   corrupted

Cloris returning from the trance
Which love and soft desire had bred,
Her timorous hand she gently laid
(Or° guided by design or chance)   either
105   Upon that fabulous Priapus,[6]
That potent god, as poets feign;
But never did young shepherdess,
Gathering of fern upon the plain,
More nimbly draw her fingers back,
110   Finding beneath the verdant leaves a snake,

Than Cloris her fair hand withdrew,
Finding that god of her desires
Disarmed of all his awful fires,
And cold as flowers bathed in the morning dew.
115   Who can the nymph's confusion guess?
The blood forsook the hinder place,
And strewed with blushes all her face,
Which both disdain and shame expressed.
And from Lysander's arms she fled,
120   Leaving him fainting on the gloomy bed.

Like lightning through the grove she hies,
Or Daphne from the Delphic god,[7]
No print upon the grassy road
She leaves, to instruct pursuing eyes.
125   The wind that wantoned in her hair,
And with her ruffled garments played,

---

4. I.e., the erect penis.
5. The unfeeling object.
6. Greek god of male fertility, often depicted as possessing
a permanent erection.
7. Apollo, who pursued the nymph Daphne until she was
turned into a laurel tree in order to escape his advances.

Discovered in the flying maid
All that the gods e'er made, if fair.
So Venus, when her love was slain,
130   With fear and haste flew o'er the fatal plain.[8]

The nymph's resentments none but I
Can well imagine or condole.
But none can guess Lysander's soul,
But those who swayed his destiny.
135   His silent griefs swell up to storms,
And not one god his fury spares;
He cursed his birth, his fate, his stars;
But more the shepherdess's charms,
Whose soft bewitching influence
140   Had damned him to the hell of impotence.

1680

COMPANION READING

John Wilmot, Earl of Rochester: The Imperfect Enjoyment[1]

Naked she lay, clasped in my longing arms,
I filled with love, and she all over charms;
Both equally inspired with eager fire,
Melting through kindness, flaming in desire.
5   With arms, legs, lips close clinging to embrace,
She clips me to her breast, and sucks me to her face.
Her nimble tongue, Love's lesser lightning, played
Within my mouth, and to my thoughts conveyed
Swift orders that I should prepare to throw
10   The all-dissolving thunderbolt below.
My fluttering soul, sprung with the pointed kiss,
Hangs hovering o'er her balmy brinks of bliss.
But whilst her busy hand would guide that part
Which should convey my soul up to her heart,
15   In liquid raptures I dissolve all o'er,
Melt into sperm, and spend at every pore.
A touch from any part of her had done 't:
Her hand, her foot, her very look's a cunt.

8. When her beloved Adonis was wounded by a boar, the goddess of love rushed to help him, but in vain.

1. John Wilmot, Earl of Rochester (1647–1680), was a lyric poet and satirist known for his many notorious escapades. Always living at odds with ordinary time, mostly ahead of it, he became Earl at age 10, when his father died, received his M.A. at Oxford at 14; conducted a Grand Tour of Europe during the next three years; tried to abduct his future wife Elizabeth Malet when he was 18, and was briefly imprisoned for the attempt; married her at 20; and died, after long libertinage and precipitate piety, at 33. Rochester's wit and beauty, the stupendous energies of his mind (erudite, inventive), of his language (droit, obscene), of his body (alcoholic, bisexual), and of his convictions (hedonistic, atheistic) fascinated the Restoration court. Before his death, Rochester asked his mother to burn his papers, and she did. Fewer than 100 poems survive. Rochester had never troubled to publish any of them himself; a pirated collection appeared a few months after his death. Yet these pieces, and the conflicting accounts of the life that produced them, have been enough to make him last. Soon after his death, Aphra Behn claimed in verse to have received a visit from his "lovely phantom." "The great, the god-like Rochester" comes be her in order both to praise and to correct her poetry. Since then he has haunted many—pietists, poets, and others—as object of veneration, or reproach, or both together.

Smiling, she chides in a kind murmuring noise,
20   And from her body wipes the clammy joys,
When, with a thousand kisses wandering o'er
My panting bosom, "Is there then no more?"
She cries. "All this to love and rapture's due;
Must we not pay a debt to pleasure too?"
25   But I, the most forlorn, lost man alive,
To show my wished obedience vainly strive:
I sigh, alas! and kiss, but cannot swive.°   *screw*
Eager desires confound my first intent,
Succeeding shame does more success prevent,
30   And rage at last confirms me impotent.
Ev'n her fair hand, which might bid heat return
To frozen age, and make cold hermits burn,
Applied to my dead cinder, warms no more
Than fire to ashes could past flames restore.
35   Trembling, confused, despairing, limber, dry,
A wishing, weak, unmoving lump I lie.
This dart of love, whose piercing point, oft tried,
With virgin blood ten thousand maids have dyed,
Which nature still directed with such art
40   That it through every cunt reached every heart—
Stiffly resolved, 'twould carelessly invade
Woman or man, nor ought° its fury stayed:°   *anything / stopped*
Where'er it pierced, a cunt it found or made—
Now languid lies in this unhappy hour,
45   Shrunk up and sapless like a withered flower.
    Thou treacherous, base deserter of my flame,
False to my passion, fatal to my fame,
Through what mistaken magic dost thou prove
So true to lewdness, so untrue to love?
50   What oyster-cinder-beggar-common whore
Didst thou e'er fail in all thy life before?
When vice, disease, and scandal lead the way,
With what officious haste doest thou obey!
Like a rude, roaring hector° in the streets   *bully*
55   Who scuffles, cuffs, and justles all he meets,
But if his king or country claim his aid,
The rakehell villain shrinks and hides his head;
Ev'n so thy brutal valor is displayed,
Breaks every stew,° does each small whore invade,   *brothel*
60   But when great Love the onset does command,
Base recreant to thy prince, thou dar'st not stand.
Worst part of me, and henceforth hated most,
Through all the town a common fucking post,
On whom each whore relieves her tingling cunt
65   As hogs on gates do rub themselves and grunt,
Mayst thou to ravenous chancres° be a prey,   *syphilis sores*
Or in consuming weepings waste away;
May strangury and stone[2] thy days attend;

---

2. Painful diseases of the bladder and urinary tract that block the flow of urine.

May'st thou never piss, who didst refuse to spend
70   When all my joys did on false thee depend.
    And may ten thousand abler pricks agree
    To do the wronged Corinna right for thee.

1680

To Lysander at the Music-Meeting

It was too much, ye gods, to see and hear,
Receiving wounds both from the eye and ear.
One charm might have secured a victory;
Both, raised the pleasure even to ecstasy.
5   So ravished lovers in each other's arms,
Faint with excess of joy, excess of charms.
Had I but gazed and fed my greedy eyes,
Perhaps you'd pleased no farther than surprise.
That heav'nly form might admiration move,
10   But, not without the music, charmed° with love: *have charmed*
At least so quick the conquest had not been;
You stormed without, and harmony within.
Nor could I listen to the sound alone,
But I alas must look—and was undone:
15   I saw the softness that composed your face,
While your attention heightened every grace:
Your mouth all full of sweetness and content,
And your fine killing eyes of languishment:
Your bosom now and then a sigh would move,
20   (For music has the same effects with love).
Your body easy and all tempting lay,
Inspiring wishes which the eyes betray,
In all that have the fate to glance that way.
A careless and a lovely negligence,
25   Did a new charm to every limb dispense.
So look young angels, listening to the sound,
When the tuned spheres glad[1] all the heav'ns around:
So raptured lie amidst the wondering crowd,
So charmingly extended on a cloud.
30   When from so many ways love's arrows storm,
Who can the heedless heart defend from harm?
Beauty and music must the soul disarm;
Since harmony, like fire to wax, does fit
The softened heart impressions to admit:
35   As the brisk sounds of war the courage move,
Music prepares and warms the soul to love.
But when the kindling sparks such fuel meet,
No wonder if the flame inspired be great.

1684

---

1. Gladden. In the Ptolemaic view of the universe that Behn invokes here, the heavens were composed of concentric crystalline spheres, whose motion produced a sublime music. Angels could hear it, humans could not.

To the Fair Clarinda, Who Made Love to Me, Imagined More than Woman

Fair lovely maid, or if that title be
Too weak, too feminine for nobler thee,
Permit a name that more approaches truth,
And let me call thee, lovely charming youth.
5   This last will justify my soft complaint,
While that may serve to lessen my constraint;
And without blushes I the youth pursue,
When so much beauteous woman is in view.
Against thy charms we struggle but in vain,
10   With thy deluding form thou giv'st us pain,
While the bright nymph betrays us to the swain.[1]
In pity to our sex sure thou wert sent,
That we might love, and yet be innocent:
For sure no crime with thee we can commit;
15   Or if we should—thy form excuses it.
For who that gathers fairest flowers believes
A snake lies hid beneath the fragrant leaves.
    Thou beauteous wonder of a different kind,
Soft Cloris with the dear Alexis[2] joined;
20   Whene'er the manly part of thee would plead
Thou tempts us with the image of the maid,
While we the noblest passions do extend
The love to Hermes, Aphrodite the friend.[3]

1688

❂ APHRA BEHN AND HER TIME ❂
Coterie Writing

To Lysander, To the Fair Clarinda, A Letter to Mr. Creech: Some of Behn's poetry, like much other verse in the seventeenth century, proffered its readers the voyeuristic sense that they were being let in on the poet's correspondence. Sometimes this was so. In literary families and in friendships, verse often served as a medium of communication. A poem might make its way first from the writer to a designated recipient, then to a larger circle of acquaintances, and finally (with or without the author's consent) to the printing press. The practice of circulating manuscripts has come to be called "coterie writing," and its antecedents were ancient. Theocritus, the Greek poet credited with inventing pastoral verse, cast many of his poems as expressions of love and friendship (sung rather than written) among shepherds and nymphs living in a Golden Age. The Greek names of these ardent Arcadians—all those swooning "Lysanders" and "Clarindas"—came down to the English poets through the *Eclogues* of Virgil, Theocritus's immeasurably influential Roman imitator. Another Roman, Horace, had pioneered the durable paradigm of the verse epistle, a wittily self-conscious poetic performance addressed to a real-life, explicitly identified contemporary. In the seventeenth century, the

---

1. The conventional pastoral term for a male lover or a country lad.
2. "Cloris" is female, "Alexis" male.

3. Named after the offspring of these two gods, a hermaphrodite combines the characteristics of both sexes.

resurgence of coterie writing began with the work of Katherine Philips, who celebrated her friendships with women in poems published to great acclaim shortly after her early death. (Behn admired Philips enormously, but reworked the tradition by addressing many of her poems to men—lovers and literary colleagues—in a boldly specific, often sexual language that contrasted sharply with Philips's celebrated chastity.) Both men and women produced poems of friendship in great numbers, but for women writers the practice appears to have held a particular attraction. In addressing other women, they could enact a solidarity, cultivate a self-discovery, define and develop a resistance otherwise muted in a male-dominated world; they often depict themselves as building from female friendship what the critic Janet Todd calls "the last buttress against the irrationality always implied in the female condition." The equivocal "privacy" of the coterie poem made it a particularly supple medium, capable of combining fact and fiction, disguise and revelation, intimacy and declamation. The three practitioners sampled here worked many variations in this pliable, powerful mode of writing.

Mary, Lady Chudleigh[1]
To the Ladies

Wife and servant are the same,
But only differ in the name:
For when that fatal knot is tied,
Which nothing, nothing can divide:
5   When she the word *obey* has said,
And man by law supreme has made,
Then all that's kind is laid aside,
And nothing left but state° and pride: dignity
Fierce as an Eastern Prince he grows,
10   And all his innate rigor shows:
Then but to look, to laugh, or speak,
Will the nuptial contract break.
Like mutes she signs alone must make,
And never any freedom take:
15   But still be governed by a nod,
And fear her husband as her God:
Him still must serve, him still obey,
And nothing act, and nothing say,
But what her haughty lord thinks fit,
20   Who with the power, has all the wit.°   intelligence
Then shun, oh! shun that wretched state,
And all the fawning flatterers hate:
Value your selves, and men despise,
You must be proud, if you'll be wise.

1703

1. Born Mary Lee, and wed at age 17 into a family as aristocratic as her own, Lady Chudleigh (1656–1710) lived and wrote in the west coast county of Devon. After years of dispatching manuscript verses among a widening circle of writing friends (including the laureate John Dryden and the pioneering feminist Mary Astell), Chudleigh made her first foray into print with *The Ladies Defense* (1701), a satiric retort to a parson who had exhorted all women (in her mocking paraphrase) to "give up their reason, and their wills resign" to the dictates of their husbands. In her *Defense*, and in the two collections of shorter poems that followed (1703, 1710), Chudleigh sought to expand her coterie into a larger collective readership consisting of "all ingenious ladies": women willing, in defiance of male presumption and social convention, "to read and think, and think and read again," and thereby to "make it our whole business to be wise."

To Almystrea[1]

1

Permit Marissa[2] in an artless lay
To speak her wonder, and her thanks repay:
Her creeping Muse can ne'er like yours ascend;
She has not strength for such a towering flight.
5   Your wit, her humble fancy does transcend;
She can but gaze at your exalted height:
Yet she believed it better to expose
    Her failures, than ungrateful prove;
        And rather chose
10   To show a want of sense, than want of love:
But taught by you, she may at length improve,
And imitate those virtues she admires.
Your bright example leaves a tract divine,
She sees a beamy brightness in each line,
15   And with ambitious warmth aspires,
Attracted by the glory of your name,
To follow you in all the lofty roads of fame.

2

Merit like yours can no resistance find,
But like a deluge overwhelms the mind;
20   Gives full possession of each part,
Subdues the soul, and captivates the heart.
Let those whom wealth, or interest[3] unite,
    Whom avarice, or kindred sway,[4]
    Who in the dregs of life delight,
25   And every dictate of their sense° obey,   *appetites*
Learn here to love at a sublimer rate,
To wish for nothing but exchange of thoughts,
    For intellectual joys,
    And pleasures more refined
30   Than earth can give, or fancy can create.
Let our vain sex be fond of glittering toys,
Of pompous titles, and affected noise,
Let envious men by barb'rous custom led
    Descant° on faults,   *expound*
35   And in detraction° find   *criticisms*
Delights unknown to a brave generous mind,
While we resolve a nobler path to tread,
    And from tyrannic custom free,
View the dark mansions of the mighty dead,
40   And all their close recesses see;
    Then from those awful shades retire,
        And take a tour above,
    And there, the shining scenes admire,
    The opera of eternal love;

1. The name is an anagram for Mary Astell, feminist author of *Some Reflections upon Marriage*.
2. Chudleigh's pen name.
3. Self-interest, desire for power and material prosperity.
4. I.e., who are motivated by greed or desire for family status.

45   View the machines,[5] on the bright actors gaze,
      Then in a holy transport, blest amaze,
      To the great Author our devotion raise,
      And let our wonder terminate in praise.

1703

Anne Finch, Countess of Winchilsea[1]
The Introduction

      Did I my lines intend for public view,
      How many censures would their faults pursue!
      Some would, because such words they do affect,
      Cry they're insipid, empty, uncorrect.
5   And many have attained, dull and untaught,
      The name of wit, only by finding fault.
      True judges might condemn their want of wit,
      And all might say they're by a woman writ.
      Alas! A woman that attempts the pen,
10   Such an intruder on the rights of men,
      Such a presumptuous creature is esteemed,
      The fault can by no virtue be redeemed.
      They tell us we mistake our sex and way;
      Good breeding, fashion, dancing, dressing, play
15   Are the accomplishments we should desire;
      To write, or read, or think, or to inquire
      Would cloud our beauty, and exhaust our time,
      And interrupt the conquests of our prime;
      Whilst the dull manage of a servile house
20   Is held by some our utmost art, and use.
          Sure 'twas not ever thus, nor are we told
      Fables,° of women that excelled of old;   *false stories*
      To whom, by the diffusive° hand of heaven   *scattering*
      Some share of wit and poetry was given.
25   On that glad day, on which the Ark returned,[2]
      The holy pledge for which the land had mourned,
      The joyful tribes attend it on the way,
      The Levites do the sacred charge convey,
      Whilst various instruments before it play;
30   Here, holy virgins in the concert join,
      The louder notes to soften, and refine,

---

5. The stage mechanisms used to move scenery and produce striking effects (including the appearances of gods and angels).

1. In the early 1680s, while serving as Maid of Honor to Mary of Modena (wife of the future James II), Anne Kingsmill (1661–1720) met and married Colonel Heneage Finch, and savored the splendors of the Stuart court. When that world vanished in the Revolution of 1688, she and her husband withdrew to his country estate, where she suffered recurrent depression, cultivated friendships, wrote poetry, and saw her work published in several miscellanies. In 1713, despite her wariness of the censures heaped on women writers, she published anonymously a collection of her own, *Miscellany Poems on Several Occasions*. (*The Introduction*, in which she most memorably confronts the censurers, remained like much of her verse unpublished until the 20th century.) The book brought her some fame in her own time and much more a century later, when William Wordsworth proclaimed his admiration for her work. Her poetry moves adroitly among polarities: city and country, satire and affection, solitude and friendship.

2. The Ark of the Covenant was a chest containing the stone tablets of the Ten Commandments. Recovered by King David, it was carried into Jerusalem by members of the Levite tribe (1 Chronicles 15).

And with alternate verse,[3] complete the hymn divine.
Lo! The young poet,[4] after God's own heart,
By Him inspired, and taught the Muse's art,
35   Returned from conquest, a bright chorus meets,
That sing his slain ten thousand in the streets.
In such loud numbers° they his acts declare,   *verses*
Proclaim the wonders of his early war,
That Saul upon the vast applause does frown,
40   And feels its mighty thunder shake the crown.[5]
What can the threatened judgment now prolong?[6]
Half of the kingdom is already gone:
The fairest half, whose influence guides the rest,
Have David's empire o'er their hearts confessed.
45   A woman[7] here leads fainting Israel on,
She fights, she wins, she triumphs with a song,
Devout, majestic, for the subject fit,
And far above her arms, exalts her wit,
Then to the peaceful, shady palm withdraws,
50   And rules the rescued nation with her laws.
How are we fal'n, fal'n by mistaken rules?
And education's, more than nature's fools,
Debarred from all improvements of the mind,
And to be dull, expected and designed°;   *intended*
55   And if someone would soar above the rest,
With warmer fancy[8] and ambition pressed,
So strong the opposing faction still appears,
The hopes to thrive can ne'er outweigh the fears.
Be cautioned then my Muse, and still retired;
60   Nor be despised, aiming to be admired;
Conscious of wants, still with contracted wing,
To some few friends and to thy sorrows sing;
For groves of laurel[9] thou wert never meant;
Be dark enough thy shades, and be thou there content.

1903

Friendship Between Ephelia and Ardelia[1]

Eph.   What friendship is, Ardelia, show.
Ard.   'Tis to love, as I love you.
Eph.   This account, so short (though kind)
         Suits not my inquiring mind.
5   Therefore farther now repeat:
         What is friendship when complete?
Ard.   'Tis to share all joy and grief;

3. Responsive singing: the male and the female choruses
sing by turns, answering line with line.
4. David, who in his youth was skilled both as a fighter,
conquering the Philistines, and as a harper, credited with
composing the Psalms.
5. Saul, first king of Israel, had made David his general
but tried to kill him after hearing the women of Israel
singing, "Saul has slain his thousands, and David his ten

thousands" (1 Samuel 18.7).
6. Postpone; the prophet Samuel had foretold an untimely end to Saul's reign.
7. Deborah, judge and prophet who led the Israelites to
victory over the Canaanites (Judges 4–5).
8. Livelier imagination.
9. Tree whose leaves were used to crown celebrated poets.
1. "Ardelia" is Finch's pastoral pen name.

'Tis to lend all due relief
  From the tongue, the heart, the hand;
10 'Tis to mortgage house and land;
  For a friend be sold a slave;
  'Tis to die upon a grave,
  If a friend therein do lie.
Eph.   This indeed, though carried high,
15 This, though more than e'er was done
  Underneath the rolling sun,
  This has all been said before.
  Can Ardelia say no more?
Ard.   Words indeed no more can show:
20 But 'tis to love, as I love you.

                                                            1713

A Ballad to Mrs. Catherine Fleming in London
from Malshanger Farm in Hampshire

From me, who whilom° sung the town,   *formerly*
  This second ballad comes;
To let you know we are got down
  From hurry, smoke, and drums:
5 And every visitor that rolls
In restless coach from Mall to Paul's,[1]
  With a fa-la-la-la-la-la.

And now were I to paint the seat[2]
  (As well-bred poets use°)   *do*
10 I should embellish our retreat,
  By favor of the Muse:
Though to no villa we pretend,
But a plain farm at the best end,
  With a fa-la etc.

15 Where innocence and quiet reigns,
  And no distrust is known;
His nightly safety none maintains,
  By ways they do in town,
Who rising loosen bolt and bar;
20 We draw the latch and out we are,
  With a fa-la etc.

For jarring sounds in London streets,
  Which still are passing by;
Where "Cowcumbers"[3] with "Sand ho" meets,
25   And for loud mastery vie:
The driver whistling to his team
Here wakes us from some rural dream,
  With a fa-la etc.

1. From Pall Mall, a fashionable promenade in London,   2. The "country seat": the farm.
to St. Paul's Cathedral.   3. Cucumbers; these are the cries of street peddlers.

30
From rising hills through distant views,
 We see the sun decline;
Whilst everywhere the eye pursues
 The grazing flocks and kine:
Which home at night the farmer brings,
And not the post's but sheep's bell rings,
35 With a fa-la etc.

We silver trouts and crayfish eat,
 Just taken from the stream;
And never think our meal complete,
 Without fresh curds and cream:
40
And as we pass by the barn floor,
We choose our supper from the door,
  With a fa-la etc.

Beneath our feet the partridge springs,
 As to the woods we go;
45
Where birds scarce stretch their painted wings,
 So little fear they show:
But when our outspread hoops° they spy,   *hoop skirts*
They look when we like them should fly,
  With a fa-la etc.

50
Through verdant circles as we stray,
 To which no end we know;
As we o'erhanging boughs survey,
 And tufted grass below:
Delight into the fancy falls,
55
And happy days and verse recalls,
  With a fa-la etc.

Oh! Why did I these shades forsake,
 And shelter of the grove;
The flowering shrub, the rustling brake,°   *thicket*
60
 The solitude I love:
Where emperors have fixed their lot,
And greatly chose to be forgot,
  With a fa-la etc.

Then how can I from hence depart,
65
 Unless my pleasing friend
Should now her sweet harmonious art
 Unto these shades extend:
And, like old Orpheus' powerful song,[4]
Draw me and all my woods along,
70
  With a fa-la etc.

So charmed like Birnam's they would rise,
And march in goodly row,[5]

4. The mythological poet's music charmed trees and stones into motion.
5. In Shakespeare's *Macbeth*, the forest of Birnam "comes" to Dunsinane (fulfilling the witches' prophecy) when soldiers carry boughs as camouflage.

But since it might the town surprise
   To see me travel so,
75 I must from soothing joys like these,
   Too soon return in open chaise°   *carriage*
     With a fa-la etc.

Meanwhile accept what I have writ,
   To show this rural scene;
80 Nor look for sharp satiric wit
   From off the balmy plain:
The country breeds no thorny bays,
   But mirth and love and honest praise,
     With a fa-la etc.

c. 1719   1929

Mary Leapor[1]
The Headache. To Aurelia

Aurelia, when your zeal makes known
Each woman's failing but your own,
How charming Silvia's teeth decay,
And Celia's hair is turning grey;
5 Yet Celia gay has sparkling eyes,
But (to your comfort) is not wise:
Methinks you take a world of pains
To tell us Celia has no brains.

  Now you wise folk, who make such a pother°   *fuss*
10 About the wit of one another,
With pleasure would your brains resign,
Did all your noddles° ache like mine.   *heads*

  Not cuckolds half my anguish know,
When budding horns[2] begin to grow;
15 Nor battered skull of wrestling Dick,
Who late was drubbed at singlestick;[3]
Nor wretches that in fevers fry,
Not Sappho[4] when her cap's awry,
E'er felt such torturing pangs as I;
20 Not forehead of Sir Jeffrey Strife,
When smiling Cynthio kissed his wife.

1. The daughter of a gardener, Mary Leapor (1722–1746) worked as a kitchen maid, read voraciously, wrote plentifully, and sustained the tradition of the social poem (complete with pastoral pseudonyms) into a new era and a new register. Her manuscripts, circulating among neighbors, brought her the attention, friendship, and support of Bridget Freemantle, who undertook to arrange their publication. Leapor died of measles at age 24 before she could see her work in print. Her *Poems upon Several Occasions* appeared in 1748; its success prompted an additional volume three years later. Though the books were marketed as (in the words of one contemporary) the work of "a most extraordinary, uncultivated genius," the poems themselves prove otherwise. They display influences absorbed from Greek and Roman classics, Restoration drama, and Augustan literature—particularly Swift and Pope. Leapor transports these elements across boundary lines of class and gender to produce a new, arresting voice speaking from an old position: that of the woman who must labor in order to live.
2. Folklore held that the husband of an unfaithful wife would sprout horns from his forehead.
3. Beaten in a fencing match using short, heavy sticks.
4. Apparently a mutual friend; the ensuing names, too, refer to either real or imaginary people, otherwise unidentified.

Not lovesick Marcia's languid eyes,
Who for her simpering Corin dies,
So sleepy look or dimly shine,
25 As these dejected eyes of mine:
Not Claudia's brow such wrinkles made
At sight of Cynthia's new brocade.

Just so, Aurelia, you complain
Of vapors, rheums, and gouty pain;
30 Yet I am patient, so should you,
For cramps and headaches are our due:
We suffer justly for our crimes,
For scandal you, and I for rhymes;
Yet we (as hardened wretches do)
35 Still the enchanting vice pursue;
Our reformation ne'er begin
But fondly hug the darling sin.

Yet there's a might difference too
Between the fate of me and you;
40 Though you with tottering age shall bow,
And wrinkles scar your lovely brow,
Your busy tongue may still proclaim
The faults of every sinful dame:
You still may prattle nor give o'er,
45 When wretched I must sin no more.
The sprightly Nine° must leave me then,   Muses
This trembling hand resign its pen:
No matron ever sweetly sung,
Apollo° only courts the young.   god of poetry
50 Then who would not (Aurelia, pray)
Enjoy his favors while they may?
Nor cramps nor headaches shall prevail:
I'll still write on, and you shall rail.

1748

Advice to Sophronia

When youth and charms have ta'en their wanton flight,
And transient beauty bids the fair good-night;
When once her sparkling eyes shall dimly roll,
Then let the matron dress her lofty soul;
5 Quit affectation, partner of her youth,
For goodness, prudence, purity, and truth.
These virtues will her lasting peace prepare,
And give a sanction to her silver hair.
These precepts let the fond Sophronia prove,
10 Nor vainly dress her blinking eyes with love.
Can roses flourish on a leafless thorn,
Or dewy woodbines grace a wintry morn?
The weeping Cupids languish in your eye;
On your brown cheek the sickly beauties die.

15 Time's rugged hand has stroked your visage o'er;
    The gay vermilion stains your lip no more.
    None can with justice now your shape admire;
    The drooping lilies on your breast expire.
    Then, dear Sophronia, leave thy foolish whims:
20 Discard your lover with your favorite sins.
    Consult your glass; then prune your wanton mind,
    Nor furnish laughter for succeeding time.
    'Tis not your own; 'tis gold's all-conquering charms
    Invite Myrtillo to your shrivelled arms:
25 And shall Sophronia, whose once-lovely eyes
    Beheld those triumphs which her heart despised,
    Who looked on merit with a haughty frown,
    At five-and-fifty take a beardless clown?
    Ye pitying Fates, this withered damsel save,
30 And bear her safely to her virgin grave.

1751

An Essay on Woman

    Woman, a pleasing but a short-lived flower,
    Too soft for business and too weak for power:
    A wife in bondage, or neglected maid;
    Despised, if ugly; if she's fair, betrayed.
5   'Tis wealth alone inspires every grace,
    And calls the raptures to her plenteous face.
    What numbers for those charming features pine,
    If blooming acres round her temples twine![1]
    Her lip the strawberry, and her eyes more bright
10 Than sparkling Venus in a frosty night;
    Pale lilies fade and, when the fair appears,
    Snow turns a negro[2] and dissolves in tears,
    And, where the charmer treads her magic toe,
    On English ground Arabian odors grow;
15 Till mighty Hymen° lifts his sceptred rod,   god of marriage
    And sinks her glories with a fatal nod,
    Dissolves her triumphs, sweeps her charms away,
    And turns the goddess to her native clay.

    But, Artemisia,[3] let your servant sing
20 What small advantage wealth and beauties bring.
    Who would be wise, that knew Pamphilia's[4] fate?
    Or who be fair, and joined to Sylvia's mate?
    Sylvia, whose cheeks are fresh as early day,
    As evening mild, and sweet as spicy May:
25 And yet that face her partial husband tires,

1. I.e., if her dowry includes valuable land.
2. I.e., seems black by comparison.
3. The name of an ancient ruler celebrated as a patron of literature; Leapor applies it to her friend and sponsor Bridget Freemantle.

4. The lines about "Pamphilia" suggest that she may serve here as Leapor's alter ego; the other pastoral names (Sylvia, Simplicus, etc.) conjure up acquaintances real or imaginary.

And those bright eyes, that all the world admires.
Pamphilia's wit who does not strive to shun,
Like death's infection or a dog-day's sun?
The damsels view her with malignant eyes,
30 The men are vexed to find a nymph so wise:
And wisdom only serves to make her know
The keen sensation of superior woe.
The secret whisper and the listening ear,
The scornful eyebrow and the hated sneer,
35 The giddy censures of her babbling kind,
With thousand ills that grate a gentle mind,
By her are tasted in the first degree,
Though overlooked by Simplicus and me.
Does thirst of gold a virgin's heart inspire,
40 Instilled by Nature or a careful sire?
Then let her quit extravagance and play,
The brisk companion and expensive tea,
To feast with Cordia in her filthy sty
On stewed potatoes or on mouldy pie;
45 Whose eager eyes stare ghastly at the poor,
And fright the beggars from her hated door;
In greasy clouts° she wraps her smokey chin,   rags
And holds that pride's a never-pardoned sin.
    If this be wealth, no matter where it falls;
50 But save, ye Muses, save your Mira's[5] walls:
Still give me pleasing indolence and ease,
A fire to warm me and a friend to please.

    Since, whether sunk in avarice or pride,
A wanton virgin or a starving bride,
55 Or° wondering crowds attend her charming tongue,   whether
Or, deemed an idiot, ever speaks the wrong;
Though Nature armed us for the growing ill
With fraudful cunning and a headstrong will;
Yet, with ten thousand follies to her charge,
60 Unhappy woman's but a slave at large.

                                                                1751

The Epistle of Deborah Dough

Dearly beloved Cousin, these
Are sent to thank you for your cheese;
The price of oats is greatly fell:
I hope your children all are well
5 (Likewise the calf you take delight in),
As I am at this present writing.
But I've no news to send you now;
Only I've lost my brindled° cow,   spotted
And that has greatly sunk my dairy.
10 But I forgot our neighbor Mary;

---

5. Leapor's pen name (derived from "Mary").

Our neighbor Mary—who, they say,
Sits scribble-scribble all the day,
And making—what—I can't remember;
But sure 'tis something like December;
15   A frosty morning—let me see—
O! Now I have it to a T:
She throws away her precious time
In scrawling nothing else but rhyme;[1]
Of which, they say, she's mighty proud,
20   And lifts her nose above the crowd;
Though my young daughter Cicely
Is taller by a foot than she,
And better learned (as people say);
Can knit a stocking in a day;
25   Can make a pudding, plump and rare;
And boil her bacon to an hair;
Will coddle° apples nice and green,   cook
And fry her pancakes—like a queen.

       But there's a man, that keeps a dairy,
30   Will clip the wings of neighbor Mary:
Things wonderful they talk of him,
But I've a notion 'tis a whim.
Howe'er, 'tis certain he can make
Your rhymes as thick as plums in cake;
35   Nay more, they say that from the pot
He'll take his porridge, scalding hot,
And drink 'em down;—and yet they tell ye
Those porridge shall not burn his belly;
A cheesecake o'er his head he'll throw,
40   And when 'tis on the stones below,
It shan't be found so much as quaking,
Provided 'tis of his wife's making.
From this some people would infer
That this good man's a conjuror:
45   But I believe it is a lie;
I never thought him so, not I,
Though Win'fred Hobble who, you know,
Is plagued with corns on every toe,
Sticks on his verse with fastening spittle,
50   And says it helps her feet a little.
Old Frances too his paper tears,
And tucks it close behind his ears;
And (as she told me t'other day)
It charmed her toothache quite away.

55   Now as thou'rt better learned than me,
Dear Cos', I leave it all to thee
To judge about this puzzling man,
And ponder wisely—for you can.

---

1. A pun on "rime" (frost), which is why her work is "like December."

60   Now Cousin, I must let you know
        That, while my name is Deborah Dough,
        I shall be always glad to see ye,
        And what I have, I'll freely gi' ye.

            'Tis one o'clock, as I'm a sinner;
        The boys are all come home to dinner,
65   And I must bid you now farewell.
        I pray remember me to Nell;
        And for your friend I'd have you know
        Your loving Cousin,
                    DEBORAH DOUGH

1751

END OF APHRA BEHN AND COTERIE WRITING

OROONOKO   "I am very ill and have been dying this twelve month," Behn wrote an acquaintance late in 1687; she suffered from degenerative arthritis and had some eighteen
months' dying still to do. Now, near the end of her writing career, she set down a narrative of
events that had predated its beginnings, a story that she claimed to recall from the months she
spent in 1663–1664 as a young woman in Surinam, an English colony on the northeastern
coast of South America. A friend records that during the intervening decades Behn had often
told the story of an African prince enslaved on the plantation where she dwelt; prompted by
his love for a slave from his own country, he mounted a rebellion against his English masters.
In *Oroonoko*, Behn displayed Surinam as a world where the appetites of trade and empire had
brought several cultures—indigenous "Indians," colonizing Europeans, abducted Africans—
into violent and precarious fusion.

Writing the narrative, Behn undertook volatile fusions of her own. On the title page, the
single name "Oroonoko" sits above two subtitles in which both hero and text are implicitly
split in two. The hero is both "royal" and a "slave"; the text's "true history" is so suffused with
fictional conventions that for a long while historians suspected that Behn had never been to
Surinam and had made the whole thing up (the truth of many of the story's details has been
neither established nor refuted). Oroonoko and his beloved Imoinda play out the love-and-loss
plot of a heroic romance—a genre favored by Restoration aristocracy—within the far more
realistic context of a world driven by bourgeois imperatives and political aspirations. Behn's
boldest fusion involves not only cultures, identities, and modes but also times. Oroonoko, "the
chief actor in this history," comes to embody the history of Stuart sovereignty, playing the
roles of all three kings to whom Behn had devoted her own obsessive loyalties: Charles I,
whose 1649 execution haunts the narrative, particularly in its last few pages; Charles II, whose
1660 Restoration Behn pointedly invokes at the celebratory moment of the African prince's
arrival at Surinam; and James II, the beleaguered Catholic king whose three-year reign was
hurtling toward its close at the very moment of *Oroonoko's* publication, and whose predicament as the embattled champion of an oppressed minority finds many echoes in the royal
slave's rebellion and his fate.

Mapping all these convergences—of culture with culture, of monarch with slave, of
man with woman—Behn places herself as narrator problematically near their center. The
story is driven by her empathy for the slave couple, for whom she acts as mentor, friend, and
advocate. Yet her empathy is complicated, perhaps even compromised. She shows less pity
for less "royal" slaves, she acknowledges the possibility of her own complicity (however
inadvertent) in her hero's pain, and she is oddly absent at the height of his suffering. She
also participates in the profitable systems that enmesh him. Even before she tells his story,

she presents herself as a kind of trader, who has brought back from Surinam butterflies for the Royal Society and exotic feathers for the dress of the "Indian Queen" in the popular heroic tragedy of that name. As the scholar Laura Brown points out, Behn's "treatment of slavery . . . is neither coherent nor fully critical." The narrative is by turns empathetic with the oppressed and complicit with the powerful; the crossing vectors of Behn's allegiance produce no conclusive sum.

In *Oroonoko*, cultural compounds prove unstable. Again and again in the story, human bodies are torn apart, and these sunderings foretell other dissolutions. Behn repeatedly reminds her readers that shortly after the events she narrates, the entire colony at Surinam disappeared: the English traded it away to the Dutch (they got New York in return). As colonist she laments this loss; as Tory, she anticipates another: the loss of James II in the parliamentary overthrow that would soon supplant the English Catholic with the Dutch Protestant William of Orange. Stuart rule, which had "ended" once with regicide, would end again (like the world of her youth in Surinam) with revolution.

Behn died shortly after publishing her narrative; she was buried in Westminster Abbey, where William would be crowned just five days later. After Behn's death, *Oroonoko* did more than any of her other works to sustain her fame. As a prose narrative and in an oft-revived dramatic adaptation, it became one of the touchstone texts for the antislavery movement that grew in England and America over the next century and a half. Only with the appearance of *Uncle Tom's Cabin* in the 1850s did the advocates of abolition find a more contemporary narrative that could take its place. Behn's intricately fictionalized "true history" had survived its initial moment, and helped shape history thereafter.

Oroonoko
or
The Royal Slave
A True History

I do not pretend, in giving you the history of this royal slave, to entertain my reader with the adventures of a feigned hero, whose life and fortunes Fancy may manage at the poet's pleasure; nor in relating the truth, design to adorn it with any accidents, but such as arrived in earnest to him. And it shall come simply into the world, recommended by its own proper merits, and natural intrigues; there being enough of reality to support it, and to render it diverting, without the addition of invention.

I was myself an eyewitness to a great part of what you will find here set down; and what I could not be witness of, I received from the mouth of the chief actor in this history, the hero himself, who gave us the whole transactions of his youth; and though I shall omit, for brevity's sake, a thousand little accidents of his life, which however pleasant to us, where history was scarce, and adventures very rare, yet might prove tedious and heavy to my reader, in a world where he finds diversions for every minute, new and strange. But we who were perfectly charmed with the character of this great man were curious to gather every circumstance of his life.

The scene of the last part of his adventures lies in a colony in America called Surinam, in the West Indies.

But before I give you the story of this gallant slave, 'tis fit I tell you the manner of bringing them to these new colonies; for those they make use of there, are not natives of the place; for those we live with in perfect amity, without daring to command them; but on the contrary, caress them with all the brotherly and friendly affection in the world, trading with them for their fish, venison, buffaloes, skins, and little rarities; as marmosets, a sort of monkey as big as a rat or weasel, but of a marvelous and delicate shape, and has face and hands like an human creature; and cousheries,[1] a little beast in the form and fashion of a lion, as big as a kitten; but so exactly made in all parts like that noble beast, that it is it in miniature. Then for little parakeets, great parrots, macaws, and a thousand other birds and beasts of wonderful and surprising forms, shapes, and colors. For skins of prodigious snakes, of which there are some threescore yards in length; as is the skin of one that may be seen at His Majesty's Antiquaries,[2] where are also some rare flies,[3] of amazing forms and colors, presented to them by myself, some as big as my fist, some less; and all of various excellencies, such as art cannot imitate. Then we trade for feathers, which they order into all shapes, make themselves little short habits of them, and glorious wreaths for their heads, necks, arms, and legs, whose tinctures are inconceivable. I had a set of these presented to me, and I gave them to the King's Theater, and it was the dress of the *Indian Queen*,[4] infinitely admired by persons of quality, and were inimitable. Besides these, a thousand little knacks and rarities in nature, and some of art; as their baskets, weapons, aprons, etc. We dealt with them with beads of all colors, knives, axes, pins, and needles, which they used only as tools to drill holes with in their ears, noses, and lips, where they hang a great many little things; as long beads, bits of tin, brass, or silver, beat thin, and any shining trinket. The beads they weave into aprons about a quarter of an ell[5] long, and of the same breadth, working them very prettily in flowers of several colors of beads; which apron they wear just before them, as Adam and Eve did the fig leaves; the men wearing a long strip of linen, which they deal with us for. They thread these beads also on long cotton threads, and make girdles to tie their aprons to, which come twenty times or more about the waist and then cross, like a shoulder-belt, both ways, and round their necks, arms, and legs. This adornment, with their long black hair, and the face painted in little specks or flowers here and there, makes them a wonderful figure to behold. Some of the beauties which indeed are finely shaped, as almost all are, and who have pretty features, are very charming and novel; for they have all that is called beauty except the color, which is a reddish yellow; or after a new oiling, which they often use to themselves, they are of the color of a new brick, but smooth, soft, and sleek. They are extreme modest and bashful, very shy, and nice[6] of being touched. And though they are all thus naked, if one lives forever among them, there is not to be seen an indecent action or glance; and being continually used to see one another so unadorned, so like our first parents before the Fall, it seems as if they had no wishes; there being nothing to heighten curiosity, but all you can see, you see at once, and every moment see; and where there is no novelty, there can be no curiosity. Not but I have seen a handsome young Indian, dying for love of a very beautiful young Indian maid; but all his courtship was, to fold his arms, pursue her with his eyes, and sighs were all his language; while she, as if no such lover were present, or rather, as if she desired none such, carefully guarded her eyes from beholding him; and never approached him, but she looked down with all the blushing modesty I have seen in the most severe and cautious of our world. And these people represented to me an absolute idea of the first state of innocence, before man knew how to sin; and 'tis most evident and plain, that simple Nature is the most harmless, inoffensive, and virtuous mistress. 'Tis she alone, if she were permitted,

---

1. Other writers mention this animal, but its identity remains uncertain.
2. Probably the "Repository" (museum) of the Royal Society.
3. Butterflies.

4. A heroic drama (1664) by Robert Howard and John Dryden, celebrated for its sumptuous costumes and design.
5. Forty-five inches.
6. Shy.

that better instructs the world than all the inventions of man; religion would here but destroy that tranquillity they possess by ignorance, and laws would but teach them to know offense, of which now they have no notion. They once made mourning and fasting for the death of the English governor, who had given his hand to come on such a day to them, and neither came, nor sent; believing, when once a man's word was past, nothing but death could or should prevent his keeping it. And when they saw he was not dead, they asked him, what name they had for a man who promised a thing he did not do? The governor told them, such a man was a liar, which was a word of infamy to a gentleman. Then one of them replied, "Governor, you are a liar, and guilty of that infamy." They have a native justice which knows no fraud, and they understand no vice, or cunning, but when they are taught by the white men. They have plurality of wives which, when they grow old, they serve those that succeed them, who are young; but with a servitude easy and respected; and unless they take slaves in war, they have no other attendants.

Those on that continent where I was had no king; but the oldest war captain was obeyed with great resignation.

A war captain is a man who has led them on to battle with conduct[7] and success, of whom I shall have occasion to speak more hereafter, and of some other of their customs and manners, as they fall in my way.

With these people, as I said, we live in perfect tranquillity and good understanding, as it behooves us to do; they knowing all the places where to seek the best food of the country, and the means of getting it; and for very small and invaluable trifles, supply us with what 'tis impossible for us to get; for they do not only in the wood, and over the savannahs, in hunting, supply the parts of hounds, by swiftly scouring through those almost impassable places, and by the mere activity of their feet, run down the nimblest deer, and other eatable beasts; but in the water, one would think they were gods of the rivers, or fellow citizens of the deep, so rare an art they have in swimming, diving, and almost living in water, by which they command the less swift inhabitants of the floods. And then for shooting, what they cannot take, or reach with their hands, they do with arrows, and have so admirable an aim, that they will split almost a hair; and at any distance that an arrow can reach, they will shoot down oranges and other fruit, and only touch the stalk with the darts' points, that they may not hurt the fruit. So that they being, on all occasions, very useful to us, we find it absolutely necessary to caress them as friends, and not to treat them as slaves; nor dare we do other, their numbers so far surpassing ours in that continent.

Those then whom we make use of to work in our plantations of sugar are Negroes, black slaves altogether, which are transported thither in this manner.

Those who want slaves make a bargain with a master, or captain of a ship, and contract to pay him so much apiece, a matter of twenty pound a head for as many as he agrees for, and to pay for them when they shall be delivered on such a plantation. So that when there arrives a ship laden with slaves, they who have so contracted go aboard, and receive their number by lot; and perhaps in one lot that may be for ten, there may happen to be three or four men; the rest, women and children; or be there more or less of either sex, you are obliged to be contented with your lot.

Coramantien,[8] a country of blacks so called, was one of those places in which they found the most advantageous trading for these slaves, and thither most of our

7. Skillful management.
8. Koromantyn, a fort and trading post on the western
coast of Africa (in modern Ghana).

great traders in that merchandise trafficked; for that nation is very warlike and brave, and having a continual campaign, being always in hostility with one neighboring prince or other, they had the fortune to take a great many captives; for all they took in battle were sold as slaves, at least, those common men who could not ransom themselves. Of these slaves so taken, the general only has all the profit; and of these generals, our captains and masters of ships buy all their freights.

The King of Coramantien was himself a man of a hundred and odd years old, and had no son, though he had many beautiful black wives; for most certainly, there are beauties that can charm of that color. In his younger years he had had many gallant men to his sons, thirteen of which died in battle, conquering when they fell; and he had only left him for his successor one grandchild, son to one of these dead victors; who, as soon as he could bear a bow in his hand, and a quiver at his back, was sent into the field, to be trained up by one of the oldest generals to war; where, from his natural inclination to arms, and the occasions given him, with the good conduct of the old general, he became, at the age of seventeen, one of the most expert captains, and bravest soldiers, that ever saw the field of Mars; so that he was adored as the wonder of all that world, and the darling of the soldiers. Besides, he was adorned with a native beauty so transcending all those of his gloomy race, that he struck an awe and reverence, even in those that knew not his quality; as he did in me, who beheld him with surprise and wonder, when afterwards he arrived in our world.

He had scarce arrived at his seventeenth year when, fighting by his side, the general was killed with an arrow in his eye, which the Prince Oroonoko (for so was this gallant Moor[9] called) very narrowly avoided; nor had he, if the general, who saw the arrow shot, and perceiving it aimed at the Prince, had not bowed his head between, on purpose to receive it in his own body rather than it should touch that of the Prince, and so saved him.

'Twas then, afflicted as Oroonoko was, that he was proclaimed general in the old man's place; and then it was, at the finishing of that war, which had continued for two years, that the Prince came to court, where he had hardly been a month together, from the time of his fifth year to that of seventeen; and 'twas amazing to imagine where it was he learned so much humanity or, to give his accomplishments a juster name, where 'twas he got that real greatness of soul, those refined notions of true honor, that absolute generosity, and that softness that was capable of the highest passions of love and gallantry, whose objects were almost continually fighting men, or those mangled or dead; who heard no sounds but those of war and groans. Some part of it we may attribute to the care of a Frenchman of wit and learning, who finding it turn to very good account to be a sort of royal tutor to this young black, and perceiving him very ready, apt, and quick of apprehension, took a great pleasure to teach him morals, language, and science, and was for it extremely beloved and valued by him. Another reason was, he loved, when he came from war, to see all the English gentlemen that traded thither, and did not only learn their language but that of the Spaniards also, with whom he traded afterwards for slaves.

I have often seen and conversed with this great man, and been a witness to many of his mighty actions, and do assure my reader, the most illustrious courts could not have produced a braver man, both for greatness of courage and mind, a judgment more solid, a wit more quick, and a conversation more sweet and diverting. He knew

9. The word originally meant "Moroccan," but was often used more generally for any person of African descent. Oroonoko's name may echo the river Orinoco in Venezuela, or the African god Oro.

almost as much as if he had read much: he had heard of, and admired the Romans; he had heard of the late Civil Wars in England, and the deplorable death of our great monarch,[1] and would discourse of it with all the sense, and abhorrence of the injustice imaginable. He had an extreme good and graceful mien, and all the civility of a well-bred great man. He had nothing of barbarity in his nature, but in all points addressed himself as if his education had been in some European court.

This great and just character of Oroonoko gave me an extreme curiosity to see him, especially when I knew he spoke French and English, and that I could talk with him. But though I had heard so much of him, I was as greatly surprised when I saw him as if I had heard nothing of him, so beyond all report I found him. He came into the room, and addressed himself to me, and some other women, with the best grace in the world. He was pretty tall, but of a shape the most exact that can be fancied; the most famous statuary[2] could not form the figure of a man more admirably turned from head to foot. His face was not of that brown, rusty black which most of that nation are, but a perfect ebony, or polished jet. His eyes were the most awful that could be seen, and very piercing, the white of them being like snow, as were his teeth. His nose was rising and Roman, instead of African and flat; his mouth, the finest shaped that could be seen, far from those great turned lips which are so natural to the rest of the Negroes. The whole proportion and air of his face was so noble and exactly formed that, bating[3] his color, there could be nothing in nature more beautiful, agreeable, and handsome. There was no one grace wanting that bears the standard of true beauty. His hair came down to his shoulders by the aids of art, which was, by pulling it out with a quill and keeping it combed, of which he took particular care. Nor did the perfections of his mind come short of those of his person, for his discourse was admirable upon almost any subject; and whoever had heard him speak, would have been convinced of their errors, that all fine wit is confined to the white men, especially to those of Christendom; and would have confessed that Oroonoko was as capable even of reigning well, and of governing as wisely, had as great a soul, as politic maxims,[4] and was as sensible of power as any prince civilized in the most refined schools of humanity and learning, or the most illustrious courts.

This Prince, such as I have described him, whose soul and body were so admirably adorned, was (while yet he was in the court of his grandfather) as I said, as capable of love as 'twas possible for a brave and gallant man to be; and in saying that, I have named the highest degree of love; for sure, great souls are most capable of that passion.

I have already said the old general was killed by the shot of an arrow, by the side of this Prince, in battle; and that Oroonoko was made general. This old dead hero had one only daughter left of his race; a beauty that, to describe her truly, one need say only, she was female to the noble male; the beautiful black Venus to our young Mars; as charming in her person as he, and of delicate virtues. I have seen an hundred white men sighing after her, and making a thousand vows at her feet, all vain and unsuccessful; and she was, indeed, too great for any but a prince of her own nation to adore.

Oroonoko coming from the wars (which were now ended) after he had made his court to his grandfather, he thought in honor he ought to make a visit to Imoinda, the daughter of his foster-father, the dead general; and to make some excuses to her, because his preservation was the occasion of her father's death; and to present her

1. Charles I, whose beheading in 1649 by sentence of the House of Commons marked the culmination of the wars between Royalists and Parliament.
2. Sculptor.
3. Excepting.
4. Shrewd principles or sayings.

with those slaves that had been taken in this last battle, as the trophies of her father's victories. When he came, attended by all the young soldiers of any merit, he was infinitely surprised at the beauty of this fair Queen of Night, whose face and person was so exceeding all he had ever beheld; that lovely modesty with which she received him, that softness in her look and sighs, upon the melancholy occasion of this honor that was done by so great a man as Oroonoko, and a prince of whom she had heard such admirable things; the awfulness[5] wherewith she received him, and the sweetness of her words and behavior while he stayed, gained a perfect conquest over his fierce heart, and made him feel the victor could be subdued. So that having made his first compliments, and presented her a hundred and fifty slaves in fetters, he told her with his eyes that he was not insensible of her charms; while Imoinda, who wished for nothing more than so glorious a conquest, was pleased to believe she understood that silent language of new-born love; and from that moment, put on all her additions to beauty.

The Prince returned to court with quite another humor[6] than before; and though he did not speak much of the fair Imoinda, he had the pleasure to hear all his followers speak of nothing but the charms of that maid; insomuch that, even in the presence of the old king, they were extolling her, and heightening, if possible, the beauties they had found in her; so that nothing else was talked of, no other sound was heard in every corner where there were whisperers, but "Imoinda! Imoinda!"

'Twill be imagined Oroonoko stayed not long before he made his second visit; nor, considering his quality, not much longer before he told her he adored her. I have often heard him say that he admired by what strange inspiration he came to talk things so soft and so passionate, who never knew love, nor was used to the conversation of women; but (to use his own words) he said, most happily, some new, and till then unknown power instructed his heart and tongue in the language of love, and at the same time, in favor of him, inspired Imoinda with a sense of his passion. She was touched with what he said, and returned it all in such answers as went to his very heart, with a pleasure unknown before. Nor did he use those obligations ill that love had done him; but turned all his happy moments to the best advantage; and as he knew no vice, his flame aimed at nothing but honor, if such a distinction may be made in love; and especially in that country, where men take to themselves as many as they can maintain, and where the only crime and sin with woman is to turn her off, to abandon her to want, shame, and misery. Such ill morals are only practiced in Christian countries, where they prefer the bare name of religion; and, without virtue or morality, think that's sufficient. But Oroonoko was none of those professors; but as he had right notions of honor, so he made her such propositions as were not only and barely such; but, contrary to the custom of his country, he made her vows she should be the only woman he would possess while he lived; that no age or wrinkles should incline him to change, for her soul would be always fine, and always young; and he should have an eternal idea in his mind of the charms she now bore, and should look into his heart for that idea, when he could find it no longer in her face.

After a thousand assurances of his lasting flame, and her eternal empire over him, she condescended to receive him for her husband; or rather, received him, as the greatest honor the gods could do her.

There is a certain ceremony in these cases to be observed, which I forgot to ask him how performed; but 'twas concluded on both sides that, in obedience to him, the grandfather was to be first made acquainted with the design; for they pay a most absolute resignation to the monarch, especially when he is a parent also.

On the other side, the old king, who had many wives, and many concubines, wanted not court flatterers to insinuate in his heart a thousand tender thoughts for this young beauty; and who represented her to his fancy as the most charming he had ever possessed in all the long race of his numerous years. At this character his old heart, like an extinguished brand, most apt to take fire, felt new sparks of love and began to kindle; and now grown to his second childhood, longed with impatience to behold this gay thing, with whom, alas, he could but innocently play. But how he should be confirmed she was this wonder, before he used his power to call her to court (where maidens never came, unless for the King's private use) he was next to consider; and while he was so doing, he had intelligence brought him, that Imoinda was most certainly mistress to the Prince Oroonoko. This gave him some chagrin; however, it gave him also an opportunity, one day, when the Prince was a-hunting, to wait on a man of quality, as his slave and attendant, who should go and make a present to Imoinda, as from the Prince; he should then, unknown, see this fair maid, and have an opportunity to hear what message she would return the Prince for his present; and from thence gather the state of her heart, and degree of her inclination. This was put in execution, and the old monarch saw, and burned; he found her all he had heard, and would not delay his happiness, but found he should have some obstacle to overcome her heart; for she expressed her sense of the present the Prince had sent her, in terms so sweet, so soft and pretty, with an air of love and joy that could not be dissembled, insomuch that 'twas past doubt whether she loved Oroonoko entirely. This gave the old king some affliction, but he salved it with this, that the obedience the people pay their king was not at all inferior to what they paid their gods, and what love would not oblige Imoinda to do, duty would compel her to.

He was therefore no sooner got to his apartment, but he sent the royal veil to Imoinda, that is, the ceremony of invitation; he sends the lady, he has a mind to honor with his bed, a veil, with which she is covered and secured for the King's use; and 'tis death to disobey; besides, held a most impious disobedience.

'Tis not to be imagined the surprise and grief that seized this lovely maid at this news and sight. However, as delays in these cases are dangerous, and pleading worse than treason, trembling and almost fainting, she was obliged to suffer herself to be covered and led away.

They brought her thus to court; and the King, who had caused a very rich bath to be prepared, was led into it, where he sat under a canopy in state, to receive this longed for virgin; whom he having commanded should be brought to him, they (after disrobing her) led her to the bath and, making fast the doors, left her to descend. The King, without more courtship, bade her throw off her mantle and come to his arms. But Imoinda, all in tears, threw herself on the marble on the brink of the bath, and besought him to hear her. She told him, as she was a maid, how proud of the divine glory she should have been of having it in her power to oblige her king; but as by the laws he could not, and from his royal goodness would not take from any man his wedded wife, so she believed she should be the occasion of making him commit a great sin, if she did not reveal her state and condition, and tell him she was another's, and could not be so happy to be his.

The King, enraged at this delay, hastily demanded the name of the bold man that had married a woman of her degree without his consent. Imoinda, seeing his eyes fierce and his hands tremble, whether with age or anger I know not, but she fancied the last, almost repented she had said so much, for now she feared the storm would fall on the Prince; she therefore said a thousand things to appease the raging of his flame, and to prepare him to hear who it was with calmness; but before she spoke, he imagined who she meant, but would not seem to do so, but commanded her to lay aside her mantle and suffer herself to receive his caresses; or by his gods, he swore, that happy man whom she was going to name should die, though it were even Oroonoko himself. "Therefore," said he, "deny this marriage, and swear thyself a maid." "That," replied Imoinda, "by all our powers I do, for I am not yet known to my husband." "'Tis enough," said the King, "'tis enough to satisfy both my conscience and my heart." And rising from his seat, he went and led her into the bath, it being in vain for her to resist.

In this time the Prince, who was returned from hunting, went to visit his Imoinda, but found her gone; and not only so, but heard she had received the royal veil. This raised him to a storm, and in his madness they had much ado to save him from laying violent hands on himself. Force first prevailed, and then reason. They urged all to him that might oppose his rage; but nothing weighed so greatly with him as the King's old age, incapable of injuring him with Imoinda. He would give way to that hope, because it pleased him most, and flattered best his heart. Yet this served not altogether to make him cease his different passions, which sometimes raged within him, and sometimes softened into showers. 'Twas not enough to appease him, to tell him his grandfather was old, and could not that way injure him, while he retained that awful[7] duty which the young men are used there to pay to their grave relations. He could not be convinced he had no cause to sigh and mourn for the loss of a mistress he could not with all his strength and courage retrieve. And he would often cry, "O my friends! Were she in walled cities, or confined from me in fortifications of the greatest strength; did enchantments or monsters detain her from me, I would venture through any hazard to free her. But here, in the arms of a feeble old man, my youth, my violent love, my trade in arms, and all my vast desire of glory avail me nothing. Imoinda is as irrecoverably lost to me as if she were snatched by the cold arms of death. Oh! she is never to be retrieved. If I would wait tedious years, till fate should bow the old King to his grave, even that would not leave me Imoinda free; but still that custom that makes it so vile a crime for a son to marry his father's wives or mistress would hinder my happiness; unless I would either ignobly set an ill precedent to my successors, or abandon my country and fly with her to some unknown world, who never heard our story."

But it was objected to him that his case was not the same; for Imoinda being his lawful wife, by solemn contract, 'twas he was the injured man, and might, if he so pleased, take Imoinda back, the breach of the law being on his grandfather's side; and that if he could circumvent him, and redeem her from the otan, which is the palace of the King's women, a sort of seraglio, it was both just and lawful for him so to do.

This reasoning had some force upon him, and he should have been entirely comforted, but for the thought that she was possessed by his grandfather. However, he loved so well that he was resolved to believe what most favored his hope, and to endeavor to learn from Imoinda's own mouth what only she could satisfy him in: whether she was robbed of that blessing, which was only due to his faith and love. But as it was very hard to get a sight of the women, for no men ever entered into the otan but when the King went to entertain himself with some one of his wives or mistresses, and 'twas death at any other time for any other to go in, so he knew not how to contrive to get a sight of her.

7. Reverential.

While Oroonoko felt all the agonies of love, and suffered under a torment the most painful in the world, the old king was not exempted from his share of affliction. He was troubled for having been forced by an irresistible passion to rob his son of a treasure he knew could not but be extremely dear to him, since she was the most beautiful that ever had been seen; and had besides all the sweetness and innocence of youth and modesty, with a charm of wit surpassing all. He found that however she was forced to expose her lovely person to his withered arms, she could only sigh and weep there, and think of Oroonoko; and oftentimes could not forbear speaking of him, though her life were, by custom, forfeited by owning her passion. But she spoke not of a lover only, but of a prince dear to him to whom she spoke; and of the praises of a man, who, till now, filled the old man's soul with joy at every recital of his bravery, or even his name. And 'twas this dotage on our young hero that gave Imoinda a thousand privileges to speak of him without offending, and this condescension in the old king that made her take the satisfaction of speaking of him so very often.

Besides, he many times inquired how the Prince bore himself; and those of whom he asked, being entirely slaves to the merits and virtues of the Prince, still answered what they thought conduced best to his service; which was, to make the old king fancy that the Prince had no more interest in Imoinda, and had resigned her willingly to the pleasure of the king; that he diverted himself with his mathematicians, his fortifications, his officers, and his hunting.

This pleased the old lover, who failed not to report these things again to Imoinda, that she might, by the example of her young lover, withdraw her heart and rest better contented in his arms. But however she was forced to receive this unwelcome news, in all appearance, with unconcern and content, her heart was bursting within, and she was only happy when she could get alone, to vent her griefs and moans with sighs and tears.

What reports of the Prince's conduct were made to the King, he thought good to justify as far as possibly he could by his actions; and when he appeared in the presence of the King, he showed a face not at all betraying his heart; so that in a little time the old man, being entirely convinced that he was no longer a lover of Imoinda, he carried him with him, in his train to the otan, often to banquet with his mistress. But as soon as he entered one day into the apartment of Imoinda with the King, at the first glance from her eyes, notwithstanding all his determined resolution, he was ready to sink in the place where he stood; and had certainly done so, but for the support of Aboan, a young man who was next to him; which, with his change of countenance, had betrayed him, had the King chanced to look that way. And I have observed, 'tis a very great error in those who laugh when one says a Negro can change color; for I have seen them as frequently blush, and look pale, and that as visibly as ever I saw in the most beautiful white. And 'tis certain that both these changes were evident, this day, in both these lovers. And Imoinda, who saw with some joy the change in the Prince's face, and found it in her own, strove to divert the King from beholding either, by a forced caress, with which she met him, which was a new wound in the heart of the poor dying Prince. But as soon as the King was busied in looking on some fine thing of Imoinda's making, she had time to tell the Prince with her angry but love-darting eyes, that she resented his coldness, and bemoaned her own miserable captivity. Nor were his eyes silent, but answered hers again, as much as eyes could do, instructed by the most tender and most passionate heart that ever loved. And they spoke so well, and so effectually, as Imoinda no longer doubted but she was the only delight, and the darling of that soul she found pleading in them its right of love, which none was more willing to resign than she. And 'twas this powerful language alone that in an instant conveyed all the thoughts of their souls to each other, that they both found there wanted but opportunity to make them both entirely happy. But when he saw another door opened by Onahal, a former old wife of the King's who now had charge of Imoinda, and saw the prospect of a bed of state made ready with sweets and flowers for the dalliance of the King, who immediately led the trembling victim from his sight into that prepared repose, what rage, what wild frenzies seized his heart! Which forcing to keep within bounds, and to suffer without noise, it became the more insupportable and rent his soul with ten thousand pains. He was forced to retire to vent his groans, where he fell down on a carpet, and lay struggling a long time, and only breathing now and then, "O Imoinda!" When Onahal had finished her necessary affair within, shutting the door, she came forth to wait till the King called; and hearing some one sighing in the other room, she passed on, and found the Prince in that deplorable condition which she thought needed her aid. She gave him cordials but all in vain, till finding the nature of his disease by his sighs, and naming Imoinda, she told him he had not so much cause as he imagined to afflict himself; for if he knew the King so well as she did, he would not lose a moment in jealousy, and that she was confident that Imoinda bore, at this minute, part in his affliction. Aboan was of the same opinion; and both together persuaded him to reassume his courage; and all sitting down on the carpet, the Prince said so many obliging things to Onahal, that he half persuaded her to be of his party. And she promised him she would thus far comply with his just desires, that she would let Imoinda know how faithful he was, what he suffered, and what he said.

This discourse lasted till the King called, which gave Oroonoko a certain satisfaction; and with the hope Onahal had made him conceive, he assumed a look as gay as 'twas possible a man in his circumstances could do; and presently after, he was called in with the rest who waited without. The King commanded music to be brought, and several of his young wives and mistresses came all together by his command, to dance before him, where Imoinda performed her part with an air and grace so passing all the rest as her beauty was above them, and received the present ordained as a prize. The Prince was every moment more charmed with the new beauties and graces he beheld in this fair one; and while he gazed and she danced, Onahal was retired to a window with Aboan.

This Onahal, as I said, was one of the past mistresses of the old king; and 'twas these (now past their beauty) that were made guardians, or governants, to the new and the young ones; and whose business it was, to teach them all those wanton arts of love with which they prevailed and charmed heretofore in their turn; and who now treated the triumphing happy ones with all the severity, as to liberty and freedom, that was possible, in revenge of those honors they rob them of; envying them those satisfactions, those gallantries and presents, that were once made to themselves, while youth and beauty lasted, and which they now saw pass regardless by, and paid only to the bloomings. And certainly, nothing is more afflicting to a decayed beauty than to behold in itself declining charms that were once adored, and to find those caresses paid to new beauties to which once she laid a claim; to hear them whisper as she passes by, "That once was a delicate woman." These abandoned ladies therefore endeavor to revenge all the despites and decays of time on these flourishing happy ones. And 'twas this severity that gave Oroonoko a thousand fears he should never prevail with Onahal to see Imoinda. But, as I said, she was now retired to a window with Aboan.

This young man was not only one of the best quality, but a man extremely well made and beautiful; and coming often to attend the King to the otan, he had subdued the heart of the antiquated Onahal, which had not forgot how pleasant it was to be in love. And though she had some decays in her face, she had none in her sense and wit; she was there agreeable still, even to Aboan's youth, so that he took pleasure in entertaining her with discourses of love. He knew also, that to make his court to these she-favorites was the way to be great; these being the persons that do all affairs and business at court. He had also observed that she had given him glances more tender and inviting than she had done to others of his quality. And now, when he saw that her favor could so absolutely oblige the Prince, he failed not to sigh in her ear, and to look with eyes all soft upon her, and give her hope that she had made some impressions on his heart. He found her pleased at this, and making a thousand advances to him; but the ceremony ending, and the King departing, broke up the company for that day, and his conversation.

Aboan failed not that night to tell the Prince of his success, and how advantageous the service of Onahal might be to his amour with Imoinda. The Prince was overjoyed with this good news, and besought him, if it were possible, to caress her, so as to engage her entirely; which he could not fail to do, if he complied with her desires. "For then," said the Prince, "her life lying at your mercy, she must grant you the request you make in my behalf." Aboan understood him, and assured him he would make love so effectually, that he would defy the most expert mistress of the art to find out whether he dissembled it or had it really. And 'twas with impatience they waited the next opportunity of going to the otan.

The wars came on, the time of taking the field approached, and 'twas impossible for the Prince to delay his going at the head of his army to encounter the enemy; so that every day seemed a tedious year, till he saw his Imoinda, for he believed he could not live if he were forced away without being so happy. 'Twas with impatience therefore that he expected the next visit the King would make; and, according to his wish, it was not long.

The parley of the eyes of these two lovers had not passed so secretly, but an old jealous lover could spy it; or rather, he wanted not flatterers who told him they observed it. So that the Prince was hastened to the camp, and this was the last visit he found he should make to the otan; he therefore urged Aboan to make the best of this last effort, and to explain himself so to Onahal, that she, deferring her enjoyment of her young lover no longer, might make way for the Prince to speak to Imoinda.

The whole affair being agreed on between the Prince and Aboan, they attended the King, as the custom was, to the otan; where, while the whole company was taken up in beholding the dancing and antic[8] postures the women royal made to divert the King, Onahal singled out Aboan, whom she found most pliable to her wish. When she had him where she believed she could not be heard, she sighed to him, and softly cried, "Ah, Aboan! When will you be sensible of my passion? I confess it with my mouth, because I would not give my eyes the lie; and you have but too much already perceived they have confessed my flame. Nor would I have you believe that because I am the abandoned mistress of a king I esteem myself altogether divested of charms. No, Aboan; I have still a rest of beauty enough engaging, and have learned to please too well, not to be desirable. I can have lovers still, but will have none but Aboan." "Madam," replied the half-feigning youth, "you have already, by my eyes, found you can still conquer; and I believe 'tis in pity of me, you condescend to this kind confession. But, Madam, words are used to be

8. Fantastic or grotesque.

so small a part of our country courtship, that 'tis rare one can get so happy an opportunity as to tell one's heart; and those few minutes we have are forced to be snatched for more certain proofs of love than speaking and sighing; and such I languish for."

He spoke this with such a tone that she hoped it true, and could not forbear believing it; and being wholly transported with joy, for having subdued the finest of all the King's subjects to her desires, she took from her ears two large pearls and commanded him to wear them in his. He would have refused them, crying, "Madam, these are not the proofs of your love that I expect; 'tis opportunity, 'tis a lone hour only, that can make me happy." But forcing the pearls into his hand, she whispered softly to him, "Oh! Do not fear a woman's invention when love sets her a-thinking." And pressing his hand she cried, "This night you shall be happy. Come to the gate of the orange groves, behind the otan, and I will be ready, about midnight, to receive you." 'Twas thus agreed, and she left him, that no notice might be taken of their speaking together.

The ladies were still dancing, and the King, laid on a carpet, with a great deal of pleasure was beholding them, especially Imoinda, who that day appeared more lovely than ever, being enlivened with the good tidings Onahal had brought her of the constant passion the Prince had for her. The Prince was laid on another carpet at the other end of the room, with his eyes fixed on the object of his soul; and as she turned or moved so did they; and she alone gave his eyes and soul their motions. Nor did Imoinda employ her eyes to any other use than in beholding with infinite pleasure the joy she produced in those of the Prince. But while she was more regarding him than the steps she took, she chanced to fall, and so near him as that leaping with extreme force from the carpet, he caught her in his arms as she fell; and 'twas visible to the whole presence, the joy wherewith he received her. He clasped her close to his bosom, and quite forgot that reverence that was due to the mistress of a king, and that punishment that is the reward of a boldness of this nature; and had not the presence of mind of Imoinda (fonder of his safety than her own) befriended him in making her spring from his arms and fall into her dance again, he had at that instant met his death; for the old king, jealous to the last degree, rose up in rage, broke all the diversion, and led Imoinda to her apartment, and sent out word to the Prince to go immediately to the camp; and that if he were found another night in court, he should suffer the death ordained for disobedient offenders.

You may imagine how welcome this news was to Oroonoko, whose unseasonable transport and caress of Imoinda was blamed by all men that loved him; and now he perceived his fault, yet cried that for such another moment, he would be content to die.

All the otan was in disorder about this accident; and Onahal was particularly concerned, because on the Prince's stay depended her happiness, for she could no longer expect that of Aboan. So that e'er they departed, they contrived it so that the Prince and he should come both that night to the grove of the otan, which was all of oranges and citrons, and that there they should wait her orders.

They parted thus, with grief enough, till night, leaving the King in possession of the lovely maid. But nothing could appease the jealousy of the old lover. He would not be imposed on, but would have it that Imoinda made a false step on purpose to fall into Oroonoko's bosom, and that all things looked like a design on both sides, and 'twas in vain she protested her innocence. He was old and obstinate, and left her more than half assured that his fear was true.

The King going to his apartment, sent to know where the Prince was, and if he intended to obey his command. The messenger returned and told him he found the Prince pensive, and altogether unpreparing for the campaign; that he lay negligently on the ground, and answered very little. This confirmed the jealousy of the King, and he commanded that they should very narrowly and privately watch his motions; and that he should not stir from his apartment, but one spy or other should be employed to watch him. So that the hour approaching, wherein he was to go to the citron grove, and taking only Aboan along with him, he leaves his apartment, and was watched to the very gate of the otan, where he was seen to enter, and where they left him, to carry back the tidings to the King.

Oroonoko and Aboan were no sooner entered but Onahal led the Prince to the apartment of Imoinda, who, not knowing anything of her happiness, was laid in bed. But Onahal only left him in her chamber to make the best of his opportunity, and took her dear Aboan to her own, where he showed the height of complaisance[9] for his prince, when, to give him an opportunity, he suffered himself to be caressed in bed by Onahal.

The Prince softly wakened Imoinda, who was not a little surprised with joy to find him there, and yet she trembled with a thousand fears. I believe he omitted saying nothing to this young maid that might persuade her to suffer him to seize his own and take the rights of love; and I believe she was not long resisting those arms where she so longed to be; and having opportunity, night and silence, youth, love and desire, he soon prevailed, and ravished in a moment what his old grandfather had been endeavoring for so many months.

'Tis not to be imagined the satisfaction of these two young lovers; nor the vows she made him, that she remained a spotless maid till that night; and that what she did with his grandfather had robbed him of no part of her virgin honor, the gods in mercy and justice having reserved that for her plighted lord, to whom of right it belonged. And 'tis impossible to express the transports he suffered while he listened to a discourse so charming from her loved lips, and clasped that body in his arms for whom he had so long languished; and nothing now afflicted him but his sudden departure from her; for he told her the necessity and his commands; but should depart satisfied in this, that since the old king had hitherto not been able to deprive him of those enjoyments which only belonged to him, he believed for the future he would be less able to injure him. So that abating the scandal of the veil, which was no otherwise so than that she was wife to another, he believed her safe even in the arms of the King, and innocent; yet would he have ventured at the conquest of the world, and have given it all, to have had her avoided that honor of receiving the royal veil. 'Twas thus, between a thousand caresses, that both bemoaned the hard fate of youth and beauty, so liable to that cruel promotion; 'twas a glory that could well have been spared here, though desired and aimed at by all the young females of that kingdom.

But while they were thus fondly employed, forgetting how time ran on and that the dawn must conduct him far away from his only happiness, they heard a great noise in the otan, and unusual voices of men; at which the Prince, starting from the arms of the frighted Imoinda, ran to a little battle-ax he used to wear by his side; and having not so much leisure as to put on his habit, he opposed himself against some who were already opening the door; which they did with so much violence that Oroonoko was not able to defend it, but was forced to cry out with a commanding voice, "Whoever ye are that have the boldness to attempt to approach this apartment thus rudely, know that I, the Prince Oroonoko, will revenge it with the certain death of him that first enters. Therefore stand back, and know this place is sacred to love and me this night; tomorrow 'tis the King's."

9. Desire to please.

This he spoke with a voice so resolved and assured that they soon retired from the door, but cried, "'Tis by the King's command we are come; and being satisfied by thy voice, O Prince, as much as if we had entered, we can report to the King the truth of all his fears, and leave thee to provide for thy own safety, as thou art advised by thy friends."

At these words they departed, and left the Prince to take a short and sad leave of his Imoinda; who trusting in the strength of her charms, believed she should appease the fury of a jealous king by saying she was surprised, and that it was by force of arms he got into her apartment. All her concern now was for his life, and therefore she hastened him to the camp, and with much ado prevailed on him to go. Nor was it she alone that prevailed; Aboan and Onahal both pleaded, and both assured him of a lie that should be well enough contrived to secure Imoinda. So that at last, with a heart sad as death, dying eyes, and sighing soul, Oroonoko departed, and took his way to the camp.

It was not long after the King in person came to the otan, where beholding Imoinda with rage in his eyes, he upbraided her wickedness and perfidy, and threatening her royal lover, she fell on her face at his feet, bedewing the floor with her tears and imploring his pardon for a fault which she had not with her will committed, as Onahal, who was also prostrate with her, could testify that, unknown to her, he had broke into her apartment, and ravished her. She spoke this much against her conscience; but to save her own life, 'twas absolutely necessary she should feign this falsity. She knew it could not injure the Prince, he being fled to an army that would stand by him against any injuries that should assault him. However, this last thought of Imoinda's being ravished changed the measures of his revenge, and whereas before he designed to be himself her executioner, he now resolved she should not die. But as it is the greatest crime in nature amongst them to touch a woman after having been possessed by a son, a father, or a brother, so now he looked on Imoinda as a polluted thing, wholly unfit for his embrace; nor would he resign her to his grandson, because she had received the royal veil. He therefore removes her from the otan, with Onahal, whom he put into safe hands, with order they should be both sold off as slaves to another country, either Christian or heathen; 'twas no matter where.

This cruel sentence, worse than death, they implored might be reversed; but their prayers were vain, and it was put in execution accordingly, and that with so much secrecy that none, either without or within the otan, knew anything of their absence or their destiny.

The old king, nevertheless, executed this with a great deal of reluctance; but he believed he had made a very great conquest over himself when he had once resolved, and had performed what he resolved. He believed now that his love had been unjust, and that he could not expect the gods, or Captain of the Clouds (as they call the unknown power) should suffer a better consequence from so ill a cause. He now begins to hold Oroonoko excused and to say he had reason for what he did; and now everybody could assure the King, how passionately Imoinda was beloved by the Prince; even those confessed it now who said the contrary before his flame was abated. So that the King being old and not able to defend himself in war, and having no sons of all his race remaining alive but only this to maintain him on the throne; and looking on this as a man disobliged, first by the rape of his mistress, or rather, wife, and now by depriving him wholly of her, he feared, might make him desperate, and do some cruel thing, either to himself, or his old grandfather the offender; he began to repent him extremely of the contempt he had, in his rage, put on Imoinda.

Besides, he considered he ought in honor to have killed her for this offense, if it had been one. He ought to have had so much value and consideration for a maid of her quality, as to have nobly put her to death, and not to have sold her like a common slave, the greatest revenge, and the most disgraceful of any, and to which they a thousand times prefer death, and implore it as Imoinda did, but could not obtain that honor. Seeing therefore it was certain that Oroonoko would highly resent this affront, he thought good to make some excuse for his rashness to him, and to that end he sent a messenger to the camp with orders to treat with him about the matter, to gain his pardon, and to endeavor to mitigate his grief; but that by no means he should tell him she was sold, but secretly put to death; for he knew he should never obtain his pardon for the other.

When the messenger came, he found the Prince upon the point of engaging with the enemy, but as soon as he heard of the arrival of the messenger he commanded him to his tent, where he embraced him and received him with joy; which was soon abated, by the downcast looks of the messenger, who was instantly demanded the cause by Oroonoko, who, impatient of delay, asked a thousand questions in a breath, and all concerning Imoinda. But there needed little return, for he could almost answer himself of all he demanded from his sighs and eyes. At last, the messenger casting himself at the Prince's feet and kissing them with all the submission of a man that had something to implore which he dreaded to utter, he besought him to hear with calmness what he had to deliver to him, and to call up all his noble and heroic courage to encounter with his words, and defend himself against the ungrateful things he must relate. Oroonoko replied, with a deep sigh and a languishing voice, "I am armed against their worst efforts—for I know they will tell me, Imoinda is no more—and after that, you may spare the rest." Then, commanding him to rise, he laid himself on a carpet under a rich pavilion, and remained a good while silent, and was hardly heard to sigh. When he was come a little to himself, the messenger asked him leave to deliver that part of his embassy which the Prince had not yet divined, and the Prince cried, "I permit thee." Then he told him the affliction the old king was in for the rashness he had committed in his cruelty to Imoinda, and how he deigned to ask pardon for his offense, and to implore the Prince would not suffer that loss to touch his heart too sensibly which now all the gods could not restore him, but might recompense him in glory which he begged he would pursue; and that death, that common revenger of all injuries, would soon even the account between him and a feeble old man.

Oroonoko bade him return his duty to his lord and master, and to assure him there was no account of revenge to be adjusted between them; if there were, 'twas he was the aggressor, and that death would be just, and, maugre[1] his age, would see him righted; and he was contented to leave his share of glory to youths more fortunate, and worthy of that favor from the gods. That henceforth he would never lift a weapon, or draw a bow, but abandon the small remains of his life to sighs and tears, and the continual thoughts of what his lord and grandfather had thought good to send out of the world, with all that youth, that innocence, and beauty.

After having spoken this, whatever his greatest officers and men of the best rank could do, they could not raise him from the carpet, or persuade him to action and resolutions of life, but commanding all to retire, he shut himself into his pavilion all that day,

---

1. In spite of; i.e., despite Oroonoko's youth, death will avenge the king by taking Oroonoko first.

while the enemy was ready to engage; and wondering at the delay, the whole body of the chief of the army then addressed themselves to him, and to whom they had much ado to get admittance. They fell on their faces at the foot of his carpet, where they lay, and besought him with earnest prayers and tears to lead them forth to battle, and not let the enemy take advantages of them; and implored him to have regard to his glory, and to the world that depended on his courage and conduct. But he made no other reply to all their supplications but this, that he had now no more business for glory; and for the world, it was a trifle not worth his care. "Go," continued he, sighing, "and divide it amongst you; and reap with joy what you so vainly prize, and leave me to my more welcome destiny."

They then demanded what they should do, and whom he would constitute in his room, that the confusion of ambitious youth and power might not ruin their order, and make them a prey to the enemy. He replied, he would not give himself the trouble; but wished them to choose the bravest man amongst them, let his quality or birth be what it would. "For, O my friends!" said he, "it is not titles make men brave, or good; or birth that bestows courage and generosity, or makes the owner happy. Believe this, when you behold Oroonoko, the most wretched, and abandoned by fortune of all the creation of the gods." So turning himself about, he would make no more reply to all they could urge or implore.

The army beholding their officers return unsuccessful, with sad faces and ominous looks that presaged no good luck, suffered a thousand fears to take possession of their hearts, and the enemy to come even upon them, before they would provide for their safety by any defense; and though they were assured by some, who had a mind to animate them, that they should be immediately headed by the Prince, and that in the meantime Aboan had orders to command as general, yet they were so dismayed for want of that great example of bravery that they could make but a very feeble resistance, and at last downright fled before the enemy, who pursued them to the very tents, killing them. Nor could all Aboan's courage, which that day gained him immortal glory, shame them into a manly defense of themselves. The guards that were left behind about the Prince's tent, seeing the soldiers flee before the enemy and scatter themselves all over the plain in great disorder, made such outcries as roused the Prince from his amorous slumber, in which he had remained buried for two days without permitting any sustenance to approach him. But in spite of all his resolutions, he had not the constancy of grief to that degree as to make him insensible of the danger of his army; and in that instant he leapt from his couch and cried, "Come, if we must die, let us meet death the noblest way; and 'twill be more like Oroonoko to encounter him at an army's head, opposing the torrent of a conquering foe, than lazily, on a couch, to wait his lingering pleasure, and die every moment by a thousand wrecking thoughts; or be tamely taken by an enemy and led a whining, love-sick slave, to adorn the triumphs of Jamoan, that young victor, who already is entered beyond the limits I had prescribed him."

While he was speaking, he suffered his people to dress him for the field; and sallying out of his pavilion, with more life and vigor in his countenance than ever he showed, he appeared like some divine power descended to save his country from destruction; and his people had purposely put him on all things that might make him shine with most splendor, to strike a reverend awe into the beholders. He flew into the thickest of those that were pursuing his men, and being animated with despair, he fought as if he came on purpose to die, and did such things as will not be believed that human strength could perform, and such as soon inspired all the rest with new courage and new order. And now it was that they began to fight indeed, and so, as if they would not be outdone even by their adored hero, who turning the tide of the victory, changing absolutely the fate of the day, gained an entire conquest; and Oroonoko having the good fortune to single out Jamoan, he took him prisoner with his own hand, having wounded him almost to death.

This Jamoan afterwards became very dear to him, being a man very gallant and of excellent graces and fine parts, so that he never put him amongst the rank of captives, as they used to do, without distinction, for the common sale or market, but kept him in his own court, where he retained nothing of the prisoner but the name, and returned no more into his own country, so great an affection he took for Oroonoko; and by a thousand tales and adventures of love and gallantry, flattered his disease of melancholy and languishment, which I have often heard him say had certainly killed him, but for the conversation of this prince and Aboan, [and] the French governor he had from his childhood, of whom I have spoken before, and who was a man of admirable wit, great ingenuity and learning, all which he had infused into his young pupil. This Frenchman was banished out of his own country for some heretical notions he held; and though he was a man of very little religion, he had admirable morals, and a brave soul.

After the total defeat of Jamoan's army, which all fled, or were left dead upon the place, they spent some time in the camp, Oroonoko choosing rather to remain a while there in his tents, than enter into a palace, or live in a court where he had so lately suffered so great a loss. The officers therefore, who saw and knew his cause of discontent, invented all sorts of diversions and sports to entertain their prince: so that what with those amusements abroad and others at home, that is, within their tents, with the persuasions, arguments, and care of his friends and servants that he more peculiarly prized, he wore off in time a great part of that chagrin and torture of despair which the first effects of Imoinda's death had given him; insomuch as having received a thousand kind embassies from the King, and invitations to return to court, he obeyed, though with no little reluctance; and when he did so, there was a visible change in him, and for a long time he was much more melancholy than before. But time lessens all extremes, and reduces them to mediums and unconcern; but no motives or beauties, though all endeavored it, could engage him in any sort of amour, though he had all the invitations to it, both from his own youth and others' ambitions and designs.

Oroonoko was no sooner returned from this last conquest, and received at court with all the joy and magnificence that could be expressed to a young victor, who was not only returned triumphant but beloved like a deity, when there arrived in the port an English ship.

This person had often before been in these countries, and was very well known to Oroonoko, with whom he had trafficked for slaves, and had used to do the same with his predecessors.

This commander was a man of a finer sort of address and conversation, better bred and more engaging than most of that sort of men are; so that he seemed rather never to have been bred out of a court than almost all his life at sea. This captain therefore was always better received at court than most of the traders to those countries were; and especially by Oroonoko, who was more civilized, according to the European mode, than any other had been, and took more delight in the white nations, and, above all, men of parts and wit. To this captain he sold abundance of his slaves, and for the favor and esteem he had for him made him many presents, and obliged him to stay at court as long as possibly he could. Which the captain seemed to take as a very great honor done him, entertaining the Prince every day with globes and maps, and mathematical discourses and instruments; eating, drinking, hunting, and living with him with so much familiarity that it was not to be doubted but he had gained very greatly upon the heart of this gallant young man. And the captain, in return of all these mighty favors, besought the Prince to honor his vessel with his presence, some day or other, to dinner, before he should set sail; which he condescended to accept, and appointed his day. The captain, on his part, failed not to have all things in a readiness, in the most magnificent order he could possibly. And the day being come, the captain, in his boat richly adorned with carpets and velvet cushions, rowed to the shore to receive the Prince; with another longboat, where was placed all his music and trumpets, with which Oroonoko was extremely delighted, who met him on the shore, attended by his French governor, Jamoan, Aboan, and about an hundred of the noblest of the youths of the court. And after they had first carried the Prince on board, the boats fetched the rest off; where they found a very splendid treat, with all sorts of fine wines, and were as well entertained as 'twas possible in such a place to be.

The Prince having drunk hard of punch, and several sorts of wine, as did all the rest (for great care was taken they should want nothing of that part of the entertainment) was very merry, and in great admiration of the ship, for he had never been in one before; so that he was curious of beholding every place where he decently might descend. The rest, no less curious, who were not quite overcome with drinking, rambled at their pleasure fore and aft, as their fancies guided them: so that the captain, who had well laid his design before, gave the word and seized on all his guests; they clapping great irons suddenly on the Prince when he was leaped down in the hold to view that part of the vessel, and locking him fast down, secured him. The same treachery was used to all the rest; and all in one instant, in several places of the ship, were lashed fast in irons and betrayed to slavery. That great design over, they set all hands to work to hoist sail; and with as treacherous and fair a wind they made from the shore with this innocent and glorious prize, who thought of nothing less than such an entertainment.

Some have commended this act, as brave in the captain; but I will spare my sense of it, and leave it to my reader to judge as he pleases.

It may be easily guessed in what manner the Prince resented this indignity, who may be best resembled to a lion taken in a toil; so he raged, so he struggled for liberty, but all in vain; and they had so wisely managed his fetters that he could not use a hand in his defense, to quit himself of a life that would by no means endure slavery; nor could he move from the place where he was tied to any solid part of the ship against which he might have beat his head, and have finished his disgrace that way; so that being deprived of all other means, he resolved to perish for want of food. And pleased at last with that thought, and toiled and tired by rage and indignation, he laid himself down, and sullenly resolved upon dying, and refused all things that were brought him.

This did not a little vex the captain, and the more so because he found almost all of them of the same humor; so that the loss of so many brave slaves, so tall and goodly to behold, would have been very considerable. He therefore ordered one to go from him (for he would not be seen himself) to Oroonoko, and to assure him he was afflicted for having rashly done so inhospitable a deed, and which could not be now remedied, since they were far from shore; but since he resented it in so high a nature, he assured him he would revoke his resolution, and set both him and his friends ashore on the next land they should touch at; and of this the messenger gave him his oath, provided he would resolve to live. And Oroonoko, whose honor was such as he never had violated a word in his life himself, much less a solemn asseveration, believed in an instant what this man said, but replied he expected for a confirmation of this to have his shameful fetters dismissed. This demand was carried to the captain, who returned him answer that the offense had been so great which he had put upon the Prince, that he durst not trust him with liberty while he remained in the ship, for fear lest by a valor natural to him, and a revenge that would animate that valor, he might commit some outrage fatal to himself and the King his master, to whom his vessel did belong. To this Oroonoko replied, he would engage his honor to behave himself in all friendly order and manner, and obey the command of the captain, as he was lord of the King's vessel, and general of those men under his command.

This was delivered to the still doubting captain, who could not resolve to trust a heathen he said, upon his parole,[2] a man that had no sense or notion of the God that he worshipped. Oroonoko then replied he was very sorry to hear that the captain pretended to the knowledge and worship of any gods who had taught him no better principles, than not to credit as he would be credited; but they told him the difference of their faith occasioned that distrust: for the captain had protested to him upon the word of a Christian, and sworn in the name of a great God, which if he should violate, he would expect eternal torment in the world to come. "Is that all the obligation he has to be just to his oath?" replied Oroonoko. "Let him know I swear by my honor, which to violate, would not only render me contemptible and despised by all brave and honest men, and so give myself perpetual pain, but it would be eternally offending and diseasing all mankind, harming, betraying, circumventing, and outraging all men; but punishments hereafter are suffered by oneself; and the world takes no cognizances whether this god have revenged them, or not, 'tis done so secretly, and deferred so long; while the man of no honor suffers every moment the scorn and contempt of the honester world, and dies every day ignominiously in his fame, which is more valuable than life. I speak not this to move belief, but to show you how you mistake, when you imagine that he who will violate his honor will keep his word with his gods." So turning from him with a disdainful smile, he refused to answer him when he urged him to know what answer he should carry back to his captain; so that he departed without saying any more.

The captain pondering and consulting what to do, it was concluded that nothing but Oroonoko's liberty would encourage any of the rest to eat, except the Frenchman, whom the captain could not pretend to keep prisoner, but only told him he was secured because he might act something in favor of the Prince, but that he should be freed as soon as they came to land. So that they concluded it wholly necessary to free the Prince from his irons that he might show himself to the rest, that they might have an eye upon him, and that they could not fear a single man.

This being resolved, to make the obligation the greater, the captain himself went to Oroonoko; where, after many compliments, and assurances of what he had already promised, he receiving from the Prince his parole, and his hand, for his good behavior, dismissed his irons, and brought him to his own cabin; where, after having treated and reposed him a while, for he had neither eaten nor slept in four days before, he besought him to visit those obstinate people in chains, who refused all manner of sustenance; and entreated him to oblige them to eat, and assure them of their liberty the first opportunity.

Oroonoko, who was too generous not to give credit to his words, showed himself to his people, who were transported with excess of joy at the sight of their darling prince, falling at his feet, and kissing and embracing them, believing, as some divine

2. Word of honor.

oracle, all he assured them. But he besought them to bear their chains with that bravery that became those whom he had seen act so nobly in arms; and that they could not give him greater proofs of their love and friendship, since 'twas all the security the captain (his friend) could have against the revenge, he said, they might possibly justly take, for the injuries sustained by him. And they all, with one accord, assured him they could not suffer enough when it was for his repose and safety.

After this they no longer refused to eat, but took what was brought them and were pleased with their captivity, since by it they hoped to redeem the Prince, who, all the rest of the voyage, was treated with all the respect due to his birth, though nothing could divert his melancholy; and he would often sigh for Imoinda, and think this a punishment due to his misfortune, in having left that noble maid behind him that fatal night in the otan, when he fled to the camp.

Possessed with a thousand thoughts of past joys with this fair young person, and a thousand griefs for her eternal loss, he endured a tedious voyage, and at last arrived at the mouth of the river of Surinam, a colony belonging to the King of England, and where they were to deliver some part of their slaves. There the merchants and gentlemen of the country going on board to demand those lots of slaves they had already agreed on, and amongst those the overseers of those plantations where I then chanced to be, the captain, who had given the word, ordered his men to bring up those noble slaves in fetters, whom I have spoken of; and having put them, some in one, and some in other lots, with women and children (which they call pickaninnies), they sold them off as slaves to several merchants and gentlemen; not putting any two in one lot, because they would separate them far from each other; not daring to trust them together, lest rage and courage should put them upon contriving some great action, to the ruin of the colony.

Oroonoko was first seized on and sold to our overseer, who had the first lot, with seventeen more of all sorts and sizes, but not one of quality with him. When he saw this, he found what they meant; for, as I said, he understood English pretty well; and being wholly unarmed and defenseless, so as it was in vain to make any resistance, he only beheld the captain with a look all fierce and disdainful; upbraiding him with eyes that forced blushes on his guilty cheeks, he only cried in passing over the side of the ship, "Farewell, Sir! 'Tis worth my suffering to gain so true a knowledge both of you and of your gods by whom you swear." And desiring those that held him to forbear their pains, and telling them he would make no resistance, he cried, "Come, my fellow slaves, let us descend, and see if we can meet with more honor and honesty in the next world we shall touch upon." So he nimbly leapt into the boat, and showing no more concern, suffered himself to be rowed up the river with his seventeen companions.

The gentleman that bought him was a young Cornish gentleman, whose name was Trefry, a man of great wit and fine learning, and was carried into those parts by the Lord——, Governor, to manage all his affairs.[3] He reflecting on the last words of Oroonoko to the captain, and beholding the richness of his vest,[4] no sooner came into the boat, but he fixed his eyes on him; and finding something so extraordinary in his face, his shape and mien, a greatness of look, and haughtiness in his air, and finding he spoke English, had a great mind to be inquiring into his quality and fortune; which, though Oroonoko endeavored to hide by only confessing he was above the rank of common slaves, Trefry soon found he was yet something greater than he con-

3. John Treffry (?–1674) supervised the plantation at Parham for Francis, Lord Willoughby (1613?–1686), a nobleman long involved with colonization, who received from Charles II both the governorship and a grant of land in Surinam; his appointment of Behn's father to the post of lieutenant-governor appears to account for her sojourn in the colony (though her father died en route).
4. Robe.

fessed; and from that moment began to conceive so vast an esteem for him, that he ever after loved him as his dearest brother, and showed him all the civilities due to so great a man. Trefry was a very good mathematician and a linguist, could speak French and Spanish, and in the three days they remained in the boat (for so long were they going from the ship to the plantation) he entertained Oroonoko so agreeably with his art and discourse, that he was no less pleased with Trefry, than he was with the Prince; and he thought himself, at least, fortunate in this, that since he was a slave, as long as he would suffer himself to remain so, he had a man of so excellent wit and parts for a master. So that before they had finished their voyage up the river, he made no scruple of declaring to Trefry all his fortunes and most part of what I have here related, and put himself wholly into the hands of his new friend, whom he found resenting all the injuries were done him, and was charmed with all the greatnesses of his actions, which were recited with that modesty and delicate sense, as wholly vanquished him, and subdued him to his interest. And he promised him on his word and honor, he would find the means to reconduct him to his own country again; assuring him, he had a perfect abhorrence of so dishonorable an action; and that he would sooner have died, than have been the author of such a perfidy. He found the Prince was very much concerned to know what became of his friends, and how they took their slavery; and Trefry promised to take care about the inquiring after their condition, and that he should have an account of them.

Though, as Oroonoko afterwards said, he had little reason to credit the words of a backearary,[5] yet he knew not why, but he saw a kind of sincerity and awful truth in the face of Trefry; he saw an honesty in his eyes, and he found him wise and witty enough to understand honor; for it was one of his maxims, "A man of wit could not be a knave or villain."

In their passage up the river they put in at several houses for refreshment, and ever when they landed numbers of people would flock to behold this man; not but their eyes were daily entertained with the sight of slaves, but the fame of Oroonoko was gone before him, and all people were in admiration of his beauty. Besides, he had a rich habit on, in which he was taken, so different from the rest, and which the captain could not strip him of because he was forced to surprise his person in the minute he sold him. When he found his habit made him liable, as he thought, to be gazed at the more, he begged Trefry to give him something more befitting a slave; which he did, and took off his robes. Nevertheless, he shone through all and his osenbrigs (a sort of brown holland suit he had on)[6] could not conceal the graces of his looks and mien; and he had no less admirers than when he had his dazzling habit on. The royal youth appeared in spite of the slave, and people could not help treating him after a different manner without designing it; as soon as they approached him they venerated and esteemed him; his eyes insensibly commanded respect, and his behavior insinuated it into every soul. So that there was nothing talked of but this young and gallant slave, even by those who yet knew not that he was a prince.

I ought to tell you, that the Christians never buy any slaves but they give them some name of their own, their native ones being likely very barbarous, and hard to pronounce; so that Mr. Trefry gave Oroonoko that of Caesar, which name will live in that country as long as that (scarce more) glorious one of the great Roman, for 'tis

---

5. An African-derived term for "white master."
6. Osnaburg and holland were thick cotton or linen fabrics.

most evident, he wanted no part of the personal courage of that Caesar, and acted things as memorable, had they been done in some part of the world replenished with people and historians that might have given him his due. But his misfortune was to fall in an obscure world, that afforded only a female pen to celebrate his fame, though I doubt not but it had lived from others' endeavors, if the Dutch, who immediately after his time took that country,[7] had not killed, banished, and dispersed all those that were capable of giving the world this great man's life, much better than I have done. And Mr. Trefry, who designed it, died before he began it, and bemoaned himself for not having undertook it in time.

For the future therefore, I must call Oroonoko Caesar, since by that name only he was known in our western world, and by that name he was received on shore at Parham House, where he was destined a slave. But if the King himself (God bless him) had come ashore, there could not have been greater expectations by all the whole plantation, and those neighboring ones, than was on ours at that time; and he was received more like a governor than a slave. Notwithstanding, as the custom was, they assigned him his portion of land, his house, and his business, up in the plantation. But as it was more for form than any design to put him to his task, he endured no more of the slave but the name, and remained some days in the house, receiving all visits that were made him, without stirring towards that part of the plantation where the Negroes were.

At last, he would needs go view his land, his house, and the business assigned him. But he no sooner came to the houses of the slaves, which are like a little town by itself, the Negroes all having left work, but they all came forth to behold him, and found he was that prince who had, at several times, sold most of them to these parts; and, from a veneration they pay to great men, especially if they know them, and from the surprise and awe they had at the sight of him, they all cast themselves at his feet, crying out, in their language, "Live, O King! Long live, O King!" And kissing his feet, paid him even divine homage.

Several English gentlemen were with him; and what Mr. Trefry had told them was here confirmed, of which he himself before had no other witness than Caesar himself. But he was infinitely glad to find his grandeur confirmed by the adoration of all the slaves.

Caesar, troubled with their over-joy, and over-ceremony, besought them to rise, and to receive him as their fellow slave, assuring them, he was no better. At which they set up with one accord a most terrible and hideous mourning and condoling, which he and the English had much ado to appease. But at last they prevailed with them, and they prepared all their barbarous music, and everyone killed and dressed something of his own stock (for every family has their land apart, on which, at their leisure times, they breed all eatable things) and clubbing it together, made a most magnificent supper, inviting their grandee captain, their prince, to honor it with his presence, which he did, and several English with him, where they all waited on him, some playing, others dancing before him all the time, according to the manners of their several nations, and with unwearied industry endeavoring to please and delight him.

While they sat at meat Mr. Trefry told Caesar that most of these young slaves were undone in love, with a fine she-slave, whom they had had about six months on their land. The Prince, who never heard the name of love without a sigh, nor any

7. In 1667 Surinam twice changed hands. The Dutch briefly captured the colony and the English won it back, but immediately ceded it to the Dutch (in exchange for New York) at the Treaty of Breda.

mention of it without the curiosity of examining further into that tale which of all discourses was most agreeable to him, asked, how they came to be so unhappy, as to be all undone for one fair slave? Trefry, who was naturally amorous, and loved to talk of love as well as anybody, proceeded to tell him, they had the most charming black that ever was beheld on their plantation, about fifteen or sixteen years old, as he guessed; that, for his part, he had done nothing but sigh for her ever since she came; and that all the white beauties he had seen never charmed him so absolutely as this fine creature had done; and that no man of any nation ever beheld her, that did not fall in love with her; and that she had all the slaves perpetually at her feet; and the whole country resounded with the fame of Clemene, "for so," said he, "we have christened her. But she denies us all with such a noble disdain, that 'tis a miracle to see that she, who can give such eternal desires, should herself be all ice, and all unconcern. She is adorned with the most graceful modesty that ever beautified youth; the softest sigher—that, if she were capable of love, one would swear she languished for some absent happy man; and so retired, as if she feared a rape even from the God of Day,[8] or that the breezes would steal kisses from her delicate mouth. Her task of work some sighing lover every day makes it his petition to perform for her, which she accepts blushing, and with reluctance, for fear he will ask her a look for a recompense, which he dares not presume to hope, so great an awe she strikes into the hearts of her admirers." "I do not wonder," replied the Prince, "that Clemene should refuse slaves, being as you say so beautiful, but wonder how she escapes those who can entertain her as you can do. Or why, being your slave, you do not oblige her to yield." "I confess," said Trefry, "when I have, against her will, entertained her with love so long as to be transported with my passion even above decency, I have been ready to make use of those advantages of strength and force nature has given me. But oh! she disarms me, with that modesty and weeping so tender and so moving, that I retire, and thank my stars she overcame me." The company laughed at his civility to a slave, and Caesar only applauded the nobleness of his passion and nature, since that slave might be noble, or, what was better, have true notions of honor and virtue in her. Thus passed they this night, after having received from the slaves all imaginable respect and obedience.

The next day Trefry asked Caesar to walk, when the heat was allayed, and designedly carried him by the cottage of the fair slave, and told him, she whom he spoke of last night lived there retired. "But, " says he, "I would not wish you to approach, for I am sure you will be in love as soon as you behold her." Caesar assured him he was proof against all the charms of that sex, and that if he imagined his heart could be so perfidious to love again after Imoinda, he believed he should tear it from his bosom. They had no sooner spoke, but a little shock dog,[9] that Clemene had presented her, which she took great delight in, ran out, and she, not knowing anybody was there, ran to get it in again, and bolted out on those who were just speaking of her. When seeing them she would have run in again, but Trefry caught her by the hand and cried, "Clemene, however you fly a lover, you ought to pay some respect to this stranger" (pointing to Caesar). But she, as if she had resolved never to raise her eyes to the face of a man again, bent them the more to the earth when he spoke, and gave the Prince the leisure to look the more at her. There needed no long gazing or consideration to examine who this fair creature was. He soon saw Imoinda all over her; in a minute he saw her face, her shape, her air, her modesty, and all that called

---

8. The sun.   9. A thick-haired dog.

forth his soul with joy at his eyes, and left his body destitute of almost life. It stood without motion, and, for a minute, knew not that it had a being. And I believe he had never come to himself, so oppressed he was with overjoy, if he had not met with this allay,[1] that he perceived Imoinda fall dead in the hands of Trefry. This awakened him, and he ran to her aid, and caught her in his arms, where, by degrees, she came to herself; and 'tis needless to tell with what transports, what ecstasies of joy, they both a while beheld each other, without speaking, then snatched each other to their arms, then gaze again, as if they still doubted whether they possessed the blessing they grasped. But when they recovered their speech, 'tis not to be imagined what tender things they expressed to each other, wondering what strange fate had brought them again together. They soon informed each other of their fortunes, and equally bewailed their fate; but at the same time, they mutually protested that even fetters and slavery were soft and easy, and would be supported with joy and pleasure, while they could be so happy to possess each other, and to be able to make good their vows. Caesar swore he disdained the empire of the world while he could behold his Imoinda, and she despised grandeur and pomp, those vanities of her sex, when she could gaze on Oroonoko. He adored the very cottage where she resided, and said, that little inch of the world would give him more happiness than all the universe could do, and she vowed, it was a palace, while adorned with the presence of Oroonoko.

Trefry was infinitely pleased with this novel,[2] and found this Clemene was the fair mistress of whom Caesar had before spoke; and was not a little satisfied, that Heaven was so kind to the Prince as to sweeten his misfortunes by so lucky an accident, and leaving the lovers to themselves, was impatient to come down to Parham House (which was on the same plantation) to give me an account of what had happened. I was as impatient to make these lovers a visit, having already made a friendship with Caesar, and from his own mouth learned what I have related, which was confirmed by his Frenchman, who was set on shore to seek his fortunes, and of whom they could not make a slave because a Christian, and he came daily to Parham Hill to see and pay his respects to his pupil prince. So that concerning and interesting myself in all that related to Caesar, whom I had assured of liberty as soon as the governor arrived, I hasted presently to the place where the lovers were, and was infinitely glad to find this beautiful young slave (who had already gained all our esteems, for her modesty and her extraordinary prettiness) to be the same I had heard Caesar speak so much of. One may imagine then, we paid her a treble respect; and though from her being carved in fine flowers and birds all over her body, we took her to be of quality before, yet, when we knew Clemene was Imoinda, we could not enough admire her.

I had forgot to tell you, that those who are nobly born of that country are so delicately cut and raced[3] all over the fore part of the trunk of their bodies, that it looks as if it were japanned;[4] the works being raised like high point[5] round the edges of the flowers. Some are only carved with a little flower or bird at the sides of the temples, as was Caesar; and those who are so carved over the body resemble our ancient Picts,[6] that are figured in the chronicles, but these carvings are more delicate.

1. Reduction; release.
2. New development.
3. Carved.
4. Varnished with a glossy black lacquer.
5. Intricate lace.
6. Ancient inhabitants of northern Britain, possibly so named by the Romans because of the "pictures" (tattoos and other ornaments) they bore on their skin.

From that happy day Caesar took Clemene for his wife, to the general joy of all people, and there was as much magnificence as the country would afford at the celebration of this wedding. And in a very short time after she conceived with child; which made Caesar even adore her, knowing he was the last of his great race. This new accident made him more impatient of liberty, and he was every day treating with Trefry for his and Clemene's liberty; and offered either gold, or a vast quantity of slaves, which should be paid before they let him go, provided he could have any security that he should go when his ransom was paid. They fed him from day to day with promises, and delayed him, till the Lord Governor should come, so that he began to suspect them of falsehood, and that they would delay him till the time of his wife's delivery, and make a slave of that too, for all the breed is theirs to whom the parents belong. This thought made him very uneasy, and his sullenness gave them some jealousies[7] of him, so that I was obliged, by some persons who feared a mutiny (which is very fatal sometimes in those colonies that abound so with slaves that they exceed the whites in vast numbers), to discourse with Caesar, and to give him all the satisfaction I possibly could. They knew he and Clemene were scarce an hour in a day from my lodgings, that they ate with me, and that I obliged them in all things I was capable of: I entertained him with the lives of the Romans, and great men, which charmed him to my company, and her, with teaching her all the pretty works that I was mistress of, and telling her stories of nuns, and endeavoring to bring her to the knowledge of the true God. But of all discourses Caesar liked that the worst, and would never be reconciled to our notions of the Trinity, of which he ever made a jest; it was a riddle, he said, would turn his brain to conceive, and one could not make him understand what faith was. However, these conversations failed not altogether so well to divert him, that he liked the company of us women much above the men, for he could not drink, and he is but an ill companion in that country that cannot. So that obliging him to love us very well, we had all the liberty of speech with him, especially myself, whom he called his Great Mistress; and indeed my word would go a great way with him. For these reasons, I had opportunity to take notice to him, that he was not well pleased of late, as he used to be, was more retired and thoughtful, and told him, I took it ill he should suspect we would break our words with him, and not permit both him and Clemene to return to his own kingdom, which was not so long away, but when he was once on his voyage he would quickly arrive there. He made me some answers that showed a doubt in him, which made me ask him, what advantage it would be to doubt? It would but give us a fear of him, and possibly compel us to treat him so as I should be very loath to behold: that is, it might occasion his confinement. Perhaps this was not so luckily spoke of me, for I perceived he resented that word, which I strove to soften again in vain. However, he assured me, that whatsoever resolutions he should take, he would act nothing upon the white people. And as for myself, and those upon that plantation where he was, he would sooner forfeit his eternal liberty, and life itself, than lift his hand against his greatest enemy on that place. He besought me to suffer no fears upon his account, for he could do nothing that honor should not dictate, but he accused himself for having suffered slavery so long; yet he charged that weakness on love alone, who was capable of making him neglect even glory itself, and for which now he reproaches himself every moment of the day. Much more to this effect he spoke, with an air impatient enough to make me know he would not be long in bondage, and though he suffered only the name of a

---

7. Suspicions.

slave, and had nothing of the toil and labor of one, yet that was sufficient to render him uneasy, and he had been too long idle, who used to be always in action, and in arms. He had a spirit all rough and fierce, and that could not be tamed to lazy rest, and though all endeavors were used to exercise himself in such actions and sports as this world afforded, as running, wrestling, pitching the bar,[8] hunting and fishing, chasing and killing tigers of a monstrous size, which this continent affords in abundance; and wonderful snakes, such as Alexander[9] is reported to have encountered at the river of Amazons, and which Caesar took great delight to overcome; yet these were not actions great enough for his large soul, which was still panting after more renowned action.

Before I parted that day with him, I got, with much ado, a promise from him to rest yet a little longer with patience, and wait the coming of the Lord Governor, who was every day expected on our shore. He assured me he would, and this promise he desired me to know was given perfectly in complaisance to me, in whom he had an entire confidence.

After this, I neither thought it convenient to trust him much out of our view, nor did the country who feared him; but with one accord it was advised to treat him fairly, and oblige him to remain within such a compass, and that he should be permitted as seldom as could be to go up to the plantations of the Negroes; or if he did, to be accompanied by some that should be rather in appearance attendants than spies. This care was for some time taken, and Caesar looked upon it as a mark of extraordinary respect, and was glad his discontent had obliged them to be more observant to him. He received new assurance from the overseer, which was confirmed to him by the opinion of all the gentlemen of the country, who made their court to him. During this time that we had his company more frequently than hitherto we had had, it may not be unpleasant to relate to you the diversions we entertained him with, or rather he us.

My stay was to be short in that country, because my father died at sea, and never arrived to possess the honor was designed him (which was lieutenant-general of six and thirty islands, besides the continent[1] of Surinam), nor the advantages he hoped to reap by them, so that though we were obliged to continue on our voyage, we did not intend to stay upon the place. Though, in a word, I must say thus much of it, that certainly had his late Majesty,[2] of sacred memory, but seen and known what a vast and charming world he had been master of in that continent, he would never have parted so easily with it to the Dutch. 'Tis a continent whose vast extent was never yet known, and may contain more noble earth than all the universe besides; for they say it reaches from east to west, one way as far as China, and another to Peru. It affords all things both for beauty and use; 'tis there eternal spring, always the very months of April, May, and June. The shades are perpetual, the trees, bearing at once all degrees of leaves and fruit from blooming buds to ripe autumn, groves of oranges, lemons, citrons, figs, nutmegs, and noble aromatics, continually bearing their fragrancies. The trees appearing all like nosegays adorned with flowers of different kind; some are all white, some purple, some scarlet, some blue, some yellow; bearing, at the same time, ripe fruit and blooming young, or producing every day new. The very wood of all these trees have an intrinsic value above common timber, for they are,

8. Hurling a heavy rod for purposes of exercise or sport.
9. Legends surrounding Alexander the Great included his encounter with the mythical woman warriors called Amazons, and with the formidable snakes inhabiting their territories.
1. Mainland.
2. Charles II.

when cut, of different colors, glorious to behold, and bear a price considerable, to inlay withal. Besides this, they yield rich balm and gums, so that we make our candles of such an aromatic substance as does not only give a sufficient light but, as they burn, they cast their perfumes all about. Cedar is the common firing, and all the houses are built with it. The very meat we eat, when set on the table, if it be native, I mean of the country, perfumes the whole room, especially a little beast called an armadillo, a thing which I can liken to nothing so well as a rhinoceros. 'Tis all in white armor so jointed that it moves as well in it as if it had nothing on. This beast is about the bigness of a pig of six weeks old. But it were endless to give an account of all the diverse wonderful and strange things that country affords, and which we took a very great delight to go in search of, though those adventures are oftentimes fatal and at least dangerous. But while we had Caesar in our company on these designs we feared no harm, nor suffered any.

As soon as I came into the country, the best house in it was presented me, called St. John's Hill. It stood on a vast rock of white marble, at the foot of which the river ran a vast depth down, and not to be descended on that side. The little waves still dashing and washing the foot of this rock made the softest murmurs and purlings in the world, and the opposite bank was adorned with such vast quantities of different flowers eternally blowing,[3] and every day and hour new, fenced behind them with lofty trees of a thousand rare forms and colors, that the prospect was the most ravishing that sands can create. On the edge of this white rock, toward the river, was a walk or grove of orange and lemon trees, about half the length of the Mall[4] here, whose flowery and fruity branches meet at the top, and hindered the sun, whose rays are very fierce there, from entering a beam into the grove, and the cool air that came from the river made it not only fit to entertain people in at all the hottest hours of the day, but refreshed the sweet blossoms, and made it always sweet and charming, and sure the whole globe of the world cannot show so delightful a place as this grove was. Not all the gardens of boasted Italy can produce a shade to out-vie this, which Nature had joined with Art to render so exceeding fine. And 'tis a marvel to see how such vast trees, as big as English oaks, could take footing on so solid a rock, and in so little earth, as covered that rock, but all things by nature there are rare, delightful, and wonderful. But to our sports.

Sometimes we would go surprising,[5] and in search of young tigers in their dens, watching when the old ones went forth to forage for prey, and oftentimes we have been in great danger, and have fled apace for our lives, when surprised by the dams. But once, above all other times, we went on this design, and Caesar was with us, who had no sooner stolen a young tiger from her nest, but going off, we encountered the dam, bearing a buttock of a cow, which he[6] had torn off with his mighty paw, and going with it towards his den. We had only four women, Caesar, and an English gentleman, brother to Harry Martin, the great Oliverian.[7] We found there was no escaping this enraged and ravenous beast. However, we women fled as fast as we could from it, but our heels had not saved our lives if Caesar had not laid down his cub, when he found the tiger quit her prey to make the more speed towards him, and taking Mr. Martin's sword desired him to stand aside, or follow the ladies. He obeyed him, and Caesar met this monstrous beast of might, size, and vast limbs, who came

3. Blossoming.
4. A walk extending alongside London's St. James's Park.
5. I.e., surprise-attacking.
6. The "dam" is the cub's mother, but Behn has surpris-

ingly shifted the gender of the pronoun from "she" to "he"; she will do so again in reference to another tiger in the next paragraph.
7. Supporter of Oliver Cromwell.

with open jaws upon him, and fixing his awful stern eyes full upon those of the beast, and putting himself into a very steady and good aiming posture of defense, ran his sword quite through his breast down to his very heart, home to the hilt of the sword. The dying beast stretched forth her paw, and going to grasp his thigh, surprised with death in that very moment, did him no other harm than fixing her long nails in his flesh very deep, feebly wounded him, but could not grasp the flesh to tear off any. When he had done this, he hollowed to us to return, which, after some assurance of his victory, we did, and found him lugging out the sword from the bosom of the tiger, who was laid in her blood on the ground. He took up the cub, and with an uncon- cern, that had nothing of the joy or gladness of a victory, he came and laid the whelp at my feet. We all extremely wondered at his daring, and at the bigness of the beast, which was about the height of an heifer, but of mighty, great, and strong limbs.

Another time, being in the woods, he killed a tiger, which had long infested that part, and borne away abundance of sheep and oxen and other things, that were for the support of those to whom they belonged. Abundance of people assailed this beast, some affirming they had shot her with several bullets quite through the body, at several times, and some swearing they shot her through the very heart, and they believed she was a devil rather than a mortal thing. Caesar had often said he had a mind to encounter this monster, and spoke with several gentlemen who had attempted her, one crying, I shot her with so many poisoned arrows, another with his gun in this part of her, and another in that. So that he remarking all these places where she was shot, fancied still he should overcome her, by giving her another sort of a wound than any had yet done, and one day said (at the table), "What trophies and garlands, ladies, will you make me, if I bring you home the heart of this ravenous beast that eats up all your lambs and pigs?" We all promised he should be rewarded at all our hands. So taking a bow, which he chose out of a great many, he went up in the wood, with two gentlemen, where he imagined this devourer to be. They had not passed very far in it, but they heard her voice, growling and grumbling, as if she were pleased with something she was doing. When they came in view, they found her muzzling in the belly of a new ravished sheep which she had torn open, and seeing herself approached, she took fast hold of her prey with her forepaws, and set a very fierce rag- ing look on Caesar, without offering to approach him, for fear, at the same time, of losing what she had in possession. So that Caesar remained a good while, only taking aim, and getting an opportunity to shoot her where he designed. 'Twas some time before he could accomplish it, and to wound her and not kill her would but have enraged her more, and endangered him. He had a quiver of arrows at his side, so that if one failed he could be supplied. At last, retiring a little, he gave her opportunity to eat, for he found she was ravenous, and fell to as soon as she saw him retire, being more eager of her prey than of doing new mischiefs. When he going softly to one side of her, and hiding his person behind certain herbage that grew high and thick, he took so good aim that, as he intended, he shot her just into the eye, and the arrow was sent with so good a will, and so sure a hand, that it stuck in her brain, and made her caper and become mad for a moment or two, but being seconded by another arrow, he fell dead upon the prey. Caesar cut him open with a knife, to see where those wounds were that had been reported to him, and why he did not die of them. But I shall now relate a thing that possibly will find no credit among men, because 'tis a notion commonly received with us that nothing can receive a wound in the heart and live; but when the heart of this courageous animal was taken out, there were seven bullets of lead in it, and the wounds seamed up with great scars, and she lived with the bullets a great while, for it was long since they were shot. This heart the conqueror brought up to us, and 'twas a very great curiosity, which all the country came to see; and which gave Caesar occasion of many fine discourses, of accidents in war and strange escapes.

At other times he would go a-fishing, and discoursing on that diversion, he found we had in that country a very strange fish, called a numb eel[8] (an eel of which I have eaten), that while it is alive, it has a quality so cold that those who are angling, though with a line of never so great a length, with a rod at the end of it, it shall, in the same minute the bait is touched by this eel, seize him or her that holds the rod with benumbedness, that shall deprive them of sense for a while. And some have fallen into the water, and others dropped as dead on the banks of the rivers where they stood, as soon as this fish touches the bait. Caesar used to laugh at this, and believed it impossible a man could lose his force at the touch of a fish; and could not understand that philosophy, that a cold quality should be of that nature. However, he had a great curiosity to try whether it would have the same effect on him it had on others, and often tried, but in vain. At last, the sought-for fish came to the bait as he stood angling on the bank; and instead of throwing away the rod, or giving it a sudden twitch out of the water, whereby he might have caught both the eel and have dismissed the rod before it could have too much power over him for experiment sake, he grasped it but the harder, and fainting fell into the river. And being still possessed of the rod, the tide carried him senseless as he was a great way, till an Indian boat took him up, and perceived, when they touched him, a numbness seize them, and by that knew the rod was in his hand, which with a paddle (that is, a short oar) they struck away, and snatched it into the boat, eel and all. If Caesar were almost dead with the effect of this fish, he was more so with that of the water, where he had remained the space of going a league, and they found they had much ado to bring him back to life. But at last they did, and brought him home, where he was in a few hours well recovered and refreshed, and not a little ashamed to find he should be overcome by an eel, and that all the people who heard his defiance would laugh at him. But we cheered him up and he, being convinced, we had the eel at supper, which was a quarter of an ell about, and most delicate meat, and was of the more value, since it cost so dear as almost the life of so gallant a man.

About this time we were in many mortal fears about some disputes the English had with the Indians, so that we could scarce trust ourselves, without great numbers, to go to any Indian towns or place where they abode, for fear they should fall upon us, as they did immediately after my coming away, and that it was in the possession of the Dutch, who used them not so civilly as the English, so that they cut in pieces all they could take, getting into houses, and hanging up the mother, and all her children about her, and cut a footman I left behind me all in joints, and nailed him to trees.

This feud began while I was there, so that I lost half the satisfaction I proposed, in not seeing and visiting the Indian towns. But one day, bemoaning of our misfortunes upon this account, Caesar told us we need not fear, for if we had a mind to go he would undertake to be our guard. Some would, but most would not venture. About eighteen of us resolved, and took barge, and after eight days arrived near an Indian town. But approaching it, the hearts of some of our company failed, and they would not venture on shore, so we polled who would, and who would not. For my part, I said, if Caesar would, I would go. He resolved, so did my brother and my

8. An electric eel.

woman, a maid of good courage. Now none of us speaking the language of the people, and imagining we should have a half diversion in gazing only and not knowing what they said, we took a fisherman that lived at the mouth of the river, who had been a long inhabitant there, and obliged him to go with us. But because he was known to the Indians, as trading among them, and being, by long living there, become a perfect Indian in color, we, who resolved to surprise them, by making them see something they never had seen (that is, white people) resolved only myself, my brother, and woman should go. So Caesar, the fisherman, and the rest, hiding behind some thick reeds and flowers, that grew on the banks, let us pass on towards the town, which was on the bank of the river all along. A little distant from the houses, or huts, we saw some dancing, others busied in fetching and carrying of water from the river. They had no sooner spied us but they set up a loud cry, that frighted us at first. We thought it had been for those that should kill us, but it seems it was of wonder and amazement. They were all naked, and we were dressed, so as is most commode for the hot countries, very glittering and rich, so that we appeared extremely fine. My own hair was cut short, and I had a taffeta cap, with black feathers, on my head. My brother was in a stuff[9] suit, with silver loops and buttons, and abundance of green ribbon. This was all infinitely surprising to them, and because we saw them stand still, till we approached them, we took heart and advanced, came up to them, and offered them our hands, which they took, and looked on us round about, calling still for more company; who came swarming out, all wondering, and crying out *tepeeme*, taking their hair up in their hands, and spreading it wide to those they called out to, as if they would say (as indeed it signified) "numberless wonders," or not to be recounted, no more than to number the hair of their heads. By degrees they grew more bold, and from gazing upon us round, they touched us, laying their hands upon all the features of our faces, feeling our breasts and arms, taking up one petticoat, then wondering to see another, admiring our shoes and stockings, but more our garters, which we gave them, and they tied about their legs, being laced with silver lace at the ends, for they much esteem any shining things. In fine, we suffered them to survey us as they pleased, and we thought they would never have done admiring us. When Caesar and the rest saw we were received with such wonder, they came up to us, and finding the Indian trader whom they knew (for 'tis by these fishermen, called Indian traders, we hold a commerce with them; for they love not to go far from home, and we never go to them), when they saw him therefore they set up a new joy, and cried, in their language, "Oh! here's our *tiguamy*, and we shall now know whether those things can speak." So advancing to him, some of them gave him their hands, and cried, "*Amora tiguamy*," which is as much as, "How do you," or "Welcome friend," and all, with one din, began to gabble to him, and asked, If we had sense, and wit? If we could talk of affairs of life, and war, as they could do? If we could hunt, swim, and do a thousand things they use? He answered them, we could. Then they invited us into their houses, and dressed venison and buffalo for us; and, going out, gathered a leaf of a tree, called a sarumbo leaf, of six yards long, and spread it on the ground for a tablecloth, and cutting another in pieces instead of plates, setting us on little bow Indian stools, which they cut out of one entire piece of wood, and paint in a sort of japan work. They serve everyone their mess on these pieces of leaves, and it was very good, but too high seasoned with pepper. When we had eaten, my brother and I took out our flutes and played to them, which gave them new wonder, and I soon perceived, by an

9. Woolen.

admiration that is natural to these people, and by the extreme ignorance and simplicity of them, it were not difficult to establish any unknown or extravagant religion among them, and to impose any notions or fictions upon them. For seeing a kinsman of mine set some paper afire with a burning-glass, a trick they had never before seen, they were like to have adored him for a god, and begged he would give them the characters or figures of his name, that they might oppose it against winds and storms, which he did, and they held it up in those seasons, and fancied it had a charm to conquer them, and kept it like a holy relic. They are very superstitious, and called him the great *peeie*, that is, prophet. They showed us their Indian *peeie*, a youth of about sixteen years old, as handsome as Nature could make a man. They consecrate a beautiful youth from his infancy, and all arts are used to complete him in the finest manner, both in beauty and shape. He is bred to all the little arts and cunning they are capable of, to all the legerdemain tricks and sleight of hand whereby he imposes upon the rabble, and is both a doctor in physic and divinity. And by these tricks makes the sick believe he sometimes eases their pains, by drawing from the afflicted part little serpents, or odd flies, or worms, or any strange thing; and though they have besides undoubted good remedies for almost all their diseases, they cure the patient more by fancy than by medicines, and make themselves feared, loved, and reverenced. This young *peeie* had a very young wife, who seeing my brother kiss her, came running and kissed me; after this, they kissed one another, and made it a very great jest, it being so novel, and new admiration and laughing went round the multitude, that they never will forget that ceremony, never before used or known. Caesar had a mind to see and talk with their war captains, and we were conducted to one of their houses, where we beheld several of the great captains, who had been at council. But so frightful a vision it was to see them no fancy can create; no such dreams can represent so dreadful a spectacle. For my part I took them for hobgoblins, or fiends, rather than men. But however their shapes appeared, their souls were very humane and noble, but some wanted their noses, some their lips, some both noses and lips, some their ears, and others cut through each cheek, with long slashes, through which their teeth appeared; they had several other formidable wounds and scars, or rather dismemberings. They had *comitias*, or little aprons before them, and girdles of cotton, with their knives naked, stuck in it, a bow at their backs, and a quiver of arrows on their thighs, and most had feathers on their heads of diverse colors. They cried "*Amora tiguamy*" to us at our entrance, and were pleased we said as much to them. They feted us, and gave us drink of the best sort, and wondered, as much as the others had done before, to see us. Caesar was marveling as much at their faces, wondering how they should all be so wounded in war; he was impatient to know how they all came by those frightful marks of rage or malice, rather than wounds got in noble battle. They told us, by our interpreter, that when any war was waging, two men chosen out by some old captain, whose fighting was past, and who could only teach the theory of war, these two men were to stand in competition for the generalship, or Great War Captain, and being brought before the old judges, now past labor, they are asked, what they dare do to show they are worthy to lead an army? When he who is first asked, making no reply, cuts off his nose, and throws it contemptibly[1] on the ground, and the other does something to himself that he thinks surpasses him, and perhaps deprives himself of lips and an eye. So they slash on till one gives out, and many have died in this debate. And 'tis by a passive valor they show and prove their activity, a sort of

---

1. Contemptuously.

courage too brutal to be applauded by our black hero; nevertheless he expressed his esteem of them.

In this voyage Caesar begot so good an understanding between the Indians and the English, that there were no more fears or heartburnings during our stay, but we had a perfect, open, and free trade with them. Many things remarkable, and worthy reciting, we met with in this short voyage, because Caesar made it his business to search out and provide for our entertainment, especially to please his dearly adored Imoinda, who was a sharer in all our adventures; we being resolved to make her chains as easy as we could, and to compliment the Prince in that manner that most obliged him.

As we were coming up again, we met with some Indians of strange aspects, that is, of a larger size, and other sort of features, than those of our country. Our Indian slaves, that rowed us, asked them some questions, but they could not understand us, but showed us a long cotton string with several knots on it, and told us, they had been coming from the mountains so many moons as there were knots. They were habited in skins of a strange beast, and brought along with them bags of gold dust, which, as well as they could give us to understand, came streaming in little small channels down the high mountains, when the rains fell, and offered to be the convoy to anybody, or persons, that would go to the mountains. We carried these men up to Parham, where they were kept till the Lord Governor came. And because all the country was mad to be going on this golden adventure, the governor, by his letters, commanded (for they sent some of the gold to him) that a guard should be set at the mouth of the river of Amazons (a river so called, almost as broad as the river of Thames), and prohibited all people from going up that river, it conducting to those mountains of gold. But we going off for England before the project was further prosecuted, and the Governor being drowned in a hurricane, either the design died, or the Dutch have the advantage of it. And 'tis to be bemoaned what His Majesty lost by losing that part of America.

Though this digression is a little from my story, however since it contains some proofs of the curiosity and daring of this great man, I was content to omit nothing of his character.

It was thus, for some time we diverted him. But now Imoinda began to show she was with child, and did nothing but sigh and weep for the captivity of her lord, herself, and the infant yet unborn, and believed, if it were so hard to gain the liberty of two, 'twould be more difficult to get that for three. Her griefs were so many darts in the great heart of Caesar, and taking his opportunity one Sunday, when all the whites were overtaken in drink, as there were abundance of several trades, and slaves for four years,[2] that inhabited among the Negro houses, and Sunday was their day of debauch (otherwise they were a sort of spies upon Caesar), he went pretending out of goodness to them, to feast amongst them, and sent all his music, and ordered a great treat for the whole gang, about three hundred Negroes. And about a hundred and fifty were able to bear arms, such as they had, which were sufficient to do execution with spirits accordingly. For the English had none but rusty swords, that no strength could draw from a scabbard, except the people of particular quality, who took care to oil them and keep them in good order. The guns also, unless here and there one, or those newly carried from England, would do no good or harm, for 'tis the nature of that country to rust and eat up iron, or any metals but gold and silver. And they are very inexpert at the bow, which the Negroes and Indians are perfect masters of.

---

2. I.e., whites who, as punishment for crime or debt, had been forced into service for fixed periods of time.

Caesar, having singled out these men from the women and children, made a harangue to them of the miseries and ignominies of slavery; counting up all their toils and sufferings, under such loads, burdens, and drudgeries as were fitter for beasts than men, senseless brutes than human souls. He told them it was not for days, months, or years, but for eternity; there was no end to be of their misfortunes. They suffered not like men who might find a glory and fortitude in oppression, but like dogs that loved the whip and bell,[3] and fawned the more they were beaten. That they had lost the divine quality of men, and were become insensible asses, fit only to bear. Nay worse, an ass, or dog, or horse, having done his duty, could lie down in retreat, and rise to work again, and while he did his duty endured no stripes; but men, villainous, senseless men such as they, toiled on all the tedious week till black Friday, and then, whether they worked or not, whether they were faulty or meriting, they promiscuously, the innocent with the guilty, suffered the infamous whip, the sordid stripes, from their fellow slaves till their blood trickled from all parts of their body, blood whose every drop ought to be revenged with a life of some of those tyrants that impose it. "And why," said he, "my dear friends and fellow sufferers, should we be slaves to an unknown people? Have they vanquished us nobly in fight? Have they won us in honorable battle? And are we, by the chance of war, become their slaves? This would not anger a noble heart, this would not animate a soldier's soul. No, but we are bought and sold like apes, or monkeys, to be the sport of women, fools, and cowards, and the support of rogues, runagades, that have abandoned their own countries, for raping, murders, thefts, and villainies. Do you not hear every day how they upbraid each other with infamy of life below the wildest savages, and shall we render obedience to such a degenerate race, who have no one human virtue left to distinguish them from the vilest creatures? Will you, I say, suffer the lash from such hands?" They all replied, with one accord, "No, no, no; Caesar has spoke like a great captain, like a great king."

After this he would have proceeded, but was interrupted by a tall Negro of some more quality than the rest. His name was Tuscan, who bowing at the feet of Caesar, cried, "My lord, we have listened with joy and attention to what you have said, and, were we only men, would follow so great a leader through the world. But oh! consider, we are husbands and parents too, and have things more dear to us than life: our wives and children unfit for travel, in these impassable woods, mountains, and bogs. We have not only difficult lands to overcome, but rivers to wade, and monsters to encounter, ravenous beasts of prey—" To this, Caesar replied, that honor was the first principle in nature that was to be obeyed; but as no man would pretend to that, without all the acts of virtue, compassion, charity, love, justice, and reason, he found it not inconsistent with that, to take an equal care of their wives and children, as they would of themselves, and that he did not design, when he led them to freedom and glorious liberty, that they should leave that better part of themselves to perish by the hand of the tyrant's whip. But if there were a woman among them so degenerate from love and virtue to choose slavery before the pursuit of her husband, and with the hazard of her life to share with him in his fortunes, that such an one ought to be abandoned, and left as a prey to the common enemy.

To which they all agreed—and bowed. After this, he spoke of the impassable woods and rivers, and convinced them, the more danger, the more glory. He told them that he had heard of one Hannibal, a great captain, had cut his way through

---

3. Because rigorous training has taught them to cherish their punishment.

mountains of solid rocks,[4] and should a few shrubs oppose them, which they could fire before them? No, 'twas a trifling excuse to men resolved to die, or overcome. As for bogs, they are with a little labor filled and hardened, and the rivers could be no obstacle, since they swam by nature, at least by custom, from their first hour of their birth. That when the children were weary they must carry them by turns, and the woods and their own industry would afford them food. To this they all assented with joy.

Tuscan then demanded, what he would do? He said, they would travel towards the sea; plant a new colony, and defend it by their valor; and when they could find a ship, either driven by stress of weather, or guided by Providence that way, they would seize it, and make it a prize, till it had transported them to their own countries. At least, they should be made free in his kingdom, and be esteemed as his fellow sufferers, and men that had the courage and the bravery to attempt, at least, for liberty. And if they died in the attempt it would be more brave than to live in perpetual slavery.

They bowed and kissed his feet at this resolution, and with one accord vowed to follow him to death. And that night was appointed to begin their march; they made it known to their wives, and directed them to tie their hamaca[5] about their shoulder, and under their arm like a scarf; and to lead their children that could go, and carry those that could not. The wives, who pay an entire obedience to their husbands, obeyed, and stayed for them where they were appointed. The men stayed but to furnish themselves with what defensive arms they could get, and all met at the rendezvous, where Caesar made a new encouraging speech to them, and led them out.

But, as they could not march far that night, on Monday early, when the overseers went to call them all together to go to work, they were extremely surprised to find not one upon the place, but all fled with what baggage they had. You may imagine this news was not only suddenly spread all over the plantation, but soon reached the neighboring ones, and we had by noon about six hundred men, they call the militia of the county, that came to assist us in the pursuit of the fugitives. But never did one see so comical an army march forth to war. The men of any fashion would not concern themselves, though it were almost the common cause, for such revoltings are very ill examples, and have very fatal consequences oftentimes in many colonies. But they had a respect for Caesar, and all hands were against the Parhamites, as they called those of Parham Plantation, because they did not, in the first place, love the Lord Governor, and secondly, they would have it that Caesar was ill used, and baffled with.[6] And 'tis not impossible but some of the best in the country was of his counsel in this flight, and depriving us of all the slaves, so that they of the better sort would not meddle in the matter. The deputy governor,[7] of whom I have had no great occasion to speak, and who was the most fawning fair-tongued fellow in the world, and one that pretended the most friendship to Caesar, was now the only violent man against him, and though he had nothing, and so need fear nothing, yet talked and looked bigger than any man. He was a fellow whose character is not fit to be mentioned with the worst of the slaves. This fellow would lead his army forth to meet Caesar, or rather to pursue him. Most of their arms were of those sort of cruel whips they call cat-with-nine-tails; some had rusty useless guns for show; others old basket-hilts, whose blades had never seen the light in this age, and others had long staffs, and clubs. Mr. Trefry went along rather to be a

---

4. The Carthaginian general (247–182 B.C.) had accomplished this while crossing the Alps to invade Rome.
5. Hammock.
6. Cheated.

7. William Byam, who during a decade as administrator in Surinam had acquired a reputation for arrogance and severity.

mediator than a conqueror in such a battle, for he foresaw and knew, if by fighting they put the Negroes into despair, they were a sort of sullen fellows that would drown or kill themselves before they would yield, and he advised that fair means was best. But Byam was one that abounded in his own wit, and would take his own measures.

It was not hard to find these fugitives, for as they fled they were forced to fire and cut the woods before them, so that night or day they pursued them by the light they made, and by the path they had cleared. But as soon as Caesar found he was pursued, he put himself in a posture of defense, placing all the women and children in the rear, and himself, with Tuscan by his side, or next to him, all promising to die or conquer. Encouraged thus, they never stood to parley, but fell on pell-mell upon the English, and killed some, and wounded a good many, they having recourse to their whips, as the best of their weapons. And as they observed no order, they perplexed the enemy so sorely, with lashing them in the eyes. And the women and children, seeing their husbands so treated, being of fearful cowardly dispositions, and hearing the English cry out, "Yield and live, yield and be pardoned," they all ran in amongst their husbands and fathers, and hung about them, crying out, "Yield, yield, and leave Caesar to their revenge," that by degrees the slaves abandoned Caesar, and left him only Tuscan and his heroic Imoinda, who, grown big as she was, did nevertheless press near her lord, having a bow, and a quiver full of poisoned arrows, which she managed with such dexterity that she wounded several, and shot the governor into the shoulder, of which wound he had like to have died but that an Indian woman, his mistress, sucked the wound, and cleansed it from the venom. But however, he stirred not from the place till he had parleyed with Caesar, who he found was resolved to die fighting, and would not be taken; no more would Tuscan, or Imoinda. But he, more thirsting after revenge of another sort, than that of depriving him of life, now made use of all his art of talking and dissembling, and besought Caesar to yield himself upon terms which he himself should propose, and should be sacredly assented to and kept by him. He told him, it was not that he any longer feared him, or could believe the force of two men, and a young heroine, could overcome all them, with all the slaves now on their side also, but it was the vast esteem he had for his person, the desire he had to serve so gallant a man, and to hinder himself from the reproach hereafter of having been the occasion of the death of a prince, whose valor and magnanimity deserved the empire of the world. He protested to him, he looked upon this action as gallant and brave, however tending to the prejudice of his lord and master, who would by it have lost so considerable a number of slaves, that this flight of his should be looked on as a heat of youth, and rashness of a too forward courage, and an unconsidered impatience of liberty, and no more; and that he labored in vain to accomplish that which they would effectually perform, as soon as any ship arrived that would touch on his coast. "So that if you will be pleased," continued he, "to surrender yourself, all imaginable respect shall be paid you; and yourself, your wife, and child, if it be here born, shall depart free out of our land." But Caesar would hear of no composition, though Byam urged, if he pursued and went on in his design, he would inevitably perish, either by great snakes, wild beasts, or hunger, and he ought to have regard to his wife, whose condition required ease, and not the fatigues of tedious travel, where she could not be secured from being devoured. But Caesar told him, there was no faith in the white men, or the gods they adored, who instructed them in principles so false that honest men could not live amongst them; though no people professed so much, none performed so little; that he knew what he had to do, when he dealt with men of honor, but with them a man ought to be eternally on his guard, and never to eat and drink with Christians without his weapon of defense in his hand, and, for his own security, never to credit one word they spoke. As for the rashness and inconsiderateness of his action he would confess the governor is in the right, and that he was ashamed of what he had done, in endeavoring to make those free, who were by nature slaves, poor wretched rogues, fit to be used as Christians' tools; dogs, treacherous and cowardly, fit for such masters, and they wanted only but to be whipped into the knowledge of the Christian gods to be the vilest of all creeping things, to learn to worship such deities as had not power to make them just, brave, or honest. In fine, after a thousand things of this nature, not fit here to be recited, he told Byam, he had rather die than live upon the same earth with such dogs. But Trefry and Byam pleaded and protested together so much, that Trefry believing the governor to mean what he said, and speaking very cordially himself, generously put himself into Caesar's hands, and took him aside, and persuaded him, even with tears, to live, by surrendering himself, and to name his conditions. Caesar was overcome by his wit and reasons, and in consideration of Imoinda, and demanding what he desired, and that it should be ratified by their hands in writing, because he had perceived that was the common way of contract between man and man amongst the whites. All this was performed, and Tuscan's pardon was put in, and they surrender to the governor, who walked peaceably down into the plantation with them, after giving order to bury their dead. Caesar was very much toiled with the bustle of the day, for he had fought like a Fury, and what mischief was done he and Tuscan performed alone, and gave their enemies a fatal proof that they durst do anything, and feared no mortal force.

But they were no sooner arrived at the place where all the slaves receive their punishments of whipping, but they laid hands on Caesar and Tuscan, faint with heat and toil; and surprising them, bound them to two several stakes, and whipped them in a most deplorable and inhumane manner, rending the very flesh from their bones; especially Caesar, who was not perceived to make any moan, or to alter his face, only to roll his eyes on the faithless governor, and those he believed guilty, with fierceness and indignation. And, to complete his rage, he saw every one of those slaves, who, but a few days before, adored him as something more than mortal, now had a whip to give him some lashes, while he strove not to break his fetters, though if he had, it were impossible. But he pronounced a woe and revenge from his eyes, that darted fire, that 'twas at once both awful and terrible to behold.

When they thought they were sufficiently revenged on him, they untied him, almost fainting with loss of blood from a thousand wounds all over his body, from which they had rent his clothes, and led him bleeding and naked as he was, and loaded him all over with irons, and then rubbed his wounds, to complete their cruelty, with Indian pepper, which had like to have made him raving mad, and in this condition made him so fast to the ground that he could not stir, if his pains and wounds would have given him leave. They spared Imoinda, and did not let her see this barbarity committed towards her lord, but carried her down to Parham, and shut her up, which was not in kindness to her, but for fear she should die with the sight, or miscarry, and then they should lose a young slave, and perhaps the mother.

You must know, that when the news was brought on Monday morning, that Caesar had betaken himself to the woods, and carried with him all the Negroes, we were possessed with extreme fear, which no persuasions could dissipate, that he would secure himself till night, and then, that he would come down and cut all our throats. This apprehension made all the females of us fly down the river, to be secured, and while we were away, they acted this cruelty. For I suppose I had authority and interest enough there, had I suspected any such thing, to have prevented it, but we had not gone many leagues, but the news overtook us that Caesar was taken, and whipped like a common slave. We met on the river with Colonel Martin, a man of great gallantry, wit, and goodness, and, whom I have celebrated in a character of my new comedy,[8] by his own name, in memory of so brave a man. He was wise and eloquent, and, from the fineness of his parts, bore a great sway over the hearts of all the colony. He was a friend to Caesar, and resented this false dealing with him very much. We carried him back to Parham, thinking to have made an accommodation; when we came, the first news we heard was that the governor was dead of a wound Imoinda had given him, but it was not so well. But it seems he would have the pleasure of beholding the revenge he took on Caesar, and before the cruel ceremony was finished, he dropped down, and then they perceived the wound he had on his shoulder was by a venomed arrow, which, as I said, his Indian mistress healed, by sucking the wound.

We were no sooner arrived, but we went up to the plantation to see Caesar, whom we found in a very miserable and inexpressible condition, and I have a thousand times admired how he lived, in so much tormenting pain. We said all things to him that trouble, pity, and good nature could suggest, protesting our innocence of the fact, and our abhorrence of such cruelties; making a thousand professions of services to him, and begging as many pardons for the offenders, till we said so much, that he believed we had no hand in his ill treatment, but told us, he could never pardon Byam. As for Trefry, he confessed he saw his grief and sorrow for his suffering, which he could not hinder, but was like to have been beaten down by the very slaves, for speaking in his defense. But for Byam, who was their leader, their head—and should, by his justice, and honor, have been an example to them—for him, he wished to live, to take a dire revenge of him, and said, "It had been well for him if he had sacrificed me, instead of giving me the contemptible whip." He refused to talk much, but begging us to give him our hands, he took them, and protested never to lift up his, to do us any harm. He had a great respect for Colonel Martin, and always took his counsel, like that of a parent, and assured him, he would obey him in anything but his revenge on Byam. "Therefore," said he, "for his own safety, let him speedily dispatch me, for if I could dispatch myself, I would not, till that justice were done to my injured person, and the contempt of a soldier. No, I would not kill myself, even after a whipping, but will be content to live with that infamy, and be pointed at by every grinning slave, till I have completed my revenge; and then you shall see that Oroonoko scorns to live with the indignity that was put on Caesar." All we could do could get no more words from him, and we took care to have him put immediately into a healing bath, to rid him of his pepper, and ordered a chirurgeon[9] to anoint him with healing balm, which he suffered, and in some time he began to be able to walk and eat. We failed not to visit him every day, and, to that end, had him brought to an apartment at Parham.

The governor was no sooner recovered, and had heard of the menaces of Caesar, but he called his council, who (not to disgrace them, or burlesque the government there) consisted of such notorious villains as Newgate[1] never transported, and possi-

---

8. *The Younger Brother: or the Amorous Jilt*, produced posthumously in 1696.
9. Surgeon.

1. London prison from which convicts were sent to work in the colonies.

bly originally were such, who understood neither the laws of God or man, and had no sort of principles to make them worthy the name of men, but at the very council table would contradict and fight with one another, and swear so bloodily that 'twas terrible to hear and see them. (Some of them were afterwards hanged, when the Dutch took possession of the place; others sent off in chains.) But calling these special rulers of the nation together, and requiring their counsel in this weighty affair, they all concluded that (damn them) it might be their own cases, and that Caesar ought to be made an example to all the Negroes, to fright them from daring to threaten their betters, their lords and masters, and, at this rate, no man was safe from his own slaves, and concluded, *nemine contradicente*,[2] that Caesar should be hanged.

Trefry then thought it time to use his authority, and told Byam his command did not extend to his lord's plantation, and that Parham was as much exempt from the law as Whitehall; and that they ought no more to touch the servants of the Lord — (who there represented the King's person) than they could those about the King himself; and that Parham was a sanctuary, and though his lord were absent in person, his power was still in being there, which he had entrusted with him, as far as the dominions of his particular plantations reached, and all that belonged to it; the rest of the country, as Byam was lieutenant to his lord, he might exercise his tyranny upon. Trefry had others as powerful, or more, that interested themselves in Caesar's life, and absolutely said he should be defended. So turning the governor, and his wise council, out of doors (for they sat at Parham House) we set a guard upon our landing place, and would admit none but those we called friends to us and Caesar.

The governor having remained wounded at Parham till his recovery was completed, Caesar did not know but he was still there, and indeed, for the most part, his time was spent there, for he was one that loved to live at other people's expense, and if he were a day absent, he was ten present there, and used to play, and walk, and hunt, and fish, with Caesar. So that Caesar did not at all doubt, if he once recovered strength, but he should find an opportunity of being revenged on him. Though, after such a revenge, he could not hope to live, for if he escaped the fury of the English mobile,[3] who perhaps would have been glad of the occasion to have killed him, he was resolved not to survive his whipping, yet he had, some tender hours, a repenting softness, which he called his fits of coward, wherein he struggled with love for the victory of his heart, which took part with his charming Imoinda there; but, for the most part, his time was passed in melancholy thought, and black designs. He considered, if he should do this deed, and die either in the attempt, or after it, he left his lovely Imoinda a prey, or at best a slave, to the enraged multitude; his great heart could not endure that thought. "Perhaps," said he, "she may be first ravished by every brute, exposed first to their nasty lusts, and then a shameful death." No, he could not live a moment under that apprehension, too insupportable to be borne. These were his thoughts, and his silent arguments with his heart, as he told us afterwards, so that now resolving not only to kill Byam, but all those he thought had enraged him, pleasing his great heart with the fancied slaughter he should make over the whole face of the plantation, he first resolved on a deed that (however horrid it at first appeared to us all), when we had heard his reasons, we thought it brave and just. Being able to walk and, as he believed, fit for the execution of his great design, he begged Trefry to trust him into the air, believing a walk would do him good, which was granted him, and taking Imoinda with him, as he

2. No one disagreeing.   3. Mob.

used to do in his more happy and calmer days, he led her up into a wood where, after (with a thousand sighs, and long gazing silently on her face, while tears gushed, in spite of him, from his eyes), he told her his design first of killing her, and then his enemies, and next himself, and the impossibility of escaping, and therefore he told her the necessity of dying. He found the heroic wife faster pleading for death than he was to propose it, when she found his fixed resolution, and on her knees besought him not to leave her a prey to his enemies. He (grieved to death) yet pleased at her noble resolution, took her up, and embracing her with all the passion and languishment of a dying lover, drew his knife to kill this treasure of his soul, this pleasure of his eyes. While tears trickled down his cheeks, hers were smiling with joy she should die by so noble a hand, and be sent in her own country (for that's their notion of the next world) by him she so tenderly loved, and so truly adored in this, for wives have a respect for their husbands equal to what any other people pay a deity, and when a man finds any occasion to quit his wife, if he love her, she dies by his hand; if not, he sells her, or suffers some other to kill her. It being thus, you may believe the deed was soon resolved on, and 'tis not to be doubted, but the parting, the eternal leave-taking of two such lovers, so greatly born, so sensible,[4] so beautiful, so young, and so fond, must be very moving, as the relation of it was to me afterwards.

All that love could say in such cases being ended, and all the intermitting irresolutions being adjusted, the lovely, young, and adored victim lays herself down before the sacrificer, while he, with a hand resolved, and a heart breaking within, gave the fatal stroke, first cutting her throat, and then severing her yet smiling face from that delicate body, pregnant as it was with fruits of tenderest love. As soon as he had done, he laid the body decently on leaves and flowers, of which he made a bed, and concealed it under the same coverlid of nature, only her face he left yet bare to look on. But when he found she was dead, and past all retrieve, never more to bless him with her eyes and soft language, his grief swelled up to rage; he tore, he raved, he roared, like some monster of the wood, calling on the loved name of Imoinda. A thousand times he turned the fatal knife that did the deed toward his own heart, with a resolution to go immediately after her, but dire revenge, which now was a thousand times more fierce in his soul than before, prevents him, and he would cry out, "No, since I have sacrificed Imoinda to my revenge, shall I lose that glory which I have purchased so dear, as at the price of the fairest, dearest, softest creature that ever Nature made? No, no!" Then, at her name, grief would get the ascendant of rage, and he would lie down by her side, and water her face with showers of tears, which never were wont to fall from those eyes. And however bent he was on his intended slaughter, he had not power to stir from the sight of this dear object, now more beloved and more adored than ever.

He remained in this deploring condition for two days, and never rose from the ground where he had made his sad sacrifice. At last, rousing from her side, and accusing himself with living too long now Imoinda was dead, and that the deaths of those barbarous enemies were deferred too long, he resolved now to finish the great work; but offering to rise, he found his strength so decayed, that he reeled to and fro, like boughs assailed by contrary winds, so that he was forced to lie down again, and try to summon all his courage to his aid. He found his brains turn round, and his eyes were dizzy, and objects appeared not the same to him as they were wont to do; his breath

4. Sensitive.

was short, and all his limbs surprised with a faintness he had never felt before. He had not eaten in two days, which was one occasion of this feebleness, but excess of grief was the greatest; yet still he hoped he should recover vigor to act his design, and lay expecting it yet six days longer, still mourning over the dead idol of his heart, and striving every day to rise, but could not.

In all this time you may believe we were in no little affliction for Caesar and his wife. Some were of opinion he was escaped never to return; others thought some accident had happened to him. But however, we failed not to send out a hundred people several ways to search for him. A party of about forty went that way he took, among whom was Tuscan, who was perfectly reconciled to Byam. They had not gone very far into the wood, but they smelt an unusual smell, as of a dead body, for stinks must be very noisome that can be distinguished among such a quantity of natural sweets, as every inch of that land produces. So that they concluded they should find him dead, or somebody that was so. They passed on towards it, as loathsome as it was, and made such a rustling among the leaves that lie thick on the ground, by continual falling, that Caesar heard he was approached, and though he had, during the space of these eight days, endeavored to rise, but found he wanted strength, yet looking up, and seeing his pursuers, he rose, and reeled to a neighboring tree, against which he fixed his back. And being within a dozen yards of those that advanced and saw him, he called out to them, and bid them approach no nearer, if they would be safe; so that they stood still, and hardly believing their eyes, that would persuade them that it was Caesar that spoke to them, so much was he altered, they asked him what he had done with his wife, for they smelt a stink that almost struck them dead. He, pointing to the dead body, sighing, cried, "Behold her there." They put off the flowers that covered her with their sticks, and found she was killed, and cried out, "Oh monster! that hast murdered thy wife." Then asking him, why he did so cruel a deed, he replied, he had no leisure to answer impertinent questions. "You may go back," continued he, "and tell the faithless governor he may thank Fortune that I am breathing my last, and that my arm is too feeble to obey my heart in what it had designed him." But his tongue faltering, and trembling, he could scarce end what he was saying. The English taking advantage by his weakness, cried, "Let us take him alive by all means." He heard them; and, as if he had revived from a fainting, or a dream, he cried out, "No, gentlemen, you are deceived, you will find no more Caesars to be whipped, no more find a faith in me. Feeble as you think me, I have strength yet left to secure me from a second indignity." They swore all anew, and he only shook his head, and beheld them with scorn. Then they cried out, "Who will venture on this single man? Will nobody?" They stood all silent while Caesar replied, "Fatal will be the attempt to the first adventurer, let him assure himself," and, at that word, held up his knife in a menacing posture. "Look ye, ye faithless crew," said he, "'tis not life I seek, nor am I afraid of dying," and, at that word, cut a piece of flesh from his own throat, and threw it at them, "yet still I would live if I could, till I had perfected my revenge. But oh! it cannot be. I feel life gliding from my eyes and heart, and, if I make not haste, I shall yet fall a victim to the shameful whip." At that, he ripped up his own belly, and took his bowels and pulled them out, with what strength he could, while some, on their knees imploring, besought him to hold his hand. But when they saw him tottering, they cried out, "Will none venture on him?" A bold English cried, "Yes, if he were the Devil" (taking courage when he saw him almost dead) and swearing a horrid oath for his farewell to the world he rushed on. Caesar with his armed hand met him so fairly, as stuck him to the heart, and he fell dead at his feet. Tuscan seeing that, cried out, "I love thee, oh Caesar, and therefore will not let thee die, if possible." And, running to him, took him in his arms, but at the same time, warding a blow that Caesar made at his bosom, he received it quite through his arm, and Caesar having not the strength to pluck the knife forth, though he attempted it, Tuscan neither pulled it out himself, nor suffered it to be pulled out, but came down with it sticking in his arm, and the reason he gave for it was because the air should not get into the wound. They put their hands across, and carried Caesar between six of them, fainted as he was, and they thought dead, or just dying, and they brought him to Parham, and laid him on a couch, and had the chirurgeon immediately to him, who dressed his wounds, and sewed up his belly, and used means to bring him to life, which they effected. We ran all to see him; and, if before we thought him so beautiful a sight, he was now so altered that his face was like a death's head blacked over, nothing but teeth and eye-holes. For some days we suffered nobody to speak to him, but caused cordials to be poured down his throat, which sustained his life, and in six or seven days he recovered his senses. For you must know, that wounds are almost to a miracle cured in the Indies, unless wounds in the legs, which rarely ever cure.

When he was well enough to speak, we talked to him, and asked him some questions about his wife, and the reasons why he killed her. And he then told us what I have related of that resolution, and of his parting, and he besought us we would let him die, and was extremely afflicted to think it was possible he might live. He assured us, if we did not dispatch him, he would prove very fatal to a great many. We said all we could to make him live, and gave him new assurances, but he begged we would not think so poorly of him, or of his love to Imoinda, to imagine we could flatter him to life again; but the chirurgeon assured him he could not live, and therefore he need not fear. We were all (but Caesar) afflicted at this news; and the sight was gashly.[5] His discourse was sad; and the earthly smell about him so strong, that I was persuaded to leave the place for some time (being myself but sickly, and very apt to fall into fits of dangerous illness upon any extraordinary melancholy). The servants, and Trefry, and the chirurgeons, promised all to take what possible care they could of the life of Caesar, and I, taking boat, went with other company to Colonel Martin's, about three days' journey down the river; but I was no sooner gone, but the governor taking Trefry about some pretended earnest business a day's journey up the river, having communicated his design to one Banister, a wild Irishman, and one of the council, a fellow of absolute barbarity, and fit to execute any villainy, but was rich, he came up to Parham, and forcibly took Caesar, and had him carried to the same post where he was whipped, and causing him to be tied to it, and a great fire made before him, he told him he should die like a dog, as he was. Caesar replied, this was the first piece of bravery that ever Banister did, and he never spoke sense till he pronounced that word, and, if he would keep it, he would declare, in the other world, that he was the only man, of all the whites, that ever he heard speak truth. And turning to the men that bound him, he said, "My friends, am I to die, or to be whipped?" And they cried, "Whipped! no; you shall not escape so well." And then he replied, smiling, "A blessing on thee," and assured them, they need not tie him, for he would stand fixed, like a rock, and endure death so as should encourage them to die. "But if you whip me," said he, "be sure you tie me fast."

He had learned to take tobacco, and when he was assured he should die, he desired they would give him a pipe in his mouth, ready lighted, which they did, and the executioner came, and first cut off his members,[6] and threw them into the fire.

---

5. Ghastly.   6. Genitals.

After that, with an ill-favored knife, they cut his ears and his nose, and burned them; he still smoked on, as if nothing had touched him. Then they hacked off one of his arms, and still he bore up, and held his pipe. But at the cutting off the other arm, his head sunk, and his pipe dropped, and he gave up the ghost, without a groan, or a reproach. My mother and sister were by him all the while, but not suffered to save him, so rude and wild were the rabble, and so inhuman were the justices, who stood by to see the execution, who after paid dearly enough for their insolence. They cut Caesar in quarters, and sent them to several of the chief plantations. One quarter was sent to Colonel Martin, who refused it, and swore he had rather see the quarters of Banister and the governor himself than those of Caesar on his plantations, and that he could govern his Negroes without terrifying and grieving them with frightful spectacles of a mangled king.

Thus died this great man, worthy of a better fate, and a more sublime wit than mine to write his praise. Yet, I hope, the reputation of my pen is considerable enough to make his glorious name to survive to all ages, with that of the brave, the beautiful, and the constant Imoinda.

1688

━━━━◆◇▷ ━━━━

Jonathan Swift
1667–1745

Arguably the greatest prose satirist in the history of English literature, Jonathan Swift was born in Dublin, the only son of English parents, seven months after his father died. In his infancy he was kidnapped by his nurse and did not see his mother for three years. With the future dramatist William Congreve he attended the Kilkenny School (Ireland's best), and in 1682 he began six years of study at Trinity College, Dublin. He received his B.A. degree in 1686. From 1689, Swift served as secretary to Sir William Temple (1628–1699), a retired diplomat whose father had befriended Swift's family. Swift worked at Temple's estate at Moor Park in Surrey for most of the next ten years. It was at Moor Park that Swift first experienced the vertigo, nausea, and hearing impairment of Ménière's syndrome, a disturbance of the inner ear that would plague him for the rest of his life and sometimes wrongly led him (and others) to question his mental stability. While working for Temple, Swift also wrote his first poems, undistinguished compositions that do not presage the literary acclaim that was to come.

Not content with his station in life, Swift took an M.A. degree from Oxford University in 1692; three years later, he was ordained a priest in the (Anglican) Church of Ireland and appointed to the undesirable prebendary of Kilroot, where he found the local Presbyterians unsympathetic and the salary meager. Added to professional discontent was personal disappointment: Swift was rejected in his marriage proposal to Jane "Varina" Waring, the daughter of an Anglican clergyman. Swift returned to Moor Park in 1696, and, after Temple died in 1699, held a series of ecclesiastical posts in Ireland, none of which fulfilled his ambition for an important position in England. In 1702 he was made Doctor of Divinity by his alma mater, Trinity College, Dublin.

While at Moor Park, Swift began to tutor an eight-year-old girl, Esther "Stella" Johnson, daughter of Sir William's late steward. Though she was nearly fourteen years Swift's junior, "Stella" would in time become his beloved companion and his most trusted friend. When she was eighteen, Swift described her as "one of the most beautiful, graceful, and agreeable young women in London." In 1701, at Swift's request, Stella and Sir William's spinster cousin, Rebecca Dingley, moved to Dublin, where they remained for the rest of their lives. Swift and

Stella met regularly, but never alone. Although there has been much debate about the nature of their relationship, it is clear that Swift and Stella loved, trusted, and valued each other, whether or not they were ever secretly married (the evidence suggests they were not). Swift's *Journal to Stella* (composed 1710 to 1713) and the series of poems he composed for her birthdays reveal a playful intimacy and affection not seen in his more public writings.

Moor Park not only led him to Stella but was also the cradle of Swift's first major literary work: *A Tale of a Tub* (composed 1697 to 1698, published 1704), a brilliant satire on "corruptions in religion and learning," published with *The Battle of the Books*, Swift's mock-epic salvo in the debate between the Ancients and the Moderns. Like most of his subsequent works, *A Tale of a Tub* did not appear under Swift's name, though its ironic treatment of the church subsequently damaged his prospects for ecclesiastical preferment when his authorship became widely known.

In the first decade of the new century Swift placed his hopes for preferment with the Whigs, then in power, and became associated with the Whig writers Joseph Addison and Richard Steele, founder of the *Tatler*, a London periodical in which two of Swift's important early poems, *A Description of the Morning* (1709) and *A Description of a City Shower* (1710), first appeared. Swift's career as a political polemicist began when he rose to the defense of three Whig lords facing impeachment with his allegorical *Discourse of the Contests and Dissentions between the Nobles and Commons in Athens and Rome* (1701). His *Bickerstaff Papers* (1708–1709), witty parodies of the cobbler-turned-astrologer John Partridge, occasioned much laughter regardless of party allegiances. More important, Swift began to write a series of pamphlets on church affairs, including his ironical *Argument against Abolishing Christianity* (1708) and *A Letter . . . Concerning the Sacramental Test* (1709), which damaged his relationship with the Whigs.

While in London as an emissary for the Irish clergy in 1708, Swift met Esther "Vanessa" Vanhomrigh (pronounced "Vanummry") and, as with "Stella," acted as her mentor. Although his feelings for this attractive young woman (twenty-one years younger than he) clearly became more than paternal, Swift was eventually put off by her declaration of "inexpressible passion" and wrote *Cadenus and Vanessa* (composed 1713, published 1726) to cool the relationship.

Vehemently disagreeing with the Whig policies supporting the Dissenters (Protestants who were not members of the established church) because he feared they would weaken the Anglican church, Swift shifted his allegiance to the Tories in 1710 and soon became their principal spokesman and propagandist, taking charge of their weekly periodical the *Examiner* (1710–1711) and producing a series of highly effective political pamphlets, such as *The Conduct of the Allies* (1712), which called for an end to the War of Spanish Succession (1701–1713). Swift's years in London from 1710 to 1714, when he was an important lobbyist for the Church of Ireland and an influential agent of the Tory government, were the most exciting of his life.

In 1713 Swift was installed as Dean of Saint Patrick's Cathedral, Dublin—a prestigious appointment, but far short of the English bishopric he felt he deserved. Returning quickly to London, Swift became a vital presence in the Scriblerus Club—with Alexander Pope, John Arbuthnot, John Gay, Thomas Parnell, and Robert Harley, Earl of Oxford—which met in 1714. The influence of this group, with its love of parody, literary hoaxes, and the ridicule of false learning, is evident in *Gulliver's Travels*. Upon the death of Queen Anne in 1714 and the resultant fall of the Tory Ministry, Swift's hopes for further advancement were dashed, and he took up permanent residence in Ireland, where he conscientiously carried out his duties as Dean.

When Swift successfully defended Irish interests by writing *The Drapier's Letters* (1724–1725)—attacking a government plan to impose a new coin, "Wood's halfpence," that would devalue Ireland's currency and seriously damage the economy—he became a national hero. Thereafter, the people lit bonfires on his birthday and hailed him as a champion of Irish liberty, though he never ceased to regard Ireland as the land of his exile. From Dublin, he corresponded with Pope, Gay, Arbuthnot, and Henry St. John, Lord Bolingbroke; he enjoyed a long visit with his friends in England in 1726. While there, he encouraged Gay's *The Beggar's Opera* and Pope's *The Dunciad*, and arranged for the publication of his own masterpiece, *Gulliver's Travels* (1726).

When the death of George I the following year briefly created hopes of unseating "Prime Minister" Robert Walpole, Swift paid his final visit to England, where he assisted Pope in editing their joint *Miscellanies* in three volumes (1727, 1728, 1732). The years that followed in Dublin saw the production of many of Swift's finest poems, including *The Lady's Dressing Room* (1732), *A Beautiful Young Nymph Going to Bed* (1734), and *Verses on the Death of Dr. Swift* (composed 1731–1732, published 1739), his most celebrated poem. Swift continued to champion the cause of Irish political and economic freedom; with his like-minded friend Thomas Sheridan, he conducted a weekly periodical, the *Intelligencer* (1728). In 1729, he published his most famous essay, *A Modest Proposal*. Some years later, he supervised the publication of the first four volumes of his *Works* (1735) by the Dublin publisher George Faulkener.

When Swift reached his early seventies, his infirmities made him incapable of carrying out his clerical duties at Saint Patrick's; at seventy-five, he was found "of unsound mind and memory," and guardians were appointed to manage his affairs. In addition to ongoing debilities from Ménière's syndrome, he suffered from arteriosclerosis, aphasia, memory loss, and other diseases of old age; he was not insane, however, as many of his contemporaries believed. A devoted clergyman, Swift practiced the Christian charity he preached, giving more than half of his income to the needy; the founding of Ireland's first mental hospital through a generous provision in his will was the most famous of Swift's many benefactions.

Voltaire hailed Swift as the "English Rabelais," while Henry Fielding lauded him as the "English Lucian." Although the more delicate sensibilities of the nineteenth century eschewed his writings for their coarseness and truculence, twentieth-century readers have prized Swift's work for its intelligence, wit, and inventiveness. A committed champion of social justice and an untiring enemy of pride, Swift was a brilliant satirist in part because he was a thoroughgoing humanist.

A DESCRIPTION OF A CITY SHOWER   "They say 'tis the best thing I ever writ, and I think so too," boasted Swift of his *Description of a City Shower* in 1710. It was first published in the *Tatler*, No. 238, on 17 October 1710, soon after its composition. Swift's closely observed rendering of London street life playfully mocks the English imitators of Virgil, especially John Dryden and his celebrated translation, *The Works of Virgil* (1697). We see, for example, Swift's mock-heroic effects based on Virgil's *Aeneid* (29–19 B.C.), most notably in comparing the timorous "beau" trapped in his sedan chair to the fierce Greek warriors hiding inside the Trojan Horse, and in calling to mind the storm that led to Queen Dido's seduction and eventual ruin (Dryden's translation 4.231–238). The division of the poem into portents, preliminaries, and deluge closely parallels the tempest scene in Virgil's *Georgics* (36–29 B.C.; bk. 1, 431–458, 483–538 in Dryden), so that Swift uses structural and verbal elements from a classical poem extolling the virtues of agriculture and rural life to depict the teeming diversity of the contemporary urban scene.

A Description of a City Shower

Careful observers may foretell the hour
(By sure prognostics) when to dread a shower.
While rain depends,° the pensive cat gives o'er   *is impending*
Her frolics, and pursues her tail no more.
5   Returning home at night you find the sink[1]
Strike your offended sense with double stink.
If you be wise, then go not far to dine,

1. Sewer. The poem is built upon Swift's experiences in London: on 8 November 1710, Swift wrote to his beloved Stella (Esther Johnson) that "I will give ten shillings a week for my lodging; for I am almost stunk out of this with the sink, and it helps me to verses in my Shower." The parsimonious Swift normally spent around half this amount for lodgings.

You spend in coach-hire more than save in wine.
A coming shower your shooting corns² presage,
10   Old aches³ throb, your hollow tooth will rage:
Sauntering in coffee-house is Dulman seen;
He damns the climate, and complains of spleen.⁴

        Meanwhile the South,° rising with dabbled° wings,   *south wind / muddy*
A sable cloud athwart the welkin° flings;   *sky*
15   That swilled more liquor than it could contain,
And like a drunkard gives it up again.
Brisk Susan whips her linen from the rope,⁵
While the first drizzling shower is borne aslope:°   *at a slant*
Such is that sprinkling which some careless quean°   *hussy*
20   Flirts° on you from her mop, but not so clean: *flicks*
You fly, invoke the gods; then turning, stop
To rail; she singing, still whirls on her mop.
Nor yet the dust had shunned th' unequal strife,
But aided by the wind, fought still for life;
25   And wafted with its foe by violent gust,
'Twas doubtful which was rain, and which was dust.⁶
Ah! Where must needy poet seek for aid,
When dust and rain at once his coat invade?
Sole coat, where dust cemented by the rain
30   Erects the nap, and leaves a cloudy stain.
        Now in contiguous drops the flood comes down,
Threatening with deluge this devoted° town.   *doomed*
To shops in crowds the daggled° females fly,   *muddied*
Pretend to cheapen° goods, but nothing buy.   *bargain for*
35   The Templer spruce,⁷ while every spout's abroach,⁸
Stays till 'tis fair, yet seems to call a coach.
The tucked-up seamstress walks with hasty strides,
While streams run down her oiled umbrella's sides.
Here various kinds by various fortunes led,
40   Commence acquaintance underneath a shed.°   *shelter*
Triumphant Tories, and desponding Whigs,⁹
Forget their feuds, and join to save their wigs.
Boxed° in a chair¹ the beau impatient sits,   *confined*
While spouts run clattering o'er the roof by fits;
45   And ever and anon with frightful din
The leather sounds; he trembles from within.
So when Troy chairmen bore the wooden steed,
Pregnant with Greeks, impatient to be freed;
(Those bully Greeks, who, as the moderns do,
50   Instead of paying chairmen, run them through²)

2. The shooting pain in your corns.
3. Pronounced "aitches."
4. Dulman (a descriptive name) complains of melancholy or depression, then attributed to the spleen.
5. The typically named maid brings in her washing from the line.
6. Swift here parallels a line from Samuel Garth's popular satirical poem, *The Dispensary* (1699): "'Tis doubtful which is sea, and which is sky" (5.176).
7. Well-dressed lawyer.
8. Drainpipe pouring water.
9. 1710, the year this poem was written, was the first year of the Tory ministry under Queen Anne.
1. A sedan chair, carried by two men; this one has a leather roof.
2. With their swords.

Laocoon struck the outside with his spear,
And each imprisoned hero quaked for fear.[3]

Now from all parts the swelling kennels[4] flow,
And bear their trophies with them as they go:
55 Filths of all hues and odors, seem to tell
What streets they sailed from, by the sight and smell.
They, as each torrent drives with rapid force
From Smithfield, or St. Pulchre's shape their course;[5]
And in huge confluent join at Snow Hill ridge,
60 Fall from the conduit prone to Holborn Bridge.[6]
Sweepings from butchers' stalls, dung, guts, and blood,
Drowned puppies, stinking sprats,° all drenched in mud, ⎫   *small fish*
Dead cats and turnip tops come tumbling down the flood.[7] ⎭

1710   1710

STELLA'S BIRTHDAY   Between 1719 and 1727 Swift wrote seven birthday poems to "Stella," his
dear Esther Johnson. The one printed here is his first. Swift's earliest use of the name "Stella" in
verse was in the first of this series of celebratory verses, which play on the obligation of the Poet
Laureate to write an official "birthday ode" for the monarch every year. Placing himself in the role
of her laureate, Swift may have chosen the name "Stella" to highlight the difference between his
own uncontrived expressions of affection and those of the courtly Sir Philip Sidney in *Astrophil
and Stella* (1591). Like Shakespeare's Sonnet 130 ("My mistress' eyes are nothing like the sun"),
Swift's first poem on Stella's birthday violates the traditions of the conventional love lyric by calling attention to his beloved's considerable weight and age, only to suggest that his admiration of
her lies in her deeper virtues. Though more formal than the *Journal to Stella*, Swift's birthday
verses were written primarily for Stella's enjoyment and for the entertainment of their small circle
of intimate friends. Despite the private nature of these poems, Swift nevertheless authorized their
publication in the third and last volume of the Pope-Swift *Miscellanies*, which appeared in March
1728.

Stella's Birthday, 1719
WRITTEN IN THE YEAR 1718/9[1]

Stella this day is thirty-four,[2]
(We shan't dispute a year or more):
However, Stella, be not troubled,
Although thy size and years are doubled,

3. When the Trojans carried the Greek's wooden horse
into Troy, thinking that the opposing army had given up
their siege, the priest Laocoon was suspicious, and struck
the horse. See *Aeneid* 2.50–53.
4. Gutters, which were also open sewers.
5. Respectively, the cattle market and the parish west of
the Newgate prison.
6. Snow Hill ridge extended down to Holborn Bridge,
which spanned Fleet ditch, used as an open sewer; from
1343, local butchers had been given permission to dump
entrails in the Fleet.
7. These last three lines were intended against the licentious manner of modern poets, in making three rhymes
together, which they call *Triplets*; and the last of the
three was two, or sometimes more syllables longer, called
an *Alexandrian*. These *Triplets* and *Alexandrians* were

brought in by Dryden, and other poets in the reign of
Charles II. They were the mere effect of haste, idleness,
and want of money, and have been wholly avoided by the
best poets since these verses were written [Swift's note].
1. Until the calendar was reformed in 1751, the new year
legally began on the Feast of the Annunciation (sometimes called "Lady Day") on March 25, though January 1
was also commonly recognized as the start of the new
year. Therefore, to avoid confusion, it was a widely
accepted practice to write dates between January 1 and
March 24 according to both methods of reckoning:
1718/19. Since Swift's poem was composed in February or
March, we would say it was written in 1719.
2. Stella (Esther Johnson) actually celebrated her thirty-
eighth birthday on 13 March 1719.

5   Since first I saw thee at sixteen,[3]
The brightest virgin on the green.[4]
So little is thy form° declined;   *figure*
Made up° so largely in thy mind.   *compensated*

    Oh, would it please the gods to *split*
10   Thy beauty, size, and years, and wit,
No age could furnish out a pair
Of nymphs so graceful, wise, and fair:
With half the luster of your eyes,
With half your wit, your years, and size:
15   And then before it grew too late,
How should I beg of gentle fate,
(That either nymph might have her swain),
To split my worship too in twain.

1719   1728

THE LADY'S DRESSING ROOM   The first of Swift's so-called scatological poems, which have attracted much critical attention and amateur psychoanalysis, these verses enjoyed considerable popularity in Swift's lifetime, though some contemporaries condemned them as "deficient in point of delicacy, even to the highest degree." One of Swift's friends recorded in her memoirs that *The Lady's Dressing Room* made her mother "instantly" lose her lunch. Sir Walter Scott found in this poem (and other pieces by Swift) "the marks of an incipient disorder of the mind, which induced the author to dwell on degrading and disgusting subjects." If Pope's *The Rape of the Lock* describes Belinda at the "altar" of her dressing table undergoing "the sacred rites of pride" as she and her maid apply all manner of cosmetics to make her a beautiful "goddess" and arm her for the battle of the sexes, then *The Lady's Dressing Room* reveals the coarse realities of Celia's embodiment—a humorous and disturbing corrective to the pretense and false appearances on which her glorification depends. Although Swift assails the social and literary conventions that celebrate women for their superficial qualities, there is also a misogynistic quality to the poem, which may be attributable to his anger and disappointment over his beloved Stella's death in January 1728. Nevertheless, Strephon is ridiculed for being so naively idealistic about his lover and so easily deceived by appearances; once his secret investigations free him from his illusions, Strephon's permanent revulsion and rejection of all women show his inability to follow a middle course by appreciating women in their complex reality.

The Lady's Dressing Room

    Five hours (and who can do it less in?)
By haughty Celia spent in dressing;
The goddess from her chamber issues,
Arrayed in lace, brocade, and tissues:
5   Strephon,[1] who found the room was void,
And Betty[2] otherwise employed,
Stole in, and took a strict survey,
Of all the litter as it lay:

---

3. Swift first met Stella when she was eight years old; he may have "seen" her only when she grew from child to woman.
4. The village green, or common land, here implies a pastoral simplicity that suggests the natural innocence of

their relationship.
1. Strephon and Celia are names usually associated with pastoral poetry, and are therefore used mockingly here.
2. A typical maidservant's name.

Whereof, to make the matter clear,
10   An *inventory* follows here.

And first, a dirty smock appeared,
Beneath the arm-pits well besmeared;
Strephon, the rogue, displayed it wide,
And turned it round on every side.
15   In such a case few words are best,
And Strephon bids us guess the rest;
But swears how damnably the men lie,
In calling Celia sweet and cleanly.

Now listen while he next produces
20   The various combs for various uses,
Filled up with dirt so closely fixed,
No brush could force a way betwixt;
A paste of composition rare,
Sweat, dandruff, powder, lead,[3] and hair,
25   A forehead cloth with oil upon't
To smooth the wrinkles on her front;
Here alum flour[4] to stop the steams,
Exhaled from sour, unsavory streams;
There night-gloves made of Tripsy's[5] hide,
30   Bequeathed by Tripsy when she died;
With puppy water,[6] beauty's help,
Distilled from Tripsy's darling whelp.
Here gallipots° and vials placed,   *ointment jars*
Some filled with washes, some with paste;
35   Some with pomatum,° paints, and slops,   *hair ointment*
And ointments good for scabby chops.°   *lips or cheeks*
Hard° by a filthy basin stands,   *close*
Fouled with the scouring of her hands;
The basin takes whatever comes,
40   The scrapings of her teeth and gums,
A nasty compound of all hues,
For here she spits, and here she spews.

But oh! it turned poor Strephon's bowels,
When he beheld and smelt the towels;
45   Begummed, bemattered, and beslimed;
With dirt, and sweat, and ear-wax grimed.
No object Strephon's eye escapes,
Here, petticoats in frowzy° heaps;   *unkempt*
Nor be the handkerchiefs forgot,
50   All varnished o'er with snuff[7] and snot.
The stockings why should I expose,

---

3. White lead face paint, used to whiten the skin.
4. Powdered alum used like modern antiperspirant.
5. Celia's lapdog; no fashionable lady was without such a pet.
6. A recipe for this cosmetic, made from the innards of a pig or a fat puppy, was given in the "Fop's Dictionary" in

Mundus Muliebris [Womanly Make-up]: *Or, the Ladies' Dressing Room Unlocked* (1690), which Swift also used for other terms.
7. Powdered tobacco, sniffed by fashionable men and women alike.

Stained with the moisture of her toes;
Or greasy coifs and pinners° reeking,   *night caps*
Which Celia slept at least a week in?
55   A pair of tweezers next he found
To pluck her brows in arches round,
Or hairs that sink the forehead low,
Or on her chin like bristles grow.

The virtues we must not let pass
60   Of Celia's magnifying glass;
When frighted Strephon cast his eye on't,
It showed the visage of a giant:[8]
A glass that can to sight disclose
The smallest worm in Celia's nose,
65   And faithfully direct her nail
To squeeze it out from head to tail;
For catch it nicely by the head,
It must come out alive or dead.

Why, Strephon, will you tell the rest?
70   And must you needs describe the chest?
That careless wench! no creature warn her
To move it out from yonder corner,
But leave it standing full in sight,
For you to exercise your spite!
75   In vain the workman showed his wit
With rings and hinges counterfeit
To make it seem in this disguise
A cabinet to vulgar eyes;
Which Strephon ventured to look in,
80   Resolved to go through *thick and thin*;
He lifts the lid: there need no more,
He smelt it all the time before.

As, from within Pandora's box,
When Epimethus oped the locks,
85   A sudden universal crew
Of human evils upward flew;[9]
He still was comforted to find
That hope at last remained behind.

So, Strephon, lifting up the lid
90   To view what in the chest was hid,
The vapors flew from out the vent,
But Strephon cautious never meant
The bottom of the pan to grope,
And foul his hands in search of hope.

8. Cf. *Gulliver's Travels*, Part 2, "A Voyage to Brobdingnag," ch. 1: "This made me reflect upon the fair skins of
our *English* ladies, who appear so beautiful to us, only
because they are of our own size, and their defects not to
be seen but through magnifying glass, where we find by
experiment that the smoothest and whitest skins look
rough and coarse, and ill colored."
9. In Greek mythology, Epimethus, acting against advice,
opened the box Jove had given his wife Pandora, and all
the evils and vices of the world flew out, leaving only
hope in the box.

95   O! ne'er may such a vile machine°   *construction*
        Be once in Celia's chamber seen!
        O! may she better learn to keep
        "Those secrets of the hoary deep."[1]

        As mutton cutlets, prime of meat,
100   Which though with art you salt and beat
        As laws of cookery require,
        And roast them at the clearest fire;
        If from adown the hopeful chops
        The fat upon a cinder drops,
105   To stinking smoke it turns the flame
        Poisoning the flesh from whence it came;
        And up exhales a greasy stench
        For which you curse the careless wench:
        So things which must not be expressed,
110   When *plumped*° into the reeking chest,   *dropped*
        Send up an excremental smell
        To taint the parts from which they fell:
        The petticoats and gown perfume,
        And waft a stink round every room.

115   Thus finishing his grand survey,
        The swain disgusted slunk away,
        Repeating in his amorous fits,
        "Oh! Celia, Celia, Celia shits!"

        But Vengeance, goddess never sleeping,
120   Soon punished Strephon for his peeping.
        His foul imagination links
        Each dame he sees with all her stinks:
        And if unsavory odors fly,
        Conceives a lady standing by:
125   All women his description fits,
        And both ideas jump° like wits   *join together*
        By vicious fancy coupled fast,
        And still appearing in contrast.

        I pity wretched Strephon, blind
130   To all the charms of womankind;
        Should I the queen of love refuse,
        Because she rose from stinking ooze?[2]
        To him that looks behind the scene,
        Statira's but some pocky quean.[3]

135   When Celia in her glory shows,
        If Strephon would but stop his nose,
        Who now so impiously blasphemes
        Her ointments, daubs, and paints and creams;

---

1. Quoting Milton's *Paradise Lost* 2.891, in which Sin is unleashing the chaotic forces of her infernal realm.
2. Venus, Roman goddess of sexual love and physical beauty, rose from the sea.

3. One of the heroines of Nathaniel Lee's highly popular tragedy *The Rival Queens* (1677); Swift's common slattern (quean) has had either smallpox or venereal disease.

Her washes, slops, and every clout,[4]
140   With which she makes so foul a rout;[5]
He soon would learn to think like me,
And bless his ravished eyes to see
Such order from confusion sprung,
Such gaudy *tulips* raised from *dung*.

c. 1730   1732

⁂

COMPANION READING

Lady Mary Wortley Montagu: The Reasons that Induced Dr. S. to write a Poem called The Lady's Dressing Room[1]

The Doctor in a clean starched band,
His golden snuff box in his hand,
With care his diamond ring displays
And artful shows its various rays,
5   While grave he stalks down —— street
His dearest Betty —— to meet.[2]
    Long had he waited for this hour,
Nor gained admittance to the bower,
Had joked and punned, and swore and writ,
10   Tried all his gallantry and wit,[3]
Had told her oft what part he bore
In Oxford's schemes in days of yore,[4]
But bawdy,° politics, nor satire   obscenity
Could move this dull hard hearted creature.
15   Jenny her maid could taste° a rhyme   enjoy
And, grieved to see him lose his time,
Had kindly whispered in her ear,
"For twice two pound you enter here;
My lady vows without that sum
20   It is in vain you write or come."
    The destined offering now he brought,
And in a paradise of thought,

4. Washes were either treated water used for the complexion or stale urine used as a detergent; clouts were rags.
5. Both of her skin and, presumably, of the men.
1. Lady Mary Wortley Montagu (1689–1762), born Mary Pierrepont, acquired her title at age one, lost her mother at age three, and fervently pursued a plan of self-education at odds with the conventional domesticating agenda laid out for young women of her rank. In 1712 she married, against her father's wishes, Edward Wortley Mantagu, a Whig Member of Parliament who was later appointed ambassador to Turkey. Accompanying him on this assignment, she was to become fascinated by the Turkish practice of inoculating against smallpox, which she successfully championed in England on her return. She also reported eloquently in missives home on the gaps and continuities between British and Turkish culture. Her Turkish Embassy Letters, which she compiled

from her writings during this sojourn, remain the foundation of her fame. Her life as a writer also yielded essays, short fiction, and a comedy, but she worked more steadily at verse, collaborating with Alexander Pope on some poems and combating him in others, after their friendship had disintegrated into a round of bitter, witty recriminations. In her riposte to Jonathan Swift's poem, Montagu mimics his iambic tetrameter and other mannerisms.
2. In Swift's poem, Betty is the maid's name, Celia, the mistress's.
3. Montagu echoes Swift's poem *Cadenus and Vanessa*, where the clumsy lover "Had sighed and languished, / vowed, and writ, / For pastime, or to show his wit" (542–43).
4. Swift had collaborated closely in the political schemes of Robert Harley, first Earl of Oxford (1661–1724).

With a low bow approached the dame,
Who smiling heard him preach his flame.
His gold she takes (such proofs as these
Convince most unbelieving shes)
And in her trunk rose up to lock it
(Too wise to trust it in her pocket)
And then, returned with blushing grace,
Expects the doctor's warm embrace.
   But now this is the proper place
Where morals stare me in the face,
And for the sake of fine expression
I'm forced to make a small digression.
Alas for wretched humankind,
With learning mad, with wisdom blind!
The ox thinks he's for saddle fit
(As long ago friend Horace writ[5])
And men their talents still mistaking,
The stutterer fancies his is speaking.
With admiration oft we see
Hard features heightened by toupée,
The beau affects° the politician,   pretends to be
Wit is the citizen's ambition,
Poor Pope philosophy displays on
With so much rhyme and little reason,
And though he argues ne'er so long
That all is right, his head is wrong.[6]
   None strive to know their proper merit
But strain for wisdom, beauty, spirit,
And lose the praise that is their due
While they've th' impossible in view.
So have I seen the injudicious heir
To add one window the whole house impair.
   Instinct the hound does better teach,
Who never undertook to preach;
The frighted hare from dogs does run
But not attempts to bear a gun.
Here many noble thoughts occur
But I prolixity abhor,
And will pursue th' instructive tale
To show the wise in some things fail.
   The reverend lover with surprise ⎫
Peeps in her bubbies, and her eyes, ⎬
And kisses both, and tries—and tries.⎭
The evening in this hellish play,
Beside his guineas thrown away,
Provoked the priest to that degree
He swore, "The fault is not in me.
Your damned close stool° so near my nose,   chamber pot

Line numbers: 25, 30, 35, 40, 45, 50, 55, 60, 65, 70

5. "The ox desires the saddle" (Horace, *Epistles* 1.14.43).
6. Montagu ridicules Pope's conclusion to *An Essay on*   Man: "Whatever IS, is RIGHT." See page 1275.

Your dirty smock, and stinking toes
Would make a Hercules as tame
As any beau that you can name."
    The nymph grown furious roared, "By God
75 The blame lies all in sixty odd,"[7]
And scornful pointing to the door
Cried, "Fumbler, see my face no more."
"With all my heart I'll go away,
But nothing done, I'll nothing pay.
80 Give back the money." "How," cried she,
"Would you palm such a cheat on me!
For poor four pound to roar and bellow—
Why sure you want some new Prunella?"[8]
"I'll be revenged, you saucy quean"°   *whore*
85 (Replies the disappointed Dean)
"I'll so describe your dressing room
The very Irish shall not come."
She answered short, "I'm glad you'll write.
You'll furnish paper when I shite."[9]

1734

❧

GULLIVER'S TRAVELS *Travels into Several Remote Nations of the World. In Four Parts. By Lemuel Gulliver*—better known as *Gulliver's Travels*—was first published in late October 1726 and enjoyed instant success. One contemporary observer noted that "several thousands sold in a week," and Swift's London friends wrote to him in Dublin to say that everyone was reading and talking about Gulliver. Readers continue to be fascinated by Swift's masterpiece: since 1945, more than 500 books and scholarly articles have been devoted to *Gulliver's Travels*. Variously classified as an early novel, an imaginary voyage, a moral and political allegory, and even a children's story, Lemuel Gulliver's four journeys, representing the four directions of the globe, comprise a survey of the human condition: a comic, ironic, and sometimes harrowing answer to the question, "What does it mean to be a human being?"

    In the first voyage, the diminutive citizens of Lilliput represent human small-mindedness and petty ambitions. Filled with self-importance, the Lilliputians are cruel, treacherous, malicious, and destructive. The perspective is reversed in the second voyage to Brobdingnag, land of giants, where Gulliver has the stature of a Lilliputian. He is humbled by his own helplessness and, finding the huge bodies of the Brobdingnagians grotesque, he realizes how repulsive the Lilliputians must have found him. When Gulliver gives the wise king an account of the political affairs of England—which manifest hypocrisy, avarice, and hatred—the enlightened monarch concludes that most of the country's inhabitants must be "the most pernicious race of little odious vermin that Nature ever suffered to crawl upon the surface of the earth." In the third voyage (which was written last), Gulliver visits the flying island of Laputa and the metropolis of Lagado, on an adjacent continent, where he encounters the misuse of human

---

7. I.e., Swift's impotence derives not from her odors but from his age (65 at the time the poem was written).
8. "Prunella" is both a fabric used in clergy vestments (Swift was a clergyman), and the name of the promiscu-

ous, low-born heroine in Richard Estcourt's comic interlude *Prunella* (1708).
9. Compare line 118 of Swift's poem, page 1184.

reason. In Laputa, those who are supposedly "wise" lack all common sense and practical ability; at Lagado, the Academy of Projectors is staffed by professors who waste both money and intelligence on absurd endeavors. Swift aims his satire at so-called intellectuals—especially the "virtuosi," or amateur scientists of the Royal Society—who live in the world of their own speculations and so fail to use their gifts for the common good. Throughout *Gulliver's Travels* that which is admirable is held up to expose corruption in the reader's world, and that which is deplorable is identified with the institutions and practices associated with contemporary Europe, particularly Britain.

Gulliver's fourth voyage finds him on the island of the Houyhnhnms, horses endowed with reason, whose highly rational and well-ordered (though emotionally sterile) society is contrasted with the violence, selfishness, and brutality of the Yahoos, irrational beasts who bear a disconcerting resemblance to humans. In his foolish pride, Gulliver believes that he can escape the human condition and live as a stoical Houyhnhnm, even when he returns to his family in England. Of course, Gulliver is neither Houyhnhnm nor Yahoo, but a man. His time in Houyhnhnm-land does not teach him to be more rational or compassionate, but makes him more foolish, derelict in his duties as husband, father, and citizen. Instead of seeking to become a better man, Gulliver strives to become what he is not—with results that are both tragic and farcical. Although the poet Edward Young charged Swift with having "blasphemed a nature little lower than that of the angels" in satirizing the follies of humankind, *Gulliver's Travels* reveals the Dean of Saint Patrick's to be more a humanist than a misanthrope. With brilliantly modulated ironic self-awareness, Swift's painful comedy of exposure to the truth of human frailty demonstrates that there is no room for the distortions of human pride in a world where our practices are so evidently at variance with our principles. Swift advances no program of social reform, but provokes a new recognition—literally, a rethinking—of our own humanity.

from Gulliver's Travels
from Part 3. A Voyage to Laputa
CHAPTER 5

The author permitted to see the grand Academy of Logado. The Academy largely[1] described. The arts wherein the professors employ themselves.

This Academy is not an entire single building, but a continuation of several houses on both sides of a street, which growing waste,[2] was purchased and applied to that use.

I was received very kindly by the Warden, and went for many days to the Academy. Every room has in it one or more projectors,[3] and I believe I could not be[4] in fewer than five hundred rooms.

The first man I saw was of a meager aspect, with sooty hands and face, his hair and beard long, ragged and singed in several places. His clothes, shirt, and skin were all of the same color. He had been eight years upon a project for extracting sunbeams out of cucumbers,[5] which were to be put into vials hermetically sealed, and let out to warm the

---

1. In general. The academy is a satire of the Royal Society, founded in 1662 for the purpose of scientific experimentation. Though many of its members made major contributions to science, the Society had a reputation for bizarre speculation. Swift had visited the Society in 1710 and here parodies actual experiments recorded in its *Philosophical Transactions*; he is also parodying the description of "Solomon's House," an academy of science

in Francis Bacon's *New Atlantis* (1626).
2. Falling into disuse.
3. Those people undertaking the project.
4. Could not have been.
5. Stephen Hales (1677–1761), English botanist and physiologist, had recently investigated sunlight's agency in plant respiration. This and other studies were published in his *Vegetable Staticks* (1726).

air in raw, inclement summers. He told me, he did not doubt in eight years more, that he should be able to supply the Governor's gardens with sunshine at a reasonable rate; but he complained that his stock was low, and entreated me to give him something as an encouragement to ingenuity,[6] especially since this had been a very dear season for cucumbers. I made him a small present, for my Lord[7] had furnished me with money on purpose, because he knew their practice of begging from all who go to see them.

I went into another chamber, but was ready to hasten back, being almost overcome with a horrible stink. My conductor pressed me forward, conjuring me in a whisper to give no offense, which would be highly resented, and therefore I durst not so much as stop my nose. The projector of this cell was the most ancient student of the Academy. His face and beard were of a pale yellow; his hands and clothes daubed over with filth. When I was presented to him, he gave me a very close embrace (a compliment I could well have excused). His employment from his first coming into the Academy was an operation to reduce human excrement to its original food, by separating the several parts, removing the tincture which it receives from the gall, making the odor exhale, and scumming off the saliva. He had a weekly allowance from the Society of a vessel filled with human ordure,[8] about the bigness of a Bristol barrel.[9]

I saw another at work to calcine[1] ice into gunpowder, who likewise showed me a treatise he had written concerning the malleability of fire,[2] which he intended to publish.

There was a most ingenious architect who had contrived a new method for building houses, by beginning at the roof and working downwards to the foundation, which he justified to me by the like practice of those two prudent insects, the bee and the spider.

There was a man born blind, who had several apprentices in his own condition: their employment was to mix colors for painters, which their master taught them to distinguish by feeling and smelling.[3] It was indeed my misfortune to find them at that time not very perfect in their lessons, and the professor himself happened to be generally mistaken: this artist is much encouraged and esteemed by the whole fraternity.

In another apartment I was highly pleased with a projector, who had found a device of ploughing the ground with hogs, to save the charges of ploughs, cattle, and labor. The method is this; in an acre of ground you bury, at six inches distance, and eight deep, a quantity of acorns, dates, chestnuts, and other mast[4] or vegetables whereof these animals are fondest: then you drive six hundred or more of them into the field, where in a few days they will root up the whole ground in search of their food, and make it fit for sowing, at the same time manuring it with their dung; it is true upon experiment they found the charge and trouble very great, and they had little or no crop. However, it is not doubted that this invention may be capable of great improvement.

I went into another room, where the walls and ceiling were all hung round with cobwebs, except a narrow passage for the artist[5] to go in and out. At my entrance he called aloud to me not to disturb his webs. He lamented the fatal mistake the world

6. His investigative powers.
7. The warden of the Academy.
8. Excrement.
9. A medium-size barrel, holding about 37 gallons.
1. Desiccate.
2. Cf. Rabelais, *Gargantua and Pantagruel* (1532–1564), bk. 5, ch. 22: "Others were cutting fire with a knife, and drawing water up in a net."
3. Based on Robert Boyle's account in *Experiments and*

Observations Upon Colors (1665), of a blind man who could distinguish colors.
4. Nuts.
5. Modeled on both the Frenchman M. Bon, who believed silk could be made from cobwebs, and Dr. Wall, who suggested that the excreta of ants fed on plant sap could be used as dye; both suggestions were published in the *Transactions of the Royal Society*.

had been so long in of using silkworms, while we had such plenty of domestic insects, who infinitely excelled the former, because they understood how to weave as well as spin. And he proposed farther, that by employing spiders, the charge[6] of dyeing silks would be wholly saved, whereof I was fully convinced when he showed me a vast number of flies most beautifully colored, wherewith he fed his spiders, assuring us, that the webs would take a tincture from them; and as he had them of all hues, he hoped to fit everybody's fancy, as soon as he could find proper food for the flies, of certain gums, oils, and other glutinous matter to give a strength and consistence to the threads.

There was an astronomer who had undertaken to place a sundial upon the great weathercock on the Town House,[7] by adjusting the annual and diurnal motions of the earth and sun, so as to answer and coincide with all accidental turnings of the wind.

I was complaining of a small fit of the colic, upon which my conductor led me into a room, where a great physician resided, who was famous for curing that disease by contrary operations from the same instrument. He had a large pair of bellows with a long slender muzzle of ivory. This he conveyed eight inches up the anus, and drawing in the wind, he affirmed he could make the guts as lank as a dried bladder. But when the disease was more stubborn and violent, he let in the muzzle while the bellows was full of wind, which he discharged into the body of the patient, then withdrew the instrument to replenish it, clapping his thumb strongly against the orifice of the fundament; and this being repeated three or four times, the adventitious wind would rush out, bringing the noxious along with it (like water put into a pump) and the patient recover. I saw him try both experiments upon a dog, but could not discern any effect from the former. After the latter, the animal was ready to burst, and made so violent a discharge, as was very offensive to me and my companions. The dog died on the spot, and we left the doctor endeavoring to recover him by the same operation.[8]

I visited many other apartments, but shall not trouble my reader with all the curiosities I observed, being studious of brevity.

I had hitherto seen only one side of the Academy, the other being appropriated to the advancers of speculative learning, of whom I shall say something when I have mentioned one illustrious person more, who is called among them *the universal artist*.[9] He told us he had been thirty years employing his thoughts for the improvement of human life. He had two large rooms full of wonderful curiosities, and fifty men at work. Some were condensing air into a dry, tangible substance, by extracting the niter,[1] and letting the aqueous or fluid particles percolate; others softening marble for pillows and pincushions; others petrifying the hoofs of a living horse to preserve them from foundering. The artist himself was at that time busy upon two great designs: the first, to sow land with chaff, wherein he affirmed the true seminal virtue to be contained, as he demonstrated by several experiments which I was not skillful enough to comprehend. The other was, by a certain composition of gums, minerals, and vegetables outwardly applied, to prevent the growth of wool upon two young lambs; and he hoped in a reasonable time to propagate the breed of naked sheep all over the kingdom.

6. Expense.
7. Town Hall.
8. Robert Hooke (1635–1703) produced artificial respiration in a dog (1667) by blowing air into its windpipe with a pair of bellows.
9. Possibly Robert Boyle (1627–1691), whose many scientific experiments investigated the nature of air, marble, petrifaction, agriculture, and sheep breeding.
1. Air was believed to contain nitrous matter.

We crossed a walk to the other part of the Academy, where, as I have already said, the projectors in speculative learning resided.

The first professor I saw was in a very large room, with forty pupils about him. After salutation, observing me to look earnestly upon a frame, which took up the greatest part of both the length and breadth of the room, he said perhaps I might wonder to see him employed in a project for improving speculative knowledge by practical and mechanical operations. But the world would soon be sensible[2] of its usefulness, and he flattered himself that a more noble exalted thought never sprang in any other man's head. Everyone knew how laborious the usual method is of attaining to arts and sciences; whereas by his contrivance, the most ignorant person at a reasonable charge, and with a little bodily labor, may write books in philosophy, poetry, politics, law, mathematics, and theology, without the least assistance from genius or study. He then led me to the frame, about the sides whereof all his pupils stood in ranks. It was twenty foot square, placed in the middle of the room. The superficies[3] was composed of several bits of wood, about the bigness of a die,[4] but some larger than others. They were all linked together by slender wires. These bits of wood were covered on every square with papers pasted on them, and on these papers were written all the words of their language in their several moods, tenses, and declensions, but without any order. The professor then desired me to observe, for he was going to set his engine[5] at work. The pupils at his command took each of them hold of an iron handle, whereof there were forty fixed round the edges of the frame, and giving them a sudden turn, the whole disposition of the words was entirely changed. He then commanded six and thirty of the lads to read the several lines softly as they appeared upon the frame; and where they found three or four words together that might make part of a sentence, they dictated to the four remaining boys who were scribes. This work was repeated three or four times, and at every turn the engine was so contrived, that the words shifted into new places, as the square bits of wood moved upside down.

Six hours a day the young students were employed in this labor, and the professor showed me several volumes in large folio already collected, of broken sentences, which he intended to piece together, and out of those rich materials to give the world a complete body of all arts and sciences; which however might be still improved, and much expedited, if the public would raise a fund for making and employing five hundred such frames in Lagado, and oblige the managers to contribute in common their several[6] collections.

He assured me, that this invention had employed all his thoughts from his youth, that he had emptied the whole vocabulary into his frame, and made the strictest computation of the general proportion there is in books between the numbers of particles, nouns, and verbs, and other parts of speech.

I made my humblest acknowledgments to this illustrious person for his great communicativeness, and promised if ever I had the good fortune to return to my native country, that I would do him justice, as the sole inventor of this wonderful machine; the form and contrivance of which I desired leave to delineate upon paper as in the figure here annexed. I told him, although it were the custom of our learned in Europe to steal inventions from each other,[7] who had thereby at least this advantage, that it

2. Aware.
3. Surface.
4. Singular of dice.
5. Machine.
6. Individual.

7. No international patent agreement existed at this time, and the theft of inventions was common as nations competed in developing technology for commercial manufacturing and navigation on the open seas.

became a controversy which was the right owner, yet I would take such caution, that he should have the honor entire without a rival.

We next went to the school of languages, where three professors sat in consultation upon improving that of their own country.[8]

The first project was to shorten discourse by cutting polysyllables into one, and leaving out verbs and participles, because in reality all things imaginable are but nouns.

The other project was a scheme for entirely abolishing all words whatsoever; and this was urged as a great advantage in point of health as well as brevity. For, it is plain, that every word we speak is in some degree a diminution of our lungs by corrosion, and consequently contributes to the shortening of our lives. An expedient was therefore offered, that since words are only names for *things*, it would be more convenient for all men to carry about them such *things* as were necessary to express the particular business they are to discourse on.[9] And this invention would certainly have taken place, to the great ease as well as health of the subject,[1] if the women in conjunction with the vulgar and illiterate had not threatened to raise a rebellion, unless they might be allowed the liberty to speak with their tongues, after the manner of their forefathers; such constant irreconcilable enemies to science are the common people. However, many of the most learned and wise adhere to the new scheme of expressing themselves by *things*, which hath only this inconvenience attending it, that if a man's business be very great, and of various kinds, he must be obliged in proportion to carry a greater bundle of *things* upon his back, unless he can afford one or two strong servants to attend him. I have often beheld two of those sages almost sinking under the weight of their packs, like peddlers among us; who when they met in the streets would lay down their loads, open their sacks, and hold conversation for an hour together; then put up their implements, help each other to resume their burdens, and take their leave.

But for short conversations a man may carry implements in his pockets and under his arms, enough to supply him, and in his house he cannot be at a loss; therefore the room where company meet who practice this art, is full of all *things* ready at hand, requisite to furnish matter for this kind of artificial converse.[2]

Another great advantage proposed by this invention, was that it would serve as a universal language to be understood in all civilized nations, whose goods and utensils are generally of the same kind, or nearly resembling, so that their uses might easily be comprehended. And thus, ambassadors would be qualified to treat with foreign princes or ministers of state, to whose tongues they were utter strangers.

I was at the mathematical school, where the master taught his pupils after a method scarce imaginable to us in Europe. The proposition and demonstration were fairly written on a thin wafer, with ink composed of a cephalic[3] tincture. This the student was to swallow upon a fasting stomach, and for three days following eat noth-

8. The first secretary to the Royal Society, Thomas Spratt, in his *History* (1667) of that institution, recommended that such an Academy be founded, as the new style of science writing should strive to describe "so many *things* in an equal number of words." Although Swift burlesques this notion, he himself had published *Proposals for Correcting, Improving and Ascertaining the English Tongue* (1712), in which he suggested that an Academy be established with the aim of preserving culture and "fixing our language for ever."

9. The growth of scientific knowledge about the nature of the material world had encouraged suggestions that language should be made less abstract. In satirizing the projector, Swift alludes to John Locke's theory of language in Book 3 of *An Essay Concerning Human Understanding* (1690), where Locke argues that words stand for things only indirectly.

1. Both the individual practitioner and the people of the nation as a whole.

2. A reference to the Royal Society's attempt to collect one specimen or example of every thing in the world.

3. Of or for the head.

ing but bread and water. As the wafer digested, the tincture mounted to his brain, bearing the proposition along with it. But the success has not hitherto been answerable, partly by some error in the *quantum* or composition, and partly by the perverseness of lads, to whom this bolus[4] is so nauseous that they generally steal aside, and discharge it upwards before it can operate; neither have they been yet persuaded to use so long an abstinence as the prescription requires.

CHAPTER 10

The Luggnaggians commended. A particular description of the Struldbruggs, with many conversations between the author and some eminent persons upon that subject.[1]

The Luggnaggians are a polite and generous people, and although they are not without some share of that pride which is peculiar to all Eastern countries, yet they show themselves courteous to strangers, especially such who are countenanced by the Court. I had many acquaintance among persons of the best fashion, and being always attended by my interpreter, the conversation we had was not disagreeable.

One day in much good company, I was asked by a person of quality, whether I had seen any of their Struldbruggs or Immortals. I said I had not, and desired he would explain to me what he meant by such an appellation applied to a mortal creature. He told me, that sometimes, though very rarely, a child happened to be born in a family with a red circular spot in the forehead, directly over the left eyebrow, which was an infallible mark that it should never die. The spot, as he described it, was about the compass of a silver threepence, but in the course of time grew larger, and changed its color; for at twelve years old it became green, so continued till five and twenty, then turned to a deep blue; at five and forty it grew coal black, and as large as an English shilling, but never admitted any farther alteration. He said these births were so rare, that he did not believe there could be above eleven hundred Struldbruggs of both sexes in the whole kingdom, of which he computed about fifty in the metropolis, and among the rest a young girl born about three years ago. That these productions were not peculiar to any family, but a mere effect of chance, and the children of the Struldbruggs themselves, were equally mortal with the rest of the people.

I freely own myself to have been struck with inexpressible delight upon hearing this account: and the person who gave it me happening to understand the Balnibarbian language, which I spoke very well, I could not forbear breaking out into expressions perhaps a little too extravagant. I cried out as in a rapture: Happy nation where every child hath at least a chance for being immortal! Happy people who enjoy so many living examples of ancient virtue, and have masters ready to instruct them in the wisdom of all former ages! But, happiest beyond all comparison are those excellent Struldbruggs, who being born exempt from that universal calamity of human nature, have their minds free and disengaged, without the weight and depression of spirits caused by the continual apprehension of death. I discovered my admiration[2] that I had not observed any of these illustrious persons at Court, the black spot on the forehead being so remarkable a distinction, that I could not have easily overlooked it; and it was impossible that his Majesty, a most judicious prince, should not

---

4. Mass of chewed food.
1. In order to return to England, Gulliver sails west on the Pacific from Balnibarbi (the country of which Lagado is the capital) to Japan, stopping en route at the island of "Luggnagg," where he makes the following observations.
2. Expressed my surprise.

provide himself with a good number of such wise and able counselors. Yet perhaps the virtue of those reverend sages was too strict for the corrupt and libertine manners of a Court. And we often find by experience that young men are too opinionative and volatile to be guided by the sober dictates of their seniors. However, since the King was pleased to allow me access to his royal person, I was resolved upon the very first occasion to deliver my opinion to him on this matter freely, and at large, by the help of my interpreter; and whether he would please to take my advice or no, yet in one thing I was determined, that his Majesty having frequently offered me an establishment in this country, I would with great thankfulness accept the favor, and pass my life here in the conversation of those superior beings the Struldbruggs, if they would please to admit me.

The gentleman to whom I addressed my discourse, because (as I have already observed) he spoke the language of Balnibarbi, said to me with a sort of a smile, which usually ariseth from pity to the ignorant, that he was glad of any occasion to keep me among them, and desired my permission to explain to the company what I had spoke. He did so, and they talked together for some time in their own language, whereof I understood not a syllable, neither could I observe by their countenances what impression my discourse had made on them. After a short silence the same person told me, that his friends and mine (so he thought fit to express himself) were very much pleased with the judicious remarks I had made on the great happiness and advantages of immortal life, and they were desirous to know in a particular manner, what scheme of living I should have formed to myself, if it had fallen to my lot to have been born a Struldbrugg.

I answered, it was easy to be eloquent on so copious and delightful a subject, especially to me who have been often apt to amuse myself with visions of what I should do if I were a king, a general, or a great lord; and upon this very case I had frequently run over the whole system how I should employ myself, and pass the time if I were sure to live for ever.

That, if it had been my good fortune to come into the world a Struldbrugg, as soon as I could discover my own happiness by understanding the difference between life and death, I would first resolve by all arts and methods whatsoever to procure myself riches. In the pursuit of which by thrift and management, I might reasonably expect in about two hundred years, to be the wealthiest man in the kingdom. In the second place, I would from my earliest youth apply myself to the study of arts and sciences, by which I should arrive in time to excel all others in learning. Lastly I would carefully record every action and event of consequence that happened in the public,[3] impartially draw the characters of the several successions of princes, and great ministers of state, with my own observations on every point. I would exactly set down the several changes in customs, language, fashions of dress, diet and diversions. By all which acquirements, I should be a living treasury of knowledge and wisdom, and certainly become the oracle of the nation.

I would never marry after threescore, but live in an hospitable manner, yet still on the saving side. I would entertain myself in forming and directing the minds of hopeful young men, by convincing them from my own remembrance, experience, and observation, fortified by numerous examples, of the usefulness of virtue in public and private life. But, my choice and constant companions should be a set of my own immortal brotherhood, among whom I would elect a dozen from the most ancient

---

3. The state (from Latin *res publica*, the "public thing," from which derives the word *republic*).

down to my own contemporaries. Where any of these wanted[4] fortunes, I would provide them with convenient lodges round my own estate, and have some of them always at my table, only mingling a few of the most valuable among you mortals, whom length of time would harden me to lose with little or no reluctance, and treat your posterity after the same manner, just as a man diverts himself with the annual succession of pinks and tulips in his garden, without regretting the loss of those which withered the preceding year.

These Struldbruggs and I would mutually communicate our observations and memorials through the course of time, remark the several gradations by which corruption steals into the world, and oppose it in every step, by giving perpetual warning and instruction to mankind; which, added to the strong influence of our own example, would probably prevent that continual degeneracy of human nature so justly complained of in all ages.

Add to all this, the pleasure of seeing the various revolutions of states and empires, the changes in the lower and upper world,[5] ancient cities in ruins, and obscure villages become the seats of kings. Famous rivers lessening into shallow brooks, the ocean leaving one coast dry, and overwhelming another, the discovery of many countries yet unknown. Barbarity overrunning the politest nations, and the most barbarous becoming civilized. I should then see the discovery of the longitude, the perpetual motion, the universal medicine,[6] and many other great inventions brought to the utmost perfection.

What wonderful discoveries should we make in astronomy, by outliving and confirming our own predictions, by observing the progress and returns of comets, with the changes of motion in the sun, moon, and stars.

I enlarged upon many other topics, which the natural desire of endless life and sublunary[7] happiness could easily furnish me with. When I had ended, and the sum of my discourse had been interpreted as before, to the rest of the company, there was a good deal of talk among them in the language of the country, not without some laughter at my expense. At last the same gentleman who had been my interpreter said, he was desired by the rest to set me right in a few mistakes, which I had fallen into through the common imbecility of human nature, and upon that allowance was less answerable for them. That, this breed of Struldbruggs was peculiar to their country, for there were no such people either in Balnibarbi or Japan, where he had the honor to be ambassador from his Majesty, and found the natives in both those kingdoms very hard to believe[8] that the fact was possible, and it appeared from my astonishment when he first mentioned the matter to me, that I received it as a thing wholly new, and scarcely to be credited. That in the two kingdoms above-mentioned, where during his residence he had conversed very much, he observed long life to be the universal desire and wish of mankind. That whoever had one foot in the grave, was sure to hold back the other as strongly as he could. That the oldest had still hopes of living one day longer, and looked on death as the greatest evil, from which nature always prompted him to retreat; only in this island of Luggnagg, the appetite for living was not so eager, from the continual example of the Struldbruggs before their eyes.

4. Lacked.
5. On the earth and in the heavens.
6. As at Lagado, Gulliver enumerates scientific quests Swift scoffed at: for a method of determining the longitude of a ship at sea, for a perpetual motion machine, for one drug sufficient to cure all ills.
7. Earthly.
8. To convince.

That the system of living contrived by me was unreasonable and unjust, because it supposed a perpetuity of youth, health, and vigor, which no man could be so foolish to hope, however extravagant he may be in his wishes. That the question therefore was not whether a man would choose to be always in the prime of youth, attended with prosperity and health, but how he would pass a perpetual life under all the usual disadvantages which old age brings along with it. For although few men will avow their desires of being immortal upon such hard conditions, yet in the two kingdoms before-mentioned of Balnibarbi and Japan, he observed that every man desired to put off death for some time longer, let it approach ever so late, and he rarely heard of any man who died willingly, except he were incited by the extremity of grief or torture. And he appealed to me whether in those countries I had traveled, as well as my own, I had not observed the same general disposition.

After this preface he gave me a particular account of the Struldbruggs among them. He said they commonly acted like mortals, till about thirty years old, after which by degrees they grew melancholy and dejected, increasing in both till they came to fourscore. This he learned from their own confession; for otherwise there not being above two or three of that species born in an age, they were too few to form a general observation by. When they came to fourscore years, which is reckoned the extremity of living in this country, they had not only all the follies and infirmities of other old men, but many more which arose from the dreadful prospect of never dying. They were not only opinionative, peevish, covetous, morose, vain, talkative, but uncapable of friendship, and dead to all natural affection, which never descended below their grandchildren. Envy and impotent desires are their prevailing passions. But those objects against which their envy seems principally directed, are the vices of the younger sort, and the deaths of the old. By reflecting on the former, they find themselves cut off from all possibility of pleasure; and whenever they see a funeral, they lament and repine that others have gone to an harbor of rest, to which they themselves never can hope to arrive. They have no remembrance of anything but what they learned and observed in their youth and middle age, and even that is very imperfect. And for the truth or particulars of any fact, it is safer to depend on common traditions than upon their best recollections. The least miserable among them appear to be those who turn to dotage, and entirely lose their memories; these meet with more pity and assistance, because they want many bad qualities which abound in others.

If a Struldbrugg happen to marry one of his own kind, the marriage is dissolved of course by the courtesy of the kingdom, as soon as the younger of the two comes to be fourscore. For the law thinks it a reasonable indulgence, that those who are condemned without any fault of their own to a perpetual continuance in the world, should not have their misery doubled by the load of a wife.[9]

As soon as they have completed the term of eighty years, they are looked on as dead in law; their heirs immediately succeed to their estates, only a small pittance is reserved for their support, and the poor ones are maintained at the public charge. After that period they are held incapable of any employment of trust or profit, they cannot purchase lands or take leases, neither are they allowed to be witnesses in any cause, either civil or criminal, not even for the decision of meres[1] and bounds.

---

9. Swift himself never married.   1. Property lines (at issue in property disputes).

At ninety they lose their teeth and hair, they have at that age no distinction of taste, but eat and drink whatever they can get, without relish or appetite. The diseases they were subject to, still continue without increasing or diminishing. In talking they forget the common appellation of things, and the names of persons, even of those who are their nearest friends and relations. For the same reason they never can amuse themselves with reading, because their memory will not serve to carry them from the beginning of a sentence to the end; and by this defect they are deprived of the only entertainment whereof they might otherwise be capable.

The language of this country being always upon the flux, the Struldbruggs of one age do not understand those of another, neither are they able after two hundred years to hold any conversation (farther than by a few general words) with their neighbors the mortals, and thus they lie under the disadvantage of living like foreigners in their own country. This was the account given me of the Struldbruggs, as near as I can remember. I afterwards saw five or six of different ages, the youngest not above two hundred years old, who were brought to me at several times by some of my friends; but although they were told that I was a great traveler, and had seen all the world, they had not the least curiosity to ask me a question; only desired I would give them *slumskudask*, or a token of remembrance, which is a modest way of begging, to avoid the law that strictly forbids it, because they are provided for by the public, although indeed with a very scanty allowance.

They are despised and hated by all sorts of people; when one of them is born, it is reckoned ominous, and their birth is recorded very particularly; so that you may know their age by consulting the registry, which however hath not been kept above a thousand years past, or at least hath been destroyed by time or public disturbances. But the usual way of computing how old they are, is, by asking them what kings or great persons they can remember, and then consulting history, for infallibly the last prince in their mind did not begin his reign after they were fourscore years old.

They were the most mortifying sight I ever beheld, and the women more horrible than the men. Besides the usual deformities in extreme old age, they acquired an additional ghastliness in proportion to their number of years, which is not to be described, and among half a dozen I soon distinguished which was the eldest, although there were not above a century or two between them.

The reader will easily believe, that from what I had heard and seen, my keen appetite for perpetuity of life was much abated. I grew heartily ashamed of the pleasing visions I had formed, and thought no tyrant could invent a death into which I would not run with pleasure from such a life. The king heard of all that had passed between me and my friends upon this occasion, and rallied me very pleasantly, wishing I would send a couple of Struldbruggs to my own country, to arm our people against the fear of death; but this it seems is forbidden by the fundamental laws of the kingdom, or else I should have been well content with the trouble and expense of transporting them.

I could not but agree that the laws of this kingdom, relating to the Struldbruggs, were founded upon the strongest reasons, and such as any other country would be under the necessity of enacting in the like circumstances. Otherwise, as avarice is the necessary consequent of old age, those Immortals would in time become proprietors of the whole nation, and engross the civil power, which, for want of abilities to manage, must end in the ruin of the public.

from *Part 4. A Voyage to the Country of the Houyhnhnms*[1]

CHAPTER 1

The author sets out as Captain of a ship. His men conspire against him, confine him a long time to his cabin, set him on shore in an unknown land. He travels up into the country. The Yahoos,[2] a strange sort of animal, described. The author meets two Houyhnhnms.

I continued at home with my wife and children about five months in a very happy condition, if I could have learned the lesson of knowing when I was well. I left my poor wife big with child, and accepted an advantageous offer made me to be Captain of the *Adventure*,[3] a stout merchantman of 350 tons: for I understood navigation well, and being grown weary of a surgeon's employment at sea, which however I could exercise upon occasion, I took a skillful young man of that calling, one Robert Purefoy,[4] into my ship. We set sail from Portsmouth upon the seventh day of September, 1710; on the fourteenth, we met with Captain Pocock[5] of Bristol, at Teneriffe,[6] who was going to the bay of Campeche, to cut logwood. On the sixteenth, he was parted from us by a storm; I heard since my return, that his ship foundered, and none escaped, but one cabin boy. He was an honest man, and a good sailor, but a little too positive in his own opinions, which was the cause of his destruction, as it hath been of several others. For if he had followed my advice, he might at this time have been safe at home with his family as well as myself.

I had several men died in my ship of calentures,[7] so that I was forced to get recruits out of Barbados, and the Leeward Islands, where I touched by[8] the direction of the merchants who employed me, which I had soon too much cause to repent; for I found afterwards that most of them had been buccaneers. I had fifty hands on board, and my orders were, that I should trade with the Indians in the South Sea, and make what discoveries I could. These rogues whom I had picked up debauched my other men, and they all formed a conspiracy to seize the ship and secure me; which they did one morning, rushing into my cabin, and binding me hand and foot, threatening to throw me overboard, if I offered to stir. I told them, I was their prisoner, and would submit. This they made me swear to do, and then unbound me, only fastening one of my legs with a chain near my bed, and placed a sentry at my door with his piece charged,[9] who was commanded to shoot me dead, if I attempted my liberty. They sent me down victuals and drink, and took the government of the ship to themselves. Their design was to turn pirates, and plunder the Spaniards, which they could not do till they got more men. But first they resolved to sell the goods in the ship, and then go to Madagascar[1] for recruits, several among them having died since my confinement.

1. Pronounced "whinnims," to mimic the sound of a horse's whinny, though some scholars have offered more complex interpretations of this name. With characteristic irony, Swift probably chose horses to represent rational creatures because the philosopher John Locke (1632–1704) and Bishop Edward Stillingfleet (1635–1699) had argued extensively about how one might distinguish man as a rational animal from an evidently irrational animal, such as a horse.
2. The name may be derived from similarly titled African or Guianan tribes. The animals represent sinful, fallen humanity, and their juxtaposition with the Houyhnhnms is designed to question belief in the innate rationality of humankind and the superiority of humans over other creatures.
3. The name of two ships of the notorious pirate Captain

William Kidd (d. 1701). Kidd, originally commissioned to capture pirates, was also subject to a mutiny.
4. "Pure faith," associating Gulliver with the overzealous Puritans.
5. Probably modeled on the dogmatic Captain Dampier (1652–1715), who had spent three years logcutting around the Campeche Bay, on the Yucatan Peninsula, in the Gulf of Mexico. His violent disagreements with his lieutenant led to a court martial.
6. One of the Canary Islands, off the northwestern coast of Africa.
7. Tropical fevers.
8. Landed according to.
9. Gun loaded.
1. A popular meeting place for pirates.

They sailed many weeks, and traded with the Indians, but I knew not what course they took, being kept close prisoner in my cabin, and expecting nothing less than to be murdered, as they often threatened me.

Upon the ninth day of May, 1711, one James Welch came down to my cabin; and said he had orders from the Captain to set me ashore. I expostulated with him, but in vain; neither would he so much as tell me who their new captain was. They forced me into the longboat, letting me put on my best suit of clothes, which were good as new, and a small bundle of linen, but no arms except my hanger;[2] and they were so civil as not to search my pockets, into which I conveyed what money I had, with some other little necessaries. They rowed about a league; and then set me down on a strand.[3] I desired them to tell me what country it was. They all swore, they knew no more than myself, but said, that the Captain (as they called him) was resolved, after they had sold the lading,[4] to get rid of me in the first place where they discovered land. They pushed off immediately, advising me to make haste, for fear of being overtaken by the tide, and bade me farewell.

In this desolate condition I advanced forward, and soon got upon firm ground, where I sat down on a bank to rest myself, and consider what I had best to do. When I was a little refreshed, I went up into the country, resolving to deliver myself to the first savages I should meet, and purchase my life from them by some bracelets, glass rings, and other toys,[5] which sailors usually provide themselves with in those voyages, and whereof I had some about me: the land was divided by long rows of trees, not regularly planted, but naturally growing; there was great plenty of grass, and several fields of oats. I walked very circumspectly for fear of being surprised, or suddenly shot with an arrow from behind or on either side. I fell into a beaten road, where I saw many tracks of human feet, and some of cows, but most of horses. At last I beheld several animals in a field, and one or two of the same kind sitting in trees. Their shape was very singular, and deformed, which a little discomposed me, so that I lay down behind a thicket to observe them better. Some of them coming forward near the place where I lay, gave me an opportunity of distinctly marking[6] their form. Their heads and breasts were covered with a thick hair, some frizzled and others lank; they had beards like goats, and a long ridge of hair down their backs, and the foreparts of their legs and feet, but the rest of their bodies were bare, so that I might see their skins, which were of a brown buff color. They had no tails, nor any hair at all on their buttocks, except about the anus; which, I presume, Nature had placed there to defend them as they sat on the ground; for this posture they used, as well as lying down, and often stood on their hind feet. They climbed high trees, as nimbly as a squirrel, for they had strong extended claws before and behind, terminating in sharp points, and hooked. They would often spring, and bound, and leap with prodigious agility. The females were not so large as the males; they had long lank hair on their heads, and only a sort of down on the rest of their bodies, except about the anus, and pudenda.[7] Their dugs[8] hung between their forefeet, and often reached almost to the ground as they walked. The hair of both sexes was of several colors, brown, red, black, and yellow. Upon the whole, I never beheld in all my travels so disagreeable an animal, nor one against which I naturally conceived so strong an antipathy. So that thinking I had seen enough, full of contempt and aversion, I got up and pursued

---

2. A short sword, typically hung from the belt.
3. The shore; in this context, apparently a spit extending into the sea.
4. Cargo.

5. Trinkets.
6. Observing.
7. Genitals.
8. Breasts.

the beaten road, hoping it might direct me to the cabin of some Indian. I had not gone far when I met one of these creatures full in my way, and coming up directly to me. The ugly monster, when he saw me, distorted several ways every feature of his visage, and stared as at an object he had never seen before; then approaching nearer, lifted up his forepaw, whether out of curiosity or mischief, I could not tell. But I drew my hanger, and gave him a good blow with the flat side of it; for I durst not strike him with the edge, fearing the inhabitants might be provoked against me, if they should come to know, that I had killed or maimed any of their cattle. When the beast felt the smart, he drew back, and roared so loud, that a herd of at least forty came flocking about me from the next field, howling and making odious faces; but I ran to the body of a tree, and leaning my back against it, kept them off, by waving my hanger. Several of this cursed brood getting hold of the branches behind leaped up into the tree, from whence they began to discharge their excrements on my head: however, I escaped pretty well, by sticking close to the stem of the tree, but was almost stifled with the filth, which fell about me on every side.

In the midst of this distress, I observed them all to run away on a sudden as fast as they could, at which I ventured to leave the tree, and pursue the road, wondering what it was that could put them into this flight. But looking on my left hand, I saw a horse walking softly in the field, which my persecutors having sooner discovered, was the cause of their flight. The horse started a little when he came near me, but soon recovering himself, looked full in my face with manifest tokens of wonder: he viewed my hands and feet, walking round me several times. I would have pursued my journey, but he placed himself directly in the way, yet looking with a very mild aspect, never offering the least violence. We stood gazing at each other for some time; at last I took the boldness to reach my hand towards his neck, with a design to stroke it, using the common style and whistle of jockeys when they are going to handle a strange horse. But this animal, seeming to receive my civilities with disdain, shook his head, and bent his brows, softly raising up his left forefoot to remove my hand. Then he neighed three or four times, but in so different a cadence, that I almost began to think he was speaking to himself in some language of his own.

While he and I were thus employed, another horse came up; who applying[9] himself to the first in a very formal manner, they gently struck each other's right hoof before, neighing several times by turns, and varying the sound, which seemed to be almost articulate. They went some paces off, as if it were to confer together, walking side by side, backward and forward, like persons deliberating upon some affair of weight, but often turning their eyes towards me, as it were to watch that I might not escape. I was amazed to see such actions and behavior in brute beasts, and concluded with myself, that if the inhabitants of this country were endued with a proportionable degree of reason, they must needs be the wisest people upon earth. This thought gave me so much comfort, that I resolved to go forward until I could discover some house or village, or meet with any of the natives, leaving the two horses to discourse together as they pleased. But the first, who was a dapple-grey, observing me to steal off, neighed after me in so expressive a tone, that I fancied myself to understand what he meant; whereupon I turned back, and came near him, to expect[1] his farther commands. But concealing my fear as much as I could, for I began to be in some pain,[2] how this adventure might terminate; and the reader will easily believe I did not much like my present situation.

9. Addressing.
1. Await.

2. Began to be worried.

The two horses came up close to me, looking with great earnestness upon my face and hands. The grey steed rubbed my hat all round with his right forehoof, and discomposed it so much, that I was forced to adjust it better, by taking it off, and settling it again; whereat both he and his companion (who was a brown bay) appeared to be much surprised; the latter felt the lappet[3] of my coat, and finding it to hang loose about me, they both looked with new signs of wonder. He stroked my right hand, seeming to admire the softness, and color; but he squeezed it so hard between his hoof and his pastern,[4] that I was forced to roar; after which they both touched me with all possible tenderness. They were under great perplexity about my shoes and stockings, which they felt very often, neighing to each other, and using various gestures, not unlike those of a philosopher,[5] when he would attempt to solve some new and difficult phenomenon.

Upon the whole, the behavior of these animals was so orderly and rational, so acute and judicious, that I at last concluded, they must needs be magicians, who had thus metamorphosed themselves upon some design, and seeing a stranger in the way, were resolved to divert themselves with him; or perhaps were really amazed at the sight of a man so very different in habit, feature, and complexion from those who might probably live in so remote a climate.[6] Upon the strength of this reasoning, I ventured to address them in the following manner: Gentlemen, if you be conjurers, as I have good cause to believe, you can understand any language; therefore I make bold to let your Worships know, that I am a poor distressed Englishman, driven by his misfortunes upon your coast, and I entreat one of you, to let me ride upon his back, as if he were a real horse, to some house or village, where I can be relieved. In return of which favor, I will make you a present of this knife and bracelet (taking them out of my pocket). The two creatures stood silent while I spoke, seeming to listen with great attention; and when I had ended, they neighed frequently towards each other, as if they were engaged in serious conversation. I plainly observed that their language expressed the passions[7] very well, and the words might with little pains be resolved into an alphabet more easily than the Chinese.

I could frequently distinguish the word *Yahoo*, which was repeated by each of them several times; and although it were impossible for me to conjecture what it meant, yet while the two horses were busy in conversation, I endeavored to practice this word upon my tongue; and as soon as they were silent, I boldly pronounced *Yahoo* in a loud voice, imitating, at the same time, as near as I could, the neighing of a horse; at which they were both visibly surprised, and the grey repeated the same word twice, as if he meant to teach me the right accent, wherein I spoke after him as well as I could, and found myself perceivably to improve every time, although very far from any degree of perfection. Then the bay tried me with a second word, much harder to be pronounced; but reducing it to the English *orthography*,[8] may be spelled thus, *Houyhnhnm*. I did not succeed in this so well as the former, but after two or three farther trials, I had better fortune; and they both appeared amazed at my capacity.

After some farther discourse, which I then conjectured might relate to me, the two friends took their leaves, with the same compliment of striking each other's hoof; and the grey made me signs that I should walk before him; wherein I thought it prudent to comply, till I could find a better director. When I offered to slacken my pace,

3. Lapel.
4. Part of a horse's foot between the fetlock (a projection of the lower leg) and the hoof.
5. Scientist.

6. Region.
7. Emotions.
8. Spelling.

he would cry *Hhuun, Hhuun*; I guessed his meaning, and gave him to understand, as well as I could, that I was weary, and not able to walk faster; upon which, he would stand a while to let me rest.

CHAPTER 2

The author conducted by a Houyhnhnm to his house. The house described. The author's reception. The food of the Houyhnhnms. The author in distress for want of meat, is at last relieved. His manner of feeding in that country.

Having traveled about three miles, we came to a long kind of building, made of timber stuck in the ground, and wattled across;[9] the roof was low, and covered with straw. I now began to be a little comforted, and took out some toys, which travelers usually carry for presents to the savage Indians of America and other parts, in hopes the people of the house would be thereby encouraged to receive me kindly. The horse made me a sign to go in first; it was a large room with a smooth, clay floor, and a rack[1] and manger extending the whole length on one side. There were three nags,[2] and two mares, not eating, but some of them sitting down upon their hams,[3] which I very much wondered at; but wondered more to see the rest employed in domestic business. The last seemed but ordinary cattle; however, this confirmed my first opinion, that a people who could so far civilize brute animals, must needs excel in wisdom all the nations of the world. The grey came in just after, and thereby prevented any ill treatment, which the others might have given me. He neighed to them several times in a style of authority, and received answers.

Beyond this room there were three others, reaching the length of the house, to which you passed through three doors, opposite to each other, in the manner of a vista;[4] we went through the second room towards the third; here the grey walked in first, beckoning me to attend:[5] I waited in the second room, and got ready my presents, for the master and mistress of the house: they were two knives, three bracelets of false pearl, a small looking glass, and a bead necklace. The horse neighed three or four times, and I waited to hear some answers in a human voice, but I heard no other returns than in the same dialect, only one or two a little shriller than his. I began to think that this house must belong to some person of great note among them, because there appeared so much ceremony before I could gain admittance. But, that a man of quality should be served all by horses, was beyond my comprehension. I feared my brain was disturbed by my sufferings and misfortunes: I roused myself, and looked about me in the room where I was left alone; this was furnished as the first, only after a more elegant manner. I rubbed mine eyes often, but the same objects still occurred. I pinched my arms and sides, to awake myself, hoping I might be in a dream. I then absolutely concluded, that all these appearances could be nothing else but necromancy[6] and magic. But I had no time to pursue these reflections; for the grey horse came to the door, and made me a sign to follow him into the third room, where I saw a very comely mare, together with a colt and foal, sitting on their haunches, upon mats of straw, not unartfully made, and perfectly neat and clean.

---

9. Filled in with twigs and branches.
1. Hayrack for the feed.
2. Ponies.
3. Buttocks.

4. Long, narrow view (usually between rows of trees).
5. Wait.
6. Sorcery.

The mare, soon after my entrance, rose from her mat, and coming up close, after having nicely[7] observed my hands and face, gave me a most contemptuous look; then turning to the horse, I heard the word *Yahoo* often repeated betwixt them; the meaning of which word I could not then comprehend, although it were the first I had learned to pronounce; but I was soon better informed, to my everlasting mortification: for the horse beckoning to me with his head, and repeating the word *Hhuun, Hhuun,* as he did upon the road, which I understood was to attend him, led me out into a kind of court, where was another building at some distance from the house. Here we entered, and I saw three of those detestable creatures, which I first met after my landing, feeding upon roots, and the flesh of some animals, which I afterwards found to be that of asses and dogs, and now and then a cow dead by accident or disease.[8] They were all tied by the neck with strong withes,[9] fastened to a beam; they held their food between the claws of their forefeet, and tore it with their teeth.

The master horse ordered a sorrel nag, one of his servants, to untie the largest of these animals, and take him into the yard. The beast and I were brought close together, and our countenances diligently compared, both by master and servant, who thereupon repeated several times the word *Yahoo.* My horror and astonishment are not to be described, when I observed, in this abominable animal, a perfect human figure; the face of it indeed was flat and broad, the nose depressed, the lips large, and the mouth wide. But these differences are common to all savage nations, where the lineaments of the countenance are distorted by the natives suffering[1] their infants to lie groveling on the earth, or by carrying them on their backs, nuzzling with their face against the mother's shoulders. The forefeet of the Yahoo differed from my hands in nothing else but the length of the nails, the coarseness and brownness of the palms, and the hairiness on the backs. There was the same resemblance between our feet, with the same differences, which I knew very well, though the horses did not, because of my shoes and stockings; the same in every part of our bodies, except as to hairiness and color, which I have already described.

The great difficulty that seemed to stick with the two horses, was, to see the rest of my body so very different from that of a Yahoo, for which I was obliged to my clothes, whereof they had no conception: the sorrel nag offered me a root, which he held (after their manner, as we shall describe in its proper place) between his hoof and pastern; I took it in my hand, and having smelt it, returned it to him as civilly as I could. He brought out of the Yahoo's kennel a piece of ass's flesh, but it smelt so offensively that I turned from it with loathing; he then threw it to the Yahoo, by whom it was greedily devoured. He afterwards showed me a wisp of hay, and a fetlock full of oats; but I shook my head, to signify, that neither of these were food for me. And indeed, I now apprehended, that I must absolutely starve, if I did not get to some of my own species: for as to those filthy Yahoos, although there were few greater lovers of mankind, at that time, than myself; yet I confess I never saw any sensitive[2] being so detestable on all accounts; and the more I came near them, the more hateful they grew, while I stayed in that country. This the master horse observed by my behavior, and therefore sent the Yahoo back to his kennel. He then

7. Closely.
8. The Yahoos eat food listed in Leviticus (11.3, 27, 39–40) as unclean, suggesting that they exemplify the human condition distorted and debased by sin.

9. Leashes.
1. Allowing.
2. "Having sense or perception, but not reason" (Johnson's *Dictionary*).

put his forehoof to his mouth, at which I was much surprised, although he did it with ease, and with a motion that appeared perfectly natural, and made other signs to know what I would eat; but I could not return him such an answer as he was able to apprehend; and if he had understood me, I did not see how it was possible to contrive any way for finding myself nourishment. While we were thus engaged, I observed a cow passing by, whereupon I pointed to her, and expressed a desire to let me go and milk her. This had its effect; for he led me back into the house, and ordered a mare-servant to open a room, where a good store of milk lay in earthen and wooden vessels, after a very orderly and cleanly manner. She gave me a large bowl full, of which I drank very heartily, and found myself well refreshed.

About noon I saw coming towards the house a kind of vehicle drawn like a sledge by four Yahoos. There was in it an old steed, who seemed to be of quality; he alighted with his hind feet forward, having by accident got a hurt in his left forefoot. He came to dine with our horse, who received him with great civility. They dined in the best room, and had oats boiled in milk for the second course, which the old horse ate warm, but the rest cold. Their mangers were placed circular in the middle of the room, and divided into several partitions, round which they sat on their haunches upon bosses[3] of straw. In the middle was a large rack with angles answering to every partition of the manger. So that each horse and mare ate their own hay, and their own mash of oats and milk, with much decency and regularity. The behavior of the young colt and foal appeared very modest, and that of the master and mistress extremely cheerful and complaisant[4] to their guest. The grey ordered me to stand by him, and much discourse passed between him and his friend concerning me, as I found by the stranger's often looking on me, and the frequent repetition of the word Yahoo.

I happened to wear my gloves, which the master grey observing, seemed perplexed, discovering signs of wonder what I had done to my forefeet; he put his hoof three or four times to them, as if he would signify, that I should reduce them to their former shape, which I presently did, pulling off both my gloves, and putting them into my pocket. This occasioned farther talk, and I saw the company was pleased with my behavior, whereof I soon found the good effects. I was ordered to speak the few words I understood, and while they were at dinner, the master taught me the names for oats, milk, fire, water, and some others; which I could readily pronounce after him, having from my youth a great facility in learning languages.

When dinner was done, the master horse took me aside, and by signs and words made me understand the concern he was in, that I had nothing to eat. Oats in their tongue are called *hlunnh*. This word I pronounced two or three times; for although I had refused them at first, yet upon second thoughts, I considered that I could contrive to make of them a kind of bread, which might be sufficient with milk to keep me alive, till I could make my escape to some other country, and to creatures of my own species. The horse immediately ordered a white mare-servant of his family to bring me a good quantity of oats in a sort of wooden tray. These I heated before the fire as well as I could, and rubbed them till the husks came off, which I made a shift[5] to winnow from the grain; I ground and beat them between two stones, then took water, and made them into a paste or cake, which I toasted at the fire, and ate warm with milk. It was at first a very insipid diet, although common enough in many parts of Europe, but grew tolerable by time; and having been often reduced to hard fare in

3. Piles or seats.
4. Courteous.

5. Attempted.

my life, this was not the first experiment I had made how easily nature is satisfied.[6] And I cannot but observe, that I never had one hour's sickness, while I stayed in this island. 'Tis true, I sometimes made a shift to catch a rabbit, or bird, by springes[7] made of Yahoos' hairs, and I often gathered wholesome herbs, which I boiled, or ate as salads with my bread, and now and then, for a rarity, I made a little butter, and drank the whey. I was at first at a great loss for salt; but custom soon reconciled the want of it; and I am confident that the frequent use of salt among us is an effect of luxury, and was first introduced only as a provocative to drink; except where it is necessary for preserving of flesh in long voyages, or in places remote from great markets. For we observe no animal to be fond of it but man:[8] and as to myself, when I left this country, it was a great while before I could endure the taste of it in anything that I ate.

This is enough to say upon the subject of my diet, wherewith other travelers fill their books, as if the readers were personally concerned whether we fared[9] well or ill. However, it was necessary to mention this matter, lest the world should think it impossible that I could find sustenance for three years in such a country, and among such inhabitants.

When it grew towards evening, the master horse ordered a place for me to lodge in; it was but six yards from the house, and separated from the stable of the Yahoos. Here I got some straw, and covering myself with my own clothes, slept very sound. But I was in a short time better accommodated, as the reader shall know hereafter, when I come to treat more particularly about my way of living.

CHAPTER 3

The author studious to learn the language, the Houyhnhnm his master assists in teaching him. The language described. Several Houyhnhnms of quality come out of curiosity to see the author. He gives his master a short account of his voyage.

My principal endeavor was to learn the language, which my master (for so I shall henceforth call him) and his children, and every servant of his house were desirous to teach me. For they looked upon it as a prodigy that a brute animal should discover[1] such marks of a rational creature. I pointed to everything, and inquired the name of it, which I wrote down in my journal book when I was alone, and corrected my bad accent, by desiring those of the family to pronounce it often. In this employment, a sorrel nag, one of the under servants, was very ready to assist me.

In speaking, they pronounce through the nose and throat, and their language approaches nearest to the High Dutch or German, of any I know in Europe; but is much more graceful and significant.[2] The Emperor Charles V made almost the same observation, when he said, that if he were to speak to his horse, it should be in High Dutch.[3]

The curiosity and impatience of my master were so great, that he spent many hours of his leisure to instruct me. He was convinced (as he afterwards told me) that I must be a Yahoo, but my teachableness, civility, and cleanliness astonished him; which were qualities altogether so opposite to those animals. He was most perplexed

---

6. A commonplace idea in ancient satire; Swift may here be mocking it.
7. Snares.
8. This is, of course, untrue, but Gulliver's subsequent dislike of salt indicates his dislike of human society in general.

9. A pun on "fare," meaning both food and "to get along."
1. Display.
2. Expressive.
3. I.e., German; Charles V of Spain (1500–1551) was believed to have said that he would address his God in Spanish, his mistress in Italian, and his horse in German.

about my clothes, reasoning sometimes with himself, whether they were a part of my body; for I never pulled them off till the family were asleep, and got them on before they waked in the morning. My master was eager to learn from whence I came, how I acquired those appearances of reason, which I discovered in all my actions, and to know my story from my own mouth, which he hoped he should soon do by the great proficiency I made in learning and pronouncing their words and sentences. To help my memory, I formed all I learned into the English alphabet, and writ the words down with the translations. This last, after some time, I ventured to do in my master's presence. It cost me much trouble to explain to him what I was doing; for the inhabitants have not the least idea of books or literature.

In about ten weeks' time I was able to understand most of his questions, and in three months could give him some tolerable answers. He was extremely curious to know from what part of the country I came, and how I was taught to imitate a rational creature, because the Yahoos (whom he saw I exactly resembled in my head, hands, and face, that were only visible), with some appearance of cunning, and the strongest disposition to mischief, were observed to be the most unteachable of all brutes. I answered, that I came over the sea, from a far place, with many others of my own kind, in a great hollow vessel made of the bodies of trees. That my companions forced me to land on this coast, and then left me to shift for myself. It was with some difficulty, and by the help of many signs, that I brought him to understand me. He replied, that I must needs be mistaken, or that I *said the thing which was not*. (For they have no word in their language to express lying or falsehood.) He knew it was impossible[4] that there could be a country beyond the sea, or that a parcel of brutes could move a wooden vessel whither they pleased upon water. He was sure no Houyhnhnm alive could make such a vessel, or would trust Yahoos to manage it.

The word *Houyhnhnm*, in their tongue, signifies a *horse*, and in its etymology, the *Perfection of Nature*. I told my master, that I was at a loss for expression, but would improve as fast as I could; and hoped in a short time I should be able to tell him wonders: he was pleased to direct his own mare, his colt and foal, and the servants of the family to take all opportunities of instructing me, and every day for two or three hours, he was at the same pains himself: several horses and mares of quality in the neighborhood came often to our house upon the report spread of a wonderful Yahoo, that could speak like a Houyhnhnm, and seemed in his words and actions to discover some glimmerings of reason. These delighted to converse with me; they put many questions, and received such answers as I was able to return. By all which advantages, I made so great a progress, that in five months from my arrival, I understood whatever was spoke, and could express myself tolerably well.

The Houyhnhnms who came to visit my master, out of a design of seeing and talking with me, could hardly believe me to be a right[5] Yahoo, because my body had a different covering from others of my kind. They were astonished to observe me without the usual hair or skin, except on my head, face, and hands; but I discovered that secret to my master, upon an accident, which happened about a fortnight before.

I have already told the reader, that every night when the family were gone to bed, it was my custom to strip and cover myself with my clothes: it happened one morning early, that my master sent for me, by the sorrel nag, who was his valet; when

4. The Houyhnhnm thus shows himself to be so dependent on reason that he is dogmatic in his ignorance, unable (like rationalists in religion) to accept what he does not know by his own reasoning.
5. True.

he came, I was fast asleep, my clothes fallen off on one side, and my shirt above my waist. I awaked at the noise he made, and observed him to deliver his message in some disorder; after which he went to my master, and in a great fright gave him a very confused account of what he had seen: this I presently discovered; for going as soon as I was dressed, to pay my attendance upon his Honor, he asked me the meaning of what his servant had reported, that I was not the same thing when I slept as I appeared to be at other times; that his valet assured him, some part of me was white, some yellow, at least not so white, and some brown.

I had hitherto concealed the secret of my dress, in order to distinguish myself as much as possible, from that cursed race of Yahoos; but now I found it in vain to do so any longer. Besides, I considered that my clothes and shoes would soon wear out, which already were in a declining condition, and must be supplied by some contrivance from the hides of Yahoos or other brutes; whereby the whole secret would be known: I therefore told my master, that in the country from whence I came, those of my kind always covered their bodies with the hairs of certain animals prepared by art, as well for decency, as to avoid inclemencies of air both hot and cold; of which, as to my own person, I would give him immediate conviction, if he pleased to command me; only desiring his excuse, if I did not expose those parts that Nature taught us to conceal. He said my discourse was all very strange, but especially the last part; for he could not understand why Nature should teach us to conceal what Nature had given. That neither himself nor family were ashamed of any parts of their bodies; but however I might do as I pleased. Whereupon, I first unbuttoned my coat, and pulled it off. I did the same with my waistcoat;[6] I drew off my shoes, stockings, and breeches. I let my shirt down to my waist, and drew up the bottom, fastening it like a girdle about my middle to hide my nakedness.

My master observed the whole performance with great signs of curiosity and admiration. He took up all my clothes in his pastern, one piece after another, and examined them diligently; he then stroked my body very gently, and looked round me several times, after which he said, it was plain I must be a perfect Yahoo; but that I differed very much from the rest of my species, in the softness, and whiteness, and smoothness of my skin, my want of hair in several parts of my body, the shape and shortness of my claws behind and before, and my affectation of walking continually on my two hinder feet. He desired to see no more, and gave me leave to put on my clothes again, for I was shuddering with cold.

I expressed my uneasiness at his giving me so often the appellation of *Yahoo*, an odious animal, for which I had so utter an hatred and contempt; I begged he would forbear applying that word to me, and take the same order in his family, and among his friends whom he suffered to see me. I requested likewise, that the secret of my having a false covering to my body might be known to none but himself, at least as long as my present clothing should last; for, as to what the sorrel nag his valet had observed, his Honor might command him to conceal it.

All this my master very graciously consented to,[7] and thus the secret was kept till my clothes began to wear out, which I was forced to supply by several contrivances, that shall hereafter be mentioned. In the meantime, he desired I would go on with my utmost diligence to learn their language, because he was more astonished at my

6. Vest.
7. The Houyhnhnms may have no word for "lying," but they can hide the truth.

capacity for speech and reason, than at the figure of my body, whether it were covered or no; adding, that he waited with some impatience to hear the wonders which I promised to tell him.

From thenceforward he doubled the pains he had been at to instruct me; he brought me into all company, and made them treat me with civility, because, as he told them privately, this would put me into good humor, and make me more diverting.

Every day when I waited on him, beside the trouble he was at in teaching, he would ask me several questions concerning myself, which I answered as well as I could; and by those means he had already received some general ideas, though very imperfect. It would be tedious to relate the several steps, by which I advanced to a more regular conversation: but the first account I gave of myself in any order and length, was to this purpose:

That, I came from a very far country, as I already had attempted to tell him, with about fifty more of my own species; that we traveled upon the seas, in a great hollow vessel made of wood, and larger than his Honor's house. I described the ship to him in the best terms I could, and explained by the help of my handkerchief displayed, how it was driven forward by the wind. That upon a quarrel among us, I was set on shore on this coast, where I walked forward without knowing whither, till he delivered me from the persecution of those execrable Yahoos. He asked me, who made the ship, and how it was possible that the Houyhnhnms of my country would leave it to the management of brutes? My answer was, that I durst proceed no farther in my relation, unless he would give me his word and honor that he would not be offended, and then I would tell him the wonders I had so often promised. He agreed; and I went on by assuring him, that the ship was made by creatures like myself, who in all the countries I had traveled, as well as in my own, were the only governing, rational animals; and that upon my arrival hither, I was as much astonished to see the Houyhnhnms act like rational beings, as he or his friends could be in finding some marks of reason in a creature he was pleased to call a Yahoo, to which I owned my resemblance in every part, but could not account for their degenerate and brutal nature. I said farther, that if good fortune ever restored me to my native country, to relate my travels hither, as I resolved to do, everybody would believe that I *said the thing which was not;* that I invented the story out of my own head; and with all possible respect to himself, his family, and friends, and under his promise of not being offended, our countrymen would hardly think it probable, that a Houyhnhnm should be the presiding creature of a nation, and a Yahoo the brute.

CHAPTER 4

The Houyhnhnms' notion of truth and falsehood. The author's discourse disapproved by his master. The author gives a more particular account of himself, and the accidents of his voyage.

My master heard me with great appearances of uneasiness in his countenance, because *doubting* or *not believing,* are so little known in this country, that the inhabitants cannot tell how to behave themselves under such circumstances. And I remember in frequent discourses with my master concerning the nature of manhood,[8] in other parts of the world, having occasion to talk of *lying,* and *false representation,* it was with much difficulty that he comprehended what I meant, although he

---

8. Human nature.

had otherwise a most acute judgment. For he argued thus: that the use of speech was to make us understand one another, and to receive information of facts; now if any one *said the thing which was not*, these ends were defeated; because I cannot properly be said to understand him, and I am so far from receiving information, that he leaves me worse than in ignorance, for I am led to believe a thing *black* when it is *white*, and *short* when it is *long*. And these were all the notions he had concerning that faculty of *lying*, so perfectly well understood, and so universally practiced among human creatures.

To return from this digression; when I asserted that the Yahoos were the only governing animal in my country, which my master said was altogether past his conception, he desired to know, whether we had Houyhnhnms among us, and what was their employment: I told him, we had great numbers, that in summer they grazed in the fields, and in winter were kept in houses, with hay and oats, where Yahoo servants were employed to rub their skins smooth, comb their manes, pick their feet, serve them with food, and make their beds. I understand you well, said my master; it is now very plain, from all you have spoken, that whatever share of reason the Yahoos pretend to, the Houyhnhnms are your masters;[9] I heartily wish our Yahoos would be so tractable. I begged his Honor would please to excuse me from proceeding any farther, because I was very certain that the account he expected from me would be highly displeasing. But he insisted in commanding me to let him know the best and the worst: I told him, he should be obeyed. I owned, that the Houyhnhnms among us, whom we called *horses*, were the most generous and comely animal we had, that they excelled in strength and swiftness; and when they belonged to persons of quality, employed in traveling, racing, or drawing chariots, they were treated with much kindness and care, till they fell into diseases, or became foundered in the feet;[1] but then they were sold, and used to all kind of drudgery till they died; after which their skins were stripped and sold for what they were worth, and their bodies left to be devoured by dogs and birds of prey.[2] But the common race of horses had not so good fortune, being kept by farmers and carriers and other mean people, who put them to greater labor, and fed them worse. I described as well as I could, our way of riding, the shape and use of a bridle, a saddle, a spur, and a whip, of harness and wheels. I added, that we fastened plates of a certain hard substance called *iron* at the bottom of their feet, to preserve their hoofs from being broken by the stony ways on which we often traveled.

My master, after some expressions of great indignation, wondered how we dared to venture upon a Houyhnhnm's back, for he was sure that the weakest servant in his house would be able to shake off the strongest Yahoo, or by lying down, and rolling upon his back, squeeze the brute to death. I answered, that our horses were trained up from three or four years old to the several uses we intended them for; that if any of them proved intolerably vicious, they were employed for carriages; that they were severely beaten while they were young, for any mischievous tricks; that the males, designed for the common use of riding or draft, were generally *castrated* about two years after their birth, to take down their spirits, and make them more tame and gentle; that they were indeed sensible of rewards and punishments; but his Honor would please to consider, that they had not the least tincture of reason any more than the Yahoos in this country.

---

9. Possibly a satire on the English love of horses.
1. Until their feet give in from overwork.
2. Swift mockingly paraphrases the *Iliad* 1.4–6: "The souls of mighty Chiefs untimely slain; / Whose limbs unburied on the naked shore, / Devouring dogs and hungry vultures tore" (Pope's translation).

It put me to the pains of many circumlocutions to give my master a right idea of what I spoke; for their language doth not abound in variety of words, because their wants and passions are fewer than among us. But it is impossible to express his noble resentment at our savage treatment of the Houyhnhnm race, particularly after I had explained the manner and use of *castrating* horses among us, to hinder them from propagating their kind, and to render them more servile. He said, if it were possible there could be any country where Yahoos alone were endued with reason, they certainly must be the governing animal, because reason will in time always prevail against brutal strength. But, considering the frame of our bodies, and especially of mine, he thought no creature of equal bulk was so ill-contrived for employing that reason in the common offices of life; whereupon he desired to know whether those among whom I lived, resembled me or the Yahoos of his country. I assured him, that I was as well shaped as most of my age, but the younger and the females were much more soft and tender, and the skins of the latter generally as white as milk. He said, I differed indeed from other Yahoos, being much more cleanly, and not altogether so deformed, but in point of real advantage, he thought I differed for the worse. That my nails were of no use either to my fore or hinder feet; as to my forefeet, he could not properly call them by that name, for he never observed me to walk upon them; that they were too soft to bear the ground; that I generally went with them uncovered, neither was the covering I sometimes wore on them of the same shape, or so strong as that on my feet behind. That I could not walk with any security, for if either of my hinder feet slipped, I must inevitably fall. He then began to find fault with other parts of my body, the flatness of my face, the prominence of my nose, mine eyes placed directly in front, so that I could not look on either side without turning my head, that I was not able to feed myself, without lifting one of my forefeet to my mouth, and therefore Nature had placed those joints to answer that necessity. He knew not what could be the use of those several clefts and divisions in my feet behind; that these were too soft to bear the hardness and sharpness of stones without a covering made from the skin of some other brute; that my whole body wanted a fence against heat and cold, which I was forced to put on and off every day with tediousness and trouble. And lastly, that he observed every animal in this country naturally to abhor the Yahoos, whom the weaker avoided, and the stronger drove from them. So that supposing us to have the gift of reason, he could not see how it were possible to cure that natural antipathy which every creature discovered[3] against us; nor consequently, how we could tame and render them serviceable. However, he would (as he said) debate that matter no farther, because he was more desirous to know my own story, the country where I was born, and the several actions and events of my life before I came hither.

I assured him, how extremely desirous I was that he should be satisfied in every point; but I doubted much, whether it would be possible for me to explain myself on several subjects whereof his Honor could have no conception, because I saw nothing in his country to which I could resemble[4] them. That, however, I would do my best, and strive to express myself by similitudes, humbly desiring his assistance when I wanted proper words; which he was pleased to promise me.

I said, my birth was of honest parents, in an island called England, which was remote from this country, as many days' journey as the strongest of his Honor's servants could travel in the annual course of the sun. That I was bred a surgeon, whose

3. Displayed.   4. Compare.

trade it is to cure wounds and hurts in the body, got by accident or violence; that my country was governed by a female man, whom we called a *Queen*. That I left it to get riches,[5] whereby I might maintain myself and family when I should return. That in my last voyage, I was commander of the ship, and had about fifty Yahoos under me, many of which died at sea, and I was forced to supply[6] them by others picked out from several nations. That our ship was twice in danger of being sunk; the first time by a great storm, and the second, by striking against a rock. Here my master interposed, by asking me, how I could persuade strangers out of different countries to venture with me, after the losses I had sustained, and the hazards I had run. I said, they were fellows of desperate fortunes, forced to fly from the places of their birth, on account of their poverty or their crimes. Some were undone by lawsuits; others spent all they had in drinking, whoring, and gaming; others fled for treason; many for murder, theft, poisoning, robbery, perjury, forgery, coining false money, for committing rapes or sodomy, for flying from their colors,[7] or deserting to the enemy, and most of them had broken prison; none of these durst return to their native countries for fear of being hanged, or of starving in a jail; and therefore were under a necessity of seeking a livelihood in other places.

During this discourse, my master was pleased often to interrupt me. I had made use of many circumlocutions in describing to him the nature of the several crimes, for which most of our crew had been forced to fly their country. This labor took up several days' conversation before he was able to comprehend me. He was wholly at a loss to know what could be the use or necessity of practicing those vices. To clear up which I endeavored to give him some ideas of the desire of power and riches, of the terrible effects of lust, intemperance, malice, and envy. All this I was forced to define and describe by putting of cases, and making suppositions. After which, like one whose imagination was struck with something never seen or heard of before, he would lift up his eyes with amazement and indignation. Power, government, war, law, punishment, and a thousand other things had no terms, wherein that language could express them, which made the difficulty almost insuperable to give my master any conception of what I meant. But being of an excellent understanding, much improved by contemplation and converse, he at last arrived at a competent knowledge of what human nature in our parts of the world is capable to perform, and desired I would give him some particular account of that land, which we call Europe, but especially, of my own country.

from CHAPTER 5

The author at his master's commands informs him of the state of England. The causes of war among the princes of Europe. The author begins to explain the English Constitution.

The reader may please to observe, that the following extract of many conversations I had with my master, contains a summary of the most material points, which were discoursed at several times for above two years; his Honor often desiring fuller satisfaction[8] as I farther improved in the Houyhnhnm tongue. I laid before him, as well as I could, the whole state of Europe; I discoursed of trade and manufactures, of arts and sciences; and the answers I gave to all the questions he made, as they arose upon several subjects,

5. Gulliver originally stated that he undertook his second and third voyages out of a desire to travel: he now reads all human motivation in the worst possible light.
6. Replace.
7. Deserting their regiment in the army.
8. Better explanation.

were a fund of conversation not to be exhausted. But I shall here only set down the substance of what passed between us concerning my own country, reducing it into order as well as I can, without any regard to time or other circumstances, while I strictly adhere to truth. My only concern is, that I shall hardly be able to do justice to my master's arguments and expressions, which must needs suffer by my want of capacity, as well as by a translation into our barbarous English.[9]

In obedience therefore to his Honor's commands, I related to him the Revolution under the Prince of Orange,[1] the long war with France[2] entered into by the said Prince, and renewed by his successor the present Queen, wherein the greatest powers of Christendom were engaged, and which still continued: I computed, at his request, that about a million of Yahoos might have been killed in the whole progress of it, and perhaps a hundred or more cities taken, and five times as many ships burnt or sunk.

* * * And, being no stranger to the art of war, I gave him a description of cannons, culverins,[3] muskets, carabines,[4] pistols, bullets, powder, swords, bayonets, battles, sieges, retreats, attacks, undermines, countermines,[5] bombardments, seafights; ships sunk with a thousand men, twenty thousand killed on each side; dying groans, limbs flying in the air, smoke, noise, confusion, trampling to death under horses' feet; flight, pursuit, victory; fields strewed with carcasses left for food to dogs, and wolves, and birds of prey; plundering, stripping, ravishing, burning, and destroying. And to set forth the valor of my own dear countrymen, I assured him, that I had seen them blow up a hundred enemies at once in a siege, and as many in a ship, and beheld the dead bodies drop down in pieces from the clouds, to the great diversion of all the spectators.

I was going on to more particulars, when my master commanded me silence. He said, whoever understood the nature of Yahoos might easily believe it possible for so vile an animal to be capable of every action I had named, if their strength and cunning equaled their malice. But as my discourse had increased his abhorrence of the whole species, so he found it gave him a disturbance in his mind, to which he was wholly a stranger before. He thought his ears being used to such abominable words, might by degrees admit them with less detestation. That although he hated the Yahoos of this country, yet he no more blamed them for their odious qualities, than he did a *gnnayh* (a bird of prey) for its cruelty, or a sharp stone for cutting his hoof. But when a creature pretending to reason could be capable of such enormities, he dreaded lest[6] the corruption of that faculty might be worse than brutality itself. He seemed therefore confident, that instead of reason, we were only possessed of some quality fitted to increase our natural vices; as the reflection from a troubled stream returns the image of an ill-shapen body, not only *larger*, but more *distorted*.

He added, that he had heard too much upon the subject of war, both in this, and some former discourses. There was another point which a little perplexed him at present. I had said, that some of our crew left their country on account of being ruined by *law*; that I had already explained the meaning of the word; but he was at a loss how it should come to pass, that the *law* which was intended for *every* man's preservation,

9. Presumably "barbarous," because English both lacks appropriate words to express Houyhnhnm concepts and has concepts (e.g., of lust, malice, envy) for which the other language has no words.
1. The Glorious Revolution of 1688 by which William of Orange, and his wife, Mary Stuart, ascended to the English throne in 1689.
2. The War of the League of Augsburg (1689–1697) and the War of the Spanish Succession (1701–1713), which Swift (as a good Tory) opposed.
3. Large cannons.
4. Short firearms.
5. Digging under fortification walls, and counter-digging by those inside the fort to stop the besiegers.
6. Worried that.

be of no use. Wherein he agreed entirely with the sentiments of Socrates, as Plato delivers them;[8] which I mention as the highest honor I can do that prince of philosophers. I have often since reflected what destruction such a doctrine would make in the libraries of Europe, and how many paths to fame would be then shut up in the learned world.

Friendship and benevolence are the two principal virtues among the Houyhnhnms, and these not confined to particular objects,[9] but universal to the whole race. For a stranger from the remotest part is equally treated with the nearest neighbor, and wherever he goes, looks upon himself as at home. They preserve *decency* and *civility* in the highest degrees, but are altogether ignorant of *ceremony*.[1] They have no fondness for their colts or foals, but the care they take in educating them proceedeth entirely from the dictates of *Reason*. And I observed my master to show the same affection to his neighbor's issue that he had for his own.[2] They will have it that *Nature* teaches them to love the whole species, and it is *Reason* only that maketh a distinction of persons, where there is a superior degree of virtue.

When the matron Houyhnhnms have produced one of each sex, they no longer accompany with[3] their consorts, except they lose one of their issue by some casualty, which very seldom happens: but in such a case they meet again. Or when the like accident befalls a person,[4] whose wife is past bearing, some other couple bestow him one of their own colts, and then go together a second time, till the mother be pregnant. This caution is necessary to prevent the country from being overburdened with numbers.[5] But the race of inferior Houyhnhnms bred up to be servants is not so strictly limited upon this article; these are allowed to produce three of each sex, to be domestics in the noble families.

In their marriages they are exactly careful to choose such colors as will not make any disagreeable mixture in the breed.[6] *Strength* is chiefly valued in the male, and *comeliness* in the female, not upon the account of *love*, but to preserve the race from degenerating; for where a female happens to excel in *strength*, a consort is chosen with regard to *comeliness*. Courtship, love, presents, jointures,[7] settlements, have no place in their thoughts, or terms whereby to express them in their language. The young couple meet and are joined, merely because it is the determination of their parents and friends: it is what they see done every day, and they look upon it as one of the necessary actions in a reasonable being. But the violation of marriage, or any other unchastity, was never heard of, and the married pair pass their lives with the same friendship, and mutual benevolence that they bear to others of the same species who come in their way; without jealousy, fondness, quarreling, or discontent.

In educating the youth of both sexes, their method is admirable, and highly deserveth our imitation. These are not suffered to taste a grain of *oats*, except upon certain days, till eighteen years old; nor *milk*, but very rarely; and in summer they graze two hours in the morning, and as many in the evening, which their parents likewise observe, but the servants are not allowed above half that time, and a great

8. I.e., that ethics (human nature) is worth studying, while the physical world is not, as we can never have certain knowledge of it: "Socrates: I am a friend of learning—the trees and the countryside won't teach me anything, but the people in the city do" *Phaedrus* (230d3–5).
9. To other, particular Houyhnhnms.
1. As are the Utopians.
2. As do men in Plato's *Republic* (461d).
3. Have sex with.

4. A male Houyhnhnm.
5. The Utopians are under no such restriction, knowing (as the Houyhnhnms do not) of other lands to which they can send their excess population.
6. In Plato's *Republic* (458d–461e), eugenic principles also control mating.
7. Marriage settlements for wives, should they survive their husbands.

part of their grass is brought home, which they eat at the most convenient hours, when they can be best spared from work.

Temperance, industry, exercise, and *cleanliness,* are the lessons equally enjoined to the young ones of both sexes, and my master thought it monstrous in us to give the females a different kind of education from the males, except in some articles of domestic management;[8] whereby as he truly observed, one half of our natives were good for nothing but bringing children into the world, and to trust the care of their children to such useless animals, he said, was yet a greater instance of brutality.

But the Houyhnhnms train up their youth to strength, speed, and hardiness, by exercising them in running races up and down steep hills, or over hard stony grounds, and when they are all in a sweat, they are ordered to leap over head and ears into a pond or a river. Four times a year the youth of certain districts meet to show their proficiency in running, and leaping, and other feats of strength or agility, where the victor is rewarded with a song made in his or her praise. On this festival the servants drive a herd of Yahoos into the field, laden with hay, and oats, and milk for a repast to the Houyhnhnms; after which, these brutes are immediately driven back again, for fear of being noisome to the assembly.

Every fourth year, at the *vernal equinox,* there is a Representative Council of the whole nation, which meets in a plain about twenty miles from our house, and continueth about five or six days. Here they inquire into the state and condition of the several districts, whether they abound or be deficient in hay or oats, or cows or Yahoos? And wherever there is any want (which is but seldom) it is immediately supplied by unanimous consent and contribution. Here likewise the regulation of children is settled: as for instance, if a Houyhnhnm hath two males, he changeth one of them with another who hath two females: and when a child hath been lost by any casualty, where the mother is past breeding, it is determined what family in the district shall breed another to supply the loss.

CHAPTER 9

A grand debate at the general Assembly of the Houyhnhnms, and how it was determined. The learning of the Houyhnhnms. Their buildings. Their manner of burials. The defectiveness of their language.

One of these grand Assemblies was held in my time, about three months before my departure, whither my master went as the Representative of our district. In this Council was resumed their old debate, and indeed, the only debate that ever happened in their country; whereof my master after his return gave me a very particular account.

The question to be debated, was, whether the Yahoos should be exterminated from the face of the earth. One of the *members* for the affirmative offered several arguments of great strength and weight, alleging, that as the Yahoos were the most filthy, noisome, and deformed animal which Nature ever produced, so they were the most restive and indocile,[9] mischievous, and malicious: they would privately suck the teats of the Houyhnhnms' cows, kill and devour their cats, trample down their oats and grass, if they were not continually watched, and commit a thousand other extravagancies. He took notice of a general tradition, that Yahoos had not been

---

8. In both Plato's *Republic* (451e6–7) and More's *Utopia,* the sexes receive the same education; Swift also began (but never completed) an essay entitled *Of the Education*

of Ladies (c. 1728).
9. Unteachable.

always in their country, but, that many ages ago, two of these brutes appeared together upon a mountain,[1] whether produced by the heat of the sun upon corrupted mud and slime, or from the ooze and froth of the sea, was never known.[2] That these Yahoos engendered, and their brood in a short time grew so numerous as to overrun and infest the whole nation. That the Houyhnhnms, to get rid of this evil, made a general hunting, and at last enclosed the whole herd; and destroying the elder, every Houyhnhnm kept two young ones in a kennel, and brought them to such a degree of tameness, as an animal so savage by nature can be capable of acquiring; using them for draft and carriage. That there seemed to be much truth in this tradition, and that those creatures could not be *ylnhniamshy* (or *aborigines* of the land) because of the violent hatred the Houyhnhnms, as well as all other animals, bore them; which although their evil disposition sufficiently deserved, could never have arrived at so high a degree, if they had been *aborigines*, or else they would have long since been rooted out. That the inhabitants taking a fancy to use the service of the Yahoos, had very imprudently neglected to cultivate the breed of *asses*, which were a comely animal, easily kept, more tame and orderly, without any offensive smell, strong enough for labor, although they yield to the other in agility of body; and if their braying be no agreeable sound, it is far preferable to the horrible howlings of the Yahoos.[3]

Several others declared their sentiments to the same purpose, when my master proposed an expedient to the assembly, whereof he had indeed borrowed the hint from me. He approved of the tradition, mentioned by the Honorable Member who spoke before, and affirmed, that the two Yahoos said to be first seen among them had been driven thither over the sea; that coming to land, and being forsaken by their companions, they retired to the mountains, and degenerating by degrees, became in process of time, much more savage than those of their own species in the country from whence these two originals came. The reason of his assertion was, that he had now in his possession a certain wonderful[4] Yahoo (meaning myself), which most of them had heard of, and many of them had seen. He then related to them, how he first found me: that my body was all covered with an artificial composure of the skins and hairs of other animals; that I spoke in a language of my own, and had thoroughly learned theirs; that I had related to him the accidents which brought me thither; that when he saw me without my covering, I was an exact Yahoo in every part, only of a whiter color, less hairy, and with shorter claws. He added, how I had endeavored to persuade him, that in my own and other countries the Yahoos acted as the governing, rational animal, and held the Houyhnhnms in servitude; that he observed in me all the qualities of a Yahoo, only a little more civilized by some tincture of reason, which however was in a degree as far inferior to the Houyhnhnm race, as the Yahoos of their country were to me;[5] that, among other things, I mentioned a custom we had of *castrating* Houyhnhnms when they were young, in order to render them tame; that the operation was easy and safe; that it was no shame to

---

1. Probably Milton's "steep savage Hill," the garden of Eden (*Paradise Lost*, 4.172).
2. Humans are supposed to be of divine origin, but the Yahoos represent such a degraded form of humanity that they (like, it was believed, insects on the Nile's banks) were formed from the action of the sun on mud.
3. The commonplace comparison of humans to asses was

one Swift had previously used in *A Tale of a Tub* (1704) and *The Battle of the Books* (1704).
4. Amazing, unusual.
5. Gulliver falls between the Houyhnhnms and the Yahoos in reason, as he did between the Lilliputians and the Brobdingnagians in size.

learn wisdom from brutes, as industry is taught by the ant, and building by the swallow. (For so I translate the word *lyhannh*, although it be a much larger fowl.) That this invention might be practiced upon the younger Yahoos here, which, besides rendering them tractable and fitter for use, would in an age put an end to the whole species without destroying life. That, in the meantime the Houyhnhnms should be exhorted to cultivate the breed of asses, which, as they are in all respects more valuable brutes, so they have this advantage, to be fit for service at five years old, which the others are not till twelve.

This was all my master thought fit to tell me at that time, of what passed in the grand Council. But he was pleased to conceal[6] one particular, which related personally to myself, whereof I soon felt the unhappy effect, as the reader will know in its proper place, and from whence I date all the succeeding misfortunes of my life. * * *

CHAPTER 10

The author's economy[7] and happy life among the Houyhnhnms. His great improvement in virtue, by conversing with them. Their conversations. The author hath notice given him by his master that he must depart from the country. He falls into a swoon for grief, but submits. He contrives and finishes a canoe, by the help of a fellow servant, and puts to sea at a venture.[8]

I had settled my little economy to my own heart's content. My master had ordered a room to be made for me after their manner, about six yards from the house, the sides and floors of which I plastered with clay, and covered with rush mats of my own contriving; I had beaten hemp, which there grows wild, and made of it a sort of ticking;[9] this I filled with the feathers of several birds I had taken with springes made of Yahoos' hairs, and were excellent food. I had worked[1] two chairs with my knife, the sorrel nag helping me in the grosser[2] and more laborious part. When my clothes were worn to rags, I made myself others with the skins of rabbits, and of a certain beautiful animal about the same size, called *nnuhnoh,* the skin of which is covered with a fine down. Of these I likewise made very tolerable stockings. I soled my shoes with wood which I cut from a tree, and fitted to the upper leather, and when this was worn out, I supplied it with the skins of Yahoos dried in the sun. I often got honey out of hollow trees, which I mingled with water,[3] or ate it with my bread. No man could more verify the truth of these two maxims, *That nature is very easily satisfied;* and, *That necessity is the mother of invention.* I enjoyed perfect health of body and tranquillity of mind; I did not feel the treachery or inconstancy of a friend, nor the injuries of a secret or open enemy. I had no occasion of bribing, flattering, or pimping, to procure the favor of any great man or of his minion. I wanted no fence[4] against fraud or oppression; here was neither physician to destroy my body, nor lawyer to ruin my fortune; no informer to watch my words and actions, or forge accusations against me for hire; here were no jibers, censurers, backbiters, pickpockets,

---

6. Another indication that the Houyhnhnms are not completely honest or candid.
7. Method of living.
8. Without further planning.
9. Sturdy material used for making mattress covering.

1. Made.
2. Heavier, larger.
3. Honey-sweetened water was a Utopian drink.
4. Defense.

highwaymen, housebreakers, attorneys, bawds, buffoons, gamesters, politicians, wits, splenetics, tedious talkers, controvertists, ravishers, murderers, robbers, virtuosos;[5] no leaders or followers of party and faction; no encouragers to vice, by seducement or examples; no dungeon, axes, gibbets, whipping posts, or pillories; no cheating shopkeepers or mechanics;[6] no pride, vanity, or affectation; no fops, bullies, drunkards, strolling whores, or poxes;[7] no ranting, lewd, expensive wives; no stupid, proud pendants; no importunate, overbearing, quarrelsome, noisy, roaring, empty, conceited, swearing companions; no scoundrels, raised from the dust upon the merit of their vices, or nobility thrown into it on account of their virtues; no lords, fiddlers, judges, or dancing masters.[8]

I had the favor of being admitted to[9] several Houyhnhnms, who came to visit or dine with my master; where his Honor graciously suffered me to wait in the room, and listen to their discourse. Both he and his company would often descend to ask me questions, and receive my answers. I had also sometimes the honor of attending my master in his visits to others. I never presumed to speak, except in answer to a question, and then I did it with inward regret, because it was a loss of so much time for improving myself; but I was infinitely delighted with the station of a humble auditor in such conversations, where nothing passed but what was useful, expressed in the fewest and most significant words; where (as I have already said) the greatest *decency* was observed, without the least degree of ceremony; where no person spoke without being pleased himself, and pleasing his companions; where there was no interruption, tediousness, heat,[1] or difference of sentiments. They have a notion, that when people are met together, a short silence doth much improve conversation: this I found to be true, for during those little intermissions of talk, new ideas would arise in their minds, which very much enlivened the discourse. Their subjects are generally on friendship and benevolence, or order and economy, sometimes upon the visible operations of Nature, or ancient traditions, upon the bounds and limits of virtue, upon the unerring rules of reason, or upon some determinations to be taken at the next great Assembly, and often upon the various excellencies of *poetry*. I may add without vanity, that my presence often gave them sufficient matter for discourse, because it afforded my master an occasion of letting his friends into the history of me and my country, upon which they were all pleased to descant in a manner not very advantageous to humankind; and for that reason I shall not repeat what they said: only I may be allowed to observe, that his Honor, to my great admiration, appeared to understand the nature of Yahoos much better than myself. He went through all our vices and follies, and discovered many which I had never mentioned to him, by only supposing what qualities a Yahoo of their country, with a small proportion of reason, might be capable of exerting; and concluded, with too much probability, how vile as well as miserable such a creature must be.

I freely confess, that all the little knowledge I have of any value, was acquired by the lectures I received from my master, and from hearing the discourses of him

5. One knowledgeable or interested in apparently trivial "scientific" pursuits.
6. Laborers.
7. Venereal diseases.
8. That necessary tutor for the socially aspiring, the danc-

ing master (usually French), was a particular figure of fun; he usually accompanied himself on the fiddle.
9. Allowed to meet.
1. Heat of argument.

and his friends; to which I should be prouder to listen, than to dictate to the greatest and wisest assembly in Europe. I admired the strength, comeliness, and speed of the inhabitants; and such a constellation of virtues in such amiable persons produced in me the highest veneration. At first, indeed, I did not feel that natural awe which the Yahoos and all other animals bear towards them, but it grew upon me by degrees, much sooner than I imagined, and was mingled with a respectful love and gratitude, that they would condescend to distinguish me from the rest of my species.

When I thought of my family, my friends, my countrymen, or human race in general, I considered them as they really were, Yahoos in shape and disposition, perhaps a little more civilized, and qualified with the gift of speech, but making no other use of reason, than to improve and multiply those vices, whereof their brethren in this country had only the share that Nature allotted them. When I happened to behold the reflection of my own form in a lake or a fountain, I turned away my face in horror and detestation of myself,[2] and could better endure the sight of a common Yahoo, than of my own person. By conversing with the Houyhnhnms, and looking upon them with delight, I fell to imitate their gait and gesture, which is now grown into a habit, and my friends often tell me in a blunt way, that *I trot like a horse*; which, however, I take for a great compliment; neither shall I disown, that in speaking I am apt to fall into the voice and manner of the Houyhnhnms, and hear myself ridiculed on that account without the least mortification.

In the midst of all this happiness, when I looked upon myself to be fully settled for life, my master sent for me one morning a little earlier than his usual hour. I observed by his countenance that he was in some perplexity, and at a loss how to begin what he had to speak. After a short silence, he told me, he did not know how I would take what he was going to say; that in the last general Assembly, when the affair of the Yahoos was entered upon, the representatives had taken offense at his keeping a Yahoo (meaning myself) in his family more like a Houyhnhnm, than a brute animal. That he was known frequently to converse with me, as if he could receive some advantage or pleasure in my company; that such a practice was not agreeable to reason or Nature, or a thing ever heard of before among them. The Assembly did therefore *exhort* him, either to employ me like the rest of my species, or command me to swim back to the place from whence I came. That the first of these expedients was utterly rejected by all the Houyhnhnms who had ever seen me at his house or their own, for they alleged, that because I had some rudiments of reason, added to the natural pravity[3] of those animals, it was to be feared, I might be able to seduce them into the woody and mountainous parts of the country, and bring them in troops by night to destroy the Houyhnhnms' cattle, as being naturally of the ravenous[4] kind, and averse from labor.

My master added, that he was daily pressed by the Houyhnhnms of the neighborhood to have the Assembly's *exhortation* executed, which he could not put off much longer. He doubted[5] it would be impossible for me to swim to another country, and therefore wished I would contrive some sort of vehicle resembling those I had described to him, that might carry me on the sea, in which work I should have the

---

2. A mocking reversal both of a common pattern in pastoral love poetry and of the Greek myth of Narcissus.
3. Depravity.

4. Rapacious, predatory, or greedy.
5. Feared.

assistance of his own servants, as well as those of his neighbors. He concluded, that for his own part he could have been content to keep me in his service as long as I lived, because he found I had cured myself of some bad habits and dispositions, by endeavoring, as far as my inferior nature was capable, to imitate the Houyhnhnms.

I should here observe to the reader, that a decree of the general Assembly in this country is expressed by the word *hnhloayn*, which signifies an *exhortation*, as near as I can render it, for they have no conception how a rational creature can be *compelled*, but only advised, or *exhorted*, because no person can disobey reason, without giving up his claim to be a rational creature.

I was struck with the utmost grief and despair at my master's discourse, and being unable to support the agonies I was under, I fell into a swoon at his feet; when I came to myself, he told me, that he concluded I had been dead. (For these people are subject to no such imbecilities of nature.) I answered, in a faint voice, that death would have been too great an happiness; that although I could not blame the Assembly's *exhortation*, or the urgency[6] of his friends, yet in my weak and corrupt judgment, I thought it might consist[7] with reason to have been less rigorous. That I could not swim a league, and probably the nearest land to theirs might be distant above a hundred; that many materials, necessary for making a small vessel to carry me off, were wholly wanting in this country, which, however, I would attempt in obedience and gratitude to his Honor, although I concluded the thing to be impossible, and therefore looked on myself as already devoted to destruction. That the certain prospect of an unnatural death was the least of my evils: for, supposing I should escape with life by some strange adventure, how could I think with temper[8] of passing my days among Yahoos, and relapsing into my old corruptions, for want of examples to lead and keep me within the paths of virtue? That I knew too well upon what solid reasons all the determinations of the wise Houyhnhnms were founded, not to be shaken by arguments of mine, a miserable Yahoo; and therefore after presenting him with my humble thanks for the offer of his servants' assistance in making a vessel, and desiring a reasonable time for so difficult a work, I told him I would endeavor to preserve a wretched being; and, if ever I returned to England, was not without hopes of being useful to my own species, by celebrating the praises of the renowned Houyhnhnms, and proposing their virtues to the imitation of mankind.

My master in a few words made me a very gracious reply, allowed me the space of two *months* to finish my boat; and ordered the sorrel nag, my fellow servant (for so at this distance I may presume to call him) to follow my instructions, because I told my master, that his help would be sufficient, and I knew he had a tenderness for me.

In his company my first business was to go to that part of the coast, where my rebellious crew had ordered me to be set on shore. I got upon a height, and looking on every side into the sea, fancied I saw a small island, towards the northeast: I took out my pocket glass, and could then clearly distinguish it about five leagues off, as I computed; but it appeared to the sorrel nag to be only a blue cloud: for, as he had no conception of any country beside his own, so he could not be as expert in distinguishing remote objects at sea, as we who so much converse[9] in that element.

After I had discovered this island, I considered no farther; but resolved it should, if possible, be the first place of my banishment, leaving the consequence to Fortune.

6. Urging.
7. Be consistent.
8. Calmness.
9. Are familiar with.

I returned home, and consulting with the sorrel nag, we went into a copse at some distance, where I with my knife, and he with a sharp flint fastened very artificially, after their manner, to a wooden handle, cut down several oak wattles about the thickness of a walking staff, and some larger pieces. But I shall not trouble the reader with a particular description of my own mechanics; let it suffice to say, that in six weeks' time, with the help of the sorrel nag, who performed the parts that required most labor, I finished a sort of Indian canoe, but much larger, covering it with the skins of Yahoos well stitched together, with hempen threads of my own making. My sail was likewise composed of the skins of the same animal; but I made use of the youngest I could get, the older being too tough and thick, and I likewise provided myself with four paddles. I laid in a stock of boiled flesh, of rabbits and fowls, and took with me two vessels, one filled with milk, and the other with water.

I tried my canoe in a large pond near my master's house, and then corrected in it what was amiss; stopping all the chinks with Yahoos' tallow, till I found it staunch,[1] and able to bear me and my freight. And when it was as complete as I could possibly make it, I had it drawn on a carriage very gently by Yahoos, to the seaside, under the conduct of the sorrel nag, and another servant.

When all was ready, and the day came for my departure, I took leave of my master and lady, and the whole family, mine eyes flowing with tears, and my heart quite sunk with grief. But his Honor, out of curiosity, and perhaps (if I may speak it without vanity) partly out of kindness, was determined to see me in my canoe, and got several of his neighboring friends to accompany him. I was forced to wait above an hour for the tide, and then observing the wind very fortunately bearing towards the island, to which I intended to steer my course, I took a second leave of my master, but as I was going to prostrate myself to kiss his hoof, he did me the honor to raise it gently to my mouth. I am not ignorant how much I have been censured for mentioning this last particular. For my detractors are pleased to think it improbable, that so illustrious a person should descend to give so great a mark of distinction to a creature so inferior as I. Neither have I forgot, how apt some travelers are to boast of extraordinary favors they have received.[2] But if these censurers were better acquainted with the noble and courteous disposition of the Houyhnhnms, they would soon change their opinion.

I paid my respects to the rest of the Houyhnhnms in his Honor's company; then getting into my canoe, I pushed off from shore.

CHAPTER 11

The author's dangerous voyage. He arrives at New Holland, hoping to settle there. Is wounded with an arrow by one of the natives. Is seized and carried by force into a Portuguese ship. The great civilities of the captain. The author arrives at England.

I began this desperate voyage on February 15, 1715, at 9 o'clock in the morning. The wind was very favorable; however, I made use at first only of my paddles, but considering I should soon be weary, and that the wind might probably chop about,[3] I ventured to set up my little sail; and thus, with the help of the tide, I went at the rate of a league and a half an hour, as near as I could guess. My master and his friends continued[4] on

---

1. Watertight.
2. Swift heightens the absurdity of Gulliver's action, and draws attention to his later misanthropy.

3. Change direction.
4. Stayed.

the shore, till I was almost out of sight; and I often heard the sorrel nag (who always loved me) crying out, *Hnuy illa nyha maiah Yahoo*, Take care of thyself, gentle Yahoo.

My design was, if possible, to discover some small island uninhabited, yet sufficient by my labor to furnish me with the necessaries of life, which I would have thought a greater happiness than to be first minister in the politest court of Europe; so horrible was the idea I conceived of returning to live in the society and under the government of Yahoos. For in such a solitude as I desired, I could at least enjoy my own thoughts, and reflect with delight on the virtues of those inimitable Houyhnhnms, without any opportunity of degenerating into the vices and corruptions of my own species.

The reader may remember what I related when my crew conspired against me, and confined me to my cabin. How I continued there several weeks, without knowing what course we took, and when I was put ashore in the longboat, how the sailors told me with oaths, whether true or false, that they knew not in what part of the world we were. However, I did then believe us to be about ten degrees southward of the Cape of Good Hope, or about 45 degrees southern latitude, as I gathered from some general words I overheard among them, being I supposed to the southeast in their intended voyage to Madagascar. And although this were but little better than conjecture, yet I resolved to steer my course eastward, hoping to reach the southwest coast of New Holland, and perhaps some such island as I desired, lying westward of it. The wind was full west, and by six in the evening I computed I had gone eastward at least eighteen leagues, when I spied a very small island about half a league off, which I soon reached. It was nothing but a rock, with one creek, naturally arched by the force of tempests. Here I put in my canoe, and climbing a part of the rock, I could plainly discover[5] land to the east, extending from south to north. I lay all night in my canoe, and repeating my voyage early in the morning, I arrived in seven hours to the southwest point of New Holland.[6] This confirmed me in the opinion I have long entertained, that the maps and charts place this country at least three degrees more to the east than it really is;[7] which thought I communicated many years ago to my worthy friend Mr. Herman Moll, and gave him my reasons for it, although he hath rather chosen to follow other authors.[8]

I saw no inhabitants in the place where I landed, and being unarmed, I was afraid of venturing far into the country. I found some shellfish on the shore, and ate them raw, not daring to kindle a fire, for fear of being discovered by the natives. I continued three days feeding on oysters and limpets,[9] to save my own provisions, and I fortunately found a brook of excellent water, which gave me great relief.

On the fourth day, venturing out early a little too far, I saw twenty or thirty natives upon a height, not above five hundred yards from me. They were stark naked, men, women, and children, round a fire, as I could discover by the smoke. One of them spied me, and gave notice to the rest; five of them advanced towards me, leaving the women and children at the fire. I made what haste I could to the shore, and getting into my canoe, shoved off: the savages observing me retreat, ran after me; and before I could get far enough into the sea, discharged an arrow, which wounded me deeply on the inside of my left knee (I shall carry the mark to my grave). I apprehended the arrow might be

---

5. Discern.
6. New Holland was the name the explorer Abel Tasman originally gave to the western coast of Australia. Gulliver seems to place the land of the Houyhnhnms west of southwestern Australia, in which case the distance he covers to reach New Holland is improbable (1,500 to 2,000 nautical miles in 16 hours). It is possible, however, that Gulliver is meant to have landed on Tasmania, thus putting the Houyhnhnms a short distance west of this island.
7. Dampier claimed that he had found New Holland further west than indicated in Tasman's charts.
8. This geographer's *New and Correct Map of the Whole World* (1719) was probably the basis for Swift's geography in *Gulliver's Travels.*
9. Small mollusks that attach themselves to rocks.

poisoned, and paddling out of the reach of their darts (being a calm day) I made a shift to suck the wound, and dress it as well as I could.

I was at a loss what to do, for I durst not return to the same landing place, but stood[1] to the north, and was forced to paddle; for the wind though very gentle was against me, blowing northwest. As I was looking about for a secure landing place, I saw a sail to the north-north-east, which appearing every minute more visible, I was in some doubt, whether I should wait for them or no; but at last my detestation of the Yahoo race prevailed, and turning my canoe, I sailed and paddled together to the south, and got into the same creek from whence I set out in the morning, choosing rather to trust myself among these *barbarians*, than live with European Yahoos. I drew up my canoe as close as I could to the shore, and hid myself behind a stone by the little brook, which, as I have already said, was excellent water.

The ship came within a half a league of this creek, and sent out her longboat with vessels to take in fresh water (for the place it seems was very well known) but I did not observe it till the boat was almost on shore, and it was too late to seek another hiding place. The seamen at their landing observed my canoe, and rummaging it all over, easily conjectured that the owner could not be far off. Four of them well armed searched every cranny and lurking hole, till at last they found me flat on my face behind the stone. They gazed a while in admiration[2] at my strange uncouth dress, my coat made of skins, my wooden-soled shoes, and my furred stockings; from whence, however, they concluded I was not a native of the place, who all go naked. One of the seamen in Portuguese bid me rise, and asked who I was. I understood that language very well, and getting upon my feet, said, I was a poor Yahoo, banished from the Houyhnhnms, and desired they would please to let me depart. They admired to hear me answer them in their own tongue, and saw by my complexion I must be a European; but were at a loss to know what I meant by Yahoos and Houyhnhnms, and at the same time fell a laughing at my strange tone in speaking, which resembled the neighing of a horse. I trembled all the while betwixt fear and hatred: I again desired leave to depart, and was gently moving to my canoe; but they laid hold on me, desiring to know, what country I was of? whence I came? with many other questions. I told them, I was born in England, from whence I came about five years ago, and then their country and ours were at peace. I therefore hoped they would not treat me as an enemy, since I meant them no harm, but was a poor Yahoo, seeking some desolate place where to pass the remainder of his unfortunate life.

When they began to talk, I thought I never heard or saw anything so unnatural; for it appeared to me as monstrous as if a dog or a cow should speak in England, or a Yahoo in Houyhnhnmland. The honest Portuguese were equally amazed at my strange dress, and the odd manner of delivering my words, which however they understood very well. They spoke to me with great humanity, and said they were sure their captain would carry me *gratis* to Lisbon, from whence I might return to my own country; that two of the seamen would go back to the ship, to inform the captain of what they had seen, and receive his orders; in the meantime, unless I would give my solemn oath not to fly,[3] they would secure me by force. I thought it best to comply with their proposal. They were very curious to know my story, but I gave them very little satisfaction; and they all conjectured, that my misfortunes had impaired my reason. In two hours the boat, which went loaden with vessels of water,

---

1. Steered.
2. Wonder, amazement.

3. Attempt to escape.

returned with the captain's commands to fetch me on board. I fell on my knees to preserve my liberty; but all was in vain, and the men having tied me with cords, heaved me into the boat, from whence I was taken into the ship, and from thence into the captain's cabin.

His name was Pedro de Mendez; he was a very courteous and generous person; he entreated me to give some account of myself, and desired to know what I would eat or drink; said, I should be used as well as himself, and spoke so many obliging things, that I wondered to find such civilities from a Yahoo. However, I remained silent and sullen; I was ready to faint at the very smell of him and his men. At last I desired something to eat out of my own canoe; but he ordered me a chicken and some excellent wine, and then directed that I should be put to bed in a very clean cabin. I would not undress myself, but lay on the bed clothes, and in half an hour stole out, when I thought the crew was at dinner, and getting to the side of the ship was going to leap into the sea, and swim for my life, rather than continue among Yahoos. But one of the seamen prevented me, and having informed the captain, I was chained to my cabin.

After dinner Don Pedro came to me, and desired to know my reason for so desperate an attempt: assured me he only meant to do me all the service he was able, and spoke so very movingly, that at last I descended[4] to treat him like an animal which had some little portion of reason. I gave him a very short relation of my voyage, of the conspiracy against me by my own men, of the country where they set me on shore, and of my three years' residence there. All which he looked upon as if it were a dream or a vision; whereat I took great offense; for I had quite forgot the faculty of lying, so peculiar to Yahoos in all countries where they preside, and consequently the disposition of suspecting truth in others of their own species. I asked him, whether it were the custom of his country to *say the thing that was not?* I assured him I had almost forgot what he meant by falsehood, and if I had lived a thousand years in Houyhnhnmland, I should never have heard a lie from the meanest servant; that I was altogether indifferent whether he believed me or no; but however, in return for his favors, I would give so much allowance to the corruption of his nature, as to answer any objection he would please to make, and then he might easily discover the truth.

The captain, a wise man, after many endeavors to catch me tripping in some part of my story, at last began to have a better opinion of my veracity.[5] But he added, that since I professed so inviolable an attachment to truth, I must give him my word of honor to bear him company in this voyage without attempting anything against my life, or else he would continue[6] me a prisoner till we arrived at Lisbon. I gave him the promise he required; but at the same time protested that I would suffer the greatest hardships rather than return to live among Yahoos.

Our voyage passed without any considerable accident.[7] In gratitude to the captain I sometimes sat with him at his earnest request, and strove to conceal my antipathy against human kind, although it often broke out, which he suffered to pass without observation. But the greatest part of the day, I confined myself to my cabin, to avoid seeing any of the crew. The captain had often entreated me to strip myself of

---

4. Condescended.
5. In the first edition, the sentence continues: "and the rather, because he confessed, he met with a Dutch Skipper, who pretended to have landed with five others of his crew upon a certain island or continent south of New Holland, where they went for fresh water, and observed a horse driving before him several animals exactly resembling those I had described under the name of Yahoos,

with some other particulars, which the captain said he had forgot, because he then concluded them all to be lies." In 1735 Swift's Dublin publisher, George Faulkener, omitted these lines, probably because they contradicted Gulliver's later statement that no other European had visited this land.
6. Keep.
7. Incident.

my savage dress, and offered to lend me the best suit of clothes he had. This I would not be prevailed on to accept, abhorring to cover myself with anything that had been on the back of a Yahoo. I only desired he would lend me two clean shirts, which having been washed since he wore them, I believed would not so much defile me. These I changed every second day, and washed them myself.

We arrived at Lisbon, Nov. 5, 1715. At our landing the captain forced me to cover myself with his cloak, to prevent the rabble from crowding about me. I was conveyed to his own house, and at my earnest request, he led me up to the highest room backwards.[8] I conjured[9] him to conceal from all persons what I had told him of the Houyhnhnms, because the least hint of such a story would not only draw numbers of people to see me, but probably put me in danger of being imprisoned, or burnt by the Inquisition.[1] The captain persuaded me to accept a suit of clothes newly made, but I would not suffer the tailor to take my measure; however, Don Pedro being almost of my size, they fitted me well enough. He accoutered[2] me with other necessaries all new, which I aired for twenty-four hours before I would use them.

The captain had no wife, nor above three servants, none of which were suffered to attend at meals, and his whole deportment was so obliging, added to very good *human* understanding, that I really began to tolerate his company. He gained so far upon me, that I ventured to look out of the back window. By degrees I was brought into another room, from whence I peeped into the street, but drew my head back in a fright. In a week's time he seduced me down to the door. I found my terror gradually lessened, but my hatred and contempt seemed to increase. I was at last bold enough to walk the street in his company, but kept my nose well stopped with rue,[3] or sometimes with tobacco.

In ten days Don Pedro, to whom I had given some account of my domestic affairs, put it upon me as a point of honor and conscience, that I ought to return to my native country, and live at home with my wife and children. He told me, there was an English ship in the port just ready to sail, and he would furnish me with all things necessary. It would be tedious to repeat his arguments, and my contradictions. He said, it was altogether impossible to find such a solitary island as I had desired to live in; but I might command in my own house, and pass my time in a manner as recluse as I pleased.

I complied at last, finding I could not do better. I left Lisbon the 24th day of November, in an English merchantman, but who was the master I never inquired. Don Pedro accompanied me to the ship, and lent me twenty pounds. He took kind leave of me, and embraced me at parting, which I bore as well as I could. During this last voyage I had no commerce[4] with the master or any of his men, but pretending I was sick kept close in my cabin. On the fifth of December, 1715, we cast anchor in the Downs[5] about nine in the morning, and at three in the afternoon I got safe to my house at Redriff.

My wife and family received me with great surprise and joy, because they concluded me certainly dead; but I must freely confess the sight of them filled me only with hatred, disgust, and contempt, and the more by reflecting on the near alliance I

8. At the back of the house.
9. Appealed earnestly to.
1. Either because the Houyhnhnm hierarchy contradicted Genesis, in which man has dominion over the earth, or because Gulliver had been associating with diabolical powers, who could make humans appear to be horses (as

Gulliver himself had first believed).
2. Attired.
3. Strong-smelling shrub, used for medicinal purposes.
4. Interaction.
5. The sea off the North Downs in East Kent.

had to them. For, although since my unfortunate exile from the Houyhnhnm country, I had compelled myself to tolerate the sight of Yahoos, and to converse with Don Pedro de Mendez, yet my memory and imaginations were perpetually filled with the virtues and ideas of those exalted Houyhnhnms. And when I began to consider, that by copulating with one of the Yahoo species, I had become a parent of more, it struck me with the utmost shame, confusion, and horror.

As soon as I entered the house, my wife took me in her arms, and kissed me, at which, having not been used to the touch of that odious animal for so many years, I fell in a swoon for almost an hour. At the time I am writing it is five years since my last return to England: during the first year I could not endure my wife or children in my presence, the very smell of them was intolerable, much less could I suffer them to eat in the same room. To this hour they dare not presume to touch my bread, or drink out of the same cup, neither was I ever able to let one of them take me by the hand.[6] The first money I laid out was to buy two young stone-horses,[7] which I keep in a good stable, and next to them the groom is my greatest favorite; for I feel my spirits revived by the smell he contracts in the stable. My horses understand me tolerably well; I converse with them at least four hours every day. They are strangers to bridle or saddle, they live in great amity with me, and friendship to each other.

CHAPTER 12

The author's veracity. His design in publishing this work. His censure of those travelers who swerve from the truth. The author clears himself from any sinister ends in writing. An objection answered. The method of planting Colonies. His native country commended. The right of the Crown to those countries described by the author is justified. The difficulty of conquering them. The author takes his last leave of the reader, proposeth his manner of living for the future, gives good advice, and concludeth.

Thus, gentle reader,[8] I have given thee a faithful history of my travels for sixteen years, and above seven months, wherein I have not been so studious of ornament as of truth. I could perhaps like others have astonished thee with strange improbable tales; but I rather chose to relate plain matter of fact in the simplest manner and style, because my principal design was to inform, and not to amuse thee.

It is easy for us who travel into remote countries, which are seldom visited by Englishmen or other Europeans, to form descriptions of wonderful animals both at sea and land. Whereas a traveler's chief aim should be to make men wiser and better, and to improve their minds by the bad as well as good example of what they deliver concerning foreign places.[9]

I could heartily wish a law were enacted, that every traveler, before he were permitted to publish his voyages, should be obliged to make oath before the Lord High Chancellor that all he intended to print was absolutely true to the best of his knowledge; for then the world would no longer be deceived as it usually is, while some writers, to make their works pass the better upon the public, impose the grossest falsities on the unwary reader. I have perused several books of travels with great delight in my younger days; but having since gone over most parts of the globe, and been able to

---

6. Gulliver's unwillingness to share his bread or cup with his wife or children emphasizes his unchristian behavior.
7. Stallions.
8. Highly ironic, since the "gentle" readers must be Yahoos.
9. More's *Utopia* also argues that accounts of distant travels should provide useful lessons rather than fabulous tales.

contradict many fabulous accounts from my own observation, it hath given me a great disgust against this part of reading, and some indignation to see the credulity of mankind so impudently abused. Therefore since my acquaintance were pleased to think my poor endeavors might not be unacceptable to my country, I imposed on myself as a maxim, never to be swerved from, that I would *strictly adhere to truth;* neither indeed can I be ever under the least temptation to vary from it, while I retain in my mind the lectures and example of my noble master, and the other illustrious Houyhnhnms, of whom I had so long the honor to be an humble hearer.

> —*Nec si miserum Fortuna Sinonem*
> *Finxit, vanum etiam mendacemque improba finget.*[1]

I know very well how little reputation is to be got by writings which require neither genius nor learning, nor indeed any other talent, except a good memory or an exact journal. I know likewise, that writers of travels, like dictionary-makers, are sunk into oblivion by the weight and bulk of those who come last, and therefore lie uppermost.[2] And it is highly probable, that such travelers who shall hereafter visit the countries described in this work of mine, may, by detecting my errors (if there be any), and adding many new discoveries of their own, jostle me out of vogue, and stand in my place, making the world forget that ever I was an author. This indeed would be too great a mortification if I wrote for fame; but, as my sole intention was the PUBLIC GOOD,[3] I cannot be altogether disappointed. For who can read of the virtues I have mentioned in the glorious Houyhnhnms, without being ashamed of his own vices, when he considers himself as the reasoning, governing animal of his country? I shall say nothing of those remote nations where Yahoos preside, amongst which the least corrupted are the Brobdingnagians, whose wise maxims in morality and government it would be our happiness to observe. But I forbear descanting further, and rather leave the judicious reader to his own remarks and applications.

I am not a little pleased that this work of mine can possibly meet with no[4] censurers: for what objections can be made against a writer who relates only plain facts that happened in such distant countries, where we have not the least interest with respect either to trade or negotiations? I have carefully avoided every fault with which common writers of travels are often too justly charged. Besides, I meddle not the least with any *party,* but write without passion, prejudice, or ill-will against any man or number of men whatsoever. I write for the noblest end, to inform and instruct mankind, over whom I may, without breach of modesty, pretend to some superiority from the advantages I received by conversing so long among the most accomplished Houyhnhnms. I write without any view towards profit or praise. I never suffer a word to pass that may look like reflection,[5] or possibly give the least offense even to those who are most ready to take it. So that I hope I may with justice pronounce myself an author perfectly blameless, against whom the tribe of answerers, considerers, observers, reflecters, detecters, remarkers, will never be able to find matter for exercising their talents.[6]

---

1. "Nor, if cruel Fortune has made Sinon miserable, shall he also make him false and deceitful" (Virgil, *Aeneid* 2. 79–80). Swift cleverly employs the words that the Greek Sinon, the most famous liar in antiquity, used in the fraudulent tale he told to fool the Trojans into accepting *his* (wooden) horse.
2. The most current dictionary is the one most frequently used.
3. The English buccaneer and navigator William Dampi-

er professes a similar aim in the dedication to his *New Voyage Round the World* (1697).
4. Cannot possibly encounter any.
5. Criticism.
6. At this time it was common for historical and fictional accounts to be "applied" to contemporary situations or persons; by having Gulliver deny at such length that he is doing this, Swift draws attention to the possibility of making such connections.

I confess, it was whispered to me, that I was bound in duty as a subject of England, to have given in a memorial to a Secretary of State, at my first coming over; because, whatever lands are discovered by a subject belong to the Crown. But I doubt whether our conquests in the countries I treat of, would be as easy as those of Ferdinando Cortez over the naked Americans.[7] The Lilliputians, I think, are hardly worth the charge of a fleet and army to reduce them, and I question whether it might be prudent or safe to attempt the Brobdingnagians. Or whether an English army would be much at their ease with the Flying Island over their heads.[8] The Houyhnhnms, indeed, appear not to be so well prepared for war, a science to which they are perfect strangers, and especially against missive weapons.[9] However, supposing myself to be a minister of State, I could never give my advice for invading them. Their prudence, unanimity, unacquaintedness with fear, and their love of their country would amply supply all defects in the military art. Imagine twenty thousand of them breaking into the midst of an European army, confounding the ranks, overturning the carriages, battering the warriors' faces into mummy,[1] by terrible yerks[2] from their hinder hoofs. For they would well deserve the character given to Augustus; *Recalcitrat undique tutus.*[3] But instead of proposals for conquering that magnanimous nation, I rather wish they were in a capacity or disposition to send a sufficient number of their inhabitants for civilizing Europe, by teaching us the first principles of honor, justice, truth, temperance, public spirit, fortitude, chastity, friendship, benevolence, and fidelity. The *names* of all which virtues are still retained among us in most languages, and are to be met with in modern as well as ancient authors; which I am able to assert from my own small reading.

But I had another reason which made me less forward[4] to enlarge his Majesty's dominions by my discoveries. To say the truth, I had conceived a few scruples with relation to the distributive justice[5] of princes upon those occasions. For instance, a crew of pirates[6] are driven by a storm they know not whither, at length a boy discovers land from the topmast, they go on shore to rob and plunder; they see a harmless people, are entertained with kindness, they give the country a new name, they take formal possession of it for the king, they set up a rotten plank or a stone for a memorial, they murder two or three dozen of the natives, bring away a couple more by force for a sample, return home, and get their pardon. Here commences a new dominion acquired with a title by *divine right.* Ships are sent with the first opportunity, the natives driven out or destroyed, their princes tortured to discover their gold;[7] a free license given to all acts of inhumanity and lust, the earth reeking with the blood of its inhabitants; and this execrable crew of butchers employed in so pious an expedition, is a *modern colony* sent to convert and civilize an idolatrous and barbarous people.

---

7. In the 1520s, Cortés and 400 soldiers rapidly conquered the Aztec empire in Mexico.
8. These sentences refer to Gulliver's other travels: in Lilliput he encountered a miniature people; in Brobdingnag he met with giants; and in Laputa he encountered the Flying Island (able to force inhabitants below to submit either through starving them by blocking out the sun or by crushing them).
9. Anything thrown or shot through the air.
1. Pulp.
2. Kicks.
3. "He kicks back, well protected on every side" (Horace, *Satires* 2.i.20). While Gulliver refers admiringly to the horse's ability to defend itself, Swift recalls the context

for Horace's decision to use satire (rather than praise) when writing about Augustus: according to Horace, Augustus would kick out like a horse if he sensed servile flattery, so flattery was pointless. Gulliver's lavish praise of the Houyhnhnms backfires on him, not because the Houyhnhnms disliked it, but because his uncritical identification with them leaves him unable to cope with human society.
4. Eager.
5. Fairness with regard to the rights of the native people.
6. Referring to the first Spanish colonizers of America.
7. Several Aztec princes were tortured by Cortés, and the Incan emperor Atahuallpa by Pizarro (1533).

But this description, I confess, doth by no means affect the British nation, who may be an example to the whole world for their wisdom, care, and justice in planting colonies;[8] their liberal endowments for the advancement of religion and learning; their choice of devout and able pastors to propagate Christianity; their caution in stocking their provinces with people of sober lives and conversations from this the mother kingdom;[9] their strict regard to the distribution of justice, in supplying the civil administration through all their colonies with officers of the greatest abilities, utter strangers to corruption; and to crown all, by sending the most vigilant and virtuous governors, who have no other views than the happiness of the people over whom they preside, and the honor of the King their master.

But, as those countries which I have described do not appear to have any desire of being conquered, and enslaved, murdered, or driven out by colonies, nor abound either in gold, silver, sugar, or tobacco; I did humbly conceive they were by no means proper objects of our zeal, our valor, or our interest. However, if those whom it more concerns, think fit to be of another opinion, I am ready to depose, when I shall be lawfully called, that no European did ever visit those countries before me. I mean, if the inhabitants ought to be believed.[1]

But as to the formality of taking possession in my Sovereign's name, it never came once into my thoughts; and if it had, yet as my affairs then stood, I should perhaps in point of prudence and self-preservation, have put it off to a better opportunity.

Having thus answered the *only* objection that can ever be raised against me as a traveler, I here take a final leave of my courteous readers, and return to enjoy my own speculations in my little garden at Redriff, to apply those excellent lessons of virtue which I learned among the Houyhnhnms, to instruct the Yahoos of my own family as far as I shall find them docible[2] animals, to behold my figure often in a glass, and thus if possible habituate myself by time to tolerate the sight of a human creature, to lament the brutality of Houyhnhnms in my own country, but always treat their persons with respect, for the sake of my noble master, his family, his friends, and the whole Houyhnhnm race, whom these of ours[3] have the honor to resemble in all their lineaments, however their intellectuals[4] came to degenerate.

I began last week to permit my wife to sit at dinner with me, at the farthest end of a long table, and to answer (but with the utmost brevity) the few questions I ask her. Yet the smell of a Yahoo continuing very offensive, I always keep my nose well stopped with rue, lavender, or tobacco leaves. And although it be hard for a man late in life to remove old habits, I am not altogether out of hopes in some time to suffer a neighbor Yahoo in my company, without the apprehensions I am yet under of his teeth or his claws.

My reconcilement to the Yahoo-kind in general might not be so difficult if they would be content with those vices and follies only, which Nature hath entitled them to. I am not in the least provoked at the sight of a lawyer, a pickpocket, a colonel, a fool, a lord, a gamester, a politician, a whoremonger, a physician, an evidence,[5] a suborner,[6] an attorney, a traitor, or the like: this is all according to the due course of

---

8. Intended ironically.
9. Felons were commonly given a sentence of mandatory "transportation" to Britain's colonies.
1. The first edition continued: "unless a dispute may arise about the two Yahoos, said to have been seen many Ages ago on a mountain in Houyhnhnm-land, from whence the opinion is, that the race of those brutes hath descended; and these, for anything I know, may have been English, which indeed I was apt to suspect from the linea-

ments of their posterity's countenances, although very much defaced. But how far that will go to make out a title, I leave to the learned in colony law." Faulkener omitted this passage in the 1735 edition.
2. Teachable.
3. I.e., horses.
4. Intellects.
5. A (false) witness.
6. One who bribes another to commit a misdeed.

things; but when I behold a lump of deformity and diseases both in body and mind, smitten with *pride*, it immediately breaks all the measures of my patience; neither shall I be ever able to comprehend how such an animal and such a vice could tally together. The wise and virtuous Houyhnhnms, who abound in all excellencies that can adorn a rational creature, have no name for this vice in their language, which hath no terms to express anything that is evil, except those whereby they describe the detestable qualities of their Yahoos, among which they were not able to distinguish this of pride, for want of thoroughly understanding human nature, as it showeth itself in other countries, where that animal presides. But I, who had more experience, could plainly observe some rudiments of it among the wild Yahoos.

But the Houyhnhnms, who live under the government of Reason, are no more proud of the good qualities they possess, than I should be for not wanting a leg or an arm, which no man in his wits would boast of, although he must be miserable without them. I dwell the longer upon this subject from the desire I have to make the society of an English Yahoo by any means not insupportable, and therefore I here entreat those who have any tincture of this absurd vice, that they will not presume to appear in my sight.[7]

FINIS

c. 1721–1725   1726

A MODEST PROPOSAL   In a letter written to Alexander Pope in August 1729, Swift described the condition of Ireland: "There have been three terrible years' dearth of corn [i.e., wheat], and every place strewn with beggars, but dearths are common in better climates, and our evils lie much deeper. Imagine a nation the two-thirds of whose revenues are spent out of it, and who are not permitted [by Britain] to trade with the other third, and where the pride of the women will not suffer them to wear their own manufactures even where they excel what come from abroad." Two months later, Swift published what is today his most famous political essay: *A Modest Proposal.* Swift had previously written a dozen or more tracts to help free Ireland from its desperate social, economic, and political plight. In *A Modest Proposal,* however, Swift wielded two favorite weapons from his armory of satirical techniques—irony and parody—with devastating effect. In creating a persona who combines a mixture of calculating rationality and misplaced compassion but does not comprehend the enormity of his plan, Swift aims his satire not only at the political arithmeticians (forerunners of today's social engineers and economic planners) and the exploitative and predatory absentee landlords living in England but at the Irish people as well. Believing Ireland to be its own worst enemy, Swift delineates a program of commercial cannibalism that institutionalizes the country's own self-destructive tendencies. Preserving a nation through the consumption of its children is self-defeating, however demographically logical, because it undermines the understanding of humanity upon which civil society depends. Swift thus highlights the futility of financial improvement unaccompanied by social and moral reform.

A Modest Proposal

FOR PREVENTING THE CHILDREN OF POOR PEOPLE IN IRELAND
FROM BEING A BURDEN TO THEIR PARENTS OR COUNTRY,
AND FOR MAKING THEM BENEFICIAL TO THE PUBLIC

It is a melancholy object to those who walk through this great town,[1] or travel in the country, when they see the streets, the roads, and cabin doors crowded with beggars of the female sex, followed by three, four, or six children, *all in rags,* and importuning

---

7. Gulliver thus falls into pride, the very vice he rejects.   1. Dublin.

every passenger[2] for an alms. These mothers, instead of being able to work for their honest livelihood, are forced to employ all their time in strolling,[3] to beg sustenance for their helpless infants, who, as they grow up, either turn thieves for want of work, or leave their dear native country to fight for the Pretender in Spain,[4] or sell themselves to the Barbados.[5]

I think it is agreed by all parties that this prodigious number of children, in the arms, or on the backs, or at the heels of their mothers, and frequently of their fathers, is in the present deplorable state of the kingdom a very great additional grievance; and therefore whoever could find out a fair, cheap, and easy method of making these children sound, useful members of the commonwealth would deserve so well of the public, as to have his statue set up for a preserver of the nation.

But my intention is very far from being confined to provide only for the children of professed beggars; it is of a much greater extent, and shall take in the whole number of infants at a certain age who are born of parents in effect as little able to support them as those who demand our charity in the streets.

As to my own part, having turned my thoughts for many years upon this important subject, and maturely weighed the several schemes of other projectors,[6] I have always found them grossly mistaken in their computation. It is true a child just dropped from its dam may be supported by her milk for a solar year with little other nourishment, at most not above the value of two shillings, which the mother may certainly get, or the value in scraps, by her lawful occupation of begging, and it is exactly at one year old that I propose to provide for them, in such a manner as instead of being a charge upon their parents or the parish, or wanting food and raiment for the rest of their lives, they shall, on the contrary, contribute to the feeding and partly to the clothing of many thousands.

There is likewise another great advantage in my scheme, that it will prevent those voluntary abortions, and that horrid practice of women murdering their bastard children, alas, too frequent among us, sacrificing the poor innocent babes, I doubt[7] more to avoid the expense than the shame, which would move tears and pity in the most savage and inhuman breast.

The number of souls in this kingdom being usually reckoned one million and a half, of these I calculate there may be about two hundred thousand couple whose wives are breeders, from which number I subtract thirty thousand couple who are able to maintain their own children, although I apprehend there cannot be so many under the present distresses of the kingdom; but this being granted, there will remain an hundred and seventy thousand breeders. I again subtract fifty thousand for those women who miscarry, or whose children die by accident or disease within the year.[8] There only remain a hundred and twenty thousand children of poor parents annually born: the question therefore is how this number shall be reared and provided for, which, as I have already said, under the present situation of affairs, is utterly impossible by all the methods hitherto proposed: for we can neither employ them in handicraft, or agriculture; we neither build houses (I mean in the country) nor cultivate land;[9] they can very seldom pick up a livelihood by stealing till they arrive at six years old, except where they are of

2. Passerby.
3. Wandering aimlessly.
4. Catholic Ireland was loyal to the Pretender, James Francis Edward Stuart (1688–1766), son of James II, who was deposed from the English throne in 1688 because of his Catholicism. Religious ties also made the Irish ideal recruits for France and Spain in their wars against England.
5. The impoverished Irish emigrated to the West Indies

in large numbers, buying their passage by selling their labor in advance to the sugar plantations.
6. Devisers of new "projects," usually of doubtful value.
7. Believe.
8. It is telling that Swift here projects an infant mortality rate of approximately 30 percent in a child's first year.
9. The vast estates of English absentee landlords, and British retention of Irish land for grazing sheep, rather than agriculture, contributed to Ireland's poverty.

towardly parts,[1] although, I confess they learn the rudiments much earlier, during which time they can however be properly looked upon only as *probationers*, as I have been informed by a principal gentleman in the County of Cavan, who protested to me, that he never knew above one or two instances under the age of six, even in a part of the kingdom so renowned for the quickest proficiency in that art.

I am assured by our merchants that a boy or a girl, before twelve years old, is no salable commodity, and even when they come to this age, they will not yield above three pounds, or three pounds and half-a-crown at most on the Exchange,[2] which cannot turn to account[3] either to the parents or kingdom, the charge of nutriment and rags having been at least four times that value.

I shall now therefore humbly propose my own thoughts, which I hope will not be liable to the least objection.

I have been assured by a very knowing American[4] of my acquaintance in London, that a young healthy child well nursed is at a year old a most delicious, nourishing, and wholesome food, whether stewed, roasted, baked, or boiled, and I make no doubt that it will equally serve in a fricassee or ragout.[5]

I do therefore humbly offer it to public consideration, that of the hundred and twenty thousand children already computed, twenty thousand may be reserved for breed, whereof only one fourth part to be males, which is more than we allow to sheep, black cattle, or swine, and my reason is that these children are seldom the fruits of marriage, a circumstance not much regarded by our savages, therefore one male will be sufficient to serve four females. That the remaining hundred thousand may at a year old be offered in sale to the persons of quality and fortune through the kingdom, always advising the mother to let them suck plentifully in the last month, so as to render them plump, and fat for a good table. A child will make two dishes at an entertainment for friends, and when the family dines alone, the fore or hind quarter will make a reasonable dish, and seasoned with a little pepper or salt will be very good boiled on the fourth day, especially in winter.

I have reckoned upon a medium, that a child just born will weigh 12 pounds, and in a solar year if tolerably nursed increaseth to 28 pounds.

I grant this food will be somewhat dear,[6] and therefore very proper for landlords, who, as they have already devoured most of the parents, seem to have the best title to the children.

Infants' flesh will be in season throughout the year, but more plentiful in March, and a little before and after, for we are told by a grave author,[7] an eminent French physician, that fish being a prolific diet,[8] there are more children born in Roman Catholic countries about nine months after Lent than at any other season; therefore reckoning a year after Lent, the markets will be more glutted than usual, because the number of Popish infants is at least three to one in this kingdom, and therefore it will have one other collateral advantage by lessening the number of Papists among us.

I have already computed the charge of nursing a beggar's child (in which list I reckon all cottagers,[9] laborers, and four-fifths of the farmers) to be about two shillings *per annum*, rags included, and I believe no gentleman would repine to give ten shillings for the carcass of a good fat child, which, as I have said, will make four dishes

1. Precocious.
2. At the market.
3. Be of value.
4. Some of the British believed that the harsh living conditions in America made the colonists adopt "savage" practices.
5. A fricassee is meat stewed in gravy, a ragout is a highly seasoned French stew; such foreign dishes were becoming increasingly popular with fashionable Britons.
6. Both expensive and, of course, beloved.
7. The satirist François Rabelais, in *Gargantua and Pantagruel* (1532–1564), Book 5, ch. 29.
8. One increasing fertility.
9. Tenant farmers.

of excellent nutritive meat, when he hath only some particular friend or his own family to dine with him. Thus the Squire will learn to be a good landlord and grow popular among his tenants, the mother will have eight shillings net profit, and be fit for work till she produces another child.

Those who are more thrifty (as I must confess the times require) may flay the carcass, the skin of which, artificially[1] dressed, will make admirable gloves for ladies and summer boots for fine gentlemen.

As to our City of Dublin, shambles[2] may be appointed for this purpose in the most convenient parts of it, and butchers we may be assured will not be wanting, although I rather recommend buying the children alive and dressing them hot from the knife,[3] as we do roasting pigs.

A very worthy person, a true lover of his country, and whose virtues I highly esteem, was lately pleased, in discoursing on this matter, to offer a refinement upon my scheme. He said that many gentlemen of this kingdom, having of late destroyed their deer, he conceived that the want of venison might be well supplied by the bodies of young lads and maidens, not exceeding fourteen years of age nor under twelve, so great a number of both sexes in every country being now ready to starve for want of work and service;[4] and these to be disposed of by their parents if alive, or otherwise by their nearest relations. But with due deference to so excellent a friend and so deserving a patriot, I cannot be altogether in his sentiments; for as to the males, my American acquaintance assured me from frequent experience that their flesh was generally tough and lean, like that of our schoolboys, by continual exercise, and their taste disagreeable, and to fatten them would not answer the charge. Then as to the females, it would, I think with humble submission, be a loss to the public, because they soon would become breeders themselves; and besides, it is not improbable that some scrupulous people might be apt to censure such a practice (although indeed very unjustly) as a little bordering upon cruelty which, I confess, hath always been with me the strongest objection against any project, however so well intended.

But in order to justify my friend, he confessed that this expedient was put into his head by the famous Psalmanazar,[5] a native of the island Formosa, who came from thence to London above twenty years ago, and in conversation told my friend that in his country when any young person happened to be put to death, the executioner sold the carcass to persons of quality as a prime dainty, and that, in his time, the body of a plump girl of fifteen, who was crucified for an attempt to poison the emperor, was sold to his Imperial Majesty's Prime Minister of State[6] and other great Mandarins of the Court, in joints from the gibbet,[7] at four hundred crowns. Neither indeed can I deny that if the same use were made of several plump young girls in this town, who, without one single groat[8] to their fortunes, cannot stir abroad without a chair,[9] and appear at the playhouse and assemblies[1] in foreign fineries which they never will pay for, the kingdom would not be the worse.

Some persons of a desponding spirit are in great concern about that vast number of poor people who are aged, diseased, or maimed, and I have been desired to employ my thoughts what course may be taken to ease the nation of so grievous an encum-

---

1. Skillfully.
2. Places where meat is slaughtered and sold.
3. Skinning and gutting them immediately after killing.
4. Positions as servants.
5. George Psalmanazar, a Frenchman who pretended to be from Formosa (now Taiwan), wrote a book about its customs, the *Historical and Geographical Description of For-*

mosa (1704), which was quickly exposed as fraudulent.
6. A reference to Robert Walpole.
7. Gallows.
8. Silver coin (issued 1351–1662) equal to four pennies.
9. A sedan chair, carried by two men.
1. Social gatherings.

brance. But I am not in the least pain upon that matter, because it is very well known that they are every day dying, and rotting, by cold, and famine, and filth, and vermin, as fast as can be reasonably expected. And as to the younger laborers they are now in almost as hopeful a condition. They cannot get work, and consequently pine away for want of nourishment, to a degree that if at any time they are accidentally hired to common labor, they have not strength to perform it; and thus the country and themselves are in a fair way of being soon delivered from the evils to come.

I have too long digressed, and therefore shall return to my subject. I think the advantages by the proposal which I have made are obvious and many, as well as of the highest importance.

For first, as I have already observed, it would greatly lessen the number of Papists, with whom we are yearly overrun, being the principal breeders of the nation as well as our most dangerous enemies, and who stay at home on purpose with a design to deliver the kingdom to the Pretender, hoping to take their advantage by the absence of so many good Protestants, who have chosen rather to leave their country than stay at home, and pay tithes against their conscience, to an Episcopal curate.[2]

Secondly, the poorer tenants will have something valuable of their own, which by law may be made liable to distress,[3] and help to pay their landlords rent, their corn and cattle being already seized, and *money a thing unknown*.

Thirdly, whereas the maintenance of a hundred thousand children from two years old and upwards cannot be computed at less than ten shillings a piece *per annum*, the nation's stock will be thereby increased fifty thousand pounds *per annum*, besides the profit of a new dish introduced to the tables of all gentlemen of fortune in the kingdom who have any refinement in taste, and the money will circulate among ourselves, the goods being entirely of our own growth and manufacture.

Fourthly, the constant breeders, besides the gain of eight shillings sterling *per annum* by the sale of their children, will be rid of the charge of maintaining them after the first year.

Fifthly, this food would likewise bring great custom to taverns, where the vintners will certainly be so prudent as to procure the best receipts[4] for dressing it to perfection, and consequently have their houses frequented by all the fine gentlemen, who justly value themselves upon their knowledge in good eating; and a skillful cook who understands how to oblige his guests will contrive to make it as expensive as they please.

Sixthly, this would be a great inducement to marriage, which all wise nations have either encouraged by rewards or enforced by laws and penalties. It would increase the care and tenderness of mothers toward their children, when they were sure of a settlement for life to the poor babes, provided in some sort by the public to their annual profit instead of expense. We should see an honest emulation[5] among the married women, which of them could bring the fattest child to the market; men would become as fond of their wives, during the time of their pregnancy, as they are now of their mares in foal, their cows in calf, or sows when they are ready to farrow,[6] nor offer to beat or kick them (as it is too frequent a practice) for fear of a miscarriage.

Many other advantages might be enumerated: for instance, the addition of some thousand carcasses in our exportation of barreled beef;[7] the propagation of swine's flesh, and improvement in the art of making good bacon, so much wanted among us by

2. The tithes, or ecclesiastical taxes, that supported the Church were avoided by the many "good" Protestants who absented themselves from Ireland on the grounds—spurious, Swift implies—of "conscience."
3. Seizure for debt.
4. Recipes.
5. Competition.
6. Give birth.
7. Pickled beef.

the great destruction of pigs, too frequent at our tables, which are no way comparable in taste or magnificence to a well-grown, fat yearling child, which roasted whole will make a considerable figure at a Lord Mayor's feast or any other public entertainment. But this and many others I omit, being studious of brevity.

Supposing that one thousand families in this city would be constant customers for infants' flesh, besides others who might have it at merry-meetings, particularly weddings and christenings, I compute that Dublin would take off annually about twenty thousand carcasses, and the rest of the kingdom (where probably they will be sold somewhat cheaper) the remaining eighty thousand.

I can think of no one objection that will possibly be raised against this proposal, unless it should be urged that the number of people will be thereby much lessened in the kingdom. This I freely own, and was indeed one principal design in offering it to the world. I desire the reader will observe that I calculate my remedy *for this one individual Kingdom of Ireland, and for no other that ever was, is, or, I think, ever can be upon earth. Therefore let no man talk to me of other expedients:[8] Of taxing our absentees at five shillings a pound; of using neither clothes nor household furniture, except what is of our own growth and manufacture; of utterly rejecting the materials and instruments that promote foreign luxury; of curing the expensiveness of pride, vanity, idleness, and gaming in our women; of introducing a vein of parsimony, prudence, and temperance; of learning to love our country, wherein we differ even from* LAPLANDERS, *and the inhabitants of* TOPINAMBOO;[9] *of quitting our animosities and factions, nor act any longer like the Jews, who were murdering one another at the very moment their city was taken;[1] of being a little cautious not to sell our country and consciences for nothing; of teaching landlords to have at least one degree of mercy toward their tenants. Lastly, of putting a spirit of honesty, industry, and skill into our shopkeepers, who, if a resolution could now be taken to buy our native goods, would immediately unite to cheat and exact upon us in the price, the measure, and the goodness, nor could ever yet be brought to make one fair proposal of just dealing, though often and earnestly invited to it.*

Therefore I repeat, let no man talk to me of these and the like expedients till he hath at least some glimpse of hope that there will ever be some hearty and sincere attempt to put them in practice.

But as to myself, having been wearied out for many years with offering vain, idle, visionary thoughts, and at length utterly despairing of success, I fortunately fell upon this proposal, which as it is wholly new, so it hath something solid and real, of no expense and little trouble, full in our own power, and whereby we can incur no danger in *disobliging* ENGLAND. For this kind of commodity will not bear exportation, the flesh being of too tender a consistence, to admit a long continuance in salt, *although perhaps I could name a country[2] which would be glad to eat up our whole nation without it.*

After all I am not so violently bent upon my own opinion as to reject any offer proposed by wise men, which shall be found equally innocent, cheap, easy, and effectual. But before something of that kind shall be advanced in contradiction to my scheme and offering a better, I desire the author or authors will be pleased maturely to consider two points. First, as things now stand, how they will be able to find food

---

8. The kind of proposals Swift himself had made in earnest for remedying the poverty of Ireland; his *Proposal for the Universal Use of Irish Manufacture in Cloaths and Furniture . . . Utterly Rejecting and Renouncing Everything Wearable that Comes from England* (1720) is a typical example.
9. The inhabitants of the most hostile environments—

the frozen north or the Brazilian jungle—love their countries more than the Irish.
1. According to one historian, when Jerusalem was besieged and captured by the Emperor Titus in A.D. 70, factional fighting inside the city contributed to its destruction.
2. England.

and raiment for an hundred thousand useless mouths and ba~~~
being a round million of creatures in human figure throughoc~~~ And secondly, there
whole subsistence put into a common stock would leave them it's kingdom whose
pounds sterling; adding those who are beggars by profession to ~~~wo millions of
cottagers, and laborers with their wives and children, who are b~~~ of farmers,
desire those politicians who dislike my overture, and may perhap~~~ effect; I
attempt an answer, that they will first ask the parents of these mortal~~~d to
would not at this day think it a great happiness to have been sold for t~~~
old, in the manner I prescribe, and thereby have avoided such a perpetu~~~
misfortunes as they have since gone through, by the oppression of land~~~
impossibility of paying rent without money or trade, the want of commo~~~
nance, with neither house nor clothes to cover them from the inclemencies~~~
weather, and the most inevitable prospect of entailing[3] the like or greater mis~~~
upon their breed forever.

I profess in the sincerity of my heart that I have not the least personal inter
est in endeavoring to promote this necessary work, having no other motive than
the *public good of my country, by advancing our trade, providing for infants, relieving
the poor, and giving some pleasure to the rich.* I have no children by which I can propose to get a single penny; the youngest being nine years old, and my wife past
child-bearing.

1729   1729

∞

COMPANION READING

William Petty: from *Political Arithmetic*[1]

~~~n Chapter 4. How to enable the people of England and Ireland to spend 5 millions worth
~~~mmodities more than now; and how to raise the present value of the lands and goods of
~~~d from 2 to 3.

~~~to be done: 1. By bringing one million of the present 1,300 thousand of the
~~~ut of Ireland into England, though at the expense of a million of money. 2.
~~~remaining three hundred thousand left behind be all herdsmen and dairy
~~~rvants to the owners of the lands and stock transplanted into England, all
~~~en 16 and 60 years, and to quit all other trades, but that of cattle, and to
~~~ing but salt and tobacco. Neglecting all housing, but what is fittest for
~~~usand people, and this trade, though to the loss of 2 millions-worth of
~~~ a million of people be worth 70 pounds per head one with another,
~~~orth 70 millions; then the said people, reckoned as money at 5 per-
~~~l yield 3 millions and a half per annum. 3. And if Ireland send into

~~~7) represents the type of Eng-
~~~in his implicit criticism of
~~~nd in A Modest Proposal.
~~~othier and weaver, was an
~~~mist, and a charter mem-
~~~ted physician-general to
~~~ in 1652, he obtained
~~~Ireland through his
~~~forfeited by Roman
~~~bled him to devote

his attention to his economic writings and to the Royal
Society in London, though he was less than solicitous of
his tenants in Ireland. Swift's friendship with Petty's children, Lord Shelburne and Lady Kerry, did not prevent
him parodying Petty's *Political Arithmetic* (1691) in *A
Modest Proposal.* Petty's suggestion that Ireland be turned
into one huge farm to supply England by removing all the
Irish was only one of many "political arithmetic" projects
published during the Restoration and 18th century,
reflecting English interest in "scientific" programs for
social "improvement."

a half worth of effects (receiving nothing back), then England
England 1 million Ireland, and otherwise, 5 millions per annum more than now,
will be enrich˙ purchase, is worth one hundred millions of pounds sterling, as was
which, ar *
pro˙

POSTSCRIPT

...s jealous age this essay should be taxed of an evil design to waste and dispeo-
˙eland, we say that the author of it intends not to be *Felo de se*,[2] and propound
˙nething quite contrary, by saying it is naturally possible in about 25 years to double
the inhabitants of Great Britain and Ireland and make the people full as many as the
territory of those kingdoms can with tolerable labor afford a competent livelihood
unto, which I prove thus, (viz.)

1. The sixth part of the people are teeming women[3] of between 18 and 44 years old.
2. It is found by observation that but 1/3 part or between 30 and 40 of the teeming women are married.
3. That a teeming woman, at a medium, bears a child every two years and a half.
4. That in mankind at London, there are 14 males for 13 females, and because
   males are prolific[4] 40 years, and females but 25, there are in effect 560 males f˙
   325 females.
5. That out of the mass of mankind there dies one out of 30 per annum.
6. That at Paris, where the christenings and the births are the same in num˙
   christenings are above 18,000 per annum, and consequently the bir˙˙
   don, which far exceed the christenings there, cannot be less than ˙
   the burials are above 23,000.

AS FOR EXAMPLE

Of 600 people, the sixth part (viz. 100) are teeming women˙
married) might bear 40 children per annum (viz.) 20 more˙
the rate of one out of 30; and consequently in 16 years t˙
ing the whole 920. And by the same reason, in the n˙
280 more, in all 1,200, viz. double of the original n˙

Upon these principles, if there be about 19,0˙
number of the married teeming women must b˙
of the teeming women must be above 114,0˙
many viz. 684,000; which agrees well en˙
elsewhere computed to be.

To conclude it is naturally pos˙
since there are in effect 560 male˙
land can with moderate labor, f˙
people or to about 20 million˙
strated. * * *

fro˙
of c˙
Irela˙

This is˙
people o˙
That the˙
women, se˙
aged betwe˙
import noth˙
these 300 tho˙
houses. Now i˙
the whole are ˙
cent interest, wi˙

3. Bequeathing.
1. William Petty (1623–168˙
lishman Swift had in mind˙
English rapaciousness in Ire˙
Petty, the son of a London cl˙
extraordinary scholar and anat˙
ber of the Royal Society. Appoi˙
the parliamentary army in Irelan˙
considerable property holdings in˙
additional task of surveying lands˙
Catholics. His newfound fortune en˙

---

2. Suicidal; literally, "felon of (one)self."
3. Women capable of breeding.

Alexander Pope

1688–1744

"The life of a wit is a warfare upon earth; and the present spirit of the learned world is such, that to serve it . . . one must have the constancy of a martyr, and a resolution to suffer for its sake." Though still in his twenties when he wrote these words, Alexander Pope knew from painful experience their bitter truth. As a Roman Catholic, he could not vote, inherit or purchase land, attend a "public" school or a university, live within ten miles of London, hold public office, or openly practice his religion. He was obliged to pay double taxes. Such civil disenfranchisement barred him from receiving the literary patronage most talented writers depended upon for their livelihood. No wonder Pope wrote of "certain laws, by suff'rers thought unjust," by which he was "denied all posts of profit or of trust" (*Imitations of Horace, Epistle* 2.2.60–61). Despite whatever patriotism or loyalty to their country they may have felt, Catholics were widely regarded as alien and seditious. Pope's resentment of this attitude is evident in the *Epistle to Bathurst* (1733) when he calls the London Monument, which bears an inscription blaming the Great Fire of 1666 on a Papist conspiracy to destroy the capital, "a tall bully" who "lies."

Religion was not Pope's greatest impediment to success, however. When he was twelve, he contracted tuberculosis of the spine (Pott's disease), a condition that stunted his growth and left him humpbacked and deformed. At four feet six inches, he could not sit at an ordinary table with other adults unless his seat was raised. His constitution was so weakened that he frequently suffered from migraine headaches, asthma, nausea, and fevers. For much of his life, he could not hold his body upright without the help of stays, and he was unable to bathe, dress or undress, rise or go to bed by himself. Pope summarized his condition most succinctly in *An Epistle to Dr. Arbuthnot* (1735), when he wrote of "this long disease, my life."

Pope was born in London in 1688, the only child of his parents' marriage. Pope's *Epistle to Dr. Arbuthnot* includes a tribute to his father's equanimity and goodness; his mother is praised as "a noble wife." At the age of nine, Pope was sent to a school for Catholic boys but was expelled in his first year for writing a satire on his schoolmaster—a sign of things to come. When he was twelve, his family moved from the environs of London to Binfield, in the royal forest of Windsor; the effect of Windsor's "green retreats" on Pope's youthful imagination is apparent in the *Pastorals* (1709) and in *Windsor-Forest* (1713). At Binfield, he began to teach himself Greek and Latin with great determination, though the rigors of his studies made his sickness worse. Refusing to yield to his infirmity, he began, at fifteen, to journey into London to learn French and Italian. Pope spoke of these adolescent years as his "great reading period" when he "went through all the best critics, almost all the English, French, and Latin poets of any name . . . [and] Homer and some other of the Greek poets in the original." During this time Pope met his great friend John Caryll, at whose request he would write *The Rape of the Lock,* and Martha Blount, who was to become his lifelong intimate companion and to whom he addressed *Of the Characters of Women: An Epistle to a Lady* (1735).

Pope claimed that "as yet a child . . . I lisp'd in numbers [i.e., meter]." Certainly he was a precocious poet and his early efforts were encouraged by many, including the playwrights William Wycherley and William Congreve, to whom Pope dedicated his *Iliad* (1715–1720). If Pope had encouraging friends, he soon had detracting enemies as well. His first publication, the *Pastorals* (1709), occasioned a rivalry between Pope's Tory supporters and the Whig partisans of Ambrose Philips, whose *Pastorals* appeared in the same volume. Pope's next important poem, *An Essay on Criticism* (1711), brought a barrage of vituperative abuse from the critic John Dennis, who called Pope "a hunch-backed toad" and argued that his deformity was merely the outward sign of mental and moral ugliness. Undaunted, Pope continued to publish: the *Messiah* (1712), *The Rape of the Lock* (1712, substantially enlarged in 1714), *Windsor-Forest*

(1713), and *The Temple of Fame* (1715). With the publication of his *Works* (1717), Pope had proved himself master of a dazzling repertoire of poetic modes: pastoral and georgic, didactic, eclogue, mock-epic, allegorical dream-vision, heroic, and elegiac. No other living poet could display such dazzling versatility and comprehensive control.

There was still another area, however, in which Pope was proving the breathtaking range of his poetic gifts. Between 1713 and 1726, Pope devoted much of his creative energy to translating Homer's epics, the *Iliad* and the *Odyssey*, into heroic couplets. "Pope's Homer" not only won for him financial independence so that he could "live and thrive, / Indebted to no Prince or Peer alive" (*Imitations of Horace, Epistle* 2.2), it also confirmed his reputation as the presiding poetic genius of his time. While he was working on the *Odyssey*, Pope produced a six-volume edition of Shakespeare's works (1725), which, though it contained some valuable insights, was very much an amateur effort. When Lewis Theobald, the leading Shakespeare scholar of the time, rather pedantically highlighted Pope's many editorial shortcomings in *Shakespeare Restored, or, a Specimen of the Many Errors Committed . . . by Mr. Pope* (1726), Pope's revenge was not far off: two years later, he published *The Dunciad*, a savagely satirical assault on Pope's critics and the bankrupt cultural values they embodied.

In the seventeen years between Dennis's attack and the publication of *The Dunciad*, Pope's appearance, talent, and character had been assailed in print more than fifty times. His enemies accused him of being obscene, seditious, duplicitous, venal, vain, blasphemous, libelous, ignorant, and a bad poet. Theobald's rebuke was the last straw, perhaps because it was the most justified. Pope's style of comic social criticism owed much to his membership in the Scriblerus Club with John Gay, Jonathan Swift, Dr. John Arbuthnot, Thomas Parnell, and Robert Harley, Earl of Oxford. The Scriblerians originally planned to produce a series entitled *The Works of the Unlearned*; although the group regularly met only for a short while in 1714, its members remained in contact. In addition to *The Dunciad*, the fruit of their exchanges may be seen in Swift's *Gulliver's Travels* (1726), Gay's *The Beggar's Opera* (1728), Pope's *Peri Bathous: Or, the Art of Sinking in Poetry* (1728), and Arbuthnot's and Pope's *Memoirs of the Extraordinary Life, Works, and Discoveries of Martinus Scriblerus* (1741).

An *Essay on Man* (1733–1734) showcased Pope's talent for philosophical poetry. This work and four *Moral Essays* (1731–1735) were originally intended to form part of a long poetic sequence on the nature of humankind that Pope had hoped would be his greatest work, though the project was abandoned. Between 1733 and 1738, Pope published more than a dozen *Imitations of Horace*. In these loose adaptations of Horace's epistles and satires, Pope invested his modern social criticism with the classical authority of a revered Roman poet. The *Moral Essays*, or "Epistles to Several Persons" as Pope called them, also show Pope assuming the mantle of Horace by using the familiar epistle as a vehicle for social commentary. Pope's Horatian poems are his most mature, elegant, and self-assured works.

In 1737, he published an authorized version of his letters, which he doctored to improve his reputation. His last years were a time of retirement at his villa at Twickenham, famous for its grotto of "Friendship and Liberty" and for the five-acre landscape garden Pope had designed. In *The New Dunciad* (1742), Pope shifted his attack from hack writers and low culture to all forms of hypocrisy and pretense. It was his final triumph. He worked with William Warburton on a new edition of his *Works* (1751), even as his many illnesses became still more overwhelming. Though he was a self-confessed "fool to Fame" (*Arbuthnot*), he told those gathered around his deathbed: "There is nothing that is meritorious but virtue and friendship." He was, as his enemies claimed, bellicose, self-indulgent, and self-aggrandizing. He was morally and physically courageous and had a great gift for friendship. Although it is no longer fashionable to call the first half of the eighteenth century the "Age of Pope," many of his contemporaries saw him as the predominant literary genius of his time. Today, most literary historians agree that the greatest English poet between John Milton and William Wordsworth was Alexander Pope.

AN ESSAY ON CRITICISM   Pope was only twenty-one years old when he wrote *An Essay on Criticism*, which was published anonymously in 1711. This aesthetic manifesto in heroic couplets is written in the tradition of Horace's *Ars Poetica* (c. 19 B.C.), Boileau's *Art poétique* (1674), and other verse essays delineating poetic principles and practices. Pope's chief contributions to the genre are his ringing epigrams and the playful ease with which he satirizes contemporary critics who lack genuine poetic understanding. *The Essay on Criticism* is divided into three parts: the first examines the rules of taste, their relationship to Nature, and the authority of classical authors. The second (lines 201–559) considers the impediments preventing the attainment of the classical ideals outlined in part one. In the third part, Pope proposes an aesthetic and moral reformation to restore wit, sense, and taste to their former glory. While acknowledging the importance of precepts, Pope asserts the primacy of poetic genius and the power of imagination.

from An Essay on Criticism

'Tis hard to say, if greater want of skill
Appear in writing or in judging ill;
But, of the two, less dangerous is th' offense,
To tire our patience, than mislead our sense:°   *judgment*
5   Some few in that, but numbers err in this,
Ten censure wrong for one who writes amiss;
A fool might once himself alone expose,
Now one in verse makes many more in prose.[1]
   'Tis with our judgments as our watches, none
10   Go just alike, yet each believes his own.
In poets as true genius is but rare,
True taste as seldom is the critic's share;
Both must alike from Heav'n derive their light,
These born to judge, as well as those to write.
15   Let such teach others who themselves excel,
And censure freely who have written well.
Authors are partial to their wit,[2] 'tis true,
But are not critics to their judgment too?
   Yet if we look more closely, we shall find
20   Most have the seeds of judgment in their mind;
Nature affords at least a glimm'ring light;
The lines, though touched but faintly, are drawn right.
But as the slightest sketch, if justly traced, ⎤
Is by ill coloring but the more disgraced, ⎬
25   So by false learning is good sense defaced; ⎦
Some are bewildered in the maze of Schools,[3]
And some made coxcombs[4] Nature meant but fools.
In search of wit these lose their common sense,
And then turn critics in their own defense.
30   Each burns alike, who can, or cannot write,
Or° with a rival's or an eunuch's spite.[5]   *either*
All fools have still° an itching to deride,[6]   *continually*

---

1. I.e., many bad critics respond to one bad poet.
2. Both their writings and their (fancied) ability to write well.
3. Schools of criticism.
4. Conceited show-offs.
5. I.e., they either seek to compete or, knowing themselves sterile, criticize out of envy.
6. The fool's perpetual itching suggests disease.

And fain° would be upon the laughing side: *gladly*
If Maevius scribble in Apollo's spite,[7]
35   There are, who judge still worse than he can write.
Some have at first for wits,° then poets past,   *intellectuals*
Turned critics next, and proved plain fools at last;
Some neither can for wits nor critics pass,
As heavy mules are neither horse nor ass.
40   Those half-learned witlings, num'rous in our isle,
As half-formed insects on the banks of Nile;
Unfinished things, one knows not what to call,
Their generation's so equivocal:[8]
To tell° 'em, would a hundred tongues require,   *count*
45   Or one vain wit's, that might a hundred tire.
But you who seek to give and merit° fame,   *deserve*
And justly bear a critic's noble name,
Be sure yourself and your own reach° to know,   *ability*
How far your genius, taste, and learning go;
50   Launch not beyond your depth, but be discrete,
And mark° that point where sense and dullness meet.   *note*
Nature to all things fixed the limits fit,
And wisely curbed proud man's pretending° wit: *aspiring*
As on the land while here the ocean gains,
55   In other parts it leaves wide sandy plains;
Thus in the soul while memory prevails,
The solid power of understanding fails;
Where beams of warm imagination play,
The memory's soft figures melt away.
60   One science only will one genius fit;[9]
So vast is Art, so narrow human wit;°   *understanding*
Not only bounded to peculiar° arts,   *particular*
But oft in those, confined to single parts.
Like kings we lose the conquests gained before,
65   By vain ambition still to make them more:
Each might his several province well command,
Would all but stoop to what they understand.
First follow NATURE, and your judgment frame
By her just standard, which is still° the same: *always*
70   Unerring Nature, still divinely bright,
One clear, unchanged, and universal light,
Life, force, and beauty, must to all impart,
At once the source, and end, and test of art.
Art from that fund each just supply provides,
75   Works without show,[1] and without pomp presides:
In some fair body thus th' informing soul[2]
With spirits feeds, with vigor fills the whole,
Each motion guides, and every nerve sustains;

---

7. Maevius, a third-rate Roman poet, is set against Apollo, patron of good poetry.
8. Like the generation of insects on the banks of the Nile, thought to occur spontaneously, through the action of sun on mud.

9. The artist can hope only to succeed in one subject area or object of study.
1. The suggestion that art should mask its presence came from Horace.
2. The force that animates.

Itself unseen, but in th' effects, remains.
Some, to whom Heav'n in wit has been profuse,
Want° as much more, to turn it to its use;   *need*
For wit and judgment often are at strife,
Though meant each other's aid, like man and wife.
'Tis more to guide than spur the Muse's steed;[3]
Restrain his fury, than provoke his speed;
The winged courser,° like a gen'rous horse,   *swift horse*
Shows most true mettle° when you check his course.   *spirit*
  Those RULES of old discovered, not devised,
Are Nature still, but Nature *methodized;*
Nature, like Liberty, is but restrained
By the same laws which first herself ordained.
  Hear how learn'd Greece her useful rules indites,°   *composes*
When to repress, and when indulge our flights:
High on Parnassus'[4] top her sons she showed,
And pointed out° those arduous paths they trod,   *appointed*
Held from afar, aloft, th' immortal prize,
And urged the rest by equal steps to rise;
Just precepts thus from great examples giv'n,
She drew from them what they derived from Heav'n.
The gen'rous critic fanned the poet's fire,
And taught the world, with reason to admire.
Then criticism the Muse's handmaid proved,
To dress her charms,[5] and make her more beloved;
But following wits from that intention strayed;
Who could not win the mistress, wooed the maid;
Against the poets their own arms they turned,
Sure to hate most the men from whom they learned.
So modern 'pothecaries,° taught the art   *druggists*
By doctors' bills° to play the doctor's part,   *prescriptions*
Bold in the practice of mistaken° rules,   *misunderstood*
Prescribe, apply, and call their masters fools.
Some on the leaves of ancient authors prey,[6]
Nor time nor moths e'er spoiled so much as they:
Some dryly plain, without invention's° aid,   *imagination's*
Write dull receipts° how poems may be made: *recipes*
These leave the sense, their learning to display,
And those explain the meaning quite away.
  You then whose judgment the right course would steer,
Know well each ANCIENT'S proper character,[7]
His fable,° subject, scope° in every page,   *plot / intention*
Religion, country, genius of his age:
Without all these at once before your eyes,
Cavil° you may, but never criticize.   *quibble*
Be Homer's works your study, and delight,
Read them by day, and meditate by night,

80
85
90
95
100
105
110
115
120
125

3. Pegasus, the winged horse.
4. Mount Parnassus in Greece was sacred to the Muses.
5. Both dress and address, i.e., both interpret and adjust.
6. Textual commentators, depicted as literal bookworms
in continuation of the earlier insect metaphor.
7. An interest in the historical method in criticism was
on the rise.

Thence form your judgment, thence your maxims bring,
And trace the Muses upward to their spring;
Still with itself compared, his text peruse;
And let your comment be the Mantuan Muse.[8]

130   When first young Maro° in his boundless mind   *Virgil*
A work t' outlast immortal Rome designed,
Perhaps he seemed° above the critic's law,   *thought himself*
And but from Nature's fountains scorned to draw:
But when t' examine every part he came,
135   Nature and Homer were, he found, the same:
Convinced, amazed, he checks the bold design, ⎤
And rules as strict his labored work confine,   ⎬
As if the Stagyrite[9] o'erlooked each line.   ⎦
Learn hence for ancient rules a just esteem;
140   To copy Nature is to copy them. * * *

Of all the causes which conspire to blind
Man's erring judgment, and misguide the mind,
What the weak head with strongest bias[1] rules,
Is pride, the never-failing vice of fools.
205   Whatever Nature has in worth denied,
She gives in large recruits° of needful° pride;   *supplies / needed*
For as in bodies, thus in souls, we find
What wants° in blood and spirits, swelled with wind;   *is lacking*
Pride, where wit fails, steps in to our defense,
210   And fills up all the mighty void of sense!
If once right reason drives that cloud away,
Truth breaks upon us with resistless day;
Trust not yourself; but your defects to know,
Make use of every friend—and every foe.
215   A little learning is a dang'rous thing;
Drink deep, or taste not the Pierian spring:[2]
There shallow draughts[3] intoxicate the brain,
And drinking largely sobers us again.
Fired at first sight with what the Muse imparts,
220   In fearless youth we tempt° the heights of Arts,   *attempt*
While from the bounded° level of our mind,   *limited*
Short views we take, nor see the lengths behind,
But more advanced, behold with strange surprise
New, distant scenes of endless science[4] rise!
225   So pleased at first, the towering Alps we try,
Mount o'er the vales, and seem to tread the sky;
Th' eternal snows appear already past,
And the first clouds and mountains seem the last:
But those attained, we tremble to survey
230   The growing labors of the lengthened way,

8. Virgil (born near Mantua) and his *Aeneid*, which took Homer's epics as models and was the best commentary on them.
9. Aristotle, whose *Poetics* provided the basis for later rules on poetry and epic writing.

1. Not only prejudice but a kind of bowling ball. (In bowls, the bias ball is one weighted to roll obliquely.)
2. Hippocrene, the stream associated with the Muses.
3. I.e., drinking small amounts.
4. Knowledge, subjects requiring study.

Th' increasing prospect tires our wandering eyes,
Hills peep o'er hills, and Alps on Alps arise! * * *
285   Thus critics, of less judgment than caprice,
Curious,° not knowing, not exact, but nice,°   *picky / fussy*
Form short ideas; and offend in arts
(As most in manners) by a love to parts.[5]
Some to conceit[6] alone their taste confine,
290   And glitt'ring thoughts struck out at every line;
Pleased with a work where nothing's just or fit;
One glaring chaos and wild heap of wit:
Poets like painters, thus, unskilled to trace
The naked Nature and the living grace,
295   With gold and jewels cover every part,
And hide with ornaments their want° of art.   *lack*
True wit is Nature to advantage dressed,
What oft was thought, but ne'er so well expressed,
Something, whose truth convinced at sight we find,
300   That gives us back the image of our mind:
As shades° more sweetly recommend the light,   *shadows*
So modest plainness sets off sprightly wit:
For works may have more wit than does 'em good,
As bodies perish through excess of blood.[7]
305   Others for language all their care express,
And value books, as women men, for dress:
Their praise is still—The style is excellent:
The sense, they humbly take upon content.°   *trust*
Words are like leaves; and where they most abound,
310   Much fruit of sense beneath is rarely found.
False eloquence, like the prismatic glass,
Its gaudy colors spreads on every place;
The face of Nature we no more survey,°   *observe*
All glares alike, without distinction gay:
315   But true expression, like th' unchanging sun,
Clears, and improves whate'er it shines upon,
It gilds all objects, but it alters none.
Expression is the dress of thought,[8] and still
Appears more decent° as more suitable;   *correct*
320   A vile conceit° in pompous words expressed,   *idea*
Is like a clown° in regal purple dressed;   *peasant*
For different styles with different subjects sort,°   *belong*
As several garbs with Country, Town, and Court.[9]
Some by old words to fame have made pretense;[1]
325   Ancients in phrase, mere Moderns in their sense!
Such labored nothings, in so strange a style,
Amaze the unlearn'd, and make the learned smile.

5. Individual talents.
6. Extravagant use of metaphor.
7. Apoplexy, it was thought, was caused by such an excess.
8. It was generally held that a person's appearance reflected his or her inner self.
9. As various styles of dress suit country, mercantile, and courtly life.
1. Made a claim. Deliberately archaic language was used by Spenser and by a number of his 18th-century imitators.

Unlucky, as Fungoso in the play,[2]
These sparks[3] with awkward vanity display }
330   What the fine gentleman wore yesterday! }
And but so mimic ancient wits at best,
As apes our grandsires in their doublets[4] dressed.
In words, as fashions, the same rule will hold;
Alike fantastic, if too new, or old;
335   Be not the first by whom the new are tried,
Nor yet the last to lay the old aside.
    But most by numbers[5] judge a poet's song,
And smooth or rough, with them, is right or wrong;
In the bright Muse though thousand charms conspire,°   *work together*
340   Her voice is all these tuneful fools admire,
Who haunt Parnassus but to please their ear, }
Not mend their minds; as some to church repair, }
Not for the doctrine, but the music there. }
These equal syllables alone require,
345   Though oft the ear the open vowels tire,[6]
While expletives their feeble aid do join,
And ten low words oft creep in one dull line,
While they ring round the same unvaried chimes,
With sure returns of still expected rhymes.
350   Where-e'er you find the cooling western breeze,
In the next line, it whispers through the trees;
If crystal streams with pleasing murmurs creep,
The reader's threatened (not in vain) with sleep.
Then, at the last, and only couplet fraught
355   With some unmeaning thing they call a thought,
A needless Alexandrine[7] ends the song,
That like a wounded snake, drags its slow length along.
Leave such to tune their own dull rhymes, and know
What's roundly smooth, or languishingly slow;
360   And praise the easy vigor of a line,
Where Denham's strength, and Waller's sweetness join.[8]
True ease in writing comes from art, not chance,
As those move easiest who have learned to dance.
'Tis not enough no harshness gives offense,
365   The sound must seem an echo to the sense.[9]
Soft is the strain when Zephyr° gently blows,   *the west wind*
And the smooth stream in smoother numbers flows;
But when loud surges lash the sounding shore,
The hoarse, rough verse should like the torrent roar.
370   When Ajax[1] strives, some rock's vast weight to throw,

2. In Ben Jonson's *Every Man Out of His Humor* (1599), this student lagged behind the fashions.
3. Hot-blooded young men, aspiring to fame and romantic conquest.
4. Close-fitting garment for the upper body.
5. Meter of verse, patterns of sound.
6. This line, like the couplets that follow, illustrates the fault it criticizes.
7. The 12 syllables and six stresses of an Alexandrine are

illustrated in the next line.
8. Pope follows Dryden in his stylistic characterization of John Denham (1615–1669) and Edmund Waller (1606–1687), two poets greatly respected by writers of the early 18th century, especially for their work in heroic couplets.
9. The following nine lines exemplify the rule laid down here.
1. The fabulously strong Greek hero in Homer's *Iliad*.

The line too labors, and the words move slow;
Not so, when swift Camilla[2] scours the plain,
Flies o'er th' unbending corn, and skims along the main.°   *sea*
Hear how Timotheus'[3] varied lays surprise,
375   And bid alternate passions fall and rise!
While, at each change, the son of Lybian Jove[4]
Now burns with glory, and then melts with love;
Now his fierce eyes with sparkling fury glow;
Now sighs steal out, and tears begin to flow:
380   Persians and Greeks like turns of nature[5] found,
And the world's victor stood subdued by sound!
The pow'rs of music all our hearts allow;°   *admit to*
And what Timotheus was, is Dryden now.

* * *

THE RAPE OF THE LOCK   "New things are made familiar, and familiar things are made new," wrote Samuel Johnson about the most accomplished poem of Pope's younger years. "The whole detail of a female day is brought before us invested with so much art of decoration that, though nothing is disguised, everything is striking."

Only a poet with formidable imaginative powers could have made a great mock-heroic poem out of such unpromising materials. When Robert, Lord Petre, cut a love-lock from the head of Arabella Fermor without her permission, the two young people, both in their early twenties, quarreled bitterly. Their families, leading members of the Roman Catholic gentry once on the friendliest terms, became seriously estranged. Pope's friend John Caryll, who saw himself as a mediator among the group, asked him "to write a poem to make a jest of it, and laugh them together."

Pope's first effort was a poem in two cantos, *The Rape of the Locke*, printed in 1712 with some of his other pieces and the work of other poets. Two years later, Pope separately published *The Rape of the Lock*, enlarged to five cantos by the addition of the "machinery" of the sylphs and gnomes, and by the game of Ombre. The poem reached its final form in 1717 when Pope added the moralizing declamation of Clarissa (5.7–35), a parody of the speech of Sarpedon to Glaucus in the *Iliad*. The mock-epic tenor of the five-canto poem was clearly influenced by Pope's translation of the *Iliad*, his main project while most of *The Rape of the Lock* was being composed. Other influences were Homer's *Odyssey*, Virgil's *Aeneid*, Milton's *Paradise Lost*, and Boileau's *Le Lutrin* (1674, 1683), a mock-heroic satire on clerical infighting over the placement of a lectern. Yoking together the mundanely trivial and the mythically heroic as he follows the course of Belinda's day, Pope produced a vivid, yet affectionate, mockery of the fashions and sexual mores common in his own social circle.

The arming of the champion for war became the application of Belinda's (i.e., Arabella's) make-up for the battle of the sexes; the larger-than-life gods of classical mythology became miniature cartoon-like sylphs; Aeneas' voyage up the Tiber became Belinda's progress up the Thames; the depiction of Achilles' shield became the description of Belinda's petticoat; the test of single combat became the game of cards; the hero's journey to the underworld became the gnome's adventure in the Cave of Spleen; and the rape of Helen that started the Trojan War became the "rape" (stealing) of Belinda's hair that began an unpleasant social squabble. All the trappings of classical epic are here: the divine messenger appearing to the hero in a dream, the sacrifice to the gods, the inspirational speech to the troops before battle, the epic feast, the violent melee, and the final triumphant apotheosis. Throughout the poem, the enormous distance between the trivial *matter* and the heroic *manner* produces brilliantly comic results.

2. An Amazon warrior in Virgil's *Aeneid*.
3. Musician to Alexander the Great, as portrayed in Dryden's *Alexander's Feast* (1697).
4. Alexander the Great.
5. Similar changes of emotion.

The Rape of the Lock

An Heroi-Comical Poem in Five Cantos

Nolueram, Belinda, tuos violare capillos,
Sed juvat hoc precibus me tribuisse tuis.

Martial[1]

To Mrs. Arabella Fermor
   Madam,
   It will be in vain to deny that I have some regard for this piece, since I dedicate it to you. Yet you may bear me witness, it was intended only to divert a few young ladies, who have good sense and good humor enough, to laugh not only at their sex's little unguarded follies, but at their own.[2] But as it was communicated with the air of a secret, it soon found its way into the world. An imperfect copy having been offered to a bookseller, you had the good nature for my sake to consent to the publication of one more correct; this I was forced to before I had executed half my design, for the *machinery* was entirely wanting to complete it.
   The *machinery*, Madam, is a term invented by the critics, to signify that part which the deities, angels, or demons, are made to act in a poem; for the ancient poets are in one respect like many modern ladies: let an action be never so trivial in itself, they always make it appear of the utmost importance. These machines I determined to raise on a very new and odd foundation, the Rosicrucian[3] doctrine of spirits.
   I know how disagreeable it is to make use of hard words before a lady; but 'tis so much the concern of a poet to have his works understood, and particularly by your sex, that you must give me leave to explain two or three difficult terms.
   The Rosicrucians are a people I must bring you acquainted with. The best account I know of them is in a French book called *Le Comte de Gabalis*,[4] which both in its title and size is so like a novel, that many of the fair sex have read it for one by mistake. According to these gentlemen, the four elements are inhabited by spirits, which they call Sylphs, Gnomes, Nymphs, and Salamanders.[5] The Gnomes, or Demons of Earth, delight in mischief; but the Sylphs, whose habitation is in the air, are the best-conditioned[6] creatures imaginable. For they say, any mortals may enjoy the most intimate familiarities with these gentle spirits, upon a condition very easy to all true adepts, an inviolate preservation of chastity.
   As to the following cantos, all the passages of them are as fabulous,[7] as the vision at the beginning, or the transformation at the end (except the loss of your hair, which I always mention with reverence). The human persons are as fictitious as the airy ones; and the character of Belinda, as it is now managed, resembles you in nothing but in beauty.
   If this poem had as many graces as there are in your person, or in your mind, yet I could never hope it should pass through the world half so uncensured as you have done. But let its fortune be what it will, mine is happy enough, to have given me this occasion of assuring you that I am, with the truest esteem,

---

1. "I did not wish, [Belinda,] to violate your locks, but I rejoice to have yielded this to your wishes" (Martial, *Epigrams* 12.84). Pope has substituted "Belinda" for Martial's "Polytimus."
2. I.e., at their own individual follies as well.
3. A secret society of the 17th and 18th centuries, devoted to the study of ancient religious, philosophical, and mystical doctrines.

4. Written in 1670 by the Abbé de Monfaucon de Villars, its approach to Rosicrucian philosophy was lighthearted. It was printed in duodecimo, a small "pocketbook" size common to many inexpensive novels.
5. Elemental spirits living in fire.
6. Best natured, having the best character.
7. Fictional.

Madam,
Your most obedient
humble servant.
A. Pope

CANTO 1

What dire offense from am'rous causes springs,
What mighty contests rise from trivial things,
I sing[8]—This verse to Caryll, Muse! is due;
This, ev'n Belinda may vouchsafe to view:
5   Slight is the subject, but not so the praise,
If she inspire, and he approve my lays.°   *verses*
    Say what strange motive, Goddess!° could compel   *his Muse*
A well-bred lord t' assault a gentle belle?
Oh say what stranger cause, yet unexplored,
10   Could make a gentle belle reject a lord?
In tasks so bold, can little men engage,
And in soft bosoms dwells such mighty rage?
    Sol through white curtains shot a tim'rous ray,
And op'd those eyes that must eclipse the day;
15   Now lapdogs[9] give themselves the rousing shake,
And sleepless lovers, just at twelve, awake:
Thrice rung the bell, the slipper knocked the ground,[1]
And the pressed watch returned a silver sound.[2]
Belinda still her downy pillow pressed,
20   Her guardian Sylph prolonged the balmy rest.
'Twas he had summoned to her silent bed
The morning dream that hovered o'er her head.
A youth more glitt'ring than a birthnight beau,[3]
(That ev'n in slumber caused her cheek to glow)
25   Seemed to her ear his winning lips to lay,
And thus in whispers said, or seemed to say:[4]
    "Fairest of mortals, thou distinguished care
Of thousand bright inhabitants of air!
If e'er one vision touched thy infant thought,
30   Of all the nurse and all the priest have taught,[5]
Of airy elves by moonlight shadows seen,
The silver token, and the circled green,[6]
Or virgins visited by angel pow'rs,[7]
With golden crowns and wreaths of heav'nly flow'rs,
35   Hear and believe! thy own importance know,
Nor bound thy narrow views to things below.

8. Pope begins with the ancient epic formula of "proposition" of the work as a whole, and "invocation" of the gods' assistance, continuing with the traditional epic questions.
9. Small dogs imported from Asia were highly fashionable ladies' pets at this time.
1. Belinda rings the bell and then finally bangs her slipper on the floor to call her maid.
2. The popular "pressed watch" chimed the hour and quarter hours when its stem was pressed, saving its owner from striking a match to see the time.

3. On a royal birthday, courtiers' clothes were particularly extravagant.
4. His whispering recalls the serpent's temptation of Eve in Milton.
5. The nurse and priest were seen as two standard sources of superstition.
6. Withered circles in the grass and silver coins were supposed to be signs of fairies' presence.
7. Belinda is reminded of the many virgin saints, and particularly the Annunciation to the Virgin Mary.

Some secret truths from learned pride concealed,
To maids alone and children are revealed:
What though no credit doubting wits may give?[8]
40 The fair and innocent shall still believe.
Know then, unnumbered spirits round thee fly,
The light militia of the lower sky;
These, though unseen, are ever on the wing,
Hang o'er the box, and hover round the ring.[9]
45 Think what an equipage[1] thou hast in air,
And view with scorn two pages and a chair.[2]
As now your own, our beings were of old,
And once enclosed in woman's beauteous mold;
Thence, by a soft transition, we repair
50 From earthly vehicles[3] to these of air.
Think not, when woman's transient breath is fled,
That all her vanities at once are dead:
Succeeding vanities she still regards,
And though she plays no more, o'erlooks the cards.
55 Her joy in gilded chariots, when alive,
And love of Ombre,[4] after death survive.
For when the fair in all their pride expire,
To their first elements[5] their souls retire:
The sprites of fiery termagants° in flame   *scolding women*
60 Mount up, and take a salamander's name.
Soft yielding minds to water glide away,
And sip with Nymphs, their elemental tea.
The graver prude sinks downward to a Gnome,
In search of mischief still on earth to roam.
65 The light coquettes in Sylphs aloft repair,
And sport and flutter in the fields of air.
    "Know farther yet; whoever fair and chaste
Rejects mankind, is by some Sylph embraced:
For spirits, freed from mortal laws, with ease
70 Assume what sexes and what shapes they please.[6]
What guards the purity of melting maids,[7]
In courtly balls, and midnight masquerades,
Safe from the treach'rous friend, the daring spark,[8]
The glance by day, the whisper in the dark;
75 When kind occasion prompts their warm desires,
When music softens, and when dancing fires?
'Tis but their Sylph, the wise celestials know,
Though *Honor* is the word with men below.

8. Religious skepticism was on the increase.
9. The theater box and the equally fashionable drive round Hyde Park.
1. Carriage, horses, and attendants.
2. A sedan chair, carried by two chairmen.
3. Both the carriage, and the physical body.
4. Ombre (pronounced Omber) was an elaborate card game, introduced into England in the 17th century and highly fashionable in the early 18th century. Given the general tenor of the poem, Pope may also be punning on the origin of the word "Ombre," from the Spanish *hombre*, meaning "man."
5. The four elements of fire, water, earth, and air were thought to make up all things; so an individual's character was determined by whichever element dominated his or her soul.
6. Cf. *Paradise Lost*, "For spirits when they please / Can either sex assume, or both" (1.423–24).
7. I.e., the chastity of weakening virgins.
8. A bold, brash, and showy young man.

"Some nymphs there are, too conscious of their face,
For life predestined to the Gnomes' embrace.
These swell their prospects and exalt their pride,
When offers are disdained, and love denied.
Then gay ideas crowd the vacant brain;
While peers° and dukes, and all their sweeping train,   *aristocrats*
And garters, stars, and coronets[9] appear,
And in soft sounds, 'your Grace'[1] salutes their ear.
'Tis these that early taint the female soul,
Instruct the eyes of young coquettes to roll,
Teach infant cheeks a bidden° blush to know,   *deliberate*
And little hearts to flutter at a beau.
   "Oft when the world imagine women stray,
The Sylphs through mystic mazes guide their way,
Through all the giddy circle they pursue,
And old impertinence° expel by new.   *frivolity*
What tender maid but must a victim fall
To one man's treat, but for another's ball?
When Florio speaks, what virgin could withstand,
If gentle Damon did not squeeze her hand?
With varying vanities, from ev'ry part,
They shift the moving toy shop[2] of their heart;
Where wigs with wigs, with sword knots sword knots strive,[3]
Beaus banish beaus, and coaches coaches drive.[4]
This erring mortals levity may call,
Oh blind to truth! the Sylphs contrive it all.
   "Of these am I, who thy protection claim,
A watchful sprite, and Ariel is my name.
Late, as I ranged the crystal wilds of air,
In the clear mirror of thy ruling star
I saw, alas! some dread event impend,
Ere to the main° this morning sun descend.   *sea*
But Heav'n reveals not what, or how, or where:
Warned by thy Sylph, oh pious maid beware!
This to disclose is all thy guardian can.
Beware of all, but most beware of man!"
   He said; when Shock,[5] who thought she slept too long,
Leapt up, and waked his mistress with his tongue.
'Twas then Belinda! if report say true,
Thy eyes first opened on a *billet-doux*;°   *love letter*
Wounds, charms, and ardors, were no sooner read,
But all the vision vanished from thy head.
   And now, unveiled, the toilet° stands displayed,   *dressing table*
Each silver vase in mystic order laid.
First, robed in white, the nymph intent adores
With head uncovered, the cosmetic pow'rs.

Line numbers: 80, 85, 90, 95, 100, 105, 110, 115, 120

9. Emblems of noble rank.
1. Form of address for a duke or a duchess.
2. Where toys and trinkets are sold; "moving" here means easily changed, unstable.
3. Most men wore wigs in public; formally dressed men tied ribbons to the hilt of their swords.
4. In word order and versification, these two lines mimic both Homer's and Ovid's description of heroic combat.
5. The shock or shough, a long-haired Icelandic poodle, fashionable as a lapdog.

125   A heav'nly image[6] in the glass appears,
    To that she bends, to that her eyes she rears;°   *raises*
    Th' inferior priestess,[7] at her altar's side,
    Trembling, begins the sacred rites of pride.
    Unnumbered treasures ope at once, and here
130   The various off'rings of the world appear;
    From each she nicely culls with curious° toil,   *careful*
    And decks the goddess with the glitt'ring spoil.
    This casket India's glowing gems unlocks,
    And all Arabia° breathes from yonder box.   *eastern perfume*
135   The tortoise here and elephant unite,
    Transformed to combs, the speckled and the white.[8]
    Here files of pins extend their shining rows,
    Puffs, powders, patches, Bibles,[9] *billet-doux*.
    Now awful° beauty puts on all its arms;   *awe-inspiring*
140   The fair each moment rises in her charms,
    Repairs her smiles, awakens ev'ry grace,
    And calls forth all the wonders of her face;
    Sees by degrees a purer blush[1] arise,
    And keener lightnings[2] quicken in her eyes.
145   The busy Sylphs surround their darling care;
    These set the head, and those divide the hair,
    Some fold the sleeve, whilst others plait the gown;
    And Betty's praised for labors not her own.

CANTO 2

    Not with more glories, in th' ethereal plain,°   *sky*
    The sun first rises o'er the purpled main,
    Than issuing forth, the rival of his beams
    Launched on the bosom of the silver Thames.[1]
5   Fair nymphs, and well-dressed youths around her shone,
    But ev'ry eye was fixed on her alone.
    On her white breast a sparkling cross she wore,
    Which Jews might kiss, and infidels adore.[2]
    Her lively looks a sprightly mind disclose,
10   Quick as her eyes, and as unfixed as those:
    Favors to none, to all she smiles extends,
    Oft she rejects, but never once offends.
    Bright as the sun, her eyes the gazers strike,
    And, like the sun, they shine on all alike.
15   Yet graceful ease, and sweetness void of pride,
    Might hide her faults, if belles had faults to hide:
    If to her share some female errors fall,
    Look on her face, and you'll forget 'em all.

---

6. I.e., Belinda herself.
7. Belinda's maid, Betty.
8. Tortoise-shell and ivory.
9. Patches were small beauty spots of black silk, pasted onto the face to make the skin appear whiter. It was fashionable to own Bibles in very small format.
1. The even, artificial blush of rouge.
2. Caused by drops of belladonna (deadly nightshade),

which dilates the pupils.
1. Belinda takes a boat from London to Hampton Court, avoiding the dirt and squalor of the streets; her voyage compares with Aeneas's up the Tiber (*Aeneid* 7), or, alternatively, Cleopatra's up the Nile (*Antony and Cleopatra* 2.2).
2. Kissing the cross was the sign of religious conversion.

This nymph, to the destruction of mankind,
20　Nourished two locks which graceful hung behind
In equal curls, and well conspired to deck
With shining ringlets the smooth iv'ry neck.
Love in these labyrinths his slaves detains,
And mighty hearts are held in slender chains.
25　With hairy springes° we the birds betray,　　　　　　　　　　*noose traps*
Slight lines° of hair surprise the finny prey,　　　　　　　　*fishing lines*
Fair tresses man's imperial race ensnare,
And beauty draws us with a single hair.
　　Th' adventurous Baron[3] the bright locks admired,
30　He saw, he wished, and to the prize aspired:
Resolved to win, he meditates the way,
By force to ravish, or by fraud betray;
For when success a lover's toil attends,
Few ask, if fraud or force attained his ends.
35　　For this, ere Phoebus rose, he had implored
Propitious Heav'n, and ev'ry pow'r adored,°　　　　　　　　　*worshipped*
But chiefly *Love*—to *Love* an altar built,
Of twelve vast French romances, neatly gilt.
There lay three garters, half a pair of gloves;
40　And all the trophies of his former loves.
With tender *billet-doux* he lights the pyre,
And breathes three am'rous sighs to raise the fire.
Then prostrate falls, and begs with ardent eyes
Soon to obtain, and long possess the prize:
45　The pow'rs gave ear, and granted half his pray'r,
The rest the winds dispersed in empty air.[4]
　　But now secure the painted vessel glides,
The sunbeams trembling on the floating tides,
While melting music steals upon the sky,
50　And softened sounds along the waters die.
Smooth flow the waves, the zephyrs° gently play,　　　　　　　*breezes*
Belinda smiled, and all the world was gay.
All but the Sylph—with careful° thoughts oppressed,　　　　　*worried*
Th' impending woe sat heavy on his breast.
55　He summons strait his denizens[5] of air;
The lucid squadrons round the sails repair:
Soft o'er the shrouds° aerial whispers breathe,　　　　　　　　*ropes*
That seemed but zephyrs to the train beneath.
Some to the sun their insect wings unfold,
60　Waft on the breeze, or sink in clouds of gold.
Transparent forms, too fine for mortal sight,
Their fluid bodies half dissolved in light,
Loose to the wind their airy garments flew,
Thin glitt'ring textures of the filmy dew;
65　Dipped in the richest tincture of the skies,

---

3. Robert, Lord Petre (1690–1713), responsible for the original incident.
4. Cf. *The Aeneid* 2.794–95, which Dryden translated:
"Apollo heard, and granting half his pray'r, / Shuffled in winds the rest, and toss'd in empty air."
5. Naturalized foreigner.

Where light disports in ever-mingling dyes,
While ev'ry beam new transient colors flings,
Colors that change whene'er they wave their wings.
Amid the circle, on the gilded mast,
70   Superior by the head, was Ariel placed;[6]
His purple pinions opening to the sun,
He raised his azure wand, and thus begun:
    "Ye Sylphs and Sylphids,° to your chief give ear,   *female Sylphs*
Fays, Fairies, Genii, Elves, and Demons hear!
75   Ye know the spheres and various tasks assigned,
By laws eternal to th' aerial kind.
Some in the fields of purest ether[7] play,
And bask and whiten in the blaze of day.
Some guide the course of wandering orbs° on high,   *comets*
80   Or roll the planets through the boundless sky.
Some less refined, beneath the moon's pale light
Pursue the stars that shoot athwart the night,
Or suck the mists in grosser° air below,   *heavier*
Or dip their pinions in the painted bow,°   *rainbow*
85   Or brew fierce tempests on the wintry main,
Or o'er the glebe° distill the kindly rain.   *farmland*
Others on earth o'er human race preside,
Watch all their ways, and all their actions guide:
Of these the chief the care of nations own,
90   And guard with arms divine the British throne.
    "Our humbler province is to tend the fair,
Not a less pleasing, though less glorious care.
To save the powder from too rude° a gale,   *rough*
Nor let th' imprisoned essences° exhale,   *perfumes*
95   To draw fresh colors from the vernal flow'rs,
To steal from rainbows ere they drop in show'rs
A brighter wash;[8] to curl their waving hairs,
Assist their blushes, and inspire their airs;
Nay oft, in dreams, invention we bestow,
100   To change a flounce, or add a furbelow.°   *fringe*
    "This day, black omens threat the brightest fair
That e'er deserved a watchful spirit's care;
Some dire disaster, or° by force or sleight,°   *either / trick*
But what, or where, the fates have wrapped in night.
105   Whether the nymph shall break Diana's law,°   *virginity*
Or some frail China jar receive a flaw,
Or stain her honor, or her new brocade,
Forget her pray'rs, or miss a masquerade,
Or lose her heart, or necklace, at a ball;
110   Or whether Heav'n has doomed that Shock must fall.
Haste then ye spirits! to your charge° repair;   *duty*
The flutt'ring fan be Zephyretta's care;
The drops° to thee, Brillante, we consign;   *earrings*

6. Heroes of epics were typically taller than their men.   8. A cosmetic rinse.
7. Air beyond the moon.

And, Momentilla, let the watch be thine;
115   Do thou, Crispissa,[9] tend her fav'rite lock;
Ariel himself shall be the guard of Shock.
    "To fifty chosen Sylphs, of special note,
We trust th' important charge, the petticoat:
Oft have we known that sev'nfold fence[1] to fail,
120   Though stiff with hoops, and armed with ribs of whale.
Form a strong line about the silver bound,
And guard the wide circumference around.
    "Whatever spirit, careless of his charge,
His post neglects, or leaves the fair at large,
125   Shall feel sharp vengeance soon o'ertake his sins,
Be stopped in vials, or transfixed with pins;
Or plunged in lakes of bitter washes lie,
Or wedged whole ages in a bodkin's[2] eye:
Gums and pomatums° shall his flight restrain,   ointments
130   While clogged he beats his silken wings in vain;
Or alum styptics[3] with contracting power
Shrink his thin essence like a rivelled° flower.   shriveled
Or as Ixion[4] fixed, the wretch shall feel
The giddy motion of the whirling mill,[5]
135   In fumes of burning chocolate shall glow,
And tremble at the sea that froths below!"
    He spoke; the spirits from the sails descend;
Some, orb in orb, around the nymph extend,
Some thrid° the mazy ringlets of her hair,   slid through
140   Some hang upon the pendants of her ear;
With beating hearts the dire event they wait,
Anxious, and trembling for the birth of fate.

CANTO 3

Close by those meads forever crowned with flow'rs,
Where Thames with pride surveys his rising tow'rs,
There stands a structure of majestic frame,
Which from the neighb'ring Hampton takes its name.[1]
5   Here Britain's statesmen oft the fall foredoom
Of foreign tyrants, and of nymphs at home;
Here thou, great Anna! whom three realms obey,[2]
Dost sometimes counsel take—and sometimes tea.
    Hither the heroes and the nymphs resort,
10   To taste awhile the pleasures of a court;
In various talk th' instructive hours they passed,

9. The Latin *crispere* means "to curl."
1. Serving Belinda like the epic warrior's shield, her petticoat has seven layers bound together with a silver band
(cf. *Iliad* 18 or *Aeneid* 8).
2. Blunt, thick needle; the Sylph, like the camel in
Matthew 19.24, has difficulty getting through. Pope later
plays on the various meanings of "bodkin," which also
include a hair ornament and a dagger.
3. Astringents that stopped bleeding.

4. Having tried the chastity of Hera, Ixion was punished
by being tied to a revolving wheel of fire.
5. For grinding cocoa beans.
1. Hampton Court, about 15 miles upriver from London,
was built in the 16th century by Cardinal Wolsey, and by
Queen Anne's day was associated with wits as well as
with statesmen.
2. The English Crown still maintained its ancient claim
to rule France as well as Great Britain and Ireland.

    Who gave the ball, or paid the visit last:
    One speaks the glory of the British Queen,
    And one describes a charming Indian screen;
15   A third interprets motions, looks, and eyes;
    At ev'ry word a reputation dies.
    Snuff, or the fan, supply each pause of chat,
    With singing, laughing, ogling, and all that.
       Meanwhile declining from the noon of day,
20   The sun obliquely shoots his burning ray;
    The hungry judges soon the sentence sign,
    And wretches hang that jurymen may dine;
    The merchant from th' Exchange° returns in peace,   *market*
    And the long labors of the toilette cease—
25   Belinda now, whom thirst of fame invites,
    Burns to encounter two advent'rous knights,
    At Ombre[3] singly to decide their doom;
    And swells her breast with conquests yet to come.
    Straight the three bands prepare in arms to join,
30   Each band the number of the Sacred Nine.[4]
    Soon as she spreads her hand, th' aerial guard
    Descend, and sit on each important card:
    First Ariel perched upon a Matador,[5]
    Then each, according to the rank they bore;
35   For Sylphs, yet mindful of their ancient race,
    Are, as when women, wondrous fond of place.°   *rank*
       Behold, four kings in majesty revered,
    With hoary whiskers[6] and a forky beard;
    And four fair queens whose hands sustain° a flow'r,   *hold*
40   Th' expressive emblem of their softer pow'r;
    Four knaves in garbs succinct,° a trusty band,   *girded up*
    Caps on their heads, and halberds in their hand;
    And particolored troops, a shining train,
    Draw forth to combat on the velvet plain.[7]
45   The skillful nymph reviews her force with care;
    "Let spades be trumps!" she said, and trumps they were.[8]
       Now move to war her sable Matadors,
    In show like leaders of the swarthy moors.
    Spadillio first, unconquerable lord!
50   Led off two captive trumps, and swept the board.
    As many more Manillio forced to yield,
    And marched a victor from the verdant field.
    Him Basto followed, but his fate more hard
    Gained but one trump and one plebeian card.

3. A card game played with 40 cards, similar to modern bridge: three players hold nine cards each and bid for tricks, with the highest bidder becoming the "ombre" (man) and choosing trumps.
4. Pope links the nine Muses to the nine cards each player holds.
5. The Matadores are the three cards of highest value; Belinda holds all three: when trumps are black, they are the Spadillio (ace of spades), Manillio (deuce of spades),
and Basto (ace of clubs).
6. Gray mustache. The royal figures on the cards now conduct a mock-epic review of their forces, and the whole game is described as an epic battle, with the characters appearing as on the cards.
7. The green velvet card table.
8. Cf. Genesis 1.3, "Then God said, 'Let there be light'; and there was light."

55   With his broad saber next, a chief in years,
     The hoary majesty of spades appears;
     Puts forth one manly leg, to sight revealed;
     The rest his many-colored robe concealed.
     The rebel knave who dares his prince engage,
60   Proves the just victim of his royal rage.
     Ev'n mighty Pam[9] that kings and queens o'erthrew,
     And mowed down armies in the fights of Lu,
     Sad chance of war! now, destitute of aid,
     Falls undistinguished by the victor spade!
65   Thus far both armies to Belinda yield;
     Now to the Baron fate inclines the field.
     His warlike amazon her host invades,
     Th' imperial consort of the crown of spades.
     The club's black tyrant first her victim died,
70   Spite of his haughty mien and barb'rous pride:
     What boots the regal circle on his head,
     His giant limbs in state unwieldy spread?
     That long behind he trails his pompous robe,
     And of all monarchs only grasps the globe?
75   The Baron now his diamonds pours apace;
     Th' embroidered king who shows but half his face,
     And his refulgent queen, with pow'rs combined,
     Of broken troops an easy conquest find.
     Clubs, diamonds, hearts, in wild disorder seen,
80   With throngs promiscuous strew the level green.
     Thus when dispersed a routed army runs,
     Of Asia's troops and Afric's sable sons,
     With like confusion different nations fly,
     Of various habit and of various dye,
85   The pierced battalions disunited fall,
     In heaps on heaps; one fate o'erwhelms them all.
         The knave of diamonds tries his wily arts,
     And wins (oh shameful chance!) the queen of hearts.
     At this, the blood the virgin's cheek forsook,
90   A livid paleness spreads o'er all her look;
     She sees, and trembles at th' approaching ill,
     Just in the jaws of ruin, and codille.[1]
     And now (as oft in some distempered state)
     On one nice trick[2] depends the gen'ral fate.
95   An ace of hearts steps forth: the king[3] unseen
     Lurked in her hand, and mourned his captive queen.
     He springs to vengeance with an eager pace,
     And falls like thunder on the prostrate ace.
     The nymph exulting fills with shouts the sky,
100 The walls, the woods, and long canals reply.
         Oh thoughtless mortals! ever blind to fate,

---

9. The knave or jack of clubs, which took precedence
over all trumps in the game of Lu, or Loo.
1. Literally "elbow": the defeat suffered by the ombre if
another player wins more tricks.

2. Trick applies in both its technical and general senses as
Belinda makes this careful maneuver.
3. The King of Hearts.

Too soon dejected, and too soon elate!
Sudden these honors shall be snatched away,
And cursed forever this victorious day.
105   For lo! the board with cups and spoons is crowned,
The berries crackle, and the Mill turns round.[4]
On shining altars of Japan[5] they raise
The silver lamp; the fiery spirits blaze.
From silver spouts the grateful° liquors glide,   *pleasing*
110   While China's earth receives the smoking tide.
At once they gratify their scent and taste,
And frequent cups prolong the rich repast.
Straight° hover round the fair her airy band;   *immediately*
Some, as she sipped, the fuming liquor fanned,
115   Some o'er her lap their careful plumes displayed,
Trembling, and conscious of the rich brocade.
Coffee (which makes the politician wise,
And see through all things with his half-shut eyes)
Sent up in vapors[6] to the Baron's brain
120   New stratagems, the radiant lock to gain.
Ah cease rash youth! desist ere 'tis too late,
Fear the just gods, and think of Scylla's fate![7]
Changed to a bird, and sent to flit in air,
She dearly pays for Nisus' injured hair!
125   But when to mischief mortals bend their will,
How soon they find fit instruments of ill!
Just then, Clarissa drew with tempting grace
A two-edged weapon from her shining case;
So ladies in romance assist their knight,
130   Present the spear, and arm him for the fight.
He takes the gift with rev'rence, and extends
The little engine° on his fingers' ends,   *instrument*
This just behind Belinda's neck he spread,
As o'er the fragrant steams she bends her head:
135   Swift to the lock a thousand sprites repair,
A thousand wings, by turns, blow back the hair,
And thrice they twitched the diamond in her ear,
Thrice she looked back, and thrice the foe drew near.
Just in that instant, anxious Ariel sought
140   The close recesses of the virgin's thought;
As on the nosegay in her breast reclined,
He watched th' ideas rising in her mind,
Sudden he viewed, in spite of all her art,
An earthly lover° lurking at her heart.   *Lord Petre*
145   Amazed, confused, he found his pow'r expired,
Resigned to fate, and with a sigh retired.
    The peer now spreads the glitt'ring forfex° wide,   *scissors*
T' enclose the lock; now joins it, to divide.

---

4. Grinding coffee beans.
5. Lacquered tables ("Japan" was a type of varnish originating in that country).
6. Both steam and vain imaginations.

7. Scylla plucked purple hair from the head of her father, King Nisus, to offer to her lover, Minos, so destroying her father's power. Minos rejected her impiety, and Scylla was transformed into a bird.

Ev'n then, before the fatal engine closed,
150 A wretched Sylph too fondly interposed;
Fate urged the shears, and cut the Sylph in twain
(But airy substance soon unites again)[8]
The meeting points the sacred hair dissever
From the fair head, forever and forever!
155   Then flashed the living lightning from her eyes,
And screams of horror rend th' affrighted skies.
Not louder shrieks to pitying Heav'n are cast,
When husbands or when lapdogs breathe their last,
Or when rich china vessels, fall'n from high,
160 In glitt'ring dust and painted fragments lie!
     Let wreaths of triumph now my temples twine,
(The victor cried) the glorious prize is mine!
While fish in streams, or birds delight in air,
Or in a coach and six[9] the British fair,
165 As long as Atalantis[1] shall be read,
Or the small pillow grace a lady's bed,[2]
While visits shall be paid on solemn days,
When numerous wax lights[3] in bright order blaze,
While nymphs take treats, or assignations give,
170 So long my honor, name, and praise shall live!
     What time would spare, from steel receives its date,°   end
And monuments, like men, submit to fate!
Steel could the labor of the gods destroy,
And strike to dust th' imperial tow'rs of Troy;[4]
175 Steel could the works of mortal pride confound,
And hew triumphal arches to the ground.
What wonder then, fair nymph! thy hairs should feel
The conqu'ring force of unresisted steel?

CANTO 4

But anxious cares the pensive nymph oppressed,
And secret passions labored in her breast.
Not youthful kings in battle seized alive,
Not scornful virgins who their charms survive,
5 Not ardent lovers robbed of all their bliss,
Not ancient ladies when refused a kiss,
Not tyrants fierce that unrepenting die,
Not Cynthia when her manteau's° pinned awry,   gown's
E'er felt such rage, resentment, and despair,
10 As thou, sad virgin! for thy ravished hair.
     For, that sad moment, when the Sylphs withdrew,

8. *Milton* lib. 6 [Pope's note], citing *Paradise Lost*
6.329–31, "The girding sword with discontinuous
wound / Passed through him, but the ethereal substance
closed / Not long divisible. . . ."
9. A carriage drawn by six horses; a symbol of wealth and
prestige.
1. The scandalous *Atalantis: Secret Memoirs and Manners
of Several Persons of Quality* (1709), by Mary Delarivière

Manley.
2. Said to be a place where ladies hid romance novels and
other contraband.
3. Candles made of wax, rather than the cheaper tallow.
Evening social visits were an essential part of the fashionable woman's routine.
4. Even Troy, fabled to have been built by Apollo and
Poseidon, was destroyed by arms.

And Ariel weeping from Belinda flew,
Umbriel, a dusky melancholy sprite
As ever sullied the fair face of light,
15   Down to the central earth, his proper scene,
Repaired to search the gloomy Cave of Spleen.[1]
    Swift on his sooty pinions flits the Gnome,
And in a vapor[2] reached the dismal dome.
No cheerful breeze this sullen region knows,
20   The dreaded east[3] is all the wind that blows.
Here, in a grotto, sheltered close from air,
And screened in shades° from day's detested glare,   *shadows*
She sighs forever on her pensive bed,
Pain at her side, and Megrim° at her head.   *migraine*
25   Two handmaids wait the throne: alike in place,
But diff'ring far in figure and in face.
Here stood Ill-Nature like an ancient maid,
Her wrinkled form in black and white arrayed;
With store of pray'rs, for mornings, nights, and noons,
30   Her hand is filled; her bosom with lampoons.
    There Affectation with a sickly mien
Shows in her cheek the roses of eighteen,
Practiced to lisp, and hang the head aside,
Faints into airs, and languishes with pride;
35   On the rich quilt sinks with becoming woe,
Wrapped in a gown, for sickness, and for show.
The fair ones feel such maladies as these,
When each new nightdress gives a new disease.
    A constant vapor o'er the palace flies;
40   Strange phantoms rising as the mists arise;
Dreadful, as hermit's dreams in haunted shades,
Or bright as visions of expiring maids.[4]
Now glaring fiends, and snakes on rolling spires,°   *coils*
Pale specters, gaping tombs, and purple fires:
45   Now lakes of liquid gold, Elysian scenes,[5]
And crystal domes, and angels in machines.
    Unnumbered throngs on ev'ry side are seen
Of bodies changed to various forms by Spleen.[6]
Here living teapots stand, one arm held out,
50   One bent; the handle this, and that the spout:
A pipkin[7] there like Homer's tripod walks;
Here sighs a jar, and there a goose pie[8] talks;
Men prove with child, as pow'rful fancy works,
And maids, turned bottles, call aloud for corks.

---

1. Named after the bodily organ, "spleen" was the current name for the fashionable affliction of melancholy or ill-humor. Umbriel's descent into the womb-like Cave of Spleen suggests the epic commonplace of the journey to the underworld.
2. "The spleen" was also called "the vapors."
3. The east wind was supposed to induce fits of spleen.
4. Religious visions of hell and heaven.
5. Elysium was the classical paradise, but this also recalls contemporary theater, which made much of scenic spectacle and the use of machinery.
6. Hallucinations similar to those described in the following lines were common to those afflicted with spleen.
7. Small pot or pan. Hephaistos's "walking" tripods are described in the *Iliad* 18.439ff.
8. Alludes to a real fact, a Lady of distinction imagin'd herself in this condition [Pope's note].

55   Safe passed the Gnome through this fantastic band,
      A branch of healing spleenwort⁹ in his hand.
      Then thus addressed the pow'r—"Hail, wayward Queen!
      Who rule the sex to fifty from fifteen,
      Parent of vapors and of female wit,
60   Who give th' hysteric or poetic fit,
      On various tempers act by various ways,
      Make some take physic,° others scribble plays;¹   *medicine*
      Who cause the proud their visits to delay,
      And send the godly in a pet° to pray.   *ill-humor*
65   A nymph there is that all thy pow'r disdains,
      And thousands more in equal mirth maintains.
      But oh! if e'er thy Gnome could spoil a grace,
      Or raise a pimple on a beauteous face,
      Like citron-waters° matrons' cheeks inflame,   *flavored brandy*
70   Or change complexions at a losing game;
      If e'er with airy horns² I planted heads,
      Or rumpled petticoats, or tumbled beds,
      Or caused suspicion when no soul was rude,
      Or discomposed the headdress of a prude,
75   Or e'er to costive° lapdog gave disease,   *constipated*
      Which not the tears of brightest eyes could ease:
      Hear me, and touch Belinda with chagrin;
      That single act gives half the world the spleen."
          The goddess with a discontented air
80   Seems to reject him, though she grants his pray'r.
      A wondrous bag with both her hands she binds,
      Like that where once Ulysses held the winds;³
      There she collects the force of female lungs,
      Sighs, sobs, and passions, and the war of tongues.
85   A vial next she fills with fainting fears,
      Soft sorrows, melting griefs, and flowing tears.
      The Gnome rejoicing bears her gifts away,
      Spreads his black wings, and slowly mounts to day.
          Sunk in Thalestris'⁴ arms the nymph he found,
90   Her eyes dejected and her hair unbound.
      Full o'er their heads the swelling bag he rent,
      And all the furies issued at the vent.
      Belinda burns with more than mortal ire,
      And fierce Thalestris fans the rising fire.
95   "O wretched maid!" she spread her hands, and cried,
      (While Hampton's echoes "Wretched maid!" replied)
      "Was it for this you took such constant care
      The bodkin, comb, and essence to prepare;
      For this your locks in paper durance° bound,   *curling papers*
100   For this with tort'ring irons wreathed around?

9. Pope changes the golden bough that protected Aeneas
on his trip through the underworld into an herb that was
supposed to be good for the spleen.
1. Melancholy was associated with artistic creativity.
2. A sign that a husband had been cuckolded.

3. Given to him by the wind god Aeolus (*Odyssey*
10.19ff.).
4. A queen of the Amazons; here Mrs. Morley, Arabella's
second cousin.

For this with fillets[5] strained your tender head,
And bravely bore the double loads of lead?°   *wire supports*
Gods! shall the ravisher display your hair,
While the fops envy, and the ladies stare!

105   Honor forbid! at whose unrivaled shrine
Ease, pleasure, virtue, all, our sex resign.
Methinks already I your tears survey,
Already hear the horrid things they say,
Already see you a degraded toast,[6]

110   And all your honor in a whisper lost!
How shall I, then, your helpless fame defend?
'Twill then be infamy to seem your friend!
And shall this prize, th' inestimable prize,
Exposed through crystal to the gazing eyes,

115   And heightened by the diamond's circling rays,
On that rapacious hand forever blaze?[7]
Sooner shall grass in Hyde Park Circus grow,[8]
And wits take lodgings in the sound of Bow;[9]
Sooner let earth, air, sea, to Chaos fall,

120   Men, monkeys, lapdogs, parrots, perish all!"
     She said; then raging to Sir Plume[1] repairs,
And bids her beau demand the precious hairs:
(Sir Plume, of amber snuffbox justly vain,
And the nice conduct of a clouded cane[2])

125   With earnest eyes, and round unthinking face,
He first the snuffbox opened, then the case,
And thus broke out—"My Lord, why, what the devil?
Z—ds![3] damn the lock! 'fore Gad, you must be civil!
Plague on't! 'tis past a jest—nay prithee, Pox!

130   Give her the hair"—he spoke, and rapped his box.
     "It grieves me much" (replied the Peer again)
"Who speaks so well should ever speak in vain.
But by this lock, this sacred lock I swear
(Which never more shall join its parted hair,

135   Which never more its honors shall renew,
Clipped from the lovely head where late it grew)
That while my nostrils draw the vital air,
This hand which won it shall forever wear."
He spoke, and speaking, in proud triumph spread

140   The long-contended honors[4] of her head.
     But Umbriel, hateful Gnome! forbears not so;
He breaks the vial whence the sorrows flow.
Then see! the nymph in beauteous grief appears,

---

5. Headbands, with reference to priestesses in the *Aeneid*.
6. A woman whose toast is often drunk, and who by implication is all too well known to her (male) toasters: (cf. Canto 5.10, and Fielding's *Tom Jones*, where Sophia is not pleased by reports that she has been Tom's toast, bk. 13, ch. 11).
7. I.e., mounted in a ring.
8. The fashion for driving coaches around Hyde Park pre-

vented grass from growing there.
9. A commercial area around St. Mary-le-Bow, and not at all fashionable.
1. Sir George Browne, cousin of Arabella's mother.
2. Skilled use of a cane with a head of dark polished stone.
3. Zounds, a corruption of "God's wounds," a mild oath.
4. Her beautiful hair.

Her eyes half-languishing, half-drowned in tears;
145 On her heaved bosom hung her drooping head,
Which, with a sigh, she raised; and thus she said:
    "Forever cursed be this detested day,⁵
Which snatched my best, my fav'rite curl away!
Happy! ah ten times happy, had I been,
150 If Hampton Court these eyes had never seen!
Yet am not I the first mistaken maid,
By love of courts to num'rous ills betrayed.
Oh had I rather unadmired remained
In some lone isle, or distant northern land;
155 Where the gilt chariot never marks the way,
Where none learn Ombre, none e'er taste bohea!°   tea
There kept my charms concealed from mortal eye,
Like roses that in deserts bloom and die.
What moved my mind with youthful lords to roam?
160 O had I stayed, and said my pray'rs at home!
'Twas this, the morning omens seemed to tell;
Thrice from my trembling hand the patch box fell;
The tott'ring china shook without a wind,
Nay, Poll° sat mute, and Shock was most unkind!   her parrot
165 A Sylph too warned me of the threats of fate,
In mystic visions, now believed too late!
See the poor remnants of these slighted hairs!
My hands shall rend what ev'n thy rapine spares:
These, in two sable ringlets taught to break,°   divide
170 Once gave new beauties to the snowy neck.
The sister lock now sits uncouth, alone,
And in its fellow's fate foresees its own;
Uncurled it hangs, the fatal shears demands;
And tempts once more thy sacrilegious hands.
175 Oh hadst thou, cruel! been content to seize
Hairs less in sight, or any hairs but these!"

CANTO 5

She said: the pitying audience melt in tears,
But Fate and Jove had stopped the Baron's ears.
In vain Thalestris with reproach assails,
For who can move when fair Belinda fails?
5 Not half so fixed the Trojan¹ could remain,
While Anna begged and Dido raged in vain.
Then grave Clarissa² graceful waved her fan;
Silence ensued, and thus the nymph began.
    "Say, why are beauties praised and honored most,
10 The wise man's passion, and the vain man's toast?

---

5. Echoing Achilles' lament for his slain friend Patroclus
(*Iliad* 18.107ff.).
1. Aeneas, fixed on his decision to leave Carthage and
abandon Dido despite her pleas and those of her sister
Anna (*Aeneid* 4.269–449).

2. A new character introduced . . . to open more clearly
the moral of the poem, in a parody of the speech of
Sarpedon to Glaucus in Homer [Pope's note in the 1717
edition]. Sarpedon's speech (*Iliad* 12) is a famous reflection on glory.

Why decked with all that land and sea afford,
Why angels called, and angel-like adored?
Why round our coaches crowd the white-gloved beaus,
Why bows the side box from its inmost rows?[3]
15 How vain are all these glories, all our pains,
Unless good sense preserve what beauty gains:
That men may say when we the front box grace,
Behold the first in virtue as in face!
Oh! if to dance all night, and dress all day,
20 Charmed the smallpox,[4] or chased old age away;
Who would not scorn what housewife's cares produce,
Or who would learn one earthly thing of use?
To patch, nay ogle, might become a saint,
Nor could it sure be such a sin to paint.
25 But since, alas! frail beauty must decay,
Curled or uncurled, since locks will turn to gray,
Since painted or not painted, all shall fade,
And she who scorns a man, must die a maid;
What then remains, but well our pow'r to use,
30 And keep good humor still whate'er we lose?
And trust me, dear! good humor can prevail,
When airs, and flights, and screams, and scolding fail.
Beauties in vain their pretty eyes may roll;
Charms strike the sight, but merit wins the soul."
35   So spoke the dame, but no applause ensued;
Belinda frowned, Thalestris called her prude.
"To arms, to arms!" the fierce virago[5] cries,
And swift as lightning to the combat flies.
All side in parties, and begin th' attack;
40 Fans clap, silks rustle, and tough whalebones crack;
Heroes' and heroines' shouts confus'dly rise,
And bass and treble voices strike the skies.
No common weapons in their hands are found,
Like gods they fight, nor dread a mortal wound.
45   So when bold Homer makes the gods engage,
And heav'nly breasts with human passions rage;
'Gainst Pallas,° Mars; Latona,[6] Hermes arms;   Athena
And all Olympus rings with loud alarms.
Jove's thunder roars, Heav'n trembles all around;
50 Blue Neptune storms, the bellowing deeps resound;
Earth shakes her nodding tow'rs, the ground gives way;
And the pale ghosts start at the flash of day!
    Triumphant Umbriel on a sconce's[7] height
Clapped his glad wings, and sat to view the fight:
55 Propped on their bodkin spears, the sprites survey
The growing combat, or assist the fray.
    While through the press enraged Thalestris flies,

3. At the theater, gentlemen sat in the side boxes, ladies in the front boxes facing the stage.
4. A common disease, which frequently left permanent facial scars.
5. Woman who behaves like a man.
6. Mother of Diana and Apollo.
7. Candlestick attached to the wall.

And scatters deaths around from both her eyes,
A beau and witling° perished in the throng,   *little wit*
60   One died in metaphor, and one in song.
"O cruel Nymph! a living death I bear,"
Cried Dapperwit, and sunk beside his chair.
A mournful glance Sir Fopling upwards cast,
"Those eyes are made so killing"[8]—was his last:
65   Thus on Meander's flow'ry margin lies
Th' expiring swan, and as he sings he dies.[9]
     When bold Sir Plume had drawn Clarissa down,
Chloe stepped in, and killed him with a frown;
She smiled to see the doughty hero slain,
70   But at her smile the beau revived again.
     Now Jove suspends his golden scales in air,[1]
Weighs the men's wits against the lady's hair;
The doubtful beam long nods from side to side;
At length the wits mount up, the hairs subside.
75   See fierce Belinda on the Baron flies,
With more than usual lightning in her eyes;
Nor feared the chief th' unequal fight to try,
Who sought no more than on his foe to die.[2]
But this bold lord, with manly strength indued,
80   She with one finger and a thumb subdued:
Just where the breath of life his nostrils drew,
A charge of snuff the wily virgin threw;
The Gnomes direct, to ev'ry atom just,
The pungent grains of titillating dust.
85   Sudden, with starting tears each eye o'erflows,
And the high dome re-echoes to his nose.[3]
     "Now meet thy fate," incensed Belinda cried,
And drew a deadly bodkin from her side.
(The same, his ancient personage to deck,
90   Her great-great-grandsire wore about his neck
In three seal rings; which after, melted down,
Formed a vast buckle for his widow's gown:
Her infant grandame's° whistle next it grew,   *grandmother's*
The bells she jingled, and the whistle blew;
95   Then in a bodkin[4] graced her mother's hairs,
Which long she wore, and now Belinda wears.)
     "Boast not my fall" (he cried) "insulting foe!
Thou by some other shalt be laid as low.
Nor think, to die dejects my lofty mind;
100   All that I dread is leaving you behind!
Rather than so, ah let me still survive,
And burn in Cupid's flames—but burn alive."
     "Restore the lock!" she cries; and all around

---

8. A line from Giovanni Bononcini's opera, *Camilla* (1696), which at this time was popular in London.
9. Meander: a river in Asia Minor. Swans were popularly believed to sing only on their death. This simile refers to Ovid's *Heroides* 7, a lament from Dido to Aeneas.

1. To determine victory in battle; a convention found in both Homer and Virgil.
2. A standard metaphor for sexual climax.
3. Cf. his boast, 4.133–38.
4. A decorative pin, shaped like a dagger.

"Restore the lock!" the vaulted roofs rebound.
105   Not fierce Othello in so loud a strain
Roared for the handkerchief that caused his pain.
But see how oft ambitious aims are crossed,
And chiefs contend 'till all the prize is lost!
The lock, obtained with guilt, and kept with pain,
110   In ev'ry place is sought, but sought in vain:
With such a prize no mortal must be blest,
So Heav'n decrees! with Heav'n who can contest?
     Some thought it mounted to the lunar sphere,[5]
Since all things lost on earth are treasured there.
115   There heroes' wits are kept in ponderous vases,
And beaus' in snuffboxes and tweezer cases.
There broken vows and deathbed alms are found,
And lovers' hearts with ends of riband bound;
The courtier's promises, and sick man's pray'rs,
120   The smiles of harlots, and the tears of heirs,
Cages for gnats, and chains to yoke a flea;
Dried butterflies, and tomes of casuistry.[6]
     But trust the Muse—she saw it upward rise,
Though marked by none but quick poetic eyes:
125   (So Rome's great founder to the heav'ns withdrew,
To Proculus alone confessed in view.[7])
A sudden star, it shot through liquid air,
And drew behind a radiant trail of hair.
Not Berenice's locks first rose so bright,[8]
130   The heav'ns bespangling with disheveled light.
The Sylphs behold it kindling as it flies,
And pleased pursue its progress through the skies.
     This the beau monde shall from the Mall[9] survey,
And hail with music its propitious ray.
135   This, the blest lover shall for Venus° take,   *the planet*
And send up vows from Rosamonda's Lake.[1]
This Partridge[2] soon shall view in cloudless skies,
When next he looks through Galileo's eyes;[3]
And hence th' egregious wizard shall foredoom
140   The fate of Louis, and the fall of Rome.
     Then cease, bright nymph! to mourn thy ravished hair
Which adds new glory to the shining sphere!
Not all the tresses that fair head can boast
Shall draw such envy as the lock you lost.
145   For, after all the murders of your eye,

---

5. Cf. Ariosto's *Orlando Furioso* (1516–1532), in which Orlando's lost wits are sought on the moon. See also *Paradise Lost* 3.444ff.

6. Subtle reasoning (often used of arguments justifying immoral conduct).

7. When Romulus was killed mysteriously, Proculus soothed popular grief by asserting that he had been taken up to heaven.

8. The Egyptian queen Berenice made an offering of her hair after her husband returned victorious from the wars;

when it disappeared from the temple, the court astronomer claimed it had been made into a new constellation.

9. A fashionable walk in St. James's Park.

1. Where lovers met in St. James's Park.

2. John Partridge was a ridiculous star-gazer, who in his almanacs every year, never failed to predict the downfall of the Pope and the King of France, then at war with the English [Pope's note].

3. I.e., a telescope.

When, after millions slain, yourself shall die;
When those fair suns[4] shall set, as set they must,
And all those tresses shall be laid in dust;
This lock, the Muse shall consecrate to fame,
150   And mid'st the stars inscribe Belinda's name!
1711–1717   1712; 1714; 1717

from An Essay on Man

In Four Epistles to Henry St. John, Lord Bolingbroke[1]
Epistle 1

To the Reader

As the epistolary way of writing hath prevailed much of late, we have ventured to publish this piece composed some time since, and whose author chose this manner, notwithstanding his subject was high and of dignity, because of its being mixed with argument which of its nature approacheth to prose. This,[2] which we first give the reader, treats of the Nature and State of MAN, with respect to the UNIVERSAL SYSTEM;[3] the rest will treat of him with respect to his OWN SYSTEM, as an individual, and as a member of society, under one or other of which heads all ethics are included.

As he imitates no man, so he would be thought to vie with no man in these Epistles, particularly with the noted author of two lately published;[4] but this he may most surely say: that the matter of them is such as is of importance to all in general, and of offense to none in particular.

The Design

Having proposed to write some pieces on human life and manners, such as (to use my lord Bacon's expression) "come home to men's business and bosoms,"[5] I thought it more satisfactory to begin with considering Man in the abstract, his Nature and his State, since, to prove any moral duty, to enforce any moral precept, or to examine the perfection or imperfection of any creature whatsoever, it is necessary first to know what condition and relation it is placed in, and what is the proper end and purpose of its being.

The science[6] of human nature is, like all other sciences, reduced to a few clear points: there are not many *certain truths* in this world. It is therefore in the anatomy of the mind as in that of the body: more good will accrue to mankind by attending to the large, open, and perceptible parts, than by studying too much

---

4. I.e., her eyes.
1. "I believe," wrote Pope to his friend John Caryll, "that there is not in the whole course of the Scripture any precept so often and so strongly inculcated, as the trust and eternal dependence we ought to repose in that Supreme Being who is our constant preserver and benefactor." This is the theme of Pope's didactic and exhortatory *Essay on Man*, whose four epistles were published anonymously over eleven months in 1733–1734. For Pope, "to reason right is to submit" (line 164), not least because humankind occupies a middle ground—between angels and beasts—in a divinely ordered universe. Pope had intended the *Essay on Man* and the four *Moral Essays* (1731–1735) to be the first and last parts of a great poetic sequence on the nature of humankind, though he never

completed the project. The *Essay* is addressed to Henry St. John, first Viscount Bolingbroke (1678–1751), a leading Tory statesman and political writer whom Pope described as "my guide, philosopher, and friend."
2. I.e., the first Epistle.
3. I.e., within the cosmic order, ordained by God.
4. I.e., Pope himself, whose *Epistle to Bathurst* (1733) and the first *Imitation of Horace* (1733) had recently been published. The *Essay on Man* was published anonymously; Pope uses his little address to the reader both to advertise his own work and to confuse his enemies about the identity of the poem's author.
5. From Bacon's Dedicatory Epistle in the collected edition of the *Essays* (1625).
6. Knowledge.

such finer nerves and vessels, the conformations and uses of which will forever escape our observation. The disputes are all upon these last, and, I will venture to say, they have less sharpened the wits than the hearts of men against each other, and have diminished the practice more than advanced the theory of morality. If I could flatter myself that this Essay has any merit, it is in steering betwixt the extremes of doctrines seemingly opposite, in passing over terms utterly unintelligible, and in forming a temperate yet not inconsistent, and a short yet not imperfect system of ethics.

This I might have done in prose, but I chose verse, and even rhyme, for two reasons. The one will appear obvious: that principles, maxims, or precepts so written, both strike the reader more strongly at first, and are more easily retained by him afterwards. The other may seem odd, but is true: I found I could express them more shortly this way than in prose itself; and nothing is more certain, than that much of the force as well as grace of arguments or instructions depends on their conciseness. I was unable to treat this part of my subject more in detail without becoming dry and tedious, or more poetically, without sacrificing perspicuity to ornament, without wandering from the precision, or breaking the chain of reasoning. If any man can unite all these without diminution of any of them, I freely confess he will compass a thing above my capacity.

What is now published, is only to be considered as a general map of MAN, marking out no more than the greater parts, their extent, their limits, and their connection, but leaving the particular to be more fully delineated in the charts which are to follow. Consequently, these Epistles in their progress (if I have health and leisure to make any progress) will be less dry, and more susceptible of poetical ornament. I am here only opening the fountains, and clearing the passage. To deduce the rivers, to follow them in their course, and to observe their effects, may be a task more agreeable.

ARGUMENT

Of the Nature and State of Man, with respect to the UNIVERSE.

Of Man in the abstract.—I. That we can judge only with regard to our own system, being ignorant of the relations of systems and things, verses 17, etc. II. That Man is not to be deemed imperfect, but a being suited to his place and rank in the creation, agreeable to the general order of things, and conformable to ends and relations to him unknown, ver. 35, etc. III. That it is partly upon his ignorance of future events, and partly upon the hope of a future state, that all his happiness in the present depends, ver. 77, etc. IV. The pride of aiming at more knowledge, and pretending to more perfection, the cause of man's error and misery. The impiety of putting himself in the place of God, and judging of the fitness or unfitness, perfection or imperfection, justice or injustice of his dispensations, Ver. 113, etc. V. The absurdity of conceiting himself the final cause of the creation, or expecting that perfection in the *moral* world, which is not in the *natural*, Ver. 131, etc. VI. The unreasonableness of his complaints against Providence, while on the one hand he demands the perfections of the angels, and on the other the bodily qualifications of the brutes; though, to possess any of the sensitive faculties in a higher degree, would render him miserable, Ver. 173, etc. VII. That throughout the whole visible world, an universal order and gradation in the sensual and mental faculties is observed, which causes a subordination of creature to creature, and of all creatures to Man. The gradations of sense, instinct, thought, reflection, reason; that reason alone countervails all the other faculties, Ver. 207. VIII. How much farther this order and subordination of living creatures may extend, above and below us; were any part of which broken, not that part only, but the whole connected creation must be destroyed. Ver. 233. IX. The extravagance, madness, and pride of such a desire, Ver. 259. X. The consequence of all the absolute submission due to providence, both as to our present and future state, Ver. 281, etc. to the end.

	Awake, my ST. JOHN! leave all meaner° things	*base*
	To low ambition, and the pride of kings.	
	Let us (since life can little more supply	
	Than just to look about us and to die)	
5	Expatiate free[7] o'er all this scene of man;	
	A mighty maze! but not without a plan;	
	A wild, where weeds and flow'rs promiscuous° shoot,	*randomly mixed*
	Or garden, tempting with forbidden fruit.	
	Together let us beat[8] this ample field,	
10	Try what the open, what the covert yield;	
	The latent tracts, the giddy heights explore	
	Of all who blindly creep, or sightless soar;[9]	
	Eye nature's walks,° shoot folly as it flies,	*behaviors*
	And catch the manners living as they rise;	
15	Laugh where we must, be candid° where we can;	*generous*
	But vindicate the ways of God to Man.[1]	
	1. Say first, of God above, or Man below,	
	What can we reason, but from what we know?	
	Of Man what see we, but his station here,	
20	From which to reason, or to which refer?	
	Through worlds unnumbered though the God be known,	
	'Tis ours to trace him only in our own.	
	He, who through vast immensity can pierce,	
	See worlds on worlds compose one universe,	
25	Observe how system into system runs,	
	What other planets circle other suns,	
	What varied being peoples° ev'ry star,	*inhabits*
	May tell why Heav'n has made us as we are.	
	But of this frame the bearings, and the ties,	
30	The strong connections, nice dependencies,	
	Gradations just,[2] has thy° pervading soul	*the reader's*
	Looked through? or can a part contain the whole?	
	Is the great chain,[3] that draws all to agree,	
	And drawn supports, upheld by God, or thee?	

7. Wander or speak unrestrainedly.
8. "Beat," "open," "covert" are all hunting terms: Pope imagines them to be searching out game by walking back and forth across open and wooded land.
9. There is a middle way appropriate to man between ignorance and presumption.
1. Cf. *Paradise Lost*, 1.24–26: "That to the highth of this great argument / I may assert eternal providence, / And

justify the ways of God to men." Pope's mention of the "garden, tempting with forbidden fruit" (line 8) also calls to mind the opening lines of Milton's epic.
2. "Connections," "dependencies," and "gradations" were key terms of the new sciences.
3. The Great Chain of Being linked all levels of creation, at the same time maintaining a fixed hierarchy.

35   2. Presumptuous Man! the reason wouldst thou find,
        Why formed so weak, so little, and so blind!
        First, if thou canst, the harder reason guess,
        Why formed no weaker, blinder, and no less!
        Ask of thy mother earth, why oaks are made
40   Taller or stronger than the weeds they shade?
        Or ask of yonder argent fields above,
        Why Jove's satellites⁴ are less than Jove?
            Of systems possible, if 'tis confest
        That wisdom infinite must form the best,
45   Where all must full or not coherent be,⁵
        And all that rises, rise in due degree;
        Then, in the scale of reas'ning life, 'tis plain
        There must be, somewhere, such a rank as Man;
        And all the question (wrangle e'er so long)
50   Is only this, if God has placed him wrong?
            Respecting Man, whatever wrong we call,
        May, must be right, as relative to all.
        In human works, though labored on with pain,
        A thousand movements scarce one purpose gain;
55   In God's, one single can its end produce;
        Yet serves to second too some other use.
        So Man, who here seems principal alone,
        Perhaps acts second to some sphere unknown,
        Touches some wheel, or verges to some goal;
60   'Tis but a part we see, and not a whole.
            When the proud steed shall know why Man restrains
        His fiery course, or drives him o'er the plains;
        When the dull ox, why now he breaks the clod,
        Is now a victim, and now Egypt's god:⁶
65   Then shall Man's pride and dullness comprehend
        His actions', passions', being's, use and end;
        Why doing, suff'ring, checked, impelled; and why
        This hour a slave, the next a deity.
            Then say not Man's imperfect, Heav'n in fault;
70   Say rather, Man's as perfect as he ought;
        His knowledge measured to his state and place,
        His time a moment, and a point his space.
        If to be perfect in a certain sphere,°   *area of influence*
        What matter, soon or late, or here or there?
75   The blest today is as completely so,
        As who began a thousand years ago.

            3. Heav'n from all creatures hides the book of fate,
        All but the page prescribed, their present state;
        From brutes what men, from men what spirits° know: *angels*
80   Or who could suffer being here below?
        The lamb thy riot° dooms to bleed today,   *extravagance*
        Had he thy reason, would he skip and play?

---

4. Jupiter's moons. "Satellites" here has four syllables.   point.
5. The Great Chain of Being could not be broken at any   6. Apis, sacred bull of Memphis.

Pleased to the last, he crops the flow'ry food,
And licks the hand just raised to shed his blood.
85   Oh blindness to the future! kindly giv'n,
That each may fill the circle marked by Heav'n;
Who sees with equal eye, as God of all,
A hero perish, or a sparrow fall,
Atoms or systems° into ruin hurled,   *solar systems*
90   And now a bubble burst, and now a world.
    Hope humbly then; with trembling pinions soar;
Wait the great teacher death, and God adore!
What future bliss, he gives not thee to know,
But gives that hope to be thy blessing now.
95   Hope springs eternal in the human breast:
Man never *is*, but always to *be* blest:
The soul, uneasy and confined from home,[7]
Rests and expatiates in a life to come.
    Lo! the poor Indian, whose untutored mind
100   Sees God in clouds, or hears him in the wind;
His soul proud science never taught to stray
Far as the solar walk, or milky way;
Yet simple nature to his hope has giv'n,
Behind the cloud-topped hill, an humbler Heav'n;
105   Some safer world in depth of woods embraced,
Some happier island in the watry waste,
Where slaves once more their native land behold,
No fiends torment, no Christians thirst for gold![8]
To be, contents his natural desire,
110   He asks no angel's wing, no seraph's fire;[9]
But thinks, admitted to that equal sky,
His faithful dog shall bear him company.

    4. Go, wiser thou! and in thy scale of sense
Weigh thy opinion against providence;
115   Call imperfection what thou fancy'st such,
Say, here he gives too little, there too much;
Destroy all creatures for thy sport or gust,°   *appetite*
Yet cry, If Man's unhappy, God's unjust;
If Man alone engross not Heav'n's high care,
120   Alone made perfect here, immortal there:
Snatch from his hand the balance and the rod,
Rejudge his justice, be the God of God!
    In pride, in reas'ning pride, our error lies;
All quit their sphere, and rush into the skies.
125   Pride still is aiming at the blest abodes,
Men would be angels, angels would be gods.
Aspiring to be gods, if angels fell,
Aspiring to be angels, men rebel;
And who but wishes to invert the laws
130   Of ORDER, sins against th' Eternal Cause.

7. Away from its heavenly origin.
8. The Christian is meant to "thirst for God" (Psalm 42.2).
9. Seraphs were traditionally thought of as fiery.

  5. Ask for what end th' heav'nly bodies shine,
Earth for whose use? Pride answers, " 'Tis for mine:
For me kind Nature wakes her genial° pow'r,   *generating*
Suckles each herb, and spreads out ev'ry flow'r;
135   Annual for me, the grape, the rose renew
The juice nectareous, and the balmy dew;
For me, the mine a thousand treasures brings;
For me, health gushes from a thousand springs;
Seas roll to waft me, suns to light me rise;
140   My foot-stool earth, my canopy the skies."
      But errs not Nature from this gracious end,
From burning suns when livid deaths descend,
When earthquakes swallow, or when tempests sweep
Towns to one grave, whole nations to the deep?
145   "No" ('tis replied) "the first Almighty cause[1]
Acts not by partial, but by gen'ral laws;
Th' exceptions few; some change since all began,
And what created perfect?"—Why then Man?
If the great end be human happiness,
150   Then Nature deviates; and can Man do less?
As much that end a constant course requires
Of show'rs and sunshine, as of Man's desires;
As much eternal springs and cloudless skies,
As men for ever temp'rate, calm, and wise.
155   If plagues or earthquakes break not Heav'n's design,
Why then a Borgia, or a Catiline?[2]
Who knows but he, whose hand the light'ning forms,
Who heaves old ocean, and who wings the storms,
Pours fierce ambition in a Caesar's mind,
160   Or turns young Ammon[3] loose to scourge mankind?
From pride, from pride, our very reas'ning springs;
Account for moral as for nat'ral things:
Why charge we Heav'n in those, in these acquit?
In both, to reason right is to submit.
165   Better for us, perhaps, it might appear,
Were there all harmony, all virtue here;
That never air or ocean felt the wind;
That never passion discomposed the mind:
But all subsists by elemental strife;
170   And passions are the elements of life.
The gen'ral ORDER, since the whole began,
Is kept in Nature, and is kept in Man.

  6. What would this Man? Now upward will he soar,
And little less than angel, would be more;
175   Now looking downwards, just as grieved appears
To want the strength of bulls, the fur of bears.

---

1. God the Creator.
2. Cesare Borgia (1476–1507), an Italian duke from a notoriously ruthless family. Lucius Sergius Catiline (d. 62 B.C.) plotted unsuccessfully against the Roman state.

3. Alexander the Great, King of Macedonia (336–323 B.C.) and conqueror of Asia Minor, Syria, Egypt, Babylonia, and Persia.

Made for his use all creatures if he call,
Say what their use, had he the pow'rs of all?
Nature to these, without profusion kind,
180   The proper organs, proper pow'rs assigned;
Each seeming want compensated of course,[4]
Here with degrees of swiftness, there of force;
All in exact proportion to the state;
Nothing to add, and nothing to abate.
185   Each beast, each insect, happy in its own;
Is Heav'n unkind to Man, and Man alone?
Shall he alone, whom rational we call,
Be pleased with nothing, if not blessed with all?
     The bliss of Man (could pride that blessing find)
190   Is not to act or think beyond mankind;
No pow'rs of body or of soul to share,
But what his nature and his state can bear.
Why has not Man a microscopic eye?
For this plain reason, Man is not a fly.
195   Say what the use, were finer optics giv'n,
T' inspect a mite, not comprehend the Heav'n?[5]
Or touch, if tremblingly alive all o'er,
To smart and agonize at ev'ry pore?
Or quick effluvia[6] darting through the brain,
200   Die of a rose in aromatic pain?
If Nature thundered in his op'ning ears,
And stunned him with the music of the spheres,
How would he wish that Heav'n had left him still
The whisp'ring zephyr,° and the purling rill?   *breeze*
205   Who finds not providence all good and wise,
Alike in what it gives, and what denies?

     7. Far as creation's ample range extends,
The scale of sensual, mental pow'rs ascends:
Mark how it mounts, to Man's imperial race,
210   From the green myriads in the peopled grass:
What modes of sight betwixt each wide extreme,
The mole's dim curtain, and the lynx's beam:
Of smell, the headlong lioness[7] between,
And hound sagacious on the tainted[8] green:
215   Of hearing, from the life that fills the flood,
To that which warbles through the vernal wood:
The spider's touch, how exquisitely fine!
Feels at each thread, and lives along the line:
In the nice bee, what sense so subtly true
220   From pois'nous herbs extracts the healing dew:[9]

---

4. As is fitting, in the normal course of events.
5. It was commonly believed that man alone of all the animals was able to look up to Heaven.
6. Epicurus (c. 340–270 B.C.) and others believed that sensations reached the brain from the pores via streams of invisible particles.

7. Lions were, according to Pope, believed to hunt "by the ear, and not by the nostril."
8. Sagacious: of acute perception; tainted: i.e., with the smell of the hunted animal.
9. Honey had been thought to fall on flowers as dew and was used for medicinal purposes.

How instinct varies in the grov'ling swine,
Compared, half-reas'ning elephant, with thine:
'Twixt that, and reason, what a nice barrier;[1]
Forever sep'rate, yet forever near!
225   Remembrance and reflection how allied;
What thin partitions sense from thought divide:
And middle natures, how they long to join,
Yet never pass th' insuperable line!
Without this just gradation, could they be
230   Subjected these to those, or all to thee?
The pow'rs of all subdued by thee alone,
Is not thy reason all these pow'rs in one?

    8. See, through this air, this ocean, and this earth,
All matter quick,° and bursting into birth.   *living*
235   Above, how high progressive life may go!
Around, how wide! how deep extend below!
Vast chain of being, which from God began,
Natures ethereal, human, angel, Man,
Beast, bird, fish, insect! what no eye can see,
240   No glass° can reach! from infinite to thee,   *magnifying glass*
From thee to nothing!—On superior pow'rs
Were we to press, inferior might on ours:
Or in the full creation leave a void,
Where, one step broken, the great scale's destroyed:
245   From nature's chain whatever link you strike,
Tenth or ten thousandth, breaks the chain alike.
    And if each system in gradation roll,
Alike essential to th' amazing whole;
The least confusion but in one, not all
250   That system only, but the whole must fall.
Let earth unbalanced from her orbit fly,[2]
Planets and suns run lawless through the sky,
Let ruling angels from their spheres be hurled,[3]
Being on being wrecked, and world on world,
255   Heav'n's whole foundations to their center nod,
And Nature tremble to the throne of God:
All this dread ORDER break—for whom? for thee?
Vile worm!—oh madness, pride, impiety!

    9. What if the foot, ordained the dust to tread,
260   Or hand to toil, aspired to be the head?
What if the head, the eye, or ear repined
To serve mere engines to the ruling mind?
Just as absurd for any part to claim
To be another, in this gen'ral frame:
265   Just as absurd, to mourn the tasks or pains

---

1. Fine distinction. "Barrier" is pronounced "bar-REAR."
2. Cf. *Paradise Lost* 7.242, where "Earth, self-balanced, on her center hung."

3. According to Thomas Aquinas (c. 1225–1274), a sign of the end of the world.

The great directing MIND of ALL ordains.
    All are but parts of one stupendous whole,
Whose body, Nature is, and God the soul;
That, changed through all, and yet in all the same,

270   Great in the earth, as in th' ethereal frame,
Warms in the sun, refreshes in the breeze,
Glows in the stars, and blossoms in the trees,
Lives through all life, extends through all extent,
Spreads undivided, operates unspent,

275   Breathes in our soul, informs° our mortal part,   *permeates*
As full, as perfect, in a hair as heart;
As full, as perfect, in vile Man that mourns,
As the rapt seraph that adores and burns;
To him no high, no low, no great, no small;

280   He fills, he bounds, connects, and equals all.

        10. Cease then, nor ORDER imperfection name:[4]
Our proper bliss depends on what we blame.
Know thy own point: This kind, this due degree
Of blindness, weakness, Heav'n bestows on thee.

285   Submit—In this, or any other sphere,
Secure to be as blest as thou canst bear:
Safe in the hand of one disposing Pow'r,
Or° in the natal, or the mortal hour.   *either*
All nature is but art, unknown to thee;

290   All chance, direction, which thou canst not see;
All discord, harmony, not understood;[5]
All partial evil, universal good:[6]
And, spite of pride, in erring reason's spite,
One truth is clear, "Whatever IS, is RIGHT."

                                                    1733

John Gay
1685–1732

John Gay was born to hardworking, pious tradespeople in Barnstaple, a busy port town in southwestern England. Educated well but orphaned early, he moved at age eighteen to London, where he tried trade for a time, gave it up for literature, and made himself a master of the mock, at a moment when the mock mattered most.

---

4. I.e., do not call order imperfection.
5. Here, as earlier in the poem, Pope invokes the Horatian principle of *concordia discors* (Horace, *Epistles* 1.12.19), a harmony of opposites.

6. In a letter to John Caryll in 1718, Pope wrote that "true piety would make us know, that all misfortunes may as well be blessings."

In the early eighteenth century, the "mock" was not just a gesture of derision but an intricate art form, in which scenes of contemporary life, appropriated from streets, stables, salons, and other ordinary sites, were represented in grand styles first crafted for the actions of ancient heroes. In his mock-pastoral *Description of a City Shower* (1709), for example, Swift depicted the muddy chaos of an urban rainstorm in the language Virgil had devised to render the rural delights of a Golden Age; in his mock-epic *Rape of the Lock* (1712), Pope portrayed the trivial agitations of London beaux and belles in formulations absorbed from Homer. Befriended by Pope and Swift, Gay became perhaps the most supple and assiduous practitioner in their mock-heroic vein. In his early successes, he showed himself adept at devising new combinations of mode and topic, new ways of savoring both high styles and low subjects even while making fun of them. In *The Shepherd's Week* (1714), he took on both Virgil's idealism and also the ungainly "realism" attempted by some of that Roman poet's eighteenth-century imitators. He endowed his shepherds with preposterously "rustic" names (Bumkinet, Hobnelia, Bowzybeus) and a ludicrously hybrid language, alternately high-flying and homespun. But he gave them also a grace and good nature that survive the mock. The poem's closing image of a drunken swain sleeping out the sunset ("ruddy, like his face, the sun descends") reads like the poet's own benediction. In his next big work, *Trivia, or the Art of Walking the Streets of London* (1716), Gay's grandiloquent Virgilian instruction makes city walking seem not just a "trivial" chore but an "art," comic, challenging, alternately appalling and attractive.

Gay built his life as he made his art, by improvising. He earned money by his plays and poems; he lost money in that evanescent investment scheme the South Sea Bubble; he served as Commissioner of Lotteries, and as secretary, steward, and companion to several members of the nobility; and he sought for years to secure steady patronage at court, by means of flattering verse and ingratiating conduct. His frustration peaked when he published a virtuosic set of *Fables* (1727) for the four-year-old Prince William and received as reward a royal appointment as attendant to the prince's two-year-old sister. The aristocrats he courted valued him for his compliant temper and beguiling company, but they patronized him in both senses of the word.

Gay refused the royal appointment, staking his hopes instead on his new project for the stage, *The Beggar's Opera* (1728). The initial notion for the piece had come from Swift, who suggested a "Newgate pastoral"—that is, a mixture in which the "whores and thieves" who inhabited Newgate prison and its neighborhood would supplant the nymphs and shepherds frolicking on Arcadian hillsides. Swift's hint is an ordinary mock recipe: two worlds collide, one real, one fictitious. Gay built from it an intricate hall of mirrors, where many more worlds met. For his thieves he drew on two real-life models, recently executed: Jonathan Wild and Jack Sheppard. Wild had run a large criminal organization that profited him two ways: he collected money from the resale of goods stolen by his subordinates; and he collected rewards from the government for turning in his associates and rivals whenever they became too troublesome. Sheppard had acquired fame as Wild's most high-spirited and elusive prey; a brilliant thief in his own right, he had often managed to escape the prisons and predicaments into which Wild had betrayed him. In *The Beggar's Opera*, Gay resurrects the two late criminals as Mr. Peachum, who like Wild manages a lucrative double life, and Captain Macheath, who like Sheppard proves susceptible of capture and gifted at escape. Here the worlds begin to multiply. Developing a comparison then current in the political press, Gay made his criminals conjure up the most powerful politician alive: Robert Walpole, the Whig prime minister who ran his political machine (so the *Opera* insists) with the efficiency of Peachum and the self-indulgence of Macheath.

The Beggar's Opera mixed low with high in form as well as content. Like "Newgate pastoral," the phrase "beggar's opera" fuses opposites. Italian opera was the most expensive, exotic, and fashionable entertainment in London. Gay's theatrical game was to replay opera's intricacies using beggars' means. He supplanted the elaborate arias of foreign composers with the simpler tunes of British street songs; he replaced the original words to those tunes with new lyrics that voiced his characters' strong emotions; he even re-enacted a recent, much-publicized rivalry between two high-paid prima donnas, at war for the allegiance of their audience, in the contest he stages between Peachum's daughter Polly and the jailer's daughter Lucy Lockit for the devotion of fickle Captain Macheath. On Gay's stage, worlds converge with a density even Swift could not have foreseen. Opera house and street corner; Whitehall and Newgate; art and commerce; politics, business, and crime: all of these turn out to operate on the same principles of self-interest.

Reading the new piece before its premiere, Gay's well-wishers hedged their bets as to its success. "It would either take greatly," the playwright William Congreve predicted, "or be damned confoundedly." In the event, it did both. The triumph of the opening night is the stuff of theatrical legend, but it provoked a counter-chorus of condemnation from critics who saw the play as endangering opera, glorifying thieves, traducing government. Amid the debate, the play enjoyed a long run, entrancing an audience made up of the very people it mocked (including Walpole himself, who reportedly conducted an extra chorus of the play's most satiric song, "When you censure the age"). *The Beggar's Opera* offered theatergoers simple pleasures (deft performances, comic reversals, well-loved tunes) and intricate ones too: the often ironic play of Gay's new lyrics against the original words that the auditors had already in their heads; the debunking of love and marriage in sharp dialogue and the glorifying of it in sentimental song; the volatile charisma of the mock-hero Macheath, who for many observers came to seem utterly heroic by evening's end; the arresting alchemy by which Gay transmuted (as the Romantic essayist William Hazlitt later expressed it) "this motley group" of "highwaymen, turnkeys, their mistresses, wives, or daughters . . . into a set of fine gentlemen and ladies, satirists and philosophers." In his painting of the opening night (Color Plate 27), William Hogarth suggests how these transformations came to include the spectators as well. Occupying the sides of the stage, an audience of aristocrats, politicians, and theater people (Gay himself among them) observe the play in progress; they are encompassed by the same prison walls wherein Macheath and his pursuers play out their intricate transactions, in which everything and everyone—goods, votes, spouses—had become commodities, items of exchange, reckoned in account books as profit and as loss.

The Beggar's Opera brought Gay prosperity and celebrity but not security. Walpole evicted him from his subsidized lodgings and banned production of the *Opera*'s much-anticipated sequel *Polly*. When Gay died less than five years after his fabled first night, however, he was buried with elaborate ceremony in the Poet's Corner of Westminster Abbey. Friends commended the appropriateness of the site but marveled at the incongruity of the pomp. Incongruity, though, had been Gay's stock in trade, and nowhere more so than in his greatest hit. Its long run continues in theaters around the world. It spawned numberless short-lived imitations in its own time and a more durable descendant in the twentieth century: *Die Dreigroschenoper* (*The Threepenny Opera*, 1928), in which Bertolt Brecht and Kurt Weill adapted Gay's characters, plot, and critique of commerce to produce their own dark and gleeful Marxist assault on contemporary capitalism. By routes less direct, Gay's work has infused both the modern musical theater (which continues to combine operatic and popular modes) and pop culture in general—where, for example, Brecht and Weill's sardonic "Ballad of Mack the Knife" became a pop hit of the early 1960s. *The Beggar's Opera* grabbed attention first—and sustains it still—for the ironic dexterity with which it mixed things up, in full mock mode.

The Beggar's Opera

Nos haec novimus esse nihil.[1]

Dramatis Personae[2]
Men

PEACHUM
LOCKIT
MACHEATH
FILCH
JEMMY TWITCHER
CROOK-FINGERED JACK
WAT DREARY
ROBIN OF BAGSHOT   } *Macheath's Gang*
NIMMING NED
HARRY PADINGTON
MATT OF THE MINT
BEN BUDGE
BEGGAR
PLAYER
CONSTABLES, DRAWER, TURNKEY, ETC.

Women

MRS. PEACHUM
POLLY PEACHUM
LUCY LOCKIT
DIANA TRAPES
MRS. COAXER
DOLLY TRULL
MRS. VIXEN   } *Women of the Town*
BETTY DOXY
JENNY DIVER
MRS. SLAMMEKIN
SUKY TAWDRY
MOLLY BRAZEN

INTRODUCTION

[Beggar, Player]

BEGGAR: If poverty be a title[3] to poetry, I am sure nobody can dispute mine. I own myself of the Company of Beggars; and I make one at their weekly festivals at St. Giles's.[4] I have a small yearly salary for my catches,[5] and am welcome to a mock laureate dinner there whenever I please, which is more than most poets can say.

---

1. We know these things to be nothing (Martial, *Epigrams* 13.2.8).
2. Many of these names reflect the characters' low-life habits: to "peach" is to inform on, to filch is to steal, twitchers are pickpockets, nimmers are thieves, and trulls and doxies are prostitutes.
3. Deed of ownership.

4. An almshouse near the parish of St. Giles, patron saint of lepers and beggars.
5. Rounds, songs for two or more voices in which each voice starts the same melody at a different time. The form was very popular; enthusiasts assembled in "catch clubs" for whole evenings of singing.

PLAYER: As we live by the Muses, 'tis but gratitude in us to encourage poetical merit wherever we find it. The Muses, contrary to all other ladies, pay no distinction to dress, and never partially[6] mistake the pertness of embroidery for wit, nor the modesty of want for dullness. Be the author who he will, we push his play as far as it will go. So (though you are in want) I wish you success heartily.

BEGGAR: This piece I own was originally writ for the celebrating the marriage of James Chanter and Moll Lay, two most excellent ballad singers. I have introduced the similes that are in all your celebrated operas: the swallow, the moth, the bee, the ship, the flower, etc. Besides, I have a prison scene which the ladies always reckon charmingly pathetic. As to the parts, I have observed such a nice impartiality to our two ladies, that it is impossible for either of them to take offense.[7] I hope I may be forgiven, that I have not made my opera throughout unnatural, like those in vogue; for I have no recitative.[8] Excepting this, as I have consented to have neither prologue nor epilogue, it must be allowed an opera in all its forms. The piece indeed hath been heretofore frequently represented by ourselves in our great room at St. Giles's, so that I cannot too often acknowledge your charity in bringing it now on the stage.

PLAYER: But I see 'tis time for us to withdraw; the actors are preparing to begin. Play away the overture.   [Exeunt.]

ACT 1

Scene 1. Peachum's House

[Peachum sitting at a table with a large book of accounts before him.]

Air 1. An old woman clothed in gray, etc.[9]

> *Through all the employments of life*
>   *Each neighbor abuses his brother;*
> *Whore and rogue they call husband and wife:*
>   *All professions be-rogue one another.*
> *The priest calls the lawyer a cheat,*
>   *The lawyer be-knaves the divine;*
> *And the statesman, because he's so great,[1]*
>   *Thinks his trade as honest as mine.*

A lawyer is an honest employment, so is mine. Like me too he acts in a double capacity, both against rogues and for 'em; for 'tis but fitting that we should protect and encourage cheats, since we live by them.

Scene 2

[Peachum, Filch]

FILCH: Sir, Black Moll hath sent word her trial comes on in the afternoon, and she hopes you will order matters so as to bring her off.

---

6. In a prejudiced way.
7. The Beggar alludes to recent rivalries between leading ladies in Italian operas.
8. Sung speech, an operatic convention. The Beggar promises that here, by contrast, dialogue will be spoken naturally.

9. I.e., this air is to be sung to the familiar ballad tune, *An Old Woman Clothed in Gray.*
1. The word "great" was often attached to the Whig Prime Minister Robert Walpole, whom Gay's Tory party opposed vigorously in the 1720s and 1730s.

PEACHUM: Why, she may plead her belly at worst;[2] to my knowledge she hath taken care of that security. But as the wench is very active and industrious, you may satisfy her that I'll soften the evidence.

FILCH: Tom Gagg, Sir, is found guilty.

PEACHUM: A lazy dog! When I took him the time before, I told him what he would come to if he did not mend his hand. This is death without reprieve. I may venture to book him.[3] [Writes.] For Tom Gagg, forty pounds. Let Betty Sly know that I'll save her from transportation,[4] for I can get more by her staying in England.

FILCH: Betty hath brought more goods into our lock to-year than any five of the gang; and in truth, 'tis a pity to lose so good a customer.

PEACHUM: If none of the gang take her off, she may, in the common course of business, live a twelve-month longer. I love to let women scape. A good sportsman always lets the hen partridges fly, because the breed of the game depends upon them. Besides, here the law allows us no reward; there is nothing to be got by the death of woman—except our wives.[5]

FILCH: Without dispute, she is a fine woman! 'Twas to her I was obliged for my education, and (to say a bold word) she hath trained up more young fellows to the business than the gaming-table.

PEACHUM: Truly, Filch, thy observation is right. We and the surgeons[6] are more beholden to women than all the professions besides.

Air 2. The bonny gray-eyed morn, etc.

FILCH: *'Tis woman that seduces all mankind,*
By her we first were taught the wheedling arts:
Her very eyes can cheat; when most she's kind,
She tricks us of our money with our hearts.
For her, like wolves by night we roam for prey,
And practice ev'ry fraud to bribe her charms;
For suits of love, like law, are won by pay,
And beauty must be fee'd into our arms.

PEACHUM: But make haste to Newgate,[7] boy, and let my friends know what I intend; for I love to make them easy one way or other.

FILCH: When a gentleman is long kept in suspense, penitence may break his spirit ever after. Besides, certainty gives a man a good air upon his trial, and makes him risk another without fear or scruple. But I'll away, for 'tis a pleasure to be the messenger of comfort to friends in affliction.

Scene 3

[Peachum]

But 'tis now high time to look about me for a decent execution against next Sessions.[8] I hate a lazy rogue, by whom one can get nothing 'till he is hanged. A register of the gang, [reading] Crook-fingered Jack. A year and a half in the service; Let me see how much the stock owes to his industry; one, two, three, four, five

2. A pregnant woman could not be hanged.
3. I.e., enter in the books the reward for "peaching" him.
4. Convicts were often transported to the colonies.
5. Husbands inherited their wives' property.

6. Who treat venereal diseases.
7. London's main prison.
8. Of the criminal court.

gold watches, and seven silver ones. A mighty clean-handed fellow! Sixteen snuff-boxes, five of them of true gold. Six dozen of handkerchiefs, four silver-hilted swords, half a dozen of shirts, three tie-perriwigs, and a piece of broad cloth. Considering these are only the fruits of his leisure hours, I don't know a prettier fellow, for no man alive hath a more engaging presence of mind upon the road. Wat Dreary, alias Brown Will, an irregular dog, who hath an underhand way of disposing of his goods. I'll try him[9] only for a Sessions or two longer upon his good behavior. Harry Padington, a poor petty-larceny rascal, without the least genius; that fellow, though he were to live these six months, will never come to the gallows with any credit. Slippery Sam; he goes off the next Sessions, for the villain hath the impudence to have views of following his trade as a tailor, which he calls an honest employment. Mat of the Mint; lifted[1] not above a month ago, a promising sturdy fellow, and diligent in his way; somewhat too bold and hasty, and may raise good contributions on[2] the public, if he does not cut himself short by murder. Tom Tipple, a guzzling soaking sot, who is always too drunk to stand himself, or to make others stand. A cart[3] is absolutely necessary for him. Robin of Bagshot, alias Gorgon, alias Bluff Bob, alias Carbuncle, alias Bob Booty.[4]

Scene 4

[Peachum, Mrs. Peachum]

MRS. PEACHUM: What of Bob Booty, husband? I hope nothing bad hath betided him. You know, my dear, he's a favorite customer of mine. 'Twas he made me a present of this ring.

PEACHUM: I have set his name down in the blacklist, that's all, my dear; he spends his life among women, and as soon as his money is gone, one or other of the ladies will hang him for the reward, and there's forty pound lost to us forever.

MRS. PEACHUM: You know, my dear, I never meddle in matters of death; I always leave those affairs to you. Women indeed are bitter bad judges in these cases, for they are so partial to the brave that they think every man handsome who is going to the camp[5] or the gallows.

Air 3. Cold and raw, etc.

> If any wench Venus's girdle wear,
>   Though she be never so ugly;
> Lilies and roses will quickly appear,
>   And her face look wond'rous smugly.
> Beneath the left ear so fit but a cord
>   (A rope so charming a zone[6] is!),
> The youth in his cart hath the air of a lord,
>   And we cry, There dies an Adonis!

But really, husband, you should not be too hardhearted, for you never had a finer, braver set of men than at present. We have not had a murder among them all, these seven months. And truly, my dear, that is a great blessing.

9. Keep him on.
1. Enlisted.
2. From.
3. A condemned prisoner rode in a cart to his execution.

4. All names referring to the prime minister, Robert Walpole.
5. To war.
6. Belt.

PEACHUM: What a dickens is the woman always a whimpering about murder for? No gentleman is ever looked upon the worse for killing a man in his own defense; and if business cannot be carried on without it, what would you have a gentleman do?

MRS. PEACHUM: If I am in the wrong, my dear, you must excuse me, for nobody can help the frailty of an over-scrupulous conscience.

PEACHUM: Murder is as fashionable a crime as a man can be guilty of. How many fine gentlemen have we in Newgate every year, purely upon that article! If they have wherewithal to persuade the jury to bring it in[7] manslaughter, what are they the worse for it? So, my dear, have done upon this subject. Was Captain Macheath here this morning, for the bank-notes[8] he left with you last week?

MRS. PEACHUM: Yes, my dear; and though the bank hath stopped payment, he was so cheerful and so agreeable! Sure there is not a finer gentleman upon the road than the Captain! If he comes from Bagshot[9] at any reasonable hour he hath promised to make one this evening with Polly and me, and Bob Booty, at a party of quadrille.[1] Pray, my dear, is the Captain rich?

PEACHUM: The Captain keeps too good company ever to grow rich. Marybone and the chocolate-houses[2] are his undoing. The man that proposes to get money by "play" should have the education of a fine gentleman, and be trained up to it from his youth.

MRS. PEACHUM: Really, I am sorry upon Polly's account the Captain hath not more discretion. What business hath he to keep company with lords and gentlemen? He should leave them to prey upon one another.

PEACHUM: Upon Polly's account! What, a plague, does the woman mean? Upon Polly's account!

MRS. PEACHUM: Captain Macheath is very fond of the girl.

PEACHUM: And what then?

MRS. PEACHUM: If I have any skill in the ways of women, I am sure Polly thinks him a very pretty man.

PEACHUM: And what then? You would not be so mad to have the wench marry him! Gamesters and highwaymen are generally very good to their whores, but they are very devils to their wives.

MRS. PEACHUM: But if Polly should be in love, how should we help her, or how can she help herself? Poor girl, I am in the utmost concern about her.

Air 4. Why is your faithful slave disdained? etc.

If love the virgin's heart invade,
How, like a moth, the simple maid
    Still plays about the flame!
If soon she be not made a wife;
Her honor's singed, and then for life,
    She's—what I dare not name.

PEACHUM: Look ye, wife. A handsome wench in our way of business is as profitable as at the bar of a Temple coffeehouse, who looks upon it as her livelihood to grant every liberty but one. You see I would indulge the girl as far as prudently we

7. Reduce it to.
8. Bankers' checks.
9. Bagshot Heath, west of London, where many highway-

men plied their trade.
1. A fashionable card game for four.
2. Both sites of gambling.

can. In anything, but marriage! After that, my dear, how shall we be safe? Are we not then in her husband's power? For a husband hath the absolute power over all a wife's secrets but her own. If the girl had the discretion of a court lady, who can have a dozen young fellows at her ear without complying with one, I should not matter it; but Polly is tinder, and a spark will at once set her on a flame. Married! If the wench does not know her own profit, sure she knows her own pleasure better than to make herself a property! My daughter to me should be, like a court lady to a minister of state, a key to the whole gang. Married! If the affair is not already done, I'll terrify her from it, by the example of our neighbors.

MRS. PEACHUM: Mayhap, my dear, you may injure the girl. She loves to imitate the fine ladies, and she may only allow the Captain liberties in the view of interest.[3]

PEACHUM: But 'tis your duty, my dear, to warn the girl against her ruin, and to instruct her how to make the most of her beauty. I'll go to her this moment, and sift[4] her. In the meantime, wife, rip out the coronets and marks[5] of these dozen of cambric handkerchiefs, for I can dispose of them this afternoon to a chap in the city.

Scene 5

[Mrs. Peachum]

Never was a man more out of the way[6] in an argument than my husband! Why must our Polly, forsooth, differ from her sex, and love only her husband? And why must Polly's marriage, contrary to all observation, make her the less followed by other men? All men are thieves in love, and like a woman the better for being another's property.

Air 5. Of all the simple things we do, etc.

> *A maid is like the golden oar,[7]*
> *Which hath guineas intrinsical in't,*
>   *Whose worth is never known, before*
>   *It is tried and imprest[8] in the Mint.*
>   *A wife's like a guinea in gold,*
>   *Stamped with the name of her spouse;*
>   *Now here, now there; is bought, or is sold;*
>   *And is current in every house.*

Scene 6

[Mrs. Peachum, Filch]

MRS. PEACHUM: Come hither Filch. I am as fond of this child, as though my mind misgave me[9] he were my own. He hath as fine a hand at picking a pocket as a woman, and is as nimble fingered as a juggler. If an unlucky Session does not cut the rope of thy life, I pronounce, boy, thou wilt be a great man[1] in history. Where was your post last night, my boy?

---

3. Self-interest, profit.
4. Question.
5. The embroidered marks of the handkerchiefs' aristocratic owners.
6. In the wrong.

7. Ore.
8. Smelted and stamped.
9. Suspected.
1. Another jab at the prime minister, Robert Walpole.

FILCH: I plyed at the opera, Madam; and considering 'twas neither dark nor rainy, so that there was no great hurry in getting chairs and coaches, made a tolerable hand on't. These seven handkerchiefs, Madam.

MRS. PEACHUM: Colored ones, I see. They are of sure sale from our warehouse at Redriff among the seamen.

FILCH: And this snuffbox.

MRS. PEACHUM: Set in gold! A pretty encouragement this to a young beginner.

FILCH: I had a fair tug at a charming gold watch. Pox take the tailors for making the fobs[2] so deep and narrow! It stuck by the way, and I was forced to make my escape under a coach. Really, Madam, I fear I shall be cut off in the flower of my youth, so that every now and then (since I was pumped[3]) I have thoughts of taking up[4] and going to sea.

MRS. PEACHUM: You should go to Hockley in the Hole,[5] and to Marybone, child, to learn valor. These are the schools that have bred so many brave men. I thought, boy, by this time, thou hadst lost fear as well as shame. Poor lad! How little does he know as yet of the Old Baily![6] For the first fact I'll insure thee from being hanged; and going to sea, Filch, will come time enough upon a sentence of transportation. But now, since you have nothing better to do, ev'n go to your book, and learn your catechism;[7] for really a man makes but an ill figure in the ordinary's paper,[8] who cannot give a satisfactory answer to his questions. But, hark you, my lad. Don't tell me a lie; for you know I hate a liar. Do you know of anything that hath passed between Captain Macheath and our Polly?

FILCH: I beg you, Madam, don't ask me; for I must either tell a lie to you or to Miss Polly; for I promised her I would not tell.

MRS. PEACHUM: But when the honor of our family is concerned—

FILCH: I shall lead a sad life with Miss Polly, if ever she come to know that I told you. Besides, I would not willingly forfeit my own honor by betraying anybody.

MRS. PEACHUM: Yonder comes my husband and Polly. Come Filch, you shall go with me into my own room, and tell me the whole story. I'll give thee a glass of a most delicious cordial that I keep for my own drinking.

Scene 7

[Peachum, Polly]

POLLY: I know as well as any of the fine ladies how to make the most of myself and of my man too. A woman knows how to be mercenary, though she hath never been in a court or at an assembly.[9] We have it in our natures, Papa. If I allow Captain Macheath some trifling liberties, I have this watch and other visible marks of his favor to show for it. A girl who cannot grant some things, and refuse what is most material, will make but a poor hand of her beauty, and soon be thrown upon the common.

Air 6. What shall I do to show how much I love her, etc.

Virgins are like the fair flower in its luster,
  Which in the garden enamels the ground;

---

2. Watch-pockets.
3. Half-drowned under a pump (a punishment for pickpockets).
4. Reforming.
5. A site of boxing and bear-baiting.

6. London's main trial court.
7. Religious instruction.
8. The chaplain of Newgate (the Ordinary) often published the confessions of recently executed prisoners.
9. A fashionable social gathering.

Near it the bees in play flutter and cluster,
  And gaudy butterflies frolic around.
But, when once plucked, 'tis no longer alluring,
  To Covent Garden¹ 'tis sent (as yet sweet),
There fades, and shrinks, and grows past all enduring,
  Rots, stinks, and dies, and is trod under feet.

PEACHUM: You know, Polly, I am not against your toying and trifling with a customer in the way of business, or to get out a secret, or so. But if I find out that you have played the fool and are married, you jade you, I'll cut your throat, hussy. Now you know my mind.

Scene 8

[*Peachum, Polly, Mrs. Peachum*]

Air 7. Oh London is a fine town

[*Mrs. Peachum, in a very great passion.*]

Our Polly is a sad slut! nor heeds what we have taught her.
I wonder any man alive will ever rear a daughter!
For she must have both hoods and gowns, and hoops to swell her pride,
With scarves and stays,² and gloves and lace; and she will have men beside;
And when she's dressed with care and cost, all tempting, fine and gay,
As men should serve a cowcumber,³ she flings herself away.
Our Polly is a sad slut, etc.

You baggage! You hussy! You inconsiderate jade! Had you been hanged, it would not have vexed me, for that might have been your misfortune; but to do such a mad thing by choice! The wench is married, husband.

PEACHUM: Married! The Captain is a bold man, and will risk anything for money; to be sure he believes her a fortune. Do you think your mother and I should have lived comfortably so long together, if ever we had been married? Baggage!

MRS. PEACHUM: I knew she was always a proud slut; and now the wench hath played the fool and married, because forsooth she would do like the gentry. Can you support the expense of a husband, hussy, in gaming, drinking, and whoring? Have you money enough to carry on the daily quarrels of man and wife about who shall squander most? There are not many husbands and wives who can bear the charges⁴ of plaguing one another in a handsome way. If you must be married, could you introduce nobody into our family but a highwayman? Why, thou foolish jade, thou wilt be as ill-used, and as much neglected, as if thou hadst married a lord!

PEACHUM: Let not your anger, my dear, break through the rules of decency, for the Captain looks upon himself in the military capacity, as a gentleman by his profession. Besides what he hath already, I know he is in a fair way of getting, or of dying;⁵ and both these ways, let me tell you, are most excellent chances for a wife. Tell me hussy, are you ruined or no?

MRS. PEACHUM: With Polly's fortune, she might very well have gone off to a person of distinction. Yes, that you might, you pouting slut!

---

1. A London market for flowers, fruits, and vegetables; also a haunt of prostitutes.
2. Corsets.

3. A (worthless) cucumber.
4. Expense.
5. He is likely to make more or to die trying.

PEACHUM: What, is the wench dumb? Speak, or I'll make you plead by squeezing out an answer from you.[6] Are you really bound wife to him, or are you only upon liking? [*Pinches her.*]

POLLY: Oh! [*Screaming.*]

MRS. PEACHUM: How the mother is to be pitied who hath handsome daughters! Locks, bolts, bars, and lectures of morality are nothing to them. They break through them all. They have as much pleasure in cheating a father and mother, as in cheating at cards.

PEACHUM: Why, Polly, I shall soon know if you are married, by Macheath's keeping from[7] our house.

Air 8. Grim king of the ghosts, etc.

POLLY: *Can love be controlled by advice?*
　　Will Cupid our mothers obey?
　Though my heart were as frozen as ice,
　　At his flame 'twould have melted away.

When he kissed me so closely he pressed,
　'Twas so sweet that I must have complied;
So I thought it both safest and best
　To marry, for fear you should chide.

MRS. PEACHUM: Then all the hopes of our family are gone forever and ever!

PEACHUM: And Macheath may hang his father and mother-in-law, in hope to get into their daughter's fortune.

POLLY: I did not marry him (as 'tis the fashion) coolly and deliberately for honor and money. But, I love him.

MRS. PEACHUM: Love him! worse and worse! I thought the girl had been better bred. Oh husband, husband! Her folly makes me mad! My head swims! I'm distracted! I can't support myself—Oh! [*Faints.*]

PEACHUM: See, wench, to what a condition you have reduced your poor mother! A glass of cordial, this instant. How the poor woman takes it to heart!

[*Polly goes out, and returns with it.*]

Ah, hussy, now this is the only comfort your mother has left!

POLLY: Give her another glass, Sir; my mama drinks double the quantity whenever she is out of order. This, you see, fetches[8] her.

MRS. PEACHUM: The girl shows such a readiness, and so much concern, that I could almost find in my heart to forgive her.

Air 9. O Jenny, O Jenny, where hast thou been

O Polly, you might have toyed and kissed.
By keeping men off, you keep them on.

POLLY: *But he so teased me,*
　　And he so pleased me,
　What I did, you must have done.

---

6. Confessions were sometimes extracted by pressing with weights.

7. Staying away from.

8. Revives.

MRS. PEACHUM: Not with a highwayman.—You sorry slut!

PEACHUM: A word with you, wife. 'Tis no new thing for a wench to take man without consent of parents. You know 'tis the frailty of woman, my dear.

MRS. PEACHUM: Yes, indeed, the sex is frail. But the first time a woman is frail, she should be somewhat nice[9] methinks, for then or never is the time to make her fortune. After that, she hath nothing to do but guard herself from being found out, and she may do what she pleases.

PEACHUM: Make yourself a little easy; I have a thought shall soon set all matters again to rights. Why so melancholy, Polly? Since what is done cannot be undone, we must all endeavor to make the best of it.

MRS. PEACHUM: Well, Polly, as far as one woman can forgive another, I forgive thee. Your father is too fond of you, hussy.

POLLY: Then all my sorrows are at an end.

MRS. PEACHUM: A mighty likely speech in troth, for a wench who is just married!

Air 10. Thomas, I cannot, etc.

POLLY: *I, like a ship in storms, was tossed;*
Yet afraid to put into land;
For seized in the port the vessel's lost,
Whose treasure is contraband.
   The waves are laid,[1]
   My duty's paid.
O joy beyond expression!
   Thus, safe a-shore,
   I ask no more,
My all is in my possession.

PEACHUM: I hear customers in t'other room; Go, talk with 'em, Polly; but come to us again, as soon as they are gone. But, hark ye, child, if 'tis the gentleman who was here yesterday about the repeating-watch,[2] say you believe we can't get intelligence of it till tomorrow. For I lent it to Suky Straddle, to make a figure with it tonight at a tavern in Drury Lane.[3] If t'other gentleman calls for the silver-hilted sword; you know beetle-browed Jemmy hath it on, and he doth not come from Tunbridge till Tuesday night; so that it cannot be had till then.

Scene 9

[Peachum, Mrs. Peachum]

PEACHUM: Dear wife, be a little pacified. Don't let your passion run away with your senses. Polly, I grant you, hath done a rash thing.

MRS. PEACHUM: If she had had only an intrigue with the fellow, why the very best families have excused and huddled up a frailty of that sort. 'Tis marriage, husband, that makes it a blemish.

PEACHUM: But money, wife, is the true fuller's earth[4] for reputations, there is not a spot or a stain but what it can take out. A rich rogue nowadays is fit company for any gentleman; and the world, my dear, hath not such a contempt for roguery as you imagine. I tell you, wife, I can make this match turn to our advantage.

---

9. Careful, fastidious.
1. Have subsided.
2. An especially valuable timepiece: it announced the current hour and quarter-hour by a series of bells that rang at the push of a button.
3. Another haunt of prostitutes; also the location of the rival theater.
4. A mineral used as a cleaning solvent.

MRS. PEACHUM: I am very sensible,[5] husband, that Captain Macheath is worth money, but I am in doubt whether he hath not two or three wives already, and then if he should die in a Session or two, Polly's dower would come into dispute.

PEACHUM: That, indeed, is a point which ought to be considered.

Air 11. A soldier and a sailor

> *A fox may steal your hens, Sir,*
> *A whore your health and pence, Sir,*
> *Your daughter rob your chest, Sir,*
> *Your wife may steal your rest, Sir,*
>   *A thief your goods and plate.[6]*
> *But this is all but picking,*
> *With rest, pence, chest, and chicken;*
> *It ever was decreed, Sir,*
> *If lawyer's hand is fee'd, Sir,*
>   *He steals your whole estate.*

The lawyers are bitter enemies to those in our way.[7] They *don't care*[8] that anybody should get a clandestine livelihood but themselves.

Scene 10

[*Mrs. Peachum, Peachum, Polly*]

POLLY: 'Twas only Nimming Ned. He brought in a damask window curtain, a hoop petticoat, a pair of silver candlesticks, a periwig, and one silk stocking from the fire that happened last night.

PEACHUM: There is not a fellow that is cleverer in his way, and saves more goods out of the fire than Ned. But now, Polly, to your affair; for matters must not be left as they are. You are married then, it seems?

POLLY: Yes, Sir.

PEACHUM: And how do you propose to live, child?

POLLY: Like other women, Sir, upon the industry of my husband.

MRS. PEACHUM: What, is the wench turned fool? A highwayman's wife, like a soldier's, hath as little of his pay as of his company.

PEACHUM: And had not you the common views of a gentlewoman in your marriage, Polly?

POLLY: I don't know what you mean, Sir.

PEACHUM: Of a jointure,[9] and of being a widow.

POLLY: But I love him, Sir: how then could I have thoughts of parting with him?

PEACHUM: Parting with him! Why, that is the whole scheme and intention of all marriage articles. The comfortable estate of widowhood is the only hope that keeps up a wife's spirits. Where is the woman who would scruple to be a wife, if she had it in her power to be a widow whenever she pleased? If you have any views of this sort, Polly, I shall think the match not so very unreasonable.

POLLY: How I dread to hear your advice! Yet I must beg you to explain yourself.

PEACHUM: Secure what he hath got, have him peached the next Sessions, and then at once you are made a rich widow.

---

5. Well aware.
6. Utensils plated with silver or gold.
7. In our line of work.

8. Want.
9. "Estate settled on a wife to be enjoyed after her husband's decease" (Johnson's *Dictionary*).

POLLY: What, murder the man I love! The blood runs cold at my heart with the very thought of it.

PEACHUM: Fie, Polly! What hath murder to do in the affair? Since the thing sooner or later must happen, I dare say, the Captain himself would like that we should get the reward for his death sooner than a stranger. Why, Polly, the Captain knows, that as 'tis his employment to rob, so 'tis ours to take robbers; every man in his business. So that there is no malice in the case.

MRS. PEACHUM: Ay, husband, now you have nicked the matter. To have him peached is the only thing could ever make me forgive her.

Air 12. Now ponder well, ye parents dear

POLLY: *Oh, ponder well! be not severe;*
So save a wretched wife!
For on the rope that hangs my dear
Depends poor Polly's life.

MRS. PEACHUM: But your duty to your parents, hussy, obliges you to hang him. What would many a wife give for such an opportunity!

POLLY: What is a jointure, what is widowhood to me? I know my heart. I cannot survive him.

Air 13. Le printemps rappelle aux armes[1]

The turtle[2] thus with plaintive crying,
Her lover dying,
The turtle thus with plaintive crying,
Laments her dove.
Down she drops quite spent with sighing,
Paired in death, as paired in love.

Thus, Sir, it will happen to your poor Polly.

MRS. PEACHUM: What, is the fool in love in earnest then? I hate thee for being particular.[3] Why, wench, thou art a shame to thy very sex.

POLLY: But hear me, Mother. If you ever loved—

MRS. PEACHUM: Those cursed playbooks she reads have been her ruin. One word more, hussy, and I shall knock your brains out, if you have any.

PEACHUM: Keep out of the way, Polly, for fear of mischief, and consider of what is proposed to you.

MRS. PEACHUM: Away, hussy. Hang your husband, and be dutiful.

Scene 11

[Mrs. Peachum, Peachum]

[Polly listening.]

MRS. PEACHUM: The thing, husband, must and shall be done. For the sake of intelligence[4] we must take other measures, and have him peached the next Session without her consent. If she will not know her duty, we know ours.

---

1. Spring calls to arms.
2. Turtledove.
3. Odd, exceptional.

4. "Account of things distant or secret" (Johnson's *Dictionary*).

PEACHUM: But really, my dear, it grieves one's heart to take off a great man. When I consider his personal bravery, his fine stratagem, how much we have already got by him, and how much more we may get, methinks I can't find in my heart to have a hand in his death. I wish you could have made Polly undertake it.

MRS. PEACHUM: But in a case of necessity—our own lives are in danger.

PEACHUM: Then, indeed, we must comply with the customs of the world, and make gratitude give way to interest. He shall be taken off.

MRS. PEACHUM: I'll undertake to manage Polly.

PEACHUM: And I'll prepare matters for the Old Baily.

Scene 12

[Polly]

Now I'm a wretch, indeed. Methinks I see him already in the cart, sweeter and more lovely than the nosegay[5] in his hand! I hear the crowd extolling his resolution and intrepidity! What volleys of sighs are sent from the windows of Holborn,[6] that so comely a youth should be brought to disgrace! I see him at the tree![7] The whole circle are in tears! Even butchers weep! Jack Ketch[8] himself hesitates to perform his duty, and would be glad to lose his fee, by a reprieve. What then will become of Polly! As yet I may inform him of their design, and aid him in his escape. It shall be so. But then he flies, absents himself, and I bar myself from his dear dear conversation! That too will distract me.[9] If he keep out of the way, my Papa and Mama may in time relent, and we may be happy. If he stays, he is hanged, and then he is lost forever! He intended to lie concealed in my room, 'till the dusk of the evening: If they are abroad, I'll this instant let him out, lest some accident should prevent him. [Exit, and returns.]

Scene 13

[Polly, Macheath]

Air 14. Pretty Parrot, say—

MACHEATH: *Pretty Polly, say,*
                When I was away,
                Did your fancy never stray
                To some newer lover?

POLLY: *Without disguise,*
                Heaving sighs,
                Doting eyes,
                My constant heart discover.[1]
                Fondly let me loll!

MACHEATH: *O pretty, pretty Poll.*

POLLY: And are *you* as fond as ever, my dear?

MACHEATH: Suspect my honor, my courage, suspect anything but my love. May my pistols miss fire, and my mare slip her shoulder while I am pursued, if I ever forsake thee!

---

5. Bouquet, often carried by condemned prisoners.
6. The road from Newgate to Tyburn, where criminals were hanged.
7. The gallows ("Tyburn tree").
8. England's most famous hangman (d. 1686); thereafter, any hangman.
9. Make me crazy.
1. Reveal, uncover.

POLLY: Nay, my dear, I have no reason to doubt you, for I find in the romance you lent me, none of the great heroes were ever false in love.

Air 15. Pray, fair one, be kind

MACHEATH: *My heart was so free,*
It roved like the bee,
'Till Polly my passion requited;
I sipped each flower,
I changed ev'ry hour,
But here ev'ry flower is united.

POLLY: Were you sentenced to transportation, sure, my dear, you could not leave me behind you—could you?

MACHEATH: Is there any power, any force that could tear me from thee? You might sooner tear a pension out of the hands of a courtier, a fee from a lawyer, a pretty woman from a looking glass, or any woman from quadrille. But to tear me from thee is impossible!

Air 16. Over the hills and far away

Were I laid on Greenland's coast,
And in my arms embraced my lass;
Warm amidst eternal frost,
Too soon the half year's night[2] would pass.

POLLY: *Were I sold on Indian soil,*
Soon as the burning day was closed,
I could mock the sultry toil,
When on my charmer's breast reposed.
MACHEATH: *And I would love you all the day,*
POLLY: *Every night would kiss and play,*
MACHEATH: *If with me you'd fondly stray*
POLLY: *Over the hills and far away.*

POLLY: Yes, I would go with thee. But oh!—how shall I speak it? I must be torn from thee. We must part.
MACHEATH: How! Part!
POLLY: We must, we must. My Papa and Mama are set against thy life. They now, even now are in search after thee. They are preparing evidence against thee. Thy life depends upon a moment.

Air 17. Gin thou wert mine awn thing—

O what pain it is to part!
Can I leave thee, can I leave thee?
O what pain it is to part!
Can thy Polly ever leave thee?
But lest death my love should thwart,
And bring thee to the fatal cart,

2. The long dark winter of the polar regions.

> *Thus I tear thee from my bleeding heart!*
> *Fly hence, and let me leave thee.*

One kiss and then—one kiss—begone—farewell.

MACHEATH: My hand, my heart, my dear, is so riveted to thine, that I cannot unloose my hold.

POLLY: But my Papa may intercept thee, and then I should lose the very glimmering of hope. A few weeks, perhaps, may reconcile us all. Shall thy Polly hear from thee?

MACHEATH: Must I then go?

POLLY: And will not absence change your love?

MACHEATH: If you doubt it, let me stay—and be hanged.

POLLY: O how I fear! How I tremble! Go—but when safety will give you leave, you will be sure to see me again; for 'till then Polly is wretched.

Air 18. O the broom, etc.

[*Parting, and looking back at each other with fondness; he at one door, she at the other.*]

MACHEATH: *The miser thus a shilling sees,*
> *Which he's obliged to pay,*
> *With sighs resigns it by degrees,*
> *And fears 'tis gone for aye.*[3]

POLLY: *The boy, thus, when his sparrow's flown,*
> *The bird in silence eyes;*
> *But soon as out of sight 'tis gone,*
> *Whines, whimpers, sobs, and cries.*

ACT 2

Scene 1. A Tavern near Newgate

[*Jemmy Twitcher, Crook-fingered Jack, Wat Dreary, Robin of Bagshot, Nimming Ned, Henry Padington, Matt of the Mint, Ben Budge, and the rest of the gang, at the table, with wine, brandy, and tobacco.*]

BEN: But prithee, Matt, what is become of thy brother Tom? I have not seen him since my return from transportation.

MATT: Poor brother Tom had an accident this time twelvemonth, and so clever a made fellow he was, that I could not save him from those fleaing[1] rascals the surgeons; and now, poor man, he is among the otamys[2] at Surgeon's Hall.

BEN: So it seems, his time was come.

JEMMY: But the present time is ours, and nobody alive hath more. Why are the laws leveled at us? Are we more dishonest than the rest of mankind? What we win, gentlemen, is our own by the law of arms, and the right of conquest.

CROOK-FINGERED JACK: Where shall we find such another set of practical philosophers, who to a man are above the fear of death?

WAT: Sound men, and true!

ROBIN: Of tried courage, and indefatigable industry!

3. Forever.
1. Flaying, robbing.

2. Skeletons (from "anatomies"). The corpses of executed criminals were often used in medical studies.

NED: Who is there here that would not die for his friend?

HARRY: Who is there here that would betray him for his interest?

MATT: Show me a gang of courtiers that can say as much.

BEN: We are for a just partition of the world, for every man hath a right to enjoy life.

MATT: We retrench³ the superfluities of mankind. The world is avaricious, and I hate avarice. A covetous fellow, like a jackdaw, steals what he was never made to enjoy, for the sake of hiding it. These are the robbers of mankind, for money was made for the free-hearted and generous, and where is the injury of taking from another, what he hath not the heart to make use of?

JEMMY: Our several stations⁴ for the day are fixed. Good luck attend us all. Fill the glasses.

Air 19. Fill ev'ry glass, etc.

MATT: *Fill ev'ry glass, for wine inspires us,*
        And fires us
    With courage, love, and joy.
    Women and wine should life employ.
    Is there aught else on earth desirous?

CHORUS: *Fill ev'ry glass, etc.*

Scene 2

[To them enter Macheath]

MACHEATH: Gentlemen, well met. My heart hath been with you this hour; but an unexpected affair hath detained me. No ceremony, I beg you.

MATT: We were just breaking up to go upon duty. Am I to have the honor of taking the air with you, Sir, this evening upon the heath? I drink a dram now and then with the stage-coachmen in the way of friendship and intelligence; and I know that about this time there will be passengers upon the Western Road,⁵ who are worth speaking with.

MACHEATH: I was to have been of that party—but—

MATT: But what, Sir?

MACHEATH: Is there any man who suspects my courage?

MATT: We have all been witnesses of it.

MACHEATH: My honor and truth to the gang?

MATT: I'll be answerable for it.

MACHEATH: In the division of our booty, have I ever shown the least marks of avarice or injustice?

MATT: By these questions something seems to have ruffled you. Are any of us suspected?

MACHEATH: I have a fixed confidence, gentlemen, in you all, as men of honor, and as such I value and respect you. Peachum is a man that is useful to us.

MATT: Is he about to play us any foul play? I'll shoot him through the head.

MACHEATH: I beg you, gentlemen, act with conduct and discretion. A pistol is your last resort.

MATT: He knows nothing of this meeting.

---

3. Cut back, economize.
4. Our respective jobs.

5. Through Bagshot Heath, west of London.

MACHEATH: Business cannot go on without him. He is a man who knows the world, and is a necessary agent to us. We have had a slight difference, and till it is accommodated I shall be obliged to keep out of his way. Any private dispute of mine shall be of no ill consequence to my friends. You must continue to act under his direction, for the moment we break loose from him, our gang is ruined.

MATT: As a bawd[6] to a whore, I grant you, he is to us of great convenience.

MACHEATH: Make him believe I have quitted the gang, which I can never do but with life.[7] At our private quarters I will continue to meet you. A week or so will probably reconcile us.

MATT: Your instructions shall be observed. 'Tis now high time for us to repair to our several duties; so till the evening at our quarters in Moor-fields[8] we bid you farewell.

MACHEATH: I shall wish myself with you. Success attend you. [Sits down melancholy at the table.]

Air 20. March in Rinaldo, with drums and trumpets

MATT: *Let us take the road.*
Hark! I hear the sound of coaches!
The hour of attack approaches,
To your arms, brave boys, and load.
See the ball I hold!
Let the chemists[9] toil like asses,
Our fire their fire surpasses,
And turns all our lead to gold.

[The gang, ranged in the front of the stage, load their pistols, and stick them under their girdles,[1] then go off singing the first part in chorus.]

Scene 3

[Macheath, Drawer[2]]

MACHEATH: What a fool is a fond wench! Polly is most confoundedly bit.[3] I love the sex. And a man who loves money might as well be contented with one guinea, as I with one woman. The town perhaps hath been as much obliged to me, for recruiting it with free-hearted ladies, as to any recruiting officer in the army. If it were not for us and the other gentlemen of the sword, Drury Lane would be uninhabited.

Air 21. Would you have a young virgin, etc.

If the heart of a man is depressed with cares,
The mist is dispelled when a woman appears;
Like the notes of a fiddle, she sweetly, sweetly
Raises the spirits, and charms our ears,
Roses and lilies her cheeks disclose,

---

6. Pimp.
7. I.e., I will quit the gang only when I quit my life.
8. Just outside the old City wall.
9. Alchemists, who sought to turn base metals into gold.

1. Belts.
2. Bartender.
3. Ensnared.

But her ripe lips are more sweet than those.
   Press her,
   Caress her
   With blisses,
   Her kisses
Dissolve us in pleasure, and soft repose.

I must have women. There is nothing unbends[4] the mind like them. Money is not so strong a cordial for the time. Drawer! [*Enter Drawer.*] Is the porter gone for all the ladies, according to my directions?

DRAWER: I expect him back every minute. But you know, Sir, you sent him as far as Hockley in the Hole, for three of the ladies, for one in Vinegar Yard, and for the rest of them somewhere about Lewkner's Lane.[5] Sure some of them are below, for I hear the bar bell. As they come I will show them up. Coming, coming!

Scene 4

[*Macheath, Mrs. Coaxer, Dolly Trull, Mrs. Vixen, Betty Doxy, Jenny Diver, Mrs. Slammekin, Suky Tawdry, and Molly Brazen*]

MACHEATH: Dear Mrs. Coaxer, you are welcome. You look charmingly today. I hope you don't want the repairs of quality, and lay on paint.[6]—Dolly Trull! Kiss me, you slut; are you as amorous as ever, hussy? You are always so taken up with stealing hearts, that you don't allow yourself time to steal anything else. Ah Dolly, thou wilt ever be a coquette!—Mrs. Vixen, I'm yours, I always loved a woman of wit and spirit; they make charming mistresses, but plaguy wives.—Betty Doxy! Come hither, hussy. Do you drink as hard as ever? You had better stick to good wholesome beer; for in troth, Betty, strong waters[7] will in time ruin your constitution. You should leave those to your betters.—What! And my pretty Jenny Diver too! As prim and demure as ever! There is not any prude, though ever so high bred, hath a more sanctified look, with a more mischievous heart. Ah! Thou art a dear artful hypocrite.—Mrs. Slammekin! As careless and genteel as ever! All you fine ladies, who know your own beauty, affect an undress.—But see, here's Suky Tawdry come to contradict what I was saying. Everything she gets one way she lays out upon her back. Why, Suky, you must keep at least a dozen tallymen.[8]—Molly Brazen! [*She kisses him.*] That's well done. I love a free-hearted wench. Thou hast a most agreeable assurance, girl, and art as willing as a turtle. But hark! I hear music. The harper is at the door. "If music be the food of love, play on."[9] Ere you seat yourselves, ladies, what think you of a dance? Come in. [*Enter Harper.*] Play the French tune, that Mrs. Slammekin was so fond of.

[*A dance á la ronde*[1] *in the French manner; near the end of it this song and chorus.*]

Air 22. Cotillon

Youth's the season made for joys,
   Love is then our duty,
She alone who that employs,
   Well deserves her beauty.

---

4. Relaxes.
5. Both in Drury Lane.
6. I hope you do not need to paint your face as women of quality do.

7. Hard liquor.
8. Merchants who provide goods on credit.
9. The opening line of Shakespeare's *Twelfth Night*.
1. A circular dance.

> Let's be gay,
>> While we may,
> Beauty's a flower, despised in decay.
> Youth's the season etc.
>
> Let us drink and sport today,
>> Ours is not tomorrow.
> Love with youth flies swift away,
>> Age is nought but sorrow.
>>> Dance and sing,
>>> Time's on the wing,
> Life never knows the return of spring.

CHORUS: *Let us drink, etc.*

MACHEATH: Now, pray ladies, take your places. Here fellow. [*Pays the Harper.*] Bid the Drawer bring us more wine. [*Exit Harper.*] If any of the ladies choose gin, I hope they will be so free to call for it.

JENNY: You look as if you meant me. Wine is strong enough for me. Indeed, Sir, I never drink strong waters, but when I have the cholic.

MACHEATH: Just the excuse of the fine ladies! Why, a lady of quality is never without the cholic. I hope, Mrs. Coaxer, you have had good success of late in your visits among the mercers.[2]

COAXER: We have so many interlopers—yet with industry, one may still have a little picking. I carried a silver-flowered lutestring, and a piece of black padesoy[3] to Mr. Peachum's lock but last week.

VIXEN: There's Molly Brazen hath the ogle of a rattlesnake. She riveted a linen-draper's eye so fast upon her, that he was nicked[4] of three pieces of cambric before he could look off.

BRAZEN: Oh dear, Madam! But sure nothing can come up to your handling of laces! And then you have such a sweet deluding tongue! To cheat a man is nothing; but the woman must have fine parts indeed who cheats a woman!

VIXEN: Lace, Madam, lies in a small compass, and is of easy conveyance. But you are apt, Madam, to think too well of your friends.

COAXER: If any woman hath more art than another, to be sure, 'tis Jenny Diver. Though her fellow be never so agreeable, she can pick his pocket as coolly, as if money were her only pleasure. Now that is a command of the passions uncommon in a woman!

JENNY: I never go to the tavern with a man, but in the view of business. I have other hours, and other sort of men for my pleasure. But had I your address,[5] Madam—

MACHEATH: Have done with your compliments, ladies; and drink about: You are not so fond of me, Jenny, as you use to be.

JENNY: 'Tis not convenient, Sir, to show my fondness among so many rivals. 'Tis your own choice, and not the warmth of my inclination that will determine you.[6]

Air 23. All in a misty morning, etc.

> Before the barn door crowing,
>> The cock by hens attended,

---

2. Dealers in textiles.
3. Types of silk fabric.
4. Robbed.

5. Polished manner.
6. Make up your mind.

His eyes around him throwing,
  Stands for a while suspended.
Then one he singles from the crew,
  And cheers the happy hen;
With how do you do, and how do you do,
  And how do you do again.

MACHEATH: Ah Jenny! Thou art a dear slut.

TRULL: Pray, Madam, were you ever in keeping?[7]

TAWDRY: I hope, Madam, I ha'n't been so long upon the town, but I have met with some good fortunes as well as my neighbors.

TRULL: Pardon me, Madam, I meant no harm by the question; 'twas only in the way of conversation.

TAWDRY: Indeed, Madam, if I had not been a fool, I might have lived very handsomely with my last friend. But upon his missing five guineas, he turned me off. Now I never suspected he had counted them.

SLAMMEKIN: Who do you look upon, Madam, as your best sort of keepers?

TRULL: That, Madam, is thereafter as they be.[8]

SLAMMEKIN: I, Madam, was once kept by a Jew; and bating[9] their religion, to women they are a good sort of people.

TAWDRY: Now for my part, I own I like an old fellow: for we always make them pay for what they can't do.

VIXEN: A spruce prentice, let me tell you, ladies, is no ill thing, they bleed[1] freely. I have sent at least two or three dozen of them in my time to the plantations.[2]

JENNY: But to be sure, Sir, with so much good fortune as you have had upon the road, you must be grown immensely rich.

MACHEATH: The road, indeed, hath done me justice, but the gaming table hath been my ruin.

Air 24. When once I lay with another man's wife, etc.

JENNY: *The gamesters and lawyers are jugglers[3] alike,*
  If they meddle your all is in danger.
Like gypsies, if once they can finger a souse,[4]
Your pockets they pick, and they pilfer your house,
  And give your estate to a stranger.

A man of courage should never put anything to the risk, but his life. These are the tools of a man of honor. Cards and dice are only fit for cowardly cheats, who prey upon their friends. [*She takes up his pistol. Tawdry takes up the other.*]

TAWDRY: This, Sir, is fitter for your hand. Besides your loss of money, 'tis a loss to the ladies. Gaming takes you off from women. How fond could I be of you! But before company, 'tis ill bred.

MACHEATH: Wanton hussies!

JENNY: I must and will have a kiss to give my wine a zest.

---

7. A kept mistress of a wealthy gentleman.
8. It depends how they treat me.
9. Apart from.
1. Spend.

2. I.e., incited them to steal and thereby caused them to be transported to the colonies.
3. Sleight-of-hand artists.
4. Get their hands on a sou (a French penny).

[*They take him about the neck, and make signs to Peachum and the constables, who rush in upon him.*]

Scene 5
[*To them, Peachum and constables*]

PEACHUM: I seize you, Sir, as my prisoner.

MACHEATH: Was this well done, Jenny? Women are decoy ducks; who can trust them! Beasts, jades, jilts, harpies, furies, whores!

PEACHUM: Your case, Mr. Macheath is not particular. The greatest heroes have been ruined by women. But, to do them justice, I must own they are a pretty sort of creatures, if we could trust them. You must now, Sir, take your leave of the ladies, and if they have a mind to make you a visit, they will be sure to find you at home. The gentleman, ladies, lodges in Newgate. Constables, wait upon the Captain to his lodgings.

Air 25. When first I laid siege to my Chloris, etc.

MACHEATH: *At the tree I shall suffer with pleasure,*
    At the tree I shall suffer with pleasure,
      Let me go where I will,
      In all kinds of ill,
    I shall find no such furies as these are.

PEACHUM: Ladies, I'll take care the reckoning shall be discharged.[5]
              [*Exit Macheath, guarded with Peachum and constables.*]

Scene 6
[*The women remain*]

VIXEN: Look ye, Mrs. Jenny, though Mr. Peachum may have made a private bargain with you and Suky Tawdry for betraying the Captain, as we were all assisting, we ought all to share alike.

COAXER: I think, Mr. Peachum, after so long an acquaintance, might have trusted me as well as Jenny Diver.

SLAMMEKIN: I am sure at least three men of his hanging, and in a year's time too (if he did me justice) should be set down to my account.[6]

TRULL: Mrs. Slammekin, that is not fair. For you know one of them was taken in bed with me.

JENNY: As far as a bowl of punch or a treat, I believe Mrs. Suky will join with me. As for anything else, ladies, you cannot in conscience expect it.

SLAMMEKIN: Dear Madam—

TRULL: I would not for the world—

SLAMMEKIN: 'Tis impossible for me—

TRULL: As I hope to be saved, Madam—

SLAMMEKIN: Nay, then I must stay here all night—

TRULL: Since you command me.   [*Exit with great ceremony.*]

---

5. The bill shall be paid.

6. I.e., I deserve the credit for at least three men that Peachum has had hanged.

Scene 7. Newgate

[*Lockit, Turnkeys,*[7] *Macheath, Constables*]

LOCKIT: Noble Captain, you are welcome. You have not been a lodger of mine this year and half. You know the custom, Sir. Garnish,[8] Captain, garnish. Hand me down those fetters there.

MACHEATH: Those, Mr. Lockit, seem to be the heaviest of the whole set. With your leave, I should like the further pair better.

LOCKIT: Look ye, Captain, we know what is fittest for our prisoners. When a gentleman uses me with civility, I always do the best I can to please him. Hand them down I say. We have them of all prices, from one guinea to ten, and 'tis fitting every gentleman should please himself.

MACHEATH: I understand you, Sir. [*Gives money.*] The fees here are so many, and so exorbitant, that few fortunes can bear the expense of getting off[9] handsomely, or of dying like a gentleman.

LOCKIT: Those, I see, will fit the Captain better. Take down the further pair. Do but examine them, Sir. Never was better work. How genteelly they are made! They will sit as easy as a glove, and the nicest[1] man in England might not be ashamed to wear them. [*He puts on the chains.*] If I had the best gentleman in the land in my custody I could not equip him more handsomely. And so, Sir, I now leave you to your private meditations.

Scene 8

[*Macheath*]

Air 26. Courtiers, courtiers think it no harm, etc.

Man may escape from rope and gun;
Nay, some have outlived the doctor's pill:
Who takes a woman must be undone,
   That basilisk[2] *is sure to kill.*
The fly that sips treacle is lost in the sweets,
So he that tastes woman, woman, woman,
   He that tastes woman, ruin meets.

To what a woeful plight have I brought myself! Here must I (all day long, 'till I am hanged) be confined to hear the reproaches of a wench who lays her ruin at my door. I am in the custody of her father, and to be sure if he knows of the matter, I shall have a fine time on't betwixt this[3] and my execution. But I promised the wench marriage. What signifies a promise to a woman? Does not man in marriage itself promise a hundred things that he never means to perform? Do all we can, women will believe us; for they look upon a promise as an excuse for following their own inclinations. But here comes Lucy, and I cannot get from her. Would I were deaf!

7. Jailers.
8. Pay the jailer the customary bribe.
9. Escaping punishment.
1. Most discerning.

2. Mythical serpent which killed by its breath or its glance.
3. This moment.

Scene 9

[*Macheath, Lucy*]

LUCY: You base man you, how can you look me in the face after what hath passed between us? See here, perfidious wretch, how I am forced to bear about the load of infamy you have laid upon me.[4] O Macheath! Thou hast robbed me of my quiet. To see thee tortured would give me pleasure.

Air 27. A lovely lass to a friar came, etc.

> *Thus when a good housewife sees a rat*
> > *In her trap in the morning taken,*
> *With pleasure her heart goes pit a pat,*
> > *In revenge for her loss of bacon.*
> > > *Then she throws him*
> > > *To the dog or cat,*
> *To be worried, crushed, and shaken.*

MACHEATH: Have you no bowels,[5] no tenderness, my dear Lucy, to see a husband in these circumstances?
LUCY: A husband!
MACHEATH: In every respect but the form, and that, my dear, may be said over us at any time. Friends should not insist upon ceremonies. From a man of honor, his word is as good as his bond.
LUCY: 'Tis the pleasure of all you fine men to insult the women you have ruined.

Air 28. 'Twas when the sea was roaring, etc.

> *How cruel are the traitors,*
> > *Who lie and swear in jest,*
> *To cheat unguarded creatures*
> > *Of virtue, fame, and rest!*
> *Whoever steals a shilling,*
> > *Through shame the guilt conceals:*
> *In love the perjured villain*
> > *With boasts the theft reveals.*

MACHEATH: The very first opportunity, my dear (have but patience), you shall be my wife in whatever manner you please.
LUCY: Insinuating monster! And so you think I know nothing of the affair of Miss Polly Peachum. I could tear thy eyes out!
HEATH: Sure Lucy, you can't be such a fool as to be jealous of Polly!
LUCY: Are you not married to her, you brute you?
MACHEATH: Married! Very good. The wench gives it out only to vex thee, and to ruin me in thy good opinion. 'Tis true, I go to the house; I chat with the girl, I kiss her, I say a thousand things to her (as all gentlemen do) that mean nothing, to divert myself; and now the silly jade hath set it about that I am married to her, to let me know what she would be at. Indeed, my dear Lucy, these violent passions may be of ill consequence to a woman in your condition.

---

4. I.e., she is pregnant.   5. The bodily seat of tenderness, pity.

LUCY: Come, come, Captain, for all your assurance, you know that Miss Polly hath put it out of your power to do me the justice you promised me.

MACHEATH: A jealous woman believes everything her passion suggests. To convince you of my sincerity, if we can find the ordinary,[6] I shall have no scruples of making you my wife; and I know the consequence of having two at a time.

LUCY: That you are only to be hanged, and so get rid of them both.

MACHEATH: I am ready, my dear Lucy, to give you satisfaction—if you think there is any in marriage. What can a man of honor say more?

LUCY: So then it seems, you are not married to Miss Polly.

MACHEATH: You know, Lucy, the girl is prodigiously conceited. No man can say a civil thing to her, but (like other fine ladies) her vanity makes her think he's her own for ever and ever.

Air 29. The sun had loosed his weary teams, etc.

> The first time at the lookingglass
>   The mother sets her daughter,
> The image strikes the smiling lass
>   With self-love ever after.
> Each time she looks, she, fonder grown,
>   Thinks ev'ry charm grows stronger.
> But alas, vain maid, all eyes but your own
>   Can see you are not younger.

When women consider their own beauties, they are all alike unreasonable in their demands; for they expect their lovers should like them as long as they like themselves.

LUCY: Yonder is my father—perhaps this way we may light upon the ordinary, who shall try if you will be as good as your word. For I long to be made an honest woman.

Scene 10

[Peachum, Lockit with an account book]

LOCKIT: In this last affair, Brother Peachum, we are agreed. You have consented to go halves in Macheath.

PEACHUM: We shall never fall out about an execution. But as to that article, pray how stands our last year's account?

LOCKIT: If you will run your eye over it, you'll find 'tis fair and clearly stated.

PEACHUM: This long arrear[7] of the government is very hard upon us! Can it be expected that we should hang our acquaintance for nothing, when our betters will hardly save theirs without being paid for it. Unless the people in employment pay better, I promise them for the future, I shall let other rogues live besides their own.

LOCKIT: Perhaps, Brother, they are afraid these matters may be carried too far. We are treated too by them with contempt, as if our profession was not reputable.

PEACHUM: In one respect indeed, our employment may be reckoned dishonest, because like great statesmen, we encourage those who betray their friends.

LOCKIT: Such language, Brother, anywhere else, might turn to your prejudice.[8] Learn to be more guarded, I beg you.

---

6. The prison chaplain.   8. Be used against you.
7. Lateness in the payment of debts.

Air 30. How happy are we, etc.

When you censure the age,
Be cautious and sage,
Lest the courtiers offended should be:
If you mention vice or bribe,
'Tis so pat⁹ to all the tribe;
Each cries, "That was leveled at me!"

PEACHUM: Here's poor Ned Clincher's name, I see. Sure, Brother Lockit, there was a little unfair proceeding in Ned's case: for he told me in the condemned hold,¹ that for value received, you had promised him a Session or two longer without molestation.

LOCKIT: Mr. Peachum, this is the first time my honor was ever called in question.

PEACHUM: Business is at an end if once we act dishonorably.

LOCKIT: Who accuses me?

PEACHUM: You are warm,² Brother.

LOCKIT: He that attacks my honor, attacks my livelihood. And this usage, Sir, is not to be borne.

PEACHUM: Since you provoke me to speak, I must tell you too, that Mrs. Coaxer charges you with defrauding her of her information money³ for the apprehending of curl-pated Hugh. Indeed, indeed, Brother, we must punctually pay our spies, or we shall have no information.

LOCKIT: Is this language to me, Sirrah, who have saved you from the gallows, Sirrah!
[*Collaring each other.*]

PEACHUM: If I am hanged, it shall be for ridding the world of an arrant rascal.

LOCKIT: This hand shall do the office of the halter⁴ you deserve, and throttle you— you dog!—

PEACHUM: Brother, Brother, we are both in the wrong. We shall be both losers in the dispute—for you know we have it in our power to hang each other. You should not be so passionate.

LOCKIT: Nor you so provoking.

PEACHUM: 'Tis our mutual interest; 'tis for the interest of the world we should agree. If I said anything, Brother, to the prejudice of your character, I ask pardon.

LOCKIT: Brother Peachum, I can forgive as well as resent. Give me your hand. Suspicion does not become a friend.

PEACHUM: I only meant to give you occasion to justify yourself. But I must now step home, for I expect the gentleman about this snuffbox that Filch nimmed two nights ago in the park. I appointed him at this hour.

Scene 11

[*Lockit, Lucy*]

LOCKIT: Whence come you, hussy?

LUCY: My tears might answer that question.

LOCKIT: You have then been whimpering and fondling, like a spaniel, over the fellow that hath abused you.

9. Suitable.
1. Death row.
2. Angry.
3. Reward for informing on someone.
4. Noose.

LUCY: One can't help love; one can't cure it. 'Tis not in my power to obey you, and hate him.

LOCKIT: Learn to bear your husband's death like a reasonable woman. 'Tis not the fashion, nowadays, so much as to affect sorrow upon these occasions. No woman would ever marry, if she had not the chance of mortality for a release. Act like a woman of spirit, hussy, and thank your father for what he is doing.

Air 31. Of a noble race was Shenkin

LUCY: *Is then his fate decreed, Sir?*
    Such a man can I think of quitting?
When first we met, so moves me yet,
    O see how my heart is splitting!

LOCKIT: Look ye, Lucy, there is no saving him. So, I think, you must do like other widows: buy yourself weeds,[5] and be cheerful.

Air 32

You'll think ere many days ensue
    This sentence not severe;
I hang your husband, child, 'tis true,
    But with him hang your care.
        Twang dang dillo dee.

Like a good wife, go moan over your dying husband. That, child, is your duty. Consider, girl, you can't have the man and the money too—so make yourself as easy as you can, by getting all you can from him.

Scene 12

[Lucy, Macheath]

LUCY: Though the ordinary was out of the way today, I hope, my dear, you will, upon the first opportunity, quiet my scruples. Oh, Sir! My father's hard heart is not to be softened, and I am in the utmost despair.

MACHEATH: But if I could raise a small sum—would not twenty guineas, think you, move him? Of all the arguments in the way of business, the perquisite[6] is the most prevailing. Your father's perquisites for the escape of prisoners must amount to a considerable sum in the year. Money well timed, and properly applied, will do anything.

Air 33. London ladies

If you at an office solicit your due,[7]
    And would not have matters neglected;
You must quicken the clerk with the perquisite too,
    To do what his duty directed.
Or would you the frowns of a lady prevent,
    She too has this palpable failing,
The perquisite softens her into consent;
    That reason with all is prevailing.

---

5. A widow's mourning clothes.　　　　　7. Seek what is due to you.
6. Tip.

LUCY: What love or money can do shall be done: for all my comfort depends upon your safety.

Scene 13

[Lucy, Macheath, Polly]

POLLY: Where is my dear husband? Was a rope ever intended for this neck! O let me throw my arms about it, and throttle thee with love! Why dost thou turn away from me? 'Tis thy Polly. 'Tis thy wife.

MACHEATH: Was ever such an unfortunate rascal as I am!

LUCY: Was there ever such another villain!

POLLY: O Macheath! Was it for this we parted? Taken! Imprisoned! Tried! Hanged! Cruel reflection! I'll stay with thee 'till death. No force shall tear thy dear wife from thee now. What means my love? Not one kind word! Not one kind look! Think what thy Polly suffers to see thee in this condition.

Air 34. All in the downs, etc.

Thus when the swallow, seeking prey,
*   Within the sash[8] is closely pent,*
His comfort, with bemoaning lay,[9]
*   Without sits pining for th' event.*
Her chatt'ring lovers all around her skim;
She heeds them not (poor bird!) her soul's with him.

MACHEATH: I must disown her. [*Aside.*] The wench is distracted.

LUCY: Am I then bilked of my virtue? Can I have no reparation? Sure men were born to lie, and women to believe them! O villain! Villain!

POLLY: Am I not thy wife? Thy neglect of me, thy aversion to me too severely proves it. Look on me. Tell me, am I not thy wife?

LUCY: Perfidious wretch!

POLLY: Barbarous husband!

LUCY: Hadst thou been hanged five months ago, I had been happy.

POLLY: And I too. If you had been kind to me 'till death, it would not have vexed me. And that's no very unreasonable request (though from a wife) to a man who hath not above seven or eight days to live.

LUCY: Art thou then married to another? Hast thou two wives, monster?

MACHEATH: If women's tongues can cease for an answer—hear me.

LUCY: I won't. Flesh and blood can't bear my usage.

POLLY: Shall I not claim my own? Justice bids me speak.

Air 35. Have you heard of a frolicsome ditty, etc.

MACHEATH: *How happy could I be with either,*
*   Were t'other dear charmer away!*
But while you thus tease me together,
*   To neither a word will I say;*
But tol de rol, etc.

---

8. Window frame.   9. Plaintive song.

POLLY: Sure, my dear, there ought to be some preference shown to a wife! At least she may claim the appearance of it. He must be distracted with his misfortunes, or he could not use me thus!

LUCY: O villain, villain! Thou hast deceived me. I could even inform against thee with pleasure. Not a prude wishes more heartily to have facts against her intimate acquaintance, than I now wish to have facts against thee. I would have her satisfaction, and they should all out.

Air 36. Irish trot

POLLY: *I'm bubbled.*[1]
LUCY: *I'm bubbled.*
POLLY: *Oh how I am troubled!*
LUCY: *Bamboozled, and bit!*
POLLY: *My distresses are doubled.*
LUCY: *When you come to the tree, should the hangman refuse,*
    These fingers, with pleasure, could fasten the noose.
POLLY: *I'm bubbled, etc.*

MACHEATH: Be pacified, my dear Lucy. This is all a fetch[2] of Polly's, to make me desperate with[3] you in case I get off. If I am hanged, she would fain[4] the credit of being thought my widow. Really, Polly, this is no time for a dispute of this sort; for whenever you are talking of marriage, I am thinking of hanging.

POLLY: And hast thou the heart to persist in disowning me?

MACHEATH: And hast thou the heart to persist in persuading me that I am married? Why, Polly, dost thou seek to aggravate my misfortunes?

LUCY: Really, Miss Peachum, you but expose yourself. Besides, 'tis barbarous in you to worry a gentleman in his circumstances.

Air 37

POLLY: *Cease your funning;*
      Force or cunning
  Never shall my heart trapan.[5]
      All these sallies
      Are but malice
  To seduce my constant man.
    'Tis most certain,
      By their flirting
  Women oft, have envy shown;
      Pleased, to ruin
      Others' wooing;
  Never happy in their own!

POLLY: Decency, Madam, methinks might teach you to behave yourself with some reserve with the husband, while his wife is present.

MACHEATH: But seriously, Polly, this is carrying the joke a little too far.

1. Cheated, fooled.
2. Trick.
3. Ruin my hopes of having.
4. Would like.
5. Ensnare.

LUCY: If you are determined, Madam, to raise a disturbance in the prison, I shall be obliged to send for the turnkey to show you the door. I am sorry, Madam, you force me to be so ill-bred.

POLLY: Give me leave to tell you, Madam. These forward airs don't become you in the least, Madam. And my duty, Madam, obliges me to stay with my husband, Madam.

Air 38. Good-morrow, gossip Joan

LUCY: *Why how now, Madam Flirt?*
    If you thus must chatter;
  And are for flinging dirt,
    Let's try who best can spatter;
    Madam Flirt!

POLLY: *Why how now, saucy jade;*
    Sure the wench is tipsy!

[To him.] *How can you see me made*
    The scoff of such a gypsy?

[To her.] *Saucy jade!*

Scene 14

[Lucy, Macheath, Polly, Peachum]

PEACHUM: Where's my wench? Ah, hussy! Hussy! Come you home, you slut; and when your fellow is hanged, hang yourself, to make your family some amends.

POLLY: Dear, dear father, do not tear me from him—I must speak; I have more to say to him. Oh! Twist thy fetters about me, that he may not haul me from thee!

PEACHUM: Sure all women are alike! If ever they commit the folly, they are sure to commit another by exposing themselves. Away—not a word more. You are my prisoner now, hussy.

Air 39. Irish howl

POLLY: *No power on earth can e'er divide*
  The knot that sacred love hath tied.
  When parents draw against our mind,[6]
  The true-love's knot they faster bind.
    Oh, oh ray, oh Amborah, oh, oh, etc.

[Holding Macheath, Peachum pulling her.]

Scene 15

[Lucy, Macheath]

MACHEATH: I am naturally compassionate, wife, so that I could not use the wench as she deserved, which made you at first suspect there was something in what she said.

LUCY: Indeed, my dear, I was strangely puzzled.

MACHEATH: If that had been the case, her father would never have brought me into this circumstance. No, Lucy, I had rather die than be false to thee.

6. Pull against our wishes.

LUCY: How happy am I, if you say this from your heart! For I love thee so, that I could sooner bear to see thee hanged than in the arms of another.

MACHEATH: But couldst thou bear to see me hanged?

LUCY: O, Macheath, I can never live to see that day.

MACHEATH: You see, Lucy, in the account of love you are in my debt, and you must now be convinced, that I rather choose to die than be another's. Make me, if possible, love thee more, and let me owe my life to thee. If you refuse to assist me, Peachum and your father will immediately put me beyond all means of escape.

LUCY: My father, I know, hath been drinking hard with the prisoners, and I fancy he is now taking his nap in his own room. If I can procure the keys, shall I go off with thee, my dear?

MACHEATH: If we are together, 'twill be impossible to lie concealed. As soon as the search begins to be a little cool, I will send to thee. 'Till then my heart is thy prisoner.

LUCY: Come then, my dear husband, owe thy life to me, and though you love me not, be grateful. But that Polly runs in my head strangely.

MACHEATH: A moment of time may make us unhappy forever.

Air 40. The lass of Patie's mill, etc.

LUCY: *I like the fox shall grieve,*
 Whose mate hath left her side.
Whom hounds, from morn to eve,
 Chase o'er the country wide.
Where can my lover hide?
 Where cheat the weary pack?
If love be not his guide,
 He never will come back!

ACT 3

Scene 1. Newgate

[Lockit, Lucy]

LOCKIT: To be sure, wench, you must have been aiding and abetting to help him to this escape.

LUCY: Sir, here hath been Peachum and his daughter Polly, and to be sure they know the ways of Newgate as well as if they had been born and bred in the place all their lives. Why must all your suspicion light upon me?

LOCKIT: Lucy, Lucy, I will have none of these shuffling answers.

LUCY: Well then, if I know anything of him I wish I may be burnt!

LOCKIT: Keep your temper, Lucy, or I shall pronounce you guilty.

LUCY: Keep yours, Sir, I do wish I may be burned. I do—and what can I say more to convince you?

LOCKIT: Did he tip handsomely? How much did he come down with? Come hussy, don't cheat your father; and I shall not be angry with you. Perhaps you have made a better bargain with him than I could have done. How much, my good girl?

LUCY: You know, Sir, I am fond of him, and would have given money to have kept him with me.

LOCKIT: Ah, Lucy! Thy education might have put thee more upon thy guard; for a girl in the bar of an alehouse is always besieged.

LUCY: Dear Sir, mention not my education—for 'twas to that I owe my ruin.

Air 41. If love's a sweet passion, etc.

When young at the bar you first taught me to score,[1]
And bid me be free of my lips, and no more;
I was kissed by the parson, the squire, and the sot.
When the guest was departed, the kiss was forgot.
But his kiss was so sweet, and so closely he pressed,
That I languished and pined till I granted the rest.

If you can forgive me, Sir, I will make a fair confession, for to be sure he hath been a most barbarous villain to me.

LOCKIT: And so you have let him escape, hussy? Have you?

LUCY: When a woman loves, a kind look, a tender word can persuade her to anything, and I could ask no other bribe.

LOCKIT: Thou wilt always be a vulgar[2] slut, Lucy. If you would not be looked upon as a fool, you should never do anything but upon the foot of[3] interest. Those that act otherwise are their own bubbles.[4]

LUCY: But love, Sir, is a misfortune that may happen to the most discreet woman, and in love we are all fools alike. Notwithstanding all he swore, I am now fully convinced that Polly Peachum is actually his wife. Did I let him escape (fool that I was!) to go to her? Polly will wheedle herself into his money, and then Peachum will hang him, and cheat us both.

LOCKIT: So I am to be ruined, because, forsooth, you must be in love! A very pretty excuse!

LUCY: I could murder that impudent happy strumpet. I gave him his life, and that creature enjoys the sweets of it. Ungrateful Macheath!

Air 42. South Sea ballad

My love is all madness and folly,
  Alone I lie,
   Toss, tumble, and cry,
What a happy creature is Polly!
Was e'er such a wretch as I!
With rage I redden like scarlet,
That my dear inconstant varlet,
  Stark blind to my charms,
   Is lost in the arms
Of that jilt, that inveigling harlot!
  Stark blind to my charms,
   Is lost in the arms
Of that jilt, that inveigling harlot!
This, this my resentment alarms.

LOCKIT: And so, after all this mischief, I must stay here to be entertained with your caterwauling, Mistress Puss! Out of my sight, wanton strumpet! You shall fast and mortify yourself into reason, with now and then a little handsome discipline[5] to bring you to your senses. Go.

---

1. Tally, keep an account.
2. Common.
3. For the sake of.
4. Cheat themselves.
5. A beating.

Scene 2

[*Lockit*]

LOCKIT: Peachum then intends to outwit me in this affair; but I'll be even with him. The dog is leaky in his liquor,[6] so I'll ply him that way, get the secret from him, and turn this affair to my own advantage. Lions, wolves, and vultures don't live together in herds, droves, or flocks. Of all animals of prey, man is the only sociable one. Every one of us preys upon his neighbor, and yet we herd together. Peachum is my companion, my friend. According to the custom of the world, indeed, he may quote thousands of precedents for cheating me. And shall not I make use of the privilege of friendship to make him a return?

Air 43. Packington's Pound

Thus gamesters united in friendship are found,
Though they know that their industry all is a cheat;
They flock to their prey at the dicebox's sound,
And join to promote one another's deceit.
But if by mishap
They fail of a chap,[7]
To keep in their hands, they each other entrap.
Like pikes, lank with hunger, who miss of their ends,[8]
They bite their companions, and prey on their friends.

Now, Peachum, you and I, like honest tradesmen, are to have a fair trial which of us two can overreach the other.—Lucy! [*Enter Lucy.*] Are there any of Peachum's people now in the house?

LUCY: Filch, Sir, is drinking a quartern[9] of strong waters in the next room with Black Moll.

LOCKIT: Bid him come to me.

Scene 3

[*Lockit, Filch*]

LOCKIT: Why, boy, thou lookest as if thou wert half starved, like a shotten herring.[1]

FILCH: One had need have the constitution of a horse to go through the business. Since the favorite child-getter[2] was disabled by a mishap, I have picked up a little money by helping the ladies to a pregnancy against their being called down to sentence. But if a man cannot get an honest livelihood any easier way, I am sure, 'tis what I can't undertake for another Session.

LOCKIT: Truly, if that great man should tip off,[3] 'twould be an irreparable loss. The vigor and prowess of a knight-errant never saved half the ladies in distress that he hath done. But, boy, can'st thou tell me where thy master is to be found?

FILCH: At his lock,[4] Sir, at the Crooked Billet.

LOCKIT: Very well. I have nothing more with you.

[*Exit Filch.*]

---

6. Talkative when drunk.
7. Cannot get a customer (prey).
8. Fail to catch their prey.
9. Quarter-pint.
1. A herring that has spawned.

2. Begetter (i.e., Macheath).
3. Die.
4. A cant word signifying a warehouse where stolen goods are deposited [Gay's note].

I'll go to him there, for I have many important affairs to settle with him; and in the way of those transactions, I'll artfully get into his secret. So that Macheath shall not remain a day longer out of my clutches.

Scene 4. A Gaming House
[*Macheath in a fine tarnished coat, Ben Budge, Matt of the Mint*]

MACHEATH: I am sorry, gentlemen, the road was so barren of money. When my friends are in difficulties, I am always glad that my fortune can be serviceable to them. [*Gives them money.*] You see, gentlemen, I am not a mere Court friend, who professes everything and will do nothing.

Air 44. Lillibullero

The modes of the Court so common are grown,
* That a true friend can hardly be met;*
Friendship for interest is but a loan,
* Which they let out for what they can get.*
*   'Tis true, you find*
*   Some friends so kind,*
Who will give you good counsel themselves to defend.
*   In sorrowful ditty,*
*   They promise, they pity,*
But shift you[5] for money, from friend to friend.

But we, gentlemen, have still honor enough to break through the corruptions of the world. And while I can serve you, you may command me.

BEN: It grieves my heart that so generous a man should be involved in such difficulties, as oblige him to live with such ill company, and herd with gamesters.

MATT: See the partiality of mankind! One man may steal a horse, better than another look over a hedge.[6] Of all mechanics,[7] of all servile handicraftsmen, a gamester is the vilest. But yet, as many of the quality[8] are of the profession, he is admitted amongst the politest company. I wonder we are not more respected.

MACHEATH: There will be deep play tonight at Marybone, and consequently money may be picked up upon the road. Meet me there, and I'll give you the hint who is worth setting.[9]

MATT: The fellow with a brown coat with a narrow gold binding, I am told, is never without money.

MACHEATH: What do you mean, Matt? Sure you will not think of meddling with him! He's a good honest kind of a fellow, and one of us.

BEN: To be sure, Sir, we will put ourselves under your direction.

MACHEATH: Have an eye upon the moneylenders. A rouleau,[1] or two, would prove a pretty sort of an expedition. I hate extortion.

MATT: Those rouleaus are very pretty things. I hate your bank bills. There is such a hazard in putting them off.[2]

---

5. Put you off.
6. I.e., one man is permitted to steal a horse, though another is not permitted even to look at one; proverbial.
7. Tradesmen.

8. The people of quality (gentry).
9. Setting upon, robbing.
1. A packet of gold coins.
2. Getting rid of them, passing them off.

MACHEATH: There is a certain man of distinction, who in his time hath nicked me out of a great deal of the ready. He is in my cash,[3] Ben; I'll point him out to you this evening, and you shall draw upon him for the debt. The company are met; I hear the dicebox in the other room. So, gentlemen, your servant. You'll meet me at Marybone.

Scene 5. Peachum's Lock

[A *table with wine, brandy, pipes, and tobacco.*
Peachum, Lockit]

LOCKIT: The coronation account,[4] Brother Peachum, is of so intricate a nature, that I believe it will never be settled.

PEACHUM: It consists indeed of a great variety of articles. It was worth to our people, in fees of different kinds, above ten installments.[5] This is part of the account, Brother, that lies open before us.

LOCKIT: A lady's tail[6] of rich brocade—that, I see, is disposed of.

PEACHUM: To Mrs. Diana Trapes, the tallywoman,[7] and she will make a good hand[8] on't in shoes and slippers, to trick out young ladies, upon their going into keeping.

LOCKIT: But I don't see any article of the jewels.

PEACHUM: Those are so well known, that they must be sent abroad. You'll find them entered under the article of exportation. As for the snuffboxes, watches, swords, etc., I thought it best to enter them under their several heads.

LOCKIT: Seven and twenty women's pockets[9] complete; with the several things therein contained; all sealed, numbered, and entered.

PEACHUM: But, Brother, it is impossible for us now to enter upon this affair. We should have the whole day before us. Besides, the account of the last half year's plate is in a book by itself, which lies at the other office.

LOCKIT: Bring us then more liquor. Today shall be for pleasure, tomorrow for business. Ah, Brother, those daughters of ours are two slippery hussies. Keep a watchful eye upon Polly, and Macheath in a day or two shall be our own again.

Air 45. Down in the north country, etc.

LOCKIT: *What gudgeons[1] are we men!*
Ev'ry woman's easy prey.
Though we have felt the hook, again
We bite and they betray.
The bird that hath been trapped,
When he hears his calling mate,
To her he flies, again he's clapped
Within the wiry grate.

3. Owes me money.
4. A manuscript inventory of items stolen during the coronation of George II; Peachum "keeps books" like an ordinary businessman.
5. I.e., the thieves have found a single coronation more than ten times as profitable as the annual installment of the new Lord Mayor.
6. Train (of a woman's dress).
7. One who provides goods on credit.
8. Profit.
9. A pocket was a detachable bag worn outside the woman's dress.
1. "A small fish . . . easily caught, and therefore made a proverbial name for a man easily cheated" (Johnson's *Dictionary*).

PEACHUM: But what signifies catching the bird, if your daughter Lucy will set open the door of the cage?

LOCKIT: If men were answerable for the follies and frailties of their wives and daughters, no friends could keep a good correspondence together for two days. This is unkind of you, Brother; for among good friends, what they say or do goes for nothing.

[Enter a servant.]

SERVANT: Sir, here's Mrs. Diana Trapes wants to speak with you.

PEACHUM: Shall we admit her, Brother Lockit?

LOCKIT: By all means. She's a good customer, and a fine-spoken woman. And a woman who drinks and talks so freely will enliven the conversation.

PEACHUM: Desire her to walk in.

[Exit servant.]

Scene 6

[Peachum, Lockit, Mrs. Trapes]

PEACHUM: Dear Mrs. Dye, your servant. One may know by your kiss, that your gin is excellent.

TRAPES: I was always very curious[2] in my liquors.

LOCKIT: There is no perfumed breath like it. I have been long acquainted with the flavor of those lips. Han't I, Mrs. Dye?

TRAPES: Fill it up. I take as large draughts of liquor, as I did of love. I hate a flincher in either.

Air 46. A shepherd kept sheep, etc.

In the days of my youth I could bill like a dove, fa, la, la, etc.
Like a sparrow at all times was ready for love, fa, la, la, etc.
The life of all mortals in kissing should pass,
Lip to lip while we're young—then the lip to the glass, fa, la, etc.

But now, Mr. Peachum, to our business. If you have blacks[3] of any kind, brought in of late: mantoes,[4] velvet scarves, petticoats—let it be what it will—I am your chap, for all my ladies are very fond of mourning.

PEACHUM: Why, look ye, Mrs. Dye, you deal so hard with us, that we can afford to give the gentlemen, who venture their lives for the goods, little or nothing.

TRAPES: The hard times oblige me to go very near[5] in my dealing. To be sure, of late years I have been a great sufferer by the Parliament. Three thousand pounds would hardly make me amends. The act for destroying the Mint[6] was a severe cut upon our business. 'Till then, if a customer[7] stepped out of the way, we knew where to have her. No doubt you know Mrs. Coaxer. There's a wench now (till today) with a good suit of clothes of mine upon her back, and I could never set eyes upon her for three months together. Since the act too against imprisonment

2. Fastidious.
3. Black clothing.
4. Loose robes (French: manteaux).
5. To pay as little as possible.
6. The Mint was a safe haven for debtors, and hence a

gathering place for disreputable characters. The Act (10 October 1723) made it much harder to feign bankruptcy, and thereby to take refuge in the Mint.
7. Prostitute.

for small sums,[8] my loss there too hath been very considerable, and it must be so, when a lady can borrow a handsome petticoat, or a clean gown, and I not have the least hank[9] upon her! And, o' my conscience, now-a-days most ladies take a delight in cheating, when they can do it with safety.

PEACHUM: Madam, you had a handsome gold watch of us t'other day for seven guineas. Considering we must have our profit, to a gentleman upon the road, a gold watch will be scarce worth the taking.

TRAPES: Consider, Mr. Peachum, that watch was remarkable, and not of very safe sale. If you have any black velvet scarves—they are a handsome winter wear; and take with most gentlemen who deal with my customers. 'Tis I that put the ladies upon a good foot. 'Tis not youth or beauty that fixes their price. The gentlemen always pay according to their dress, from half a crown to two guineas; and yet those hussies make nothing of bilking of me. Then too, allowing for accidents. I have eleven fine customers now down under the surgeon's hands[1]—what with fees and other expenses, there are great goings-out, and no comings-in, and not a farthing to pay for at least a month's clothing. We run great risks—great risks indeed.

PEACHUM: As I remember, you said something just now of Mrs. Coaxer.

TRAPES: Yes, Sir. To be sure I stripped her of a suit of my own clothes about two hours ago; and have left her as she should be, in her shift, with a lover of hers at my house. She called him upstairs, as he was going to Marybone in a hackney coach. And I hope, for her own sake and mine, she will persuade the Captain to redeem[2] her, for the Captain is very generous to the ladies.

LOCKIT: What Captain?

TRAPES: He thought I did not know him. An intimate acquaintance of yours, Mr. Peachum—only Captain Macheath—as fine as a lord.

PEACHUM: Tomorrow, dear Mrs. Dye, you shall set your own price upon any of the goods you like. We have at least half a dozen velvet scarves, and all at your service. Will you give me leave to make you a present of this suit of nightclothes for your own wearing? But are you sure it is Captain Macheath?

TRAPES: Though he thinks I have forgot him, nobody knows him better. I have taken a great deal of the Captain's money in my time at second hand, for he always loved to have his ladies well dressed.

PEACHUM: Mr. Lockit and I have a little business with the Captain—you understand me—and we will satisfy you for Mrs. Coaxer's debt.

LOCKIT: Depend upon it. We will deal like men of honor.

TRAPES: I don't inquire after your affairs—so whatever happens, I wash my hands on't. It hath always been my maxim, that one friend should assist another. But if you please, I'll take one of the scarves home with me. 'Tis always good to have something in hand.

Scene 7. Newgate

[Lucy]

LUCY: Jealousy, rage, love, and fear are at once tearing me to pieces. How I am weather-beaten and shattered with distresses!

---

8. "An Act to Prevent Frivolous and Vexatious Arrests" (24 June 1726); "small sums" meant ten pounds if a Superior court matter, or 40 shillings if an Inferior.
9. Hold.

1. For treatment of venereal disease.
2. I.e., will help her to buy back (as at a pawn shop) her "suit of . . . clothes."

Air 47. One evening, having lost my way, etc.

I'm like a skiff on the ocean tossed,
    Now high, now low, with each billow born,
With her rudder broke, and her anchor lost,
    Deserted and all forlorn.
While thus I lie rolling and tossing all night,
That Polly lies sporting on seas of delight!
    Revenge, revenge, revenge,
Shall appease my restless sprite.

I have the ratsbane[3] ready. I run no risk; for I can lay her death upon the gin, and so many die of that naturally that I shall never be called in question. But say I were to be hanged—I never could be hanged for anything that would give me greater comfort than the poisoning that slut.

[*Enter Filch.*]

FILCH: Madam, here's our Miss Polly come to wait upon you.
LUCY: Show her in.

Scene 8

[*Lucy, Polly*]

LUCY: Dear Madam, your servant. I hope you will pardon my passion, when I was so happy to see you last. I was so overrun with the spleen,[4] that I was perfectly out of myself. And really when one hath the spleen, everything is to be excused by a friend.

Air 48. Now Roger, I'll tell thee, because thou'rt my son

When a wife's in her pout,
(As she's sometimes, no doubt)
The good husband as meek as a lamb,
    Her vapors to still,
    First grants her her will,
And the quieting draught is a dram.[5]
Poor man! And the quieting draught is a dram.

I wish all our quarrels might have so comfortable a reconciliation.
POLLY: I have no excuse for my own behavior, Madam, but my misfortunes. And really, Madam, I suffer too upon your account.
LUCY: But, Miss Polly, in the way of friendship, will you give me leave to propose a glass of cordial to you?
POLLY: Strong waters are apt to give me the headache. I hope, Madam, you will excuse me.
LUCY: Not the greatest lady in the land could have better in her closet, for her own private drinking. You seem mighty low in spirits, my dear.

3. Rat poison.
4. Generally, ill temper; more specifically, a fashionable disease resembling hypochondria, also known as "the
vapors."
5. A shot of alcohol.

POLLY: I am sorry, Madam, my health will not allow me to accept of your offer. I should not have left you in the rude manner I did when we met last, Madam, had not my Papa hauled me away so unexpectedly. I was indeed somewhat provoked, and perhaps might use some expressions that were disrespectful. But really, Madam, the Captain treated me with so much contempt and cruelty, that I deserved your pity, rather than your resentment.

LUCY: But since his escape, no doubt all matters are made up again. Ah Polly! Polly! 'Tis I am the unhappy wife; and he loves you as if you were only his mistress.

POLLY: Sure, Madam, you cannot think me so happy as to be the object of your jealousy. A man is always afraid of a woman who loves him too well—so that I must expect to be neglected and avoided.

LUCY: Then our cases, my dear Polly, are exactly alike. Both of us indeed have been too fond.

Air 49. O Bessy Bell

POLLY: *A curse attends that woman's love,*
 Who always would be pleasing.
LUCY: *The pertness of the billing dove,*
 Like tickling, is but teasing.
POLLY: *What then in love can woman do?*
LUCY: *If we grow fond they shun us.*
POLLY: *And when we fly them, they pursue.*
LUCY: *But leave us when they've won us.*

LUCY: Love is so very whimsical in both sexes, that it is impossible to be lasting. But my heart is particular,[6] and contradicts my own observation.

POLLY: But really, Mistress Lucy, by his last behavior, I think I ought to envy you. When I was forced from him, he did not show the least tenderness. But perhaps, he hath a heart not capable of it.

Air 50. Would fate to me Belinda give

Among the men, coquettes we find,
Who court by turns all womankind;
And we grant all their hearts desired,
When they are flattered, and admired.

The coquettes of both sexes are self-lovers, and that is a love no other whatever can dispossess. I fear, my dear Lucy, our husband is one of those.

LUCY: Away with these melancholy reflections; indeed, my dear Polly, we are both of us a cup too low.[7] Let me prevail upon you, to accept of my offer.

Air 51. Come, sweet lass, etc.

 Come, sweet lass,
 Let's banish sorrow
 Till tomorrow;
 Come, sweet lass,

6. In two senses: (1) preoccupied with one person (Macheath), and therefore (2) idiosyncratic—an exception to the rule she has just pronounced.
7. I.e., needing a drink.

> *Let's take a chirping*[8] *glass.*
>   *Wine can clear*
>   *The vapors of despair;*
>   *And make us light as air;*
>   *Then drink, and banish care.*

I can't bear, child, to see you in such low spirits. And I must persuade you to what I know will do you good. [*Aside.*] I shall now soon be even with the hypocritical strumpet.   [*Exit.*]

Scene 9.

[*Polly*]

All this wheedling of Lucy cannot be for nothing. At this time too! When I know she hates me! The dissembling of a woman is always the forerunner of mischief. By pouring strong waters down my throat, she thinks to pump some secrets out of me. I'll be upon my guard, and won't taste a drop of her liquor, I'm resolved.

Scene 10

[*Lucy, with strong waters; Polly*]

LUCY: Come, Miss Polly.

POLLY: Indeed, child, you have given yourself trouble to no purpose. You must, my dear, excuse me.

LUCY: Really, Miss Polly, you are so squeamishly affected about taking a cup of strong waters as a lady before company. I vow, Polly, I shall take it monstrously ill if you refuse me. Brandy and men (though women love them never so well)[9] are always taken by us with some reluctance—unless 'tis in private.

POLLY: I protest, Madam, it goes against me. What do I see! Macheath again in custody! Now every glimmering of happiness is lost. [*Drops the glass of liquor on the ground.*]

LUCY [*Aside*]: Since things are thus, I'm glad the wench hath escaped: for by this event, 'tis plain, she was not happy enough to deserve to be poisoned.

Scene 11

[*Lockit, Macheath, Peachum, Lucy, Polly*]

LOCKIT: Set your heart to rest, Captain. You have neither the chance of love or money for another escape, for you are ordered to be called down upon your trial immediately.

PEACHUM: Away, hussies! This is not a time for a man to be hampered with his wives. You see, the gentleman is in chains already.

LUCY: O husband, husband, my heart longed to see thee; but to see thee thus distracts me!

POLLY: Will not my dear husband look upon his Polly? Why hadst thou not flown to me for protection? With me thou hadst been safe.

---

8. Cheering.   9. However much women may love them.

Air 52. The last time I went o'er the moor

POLLY: *Hither, dear husband, turn your eyes.*
LUCY: *Bestow one glance to cheer me.*
POLLY: *Think with that look, thy Polly dies.*
LUCY: *O shun me not—but hear me.*
POLLY: *'Tis Polly sues.*
LUCY: *'Tis Lucy speaks.*
POLLY: *Is thus true love requited?*
LUCY: *My heart is bursting.*
POLLY: *Mine too breaks.*
LUCY: *Must I—*
POLLY: *Must I be slighted?*

MACHEATH: What would you have me say, ladies? You see, this affair will soon be at an end, without my disobliging either of you.
PEACHUM: But the settling this point, Captain, might prevent a lawsuit between your two widows.

Air 53. Tom Tinker's my true love

MACHEATH: *Which way shall I turn me? How can I decide?*
    Wives, the day of our death, are as fond as a bride.
    One wife is too much for most husbands to hear,
    But two at a time there's no mortal can bear.
    This way, and that way, and which way I will,
    What would comfort the one, t'other wife would take ill.

POLLY: But if his own misfortunes have made him insensible to mine—A father sure will be more compassionate. Dear, dear Sir, sink[1] the material evidence, and bring him off at his trial. Polly upon her knees begs it of you.

Air 54. I am a poor shepherd undone

When my hero in court appears,
    And stands arraigned for his life;
Then think of poor Polly's tears;
    For Ah! Poor Polly's his wife.
Like the sailor he holds up his hand,
    Distressed on the dashing wave.
To die a dry death at land,
    Is as bad as a wat'ry grave.
And alas, poor Polly!
Alack, and well-a-day!
Before I was in love,
    Oh! Every month was May.

LUCY: If Peachum's heart is hardened, sure you, Sir, will have more compassion on a daughter. I know the evidence is in your power. How then can you be a tyrant to me? [*Kneeling.*]

1. Suppress.

Air 55. Ianthe the lovely, etc.

When he holds up his hand arraigned for his life,
O think of your daughter, and think I'm his wife!
What are cannons, or bombs, or clashing of swords?
For death is more certain by witness's words.
Then nail up their lips; that dread thunder allay;
And each month of my life will hereafter be May.

LOCKIT: Macheath's time is come, Lucy. We know our own affairs, therefore let us have no more whimpering or whining.

Air 56. A cobbler there was, etc.

Ourselves, like the great, to secure a retreat,
When matters require it, must give up our gang:
  And good reason why,
  Or, instead of the fry,[2]
  Ev'n Peachum and I,
Like poor petty rascals, might hang, hang;
Like poor petty rascals, might hang.

PEACHUM: Set your heart at rest, Polly. Your husband is to die today. Therefore, if you are not already provided, 'tis high time to look about for another. There's comfort for you, you slut.

LOCKIT: We are ready, Sir, to conduct you to the Old Bailey.

Air 57. Bonny Dundee

MACHEATH: *The charge is prepared; the lawyers are met,*
  The judges all ranged (a terrible show!).
  I go undismayed, for death is a debt—
  A debt on demand—so take what I owe.
  Then farewell my love. Dear charmers, adieu.
  Contented I die—'tis the better for you.
  Here ends all dispute the rest of our lives,
  For this way at once I please all my wives.

Now, gentlemen, I am ready to attend you.

Scene 12

[Lucy, Polly, Filch]

POLLY: Follow them, Filch, to the court. And when the trial is over, bring me a particular account of his behavior, and of everything that happened. You'll find me here with Miss Lucy. [*Exit Filch.*] But why is all this music?

LUCY: The prisoners, whose trials are put off till next Session, are diverting themselves.

POLLY: Sure there is nothing so charming as music! I'm fond of it to distraction! But alas! Now, all mirth seems an insult upon my affliction. Let us retire, my dear Lucy, and indulge our sorrows. The noisy crew, you see, are coming upon us.   [*Exit.*]

---

2. Small fish.

[*A dance of prisoners in chains, etc.*]

Scene 13. The Condemned Hold
[*Macheath, in a melancholy posture*]

Air 58. Happy Groves

O cruel, cruel, cruel case!
Must I suffer this disgrace?

Air 59. Of all the girls that are so smart

Of all the friends in time of grief,	
When threatening death looks grimmer,	
Not one so sure can bring relief,	
As this best friend, a brimmer.[3]	[*Drinks.*]

Air 60. Britons strike home

Since I must swing, I scorn, I scorn to wince or whine.	[*Rises.*]

Air 61. Chevy Chase

But now again my spirits sink;	
I'll raise them high with wine.	[*Drinks a glass of wine.*]

Air 62. To old Sir Simon the king

But valor the stronger grows,	
The stronger liquor we're drinking.	
And how can we feel our woes,	
When we've lost the trouble of thinking?	[*Drinks.*]

Air 63. Joy to great Caesar

If thus—A man can die	
Much bolder with brandy.	[*Pours out a bumper of brandy.*]

Air 64. There was an old woman

So I drink off this bumper. And now I can stand the test.	
And my comrades shall see, that I die as brave as the best.	[*Drinks.*]

Air 65. Did you ever hear of a gallant sailor

But can I leave my pretty hussies,
Without one tear, or tender sigh?

Air 66. Why are mine eyes still flowing

Their eyes, their lips, their busses[4]
Recall my love—Ah must I die?

---

3. A cup filled to the brim.   4. Kisses.

Air 67. Green Sleeves

Since laws were made for ev'ry degree,
To curb vice in others, as well as me,
I wonder we ha'n't better company,
    Upon Tyburn tree!
But gold from law can take out the sting;
And if rich men like us were to swing,
'Twould thin the land, such numbers to string
    Upon Tyburn tree!

JAILER: Some friends of yours, Captain, desire to be admitted. I leave you together.

Scene 14

[Macheath, Ben Budge, Matt of the Mint]

MACHEATH: For my having broke[5] prison, you see, gentlemen, I am ordered immediate execution. The sheriff's officers, I believe, are now at the door. That Jemmy Twitcher should peach me, I own surprised me! 'Tis a plain proof that the world is all alike, and that even our gang can no more trust one another than other people. Therefore, I beg you, gentlemen, look well to yourselves, for in all probability you may live some months longer.

MATT: We are heartily sorry, Captain, for your misfortune. But 'tis what we must all come to.

MACHEATH: Peachum and Lockit, you know, are infamous scoundrels. Their lives are as much in your power, as yours are in theirs. Remember your dying friend. 'Tis my last request. Bring those villains to the gallows before you, and I am satisfied.

MATT: We'll do't.

JAILER: Miss Polly and Miss Lucy entreat a word with you.

MACHEATH: Gentlemen, adieu.

Scene 15

[Lucy, Macheath, Polly]

MACHEATH: My dear Lucy—my dear Polly—whatsoever hath passed between us is now at an end. If you are fond of marrying again, the best advice I can give you is to ship yourselves off for the West Indies, where you'll have a fair chance of getting a husband apiece; or by good luck, two or three, as you like best.

POLLY: How can I support this sight!

LUCY: There is nothing moves one so much as a great man in distress.

Air 68. All you that must take a leap, etc.

LUCY: *Would I might be hanged!*
POLLY: *And I would so too!*
LUCY: *To be hanged with you.*
POLLY: *My dear, with you.*
MACHEATH: *O leave me to thought! I fear! I doubt!*
    I tremble! I droop! See, my courage is out.   [*Turns up the empty bottle.*]

5. Broken out of.

POLLY: *No token of love?*
MACHEATH: *See, my courage is out.*   [*Turns up the empty pot.*]
LUCY: *No token of love?*
POLLY: *Adieu!*
LUCY: *Farewell!*
MACHEATH: *But hark! I hear the toll of the bell.*
CHORUS: *Tol de rol lol, etc.*
JAILER: Four women more, Captain, with a child a-piece! See, here they come.
   [*Enter women and children.*]
MACHEATH: What—four wives more! This is too much. Here—tell the sheriff's
   officers I am ready.

                                    [*Exit Macheath guarded.*]

                                Scene 16

                     [*To them, enter Player and Beggar*]

PLAYER: But, honest friend, I hope you don't intend that Macheath shall be really
   executed.
BEGGAR: Most certainly, Sir. To make the piece perfect, I was for doing strict poetical justice. Macheath is to be hanged; and for the other personages of the drama,
   the audience must have supposed they were all either hanged or transported.
PLAYER: Why then, friend, this is a downright deep tragedy. The catastrophe is
   manifestly wrong, for an opera must end happily.
BEGGAR: Your objection, Sir, is very just; and is easily removed. For you must
   allow, that in this kind of drama, 'tis no matter how absurdly things are brought
   about. So—you rabble there—run and cry a reprieve—let the prisoner be brought
   back to his wives in triumph.
PLAYER: All this we must do, to comply with the taste of the town.[6]
BEGGAR: Through the whole piece you may observe such a similitude of manners
   in high and low life, that it is difficult to determine whether (in the fashionable
   vices) the fine gentlemen imitate the gentlemen of the road, or the gentlemen of
   the road the fine gentlemen. Had the play remained, as I at first intended, it would
   have carried a most excellent moral. 'Twould have shown that the lower sort of
   people have their vices in a degree as well as the rich, and that they are punished
   for them.

                                Scene 17

                    [*To them, Macheath with rabble, etc.*]

MACHEATH: So, it seems, I am not left to my choice, but must have a wife at last.
   Look ye, my dears, we will have no controversy now. Let us give this day to mirth,
   and I am sure she who thinks herself my wife will testify her joy by a dance.
ALL: Come, a dance, a dance.
MACHEATH: Ladies, I hope you will give me leave to present a partner to each of
   you. And (if I may without offense) for this time, I take Polly for mine. [*To Polly.*]
   And for life, you slut, for we were really married. As for the rest—But at present
   keep your own secret.

6. The fashionable audience.

A Dance

Air 69. Lumps of pudding, etc.

Thus I stand like the Turk, with his doxies around;[7]
From all sides their glances his passion confound;
For black, brown, and fair, his inconstancy burns,
And the different beauties subdue him by turns:
Each calls forth her charms, to provoke his desires:
Though willing to all; with but one he retires.
But think of this maxim, and put off your sorrow,
The wretch of today, may be happy tomorrow.
CHORUS: *But think of this maxim, etc.*

FINIS.

1727

1728

❊ "THE BEGGAR'S OPERA" AND ITS TIME ❊

Influences and Impact

Attending performances of *The Beggar's Opera* in 1728, audiences encountered elements intensely familiar and newly mixed: old tunes supplied with new words; Newgate prison (notorious for its filth and depravity) reimagined as a site of revels, dancing, and amorous dalliance; and two famous criminals—Jonathan Wild and Jack Sheppard—reconceived as comic singers, fuddled tacticians, and intrafamilial contenders, indeed as those stock antagonists the huffy father and the sleek son-in-law.

The mix of elements proved potent long beyond the first production; the play was revived in London at least once a year for more than a century and a half. Gay's songs, scenes, and above all his central character Macheath became cultural icons, habitually referred and resorted to by many different admirers for many different purposes. The selections that follow trace some of the influences the *Opera* absorbed, and some of those it disseminated.

Thomas D'Urfey[1]
from *Wit and Mirth: or, Pills to Purge Melancholy*
WHY IS YOUR FAITHFUL SLAVE DISDAINED?[2]

Why is your faithful slave disdained?
By gentle arts my heart you gained!
   Oh, keep it by the same!
For ever shall my passion last,
5   If you will make me once possessed
   Of what I dare not name.

7. Like a Sultan in a harem.
1. In 1719, at the close of his checkered career as playwright, court poet, ballad-maker, and singer, Thomas D'Urfey (1653–1723) compiled his own edition of *Wit and Mirth*, a song anthology that had appeared, in various versions and with considerable success, over the preceding 20 years. D'Urfey's popular collection provided Gay with his principal source for both the melodies and the lyric memories by which he proposed to beguile his audience. Many of Gay's new texts push playfully and pointedly against D'Urfey's originals, reversing genders and subverting sentiments.
2. Compare *The Beggar's Opera*, Air 4: "If love the virgin's heart invade" (page 1282).

Though charming are your wit and face,
'Tis not alone to hear and gaze
    That will suffice my flame;
10 Love's infancy on hopes may live,
But you to mine full grown must give
    Of what I dare not name.

When I behold your lips, your eyes,
Those snowy breasts that fall and rise,
15   Fanning my raging flame;
That shape so made to be embraced,
What would I give I might but taste
    Of what I dare not name!

In courts I never wish to rise,
20 Both wealth and honor I despise,
    And that vain breath called fame;
By love I hope no crowns to gain.
'Tis something more I would obtain:
    'Tis what I dare not name.

WHAT SHALL I DO TO SHOW HOW MUCH I LOVE HER?[1]

What shall I do to show how much I love her?
    How many millions of sighs can suffice?
That which wins other hearts ne'er can move her,
    Those common methods of love she'll despise.
5 I will love more than man e'er loved before me,
    Gaze on her all the day, and melt all the night,
'Till for her own sake at last she'll implore me,
    To love her less to preserve our delight.

Since gods themselves could not ever[2] be loving,
10   Men must have breathing recruits[3] for new joys;
I wish my soul could be ever improving,
    Though eager love, more than sorrow, destroys.
In fair Aurelia's arms leave me expiring,
    To be embalmed with the sweets of her breath.
15 To the last moment I'll still be desiring;
    Never had hero so glorious a death.[4]

WOULD YE HAVE A YOUNG VIRGIN?[1]

Would ye have a young virgin of fifteen years?
You must tickle her fancy with *sweets* and *dears*,
Ever toying, and playing, and sweetly, sweetly,
Wittily, prettily, talk her down.
5 Chase her, and praise her, if fair or brown,
        Soothe her and smoothe her,
        And tease her, and please her,
And touch but her smicket[2], and all's your own.

---

1. Compare Air 6: "Virgins are like the fair flower in its luster" (page 1284).
2. Always.
3. I.e., pauses to catch their breath.

4. With the familiar pun on "death" as sexual fulfillment.
1. Compare Air 21: "If the heart of a man is depressed with cares" (page 1294).
2. Petticoat; undergarment.

Do ye fancy a widow well known in a man?[3]
10 With a front of assurance come boldly on.
Let her rest not an hour, but briskly, briskly,
Put her in mind how her time steals on.
Rattle and prattle although she frown,
Rouse her and touse her from morn to noon,
15 Show her some hour y'are able to grapple,
Then get but her writings[4] and all's your own.

Do ye fancy a punk[5] of a humor free,
That's kept by a fumbler of quality?[6]
You must rail at her keeper, and tell her, tell her
20   Pleasure's best charm is variety.
Swear her much fairer than all the town,
Try her, and ply her when Cully's[7] gone,
    Dog her, and jog[8] her,
    And meet her, and treat her,
25 And kiss with two guineas,[9] and all's your own.

LUMPS OF PUDDING[1]

When I was in the low country,[2]
When I was in the low country,
What slices of pudding[3] and pieces of bread
My mother gave me when I was in need.

5   My mother she killed a good fat hog,
She made such puddings would choke a dog;
And I shall ne'er forget till I dee[4]
What lumps of pudding my mother gave me.

She hung them up upon a pin,
10 The fat run out and the maggots crept in;
If you won't believe me you may go and see
What lumps of pudding my mother gave me.

And every day my mother would cry
Come stuff your belly, girl, until you die;
15 'Twould make you laugh if you were to see
What lumps of pudding my mother gave me.

I no sooner at night was got into bed,
But she all in kindness would come with speed;
She gave me such parcels I thought I should dee,
20 With eating of pudding my mother gave me.

---

3. I.e., experienced with men.
4. I.e., legal documents transferring her wealth.
5. Whore; prostitute.
6. I.e., an inept, wealthy (and probably older) lover.
7. I.e., her duped lover.
8. Push; pressure.
9. A guinea was a coin worth one shilling and one pound.

1. Compare Air 69: "Thus I stand like a Turk, with his doxies around" (page 1322).
2. A low-lying region, close to sea level.
3. The word referred to many different kinds of recipes, meat as well as dairy, savory as well as sweet.
4. Die.

At last I rambled abroad and then
I met in my frolic an honest man.
Quoth he, "My dear Phillis I'll give unto thee
Such pudding you never did see."

25 Said I, "Honest man, I thank thee most kind."
And as he told me indeed I did find;
He gave me a lump which did so agree,
One bit was worth all my mother gave me.

                                                    1719

Daniel Defoe[1]

from *The True and Genuine Account of the Life and Actions*
of the Late Jonathan Wild[2]

[PREFACE]

The several absurd and ridiculous accounts which have been published, notwith-standing early and seasonable caution given, of the life and conduct of this famous, or if you please, infamous creature, JONATHAN WILD, make a short preface to this account absolutely necessary.

It is something strange, that a man's life should be made a kind of a romance[3] before his face, and while he was upon the spot to contradict it; or, that the world should be so fond of a formal chimney-corner tale,[4] that they had rather a story should be made merry than true. The author of this short but exact account of Mr. Wild assures the world, that the greatest part of all that has hitherto appeared of this kind has been evidently invented and framed out of the heads of the scribbling authors, merely to get a penny, without regard to truth of fact, or even to probability, or with-out making any conscience of their imposing on the credulous world.

Nay, so little ground has there been for them, that except there was such a man as JONATHAN WILD, that he was born at Wolverhampton, lived in the Old Bailey, was called a thief-catcher, and was hanged at Tyburn, there is not one story printed of him that can be called truth, or that is not mingled up with so much false-hood and fable as to smother and drown that little truth which is at the bottom of it.

The following tract does not indeed make a jest of his story as they do, or pre-sent his history, which indeed is a tragedy of itself, in a style of mockery and ridicule, but in a method agreeable to the fact. They that had rather have a false-hood to laugh at, than a true account of things to inform them, had best buy the fiction, and leave the history to those who know how to distinguish good from evil.

---

1. The pioneering novelist Daniel Defoe (1660–1731) had worked as a journalist and spy before turning to fiction late in life, and he continued to write journalism while publishing fictions disguised as fact, such as *Robinson Crusoe* (1719) and *Moll Flanders* (1722). This brief account of Wild's life appeared in June 1725, less than a month after his execution. The attribution to Defoe is plausible on grounds of style but unsupported by external evidence, and has been questioned.
2. Wild (c. 1682–1725) attained an unprecedented mix of celebrity and notoriety by organizing crime more efficiently, more ruthlessly, and more profitably than any predecessor in the London underworld. His tactics for reaping gain from both robbers and their victims supplied much of the basis for Peachum's operations in *The Beggar's Opera*. (In the wake of the play's success one newspaper reported, albeit unreliably, that Wild and Gay had once actually met, and that the thief-taker had instructed the playwright in "all the knavish offices and intrigues of the thieving trade.") In the selections here, Defoe assesses Wild's impact, details his methods, and reports his execution, attending all the while to the new workings of publicity, the play of popular genres (romance, history, tragedy) around the core of facts.
3. "A tale of wild adventures in war and love" (Johnson's *Dictionary*).
4. The kind of story told at hearthside: joke, fairy tale, folktale, etc.

[TACTICS]

∗ ∗ ∗ [Wild's] method was this: When a purchase was made,[1] Jonathan inquired first where it was gotten, what house had been robbed, or who had lost the goods; and having learnt that, his next business was to have the goods deposited in proper places, always avoiding the receiving them himself, or bringing himself into any jeopardy as to the law. Then he found out proper instruments to employ to go to the persons who had been robbed, and tell them that if they could describe what they had lost, they believed they could help them to them again; for that[2] there was a parcel of stolen goods stopped by an honest broker, to whom they were offered to be sold, and if their goods were among them they might have them again for a small matter of expense.

The people who had been robbed, it may be supposed, were always willing enough to hear of their goods again, and very thankful to the discoverer, and so readily gave an account of the things they had lost, with such proper descriptions of them as were needful. The next day they should be told there was such or such part of their goods stopped among other goods, which it was supposed were stolen from other people, and so upon assurance given on both sides to make no inquiry into the particular circumstances of stopping the goods, and a consideration to the person who went between, for helping the loser to his goods again, the things were restored, and the person received abundance of thanks and acknowledgments for their honesty and kindness. And this part always fell to Jonathan, or his mistress Milliner,[3] or perhaps both, who always pretended they got nothing for their pains but the satisfaction of having helped the people to recover their own again, which was taken by a company of rogues; professing their sorrow that they had not had the good luck at the same time to detect the rogues that took them, and bring them to the punishment they deserved.

On the other hand, they acted as safe a part with the thief also; for, rating and reproving the rogue for his villainy, they would pretend to bring them to an honest restoring the goods again, taking a reasonable consideration for their honesty, and so bring them to lodge them in such a place as should be directed. And sometimes, as I have been told, he has officiously caused the thief or thieves to be taken with the goods upon them, when he has not been able to bring them to comply, and so has made himself both thief and chapman,[4] as the proverb says; getting a reward for the discovery, and bringing the poor wretch to the gallows too, and this only because he could not make his market of him to his mind.[5] ∗ ∗ ∗

It must be confessed, Jonathan Wild played a sure game in all this; and therefore it is not to be wondered at that he went on for so many years without any disaster. Nay, he acquired a strange and, indeed, unusual reputation, for a mighty honest man; till his success hardened him to put on a face of public service in it, and for that purpose to profess an open and bare correspondence among the gang of thieves. By which his house became an office of intelligence for inquiries of that kind, as if all stolen goods had been deposited with him, in order to be restored. But even this good character of his, as it did not last long, so neither did it come all at once; and some tell us (how true it is, I will not affirm) that he was obliged to give up every now and then one or two of his clients to the gallows, to support his rising reputation. In which cases, he never failed to proclaim his own credit in bringing offenders to justice, and in delivering his country from

1. Robbery was committed.
2. Because.
3. Mary Milliner, a brothel-keeper, was Wild's lover and

accomplice.
4. Purchaser.
5. I.e., draw a satisfactory profit from his thievery.

such dangerous people. Some have gone so far as to tell us the very particulars which recommended any of the gangs to him for a sacrifice, and to divide them into classes: For example, (1) such as having committed the secret of a fact⁶ to him yet would not submit their purchase to his disposal. Or (2), would not accept reasonable terms of composition for restoring the goods: Or (3), used any threatening speeches against their comrades. These he would immediately cause to be apprehended, he knowing both their haunts, and where the goods were deposited; and in such cases, none so vigilant in the discovery, or so eager in apprehending the thief. And, generally speaking, he had his ways and means to bring in others of the gang to come in and confess, that they might impeach the person so intended to be given up to justice. * * *

[EXECUTION]¹

We come now to his behavior after this condemnation, and at the place of execution; at which last place he indeed scarce said a word to God or man, being either dozed with the liquid laudanum² which he had taken, or demented and confused by the horror of what was before him, and the reflection of what was within him. Nor even before he took the dose of laudanum was he in any suitable manner sensible of his condition, or concerned about it; very little sign appeared of his having the least hope concerning his future state. But as he lived hardened, he seemed to die stupid. He declined coming to the chapel, either to the sermon or prayers, pleading his lameness by the gout, but chiefly the crowds and disorders of the people discomposing or disordering him. In the condemned hold, or place where malefactors are kept after their sentence, they had prayers as usual; and he seemed to join with them in a kind of form, but little or nothing of the penitence of a criminal, in view of death, appeared upon him. His principal inquiries seemed to be about what kind of state was to be expected after death, and how the invisible world was to be described; but nothing of the most certain judgment which is there to be expected, righteous and terrible, according to the deeds done in the body, or of a savior to whom to have recourse, as the slayer in the old law had to the city of refuge, to save him from the avenger of blood. As his time shortened he seemed more and more confused, and then began to entertain discourses of the lawfulness of dismissing ourselves out of the present misery after the example of the ancient Romans,³ which, as he said, was then esteemed as an act of bravery and gallantry, and recorded to their honor.

This kind of discourse was indeed sufficient to have caused the keepers to have had an eye to him, so as to prevent any violence he might offer to himself, and they did watch him as narrowly as they could. However, he so far deceived them, as that the day before his execution he found means to have a small bottle with the liquid laudanum conveyed to him unseen, of which he took so large a quantity, that it was soon perceived by the change it made upon him, for he was so drowsy that he could not hold up his head, or keep open his eyes, at the time of reading the prayers. Upon this two of his fellow prisoners endeavored to rouse him (not suspecting that he had taken enough to hurt him), and taking him by the hands, they persuaded him to stand up, and walk a little about the room, which he could not do without help because of

---

6. Crime; robbery.
1. In 1725, Wild's long series of successes came to an end, when he was forced to stand trial under a new law (nicknamed the "Jonathan Wild Act") that made it a capital crime to accept money for the recovery of stolen proper-

ty. Former associates, disenchanted by his treacheries, testified against him.
2. A solution containing opium.
3. I.e., of committing suicide, a practice regarded in Rome as an honorable response to failure or disgrace.

his gout.[4] This walking, though it did a little waken him, had several other operations at the same time. For first it changed his countenance, turning it to be exceeding pale, then it put him into a violent sweat, which made them apprehend he would
faint, upon which they offered to give him something to keep up his spirits, but he
refused it, telling them he was very sick; soon after which he vomited very violently,
and this in all probability prolonged his life for the execution, for by their stirring
him, and making him vomit, he brought up the greatest part of the laudanum which
he had taken, before it had been long enough in his stomach to mix with the animal
spirits or blood, which if it had done but one hour more, he would certainly have tak-
en his last sleep in the prison. But nature, having thus discharged itself of the load, he
revived again, and though still dozed and insensible of what he said or did, yet he was
able to walk about, speak, and act sufficiently for the part that remained to him,
namely, for the last scene of his life at the gallows.

Accordingly, on Monday the 24th of May, he was conveyed in a cart to Tyburn,
and though it was apparent he was still under the operation of the laudanum, and
that which was left in his stomach had so far seized upon his spirits as to make him
almost stupid, yet it began to go off, and nature getting the mastery of it, he began
to be more sensible of what he was going about; but the scene was then short, and
he had little to do but to stand up in the cart, and, the needful apparatus being
made, be turned off with the rest, which was done about 3 o'clock in the afternoon.
The rudeness of the mob to him, both at his first going into the cart, and all the way
from thence to the place of execution, is not to be expressed, and shows how notorious his life had been, and what impression his known villainies had made on the
minds of the people. For, contrary to the general behavior of the street in such cases, instead of compassionate expressions, and a general cast of pity, which ordinarily
sits on the countenances of the people, when they see the miserable objects of justice go to their execution; here was nothing to be heard but cursings and execrations. Abhorring the crimes and the very name of the man, throwing stones and dirt
at him all the way, and even at the place of execution; the other malefactors being
all ready to be turned off, but the hangman giving him leave to take his own time,
and he continuing setting down in the cart, the mob impatient, and fearing a
reprieve, though they had no occasion for it, called furiously upon the hangman to
dispatch him, and at last threatened to tear him to pieces, if he did not tie him up
immediately.

In short there was a kind of an universal rage against him, which nothing but his
death could satisfy, or put an end to, and if a reprieve had come, it would have, 'twas
thought, been difficult for the officers to have brought him back again without his
receiving some mischief, if not his death's wound, from the rabble. So detestable had
he made himself by his notorious crimes, and to such a height were his wicked practices come.

Thus ended the tragedy, and thus was a life of horrid and inimitable wickedness
finished at the gallows, the very same place where, according to some, above 120
miserable creatures had been hanged whose blood in great measure may be said to lie
at his door, either in their being first brought into the thieving trade, or led on in it
by his encouragement and assistance; and many of them at last betrayed and brought
to justice by his means, upon which worst sort of murder he valued himself, and
would have had it passed for merit, even with the government itself.

1725

---

4. A disease, common at the time, entailing painful inflammation of the joints in hands and feet.

Henry Fielding[1]
from *The Life of Mr. Jonathan Wild the Great*
["An Adventure Where Wild, in the Division of the Booty,
Exhibits an Astonishing Instance of Greatness"]

Mr. Wild and Mr. Bagshot[2] went together to the tavern, where Mr. Bagshot (generously, as he thought) offered to share the booty, and, having divided the money into two unequal heaps, and added a golden snuff-box[3] to the lesser heap, he desired Mr. Wild to take his choice.

Mr. Wild immediately conveyed the larger share of the ready into his pocket, according to an excellent maxim of his: "First secure what share you can before you wrangle for the rest"; and then, turning to his companion, he asked him with a stern countenance whether he intended to keep all that sum to himself? Mr. Bagshot answered, with some surprise, that he thought Mr. Wild had no reason to complain; for it was surely fair, at least on his part, to content himself with an equal share of the booty, who had taken the whole. "I grant you took it," replied Wild; "but, pray, who proposed or counseled the taking it? Can you say that you have done more than executed my scheme? and might not I, if I had pleased, have employed another, since you well know there was not a gentleman in the room but would have taken the money if he had known how, conveniently and safely, to do it?" "That is very true," returned Bagshot, "but did not I execute the scheme, did not I run the whole risk? Should not I have suffered the whole punishment if I had been taken, and is not the laborer worthy of his hire?"[4] "Doubtless," says Jonathan, "he is so, and your hire I shall not refuse you, which is all that the laborer is entitled to or ever enjoys. I remember when I was at school to have heard some verses which for the excellence of their doctrine made an impression on me, purporting that the birds of the air and the beasts of the field work not for themselves.[5] It is true, the farmer allows fodder to his oxen and pasture to his sheep; but it is for his own service, not theirs. In the same manner the ploughman, the shepherd, the weaver, the builder, and the soldier work not for themselves but others; they are contented with a poor pittance (the laborer's hire), and permit us, the GREAT, to enjoy the fruits of their labors. Aristotle, as my master told us, hath plainly proved, in the first book of his politics, that the low, mean, useful part of mankind are born slaves to the wills of their superiors, and are indeed as much their property as the cattle.[6] It is well said of us, the higher order of mortals, that we are born only to devour the fruits of the earth; and it may be as well said of the lower class, that they are born only to produce them for us. Is not the battle gained by the sweat and danger of the common soldier? Are not the honor and

1. Over the course of a short life, Henry Fielding (1707–1754) sustained several brilliant careers, as playwright, journalist, polemicist, novelist, lawyer, magistrate. *Jonathan Wild* combines components of many of them. By the time it appeared, in 1743, Walpole had been stripped of power for one year and Wild had been dead for almost twenty. But Fielding, like Gay and others before him, pointedly conflates the politician and the criminal. The epithet "the great man," which Fielding applies to Wild on nearly every page, had in real life adhered to Walpole throughout his tenure as prime minister. By such echoes and displacements, Fielding anatomizes with sometimes heavy irony the ways in which a powerfully seductive leader can persuade his followers to collude in their own exploitation.
2. Fielding borrowed the name of Wild's accomplice from Gay's *Opera*: Peachum, combing his catalogue of criminals eligible for the gallows, mentions one "Robin

Bagshot, alias Gorgon, alias Bluff Bob, alias Carbuncle, alias Bob Booty" (1.3). All those aliases riff wittily on the reputation and nicknames of Robert Walpole—though in Fielding's anecdote it is Wild, and not Bagshot, who will expound Walpole's methods. At this juncture in the story, Bagshot, acting on Wild's instructions, has just robbed a rich gambler at gunpoint.
3. Snuff was powdered tobacco, enjoyed as a stimulant and sneeze-inducer; the pocket-cases in which it was carried were often ornate and expensive.
4. I.e., his wages (Bagshot echoes Luke 10.7).
5. Wild, trumping one scriptural quotation with another, here echoes Matthew 6.26.
6. "For that [person who] can foresee by the exercise of mind is by nature intended to be lord and master, and that which can with its body give effect to such foresight is a subject, and by nature a slave; hence master and slave have the same interest" (Aristotle, *Politics* 1.2).

fruits of the victory the general's who laid the scheme? Is not the house built by the labor of the carpenter and the bricklayer? Is it not built for the profit of the architect and for the use of the inhabitant, who could not easily have placed one brick upon another? Is not the cloth or the silk wrought into its form and variegated with all the beauty of colors by those who are forced to content themselves with the coarsest and vilest part of their work, while the profit and enjoyment of their labors fall to the share of others? Cast your eye abroad, and see who is it lives in the most magnificent buildings, feasts his palate with the most luxurious dainties, his eyes with the most beautiful sculptures and delicate paintings, and clothes himself in the finest and richest apparel; and tell me if all these do not fall to his lot who had not any the least share in producing all these conveniences, nor the least ability so to do? Why then should the state of a prig[7] differ from all others? Or why should you, who are the laborer only, the executor of my scheme, expect a share in the profit? Be advised, therefore; deliver the whole booty to me, and trust to my bounty for your reward." Mr Bagshot was some time silent, and looked like a man thunderstruck, but at last, recovering himself from his surprise, he thus began: "If you think, Mr. Wild, by the force of your arguments, to get the money out of my pocket, you are greatly mistaken. What is all this stuff to me? D—n me, I am a man of honor, and, though I can't talk as well as you, by G— you shall not make a fool of me; and if you take me for one, I must tell you, you are a rascal." At which words he laid his hand to his pistol. Wild, perceiving the little success the great strength of his arguments had met with, and the hasty temper of his friend, gave over his design for the present, and told Bagshot he was only in jest. But this coolness with which he treated the other's flame had rather the effect of oil than of water. Bagshot replied in a rage: "D—n me, I don't like such jests; I see you are a pitiful rascal and a scoundrel." Wild, with a philosophy worthy of great admiration, returned: "As for your abuse, I have no regard to it; but, to convince you I am not afraid of you, let us lay the whole booty on the table, and let the conqueror take it all." And having so said, he drew out his shining hanger,[8] whose glittering so dazzled the eyes of Bagshot, that, in a tone entirely altered, he said: "No! he was contented with what he had already; that it was mighty ridiculous in them to quarrel among themselves; that they had common enemies enough abroad, against whom they should unite their common force; that if he had mistaken Wild he was sorry for it; and that as for a jest, he could take a jest as well as another." Wild, who had a wonderful knack of discovering and applying the passions of men, beginning now to have a little insight into his friend, and to conceive what arguments would make the quickest impression on him, cried out in a loud voice: "That he had bullied him into drawing his hanger, and, since it was out, he would not put it up without satisfaction." "What satisfaction would you have?" answered the other. "Your money or your blood," said Wild. "Why, look ye, Mr. Wild," said Bagshot, "if you want to borrow a little of my part, since I know you to be a man of honor, I don't care if I lend you; for, though I am not afraid of any man living, yet rather than break with a friend, and as it may be necessary for your occasions—" Wild, who often declared that he looked upon borrowing to be as good a way of taking as any, and, as he called it, the genteelest kind of sneaking-budge,[9] putting up his hanger, and shaking his friend by the hand, told him he had hit the nail on the head; it was really his present necessity only that prevailed with him against his will, for that his honor was concerned to pay a considerable sum the next morning. Upon which, contenting himself with one half of Bagshot's share, so that he had three parts in four of the whole, he took leave of his companion and retired to rest.

7. Thief.
8. A short sword.

9. Robbing-scheme; scam.

["THE MASTER OF THE SHOW"]

* * * The stage of the world differs from that in Drury Lane[1] principally in this—that whereas, on the latter, the hero or chief figure is almost continually before your eyes, while the under-actors are not seen above once in an evening; now, on the former, the hero or great man is always behind the curtain, and seldom or never appears or doth anything in his own person. He doth indeed, in this GRAND DRAMA, rather perform the part of the prompter, and doth instruct the well-drest figures, who are strutting in public on the stage, what to say and do. To say the truth, a puppet-show will illustrate our meaning better, where it is the master of the show (the great man) who dances and moves everything, whether it be the King of Muscovy[2] or whatever other potentate *alias* puppet which we behold on the stage; but he himself keeps wisely out of sight: for, should he once appear, the whole motion would be at an end. Not that any one is ignorant of his being there, or supposes that the puppets are not mere sticks of wood, and he himself the sole mover; but as this (though every one knows it) doth not appear visibly, i.e., to their eyes, no one is ashamed of consenting to be imposed upon; of helping on the drama, by calling the several sticks or puppets by the names which the master hath allotted to them, and by assigning to each the character which the great man is pleased they shall move in, or rather in which he himself is pleased to move them.

It would be to suppose thee, gentle reader, one of very little knowledge in this world, to imagine thou hast never seen some of these puppet-shows which are so frequently acted on the great stage; but though thou shouldst have resided all thy days in those remote parts of this island which great men seldom visit, yet, if thou hast any penetration, thou must have had some occasions to admire both the solemnity of countenance in the actor and the gravity in the spectator, while some of those farces are carried on which are acted almost daily in every village in the kingdom. He must have a very despicable opinion of mankind indeed who can conceive them to be imposed on as often as they appear to be so. The truth is, they are in the same situation with the readers of romances;[3] who, though they know the whole to be one entire fiction, nevertheless agree to be deceived; and, as these find amusement, so do the others find ease and convenience in this concurrence. * * *

1743

from *A Narrative of All the Robberies, Escapes, &c. of John Sheppard*[1]
[ON THIEF-CATCHING]

I have often lamented the scandalous practice of thief-catching, as it is called, and the public manner of offering rewards for stolen goods, in defiance of two several acts of parliament—the thief-catchers living sumptuously, and keeping public offices of intelligence. These who forfeit their lives every day they breathe,[2] and deserve the

1. Drury Lane was the site and name of one of the two foremost playhouses in London; several of Fielding's own comedies had been produced there.
2. A powerful principality in Russia (Moscow was its capital).
3. The term was applied loosely and variously to novels and other, more fantastical prose fictions.
1. John Sheppard (1702–1724), widely and familiarly known as Jack, was an accomplished thief, a promiscuous seducer, the greatest escape artist of his time, and the chief inspiration behind Gay's Macheath. Jonathan Wild, goaded by Sheppard's audacity, celebrity, and independence, tried time and again to have him caught and

hung, but Sheppard repeatedly broke out of the most elaborate confinements the Newgate specialists could devise for him. During his last imprisonment, his jailers charged sightseers special admission for the privilege of simply looking at the doomed but dapper convict. By this time, Sheppard's popularity was sufficient to turn the tables: the public, favoring him, began to revile his nemesis Wild. The present *Narrative*, purportedly an autobiography, went on sale the day after Sheppard's execution. It was for a long time attributed to Defoe, but is probably the work of some less eminent ghostwriter.
2. I.e., they commit crimes deserving such forfeiture.

gallows as richly as any of the thieves, send us as their representatives to Tyburn,[3] once a month. Thus they hang by proxy, while we do it fairly in person.

I never corresponded with any of them. I was indeed twice at a thief-catcher's *levée*,[4] and must confess the man treated me civilly. He complimented me on my successes, said he heard that I had both an hand and head admirably well turned to *business*, and that I and my friends *should be always welcome to him*. But caring not for his acquaintance, I never troubled him, nor had we any dealings together.

[THE GREAT ESCAPE]

As my last escape from Newgate out of the strong room called the Castle[1] has made a greater noise in the world than any other action of my life, I shall relate every minute circumstance thereof as far as I am able to remember, intending thereby to satisfy the curious and do justice to the innocent. * * *

* * * As near as can be remembered, just before three in the afternoon I went to work, taking off first my handcuffs;[2] next with main strength I twisted a small iron link of the chain between my legs asunder, and the broken pieces proved extreme useful to me in my design. The fett-locks[3] I drew up to the calves of my legs, taking off before that my stockings, and with my garters made them firm to my body, to prevent their shackling.[4] I then proceeded to make a hole in the chimney of the Castle about three foot wide, and six foot high from the floor, and with the help of the broken links aforesaid wrenched an iron bar out of the chimney, of about two feet and a half in length, and an inch square: a most notable implement. I immediately entered the Red Room directly over the Castle, where some of the Preston rebels[5] had been kept a long time agone. And, as the keepers say, the door had not been unlocked for seven years; but I intended not to be seven years in opening it, though they had. I went to work upon the nut of the lock, and with little difficulty got it off, and made the door fly before me. In this room I found a large nail, which proved of great use in my farther progress. The door of the entry between the Red Room and the Chapel proved an hard task, it being a laborious piece of work; for here I was forced to break away the wall, and dislodge the bolt which was fastened on the other side. This occasioned much noise, and I was very fearful of being heard by the Master-side debtors.[6] Being got to the Chapel, I climbed over the iron spikes, and with ease broke one of them off for my further purposes, and opened the door on the inside. The door going out of the Chapel to the leads,[7] I stripped the nut from off the lock, as I had done before from that of the Red Room, and then got into the entry between the Chapel and the leads; and came to another strong door, which being fastened by a very strong lock, there I had like to have stopped, and it being full dark, my spirits began to fail me, as greatly doubting of succeeding. But cheering up, I wrought on with great diligence, and in less than half an hour, with the main help of the nail from the Red Room, and the spike from the Chapel, wrenched the box off, and so made the door my humble servant.

1724

3. The site of public executions, which were regarded also as edifying public entertainments. A crowd of about 200,000 saw Sheppard die there.

4. A social gathering, customarily held before noon; "the concourse of those who crowd round a man of power in a morning" (Johnson's *Dictionary*).

1. The prison's most formidable cell, where Sheppard was secured "with my legs chained together, loaded with heavy irons, and stapled down to the floor."

2. Sheppard has earlier discovered that he can remove these with his teeth.

3. The shackles around his feet.

4. I.e., to prevent their falling back down to his feet and encumbering him.

5. Prisoners taken during the failed Jacobite uprising at Preston, November 1715.

6. I.e., convicts (mostly debtors) confined in Newgate's Master's Ward, where the wealthiest prisoners could purchase the most comfortable accommodations.

7. I.e., the prison roof, made of lead tiles, across which Sheppard will eventually make his escape from Newgate to the rooftop of a neighboring house.

John Thurmond
from *Harlequin Sheppard*[1]
[SHEPPARD RECAPTURED][2]

The scene changes to Clare Market,[3] and discovers[4] a butcher's shop. SHEPPARD comes in very merry, and goes to purchase some of the meat. While he is employed with the butcher, an alehouse boy[5] comes in, with pots over his shoulder and, discovering SHEPPARD, retires. SHEPPARD and the butcher go off together.

The scene changes to a room in an alehouse. FRISKY MOLL[6] enters, and seems to be pleased,[7] as having heard of SHEPPARD's escape. SHEPPARD comes in, and discovering himself to her, she's mightily rejoiced. They drink together, and after some time dance. While they are in high mirth, the alehouse boy appears with the constable and others, and seize SHEPPARD. FRISKY MOLL makes resistance, but they carry him off. And the entertainment concludes with

A CANTING SONG[8]

Sung by FRISKY MOLL

From prigs that snaffle the prancers strong[9]
    To you of the Peter lay,[1]
I pray now listen a while to my song,
    How my boman he hicked away.[2]

5   He broke through all rubs in the whitt,[3]
    And chived his darbies in twain;[4]
But filing of a rumbo ken,[5]
    My boman is snabbled again.[6]

I, Frisky Moll, with my rum coll,[7]
10   Would grub in a bowzing ken;[8]
But ere for the scran he had tipped the cole,[9]
    The harman,[1] he came in.

---

1. The word "harlequin" in a play's title promised a pantomime, a short show with music and songs but no dialogue, presented at the playhouses as part of an evening's entertainment. *Harlequin Sheppard*, purporting to display Sheppard's celebrated escape and ultimate capture, was performed at the Theater Royal in Drury Lane 12 days after his execution. Since it was booed off the stage on its first night (28 November 1724), the audience may not have witnessed its final scene, reprinted here.
2. After his famous escape from the Castle on 15 October 1724, Sheppard remained free for two weeks; on 31 October he was recognized and arrested in Drury Lane, not far from the playhouse where *Harlequin Sheppard* appeared a month later.
3. A market specializing in butchers' shops; Sheppard's mother and several of his mistress/accomplices lived nearby.
4. Reveals.
5. I.e., tavern-servant.
6. A woman named "Moll Frisky" figures in several accounts of Sheppard's last days. Notorious as a ladies' man, Sheppard had earlier been betrayed back into custody by a longtime lover called Edgworth Bess.
7. The word "seems" does not imply falsity or connivance on Moll's part; it is instead a conventional pantomime stage direction, instructing the actor to display the specified emotion.
8. Cant is jargon, here the specialized slang of London's underworld. For more than a century, writers of criminal literature had managed to please an enormous readership by deploying and explaining this "secret" language. In its original edition, *Harlequin Sheppard* included footnotes for all the cant terms in this song; those glosses appear in quotation marks in the notes that follow here.
9. "Gentlemen of the pad"; i.e., horse-stealers. Prigs: thieves; snaffle: bridle; prancers: horses; pad: path, road.
1. "Those that break shop-glasses [i.e., windows], or cut portmanteaus [i.e., large, well-packed pieces of luggage] behind coaches." Lay: trick, scam.
2. "Her rogue had got away."
3. Rubs: obstacles; whitt: "Newgate, or any other prison."
4. "Sawed his chains in two."
5. "Robbing a pawnbroker's shop." Sheppard had in fact committed such a crime shortly after his great escape.
6. "Taken again."
7. "Clever thief."
8. "Would eat in an alehouse."
9. "Before the reckoning [i.e., tavern bill] was paid"; cole: cash.
1. "Constable."

> A famble, a tattle, and two pops,[2]
>   Had my boman when he was ta'en;
> 15   But had he not bowzed in the diddle-shops,[3]
>   He'd still been in Drury Lane.

1724

Charlotte Charke[1]

from *A Narrative of the Life of Mrs. Charlotte Charke*

[A MACHEATH "PERFORMED IN CHARACTER"]

We waited in court, expecting every moment to be called upon, and dismissed with a slight reprimand. But alas! 'twas not so easy as we thought, for we were beckoned to the other end of the court, and told, that the keeper of the prison insisted on our going to jail, only for a show, and to say we had been under lock and key. An honor, I confess, I was not in the least ambitious of; and for the show, I thought 'twould never be over, for it lasted from nine in the morning 'til the same hour of the next; and had it not been for the generous and friendly assistance of the before-mentioned gentleman,[2] I believe would have held out 'til *Doomsday* with me, for another day must have absolutely put an end to my life. ∗ ∗ ∗

The evening wore apace, and the clock struck eight, the dreadful signal for the gates to be locked up for the night.

I offered half a guinea apiece for beds,[3] but was denied them; and, if I had not fortunately been acquainted with the turnkey, who was a very good-natured fellow, we must have been turned into a place to lie upon the bare ground, and have mixed among the felons, whose chains were rattling all night long, and made the most hideous noise I ever heard, there being upwards of two hundred men and boys under the different sentences of death and transportation.

Their rags and misery gave me so shocking an idea, I begged the man, in pity, to hang us all three, rather than put us among such a dreadful crew. The very stench of them would have been a sufficient remedy against any future ills that could have happened to me; but those dreadful apprehensions were soon ended, by the young fellow who was our warder for the night, making interest with a couple of shoemakers, who were imprisoned in the women's condemned-hole; which, till they came, had not been occupied for a considerable time.

These two persons were confined, one for debt, the other for having left his family, with a design to impose his wife and children on the parish.[4]

Extremely glad were we to be admitted into the dismal cell; which, though the walls and flooring were formed of flint, at that time I was proud of entering, as the men were neat, and their bed (which my companions only took part of) entirely clean.

2. "A ring, a watch, and a pair of pistols."

3. "Gevena-shops," i.e., gin-shops, taverns.

1. Charlotte Charke (1713–1760) was a strolling player, an actor who spent much of her life traveling and performing with makeshift companies in English provincial towns. Her distinction derived in part from her lineage (her father was Colley Cibber, one of the central figures in the London theater early in the eighteenth century); in part from her gift for cross-dressing, for assuming masculine roles and costume both onstage and off (she "passed" as a man for long periods of her life); but most of all from her autobiography, in which she proclaims her aspirations, disappointments, and eccentricities with hypnotic fervor. In the excerpt here, she tells of being arrested and briefly confined in a local jail, along with a few of her fellow actors, on false charges whose chief purpose was to force the players to buy back their freedom by paying off the authorities.

2. A benefactor who later came to the players' rescue.

3. In prisons at this period, even the most basic comforts were obtainable only by bribery; compare Lockit's enthusiasm for "garnish" (payment; *Beggar's Opera* 2.7).

4. The parish, or local governing body, was obliged to support all legal residents who were thus abandoned.

The two gentlemen of the craft had, the day we were brought in, furnished themselves with each a skin, for under-leathers; which, being hollow, one within the other, I chose for my dormitory,[5] and having a pair of boots on and a great coat, rolled into my leathern couch, secure from every evil that might occur from such a place, except a cold, which I got, occasioned by the dampness of my bedchamber.

As we were not there for any crime, *but that committed by those who informed against us*, I had the good fortune to prevail on my friend the turnkey to permit me to send for candles and some good liquor, to reward our kind hosts, and preserve us from the dreadful apprehensions of getting each an ague[6] in our petrified apartment.

I continued, for the most part of the night, very low spirited and in very ill humor, 'til I was roused by the drollery of one Mr. Maxfield, my fellow-sufferer, a good-natured man, and of an odd turn of humor; who would not let me indulge my melancholy, which he saw had strongly possessed me, and insisted, as he had often seen me exhibit Captain Macheath in a sham-prison, I should, as I was then actually in the condemned-hold, sing all the bead-roll of songs in the last act,[7] that he might have the pleasure of saying, I had once performed IN CHARACTER.

1755

James Boswell
from London Journal[1]
[ENTRIES ON MACHEATH]

TUESDAY 3 MAY 1763.[2] * * * I thought I should see prisoners of one kind or other, so went to Newgate. I stepped into a sort of court before the cells. They are surely most dismal places. There are three rows of 'em, four in a row, all above each other. They have double iron windows, and within these, strong iron rails; and in these dark mansions are the unhappy criminals confined. I did not go in, but stood in the court, where were a number of strange blackguard beings with sad countenances, most of them being friends and acquaintances of those under sentence of death. Mr. Rice the broker was confined in another part of the house. In the cells were Paul Lewis for robbery and Hannah Diego for theft. I saw them pass by to chapel. The woman was a big unconcerned being. Paul, who had been in the sea-service and was called Captain, was a genteel, spirited young fellow. He was just a Macheath. He was dressed in a white coat and blue silk vest and silver, with his hair neatly queued[3] and a silver-laced hat, smartly cocked. An acquaintance asked him how he was. He said, "Very well"; quite resigned. Poor fellow! I really took a great concern for him, and wished to relieve him. He walked firmly and with a good air, with his chains rattling upon him, to the chapel.[4] * * *

THURSDAY 19 MAY 1763. * * * I then sallied forth to the Piazzas in rich flow of animal spirits and burning with fierce desire. I met two very pretty little girls who asked me to take them with me. "My dear girls," said I, "I am a poor fellow. I can give you no money. But if you choose to have a glass of wine and my company and let us be gay and obliging to each other without money, I am your man." They agreed with great good humor. So back to the Shakespeare[5] I went. "Waiter," said I, "I have got

---

5. Bed; sleeping-place.
6. A cold.
7. I.e., the medley of tunes Macheath sings "in a melancholy posture" as he contemplates his imminent execution (*Beggar's Opera* 3.13, page 1319).
1. For James Boswell, see pages 1398–1400. As a young man, Boswell played Macheath in an amateur household production of *The Beggar's Opera*. As the following excerpts from his journals suggest, he remained preoccupied with the character and the play throughout his life.

2. At this point, Boswell is 22 years old, living in London at a deliberate distance from his family in Scotland, trying to choose a career and a destiny, and sightseeing and journal-writing all the while.
3. I.e., arranged in a braided ponytail.
4. Like Macheath and other Newgate convicts in *The Beggar's Opera* (3.12–15).
5. I.e., the Shakespeare's Head tavern in Covent Garden, an area teeming with brothels and gambling houses.

here a couple of human beings; I don't know how they'll do." "I'll look, your Honor," cried he, and with inimitable effrontery stared them in the face and then cried, "They'll do very well." "What," said I, "are they good fellow-creatures? Bring them up, then." We were shown into a good room and had a bottle of sherry before us in a minute. I surveyed my seraglio[6] and found them both good subjects for amorous play. I toyed with them and drank about and sung *Youth's the Season*[7] and thought myself Captain Macheath; and then I solaced my existence with them, one after the other, according to their seniority. I was quite *raised*, as the phrase is: thought I was in a London tavern, the Shakespeare's Head, enjoying high debauchery after my sober winter. I parted with my ladies politely and came home in a glow of spirits.

WEDNESDAY 15 FEBRUARY 1775.[8] * * * Drank tea first at home, then at Captain Schaw's; went with him and Mrs. Schaw to *The Beggar's Opera*, performed by desire of several ladies of quality. There was an elegant audience. Digges[9] looked and sung as well as ever. I was quite in London.[1] A girl from Ireland who played Polly, by the name of Mistress Ramsay, pleased me very well. Only her notes were sometimes not sweet enough, but like the cry of a peacock. I sat between Lady Betty Cochrane and Mrs. Schaw in one of the rows of the pit taken by Lady Dundonald. I was cheerful and happy, having no pretensions, being very well established as an agreeable companion, and being a married man. Life is like a road, the first part of which is a hill. A man must for a while be constantly pulling that he may get forward, and not run back. When he has got beyond the steep, and on smooth ground—that is, when his character is fixed—he goes on smoothly upon level ground. I could not help indulging Asiatic ideas as I viewed such a number of pretty women some of them young gay creatures with their hair dressed with flowers.[2] But thoughts of mortality and change came upon me, and then I was glad to feel indifference.

END OF "THE BEGGAR'S OPERA," INFLUENCES AND IMPACT

William Hogarth
1697–1764

"I had naturally a good eye," William Hogarth remembered near his life's end. "Shows of all sorts gave me uncommon pleasure when an infant." The "shows" (spectacles) that filled his eye in the turbulent London neighborhood of Smithfield where he grew up suffused his art for

---

6. Harem. Compare Macheath's final song: "Thus I stand like the Turk, with his doxies around" (3.17).

7. The song accompanies Macheath's dance among his "free-hearted ladies" (2.4).

8. Boswell is now married with two daughters, living in Edinburgh and working as a lawyer.

9. West Digges, eminent Edinburgh actor, whose performances as Macheath had entranced Boswell since boyhood.

1. I.e., transported in mind and memory by several

means: by the setting of the *Opera*; by the echoes of London theatrical life; by the recollection of his former Macheath-like "high debauchery" in the city, and of his youthful idolatry of Digges.

2. Perhaps an echo of Macheath's amorous line "But here ev'ry flower is united" (1.13). The song mingles memories of promiscuity with pledges of fidelity; the line reappears throughout Boswell's journals. By "Asiatic ideas," Boswell means both Old Testament polygamy and fantasies of the harem.

life: the antics of actors and the raucousness of audiences at Bartholomew Fair; the chicanery and pathos of prostitutes and thieves; the casual injustice of constables and magistrates. Above all, he watched his father fail. Richard Hogarth, a classical scholar, spent four years as a prisoner for debt, when his coffeehouse (catering to learned men and specializing in Latin conversation) failed to cover its own expenses. The debtor's family was effectually imprisoned too, and Hogarth, in his early teens during the ordeal, never forgot. "The emphasis throughout his work" (notes his biographer Ronald Paulson) "is on prisons, real and metaphorical. Even when he is not dealing with people who are in a prison . . . he portrays rooms that are more like prison cells than boudoirs or parlors."

At age seventeen, Hogarth was apprenticed to a silver engraver, ornamenting platters, rings, tableware, and the like. Finding the work dull, he switched to copper engraving, the technique by which book illustrators and printmakers created and reproduced their pictures. Late in his twenties he commenced his career as painter. His first great successes combined both craft and art. Hogarth produced the series of six pictures that make up A Harlot's Progress first as a set of paintings in oil, then as a sequence of copper engravings aimed at wider distribution. If A Harlot's Progress launched his popularity, A Rake's Progress (engraved in 1735 from canvases painted the year before) clinched his reputation as Britain's most masterly, mocking delineator of contemporary vice and folly. Though he continued for a while to nurture conventional ambitions as a painter of portraits and historical subjects catering to aristocratic tastes, Hogarth came gradually to recognize the originality, force, and commercial viability of his satrical engravings. As he later expressed it (in his own idiosyncratic syntax), he had discovered a style pitched between "the sublime and the grotesque," and had devised "a more new way of proceeding, viz. painting and engraving modern moral subjects, a field unbroke up in any country or any age. . . . Provided I could strike the passions, and by small sums from many, by means of prints which I could engrave from my pictures myself, I could secure my property to myself." Hogarth managed to "strike the passions" both ways: by depicting them vividly in the countenance of his characters, and by igniting them in his audience. He also managed, better than any predecessor, to "secure his property to himself." He petitioned Parliament to pass the Engraver's Copyright Act (often called "Hogarth's Act"), which protected printmakers from the then rampant piratical reproduction of their work, and which thereby (in Ho-garth's proud words) "made prints a considerable article and trade in this country, there being more business of that kind done in this town than in Paris or anywhere else." The engravings of A Rake's Progress were first published, pointedly, the day after Hogarth's Act became the law of the land.

Early in his career, Hogarth had been praised as a "Shakespeare in painting," and admirers noted repeatedly the literary force of his graphic art; only he, wrote one, could "teach pictures to speak and to think." Hogarth had appropriated the very idea of an instructive moral "progress" from John Bunyan's phenomenally popular religious narrative Pilgrim's Progress, but he made the journey at once darker and more satiric. Bunyan's Mr. Christian progresses through Vanity Fair and other dangers toward the Celestial City; Hogarth's protagonists remain mired within the Vanity Fair of contemporary London; their "progress" takes them downward to degradation and death. His art also helped shape a newer form of narrative, the novel. Like the novel, Hogarth's sequences abound in suggestive subplots, telling asides, and startling revelations, played out in the tiniest details carefully placed. Novelists as different from one another as Samuel Richardson, Henry Fielding, and Laurence Sterne valued him as a friend, sought him as a collaborator, and embraced him as a past master in their own moral and narrative mode. "I almost dare affirm," wrote Fielding, "that those two works of his, which he calls The Rake's and The Harlot's Progress, are calculated more to serve the cause of virtue, and for the preservation of mankind, than all the folios of morality which have ever been written."

A Rake's Progress

Plate 1   Tom Rakewell's father (depicted in the portrait above the mantle) has recently died. The old man was miserly: he wore a coat and fur hat indoors so as not to incur the costs of a fire; he saved broken junk (in the open chest); he nearly starved his housecat (lower left). The young man is profligate: he has torn open doors and cabinets in search of sequestered wealth; he is being measured for new and ostentatious clothes; he is trying to pay off the raging mother of Sarah Young, the weeping woman (at right) whom he has made pregnant.

Plate 2   Nearly unrecognizable in his new elegance, Rakewell (the tallest figure in the picture) surrounds himself with instructors and tradespeople eager to sell their services. In the foreground (from left to right) are a composer, a fencing master, a dance teacher (with fiddle), a hired killer (in black; the note in Tom's hand, from "William Stab," vouches for the assassin as "a man of honor"); a huntsman (with horn); and a jockey, whose trophy cup bears the suggestive name of the winning horse: "Silly Tom." The two moping Englishmen at the back may be miffed to find themselves supplanted by the fashionable foreigners in front of them. The painting above the mantle depicts the Judgment of Paris, that indolent princeling whose unrestrained desires precipitated the catastrophe of the Trojan War.

Plate 3   Rakewell (sprawled at left) has bought himself an orgy. All the Roman portraits in the upper right corner have been defaced, except that of the emperor Nero, who looks out over the havoc like some patron saint of vandalism (his reputed incendarism is re-enacted by the woman standing at the back near the shattered mirror, holding a candle flame to the map of the world). One prostitute caresses Tom while conveying away his watch; in the foreground opposite, a woman disrobes in preparation for an obscene dance that will likely involve the reflective platter and large candle held by the cross-eyed lackey in the doorway. Admonitions to the orgiasts lie at hand, in the form of the chicken's carcass (lower right corner), stripped and forked; and in the person of the ballad singer, tattered, pregnant, and ignored, whose song bears the telling title "Black Joke."

Plate 4   Carried in his sedan chair to a night of gaming at White's Chocolate House and gambling club (rear left), Tom is stopped by a bailiff who serves him with a notice of arrest for debt. He receives aid not from the revellers in the distance but from Sarah Young, the abandoned lover whose mother he tried to buy off in Plate 1. Reversing that gesture, she seeks to secure his release by offering the money she has earned by making ribbons and caps (sample wares hang at her side). On a ladder a lamplighter, distracted by the goings-on, carelessly (and emblematically) spills his flammable fluid onto Rakewell's head. Hogarth reworked this picture more often than any other in the series. In this late version, a lightning bolt aims pointedly at the gambling house, upper left, while at the lower right, a group of urchins in the open air has made an early start at playing comparably dangerous games.

Plate 5   Intent on wealth, not the love Sarah offers, Rakewell weds an old woman in a dim, disintegrating church where light and faith are in scant supply. On the left, the Poor's Box," receptacle of charity, has long been shut (a cobweb covers its lid); on the right wall, the table of commandments is cracked. The one-eyed bride appears to wink at the grim parson; Rakewell proffers her the ring while eying her maid. On the floor, a canine couple parodies the human ceremony; in the back, a woman with churchkeys flailing tries to prevent the intrusion of Sarah Young, holding the child Rakewell has sired. Sarah's mother does vigorous but unavailing battle.

Plate 6   During a night of gambling, Rakewell has evidently lost the fortune he acquired by his calculating marriage. Wigless, frantic, he falls to one knee and curses his lot; his rage is replicated (as were his nuptials) by a dog on the floor to his right. The croupier at rear center, carrying the candles, echoes the "world-burning" woman in Plate 3. This time, though, the building is actually on fire. The lantern-bearing watchman at left has come to give warning. Most of the gamblers are too immersed in their own operations to notice either Rakewell's anguish or their own danger.

Plate 7   In the wake of his losses, Rakewell has at last been imprisoned for debt, unable to pay the "garnish" (or customary bribe) that the jailer behind him expects, or even the cost of a beer. The note on the table—"I have read your play and find it will not do"—rejects his last poor, literary attempt at solvency. His wife rails, Sarah faints, his daughter tugs at Sarah's skirts, and his cellmates embody futilities even more preposterous than his own playwriting. The impoverished man at left has devised "a new scheme for paying the debts of the nation." The man seated at the stove is an alchemist, vainly trying to transmute base metals into gold; before his imprisonment, he also built himself a pair of wings (upper left), but they, like Rakewell's upward aspirations, have produced only debt and confinement, not flight and freedom.

Plate 8   Rakewell has been moved from debtor's prison to Bethlehem Royal Hospital (better known as Bedlam), London's asylum for the insane. Grinning outright for the first time in the series, Tom claws at his head while guards restrain him. Sarah Young, weeping, has come to give him comfort. The other two women are here to amuse themselves (at the cost of two pence per visit, Bedlam had become one of London's most popular entertainments). Some inmates display lunatic religious zeal; others have gone mad in pursuit of science. The man drawing the world on the wall seeks a solution to the longitude, the navigational problem that had obsessed Britons for many decades. Behind the open door of the central cell, a naked madman sits and thinks he's king. In this final revision of the plate (1763), Hogarth has superimposed upon the longitudinist's globe an emblem of Britannia, as though empire and madhouse were now one.

═╬ PERSPECTIVES ╬═
Mind and God

Nature, and Nature's Laws lay hid in Night.
God said, *Let Newton be!* and All was *Light*.

So wrote Alexander Pope, capturing in a couplet the awe with which many of his contemporaries regarded the accomplishments of Isaac Newton. The lines, intended for Newton's tomb, compass his whole career. Pope's last word evokes one of the scientist's early breakthroughs: the discovery that sunlight, for all its seeming "whiteness," teemed with colors, whose operations could be mathematically described. Later, in his masterwork *Naturalis Philosophiae Principia Mathematica* (The Mathematical Principles of Natural Philosophy, 1687), Newton had expounded "Nature's Laws" on a scale and with a precision heretofore unmatched, pinpointing, in compact mathematical formulas, the laws governing gravity and motion, both on earth and throughout the heavens. In Pope's replaying of Genesis, Newton himself becomes a principle, not merely the interpreter of Creation but virtually synonymous with it: God's luminous word, from which revelation follows. For numberless admirers, the name of Newton figured forth not only the intricate simplicities of "Nature's Laws," but also the astonishing, hitherto unsuspected capacity of the human mind to shed light upon the works of God.

The human mind itself promptly became the object of new investigation, Newtonian in its ambitions and its methods. Two years after the *Principia* appeared, John Locke published his *Essay Concerning Human Understanding* (1689), a work comparably influential, in which he sought answers to key questions of epistemology: what do we know? and by what means do we come to know it? Locke, like Newton, brought luster to the scientific approach championed by the Royal Society (of which both men were members): empiricism, the conviction that truth could be attained solely through experiment and experience. The intimate interplay of those two crucial elements is nicely registered in Albert Einstein's account of the way that Newton did his work: "The conceptions which he used to reduce the material of experience to order seemed to flow spontaneously from experience itself, from the beautiful experiments which he ranged in order like playthings and describes with an affectionate wealth of detail." Locke imported empiricism from the physical sciences into the realms of philosophy and psychology. Striving to found a science of mind, to make sense of the running encounter between the material world and human perception, Locke and his successors found in experience both a method for investigating epistemological problems and the core of their solution: for these thinkers, experience is how we know, it is what we know, and it is how we can learn more about the processes of our knowing. The human mind is intrinsically (though not methodically) empiricist in its ways of gathering its "wealth of detail" about the world.

Under the mind's new scrutinies, God's place and primacy fell open to new questions. Empiricism itself was seen to cut two ways. On the one hand, as Newton and the vast majority of his followers delightedly proclaimed, experimental observation was revealing a universal architecture so exquisite as to prove both the existence and the matchless artistry of God the architect; this route from reason to religious faith became known as the "argument from design." On the other hand, discovery was beginning to conjure up alternative possibilities unsettling to faith: of a God not wholly supreme but subject to nature's inexorable laws; or of laws so efficiently self-sustaining that they needed no God to enforce them. In some of its modes, empiricism itself could be seen to imperil faith, since direct experience or demonstration of the divine proved elusive in a science that limited itself to the observation of material, mechanical causes and effects. For Newton, Locke, and countless other inquirers, empiricism promised to explain the ways of God; but they had begun a process which, in other hands, might threaten to explain God away.

The clash between science and theology gathered force in the mid-nineteenth century, when discoveries in geology (the age of the Earth) and biology (evolution) rendered Scripture strongly suspect. But contention between faith and science was manifest much earlier. At the start of the nineteenth century, William Blake briefly sketched the lines of struggle in his private notebook. "Newton's particles of light," he wrote

> Are sands upon the Red sea shore,
> Where Israel's tents do shine so bright.

Against the arrogance of inquiry, Blake insists upon humility and awe; biblical revelation trumps all the small advancements of human knowledge. Pope had gestured in this direction some seven decades earlier. He suggested, in his *Essay on Man,* that for "superior beings" (angels, God), the sight of Newton unfolding "all Nature's law" might provide the same kind of amazement and amusement that we mortals derive from the antics of a performing ape—a creature who knows more than we might expect, but far less than we ourselves. So great (Pope argues) is the difference between human and divine capacities. Throughout the eighteenth century, in works suffused by the concepts of Newton and of Locke, the relations between mind and God were brilliantly explicated and newly contested, as poets and philosophers undertook, from varying vantages and factions, to sing God's praise, to parse his ways, to work toward him by reason or (in rare instances) to reason him out of existence altogether.

+•+ ≡◆≡ +•+

Isaac Newton
1642–1727

Albert Einstein summed up Newton's abilities as follows: "In one person, he combined the experimenter, the theorist, the mechanic, and, not least, the artist in exposition." Einstein praises magnificently, and omits much. Newton also combined in his one person a supreme mathematician, an obsessive alchemist, a forceful administrator, and (perhaps most important, in his own view) an ardent theologian, eager to discover and expound the place of God in his creation. His voluminous, unorthodox writings on the subject remained unpublished in his lifetime. By denying the full divinity of Christ, Newton accorded God *more* authority than did conventional Anglicanism. His views, if known, would have toppled him from the public eminences he enjoyed: as Lucasian Professor of Mathematics at Cambridge, as Master of the Mint in London, as President of the Royal Society. Still, Newton's first admirers found in his scientific work exhilarating support for a more mainstream theology: the strongest foundation yet for the argument from design. It was the business of natural philosophy, Newton repeatedly insisted, "to deduce causes from effects, until we come to the First Cause, which is certainly not mechanical." Newton's own scientific revelations gave rise to a passionate interest in "natural religion"—a faith in God's existence and benevolence, grounded in the orderliness and beauty of the natural world. One of that faith's adherents was the ambitious young classicist and clergyman Richard Bentley (1662–1742), who, having been commissioned to deliver a series of lectures defending Christianity against atheism, found in Newton's recently published *Principia* abundant new evidence for his own arguments about the divine "origin and frame of the universe." While preparing his lectures for the press, Bentley sent Newton a set of questions, in order to make sure that he was correctly understanding and deploying the *Principia.* Newton's four replies (the first is excerpted here) map the convergence that interests him most, between the discoveries of science and the majesty of God.

from **Letter to Richard Bentley**

10 December 1692

Sir,

When I wrote my treatise about our system, I had an eye upon such principles as might work with considering men for the belief of a Deity, and nothing can rejoice me more than to find it useful for that purpose. But if I have done the public any service this way, 'tis due to nothing but industry and a patient thought.

As to your first query, it seems to me, that if the matter of our sun and planets and all the matter in the universe was evenly scattered throughout all the heavens, and every particle had an innate gravity towards all the rest,[1] and the whole space throughout which this matter was scattered was but finite, the matter on the outside of this space would by its gravity tend towards all the matter on the inside, and by consequence fall down to the middle of the whole space, and there compose one great spherical mass. But if the matter was evenly diffused through an infinite space, it would never convene into one mass, but some of it convene into one mass and some into another so as to make an infinite number of great masses scattered at great distances from one to another throughout all that infinite space. And thus might the sun and fixed stars be formed, supposing the matter were of a lucid[2] nature. But how the matter should divide itself into two sorts, and that part of it which is fit to compose a shining body should fall down into one mass and make a sun, and the rest which is fit to compose an opaque body should coalesce not into one great body like the shining matter but into many little ones; or, if the sun was at first an opaque body like the planets, or the planets lucid bodies like the sun, how he alone should be changed into a shining body whilst all they continue opaque, or all they be changed into opaque ones whilst he remains unchanged, I do not think explicable by mere natural causes but am forced to ascribe it to the counsel[3] and contrivance of a voluntary agent. The same power, whether natural or supernatural, which placed the sun in the center of the orbs[4] of the six primary planets, placed Saturn in the center of the orbs of his five secondary planets,[5] and Jupiter in the center of the orbs of his four secondary ones, and the Earth in the center of the moon's orb; and therefore, had this cause been a blind one without contrivance and design, the sun would have been a body of the same kind with Saturn, Jupiter and the Earth; that is without light and heat. Why there is one body in our system qualified to give light and heat to all the rest I know no reason but because the author of the system thought it convenient, and why there is but one body of this kind I know no reason but because one was sufficient to warm and enlighten all the rest. For the Cartesian hypothesis[6] of suns losing their light and then turning into comets and comets into planets can have no place in my system and is plainly erroneous, because it's certain that comets as often as they appear to us descend into the system of our planets lower than the orb of Jupiter and sometimes lower than the orbs of Venus and Mercury, and yet never stay here but always return from the sun with the same degrees of motion by which they approached him.

1. Newton did not endorse this premise. "You sometimes speak," he wrote Bentley in his second letter, "of gravity as essential and inherent to matter: pray do not ascribe that notion to me, for the cause of gravity is what I do not pretend to know."
2. Light-producing.
3. Deliberate design.

4. Orbits.
5. I.e., Saturn's moons; Newton states the numbers of planets and their moons then known.
6. A theory put forth by the French mathematician and philosopher René Descartes (1596–1650) in his highly influential treatises on physics, which Newton's *Principia* had challenged.

To your second query I answer that the motions which the planets now have could not spring from any natural cause alone but were impressed by an intelligent agent. For since comets descend into the region of our planets and here move all manner of ways, going sometimes the same way with the planets, sometimes the contrary way, and sometimes in cross ways in planes inclined to the plane of the ecliptic at all kinds of angles, it's plain that there is no natural cause which could determine all the planets both primary and secondary to move the same way and in the same plane without any considerable variation.[7] This must have been the effect of counsel. Nor is there any natural cause which could give the planets those just degrees of velocity in proportion to their distances from the sun and other central bodies about which they move and to the quantity of matter contained in those bodies, which were requisite to make them move in concentric orbs about those bodies. Had the planets been as swift as comets in proportion to their distances from the sun (as they would have been, had their motions been caused by their gravity, whereby the matter at the first formation of the planets might fall from the remotest regions towards the sun), they would not move in concentric orbs but in such eccentric ones as the comets move in. Were all the planets as swift as Mercury or as slow as Saturn or his satellites, or were their several velocities otherwise much greater or less than they are (as they might have been had they arose from any other cause than their gravity), or had their distances from the centers about which they move been greater or less than they are with the same velocities; or had the quantity of matter in the sun or in Saturn, Jupiter, and the Earth and by consequence their gravitating power been greater or less than it is, the primary planets could not have revolved about the sun nor the secondary ones about Saturn, Jupiter and the Earth in concentric circles as they do, but would have moved in hyperbolas or parabolas or in ellipses very eccentric. To make this system therefore, with all its motions, required a cause which understood and compared together the quantities of matter in the several bodies of the sun and planets and the gravitating powers resulting from thence, the several distances of the primary planets from the sun and secondary ones from Saturn, Jupiter, and the Earth, and the velocities with which these planets could revolve at those distances about those quantities of matter in the central bodies. And to compare and adjust all these things together in so great a variety of bodies argues that cause to be not blind and fortuitous, but very well skilled in mechanics and geometry.

To your third query I answer that it may be represented that the sun may, by heating those planets most which are nearest to him, cause them to be better concocted[8] and more condensed by concoction. But when I consider that our Earth is much more heated in its bowels below the upper crust by subterraneous fermentations of mineral bodies than by the sun, I see not why the interior parts of Jupiter and Saturn might not be as much heated, concocted, and coagulated by those fermentations as our Earth is, and therefore this various density should have some other cause than the various distances of the planets from the sun; and I am confirmed in this opinion by considering that the planets of Jupiter and Saturn, as they are rarer[9] than

7. Newton oversimplifies: the planes of the planets actually incline to each other by as much as five degrees. Newton's arguments in this letter, suggests his biographer Richard Westfall, "reveal above all a determination to find God in nature," even to impose God upon nature. All the phenomena that Newton here attributes to the intervention of divine "counsel" and "skill" were explained scientifically over the course of the next century by physicists applying and extending Newton's own system, so that (as the most brilliant of the extenders, Pierre Simon Laplace, is said to have remarked to Napoleon) the hypothesis of divine intervention was no longer necessary.
8. Purified by heat (and hence made denser by the absence of the extraneous matter that the heat has annihilated).
9. Less dense.

the rest, so they are vastly greater and contain a far greater quantity of matter and have many satellites about them, which qualifications surely arose not from their being placed at so great a distance from the sun, but were rather the cause why the Creator placed them at that great distance. For by their gravitating powers they disturb one another's motions very sensibly, as I find by some late observations of Mr. Flamsteed,[1] and had they been placed much nearer to the sun and to one another they would by the same powers have caused a considerable disturbance in the whole system. * * *

Lastly, I see nothing extraordinary in the inclination of the Earth's axis for proving a Deity unless you will urge it as a contrivance for winter and summer and for making the Earth habitable towards the poles, and that the diurnal rotations of the sun and planets, as they could hardly arise from any cause purely mechanical, so by being determined all the same way with the annual and menstrual[2] motions they seem to make up that harmony in the system which (as I explained above) was the effect of choice rather than of chance.

There is yet another argument for a Deity which I take to be a very strong one, but till the principles on which 'tis grounded be better received I think it more advisable to let it sleep. I am

Your most humble servant to command
Is. NEWTON

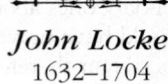

John Locke
1632–1704

In the preface to his *Essay Concerning Human Understanding*, Locke depicts "the incomparable Mr. Newton" as one of the "master builders" of the new science, and himself as a mere "under-laborer," busy "clearing the ground a little, and removing some of the rubbish that lies in the way to knowledge." The eighteenth century, though, tended to venerate the two thinkers equally, Newton as master explicator of the cosmos, Locke as master inquirer into the mind. Starting from the claim that "simple ideas," acquired early, constituted the building blocks of thought, Locke constructed a system of the mind of comparable in intricacy with Newton's universe, but of greater idiosyncrasy (since the content of consciousness differed from person to person, and indeed determined individual identity). Part of Locke's appeal lay in the comparative accessibility of his empiricism. His experiments, unlike Newton's, required neither telescope nor prism, calculus nor genius: readers could perform them (as Locke repeatedly suggested) in the laboratories of their minds, using their own perceptions and memories as raw material. More than any other text, Locke's *Essay* spurred that fascination with the first person which suffuses so much eighteenth-century writing: autobiographies, essays, diaries, travel journals, philosophic treatises, novels. Locke described the workings of the mind so persuasively that in effect he changed them too, prompting an analytic self-consciousness that had not obtained in the same kind and to the same degree before his book appeared.

---

1. John Flamsteed (1646–1719), astronomer and director of the Royal Greenwich Observatory, had recently supplied Newton with these data; the two men later quarrelled bitterly over Flamsteed's reluctance to make available the immense, precise, and urgently needed records of his celestial observations.
2. Monthly.

from An Essay Concerning Human Understanding
[ON IDEAS[1]]

Every man being conscious to himself that he thinks, and that which his mind is employed about whilst thinking being the *ideas* that are there, 'tis past doubt, that men have in their minds several *ideas*, such as are those expressed by the words *whiteness, hardness, sweetness, thinking, motion, man, elephant, army, drunkenness*, and others. It is in the first place then to be inquired, how he comes by them? I know it is a received doctrine, that men have native *ideas* and original characters[2] stamped upon their minds, in their very first being. This opinion I have at large examined already, and I suppose what I have said in the foregoing book[3] will be much more easily admitted, when I have shown whence the understanding may get all the *ideas* it has, and by what ways and degrees they may come into the mind; for which I shall appeal to everyone's own observation and experience.

Let us then suppose the mind to be, as we say, white paper, void of all characters, without any *ideas*. How comes it to be furnished? Whence comes it by that vast store, which the busy and boundless fancy of man has painted on it, with an almost endless variety? Whence has it all the materials of reason and knowledge? To this I answer, in one word, from *experience*. In that, all our knowledge is founded, and from that it ultimately derives itself. Our observation employed either about *external, sensible objects, or about the internal operations of our minds, perceived and reflected on by ourselves, is that which supplies our understandings with all the materials of thinking*. These two are the fountains of knowledge, from whence all the *ideas* we have, or can naturally have, do spring.

First, *our senses*, conversant about particular sensible objects, do *convey into the mind*, several distinct *perceptions* of things, according to those various ways, wherein those objects do affect them; and thus we come by those *ideas* we have of *yellow, white, heat, cold, soft, hard, bitter, sweet*, and all those which we call sensible qualities, which when I say the senses convey into the mind, I mean, they from external objects convey into the mind what produces there those *perceptions*. This great source of most of the *ideas* we have, depending wholly upon our senses and derived by them to the understanding, I call SENSATION.

Secondly, the other fountain from which experience furnisheth the understanding with *ideas* is the *perception of the operations of our own minds* within us, as it is employed about the *ideas* it has got; which operations, when the soul comes to reflect on, and consider, do furnish the understanding with another set of *ideas*, which could not be had from things without; and such are *perception, thinking, doubting, believing, reasoning, knowing, willing*, and all the different actings of our own minds; which we being conscious of, and observing in ourselves, do from these receive into our understandings, as distinct *ideas*, as we do from bodies affecting our senses. This source of *ideas* every man has wholly in himself. And though it be not sense, as having nothing to do with external objects, yet it is very like it, and might properly enough be called internal sense. But as I call the other *sensation*, so I call this REFLECTION, the *ideas* it affords being such only, as the mind gets by reflecting on its own operations within itself. By REFLECTION then, in the following part of this discourse, I would be understood to mean, that notice

---

1. All selections are from Book 2, "Of Ideas"; chapter and section numbers follow each section, in brackets. Most of Locke's italics have been retained.

2. Inscriptions.

3. In which Locke denied the existence of "innate principles," received by the soul "in its very first being" (1.2.1).

which the mind takes of its own operations, and the manner of them, by reason whereof there come to be *ideas* of these operations in the understanding. These two, I say, *viz.* external, material things, as the objects of SENSATION, and the operations of our own minds within, as the objects of REFLECTION, are, to me, the only originals,[4] from whence all our *ideas* take their beginnings. The term *operations* here I use in a large sense, as comprehending not barely the actions of the mind about its *ideas*, but some sort of passions arising sometimes from them, such as is the satisfaction or uneasiness arising from any thought.

The understanding seems to me not to have the least glimmering of any *ideas*, which it doth not receive from one of these two. *External objects furnish the mind with the ideas of sensible qualities*, which are all those different perceptions they produce in us; and the *mind furnishes the understanding with* ideas *of its own operations*.

These, when we have taken a full survey of them, and their several modes, combinations, and relations, we shall find to contain all our whole stock of *ideas*; and that we have nothing in our minds which did not come in one of these two ways. Let anyone examine his own thoughts, and thoroughly search into his understanding, and then let him tell me, whether all the original *ideas* he has there are any other than of the objects of his *senses*, or of the operations of his mind, considered as objects of his *reflection*; and how great a mass of knowledge soever he imagines to be lodged there, he will, upon taking a strict view, see that he has *not any idea in his mind, but what one of these two have imprinted*; though, perhaps, with infinite variety compounded and enlarged by the understanding, as we shall see hereafter.

He that attentively considers the state of a *child*, at his first coming into the world, will have little reason to think him stored with plenty of *ideas*, that are to be the matter of his future knowledge. 'Tis by degrees he comes to be furnished with them. And though the *ideas* of obvious and familiar qualities imprint themselves before the memory begins to keep a register of time and order, yet 'tis often so late, before some unusual qualities come in the way, that there are few men that cannot recollect the beginning of their acquaintance with them; and if it were worthwhile, no doubt a child might be so ordered as to have but a very few, even of the ordinary *ideas*, till he were grown up to a man. But all that are born into the world being surrounded with bodies that perpetually and diversely affect them, variety of *ideas*, whether care be taken about it or no, are imprinted on the minds of children. *Light* and *colors* are busy at hand everywhere, when the eye is but open; *sounds* and some *tangible qualities* fail not to solicit their proper senses, and force an entrance to the mind; but yet, I think, it will be granted easily, that if a child were kept in a place where he never saw any other but black and white till he were a man, he would have no more *ideas* of scarlet or green, than he that from his childhood never tasted an oyster, or a pineapple, has of those particular relishes.

Men then come to be furnished with fewer or more simple *ideas* from without, according as the *objects* they converse with[5] afford greater or less variety; and from the operation of their minds within, according as they more or less *reflect* on them. For, though he that contemplates the operations of his mind cannot but have plain and clear *ideas* of them; yet unless he turn his thoughts that way, and considers them *attentively*, he will no more have clear and distinct *ideas* of all the *operations of his mind*, and all that may be observed therein, than he will have all the particular *ideas* of any landscape, or of the parts and motions of a clock, who will not turn his eyes to it, and with attention heed all the parts of it. The picture or clock may be so placed that they may come in his way every day; but yet he will have but a confused *idea* of all the parts they are made up of, till he *applies himself with attention,* to consider them each in particular. [1.1–7]

* * *

But to return to the matter in hand, the *ideas* we have of substances, and the ways we come by them; I say *our specific* ideas *of substances* are nothing else but *a collection of a certain number of simple ideas, considered as united in one thing.* These *ideas* of substances, though they are commonly called simple apprehensions, and the names of them simple terms, yet in effect, are complex and compounded. Thus the *idea* which an *Englishman* signifies by the name *swan* is white color, long neck, red beak, black legs, and whole feet, and all these of a certain size, with a power of swimming in the water, and making a certain kind of noise, and, perhaps, to a man who has long observed those kind of birds, some other properties, which all terminate in sensible simple *ideas,* all united in one common subject.

Besides the complex *ideas* we have of material sensible substances, of which I have last spoken, by the simple *ideas* we have taken from those operations of our own minds, which we experiment[6] daily in ourselves, as thinking, understanding, willing, knowing, and power of beginning motion, etc. co-existing in some substance, we are able to frame *the complex* idea *of an immaterial spirit.* And thus by putting together the *ideas* of thinking, perceiving, liberty, and power of moving themselves and other things, we have as clear a perception and notion of immaterial substances, as we have of material. For putting together the *ideas* of thinking and willing, or the power of moving or quieting corporeal motion, joined to substance, of which we have no distinct *idea,* we have the *idea* of an immaterial spirit; and by putting together the *ideas* of coherent solid parts, and a power of being moved, joined with substance, of which likewise we have no positive *idea,* we have the *idea* of matter. The one is as clear and distinct an *idea,* as the other: the *idea* of thinking, and moving a body, being as clear and distinct *ideas,* as the *ideas* of extension, solidity, and being moved. [23.14–15]

* * *

If we examine the *idea* we have of the incomprehensible Supreme Being, we shall find that we come by it the same way; and that the complex *ideas* we have both of God, and separate spirits, are made up of the simple *ideas* we receive from *reflection; v.g.* having, from what we experiment in ourselves, got the *ideas* of existence and duration; of knowledge and power; of pleasure and happiness; and of several other qualities and powers, which it is better to have than to be without; when we would frame an *idea* the most suitable we can to the Supreme Being, we enlarge every one of these with our *idea* of infinity; and so putting them together, make our complex *idea* of God. For that the mind has such a power of enlarging some of its *ideas,* received from sensation and reflection, has been already showed. [23.33]

[ON IDENTITY]

Personal identity consists, not in the identity of substance, but, as I have said, in the identity of *consciousness,* wherein, if Socrates and the present Mayor of Queenborough agree, they are the same person. If the same Socrates waking and sleeping do not partake of the same *consciousness,* Socrates waking and sleeping is not the same person. And to punish Socrates waking, for what sleeping Socrates thought, and

---

6. Experience.

waking Socrates was never conscious of, would be no more of right, than to punish one twin for what his brother-twin did, whereof he knew nothing, because their outsides were so like that they could not be distinguished; for such twins have been seen.

But yet possibly it will still be objected, suppose I wholly lose the memory of some parts of my life, beyond a possibility of retrieving them, so that perhaps I shall never be conscious of them again; yet am I not the same person that did those actions, had those thoughts, that I was once conscious of, though I have now forgot them? To which I answer, that we must here take notice what the word *I* is applied to, which in this case is the man only. And the same man being presumed to be the same person, *I* is easily here supposed to stand also for the same person. But if it be possible for the same man to have distinct incommunicable consciousness at different times, it is past doubt the same man would at different times make different persons; which, we see, is the sense of mankind in the solemnest declaration of their opinions, human laws not punishing the *mad man* for the *sober man's* actions, nor the *sober man* for what the *mad man* did, thereby making them two persons; which is somewhat explained by our way of speaking in *English*, when we say such an one *is not himself*, or is *besides himself*; in which phrases it is insinuated, as if those who now, or, at least, first used them, thought, that *self* was changed, the *self* same person was no longer in that man.

But yet 'tis hard to conceive that Socrates the same individual man should be two persons. To help us a little in this, we must consider what is meant by *Socrates*, or the same individual *man*.

First, it must be either the same individual, immaterial, thinking substance: in short, the same numerical soul, and nothing else.

Secondly, or the same animal,[7] without any regard to an immaterial soul.

Thirdly, or the same immaterial spirit united to the same animal.

Now take which of these suppositions you please, it is impossible to make personal identity to consist in anything but consciousness, or reach any farther than that does.

For by the first of them, it must be allowed possible that a man born of different women, and in distant times, may be the same man. A way of speaking, which whoever admits, must allow it possible for the same man to be two distinct persons, as any two that have lived in different ages without the knowledge of one another's thoughts.

By the second and third, Socrates in this life, and after it, cannot be the same man any way, but by the same consciousness; and so making *human identity* to consist in the same thing wherein we place *personal identity*, there will be no difficulty to allow the same man to be the same person. But then they who place *human identity* in consciousness only, and not in something else, must consider how they will make the infant Socrates the same man with Socrates after the resurrection. But whatsoever to some men makes a *man*, and consequently the same individual man, wherein perhaps few are agreed, personal identity can by us be placed in nothing but consciousness (which is that alone which makes what we call *self*) without involving us in great absurdities.

But is not a man drunk and sober the same person? Why else is he punished for the fact[8] he commits when drunk, though he be never afterwards conscious of it? Just as much the same person, as a man that walks, and does other things in his sleep, is

7. Physical, living body.   8. Deed.

the same person, and is answerable for any mischief he shall do in it. Human laws punish both with a justice suitable to their way of knowledge: because in these cases, they cannot distinguish certainly what is real, what counterfeit; and so the ignorance in drunkeness or sleep is not admitted as a plea. For though punishment be annexed to personality, and personality to consciousness, and the drunkard perhaps be not conscious of what he did, yet human judicatures justly punish him; because the fact is proved against him, but what of consciousness cannot be proved for him. But in the great day,[9] wherein the secrets of all hearts shall be laid open, it may be reasonable to think, no one shall be made to answer for what he knows nothing of; but shall receive his doom, his conscience accusing or excusing him. [27.19–22]

1671–1689   1689

━━━ ≍✦≍ ━━━

Isaac Watts
1674–1748

"As his mind was capacious, his curiosity excursive, and his industry continual," wrote Samuel Johnson in praise of the dissenting minister Isaac Watts, "his writings are very numerous." Watts produced books of poetry, logic, theology, philosophy, and science, but the writings that have mattered most are the hymns and psalm translations (about seven hundred in all) that he began composing in his early twenties. In his philosophical writings, Watts worked hard to absorb the innovations of Newton's physics and Locke's psychology; in his hymns, an older structure of piety prevails. One of empiricism's chief effects was to entangle truth with time, to make knowledge a consequence of *process* (a series of experiments, a sequence of ideas). In Watts's hymns, truth is eternal; the mind's chief tasks are to register God's greatness and to praise it aright. The singing of hymns, and of psalms awkwardly translated from the Hebrew, had been a practice of long standing in Protestant congregations. Watts brought to these forms a new clarity and grace, in verses he carefully crafted, week after week, for the immediate use and pleasure of his congregants. He sought (he once explained) to achieve an "ease of numbers [i.e., meter] and smoothness of sound, and . . . to make the sense plain and obvious." In print, the simplicity of his style gradually won a wider attention, extending far beyond local circles of dissent. As the religious historian and poet Donald Davie has pointed out, Watts's hymns and psalms probably touched more minds (and certainly resounded in more throats) over the course of the eighteenth century than any of the texts we now deem greater hits: *Gulliver's Travels*, Johnson's *Dictionary*, Thomson's *Seasons*. In his lifetime and for more than a century after, Watts was reckoned the English, Christian successor to that ancient king of Israel traditionally credited with creating the Psalms. "Were David to speak English," Watts's brother once remarked to him, "he would choose to make use of your style."

A Prospect of Heaven Makes Death Easy[1]

There is a land of pure delight
    Where saints immortal reign;
Infinite day excludes the night,
    And pleasures banish pain.

5   There everlasting spring abides,
    And never-withering flowers:

---

9. I.e., Judgment Day.   1. From *Hymns and Spiritual Songs* (1707).

Death like a narrow sea divides
    This heav'nly land from ours.

Sweet fields beyond the swelling flood
10   Stand dressed in living green:
So to the Jews old Canaan stood,
    While Jordan rolled between.[2]

But timorous mortals start° and shrink   *tremble*
    To cross this narrow sea,
15 And linger shivering on the brink,
    And fear to launch away.

O! could we make our doubts remove,°   *withdraw*
    Those gloomy doubts that rise,
And see the Canaan that we love,
20   With unbeclouded eyes:

Could we but climb where Moses stood,[3]
    And view the landskip° o'er,   *landscape*
Not Jordan's stream, nor death's cold flood
    Should fright us from the shore.

1707

The Hurry of the Spirits, in a Fever and Nervous Disorders[1]

My frame of nature is a ruffled sea,
And my disease the tempest. Nature feels
A strange commotion to her inmost center;
The throne of reason shakes. "Be still, my thoughts;
5 Peace and be still." In vain my reason gives
The peaceful word, my spirit strives in vain
To calm the tumult and command my thoughts.
This flesh, this circling blood, these brutal powers
Made to obey, turn rebels to the mind,
10 Nor hear its laws. The engine° rules the man.   *body*
Unhappy change! When nature's meaner springs,
Fired to impetuous ferments, break all order;
When little restless atoms rise and reign
Tyrants in sovereign uproar, and impose
15 Ideas on the mind; confused ideas
Of non-existents and impossibles,
Who can describe them? Fragments of old dreams,
Borrowed from midnight, torn from fairy fields
And fairy skies, and regions of the dead,
20 Abrupt, ill-sorted. O 'tis all confusion!
If I but close my eyes, strange images

---

2. In Joshua 3, the children of Israel, at the end of their 40-year journey in the desert, see the promised land of Canaan across the River Jordan.
3. Having led the Israelites to the end of their desert journey, Moses on his last day of life climbed the mountain of Nebo, and surveyed the entire promised land (Deuteron-

omy 34.1–4).
1. Not a hymn but an autobiographical poem, the first in a sequence entitled *Thoughts and Meditations in a Long Sickness, 1712 and 1713*, published decades later in Watts' *Reliquiae Juveniles* (writings in youth).

In thousand forms and thousand colors rise,
Stars, rainbows, moons, green dragons, bears and ghosts,
An endless medley rush upon the stage
25   And dance and riot wild in reason's court
Above control. I'm in a raging storm,
Where seas and skies are blended, while my soul
Like some light worthless chip of floating cork
Is tossed from wave to wave: now overwhelmed
30   With breaking floods, I drown, and seem to lose
All being; now high-mounted on the ridge
Of tall foaming surge, I'm all at once
Caught up into the storm, and ride the wind,
The whistling wind; unmanageable steed,
35   And feeble rider! Hurried many a league
Over the rising hills of roaring brine,
Through airy wilds unknown, with dreadful speed
And infinite surprise, till some few minutes
Have spent the blast, and then perhaps I drop
40   Near to the peaceful coast. Some friendly billow
Lodges me on the beach, and I find rest.
Short rest I find; for the next rolling wave
Snatches me back again; then ebbing far
Sets me adrift, and I am borne off to sea,
45   Helpless, amidst the bluster of the winds,
Beyond the ken of shore.

    Ah, when will these tumultuous scenes be gone?
When shall this weary spirit, tossed with tempests,
Harassed and broken, reach the ports of rest,
50   And hold it firm? When shall this wayward flesh
With all th' irregular springs of vital movement
Ungovernable, return to sacred order,
And pay their duties to the ruling mind?

1712   1734

Against Idleness and Mischief[1]

How doth the little busy bee
    Improve each shining hour,
And gather honey all the day
    From every opening flower!

5   How skillfully she builds her cell!
    How neat she spreads the wax!
And labors hard to store it well
    With the sweet food she makes.

In works of labor, or of skill,
10   I would be busy too;

---

1. From *Divine Songs Attempted in Easy Language, for the Use of Children*. The poems in this durable little collection were memorized by numberless children in the 18th and 19th centuries, including Lewis Caroll's Alice. Wandering through Wonderland, she is commanded by its inhabitants (as she doubtless was in school) to recite these verses, and discovers to her dismay that the lines come out all wrong.

For Satan finds some mischief still°   *always*
    For idle hands to do.

In books, or work, or healthful play,
    Let my first years be passed.
15 That I may give for every day
    Some good account at last.

                                                    1715

Man Frail, and God Eternal[1]

Our God, our help in ages past,
    Our hope for years to come,
Our shelter from the stormy blast,
    And our eternal home.

5   Under the shadow of thy throne
        Thy saints have dwelt secure.
    Sufficient is thine arm alone,
        And our defense is sure.

    Before the hills in order stood,
10   Or earth received her frame,
    From everlasting thou art God,
        To endless years the same.

    Thy word commands our flesh to dust,
        Return, ye sons of men.
15 All nations rose from earth at first,
        And turn to earth again.

    A thousand ages in thy sight
        Are like an evening gone;
    Short as the watch that ends the night,
20   Before the rising sun.

    The busy tribes of flesh and blood
        With all their lives and cares
    Are carried downwards by thy flood,
        And lost in following years.

25 Time, like an ever-rolling stream
        Bears all its sons away.
    They fly forgotten, as a dream
        Dies at the opening day.

    Like flowery fields the nations stand
30   Pleased with the morning light.
    The flowers beneath the mower's hand
        Lie withering ere 'tis night.

---

1. An imitation of Psalm 90, lines 1–6. This and the next poem are from *The Psalms of David Imitated in the Language of the New Testament, and Applied to the Christian State and Worship*. As the title indicates, Watts intended not merely to translate the Psalms, but to recast them. In his preface, he declares himself "the first who hath brought down the royal author [King David] into the common affairs of the Christian life, and let the psalmist of Israel into the Church of Christ, without anything of a Jew about him."

Our God, our help in ages past,
Our hope for years to come,
35   Be thou our guard while troubles last,
And our eternal home.

1719

Miracles Attending Israel's Journey[1]

When Israel, freed from Pharaoh's hand,
Left the proud tyrant and his land,
The tribes with cheerful homage own[2]
Their king, and Judah[3] was his throne.

5   Across the deep[4] their journey lay;
The deep divides to make them way.
Jordan beheld their march, and fled
With backward current to his head.[5]

The mountains shook like frighted sheep.
10   Like lambs the little hillocks leap.[6]
Not Sinai[7] on her base could stand,
Conscious of sovereign power at hand.

What power could make the deep divide?
Make Jordan backward roll his tide?
15   Why did ye leap, ye little hills?
And whence the fright that Sinai feels?

Let every mountain, every flood,
Retire, and know th'approaching God,
The king of Israel. See him here.
20   Tremble thou earth, adore, and fear.

He thunders, and all nature mourns.
The rock to standing pool he turns.
Flints spring with fountains at his word,[8]
And fires and seas confess the Lord.

1719

---

1. An imitation of Psalm 114. In 1712, Watts sent a version of this poem to the *Spectator*, where it appeared (No. 461, Tuesday, 19 August 1712) along with a letter from the poet explaining a discovery he had made while translating: "As I was describing the journey of Israel from Egypt, and added the Divine Presence amongst them, I perceived a beauty in the Psalm which was entirely new to me, and which I was going to lose; and that is, that the poet utterly conceals the presence of God in the beginning of it. . . . The reason now seems evident, and this conduct necessary. For if God had appeared before [i.e., at the start of the poem], there could be no wonder why the mountains should leap and the sea retire; therefore that this convulsion of nature may be brought in with due surprise, his name is not mentioned till afterward, and then with a very agreeable turn of thought God is introduced at once in all his majesty."
2. Acknowledged (God as their king).
3. A portion of the land promised by God to the

Israelites; here the name is used to designate the entire promised land.
4. The Red Sea, whose miraculous parting made possible the Israelites' escape from Egypt (Exodus 14.21–31).
5. Alludes to a second, similar miracle later in the journey: God makes the waters of the river Jordan "stand upon an heap," so that the Israelites can pass "clean over" dry ground, into the promised land (Joshua 3.14–17).
6. Lines 9–10 may refer (in the original Psalm) to the hills and mountains of the promised land, the dwelling places of local gods who tremble at Israel's advent.
7. The sacred mountain on which Moses received from the Lord the Ten Commandments. At the Lord's approach, "the whole mount quaked greatly" (Exodus 19.18).
8. In the Book of Numbers (20.8–11), God miraculously produces water from rock in order to sustain the Israelites during their journey.

⊶ ⋹✦⋺ ⊷

David Hume
1711–1776

As he lay dying at home in his native city of Edinburgh, David Hume entertained a visitor by conjuring up, with characteristic cheerfulness, a scenario in the afterlife. He imagined himself begging the fatal ferryman Charon for a little more time: "Have a little patience, good Charon, I have been endeavoring to open the eyes of the public. If I live a few years longer, I may have the satisfaction of seeing the downfall of some of the prevailing systems of superstition." The "prevailing system" which Hume had become most notorious for attacking was the Christian religion, whose favorite tenets—providence, miracles, the argument from design, the afterlife itself—he had called into question, with increasing audacity, over the course of his work. But he had also done much damage to newer systems of thought, notably Locke's. Locke had regarded personal identity as coherent and continuous, the consequence of lifelong experiences and ideas accumulated in the memory. Hume, in his early, massive *Treatise of Human Nature* (1739–1740), waived all this away as an arrant fiction—though perhaps a necessary one, since empiricism properly pursued reveals so radical an incoherence in mortal minds that empiricists themselves must intermittently abandon philosophy in order to go about their daily lives. Like many of his empiric predecessors, Hume argued that knowledge of the real world "must be founded entirely on experience"; more than any predecessor he was willing to entertain (and to entertain with) the doubts and demolitions arising from that premise. In his own lifetime, his skepticism did not prove as contagious as he had hoped. The *Treatise*, he recalled wryly, "fell *deadborn from the press*, without reaching such distinction as even to excite a murmur among the zealots." Though his attempt to recast his chief arguments more succinctly in *An Enquiry Concerning Human Understanding* (1748) prompted a somewhat livelier response, he eventually made his fortune not as a philosopher but as author of the highly successful *History of England* (1754–1763). He faced the general indifference or hostility to his arguments as blithely as he later greeted death, continually refining his views and revising his prose. He knew himself out of sync with his times. When, in his fantasy, he forecasts to Charon the imminent downfall of superstition, the ferryman responds, "You loitering rogue, that will not happen these many hundred years. Do you fancy I will grant you a lease for so long a term? Get into the boat this instant, you lazy loitering rogue." More than two hundred years later, the artful mischief of Hume's work has secured him some such lease. His writings, lucid and elusive, forthright and sly, demand (and receive) continual reassessment; his skepticism has proven more powerful than his contemporaries suspected, and he figures as perhaps the wittiest and most self-possessed philosophical troublemaker since Socrates.

from A Treatise of Human Nature
[The Mind as Theater[1]]

There are some philosophers,[2] who imagine we are every moment intimately conscious of what we call our *self*; that we feel its existence and its continuance in existence; and are certain, beyond the evidence of a demonstration, both of its perfect identity and simplicity. The strongest sensation, the most violent passion, say they, instead of distracting us from this view, only fix it the more intensely, and make us consider their influence on *self* either by their pain or pleasure. To attempt a farther

1. From Book 1, section 6, "Of Personal Identity."
2. Notably Joseph Butler, an Anglican bishop who argued in *The Analogy of Religion* (1736) that the existence of the

self is a truth of which every person is continually (and correctly) certain.

proof of this were to weaken its evidence; since no proof can be derived from any fact, of which we are so intimately conscious; nor is there anything of which we can be certain, if we doubt of this.

Unluckily all these positive assertions are contrary to that very experience which is pleaded for them, nor have we any idea of *self*, after the manner it is here explained. For from what impression could this idea be derived? This question 'tis impossible to answer without a manifest contradiction and absurdity; and yet 'tis a question, which must necessarily be answered, if we would have the idea of self pass for clear and intelligible. It must be some one impression, that gives rise to every real idea. But self or person is not any one impression, but that to which our several impressions and ideas are supposed to have a reference. If any impression gives rise to the idea of self, that impression must continue invariably the same through the whole course of our lives, since self is supposed to exist after that manner. But there is no impression constant and invariable. Pain and pleasure, grief and joy, passions and sensations succeed each other, and never all exist at the same time. It cannot, therefore, be from any of these impressions, or from any other, that the idea of self is derived; and consequently there is no such idea.

But farther, what must become of all our particular perceptions upon this hypothesis? All these are different, and distinguishable, and separable from each other, and may be separately considered, and may exist separately, and have no need of anything to support their existence. After what manner, therefore, do they belong to self; and how are they connected with it? For my part, when I enter most intimately into what I call *myself*, I always stumble on some particular perception or other, of heat or cold, light or shade, love or hatred, pain or pleasure. I never can catch *myself* at any time without a perception, and never can observe anything but the perception. When my perceptions are removed for any time, as by sound sleep, so long am I insensible of *myself*, and may truly be said not to exist. And were all my perceptions removed by death, and could I neither think, nor feel, nor see, nor love, nor hate after the dissolution of my body, I should be entirely annihilated, nor do I conceive what is farther requisite to make me a perfect nonentity. If anyone upon serious and unprejudiced reflection, thinks he has a different notion of *himself*, I must confess I can reason no longer with him. All I can allow him is, that he may be in the right as well as I, and that we are essentially different in this particular. He may, perhaps, perceive something simple and continued, which he calls *himself*; though I am certain there is no such principle in me.

But setting aside some metaphysicians of this kind, I may venture to affirm of the rest of mankind, that they are nothing but a bundle or collection of different perceptions, which succeed each other with an inconceivable rapidity, and are in a perpetual flux and movement. Our eyes cannot turn in their sockets without varying our perceptions. Our thought is still more variable than our sight; and all our other senses and faculties contribute to this change; nor is there any single power of the soul which remains unalterably the same, perhaps for one moment. The mind is a kind of theater, where several perceptions successively make their appearance: pass, re-pass, glide away, and mingle in an infinite variety of postures and situations. There is properly no *simplicity* in it at one time, nor *identity* in different; whatever natural propension we may have to imagine that simplicity and identity. The comparison of the theater must not mislead us. They are the successive perceptions only, that constitute the mind; nor have we the most distant notion of the place where these scenes are represented, or of the materials, of which it is composed. * * *

[PHILOSOPHY AND COMMON LIFE[3]]

But what have I here said, that reflections very refined and metaphysical have little or no influence upon us? This opinion I can scarce forbear retracting, and condemning from my present feeling and experience. The *intense* view of these manifold contradictions and imperfections in human reason has so wrought upon me, and heated my brain, that I am ready to reject all belief and reasoning, and can look upon no opinion even as more probable or likely than another. Where am I, or what? From what causes do I derive my existence, and to what condition shall I return? Whose favor shall I court, and whose anger must I dread? What beings surround me? and on whom have I any influence, or who have any influence on me? I am confounded with all these questions, and begin to fancy myself in the most deplorable condition imaginable, environed with the deepest darkness, and utterly deprived of the use of every member and faculty.

Most fortunately it happens, that since reason is incapable of dispelling these clouds, nature herself suffices to that purpose, and cures me of this philosophical melancholy and delirium, either by relaxing this bent of mind, or by some avocation and lively impression of my senses, which obliterate all these chimeras. I dine, I play a game of backgammon, I converse, and am merry with my friends; and when after three or four hour's amusement, I would return to these speculations, they appear so cold, and strained, and ridiculous, that I cannot find in my heart to enter into them any farther.

Here then I find myself absolutely and necessarily determined to live, and talk, and act like other people in the common affairs of life. But notwithstanding that my natural propensity, and the course of my animal spirits and passions, reduce me to this indolent belief in the general maxims of the world, I still feel such remains of my former disposition, that I am ready to throw all my books and papers into the fire, and resolve never more to renounce the pleasures of life for the sake of reasoning and philosophy. For these are my sentiments in that splenetic[4] humor, which governs me at present. I may, nay I must yield to the current of nature, in submitting to my senses and understanding; and in this blind submission I show most perfectly my skeptical disposition and principles. But does it follow, that I must strive against the current of nature, which leads me to indolence and pleasure; that I must seclude myself, in some measure, from the commerce and society of men, which is so agreeable; and that I must torture my brain with subtleties and sophistries, at the very time that I cannot satisfy myself concerning the reasonableness of so painful an application, nor have any tolerable prospect of arriving by its means at truth and certainty? Under what obligation do I lie of making such an abuse of time? And to what end can it serve either for the service of mankind, or for my own private interest? No: if I must be a fool, as well as those who reason or believe anything *certainly* are, my follies shall at least be natural and agreeable. Where I strive against my inclination, I shall have a good reason for my resistance; and will no more be led a wandering into such dreary solitudes, and rough passages, as I have hitherto met with.

---

3. From Book 1, Section 7: "Conclusion of This Book." The first book of the *Treatise* serves as a long prelude to the whole; in concluding it, Hume considers the "manifest contradictions" between the assumptions on which ordinary people lead their lives, and the volatile questions raised by "refined reasoning" (rigorous philosophic inquiry). Pinpointing these contradictions in himself, he contemplates the precariousness of his enterprise, and the intricacy of his motives for undertaking it.
4. Depressive, irritable.

There are the sentiments of my spleen[5] and indolence; and indeed I must confess, that philosophy has nothing to oppose to them, and expects a victory more from the returns of a serious good-humored disposition, than from the force of reason and conviction. In all the incidents of life we ought still to preserve our skepticism. If we believe, that fire warms, or water refreshes, 'tis only because it costs us too much pains to think otherwise. Nay if we are philosophers, it ought only to be upon skeptical principles, and from an inclination, which we feel to the employing ourselves after that manner. Where reason is lively, and mixes itself with some propensity, it ought to be assented to. Where it does not, it never can have any title to operate upon us.

At the time, therefore, that I am tired with amusement and company, and have indulged a *reverie* in my chamber, or in a solitary walk by a riverside, I feel my mind all collected within itself, and am naturally *inclined* to carry my view into all those subjects, about which I have met with so many disputes in the course of my reading and conversation.[6] I cannot forbear having a curiosity to be acquainted with the principles of moral good and evil, the nature and foundation of government, and the cause of those several passions and inclinations, which actuate and govern me. I am uneasy to think I approve of one object, and disapprove of another; call one thing beautiful, and another deformed; decide concerning truth and falsehood, reason and folly, without knowing upon what principles I proceed. I am concerned for the condition of the learned world, which lies under such a deplorable ignorance in all these particulars. I feel an ambition to arise in me of contributing to the instruction of mankind, and of acquiring a name by my inventions and discoveries. These sentiments spring up naturally in my present disposition; and should I endeavor to banish them, by attaching myself to any other business or diversion, I *feel* I should be a loser in point of pleasure; and this is the origin of my philosophy.

1734–1737   1739–1740

from An Enquiry Concerning Human Understanding[1]
from Section 10: Of Miracles

A miracle is a violation of the laws of nature; and as a firm and unalterable experience has established these laws, the proof against a miracle, from the very nature of the fact, is as entire as any argument from experience can possibly be imagined. Why is it more than probable that all men must die; that lead cannot, of itself, remain suspended in the air; that fire consumes wood, and is extinguished by water; unless it be, that these events are found agreeable to the laws of nature, and there is required a violation of these laws, or in other words, a miracle to prevent them? Nothing is esteemed a miracle, if it ever happen in the common course of nature. It is no miracle that a man, seemingly in good health, should die on a sudden; because such a kind of death, though more unusual than any other, has yet been frequently observed to happen. But it is a miracle that a dead man should come to life; because that has never been observed in any age or country. There must, therefore, be a uniform experience

5. Despondency.
6. In the list that follows, Hume names many of the topics he will take up later in the *Treatise*.
1. Hume wrote this essay in the mid-1730s, intending to include it in his *Treatise*; conscious of its volatility, he withheld it for a dozen years, publishing it for the first time in his *Philosophical Essays Concerning Human Understanding* (1748); ten years later a revised version of the work appeared, under the new title *An Enquiry. . . . The* essay proved at least as explosive as he had anticipated, prompting a spate of refutations.

against every miraculous event, otherwise the event would not merit that appellation. And as a uniform experience amounts to a proof, there is here a direct and full *proof*, from the nature of the fact, against the existence of any miracle; nor can such a proof be destroyed, or the miracle rendered credible, but by an opposite proof, which is superior.

The plain consequence is (and it is a general maxim worthy of our attention), "That no testimony is sufficient to establish a miracle, unless the testimony be of such a kind, that its falsehood would be more miraculous than the fact which it endeavors to establish; and even in that case there is a mutual destruction of arguments, and the superior only gives us an assurance suitable to that degree of force which remains after deducting the inferior." When anyone tells me, that he saw a dead man restored to life, I immediately consider with myself, whether it be more probable, that this person should either deceive or be deceived, or that the fact, which he relates, should really have happened. I weigh the one miracle against the other; and according to the superiority which I discover, I pronounce my decision, and always reject the greater miracle. If the falsehood of his testimony would be more miraculous than the event which he relates, then, and not till then, can he pretend to command my belief or opinion.

In the foregoing reasoning we have supposed, that the testimony, upon which a miracle is founded, may possibly amount to an entire proof, and that the falsehood of that testimony would be a real prodigy. But it is easy to show that we have been a great deal too liberal in our concession, and that there never was a miraculous event established on so full an evidence.

For *first*, there is not to be found, in all history, any miracle attested by a sufficient number of men, of such unquestioned good sense, education, and learning, as to secure us against all delusion in themselves; of such undoubted integrity, as to place them beyond all suspicion of any design to deceive others; of such credit and reputation in the eyes of mankind, as to have a great deal to lose in case of their being detected in any falsehood; and at the same time, attesting facts performed in such a public manner and in so celebrated a part of the world, as to render the detection unavoidable. All which circumstances are requisite to give us a full assurance in the testimony of men.

Secondly. We may observe in human nature a principle which, if strictly examined, will be found to diminish extremely the assurance which we might, from human testimony, have, in any kind of prodigy. The maxim by which we commonly conduct ourselves in our reasonings is that the objects of which we have no experience resemble those of which we have; that what we have found to be most usual is always most probable; and that where there is an opposition of arguments, we ought to give the preference to such as are founded on the greatest number of past observations. But though, in proceeding by this rule, we readily reject any fact which is unusual and incredible in an ordinary degree; yet in advancing farther, the mind observes not always the same rule; but when anything is affirmed utterly absurd and miraculous, it rather the more readily admits of such a fact, upon account of that very circumstance which ought to destroy all its authority. The passion of *surprise* and *wonder,* arising from miracles, being an agreeable emotion, gives a sensible tendency towards the belief of those events from which it is derived. And this goes so far, that even those who cannot enjoy this pleasure immediately, nor can believe those miraculous events, of which they are informed, yet love to partake of the satisfaction at second-hand or by rebound, and place a pride and delight in exciting the admiration of others.

With what greediness are the miraculous accounts of travelers received, their descriptions of sea and land monsters, their relations of wonderful adventures, strange men, and uncouth manners? But if the spirit of religion join itself to the love of wonder, there is an end of common sense; and human testimony, in these circumstances, loses all pretensions to authority. A religionist may be an enthusiast,[2] and imagine he sees what has no reality. He may know his narrative to be false, and yet persevere in it, with the best intentions in the world, for the sake of promoting so holy a cause; or even where this delusion has not place, vanity, excited by so strong a temptation, operates on him more powerfully than on the rest of mankind in any other circumstances; and self-interest with equal force. His auditors may not have, and commonly have not, sufficient judgment to canvass his evidence. What judgment they have, they renounce by principle, in these sublime and mysterious subjects; or if they were ever so willing to employ it, passion and a heated imagination disturb the regularity of its operations. Their credulity increases his impudence; and his impudence overpowers their credulity. * * *

Thirdly. It forms a strong presumption against all supernatural and miraculous relations, that they are observed chiefly to abound among ignorant and barbarous nations; or if a civilized people has ever given admission to any of them, that people will be found to have received them from ignorant and barbarous ancestors, who transmitted them with that inviolable sanction and authority, which always attend received opinions. When we peruse the first histories of all nations, we are apt to imagine ourselves transported into some new world, where the whole frame of nature is disjointed, and every element performs its operations in a different manner from what it does at present. Battles, revolutions, pestilence, famine, and death are never the effect of those natural causes which we experience. Prodigies, omens, oracles, judgments, quite obscure the few natural events that are intermingled with them. But as the former grow thinner every page, in proportion as we advance nearer the enlightened ages, we soon learn that there is nothing mysterious or supernatural in the case, but that all proceeds from the usual propensity of mankind towards the marvelous, and that, though this inclination may at intervals receive a check from sense and learning, it can never be thoroughly extirpated from human nature. * * *

Upon the whole, then, it appears that no testimony for any kind of miracle has ever amounted to a probability, much less to a proof; and that, even supposing it amounted to a proof, it would be opposed by another proof; derived from the very nature of the fact, which it would endeavor to establish. It is experience only which gives authority to human testimony; and it is the same experience which assures us of the laws of nature. When, therefore, these two kinds of experience are contrary, we have nothing to do but subtract the one from the other, and embrace an opinion, either on one side or the other, with that assurance which arises from the remainder. But according to the principle here explained, this subtraction, with regard to all popular religions, amounts to an entire annihilation; and therefore we may establish it as a maxim, that no human testimony can have such force as to prove a miracle, and make it a just foundation for any such system of religion. * * *

What we have said of miracles may be applied, without any variation, to prophecies; and indeed, all prophecies are real miracles, and as such only can be admitted as proofs of any revelation. If it did not exceed the capacity of human nature to foretell future events, it would be absurd to employ any prophecy as an argument for a divine

2. Fanatic.

mission or authority from heaven. So that, upon the whole, we may conclude, that the *Christian religion* not only was at first attended with miracles, but even at this day cannot be believed by any reasonable person without one. Mere reason is insufficient to convince us of its veracity. And whoever is moved by *faith* to assent to it, is conscious of a continued miracle in his own person, which subverts all the principles of his understanding, and gives him a determination to believe what is most contrary to custom and experience.

c. 1736   1748

Christopher Smart
1722–1771

"Newton . . . is more of error than of the truth, but I am of the Word of God," wrote Christopher Smart in his astonishing poem *Jubilate Agno* ("Rejoice in the Lamb"). For Smart, as for a growing number of Christians in the century's second half, the Newtonian "error" consisted in a commitment to materialist science, to an empiricism that investigated the physical world and sought its seeming system, rather than submitting to faith in a God who worked by will and sometimes by miracle, free of any fixed laws of nature. Smart composed *Jubilate Agno* in his late thirties, while confined in a madhouse; after a brilliant career as a classical scholar at Cambridge, and an auspicious start in London as a literary adventurer (poet, editor, translator, essayist), he suffered a derangement whose chief symptom was his compulsion to pray spontaneously in public places (he was too much "of the Word of God" to be socially acceptable). Released from the asylum after five years, Smart recast much material from the *Jubilate Agno* in his *Song of David* (1763); following Watts's precedent, he published a translation of the Psalms (1767) and (while imprisoned for debt at the very end of his life) a book of *Hymns for the Amusement of Children* (1771). *Jubilate Agno* remained in manuscript and unknown for a century and a half after the poet's death. Smart called it "my Magnificat," *magnificat* being the title of the liturgical hymn first uttered by the Virgin Mary upon learning that she would conceive a son: "My Soul doth magnify the Lord" (Luke 1.46–55). Structured like a responsive prayer, Smart's poem moves rapidly across a wide range of reference, from the scriptural and mystical to the local and the homely ("God be gracious to Baumgarden"—a London bassoon player). But Smart returns repeatedly to a preoccupation touched on in the poem's title: to the animal world as emblem and embodiment of God's grace and greatness (in Smart's time natural history was among the branches of knowledge least touched by the new science, and most inflected by faith and folklore). In the excerpts that follow, Smart punningly pinpoints the animal essences of languages ancient and modern, then depicts the feline who kept him company during his years of confinement, singing Jeoffry's praises with such exuberance as to make *magnificat* seem a latent, sacred, and affectionate pun.

from Jubilate Agno
[ANIMALS IN LANGUAGE[1]]

625   For the power of some animal is predominant in every language.
        For the power and spirit of a CAT is in the Greek.

---

1. These selections come from Fragment B of Smart's manuscript. Some pages of Smart's manuscript contain long sequences of lines beginning "Let"; other pages contain lines beginning "For," with clear enough indications that the "Let" and "For" lines were meant to be dovetailed and read alternately, in the form of responsive prayer. For the two excerpts printed here, though, lines beginning "Let" have not been found—and may never have been written.

For the sound of a cat is in the most useful preposition κατ' ευχην.[2]

For the pleasantry of a cat at pranks is in the language ten thousand times over.[3]

For JACK UPON PRANCK is in the performance of περι together or separate.[4]

630 For Clapperclaw[5] is in the grappling of the words upon one another in all the modes of versification.

For the sleekness of a Cat is in his αγλαιηφι.[6]

For the Greek is thrown from heaven and falls upon its feet.[7]

For the Greek when distracted from the line is sooner restored to rank and rallied into some form than any other.

For the purring of a Cat is his τρυζει.[8]

635 For his cry is in ουαι,[9] which I am sorry for.

For the Mouse (Mus) prevails in the Latin.[1]

For *Edi-mus, bibi-mus, vivi-mus—ore-mus.*[2]

For the Mouse is a creature of great personal valor.

For—this is a true case—Cat takes female mouse from the company of male—male mouse will not depart, but stands threat'ning and daring.

640 For this is as much as to challenge, if you will let her go, I will engage you, as prodigious a creature as you are.

For the Mouse is of an hospitable disposition.

For bravery and hospitality were said and done by the Romans rather than others.

For two creatures the Bull and the Dog prevail in the English.

For all the words ending in -ble are in the creature. Invisi-ble, Incompre-hensi-ble, ineffa-ble, A-ble.

645 For the Greek and Latin are not dead languages, but taken up and accepted for the sake of him that spoke them.

For can is (*canis*[3]) is cause and effect a dog.

For the English is concise and strong. Dog and Bull again.

For Newton's notion of colors is αλογοξ,[4] unphilosophical.

[MY CAT JEOFFRY]

695 For I will consider my Cat Jeoffry.

For he is the servant of the Living God duly and daily serving him.

For at the first glance of the glory of God in the East he worships in his way.

For is this done by wreathing his body seven times round with elegant quickness.

For then he leaps up to catch the musk, which is the blessing of God upon his prayer.

700 For he rolls upon prank to work it in.

For having done duty and received blessing he begins to consider himself.

For this he performs in ten degrees.

For first he looks upon his fore-paws to see if they are clean.

For secondly he kicks up behind to clear away there.

---

2. Greek *kat' euchen*: "according to prayer."
3. The syllable *kat* appears in many word forms.
4. Greek *perikato* means "upside down" (as, probably, does "Jack Upon Pranck").
5. To claw, scratch.
6. *Aglaiefi*: "beauty."
7. Perhaps an allusion to the Greek poetic term *catalexis*, the shortening or omission of a "foot" from a line of verse; the prefix *cata-* means "down."

8. *Truzei*: "murmur."
9. *Ouai*: exclamation of lament ("ah!").
1. Partly because (as Smart illustrates in line 637), the syllable *mus* means "mouse" and is also the suffix for first person plural present-tense conjugations.
2. "We eat, we drink, we live—let us pray."
3. Latin: dog.
4. *Alogos*: literally, "without the Word."

705   For thirdly he works it upon stretch with the fore-paws extended.
    For fourthly he sharpens his paws by wood.
    For fifthly he washes himself.
    For sixthly he rolls upon wash.
    For seventhly he fleas himself, that he may not be interrupted upon the beat.
710   For eighthly he rubs himself against a post.
    For ninthly he looks up for his instructions.
    For tenthly he goes in quest of food.
    For having considered God and himself he will consider his neighbor.
    For if he meets another cat he will kiss her in kindness.
715   For when he takes his prey he plays with it to give it chance.
    For one mouse in seven escapes by his dallying.
    For when his day's work is done his business more properly begins.
    For he keeps the Lord's watch in the night against the adversary.
    For he counteracts the powers of darkness by his electrical skin and glar-
        ing eyes.
720   For he counteracts the Devil, who is death, by brisking about the life.
    For in his morning orisons he loves the sun and the sun loves him.
    For he is of the tribe of Tiger.
    For the Cherub Cat is a term of the Angel Tiger.
    For he has the subtlety and hissing of a serpent, which in goodness he
        suppresses.
725   For he will not do destruction, if he is well-fed, neither will he spit without
        provocation.
    For he purrs in thankfulness, when God tells him he's a good Cat.
    For he is an instrument for the children to learn benevolence upon.
    For every house is incomplete without him and a blessing is lacking in
        the spirit.
    For the Lord commanded Moses concerning the cats at the departure of the
        Children of Israel from Egypt.[5]
730   For every family had one cat at least in the bag.
    For the English Cats are the best in Europe.
    For he is the cleanest in the use of his fore-paws of any quadrupede.
    For the dexterity of his defense is an instance of the love of God to him
        exceedingly.
    For he is the quickest to his mark of any creature.
735   For he is tenacious of his point.
    For he is a mixture of gravity and waggery.
    For he knows that God is his Savior.
    For there is nothing sweeter than his peace when at rest.
    For there is nothing brisker than his life when in motion.
740   For he is of the Lord's poor and so indeed is he called by benevolence per-
        petually—Poor Jeoffry! poor Jeoffry! the rat has bit thy throat.
    For I bless the name of the Lord Jesus that Jeoffry is better.
    For the divine spirit comes about his body to sustain it in complete cat.
    For his tongue is exceeding pure so that it has in purity what it wants in music.
    For he is docile and can learn certain things.
745   For he can set up with gravity which is patience upon approbation.

---

5. "Take your flocks and your herds," says the Egyptian Pharaoh when demanding the Israelites' departure (Exodus 12.32); Smart adds the Lord and the cats.

For he can fetch and carry, which is patience in employment.
For he can jump over a stick which is patience upon proof positive.
For he can spraggle° upon waggle at the word of command.   *sprawl*
For he can jump from an eminence into his master's bosom.
750 For he can catch the cork and toss it again.
For he is hated by the hypocrite and miser.
For the former is afraid of detection.
For the latter refuses the charge.
For he camels his back to bear the first notion of business.
755 For he is good to think on, if a man would express himself neatly.
For he made a great figure in Egypt for his signal services.
For he killed the Ichneumon-rat° very pernicious by land.   *mongoose*
For his ears are so acute that they sting again.
For from this proceeds the passing quickness of his attention.
760 For by stroking of him I have found out electricity.
For I perceived God's light about him both wax and fire.
For the Electrical fire is the spiritual substance, which God sends from
     heaven to sustain the bodies both of man and beast.
For God has blessed him in the variety of his movements.
For, though he cannot fly, he is an excellent clamberer.
765 For his motions upon the face of the earth are more than any other
     quadrupede.
For he can tread to all the measures upon the music.
For he can swim for life.
For he can creep.
c. 1758–1763   1939

William Cowper
1731–1800

Like Christopher Smart, William Cowper suffered madness, loved animals, wrote hymns, and invented capacious new structures for religious verse. But where Smart wrote to celebrate his sure salvation, Cowper wrote out of the certainty that he was damned—unworthy of redemption and predestined for hellfire. The conviction first took hold in 1763, when a paralyzing panic cut him off from impending attachments (to a new job he was about to secure, a beloved woman he was soon to marry) and prompted several attempts at suicide. The course of recovery took him first to an asylum, then through a conversion to Calvinism, then to the household of Mary Unwin, who loved and looked after him for the next four decades, and finally into partnership with Unwin's neighbor, the austere hymn-writer John Newton, with whom Cowper collaborated for years on a new collection of religious song, the *Olney Hymns* (it included, along with several of Cowper's still-sung texts, Newton's perdurable *Amazing Grace*). A second, sharper attack of madness, ten years after the first, deepened Cowper's conviction of his doom but also ushered in years of plentiful poetic composition. Seizing any small occasion (a fish dinner, the death of a pet bird) to produce a short, often comic piece of verse, Cowper wrote poems to hold terror at bay. As his output increased, his ambition did too. *The Task*, a massive mock epic grounded in the comforts of Cowper's rural retirement (sofa, garden, seasons) but ranging satirically over the whole wide world, surprised even its author by its scope and popularity. Spurred by its success, Cowper undertook to translate Homer's epics, hoping to surpass Pope's attempts earlier in the century. In a passage near the midpoint of *The Task* (printed here), Newton appears briefly as the embodiment of Cowper's deepest hope, that the mind might merge with God through a science immersed in faith—"philosophy baptized." In his last, autobiographical poem, *The Cast-away*, Cowper draws a darker picture, of a mind sundered from its maker by distance and despair.

Light Shining out of Darkness[1]

God moves in a mysterious way,
    His wonders to perform;
He plants his footsteps in the sea,
    And rides upon the storm.

5   Deep in unfathomable mines
        Of never-failing skill,
He treasures up his bright designs,
    And works his sov'reign will.

Ye fearful saints[2] fresh courage take,
10   The clouds ye so much dread
Are big with mercy, and shall break
    In blessings on your head.

Judge not the Lord by feeble sense,
    But trust him for his grace;
15   Behind a frowning providence,
    He hides a smiling face.

His purposes will ripen fast,
    Unfolding every hour;
The bud may have a bitter taste,
20   But sweet will be the flower.

Blind unbelief is sure to err,
    And scan his work in vain;
God is his own interpreter,
    And he will make it plain.

c. 1773   1774

from The Task
["PHILOSOPHY BAPTIZED"[1]]

God never meant that man should scale the heav'ns
By strides of human wisdom. In his works
Though wond'rous, he commands us in his word
To seek *him* rather, where his mercy shines.
225   The mind indeed enlightened from above
Views him in all. Ascribes to the grand cause
The grand effect. Acknowledges with joy
His manner, and with rapture tastes his style.
But never yet did philosophic° tube   *scientific*

---

1. Written and first published during the period of Cowper's collaboration with John Newton; later included in their *Olney Hymns* (1779).

2. Cowper addresses those who (according to Calvinist theology) are predestined for salvation.
1. From Book 3, "The Garden."

230   That brings the planets home into the eye
      Of observation, and discovers, else°   *otherwise*
      Not visible, his family of worlds,
      Discover him that rules them; such a veil
      Hangs over mortal eyes, blind from the birth
235   And dark in things divine. Full often too
      Our wayward intellect, the more we learn
      Of nature, overlooks her author more,
      From instrumental causes proud to draw
      Conclusions retrograde and mad mistake.
240   But if his word once teach us, shoot a ray
      Through all the heart's dark chambers, and reveal
      Truths undiscerned but by that holy light,
      Then all is plain. Philosophy baptized
      In the pure fountain of eternal love
245   Has eyes indeed; and viewing all she sees
      As meant to indicate a God to man,
      Gives *him* his praise, and forfeits not her own.
      Learning has borne such fruit in other days
      On all her branches. Piety has found
250   Friends in the friends of science, and true prayer
      Has flowed from lips wet with Castalian dews.[2]
      Such was thy wisdom, Newton, childlike sage!
      Sagacious reader of the works of God,
      And in his word sagacious. * * *

1783–1785   1785

The Cast-away[1]

      Obscurest night involved° the sky,   *encompassed*
          Th' Atlantic billows roared,
      When such a destined° wretch as I   *doomed*
          Washed headlong from on board
5   Of friends, of hope, of all beret,
      His floating home for ever left.

      No braver chief[2] could Albion° boast   *Britain*
          Than he with whom he went,
      Nor ever ship left Albion's coast
10   With warmer wishes sent.
      He loved them both, but both in vain,
      Nor him beheld, nor her again.

      Not long beneath the whelming brine
          Expert to swim, he lay,

2. I.e., from poets (who have drunk of the inspirational Castalian spring on the mountain of the Muses).
1. Cowper based this poem on a mariner's account, in a popular travel book, of having watched helplessly as a shipmate was hurled overboard during a storm: "We were the more grieved at his unhappy fate, as we . . . conceived from the manner in which he swam that he might continue sensible, for a considerable time longer, of the hor-

ror attending his irretrievable situation." Cowper collates the doomed man's situation with his own, which he conceived as also "irretrievable"; the poem, left in manuscript at his death, is his last surviving original poem in English.
2. George Anson, commander of the naval squadron in which the sailor was lost.

15 Nor soon he felt his strength decline
  Or courage die away;
 But waged with Death a lasting strife
 Supported by despair of life.

 He shouted, nor his friends had failed
20 To check the vessel's course,
 But so the furious blast prevailed
  That, pitiless perforce,
 They left their outcast mate behind,
 And scudded still before the wind.

25 Some succor yet they could afford,
  And, such as storms allow,
 The cask, the coop, the floated cord
  Delayed not to bestow;
 But he, they knew, nor ship nor shore,
30 Whate'er they gave, should visit more.

 Nor, cruel as it seemed, could he
  Their haste, himself, condemn,
 Aware that flight, in such a sea,
  Alone could rescue them;
35 Yet bitter felt it still to die
 Deserted, and his friends so nigh.

 He long survives who lives an hour
  In ocean, self-upheld,
 And so long he, with unspent power,
40 His destiny repelled,
 And ever, as the minutes flew,
 Entreated help, or cried, Adieu!

 At length, his transient respite past,
  His comrades, who before
45 Had heard his voice in every blast,
  Could catch the sound no more;
 For then, by toil subdued, he drank
 The stifling wave, and then he sank.

 No poet wept him: but the page
50 Of narrative[3] sincere
 That tells his name, his worth,° his age,   *rank*
  Is wet with Anson's tear,
 And tears by bards or heroes shed
 Alike immortalize the dead.

55 I therefore purpose not or dream,
  Descanting on his fate,
 To give the melancholy theme
  A more enduring date,

3. The log book of the ship from which he fell.

But misery still delights to trace
60   Its semblance in another's case.

No voice divine the storm allayed,
   No light propitious shone,
When, snatched from all effectual aid,
   We perished, each, alone;
65   But I beneath a rougher sea,
And whelmed in deeper gulphs than he.

1799   1804

━━╃ END OF PERSPECTIVES: MIND AND GOD ╄━━

⊶ ⋈✦⋈ ⊷

Thomas Gray
1716–1771

Toward the end of his most famous poem, *Elegy Written in a Country Churchyard,* Thomas Gray
commends the quietude with which the villagers have led their ordinary lives:

Along the cool sequestered vale of life
They kept the noiseless tenor of their way.

Tenor here means "course," and the line incorporates a notable revision: Gray had originally
written "silent tenor," and then written the new adjective "noiseless" above the old, without
crossing out "silent." In retrospect, this manuscript moment of alternate possibilities looks
emblematic. Sickly, shy, and melancholic, Gray was often drawn toward silence but never settled there. Words—in ancient literature and in modern history, in talk and correspondence
with his friends, in the varied idioms of his own compelling poems—exerted too strong a fascination. The fascination started early. At age nine, having weathered a bleak childhood in the
troubled London household of his irascible father and doting mother, he entered the privileged
precincts of Eton College, where his uncles worked and where he hit upon the satisfactions
that would fill his life: passionate reading (in the classics first and foremost) and passionate
friendships, with three schoolmates in particular: Richard West, Thomas Ashton, and Horace
Walpole, son of the notorious prime minister Robert Walpole. Dubbing themselves the
Quadruple Alliance, the four friends piqued themselves on a collective erudition, refinement,
and wit that set them off from their contemporaries. The links among them mattered enormously in Gray's life of writing: West inspired his poems; Walpole sponsored their publication;
and all Gray's friendships, at Eton and beyond, drew from Gray a steady flow of virtuosic letters, in which the voice of the "Alliance," at once antic and vulnerable, never abated. "His letters," remarked Walpole (whose own letters have evoked similar praise), "were the best I ever
saw, and had more novelty and wit." Gray's affections took form and motion partly from their
containment. He was homosexual; yet there is no evidence that he ever physically consummated the great passions of his life—for Walpole, for West, and, in his last years, for the young
Swiss scion Charles-Victor de Bonstatten.

   After nine years at Eton, Gray was admitted to Cambridge. He found university life far less
pleasing, with its drudgeries, pressures, and solitudes, but Cambridge ultimately afforded him a few
new friendships and a permanent sanctuary. After a Grand Tour of Europe, undertaken in

Walpole's company (the two men quarreled en route, after which they were estranged for five years), Gray returned to the university, ostensibly to learn law, but in fact to pursue his own private program of study. He read widely, copiously, and systematically in many subjects (botany, zoology, and music, as well as literature and history), making himself one of the most learned scholars alive, and eventually becoming (in 1768) Regius Professor of Modern History. He never delivered a lecture, and continued to spend much of his time alone reading, but thoroughgoing privacy had long ceased to be an option. In his late thirties, Gray had stumbled, reluctantly, into enormous poetic fame. He had written Latin verse when young; in 1742, the year his beloved West died of tuberculosis, he commenced English poetry in earnest. The *Elegy*'s completion took five years or more; its publication in 1751 (a "distress" the poet had hoped to avoid) brought upon Gray an instantaneous, massive, and baffling celebrity. As if in recoil, he veered onto an alternate poetic path, carefully crafting over the ensuing years a set of intricate Pindaric odes, including *The Bard* and *The Progress of Poesy*; the two poems were printed, on Walpole's own press, in 1757. They provoked both admiration, as a new embodiment of poetic sublimity, and derision, as gratuitously labored, showily obscure. In the years following their murky reception, Gray wrote only a few poems and published none. He pursued other studies (including Norse literature); fell in love one final time; and died abruptly, mourned deeply by his friends and widely by a public whose thoughts and feelings about death itself he had done much to shape. In one early version of the *Elegy* the line about silence appears as an admonition addressed by the poet to himself: "Pursue the silent tenor of thy doom." In his letters (published posthumously) and in his poems, Gray worked for that doom a delicate but decisive reversal.

Elegy Written in a Country Churchyard

The curfew tolls the knell of parting day,
The lowing herd wind slowly o'er the lea,
The plowman homeward plods his weary way,
And leaves the world to darkness and to me.

5 Now fades the glimmering landscape on the sight,
And all the air a solemn stillness holds,
Save where the beetle wheels his droning flight,
And drowsy tinklings lull the distant folds;

Save that from yonder ivy-mantled tower
10 The moping owl does to the moon complain
Of such as, wand'ring near her secret bower,
Molest her ancient solitary reign.

Beneath those rugged elms, that yew-tree's shade,
Where heaves the turf in many a mouldering heap,
15 Each in his narrow cell for ever laid,
The rude forefathers of the hamlet sleep.

The breezy call of incense-breathing morn,
The swallow twitt'ring from the straw-built shed,
The cock's shrill clarion, or the echoing horn,
20 No more shall rouse them from their lowly bed.

For them no more the blazing hearth shall burn,
Or busy housewife ply her evening care:
No children run to lisp their sire's return,
Or climb his knees the envied kiss to share.

25 Oft did the harvest to their sickle yield,
 Their furrow oft the stubborn glebe° has broke;   *clod of earth*
 How jocund did they drive their team afield!
 How bowed the woods beneath their sturdy stroke!

 Let not Ambition mock their useful toil,
30 Their homely joys, and destiny obscure;
 Nor Grandeur hear, with a disdainful smile,
 The short and simple annals of the poor.

 The boast of heraldry, the pomp of power,
 And all that beauty, all that wealth e'er gave,
35 Awaits alike th' inevitable hour.
 The paths of glory lead but to the grave.

 Nor you, ye Proud, impute to these the fault,
 If Mem'ry o'er their tomb no trophies raise,
 Where through the long-drawn aisle and fretted vault
40 The pealing anthem swells the note of praise.

 Can storied urn or animated bust
 Back to its mansion call the fleeting breath?
 Can Honor's voice provoke the silent dust,
 Or Flatt'ry soothe the dull cold ear of Death?

45 Perhaps in this neglected spot is laid
 Some heart once pregnant with celestial fire;
 Hands that the rod of empire might have swayed,
 Or waked to ecstasy the living lyre.

 But Knowledge to their eyes her ample page
50 Rich with the spoils of time did ne'er unroll;
 Chill Penury repressed their noble rage,
 And froze the genial current of the soul.

 Full many a gem of purest ray serene,
 The dark unfathomed caves of ocean bear:
55 Full many a flower is born to blush unseen,
 And waste its sweetness on the desert air.

 Some village-Hampden[1] that with dauntless breast
 The little tyrant of his fields withstood;
 Some mute inglorious Milton here may rest,
60 Some Cromwell guiltless of his country's blood.

 Th' applause of listening senates to command,
 The threats of pain and ruin to despise,
 To scatter plenty o'er a smiling land,
 And read their history in a nation's eyes,

65 Their lot forbade: nor circumscribed alone
 Their growing virtues, but their crimes confined;

1. John Hampden (1594–1643), Parliamentary statesman and general in the Civil Wars, famed for his firm defiance of
Charles I.

Forbade to wade through slaughter to a throne,
And shut the gates of mercy on mankind,

The struggling pangs of conscious truth to hide,
70   To quench the blushes of ingenuous shame,
Or heap the shrine of Luxury and Pride
With incense kindled at the Muse's flame.[2]

Far from the madding crowd's ignoble strife,
Their sober wishes never learned to stray;
75   Along the cool sequestered vale of life
They kept the noiseless tenor of their way.

Yet ev'n these bones from insult to protect
Some frail memorial still erected nigh,
With uncouth rhymes and shapeless sculpture decked,
80   Implores the passing tribute of a sigh.

Their name, their years, spelt by th' unlettered muse,
The place of fame and elegy supply:
And many a holy text around she strews,
That teach the rustic moralist to die.

85   For who to dumb Forgetfulness a prey,
This pleasing anxious being e'er resigned,
Left the warm precincts of the cheerful day,
Nor cast one longing ling'ring look behind?

On some fond breast the parting soul relies,
90   Some pious drops the closing eye requires;
Ev'n from the tomb the voice of nature cries,
Ev'n in our ashes live their wonted fires.

For thee, who mindful of th' unhonored dead
Dost in these lines their artless tale relate;
95   If chance, by lonely Contemplation led,
Some kindred spirit shall inquire thy fate,

Haply some hoary-headed swain may say,
"Oft have we seen him at the peep of dawn
Brushing with hasty steps the dews away
100   To meet the sun upon the upland lawn.

"There at the foot of yonder nodding beech
That wreathes its old fantastic roots so high,

---

2. According to Gray's friend William Mason, the poem originally concluded at this juncture with the following four stanzas, preserved in a manuscript at Eton College:

The thoughtless world to majesty may bow
Exalt the brave, and idolize success,
But more to innocence their safety owe
Than power and genius e'er conspired to bless.

And thou, who mindful of the unhonored dead
Dost in these notes their artless tale relate
By night and lonely contemplation led

To linger in the gloomy walks of fate,

Hark how the sacred calm, that broods around
Bids ev'ry fierce tumultuous passion cease
In still small accents whisp'ring from the ground
A grateful earnest of eternal peace.

No more with reason and thyself at strife;
Give anxious cares and endless wishes room
But through the cool sequestered vale of life
Pursue the silent tenor of thy doom.

His listless length at noontide would he stretch,
And pore upon the brook that babbles by.

105 "Hard by yon wood, now smiling as in scorn,
Mutt'ring his wayward fancies he would rove,
Now drooping, woeful wan, like one forlorn,
Or crazed with care, or crossed in hopeless love.

"One morn I missed him on the 'customed hill,
110 Along the heath and near his favorite tree;
Another came; nor yet beside the rill,
Nor up the lawn, nor at the wood was he;

"The next with dirges due in sad array
Slow through the church-way path we saw him borne.
115 Approach and read (for thou can'st read) the lay,
Graved on the stone beneath yon aged thorn."

The Epitaph

Here rests his head upon the lap of earth
A youth to fortune and to fame unknown.
Fair Science frowned not on his humble birth,
120 *And Melancholy marked him for her own.*

Large was his bounty, and his soul sincere,
Heaven did a recompense as largely send:
He gave to Mis'ry all he had, a tear,
He gained from Heav'n ('twas all he wished) a friend.

125 *No farther seek his merits to disclose,*
Or draw his frailties from their dread abode,
(There they alike in trembling hope repose)
The bosom of his Father and his God.

1746–1750   1751

Samuel Johnson
1709–1784

Samuel Johnson was born among books—his father sold them, not very successfully, at the family's combined home and shop in the market town of Lichfield. The son went on to create some of the most celebrated books of his age: an entire *Dictionary*, an edition of Shakespeare, a travel book, philosophical fictions, two eminent series of essays, a thick cluster of biographies. Despite his output, Johnson suffered from a chronic sense that he was underusing his talent, and throughout his *oeuvre* he wrote about "human unsuccess" (in W. H. Auden's phrase) with an empathy and acuity that few have matched before or since.

Johnson's struggles began early. An infection in infancy, followed by an attack of scrofula at age two, left his face scarred and his sight and hearing permanently impaired; by the age of eight a nervous disorder, probably Tourette's syndrome, brought on the compulsive gesticulations and intermittent muttering that would afflict him throughout his life, making him appear bizarre or even repellent at first encounter—until (as many testified) the stunning moment when he would begin to speak. His impressiveness had begun early, too. In childhood, the speed with which he acquired knowledge and the force with which he retained it astonished classmates and teachers, and also his parents, whose desire to show off his attainments often made him miserable. Johnson found more congenial mentors in his cousin, the rakish but learned young clergyman Cornelius Ford, at whose home he spent about half a year at age sixteen, and in Gilbert Walmesley, a middle-aged Lichfield lawyer, who welcomed Johnson often to his ample table and to the intelligent, disputatious company there assembled. Under Ford's and Walmesley's influence, Johnson undertook an intense but improvisatory program of reading, mostly in his father's shop. He read with a ferocious concentration that locked the texts into lifelong memory. "In this irregular manner," he later recalled, "I had looked into a great many books, which were not commonly known at the university, where they seldom read any books but what are put into their hands by their tutors; so that when I came to Oxford, Dr. Adams, now master of Pembroke College, told me, I was the best qualified for the university that he had ever known come there."

Despite such qualifications, Johnson's time at Oxford ushered in not triumph but frustration, and an oppressive sense of failure. Though he continued to be admired for his reading, and began to be noted for his writing, Johnson left the university after only thirteen months, "miserably poor" and unable to pay the fees, unbearably depressed and incapable of envisioning a viable future. After a melancholy year at home, during which his father died in debt, Johnson tried his hand at a variety of jobs beneath his earlier expectations: as assistant at a grammar school (he applied for three such positions, secured one, and left it in disgust after six months), and as occasional contributor to *The Birmingham Journal*. At Birmingham, he befriended the merchant Harry Porter and his wife Elizabeth ("Tetty"); she saw past his awkwardness at their first encounter, remarking to her daughter, "This is the most sensible man that I ever saw in my life." In 1735, ten months after her husband's death, she and Johnson married, despite wariness in both families at their difference in age (she was twenty years his senior). The new husband and wife tried to start a country boarding school, but it attracted only a handful of students. Early in 1737, Johnson decided to try something new: the life of a freelance writer in London.

The generic term for such a life was "Grub Street": it identified both an actual London street where some writers lived and plied their trade, and also the painful state of mind in which almost all of them did so, eking out precarious incomes from whatever assignments they could drum up. From the first, Johnson fared a little better than most. He attached himself immediately to Edward Cave, founder of the flourishing *Gentleman's Magazine*, in which Johnson's writing appeared plentifully over the next decade: essays, poems, short biographies, reviews, and voluminous, ingeniously fictionalized reports of debates in Parliament (authentic transcriptions were prohibited by law). The work provided some security but no prosperity: Johnson and his wife lived in poverty for many years. The struggle fueled articulate rage: in his poem *London* (1738), Johnson inveighed against the corruption of Robert Walpole's government and the cruelties of the city. Among his Grub Street colleagues he found a friend who, far more than himself, had made a sense of injury the basis of both life and art. The poet Richard Savage, generous, brilliant, and unstable, believed himself the abandoned offspring of a wealthy countess, and squandered much of his short life in the vain pursuit of recognition and redress. In *The Life of Richard Savage* (1744), published soon after his friend's early death, Johnson for the first time orchestrated many of the elements that would make his own work great: a commitment to biographical precision rather than routine panegyric; an analysis of expectation, self-delusion, and disappointment; a deep sympathy combined with nuanced judgment.

Savage was a memoir of Grub Street, but not yet for Johnson a valedictory. For two more years he continued his life of anonymous publication, narrow income, and declining spirits—

"lost," as a friend lamented, "both to himself and the world." Then a new project found him. In 1746, the bookseller Robert Dodsley, struck by the erudition evident in Johnson's unsigned pieces, persuaded him to create a new dictionary of English, and assembled a consortium of publishers to finance (and profit from) the enormous undertaking. Johnson and his wife promptly moved from cramped and squalid quarters to a three-story house complete with a well-lit garret. There, with the help of six part-time assistants, Johnson made his lexicon, compiling word lists, tracking shifts and gradations of meaning, devising definitions, and illustrating them with quotations culled from the authors he most admired. The writer who (as Adam Smith later testified) "knew more books than any man alive" now decanted them discriminatingly into the two folio volumes of his *Dictionary* (1755), so as to make the work not only a standard reference for the language but also a compendium of its literature and its learning. The task took Johnson longer than he had anticipated—seven years, not three—but during this span he had busied himself in other ways as well: publishing *The Vanity of Human Wishes* (1749), a long poem on the pain of disillusion; witnessing the long-postponed production of his tragedy *Irene* (which brought him welcome added income); and composing, twice a week for two years, the periodical essay called *The Rambler* (1750–1752), the most formidable and famous instance of the genre since Addison and Steele had set down the *Spectator* forty years before. Johnson had embarked on the *Dictionary* as a virtual unknown; he emerged from the project with lasting fame and a double measure of celebratory sobriquets: he was widely known as "Dictionary Johnson," and was sometimes referred to simply (without surname) as "the Rambler."

As an epitome of his character the second label was perhaps more apt. A restlessness closely connected with loneliness had marked Johnson's mind since childhood. During the years of the *Dictionary*'s making, the loneliness had deepened. In 1752 Tetty died, and despite the strains in a marriage that had been differently difficult for both of them, Johnson mourned her obsessively for the rest of his days. He also contrived new sources of companionship, at home and in the wider world. He housed under his roof a group of eccentric, often difficult characters, including the ungainly man of medicine Robert Levet; the Jamaican servant Francis Barber; the blind Anna Williams, who waited up late every night to keep him company in his final cup of tea, often after he had spent long hours in more elevated society. He established what amounted to a second residence in the more polished household of the brewer Henry Thrale and his witty wife Hester, who welcomed and pampered not only Johnson but also the accomplished people who now rejoiced to rotate in his orbit: the actor David Garrick (who had been his pupil in the failed school and his companion on the road to London); the painter Joshua Reynolds; the politician and orator Edmund Burke; the writer Oliver Goldsmith; and Johnson's ardent young protégé and future biographer James Boswell. At the Thrales' country seat, and at the London clubs he formed to stave off solitude, Johnson sat surrounded by luminaries, savoring and often dominating the conversation. He talked (as Boswell noted) "for victory," and he generally secured it by a kind of surprise attack, a witty demolition of his companions' most familiar premises and casual assumptions. He won his listeners over by texture as well as text: by the spontaneous clarity and force of his utterance (as lexicographer he had defined every word he spoke); by the depth and energy of his voice.

Writing was by contrast largely solitary. Johnson's work pattern in the decade after the *Dictionary* recapitulated that of the one before: one ambitious, overarching project—this time an edition of all Shakespeare's plays (1765)—punctuated by shorter writings of lasting significance: a new periodical essay called *The Idler* (1758–1760); the philosophical tale *Rasselas, Prince of Abyssinia* (1759). In 1762 Johnson received a royal pension from George III in recognition of the *Dictionary*, assuring him an income of £300 a year for the remainder of his life. The pension brought Johnson a new security, along with the occasional accusation that his subsequent political pamphlets, generally favorable to the regime, amounted to paid propaganda. In fact, Johnson's politics throughout his life correlated fairly well with the views he implicitly espoused in the distinction he once drew for Boswell: "The prejudice of the Tory is for establishment; the prejudice of the Whig is for innovation." Born into a world where Whigs had long prevailed,

Johnson early committed himself to Tory ways of thought: he cherished precedent, defended "subordination" (social hierarchy), and opposed Whiggish innovation with seriocomic fervor. What remained most notable about his politics was their compassion. "From first to last," John Wain remarks, Johnson "rooted his life among the poor and outcast"; in his work he argued the causes of prostitutes and slaves, of anyone sunk by the "want of necessaries" into "motionless despondence."

In the wake of his pension, Johnson's writing grew sparser, and markedly more social, compassing gestures to and for people he valued. He continued an ingrained habit of churning out prose for his friends to use under their own names: dictating law briefs for lawyers, composing sermons for preachers. He carried on an abundant and affectionate correspondence with Hester Thrale. With Boswell as companion, he traveled to the Scottish Highlands, and on his return published his account of that gregarious trip, *A Journey to the Western Islands* (1775). His final large work was social in a different sense. He accepted a commission to provide *Prefaces Biographical and Critical* for an anthology of English poets of the past hundred and fifty years. These included predecessors who had influenced him, contemporaries he had known, successors he regarded with admiration or alarm. To write their biographies, to analyze their works, was in a sense to live over his own literary life, and to reenter, at length and for the last time, the world of reading and of writing in which he'd now made his way for almost seven decades.

"Our social comforts drop away," Johnson lamented when his friend Levet died in 1782; his own last years were marred by loss. Successive deaths shrunk his contentious household; his friendship with Hester Thrale disintegrated under the pressure of her passion for a man of whom Johnson disapproved; a stroke temporarily deprived him of speech and ushered in his final difficult illness. At his death, an admirer remarked that Johnson had left "a chasm, which not only nothing can fill up, but which nothing has a tendency to fill up. Johnson is dead. Let us go to the next best:—there is nobody: no man can be said to put you in mind of Johnson." Biographers rushed in to fill the chasm, with the testimony of friends and of detractors, and with transcriptions of the hypnotic talk that many of them (notably Boswell and Thrale) had begun to record decades before. For most of the nineteenth century the fame of Johnson's talk far surpassed that of his writing. In recent decades scholars and readers have redressed the balance, finding in Johnson's prose and verse the richest repositories of his thought. Throughout a life of arduous struggle, prodigious accomplishment, and (in the end) near-matchless celebrity, Johnson wrote most eloquently and most feelingly—even in the *Dictionary*, even in literary criticism—of human vulnerabilities: to hope and disappointment, suffering and loss.

THE RAMBLER   In the midst of working on his *Dictionary*, Johnson took on an ambitious additional task: he wrote *The Rambler*, a twice-weekly periodical essay which he sustained for two full years (1750–1752). The project brought him needed income and also a useful respite from the strains of lexicography. *The Rambler*'s most famous antecedent was Addison and Steele's the *Spectator* (1711–1713), and though Johnson would later praise Addison's prose as a "model of the middle style . . . always equable and always easy," he chose for his own essays a mode more astringent: a large, often Latinate vocabulary, intricately balanced sentences, a steady alertness to the human propensity for self-delusion, a willingness to confront rather than ingratiate. Pressures of production could run high (Johnson later claimed that he sometimes wrote his essay with the printer's messenger standing at his side, waiting to take the text to the press), and speed of output may have helped shape the results. Many *Ramblers*, with their formidably wrought prose and surprising turns of thought, manage to seem imposing and improvisatory at the same time. Free to choose his topics, working under relentlessly recurrent deadlines, Johnson drew on four decades dense with reading and thought, during which (in the words of his biographer John Hawkins) he had "accumulated a fund of moral science that was more than sufficient for such an undertaking," and had become "in a very eminent degree qualified for the office of an instructor of mankind in their greatest and most important concerns." Readers proved eager for the instruction. More than any of his earlier writings, *The Rambler* established Johnson's style, his substance, and his fame.

Rambler No. 4

[ON FICTION]

Saturday, 31 March 1750

Simul et jucunda et idonea dicere vitae.

Horace, *Ars Poetica* 1.334

And join both profit and delight in one.

Creech

The works of fiction with which the present generation seems more particularly delighted are such as exhibit life in its true state, diversified only by accidents that daily happen in the world, and influenced by passions and qualities which are really to be found in conversing with mankind.

This kind of writing may be termed not improperly the comedy of romance, and is to be conducted nearly by the rules of comic poetry. Its province is to bring about natural events by easy means, and to keep up curiosity without the help of wonder: it is therefore precluded from the machines[1] and expedients of the heroic romance, and can neither employ giants to snatch away a lady from the nuptial rites, nor knights to bring her back from captivity; it can neither bewilder its personages in deserts, nor lodge them in imaginary castles.

I remember a remark made by Scaliger upon Pontanus,[2] that all his writings are filled with the same images; and that if you take from him his lillies and his roses, his satyrs and his dryads, he will have nothing left that can be called poetry. In like manner, almost all the fictions of the last age will vanish, if you deprive them of a hermit and a wood, a battle and a shipwreck.

Why this wild strain of imagination found reception so long, in polite and learned ages, it is not easy to conceive; but we cannot wonder that, while readers could be procured, the authors were willing to continue it: for when a man had by practice gained some fluency of language, he had no further care than to retire to his closet,[3] let loose his invention, and heat his mind with incredibilities; a book was thus produced without fear of criticism, without the toil of study, without knowledge of nature, or acquaintance with life.

The task of our present writers is very different; it requires, together with that learning which is to be gained from books, that experience which can never be attained by solitary diligence, but must arise from general converse, and accurate observation of the living world. Their performances have, as Horace expresses it, *plus oneris quantum veniae minus*, little indulgence, and therefore more difficulty.[4] They are engaged in portraits of which every one knows the original, and can detect any deviation from exactness of resemblance. Other writings are safe, except from the malice of learning, but

1. "Supernatural agency in poems" (Johnson's *Dictionary*).
2. The Renaissance humanist Julius Caesar Scaliger (1484–1558) criticized the poetry of Giovanni Pontano

(1426–1503).
3. Study.
4. Horace, *Epistles* 2.1.170.

these are in danger from every common reader; as the slipper ill executed was censured by a shoemaker who happened to stop in his way at the Venus of Apelles.[5]

But the fear of not being approved as just copiers of human manners, is not the most important concern that an author of this sort ought to have before him. These books are written chiefly to the young, the ignorant, and the idle, to whom they serve as lectures of conduct, and introductions into life. They are the entertainment of minds unfurnished with ideas, and therefore easily susceptible of impressions; not fixed by principles, and therefore easily following the current of fancy; not informed by experience, and consequently open to every false suggestion and partial account.

That the highest degree of reverence should be paid to youth, and that nothing indecent should be suffered to approach their eyes or ears, are precepts extorted by sense and virtue from an ancient writer, by no means eminent for chastity of thought.[6] The same kind, though not the same degree of caution, is required in every thing which is laid before them, to secure them from unjust prejudices, perverse opinions, and incongruous combinations of images.

In the romances formerly written, every transaction and sentiment was so remote from all that passes among men, that the reader was in very little danger of making any applications to himself; the virtues and crimes were equally beyond his sphere of activity; and he amused himself with heroes and with traitors, deliverers and persecutors, as with beings of another species, whose actions were regulated upon motives of their own, and who had neither faults nor excellencies in common with himself.

But when an adventurer is leveled with the rest of the world, and acts in such scenes of the universal drama, as may be the lot of any other man, young spectators fix their eyes upon him with closer attention, and hope by observing his behavior and success to regulate their own practices, when they shall be engaged in the like part.

For this reason these familiar histories may perhaps be made of greater use than the solemnities of professed morality, and convey the knowledge of vice and virtue with more efficacy than axioms and definitions. But if the power of example is so great, as to take possession of the memory by a kind of violence, and produce effects almost without the intervention of the will, care ought to be taken that, when the choice is unrestrained, the best examples only should be exhibited; and that which is likely to operate so strongly, should not be mischievous or uncertain in its effects.

The chief advantage which these fictions have over real life is, that their authors are at liberty, though not to invent, yet to select objects, and to cull from the mass of mankind those individuals upon which the attention ought most to be employed; as a diamond, though it cannot be made, may be polished by art, and placed in such a situation as to display that lustre which before was buried among common stones.

It is justly considered as the greatest excellency of art, to imitate nature; but it is necessary to distinguish those parts of nature, which are most proper for imitation: greater care is still required in representing life, which is so often discolored by passion, or deformed by wickedness. If the world be promiscuously[7] described, I cannot see of what use it can be to read the account; or why it may not be as safe to turn the eye immediately upon mankind, as upon a mirror which shows all that presents itself without discrimination.

It is therefore not a sufficient vindication of a character, that it is drawn as it appears, for many characters ought never to be drawn; nor of a narrative, that the

---

5. In his *Natural History*, Pliny the Elder tells this story of the famous painter Apelles.
6. Johnson refers to the opening lines of Juvenal's four-

teenth satire.
7. Indiscriminately.

train of events is agreeable to observation and experience, for that observation which is called knowledge of the world will be found much more frequently to make men cunning than good. The purpose of these writings is surely not only to show mankind, but to provide that they may be seen hereafter with less hazard; to teach the means of avoiding the snares which are laid by Treachery for Innocence, without infusing any wish for that superiority with which the betrayer flatters his vanity; to give the power of counteracting fraud, without the temptation to practice it; to initiate youth by mock encounters in the art of necessary defense, and to increase prudence without impairing virtue.

Many writers, for the sake of following nature, so mingle good and bad qualities in their principal personages, that they are both equally conspicuous; and as we accompany them through their adventures with delight, and are led by degrees to interest ourselves in their favor, we lose the abhorrence of their faults, because they do not hinder our pleasure, or, perhaps, regard them with some kindness for being united with so much merit.

There have been men indeed splendidly wicked, whose endowments threw a brightness on their crimes, and whom scarce any villainy made perfectly detestable, because they never could be wholly divested of their excellencies; but such have been in all ages the great corrupters of the world, and their resemblance ought no more to be preserved, than the art of murdering without pain.

Some have advanced, without due attention to the consequences of this notion, that certain virtues have their correspondent faults, and therefore that to exhibit either apart is to deviate from probability. Thus men are observed by Swift to be "grateful in the same degree as they are resentful."[8] This principle, with others of the same kind, supposes man to act from a brute impulse, and pursue a certain degree of inclination, without any choice of the object; for otherwise, though it should be allowed that gratitude and resentment arise from the same constitution of the passions, it follows not that they will be equally indulged when reason is consulted; yet unless that consequence be admitted, this sagacious maxim becomes an empty sound, without any relation to practice or to life.

Nor is it evident, that even the first motions to these effects are always in the same proportion. For pride, which produces quickness of resentment, will obstruct gratitude, by unwillingness to admit that inferiority which obligation implies; and it is very unlikely that he who cannot think he receives a favor will acknowledge or repay it.

It is of the utmost importance to mankind that positions of this tendency should be laid open and confuted; for while men consider good and evil as springing from the same root, they will spare the one for the sake of the other, and in judging, if not of others at least of themselves, will be apt to estimate their virtues by their vices. To this fatal error all those will contribute, who confound the colors of right and wrong, and instead of helping to settle their boundaries, mix them with so much art, that no common mind is able to disunite them.

In narratives where historical veracity has no place, I cannot discover why there should not be exhibited the most perfect idea of virtue; of virtue not angelical, nor above probability, for what we cannot credit we shall never imitate, but the highest and purest that humanity can reach, which, exercised in such trials as the various revolutions of things shall bring upon it, may, by conquering some calamities, and enduring others, teach us what we may hope, and what we can perform. Vice, for vice is necessary

---

8. In fact, it was Pope who made this observation, in the *Miscellanies* he coauthored with Swift.

to be shown, should always disgust; nor should the graces of gaiety, or the dignity of courage, be so united with it, as to reconcile it to the mind. Wherever it appears, it should raise hatred by the malignity of its practices, and contempt by the meanness of its stratagems; for while it is supported by either parts[9] or spirit, it will be seldom heartily abhorred. The Roman tyrant was content to be hated, if he was but feared;[1] and there are thousands of the readers of romances willing to be thought wicked, if they may be allowed to be wits. It is therefore to be steadily inculcated, that virtue is the highest proof of understanding, and the only solid basis of greatness; and that vice is the natural consequence of narrow thoughts, that it begins in mistake, and ends in ignominy.

Rambler No. 60

[ON BIOGRAPHY]

Saturday, 13 October 1750

—*Quid sit pulchrum, quid turpe, quid utile, quid non,*
Plenius et melius Chrysippo et Crantore dicit.

Horace, *Epistles* 1.2.3–4

Whose works the beautiful and base contain;
Of vice and virtue more instructive rules,
Than all the sober sages of the schools.

Francis

All joy or sorrow for the happiness or calamities of others is produced by an act of the imagination, that realizes the event however fictitious, or approximates[1] it however remote, by placing us, for a time, in the condition of him whose fortune we contemplate; so that we feel, while the deception lasts, whatever motions would be excited by the same good or evil happening to ourselves.

Our passions are therefore more strongly moved, in proportion as we can more readily adopt the pains or pleasures proposed to our minds, by recognizing them as once our own, or considering them as naturally incident to our state of life. It is not easy for the most artful writer to give us an interest in happiness or misery, which we think ourselves never likely to feel, and with which we have never yet been made acquainted. Histories of the downfall of kingdoms, and revolutions of empires, are read with great tranquility; the imperial tragedy pleases common auditors only by its pomp of ornament, and grandeur of ideas; and the man whose faculties have been engrossed by business, and whose heart never fluttered but at the rise or fall of stocks, wonders how the attention can be seized, or the affections agitated by a tale of love.

Those parallel circumstances, and kindred images, to which we readily conform our minds, are, above all other writings, to be found in narratives of the lives of particular persons; and therefore no species of writing seems more worthy of cultivation than biography, since none can be more delightful or more useful, none can more certainly enchain the heart by irresistible interest, or more widely diffuse instruction to every diversity of condition.

The general and rapid narratives of history, which involve a thousand fortunes in the business of a day, and complicate innumerable incidents in one great transaction,

9. Abilities.
1. The Roman historian Suetonius reports this of the emperor Caligula.
1. Bring close.

afford few lessons applicable to private life, which derives its comforts and its wretchedness from the right or wrong management of things which nothing but their frequency makes considerable, *parva, si non fiant quotidie*, says Pliny,[2] and which can have no place in those relations which never descend below the consultation of senates, the motions of armies, and the schemes of conspirators.

I have often thought that there has rarely passed a life of which a judicious and faithful narrative would not be useful. For, not only every man has, in the mighty mass of the world, great numbers in the same condition with himself, to whom his mistakes and miscarriages, escapes and expedients, would be of immediate and apparent use; but there is such an uniformity in the state of man, considered apart from adventitious and separable decorations and disguises, that there is scarce any possibility of good or ill, but is common to humankind. A great part of the time of those who are placed at the greatest distance by fortune, or by temper, must unavoidably pass in the same manner; and though, when the claims of nature are satisfied, caprice, and vanity, and accident, begin to produce discriminations and peculiarities, yet the eye is not very heedful, or quick, which cannot discover the same causes still terminating their influence in the same effects, though sometimes accelerated, sometimes retarded, or perplexed by multiplied combinations. We are all prompted by the same motives, all deceived by the same fallacies, all animated by hope, obstructed by danger, entangled by desire, and seduced by pleasure.

It is frequently objected to relations of particular lives, that they are not distinguished by any striking or wonderful vicissitudes. The scholar who passed his life among his books, the merchant who conducted only his own affairs, the priest, whose sphere of action was not extended beyond that of his duty, are considered as no proper objects of public regard, however they might have excelled in their several stations, whatever might have been their learning, integrity, and piety. But this notion arises from false measures of excellence and dignity, and must be eradicated by considering that, in the esteem of uncorrupted reason, what is of most use is of most value.

It is, indeed, not improper to take honest advantages of prejudice, and to gain attention by a celebrated name; but the business of the biographer is often to pass slightly over those performances and incidents, which produce vulgar greatness, to lead the thoughts into domestic privacies, and display the minute details of daily life, where exterior appendages are cast aside, and men excel each other only by prudence and by virtue. The account of Thuanus is, with great propriety, said by its author to have been written, that it might lay open to posterity the private and familiar character of that man, *cujus ingenium et candorem ex ipsius scriptis sunt olim semper miraturi*,[3] whose candor and genius will to the end of time be by his writings preserved in admiration.

There are many invisible circumstances which, whether we read as inquirers after natural or moral knowledge, whether we intend to enlarge our science,[4] or increase our virtue, are more important than public occurrences. Thus Sallust, the great master of nature, has not forgot, in his account of Catiline, to remark that "his walk was now quick, and again slow," as an indication of a mind revolving something with violent commotion.[5] Thus the story of Melancthon[6] affords a striking lecture on the value of time, by informing us, that when he made an appointment, he expected not only the hour, but the minute to be fixed, that the day might not run out in the

---

2. "Matters which would be trivial were they not part of a daily routine" (Pliny the Younger, *Epistles* 3.1).

3. Johnson quotes from a commentary affixed by Nicolas Rigault to the *History of His Own Time* by the French historian Jacques-Auguste de Thou (1553–1617). The Latin is translated by the words that follow.

4. Knowledge.

5. Johnson quotes from an account by the Roman historian Sallust of Catiline's conspiracy against Rome.

6. Johnson quotes from a biography of the Protestant theologian Philip Melancthon (1497–1560) by Joachim Camerarius.

idleness of suspense; and all the plans and enterprises of De Witt are now of less importance to the world, than that part of his personal character which represents him as "careful of his health, and negligent of his life."[7]

But biography has often been allotted to writers who seem very little acquainted with the nature of their task, or very negligent about the performance. They rarely afford any other account than might be collected from public papers, but imagine themselves writing a life when they exhibit a chronological series of actions or preferments; and so little regard the manners or behavior of their heroes, that more knowledge may be gained of a man's real character, by a short conversation with one of his servants, than from a formal and studied narrative, begun with his pedigree, and ended with his funeral.

If now and then they condescend to inform the world of particular facts, they are not always so happy as to select the most important. I know not well what advantage posterity can receive from the only circumstance by which Tickell has distinguished Addison from the rest of mankind, the irregularity of his pulse:[8] nor can I think myself overpaid for the time spent in reading the life of Malherb,[9] by being enabled to relate, after the learned biographer, that Malherb had two predominant opinions; one, that the looseness of a single woman might destroy all her boast of ancient descent; the other, that the French beggars made use very improperly and barbarously of the phrase "noble gentleman," because either word included the sense of both.

There are, indeed, some natural reasons why these narratives are often written by such as were not likely to give much instruction or delight, and why most accounts of particular persons are barren and useless. If a life be delayed till interest and envy are at an end, we may hope for impartiality, but must expect little intelligence; for the incidents which give excellence to biography are of a volatile and evanescent kind, such as soon escape the memory, and are rarely transmitted by tradition. We know how few can portray a living acquaintance, except by his most prominent and observable particularities, and the grosser features of his mind; and it may be easily imagined how much of this little knowledge may be lost in imparting it, and how soon a succession of copies will lose all resemblance of the original.

If the biographer writes from personal knowledge, and makes haste to gratify the public curiosity, there is danger lest his interest, his fear, his gratitude, or his tenderness, overpower his fidelity, and tempt him to conceal, if not to invent. There are many who think it an act of piety to hide the faults or failings of their friends, even when they can no longer suffer by their detection; we therefore see whole ranks of characters adorned with uniform panegyric, and not to be known from one another, but by extrinsic and casual circumstances. "Let me remember," says Hale, "when I find myself inclined to pity a criminal, that there is likewise a pity due to the country."[1] If we owe regard to the memory of the dead, there is yet more respect to be paid to knowledge, to virtue, and to truth.

7. Johnson quotes the essayist Sir William Temple's verdict on the Dutch statesman Jan de Witt (1625–1672).
8. Thomas Tickell prefixed a biography of Joseph Addison to his edition of Addison's Works (1721).
9. Johnson refers to the biography of the French poet Francois de Malherbe (1555–1628) by the Marquis de Racan.
1. Johnson quotes from the biography of Sir Matthew Hale (1609–1676), eminent jurist and religious writer, by Gilbert Burnet.

Idler No. 31[1]

[ON IDLENESS]

Saturday, 18 November 1758

Many moralists have remarked, that pride has of all human vices the widest dominion, appears in the greatest multiplicity of forms, and lies hid under the greatest variety of disguises; of disguises, which, like the moon's "veil of brightness," are both its "luster and its shade,"[2] and betray it to others, though they hide it from ourselves.

It is not my intention to degrade pride from this pre-eminence of mischief, yet I know not whether idleness may not maintain a very doubtful and obstinate competition.

There are some that profess idleness in its full dignity, who call themselves the Idle, as Busiris in the play "calls himself the Proud";[3] who boast that they do nothing, and thank their stars that they have nothing to do; who sleep every night till they can sleep no longer, and rise only that exercise may enable them to sleep again; who prolong the reign of darkness by double curtains, and never see the sun but to "tell him how they hate his beams";[4] whose whole labor is to vary the postures of indulgence, and whose day differs from their night but as a couch or chair differs from a bed.

These are the true and open votaries of idleness, for whom she weaves the garlands of poppies, and into whose cup she pours the waters of oblivion; who exist in a state of unruffled stupidity,[5] forgetting and forgotten; who have long ceased to live, and at whose death the survivors can only say, that they have ceased to breathe.

But idleness predominates in many lives where it is not suspected, for, being a vice which terminates in itself, it may be enjoyed without injury to others, and is therefore not watched like fraud, which endangers property, or like pride, which naturally seeks its gratifications in another's inferiority. Idleness is a silent and peaceful quality, that neither raises envy by ostentation, nor hatred by opposition; and therefore nobody is busy to censure or detect it.

As pride sometimes is hid under humility, idleness is often covered by turbulence and hurry. He that neglects his known duty and real employment, naturally endeavors to crowd his mind with something that may bar out the remembrance of his own folly, and does any thing but what he ought to do with eager diligence, that he may keep himself in his own favor.

Some are always in a state of preparation, occupied in previous measures, forming plans, accumulating materials, and providing for the main affair. These are certainly under the secret power of idleness. Nothing is to be expected from the workman whose

---

1. *The Idler* (1758–1760) bears a more self-deprecating title than *The Rambler;* other circumstances, too, suggest that Johnson intended a less imposing performance in this series of periodical essay than in its predecessor. The new pieces appeared not twice but once a week, and not as an independent sheet but as a department within a weekly newspaper called *The Universal Chronicle* (which achieved little eminence apart from Johnson's contribution). The *Idlers* were shorter than the *Ramblers,* and dealt more often in light topics and comic touches.

Boswell opined that the second series had "less body and more spirit . . . more variety of real life, and greater facility of language." His judgment is hardly definitive; the comparison has been assayed, with varying results, many times since.

2. Both quotations come from Samuel Butler's poem *Hudibras* (1663–1678) 2.1.905 and 908.

3. *Busiris* (1719) by Edward Young.

4. Milton, *Paradise Lost* 4.37.

5. Stupor.

tools are forever to be sought. I was once told by a great master, that no man ever excelled in painting, who was eminently curious[6] about pencils[7] and colors.

There are others to whom idleness dictates another expedient, by which life may be passed unprofitably away without the tediousness of many vacant hours. The art is, to fill the day with petty business, to have always something in hand which may raise curiosity, but not solicitude, and keep the mind in a state of action, but not of labor.

This art has for many years been practiced by my old friend Sober,[8] with wonderful success. Sober is a man of strong desires and quick imagination, so exactly balanced by the love of ease, that they can seldom stimulate him to any difficult undertaking; they have, however, so much power, that they will not suffer him to lie quite at rest, and though they do not make him sufficiently useful to others, they make him at least weary of himself.

Mr. Sober's chief pleasure is conversation; there is no end of his talk or his attention; to speak or to hear is equally pleasing; for he still fancies that he is teaching or learning something, and is free for the time from his own reproaches.

But there is one time at night when he must go home, that his friends may sleep; and another time in the morning, when all the world agrees to shut out interruption. These are the moments of which poor Sober trembles at the thought. But the misery of these tiresome intervals, he has many means of alleviating. He has persuaded himself that the manual arts are undeservedly overlooked; he has observed in many trades the effects of close thought, and just ratiocination. From speculation he proceeded to practice, and supplied himself with the tools of a carpenter, with which he mended his coal-box very successfully, and which he still continues to employ, as he finds occasion.

He has attempted at other times the crafts of the shoemaker, tinman, plumber, and potter; in all these arts he has failed, and resolves to qualify himself for them by better information. But his daily amusement is chemistry. He has a small furnace, which he employs in distillation, and which has long been the solace of his life. He draws oils and waters, and essences and spirits, which he knows to be of no use; sits and counts the drops as they come from his retort, and forgets that, while a drop is falling, a moment flies away.

Poor Sober! I have often teased him with reproof, and he has often promised reformation; for no man is so much open to conviction as the idler, but there is none on whom it operates so little. What will be the effect of this paper I know not; perhaps he will read it and laugh, and light the fire in his furnace; but my hope is that he will quit his trifles, and betake himself to rational and useful diligence.

Idler No. 32
[ON SLEEP]

Saturday, 25 November 1758

Among the innumerable mortifications that waylay human arrogance on every side may well be reckoned our ignorance of the most common objects and effects, a defect of which we become more sensible by every attempt to supply it. Vulgar and inactive minds confound familiarity with knowledge, and conceive themselves informed of the

6. "Difficult to please" (Johnson's *Dictionary*).
7. Brushes.

8. Johnson's friends believed that the portrait of Sober was autobiographical.

whole nature of things when they are shown their form or told their use; but the speculatist, who is not content with superficial views, harasses himself with fruitless curiosity, and still as he inquires more perceives only that he knows less.

Sleep is a state in which a great part of every life is passed. No animal has been yet discovered, whose existence is not varied with intervals of insensibility; and some late philosophers have extended the empire of sleep over the vegetable world.

Yet of this change so frequent, so great, so general, and so necessary, no searcher has yet found either the efficient or final cause; or can tell by what power the mind and body are thus chained down in irresistible stupefaction; or what benefits the animal receives from this alternate suspension of its active powers.

Whatever may be the multiplicity or contrariety of opinions upon this subject, nature has taken sufficient care that theory shall have little influence on practice. The most diligent inquirer is not able long to keep his eyes open; the most eager disputant will begin about midnight to desert his argument, and once in four and twenty hours, the gay and the gloomy, the witty and the dull, the clamorous and the silent, the busy and the idle, are all overpowered by the gentle tyrant, and all lie down in the equality of sleep.

Philosophy has often attempted to repress insolence by asserting that all conditions are leveled by death; a position which, however it may deject the happy, will seldom afford much comfort to the wretched. It is far more pleasing to consider that sleep is equally a leveler with death; that the time is never at a great distance, when the balm of rest shall be effused alike upon every head, when the diversities of life shall stop their operation, and the high and the low shall lie down together.

It is somewhere recorded of Alexander, that in the pride of conquests, and intoxication of flattery, he declared that he only perceived himself to be a man by the necessity of sleep. Whether he considered sleep as necessary to his mind or body it was indeed a sufficient evidence of human infirmity; the body which required such frequency of renovation gave but faint promises of immortality; and the mind which, from time to time, sunk gladly into insensibility had made no very near approaches to the felicity of the supreme and self-sufficient nature.

I know not what can tend more to repress all the passions that disturb the peace of the world than the consideration that there is no height of happiness or honor from which man does not eagerly descend to a state of unconscious repose; that the best condition of life is such that we contentedly quit its good to be disentangled from its evils; that in a few hours splendor fades before the eye and praise itself deadens in the ear; the senses withdraw from their objects, and reason favors the retreat.

What then are the hopes and prospects of covetousness, ambition and rapacity? Let him that desires most have all his desires gratified, he never shall attain a state which he can, for a day and a night, contemplate with satisfaction, or from which, if he had the power of perpetual vigilance, he would not long for periodical separations.

All envy would be extinguished if it were universally known that there are none to be envied, and surely none can be much envied who are not pleased with themselves. There is reason to suspect that the distinctions of mankind have more show than value when it is found that all agree to be weary alike of pleasures and of cares, that the powerful and the weak, the celebrated and obscure, join in one common wish, and implore from nature's hand the nectar of oblivion.

Such is our desire of abstraction from ourselves that very few are satisfied with the quantity of stupefaction which the needs of the body force upon the mind. Alexander himself added intemperance to sleep, and solaced with the fumes of wine the sovereignty of the world. And almost every man has some art by which he steals his thoughts away from his present state.

It is not much of life that is spent in close attention to any important duty. Many hours of every day are suffered to fly away without any traces left upon the intellects. We suffer phantoms to rise up before us, and amuse ourselves with the dance of airy images, which after a time we dismiss forever, and know not how we have been busied.

Many have no happier moments than those that they pass in solitude, abandoned to their own imagination, which sometimes puts sceptres in their hands or mitres on their heads, shifts the scene of pleasure with endless variety, bids all the forms of beauty sparkle before them, and gluts them with every change of visionary luxury.

It is easy in these semi-slumbers to collect all the possibilities of happiness, to alter the course of the sun, to bring back the past, and anticipate the future, to unite all the beauties of all seasons, and all the blessings of all climates, to receive and bestow felicity, and forget that misery is the lot of man. All this is a voluntary dream, a temporary recession from the realities of life to airy fictions; an habitual subjection of reason to fancy.

Others are afraid to be alone, and amuse themselves by a perpetual succession of companions, but the difference is not great; in solitude we have our dreams to ourselves, and in company we agree to dream in concert. The end sought in both is forgetfulness of ourselves.

A DICTIONARY OF THE ENGLISH LANGUAGE   Johnson's *Dictionary* struck its first readers as a nearly superhuman accomplishment; it seems one still. "A dictionary of the English language," observed one early reviewer, had never before "been attempted with the least degree of success"; the closest antecedents to Johnson's project were the national dictionaries of France and Italy, and these had been composed by whole academies of scholars, working collectively over the course of decades. Here, by contrast, was the seven years' labor of a single author (aided only by six part-time amanuenses): 40,000 words defined with unprecedented exactitude, and illustrated with more than 114,000 passages drawn from English prose and poetry of the previous 250 years. Ninety years earlier, members of the newly founded Royal Society for Improving Natural Knowledge had dreamed of such a resource; Johnson produced it by empirical methods much like the ones they promulgated. He spent his first years on the project accumulating data, rereading the English writers he valued most, marking any passage that strikingly illuminated the workings of a particular word. He then worked from this heap of collected evidence to the fine-honed, sharply distinguished conclusions of his definitions. The results have been variously and accurately described as the first standard English dictionary; as one of the final fruits of Renaissance humanism; as a commonplace-book (or database) of important English writing from Sidney to Pope; as a massive map of its author's mind. The key to that map resides in the *Dictionary's* Preface, where Johnson measures the grandeur of his aspirations against the limitations of his achievement. In this mix of personal memoir and linguistic meditation, lexicography becomes a local instance of the vanity of human wishes. Human language, massive, metamorphic, and intractable, overmatches the human desire to codify and contain it, to fix it once and for all.

from A Dictionary of the English Language
from *Preface*
[ON METHOD]

It is the fate of those who toil at the lower employments of life to be rather driven by the fear of evil than attracted by the prospect of good; to be exposed to censure, without hope of praise; to be disgraced by miscarriage or punished for neglect, where success would have been without applause and diligence without reward.

Among these unhappy mortals is the writer of dictionaries; whom mankind have considered not as the pupil but the slave of science, the pioneer[1] of literature, doomed only to remove rubbish and clear obstructions from the paths through which learning and genius press forward to conquest and glory, without bestowing a smile on the humble drudge that facilitates their progress. Every other author may aspire to praise; the lexicographer can only hope to escape reproach, and even this negative recompense has been yet granted to very few.

I have, notwithstanding this discouragement, attempted a dictionary of the English language which, while it was employed in the cultivation of every species of literature, has itself been hitherto neglected; suffered to spread, under the direction of chance, into wild exuberance; resigned to the tyranny of time and fashion, exposed to the corruptions of ignorance, and caprices of innovation.

When I took the first survey of my undertaking, I found our speech copious order, and energetic without rules: wherever I turned my view, there was to be disentangled and confusion to be regulated; choice was to be made out variety, without any established principle of selection; adulterations were without a settled test of purity; and modes of expression to be rejected or out the suffrages[2] of any writers of classical reputation or acknowledged

Having therefore no assistance but from general grammar, I applied perusal of our writers; and, noting whatever might be of use to ascertain any word or phrase, accumulated in time the materials of a dictionary degrees, I reduced to method, establishing to myself in the progress rules as experience and analogy suggested to me; experience, observation were continually increasing; and analogy, which, obscure, was evident in others.

[ON DEFINITIONS AND EXAMPLES]

That part of my work on which I expect malignity most explanation; in which I cannot hope to satisfy those who be pleased, since I have not always been able to satisfy guage by itself is very difficult; many words cannot because the idea signified by them has not more than phrase, because simple ideas cannot be described. unknown, or the notion unsettled and indefinite, and words by which such notions are conveyed or such ous and perplexed. And such is the fate of hapless ness, but light, impedes and distresses it; things

1. "One whose business is to level the road, throw up works, or sink mines in military operations" (Johnson's
2. V

much known, to be happily illustrated. To explain requires the use of terms less abstruse than that which is to be explained, and such terms cannot always be found; for as nothing can be proved but by supposing something intuitively known and evident without proof, so nothing can be defined but by the use of words too plain to admit a definition.

Other words there are, of which the sense is too subtle and evanescent to be fixed in a paraphrase; such are all those which are by the grammarians termed expletives, and, in dead languages, are suffered to pass for empty sounds, of no other use than to fill a verse or to modulate a period,[1] but which are easily perceived in living tongues to have power and emphasis, though it be sometimes such as no other form of expression can convey. * * *

The solution of all difficulties and the supply of all defects must be sought in the examples subjoined to the various senses of each word, and ranged according to the time of their authors.

When first I collected these authorities, I was desirous that every quotation should be useful to some other end than the illustration of a word; I therefore extracted from philosophers principles of science; from historians remarkable facts; from chemists complete processes; from divines striking exhortations; and from poets beautiful descriptions. Such is design while it is yet at a distance from execution. When the time called upon me to range this accumulation of elegance and wisdom into an alphabetical series, I soon discovered that the bulk of my volumes would fright away the student, and was forced to depart from my scheme of including all that was pleasing or useful in English literature, and reduce my transcripts very often to clusters of words in which scarcely any meaning is retained; thus to the weariness of copying, I was condemned to add the vexation of expunging. Some passages I have yet spared which may relieve the labor of verbal searches, and intersperse with verdure and flowers the dusty deserts of barren philology.

The examples, thus mutilated, are no longer to be considered as conveying the sentiments or doctrine of their authors; the word for the sake of which they are inserted, with all its appendant clauses, has been carefully preserved; but it may sometimes happen, by hasty detruncation, that the general tendency of the sentence may be changed: the divine may desert his tenets, or the philosopher his system. * * *

[CONCLUSION]

[A w]ork is difficult because it is large, even though all its parts might singly be [performed] with facility; where there are many things to be done, each must be [allowed its] share of time and labor in the proportion only which it bears to the [whole; nor] can it be expected that the stones which form the dome of a temple [should be sq]uared and polished like the diamond of a ring.

[Of the event] of this work, for which, having labored it with so much application, [I cannot but h]ave some degree of parental fondness, it is natural to form conjectures. [Those who have] been persuaded to think well of my design will require that it should [fix our language] and put a stop to those alterations which time and chance have [hitherto su]ffered to make in it without opposition. With this consequence I will [confess that I flat]tered myself for a while; but now begin to fear that I have indulged [expectation which] neither reason nor experience can justify. When we see men grow [old and die at a cer]tain time one after another, from century to century, we laugh at [the elixir that prom]ises to prolong life to a thousand years; and with equal justice may the lexicographer be derided, who being able to produce no example of a nation that has preserved their words and phrases from mutability, shall imagine that his dictionary can embalm his language and secure it from corruption and decay, that it is in his power to change sublunary nature, and clear the world at once from folly, vanity, and affectation. * * *

The great pest of speech is frequency of translation. No book was ever turned from one language into another without imparting something of its native idiom; this is the most mischievous and comprehensive innovation; single words may enter by thousands and the fabric of the tongue continue the same, but new phraseology changes much at once; it alters not the single stones of the building but the order of the columns.[1] If an academy should be established for the cultivation of our style, which I, who can never wish to see dependence multiplied, hope the spirit of English liberty will hinder or destroy, let them, instead of compiling grammars and dictionaries, endeavor, with all their influence, to stop the license of translators, whose idleness and ignorance, if it be suffered to proceed, will reduce us to babble a dialect of France.

If the changes that we fear be thus irresistible, what remains but to acquiesce with silence, as in the other insurmountable distresses of humanity? It remains that we retard what we cannot repel, that we palliate what we cannot cure. Life may be lengthened by care, though death cannot be ultimately defeated: tongues, like governments, have a natural tendency to degeneration; we have long preserved our constitution, let us make some struggles for our language.

In hope of giving longevity to that which its own nature forbids to be immortal, I have devoted this book, the labor of years, to the honor of my country, that we may no longer yield the palm[2] of philology without a contest to the nations of the Continent. The chief glory of every people arises from its authors: whether I shall add anything by my own writings to the reputation of English literature must be left to time: much of my life has been lost under the pressures of disease; much has been trifled away; and much has always been spent in provision for the day that was passing over me; but I shall not think my employment useless or ignoble if by my assistance foreign nations and distant ages gain access to the propagators of knowledge, and understand the teachers of truth; if my labors afford light to the repositories of science, and add celebrity to Bacon, to Hooker, to Milton, and to Boyle.

When I am animated by this wish, I look with pleasure on my book, however defective, and deliver it to the world with the spirit of a man that has endeavored well. That it will immediately become popular I have not promised to myself: a few wild blunders and risible absurdities, from which no work of such multiplicity was ever free, may for a time furnish folly with laughter, and harden ignorance in contempt; but useful diligence will at last prevail, and there never can be wanting some who distinguish desert,[3] who will consider that no dictionary of a living tongue ever can be perfect, since while it is hastening to publication some words are budding and some falling away; that a whole life cannot be spent upon syntax and etymology, and that even a whole life would not be sufficient; that he whose design includes whatever language can express, must often speak of what he does not understand; that a writer will sometimes be hurried by eagerness to the end, and sometimes faint with weariness under a task, which Scaliger compares to the labors of the anvil and the mine;[4] that what is obvious is not always known, and what is known is not always

---

1. In classical architecture, the five "orders" are Doric, Ionic, Corinthian, Tuscan, and Composite.
2. Crown (symbol of victory).
3. Merit.

4. Johnson refers to a poem, *Against the Compilers of the Lexicons*, by the great Renaissance scholar Joseph Justus Scaliger.

present; that sudden fits of inadvertency will surprise vigilance, slight avocations will seduce attention, and casual eclipses of the mind will darken learning; and that the writer shall often in vain trace his memory at the moment of need for that which yesterday he knew with intuitive readiness, and which will come uncalled into his thoughts tomorrow.

In this work, when it shall be found that much is omitted, let it not be forgotten that much likewise is performed; and though no book was ever spared out of tenderness to the author, and the world is little solicitous to know whence proceeded the faults of that which it condemns; yet it may gratify curiosity to inform it, that the *English Dictionary* was written with little assistance of the learned, and without any patronage of the great; not in the soft obscurities of retirement or under the shelter of academic bowers, but amidst inconvenience and distraction, in sickness and in sorrow. It may repress the triumph of malignant criticism to observe that if our language is not here fully displayed, I have only failed in an attempt which no human powers have hitherto completed. If the lexicons of ancient tongues, now immutably fixed and comprised in a few volumes, are yet, after the toil of successive ages, inadequate and delusive; if the aggregated knowledge, and cooperating diligence of the Italian academicians did not secure them from the censure of Beni;[5] if the embodied critics of France, when fifty years had been spent upon their work, were obliged to change its economy and give their second edition another form, I may surely be contented without the praise of perfection, which, if I could obtain, in this gloom of solitude, what would it avail me? I have protracted my work till most of those whom I wished to please have sunk into the grave, and success and miscarriage are empty sounds: I therefore dismiss it with frigid tranquillity, having little to fear or hope from censure or from praise.

[SOME ENTRIES][1]

FUNK. n.s. A stink. A low word.

IMAGINÁTION. n.s. [*imaginatio*, Lat. *imagination*, Fr. from *imagine*.]

1. Fancy; the power of forming ideal pictures; the power of representing things absent to one's self or others.

> *Imagination* I understand to be the representation of an individual thought. *Imagination* is of three kinds: joined with belief of that which is to come; joined with memory of that which is past; and of things present, or as if they were present: for I comprehend in this imagination feigned and at pleasure, as if one should imagine such a man to be in the vestments of a pope, or to have wings.
> —Bacon

> Our simple apprehension of corporal objects, if present, is sense; if absent, *imagination*: when we would perceive a material object, our fancies present us with its idea.
> —Glanville

5. Paolo Beni criticized the Italian dictionary published in 1612 by the Accademia della Crusca.
1. All entries are from the fourth edition of Johnson's *Dictionary* (1773), the last that Johnson prepared. Each entry is presented complete, with etymology, definitions, illustrations.

O whither shall I run, or which way fly
The sight of this so horrid spectacle,
Which erst my eyes beheld, and yet behold!
For dire *imagination* still pursues me.

—Milton

Where beams of warm *imagination* play,
The memory's soft figures melt away.

—Pope

2. Conception; image in the mind; idea.

Sometimes despair darkens all her *imaginations*; sometimes the active passion of love cheers and clears her invention.

—Sidney

Princes have but their titles for their glories,
An outward honor for an inward toil;
And, for unfelt *imaginations*,
They often feel a world of restless cares.

—Shakespeare, *Richard III*

Better I were distract,
So should my thoughts be severed from my griefs;
And woes, by wrong *imaginations*, lose
The knowledge of themselves.

—Shakespeare, *King Lear*

His *imaginations* were often as just as they were bold and strong.

—Dennis

3. Contrivance; scheme.

Thou hast seen all their vengeance, and all their *imaginations* against me.

—Bible (Lamentations 3.60)

4. An unsolid or fanciful opinion.

We are apt to think that space, in itself, is actually boundless; to which *imagination*, the idea of space, of itself leads us.

—Locke

JÚDGMENT. n.s. [*jugement*, Fr.]

1. The power of discerning the relations between one term or one proposition and another.

O *judgment!* thou art fled to brutish beasts,
And men have lost their reason.

—Shakespeare, *Julius Caesar*

The faculty, which God has given man to supply the want of certain knowledge, is *judgment*, whereby the mind takes any proposition to be true or false, without perceiving a demonstrative evidence in the proofs.

—Locke

Judgment is that whereby we join ideas together by affirmation or negation; so, this tree is high.

—Watts

2. Doom; the right or power of passing judgment.

> If my suspect be false, forgive me, God;
> For *judgment* only doth belong to thee.
>
> —Shakespeare, *Henry VI*

3. The act of exercising judicature; judicatory.

> They gave *judgment* upon him.
>
> —Bible (2 Kings)

> When thou, O Lord, shalt stand disclosed
> In majesty severe,
> And sit in *judgment* on my soul,
> O how shall I appear?
>
> —Addison's *Spectator*

4. Determination; decision.

> Where distinctions or identities are purely material, the *judgment* is made by the
> imagination, otherwise by the understanding.
>
> —Glanville's *Scepsis*

> We shall make a certain *judgment* what kind of dissolution that earth was capable of.
>
> —Burnet's *Theory*

> Reason ought to accompany the exercise of our senses, whenever we would form a
> just *judgment* of things proposed to our inquiry.
>
> —Watts

5. The quality of distinguishing propriety and impropriety; criticism.

> *Judgment*, a cool and slow faculty, attends not a man in the rapture of poetical com-
> position.
>
> —Dennis

> 'Tis with our *judgments* as our watches, none
> Go just alike; yet each believes his own.
>
> —Pope

6. Opinion; notion.

> I see men's *judgments* are
> A parcel of their fortunes, and things outward
> Draw the inward quality after them,
> To suffer all alike.
>
> —Shakespeare, *Antony and Cleopatra*

> When she did think my master loved her well,
> She, in my *judgment*, was as fair as you.
>
> —Shakespeare

7. Sentence against a criminal.

> When he was brought again to th' bar, to hear
> His knell rung out, his *judgment*, he was stirred
> With agony.
>
> —Shakespeare, *Henry VIII*

> The chief priests informed me, desiring to have *judgment* against him.
>
> —Bible (Acts 25.15)

On Adam last this *judgment* he pronounced.

—Milton

8. Condemnation. This is a theological use.

The *judgment* was by one to condemnation; but the free gift is of many offenses unto justification.

—Bible (Romans 5.16)

The precepts, promises, and threatenings of the Gospel will rise up in *judgment* against us, and the articles of our faith will be so many articles of accusation.

—Tillotson

9. Punishment inflicted by Providence, with reference to some particular crime.

This *judgment* of the heavens that makes us tremble,
Touches us not with pity.

—Shakespeare, *King Lear*

We cannot be guilty of greater uncharitableness, than to interpret afflictions as punishments and *judgments*: it aggravates the evil to him who suffers, when he looks upon himself as the mark of divine vengeance.

—Addison's *Spectator*

10. Distribution of justice.

The Jews made insurrection against Paul, and brought him to the *judgment* seat.

—Bible (Acts 18.12)

Your dishonor
Mangles true *judgment*, and bereaves the state
Of that integrity which should become it.

—Shakespeare, *Coriolanus*

In *judgments* between rich and poor, consider not what the poor man needs, but what is his own.

—Taylor

A bold and wise petitioner goes strait to the throne and *judgment* seat of the monarch.

—Arbuthnot and Pope

11. Judiciary law; statute.

If ye hearken to these *judgments*, and keep and do them, the Lord thy God shall keep unto thee the covenant.

—Bible (Deuteronomy)

12. The last doom.

The dreadful *judgment* day
So dreadful will not be as was his sight.

—Shakespeare, *Henry VI*

LEXICÓGRAPHER. n.s. [λεξικον and γραφειν; *lexicographe,* Fr.] A writer of dictionaries; a harmless drudge, that busies himself in tracing the original, and detailing the signification of words.

> Commentators and *lexicographers* acquainted with the Syriac language, have given these hints in their writings on scripture.
>
> —Watt's *Improvement of the Mind*

VACÚITY. n.s. [*vacuitas;* from *vacuus,* Lat. *vacuité,* Fr.]

1. Emptiness; state of being unfilled.

> Hunger is such a state of *vacuity,* as to require a fresh supply of aliment.
>
> —Arbuthnot

2. Space unfilled; space unoccupied.

> In filling up *vacuities,* turning out shadows and ceremonies, by explicit prescription of substantial duties, which those shadows did obscurely represent.
>
> —Hammond's *Fund*

> He, that seat soon failing, meets
> A vast *vacuity.*
>
> —Milton

> Body and space are quite different things, and a *vacuity* is interspersed among the particles of matter.
>
> —Bentley

> God, who alone can answer all our longings, and fill every *vacuity* of our soul, should entirely possess our heart.
>
> —Rogers

> Redeeming still at night these *vacuities* of the day.
>
> —Fell

3. Inanity; want of reality.

> The soul is seen, like other things, in the mirror of its effects: but if they'll run behind the glass to catch at it, their expectations will meet with *vacuity* and emptiness.
>
> —Glanville

James Boswell
1740–1795

"I have discovered," James Boswell announced at age twenty-two in the journal he had just commenced, "that we may be in some degree whatever character we choose." The possibilities opened up by this discovery both exhilarated and troubled him. Neither the "choosing" nor the "being" turned out to be as simple as he expected, in part because some alternate choice always beckoned. In the pages of his journal, Boswell performed his excited choices and anxious reconsiderations. The oscillation did much to drive the intricate comedy and intermittent pathos, the energetic posing and fervent self-scrutiny of the diaries he kept all his adult life, and of the published books he crafted from them.

Boswell's parents had chosen their own characters early, and had stuck to them assiduously. His father was a Scots laird—heir to an ancient family and a landed estate—and a distinguished jurist, serving as justice on Scotland's highest courts. His mother was an impassioned Calvinist, who numbered among her many strictures an abhorrence of the theater; the actors' freedom of character-choice, which made the playhouse for her a place of sinful deception, would make it the site of a lifelong enchantment for her son. Boswell's parents had chosen firmly for their first-born too. James was to become, like his father, an eminent lawyer and respectable landowner.

Boswell chafed at the narrowness of the scheme. Struggling (he later recalled) "against paternal affection, ambition, interest," he ran away to London for a short spell at age eighteen and returned there at twenty-two, seeking a commission as a soldier with the king's personal bodyguard, a post that would have secured him lifelong residence in the city, flashy uniforms, and ample opportunities to display himself in them. While Boswell waited for this prospect to materialize (it never did), he found his real calling. He started to keep a copious journal, narrating each day in succession, dispatching the text in weekly packets to his friend John Johnston back home in Scotland. After Samuel Johnson befriended the young diarist, six months into his London stay, the friendship gave Boswell's journal a new purpose (to record the conversations of this dazzling talker) and his life a new direction. Returning to Scotland in 1766, Boswell took up the life his father had mapped for him, settling in Edinburgh, and becoming (as he haughtily informed his disreputable friend John Wilkes) "a Scottish lawyer, a Scottish laird, and a Scottish married man." In each of these roles, though, he repeatedly broke character. He went down to London almost every spring, ostensibly to cultivate his legal practice but really to renew his old absorptions: in theater, in sexual adventure, in the spellbinding company of Johnson and the group of artists, writers, and thinkers who surrounded him.

Boswell yearned to join their number not merely as admirer but as eminent author, and he soon did. Over the ensuing years, he produced much journalism and some verse, as well as three books in which he explored with increasing audacity the potential of his own diary as a public text—as a vehicle of entertainment, instruction, profit, and fame. He pursued for the journal form a print authority it had not previously possessed, devising ways for it to encroach upon, even to colonize, territory and tasks traditionally reserved to other genres: travel book, "character" sketch, biography. In his first attempt, *An Account of Corsica . . . and Memoirs of Pascal Paoli* (1769), he recast his original travel journal (rearranging the entries, dropping the dates) to produce a heroic portrait of his friend the liberator. In his second experiment, *A Journal of a Tour to the Hebrides with Samuel Johnson* (1785), which appeared the year after Johnson's death, the imperative to portraiture was even more pronounced. The public craved accounts of the lost titan, and this time Boswell met that demand a different way. He presented his journal *as* a journal, with scrupulously dated, plentifully narrated consecutive entries rich in the "minute details of daily life" that Johnson himself had stipulated as the criteria for good biography. The book struck readers as startlingly new. Some mocked it for its minutiae ("How are we all with rapture touched," exclaimed one versifier, "to see / Where, when, and at what hour, you swallowed tea!"), while many praised its veracity and abundance.

There was much more where that came from. In *The Life of Samuel Johnson, LL.D.* (1791), Boswell deployed the *Tour*'s techniques on a massive scale. Drawing on his diaries, and on years of arduous research among Johnson's many acquaintances, Boswell built a thousand-page biography that is largely a book of talk, of conversations diligently recorded and deftly dramatized, the culmination of the textual theater that Boswell had long practiced in manuscript. Johnson's capacious mind and imposing presence find embodiment in a text dense with accumulated time, told and retold over the span of almost three decades that stretches from Boswell's first

Johnsonian journal entry to the biography's publication. Pleased with the book's commercial success, stung by charges that he had been either too partial to Johnson or too critical of him, Boswell worked at two further editions (in which his footnotes swelled with new information and rebuttals). He died at fifty-five, unmade by alcoholism, by venereal disease, and by the violent depressions that accompanied his ongoing uncertainty as to what he might "be" and had become.

His books sustained his fame, though ever since the *Life*'s first appearance, readers have debated the degree of its accuracy and the merits of its portraiture. Two centuries later, Boswell's biography has become a touchstone text for the problem of the "documentary"—the question of how art and "fact" should merge in representations of historical events. Over the past eighty years the debate has been deepened by the unexpected recovery of Boswell's original papers, including the diaries that he drew on and boasted of in his published books. The papers had long been given up for lost, but masses of them had actually been stashed and forgotten by various descendants in odd receptacles (cabinet, croquet box, grain loft) on estates scattered across Scotland and Ireland. The papers' recovery took more than twenty years; the process of their publication continues. Taken together, Boswell's papers and his published works make it possible to trace the intricate course by which the flux of his energetic, agitated life became fixed in text.

from The Life of Samuel Johnson, LL.D.

[INTRODUCTION; BOSWELL'S METHOD]

To write the Life of him who excelled all mankind in writing the lives of others, and who, whether we consider his extraordinary endowments or his various works, has been equaled by few in any age, is an arduous, and may be reckoned in me a presumptuous task.

Had Dr. Johnson written his own life, in conformity with the opinion which he has given, that every man's life may be best written by himself;[1] had he employed in the preservation of his own history, that clearness of narration and elegance of language in which he has embalmed so many eminent persons, the world would probably have had the most perfect example of biography that was ever exhibited. But although he at different times, in a desultory manner, committed to writing many particulars of the progress of his mind and fortunes, he never had preserving diligence enough to form them into a regular composition. Of these memorials a few have been preserved; but the greater part was consigned by him to the flames, a few days before his death.

As I had the honor and happiness of enjoying his friendship for upwards of twenty years; as I had the scheme of writing his life constantly in view; as he was well apprised of this circumstance, and from time to time obligingly satisfied my inquiries, by communicating to me the incidents of his early years; as I acquired a facility in recollecting, and was very assiduous in recording, his conversation, of which the extraordinary vigor and vivacity constituted one of the first features of his character; and as I have spared no pains in obtaining materials concerning him, from every quarter where I could discover that they were to be found, and have been favored with the most liberal communications by his friends; I flatter myself that few biographers have entered upon such a work as this with more advantages; independent of literary abilities, in which I am not vain enough to compare myself with some great names who have gone before me in this kind of writing. * * *

Instead of melting down my materials into one mass, and constantly speaking in my own person, by which I might have appeared to have more merit in the exe-

1. In *Idler* No. 84.

cution of the work, I have resolved to adopt and enlarge upon the excellent plan of Mr. Mason, in his *Memoirs* of Gray.[2] Wherever narrative is necessary to explain, connect, and supply, I furnish it to the best of my abilities; but in the chronological series of Johnson's life, which I trace as distinctly as I can, year by year, I produce, wherever it is in my power, his own minutes,[3] letters, or conversation, being convinced that this mode is more lively, and will make my readers better acquainted with him, than even most of those were who actually knew him, but could know him only partially; whereas there is here an accumulation of intelligence from various points, by which his character is more fully understood and illustrated.

Indeed I cannot conceive a more perfect mode of writing any man's life than not only relating all the most important events of it in their order, but interweaving what he privately wrote, and said, and thought; by which mankind are enabled as it were to see him live, and to "live o'er each scene"[4] with him, as he actually advanced through the several stages of his life. Had his other friends been as diligent and ardent as I was, he might have been almost entirely preserved. As it is, I will venture to say that he will be seen in this work more completely than any man who has ever yet lived.

And he will be seen as he really was; for I profess to write, not his panegyric, which must be all praise, but his Life; which, great and good as he was, must not be supposed to be entirely perfect. To be as he was, is indeed subject of panegyric enough to any man in this state of being; but in every picture there should be shade as well as light, and when I delineate him without reserve, I do what he himself recommended, both by his precept[5] and his example. * * *

What I consider as the peculiar value of the following work is the quantity that it contains of Johnson's conversation; which is universally acknowledged to have been eminently instructive and entertaining; and of which the specimens that I have given upon a former occasion have been received with so much approbation that I have good grounds for supposing that the world will not be indifferent to more ample communications of a similar nature. * * *

I am fully aware of the objections which may be made to the minuteness on some occasions of my detail of Johnson's conversation, and how happily it is adapted for the petty exercise of ridicule, by men of superficial understanding and ludicrous fancy;[6] but I remain firm and confident in my opinion, that minute particulars are frequently characteristic,[7] and always amusing, when they relate to a distinguished man. I am therefore exceedingly unwilling that anything, however slight, which my illustrious friend thought it worth his while to express, with any degree of point,[8] should perish. * * *

Of one thing I am certain, that considering how highly the small portion which we have of the table talk and other anecdotes of our celebrated writers[9] is valued, and how earnestly it is regretted that we have not more, I am justified in preserving rather

2. William Mason constructed his *Memoirs* of Thomas Gray (1775) around a selection of the poet's letters.
3. Memoranda.
4. "To wake the soul by tender strokes of art, / To raise the genius, and to mend the heart, / To make mankind in conscious virtue bold, / Live o'er each scene, and be what they behold" (lines 1–4 of Pope's prologue to Addison's *Cato*).
5. Boswell proceeds to quote from *Rambler* No. 60 (see page 1384) in which Johnson articulates his biographical principles.
6. Boswell's Hebridean journal had already been parodied in print for its "minuteness" and "detail."
7. Revealing of character.
8. "Remarkable turn of words or thought" (Johnson's *Dictionary*).
9. E.g., Joseph Spence's *Anecdotes, Observations and Characters of Books and Men, Collected from the Conversation of Mr. Pope*, which (though unpublished until 1820) Johnson drew on for his *Life* of Pope.

too many of Johnson's sayings than too few; especially as from the diversity of dispositions it cannot be known with certainty beforehand, whether what may seem trifling to some, and perhaps to the collector himself, may not be most agreeable to many; and the greater number that an author can please in any degree, the more pleasure does there arise to a benevolent mind.

To those who are weak enough to think this a degrading task, and the time and labor which have been devoted to it misemployed, I shall content myself with opposing the authority of the greatest man of any age, Julius Caesar, of whom Bacon observes, that "in his book of Apothegms which he collected, we see that he esteemed it more honor to make himself but a pair of tables, to take the wise and pithy words of others, than to have every word of his own to be made an apothegm or an oracle."

Having said thus much by way of introduction, I commit the following pages to the candor of the Public.

[DINNER WITH WILKES]

[May 1776] I am now to record a very curious incident in Dr. Johnson's life, which fell under my own observation; of which *pars magna fui*,[1] and which I am persuaded will, with the liberal-minded, be much to his credit.

My desire of being acquainted with celebrated men of every description had made me, much about the same time, obtain an introduction to Dr. Samuel Johnson and to John Wilkes, Esq.[2] Two men more different could perhaps not be selected out of all mankind. They had even attacked one another with some asperity in their writings; yet I lived in habits of friendship with both. I could fully relish the excellence of each; for I have ever delighted in that intellectual chemistry which can separate good qualities from evil in the same person.

Sir John Pringle,[3] "mine own friend and my Father's friend," between whom and Dr. Johnson I in vain wished to establish an acquaintance, as I respected and lived in intimacy with both of them, observed to me once, very ingeniously, "It is not in friendship as in mathematics, where two things, each equal to a third, are equal between themselves. You agree with Johnson as a middle quality, and you agree with me as a middle quality; but Johnson and I should not agree." Sir John was not sufficiently flexible, so I desisted, knowing, indeed, that the repulsion was equally strong on the part of Johnson, who, I know not from what cause, unless his being a Scotchman, had formed a very erroneous opinion of Sir John. But I conceived an irresistible wish, if possible, to bring Dr. Johnson and Mr. Wilkes together. How to manage it was a nice[4] and difficult matter.

My worthy booksellers[5] and friends, Messieurs Dilly in the Poultry, at whose hospitable and well-covered table I have seen a greater number of literary men than at any other, except that of Sir Joshua Reynolds, had invited me to meet Mr. Wilkes and some more gentlemen on Wednesday, May 15. "Pray," said I, "let us have Dr. Johnson."—"What, with Mr. Wilkes? not for the world," said Mr. Edward Dilly, "Dr. Johnson would never forgive me."—"Come," said I, "if you'll let me negotiate for

---

1. "I was no small part." (Virgil, *Aeneid* 2.5).
2. John Wilkes (1727–1797), libertine, satirist, and radical politician, had been expelled from Parliament for blasphemous and seditious libel. Johnson considered Wilkes an unprincipled philanderer and demagogue.
3. John Pringle (1707–1782), distinguished physician and president of the Royal Society. Johnson disliked Pringle's freethinking religious views and his pro-American political convictions.
4. Delicate.
5. Publishers.

you, I will be answerable that all shall go well." DILLY: "Nay, if you will take it upon you, I am sure I shall be very happy to see them both here."

Notwithstanding the high veneration which I entertained for Dr. Johnson, I was sensible that he was sometimes a little actuated by the spirit of contradiction, and by means of that I hoped I should gain my point. I was persuaded that if I had come upon him with a direct proposal, "Sir, will you dine in company with Jack Wilkes?" he would have flown into a passion, and would probably have answered, "Dine with Jack Wilkes, Sir! I'd as soon dine with Jack Ketch."[6] I therefore, while we were sitting quietly by ourselves at his house in an evening, took occasion to open my plan thus:—"Mr. Dilly, Sir, sends his respectful compliments to you, and would be happy if you would do him the honor to dine with him on Wednesday next along with me, as I must soon go to Scotland." JOHNSON: "Sir, I am obliged to Mr. Dilly. I will wait upon him:" BOSWELL: "Provided, Sir, I suppose, that the company which he is to have is agreeable to you." JOHNSON: "What do you mean, Sir? What do you take me for? Do you think I am so ignorant of the world, as to imagine that I am to prescribe to a gentleman what company he is to have at his table?" BOSWELL: "I beg your pardon, Sir, for wishing to prevent you from meeting people whom you might not like. Perhaps he may have some of what he calls his patriotic[7] friends with him." JOHNSON: "Well, Sir, and what then? What care I for his *patriotic friends?* Poh!" BOSWELL: "I should not be surprised to find Jack Wilkes there." JOHNSON: "And if Jack Wilkes *should* be there, what is that to *me,* Sir? My dear friend, let us have no more of this. I am sorry to be angry with you; but really it is treating me strangely to talk to me as if I could not meet any company whatever, occasionally." BOSWELL: "Pray forgive me, Sir. I meant well. But you shall meet whoever comes, for me." Thus I secured him, and told Dilly that he would find him very well pleased to be one of his guests on the day appointed.

Upon the much-expected Wednesday, I called on him about half an hour before dinner, as I often did when we were to dine out together, to see that he was ready in time, and to accompany him. I found him buffeting[8] his books, as upon a former occasion, covered with dust and making no preparation for going abroad. "How is this, Sir?" said I. "Don't you recollect that you are to dine at Mr. Dilly's?" JOHNSON: "Sir, I did not think of going to Dilly's: it went out of my head. I have ordered dinner at home with Mrs. Williams."[9] BOSWELL: "But, my dear Sir, you know you were engaged to Mr. Dilly, and I told him so. He will expect you, and will be much disappointed if you don't come." JOHNSON: "You must talk to Mrs. Williams about this."

Here was a sad dilemma. I feared that what I was so confident I had secured would yet be frustrated. He had accustomed himself to show Mrs. Williams such a degree of humane attention, as frequently imposed some restraint upon him; and I knew that if she should be obstinate, he would not stir. I hastened downstairs to the blind lady's room and told her I was in great uneasiness, for Dr. Johnson had engaged to me to dine this day at Mr. Dilly's, but that he had told me he had forgotten his engagement, and had ordered dinner at home. "Yes, Sir," said she, pretty peevishly, "Dr. Johnson is to dine at home." "Madam," said I "his respect for you is such that I

6. Famous 17th-century hangman.
7. Those in favor of diminishing the power of the monarch and supporting the rights of the American colonists. Johnson had recently written a political tract called *The Patriot* (1774) in which he attacked Wilkes

and his supporters.
8. Vigorously cleaning.
9. An elderly blind woman who lived in Johnson's house as one of several dependents.

know he will not leave you unless you absolutely desire it. But as you have so much of his company, I hope you will be good enough to forgo it for a day; as Mr. Dilly is a very worthy man, has frequently had agreeable parties at his house for Dr. Johnson, and will be vexed if the Doctor neglects him today. And then, Madam, be pleased to consider my situation; I carried the message, and I assured Mr. Dilly that Dr. Johnson was to come, and no doubt he has made a dinner, and invited a company, and boasted of the honor he expected to have. I shall be quite disgraced if the Doctor is not there." She gradually softened to my solicitations, which were certainly as earnest as most entreaties to ladies upon any occasion, and was graciously pleased to empower me to tell Dr. Johnson, "That all things considered, she thought he should certainly go." I flew back to him, still in dust, and careless of what should be the event,[1] "indifferent in his choice to go or stay";[2] but as soon as I had announced to him Mrs. Williams's consent, he roared, "Frank, a clean shirt," and was very soon dressed. When I had him fairly[3] seated in a hackney coach with me, I exulted as much as a fortune hunter who has got an heiress into a post chaise with him to set out for Gretna Green.[4]

When we entered Mr. Dilly's drawing room, he found himself in the midst of a company he did not know. I kept myself snug and silent, watching how he would conduct himself. I observed him whispering to Mr. Dilly, "Who is that gentleman, Sir?"—"Mr. Arthur Lee."—JOHNSON: "Too, too, too" (under his breath), which was one of his habitual mutterings. Mr. Arthur Lee could not but be very obnoxious to Johnson, for he was not only a *patriot* but an *American*. He was afterwards minister from the United States at the court of Madrid. "And who is the gentleman in lace?"—"Mr. Wilkes, Sir." This information confounded him still more; he had some difficulty to restrain himself, and taking up a book, sat down upon a window seat and read, or at least kept his eye upon it intently for some time, till he composed himself. His feelings, I dare say, were awkward enough. But he no doubt recollected his having rated[5] me for supposing that he could be at all disconcerted by any company, and he, therefore, resolutely set himself to behave quite as an easy man of the world, who could adapt himself at once to the disposition and manners of those whom he might chance to meet.

The cheering sound of "Dinner is upon the table" dissolved his reverie, and we *all* sat down without any symptom of ill humor. There were present, besides Mr. Wilkes, and Mr. Arthur Lee, who was an old companion of mine when he studied physics at Edinburgh, Mr. (now Sir John) Miller, Dr. Lettsom, and Mr. Slater, the druggist. Mr. Wilkes placed himself next to Dr. Johnson and behaved to him with so much attention and politeness that he gained upon him insensibly.[6] No man eat[7] more heartily than Johnson, or loved better what was nice and delicate. Mr. Wilkes was very assiduous in helping him to some fine veal. "Pray give me leave, Sir—It is better here—A little of the brown—Some fat, Sir—A little of the stuffing—Some gravy—Let me have the pleasure of giving you some butter—Allow me to recommend a squeeze of this orange, or the lemon, perhaps, may have more zest."—"Sir, Sir, I am obliged to you, Sir," cried Johnson, bowing, and turning his head to him with a look for some time of "surly virtue,"[8] but, in a short while, of complacency.

---

1. Not caring how the matter turned out.
2. Boswell adapts a line from Addison's *Cato*: "Indiff'rent in his choice to sleep or die" (5.1).
3. Securely.
4. A village just across the border in Scotland; it was the common destination of eloping couples, who could there-

by bypass the formalities and restrictions of the Anglican Church.
5. Chided.
6. Imperceptibly.
7. Ate (pronounced "ett").
8. Boswell quotes from Johnson's poem *London*.

Foote being mentioned, Johnson said, "He is not a good mimic." One of the company added, "A merry Andrew, a buffoon." JOHNSON: "But he has wit[9] too, and is not deficient in ideas, or in fertility and variety of imagery, and not empty of reading;[1] he has knowledge enough to fill up his part. One species of wit he has in an eminent degree, that of escape. You drive him into a corner with both hands; but he's gone, Sir, when you think you have got him—like an animal that jumps over your head. Then he has a great range for his wit; he never lets truth stand between him and a jest, and he is sometimes mighty coarse. Garrick is under many restraints from which Foote is free." WILKES: "Garrick's wit is more like Lord Chesterfield's." JOHNSON: "The first time I was in company with Foote was at Fitzherbert's.[2] Having no good opinion of the fellow, I was resolved not to be pleased; and it is very difficult to please a man against his will. I went on eating my dinner pretty sullenly, affecting not to mind him. But the dog was so very comical, that I was obliged to lay down my knife and fork, throw myself back upon my chair, and fairly laugh it out. No, Sir, he was irresistible. He upon one occasion experienced, in an extraordinary degree, the efficacy of his powers of entertaining. Among the many and various modes which he tried of getting money, he became a partner with a small-beer brewer, and he was to have a share of the profits for procuring customers among his numerous acquaintance. Fitzherbert was one who took his small beer;[3] but it was so bad that the servants resolved not to drink it. They were at some loss how to notify[4] their resolution, being afraid of offending their master, who they knew liked Foote much as a companion. At last they fixed upon a little black boy, who was rather a favorite, to be their deputy and deliver their remonstrance; and having invested him with the whole authority of the kitchen, he was to inform Mr. Fitzherbert, in all their names, upon a certain day, that they would drink Foote's small beer no longer. On that day Foote happened to dine at Fitzherbert's, and this boy served at table; he was so delighted with Foote's stories, and merriment, and grimace,[5] that when he went downstairs, he told them, 'This is the finest man I have ever seen. I will not deliver your message. I will drink his small beer.'"

Somebody observed that Garrick could not have done this. WILKES: "Garrick would have made the small beer still smaller. He is now leaving the stage; but he will play Scrub[6] all his life." I knew that Johnson would let nobody attack Garrick but himself, as Garrick once said to me, and I had heard him praise his liberality; so to bring out his commendation of his celebrated pupil, I said, loudly, "I have heard Garrick is liberal." JOHNSON: "Yes, Sir, I know that Garrick has given away more money than any man in England that I am acquainted with, and that not from ostentatious views. Garrick was very poor when he began life; so when he came to have money, he probably was very unskillful in giving away, and saved when he should not. But Garrick began to be liberal as soon as he could; and I am of opinion, the reputation of avarice which he has had, has been very lucky for him and prevented his having many enemies. You despise a man for avarice, but do not hate him. Garrick might have been much better attacked for living with more splendor than is suitable to a player: if they had had the wit to have assaulted him in that quarter, they might have galled him more. But they have kept clamoring about his avarice, which has rescued him from much obloquy and envy."

---

9. Intelligence, cleverness.
1. Devoid of learning.
2. William Fitzherbert (1712–1772), landowner and politician.
3. Weak beer.

4. Express.
5. Exaggerated facial expressions (Foote specialized in caricatures of his contemporaries).
6. A character in George Farquhar's comedy, *The Beaux' Stratagem*.

Talking of the great difficulty of obtaining authentic information for biography, Johnson told us, "When I was a young fellow I wanted to write the *Life of Dryden*, and in order to get materials, I applied to the only two persons then alive who had seen him; these were old Swinney, and old Cibber.[7] Swinney's information was no more than this, "That at Will's coffeehouse Dryden had a particular chair for himself, which was set by the fire in winter, and was then called his winter-chair; and that it was carried out for him to the balcony in summer, and was then called his summer-chair." Cibber could tell no more but "that he remembered him a decent old man, arbiter of critical disputes at Will's." You are to consider that Cibber was then at a great distance from Dryden, had perhaps one leg only in the room, and durst not draw in the other." BOSWELL: "Yet Cibber was a man of observation?" JOHNSON: "I think not." BOSWELL: "You will allow his *Apology* to be well done." JOHNSON: "Very well done, to be sure, Sir. That book is a striking proof of the justice of Pope's remark:

> Each might his several province well command,
> Would all but stoop to what they understand."[8]

BOSWELL: "And his plays are good." JOHNSON: "Yes; but that was his trade; *l'esprit du corps:* he had been all his life among players and play-writers. I wondered that he had so little to say in conversation, for he had kept the best company, and learnt all that can be got by the ear. He abused Pindar[9] to me, and then showed me an ode of his own, with an absurd couplet, making a linnet soar on an eagle's wing. I told him that when the ancients made a simile, they always made it like something real."

Mr. Wilkes remarked, that "among all the bold flights of Shakespeare's imagination, the boldest was making Birnam Wood march to Dunsinane,[1] creating a wood where there never was a shrub; a wood in Scotland! ha! ha! ha!" And he also observed that "the clannish slavery of the Highlands of Scotland was the single exception to Milton's remark[2] of 'The mountain nymph, sweet Liberty,' being worshipped in all hilly countries." "When I was at Inverary," said he, "on a visit to my old friend, Archibald, Duke of Argyle, his dependents congratulated me on being such a favorite of his Grace. I said, 'It is then, gentlemen, truly lucky for me; for if I had displeased the Duke, and he had wished it, there is not a Campbell among you but would have been ready to bring John Wilkes's head to him in a charger. It would have been only

> Off with his head! So much for Aylesbury.[3]

I was then member[4] for Aylesbury." * * *

Mr. Arthur Lee mentioned some Scotch who had taken possession of a barren part of America, and wondered why they should choose it. JOHNSON: "Why, Sir, all barrenness is comparative. The *Scotch* would not know it to be barren." BOSWELL: "Come, come, he is flattering the English. You have now been in Scotland, Sir, and say if you did not see meat and drink enough there." JOHNSON: "Why yes, Sir; meat and drink enough

7. Owen Mac Swiney and Colley Cibber, actors from the first half of the 18th century. Cibber was also a poet, playwright, and the author of a widely read autobiography (his *Apology*).
8. Pope, *Essay on Criticism*, lines 66–67.
9. Spoke disparagingly of the ancient Greek poet Pindar, famous for his odes.
1. In Act 5 of *Macbeth*. In his *Journey to the Western*

Islands (1775), Johnson had commented repeatedly on the treelessness of Scotland.
2. In his poem *L'Allegro* (36).
3. Wilkes adapts Colley Cibber's popular version of Shakespeare's *Richard III*, which contains the line, "Off with his head. So much for Buckingham."
4. Of Parliament.

to give the inhabitants sufficient strength to run away from home." All these quick and lively sallies were said sportively, quite in jest, and with a smile, which showed that he meant only wit. Upon this topic he and Mr. Wilkes could perfectly assimilate; here was a bond of union between them, and I was conscious that as both of them had visited Caledonia,[5] both were fully satisfied of the strange narrow ignorance of those who imagine that it is a land of famine. But they amused themselves with persevering in the old jokes. When I claimed a superiority for Scotland over England in one respect, that no man can be arrested there for a debt merely because another swears it against him; but there must first be the judgment of a court of law ascertaining its justice; and that a seizure of the person, before judgment is obtained, can take place only if his creditor should swear that he is about to fly from the country, or, as it is technically expressed, is *in meditatione fugae*. WILKES: "That, I should think, may be safely sworn of all the Scotch nation." JOHNSON (to Mr. Wilkes): "You must know, Sir, I lately took my friend Boswell and showed him genuine civilized life in an English provincial town. I turned him loose at Lichfield, my native city, that he might see for once real civility: for you know he lives among savages in Scotland, and among rakes in London." WILKES: "Except when he is with grave, sober, decent people like you and me." JOHNSON (smiling): "And we ashamed of him."

They were quite frank and easy. Johnson told the story of his asking Mrs. Macaulay[6] to allow her footman to sit down with them, to prove the ridiculousness of the argument for the equality of mankind; and he said to me afterwards, with a nod of satisfaction, "You saw Mr. Wilkes acquiesced." Wilkes talked with all imaginable freedom of the ludicrous title given to the Attorney General, *Diabolus Regis*,[7] adding, "I have reason to know something about that officer; for I was prosecuted for a libel."[8] Johnson, who many people would have supposed must have been furiously angry at hearing this talked of so lightly, said not a word. He was now, *indeed*, "a good-humored fellow."

After dinner we had an accession[9] of Mrs. Knowles, the Quaker lady, well known for her various talents, and of Mr. Alderman Lee. Amidst some patriotic groans, somebody (I think the Alderman) said, "Poor old England is lost." JOHNSON: "Sir, it is not so much to be lamented that Old England is lost, as that the Scotch have found it."[1] WILKES: "Had Lord Bute governed Scotland only, I should not have taken the trouble to write his eulogy, and dedicate *Mortimer* to him."[2]

Mr. Wilkes held a candle to show a fine print of a beautiful female figure which hung in the room, and pointed out the elegant contour of the bosom with the finger of an arch connoisseur. He afterwards, in a conversation with me, waggishly insisted that all the time Johnson showed visible signs of a fervent admiration of the corresponding charms of the fair Quaker.

This record, though by no means so perfect as I could wish, will serve to give a notion of a very curious interview, which was not only pleasing at the time, but had the agreeable and benignant effect of reconciling any animosity, and sweetening any

5. Scotland (from the Roman name for North Britain).
6. Catherine Macaulay, author of a controversial *History of England* (1763–1783). In order to test her egalitarian principles, Johnson had proposed that she invite her footman to join them at dinner. "I thus, Sir, showed her the absurdity of the leveling doctrine," he told Boswell. "She has never liked me since."
7. The King's Devil.
8. See n 2, page 1402.
9. I.e., these additional guests arrived: Mary Morris Knowles (1733–1807), a highly accomplished needlewoman whose "sutile pictures" Johnson praised in a letter to Mrs. Thrale; and William Lee (1739–1795), merchant, diplomat, and the only American ever elected an alderman of London.
1. Soon after succeeding to the throne in 1760, George III made his former tutor, the Scottish Earl of Bute, Prime Minister of Britain. The appointment unleashed a flood of anti-Scottish propaganda.
2. As part of a sustained campaign against Bute's government, Wilkes had chosen to reprint a 1731 play called *The Fall of Mortimer* and had prefaced it with a mock-respectful dedication to the prime minister.

acidity, which in the various bustle of political contest, had been produced in the minds of two men, who though widely different, had so many things in common—classical learning, modern literature, wit, and humor, and ready repartee—that it would have been much to be regretted if they had been forever at a distance from each other.

Mr. Burke gave me much credit for this successful *negotiation* and pleasantly said that "there was nothing to equal it in the whole history of the *Corps Diplomatique*."

I attended Dr. Johnson home, and had the satisfaction to hear him tell Mrs. Williams how much he had been pleased with Mr. Wilkes's company, and what an agreeable day he had passed.

+→═◆═←+

Hester Salusbury Thrale Piozzi
1740–1821

Hester Salusbury Thrale Piozzi: the litany of last names tells some of her story. She was born to the Salusburys, an aristocratic and in some branches wealthy Welsh family; both her parents could claim the bloodline, neither of them the wealth. So she was wed at age twenty-three to Henry Thrale, a successful English brewer twelve years her senior, for whom she neither felt nor feigned love. She accepted his proposal in order to secure for her family a large bequest that hinged on her being married. Nonetheless, she threw herself with a will into domestic life at Streatham, Henry's estate six miles outside London. She bore twelve children and mourned eight of them, dead in infancy or childhood. She worked hard helping her husband to advance his endless commercial and political aspirations. And she hosted frequent gatherings of eminent houseguests, with Samuel Johnson the most frequent and most eminent of them all. Johnson had met the Thrales in 1765 and valued them both, Henry for his affability, Hester for her wide curiosity, sharp conversation, and attentive care. For nearly two decades she made Streatham Johnson's second home, and a center of British intellectual life.

Hester Thrale had always read and written plentifully, and in her early twenties had published some short verse in newspapers. During her marriage to Thrale her writing remained mostly a matter of manuscript—occasional poems, innumerable letters, and two sustained autobiographical documents: *The Family Book*, in which she recorded the progress of her offspring, and *Thraliana*, a text more her own, in which she recorded talk, thought, experience, feeling, "and in fine, every thing that struck me at the time." Johnson had recommended the practice, and her husband had given her the handsomely bound blank books in which to pursue it. In those volumes she detailed (among many other things) her intricate connection and her frequent exasperation with both men.

At Henry's death in 1781, much changed. Helped by Johnson, Hester Thrale managed and then sold the brewery. Despite objections by Johnson, and by almost all her family and friends, she fell deeply in love for the only time in her life, with the Italian musician Gabriel Piozzi. Foreign, Roman Catholic, irascible, and not rich, Piozzi combined traits that alienated virtually everyone in Thrale's once cohesive world. Friends marveled at the sudden prevalence of passion in a woman who had once been, as one of them lamented, "the best mother, the best wife, the best friend, the most amiable member of society. . . . I am myself convinced that the poor woman is mad." So were many others, but in the summer of 1784, the "poor woman" married her beloved and departed with him for Italy, leaving in her wake a cacophony, in gossip and newsprint, of scandal and scorn.

In her new marriage and new country, Hester Piozzi launched her career as published author. She produced *Anecdotes of the Late Samuel Johnson* (1786), culled from *Thraliana*; a collection of Johnson's *Letters* (1788); *Observations and Reflections* (1789), reworked from her journal of a tour through Europe; and *British Synonymy* (1794), an anecdotal survey of the overlapping meanings of English words. Piozzi's books brought her equivocal fame at best, heavily mixed with retrospectives on her history as celebrated hostess and social renegade. She spent her last decades in England, Wales, and (after Piozzi's death) at Bath, where she once reported with amusement that a tourist had "brought his son here, that he might see the *first woman in England*. So I am now grown one of the curiosities of Bath, it seems, and *one of the Antiquities*." Her writing, though, has too much edge to pass as harmless "curiosity." When her *Anecdotes of Johnson* first appeared, Horace Walpole voiced a common complaint: "Her panegyric is loud in praise of her hero; and almost every fact she relates disgraces him." Walpole exaggerates, but the push-pull that he points to is one element that makes her work still fascinating. Again and again she immerses herself energetically in the conventional roles assigned to women ("best mother," "best wife," "best friend"), then steps aside to examine them askance, to question, to debunk, even to renounce them. Vibrating between acquiescence and anger, sentimentality and acerbity, Hester Salusbury Thrale Piozzi struck a note of her own, making for herself an interesting life, and a various and idiosyncratic body of work.

from Thraliana

[FIRST ENTRIES]

It is many years since Doctor Samuel Johnson advised me to get a little book, and write in it all the little anecdotes which might come to my knowledge, all the observations I might make or hear; all the verses never likely to be published, and in fine every thing which struck me at the time. Mr. Thrale has now treated me with a repository, and provided it with the pompous title of Thraliana.[1] I must endeavor to fill it with nonsense new and old. 15 September 1776.

Bob Lloyd[2] used to say that a parent or other person devoted to the care and instruction of youth, led the life of a finger post, still fixed to one disagreeable spot himself, while his whole business was only to direct others in the way.

An old man's child, says Johnson, leads much the same sort of life as a child's dog, teased like that with fondness through folly, and exhibited like that to every company, through idle and empty vanity.

I have heard Johnson observe that as education is often compared to agriculture, so it resembles it chiefly in this: that though no one can tell whether the crop may answer the culture,[3] yet if nothing be sowed, we all see that no crop can be obtained.

* * *

[Brighton, July–August 1780] I have picked up Piozzi[4] here, the great Italian singer; he shall teach Hester. She will have some powers in the musical way I believe. Her voice though not strong is sweet and flexible, her taste correct, and her expression pleasing. The other two girls leave me tomorrow; they will do very well; Susan is three parts a Beauty, and quite a Scholar for ten Years old. * * *

I dread the general election more than ever. Mr. Thrale is now well enough to canvass in person, and 'twill kill him.[5] Had it happened when he *could not absolutely*

1. He had given his wife six leather-bound blank volumes, each displaying the "pompous title" on its cover, on a red label stamped with gold lettering.
2. A poet.
3. I.e., will prove worth the care expended on it.
4. "He is amazingly like my father" [Thrale's note]. Born near Venice, Gabriel Piozzi (1740–1809) had now lived in England for about four years, giving concerts and teaching voice.
5. Henry Thrale was running for Parliament; he ended up finishing third in a field of three.

have stirred, we would have done it for him, but now! Well! One should not however anticipate misfortunes, they will come time enough.

* * *

[8 August 1780] Piozzi is become a prodigious favorite with me. He is so intelligent a creature, so discerning, one can't help wishing for his good opinion. His singing surpasses everybody's for taste, tenderness, and true elegance. His hand on the fortepiano too is so soft, so sweet, so delicate, every tone goes to one's heart I think, and fills the mind with emotions one would not be without, though inconvenient enough sometimes. I made him sing yesterday, and though he says his voice is gone, I cannot somehow or other get it out of my ears—odd enough!

These were the Verses he sung to me.

> Amor—non sò che sia,
> Ma sò che è un traditor;
> Cosa è la gelosia?
> Non l'hò provato ancor.
>
> La donna mi vien detto
> Fà molto sospirar;
> Ed Io poveretto,
> Men' voglio innamorar.

I instantly translated them for him, and made him sing them in English thus all'Improviso.

> For Love—I can't abide it,
> The treacherous rogue I know;
> Distrust!—I never tried it
> Whether t'would sting or no.
>
> For Flavia many sighs are,
> Sent up by sad despair.
> And yet poor simple I Sir
> Am hasting to the snare.

[October–November 1780] Here is Sophy Streatfield again, handsomer than ever, and flushed with new conquests: the Bishop of Chester feels her power I am sure. She showed me a letter from him that was as tender, and had all the *tokens* upon it as strong as ever I remember to have seen 'em. I repeated to her out of Pope's Homer. "Very well Sophy," says I,

> "Range undisturbed among the hostile crew,
> But touch not *Hinchliffe*, Hinchliffe is *my* due."[6]

"Miss Streatfield," says my Master, "could have quoted these lines *in the Greek*." His saying so piqued me; and piqued me because it was true. I wish I understood Greek! Mr. Thrale's preference of her to me never vexed me so much as my consciousness—or fear at least—that he had *reason* for his preference. She has ten times my beauty, and five times my scholarship. Wit and knowledge has she none.

---

6. "Rage uncontrolled through all the hostile crew / But touch not Hector; Hector is my due"; Achilles's instructions to Patroclus in Pope's translation of Homer's *Iliad* (16.113). John Hinchliffe was Bishop of Peterborough and a friend of the family.

How fond some people are of riding in a carriage! Those most I think who had from beginning least chance of keeping one. Johnson dotes on a coach; so do many people indeed. I never get into any vehicle, but for the sake of being conveyed to some place, or some person. The motion is unpleasing to me in itself, and the straitness[7] of the room makes it inconvenient. Conversation too is almost wholly precluded, the grinding of the wheels hinders one from hearing, and the necessity of raising one's voice makes it less comfortable to talk. A book is better than a friend in a carriage—and a carriage is the only place where it is so.

* * *

[10 December 1780] We have got a sort of literary curiosity amongst us; the foul copy of Pope's Homer,[8] with all his old intended verses, sketches, emendations etc. Strange that a man should keep such things! Stranger still that a woman should write such a book as this; put down every occurrence of her life, every emotion of her heart, and call it a *Thraliana* forsooth—but then I mean to destroy it.

All wood and wire behind the scenes[9] sure enough! One sees that Pope labored as hard—

as if the Stagyrite o'erlooked each line[1]

indeed, and how very little effect those glorious verses at the end of the 8th book of the *Iliad* have upon one, when one sees 'em all in their cradles and clouts;[2] and "light" changed for "bright"—and then the whole altered again, and the line must end with "night"—and Oh Dear! thus—*torturing one poor word a thousand ways.*[3]

Johnson says 'tis pleasant to see the progress of such a mind. True; but 'tis a malicious pleasure, such as men feel when they watch a woman at her toilet[4] and

see by degrees a purer blush arise, *etc.*[5]

Wood and wire once more! Wood and wire!—

* * *

[January 1781] What an odd partiality I have for a rough character! and even for the hard parts of a soft one! Fanny Burney[6] has secured my heart. I now love her with a fond and firm affection, besides my esteem of her parts,[7] and my regard for her father. Her lofty spirit—dear Creature!—has quite subdued mine; and I adore her for the pride which once revolted me. There is no true affection, no friendship in the sneakers and fawners. 'Tis not for obsequious civility that I delight in Johnson or Hinchliffe, Sir Richard Jebb or Piozzi, who has as much spirit *in his way* as the best of them—great solidity of mind too I think, some sarcasm, and wonderful discernment in that rough Italian. I will do him all the service I can.

[10 January 1781] I will now write out the Characters of the people who are intended to have their portraits hung up in the Library here at Streatham.[8] * * *

---

7. Narrowness
8. The manuscript draft of Pope's translation of the *Iliad*. Johnson was consulting it for his biography of Pope.
9. I.e., backstage at a theater.
1. Pope's *Essay on Criticism* (line 138). The "Stagyrite" is Aristotle, the Greek philosopher Pope here invokes as the ultimate arbiter of literary judgment.
2. Diapers.
3. Dryden, *Mac Flecknoe* (line 208).
4. Dressing table.
5. From Pope's description of Belinda in *The Rape of the Lock* (1.143).

6. Frances Burney (1752–1840), diarist and novelist. Her first novel, *Evelina, or a Young Lady's Entrance into the World* (1778), brought her to the attention and admiration of the Streatham circle.
7. Intellect.
8. The 13 paintings, by Sir Joshua Reynolds, had been commissioned by Henry Thrale. They depicted his wife, daughter, and distinguished friends, including Johnson, Burke, Baretti, and Reynolds himself. A "character" is a word portrait; Hester Thrale wrote one in verse for each person Reynolds depicted.

My own and my eldest daughter's portraits in one picture come next, and are to be placed over the chimney.[9]

> In features so placid, so smooth, so serene,
> What trace of the wit or the Welsh-woman's seen?
> Of the temper sarcastic, the flattering tongue,
> The sentiment right—with th' occasion still wrong.
> What trace of the tender, the rough, the refined,
> The soul in which all contrarieties joined?
> Where though merriment loves over method to rule,
> Religion resides, and the virtues keep school;
> Till when tired we condemn her dogmatical air,
> Like a rocket she rises, and leaves us to stare.
> To such contradictions d'ye wish for a clue?
> Keep vanity still—that vile passion—in view.
> For 'tis thus the slow miner his fortune to make,
> Of arsenic thin scattered pursues the pale track;
> Secure where that poison pollutes the rich ground,
> That it points to the soil where some silver is found.

The portrait of my eldest daughter deserves better lines than these which follow. She is a valuable girl.

> Of a virgin so tender the face or the fame,
> Alike would be injured by praise or by blame.
> To the world's fiery trial too early consigned,
> She soon shall experience it, cruel or kind.
>
> His concern thus the anxious enameller hides,
> And his well finished work to the furnace confides;
> But jocund resumes it secure from decay,
> If the colors stand firm on the dangerous day.

* * *

One Page more I see ends the 3d Volume of Thraliana! strange farrago as it is of sense, nonsense, public, private follies—but chiefly my own—and I the little Hero etc. Well! but who should be the Hero of an *Ana*? Let me vindicate my own vanity if it be with my last pen. This volume will be finished at Streatham and be left there—where I may never more return to dwell!

Mr. Thrale *may die*,[1] and not leave me sufficient to keep Streatham open as it has been kept, and I shall hate to live in it with more thought about expenses than I have done. I *may* indeed be left sole mistress of the brewhouse to manage for my girls, but that I hardly think will be the case; and if not so, why Farewell pretty Streatham, where I have spent many a merry hour, and many a sad one.

My poor little old Aunt at Bath is dying too, and I am dolt enough to be sincerely sorry, the more as her past kindnesses claim that personal attendance from me, which Mr. Thrale will not permit me to pay her—poor, little, old, insipid, useless creature! May God Almighty in his mercy, pity, receive and bless her, as a most inoffensive atom of humanity—for whom his only Son consented to be crucified, and among whose flock she has most innocently fed for sixty or seventy years.—

---

9. Her verse self-portrait follows.   1. He had suffered a series of strokes.

Here closes the third volume

Streatham

Monday 29 January 1781.

[The Death of Henry Thrale; Marriage to Gabriel Piozzi]

[Sunday 18 March 1781] Well! Now I have experienced the delights of a London winter spent in the bosom of flattery, gaiety, and Grosvenor Square. 'Tis a poor thing however, and leaves a void in the mind; but I have had my compting-house[1] duties to attend, my sick Master to watch, my little children to look after—and how much good have I done in any way? Not a scrap as I can see. The pecuniary affairs have gone on perversely: how should they choose when the sole proprietor is incapable of giving orders, yet not so far incapable as to be set aside! Distress, fraud, folly meet me at every turn, and I am not able to fight against them all, though endued with an iron constitution which shakes not by sleepless nights, or days severely fretted. Mr. Thrale talks now of going to Spa and Italy again. How shall we drag him thither? A man who cannot keep awake four hours at a stroke, who can scarce retain the Feces etc. Well! This will indeed be a trial of one's patience; and who must go with us on this expedition? Mr. Johnson! He will indeed be the only happy person of the party. He values nothing under heaven but his own mind, which is a spark *from* Heaven; and *that* will be invigorated by the addition of new ideas. If Mr. Thrale dies on the road, Johnson will console himself by learning *how it is* to travel with a corpse—and after all, such reasoning is the true philosophy—one's heart is a mere encumbrance. Would I could leave mine behind. The children shall go to their sisters at Kensington. Mrs. Cumyns[2] may take care of 'em all. God grant us a happy Meeting! Some *where* and some *time!*

Baretti should attend I think. There is no man who has so much of *every* language, and can manage so well with Johnson, and is so tidy on the road, so active too to obtain good accommodations. He is the man in the world I think whom I most abhor, and who hates, and professes to hate me the most. But what does that signify? He will be careful of Mr. Thrale and Hester whom he *does* love—and he won't strangle me I suppose. It will be very convenient to have him. Somebody we must have. Croza would court our Daughter, and Piozzi could not talk to Johnson, nor I suppose do one any good, but sing to one—and how should we sing *songs in a strange land?* Baretti must be the man, and I will beg it of him as a favor. Oh the triumph he will have! and the lies that he will tell!

If I die abroad I shall leave all my papers in charge with Fanny Burney. I have at length conquered all her scruples, and won her confidence and her heart. 'Tis the most valuable conquest I ever *did* make, and dearly, very dearly, do I love my little *Tayo,* so the people at Otaheite[3] call a *bosom friend.* She is now satisfied of my affection, and has no reserves, no ill opinion, no further notion I shall insult her sweetness. I now respect her caution, and esteem her above all living women. Mrs. Byron will half break her heart at my going. Mrs. Lambart is going herself.[4]

No danger of all these distresses it seems. Mr. Thrale died on the 4th of April 1781.[5]

* * *

---

1. Bookkeeping. During her husband's final illness, Thrale was helping to manage the brewery.
2. A childhood friend, who now ran a school which Sophia and Susan Thrale attended.
3. Tahiti, where Burney's brother James had traveled on

one of Captain James Cook's expeditions.
4. Sophia Byron and Elizabeth Lambart were Thrale's close friends and frequent correpondents.
5. Thrale set down these two sentences at the center of a blank page.

[20 September 1782] Now! That little dear discerning creature Fanny Burney says I'm in love with Piozzi—very likely! He is so amiable, so honorable, so much above his situation by his abilities, that if

> Fate hadn't fast bound her
> With Styx nine times round her
> Sure Music and Love were victorious.[6]

But if he is ever so worthy, ever so lovely, he is *below me* forsooth. In what is he below me? In virtue—I would I were above him. In understanding—I would mine were from this instant under the guardianship of his. In birth—to be sure, he is below me in birth, and so is almost every man I know, or have a chance to know. But he is below me in fortune—is mine sufficient for us both? More than amply so. Does he deserve it by his conduct in which he has always united warm notions of honor with cool attention to economy, the spirit of a gentleman with the talents of a professor? How shall any man deserve fortune if he does not? But I am the guardian of five daughters by Mr. Thrale, and must not disgrace their name and family. Was then the man my mother chose for me of higher extraction than him I have chosen for myself? No. But his fortune was higher. I wanted fortune then perhaps, do I want it now? Not at all. But I am not to think about myself. I married the first time to please my mother, I must marry the second time to please my daughter.[7] I have always sacrificed my own choice to that of others, so I must sacrifice it again. But why? Oh because I am a woman of superior understanding, and must not for the world degrade myself from my situation in life. But if I have superior understanding, let me at least make use of it for once, and rise to the rank of a human being conscious of its own power to discern good from ill. The person who has uniformly acted by the will of others, has hardly that dignity to boast. * * *

[4 November 1782] Sir Richard Musgrave[8] has sent me proposals of marriage from Ireland. His wife is dying at least if not dead, and he is in haste for a better. He will get *me* to be sure!! a likely matter! when my head is full of nothing but my children—my heart of my beloved Piozzi! * * *

[Brighthelmstone, Saturday, 16 November 1782] For him I have been contented to reverse the laws of Nature, and request of my child that concurrence which at my age (and a widow) I am not required either by divine or human institutions to ask even of a parent. The life I gave her she may now more than repay, only by agreeing to what she will with difficulty prevent, and which if she does prevent, will give her lasting remorse—for those who stab *me* shall hear me groan—whereas if she will—but how can she?—gracefully, or even compassionately consent, if she will go abroad with me upon the chance of his death or mine preventing our union, and live with me till she is of age—perhaps there is no heart so callous by avarice, no soul so poisoned by prejudice, no head so feathered by foppery, that will forbear to excuse her when she returns to the rich and the gay, for having saved the life of a mother through compliance extorted by anguish, contrary to the received opinions of the world.

---

6. Pope, *Ode for Music, on St. Cecelia's Day* (lines 90–92). The passage describes Eurydice, momentarily freed from her imprisonment in the underworld by the enchanting music of her lover Orpheus.

7. Queeney, who objected vehemently to the prospect of her mother's marriage to Piozzi.

8. Irish baronet and member of Parliament, whom Thrale had met at Bath in 1776.

[Brighthelmstone, 19 November 1782] What is above written, though intended only to unload my heart by writing it, I showed in a transport of passion to Queeney and to Burney. Sweet Fanny Burney cried herself half blind over it, said there was no resisting such pathetic eloquence, and that if she was the daughter instead of the friend, she should be even tempted to attend me to the altar. But that while she possessed her reason, nothing should seduce her to approve what reason itself would condemn: that children, religion, situation, country and character—besides the diminution of fortune by the certain loss of £800 a year were too much to sacrifice to any *one* man. If however I were resolved to make the sacrifice, *à la bonne heure!*[9] It was an astonishing proof of an attachment, very difficult for mortal man to repay.

I will talk no more of it.

* * *

[29 January 1783] Adieu to all that's dear, to all that's lovely. I am parted from my Life, my Soul! my Piozzi: *Sposo promesso! Amante adorato! Amico senza equale.*[1] If I can get health and strength to write my story here, 'tis all I wish for now! Oh Misery!

The cold dislike of my eldest daughter I thought might wear away by familiarity with his merit, and that we might live tolerably together or at least part friends, but no. Her aversion increased daily, and she communicated it to the others. They treated *me* insolently, and *him* very strangely—running away whenever he came as if they saw a serpent, and plotting with their governess, a cunning Italian, how to invent lies to make me hate him, and twenty such narrow tricks. By these means the notion of my partiality took air—and whether Miss Thrale sent him word slyly, or not I cannot tell; but on the 25 January 1783 Mr. Crutchley[2] came hither to *conjure* me not to go to Italy: he had heard *such* things he said, and by *means* next to *miraculous*. The next day, Sunday 26, Fanny Burney came, said I must marry him instantly, or give him up; that my reputation would be lost else. I actually groaned with anguish, threw myself on the bed in an agony which my fair daughter beheld with frigid indifference. She had indeed never by one tender word endeavored to dissuade me from the match, but said coldly that if I *would* abandon my children, I *must*; that their father had not deserved such treatment from me; that I should be punished by Piozzi's neglect, for that she knew he hated me, and that I turned out my offspring to chance for his sake like puppies in a pond to swim or drown according as Providence pleased; that for her part she must look herself out a place like the other servants, for my face would she never see more. "Nor write to me?" said I. "I shall not Madam," replied she with a cold sneer, "easily find *out your address,* for you are going you know not whither I believe." Susan and Sophy said nothing at all, but they taught the two little ones to cry, "Where are you going Mama? Will you leave us, and die as our poor papa did?" There was no standing *that,* so I wrote my lover word that my mind was all distraction, and bid him come to me the next morning my birthday, 27 January. Mean time I took a vomit, and spent the Sunday night in torture not to be described. My falsehood to my Piozzi, my strong affection for him, the incapacity I felt in myself to resign the man I so adored, the hopes I had so cherished, inclined me strongly to set them all at defiance, and go with him to Church to sanctify the promises I had so often made him, while the idea of

9. Fine! Good for you! (French.)
1. Promised husband, adored lover, friend without equal.

2. Jeremiah Crutchley, one of the executors of Henry Thrale's will.

abandoning the children of my first husband, who left me so nobly provided for, and who depended on my attachment to his offspring, awakened the voice of conscience, and threw me on my knees to pray for *his* direction who was hereafter to judge my conduct.

His grace illuminated me, his power strengthened me; and I flew to my daughter's bed in the morning and told, told her my resolution to resign my own, my dear, my favorite purposes; and to prefer my children's interest to my love. She questioned my ability to make the sacrifice; said one word from him would undo all my[3] * * *

[27 June 1784] My daughters parted with me at last prettily enough *considering* (as the phrase is). We shall perhaps be still better friends apart than together. Promises of correspondence and kindness were very sweetly reciprocated, and the eldest wished for Piozzi's safe return obligingly.[4]

I fancy two days more will absolutely bring him to Bath—The present moments are critical and dreadful, and would shake stronger nerves than mine. Oh Lord strengthen me to do thy will I pray.

[28 June] I am not *yet sure* of seeing him again—not *sure* he lives, not *sure* he loves me, *yet*. Should any thing happen *now!!* Oh I will not trust myself with such a fancy—it will either kill me, or drive me distracted.

[2 July] The happiest day of my whole life I think. Yes, *quite* the happiest. My Piozzi came home yesterday and dined with me. But my spirits were too much agitated, my heart too much dilated, I was too painfully happy *then*. My sensations are more quiet today, and my felicity less tumultuous. I have spent the night as I ought in prayer and Thanksgiving. Could I have slept, I had not deserved such blessings. May the Almighty but preserve them to me! He lodges at our old house on the South Parade. His companion Mecci[5] is a faithless treacherous fellow—but no matter! 'Tis all over now.

[Bath, 25 July] I am returned from church the happy wife of my lovely, my faithful Piozzi, subject of my prayers, object of my wishes, my sighs, my reverence, my esteem.

His nerves have been horribly shaken, but he lives, he loves me, and will be mine *for ever*. He has sworn it in the face of God and the whole Christian Church: Catholics, Protestants, all are witnesses. May he who has preserved us thus long for each other give us a long life together—and so I hope and trust he will through the merits of Jesus Christ. Amen.

[London, 3 September] I have now been six weeks married, and enjoyed greater and longer felicity than I ever yet experienced. To crown all, my dear daughters Susanna and Sophia have spent the day with myself and my amiable husband. We part in peace, and love, and harmony, and tomorrow I set off for the finest country in the world, in company with the most excellent man in it.

Some natural tears they dropped, but wiped 'em soon. Milton.[6]

* * *

3. The remainder of the entry is lost, because the next page is missing. Informed of Thrale's decision, Piozzi left for Italy. Negotiations between mother and daughter continued for another year, until Queeney finally capitulated on the grounds that Thrale's agitation was endangering her health. The daughters were to remain in England, looked after by the trustees of their father's estate;

the mother would reside with her new husband in Italy.
4. He was now returning from Italy to England.
5. Francesco Mecci, a teacher of Italian, whom Thrale apparently suspected of trying to prevent the marriage.
6. From the description of Adam and Eve as they prepare to depart from paradise (*Paradise Lost* 12.645).

[THE DEATH OF JOHNSON]

[Milan, January 1785] The new year is begun. May God prosper it to my husband, my children, and myself. I went to church and prayed most fervently for their happiness.

My Piozzi is not well. He has no disorder though that shortens life, notwithstanding the uneasiness it occasions him. Strong fibers with weak nerves produce all his sufferings, and add to his natural irritability. The constant complaints too which he makes of his health take off from the envy his situation would otherwise provoke, but he is best on a journey. I shall like to go to Venice in the spring—if nothing prevents me, *which I should like still better*. Praying for children is wrong however, and I will do it no more. I used to weary Heaven with requests for pregnancy, and now!! all I begged for are in the grave almost, and those that are left, love not *me*.

I had letters the other day indeed of which I ought not to complain. Susan and Sophy's kindness *should* compensate for the frigidity of their elder sister, and Mr. Cator says all of them are well.

Oh poor Dr. Johnson!!![7]

[25 January 1785] I have recovered myself sufficiently to think what will be the consequence to me of Johnson's death, but must wait the event as all thoughts on the future in this world are vain.

Six people have already undertaken to write his life I hear, of which Sir John Hawkins, Mr. Boswell, Tom Davies, and Dr. Kippis are four. Piozzi says he would have me add to the number, and so I would; but that I think my anecdotes too few, and am afraid of saucy answers if I send to England for others. The saucy answers *I* should disregard, but my heart is made vulnerable by my late marriage, and I am certain that to spite me, they would insult my husband. Poor Johnson! I see they will leave *nothing untold* that I labored so long to keep secret; and I was so very delicate in trying to conceal his fancied insanity,[8] that I retained no proofs of it—or hardly any—nor ever mentioned it in these books, lest by dying first *they* might be printed and the secret (for such I thought it) discovered.

I used to tell him in jest that his biographers would be at a loss concerning some orange peel he used to keep in his pocket,[9] and many a joke we had about the Lives that would be published. "Rescue me out of all their hands, my dear, and do it *yourself*," said he. "Taylor, Adams, and Hector[1] will furnish you with juvenile anecdotes, and Baretti will give you all the rest that you have not already—for I think Baretti is a liar only when he speaks of himself." "Oh!" said I, "Baretti told me yesterday that you got by heart six pages of Machiavel's *History*[2] once, and repeated 'em thirty years afterwards word for word." "O why this indeed is a *gross* lie," says Johnson. "I never read the book at all." "Baretti too told me of *you*" (said I) "that you once kept sixteen cats in your chamber, and yet they scratched your legs to such a degree, you were forced to use mercurial plasters[3] for some time after." "Why this" (replied Johnson) "is an unprovoked lie indeed. I thought the fellow would not have broken through divine and human laws thus, to make Puss his heroine. But I see I was mistaken."

1776–1808   1951

---

7. He had died 13 December 1785.
8. Johnson had confided to her more than to others how deeply and how often he feared the loss of his faculties.
9. He used it as a laxative.

1. Johnson's childhood friends.
2. Niccolò Machiavelli's history of Florence, *Storie Fiorentine* (1520–1525).
3. Bandages soaked in mercury.

POLITICAL AND RELIGIOUS ORDERS

One political order that cannot be ignored by readers of British literature and history is the monarchy, since it provides the terms by which historical periods are even today divided up. Thus much of the nineteenth century is often spoken of as the "Victorian" age or period, after Queen Victoria (reigned 1837–1901), and the writing of the period is given the name Victorian literature. By the same token, writing of the period 1559–1603 is often called "Elizabethan" after Elizabeth I, and that of 1901–1910 "Edwardian" after Edward VII. This system however is based more on convention than logic, since few would call the history (or literature) of late twentieth-century Britain "Elizabethan" any more than they would call the history and literature of the eighteenth century "Georgian," though four king Georges reigned between 1714 and 1820. Where other, better terms exist these are generally adopted.

As these notes suggest, however, it is still common to think of British history in terms of the dates of the reigning monarch, even though the political influence of the monarchy has been strictly limited since the seventeenth century. Thus, where an outstanding political figure has emerged it is he or she who tends to name the period of a decade or longer; for the British, for example, the 1980s was the decade of "Thatcherism" as for Americans it was the period of "Reaganomics." The monarchy, though, still provides a point of common reference and has up to now shown a remarkable historical persistence, transforming itself as occasion dictates to fit new social circumstances. Thus, while most of the other European monarchies disappeared early in the twentieth century, if they had not already done so, the British institution managed to transform itself from imperial monarchy, a role adopted in the nineteenth century, to become the head of a welfare state and member of the European Union. Few of the titles gathered by Queen Victoria, such as Empress of India, remain to Elizabeth II (reigns 1952–), whose responsibilities now extend only to the British Isles with some vestigial role in Australia, Canada, and New Zealand among other places.

The monarchy's political power, like that of the aristocracy, has been successively diminished over the past several centuries, with the result that today both monarch and aristocracy have only formal authority. This withered state of today's institutions, however, should not blind us to the very real power they wielded in earlier centuries. Though the medieval monarch King John had famously been obliged to recognize the rule of law by signing the Magna Carta ("Great Charter") in 1215, thus ending arbitrary rule, the sixteenth- and seventeenth-century English monarchs still officially ruled by "divine right" and were under no obligation to attend to the wishes of Parliament. Charles I in the 1630s reigned mostly without summoning a parliament, and the concept of a "constitutional monarchy," being one whose powers were formally bound by statute, was introduced only when King William agreed to the Declaration of Right in 1689. This document, together with the contemporaneous Bill of Rights, while recognizing that sovereignty still rests in the monarch, formally transferred executive and legislative powers to Parliament. Bills still have to receive Royal Assent, though this was last denied by Queen Anne in 1707; the monarch still holds "prerogative" powers, though these, which include the appointment of certain officials, the dissolution of Parliament and so on, are, in practice wielded by the prime minister. Further information on the political character of various historical periods can be found in the period introductions.

Political power in Britain is thus held by the prime minister and his or her cabinet, members of which are also members of the governing party in the House of Commons. As long as the government is able to command a majority in the House of Commons, sometimes by a coalition of several parties but more usually by the absolute majority of one, it both makes the laws and carries them out. The situation is therefore very different from the American doctrine of the "Separation of Powers," in which Congress is independent of the President and can even be controlled by the opposing party. The British state of affairs has led to the office of prime minister being compared to that of an "elected dictatorship" with surprising frequency over the past several hundred years.

British government is bicameral, having both an upper and a lower house. Unlike other bicameral systems, however, the upper house, the House of Lords, is not elected, its membership being largely hereditary. Membership can come about in four main ways: (1) by birth, (2) by appointment by the current prime minister often in consultation with the Leader of the Opposition, (3) by virtue of holding a senior position in the judiciary, and (4) by being a bishop of the Established Church (the Church of England). In the House of Commons, the lower house, the particular features of the British electoral system have meant that there are never more than two large parties, one of which is in power. These are, together, "Her Majesty's Government and Opposition." Local conditions in Northern Ireland and Scotland have meant that these areas sometimes send members to Parliament in London who are members neither of the Conservative nor of the Labour parties; in general, however, the only other group in the Commons is the small Liberal Party.

Taking these categories in turn, all members of the hereditary aristocracy (the "peerage") have a seat in the House of Lords. The British aristocracy, unlike those of other European countries, was never formally dispossessed of political power (for example by a revolution), and though their influence is now limited, nevertheless all holders of hereditary title—dukes, marquesses, earls, viscounts and barons, in that order of precedence—sit in the Lords. Some continue to do political work and may be members of the Government or of the Opposition, though today it would be considered unusual for a senior member of government to sit in the House of Lords. The presence of the hereditary element in the Lords tends to give the institution a conservative tone, though the presence of the other members ensures this is by no means always the case. Secondly there are "life peers," who are created by the monarch on the prime minister's recommendation under legislation dating from 1958. They are generally individuals who have distinguished themselves in one field or another; retiring senior politicians from the Commons are generally elevated to the Lords, for example, as are some senior civil servants, diplomats, business and trade union leaders, academics, figures in the arts, retiring archbishops, and members of the military. Some of these take on formal political responsibilities and others do not. Finally, senior members of the judiciary sit in the Lords as Law Lords, while senior members of the Church of England hierarchy also sit in the Lords and frequently intervene in political matters. It has been a matter of some controversy whether senior members of other religious denominations, or religions, should also sit in the House of Lords. Within the constitution (by the Parliament Act of 1911 and other acts) the powers of the House of Lords are limited mostly to the amendment and delay of legislation; from time to time the question of its reform or abolition is raised.

In addition, there are minor orders of nobility that should be mentioned. A baronet is a holder of a hereditary title, but he is not a member of the peerage; the style is Sir (followed by his first and last names), Baronet (usually abbreviated as Bart. or Bt.). A knight is a member of one of the various orders of British knighthood, the oldest of which dates back to the Middle Ages (the Order of the Garter), the majority to the eighteenth or nineteenth centuries (the Order of the Thistle, the Bath, Saint Michael, and Saint George, etc.). The title is nonhereditary and is given for various services; it is marked by various initials coming after the name. K.C.B., for example, stands for "Knight Commander of the Bath," and there are many others.

In the House of Commons itself, the outstanding feature is the dominance of the party system. Party labels, such as "Whigs" and "Tories," were first used from the late seventeenth century, when groups of members began to form opposing factions in a Parliament now freed of much of the power of the king. The "Tories," for example, a name now used to refer to the modern Conservative Party, were originally members of that faction that supported James II (exiled in 1689); the word "Tory" comes from the Irish (Gaelic) for outlaw or thief. The "Whigs," on the other hand, supported the constitutional reforms associated with the 1689 Glorious Revolution; the word "whig" is obscurely related to the idea of regicide. The Whig faction largely dominated the political history of the eighteenth century, though the electorate was too small, and politics too controlled by the patronage of the great aristocratic families, for much of a party system to develop. It was only in the middle decades of the nineteenth century that the familiar party system in parliament and the associated electioneering organization in the country at large came into being. The Whigs were replaced by the Liberal Party around the mid-century, as the Liberals were to be replaced by the Labour Party in the early decades of the twentieth century; the Tories had become firm Conservatives by the time of Lord Derby's administrations in the mid-nineteenth century.

The party system has always been fertile ground for a certain amount of parliamentary theater, and it has fostered the emergence of some powerful personalities. Whereas the eighteenth-century Whig prime minister Sir Robert Walpole owed his authority to a mixture of personal patronage and the power made available through the alliances of powerful families, nineteenth-century figures such as Benjamin Disraeli (Conservative prime minister 1868, 1874–1880) and William Ewart Gladstone (Liberal prime minister 1868–1874; 1880–1885; 1885; 1892–1894), were at the apex of their respective party machines. Disraeli, theatrical, personable and with a keen eye for publicity (he was, among other things, a close personal friend of Queen Viotoria), formed a great contrast to the massive moral appeals of his parliamentary opponent Gladstone. One earlier figure, William Pitt (1759–1806), prime minister at twenty-four and leader of the country during the French Revolution and earlier Napoleonic wars, stands comparison with these in the historical record; of twentieth-century political figures, David Lloyd-George, Liberal prime minister during World War I, and Winston Churchill, Conservative, during World War II, deserve special mention.

Though political power in the United Kingdom now rests with Parliament at Westminster in London, this has not always been the only case. Wales, which is now formally a principality within the political construction. "England and Wales," was conquered by the English toward the end of the thirteenth century—too early for indigenous representative institutions to have fallen into place. Scotland, on the other hand, which from 1603 was linked with England under a joint monarchy but only became part of the same political entity with the Act of Union in 1707, did develop discrete institutions. Recent votes in both Scotland and Wales are leading toward greater local legislative control over domestic issues in both Scotland and Wales. Many Scottish institutions—for example, the legal and educational systems—are substantially different from those of England, which is not true in the case of Wales. The Church of Scotland in particular has no link with the Church of England, having been separately established in 1690 on a Presbyterian basis; this means that authority in the Scottish church is vested in elected pastors and lay elders and not in an ecclesiastical hierarchy of priests and bishops. But the most vexed of the relationships within the union has undoubtedly been that between England and Ireland.

There has been an English presence in Ireland from the Middle Ages on, and this became dominant in the later sixteenth century when English policy was deliberately to conquer and colonize the rest of the country. The consequence of this policy, however, was that an Irish Protestant "Ascendancy" came to rule over a largely dispossessed Catholic Irish peasantry; in 1689 at the Battle of the Boyne this state of affairs was made permanent, as Irish Catholic support for the exiled and Catholic-sympathizing James II was routed by the invading troops of the new Protestant king, William III. An Irish parliament met in Dublin, but this was restricted to Protestants; the Church of Ireland was the established Protestant church in a country where most of the population was Catholic. Irish political representation was shifted to Westminster by Pitt in 1800 under the formal Act of Union with Ireland; the Church of Ireland was disestablished by Gladstone later in the century. In the twentieth century, continuing agitation in the Catholic south of the country first for Home Rule and subsequently for independence from Britain—agitation that had been a feature of almost the whole nineteenth century at greater or lesser levels of intensity—led to the establishment first of the Irish Free State (1922) and later of the Republic (1948). In the Protestant North of the country, a local parliament met from 1922 within the common framework of the United Kingdom, but this was suspended in 1972 and representation returned to Westminster, as renewed violence in the province threatened local institutions. In Northern Ireland several hundred years of conflict between Protestants, who form the majority of the population in the province, and Catholics have led to continuing political problems.

Since the Reformation in the sixteenth century Britain has officially been a Protestant country with a national church headed by the monarch. This "Established Church," the Church of England or Anglican Church, has its own body of doctrine in the Thirty-Nine Articles and elsewhere, its own order of services in the Book of Common Prayer, and its own translation of the Bible (the "Authorized Version"), commissioned by James I (reigned 1603–1625) as Head of the Church. There is an extensive ecclesiastical hierarchy and a worldwide communion that includes the American Episcopalian Church.

The Reformation in England was not an easy business, and it has certain negative consequences even today. Some of these have been touched upon above in the case of Ireland. Those professing Roman Catholicism were excluded from political office and suffered other penalties until 1829, and a Catholic hierarchy parallel to that of the Church of England only came into being in Britain in the later nineteenth century. Though many of the restrictions on Roman Catholics enacted by Act of Parliament at the end of the seventeenth century were considerably softened in the course of the eighteenth, nevertheless they were very real.

English Protestantism, however, is far from being all of a piece. As early as the sixteenth century, many saw the substitution of the King's authority and that of the national ecclesiastical hierarchy for that of the Pope to be no genuine Protestant Reformation, which they thought demanded local autonomy and individual judgment. In the seventeenth century many "dissenting" or "Non-Conformist" Protestant sects thus grew up or gathered strength (many becoming "Puritans"), and these rejected the authority of the national church and its bishops and so the authority of the king. They had a brief moment of freedom during the Civil War and the Commonwealth (1649–1660) following the execution of Charles I, when there was a flowering of sects from Baptists and Quakers, which still exist today, to Ranters, Shakers, Anabaptists, Muggletonians, etc., which in the main do not (except for some sects in the United States). The monarchy and the Church were decisively reestablished in 1660, but subsequent legislation, most importantly the Act of Toleration (1689), suspended laws against dissenters on certain conditions.

Religious dissent or nonconformity remained powerful social movements over the following centuries and received new stimulus from the "New Dissenting" revivalist movements of the eighteenth century (particularly Methodism, though there was also a growth in the Congregationalist and Baptist churches). By the nineteenth century, the social character and geographical pattern of English dissent had been established: religious nonconformity was a feature of the new working classes brought into being by the Industrial Revolution in the towns of the Midlands and North of England. Anglicanism, which was associated with the pre-industrial traditional order, was rejected also by many among the rising bourgeoisie and lower middle classes; almost every major English novel of the mid-nineteenth century and beyond is written against a background of religious nonconformity or dissent, which had complex social and political meanings. Nonconformity was also a particular feature of Welsh society.

Under legislation enacted by Edward I in 1290, the Jews were expelled from England, and there were few of them in the country until the end of the seventeenth century, when well-established Jewish communities began to appear in London (the medieval legislation was repealed under the Commonwealth in the 1650s). Restrictions on Jews holding public office continued until the mid-nineteenth century, and at the end of the century large Jewish communities were formed in many English cities by refugees from Central and Eastern European anti-Semitism.

Britain today is a multicultural country and significant proportions of the population, many of whom came to Britain from former British Empire territories, profess Hinduism or Islam, among other religions. The United Kingdom has been a member of the European Union since the early 1970s, and this has further loosened ties between Britain and former empire territories or dominions, many of which are still linked to Britain by virtue of the fact that the British monarch is Head of the "Commonwealth," an organization to which many of them belong. In some cases, the British monarch is also Head of State. Most importantly, however, British membership of the European Union has meant that powers formerly held by the national parliament have been transferred either to the European Parliament in Strasbourg, France, or to the European Commission, the executive agency in Brussels, Belgium, or, in the case of judicial review and appeal, to the European Court of Justice. This process seems set to generate tensions in Britain for some years to come.

David Tresilian

ENGLISH MONARCHS

Before the Norman conquest (1066), these included:

Alfred the Great	871–899
Edmund I	940–946
Ethelred the Unready	948–1016
Edward the Confessor	1042–1066
Harold II	1066

The following monarchs are divided by the dynasty ("House") to which they belong:

Normandy

William I the Conqueror	1066–1087
William II, Rufus	1087–1100
Henry I	1100–1135

Blois

Stephen	1135–1154

Plantagenet

Henry II	1154–1189
Richard I "Coeur de Lion"	1189–1199
John	1199–1216
Henry III	1216–1272
Edward I	1272–1307
Edward II	1307–1327
Edward III	1327–1377
Richard II	1377–1399

Lancaster

Henry IV	1399–1413
Henry V	1413–1422
Henry VI	1422–1471

York

Edward IV	1461–1483
Edward V	1483
Richard III	1483–1485

Tudor

Henry VII	1485–1509
Henry VIII	1509–1547
Edward VI	1547–1553
Mary I	1553–1558
Elizabeth I	1558–1603

Kings of England and of Scotland:

Stuart

James I (James VI of Scotland)	1603–1625
Charles I	1625–1649
Commonwealth (Republic)	
Council of State	1649–1653
Oliver Cromwell, Lord Protector	1653–1658
Richard Cromwell	1658–1660

Stuart

Charles II	1660–1685
James II	1685–1688
(Interregnum 1688–1689)	
William III and Mary II	1685–1701 (Mary dies 1694)
Anne	1702–1714

Hanover

George I	1714–1727
George II	1727–1760
George III	1760–1820
George IV	1820–1830
William IV	1830–1837
Victoria	1837–1901

Saxe-Coburg and Gotha

Edward VII	1901–1910

Windsor

George V	1910–1936
Edward VIII	1936
George VI	1936–1952
Elizabeth II	1952–

MONEY, WEIGHTS, AND MEASURES

The possibility of confusion by the British monetary system has considerably decreased since 1971, when decimalization of the currency took place. There are now 100 pence to a pound (worth about $1.60 in the late 1990s). Prior to this date the currency featured a gallery of other units as well. These coins—shillings, crowns, half-crowns, florins, threepenny-bits, and far-things—were contemporary survivals of the currency's historical development. As such they had a familiar presence in the culture, which was reflected in the slang terms used to refer to them in the spoken language. At least one of these terms, that of a "quid" for a pound, is still in use today.

The old currency divided the pound into 20 shillings, each of which contained 12 pence. There were, therefore, 240 pence in 1 pound. Five shillings made a crown, a half-crown was $2\frac{1}{2}$ shillings, and a florin was 2 shillings; there was also a sixpence, a threepenny-bit, and a far-thing (a quarter of a penny). In slang, a shilling was a "bob," a sixpence a "tanner," and a penny a "copper." Sums were written as, for example, £12. 6s. 6d. or £12/6/6 (12 pounds, 6 shillings, and 6 pence; the "d." stands for "denarius," from the Latin). Figures up to £5 were often expressed in shillings alone: the father of the novelist D. H. Lawrence, for instance, who was a coal miner, was paid around 35 shillings a week at the beginning of the twentieth century— i.e., 1 pound and 15 shillings, or £1/15/-. At this time two gold coins were also still in circula-tion, the sovereign (£1) and the half-sovereign (10s.), which had been the principal coins of the nineteenth century; the largest silver coin was the half-crown (2 / 6). Later all coins were composed either of copper or an alloy of copper and nickel. The guinea was £1/1/- (1 pound and 1 shilling, or 21 shillings); though the actual coin had not been minted since the begin-ning of the nineteenth century, the term was still used well into the twentieth to price luxury items and to pay professional fees.

The number of dollars that a pound could buy has fluctuated with British economic for-tunes. The current figure has been noted above; in 1912 it was about $5.00. To get a sense of how much the pound was worth to those who used it as an everyday index of value, however, we have to look at what it could buy within the system in which it was used. To continue the Lawrence example, a coal miner may have been earning 35 shillings a week in the early years of the twentieth century, but of this he would have to have paid six shillings as rent on the family house; his son, by contrast, could command a figure of £300 as a publisher's advance on his novel *The Rainbow* (pub. 1915), a sum which alone would have placed him somewhere in the middle class. In *A Room of One's Own* (1928) Virginia Woolf recommended the figure of £500 a year as necessary if a woman were to write; at today's values this would be worth around £25,000 ($41,000)—considerably more than the pay of, for example, a junior faculty member at a British university, either then or now.

In earlier periods an idea of the worth of the currency, being the relation between wages and prices, can similarly be established by taking samples from across the country at specific dates. Toward the end of the seventeenth century, for example, Poor Law records tell us that a family of five could be considered to subsist on an annual income of £13/14/-, which included £9/14/- spent on food. At the same time an agricultural laborer earned around £15/12/- annu-ally, while at the upper end of the social scale, the aristocracy dramatically recovered and increased their wealth in the period after the restoration of the monarchy in 1660. By 1672 the early industrialist Lord Wharton was realizing an annual profit of £3,200 on his lead mine and smelting plant in the north of England; landed aristocratic families such as the Russells, spon-sors of the 1689 Glorious Revolution and later dukes of Bedford, were already worth £10,000 a year in 1660. Such details allow us to form some idea of the value of the £10 the poet John Milton received for *Paradise Lost* (pub. 1667), as well as to see the great wealth that went into building the eighteenth-century estates that now dot the English countryside.

By extending the same method to the analysis of wage-values during the Industrial Revolution over a century and a half later, the economic background to incidents of public disorder in the period, such as the 1819 "Peterloo Massacre" in London, can be reconstructed, as can the background to the poems of Wordsworth, for example, many of which concern vagrancy and the lives of the rural poor. Thus the essayist William Cobbett calculated in the 1820s that £1/4/– a week was needed to support a family of five, though actual average earnings were less than half this sum. By contrast, Wordsworth's projection of "a volume which consisting of 160 pages might be sold at 5 shillings" (1806)—part of the negotiations for his *Poems in Two Volumes* (1807)—firmly establishes the book as a luxury item. Jane Austen's contemporaneous novel *Mansfield Park* (1814), which gives many details about the economic affairs of the English rural gentry, suggests that at least £1000 a year is a desirable income.

Today's pound sterling, though still cited on the international exchanges with the dollar, the deutsche mark, and the yen, decisively lost to the dollar after World War I as the central currency in the international system. At present it seems highly likely that, with some other European national currencies, it will shortly cease to exist as the currency unit of the European Union is adopted as a single currency in the constituent countries of the Union.

British weights and measures present less difficulty to American readers since the vast inertia permeating industry and commerce following the separation of the United States from Britain prevented the reform of American weights and measures along metric lines, which had taken place where the monetary system was concerned. Thus the British "Imperial" system, with some minor local differences, was in place in both countries until decimalization of the British system began in stages from the early 1970s on. Today all British weights and measures, with the exception of road signs, which still generally give distances in miles, are metric in order to bring Britain into line with European Union standards. Though it is still possible to hear especially older people measuring area in acres and not in hectares, distances in miles and not in kilometers, or feet and yards and not centimeters and meters, weight in pounds and ounces and not in grams and kilograms, and temperature in Fahrenheit and not in centigrade, etc., it is becoming increasingly uncommon. Measures of distance that might be found in older texts—such as the league (three miles, but never in regular use), the furlong (220 yards), and the ell (45 inches)—are now all obsolete; the only measure still heard in current use is the stone (14 pounds), and this is generally used for body weight.

David Tresilian

BIBLIOGRAPHIES

The Middle Ages

Dictionaries, Encyclopedias • Miranda Green, ed., *Dictionary of Celtic Mythology*, 1992. • Hans Kurath et al., eds., *The Middle English Dictionary*, 1952–. • Norris J. Lacy, ed., *The New Arthurian Encyclopedia*, 1991. • Paul E. Szarmach, M. Teresa Tavormina, Joel T. Rosenthal, eds., *Medieval England: an encyclopedia*, 1998 • Joseph Strayer, gen. ed., *The Dictionary of the Middle Ages*, 13 vols., 1982–1989. • David Wallace, ed., *The Cambridge History of Medieval English Literature*, 1999.

Journals • *Celtica* • *Exemplaria: A Journal of Theory in Medieval and Renaissance Studies* • *Medium Aevum* • *Speculum*, vol. 1–64 (1926–1989) available on-line through JSTOR ("Journal Storage"): http://www.jstor.org

On-Line Sources • Reference material and on-line texts: • Internet Medieval Sourcebook (IMS) (historical and literary texts, both extracts and complete works, some in out-of-date translations): www.fordham.edu/halsall/sbook.html • The Labyrinth: Resources for Medieval Studies (the best clearing-house for access to more specialized sites): www.georgetown.edu/labyrinth/ • *The Medieval Review* (book review journal): http://www.hti.umich.edu/t/tmr/ • The Online Reference Book for Medieval Studies (ORB): http://orb.rhodes.edu/ • NetSERF: The Internet Connection for Medieval Resources: http://netserf.cua.edu

Images From Medieval Manuscripts and Entire Digitized Manuscripts: • Pages from the Beowulf manuscript in color facsimile: http://www.uky.edu/~kiernan/eBeowulf/main.htm • The pages run by the Bibliothèque Nationale (Paris) are especially good, and can be searched by subject: http://www.bnf.fr/enluminures/aaccueil.htm • Medieval Illuminated Manuscripts, a joint project of the National Library of the Netherlands and the Museum Meermanno: http://www.kb.nl/kb/manuscripts/ • The Danish Royal Library at Copenhagen (Det Kongelige Bibliotek) has digitized a number of its manuscripts in their entireties, including several of English origin: http://www.kb.dk/kb/dept/nbo/ha/manuskripter/index2-en.htm • The *Très Riches Heures* of Jean, Duc de Berry, is a wonderful trove of images of courtly life, agriculture, and later medieval piety. Much of it is at: http://metalab.unc.edu/wm/rh • All the calendar pages, with some introduction, are at: http://humanities.uchicago.edu/images/heures/heures.html • The late fourteenth-century *Petites Heures* is at: http://www.bnf.fr/enluminures/texte/atx3_02.htm • A famous 13th-century English manuscript of an Anglo-Norman verse life of King Edward "The Confessor," densely illustrated: http://www.lib.cam.ac.uk/MSS/Ee.3.59 • The 12th-century "Aberdeen Bestiary," in a beautifully designed and educational site: http://www.clues.abdn.ac.uk:8080/besttest/firstpag.html

The British Isles Before the Norman Conquest

• D. A. Binchy, *Celtic and Anglo-Saxon Kingship*, 1970. • Peter Hunter Blair, *Roman Britain and Early England, 55 B.C.–A.D. 871*, 1963. • Peter Hunter Blair, *Introduction to Anglo-Saxon England*, 2nd ed., 1977. • H. M. Chadwick, *The Heroic Age*, 1912. • Nora K. Chadwick, *The Celts*, 1970. • Liam de Paor, *The Peoples of Ireland*, 1986. • Myles Dillon and Nora K. Chadwick, *The Celtic Realms*, 1972. • *English Historical Documents*, vol. I, c. 500–1042, ed. Dorothy Whitelock, 1953. [Primary sources in English translation; introductions provide excellent context.] • Nicholas Howe, *Migration and Mythmaking in Anglo-Saxon England*, 1989. • Hugh A. MacDougall, *Racial Myth in English History: Trojans, Teutons, and Anglo-Saxons*, 1982. • Kim McCone, *Pagan past and Christian present in early Irish literature*, 1990. • Nerys Patterson, *Cattle Lords and Clansmen: The Social Structure of Early Ireland*, 2nd ed., 1996. • Frank M. Stenton, "Anglo-Saxon England," *The Oxford History of England*, vol. 2, 1971. • Dorothy Whitelock, *The Beginnings of English Society*, 1952. • David M. Wilson, *The Anglo-Saxons*, 1960. • Charles D. Wright, *The Irish Tradition in Old English Literature*, 1993.

The Norman Conquest and Its Impact • Jonathan Alexander and Paul Binski, *Age of Chivalry: Art in Plantagenet England 1200–1400*, 1987. • Christopher Brooke, *From Alfred to Henry III, 871–1272*, 1961. • R. Allen Brown, *The Normans*, 1984. • Marjorie Chibnall, *Anglo-Norman England, 1066–1166*, 1984. • Michael Clanchy, *England and Its Rulers, 1066–1307*, 1983. • *English Historical Documents*, vol. II, *1042–1189*, eds. David C. Douglas and George W. Greenaway, 1953; vol. III, *1189–1327*, ed. Harry Rothwell, 1975. • Elizabeth Hallam, *Plantagenet Chronicles*, 1986. Chronicle sources, fine illustrations. • H. W. Koch, *Medieval Warfare*, 1978. • A. L. Poole, *From Domesday Book to Magna Carta*, The Oxford History of England, 1955. • F. M. Powicke, *The Thirteenth Century, 1216–1307*, The Oxford History of England, vol. 4, 1953. • Pauline Stafford, *Unification and Conquest: A Political and Social History of England in the Tenth and Eleventh Centuries*, 1989. • Philip Warner, *The Medieval Castle*, 1971.

Continental and Insular Cultures • Judson B. Allen, *The Friar as Critic: Literary Attitudes in the Later Middle Ages*, 1971. • Erich Auerbach, *Mimesis: The Representation of Reality in Western Literature*, trans. Willard R. Trask, 1957. • William Calin, *The French Tradition and the Literature of Medieval England*, 1994. • Marcia Colish, *The Mirror of Language*, rev. ed., 1983. • Ernst Robert Curtius, *European Literature and the Latin Middle Ages*, trans. Willard R. Trask, 1953. • Peter Dronke, *Medieval Latin and the Rise of the European Love Lyric*, 2nd ed., 2 vols., 1968. • Robert W. Hanning, *The Individual in Twelfth-Century Romance*, 1978. • Johan Huizinga, *The Autumn of the Middle Ages*, trans. Rodney J. Payton and Ulrich Mammitzsch, 1996. • W. P. Ker, *Epic and Romance*, 1957. • C. S. Lewis, *The Discarded Image: An Introduction to Medieval and Renaissance Literature*, 1964. • A. J. Minnis, *Medieval Theory of Authorship: Scholastic Literary Attitudes in the Later Middle Ages*, 2nd ed., 1988. • Nigel Saul, ed., *England in Europe 1066–1453*, 1994. • Rosamund Tuve, *Allegorical Imagery: Some Medieval Books and their Posterity*, 1966.

Politics and Society in the Fourteenth and Fifteenth Centuries • David Aers, ed., *Culture and History, 1350–1600*, 1992. • R. B. Dobson, *The Peasants' Revolt of 1381*, 2nd ed., 1983. • *English Historical Documents*, vol. IV, *1327–1485*, ed. A. R. Myers, 1969. • Chris Given-Wilson, *The English Nobility in the Late Middle Ages*, 1987. • Rodney H. Hilton, *Bond Men Made Free: Medieval Peasant Movements and the English Rising of 1381*, 1973. • Ernest F. Jacob, "The Fifteenth Century," *The Oxford History of England*, vol. 6, 1961. • Maurice Keen, *English Society in the Later Middle Ages*, 1990. • Gordon Leff, *The Dissolution of the Medieval Outlook: An Essay on Intellectual and Spiritual Change in the Fourteenth Century*, 1976. • Gervase Matthew, *The Court of Richard II*, 1968. • May McKisack, *The Fourteenth Century, 1307–1399*, 1959. • Colin Platt, *The English Medieval Town*, 1976. • Paul Strohm, *England's empty throne: usurpation and the language of legitimation, 1399–1422*, 1998. • Juliet Vale, *Edward III and Chivalry: Chivalric Society and Its Context 1270–1350*, 1982. • David Wallace, ed., *Bodies and Disciplines: Intersections of Literature and History in Fifteenth-Century England*, 1996. • Scott L. Waugh, *England in the Reign of Edward III*, 1991. [extensive and helpful bibliography]

Religious Institutions and Cultures • Margaret Aston, *Lollards and Reformers*, 1994. • Renate Blumenfeld-Kosinski and Timea Szell, eds., *Images of Sainthood in Medieval Europe*, 1991. • Janet Burton, *Monastic and Religious Orders in Britain, 1000–1300*, 1994. • M. D. Chenu, *Nature, Man, and Society in the Twelfth Century*, eds. and trans. Jerome Taylor and Lester K. Little, 1968. • Ronald C. Finucane, *Miracles and Pilgrims: Popular Beliefs in Medieval England*, 1977. • Thomas Heffernan, *Sacred Biography: Saints and Their Biographers in the Middle Ages*, 1988. • Anne Hudson, *The Premature Reformation: Wycliffite Texts and Lollard History*, 1988. • W. A. Pantin, *The English Church in the Fourteenth Century*, 1980.

Gender, Sexuality, Courtliness, Marriage • John Boswell, *Christianity, Social Tolerance, and Homosexuality: Gay People in Western Europe from the Beginning of the Christian Era to the Fourteenth Century*, 1980. • Christopher Brooke, *The Medieval Idea of Marriage*, 1989. • Glenn Burger and Steven F. Krueger, eds., *Queering the Middle Ages*, 2001. • Jeffrey J. Cohen and Bonnie Wheeler, eds., *Becoming male in the Middle Ages*, 1997. • Susan Crane, *Insular Romance: Politics, Faith, and Culture in Anglo-Norman and Middle English Literature*, 1986. • Georges Duby, *The Knight, the Lady, and the Priest: The Making of Modern Marriage* *in Medieval France*, trans. Barbara Bray, 1983. • Frances and Joseph Gies, *Marriage and the Family in the Middle Ages*, 1987. • Henry A. Kelly, *Love and Marriage in the Age of Chaucer*, 1975. • Clare A. Lees, ed., *Medieval Masculinities: Regarding Men in the Middle Ages*, 1994. • C. S. Lewis, *The Allegory of Love*, 1938. • V. J. Scattergood and J. W. Sherborne, eds., *English Court Culture in the Later Middle Ages*, 1983.

Women, Work, and Religion • Judith Bennett, *Women in the Medieval English Countryside*, 1986. • Caroline Walker Bynum, *Holy Feast and Holy Fast: The Religious Significance of Food to Medieval Women*, 1987. • Sharon Elkins, *Holy Women of Twelfth Century England*, 1988. • Mary Erler and Maryanne Kowaleski, eds., *Women and Power in the Middle Ages*, 1988. • Christine Fell, *Women in Anglo-Saxon England*, 1986. • Penny Schine Gold, *The Lady and the Virgin: Image, Attitude, and Experience in Twelfth-Century France*, 1985. • Barbara Hanawalt, ed., *Women and Work in Preindustrial Europe*, 1986. • Martha Howell, *Women, Production and Patriarchy in Late Medieval Cities*, 1986. • C. E. Meek and M. K. Simms, eds., *The Fragility of Her Sex? Medieval Irish Women in Their European Context*, 1995. • Barbara Newman, *From Virile Woman to Woman Christ: Studies in Medieval Religion and Literature*, 1995. • Lesley Smith and Jane H. M. Taylor, eds., *Women, the Book, and the Godly*, 1995. • Pauline Stafford, *Queens, Concubines, and Dowagers: The King's Wife in the Early Middle Ages*, 1983. • Ulrike Wiethaus, ed., *Maps of Flesh and Light: The Religious Experience of Medieval Women Mystics*, 1993. • Jocelyn Wogan-Browne, *Saints' lives and women's literary culture c. 1150–1300 : virginity and its authorizations*, 2001.

Modes of Transmission: Orality, Literacy, Manuscripts, Languages • Janet Backhouse, *Books of Hours*, 1985. • Mary Carruthers, *The Book of Memory: A Study of Memory in Medieval Culture*, 1990. • Roger Chartier, ed., *The Culture of Print: Power and the Uses of Print in Early Modern Europe*, 1989. • M. T. Clanchy, *From Memory to Written Record: England, 1066–1307*, 2nd ed., 1993. • Janet Coleman, *Medieval Readers and Writers, 1350–1400*, 1981. • Joyce Coleman, *Public Reading and the Reading Public in Late Medieval England and France*, 1996. • Christopher de Hamel, *A History of Illuminated Manuscripts*, 1986. •

John H. Fisher, *The Emergence of Standard English*, 1996. • John Miles Foley, *The Theory of Oral Composition: History and Methodology*, 1988. • Jeremy Griffiths and Derek Pearsall, eds., *Book Production and Publishing in Britain, 1375–1475*, 1989. • Seth Lerer, *Literacy and Power in Anglo-Saxon England*, 1991. • Jeff Opland, *Anglo-Saxon Oral Poetry: A Study of the Traditions*, 1979. • Nicholas Orme, *From Childhood to Chivalry: The Education of the English Kings and Aristocracy 1066–1530*, 1984.

Old English Literature • Journals. • *Anglo-Saxon England* • *Old English Newsletter*

Bibliography. • Stanley B. Greenfield and Fred C. Robinson, *Bibliography of Publications on Old English Literature*, 1980.

Studies and Guides. • Michael Alexander, *Old English Literature*, 1983. • Jess B. Bessinger and Stanley J. Kahrl, eds., *Essential Articles for the Study of Old English Poetry*, 1968. • Jane Chance, *Woman as Hero in Old English Literature*, 1986. • Helen Damico and Alexandra Hennessey Olsen, eds., *New Readings on Women in Old English Literature*, 1990. • Allen J. Franzten, *The Desire for Origins: New Language, Old English, and Teaching the Tradition*, 1990. • Allen J. Franzten, ed., *Speaking Two Languages: Traditional Disciplines and Contemporary Theory in Medieval Studies*, 1991. • Malcolm Godden and Michael Lapidge, eds., *The Cambridge Companion to Old English Literature*, 1991. • Stanley B. Greenfield, *Hero and Exile: The Art of Old English Poetry*, 1989. • Stanley B. Greenfield and Daniel G. Calder, *A New Critical History of Old English Literature*, 1986. • Britton J. Harwood and Gillian Overing, eds., *Class and Gender in Early English Literature: Intersections*, 1994. • Katherine O'Brien O'Keeffe, ed., *Old English Shorter Poems: Basic Readings*, 1994. • Charles D. Wright, *The Irish Tradition in Old English Literature*, 1993.

Middle English Language and Literature • Middle English Grammar. • John A. Burrow and Thorlac Turville-Petre, *A Book of Middle English*, 1996. • Joseph Wright and Elizabeth Mary Wright, *An Elementary Middle English Grammar*, 1979.

On-Line Sources. • TEAMS (The Consortium for the Teaching of the Middle Ages) publishes a series of Middle English texts, also available on-line: http://www.lib.rochester.edu/camelot/teams/tmsmenu.htm • The "Middle

English Compendium" contains texts, a hyper-bibliography, and the *Middle English Dictionary* on-line: http://ets.umdl.umich.edu/m/mec/

Texts. • Jocelyn Wogan-Browne et al., eds., *The Idea of the Vernacular: An Anthology of Middle English Literary Theory, 1280–1520*, 1999.

Studies. • David Aers, *Community, Gender, and Individual Identity: English Writing 1360–1430*, 1988. • H. S. Bennett, "Chaucer and the Fifteenth Century," *The Oxford History of English Literature*, vol. 2, part 1, 1947. • J. A. W. Bennett and Douglas Gray, "Middle English Literature," *The Oxford History of English Literature*, vol. 1, part 2, 1986. • J. A. Burrow, *Ricardian Poetry: Chaucer, Gower, Langland, and the Gawain*, 1971. • William Calin, *The French Tradition and the Literature of Medieval England*, 1994. • Rita Copeland, ed., *Criticism and Dissent in the Middle Ages*, 1996. • E. K. Chambers, "English Literature at the Close of the Middle Ages," *The Oxford History of English Literature*, vol. 2, part 2, 1961. • Basil Cottle, *The Triumph of English 1350–1400*, 1969. • Carolyn Dinshaw, *Getting Medieval: Sexualities and Communities, Pre- and Postmodern*, 1999. • A. S. G. Edwards, *Middle English Prose: A Critical Guide to Major Authors and Genres*, 1984. • Ruth Evans and Lesley Johnson, eds., *Feminist Readings in Middle English Literature: The Wife of Bath and All Her Sect*, 1994. • Laurie A. Finke and Martin B. Schichtman, eds., *Medieval Texts and Contemporary Readers*, 1987. • Richard Firth Green, *A Crisis of Truth: Literature and Law in Ricardian England*, 1999. • Boris Ford, *Medieval Literature: Chaucer and the Alliterative Tradition*, 1982. • Stephen Justice, *Writing and Rebellion: England in 1381*, 1994. • Karma Lochrie, *Covert Operations: The Medieval Uses of Secrecy*, 1999. • Carol M. Meale, ed., *Women and Literature in Britain, c. 1150–1500*, 1993. • Charles Muscatine, *Poetry and Crisis in the Age of Chaucer*, 1972. • Glending Olson, *Literature as Recreation in the Later Middle Ages*, 1982. • Lee Patterson, ed., *Literary Practice and Social Change in Britain, 1380–1530*, 1990. • Lee Patterson, *Negotiating the Past: The Historical Understanding of Medieval Literature*, 1987. • Larry Scanlon, *Narrative, Authority, and Power: The Medieval Exemplum and the Chaucerian Tradition*, 1994. • A. C. Spearing, *Readings in Medieval Poetry*, 1987. • Paul Strohm, *Hochon's Arrow: The Social Imagination of Fourteenth-Century Texts*, 1992. • Thorlac Turville-Petre, *The Alliterative Revival*, 1977. • Thorlac Turville-Petre, *England*

the Nation: Language, Literature, and National Identity, 1290–1340, 1996.

Celtic Culture and Literature • Bibliography. • Rachel Bromwich, *Medieval Celtic Literature: A Select Bibliography*, 1974.

Studies. • Miranda J. Green, ed., *Celtic Goddesses: Warriors, Virgins, and Mothers*, 1995. • Miranda J. Green, ed., *The Celtic World*, 1995.

Irish Culture and Literature (including Early Irish Verse) • Translations. • James Carney, *Medieval Irish Lyrics with "The Irish Bardic Poet,"* 1985. • Tom Peete Cross and Clark Harris Slover, eds., *Ancient Irish Tales*, 1936; repr. with updated bibliography, 1969. • Patrick K. Ford, trans., *The Celtic poets: songs and tales from early Ireland and Wales*, 1999. • Jeffrey Gantz, *Early Irish Myths and Sagas*, 1981. • Kenneth Hurlstone Jackson, *A Celtic Miscellany: Translations from the Celtic Literatures*, 1951. • Kuno Meyer, trans., *Ancient Irish Poetry*, 1994. • Frank O'Connor, trans., *Kings, Lords, and Commons: An Anthology from the Irish*, 1959. • H. P. A. Oskamp, ed. and trans., [translation used], *The Voyage of Máel Dúin*, 1970.

Studies. • Lisa M. Bitel, *Isle of the saints: monastic settlement and Christian community in early Ireland*, 1990. • Lisa M. Bitel, *Land of women: tales of sex and gender from early Ireland*, 1996. • James Carney, *Studies in Irish Literature and History*, 1979. • Doris Edel, ed., *Cultural Identity and Cultural Integration: Ireland and Europe in the Early Middle Ages*, 1995. • Jeffrey Gantz, *Early Irish Myths and Sagas*, 1981. • Kim McKone, *Pagan Past and Christian Present in Early Irish Literature*, 1990. • Brian Murdoch, *In Pursuit of the Caillech Berre: An Early Irish Poem and the Medievalist at Large*, Zeitschrift fur celtische Philologie 44 (1991): 80–127. • Donncha Ó hAodha, *The Lament of the Old Woman of Beare*, in Donnchadh Ó Corráin et al., eds., *Sages, Saints, and Storytellers: Celtic Studies in Honor of Professor James Carney*, 1989, pp. 308–31. • Nerys Patterson, *Cattle Lords and Clansmen: The Social Structure of Early Ireland*, 2nd ed., 1996. • Alwyn Rees and Brinley Rees, *Celtic Heritage*, 1961. • J. E. Caerwyn Williams and Patrick K. Ford, *The Irish Literary Tradition*, 1992.

Scottish Culture and Literature • Adam J. Aitken et al., eds., *Bards and Makars: Scottish Language and Literature, Medieval and Renaissance*, 1977.

Welsh Culture and Literature • Translations. • Joseph Clancy, *The Earliest Welsh Poetry*, 1970. • Anthony Conran, *The Penguin Book of Welsh Verse*, 1967. • D. Johnston, ed. and trans., *Medieval Welsh Erotic Poetry*, 1991.

Bibliography. • Rachel Bromwich, *Medieval Celtic Literature: A Select Bibliography*, 1974.

Studies. • Stephen S. Evans, *The Heroic Poetry of Dark-Age Britain*, 1997. • Kenneth Jackson, *Language and History in Early Britain*, 1953. • A. O. H. Jarman, *The Cynfeirdd: Early Welsh Poets and Poetry*, 1981. • A. O. H. Jarman and Gwilym Rees Hughes, eds., *A Guide to Welsh Literature*, vol. I, 1976. • A. T. E. Matonis, "Traditions of Panegyric in Welsh Poetry: The Heroic and the Chivalric," *Speculum* 53 (1978): 667–87. • Jenny Rowland, *Early Welsh Saga Poetry*, 1990. • Sir Ifor Williams, *The Beginnings of Welsh Poetry: Studies*, 1980. • J. E. C. Williams, *The Poet of the Welsh Princes*, 1994.

Perspectives: Arthurian Myth in the History of Britain • Translations. • Geoffrey of Monmouth, *History of the Kings of Britain*, trans. Lewis Thorpe, 1966. • Gerald of Wales, *The Journey through Wales and The Description of Wales*, trans. L. Thorpe, 1978. • E. L. G. Stones, ed. and trans., *Anglo-Scottish Relations 1174–1328: Some Selected Documents*, 1965.

Studies. • Christopher Brooke, "Geoffrey of Monmouth as a Historian," in C. Brooke et al., eds., *Church and Government in the Middle Ages*, 1976. • Michael J. Curley, *Geoffrey of Monmouth*, 1994. • John Gillingham, *The Context and Purposes of Geoffrey of Monmouth's History of the Kings of Britain, Anglo-Norman Studies*, vol. 13, 1990. • Robert W. Hanning, *The Vision of History in Early Britain: From Gildas to Geoffrey of Monmouth*, 1966. • Francis Ingledew, "The Book of Troy and the Genealogical Construction of History: The Case of Geoffrey of Monmouth's Historia Regum Britanniae," *Speculum* 69(1994): 665–704. • Roger Sherman Loomis, ed., *Arthurian Literature in the Middle Ages*, 1959. • Monika Otter, *Inventiones: Fiction and Referentiality in Twelfth-Century Historical Writing*, 1996. • Michael Prestwich, *Edward the First*, 1988. • E. L. G. Stones, *Edward I*, 1968. • J. S. P. Tatlock, *The Legendary History of Britain*, 1950.

Arthurian Romance • Bibliography. • Norris J. Lacy, ed., *Medieval Arthurian Literature: A Guide to Recent Research*, 1996.

Encyclopedia. • Norris J. Lacy, ed., *The New Arthurian Encyclopedia*, 1991.

Journals. • *Arthuriana*: http://www2.smu.edu/arthuriana • *Arthurian Literature*

Studies. • John Darrah, *Paganism in Arthurian Romance*, 1994. • Thelma Fenster, ed., *Arthurian Women: A Casebook*, 1996. • Maureen Fries and Jeanie Watson, eds., *Approaches to Teaching the Arthurian Tradition*, 1992. • Edward D. Kennedy, ed., *King Arthur: A Casebook*, 1996. • Stephen Knight, *Arthurian Literature and Society*, 1983. • Roger Sherman Loomis, ed., *Arthurian Literature in the Middle Ages: A Collaborative History*, 1969. • Martin Schichtman and James Carley, eds., *Culture and the King: the Social Implications of the Arthurian Legend*, 1994. • Eugene Vinaver, *The Rise of Romance*, 1984.

Medieval Drama • Studies. • *Contexts for Early English Drama*, eds. Marianne Briscoe and John Coldewey, 1989. • John D. Cox and David Scott Kastan, eds., *A New History of Early English Drama*, 1997. • Clifford Davidson and John Stroupe, eds., *Drama in the Middle Ages*, 1982 • Jody Enders, *The Medieval Theater of Cruelty: Rhetoric, Memory, Violence*, 1999. • Claire Sponsler, *Drama and Resistance: Bodies, Goods, and Theatricality in Late Medieval England*, 1997. • Rosemary Woolf, *The English Mystery Plays*, 1972.

Middle Scots Poetry • Walter Scheps and J. Anna Looney, eds., *Middle Scots Poets: A Reference Guide to James I of Scotland, Robert Henryson, William Dunbar, and Gavin Douglas*, 1986.

Mystical Writings • Bibliography. • Michael E. Sawyer, *A Bibliographical Index of Five English Mystics: Richard Rolle, Julian of Norwich, the Author of The Cloud of Unknowing, Walter Hilton, Margery Kempe*, 1978.

General Studies. • David Aers and Lynn Staley, *The Powers of the Holy: Religion, Politics, and Gender in Late Medieval English Culture*, 1996. • Sarah Beckwith, *Christ's Body: Identity, Culture, and Society in Late Medieval Writings*, 1993. • Frances Beer, *Women and Mystical Experience in the Middle Ages*, 1992. • Marion Glasscoe, *English Medieval Mystics: Games of Faith*, 1993. • Marion Glasscoe, ed., *The Medieval Mystical Tradition in England*, Exeter Symposium, vols. 1–5, 1980–1992. • Wolfgang Riehle, *The Middle English Mystics*, trans. Bernard Standring, 1981. • Paul Szarmach, ed., *An Introduction to the Medieval Mystics of Europe*, 1984. • A. K. Warren,

Anchorites and their Patrons in Medieval England, 1985.

Vernacular Religion and Repression • Texts. • Anne Hudson and H. L. Spencer, "Old Author, New Work: the Sermons of MS Longleat 4," *Medium Aevum* 53 (1984), pp. 231–32 [source for "Preaching and Teaching in the Vernacular"] • Jocelyn Wogan-Browne et al., eds., *The Idea of the Vernacular: An Anthology of Middle English Literary Theory, 1280–1520,* 1999 [source for "The Holy Prophet David"] • Anne Hudson, ed., *Selections from English Wycliffite Writings,* 1997 [source for several modernized texts]. • William Matthews, *Later Medieval English Prose,* 1963 [source for Mirk, *Festial*] • Michael Sargent, ed., *Nicholas Love's "Mirrour of the Blessed Lyf of Jesus Christ Oure Lord,"* 1992 [source used].

Studies. • Rita Copeland, *Pedagogy, Intellectuals, and Dissent in the Later Middle Ages,* 2001 • Anne Hudson, *The Premature Reformation: Wycliffite Texts and Lollard History,* 1988. • Anthony Kenny, *Wyclif,* 1985. • K. B. McFarlane, *Lancastrian Kings and Lollard Knights,* 1972.

King Alfred and Asser's *Life of Alfred* • Translations. • Kevin Crossley-Holland, ed., *The Anglo-Saxon World: An Anthology,* 1983. [translation used] • L. C. Jane, trans., *Asser's Life of King Alfred,* 1926. [translation used] • Simon Keynes and Michael Lapidge, trans., *Alfred the Great: Asser's Life of King Alfred and Other Contemporary Sources,* 1983.

Studies. • Alfred P. Smyth, *King Alfred the Great,* 1995. • David J. Sturdy, *Alfred the Great,* 1995. • Dorothy Whitelock, *The Genuine Asser,* 1968.

The Anglo-Saxon Chronicle • Translation. • Anne Savage, trans., *The Anglo-Saxon Chronicles,* 1982.

Study. • Stephen Morillo, ed., *The Battle of Hastings: Sources and Interpretations,* 1996.

Bede • Translation. • Bertram Colgrave and R. A. B. Mynors, eds. and trans., *Bede's Ecclesiastical History of the English People,* 1969.

Studies. • Peter Hunter Blair, *The World of Bede,* 1970. • George H. Brown, *Bede, the Venerable,* 1987. • Robert T. Farrell, ed., *Bede and Anglo-Saxon England,* 1978. • J. M. Wallace-

Hadrill, *Bede's Ecclesiastical History of the English People: A Historical Commentary,* 1993. • Benedicta Ward, *The Venerable Bede,* 1990.

Beowulf • Edition. • Frederick Klaeber, ed., *Beowulf and the Fight at Finnsburg,* rev. W. F. Bolton, 1973. [standard edition]

Translations. • Howell D. Chickering, Jr., trans., *Beowulf: A Dual-Language Edition,* 1977. • Kevin Crossley-Holland, trans., *Beowulf,* 1968. • E. T. Donaldson, trans., *Beowulf,* ed. Joseph E. Tuso, 1975. [Norton Critical Edition] • Seamus Heaney, trans. *Beowulf: A New Verse Translation,* 2000. • Alan Sullivan and Timothy Murphy, trans., *Beowulf,* 2003. [translation used]

Bibliography. • Robert J. Hasenfratz, *Beowulf Scholarship: An Annotated Bibliography, 1979–1990,* 1993.

Studies. • Peter S. Baker, *Beowulf: Basic Readings,* 1995. • Adrien Bonjour, *The Digressions in Beowulf,* 1950. • R. W. Chambers, *Beowulf: An Introduction to the Study of the Poem,* 3rd ed., suppl. C. L. Wrenn, 1959. • George Clark, *Beowulf,* 1990. • John Miles Foley, *Traditional Oral Epic: The Odyssey, Beowulf, and the Serbo-Croatian Return Song,* 1990. • Donald K. Fry, ed. *The Beowulf Poet,* 1968. • R. D. Fulk, ed., *Interpretations of Beowulf: A Critical Anthology,* 1991. • Edward B. Irving, Jr., *Rereading Beowulf,* 1989. • J. D. A. Ogilvy and Donald C. Baker, *Reading Beowulf: An Introduction to the Poem, Its Background, and Its Style,* 1983. • Gillian Overing, *Language, Sign, and Gender in Beowulf,* 1990. • Fred C. Robinson, *Beowulf and the Appositive Style,* 1985. • J. R. R. Tolkien, *Beowulf, the Monsters, and the Critics,* 1937.

Chaucer • Editions. • E. Talbot Donaldson, ed., *Chaucer's Poetry,* 1957. [edition used] • Larry D. Benson, gen. ed., *The Riverside Chaucer,* 3rd ed., 1987. [standard edition] • V. A. Kolve and Glending Olson, eds., *The Canterbury Tales: Nine Tales and the "General Prologe,"* 1989. [Norton Critical Edition] • Peter G. Beidler, ed., *Geoffrey Chaucer: "The Wife of Bath": Complete, Authoritative Text with Biographical and Historical Context, Critical History, and Essays from Five Contemporary Critical Perspectives,* 1996.

On-Line Sources. • Chaucer Metapage: http://www.unc.edu/depts/chaucer/ • Harvard

Chaucer Page: http://icg.fas.harvard.edu/ ~chaucer/ • Text with electronic glosses: http://www.librarius.com • The Wife of Bath's Portrait, from the Ellesmere Chaucer, is at http://www.huntington.org/LibraryDiv/ ChaucerPict.html

Electronic Editions. • *Chaucer: Life and Times*, CD-ROM, Primary Sources Media 1995. [with full text from *The Riverside Chaucer*; notes and glosses in pull-down windows] • Peter Robinson, ed., *The Wife of Bath's Prologue*, Cambridge University Press 1996. [challenging format, but complete survey of manuscripts]

Biographies. • Martin M. Crow and C. Olson, eds., *Chaucer Life-Records*, 1966. • Donald R. Howard, *Chaucer: His Life, His Works, His World*, 1987. • Derek Pearsall, *The Life of Geoffrey Chaucer*, 1992.

Bibliography. • "An Annotated Chaucer Bibliography," annually in *Studies in the Age of Chaucer*; most recent, for 1999, compiled and edited by Mark Allen and Bege K. Bowers, SAC 23 (2001): 615–99. • John Leyerle and Anne Quick, *Chaucer: A Bibliographical Introduction*, 1986.

Journals. • *Studies in the Age of Chaucer* • *Chaucer Review* • *Chaucer Yearbook: A Journal of Late Medieval Studies*

Handbooks and Source Collections. • Larry D. Benson and Theodore Anderson, eds., *The Literary Context of Chaucer's Fabliaux*, 1971. • Piero Boitani and Jill Mann, eds., *Cambridge Chaucer Companion*, 1986. • Robert P. Miller, ed., *Chaucer: Sources and Backgrounds*, 1977. • Beryl Rowland, ed., *Companion to Chaucer Studies*, 2nd ed., rev. 1979.

General Studies. • Susan Crane, *Gender and Romance in Chaucer's Canterbury Tales*, 1994. • Alfred David, *The Strumpet Muse: Art and Morals in Chaucer's Poetry*, 1976. • Carolyn Dinshaw, *Chaucer's Sexual Poetics*, 1989. • E. Talbot Donaldson, *Speaking of Chaucer*, 1970. • John M. Fyler, *Chaucer and Ovid*, 1979. • John Ganim, *Chaucerian Theatricality*, 1990. • Peggy Knapp, *Chaucer and the Social Contest*, 1990. • Stephen Knight, *Geoffrey Chaucer*, 1986. • V. A. Kolve, *Chaucer and the Imagery of Narrative*, 1984. • Seth Lerer, *Chaucer and His Readers: Imagining the Author in Late-Medieval England*, 1993. • A. J. Minnis, *Chaucer and Pagan Antiquity*,

1982. • Charles Muscatine, *Chaucer and the French Tradition*, 1957. • Paul A. Olson, *The Canterbury Tales and the Good Society*, 1986. • Lee Patterson, *Chaucer and the Subject of History*, 1991. • D. W. Robertson Jr., *Chaucer's London*, 1968. • D. W. Robertson Jr., *A Preface to Chaucer*, 1962. • Donald M. Rose, ed., *New Perspectives in Chaucer Criticism*, 1981. • Paul Strohm, *Social Chaucer*, 1989. • David Wallace, *Chaucerian Polity: Absolutist Lineages and Associational Forms in England and Italy*, 1997.

Studies, *Canterbury Tales*. • C. David Benson, *Chaucer's Drama of Style: Poetic Variety and Contrast in* The Canterbury Tales, 1986. • Muriel Bowden, *A Commentary on the General Prologue to* The Canterbury Tales, 1948. • Donald R. Howard, *The Idea of* The Canterbury Tales, 1976. • H. Marshall Leicester Jr., *The Disenchanted Self: Representing the Subject in* The Canterbury Tales, 1990. • Carl Lindahl, *Earnest Games: Folkloric Patterns in* The Canterbury Tales, 1987. • Jill Mann, *Chaucer and the Medieval Estates Satire*, 1973. • Paul A. Olson, *The Canterbury Tales and the Good Society*, 1986. • Winthrop Wetherbee, *Geoffrey Chaucer: The Canterbury Tales*, 1989.

Dayfydd ap Gwilym • Translations. • Rolfe Humphries, trans., *Nine Thorny Thickets: Selected Poems by Dafydd ap Gwilym in New Arrangements by Jon Roush*, 1969. [edition used] • Rachel Bromwich, trans., *Dafydd ap Gwilym: A Selection of Poems*, 1982. • Richard Morgan Loomis, trans., *Dafydd ap Gwilym: The Poems*, 1982.

Studies. • Rachel Bromwich, *Aspects of the Poetry of Dafydd ap Gwilym: Collected Papers*, 1986. • Helen Fulton, *Dafydd ap Gwilym and the European Context*, 1989.

The Dream of the Rood • Edition. • *The Dream of the Rood*, ed. Michael Swanton, 1970.

Translation. • Kevin Crossley-Holland, ed., *The Anglo-Saxon World: An Anthology*, 1983.

Studies. • Martin Irvine, "Anglo-Saxon Literary Theory Exemplified in Old English Poems: Interpreting the Cross in *The Dream of the Rood* and *Elene*," *Old English Shorter Poems*, ed. Katherine O'Brien O'Keeffe, 1994. • Rosemary Woolf, "Doctrinal Influences in *The Dream of the Rood*," *Medium Aevum*, vol. 27, 1958.

William Dunbar • Edition. • *William Dunbar: Poems*, ed. James Kinsley, 1958.

Studies. • Priscilla Bawcutt, *Dunbar the Maker*, 1992. • Edmund Reiss, *William Dunbar*, 1978. • Florence Ridley, "Studies in Dunbar and Henryson: The Present Situation," *Fifteenth-Century Studies: Recent Essays*, ed. Robert F. Yeager, 1984. • Ian Simpson Ross, *William Dunbar*, 1981.

Judith • Edition. • *Judith*, ed. B. J. Timmer, 1966.

Translation. • S. A. J. Bradley, trans., *Anglo-Saxon Poetry*, 1982.

Studies. • Karma Lochrie, "Gender, Sexual Violence, and the Politics of War in the Old English *Judith*," *Class and Gender in Early English Literature*, eds. Britton J. Harwood and Gillian Overing, 1994. • Helen Damico, "The Valkyrie Reflex in Old English Literature," *New Readings on Women in Old English Literature*, eds. Helen Damico and Alexandra Hennessey Olsen, 1990.

The Mabinogi • Translation. • Patrick Ford, trans., *The Mabinogi and Other Medieval Welsh Tales*, 1977. [translation used] • Gwyn and Thomas Jones, trans., *The Mabinogion*, 1949.

Studies. • W. J. Gruffyd, *Folklore and Myth in The Mabinogion*, 1994. • Sioned Davies, *The Four Branches of The Mabinogi*, 1993. • Proinsias MacCana, *The Mabinogi*, 1992. • Caitlin Matthews, *Mabon and the Mysteries of Britain: An Exploration of The Mabinogion*, 1987.

Sir Thomas Malory • Editions. • Thomas Malory, *Le Morte d'Arthur*, ed. Janet Cowen, intro. John Lawlor, 2 vols., 1969. • Thomas Malory, *King Arthur and his Knights: Selected Tales*, ed. E. Vinaver, 1975. [edition used] • *The Works of Sir Thomas Malory*, ed. Eugene Vinaver, 1977.

Guides and Studies. • Elizabeth Archibald and A. S. G. Edwards, *A Companion to Malory*, 1996. • Larry D. Benson, *Malory's Morte Darthur*, 1976. • Burt Dillon, *A Malory Handbook*, 1978. • P. J. C. Field, *The Life and Times of Sir Thomas Malory*, 1993. • Beverly Kennedy, *Knighthood in the Morte d'Arthur*, 1985. • Terence McCarthy, *An Introduction to Malory*, rev. ed., 1991. • William Matthews, *The Ill-Framed Knight: A Skeptical Inquiry into the Identity of Sir Thomas Malory*, 1966. • Charles Moorman, *The Book of Kyng Arthur: The Unity of Malory's Morte Darthur*, 1965. •

Felicity Riddy, *Sir Thomas Malory*, 1987. • Toshiyuki Takamiya and Derek Brewer, eds., *Aspects of Malory*, 1981. • Muriel Whitaker, *Arthur's Kingdom of Adventure: The World of Malory's Morte Darthur*, 1984.

Marie de France • Translations. • Glyn S. Burgess and Keith Busby, trans., *The Lais of Marie de France*, 1986. • Robert Hanning and Joan Ferrante, *The Lais of Marie de France*, 1978. [translation used]

Bibliography. • Glyn S. Burgess, *Marie de France: An Analytical Bibliography*, 1977; suppl. no. 1, 1986.

Studies. • Margaret M. Boland, *Architectural Structure in the Lais of Marie de France*, 1995. • Glyn S. Burgess, *The Lais of Marie de France: Text and Context*, 1987. • Paula M. Clifford, *Marie de France, Lais*, 1982. • Emanuel J. Mickel, *Marie de France*, 1974.

Middle English Lyrics • Editions. • Maxwell S. Luria and Richard L. Hoffman, eds., *Middle English Lyrics*, 1974. [Norton Critical Edition; edition used] • R. T. Davies, *Medieval English Lyrics: A Critical Anthology*, 1963. [edition used] • Theodore Silverstein, ed., *English Lyrics Before 1500*, 1971. • Celia Sisam and Kenneth Sisam, eds., *The Oxford Book of Medieval English Verse*, 1970.

Translations. • Frederick Goldin, trans., *The Lyrics of the Troubadours and Trouvères: Original Texts, with Translations and Introductions*, 1973. • James J. Wilhelm, *Lyrics of the Middle Ages: An Anthology*, 1990.

Studies. • Peter Dronke, *The Medieval Lyric*, 3rd ed., 1996. • Douglas Gray, *Themes and Images in the Medieval English Religious Lyric*, 1972. • David L. Jeffrey, *The Early English Lyric and Franciscan Spirituality*, 1975. • John F. Plummer, ed., *Vox Feminae: Studies in Medieval Woman's Song*, 1981. • Rosemary Woolf, *The English Religious Lyric in the Middle Ages*, 1968.

Ohthere's Journey • Translation and Study. • Niels Lund, ed., and Christine Fell, trans., *Two Voyagers at the Court of King Alfred: The Ventures of Ohthere and Wulfstan*, 1984.

Second Play of the Shepherds • Editions. • Peter Happé, *English Mystery Plays: A Selection*,

1975. [edition used] • David Bevington, ed., *Medieval Drama*, 1975. • Martin Stevens and A. C. Cawley, eds., *The Townley Plays*, 2 vols., 1994.

Bibliography. • Sidney E. Berger, ed., *Medieval English Drama: An Annotated Bibliography of Recent Criticism*, 1990.

Studies and Guides. • Richard Beadle, ed., *The Cambridge Companion to Medieval English Theatre*, 1994. • Richard K. Emmerson, ed., and V. A. Kolve, intro., *Approaches to Teaching Medieval English Drama*, 1990. • O. B. Hardison Jr., *Christian Rite and Christian Drama in the Middle Ages*, 1965. • V. A. Kolve, *The Play Called Corpus Christi*, 1966. • Martin Stevens, *Four Middle English Mystery Cycles: Textual, Contextual, and Critical Interpretations*, 1987.

Sir Gawain and the Green Knight • Translations. • J. R. R. Tolkien, trans., *Sir Gawain and the Green Knight*, 1965. [translation used] • W. R. J. Barron, ed. and trans., *Sir Gawain and the Green Knight*, 1974.

Bibliography. • Malcolm Andrew, *The Gawain-Poet: An Annotated Bibliography, 1839–1977*, 1979.

Guides and Studies. • Ross Arthur, *Medieval Sign Theory and Sir Gawain and the Green Knight*, 1987. • Larry D. Benson, *Art and Tradition in Sir Gawain and the Green Knight*, 1965. • Robert J. Blanch et al., eds., *Text and Matter: New Critical Perspectives of the Pearl-Poet*, 1991. • Robert J. Blanch and Julian Wasserman, *From Pearl to Gawain: Forme to Fynisment*, 1995. • Marie Borroff, *Sir Gawain and the Green Knight: A Stylistic and Metrical Study*, 1973. • Derek Brewer and Jonathan Gibson, eds., *A Companion to the Gawain-Poet*, 1997. • Elisabeth Brewer, comp., *Sir Gawain and the Green Knight: Sources and Analogues*, 1992. • John Burrow, *A Reading of Sir Gawain and the Green Knight*, 1966. • Wendy Clein, *Concepts of Chivalry in Sir Gawain and the Green Knight*, 1987. • Lynn Staley Johnson, *The Voice of the Gawain-Poet*, 1984. • Sandra Pierson Prior, *The Pearl Poet Revisited*, 1994. • Ad Putter, *An Introduction to the Gawain-Poet*, 1996. • Allen Shoaf, *The Poem as Green Girdle: Commercium in Sir Gawain and the Green Knight*, 1984. • A. C. Spearing, *The Gawain-Poet: a Critical Study*,

1970. • Meg Stainsby, *Sir Gawain and the Green Knight: An Annotated Bibliography, 1978–1989*, 1992.

Taliesin • Translation. • Ifor and J. Caerwyn Williams, trans., *The Poems of Taliesin*, 1968.

Study. • J. E. Caerwyn Williams, *The Poets of the Welsh Princes*, 1994.

The Wanderer • Editions. • T. P. Dunning and A. J. Bliss, eds., *The Wanderer*, 1969. • Anne L. Klinck, *The Old English Elegies: A Critical Edition and Genre Study*, 1992.

Translation. • Kevin Crossley-Holland, ed., *The Anglo-Saxon World: An Anthology*, 1983.

Study. • Martin Green, ed., *The Old English Elegies: New Essays in Criticism and Research*, 1983.

The Wife's Lament • Edition. • Anne L. Klinck, *The Old English Elegies: A Critical Edition and Genre Study*, 1992.

Translation. • Kevin Crossley-Holland, ed., *The Anglo-Saxon World: An Anthology*, 1983.

Studies. • Helen T. Bennett, "Exile and the Semiosis of Gender in Old English Elegies," *Class and Gender in Early English Literature*, eds. Britton J. Harwood and Gillian Overing, 1994. • Barrie Ruth Strauss, "Women's Words as Weapons in *The Wife's Lament*," *Old English Shorter Poems*, ed. Katharine O'Brien O'Keeffe, 1994.

Wulf and Eadwacer • Edition. • Anne L. Klinck, *The Old English Elegies: A Critical Edition and Genre Study*, 1992.

Translation. • Kevin Crossley-Holland, ed., *The Anglo-Saxon World: An Anthology*, 1983.

Studies. • Helen T. Bennett, "Exile and the Semiosis of Gender in Old English Elegies" *Class and Gender in Early English Literature*, ed. Britton J. Harwood and Gillian Overing, 1994. • Pat Bellanoff, "Women's Songs, Women's Language: *Wulf and Eadwacer* and *The Wife's Lament*," *New Readings on Women in Old English Literature*, eds. Helen Damico and Alexandra Hennessey Olsen, 1990. • Marilyn Desmond, "The Voice of Exile: Feminist Literary History and the Anonymous Anglo-Saxon Elegy," *Critical Inquiry*, vol. 16, 1990.

The Early Modern Period

Bibliographies • *English Literary Renaissance*, 1971 to present. • Alfred Harbage, ed., S. Schoenbaum, rev., *Annals of English Drama, 975–1700*, 3 vols. • *New Cambridge Bibliography of English Literature, 600–1600*, 1969. • S. A. and D. R. Tannenbaum, eds., *Elizabethan Bibliographies*, 10 vols., 1967.

Guides to Research • A. R. Braunmuller and Michael Hattaway, *The Cambridge Companion to English Renaissance Drama*, 1990. • Douglas Bush, *English Literature in the Earlier Seventeenth Century 1600–1660*, 1962. • C. S. Lewis, *English Literature in the Sixteenth Century*, 1954. • A. W. Ward and A. R. Waller, eds., *The Cambridge History of English Literature*, 15 vols., vols. 3–6, 1909. Steven N. Zwicker, ed. *The Cambridge Companion to English Literature, 1650–1740*, 1998.

Drama, Poetry, and Prose • David Bevington, *Tudor Drama and Politics*, 1968. • Rebecca Bushnell, *Tragedies of Tyrants*, 1990. Karen Cunningham, *Imaginary Betrayals: Subjectivity and the Discourses of Treason in Early Modern England*, 2002. Heather Dubrow, *Echoes of Desire: English Petrarchanism and Its Counterdiscourses*, 1995. • Jonathan Dollimore, *Radical Tragedy. Religion, Ideology and Power in the Drama of Shakespeare and His Contemporaries*, 1985. • Martin Elsky, *Authorizing Words: Speech, Writing and Print in the Renaissance*, 1989. • Anne Ferry, *"The Inward Language": Sonnets of Wyatt, Sidney, Shakespeare and Donne*, 1983. • Ernest B. Gilman, *Iconoclasm and Poetry in the English Reformation*, 1986. • Stephen Greenblatt, *Renaissance Self-Fashioning*, 1980. • Thomas M. Greene, *The Light in Troy: Imitation and Discovery in Renaissance Poetry*, 1982. • Andrew Gurr, *Playgoing in Shakespeare's London*, 1987. Andrew Hadfield, *Literature, Politics, and National Identity: Reformation to Renaissance*, 1994. Elizabeth Hanson, *Discovering The Subject in Renaissance England*, 1998. • Peter Herman, ed., *Rethinking the Henrician Age: Essays on Early Tudor Texts and Contexts*, 1994. John King, *English Reformation Literature: The Tudor Origins of the Protestant Tradition*, 1982. Claire McEachern, *The Poetics of English Nationhood 1590–1612*, 1996. • Janel Mueller, *The Native Tongue and the Word: Developments in English Prose Style, 1380–1580*, 1984. • Steven Mullaney, *The Place of the Stage: License, Place and Power in*

Renaissance England, 1988. • David Norbrook, *Poetry and Politics in the English Renaissance*, 1984. Michael O'Connell, *The Idolatrous Eye: Iconoclasm and Theater in Renaissance England*, 2000. • Stephen Orgel, *The Illusion of Power: Political Theater in the English Renaissance*, 1971. • Patricia Parker, *Inescapable Romance*, 1979. • David Quint, *Epic and Empire*, 1993. • Wayne Rebhorn, *The Emperor of Men's Minds: Literature and the Renaissance Discourse of Rhetoric*, 1995. • Kevin Sharpe, *Reading Revolutions: The Politics of Reading in Early Modern England*, 2000. • Rosemund Tuve, *Elizabethan and Metaphysical Imagery*, 1947. • R. S. White, *Natural Law in English Renaissance Literature*, 1996. • Luke Wilson, *Theaters of Intention: Drama and the Law in Early Modern England*, 2000.

History, Religion, and Political Thought • Sharon Achinstein, *Milton and the Revolutionary Reader*, 1994. • Brandon Bradshaw and Peter Roberts, eds., *British Consciousness and Identity*, 1998. • Glenn Burgess, *Absolute Monarchy and the Stuart Constitution*, 1996. • Cyndia Clegg, *Press Censorship in Elizabethan England*, 1997. • ———, *Press Censorship in Jacobean England*, 2001. • Patrick Collinson, *The Elizabethan Puritan Movement*, 1967. • John Guy, *Tudor England*, 1988. • Richard Helgerson, *Forms of Nationhood: The Elizabethan Writing of England*, 1992. • E. J. Levy, *Tudor Historical Thought*, 1967. • Lawrence Manley, *Literature and Culture in Early Modern London*, 1995. • David Norbrook, *Writing the English Republic: Poetry Rhetoric, Politics 1627–1660*, 1999. • Annabel Patterson, *Reading Holinshed's Cronicles*, 1994. • Linda Levy Peck, ed., *The Mental World of the Jacobean Court*, 1991. • Conrad Russell, *The Crisis of Parliaments: English History 1509–1660*, 1971. • Quentin Skinner, *The Foundations of Modern Political Thought*, 2 vols., 1978. • J. P. Sommerville, *Politics and Ideology in England, 1608–1640*, 1986. • Debora Shuger, *The Renaissance Bible: Scholarship, Sacrifice, and Subjectivity*, 1994. • D. W. Woolf, *The Idea of History in Early Stuart England*, 1990.

Humanism • Douglas Bush, *The Renaissance and English Humanism*, 1939. • Kathy Eden, *Hermeneutics and the Rhetorical Tradition: Chapters in the Ancient Legacy and Its Humanist Reception*, 1997. • William Kerrigan and Gordon Braden, *The Idea of the Renaissance*, 1989. • Arthur

Kinney, *Humanist Poetics*, 1986. • Charles Schmitt and Quentin Skinner, eds., *The Cambridge History of Renaissance Philosophy*, 1988.

Science and Exploration • David Cressy, *Coming Over: Migration and Communication between England and New England in the Seventeenth Century*, 1987. • Stephen Greenblatt, *Marvelous Possessions: The Wonder of the New World*, 1991. • Stephen Greenblatt, ed., *New World Encounters*, 1993. • Jeffrey Knapp, *An Empire Nowhere: England, America, and Literature from Utopia to The Tempest*, 1995. • Thomas Laqueur, *Making Sex: Body and Gender from the Greeks to Freud*, 1990. • Frank Lestrigant, *Mapping the Renaissance World*, 1991. • Wayne Shumaker, *The Occult Sciences in the Renaissance*, 1972. • Nancy G. Siraisi, *Medieval and Early Renaissance Science*, 1990. • Keith Thomas, *Religion and the Decline of Magic*, 1971. • Michael Witmore, *Culture of Accidents: Unexpected Knowledge in Early Modern England*, 2001.

Social Settings and Gender Roles • Susan Dwyer Amussen, *An Ordered Society: Gender and Class in Early Modern England*, 1988. • Elaine V. Beilin, *Redeeming Eve: Women Writers of the English Renaissance*, 1987. • Alan Bray, *Homosexuality in Renaissance England*, 1982. • Anthony Fletcher, *Gender, Sex, and Subordination in England, 1500–1800*, 1995. • Kim F. Hall, *Things of Darkness: Economies of Race and Gender in Early Modern England*, 1995. • Margo Hendricks and Patricia Parker, eds., *Women, "Race" and Writing in the Early Modern Period*, 1994. • Daniel Javitch, *Poetry and Courtliness in Renaissance England*, 1976. • Constance Jordan, *Renaissance Feminism: Literary Texts and Political Models*, 1990. • Peter Laslett, *The World We Have Lost—Further Explored*, 1983. • Barbara Kiefer Lewalski, *Writing Women in Jacobean England*, 1993. • Ian Maclean, *The Renaissance Notion of Woman*, 1980. • Lawrence Manley, *Literature and Culture in Early Modern London*, 1995. • Steve Rappaport, *Worlds within Worlds: Structures of Life in Sixteenth-Century London*, 1989. • Mary Beth Rose, *Gender and Heroism in Early Modern English Literature*, 2002. • Bruce R. Smith, *Homosexual Desire in Shakespeare's England: A Cultural Poetics*, 1991. • Eve Sanders, *Gender and Literacy on Stage in Early Modern England*, 1998. • Lawrence Stone, *The Family, Sex, and Marriage, 1500–1800*, 1965. • Linda Woodbridge, *Women and the English Renaissance: Literature and the Nature of Womankind, 1540–1640*, 1984.

Perspectives: The Civil War, or the Wars of Three Kingdoms • Texts. • Thomas Carlyle, ed., *Oliver Cromwell's Letters and Speeches: With Elucidations*, 2 vols., 1904. • Pádraig De Brún, Breandán Ó Buachalla, and Tomás Ó Concheanainn, eds., *Nua-Dhuanaire*, vol. 1., 1971. • "John O'Dwyer of the Glenn" in *Irish Mistrelsy or the Bardic Remains of Ireland*, ed. James Hardiman, 2 vols., 1831. • Philip A. Knachel, ed., *Eikon Basilike*, 1966. • John Lilburne, *Englands New Chains Discoverd. The Leveller Tracts, 1647–1653*, ed. Godfrey Davies Haller, 1944. • W. Dunn Macray, ed., *History of the Rebellion and Civil Wars in England: Begun in the Year 1641 by Edward, Earl of Clarendon*, 1888. • "The Petition of the Gentlewomen and Tradesmen's Wives" in *English Women's Voices 1540–1700*, ed. Charlotte F. Otten, 1992.

Criticism and History. • Martyn Bennett, *The Civil Wars in Britain and Ireland: 1638–1651*, 1997. • Martyn Bennett, *The English Civil War: 1640–1649*, 1995. • Christopher Hill, *The World Turned Upside Down: Radical Ideas During the English Revolution*, 1972. • Jane Ohlmeyer, ed., *Ireland from Independence to Occupation, 1641–1660*, 1995. • Nigel Smith, *Literature and Revolution in England, 1640–1660*, 1994. • Keith Thomas, "Women and the Civil War Sects," *Past and Present*, 1958.

Perspectives: Government and Self-Government • Editions. • Roger Ascham, *The Schoolmaster*, 1570, ed. Lawrence Ryan. • Baldassare Castiglione, *The Book of the Courtier*, trans. Sir Thomas Hoby, 1966. • Sir Thomas Elyot, *The Book Named the Governor*, ed. S. E. Lehmberg, 1963. • Sir Thomas Elyot, *The Defence of Good Women*, ed. Edwin Johnson Howard, 1940. • John Foxe, *The Acts and Monuments of John Foxe*, ed. Stephen Cattley, 8 vols., 1843–1847, repr. 1965. • Richard Hooker, *The Folger Library Edition of the Works of Richard Hooker*, ed. W. Speed Hill, 8 vols., 1977. • James VI and I, *Political Writings*, ed. Johann P. Sommerville, 1994. • Richard Mulcaster, *Elementarie*, ed. E. T. Compagnac, 1925. • Thomas Russell, ed., *The Works of the English Reformers: William Tyndale and John Frith*, 3 vols., 1831. • Juan Luis Vives, *The Instruction of a Christen Woman*, trans. Richard Hyrde, 1540.

Perspectives: Tracts on Women and Gender • Editions. • Desiderius Erasmus, *A Ryght Frutefull Epistle Devised in Laude and Praise of Matrimony*, trans. Richard Tavernour, 1534. • Haec

Vir: Or, The Womanish Man, 1620. • *Hic Mulier: Or The Man-Woman,* 1620. • Barbara Kiefer Lewalski, ed., *The Polemics and Poems of Rachel Speght,* 1996. • Randall Martin, *Women Writers in Renaissance England,* 1997. • Charlotte F. Otten, ed., *English Women's Voices, 1540–1700,* 1992. • Barnabe Riche, *My Ladies Looking-Glasse,* 1616. • Simon Shepherd, ed., *The Women's Sharp Revenge: Five Women's Pamphlets from the Renaissance,* 1985. • Esther Soweram, *Ester Hath Hang'd Haman,* 1617. • Rachel Speght, *A Mouzell for Melastomus,* 1617. • Joseph Swetnam, *The Araignment of Lewde, Idle, Froward, and Unconstant Women,* 1615. • Betty Travitsky, ed., *The Paradise of Women: Writings by Englishwomen of the Renaissance,* 1981. • Margaret Tyler, *The Mirrour of Princely Deedes and Knighthood, Book I,* 1578.

Criticism. • Elaine Beilin, *Redeeming Eve: Women Writers of the English Renaissance,* 1987. • Ann Rosalind Jones, "Counterattacks on 'the Bayter of Women': Three Pamphleteers of the Early Seventeenth Century," in *The Renaissance Englishwoman in Print,* eds. Anne Hazelcorn and Betty Travitsky, 1990. • Constance Jordan, *Renaissance Feminism: Literary Texts and Political Models,* 1990. • Barbara Kiefer Lewalski, *Writing Women in Jacobean England,* 1993. • R. Valerie Lucas, "Hic Mulier: The Female Transvestite in Early Modern England," *Renaissance and Reformation,* vol. XXIV, no. 1, 1988. • Megan Matchinske, "Legislating 'Middle-Class' Morality in the Marriage Market: Ester Sowernam's, *Ester Hath Hang'd Haman,*" *English Literary Renaissance,* vol. 24, no. 1, 1994. • Linda Woodbridge, *Women and the English Renaissance: Literature and the Nature of Womankind, 1540–1620,* 1986.

John Donne • Editions. • John Carey, ed., *John Donne: Selected Poetry,* 1996. • Helen Gardner, ed., *John Donne: The Divine Poems,* 1952. • Helen Gardner, ed., *John Donne: The Elegies and The Songs and Sonnets,* 1965. • H. J. C. Grierson, ed., *The Poems of John Donne,* 1912. • G. R. Peter and Evelyn Simpson, eds., *Sermons,* 10 vols., 1953–1962. • Neil Rhodes, ed., *Prose Works: Selections,* 1987. • A. J. Smith, ed., *John Donne: The Complete English Poems,* 1971. • Gary A. Stringer, ed., *The Variorum Edition of the Poetry of John Donne,* 1995.

Biography. • R. C. Bald, *John Donne: A Life.* 1970. • John Carey, *John Donne: Life, Mind and Art,* 1981. • Izaac Walton, *Life of Dr. John Donne,* ed. G. Saintsbury, 1927. • Frank J. Warnke, *John Donne,* 1987.

Criticism. • James S. Baumlin, *John Donne and the Rhetorics of Renaissance Discourse,* 1991. • Harold Bloom, ed., *John Donne and the Seventeenth-Century Metaphysical Poets,* 1986. • Cleanth Brooks, *The Well Wrought Urn,* 1949. • Meg Lotta Brown, *Donne and the Politics of Conscience,* 1995. • Naresh Chandra, *John Donne and Metaphysical Poetry,* 1990. • Denis Flynn, *John Donne and the Ancient Catholic Nobility,* 1995. • T. S. Eliot, *The Varieties of Metaphysical Poetry,* ed. Ronald Schuchard, 1993. • Barbara L. Estrin, *Laura: Uncovering Gender and Genre in Wyatt, Donne, and Marvell,* 1994. • Pierre Legouis, *Donne the Craftsman,* 1928. • Arthur F. Marotti, ed., *Critical Essays on John Donne,* 1994. • Arthur Marotti, *John Donne, a Coterie Poet,* 1986. • Murray Roston, *The Soul of Wit,* 1974. • A. J. Smith, ed., *John Donne: The Critical Heritage,* 1975–1996. • A. J. Smith, ed., *John Donne: Essays in Celebration,* 1972. • Helen Wilcox, Richard Todd, and Alasdair MacDonald, eds., *Sacred and Profane: Secular and Devotional Interplay in Early Modern British Literature,* 1996. • William Zunder, *The Poetry of John Donne: Literature and Culture in the Elizabethan and Jacobean Period,* 1982.

Our Texts. • Helen Gardner, ed., *John Donne: The Divine Poems,* 1952. • H. J. C. Grierson, ed., *The Poems of John Donne,* 1912. • G. R. Peter and Evelyn Simpson, eds., *Sermons,* 10 vols., 1953–1962. • J. Sparrow, ed., *Devotions Upon Emergent Occasions,* 1923.

Queen Elizabeth I • Editions. • Leicester Bradner, ed., *The Poems of Elizabeth I,* 1964. • Leah S. Marcus, Janel Mueller, and Mary Beth Rose, ed., *Elizabeth I: Collected Works,* 2000. • Caroline Pemberton, ed., *Queen Elizabeth's Englishings of Boethius,* De Consolatione Philosophiae, A.D. 1593, 1889, repr. 1973.

Biography. • Christopher Haigh, *Elizabeth I,* 1988. • Christopher Hibbert, *Elizabeth I: Genius of the Golden Age,* 1991. • Wallace MacCaffrey, *Elizabeth I,* 1993. • J. E. Neale, *Queen Elizabeth I,* 1934. • Maria Perry, *The Word of a Prince: The Life of Elizabeth from Contemporary Documents,* 1990.

Criticism. • Marie Axton, *The Queen's Two Bodies: Drama and Elizabethan Succession,* 1977. • Philippa Berry, *Of Chastity and Power: Elizabethan Literature and the Unmarried*

Queen, 1989. • Susan Frye, *Elizabeth I: The Competition for Representation*, 1993. • Helen Hackett, *Virgin Mother, Maiden Queen: Elizabeth I and the Cult of the Virgin Mary*, 1995. • Lisa Hopkins, *Queen Elizabeth and Her Court*, 1990. • J. E. Neale, *Elizabeth and Her Parliaments*, 2 vols., 1953 • Frances Yates, *Astraea: The Imperial Theme*, 1973.

Edmund Spenser • Editions. • Edwin A. Greenlaw et al., eds., *The Works of Edmund Spenser, a Variorum Edition*, 10 vols., 1932–1949. • Andrew Hadfield, ed., *The Cambridge Companion to Spenser*, 2001. • A. C. Hamilton, ed., *The Faerie Queene*, 1980. • William Oram et al., eds., *The Yale Edition of the Shorter Poems of Edmund Spenser*, 1989. • Thomas P. Roche, Jr. and C. Patrick O'Donell, eds., *Edmund Spenser: The Faerie Queene*, 1981. • J. C. Smith and E. De Selincourt, eds., *Complete Poetical Works*, 1970.

Biography. • Judith H. Anderson, Donald Cheney, and David A. Richardson, eds., *Spenser's Life and the Subject of Biography*, 1996. • Patrick Cheney, *Spenser's Famous Flight: A Renaissance Idea of a Literary Career*, 1993. • Richard Rambuss, *Spenser's Secret Career*, 1993.

Criticism. • Paul Alpers, *The Poetry of* The Faerie Queene, 1967. • Harry Berger, *The Allegorical Temper*, 1957. • Harry Berger, *Revisionary Play: Studies in the Spenserian Dynamics*, 1988. • Sheila Cavanagh, *Wanton Eyes and Chaste Desires*, 1994. • Patricia Coughlan, ed., *Spenser and Ireland: An Interdisciplinary Perspective*, 1989. • Jonathan Goldberg, *Endlesse Worke: Spenser and the Structures of Discourse*, 1981. • Kenneth Gross, *Spenserian Poetics: Idolatry, Iconoclasm, and Magic*, 1985. • John Guillory, *Poetic Authority: Spenser, Milton, and Literary History*, 1983. • Andrew Hadfield, *Edmund Spenser's Irish Experience*, 1997. • A. C. Hamilton, *The Spenser Encyclopedia*, 1990. • John N. King, *Spenser's Poetry and the Reformation Tradition*, 1990. • Theresa M. Krier, *Gazing on Secret Sights: Spenser, Classical Imitation, and the Decorums of Vision*, 1990. • Isabel G. MacCaffrey, *Spenser's Allegory: The Anatomy of the Imagination*, 1976. • David Lee Miller, *The Poem's Two Bodies: The Poetics of the 1590 Faerie Queene*, 1988. • James Nohrnberg, *The Analogy of* The Faerie Queene, 1976. • Thomas P. Roche, Jr., *The Kindly Flame: A Study of the Third and Fourth Books of Spenser's* Faerie Queene, 1964. • John Rooks, *Love's Courtly Ethic in* The Faerie Queene: *From Garden to Wilderness*, 1992. • David R. Shore,

Spenser and the Poetics of Pastoral, 1985. • Susan Snyder, *Pastoral Process: Spenser, Marvell, Milton*, 1998. • John Watkins, *The Spectre of Dido: Spenser and Virgilian epic*, 1995. • Kathleen Williams, *Spenser's World of Glass: A Reading of* The Faerie Queene, 1966.

George Herbert • Editions. • Mario Di Cesare, ed., *George Herbert and the Seventeenth-Century Religious Poets*, 1978. • F. E. Hutchinson, ed., *The Works of George Herbert*, 1941. • C. A. Patrides, ed., *The English Poems of George Herbert*, 1974.

Biography. • Amy M. Charles, *Life of George Herbert*, 1977. • Stanley Stewart, *George Herbert*, 1986.

Criticism. • Stanley Fish, *The Living Temple: George Herbert and Catechizing*, 1978. • Barbara Leah Harman, *Costly Monuments: Representations of the Self in George Herbert's Poetry*, 1982. • Seamus Heaney, *The Redress of Poetry*, 1990. • Christopher Hodgkins, *Authority, Church, and Society in George Herbert: Return to the Middle Way*, 1993 • C. A. Patrides, ed., *George Herbert: The Critical Heritage*, 1983. • Terry Sherwood, *Herbert's Prayerful Art*, 1989. • Marion White Singleton, *God's Courtier: Configuring a Different Grace in George Herbert's Temple*, 1987. • J. H. Summers, *George Herbert: His Religion and Art*, 1954. • Rosemond Tuve, *A Reading of George Herbert*, 1952. • Helen Vendler, *The Poetry of George Herbert*, 1975.

Robert Herrick • Editions. • L. C. Martin, ed., *Poetical Works*, 1956. • J. Max Patrick, ed., *Complete Poetry*, 1963.

Biography. • Roger B. Rollin, *Robert Herrick*, 1966. • George Walton Scott, *Robert Herrick*, 1974.

Criticism. • Robert Deming, *Ceremony and Art*, 1974. • A. Leigh Deneef, *"This Poetick Liturgy": Robert Herrick's Ceremonial Mode*, 1974. • Leah Marcus, *The Politics of Mirth: Jonson, Herrick, Milton, Marvell, and the Defense of Old Holiday Pastimes*, 1986. • Roger B. Rollin and J. Max Patrick, eds., *"Trust To Good Verses": Herrick Tercentenary Essays*, 1978. • L. E. Semler, "Robert Herrick, the Human Figure, and the English Mannerist Aesthetic," *Studies in English Literature*, vol. 35, no. 1 (Winter), 1995.

Ben Jonson • Editions. • Robert Adams, ed., *Ben Jonson's Plays and Masques*, 1979. • Ian Donaldson, ed., *Ben Jonson*, 1985. • C. H. Herford,

Percy Simspon, and Evelyn Simpson, eds., *The Works of Ben Jonson*, 11 vols., 1925–1952. • Stephen Orgel, ed., *Complete Masques*, 1969. • Helen Ostovich, ed., *Jonson, Four Comedies*, 1997.

Biography. • David Riggs, *Ben Jonson: A Life*, 1989. • George E. Rowe, *Distinguishing Jonson*, 1988.

Criticism. • Richard Burt, *Licensed by Authority: Ben Jonson and the Discourses of Censorship*, 1993. • Ian Donaldson, *The World Upside Down*, 1970. • Jonathan Haynes, *The Social Relations of Jonson's Theater*, 1992. • Richard Helgerson, *Self-Crowned Laureates*, 1983. • James Hirsh, ed., *New Perspectives on Ben Jonson*, 1997. • G. B. Jackson, *Vision and Judgment in Ben Jonson's Drama*, 1968. • Alexander Leggatt, *Ben Jonson, His Vision and His Art*, 1981. • Katharine Eisaman Maus, *Ben Jonson and the Roman Frame of Mind*, 1984. • David C. McPherson, *Shakespeare, Jonson and the Myth of Venice*, 1990. • Rosalind Miles, *Ben Jonson, His Craft and Art*, 1990. • Stephen Orgel, *The Jonsonian Masque*, 1965. • Stephen Orgel and Roy Strong, *Inigo Jones: The Theatre of the Stuart Court*, 1973. • E. B. Patridge, *The Broken Compass*, 1958. • William W. E. Slights, *Ben Jonson and the Art of Secrecy*, 1994. John Gordon Sweeney, *Jonson and the Psychology of the Public Theater*, 1985. • Robert N. Watson, *Ben Jonson's Parodic Strategy*, 1987. • Don E. Wayne, *Penshurst: The Semiotics of Place and the Poetics of History*, 1984.

Our Text. • C. H. Herford, Percy Simspon, and Eveyln Simpson, eds., *The Works of Ben Jonson*, 11 vols., 1925–1952.

Aemilia Lanyer • Editions. • A. L. Rowse, ed., *The Poems of Shakespeare's Dark Lady: Salve Deus Rex Judaeorum*, 1979. • Susanne Woods, ed., *The Poems of Aemilia Lanyer: Salve Deus Rex Judaeorum*, 1993.

Criticism. • Barbara Kiefer Lewalski, *Writing Women in Jacobean England*, 1993. • Lisa Schnell, "'So Great a Diffrence Is There in Degree': Aemilia Lanyer and the Aims of Feminist Criticism," *Modern Language Quarterly*, vol. 57, no. 1, 1996.

Andrew Marvell • Editions. • Elizabeth Story Donno, ed., *The Complete Poems*, 1985. • Frank Kermode and Keith Walker, eds., *Poems. Selections*, 1994. • M. Margoliouth, ed., *Poems and Letters*, 1927, rev. Pierre Legouis and E. E. Duncan-Jones, 1971.

Biography. • John Dixon Hunt, *Andrew Marvell: His Life and Writings*, 1978. • Patsy Griffin, *The Modest Ambition of Andrew Marvell: A Study of Marvell and His Relation to Lovelace, Fairfax, Cromwell, and Milton*, 1995. • Thomas Wheeler, *Andrew Marvell Revisited*, 1996.

Criticism. • Philip Brockbank, *Approaches to Marvell*, ed. C. A. Patrides, 1978. • Warren L. Chernaik, *The Poet's Time: Politics and Religion in the Work of Andrew Marvell*, 1983. • Rosalie Colie, *My Echoing Song*, 1970. • Conal Condren and A. D. Cousins, eds., *The Political Identity of Andrew Marvell*, 1990. • Patrick Cullen, *Spenser, Marvell, and Renaissance Pastoral*, 1970. • E. S. Donno, ed., *Andrew Marvell: The Critical Heritage*, 1978. • Annabel Patterson, *Marvell and the Civic Crown*, 1978. • Allan Pritchard, "Marvell's 'The Garden': A Restoration Poem?" *Studies in English Literature*, vol. 23, no. 3 (Summer), 1983. • Robert Wilcher, *Andrew Marvell*, 1985.

Our Text. • M. Margoliouth, ed., *Poems and Letters*, 1927.

Christopher Marlowe • Editions. • David Bevington and Eric Rasmussen, eds., *Doctor Faustus A-and B-Texts (1604, 1616): Christopher Marlowe and his Collaborator and Revisers*, 1993. • Fredson Bowers, *The Complete Works of Christopher Marlowe*, 2 vols., 1981. • Stephen Orgel, *The Complete Poems and Translations of Christopher Marlowe*, 1971.

Biography. • John Bakeless, *The Tragicall History of Christopher Marlowe*, 2 vols., 1942. • Charles Nicholl, *The Reckoning: The Murder of Christopher Marlowe*, 1992.

Criticism. • C. L. Barber, *Creating Elizabethan Tragedy: The Theater of Marlowe and Kyd*, 1988. • Douglas Cole, *Suffering and Evil in the Plays of Christopher Marlowe*, 1962. • Roma Gill, *The Plays of Christopher Marlowe*, 1971. • Darryll Grantley and Peter Roberts, eds., *Christopher Marlowe and English Renaissance Culture*, 1996. • Clark Hulse, *Metamorphic Verse: The Elizabethan Minor Epic*, 1981. • William Keach, *Elizabethan Erotic Narratives*, 1977. • Harry Levin, *The Overreacher: A Study of Christopher Marlowe*, 1952. • Simon Shepherd, *Marlowe and the Politics of Elizabethan Theater*, 1986. • Vivien Thomas and William Tydeman, eds., *Christopher Marlowe: The Plays and Their Sources*, 1994.

John Milton • Editions. • John Carey and Alastair Fowler, eds., *The Poems of John Milton*,

1968. • Alastair Fowler, ed., *John Milton: Paradise Lost*, 1968. • Merritt Y. Hughes, ed., *Complete Poetry and Major Prose*, 1957. • C. A. Patrides, ed., *John Milton: Selected Prose*, 1985. • F. A. Patterson et al., eds., *The Works of John Milton*, 1931–1938. • Don M. Wolfe, ed., *The Complete Prose Works of John Milton*, 1953–1982.

Biography. • Douglas Bush, *John Milton*, 1964. • Joseph M. French, *The Life Records of John Milton*, 1949–1958. • W. R. Parker, *Milton: A Biography*, 1968. • A. N. Wilson, *The Life of John Milton*, 1983.

Criticism. • Arthur Barker, *Milton and the Puritan Dilemma, 1641–1660*, 1942. • Joan S. Bennett, *Reviving Liberty: Radical Christian Humanism in Milton's Great Poems*, 1989. • Lana Cable, *Carnal Rhetoric: Milton's Iconoclasm and the Poetics of Desire*, 1995. • Dennis Danielson, ed., *The Cambridge Companion to Milton*, 1989. • Mario Di Cesare, ed., *Milton in Italy*, 1991. • William Empson, *Milton's God*, 1965. • Stanley Fish, *Surprised by Sin: The Argument of* Paradise Lost, 1971. • Christopher Hill, *Milton and the English Revolution*, 1977. • Frank Kermode, *The Living Milton*, 1960. • Barbara K. Lewalski, Paradise Lost *and the Rhetoric of Literary Forms*, 1985. • C. S. Lewis, *A Preface to* Paradise Lost, 1942. • David Lowenstein and James Grantham Turner, *Politics, Poetics, and Hermeneutics in Milton's Prose*, 1990. • Kristin McColgan and Charles Durham, eds., *Arenas of Conflict: Milton and the Unfettered Mind*, 1996. • Marjorie Nicolson, *John Milton: A Reader's Guide to His Poetry*, 1963. • Mary Nyquist and Margaret Ferguson, eds., *Remembering Milton: Essays on the Texts and Traditions*, 1988. • W. R. Parker, *Milton's Debt to Greek Tragedy in Samson Agonistes*, 1937. • Annabel Patterson, ed., *John Milton*, 1992. • Maureen Quilligan, *Milton's Spenser: The Politics of Reading*, 1983. • Mary Ann Radzinowicz, *Toward Samson Agonistes*, 1978. • B. Rajan, *Paradise Lost and the Seventeenth-Century Reader*, 1962. • John Rogers, *The Matter of Revolution: Science, Poetry and Politics in the Age of Milton*, 1996. • John P. Rumrich, *Milton Unbound: Controversy and Reinterpretation*, 1996. • John T. Shawcross, *John Milton: The Self and the World*, 1993. • John Steadman, *Epic and Tragic Structure in* Paradise Lost, 1976. • Paul Stevens, *Imagination and the Presence of Shakespeare in* Paradise Lost, 1985. • Joseph Summers, *The Muse's Method: An Introduction to* Paradise Lost, 1962. • Joseph Wittreich, *Interpreting* Samson Agonistes, 1986.

Our Text. • Merrit Y. Hughes, ed., *Complete Poetry and Major Prose*, 1957.

Annotations Based On. • John Carey and Alastair Fowler, eds., *The Poems of John Milton*, 1968. • Alastair Fowler, ed., *John Milton: Paradise Lost*, 1968.

Katherine Philips • Editions. • George Saintsbury, ed., *Minor Poets of the Caroline Period*, 1905. • Patrick Thomas, ed., *The Collected Works of Katherine Philips: The Matchless Orinda*, 1993.

Biography. • Philip Webster Souers, *The Matchless Orinda*, 1931. • Patrick Thomas, *Katherine Philips* (Orinda), 1988.

Criticism. • Harriette Andreadis, "The Sapphic-Platonics of Katherine Philips, 1632–1664," *Signs*, vol. 15, no. 1 (Autumn), 1989. • Celia A. Easton, "Excusing the Breach of Nature's Laws: The Discourse of Denial and Disguise in Katherine Philips' Friendship Poetry," *Restoration Studies in English Literary Culture, 1660–1700*, vol. 14, no. 1 (Spring), 1990. • Elizabeth Hageman, "Katherine Philips: The Matchless Orinda," in Katharina M. Wilson, ed., *Women Writers of the Renaissance and Reformation*, 1987. • Claudia A. Limbert, "The Poetry of Katherine Philips: Holographs, Manuscripts, and Early Printed Texts," *Philological Quarterly*, vol. 70, no. 2 (Spring), 1991. • Dorothy Mermin, "Women Becoming Poets: Katherine Philips, Aphra Behn, Anne Finch," *English Literary History*, vol. 57, no. 2 (Summer), 1990. • Ellen Moody, "Orinda, Rosania, Lucasia et Aliae: Towards a New Edition of the Works of Katherine Philips," *Philological Quarterly*, vol. 66, no. 3 (Summer), 1987. • Arlene Stiebel, "Subversive Sexuality: Masking the Erotic in Poems by Katherine Philips and Aphra Behn," *Renaissance Discourses of Desire*, eds. Claude J. Summers and Ted Larry Pebworth, 1993.

Our Text. • Katherine Philips, *Poems by the Most Deservedly Admired Mrs. Katherine Philips The Matchless Orinda*, 1669.

Sir Walter Raleigh • Editions. • A. M. C. Latham, ed., *Poems*, 1950. • William Oldys and Thomas Birch, eds., *The Works of Sir Walter Raleigh*, 8 vols., 1829, repr. 1968.

Biography. • Willard Wallace, *Sir Walter Raleigh*, 1959.

Criticism. • Philip Edwards, *Sir Walter Ralegh*, 1953, repr. 1976. • Stephen J. Greenblatt, *Sir Walter Ralegh: The Renaissance Man and His*

Roles, 1973. • David B. Quinn, *Ralegh and the British Empire*, 1947, repr. 1962. • E. A. Strathmann, *Sir Walter Ralegh: A Study in Elizabethan Skepticism*, 1951.

The Discovery in Context: Voyage Literature • Editions. • Arthur Barlow, in Richard Hakluyt, *The Principal Navigations, Voyages, Traffiques, and Discoveries of the English Nation*, 8 vols., 1907. • Richard Hakluyt, *Divers Voyages Touching the Discoverie of America*, 1580. • Thomas Hariot, *Briefe and True Report of the Newfoundland Land of Virginia*, 1580; facs., 1931. • René Landonnière in Richard Hakluyt, *The Principal Navigations, Voyages, Traffiques, and Discoveries of the English Nation*, 8 vols., 1907. • Michel de Montaigne, *Essays*, trans. John Florio, 3 vols., 1910, repr. 1928.

William Shakespeare: *Twelfth Night* • Editions. • David Bevington, ed., *The Complete Works of Shakespeare*, 1992. • John Russell Brown, ed., *Twelfth Night*, 2001. • George Lyman Kittredge, ed., *Twelfth Night*, 1941. • John Maule Lothian and T. W. Craik, eds., *Twelfth Night*, 1975.

Criticism. • Barry B. Adams, "Orsino and the Spirit of Love: Text, Syntax, and Sense in Twelfth Night, I.i.1–15," *Shakespeare Quarterly*, vol. 29, 1978. • John Russell Brown, *Shakespeare's Dramatic Style: Romeo and Juliet, As You Like It, Julius Caesar, Twelfth Night, Macbeth*, 1971. • Jonathan Crewe, "In the Field of Dreams: Transvestism in *Twelfth Night* and *The Crying Game*," Representations, (Spring, 1995). • Paul Dean, "'Comfortable Doctrine': Twelfth Night and the Trinity," *Review of English Studies: A Quarterly Journal of English Literature and the English Language*, vol. 52, no. 208 (Nov.), 2001. • Jean E. Howard, "Crossdressing, the Theatre, and Gender Struggle in Early Modern England," *Shakespeare Quarterly*, vol. 39, no. 4 (Winter), 1988. • Keir Elam, "The Fertile Eunuch: Twelfth Night, Early Modern Intercourse, and the Fruits of Castration," *Shakespeare Quarterly*, vol. 47, no. 1 (Spring), 1996. • Yu Jin Ko, "The Comic Close of Twelfth Night and Viola's Noli Me Tangere," *Shakespeare Quarterly*, vol. 48, no. 4 (Winter), 1997. • Joseph Pequigney, "The Two Antonios and Same-Sex Love in Twelfth Night and The Merchant Of Venice," *English Literary Renaissance*, vol. 22, no. 2 (Spring), 1992. • Dennis R. Preston, "The Minor Characters in Twelfth Night," *Shakespeare Quarterly*, vol. 21, 1970. • Phyllis Rackin, "Androgyny, Mimesis, and the Mar-

riage of the Boy Heroine on the English Renaissance Stage," *PMLA: Publications of the Modern Language Association of America*, vol. 102, no. 1 (Jan.), 1987. • Stanley Wells, ed., *Twelfth Night: Critical Essays*, 1986. • R. S. White, ed., *Twelfth Night*, 1996.

Our Text. • David Bevington, ed., *The Complete Works of Shakespeare*, 1992.

Sir Philip Sidney • Editions. • Katherine Duncan-Jones, ed., *The Countess of Pembroke's* Arcadia (The Old Arcadia), 1985. • Katherine Duncan-Jones and Jan van Dorsten, eds., *Miscellaneous Prose of Sir Philip Sidney*, 1973. • Maurice Evans, ed., *The Countess of Pembroke's* Arcadia, 1977. • Albert Feuillerat, ed., *The Complete Works*, 4 vols., 1922–1926. • Robert Kimbrough, ed., *Sir Philip Sidney: Selected Prose and Poetry*, 1983. • William Ringler, ed., *Poetry*, 1962. • Jean Robertson, *The Countess of Pembroke's* Arcadia (The Old Arcadia), 1973. • J. A. Van Dorsten, ed., *A Defence of Poetry*, 1966.

Biography. • John Buxton, *Sir Philip Sidney and the English Renaissance*, 1964. • Katharine Duncan-Jones, *Sir Philip Sidney, Courtier Poet*, 1991. • A. C. Hamilton, *Sir Philip Sidney: A Study of His Life and Works*, 1977. • James M. Osborn, *Young Philip Sidney, 1572–1577*, 1972.

Criticism. • Dorothy Connell, *Sir Philip Sidney: The Maker's Mind*, 1977. • David Kalstone, *Sidney's Poetry: Contexts and Interpretations*, 1965. • Dennis Kay, ed., *Sir Philip Sidney: An Anthology of Modern Criticism*, 1987. • Arthur F. Kinney, ed., *Sidney in Retrospect: Selections from English Literary Renaissance*, 1988. • Jon S. Lawry, *Sidney's Two Arcadias; Pattern and Proceeding*, 1972. • Richard C. McCoy, *Sir Philip Sidney: Rebellion in Arcadia*, 1978. • Gary F. Waller and Michael D. Moore, *Sir Philip Sidney and the Interpretation of Renaissance Culture: A Collection of Critical and Scholarly Essays*, 1984. • Andrew D. Weiner, *Sir Philip Sidney and the Poetics of Protestantism: A Study of Contexts*, 1978. • Blair Worden, *The Sound of Virtue: Philip Sidney's Arcadia and Elizabethan Politics*, 1996.

The Apology in Context: The Art of Poetry • Editions. • Samuel Daniel, *A Defence of Ryme*, ed. G. B. Harrison, 1966. • George Gascoigne, *The Complete Works*, ed. John Cunliffe, 2 vols., 1907, 1910. • Stephen Gosson, *The School of Abuse*, ed. Edward Arber, 1869. • George Puttenham, *The Arte of English Poesie*, eds. Gladys Dodge Willcock and Alice Walker, 1970.

Criticism. • Margaret W. Ferguson, *Trials of Desire: Renaissance Defenses of Poetry*, 1983. • Peter C. Herman, *Squitter-Wits and Muse-Haters: Sidney, Spenser, Milton and Renaissance Antipoetic Sentiment*, 1996.

John Skelton • Editions. • Robert S. Kinsman, ed., *Poems*, 1969. • John Scattergood, ed., *Complete English Poems*, 1983.

Biography. • Nan Cooke Carpenter, *John Skelton*, 1967.

Criticism. • Stanley Fish, *John Skelton's Poetry*, 1965. • Richard Halpern, *The Poetics of Primitive Accumulation: English Renaissance Culture and the Genealogy of Capital*, 1991. • Arthur F. Kinney, *John Skelton: Priest as Poet, Seasons of Discovery*, 1987. • Greg Walker, *John Skelton and the Politics of the 1520s*, 1988.

Isabella Whitney • Editions. • Michael David Felder, *The Poems of Isabella Whitney: A Critical Edition*.

Criticism. • Elaine V. Beilin, "Writing Public Poetry: Humanism and the Woman Writer," *Modern Language Quarterly*, vol. 51, 1990. • Ann Rosalind Jones, "Nets and Bridles: Early Modern Conduct Books and Sixteenth-Century Women's Lyrics," *The Ideology of Conduct: Essays on Literature and the History of Sexuality*, eds. Nancy Armstrong and Leonard Tennenhouse, 1987. • Wendy Wall, "Isabella Whitney and the Female Legacy," *English Literary History*, vol. 58, 1991.

Lady Mary Wroth • Editions. • R. E. Pritchard, ed., *Poems: A Modernized Edition*, 1996. • Josephine A. Roberts, ed., *The Poems of Lady Mary Wroth*, 1983. • Josephine A. Roberts, ed., *The First Part of the Countess of Montgomery's* Urania *by Lady Mary Wroth*, 1995. • G. F. Waller, ed., *Pamphilia to Amphilanthus*, 1977.

Biography. • Kim Walker, *Women Writers of the English Renaissance*, 1996.

Criticism. • Naomi J. Miller, *Changing the Subject: Mary Wroth and the Figurations of Gender in Early Modern England*, 1996. • Naomi J. Miller and Gary Waller, eds., *Reading Mary Wroth: Representing Alternatives in Early Modern England*, 1991. • May Nelson Paulissen, *The Love Sonnets of Lady Mary Wroth: A Critical Introduction*, 1982. • Gary Waller, *The Sidney Family Romance: Mary Wroth, William Herbert, and the Early Modern Construction of Gender*, 1993. • Anne Hazelcorn and Betty Travitsky, eds., *The Renaissance Englishwoman in Print*, 1990.

Sir Thomas Wyatt • Editions. • Kenneth Muir and Patricia Thomson, *Collected Poems of Sir Thomas Wyatt*, 1693. • Richard Harrier, *The Canon of Sir Thomas Wyatt's Poetry*, 1975.

Biography. • Stephen Foley, *Sir Thomas Wyatt*, 1990.

Criticism. • Jonathan Crewe, *Trials of Authorship: Anterior Forms and Poetic Reconstruction from Wyatt to Shakespeare*, 1990. • Barbara Estrin, *Laura: Uncovering Gender and Genre in Wyatt, Donne and Marvell*, 1994. • Thomas M. Greene, *The Light in Troy: Imitation and Discovery in Renaissance Poetry*, 1982. • Elizabeth Heale, *Wyatt, Surrey, and Early Tudor Poetry*, 1998.

The Restoration and the Eighteenth Century

Bibliographies and Guides to Research • Robin Alston et al., *The Eighteenth-Century Short-Title Catalogue (ESTC)*, online and on CD-ROM. • Margaret M. Duggan, *English Literature and Backgrounds, 1660–1700: A Selective Critical Guide*, 2 vols., 1990. • *The Eighteenth Century: A Current Bibliography for [1925–]*, annual. The bibliographies for 1925–1970 have been reprinted as *English Literature, 1660–1800: A Bibliography of Modern Studies*, 1950–1972. • Waldo Sumner Glock, *Eighteenth-Century English Literary Studies: A Bibliography*, 1984. • Roger D. Lund, *Restoration and Early Eighteenth-* *Century English Literature, 1660–1740: A Selected Bibliography of Resource Materials*, 1980. • Joanne Shattock, ed., *The Cambridge Bibliography of English Literature*, vol. 2, 1660–1800, 2003. • R. D. Spector, *Backgrounds to Restoration and Eighteenth-Century English Literature: An Annotated Bibliographical Guide to Modern Scholarship*, 1989. • *Studies in English Literature*, Annual review of "Recent Studies in the Restoration and Eighteenth Century" (Summer issue), 1961–.

On-Line Resources • Alan Liu et al., eds., *Voice of the Shuttle: Restoration and Eighteenth Century:*

http://vos.ucsb.edu • Jack Lynch, ed., *Eighteenth-Century Resources*: http://andromeda.rutgers.edu/~jlynch/18th/ • James E. May, *The C-18L Bibliographies: Resources for Eighteenth-Century Studies across the Disciplines*: http://www.personal.psu.edu/special/C18/maytools.htm

Cultural and Intellectual Background • John Brewer, *The Pleasures of the Imagination: English Culture in the Eighteenth Century*, 1997. • James Engell, *The Creative Imagination: Enlightenment to Romanticism*, 1981. • James Engell, *Forming the Critical Mind: Dryden to Coleridge*, 1989. • Northrop Frye, "Towards Defining an Age of Sensibility," *English Literary History*, vol. 23, 1956; repr. in *Backgrounds to Eighteenth-Century Literature*, ed. Kathleen Williams, 1971. • Donald Greene, *The Age of Exuberance: Backgrounds to Eighteenth-Century English Literature*, 1970. • Jürgen Habermas, *The Structural Transformation of the Public Sphere*, 1962; trans., Thomas Burger, 1989. • Jean H. Hagstrum, *Sex and Sensibility: Ideal and Erotic Love from Milton to Mozart*, 1980. • Tim Harris, *Popular Culture in Restoration England*, c. 1500–1800, 1995. • Lawrence Lipking, *The Ordering of the Arts in Eighteenth-Century England*, 1970. • Gerald MacLean, ed., *Culture and Society in the Stuart Restoration: Literature, Drama, History*, 1995. • C. A. Moore, *Backgrounds of English Literature, 1700–1760*, 1953. • John Mullan and Christopher Reid, eds., *Eighteenth-Century Popular Culture: A Selection*, 2000. • Ronald Paulson, *Breaking and Remaking: Aesthetic Practice in England, 1700–1820*, 1989. • Roy Porter, *The Creation of the Modern World: The British Enlightenment*, 2000. • Pat Rogers, ed., *The Context of English Literature: The Eighteenth Century*, 1978. • Pat Rogers, *Grub Street: Studies in a Subculture*, 1972. • James Sambrook, *The Eighteenth Century: The Intellectual and Cultural Context of English Literature, 1700–1789*, 2nd ed., 1993. • J. W. Yolton et al., eds., *The Blackwell Companion to the Enlightenment*, 1991. • Steven N. Zwicker, *The Cambridge Companion to English Literature, 1650–1740*, 1998.

History, Religion, and Political Thought • Jeremy Black, *An Illustrated History of Eighteenth-Century Britain*, 1996. • John Brewer, *The Sinews of Power: War, Money, and the English State, 1688–1783*, 1989. • J. C. D. Clark, *English Society, 1688–1832*, 1985. • Linda Colley, *Britons: Forging the Nation, 1707–1837*, 1992. • Peter Earle, *The Making of the English Middle Class*, 1989. • Jeremy Gregory and John Stevenson, *Britain in the Eighteenth Century, 1688–1820*, 2000. • Tim Harris, *Politics Under the Later Stuarts*, 1993. • Tim Harris, *The Politics of Religion in Restoration England*, 1990. • T. W. Heyck, *The Peoples of the British Isles*, vol. 2, 1688–1870, 1992. • Ronald Hutton, *Charles II*, 1989. • Ronald Hutton, *The Restoration*, 1985. • J. P. Kenyon, *The Stuart Constitution*, 2nd ed., 1986. • Mark Kishlansky, *A Monarchy Transformed: Britain 1603–1714*, 1996. • Paul Langford, *A Polite and Commercial People: England 1727–1783*, 1989. • Dorothy Marshall, *Eighteenth Century England*, 2nd. ed., 1962. • Neil McKendrick, John Brewer, and J. H. Plumb, *The Birth of a Consumer Society: The Commercialization of Eighteenth-Century Britain*, 1982. • J. H. Plumb, *England in the Eighteenth Century*, 1972. • J. G. A. Pocock, *Politics, Language, and Time: Essays on Political Thought and History*, 1989. • J. G. A. Pocock, *Virtue, Commerce, and History*, 1985. • Roy Porter, *English Society in the Eighteenth Century*, rev. ed., 1990. • Isabel Rivers, *Reason, Grace, and Sentiment: A Study of the Language of Religion and Ethics in England, 1660–1780*, vol. 1, *Whichcote to Wesley*, 1991. • Richard B. Schwartz, *Daily Life in Johnson's London*, 1983. • W. A. Speck, *Stability and Strife: England, 1714–1760*, 1977. • John Spurr, *The Restoration Church of England*, 1991. • E. P. Thompson, *Albion's Fatal Tree: Crime and Society in Eighteenth-Century England*, 1976. • E. P. Thompson, *Customs in Common*, 1991. • John Wroughton, *The Longman Companion to the Stuart Age 1603–1714*, 1997.

Women, Writing, Politics, and Culture • George Ballard, *Memoirs of Several Ladies of Great Britain Who Have Been Celebrated for Their Writings or Skill in the Learned Languages, Arts, and Sciences*, 1752; ed. Ruth Perry, 1985. • Margaret J. M. Ezell, *Writing Women's Literary History*, 1993. • Catherine Gallagher, *Nobody's Story: The Vanishing Acts of Women Writers in the Marketplace, 1670–1820*, 1994. • Susan Greenfield and Carol Barash, eds., *Inventing Maternity*, 1999. • Isobel Grundy and Susan Wiseman, eds., *Women, Writing, and History: 1640–1799*, 1992. • Bridget Hill, *Eighteenth-Century Women: An Anthology*, 1984. • Bridget Hill, *Women, Work, and Sexual Politics in Eighteenth-Century England*, 1989. • Sylvia Meyers, *The Bluestocking Circle*, 1990. • Anita Pacheco, ed., *Early Women Writers:*

1660–1720, 1998. • Myra Reynolds, *The Learned Lady in England, 1650–1760*, 1920. • Mona Scheuermann, *Her Bread to Earn: Women, Money, and Society from Defoe to Austen*, 1993. • Hilda Smith, *Reason's Disciples: Seventeenth-Century English Feminists*, 1982. • Susan Staves, *Married Women's Separate Property in England, 1660–1833*, 1990. • Beth Fawkes Tobin, *History, Gender, and Eighteenth-Century Literature*, 1994. • Janet Todd, ed., *A Dictionary of British and American Women Writers, 1660–1800*, 1985. • Janet Todd, *The Sign of Angellica: Women, Writing, and Fiction, 1660–1800*, 1989. • Katherine Wilson and Frank J. Warnke, eds., *Women Writers of the Seventeenth Century*, 1989.

General Literature • Martin C. Battestin, *The Providence of Wit: Aspects of Form in Augustan Literature and the Arts*, 1974. • Richard Braverman, *Plots and Counterplots: Sexual Politics and the Body Politic in English Literature, 1660–1730*. • John Butt and Geoffrey Carnall, *English Literature in the Mid-Eighteenth Century*, 1979. • James L. Clifford, ed., *Eighteenth-Century English Literature: Modern Essays in Criticism*, 1959. • Leopold Damrosch, Jr., ed., *Modern Essays on Eighteenth-Century Literature*, 1988. • Robert DeMaria, Jr., ed., *British Literature, 11640–1789: A Critical Reader*, 1999. • Bonamy Dobrée, *English Literature in the Early Eighteenth Century, 1700–1740*, 1959. • Paul Fussell, *The Rhetorical World of Augustan Humanism*, 1965. • Roger Lonsdale, ed., *The Sphere History of Literature*, vol. 4, *Dryden to Johnson*, rev. ed., 1987. • Felicity Nussbaum and Laura Brown, eds., *The New Eighteenth Century: Theory, Politics, English Literature*, 1987. • Ronald Paulson, *Popular and Polite Art in the Age of Hogarth and Fielding*, 1979. • Martin Price, *To the Palace of Wisdom: Studies in Order and Energy from Dryden to Blake*, 1964. • Isabel Rivers, ed., *Books and Their Readers in Eighteenth-Century England*, 1982. • Isabel Rivers, ed., *Books and Their Readers in Eighteenth-Century England: New Essays*, 2002. • John Sitter, *Literary Loneliness in Mid-Eighteenth-Century England*, 1982. • James Sutherland, *English Literature of the Late Seventeenth Century*, 1969. • Howard Weinbrot, *Britannia's Issue: The Rise of British Literature from Dryden to Ossian*, 1993. • David Womersley, ed., *A Companion to Literature from Milton to Blake*, 2000. • Steven N. Zwicker, *Lines of Authority: Politics and English Literary Culture, 1649–1689*, 1993.

Drama • R. W. Bevis, *English Drama: Restoration and Eighteenth Century, 1660–1789*, 1988. Laura Brown, *English Dramatic Form, 1660–1760*, 1981. • J. Douglas Canfield and Deborah C. Payne, eds., *Cultural Readings of Restoration and Eighteenth-Century English Theater*, 1995. • T. W. Craik et al., eds., *The Revels History of Drama in English*, vol. 5, 1660–1750. • Deborah Payne Fiske, ed., *The Cambridge Companion to English Restoration Theatre*, Cambridge 2000. • Pat Gill, *Interpreting Ladies: Women, Wit, and Morality in the Restoration Comedy of Manners*, 1994. • John T. Harwood, *Critics, Values, and Restoration Comedy*, 1982. • Derek Hughes, *English Drama 1660–1700*, 1996. • Robert D. Hume, *The Development of English Drama in the Late Seventeenth Century*, 1976. • Robert D. Hume, *The Rakish Stage: Studies in English Drama, 1660–1800*, 1983. • John Loftis, ed., *Restoration Drama*, 1966. • Robert Markley, *Two-Edg'd Weapons: Style and Ideology in the Comedies of Etherege, Wycherley, and Congreve*, 1988. • Earl Miner, ed., *Restoration Dramatists*, 1966. • Allardyce Nicoll, *A History of English Drama, 1660–1900*, vols. 1–3 (1660–1800) 1952. • Susan J. Owen, ed. *A Companion to Restoration Drama*, 2001. • David Roberts, *The Ladies: Female Patronage of Restoration Drama, 1660–1700*, 1989.

Fiction • Nancy Armstrong, *Desire and Domestic Fiction*, 1989. • Jerry C. Beasley, *English Fiction, 1660–1800: A Guide to Information Sources*, 1978. • John Bender, *Imaging the Penitentiary*, 1987. • Terry Castle, *Masquerade and Civilization*, 1986. • Leopold Damrosch, *God's Plot and Man's Stories*, 1985. • Lennard J. Davis, *Factual Fictions: The Origins of the English Novel*, 1983. • Margaret Anne Doody, *The True Story of the Novel*, 1996. • Christopher Flint, *Family Fictions: Narrative and Domestic Relations in Britain, 1688–1789*, 2000. • J. Paul Hunter, *Before Novels*, 1990. • Deidre Shauna Lynch, *The Economy of Character: Novels, Market Culture, and the Business of Inner Meaning*, 1998. • Michael McKeon, *The Origins of the English Novel, 1660–1740*, 1987. • John Richetti, ed., *The Cambridge Companion to the Eighteenth-Century Novel*, 1996. • John Richetti, *The English Novel in History 1700–1780*, 1999. • John Richetti, *Popular Fiction Before Richardson*, 1969. • Paul Salzman, *English Prose Fiction, 1558–1700: A Critical History*, 1985. • Mary Ann Schofield and Cecelia Macheski, *Fetter'd or Free? British Women Novelists, 1670–1815*, 1986. • Jane

Spencer, *The Rise of the Woman Novelist*, 1986. • Ian Watt, *The Rise of the Novel: Studies in Defoe, Richardson, and Fielding*, 1957.

Poetry • Carol Barash, *English Women's Poetry, 1649–1714: Politics, Community, and Linguistic Authority*, 1997. • Margaret Doody, *The Daring Muse: Augustan Poetry Reconsidered*, 1985. • Germaine Greer et al., eds., *Kissing the Rod: An Anthology of Seventeenth-Century Women's Verse*, 1988. • Jean Hagstrum, *The Sister Arts: The Tradition of Literary Pictorialism and English Poetry from Dryden to Gray*, 1958. • Ian Jack, *Augustan Satire: Intention and Idiom in English Poetry, 1660–1750*, 1952. • Donna Landry, *The Muses of Resistance: Laboring-Class Women's Poetry in Britain, 1739–1796*, 1990. • Roger Lonsdale, ed., *The New Oxford Book of Eighteenth-Century Verse*, 1984. • Roger Lonsdale, ed., *Eighteenth-Century Women Poets*, 1990. • Eric Rothstein, *Restoration and Eighteenth-Century Poetry, 1660–1800*, 1981. • Patricia Spacks, *The Poetry of Vision*, 1967. • James Sutherland, *A Preface to Eighteenth-Century Poetry*, 1948. • Howard Weinbrot, *The Formal Strain: Studies in Augustan Imitation and Satire*, 1969.

Satire • Ronald Paulson, *The Fictions of Satire*, 1967. • Claude Rawson, ed., *English Satire and the Satiric Tradition*, 1984. • Claude Rawson, *Order from Confusion Sprung*, 1985. • Michael Seidel, *Satiric Inheritance: Rabelais to Sterne*, 1979.

Letters, Diaries, Autobiography, Biography • Howard Anderson, Philip B. Daghlian, and Irvin Ehrenpreis, eds., *The Familiar Letter in the Eighteenth Century*, 1966. • William Epstein, *Recognizing Biography*, 1987. • Michael Mascuch, *Origins of the Individualist Self: Autobiography and Self-Identity in England, 1591–1791*, 1996. • Felicity Nussbaum, *The Autobiographical Subject: Gender and Ideology in Eighteenth-Century England*, 1989. • Bruce Redford, *The Converse of the Pen: Acts of Intimacy in the Eighteenth-Century Familiar Letter*, 1987. • Stuart Sherman, *Telling Time: Clocks, Diaries, and English Diurnal Form, 1660–1785*, 1996. • Patricia Meyer Spacks, *Imagining a Self: Autobiography and Novel in Eighteenth-Century England*, 1976. • Richard Wendorf, *The Elements of Life: Biography and Portrait Painting in Stuart and Georgian England*, 1990.

Perspectives: Mind and God (See also "Cultural and Intellectual Backgrounds") • Jonathan Bennett, *Locke, Berkeley, Hume: Central Themes*, 1971. • James Collins, *The British Empiricists*, 1967. • Peter Gay, ed., *The Enlightenment: A Comprehensive Anthology*, 1973. • John J. Richetti, *Philosophical Writing: Locke, Berkeley, Hume*, 1983. • Keith Thomas, ed., *The British Empricists*, 1992. • Richard S. Westfall, *Science and Religion in Seventeenth-Century England*, 1958. • R. S. Woolhouse, *The Empiricists*, 1988. • John W. Yolton, *Perception and Reality: A History from Descartes to Kant*, 1996. • John W. Yolton, ed., *Philosophy, Religion, and Science in the Seventeenth and Eighteenth Centuries*, 1990.

Perspectives: The Royal Society and the New Science • I. Bernard Cohen with K. E. Duffin and Stuart Strickland, eds., *Puritanism and the Rise of Modern Science: The Merton Thesis*, 1990. • Michael Hunter, *Science and Society in Restoration England*, 1981. • Michael Hunter, *Science and the Shape of Orthodoxy: Intellectual Change in Late Seventeenth-Century Britain*, 1995. • Michael Hunter, *The Royal Society and Its Fellows, 1660–1700: The Morphology of an Early Scientific Institution*, 2nd ed., 1994. • Lisa Jardine, *Ingenious Pursuits: Building the Scientific Revolution*, 2000. • Londa Schiebinger, *The Mind Has No Sex: Women in the Origins of Modern Science*, 1989. • Londa Schiebinger, *Nature's Body: Gender in the Making of Modern Science*, 1993. • Steven Shapin and Simon Schaffer, *Leviathan and the Air-Pump: Hobbes, Boyle, and the Experimental Life*, 1985. • Steven Shapin, *The Scientific Revolution*, 1996. • Steven Shapin, *A Social History of Truth: Civility and Science in Seventeenth-Century England*, 1994. • Larry R. Stewart, *The Rise of Public Science: Rhetoric, Technology and Natural Philosophy in Newtonian Britain, 1660–1750*, 1992. • Geoffrey V. Sutton, *Science for a Polite Society: Gender, Culture, and the Demonstration of Enlightenment*, 1995. • Catherine Wilson, *The Invisible World: Early Modern Philosophy and the Invention of the Microscope*, 1995. • John W. Yolton, ed., *Philosophy, Religion, and Science in the Seventeenth and Eighteenth Centuries*, 1990.

Aphra Behn • Editions. • Catherine Gallagher, ed., *Oroonoko*, 2000. • Joanna Lipking, ed., *Oroonoko: An Authoritative Text, Historical Backgrounds, Criticism*, 1997. • Janet Todd, ed., *Oroonoko, The Rover, and other Works*, 1992. • Janet Todd, ed., *The Works of Aphra Behn*, 7 vols., 1992–1996.

Biography. • Janet Todd, *The Secret Life of Aphra Behn*, 1997.

Criticism. • Laura Brown, "The Romance of Empire: Oroonoko and the Trade in Slaves," *The New Eighteenth Century*, eds. Felicity Nussbaum and Laura Brown, 1987. • Margaret W. Ferguson, "Juggling the Categories of Race, Class and Gender: Aphra Behn's Oroonoko," *Women's Studies*, vol. 19, 1991. • Oddvar Holmesland, "Aphra Behn's Oroonoko: Cultural Dialectics and the Novel," *ELH*, vol. 68, 2001. • Catherine Gallagher, "The Author-Monarch and the Royal Slave: Oroonoko and the Blackness of Representation," *Nobody's Story: The Vanishing Acts of Women Writers in the Marketplace, 1670–1820*, 1994. • Heidi Hutner, ed., *Rereading Aphra Behn*, 1993. • Sara Heller Mendelson, *The Mental World of Stuart Women: Three Studies*, 1987. • Mary Ann O'Donnell, *Aphra Behn: An Annotated Bibliography*, 1986. • M. I. Stapleton, "Aphra Behn, Libertine," *Restoration*, vol. 24, 2000. • Janet Todd, ed., *Aphra Behn Studies*, 1996.

James Boswell • Editions. • R. W. Chapman, ed., *Life of Johnson*, rev. J. D. Fleeman. 1970. • G. B. Hill and L. F. Powell, eds., *Boswell's Life of Johnson*, 6 vols., 1934–1964. • Frederick A. Pottle, et al., eds., *The Yale Editions of the Private Papers of James Boswell*, 1950–. • Frederick A. Pottle, ed., *Boswell's London Journal, 1762–1763*, 1950. • Frederick A. Pottle and Charles H. Bennett, eds., *Boswell's Journal of a Tour to the Hebrides with Samuel Johnson*, 1773, 1963. • John Wain, ed., *The Journals of James Boswell, 1762–1795*, 1991.

Biographies. • Frank Brady, *James Boswell, the Later Years, 1769–1795*, 1984. • Mary Hyde, *The Impossible Friendship: Boswell and Mrs. Thrale*, 1972. • Peter Martin, *A Life of James Boswell*, 2000. • Frederick A. Pottle, *James Boswell, the Earlier Years, 1740–1769*, 1985. • Frederick A. Pottle, *The Literary Career of James Boswell*, 1929.

Criticism. • (See Also the Listings of Criticism on Samuel Johnson). • Hamilton Cochrane, *Boswell's Literary Art: An Annotated Bibliography of Critical Studies*, 1992. • James L. Clifford, ed., *Twentieth Century Interpretations of Boswell's Life of Johnson*, 1970. • Greg Clingham, ed., *New Light on Boswell: Critical and Historical Essays on the Occasion of the Bicentenary of The Life of Johnson*, 1991. • Irma S. Lustig, ed., *Boswell: Citizen of the World, Man of Letters*, 1995 • Adam Sisman, *Boswell's Presumptuous Task*, 2001. • John A. Vance, ed., *Boswell's Life of Johnson: New Questions, New Answers*, 1995.

Margaret Lucas Cavendish, Duchess of Newcastle • Editions. • Kate Lilley, ed., *The Blazing World and Other Writings*, 1994. • Paul Salzman, ed. The Blazing World, *An Anthology of Seventeenth-Century Fiction*, 1991.

Biography. • Kathleen Jones, *A Glorious Fame: The Life of Margaret Cavendish, Duchess of Newcastle*, 1988.

Criticism • Anna Battigelli, *Margaret Cavendish and the Exiles of the Mind*, 1998. • Catherine Gallagher, "Embracing the Absolute: The Politics of the Female Subject in Seventeenth-Century England," *Genders*, vol. 1, 1988. • Rosemary Kegl, "The World I Have Made: Margaret Cavendish, Feminism, and the Blazing World," *Feminist Readings of Early Modern Culture*, eds. Valerie Traub, M. Lindsay Kaplan, and Dympna Callaghan, 1996. • Eve Keller, "Producing Petty Gods: Margaret Cavendish's Critique of Experimental Science," *English Literary History*, vol. 64, no. 2, 1997. • Sara Heller Mendelson, *The Mental World of Stuart Women: Three Studies*, 1987. • John Rogers, *The Matter of Revolution: Science, Poetry, and Politics in the Age of Milton*, 1996.

Mary, Lady Chudleigh • Edition. • Margaret J. M. Ezell, ed., *The Poems and Prose of Mary, Lady Chudleigh*, 1993.

Criticism. • Carol Barash, *"The Native Liberty."*

William Cowper • Editions. • John D. Baird and Charles Ryskamp, eds., *The Poems of William Cowper*, 3 vols., 1980–1995. • James King and Charles Ryskamp, eds., *The Letters and Prose Writings of William Cowper*, 5 vols., 1979–1986. • James Sambrook, ed., *"The Task" and Selected Other Poems*, 1994.

Biography. • James King, *William Cowper: A Biography*, 1986. • Charles Ryskamp, *William Cowper of the Inner Temple, Esq.*, 1959.

Criticism. • Morris Golden, *In Search of Stability: The Poetry of William Cowper*, 1960. • Vincent Newey, *Cowper's Poetry: A Critical Study and Reassessment*, 1982.

Daniel Defoe • Editions. • Paula Backscheider, ed., *A Journal of the Plague Year*, 1992. • P. N. Furbank and W. R. Owens, eds., The True-

Born Englishman *and Other Writings*, 1997. • Louis Landa and David Roberts, eds., A Journal of the Plague Year: *Text, Backgrounds, Criticism*, 1990. • William L. Payne, ed., *The Best of Defoe's* Review: *An Anthology*, 1951. • Manuel Schonhorn, *Accounts of the Apparition of Mrs. Veal*, 1965.

Biography. • Paula R. Backscheider, *Daniel Defoe: His Life*, 1989. • Maximillian E. Novak, *Daniel Defoe, Master of Fictions*, 2001.

Criticism. • Paula R. Backscheider, *Daniel Defoe: Ambition and Innovation*, 1986. • Rodney Baine, *Daniel Defoe and the Supernatural*, 1979. • David Blewett, *Defoe's Art of Fiction*, 1979. • Lincoln B. Faller, *Crime and Defoe: A New Kind of Writing*, 1993. • P. N. Furbank and W. R. Owens, *The Canonisation of Daniel Defoe*, 1988. • J. Paul Hunter, *The Reluctant Pilgrim: Defoe's Emblematic Method and Quest for Form* in Robinson Crusoe, 1966. • Roger D. Lund, ed., *Critical Essays on Daniel Defoe*, 1997. • Watson Nicholson, *The Historical Sources of Defoe's* Journal of the Plague Year, 1919. • Watson Nicholson, *Realism, Myth and History in Defoe's Fiction*, 1983. • Maximillian E. Novak, *Economics and the Fiction of Daniel Defoe*, 1962. • Maximillian E. Novak, *Realism, Myth, and History in Defoe's Fiction*, 1983. • William Payne, Mr. *Review: Daniel Defoe as the Author of the* Review, 1961. • John J. Richetti, *Daniel Defoe*, 1987. • John J. Richetti, *Defoe's Narratives*, 1975. • Pat Rogers, ed., *Defoe, the Critical Heritage*, 1972.

John Dryden • Editions. • Paul Hammond, *The Poems of John Dryden*, 1995–. • James Kinsley, ed., *The Poems and Fables of John Dryden*, 1962. • H. T. Swedenberg, Jr. and Edward Niles Hooker, eds., *Works*, 20 vols., 1961–. • Keith Walker, ed., *John Dryden*, 1987. • George Watson, ed., *"Of Dramatick Poesy" and Other Critical Essays*, 2 vols., 1962. • Steven N. Zwicker, ed., *Selected Poems*, 2002.

Biographies. • Paul Hammond, *John Dryden: A Literary Life*, 1991. • James Anderson Winn, *John Dryden and His World*, 1987.

Criticism. • Reuben Brower, "An Allusion to Europe: Dryden and Poetic Tradition," *English Literary History*, vol. 19, 1952. • David A. Bywaters, *Dryden in Revolutionary England*, 1991. • Michael Werth Gelber, *The Just and the Lively: The Literary Criticism of John Dryden*, 1999. • Phillip Harth, *Contexts of Dryden's Thought*, 1968. • Geoffrey Hill, *The Enemy's Country*, 1991. • David Hopkins, *John Dryden*,

1986. • Robert Hume, *Dryden's Criticism*, 1970. • James and Helen Kinsley, *Dryden: The Critical Heritage*, 1971. • Earl Miner, *Dryden's Poetry*, 1967. • Earl Miner, ed., *John Dryden*, 1972. • H. T. Swedenborg, ed., *Essential Articles for the Study of John Dryden*, 1966. • James A. Winn, ed., *Critical Essays on John Dryden*, 1997. • David Wykes, *A Preface to Dryden*, 1977. • Steven N. Zwicker, *Dryden's Political Poetry: The Typology of King and Nation*, 1972. • Steven N. Zwicker, *Politics and Language in Dryden's Poetry: The Arts of Disguise*, 1984.

John Evelyn • Editions. • John Bowie, *The Diary of John Evelyn*, 1983. • E. S. de Beer, *The Diary of John Evelyn*, 6 vols., 1955.

Biography. • John Bowie, *John Evelyn and His World*, 1981.

Anne Finch, Countess of Winchilsea • Editions. • Myra Reynolds, ed., *The Poems of Anne, Countess of Winchilsea*, 1903. • Katherine M. Rogers, ed., *Selected Poems of Anne Finch, Countess of Winchilsea*, 1979.

Biography. • Barbara McGovern, *Anne Finch and Her Poetry: A Critical Biography*, 1992.

Criticism. • Charles H. Hinnant, *The Poetry of Anne Finch*, 1994.

John Gay • Editions. • Vinton A. Dearing and Charles Beckwith, eds., *John Gay: Poetry and Prose*, 2 vols., 1974. • John Fuller, *John Gay: Dramatic Works*, 2 vols., 1983. • Bryan Loughery and T. O. Treadwell, eds., *The Beggar's Opera*, 1987. • Edgar V. Roberts, ed., *The Beggar's Opera*, 1969.

Biography. • David Nokes, *John Gay: A Profession of Friendship*, 1995.

Criticism. • Sven Armens, *John Gay, Social Critic*, 1954. Dianne Dugaw, *"Deep Play": John Gay and the Invention of Modernity*, 2001. • William Empson, "*The Beggar's Opera*: Mock-Pastoral as the Cult of Independence," *Some Versions of Pastoral*, 1935. • Michael Friedman, "He Was Just a Macheath: Boswell and *The Beggar's Opera*," *Age of Johnson*, vol. 4, 1991. • Peter Elfed Lewis, *John Gay: The Beggar's Opera*, 1976. • Peter Lewis and Nigel Wood, eds., *John Gay and the Scriblerians*, 1988. • Yvonne Noble, ed., *Twentieth-Century Interpretations of* The Beggar's Opera: *A Collection of Critical Essays*, 1975. • Calhoun Winton, *John Gay and the London Theatre*, 1993.

Thomas Gray • Editions. • Roger Lonsdale, ed., *The Poems of Gray, Collins and Goldsmith*, 1969. • Alastair Macdonald, ed., *An Elegy Wrote in a Country Church Yard*, 1976. • H. W. Starr and J. R. Hendrickson, eds., *The Complete Poems of Thomas Gray: English, Latin and Greek*, 1966. • Paget Toynbee and Leonard Whibley, eds., *The Correspondence of Thomas Gray*, rev. ed., 1971.

Biography. • Robert L. Mack, *Thomas Gray: A Life*, 2000. • R. W. Ketton-Cremer, *Thomas Gray*, 1955.

Criticism. • F. W. Hilles and Harold Bloom, eds., *From Sensibility to Romanticism*, 1965. • James Downey and Ben Jones, eds., *Fearful Joy: Papers from the Thomas Gray Bicentenary Conference*, 1974. • Robert F. Gleckner, *Gray Agonistes: Thomas Gray and Masculine Friendship*, 1997. • Morris Golden, *Thomas Gray*, 1988. • W. B. Hutchings and William Ruddick, eds., *Thomas Gray: Contemporary Essays*, 1993. • Suvir Kaul, *Thomas Gray and Literary Authority: A Study in Ideology and Poetics*, 1992. • Vincent Newey, "The Selving of Thomas Gray," *Centring the Self: Subjectivity, Society, and Reading from Thomas Gray to Thomas Hardy*, 1995. • Herbert W. Starr, *Twentieth-Century Interpretations of Gray's Elegy*, 1968. • Frank A. Vaughan, *Again to the Life of Eternity: William Blake's Illustrations of the Poems of Thomas Gray*, 1995. • Henry Winefield, *The Poet Without a Name: Gray's Elegy and the Problem of History*, 1991.

William Hogarth • Editions. • Ronald Paulson, ed., *The Analysis of Beauty*, 1998. • Ronald Paulson, ed., *Hogarth's Graphic Works*, 3rd ed., 1989. • Sean Shesgreen, ed., *Engravings by Hogarth*, 1973.

Biographies. • Ronald Paulson, *Hogarth*, 3 vols., 1991–1993. • Jenny Uglow, *Hogarth: A Life and a World*, 1997.

Criticism. • David Bindman, *Hogarth*, 1981. • David Dabydeen, *Hogarth, Walpole, and Commercial Britain*, 1987. • Bernadette Fort and Angela Rosenthal, eds., *The Other Hogarth: Aesthetics of Difference*, 2001. • Ronald Paulson, *The Art of Hogarth*, 1975.

Robert Hooke • Criticism. • Ellen Tan Drake, *Restless Genius: Robert Hooke and his Earthly Thoughts*, 1996. • Michael Hunter and Simon Schaffer, eds., *Robert Hooke: New Studies*, 1989.

David Hume • Editions. • Antony Flew, ed., *An Enquiry Concerning Human Understanding*, 1988. • Selby-Bigge and P. H. Nidditch, eds., *Enquiries Concerning Human Understanding and Concerning the Principles of Morals*, 3rd ed., 1975. • Selby-Bigge and P. H. Nidditch, eds., *A Treatise of Human Nature*, 2nd ed., 1978.

Biography. • E. E. Mossner, *The Life of David Hume*, 1954.

Criticism. • A. J. Ayer, *Hume*, 1980. • John Bricke, *Hume's Philosophy of Mind*, 1980. • V. C. Chappell, ed., *Hume*, 1966. • Jerome Christensen, *Practicing Enlightenment: Hume and the Formation of a Literary Career*, 1987. • Antony Flew, *David Hume, Philosopher of Moral Science*, 1986. • J. C. A. Gaskin, *Hume's Philosophy of Religion*, rev. ed. 1988. • Norman Kemp Smith, *The Philosophy of David Hume*, 1941. • David Fate Norton, ed., *The Cambridge Companion to Hume*, 1993.

Samuel Johnson • Editions. • Frank Brady and W. K. Wimsatt, eds., *Selected Poetry and Prose*, 1977. • J. D. Fleeman, *A Journey to the Western Islands of Scotland*, 1985. • Donald Greene, ed., *Samuel Johnson*, 1984. • G. B. Hill, ed., *Johnson's Lives of the English Poets*, 3 vols., 1905. • Peter Levi, *A Journey to the Western Islands of Scotland* and *The Journal of a Tour to the Hebrides*, 1984. • E. L. McAdam, Jr. and George Milne, *Johnson's Dictionary: A Modern Selection*, 1963. • E. L. McAdam, Jr. et al., eds., *The Yale Edition of the Works of Samuel Johnson*, 14 vols., 1958–. • Anne McDermott, ed., *A Dictionary of the English Language* on CD-ROM [computer file], 1996. • Bruce Redford, ed., *The Letters of Samuel Johnson*, 5 vols., 1992–1994. • Pat Rogers, *Johnson and Boswell in Scotland: A Journey to the Hebrides*, 1993.

Biographies. • Walter Jackson Bate, *Samuel Johnson*, 1977. • James Boswell, *Boswell's Life of Johnson*, eds. G. B. Hill and L. F. Powell, 6 vols., 1934–1964. • O. M. Brack, Jr. and Robert E. Kelley, *The Early Biographies of Samuel Johnson*, 1974. • James L. Clifford, *Dictionary Johnson: The Middle Years of Samuel Johnson*, 1979. • James L. Clifford, *Young Sam Johnson*, 1955. • Robert DeMaria, Jr., *The Life of Samuel Johnson: A Critical Biography*, 1993. • John Hawkins, *The Life of Samuel Johnson, LL.D.*, ed. Bertram Davis, 1961. • G. B. Hill, ed., *Johnsonian Miscellanies*, 2 vols., 1897. • Thomas Kaminski, *The Early Career of Samuel Johnson*, 1987. • Lawrence I. Lipking,

Samuel Johnson: The Life of an Author, 2000. • John Wain, *Samuel Johnson*, 1974.

Criticism. • Walter Jackson Bate, *The Achievement of Samuel Johnson*, 1955. • Harold Bloom, ed., *Modern Critical Views: Dr. Samuel Johnson and James Boswell*, 1986. • James T. Boulton, ed., *Johnson, the Critical Heritage*, 1971. • Jonathan Clark and Howard Erskine-Hill, eds., *Samuel Johnson in Historical Context*, 2002. • James L. Clifford and Donald Greene, *Johnsonian Studies, 1887–1950: A Survey and Bibliography*, 1951. • Greg Clingham, *The Cambridge Companion to Samuel Johnson*, 1997. • Leopold Damrosch, *The Uses of Johnson's Criticism*, 1976. • Philip Davis, *In Mind of Johnson: A Study of Johnson the Rambler*, 1989. • Robert DeMaria, Jr., *Johnson's, Dictionary, and the Language of Learning*, 1986. • Robert DeMaria, Jr., *Samuel Johnson and the Life of Reading*, 1997. • Robert Folkenflik, *Samuel Johnson, Biographer*, 1978. • Paul Fussell, *Samuel Johnson and the Life of Writing*, 1971. • Donald Greene, *The Politics of Samuel Johnson*, 2nd ed., 1990. • Donald Greene and John A. Vance, *A Bibliography of Johnsonian Studies, 1970–1985*, 1987. • Isobel Grundy, ed., *Samuel Johnson: New Critical Essays*, 1984. • Jean H. Hagstrum, *Samuel Johnson's Literary Criticism*, 1967. • Kevin Hart, *Samuel Johnson and the Culture of Property*, 1999. • Nicholas Hudson, *Samuel Johnson and Eighteenth-Century Thought*, 1988. • Paul J. Korshin, ed., *Johnson after Two Hundred Years*, 1986. • Jack Lynch, *A Bibliography of Johnson Studies, 1986–1998*, 2000. • G. F. Parker, *Johnson's Shakespeare*, 1989. • Allen Reddick, *The Making of Johnson's Dictionary, 1746–1773*, 1996. • Pat Rogers, *Johnson and Boswell: The Transit of Caledonia*, 1995. • Pat Rogers, *The Samuel Johnson Encyclopedia*, 1996. • Arthur Sherbo, *Samuel Johnson's Critical Opinions: A Reexamination*, 1995. • James H. Sledd and Gwin J. Kolb, *Dr. Johnson's Dictionary: Essays in the Biography of a Book*, 1955. • Robert D. Spector, *Samuel Johnson and the Essay*, 1997. • David F. Venturo, *Johnson the Poet*, 1999. David Wheeler, ed., *Domestick Privacies*, 1987. • William K. Wimsatt, *Philosophic Words: A Study of Style and Meaning in the Rambler and Dictionary of Samuel Johnson*, 1948. • William K. Wimsatt, *The Prose Style of Samuel Johnson*, 1941. • Thomas M. Woodman, *A Preface to Samuel Johnson*, 1993.

Mary Leapor • Biography and Criticism. • Richard Greene, *Mary Leapor: A Study in Eighteenth-Century Women's Poetry*, 1993.

John Locke • Editions. • Peter H. Nidditch, ed., *An Essay Concerning Human Understanding*, 1975. • J. W. Yolton, *The Locke Reader*, 1977.

Criticism. • R. I. Aaron, *John Locke*, rev. ed., 1955. • Vere Chappell, ed., *The Cambridge Companion to Locke*, 1994. • John Dunn, *Locke*, 1984. • Christopher Fox, *Locke and the Scriblerians: Identity and Consciousness in Early Eighteenth-Century Britain*, 1988. • W. M. Spellman, *John Locke*, 1997. • John W. Yolton, *Locke: An Introduction*, 1985.

Lady Mary Wortley Montagu • Editions. • Robert Halsband, ed., *The Complete Letters of Lady Mary Wortley Montagu*, 1965–1967. • Robert Halsband and Isobel Grundy, eds., *Essays and Poems and Simplicity, a Comedy*, 1977. • Malcolm Jack, ed., *Turkish Embassy Letters*, 1993.

Biography. • Robert Halsband, *The Life of Lady Mary Wortley Montagu*, 1956.

Criticism. • Jill Campbell, "Lady Mary Wortley Montagu and the Historical Machinery of Female Identity," *History, Gender, and Eighteenth-Century Literature*, ed. Beth Fawkes Tobin, 1994. • Cynthia Lowenthal, *Lady Mary Wortley Montagu and the Eighteenth-Century Familiar Letter*, 1994. • Ruth Bernard Yeazell, "Public Baths and Private Harems: Lady Mary Wortley Montagu and the Origins of Ingres's *Bain Turc*," *Yale Journal of Criticism*, vol. 7, no. 1, 1994.

Sir Isaac Newton • Editions. • I. Bernard Cohen and Richard S. Westfall, eds., *Newton: Texts, Backgrounds, Commentaries*, 1995. • H. W. Turnbull, *The Correspondence of Isaac Newton*, 7 vols., 1959–1977.

Biography. • Richard S. Westfall, *Never at Rest*, 1980.

Criticism. • D. Gjertsen, *The Newton Handbook*, 1986. • F. E. Manuel, *The Religion of Isaac Newton*, 1974. • Marjorie Hope Nicolson, *Newton Demands the Muse: Newton's Opticks and the Eighteenth-Century Poets*, 1946.

Samuel Pepys • Editions. • Robert Latham, ed., *The Illustrated Pepys*, 1983. • Robert Latham, ed., *The Shorter Pepys*, 1985. • Robert Latham and William Matthews, eds., *The Diary of Samuel Pepys*, 11 vols., 1970–1983.

Biographies. • Arthur Bryant, *Samuel Pepys*, 3

vols., 3rd ed., 1967. • Richard Ollard, *Pepys: A Biography*, 1975. • J. R. Tanner, *Samuel Pepys and the Royal Navy*, 1920.

Criticism. • Francis Barker, *The Tremulous Private Body: Essays on Subjection*, rev. ed., 1995. • Harry Berger, Jr., "The Pepys Show: Ghost-Writing and Documentary Desire in the Diary," *ELH*, vol. 65, 1998. • Marjorie Hope Nicolson, *Pepys' Diary and the New Science*, 1965. • Robert Louis Stevenson, "Samuel Pepys," *Familiar Studies of Men and Books*, 1895. • Stuart Sherman, " 'In the Fullness of Time': Pepys and His Predecessors" and " 'With My Minute Wach in My Hand': The Diary as Timekeeper," *Telling Time: Clocks, Diaries, and English Diurnal Form, 1660–1785*, 1996. • James Grantham Turner, "Pepys and the Private Parts of Monarchy," in *Culture and Society in the Restoration*, ed. Gerald MacLean, 1995.

Hester Lynch Thrale Piozzi • Editions. • Katherine C. Balderston, ed., *Thraliana; the Diary of Mrs. Hester Lynch Thrale (later Mrs. Piozzi) 1776–1809*, 2nd ed., 1951. • Edward A. Bloom and Lillian D. Bloom, eds., *The Piozzi Letters*, 1989–. • A. Hayward, ed., *Autobiography, Letters and Literary Remains of Mrs. Piozzi (Thrale)*, 2 vols., 1975. • Mary Hyde, ed., *The Thrales of Streatham Park*, 1977.

Biographies. • James L. Clifford, *Hester Lynch Piozzi (Mrs. Thrale)*, rev. ed., 1968. • William McCarthy, *Hester Thrale Piozzi, Portrait of a Literary Woman*, 1985.

Criticism. • Martine Watson Brownely, "Eighteenth-Century Women's Images and Roles: The Case of Hester Thrale Piozzi," *Biography*, vol. 3, 1980. • Felicity A. Nussbaum, "Managing Women: Thrale's *Family Book* and *Thraliana*," *The Autobiographical Subject: Gender and Ideology in Eighteenth-Century England*, 1989. • John Riely, "Johnson and Mrs. Thrale: The Beginning and the End," *Johnson and His Age*, ed. James Engell, 1984. • Judy Simons, "The Unfixed Text: Narrative and Identity in Women's Private Writings," *The Representation of the Self in Women's Autobiography*, eds. Vita Fortunati and Gabriella Morisco, 1993.

Alexander Pope • Editions. • John Butt et al., eds., *The Twickenham Edition of the Poems of Alexander Pope*, 11 vols., 1940–1969. • John Butt, ed., *The Poems of Alexander Pope*,

1963. • George Sherburn, ed., *The Correspondence of Alexander Pope*, 5 vols., 1956. • Cynthia Wall, ed., *The Rape of the Lock*, 1998. • Aubrey Williams, ed., *Poetry and Prose of Alexander Pope*, 1969.

Biographies. • Maynard Mack, *Alexander Pope: A Life*, 1985. • George Sherburn, *The Early Career of Alexander Pope*, 1934. • Joseph Spence, *Observations, Anecdotes, and Characters of Books and Men*, ed. James M. Osborn, 2 vols., 1966.

Criticism. • Paul Baines, *The Complete Critical Guide to Alexander Pope*, 2001. • Reuben Brower, *Alexander Pope: The Poetry of Allusion*, 1959. • Laura Brown, *Alexander Pope*, 1985. • Morris Brownell, *Alexander Pope and the Arts of Georgian England*, 1978. • Helen Deutsch, *Resemblance and Disgrace: Alexander Pope and the Deformation of Culture*, 1996. • Howard Erskine-Hill, ed., *Alexander Pope: World and Word*, 1998. • Howard Erskine-Hill, *The Social Milieu of Alexander Pope*, 1978. • David Fairer, ed., *Pope: New Contexts*, 1990. • David Fairer, *Pope's Imagination*, 1984. • David F. Foxon, *Pope and the Eighteenth-Century Book Trade*, 1991. • Bertrand A. Goldgar, *Literary Criticism of Alexander Pope*, 1965. • Dustin Griffin, *Alexander Pope: The Poet in the Poems*, 1978. • Brean Hammond, ed., *Longman Critical Readers: Pope*, 1966. • J. Paul Hunter, "Pope and the Ideology of the Couplet," *Ideas*, vol. 4, no. 1, 1996. • Maynard Mack, *The Garden and the City: Retirement and Politics in the Later Poetry of Pope*, 1969. • Maynard Mack, ed., *Essential Articles for the Study of Alexander Pope*, 1968. • Maynard Mack and James Winn, eds., *Pope: Recent Essays by Several Hands*, 1980. • David B. Morris, *Alexander Pope: The Genius of Sense*, 1984. • Marjorie Hope Nicolson and G. S. Rousseau, *"This Long Disease, My Life": Alexander Pope and the Sciences*, 1968. • Valerie Rumbold, *Women's Place in Pope's World*, 1989. • Geoffrey Tillotson, *On the Poetry of Pope*, 2nd. ed., 1950. • Howard Weinbrot, *Alexander Pope and the Tradition of Formal Verse Satire*, 1982. • Aubrey L. Williams, *Pope's Dunciad: A Study of Its Meaning*, 1955.

Christopher Smart • Editions. • Karina Williamson, ed., *The Poetical Works of Christopher Smart*, 5 vols., 1980–1996. • Karina Williamson and Marcus Walsh, eds., *Selected Poems*, 1990.

Biographies. • Christopher Devlin, *Poor Kit Smart*, 1961. • Arthur Sherbo, *Christopher Smart, Scholar of the University*, 1967.

Criticism. • Moira Dearnely, *The Poetry of Christopher Smart*, 1967. • Harriet Guest, *A Form of Sound Words: The Religious Poetry of Christopher Smart*, 1989. • Geoffrey H. Hartmann, "Christopher Smart's, 'Magnificat',: Towards a Theory of Representation," *English Literary History*, vol. 41, 1974. • Clement Hawes, *Mania and Literary Style: The Rhetoric of Enthusiasm from the Ranters to Christopher Smart*, 1996.

Jonathan Swift • Editions. • Herbert Davis, ed., *The Prose Works of Jonathan Swift*, 14 vols., 1939–1968. • Christopher Fox, ed., *Gulliver's Travels: Complete, Authoritative Text with Biographical and Historical Contexts, Critical History, and Essays from Five Contemporary Critical Perspectives*, 1995. • A. C. Guthkelch and D. Nichol Smith, eds., *"A Tale of a Tub," to Which Is Added "The Battle of the Books," and the "Mechanical Operation of the Spirit,"* 2nd ed., 1958. • Pat Rogers, ed., *The Complete Poems*, 1983. • Harold Williams, ed., *The Correspondence of Jonathan Swift*, 5 vols., 1963–1965. • Harold Williams, ed., *Journal to Stella*, 2 vols., 1948. • Harold Williams, ed., *The Poems of Jonathan Swift*, 2nd ed., 3 vols., 1958.

Biographies. • Irvin Ehrenpreis, *Swift: The Man, His Works, and the Age*, 3 vols., 1962–1983. • Victoria Glendinning, *Jonathan Swift: A Portrait*, 1999. • David Nokes, *Jonathan Swift, A Hypocrite Reversed: A Critical Biography*, 1985.

Criticism. • Frank Boyle, *Swift as Nemesis: Modernity and Its Satirist*, 2000. • J. A. Downie, *Jonathan Swift: Political Writer*, 1985. • Robert C. Elliott, *The Power of Satire: Magic, Ritual, Art*, 1960. • Oliver W. Ferguson, *Jonathan Swift and Ireland*, 1962. • H. J. Real Fischer and J. Wooley, eds., *Swift and His Contexts*, 1989. • John Irwin Fischer and Donald C. Mell Jr., eds., *Contemporary Studies of Swift's Poetry*, 1980. • Carol Houlihan Flynn, *The Body in Swift and Defoe*, 1990. • Christopher Fox, ed., *Walking Naboth's Vineyard: New Studies of Swift*, 1995. • Nora Crow Jaffe, *The Poet Swift*, 1977. • Ellen Pollak, *The Poetics of Sexual Myth: Gender and Ideology in the Verse of Swift and Pope*, 1985. • Martin Price, *Swift's Rhetorical Art: A Study in Structure and Meaning*, 1953. • C. J. Rawson, ed., *The Character of Swift's Satire*, 1983. • Richard H. Rodino, *Swift Studies, 1965–1980: An Annotated Bibliography*, 1984. • Edward W. Rosenheim, *Swift*

and the Satirist's Art, 1963. • Edward W. Said, "Swift as Intellectual" and "Swift's Tory Anarchy," *The World, the Text, and the Critic*, 1983. • Brian Vickers, ed., *The World of Jonathan Swift: Essays for the Tercentenary*, 1968. • David M. Vieth, *Swift's Poetry 1900–1980: An Annotated Bibliography of Studies*, 1982. • Kathleen Williams, ed., *Swift: The Critical Heritage*, 1970.

Isaac Watts • Editions. • Bennett A. Brockman, ed., *Divine Songs Attempted in an Easy Language for the Use of Children*, 1978. • Bennett A. Brockman, *The Psalms and Hymns of Isaac Watts: With All the Additional Hymns and Complete Indexes*, 1997.

Biography. • Arthur Paul Davis, *Isaac Watts: His Life and Work*, 1943.

Criticism. • Donald Davie, *The Eighteenth-Century Hymn in England*, 1993. • Madeleine Forell Marshall and Janet Todd, *English Congregational Hymns in the Eighteenth Century*, 1982. • J. R. Watson, *The English Hymn: A Critical and Historical Study*, 1997.

John Wilmot, Earl of Rochester • Editions. • Frank H. Ellis, ed., *The Complete Works*, 1994. • Jeremy Treglown, *The Letters of John Wilmot, Earl of Rochester*, 1980. • David M. Vieth, ed., *The Complete Poems of John Wilmot, Earl of Rochester*, 1968. • Keith Walker, ed., *The Poems of John Wilmot, Earl of Rochester*, 1984.

Biographies. • John Adlard, *The Debt to Pleasure*, 1974. • Graham Greene, *Lord Rochester's Monkey; Being the Life of John Wilmot, Second Earl of Rochester*, 1974. • Jeremy Lamb, *So Idle a Rogue: The Life and Death of Lord Rochester*, 1993. • Vivian de Sola Pinto, *Enthusiast in Wit: A Portrait of John Wilmot, Earl of Rochester*, 1962.

Criticism. • David Farley-Hills, *Rochester's Poetry*, 1978. • David Farley-Hills, ed., *Rochester: The Critical Heritage*, 1972. • Nicholas Fisher, ed., *That Second Bottle: Essays on John Wilmot, Earl of Rochester*, 2000. • Dustin Griffin, *Satires Against Man: The Poems of Rochester*, 1973. • Marianne Thormählen, *Rochester: The Poems in Context*, 1993. • Jeremy Treglown, ed., *Spirit of Wit: Reconsiderations of Rochester*, 1982. • David M. Vieth, ed., *John Wilmot, Earl of Rochester: Critical Essays*, 1988.

CREDITS

TEXT CREDITS

Bede: From BEDE'S ECCLESIASTICAL HISTORY OF THE ENGLISH PEOPLE edited by Bertram Colgrave and R. A. B. Mynors (1969). Reprinted by permission of Oxford University Press.

BEOWULF, translated by Alan Sullivan. Reprinted by permission of Longman Publishers.

Boland, Eavan: "From the Irish of Pangur the Cat" from AN ORIGIN LIKE WATER: COLLECTED POEMS 1967–1987 by Eavan Boland. Copyright © 1996 by Eavan Boland. Used by permission of W. W. Norton & Company.

Chaucer, Geoffrey: from CHAUCER'S POETRY, selected and edited by E. T. Donaldson. Copyright © 1958, 1975 HarperCollins Publishers. Reprinted by permission of Pearson Education, Inc.

Lady Chudleigh, Mary: "To Almystrea," "To The Ladies" from THE POEMS AND PROSE OF MARY, LADY CHUDLEIGH edited by Margaret J. M. Ezell. Copyright © 1993 by Oxford University Press, Inc. Reprinted by permission.

Dafydd ap Gwilym: "One Saving Place," "The Hateful Husband," "The Winter," "The Ruin," from NINE THORNY THICKETS: SELECTED POEMS BY DAFYDD AP GWILYM, arrangements by Rolfe Humphries. Copyright © 1969 Rolfe Humphries. Reprinted by permission of Kent State University Press.

"The Dream of the Rood," "The Wanderer," "Wulf and Eadwacer," and "The Wife's Lament" translated by Kevin Crossley-Holland from THE EXETER BOOK RIDDLES, 1993. Copyright © 1993 Kevin Crossley-Holland. Reproduced by permission of the author c/o Rogers, Coleridge & White Ltd., 20 Powis Mews, London W11 1JN.

Dryden, John. Introduction, edited text and editorial matter © by Keith Walker 1987. Reprinted from JOHN DRYDEN edited by Keith Walker (The Oxford Authors, 1987) by permission of Oxford University Press. From THE POEMS AND FABLES OF JOHN DRYDEN edited by James Kinsley (1962). Reprinted by permission of Oxford University Press.

"Ebbing" and "Findabair Remembers Fróech" from MEDIEVAL IRISH LYRICS, translations from the Irish by James Carney (Dolmen Press, 1967). Reproduced by permission of Colin Smythe Ltd.

Evelyn, John: Excerpt from THE DIARY OF JOHN EVELYN edited by E. S. de Beer. Copyright © 1955 Oxford University Press. Reprinted by permission of Oxford University Press, England.

Gay, John: "The Beggar's Opera" from John Gay: DRAMATIC WORKS, Volume II edited by John Fuller (1983). Reprinted by permission of Oxford University Press.

Geoffrey of Monmouth: From HISTORY OF KINGS OF BRITAIN by Geoffrey of Monmouth, translated by Lewis Thorpe. (Penguin Classics, 1966) Translation copyright © Lewis Thorpe, 1966.

Gerald of Wales: Excerpts from GERALD OF WALES: THE JOURNEY THROUGH WALES AND THE DESCRIPTION OF WALES translated by Lewis Thorpe. Middlesex, England: Penguin Books Ltd., 1978.

Gray, Thomas: "Letter to Thomas Wharton" by Thomas Gray from CORRESPONDENCE OF THOMAS GRAY edited by Paget Toynbee and Leonard Whibley. Copyright 1935 Oxford University Press. Reprinted by permission of Oxford University Press, England.

Johnson, Samuel: "Anoch" from SAMUEL JOHNSON: A JOURNEY TO THE WESTERN ISLANDS OF SCOTLAND edited by Mary Lascelles. Copyright © 1971 by Yale University. Reprinted by permission of Yale University Press. Excerpt from SAMUEL JOHNSON: DIARIES, PRAYERS, AND ANNALS edited by E. L. McAdam, Jr., et al. Copyright © 1958 by Yale University Press, Inc. Reprinted by permission of Yale University Press.

"Judith" from ANGLO-SAXON POETRY: AN ANTHOLOGY OF OLD ENGLISH POEMS, translated by S. A. J. Bradley. Copyright © 1982 by David Campbell Publishers Ltd. Reprinted by permission of David Campbell Publishers Ltd.

Malory, Sir Thomas: From KING ARTHUR AND HIS KNIGHTS: SELECTED TALES FROM SIR THOMAS MALORY, edited by Eugene Vinaver, copyright © 1975, 1968, 1956 by Eugene Vinaver. Used by permission of Oxford University Press. Excerpt from CAXTON'S MALORY: A NEW EDITION OF SIR THOMAS MALORY'S LE MORTE DARTHUR translated & edited by James W. Spisak & William Matthews. Copyright © 1983 The Regents of the University of California. Reprinted by permission of University of California Press.

Marie de France: From THE LAIS OF MARIE DE FRANCE by Robert Hanning and Joan Ferrante. Reprinted by permission of Baker Book House Company.

Milton, John: Adapted and abridged excerpts from Alastair Fowler's notes from PARADISE LOST by Milton. Copyright © 1968 Longman Group Limited. Reprinted by permission of Addison Wesley Longman, Essex, England.

ILLUSTRATION CREDITS

INDEX